Contemporary Authors

Contemporary Authors

**A Bio-Bibliographical Guide to
Current Writers in Fiction, General Nonfiction,
Poetry, Journalism, Drama, Motion Pictures,
Television and Other Fields**

JANE A. BOWDEN
Editor

volumes **65-68**

GALE RESEARCH COMPANY • BOOK TOWER • DETROIT, MICHIGAN 48226

CONTEMPORARY AUTHORS

Published by
Gale Research Company, Book Tower, Detroit, Michigan 48226
Each Year's Volumes Are Cumulated and Revised About Five Years Later

Frederick G. Ruffner, *Publisher*   James M. Ethridge, *Editorial Director*

STAFF

Jane A. Bowden, *Editor*
Frances Carol Locher, *Associate Editor*
James Carleton Obrecht, Frank Michael Soley,
Susan A. Stefani, and Barbara Welch, *Assistant Editors*
Johanna P. Zecker, *Research Assistant*

Alan E. Abrams, *Consultant*
Eunice Bergin, *Copy Editor*
Linda Cairo, Laurlyn Niebuhr, Arlene True,
and Benjamin True, *Sketchwriters*
Norma Sawaya and Shirley Seip, *Editorial Assistants*
Laura Bryant, *Operations Supervisor*
Michaeline Nowinski, *Production Manager*

Copyright © 1977
GALE RESEARCH COMPANY

ISBN 0-8103-0029-X

Preface

Authors, as persons who express opinions or report facts which influence the actions of others, or who tell tales which stimulate the minds of others, have always had a special interest for everyone who read their works.

Until recently, it was writers of books who had primary interest for readers. Now, however, the newspaper reporter who is famous in his own right, the television anchorperson or correspondent, the influential editor or columnist of a popular magazine, and many other persons active in communications have an equal claim on the interest of the public. In fact, individuals often move rapidly from one area of communications to another and the medium is of less significance than the communicator.

CA Has Changed Its Scope

Therefore, with this issue *Contemporary Authors* has changed its scope to include significant personalities from all media—books, magazines, newspapers, TV, radio, films, etc. The title page has a new subtitle to reflect this change:

Contemporary Authors:
A Bio-Bibliographical Guide to Current Writers in Fiction,
General Nonfiction, Poetry, Journalism, Drama, Motion Pictures,
Television, and Other Fields.

Besides authors of books of a nontechnical nature, *CA* now includes newspaper and TV reporters, columnists, prominent newspaper and periodical editors, syndicated cartoonists, screenwriters, TV scriptwriters, and other media people.

Among the media people in this volume are Barbara Walters, Daniel Schorr, Earl Wilson, Federico Fellini, Mike Wallace, Sally Quinn, Mel Brooks, John Scali, Max Frankel, and Marlene Sanders. Also covered are major TV Capitol and foreign correspondents, wire service reporters and bureau chiefs, important by-line contributors to newspapers and magazines, and other writers of interest to the public.

Further Suggestions Are Welcome

Interest in media people on the part of librarians and users of *CA* is very high, as indicated by the numerous suggestions *CA* has received in recent years concerning the need for a reliable, on-going source of information on non-book and non-print communicators. Suggestions and comments in both individual letters and responses to our surveys have been very helpful in planning the present change.

CA will, of course, continue to focus primarily on persons whose work appears in book form, but the editors believe the addition of other media people will make *CA* even more useful.

Further comments from users will be welcome.

CONTEMPORARY AUTHORS

*Indicates that a listing has been compiled from secondary sources believed to be reliable,
but has not been personally verified for this edition by the author sketched.*

AALTO, (Hugo) Alvar (Henrik) 1898-1976

February 3, 1898—May 11, 1976; Finnish architect, educator, and writer. Obituaries: *New York Times,* May 13, 1976; *Washington Post,* May 13, 1976; *Current Biography,* July, 1976.

* * *

ABAJIAN, James De Tar 1914-

PERSONAL: Born May 30, 1914, in Sacramento, Calif.; son of James Claude and Elizabeth (Engelhardt) De Tar Abajian. *Education:* University of Wisconsin, Madison, B.S., 1936, graduate study, 1936-38; University of Michigan, Ann Arbor, further graduate study, 1939-42. *Home:* 4801 17th St., San Francisco, Calif. 94117. *Office:* California Historical Society, 2090 Jackson St., San Francisco, Calif. 94109.

CAREER: State Historical Society of Wisconsin, Madison, assistant in manuscripts division, 1933-38, assistant curator of manuscripts, 1943; University of Michigan, Ann Arbor, assistant curator of rare books, 1939-43; California Historical Society, San Francisco, chief librarian, 1949-68; San Francisco Public Library, San Francisco, director of Martin Luther King, Jr. Special Collection, 1969-71. *Military service:* U.S. Army, Signal Corps, 1943-44. *Member:* San Francisco African American Historical and Cultural Society.

WRITINGS: (With Elizabeth Parker) *The Black Presence in San Francisco* (pamphlet), San Francisco African American Historical and Cultural Society, 1974; (editor) *Blacks and Their Contributions to the American West: A Bibliography and Union List of Holdings through 1970,* G. K. Hall, 1974; *Blacks in Selected Newspapers, Censuses, and Other Sources: An Index to Names and Subjects,* three volumes, G. K. Hall, in press. Contributor to professional journals. Member of advisory committee for Afro-American Publishing, 1968-70, and *Living Webster Dictionary of the English Language,* 1970-71.

WORK IN PROGRESS: Dictionary of Photographers in California and Nevada Before 1900, publication expected in 1979; research on California artists before 1920 and on general history of California and the American West.

ABARBANEL, Karin 1950-

PERSONAL: Born February 23, 1950, in Long Branch, N.J.; daughter of Albert (a writer and psychologist) and Dorothy (a business manager; maiden name, Fennell) Abarbanel. *Education:* Middlebury College, B.A. (magna cum laude), 1971; Columbia University, M.A., 1972. *Politics:* None. *Religion:* None. *Residence:* New York, N.Y. *Agent:* Ruth Aley, 145 East 35th St., New York, N.Y. *Office: Foundation News,* 888 Seventh Ave., New York, N.Y. 10019.

CAREER: American Film Theatre, New York City, education coordinator, 1973-74; Janice LaRouche Associates, New York City, resume and career counselor, 1974—; *Foundation News,* New York City, associate editor, 1976—. Lecturer to academic and business organizations. *Member:* National Association of Female Executives (member of editorial board), Committee of Small Magazine Editors and Publishers, Advertising Women of New York, Columbia University Alumni Association, Phi Beta Kappa.

WRITINGS: (With Gonnie M. Siegel) *The Woman's Work Book* (career guide and national directory of employment resources), Praeger, 1975; (with Howard Hillman) *The Art of Winning Foundation Grants,* Vanguard, 1975. Contributor to magazines, newsletters, and women's news media.

WORK IN PROGRESS: Research and feature writing on community development, Southern rural renaissance, public interest firms, the monitoring of government policy, on medical education, and on resumes and careers for women.

* * *

ABBOTT, Carl (John) 1944-

PERSONAL: Born December 3, 1944, in Knoxville, Tenn.; son of Lyndon E. (a college professor) and Mildred (Schaeffer) Abbott; married Margery Post (a city planner), August 5, 1967. *Education:* Swarthmore College, B.A., 1966; University of Chicago, M.A., 1967, Ph.D., 1971. *Religion:* Society of Friends (Quakers). *Home:* 726 Delaware Ave., Norfolk, Va. 23508. *Office:* Department of History, Old Dominion University, Norfolk, Va. 23508.

CAREER: University of Denver, Denver, Colo., assistant professor of history, 1971-72; Old Dominion University, Norfolk, Va., assistant professor of history and urban studies, 1972—. *Member:* American Historical Association,

Organization of American Historians, Social Science History Association, Western History Association.

WRITINGS: The Human and Environmental Costs of American Growth, Forum Press, 1974; (editor and contributor) *Colonial Place, Norfolk: The Evolution of an Urban Neighborhood,* Institute of Government, University of Virginia, 1975; *Colorado: The History of the Centennial State,* Colorado Associated University Press, 1976. Contributor of articles and reviews to history journals, regional magazines, and newspapers.

WORK IN PROGRESS: Research on the American West and American cities.

*   *   *

ABE, Kobo   1924-

PERSONAL: Born March 7, 1924, in Tokyo, Japan; son of Asakichi (a doctor) and Yorimi Abe; married Machi Yamada (an artist), March, 1947; children: Neri (daughter). *Education:* Tokyo University, M.D., 1948. *Home:* 1-22-10 Wakaba Cho, Chofu City, Tokyo, Japan.

CAREER: Novelist and playwright. Director and producer of the Kobo Theatre Workshop in Tokyo, Japan, 1973—. *Awards, honors:* Post-war literature prize, 1950; Akutagawa prize, 1951, for *Kabe-S karumashi no hanzai;* Kishida prize for drama, 1958; Yomiuri literature prize, 1962; special jury prize from Cannes Film Festival, 1964, for film, "Woman in the Dunes"; Tanizaki prize for drama, 1967.

WRITINGS—Novels in English translation; all translated by E. Dale Saunders: *Daiyon Kampyoki,* Kodan-sha, 1959, translation published as *Inter Ice Age Four,* Knopf, 1970; *Suna no onna,* Shincho-sha, 1962, translation published as *Woman in the Dunes,* Knopf, 1964, adapted screenplay with Hiroshi Teshigahara published under same title, Phaedra, 1966, 2nd edition, 1971; *Tanin no kao,* Kodan-sha, 1964, translation published as *The Face of Another,* Knopf, 1966; *Moetsukita chizu,* Shincho-sha, 1967, translation published as *The Ruined Map,* Knopf, 1969; *Hakootoko,* Shincho-sha, 1973, translation published as *The Box Man,* Knopf, 1975.

Other novels: *Owarishi michino shirubeni* (title means "The Road Sign at the End of the Road"), Shinzenbi-sha, 1948; *Kabe-S karumashi no hanzai* (title means "The Crimes of S. Karma"), Getsuyo-syobo, 1951; *Kiga domei* (title means "Hunger Union"), Kodan-sha, 1954; *Kemonotachi wa kokyo o mezasu* (title means "Animals Are Forwarding to their Natives"), Kodan-sha, 1957; *Ishi no me* (title means "Eyes of Stone"), Shincho-sha, 1960; *Omaenimo tsumi ga aru* (title means "You Are Guilty Too"), Gakusyukenkyu-sha, 1965; *Enomoto Buyo* (title means "Enomoto Buyo"), Tyuokaron-sha, 1965.

Plays in English translation: *Tomodachi, Enemoto Takeaki,* Kawade-syobo, 1967, translation by Donald Keene published as *Friends,* Grove, 1969; *Bo ni natta otoko,* Shincho-sha, 1969, translation by Keene published as *The Man Who Turned into a Stick,* University of Tokyo Press, 1975.

Other plays: *Seifuku* (title means "The Uniform"), Aoki-syoten, 1955; *Yurei wa kokoniiru* (title means "Here is a Ghost"), Shincho-sha, 1959; *Abe Kobe gikyoku zenshu* (title means "The Collected Plays of Kobo Abe"), Shincho-sha, 1970; *Mihitsu no koi* (title means "Willful Negligence"), Shincho-sha, 1971; *Ai no megane wa irogarasu* (title means "Love's Spectacles Are Colored Glass"), Shincho-sha, 1973; *Midoriiro no stocking* (title means "Green Stocking"), Shincho-sha, 1974; *Ue* (title means "The Cry of the Fierce Animals"), Shincho-sha, 1975.

Other works: *Suichu toshi* (short stories; title means "The City in Water"), Togen-sha, 1964; *Yume no tobo* (short stories; title means "Runaway in the Dream"), Tokuma-syoten, 1968; *Uchinaro henkyo* (essays; title means "Inner Border"), Tyuokoron-sha, 1971; *Abe Kobo zensakuhin* (title means "The Collected Works of Kobo Abe"), fifteen volumes, Shincho-sha, 1972-73; *Han gekiteki ningen* (collected lectures; title means "Anti-Dramatic Man") Tyuokoron-sha, 1973; *Hasso no shuhen* (lectures; title means "Circumference of Inspiration"), Shincho-sha, 1974; *Warau Tsuki* (short stories; title means "The Laughing Moon"), Shincho-sha, 1975.

WORK IN PROGRESS: A novel, working title means "The Secret Meeting."

SIDELIGHTS: Kobo Abe wrote and sold his first novel while a student in medical school. After graduation he did not practice medicine but rather used his medical knowledge in writing and play direction. Many critics comment on the strong use of that educational background for the convincing technicalities in his fiction. Alan Levy said: "In those days, Abe was known as a surrealist. It was only in the nineteen-fifties that he began to create a metaphoric reality. Then, from Abe's pen in the nineteen-sixties, there came a trilogy of psychological novels that chart, like no other modern writing by one man that I've read, the walls and masks of everyday life. . . ."

The uniqueness of Abe was also asserted by Shane Stevens. "Like Abe's earlier, widely acclaimed 'Woman in the Dunes,' 'The Ruined Map' is also very experimental in its handling of material and owes more to the French modernists than to contemporary Japanese literary style. That is to say, although the roots of Abe's work are found in Japanese literary tradition going back to the 13th century his experimentations go beyond current Japanese literary modes.

"'The Ruined Map' is a brilliant display of pyrotechnics, a compelling tour de force that seems to have been built lovingly, word by word, sentence by sentence, by a master jeweler of polished prose. In one specific kind of craftsmanship—a blending of introspection with a great attention to the minutiae of life, always a trademark of the literary avant-garde—I find him to have absolutely no peers among contemporary Japanese novelists, and here I would include even the incandescent Kawabata, Japan's first Nobel Laureate." Of course, not all critics agree. Thomas Fitzsimmons feels that Abe faulters with "what seems to me one of the weaknesses of much current Japanese prose fiction (the poets are bolder): The seeming inability to present interior states with a few bold strokes of imagery, scene, and rhythm, the reliance upon textbook psychology to painstakingly (and painfully) expound, explain, and exhaust whatever aspects of being can be reduced to linear discourse."

Abe has little concern for the investigation of his Japanese roots. In 1966 he wrote his last biographical note: "I was born in Tokyo and brought up in Manchuria. The place of family origin on my papers, however, is in Hokkaido, and I have lived there for a few years. In short, my place of birth, the place where I was brought up, and my place of family origin are three different places on the map. Thanks to this fact, it is a difficult matter for me to write even an abbreviated list of important dates in my life. Essentially, I am a man without a hometown." Andrew Horvat contends this alienation is one answer to Abe's success outside Japan. "This particular situation is not exotic to foreign readers. The interest that Abe commands among readers living in other industrialized nations comes from the author's positive attitude toward having no roots—*of living in limbo, but enjoying it!*"

Abe is better known in Japan for his highly successful dramatic work than for his fiction. Harold Pinter clears all his Japanese productions through him. Abe directs and produces his own plays (along with some occasional work by others) with his own company in his own theatre. He once told Alan Levy: "Labor should produce some joy, but novels are not necessarily the work of joy. Perhaps that's why I enjoy producing and directing plays so much. It is, you see, my revenge against writing novels—or maybe my straw of survival. The novel is an approach to death; the theater brings things to life."

He seldom answers the phone or reads his mail and has said, "Asking a novelist to talk about his writing is like asking him to describe his coffin." He reads and writes German and English.

BIOGRAPHICAL/CRITICAL SOURCES: New York Times Magazine, November 17, 1974.

* * *

ABEL, Bob 1931-

PERSONAL: Born January 22, 1931, in Middletown, Conn.; son of Frank E. (an insurance agent) and Grace (Gordon) Abel; married wife, Carole (a literary agent), May 9, 1969; children: Douglas William, David Warren. *Education:* University of Connecticut, B.A., 1953; Boston University, B.S. (summa cum laude), 1956; also attended New School for Social Research, 1957-60. *Home:* 160 West 87th Street, New York, N.Y. 10024. *Agent:* Freya Manston, 639 Carlton Ave., Brooklyn, N.Y. 11238. *Politics:* Radical liberal. *Religion:* "To teach my children to be good and kind people."

CAREER: Drug Trade News, New York City, associate editor, 1956-59; *Ad-Lib,* New York City, editor in chief, 1961-62; *Realist,* New York City, managing editor, 1962-66; Dell Publishing Co., New York City, senior editor, 1968-72; Warner Books, New York City, executive editor, 1972-75; free-lance writer. Consultant to Irwin Swann Collection of Caricature & Art, 1974—. *Military service:* U.S. Army, 1953-55. *Member:* American Society of Journalists and Authors; Upper West Side Made Redundant Editor's & Writer's Wednesday Luncheon Club (co-founder).

WRITINGS: (Editor with David Manning White) *The Funnies: An American Idiom,* Free Press of Glencoe, 1963; (editor) *The American Cartoon Album,* Dodd, 1974; *The Book of Beer,* Regnery, 1976. Contributor to magazines. Contributing editor, *Cavalier,* 1967-70.

WORK IN PROGRESS: A study of drinking for Little, Brown, publication expected in 1977; writing two books, one with Henry Rothblatt, one with Marilyn Rosanes-Berrett.

SIDELIGHTS: "I write satire on occasion," Abel says, "to prove that life is constantly imitating satire. Writing is painfully hard work—instant backaches, sudden needs for a cup of tea, et al—but there are lovely moments when the moon (I, a Night Person) is right or something, and it all comes out right—and those help—just barely, sometimes, make up for rewrites and late payment and all the other unpleasant business connected with the profession. Having been an editor, the complexity of those folks' problems come as no surprise to me, but a bit more of sweet reasonableness on both sides would make for better work and more agreeable relationships."

ABRAHAMSEN, David 1903-

PERSONAL: Born June 23, 1903, in Trondheim, Norway; came to the United States in 1940, naturalized citizen, 1946; son of Salomon and Marie (Fischer) Abrahamsen; married Lova Katz, May 5, 1932; children: Inger (Mrs. Osborne Elliott), Anne-Marie (Mrs. William J. Foltz). *Education:* Royal Frederick University, M.D., 1929; London School of Economics and Political Science, postdoctoral study, 1936-37; State University of New York, M.D., 1943. *Office:* 1035 Fifth Ave., New York, N.Y. 10028.

CAREER: Private practice of medicine in Norway, 1929-31; University of Oslo, Oslo, Norway, intern at Royal Norwegian Clinics, 1931-32; Psychiatric Clinic, Oslo, Norway, resident and assistant physician in neurology and psychiatry, 1932-36; Department of Justice, Oslo, psychiatrist, 1938-40; St. Elizabeth's Hospital, Washington, D.C., psychiatrist, 1940-41; psychiatrist at Illinois State Penitentiary, 1941-42; Menninger Clinic, Topeka, Kan., research associate, 1942-43; Bellevue Hospital, New York, N.Y., psychiatrist, 1943-44; Columbia University, New York, N.Y., research associate in psychiatry, 1944-53, director of child guidance and mental hygiene, 1950-53. Diplomate of American Board of Psychiatry and Neurology, 1947. Visiting professor at Yale University, 1949-50, and New School for Social Research, 1959-61. Distinguished public health officer in Norway, 1929-31; director and supervisor of Oslo Children's Home, 1934-36; director of research on treatment of behavior disorders in children at New York City's Psychiatric Institute, 1944-48; director of scientific research for New York State Department of Mental Hygiene, 1948-52; organizer and director of Psychiatric Forum, Inc., 1946—. Member of board of directors of Home Advisory Council and Home Term Court, 1953—; member of board of directors and advisory board of Music Therapy Organization, 1954—; member of New York governor's committee to propose new legislation on the definition of legal insanity, 1957-62; member of board of overseers of Lemberg Center for the Study of Violence, at Brandeis University, 1966-72. *Military service:* Norwegian Army, 1940.

MEMBER: International P.E.N., American Medical Association (fellow), American Psychiatric Association (fellow), American College of Psychoanalysis, American Society for Criminology, American Psychopathological Association, Authors League of America, Norwegian Medical Association, Eastern Psychoanalytic Association, New York Academy of Medicine (fellow), New York County Medical Society, New York Society for Clinical Psychiatry.

WRITINGS: Crime and the Human Mind, Columbia University Press, 1944; *Men, Mind, and Power,* Columbia University Press, 1945; *The Mind and Death of a Genius,* Columbia University Press, 1946; *Report on the Study of One Hundred Two Sex Offenders at Sing Sing Prison as Submitted to Governor Thomas E. Dewey,* State Hospital Press (Albany), 1950; *Who Are the Guilty?: A Study of Education and Crime,* Rinehart, 1958; *The Road to Emotional Maturity,* Prentice-Hall, 1960; *The Psychology of Crime,* Columbia University Press, 1969; *The Emotional Care of Your Child,* Simon & Schuster, 1970; *Our Violent Society,* Funk, 1973; *The Murdering Mind,* Harper, 1977; *Nixon versus Nixon,* Farrar, Strauss, in press. Contributor to scientific and medical journals.

SIDELIGHTS: Some of Abrahamsen's books have appeared in French, German, Persian, Spanish, and Swedish editions.

ABU-LUGHOD, Janet L(ouise) 1928-

PERSONAL: Born August 3, 1928, in Newark, N.J.; daughter of Irving Otto (a businessman) and Tessie Lippman; married Ibrahim Abu-Lughod (a professor), December 8, 1951; children: Lila, Mariam, Deena, Jawad. *Education:* University of Chicago, B.A., 1947, M.A., 1950; University of Massachusetts, Ph.D., 1966. *Home:* 908 Ashland Ave., Wilmette, Ill. 60091. *Office:* Department of Sociology, Northwestern University, Evanston, Ill. 60201.

CAREER: American Society of Planning Officials, Chicago, Ill., director of research, 1950-52; American Council to Improve Our Neighborhoods, New York City, consulting sociologist in New York City and Philadelphia, 1954-57; American University in Cairo, Cairo, Egypt, assistant professor of sociology, 1958-60; Northwestern University, Evanston, Ill., associate professor, 1967-71; professor of sociology, 1971—. *Member:* American Sociological Association, Social Science History Association, Phi Beta Kappa. *Awards, honors:* Radcliffe Institute fellow, 1963-64; Ford Foundation faculty fellow, 1971-72; Guggenheim fellowship, 1976-77.

WRITINGS: (With Nelson Foote and others) *Housing Choices and Constraints,* McGraw, 1960; (with Ezz Eddin Attiya) *Cairo Fact Book,* American University of Cairo, 1963; *Cairo: 1001 Years of the City Victorious,* Princeton University Press, 1971; *Third World Urbanization,* Maaroufa Press, 1977.

Contributor: Ira M. Lapidus, editor, *Middle Eastern Cities: A Symposium on Ancient, Islamic, and Contemporary Middle Eastern Urbanism,* University of California Press, 1969; Ibrahim Abu-Lughod, editor, *The Transformation of Palestine,* Northwestern University Press, 1971; Richard T. Antoun and Ilya Harik, editors, *Rural Politics and Social Change in the Middle East,* Indiana University Press, 1972; L. Carl Brown, editor, *From Madina to Metropolis: Heritage and Change in the Near Eastern City,* Darwin Press, 1973; K. Hapgood and J. Getzels, editors, *Planning, Women, and Change,* American Society of Planning Officials (Chicago), 1974; I. Abu-Lughod, editor, *African Themes,* Northwestern University Press, 1975; Helen I. Safa and Brian M. Du Toit, editors, *Migration and Urbanization,* Aldine, 1975; J. Walton and L. H. Masotti, editors, *The City in Comparative Perspective,* Halsted, 1976. Contributor to journals in the social sciences.

WORK IN PROGRESS: A book on Moroccan urbanization.

*   *   *

ADAMS, Ramon Frederick 1889-1976

1889—April 29, 1976; American musician, folklorist, and author of books on Western Americana. Obituaries: *AB Bookman's Weekly,* May 31, 1976.

*   *   *

ADCOCK, Almey St. John 1894-
  (Hilary March)

PERSONAL: Born March 15, 1894, in Neasden, Middlesex, England; daughter of Arthur St. John (a poet, writer, and editor) and Marion Louise (Taylor) Adcock; married Eric Shelton Arundel (a patent office examiner), August 15, 1931. *Education:* Privately educated. *Politics:* Labour. *Home:* 20 Ebrington Rd., West Malvern, Worcestershire, England.

CAREER: Novelist and radio dramatist. *Member:* P.E.N.

WRITINGS: The Man Who Lived Alone, Jarrolds, 1923; *This Above All,* Harrap, 1924; *Winter Wheat,* Doran, 1926; *Master Where He Will,* Faber, 1926, published as *Love Is Master,* Little, Brown, 1928; *The Judas Tree,* Hodder & Stoughton, 1928; *Poacher's Moon,* Hodder & Stoughton, 1929; *The Street Paved with Water,* Hodder & Stoughton, 1930; *Up Hill,* Hodder & Stoughton, 1932; *The Woman at Iron Crag: A Story of the English Lakes,* Hodder & Stoughton, 1934; (editor) *Wonderful London: The World's Greatest City Described by Its Best Writers and Pictured by Its Finest Photographers,* revised edition (Almey St. John Adcock was not associated with previous edition), Amalgamated Press, 1935; *Tin Town,* Jarrolds, 1939; *The Warped Mirror: The Story of Maria Marten,* Jarrolds, 1948.

Novels; under pseudonym Hilary March: *Wet Weather,* J. H. Sears & Co., 1927; *Simon Wisdom,* Besant, 1929; *A Widow on Richmond Green,* Besant, 1930; *Either/or,* Secker & Warburg, 1966, published as *A Question of Love,* Simon & Schuster, 1967.

Also author of radio plays, "You Can't Live for Ever," "Cleopatra and the Cut," "The Old Flame," "The Happy Return," and "The Good Son."*

*   *   *

ADER, Paul (Fassett) 1919-
  (James Allen)

PERSONAL: Born October 20, 1919, in Asheville, N.C.; son of Olin P. (a Methodist clergyman) and Estella (Fassett) Ader; married Cicely Peeples, June 7, 1949; children: Donald, Rosalind, Alison. *Education:* Duke University, B.A., 1940; University of North Carolina, M.A., 1949. *Religion:* Protestant. *Home:* 519 Serenade Dr., San Antonio, Tex. 78216.

CAREER: U.S. Army Air Forces, radar officer in England, 1942-45; free-lance writer, 1946-47; U.S. Air Force, Security Service, career officer, 1951-69, retiring as lieutenant colonel; free-lance writer, 1970—. Site manager of Comprehensive Nutrition Program for Senior Citizens. *Member:* Phi Beta Kappa.

WRITINGS: (Under pseudonym James Allen) *We Always Come Back* (novel), W. H. Allen, 1945; *The Leaf Against the Sky* (novel), Crown, 1947; *How to Make a Million at the Track,* Regnery, 1977.

WORK IN PROGRESS: The Million-Dollar Rip-Off at Belmont Park, a novel.

BIOGRAPHICAL/CRITICAL SOURCES: Harry R. Warfel, editor, *American Novelist of Today,* American Book Co., 1951.

*   *   *

ADKINS, Nelson F(rederick) 1897-1976

February 3, 1897—July 27,1976; American educator and author of books on English and American literature. Obituaries: *New York Times,* July 30, 1976.

*   *   *

ADLARD, (P.) Mark 1932-

PERSONAL: Born June 19, 1932, in England; son of A. M. (an auctioneer) and E. (Leech) Adlard; married Sheila Rosemary Skuse, October 19, 1968; children: Vanessa, Robert. *Education:* Trinity College, Cambridge, B.A., 1954. *Home:* 12 The Green, Seaton Carew, Hartlepool, Cleveland TS25 1AS, England. *Agent:* John Farquharson Ltd., 15 Red Lion Sq., London WC1R 4QW, England.

CAREER: In industrial business management in England, 1956-76.

WRITINGS—Science fiction novels: *Interface,* Sidgwick & Jackson, 1971, Futura Publishing, in press; *Volteface,* Sidgwick & Jackson, 1972, Futura Publishing, in press; *Multiface,* Sidgwick & Jackson, 1975, Futura Publishing, in press.

WORK IN PROGRESS: Wood and Black Skin, a novel, "with a background derived from Arctic whaling in the early nineteenth century."

SIDELIGHTS: Adlard writes: "One of my main preoccupations is with the way economic activity can somehow give meaning or significance to individual lives, and why it often fails to do so. My three novels looked at this in a science fiction context, set in the twenty-second century when work has become a therapy. In my next novels I shall be looking at the past."

* * *

ADLER, Mortimer Jerome 1902-

PERSONAL: Born December 28, 1902, in New York, N.Y.; son of Ignatz (a jewelry salesman) and Clarissa (a school teacher; maiden name, Manheim) Adler; married Helen Leavenworth Boyton, May 2, 1927 (divorced, 1961); married Caroline Sage Pring, 1963; children: (first marriage) Mark Arthur, Michael Boynton; (second marriage) Douglas Robert, Philip Pring. *Education:* Columbia University, Ph.D., 1928. *Office:* Institute for Philosophical Research, 201 East Erie St., Chicago, Ill. 60611.

CAREER: New York Sun, New York City, secretary to editor, 1915-17; Columbia University, New York City, instructor in psychology, 1923-30; University of Chicago, Chicago, Ill., associate professor, 1930-42, professor of philosophy of law, 1942-52; Institute for Philosophical Research, Chicago, president and director, 1952—; San Francisco Productions, Inc., Chicago, president, 1954—. Lecturer and assistant director of People's Institute (New York City), 1927-29; visiting lecturer, City College (now of the City University of New York), 1927, St. John's College (Annapolis, Md.), 1936, and University of Chicago, 1963-68; lecturer for U.S. Air Transport Command. Consultant to Ford Foundation, 1952-56. Honorary trustee, Aspen Institute for Humanistic Studies, 1974—. American Catholic Philosophical Association, American Philosophical Association, Phi Beta Kappa.

WRITINGS: Dialectic, Harcourt, 1927; (with Jerome Michael) *Crime, Law, and Social Science,* Harcourt, 1933, reprint, Patterson Smith, 1971; (with Maude Phelps Hutchins) *Diagrammatics,* Random House, 1935; *Art and Prudence: A Study in Practical Philosophy,* Longmans, Green, 1937, revised edition published as *Poetry and Politics,* Duquesne University Press, 1965; *What Man Has Made of Man: A Study of the Consequences of Platonism and Positivism in Psychology,* Longmans, Green, 1937; *Saint Thomas and the Gentiles,* Marquette University Press, 1938.

Problems for Thomists: The Problem of Species, Sheed, 1940; (editor) *The Philosophy and Science of Man as a Foundation for Ethics and Politics,* University of Chicago, 1940; *How to Read a Book: The Art of Getting a Liberal Education,* Simon & Schuster, 1940, revised edition (with Charles Van Doren), 1972; *Hierarchy,* College of St. Thomas (St. Paul, Minn.), 1940; *A Dialetic of Morals: Toward the Foundations of Political Philosophy,* University of Notre Dame, 1941; *How to Think About War and Peace,*

Simon & Schuster, 1944; (associate editor) *The Great Ideas: A Syntopicon of Great Books of the Western World,* two volumes, Encyclopaedia Britannica, 1952; *The Democratic Revolution,* Industrial Indemnity Co., 1956; *The Capitalistic Revolution,* Industrial Indemnity Co., 1957; *Liberal Education in an Industrial Democracy,* Industrial Indemnity Co., 1957; (with Louis O. Kelso) *The Capitalist Manifesto,* Random House, 1958; (with Milton Mayer) *The Revolution in Education,* University of Chicago Press, 1958; *The Idea of Freedom,* Doubleday, Volume I: *A Dialectical Examination of the Conceptions of Freedom,* 1958, Volume II: *A Dialectical Examination of the Controversies About Freedom,* 1961; *Family Participation Plan for Reading and Discussing the Great Books of the Western World,* with reading guides, Encyclopaedia Britannica, 1959.

(With Kelso) *The New Capitalists: A Proposal to Free Economic Growth from the Slavery of Savings,* Random House, 1961; *The Conditions of Philosophy: Its Checkered Past, Its Present Disorder, and Its Future Promise,* Atheneum, 1965; *The Greeks, the West, and World Culture,* New York Public Library, 1966; *The Difference of Man and the Difference It Makes,* Holt, 1967; *Freedom: A Study of the Development of the Concept in the English and American Traditions of Philosophy,* Magi Books, 1968; (editor with Van Doren) *The Negro in American History,* three volumes, Encyclopaedia Britannica Educational Corp., 1969; *The Time of Our Lives: The Ethics of Common Sense,* Holt, 1970; *The Common Sense of Politics,* Holt, 1971; (with William Gorman) *The American Testament,* Praeger, 1975, *Some Questions about Language,* Open Court, 1976.

"The Great Ideas Program," series published by Encyclopaedia Britannica: Volume 1: (with Peter Wolff) *A General Introduction to the Great Books and to a Liberal Education,* 1959; Volume 2: (with Wolff) *The Development of Political Theory and Government,* 1959; Volume 3: (with Wolff) *Foundations of Science and Mathematics,* 1960; Volume 4: (with Seymour Cain) *Religion and Theology,* 1961; Volume 5: (with Wolff) *Philosophy of Law and Jurisprudence,* 1961; Volume 6: (with Cain) *Imaginative Literature I: From Homer to Shakespeare,* 1961; Volume 7: (with Cain) *Imaginative Literature II: From Cervantes to Dostoevsky,* 1962; Volume 8: (with Cain) *Ethics: The Study of Moral Values,* 1962; Volume 9: (with V. J. McGill) *Biology, Psychology, and Medicine,* 1963; Volume 10: (with Cain) *Philosophy,* 1963.

Associate editor, "Great Books of the Western World" series, fifty-four volumes, Encyclopaedia Britannica, 1952; editor-in-chief with Robert M. Hutchins, "The Great Ideas Today" series, Encyclopaedia Britannica, 1961—; editor with Hutchins, "Gateway to the Great Books" series, ten volumes, Encyclopaedia Britannica, 1963; editor, "The Annals of America" series, twenty-three volumes, Encyclopaedia Britannica, 1968—. Contributor to professional journals and popular magazines, including *Commonweal, Social Frontier, New Scholasticism, Thomist, Review of Literature, Harper's,* and *Ladies' Home Journal.* Encyclopaedia Britannica, director of editorial planning, 1966—, chairman of editorial board, 1974—.

* * *

AGAN, Patrick 1943-

PERSONAL: Born March 6, 1943, in Elmira, N.Y.; son of Eugene Francis (a stockbroker) and Marjorie (Manley) Agan. *Education:* Attended St. Bonaventure University, 1961-62, and Pratt Institute, 1962-64. *Religion:* Roman Catholic. *Home:* 49 Remsen St., Brooklyn Heights, N.Y. 11201. *Agent:* Garon-Brooke Associates, 415 Central Park West, New York, N.Y. 10025.

CAREER: Worked as display designer and showroom salesman in New York, N.Y., 1966-70; Stendig Furniture Co., New York, N.Y., manager of showroom, 1970-72; free-lance magazine writer, 1973—. Member of original production of "Man of La Mancha," 1965. *Member:* National Trust for Historic Preservation.

WRITINGS: Whatever Happened To . . .?, Ace Books, 1974; *Clint Eastwood, the Man Behind the Myth,* Pyramid Books, 1975; *Is That Who I Think It Is?,* Ace Books, two volumes, 1975. Columnist for *Screen Stars, Modern Movies,* and *Movie World,* all 1973—. Contributing editor, *Celebrity,* 1975—.

WORK IN PROGRESS: Volume III of *Is That Who I Think It Is?;* a novel about the new Hollywood and a screenplay based on this novel; two separate television series formats; an astrological guide to beauty and health.

SIDELIGHTS: Patrick Agan writes: "My writing can best be described as commercially entertaining, which is just the way I want it. In my work as a movie columnist, interviewer, tracer of personalities past and present, I try to interest and entertain on the level that I most enjoy being entertained. Celebrity, the phenomenon of it, has interested me from the first day I picked up a movie magazine, and I frankly feel that our society today is basically one big gossip column. . . . If that sounds like hype, it is, as the first lesson I've learned about writing is that if no one sees it, you might just as well leave it in the typewriter. As Barnum said, 'Give the people what they want.' And as Louis B. Mayer said, 'Leave the message to Western Union.' And I say when you read Patrick Agan, you'll have a few laughs mixed in among the straight facts. Here's to getting the words out!"

*　　*　　*

AGAR, Herbert (Sebastian) 1897-

PERSONAL: Born September 29, 1897, in New Rochelle, N.Y.; son of John Giraud and Agnes Louise (Macdonough) Agar; married Adeline Scott, February 6, 1918 (divorced, 1933); married Eleanor Chilton, April 11, 1933 (divorced, 1945); married Barbara Lutyens Wallace, June, 1945; children: (first marriage) William Scott, Agnes. *Education:* Columbia University, B.A., 1919; Princeton University, M.A., 1920, Ph.D., 1922. *Home:* Beechwood, Petworth, Sussex, England. *Office:* New Mexico Military Institute, Roswell, N.M. 88206.

CAREER: Correspondent from London, England, for *Louisville Courier-Journal* and *Louisville Times,* 1929-34; *Louisville Courier-Journal,* Louisville, Ky., daily columnist, 1935-39, editor, 1940-42; Office of War Information, London, England, director of British Division, 1943-46; Rupert Hart-Davis (publisher), London, England, director, 1951-63; T.W.W. Ltd. (Independent Television South Wales and West of England), London, England, director, 1953-65. Special assistant to American ambassador in London, 1943-46, counsellor for public affairs at U.S. Embassy in England, 1946. Founder of Freedom House in 1941, and its first president. *Military service:* U.S. Naval Reserve, active duty, 1917-18, 1942; became lieutenant commander.

MEMBER: National Arts Club, Phi Beta Kappa, Century Club, Savile Club. *Awards, honors:* Pulitzer Prize for history, 1933, for *The People's Choice;* Litt.D. from Southwestern University, Memphis, Tenn., 1936; LL.D. from Boston University, 1941.

WRITINGS: Milton and Plato, Princeton University Press, 1928; (with Eleanor Carroll Chilton and Willis Fisher) *Fire and Sleet and Candlelight* (poems), John Day, 1928; (with Chilton) *The Garment of Praise* (study of English poetry), Doubleday, 1929; *Bread and Circuses,* Eyre & Spottiswoode, 1930; (with Chilton) *Healthy, Wealthy, and Wise,* E. & L. Rosenfield, 1930; *The Defeat of Baudelaire,* Hogarth Press, 1932; *The People's Choice from Washington to Harding: A Study in Democracy,* Houghton, 1933 (published in England as *The American Presidents from Washington to Harding: A Study in Democracy,* Eyre & Spottiswoode, 1933), reprinted, Norman S. Berg, 1968; *Land of the Free,* Houghton, 1935; (editor with Allen Tate) *Who Owns America?: A New Declaration of Independence,* Houghton, 1936, reprinted, Books for Libraries, 1970; *What Is America?,* Eyre & Spottiswoode, 1936; *Pursuit of Happiness: The Story of American Democracy,* Houghton, 1938.

(With Helen Hill) *Beyond German Victory,* Reynal & Hitchcock, 1940; (co-author) *The City of Man,* Viking, 1940; (with Lewis Mumford and Frank Kingdon) *World-Wide Civil War,* Freedom House, 1942; *A Time for Greatness,* Little, Brown, 1942; (editor) Henry Adams, *The Formative Years,* two volumes, Houghton, 1947, reprinted, Greenwood Press, 1974; *The Price of Union,* Houghton, 1950, (published in England as *The United States: The Presidents, the Parties, and the Constitution,* Eyre & Spottiswoode, 1950, 2nd edition, Houghton, 1966; *A Declaration of Faith,* Houghton, 1952; *Abraham Lincoln,* Macmillan, 1952; *The Price of Power: America Since 1945,* University of Chicago Press, 1957; *The Unquiet Years: U.S.A., 1945-1955,* Hart-Davis, 1957.

The Saving Remnant: An Account of Jewish Survival Since 1914, Viking, 1960; *The Americans: Ways of Life and Thought* (collected from British Broadcasting Corp. broadcasts), Cohen & West, 1956, Dufour, 1962; *The Perils of Democracy,* Bodley Head, 1965, Dufour, 1966; *Britain Alone, June 1940-June 1941,* Bodley Head, 1972, published as *The Darkest Year: Britain Alone, June 1940-June 1941,* Doubleday, 1973.

Columnist, "Time and Tide" column, syndicated by *Louisville Courier-Journal,* 1935-39.

Contributor to scholarly journals. Literary editor of *English Review,* 1930-34; editor of *Free America,* 1937-47.

SIDELIGHTS: Agar's writings strongly urged the United States to enter World War II. In 1941, he helped to organize Freedom House to promote peace and international cooperation.

*　　*　　*

AHOKAS, Jaakko (Alfred) 1923-

PERSONAL: Born August 16, 1923, in Kangasala, Finland; came to the United States in 1964; son of Viljo Jaakko (an ambassador) and Laila (Liuksiala) Ahokas; married Marita Amberla, December 7, 1946 (divorced, 1957); married Elda Roveda (a language teacher), August 17, 1957; children: Yrjoe Jaakko Arthur, Laila Kaarina. *Education:* Helsinki University, M.A., 1952, Ph.D., 1959. *Religion:* Lutheran.

CAREER: State Department, Helsinki, Finland, translator, 1949-64; Indiana University, Bloomington, visiting professor of Finnish civilization, 1964-66; John J. Pershing College, Beatrice, Neb., associate professor of French, 1966-67; Indiana University, associate professor of Finnish literature and civilization, 1967-71; Temple University, Philadelphia, Pa., associate professor of French, 1971-73; currently teaching in Finland. Instructor at Turku University, Turku, Finland, 1963-64. Chairperson of International Writers' Seminar (Finland), 1964. *Military service:* Finnish Army, 1941-44.

MEMBER: International Federation of Translators (member of council, 1963-65), Modern Language Association of America, Association for Computing Machinery, Finnish Society of Translators (founding member; chairperson, 1955-64; honorary member), Modern Language Society of Finland, Finnish Society for Literary Research, Societe de Linguistique Romane. *Awards, honors:* Prix Halperine-Kaminsky, 1957, for translation of *Soldats Inconnus;* Wihuri Foundation grant, 1959-60; Italian Government grant, 1959-60; Helander Foundation grant, 1961; French Government grant, 1961; Finnish Academy of Science grant, 1963; arts and letters award from New York Metropolitan chapter of Finlandia Foundation, 1974.

WRITINGS: (Co-translator from Finnish into French) Vaeinoe Linna, *Soldats Inconnus,* Robert Laffont, 1957; *Essai d'un Glossaire genevoic d'apres les registres du Conseil de la ville de 1409 a 1536,* Societe Neophilologique de Helsinki, 1959; (translator from Finnish into French) Joel Lehtonen, *La Combe aux Mauvaises Herbes,* Mondiales, 1962; *Esseitae 63,* Tajo Oy, 1963; *History of Finnish Literature from the Origins to Our Days,* American-Scandinavian Foundation, 1973; (editor and translator from Finnish into French) *Anthologie de la Prose Finlandaise,* Pierre Seghers, 1974. Contributor to *Encyclopedia of World Literature in the Twentieth Century* and to language and literature journals in the United States and abroad.

SIDELIGHTS: Ahokas speaks Swedish, French, Italian, and German, and has studied Latin, Spanish, and Russian. *Avocational interests:* Theater, music, architecture.

* * *

AIKMAN, David (B. T.) 1944-

PERSONAL: Born June 6, 1944, in England; son of Barry Thomson (a travel agent) and Joyce (Carter) Aikman; married Maria Veronica Devera Tan, October 27, 1974. *Education:* Earned B.A. (honors) from Worcester College, Oxford; University of Washington, Seattle, earned M.A., currently a doctoral student. *Religion:* Christian. *Office:* Time, Rockefeller Center, New York, N.Y. 10020.

CAREER/WRITINGS: Tourist guide in Europe, 1964-65; Barclays Bank International, London, England, trainee in London and New York City, 1965-66; University of Washington, Seattle, instructor in Russian language and modern Asian history, 1966-71; *Time,* New York City, correspondent in New York City, Washington, D.C., Hong Kong, and correspondent in Berlin, 1977—. Member of International English (Christian) Fellowship (Hong Kong). *Member:* Foreign Correspondents Club (Hong Kong), Travellers Club (London).

WORK IN PROGRESS: A Garden of Chinese Memories, with Mabel Broadbridge, in press.

SIDELIGHTS: Aikman writes: "Both before and while being a journalist I have traveled very extensively in the world and consider myself by training and inclination a foreign correspondent. I speak, with varying clumsiness or facility, Russian, French, German, Mongolian, Turkish, Chinese. I always wanted to be a diplomat and fell into journalism through a highly unusual series of accidents which has always suggested the hand of the Lord at work. I prefer analytical and descriptive writing to running news stories,

which I have never been very good at. I have a great love for China and the Chinese people but not for the Communist idealogy." Aikman has made three trips to China, and covered the last weeks of South Vietnam and Cambodia, interviewing Souvanna Phouma and others. He also interviewed Philippine Moslem rebels and Philippine President Marcos.

* * *

AKHMADULINA, Bella Akhatovna 1937-

PERSONAL: Born April 10, 1937, in Moscow, U.S.S.R.; married Yevgeny Yevtushenko (a poet), 1954 (divorced); married Yuri Navigin (a story and screen writer). *Education:* Attended A. M. Gorky Institute of World Literature, Moscow, in mid 1950's. *Office:* Soyuz Pisateley, S.S.S.R., Ulitsa Vorovskogo 52, Moscow, U.S.S.R.

CAREER: Poet, 1962—. Delegate to the Second All-Russian Congress of Writers, 1965.

WRITINGS—Poems: *Struna* (title means "The String"), Sovetskii Pisatel, 1962; *Oznob* (includes prose pieces), 1968, translation by Geoffrey Dutton and Igor Mezhakoff-Koriakin, introduction by Yevgeny Yevtushenko, published as *Fever and Other Poems,* Morrow, 1969; *Uroki muzyki* (title means "Music Lessons"), Sovetskii Pisatel, 1969.

Poems represented in anthologies including: *Penguin Book of Russian Verse,* edited by Dimitri Obolensky, Penguin, 1962; *Russia's Other Poets,* translated and edited by Keith Bosley, Longmans, 1968; *The New Russian Poets, 1953-1966* (bilingual edition) edited by George Reavey, October House, 1968.

Also author of *Skazka o dozhde* (title means "The Rain), 1963; *Moya rodoslovnaya* (title means "My Ancestry"), 1964; and a collection in Russian, title means "Summer Leaves," 1968. Author of film script, "Clear Ponds," 1965, and of stories for *Yunost* (a journal; title means "Youth").

SIDELIGHTS: Bella Akhmadulina has been called one of the most brilliant female poets in Russia today. She has written poems on very untraditional subjects such as catching a cold or buying a carbonated drink from a machine. The early poems are mainly short and written in a simple, direct style. Some of her later poems have been longer, particularly those included in *Fever and Other Poems.**

* * *

ALBANESE, Catherine L(ouise) 1940-

PERSONAL: Born August 21, 1940, in Philadelphia, Pa.; daughter of Louis and Theresa (Spirizi) Albanese. *Education:* Chestnut Hill College, A.B., 1962; Duquesne University, M.A. (history), 1968; University of Chicago, M.A. (history of Christianity), 1970, Ph.D., 1972. *Office:* Department of Religious Studies, Pennsylvania State University, University Park, Pa.

CAREER: Wright State University, Dayton, Ohio, assistant professor, 1972-76, associate professor of religion, 1976—. Visiting associate professor at Pennsylvania State University, 1976-77. *Member:* American Academy of Religion, American Society of Church History, American Historical Association, American Studies Association, Popular Culture Association, Ohio Academy of Religion (vice-president, 1974-75; president, 1975-76), Phi Alpha Theta. *Awards, honors:* National Endowment for the Humanities stipend, summer, 1975.

WRITINGS: Sons of the Fathers: The Civil Religion of the

American Revolution, Temple University Press, 1976; *Corresponding Motion: Transcendental Religion and the New America*, Temple University Press, in press; (contributor) Nicholas Piediscalzi and William Collie, editors, *Ways to Teach About Religion in the Public Schools*, Argus Communications, in press; (contributor) R. Pierce Beaver, editor, *Papers of the American Society of Missiology*, William Carey Library, in press. Contributor of more than twenty articles and reviews to academic journals. Member of editorial board of *Environmental Review*.

WORK IN PROGRESS: Nature Religion and Civil Religion in America.

* * *

ALBERS, Josef 1888-1976

March 19, 1888—March 25, 1976; German-born American painter, color theorist, educator, poet, and author. Obituaries: *New York Times*, March 26, 1976; *Newsweek*, April 5, 1976; *Time*, April 5, 1976; *Current Biography*, May, 1976. (See index for previous *CA* sketch)

* * *

ALBRIGHT, John Brannon 1930-

PERSONAL: Born May 8, 1930, in Los Angeles, Calif.; son of Fred, Jr. (a businessman) and Lestelle (Mullins) Albright; married Janice Rose Wylie, September 8, 1951 (divorced, 1952). *Education:* University of Southern California, B.A., 1952. *Politics:* Democrat. *Religion:* Protestant. *Office: New York Times,* 229 West 43rd St., New York, N.Y. 10036.

CAREER: Glendale Independent, Glendale, Calif., associate editor, 1952-56; *Valley Press,* Palmdale, Calif., managing editor, 1956-59; *New York World-Telegram & Sun,* New York, N.Y., copy editor, 1959-66; *New York Times,* New York City, copy editor of travel section, 1966—. *Member:* Society of American Travel Writers, New York City Deadline Club, University of Southern California School of Journalism Alumni Association, Society of Professional Journalists (Sigma Delta Chi).

WRITINGS: (With Frances Cerra, Henry Gilgoff, April Klimley, and others) *Better Times,* Doubleday, 1975. Co-author of "Travel Notes," a weekly column in *New York Times.*

* * *

ALDEN, Robert L(eslie) 1937-

PERSONAL: Born December 10, 1937, in Brockton, Mass.; son of Allen Nathan (a painter) and Apollonia Eva (Simon) Alden; married Mary Jane Emilie Hauck, June 4, 1966; children: John Simon, Grace Anne Byrd. *Education:* Barrington College, B.A., 1959; Westminster Theological Seminary, Philadelphia, Pa., B.D., 1962; Hebrew Union College, Ph.D., 1966. *Politics:* Republican. *Home:* 3575 Arapahoe Pl., Littleton, Colo. 80122. *Office address:* Conservative Baptist Theological Seminary, Box 10,000 UPS, Denver, Colo. 80210.

CAREER: Ordained Baptist minister, 1966; Conservative Baptist Theological Seminary, Denver, Colo., assistant professor, 1966-72, associate professor of Old Testament, 1972—. *Member:* Near East Archaeological Society, American Schools of Oriental Research, American Oriental Society, Evangelical Theological Society, Catholic Biblical Society. *Awards, honors:* Interfaith fellow of Hebrew Union College-Jewish Institute of Religion, 1962-66.

WRITINGS: Psalms: Songs of Devotion, Moody, 1975; *Psalms: Songs of Dedication,* Moody, 1975; *Psalms: Songs of Discipleship,* Moody, 1976. Also contributor of translations to *New International Version of the Bible,* sponsored by New York Bible Society. Contributor to *Zondervan Pictorial Encyclopedia of the Bible* and to journals.

WORK IN PROGRESS: Contributions to four books, *Theological Word Book of the Old Testament, Tyndale Family Bible Encyclopedia, Expositor's Bible Commentary,* edited by Frank Gaebelein, and *The Englishman's Hebrew-English Old Testament,* edited by Joseph Magil.

SIDELIGHTS: "As transplanted Easterners we have fallen in love with Colorado," Alden wrote *CA.* "My interest in model railroading was heightened by the complex and fascinating history of railroading in the mining era of Colorado. And our love for the mountains has grown over the years.

"On my sabbatical leave in 1972 we traveled through Africa and the Middle East visiting missionary friends, but most of the time was spent in Israel where I studied Hebrew at the American Institute of Holy Land Studies on Mount Zion in Jerusalem. It also afforded me longer and deeper views of the land which I had visited a half dozen times before."

* * *

ALDERSON, Jo(anne) Bartels 1930-

PERSONAL: Born September 21, 1930, in Janesville, Wis.; daughter of Frederick Carl and Rose (Griesbach) Bartels; married James Michael Alderson, June 21, 1952; children: James Michael, Kaye Joanne, Jaye Marie, Ann Julia, Erica Jane. *Education:* Milton College, B.A. (cum laude), 1952; University of Wisconsin, graduate study, 1952, 1959-60. *Home:* 1950 Georgia St., Oshkosh, Wis. 54901.

CAREER: Janesville Daily Gazette, Janesville, Wis., reporter, 1949-52; free-lance writer, 1952-68; *Paper for Central Wisconsin,* Oshkosh, proofreader and writer, 1968-70; free-lance writer, 1970—. Co-founder of Greenroom Experimental Drama Group of the Oshkosh Community Players; drama teacher and director for Oshkosh high school, recreation department, Community Players, Junior Theater, and Mask and Wig Theater. Has performed in productions of her own plays. Member of Wisconsin Arts Council study group, 1966-67; president and member of board of directors of Grand Opera House Committee.

MEMBER: National League of American Pen Women, Wisconsin Fellowship of Poets (president and member of board of directors), Council for Wisconsin Writers (president and member of board of directors), Wisconsin Press Women, Wisconsin Regional Writers, Fox Valley Artists Association, Sigma Phi Zeta.

WRITINGS: (Editor with husband, J. Michael Alderson) *Poems Out of Wisconsin III,* Wisconsin Fellowship of Poets, 1967; (with J. Michael Alderson) *The Man Mazzuchelli: Pioneer Priest,* Wisconsin House, 1974.

Plays: "Day of Revenge" (one-act), first produced at Oshkosh Community Players Playhouse, March 14, 1961; "Fire and Ice" (three-act), first produced at Oshkosh Grand Theatre, June 17, 1968; "A Dialogue with the Brownings," first produced in Green Lake, Wis., April 12, 1969; "Interview with Emily," first produced in Madison, Wis., at Edgewood College, June 9, 1971. Contributor of articles and poems to magazines and newspapers.

* * *

ALEXANDER, Frank 1943-

PERSONAL: Born February 20, 1943, in San Diego, Calif.;

son of Claud E. (an aircraft assembly foreman) and Bette (Wheir) Alexander. *Education:* Utah State University, B.A., 1965; Stanford University, M.A., 1968. *Home and office:* 564 Central Ave., Suite 217, Alameda, Calif. 94501.

CAREER: Jobs Corps, Clinton, Iowa, curriculum writer and job counselor, 1968-69; Job Corps, Astoria, Ore., reading and mathematics instructor, 1969-71; Galileo Spaghetti Restaurants, Oklahoma City, Okla., partner, 1972-73; Professional Development Systems, Berkeley, Calif., writer, 1973-74; Front Row Experience (educational publishing company), Alameda, Calif., editor and manager, 1974—. *Member:* Sierra Club (San Francisco Bay chapter).

WRITINGS: (Editor) *Perceptual-Motor Lesson Plans,* Front Row Experience, 1975; *I'm in Love with a Mannequin* (poems), Cocono, 1976.

WORK IN PROGRESS: A second book of poems.

SIDELIGHTS: Alexander writes that he enjoys writing "old-fashioned sing-song tongue-in-cheek poetry" that has come out of "my many experiences as a fire fighter for the U.S. Forest Service, bus boy, dish washer, sandwich maker, fast food cashier, assistant motel manager, bell hop, free-lance salesman, free-lance newspaper reporter, teacher, job counselor, curriculum writer, editor, office manager, factory worker, Peace Corps volunteer, etc."

BIOGRAPHICAL/CRITICAL SOURCES: Oakland Tribune, July 30, 1976.

* * *

ALEXANDER, Thomas G(len) 1935-

PERSONAL: Born August 8, 1935, in Logan, Utah; son of Glen M. (a professor) and Violet (Bird) Alexander; married Marilyn Johns (a teacher), August 15, 1959; children: Brooke Ann, Brenda Lynn, Tracy Lee, Mark Thomas. *Education:* Weber State College, A.S., 1955; University of Utah, student, 1955; Utah State University, B.S., 1960, M.S., 1961; University of California, Berkeley, Ph.D., 1965. *Office:* Charles Redd Center for Western Studies, Brigham Young University, Provo, Utah 84602.

CAREER: Brigham Young University, Provo, Utah, assistant professor, 1964-68, associate professor, 1968-73, professor of history, 1973—, assistant director of Charles Redd Center for Western Studies, 1972-73, associate director, 1973—. Visiting research professor at Utah State University, summer, 1965; visiting instructor at Kearney State College, summer, 1966; instructor at Brigham Young University Summer Abroad Program (Salzburg), 1968; adjunct associate professor at Southern Illinois University, 1970-71. Member of history committee of Utah Heritage Foundation, 1966-68; member of advisory council of Denver Records Council of National Archives & Records Service, 1969-74, member of its board of directors, 1969-71; member of awards committee of Utah Academy of Arts, Sciences, and Letters, 1975-76, chairman, 1976.

MEMBER: Organization of American Historians, Agricultural History Society, Mormon History Association (member of board of directors, 1970-73, 1975-76; first vice-president, 1973-74; president, 1974-75), Western History Association, Utah State Historical Society (Utah Valley branch; member of board of directors, 1965-68), Phi Alpha Theta, Pi Sigma Alpha, Phi Kappa Phi. *Awards, honors:* Woodrow Wilson fellowship, 1963; award from Mormon History Association, 1968, for best article on Mormon history; Morris Rosenblatt Award from *Utah Historical Quarterly,* 1969; National Historical Publications Commission fellowship, 1970-71; Karl G. Maeser Research Award, 1976.

WRITINGS: (With Leonard Arrington) *Water for Urban Reclamation: The Provo River Project* (monograph), Utah Agricultural Experiment Station, 1966; (contributor) John Porter Bloom, editor, *The American Territorial System,* Ohio University Press, 1973; (editor) *Essays on the American West,* Brigham Young University Press, Volume III: *1972-1973,* 1974, Volume V: *1973-1974,* 1975, Volume VI: *1974-1975,* 1976; (with James B. Allen) *Manchester Mormons: The Journal of William Clayton, 1840-1842,* Peregrine Smith, 1974; (with Arrington) *A Dependent Commonwealth: Utah's Economy from Statehood to the Great Depression,* Brigham Young University Press, 1974.

Assistant editor of *The Papers of Ulysses S. Grant,* Southern Illinois Press, Volume V, 1971-73. Contributor of more than fifty articles and reviews to history journals and Mormon periodicals. Member of advisory editorial board of Utah State Historical Society, 1968—, guest editor, summer, 1971; member of advisory board of *Courage: A Journal of History, Thought, and Action,* 1972-73; editor of *Newsletter of the Mormon History Association,* 1973-74; associate editor of *Journal of Mormon History,* 1973-74.

WORK IN PROGRESS: The Interior Department, Congress, and the Intermountain West, 1863-1896, publication expected by Brigham Young University Press; a textbook on Utah history with others; a history of the Latter-day Saints Church, 1900-1930.

* * *

ALIANO, Richard Anthony 1946-

PERSONAL: Born October 26, 1946, in New York, N.Y.; son of Albert Anthony and Ann (Barbera) Aliano. *Education:* Queens College of the City University of New York, B.A. (magna cum laude), 1968, M.A., 1969; City University of New York, Ph.D., 1973. *Politics:* Republican. *Religion:* Roman Catholic. *Home:* 75-08 249th St., Bellerose, N.Y. 11426. *Office:* Department of Political Science, Queens College of the City University of New York, Flushing, N.Y. 11367.

CAREER: Queens College of the City University of New York, Flushing, N.Y., lecturer, 1969-73, assistant professor of political science, 1973—. *Military service:* Army National Guard, 1969-75; became sergeant. *Member:* American Political Science Association, American Association of University Professors, Northeast Political Science Association, Association of Italian-American Faculty of the City University of New York, Phi Beta Kappa.

WRITINGS: American Defense Policy from Eisenhower to Kennedy: The Politics of Changing Military Requirements, 1957-1961, Ohio University Press, 1975. Contributor to political science and military journals.

WORK IN PROGRESS: The Crime of World Power: Politics Without Government in the International System; Introduction to Politics, with Norman Bailey.

* * *

ALIBRANDI, Tom 1941-

PERSONAL: Born August 10, 1941, in Syracuse, N.Y.; son of John G. (in construction) and Elsya (Wilson) Alibrandi; married Lucinda Westholt (a psychologist), June 23, 1973; children: John, Timothy. *Education:* University of Arizona, student, 1959-61; Syracuse University, B.A., 1963; University of California, Los Angeles, counseling certificate, 1974. *Home and office address:* P.O. Box 1109, Laguna Beach, Calif. 92652.

CAREER: Employed in construction management in Syracuse, N.Y., Los Angeles, Calif., and Montreal, Quebec, 1963-71; carpenter in Orange County, Calif., 1971-74; Family Development Program, Laguna Beach, Calif., counselor, 1975—. Director of youth programs for Orange County Alcoholism Program, 1975—. *Awards, honors:* Grant from Orange County, Calif., 1976.

WRITINGS: Free Yourself, Major Books, 1975; *The Meditation Handbook,* Major Books, 1976; *Biorhythm: Get the Most Out of Your Life,* Major Books, 1976. Contributor to *Alcoholism Digest, Grapevine,* and *Modern People Newsweekly.*

WORK IN PROGRESS: The Constructor, a novel; a book on adolescent alcohol abuse; *Killshot,* a novel.

SIDELIGHTS: Alibrandi comments that he "started writing three years ago after I hurt my back on a construction project. My hope is to alternate between fiction and non-fiction works. And do a lot of traveling."

BIOGRAPHICAL/CRITICAL SOURCES: Los Angeles Times, December 12, 1975; *Orange County Register,* June 13, 1976; *Orange County Daily Pilot,* September 12, 1976.

* * *

ALLARD, Michel (Adrien) 1924-1976

January 27, 1924—1976; French educator, scholar, and author of books on Islamic religious philosophy. Obituaries: *AB Bookman's Weekly,* March 1, 1976.

* * *

ALLEN, Ira R. 1948-

PERSONAL: Born January 16, 1948, in Portland, Ore.; son of Arthur (a management analyst) and Mynne (Leites) Allen; married Marin Pearson (a university instructor), June 16, 1974; children: Jonathan J. M. *Education:* University of Maryland, B.S., 1970. *Religion:* Jewish. *Home:* 8810 Maywood Ave., Silver Spring, Md. 20910. *Office:* United Press International, 315 National Press Building, Washington, D.C. 20045.

CAREER/WRITINGS: Baltimore Evening Sun, Baltimore, Md., reporter, 1969; United Press International (UPI), reporter in Baltimore, Md., 1970-71, broadcast writer in Chicago, Ill., 1971-72, reporter in Washington, D.C., 1972—. Member of board of directors of Maryland Media, Inc., 1974—. *Member:* Washington Press Club, University of Maryland Young Alumni Club (member of board of directors, 1973—), Sigma Delta Chi.

* * *

ALLEN, James
See ADER, Paul (Fassett)

* * *

ALLEN, Leroy 1912-

PERSONAL: Born July 13, 1912, in McLeansboro, Ill.; son of Arden W. (a carpenter) and Eliza (Pierce) Allen; married Rita Kole (an artist), on April 7, 1961. *Education:* "Higher education by self-study. Have earned some college credits by attending night classes and taking correspondence courses." *Politics:* Republican (but not "hardshell"). *Religion:* Protestant. *Home:* 1207 Bryson Avenue, Simi Valley, Calif. 93065. *Agent:* Marie Wilkerson, Park Avenue Literary Agency, New York, N.Y. 10017.

CAREER: U.S. Navy, chief yeoman, 1931-75; first joined Navy in 1931, left after four years, worked ensuing six years as warehouseman in Los Angeles. "Went back in Navy in World War II, served from February, 1942-September, 1945, saw action in Pacific Theater. Returned to Los Angeles and worked at several jobs until 1951, when I rejoined the Navy, served until retired this year. First ship was battleship, *USS West Virginia,* but served thereafter mostly on destroyers. Have sailed every ocean and been 'on liberty' in every continent." *Member:* American Legion, Veterans of Foreign Wars, Fleet Reserve Association, Toastmasters International. *Awards, honors:* Freedoms Foundation Award, for essays, won three times.

WRITINGS: Desires of the Heart, Zondervan, 1951; *Across the Seas,* Zondervan, 1952; *Shawnee Lance,* Dell, 1970. Also author of booklet, *Barabbas.*

WORK IN PROGRESS: The Lonely Time; a book with Civil War background, featuring a white boy and a young Negro slave who are "on their own" together in the Arkansas backwoods.

SIDELIGHTS: Allen writes: "My motivation is the belief that even a minor talent should not be left unexpressed. My major areas of interest for writing purposes are the Navy, Indian life at any time frame/any geographical area, and adventure in general.

"I have moderate fluency in French and Spanish (enough to get along in those countries). I am deeply interested in history, am a sports enthusiast (spectator mostly), and am probably the most happily married man you'll ever meet."

Across the Seas has been reprinted in magazines and read over radio in Chicago.

* * *

ALLEN, Phyllis (Greig)

PERSONAL: Maiden name, Kensington; widowed. *Education:* Attended Stockwell College, London, and London School of Economics and Political Science. *Home:* Lookout, Honey Lane, Selborne, Alton, Hampshire, England.

CAREER: Building Research Station, Garston, Watford, England, member of staff, 1951-68.

WRITINGS: (With William Mullins) *Student Housing: Architectural and Social Aspects,* Praeger, 1971.

* * *

ALLEN, Phyllis S(loan) 1908-

PERSONAL: Born April 14, 1908, in Cardston, Alberta, Canada; daughter of John Samuel (a farmer) and Grace (Kearl) Sloan; married Mark Knight Allen (a psychology professor), January 18, 1934; children: Barbara A. Crockett, Mary Inez, James Sloan, Grace Jean. *Education:* University of California, Berkeley, B.A., 1931. *Politics:* Republican. *Religion:* Church of Jesus Christ of Latter-day Saints (Mormons). *Home:* 836 North 1100 East, Provo, Utah 84601. *Office:* 233 Brimhall, Brigham Young University, Provo, Utah 84602.

CAREER: Worked professionally in the field of interior design in Salt Lake City, Utah, in Dinwoodey's, 1931-32, and ZCMI, 1932-33, and in Breuhner's, Sacramento, Calif., 1933-34; Brigham Young University, Provo, Utah, instructor in interior design, 1961-72, chairman of department of interior environment, 1972-75, member of department faculty, 1975—. Member, state board of Utah Heritage Foundation. *Member:* American Society of Interior Designers (associate member), Interior Design Society, Interior Design Educator's Council. *Awards, honors:* Attingham grant from American Society of Interior Designers, 1975.

WRITINGS: Beginnings of Interior Environment, Brigham Young University Press, 1972, revised edition, 1976; *The Young Decorator,* Brigham Young University Press, 1975. Contributor of articles to local publications.

WORK IN PROGRESS: A book for children.

* * *

ALLEN, (Alexander) Richard 1929-

PERSONAL: Born February 10, 1929, in Vancouver, British Columbia, Canada; son of Harold Tuttle (a clergyman) and Ruby (a nurse; maiden name, Reilly) Allen; married Margaret Ritchie, July 14, 1951 (divorced, 1964); married Nettie Shewchuk, April 24, 1965; children: (second marriage) Daniel Richard, Philip Andrew. *Education:* Attended University of British Columbia, 1947-48, 1949-50; University of Toronto, B.A. (honors), 1956; University of Saskatchewan, M.A., 1961; Duke University, Ph.D., 1967. *Politics:* New Democratic Party. *Religion:* Protestant. *Home:* 85 Haddon Ave. N., Hamilton, Ontario, Canada L85 4A4. *Office:* Department of History, McMaster University, Hamilton, Ontario, Canada L85 4L9.

CAREER: Elementary teacher in public schools of Ottawa, Ontario, 1954-55, and Crystal Bay, Ontario, 1956-57; University of Saskatchewan, Regina, general secretary of student Christian movement, 1957-61, special lecturer, 1964-67, assistant professor, 1967-70, associate professor of history, 1970-74, chairman of Canadian Plains Area Studies Program, 1967-70, 1972-74; McMaster University, Hamilton, Ontario, associate professor of history, 1974—. *Member:* Canadian Historical Association (council member, 1974—). *Awards, honors:* Canada Council senior leave fellow, 1970-71.

WRITINGS: The Social Passion, Religion and Social Reform in Canada, 1914-1928, University of Toronto Press, 1971; (editor) *A Region of the Mind: Interpreting the Western Canadian Plains,* Canadian Plains Studies Centre, 1973; (editor) *The Social Gospel in Canada* (conference papers), National Museum of Man, 1975. Contributor to historical journals. Editor of *Canadian Plains Studies,* 1972-75.

WORK IN PROGRESS: A biography of Salem Goldworth Bland; editing *Man and Nature on the Prairies.*

* * *

ALLEN, Rupert C(lyde) 1927-

PERSONAL: Born October 1, 1927, in Tucson, Ariz.; son of Rupert (a barber) and Eula (Lyle) Allen; married Emilia Erickson (a teacher), December 14, 1953; children: Eric, Catherine, Mark, Elizabeth. *Education:* University of California, Berkeley, A.B., 1951, M.A., 1953, Ph.D., 1960. *Home:* 4145 East Burns, Tucson, Ariz. 85711. *Office:* Department of Romance Languages, University of Arizona, Building 67, Tucson, Ariz. 85721.

CAREER: University of Pittsburgh, Pittsburgh, Pa., assistant professor of Spanish, 1959-60; University of Arizona, Tucson, assistant professor, 1961-63, associate professor, 1964-69, professor of Spanish, 1969—. *Military service:* U.S. Army Air Forces, 1946-47.

WRITINGS: The Symbolic World of Federico Garcia Lorca, University of New Mexico Press, 1972; *Psyche and Symbol in the Theater of Federico Garcia Lorca,* University of Texas Press, 1974.

WORK IN PROGRESS: Symbolic Experience: A Study of Poems by Pedro Salinas; The Poetry behind Poetry: A Study of Taoism, Haiku, and Modern Spanish Poetry.

* * *

ALLEN, William 1940-

PERSONAL: Born September 8, 1940, in Dallas, Tex.; son of William Walter, Jr. (a carpenter) and Loraine (Stark) Allen. *Education:* Attended North Texas State University, 1960-63; California State University, Long Beach, B.A., 1968; University of Iowa, M.F.A., 1970. *Home:* 666 Mohawk, Columbus, Ohio 43206. *Office:* Department of English, Ohio State University, 164 West 17th Ave., Columbus, Ohio 43210.

CAREER: Ohio State University, Columbus, visiting instructor, 1972-73, assistant professor of English, 1973—. Coordinator of Vandewater Poetry Contest, Academy of American Poets Contest, and Jacobsen Short Story Contest, 1973—; judge for Poetry Society of Texas. *Military service:* U.S. Army, Signal Corps, 1958-60. *Awards, honors:* Los Angeles Newspaper Guild award, 1967, as California State, Long Beach journalist of the year.

WRITINGS: Starkweather (non-fiction), Houghton, 1976; *To Tojo from Billy-Bob Jones* (novel), Houghton, 1977.

Contributor: Min S. Yee, editor, *The Great Escape,* Bantam, 1974; Earle Wallace and Andrew M. Scott, editors, *Politics U.S.A.,* Macmillan, 1974; Mark Schorer, Philip Durham, Everett L. Jones, editors, *Harbrace College Reader,* Harcourt, 1976. Contributor of short stories, articles, and reviews to newspapers and magazines, including *Antioch Review, Reader's Digest, Saturday Review, New York Times, Westways, Audience,* and *Columbus Dispatch.* Editor of *Ohio Journal* (literary magazine), 1973—.

WORK IN PROGRESS: A novel set in Texas during the nineteen-twenties.

SIDELIGHTS: Allen has been writing since the age of twelve. He is interested in fiction and non-fiction, especially recent American history, humor, and writing about his regional Texas background. Concerning literary theory he says, "Every good story should have at least one chicken in it."

* * *

ALLRED, Dorald M(ervin) 1923-

PERSONAL: Born July 11, 1923, in Lehi, Utah; son of Robert Mitchell (a farmer) and Hazel (a farmer; maiden name, Beck) Allred; married Berna Brown, 1952; children: Kevin, Anita (Mrs. David Rawlinson), Kyle, Darin, Lori. *Education:* Brigham Young University, B.A., 1950, M.A., 1951; University of Utah, Ph.D., 1954. *Religion:* Church of Jesus Christ of Latter-day Saints (Mormons). *Office:* Department of Zoology, Brigham Young University, Provo, Utah 84602.

CAREER: Chief of entomology and arachnoid section at Dugway Proving Ground, 1954-56; Brigham Young University, Provo, Utah, assistant professor, 1956-63, associate professor, 1963-68, professor of zoology, 1968—, assistant to dean of College of Biology and Agriculture, 1974—, associate director of Life Science Museum, 1976—. *Military service:* U.S. Navy, 1943-46. *Member:* World Wildlife Federation, Entomological Society of America, American Forestry Federation, Ecological Society of America, American Institute of Biological Sciences, American Association for the Advancement of Science, American Arachnoid Society,

American Society of Parasitology, American Nature Study Society, National Audubon Society, American Microscopical Society, Wildlife Disease Association, Utah Academy of Science, Sigma Xi. *Awards, honors:* Karl G. Maeser research award from Brigham Young University, 1967.

WRITINGS: Living Things: An Introduction to Natural History, Brigham Young University Press, 1974. Contributor of more than a hundred articles to scientific journals.

WORK IN PROGRESS: Research on arthropod ecology and natural history.

* * *

ALOTTA, Robert I(gnatius) 1937-

PERSONAL: Born February 26, 1937, in Philadelphia, Pa.; son of Peter (a driver and salesman) and Jean (a secretary; maiden name, Sacchetti) Alotta; married Alice J. Danley, October 1, 1960; children: Peter A., Amy L. *Education:* La Salle College, B.A., 1959. *Politics:* "I vote the man, not the party." *Religion:* "Christian Existentialist." *Home:* 315 South 12th St., Philadelphia, Pa. 19107. *Office:* Philadelphia Housing Authority, 2012 Chestnut St., Philadelphia, Pa. 19103.

CAREER: Triangle Publications, Philadelphia, Pa., merchandising manager in *Inquirer* division, 1959-63, manager of customer service department in *Inquirer-Daily News* divisions, 1963-66, new business coordinator in *Daily News* division, 1966-67; Penn Central Transportation Co., Philadelphia, manager of special projects, 1967-72; Philadelphia Housing Authority, Philadelphia, director of public information, 1972—. Has made regular appearances on "Captain Noah Show," on WPVI-Television, 1971-76, and other radio and television programs. President of Delaware Valley department of Council on Abandoned Military Posts, 1970—; member of board of directors and executive committee of Philadelphia Council for International Visitors, 1975—; member of president's council of advisers at La Salle College. *Military service:* U.S. Army, Security Agency, 1960-61.

MEMBER: American Association for State and Local History, National Association of Housing and Redevelopment Officials, Company of Military Historians (treasurer of Philadelphia area chapter), Historical Society of Pennsylvania, Shackamaxon Society (president, 1965—), Friends of the Philadelphia Free Library, Tau Alpha Pi.

AWARDS, HONORS: Philadelphia Copy Club annual award, 1961; Foundation for Community Health citation, 1963; certificate of excellence from Philadelphia Art Directors' Club, 1965; National Retail Merchants Association gold medal, 1965, silver medal, 1966; George Washington Honor Medal from Freedoms Foundation, 1970, and George Washington Honor Certificate, 1973, both for "A Fort Mifflin Diary"; Valley Forge Honor Certificate, 1974, for "Old Fort Mifflin: The Defenders"; America the Beautiful Award from *Holiday,* 1971; recognized by Pennsylvania House of Representatives, 1972, and by Governor of Pennsylvania, 1974; Legion of Honor from Chapel of the Four Chaplains, 1975; Colonial Dames state award, 1975, and national award, 1976, and Daughters of the American Revolution national bicentennial award, 1976, all for *Street Names of Philadelphia.*

WRITINGS: Street Names of Philadelphia, Temple University Press, 1975. Author of pamphlets: "Historic Churches of Pennsylvania," 1965, "The Men of Mifflin," 1970, "The Spirit of the Men of Mifflin," 1971, "A Glossary of Fortification Terms," 1972, "A Fort Mifflin Diary," 1973, "Old Fort Mifflin: "The Defenders," 1974, "Just Some Girl" (poems), 1974, and "Old Fort Mifflin: The Buildings and Structures," 1976.

Author of "Past Prolog" scripts on American history, for WCAU-FM Radio, 1976. Contributor to local and national history journals.

WORK IN PROGRESS: Research for *Stop the Evil,* a nonfiction account of a Civil War deserter who was hanged for desertion and murder.

SIDELIGHTS: Alotta writes: "I hated history when I was in school, perhaps because I couldn't remember all the dates. So, I decided to write history as I felt it should be written—sort of putting my money where my mouth is. Maybe I've been lucky as a writer."

His attempts to make history more interesting include his association with The Shackamaxon Society, which he founded to care for Old Fort Mifflin, an abandoned structure in southwest Philadelphia, and his creation of the Old Fort Mifflin Guard, a Revolutionary War re-enactment group for young men and boys. Civic activities of a more light-hearted nature include his W. C. Fields Birthday Party, Philadelphia-New York Hoagie Competition and Eat, and Penn's Landing Celebration. He has also served as a judge for Philadelphia's Mummer's Day Parade. Recently, he has been working with the Free Library of Philadelphia on a program for school-age children, "Touch the Author."

* * *

ALTHER, Lisa 1944-

PERSONAL: Born July 23, 1944, in Tennessee; daughter of John Shelton (a surgeon) and Alice Margaret (Greene) Reed; married Richard Philip Alther (a painter), August 26, 1966; children: Sara Halsey. *Education:* Wellesley College, B.A., 1966. *Politics:* None. *Religion:* None. *Address:* c/o Alfred A. Knopf, Inc., 201 East 50th St., New York, N.Y. 10022.

CAREER: Atheneum Publishers, New York, N.Y., secretary and editorial assistant, 1967; free-lance writer, 1967—. Writer for Garden Way, Inc., Charlotte, Vt., 1970-71. Member of board of directors of Planned Parenthood of Champlain Valley, 1972. *Member:* Authors Guild of Authors League of America, P.E.N.

WRITINGS: Kinflicks (novel), Knopf, 1976. Contributor of articles and stories to national magazines, including *Vogue, McCall's, Cosmopolitan, Natural History, New Society, Yankee, Vermont Freeman, New Englander, New Times,* and *Mankind.*

WORK IN PROGRESS: A novel.

* * *

ALTMAN, Frances 1937-

PERSONAL: Born September 5, 1937, in Los Angeles, Calif.; daughter of W. F. and Ethel (Baker) Green; married Charles O. Altman, 1958. *Education:* Attended University of Tulsa. *Home:* 415 West Braeside, Arlington Heights, Ill. 60004. *Office:* 400 West Madison, Chicago, Ill. 60606.

CAREER: Day Publications, Chicago, Ill., special features editor, 1967-70; Paddock Publications, Arlington Heights, Ill., promotions director, 1970-72; *Suburban Week,* Chicago, Ill., managing editor, 1972-74; *Countryside Living,* Barrington, Ill., editor, 1975—; National Hot Dog and Sausage Council, Chicago, Ill., public relations work, 1976—.

MEMBER: National Woman's Press Association (vice-president, 1975-76), National League of American Pen Women, National Federation of Press Women, Midwest Writer's Association, Illinois Woman's Press Association, Chicago Children's Roundtable. *Awards, honors:* Alma Award from National Appliance Industry, 1969, 1970; National Federation of Press Women feature story awards, 1971, 1974, and 1976, news story award, 1972, news and features award, 1973, promotion award, 1973; John Cotton Cana Award from Northern Illinois Library Association, 1973; also awards from Illinois Press Woman's Association.

WRITINGS—For children: *Reggie the Goat*, Denison, 1966; *George Gershwin, Composer*, Denison, 1968; *Herbert V. Prochnow, Banker*, Denison, 1969; *The Something Egg*, Denison, 1970; *Dwight D. Eisenhower, Crusader for Peace*, Denison, 1970; *Douglas A. MacArthur, Soldier*, Denison, 1974.

Author of scripts for "Mr. Stibbs" documentary film, 1974, and "Antique World" tape recording for WRN Agency and Comptron Corp., 1975. Contributor to trade journals, children's magazines, and national periodicals, including *Business Week, Lady's Circle,* and *Press Woman*.

*   *   *

ALUKO, Timothy Mofolorunso 1918-

PERSONAL: Born June 14, 1918, in Ilesha, West Nigeria; married Janet Adebisi Fajemisin, 1950; children: six. *Education:* Attended Government College, Ibadan, 1933-38, and University of Lagos; University of London, B.Sc., 1950, Diploma in Town Planning, 1950; University of Newcastle upon Tyne, M.Sc., 1969. *Office:* Faculty of Engineering, University of Lagos, Lagos, Nigeria.

CAREER: Employed in public works department, Lagos, Nigeria, 1943-46; executive engineer in public works department, Ibadan, Nigeria, and Lagos, 1950-56; town engineer, Lagos Town Council, Lagos, 1956-60; director and permanent secretary, Ministry of Works and Transport, Western Region, Nigeria, 1960-66; University of Ibadan, Ibadan, Nigeria, senior lecturer, 1966; University of Lagos, Lagos, research fellow in municipal engineering, 1966—. *Member:* Institution of Civil Engineers (fellow), Institution of Municipal Engineers, Nigerian Society of Engineers. *Awards, honors:* Officer, Order of the British Empire, 1963; Officer, Order of the Niger, 1964.

WRITINGS—Novels: *One Man One Wife*, Nigerian Printing and Publishing Co., 1959, Humanities Press, 1968; *One Man, One Matchet*, Heinemann, 1964, Verrey, 1965; *Kinsman and Foreman*, Heinemann, 1966; *Chief the Honourable Minister*, Humanities Press, 1970; *His Worshipful Majesty*, Heinemann, 1972. Work included in *African New Writing*, Lutterworth Press, 1947. Contributor of short stories to *West African Review*.

SIDELIGHTS: Timothy Aluko is from Yoruba country, and as the Yoruba, unlike most of their neighbors, have a lengthy tradition of dwelling in towns, it is fitting that he should have specialized in town planning. He began to write in his 'twenties, and some of his short stories were broadcast on a BBC program, *Calling Africa*.

BIOGRAPHICAL/CRITICAL SOURCES: Margaret Laurence, *Long Drums and Cannons*, Macmillan, 1968.*

*   *   *

ALVERSON, Donna 1933-

PERSONAL: Born March 21, 1933, in Watseka, Ill.; daughter of W. Howard (a rancher) and Donna (Rosenberger) Walker; married Jimmie F. Alverson (a rancher and owner of an animal serum company), December 27, 1950 (divorced, December, 1965); children: Jimmie F., Jr. *Education:* Attended Cherry Hill Business Academy. *Home:* Honeycutt Farm, 51 Grassy Lake Rd., Archer, Fla. 32618. *Agent:* Hoffman/Sheedy, 145 West 86th St., New York, N.Y. 10024.

CAREER: Professional barrel racer in rodeos, 1947-62; Office of the District Attorney, Fort Worth, Tex., legal secretary, 1962-65; district court clerk for Tarrant County, Tex., 1965-67; *Quarter Racing Record,* Fort Worth, Tex., editor, 1967-70; Pratt & Whitney Aircraft, Fort Worth, legal secretary, 1970-71; *Florida Horse*, Ocala, Fla., editor, 1972-74; breeder of thoroughbred horses and Santa Gertrudis cattle, 1972—. Public relations representative for Ocala Breeders Sales Co., 1974-75.

MEMBER: American Quarter Horse Association, Rodeo Cowboys Association, Girls Rodeo Association, Florida Thoroughbred Breeders Association, Marion County Art League, Committee of One Hundred (Ocala). *Awards, honors:* First person award from *Reader's Digest*, for "The Story of Jeep Honeycutt, an American Quarter Horse."

WRITINGS: Drum Runnin' Fool (novel), Reader's Digest Press, 1976. Contributor of stories and articles to horseman's journals.

WORK IN PROGRESS: The Fires of Summer; Nasrullah's Song; The Passing of Spring, completion expected in 1978; research for *Thoroughbred and Quarter Horse Cross.*

SIDELIGHTS: Donna Alverson writes: "*Drum Runnin' Fool* is not a children's book. It can be read by teen-agers, which in today's market is a feat not easily accomplished. . . . [It] is the story of one of the finest American Quarter Horses that I have been privileged to own. . . . I drew upon my experiences in the arena, and my sister's, to create the character of Anna Norman. . . . The novels on which I am currently working all reflect my love of the south, its people and the out-of-doors. One, in particular, *Nasrullah's Song*, is the story of an industry built on the horse, the American Thoroughbred. . . . I grew up with fine horses, courageous men and stubborn women . . . and thousands of acres over which to ride and work cattle. We were working ranch people, born with a love for the land and a grass roots philosophy of people and things that has somehow been pushed aside in the last few decades. Perhaps the current generation's tentative reachings toward the land and agriculture will restore some of the camaraderie that is so elusive and lacking within today's cutthroat business world."

AVOCATIONAL INTERESTS: Travel, oil painting, making pen and ink drawings, caring for "stray dogs and cats, poor calves, and thin horses."

BIOGRAPHICAL/CRITICAL SOURCES: Kirkus, September 15, 1976.

*   *   *

AMIN, Ali 1913(?)-1976

1913(?)—April 3, 1976; Egyptian journalist and founder of newspapers. Obituaries: *New York Times*, April 4, 1976.

*   *   *

AMIS, Martin 1949-

PERSONAL: Born August 25, 1949, in Oxford, England;

son of Kingsley William (the writer) and Hilary (Bardwell) Amis. *Education:* Oxford University, B.A. (honors), 1971. *Home:* 14 Kensington Gardens Sq., London W.2, England. *Agent:* A. D. Peters, 10 Buckingham St., Adelphi, London W.C.2, England. *Office: New Statesman,* 10 GT Turnstile, London W.C.2, England.

CAREER: Times Literary Supplement, London, England, editorial assistant, 1972-75; *New Statesman,* London, assistant literary editor, 1975—. *Awards, honors:* Somerset Maugham Award from National Book League, 1974, for *The Rachel Papers.*

WRITINGS—Novels: *The Rachel Papers,* J. Cape, 1973, Knopf, 1974; *Dead Babies,* J. Cape, 1975, Knopf, 1976. Contributor to London newspapers.

WORK IN PROGRESS: A novel, *Success.*

BIOGRAPHICAL/CRITICAL SOURCES: Contemporary Literary Criticism, Volume IV, Gale, 1975.

* * *

ANAND, Mulk Raj 1905-

PERSONAL: Born December 12, 1905, in Peshawar, India; son of Lal Chand (a coppersmith and soldier) and Ishwar (Kaur) Anand; married Kathleen Van Gelder (an actress), 1939 (divorced, 1948); married Shirin Vajifdar (a classical dancer), 1949; children: one daughter. *Education:* University of Punjab, B.A. (with honors), 1924; University College, London, Ph.D., 1929; additional study at Cambridge University, 1929-30. *Home:* 25 Cuffe Parade, Colaba, Bombay 5, India. *Agent:* David Hingham, 5-8, Lower John St., Golden Sq., London W1R 4HA, England. *Office:* MARG Publications, Army & Navy Building, 148, Mahatma Gandhi Rd., Bombay 400023, India.

CAREER: Novelist, essayist, and lecturer. Fought with Republicans in Spanish Civil War, 1937-38; helped found the Progressive Writer's Movement in India, 1938; lecturer in literature and philosophy at London County Council Adult Education Schools and worked as broadcaster and scriptwriter in films division for British Broadcasting Corp., 1939-45; lecturer at various Indian universities, 1948-63; Tagore Professor of Fine Arts at University of Punjab, 1963-66; visiting professor at Institute of Advanced Studies in Simla, 1967-68; president of Lokayata Trust (an organization developing community and cultural centers in India), 1970—. *Member:* Indian National Academy of Art (fine arts chairman, 1965-70), Indian National Academy of Letters, Sahitya Academy, National Book Trust of India, Arts Theatre Club (London). *Awards, honors:* Leverhulme fellow, 1940-42; International Peace Prize from World Council of Peace, 1952, for promoting understanding among nations; Padma Bhusan, 1968.

WRITINGS—Novels: *Untouchable,* preface by E. M. Forster, Wishart, 1935, Hutchinson, 1947, revised edition, Bodley Head, 1970; *Coolie,* Lawrence & Wishart, 1936, Liberty Press, 1952, new revised edition, Bodley Head, 1972; *Two Leaves and a Bud,* Lawrence & Wishart, 1937, Liberty Press, 1954; *Lament on the Death of a Master of Arts,* Naya Sansar (Lucknow, India), 1938; *The Village,* J. Cape, 1939; *Across the Black Waters,* J. Cape, 1940; *The Sword and the Sickle,* J. Cape, 1942; *The Big Heart,* Hutchinson, 1945; *Seven Summers: The Story of an Indian Childhood* (Book I of septet, "Seven Ages of Man"), Hutchinson, 1951; *Private Life of an Indian Prince,* Hutchinson, 1953, revised edition, Bodley Head, 1970; *The Old Woman and the Cow,* Kutub-Popular (Bombay, India), 1960; *The*

Road, Sterling (New Delhi, India), 1961; *Death of a Hero: Epitaph for Maqbool Sherwani,* Kutub-Popular, 1963; *Morning Face* (Book II of septet, "Seven Ages of Man") Kutub-Popular, 1968. Also author of *Confessions of a Lover* (Book III of the septet), Arnold-Heinemann (New Delhi, India).

Stories: *The Lost Child and Other Stories,* J. A. Allen, 1934; *The Barber's Trade Union and Other Stories,* J. Cape, 1944; *Indian Fairy Tales* [*Retold*], Kutub-Popular, 1946, 2nd edition, 1966; *The Tractor and the Corn Goddess and Other Stories,* Thacker (Bombay), 1947; *Reflections on the Golden Bed and Other Stories,* Current Book House (Bombay), 1954; *The Power of Darkness and Other Stories,* Jaico (Bombay), 1959; *More Indian Fairy Tales,* Kutub-Popular, 1961; *Lajwanti and Other Stories,* Jaico, 1966; *Between Tears and Laughter and Other Stories,* Sterling, 1973.

Nonfiction: *Persian Painting,* Faber, 1931; *Curries and Other Indian Dishes,* Harmsworth, 1932; *The Golden Breath: Studies in Five Poets of the New India,* Dutton, 1933; *The Hindu View of Art,* Allen & Unwin, 1933, 2nd edition published as *The Hindu View of Art With an Introductory Essay on Art and Reality by Eric Gill,* Asia Publishing House, 1957; *Apology for Heroism: A Brief Autobiography of Ideas,* Drummond, 1934, 2nd edition, Kutub-Popular, 1957; *Letters on India,* Transatlantic, 1942; *Homage to Tagore,* Sangam (Lahore, India), 1946; (with Krishna Hutheesing) *The Bride's Book of Beauty,* Kutub-Popular, 1947; *On Education,* Hind Kitabs (Bombay), 1947; *The Story of India* (juvenile history), Kutub-Popular, 1948; *The King-Emperor's English; or, The Role of the English Language in Free India,* Hind Kitabs, 1948; *Lines Written to an Indian Air: Essays,* Nalanda (Bombay), 1949; *The Indian Theatre,* Dobson, 1950, Roy, 1951; *The Story of Man* (juvenile natural history) Sikh (Delhi), 1954; *The Dancing Foot,* Publications Division, Indian Ministry of Information & Broadcasting (Delhi), 1957; *Kama Kala: Some Notes on the Philosophical Basis of Hindu Erotic Sculpture,* Nagel, 1958; (author of introduction and text) *India in Color,* McGraw, 1958.

(With Stella Kramrisch) *Homage to Khajuraho,* Marg Publications (Bombay), 1960, 2nd edition, 1962; *Is There a Contemporary Indian Civilisation?,* Asia Publishing House, 1963; *The Third Eye: A Lecture on the Appreciation of Art,* edited by Diwan Chand Sharma, privately printed for the University of Punjab, 1963; (with Hebbar) *The Singing Line,* Western Printers & Publishers, 1964; (with others) *Inde, Napal, Ceylan* (French guidebook), Editions Vilo (Paris), 1965; *Bombay,* Marg Publications, 1965; *Design for Living,* Marg Publications, 1967; *The Volcano: Some Comments on the Development of Rabindranath Tagore's Aesthetic Theories and Art Practice,* Maharaja Sayajirao University of Baroda, 1967; *The Humanism of M. K. Gandhi, Three Lectures,* University of Punjab, 1967; (with others) *Konarak,* Marg Publications, 1968; (author of text) *Ajanta,* Marg Publications, 1971; *Album of Indian Paintings,* National Book Trust (New Delhi), 1973.

Editor: *Marx and Engels on India,* Socialist Book Club (Allahabad, India), 1933; (with Iqbal Singh) *Indian Short Stories,* New India (London), 1946; Ananda Kentish Coomaraswamy, *Introduction to Indian Art,* Theosophical Publishing, 1956; *Delhi, Agra,* [*and*] *Sikri,* Marg Publications, 1960; *Annals of Childhood,* Kranchalson (Agra, India), 1968; *Experiments: Contemporary Indian Short Stories,* Kranchalson, 1968; *Grassroots* (short stories), Kranchalson, 1968; *Contemporary World Sculpture,* Marg Publications, 1968.

Editor of numerous magazines and journals, 1930—, including *Marg* (Indian art quarterly), 1946—.

WORK IN PROGRESS: Remaining four books of septet, "Seven Ages of Man," tentatively titled *The Bubble, And So He Plays His Part, A World Too Wide,* and *Last Scene;* a book on the appreciation of art, *Seven Little Known Birds of the Inner Eye; or, How to Taste a Picture,* for Charles E. Tuttle (Tokyo); Tagore lecture on Indian fiction, *A Novel Form in the Ocean of Story,* for Punjab University Publication Bureau.

SIDELIGHTS: Anand told *CA:* "I believe in the only ism possible in our age—humanism. I feel that man can grow into the highest consciousness from insights into the nature of human experience derived through creative art and literature. The piling up of these insights may make a man survive at some level of the quality of life, in our tragic age.

"I believe in co-existence among human beings and co-discovery of cultures. I believe the world must end the arms race and get five percent disarmament to give resources for building basic plenty throughout the world by the year 2000.

"I believe, though man has fallen very low at various times in history, he is not so bad that he will not survive on this planet—as long as the earth does not grow cold. I always dream the earth is not flat, but round."

BIOGRAPHICAL/CRITICAL SOURCES: Scrutiny, June, 1935; Jack Lindsay, *The Lotus and the Elephant,* Kutub-Popular, 1954; K. R. Srinivasa Iyengar, *Indian Writing in English,* Asia Publishing House, 1962; *Contemporary Indian Literature,* December, 1965; D. Riemenschneider, *The Ideal of Man in Anand's Novels,* Kutub-Popular, 1969; Margaret Berry, *Mulk Raj Anand: Man and Novelist,* Beale (Amsterdam), 1970.

*   *   *

ANDERSEN, Marianne S(inger) 1934-

PERSONAL: Born June 24, 1934, in Austria; came to the United States in 1940, naturalized citizen, 1944; daughter of Richard (a physician) and Jolanthe (an opera singer; maiden name, Garda) Singer; married Arnold Andersen (a diplomat and publishing executive; separated); children: Richard Esten. *Education:* Hunter College of the City University of New York, B.A., 1954, M.A., 1974; further graduate study at International Graduate University, 1974—. *Home:* 60 West 57th St., New York, N.Y. 10019. *Office:* School of Behavioral Science, International Graduate University, 205 West End Ave., Suite 1P, New York, N.Y. 10023.

CAREER: Free-lance editor and writer in New York City; Jarrow Press, Inc., Boston, Mass., trade book editor, 1970-72; Collins Associates, New York City, trade book editor and writer, 1972-74; International Graduate University, New York, N.Y., director of administration, 1974—. Research and editorial associate of Institute for Research in Hypnosis, 1974—. Former member of United Nations Hospitality Committee. *Member:* American Psychological Association (associate member), Society for Clinical and Experimental Hypnosis (student affiliate member).

WRITINGS: (Editor) *Sterling Guide to Summer Jobs,* Sterling, 1956; (with Louis M. Savary) *Passages: A Guide for Pilgrims of the Mind,* Harper, 1972. Managing editor of *Freelancer's Newsletter,* 1970-72.

WORK IN PROGRESS: Research on the management of hypertension by hypnotherapy and on obesity, stress, and general psychosomatic subjects.

SIDELIGHTS: Marianne Andersen writes: "Writing/editing and psychology have always been my dominant interests. In my publishing career these were combined, through my specialization in books in the mental health field. I plan to resume writing for the trade market, since I am strongly committed to the dissemination of accurate information—especially on my specialty of hypnosis and hypnotherapy." *Avocational interests:* Music.

*   *   *

ANDERSON, Charles Burroughs 1905-

PERSONAL: Born March 4, 1905, in Washington, Iowa; son of Marion Thompson (a salesman) and Lucy (a church organist; maiden name, Burroughs) Anderson; married Herta Lindke, August 20, 1938 (divorced, 1946); married Frances Louise Wallace, May 27, 1946. *Education:* University of Chicago, Ph.B., 1926; Columbia University, M.A., 1929; University of Paris, further graduate study, 1931; University of Berlin, diploma, 1933. *Politics:* Independent. *Religion:* "No formal affiliation." *Home:* 554 Riverside Dr., Ormond Beach, Fla. 32074. *Office:* Anderson's Book Shop, 96-98 Chatsworth Ave., Larchmont, N.Y. 10538.

CAREER: Secondary school teacher in Greenwich, Conn., 1926-28; Columbia University, New York, N.Y., instructor in English, 1929-31; Berlitz Institute, Berlin, Germany, teacher of English, 1933; teacher of English and German at Horace Mann School, New York, N.Y., 1934-45; Anderson's Book Shop, Larchmont, N.Y., owner, 1946—. Lecturer at New York University, 1959-62. Supervisor for College Entrance Examination Board, 1933-39.

MEMBER: American Booksellers Association (honorary life member; member of board of directors, 1954-62, 1964-73, chairman of board, 1960-62; president, 1958-60), Library Club of America (member of board of directors, 1959), National Committee for Florence Agreement (member of board of directors, 1960-68), English Graduate Union (Columbia University), Princeton University Club, Alpha Delta Phi, Lions Club.

WRITINGS: Common Errors in English Corrected, Van Nostrand, 1931; *Rapid Vocabulary Builder,* Van Nostrand, 1931; *Guide to Good Pronunciation,* Van Nostrand, 1931; (translator with Bessie Schonberg) Curt Sachs, *World History of the Dance,* Norton, 1939; (editor) *A Manual on Bookselling,* Crown, 1974; (editor) *Bookselling in America and the World,* Quadrangle, 1975. Contributor to magazines. Editor-in-chief for American Booksellers Association, 1972-75.

*   *   *

ANDERSON, H(obson) Dewey 1897-1975

PERSONAL: Born January 14, 1897, in Grand Forks, N.D.; son of Hans D. and Amalia B. (Peterson) Anderson; married Erma Sams, June 30, 1920; married second wife, Shirley Charles Nichols, November 14, 1969; children: (first marriage) Harry, June Anderson Jensen; (second marriage—stepchildren) Isabel Swisher, Alan Nichols. *Education:* Stanford University, A.B., 1927, M.A., 1928, Ph.D., 1932. *Politics:* Democrat. *Religion:* Methodist. *Residence:* Carmel, Calif.

CAREER: Executive of Prisoner of War Work and Relief in Poland and the Baltic countries, 1921-24; executive of American section of European Student Relief in Russia, 1924-27; Stanford University, Stanford, Calif., faculty member and director of Stanford-Alaska Educational Study, 1930-34;

member of California state assembly, 1935-37; appointed budgeteer by California governor-elect, 1938-39; administrator of California State Relief Administration, 1939; Temporary National Economic Committee, Washington, D.C., economic counsel and executive secretary, 1939-41; Board of Economic Warfare, Washington, D.C., chief of American Hemisphere Division, 1942; U.S. Department of State, Washington, D.C., chief of Supply and Transport Division in Office of Foreign Relief and Rehabilitation, 1943; War Food Administration, Washington, D.C., member of food advisory committee, 1943; founding member and chief of field operations for United Nations Relief and Rehabilitation Administration, 1944; U.S. Senate, Washington, D.C., executive secretary of Small Business Committee, 1945; writer, economist, and cattle rancher, 1945-75. Former executive director of Public Affairs Institute and member of board of directors of Citizens Committee on Natural Resources. Senior physical director of Coast Defenses for Puget Sound, 1917-18; director of research on economic problems for John Randolph and Dora Haynes Foundation, 1936-38; co-director of Stanford University's Institute for Occupational Research. President of California Conference on Social Work, 1938-39.

MEMBER: American Economic Association, American Political Science Association, National Press Club, Phi Beta Kappa, Phi Delta Kappa (president; national council delegate).

WRITINGS: (With Percy E. Davidson) *Occupational Trends in the United States,* Stanford University Press, 1940; *California State Government,* Stanford University Press, 1942; (with Davidson) *Ballots and the Democratic Class Struggle: A Study in the Background of Political Education,* Stanford University Press, 1943; (with Davidson) *Recent Occupational Trends in American Labor* (supplement to *Occupational Trends in the United States*), Stanford University Press, 1945; (with others) *The Future of Independent Business,* U.S. Government Printing Office, 1947; (with Michael Marks Davis) *Medical Care for the Individual and the Issue of Compulsory Health Insurance,* U.S. Government Printing Office, 1948; *An Action Program for the Redwood Forest of California,* Public Affairs Institute, 1949.

(With Hilmar Stephen Raushenbush) *A Policy and Program for Success,* Public Affairs Institute, 1950; *Aluminum for Defense and Prosperity,* Public Affairs Institute, 1951; (with others) *The Arab Refugee Problem, How It Can Be Solved: Proposals Submitted to the General Assembly of the United Nations,* privately printed, 1951; (with others) *The Defense of America,* Public Affairs Institute, 1951; (with Raushenbush) *To Make a Free World: An Exploration of a New Foreign Policy,* Public Affairs Institute, 1955; *The Present Day Doctor of Chiropractic,* Public Affairs Institute, 1956; *Health Service Is a Basic Right of All the People,* Public Affairs Institute, 1956; *Meeting California's Water Needs,* Public Affairs Institute, 1958; *Voting in California: Tabulations and Comments on Registration, Senatorial and Gubernatorial Elections, 1932-1956, with Application to the 1958 Elections,* Public Affairs Institute, 1958; (with others) *Natural Resources: Their Protection and Development,* Public Affairs Institute, 1959.

(With others) *The People and 1960: Statements of Facts and Opinion on Twenty-Four of the Most Important Issues Confronting the American People Today,* Public Affairs Institute, 1960.

Always to Start Anew: The Making of a Public Activist, Vantage, 1970.

OBITUARIES: Washington Post, August 10, 1975.*

(Died August 4, 1975, in Lassen County, Calif.)

*   *   *

ANDERSON, Joan Wester 1938-

PERSONAL: Born August 12, 1938, in Evanston, Ill.; daughter of Theodore (an electronics engineer) and Monica (Noesges) Wester; married William H. Anderson (an insurance agent), August 20, 1960; children: Christopher, Timothy, William, Brian, Nancy. *Education:* Attended Mount Mary College. *Religion:* Roman Catholic. *Home:* 811 North Hickory, Arlington Heights, Ill. 60004.

CAREER: WIND-Radio, Chicago, Ill., music librarian, 1959-61; free-lance writer, 1973—. Performed in local little theater productions and directed and performed in a quartet accompanying vocalists on record albums, both 1959-61.

WRITINGS: (With Ann Toland Serb) *Love, Lollipops and Laundry* (humor), Our Sunday Visitor Press, 1976. Contributor of more than one hundred-forty articles to magazines, including *Catholic Digest, Life and Health, Day Care and Early Education,* and *True Romance,* and to newspapers. Guest columnist in *Marriage.*

WORK IN PROGRESS: A sequel to *Love, Lollipops and Laundry,* with Ann Toland Serb; preparing a weekly humor column.

SIDELIGHTS: Joan Anderson writes: "As a full-time housewife, I believe that we are perhaps the most ignored minority group in society today. To counteract the effects of the media, I began my writing career by directing uplifting and humorous material to housewives, reinforcing their own feelings of self-worth. I later branched out into interview and research pieces, but my housewife-oriented material, as seen in *Love, Lollipops and Laundry,* remains the favorite among my readers, judging by my mail. Believing strongly that there is life after motherhood, I strongly urge all housebound women to take advantage of their situation by developing their potential and personal interests within their family structure. If I can do it, anyone can!"

*   *   *

ANDERSON, Luther A(dolph)

PERSONAL: Born in Ironwood, Mich.; son of Peter Edward and Carolina (Gustafson) Anderson; married Ethel Marie Martin (a teacher), August 1, 1938. *Education:* DePaul College of Commerce, B.C.S., 1924; University of Chicago, Ph.B., 1927. *Home and office:* 139 South Curry St., Ironwood, Mich. 49938. *Agent:* Dominick Abel Literary Services, 529 South Wabash, Chicago, Ill. 60605.

CAREER: Haskins & Sells (an accounting firm), Chicago, Ill., public accountant, 1928-29; Price Waterhouse & Co. (an accounting firm), Milwaukee, Wis., public accountant, 1930-31; Armour & Co. (meat packers), Ironwood, Mich., private accountant, 1931-63; writer, 1963—.

WRITINGS: Hunting, Fishing, and Camping, Macmillan, 1945; *Hunting the American Game Field,* Ziff-Davis, 1949; *How to Hunt Deer and Small Game,* Ronald, 1959; *How to Hunt Whitetail Deer,* Funk, 1968; *How to Hunt American Small Game,* Funk, 1969; *A Guide to Canoe Camping,* Reilly & Lee, 1969; *Hunting the Uplands with Shotgun and Rifle,* Winchester Press, 1976.

*   *   *

ANDERSON, Ray Sherman 1925-

PERSONAL: Born August 22, 1925, in South Dakota; son

of Albert Sherman (a farmer) and Alma H. (Christensen) Anderson; married Mildred Mary Babb, August 28, 1946; children: Carol (Mrs. Timothy Purga), Jollene, Ruth. *Education:* South Dakota State University, B.S., 1949; Fuller Theological Seminary, B.D., 1959; University of Edinburgh, Ph.D., 1972. *Home:* 2182 Sycamore Canyon, Santa Barbara, Calif. 93108. *Office:* Department of Theology, Fuller Theological Seminary, 135 North Oakland, Pasadena, Calif. 91101.

CAREER: Pastor of Evangelical Free Church in Covina, Calif., 1959-70; Westmont College, Santa Barbara, Calif., assistant professor of theology, 1972-76; Fuller Theological Seminary, Pasadena, Calif., associate professor of theology and assistant dean, 1976—. *Military service:* U.S. Army Air Forces, navigator, 1943-45; became first lieutenant. *Awards, honors:* Fellow of Case Study Institute, Cambridge, 1976.

WRITINGS: Like Living Stones, Free Church Publications, 1964; *Historical Transcendence and the Reality of God,* Eerdmans, 1975.

WORK IN PROGRESS: Theological Foundations for Ministry: Selected Readings for a Theology of the Church in Ministry.

SIDELIGHTS: Anderson writes: "I discovered the relevance of theology while involved in ministry, and am now exploring the relevance of ministry for theology!"

* * *

ANDERSON, Shirley Lord 1934-
(Shirley Lord)

PERSONAL: Born August 28, 1934, in London, England; came to the United States in 1971; daughter of Francis James (a company director) and Mabel (Williamson) Stringer; married: Cyril Lord, January 17, 1960 (divorced, December, 1973); married David Jean Anderson (a business consultant), August 3, 1974; *Education:* Attended secondary school in Essex, England. *Politics:* Conservative. *Religion:* Roman Catholic. *Home:* 1 PeatHole Lane, Bellport, N.Y. *Office:* Helena Rubinstein, 300 Park Ave., New York, N.Y. 10022.

CAREER: London Star, London, England, woman's editor, 1960-61; *Evening Standard,* London, woman's editor, 1961-63; *Harper's Bazaar,* London and New York, N.Y., beauty and health editor, 1963-73; *Vogue,* New York City, beauty and health editor, 1973-75; Helena Rubinstein, New York City, vice-president for Corporate Relations, 1975—. "Be Beautiful," a column syndicated by Field Syndicate, 1975—, appears in about fifty newspapers. Professional tours in England and the United States include "Shirley Lord Show" and Shirley Lord Beauty Breakfast." City commissioner for Craigavan, Northern Ireland.

WRITINGS: Small Beer at Claridge's (autobiography), M. Joseph, 1968; *The Easy Way to Good Looks,* Crowell, 1976. Woman's editor for London's Evening News, *1963-67.*

WORK IN PROGRESS: A series of twelve books on beauty, health, and psyche; a radio series on teenage beauty; a novel.

* * *

ANDERTON, David A(lbin) 1919-

PERSONAL: Born May 7, 1919, in Paterson, N.J.; son of John T. (a silk mill owner) and Helen (Smith) Anderton; married: Katherine Meili, June 13, 1942; children: Bruce David, Craig Douglas. *Education:* Rensselaer Polytechnic

Institute, B.A.E., 1941. *Home and office:* 30 South Murray Ave., Ridgewood, N.J. 07450.

CAREER: Grumman Aircraft, Bethpage, N.Y., engineer, 1941-46; General Electric Co., Schenectady, N.Y., project engineer, 1946-50; *Aviation Week,* New York, N.Y., technical editor, 1950-63; free-lance writer and photographer, 1963—. Has lectured on aerospace, travel, and jazz, and taught courses in aerodynamics. *Member:* American Society of Journalists and Authors, American Society of Magazine Photographers, Professional Photographers of America, American Institute of Aeronautics and Astronautics, Aviation/Space Writers Association.

WRITINGS: Strategic Air Command, Ian Allen, 1975, Scribner, 1976. Contributor to technical and trade journals in the United States and abroad.

WORK IN PROGRESS: Laboratory in Space: The Story of Skylab, for National Aeronautics and Space Administration (NASA); *Superfortress at War,* publication expected by Ian Allan.

SIDELIGHTS: Anderton writes: "I write for fun and I write for money, and as long as there is some of both on any given assignment, I'm happy. I approach my photographic assignments the same way. I like to believe in the subjects I write about, which tends sometimes to be limiting, but I sleep well." *Avocational interests:* "I play drums in, and manage, two bands. One is a big (seventeen-piece) swing-era band, and the other is a traditional jazz sextette," building models (especially airplanes), collecting aviation classics and old books, collecting jazz records.

* * *

ANDONIAN, Jeanne (Beghian) 1891(?)-1976

1891(?)—March 3, 1976; educator, lecturer, and novelist under pseudonym Janine May. Obituaries: *New York Times,* March 5, 1976.

* * *

ANDREASEN, Alan R(obert) 1934-

PERSONAL: Born December 1, 1934, in Toronto, Ontario, Canada; came to the United States in 1962; son of Oho William and Marjorie Gertrude Andreasen; married Margaret Clare Schlaeger, August 7, 1965; children: Elizabeth Maia. *Education:* University of Western Ontario, B.A., 1956; Columbia University, M.S., 1959, Ph.D., 1964. *Home:* 13 Persimmon Circle, Urbana, Ill. 61801. *Office:* Survey Research Laboratory, University of Illinois, Urbana, Ill. 61822.

CAREER: State University of New York at Buffalo, lecturer, 1962-64, assistant professor, 1964-66, associate professor, 1966-72, professor of marketing and environmental analysis and policy, 1972-73; University of Illinois, Urbana—Champaign, professor of business administration and research professor at Survey Research Laboratory, 1974—. Visiting professor at Indian Institute of Management, summer, 1972; visiting associate professor at University of California, Los Angeles, 1973. Research associate of Marketing Science Institute, summers, 1964, 1965; director of Reckful Consultants, Inc., 1967-72; director of Champaign County Arts and Humanities Council, 1975—. *Member:* American Marketing Association, American Sociological Association, American Association for Public Opinion Research, Association for Consumer Research.

WRITINGS: Inner City Business: A Case Study of Buffalo, New York, Praeger, 1971; (editor and contributor) *Im-*

proving Inner City Marketing, American Marketing Association, 1972; *The Disadvantaged Consumer,* Free Press, 1975; (editor with Seymour Sudman) *Public Policy and Marketing Thought,* American Marketing Association, in press.

Contributor: Peter D. Bennett, editor, *Marketing and Economic Development,* American Marketing Association, 1965; David Kollatt and others, editors, *Research in Consumer Behavior,* Holt, 1970; Herman J. Peters, editor, *Vocational Guidance and Career Development,* 2nd edition (Andreasen was not included in 1st edition), Macmillan, 1970; Ralph Day and Thomas Ness, editors, *Models in Marketing: Behavioral Science Applications,* Intext Educational, 1971; Scott Ward and Peter Wright, editors, *Advances in Consumer Research,* Volume I, Association for Consumer Research, 1974. Contributor of about twenty-five articles and reviews to marketing and management journals. Member of editorial review board of *Journal of Marketing,* 1970—.

* * *

ANDRESKI, Iris
    See GILLESPIE, I(ris) S(ylvia)

* * *

ANDREW, J(ames) Dudley   1945-

PERSONAL: Born July 28, 1945, in Evansville, Ind.; son of James D. (an electronics engineer) and Lois J. (Zurlinden) Andrew; married Stephanie Phalen, February 1, 1969; children: Brigid Catherine, Ellen Jeannette, James Dudley. *Education:* University of Notre Dame, A.B., 1967; Columbia University, M.F.A., 1969; University of Iowa, Ph.D., 1972. *Religion:* Roman Catholic. *Home:* 1157 Court St., Iowa City, Iowa 52240. *Office:* Division of Broadcasting and Film, University of Iowa, 102 Old Armory, Iowa City, Iowa 52242.

CAREER: University of Iowa, Iowa City, instructor, 1969-72, assistant professor, 1972-75, associate professor of English and speech and dramatic art, 1975—, head of film division, 1972—. Visiting professor at Colorado College, summers, 1970, 1974-76. Director of summer seminar, National Endowment for the Humanities, 1977. *Member:* Council on International Educational Exchange (member of directorial board of Paris film program), Society for Cinema Studies, Speech Communication Association of America, American Film Institute, Committee on Institutional Cooperation (member of film panel), Midwest Modern Language Association (founder of film and literature section). *Awards, honors:* Woodrow Wilson fellowship, 1967; Danforth fellow, 1967-72; Old Gold summer fellowship, 1972; National Endowment for the Humanities fellowship for younger humanists, 1973-74.

WRITINGS: The Major Film Theorists, Oxford University Press, 1976; *Andre Bazin: His Life and Work,* Oxford University Press, in press. Guest editor, *Quarterly Review of Film Studies;* member of editorial boards of *Quarterly Journal of Speech* and *Research in Film.*

* * *

ANDREWS, Bart   1945-

PERSONAL: Name originally Andrew Stephen Ferreri; name legally changed, 1964; born February 25, 1945, in Brooklyn, N.Y.; son of Joseph (a businessman) and Camille (Sollecito) Ferreri; divorced. *Education:* New York University, B.A., 1963. *Home address:* P.O. Box 727, Hollywood,

Calif. 90028. *Agent:* James Trupin, P.O. Box 276, Hastings-on-Hudson, N.Y. 10706.

CAREER: Prospect House (resort hotel), Lake Bomoseen, Vt.; social director, 1959-63; Columbia Broadcasting System (CBS), New York, N.Y., writer, 1963-64; free-lance television writer in Hollywood, Calif., 1964—. *Member:* American Society of Composers, Authors and Publishers, Authors Guild of Authors League of America, Writers Guild of America (West).

WRITINGS: Different Spokes for Different Folks (humor), Serendipity Press, 1973; *Official TV Trivia Quiz Book.* New American Library, 1975; *Yankee Doodle Dandies* (humor), New American Library, 1975; *Official Movie Trivia Quiz Book,* New American Library, 1976; *Official TV Trivia Quiz Book, #2,* New American Library, 1976; *Lucy and Ricky and Fred and Ethel,* Dutton, 1976.

Author of some thirty television comedy scripts, including material for Bob Newhart, Carol Burnett, Soupy Sales, Paul Lynde, and Phyllis Diller. Co-author of libretto for "Ape Over Broadway" (musical comedy), first produced in New York at Bert Wheeler Theatre, March 12, 1975.

WORK IN PROGRESS: TV or Not TV, humor, for New American Library; *Official Movie Trivia Quiz Book, #2,* New American Library; *The Paul Lynde Story,* Popular Library; *Televisionland* (tentative title), Dutton.

* * *

ANDREWS, Bart   1945-

PERSONAL: Name originally Andrew Stephen Ferreri; name legally changed, 1964; born February 25, 1945, in Brooklyn, N.Y.; son of Joseph (a businessman) and Camille (Sollecito) Ferreri; divorced. *Education:* New York University, B.A., 1963. *Home address:* P.O. Box 727, Hollywood, Calif. 90028. *Agent:* James Trupin, P.O. Box 276, Hastings-on-Hudson, N.Y. 10706.

CAREER: Prospect House (resort hotel), Lake Bomoseen, Vt., social director, 1959-63; Columbia Broadcasting System (CBS), New York, N.Y., writer, 1963-64; free-lance television writer in Hollywood, Calif., 1964—. *Member:* American Society of Composers, Authors and Publishers, Authors Guild of Authors League of America, Writers Guild of America (West).

WRITINGS: Different Spokes for Different Folks (humor), Serendipity Press, 1973; *Official TV Trivia Quiz Book,* New American Library, 1975; *Yankee Doodle Dandies* (humor), New American Library, 1975; *Official Movie Trivia Quiz Book,* New American Library, 1976; *Official TV Trivia Quiz Book, #2,* New American Library, 1976; *Lucy and Ricky and Fred and Ethel,* Dutton, 1976.

Author of about thirty television comedy scripts, including material for Bob Newhart, Carol Burnett, Soupy Sales, Paul Lynde, and Phyllis Diller.

Co-author of libretto for "Ape Over Broadway" (musical comedy), first produced in New York, at Bert Wheeler Theatre, March 12, 1975.

WORK IN PROGRESS: TV Or Not TV, humor, for New American Library; *Official Movie Trivia Quiz Book, #2,* New American Library; *The Paul Lynde Story,* Popular Library; *Televisionland* (tentative title), Dutton.

SIDELIGHTS: Andrews told *CA,* "My motivation is simply sitting down on a chair every morning and starting. I don't consider it fun, but something I *must* do. I can't think of anything else I could do, or would be capable of doing. I write material that is entertainment that in which the general public is interested. I would never, for instance, write a book about world crises. I love show business and most of my writing, in some way, deals with this."

* * *

ANDREWS, George F(redrick) 1918-

PERSONAL: Born September 24, 1918, in Minneapolis, Minn.; son of Frederick S. (a salesman) and Kathryn (Chesher) Andrews; married Geraldine M. Dolphin, November 5, 1945; children: Alan A. *Education:* University of Michigan, B.Arch., 1941; also studied at Pennsylvania State University. *Home:* 3205 Olive St., Eugene, Ore. 97405. *Office:* School of Architecture and Allied Arts, University of Oregon, Eugene, Ore. 97403.

CAREER: Registered architect in Oregon; Smith, Hinchman & Grylls (architects), Detroit, Mich., draftsman-designer, 1941-45; Perkins & Will (architects), Chicago, Ill., designer and associate, 1945-48; University of Oregon, Eugene, assistant professor, 1948-53, associate professor, 1953-62, professor of architecture, 1962—. Fulbright lecturer at Technical University of Helsinki, 1962-63. Has conducted field research at more than seventy Maya sites in Mexico, Guatemala, Honduras, Belice, and British Honduras; director of summer field research projects at Comalcalco, Tabasco, Mexico, 1966, and Edzna, Campeche, Mexico, 1968. His exhibits include "Maya Cities," 1965, and "Maya Art and Architecture," 1973, both at University of Oregon, and "Maya Art and Architecture" at a gallery in Medford, Ore., 1974. *Awards, honors:* Award of merit from *House and Home*, 1959; grant from National Science Foundation, 1972; senior fellowship from National Endowment for the Humanities, 1973-74.

WRITINGS: Comalcalco, Tabasco, Mexico: An Architectonic Survey, University of Oregon, 1967; *Edzna, Campeche, Mexico: Settlement Patterns and Monumental Architecture,* University of Oregon, 1969; *Maya Cities: Placemaking and Urbanization,* University of Oklahoma Press, 1975. Contributor to architecture journals.

WORK IN PROGRESS: Maya Architecture: Forms and Functions.

SIDELIGHTS: Andrews writes: "In support of my teaching, I have spent three years in northern Europe, primarily engaged in research focusing on housing and urban growth. For the past eighteen years I have pursued a dual career, dividing my time between my main vocation as an architect and teacher and my 'love affair' with the ancient Maya.... The bulk of my efforts as a writer are associated with a continuing investigation of the nature of [Maya] settlements and the relationships between culture and the man made environment." Andrews has traveled and studied in Scandinavia, Germany, the Netherlands, France, and Italy.

BIOGRAPHICAL/CRITICAL SOURCES: Eugene Register-Guard, July 18, 1972; *Oregonian,* December 18, 1974; *Willamette Week,* December 8, 1975.

* * *

ANDREWS, Lewis M. 1946-

PERSONAL: Born July 17, 1946, in New York, N.Y. *Education:* Princeton University, A.B., 1968; Stanford University, M.A., 1970; Union Graduate School, Ph.D., 1976. *Agent:* John Sterling, Paul R. Reynolds, Inc., 13 East 41st St., New York, N.Y. 10017.

CAREER: University of South Florida, Tampa, lecturer in

management, 1975; Bee Line Co., Davenport, Iowa, director, 1975—. *Member:* Association for Humanistic Psychology, Sierra Club.

WRITINGS: (With Marv Karlins) *Requiem for Democracy?,* Holt, 1971; (with Karlins) *Psychology: What's in It for Us?,* Random House, 1973, 2nd edition, 1975; (with Karlins) *Man Controlled,* Free Press, 1972; (with Karlins) *Biofeedback: Turning on the Power of Your Mind,* Lippincott, 1972; (with Karlins) *Gomorrah* (novel), Doubleday, 1974. Contributor to psychology journals, and to *Nation, Saturday Review, Cosmopolitan, Current,* and *Wall Street Journal.*

WORK IN PROGRESS: "Whimper," a screenplay.

* * *

ANDRUS, Paul 1931-

PERSONAL: Born September 14, 1931, in Rochester, N.Y.; son of Fred C. (a toolmaker) and Gertrude (Curtis) Andrus; married M. Joyce Bevan, June 5, 1954; children: Debra Joy, Susan Lynn, Wendy Jeanne, Robert Paul. *Education:* Bucknell University, B.S., 1954; Emory University, M.Div., 1970, S.T.D., 1973. *Home:* 8870 Southwest 49th Court, Cooper City, Fla. 33328. *Office:* Davie United Methodist Church, 6500 Southwest 47th St., Davie, Fla. 33314.

CAREER: Pratt & Whitney Aircraft, East Hartford, Conn., experimental test engineer, 1954-56; Stromberg Carlson Co., Rochester, N.Y., design engineer, 1956-59; Honeywell, Inc., St. Petersburg, Fla., senior development engineer, 1959-67; ordained United Methodist minister, 1968; pastor of United Methodist church in Lawrenceville, Ga., 1967-71, associate pastor of community church in St. Petersburg, Fla., 1971-75; Davie United Methodist Church, Davie, Fla., pastor, 1975—. Member of board of directors of Pinellas County Youth Symphony, 1972-73.

WRITINGS: Why Me? Why Mine?, Abingdon, 1975.

WORK IN PROGRESS: Tough-Minded Christians (tentative title), on Christian understanding of love, forgiveness, and hope.

SIDELIGHTS: Andrus writes: "*Why Me? Why Mine?* attempts to give an answer to the riddle of undeserved suffering. I am drawn to the consideration of some of these more perplexing issues through the disciplines of religion and theology because I believe the business of religion is meaning. Never have more people sought meaning in life. It is the responsibility of theology to address these issues."

* * *

ANGELL, Madeline 1919-

PERSONAL: Born January 6, 1919, in Devils Lake, N.D.; daughter of Bernard Oscar and Evelyn (Smith) Angell; married Kenneth F. Johnson (a vice-president in men's retail clothing business), August 31, 1940; children: Mark Frederick, Randall David. *Education:* University of Minnesota, B.S., 1940. *Politics:* Independent. *Religion:* Lutheran. *Home and office address:* R.R.4, Cardinal Dr., Red Wing, Minn. 55066.

CAREER: Sears, Roebuck & Co., Duluth, Minn., advertising manager, 1944-45; writer. Former co-chairman of local mayor's citizens committee for the state training school. *Member:* American Association of University Women (co-president, 1956-58). *Awards, honors:* Humanities award from McKnight Foundation, 1966, for unpublished novel *The October Horse.*

WRITINGS: One Hundred Twenty Questions and Answers About Birds, Bobbs-Merrill, 1973; *America's Best Loved Wild Animals,* Bobbs-Merrill, 1975; *The Fantastic Variety of Marine Animals,* Bobbs-Merrill, 1976. Contributor to popular magazines, including *Parents' Magazine, Better Homes and Gardens,* and *Science World.*

WORK IN PROGRESS: A history of Red Wing, Minn., for Dillon; a biography of J. W. Hancock, the first permanent white settler in Red Wing, with Mary Miller; *Red Wing's River: Touching Our Lives.*

AVOCATIONAL INTERESTS: Nature study and natural history, biking, bridge, reading (biography, history, fiction), European travel.

* * *

ANGELOU, Maya 1928-

PERSONAL: Given name, Marguerita; born April 4, 1928, in St. Louis, Mo.; daughter of Bailey (a naval dietician) and Vivian (Baxter) Johnson; married Paul Du Feu, December, 1973; children: Guy. *Education:* Attended public schools in Arkansas and California; studied music privately, dance with Martha Graham, Pearl Primus, and Ann Halprin, and drama with Frank Silvera and Gene Frankel. *Residence:* Sonoma, Calif. *Agent:* Gerald W. Purcell Associates Ltd., 133 Fifth Ave., New York, N.Y. 10003.

CAREER: Author, poet, playwright, professional stage and screen performer and singer. Appeared in "Porgy and Bess" on twenty-two nation tour sponsored by the U.S. Department of State, 1954-55; appeared in Off-Broadway plays, "Calypso Heatwave," 1957, and "The Blacks," 1960; with Godfrey Cambridge wrote, produced, and performed in "Cabaret for Freedom," Off-Broadway, 1960; appeared in "Mother Courage" at University of Ghana, 1964, and in "Meda" in Hollywood, 1966; made Broadway debut in "Look Away," 1973; directed film, "All Day Long," 1974; directed her play, "And Still I Rise," in California, 1976. *Arab Observer* (English-language newsweekly), Cairo, Egypt, associate editor, 1961-62; University of Ghana, Institute of African Studies, Legon-Accra, Ghana, assistant administrator of School of Music and Drama, 1963-66; freelance writer for *Ghanaian Times* and Ghanaian Broadcasting Corp., 1963-65; *African Review,* Accra, Ghana, feature editor, 1964-66. Lecturer, University of California, Los Angeles, 1966; writer-in-residence, University of Kansas, 1970; distinguished visiting professor, Wake Forest University, 1974, Wichita State University, 1974, California State University, Sacramento, 1974. Northern coordinator, Southern Christian Leadership Conference, 1959-60; appointed member of American Revolution Bicentennial Council by President Ford, 1975-76. Television narrator, interviewer, and host for Afro-American specials and theatre series, 1972—.

MEMBER: American Film Institute (member of board of trustees, 1975—), Directors Guild of America, Equity, American Federation of Television and Radio Artists, Women's Prison Association (member of advisory board). *Awards, honors:* Nominated for National Book Award, 1970, for *I Know Why the Caged Bird Sings;* Pulitzer Prize nomination, 1972, for *Just Give Me a Cool Drink of Water 'Fore I Diiie;* Tony Award nomination, 1973, for performance in "Look Away"; named Woman of the Year in Communications by *Ladies Home Journal,* 1976. Yale University fellowship, 1970; Rockefeller Foundation scholar in Italy, 1975; honorary degrees from Smith College, 1975, Mills College, 1975, Lawrence University, 1976.

WRITINGS—Books: I Know Why the Caged Bird Sings (autobiography; Book of the Month Club selection), Random House, 1970; *Just Give Me a Cool Drink of Water 'Fore I Diiie* (poetry), Random House, 1971; *Gather Together in My Name* (autobiography; Book of the Month Club selection), Random House, 1974; *Oh Pray My Wings Are Gonna Fit Me Well,* Randon House, 1975; *Singin' and Swingin' and Gettin' Merry Like Christmas* (Book of the Month Club selection), Random House, 1976.

Plays: (With Godfrey Cambridge) "Cabaret for Freedom" (musical revue), first produced in New York at Village Gate Theatre, 1960; "The Least of These" (two-act drama), first produced in Los Angeles, 1966; (adaptator) Sophocles, "Ajax" (two-act drama), first produced in Los Angeles at Mark Taper Forum, 1974; "And Still I Rise" (one-act musical), first produced in Oakland, Calif., at Ensemble Theatre, 1976. Also author of two-act drama, "The Clawing Within," 1966, and of two-act musical, "Adjoa Amissah," 1967, both as yet unproduced.

Screenplays: "Georgia, Georgia," Independent-Cinerama, 1972; "All Day Long," American Film Institute, 1974.

Television: "Blacks, Blues, Black" (ten one-hour programs), National Educational Television, 1968; "Assignment America" (six one-half-hour programs), 1975; "The Legacy" and "The Inheritors" (two Afro-American specials), 1976.

Recordings: "Miss Calypso" (songs), Liberty Records, 1957; "The Poetry of Maya Angelou," GWP Records, 1969.

Composer of songs, including two songs for movie, "For Love of Ivy," and composer of musical scores for both her screenplays. Contributor of articles, short stories, and poems to national periodicals, including *Harper's, Ebony, Mademoiselle, Redbook,* and *Black Scholar.*

SIDELIGHTS: Ms. Angelou speaks French, Spanish, Italian, Arabic, and Fanti.

BIOGRAPHICAL/CRITICAL SOURCES: Maya Angelou, *I Know Why the Caged Bird Sings,* Random House, 1970; *New York Post,* November 5, 1971; *New York Times,* March 24, 1972; *Harper's Bazaar,* November, 1972; *Viva,* March, 1974; Angelou, *Gather Together in My Name,* Random House, 1974; *Writers Digest,* January, 1975.

* * *

ANGERMANN, Gerhard O(tto) 1904-

PERSONAL: Born February 7, 1904, in Germany; came to the United States in 1907, naturalized citizen, 1912; son of Otto Linus and Martha (Kuhn) Angermann; married Emma Ellis, July 10, 1930; children: Gerhard, Jr., Kathryn (Mrs. William Comstock), William E. *Education:* University of Pennsylvania, B.S., 1925. *Politics:* Independent. *Home:* 8339 Thomson Rd., Philadelphia, Pa. 19117; P.O. Box 134, Delta, Ontario, Canada (summer).

CAREER: High school English teacher in Darby, Pa., 1925-27, and in Philadelphia, Pa., 1927-63, director of advanced placement program, 1953-63; supervisor of local and nationally funded smoking and health research project, 1965-68. *Member:* Oak Lane Community Club (president, 1945), Lake Beverly Protective Association (president, 1969).

WRITINGS: The Third Act (play), Samuel French, 1932; (with William Fackler and William Allen) *Learning to Live Without Cigarettes,* Doubleday, 1969. Contributor to *Reader's Digest.*

WORK IN PROGRESS: How to Pray: Or, Why Your Prayers Aren't Being Answered; Confessions of a Sex Therapist.

SIDELIGHTS: Learning to Live Without Cigarettes has sold more than one hundred thousand copies. Avocational interests: Wintering in Mexico, summering on an island in Ontario.

* * *

ANTHONY, Gordon
See STANNUS, (James) Gordon (Dawson)

* * *

ANTOUN, Richard T(aft) 1932-

PERSONAL: Born March 31, 1932, in Massachusetts; son of Taft A. (a physician) and Nelly (Haddad) Antoun; married Elize Botha (a psychologist), September 29, 1966; children: Nicholas T. Education: Williams College, B.A., 1953; Johns Hopkins University, M.A., 1955; Harvard University, Ph.D., 1963. Office: Department of Anthropology, State University of New York at Binghamton, Binghamton, N.Y. 13901.

CAREER: Manchester University, Manchester, England, research associate in anthropology, 1960-62; Indiana University, Bloomington, assistant professor of anthropology, 1963-65; American University of Beirut, Beirut, Lebanon, visiting lecturer, 1965-67; Indiana University, associate professor of anthropology, 1965-67; State University of New York at Binghamton, associate professor of anthropology, 1970—. Member: American Anthropological Association, Middle East Studies Association, Phi Beta Kappa. Awards, honors: Fulbright scholarship to Egypt, 1955-56.

WRITINGS: Arb Village: A Social Structural Study of a Transjordanian Peasant Community, Indiana University Press, 1972; (with Iliya F. Harik) Rural Politics and Social Change in the Middle East, Indiana University Press, 1972; Low Key Politics: A Middle Eastern Case Study of Local-level Leadership and Change, State University of New York Press, in press.

WORK IN PROGRESS: The Gentry of a Traditional Peasant Community Undergoing Rapid Technological Change: An Iranian Case Study; a paper studying the social organization of tradition in Islam, including analyses of the roles played and sermons delivered by Muslim preachers in peasant villages.

* * *

ANWEILER, Oskar 1925-

PERSONAL: Born September 29, 1925, in Rawicz, Poland; son of Sigmund (a head clerk) and Helene (Kolb) Anweiler; married Gerda Timmermann, June 4, 1949. Education: University of Hamburg, Dr. Phil., 1954. Home: Gutenbergstrasse 10, Bochum, Germany D463. Office: University of Bochum, Bochum, Germany D463.

CAREER: University of Hamburg, Hamburg, Germany, lecturer, 1963-64; University of Bochum, Bochum, Germany, professor of comparative education, 1964—, dean of faculty of philosophy, education, and psychology, 1966-67, 1975-76. Visiting professor in New Zealand and Canada, 1973, 1974. Deputy member of governing board, UNESCO Institute of Education, Hamburg, 1967—. Member: Comparative Education Society in Europe (vice-president, 1973—), Deutsche Gesellschaft fuer Osteuropakunde (vice-president, 1974—), Ostkolleg der Bundeszentrale fuer Politische Bildung (member of governing board, 1971—).

WRITINGS: Die Raetebewegung in Russland, 1905-1921, E. J. Brill, 1958, translation by Ruth Hein published as The Soviets: The Russian Workers, Peasants, and Soldiers Councils, 1905-1921, Pantheon, 1975; (editor with Klaus Meyer) Die sowjetische Bildungspolitik seit 1917: Dokumente und Texte, Quelle & Meyer, 1961; Geschichte der Schule und Paedogogik in Russland vom Ende des Zarenreiches bis zum Beginn der Stalin-Aera, Quelle & Meyer, 1964; Die Sowjetpaedagogik in der Welt von heute, Quelle & Meyer, 1968; (editor) Bildungsreformen in Osteuropa, Kohlhammer, 1969; (editor with K. H. Ruffman) Kulturpolitik der Sowjetunion, Kroener, 1973; (editor with F. Kuebart and K. Meyer) Die Sowjetische Bildungspolitik, 1958-1973: Dokumente und Texte, [Berlin], 1976.

Contributor: Richard Pipes, editor, Revolutionary Russia, Harvard University Press, 1968; George Katkov and others, editors, Russia Enters the Twentieth Century, Temple Smith, 1971; Boris Meissner, editor, Social Change in the Soviet Union, University of Notre Dame Press, 1972; Hans Steffen, editor, Bildung und Gesellschaft, Vandenhoeck & Ruprecht, 1972; A. S. Makarenko, Ein paedagogisches Poem, Ullstein, 1972; Reginald Edwards and others, editors, Relevant Methods in Comparative Education, UNESCO Institute for Education (Hamburg), 1973, Unipub, 1974.

Co-editor: "Erziehungswissenschaftliche Veroeffentlichungen des Osteuropa-Instituts an der Freien Universitaet Berlin" series. Contributor to encyclopedias, including Encyclopaedia Britannica, Lexikon der Paedagogik, and Marxism, Communism, and Western Society: A Comparative Encyclopedia; contributor to journals including School and Society, International Review of Education, and Zeitschrift fuer Paedogogik. Co-editor, Bildung und Erziehung.

* * *

APPLEBAUM, Samuel 1904-

PERSONAL: Born January 15, 1904, in Passaic, N.J.; son of Michael (a rabbi) and Fanny (Levine) Applebaum; married Sada Rothman (a writer), August 14, 1927; children: Michael, Lois May Applebaum Leibow. Education: Juilliard School of Music, diploma, 1928; also attended Columbia University. Religion: Jewish. Home and studio: 23 North Ter., Maplewood, N.J. 07040.

CAREER: Musician, educator, and writer. Manhattan School of Music, New York, N.Y., professor of music, 1954—. Recorded nine records in clinician series for Golden Crest Records. Lecturer at Fairleigh Dickinson University and at Douglass College (of Rutgers University). Member of Governing Arts Council of New Jersey and of Maplewood Arts Council.

MEMBER: International Music Honor Society, American String Teachers Association, Music Educators National Conference, Music Teachers National Association, National Federation of Music Clubs (past vice-president), New Jersey Music Educators (past president). Awards, honors: Award from National Federation of Music Clubs, 1957; named Distinguished Teacher of the Year by American String Teachers Association, 1967; Ph.D., Gettysburg College, 1973, Southwestern College, Winfield, Kan., 1976.

WRITINGS: (With wife, Sada Applebaum) With the Artists: World Famous String Players Discuss Their Art, J. Markert, 1955; The Belwin String Builder, five volumes and teachers manual, Belwin, 1960; (with S. Applebaum) The Way They Play, four books, Crown, 1972-76. Also author of Samuel Applebaum String Course, three volumes, Building Technic, four volumes, and University String Builder. Author of scripts of music teaching films for University of Wisconsin Extension and Belwin. American editor with daughter, Lois A. Leibow, of *Strad* magazine. Contributor of articles to music publications.

WORK IN PROGRESS: Book V of *The Way They Play,* to be called *The Role of Music and Art in the Personality; 1001 Questions and Answers on How to Teach Stringed Instruments.*

SIDELIGHTS: In addition to the recordings for Golden Crest, Applebaum has made a number of recordings for Music Minus One (MMO) which include duet books.

*   *   *

ARCHDEACON, Thomas J(ohn)   1942-

PERSONAL: Born July 5, 1942, in New York, N.Y.; son of Daniel Joseph (an elevator operator) and Elizabeth (O'Callaghan) Archdeacon; married Marilyn Lavin (a writer), September 7, 1968; children: Meghan, Patrick, Caitlin. *Education:* Fordham University, A.B., 1964; Columbia University, M.A., 1965, Ph.D., 1971. *Religion:* Roman Catholic. *Residence:* Madison, Wis. *Office:* Department of History, University of Wisconsin, Madison, Wis. 53706.

CAREER: University of Wisconsin, Madison, assistant professor of history, 1972—. *Military service:* U.S. Army, assistant professor at U.S. Military Academy, 1969-72; became captain. *Member:* Social Science History Association.

WRITINGS: New York City, 1664-1710: Conquest and Change, Cornell University Press, 1976.

WORK IN PROGRESS: Research on New York City at the time of the American Revolution and on New York's Yorkville neighborhood in the nineteenth and twentieth centuries.

*   *   *

ARCHER, Gleason Leonard, Jr.   1916-

PERSONAL: Born May 22, 1916, in Norwell, Mass.; son of Gleason Leonard (an educator) and Elizabeth (Snyder) Archer; married L. Virginia Atkinson, May 11, 1939 (died August 24, 1962); married Sandra P. Larsen, March 21, 1964; children: (first marriage) Gleason Leonard III, Jonathan A., Heather M.; (second marriage) Laurel E., Elizabeth S. *Education:* Harvard University, B.A. (summa cum laude), 1938, M.A., 1940, Ph.D., 1944; Suffolk University, LL.B., 1939; Princeton Theological Seminary, B.D., 1945. *Politics:* Republican. *Home:* 812 Castlewood Lane, Deerfield, Ill. 60015. *Office:* Trinity Evangelical Divinity School, Deerfield, Ill. 60015.

CAREER: Ordained Presbyterian minister, 1945; student pastor at Presbyterian churches in Jacksonville and Providence, N.J., 1942-45; assistant pastor of church in Boston, Mass., 1945-48; Fuller Seminary, Pasadena, Calif., professor of Biblical languages, 1948-65; Trinity Evangelical Divinity School, Deerfield, Ill., professor of Old Testament and Semitic languages, 1965—. Trustee of Suffolk University, 1946-49.

MEMBER: National Association of Biblical Instructors, National Association of Evangelicals, Evangelical Theological Society, Evangelical Free Church Ministerium, American Numismatic Association, American Israel Numismatic Association, Phi Beta Kappa. *Awards, honors:* Christian Research Foundation award, 1957.

WRITINGS: In the Shadow of the Cross, Zondervan, 1957; *The Epistle to the Hebrews: A Study Manual,* Baker Book,

1957; (translator from the Latin) *Jerome's Commentary on Daniel,* Baker Book, 1958; *The Epistle to the Romans: A Study Manual,* Baker Book, 1959; *A Survey of Old Testament Introduction,* Moody, 1964, revised edition, 1974.

Contributor: C.F.H. Henry, editor, *The Biblical Expositor,* Volume II, A. J. Holman, 1960; *Wycliffe Bible Commentary,* Moody, 1962; C. H. Roddy, editor, *Things Most Surely Believed,* Revell, 1963; D. Guthrie, J. A. Moyter, A. M. Stibbs and D. J. Wiseman, editors, *New Bible Commentary,* Inter-Varsity Press, revised edition (Archer was not associated with earlier edition), 1970; J. B. Payne, editor, *New Perspectives on the O.T.,* Word Inc., 1970; John H. Skilton, editor, *The Law and The Prophets,* Presbyterian & Reformed, 1974. Contributor to *Baker's Dictionary of Theology, The Pictorial Bible Dictionary, World Book Encyclopedia,* and *Baker's Dictionary of Christian Ethics.* Contributor to theology journals. Associate editor, *The Zondervan Pictorial Encyclopedia of the Bible,* 1975, and *A Theological Workbook of the Old Testament,* Moody.

WORK IN PROGRESS: A commentary on *Daniel* for *Expositor's Bible Commentary,* edited by Frank E. Gaebelein, for Zondervan; contributions for *Tyndale Family Bible Encyclopedia,* and *A Theological Workbook of the O.T.,* publication by Moody expected in 1977 or 1978.

SIDELIGHTS: Archer has made the sound recordings "I Chronicles—II Chronicles—Malachi," "Ecclesiastes," and "Song of Solomon," for the "Audio Bible College" series division of Sacred Records, Inc., in 1957.

*   *   *

ARGAN, Giulio Carlo   1909-

PERSONAL: Born May 17, 1909, in Turin, Italy; son of Valerio and Libera (Roncardi) Argan; married Anna Mazzucchelli, December 28, 1939; children: Paola. *Education:* University of Turin, laureato in lettere, 1931. *Home:* Via Filippo Casini 16, Rome 00153, Italy. *Office:* Via Gaetano Sacchi 20, Rome 00153, Italy.

CAREER: University of Rome, Rome, Italy, university lecturer in medieval and modern art, 1934-39; Office of the Director General of Fine Arts, Rome, Italy, inspector, 1933-39, superintendent and head inspector for state galleries and museums, 1939-55; University of Palermo, Palermo, Italy, professor of history of modern art, 1955-59; University of Rome, Rome, Italy, professor of history of modern art, 1959—. President of 2nd session of Consiglio Superiore delle Antichita e Belle Arti, 1970. *Member:* Associazione Internazionale dei Critici d'Arte (AICA; past president; now honorary president), Accademia di San Luca, Accademia dei Lincei, Accademia delle Scienze di Torino, Accademia di Scienze e Lettere di Palermo, Accademia Clementina di Bologna.

AWARDS, HONORS: Premio Feltrinelli, 1959, for art criticism; Premio Europeo Cortina-Ulisse, 1968, for architecture criticism; Diploma di Benemerenza d: 1 Classe per la Scuola e la cultura.

WRITINGS: L'architettura protocristiana preromanica e romanica, Novissima enciclopedia monografica illustrata (Florence), 1936, 2nd edition, 1945; *L'architettura del duecento e trecento in Italia,* Novissima enciclopedia monografica illustrata, 1937, 2nd edition, 1943; *Storia dell'arte italiana,* two volumes, Perrella (Naples), 1937; *Arturo Tosi,* Le Monnier (Florence), 1938; *Henry Moore,* De Silva (Turin), 1948.

Walter Gropius e la Bauhaus, Einaudi (Turin), 1951; *Bor-*

romini, Mondadori (Milan), 1952; *Scultura di Picasso* (text in English and Italian), Alfieri (Venice), 1953; *Umberto Boccioni*, edited by Maurizio Calvesi, De Luca (Rome), 1953; *Studi e note*, Fratelli Bocca (Rome), 1955; *Fra Angelico: Biographical and Critical Study*, translated by James Emmons, Skira, 1955; *Pier Luigi Nervi*, Il Balcone (Milan), 1955; (with others) *Arte d'Italia*, Instituto editoriale italiano (Milan), 1955; (with Jacques Lassaigne) *The Fifteenth Century, From Van Eyck to Botticelli*, translated by Stuart Gilbert, Skira, 1955; *Arturo Martini* (text in French, English, German, and Dutch), Kiepenheuer & Witsch (Cologne), 1956, Universe Books, 1959; *Botticelli: Biographical and Critical Study*, translated by James Emmons, Skira, 1957; *Marcel Breuer, disegno industriale e architettura* (text in Italian and English), Goerlich (Milan), 1957; *L'architettura barocca in Italia*, Garzanti (Milan), 1957, 3rd edition, 1963; *Umberto Mastroianni*, Cavallino (Venice), 1958.

Fautrier: "Matiere e memoire" (text in Italian, French, English, and German), Edizioni Apollinaire (Milan), 1960; *L'architettura barocca i Italia: Appunti delle lezioni tenute durante l'anno accademico 1959-60*, compiled by Maurizio Bonicatti, Edizioni dell'Ateneo (Rome), 1960; *Pietro Consagra* (text in German and English), translated by Haakon Chevalier and Felix Baumann, Editions du Griffon (Neuchatel), 1962; *Paulucci*, La Bussola (Turin), 1963; *Salvezza e caduta nell'arte moderna*, Il Saggiatore (Milan), 1964; *L'Europa delle Capitali, 1600-1700*, Skira, 1964, translation by Anthony Rhodes published as *The Europe of the Capitals, 1600-1700*, 1965; *La pittura dell'Illuminismo in Inghilterra*, compiled by Maurizio Fagiolo dell'Arco, Bulzoni (Rome), 1965; *Progetto e destino*, Il Saggiatore, 1965, 2nd edition, 1968; *Il primo rinascimento: Esempi di metodolgia per una lettura critical dell'opera d'arte*, edited by Maurizio Fagiolo dell'Arco, Bulzoni, 1966; (with others) *Leonardo Savioli*, Edizione centro proposte (Florence), 1966; *Esempi di critica sulle tecniche artistiche*, edited by Maurizio Fagiolo dell'Arco, Bulzoni, 1967; *Il neoclassicismo*, edited by Maurizio Fagiolo dell'Arco, Bulzoni, 1968; *Storia dell'arte italiana*, three volumes, Sansoni (Florence), 1968-70; *Renaissance Painting*, translated by Robert Allen and edited by Hans Jaffe, Dell, 1968 (published in England as *The Renaissance*, Thames & Hudson, 1969); *Antonio Canova*, edited by Elisa Debenedetti, Bulzoni, 1969; (with Manfred de La Motte) *G. Hoehme* (text in English, German, and Italian), L'attico/Senior (Rome), 1969; *The Renaissance City*, translated by Susan Edna Bassnett, Studio Vista, 1969, Braziller, 1970.

Studi e note dal Bramante al Canova, Bulzoni, 1970; *L'arte moderna 1770/1970*, Sansoni, 1970, 2nd edition, 1971; *Mastroianni*, Cassa di risparmio di Cuneo, 1971; *Henry Moore*, Fabbri (Milan), 1971, translation by Daniel Dichter published under same title, Abrams, 1973; (with others) *Antonio Corpora* (text in French, English, and Italian), Villand & Galanis (Paris), 1972; (with Maurizio Fagiolo dell'Arco) *Guida alla storia dell'arte*, Sansoni, 1974; *Antonio Scordia: Opere recenti, 1970-74*, Il collezionista d'arte contemporanea (Rome), 1974; *Libera*, [Rome], 1975.

Editor: Giacomo Manzu, *Disegni*, Istituto italiano d'arti grafiche (Bergamo), 1948; *Bruelleschi: 92 Tavole in nero*, Mondadori, 1955; *I maestri della pittura italiana*, Mondadori, 1959; *La litografia*, Editalia (Rome), 1963; *Capogrossi*, Editalia, 1967; *Man Ray, Rayograph*, Martano (Turin), 1970; *Il Revival*, Mazzotta (Milan), 1974.

Contributor: Filiberto Menna, *Industrial Design*, Villar (Rome), 1962; Paolo Portoghesi and others, editors, *Michelangiolo architetto*, Einaudi, 1964; Vittorio Viale, editor, *I*

sei di Torino, 1929-32, Galleria d'arte moderna (Turin), 1965; Giuseppe Maria Pilo and others, editors, *Michelangelo Grigoletti e il suo tempo*, Electa (Milan), 1971; Lara Vinca Masini and Charles Spencer, editors, *Ciussi, 64-74* (text in English and Italian), Grafiche Tirelli, 1974.

Author of introduction or preface: Tiziano Vecelli, *L'amor sacro e l'amor profano*, Bompiani (Milan), 1949; Pier Carlo Santini, editor, *Ignazio Gardella*, Edizioni di Comunita (Milan), 1959; *Art Treasures in Italy: Monuments, Masterpieces, Commissions, and Collections*, McGraw, 1969; *Bonalumi-Modena*, Galleria civica d'arte moderna (Modena), 1975.

Founding editor, *Storia dell'Arte*, 1969—; co-editor, *L'Arte*, 1968-72.

WORK IN PROGRESS: L'arte Moderna: 1880-1940.

* * *

ARKIN, Frieda 1917-

PERSONAL: Born September 4, 1917, in Brooklyn, N.Y.; daughter of Chaim (a merchant) and Anna (Gamsu) Weitzman; married; children: Thomas, Constance. *Education:* Attended Juilliard School of Music, 1936-37, and University of Missouri, 1937-38; University of Chicago, B.A., 1940; Columbia University, M.A., 1947. *Religion:* None. *Home:* 600 West 116th St., New York, N.Y. 10027. *Agent:* A. L. Hart, Fox Chase Agency, 419 East 57th St., New York, N.Y. 10022.

CAREER: Hofstra College (now University), Hempstead, N.Y., lecturer in anthropology, summer, 1947; Hunter College (now of the City University of New York), New York, N.Y., lecturer in physical anthropology, 1947-54; writer, 1957—.

WRITINGS: The Cook's Companion: Dictionary of Culinary Tips and Terms, Doubleday, 1968; *The Dorp* (novel), Dial, 1969; *Kitchen Wisdom*, Holt, in press.

Short stories have been anthologized in *Best American Short Stories 1962*, edited by Martha Foley and David Burnett, Houghton, 1962; *Best American Short Stories 1964*, edited by Foley and Burnett, Houghton, 1964.

Contributor of stories to literary magazines, including *Yale Review, New Mexico Quarterly, Colorado Quarterly, Kenyon Review, Georgia Review, Transatlantic Review*, and *Massachusetts Review*.

WORK IN PROGRESS: A novel.

SIDELIGHTS: Frieda Arkin writes: "Thornton Wilder, during the fifteen years before his death, generously gave me much valuable critical advice. I am enormously indebted to him. I am indebted also to Martha Foley, a woman of astute literary judgment. I started writing fiction very late in life, at a time when most writers are at the peak of their powers. I run panting."

* * *

ARMER, Laura (Adams) 1874-1963

PERSONAL: Born January 12, 1874, in Sacramento, Calif.; married Sidney Armer (an artist), in 1902; children: Austin. *Home:* Fortuna, California.

CAREER: Writer, artist. *Awards, honors:* Newberry Medal, 1932, for *Waterless Mountain; The Forest Pool* named Caldecott Honor Book, 1939.

WRITINGS: (Self-illustrated; with husband, Sidney Armer) *Waterless Mountain*, Longmans, Green, 1931; (illustrated by husband) *Dark Circle of Branches*, Longmans, Green, 1933; (illustrated by husband) *Cactus*, Stokes, 1934; (self-illustrated) *Southwest*, Longmans, Green, 1935; (self-illustrated with husband) *The Traders' Children*, Longmans, Green, 1937; (self-illustrated) *The Forest Pool*, Longmans, Green, 1938; (illustrated by husband) *Farthest West*, Longmans, Green, 1939; (self-illustrated with husband and son, Austin Armer) *In Navajo Land*, McKay, 1962.

SIDELIGHTS: Laura Armer wrote: "Everyone gets born of course, and doesn't know much about it. His parents mark the date for him if he is civilized, so called, and record a certificate of birth in the city hall of his village. Mine was recorded in Sacramento, California.

"My parents soon moved to San Francisco, and there I went to public school, private school, and home school—the last for the reason that I was not very strong, and couldn't stand the daily contact with forty-nine husky children of every nationality. San Francisco has always been known as a cosmopolitan center, and of necessity its children came from Italian, Irish, German, French, Jewish, Chinese, and Japanese families.

"Very early in life I became interested in a Chinese family who ran a laundry near where I lived. I liked the little children, dressed with bright colored aprons, over their padded coats. When I grew up and studied Chinese art and literature with its legends and symbolism, I always recalled the two almond-eyed, smooth-skinned babies of the laundryman. Come to think of it, those little children may have started me on the study of Indian children, long after I had raised my own son, Austin.

"I must tell you about Austin. Of course he was the most beautiful and interesting child ever, and many of the pretty things he did on his way to being a man have been recorded in *Waterless Mountain*. All the other dream happenings came from my own childhood. I believe that every boy and girl born into the world 'comes trailing clouds of glory,' which most grown-ups have forgotten. I remembered the beautiful visions of another world, and I saw them come true in my own child, who loved all beauty. We had such a glorious time together learning about birds, butterflies, flowers, and ferns, rocks, and even stars. When Austin was not quite three he said to me one night, 'I want a paper bag and a ladder. I'm going to climb to the sky and get a bagful of stars for you, mumsey.'

"He did get me a bagful of stars, which shine for me this minute while I am telling you about them. His father, Sidney Armer, who married me, so the records say, in San Francisco in 1902, considers Austin the brightest star of all.

"Perhaps there are some children who dream as I dreamed when a very little girl, about all the things grown-ups laugh at. I am sure that everyone has dreamed of flying, so soaring so easily in the air and being sure that he could teach others how to do it.

"There were no flying machines when I was a child, but men were trying to invent them. There were no horseless carriages, but men did make them. So I have seen many dreams of the impossible come true. That is why I still hope that men will learn how not to go to war, how not to be so greedy for money that they enslave their brothers to toil and grow sick with producing for profit instead of making what they need for happiness.

"I have the hope of that dream coming true for all the people of the earth, because so many beautiful things have happened in the sixty years that I have been 'walking to and fro and up and down the earth.'

"Of course I know the terrible things that have happened. I do not close my eyes to war and poverty. I can talk about tragedy first hand because I have lived through as much sorrow as anyone, but I do not wish to talk about those bad things, simply because I am much more interested in the 'clouds of glory' that all little children know about. Yonger Brother knew about them and he sprinkled pollen on them when he sought the gods on their summits, with a prayer within his heart.

"'In your heart are secrets you cannot name, songs you cannot hear, and words that you must not speak.' I will speak them for you, I will sing them for you, for I know all about those secrets deep in your hearts, those beautiful, unnamable dreams which have come with you out of the long past. They are born through all the experience of all the people who walked the earth before you. They are precious and not to be wasted. You are happiest when you hear them singing in your heart.

>   A bag of stars and a ladder to climb,
>   A merry hunt for rainbow's end,

and then a book which makes you sure that dreams of beauty are more real than acts that are ugly and sorrowful."

BIOGRAPHICAL/CRITICAL SOURCES: Kunitz and Haycraft, editors, *Junior Book of Authors*, H. W. Wilson, 1934, 2nd edition, 1951; *Illustrators of Children's Books: 1744-1945*, Horn Book, 1947; Miller and Field, editors, *Newberry Medal Books: 1922-1955*, Horn Book, 1955.

(Died March 3, 1963)

*   *   *

ARMS, Johnson
   See HALLIWELL, David (William)

*   *   *

ARMSTRONG, John Byron   1917-1976
   (John Byron, Charles Willard)

September 20, 1917—February 29, 1976; American newspaperman, businessman, bookseller, and author. Obituaries: *AB Bookman's Weekly*, May 17, 1976. (See index for previous *CA* sketch)

*   *   *

ARNOLD, Charles Harvey   1920-

PERSONAL: Born May 25, 1920, in Atlanta, Ga.; son of Charles Hill (a deputy marshal) and Ida (Ashley) Arnold; married Patricia Streeter (a school teacher), June 18, 1945; children: Erich, Jan, Lauren Arnold Pokorny, Gregory, Lisa, Lael, Jon, Jonathan. *Education:* David Lipscomb College, A.A., 1943; attended University of Georgia, 1943-44, and Transylvania College, 1944-45; University of Chicago, B.D., 1950, M.A., 1961. *Politics:* Democrat. *Home and office:* 5715 Harper Ave., Chicago, Ill. 60637.

CAREER: Ordained minister of the Congregational Church, 1944; pastor in Fox Lake, Ill.; Chicago Theological Seminary, Chicago, Ill., assistant librarian, 1956-57, librarian, 1957-62; University of Chicago, Chicago, bibliographer in religion and philosophy, 1962-73; St. Andrew Crawford United Church of Christ, Chicago, minister, 1975—. *Member:* American Theological Library Association, American Academy of Religion.

WRITINGS: *Near the Edge of Battle*, Divinity School Association, 1966; *God Before You and Behind You*, Brethren Press, 1974. Editor of "Philosophy and Religion" series, Gale, 1971.

WORK IN PROGRESS: A book on the relationship of religion to American democracy.

* * *

ARNOLD, Mary Ann 1918-

PERSONAL: Born February 20, 1918, in Clyde, Ohio; daughter of Paul A. (a steel rule die maker) and Nellie (a nurse; maiden name, Simpson) Bauman; married Delmar W. Arnold (a group claims consultant), March 1, 1942; children: Delmar W., Jr. *Education:* Attended Cleveland Institute of Art, 1939-42. *Politics:* Republican. *Religion:* Episcopalian. *Home and office:* 2782 10th St., Cuyahoga Falls, Ohio 44221.

CAREER: Free-lance artist and writer. Docent of Akron Institute of Art. *Member:* Ohio Arts and Crafts, Tri-County Society of Fine Arts, Women's Art League (Akron, Ohio), Cleveland Institute of Art Alumni Association.

WRITINGS—For children; all self-illustrated: *Going to the Hospital* (coloring book), Herriott Printing Co., 1968; *My Chapel Hill Coloring Book,* Chapel Hill Mall, 1970.

WORK IN PROGRESS: Fifty-Two Years of Diabetes.

* * *

ARNOLD-FORSTER, Mark 1920-

PERSONAL: Born April 16, 1920, in Swindon, England; son of William Edward (a painter) and Katherine (Laird) Arnold-Forster; married Valentine Mitchison, January 13, 1955; children: Kate, Sam, Joshua, Mary, Jacob. *Education:* Attended school in England. *Religion:* Church of England. *Home:* 50 Clarendon Road, London W.11, England. *Agent:* A. P. Watt & Son, 10 Norfolk St., London W.C.2, England. *Office: Guardian,* 192 Grays Inn Road, London W.C.1, England.

CAREER: Journalist with *Guardian,* London, England. *Military Service:* Royal Navy, 1940-46; received Distinguished Service Order and Distinguished Service Cross; mentioned in dispatches.

WRITINGS: The World at War, Stein & Day, 1974.

SIDELIGHTS: The World at War is based on the twenty six hour television series of the same name, produced by Thames Television, London. In writing his book, Arnold-Forster had access to the records of the Foreign Office and the minutes of the cabinet meetings under Chamberlain, which had recently been opened for inspection by scholars.

* * *

ARNOTHY, Christine 1930-

PERSONAL: Born November 20, 1930, in Budapest, Hungary; daughter of Antoine (a professor) and Irene (Achs) Kovach de Szendroe; married Claude Bellanger (director general of *Le Parisien Libere*); children: Christiane Swire, Pierre, Francois. *Home:* 168 Avenue Victor Hugo, Paris 75116, France. *Agent:* Maximilian Becker, 115 East 82nd St., New York, N.Y. 10028.

CAREER: Writer. *Awards, honors:* Grand prix verite, 1954; Prix de quatre jurys, 1967; named chevalier of Ordre National du Merite, 1971, and officier des arts et lettres of Ministere des Affaires Culturelles, 1974; Grand prix de la nouvelle from Academie Francaise, 1976.

WRITINGS—In English translation: *J'ai quinze ans et je ne veux pas mourir,* Fayard, 1955, translation by Antonia White published as *I Am Fifteen and I Don't Want to Die,* Dutton, 1956, published as *I Am Fifteen and I Don't Want*

To Die: An Unforgettable True Story of the Horrors of War, Popular Library, 1957; *Dieu est en retard,* Gallimard, 1955, translation by Anne Green published as *God Is Late,* Dutton, 1957; *Il n'est pas si facile de vivre,* Fayard, 1957, translation by White published as *It Is Not So Easy to Live,* Collins, 1958, Dutton, 1960; *Those Who Wait,* translated by White, Collins, 1957; *Le Guerisseur,* Fayard, 1958, translation by White published as *The Charlatan,* Dutton, 1959; *Women of Japan,* translated by Diana Athill, Deutsch, 1959.

Pique-nique en Sologne, Julliard, 1960, translation by White published as *The Serpent's Bite,* Collins, 1961; *Le Cardinal prisonnier,* Julliard, 1962, translation by White published as *The Captive Cardinal,* Doubleday, 1964; *Le Jardin noir,* Julliard, 1966, translation by Robert Baldick published as *The Black Garden,* Holt, 1969; *Aviva,* Flammarion, 1968, translation by Monroe Stearns published as *Shalom Aviva!,* McKay, 1970; *Un Type merveilleux,* Flammarion, 1972, translation by Frances Thompson and Charles Lam Markmann published as *Anouk in Love,* Doubleday, 1975.

Other works: *La Saison des Americains* (novel), Julliard, 1964; *Jouer a l'ete* (novel), Julliard, 1967; *Chiche!* (novel), Flammarion, 1970; *Lettre ouverte aux rois nus,* Michel, 1974; *Le Cavalier Mongol* (short stories; title means "The Mongolian Riders"), Flammarion, 1976.

* * *

ART, Robert (Jeffrey) 1942-

PERSONAL: Born August 24, 1942, in Canton, Ohio; son of Herbert (a businessman) and Dorothy Art; married Suzanne Strauss; children: David, Robyn. *Education:* Columbia University, A.B. (summa cum laude), 1964; Harvard University, Ph.D., 1967. *Residence:* Lincoln, Mass. *Office:* Department of Political Science, Brandeis University, Waltham, Mass. 02154.

CAREER: Harvard University, Cambridge, Mass., research fellow at Center for International Affairs, 1967—; Brandeis University, Waltham, Mass., associate professor of politics, 1972—. *Member:* American Political Science Association, Phi Beta Kappa. *Awards, honors:* Woodrow Wilson fellow, 1964-65, 1966-67; Council on Foreign Relations international affairs fellow, 1970-71; Guggenheim fellow, 1975-76.

WRITINGS: TFX Decision: McNamara and the Military, Little, Brown, 1968; (editor with Kenneth N. Waltz) *The Use of Force,* Little, Brown, 1971; (editor with Robert Jervis) *International Politics,* Little, Brown, 1973. Contributor to professional journals.

WORK IN PROGRESS: A book on American defense policy from 1957 to 1976; *The Quest for Security,* completion expected in 1978; *From Containment to Detente: American Foreign Policy, 1945-1978,* completion expected in 1979.

* * *

ARVILL, Robert
See BOOTE, Robert Edward

* * *

ARVIN, Kay K(rehbiel) 1922-

PERSONAL: Born June 7, 1922, in Cullison, Kan.; daughter of Arthur J. and Rozella (Richardson) Krehbiel; married Lester Cave Arvin (a lawyer), May 13, 1945; children: Scott Brentwood, Reed Richardson. *Education:* University of Ottawa, A.B., 1943; Washburn University, J.D., 1951, LL.B., 1952. *Religion:* Baptist. *Home:* 8 Cypress Dr., Wichita, Kan. 67206. *Office:* Arvin, Arvin, Busey & Thomas, 814 Century Plaza Bldg., Wichita, Kan. 67202.

CAREER: Civilian in military intelligence department in Honolulu, Hawaii, 1943-45; admitted to Kansas Bar, 1951; attorney, specializing in marriage counseling and domestics relations law, 1951—; Arvin, Arvin, Busey & Thomas, Wichita, Kan., partner, 1951—. Member of board of directors of Monica House (rehabilitation center for girls) and Kansas Foundation for the Blind. Past director of Family Consultation Services (Wichita).

MEMBER: International Platform Association, American Bar Association, American Academy of Matrimonial Lawyers (fellow), National Council of Juvenile Judges (associate member), Future Home Makers of America (honorary life member), Kansas Bar Association, Kansas Press Women's Association (patron), Wichita Area Chamber of Commerce (member of board of directors), Wichita Bar Association (honorary life member), Soroptimist Club.

WRITINGS: Golden Spindle of Love, Mennonite Press, 1963; *One Plus One Equals One: How to Have a Happy and Successful Marriage,* Broadman, 1969. Contributor to magazines and newspapers.

*   *   *

ASHE, Arthur 1943-

PERSONAL: Born July 10, 1943, in Richmond, Va.; son of Arthur (a parks department guard) and M. C. Ashe. *Education:* University of California, Los Angeles, B.S., 1966. *Home:* 4400 Northwest 87th Ave., Miami, Fla. 33148. *Office:* 888 17th St. N.W., Washington, D.C. 20006.

CAREER: Tennis player since 1968. President of Players Enterprises, Inc., 1969—. Member of U.S. Davis Cup Tennis Team, 1967—; numerous tennis championships include National Indoor Junior Tennis Championship, 1960, 1961, U.S. Men's Hard Court Championship, 1963, U.S. intercollegiate championships, 1965, U.S. Men's Clay Court Championship, 1967, U.S. Amateur Title, 1968, U.S. Open Championship, 1968, Australian Open Championship, 1970, and Wimbledon Championship, 1975. *Military service:* U.S. Army, 1967-69.

WRITINGS: (With Frank Deford) *Arthur Ashe: Portrait in Motion,* Houghton, 1975. Contributor to tennis magazines.

SIDELIGHTS: Ashe first played tennis at the age of seven, with a borrowed racket on a segregated court; ten years later he won the national junior championship. He is the first Black named to a U.S. Davis Cup team.

BIOGRAPHICAL/CRITICAL SOURCES: John McPhee, *Levels of the Game,* Farrar, Straus, 1969; Louie Robinson, Jr., *Arthur Ashe: Tennis Champion,* Doubleday, 1970.

*   *   *

ASHFORD, (H.) Ray 1926-

PERSONAL: Born July 22, 1926, in Princeton, British Columbia, Canada; son of Herbert E. D. (a clergyman) and Evelyn M. (Jackson) Ashford; married Phyllis Arlyne Sharpe, August 31, 1948; children: Hugh, Heather (Mrs. David Dillenbeck), Elizabeth, Timothy. *Education:* Mount Allison University, B.A., 1947; St. Andrew's College, Saskatoon, Saskatchewan, B.D., 1950; Columbia University, M.A., 1975. *Home:* 2506 Chilver Rd., Windsor, Ontario, Canada N8W 2V9. *Office:* 897 Windermer Rd., Windsor, Ontario, Canada N8Y 3E3.

CAREER: Ordained pastor of United Church of Canada, 1950; pastor of United Churches of Canada in Calgary, Alberta, Sudbury, Ontario, Toronto, Ontario, and Montreal, Quebec, 1950-70; Fanshawe College, London, Ontario, chairman of department of student services, 1970-73; United Church of Canada, Windsor, Ontario, pastor, 1973—. *Military service:* Royal Canadian Naval Volunteer Reserve, 1945.

WRITINGS: Take It Easy, Fortress, 1976; *Loving Ourselves,* Fortress, in press.

*   *   *

ASHLEY, Nova Trimble 1911-

PERSONAL: Born July 10, 1911, in Selden, Kan.; daughter of Rufus William (in real estate and insurance) and Margaret (Lipton) Trimble; married James Ercle Ashley (a teacher), August 20, 1929; children: Keith, Kenneth L., James K. (deceased), Joyce (Mrs. Donald C. Olson). *Education:* Has studied at Wichita State University. *Politics:* Republican. *Religion:* United Methodist. *Home:* 2101 South Glendale, Wichita, Kan. 67218.

CAREER: Wesley Medical Center, Wichita, Kan., supervisor of insurance, 1950-70; free-lance writer, 1970—. Taught creative writing for Twentieth Century Club, 1961-72.

MEMBER: National League of American Pen Women (Kansas president, 1974-76; Wichita president, 1973-76), National Federation of Press Women, Chaparral Poets (member of board of directors), Kansas Press Women, Kansas Authors Club, Wichita Press Women, Wichita Line Women, Saturday Scribes (chairperson, 1964-70). *Awards, honors:* More than two hundred literary awards from organizations, including Pennsylvania Poetry Society, Kansas Authors Club, National League of American Pen Women, Phoenix Poetry Club, and Ozark Writers and Artists Guild; named Kansas poet of the year by Chaparral Poets, 1969, 1970, 1971.

WRITINGS—Books of poems: *Through an Ocean of Gold,* Triangle, 1962; *Coffee with Nova,* Robbins, 1966; *Loquacious Mood,* Golden Quill, 1970; *Haps and Mishaps,* Branden Press, 1973; *Hang in There, Mom,* C. R. Gibson, 1976; *Chin Up, Dad,* C. R. Gibson, 1976. Contributor to more than a hundred magazines and newspapers, including *Good Housekeeping* and *McCall's.*

WORK IN PROGRESS: A book of poems about grandmothers, for C. R. Gibson.

*   *   *

ASKEW, Jack
See HIVNOR, Robert

*   *   *

ASTER, Sidney 1942-

PERSONAL: Born May 24, 1942, in Montreal, Quebec, Canada; son of Sam and Ida (Rothman) Aster; married: Joyce Nora Bercovitch (a batikist), January 28, 1965; children: Andrea Zoe, Dylan Mark. *Education:* McGill University, B.A., 1963, M.A., 1965; London School of Economics and Political Science, University of London, Ph.D., 1968. *Home address:* R.R.3, Georgetown, Ontario, Canada L7G 4S6. *Office:* Erindale College, University of Toronto, Mississauga, Ontario, Canada.

CAREER: Writer; assistant professor at University of Toronto, 1976—.

WRITINGS: (Contributor) A.J.P. Taylor, editor, *Lloyd George: Twelve Essays*, Hamish Hamilton, 1971; *1939: The Making of the Second World War*, Deutsch, 1973; (editor) *The "X" Documents: The Secret History of Foreign Office Contacts with the German Resistance of 1937-1939*, Deutsch, 1974; *Anthony Eden*, Weidenfeld & Nicolson, 1976.

WORK IN PROGRESS: *Lord Salter: A Biography*, completion expected in 1978.

BIOGRAPHICAL/CRITICAL SOURCES: *Montreal Star*, August 31, 1973.

* * *

ASTLEY, Thea Beatrice May 1925-

PERSONAL: Born August 25, 1925, in Brisbane, Queensland, Australia; daughter of Cecil and Eileen (Lindsay) Astley; married Edmund John Gregson, August 27, 1948; children: one son. *Education:* University of Queensland, graduated, 1947. *Office:* Department of English, Macquarie University, North Ryde, Sydney, New South Wales, Australia 2113.

CAREER: Teacher of English in Queensland, Australia, 1944-48, and in New South Wales, Australia, 1948-67; Macquarie University, Sydney, senior tutor in department of English, 1968—. *Awards, honors:* Commonwealth Literary Fund fellowships, 1961, 1964; Miles Franklin Awards for *The Well-Dressed Explorer*, 1962, *The Slow Natives*, 1965, and *The Acolyte*, 1973; Moomba Award, 1965, for *The Slow Natives;* Age Newspaper book-of-the-year award, 1975, for *A Kindness Cup*.

WRITINGS—Novels: *Girl With a Monkey*, Angus & Robertson, 1958; *A Descant for Gossips*, Angus & Robertson, 1960; *The Well-Dressed Explorer*, Angus & Robertson, 1962; *The Slow Natives*, Angus & Robertson, 1965, M. Evans, 1967; *A Boatload of Home Folk*, Angus & Robertson, 1968; *The Acolyte*, Angus & Robertson, 1972; *A Kindness Cup*, Thomas Nelson, 1975. Short stories have been included in anthology, *Coast to Coast*, Angus & Robertson, 1961, 1963, and 1965. Contributor of poems to anthologies and periodicals. Editor, *Coast to Coast*, 1969-70.

WORK IN PROGRESS: Another novel.

SIDELIGHTS: *The Slow Natives* is Thea Astley's only novel published in the United States to date. While comparing Astley to "Australia's over-mannered senior novelist Patrick White" and calling her the best Australian woman novelist since Christine Stead, a reviewer for *Time* made yet another comparison. He writes, "There is a convent near Brisbane, Australia, where the nuns serve visitors a specialty of their religious house: confiture of prickly pear. This exotic jam might well symbolize the theme of Thea Astley's novel, in which the harsh products of Australian soil undergo the painful process of civilization.

"The scene is subtropical Brisbane, where a family of intellectual pioneers tests its illusions against a philistine, no-nonsense, somewhat raffish society." He goes on to say that "The author's feminine eye and ear for antipodean Babbittry and for significant styles in decor, clothes, deportment and accent make her a lively social satirist. But her book should not be mistaken for a mere gibe at the gaucheries of a raw culture. She is also dealing with the moral fate of a painfully recognizable family."

Writing about Thea Astley's style in *The Slow Natives*, William J. Lynch said "Miss Astley's novel is remarkable for its tight structure and its verbal economy. She manipulates and

interweaves the lives of several pivotal characters without losing grip on any of them. . . . Her belief in the regenerative power of human love gives a positive tone to this book which is lacking in so many of the current pseudo-existentialist dronings on the triviality of human existence. . . . It is a good indication of the power that artistically controlled writing can still exert on the reader."

AVOCATIONAL INTERESTS: Music, friends, conversation.

BIOGRAPHICAL/CRITICAL SOURCES: *Time*, October 20, 1967; *Best Sellers*, December 1, 1967; L. J. Blake, *Australian Writers*, Rigby, 1968; *Southerly* (Sydney), Number 1, 1970.

* * *

ATKIN, William Wilson 1912(?)-1976

1912(?)—February 6, 1976; American architectural writer and editor, publisher, and author. Obituaries: *New York Times*, February 8, 1976.

* * *

AUKOFER, Frank A(lexander) 1935-

PERSONAL: Born April 6, 1935, in Milwaukee, Wis.; son of Herbert A. (a printer) and Wanda M. (Kaminski) Aukofer; married D. Sharlene Talatzko (an airline agent), August 6, 1960; children: Juliann, Matthew, Becky, Joseph. *Education:* Marquette University, B.A., 1960; Northwestern University, graduate study, 1966-67. *Religion:* Roman Catholic. *Home:* 4015 Thornton St., Annandale, Va. 22003. *Agent:* Larry Sternig, 742 Robertson St., Milwaukee, Wis. 53213. *Office:* *Milwaukee Journal*, 734 National Press Building, Washington, D.C. 20045.

CAREER: Wisconsin Cuneo Press, Milwaukee, began as apprentice, became journeyman compositor, 1953-58; *Milwaukee Journal*, Milwaukee, Wis., compositor, 1958-60, reporter and automobile editor, 1960-69, assistant city editor, 1969-70, Washington correspondent, 1970—. Notable assignments include the civil rights movements of the 1960's, the Watergate hearings, and Richard Nixon's resignation from the presidency. Advertising manager of Marquette University Press, 1959-60. *Military service:* U.S. Air Force Reserve, 1952-60. *Member:* National Press Club (vice-president, 1977), Sigma Delta Chi. *Awards, honors:* Received four awards from Milwaukee Press Club and two traffic safety writing awards from American Trucking Associations.

WRITINGS: *City with a Chance* (history of the civil rights movement in Wisconsin), Bruce Books, 1968. Milwaukee correspondent for *Newsweek*. Contributor to magazines and newspapers, including *Life*.

SIDELIGHTS: Aukofer writes: "As a reporter, I am convinced that the best kind of journalism is that which communicates well to the largest number. I am also committed to the conviction that no one has a corner on the truth; that probably everyone has some piece of it. Therefore, my commitment as a newspaperman is to communicate as accurately and fairly as possible the varying opinions and interpretations of the truth as expressed by those whom I cover. That, of course, does not mean that I am willing to accept a version of the truth that is completely at odds with experience or fundamental morality. I believe that newspaper reporters and editors must make judgments, but I do not believe that their role is to substitute their judgments for fair and accurate reporting." *Avocational interests:* Travel, automobiles.

AULTMAN, Richard E(ugene) 1933-

PERSONAL: Born December 21, 1933, in Moline, Ill.; son of Chester Clyde and Margaret Augusta (Klouser) Aultman; married Marjorie Katherine Kirk, November 4, 1974; children: Kimberly Ann, Michael Stewart. *Education:* Northwestern University, B.A., 1956, M.S., 1957. *Religion:* Congregationalist. *Home:* 2 Cedar Lane, Weston, Conn. 06880.

CAREER: Decatur Herald-Review, Decatur, Ill., sports reporter, 1957-59; *Chicago Sun-Times,* Chicago, Ill., copy editor, 1959; *Golf Digest,* Norwalk, Conn., associate editor, 1959-61, executive editor, 1961-64, editor, 1964-73, contributing editor, 1973—. *Member:* Golf Writers Association of America, Beta Theta Pi. *Awards, honors:* MacGregor-Brunswick golf writers' award in Magazine Division, from National Golf Writers Championship, 1963.

WRITINGS: (With Gary Player) *Golf Secrets,* Prentice-Hall, 1962; *Learn to Play Golf,* Rand-McNally, 1966; *Square-to-Square Golf Swing: Model Method for the Modern Player,* Golf Digest, 1970; (with Bob Toski) *Touch System for Better Golf,* Golf Digest, 1971; (with Eddie Merrins) *Swing the Handle, Not the Clubhead,* Golf Digest, 1973; (with Jack Grout) *Play Golf As I Taught Jack Nicklaus,* Atheneum, 1975; (with Ken Bowden) *Methods of Golf's Masters,* Coward, 1975. Co-author of syndicated column, "Golfing with Arnold Palmer," 1964—. Contributor to sports magazines.

WORK IN PROGRESS: A golf instruction book, with Lee Trevino, for Atheneum.

SIDELIGHTS: Aultman has played golf since he was about four years old; presently he teaches golf.

*　　*　　*

AUSTER, Nancy (Eileen) R(oss) 1926-

PERSONAL: Born August 19, 1926, in New York, N.Y.; daughter of Norman Lask (a dentist) and Edith Cornelia (Jacobson) Ross; married Donald Auster (a college professor), August 18, 1946; children: Carol Jean, Ellen Ruth. *Education:* Barnard College, A.B., 1948; Indiana University, M.B.A., 1954; additional study at St. Lawrence University, 1960-62 and 1971, and State University of New York College at Potsdam, 1968 and 1970. *Religion:* Unitarian-Universalist. *Home:* 21 Craig Dr., Canton, N.Y. 13617. *Office:* Social Science Department, State University of New York Agricultural and Technical College, Canton, N.Y. 13617.

CAREER: Conference Board, Inc., New York City, research associate, 1948-51; American Home Products Corp., New York City, assistant to budget director, 1951; Indiana University, Bloomington, research assistant in School of Business, 1952-54, editor of publications of Bureau of Business Research, 1954-56; research associate and statistical analyst, 1961-62; St. Lawrence University, Canton, N.Y., lecturer in economics department, 1962-66; State University of New York Agricultural and Technical College, Canton, assistant professor, 1966-70, associate professor, 1970-73, professor of economics, 1973—, acting chairperson of social science department. *Member:* American Economics Association, American Statistical Association, League of Women Voters (executive board member of Canton-Potsdam chapter, 1960-62), Eastern Economics Association, North Country Economics Association (executive committee member, 1975—), New York State Economics Association (secretary-treasurer, 1970-71), New York Association of Junior Colleges, Phi Delta Kappa, Delta Kappa Gamma, Beta Gamma Sigma.

WRITINGS: (Editor with Lucy Earisman) *Production Manual: Editorial Division, Bureau of Business Research,* Bureau of Business Research, Indiana University, 1956; (with husband, Donald Auster) *Men Who Enter Nursing: A Sociological Analysis* (monograph), U.S. Public Health Service, 1970. Contributor to *Conference Board Record.* Editor of *Faculty Senate Bulletin* of State University of New York, 1973-75.

*　　*　　*

AUSTIN, Lettie J(ane) 1925-

PERSONAL: Born March 21, 1925, in Joplin, Mo.; married Lewis H. Fenderson, 1965. *Education:* Lincoln University, Jefferson City, Mo., B.A., 1946; Kansas State College of Agriculture and Applied Science (now Kansas State University), M.A., 1947; Stanford University, Ed.D., 1952; University of Nottingham, M.A., 1954; Howard University, M.S., 1963. *Office:* Department of English, Howard University, Washington, D.C., 20001.

CAREER: Howard University, Washington, D.C., instructor in English, 1947-50; New York University, New York, N.Y., instructor, 1949-50; University of Maryland, lecturer in American literature in overseas program, 1952-53; Howard University, assistant professor, 1954-57, associate professor, 1958-67, professor of English, 1968—. Institute for Teachers of English, Texas Southern University, associate director, summer, 1961-64, assistant director, summer, 1965-66. Curriculum preparation specialist, Educational Services, Inc., 1964-65; reader, Educational Testing Service, 1966—. Consultant to Texas Southern University, 1955-56, Temple University, 1955, Peace Corps in Togo and Senegal, summer, 1971, Norfolk State College, 1971-72, and Phelps-Stokes Foundation, 1972—. *Member:* National Council of Teachers of English, College Association of Reading Teachers, American Psychological Association. *Awards, honors:* Fulbright grant, 1952-54.

WRITINGS: (With Alice W. Grant and others) *College Reading Skills,* Knopf, 1966; (editor with husband, Lewis H. Fenderson, and Sophia P. Nelson) *The Black Man and the Promise of America,* Scott, Foresman, 1970. Contributor of articles to professional journals, including *College Language Association Journal, Personality and Social Psychology,* and *Journal of Reading.**

*　　*　　*

AWOLOWO, Obafemi Awo 1909-

PERSONAL: Born March 6, 1909, in Ikenne, Western Nigeria; son of David Sopulu (a Yoruba farmer) and Mary (Efunyela) Awolowo; married Hannah Idowu Dideolu, December 26, 1937; children: two sons, three daughters. *Education:* Wesley College, Ibadan, Nigeria, graduate, 1927; University of London, B.Com. (with honors), 1944, LL.B., 1946. *Religion:* Protestant. *Home:* Ikenne, Ijebu Remo, Nigeria. *Office:* Office of the Chancellor, Ahmadu Bello University, Zaria, Nigeria.

CAREER: School teacher in Ogbe, Abeokuta, Nigeria, 1928-29; stenographer in Lagos, Nigeria, 1930-32; Wesley College, Ibadan, Nigeria, clerk-stenographer, 1932-34; Nigerian *Daily Times,* reporter, 1934-35; Nigerian Motor Transport Union, assistant secretary, 1936-40, general secretary, 1941-44; editor, *Nigerian Worker,* 1939-44; called to the Bar at Inner Temple, 1947; solicitor and advocate of the Supreme Court of Nigeria in Ibadan, 1946-52; cabinet minister and leader of government business, Western Region of Nigeria, 1952-54, premier of the Western Region, 1954-59;

leader of the opposition in Federal Parliament, Lagos, Nigeria, 1960-62; elected leader of the Yoruba people, 1966; Government of Nigeria, vice-chairman of the Federal Executive Council and head of the Ministry of Finance, 1967-71; University of Ife, Ile-Ife, Nigeria, chancellor, 1969-75; Ahmadu Bello University, Zaria, Nigeria, chancellor, 1975—. Member of Nigerian Youth Movement (leading efforts to reform Ibadan Native Authority council), 1940-43; co-founder, Trades Union Congress of Nigeria, 1943; founder of Egbe Omo Oduduwa (Yoruba cultural movement) in London, England, 1945, general secretary, 1948-51; founder of Action Group of Nigeria (a political party), 1951. *Awards, honors:* LL.D. from University of Nigeria, 1961, University of Ibadan, 1973, and Ahmadu Bello University, 1975; D.Sc. from University of Ife, 1967; D.Litt. from University of Lagos, 1970.

WRITINGS: Path to Nigerian Freedom, Faber, 1947; *Forward to a New Nigeria,* Western Nigeria Information Services, 1957; *Awo: The Chief Autobiography of Chief Obafemi Awolowo,* Cambridge University Press, 1960; *Anglo-Nigerian Military Pact Agreement,* Action Group Bureau of Information, 1960; *Presidential Address Delivered by Chief the Honourable Obafemi Awolowo, Federal President of the Action Group and Leader of the Opposition in the Federal House of Representatives at the Seventh Congress of the Action Group Held at the Abalabi Club, Mushin, on Monday, 19th September, 1960,* African Press, 1960; *Forward with Democratic Socialism: A Message by Chief Awolowo from Broad Street Prison, Lagos,* Action Group of Nigeria, 1961; *Thoughts on Nigerian Constitution,* Oxford University Press, 1966; *An Address Delivered by Chief Obafemi Awolowo on the Occasion of His Installation as the First Chancellor of the University of Ife at Ile-Ife on Monday, 15 May, 1967,* Ibadan University Press, 1967; *Blueprint for Post-War Reconstruction,* Nigerian Federal Ministry of Information, 1967; *My Early Life,* J. West Publications, 1968; *The Path to Economic Freedom in Developing Countries,* University of Lagos, 1968; *The People's Republic,* Oxford University Press, 1968; *The Strategy and Tactics of the People's Republic of Nigeria,* Macmillan, 1970. Also author of *Action Group Fourteen-Point Programme,* 1959; *African Unity,* 1961; and *Lecture on the Financing of the Nigerian Civil War and Its Implications for the Future Economy of the Nation,* 1970. Contributor to newspapers. Founder, *Nigerian Tribune,* 1949.

SIDELIGHTS: With considerable financial difficulty, Awolowo, whose inherited titles as a descendant of Oduduwo (founder of the Yoruba kingdom) include Ashiwaju of Ijebu-Remo, Losi of Ikenne, Lisa of Ijeun, Apesin of Oshogbo, Odole of Ife, Ajagunla of Ado Ekiti, Odofin of Owo, and Obing Ikpan Isong of Ibibioland, educated himself in Nigeria and later in England. He also has been conferred with Chieftancy titles in other parts of Nigeria. His political activities began while a student in London. His party positions were moderate at first, later moved toward the left in order to accommodate other members of the party and maintain political unity. He was able to visit India in 1952 and 1953 for political discussions with Nehru (whom Awolowo admired) and other Indian leaders, and to study India's system of symbol voting. Later, as premier of Nigeria's Western Region, Awolowo toured England, the United States, West Germany, Italy, and Japan to promote interest in trade and investment operations in Nigeria.

During a dispute with leaders inside his political party, Awolowo and several others were arrested in 1962, Awolowo himself was "detained" and tried for "treasonable felony

and conspiracy," convicted, and sentenced to ten years in prison, all in 1962-63. He was imprisoned until 1966, when he was pardoned and released; and whereupon he resumed his political career.

BIOGRAPHICAL/CRITICAL SOURCES: John Gunther, *Inside Africa,* Harper, 1955; *Time,* February 16, 1959; *U.S. News,* July 4, 1960; Edna Mason Kaula, *Leaders of the New Africa* (juvenile), World Publishing, 1966; *The New Africans,* Putnam, 1967; Adrian A. Roscoe, editor, *Mother Is Gold: West African Literature,* Cambridge University Press, 1971.

* * *

AXELROD, George 1922-

PERSONAL: Born June 9, 1922, in New York, N.Y.; son of Herman (in real estate) and Beatrice Carpenter (a silent picture actress); married Gloria Washburn, February 28, 1942 (divorced June, 1954); married Joan Stanton, October, 1954; children: (first marriage) Peter, Steven; (second marriage) Nina. *Residence:* Beverly Hills, Calif. *Agent:* Irving Paul Lazar, 211 S. Beverly Dr., Beverly Hills, Calif.

CAREER: Playwright, screenwriter, and novelist. Stage manager and actor in summer stock, 1940-41; writer of scripts for radio shows, including "The Shadow," "Midnight," and "Grand Ole Opry," and television scriptwriter for "Celebrity Time," 1941-52; scriptwriter for films and television, 1952—; producer and director of stage and films, including his own work, 1955—. *Military service:* U.S. Army, Signal Corps. *Member:* Authors League of America, Dramatists Guild.

WRITINGS—Novels: *Beggar's Choice,* Howell, Soskin, 1947 (published in England as *Hobson's Choice,* Elek, 1951); *Blackmailer,* Fawcett, 1952; *Where Am I Now-When I Need Me?,* Viking, 1971, published as *Where Am I Now That I Need Me?,* Pocket Books, 1972.

Plays: *The Seven Year Itch: A Romantic Comedy* (three-act; produced in New York at Fulton (now Helen Hayes) Theatre, 1952), Random House, 1953; *Will Success Spoil Rock Hunter? A New Comedy* (three-act; first produced in New York at Belasco Theatre, 1955), Random House, 1956; *Goodbye Charlie* (two-act; first produced in New York at Longacre Theatre, 1959), Samuel French, 1959.

Screenplays: "Phffft," Columbia, 1954; (with Billy (Wilder) "The Seven Year Itch," Twentieth Century-Fox, 1955; "Bus Stop," Twentieth Century-Fox, 1956; "Breakfast at Tiffany's," Paramount, 1961; "The Manchurian Candidate," United Artists, 1962; "Paris When It Sizzles," Paramount, 1964; "How to Murder Your Wife," United Artists, 1965; (with Larry H. Johnson) "Lord Love a Duck," United Artists, 1966; "The Secret Life of an American Wife," Twentieth Century-Fox, 1968.

Contributor of sketches to "Small Wonder," a revue, 1948; writer of night club musical, "All About Love," 1951.

* * *

AYER, Margaret

PERSONAL: Born in New York, N.Y.; daughter of Ira (a physician) and Louise (Foster) Ayer; married Alfred Babbington Smith (a banker). *Education:* Attended Philadelphia Museum School of Industrial Art; studied art privately in Paris and Rome. *Home:* 18492 Capricorn Ct., Castro Valley, Calif. 94546.

CAREER: Free-lance writer, artist, and illustrator.

Member: Society of Illustrators, Asia Society, Women's National Book Association, Artists Guild of New York (past vice-president).

WRITINGS—All self-illustrated books for children: *The Elves Service Station,* Abelard, 1951; *The Wish That Went Wild,* Abelard, 1952; *Getting to Know Thailand,* Coward, 1959, revised edition, 1972; *Made in Thailand,* Knopf, 1964; *Animals of Southeast Asia,* St. Martin's, 1970. Also author and illustrator of six books of bible stories published by Gibson, 1958-65.

Illustrator of more than one hundred books, including: Margaret Landon, *Anna and the King of Siam,* John Day, 1944, new edition published as *Anna and the King,* 1947; Jean Bothwell, *Little Flute Player,* Morrow, 1949; Muriel Fuller, editor, *Favorite Old Fairy Tales,* Nelson, 1949; Phyllis Ayer Sowers, *Elephant Boy of the Teak Forest,* Messner, 1949; Bothwell, *Onions without Tears: A Collection of Intriguing Recipes,* Hastings House, 1950; Frances Fitzpatrick Wright, *Surprise at Sampey Place,* 1950; Bothwell, *Sword of a Warrior,* Harcourt, 1951; Bothwell, *Paddy and Sam,* Abelard, 1952; and Wright, *Poplar Street Park,* Abingdon, 1952.

SIDELIGHTS: Margaret Ayer told *CA:* "I was pleased to find that *The Elves Service Station* was used so much by children in a hospital that it was falling to pieces and held together by adhesive tape."

* * *

BABCOCK, Dorothy E(llen) 1931-

PERSONAL: Born July 20, 1931, in Philadelphia, Pa.; daughter of Peter Joseph (a mechanic) and Dorothy (Muldowney) Kreinbihl; married Clarence O. Babcock (a mining research engineer), June 28, 1958; children: Donna Rita, Phyllis Anne, Karen Denise. *Education:* University of Pennsylvania, B.S.N.Ed., 1956; Catholic University of America, M.S.N., 1958; University of Colorado, further graduate study, 1967-68. *Politics:* Democrat. *Home:* 5 South Flower St., Lakewood, Colo. 80226. *Office:* Colorado Group and Family Center, 609 West Littleton Blvd., Littleton, Colo. 80120.

CAREER: Denver General Hospital, Denver, Colo., clinical specialist in psychiatric mental health nursing, and therapist, 1969-76; Metropolitan State College, Denver, Colo., adjunct faculty member of psychiatric nursing, 1976—. Clinical instructor at University of Colorado and adjunct faculty member at UWW Loretto Heights, Denver, Colo., both 1974—. *Member:* International Transactional Analysis Association, Mental Health Association, Denver Area Transactional Analysis Seminar (president, 1972-73), Colorado Nursing Association, Colorado Mental Health Association (member of licensure subcommittee), Pi Gamma Mu, Sigma Theta Tau.

WRITINGS: Introduction to Growth Development and Family Life, F. A. Davis, 1962, 3rd edition, 1972; (with Terry Keepers) *Raising Kids OK,* Grove, 1976. Contributor to nursing and transactional analysis journals.

SIDELIGHTS: Dorothy Babcock comments briefly: "I like to work with parents and help them become more self-confident; feeling o.k. about themselves, and able to pass on that to their children."

* * *

BAER, Walter S. III 1937-

PERSONAL: Born July 27, 1937, in Chicago, Ill.; son of Walter S., Jr. (a business executive) and Margaret S. (Mayer) Baer; married Miriam R. Schenker (a school administrator), June 18, 1959; children: David W., Alan B. *Education:* California Institute of Technology, B.S., 1959; University of Wisconsin, Madison, Ph.D., 1964. *Politics:* Democrat. *Home:* 560 Latimer Rd., Santa Monica, Calif. 90402. *Office:* 1700 Main St., Santa Monica, Calif. 90406.

CAREER: Bell Telephone Laboratories, Murray Hill, N.J., research physicist, 1964-66; White House, Washington, D.C., White House fellow, 1966-67; Office of Science and Technology, member of scientific advisory staff, 1967-69; Laird Systems, Los Angeles, Calif., senior staff member, 1969-70; self-employed consultant in Santa Monica, Calif., 1970-74; Rand Corp., Santa Monica, Calif., associate director of Energy Policy Program, 1974—. Director of Aspen (Colorado) cable television workshop, 1972-73; member of cable television advisory committee of Federal Communications Commission, 1972-75. Member of computer science board of National Academy of Sciences, 1969-72; member of technical advisory council of General Telephone & Electronics Corp., 1971-74. Trustee of St. Augustine's School; director of California Institute of Technology's Young Men's Christian Association (YMCA).

MEMBER: American Association for the Advancement of Science, American Physical Society, Association for Computing Machinery, New York Academy of Science, Sigma Xi. *Awards, honors:* Preceptor Award from Broadcast Industry Conference, 1975.

WRITINGS: Interactive Television, Rand Corp., 1971; (with Richard Adler) *Cable and Continuing Education,* Praeger, 1973; (editor with Adler) *The Electronic Box Office,* Praeger, 1974; *Cable Television: A Handbook for Decisionmaking,* Crane, Russak, 1974. Editor of "Rand Cable Television Series," four volumes, Crane, Russak, 1974. Contributor to scientific and technical journals.

WORK IN PROGRESS: Research on U.S. energy policy, telecommunications, and policies for science and technology.

* * *

BAGG, Robert Ely 1935-

PERSONAL: Born September 21, 1935, in Orange, N.J.; son of Theodore Ely and Elma Hague (White) Bagg; married Sarah Frances Robinson, August 24, 1957; children: Theodore Antibes Ariel, Christopher Augustus, Jonathan, Melissa, Robert. *Education:* Amherst College, A.B., 1957; Harvard University, graduate study, 1960; University of Connecticut, M.A., 1961, Ph.D., 1965. *Home:* 32 Barrett Pl., Northampton, Mass. 01060. *Office:* Department of English, University of Massachusetts, Amherst, Mass. 01002.

CAREER: University of Washington, Seattle, instructor in English, 1963-65; University of Massachusetts, Amherst, assistant professor, 1965-70, associate professor, 1970—. Lecturer at Smith College, 1967; visiting associate professor at University of Texas, 1971. Fellow of National Translation Center, 1969, and of American Academy in Rome. *Member:* Modern Language Association of America, Phi Kappa Phi, Phi Alpha Psi. *Awards, honors:* Armstrong Poetry Prize, 1956 and 1957; Glascock Poetry Prize, 1957; Simpson fellowship, 1957-58; Prix de Rome from American Academy of Arts and Letters, 1958-59.

WRITINGS: Poems, 1956-1957, Grosvenor House and Amherst Journal Record, 1957; *Madonna of the Cello* (poems), Wesleyan University Press, 1961; *Liberations* (three-act plays), Spiritus Mundi Press, 1969; (translator) *Euripides' Hippolytus*, Oxford University Press, 1971; *The Scrawny Sonnets and Other Narratives* (poems), University of Illinois Press, 1973. Contributor to poetry magazines, including *Arion* and *Mosaic*.*

* * *

BAHR, Edith-Jane 1926-

PERSONAL: Born June 14, 1926, in New Jersey; daughter of Thomas (an accountant) and Bertha (Thorpe) White; married Edward E. Bahr (a contractor), May 11, 1950; children: Diane (Mrs. Paul Schulman), Thomas C., Cynthia A., Barbara J. *Education:* Attended University of Maryland, 1944-46; Newark State College, B.A., 1972, M.A., 1974. *Politics:* "Hesitant Republican." *Religion:* Presbyterian. *Home:* 624 Riverside Dr., Cranford, N.J. 07016. *Agent:* Curtis Brown Ltd., 575 Madison Ave., New York, N.Y. 10022. *Office:* Bureau of Children's Shelters, 1052 Plainfield Ave., Berkeley Heights, N.J.

CAREER: Mount Carmel Guild Special Classes, Cranford, N.J., special education teacher, 1971-75; Ro-Sher Academy, Newark, N.J., director of education, 1975-76; Bureau of Children's Shelters, Berkeley Heights, N.J., educational coordinator, 1976—. *Member:* Authors Guild of Authors League of America. *Awards, honors:* Opie humor award, 1969, for *Everybody Wins, Nobody Loses.*

WRITINGS: Everybody Wins, Nobody Loses (humor), McKay, 1969; *A Nice Neighborhood* (mystery), Collins, 1974, Dell, 1975; *Help, Please* (mystery), Doubleday, 1975. Contributor of stories and articles to *Ladies' Home Journal* and *Good Housekeeping.*

WORK IN PROGRESS: Mysteries, *Fear Itself* and *Hoax?*

SIDELIGHTS: Edith-Jane Bahr writes: "I have always had a deep concern for children and young people—especially those unfortunate enough to be labeled 'retarded,' 'emotionally disturbed,' 'disadvantaged' (a word I loathe) and so on. I do enjoy working with and teaching these young people." *Avocational interests:* Travel, playing bridge.

* * *

BAHR, Robert 1940-

PERSONAL: Born October 29, 1940, in Newark, N.J.; son of Robert (an electrician) and Catherine (Kuebler) Bahr; married Alice Harrison (a librarian), 1971; children: Keith. *Education:* King's College, Briarcliff Manor, N.Y., B.A., 1964. *Agent:* Roberta Kent, W. B. Agency, 156 East 52nd St., New York, N.Y. 10022. *Office:* 1104 Walnut St., Allentown, Pa. 18102.

CAREER: Rodale Press, Emmaus Pa., editor, 1964-72; free-lance writer, 1972—. Lecturer. *Member:* National Association of Science Writers, American Society of Journalists and Authors, Society for the Scientific Study of Sex.

WRITINGS: (Compiler) *The Natural Way to a Healthy Skin*, Rodale Press, 1972; *The Virility Factor*, Putnam, 1976; *Healing and Hormones*, Dutton, 1977. Contributor to *Coronet, Sports Illustrated, TV Guide, Let's Live, Prevention*, and other periodicals.

WORK IN PROGRESS: Research on health, sex, and physical fitness.

SIDELIGHTS: Bahr wrote: "Although for several years I simply reported research findings in health, physical fitness, and medicine, I've been delving more and more in recent years into interpretive reporting, a kind of philosophy of these subjects. I've done that to a great extent in my recent book, *The Virility Factor*, and I expect to do it more extensively in future books. In other words, I intend to be opinionated. It seems to me people who are not specialists in these subjects want to know more than what the studies prove, they want to know what the proof indicates in the overall context of research."

* * *

BAIER, Kurt Erich 1917-

PERSONAL: Born January 26, 1917, in Vienna, Austria; came to United States in 1962; son of Emil and Maria (Hunna) Baier; married Annette Stoop, December 28, 1958. *Education:* University of Vienna, student, 1935-38; University of Melbourne, B.A., 1944, M.A., 1946; Oxford University, D.Phil., 1952. *Home:* 100 Maple Heights Rd., Pittsburgh, Pa. 15232. *Office:* Department of Philosophy, University of Pittsburgh, Pittsburgh, Pa. 15213.

CAREER: University of Melbourne, Melbourne, Australia, lecturer in philosophy, 1948-56; Australian National University, Canberra, professor of philosophy, 1956-62; University of Pittsburgh, Pittsburgh, Pa., professor of philosophy, 1962—, chairman of department, 1962-67. *Member:* Australian Humanities Research Council, Australian Association of Philosophy (president, 1961), American Association of Philosophy (president of Eastern Division, 1977), American Academy of Arts and Sciences.

WRITINGS: The Moral Point of View: A Rational Basis of Ethics, Cornell University Press, 1958, abridged edition with new preface, Random House, 1965; (editor with Nicholas Rescher, and contributor) *Values and the Future: The Impact of Technological Change on American Values*, Free Press, 1969.

Contributor: R. T. DeGeorge, editor, *Ethics and Society*, Doubleday, 1966; Sidney Hook, editor, *Human Value and Economic Policy*, New York University Press, 1967; P. W. Kurtz, editor, *Moral Problems in Contemporary Society*, Prentice-Hall, 1969; Howard Keifer and Milton K. Munik, editors, *Contemporary Philosophic Thought*, Volume IV, State University of New York Press, 1970; Myles Brand, editor, *The Nature of Human Action*, Scott-Foresman, 1970; R. Pennock and J. Chapman, editors, *Political Obligation*, Atherton Press, 1970; C. M. Beck, B. S. Crittenden, and E. V. Sullivan, editors, *Moral Education: Interdisciplinary Approaches*, University of Toronto Press, 1971; Peter A. French, *Individual and Collective Responsibility: My-Lai*, Schenkman, 1972; James F. Doyle, editor, *Educational Judgments*, Routledge & Kegan Paul, 1973; Glenn Langford and D. J. O'Connor, editors *New Essays in the Philosophy of Education*, Routledge & Kegan Paul, 1973; R. O. Clarke and Peter C. List, editors, *Environmental Spectrum*, Van Nostrand, 1974. Contributor to professional journals.

* * *

BAILEY, Chris H(arvey) 1946-

PERSONAL: Born August 4, 1946, in Robinson, Ill.; son of Ray Kenneth (a maintenance engineer) and Imogene (Roberts) Bailey. *Education:* Brigham Young University, A.S., 1966, B.S., 1970. *Religion:* Church of Jesus Christ of Latter-day Saints. *Home:* "Castle Largo," 230 Center St., Bristol, Conn. 06010. *Office:* American Clock & Watch Museum, Inc., 100 Maple St., Bristol, Conn. 06010.

CAREER: Brigham Young University, Provo, Utah, research associate, 1970-72, part-time instructor in historical research technology, 1971-72; American Clock & Watch Museum, Bristol, Conn., curator, 1972-73, managing director, 1973—; writer. Lecturer on clockmaking in the United States. *Military service:* U.S. Army National Guard, 1970-76. *Member:* National Association of Watch and Clock Collectors (director, 1975-79), Antiquarian Horological Society, American Association of Museums, American Association for State and Local History, Vintage Phonograph Society of New Zealand, Connecticut Historical Society, Utah Genealogical Society (charter member), Connecticut League of Historical Societies, Illinois State Genealogical Society (charter member), Crawford County Historical Society (Ill.), City of London Phonograph and Gramophone Society, Atlantic Region Rolls Royce Owner's Club, Society for Local History and Genealogy (Brigham Young University).

WRITINGS: Highsmiths in America, privately printed, 1971; *Two Hundred Years of American Clocks and Watches,* Prentice-Hall, 1975. Contributor to journals in his field. Contributing editor, *Genealogical Society Quarterly,* 1972-76. Author of column, "Old Crawford County," in *Argus,* 1970-72.

WORK IN PROGRESS: Researching wooden movement clockmakers of America; a book *Victorian America's Clocks.*

AVOCATIONAL INTERESTS: Restoring a castellated Victorian mansion built in 1880.

* * *

BAIRD, Duncan H. 1917-

PERSONAL: Born October 26, 1917, in New Jersey; son of Julian Braden (a banker) and Helen (Hall) Baird; married first wife, Jean M., February 23, 1943 (divorced November 15, 1965); married Mary Bowlby (a teacher), June 24, 1966; children: (first marriage) Ann, Jane, Elizabeth (Mrs. Conrad Newburgh). *Education:* Yale University, B.A., 1939; University of Michigan, LL.B., 1942; University of Minnesota, Ph.D., 1962. *Politics:* Republican. *Religion:* Unitarian-Universalist. *Home:* 2144 Charlton, St. Paul, Minn. 55118. *Office:* Macalester College, St. Paul, Minn. 55105.

CAREER: Doherty, Rumble & Butler (attorneys), St. Paul, Minn., associate, 1946-56; Macalester College, St. Paul, Minn., assistant professor, 1961-73, associate professor of political science, 1973—. Family Service of St. Paul, member of board of directors, 1950-56, president, 1954-55. *Military service:* U.S. Naval Reserve, active duty, 1942-46; became lieutenant. *Member:* Law and Society Association, University Club of St. Paul.

WRITINGS: (With Dorothy Dodge) *Continuities and Discontinuities,* Schenkman, 1975. Contributor to *Minnesota Law Review.*

* * *

BAKELY, Don(ald Carlisle) 1928-

PERSONAL: Born August 23, 1928, in Elwood, N.J.; son of Edwin P. and Margaret (Decker) Bakely; married Jeanne Flagg, 1949; children: Paul, Stephen, Claudia, Peter, Matthew, Lois, Bethany. *Education:* Attended West Virginia Wesleyan College, 1948-49; Temple University, B.Sc.Ed., 1952, M.Div., 1955; further graduate study, Mount Airy Lutheran Seminary, 1960-65. *Home:* 1708 Southwest Blvd., Kansas City, Kan. 66103. *Office:* Cross-Lines Cooperative Council, 1620 South 37th St., Kansas City, Kan. 66106.

CAREER: Assistant pastor of Methodist church in Camden, N.J., 1949-50; pastor in Camden, 1950-53, 1958-65, and Brooklawn, N.J., 1953-58; Cross-Lines Cooperative Council, Kansas City, Kan., executive director, director of Cross-Lines Homes and Cross-Lines Retirement Center, and president of Cross-Lines Towers, 1965—. Consultant to Vista and Office of Economic Opportunity. *Military service:* U.S. Army, paratrooper and member of President Truman's Honor Guard, 1946-49. *Awards, honors:* Citizens award from Wyandotte County Bar Association, 1971; commendation from President Gerald Ford and from National Jaycees, both 1976.

WRITINGS: If: A Big Word with the Poor, Faith & Life, 1976.

WORK IN PROGRESS: My People Hurt; Bethany; Cross-Lines.

SIDELIGHTS: Bakely writes that he grew up in poverty. As a clergyman in New Jersey, identifying strongly with the poor, he integrated his congregation, opening doors to a new life for the previously unwanted members of the neighborhood. Cross-Lines Cooperative Council, which he heads, is a new approach to inner-city, suburban, church, and business people of different races and religious backgrounds, aimed at helping them to pool their resources to meet problems caused by poverty and ignorance. It is backed by churches representing more than thirty religious denominations and is staffed by several hundred volunteer workers who deal with poverty, education, housing, health, religion, legal needs, recreation, community organization, team ministries, financial matters, employment counseling, job training, and legislation.

BIOGRAPHICAL/CRITICAL SOURCES: Ralph Creger, *The Lord Will Wipe Them Out,* Lyle Stuart, 1976.

* * *

BAKER, Elsie 1929-
(Meg Woodson)

PERSONAL: Born May 17, 1929, in New York, N.Y.; daughter of Andrew C. (a plumber) and Iris (Cox) Blucher; married Clinton C. Baker (a clergyman), May 29, 1954; children: Elizabeth, Timothy (deceased). *Education:* Queens College (now of the City University of New York), B.A., 1951; New York Theological Seminary, M.R.E., 1954. *Politics:* Republican. *Religion:* Reformed Church in America. *Home:* 6816 Greenbriar Dr., Parma Heights, Ohio 44130.

CAREER: Writer. *Member:* St. David's Christian Writers Association. *Awards, honors:* Third prize from Evangelical Press Association, 1972, for "From Frustration to Fulfillment"; first prize from Evangelical Press Association, 1973, for "The Voice on the Waters"; book of the year award from Campus Life, 1976, for *If I Die at Thirty.*

WRITINGS: (Under pseudonym Meg Woodson) *If I Die at Thirty,* Zondervan, 1966. Contributor to religious magazines, under pseudonym Meg Woodson.

WORK IN PROGRESS: Following Joey Home, nonfiction; *Mourning Light* (tentative title).

SIDELIGHTS: "I write for two primary, all-encompassing purposes," Baker told *CA,* "to honor God and to be of help to the people of God. Most of my writing to date has been centered around the illness (cystic fibrosis) of both of my children, and the death of our son. I find it rewarding indeed to be able to take the personal circumstances of my life and through my writing give them a purpose as large as the universe itself."

BAKER, F(rederick) Sherman   1902-1976

September 15, 1902—April 8, 1976; American editor and publisher of novels. Obituaries: *Publishers Weekly,* May 3, 1976.

* * *

BAKER, Lucinda   1916-

PERSONAL: Born July 10, 1916, in Atlanta, Ill.; daughter of Hazle Howard (an Indian trader) and Adah Rebecca (a teacher; maiden name, Mason) Baker; married Willard Alan Greiner (a singer), June 27, 1946. *Education:* Attended Arizona State College (now Northern Arizona University), 1934-38. *Politics:* Democrat. *Home address:* P.O. Box 418, Sedona, Ariz. 86336. *Agent:* Lurton Blassingame, 60 East 42nd St., New York, N.Y. 10017.

CAREER: Free-lance writer, 1936—. *Member:* Authors Guild of Authors League of America, Mystery Writers of America. *Awards, honors:* First prize in National Pan-Hellenic Essay Contest, 1937.

WRITINGS: The Place of Devils (mystery novel), Putnam, 1976; *Walk the Night Unseen* (mystery novel), Putnam, in press. Contributor of about two thousand stories to magazines in the United States and abroad, including *Redbook, Ladies' Home Journal, Family Circle,* and *Ingenue.*

WORK IN PROGRESS: A historical novel set in Arizona; several gothic novels.

SIDELIGHTS: Lucinda Baker writes: "I consider myself, first and foremost, a story-teller. I never wanted to be anything else. It has been a joyful life. I was brought to Las Vegas, N.M., when I was ten, and after that my father took us to Arizona, where he worked on the Indian reservation, buying hides, wool and furs, rugs, etc., and selling hardware, dry goods, tools, etc. to traders for sale in trading posts. Our family moved frequently, and I attended sixteen schools before I was seventeen. I left college to write children's radio plays in Hollywood, but this only lasted a few months. During World War Two I wrote and lived in Hollywood, San Francisco and Chicago—so all of them are, in a way, home to me."

* * *

BAKER, W(illiam) W(allace)   1921-

PERSONAL: Born July 2, 1921, in Kansas City, Mo.; son of William Reaune (a lawyer) and Grace (Wallace) Baker; married Virginia Elizabeth Graham, December 21, 1941; children: William W., Jr. (deceased). *Education:* University of Michigan, A.B., 1947. *Religion:* Episcopalian. *Home:* 4900 West 64th St., Prairie Village, Kan. 66208. *Office: Kansas City Star and Times,* 18th and Grand, Kansas City, Mo. 64108.

CAREER/WRITINGS: Kansas City Star and Times, Kansas City, Mo., reporter, 1947, copy editor, 1947-51, makeup editor, 1951-56, editorial writer, 1956-63, associate editor, 1953-67, editor, 1967—, member of board of directors, 1965—, executive vice-president, 1971-75, president, 1975—. Trustee of University of Missouri at Kansas City, William Allen White Foundation, and Episcopal Diocese of Kansas; regent of Rockhurst College. *Military service:* U.S. Army, 1941-45; became master sergeant; received Bronze Star. *Member:* American Newspaper Publishers Association, American Society of Newspaper Editors, National Conference of Editorial Writers, Kansas City Press Club, Sigma Delta Chi.

BAKKEN, Henry Harrison   1896-

PERSONAL: Born March 24, 1896, in Arena, Wis.; son of Halvor and Malla (Nelson) Bakken; married Clara K. Grimstad, September 2, 1922; children: Hugh R., James F., David C., Haakon R. *Education:* University of Wisconsin, Madison, B.A., 1922, M.A., 1924; Harvard University, further graduate study, 1929-30. *Home:* 2218 Chadbourne Ave., Madison, Wis. 53705.

CAREER: U.S. Department of Agriculture, Washington, D.C., economist in Cost of Marketing Division of Bureau of Agricultural Economics, 1922-23; University of Wisconsin, Madison, assistant agricultural economist, 1923-24, assistant professor, 1924-32, associate professor, 1932-43, 1947-53, professor of agricultural economics, 1953-66, professor emeritus, 1966—. Agricultural economist for Food Price Division of Office of Price Administration, 1943-44; price control officer for Allied Control Commission of Foreign Economic Administration (Rome), 1944-45; agricultural specialist in London and Oslo, 1945; agricultural adviser in Field Service attached to American Embassy in Oslo, 1945-46; economic consultant to Headquarters of Supreme Commander of the Allied Powers in Japan, 1946-47. Research consultant to University of Puerto Rico Experiment Station, 1953, lecturer at Extension Division, 1954; Smith-Mundt Exchange Professor at University of Chile, 1957; Fulbright lecturer in Finland and Norway, 1962-63. Owner and manager of Mimir Publishers. Member of Organization of American States agrarian reform team in Honduras and Puerto Rico, 1961; conducted research project in western Africa, 1967-69. Chairman of educational advisory committee of Chicago Board of Trade, 1960-63. *Military service:* U.S. Army, 1916-17.

MEMBER: American Economic Association, American Farm Economic Association, Royal Economic Association, Acacia, Masons, Shriners.

WRITINGS: (With Marvin A. Schaars) *The Economics of Cooperative Marketing,* McGraw, 1937; *Cooperation to the Finnish,* Mimir Publishers, 1939; *Theory of Markets and Marketing,* Mimir Publishers, 1953; (with George Max Beal) *Fluid Milk Marketing,* Mimir Publishers, 1956; (with Elmer E. Zank) *Light and Power: Rates and Costs of Service in Wisconsin REA Cooperatives,* University of Wisconsin Press, 1959; *Futures Trading Seminar,* Mimir Publishers, (with others) Volume I: *History and Development,* 1960; (editor) Volume II: *Environmental Factors,* 1963, (with others) Volume III: *A Commodity Market Forum for College Teachers of Economics,* 1966, (editor with others) Volume IV: *Futures Trading in Livestock: Origins and Concepts,* 1970; (with Holbrook Working, E. B. Harris, Gene Futrell, Roger Gray, Robert E. Schneider, and Don Paarlberg) *Informa Oficial de la Mision 105 de Asistencia Tecnica Directa a Honduras Sobre Reforma Agraria y Desarrollo Agricola* (title means "Official Report on Agrarian Reform for Honduras"), three volumes, Organization of American States, 1962; *Basic Concepts, Principles, and Practices of Cooperation,* Mimir Publishers, 1963; (with John Sharp, W. P. Mortenson, and John F. Heimovics) *Marketing and Storage Facilities for Selected Crops: Honduras,* Weitz-Hettelsater Engineers, 1965; (with Fernando Cavada, John C. White, Henry O. Heckman, and William S. Farris) *A Grain Stabilization Study of the Entente States and Ghana of West Africa,* Weitz-Hettelsater Engineers, 1969; *The Hills of Home: A Family History,* Mimir Publishers, 1976. Contributor to professional journals.

WORK IN PROGRESS: An autobiography.

BALABAN, John 1943-

PERSONAL: Born December 2, 1943, in Philadelphia, Pa.; son of Phillip and Alice (Georgies) Balaban; married Lana Flanagan (a teacher), November 27, 1970. *Education:* Pennsylvania State University, B.A., 1966; Harvard University, M.A., 1967. *Home:* 306 South Gill St., State College, Pa. 16801. *Office:* Department of English, Pennsylvania State University, University Park, Pa. 16802.

CAREER: Pennsylvania State University, University Park, assistant professor of English, 1970—. Fulbright senior lecturer in Romania, 1976-77. Has given readings of his poetry at colleges and universities all over the United States and in England, as well as on radio programs. *Wartime service:* Instructor in literature and descriptive linguistics at University of Can Tho, 1967-68, and Committee of Responsibility to Save War-Injured Children, field representative in South Vietnam, 1968-69, as alternative to military service. *Awards, honors:* Woodrow Wilson fellowship, 1966-67; Fulbright-Hays travel grant to Vietnam, 1971-72; National Endowment for the Humanities younger humanist fellowship, 1971-72; Lamont Award from Academy of American Poets, 1974, for *After Our War;* nominated for National Book Award, 1975, for *After Our War.*

WRITINGS: Vietnam Poems (chapbook), Carcanet, 1970; (editor) *Vietnamese Folk Poetry,* Unicorn Press, 1974; *After Our War* (poems), University of Pittsburgh Press, 1974.

Documentary film: (With Peter H. Wolff) "Children of the Evil Hour," Committee of Responsibility, Inc., 1969.

Poems have been anthologized in *Making It New,* edited by John Chase, Harper, 1972; *Directions in Literary Criticism,* edited by Stanley Weintraub and Phillip Young, Pennsylvania State University Press, 1973; *Eating the Menu,* edited by Bruce Edward Taylor, Kendall-Hunt, 1974. Contributor of about thirty-five poems, articles, translations, and reviews to literary journals, including *American Poetry Review, American Scholar, Prairie Schooner, Chelsea, Nation, Poetry Now,* and *New Letters.*

WORK IN PROGRESS: Poems; translations of Vietnamese poetry.

SIDELIGHTS: Balaban writes: "Dante wrote that the fit subjects for poetry are love, virtue, and war. I pursue these three topics with the belief that they are really one."

BIOGRAPHICAL/CRITICAL SOURCES: Saturday Review—World, October 10, 1972.

* * *

BALL, David 1937-

PERSONAL: Born February 27, 1937, in New York, N.Y.; son of Harry (a teacher) and Ethel (a teacher; maiden name, Kaplan) Ball; married Ellen Lapidus, June, 1958 (divorced, 1961); married Nicole Binder (a teacher), June 13, 1966; children: Samuel, Julian. *Education:* Brandeis University, B.A., 1959; Sorbonne, University of Paris, Licence es Lettres, 1964, Docteur en Literature Generale et Comparee, 1971. *Politics:* "Skeptical socialist." *Residence:* Northampton, Mass. *Office:* Department of French, Smith College, Northampton, Mass. 01063.

CAREER: Smith College, Northampton, Mass., lecturer, 1969-71, assistant professor, 1971-76, associate professor of French, 1976—. Poet. *Member:* American Society for Eighteenth-Century Studies, Amnesty International. *Awards, honors:* Fulbright scholar, 1959; French Government fellowship, 1967 and 1968; Eugene M. Warren Poetry Prize from Brandeis University, 1957.

WRITINGS: Two Poems, Matrix Press (London), 1964; *New Topoi,* Buffalo Press, 1972; *The Mutant Daughter,* Buffalo Press, 1975; *Praise of Crazy,* Diana's Bi-Monthly (Providence, R.I.), 1975; *The Garbage Poems: From the New Zone,* Burning Deck, (Providence), 1976. Work represented in anthology, *Jazz Poems,* edited by Anselm Hollo, Vista Books, 1963. Contributor of poems, translations, and articles to periodicals and journals, including *World, Locus Solus, New Republic, Massachusetts Review, Atlantic Monthly, Etudes Anglaises,* and *Revue de Litterature Comparee.* Editor of *Blue Pig* (magazine).

WORK IN PROGRESS: Poetry; research in Greek civilization, European medieval culture, and eighteenth century France; more poems.

SIDELIGHTS: Ball told *CA:* "My goal in writing, as far as I can tell (for who knows, really?), is to record fragments of experience in beautiful, ugly, or amusing form. I write letters (feeling silly as I do so) to try, pathetically, to stop the general spread of torture and fascism."

* * *

BALLANTYNE, David (Watt) 1924-

PERSONAL: Born June 14, 1924, in Auckland, New Zealand; son of David Watt (a carpenter) and Iris Joyce (a cook; maiden name, Foley) Ballantyne; married Vivienne Jean Margaret Heise (a librarian), March 18, 1949; children: Stephen James. *Education:* Attended secondary school in Gisborne, New Zealand. *Home:* 4 Lincoln St., Auckland 2, New Zealand. *Office: Auckland Star,* P.O. Box 3697, Auckland, New Zealand.

CAREER: Auckland Star, Auckland, New Zealand, reporter, 1943-47; *Southern Cross,* Wellington, New Zealand, reporter, 1947-48; *Auckland Star,* reporter and film critic, 1949-54; *Evening News,* London, England, reporter and feature writer, 1955-63; *Finding Out,* London, editor, 1964; *Evening Standard,* London, reporter, 1965; *Auckland Star,* feature writer, literary editor, and author of column "Saturday Viewpoint," 1966—. *Military service:* New Zealand Army, 1942-43.

MEMBER: P.E.N. International (executive member of Auckland branch), New Zealand Producers, Directors, and Writers Guild. *Awards, honors:* Hubert Church Memorial Award from P.E.N. Centre, New Zealand, 1949, for *The Cunninghams;* prize from Associated Television, 1961, for the television drama "Passing Through"; New Zealand Scholarship in Letters, 1968.

WRITINGS: The Cunninghams (novel), Vanguard, 1948, Whitcoulls, 1976; *The Last Pioneer* (novel), Whitcombe & Tombs, 1963; *And the Glory* (stories), Whitcombe & Tombs, 1963; (editor) *Around the World: Looking at Other Lands* (juvenile), Purnell, 1965, Ginn, 1966; *A Friend of the Family* (novel), Whitcombe & Tombs, 1966; *Sydney Bridge Upside Down* (novel), Whitcombe & Tombs, 1968. Also author of television plays, including "Passing Through," produced in United Kingdom, 1963, "Night of the Leopard," 1963, "Twice upon a Time," 1965, "Frances Hodgkins" (documentary), 1969, and "Arthur K. Frupp," 1970.

Work has been represented in anthologies, including *Speaking for Ourselves,* edited by Frank Sargeson, Caxton, 1945; *New Zealand Short Stories,* edited by D. M. Davin, Oxford University Press, 1953, 2nd edition, edited by C. K. Stead, 1966; *Last Adventure and Other New Zealand Stories,* edited by Frank Auerbach, Horst Erdmann Verlag, 1972; and *Short Stories by New Zealanders,* edited by Phoebe C. Meikle, Longman, 1972.

Contributor to *World Book Encyclopedia* and to periodicals, including *Kenyon Review, Landfall,* and *Pacific.*

WORK IN PROGRESS: The Talkback Man, a novel; dramatizing novels by Ngaio Marsh for New Zealand television.

SIDELIGHTS: Ballantyne told *CA:* "I have always been a writer. As a child, I wrote stories and hand-printed and bound magazines for family circulation. I wanted to be a full-time writer of fiction, but I haven't regretted the need to stay in daily journalism. I like deadlines. My assignments have taken me to Leningrad, Rome, Paris, Hollywood, the South Pole and many other places. My favourite city is London, where I lived for eleven wonderful years. But I feel compelled to live in my own country and to write about it. My big book is yet to come."

BIOGRAPHICAL/CRITICAL SOURCES: E. H. McCormick *New Zealand Literature,* Oxford University Press, 1959; Joan Stevens, *The New Zealand Novel,* A. H. & A. W. Reed, 1961; M. H. Holcroft, *Islands of Innocence,* A. H. & A. W. Reed, 1964; H. Winston Rhodes, *New Zealand Fiction since 1945,* McIndoe, 1968; Rhodes, *New Zealand Novels,* University of New Zealand Press, 1969.

* * *

BALTAZZI, Evan Serge 1919-

PERSONAL: Born April 11, 1919, in Smyrna; came to the United States in 1959, naturalized citizen, 1964; son of Phocion (a civil engineer) and Agnes (Varda) Baltazzi; married Nellie Biorlaro, July 17, 1945; children: Agnes Sylvie (Mrs. William Brewenga), James Philip, Marie Irene. *Education:* University of Athens, diploma in industrial chemistry, 1945; Sorbonne, University of Paris, certificate for higher studies in biochemistry, 1946, D.Sc. (magna cum laude), 1949; School of Industrial Heating, Paris, certificate, 1948; Oxford University, D.Phil., 1954; Northwestern University, additional study, 1966. *Home and office:* 825 Greengate Oval, Northfield, Ohio 44067.

CAREER: French National Research Center, Paris, France, assistant professor, 1949-53, associate professor of research, 1953-59; Nalco Chemical Co., Chicago, Ill., senior group leader in organic chemistry research, 1960-62; Illinois Institute of Technology, Research Institute, Chicago, manager of organic and analytical chemistry department, 1962-64; Addressograph Multigraph Co., Multigraphics Development Center, Warrenville Heights, Ohio, director of research and development, 1964—. Young Men's Christian Association (YMCA), judo instructor, 1965—; member, Amateur Athletic Union national committee for judo, 1965-71, U.S. Olympic judo committee, 1966-72. Chairman of national and international research symposia and conferences. Holder of twenty-seven patents, including those covering a system of chemical shorthand and a program of self-defense.

MEMBER: American Self-Protection Association (president and chairman of board of directors, 1965—), American Chemical Society, American Institute of Chemists (fellow), American Management Association, Society of Photographic Scientists and Engineers (director, 1974—), Societe Chimique de France, Chemical Society (England), Masons. *Awards, honors:* Fellow of National Research Council of Canada, 1955-56.

WRITINGS: Basic ASP, privately printed, 1972; *Kickboxing,* Tuttle, 1976.

WORK IN PROGRESS: A Stick for Self-Defense; Winning Kickboxing Combinations for Competition and Self-Defense; Self-Defense for Laymen and Black Belts.

SIDELIGHTS: Baltazzi has trained in various forms of the martial arts since the age of thirteen, and was captain of the Oxford University judo team in the early 1950's. On demonstrations of fighting techniques he was struck by the public's ignorance and he resolved to make the benefits of fighting sports more accessible to the average person. Baltazzi worked on a new system applicable to all combative arts and new teaching methods for eleven and one half years. The result of his work is now available in a program called American Self-Protection (ASP).

Baltazzi told *CA:* "ASP is a general systematic method for developing motor skills particularly suited for the combative arts. [It is] ideal for training normal and handicapped people by mobilizing the basic self-preservation instincts and training the subject to utilize universally applicable principles.

"At the basic level," he continued, "ASP makes use of very few versatile elements of motion which by repetition become conditioned reflexes. . . . [These] techniques of body shifting and getting out of the way of an attack must be mastered first, *with little or no emphasis on retaliation.* Striking and kicking techniques are then studied systematically, only *after* body shifting is mastered. . . . Getting out of the way of an attack first, by appropriate motion of the body is the essence of self-protection. Retaliation should follow, only when necessary. Many more people can be taught to evade an attack, than to retaliate efficiently. Several would not want to retaliate, even if they know how. All, however, would want to evade an attack."

AVOCATIONAL INTERESTS: Fishing, big and small game hunting, boating, camping, history, classical music, handwriting analysis.

* * *

BANKS, Jane 1913-
(Taylor Banks)

PERSONAL: Born April 20, 1913, in Milwaukee, Wis.; daughter of Albert Ruger (a grain executive) and Grace (Tweeden) Taylor; married Elliot Marshall III, September 21, 1936 (divorced, 1943); married Charles Louis Banks (an airline executive), September 6, 1947; children: (second marriage) Alexandra (Mrs. Jonathan Kennedy). *Education:* Attended Milwaukee Downer Seminary, Sophie Newcomb College, and Chicago Art Institute. *Politics:* Democrat. *Home:* 210 San Rafael Ave., Belvedere, Calif. 94920. *Agent:* Mrs. Rhoda Weyr, William Morris Agency, 1350 Avenue of the Americas, New York, N.Y. 10019.

CAREER: Fashion publicist for Columbia Pictures, 1946-47; painter and interior designer, 1962—. *Military service:* U.S. Navy, Waves, 1942-45; became lieutenant junior grade. *Member:* Junior League.

WRITINGS: (With Collin Dong) *The Arthritic's Cookbook,* Crowell, 1973; (with Dong) *New Hope for the Arthritic,* Crowell, 1975. Contributor of short stories to magazines, under pseudonym Taylor Banks.

WORK IN PROGRESS: A book on aging in women; research for a book on vitamins and trace minerals in diet.

* * *

BANKS, Russell 1940-

PERSONAL: Born March 28, 1940, in Newton, Mass.; son of Earl and Florence Banks; married Darlene Bennett, June, 1960 (divorced, February, 1962); married Mary Gunst (a poet), October 29, 1962; children: Leona Stamm, Caerthan,

Maia, Danis (all daughters). *Education:* Attended Colgate University, 1958; University of North Carolina, A.B., 1967. *Home and office address:* R.F.D.1, Northwood Narrows, N.H. 03261. *Agent:* Curtis Brown Ltd., 575 Madison Ave., New York, N.Y. 10022.

CAREER: Lillabulero Press, Inc., publisher and editor, 1966-75; writer, 1975—. Instructor at University of New Hampshire, 1972—; visiting professor at New England College, 1975. Writer-in-residence at Emerson College, 1971, 1976. *Member:* International P.E.N., Coordinating Council of Literary Magazines (member of board of directors, 1967-73), Phi Beta Kappa. *Awards, honors:* Woodrow Wilson fellowship, 1968; Guggenheim fellowship, 1976; St. Lawrence Award for Fiction from St. Lawrence University and *Fiction International,* 1976; recipient of Fels Award, O. Henry Prize, and other short story awards.

WRITINGS: Waiting to Freeze, Lillabulero Press, 1967; *Snow,* Granite Press, 1975; *Searching for Survivors,* Fiction Collective, 1975; *Family Life,* Avon, 1975. Also author of *The New World* (stories), 1976, and *Hamilton Stark* (novel), 1976. Co-editor of *Lillabulero.*

* * *

BANKS, Taylor
  See BANKS, Jane

* * *

BARBER, Bernard 1918-

PERSONAL: Born January 29, 1918, in Boston, Mass.; son of Albert and Jennie (Lieberman) Barber; married Elinor Gellert, September 25, 1948; children: Leslie Marianne, Christine Ruth, Philip Gellert, John Robert. *Education:* Harvard University, A.B., 1939, A.M., 1942, Ph.D., 1949. *Home address:* Braeside Lane, Dobbs Ferry, N.Y. 10522. *Office:* Department of Sociology, Barnard College, Columbia University, New York, N.Y. 10027.

CAREER: Smith College, Northampton, Mass., instructor, 1948-49, assistant professor of sociology, 1949-52; Columbia University, Barnard College, New York, N.Y., assistant professor, 1952-55, associate professor, 1955-61, professor of sociology, 1961—, chairman of department, 1962-65, 1968—. Member of drug research board of National Academy of Sciences, 1966-70. *Military service:* U.S. Naval Reserve, active duty, 1942-46; became lieutenant senior grade.

WRITINGS: Science and the Social Order, Free Press of Glencoe, 1952; *Social Stratification: A Comparative Analysis of Structure and Process,* Harcourt, 1957; (editor with Walter Hirsch) *The Sociology of Science,* Free Press of Glencoe, 1962; (contributor) E. A. Tiryakian, editor, *Sociocultural Theory, Values, and Sociocultural Change: Essays in Honor of Pitirim A. Sorokin,* Free Press of Glencoe, 1963; (with wife, Elinor G. Barber) *European Social Class: Stability and Change,* Macmillan, 1965; *Drugs and Society,* Russell Sage Foundation, 1967; (editor) *L. J. Henderson on the Social System,* University of Chicago Press, 1970; (editor with Alex Inkeles) *Stability and Social Change,* Little, Brown, 1971; (with John Lally, Julia Makarushka, and Daniel Sullivan) *Research on Human Subjects: Problems of Social Control in Medical Experimentation,* Russell Sage Foundation, 1973.

* * *

BARBER, Cyril John 1934-

PERSONAL: Born May 18, 1934, in Pretoria, South Africa;

naturalized U.S. citizen, 1976; son of Charles Stanley and Muriel Radford (Cook) Barber; married Aldyth Ayleen Aereboe, April 13, 1957; children: Allan Marlin, Stephen Marlin. *Education:* Dallas Theological Seminary, M.Th., 1967; Rosary College, M.A.L.S., 1971. *Religion:* Independent Baptist. *Home:* 2729 Fragancia Ave., Hacienda Heights, Calif. 91745. *Office:* Rosemead Graduate School of Psychology, P.O. Box 6000, Rosemead, Calif. 91770.

CAREER: South Africa Mutual Life Insurance Society, Johannesburg, accountant, 1950-62; Dallas Theological Seminary, Dallas, Tex., acquisitions librarian and manager of bookstore, 1962-67; Winnipeg Bible College, Winnipeg, Manitoba, librarian and chairman of department of Bible exposition, 1967-69; Trinity Evangelical Divinity School, Deerfield, Ill., head librarian and instructor in New Testament, 1969-72; Rosemead Graduate School of Psychology, Rosemead, Calif., assistant professor, 1972-74, associate professor of psychological bibliography and systematic theology, 1974—, director of library, 1972—. *Member:* American Library Association, American Theological Library Association, Evangelical Theological Society, Society of Biblical Literature, Royal Society of Literature, Royal Geographical Society, Philosophical Society of Great Britain, California Library Association, California Writers Guild, Beta Phi Mu. *Awards, honors:* D.Lit. from University of London.

WRITINGS: (With Elmer Towns) *Successful Church Libraries,* Baker Book, 1970; *God Has the Answer . . .,* Baker Book, 1974; *Love Unlimited,* Narramore Christian Foundation, 1974; *The Minister's Library,* Baker Book, 1974, supplement, 1976; *Work: The Subtle Addiction,* Narramore Christian Foundation, 1974; *Searching for Identity,* Moody, 1975; *Read for Your Life,* Rosemead Graduate School of Psychology, 1975; *Nehemiah and the Dynamics of Effective Leadership,* Loizeaux Brothers, 1976. Also author of forewords. Contributor to *Zondervan's Pictorial Encyclopedia of the Bible* and *Tyndale Family Bible Encyclopedia* and of articles and reviews to theology journals. Contributing editor of *Journal of Psychology and Theology,* 1972—.

WORK IN PROGRESS: Your Children Have Real Possibilities, with Gary Strauss; *Your Marriage Has Real Possibilities,* based on the book of Genesis, with wife, Aldyth Barber; expository studies of First Samuel and Matthew.

SIDELIGHTS: Barber writes: "One man I worked under was noted for his slogans. Two deeply impressed me. 'The price of success is effort,' and 'Do it now.'"

* * *

BARD of Avondale
  See JACOBS, Howard

* * *

BARKER, Bill
  See BARKER, William J(ohn)

* * *

BARKER, Jane Valentine 1930-

PERSONAL: Born May 17, 1930, in Boulder, Colo.; daughter of John Burr (in hardware) and Roberta (Beckwith) Valentine; married Richard T. Barker, September 11, 1952; children: Richard Valentine, Bruce Thomas. *Education:* University of Colorado, B.A. *Religion:* Presbyterian. *Home and office:* 860 Sixth St., Boulder, Colo.

CAREER: Boulder Daily Camera, Boulder, Colo., columnist and feature writer, 1967—. *Member:* National Federation of Press Women, Colorado Press Women, Boulder Writers Club, Boulder Writers Workshop, University of Colorado Boulder Area Alumni Club (president, 1964).

WRITINGS: Seventy-Six Historic Homes of Boulder, Pruett, 1976.

WORK IN PROGRESS: A sequel to *Seventy-Six Historic Homes of Boulder,* a history of the town and its pioneer families.

* * *

BARKER, Ronald 1921(?)-1976

1921(?)—May 22, 1976; British publishers association executive, literary agent, and author of thriller novels, sometimes under pseudonym E. B. Ronald. Obituaries: *Publishers Weekly,* June 14, 1976.

* * *

BARKER, William J(ohn)
(Bill Barker)

PERSONAL: Born in Denver, Colo.; son of John Elliott (a utilities executive) and Jessie F. (Kennedy) Barker; married Lydia Day Downer; children: William J., Jr., Richard G. Downer, Robin Downer Magnuson, Patricia Raine. *Education:* Attended University of Colorado and Harvard University. *Residence:* Denver, Colo. *Office:* KOA-Radio/Television, 1044 Lincoln St., Denver, Colo. 80203.

CAREER: Denver Post, Denver, Colo., feature writer and author of column "The Wayward West," and "The Wayward Reporter," 1949-59; KOA-Radio/Television, Denver, Colo., host of talk show "The Bill Barker Show," 1959—. Has also worked as advertising account executive and film set designer. *Military service:* U.S. Army, Infantry, 1944-46; served in European theater; received Bronze Star with oak leaf cluster and two battle stars. *Member:* American Federation of Television and Radio Artists, Colorado Authors League, Denver Press Club. *Awards, honors:* "Big Story" television show award, 1956, for reporting "The Bridey Murphy" reincarnation story.

WRITINGS: The Wayward West, Doubleday, 1959; (contributor) Morey Bernstein, *The Search for Bridey Murphy,* Doubleday, revised edition (Barker was not associated with first edition), 1965; (with Jackie Lewin) *Denver!,* Doubleday, 1972.

Work has been anthologized in *Rocky Mountain Empire,* edited by Elvin Howe, Doubleday, 1950. Author of shop manuals for Remington Arms Co. Author of "Barker," a column in *Rocky Mountain Journal,* 1973—. Combat correspondent for U.S. Army, 1944-46. Contributor to sports car magazines and to *Empire,* and *Town and Country.* Editor of *Rocky Mountain Life,* 1946-47.

WORK IN PROGRESS: The Hereafter and the Heretofore, a study of medical hypnosis and reincarnation; *Cars That Have Owned Me,* "misadventures with exotic cars."

SIDELIGHTS: Barker writes: "To me, the creative arts are all related. As an undergraduate cartooning for the *Harvard Lampoon,* it never occurred to me there was anything else as a career—till I starved as an artist in the real world. I took up writing because it was easier to sell. For awhile I was an actor because it was easier to use other peoples' words than write my own. And I became a talk show host because I neither had to write, draw, nor memorize the writings of others. You're looking at a jack of all trades and master of?. . ."

BARMAN, Alicerose 1919-

PERSONAL: Born May 14, 1919, in Chicago, Ill.; daughter of Edgar L. and Nell (Fackson) Schnadig; married Matthew J. Barman (a retail shopowner), December 17, 1939; children: Thomas P., Charles A. *Education:* Pestalozzi Froebel Teacher's College, B.Ed., 1940; University of Chicago, M.A., 1944. *Politics:* Independent. *Religion:* Jewish. *Home:* 730 Lexington Court, Northbrook, Ill. 60062. *Office:* School District 108, Highland Park, Ill. 60035.

CAREER: Association for Family Living, Chicago, Ill., group leader for parent education groups, 1949-56; elementary school teacher in Northbrook, Ill., 1956-57; Loop College of Chicago City Colleges, Chicago, instructor in child development, 1965-69; Northeastern Illinois University, Chicago, member of extension faculty, 1969-75; National College of Education, Evanston, Ill., instructor in child development, 1975-76; writer, 1975—. High school guidance counselor, 1956-65; consultant. Associate director of Irene Josselyn Clinic, 1960-71; member of Northfield Township Mental Health Commission. Has appeared on Chicago television programs.

MEMBER: National Association for Childhood Education, American Orthopsychiatric Association (fellow), Illinois Association of Community Mental Health Agencies (honorary member), North Shore Mental Health Association (associate director, 1960-71), Sigma Delta Tau.

WRITINGS: (Contributor) Joan Wylie, editor, *A Creative Guide for Pre-School Teachers,* Western Publishing, 1967; *Mental Health in Classroom and Corridor,* Western Publishing, 1968. Author of pamphlets on child care and development. Contributor to magazines, including *American Home, American Family, Your Baby,* and *Parents' Magazine,* and to newspapers.

* * *

BARNES, Peter 1931-

PERSONAL: Born January 10, 1931, in London, England; son of Frederick and Martha (Miller) Barnes; married Charlotte Beck, 1960. *Home:* 7 Archery Close, Connaught St., London W. 2, England. *Agent:* Margaret Ramsay Ltd., 14a Goodwin's Court, London W.C. 2, England.

CAREER: Films and Filming magazine, London, England, critic, 1954; Warwick Film Productions Ltd., London, story editor, 1956; playwright, 1963—; stage director, 1970—.

AWARDS, HONORS: John Whiting Playwrights Award, 1968, for *The Ruling Class; Evening Standard* Annual Drama Award for most promising playwright, 1969.

WRITINGS—Plays: "The Time of the Barracudas" (two-act), first produced in San Francisco at Curran Theatre, 1963; "Sclerosis" (one-act), first produced in Edinburgh, Scotland at Traverse Theatre, 1963; *The Ruling Class* (two-act; first produced in Nottingham, England at Playhouse Theatre, 1968, produced in Washington, D.C. at Kreeger Theatre, 1971), Grove, 1969; *Leonardo's Last Supper and Noonday Demons* (two one-act plays; both first produced in London at Open Space Theatre, 1969), Heinemann, 1970; *Lulu* (adaptation and consolidation of two plays by Frank Wedekind; two-act; first produced in Nottingham at Playhouse Theatre, 1970), Heinemann, 1971; "The Devil Is an Ass" (adaptation of play by Ben Jonson; two-act), first produced in Nottingham at Playhouse Theatre, 1973; *The Bewitched* (two-act; first produced in London by Royal Shakespeare Company at Aldwych Theatre, 1974), Heinemann, 1974.

Screenplays: "Violent Moment," Anglo Amalgamated, 1958; "The White Trap," Anglo Amalgamated, 1959; "Breakout," Anglo Amalgamated, 1959; "The Professionals," Anglo Amalgamated, 1961; "Off Beat," British Lion, 1961; "Ring of Spies," British Lion, 1965; "Not With My Wife, You Don't," Warner Bros., 1966; "The Ruling Class" (adapted from own play), United Artists, 1972.

SIDELIGHTS: David William, director of the American premier of Barnes' award winning drama *The Ruling Class* wrote: "Just as *Streetcar* [*Named Desire*] is about America, although not only about America, so *The Ruling Class* is about England, although not only England. England provides the local habitation and the name. But beneath the vivid, specific narrative surface of the play swirl the dangerous currents of fantasy and the subconscious. One of the special triumphs of the play is the vision and the wit with which the dramatist has incarnated the life of the psyche: its tensions and paradox, hilarity and horror. For the play is both funny and frightening: a playful nightmare.

"The appalling injury that can be done by society and the individual (or both, acting in some dreadful collusion) to society and the individual in order to perpetuate a status quo regardless of the demands of humanity and truth—this is the material out of which Peter Barnes has shaped a swift and resonant play. The silhouette never shrinks to one of propaganda; the spell is the artist's, unique and surprising."

BIOGRAPHICAL/CRITICAL SOURCES: Carolyn Riley and Phyllis Mendelson, editors, *Contemporary Literary Criticism*, Volume V, Gale, 1976.

*   *   *

BARNESS, Richard 1917-

PERSONAL: Born September 1, 1917, in Fertile, Minn.; son of Mandel and Mae Barness; married, 1945 (wife deceased.) children: Gloria, Sharon. *Education:* Educated in Minnesota. *Politics:* Democrat Farmer-Labor. *Religion:* Lutheran. *Home:* 1009 Nicollet Ave., Minneapolis, Minn. 55403.

CAREER: Has worked as an employment counselor in Minneapolis, Minn., 1969-74; H.I.R.E.D. (city employment agency), Minneapolis, in public relations, 1974—. *Member:* Minneapolis Writers Club.

WRITINGS: *Graystone College*, Lerner, 1973; *Listen to Me*, Lerner, 1976. Contributor of over 600 articles and short stories to church publications, confessional magazines, and other periodicals.

WORK IN PROGRESS: *Thirty Years Hath September*, a murder mystery; *Shadows Leave No Footprints*, a teenage mystery.

SIDELIGHTS: Barness writes that he began a career in writing in 1962, while serving time in a state prison for robbery. He started writing for church publications and then branched out to write inspirational and historical articles. He told *CA:* "In my first book, *Graystone College*, I take a young man from a robbery through jail, court, to state prison, and finally to parole. My second book, *Listen to Me*, is a story of a young girl on drugs who finally winds up in a prison."

*   *   *

BARON, Oscar 1908(?)-1976

1908(?)—February 16, 1976; American antiquarian bookseller, publisher, and author, sometimes under pseudonym

Orson T. Borden. Obituaries: *New York Times*, March 20, 1976; *AB Bookman's Weekly*, May 17, 1976.

*   *   *

BARRAX, Gerald William 1933-

PERSONAL: Born June 21, 1933, in Attalla, Ala.; son of Aaron (a custodian) and Dorthera (Hedrick) Barrax; married Joan Dellimore; children: Dennis Scott, Gerald William, Joshua Cameron. *Education:* Duquesne University, B.A., 1963; University of Pittsburgh, M.A., 1969. *Home:* 808 Cooper Rd., Raleigh, N.C. 27610. *Office:* Department of English, North Carolina State University, Raleigh, N.C. 27607.

CAREER: U.S. Post Office, Pittsburgh, Pa., clerk and carrier, 1958-67; North Carolina Central University, Durham, instructor, 1969-70; North Carolina State University, Raleigh, special instructor, 1970—. *Military service:* U.S. Air Force, 1953-57; became airman first class.

WRITINGS: *Another Kind of Rain* (poetry), University of Pittsburgh Press, 1970. Represented in anthologies, including *Kaleidoscope: Poems by American Negro Poets*, edited by Robert Hayden, Harcourt, 1968. Contributor of poetry to periodicals, including *Poetry, Four Quarters*, and *Spirit*.

*   *   *

BARRETT, Leonard E(manuel) 1920-

PERSONAL: Born January 26, 1920, in Jamaica, West Indies; came to United States, 1957; naturalized U.S. citizen, 1963; son of Jeremiah and Leela Barrett; married Theodora Jackson, August 12, 1950; children: Linda Diane, Leonard E., Jr., Terry Lee. *Education:* Earned B.A. from Albright College; Temple University, M.A., 1962, Ph.D., 1967. *Politics:* Democrat. *Home:* 1536 Coolidge Ave., Roslyn, Pa. 19001. *Office:* Department of Religion and Inter-Cultural Studies, Trinity College, Hartford, Conn. 06106.

CAREER: Tailor in Jamaica in the 1940's; Bethel College, St. Mary, Jamaica, principal, 1955-57; pastor of United Methodist churches in Germantown, 1958-67; Inter American University of Puerto Rico, San German, assistant professor, 1965-66; associate professor of religion and philosophy, 1966-67; Temple University, Philadelphia, Pa., associate professor of religion, 1967-76; Trinity College, Hartford, Conn., Charles A. Dana Professor of Religion and Inter-Cultural Studies, 1977—. *Member:* American Academy of Religion. *Awards, honors:* Bert Flinchbaugh Prize for Semitic Languages from United Theological Seminary, 1950.

WRITINGS: *The Rastafarians: Messianic Cultism in Jamaica*, Institute of Caribbean Studies, University of Puerto Rico, 1968; *Soul Force: African Heritage in Afro-American Religion*, Doubleday, 1974; (contributor) C. Eric Lincoln, editor, *The Black Experience in Religion: A Collection of Readings*, Doubleday, 1974; *The Sun and the Drum: African Roots in Jamaican Folk Tradition*, Heinemann, 1976; (contributor) Wayland B. Hand, editor, *American Folk Medicine: A Symposium*, University of California Press, 1976; *The Rastafarians: Sounds of Cultural Dissonance in Jamaica*, Beacon Press, 1977.

WORK IN PROGRESS: *Primitive Religion*, for Dickenson; *Domination and Resistance in the Caribbean*, Heinemann.

SIDELIGHTS: Barrett told *CA* that his goal is "to discover those African dynamics that caused Black Folks to persist in the New World. To discover their religions, words, and behavior patterns which are African.'' He has made three trips to Africa to verify the results of his research, and has learned some of the Twi language.

BIOGRAPHICAL/CRITICAL SOURCES: Philadelphia Bulletin, November 21, 1976.

* * *

BARRIAULT, Arthur 1915(?)-1976

1915(?)—June 30, 1976; American journalist and author. Obituaries: *Washington Post*, July 6, 1976.

* * *

BARROW, Robin 1944-

PERSONAL: Born November 18, 1944, in Oxford, England; son of Arthur Hugh Duncan (a businessman) and Audry Gilchrist (Wrightson) Barrow; married Lynn Carlier Hansen, July 5, 1975. *Education:* Christ Church, Oxford, B.A., 1967; University of London, Ph.D., 1972. *Home:* 8 Hamble Rd., Oadby, Leicester, England. *Office:* School of Education, University of Leicester, Leicester, England.

CAREER: City of London School for Boys, London, England, assistant master in classics, 1969-72; University of Leicester, Leicester, England, lecturer in philosophy of education, 1972—.

WRITINGS: Athenian Democracy, Macmillan, 1973; *Plato Utilitarianism and Education*, Routledge & Kegan Paul, 1975; (with R. G. Woods) *Introduction to Philosophy of Education*, Methuen, 1975; *Moral Philosophy for Education*, Allen & Unwin, 1975; *Sparta*, Allen & Unwin, 1975; *Greek and Roman Education*, Macmillan, 1976; *Common Sense and the Curriculum*, Allen & Unwin, 1976; *Plato and Education*, Routledge & Kegan Paul, 1976; *Plato's Apology: A Philosophical Commentary*, Joint Association of Classical Teachers, 1976. Editor of *Didaskalos*, 1975-77.

* * *

BARSOTTI, C(harles) 1933-

PERSONAL: Born September 28, 1933, in San Marcos, Tex.; son of Howard Joseph and Dicey Belle (Branum) Barsotti; married Jo Ann Zimmerman, September 5, 1964 (divorced, December, 1974); children: Kerry Ann, Sharon Elaine, Susan Lea, Charles Michael. *Education:* Southwest Texas State University, B.A., 1955. *Home and office:* 7122 Eby, #102, Mirriam, Kan. 66204.

CAREER: Brown Schools, Austin, Tex., administrative director, 1957-63; Hallmark Cards, Kansas City, Mo., writer, artist, and editor, 1963-67; *Saturday Evening Post*, New York, N.Y., cartoonist and cartoon editor, 1967-69; free-lance cartoonist, 1969—. Creator of comic strip "Sally Bananas" and cartoon panel "Broadsides," both for Los Angeles Times Syndicate. *Military service:* U.S. Army, 1955-57. *Member:* Cartoonist Guild.

WRITINGS: A Girl Needs a Little Action, Harper, 1969. Contributor of cartoons to popular magazines, including *New Yorker* and *Playboy*.

* * *

BART, Lionel 1930-

PERSONAL: Name originally Lionel Begleiter; born August 1, 1930, in London, England; son of Maurice (a tailor) and Yetta Begleiter. *Education:* Attended St. Martin's School of Art, London, 1943-49.

CAREER: Worked as director of commercial art studios; composer, lyricist, and songwriter, 1959—. Founder and chief operating officer, Bart Consolidated (entertainment production-management firm), London, England. *Military service:* Royal Air Force. *Member:* Dramatists Guild, Songwriters Guild of Great Britain, Music Publishers Association, Performing Right Society. *Awards, honors:* Ivor Novello awards from Songwriters Guild of Great Britain, three in 1957, four in 1959, two in 1960, and two in 1962; Variety Club (London) Show Business Personality of the Year, 1962; Antoinette Perry (Tony) Award, 1963, for "Oliver!"; Gold disc, 1969, for soundtrack of "Oliver!"

WRITINGS—Stage musicals: (Music and lyrics; book by Frank Norman) *Fings Ain't Wot They Used T'Be* (first produced in Stratford, England at Theatre Royal, 1959), Secker & Warburg, 1960, Grove, 1962; (lyrics; music by Laurie Johnson; book by Bernard Miles) *Lock Up Your Daughters* (first produced in London at Mermaid Theatre, May 28, 1959), Samuel French, 1967; (music, lyrics, and book) "Oliver!," first produced in London at New Theatre, June 30, 1960, produced in New York at Imperial Theatre, January 6, 1963; (music and lyrics, and book with Joan Maitland) "Blitz!," first produced in London at Aldelphi Theatre, May 8, 1962; (music and lyrics with others) "Merry Rooster Panto," first produced in London at Wyndham's Theatre, December 17, 1963; (music and lyrics; book by Alun Owen) "Maggie May," first produced in London at Adelphi Theatre, September 22, 1964; (music, lyrics, and book) "Twang!," first produced in London at Shaftesbury Theatre, December 20, 1965; (music and lyrics; book by Charles K. Peck, Jr.) "La Strada," first produced in Detroit, Mich., at Fisher Theatre, October 27, 1969, produced in New York at Lunt-Fontanne Theatre, December 14, 1969.

Author of screenplay, "The Duke Wore Jeans," 1958, and of television script, "The Golden Year," broadcast by British Broadcasting Corp., 1957. Composer of music and theme songs for over twelve films, including "The Duke Wore Jeans," 1958, "Sparrows Can't Sing," 1963, "From Russia with Love," 1963, and "Man in the Middle," 1964.

SIDELIGHTS: Bart's "Oliver!," a free adaptation of Charles Dicken's *Oliver Twist*, was itself adapted for two juvenile novels by Mary Hastings. It was also filmed by Columbia Pictures in 1968.*

* * *

BARTH, Fredrik 1928-

PERSONAL: Born December 22, 1928, in Leipzig, Germany; son of Thomas Fredrik (a professor) and Randi (Thomassen) Barth; married Unni Wikan (an anthropologist), January 30, 1974. *Education:* University of Chicago, M.A., 1949; Cambridge University, Ph.D., 1957. *Home:* Roedkleivfaret 16, Oslo 3, Norway. *Office:* Ethnographic Museum, Frederiks Gt. 2B, Oslo 1, Norway.

CAREER: University of Bergen, Bergen, Norway, professor of social anthropology, 1961-72; University of Oslo, Oslo, Norway, professor of ethnography, 1973—. Visiting professor at Columbia University, 1961, University of Khartoum, 1963-64, and at Yale University, 1972. Consultant to UNESCO, Food and Agriculture Organization, and United Nations Development Programme. *Member:* Royal Anthropological Institute of Great Britain (life member), Norwegian Academy of Sciences, Danish Academy of Science, Association of Social Anthropologists of the Commonwealth, Phi Beta Kappa.

WRITINGS: Principles of Social Organization in Southern Kurdistan, University of Oslo Press, 1953; Political Leadership among Swat Pathans, Athlone Press, 1959; Nomads of South Persia, Little, Brown, 1961; Ethnic Groups and Boundaries, Allen & Unwin, 1969; Ritual and Knowledge among the Baktaman of New Guinea, Yale University Press, 1975. Contributor to journals.

WORK IN PROGRESS: Editing Symposium on Scale in Social Organization; a monograph on field material from Oman.

*   *   *

BARTHELMES, (Albert) Wes(ley, Jr.)   1922-1976

May 10, 1922—June 22, 1976; American civil servant, journalist, and writer, sometimes under pseudonym Sisyphus. Obituaries: Washington Post, June 24, 1976.

*   *   *

BARTON, Roger A(very)   1903-1976

December 27, 1903—June 16, 1976; American advertising executive, editor, newspaperman, lecturer, and author. Obituaries: New York Times, June 19, 1976.

*   *   *

BASHAM, Don W(ilson)   1926-

PERSONAL: Born September 17, 1926, in Texas; son of Hal J. (an oil company executive) and Eileen (Hicks) Basham; married Alice Roling, December 4, 1949; children: Cindi (Mrs. W. Richard Leggatt), Shari (Mrs. George Gundlach), Glenn, Lisa, Laura. Education: Phillips University, B.A., 1954, B.D., 1957. Home: 441 Northeast Second St., Pompano Beach, Fla. 33060. Office address: New Wine, P.O. Box 22888, Fort Lauderdale, Fla. 33315.

CAREER: Ordained Disciples of Christ clergyman, 1956; pastor of Christian churches in Washington, D.C., 1957-61, Toronto, Ontario, 1961-64, and Sharon, Pa., 1964-67; freelance writer, 1967-75; New Wine (magazine), Fort Lauderdale, Fla., editor, 1976—.

WRITINGS: Face Up with a Miracle, Whitaker House, 1967; Handbook on Holy Spirit Baptism, Whitaker House, 1968; Ministering the Baptism in the Holy Spirit, Whitaker House, 1969; Can a Christian Have a Demon?, Whitaker House, 1970; Handbook on Tongues, Interpretation, and Prophecy, Whitaker House, 1970; Deliver Us from Evil, Chosen Books, 1972; True and False Prophets, Manna Books, 1973; Miracle of Tongues, Revell, 1974; Manual for Spiritual Warfare, Manna Books, 1974; (with Richard Leggatt) The Most Dangerous Game, Manna Books, 1974; How God Guides Us, Manna Books, 1975; Beyond Blessing to Obedience, Christian Growth Ministries, 1976.

WORK IN PROGRESS: Understanding Spiritual Authority (tentative title).

SIDELIGHTS: Basham has conducted a Bible teaching ministry in sixteen countries, including England, Ireland, Germany, Italy, Austria, Hungary, Yugoslavia, New Zealand, and Jamaica.

*   *   *

BASSANI, Giorgio   1916-
(Giacomo Marchi)

PERSONAL: Born April 4, 1916, in Bologna, Italy. Education: Attended University of Bologna. Home: Via G. B. DeRossi 33, Rome, Italy.

CAREER: Novelist and poet. Accademia Nazionale d'Arte Drammatica, Rome, Italy, instructor in history of theatre, 1957-68; Radio Televisione Italiana, Rome, vice-president, 1964-65. Awards, honors: Charles Veillon prize in Italian literature, 1955, for Gli ultimi anni di Clelia Trotti; Strega prize, 1956, for Cinque storie ferraresi; Viareggio prize, 1962, for Il giardino dei Finzi-Contini; Campiello prize, 1969; Nelly Sachs prize, 1969; also recipient of Premi Roma.

WRITINGS: (Under pseudonym Giacomo Marchi) Una citta di Pianura, [Italy], 1940; Storie dei poveri amanti e altri verse (poetry), Astrolabio (Rome), 1946; Te lucis anti (poetry), [Italy], 1947; Un' altra liberta (poetry), [Italy], 1951; (author of introduction) Giovanni Omiccioli, De Luca (Rome), 1952; Gli ultimi anni di Clelia Trotti (novella), Nistri-Lischi (Pisa), 1955; Cinque storie ferraresi (short stories), Einaudi (Rome), 1956, translation by Isabel Quigly published as A Prospect of Ferrara, Faber, 1962, translation by William Weaver published as Five Stories of Ferrara, Harcourt, 1971; Gli occhiali d'oro (novel), Einaudi, 1958, 2nd edition, 1962, translation by Isabel Quigly published as The Gold-Rimmed Spectacles, Atheneum, 1960.

Le storie ferraresi (collected novellas; includes Gli ultimi anni di Clelia Trotti), Einaudi, 1960; Una notte del '43 (novella), Einaudi, 1960; (author of introduction) Mimi Quilici Buzzacchi, Paesaggio di Spuna, De Luca, 1962; Il giardino dei Finzi-Contini (novel), Einaudi, 1962, translation by Isabel Quigly published as The Garden of the Finzi-Continis, Atheneum, 1965; L'alba ai vetri: Poesie 1942-1950, Einaudi, 1963; Dietro la porta (novel), Einaudi, 1964, translation by William Weaver published as Behind the Door, Harcourt, 1972; Due novelle, Stamperia di Venezia (Venice), 1965; Le parole preparate, e altri seritti di letteratura, Einaudi, 1966; L'airone (novel), Mondadori (Milan), 1968, translation by William Weaver published as The Heron, Harcourt, 1970; Giorgio Bassani: Ansprachen und Dokumente zur Verleihung des Kulturpreises der Stadt Dortmund, Nelly-Sachs-Preis, am 7. Dezember 1969, Stadt- und Landesbibliothek (Dortmund), 1971; L'odore del fieno, Mondadori, 1972.*

*   *   *

BASSO, Aldo P(eter)   1922-

PERSONAL: Born December 22, 1922, in San Mateo, Calif.; son of Peter (a grocer) and Antonietta (Orecchia) Basso; married Natividad Mercedes Martinez de Corrales, August 18, 1958. Education: Attended College of San Mateo, 1941-42. Politics: Democrat. Religion: Roman Catholic. Home: 2031 M. H. del Pilar, No. 322, Malate, Manila, Philippines.

CAREER: Free-lance photographer; professional numismatist, 1959—. Military service: U.S. Army Air Forces, 1942-45; became sergeant. Member: American Numismatic Association, Philippine Numismatic and Antiquarian Society (former member of board of directors), California State Numismatic Association, Northern California Numismatic Association (president, 1969-70).

WRITINGS: Coins, Medals, and Tokens of the Philippines, Chenby (Menlo Park, Calif.), 1968, 2nd edition published as Coins, Medals, and Tokens of the Philippines, 1728-1974, privately printed, 1975.

WORK IN PROGRESS: Medals, Decorations, and Orders of the Philippines.

*   *   *

BAUGHMAN, Dorothy   1940-

PERSONAL: Surname is pronounced Bock-man; born July

13, 1940, in Prattville, Ala.; daughter of Charles Ross (a pharmacist) and Thelma (Cooper) McCartney; married James Baughman (a water company superintendent), April 22, 1960; children: James, Jr., Vicki Lynn, Toni Marie. *Education:* Attended high school in Elmore County, Ala. *Religion:* Baptist. *Home address:* P.O. Box 176, Eclectic, Ala. 36024.

CAREER: Telephone switchboard operator in Montgomery, Ala., 1959-61; Elmore County Hospital, Wetumpka, Ala., cardiogram technician, 1968-73; free-lance writer, 1973—. Member of local Community Council. *Member:* Creative Writer's Club (Montgomery, Ala.). *Awards, honors:* First prizes in juvenile pen woman's contest sponsored by Alabama Pen Women and Press and Authors Club, 1975, for "Chester the Fraidy Cat," and juvenile pen woman's bicentennial contest sponsored by Alabama Pen Women, 1975, for "The Golden Locket."

WRITINGS: Piney's Summer (juvenile), Coward, 1976. Contributor of articles and stories to popular magazines for adults and children, including *Harper's Weekly, Woman's Circle, Home Life, Antique Trader, Children's Playmate,* and *Jack and Jill.*

WORK IN PROGRESS—Juvenile: *Who Wants to Be a Lady, Anyway?; Peck and the Gold Mine; Fire, Fire!;* revising five mystery books, manuscripts for picture books, and short stories.

SIDELIGHTS: Dorothy Baughman writes that *Piney's Summer* is based on her own childhood. "I am basically nostalgic, and loved my simple childhood and that of my mother's growing up in a small southern town, the one I still live in."

BIOGRAPHICAL/CRITICAL SOURCES: Montgomery Advertiser, February 15, 1976, October 15, 1976.

*   *   *

BAUKHAGE, Hilmar Robert   1889-1976

American newsman, radio commentator, and author. Obituaries: *Time,* February 16, 1976.

*   *   *

BAUM, Thomas   1940-

PERSONAL: Born June 1, 1940, in New York; son of Otto Sigmund (a physician) and Margaret (Moore) Baum; married Carol Friedland (a story editor), September 1, 1963; children: William, Freddy. *Education:* Harvard University, B.A., 1961.

CAREER: National Broadcasting Co. (NBC), New York, N.Y., copywriter and speechwriter, 1964-68; free-lance writer, 1968—.

WRITINGS: Counterparts, Dial, 1970; *It Looks Alive to Me!,* Harper, 1976; *Hugo the Hippo,* Harcourt, 1976.

Author of teleplays for young people, "The Amazing Cosmic Awareness of Duffy Moon," American Broadcasting Corp., 1976, and "P. J. and the President's Son," ABC-TV, 1976, and of the script for "You're a Poet and Don't Know It: The Poetry Power Hour," Columbia Broadcasting System, 1976. Author of screenplays "Hugo the Hippo" and "Carny." Contributor of stories to *Playboy, Playgirl,* and *Transatlantic Review.*

*   *   *

BAX, Martin C(harles) O(wen)   1933-

PERSONAL: Born August 13, 1933, in England; married Judith Mary Osborn (a school teacher); children: Timothy, Benjamin, Alexander. *Education:* Attended New College, Oxford, 1952-56, and Guy's Hospital Medical School, 1956-59. *Home:* 17 Priory Gardens, London N6 5QY, England.

CAREER: University of London, London, England, lecturer in education, 1965—. Medical officer at Salomon Centre of Guy's Hospital, 1969-74; research community pediatrician for Thomas Coram Foundation, 1974—. *Member:* Royal Society of Medicine, British Pediatric Association, American Academy for Cerebral Palsy and Developmental Medicine.

WRITINGS: (With Judy Bernal) *Your Child's First Five Years,* St. Martin's, 1974; *The Hospital Ship* (novel), New Directions, 1976. General editor of "Clinics in Developmental Medicine," Spastics International Medical Publications. Editor of *Developmental Medicine and Child Neurology,* 1959-69, and of *Ambit.* Member of editorial board of Spastics International Medical Publications and William Heinemann Medical Books.

WORK IN PROGRESS: A second novel.

*   *   *

BAXTER, James Finney III   1893-1975

PERSONAL: Born February 15, 1893, in Portland, Me.; son of James Finney, Jr. (an industrialist, banker, and writer) and Nelly Furbish (Carpenter) Baxter; married Anne Holden Strang, June 21, 1919 (died May, 1962); children: James Finney IV, Arthur Brown, Steven Bartow. *Education:* Williams College, A.B. (summa cum laude), 1914, A.M., 1921; Harvard University, A.M., 1923, Ph.D., 1926. *Politics:* Republican. *Religion:* Episcopalian.

CAREER: Industrial Finance Corp., New York, N.Y., member of staff, 1914-15; Colorado College, Colorado Springs, instructor in history, 1921-22; Harvard University, Cambridge, Mass., instructor, 1925-27, assistant professor, 1927-31, associate professor, 1931-36, professor of history, 1936-37, master of Adams House, 1931-37; Williams College, Williamstown, Mass., president, 1937-61, president emeritus, 1961-75. Lecturer at Lowell Institute, 1931, Naval War College, 1932, Cambridge University, 1936, and Army War College, 1946; educational adviser to U.S. Military Academy. Director of research and analysis for Office of the Coordinator of Information (later Office of Strategic Services), 1941-42, deputy director of Office of Strategic Services, 1942-43, historian of Office of Scientific Research and Development, 1943-46. Member of Gaither Commission (to study the "cold war") in the 1950's; senior fellow of the Council on Foreign Relations, 1961-65. Trustee of Williams College, 1934-37, Teachers Insurance and Annuity Association, 1955-59, also of World Peace Foundation, Phillips Andover Academy, Radcliffe College, and American Military Institute; member of board of overseers of Harvard University; term trustee of Massachusetts Institute of Technology, 1956-61. Member of board of directors of State Mutual Life Insurance Co. (Worcester, Mass.).

MEMBER: American Association for the Advancement of Science (fellow), Association of American Colleges (president, 1945), American Council on Education, American Historical Association (member of executive committee, 1937-38), American Antiquarian Society, American Society of International Law, American Political Science Association, Naval Historical Society, Society of American Historians (president, 1945-46), American Academy of Arts and Sciences (fellow), Colonial Society of Massachusetts, Massachusetts Historical Society, Maine Historical Society, Phi

Beta Kappa, Kappa Alpha, Gargoyle Society, Harvard Club, Tavern Club (Boston), Century Club, Williams Club (New York City). *Awards, honors:* LL.D. from Harvard University and Amherst College, both 1938, University of Maine and Wesleyan University, both 1939, Hobart College, 1942, and Bowdoin College, 1944; Litt.D. from Syracuse University, 1945; L.H.D. from Case Institute of Technology (now Case Western Reserve University), 1948, and American International College, 1954; LL.D. from Williams College, 1947, Kenyon College, 1949, Columbia University, 1954, Brown University, 1956, and University of Rochester, 1960; D.Sc. from Union College, 1949; Pulitzer Prize in history, 1947, for *Scientists Against Time;* Presidential Certificate of Merit.

WRITINGS: The Introduction of the Ironclad Warship, Harvard University Press, 1933, Archon, 1968; *Scientists Against Time,* Little, Brown, 1946, M.I.T. Press, 1968. Contributor to history and law journals.

BIOGRAPHICAL/CRITICAL SOURCES: New York Times, June 19, 1975; *Washington Post,* June 19, 1975; *Time,* June 30, 1975.*

(Died June 17, 1975, in Williamstown, Mass.)

*   *   *

BEADLE, Leigh P(atric)   1941-

PERSONAL: Born December 1, 1941, in Bedford, England; son of Walter Lester and Anne Louis (Searle) Beadle; married Rebecca W. Wells (a cardiovascular nursing instructor), January 1, 1965. *Education:* University of North Carolina, B.A., 1964. *Home:* Tenney Circle, Chapel Hill, N.C. 27514. *Agent:* George Scheer, King Mill Rd., Chapel Hill, N.C. 27514. *Office address:* Specialty Products International, Box 784, Chapel Hill, N.C. 27514.

CAREER: Specialty Products International, Chapel Hill, N.C., president, 1970—. *Military service:* U.S. Air Force, 1964-68. U.S. Air Force Reserve, 1968—; current rank, captain. *Member:* National Rifle Association, Ercoupe Owners Club. *Awards, honors:* Three national records in the fifty meter free-rifle.

WRITINGS: Brew It Yourself, Farrar, Straus, 1971, revised edition, 1975; *Making Fine Wines and Liqueurs at Home,* Farrar, Straus, 1972.

*   *   *

BEALL, James Lee   1924-

PERSONAL: Born December 13, 1924, in Detroit, Mich.; son of Harry (a millwright) and Myrtle (a minister; maiden name, Monville) Beall; married Anne Broyles, July 3, 1946; children: James Lee, Jr., Analee, John Patrick. *Home:* 9424 East Outer Dr., Detroit, Mich. 48213. *Office:* Bethesda Temple, Inc., 7616 East Nevada, Detroit, Mich. 48234.

CAREER: Bethesda Missionary Temple, Detroit, Mich., minister, 1947—, currently pastor. Lecturer. *Military service:* U.S. Navy, 1943-46. *Awards, honors:* Th.D., Pioneer Theological Seminary, 1954; D.D., National Bible College, 1956.

WRITINGS: The School of the Holy Spirit, Whitaker House, 1971; *Let Us Make Man,* Whitaker House, 1972; *Rise to Newness of Life,* Evangel, 1974; *The Adventure of Fasting,* Revell, 1974; *Strong in the Spirit,* Revell, 1975. Contributing editor, *Logos,* 1975—.

WORK IN PROGRESS: The Foundation Stones; Pastoral Charisma.

AVOCATIONAL INTERESTS: Golf, tennis, racquetball.

BEAMISH, Tufton Victor Hamilton
See CHELWOOD, Tufton Victor Hamilton

*   *   *

BEASLEY-MURRAY, George Raymond   1916-

PERSONAL: Born October 10, 1916; son of George Alfred and Kathleen Lydia Beasley; married Ruth Weston, 1942; children: Paul, Elizabeth, Stephan, Andrew. *Education:* Spurgeon's College, London, B.D., 1941; King's College, London, M.Th., 1945, Ph.D., 1952, D.D., 1964; Jesus College, Cambridge, M.A., 1950. *Office:* Southern Baptist Theological Seminary, 2825 Lexinton Rd., Louisville, Ky. 40206.

CAREER: Ordained Baptist minister, 1941; pastor of Baptist churches in Ilford, England, 1941-48, and Cambridge, England, 1948-50; Spurgeon's College, London, England, lecturer in New Testament, 1950-56; Baptist Theological College, Zurich, Switzerland, professor of New Testament, 1956-58; Spurgeon's College, principal and lecturer in New Testament literature and theology, 1958-73; Southern Baptist Theological Seminary, Louisville, Ky., professor of New Testament, 1973—. President of Baptist Union of Great Britain and Ireland, 1968-69, chairperson of council, 1969-71.

WRITINGS: Christ is Alive, Lutterworth Press, 1947; *The News No One Knows,* Carey Kingsgate Press, 1952; *Jesus and the Future: An Examination of the Criiticism of the Eschatological Discourse,* St. Martin's, 1954; *Preaching the Gospel from the Gospels,* Judson, 1956, revised edition, Epworth, 1965; *A Commentary on Mark Thirteen,* Macmillan, 1957.

Baptism in the New Testament, St. Martin's, 1962, Eerdmans, 1973; (translator and author of introduction) Kurt Aland, *Did the Early Church Baptize Infants?,* SCM Press, 1963; (translator) Rudolph Schnackenburg, *Baptism in the Thought of St. Paul,* Basil Blackwell, 1964; *The Resurrection of Jesus Christ,* Oliphants, 1964; *The Servant of God,* Carey Kingsgate Press, 1965; *The General Epistles: James, I Peter, Jude, II Peter,* Abingdon, 1965; *Baptism Today and Tomorrow,* St. Martin's, 1966; *Reflections on the Ecumenical Movement,* Baptist Union of Great Britain and Ireland, 1966; *Renewed for Mission,* Baptist Union of Great Britain and Ireland, 1968.

(Editor and translator with R.W.W. Hoare) Rudolph Bultman, *The Gospel of St. John: A Commentary,* Basil Blackwell, 1971; *Commentary on 2 Corinthians: Broadman Bible Commentary,* Broadman, 1971; *Highlights of the Book of Revelation,* Broadman, 1971; *Commentary on Revelation: New Century Bible,* Attic Press, 1974. Also author, with Robert M. Brown, of *Layman's Theological Library,* 1965.

AVOCATIONAL INTERESTS: Music.

*   *   *

BEAUFRE, Andre   1902-1975

PERSONAL: Born January 25, 1902, in Neuilly sur Seine, France; son of Paul and Marie (Farines) Beaufre; married Genevieve Douvry, December 21, 1948; children: Florence, Roland. *Education:* Attended military academies, Free School of Political Science, and Ecole de guerre. *Home:* 27 avenue de Marigny, Paris 75008, France.

CAREER: French Army officer. Served in North Africa, 1930-42, with Algerian sharpshooters in Riff and Moroccan campaigns, as permanent secretary of national defense in Algeria, 1940-41, and as bureau chief to the commander-in-chief of North Africa, 1942; attended military missions to Soviet Union, 1939, and to United States, Canada, and England, 1943; served in Italy, France, and Alsace, 1944; head of Third Bureau in German campaign, 1945; served in Indochina, 1946-49, as a division commander and executive officer for General de Tassigny, 1946, as commander of operations in North Tonkin, 1947, and as deputy commander of Cochin China-Cambodia troops, 1948; became head of Third Bureau and deputy chief of staff for the commander-in-chief of the armies of Western Europe, 1949; returned to Indochina as commander of operations in Tonkin, 1951; director of Interallied Group Tactical Studies, 1952; commander of 2nd Motorized Infantry Division in France, 1954, of Operational Zone Kabilie, 1955, and of East Constantnois, 1955-56; commander of landing force at Port Said, Egypt, during Anglo-French invasion of the Suez Canal, 1956; deputy to the commander-in-chief of French forces in Germany, 1957; deputy chief of staff in charge of logistics and administration for Supreme Headquarters of the Allied Powers in Europe (SHAPE), 1958-60; French representative to the North Atlantic Treaty Organization (NATO) permanent council in Washington, D.C., 1960; retired from military service with rank of general of the army, 1961. Military historian and writer, 1961-75. President of the committee of the flame under the Arc de Triomphe, 1971-75; attended Yugoslav Armed Forces Scientific Activities Council, 1975.

AWARDS, HONORS—Literary: Prix Vauban, 1973, for *Strategie pour domain.* Military: Grand croix de la Legion d'honneur; Croix de guerre; Croix de la valeur militaire; Medaille de la Resistance; Medaille des evades; companion of Order of the Bath; Legion of Merit; Silver Star.

WRITINGS: Introduction a la strategie, A. Colin, 1963, translation by Richard H. Barry published as *An Introduction to Strategy: With Particular Reference to Problems of Defense, Politics, Economics, and Diplomacy in the Nuclear Age,* Praeger, 1965; *Dissuasion et strategie,* A. Colin, 1964, translation by Barry published as *Deterrence and Strategy,* Faber, 1965, Praeger, 1966; *Le drame de 1940,* Plon, 1965, translation by Desmond Flower published as *1940: The Fall of France,* Cassell, 1967, Knopf, 1968; *L'O.T.A.N. et l'Europe,* Calmann-Levy, 1966, translation by Joseph Green published as *NATO and Europe,* Knopf, 1966; *Strategie de l'action,* A. Colin, 1966, translation by Barry published as *Strategy of Action,* Praeger, 1967; *Le Revanche de 1945,* Plon, 1966; *Batir l'avenir,* Calmann-Levy, 1967; *L'Expedition de Suez,* Grasset, 1967, translation by Barry published as *The Suez Expedition, 1956,* Praeger, 1969; *L'Enjeu du desordre,* Grasset, 1969; *Laerdomar av Vietnamkriget,* Utrikespolitiska Institutet, 1969; *Memoires, 1920-1940-1945,* Presses de la Cite, 1969; *La Nature des choses,* Plon, 1969; (with Jean Offredo) *Le Sens du futur,* Editions Universitaires, 1971; *La France de la grande guerre, 1914-1919,* Culture, Art, Loisirs, 1971; *La Guerre revolutionnaire: Les Formes nouvelles de la guerre,* Fayard, 1972; (with Jean-Francois Genest and others) *La France Combattante, 1939-1945,* Culture, Art, Loisirs, 1972; *Strategie pour demain: Les Problemes militaires de la guerre moderne,* Plon, 1972, translation published as *Strategy for Tomorrow,* Crane, Russak, 1974; *Crises et guerres: Sept ans au Figaro,* Presses de la Cite, 1974; *La Nature de l'histoire,* Plon, 1974; (editor) *Strategy for the West,* Crane, Russak, 1974.

Correspondent on military affairs, *Le Figaro,* 1966-75. Publisher of *Historia Deuxieme Guerre Mondiale,* 1967-75.

SIDELIGHTS: Beaufre was imprisoned by the Vichy Gov-

ernment for a brief period in 1942 for helping the Resistance to plan logistics needs for the French Army in aiding Allied landings in North Africa. He escaped from France, went on to North Africa, and continued fighting. At the time of his retirement, Beaufre was publicly disagreeing with General de Gaulle's policies toward Algeria, the French Army, and the North Atlantic Treaty Organization.*

(Died February 13, 1975, in Belgrade, Yugoslavia; buried in France)

* * *

BEAUMONT, Cyril William 1891-1976

November 1, 1891—May 24, 1976; British ballet historian and critic, bookseller, publisher, and author. Obituaries: *New York Times,* June 1, 1976. (See index for previous *CA* sketch)

* * *

BEAUMONT, Roger A(lban) 1935-

PERSONAL: Born October 2, 1935, in Milwaukee, Wis.; son of Spencer A. and Claire (Poser) Beaumont; married Jean Prentice, 1974; children: Eric, Anne. *Education:* University of Wisconsin, Milwaukee, student, 1953-55; University of Wisconsin, Madison, B.S., 1957, M.S., 1960; Kansas State University, Ph.D., 1973. *Home:* 2002 Briar Oaks, Bryan, Tex. 77801. *Agent:* Charles Neighbors, 240 Waverly Pl., New York, N.Y. 10014. *Office:* Department of History, Texas A & M University, College Station, Tex. 77843.

CAREER: Assistant director of Center for Advanced Study in Organizational Science at University of Wisconsin, 1965-67; Wisconsin State University, Oshkosh, instructor in history, 1968-69; vice-president of administration, Civil Police (watchman service), 1969; University of Wisconsin Center for Advanced Study of Organizational Science, associate director, 1970-73, associate professor of organizational science and health systems administration, 1973-74; Texas A & M University, College Station, associate professor of history, 1974—. *Military service:* U.S. Army Reserve, 1954-62, active duty, 1957-59; became captain.

MEMBER: International Institute for Strategic Studies, American Historical Association, Science Fiction Writers Association, American Military Institute (member of advisory board), U.S. Naval Institute, Association of the U.S. Army, Inter-University Seminar on the Armed Forces in Society (fellow), Phi Alpha Theta.

WRITINGS: Military Elites, Bobbs-Merrill, 1975; (editor with Martin Edwards) *War in the Next Decade,* University Press of Kentucky, 1975; *Sword of the Raj,* Bobbs-Merrill, 1977; (contributor) B. Franklin Cooling, editor, *The Military Industrial Complex: Mars, Business, and American Society,* Kennikat, in press. Contributor to military journals and to *Horizon.*

WORK IN PROGRESS: A history of strategic bombing; revising two novels.

SIDELIGHTS: Beaumont told *CA:* "To me writing is a craft which I learned from reading biographies of writers (my favorites Kipling, Forester, Deighton, Masters, Macaulay, Burckhardt, Alain Fournier, St. Exupery, i.e., shameless storytellers), and from many teachers most of whom are gone . . . from three years of the public relations grind . . . I started at age eight, and just kept hacking away, more as an artisan than artist.''

BECK, Marilyn (Mohr) 1928-

PERSONAL: Born December 17, 1928; daughter of Max and Rose (Lieberman) Mohr; divorced, 1974; children: Mark Elliott, Andrea. *Education:* University of Southern California, A.A., 1948. *Home and office address:* P.O. Box 655, Beverly Hills, Calif. 90213. *Agent:* Arthur Pine Associates, Inc., 1780 Broadway, New York, N.Y. 10019; and Toni Mendez, Inc., 140 East 56th St., New York, N.Y. 10022.

CAREER: Free-lance writer, 1959-63; Sterling Magazines, Hollywood, Calif., West Coast editor, 1963-74. Hollywood columnist featured in *Hollywood Valley Times* and *Hollywood Citizen News,* 1963-65; free-lance entertainment writer featured in *Los Angeles Times,* 1965-67; Bell-McClure Syndicate, syndicated Hollywood columnist, 1967-72, also chief of West Coast bureau; syndicated Hollywood columnist, North American Newspaper Alliance, 1967-72, New York Times Special Features, 1972—. Created and hosted "Hollywood Outtakes," a National Broadcasting Co. (NBC) "Big Event" special, 1977. *Member:* Hollywood Women's Press Club.

WRITINGS: Marilyn Beck's Hollywood, Hawthorn, 1973.

SIDELIGHTS: Marilyn Beck has said: "I hate the word 'gossip.' I cover Hollywood as a news beat. News, based on the lives and doings of the filmland personalities, will continue as long as there's a Hollywood. . . . As long as we live in an era when celebrities themselves appear on national television and speak out on every subject, from evolution to revolution, write books, and appear in movies that reveal the intimate and often lurid details of their lives, a columnist must be just as candid. And that doesn't mean merely reporting what the stars are doing, but also why, when, and even how. I refuse to ingratiate myself with the studios by running those dull, trade-y items such as who's signed for what pictures and so-and-so's holding out for more money. All that drivel may be of interest to those in the industry, but the public couldn't care less."

BIOGRAPHICAL/CRITICAL SOURCES: Editor and Publisher, September 27, 1975.

* * *

BECKER, A(dolph) C(arl), Jr. 1920-

PERSONAL: Born December 1, 1920, in Galveston, Tex.; son of Adolph Carl (a newspaperman) and Emma (Fiesel) Becker; married June L. Hempel (an educational secretary), November 27, 1945; children: Stancie Lee (Mrs. Charles Savino), Adolph Carl III, Christine Ann, Laura Jane. *Education:* University of Texas, B.J., 1942; Columbia University, graduate study, 1970. *Politics:* "Independent with leaning to democratic." *Religion:* Roman Catholic. *Home:* 1625 Ave. M½, Galveston, Tex. 77550. *Office: Galveston Daily News,* 8522 Teichman, Galveston, Tex. 77550.

CAREER: Galveston Daily News, Galveston, Tex., sports and outdoor editor, 1946—. *Military service:* U.S. Army, 1943-46; in public relations and education. *Member:* Outdoor Writers Association of America, Texas Outdoor Writers Association (charter member; past member of board of directors), Galveston County Press Club (past president), Sigma Delta Chi. *Awards, honors:* Associated Press awards for sports writing and color photography, 1966 and 1971.

WRITINGS: Waterfowl in the Marshes, A. S. Barnes, 1969; *Lure Fishing,* A. S. Barnes, 1970; *Gulf Coast Fishing,* A. S. Barnes, 1970; *Big Red: Channel Bass Fishing,* A. S. Barnes, 1971; *Game and Bird Calling,* A. S. Barnes, 1971;

Decoying Waterfowl, A. S. Barnes, 1973; *Fishing the Texas Coast,* Cordovan, 1975; *Texas Saltwater Big Three,* Cordovan, 1975; *All About Fishing,* A. S. Barnes, in press; *Texas Fisherman's Guide,* Cordovan, in press. Author of "The Coastal Fisherman," column in *Texas Fisherman,* 1974—, "Texas Dock Lines," *Southern Yachting News,* 1974—, and "Upper Coast Outlook," *Texas Sportsman,* 1976—. Contributor of more than seven hundred articles to national and regional magazines. Field editor of *Texas Sportsman,* 1976—.

WORK IN PROGRESS: Three books.

SIDELIGHTS: Becker has become a free-lance photographer and has taught photography classes.

* * *

BECKER, B. Jay 1904-

PERSONAL: Born May 5, 1904, in Philadelphia, Pa.; son of Morris L. (a merchant) and Freda R. Becker; married Esther Elkins, January 2, 1933; children: Steve, Jean, Michael. *Education:* Temple University, LL.B., 1929. *Politics:* Independent. *Office:* King Features Syndicate, 235 East 45th St., New York, N.Y. 10017.

CAREER: Attorney in private practice in Philadelphia, Pa., 1929-37; King Features Syndicate, New York, N.Y., writer of column, "Contract Bridge by B. Jay Becker," 1956—. Lecturer. Member of Contract Bridge National Laws Commission. *Member:* Regency Club, Cavendish Club.

WRITINGS: Becker on Bridge, Grosset, 1971.

SIDELIGHTS: Becker left his law practice in 1937 to move to New York, so he could devote all his time professionally to contract bridge. He has won two world championships, thirty-five national championships, and hundreds of other titles. About one-third of the three hundred newspapers that carry his column are in foreign countries. He and his wife travel on cruises where he is the "bridge maestro aboard."

* * *

BECKETT, Kenneth A(lbert) 1929-
(Keith Bower)

PERSONAL: Born January 12, 1929, in Brighton, England; son of Albert Henry (a tax inspector) and Gladys (a secretary; maiden name, Bower) Beckett; married Gillian Tuck (a writer and editor), August 1, 1973; children: Keith Christopher. *Education:* Royal Horticultural Society School of Horticulture, diploma, 1953. *Home and office:* Bromley Cottage, Stanhoe, King's Lynn, Norfolk PE31, 8QF, England.

CAREER: St. Louis Botanic Garden, St. Louis, Mo., horticulturist, 1954; John Innes Research Institute, Bayfordburg, England, technical assistant, 1955-63; Glasgow Botanic Garden, Glasgow, Scotland, assistant curator, 1963-65; *Gardeners' Chronicle,* London, England, technical editor, 1965-69; free-lance writer, 1969—. *Military service:* British Army, 1947-49. *Member:* American Rock Garden Society, Botanical Society of the British Isles, British Pteridological Society, Botanical Society of South Africa, Hardy Plant Society, Alpine Garden Society, Canterbury Alpine Garden Society (New Zealand).

WRITINGS: The Love of Trees, Octopus, 1974; (with wife, Gillian Beckett, and Roy Hay) *Dictionary of House Plants,* Rainbird, 1975; (with G. Beckett) *Illustrated Encyclopaedia of Indoor Plants,* Doubleday, 1976; *Illustrated Dictionary of Botany,* Sampson Law, in press.

Garden booklets series; all published by Charles Letts; all 1976: *Let's Grow Chrysanthemums; . . . Dahlias; . . . Handy Bulbs; . . . House Plants; . . . Gladioli; . . . Lilies; . . . Sweet Peas; . . . Roses; . . . Plants in Window Boxes.*

Contributor of horticulture articles to magazines, sometimes under pseudonym Keith Bower. Editor of *News Bulletin* of the Botanical Society of the British Isles and *Bulletin* of the Hardy Plant Society.

WORK IN PROGRESS: Encyclopaedia of Gardening.

SIDELIGHTS: Beckett's particular interest is in seeing plants in their natural habitats. He participated in a plant hunting expedition to Chile in 1971 and 1972, and has also visited New Zealand, Hawaii, Tahiti, Easter Island, Japan, and much of Europe. He grows a large collection of his own plants, as well.

* * *

BEECHER, William (M.) 1933-

PERSONAL: Born May 27, 1933, in Massachusetts; son of Samuel and Gertrude (Kradelman) Beecher; married Eileen Brick (a teacher); children: Debbie, Diane, Lori, Nancy. *Education:* Harvard University, B.A., 1955; Columbia University, M.S., 1956. *Home:* 7911 Robison Rd., Bethesda, Md. 20034. *Office: Boston Globe,* 1750 Pennsylvania Ave. N.W., Washington, D.C. 20006.

CAREER/WRITINGS: St. Louis Globe-Democrat, St. Louis, Mo., reporter, 1956-59; Fairchild Publications, Washington, D.C., reporter, 1959-60; *Wall Street Journal,* New York, N.Y., correspondent from Washington, D.C., 1960-66; *New York Times,* New York City, Washington correspondent, 1966-73; U.S. Department of Defense, Washington, D.C., deputy assistant secretary of defense, 1973-75; *Boston Globe,* Boston, Mass., diplomatic correspondent from Washington, D.C., 1975—. Contributor to magazines, including *New York Times Magazine.* Reporting assignments have taken him to Vietnam and the Far East, the Middle East, and Europe. *Military service:* U.S. Army, Artillery, 1956; became captain in Reserves. *Member:* National Press Club, State Department Correspondents Association, White House Correspondents Association, Aviation/Space Writers Association (president, 1970-71), Harvard Club (Washington, D.C.). *Awards, honors:* Mark Watson Award for Distinguished Military Writing, 1968; citation from Overseas Press Club of America, 1975, for excellence of diplomatic reporting.

* * *

BEEKS, Graydon 1919-

PERSONAL: Born December 5, 1919, in Long Beach, Calif.; son of Graydon F. (a probation officer) and Hortense C. (a librarian; maiden name, Bright) Beeks; married Doris A. White (an accountant), February 12, 1959; children: Robert G., Jay Cooper, Aeloa. *Education:* Pomona College, B.A., 1947; University of Arizona, LL.B., 1950; University of Oregon, further study, 1968-69. *Home:* 5699 Riverdale Road S., Salem, Ore. 97302.

CAREER: Private law practice in Tucson, Ariz., 1950-59; Bernice P. Bishop Estate, Honolulu, Hawaii, member of legal staff, 1960-64; Quadrant Corp., Bellevue, Wash., planning director, 1965-69; zoning examiner for King County, Seattle, Wash., 1971-72; free-lance writer, 1972—. *Military service:* U.S. Army, 1942-45. *Member:* Freelance Writers of Seattle. *Awards, honors:* Writer's award from the governor of Washington, 1976, for *Hosea Globe and the Fantastical Peg-Legged Chu.*

WRITINGS: Hosea Globe and the Fantastical Peg-Legged Chu (juvenile fiction), Atheneum, 1975.

WORK IN PROGRESS: A juvenile science fiction novel and other fiction.

* * *

BEHRMAN, Daniel 1923-

PERSONAL: Born June 20, 1923, in New York, N.Y.; son of Emanuel (a businessman) and Miriam (Adelson) Behrman; married Lida Schechtmann, April 27, 1948 (divorced, December, 1974); married Madeleine de Sinety (a photographer), July 28, 1975; children: Dan Alain, Thomas. *Education:* University of Michigan, A.B., 1943. *Religion:* "Jewish by birth." *Home:* 4 Rue Joseph Bara, Paris 75006, France. *Agent:* A. J. Hart, 419 East 57th St., New York, N.Y. 10022. *Office:* UNESCO, Place de Fontenoy, Paris 75007, France.

CAREER: Long Island Daily Press, Jamaica, N.Y., reporter, 1945-46; *Newark Star-Ledger,* Newark, N.J., picture editor, 1947; *Long Island Daily Press,* Jamaica, N.Y., reporter, makeup and Sunday editor, 1947-48; *Paris Herald Tribune,* Paris, France, reporter, 1948; UNESCO, Paris, France, writer, 1949; *Paris Herald-Tribune,* Paris, reporter, 1950; UNESCO, Paris, writer, 1950-61, English editor, 1961-72, science writer, 1972—. *Military service:* U.S. Army, 1943-45. *Member:* International Science Writers Association.

WRITINGS: The New World of the Oceans, Little Brown, 1969; *The Man Who Loved Bicycles* (nonfiction), Harper's Magazine Press, 1973; *Solar Energy: The Awakening Science,* Little, Brown, 1976. Contributor to magazines, including American edition of *Realites, Oceans, Bike World, Railroad, Parade,* and *Catholic Digest.*

WORK IN PROGRESS: A book of photographs, based on the life of a seventy-two-year-old farmer in Brittany, with wife, Madeleine Behrman.

SIDELIGHTS: Behrman writes that he is "convinced that man, beginning with me, finds his identify through his work. If he is 'leisure' oriented, then he's got an identity problem." He adds that, with his wife, he "would like to explore further this identification with work (the basis of our writing and picture-taking around and about steam railroads) . . . perhaps to seek a way in which everyone—not just the Sierra Club—could live without destroying where they live." Behrman comments that he is "happiest when . . . doing twelve hundred words and fifty miles a day on a bicycle."

* * *

BEISSEL, Henry Eric 1929-

PERSONAL: Surname is pronounced *By*-sell; born April 12, 1929, in Cologne, Germany; emigrated to Canada in 1951, naturalized citizen, 1956; married; children: three. *Education:* Attended University of Cologne, 1950-51, and University of London, 1951; University of Toronto, B.A., 1958, M.A., 1960. *Residence:* Alexandria, Ontario, Canada (country); and Montreal, Quebec, Canada (city). *Office:* 1455 de Maisoneuve W., Montreal H3G 1M8, Quebec, Canada.

CAREER: Canadian Broadcasting Corp. (CBC)–Television, Toronto, Ontario, stage hand, 1953-54, filmmaker, 1954-55; University of Munich, Munich, Germany, lecturer in English literature, 1960-62; University of Alberta, Edmonton, lecturer in department of English, 1962-64; University of the West Indies, Trinidad, visiting professor in department of English, 1964-66; Sir George Williams University, Montreal, Quebec, associate professor of English, 1966-69; Concordia University, Montreal, associate professor, 1969-76, professor of English, 1976—. Chairman of board of directors of Montreal Theatre Laboratory.

MEMBER: International Academy of Poets, League of Canadian Poets (Quebec representative), Canadian Association of Composers and Authors, Association of Canadian University Teachers of English, Canadian Association of University Teachers, Canadian Comparative Literature Association, Playwrights Cooperative. *Awards, honors:* University of Toronto Norma Epstein poetry award, 1958; Frederic Davidson Award in Creative Writing, 1959, for a sonnet cycle, "The Trial"; Canada Council grants, 1967, 1968, 1969, 1972, 1973, 1975; grants from Ministere des Affaires culturelles, 1972, 1975.

WRITINGS: Witness the Heart (poems), Green Willow Press, 1963; *New Wings for Icarus* (poems), Coach House Press, 1966; *The World Is a Rainbow* (poems for children, with music), Canada Music Centre, 1968; (translator) Walter Bauer, *The Price of Morning,* Prism International Press, 1969; *Face on the Dark* (poems), New Press, 1970; *The Salt I Taste* (poems), D. C. Books (Montreal), 1975; (translator) Bauer, *A Different Sun* (poems), Oberon Press, 1976; (editor) *Cues and Entrances* (anthology of Canadian plays), Gage, 1977.

Plays: "Mister Skinflint" (play for marionettes), first produced in Montreal at Theatre Gesu, May 10, 1969; *Inook and the Sun* (ten-episode; first produced in Stratford, Ontario, at The Third Stage, August 1, 1973), Playwrights Co-op (Toronto), 1974; "For Crying Out Loud" (one-act play for young people), first produced in Williamstown, Ontario, at CharLan Theatre Workshop, June 4, 1975; "Goya," first produced in Montreal at Montreal Theatre Laboratory, October 27, 1976. Also author of plays as yet neither published nor produced, "Salvador," 1973, and "Improvisations for Mr. X," 1974.

Translator of plays: Tankard Dorst, "The Curve" (one-act), first produced in Edmonton, Alberta, at University of Alberta Studio Theatre, November 29, 1963; (and editor) Dorst, *A Trumpet for Nap,* Playwrights Co-op, 1973. Also translator of plays as yet neither published nor produced: Dorst, "Grand Tirade at the Town-Wall," 1965; Louis-Dominique Lavigne, "Are You Afraid of Thieves?," 1975; (with Arlette Franciere) Andre Simand, "Waiting for Gaudreault," 1975.

Work appears in anthologies, including *Modern Canadian Verse,* edited by A.J.M. Smith, Oxford University Press, 1967; *The Blasted Pine,* edited by F. C. Scott, Macmillan, 1967; *The Enchanted Land,* edited by T. R. Lower and F. W. Cogswell, Gage, 1967; *The Wind Has Wings,* edited by M. A. Downie and Barbara Robertson, Oxford University Press, 1968; *Sleepingbags and Flying Machines,* edited by John McInnes and Emily Hearn, Thomas Nelson, 1973; *For Neruda, for Chile,* edited by Walter Lowenfels, Beacon Press, 1975; *Mirrors,* edited by Lou Pearce, Gage, 1975; *The Penguin Book of Canadian Verse,* edited by Ralph Gustafson, Penguin, 1975.

Contributor to literary journals, including *Canadian Forum, Voices, Tamarack Review, Quarry, Prism International, Northern Journey, Laomedan Review,* and *West Coast Review,* and to newspapers. Editor and publisher of *Edge,* 1963-69.

WORK IN PROGRESS: A novel, *Winter Crossing;* a book of poems, *Northern Suite;* a confessional novel; translations of poems by Pablo Neruda, *Quays of Sadness,* and poems by Peter Huchel, *A Thistle in His Mouth.*

SIDELIGHTS: Beissel told *CA:* "Writing for me is a way of understanding and of coming to terms with the contradictions of reality. It is also the only way I know in which to preserve my sanity as a member of a species with such potential grandeur hell-bent on destroying itself. My commitment is unambiguously on the side of all the creative forces in the world." His work has been translated into French, Spanish, Serbo-Croatian, German, Hungarian, and Japanese.

AVOCATIONAL INTERESTS: Literature, music, painting, astronomy, neurology, anthropology, history.

* * *

BELKIN, Samuel 1911-1976

December 12, 1911—April 18, 1976; Polish-born American educator, scholar, university administrator, and author of books on Jewish philosophy and related topics. Obituaries: *New York Times,* April 19, 1976; *Time,* May 3, 1976; *AB Bookman's Weekly,* June 28, 1976; *Current Biography,* June, 1976. (See index for previous *CA* sketch)

* * *

BELL, Stephen (Scott) 1935-

PERSONAL: Born December 9, 1935, in Oskaloosa, Iowa; son of Howard A. (a merchant) and Florence (a teacher; maiden name, Scott) Bell; married Joyce Dillavou (a musician), June 16, 1957; children: Allison Kay, Hilary Ann. *Education:* Central College (now Central University of Iowa), B.A., 1959; Northwestern University, M.S.J., 1963. *Office:* ABC News, American Broadcasting Co., 1124 Connecticut Ave. N.W., Washington, D.C. 20036.

CAREER/WRITINGS: KBOE Radio, Oskaloosa, Iowa, announcer and news reporter, 1955-59; WOI Radio-TV, Ames, Iowa, reporter, 1959-60; WGN Radio-TV, Chicago, Ill., news writer and reporter, 1960-61; WOW Radio-TV, Omaha, Neb., writer, chief newscaster, producer and narrator of own documentary series, "The Outsider," 1962-65; WNEW Radio, New York City, reporter and newscaster, 1965-67; American Broadcasting Co. (ABC), New York City, radio news correspondent in New York, 1967-70, combat correspondent in Saigon, 1970-71, chief Asian correspondent based in Hong Kong, 1972-74, writer and co-producer, with Ted Koppel, of documentary, "The People of People's China," 1973, White House correspondent, 1974—, co-anchor, with Margaret Osmer, of "Good Morning America" news segments, 1975—. Notable assignments include Robert Kennedy assassination, President Nixon's world trip, Vietnam conflict, release of U.S. prisoners from Hanoi, and Watergate transition. Writer of news scripts for television broadcasts.

MEMBER: Washington Radio and Television Correspondents Association, White House Correspondents Association, Hong Kong Foreign Correspondents Association. *Awards, honors:* Emmy nominations from National Academy of Television Arts and Sciences, 1964, for "The Outsiders," and 1973, for "ABC Evening News" reports from China; Overseas Press Club award, 1969; National Headliners documentary award, 1976, for "Lawyers: Guilty as Charged?."

SIDELIGHTS: During Bell's assignment as combat correspondent with the ABC News Saigon Bureau, he frequently found himself in the thick of the action throughout southeast

Asia. Following an encounter with the Viet Cong in April, 1970, Bell and his crew were captured and held prisoner in Cambodia for nearly an hour at gunpoint. Despite the danger, Bell turned on his tape recorder and taped a report of the incident.

* * *

BELLAMY, Guy 1935-

PERSONAL: Born March 21, 1935, in Bristol, England; son of James Eric and Audrey Mary (Shern) Bellamy. *Education:* Attended school in Farnham, Surrey, England. *Home:* 28 Pilgrims Close, Farnham, Surrey, England. *Agent:* John Farquharson Ltd., 15 Red Lion Sq., London W.C.1, England.

CAREER: Currently a sub-editor for *Sun,* London, England. *Military service:* Royal Air Force; served in Germany.

WRITINGS: The Secret Lemonade Drinker (novel), Holt, 1977.

WORK IN PROGRESS: Cardboard Fred (tentative title), a novel.

SIDELIGHTS: Bellamy comments: "I have never been able to understand why British novels, aside from those of Graham Greene, are so shoddily written alongside the contemporary American product."

* * *

BELZ, Herman (Julius) 1937-

PERSONAL: Born September 13, 1937, in Camden, N.J.; son of Irvin Carl and Ella (Engler) Belz; married Mary Martin (a social worker), August 5, 1961; children: Kristin, Aaron. *Education:* Princeton University, B.A., 1959; University of Washington, Seattle, M.A., 1963, Ph.D., 1966. *Politics:* "Neo-conservative." *Home:* 433 Branch Dr., Silver Spring, Md. 20901. *Office:* Department of History, University of Maryland, College Park, Md. 20742.

CAREER: University of Maryland, College Park, assistant professor, 1966-68, associate professor of American history, 1968—. Associate professor at University of Colorado, summer, 1969. *Military service:* U.S. Naval Reserve, 1959-65, active duty, 1959-61; became lieutenant junior grade. *Member:* American Historical Association, Organization of American Historians, American Society for Legal History, Academy of Political Science, Southern Historical Association. *Awards, honors:* Albert J. Beveridge Award from American Historical Association, 1966.

WRITINGS: Reconstructing the Union: Theory and Policy during the Civil War, Cornell University Press, 1969; *A New Birth of Freedom: The Republican Party and Freedmen's Rights, 1861 to 1866,* Greenwood Press, 1976. Contributor to history journals.

WORK IN PROGRESS: A history of constitutionalism in the United States, as an aspect of American political thought and theory.

SIDELIGHTS: Belz writes: "I was influenced in graduate school by Arthur Bestor, and in subsequent writing by the work of David Potter. Vaguely on the left in earlier years, I have become more concerned with problems of constitutionalism and have moved away from earlier sympathies and identifications."

* * *

BENDER, John B(ryant) 1940-

PERSONAL: Born July 19, 1940, in Tulsa, Okla.; son of J. B. (a businessman) and Lilly (Cook) Bender; married Ann Williams (an attorney), August 15, 1967. *Education:* Princeton University, B.A., 1962; Yale University, graduate study, 1962-63; Cornell University, Ph.D., 1967. *Office:* Department of English, Stanford University, Stanford, Calif. 94305.

CAREER: Stanford University, Stanford, Calif., assistant professor, 1967-73, associate professor of English, 1973—. *Member:* Modern Language Association of America, Renaissance Society of America, American Society for Eighteenth-Century Studies. *Awards, honors:* Fellowships from American Council of Learned Societies, 1975, and Huntington Library, 1976.

WRITINGS: Spenser and Literary Pictorialism, Princeton University Press, 1972. Contributor to language, art, and opera journals.

WORK IN PROGRESS: "The Tempest" at the Court of James I; Images of Prison in Eighteenth-Century Art and Literature.

* * *

BENNETT, A(bram) E(lting Hasbrouck) 1898-

PERSONAL: Born January 12, 1898, in Alliance, Neb.; son of Charles Elting and Bertha (Kinsey) Bennett; children: Foster (deceased), Ann (deceased), Jeanne. *Education:* University of Nebraska, B.S., 1919, M.D., 1921. *Home:* 668 Moraga Rd., Moraga, Calif. 94556. *Office:* 2000 Dwight Way, Berkeley, Calif. 94704.

CAREER: University of Nebraska Hospital, Omaha, intern, 1920-21; Philadelphia General Hospital, Philadelphia, Pa., intern, 1922-23; Philadelphia Orthopedic Hospital and Nervous Infirmary, Philadelphia, resident in neurology, 1923; Johns Hopkins University, Phipps Psychiatric Clinic, Baltimore, Md., resident in neurology, 1924; private practice, specializing in neurology and psychiatry, in Omaha, 1924-48, and Berkeley, Calif., 1948—. Diplomate of National Board of Medical Examiners and American Board of Psychiatry and Neurology. Instructor and assistant professor at University of Nebraska, 1925-47; professor, chairman of neurology and psychiatry, and founder and head of department of psychiatry at Herrick Memorial Hospital, Berkeley, 1948-63; associate clinical professor in psychiatry at University of California. Founder and director of A. E. Bennett Neuropsychiatric Research Foundation, 1945—. Consultant in psychiatry, Veteran's Administration, Martinez, Calif., 1949-66.

MEMBER: American Association for the Advancement of Science (fellow), American Psychiatric Association (life fellow), American Medical Association (fellow; council member, 1948; section vice-chairman, 1949-50), American Neurological Association (fellow), Society for Biological Psychiatry (honorary member and president, 1952), National Huguenot Society (surgeon general, 1974—), Royal College of Psychiatry (founding fellow), Argentina Society for Biological Psychiatry (honory member), Central Society for Clinical Research, Central Neuro-Psychiatric Association (president, 1945), California Medical Association (section chairman, 1953), Northern California Huguenot Society (vice-president, 1968—), Alameda County Medical Association, Alpha Omega Alpha, Phi Rho Sigma, Elks, Rotary International, Berkeley City Commons Club (president, 1959-60). *Awards, honors:* American Medical Association awards for science exhibits, 1940, 1946, 1958; gold medal from Society for Biological Psychiatry, 1973. The Dr. A. E. Bennett Psychiatric Pavilion at Herrick Memorial Hospital is named for the author.

WRITINGS: (With Avis B. Purdy) *Psychiatric Nursing Technic,* F. A. Davis, 1940; (with E. A. Hargrove and Bernice Engel) *The Practice of Psychiatry in General Hospitals,* University of California Press, 1956; *Fifty Years in Neurology and Psychiatry* (autobiographical), Intercontinental Medical Book Corp., 1972; *Alcoholism and the Brain,* Intercontinental Medical Book Corp., 1976. Contributor to medical journals. Associate editor of *Diseases of the Nervous System, Quarterly Review of Psychiatry and Neurology,* and *Psychiatry in General Practice.*

SIDELIGHTS: Bennett has pioneered in several areas of psychiatric research and artificial fever therapy, including effective use of convulsive shock in depressive disorders, use of curare, modern therapy for the mentally ill in general hospitals, and research in the treatment of alcoholic brain disease. He was a founding member of the World Federation of Biological Psychiatry and of the World Psychiatric Association.

*   *   *

BENSON, Maxine (Frances) 1939-

PERSONAL: Born September 5, 1939, in Boulder, Colo.; daughter of Mac Walden (a businessman) and Frances (a legal secretary; maiden name, Ladwig) Benson. *Education:* University of Colorado, B.A. (magna cum laude), 1961, M.A., 1962, Ph.D., 1968; University of Denver, M.A., 1973. *Home:* 2880 South Locust, Denver, Colo. 80222. *Office:* State Historical Society of Colorado, 1300 Broadway, Denver, Colo. 80203.

CAREER: State Historical Society of Colorado, Denver, deputy state historian, 1964-65, 1966-67, state historian, 1967-71, curator of documentary resources, 1972—. Visiting lecturer at University of Denver, summers, 1969-71, 1975, and Metropolitan State College, spring, 1970, 1977; visiting postdoctoral research associate at Smithsonian Institution, 1971-72.

MEMBER: American Historical Association, Organization of American Historians, American Association for State and Local History, Victorian Society in America, Western History Association, Colorado Authors League, Colorado Corral of the Westerners, Phi Beta Kappa, Phi Alpha Theta, Alpha Omicron Pi. *Awards, honors:* Fellowship from National Historical Publications Commission, 1971.

WRITINGS: (With Carl Ubbelohde and Duane A. Smith) *A Colorado History,* revised edition (Benson was not associated with 1965 edition), Pruett, 1972, centennial edition, 1976. Contributor to history journals and regional magazines. Editor of *Colorado,* 1967-71, advisory editor, 1972—.

WORK IN PROGRESS: A book on the history of the State Historical Society of Colorado, 1879-1979, publication expected in 1979; research on Edwin James.

AVOCATIONAL INTERESTS: Music (especially listening to opera), investing in the stock market, travel.

*   *   *

BENTLEY, Nicolas Clerihew 1907-

PERSONAL: Born June 14, 1907, in London, England; son of Edmund Clerihew (a writer) and Violet (Boileau) Bentley; married Barbara Hastings, 1934; children: one daughter. *Education:* Attended Heatherly School of Art. *Home:* Old School, Downhead, Shepton Mallet, Somerset, England.

CAREER: Artist and writer. Director of Andre Deutsch (publisher), 1951—. *Member:* Society of Industrial Artists and Designers, (fellow), Garrick Club.

WRITINGS: Die? I Thought I'd Laugh: A Book of Pictures, Methuen, 1936; *Ballet Hoo,* Cresset Press, 1937; *Le Sport,* V. Gallancz, 1939; *Second Thoughts and Other Poems,* Joseph, 1939; *Animal, Vegetable, and South Kensington,* Methuen, 1940; *The Tongue-Tied Canary* (thriller), Joseph, 1949; *The Floating Dutchman* (thriller), Joseph, 1950, Panther, 1971; *How Can You Bear to Be Human?,* Deutsch, 1957, Dutton, 1958; *A Version of the Truth,* Deutsch, 1960; *Third Party Risk,* Penguin, 1961; *Book of Birds,* Transatlantic, 1965; *The Victorian Scene: A Picture Book of the Period, 1837-1901,* New York Graphic Society, 1968, Spring Books, 1971; *Don't Do-It-Yourself: A Fantasy for Exporters* (self-illustrated), British National Export Council, 1970; *Golden Sovereigns, and Some of Lesser Value: From Boadicea to Elizabeth II,* Mitchell Beazley, 1970; *The Events of That Week,* St. Martin's, 1972; *Nicolas Bentley's Tales from Shakespeare,* Mitchell Beazley, 1972, Simon & Schuster, 1973; *Edwardian Album: A Photographic Excursion into a Lost Age of Innocence,* Viking, 1974; *Inside Information,* Deutsch, 1974. Also author of *The Time of My Life,* 1937, *Gammon and Espionage,* 1938, and *Pay Bed,* 1976.

Editor: (With Leonard Russell) The English Comic Album, Joseph, 1948; Frederick Bason, *Diary,* Wingate, 1950; Evan Esar, *Treasury of Humorous Comic Quotations,* Phoenix House, 1951; *The Pick of Punch* (multi-volume work), Deutsch, 1955-57; *A Choice of Ornaments,* Deutsch, 1959; Bergen Evans, *Comfortable Words,* Random House, 1962; W. H. Russell, *Dispatches from the Crimea, 1854-1856,* Hill & Wang, 1976. Also editor of *Reminiscences* by Captain Gronau, 1977, and *Images of Elsewhere,* 1977.

Also illustrator of books by others, including Thomas Stearns Eliot, Hilaire Belloc, and Roy Fuller.

AVOCATIONAL INTERESTS: Music, looking at paintings, travel.

*   *   *

BENVENISTI, Meron (Shmuel) 1934-

PERSONAL: Born April 21, 1934, in Jerusalem, Israel; son of David and Lea (Friedman) Benvenisti; married Shoshana Lahav (a teacher), January 4, 1968; children: Eyal, Yuval, Sharon. *Education:* Hebrew University of Jerusalem, B.A. and B.Sc., 1961. *Politics:* Israel Labour Party. *Religion:* Jewish. *Home:* Ein Rogel 22, Jerusalem, Israel. *Office:* Jerusalem Municipality, 22 Jaffa Rd., Jerusalem, Israel.

CAREER: Israeli Government, Jerusalem, director of economic and development department in Ministry of Tourism, 1960-65, administrator of Old City and East Jerusalem, 1967-71, city councillor of Jerusalem municipality, 1969-74, deputy mayor, 1974—. *Military service:* Israel Defense Force, 1951-53.

WRITINGS: Mivtsarei Hatsalbanim B'Israel (title means "Crusader Castles in Israel"), Kiriyat Sepher (Jerusalem), 1965; *The Crusaders in the Holy Land,* translated by Pamela Fitton, Israel Universities Press, 1970, Macmillan, 1972; *Mul Hahoma Hasegura,* Weidenfeld & Nicolson, 1973, translation by Peretz Kidron published as *Jerusalem: The Torn City,* University of Minnesota Press, 1977. Contributor of map of crusader Palestine to atlas of Israel, 1960, 2nd edition, 1973.

WORK IN PROGRESS: Urban planning of Jerusalem.

AVOCATIONAL INTERESTS: Boating.

BEQUAERT, Lucia H(umes)

PERSONAL: Born in Springfield, Mass.; daughter of Jo Allison (a stockbroker) and Lucia H. Kingsbury (Coy) Humes; married second husband, Frank C. Bequaert (a businessman and writer), 1968; children: William, Rebekah, Andrew, Michael. *Education:* Wellesley College, student; Northeastern University, B.S. (summa cum laude), 1969; Harvard University, Ed.M., 1972. *Home:* 44 Bertwell Rd., Lexington, Mass. 02173.

CAREER: Northeastern University, Boston, Mass., assistant to the director of adult day programs, 1966-69; community mental health project coordinator in Boston and Brookline, Mass., 1970-71; Tufts University, Medford, Mass., staff member of Study Group on Continuing Education for Urban Women, 1972-73; NEW Associates (consultants for women's education and career development), Arlington, Mass., co-founder and co-director, 1973-75; counselor, providing vocational guidance to women, 1975—. Member of Council on Higher Education for Urban Women, 1974. Member of board of directors of Fernboro Street Association, 1965-70, and Winners (also past president); executive director of Girls Club (Lynn, Mass.), 1976—. *Member:* League of Women Voters, Adult Education Association of the United States of America, Massachusetts Personnel and Guidance Association.

WRITINGS: (Editor) *Directory of Community Resources,* Massachusetts Mental Health Area Board, 1970; (editor with Suzanne Lipsky and Rosamund Rosenmaeir, and contributor) *Report of the Boston Conference on Higher Education for Urban Women,* John Hay Whitney Foundation, 1973; (editor with Linda Letty and Barbara Williams) *Urban Women's Guide to Higher Education,* John Hay Whitney Foundation, 1973; *Single Women: Alone and Together,* Beacon Press, 1976.

WORK IN PROGRESS: A book about blue-collar girls and their life plans.

SIDELIGHTS: Lucia Bequaert states that her career objectives are "to provide professional services to education, research and development programs, in the areas of career planning and life planning for educational and directional counseling; continuing education. Special interests include women's education and career development; urban and inner-city family life; and the development and implementation of sound management policies for private, non-profit social service organizations.

*   *   *

BERCHEN, Ursula 1919-

PERSONAL: Born May 12, 1919, in Vancouver, British Columbia, Canada; daughter of Edward Alfred (in the Canadian Army) and Isabelle Francoise (a teacher; maiden name, Masse) Townsend; married William Berchen (a photographer), April 1, 1944; children: Robert, Julie, Christine. *Education:* Royal College of Music, A.R.C.M., 1939. *Home:* 169 Taylor St., Pembroke, Mass. 02359. *Office:* Thomas Crane Library, Washington St., Quincy, Mass. 02359.

CAREER: Thomas Crane Public Library, Quincy, Mass., senior assistant, 1966—.

WRITINGS: (With husband, William Berchen) *Aspects of Boston,* Houghton, 1975; (with William Berchen) *Bermuda Impressions* (photographs by William Berchen), Hastings House, 1976.

BERCHEN, William 1920-

PERSONAL: Born March 10, 1920, in Germany; came to United States, 1921; naturalized citizen, 1960; son of Peter and Helen (Menken) Berchen; married Ursula Townsend (a librarian), April 1, 1944; children: Robert, Julie (Mrs. Paul Morway), Christine. *Education:* Attended New York University and University of Arkansas. *Home and office:* 169 Taylor St., Pembroke, Mass. 02359.

CAREER: Professional photographer, 1946—; has had several solo exhibitions of photographs in the Boston area and in New York City. *Military service:* U.S. Army, 1940-46; served in Bermuda. *Member:* American Society of Magazine Photographers.

WRITINGS—With his own photographs: *Maine,* Houghton, 1973; (with wife, Ursula Berchen) *Aspects of Boston,* Houghton, 1975.

Photographic illustrator: Monica Dickens, *Cape Cod,* Viking, 1972; Ursula Berchen, *Bermuda Impressions,* Hastings House, 1976. Filmed "Spring" for Boston's public television network, 1971.

WORK IN PROGRESS: A book of photographs of New England.

*   *   *

BERCK, Martin G(ans) 1928-

PERSONAL: Born February 25, 1928, in New York, N.Y.; son of Samuel and Florence (Gans) Berck; married Lenore Firestein (an arts administrator), July 12, 1953; children: Jonathan, Judith, David. *Education:* New York University, A.B., 1947; Columbia University, M.S., 1953. *Home:* 604 Ramapo Rd., Teaneck, N.J. 07666. *Office:* Newsday, 550 Stewart Ave., Garden City, N.Y. 11530.

CAREER/WRITINGS: Pan American Airways, New York City, editor of company information and training manuals, 1949-50; Associated Press (AP), Cleveland, Ohio, editor, reporter, rewrite man, and feature writer, 1953-56; *New York Herald Tribune,* New York City, reporter, rewrite man, special correspondent from the Middle East and Europe, United Nations correspondent, and national news editor, 1956-66; National Broadcasting Co. (NBC) News, New York City, writer, editor, political specialist, field producer, feature editor, assignment editor, special reports editor, editorial coordinator of United Nations Bureau, reporter and producer for television news, and supervisor of WNBC-Radio news, 1966-72; *Newsday,* New York City, United Nations correspondent and foreign editor, 1972—. Contributor of articles and reviews to magazines. Adjunct associate professor at New York University. *Military service:* U.S. Army, combat correspondent in Korea, 1950-52.

*   *   *

BERE, Rennie Montague 1907-

PERSONAL: Born November 28, 1907, in Bere Regis, Dorset, England; son of Montague A. (a clergyman) and Sarah Lucy (Troyte) Bere; married Anne Maree Barber, 1936. *Education:* Attended Marlborough College, 1921-26; Selwyn College, Cambridge, B.A., 1929, M.A., 1943. *Home:* West Cottage, Bude, North Cornwall, England.

CAREER: Her Majesty's Overseas Service, colonial administrative service in Uganda, assistant district officer, 1930-42, district officer, 1942-51, provincial commissioner, 1951-55; director and chief warden of Uganda National Parks, 1955-60; free-lance writer, 1960—. Cornwall Naturalists' Trust, council member, 1960, president, 1967-70. Commandant of Polish Refugee Settlements, 1943-44.

MEMBER: Royal Commonwealth Society, Alpine Club, Uganda Kobs (past president). *Awards, honors:* Commander of the Order of St. Michael and St. George, 1957.

WRITINGS: The Wild Mammals of Uganda and Neighbouring Regions of East Africa, Longmans, Green, 1962; *The African Elephant,* Golden Press, 1966; *Wild Animals in an African National Park,* Deutsch, 1966; *The Way to the Mountains of the Moon,* Arthur Barker, 1966; *Birds in an African National Park,* Deutsch, 1969; *Antelopes,* Arco, 1970; *The Life of Antelopes,* Bodley Head, 1970; *Wild Life in Cornwall: A Naturalist's View of the Southwestern Peninsula,* D. B. Barton, 1970; *Crocodile's Eggs for Supper,* Deutsch, 1973; *The Mammals of East and Central Africa,* Longman, 1975. Contributor to wildlife, anthropology, and mountaineering journals.

AVOCATIONAL INTERESTS: Game and bird watching, cricket, mountaineering.

*   *   *

BERLIN, Ellin (Mackay) 1904-

PERSONAL: Born in 1904 in Roslyn, N.Y.; daughter of Clarence Hungerford (a corporation president) and Katherine Alexander (a writer; maiden name, Duer) Mackay; married Irving Berlin (the songwriter), January 4, 1926; children: Mary Ellin, Linda Louise, Elizabeth Irving, Irving, Jr. (deceased). *Education:* Attended Barnard College.

CAREER: Journalist and magazine writer.

WRITINGS: Land I Have Chosen (novel), Doubleday, 1944; *Lace Curtains,* Doubleday, 1948; *Silver Platter* (biography), Doubleday, 1957; *The Best of Families,* Doubleday, 1970. Contributor of short stories and articles to popular magazines, including *New Yorker, Saturday Evening Post,* and *Ladies' Home Journal.*

SIDELIGHTS: Warner Brothers has purchased motion picture rights for the novel *Land I Have Chosen.**

*   *   *

BERMAN, Susan 1945-

PERSONAL: Born May 18, 1945, in Minneapolis, Minn.; daughter of Dave (a hotel owner) and Lynell (a dancer; maiden name, Ewald) Berman. *Education:* University of California, Los Angeles, B.A., 1967; University of California, Berkeley, M.A., 1969. *Politics:* Democrat. *Religion:* Jewish. *Home:* 3002 Clay St., San Francisco, Calif. *Agent:* Rhoda Weyr, William Morris Agency, 1350 Avenue of the Americas, New York, N.Y. 10019.

CAREER: San Francisco Examiner, San Francisco, Calif., reporter, 1971-74; *City,* San Francisco, Calif., associate editor, 1975; KPIX-Television, San Francisco, Calif., writer for "Evening Show," 1976—.

WRITINGS: Underground Guide to the College of Your Choice, Signet, 1971; *Driver, Give a Soldier a Lift* (novel), Putnam, 1976.

SIDELIGHTS: Susan Berman told *CA:* "Although the word at this point is a cliche, interactions are what I write about. I include much about my feelings and perceptions to help the reader identify with my pieces. I was born to write. I grew up in Las Vegas and I handicapped the Academy Awards for my block when I was nine."

BERTRAM, James Munro 1910-

PERSONAL: Born August 11, 1910, in Auckland, New Zealand; son of Ivo Edgar (a clergyman) and Evelyn (Bruce) Bertram; married Jean Ellen Stevenson (a writer), March 14, 1947. *Education:* University of Auckland, M.A., 1932; New College, Oxford, M.A., 1935; also studied at Yenching University, 1936. *Politics:* Liberal. *Religion:* Presbyterian. *Home:* 30 Park Rd., Belmont, Lower Hutt, New Zealand.

CAREER: London Times, London, England, sub-editor, 1935; China Defence League, Hong Kong, secretary, 1938-40; British Embassy, Chungking, China, press attache, 1941; Far Eastern Commission, Tokyo, Japan, adviser to the New Zealand delegation, 1945-46; Victoria University of Wellington, Wellington, New Zealand, senior lecturer, 1947-65, associate professor, 1966-72, professor of English, 1973-76, professor emeritus, 1976—; writer, 1976—. *Military service:* Hong Kong Volunteer Defence Corps, gunner, 1941-45. *Member:* International P.E.N. (New Zealand center), New Zealand China Society (patron).

WRITINGS: Crisis in China, Macmillan, 1937, published as *First Act in China,* Viking, 1938; *Unconquered,* John Day, 1939 (published in England as *North China Front,* Macmillan, 1939); *Beneath the Shadow,* John Day, 1947 (published in England as *The Shadow of a War,* Gollancz, 1947); *Return to China,* Heinemann, 1957; *The Young Traveller in China Today,* Phoenix House, 1961; (editor) *New Zealand Letters of Thomas Arnold the Younger,* Auckland & Oxford, 1966; *Occasional Verses,* Wai-te-ata Press, 1970; *Charles Brasch,* Oxford University Press, 1976. Author and narrator of script for "Hunting Horns," Pacific Films, 1976. Contributor to scholarly journals, and to *New Zealand Listener, Landfall,* and *Islands.*

WORK IN PROGRESS: Editing *Letters of Thomas Arnold the Younger,* Volume II, for Auckland & Oxford; *Dan Davin,* on New Zealand writers and their work; studying the poetry of Arthur Hugh Clough.

SIDELIGHTS: Bertram spent the years 1941-45 as a prisoner of war in Hong Kong and Tokyo. He told *CA:* "This experience of working as a coolie in Asia gave me a new understanding of social and natural revolutionary movements in East Asia."

BIOGRAPHICAL/CRITICAL SOURCES: Islands, summer, 1975.

*   *   *

BESSER, Milton 1911-1976

January 12, 1911—July 22, 1976; American educator, journalist, and writer. Obituaries: *New York Times,* July 24, 1976.

*   *   *

BESSY, Maurice 1910-

PERSONAL: Born December 4, 1910, in Nice, France; son of Pierre and Emilie (Labiche) Bessy; married Simone Voisin, March 25, 1949. *Education:* Attended Lycee de Nice for seven years. *Home:* 9 Avenue Mozart, Paris 75016, France. *Office:* 71 rue du Faubourg-Saint-Honore, Paris 75008, France.

CAREER: Publisher of motion picture magazines and trade papers, including *Cinemonde,* 1928-66, and *Film Francais, Une semaine de Paris, Paris-Theatre,* and *Bulletin du Festival de Cannes,* all 1946-66; International Film Festival, Cannes, France, general delegate, 1971—. Founder and president, Prix Louis-Delluc, 1937—; president of board of television, 1960. Member of consulting commission on cinema, 1958. *Member:* Societe des ecrivains du cinema et de television (president, 1958—). *Awards, honors:* Named Officier de la Legion d'honneur.

WRITINGS: (With Guiseppe Lo Duca and Georges Melies) *Georges Melies, mage [et] Mes Memoirs* (the former by Bessy and Lo Duca, the latter by Melies; title means "Georges Melies, Magus"), Prisma (Paris), 1945; (with Lo Duca) *Louis Lumiere, inventeur* (title means "Louis Lumiere, Inventor"), Prisma, 1948; *Le Contre Memorial de Sainte-Helene,* Fasquelle, 1949.

Les truquages au cinema (preface by Orson Welles; title means "Movie Tricks"), Prisma, 1951; (with Robert Florey) *Monsieur Chaplin; ou, Le rire dans la nuit* (title means "Mr. Chaplin; or, Laughter in the Dark"), J. Damase (Paris), 1952.

Imprecis d'erotisme (title means "Imprecise Eroticism"), J. J. Pauvert, 1961; *Histoire en mille images de la magie,* Pont Royal, 1961, translation by Margaret Crosland and Alan Daventry published as *A Pictorial History of Magic and the Supernatural,* Spring Books, 1963; *Histoire en mille images du cinema* (title means "A Pictorial History of Motion Pictures"), Pont Royal, 1962; *Orson Welles,* Seghers, 1963, translation by Ciba Vaughan published under same title, Crown, 1971; *Bilan de la magie* (title means "Magic Schedule"), Albin Michel, 1964; (with Jean-Louis Chardans) *Dictionnaire du cinema et de la television* (title means "Dictionary of Motion Pictures and Television"), four volumes, J. J. Pauvert, 1965-71; *Melies,* Anthologie du Cinema, 1966.

Walt Disney, Seghers, 1970; (with Robin Livio) *Charlie Chaplin,* Denoel (Paris), 1972; *Bourvil,* Denoel, 1972; *Les Passagers du Souvenir,* Albin Michel, 1977. Also translator of two novels, both by Orson Welles, *Mr. Arkadin,* 1953, and *V.I.P.,* 1955.

Novels: *Gueule de soleil* (title means "Sunny Mouth"), Fasquelle, 1934; *Sang nouveau* (title means "New Blood"), Fasquelle, 1938; *Buisson ardent* (title means "Burning Bush"), Fasquelle, 1944; *Car c'est Dieu qu'on enterre* (title means "Because God Is Buried"), Albin Michel, 1960.

Screenplays: "Le carrefour des Enfants perdus" (title means "Lost Children Crossroads"), released by M.A.I.C., 1943; *Voici le temps des assassins* (title means "Here Is the Time of Murderers"; released by Filmsonor, 1956), Editions France Empire, 1956; "Le Diable et les 10 commandements" (title means "The Devil and the Ten Commandments"), released by Filmsonar, 1962.

WORK IN PROGRESS: Permanence du neant (title means "The Permanence of Nothingness"); a French translation of Orson Welles' novel, *Two by Two.*

*　　*　　*

BIANCOLLI, Louis Leopold 1907-

PERSONAL: Born April 17, 1907, in New York, N.Y.; son of Carmine and Achilla (Montesano) Biancolli; married Edith Rattner, 1933 (died, 1957); married Jeanne Mitchell, 1958; children: (first marriage) Margaret (Mrs. Murray Weissbach); (second marriage) Lucy, Amy. *Education:* New York University, A.B., 1935, A.M., 1936; Columbia University, further graduate study, 1936-38. *Home:* New Preston, Conn. 06777.

CAREER: New York World-Telegram & Sun, New York, N.Y., music critic, 1928-66; free-lance writer and translator,

1966—. Radio commentator on concert music and opera. *Member:* Music Critics Circle, Phi Beta Kappa.

WRITINGS: (With Robert Bagar) *The Concert Companion: A Comprehensive Guide to Symphonic Music,* Whittlesey House, 1947, reissued as *The Complete Guide to Orchestral Music,* Grosset, 1955; (editor) *The Book of Great Conversations: Edited from Historical Sources in Dramatic Form and with Biographical Sketches,* Simon & Schuster, 1948; (editor with Bagar) *The Victor Book of Operas,* Simon & Schuster, 1949, revised edition, 1953; (editor) *The Analytical Concert Guide,* Doubleday, 1951, 3rd edition (with William S. Mann), Cassell, 1964, Greenwood Press, 1971; (with Mary Garden) *Mary Garden's Story,* Simon & Schuster, 1951; *The Flagstad Manuscript,* Putnam, 1952; (editor) *The Opera Reader,* McGraw, 1953; (editor) *The Mozart Handbook: A Guide to the Man and His Music,* World Publishing, 1954, Grosset, 1962, Greenwood Press, 1975; (editor with Herbert F. Peyser) *Masters of the Orchestra from Bach to Prokofieff,* Putnam, 1954, Greenwood Press, 1969; (with Ruth Slenczynska) *Forbidden Childhood,* Doubleday, 1957.

(Translator) Dante Alighieri, *The Divine Comedy,* Washington Square Press, 1966; (with Roberta Peters) *A Debut at the Met,* Meredith Corp., 1967; (editor with Thomas Scherman) *The Beethoven Companion,* Doubleday, 1972. Translator of librettos from Russian and Italian. Author of annotations for the New York Philharmonic Society, 1941-49. Contributor to magazines and music brochures.

SIDELIGHTS: Biancolli told *CA:* "Of course, as you probably suspect, the real me is nowhere in this labyrinth of research, scholarship, editing, analyzing. That real me was intended by a Carmelite nun aunt of mine for the priesthood, fell in love at 17, and later married a Chassidic rabbi's daughter, lost her after two gruelling open heart operations, is now married to a lapsed Episcopalian, has served with Hebrew finesse of diction at a grand-daughter's Bat-mitzvah (with three more to go!), fought Fascism in Little Italy and everywhere else long before the war, was slated to be parachuted by the OSS near Naples because of his mastery of Neapolitan, and now teaches Yiddish and Hebrew to a 90-year-old writer Helen L. Naufmann who adopted him seven years ago to replace a son she lost in the war! Forgive this idle chatter," he continued. "I do it these days in Yiddish, Hebrew, Italian, Spanish, German, Greek, Russian, Polish, French, Latin, Neapolitan, and as you can see, even in English. I teach them around here to anyone who cares to learn. I also teach youngsters bag-punching, having once been unofficial sparring partner of the Italian heavy-weight fighter who fought the champ Big Jim Braddock to a draw! Girls, believe it or not, pick up the rhythm and intervals of bag-punching faster than boys. They have the built-in rhythms of life, bless them. If I have a hang-up, it's the ladies—properly, of course!"

Biancolli concluded, "At seventy, more than ever, I believe in Life, Love, Laughter, and Learning. Next to my wife and three daughters, I worship Beethoven. My only religion is humanity."

*　　*　　*

BIBB, (David) Porter III 1937-

PERSONAL: Born April 2, 1937, in Louisville, Ky.; son of David Porter, Jr. (a financier) and Margot (a teacher; maiden name, Clark) Bibb; married Judith Boddie Walker, May 13, 1961 (divorced, 1967); children: Hilary Walker, Addison Porter. *Education:* Yale University, B.A., 1959;

graduate study at London School of Economics and Political Science, 1961-62, and Harvard University, 1966; New York University, M.F.A., 1968. *Politics:* Independent. *Home and office:* 45 East 89th St., New York, N.Y. 10028. *Agent:* Lizer Lerner, 36 East 68th St., New York, N.Y. 10021.

CAREER: Newsweek, New York City, correspondent, 1957-59; employed by J. P. Morgan (banking), New York City, 1960-61; Interbro, Ltd. (economic and marketing consultancy), London, England, co-founder and executive, 1961-65; *Newsweek,* New York City, assistant to president, 1965-66, international marketing director, 1966-68; independent film and television producer and writer or producer of over two dozen network documentaries, specials, and movies for television, including the feature films, "Salesman," and "Gimme Shelter," 1969-70; *Rolling Stone,* San Francisco, Calif., publisher, 1971-72; communications and financial consultant for businesses and publications, including, *Kids, Andy Warhol's InterView, More, Children's Express,* and *Working Woman,* 1973—. *Military service:* U.S. Marine Corps, 1960-61. *Member:* National Press Club, Institute of Directors, Motion Picture Producers Association, University Club. *Awards, honors:* Best film award from Venice Film Festival, 1969, for "Salesman"; best documentary feature award from Berlin Film Festival and from Moscow Film Festival, both 1972, both for "Year of the Woman."

WRITINGS: CB Bible, Doubleday, 1976. Also author of the feature film, "End of the Game," Warner Brothers, 1969. Contributor of articles to national periodicals, including *Esquire, Good Housekeeping,* and *Family Circle.*

WORK IN PROGRESS: A screen play on the life of blues singer, Bessie Smith; a novel, *M.O.R.*

*   *   *

BICKLEY, R(obert) Bruce, Jr. 1942-

PERSONAL: Born August 20, 1942, in New Rochelle, N.Y.; son of Robert Bruce (a sales representative) and Jean (Wolcott) Bickley; married Karen Luce, July 2, 1966; children: Kathryn, David. *Education:* University of Virginia, B.A., 1964; Duke University, M.A., 1965, Ph.D., 1969. *Religion:* Protestant. *Home:* 3421 Robinhood Rd., Tallahassee, Fla. 32303. *Office:* Department of English, Florida State University, Tallahassee, Fla. 32306.

CAREER: Florida State University, Tallahassee, assistant professor, 1969-75, associate professor of English, 1975—. *Member:* Modern Language Association of America, Phi Beta Kappa. *Awards, honors:* Woodrow Wilson fellow, 1965-66; Danforth fellow, 1966-68.

WRITINGS: The Method of Melville's Short Fiction, Duke University Press, 1975. Contributor to journals, including *American Literary Realism* and *Studies in American Humor.*

WORK IN PROGRESS: Two books on Joel Chandler Harris, one a critical study, the other an annotated secondary bibliography.

*   *   *

BINDER, David 1931-

PERSONAL: Born February 22, 1931, in London, England; son of Carroll (a newspaperman) and Dorothy (Walton) Binder; married Helga Wagner (a physician), October 9, 1959; children: Julia, Andrea, Alena. *Education:* Harvard University, A.B. (cum laude), 1953; University of Cologne, graduate study, 1953-54. *Politics:* "Center-left." *Religion:*

Society of Friends. *Residence:* Chevy Chase, Md. *Office: New York Times,* 1920 L St., Washington, D.C. 20036.

CAREER: Louisville Times, Louisville, Ky., reporter, 1954-56; Institute of Current World Affairs, New York, N.Y., fellow in Germany, 1957-59; *Daily Mail,* London, England, reporter in Berlin, 1959-60; *Minneapolis Tribune,* Minneapolis, Minn., copy editor, 1960-61; *New York Times,* New York City, reporter, 1961—. *Member:* Foreign Press Association (Bonn, Germany; chairman, 1969-70).

WRITINGS: Berlin East and West, Sterling, 1962; *The Other German,* New Republic Books, 1975. Contributor to magazines in the United States and Germany, including *Reporter, Nation,* and *New Republic.*

WORK IN PROGRESS: Research on Vlachs.

SIDELIGHTS: Binder notes that he is motivated by "death, misery, guilt, spite, lust, contempt, and thirst." His main professional interest is in small nations.

*   *   *

BINGER, Carl A(lfred) L(anning) 1889-1976

August 26, 1889—March 22, 1976; American physician, psychiatrist, educator, and author. Obituaries: *New York Times,* March 24, 1976; *AB Bookman's Weekly,* April 12, 1976.

*   *   *

BINGHAM, Evangeline M(arguerite) L(adys) (Elliot) 1899-
(Geraldine Elliot)

PERSONAL: Born November 8, 1899, in Daharmsala, India; daughter of William Henry Wilson (a colonel) and Charlotte (Furber) Bingham; married Humphrey Francis Bingham (an administrator), November 15, 1927. *Education:* Educated in Bath, England. *Home:* Quintons, East Bergholt, Colchester, Essex, England. *Agent:* Laurence Pollinger Ltd., 18 Maddox St., London W.1, England.

CAREER: British Broadcasting Corp., London, England, member of program staff, played "Aunt Geraldine" on radio program "Children's Hour," 1923-27; Rhodesia Centre of the St. John Ambulance Association, Salisbury, South Rhodesia, centre secretary, 1941-44. Representative from Nyasaland to International Council of Women Conference, 1949; trustee, Nyasaland (now Malawi) Society for the Blind, 1951-55. *Member:* Royal Commonwealth Society for the Blind (honorary life member), Royal Commonwealth Society, Royal Horticultural Society.

WRITINGS—Under pseudonym Geraldine Elliot: *New Tales for Old,* Elkin, Matthews & Marrot, 1932; *The Long Grass Whispers: A Book of African Folktales,* Routledge & Kegan Paul, 1938, reprinted, Schocken, 1968; *Where the Leopard Passes: A Book of African Folktales* (includes *New Tales for Old*), Routledge & Kegan Paul, 1949, reprinted, Schocken, 1968; *The Hunter's Cave,* Routledge & Kegan Paul, 1951; *The Singing Chameleon: A Book of African Stories Based on Local Custom, Proverbs, and Folk-Lore,* Routledge & Kegan Paul, 1957, reprinted, 1971. Also author of stories, plays, and scripts for broadcast.

SIDELIGHTS: Mrs. Bingham collected folk tales and legends while living in Africa 1930-1955, where her husband was an administrator in Nyasaland (now Malawi). Some of her animal stories are based on her experience of raising wild animals as pets. Her book, *The Long Grass Whispers* was published in Zulu. *Avocational interests:* Landscape gardening, flower arrangement, theatre.

BIOW, Milton H. 1882(?)-1976

1882(?)—February 1, 1976; American advertising executive and author. Obituaries: *New York Times,* February 3, 1976.

* * *

BIRCH, Bruce C(harles) 1941-

PERSONAL: Born December 3, 1941, in Wichita, Kan.; son of Lauren (a machinist) and Marjory (Roberts) Birch; married Judith LeeAnn Brown, August 18, 1962; children: Jeremy. *Education:* Southwestern College, B.A., 1962; Southern Methodist University, B.D. (honors), 1965; Yale University, M.A., 1967, M.Phil., 1968, Ph.D., 1970. *Home:* 1646 Primrose Rd. N.W., Washington, D.C. 20012. *Office:* Department of Old Testament, Wesley Theological Seminary, 4400 Massachusetts Ave. N.W., Washington, D.C. 20016.

CAREER: Ordained clergyman of United Methodist Church; Iowa Wesleyan College, Mount Pleasant, instructor, 1968-69, assistant professor of religion, 1969-70; Erskine College, Due West, S.C., assistant professor of Bible and religion, 1970-71; Wesley Theological Seminary, Washington, D.C., assistant professor, 1971-73, associate professor, 1973-76, professor of Old Testament, 1976—. Palmer Lecturer at University of Puget Sound, 1976. Chairman of National Interseminary Council, 1964-67; member of national faculty advisory committee to the Bishops' Call for Peace and Self-Development of Peoples (chairman, 1974—); member of United Methodist Board of Ministry, 1975—. Member of board of directors of Washington International College, 1971-74, and International Program for Human Resources Development, 1975—; member of North American regional committee for St. George's College (Jerusalem), 1976—.

MEMBER: Society of Biblical Literature (president of Chesapeake Bay region, 1975-76), American Academy of Religion, Society for the Advancement of Continuing Education for Ministry. *Awards, honors:* Woodrow Wilson fellowships, 1965-66, 1967-68.

WRITINGS: (With Larry Rasmussen) *Bible and Ethics in the Christian Life,* Augsburg, 1976; *The Rise of the Israelite Monarchy: The Growth and Development of First Samuel, 7-15* (monograph), Scholar's Press (Missoula, Mont.), 1976. Contributor to *New International Standard Bible Encyclopedia.* Contributor of articles and reviews to theology journals.

WORK IN PROGRESS: The Church and World Resources: Biblical and Theological Perspectives, with Larry Rasmussen, for Westminster.

BIOGRAPHICAL/CRITICAL SOURCES: U.S. News and World Report, February 9, 1976; *United Methodist Reporter,* February 20, 1976.

* * *

BISHOP, John 1908-

PERSONAL: Born February 10, 1908, in Liverpool, England; son of George (a shoemaker) and Sarah Ann (Brown) Bishop; married Constance Wilson, August 13, 1935. *Education:* Birmingham University, B.A., 1931; Bristol University, M.A., 1948; Drew University, Ph.D., 1958. *Home:* 40 Wiggins St., Princeton, N.J. 08540.

CAREER: Ordained minister of Methodist Church, 1931; served as minister in England, 1931-54; Northern New Jersey Conference of United Methodist Church, minister,

1954-73. Teaching fellow at Drew Seminary, Madison, N.J., 1954-58; visiting lecturer in homiletics at Princeton Seminary, 1959-60, 1962; visiting lecturer in homiletics at Biblical Seminary, New York, N.Y., 1961; visiting professor of preaching and worship at Ashbury Theological Seminary, 1964. Writer on religion.

WRITINGS: Study Notes on Preaching and Worship, Epworth Press (London), 1949; *Methodist Worship in Relation to Free Church Worship,* Epworth Press, 1950, revised and enlarged edition, Scholars Studies Press, 1975; *The Man in the Manse,* Epworth Press, 1952; *Through the Christian Year,* National Sunday School Union, 1962; *Seeing Jesus Today,* James, 1969; *Seeing Ourselves in the Bible,* James, 1971; *Courage to Live,* Judson Press, 1976. Contributor to religious journals.

WORK IN PROGRESS: A Word in Season, sermons of the church year; *British Preachers and Their Methods; American Preachers and Their Methods.*

SIDELIGHTS: Rev. Bishop has travelled extensively in Europe, the Middle East, West Indies, and Japan. Among his chief interests are homiletics, worship, hymnology, music, poetry, drama and English literature. He is still lecturing and preaching in his retirement.

* * *

BJORNEBOE, Jens 1920-1976

1920—May 10, 1976; Norwegian playwright, painter, educator, essayist, poet, and novelist. Obituaries: *Washington Post,* May 12, 1976; *New York Times,* May 15, 1976; *AB Bookman's Weekly,* June 28, 1976.

* * *

BLACKALL, Eric Albert 1914-

PERSONAL: Born October 19, 1914, in London, England, naturalized U.S. citizen, 1965; son of Frederick and Lillie Blackall; married Jean Hargrave Frantz, June 25, 1960; children: Roger Nicholas. *Education:* Cambridge University, B.A. (first class honors), 1936, M.A., 1940; University of Vienna, D.Phil. (with distinction), 1938. *Home:* 811 Triphammer Rd., Ithaca, N.Y. 14850. *Office:* Department of German Literature, Cornell University, Ithaca, N.Y. 14850.

CAREER: University of Basel, Basel, Switzerland, lector in English language and literature, 1938-39; Cambridge University, Cambridge, England, assistant lecturer, 1939-45, lecturer in German, 1945-58, fellow of Gonville and Caius College, 1945-58; Cornell University, Ithaca, N.Y., professor of German literature, 1958-65, Avalon Foundation Professor of the Humanities, 1965-67, Jacob Gould Schurman Professor of German Literature, 1967—, chairman of department, 1958-65. Visiting professor at Cornell University, autumn, 1957, and University of Heidelberg, summer, 1968; lecturer at more than twenty-five colleges and universities in the United States and abroad.

MEMBER: International Association of Germanists, Modern Language Association of America, American Association of Teachers of German, American Association of University Professors, American Academy of Arts and Sciences (fellow), American Philosophical Society (member of council), English Goethe Society, Arthur Schnitzler Research Association, Deutscher Germanistenverband, Hugo von Hofmannsthal Gesellschaft, Society for the Humanities (Cornell University; acting director, spring, 1975), Phi Beta Kappa. *Awards, honors:* Litt.D. from Cambridge University, 1960; J. G. Robertson Prize from University of London, 1962; Guggenheim fellowship, 1965; decorated with Oesterreisches Ehrenkreuz fuer Kunst und Wissenschaft, First Class, 1973.

WRITINGS: Adalbert Stifter: A Critical Study, Cambridge University Press, 1948; (translator with Vida Harford) Alban Berg, *Wozzeck* (opera), Alfred A. Kalmus, 1952; (editor) Adalbert Stifter, *Kalkstein,* Cambridge University Press, 1956; *The Emergence of German as a Literary Language, 1700-1775,* Cambridge University Press, 1959, revised edition, Cornell University Press, in press; (contributor) P. F. Ganz, editor, *The Discontinuous Tradition,* Oxford University Press, 1970; *Goethe and the Novel,* Cornell University Press, 1976. Contributor to *Encyclopedia Americana.* Contributor of articles and reviews to language and literature journals. Member of editorial board of *PMLA,* 1973-76.

*   *   *

BLADES, James 1901-

PERSONAL: Born September 9, 1901, in Peterborough, England; son of Thomas Weston and Catherine Blades; married, January 27, 1927; married Joan Goosens, June 17, 1948; children: Douglas Hewitt. *Education:* Educated in England. *Home:* 191 Sandy Lane, Cheam, Surrey, England. *Office:* Royal Academy of Music, London, England.

CAREER: Professional timpanist, 1922—. Radio and television broadcaster for British Broadcasting Corp. (BBC), 1945—; professor of timpani and percussion, Royal Academy of Music, London, England, 1956—. Member, Music from the Movies Orchestra, 1930-50, Piccadilly Hotel Dance Band, 1939-40, London Symphony Orchestra, 1939-48, English Opera Group, 1955-73, English Chamber Orchestra, 1955-73, and Melos Ensemble, 1956-73. Lecturer, 1953—. Chairman of Wingfield Music Club for the Handicapped; member of music panel of Disabled Living Foundation. *Member:* Royal Academy of Music, Royal Institution of Great Britain, Percussive Arts Society of America, London Orchestral Association. *Awards, honors:* Officer of the Order of the British Empire, 1970; M.Mus., University of Surrey, 1976.

WRITINGS: Orchestral Percussion Technique, Oxford University Press, 1961, 2nd edition, 1973; *Percussion Instruments and Their History,* Praeger, 1970.

*   *   *

BLAINE, William L(ee) 1931-

PERSONAL: Born October 5, 1931, in Dyersville, Iowa; son of Raymond V. L. (a businessman) and Ida M. (Fischer) Blaine; married Mary Lou Curry, August, 1965 (divorced, 1975); children: Thomas Curry, Alexandra Curry. *Education:* Loras College, student, 1949-51; University of Denver, B.A., 1953; Harvard University, J.D., 1958; also attended University of Colorado. *Politics:* "Liberal moving right with age." *Religion:* "Unenthusiastic Unitarian." *Home:* 255 Yale Ave., Kensington, Calif. 94708. *Office:* California Continuing Education of the Bar, 2150 Shattuck Ave., Berkeley, Calif. 94704.

CAREER: Attorney with practice in business law, 1958—. Publisher of law books for California Continuing Education of the Bar, 1963-67, 1971—, and McGraw-Hill Book Co., 1967-71. President of San Francisco Gilbert and Sullivan Repertory Co., 1963-67. *Military service:* U.S. Army, 1953-55. *Member:* California Bar Association.

WRITINGS: (With John Bishop) *Practical Guide for the*

Unmarried Couple, Two Continents Publishing, 1975; *Where to Practice Law in California: Statistics on Lawyers' Work,* California Continuing Education of the Bar (CEB), 1976. Contributor to law journals and to *Bike World.*

WORK IN PROGRESS: A textbook for high schools and colleges on law as it can be used by laymen in society; a juvenile book; research on methods of access to information.

SIDELIGHTS: Blaine writes that his career has been sidetracked by the necessity of rearing two children as a single parent, but that his professional interest is "the theory of the structuring of information (or access devices) in such a way as to make access most efficient. As a writer/editor of expository material, I'm always interested in analyzing and trying to clarify muddy thought; many social situations could be improved by reanalysis and challenging assumptions."

*   *   *

BLAIR, Don 1933-

PERSONAL: Born March 3, 1933, in Newark, N.J.; son of James R. (an engineer) and Ruth M. Blair; married wife, Donna, August 1, 1954 (divorced August, 1963); married wife, Patricia (a dental office manager), December 12, 1964; children: (first marriage) Cynthia, Glenn; (second marriage) Deborah. *Education:* Attended Cambridge School of Radio and Television. *Home:* 48 Hilton St., Darien, Conn. 06820. *Office:* National Broadcasting Co. Radio Network, 30 Rockefeller Plaza, New York, N.Y. 10020.

CAREER/WRITINGS: WHNB-Television, West Hartford, Conn., news and sports commentator, 1962-65; Mutual Broadcasting System, New York City, newscaster, 1965-72; American Broadcasting Co. (ABC) Radio, New York City, newscaster, 1973—; National Broadcasting Co. (NBC) Radio, New York City, host of series "Consumers Corner," 1974—. Notable assignments include coverage of Gemini 9, 10, and 11, and Apollo 11 and 15. Newscaster on WCBS-Radio, 1972-74. Contributor to Connecticut newspapers. *Military service:* U.S. Army, 1953-55.

WORK IN PROGRESS: A book based on the news program "Consumers Corners."

SIDELIGHTS: Blair's voice was the only one used for Apollo 11 coverage. He reports that it was carried by all networks, broadcast groups, Armed Forces Radio, and Radio Free Europe, possibly one of the largest listening audiences of all time.

On his favorite form of recreation, Blair writes: "Home building has become my #1 hobby. I have added the dormer to my Connecticut home and built two vacation retreats in southern Vermont. I sold one late last year but use the first-built often for skiing and relaxation."

BIOGRAPHICAL/CRITICAL SOURCES: Darien Review, December 3, 1976.

*   *   *

BLAISDELL, Harold F. 1914-

PERSONAL: Born February 27, 1914, in Piermont, N.H.; son of Fred D. and Della (Clement) Blaisdell; married Edna Price, April 28, 1939; children: Michael P. *Education:* Attended Middlebury College and Lyndon Teachers College. *Home address:* P.O. Box 174, Pittsford, Vt.

CAREER: Caverly Child Health Center, Pittsford, Vt., teacher, 1956—. *Military service:* U.S. Army, 1944-45.

WRITINGS: Tricks That Take Fish, Holt, 1954; *Philosophical Fisherman,* Houghton, 1969; *Trout Fishing in New*

England, Stone Wall Press, 1973. Also author of fishing booklet for private industry and of syndicated newspaper column. Contributor of about one hundred stories to men's magazines and outdoor publications.

WORK IN PROGRESS: Articles based on summer fishing, including a trip to northern Labrador.

SIDELIGHTS: Blaisdell writes that he is "experienced in nearly all phases of hunting and fishing. Do my own photography and specialize in cooperating with camp owners in publicizing their regions through magazine articles."*

* * *

BLAKE, Bud
See BLAKE, Julian Watson

* * *

BLAKE, Julian Watson 1918-
(Bud Blake)

PERSONAL: Born February 13, 1918, in Nutley, N.J.; son of George (an art director) and Hazel (Metcalfe) Blake; married Doris Gaskill (an editorial assistant), January 4, 1941; children: Julian Gaskill, Mariana (Mrs. James Heath). *Education:* Attended National Academy of Design, 1934. *Residence:* Rumson, N.J. 07760. *Office:* King Features, 235 East 45th St., New York, N.Y. 10016.

CAREER: Kudner Agency (advertising agency), New York City, began as paste-up boy, became executive art director, 1937-43, 1946-54; King Features, New York City, drew cartoon panel "Ever Happen to You?," 1954-65; author of comic strip "Tiger" (syndicated to about five hundred newspapers), 1965—. *Military service:* U.S. Army, Infantry, 1943-46; became technical sergeant. *Member:* National Cartoonists Society, National Comics Council. *Awards, honors:* Award from National Cartoonists Society, 1970, for "Tiger."

WRITINGS—Under name Bud Blake; cartoon books: *Ever Happen to You?*, Avon, 1963; *Tiger*, Grosset, 1969; *Tiger Turns On*, Grosset, 1970. Contributor of articles and cartoons to national magazines, including *Business Week, Pictorial Review, Family Circle,* and *Woman's Day*.

BIOGRAPHICAL/CRITICAL SOURCES: Cartoonist Profiles, March, 1976.

* * *

BLAKE, Peter (Jost) 1920-

PERSONAL: Born September 20, 1920, in Berlin, Germany; naturalized U.S. citizen. *Education:* Attended University of London, 1939, Regent Street Polytechnic School of Architecture, and University of Pennsylvania, 1940; Pratt Institute, B.Arch., 1948. *Home:* 55 West 55th St., New York, N.Y. 10019.

CAREER: Architectural Forum, New York City, writer, 1942-43, associate editor, 1950-54 and 1958-61, managing editor, 1961-64, editor, 1964-72; Museum of Modern Art, New York City, curator of architecture and design, 1948-50; *House and Home*, architecture editor, 1955-57; worked in partnership with Julian Neski, 1958-61; James Baker & Peter Blake (architects), New York City, partner, 1964—; *Architecture Plus*, editor-in-chief, 1972—. Member of board of directors of Interior Design Conference (Aspen, Colo.), 1965-70.

MEMBER: American Institute of Architects (fellow), Architectural League (New York City; vice-president in archi-

tecture, 1966-68; president, 1971-72), Regional Planning Association. *Awards, honors:* Citation, 1958, for design of American Architecture Exhibition sent to tour iron curtain countries; Howard Myers Award from *Architectural Journal*, 1960.

WRITINGS: Marcel Breuer, Architect and Designer, Museum of Modern Art, 1949; (editor) *An American Synagogue for Today and Tomorrow: A Guide Book to Synagogue Design and Construction,* Union of American Hebrew Congregations, 1954; (editor) Breuer, *Sun and Shadow: The Philosophy of an Architect,* Dodd, 1955; *The Master Builders,* Knopf, 1960; *Le Corbusier: Architecture and Form,* Penguin, 1963; (with Robert Osborn) *The Everlasting Cocktail Party: A Layman's Guide to Culture Climbing,* Dial, 1964; *Frank Lloyd Wright: Architecture and Space,* Penguin, 1964; *God's Own Junkyard: The Planned Deterioration of America's Landscape,* Holt, 1964; *Mies van der Rohe: Architecture and Structure,* Penguin, 1964; *The New Forces,* Royal Australian Institute of Architects, 1971; *Architecture for the New World: The Work of Harry Seidler,* Wittenborn, 1973; *Our Housing Mess, and What Can Be Done About It,* Institute of Human Relations Press, 1974. Contributor to architecture journals, to popular magazines, and to newspapers.*

* * *

BLAKER, Alfred A(rthur) 1928-

PERSONAL: Born May 18, 1928, in Worcester, Mass.; son of John A. (a machine toolmaker) and Edith (Jeffrey) Blaker; married Sally Aiman (a teacher of classical guitar), April 6, 1956; children: John, Frances, Barbara, Elizabeth, Harry, William. *Education:* San Francisco State College (now University), B.A. (honors), 1957, graduate study, 1957-58. *Politics:* "Generally liberal, no party affiliation." *Religion:* "Nonspecific Protestant." *Home:* 2050 Blackwood Dr., Walnut Creek, Calif. 94596.

CAREER: University of California, Berkeley, head of scientific photographic laboratory, 1958-72, lecturer in photography at extension, 1966—. *Military service:* U.S. Army, Corps of Military Police, 1946-52; served in Japan, China, and Philippines.

WRITINGS: Photography for Scientific Publication, W. H. Freeman, 1965; *Field Photography: Beginning and Advanced Techniques,* W. H. Freeman, 1976; *Introduction to Scientific Photography,* W. H. Freeman, in press.

Illustrator: Dorothy Jean Ray. *Eskimo Masks: Art and Ceremony,* University of Washington Press, 1968. Contributor to photographic journals, and to *Veliger* and *Memo*.

WORK IN PROGRESS: Anthropological Photography: Humankind, Sites and, Artifacts, publication by W. H. Freeman expected in 1978; *Aircraft of the Thirties* and *Soldier's Payroll,* both novels.

* * *

BLAMIRES, David (Malcolm) 1936-

PERSONAL: Born May 4, 1936, in Heckmondwike, England; son of Clifford and Amy (Firth) Blamires. *Education:* Christ's College, Cambridge, B.A., 1957, M.A. and Ph.D., both 1963; also studied at Free University of Berlin, 1958. *Religion:* Society of Friends (Quakers). *Home:* 136 Wellington Rd., Manchester M14 6AR, England. *Office:* Department of German, University of Manchester, Manchester M13 9PL, England.

CAREER: University of Manchester, Manchester, England, assistant lecturer, 1960-63, lecturer, 1963-69, senior lecturer, 1969-73, reader in German, 1973—. *Member:* International Arthurian Society (member of committee of British branch, 1969-74), Modern Humanities Research Association, Association of University Teachers of German of Great Britain and Ireland, David Jones Society (honorary secretary), Friends' Historical Society.

WRITINGS: An Echoing Death (poems), privately printed, 1965; *Characterization and Individuality in Wolfram's "Parzival",* Cambridge University Press, 1966; *The Bible Half Hour* (essays), Beacon Hill Friends House, 1968; *David Jones: Artist and Writer,* Manchester University Press, 1971; *Homosexuality from the Inside,* Social Responsibility Council, Religious Society of Friends, 1973; *A History of Quakerism in Liversedge and Scholes,* privately printed, 1973; (translator, with Peter Rickard, Alan Deyermond, Peter King, Michael Lapidge, and Derek Brewer) *Medieval Comic Tales,* D. S. Brewer, 1973; (author of introduction) Gerardus Cambrensis, *South Wales Echo,* Enitharmon Press, 1973; *Schoepferisches Zuhoeren* (title means "Creative Listening"), Religioese Gesellschaft der Freunde (Quaeker), 1974. Contributor of articles and reviews to religious and literary journals, including *Modern Language Review, German Life and Letters, Anglo-Welsh Review, Poetry Wales, Review of English Literature, Critical Quarterly,* and *Friends Quarterly.*

AVOCATIONAL INTERESTS: Topography (especially Orkney, Shetland, Yorkshire), travel (Europe, Australia, Canada, United States).

* * *

BLIZZARD, S(amuel) W(ilson, Jr.) 1914(?)-1976

1914(?)—April 6, 1976; American educator and author of books on sociology and other topics. Obituaries: *New York Times,* April 9, 1976.

* * *

BLOCHER, Henri (Arthur) 1937-

PERSONAL: Surname is pronounced Blow-*shay;* born September 3, 1937, in Leiden, the Netherlands; son of Arthur Jacques (a clergyman) and Elizabeth (Van Nes) Blocher; married Henriette Coulon, January 19, 1961; children: Jacques Emile, Francois Henri, Agnes Louise. *Education:* Sorbonne, University of Paris, certificat d'Etudes Litteraires Generales, 1956; London Bible College, student, 1956-57; Gordon Divinity School, B.D. (summa cum laude), 1959; Faculte Libre de Theologie Protestante de Paris, diplome d'Etudes Superieures de Theologie, 1974. *Religion:* Baptist. *Home:* 16 Avenue du Marechal Joffre, Meulan 78, France. *Office:* Faculte de Theologie Evangelique, 85 Avenue de Cherbourg, Vaux-sur-Seine 78740, France.

CAREER: Institut Biblique, Nogent-sur-Marne, France, lecturer in Biblical and theological studies, 1961—; Faculte Libre de Theologie Evangelique, Vaux-sur-Seine, professor and head of department of systematic theology, 1965—. *Military service:* French Army, chaplain, 1959-61. *Member:* Comite Biblique Francais, Lausanne Continuation Committee for World Evangelism, Phi Alpha Xi.

WRITINGS: Les trois amis (title means "The Three Friends"), Ligue pour la lecture de la Bible, 1966; *The Songs of the Servant,* Inter-Varsity Press, 1975. Contributor to French periodicals and of chapter to conference proceedings. Joint editor of *Ichthus,* 1970—.

WORK IN PROGRESS: Au commencement (title means "In the Beginning"), a short expository work on Genesis; research on the theology of the Sacraments.

SIDELIGHTS: Blocher writes: "I wish to bring the resources of modern scholarship into the service of an uncompromising Christian faith: the emphasis being on radicality and integrality (the Biblical Word of God is the root of a total world-view), with the help of Calvin's heritage ..." He reads Hebrew, Greek, Latin, Spanish, and German. *Avocational interests:* Playing the clarinet.

* * *

BLOOMFIELD, Arthur (John) 1931-

PERSONAL: Born January 3, 1931, in San Francisco, Calif.; son of Arthur L. (a physician and professor of medicine) and Julia (Mayer) Bloomfield; married Anne Buenger, July 14, 1956; children: John, Cecily, Alison. *Education:* Stanford University, A.B., 1951. *Home:* 2229 Webster St., San Francisco, Calif. 94115. *Office: San Francisco Examiner,* 110 Fifth St., San Francisco, Calif. 94103.

CAREER: San Francisco Call-Bulletin, San Francisco, Calif., music and art critic, 1958-59; *San Francisco News-Call Bulletin,* San Francisco, music and art critic, 1962-65; *San Francisco Examiner,* San Francisco, music and art critic, 1965—. San Francisco correspondent to *Musical America,* 1958-61, 1963-64, and *Opera,* 1964—. Member of artistic advertising committee of Spring Opera San Francisco, 1960-62. *Military service:* U.S. Army, 1953-55. *Member:* San Francisco Chamber Music Society.

WRITINGS: The San Francisco Opera, 1923-61, Saunders, 1961; *Fifty Years of the San Francisco Opera,* San Francisco Book Co., 1972; *Arthur Bloomfield's Guide to San Francisco Restaurants,* Comstock, 1975.

* * *

BLUESTEIN, Daniel Thomas 1943- (Daniel B. Thomas)

PERSONAL: Born January 20, 1943, in Bronx, N.Y.; son of Abraham (a manager of cooperative housing) and Selma (an artist; maiden name, Cohen) Bluestine. *Education:* Attended State University of New York at Buffalo, 1961-64; City College of the City University of New York, B.A., 1966; Bernard M. Baruch College of the City University of New York, M.B.A., 1971. *Politics:* Democrat. *Religion:* Jewish. *Home:* 12 Park Trail, Croton-on-Hudson, N.Y. 10520. *Office:* Bridge Plaza Treatment and Rehabilitation Clinic, 41-21 27th St., Long Island City, N.Y. 11101.

CAREER: Elementary teacher in private school in New York City, 1966-69, 1971-72; New York City Methadone Maintenance Treatment Program, New York City, counselor, 1972-73; teacher in private school in New York City, 1973-74; Bridge Plaza Treatment and Rehabilitation Clinic, New York City, counselor on narcotics addiction, 1974—. Has given poetry readings in New York. Member of Croton Council on the Arts. *Member:* East Coast Writers.

WRITINGS—Under pseudonym Daniel B. Thomas: *Momma, I Know Why* (poems), Barlenmir House, 1974. Work represented in *East Coast Writers Anthology,* edited by Ruth Lisa Schechter and Elsa Colligan, East Coast Writers, 1975. Contributor of poems and stories for adults and children to literary journals, including *Kansas Quarterly* and *Stonecloud.*

WORK IN PROGRESS: In Spiked Shoes, poems; two verse plays; a collection of short stories; a collection of children's stories; five novels.

BLUMBERG, Rhoda 1917-

PERSONAL: Born December 14, 1917, in New York; daughter of Abraham and Irena (Fromberg) Shapiro; married Gerald Blumberg (a lawyer), January 7, 1945; children: Lawrence, Rena, Alice, Leda. *Education:* Adelphi College, B.A., 1938. *Residence:* Yorktown Heights, N.Y. *Office:* 1 Rockefeller Plaza, New York, N.Y. 10020.

CAREER: Free-lance writer. Member of board of directors of Westchester Jewish Community Services and Federation of Jewish Philanthropy (Westchester County). *Member:* Authors Guild of Authors League of America.

WRITINGS: Simon & Schuster Travel Guides, Cornerstone Library, 1974; *Firefighters,* F. Watts, 1976; *Sharks,* F. Watts, 1976; *UFO,* F. Watts, 1977; *First Ladies,* F. Watts, in press. Has written scripts for radio interviews and documentary presentations. Contributor of articles to magazines.

WORK IN PROGRESS: Quackery in America, completion expected in 1978.

* * *

BLUMIN, Stuart M(ack) 1940-

PERSONAL: Born March 29, 1940, in Miami, Fla.; son of Harry (a certified public accountant) and Faye (Silverman) Blumin; married Deborah Adelman (a criminologist), June 12, 1965. *Education:* University of Pennsylvania, B.A., 1962, M.A., 1963, Ph.D., 1968. *Residence:* Ithaca, N.Y. *Office:* Department of History, Cornell University, Ithaca, N.Y. 14853.

CAREER: Skidmore College, Saratoga Springs, N.Y., assistant professor of American studies, 1967-69; Massachusetts Institute of Technology, Cambridge, assistant professor of history, 1969-73; Cornell University, Ithaca, N.Y., assistant professor of history, 1974—. Research fellow at Harvard University, 1971-72; visiting lecturer at Brandeis University, 1972. *Member:* American Historical Association, Organization of American Historians, American Studies Association. *Awards, honors:* Ford Foundation grants, 1970, 1971; American Council of Learned Societies grants, 1971, 1973; fellowship from Old Dominion Foundation, 1972.

WRITINGS: (Contributor) Stephan Thernstrom and Richard Sennett, editors, *Nineteenth-Century Cities: Essays in the New Urban History,* Yale University Press, 1959; (contributor) Michael Drake, editor, *Applied Historical Studies,* Methuen, 1973; (contributor) Allen F. Davis and Mark H. Haller, editors, *The People of Philadelphia: A History of Ethnic Groups and Lower-Class Life, 1790-1940,* Temple University Press, 1973; *The Urban Threshold: Growth and Change in a Nineteenth-Century American Community,* University of Chicago Press, 1976; (contributor) Sander L. Gilman, editor, *The City and Sense of Community,* Center for Urban Development Research, Cornell University, 1976. Contributor to history journals.

WORK IN PROGRESS: The American Middle Class in the "Age of the Common Man": A Research Agenda.

* * *

BLYTH, Jeffrey 1926-

PERSONAL: Born March 20, 1926, in England; came to the United States in 1957; son of Herbert Robinson and Winifred Alice (Potts) Blyth; married Myrna Greenstein (a writer), 1963; children: Jonathan, Graham. *Education:* University of London, student, 1942. *Office:* 400 Madison Ave., New York, N.Y. 10017.

CAREER/WRITINGS: Daily Mail, London, England, chief foreign correspondent, 1950-70, chief U.S. correspondent, 1957-70; British Broadcasting Corp. (BBC), London, correspondent from New York, N.Y., for "P.M." and "The World at One," 1972—. Editor and publisher of Interpress of London, 1970—. *Military service:* British Army war correspondent in Italy and North Africa, 1944-47. *Member:* Foreign Press Association of America (president, 1967-68), London Press Club.

* * *

BLYTH, Myrna 1940-

PERSONAL: Born March 22, 1940, in New York, N.Y.; daughter of Benjamin (a textile manufacturer) and Betty (Austin) Greenstein; married Jeffrey Blyth (a journalist), November 25, 1962; children: Jonathan, Graham. *Education:* Bennington College, B.A., 1960. *Home:* 90 Riverside Dr., New York, N.Y. *Agent:* Emilie Jacobson, Curtis Brown Ltd., 60 East 56th St., New York, N.Y. 10022.

CAREER: Datebook, New York City, senior editor, 1960-63; *Ingenue,* New York City, book and fiction editor, 1963-72; *Family Health,* New York City, senior editor, 1972-74; *Family Circle,* New York City, book and fiction editor, 1973—.

WRITINGS: Cousin Suzanne (novel), Mason Publishing, 1975. Contributor of short stories and articles to *New Yorker, Redbook, Cosmopolitan, McCall's, Woman's Day, Family Circle, Reader's Digest, Ms., Ingenue,* and magazines in England, Holland, Scandinavia, South Africa, and Italy.

WORK IN PROGRESS: A novel.

* * *

BODDIE, Charles Emerson 1911-

PERSONAL: Born June 13, 1911, in New Rochelle, N.Y.; son of Jacob Benjamin (a Baptist clergyman) and Gertrude (a teacher; maiden name, Smith) Boddie; married Mary Lavinia Johnson, September 9, 1935; married Mabel Bell Crooks, July 4, 1970; children: (first marriage) Wilma, Richard; (second marriage) Camara and Shauree (stepdaughters). *Education:* Syracuse University, B.A., 1933; Colgate Rochester Divinity School, B.D., 1936; University of Rochester, M.A., 1949; Keuka College, D.D., 1951. *Office:* American Baptist Theological Seminary, 1800 Whites Creek Pike, Nashville, Tenn. 37207.

CAREER: Ordained Baptist minister, 1932; pastor of Baptist churches in Elmira, N.Y., 1935-39, Huntington, W.Va., 1939-42, and Rochester, N.Y., 1942-56; American Baptist Foreign Mission Societies, member of staff in missionary personnel department, 1956-61, secretary in public relations department, 1961-63; American Baptist Theological Seminary, Nashville, Tenn., president, 1963—. Lane Lecturer at New Orleans Baptist Theological Seminary, 1965; Faulkner Lecturer at Tennessee State University, 1968; preacher in Rhodesia, 1970, and Edmonton, Alberta, 1974; chapel speaker at Bucknell University and other colleges and universities; has spoken at summer camps and chautauquas. Member of board of education and publication of American Baptist Convention; member of Southern Baptist Convention Africa Baptist Evangelistic Campaigns, 1970; member of national board of directors of National Conference of Christians and Jews, 1974—. Member of board of directors of Rochester chapter of American Red Cross.

MEMBER: International Platform Association, American Guild of Organists, Rochester Advertising Club, Theta Beta Phi, Phi Kappa Phi, Omega Psi Phi, Tambourine and Bones, Ten Gallon Club.

WRITINGS: God's Bad Boys (biographies of black preachers), Judson Press, 1972. Also author of *Giant in the Earth.* Contributor to journals.

SIDELIGHTS: While with the American Baptist Foreign Mission Societies, Boddie traveled all over the world, inspecting mission stations.

* * *

BODIN, Paul 1909-

PERSONAL: Born April 16, 1909, in Paris, France; son of Eugene (a merchant) and Augustine (Gauthier) Bodin; married Suzanne Jubalt (divorced); children: Pierre. *Education:* Faculte des Lettres de Paris, diplome d'etudes superieures, 1935; Institut de Psychologie de Paris, diplome, 1940. *Home:* 12 rue de l'Etoile, Paris 75017, France. *Office:* Maison de l'O.R.T.F., 116 avenue du President Kennedy, Paris, 75016, France.

CAREER: Journalist and writer, 1932-40; *Combat* magazine, war correspondent, 1944, editor in chief, 1947-49; Paris Information Agency, Paris, director, 1949; *Entreprise* magazine, Paris, secretary general, 1953-54; French Government, Paris, secretary to minister of industry and commerce, 1954-55, chief assistant to secretary of state for arts and letters, 1956-57, member of cabinet of minister of national education, 1957-58, counselor to president of National Council, Andre Malraux, 1958, counselor in ministry of information, 1960; editor in chief of *Journal parle,* 1958; Office de Radio Television Francaise (O.R.T.F.), Paris, secretary general of information, 1958-60, inspector general, 1960—. Director of information, French Radical Party, 1955. *Military service:* Correspondent in World War II, 1939-45; covered events in France, Belgium, and Germany. *Member:* Association of French Reporters, French Society of Dramatic Authors, French Society of Letters, French Society of Psychology. *Awards, honors:* Medaille du combattant voluntaire de la Resistance, 1944; Chevalier des Arts et des Lettres, 1956; Officier, Legion d'honneur, 1969; received Croix de guerre and Croix du combattant.

WRITINGS—Novels: *Anne-Marie,* Gallimard, 1945; *Les Aventures extraordinaires de Didier Lambert,* Editions du Seuil, 1945; *Le Voyage sentimental,* Gallimard, 1946; *De Notre envoye special,* Correa, 1950; *Les Amants du Theil,* La Table Ronde, 1952, translation by Pamela Morris published as *The Sign of Eros,* Putnam, 1953 (published in England as *The Lovers Dilemma,* Bodley Head, 1954); *Une Jeune femme,* Laffont, 1966; translation by Herma Briffault published as *A Young Woman,* Crown, 1969; *Destin d'un couple,* La Table Ronde, 1968, translation published as *Woman's Destiny,* Avon, 1971.

Nonfiction: *L'Adaptation de l'enfant au milieu scolaire* (psychological study), Presses Universitaires de France, 1945; (with Jean Rostand) *Life, the Great Adventure* (discussions), Hutchinson, 1955, Scribner, 1956.

Also author of volume of poetry, *Monde plein d'aventures,* 1940, and of television dramas, "Pour l'honneur de Carlotta," 1960, and "Un Homme superieur," 1961.

WORK IN PROGRESS: A novel, *Le Psy;* an essay, *Eros au masculin.*

BOGATYRYOV, Konstantin 1924(?)-1976

1924(?)—June 17(?), 1976; Russian poet and translator. Obituaries: *New York Times,* June 19, 1976.

* * *

BOILES, Charles Lafayette (Jr.) 1932-
(Carlos Lafayette)

PERSONAL: Surname is pronounced Bwa-*leh;* born June 15, 1932, in Ada, Okla.; son of Charles Lafayette (in the supermarket business) and Pearl Lovenia (a nurse; maiden name, Webb) Boiles; married Maria Christina Vasquez, December 16, 1962; children: Claudia Iztacu, Paloma Valentina Teoxihuitl. *Education:* Juilliard School of Music, B.S., 1956, graduate study, 1958-60; Tulane University, Ph.D., 1969. *Religion:* "Monist seeker." *Residence:* Bloomington, Ind. *Office:* Faculty of Music, University of Montreal, Montreal, Quebec, Canada.

CAREER: Western Military Academy, Alton, Ill., piano teacher, 1950-51; New York Schools of Music, New York City, piano teacher, 1951-52; organist and choirmaster for Methodist church in New York City, 1959-60; Arte Asociacion Civil, Monterrey, Mexico, director, 1961; Universidad Veracruzana, Jalapa, Mexico, instructor in musical theory, 1962, staff ethnomusicologist, 1963-67, summer school lecturer, 1964-70; Indiana University, Bloomington, associate professor of ethnomusicology, 1969-76; University of Montreal, Montreal, Quebec, associate professor of ethnomusicology, 1976—. Assistant director of Tulane University's Inter-American Institute for Musical Research, 1966-69. Has conducted extensive field research on music and dance in Veracruz, Mexico. *Military service:* U.S. Army, member of Twenty-Fifth Division Band and band instructor, 1956-58; became sergeant.

MEMBER: Society for Ethnomusicology (member of council, 1974-77). *Awards, honors:* Jaap Kunst Prize from Society for Ethnomusicology, 1966.

WRITINGS: (Translator with Fernando Horcasitas) Miguel Leon-Portilla, *Time and Reality in the Thought of the Maya,* Beacon Press, 1973; *Man, Magic, and Musical Occasions,* Collegiate Publishing, 1975. Contributor of articles and reviews to professional journals. Book review editor of *Journal for Ethnomusicology,* 1970-72.

WORK IN PROGRESS: Paradigmatics of Ethnomusicology, a new approach to musical analysis; *International Cuisine for Restaurateurs and Caterers,* under pseudonym Carlos Lafayette; a world survey of music, for Prentice-Hall.

SIDELIGHTS: Boiles writes: "Although I shall continue to study the wealth of data I have collected in Mexico, in the future I should like to broaden my understanding of musical phenomena by making studies of other musics of the world, expecially of those musical systems which contrast greatly with those of Latin America. Part of this research will be involved with solving problems of musical acculturation and the way in which traditions are continued or changed. Much of my future research will be oriented toward discovering those elements functioning as musical signifiers in systems of music around the world."

AVOCATIONAL INTERESTS: International cuisine (former owner of a restaurant serving international foods).

* * *

BOKSER, Ben Zion 1907-

PERSONAL: Born July 4, 1907, in Lubomi, Poland; came

to United States in 1920; son of Elie Morris (a businessman) and Gittel (Katz) Bokser; married Kallia Halpern (a radio commentator), July 21, 1940; children: Miriam (Mrs. Wayne Caravella), Baruch. *Education:* City College (now of the City University of New York), B.A., 1928; Jewish Theological Seminary, rabbi, 1931; Columbia University, M.A., 1931, Ph.D., 1935. *Home:* 110-40 70th Ave., Forest Hills, N.Y. *Office:* 106-06 Queens Blvd., Forest Hills, N.Y.

CAREER: Rabbi of Jewish congregations in Bronx, N.Y., 1931-32, and Vancouver, British Columbia, 1932-33; Forest Hills Jewish Center, Forest Hills, N.Y., rabbi, 1934—. Adjunct professor at Queens College of the City University of New York, 1971—; visiting professor at Jewish Theological Seminary, 1952, lecturer, 1953—. Editor of radio program "Eternal Light" for Jewish Theological Seminary and National Broadcasting Corp., 1950. Member of Conference on Science, Philosophy, and Religion. *Military service:* U.S. Army, chaplain, 1944-46. *Member:* Phi Beta Kappa. *Awards, honors:* D.D. from Jewish Theological Seminary, 1964.

WRITINGS: Pharisaic Judaism in Transition, Bloch Publishing, 1935; *The Legacy of Maimonides,* Philosophical Library, 1950; *The Wisdom of the Talmud,* Philosophical Library, 1951; *From the World of the Cabbalah,* Philosophical Library, 1954; *The Gift of Life,* Abelard, 1956; *Judaism and the Modern Man,* Philosophical Library, 1957; (editor and translator) *Jewish High Holy Day Prayer Book,* Hebrew Publishing, 1957; (editor and translator) *Jewish Daily and Festival Prayer Book,* Hebrew Publishing, 1959; *Judaism: Profile of a Faith,* Knopf, 1963; *Judaism and the Christian Predicament,* Knopf, 1966; *Jews, Judaism, and the State of Israel,* Herzl Press, 1973; (editor and translator) Moshe Silberg, *Talmudic Law and the Modern State,* Burning Bush Press, 1973; *The Gifts of Life and Love,* Hebrew Publishing, 1975. Contributor to *Encyclopaedia Britannica* and *Encyclopedia Judaica.* Contributing editor of *Encyclopedia of Religion.*

WORK IN PROGRESS: Compiling a reader on Jewish mysticism.

*　　*　　*

BOLKOSKY, Sidney M(arvin) 1944-

PERSONAL: Born February 1, 1944, in Rochester, N.Y.; son of Gus (a salesman) and Freda (Rotman) Bolkosky; married Lorraine Aroesty, May 30, 1965; children: Miriam, Gabriel. *Education:* University of Rochester, B.A., 1965; Wayne State University, M.A., 1966; State University of New York at Binghamton, Ph.D., 1972. *Politics:* "Rad-lib." *Religion:* Jewish. *Office:* Western Culture Program, University of Michigan—Dearborn, Dearborn, Mich. 48128.

CAREER: Hobart & William Smith College, Geneva, N.Y., instructor in history, 1969-72; University of Michigan—Dearborn, assistant professor of history and chairman of Western culture program, 1972—. Instructor at Detroit Psychiatric Institute, 1973-75. *Awards, honors:* Grant from Michigan Council for the Humanities, 1975-76.

WRITINGS: The Distorted Image: German Jewish Perceptions of Germans and Germany, 1918-1935, American Elsevier, 1975.

WORK IN PROGRESS: A book on "Weimar culture"; an article on Thomas Mann and one on Hitler's mythical *Mein Kampf;* research in the area of applied psychoanalysis.

SIDELIGHTS: Bolkosky writes: "My interests and research have led me to a revaluation of the possibilities of studying historical motivation with the aid of psychoanalytic theory, to a reconsideration of mythopoesis and cognitive anthropology, until I have now come to believe that the motivations of psychoanalysis can be better understood by considering historical circumstances, anthropology (especially pre-civilized thought and social organization) and placing them in a context of western civilization beginning with the Greeks. This might hopefully produce a new form of psychoanalytic therapy that is more sympathetic to human needs, historical and social circumstances. It seems clear that analysis has more to learn from history and anthropology than the reverse."

*　　*　　*

BOLLES, Don 1929(?)-1976

1929(?)—June 13, 1976; American journalist and writer. Obituaries: *Washington Post,* June 14, 1976.

*　　*　　*

BOLT, Bruce A(lan) 1930-

PERSONAL: Born February 15, 1930, in Australia; came to United States, 1963, naturalized, 1972; son of Donald Frank (an engineer) and Arline (Myra) Bolt; married Beverley Bentley (a science editor), February 11, 1956; children: Gillian, Robert, Helen, Margaret. *Education:* University of Sydney, B.Sc. (honors), 1952, M.Sc., 1956, Ph.D., 1959, D.Sc., 1972. *Home:* 1508 Le Roy Ave., Berkeley, Calif. 94708. *Office:* Seismographic Station, Department of Geology and Geophysics, University of California, Berkeley, Calif. 94720.

CAREER: University of Sydney, Sydney, Australia, lecturer, 1954-61, senior lecturer in applied mathematics, 1961-62; University of California, Seismographic Station, Berkeley, professor of seismology and director of department of geology and geophysics, 1963—. Fulbright research scientist at Lamont Geological Observatory, 1960; visiting professor at Tokyo and Kyoto Universities, summer, 1972, at Cambridge University, 1973; visiting summer lecturer at Academia Sinica, People's Republic of China, 1973. Consultant to United Kingdom Atomic Energy Authority, Seismic Research Group, 1961. *Member:* Royal Society of New South Wales (council member, 1959), Seismological Society of America (president, 1975), Royal Astronomical Society (fellow), American Geophysical Union (fellow), Earthquake Engineering Research Institute (fellow), California Academy of Sciences (fellow). *Awards, honors:* Fulbright research scholar, 1960; H. O. Wood Award, 1967, 1972.

WRITINGS: (Editor) *Seismology: Body Waves and Sources,* Academic Press, 1972; (editor) *Seismology: Surface Waves and Earth Oscillations,* Academic Press, 1972; (editor) *Geophysics,* Academic Press, 1973; (with W. L. Horn, G. A. Macdonald, and R. F. Scott) *Geological Hazards,* Springer, 1975; *Nuclear Explosions and Earthquakes: The Parted Veil,* W. H. Freeman, 1975.

Editor of *Bulletin of Seismological Society of America,* 1965-71.

WORK IN PROGRESS: Earthquakes: A Primer, for W. H. Freeman.

*　　*　　*

BOND, Harold 1939-

PERSONAL: Born December 2, 1939, in Boston, Mass.; son of Khorin (a cook) and Ovsanna (Avakian) Bond. *Edu-*

cation: Northeastern University, A.B., 1962; University of Iowa, M.F.A., 1967. *Home:* 11 Chestnut St., Melrose, Mass. 02176.

CAREER: Poet. Production editor, Horizon House (magazine publishers), Dedham, Mass., 1962-65; production editor, Allyn & Bacon (textbook publishers), Boston, Mass., 1967-69; copy editor, *Boston Globe,* Boston, 1969-71. Instructor for poetry workshops at Cambridge Center for Adult Education, Cambridge, Mass., 1968—, for poets-in-the-schools programs in Massachusetts, 1971-74, and in New Hampshire, 1973—, and for Boston's Model Cities higher education program, 1972. Has given readings from his works at American colleges and universities, and on radio programs in Boston and Iowa City. *Member:* Poets Who Teach (Massachusetts). *Awards, honors:* First prizes from Armenian Allied Arts Association of America poetry competitions, 1963, 1964, 1965, and from *Kansas City Star,* 1967, 1968; National Endowment for the Arts creative writing fellowship, 1976.

WRITINGS—Poems: (With Harry Barba and Leo Hamalian) *3x3,* Harian Press, 1969; *The Northern Wall,* Northeastern University Press, 1969; *Dancing on Water,* Cummington Press, 1970; *America,* St. Vartan Press, 1976.

Poems have been anthologized in *The Young American Poets,* edited by Paul Carroll, Follett, 1968; *Speaking for Ourselves: American Ethnic Writing,* edited by Lillian Faderman and Barbara Bradshaw, Scott, Foresman, 1969, 2nd edition, 1975; *The New Yorker Book of Poems,* Viking, 1969; *Ararat: A Decade of Armenian-American Writing,* edited by Jack Antreassian, Armenian General Benevolent Union of America, 1969; *Eleven Boston Poets,* Harvard Advocate, 1970; *East Coast Poets,* edited by Ray Amorosi, Quixote Press, 1971; *Getting Into Poetry,* edited by Morris Sweetkind, Holbrook, 1972; *New Voices in American Poetry,* edited by David Allan Evans, Winthrop Publishing, 1973; *Outside/Inside,* edited by Laurie Urbscheit and Jerrod Brumfield, Holt, 1973; *Shake the Kaleidoscope: A New Anthology of Modern Poetry,* edited by Milton Klonsky, Pocket Books, 1973; *The Blacksmith,* edited by Gail Mazur, Blacksmith Press, 1975; *Writing a Poem,* edited by Florence Trefethen, Writer, 2nd edition (Bond was not associated with earlier edition), 1975; *Armenian-American Poets: A Bilingual Anthology,* edited by Garig Basmadjian, Armenian General Benevolent Union of America, 1976; *Pride & Protest: American Ethnic Literature,* edited by Jay Schulman, Aubrey Shatter, and Rosalie Ehrlich, Dell, 1976; *Traveling America: With Today's Poets,* edited by David Kherdian, Macmillan, in press.

Contributor of poems to national magazines, including *New Yorker, Harper's Saturday Review,* and *New Republic,* and to literary journals, including *North American Review, Iowa Review, Carleton Miscellany, Shenandoah, Choice, Sumac,* and *Beloit Poetry Journal.* Member of editorial board of *Ararat.*

WORK IN PROGRESS: A book of poems, *America.*

*   *   *

BOND, Nancy (Barbara)   1945-

PERSONAL: Born January 8, 1945, in Bethesda, Md.; daughter of William H. (a librarian) and Helen L. (an elementary school teacher; maiden name, Lynch) Bond. *Education:* Mount Holyoke College, B.A., 1966."ollege of Librarianship, Aberystwyth, Cardiganshire, Wales, Dip.Lib., 1972. *Politics:* Independent. *Religion:* "Informal." *Home:* 109 Valley Road, Concord, Mass. 01742.

CAREER: Oxford University Press, London, England, member of promotional staff, 1967-68; Lincoln Public Library, Lincoln, Mass., assistant children's librarian, 1969-71; Gardner Public Library, Gardner, Mass., director, 1973-75; Massachusetts Audubon Society, Lincoln, administrative assistant, 1976—. *Member:* Library Association (England), National Audubon Society, Jersey Wildlife Preservation Trust. *Awards, honors:* Hornbook award, 1976, for *A String in the Harp.*

WRITINGS: A String in the Harp (juvenile), Antheneum, 1976.

WORK IN PROGRESS: Writing juvenile and adult fiction.

SIDELIGHTS: Nancy Bond told *CA,* "Children's books are one of my greatest loves and always have been. I was much encouraged to find some fifteen years ago that I did not in fact ever have to outgrow them. But it took me rather a long time to realize I could do more than simply read them. There is a lot of very exciting fiction being written and published ostensibly for children! I wage a constant campaign to introduce it to other adults.

"My other deep interest is natural history. I am involved with organizations active in conservation, but more fundamental, I have a real conviction that men are only a part of the natural pattern and that much of what we do to the environment is senseless, thoughtless, and tragic. Only by pausing to look and make ourselves truly aware that all the parts fit, even though we may not understand how, can we preserve and protect the balance of the whole. It is therefore essential to me that we encourage by word and deed attention to minutiae, wonder at detail, and respect life in all forms."

*   *   *

BONDANELLA, Peter Eugene   1943-

PERSONAL: Born December 20, 1943, in Pinehurst, N.C.; son of Frank Patrick (a teacher) and Dorothy (a librarian; maiden name, McKenzie) Bondanella; married Julia Conaway (a professor), June 13, 1969. *Education:* Davidson College, A.B. (cum laude), 1966; Stanford University, M.A., 1967; University of Oregon, Ph.D., 1970. *Home:* 1927 South High St., Bloomington, Ind. 47401. *Office:* Department of French and Italian, Indiana University, Bloomington, Ind. 47401.

CAREER: Wayne State University, Detroit, Mich., assistant professor of Italian, 1970-72; Indiana University, Bloomington, associate professor of French and Italian, 1972—. *Member:* Modern Language Association of America, American Comparative Literature Association, American Association of Teachers of Italian, Renaissance Society of America, Midwest Modern Language Association. *Awards, honors:* National Endowment for the Humanities younger humanist fellowship, 1972-73.

WRITINGS: Machiavelli and the Art of Renaissance History, Wayne State University Press, 1973; *Francesco Guicciardini,* Twayne, 1976; (editor) *Federico Fellini: Essays in Criticism,* Oxford University Press, in press; (editor and translator, with Mark Musa) *The Decameron: A Norton Critical Edition,* Norton, in press. Contributor to language, literature, and philology journals.

WORK IN PROGRESS: Editing *The Dictionary of Italian Literature,* with wife, Julia Conaway Bondanella, for Greenwood Press; editing and translating *The Viking Portable Machiavelli,* with Mark Musa, for Viking; a complete translation and critical commentary on Boccaccio's *Decameron,* with Musa.

SIDELIGHTS: Bondanella told *CA* that his commitment to teaching and research in Italian and comparative literature is based on its "crucial contribution to the formation of the very idea of the humanities itself, beginning with the early humanists and continuing until the present day. This rich cultural continuity is particularly important for an assessment of the role the humanities must play in our modern world. One of my chief concerns is that his legacy from Italy's past not be confined to the museum or the pedagogue's study but, instead, that it be placed in a specifically contemporary context. To that end, I am interested in new critical perspectives on older literatures, as well as examing the mutual illumination of literature and the other arts, especially the Italian cinema. My hope is that Italian language and literature departments in America will broaden their horizons to include such areas of interest as Italian cinema, Italian-American relationships, folklore, and history so that departments of Italian studies will be established."

* * *

BONI, Albert 1892-

PERSONAL: Born October 21, 1892, in New York, N.Y.; son of Charles (an insurance company executive) and Bertha (Saslavsky) Boni; married Nell van Leeuwen, September 14, 1917; children: William F. *Education:* Attended Cornell University, 1909-10, and Harvard University, 1910-13. *Politics:* Socialist. *Religion:* None. *Residence:* Ormond Beach, Fla. 32074. *Office:* Readex Microprint Corp., 101 Fifth Ave., New York, N.Y. 10003.

CAREER: Book-seller and publisher, 1913—. Founded Washington Square Players (later Theatre Guild), 1915; established Little Leather Library, 1915-17, and Modern Library, 1917; vice-president of Boni & Liveright (publishers), 1917-20; president of Albert & Charles Boni, Inc., 1923-35; Readex Microprint Corp., New York, N.Y., and Chester, Vt., president, 1940-74, chairman of board of directors, 1974—. Invented Microprint and Readex reading projector, and Microprint technique. Board chairman, Readex Microprint Corp., United Kingdom.

MEMBER: National Microfilm Association (fellow), American Documentation Institute, American Library Association, American Institute of Physics, Optical Society of America, Royal Photographic Society of Great Britain, Society of Motion Picture and Television Engineers, Society of Photographic Scientists and Engineers, Rochester Museum of Arts and Sciences (N.Y.; fellow). *Awards, honors:* Rochester Museum of Arts and Sciences citation, 1944; National Microfilm Association pioneer medal, 1961.

WRITINGS—Editor: Modern Book of French Verse, Boni & Liveright, 1920; *A Guide to the Literature of Photography and Related Subjects,* Morgan & Morgan, 1943; (with Hubbard Ballou and others) *Photographic Literature: An International Bibliographic Guide to General and Specialized Literature on Photographic Processes, Techniques, Theory, Chemistry, Physics, Apparatus, Materials and Applications, Industry, History, Aesthetics,* Morgan & Morgan, 1962, supplement: *Photographic Literature 1960-1970,* 1972.

* * *

BONTECOU, Eleanor 1890(?)-1976

1890(?)—March 19, 1976; American lawyer, educator, and author of books in her field. Obituaries: *Washington Post,* March 25, 1976.

BONTRAGER, John K(enneth) 1923-

PERSONAL: Born February 15, 1923, in West Lafayette, Ohio; son of Charles Marion and Marguerite (Fishbaugh) Bontrager; married Vestal McConnell, August 25, 1943; children: Gloria (Mrs. Stephen P. Gaines), Janiece (Mrs. Roy Striplin, Jr.), Mary. *Education:* Heidelberg College, A.B., 1949; Oberlin College, B.D., 1952; Vanderbilt University, M.Div., 1973; Claremont School of Theology, D.Min. candidate. *Home:* 1442 Melrose Ave., Chula Vista, Calif. 92011. *Office:* Old San Diego Community Church, 2444 Congress, San Diego, Calif. 92110.

CAREER: Ordained minister of United Church of Christ, 1952; pastor in Wellington, Ohio, 1950-52, and in Millersburg and Glenmont, Ohio, 1952-55; U.S. Navy, chaplain, 1955-75, retiring as captain; pastor in San Diego, Calif., 1975—. *Military service:* U.S. Coast Guard, 1942-46. *Member:* International Transactional Analysis Association, Rotary International, Kiwanis, Toastmasters. *Awards, honors*—Military: Viet Nam Cross of Gallantry, Viet Nam Service Medal with six stars, China Service Medal, Navy Commendation Medal with combat V.

WRITINGS: Sea Rations, Upper Room Press, 1964; *Free the Child in You,* United Church Press, 1974.

* * *

BOOTE, Robert Edward 1920-
(Robert Arvill)

PERSONAL: Born February 6, 1920, in Stoke-on-Trent, England; son of Ernest Haydn and Helen Rose Boote; married Vera Badian, 1948; children: Karin Verli, Anthony Robert. *Education:* University of London, D.P.A., 1950, B.Sc., 1952. *Home:* 27 Woodhayes Rd., Wimbledon Common, London SW19 4RF, England.

CAREER: City of Stoke-on-Trent, England, administrative officer, 1946-48; Staffordshire County Planning and Development Department, Staffordshire, England, chief administrative officer, 1948-54; Nature Conservancy, principal, 1954-64, deputy director, 1964-73. United Kingdom delegation to Council of Europe, member of committee for conservation of nature and natural resources, 1963-71, chairman of European Committee, 1969-71, chairman of preparatory group for Conservation Year, 1970, chairman of organizing committee for European Conservation Conference and vice-president of conference, 1970, consultant for European Architectural Heritage Year, 1973-75. *Military service:* British Army, Royal Artillery, 1939-46; became acting lieutenant colonel; received Greek distinguished service medal, 1946.

MEMBER: Chartered Institute of Secretaries (fellow), Institute of Landscape Architects (honorary member), Atheneum Club. *Awards, honors:* Commander of Royal Victorian Order, 1971.

WRITINGS: (Under pseudonym Robert Arvill) *Man and Environment: Crisis and the Strategy of Choice,* Penguin, 1967, 4th edition, 1976; (contributor) John Rose, editor, *Technological Injury: Effect of Technological Advance on Environment, Life, and Society,* Gordon & Breach Science Publishers, 1969. Contributor to magazines.

AVOCATIONAL INTERESTS: Walking, music.

* * *

BORGO, Ludovico 1930-

PERSONAL: Born August 30, 1930, in Naples, Italy; came to the United States in 1953, naturalized citizen, 1958; son of

Luigi (a lawyer) and Lucia (Gianni) Borgo; married Margot Blue, November 28, 1952; children: Damon, Louis Avon. *Education:* Washington University, St. Louis, Mo., B.A., 1959; Harvard University, Ph.D., 1968. *Office:* Department of Fine Arts, Brandeis University, Waltham, Mass. 02154.

CAREER: University of Michigan, Ann Arbor, assistant professor of art history, 1965-66; Washington University, St. Louis, Mo., assistant professor of art history, 1966-69; Brandeis University, Waltham, Mass., associate professor of art history, 1969—.

WRITINGS: The Works of Mariotto Albertinelli, Garland Publishing, 1976. Contributor to *Burlington.* Editorial consultant for *The New Century Italian Renaissance Encyclopedia.*

WORK IN PROGRESS: Portraits of Rulers during the Renaissance.

SIDELIGHTS: Borgo writes: "My main motivation is to acquire as great as possible an understanding of the arts of the Renaissance so that I can pass it on to my professional colleagues and to my students. No matter how hard an historian tries to be objective, he is still liable to accept and repeat ignorant presumptions that have been formulated in the past. My duty as an historian is to dispel as many as possible of these presumptions."

*   *   *

BORROFF, Edith   1925-

PERSONAL: Born August 2, 1925, in New York, N.Y.; daughter of Albert Ramon and Marie (a pianist; maiden name, Bergersen) Borroff. *Education:* Attended Oberlin Conservatory of Music, 1943-45; American Conservatory of Music, Mus.B., 1946, Mus.M., 1948; University of Michigan, Ph.D., 1958. *Home:* 900 Lehigh Ave., Binghamton, N.Y. 13903. *Office:* Department of Music, State University of New York at Binghamton, Binghamton, N.Y. 13901.

CAREER: Milwaukee-Downer College, Milwaukee, Wis., instructor in music, 1950-54; Hillsdale College, Hillsdale, Mich., associate professor, 1958-60, professor of music, 1960-62; University of Wisconsin, Milwaukee, associate professor of music, 1962-66; Eastern Michigan University, Ypsilanti, professor of music, 1966-72; University of North Carolina, Chapel Hill, visiting professor of music, 1972-73; State University of New York at Binghamton, professor of music, 1973—.

MEMBER: American Musicological Society (member of national council), College Music Society (member of national council), Music Teachers National Association, Renaissance Society of America, Mu Phi Epsilon. *Awards, honors:* Andrew W. Mellon Postdoctoral Award, 1960-61; research grants from University of Wisconsin, 1966, and from Research Foundation of State University of New York, 1975-76.

WRITINGS: Elisabeth Jacquet de La Guerre, Institute of Medieval Music, 1966; *Music of the Baroque,* W. C. Brown, 1970; *Music in Europe and the United States: A History,* Prentice-Hall, 1971; *Notations and Editions: A Book in Honor of Louise Cuyler,* W. C. Brown, 1974; (with Marjory Irvin) *Music in Perspective,* Harcourt, 1976; *The Arts in the West,* General Learning Corp., in press.

Editor: *Mondonville's Jubilate,* University of Pittsburgh Press, 1961; Jean-Ferry Rebel, *Sonata in G Minor, 1713,* University of Pittsburgh Press, 1961; Elisabeth Jacquet de La Guerre, *Sonata in D Major, 1707,* University of Pittsburgh Press, 1961; (contributor) Louise Cuyler, *Maximilian*

the Great and Music, Part II, Oxford University Press, 1973.

Compositions: "Variations and Theme for Oboe and Piano," Fox Publishing, 1962; "Sonata for Horn and Piano," King (Boston, Mass.), 1970; also "Piano Teaching Pieces," "The Poet," and "String Quartet #3." Author of program notes for South Bend Symphony Orchestra. Contributor to *New Catholic Encyclopedia, Encyclopedia Americana,* and *Grove's Dictionary of Music and Musicians.* Contributor of about forty articles to music journals. Music critic for *Ann Arbor News,* 1966-72.

WORK IN PROGRESS: Three American Composers, on Fischer, Finney, and Crumb; *Logical Processes in the Arts; A Book of Sounds,* for children; *The Heart and the Unicorn: A Geometry,* a definition of man.

SIDELIGHTS: Edith Borroff's specialization is French music from 1650 to the Revolution, with other interests in American music and in the general study of history ("the study of how events occur in time"), and in the arts. *Avocational interests:* Painting and heraldic renderings (had a one-woman exhibition of heraldic drawings at Milwaukee-Downer College, 1952).

*   *   *

BORTH, Christian C.   1895(?)-1976

1895(?)—March 22, 1976; American association executive, automotive historian, journalist, and author of books in his field. Obituaries: *New York Times,* March 25, 1976; *AB Bookman's Weekly,* July 5, 1976.

*   *   *

BORTOLI, Georges   1923-

PERSONAL: Born June 28, 1923, in Casablanca, Morocco; son of Gabriel and Wilhelmine (Barnaud) Bortoli; married Catherine Perzinsky, November 24, 1948; children: Anne, Stephane, Catherine. *Education:* University of Algiers, Graduate in letters, 1948. *Home:* 40 bis, rue de Sevigne, 75003 Paris, France. *Office:* "Antenna 2," 5 rue de Montessuy, 75007 Paris, France.

CAREER: Radiodiffusion-Television francaise, Paris, journalist, 1957-66, Moscow bureau chief, 1966-69; France-Inter, deputy director, 1969-71; Societe nationale de television "Antenne 2," Paris, journalist and producer, 1972—. Writer. *Military service:* French Army, 1942-44. *Member:* P.E.N. Club, Societe des Gens de Lettres de France. *Awards, honors:* Prix des Maisons de la Presse, 1973, for *The Death of Stalin.*

WRITINGS: Vivre a Moscou, Robert Laffont, 1969; *The Death of Stalin,* Praeger, 1975; *Moscow and Leningrad Observed,* Oxford University Press, 1975.

WORK IN PROGRESS: Mille ans de Russie, publication by Robert Laffont expected in 1977.

SIDELIGHTS: Bortoli has traveled the length of Russia from the Baltic Sea to the Pacific several times since 1960. He resided in Moscow with his family for three years, and is one of the best known French specialists on Soviet affairs.

*   *   *

BOSCO, (Fernand Joseph Marius) Henri   1888-1976

November 16, 1888—May 4, 1976; French poet, educator, and regional novelist. Obituaries: *New York Times,* May 6, 1976; *Washington Post,* May 8, 1976; *AB Bookman's Weekly,* May 31, 1976.

BOSTON, Robert 1940-

PERSONAL: Born February 11, 1940, in Webster City, Iowa; son of Howard B. (an Army officer) and Ardys (a computer programmer; maiden name, Hupp) Boston; married DiAnne Gassmann, December 26, 1959 (divorced December 30, 1963); married Sharon Heichel (an office manager), June 20, 1964; children: (first marriage) Laura Marie; (second marriage) Irish Jean. Education: Iowa State University, B.S., 1962, M.A., 1972. Politics: Independent. Religion: "No affiliation." Home address: Route 2, Boone, Iowa 50036. Office: 243 Ross Hall, Iowa State University, Ames, Iowa 50011.

CAREER: Punch press operator in Ames, Iowa, 1958-60; Iowa Highway Commission, Ames, data coder, 1960-63; Ford Motor Co., Dallas, Tex., zone manager, 1964-67; Iowa State University, Ames, instructor in English, 1969—, chairperson of creative writing, 1975—. Musician, 1958-68. Member: Authors Guild of Authors League of America, John Steinbeck Society. Awards, honors: Award from Friends of American Writers, 1974, for A Thorn for the Flesh.

WRITINGS: A Thorn for the Flesh (novel), Harper, 1973. Contributor of articles to journals in his field.

WORK IN PROGRESS: A novel; a critical book on John Steinbeck.

SIDELIGHTS: Boston writes: "I don't consider myself to be a writer. I don't have the discipline or the drive of the writers I know. I'll probably never write for a living, and in some ways that's fortunate. I can write what, when, and how I want to without being pressured. On the other hand, I fear that I'll never produce as much as I should."

*   *   *

BOUISSAC, Paul (Antoine Rene) 1934-

PERSONAL: Born January 17, 1934, in France; son of Antoine Louis (a businessman) and Marguerite Marie (Frene) Bouissac. Education: Sorbonne, University of Paris, Licence-en-lettres, 1956, D.E.S., 1957; Ecole Pratique des Hautes Etudes, Doctorat, 1970. Office: Department of French, Victoria College, University of Toronto, 73 Queen's Park Cres. E., Toronto, Ontario, Canada M5S 1K7.

CAREER: University of Toronto, Victoria College, Toronto, Ontario, lecturer, 1962-65, assistant professor, 1965-69, associate professor, 1969-74, professor of French literature and semiotics, 1974—. Founder and manager of Debord Circus, 1964-66. Member: International Association for Semiotic Study (member of executive committee, 1972—), Semiotic Society of America (member of executive committee, 1976-78), Modern Language Association of America, Linguistic Society of America, American Anthropological Association. Awards, honors: Fellow of the Netherlands Institute for Advanced Study, 1972-73; Guggenheim fellowship, 1973-74.

WRITINGS: Les demoiselles (novel; title means "The Maidens"), Editions de Minuit, 1970; La Mesure des gestes: Prolegomenes a une semiotique gestuelle (title means "The Measurement of Gestures: Prolegomena to the Semiotics of Body Motions"), Mouton & Co., 1973; Circus and Culture: A Semiotic Approach, Indiana University Press, 1976. Contributor to linguistic and French studies journals.

WORK IN PROGRESS: A book on circus clowns.

SIDELIGHTS: Professionally, Bouissac is interested in "research in literary experiments, systems of communication and signification, and teaching related to these fields." His other interest is "the circus as a form of art, as a business, and as an object of study."

*   *   *

BOULTON, Jane 1921-

PERSONAL: Born September 25, 1921, in Indiana; daughter of John W. (an engineer) and Martha (a pianist; maiden name, Morris) Balch; married Peter Boulton (a businessman and sheep farmer), February 6, 1942; children: Ann, Michael, Barbara. Education: Attended Rollins College and Katherine Gibbs Secretarial School. Residence: Innisfail, Alberta, Canada.

CAREER: Writer and sculptor.

WRITINGS: Opal, Macmillan, 1976.

WORK IN PROGRESS: "The Search for Opal," a television script made from the book Opal; a novel; a journal.

*   *   *

BOULTON, Marjorie 1924-

PERSONAL: Born May 7, 1924, in Teddington, England; daughter of Harry (a teacher) and Evelyn Maud (a teacher; maiden name, Cartlidge) Boulton. Education: Somerville College, Oxford, B.A., 1944, M.A., 1947, B.Litt., 1948, currently candidate for D.Phil. Politics: "Anti-totalitarian, whether right or left." Home: 36 Stockmore St., Oxford OX4 1JT, England. Agent: John Johnson, 51/54 Goschen Bldg., 12/13 Henrietta St., London WC2E 8LF, England.

CAREER: Assistant English mistress in girl's high school, Westcliffe, England, 1944-46; Drake Hall Emergency Training College, Stafford, England, lecturer in English, 1948-50; Northern Counties College, Hexham, England, lecturer in English and speech training and librarian, 1950-62; Charlotte Mason College, Ambleside, England, vice-principal, 1955-62, principal, 1962-70. Professional examiner for public examinations. Member: Society of Authors, National Association for the Teaching of English, Universal Esperanto Association, British Esperanto Association, National Federation for the Self-Employed, Oxford Literary Society, Esperanto Teachers Association, Esperanto Academy, Oxford Union Society. Awards, honors: Matthew Arnold prize, Oxford University, 1947; John Buchanan prize, Liverpool University, 1958; named Esperanto Author of the Year, 1958.

WRITINGS: In English: Preliminaries (poems), Fortune Press, 1949; The Anatomy of Poetry (critical study), Routledge & Kegan Paul, 1953; The Anatomy of Prose, Routledge & Kegan Paul, 1954; Saying What We Mean, Routledge & Kegan Paul, 1959, published as The Anatomy of Language; The Anatomy of Drama, Routledge & Kegan Paul, 1960; Zamenhof, Creator of Esperanto, Routledge & Kegan Paul, 1960, Esperanto translation by the author, enlarged, Stafeto (La Laguna, Canary Isles), 1962; Words in Real Life, St. Martin's, 1965; Reading for Real Life, Macmillan, 1971; The Anatomy of the Novel, Routledge & Kegan Paul, 1975.

In Esperanto: Kontralte (poetry), Stafeto, 1955; Kvarpieda Kamarado (autobiographical), privately printed, 1956; Cent Gojkantoj (poetry), privately printed, 1957; Eroj (poetry), Stafeto, 1959; Virino Ce La Landlimo (one-act plays), Komuna Konversacia Klubo (Copenhagen), 1959; Dekdu Piedetoj (autobiographical), privately printed, 1964; Okuloj (short stories), Stafeto, 1967; Nia Sango (one-act play),

British Esperanto Association, 1970; *Ni Aktoras* (three one-act plays), Dansk Esperanto-Forlag (Aabyhoj, Denmark), 1971.

Polish: *List Zza Grobu* (fiction), translated from the English manuscript by Zofia Krajewska, Slask (Katowice, Poland), 1959; *Szantaz* (fiction), translation from the English manuscript by Krajewska, Slask, 1960.

Translator: (From the Hindi with R. S. Vyas) H. R. Bachchan, *The House of Wine,* Fortune Press, 1950; (from the French) Jules Supervielle, *The Shell and the Ear,* Lotus Press, 1951; (from the Croatian) Vlasta Ursic, *Wild Chestnuts* [and] *The House at the Toll-Gate,* privately printed, 1954; (from the English) *Angla Antologio* (anthology), Universala Esperanto-Asocio, 1957; (from the Esperanto) Tibor Sekelj, *Window on Nepal,* R. Hale, 1959; (from the English) Charles Carter, *Pri Sentemo Pri Cies Situacio,* Quaker Esperanto Society (Gloucester, England), 1972.

Contributor to *Encyclopaedia Britannica* and of articles, short stories, and poetry in English and Esperanto to magazines.

WORK IN PROGRESS: A book on Charles Reade's literary achievement; second volume of *Angla Antologio;* several other books.

SIDELIGHTS: Marjorie Boulton told *CA:* "For some years my creative writing has been mostly in Esperanto, and in English I have written mostly simple books of literary criticism, intended to help relatively inexperienced students of literature. Now, however, that I hope to live, though frugally, as a full-time writer, or nearly so, I am anxious to write more imaginatively also in English." In addition to her knowledge of Esperanto, Miss Boulton knows French, Italian, and Latin, and a smattering of German and Swedish. *Avocational interests:* Cooking, "growing as much of my own food as possible."

*   *   *

BOURAOUI, H(edi) A(ndre)   1932-

PERSONAL: Born July 16, 1932, in Sfax, Tunisia; came to Canada, 1966; naturalized Canadian citizen, 1971. *Education:* University of Toulouse, licence es lettres, 1958; Indiana University, M.S., 1960; Cornell University, Ph.D., 1966. *Home:* 2911 Bayview Ave., Apt. 214J, Willowdale, Ontario, Canada M2K 1E8. *Office:* Founders 127, York University, 4700 Keele St., Downsview, Ontario, Canada M3J 1P3.

CAREER: Wells College, Aurora, N.Y., instructor, 1962-65, assistant professor of French, 1965-66; York University, Toronto, Ontario, assistant professor, 1966-68, associate professor, 1968-73, professor of French, 1973—. Consultant to Encyclopaedia Britannica Educational Corp., 1967-70; foreign language consultant to Rand McNally, 1972—. *Member:* Modern Language Association of America, American Association of Teachers of French (president of Toronto chapter, 1969-74), American Association of African Studies, Canadian Association of University Teachers, Association of Canadian University Teachers of French, Canadian Association of American Studies, Canadian Comparative Literature Association, Canadian Association of African Studies. *Awards, honors:* Canada Council grants, 1968, 1969, 1975, 1976; Polish Government grant, 1973.

WRITINGS: Musocktail (poems), Tower Associates (Wheaton, Ill.), 1966; *Tremble* (poems), Saint Germain des Pres, 1969; *Immensement croises* (dramatic poem; title means "Immensely Crossed"; produced in Toronto at York

University Theatre, March, 1972), Saint Germain des Pres, 1969; *Creaculture I* (essays), Center for Curriculum Development (Philadelphia), 1971; *Creaculture II: Parole et action* (essays), Center for Curriculum Development, 1971; *Eclate module* (poems), Cosmos (Montreal), 1972; *Vesuviade* (poems), Saint Germain des Pres, 1976; *Structure intentionnelle du Grand Meaulnes: Vers le poeme romance* (literary criticism; title means "Intentional Structure of LeGrand Meaulnes: Towards the Poem-Novel"), A. G. Nizet, 1976.

Contributor of critical articles in English to literary journals, including *French Review, Novel, Modern Fiction Studies, Contact* (Tunisia), and *Teatr* (Poland). Editor, *Waves,* 1968—; consultant to *Presence Francophone.*

WORK IN PROGRESS: A novel, *L'Iconaison;* books of poems, *Haituvois* and *Interdiagonales;* a book of translations of his poems, *Iconoclastics;* a book of essays, *The Sexual Equation; Mediatrix.*

SIDELIGHTS: Bouraoui told *CA:* "I was born in North Africa, raised and educated in the south of France, and my graduate work took place in the United States. At present I live, write, and teach in Toronto. My situation as a Francophone writer living in an Anglophone society and my cosmopolitan background have been important to my career and my cast of thought. As a result of my breadth of cultural experience, I have attempted to disperse my publications in as wide a geographical sense as possible: the United States, Canada, France, Belgium, North Africa, Australia, Poland, etc.

"My criticism is mostly written in English, my creative work in French. I am primarily interested, however, in a world view which is not confined to a single language or nation. Thus I have written critical pieces on experimental theatre in Poland (also English and Italian experimental theatre), comparative culture in France and the United States, Francophone North African literature, the contemporary novel—the French nouveau roman, the American novel, Latin American, Egyptian, Moroccan, Algerian, Tunisian.

"Especially in my creative writing, I have tried to capture the ikons and images of a world exploding at the seams, revealed in the transmutations of my metaphors and in the explosion of my thematic explorations. As *Le Figaro litteraire* wrote, 'The striking power of these texts stuffed with puns, with deliberately grating sonorities, and with popular elements is undeniable. The poet utilizes it to denounce the faults of a pasteurized society.' I have been much concerned with the creation of new genres, trying to rejuvenate existing forms and to convert the *roman* into a *poeme romance,* the *poeme* into a *poeme-essai,* or a *poeme dramatique.*

"If I have an axe to grind, it is that both the public and critics have a tendency to catalogue artists by genre, politics, nationalism. If a writer rejects such categorization, he risks remaining somehow outside the structures of literary history. Since I have traveled extensively in Great Britain, Italy, Poland, Hungary, Germany, Australia, New Zealand, Switzerland, Belgium, Tunisia, Algeria, and Morocco, and speak four languages, French, English, Spanish, and Italian, I have come to believe in open spiritual frontiers, in democracy and, in a sense, universalism. To this end I have tried to promote fellow writers in countries outside their own and whenever possible. I would like to break the barriers between nations, and between creation and criticism. I look towards a day of complete permeability to others whoever he/she is, of whatever nationality, color, race, creed, sex—all of those artificial barriers society has created in order to separate men. For this reason I strive to create and promote a notion of comparative culture—I invented the term 'Creaculture' to describe the creative interaction of man with his milieu—and especially to develop and encourage an art which crosses cultural boundaries.''

BIOGRAPHICAL/CRITICAL SOURCES: Le Figaro littéraire, March 2-8, 1970; *Research Studies,* December, 1972; *Journal of Popular Culture,* summer, 1974.

* * *

BOWER, Keith
See BECKETT, Kenneth A(lbert)

* * *

BOWER, Sharon Anthony 1932-

PERSONAL: Born December 9, 1932, in Minneapolis, Minn.; daughter of L. O. (a lawyer) and Lois (Dahl) Anthony; married Gordon H. Bower (a professor of psychology), January 30, 1957; children: Lori, Anthony, Julia. *Education:* Gustavus Adolphus College, B.A., 1954; Northwestern University, M.A. (theater arts), 1955; Stanford University, M.A. (counseling and guidance), 1972. *Home:* 750 Mayfield Ave., Stanford, Calif. 94305.

CAREER: Louisiana State University, Baton Rouge, instructor in speech and drama, 1955-57; Quinnipiac College, Hamden, Conn., instructor in speech and drama, 1957-60; San Jose State University, San Jose, Calif., instructor in speech and drama, 1960-62; Stanford Repertory Theatre, Stanford, Calif., instructor in creative dramatics, director of Children's Theatre, and publicity promoter, 1962-71; Foothill College, Los Altos Hills, Calif., instructor in assertiveness training, 1971—. Instructor at Stanford University and De Anza College, 1972—. *Member:* American Behavior Therapy Association, American Personnel and Guidance Association, California Personnel and Guidance Association.

WRITINGS: Asserting Yourself: A Practical Guide for Positive Change, Addison-Wesley, 1976.

WORK IN PROGRESS: A "self-help" book on speaking anxiety.

BIOGRAPHICAL/CRITICAL SOURCES: Woman's Day, April, 1975; *Reader's Digest,* October, 1975.

* * *

BOWKER, R(obin) M(arsland) 1920-

PERSONAL: Born February 15, 1920, in Manchester, England; son of Joseph Maximilian (a cotton spinner) and Ethel Freda (Allen) Bowker; married Mary Pace (a teacher), 1956; children: four. *Education:* Attended private school in Godalming, England. *Home and office:* Whitewalls, Harbour Way, Old Bosham, Sussex, England.

CAREER: Writer. Has worked as a yacht yard proprietor, a sailmaker, and as managing director of a marine publisher. *Member:* Royal Ocean Racing Club, Royal London Yacht Club.

WRITINGS: (With S. A. Budd) *Make Your Own Sails,* Macmillan, 1957; *A Boat of Your Own,* St. Martin's, 1959; (author of postscript) Erskine Caldwell, *The Riddle of the Sands,* Bowker, 1976; *The Channel Handbook,* Volume I, Bowker, 1976. Contributor of more than one hundred articles to magazines and newspapers in twelve countries.

WORK IN PROGRESS: The Channel Handbook, Volume II.

BOWMAN, Bruce 1938-

PERSONAL: Born November 23, 1938, in Dayton, Ohio; son of Murray E. Bowman and Mildred Moler Bowman Elleman; married Julie Gosselin (an educational consultant), January 31, 1969; children: Carrie Lynn. *Education:* San Diego City College, A.A., 1962; California State College, Los Angeles, B.A., 1964, M.A., 1968. *Home:* 3870 Rambla Orienta, Malibu, Calif. 90265.

CAREER: Art teacher in public schools in Los Angeles, Calif., 1965-76; Cypress College, Cypress, Calif., instructor in art, 1976—. Part-time instructor at North Hollywood Adult School, 1966-68, and West Los Angeles College, 1969—. *Military service:* U.S. Navy, 1957-61.

WRITINGS—Both self-illustrated: *Shaped Canvas,* Sterling, 1976; *Toothpick Sculpture and Ice-Cream Stick Art,* Sterling, 1976. Contributor of articles to art and education journals.

WORK IN PROGRESS: Murals and Super Graphics; Children's Book of Art; a novel; a screenplay; illustrating and writing two children's books.

* * *

BOWMAN, Herbert E(ugene) 1917-

PERSONAL: Born February 8, 1917, in Harrisburg, Pa.; son of Claude Charelton (in railroad industry) and Jane (Sprout) Bowman. *Education:* University of Pennsylvania, A.B., 1938; University of Lille, diploma, 1939; Harvard University, M.A., 1941, Ph.D., 1950. *Politics:* Democrat. *Religion:* Protestant. *Home:* 85 Lowther Ave., Toronto 5, Ontario, Canada. *Office:* Department of Slavic Languages and Literatures, University of Toronto, 21 Sussex Ave., Toronto 181, Ontario, Canada.

CAREER: Harvard University, Cambridge, Mass., instructor in Russian literature, 1950-53; University of Oregon, Eugene, assistant professor, 1953-58, associate professor of Russian literature, 1958-61; University of Toronto, Toronto, Ontario, professor of Russian literature, 1961—. *Military service:* U.S. Army, Intelligence, 1942-45; became technical sergeant. *Member:* Modern Language Association of America, American Association for the Advancement of Slavic Studies, American Association of Teachers of Slavic and East European Languages, Phi Beta Kappa.

WRITINGS: Vissarion Belinski, 1811-1848: A Study in the Origins of Social Criticism in Russia, Harvard University Press, 1954, reprinted, Russell, 1969.

WORK IN PROGRESS: Research on nineteenth-century Russian and European literature and literary criticism.

SIDELIGHTS: Bowman has traveled in France and the Soviet Union.

* * *

BOYAJIAN, Cecile
See STARR, Cecile

* * *

BOYD, Julian P(arks) 1903-

PERSONAL: Born November 3, 1903, in Converse, S.C.; son of Robert Jay and Melona (Parks) Boyd; married Grace Wiggins Welch, December 21, 1927; children: Kenneth Miles. *Education:* Duke University, A.B., 1925, A.M., 1926; University of Pennsylvania, further graduate study, 1927-28. *Home address:* R.D. 1, Titusville, N.J. 08560. *Office:* Firestone Library, Princeton University, Princeton, N.J. 08540.

CAREER: Wyoming Historical and Geological Society, Wilkes Barre, Pa., editor, 1928-32; New York State Historical Association, Cooperstown, director, 1932-34; Historical Society of Pennsylvania, Philadelphia, assistant librarian, 1934-35, librarian, 1935-40; Princeton University, Princeton, N.J., librarian, 1940-52, professor of history, 1952-72, professor emeritus, 1972—, senior research historian, 1972—. Member of National Historical Publications Commission, 1951-64; Harry S. Truman Library Institute, 1957—; National Portrait Gallery Commission, 1963-69; member of board of directors of Institute for Advanced Study, 1964-68.

MEMBER: American Antiquarian Society, American Historical Association (president, 1964), American Philosophical Society (president, 1973-76), Society of American Archivists, Massachusetts Historical Society, New York Historical Society, Historical Society of Pennsylvania, Virginia Historical Society, Phi Beta Kappa. *Awards, honors:* Honorary degrees include D.Litt. from Franklin & Marshall College, 1939, Duke University, 1951, Bucknell University, 1952, and Rutgers University, 1956; L.H.D. from Washington & Jefferson College, 1952, Yale University, 1964, and Lehigh University, 1966.

WRITINGS: (Editor) *The Susquehannah Company Papers,* five volumes, Wyoming Historical and Geological Society, 1928-32; (editor) *Miner's Essays of Poor Robert the Scribe,* [Wilkes-Barre], 1930; *The Susquehannah Company: Connecticut's Experiment in Expansion,* Yale University Press, 1935; (author of notes, with Carl Van Doren) *Indian Treaties Printed by Benjamin Franklin, 1736-1762,* Historical Society of Pennsylvania, 1938; *Anglo-American Union: Joseph Galloway's Plans to Preserve the British Empire, 1774-1788,* University of Pennsylvania Press, 1941, Octagon, 1970; *The Declaration of Independence: The Evolution of the Text as Shown in Facsimiles of Various Drafts by Its Author,* Library of Congress, 1943, revised edition, Princeton, Princeton University Press, 1945; (editor) *The Papers of Thomas Jefferson,* nineteen volumes, Princeton University Press, 1950-76; (editor) *The Articles of Confederation and Perpetual Union,* Old South Association, 1960; (editor) *Fundamental Laws and Constitutions of New Jersey, 1664-1964,* Van Nostrand, 1964; *Number Seven: Alexander Hamilton's Secret Attempts to Control American Foreign Policy,* Princeton University Press, 1964. Contributor of articles to the proceedings of American Philosophical Society and American Antiquarian Society, and to professional journals, including *William and Mary Quarterly* and *American Archivist.*

WORK IN PROGRESS: Editing forty-one more volumes of *The Papers of Thomas Jefferson.*

BIOGRAPHICAL/CRITICAL SOURCES: Julian P. Boyd: A Bibliographical Record Compiled and Offered by His Friends on the Occasion of His Tenth Anniversary as Librarian at Princeton University, Princeton University Library, 1950.

*   *   *

BOYD, Sue Abbott

PERSONAL: Born in Cedar Rapids, Iowa; daughter of Calvin Eugene and Rose Lillian (Schultz) Abbott; married Arnold Boyd, August 28, 1943 (divorced, March, 1954); children: Walter Stanley. *Education:* New School for Social Research, student, 1949-50.

CAREER: South and West, Inc., Fort Smith, Ark., founder, president, and editor, 1962—. Founder of Fort Smith Affiliation of Arts, 1963. *Military service:* Women's Army

Corps, 1943-45. *Member:* United Poets Laureate International (member of international hall of fame), Poetry Society of America, National Federation of State Poetry Societies (chancellor, 1964-68). *Awards, honors:* Hatshakers Award, 1967; Litt.D. from University of Free Asia, 1968; gold plaque from Poetry Society of Oklahoma, 1968.

WRITINGS—Poems: *Decanter: Poems, 1952-1962,* South and West, 1962; *The Sample Stage,* South and West, 1964; *Fort Smith and Other Poems,* Border Press, 1965; *How It Is: Selected Poems, 1952-1968,* Olivant, 1968; (contributor) Jo McDougall, editor, *The New Look Trio,* South and West, 1970; *A Portion of the Fort Roots Poems: Volume I, Act 1,* South and West, 1973. Also author of *Of Sun and Stone,* 1959. Publisher of *Discourses on Poetry,* 1965, 1966, 1967, 1968, 1970; founder of *Voices International,* 1966—; guest editor of *Poet* (international magazine from India), 1967; founder and adviser to *Tulsa Poetry Quarterly,* 1968—.

SIDELIGHTS: Sue Boyd is particularly interested in working in prisons.*

*   *   *

BOYER, Carl B(enjamin)   1906-1976

November 3, 1906—April 26, 1976; American educator, historian, and author of books in his field. Obituaries: *New York Times,* April 27, 1976.

*   *   *

BOYER, Dwight   1912-

PERSONAL: Born November 18, 1912, in Elyria, Ohio; son of Lawrence (an office manager) and Susan (Mortimer) Boyer; married Virginia Stokes, July 22, 1937; children: Lawrence H. *Politics:* Democrat. *Religion:* Protestant. *Home:* 7188 Maple Street, Mentor, Ohio 44060. *Office:* 1801 Superior, Cleveland, Ohio 44114.

CAREER: Toledo Blade, Toledo, Ohio, writer, 1944-54; *Cleveland Plain Dealer,* Cleveland, Ohio, 1954—, feature writer. *Member:* Great Lakes Historical Society (trustee), Fairport Harbor Historical Society (trustee), Sigma Delta Chi. *Awards, honors:* News media award from Ohio Optometric Association, 1975; Heywood Broun award from Cleveland Newspaper Guild for feature writing; award from Press Club of Cleveland.

WRITINGS—All published by Dodd, Mead: *Great Stories of the Great Lakes,* 1966; *Ghost Ships of the Great Lakes,* 1968; *True Tales of the Great Lakes,* 1971; *Strange Adventures of the Great Lakes,* 1974.

WORK IN PROGRESS: A fifth Great Lakes book.

SIDELIGHTS: Boyer told *CA* that he is "motivated by the fact that history has overlooked the Great Lakes. Much of the material is about shipwrecks, all of which is thoroughly researched and documented. Formal school history all but ignores the Great Lakes . . . historians are guilty of crimes of omission of facts. I am trying to change this." He complains that "the Great Lakes are recognized only in times of national emergency when their shipping lanes make possible the wedding of natural resources and industry. The great industrial cities of the lower lakes, Buffalo, Cleveland, Lorain, Detroit and Chicago became great and remain great because of the lakes. But this 'arsenal of Democracy' as it is termed in times of war, is quickly forgotten when the supply emergency is over. Making the industry of Great Lakes shipping what it is are the sailors who 'put it all together' and the vessels they sail, some of them among the largest in the American Merchant Marine."

BRADBURY, Peggy 1930-

PERSONAL: Born October 30, 1930, in Davenport, Iowa; daughter of Donald R. (a U.S. Army colonel) and Valeda (Boltz) Patterson; married Donald F. Friedrich, January 30, 1963 (divorced August 13, 1968); married Charles Bradbury (a procurement manager), September 30, 1968; children: (first marriage) Herbert D. *Education:* Stephens College, A.A., 1950. *Religion:* Episcopal. *Home and office:* 7010 Mark Dr., San Antonio, Tex. 78218.

CAREER: Writer; has also worked as editor of military training material and military history; radio continuity writer in Norfolk, Va., 1950-52. Staff member of Southwest Writers' Conference at University of Houston; founder and director of South Texas Writers' Rally. *Member:* Circus Fans Association of America, National Writers' Club, Society of Children's Book Writers (regional adviser, 1975—).

WRITINGS: Buying Your First Horse, Cordovan Corp., 1973; *Transcriber's Guide to Medical Terminology,* Medical Examination Publishing Co., 1973; (with Steve Werk) *Horse Nutrition Handbook,* Cordovan Corp., 1974; *The Snake That Couldn't Slither* (juvenile), Putnam, 1976; *The Horseman Book of Horse Safety,* Cordovan Corp., in press. Contributor to horseman's journals and children's magazines, including *Humpty Dumpty's* and *Summer Weekly Reader.*

WORK IN PROGRESS: Research on circus topics, especially animal training.

SIDELIGHTS: Peggy Bradbury writes: "As daughter of an Army officer, I reached a saturation point on travel. I lived in Italy, Austria, and Okinawa; traveled throughout western Europe and in Japan and Hong Kong. Since moving to San Antonio I rarely leave the state.

"Although I have been interested in horses most of my life and write on related topics, my primary writing interest is in children's literature. For children, I am especially researching circus history and present-day circus life and animal information.

"Writing for young readers is both a pleasure and a responsibility. Adult readers who will tolerate poor writing deserve it; children should be given the best quality possible.

"In addition to writing, I have a strong interest in writer education. I feel that too many 'creative writing' courses are devoted to 'art for its own sake' writing and encourage extensive effort in writing forms for which there is little hope of publication. I support and encourage market-oriented writing instruction (academic and otherwise)."

* * *

BRADLEY, Hassell 1930-

PERSONAL: Given name is accented on first syllable; born June 29, 1930, in Paris, Tex.; daughter of William Frank (a college president) and Kathryn Lynn (a university professor; maiden name, Ellis) Grimes; married Joe A. Bradley (a geologist), July 8, 1951; children: William Stanton, Margaret Lynn. *Education:* University of Oklahoma, B.A., 1951. *Home:* 6474 South Sycamore St., Littleton, Colo. 80120. *Office:* Sentinel Newspapers, P.O. Box 16008, Denver, Colo. 80216; and KOA-Television, Channel 4, 1044 Lincoln St., Denver, Colo.

CAREER: Oklahoman and Times, Oklahoma City, campus correspondent, 1949; *Woodward Daily Press,* Woodward, Okla., society editor, 1949; *Paris News,* Paris, Tex., feature writer, 1950-52; *Newport Daily News,* Newport, R.I., reporter, 1952; free-lance writer, 1952-65; *Wichita Eagle and Beacon,* Wichita, Kan., feature writer, 1965-66; *Oklahoman and Times,* home and garden writer, 1967; *Wichita Eagle and Beacon,* feature writer, 1968; free-lance public relations work, 1968-71; *University Park News,* Denver, Colo., editor, 1971-73; Sentinel Newspapers, Denver, Colo., food editor, 1973—. Adult education teacher at Arapahoe Community College, 1973-74. Food editor, "Denver Today," on KOA-TV, 1976—. Member of Colorado Nutrition Council. Former member of board of directors of Corp. for Hospital Alternative Plan for Bethesda Community Mental Health Center.

MEMBER: National Press Women, Home Economists in Business (national and Denver chapters), American Home Economics Association, Authors League of America, Colorado Press Women, Colorado Home Economics Association, Denver Woman's Press Club, Alpha Chi Omega. *Awards, honors:* Headliner award from Denver chapter of Women in Communications, 1974; woman of achievement awards from Colorado Press Women, 1976, 1977; awards from Kansas Press Women and Colorado Press Women for features, historical and news writing, interviews, and food writing.

WRITINGS: Keeping Food Safe: The Complete Guide to Safeguarding Your Family's Health While Handling, Preparing, Preserving, Freezing, and Storing Food at Home, Doubleday, 1975. Author of syndicated column "Hassell in the Kitchen," 1976—. Contributor to *Colorado Woman Digest.*

WORK IN PROGRESS: A historical novel about a little-known hero from Texas history; essays and speeches on the importance of the family in contemporary society.

* * *

BRADY, John 1942-

PERSONAL: Born May 15, 1942, in Yonkers, N.Y.; son of Francis (a security agent) and Leona (a dental nurse; maiden name, Beiling) Brady; married: Lilia N. Felix (a teacher), December 31, 1965. *Education:* King's College, Wilkes-Barre, Pa., B.A. (cum laude), 1964; Bradley University, M.A., 1966. *Residence:* Cincinnati, Ohio. *Agent:* Philip Spitzer, 111-25 76th Ave., Forest Hills, N.Y. 11375. *Office:* 9933 Alliance Rd., Cincinnati, Ohio 45242.

CAREER: Indiana State University, Terre Haute, assistant professor of journalism, 1967-75; *Writer's Digest,* Cincinnati, Ohio, book editor, 1975, editor, 1975—, editorial director, 1976—. Correspondent for *New Times,* 1973—; has held in-depth interviews with national personalities, including Gay Talese, Gloria Steinem, A. E. Hotchner, Jessica Mitford, and Bob Thomas. *Member:* Cincinnati Editors Association, Sigma Delta Chi, Phi Kappa Phi, Pi Delta Epsilon.

WRITINGS: (Editor with James Hall) *Sports Literature,* McGraw, 1974; *The Craft of Interviewing,* Writer's Digest, 1976. Contributor to magazines, including *New York,* and to newspapers.

WORK IN PROGRESS: A book on screenwriters, for Scribner.

SIDELIGHTS: Brady writes: "I consider myself—in the Liebling sense—a Careful Editor. A word man. Also a good interviewer, specializing in the best and the brightest writers of the day."

* * *

BRAIDER, Donald 1923-1976

April 30, 1923—June 22, 1976; American businessman,

bookseller, educator, novelist, and author of books on art and other topics. *Obituaries: New York Times,* June 25, 1976. (See index for previous *CA* sketch)

*   *   *

BRAINARD, Joe 1942-

PERSONAL: Born March 11, 1942, in Salem, Ark. *Home:* 8 Greene St., New York, N.Y. 10013. *Agent:* Fischbach Gallery, 29 West 57th St., New York, N.Y. 10019 (paintings).

CAREER: Painter.

WRITINGS: Bolinas Journal, Big Sky, 1971; *Selected Writings,* Kulchur Foundation, 1971; *New Work,* Black Sparrow Press, 1973; *I Remember Christmas,* Museum of Modern Art, 1973; *I Remember,* Full Court Press, 1975.

*   *   *

BRAM, Elizabeth 1948-

PERSONAL: Born December 5, 1948, in New York, N.Y.; daughter of Joseph (a professor of anthropology) and Jean (a professor of classics; maiden name, Rhys) Bram. *Education:* Attended New York University, 1966-67, and Silvermine College of Art. *Home:* 4 Prospect St., Baldwin, N.Y. 11510.

CAREER: Artist (paints large murals) and writer. *Member:* Authors Guild of Authors League of America.

WRITINGS—All self-illustrated children's books: *The Door in the Tree,* Greenwillow Books, 1976; *A Dinosaur Is Too Big,* Greenwillow Books, in press; *The Man on the Unicycle and Other Stories,* Greenwillow Books, in press; *I Don't Want to Go to School,* Greenwillow Books, in press.

WORK IN PROGRESS: A self-illustrated anthology of new poems and stories, for Greenwillow Books.

AVOCATIONAL INTERESTS: Playing classical flute, singing and playing the guitar, modern dance, studying natural healing and nutrition.

*   *   *

BRAMMELL, P(aris) Roy 1900-

PERSONAL: Born December 11, 1900, in Ozawakie, Kan.; son of Harvey L. (a farmer and country preacher) and Judith Jane (Harnish) Brammell; married Naomi H. Metzger, July 8, 1930; children: Naomi Helene (Mrs. Roe E. Willis), Homer Leon. *Education:* McPherson College, A.B., 1923; University of Michigan, M.A., 1928; University of Washington, Seattle, Ph.D., 1930; Stanford University, post-doctoral study, 1939-40. *Politics:* "Registered Republican, independent voter." *Religion:* Protestant. *Home:* 2323 Marlborough Rd., Colorado Springs, Colo. 80909.

CAREER: Teacher in a one-room school in rural Kansas, 1918-19; high school English and history teacher in Ozawakie, Kan., 1923-27, principal, 1925-27; National Survey of Secondary Education, Washington, D.C., staff member, 1930-32; University of Connecticut, Storrs, assistant professor, 1932-35, associate professor, 1935-39, professor of education and dean of School of Education, 1939-60, acting dean of Graduate School, 1942-45; Southern Illinois University, Carbondale, professor of educational administration, 1960-69, assistant dean of graduate studies in education, 1966-68; writer, 1969—. Visiting professor at University of Colorado, 1948-49, and University of Washington, Seattle, 1949. Member of National Council for Accreditation of Teacher Education, 1954—.

MEMBER: American Association for Higher Education, American Association of University Professors, Phi Beta Kappa, Phi Kappa Phi, Phi Delta Kappa. *Awards, honors:* Barnard fellowship, University of Connecticut, 1973.

WRITINGS: Your Schools and Mine, Ronald, 1952; *Brother Harvey,* Brethren Press, 1976. Also author of *Three Hundred Years of Education in Connecticut,* 1935, and monographs for National Survey of Secondary Education. Contributor to academic journals.

WORK IN PROGRESS: "A combined prose and verse project, somewhat autobiographical but more particularly a tribute to my wife."

SIDELIGHTS: Brammell writes: "Some of the qualities and life styles of an earlier generation are recorded in my recent small book. As time passes I am more and more convinced that if we are to remain a stable nation some of these qualities must be revived, re-taught, and practiced, not for the purpose of glorifying the past, but to secure the future."

*   *   *

BRANDRETH, Gyles 1948-

PERSONAL: Born March 8, 1948, in England; son of Charles (a lawyer) and Alice (a teacher; maiden name, Addison) Brandreth; married Michele Brown (a writer), 1973. *Education:* New College, Oxford, B.A., 1970. *Agent:* Irene Josephy, 35 Craven St., London WC2N 5NG, England.

CAREER: Writer, 1970—. Has presented television and radio programs all over England, and in Australia and the United States; theatrical productions include "Son et Lumiere" At Royal Greenwich, and "The Little Hut", "The Dame of Sark", and "Dear Daddy" in London's West End; artistic director of Oxford Theatre Festival, 1974—. *Member:* British Pantomime Association (founder).

WRITINGS—For children: *Cinderella,* Davis-Poynter, 1973; *Aladdin,* David-Poynter, 1973; *Knight Book of Christmas Fun,* Knight, 1974; *Mother Goose,* Macmillan, 1974; *Knight Book of Party Games,* Knight, 1974; *Knight Book of Scrabble,* Knight, 1974; *Games for Trains, Planes, and Wet Days,* William Luscombe, 1974; *Domino Games and Puzzles,* Carousel, 1975; *Knight Book of Mazes,* Knight, 1975; *Knight Book of Hospital Fun and Games,* Knight, 1975; *Knight Book of Holiday Fun and Games,* Knight, 1975; *Knight Book of Easter Fun,* Knight, 1975; *Pencil and Paper Games and Puzzles,* Carousel, 1976; *Games and Puzzles with Coins and Matches,* Carousel, 1976; *Knight Book of Fun and Games for Journeys,* Knight, 1976; *Knight Book of Fun and Games for a Rainy Day,* Knight, 1976; *The How and Why Bumper Wonder Book,* Transworld, 1976; *The Royal Quiz Book,* Carousel, 1976; *Hotchpotch,* Carousel, 1976; *Fun for Every Day of the Year,* Knight, 1976.

For adults: *Brandreth's Party Games,* Eyre Methuen, 1972; *Created in Captivity,* Hodder & Stoughton, 1972; *Brandreth's Bedroom Book,* Eyre Methuen, 1973; *Discovering Pantomime,* Shire, 1973; *Complete Book of Home Entertainment,* Shire, 1974; *I Scream for Ice Cream,* Eyre Methuen, 1974; *Brandreth's Book of Waiting Games,* Hodder & Stoughton, 1975; *Brandreth's Christmas Book,* Van Nostrand, 1975; *Knight Book of Home Entertainment,* Knight, 1976; *The Generation Quiz Book,* Fontana, 1976; *Pears Family Quiz Book,* Pelham, 1976; *Scrambled Exits: The Greatest Maze Book Ever,* Dempsey & Squires, 1976; *Yarooh!: A Feast of Frank Richards,* Eyre Methuen, 1976; *A Royal Scrapbook: My Twenty-five Years on the Throne,* M. Joseph, 1976.

Author of columns in *Manchester Evening News,* 1970-72,

Honey, 1969-70, and *Woman*, 1972-73. Contributor to magazines, including *Spectator, Punch, Homes and Gardens, Nova, She*, and *Woman's Own*, and to newspapers. Editor of *Isis*, 1970—.

SIDELIGHTS: Brandreth created the National Scrabble Championships in England in 1971. He was European Monopoly Champion in 1974 and has participated in international Monopoly championships. In 1976 he was represented in the *Guinness Book of World Records* for making the longest after-dinner speech in the world. In addition to his literary achievements, he has created greeting cards, wrapping paper, stationery, records, and children's board games, including "Gyles Brandreth's Fun and Games Diary," "The Treasure Island Game," "The Alice in Wonderland Game," and "Eight Pantomime Cards."

*   *   *

BRANNIGAN, Bill
  See BRANNIGAN, William

*   *   *

BRANNIGAN, William   1936-
  (Bill Brannigan)

PERSONAL: Born January 12, 1936, in Long Island, N.Y.; son of James W. (an insurance broker) and Viola (a teacher; maiden name, Perkins) Brannigan; married Rosalind B. Prophet (in human relations training), February 12, 1972. *Education:* Tufts University, B.A., 1957; Columbia University, graduate study, 1969-70. *Religion:* Roman Catholic. *Agent:* N. S. Bienstock, Inc., 10 Columbus Circle, Suite 1270, New York, N.Y. 10019. *Office:* American Broadcasting Co.—News, P.O. Box 2641, Cairo, Egypt.

CAREER/WRITINGS: New York World Telegram & Sun, New York, N.Y., reporter trainee, 1962-63; United Press International (UPI), New York City, reporter for "Newsfilm," 1963-65; American Broadcasting Co. (ABC) News, New York City, television and radio correspondent in Saigon, 1966-68, Los Angeles, 1969, Tel Aviv, 1970-71, and New York City, 1971-73, bureau chief in Nairobi, 1973-76, and Cairo, 1976—. Notable assignments include the Tet Offensive from Vietnam, elections in South Africa, the U.S.S. *Pueblo* hearings in San Diego, the death of Nasser, and interviews of Anwar El Sadat. *Military service:* U.S. Naval Reserve, actisve duty, 1957-62; became lieutenant. *Member:* Overseas Press Club, Foreign Correspondents Club (Hong Kong; Nairobi; Cairo). *Awards, honors:* Press fellow of the Council on Foreign Relations, 1969-70.

*   *   *

BRATHWAITE, Errol (Freeman)   1924-

PERSONAL: Born April 3, 1924, in Clive, New Zealand; son of Jack Lister and Dorathea Beatrice (Anstis) Brathwaite; married Alison Irene Whyte, March 20, 1948; children: Michael John, Pamela Ann. *Education:* Attended secondary schools in New Zealand. *Religion:* Church of England. *Home:* 12 Fulton Ave., Christchurch 1, New Zealand.

CAREER: New Zealand Railways, Napier, cadet, 1940-42, 1945; Rehabilitation Department, King Country, Tekuiti, New Zealand, farm trainee (shepherd), 1946-47; New Zealand Broadcasting Corp., Christchurch, advertising copywriter, 1959-62; Dobbs, Wiggins-McCann, Erikson, Christchurch, advertising copywriter, 1962-67; Carlton-Carruthers du Chateau, Christchurch, advertising copy-

writer, 1968-72, manager, 1972—. *Military service:* New Zealand Army, Wellington Regiment, 1942-43, New Zealand Signals, 1955-58. Royal New Zealand Air Force, 1943-45, 1947-55, airgunner in No. 3 Bomber Reconnaissance Squadron, 1943-45; received Pacific Star, Empire War Medal, and New Zealand War Medal.

MEMBER: International P.E.N., Brevet Club. *Awards, honors:* Winner of centennial novel contest sponsored by *Otago Daily Times*, 1961, and New Zealand Literary Fund Award, 1962, both for *An Affair of Men*.

WRITINGS: Fear in the Night (novel), Caxton Press, 1959; *An Affair of Men* (novel), Collins, 1961, St. Martin's, 1962; *Long Way Home* (novel), Caxton Press, 1963; *The Flying Fish* (novel; first volume of trilogy), Collins, 1963, Tri-Ocean, 1969; *The Needle's Eye* (novel; second volume of trilogy), Collins, 1965, Tri-Ocean, 1969; *The Evil Day* (novel; third volume of trilogy), Collins, 1967, Tri-Ocean, 1969; *The Companion Guide to the North Island of New Zealand*, Collins, 1969; *The Companion Guide to the South Island of New Zealand*, Collins, 1971; *New Zealand and Its People*, Government Printer (New Zealand), 1973; *The Beauty of New Zealand*, Golden Press, 1973; *The Flame Box* (fairy tale fantasy), Collins, 1976. Author of radio play adaptations of *An Affair of Men, Long Way Home*, and *The Needle's Eye*, all for New Zealand Broadcasting Corp.

WORK IN PROGRESS: A Definitive History of the Royal New Zealand Air Force; A History of BP (New Zealand) Limited; a fictional saga of a New Zealand family.

SIDELIGHTS: Brathwaite's work has been translated for publication in Finland, the Netherlands, Germany, and France. *Avocational interests:* Aviation, military history.

*   *   *

BRATTER, Herbert Max   1900-1976

January 22, 1900—February 19, 1976; American economist, businessman, and author. Obituaries: *Washington Post*, March 1, 1976.

*   *   *

BRAUDY, Susan (Orr)   1941-

PERSONAL: Born August 8, 1941, in Philadelphia, Pa.; daughter of Bernard (a public service executive) and Blanche (a teacher; maiden name, Malin) Orr. *Education:* Bryn Mawr College, B.A., 1959-63; graduate study, University of Pennsylvania, 1963-64, and Yale University. *Home:* 240 Central Park S., New York, N.Y. 10019. *Agent:* Erica Spellman, International Creative Management, 40 W. 57th St., New York, N.Y. *Office: Ms.* Magazine, 370 Lexington Ave., New York, N.Y.

CAREER: Yale University, New Haven, Conn., contributing and associate editor of the *New Journal*, 1967-70; *Glamour* magazine, New York City, contributing editor, 1970-71; *Newsweek*, New York City, associate editor, 1971-72; *Ms.* magazine, New York City, contributing editor, 1972—. Consultant to Ford Foundation, 1973; advanced writing teacher, Brooklyn College, 1974-75. *Member:* Authors Guild, Modern Language Association of America.

WRITINGS: Between Marriage and Divorce, Morrow, 1975. Writer, with Mary Thom, of "Ms. Gazette." Contributor of articles to *Ms., New York Times Magazine, Atlantic, Harper's, New York*, and to *Village Voice*.

BRAUN, Sidney D(avid) 1912-

PERSONAL: Born May 10, 1912, in New York, N.Y.; son of Max and Helen (Brown) Braun; married Miriam Kadish (a teacher), June 8, 1941. *Education:* Sorbonne, University of Paris, diplome, 1932; New York University, A.B., 1934, A.M., 1935, Ph.D., 1945; additional study at University of Mexico City, Columbia University, and Middlebury Spanish School. *Home:* 90 LaSalle St., New York, N.Y. *Office:* Department of Romance Languages, Herbert H. Lehman College of the City University of New York, Bedford Park Blvd. W., Bronx, N.Y. 10468.

CAREER: Yeshiva University, New York, N.Y., associate professor, 1936-52, professor of French, 1952-65; Wayne State University, Detroit, Mich., professor of French, 1965-68; Herbert H. Lehman College and Graduate Center of the City University of New York, Bronx, N.Y., professor of French, 1968—, chairman of department of Romance languages, 1969-70. Charge de cours, Universite Francaise de New York, 1955—. Visiting associate professor, Long Island University, 1945-49; visiting professor, University of Washington, 1963-64, University of Illinois, fall, 1964, and Hebrew University of Jerusalem, spring, 1972.

MEMBER: Association Internationale des Etudes Francaises, Modern Language Association (section chairman, 1964; committee chairman, 1965), Modern Humanities Research Association, American Association of Teachers of French, American Association of University Professors, Societe des Professeurs Francais en Amerique (associate member), Societe d'Histoire du Theatre. *Awards, honors:* Modern Language Association grant, c. 1957; Yeshiva University research grant to France, 1960; Grande Medaille d'Argent de la Ville de Paris, 1960; Chevalier dans l'ordre des Palmes Academiques, 1960; Fulbright research scholar in France, 1965.

WRITINGS: The 'Courtisane' in the French Theatre from Hugo to Becque (1831-1885), Johns Hopkins Press, 1947; (editor and contributor) *Dictionary of French Literature,* Philosophical Library, 1958; (editor with Germaine Bree) Anatole France, *Le Crime de Sylvestre Bonnard,* Holt, 1958; (author of preface and notes) Andre Gide, *Correspondance, 1908-1920: Andre Gide* [et] *Andre Suares,* Gallimard, 1963; (contributor) H. H. Golden, editor, *Studies in Honor of S. M. Waxman,* Boston University Press, 1969.

Contributor to *Encyclopedia Americana,* 1964. Contributor of articles and book reviews to journals, including *Criticism, Kentucky Romance Quarterly, Europe,* and *Symposium.* Assistant literary editor and contributor, *French Review,* 1968-74; editorial consultant and contributor, *PMLA,* 1958—; member of advisory board, *Nineteenth Century French Studies,* 1974—.

WORK IN PROGRESS: Books on Dumas *fils* and on Andre Suares.

*   *   *

BRENT, Peter (Ludwig) 1931-
(Ludovic Peters)

PERSONAL: Born July 26, 1931, in Beuthen, Germany; divorced. *Education:* Attended secondary school in England. *Agent:* Jonathan Clowes, 19 Jeffreys Pl., London NW1 9PP, England.

CAREER: Worked as cleaner, industrial editor, gardener, film extra, kitchen porter, post office sorter, teacher, doorman, and dishwasher before becoming full-time writer.

WRITINGS—Nonfiction, except as indicated: *Exit* (novel),

Faber, 1960; *A Kind of Wild Justice* (novel), Bodley Head, 1962; (editor) *Young Commonwealth Poets '65* (poetry), Heinemann, 1965; *No Way Back from Prague* (novel), Hodder & Stoughton, 1969; *The Edwardians,* BBC Publications, 1972; *Godmen of India,* Quadrangle, 1972; *Captain Scott,* Saturday Review Press, 1974; *Lord Byron,* Weidenfeld & Nicolson, 1974; *T. E. Lawrence,* Putnam, 1975; *The Viking Saga,* Putnam, 1975; *The Mongol Empire,* Weidenfeld & Nicolson, 1976, published as *Genghis Khan,* McGraw, 1976; *Black Nile: Mungo Park and the Quest for the Niger,* Athenaeum, in press.

Suspense novels; all under pseudonym Ludovic Peters: *Cry Vengeance,* Abelard, 1961; *A Snatch of Music,* Abelard, 1962; *Two Sets to Murder,* Coward, 1963; *Out by the River,* Walker & Co., 1964; *Two After Malic,* Walker & Co., 1965; *Riot '71,* Walker & Co., 1967; *Double-Take,* Hodder & Stoughton, 1968; *Fall of Terror,* Hodder & Stoughton, 1968; *The Killing Game,* Hodder & Stoughton, 1969.

Author of radio and television plays for British Broadcasting Corp., and the film script "Makarios: The Long Journey," 1977.

WORK IN PROGRESS: Far Arabia, for Weidenfeld & Nicolson; *Healers of India,* publication by Harcourt expected in 1978; research for *Thieves of Certainty,* dealing with "reasons why the West is searching for gurus, Sufis, etc."; *The Uses of Ecstasy,* a sequel to *Thieves of Certainty; Sufis Today.*

SIDELIGHTS: Brent writes: "Like many others, I am increasingly convinced that the West is at the end of an intellectual cycle. Am concerned, however, to see it rushing off in all directions, searching for instant answers. If new directions are to be discovered, the search will be long and the choices painful. I would like to have some hand in the process, since it is the most vital of any we engage in. Am fascinated by what other societies may have to teach us."

*   *   *

BRETNOR, Reginald 1911-
(Grendel Briarton)

PERSONAL: Born July 30, 1911, in Vladivostok, Russia; came to United States, 1920; naturalized citizen; married Helen Harding, March 9, 1949 (died, 1967); married Rosalie Leveille (a writer), October 7, 1969. *Education:* Attended colleges in California and New Mexico. *Home address:* P.O. Box 1481, Medford, Ore. 97501.

CAREER: U.S. Office of War Information and U.S. State Department Office of International Information and Cultural Affairs, writer, 1943-47; free-lance writer, 1947—. Lecturer at Mills College, University of California, Belleville College, San Quentin Prison, and has appeared on television and radio programs. *Member:* Science Fiction Writers of America, Mystery Writers of America, National Rifle Association, Japanese Sword Society of the United States, California Society for Psychical Study.

WRITINGS: (Editor and contributor) *Modern Science Fiction: Its Meaning and Its Future,* Coward, 1953; (translator) Francois-Augustin Paradis de Moncrif, *Les Chats,* A. S. Barnes, 1962; (under pseudonym Grendel Briarton) *Through Time and Space with Ferdinand Feghoot* (a collection of puns and spoonerisms), Paradox Press, 1962, revised edition published as *The Compleat Feghoot,* Mirage Press, 1972; *Decisive Warfare: A Study in Military Theory,* Stackpole, 1969; (editor and contributor) *Science Fiction Today and Tomorrow,* Harper, 1974; *The Craft of Science Fiction,*

Harper, 1976. Contributor to *Encyclopaedia Britannica.* Contributor of fiction to *Harper's, Esquire, Fantasy and Science Fiction, Ellery Queen's Mystery Magazine,* and others. Contributor of non-fiction to *Modern Age, Military Review, Michigan Quarterly Review,* and other periodicals.

WORK IN PROGRESS: Preparing a book on the semantics of conflict; a science fiction novel; a book about cats.

AVOCATIONAL INTERESTS: Military and naval history; antique and modern weapons (has patented an automatic mortar); Japanese swords and art.

* * *

BREWER, Sam Pope 1909(?)-1976

1909(?)—April 21, 1976; American journalist and writer. Obituaries: *Washington Post,* April 24, 1976.

* * *

BRIDGE, Ann
See O'MALLEY, Mary Dolling (Sanders)

* * *

BRIDGER, Gordon (Frederick) 1932-

PERSONAL: Born February 5, 1932, in Cricklewood, London, England; son of John Dell (a physician) and Hilda (Piddington) Bridger; married Elizabeth Bewes, September 29, 1962; children: Rachael, Sarah, Mary. *Education:* Selwyn College, Cambridge, B.A. (honors), 1953, Ridley Hall, M.A. (honors), 1955. *Home:* Holy Trinity Rectory, Essex St., Norwich, Norfolk, England.

CAREER: Ordained minister of Church of England, 1956; curate in London, England, 1956-59, and in Cambridge, England, 1959-62; vicar in London, England, 1962-69; rector in Edinburgh, Scotland, 1969-72; Holy Trinity Church, Heigham, Norwich, England, rector, 1976—.

WRITINGS: The Man from Outside (nonfiction), Inter-Varsity Press, 1969; *A Day That Changed the World* (nonfiction), Inter-Varsity Press, 1975.

WORK IN PROGRESS: A small, popular commentary on I Corinthians.

* * *

BRIDGERS, Sue Ellen 1942-

PERSONAL: Born September 20, 1942, in Greenville, N.C.; daughter of Wayland L. (a farmer) and Elizabeth (Abbott) Hunsucker; married Ben Oshel Bridgers (an attorney), March 17, 1963; children: Elizabeth Abbott, Jane Bennett, Sean Mackenzie. *Education:* Western Carolina University, B.A., 1976. *Home:* 64 Savannah Dr., Sylva, N.C. 28779. *Office address:* P.O. Box 248, Sylva, N.C. 28779.

CAREER: Writer, 1970—.

WRITINGS: Home Before Dark (novel), Knopf, 1976. Contributor of stories to magazines, including *Redbook, Ingenue, Carolina Quarterly,* and *Mountain Living.*

WORK IN PROGRESS: A novel about women in one particular Southern family.

SIDELIGHTS: Bridgers told *CA:* "My writing seems to find its expression in nostalgia. My personal childhood experiences and the setting of a small southern town combine with a sense of the inevitable loss of that way of life. I feel very close to my roots when I'm working, as if the writing itself, although not autobiographical, is taking me back in time and is revealing some of the complexities of what seems to be a simple agrarian way of life.

"I am also interested in family relationships," Bridgers continued, "especially the tradition of the southern woman's two faces—gentility and power—as portrayed in a domestic setting."

* * *

BRIGGS, Ellis O(rmsbee) 1899-1976

December 1, 1899—February 21, 1976; American diplomat and author. Obituaries: *New York Times,* February 23, 1976; *Washington Post,* February 23, 1976; *AB Bookman's Weekly,* April 12, 1976; *Current Biography,* April, 1976.

* * *

BRILLIANT, Ashleigh 1933-

PERSONAL: Born December 9, 1933, in London, England; son of Victor (a British civil servant) and Amelia (Adler) Brilliant; married: Dorothy Tucker (vice-president of family business), June 28, 1968. *Education:* University of London, B.A., 1955; Claremont Graduate School, M.A., 1957; University of California, Berkeley, Ph.D., 1964. *Home and office:* 117 W. Valerio St., Santa Barbara, Calif. 93101.

CAREER: Edgware Gazette, Edgware, Middlesex, England, foreign correspondent, 1951; Central Oregon Community College, Bend, professor of history, 1964-65; Chapman College, Orange, Calif., professor of history, 1965-67; Brilliant Enterprises (publishers), Santa Barbara, Calif., founder and president, 1967—. Writer and cartoonist. Columnist and reporter for *Midtown Record,* San Francisco, Calif., 1967-69. Professor of history at Santa Barbara Community College, 1973-74.

MEMBER: International Platform Association, National Association of Television Arts and Sciences, Newspaper Comics Council, Northern California Cartoonists, Group Against Smoking Polution (GASP), Human Understanding of Sound and Hearing (HUSH). *Awards, honors:* United Nations population cartoon competition runner up, 1976.

WRITINGS: Unpoemed Titles, C.O.C. Press, 1965; *The Haight-Ashbury Songbook,* H-B Publications, 1967; *Pot Shots,* Brilliant Enterprises, 1968. Writer of column, "Trash From Ash", appearing in *San Francisco Midtown Record,* 1967-69, and syndicated feature panel cartoon, "Pot Shots," appearing in over thirty newspapers, including *Chicago Tribune* and *Detroit Free Press.*

SIDELIGHTS: Brilliant, who says he prefers to think of himself as a "philosopher-prophet-poet rather than a cartoonist," is best known for his widely syndicated captioned drawings. The success of his "Pot Shots," as they are called, began as an unexpected result of Brilliant's first painting exhibit. While only a few of the paintings were sold, their odd titles aroused much attention. "Soon," Brilliant recalls, "I was making lists of titles for pictures I had not yet painted." His idea quickly caught on and now, as Mary Scarpinato has observed, "Pot Shots" are being "used to illustrate everything from French grammar books to Japanese shopping bags."

Brilliant, who admits that he would like to win the Nobel Prize, finds parallels between his "Pot Shots" and Japanese Haiku poems. Both, he feels, illustrate a way to "reduce literature to its pure essential." He describes "Pot Shots" as "very concise descriptions of reality," and feels that they are simultaneously simple and complex. He explains, "It's however you choose to interpret it—like a poem. And that's what I'd like to win the Nobel Prize in Literature for—for creating a new genre of poetry."

BIOGRAPHICAL/CRITICAL SOURCES: New Zealand Herald, March 31, 1973.

*   *   *

BRINCKLOE, Julie (Lorraine) 1950-

PERSONAL: Born April 25, 1950, in California; daughter of William Draper (a professor and writer) and Josephine (a portrait artist; maiden name, O'Brien) Brinckloe; married Michael Scott Worobec, February 17, 1974 (divorced, December, 1975). Education: Attended Sweet Briar College and Art Students League; Carnegie-Mellon University, B.F.A., 1972. Home: 588 Dorseyville Rd., Pittsburgh, Pa. 15238.

CAREER: Free-lance writer, illustrator, and photographer. Founder of Grumpkin Press, 1974. Art teacher at St. Edmund's Academy, 1975-76. Art work includes wildlife drawings for schools and Christmas cards for the Animal Rescue League. Member: Fund for Animals.

WRITINGS—All self-illustrated children's books: The Spider Web, Doubleday, 1974; Gordon Goes Camping, Doubleday, 1975; Gordon's House, Doubleday, 1976.

Illustrator: Claude Aubry, Agouhanna, Doubleday, 1971; Herbert Gold, The Young Prince and the Magic Cone, Doubleday, 1973; Theodore Roethke, Dirty Dinky, Doubleday, 1973; Art Buchwald, The Bollo Caper, Doubleday, 1974; Alice Cromie, Nobody Wanted to Scare Her, Doubleday, 1974; Lucy Freeman, The Eleven Steps, Doubleday, 1974; William D. Brinckloe and Mary Coughlin, Managing Organizations, Glencoe Press, 1977.

Author of filmstrip series "Women in Management," Westinghouse, 1973. Contributor of poems and illustrations to Family, Wilson Library Bulletin, Pittsburgh Renaissance, and Misterogers Neighborhood.

WORK IN PROGRESS: Another children's book in the "Gordon" series, for Doubleday.

SIDELIGHTS: Julie Brinckloe writes: "My grandmother's cousin . . . was traveling secretary and model to Howard Pyle. . . . His books filled our home and I grew to love his work. I have also admired such writer-artists as Edward Lear, Arthur Rackham, Edward Gorey, Henry C. Pitz, Walt Disney, and numerous writers of adult fiction and nonfiction. . . ."

*   *   *

BROLIN, Brent C(ruse) 1940-

PERSONAL: Born August 13, 1940, in Fort Wayne, Ind.; son of Edward R. (a chemical engineer) and Benetta (Cruse) Brolin; married Jean Richards (an actress), June 1, 1969. Education: Yale University, B.A., 1962, M.Arch., 1968. Residence: New York, N.Y. Agent: Georges Borchardt, Inc., 145 East 52nd St., New York, N.Y. 10022.

CAREER: Brolin-Zeisel Research and Design, New York City, partner, 1969-73; self-employed architect, photographer, and writer, 1973—. Among his designs are private homes in the West Indies, a resort village in Jamaica, a planned working-class community in South Carolina, and renovations of tenements and brownstones in New York City. Awards, honors: Medal of excellence in architecture from American Institute of Architects, 1968.

WRITINGS: (Contributor) Gary Moore, editor, Emerging Methods in Environmental Design, M.I.T. Press, 1971; The Failure of Modern Architecture, Van Nostrand, 1976.

Work represented in anthologies. Contributor to Smithsonian, Architectural Forum, and Urban Design.

WORK IN PROGRESS: In Context: A Primer for Architectural Fit-In; writing on the "present state of architecture" and on Western technology in Yemen.

SIDELIGHTS: Brolin writes: "I feel that modern architecture has failed both socially and esthetically in the U.S.A. and abroad. We are now at a turning point. I hope that my writing will help free architects and laymen from the bonds of the rules of modern architecture, to face the future with a different state of mind."

AVOCATIONAL INTERESTS: Playing Baroque and Renaissance recorders, travel (Europe, the Middle East, India, Japan).

*   *   *

BROMBERG, Walter 1900-

PERSONAL: Born December 16, 1900, in New York, N.Y.; son of Zachar George (a jeweler) and Anna (Scholtz) Bromberg; married Ilyana Fatow, December 27, 1927 (deceased); married Esther Boyd (a psychiatric social worker), March 11, 1942; children: (first marriage) Joan Lisa, David Hahnon, (second marriage) Mark Boyd. Education: University of Cincinnati, B.S., 1925; State University of New York Downstate Medical Center, M.D., 1926. Religion: Jewish. Home and office: 3353 Cottage Way, Sacramento, Calif. 95825. Agent: Barthold Fles Literary Agency, 507 Fifth Ave., New York, N.Y. 10017.

CAREER: Neuro-psychiatrist. Senior psychiatrist at Sutter Community Hospital and American River Hospital. University of the Pacific, Stockton, Calif., adjunct professor of legal medicine, 1970—. Member of board of directors of Committee for Alcoholic Rehabilitation of Sacramento County, 1973—. Military service: U.S. Naval Reserve Medical Corps, 1942-46; served as commander.

MEMBER: American Medical Association, American Society of Social Psychiatry, American Psychiatric Association (life fellow), American Academy of Psychiatry and Law, California Medical Association, Sacramento Medical Society. Awards, honors: Golden Apple from American Academy of Psychiatry and Law, 1973, for distinguished contributions to the field.

WRITINGS: Mind of Man, Harper, 1937; (with John Winkler) Mind Explorers, Reynal & Hitchcock, 1939; Man Above Humanity, Lippincott, 1948; Mold of Murder, Grune, 1961; The Nature of Psychotherapy, Grune, 1962; Crime and the Mind, Macmillan, 1965; How to Keep Out of Jail, Franklin Watts, 1966; From Shaman to Psychotherapist, Regnery, 1975. Contributor of over eighty articles to professional and popular journals.

WORK IN PROGRESS: Murder by the Millions, analyses of motives in three hundred murders, for lay readers.

SIDELIGHTS: Bromberg writes: "After a thorough grounding in neurology, psychiatry, and psychoanalysis, as well as group and individual therapy, my present interest is in social psychiatry, including criminology. My goal is to present the human side of psychopathology in dramatic terms in such a way as to bring therapy out of the ivory towers into the media." Avocational interests: Writing, ranching.

*   *   *

BRONSON, William (Knox) 1926-1976

October 30, 1926—July 13, 1976; American editor and author of books on conservation. Obituaries: New York Times, July 15, 1976. (See index for previous CA sketch)

BRONSTEIN, Leo 1903(?)-1976

1903(?)—June 1, 1976; Polish-born American educator and author of books on fine arts. Obituaries: *New York Times,* June 4, 1976.

* * *

BROOKS, Janice Young 1943-
(Amanda Singer)

PERSONAL: Born January 11, 1943, in Kansas City, Mo.; daughter of J. W. (a surgeon) and Louise (Jones) Young; married Lawrence E. Brooks, February 2, 1965; children: David Lawrence, Amy Louise. *Education:* University of Kansas, B.S.Ed., 1965; graduate study at University of Missouri at Kansas City, 1965-67. *Home:* 5410 Aberdeen, Fairway, Kan. 66205.

CAREER: Elementary teacher in the public schools of Turner, Kan., 1965-68; writer. *Member:* Mensa.

WRITINGS: Kings and Queens: The Plantagenets of England, Thomas Nelson, 1975; (under pseudonym Amanda Singer) *Ozark Legacy* (gothic novel), Bouregy, 1975. Contributor to *Woman's Day, Baby Talk,* and other women's magazines.

WORK IN PROGRESS: Research on King John, for a historical novel; a historical novel on Margaret of Anjou; a second volume on English monarchy.

* * *

BROOKS, John
See SUGAR, Bert Randolph

* * *

BROOKS, Mel 1926-

PERSONAL: Real name, Melvin Kaminsky; born June 28, 1926, in Brooklyn, N.Y.; son of Max (a process server) and Kate (a garment worker; maiden name, Brookman) Kaminsky; married Florence Baum (a dancer), 1952 (divorced, 1959); married Anna Maria Italiano (an actress; stage name, Anne Bancroft), August, 1964; children: (first marriage) Stefanie, Nicky, Edward; (second marriage) Maximilian. *Education:* Attended Virginia Military Institute, 1944. *Representative:* Howard Rothberg, 1706 North Doheny Dr., Los Angeles, Calif. 90069.

CAREER: Comic writer, film director, and actor. Worked as stand-up comedian and as handyman, musician, and social director in Catskill Mountains resort area after World War II; sketch writer for television comic, Sid Caesar, collaborating on the television shows, "Broadway Revue," for National Broadcasting Co., 1949-50, "Your Show of Shows," NBC-TV, 1950-54, "Caesar's Hour," NBC-TV, 1954-57, and "Sid Caesar Invites You," American Broadcasting Co., 1957-58; writer for television specials starring such performers as Andy Williams, Jerry Lewis, Victor Borge, and Anne Bancroft, 1958-70; recorded a series of comic record albums with Carl Reiner, 1960-61 and 1973; wrote and narrated cartoon short, "The Critic," 1963; created television series, "Get Smart," with Buck Henry, for NBC-TV, 1965, and "When Things Were Rotten," with John Boni, Norman Steinberg, and Norman Stiles, for ABC-TV, 1975; film director of collaborated and own screenplays, 1968—. *Military service:* U.S. Army, Combat Engineers, 1944-46; served in European theatre of operations. *Member:* Directors Guild of America, Writers Guild of America. *Awards, honors:* Academy Awards, 1963, for "The Critic," and 1968, for "The Producers"; Writers Guild Awards for best original screenplay, 1968, for "The Producers," 1975, for "Blazing Saddles," and 1976, for "Young Frankenstein"; Nebula Award for dramatic writing, 1976, for "Young Frankenstein."

WRITINGS—Film scripts: "The Critic" (cartoon short subject), Pintoff-Crossbow Productions, 1963; "The Producers," Embassy, 1968; "The Twelve Chairs" (adaption from novel by Ilf and Petrov), UMC Pictures, 1970; (with Andrew Bergman, Richard Pryor, Norman Steinberg, and Alan Uger) "Blazing Saddles," Warner Bros., 1974; (with Gene Wilder) "Young Frankenstein," Twentieth Century-Fox, 1975; (with Ron Clark, Rudy DeLuca, and Barry Levinson) "Silent Movie," Twentieth Century-Fox, 1976.

Recorded comedy albums; all with Carl Reiner: "2,000 Years," Capitol, 1960; "2,000 and One Years," Capitol, 1961; "At the Cannes Film Festival," Capitol, 1961; "2,000 and Thirteen," Warner Brothers Records, 1973.

Books for musicals: (With Joe Darion) "Shinbone Alley" (adapted from Archy and Mehitabel stories by Don Marquis), first produced in New York at Broadway Theatre, April 13, 1957; "All American," first produced in New York at Winter Garden Theatre, March 19, 1962.

Contributor to broadway revue, "New Faces of 1952," first produced in New York at Royale Theatre, May 16, 1952. Writer of numerous television scripts and of commercial advertising campaigns.

SIDELIGHTS: "Ladies and gentlemen, now for the news. Our roving correspondent has just discovered a jungle boy, raised by lions in Africa, walking the streets of New York City."

"Sir, how do you survive in New York City?"

"Survive?"

"What do you eat?"

"Pigeon."

"Don't the pigeons object?"

"Only for a minute."

"What are you afraid of more than anything?"

"Buick."

"You're afraid of a Buick?"

"Yes, Buick can win in death struggle. Must sneak up on parked Buick, punch grille hard. Buick die." That comedy skit, appearing on an early Sid Caesar show, introduced Mel Brooks to the world as a comedy writer.

Playboy magazine describes Brooks as "an American Rabelais. Short and blocky, he has a nose once described as 'a small mudslide,' a grin that loops almost from ear to ear like a tenement laundry line and the flat-out energy of a buffalo stampede. His imagination is violent and boundless; and in the opinion of other comedy writers, no brain on the planet contains such a churning profusion of wildly funny ideas." That imagination and "churning profusion of wildly funny ideas" has made Brooks, along with Woody Allen, responsible for a comic film renaissance which has already been compared to America's golden age of comedy.

"I think he's the only person living today who's a direct link, an active, direct link with the golden age of comedy," agrees Ron Moody, one of the stars in Brooks' film, "Twelve Chairs." Moody explained, "I was brought up soon after the great clowns had been performing in America on film—Buster Keaton and Chaplin, the Keystone stuff, Laurel and Hardy. And then there was a great gap, and it turned into insult comedy, straight-acting comedy, high comedy. And nobody really had any success, except maybe Jacques Tati, or Pierre Etaix in France. Nobody succeeded in getting anywhere near the brilliance and quality of those days; and to me, Mel Brooks is the one man today who has rediscovered this marvelous vein of inventive comedy."

Brooks received his training in the Catskill's Borscht Belt and in early television. He recalled the talent assembled in the scriptroom of the Caesar shows: "There were seven comedy writers in that room, seven brilliant comedic brains. There was Mel Tolkin and Lucille Kallen. Then I came in. And spoiled everything. Then Joe Stein, who later wrote *Fiddler on the Roof,* and Larry Gelbart, who created, wrote, and produced *M*A*S*H* for television. Mike Stewart typed for us. Imagine! Our *typist* later wrote *Bye Bye Birdie* and *Hello, Dolly!* Later on Mike was replaced at the typewriter by somebody named Woody Allen. Neil and Danny Simon were there, too. . . . Seven rats in a cage. The pitch sessions were lethal. In that room, you had to fight to stay alive." In the fiercely critical and competitive vocal sessions Brooks was obsessed: "It wasn't only competition to be funnier than they were. I had to get to the ultimate punch line, you know, the cosmic joke that all the other jokes came out of. I had to hit all the walls. I was immensely ambitious. It was like I was screaming at the universe to pay attention. Like I had to make *God* laugh." Carl Reiner remembers one test illustrating that enormous competitive drive: "Late one day, he started fooling with the word 'carrot.' Someone groaned, 'Not another one of those dumb eyesight jokes.' Mel was up against the wall but he was going to deliver the best carrot joke of all time. Finally, he blurted out, 'He ate so many carrots he couldn't go to sleep because he could see through his eyelids.' The joke was used on the show."

Much of his ambition is derived from the artists he has set his sights on emulating. Besides Chaplin, Keaton, Fields, and Laurel and Hardy, Brooks sees strains of Tolstoy, Dostoevsky, and Gogol in his vision of that great cosmic joke. "The Russian novelists made me realize it's a bigger ball park than the *Bilko* show," he admitted. "I wanted to be the American Moliere, the new Aristophanes." Gene Wilder believes Mel's ambition has shown itself as the desire to create a lasting expression of humor everyone will understand: "Mel's interested in what's funny about the human condition. He punctures our greed, our frustrations, our contradictions—our desire for money and purity, domestic love and battalions of lovers, great food but slim and beautiful figures. He's after comedy which will still be understood in 200 years."

Brooks' career has not always been success and bright lights. Rising from an average family income of 35 dollars a week to 5,000 dollars a show was a psychological trauma that went far enough to cause physical problems, and on top of that, being unable to find a job for five years after the Caesar show went off the air, taught him there is much that is not funny in the human condition. Add the influence of the Russian novelists and one may see a large shaping force in Mel Brooks' approach to his work in film. "There's one thing you've got to understand before you can direct comedy," he believes. "Comedy is serious—deadly serious. Never, never try to be funny! The actors must be serious. Only the situation must be absurd. Funny is in the writing, not in the performing. If the situation isn't absurd, no amount of hoke will help. And another thing, the more serious the situation, the funnier the comedy can be. The greatest comedy plays against the greatest tragedy. Comedy is a red-rubber ball and if you throw it against a soft, funny wall, it will not come back. But if you throw it against the hard wall of ultimate reality, it will bounce back and be very lively."

When Brooks says he is "directing comedy" he may be a bit misleading. His competitive ambition combined with his unrestrainable energy and his "violent and boundless" imagination makes him more of a dynamo than a director on a film set. Dom De Luise, a veteran Brooksian, has observed him at work: "He can't keep his fingers out of anything because he knows; he literally knows. I've seen him crush up a pillow. A director of a big film doesn't have to do that. He'll come over and mess my hair up. A little more here. He'll take some snow—he'll put it here. . . . In order to make a train effect you've got to have somebody jumping up on the train. Who do you think was jumping up and down? It was Mel. Mel! Nobody can shake the train good enough for Mel. He's the director, the writer, he plays a role in this, and he still shakes the train himself!" His total control, over every step in the production of his films, is jealously guarded by Brooks. As De Luise mentioned, he not only writes, directs, and appears in a cameo role, but he also edits and does the casting. He does all this and he keeps to his schedule and budget. If he had his way, he would also sell the tickets, tear the tickets at the door, pull the curtain, turn on the projector, and possibly even clean the theatre after the show. "If I could get the same control over my films that a novelist has over the written page or the artist has over his canvas," muses Brooks, "I'd be a happy man."

He occasionally enters a theatre where one of his films is playing to see how the people will respond. In spite of his long experience in television, he still needs to hear and feel an audience response: "That kind of laughter is felt as love by a comedian. It bursts from the gut. It is absolutely without compromise. It's a vocal hug, a special caring." What does Mel Brooks suggest when one goes to see his films? "Enjoy! Revel! Live! Have yourselves one sweetheart of a good time. That's what my films are saying. That's what they're all about."

BIOGRAPHICAL/CRITICAL SOURCES: Show, September 17, 1970; *Playboy,* February, 1975; *Commonweal,* March 22, 1974; *Newsweek,* April 22, 1974, February 17, 1975; *Saturday Review World,* November 2, 1974; *Time,* January 13, 1975; *New York Times Magazine,* March 30, 1975.

*   *   *

BROOKS, Robert A(ngus)   1920-1976

October 16, 1920—April 11, 1976; American educator, management consultant, museum administrator, and author. Obituaries: *New York Times,* April 12, 1976.

*   *   *

BROPHY, James J(oseph)   1912-
(Jim Brophy)

PERSONAL: Born July 21, 1912, in Chicago, Ill.; son of Daniel P. (in insurance) and Agnes (Hogan) Brophy; married Mary Kromand, December 30, 1933 (divorced October 17, 1967); married Barbara Black, February 17, 1972; children: James, Jr., Jack W., Jerome P., M. Joan Brophy Richards, Joseph D., Jan Brophy Gore, Jean, Joyce, Teri J., Ronald J. *Education:* Attended DePaul University, 1934-37; University of Illinois, C.P.A., 1937. *Home:* 6423 Linden Lane, Dallas, Tex. 75230. *Office:* Brophy, Brophy & Co., 7928A Royal Lane, Dallas, Tex. 75230.

CAREER: Price, Waterhouse & Co., Chicago, Ill., accountant, 1933-41; U.S. Steel Co., Pittsburgh, Pa., audit supervisor, 1941-46; Peat, Marwick, Mitchell, & Co., Dallas, Tex., manager, 1946-51; James J. Brophy & Co., Dallas, owner, 1951-73; Dallas Land Investors, Inc., Dallas, president. Sponsor of Baylor University House of Poetry.

WRITINGS—Under name Jim Brophy: Taking a Stand, Prairie Press Books, 1971.

WORK IN PROGRESS: Poems.

AVOCATIONAL INTERESTS: Coin collecting, treasure hunting.

* * *

BROPHY, Jim
    See BROPHY, James J(oseph)

* * *

BROWN, Christopher P(aterson) 1939-

PERSONAL: Born July 20, 1939, in Niagara Falls, N.Y.; son of Harry Paterson (an executive) and Katharine (Culbertson) Brown; married Barbara A. Shafer (a consultant to the World Health Organization), July 1, 1966; children: Christopher Denny, Katharine Ann. Education: Cornell University, B.A., 1961; University of Pennsylvania, M.B.A., 1965; Oxford University, D.Phil., 1968. Religion: "No formal religion." Home address: Wytham Woods, Elk Ridge Rd., R.D.3, Oxford, Pa. 19363. Office: Commodities Division, United National Conference on Trade and Development, Palais des Nations, CH-1211 Geneva, Switzerland.

CAREER: Oxford Polytechnic, Oxford, England, lecturer in economics, 1966-68; Oxford University, Institute of Economics and Statistics, Oxford, researcher, 1968; University of Malawi, Chancellor College, Zomba, lecturer in economics, 1968-70; University of Malaya, Lembah Pantai, Kuala Lumpur, lecturer in economics, 1970-74; writer, researcher, and farmer, 1975; United Nations Conference on Trade and Development, Geneva, Switzerland, economic affairs officer, 1976—. Military service: U.S. Army, Counter Intelligence, 1961-63. Member: Merion Cricket Club, Oxford and Cambridge Club.

WRITINGS: Primary Commodity Control, Oxford University Press, 1975; (contributor) David Lim, editor, Readings on Malaysian Economic Development, Oxford University Press, 1975. Contributor to economic journals.

WORK IN PROGRESS: Developing a comprehensive primary commodity control simulation model, with cost-benefit provisions; writing a book on the United Nations Conference on Trade and Development (UNCTAD) Integrated Program for Commodities, with publication expected to result.

* * *

BROWN, James 1934-

PERSONAL: Born May 1, 1934, in Boston, Mass.; son of Constantine (a businessman) and Sophia (Lucas) Brown; married Bonnie Jo Russell (a piano teacher), November 26, 1964; children: Shannon Sophia. Education: Texas Christian University, B.A., 1960, M.A., 1962; State University of New York at Buffalo, M.A., 1969, Ph.D., 1971. Home: 2733 Rosedale, Dallas, Tex. 75205. Office: Department of Political Science, Southern Methodist University, Dallas, Tex. 75275.

CAREER: Southern Methodist University, Dallas, Tex.,

instructor, 1962-67, 1969-70, assistant professor, 1970-74, associate professor of political science, 1974—, established Political Data Bank, 1973. Regional area/center manager of News Election Service, 1974 and 1976; member of national selection committee of Institute of International Education. Military service: U.S. Army, Chemical Corps, 1954-57; became sergeant.

MEMBER: American Political Science Association, American Association of University Professors, Modern Greek Studies Association, Southern Political Science Association, Southwestern Political Science Association, Inter-University Seminar on Armed Forces and Society, Pi Sigma Alpha. Awards, honors: National Science Foundation grants, 1971 and 1973 (for travel to Greece); Arnold Foundation grant, 1971; scholar of U.S. State Department's Diplomat Program, 1971 and 1975.

WRITINGS: (Contributor) Gerald A. Dorfman and Steffan W. Schmidt, editors, The Military in Politics, Geron-X, 1974; (with Philip Seib) The Art of Politics: Electoral Strategies and Campaign Management, Alfred Publishing, 1976. Contributor to journals in the social sciences.

WORK IN PROGRESS: The Military and the Politics of Modern Greece; The Politics of America: A State and Local Perspective, for Alfred Publishing; research funded by NASA on the decision-making sequence related to the design of the Dallas/Fort Worth Regional Airport.

* * *

BROWN, Joe David 1915-1976

May 12, 1915—April 22, 1976; American journalist, novelist, and author of books on a variety of subjects. Obituaries: New York Times, April 24, 1976; Washington Post, April 24, 1976; Newsweek, May 3, 1976; Time, May 3, 1976; AB Bookman's Weekly, June 28, 1976. (See index for previous CA sketch)

* * *

BROWN, L(aurence) B(inet) 1927-

PERSONAL: Born August 13, 1927, in New Zealand; married Dorothy Fay Wood (a lecturer), December, 1950. Education: University of New Zealand, B.A., 1950, M.A. (honors), 1951, diploma in education, 1952; University of London, Ph.D., 1954. Home: 16 Mount St., Hunter's Hill, New South Wales 2110, Australia. Office: School of Psychology, University of New South Wales, Sydney, New South Wales 2033, Australia.

CAREER: Psychologist in Defense Scientific Corps., 1951-57; University of Adelaide, Adelaide, Australia, lecturer in psychology, 1957-63; Massey University, Palmerston North, New Zealand, professor of psychology, 1963-66; University of Wellington, Wellington, New Zealand, professor of psychology, 1967-74; University of New South Wales, Sydney, Australia, professor of psychology, 1974—.

WRITINGS: Psychology and Religion, Pelican, 1973, Penguin, 1974; Ideology, Pelican, 1973, Penguin, 1974. Editor of New Zealand Psychologist, 1972-74.

WORK IN PROGRESS: Further research on psychology of religion.

* * *

BROWN, Leigh

PERSONAL: Born in Newark, N.J.; daughter of Edward V. (in advertising) and Dorothy (Mears) Prescott; married

Robert Siroka, January 4, 1958 (divorced, 1964); children: Elizabeth. *Education:* Attended Montclair State College, 1957-58. *Politics:* "Redneck." *Religion:* "Plenty." *Residence:* Washington, N.J. *Office:* WOR-Radio, 1440 Broadway, New York, N.Y. 10018.

CAREER: Rider and trainer of horses; worked at Belmont Park and Monmouth Park race tracks, both during 1950s; producer for WOR-Radio, 1961—. *Member:* Professional Horsemans Association.

WRITINGS: The Show Gypsies (novel), Mason-Charter, 1976.

WORK IN PROGRESS: Playday, a novel "anti-Womens' Lib, proving goat ropers need love, too," completion expected in 1978.

SIDELIGHTS: Ms. Brown writes: "I raise dogs (miniature dachshunds), can also sing, act, type fast, paint houses. . . . Have produced legit theater shows (Carnegie Hall). Travels to Ireland, Alaska, Hawaii, West Indies, Caracas, Mexico. Still ride horses—like that better than painting houses."

*   *   *

BROWN, Ned   1882(?)-1976

1882(?)—April 18, 1976; American sports newswriter. Obituaries: *New York Times,* April 26, 1976.

*   *   *

BROWN, Robert Edward   1945-

PERSONAL: Born January 11, 1945, in New York, N.Y.; son of Sam L. (a businessman) and Jane (a businesswoman; maiden name, Bernheimer) Brown; married Elizabeth Tulsky (a poet and editor), May 24, 1970 (died, October, 1974). *Education:* University of Pennsylvania, B.S., 1966; University of Rochester, Ph.D., 1970. *Religion:* Jewish. *Home:* 1706 Nichols Canyon Rd., #2, Los Angeles, Calif. 90046. *Office: Mankind,* 8060 Melrose Ave., Los Angeles, Calif. 90046.

CAREER: California State University, Los Angeles, assistant professor of English and American studies, 1970-73; *Los Angeles Free Press,* Los Angeles, reporter and writer of feature series on "sexual politics," 1973; *Mankind,* Los Angeles, editor, 1975—. Publisher, Laurel Press/Open Spaces. Lecturer at Ithaca College, 1973, and at University of Southern California and University of California, Los Angeles, both 1976. *Member:* Modern Language Association of America, Smithsonian Institution, Center for Democratic Study, Society of American Travel Writers, Los Angeles Press Club.

WRITINGS: Gathering the Light (poetry), Red Hill, 1976. Contributor of articles and reviews to *Westways, Human Behavior, Los Angeles,* and other periodicals.

WORK IN PROGRESS: Radical Cynicism/Radical Faith, essays on contemporary American values and beliefs; *The Worldly Tradition in American Poetry,* criticism and literary history of poets in the world; *The Cosmological Vision,* criticism of twelve modern and contemporary visionaries; *Poems, 1967-1977,* a collection; *A Dream of New Zealand,* prose poetry.

SIDELIGHTS: Brown wrote, "For me, the more deeply personal the writing is, the more valuable, ultimately, it can be to the community. I publish 'small press' books as an avocation, books of poetry, fiction, and nonfiction. Quality, the criterion."

BROWN, Roy (Frederick)   1921-

PERSONAL: Born December 10, 1921, in Vancouver, British Columbia, Canada; *Home:* 13, Clarence Pl., Gravesend, Kent, England.

CAREER: Primary school teacher, 1946-69; Helen Allison School for Autistic Children, Gravesend, England, deputy headmaster, 1969-75.

WRITINGS—For children: *A Saturday in Pudney,* Abelard, 1966, new edition, Hutchinson, 1968; *The Viaduct,* Abelard, 1967, Macmillan, 1968; *The Day of the Pigeons,* Macmillan, 1968; *The Saturday Man: As Told on "Jackanory" by Joe Melia,* British Broadcasting Corp., 1969; (editor) Joseph Jacobs, *Reynard the Fox,* Abelard, 1969; *The River,* Abelard, 1970, published as *Escape the River,* Seabury, 1972; *The Battle of Saint Street,* Macmillan, 1971; *Flight of Sparrows,* Macmillan, 1972; *Bolt Hole,* Abelard, 1973, published as *No Through Road,* Seabury, 1974; *The White Sparrow,* Seabury, 1975; *The Siblings,* Abelard, 1976, published as *Find Debbie,* Seabury, 1976; *The Cage,* Abelard, in press. Also author of more than ten other books for children, 1959-71.

*   *   *

BROWN, Seyom   1933-

PERSONAL: Born May 28, 1933, in Hightstown, N.J.; son of Benjamin (a community planner) and Sarah (Sokolow) Brown; married Rose Samuels, February, 1963 (died, August, 1974); married Martha Morelock (a folksinger), January 16, 1976; children: (first marriage) Lisa, Steven, Elliot, Nell, Christina, Benjamin. *Education:* University of Southern California, B.A., 1955, M.A., 1957; University of Chicago, Ph.D., 1963. *Home:* 12701 Circle Dr., Rockville, Md. 20850. *Office:* Foreign Policy Studies Program, Brookings Institution, 1775 Massachusetts Ave. N.W., Washington, D.C. 20036.

CAREER: University of Southern California, Los Angeles, lecturer, 1958-59; University of Chicago, Chicago, Ill., instructor, 1960-61; RAND Corp., Santa Monica, Calif., social scientist, 1962-69; Brookings Institution, Washington, D.C., senior fellow in foreign policy studies, 1969—. Visiting lecturer at University of California, Los Angeles, 1963-65, and Johns Hopkins School of Advanced International Studies, 1966-69; visiting professor at University of Southern California, summer, 1970; adjunct professor at Johns Hopkins School of Advanced International Studies, 1970—. Research at Johns Hopkins University's Washington Center of Foreign Policy Research, 1965-66. Speaker for Educational Resource Network of the Institute for World Order. Consultant to U.S. Department of State, U.S. Department of Defense, and U.S. Navy.

MEMBER: International Political Science Association, Amnesty International, International Studies Association, American Political Science Association, Council on Foreign Relations, Council on Religion and International Affairs, United Nations Association, Phi Beta Kappa. *Awards, honors:* Fulbright scholarship to India, 1957-58.

WRITINGS: (With B. Hyink and E. Thacker) *Politics and Government in California,* Crowell, 1959, new edition, 1975; (contributor) E. S. Quade and W. I. Boucher, editors, *Systems Analysis and Policy Planning,* Elsevier, 1968; *The Faces of Power: Constancy and Change in United States Foreign Policy from Truman to Johnson,* Columbia University Press, 1968, revised edition, 1969; (with P. Hammond, W. Jones, and R. Patrick) *An Information System for the*

National Security Community, RAND Corp., 1969; (contributor) Sam Brown and Len Ackland, editors, *Why Are We Still in Vietnam?,* Random House, 1970; (contributor) Henry Owen, editor, *The Next Phase in Foreign Policy,* Brookings Institution, 1973; *New Forces in World Politics,* Brookings Institution, 1974; (contributor) James Chace and Earl Ravenal, editors, *Atlantis Lost: The U.S./European Relationship,* New York University Press, 1976. Contributor to *Saturday Review, Reporter,* international studies journals, and newspapers.

WORK IN PROGRESS: Regimes for the Ocean, Outerspace, and the Weather, with Nina Cornell, Larry L. Fabian, and Edith Brown Weiss, for Brookings Institution; *The Superpowers at Sea: Dangers and Opportunities;* a book on U.S. foreign policy during the Kissinger years; research on U.S.-Soviet relations.

* * *

BROWN, Weldon A(mzy)   1911-

PERSONAL: Born January 29, 1911, in Cycle, N.C.; son of William Vincent (a farmer and clergyman) and Sarah Anne (Allred) Brown; married El Rita Wachs, March 31, 1933; children: James Edward. *Education:* Dartmouth College, A.B., 1933; University of North Carolina, M.A., 1934, Ph.D., 1936. *Home:* 804 South Main St., Blacksburg, Va. 24060. *Office:* Department of History, Virginia Polytechnic Institute and State University, Blacksburg, Va. 24061.

CAREER: University of Alabama, Decatur, instructor in history and director of Decatur Center, 1936-38; University of Alabama, Tuscaloosa, instructor in history, 1938-39; Virginia Polytechnic Institute and State University, Blacksburg, assistant professor, 1939-41, associate professor, 1941-57, professor of history, 1957—. President of Blacksburg Community Federation, 1946-47. *Member:* American Historical Association, Organization of American Historians.

WRITINGS: Empire or Independence: A Study in the Failure of Reconciliation, 1774-1783, Louisiana State University Press, 1941, Kennikat, 1966; *Democracy: Man's Great Opportunity,* Riverside Press, 1949; *The Common Cause: Collectivism Menace or Challenge,* Riverside Press, 1949; *Prelude to Disaster: The American Role in Vietram, 1940-1963,* Kennikat, 1975; *The Last Chopper: The Denouement of the American Role in Vietnam, 1963-1975,* Kennikat, 1976. Contributor to history journals.

WORK IN PROGRESS: Research on the evolution of democratic freedom, especially in the colonial and revolutionary period of American history.

SIDELIGHTS: Brown writes: "The prime motivation of my life has been a love of freedom in all its aspects. . . . I became a firm believer, and still am, of the danger of all totalitarian systems—fascist, communist, or any elite minority regime. I am equally convinced that all just governments still must rest upon the consent of the governed. However, I realize that people today can act collectively through democratic processes to achieve virtually everything brutal dictatorships can. . . . Rousseau once said freedom and democracy were for angels. I am not that pessimistic. My studies of our involvement in Vietnam persuaded me that . . . we were merely anticommunist when we should have been profreedom. . . . It was most difficult to accept the avowed affirmation that we fought for freedom in Korea and South Vietnam, when the governments of those countries were as brutal as their opponents. This was our crime, to be shoring up, subsidizing, and dying for such brutal systems and covering it with the propaganda spread here of profreedom. Leadership that contributed to that was guilty of deception."

BROWNE, Roland A.   1910-

PERSONAL: Born September 18, 1910, in Coppercliff, Ontario, Canada; son of David Henry (a metallurgist) and Sara May (Davis) Browne; married Emily Catherine Williams, 1932 (divorced, 1947); married Emma Le Dortch (an elementary school teacher), July 28, 1948 (died December 20, 1975); children: (second marriage) David Michael, John Dennis. *Education:* Queen's University, Kingston, Ontario, B.A. (honors), 1933, M.A., 1935; also studied at University of Paris, 1935-36, University of Heidelberg, summer, 1936, University of Grenoble, 1936-37, and University of Cincinnati, 1939-42. *Politics:* Democrat. *Religion:* Episcopalian. *Home:* 256 Spartan Dr., Maitland, Fla. 32751. *Agent:* Wendy Weil, Julian Bach Literary Agency, 3 East 48th St., New York, N.Y. 10017. *Office:* Department of English, Florida Technological University, Orlando, Fla. 32618.

CAREER: Editorial assistant for American Council on Education, working on *Guide to Colleges, Universities, and Professional Schools,* and for McGraw-Hill, *Dictionary of Education,* both 1945; Radford College, Radford, Va., assistant professor of English, 1947-48; U.S. Army, Fort Campbell, Ky., civilian education officer, 1948-62; Austin Peay State University, Clarkesville, Tenn., assistant professor of English, 1962-68; Florida Technological University, Orlando, professor of writing, 1968—. Director of Florida Technological University Press, 1973—. Former horticultural director of Clarkesville Municipal Rose Garden. *Military service:* U.S. Army, intelligence agent, 1942-44; served in England and Normandy; became staff sergeant; received Bronze Star.

WRITINGS: For Better Gardens, Doubleday, 1964; *The Intelligent Dog's Guide to People-Owning,* Funk, 1967; *The Commonsense Guide to Flower Gardening,* Funk, 1968; *The Rose-Lover's Guide,* Atheneum, 1974; (translator from old French, and author of annotations) *The Holy Jerusalem Voyage of Ogier d'Anglure,* University Presses of Florida, 1975. Contributor of articles, stories, satire, and poems to magazines, including *Collier's, Queen's Quarterly, Tower, Florida Review,* and *Miami.* Gardening editor of *Woman's Day,* 1959-68.

WORK IN PROGRESS: My Brother, Dying: Selected Poems, 1960-1975; White Water, a novel.

AVOCATIONAL INTERESTS: Designing small sailing craft, gardening, reading, raising dogs, listening to Baroque music, designing and working crewel embroidery pieces.

* * *

BROWNELL, Blaine Allison   1942-

PERSONAL: Born November 12, 1942, in Birmingham, Ala.; son of Blaine, Jr. (an automobile dealer) and Annette (Holmes) Brownell; married Mardi Taylor, August 21, 1964; children: Blaine Erickson, Allison Wynne. *Education:* Washington & Lee University, B.A., 1965; University of North Carolina, M.A., 1967, Ph.D., 1969. *Home:* 4401 Overlook Rd., Birmingham, Ala. 35222. *Office:* Department of Urban Studies, University of Alabama, Birmingham, Ala. 35294.

CAREER: Purdue University, West Lafayette, Ind., assistant professor of history and American studies, 1969-74; University of Alabama, Birmingham, associate professor of urban studies and history and chairman of department, 1974—, director of urban affairs, 1975—. Member of Birmingham Planning Commission and Jefferson County Planning and Zoning Commission.

MEMBER: American Historical Association, Organization of American Historians, American Studies Association, History of Planning Group, Southern Historical Association. *Awards, honors:* Senior fellowship from Institute of Southern History at Johns Hopkins University, 1971-72.

WRITINGS: (Editor with Warren E. Stickle) *Bosses and Reformers: Urban Politics in America, 1880-1920,* Houghton, 1973; *The Urban Ethos in the South, 1920-1930,* Louisiana State University Press, 1975; (editor with David R. Goldfield, and contributor) *The City in Southern History,* Kennikat, 1977. Contributor to history, popular culture, and urban affairs journals. Editor of *Journal of Urban History.*

WORK IN PROGRESS: From Downtown to No-Town, a textbook, for Houghton, completion expected in 1978; research on the impact of the automobile on cities in the United States from 1910 to 1935.

SIDELIGHTS: Brownell told *CA:* "I have always been interested in writing, and at one time pondered a career in journalism. My ultimate commitment to the history of the United States was largely the result of my fascination with and appreciation of written history as art as well as analysis. Over the past six or seven years I have been especially interested in interdisciplinary work, both in American Studies and urban studies, and this interest has been reflected—for good or ill—in my publications. My involvement with urban affairs in recent years has convinced me of the essential worth of a historical perspective in the development of public policy, especially at the local level."

*   *   *

BROWNLEE, O(swald) H(arvey)   1917-

PERSONAL: Born April 14, 1917, in Moccasin, Mont.; son of William and Sarah Brownlee; married Lela McDonald, 1939. *Education:* Iowa State College (now Iowa State University), Ph.D., 1945. *Office:* Department of Economics, 271 19th Ave. S., University of Minnesota, Minneapolis, Minn. 55455.

CAREER: Iowa State College (now Iowa State University), Ames, assistant professor of economics, 1942-47, research associate, 1942-47; Carnegie Institute of Technology (now Carnegie-Mellon University), Pittsburgh, Pa., assistant professor of economics, 1947-48; University of Chicago, Chicago, Ill., assistant professor of economics, 1948-50; University of Minnesota, Minneapolis, professor of economics, 1950-56; International Cooperation Administration, Santiago, Chile, economist, 1956-57; University of Minnesota, professor of economics, 1957—, head of department, 1964-67. Visiting professor at Catholic University of Chile, 1967-69, Colgate University, 1972, and Institute of Fiscal Studies, Madrid, 1973. Deputy assistant secretary for U.S. Treasury, Washington, D.C., 1973-74.

WRITINGS: (With F. M. Boddy and others) *Applied Economic Analysis,* Putnam, 1948; (with A. G. Hart and others) *Financing Defense,* Blakiston Co., 1951; *The Economics of Public Finance,* Prentice-Hall, 1953; *Estimated Distribution of Minnesota Taxes and Public Expenditure Benefits* (pamphlet), University of Minnesota Press, 1960; (contributor) J. M. Buchanan, editor, *Public Finance: Needs, Sources, and Utilization,* Princeton University Press, 1961; (with J. A. Buttrick) *Producer, Consumer and Social Welfare,* McGraw, 1968; *State Aid to Local Government in Minnesota* (pamphlet), Minnesota State Planning Agency, 1970; *An Analysis of the Effects of the Minnesota Property Tax Reform and Relief Act on the Financial Positions of Local Government* (pamphlet), Minnesota State Planning Agency,

1970; (contributor) F. A. Harper, editor, *Toward Liberty,* Institute for Humane Studies, 1971; (contributor) Yung-Ping Chen, editor, *Understanding Economics,* Little, Brown, 1974; (with G. C. Hufbauer, Wilson E. Schmidt, Norman B. Ture, and Dan Throop Smith) *U.S. Taxation of American Business Abroad,* American Enterprise Institute-Hoover Institute, 1975. Contributor to *Encyclopaedia Britannica,* proceedings, and economic journals.

*   *   *

BROXHOLME, John Franklin   1930-
(Duncan Kyle)

PERSONAL: Born June 11, 1930, in Bradford, England; son of Norman (a valuer) and Margaret (Smith) Broxholme; married Alison Millar Hair (a teacher), September 22, 1956; children: Helen, Christopher, Lindsay. *Education:* Educated in Bradford, England. *Home and office:* Oak Lodge, Valley Farm Rd., Newton, Sudbury, Suffolk, England. *Agent:* Rupert Crew Ltd., 1A King's Mews, Gray's Inn Rd., London W.C.1, England.

CAREER: Telegraph & Argus (newspaper), Bradford, England, reporter, 1946-53; *Yorkshire Post,* Leeds, England, member of staff in features department, 1955-57; *John Bull* Magazine and *Today* Magazine, London, England, assistant editor, 1957-68; Odhams Magazines Ltd., London, editorial director, 1968-69; novelist, 1970—. *Military service:* British Army Intelligence Corps, 1948-50. *Member:* Crime Writers' Association (chairman, 1976-77).

WRITINGS—All under pseudonym Duncan Kyle, except as indicated: (Contributor, under name John F. Broxholme) John Dodge, editor, *The Practice of Journalism,* Heineman, 1968; *A Cage of Ice,* St. Martin's, 1970; *Flight Into Fear,* St. Martin's, 1972; *The Suvarov Adventure,* St. Martin's, 1974; *Terror's Cradle,* St. Martin's, 1975; *Whiteout,* St. Martin's, 1976.

WORK IN PROGRESS: Another book.

*   *   *

BRUCE, George   1909-

PERSONAL: Born March 10, 1909, in Fraserburgh, Scotland; son of Henry George Bruce (a herring curer) and Jeannie (Gray) Bruce; married Elizabeth Craven Duncan, July 25, 1935; children: David, Marjorie Anne (Mrs. Chilton Richard Inglis). *Education:* University of Aberdeen, M.A. (first class honors), 1932, teaching certification, 1933. *Religion:* Christian. *Home:* 25 Warriston Cres., Edinburgh EH3 5LB, Scotland. *Office:* Department of English, College of Wooster, Wooster, Ohio 44691.

CAREER: High school teacher of English and history in Dundee, Scotland, 1934-46; British Broadcasting Corp. (BBC), London, England, radio producer in Aberdeen, Scotland, 1946-56, talks documentary producer in Edinburgh, Scotland, 1956-70; University of Glasgow, Glasgow, Scotland, fellow in creative writing, 1971-73; writer, 1973—. Visiting professor at Union Theological Seminary, winter, 1974, and College of Wooster, 1976-77. *Member:* Cockburn Association (honorary member), Saltire Society (vice-chairman, 1973—). *Awards, honors:* Publications award from Scottish Arts Council, 1968, for *Landscapes and Figures,* and 1971, for *The Collected Poems of George Bruce.*

WRITINGS: Sea Talk (poems), Maclellan, 1944; (with T. S. Halliday) *Scottish Sculpture Today,* Findlay, Dundee, 1947; *Selected Poems,* Oliver & Boyd, 1947; (contributor) William Montgomerie, editor, *New Judgments: Robert*

Burns, Maclellan, 1947; (editor with Maurice Lindsay and Edwin Morgan) *Scottish Poetry,* Volumes I-VI, Edinburgh University Press, 1966-72; *Landscapes and Figures: A Selection of Poems,* Akros Publications, 1967; (editor) *The Scottish Literary Revival: An Anthology of Twentieth Century Poetry,* Macmillan, 1968; *The Collected Poems of George Bruce,* Edinburgh University Press, 1970; *Neil M. Gunn* (biographical/critical comment), National Library of Scotland, 1971; (contributor) Alexander Scott and Douglas Gifford, editors, *Neil M. Gunn: The Man and the Writer,* Harper, 1973; *Anne Redpath* (monograph), Edinburgh University Press, 1974; *The City of Edinburgh* (historical guide), Pitkin, 1974; *Festival in the North: The Story of the Edinburgh Festival,* R. Hale, 1975; *Some Practical Good* (conservation in Edinburgh, 1875-1975), Cockburn Association, 1975; (contributor) Robert Underwood, editor, *Scotland and the Future,* Croom helme, 1977.

Poems represented in anthologies, including *The Oxford Book of Scottish Verse,* edited by John MacQueen and Tom Scott, Oxford University Press, 1966; *Poetry of the Forties,* edited by Robin Skelton, Penguin, 1968; *Voices of Our Kind,* edited by Morven Cameron, Saltire Society and Scottish Civic Trust, 1974, 2nd edition, 1975; and *Poetry of Northeast Scotland,* edited by James Alison, Heinemann Educational Books, 1976.

Executive editor of *Scottish Review,* 1975-76.

WORK IN PROGRESS: Another collection of poems.

SIDELIGHTS: Bruce writes: "In the midst of despair at the consummation of evil in 1939, image upon image of the enduring rock of my coastal home-town associated with the enduring skill and character of the fishermen there presented themselves. Hence my first book. I also acknowledge the sensitive technical achievement of Ezra Pound as guide to the realisation in poetry of the images."

BIOGRAPHICAL/CRITICAL SOURCES: Kurt Wittig, *The Scottish Tradition in Literature,* Oliver & Boyd, 1958; John Speirs, *The Scots Literary Tradition,* revised edition, Faber, 1970; *Akros,* December, 1975.

* * *

BRUCKER, Roger W(arren) 1929-
(Warren Rogers)

PERSONAL: Born July 27, 1929, in Shelby, Ohio; son of Franklin Henry and Marian Jane (a social worker; maiden name, Love) Brucker; married Joan Wagner (a school librarian), September 9, 1951; children: Thomas Alan, Ellen, Jane Corson, Emily Lenore. *Education:* Oberlin College, B.A., 1951. *Politics:* Democrat. *Religion:* Society of Friends (Quakers). *Home:* 445 West South College St., Yellow Springs, Ohio 45387. *Agent:* Roberta Pryor, International Management Corp., 1301 Avenue of the Americas, New York, N.Y. 10019. *Office:* Odiorne Industrial Advertising, P.O. Box 280, Yellow Springs, Ohio 45387.

CAREER: Odiorne Industrial Advertising, Yellow Springs, Ohio, account executive, 1955-71, president, 1971—. Adjunct assistant professor at Wright State University, 1975—. Chairman of Yellow Springs Planning Commission, 1964-70, and Board of Zoning Appeals, 1970—. Member of board of directors of Cave Research Foundation, 1957—. *Military service:* U.S. Air Force, 1951-55; became staff sergeant. *Member:* National Speleological Society (honorary life fellow; governor, 1954-56), Central Ohio Industrial Marketers (president, 1968), Engineers Club of Dayton.

WRITINGS: (With Joe Lawrence, Jr.) *The Caves Beyond,*

Funk, 1955, Zephyrus Press, 1975; *Film Planning and Production,* U.S. Air Force, 1956; (with Richard A. Watson) *The Longest Cave,* Knopf, 1976.

Author of libretto for the opera "The Proposal," Mills Music, 1955. Author of film scripts for U.S. Air Force. Contributor of articles to marketing and advertising journals, and (sometimes under pseudonym Warren Rogers) to speleological journals. Editor of *National Speleological Bulletin,* 1956-58; member of editorial board of Zephyrus Press.

WORK IN PROGRESS: Biographies of Stephen Bishop and Floyd Collins; a chapter to be included in *Hydrology of the Central Kentucky Karst,* edited by William B. White; marketing and advertising research.

* * *

BRULLER, Jean Marcel 1902-
(Vercors)

PERSONAL: Born February 26, 1902, in Paris, France; son of Louis and Ernestine (Bourbon) Bruller; married Jeanne Barusseaud, 1931 (divorced); married Rita Barisse, 1957; children: Francois, Jean-Louis, Bertrand. *Education:* Attended University of Paris, and a technical college, received diploma in electrical engineering; studied art in Paris after military service. *Home:* Moulin des Iles, 77120 St. Augustin, France.

CAREER: Novelist, essayist, and artist specializing in graphic art and engraving; founder with Pierre de Lescure of Editions de Minuit (publishing house for French Resistance movement), 1941; lecturer, 1945—. *Military service:* French Army, served in Alpine regiment in Tunis, 1940; became lieutenant. *Member:* P.E.N., French section (vice-president), Comite National des Ecrivans (honorary president). *Awards, honors:* Legion d'honneur; medaille de la Resistance.

WRITINGS—All under pseudonym Vercors: *Le Silence de la mer,* Editions de Minuit (Paris), 1941, published as *Les Silences de la mer,* Pantheon, 1943, translation by Cyril Connolly published as *The Silence of the Sea,* Macmillan, 1944 (published in England as *Put Out the Light*), illustrated enlarged edition published as *Le Silence de la Mer,* Club des Libraries de France (Paris), 1964; *La Marche a l'Etoile,* Editions de Minuit, 1943, Pantheon, 1946, translation by Eric Sutton published as *Guiding Star,* Macmillan, 1946; *Le Songe,* Editions de Minuit, 1945; *Souffrance de mon pays,* Emile-Paul, 1945; *Le Sable du temps,* Emile-Paul, 1946; (author of introduction) Diego Brosset, *Un Homme sans l'Occident,* Editions de Minuit, 1946; *Les Armes de la nuit,* Editions de Minuit, 1946; *L'Imprimerie de Verdun,* Bibliotheque francaise, 1947; *Les Mots,* Editions de minuit, 1947; *Les Yeux et la lumiere: Mystere a six voix,* A. Michel (Paris), 1950.

Plus ou moins homme (essays), A. Michel, 1950; *La Puissance du jour,* A. Michel, 1951; *Les Animaux denatures* (novel), A. Michel, 1952, translation by wife, Rita Barisse published as *You Shall Know Them,* Little, Brown, 1953 (published in England as *Borderline,* Macmillan, 1954), published as *The Murder of the Missing Link,* Pocket Books, 1958; *Portrait d'une amitie, et autres morts memorables,* A. Michel, 1954; *Les Pas dans le sable: l'Amerique, la Chine, et la France,* A. Michel, 1954; *Coleres* (novel), A. Michel, 1956, translation by Barisse published as *The Insurgents,* Harcourt, 1956; *Les Divagations d'un Francais en Chine* (self-illustrated), A. Michel, 1956; *P.P.C.; ou Le Concours de Blois,* A. Michel, 1957, translation by Jonathan Griffin published as *For the Time Being,* Hutchinson, 1960;

Goetz, Musee de Poche, 1958; *Sur ce Rivage,* A. Michel, Volume I: *Le Periple,* 1958, Volume II: *Monsieur Prousthe: Un Souvenir,* 1958, Volume III: *La Liberte de decembre, suivi de Clementine,* 1960, translation of volumes II and III by Barisse published as *Paths of Love,* Putnam, 1961, published in England as *Freedom in December,* Hutchinson, 1961; (editor) *Morale chretienne et morale marxiste,* La Palatine (Paris), 1960.

Sylva (novel), B. Grasset, 1961, translation by Barisse published as *Sylva,* Putnam, 1962; (with Paul Misraki) *Les Chemins de l'Etre: Une Discussion,* A. Michel, 1965; (translator and illustrator) William Shakespeare, *Hamlet: Une Tragedie en cinq actes,* Editions Vialetay, 1965; (with Paul Silva-Coronel) *Quota, ou, Les Plethoriens* (novel), Stock, 1966, translation by Barisse published as *Quota,* Putnam, 1966; *La Bataille du silence: Souvenirs de minuit,* Presses de la Cite (Paris), 1967, translation by Barisse published as *The Battle of Silence,* Holt, 1968; *Le Radeau de la Meduse* (novel), Presses de la Cite, 1969, translation by Audrey C. Foote published as *The Raft of the Medusa,* McCall, 1971.

Liberte ou fatalite? Oedipe et Hamlet, Perrin (Paris), 1970; *Contes des Cataplasmes,* Editions G. P. (Paris), 1971; *Sillages* (novel), Presses de la Cite, 1972; *Sept Sentiers du desert,* Presses de la Cite, 1972; *Questions sur la vie a MM les biologists,* Stock, 1973; *Comme un Frere,* Plon (Paris), 1973; *Tendre Naufrage* (novel), Presses de la Cite, 1974; *Ce que je crois* (essay), B. Grasset, 1975.

Collections: *Three Short Novels* (includes "Guiding Star," "Night and Fog," and "The Verdun Press"), Little, Brown, 1947; *Le Songe precede de Ce Jour-la,* P. Seghers, 1950; *Le Silence de la mer et autres recits,* A. Michel, 1951; *Les Armes de la nuit et La Puissance du jour,* A. Michel, 1951; *Les Animaux denatures suivi de La Marche a l'Etoile,* Livre de Poche, 1956.

Plays: *Zoo; ou L'Assassin philanthrope* (based on *Les Animaux denatures;* first produced in Carcassonne, France, 1963), Theatre National Populaire, 1964, translation by James Clancy produced as "Zoo, or, The Philanthropic Assassin by Vercors: A Judicial, Zoological, and Moral Comedy in Three Acts," in Ithaca, N.Y., at Cornell University, March, 1968; "Le Fer et le Velours," produced at Nimes, 1969; (adaptor) "Oedipe-Roi" (based on work by Sophocles), first produced in La Rochelle, 1967, produced in Paris, 1970.

Collections of art work under name Jean Bruller: "21 Recettes de Mort Violente," 1926, published as *21 Delightful Ways of Committing Suicide for the Use of Persons Who are Discouraged or Disgusted with Life for Reasons which do not Concern Us,* Covici, Friede, 1930; "Hypotheses sur les amateurs de peinture" (title means "Hypotheses on Art Lovers"), 1927; "Un Homme coupe en tranches" (title means "A Man Cut Up in Slices"), 1929; "Les Releves trimestriels," 1932-38; "Nouvelle cle des songes" (title means "A New Key to Dreams"), 1934; "L'Enfer" (title means "This is Hell"), 1935; "Visions intimes et rassurantes de la Guerre" (title means "Comforting Visions of the War"), 1936; "Silences," 1937; "La Danse des vivants" (title means "The Dance of the Living"), 1938. Art work has been exhibited world-wide, including Vienna, 1970, and Budapest and Cologne, 1971. Also illustrator of editions of Kipling, Racine and others, and of children's books.

WORK IN PROGRESS: Cent et une Merveilles de la Gastronomie francaise (title means "One-Hundred-One Marvels of French Gastronomy"), for P. Seghers.

SIDELIGHTS: During the Nazi Occupation of France,

Jean Bruller, a then little known artist, co-founded a clandestine publishing house for the Resistance in Paris to, in Bruller's words "show world opinion that France, amid misfortune and violence, was able to keep faith with her highest purpose: her claim to think straight." Editions de Minuit, or the Midnight Press published and distributed over twenty volumes of contemporary literature in direct defiance of both the German and Vichy governments. The first of these "midnight editions" was *The Silence of the Sea* by Bruller himself under the pseudonym Vercors. The short novel was widely read and translated into some thirty languages. Its publication in the United States is said to have aroused much fervent anti-Nazi sentiment. Each copy of the original edition included the following statement. "Propaganda is not our domain. We mean to safeguard our inner life and freely serve our art. The names matter little. It is no longer a question of petty personal fame."

The Battle of Silence is Bruller's story of the founding and operation of the Midnight Press. Reviewer John Toland writes, "The activities of Vercors and the Midnight Press make for an underground tale with a difference. There is very little derring-do, no wild escapes, violent clashes or bloody scenes of torture. It is rather, as Bruller writes, 'basically a spiritual adventure,' the experience of one man 'caught up in the whirlwind of a vast cataclysm who, together with a few friends, attempted at the risk of their lives to save something that matters to them more than life.'"

BIOGRAPHICAL/CRITICAL SOURCES: New Yorker, March 9, 1946, November 8, 1969; *New York Herald Tribune Book Review,* June 28, 1953; *Atlantic,* February, 1969; *New York Times Book Review,* October 24, 1971.

*   *   *

BRUNO, Vincent J. 1926-

PERSONAL: Born February 8, 1926, in New York, N.Y.; son of Anthony J. (an administrator) and Inez (D'Antoni) Bruno; divorced. *Education:* Academie Julian, certificat, 1949; Kenyon College, B.A., 1951; Columbia University, M.A., 1962, Ph.D., 1969. *Office:* Department of Art and Art History, State University of New York at Binghamton, Binghamton, N.Y. 13901.

CAREER: U.S. Information Agency, Washington, D.C., served as cultural affairs officer in Pusan, Korea, and as acting public affairs officer in Algiers, Algeria; Colgate University, Hamilton, N.Y., instructor in art history, 1957-58; Bennett College, Greensboro, N.C., instructor in art history, 1958-60; Wellesley College, Wellesley, Mass., instructor in art history, 1964-65; Long Island University, C. W. Post College, Greenvale, N.Y., associate professor of art history, 1965-66; State University of New York at Binghamton, assistant professor, 1966-70, associate professor of art history, 1970—. Participates in annual excavations at Cosa (Italy), for American Academy in Rome. *Military service:* U.S. Army Air Forces, air cadet, 1943-45. *Awards, honors:* Grants from National Endowment for the Humanities, 1968-71, from Link Foundation, 1972, and Atlantic Foundation, 1974.

WRITINGS: (Editor and author of introduction) *The Parthenon: Norton Critical Studies in the History of Art,* Norton, 1974; *Form and Color in Greek Painting* (monograph), Norton, 1976. Contributor to *Princeton Encyclopedia of Classical Sites,* and to archaeology journals.

WORK IN PROGRESS: State University of New York House at Cosa, the final report on the Cosa excavations, reports on finds collected in two recent underwater research projects in the Tyrrhenian, one in the waters near the island of Ponza, the other in the Gulf of Talamone.

SIDELIGHTS: Bruno writes: "Beginning as a graduate student at Columbia, I have been a participant in the annual season of excavations at Cosa. . . . I was assigned the supervision of an area of the site and have completed the excavation of a large town house and surrounding ancient streets. . . . The excavations are now complete and one of the areas excavated, the town house and its garden, has been restored to form a permanent exhibition that is now open to the public along with excavated areas of the sanctuary and forum."

BIOGRAPHICAL/CRITICAL SOURCES: A. G. McKay, *Houses, Villas and Palaces in the Roman World,* Cornell University Press, 1975.

*   *   *

BUCHAN, Alastair (Francis)   1918-1976

September 9, 1918—February 3, 1976; British military expert, scholar, educator, journalist, and author of books on strategic affairs and other topics. Obituaries: *Washington Post,* February 5, 1976; *New York Times,* February 7, 1976; *AB Bookman's Weekly,* March 1, 1976.

*   *   *

BUCHANAN, Marie
(Rhona Petrie)

PERSONAL: Born in Hastings, England; married Jimmy Duell; children: Karen, Lois, Fergus. *Education:* University of London, B.A. (honors) and associateship of King's College, 1944. *Religion:* Christian. *Politics:* None. *Residence:* Gerrards Cross, Buckinghamshire, England. *Agent:* Jackie Baldick, London Management, 235-241 Regent St., London W1A 2JT, England; and Elaine Markson Literary Agency, 44 Greenwich Ave., New York, N.Y. 10011.

CAREER: Has worked as interpreter, translator, language teacher, lecturer, and social secretary in various European countries; now full-time writer. *Member:* Crime Writers Association, Writers Action Group, Oxford Book Association.

WRITINGS—Novels: *Anima,* St. Martin's, 1972 (published in England as *Greenshards,* Gollancz, 1972); *An Unofficial Breath,* St. Martin's, 1973; *The Dark Backward,* Coward, 1975; *Morgana,* Doubleday, 1977.

Crime novels, under pseudonym Rhona Petrie; all published by Gollancz, except as noted: *Death in Deakins Wood,* Dodd, 1963; *Murder by Precedent,* 1964; *Running Deep,* 1965; *Dead Loss,* 1966; *Foreign Bodies,* 1967; *Maclurg Goes West,* 1968; *Despatch of a Dove,* 1969; *Come Hell and High Water,* 1970; *Thorne in the Flesh,* 1971.

Contributor to American mystery magazines.

WORK IN PROGRESS: A second, as yet untitled, novel of seventeenth century Europe, to follow *Morgana,* for Doubleday.

SIDELIGHTS: Marie Buchanan feels that "psychology is the subject matter of the novel and also the key to its individual communication" since "observation at the subconscious level is shaped and organised at the conscious level." Writing crime novels, she finds, is a valuable discipline allowing her to place a "subjective presentation inside an objective narrative framework." Judging the success of her method, Maurice Prior wrote that Miss Buchanan engages "in much character-involvement and following-up, the con-

sequence being that the story is always mobile and extremely colourful and the build-up to the climax sound and convincing. Very good characterisation, good sleuthing and plot-manipulation and in toto well-told and a very well-rounded engrossing tale." Writing of *The Dark Backward,* a *New York Times* reviewer remarked: "Marie Buchanan treats this psychic trip without the heavy breathing and hyperbole characteristic of so many writers on spookly phenomena. The real magic is in her delightful style, which attends to reality with a sophistication that encourages belief in the author's airier speculations."

Ms. Buchanan describes herself as an avid reader, but one who dislikes category fiction, appreciating form but despairing of formula. She says she particularly admires the work of Carl Jung, Marcel Proust, William Faulkner, Arthur Koestler, Arthur Guirdham, and Jean Rhys. In the literary sense, she hopes never to "arrive, but for long to remain hopefully travelling." Ms. Buchanan told *CA* that as a student, her subjects were European languages and psychology, two aspects of communication which she feels provide the fabric and the theme of her novels. In each of her stories she claims to offer alternative levels of interpretation: Was the phenomenon of *Anima* supernatural, psychopathic, or the outcome of a skilled and criminal confidence trick? In *Unofficial Breath,* was Lorna Beckett really dead or alive, highly perceptive or mentally deranged? Her characters, in crisis, stand on the familiar precipices of nightmare, and run through what she describes as archetypal corridors of horror. Hence, Ms. Buchanan notes that her subject is the subconscious experience externalized and objectively organized; and, she points out, whether involved in the fertility rites of a High Priest of Ishtar (*The Dark Backward*), or in the metaphysics of the seventeenth century, her characters' minds undergo experiences that touch chillingly on our own lives, and their feet are as firmly on earth's crust as are ours at the present day. In human terms, Ms. Buchanan is certain, time is a dimension one can slip free of.

*   *   *

BUCK, Peggy S(ullivan)   1930-

PERSONAL: Born August 3, 1930, in North Augusta, S.C.; daughter of Charles Edmund and Ethlene (Peacock) Sullivan; married William D. Buck, October 18, 1954 (divorced, 1962); children: Wilson E., Deborah Ann. *Education:* Earned A.B. at Coker College; Appalachian State University, M.A., 1976. *Religion:* Episcopalian. *Home:* 109 West 15th St., Lumberton, N.C. 28358. *Office:* Fort Bragg Dependents Schools, Drawer A, Fort Bragg, N.C.

CAREER: Butler Elementary School, Fort Bragg, N.C., sixth grade teacher, 1965—. *Member:* National Education Association, North Carolina Association of Educators.

WRITINGS: I'm Divorced: Are You Listening, Lord? (poems), Judson, 1976.

WORK IN PROGRESS: Valium and God, for Judson, and *Thistles and Little Toy Whistles,* both books of poems; *Thoughts from the Ancients for Young Thinkers,* for children.

SIDELIGHTS: Peggy Buck writes: "I have experienced two divorces. My second marriage was very brief ending a short time ago. Out of my personal tragedy came a desire to speak out about the difficulties divorced people face in today's society and to work with and for divorced people. I went back to school obtaining a graduate degree in guidance and counseling in an effort to better understand myself and in the hope of using these skills to help others. I feel very blessed in that so much constructive has grown from such a destructive experience.

"Poetry is the form of literature that I love best (and love is the word I meant to use). Poetry to me is the form of literature most adaptable to human needs. It can become a very personal expression of one person's joy or sorrow even though written by someone not known to you personally. It should be the language of the people, the language of the human heart. Too often it is not—but it could be! I won't be 'happy' until poetry sells as well as the mystery or the gothic novel."

* * *

BUCK, Philip W(allenstein) 1900-

PERSONAL: Born May 29, 1900, in Rapid City, S.D.; son of Joseph Peter (a farmer) and Helen M. (a school teacher; maiden name, Bangs) Buck; married Barbara A. Jacobs, June 24, 1926; children: Priscilla B. Buck Alfandre, Olwen Margaret Buck Wymark, Constance Eleanor Buck Kuruppu. *Education:* University of Idaho, B.A., 1923; Oxford University, B.A., 1926; University of California, Berkeley, Ph.D., 1933. *Politics:* Democrat. *Religion:* Episcopal. *Office:* Department of Political Science, Stanford University, Stanford, Calif. 94305.

CAREER: Mills College, Oakland, Calif., assistant professor of history and government, 1926-34; Stanford University, Stanford, Calif., instructor, 1934-35, assistant professor, 1935-37, associate professor, 1937-41, professor of political science, 1941-65, professor emeritus, 1965—; Pennsylvania State University, University Park, visiting professor of political science, 1965-66; California State College, Dominguez Hills, professor of political science, 1966-70; writer, 1970—. Member of summer school faculty at University of Oregon, 1938, 1939, and University of California, 1943; member of faculty of Salzburg Seminar in American Studies, 1952. Has conducted research in England, France, Germany, and Austria.

MEMBER: American Political Science Association, Phi Beta Kappa, Phi Gamma Delta. *Awards, honors:* Rhodes scholar, 1923-26; Ford Foundation grant, 1954-58.

WRITINGS: The Politics of Mercantilism, Holt, 1942, Octagon, 1964; (with John W. Masland) *The Governments of Foreign Powers,* Holt, 1947, revised edition, 1950; (editor with Martin B. Travis, Jr., and contributor) *Control of Foreign Relations in Modern Nations,* Morrow, 1958; *Amateurs and Professionals in British Politics, 1918-1959,* University of Chicago Press, 1963; *How Conservatives Think,* Penguin, 1975. Contributor to political science journals.

WORK IN PROGRESS: An account of his own experiences.

* * *

BUCKMAN, Peter 1941-

PERSONAL: Born August 18, 1941, in Amersham, England; son of Bernard (a businessman) and Irene (a barrister; maiden name, Amiel) Buckman; married Rosemary Waeny (a literary agent), December 12, 1969; children: Jessica, Sasha. *Education:* Attended Sorbonne, University of Paris, 1959; Balliol College, Oxford, M.A., 1962. *Home:* Rynan's Cottage, Little Tew, Oxfordshire, England. *Agent:* Georges Borchardt, Inc., 145 East 52nd St., New York, N.Y. 10022.

CAREER: Penguin Books, Ltd., Harmondsworth, Middlesex, England, member of editorial board, 1962-64; New American Library, Inc., New York, N.Y., member of edi-

torial board, 1964-65; McGraw-Hill, Inc., New York, N.Y., European editor, 1966-68; full-time free-lance writer.

WRITINGS: The Limits of Protest, Bobbs-Merrill, 1970; *Playground,* Macmillan, 1971; *Education without Schools,* Souvenir Press, 1973. Contributor of television reviews to *Listener,* 1974—; contributor of book reviews to *Punch.* Advisory editor of *Paris Review,* 1965-69, and *Ramparts,* 1966-69.

WORK IN PROGRESS: A biography, *Lafayette;* an historical novel, *The Maroons;* plays for television and stage.

* * *

BUDIMIR, (Simo) Velimir 1926-

PERSONAL: Born November 1, 1926, in Mrkonjic, Yugoslavia; son of Simo and Saveta (Cebedzie) Budimir; married Andja Dimitrijevic, January 28, 1953. *Education:* Attended secondary school in Belgrade, Yugoslavia. *Home:* 730 24th St. N.W., Washington, D.C. 20037. *Office:* Tanjug, 950 National Press Building, Washington, D.C. 20045.

CAREER/WRITINGS: Tanjug, Washington, D.C., employed at foreign desk in Belgrade, Yugoslavia, 1947-53, correspondent from London, England, 1953-54, diplomatic correspondent in Belgrade, 1954-57, correspondent from Sophia, Bulgaria, 1957-60, foreign editor in Belgrade, 1960-66, correspondent from Prague, Czechoslovakia, 1966-71, diplomatic correspondent in Belgrade, 1971-75, correspondent from Washington, D.C., 1975—. *Military service:* Yugoslavian Army, 1944-46. *Member:* Union of Journalists of Yugoslavia, Press Club (Washington, D.C.). *Awards, honors:* Decorated by Government of Yugoslavia.

* * *

BULLOCK, Barbara
See BULLOCK-WILSON, Barbara

* * *

BULLOCK-WILSON, Barbara 1945-
(Barbara Bullock)

PERSONAL: Born April 13, 1945, in Santa Maria, Calif.; daughter of Wynn (a photographer and philosopher) and Edna (a home economics teacher; maiden name, Earle) Bullock; married Gene Wilson (an administrator and teacher), October 13, 1972; children: (stepchildren) Steve, Karan, Debra, Bob, Lisa. *Education:* Monterey Peninsula College, A.A., 1965; University of California, Santa Cruz, B.A., 1967, graduate study, 1970; Stanford University, A.M., 1970. *Residence:* Falmouth, Mass. *Office address:* P.O. Box 697, East Falmouth, Mass. 02536.

CAREER: CTB/McGraw-Hill, Monterey, Calif., assistant editor for test materials, 1969-70; Santa Catalina School for Girls, Monterey, Calif., librarian, 1970-71; self-employed educational consultant, 1971-73; Small World School, Falmouth, Mass., teacher and program planner, 1974—. Photographic assistant to her father, Wynn Bullock, 1959-65; program planner for Falmouth public schools, 1974; volunteer worker for Falmouth Family Planning Service, 1973—, co-director, 1975. *Awards, honors: Wynn Bullock* was named among the fifty best books of 1971 by American Institute of Graphic Arts.

WRITINGS—Under name Barbara Bullock: *Wynn Bullock,* San Francisco Museum of Art, 1969; *Wynn Bullock,* Scrimshaw Press (Berkeley, Calif.), 1971; *Increasing the Facilitation of Learning: A Systems Approach,* Interactive Education, 1971; (with Eugene Wilson) *The Instep System for Improving the Teaching/Learning Process,* Interactive Education, 1971.

Under name Barbara Bullock-Wilson: *Wynn Bullock: Photography, a Way of Life,* Morgan & Morgan, 1973; *Small World School,* Small World School, 1976. Contributor to photography and conservation magazines.

WORK IN PROGRESS: A book on Bullock nudes, with her mother, Edna Bullock; an essay on photography; research on the life and work of her father, Wynn Bullock; developing an integrated curriculum for a small, private developmental school; developing an early childhood education program for public high school students; research for a comprehensive curriculum project centering around "man's search for meaning."

AVOCATIONAL INTERESTS: Gourmet cooking, handcrafts, dancing, hiking, camping, music, indoor gardening, whales.

* * *

BULTMANN, Rudolf Karl   1884-1976

August 20, 1884—July 30, 1976; German Protestant theologian, educator, and author of books in his field. Obituaries: *New York Times,* August 1, 1976; *Washington Post,* August 2, 1976; *Current Biography,* September, 1976. (See index for previous *CA* sketch)

* * *

BUMPUS, Jerry   1937-

PERSONAL: Born January 29, 1937, in Mount Vernon, Ill.; son of Carl Lester and Opal (Gibbs) Bumpus; married Bettie McShane (a genealogist), November 11, 1961; children: Margot, Prudence. *Education:* University of Missouri, B.A., 1958; University of Iowa, M.F.A., 1960. *Politics:* "Revisionist." *Religion:* "Pantheist." *Home:* 4730 College, San Diego, Calif. 92115. *Office:* School of Literature, San Diego State University, San Diego, Calif. 92115.

CAREER: Eastern Washington State College, Cheney, assistant professor of English, 1968-71; San Diego State University, San Diego, Calif., associate professor of literature, 1971—. *Awards, honors:* Illinois Arts Council Award, 1973, for "Travelin Blues;" Fels Foundation award, 1975, for story "In the Mood of Zebras."

WRITINGS: Anaconda (novel), December Press, 1967; *Things in Place* (short stories), Fiction Collective, 1975.

Stories represented in anthologies, *Best Little Magazine Fiction, 1970,* edited by Curt Johnson, New York University Press, 1970; *The Secret Life of Our Time,* edited by Gordon Lish, Doubleday, 1973; *Cutting Edges,* edited by Jack Hicks, Holt, 1973; *Best American Short Sie , 1974,* edited by Martha Foley, Houghton, 1974; *Best American Short Stories, 1975,* edited by Foley, Houghton, 1975; *O. Henry Prize Stories,* edited by William Abrahams, Doubleday, 1976. Contributor of about fifty stories to literary journals, including *December, Transatlantic, Epoch, Triquarterly, Vagabond,* and *Lillabulero,* and to *Esquire.*

WORK IN PROGRESS: Three short novels and one long one; short stories.

* * *

BURDETTE, Franklin L.   1911-1975

PERSONAL: Born December 7, 1911, in Huntington, W.Va.; son of Frank Lee and Laura (Buckner) Burdette; married Evelyn Spruill Page, June 28, 1938; children: Franklin Page, Joseph Bryan. *Education:* Marshall College, A.B. (summa cum laude), 1934; University of Nebraska, A.M., 1935; further graduate study at University of North Carolina, 1935-36, and University of Chicago, 1936; Princeton University, A.M., 1937, Ph.D., 1938. *Religion:* Baptist. *Residence:* Bethesda, Md.

CAREER: Princeton University, Princeton, N.J., instructor in politics, 1936-37, fellow, 1937-38, instructor, 1938-39, research associate with Princeton Local Government Survey, 1939-40; Butler University, Indianapolis, Ind., 1940-46, began as assistant professor, became associate professor; University of Maryland, College Park, associate professor, 1946-47, professor of government and politics, 1947-75, head of department, 1950-54, director of Bureau of Governmental Research, 1956-75. Lecturer at American University, 1948-49. Executive secretary of National Foundation for Education in American Citizenship, 1940-46, editor of publications, 1946-50; member of board of directors of Operations and Policy Research, Inc. Member of Indiana War History Commission, 1943-46. Member of board of directors of Institute for American Universities at University of Aix-Marseille, 1958-75. Chief of Information Center Service of U.S. Information Agency, 1954-56; chairman of Maryland governor's Commission on the Reapportionment of the Legislature, 1962-64; member of Maryland State Constitutional Convention Commission, 1965-67, delegate to the convention, 1967-68. Trustee of Westminster Choir College and Montgomery College.

MEMBER: Foreign Policy Association (member of Indianapolis branch), American Society for International Law, American Historical Association, American Political Science Association (president of Washington chapter, 1950-51; member of national council, 1962-64), American Society for Public Administration (official observer in Iraq, 1957; president of Maryland chapter, 1958-59), National Civil Service League (member of council), National Municipal League, Sons of the American Revolution (vice-president general of national society, 1933-38), Association of College Honor Societies (president, 1969-71), Council on Islamic Affairs (member of board of directors, 1957-60), Middle States Council for the Social Studies (president, 1953-54), Southern Political Science Association (vice-president, 1952), Indiana Merit Association (member of board of directors, 1941-46), Kappa Delta Pi, Phi Alpha Theta, Phi Kappa Phi, Pi Sigma Alpha (national president, 1956-58; national director, 1960-75), Masons. *Awards, honors:* LL.D. from Marshall College, 1959.

WRITINGS: Filibustering in the Senate, Princeton University Press, 1940, Russell, 1965; (editor) *Education for Citizen Responsibilities: The Roles of Anthropology, Economics, Geography, History, Philosophy, Political Science, Psychology, Sociology,* Princeton University, for National Foundation for Education in American Citizenship, 1942; *Education for Citizenship,* American Council on Public Affairs, 1942; *Political Parties: An American Way,* National Foundation for Education in American Citizenship and Public Affairs Committee, 1945; *Lobbyists in Action: How Strings Are Pulled,* National Capitol Publishers, 1950; *Election Processes in Maryland,* Bureau of Public Administration, University of Maryland, 1950; *The West Virginia Delegation to the Republican National Convention,* Department of Government and Politics, University of Maryland, 1953; (editor) *Readings for Republicans,* Oceana, 1960; *Political Science: A Selected Bibliography of Books in Print,* Bureau of Governmental Research, University of Maryland, 1961;

The Republican Party: A Short History, Van Nostrand, 1968, 2nd edition, 1972.

Editor of political science series for Van Nostrand, 1948-75; co-editor of historical monographs on religion and American institutions, 1947-49. Contributor to political science journals. Editor of *Biographical Directory* of the American Political Science Association, 1945-48, 1961; member of editorial board of *American Political Science Review,* 1948-49; chairman of editorial board of *World Affairs,* 1965-75; advisory editor of *Encyclopedia Americana,* 1968-75.

OBITUARIES: Washington Post, August 12, 1975.*

(Died August 8, 1975, in Maryland)

*   *   *

BURGE, Ethel   1916-

PERSONAL: Born February 5, 1916, in Chicago, Ill.; daughter of Lon Freeze (an electrician) and Alma (Paape) Corriher; married: Floyd Burge (an electrical engineer), June 28, 1941; children: Jeffery L., Jon G. *Education:* Attended Chicago College of Commerce and Northwestern University. *Politics:* Independent. *Religion:* Unitarian-Universalist. *Home and office:* 5 East 103 Carriage Way, Hazel Crest, Ill. 60429. *Agent:* Eleanor Langdon, 457 West Oakdale, Chicago, Ill. 60657.

CAREER: Woman's Whirl, Chicago, Ill., executive director, 1958-62; *Chicago Daily News,* Chicago, Ill., columnist, 1963-65; Dartnell Publishing Co., Chicago, Ill., fashion editor, 1970—.

WRITINGS: This Business of Dressing, Dartnell, 1972. Author of columns, "Feminine Spotlight," 1957-63, for Lerner papers, and "The Fashion Strip," 1970, and "Peacock Alley," 1974, both for Dartnell Publishing, Co.

WORK IN PROGRESS: Two books, *The Personal Colorscope* and *What is Your Success Quotient?*

*   *   *

BURK, Bill E(ugene)   1932-

PERSONAL: Born November 11, 1932, in Memphis, Tenn.; son of Earnest Coy (a dairy salesperson) and Josephine (Passene) Burk; married: Frances Waters (an editor), August 24, 1956; children: Gary, Michael, Jennifer, Randall. *Education:* Memphis State University, B.S., 1957. *Politics:* Independent. *Religion:* Roman Catholic. *Residence:* Memphis, Tenn. *Office: Memphis Press-Scimitar,* 495 Union, Memphis, Tenn. 38101.

CAREER: Pacific Stars & Stripes, Tokyo, Japan, sports writer, 1953-54; United Press International (UPI), Memphis, Tenn., writer, 1955-57; *Memphis Press-Scimitar,* Memphis, Tenn., author of column "Good Evening," 1957—. Editor of *Propwash,* 1961—; covered the civil rights movement from 1962 to 1968, including the riots at the University of Mississippi and the assassination of Martin Luther King, Jr. *Military service:* U.S. Air National Guard, 1951—, active duty, with U.S. Air Force, 1951-54; served in Vietnam; received Air Medal and commendation medal.

MEMBER: Aircraft Owners and Pilots Association, National Guard Association of the United States. *Awards, honors:* Named aviation man of the year by local chapter of Experimental Aircraft Association, 1965, and by state chapter of Ninety-Nines, 1976.

WRITINGS: (With Dean Sylvester) *One-on-One* (nonfiction), Murdock, 1974. Contributor to airline and aviation magazines, including *Flying* and *AOPA Pilot,* and to *Sporting News.*

WORK IN PROGRESS: Research for biographies of three well-known industry leaders.

SIDELIGHTS: Burk is a pilot with more than seventy-five hundred hours in the air. He has flown over and traveled in every continent except Australia. *Avocational interests:* Sports, coaching baseball.

*   *   *

BURKE, Carol   1950-

PERSONAL: Born February 12, 1950, in Tahawus, N.Y.; daughter of Raymond and Grace (a teacher; maiden name, Sayer) Burke; married Jerome Christensen (a college professor), August 17, 1974. *Education:* Attended University of Durham, 1968, and Simmons College, 1968-69; Earlham College, B.A. (honors), 1972; Cornell University, M.F.A., 1974. *Home:* 1571 West State St., West Lafayette, Ind. 47906.

CAREER: Cornell University, Ithaca, N.Y., instructor in English and women's studies, 1973-75; Purdue University, West Lafayette, Ind., instructor in English, 1975—. Instructor at State University of New York College at Cortland, 1975. Poet-in-residence of Indiana Arts Commission, 1975—. Has given readings from her own works.

WRITINGS: Close Quarters (poems), Ithaca House, 1975; (editor) *Do You Have to Listen to Everything* (writing ideas for teaching creative writing), PITS Press, 1976. Contributor of poems to literary journals, including *Hiram Review, Remington Review, North Stone Review, Epoch, Rapport,* and *Penny Dreadful.* Associate editor, *Indiana Writes,* 1976—.

WORK IN PROGRESS: A second book of poems; a book on teaching creative writing; editing an anthology of children's writing.

SIDELIGHTS: Carol Burke writes: "As an undergraduate I attended a Quaker college, one which convinced me to change from a pre-med student to an English major. Despite such a change, the human body has remained an important source of imagery for my poems (as it is for many women poets)." *Avocational interests:* Travel (Europe, Northern and Western Africa).

*   *   *

BURKE, J(ackson) F.   1915-

PERSONAL: Born August 6, 1915, in Alameda, Calif.; son of Francis Frederick (an actor) and Elizabeth (Wood) Burke; married Rose de Sa Aleixo (a writer), December 25, 1958. *Education:* University of California, Berkeley, B.A., 1944. *Religion:* Roman Catholic. *Home:* 301 Forepeak Ave., Beachwood, N.J. 08722. *Agent:* Oscar Collier, Seligmann & Collier, 280 Madison Ave., New York, N.Y. 10016.

CAREER: University of California, Berkeley, member of faculty; magazine editor.

WRITINGS: Noah (novel), Bantam, 1969; *Location Shots* (novel), Harper, 1974; *Death Trick* (novel), Harper, 1975. Contributor of more than one hundred stories and poems to magazines.

WORK IN PROGRESS: Juana, a novel based on the life of Sor Juana Ines de la Cruz, the seventeenth-century Mexican poet and first defender of women's rights in the New World.

SIDELIGHTS: Burke writes: "When I was eighteen my teachers told me I was a poet, so I abandoned plans for a career in science and pursued poetry. During the 1930's I wrote a lot of formal verse. Meanwhile I came to recognize my interest in prose narrative, and by 1945 I had written a novel. Another in 1947. Alan Swallow bought them.''

* * *

BURKETT, David (Young III) 1934-

PERSONAL: Born July 7, 1934, in Pittsburgh, Pa.; son of David Young, Jr. and Faith (Espy) Burkett. *Education:* Northwestern University, B.S.J., 1956, M.S.J. (with highest distinction), 1957; graduate study at U.S. Department of State Foreign Service Institute, 1959. *Religion:* Lutheran. *Home:* 1235 East Mulberry, #305F, San Antonio, Tex. 78209. *Office:* Department of Journalism, Broadcasting, and Film, Trinity University, 715 Stadium Dr., San Antonio, Tex. 78284.

CAREER: Valley Daily News, Tarentum, Pa., reporter, 1956-57; *Black Diamond* (magazine), Chicago, Ill., writer, 1957; KITE, San Antonio, Tex., newscaster, 1965-69; Trinity University, San Antonio, Tex., public relations agent, 1960-70, instructor, 1960-70, assistant professor, 1970-75, associate professor of communication, 1975—. Member of faculty of Short Course for Professional Writers, University of Oklahoma, 1973-75. Consultant to business and to Texas Commission on Alcoholism, and Office of Education Drug Rehabilitation Program. *Military service:* U.S. Air Force, chief of internal information, Air Training Command, 1957-60. U.S. Air Force Reserves, chief of information for Central Air Force Reserve Region, 1960—; current rank, major.

MEMBER: International Communication Association, International Association of Business Communicators, Association for Education in Journalism, American College Public Relations Association, Association for Humanistic Psychology, Reserve Officers Association of the United States, Alamo Business Communicators, Armed Forces Information Council of San Antonio, Sigma Delta Chi. *Awards, honors:* Reserve Information Officer of the Year in the United States, 1973.

WRITINGS: Declare Yourself: Discovering the Me in Relationships, Spectrum, 1975. Contributor to *San Antonio, Techniques, Quill, Airman, Mirage,* and public relations and journalism periodicals.

WORK IN PROGRESS: Two books, one on humanistic approaches to teaching journalism and communication on the high school and college level and the other on the re-exploration of creativity among high school and college students.

* * *

BURNHAM, Dorothy E(dith) 1921-

PERSONAL: Born October 23, 1921, in New Haven, Conn.; daughter of Henry (a farmer and builder) and Charlotte (Zimmerman) Steller; married Ernest W. Bemis, September 11, 1948 (divorced, 1958); married Lawrence E. Burnham (a salesman), February 16, 1963; children: (first marriage) Nancy Jean (Mrs. Thomas Anspach). *Education:* Completed elementary school. *Politics:* Republican. *Religion:* Congregationalist. *Home:* 138 Carl Ave., Brockton, Mass. 02402.

CAREER: Writer.

WRITINGS: Life's Adventures in Poetry, Branden Press, 1975.

WORK IN PROGRESS: Poems.

SIDELIGHTS: Mrs. Burnham told *CA:* "The disappoint-

ments in my life have been deep and personal, and my poetry has, as I understand it now, given me the means not only to endure the hurts but also to prevail, to win over all, to find a greater strength inside to live in faith and relative pleasure. The value of my writing is in the sincerity of its truth; and because that truth captures the heart of the common man, its universality is in its simple capacity to express the sorrows and joys of the Everyman, to let him understand he's not alone after all.''

AVOCATIONAL INTERESTS: Snow skiing, winter camping, rock-hunting, gardening, bird-watching, knitting, crocheting, sewing, carpentry, upholstering, leather working, electrical work, mechanical work.

* * *

BURNS, Joan Simpson 1927-

PERSONAL: Born September 20, 1927, in Boulder, Colo.; daughter of George Gaylord ("an evolutionist") and Anne (a psychologist; maiden name, Roe) Simpson; married James MacGregor Burns (a political scientist), September 7, 1969; children: Trienah Anne Meyers, Peter Alexander Meyers. *Education:* University of Michigan, B.A., 1950. *Home and office:* High Mowing, Bee Hill Rd., Williamstown, Mass. 02167.

CAREER: Partisan Review, New York, N.Y., member of staff, 1959-60; Readers' Subscription Book Club, New York City, managing editor, 1961-63; Basic Books, New York City, editor, 1961-63; Columbia Broadcasting System-Columbia Records, New York City, special projects editor, 1963-65; Harcourt, Brace, Jovanovich, Inc., New York City, trade editor, 1966-67; full-time writer, 1967—. Member of board of directors of Massachusetts Arts and Humanities Foundation, 1976—. *Member:* Authors Guild of Authors League of America.

WRITINGS: (Editor) *John Fitzgerald Kennedy As We Remember Him,* Atheneum, 1965; *Poems and a Libretto,* Swallow Press, 1965; (with George Whitaker) *Dinosaur Hunt* (non-fiction), Harcourt, 1965; *The Awkward Embrace* (non-fiction), Knopf, 1975. Contributor of articles, short stories and poems to journals, including *Berkshire Review, American Scholar, Upcountry,* and *Berkshire Eagle.* Consultant to *Cultural Affairs,* journal of the Associated Arts Council, 1966.

WORK IN PROGRESS: Cloud, fiction; *Properties,* fiction, completion expected in 1980; poems.

* * *

BURNSIDE, Wesley M(ason) 1918-

PERSONAL: Born November 6, 1918, in Mount Pleasant, Utah; son of Mason N. and Fannie (Bills) Burnside. *Education:* Brigham Young University, B.S., 1941, M.S., 1949; further study at Art Institute of Chicago, 1946, Art Students League, 1949, and University of California, Los Angeles, 1955-58; Ohio State University, Ph.D., 1970. *Politics:* Republican. *Religion:* Church of Jesus Christ of Latter-Day Saints (Mormons). *Home:* 605 Sagewood, Provo, Utah 84601. *Office:* Department of Art and Design, Brigham Young University, Provo, Utah 84602.

CAREER: High school art teacher in Sterling, Colo., 1947-48; Idaho State University, Pocatello, instructor in art history, 1948-55; Brigham Young University, Provo, Utah, professor of art history, 1958—. *Military service:* U.S. Army Air Forces, 1943-46; served in the South Pacific.

WRITINGS: Maynard Dixon: Artist of the West, Brigham Young University Press, 1974.

WORK IN PROGRESS: Ebon Comins: Painter of Indians; research on the history of early Utah artists.

* * *

BURROUGHS, Ben(jamin F.) 1918-

PERSONAL: Born May 27, 1918, in Philadelphia, Pa.; son of Samie Burroughs; married wife, Grace, December 5, 1949; children: Carol Ellen, Kenneth Hough, Mark Van Leuven. *Home:* 137 Valley Run Dr., Cherry Hill, N.J. 08034. *Office:* 250 Park Ave., New York, N.Y. 10017.

CAREER: Writer of verse, 1947—. Worked as coppersmith in Philadelphia Naval Yard, Philadelphia, Pa., and as government employee at Philadelphia Defense Personnel Support Center, Philadelphia. *Military service:* U.S. Army Air Forces.

WRITINGS: Sketches, Fleet Press, 1968; *New Sketches,* Fleet Press, 1969; *Treasury of Sketches,* Fleet Press, 1970; *Things of the Heart* (includes *Sketches* and *New Sketches*), Fleet Press, 1973.

Writer of syndicated daily verse feature, "Sketches," 1948—.

SIDELIGHTS: Ben Burroughs told *CA* that his syndicated verse appears daily in some seventy newspapers. He estimates that he has written over eight thousand verses in his more than twenty five years in steady publication.

BIOGRAPHICAL/CRITICAL SOURCES: Writer's Digest, October, 1970.*

* * *

BURROUGHS, Jean Mitchel 1908-

PERSONAL: Born December 4, 1908, in Bonham, Tex.; daughter of Harry H. (a dentist) and Jane Read (Page) Mitchell; married John Burroughs (a radio executive), June 14, 1935; children: Jane (Mrs. Robert Downs), Nan (Mrs. John Anthony), Karen (Mrs. Herbert Marchman), Belinda. *Education:* Texas Technological University, student, 1928-29; Texas Woman's University, B.A., 1930; graduate study at University of Texas, 1935, and Eastern New Mexico University, 1957-58. *Politics:* Democrat. *Religion:* Presbyterian. *Home:* 1505 South Abilene, Portales, N.M. 88130.

CAREER: Eastern New Mexico University, Portales, adjunct professor of local and oral history, 1972—. Member of board of directors of New Mexico Garden Clubs (past president), and National Council of State Garden Clubs. *Member:* National League of American Pen Women (Albuquerque vice-president, 1975-76), Western Writers of America, New Mexico Poetry Society (vice-president, 1975-76), Roosevelt Historical Society (president), Portales Garden Club (past president), Portales Woman's Club (president). *Awards, honors:* National League of American Pen Women, first place in poetry from southwest region, 1971, second place in children's literature, 1976, for *Children of Destiny;* finalist for Spur award from Western Writers of America, 1976, for *Children of Destiny.*

WRITINGS: Children of Destiny (juvenile), Sunstone Press, 1975; (editor) *Roosevelt County: History and Heritage,* Bishop, 1975. Contributor to regional, gardening, and juvenile magazines, including *Young World, Highlights for Children,* and *Wee Wisdom,* and to *Viva.* Member of board of directors of *Southwest Heritage.*

WORK IN PROGRESS: A historical novel, based on the Mexican War, 1846-47; a biography of trail drivers in New Mexico and Texas in the late 1870's.

SIDELIGHTS: Jean Burroughs writes: "I am quite involved in research, writing and speaking on early history of this area of New Mexico where I have lived the last thirty years. My husband's term as governor of the state awoke my interest in the remarkable history of this state where Indian, Spanish and Anglo cultures live in harmony. I began writing . . . when my family of girls were living and working elsewhere."

* * *

BURROWS, William E. 1937-

PERSONAL: Born March 27, 1937, in Philadelphia, Pa.; son of Eli and Helen (Marino) Burrows; married Joelle Hodgson (an art historian), November 19, 1966; children: Lara. *Education:* Columbia University, B.A., 1960, M.A., 1962. *Politics:* "Ultra right-wing liberal." *Home:* 154 Burns St., Forest Hills, N.Y. 11375. *Office:* Department of Journalism, New York University, 100 Washington Sq. East, New York, N.Y. 10003.

CAREER: New York Times, New York, N.Y., news assistant, 1962-65; *Richmond Times-Dispatch,* Richmond, Va., reporter, 1965-66; *Washington Post,* Washington, D.C., reporter, 1966-67; *New York Times,* New York City, reporter, 1967-68; *Wall Street Journal,* New York City, reporter, 1968-70; Puerto de Pollensa, Mallorca, Spain, travel writer, 1971-73; New York University, New York City, assistant professor of journalism, 1974—. *Member:* American Academy of Political and Social Science, Authors Guild, Association for Education in Journalism, National Political Science Honor Society, Pi Sigma Alpha, Kappa Tau Alpha.

WRITINGS: Richthofen (Military Book Club selection), Harcourt, 1969; *Vigilante!,* Harcourt, 1976; *On Reporting the News,* New York University Press, 1977. Contributor of articles to *New York Times, New York, Holiday, Potomac, Harvard,* and other periodicals.

SIDELIGHTS: "My primary motivations," Burrows told *CA,* "are to contribute to my society while challenging myself through my writing and teaching. That means trying to get the best out of myself all the time. I have come to understand in the course of my professional life that ultimate competition is not with others, but with myself, and that is the toughest competition imaginable. I have to live with myself and be responsible to myself, so if I care about my integrity as an artist and a human being, I need to push up my level of competence all the time. I try to do that by avoiding what is easy or only commercial, and instead attacking what is important and challenging."

* * *

BURTON, (Alice) Elizabeth 1908-
(Susan Alice Kerby)

PERSONAL: Born October 4, 1908, in Cairo, Egypt; daughter of Richard and A.S.G. (Kerby) Burton; married John Theodore Aitken (divorced). *Politics:* Liberal. *Religion:* Church of England. *Agent:* John Farquharson Ltd., 15 Red Lion Sq., London WC1R 4QW, England.

CAREER: Writer.

WRITINGS: Cling to Her, Waiting (novel), Andrew Dakers, 1939; *The Elizabethans at Home: On Everyday Life in the Time of Elizabeth I,* Secker & Warburg, 1958, published as *The Pageant of Elizabethan England,* Scribner, 1959; *The Pageant of Stuart England,* Scribner, 1962 (published in England as *The Jacobeans at Home,* Secker & Warburg, 1962); *Here Is England,* Farrar, Straus, 1965; *The Geor-*

gians at Home, 1714-1830, Longmans, Green, 1967, published as *The Pageant of Georgian England*, Scribner, 1968; *The Pageant of Early Victorian England, 1837-1861*, Scribner, 1972 (published in England as *The Early Victorians at Home*, Longman, 1972); *The Early Tudors at Home*, Alan Lane, 1976, published as *The Pageant of Early Tudor England*, Scribner, in press.

Novels; under pseudonym Susan Alice Kerby: *Fortnight in Frascati*, Andrew Dakers, 1940; *Miss Carter and the Ifrit*, Hutchinson, 1945; *Many Strange Birds*, Hutchinson, 1947; *Fortune's Gift*, Dodd, 1947; *The Roaring Dove*, Dodd, 1948 (published in England as *Gone to Grass*, Hutchinson, 1948); *Mr. Kronion*, Werner Laurie, 1949.

Contributor to magazines and newspapers.

WORK IN PROGRESS: A history of health from primitive man to the present day.

* * *

BURTON, John A(ndrew)   1944-

PERSONAL: Born April 2, 1944, in London, England; son of Andrew (a portrait painter) and Edna (Ede) Burton. *Education:* Educated in public school in London, England. *Religion:* Atheist. *Home:* 28A Filmer Rd., London S.W.6, England. *Agent:* Murray Pollinger, Murray Pollinger Ltd., 4 Garrick St., London WC2E 9BH, England. *Office:* Fauna Preservation Society, Zoological Gardens, Regents Park, London N.W.1, England.

CAREER: British Museum of Natural History, London, England, assistant information officer, 1963-69; assistant editor, *Birds of the World*, 1969-71, *Animals*, 1971-72; editor, *Birds International* (journal of British section of International Council for Bird Preservation), 1972-75; Fauna Preservation Society, London, assistant secretary, 1975—. Director of Foe Publicity. Natural history consultant to Friends of the Furth Ltd. *Member:* International Union for the Conservation of Nature and Natural Resources, British Ornithological Union, Society for the Study of Amphibians and Reptiles, Mammal Society, Linnean Society (fellow), Otter Trust (council member), Tetrapods Club.

WRITINGS: The How and Why of Extinct Animals, Transworld, 1972, Wonder, 1974; *Birds of the Tropics*, Crown, 1973; (editor) *Owls of the World*, Dutton, 1973; *Naturalist in London*, David & Charles, 1974; *The How and Why Book of Fossils*, Transworld, 1974, Grosset, 1976; (with John Sparks) *Worlds Apart: Nature in the City*, Doubleday, 1976; *Musical Instruments from Odds and Ends*, Carousel, 1976; (with E. N. Arnold and Denys Ovenden) *Field Guide to Reptiles and Amphibians of Europe*, Collins, in press. Contributor to science magazines and conservation journals, including *New Scientist* and *Birds International*.

WORK IN PROGRESS: Research on wildlife and wildlife conservation.

* * *

BURTON, Maurice   1898-

PERSONAL: Born March 28, 1898, in London, England; son of William Francis and Jane Burton; married Margaret Rosalie Maclean, 1928; children: Richard Francis, Jane Mary, Robert Wellesley. *Education:* University of London, D.Sc., 1934. *Home:* Weston House, Albury, Guildford, Surrey GU5 9AE, England.

CAREER: Latymer Foundation, Hammersmith, London, England, biology master, 1924-27; British Museum of Nat-

ural History, London, 1927-58, began as assistant keeper, became deputy keeper in zoology department; free-lance writer, 1928—. *Member:* Royal Society of Arts (fellow), Zoological Society (fellow).

WRITINGS—Adult books: (Co-author) *The Science of Living Things*, Odhams, 1928; (co-editor and contributor) *Standard Natural History*, Warne, 1931; (editor) Jan Vlasak and Josef Seget, *Snow White: Story of a Polar Bear Cub*, Hodge, 1949, published as *Snowy: Story of a Polar Bear Cub*, Schuman, 1951; *The Story of Animal Life*, two volumes, Elsevier, 1949.

Curiosities of Animal Life, Ward Lock, 1952, R. M. McBride, 1956, revised edition, 1959; *Animal Courtship*, Hutchinson, 1953, Praeger, 1954; *Margins of the Sea*, Harper, 1954; *Living Fossils*, Thames & Hudson, 1954; *Animal Legends*, Muller, 1955, Coward, 1957; *Infancy in Animals*, Roy, 1956; *Phoenix Re-Born*, Hutchinson, 1959; *More Animal Legends*, Muller, 1959; *Sponges*, British Museum, 1959.

Under the Sea, F. Watts, 1960; *Wild Animals of the British Isles: A Guide to the Mammals, Reptiles, and Batrachians of Wayside and Woodland*, Warne, 1960; (co-author) *The Glorious Oyster*, Sidgwick & Jackson, 1960; *Animal Senses*, Routledge & Kegan Paul, 1961; *The Elusive Monster: An Analysis of the Evidence from Loch Ness*, Hart-Davies, 1961; *Introducing Life under the Sea*, Spring Books, 1961; *Systematic Dictionary of Mammals of the World*, Crowell, 1962, published as *University Dictionary of Mammals of the World*, 1968 (2nd edition published in England as *Dictionary of the World's Mammals*, Sphere, 1970); (with K. Nixon) *Bird Families*, Warne, 1962; *A Revision of the Classification of the Calcareous Sponges*, British Museum of Natural History, 1963; *Meadows and the Forest Margin*, Doubleday, 1965; *Nature in Motion*, Doubleday, 1966; (editor and contributor) *Nature: The Realm of Animals and Plants*, Grolier, 1966; *Weapons*, Doubleday, 1966; *Nature's Architects*, Doubleday, 1967; (co-editor and contributor) *Larousse Encyclopedia of Animal Life*, Hamlyn, 1967; *Wild Animals of the British Isles*, Warne, 1968; *The Hedgehog*, Deutsch, 1969, Transatlantic, 1970.

(Editor) *The Shell Natural History of Britain*, Rainbird, 1970; *Observer's Book of Wild Animals*, Warne, 1971; (editor) *World of Wildlife*, Orbis, 1971; (editor) *Encyclopedia of the Animal World*, Elsevier, 1972; (editor) *Encyclopedia of Animals in Colour*, Octopus, 1972; *The Sixth Sense of Animals*, Taplinger, 1973; *Animals of Europe: The Ecology of the Wildlife*, Holt, 1973; *The World of Reptiles and Amphibians*, Crown, 1973; (with Jane Burton) *The Colourful World of Animals*, Sundial, 1974; *How Mammals Live*, Elsevier, 1975; *Maurice Burton's The Daily Telegraph Nature Book*, David & Charles, 1975.

Juveniles: *Animals and Their Behaviour*, Arnold, 1950; *The Elephant*, Gawthorn Press, 1951; *The Ox*, Gawthorn Press, 1951; *The Reindeer*, Gawthorn Press, 1951; *The Camel*, Gawthorn Press, 1951; *The Ass*, Gawthorn Press, 1951; *The Sheep*, Gawthorn Press, 1951; *When Dumb Animals Talk*, Hutchinson, 1955; *The True Book about Animals*, Muller, 1956; *Animal Families*, Routledge & Kegan Paul, 1958; *British Mammals*, Oxford University Press, 1958; *Life in the Deep*, Roy, 1958; *The True Book about the Seas*, Muller, 1959.

(Editor and contributor) *The Wonder Book of Animals*, Ward Lock, 1960; *In Their Element: The Story of Water Mammals*, Abelard, 1960; *Mammals of the Countryside*, Wheaton, 1960; *Wild Animals and Birds of the World*, Longacre Press, 1960; *Birds and Beasts of Field and Jungle,* Odhams, 1960; *The True Book about Prehistoric Animals,* Muller, 1961, 2nd edition published as *Prehistoric Animals,* International Publications Service, 1974; *The True Book about Deserts,* Muller, 1961, 2nd edition published as *Deserts,* International Publications Service, 1974; *More Mammals of the Countryside,* Wheaton, 1961; *Water Creatures,* Longacre Press, 1961; *Baby Animals,* Longacre Press, 1961; *Birds,* Gawthorn Press, 1961; *Mammals,* Gawthorn Press, 1961; (with E. W. Groves) *The Wonder Book of Nature,* Ward Lock, 1961; *Reptiles and Amphibians of the World,* Longacre Press, 1962, 2nd edition, 1971; *Birds of Britain,* Odhams, 1962, 2nd edition, 1971; *Mammals of Great Britain,* Odhams, 1962; *The True Book of the Seashore,* Muller, 1963; (with W. B. Shepherd) *The Wonder Book of Our Earth,* Ward Lock, 1963; *Young Animals,* Hamlyn, 1964; *The Zoo Book,* Bancroft, 1966; (editor) *Animal World in Colour,* Volume 1: *Artists and Entertainers,* Volume 2: *Explorers and Wanderers,* Volume 3: *Animal Eccentrics,* Volume 4: *Animal Oddities,* Volume 5: *Builders and Breakers,* Volume 6: *Comrades and Companions,* Volume 7: *Hunters: Mammals,* Volume 8: *Hunters: Birds, Fish, and Amphibians,* Volume 9: *Hunters: Reptiles, Insects, and Invertebrates,* Volume 10: *Animal Specialists,* Volume 11: *Unusual Feeders,* Volume 12: *Sleep and Hibernation,* Odhams, 1966, Children's Press, 1969; *Animals,* Oxford University Press, 1966, F. Watts, 1968; *The Animal World: Birds, Fish, Reptiles [and] Insects,* F. Watts, 1968; *The Sea's Inhabitants,* Golden Press, 1968; *More Animals,* F. Watts, 1968; *Animal Partnerships,* Warne, 1969; *Animals of Australia,* Abedlard, 1969.

Maurice Burton's Book of Nature, Purnell, 1971, 3rd edition, 1974; *The Life of Birds,* edited by Angela Littler, Macdonald, 1972, Golden Press, 1974; *The Life of Fishes,* edited by Littler, Macdonald, 1972, Golden Press, 1974; *The Life of Insects,* Macdonald, 1972, Golden Press, 1974; *The Life of Meat Eaters,* Macdonald, 1973, Golden Press, 1974; *The Life of Reptiles and Amphibians,* Golden Press, 1974; *First Encyclopedia of Animals,* Purnell, 1974.

General editor, *Oxford Junior Encyclopaedia,* Volume II: *Natural History,* 1949; general editor with Robert Burton, and contributor: *Purnell's Encyclopedia of Animal Life,* BPC Publishing, 1968-70, published as *The International Wildlife Encyclopedia,* 1970, four volume edition, Octopus, 1974; general editor, *The World Encyclopedia of Animals,* 1972. Nature correspondent for *Daily Telegraph,* 1949—. Contributor to *Junior Science Encyclopedia* and to scientific journals. Science editor, *Illustrated London News,* 1946-64.

AVOCATIONAL INTERESTS: Gardening.

BIOGRAPHICAL/CRITICAL SOURCES: Observer, February 8, 1970.

*   *   *

BUSBY, F. M. 1921-

PERSONAL: Born March 11, 1921, in Indianapolis, Ind.; son of F. M., Sr. (a teacher) and Clara (a teacher; maiden name, Nye) Busby; married Elinor Doub (a medical secretary), April 28, 1954; children: Michele B. *Education:* Washington State University, B.Sc., 1946, B.Sc.E.E., 1947. *Politics:* "Eclectic; consider issues individually." *Religion:* "Much the same...." *Home and office:* 2852 14th Ave. W., Seattle, Wash. 98119.

CAREER: Alaska Communication System, Headquarters, Seattle, Wash., "trick chief" and project supervisor, 1947-53, telegraph engineer, 1953-70; writer, 1970—. *Military service:* National Guard, active Army duty, 1940-41. U.S.

Army, 1943-45. *Member:* Science Fiction Writers of America (vice-president, 1974-76), Authors Guild and Authors League of America, Seattle Freelances.

WRITINGS—All science fiction: *Cage a Man* (Science Fiction Book Club selection), New American Library, 1974; *The Proud Enemy,* Berkley, 1975; *Rissa Kerguelen,* Putnam, 1976; *The Long View,* Putnam, 1976; *All These Earths,* Putnam, in press.

Anthologized in *New Dimensions 3,* edited by Robert Silverberg, New American Library, 1973; *Best Science Fiction of the Year,* edited by Terry Carr, Ballantine, 1974; *Universe 5,* edited by Terry Carr, Random House, 1974; *Golden Age,* second series, edited by Brian Aldiss, Futura (London), 1975; *Best Science Fiction of the Year,* edited by Lester del Ray, Dutton, 1976.

Contributor of about thirty stories to science fiction magazines and story collections.

WORK IN PROGRESS: Zelde M'Tana, a science fiction novel; short stories.

SIDELIGHTS: Busby writes: "I 'played' with writing off-and-on for years before the chance came to take early retirement and try it in earnest. I like to deal with characters who are pushed hard by necessity and who generally manage to cope, more than not. Science fiction allows me to put characters into predicaments that could not exist in our own past and present; I like the challenge, and enjoy working with it."

*   *   *

BUSH, Eric 1899-

PERSONAL: Born August 12, 1899, in Simla, India; son of Herbert Wheeler (a clergyman and military chaplain) and Edith Cornelia (Cardew) Bush; married Mollie Noel Watts, 1938; children: Mark Eric Wheeler, Phillip John Wheeler. *Education:* Attended Royal Navy Colleges at Osborne and Dartmouth, 1912-14. *Politics:* Conservative. *Religion:* Church of England. *Home:* Hunters, Langton Green, Kent, England.

CAREER: Royal Navy, career officer; served in the North Sea and the Mediterranean until 1918, participated in the surrender of the German fleet in 1918, served in the Baltic, sometimes as Hindustani interpreter, and in the Orient, 1918-37, commanded cruiser H.M.S. *Devonshire,* 1937-39, commanded cruiser H.M.S. *Euryalus,* 1941-45, commanded battleship H.M.S. *Malaya* in Normandy and later in the Far East, during 1940's, participated in signing the surrender of Japanese forces, commanded the training ship H.M.S. *Ganges,* and retired as captain; served as commander of Sea Corps Cadets, and as general manager of Red Ensign Club, Stepney, London, England; full-time writer, 1971—. Has appeared on British Broadcasting Corp. (BBC) radio and television broadcasts. *Member:* Burma Star Association. *Awards, honors*—Military: Distinguished Service Order with two bars; mentioned in dispatches.

WRITINGS: How to Become a Naval Officer, Gieves, 1926, Allen & Unwin, 1963; *Bless Our Ship* (Book Society recommendation), Allen & Unwin, 1958; *The Flowers of the Sea,* Allen & Unwin, 1962, Naval Institute Press, 1970; *Salute the Soldier,* Allen & Unwin, 1966; *Gallipoli,* Allen & Unwin, 1975.

AVOCATIONAL INTERESTS: Yachting (won five Fastnet Ocean Races).

*   *   *

BUSH, Sargent, Jr. 1937-

PERSONAL: Born September 22, 1937, in Flemington,

N.J.; son of Sargent (a clergyman) and Marion L. (Roberts) Bush; married Cynthia Bird Greig, June 18, 1960; children: Charles Sargent, James Jonathan. *Education:* Princeton University, A.B., 1959; University of Iowa, M.A., 1964, Ph.D., 1967. *Religion:* Presbyterian. *Residence:* Madison, Wis. *Office:* Department of English, University of Wisconsin, Madison, Wis. 53706.

CAREER: Washington & Lee University, Lexington, Va., assistant professor of English, 1967-71; University of Wisconsin, Madison, assistant professor, 1971-73, associate professor of English, 1973—. *Military service:* U.S. Army Reserve, active duty, 1959-60, 1961-62. *Member:* Modern Language Association of America, Nathaniel Hawthorne Society, Connecticut Historical Society. *Awards, honors:* National Endowment for the Humanities grant, summer, 1969; fellow of Cooperative Program in the Humanities, 1969-70; American Council of Learned Societies fellowship, 1974.

WRITINGS: (Editor and contributor) *Thomas Hooker: Writings in England and Holland, 1626-1633,* Harvard University Press, 1975. Contributor to literature and history journals. Member of editorial advisory board of *Literary Monographs* and *Resources for American Literary Study.*

WORK IN PROGRESS: Research on American Puritan literature, especially on the work of Thomas Hooker; research on the life and literary career of Nathaniel Hawthorne.

* * *

BUSKIN, Martin 1930-1976

July 9, 1930—February 8, 1976; American prize-winning educational editor, educator, journalist, and author. Obituaries: *New York Times,* February 9, 1976.

* * *

BUSTARD, Robert 1938-

PERSONAL: Born August 26, 1938, in Hong Kong; son of Harold Cecil and Rachel Murdoch (Reid) Bustard. *Education:* University of St. Andrews, B.Sc. (honors), 1961; Australian National University, Ph.D., 1965. *Home:* Airlie Brae, Alyth, Perthshire PH11 8AX, Scotland. *Office:* Food and Agriculture Organization 55, Lodi Estate, New Delhi 110003, India.

CAREER: Australian National University, Canberra, research fellow in population ecology, 1963-70; chairman and managing director of Australian Government companies, 1970-74; United Nations Food and Agriculture Organization, New Delhi, India, consultant and senior technical advisor, 1975—. *Member:* Australian Society of Authors, American Society of Ichthyologists, Herpetologists League (fellow), Fauna Preservation Society, British Herpetological Society. British Ecological Society, Wildlife Preservation Society of India, Bombay Natural History Society. *Awards, honors:* Robert B. Brown Literary Award, 1974, for *Sea Turtles.*

WRITINGS: Australian Lizards, Collins, 1970; *Sea Turtles,* Taplinger, 1973 (published in Australia as *Australian Sea Turtles,* Collins, 1973); *Kay's Turtles,* Collins, 1973. Contributor of several hundred popular articles and seventy scholarly papers to magazines and journals in his field.

WORK IN PROGRESS: Operating an Indian conservation program to save the crocodilian gharial from extinction, with published material expected to result; books to follow *Kay's Turtles.*

BUTLER, Jeffrey (Ernest) 1922-

PERSONAL: Born September 27, 1922, in Cradock, South Africa; came to the United States in 1957, naturalized citizen, 1966; son of Ernest Collett (a newspaper owner) and Alison (Stringer) Butler; married Valerie Joy de la Harpe, November 27, 1947; children: Katherine, Peter, Jonathan. *Education:* Rhodes University, B.A., 1947; Oxford University, M.A., 1956, D.Phil., 1963. *Home:* 296 Pine St., Middletown, Conn. 06457. *Office:* Department of History, Wesleyan University, Middletown, Conn. 06457.

CAREER: High school teacher of science in South Africa, 1947-50; Oxford University, Oxford, England, tutor for adult education classes, 1953-57; Boston University, Boston, Mass., assistant professor of government and research associate in African studies, 1957-64; Wesleyan University, Middletown, Conn., associate professor, 1964-68, professor of history, 1968—. Lecturer at Wellesley College, 1960-64; visiting associate professor of history at University of California, Los Angeles, 1964. *Military service:* South African Army, 1943-45; served in the Middle East and Italy. *Member:* American Historical Association, African Studies Association (fellow).

WRITINGS: The Liberal Party and the Jameson Raid, Clarendon Press, 1968; (editor with Leonard Thompson) *Change in Contemporary South Africa,* University of California Press, 1975; (with Robert Rolberg and John Adams) *The Black Homelands of South Africa,* University of California Press, 1977. Former editor of ''Boston University Papers on African History.''

WORK IN PROGRESS: A history of a South African town; editing memoirs of South African official, Sir Graham Bower, 1881-1897.

* * *

BUTLER, Jerry P. 1944-

PERSONAL: Born October 23, 1944, in Little Rock, Ark.; son of Coy Phillips (a utilities executive) and Florene (an executive secretary; maiden name, Mullens) Butler; married Ruth Sharon, March 30, 1962; children: Kinsey, Kyle, Koy. *Education:* Freed-Hardeman College, A.A., 1961; Harding College, B.A., 1963; Southern Illinois University, M.S., 1964, Ph.D., 1969; additional study at Wesleyan University. *Home:* 10312 Milkyway Dr., Mabelvale, Ark. 72103. *Office:* Department of Speech Communication, University of Arkansas at Little Rock, 33rd and University, Little Rock, Ark. 72204.

CAREER: High school teacher in West Frankfort, Ill., 1964-67; University of Arkansas, Little Rock, associate professor of speech communication, 1970—. *Member:* American Forensic Association, Speech Communication Association, Southern Speech Communication Association, Arkansas Speech Communication Association (president, 1974-75).

WRITINGS: Swift to Hear, Slow to Speak, Quality Printing, 1975.

AVOCATIONAL INTERESTS: Foster care programs, electrical work, community activities, fishing, camping, bicycling.

* * *

BUTLER, Joyce 1933-

PERSONAL: Born June 27, 1933, in Portland, Maine; daughter of Charles William Eaton (an accountant) and

Dorothy (King) Kelley; married G. Robert Butler (in retail sales), March 22, 1954; children: Leslie Joyce, Stephanie Sydna, James Kelley. *Education:* Westbrook College, A.A., 1953; Boston University, A.B., 1955. *Politics:* Republican. *Religion:* Protestant. *Home address:* Durrell's Bridge Rd., Kennebunk, Me. 04043.

CAREER: Writer. *Member:* Kennebunk Historical Society (curator, 1975—). *Awards, honors:* Hart Crane and Alice Crane Williams Memorial Fund Award from American Weave Press, 1969, for poem "Red Fox on Snow."

WRITINGS: Pages from a Journal, Mercer House Press, 1976. Author of pamphlet "The outh Congregational Church: An Architectural History," 1973. Columnist, "Pages from a Journal," 1968—, and "Kennebunkport Scrapbook," 1974—, both in *York County Coast Star.* Contributor to *Down East, Lady's Circle,* and *Christian Science Monitor.* Member of board of trustees of *Salt* (magazine).

WORK IN PROGRESS: Research for a book on the 1947 forest fires in Maine, for Durrell, completion expected in 1978.

SIDELIGHTS: Joyce Butler writes: "I am a writer who chose first to be a housewife/mother, with all the dedication, hard work, and community involvement that is a part of that vocation. My column is a recounting of my experiences in that job. Although *Pages* was begun to fulfill my need and desire to be a writer, it soon became important to me as a positive statement about the everyday life of the American family, which is more often portrayed as emotionally unhealthy and foundering. The ordinariness of my subject matter is its strength; my readers delight in finding their own experiences mirrored in those of my family. My ambition is to write fiction: short stories and children's books about 'real' people as opposed to romantic figures and anthropomorphic animals. It is my wish that all my writing reflect my belief in the importance and dignity of the commonplace."

AVOCATIONAL INTERESTS: Flower gardening, antiques (including houses), needlework.

*   *   *

BUTTACI, Sal(vatore) St. John   1941-

PERSONAL: Born June 12, 1941, in Corona, N.Y.; son of Michael S. (a welder) and Josephine (Amico) Buttaci; married Susan Linda Gerstle (a teacher and editor), March 9, 1974. *Education:* Seton Hall University, B.A. (cum laude), 1965; Montclair State College, teacher certification, 1970. *Politics:* Democrat. *Religion:* Roman Catholic (Charismatic Christian). *Home:* 100 Maple St., Apt. 21, Garfield, N.J. 07026.

CAREER: St. Anne's Elementary School, Fair Lawn, N.J., teacher of English and history, 1966-68, vice-principal, 1968-70, principal, 1970-71; public school teacher in Saddle Brook, N.J., 1971—. President, Carlin-Bennett Associates, Saddle Brook, 1975—. *Member:* Committee of Small Magazine Editors and Publishers, New Jersey Education Association, Saddle Brook Education Association.

WRITINGS: "For Heaven's Sake, Sweeney." (three-act play), first produced in Paramus, N.J., 1970; *Coming-Home Poems: Stops and Pauses on the Scrapbook Express,* New Worlds Unlimited, 1974; (editor with wife, Susan Linda Gerstle) *Echoes of the Unlocked Odyssey* (poetry anthology), New Worlds Unlimited, 1974; (editor with S. L. Gerstle) *Shadows of the Elusive Dream* (poetry anthology), New Worlds Unlimited, 1975; (with S. L. Gerstle) *Reflections of the Inward Silence* (poetry anthology), New Worlds

Unlimited, 1976. Also author of two-act play, "The Party," as yet neither published nor produced. Contributor of poems to *English Journal, Gallery Series IV, The Archer, Davidson Review* and other periodicals.

WORK IN PROGRESS: Editing another poetry anthology, with wife, Susan Linda Gerstle.

SIDELIGHTS: Buttaci told *CA:* "Writing is only half the hitch in the writing talent: the other half is needing others to love you through your work. This is my reason for wanting to write. The need for someone—anyone!—to read me in a poem, find where my blood flows and my heart pounds, and in finding, love me in a few kind words."

After an automobile accident, Buttaci was paralyzed for several months, a condition that he reported as cured following healing by Evangelist Kathryn Kuhlman.

*   *   *

BUXTON, Charles R(oberts)   1913-

PERSONAL: Born March 20, 1913, in Corvallis, Ore.; son of Harry E. and Lucille (Roberts) Buxton; married Janet Millard, September 12, 1937; children: Cynda Lou (Mrs. Philip Wilcox, Jr.), Charles R., Richard M., Janet. *Education:* Oregon State University, B.A., 1935. *Religion:* Presbyterian. *Home:* 5215 Sky Trail, Littleton, Colo. 80123. *Office: Denver Post,* 650 15th St., Denver, Colo. 80201.

CAREER/WRITINGS: Oregonian, Portland, Ore., reporter, 1935-37, sports news editor, 1937, picture editor, 1938, assistant news editor, 1939-40, night city editor, 1940-46; *Denver Post,* Denver, Colo., assistant business manager, 1946-50, advertising director, 1950-51, business manager, 1951-65, general manager, 1965-70, editor and publisher, 1970—, executive vice-president, 1971—. Member of board of directors of Denver Center for the Performing Arts, Denver Convention and Visitors' Bureau, Denver Research Institute (at University of Denver), Frederick G. Bonfils Foundation, Helen G. Bonfils Foundation, Institute of International Education, Listen Foundation, National Salvation Army Advisory Council, and National Conference of Christians and Jews; member of board of trustees of Denver Post Employees Stock Trust (president of board), and Midwest Research Institute; member of Association of Nieman Foundation. Past member of board of directors of Sunday Metro Newspapers, Institute of Newspaper Operations, Gravure Research Institute, and Gravure Technical Association. *Military service:* U.S. Army, Infantry, 1940-45; became lieutenant colonel; received Bronze Star and Silver Star with oak leaf cluster.

MEMBER: Inter-American Press Association, American Society of Newspaper Editors, American Newspaper Publishers Association (member of board of directors of its Newspaper Advertising Bureau), American Press Institute, United Service Organizations, National Committee of Newspaper Publishers for Savings Bonds (chairman), American Legion, Veterans of Foreign Wars, Sigma Delta Chi, Phi Kappa Phi, Kiwanis, Cherry Hills Country Club, Denver Country Club, Denver Athletic Club, Denver Club, Cactus Club. *Awards, honors:* Outstanding service award from Oregon State University, 1976.

*   *   *

BYRD, Bobby
See BYRD, Robert James

BYRD, Robert James 1942-
(Bobby Byrd)

PERSONAL: Born April 15, 1942, in Memphis, Tenn.; son of Billy Hudson (a pilot) and Charlotte (a realtor; maiden name, Stanage) Byrd; married Lee Merrill; children: Susannah Mississippi, John William, Andrew Merrill. *Education:* University of Arizona, B.A., 1965; University of Washington, Seattle, M.A., 1967. *Religion:* Episcopalian. *Home and office:* 1330 Gardner, Las Cruces, N.M. 88001.

CAREER: Has worked variously as laborer, taxi driver, salesman, and instructor in English at Memphis State University, Memphis, Tenn., and Adams State College of Colorado, Alamosa, Colo.; now a technical writer for Lockheed Electronics Co.

WRITINGS—Under name Bobby Byrd; all poems: *Places Is and Memphis Poems*, Grosseteste Press, 1971; *Here*, North Atlantic Books, 1975; *The Bright Sun*, Blackberry Press, 1976. Also author of plays, "The Death and Life of Dandy" (three-act), "Today We'll Make a New World" (two-act), and "The Day the Clown Became a Man" (one-act), all as yet neither published nor produced.

WORK IN PROGRESS: A book of poems, *This Is Who I Am Now*; *The Crazy-Assed Dervish*, completion expected in 1976.

SIDELIGHTS: Byrd told *CA:* "For the last four years, under the instruction of a teacher, I have studied the ideas of Gurdjieff. Because of the discipline of this teaching, I have come to realize that the purpose of one's life, and one's art, is to demonstrate that, through the study of oneself and of the essential laws providing for us, one can enter into a higher and more objective understanding of the worlds in which we live."

*　　*　　*

BYRNE, Peter 1925-

PERSONAL: Born in August, 1925, in Dublin, Ireland; came to United States in 1970; son of Cyril John and Winifred Edith (Pringuer-Drysdale) Byrne. *Education:* Educated in public schools in England and Ireland. *Residence:* The Dalles, Ore. *Office address:* P.O. Box 632, The Dalles, Ore. 97058.

CAREER: Dooars Tea Co., Eastcheap, London, England, tea planter in Bengal, India, 1948-52; Nepal Safaris, Inc., Kathmandu, Nepal, owner, operator, and big game safari guide, 1953-68; International Wildlife Conservation Society, Washington, D.C., co-founder and executive director, 1968-70; since 1971, director of Academy of Applied Science of the Pacific Northwest "Bigfoot" Investigation Project. *Military service:* Royal Air Force, Air Sea Rescue Service of Coastal Command, 1943-47; served in Southeast Asia; received three campaign medals.

MEMBER: Academy of Applied Science, Bombay Natural History Society, Himalayan Club, East African Professional Hunters Association (honorary member), Explorers Club, East India Club (London).

WRITINGS: The Search for Bigfoot: Man, Myth, or Monster?, Acropolis, 1974, new edition, 1975. Co-editor and publisher, *Bigfoot News* (newsletter of the Bigfoot Information Center), 1973—.

WORK IN PROGRESS: Jim Corbett and the Maneating Tigers of Kumaon, completion expected in 1977; *Gone are the Days*, an autobiographical account of Byrne's safari career told from a conservationist's point of view; *The Yeti*, a book about Himalayan expeditions; *The Wildlife of Nepal*, completion expected in 1977.

SIDELIGHTS: Byrne's current investigations are being conducted on behalf of the International Wildlife Conservation Society and the Academy of Applied Science. They are a direct result of the Himalayan Yeti (Abominable Snowman) expeditions. Byrne has participated in private expeditions into Sikkim and Bhutan in 1949 and 1953, and organized the first U.S. expedition reconnaissance in 1957. He led Slick-Johnson expeditions in 1958 and 1959, and led the first California Bigfoot Expedition in 1960. One of the projects he founded with the International Wildlife Conservation Society was the establishment in Nepal of the Sukla Phanta Tiger Sanctuary, which was the world's first tiger sanctuary.

AVOCATIONAL INTERESTS: Photography (mainly of wildlife), natural history of the Pacific Northwest, mountaineering, rock climbing.

*　　*　　*

CADY, Jack A(ndrew) 1932-

PERSONAL: Born March 20, 1932, in Columbus, Ohio; son of Donald Victor (an auctioneer) and Paulina (a teacher and businesswoman; maiden name, Schmidt) Cady; married Pat Distlehurst, March, 1966 (divorced, January, 1972); married Deb Robson (a writer and weaver), August, 1973. *Education:* University of Louisville, B.S., 1961. *Home:* 933 Tyler St., Port Townsend, Wash. 98368.

CAREER: Auctioneer in Louisville, Ky., 1956-61; U.S. Department of Health, Education and Welfare, Corbin, Ky., Social Security claims representative, 1961-62; truck driver in the southeastern United States, 1962-65; tree high climber in Arlington, Mass., 1965-66; landscape foreman in San Francisco, Calif., 1966-67; University of Washington, Seattle, assistant professor of English, 1968-72; Knox College, Galesburg, Ill., visiting writer, 1973; Cady-Robson Landscaping, Port Townsend, Wash., in landscape construction, 1974—. *Military service:* U.S. Coast Guard, 1952-56. *Awards, honors:* First award from *Atlantic Monthly*, 1965, for story "The Burning"; National Literary Award from National Council of the Arts, 1971, for story "The Shark"; Washington Governor's Award and Iowa Award for Short Fiction from University of Iowa Press, both 1972, both for *The Burning and Other Stories*.

WRITINGS: The Burning and Other Stories, University of Iowa Press, 1973; *House of Time* (novel), edited by Lester del Rey, Ballantine, in press.

Work anthologized in *Best American Short Stories*, edited by Martha Foley, Houghton, 1966, 1969, 1970, 1971; *American Literary Anthology*, edited by George Plimpton, Viking, 1971. Contributor of stories to literary magazines, including *Atlantic Monthly* and *Yale Review*.

WORK IN PROGRESS: The Man Who Could Make Things Vanish, a novel; continuing research on the development of religion in colonial America.

SIDELIGHTS: Cady writes: "Art and writing, when it attains to the condition of literature, is non-secular. Politics, religion, economies have nothing to do with good writing. The writer has nothing to sell. All he does is try to discover a true thing and then say it truly. That is the whole job. Art allows humans to be humane in human affairs. It sustains. It seeks not idealism but rather, continues to discover and bring to light the ideal. To do this one must assume the highest standards and pursue them relentlessly. Writing is only one of the arts. It is not greater or substantially different than painting, sculpture, teaching, acting, or the composition of music. The guy who works at it is not an artist. Instead, he works as hard as he can at what he's doing and it may be that the result attains to a condition greater than himself."

* * *

CAGLE, William R(ea) 1933-

PERSONAL: Born November 15, 1933 in Hollywood, Calif. son of Howard C. (a journalist) and Eunice (Colcord) Cagle; married Dorothy L. Stewart, August, 1957 (divorced, December, 1974); married Terry L. Conrad, January 17, 1975; children: Michael Stewart, Chantal Gabrielle, Mark Christopher, Monique Antoinette. *Education:* University of California, Los Angeles, B.A., 1956, M.L.S., 1962; attended Oxford University, 1959-60. *Politics:* Independent. *Religion:* None. *Home:* 426 East 15th St., Apt. 9, Bloomington, Ind. 47401. *Office:* Lilly Library, Indiana University, Bloomington, Ind. 47401.

CAREER: Huntington Library, San Marino, Calif., assistant to the librarian, 1960-62; University of Indiana, Bloomington, English librarian, 1962-67, assistant Lilly librarian, 1967-75, acting Lilly librarian, 1975—. Advisory board member for University of Pittsburgh series of bibliography. *Military service:* U.S. Army, 1956-59, became sergeant. *Member:* Modern Language Association of America, Lincoln Society (Oxford), Grolier Club, Caxton Club.

WRITINGS: (Co-author with C. K. Byrd) *One Hundred and Fifty Years of Indiana Statehood,* Lilly Library, 1966.

Contributor: Howard Anderson, and others, editors, *The Familiar Letter in the Eighteenth Century,* University of Kansas Press; John Carter and Percy Muir, editors, *Printing and the Mind of Man,* Holt, 1967.

WORK IN PROGRESS: A bibliography of the writings of Joseph Conrad for Oxford University Press Soho Bibliographics.

* * *

CAIN, Bob
See CAIN, Robert Owen

* * *

CAIN, Robert Owen 1934-
(Bob Cain)

PERSONAL: Born August 11, 1934, in O'Neill, Neb.; son of Lawrence Owen (an accountant) and Rosalie (an institutional administrator; maiden name, Hartlieb) Cain; married second wife, Anne Walsh (a writer), January 20, 1968; children: Robert, Julie, John, Stephanie. *Education:* Attended Creighton University, 1952-53, and Brown University, 1969-71. *Residence:* New York, N.Y. *Office:* National Broadcasting Co.—News, 30 Rockefeller Plaza, New York, N.Y. 10020.

CAREER/WRITINGS: Associated with small local radio stations, 1952-62; WJAR-Television, Providence, R.I., anchor man on news program, 1962-67; WPRI-Television, Providence, R.I., anchor man on news program, 1968-71; National Broadcasting Co. (NBC) News, New York, N.Y., correspondent, 1971—. Reporter for National Broadcasting Co.—Radio news; presents weekly consumer reports on "Consumer's Challenge," for NBC. *Awards, honors:* Gavel award from Rhode Island Toastmasters, 1966; award from New York Council of Churches, 1972, for documentary program on welfare mothers; George Foster Peabody

Award from University of Georgia, 1974, for "Second Sunday" documentary presentation on Vietnam.

SIDELIGHTS: Cain writes that he is "motivated by desire for instrumentality through informed reportage of news, and meaningful interpretation where appropriate. I desire to offer the public an in-depth mirroring of facts and trends in a monumentally complex (world) society. I am concerned, especially, about the status of American Indians, about political extremism, and about the danger of a somnambulistic citizenry posed by cliche reporting of 'handout' 'news.' I like my work. The work of a network news reporter, with few exceptions, is not glamorous. It is workaday. But it is good work, whose challenge and rewards are limited only by the competence and devotion of its practitioners and the topography of current events."

AVOCATIONAL INTERESTS: Photography, folk guitar, reading.

* * *

CALDER, Robert Lorin 1941-

PERSONAL: Born April 3, 1941, in Moose Jaw, Saskatchewan, Canada; son of Earl (a laborer) and Mildred (a receptionist; maiden name, Remey) Calder; married Barbara Lynn Sinclair (a nurse), August 16, 1965; children: Alison, Kevin, Lorin. *Education:* University of Saskatchewan, B.A. (honors), 1964, M.A., 1965; University of Leeds, Ph.D., 1970. *Home:* 1228 Elliott St., Saskatoon, Saskatchewan, Canada. *Office:* Department of English, University of Saskatchewan, Saskatoon, Saskatchewan, Canada S7N 0W0.

CAREER: University of Saskatchewan, Saskatoon, instructor, 1965-67, lecturer, 1970-71, assistant professor, 1971-75, associate professor of English literature, 1975—. *Member:* Association of Canadian University Teachers of English, Canadian Association of University Teachers. *Awards, honors:* Canada Council fellowship, University of Leeds, 1967-70.

WRITINGS: W. Somerset Maugham and the Quest for Freedom, Heinemann, 1972, Doubleday, 1973.

WORK IN PROGRESS: A biography of W. Somerset Maugham; studying the writing of D. H. Lawrence, Golding, and Cary.

SIDELIGHTS: "Having grown up in Saskatchewan," Calder told *CA,* "I have been shaped by the prairie mystique and am aware of my strong roots in Western Canada. My professional interests, however, are largely in British literature; my doctoral work was done in England, and my research has been mainly on W. S. Maugham. I feel therefore that I am part of two worlds—a situation with stresses and riches. I would like to be able to show that one does not need to live in the great cosmopolitan parts of the world to produce significant work on major international literary figures. Through teaching I hope to be able to return what I have taken along the way."

* * *

CALDWELL, Edward S(abiston) 1928-

PERSONAL: Born September 18, 1928, in Seattle, Wash.; son of Henry P. (a lumber wholesaler) and Rose (Money) Caldwell; married Clara Neeley, March 29, 1948; children: Robert, Mark, James, Scott. *Education:* Northwest College of the Assemblies of God, diploma, 1949; also attended Northwest Nazarene College. *Home:* 216 West Logan, Republic, Mo. 65738. *Office:* Glad Tidings Assembly of God, 1301 West Atlantic, Springfield, Mo. 65803.

CAREER: Ordained minister, 1952; pastor in Mackay, Idaho, 1949-51, and in Firth, Idaho, 1951-53; Credit Bureaus, Inc., Salem, Ore., representative, 1953-57; pastor of Assembly of God in Caldwell, Idaho, 1957-66; General Council of Assemblies of God, Springfield, Mo., publicity director in radio-television department, 1966—. Pastor of Assembly of God in Springfield, Mo., 1974—; president of Ministerial Alliance (Caldwell, Idaho), 1964.

WRITINGS: (Editor with Richard Champion and Gary Leggett) *Our Mission in Today's World,* Gospel Publishing, 1968; *Only One Life* (novel), Gospel Publishing, 1974; *She's Gone!* (novel), Gospel Publishing, 1976. Contributor to education journals and church publications.

WORK IN PROGRESS: A play, "The Dream of Pilate's Wife."

* * *

CALDWELL, Robert G(ranville) 1882-1976

1882—May 8, 1976; American educator, diplomat, and author. Obituaries: *New York Times,* May 9, 1976.

* * *

CALHOUN, Daniel F(airchild) 1929-

PERSONAL: Born June 21, 1929, in Fairfield, Conn.; son of Philo Clarke (an attorney) and Doris Antoinette (Wheeler) Calhoun; married Janet Montgomery McGovern (a teacher), July 12, 1952; children: Carol Victoria, Philo Clarke, Virginia Stuart Blair. *Education:* Williams College, B.A., 1950; University of Chicago, M.A., 1951, Ph.D., 1959. *Politics:* Democrat. *Religion:* Episcopalian. *Home:* 1150 North Bever St., Wooster, Ohio 44691. *Office:* Department of History, College of Wooster, Wooster, Ohio 44691.

CAREER: College of Wooster, Wooster, Ohio, instructor, 1956-60, assistant professor, 1960-63, associate professor, 1963-66, professor of history, 1966—, chairman of department, 1969-72. *Member:* American Historical Association, American Association of University Professors, Ohio Academy of History, Phi Beta Kappa.

WRITINGS: The United Front: The T.U.C. and the Russians, 1923-1928, Cambridge University Press, 1976.

WORK IN PROGRESS: The Suez Crisis, 1956.

* * *

CALLAHAN, John
See GALLUN, Raymond Z. 1911-

* * *

CALLAWAY, Joseph A(tlee) 1920-

PERSONAL: Born March 31, 1920, in Warren, Arkansas; son of Charles Wade and Lizzie (Milholland) Callaway; married Sara Tullos, October 5, 1940; children: Linda Anne, William Joseph. *Education:* Ouachita College, B.A., 1952; Southern Baptist Seminary, M.Div., 1954, Ph.D., 1957; postdoctoral study at University of London, 1961-62. *Home:* 3236 Lexington Rd., Louisville, Ky. 40206. *Office:* Southern Baptist Theological Seminary, 2825 Lexington Rd., Louisville, Ky. 40206.

CAREER: Southern Baptist Seminary, Louisville, Ky., instructor in Old Testament Hebrew, 1956-57; Furman University, Greenville, S.C., assistant professor, 1957-58; Southern Baptist Seminary, Louisville, associate professor of Old Testament interpretation, 1958-59, associate professor of Biblical archaeology, 1959-61, professor of Biblical

archaeology, 1967—. Supervisor on archaeological expeditions in Israel, 1960-64; director of Ai (et-Tell) excavation, 1964—. American School of Oriental Research, trustee, 1966-67, research associate, 1968-69, research professor, 1972-73 and 1976-77; Albright Institute of Archaeological Research, trustee, 1970—, 2nd vice-president of board of trustees, 1975—. *Member:* Society of Biblical Literature, American Schools of Oriental Research, Archaeological Institute of America, Palestine Exploration Fund, World Union of Jewish Studies. *Awards, honors:* Fellowships from American Association of Theological Schools, 1961-62, and Guggenheim Foundation, 1974; grants from American Philosophical Society, 1968 and 1970, National Endowment for the Humanities, 1971-75.

WRITINGS: Pottery from the Tombs at Ai (et-Tell), Quaritch, 1964; (editor with J. McKee Adams) *Biblical Backgrounds,* Broadman, 1965, revised edition published as *A Guide to Biblical Backgrounds,* 1966; *The Early Bronze Age Sanctuary at Ai (et-Tell),* Quaritch, 1972. Contributor to *Encyclopedia of Archaeological Excavations in the Holy Land* and of articles to learned journals.

WORK IN PROGRESS: Two excavation reports, *The Early Bronze Age Citadel and Lower City at Ai (et-Tell)* and *The Iron Age Village at Ai (et-Tell);* articles and preliminary excavation reports.

* * *

CALLMANN, Rudolf 1892-1976

September 29, 1892—March 12, 1976; German-born American lawyer and author of books in his field. Obituaries: *New York Times,* March 15, 1976.

* * *

CALVOCORESSI, Peter (John Ambrose) 1912-

PERSONAL: Born November 17, 1912; son of Pandia and Irene (Ralli) Calvocoressi; married Barbara Dorothy Eden, 1938; children: two sons. *Education:* Attended Balliol College, Oxford. *Home:* Guise House, Aspley Guise, Milton Keynes MK17 8HQ, England.

CAREER: Called to the Bar, 1935; contested liberal seat for Nuneaton, 1945; at Nuremberg trials, 1945-46; Royal Institute of International Affairs, London, England, writer, 1949-54, council member, 1955-70; Penguin Books, London, editorial director, 1972-73, publisher and chief executive, 1973-75. Reader in international relations at University of Sussex, part-time, 1965-71. Director of Chatto & Windus and of Hogarth Press, 1954-65. Member of council of Institute for Strategic Studies, 1961-71; member of United Nations Sub-Commission on the Prevention of Discrimination and Protection of Minorities, 1962-71; chairman of Africa Bureau, 1963-71; deputy chairman of North Metropolitan Conciliation Committee, 1967-71; member of council of Institute of Race Relations, 1970-71; chairman of London Library, 1970-73. *Military service:* Royal Air Force, Intelligence Service, 1940-45; became wing commander. *Member:* Garrick Club.

WRITINGS: Nuremberg: The Facts, the Law, and the Consequences, Chatto & Windus, 1947, Macmillan, 1948; (with Guy Wint) *Middle East Crisis,* Penguin, 1957; *South Africa and World Opinion,* Oxford University Press, 1961; *World Order and New States: Problems of Keeping the Peace,* Praeger for the Institute for Strategic Studies, 1962; *Suez Ten Years After,* Pantheon, 1967; *International Politics since 1945,* Praeger, 1968 (published in England as *World Politics since 1945,* Longmans, Green, 1968, 3rd edition, 1976); (with Wint) *Total War: The Story of World War II*, Pantheon, 1972 (published in England as *Total War: Causes and Courses of the Second World War*, Penguin, 1972). Also author of five volumes of "Annual Survey of International Affairs" series, Royal Institute of International Affairs, 1949-54.

WORK IN PROGRESS: England, 1945-1975.

AVOCATIONAL INTERESTS: Tennis.

*   *   *

CAMMER, Leonard 1913-

PERSONAL: Born March 7, 1913, in New York, N.Y.; son of Harry (a presser) and Anna (Boriskin) Cammer; married Beatrice Berman (an artist), January 24, 1942. *Education:* College of the City of New York (now City College of the City University of New York), B.S., 1933; University of Buffalo, M.A., 1937, M.D., 1939. *Politics:* Independent. *Residence:* New York, N.Y.; and Pawling, N.Y. *Office:* 110 East 82nd St., New York, N.Y. 10028.

CAREER: City Hospital, New York, N.Y., rotating intern, 1939-41; Institute of Pennsylvania Hospital and Pennsylvania Hospital for Nervous and Mental Diseases, both Philadelphia, Pa., psychiatric trainee, 1945-47; New York State Psychiatric Institute and Hospital, New York City, psychiatric trainee, 1947-48; private practice of general psychiatry in New York City, 1948—. Diplomate of National Board of Medical Examiners and American Board of Psychiatry and Neurology (assistant examiner, 1965—); licensed to practice medicine in New York and Arizona. Founder and first medical director of Gracie Square Hospital, 1959-60; associate attending psychiatrist at Flower and Fifth Avenue Hospitals and Metropolitan Hospital, 1948—. Instructor at University of Buffalo, 1934-38; clinical associate professor at New York Medical College, 1948—; instructor at New York Academy of Medicine, 1963-70; lecturer at Cooper Union for the Advancement of Science and Art, 1969-71, and Post Graduate Center for Mental Health, 1970—. Has made more than one hundred-fifty national and local television and radio appearances. *Military service:* U.S. Naval Reserve, active duty in Medical Corps, 1941-46; became commander.

MEMBER: International Psychiatric Association for the Advancement of Electrotherapy (president), World Psychiatric Association, American Psychiatric Association (life fellow), American College of Psychiatrists (fellow), Academy of Psychosomatic Medicine (fellow), American Medical Association, Pavlovian Society, Society of Biological Psychiatry, American Society of Medical Writers, Institute of Clinical Analysis (member of advisory board), Eastern Psychiatric Research Association, New York Society for Clinical Psychiatry (life fellow), New York State Medical Society (chairman of Psychiatry Section, 1973-74), New York Academy of Sciences, New York County Medical Society, University of Buffalo Alumni Association, City Hospital Alumni Association, New York State Psychiatric Institute Alumni Association, Sigma Xi (associate member).

WRITINGS: Outline of Psychiatry, McGraw, 1962; *Up from Depression*, Simon & Schuster, 1969; *Freedom from Compulsion*, Simon & Schuster, 1976. Contributor of more than thirty articles to medical journals.

WORK IN PROGRESS: A review of current techniques, and research on the development of new techniques for behavior modification, with emphasis on the application of learning and conditioning principles and the effect of the personality of the therapist or teacher upon the subject.

SIDELIGHTS: Cammer writes: "Underlying all my writings I endeavor to express the urgent need to overcome the destructive, violent and 'selfish' impulses of man and to further those traits that make him 'human'—cooperative endeavor, concern for protecting the environment, belongingness and love. I believe that man's survival is conditional upon learning how to live and integrate with his fellow man and his cultural and physical surroundings."

AVOCATIONAL INTERESTS: Playing folk guitar, landscaping, salvaging materials ("I dislike waste of any kind"), repairing things, travel (the Orient, Europe, the Middle East, Africa).

*   *   *

CAMPBELL, George F(rederick) 1915-

PERSONAL: Born July 27, 1915, in England; son of Joseph (a shipwright) and Edith McSorley (Jones) Campbell; married Elizabeth L. Knox (a copywriter), August 29, 1942; children: Roger, Isabel, Roy. *Education:* Birkenhead Institute of Technology, national certificate in naval architecture, 1937. *Politics:* Liberal. *Religion:* Church of England. *Home address:* Hotel Bossert, Apt. 629, 98 Montague St., Brooklyn, N.Y. 11201. *Office:* American Museum of Natural History, Central Park W., New York, N.Y.

CAREER: Royal Mail Lines, London, England, assistant naval architect, 1939-55; London County Council, London, England, naval architect, 1955-61; Elliot Automation, Rochester, England, technical illustrator, 1961-63; Art Model Studios, Mt. Vernon, N.Y., ship model maker, 1963-65; Chemplant Designs, New York City, model maker, 1965-67; American Museum of Natural History, New York City, diorama designer and maker, 1967—. Designer-consultant for "Cutty Sark" Preservation Society; consultant to maritime museums and organizations. *Member:* Royal Institution of Naval Architects.

WRITINGS: (With Prosper Dowden) *Ships of the Royal Mail Lines*, Adlard Coles, 1953; *China Tea Clippers*, Adlard Coles, 1955, revised edition, McKay, 1974. Contributor to *Sea Breezes* and *Ship & Boat Builder*.

WORK IN PROGRESS: Research on Elizabethan and seventeenth-century English shipbuilding techniques for *Sovereign of the Seas;* research on the ancient city of Alexandria with special reference to sea frontage and the lighthouse, Pharos; studying marine paintings of historical ships.

SIDELIGHTS: Campbell writes that he has had a "close and active association with shipbuilding and shipping since childhood through family connections, as second best to a seagoing career thwarted by polio. An understanding of the technicalities of shipbuilding, and of the aesthetic expression of the designers of ships, past and present, inspires me to present these men on a level with the more universally acclaimed civil architects; and to achieve this end by writing, illustrating and painting in the traditional manner, whereby the truth of the subtlety of ship shapes can be shown and their beauty appreciated."

*   *   *

CAMPBELL, Ian 1942-

PERSONAL: Born August 25, 1942, in Lausanne, Switzerland; son of Donald (a clergyman) and Mary (a school teacher; maiden name, Cruickshank) Campbell. *Education:* University of Aberdeen, M.A., 1964; University of Edinburgh, Ph.D., 1970. *Politics:* "Unaligned." *Religion:* Presbyterian. *Home:* 12A St. Catherine's Pl., Edinburgh EH9

1NU, Scotland. *Office:* Department of English, University of Edinburgh, Edinburgh EH8 9JX, Scotland.

CAREER: University of Edinburgh, Edinburgh, Scotland, lecturer in English literature, 1967—. Visiting professor, University of Guelph, summer, 1973; British Council visiting lecturer, Hamburg, summer, 1971. *Member:* Association of Scottish Literary Studies (council member), Universities' Committee of Scottish Literature, Light Railway Transport League (council member), Carlyle Society (Edinburgh; vice-president), English Association (Edinburgh; council member).

WRITINGS: (Editor with R. D. S. Jack) Robert McLellan, *Jamie the Saxt,* J. Calder, 1970; (editor with C. R. Sanders, K. J. Fielding, and others) *The Duke-Edinburgh Edition of the Letters of Thomas and Jane Welsh Carlyle,* Duke University Press, 1970, Volumes I-IV, 1970, Volumes V-VII, in press; (editor) Thomas Carlyle, *Reminiscences,* Everyman, 1971; (editor) Carlyle, *Selected Essays,* Everyman, 1972; *Thomas Carlyle,* Hamish Hamilton, 1974, Scribner, 1975.

Contributor to educational scripts for British Broadcasting Corp. and commercial television stations. Contributor to literature journals, including *Nineteenth Century Fiction, Studies in Scottish Literature, Criticism, Modern Language Review, English Language Notes,* and *Notes and Queries.*

WORK IN PROGRESS: Articles on English and Scottish literature, and on the history of science; editing *The Duke-Edinburgh Editions of the Letters of Thomas and Jane Welsh Carlyle,* with C. R. Sanders, K. J. Fielding, and others, about forty volumes, for Duke University Press; editing an anthology of essays on nineteenth-century Scottish fiction; editing a selected version of Carlyle letters.

SIDELIGHTS: Campbell writes: "Being born and brought up in Switzerland I have always enjoyed contacts with other countries to avoid too narrow a Scottishness or Britishness, and frequent travel is an important stimulus to my teaching and writing life. North America is a frequent feature of this travel. I try very much to incorporate an awareness of as much as possible of life and society into teaching. Scotland's possible devolution to a limited political autonomy is an important political argument just now in Great Britain, and my work here in Scotland's capital and its University has a lot to do with educating classes critically in Scottish cultural and literary values, above all in the context of their own past, and what other countries can teach us."

AVOCATIONAL INTERESTS: Railed transport "of any kind," music (organist), travel.

*   *   *

CAMPBELL-JOHNSON, Alan 1913-

PERSONAL: Born July 16, 1913, in London, England; son of James Alexander and Gladys Susannah (Geering) Campbell-Johnson; married Imogen Fay de la Tour Dunlap, October 8, 1938; children: Virginia (Mrs. Giorgio Valentini), Keith (deceased). *Education:* Christ Church, Oxford, B.A. (2nd class honors), 1935, M.A., 1956. *Politics:* Liberal. *Religion:* Church of England. *Home:* 21 Ashley Gardens, Ambrosden Ave., London SWIP 1QD, England. *Agent:* David Higham Associates, 5-8 Lower John St., Golden Sq., London W1R 4HA, England. *Office:* 16 Bolton St., London W1Y 8HX, England.

CAREER: London Press Exchange, London, England, personal assistant to manager of public relations department, 1937-39; political secretary to leader of Liberal Party, 1938-40; Liberal candidate for Salisbury and South Wilts in Parlia-

mentary elections, 1945, 1950; press attache to viceroy and governor-general of India, 1947-48; public relations consultant, 1948—; Campbell-Johnson Group Ltd. (public relations consultants), London, chairman and managing director, 1953—. *Military service:* Royal Air Force, 1941-46; became wing-commander. *Member:* Royal Institute of International Affairs, Royal Society of Arts (fellow), Institute of Public Relations (president, 1958), National Liberal Club, Brooks's Club. *Awards, honors:* Officer of the Order of the British Empire, 1946; Companion of the Order of the Indian Empire, 1947; Officer of the Legion of Merit, 1947.

WRITINGS: (Editor) *Growing Opinions: A Symposium of British Youth Outlook,* Methuen, 1935; *Peace Offering,* Methuen, 1936; *Anthony Eden: A Biography,* R. Hale, 1938, Washburn, 1939, revised edition, R. Hale, 1955, published as *Eden: The Making of a Statesman,* Washburn, 1955; *Viscount Halifax: A Biography,* Washburn, 1941; *Mission with Mountbatten,* R. Hale, 1951, Dutton, 1953, 2nd edition, foreword by Earl Mountbatten of Burma, R. Hale, 1972.

*   *   *

CAMUS, Raoul Francois 1930-

PERSONAL: Born December 5, 1930, in Buffalo, N.Y.; son of Raymond V. (a pastry chef) and Gurli (Lowerling) Camus; married Joyce Gruber, September 27, 1952 (divorced, 1955); married Amy E. Platt (a musician and teacher), February 10, 1963; children: Colette (Mrs. Donald Polsky), Henry R., Renee E. *Education:* Queens College (now of the City University of New York), B.A., 1952; Columbia University, M.A., 1956; New York University, Ph.D., 1969. *Home:* 14-34 155th St., Whitestone, N.Y. 11357. *Office:* Department of Music, Queensborough Community College of the City University of New York, Bayside, N.Y. 11364.

CAREER: High school teacher of instrumental music in New York, N.Y., 1959-70; Queensborough Community College of the City University of New York, Bayside, N.Y., assistant professor, 1970-75, associate professor of music, 1975—. Director of Queensborough Symphony Band. *Military service:* U.S. Army National Guard, bandmaster, 1947-74; became chief warrant officer. *Member:* American Musicological Society, College Band Directors National Association, Company of Military Historians, Armed Forces Bandmasters Association of the United States, Sonneck Society.

WRITINGS: Military Music of the American Revolution, University of North Carolina Press, 1976.

WORK IN PROGRESS: A history of bands, 1783-1865; a project to develop a computer index of eighteenth-century secular tunes.

*   *   *

CANDLER, Julie 1919-

PERSONAL: Born December 28, 1919, in Illinois; daughter of Frank C. H. (an auto dealer) and Edith (a department store buyer; maiden name, Rickey) Jennings; married: William Robert Candler III (a manufacturer's representative), May, 1943 (divorced, 1965); married John W. Fisher (a public relations director), October, 1970 (divorced, 1972); children: Carolyn (Mrs. Joseph Solaka), William Robert IV, Rickey. *Education:* Attended Wayne State University and University of Michigan. *Politics:* Democrat. *Religion:* Unitarian-Universalist. *Home:* 229 Euclid, Birmingham, Mich. 48009. *Agent:* McIntosh & Otis, Inc., 475 Fifth Ave.,

New York, N.Y. 10017. *Office:* Julie Candler & Associates, 430 North Woodward, Birmingham, Mich. 48011.

CAREER: Dodge News Bureau, Detroit, Mich., secretary and writer, 1954; *Birmingham Eccentric* (newspaper), Birmingham, Mich., news editor, 1955-60; Julie Candler & Associates (public relations consultants), Birmingham, Mich., owner, 1960—. *Woman's Day* magazine, author of column" Woman at the Wheel," 1964—. Member of National Motor Vehicle Safety Advisory Council.

MEMBER: American Association for Automotive Medicine, American Society of Journalists and Authors, Outdoor Writers Association of America, Authors League of America, Women in Communications, Women's Advertising Club of Detroit (member of board of directors), Detroit Auto Writer's Group (member of board of directors), Action for Child Transportation Safety (member of board of directors). *Awards, honors:* Public service award from National Safety Council, 1967; headliner award from local chapter of Women in Communications, 1967; journalism safety award from Uniroyal, 1974; writers award from Recreational Vehicle Association, 1974; Deep Woods Award from Outdoor Writers Association of America, 1974.

WRITINGS: Woman at the Wheel, Paperback Library, 1967. Contributor to *Rudder* magazine.

WORK IN PROGRESS: A novel in collaboration with Allan Hayes.

SIDELIGHTS: Julie Candler writes: "I like to write about the things that interest me: cars, because I'm a Detroiter and this town lives and breathes car talk; camping, travel, backpacking, tennis, and boating, all of which I participate in and enjoy. Fiction writing is another interest that has resulted in a novel. . . . As for causes, it pains me that auto occupants, particularly young people, are dying needlessly because of the failure of the auto industry, government, and educators to convince them of the necessity to use safety belts every time they ride in cars."

*   *   *

CAPUTO, David A(rmand) 1943-

PERSONAL: Born August 30, 1943, in Brownsville, Pa.; son of Armand (an investment counselor) and Marie (Smalstig) Caputo; married Alice Glotfelty, June 27, 1964; children: Christopher, Elizabeth, Jeffrey. *Education:* Miami University, Oxford, Ohio, B.A., 1965; Yale University, M.A., 1967, M.Phil., 1968, Ph.D., 1970. *Office:* Department of Political Science, Purdue University, West Lafayette, Ind. 47907.

CAREER: Purdue University, West Lafayette, Ind., assistant professor, 1969-73, associate professor, 1974-76, professor of political science, 1977—. *Member:* Phi Beta Kappa. *Awards, honors:* Woodrow Wilson fellowship, 1965-66; National Science Foundation science fellowship, 1977.

WRITINGS: American Politics and Public Policy, Lippincott, 1974; (with Richard Cole) *Urban Politics and Political Decentralization: The Case of General Revenue Sharing,* Lexington Books, 1974; *Urban America: The Policy Alternatives,* W. H. Freeman, 1976; (editor with Cole) *Revenue-Sharing: Methodological Approaches and Problems,* Lexington Books, 1976; (editor) *The Politics of Public Policy-Making in America: Five Case Studies,* W. H. Freeman, in press. Contributor to scholarly journals.

WORK IN PROGRESS: Evaluation of the New Federalism, with Richard Cole.

CARBAUGH, Robert J(ohn) 1946-

PERSONAL: Born October 20, 1946, in Spokane, Wash.; son of A. B. (a businessman) and E. J. (Eisenman) Carbaugh; married Catherine J. Charette. *Education:* Gonzaga University, B.B.A., 1969; Colorado State University, M.S., 1972, Ph.D., 1974. *Residence:* Eau Claire, Wis. *Office:* Department of Economics, University of Wisconsin, Eau Claire, Wis. 54701.

CAREER: Colorado State University, Fort Collins, instructor in economics, spring, 1974; South Dakota State University, Brookings, assistant professor of economics, 1974-75; University of Wisconsin, Eau Claire, assistant professor of economics, 1975—. *Member:* American Economic Association, Phi Beta Kappa, Sigma Xi, Alpha Sigma Nu, Phi Kappa Phi, Omicron Delta Epsilon.

WRITINGS: (With Liang-Shing Fan) *The International Monetary System,* University Press of Kansas, 1976. Contributor to economics journals.

WORK IN PROGRESS: An undergraduate textbook on international economics, completion expected in 1978.

SIDELIGHTS: "My basic motivation for writing and conducting research into economics," Carbaugh told *CA,* "is to present topics at a level the typical undergraduate economics student can readily comprehend. With respect to my textbook writing, I have tried to adhere to the principle that 'a good textbook should be capable of teaching itself.'

The above philosophy not only relates to my writing, but also to my teaching. My research is primarily intended to be shared with my students, as well as to make me a more learned individual and capable instructor. The greatest enjoyment I receive from my work is seeing my undergraduate students develop a keen interest in economics, and wanting to pursue it further after graduating from college.

It is my belief that economic theory can and should be presented to the economics major and nonmajor in an understandable and relevant style. As a result, my writing and teaching is primarily issue-oriented. By this I mean that I concentrate on using introductory and intermediate economic theory to explain and analyse contemporary economic problems."

*   *   *

CAREY, Michael L(awrence) 1948-

PERSONAL: Born October 1, 1948, in Oakland, Calif.; son of Harold L. (a shipbuilder) and Margaret (a teacher; maiden name, Ryan) Carey; married Diane McCarthy (a registered nurse), August 5, 1972. *Education:* University of San Francisco, B.A. (cum laude), 1970; Dominican College of San Rafael, M.A., 1976. *Religion:* Roman Catholic. *Home:* 3537 Sleepy Hollow Dr., Santa Rosa, Calif. 95404.

CAREER: Yulupa School, Santa Rosa, Calif., teacher, 1974—. Summer school principal in Bennett Valley Union School District of Santa Rosa, 1976. *Member:* California Teachers Association, Alpha Sigma Nu, Sigma Alpha Epsilon. *Awards, honors:* Named man of the year by *San Francisco Sporting News,* 1971.

WRITINGS: Awards, Academic Therapy Publications, 1975; *Wooden School Houses of Sonoma County* (sketch book), Jallen Publications, 1975.

SIDELIGHTS: Carey writes: "One thing we all need is success; and success is what you're told, not necessarily what you do. *Awards* gives people a chance to feel good about themselves and others, for whatever we do well, we want to share. The contents of this book allow people to recognize others." *Avocational interests:* Calligraphy, sports writing, stained glass.

* * *

CARLSON, Rick J. 1940-

PERSONAL: Born November 17, 1940, in Minneapolis, Minn.; son of John and Ethel (Anderson) Carlson; married Meg Dredge, September 4, 1965; children: Rebekah, Joshua. *Education:* St. Olaf College, B.A., 1962; University of Minnesota, J.D., 1965. *Home:* 75 Upper Alcatraz, Mill Valley, Calif. 94941.

CAREER: Howard, Lefevere, Lefler, Hamilton & Pearson, Minneapolis, Minn., attorney, 1965-69; Health Services Research Center InterStudy, Minneapolis, Minn., research attorney, 1969-72; writer, 1972—. Senior research associate of National Academy of Sciences' Institute of Medicine; vice-president and senior associate of Policy Center, Inc. (Denver) and Spectrum Research, Inc. (Washington, D.C.); research associate of University of California, San Francisco; adjunct assistant professor at Boston University. Instructor at University of Minnesota, 1970; visiting fellow at Center for the Study of Democratic Institutions, 1972-73.

WRITINGS: The Need to Study Laws Relating to Health Manpower, InterStudy, 1970; (with Paul M. Ellwood, Jr. and others) *Assuring the Quality of Health Care,* InterStudy, 1973; *The End of Medicine,* Wiley, 1975; *The Dilemmas of Corrections,* Lexington Books, 1976; (editor) *The Frontiers of Science and Medicine,* Wildwood House, 1975, Regnery, in press; (editor) *A New Medicine: Holistic Approaches to Health,* Ballinger, in press. Contributor to medical and legal journals, and to *Center, Center Report,* and *Futures Conditional.*

WORK IN PROGRESS: Steps to a New Medicine: Inovations in Health and the Implications for Public Policy.

* * *

CARNELL, Corbin Scott 1929-

PERSONAL: Born July 7, 1929, in Ormond Beach, Fla.; son of Stanley C. and Doris (Scott) Carnell; married Carol Young (a part-time teacher), June 16, 1951; children: Richard, Alan, Stephen, Peter. *Education:* Wheaton College, Wheaton, Ill., B.A., 1952; Columbia University, M.A., 1953; University of Florida, Ph.D., 1960. *Politics:* Democrat. *Religion:* Episcopalian. *Home:* 1708 Southwest 43rd Ave., Gainesville, Fla. 32608. *Office:* English Department, University of Florida, Gainesville, Fla. 32611.

CAREER: Bethany College, Bethany, W.Va., instructor in English, 1953-56; University of Florida, Gainesville, assistant professor, 1960-68, associate professor, 1968-76, professor of English, 1976—. Visiting summer professor at Georgetown University, 1961, Eckerd College, 1968, Young Life Graduate Ecumenical Institute, 1972, 1973, 1975, and University of British Columbia, 1975. Member of national advisory council of Danforth Foundation, 1967-70. *Member:* Modern Language Association of America, American Academy of Religion, Conference on Christianity and Literature (vice-president, 1964-65; president, 1974-77), American Association of University Professors, Common Cause.

WRITINGS: Two Short Novels by Henry James: Adapted with Notes and Exercises for Students of English as a Second Language, Prentice-Hall, 1963; (contributor) C. A. Huttar, editor, *Imagination and the Spirit,* Eerdmans, 1971; (editor and author of introduction) *A Slow, Soft River: Seven Stories by Lawrence Dorr,* Eerdmans, 1973; *Bright Shadow of Reality: C. S. Lewis and the Feeling Intellect,* Eerdmans, 1974. Contributor to professional journals.

WORK IN PROGRESS: A book on mythic consciousness.

* * *

CARNOY, Martin 1938-

PERSONAL: Born in 1938, in Warsaw, Poland; came to the United States in 1940, naturalized citizen, 1945; son of Alan L. and Teresa Carnoy; married Judith Merle Milgrom (an actress), August 6, 1961; children: David, Jonathan. *Education:* California Institute of Technology, B.S., 1960; University of Chicago, M.A., 1961, Ph.D., 1964. *Home:* 2378 Branner Dr., Menlo Park, Calif. 94025. *Office:* School of Education, Stanford University, Stanford, Calif. 94305.

CAREER: Brookings Institution, Washington, D.C., research associate in economics, 1964-68; Stanford University, Stanford, Calif., assistant professor, 1968-71, associate professor of economics and education, 1971—, director of Latin American fellowship program, 1970—. Director of Center for Economic Studies (Palo Alto, Calif.). Consultant to Organization for Economic Cooperation and Development, World Bank, Venezuelan Ministry of Education, and Organization of American States.

MEMBER: Latin American Studies Association, Negative Population Growth (member of national advisory board), Comparative and International Education Society, Union of Radical Political Economists, Concerned Citizens for Peace (founder; co-chairman, 1966-68).

WRITINGS: (With Donald W. Baerrensen and Joseph Grunwald) *Latin American Trade Patterns,* Brookings Institution, 1965; *Industrialization in a Latin American Common Market,* Brookings Institution, 1971; (with Grunwald and Miguel Wionczek) *The United States and a Latin American Common Market,* Brookings Institution, 1971; (with Hans Thias) *Cost-Benefit Analysis in Education: A Case Study of Kenya,* Johns Hopkins Press, 1972; (editor and contributor) *Schooling in a Corporate Society,* McKay, 1972, 2nd edition, 1975; (with Grunwald and Wionczek) *La Integracion Economica Latinoamericana y la Politica de Estados Unidos* (translation by Miguel Wionczek; title means "Latin American Integration and U.S. Policy"), Centro de Estudios Monetarios Latinoamericanos, 1973; *Education As Cultural Imperialism,* McKay, 1974; (with Henry Levin) *The Limits of Educational Reform,* McKay, 1975; (with Thias and Richard Sack) *Systems Analysis in Education: A Case Study of Tunisian Secondary Schools,* Johns Hopkins Press, in press.

Monographs: *The Economics of Schooling and International Development,* Centro Intercultural de Documentacion, 1971; *The Social Benefits of Better Schooling,* School of Education, Stanford University, 1972; (with Michael Carter) *Theories of Labor Markets and Worker Productivity,* Center for Economic Studies (Palo Alto, Calif.), 1974.

Contributor: Ronald Hilton, editor, *The Movement for Latin Unity,* Praeger, 1970; Kan Chen, editor, *National Priorities,* San Francisco Press, 1970; Roberto Esqaenazi-Mayo and Michael Meyer, editors, *Latin American Scholarship Since World War Two,* University of Nebraska Press, 1971; Thomas LaBelle, editor, *Education in Latin America and the Caribbean,* Latin American Center, University of California, Los Angeles, 1972; Leopoldo Solis, editor, *La Economia Mexicana II: Politica y Desarrollo* (title means "The Mexican Economy II: Policy and Development"),

Fondo de Cultura Economia, 1973; Frank Donilla and Robert Girling, editors, *Structures of Dependency*, Institute of Political Studies, Stanford University, 1973; Hector Correa, editor, *Analytical Methods in Educational Planning and Administration*, McKay, 1975. Contributor to professional journals.

WORK IN PROGRESS: A study of the relationship between the alternative forms of work organization and the educational system.

*   *   *

CARPENTER, John 1936-

PERSONAL: Born April 14, 1936, in Cambridge, Mass.; son of Frederic Ives (a writer) and Lillian (a psychologist; maiden name, Cook) Carpenter; married Bogdana Chetkowska (a professor), April 15, 1963; children: Michael. *Education:* Harvard University, B.A. (cum laude), 1958; Sorbonne, University of Paris, Dr. d'universite, 1964. *Politics:* Independent. *Home:* 2409 East Roanoke St., Seattle, Wash. 98112.

CAREER: Poet, translator, and critic. Co-organizer of "Seattle Poetry," a series of readings. Member of Berkeley Civic Arts Commission, 1968-73; artist-in-residence for Seattle Arts Commission, 1975. *Military service:* U.S. Air Force Reserve, 1960-62. *Awards, honors:* National Endowment for the Arts fellowship, 1976-77.

WRITINGS: Histoire de la litterature francaise sur la Louisiane, 1683-1763 (title means "History of the French Literature of Lousiana, 1683-1763"), Nizet, 1965; *Putting the Loon Together* (poems), Seattle Arts Commission, 1975; (translator, editor, and author of introduction) Zbigniew Herbert, *Selected Poems*, Oxford University Press, in press.

Poems and translations have been anthologized in *The New York Times Book of Verse*, edited by Thomas Lask, Macmillan, 1972; *Selected Poems of Czeslaw Milosz*, Seabury Press, 1974. Contributor of poems, translations, and articles to literary journals, including *Poetry, London, The Seventies, Encounter, Modern Poetry in Translation, Poetry Northwest, Epoch,* and *Perspective,* and to newspapers.

WORK IN PROGRESS: A collection of poems previously published in journals; two books of new poems.

SIDELIGHTS: Carpenter writes: "As a poet my ambition is probably to be the least 'popular' poet writing in the United States—a moralist. No one loves a moralist. At the same time, I am interested in what might be loosely called avant-garde or experimental techniques. I find absolutely no conflict between the two, as the kind of moral exploration which interests me must also be experimental, 're-valued' (in the Nietzschean sense), tentative, and modest. The Second World War, the Holocaust, has changed the orientation and values of European poetry; American poetry lags behind, I think, and I am especially interested in the exploration of Polish poets like Herbert and Rozewicz, of Greek poets like Ritsos. What I dislike most is the poet who writes to show how beautiful his personality is; this is not why I write, and if I tried to write in this way, I would surely fail." Carpenter supplements his income by teaching, and by doing construction work on houses.

*   *   *

CARPENTIER (Y VALMONT), Alejo 1904-

PERSONAL: Born December 26, 1904, in Havana, Cuba; son of Jorge Julian Carpentier y Valmont (an architect);

married Andrea Esteban. *Education:* Attended Universidad de Habana. *Home:* Apartado 6153, Havana, Cuba. *Office:* Embassy of Cuba, 3 rue Scribe, Paris 4e, France.

CAREER: Worked as a commercial journalist in Havana, Cuba, 1921-24; *Cartels* magazine, Havana, editor-in-chief, 1924-28; Foniric Studios, Paris, France, director and producer of spoken arts programs and recordings, 1928-39; CMZ radio, Havana, writer and producer, 1939-41; Conservatorio Nacional, Havana, professor of history of music, 1941-43; traveled in Haiti, Europe, the United States and South America, 1943-59; Cuban Publishing House, Havana, director, 1960-67; Embassy of Cuba, Paris, France, cultural attache.

WRITINGS—All novels except as indicated: *Poemes des Antilles* (poetry), Paris, 1929; *Ecue-yambo-o*, Paris, 1933, Editorial Xanadu (Buenos Aires), 1968; *La musica en Cuba* (music history), Fondo de cultura economica (Mexico), 1946, Havana, 1961; *El reino de este mundo*, 1949, Organizacion Continental de los Festivales del Libro (Havana), c.1958, translation by Harriet de Onis published as *The Kingdom of this World*, Knopf, 1957; *Los pasos perdidos*, Ibero Americana de Publicaciones (Mexico), 1953, Organizacion Continential de los Festivales del Libro, 1960, translation by de Onis published as *The Lost Steps*, Knopf, 1956, new edition with introduction by J. B. Priestly, Knopf, 1967; *El acoso*, Editorial Losada (Buenos Aires), 1956, Instituto del Libro (Havana), 1969, new edition with introduction by Mercedes Rein, Biblioteca de Marcha (Montevideo), 1972; *El siglo de las luces*, Compania General de Ediciones (Mexico), 1962, Ediciones Revolucion (Havana), 1963, translation by John Sturrock published as *Explosion in a Cathedral*, Little, Brown, 1963; *El camino de Santiago* (short story), Editorial Galerna (Buenos Aires), 1967; *Literatura y conciencia politica en America Latina* (essays), edited by A. Corazon, Madrid, 1969; (author of text) *La ciudad de las columnas* (architectural study of Havana; photographs by Paolo Gasparini), Editorial Lumen (Barcelona), 1970; *El derecho de asilo; dibujos de Marcel Berges*, Editorial Lumen, 1972; *Los convidados de plata*, Sandino (Montevideo), 1972.

Author of "La Passion noire" (oratorio), first performed in Paris, 192(?); also writer of librettas. Contributor of articles on politics, literature and musicology to magazines, including *Revolutions Surrealist,* and other publications. Former editor of fashion section of Havana publication under pseudonym Jacqueline; former columnist for *El Nationale* (Caracas); former editor, *Iman* (Paris).

SIDELIGHTS: In a review of *The War of Time*, a writer for *Spectator* said: "Carpentier is a highly cultivated and self-conscious writer. His grand canvases, crowded with events, richly baroque in detail, are controlled at every point by their author's fastidious learning and tone of faintly mocking detachment, so that he often seems the nearest heir to Thomas Mann. True, his favourite theme is disturbance and revolution, whether personal or collective, but his standpoint is scarcely that one associates with a committed revolutionary, since the invariable outcome of revolution in his work is the state of corruption and stagnation which originally caused it."

BIOGRAPHICAL/CRITICAL SOURCES: Books Abroad, Spring, 1959; *PMLA*, Spring, 1963; E. Rodriguez Monegal, *Narradores de America*, 1966; Luis Harss and Barbara Dohmann, *Into the Mainstream*, Harper, 1967; *UNESCO Courier*, January, 1972, June, 1973.*

CARR, C(harles) T(elford) 1905-1976

1905—March 10, 1976; British educator, scholar, and author. Obituaries: *AB Bookman's Weekly,* April 5, 1976.

* * *

CARR, Pat M(oore) 1932-
(Pat M. Esslinger)

PERSONAL: Born March 13, 1932, in Grass Creek, Wyo.; daughter of Stanley (an oil camp supervisor) and Bea (Parker) Moore; married Jack H. Esslinger, June 4, 1955 (divorced, July, 1970); married Duane Carr (a professor and writer), March 26, 1971; children: Stephanie, Shelley, Sean, Jennifer. *Education:* Rice University, B.A., 1954, M.A., 1955; Tulane University, Ph.D., 1960. *Home:* 1029 Kelly Way, El Paso, Tex. 79902. *Agent:* Frances Collin, 141 East 55th St., New York, N.Y. 10022. *Office:* Department of English, University of Texas at El Paso, El Paso, Tex. 79968.

CAREER: Texas Southern University, Houston, Tex., instructor in English, 1956-58; Dillard University, New Orleans, La., assistant professor of English, 1960-61; Louisiana State University, New Orleans, assistant professor of English, 1961-62, 1965-69; University of Texas at El Paso, assistant professor, 1969-72, associate professor of English, 1972—. *Member:* Phi Beta Kappa. *Awards, honors:* Mark IV Award from Library of Congress, 1970, for *Beneath the Hill of the Three Crosses;* National Endowment for the Humanities grant, 1973.

WRITINGS: (Under name Pat M. Esslinger) *Beneath the Hill of the Three Crosses* (stories), South & West Press, 1970; *The Grass Creek Chronicle* (novel), Endeavors in Humanity, 1976; *Bernard Shaw,* Ungar, 1976. Contributor to *Encyclopedia of World Literature.* Contributor of articles and stories (before 1971, under name Pat M. Esslinger) to literary journals and to *Afro-American Forum* and *Western Humanities Review.*

WORK IN PROGRESS: The Village of Women, a novel about *la violencia* in Colombia; *The Women in the Mirror,* short stories; a book on Mimbres Indian mythology.

SIDELIGHTS: Pat Carr writes: "I've studied six languages. I've been to Europe and have seen Central and South America from Mexico to Argentina. I am committed to writing from a woman's point of view since the female experience has not yet been dealt with honestly by more than a handful of female writers."

* * *

CARROL, Shana
See NEWCOMB, Kerry and SCHAEFER, Frank

* * *

CARTER, Dan T. 1940-

PERSONAL: Born June 17, 1940, in Florence, S.C.; son of Dewey L. and Lalla (Lawhon) Carter; married Jane Winkler, August 29, 1964; children: Alicia Lee, David Charles. *Education:* University of South Carolina, B.A., 1962; University of Wisconsin, M.A., 1964; University of North Carolina, Ph.D., 1967. *Religion:* Presbyterian. *Home:* 1121 Springdale Road, N.E., Atlanta, Ga. 30306. *Office:* Department of History, Emory University Atlanta, Ga. 30322.

CAREER: University of Maryland, College Park, assistant professor, 1967-69, associate professor, 1970-71, professor of history, 1971-75; Emory University, Atlanta, Ga., Andrew W. Mellon Professor of History, 1976—. Visiting professor at University of Wisconsin, 1969-70. *Member:* Society of American Historians, Organization of American Historians, Southern Historical Association. *Awards, honors:* Bancroft Prize, 1969; Ainsfield-Wolfe Award, 1969; Lillian Smith Award, 1969; Jules Landry Prize, 1970.

WRITINGS: A Reasonable Doubt, American Heritage, 1968; *Scottsboro: A Tragedy of the American South,* Louisiana State University Press, 1969.

WORK IN PROGRESS: A study of the immediate post-Civil War South.

* * *

CARTER, Lonnie 1942-

PERSONAL: Born October 25, 1942, in Chicago, Ill.; son of Harold and Evelyn (Lipsey) Carter; married Marilyn Smutko, 1966 (divorced, 1972). *Education:* Marquette University, B.A., 1964, M.A., 1966; Yale University, M.F.A., 1969. *Home:* Cream Hill Rd., West Cornwall, Conn. 16796.

CAREER: Playwright, 1966—. Teacher of playwriting, Yale University School of Drama, 1974-75. *Awards, honors:* Molly Kazan Award, 1967, for "Another Quiet Evening at Home"; Schubert fellowship, 1968-69; Peg Santvoord fellowships, 1970, 1971, 1973; Berkshire Theatre Festival prize, 1971, for "Plumb Loco"; Guggenheim fellowship, 1971-72; National Endowment for the Arts grant, 1974; CBS Foundation grant, 1974-75; Connecticut Commission on the Arts grant, 1976.

WRITINGS—All plays: "Adam" (two-act), first produced in Milwaukee, Wis., at Marquette University, March, 1966; "Another Quiet Evening at Home" (one-act), first produced in New Haven, Conn., at Yale University, May, 1967; "If Beauty's in the Eye of the Beholder, Truth is in the Pupil Somewhere, Too" (one-act), first produced in New Haven, at Yale University, March, 1969; "Workday" (two-act), first presented as reading in New Haven, at Yale University, January, 1970; "Iz She Izzy or Iz He Ain'tzy or Iz They Both" (one-act; music by Robert Montgomery), first produced in New Haven, at Yale Repertory Theatre, March, 1970, produced in New York at St. Clement's Theatre, April, 1972; "More War in Store with Peace as Chief of Police" (one-act) [and] "If Time Must Have a Stop, Space is Where It's at Here at Dead Center of America" (one-act), first produced in New York at Old Reliable, September, 1970; "Plumb Loco" (one-act), first presented as reading in Stockbridge, Mass., at Berkshire Theatre, December, 1970.

"The Big House" (two-act), first produced in New Haven, at Yale Repertory Theatre, October, 1971; "Smoky Links" (two-act), first presented as reading in New York at American Place Theatre, December, 1972; "Watergate Classics" (three sketches), first produced in New Haven, at Yale Repertory Theatre, November, 1973; "Cream Cheese" (two-act), first produced in New York at American Place Theatre, March, 1974; "Trade-Offs" (three-act), first presented as reading in New Haven, at Yale Repertory Theatre, March, 1976. Also author of television script "From the Top," for public television. Contributor to *Yale/Theatre* and to *Scripts.*

WORK IN PROGRESS: Completing a trilogy of plays, to include "Trade-Offs," "Biccelleta, or; The Agony of the Pomegranates in the Garden," and "Rope."

CARTER, Mary Kennedy

PERSONAL: Born in Franklin, Ohio; daughter of Leon Robert and Cara Lee (Atkins) Kennedy; married Donald Wesley (a businessman), 1967; children: Keith Barrett Carter. Education: Ohio State University, B.S., 1956; Columbia University, M.A., 1964; further graduate study at University of London, 1964, and Makerere University, 1965. Home: 156 Craig Ave., Freeport, N.Y. 11520.

CAREER: Elementary school teacher in public schools in Cleveland, Ohio, 1956-60; demonstration teacher in public schools in San Diego, Calif., 1961-63; Uganda Ministry of Education, Lira, Uganda, tutor and supervisor under auspices of Columbia University, 1964-66; McGraw-Hill Book Co., New York, N.Y., project editor and writer, 1967-69; Roosevelt School District, Roosevelt, N.Y., district coordinator and teacher of Black studies, 1969-72; Adelphi University, Garden City, N.Y., instructor in Afro-American studies, 1972; curriculum writer, Mind, Inc., 1973; free-lance writer, 1973—. Member: Pi Lambda Theta, Alpha Kappa Alpha. Awards, honors: Afro-Anglo-American fellowship from Carnegie Foundation and Columbia University, 1963.

WRITINGS: Okelo and Akelo (African reader), Longmans, Green, 1964; Count on Me, American Book Co., 1970; On to Freedom (historical fiction), Hill & Wang, 1970.

WORK IN PROGRESS: A book on sub-Sahara Africa.

* * *

CARUBA, Alan 1937-
(Monica Jordan)

PERSONAL: Born October 9, 1937, in Newark, N.J.; son of Robert (a certified public accountant) and Rebecca (an author; maiden name, Friedlander) Caruba. Education: University of Miami, Coral Gables, Fla., B.A., 1959. Home: 9 Brookside Rd., Maplewood, N.J. 07040. Office address: Interlude Productions, P.O. Box 40, Maplewood, N.J. 07040.

CAREER: New York Times, New York, N.Y., regular contributor to New Jersey page, 1976; Interlude Productions, Maplewood, N.J., self-syndicator of weekly column, "Bookviews," 1973—. Free-lance writer of consumer and trade publications; writer for clients including wire services, government agencies, business and educational institutions since 1959. Military service: U.S. Army, 1960-62. Member: National Book Critics Circle (charter member), Overseas Press Club, American Society of Journalists and Authors, National Rifle Association, American Civil Liberties Union, Authors League of America. Awards, honors: Award of excellence from Communications Association of New Jersey, 1975.

WRITINGS: People Touch (novel), Pocket Books, 1972; (under pseudonym Monica Jordan) Angelface, Dell, 1976. Book reviewer for Popular Guns.

WORK IN PROGRESS: Two novels, The Caller and Moses Jordan; Rescue One, a book about firefighting; The National Hotline Handbook; and Becoming the Person You Want to Be, with Marjabelle Stweart.

SIDELIGHTS: Caruba wrote: "I have never lost the love of doing a good story for a newspaper. . . . My syndicated book news-and-reviews column allows me to indulge my vast reading habits and reach out to an audience at the same time. I am keen, as well, on my new writing ventures into fiction. I welcome all kinds of writing assignments."

CASEBIER, Allan (Frank) 1934-

PERSONAL: Born October 1, 1934, in Los Angeles, Calif.; son of Edwin (a salesman) and Vernice (McCord) Casebier; married Janet Jenks (a university librarian), 1970. Education: University of California, Los Angeles, B.A., 1958, M.A., 1964; University of Michigan, Ph.D., 1969. Agent: Max Gartenberg, 331 Madison Ave., New York, N.Y. 10017. Office: Department of Cinema, University of Southern California, Los Angeles, Calif. 90007.

CAREER: University of Michigan, Ann Arbor, instructor in philosophy, 1966-67; University of Illinois, Urbana, assistant professor of philosophy, 1967-68; University of Southern California, Los Angeles, assistant professor, 1968-76, associate professor of cinema, 1977—. Visiting professor at University of California, Los Angeles, 1974; director of National Conference on Media Responsibility, 1975. Military service: U.S. Army Reserve, Adjutant General Corps, active duty, 1956-57. Member: American Philosophical Association, Society for Cinema Studies, American Society for Aesthetics.

WRITINGS: Film Appreciation, Harcourt, 1976. Contributor to art and aesthetics journals and to Personalist.

WORK IN PROGRESS: Research on Japanese film and culture.

SIDELIGHTS: Casebier told CA his research will set the motion picture in the Japanese cultural background (aesthetic and philosophic) and relate it to the philosophical movement known as phenomenology.

* * *

CASEY, Michael 1947-

PERSONAL: Born in 1947, in Lowell, Mass.; son of Thomas Garrett (a teacher) and Louise (a claims representative; maiden name, Depoian) Casey; married Kathleen Davey (a teacher), July 26, 1975. Education: Lowell Technological Institute, B.S., 1968; State University of New York at Buffalo, M.A., 1973.

CAREER: Security guard at a research facility, 1973-74; civil servant (claims examiner), 1974—. Military service: U.S. Army, 1968-70. Member: Armenian-American Veterans. Awards, honors: Younger poet award from Yale University Press, 1972, for Obscenities.

WRITINGS: Obscenities (poems), Yale University Press, 1972. Guest editor of Rapport, 1973; member of editorial advisory board of Alice James Press.

WORK IN PROGRESS: Mill, a book on the factory of a New England mill town.

* * *

CASEY, Richard Gardiner 1890-1976

August 29, 1890—June 17, 1976; Australian government official and author. Obituaries: New York Times, June 18, 1976; Current Biography, August, 1976. (See index for previous CA sketch)

* * *

CASEY, Rosemary 1904-1976

December 21, 1904—March 22, 1976; American prize-winning playwright and author. Obituaries: New York Times, March 24, 1976.

CASPER, Joseph Andrew 1941-

PERSONAL: Born May 27, 1941, in Philadelphia, Pa.; son of Joseph Peter (a stevedore) and Antoinette Marie (Pascoe) Casper. *Education:* Fordham University, B.A., 1965, M.A., 1966; Woodstock College, M.Div., 1970; University of Southern California, Ph.D., 1973. *Office:* Division of Cinema, University of Southern California, Los Angeles, Calif. 90007.

CAREER: University of Scranton, Scranton, Pa., instructor in English, 1966-67; University of Southern California, Los Angeles, assistant professor of cinema, 1972—.

WRITINGS: Vincente Minnelli and the Film Musical, A. S. Barnes, 1976. Contributor of "Las Vegas Reviews" to *East-West.*

WORK IN PROGRESS: The Dark Comedies of Billy Wilder; The Oeuvre of Stanley Donen.

AVOCATIONAL INTERESTS: Gymnastics, swimming, bicycling, musical comedy.

* * *

CASSERLEY, H(enry) C(yril) 1903-

PERSONAL: Born June 12, 1903, in London, England; son of Edward and Sarah Casserley; married wife, Kathleen Mary, July, 1931; children: one son. *Education:* Attended Emanuel College, London. *Politics:* Conservative. *Religion:* Church of England. *Residence:* Berkhamsted, Hertfordshire, England.

CAREER: In insurance business, 1920-64; free-lance journalist on railway history, 1964—. *Military service:* British Army, 1942-44. *Member:* Stephenson Locomotive Society (general secretary, 1944-62).

WRITINGS: Locomotive Calvalcade: A Comprehensive Review Year by Year of the Changes in Steam Locomotive Development and Design which Have Taken Place on the Railways of the British Isles between the Years 1920 and 1951, Herts, 1952; (editor) *Service Suspended: A Pictorial Souvenir of British Passenger Services that Are No Longer in Operation,* Ian Allan, 1952; (with L. L. Asher) *Locomotives of British Railways: London, Midland, and Scottish Group* (also see below), A. Dakers, 1955; (with Asher) *Locomotives of British Railways: London and North Eastern Group,* (also see below), A. Dakers, 1957; (with Asher) *Locomotives of British Railways: Great Western Group* (also see below), A. Dakers, 1958; (editor) *The Observer's Book of Railway Locomotives of Britain,* revised edition (Casserley not associated with earlier edition), Warne, 1958, 5th edition, 1966.

The Historic Locomotive Pocketbook: From the "Rocket" to the End of Steam, Batsford, 1960; *British Locomotive Names of the Twentieth Century,* Ian Allan, 1963, revised edition, 1967; (with Asher) *Locomotives of British Railways: A Pictorial Record,* Spring Books, 1963, published as *Steam Locomotives of British Railways* (also includes *Locomotives of British Railways: London, Midland, and Scottish Group, ...London and North Eastern Group,* and *...Great Western Group),* Hamlyn, 1973; (with Stuart W. Johnston) *Locomotives at the Grouping,* Ian Allan, 1965; *Britain's Joint Lines,* Ian Allan, 1968; (with C. C. Dorman) *Midland Album,* Ian Allan, 1967, published as *Railway History in Pictures: The Midlands,* A. M. Kelley, 1969; *Preserved Locomotives,* Ian Allan, 1968, 4th edition, 1976.

Railway History in Pictures: Wales and the Welsh Border Counties, David & Charles, 1970; *London & South Western Locomotives,* Ian Allan, 1971; *Railways between the Wars,* David & Charles, 1971; *Famous Railway Photographers: H. C. Casserley,* David & Charles, 1972; *Railways since 1939,* David & Charles, 1972; *Outline of Irish Railway History,* David & Charles, 1974; *LMSR Steam, 1923-1948,* Barton, 1975; *Wessex,* David & Charles, 1976; *LMSR Locomotives, 1923-1948,* three volumes, Barton, 1976; *LNER Steam, 1923-1948,* Barton, 1976; *LNER Locomotives, 1923-1948,* Barton, 1976; *Recollections of the Southern Railway between the Wars,* Barton, 1976.

BIOGRAPHICAL/CRITICAL SOURCES: H. C. Casserley, *Famous Railway Photographers: H. C. Casserley,* David & Charles, 1972.

* * *

CASSIN, Rene Samuel 1887-1976

October 5, 1887—February 20, 1976; French statesman, educator, and author. Obituaries: *Washington Post,* February 21, 1976; *Time,* March 1, 1976.

* * *

CATLIN, Wynelle 1930-

PERSONAL: Born July 29, 1930, in Texas; daughter of George W. (a farmer) and Dovie (Powell) Smith; married L. E. Catlin (an oilfield worker), July 11, 1947; children: Karen (Mrs. Steve Barr), James, Laura, William. *Education:* Attended high school in Jacksboro, Tex. *Home address:* Route 2, Jacksboro, Tex. 76056.

CAREER: Worked various jobs on *Jack County Herald,* Jacksboro, Tex., 1959-71; Wee Care Nursery, Jacksboro, owner and director, 1962-67; Methodist Day Care Center, Jacksboro, director, 1967-69; free-lance writer, 1970—. Founder and co-chairman, Jack County Senior Citizens Activities Committee, 1974-76. *Member:* Author's Guild, Society of Children's Book Writers, Western Writers of America, Jack County Historical Society (treasurer, 1957-58), Abilene Writers Guild.

WRITINGS: Old Wattles (juvenile), Doubleday, 1975. Contributor to western and juvenile magazines including *Cattleman, Great West,* and *Discovery.*

WORK IN PROGRESS: Two adult books, *The Honeysuckle Vine* and *Aunt Mary's Cookbook;* four books for juveniles, *Nell's Calf, Hurry to the Fort, Guilty Or Not Guilty,* and *Where Is Billy?;* two western books.

SIDELIGHTS: Ms. Catlin told *CA,* "What motivates a writer who wants to share the way of life characteristic of a particular region? . . . Perhaps I am motivated by pride in my great-great-grandfather and the others who settled Jack County in the 1850's and want to share my admiration for their courage and perseverance, essential traits for homesteaders. . . . Or, perhaps, life here is all I know, and if I am to write, I must, of necessity, write about it."

AVOCATIONAL INTERESTS: Knitting, sewing, crocheting, patchworking, refinishing furniture, home decorating.

* * *

CAULEY, John R(owan) 1908-1976

April 25, 1908—May 17, 1976; American journalist and writer. Obituaries: *Washington Post,* May 18, 1976.

* * *

CAVALLO, Robert M. 1932-

PERSONAL: Born December 8, 1932, in New York, N.Y.;

son of Dominick and Mary (DiStefano) Cavallo; married Ellen Beach (an actress under name Ellen Evans), November 6, 1963; children: Robert Beach. *Education:* Manhattan College, B.S., 1954; St. John's University, Jamaica, N.Y., LL.B., 1957. *Home and office:* 1065 Park Ave., New York, N.Y. 10028.

CAREER: Thomas J. Flood (attorneys), New York, N.Y., associate, 1958-61; James I. Lysaght (attorneys), New York City, associate, 1961-62; private practice of law in New York City, 1962—. Instructor in law at New York University, 1975—. *Member:* Federal Bar Council, New York State Bar Association, Columbian Lawyers Association. *Awards, honors:* Res Gesta Award and Moot Court Award, both from St. John's University, both, 1957.

WRITINGS: (With Stuart Kahan) *Photography: What's the Law?*, Crown, 1976. Contributor of articles on photography law to magazines.

WORK IN PROGRESS: A book on the business of photography.

* * *

CAZDEN, Elizabeth 1950-

PERSONAL: Born February 6, 1950, in Ann Arbor, Mich.; daughter of Norman (a professor of music) and Courtney (a professor of education; maiden name, Borden) Cazden. *Education:* Oberlin College, B.A., 1971. *Religion:* Religious Society of Friends. *Residence:* Cambridge, Mass.

CAREER: Religious Society of Friends, member of Swarthmore community near Clinton, N.Y., 1970-73; free-lance clerical worker, 1973—. Writer.

WRITINGS: Biography of Antoinette Brown Blackwell, Feminist Press, 1977. Contributor of articles to religious periodicals, including *Quaker Life* and *Friends Journal.* Editor of *Quaker Action,* 1972-73.

WORK IN PROGRESS: A study of Quaker history.

SIDELIGHTS: Elizabeth Cazden has traveled extensively throughout the northeastern states and Canada. She has also traveled in Europe, staying at youth workcamps in Spain and Yugoslavia, and visiting religious communities in France. Currently, she is intent on entering law school.

* * *

CESAIRE, Aime Fernand 1913-

PERSONAL: Born June 25, 1913, in Basse-Pointe, Martinique, West Indies; son of Fernand (a comptroller with the revenue service) and Marie (Hermine) Cesaire; married Suzanne Roussi (a teacher), July 10, 1937; children: Jacques, Jean-Paul, Francis, Ina, Marc, Michelle. *Education:* Attended Ecole Normale Superieure, Paris; Sorbonne, University of Paris, licencie es lettres. *Address:* Assemblee Nationale, Paris, 7eme, France; and Mairie de Fort-de-France, Martinique, West Indies.

CAREER: Teacher at the Lycee of Fort-de-France, Martinique, 1940-45; member of the two French constituent assemblies, 1945-46; deputy for Martinique in the French National Assembly, 1946—; member of the Communist bloc in the Assembly from 1946-56, affiliated to the Parti du Regroupement Africain et des Federalistes from 1958-59, independent since 1959. Mayor of Fort-de-France, Martinique; conseiller general for the 4th canton (district) of Fort-de-France; president of the Parti Progressiste Martiniquais.

WRITINGS—Poems: Les armes miraculeuses (title means "The Miracle Weapons"), Gallimard, 1946, reprinted, 1970; *Soleil Cou-Coupe* (title means "Beheaded Sun"), K (Paris), 1948, reprinted, with *Antilles a main armee* by Charles Calixte, Kraus, 1970; *Cahier d'un retour au pays natal* (first published in *Parisian Review*), Presence Africaine, 1956, 2nd edition, 1960, translation by Emil Snyders, with parallel French and English texts, published as *Return to My Native Land,* Presence Africaine, 1968, translation by John Berger and Anna Bostock also published as *Return to My Native Land,* Penguin Books, 1969; *Ferrements* (title means "Shackles"), Editions du Seuil, 1960; *Cadastre,* Editions du Seuil, 1961, translation by Gregson Davis published under the same title, Third Press, 1972, translation by Emil Snyders and Sanford Upson published under the same title, Third Press, 1973; *State of the Union,* translation by Clayton Eshleman and Dennis Kelly of selected poems from *Les armes miraculeuses, Ferrements,* and *Cadastre,* [Bloomington, Ill.], 1966. Also author of *Corps perdu* (title means "Lost Body"), illustrated by Picasso, 1949.

Plays: *Et les chiens se taisaient: Tragedie* (title means "And the Dogs Were Silent: A Tragedy"), Presence Africaine, 1956; *La tragedie du roi Christophe,* Presence Africaine, 1963, translation by Ralph Manheim published as *The Tragedy of King Christophe,* Grove, 1970, revised French edition, 1973; *Une saison au Congo,* Editions du Seuil, 1966, translation by Manheim published as *A Season in the Congo* (produced in New York at Paperback Studio Theatre, July, 1970), Grove, 1969; *Une tempete: d'apres "La tempete" de Shakespeare. Adaptation pour un theatre negre* (title means "A Tempest: After 'The Tempest' by Shakespeare. Adaptation for the Negro Theatre"), Editions du Seuil, 1969.

Other: (With Gaston Monnerville and Leopold Sedar-Senghor) *Commemoration du centenaire de l'abolition de l'esclavage: Discours prononces a la Sorbonne le 27 avril 1948* (title means "Commemoration of the Centenary of the Abolition of Slavery: Speeches Given at the Sorbonne on April 27, 1948"), Presses Universitaires de France, 1948; *Discours sur le colonialisme,* Reclame, 1950, 5th edition, Presence Africaine, 1970, translation by Joan Pinkham published as *Discourse on Colonialism,* Monthly Review Press, 1972; *Lettre a Maurice Thorez,* 3rd edition, Presence Africaine, 1956, translation published as *Letter to Maurice Thorez,* Presence Africaine, 1957; *Toussaint Louverture: la revolution francaise et le probleme coloniale* (title means "Toussaint Louverture: The French Revolution and the Colonial Problem"), Club Francais du Livre, 1960, revised edition, Presence Africaine, 1962.

Editor of *L'Afrique.*

SIDELIGHTS: The Ghanaian writer Kofi Awoonor wrote: "Cesaire's meeting with Leopold Sedar Senghor before the Second World War signaled the beginning of one of those rare literary unions prominent in history. It produced not only a large crop of creative work, but, more important, the theoretical formulations that launched negritude as a literary movement and an important twentieth century phenomenon." Harry T. More added: "Cesaire has been one of the great exponents of what the French call negritude, the celebration of the condition of being a Negro and the demand for freedom from colonial and other bonds; in his more recent work, however, Cesaire is less the poet of negritude than of all humanity."

Prescott Nichols explained one way Cesaire has split from the negritude mainstream: "Whereas negritude, as it is sometimes espoused by Senghor and others, does frequently look to the African civilizations and cultures of the past, Cesaire, the prophet of the Third World, is continually thrusting toward the future.'' Judith Gleason explained further: ''When in 1939, at the age of 26, Cesaire left Paris for his native Martinique, the Poem he wrote about this decision made cultural history.

''Cesaire's location on that island is what distinguishes his poetry from that of his predecessors among the French symbolists and surrealists, from that of his contemporaries of African origin. His geographical position—a moral position, a rhetorical stance—is the first metaphorical premise of his poetic work.'' She continued: ''A surrealist prophet of the strong breed, Cesaire is Mosaic in his ability to perform real miracles with language because, grounded in the historical sufferings of a chosen people, his is an angry, authentic vision of the promised land. But his visionary landscapes would lack their fierce precision had not nature itself tried his descriptive powers to the breaking point. Which is again to say that the relation between his images and his environment, the ecology of his poetry, cannot be ignored.''

BIOGRAPHICAL/CRITICAL SOURCES: Lilyan Kesteloot, *Aime Cesaire,* P. Seghers, 1963, new edition, 1970; *Aime Cesaire, ecrivain Martiniquais,* Fernand Nathan, 1967; *Negro Digest,* January, 1970; *Twentieth Century Literature,* July, 1972.*

* * *

CHAMBERLIN, Waldo 1905-

PERSONAL: Born October 13, 1905, in Rockford, Ill.; son of Daniel Upham (a merchant) and Elizabeth (Coggeshall) Chamberlin; married Kathryn Rogers (an executive secretary), August 2, 1940; children: John R., David W. *Education:* University of Washington, Seattle, A.B., 1927, M.A., 1936; Stanford University, Ph.D., 1939. *Politics:* Democrat. *Religion:* Congregationalist. *Home:* 14 Conant Rd., Hanover, N.H. 03755.

CAREER: Worked in shipping and exporting business in Seattle, Wash., San Francisco, Calif., Alaska, and Far East, 1928-36; Stanford University, Stanford, Calif., research associate of Hoover Library, 1936-41; Library of Congress, Washington, D.C., fellow in naval history, 1941-42; U.S. Department of State, Washington, D.C., senior divisional assistant in Division of International Security and Organization, 1942-44; U.S. War Shipping Administration, executive assistant to chairman of Pacific Coast Maritime Industry Board, 1944-45; United Nations, documents officer at San Francisco Conference and at Preparatory Commission in London, 1945-46, deputy director of Documents Division, 1946-48; New York University, New York, N.Y., professor of government, 1948-61; Dartmouth College, Hanover, N.H., dean of summer programs, 1961-69, professor of history, 1969-71, professor emeritus, 1971—. Researcher, Brookings Institution, 1954-59. Chairman of committee on international understanding, New York State Board of Regents, 1950—; trustee, Manhasset Public Library, 1954-61. Consultant to president of Carnegie Endowment for International Peace, 1949-52. *Military service:* U.S. Naval Reserve, 1937-41; became lieutenant, junior grade. *Member:* Commission to Study the Organization of Peace. *Awards, honors:* M.A., Dartmouth College, 1962.

WRITINGS: Industrial Relations in Wartime: Great Britain, 1914-1918, An Annotated Bibliography, Stanford University Press, 1940; *Industrial Relations in Germany, 1914-1940: An Annotated Bibliography,* Stanford University Press, 1941; *Enabling Instruments of Members of the United Nations,* Carnegie Endowment for International Peace, 1951; (with Carol Carter Moore) *How to Use United Nations Documents,* New York University Press, 1952; (compiler of general index) *Documents of the United Nations Conference on International Organization,* Volume 21 and Volume 22, United Nations, 1955; (with Thomas Hovet, Jr. and Richard N. Swift) *A Chronology and Fact Book of the United Nations,* Oceana, 1959, 3rd edition (with Thomas Hovet, Jr. and Erica Hovet), 1970; (with Brenda Brimmer, Linwood Wall, and Thomas Hovet, Jr.) *A Guide to the Use of UN Documents, including References to the Specialized Agencies and Special UN Bodies,* Oceana, 1962; (contributor) Franz B. Gross, editor, *The United States and the United Nations,* University of Oklahoma Press, 1964.

Editor or co-editor, *Annual Review of UN Affairs,* Oceana, 1954, 1957, 1959. Contributor to *Encyclopedia Americana* and *Britannica Yearbook;* contributor of more than thirty articles and reviews to journals.

WORK IN PROGRESS: We Were the United Nations, a largely-autobiographical book; *History of International Government; Who Represents the Palestinians?*

* * *

CHANT, Barry (Mostyn) 1938-

PERSONAL: Born October 23, 1938, in Adelaide, South Australia; son of James Oswald (a teacher) and Vera (Penno) Chant; married Vanessa Bennett, January 23, 1960; children: Rebekah, Michael, Clinton. *Education:* University of Adelaide, B.A. (honors, 1959, diploma in education, 1962; Melbourne College of Divinity, B.D., 1968. *Home:* 88A Fisher St., Fullarton, South Australia 5063. *Office:* Adelaide Crusade Center, 27 Sturt St., Adelaide, South Australia 5000.

CAREER: Teacher of English, history, and social studies in secondary school in Murray Bridge, South Australia, 1960-63; ordained to ministry, 1961; pastor of Pentecostal church in Adelaide, South Australia, 1964-75; Crusade Bible College, Adelaide, dean, 1964—. Partner of Luke Publications, 1974—; Chairman of Christian Revival Crusade (South Australia), 1974—.

WRITINGS: Upon Dry Ground, Crusade Publications, 1969, reprinted as *Your Pocket Guide to the Power of God,* 1975; *Fact or Fantasy,* Crusade Publications, 1970; *The Secret Is Out,* Crusade Publications, 1971; *Heart of Fire: The Story of Australian Pentecostalism,* Luke Publications, 1974, revised edition, 1976; *Spindles of the Dusty Range* (children's stories), Luke Publications, 1975; *Straight Talk About Sex,* Luke Publications, 1976; *Spindles and Eagles,* Luke Publications, 1976. Associate editor and feature writer for *Impact* (formerly *Revivalist*), 1964—.

WORK IN PROGRESS: A book on marriage.

* * *

CHAPMAN, Charles F(rederic) 1881-1976

January 4, 1881—March 21, 1976; American magazine publisher and author. Obituaries: *New York Times,* March 23, 1976; *AB Bookman's Weekly,* June 28, 1976.

* * *

CHAPMAN, Hester W(olferstan) 1899-1976

November 26, 1899—April 6, 1976; British historical novelist and biographer. Obituaries: *AB Bookman's Weekly,* May 31, 1976. (See index for previous *CA* sketch)

CHAPMAN, Karen C. 1942-

PERSONAL: Born December 5, 1942, in Berkeley, Calif.; daughter of George A. (a professor) and Marguerite (Rodoani) Carbone. *Education:* University of Oregon, B.A., 1964; University of Denver, M.A., 1965, Ph.D., 1969. *Office:* Department of English, Oregon State University, Corvallis, Ore. 97331.

CAREER: Oregon State University, Corvallis, Ore., associate professor of comparative literature, 1975—, assistant dean of College of Liberal Arts. *Member:* Modern Language Association of America, American Association of University Professors, Western Association of Africanists, Rocky Mountain Modern Language Association.

WRITINGS: (Translator) *Climbie* (novel; title means ''Some Other Day''), Heinemann, 1970, Africana Publishing, 1971; (author of introduction) Ama Ata Aidoo, *Dilemma of a Ghost* (play), Collier, 1971.

WORK IN PROGRESS: Translating *Le Pagne Noir*, a collection of African folktales by Bernard Dadie.

SIDELIGHTS: Karen Chapman has traveled extensively in Italy and France.

* * *

CHAPNICK, Howard 1922-

PERSONAL: Born February 13, 1922, in New York, N.Y.; son of Murray B. (a merchant) and Frieda (Bernstein) Chapnick; married Jeanette Ebenstein (a bookkeeper), February 24, 1946; children: Denise (Mrs. Lawrence J. Ploetz), Ilene (Mrs. Thomas C. Todd). *Education:* Attended University of Pennsylvania, 1936-37; New York University, B.C.S., 1942. *Politics:* Democrat. *Religion:* Hebrew. *Home:* 145 East 27th St., New York, N.Y. 10016. *Agent:* George Dawson, Interlit Agency, 11 Hayden Pl., Wellesley Hills, Mass. 02101. *Office:* Black Star Publishing Co., 450 Park Ave. S., New York, N.Y. 10016.

CAREER: Black Star Publishing Co., New York, N.Y., president, 1946—. Instructor at University of Missouri, 1964—, and at photographic workshop of New School of Social Research, 1973—. Photographic consultant, American Iron and Steel Institute, 1976—. *Military service:* U.S. Army, 1942-46; became technical sergeant. *Member:* International Center of Photography, National Press Photographers Association, Thoreau Lyceum.

WRITINGS: (Editor) *The Illustrated Leaves of Grass*, Grosset, 1971; (editor) *The Illustrated World of Thoreau*, Grosset, 1974; *The Illustrated Eternal Sea*, Grosset, 1976; *Night Train at Wiscasset*, Doubleday, in press. Columnist for *Popular Photography*, 1976—.

* * *

CHAPPELL, Clovis G(illham) 1882-1972

PERSONAL: Born January 8, 1882, in Flatwoods, Tenn.; son of William B. (a farmer) and Mary (Gillham) Chappell; married Cecil Hart, April 15, 1908; children: Clovis G., Jr., Robert Hart. *Education:* Attended Duke University, 1902-03, and Harvard University, 1904-05. *Residence:* Waverly, Tenn.

CAREER: Ordained minister of Methodist Episcopal Church of the South, 1908; pastor in Texas, Oklahoma, Washington, D.C., and Tennessee, 1908-32, and in Birmingham, Ala., 1932-36, Oklahoma City, Okla., 1936-41, Jackson, Miss., 1941-45, and Charlotte, N.C., 1945-49; retired, 1949-72. *Awards, honors:* D.D. from Duke University and Centenary College of Louisiana, both 1920; D.Litt. from Birmingham-Southern College, 1936.

WRITINGS: The Village Tragedy, and Other Sermons, Williams & Wilkins, 1921; *Sermons on Biblical Characters*, George H. Doran Co., 1922; *More Sermons on Biblical Characters*, George H. Doran Co., 1923; *Sermons on New Testament Characters*, George H. Doran Co., 1924; *Sermons on Old Testament Characters*, George H. Doran Co., 1925; *Home Folks*, Cokesbury Press, 1926; *Familiar Failures*, George H. Doran Co., 1927; *Christ and the New Woman*, Cokesbury Press, 1928; *Men That Count*, Doubleday, Doran & Co., 1929.

All published by Cokesbury Press: *The Sermon on the Mount*, 1930; *Sermons from the Psalms*, 1931; *Sermons from the Parables*, 1933; *Sermons on the Lord's Prayer and Other Prayers of Jesus*, 1934; *Chappell's Special Day Sermons*, 1936; *Sermons from the Miracles*, 1937; *Ten Rules for Living*, 1938; *Values that Last*, 1939; *The Road to Certainty*, 1940.

All published by Abingdon-Cokesbury Press: *Faces about the Cross*, 1941; *Feminine Faces*, 1942; *Sermons from Revelation*, 1943; *Living Zestfully*, 1944; *If I Were Young*, 1945; *And the Prophets ...*, 1946; *Questions Jesus Asked*, 1948; *When the Church Was Young*, 1950; *Annointed to Preach*, 1951; *The Seven Words*, 1952; *In Parables*, 1953.

All published by Abingdon Press: *Meet These Men*, 1956; *Sermons from Job*, 1957; *Sermons on Simon Peter*, 1959; *The Cross before Calvary*, 1960; *Living with Royalty*, 1962; *Surprises in the Bible*, 1967; *Evangelistic Sermons of Clovis G. Chappell*, 1973.

(Died, 1972)

[Information supplied by author before death]

* * *

CHARLES, Robert
See SMITH, Robert Charles

* * *

CHARQUES, Dorothy (Taylor) 1899-1976

June 4, 1899—March 20, 1976; British biographer and novelist. Obituaries: *AB Bookman's Weekly*, May 17, 1976.

* * *

CHASE, Stuart 1888-

PERSONAL: Born March 8, 1888, in Somersworth, N.H.; son of Harvey Stuart (a certified public accountant) and Aaronette (Rowe) Chase; married Margaret Hatfield, July 5, 1914 (divorced); married Marian Tyler, 1930; children: (first marriage) Robert Hatfield, Sonia Hatfield. *Education:* Massachusetts Institute of Technology, student, 1907-08; Harvard University, S.B. (cum laude), 1910. *Home address:* P.O. Box 422, Georgetown, Conn. 06829.

CAREER: Certified public accountant, 1916; Harvey S. Chase Co. (certified public accountants), Boston, Mass., partner until 1917; Federal Trade Commission, Washington, D.C., conducted investigations of meat packers and the meat industry, 1917-22; Labor Bureau, Inc., New York City, partner in charge of auditing and accounting, 1922-39. Worked for U.S. Food Administration, 1918. Member of Technical Alliance (New York City), 1921; co-founder of Consumers' Research. Consultant to Securities Exchange Commission, Tennessee Valley Authority, UNESCO, government of Puerto Rico, and other organizations. *Member:*

National Institute of Arts and Letters, Phi Beta Kappa, Phi Gamma Delta. *Awards, honors:* Prize from *Life,* 1924, for article "Recipe for Bigger and Better Wars"; Litt.D. from American University, 1949; H.H.D. from Emerson College, 1970; received Boni & Liveright Prize; received Dr.Humane Letters from University of New Haven.

WRITINGS: (With first wife, Margaret H. Chase) *A Honeymoon Experiment,* Houghton, 1916; *The Tragedy of Waste,* Macmillan, 1925; (with F. J. Schlink) *Your Money's Worth: A Study in the Waste of the Consumer's Dollar* (Book of the Month selection), Macmillan, 1927; *Men and Machines,* Macmillan, 1929; *Prosperity: Fact Or Myth,* C. Boni, 1929; (with second wife, Marian Tyler) *Mexico: A Study of Two Americas* (Literary Guild selection), Macmillan, 1931; *A New Deal,* Macmillan, 1932; *The Economy of Abundance,* Macmillan, *Government in Business,* Macmillan, 1935; *Rich Land, Poor Land: A Study of Waste in the Natural Resources of America,* McGraw, 1936; *The Tyranny of Words,* Harcourt, 1938; *The New Western Front,* Harcourt, 1939.

Idle Money Idle Men, Harcourt, 1940; *The Nemesis of American Business and Other Essays,* Macmillan, 1941; *A Primer of Economics,* Row, Peterson & Co., 1941; *The Road We Are Traveling, 1914-1942,* Twentieth Century Fund, 1942; *Goals for America,* Twentieth Century Fund, 1942; *Where's the Money Coming From?,* Twentieth Century Fund, 1943; *Democracy Under Pressure,* Twentieth Century Fund, 1945; *Tomorrow's Trade,* Twentieth Century Fund, 1945; *Men at Work,* Harcourt, 1945; *For This We Fought,* Twentieth Century Fund, 1946; (with Edmund de S. Brunner) *The Proper Study of Mankind: An Inquiry into the Science of Human Relations,* Harper, 1948, revised edition, 1956; (with Marian T. Chase) *Roads to Agreement: Successful Methods in the Science of Human Relations,* Harper, 1951; (with Marian T. Chase) *Power of Words,* Harcourt, 1954; *Guides to Straight Thinking,* Harper, 1956; *Some Things Worth Knowing: A Generalist's Guide to Useful Knowledge,* Harper, 1958; *Live and Let Live,* Harper, 1959; *American Credos,* Harper, 1962; *Money to Grow On,* Harper, 1964; *The Most Probable World,* Harper, 1968; *Danger—Men Talking: A Background Book on Semantics and Communication,* Parents' Magazine Press, 1969.

Contributor to magazines.

SIDELIGHTS: Chase's interest in social problems developed under the influence of Henry George, Thorsten Veblen, R. H. Tawney, and Edward Bellamy, especially those relating to consumer education, industrial waste, labor problems, and conservation. He has said: "My interests, changing with time and history, veer farther than ever away from ideologies. These always seemed less important to me than practical measures to abolish poverty. Economics now seems less important than the broader field of social science, where I have undertaken an assignment as a sort of integrator—a non-specialist who tries to fit his specialties together and interpret their achievements."

AVOCATIONAL INTERESTS: Sketching, tennis, skiing. He adds: "I like good conversation, white wine, Mexican Indians, high mountains, Fire Island, mighty bridges, pine forests, clean-cut thinking, Russian folk songs, Charles Chaplin . . . I do not like billboards, hot dogs, high-pressure selling, radios, chambers of commerce, the stock exchange or Radio City."

BIOGRAPHICAL/CRITICAL SOURCES: Saturday Review of Literature, January 22, 1938; *Newsweek,* January 24, 1938; *New Republic,* January 25, 1939; *New York Herald Tribune,* August 25, 1940.

CHATELAIN, Nicolas 1913-1976

May 28, 1913—May 7, 1976; French journalist and author. Obituaries: *New York Times,* May 9, 1976.

* * *

CHAVES, Jonathan 1943-

PERSONAL: Born June 8, 1943, in Brooklyn, N.Y.; son of Aaron David (a doctor) and Frieda (Perskey) Chaves; married Anna Caraveli (a Ph.D. candidate), November 27, 1974; children: Ian, Colin, Rachel. *Education:* Brooklyn College of the City University of New York, B.A., 1965; Columbia University, M.A., 1966, Ph.D., 1971. *Office:* Department of Comparative Literature, State University of New York, Binghamton, N.Y. 13901.

CAREER: Brooklyn College of the City University of New York, Brooklyn, N.Y., instructor, 1970-71, assistant professor of Chinese language and literature, 1971-73; State University of New York, Binghamton, assistant professor of classical Chinese language and literature, Chinese art, and Japanese literature, 1973—. *Member:* Association for Asian Studies. *Awards, honors:* American Council of Learned Societies grant, summer, 1973, for study in Taiwan; Asian Literature Program grant from Asia Society, 1976.

WRITINGS: (Contributor) Tseng Yu-ho Ecke, editor, *Chinese Calligraphy,* Philadelphia Museum of Art, 1971; (contributor) Liu Wu-chi and Irving Yucheng Lo, editors, *Sunflower Splendor,* Indiana University Press, 1975; (translator and author of introduction) *Heaven My Blanket, Earth My Pillow: Poems from Sung Dynasty China by Yang Wan-li,* Weatherhill, 1975; *Mei Yao-ch'en and the Development of Early Sung Poetry,* Columbia University Press, 1976. Contributor of articles and translations to art and literature journals.

WORK IN PROGRESS: Studying Chinese calligraphy and its relationship with poetry.

SIDELIGHTS: Chaves has studied in India and Japan. His specialty is *Shih* poetry of the Sung dynasty. He is also interested in Japanese and Indian literature, and the "literatures of the primitive world."

* * *

CHAYES, Abram 1922-

PERSONAL: Born July 18, 1922, in Chicago, Ill.; son of Edward and Kitty (Torch) Chayes; married Antonia Handler, December 24, 1947; children: Eva, Abigail, Lincoln, Sarah Prudence, Angelica. *Education:* Harvard University, A.B., 1943, LL.B., 1949. *Home:* 3 Hubbard Park, Cambridge, Mass. 02138. *Office:* Harvard Law School, Cambridge, Mass. 02138.

CAREER: Admitted to the Bar of Connecticut, 1950, District of Columbia, 1953, and Massachusetts, 1958; legal adviser to the governor of Connecticut, 1949-50; general counsel for U.S. President's Materials Policy Commission, 1950-51; legal clerk to Supreme Court Justice Felix Frankfurter, 1951-52; Covington & Burling (law firm), Washington, D.C., associate attorney, 1952-55; Harvard University, Cambridge, Mass., assistant professor, 1955-58, professor of law, 1958-61; U.S. Department of State, legal adviser to the assistant secretary, 1961-64; Gingburg & Feldman (law firm), Washington, D.C., associate attorney, 1964-65; Harvard University, professor of law, 1965—. Staff director of Democratic Platform Committee, 1960; director of foreign policy task force of Democratic campaign, 1972. *Military service:* U.S. Army, field artillery, 1943-46; became captain;

received Bronze Star. *Member:* American Academy of Arts and Sciences (fellow), Phi Beta Kappa. *Awards, honors:* Carnegie Corporation grant, 1965-66.

WRITINGS: Closed Corporation Seminar Materials, Harvard Law School, c. 1958; (editor) Patricia M. Wald, *Law and Poverty, 1965,* U.S. Government Printing Office, 1965; (editor with R. R. Baxter) *Materials for the Carnegie-Harvard Seminar, 1966,* [Cambridge, Mass.], 1966; (compiler with Thomas Ehrlich and Andreas F. Lowenfeld) *International Legal Process: Materials for an Introductory Course,* two volumes, Little, Brown, 1968-69; (editor with Jerome B. Wiesner) *ABM: An Evaluation of the Decision to Deploy an Anti-Ballistic Missile System,* introduction by Edward M. Kennedy, Harper, 1969; (with others) *Satellite Broadcasting,* Oxford University Press, 1973. Contributor of articles to legal journals.*

*   *   *

CHELWOOD, Tufton Victor Hamilton 1917-
(Tufton Victor Hamilton Beamish)

PERSONAL: Born January 27, 1917, son of T.P.H. (a rear admiral in the Royal Navy) and Margaret Antonia Beamish; married Janet McMillan Stevenson, 1950 (divorced, 1973); married Pia McHenry, 1975; children: two daughters. *Education:* Attended Royal Military College, Sandhurst. *Home:* Chelworth House, Chelwood Gate, Sussex, England.

CAREER: British Parliament, London, England, Conservative member of House of Commons from Lewes Division of East Sussex, 1945-74, member of House of Lords, 1974—, vice-chairman of British Group Inter-Parliamentary Union, 1952-54, and of Conservative and Unionist members' committee, 1958-74, chairman of Conservative Foreign Affairs Committee, 1960-64, opposition defense spokesman, 1965-67, chairman of Conservative Group for Europe, 1970-73, member of Monnet Action Committee for United States of Europe, 1971, joint deputy leader of British delegation to European Parliment, 1973-74. Delegate to Council of Europe and chairman of assembly committee, 1951-54. Member of Church of England Council of Inter-Church Relations, 1950-60; president of Sussex Trust for Nature Conservation, 1968—. Member of board of directors of businesses in Sussex, 1970—; governor of Stowe School. Honorary freeman of Borough of Lewes, 1970. *Military service:* British Army, Royal Northumberland Fusiliers, 1937-45; served in Palestine, France, Belgium, Malaya, India, Burma, North Africa, and Italy; became captain and honorary colonel (TA); mentioned in dispatches; received Military Cross.

MEMBER: Royal Society for the Protection of Birds (president, 1967-70), Salmon and Trout Association, Society of Authors. *Awards, honors:* Deputy Lieutenant for East Sussex, 1970; Golden Cross of Merit, 1944; commander of the Order of the Phoenix (Greece), 1949; Polonia Restituta (Poland); Order of the Cedar (Lebanon), 1969; created knight, 1961, created Baron of Lewes (Life Peer), 1974.

WRITINGS—All under name Tufton Victor Hamilton Beamish: *Must Night Fall?* (analysis of Marxism in Eastern Europe), Hollis & Carter, 1950; *Battle Royal: A New Account of Simon de Montfort's Struggle against King Henry III,* Muller, 1965, Barnes & Nobel, 1966; (with Philip Goodhart) *Twice a Citizen: The Future of the Territorials,* Conservative Political Centre, 1969; *Half Marx* (on a Marxist threat to England via the Labour Party), Tom Stacey, 1970; (with Norman St. John-Stevas) *Sovereignty: Shadow or Substance,* Conservative Political Centre, 1971. Contributor to magazines and newspapers.

AVOCATIONAL INTERESTS: Shooting, fishing, ornithology, photography, music.

*   *   *

CHERRYH, C(arolyn) J(anice) 1942-

PERSONAL: Born September 1, 1942, in St. Louis, Mo.; daughter of Basil (a Social Security representative) and Lois (Van Deventer) Cherry. *Education:* University of Oklahoma, B.A., 1964; Johns Hopkins University, M.A., 1965. *Religion:* Christian. *Home:* Oklahoma City, Okla. 73114.

CAREER: Oklahoma City Public Schools, Oklahoma City, Okla., teacher of Latin and ancient history, 1965—. *Member:* Science Fiction Writers of America, American Classical League, Oklahoma City Writers, Phi Beta Kappa. *Awards, honors:* Woodrow Wilson fellow, 1965-66.

WRITINGS: Gate of Ivrel, Daw Books, 1976; *Brothers of Earth,* Daw Books, 1976.

WORK IN PROGRESS: Hunter of Worlds, Daw Books, expected date of publication 1977; a trilogy; a sequel to *Gate of Ivrel.*

SIDELIGHTS: Cherryh told *CA:* "I write science fiction and adult fantasy of an essentially anthropological slant—speculations on the essence of humanity and the possibilities of non-human intelligence and non-human society.

My classical education includes Latin, Greek, anthropology, archaeology and ancient history, with sidelines in Bronze Age myth and society; art; geology and climatology. Also in keeping with an essentially Renaissance education, I have studied literature, religion, music, astronomy; am a passable artist; know French and Italian, with some German and Russian; know the art of fencing and archery and enjoy riding.

I have retraced Caesar's campaigns in travels in England, France, Switzerland and Italy; have hiked about the hills of ancient Thebes and Mycenae in Greece; climbed Mt. Dicte on Crete, where Zeus was born; walked the dead cities of Pompeii, Troy, Ephesus, and Cnossos; have visited Rome and Istanbul, Pergamum, Athens and Delphi, lived a week in Sparta; have sailed the Adriatic past Ithaca—all of this while taking photographs and historical notes.

In the interest of authenticity in my writing I have tried camel-riding and small-craft sailing, horse-cabs and hovercraft, have explored ancient prisons and studied computer science and ancient weaponry. Things I have yet to do include as favorite dreams: to see the pyramids of Egypt and trace the Nile by boat; to sail the routes of Jason and Odysseus; to travel the route of Alexander the Great as far as India and back again; to see Mt. Erebus in Antarctica and the Great Wall of China; to be on the first commercial flight into space."

*   *   *

CHESSEX, Jacques 1934-

PERSONAL: Born March 1, 1934, in Payerne, Switzerland; son of Pierre (a writer) and Lucienne (Vallotton) Chessex; married Elisabeth Reichenbach, July 3, 1975. *Education:* University of Lausanne, License es lettres, 1960. *Home:* 1 Mercerie, 1003 Lausanne, Switzerland. *Office:* Department of French Literature, University of Lausanne, Lausanne, Switzerland.

CAREER: University of Lausanne, Lausanne, Switzerland, professor of French literature, 1960—.

WRITINGS—In translation: *A Father's Love,* translated by Martin Sokolinsky, Bobbs-Merrill, 1975.

Works in French: *Le Jour proche* (poetry), Aux miroirs partages, 1954; *Chant de printemps* (poetry), [Geneva], 1955; *Une Voix la nuit* (poetry), Mermod, 1957; (editor) *Hommage a Gustave Roud,* [Lausanne], 1957; *Batailles dans l'air* (poetry), Mermod, 1959; (author of biography) Pablo Picasso, *Dessins, epoques bleue et rose,* Mermod, 1960; *Le Tete ouverte,* Gallimard, 1962; (with Bertil Galland) *Ecriture: Cahier de litterature et de poesie,* Cahiers de la Renaissance Vaudoise (Lausanne), 1964—; *Le Jeune de huit nuits* (poetry), Payot, 1966; *La Confession du pasteur Burg,* Bourgois, 1967, reprinted with new preface, Union Generale d'Editions, 1974; *L'Ouvert obscur* (poetry), L'Age d'homme, 1967; *Reste avec nous, precede de Carnet de terre,* Cahiers de la Renaissance Vaudoise, 1967; (editor) *Charles-Albert Cingria,* Seghers, 1967; (author of text) Marcel Imsand, *1000 Lausanne,* Payot, 1969; *Portrait des Vaudois,* Cahiers de la Renaissance Vaudoise, 1969; *Carabas* (autobiographical), Grasset, 1971; *Les Saintes Ecritures,* Galland, 1972; *L'Ogre* (novel), Grasset, 1973; (author of text) *Les Dessins d'Etienne Delessert,* Galland, 1974; *Le Renard qui disait non a la lune,* Gasset, 1974; *L'Ardent royaume,* B. Grasset, 1975.

WORK IN PROGRESS: Elegie soleil du Regret (poems); *Breviaire* (poems and prose).

* * *

CHESTER, Laura 1949-

PERSONAL: Born April 13, 1949, in Cambridge, Mass.; daughter of George Miller (a lawyer) and Margaret (Sheftall) Chester; married Geoffrey M. Young (a writer and editor), August 28, 1969; children: Clovis Chester-Young. *Education:* Attended Skidmore College, 1967-69; University of New Mexico, B.A., 1972. *Home:* 2016 Cedar, Berkeley, Calif. 94709.

CAREER: Stooge (magazine), Albuquerque, N.M., co-editor, 1969-74; The Figures (small press), Berkeley, Calif., co-editor, 1975—. *Awards, honors:* Steloff Poetry Prize from Skidmore College, 1969; Kappa Alpha Theta poetry award from University of New Mexico, 1970.

WRITINGS—Poetry, sometimes with journals and prose added: *Tiny Talk,* Roundhouse, 1972; (with husband, Geoffrey M. Young) *The All Night Salt Lick,* Tribal Press, 1972; (editor with Sharon Barb) *Rising Tides: Twentieth Century American Women Poets,* Simon & Schuster, 1973; *Nightlatch,* Tribal Press, 1974; *Primagravida,* Christopher Books, 1975; *Proud and Ashamed,* Christopher Books, in press. Contributor of more than a hundred articles and poems to literary magazines. Co-editor of *Best Friends.*

WORK IN PROGRESS: Watermark, a novel; *My Life with Horses,* stories and poems; *Julian Surrender,* a novel.

SIDELIGHTS: Laura Chester writes: "My work reflects my life, its immediacy and its unconscious passageways, while embellishing, molding and transforming, what is given, what I see and sense and know. I am a feminist, a country girl and a Parisian at heart, but in general find myself becoming more and more apolitical, leading the rather selfish self-sufficient life of a woman of words, concerned foremost with my art and the difficult demanding task of its perfection—a place I have yet to reach."

* * *

CHIANG Yee 1903-

PERSONAL: Born May 19, 1903, in Kiu-chiang, China; came to United States, 1955; naturalized U.S. citizen, 1966; son of Chiang Ho-an (an artist) and Tsai Hsiang-Lin; married Tseng Yun, June 3, 1924; children: Chiang Hsiao-Yen, Chiang Chien-Fei, Chiang Chien-Lan, Chaing Chien Kou. *Education:* National Southeastern University, Nanking, China, B.Sc., 1925. *Home:* 520 West 123rd St., New York, N.Y. 10027. *Office:* Columbia University, New York, N.Y. 10027.

CAREER: Teacher of chemistry in middle schools in China; lecturer in chemistry at National Chi-Nan University in China; assistant editor of a daily newspaper in Hangchow, Chekiang, China; district governor of districts of Chiuchiang, Yushan, Tangtu, and Wu-Hu, China; University of London, School of Oriental and African Studies, London, England, lecturer in Chinese, 1935-38; Wellcome Museum of Medical Science, London, in charge of Chinese section, 1938-40; designer of decor and costumes for "The Birds," performed by the Sadler Wells Ballet, 1942; Peabody Museum, Salem, Mass., curator of Chinese ethnology, beginning 1956; Columbia University, New York, N.Y., associate professor, 1959-68, professor of Chinese, 1968-71, professor emeritus, 1971—. Visiting professor, Chinese University at Hong Kong, 1971, and Australian National University, 1972-73. *Military service:* Served in Chinese Army for one year. *Member:* American Academy of Arts and Sciences, National Society of Literature and the Arts, Royal Society of Arts (fellow), Century Association of New York. *Awards, honors:* Emerson fellow at Harvard University, 1958-59; senior specialist award from East-West Center (Honolulu), 1967; named honorary mayor of Oklahoma City, Okla., 1969; H.L.D., Hofstra University, 1970; D.Litt., Australian National University, 1972; D.Arts from Rider College; Leverhulme Fellow, University of West Australia, 1976.

WRITINGS: The Chinese Eye: An Interpretation of Chinese Painting, Methuen, 1935, 4th edition, Norton, 1960; *Chinese Calligraphy: An Introduction to Its Aesthetic and Technique,* Methuen, 1938, 3rd edition, revised and enlarged, Harvard University Press, 1973; *The Silent Traveller: A Chinese Artist in Lakeland,* Scribner, 1938; *Chinpao and the Giant Pandas,* Country Life (London), 1939; *The Silent Traveller in London,* Scribner, 1939, new edition, Transatlantic Arts, 1951; *The Silent Traveller in War Time,* Country Life, 1939; *A Chinese Childhood,* Methuen, 1940, 3rd edition, 1946, John Day, 1952; *The Silent Traveller in the Yorkshire Dales,* Methuen, 1941; *The Men of the Burma Road,* 3rd edition, Transatlantic Arts, 1942; *The Silent Traveller in Oxford,* Methuen, 1944, 2nd edition, 1945; *The Silent Traveller in Edinburgh,* Methuen, 1948, 2nd edition, 1950; *The Silent Traveller in New York,* preface by Van Wyck Brooks, Methuen, 1950, John Day, 1953; *The Silent Traveller in Dublin,* John Day, 1953; *The Silent Traveller in Paris,* Norton, 1956; *The Silent Traveller in Boston,* Norton, 1959; *The Silent Traveller in San Francisco,* Norton, 1964; *The Silent Traveller in Japan,* Norton, 1972. Also author of books in the Chinese language.

WORK IN PROGRESS: The Silent Traveller in Australia.

* * *

CHILDRESS, James Franklin 1940-

PERSONAL: Born October 4, 1940, in Mt. Airy, N.C.; son of Roscoe Franklin (a salesman) and Zella (a teacher; maiden name, Wagoner) Childress; married Georgia Harrell (a teacher), December 21, 1958; children: Albert Franklin and James Frederic (twins). *Education:* Guilford College, B.A., 1962; Yale Divinity School, B.D. (cum laude), 1965;

Yale University, M.A., 1967, Ph.D., 1968. *Religion:* Society of Friends. *Home:* 4103 Sycamore St., Chevy Chase, Md. 20015. *Office:* Center for Bioethics, Kennedy Institute, Georgetown University, Washington, D.C. 20057.

CAREER: University of Virginia, Charlottesville, assistant professor, 1968-71, associate professor, 1971-75, professor of religious studies, 1975, acting chairman of department, 1970-71, chairman, 1972-75; Georgetown University, Kennedy Institute, Center for Bioethics, Washington, D.C., Joseph P. Kennedy Senior Professor of Christian Ethics, 1975—. Adjunct professor of Christian ethics at Union Theological Seminary, Richmond, Va., 1969. *Member:* Society for Values in Higher Education, American Society of Christian Ethics (member of board of directors, 1972-76), American Academy of Religion, American Society for Social and Political Philosophy, Inter-University Seminar on Armed Forces and Society. *Awards, honors:* American Council of Learned Societies study fellowship, 1972-73; Harvard University fellow in law and religion, 1972-73; Huntington Library research award, summer, 1974.

WRITINGS: (Editor with David Harned) *Secularization and the Protestant Prospect,* Westminster, 1970; *Civil Disobedience and Political Obligation: A Study in Christian Social Ethics,* Yale University Press, 1971.

Contributor: Claude A. Frazier, editor, *Should Doctors Play God?,* Broadman, 1971; Richard W. Wertz, editor, *Readings on Ethical and Social Issues in Bio-Medicine,* Prentice-Hall, 1973; Robert Veatch and Roy Branson, editors, *Ethics and Health Care,* Ballinger, 1976; Furman Stough and Urban Holmes, editors, *Realities and Visions,* Seabury, 1976.

Editor of "Studies in Religious Ethics" monograph series for American Academy of Religion. Contributor of articles and reviews to encyclopedias and journals. Associate editor, *Journal of Religious Ethics,* 1975.

WORK IN PROGRESS: The Imago Dei in John Calvin's Ethics; Biomedical Ethics; a textbook and anthology, *Religious Social Ethics,* for Prentice-Hall; a book on violence, nonviolence, and the crisis of conscience; essays on justice and the allocation of scarce resources in health care, on compensatory justice, and on triage.

*   *   *

CHIRENJE, J. Mutero 1935-

PERSONAL: Born July 10, 1935, in Chihota, Rhodesia; son of Obed Musariri (a farmer) and Nakura (a farmer; maiden name, Rukwambaire) Chirenje; married Jemima Clarke (a nurse); children: Musariri (son). *Education:* Boston University, B.A., 1965; University of California, Los Angeles, M.A., 1967; University of London, Ph.D., 1973. *Home:* 15 Fernald Dr., #22, Cambridge, Mass. 02138. *Office:* Department of Afro-American Studies, Harvard University, 77 Dunster St., Cambridge, Mass. 02138.

CAREER: Harvard University, Cambridge, Mass., instructor, 1970-73, assistant professor of history, 1973—. *Member:* American Historical Association, African Studies Association, Association for the Study of Afro-American Life and History. *Awards, honors:* Commonwealth scholar, University of London, 1967-70.

WRITINGS: A History of Northern Botswana, 1850-1910, Associated University Presses of New Jersey, 1977; *Chief Kgama and His Times, 1835-1923* (biography), Collins, 1977. Contributor to African studies journals.

WORK IN PROGRESS: Rugande Stronger than Rope, a novel; *Ethiopianism and Afro-Americans in Southern Africa, 1884-1916.*

*   *   *

CHODOROV, Jerome 1911-

PERSONAL: Born August 10, 1911, in New York, N.Y.; son of Harry (an actor and businessman) and Lena (Simmons) Chodorov; married Rhea Grand, November 19, 1932; children: Susan. *Education:* Attended public schools in New York City. *Residence:* New York, N.Y. *Agent:* International Creative Management, 40 West 57th St., New York, N.Y. 10019.

CAREER: Journalist on *New York World,* 1930; scenarist in Hollywood, Calif., working on more than fifty films, 1933-60; playwright and screenwriter, 1935—. Stage director of plays in New York, including "Make a Million" and "The Gazebo," 1958-59, and "Blood, Sweat, and Stanley Poole," 1961. Playwright in residence, State University of New York, 1972-73. *Military service:* U.S. Army Air Forces, 1942-45; became captain. *Member:* Dramatists Guild of America (council member, 1949-55), Authors League of America, Directors Guild of America. *Awards, honors:* New York Drama Critics Circle Award and Outer Circle Award, both 1953, for *Wonderful Town.*

WRITINGS—Comedy plays, except as noted: "Barnaby and Mr. O'Malley," first produced in Wilmington, Del., at Ford Theatre, 1945; "I Had a Ball" (musical), first produced in New York at Martin Bear Theatre, December 15, 1964; *Three Bags Full* (based on play by Claude Magnier; first produced in New York at Henry Miller's Theatre, March 6, 1966), Samuel French, 1966; "Dumas and Son," first produced by Los Angeles Civic Light Opera at Pavilion Theatre, August, 1967; "A Community of Two," first produced in Washington, D.C. at National Theatre, January 15, 1974. Also reviser of two plays, "The Great Waltz," 1965, and "The Student Prince," 1966, for Los Angeles Civic Light Opera.

Plays with Joseph Fields: "Schoolhouse on the Lot," first produced in New York at Ritz Theatre, March 22, 1938; "My Sister Eileen" (based on stories by Ruth McKenney), first produced in New York at Biltmore Theatre, December 26, 1940; *Junior Miss* (based an stories by Sally Benson; first produced in New York at Lyceum Theatre, November 18, 1941), Random House, 1942; "The French Touch," first produced in New York at Cort Theatre, December 8, 1945, *Anniversary Waltz* (first produced in New York at Broadhurst Theatre, April 7, 1954), Random House, 1954; *The Ponder Heart* (adapted from novel by Eudora Welty; first produced in New York at Music Box Theatre, February 16, 1956), Random House, 1956.

Books for musicals: "Pretty Penny," first produced in New Hope, Pa., at Bucks County Playhouse, summer, 1940; (with Fields) *Wonderful Town* (based on stories by Ruth McKenny; first produced in New York at Winter Garden Theatre, February 25, 1953), Random House, 1953; (with Fields) "The Girl in Pink Tights," first produced at Mark Hellinger Theatre, March 5, 1954.

Screenplays: "The Case of the Lucky Legs," Warner Bros., 1935; "Dancing Feet," Republic, 1936; "Gentleman from Louisiana," Republic, 1936; "All Over Town," Republic, 1937; "Devil's Playground," Columbia, 1937; "Reported Missing," Universal, 1937; "Rich Man, Poor Girl," Metro-Goldwyn-Mayer, 1938; "Blonde Inspiration," Metro-Goldwyn-Mayer, 1938; "Conspiracy," RKO, 1939; "Two Girls on Broadway," Metro-Goldwyn-Mayer, 1939; "Dulcy," Metro-Goldwyn-Mayer, 1939; "Murder in the Big House," Warner Bros., 1942; "Louisiana Purchase," Paramount, 1942; "Those Endearing Young Charms," RKO, 1945; "Man From Texas," Eagle Lion, 1948. Also adapter, with Joseph Fields, of their plays, "My Sister Eileen," Columbia, 1942; "Junior Miss," Twentieth Century-Fox, 1945; and "Happy Anniversary," United Artists, 1959.

WORK IN PROGRESS: "Bech," based on the work of John Updike; a new musical, as yet untitled, for Los Angeles Civic Light Opera, completion expected in 1977.

* * *

CHOURAQUI, Andre (Nathanael) 1917-

PERSONAL: Born August 11, 1917, in Ain Temouchent, Algeria; came to Israel, 1958; son of Isaac (a merchant) and Meleha (Meyer) Chouraqui; married Annette Levy, November 16, 1958; children: Emmanuel, Elisabeth, Yael, David, Mikhal. *Education:* University of Paris, Ph.D., 1938; Paris School of Law, Docteur en droit, 1948; additional study at Sorbonne, University of Paris, Rabbinic School of France, College de France, and University of Algiers. *Home:* 8 Ain-Roguel, Jerusalem, Israel. *Office:* Alliance israelite universelle, 45 rue La Bruyere, 75009 Paris, France; and 4 Shelomoh Molko, Jerusalem, Israel.

CAREER: Lawyer, then magistrate, of Algiers District Court of Appeals in Michelet, Algeria, and Bou-Saada, Algeria, 1945-47; Alliance israelite universelle, Paris, France, assistant secretary general, 1947-53, permanent delegate, 1953—. Vice-president of Committee for Non-Government Organization of United Nations Children's Fund (UNICEF)-United Nations Appeal for Children (UNAC), 1950-56; president and municipal councillor, Commission of Culture of Jerusalem, 1969-73; president, Israel Interfaith Committee. Member of board of directors, Mikveh Israel Agricultural Institute, and Lycees of Ramat Aviv and Jerusalem. Counsellor to Prime Minister David Ben-Gurion, 1959-63; deputy mayor of Jerusalem, 1965-73. Lecturer in more than eighty countries. *Wartime service:* Served in French Resistance, 1940-45.

MEMBER: World Zionist Organization (member of tribunal), Brith Ivrit Olamit (president of French section, 1955-60), Association of Immigrants from North Africa, Association of Immigrants from Algeria (honorary president), Friends of Alliance Israelite Universelle (vice-president). *Awards, honors:* Zadoc Kahn Foundation prize, 1952; Prix du Cercle Intellectuel, 1952, for *Les Devoirs des coeurs;* Academie des Sciences Morales et politiques Audiffred prize, 1952, for *La Condition juridique de l'Israelite marocain,* and Louis Marin prize, 1956, for *L'Alliance israelite universelle;* chevalier de la Legion d'honneur, 1964; Fighter against Nazism decoration, 1964; Fighter for the National Liberation decoration, 1964; officier de l'Ordre Nationale de la Cote d'Ivoire, 1969; Prix Sevigne, 1970, for *Lettre a mon ami arabe.*

WRITINGS: La Condition juridique de l'Israelite marocain (juridical studies), preface by Rene Cassin, Presses du livre Francais (Paris), 1950, translation published as *The Social and Legal Status of the Jews of French Morocco,* preface by Jacob Blaustein, American Jewish Committee (New York), 1953; (translator and editor) Bahya ben Joseph ibn Pakuda, *Introduction aux devoirs des coeurs* (title means "The Duties of the Hearts"), preface by Jacques Maritain, Desclee de Brouwer, 1950, new edition published as *Les Devoirs du coeur,* 1972; *Les Juifs d'Afrique du Nord: Marche vers l'Occident,* Presses universitaires de France, 1952, transla-

tion by Michael M. Bernet published as *Between East and West: A History of the Jews of North Africa,* Jewish Publication Society, 1968, original French edition reissued as *La Saga des Juifs en Afrique du Nord,* Librairie Hachette (Paris), 1972; (translator) Salomon Ibn Gabirol, *La Couronne du Royaume* (title means "The Crown of the Realm"), Revue Thomiste (Paris), 1952; *L'Etat d'Israel* (title means "The State of Israel"), Presses universitaires de France, 1955, 7th edition, 1975; (translator) *Les Psaumes* (title means "The Psalms"), Presses universitaires de France, 1956; *Histoire du judaisme,* Presses universitaires de France, 1957, translation by Yvette Wiener published as *A History of Judaism,* Walker & Co., 1963, 4th French edition, Presses universitaires de France, 1968.

Cantique pour Nathanael (poems; title means "Song for Nathanael"), Jose Corti (Paris), 1960; *Theodore Herzl: Inventeur de l'Etat d'Israel* (biography), Editions du Seuil, 1960, translation published as *A Man Alone: The Life of Theodor Herzl,* Keter Books (Jerusalem), 1970; *L'Alliance israelite universelle et la renaissance juive contemporaine, 1860-1960: Cent ans d'histoire* (title means "Israeli Universal Alliance and the Jewish Contemporary Revival, 1860-1960: One Hundred Years of History"), preface by Rene Cassin, Presses universitaires de France, 1965; *Contributions a l'histoire juive contemporaine* (title means "Contribution to Contemporary Jewish History"), Volume II (Chouraqui not associated with Volume I), Editions de l'Institut de sociologie de l'Universite libre de Bruxelles, 1965; *La Pensee juive* (essays; title means "Jewish Thought"), Presses universitaires de France, 1965, 2nd edition, 1968; (with Jean Danielou) *Les Juifs: Dialogue entre Jean Danielou et Andre Chouraqui* (essays), Editions Beauchesne, 1966, translation published as *The Jews: Views and Counterviews; A Dialogue between Jean Danielou and Andre Chouraqui,* Newman Press, 1967; *Lettre a un ami arabe* (essays), Maison Mame (Tours), 1969, translation by William V. Gugli published as *Letter to an Arab Friend,* University of Massachusetts Press, 1972.

(Translator) *Le Cantique des cantiques* (title means "Song of Songs"), Presses universitaires de France, 1970; *Lettres a un ami chretien* (essays; title means "Letter to a Christian Friend"), Editions Fayard, 1971; *La vie quotidienne des Hebreux au temps de la Bible: Rois et prophetes* (history), Librairie Hachette, 1971, translation by Gugli published as *The People and the Faith of the Bible,* University of Massachusetts Press, 1975; *Vivre pour Jerusalem* (title means "Living for Jerusalem"), Desclee de Brouwer, 1973; (translator) *La Bible,* 24 volumes, Desclee de Brouwer, 1974-75; (contributor) *Salo Wittmeyer Baron Jubilee Volume,* Volume I, Columbia University Press, 1974. Also translator *The New Testament,* two volumes, 1976.

Director of "Sinai" series, Presses universitaires de France, 1954—.

* * *

CHRISTGAU, Robert (Thomas) 1942-

PERSONAL: Born April 18, 1942, in New York, N.Y.; son of George Henry (a fireman and teacher) and Virginia (a secretary; maiden name, Snyder) Christgau; married Carola Dibbell (a writer), December 21, 1974. *Education:* Dartmouth College, B.A., 1962. *Politics:* "American-identified radical." *Religion:* Atheist. *Home:* 193 Second Ave., New York, N.Y. 10003. *Office: Village Voice,* 80 University Pl., New York, N.Y. 10003.

CAREER: California Institute of the Arts, Burbank, instructor, 1970-71; Richmond College, Staten Island, N.Y., instructor, 1971-72; *Newsday,* Garden City, N.Y., music critic, 1972-74; *Village Voice,* New York, N.Y., editor and columnist, 1974—.

WRITINGS: Any Old Way You Choose It: Rock and Other Pop Music, 1967-1973, Penguin, 1973. Columnist, "Rock & Roll &" column, 1969-72, and "Consumer Guide" column, 1974—, both in *Village Voice,* "Consumer Guide" column in *Creem,* and "Secular Music" column in *Esquire.* Film critic for *Cheetah* and *Fusion.*

SIDELIGHTS: Christgau writes: "I am interested in those places where popular culture and avant-garde culture intersect. As a critic, I want to achieve a new understanding of culture in both its aesthetic and political aspects; as a journalist, I want to suggest whatever I figure out to an audience in an entertaining and provocative way."

*   *   *

CHRISTIAN, George (Eastland)   1927-

PERSONAL: Born January 1, 1927, in Austin, Tex.; son of George Eastland and Ruby (Scott) Christian; married Elizabeth Anne Brown, July 30, 1950 (died, 1957); married Jo Anne Martin, June 20, 1959; children: Elizabeth, Susan, George Scott, Robert Bruce, John, Brian. *Education:* University of Texas, B.Journalism, 1949. *Politics:* Democrat. *Religion:* Episcopalian. *Home:* 6800 Rockledge Cove, Austin, Tex. 78731. *Office:* American National Bank Tower, Austin, Tex. 78701.

CAREER: Temple Daily Telegram, Temple, Tex., sports editor, 1949; political correspondent, International News Service, 1949-56; assistant to Senator Price Daniel, Washington, D.C., 1956, to Governor Price Daniel, Austin, Tex., 1957-63, to Governor John Connally, Austin, Tex., 1963-66; press secretary and special assistant to President Lyndon B. Johnson, Washington, D.C., 1966-69; George Christian & Associates, Austin, Tex., president, 1969—. *Military service:* U.S. Marine Corps, 1944-46. *Member:* Sigma Delta Chi, Citadel Club (Austin), Headliners Club (Austin), Federal City Club (Washington).

WRITINGS: The President Steps Down: A Personal Memoir of the Transfer of Power, Macmillan, 1970.

*   *   *

CHRISTIAN, Louise
See GRILL, Nannette L.

*   *   *

CHRISTIE, John Aldrich   1920-

PERSONAL: Born April 12, 1920, in Northampton, Mass.; son of Ralph A. and Isabel C. (Sutherland) Christie; married Dorothy Sexton, August 22, 1946; children: David Brooks, John Sutherland, Roderick Graham. *Education:* Oberlin College, A.B., 1942; Wesleyan University, A.M., 1943; Yale University, M.A., 1946; Duke University, Ph.D., 1955. *Office:* Department of English, Vassar College, Poughkeepsie, N.Y. 12601.

CAREER: University of Illinois, Urbana, instructor in English, 1943-44; Vassar College, Poughkeepsie, N.Y., member of faculty, 1946—, professor of English, 1965—, director of multidisciplinary studies in changing American culture, 1973—. Fulbright professor of American literature at Delhi University, 1966, and at American Studies Research Centre, Hyderabad, 1968; member of advisory committee on international exchange persons, Fulbright

Commission, 1966—; trustee of Poughkeepsie Day School, 1964-67. *Member:* American Association of University Professors (national council member, 1964-67; chairman of committee on professional ethics, 1967-71).

WRITINGS: Thoreau as World Traveler, Columbia University Press, 1965; (with Robert Guterman) *Lowell: Employment and the Industrial Mix,* Lowell Model Cities Agency, 1970.*

*   *   *

CHRISTMAN, Henry Max   1932-

PERSONAL: Born January 21, 1932, in Kansas City, Mo.; son of Henry Max and Irene Blanche (McBride) Christman. *Education:* University of Missouri, B.A., 1953; University of Belgrade, Ph.D., 1971. *Home:* 453 Franklin D. Roosevelt Dr., New York, N.Y. 10002. *Office:* Municipal Building, New York, N.Y. 10007.

CAREER: Fund for the Republic, Santa Barbara, Calif., public information consultant, 1956-62; City of New York, N.Y., director of city records, 1966—; Long Island University, Brookville, N.Y., adjunct professor of political science, 1971—. Editorial consultant to Macmillan Company; former editor of *Progressive* magazine; member of candidates committee of Citizens Union of the City of New York, 1961-66; member of committee-at-large of Liberal Party.

MEMBER: League of Industrial Democracy (director of national council, 1969—); Americans for Democratic Action (New York State vice-chairman, 1963-67; director and chairman of Greenwich Village chapter, 1965-66), American Ethical Union, Society of American Historians, Overseas Press Club, Deadline Club, P.E.N., Authors League of America, International Typographers Union, American Association of University Professors, American Political Science Association, Phi Alpha Theta, Pi Gamma Mu, Sigma Delta Chi.

WRITINGS—Editor: The Public Papers of Chief Justice Earl Warren, Capricorn Press, 1959, 2nd edition, 1966; *The Mind and Spirit of John Peter Altgeld: Selected Writings and Addresses,* University of Illinois Press, 1960; (and reviser) Gustavus Myers, *History of Bigotry in the United States,* Capricorn Press, 1960; *A View of the Nation: An Anthology, 1955-1959,* Grove Press, 1960, reprinted, Books for Libraries, 1970; (and author of introduction) Walter Reuther, *Selected Papers,* Macmillan, 1961; (and author of introduction) Golda Meir, *This Is Our Strength: Selected Papers,* Macmillan, 1962; (and author of introduction) Hamlin Garland, *A Son of the Middle Border,* Macmillan, 1962; *Walt Whitman's New York: From Manhattan to Montauk,* Macmillan, 1963; *Peace and Arms: Reports from The Nation,* Sheed, 1964; (and author of introduction) John R. Dennett, *The South As It Is, 1865-1866,* Sidgwick & Jackson, 1965; (with Abraham Feldman) *One Hundred Years of the Nation: A Centennial Anthology,* Macmillan, 1965.

(And author of introduction) *Essential Works of Lenin,* Bantam, 1966; *The American Journalism of Marx & Engels: A Selection from the New York Daily Tribune,* New American Library, 1966; (and author of introduction) *Communism in Action: A Documentary History,* Bantam, 1969; (and author of introduction) Levi Eshkol, *State Papers,* Funk, 1969; (and author of introduction) *The Essential Tito,* St. Martin's, 1970; *Neither East nor West: The Basic Documents of Non-Alignment,* Sheed, 1973; *Indira Gandhi Speaks on Democracy, Socialism, and Third World Non-Alignment,* Taplinger, 1974.

Author of introduction: Fiorello H. La Guardia, *The Making of an Insurgent: An Autobiography,* Capricorn Press, 1961.

Contributor of articles to professional journals and magazines.*

* * *

CHRISTOPHER, Maurine (Brooks)

PERSONAL: Born in Three Springs, Tenn.; daughter of John Davis (a farmer) and Zula (a teacher and artist; maiden name, Pangle) Brooks; married Milbourne Christopher (a magician and writer), June 25, 1949. *Education:* Tusculum College, B.A. *Home:* 333 Central Park W., New York, N.Y. 10025. *Office: Advertising Age,* 708 Third Ave., New York, N.Y. 10017.

CAREER: Kingsport Times, Kingsport, Tenn., reporter, 1941-43; *Baltimore Sun,* Baltimore, Md., reporter, 1943-45; free-lance writer, 1945-47; *Advertising Age,* New York, N.Y., television-radio editor, 1947—. Moderator and producer of "Adbeat," on WHN-Radio, 1971—. *Member:* Association for the Study of Afro-American Life and History, American Women in Radio and Television (president of New York City chapter, 1974-75).

WRITINGS: America's Black Congressmen, Crowell, 1971, expanded and updated edition published as *Black Americans in Congress,* 1976. Author of television script "I Married a Magician." Contributor to *Nation.*

* * *

CHRISTOWE, Stoyan 1898-

PERSONAL: Born September 1, 1898, in Macedonia; came to United States, 1911; naturalized U.S. citizen, 1924; son of Christo (a merchant) and Mirtra (Koteva) Naumoff; married Margaret Wooters, August 30, 1937. *Education:* Attended Valparaiso University, 1918-22. *Politics:* Independent Republican. *Home:* West Dover, Vt. 05356. *Agent:* Blanche Gregory, 2 Tudor City Pl., New York, N.Y. 10017.

CAREER: Worked in factories and roundhouses in St. Louis and later on railways in Montana; Valentine Valspar Co., Chicago, Ill., editor of house organ, 1922-25; *Chicago Daily News,* Chicago, reporter in Chicago, 1925-27, correspondent in the Balkans, 1927-29; free-lance writer in New York, 1929-41, and in Vermont, 1941—; Balkans correspondent for North American Newspaper Alliance (NANA), 1952-53; elected to Vermont State House of Representatives, 1960; ran for Senate seat, 1964; Vermont State Senator, 1964-73, served as chairman of Health and Welfare Committee, of Joint Higher Education Study Committee, and of Joint Drug Study Committee, and as commissioner of Education Commission of the States. Author and lecturer. Vermont State Library Board, chairman, 1963-68, member, 1976—. *Military service:* Analyst and lecturer on Balkan guerrilla warfare in the Pentagon during World War II. *Awards, honors:* Distinguished service awards from National Council of Senior Citizens, 1970, and from Vermont Hospital Association, 1972.

WRITINGS: Heroes and Assassins, Robert McBride, 1935; *Mara* (novel), Crowell, 1937; *This Is My Country* (autobiography), Carrick & Evans, 1938; *The Lion of Yanina,* Modern Age, 1941; *My American Pilgrimage,* Atlantic, 1947; *The Eagle and the Stork* (memoirs), Harper's Magazine Press, 1976.

Work represented in anthologies, including *Good Will Days,* edited by Hilah Paulmier and Robert Schauffler, Dodd,

1947; *Ourselves and Others,* edited by Harold Wagenheim, Elizabeth Brattig, and Matthew Dolkey, Henry Holt, 1956; *American Backgrounds,* edited by Jeanne Hale and Muriel Johnstone, E. M. Hale, 1958; and *Workin' on the Railroad,* edited by Richard Reinhardt, American West, 1970.

WORK IN PROGRESS: A sequel to *The Eagle and the Stork.*

SIDELIGHTS: Christowe's autobiography, *This Is My Country,* was the only book of general reading found on President Roosevelt's desk at the time of his death. In recognition of his work, which has been translated into Macedonian, Bulgarian, Slovenian, German, French, and Serbo-Croatian, Christowe was received in private audience twice by King Boris of Bulgaria, 1928 and 1934, and by Marshall Tito in 1953.

* * *

CHRISTY, Marian 1932-

PERSONAL: Born November 9, 1932, in Ridgefield, Conn.; daughter of Peter and Anna (Saba) Christy. *Education:* Boston University, associates degree, 1957. *Residence:* Lexington, Mass. *Agent:* Bill Cooper Associates, 16 East 52nd St., New York, N.Y. 10022. *Office: Boston Globe,* Boston, Mass. 02107.

CAREER/WRITINGS: Department of Commerce, Boston, Mass., consultant, 1952-59; *Women's Wear Daily,* Boston, Mass., reporter, 1959-65; *Boston Globe,* Boston, Mass., fashion editor and author of column "Lifestyle," 1965—. "Lifestyle" is also syndicated by United Feature Syndicate to more than a hundred newspapers in the United States and Australia. Fashion news reporter for WBZ-Television in the late 1960's; commentator on WNAC-Television, 1974-75. Contributor to popular magazines, including *Harper's Bazaar* and *Reader's Digest.*

AWARDS, HONORS: About thirty-five awards, including eleven from Men's Fashion Association of New York, 1965-72, eleven from American Footwear Association of New York, 1966-72, and three J. C. Penney Journalism Awards from University of Missouri, 1966-70; Fashion Reporters Award from New York Couture Business Council, 1967; Prestige Award from French Lace Federation and Lace Importers Association, 1969; humor prize from United Press International (UPI), 1972, for "Putting on the Ritz"; named first lady of fashion by National Association of Cystic Fibrosis, 1972; named woman of the year by *New Woman,* 1973; cavaliere, Al Merito della Republica Italiana, 1973; March of Dimes Award for international correspondent of the year, 1974.

SIDELIGHTS: Marian Christy has traveled with Mrs. Richard Nixon; she has also had private interviews with well-known people, including the Empress of Iran, Mrs. Anwar El Sadat, and Lord Snowdon. She spends part of each year in Rome, Spain, Paris, and Ireland.

* * *

CHUN, Richard 1935-

PERSONAL: Born February 22, 1935, in Korea; son of Byung Hoon and Shin Sung (Hahn) Chun; married Kwang Hae Kim, February 20, 1971; children: Kyung Mee, Yong Taik. *Education:* Yon Sei University, B.A., 1957; Long Island University, M.B.A., 1966. *Home:* 435 East 77th St., New York, N.Y. 10021. *Office:* 163 East 86th St., New York, N.Y. 10028.

CAREER: Martial art international master instructor;

Richard Chun Tae Kwon Do Center, New York City, president, 1965—; Richard Chun Karate Center, New York City, president, 1965—; Life Sportsman Co., New York City, president, 1972—. Assistant professor, Hunter College of the City University of New York, 1974—. *Member:* World Tae Kwon Do Federation, International Lions Club, Amateur Athletic Union (East Coast regional chairman of Tae Kwon Do committee, 1974—). *Awards, honors:* Master Instructor of the Year from Moo Duk Kwan Association of Korea, 1975; awards from International Lions Club, 1975, 1976.

WRITINGS: Moo Duk Kwan: The Art of Self-Defense, Ohara Publications, 1975; *Moo Duk Kwan II: The Art of Self-Defense,* Ohara Publications, 1976; *Tae Kwon Do: Korean Martial Art,* Harper, 1976. Author of "Self-Defense Courses for Home Study," recorded by Conversa-Phone Institute, 1977. Contributor to *Black Belt, Karate Illustrated, Official Karate Magazine,* and *Traditional Tae Kwon Do.*

WORK IN PROGRESS: Two books, *Self-Defense for Women* and *Karate for Boys.*

SIDELIGHTS: Chun was head coach of the U.S. team to the first World Karate Tae Kwon Do Championship in Seoul, Korea, 1973. *Avocational interests:* Travel, music, reading.

BIOGRAPHICAL/CRITICAL SOURCES: Official Karate Magazine, April, 1976; *Karate Illustrated,* May, 1976; *Black Belt,* November, 1976.

* * *

CICCORELLA, Aubra Dair

PERSONAL: Born in Oil Springs, Ky.; daughter of L. E. (a clergyman) and Mary (Pendleton) Williams; married Stephen Ciccorella (a teacher; divorced, 1952); children: Patricia Lee. *Education:* Asbury College, A.B., 1927; Boston University, graduate study, 1934; University of Kentucky, M.A., 1952. *Politics:* Democrat. *Religion:* United Methodist. *Home and office:* 102 South Walnut St., Wilmore, Ky. 40390.

CAREER: Asbury College, Wilmore, Ky., teacher of speech, 1951-53, assistant professor of history, 1953-75; writer, 1975—. Visiting head of department of history at Houghton College, summer, 1965. *Member:* American Historical Association, American Academy of Political and Social Science, League of Women Voters.

WRITINGS: Alcohol and Other Narcotics, Nebraska State Department of Education, 1933; (with Cora Frances Stoddard) *The Scientist Looks at Alcohol,* Signal Press, 1934; (with daughter, Patricia Lee Ciccorella) *Crossing the Crest: The Apex and Decline of Liberalism,* Branden Press, 1975.

WORK IN PROGRESS: Crying Peace Where There Is No Peace: The Undeclared War by the United States and Allies on Soviet Russia, 1919.

SIDELIGHTS: Aubra Ciccorella writes that she was "conditioned early to reform movements and political activism." She adds that travel in Europe "has been my particular pleasure. . . . The study of various cultures, especially European cultures with stress on art and architecture has led me to far places frequently."

* * *

CIRINO, Linda D(avis)   1941-

PERSONAL: Born April 10, 1941, in New York, N.Y.; daughter of Harold (a lawyer) and Sylvia (Hyman) Davis; married Antonio Cirino (a journalist), December 18, 1966; children: Paul, Mark. *Education:* Bryn Mawr College, B.A., 1962. *Residence:* Leonia, N.J. *Agent:* Wendy Weil, Julian Bach Agency, 3 East 48th St., New York, N.Y. 10017.

CAREER: Action, Inc., New York City, editor, researcher, and writer, 1963-65; Vollmer Associates, New York City, editor, researcher, and writer, 1966-67; free-lance writer, 1967—.

WRITINGS: (With Susan Edmiston) *Literary New York: A History and a Guide,* Houghton, 1976.

WORK IN PROGRESS: Articles on a Russian immigrant family and a fashion photographer.

SIDELIGHTS: Linda Cirino comments briefly: "I am interested in translating from Italian and improving the status of translators in this country. Also I would also like to see a revival of the 'little' magazine."

* * *

CLARK, Ellery Harding, Jr.   1909-

PERSONAL: Born August 6, 1909, in Cohasset, Mass.; son of Ellery Harding (a lawyer and writer) and Victoria Maddalena (a decorator) Clark; married Grace Gelinas (a ballet instructor and choreographer), November 24, 1934; children: Grace Victoria Clark Waidner, William E., Susan E. *Education:* Harvard University, A.B. (cum laude), 1933; Boston University, A.M., 1950. *Politics:* "For best men!" *Home:* 25 Franklin St., Annapolis, Md. 21401. *Office:* Department of History, U.S. Naval Academy, Annapolis, Md. 21402.

CAREER: U.S. Navy, 1933-46, damage control officer of attack carrier "U.S.S. Randolph," leaving service as captain; U.S. Naval Academy, Annapolis, Md., instructor in history, 1946—. Former member of Secretary of the Navy's Committee for Reorganization of the Navy. Volunteer baseball coach for Annapolis farm league team. *Member:* U.S. Naval Institute, Society for North American Sports History, Society for American Baseball Research, Arsenal Football Club of London, Notts County Football Club, Nottingham Forest Football Club. *Awards, honors*—Military: Received Navy Commendation with Combat V.

WRITINGS: (Editor with Elmer Belmont Potter, and contributor) *The United States and World Sea Power,* Prentice-Hall, 1965; (editor with Chester Nimitz and Potter, and contributor) *Sea Power,* Prentice-Hall, 1970, revised edition, 1973; *The Boston Red Sox: Seventy-Fifth Anniversary History, 1901-1975,* privately printed, 1975. Contributor to *Dictionary of American History* and *Collier's Encyclopedia.* Contributor to sports magazines and military journals. Founder of U.S. Naval Institute's *Naval Review.*

WORK IN PROGRESS: The Significance of Boston Professional Baseball, 1871-1900; an evaluation of Grossadmiral Karı Donitz, commander-in-chief of German Navy in World War Two.

SIDELIGHTS: Clark has spent more than fifty years preparing his history of the Boston Red Sox. He has a collection of early Red Sox player cards, photographs, scorecards, and personal letters. This collection was exhibited at Northeastern University as part of the Boston Bicentennial celebration. He has coached cross country, indoor and outdoor track teams with an excellent record of winning scores. *Avocational interests:* Collecting East-coast duck decoys, professional soccer.

CLARK, George Norman 1890-

PERSONAL: Born February 27, 1890, in Halifax, England; son of James Walker and Mary (Midgley) Clark; married Barbara Keen, 1919; children: Martin, Patience (Mrs. Peter Charles Bayley). *Education:* Balliol College, Oxford, M.A., 1915. *Home:* 7 Ethelred Court, Dunstan Rd., Headington, Oxford OX3 9DA, England.

CAREER: Oxford University, Oriel College, Oxford, England, lecturer in modern history and fellow, 1919-31, tutor, 1922, university lecturer, 1927-31, proctor, 1929-30, Chichele Professor of Economic History, 1931-43; Cambridge University, Cambridge, England, Regius Professor of Modern History and fellow of Trinity College, 1943-47; Oxford University, provost of Oriel College, 1947-57. Creighton Lecturer at University of London, 1948; Ford's Lecturer at Oxford University, 1949-50; Murray Lecturer at University of Glasgow, 1952; Wiles Lecturer at Queen's University, Belfast, 1956; Donnellan Lecturer at Trinity College, Dublin, 1960; Whidden Lecturer at McMaster University, 1960; Leslie Stephen Lecturer at Cambridge University, 1965. Fellow of All Souls College, Oxford, 1912-19, 1931-43, 1960-75; honorary fellow of Trinity College, Dublin, 1953, Trinity College, Cambridge, 1955, and Balliol and Oriel Colleges, Oxford, 1957. Trustee of the British Museum, 1949-60. *Military service:* British Army, 1914-20; served in France; wounded twice; was prisoner of war; became captain. During World War II served as deputy director of Foreign Research and Press Service, 1939-42, and with other departments concerned with Netherlands and Belgium, 1942-45.

MEMBER: Royal College of Physicians (honorary fellow), British Academy (fellow; president, 1954-58), American Historical Association (honorary fellow), American Academy of Arts and Sciences (foreign honorary member), Royal Danish Academy of Sciences (foreign member), Royal Netherlands Academy of Sciences (foreign member), Hollandische Maatschappij der Wetenschappen (foreign member), Athenaeum Club. *Awards, honors:* Honorary degrees include LL.D. from University of Aberdeen, 1936; Litt.D. from University of Utrecht, 1936, University of Dublin, 1950, and Cambridge University, 1961; D.Litt. from University of Durham, 1950, University of Sheffield, 1951, Columbia University, 1954, and University of Hull, 1955; named commander of the Order of Orange Nassau (Netherlands), 1950; created knight, 1953.

WRITINGS: Unifying the World, Harcourt, 1920; *The Dutch Alliance and the War Against French Trade, 1688-1697,* Longmans, Green, 1923, Russell & Russell, 1971; (with F. W. Weaver) *Churchwarden's Accounts of Marston,* Oxfordshire Record Society, 1925; *The Manor of Elsfield,* privately printed, 1927; *The Seventeenth Century,* Clarendon Press, 1929, 2nd edition, 1947; *The Later Stuarts, 1660-1714,* Clarendon Press, 1934, 2nd edition, 1955; *Science and Social Welfare in the Age of Newton,* Clarendon Press, 1937, 2nd edition, 1949; (with Barbara M. Franks) *Guide to Commercial Statistics, 1696-1782,* Royal Historical Society, 1938.

(With W.J.M. van Eysinga) *The Colonial Conferences between England and the Netherlands in 1613 and 1615,* E. J. Brill, Volume I, 1940, Volume II, 1951; *Holland and the War,* Clarendon Press, 1941; *Belgium and the War,* Oxford University Press, 1942; *Historical Scholarship and Historical Thought,* Cambridge University Press, 1944; *The Wealth of England from 1496 to 1760,* Oxford University Press, 1946; *The Birth of the Dutch Republic,* Oxford University Press, 1947; *The Cycle of War and Peace in Modern History,* Cambridge University Press, 1949; *The Idea of the Industrial Revolution,* Jackson (Glasgow), 1953, University of Glasgow, 1970; *Early Modern Europe from about 1450 to about 1720,* Oxford University Press, 1957; *War and Society in the Seventeenth Century,* Cambridge University Press, 1958; (editor) *The Campden Wonder,* Oxford University Press, 1959.

Three Aspects of Stuart England, Oxford University Press, 1960; *A History of the Royal College of Physicians of London,* Clarendon Press, Volume I, 1964, Volume II, 1966; *English History: A Survey,* Clarendon Press, 1971.

Editor, *The Oxford History of England,* 15 volumes, Clarendon Press, 1934-65. Editor of *English Historical Review,* 1920-26, 1938-39.

*   *   *

CLARK, James Anthony 1907-

PERSONAL: Born September 7, 1907, in Abita Springs, La.; son of Edward Arlie (a lumberman) and Laura (Page) Clark; married Estelle Walton, April 8, 1934. *Education:* Attended South Park Junior College, Beaumont, Tex., 1927-28. *Politics:* Conservative independent. *Religion:* Roman Catholic. *Home:* 2171 University Blvd., Houston, Tex. 77030. *Office:* Energy Research and Education Foundation, Fondren Library, Room B49, Rice University, Houston, Tex. 77001.

CAREER: Beaumont Enterprises, Beaumont, Tex., news writer, 1923-27; *Galveston News,* Galveston, Tex., sports editor, 1927-36; *Town Topix* (weekly newspaper), Beaumont, publisher, 1928-31; *Beaumont Journal,* Beaumont, member of staff, 1931-35; worked on Governor's assignments, State of Texas, 1935-37; *Houston Press,* Houston, Tex., oil editor, 1937-39; Beaumont Natural Gas Co., Beaumont, general manager, 1939-41; news correspondent in Washington, D.C., 1946-47; Glenn H. McCarthy (public relations), Houston, member of promotional staff, 1947-51; James A. Clark Co., Houston, founder and partner, 1952—; Clark Book Co., Houston, president, 1961—; Energy Research and Education Foundation, Houston, founding member, 1969—, president and member of board of directors, 1970-76, chairman of board of directors, 1976—. Manager, Frank Williams and His Oklahomans Orchestra, 1931; trustee, Houston Museum of Natural Science, 1953—. *Military service:* U.S. Army, 1941-46; received Bronze Star.

MEMBER: Authors Guild, Authors League of America, Society of Professional Journalists, Retired Officers Association, Reserve Officers Association, Gulf Coast Historical Association (secretary, 1954-76), National Press Club, Houston Club. *Awards, honors:* American Association of Petroleum Geologists journalism award, 1972.

WRITINGS: (With Michel T. Halbouty) *Spindletop,* Random House, 1952; *Three Stars for the Colonel,* Random House, 1954; (with Weldon Hart) *The Tactful Texan,* Random House, 1958; *A Geography of Oil,* Gulf Publishing, 1959; (with Nathan Brock) *A Biography of Robert Alonza Welch,* Clark Book Co.; *Founders of the Oil Industry,* Schlumberger, 1967; *Marrs McLean: A Biography,* Clark Book Co., 1969; (with Halbouty) *The Last Boom,* Random House, 1972; *An Oilman's Oilman,* Gulf Publishing, 1976. Writer of syndicated columns "Tales of the Oil Country," and "Jim Clark Comments," 1952-65; writer of columns "Gassing Game" for *Energy News,* 1963-70, and "Energyscope" for *Pipeline Industry,* 1971—.

SIDELIGHTS: Clark told *CA:* "I have written about petroleum events and people I considered worth writing about and about whom no one else seemed interested in writing. The real motivation has been to make a living, become better known as a writer and to let the readers know about my subjects. I haven't tried to change the world and have succeeded in not doing so."

*   *   *

CLARK, John Grahame Douglas 1907-

PERSONAL: Born July 28, 1907, in Shortlands, Kent, England; son of Charles Douglas (a military officer) and Maude Ethel Grahame (Shaw) Clark; married Gwladys Maud White, 1936; children: William Grahame Douglas, Philip Charles Llewelyn, Margaret Helen (Mrs. John Nandris). *Education:* Marlborough College and Peterhouse, Cambridge, M.A., 1932, Ph.D., 1933. *Home:* 19 Wilberforce Rd., Cambridge, England.

CAREER: Cambridge University, Cambridge, England, assistant lecturer, 1935-46, lecturer, 1946-52, Disney Professor of Archaeology, 1952-74, head of department of archaeology and anthropology, 1956-61, 1968, master of Peterhouse, 1973—, fellow of Peterhouse, 1950—. Munro Lecturer at University of Edinburgh, 1949; Reckitt Lecturer at British Academy, 1954; Dalrymple Lecturer at University of Glasgow, 1955; G. Grant MacCurdy Lecturer at Harvard University, 1957; William Evans visiting professor at University of Otago, 1964; Commonwealth visiting fellow in Australia, 1964; Hitchcock Professor at University of California, Berkeley, 1969; Leverhulme visiting professor at University of Uppsala, 1972. Member of Royal Commission on Ancient Monuments, 1957-69, and of Ancient Monuments Board. Trustee of British Museum, 1975. *Military service:* Royal Air Force Volunteer Reserve, squadron leader, in photographic interpretation for Central Interpretation Unit, 1941-44, and for Air Historical Branch, Air Ministry, 1944-46.

MEMBER: Prehistoric Society (president, 1959-62), Society of Antiquaries (vice-president, 1960-62), Royal Irish Academy (honorary member), American Academy of Arts and Sciences (honorary foreign member), National Academy of Sciences (foreign associate), Royal Society of Northern Antiquaries (Copenhagen; honorary corresponding member), Swiss Prehistoric Society (honorary corresponding member), German Archaeological Institute (fellow), Finnish Archaeological Society (foreign member), Royal Danish Academy of Sciences (honorary foreign member), Royal Netherlands Academy of Sciences (honorary foreign member), Royal Society of Sciences (Uppsala; foreign fellow). *Awards, honors:* D.Sc. from Cambridge University, 1954; named commander of the Order of Dannebrog, 1961; Hodgkins Medal from Smithsonian Institution, 1967; named Commander of the Order of the British Empire, 1971; D.Litt. from University of Sheffield, 1971, and from National University of Ireland, 1976; Viking Medal from Wenner-Gren Foundation, 1972; Drexel Medal from University of Pennsylvania Museum, 1975.

WRITINGS: The Mesolithic Age in Britain, Cambridge University Press, 1932; *The Mesolithic Settlement of Northern Europe: A Study of the Food-Gathering Peoples of Northern Europe During the Early Post-Glacial Period,* Cambridge University Press, 1936, Greenwood Press, 1969; *Archaeology and Society,* Methuen, 1939, 3rd edition published as *Archaeology and Society: Reconstructing the Prehistoric Past,* Harvard University Press, 1957, 3rd revised

edition, Barnes & Noble, 1965; *Prehistoric England,* Batsford, 1940, 4th edition, 1948; *From Savagery to Civilization,* Cobbett Press, 1946, H. Schuman, 1953.

Prehistoric Europe: The Economic Basis, Philosophical Library, 1952; *Excavations at Star Carr: An Early Mesolithic Site at Seamer near Scarborough, Yorkshire,* Cambridge University Press, 1954, new edition, 1971; *The Study of Prehistory: An Inaugural Lecture,* Cambridge University Press, 1954; *World Prehistory: An Outline,* Cambridge University Press, 1961, 2nd edition published as *World Prehistory: A New Outline,* 1969, 3rd edition published as *World Prehistory in New Perspective,* in press; (contributor) Stuart Piggott, editor, *The Dawn of Civilization: The First World Survey of Human Cultures in Early Times,* McGraw, 1961; (with Piggott) *Prehistoric Societies,* Hutchinson, 1965; *The Stone Age Hunters,* Thames & Hudson, 1967.

Aspects of Prehistory, University of California Press, 1970; *The Early Stone Age Settlement of Scandinavia,* Cambridge University Press, 1975. Contributor to archaeology journals. Honorary editor of *Proceedings of the Prehistoric Society,* 1935-70.

SIDELIGHTS: Clark's books have been translated into Czech, Dutch, French, German, Hungarian, Italian, Japanese, Polish, Portuguese, Russian, Spanish, and Swedish. *Avocational interests:* Gardening, travel, contemporary art, sailing, oriental ceramics.

*   *   *

CLARK, John Pepper 1935-

PERSONAL: Born April 6, 1935, in Kiagbodo, Nigeria. *Education:* University of Ibadan, B.A. (honors), 1960. *Agent:* Curtis Brown Ltd., One Craven Hill, London W2 E3W, England. *Office:* Department of English, University of Lagos, Lagos, Nigeria.

CAREER: Nigerian Federal Government, information officer, 1960-61; *Daily Express,* Lagos, Nigeria, head of features and editorial writer, 1961-62; University of Lagos, Lagos, research fellow, 1964-66, professor of African literature and instructor in English, 1966—. Poet, playwright, and filmmaker. *Member:* Society of Nigerian Authors (founding member). *Awards, honors:* Institute of African Studies research fellow, 1961-62 and 1963-64; Parvin fellow at Princeton University, 1962-63.

WRITINGS: Song of a Goat (play; first produced at Ibadan University, 1961), Mbari Writers Club, 1961; *Poems,* Mbari Press (Ibadan), 1962; *Three Plays: Song of a Goat, The Masquerade, The Raft,* Oxford University Press, 1964; *America, Their America* (nonfiction), Deutsch, 1964, Africana Publishing, 1969; *A Reed in the Tide,* Longmans, Green, 1965, 2nd edition published as *A Reed in the Tide: A Selection of Poems,* Humanities, 1970; *Ozidi: A Play,* Oxford University Press, 1966; *Casualties: Poems, 1966-68,* Africana Publishing, 1970; *The Example of Shakespeare: Critical Essays on African Literature,* Northwestern University Press, 1970.

Work represented in anthologies, including *Seven African Writers,* edited by Gerald Moore, Oxford University Press, 1962; *A Book of African Verse,* edited by John Reed and Clive Wake, Heinemann, 1964; *West African Verse: An Anthology,* Longmans, Green, 1967. Author of screenplays, director, and producer of the two documentary films, "The Ozidi of Atazi" and "The Ghost Town." Founder and editor of *The Horn* (literary magazine; Ibadan); co-editor of *Black Orpheus,* 1968—. Contributor of literary criticism to

Presence Africaine, Nigeria, Transition, African Forum, Black Orpheus, and other journals.*

* * *

CLARK, Lindley H(oag), Jr. 1920-

PERSONAL: Born May 11, 1920, in Indianapolis, Ind.; son of Lindley Hoag (a business executive) and Genevieve (Nesbitt) Clark; married Dorothy Spurgeon (a librarian), October 15, 1949; children: Catherine. *Education:* Earlham College, B.A., 1948; University of Chicago, M.A., 1949. *Politics:* Republican. *Religion:* Society of Friends. *Home:* 21 Canterbury Lane, Westfield, N.J. 07090. *Office: Wall Street Journal,* 22 Cortlandt St., New York, N.Y., 10007.

CAREER: Wall Street Journal, New York, N.Y., copy editor, 1949-51, reporter, 1951-54, rewrite man, 1954-56, front-page editor, 1956-61, editorial writer, 1961-72, economic news editor, 1972—, author of column "Speaking of Business," 1969—. *Military service:* U.S. Navy, chief storekeeper, 1941-46. *Member:* Westfield Tennis Club, Echo Lake Country Club.

WRITINGS: The Secret Tax, Dow Jones-Irwin, 1976.

WORK IN PROGRESS: Milton Friedman: His Life and Our Times (tentative title), publication expected in 1978.

SIDELIGHTS: Clark comments briefly: "My chief writing interest, both at the *Journal* and otherwise, is to take business and economic subjects and make them as understandable and interesting as possible."

* * *

CLARKE, Brenda Margaret Lilian 1926-
(Brenda Honeyman)

PERSONAL: Born July 30, 1926, in Bristol, England; daughter of Edward (an insurance agent) and Lilian Rose (Brown) Honeyman; married Ronald John Clarke (a civil servant), March 5, 1955; children: Roger Stephen, Gwithian Margaret. *Education:* Cambridge University, school certificate, 1942. *Politics:* Socialist. *Religion:* Methodist. *Home:* 25 Torridge Rd., Keynsham, Bristol, Avon BS18 1QQ, England.

CAREER: British Civil Service, Ministry of Labour, Bristol, England, clerical officer, 1942-55; writer, 1968—. Section leader for British Red Cross, 1941-45. *Member:* Society of Authors, Wessex Writers' Association.

WRITINGS—All under name Brenda Honeyman; all published by R. Hale, except as indicated: *Richard by Grace of God,* 1968; *The Kingmaker,* 1969; *Richmond and Elizabeth,* 1970, Pinnacle, 1973; *Harry the King,* 1971, published as *The Warrior King,* Pinnacle, 1972; *Brother Bedford,* 1972; *Good Duke Humphrey,* 1973; *The King's Minions,* 1974; *The Queen and Mortimer,* 1974; *Edward the Warrior,* 1975; *All the King's Sons,* 1976; *The Golden Griffin,* 1976.

WORK IN PROGRESS: A trilogy covering the reign of Edward III; research on the life of Richard II.

SIDELIGHTS: Brenda Clarke told *CA,* "I find writing historical novels very comforting; not because things are so much better nowadays, but because, basically, very little has changed. Fire, flood, famine, plague, man's incredible inhumanity to man; we have experienced them all time and time again, *and we have survived!* (The devastation resulting from the Black Death in England in 1348 was greater than that resulting today from a nuclear attack.)" Brenda Clarke writes her books in a sequence, and her first six books cover fifteenth century English history. She is currently completing a seven book series on the fourteenth century.

AVOCATIONAL INTERESTS: Theatre, reading.

* * *

CLAWSON, Marion 1905-

PERSONAL: Born August 10, 1905, in Elko, Nev.; son of William Ennes and Agnes (Thompson) Clawson; married Clara Partridge, January 1, 1931 (divorced, 1947); married Mary Montgomery, September 27, 1947 (divorced, 1973); married Nora Roots, April 8, 1973; children: (first marriage) Robert Marion, Nancy Agnes; (second marriage) Daniel Conness, Patrick Lyell. *Education:* University of Nevada, B.S., 1926, M.S., 1929; further graduate study at University of California and American University; Harvard University, Ph.D., 1943. *Politics:* Democrat. *Home:* 5711 Ridgefield Rd., Bethesda, Md. 20016. *Office:* 1755 Massachusetts Ave. N.W., Washington, D.C. 20036.

CAREER: University of Nevada, Reno, agricultural economist at agricultural experiment station, 1926-29; U.S. Department of Agriculture, Washington, D.C., agricultural economist at Bureau of Agricultural Economics in Washington, 1929-38, and at Bureau in Berkeley, Calif., 1938-47, head of research and planning studies on the Columbia Basin, 1940-42, and in Central Valley, Calif., 1942-45; U.S. Department of the Interior, Bureau of Land Management, San Francisco, Calif., regional administrator, 1947-48, director of Bureau in Washington, D.C., 1948-53, member of economic advisory staff in Jerusalem, Israel, 1953-55; Resources for the Future, Inc., Washington, D.C., director of land use and management program, 1955-73, acting president, 1974-75, vice-president, 1975, consultant, 1976—. *Member:* American Agricultural Economics Association (fellow; vice-president, 1947), American Society for Range Management, Society for International Development (executive secretary, 1959-62; vice-president, 1963-66), Western Agricultural Economics Association (president, 1945-46).

WRITINGS: (With John Black, C. R. Sayre, and Walter W. Wilcox) *Farm Management,* Macmillan, 1947.

(Contributor) Eugene D. Gardner, editor, *Guide to Prospecting for Lode Gold,* U.S. Bureau of Mines, 1950; *The Western Range Livestock Industry,* McGraw, 1950; *Uncle Sam's Acres,* Dodd, 1951, Greenwood Press, 1970; (with R. Burnell Held) *The Federal Lands: Their Use and Management,* Johns Hopkins Press, 1957; *Analisis general del programa y de la administracion del Instituto Agrario Nacional* (title means "General Analysis of the Program and Administration of the National Agrarian Institute"), Consejo de Bienestar Rural (Caracas, Venezuela), 1959.

(With Held and Charles H. Stoddard) *Land for the Future,* Johns Hopkins Press, 1960; *Private and Public Provision of Outdoor Recreation Opportunity,* U.S. Outdoor Recreation Resources Review Commission, 1962; *Land and Water for Recreation: Opportunities, Problems, and Policies,* Rand McNally, 1963; *Land for Americans: Trends, Prospects, and Problems,* Rand McNally, 1963; (with Jack L. Knetsch) *Outdoor Recreation Research: Some Concepts and Suggested Areas of Study,* Resources for the Future, Inc., 1963; *Man and Land in the United States,* University of Nebraska Press, 1964; (editor) *Natural Resources and International Development,* Johns Hopkins Press, 1964; *The Public Lands,* Resources for the Future, Inc. and American Forestry Association, 1965; (with Held) *Soil Conservation in Perspective,* Johns Hopkins Press, 1965; (with Knetsch) *Economics of Outdoor Recreation,* Johns Hopkins Press, 1966; *Whither American Agriculture?,* two volumes, Resources for the Future, Inc., 1966; (with Charles L. Stewart)

Land Use Information: A Critical Survey of U.S. Statistics Including Possibilities for Greater Uniformity, Johns Hopkins Press, 1966; *The Federal Lands since 1956: Recent Trends in Use and Management*, Johns Hopkins Press, 1967; *The Land System of the United States: An Introduction to the History and Practice of Land Use and Land Tenure*, University of Nebraska Press, 1968; *Policy Directions for U.S. Agriculture: Long-Range Choices in Farming and Rural Living*, Johns Hopkins Press, 1968.

The Bureau of Land Management, Praeger, 1971; *Resources, Economic Development, and Environmental Quality*, Center for Resources Development, University of Guelph, 1971; *Suburban Land Conversion in the United States: An Economic and Governmental Process*, Johns Hopkins Press, 1971; (with Hans H. Landsberg and Lyle T. Alexander) *The Agricultural Potential of the Middle East*, American Elsevier, 1971; *America's Land and Its Uses*, Johns Hopkins Press, 1972; (editor with Landsberg) *Desalting Seawater: Achievements and Prospects*, Gordon & Breach, 1972; (with Peter Hall) *Planning and Urban Growth: An Anglo-American Comparison*, Johns Hopkins Press, 1973; (editor) *Modernizing Urban Land Policy*, Johns Hopkins Press, 1973; (editor) *Forest Policy for the Future: Conflict, Compromise, Consensus*, Johns Hopkins Press, 1974; *Forests for Whom and for What?*, Johns Hopkins Press, 1975.

Contributor to professional journals.

*   *   *

CLAYTON, Donald D(elbert) 1935-

PERSONAL: Born March 18, 1935, in Shenandoah, Iowa; son of Delbert Homer (an airline pilot) and Avis (Kembery) Clayton; married Annette Hildebrand (a painter), May 23, 1972; children: (previous marriage) Donald, Devon. *Education:* Southern Methodist University, B.S., 1956; California Institute of Technology, Ph.D., 1962. *Office:* Department of Space Physics and Astronomy, Rice University, Houston, Tex. 77001.

CAREER: Aerospace Corp., El Segundo, Calif., staff scientist, 1961-63; Rice University, Houston, Tex., assistant professor, 1963-65, associate professor, 1965-69, professor of astrophysics, 1969—, Andrew Hays Buchanan Professor of Astrophysics, 1975—. Professor at Weiss College, 1969—; visiting professor at University of Wales, summers, 1975-76. Research fellow at California Institute of Technology, 1961-63, visiting associate, 1966-67; visiting fellow at Institute of Theoretical Astronomy of Cambridge University, summers, 1967-72. Member of physics and astrophysics committees of National Research Council, 1970—.

MEMBER: International Astronomical Union, American Physical Society (fellow; member of executive committee of Division of Cosmic Physics, 1974-76), American Astronomical Society, American Meteoritical Society, American Association for the Advancement of Science, Phi Beta Kappa, Sigma Xi. *Awards, honors:* Alfred P. Sloan Foundation fellowship, 1966-70; Alexander von Humbolt Foundation award, 1977.

WRITINGS: Principles of Stellar Evolution and Nucleosynthesis, McGraw, 1968; *The Dark Night Sky: A Personal Adventure in Cosmology*, Quadrangle, 1975. Contributor of about seventy-five articles to scientific journals.

WORK IN PROGRESS: The Joshua Factor, a scientific novel; research on the origins of the chemical elements in stars and on the origin of the solar system.

SIDELIGHTS: Clayton writes: "The impetus of my writing for the public is the motive to share the sense of adventure that accompanies a life in astrophysics and cosmology. . . . The attempt to understand the circumstances and meaning of mankind pervade my work . . ."

*   *   *

CLAYTON, Howard 1929-

PERSONAL: Born March 8, 1929, in Leonardsville, Kan.; son of C. W. (a clergyman) and Minnie Belle (Vandiver) Clayton; married Wilma Jean Pennington, 1949; children: Caren Jean (Mrs. Walter Hallinkowski), Curtiss Howard. *Education:* Attended American Conservatory of Music, 1949-53, earned B.M. and M.M.; Kansas State Teachers College, Emporia, B.Ed., 1954, M.S.L.S., 1957; University of Oklahoma, Ph.D., 1965. *Religion:* Methodist. *Home:* 1514 Rowena Lane, Norman, Okla. 73069. *Office:* Library-College Associates, Inc., P.O. Box 956, Norman, Okla. 73070.

CAREER: Western Illinois University, Macomb, assistant librarian, 1957-59; Kansas State College, Pittsburgh, public service librarian, 1959-62; Southwestern College, Winfield, Kan., librarian and head of library department, 1962-64; State University of New York College at Brockport, head of library department, 1965-68; University of Oklahoma, Norman, associate professor of library sciences, 1968-77. Special instructor, University of Oklahoma, 1965. *Member:* American Library Association, Library-College Associates (executive secretary), Oklahoma Library Association, Masons, Kiwanis, Lions.

WRITINGS: (Editor) *The Teacher: Key to Library-Centered Learning*, Library-College Associates, 1976; *Elevating the Higher Learning*, Greenwood Press, in press. Editor of "Learning for Living" book series. Columnist, "The Scholiast" column in *Learning Today*. Contributor to education journals. Editor of *Learning Today, Library-College Omnibus*, and *Library-College Experimenter*.

*   *   *

CLEAGE, Albert B., Jr. 1911-

PERSONAL: Born June 13, 1911, in Indianapolis, Ind.; son of Albert B. Cleage; married Doris Graham; children: Kristin, Pearl. *Education:* Wayne State University, A.B., 1957, and graduate study; B.D. from Oberlin School of Theology; also attended University of Southern California. *Home:* 2042 Calvert, Detroit, Mich.

CAREER: Department of Public Welfare, Detroit, Mich., social case worker, 1931-38; ordained minister of United Church of Christ; pastor of churches in Lexington, Ky., 1942-43, in San Francisco, Calif., 1943-44, in Springfield, Mass., 1946-51, and in Detroit, Mich., 1951-52; Shrine of the Black Madonna, Detroit, Mich., pastor, 1952—. Co-chairman of Operation Connection to Aid Urban Blacks, 1968; member of Michigan State Commission of Freedom Now Political Party. *Member:* National Association for the Advancement of Colored People.

WRITINGS: The Black Messiah (collection of sermons), Sheed, 1968; (with George Brietman) *Myths About Malcolm X: Two Views*, Merit Publishers, 1968; (contributor) Clyde Manschreck, editor, *Erosion of Authority*, Abingdon, 1971; *Black Christian Nationalism: New Directions for the Black Church* (edited by George Bell), Morrow, 1972.

BIOGRAPHICAL/CRITICAL SOURCES: Washington Post, May 17, 1969; *Commonweal*, July 11, 1969.*

CLEARE, John 1936-

PERSONAL: Born May 2, 1936, in London, England; son of Franklin John (an engineer) and Marjorie (a teacher; maiden name, Silvey) Cleare; divorced; children: Jocelyn. *Education:* Attended Guildford School of Photography, 1957-60. *Home and office:* 67 Vanbrugh Park, Blackheath, London 5E3 7JQ, England.

CAREER: Queen (fashion magazine), London, England, staff photographer, 1960-61; Gamma Group, Lloyd Gamma Films, & Sargent Gamma (three firms working together as photography, film, and design partnership), London, England, co-founder, director, and photographer, 1962-69; freelance photographer, film cameraman, writer, lecturer, and mountaineer, 1969—. Director of Alpina Technica Productions, 1969-73. Member of management committee of British Mountaineering Council, 1972-75, member of executive committee, 1974-75. Has filmed live climbing and mountaineering broadcasts for British Broadcasting Corp. and Independent Television Network (ITV), and worked as cameraman for documentary films and advertising commercials. Has lectured in England, Kenya, Uganda, and the United States. *Military service:* British Army, Artillery officer, 1954-56; became lieutenant.

MEMBER: Alpine Club (member of committee, 1968—), Alpine Climbing Group (member of committee, 1966-67), Climbers Club. *Awards, honors:* 35mm. prize from Trento Film Festival, 1970, as cameraman for "The Climbers."

WRITINGS—All with own photographs: (With Tony Smythe) *Rock-Climbers in Action in Snowdonia,* Secker & Warburg, 1966; (with Robin Collomb) *Sea Cliff Climbing in Britain,* Constable, 1973; *Mountains,* Crown, 1975. Contributor of articles and photographs to magazines in England, the United States, and Europe. Co-editor of *Mountain Life,* 1973-75.

WORK IN PROGRESS: White Water: River Running World-Wide; a guide book to sea-stacks in the United Kingdom; a picture book on landscape and climbing in the Himalayas; a picture book with text on mountaineering in North America.

SIDELIGHTS: Cleare became interested in photography as an adult, but his love for the mountains began in early childhood, and he began climbing seriously at about thirteen. In 1971, he was a member of the International Himalayan expedition to climb the southwest face of Mount Everest. He has also done a lot of climbing in the European Alps, Ganesh Himal, Mounts Kenya and Kilimanjaro, in the California Sierra, and elsewhere in the U.S., and in Uganda and Zaire. He has also made kayak and raft descents of rivers in the western United States.

Combining his career with his life-long hobby, he has worked as cameraman on films including "Climb Up to Hell," "Last Blue Mountain," "The Waiting Face," "The Climbers," "Surrender to Everest," and most recently, the feature film "The Eiger Sanction," 1974. He writes: "Communicating in four different fields is interesting: the spoken word is so important because it involves the techniques of acting while the written word invokes the mechanical skills and different thought patterns. This is reflected in the visual media—the different approach to film from stills, the one containing a mechanical and a time element and the other purely graphic shape and tone. I would hate to be lumbered with only one media in which to work."

BIOGRAPHICAL/CRITICAL SOURCES: Walt Unsworth, *Encyclopaedia of Mountaineering,* R. Hale, 1975.

CLEMO, Richard F(rederick) 1920-1976

September 23, 1920—March 8, 1976; American college administrator, educator, and author. Obituaries: *New York Times,* March 10, 1976.

* * *

CLERICI, Gianni 1930-

PERSONAL: Born July 24, 1930, in Como, Italy; son of Luigi (an oilman) and Lucia (Castelli) Clerici; married Annamaria Gilardoni (a gardener), February 1, 1964; children: Carlotta, Luigi. *Education:* Attended Universities of Milan and Urbino. *Home:* Salita Peltrera 34, Como 22100, Italy. *Agent:* Erich Linder, Corso Matteotti 3, Milan 20100, Italy. *Office: Il Giorno,* Via Fava 20, Milan 20100, Italy.

CAREER: Il Giorno (national daily newspaper), Milan, Italy, author of column "Tennis," 1956—. *Military service:* Italian Army, mule driver for Alpine Troops, 1956. *Awards, honors:* Named best Italian journalist of the month by *Il Premiolino,* 1964; premio coni from Italian Olympic Committee, 1974, for best sports book, *Il Tennis Facile.*

WRITINGS: Il Vero Tennis (title means "The True Tennis"), Longanesi, 1965; *Fuori Rosa* (novel; title means "Out of a Rose"), Vallecchi, 1966; *Il Tennis Facile* (title means "Easy Tennis"), Mondadori, 1972; *500 Anni di Tennis,* Mondadori, 1974, translation published as *The Ultimate Tennis Book,* Follett, 1975; *Quando Viene il Lunedi* (a trilogy of novels; title means "When Monday Comes"), Mondadori, 1974.

WORK IN PROGRESS: A novel about five monkeys; research on the Italian Renaissance at the end of the fifteenth century, especially on the Dukedom of Milan; research on old tennis champions.

SIDELIGHTS: Clerici writes: "Having been a good tennis player, and very lazy at the University, I tried to write to have some money without really working. Poor results and a love for sports produced an unintentionally successful journalist."

* * *

CLEWS, Roy 1937-

PERSONAL: Born May 11, 1937, in London, England; married Olwen Jones, January 17, 1970; children: Nicholas, Sara Elizabeth. *Education:* Attended secondary school in Redditch County, England. *Politics:* "Patriot." *Religion:* Church of England. *Home and office:* 74 Flyford Close, Lodge Park, Redditch, Worcestershire, England. *Agent:* Laurence Pollinger, 18 Maddox St., London W.1, England.

CAREER: Professional soldier with Royal Marine Commando in Cyprus, 1955-58, and with Parachute Regiment, 1958-59; served with Spanish Foreign Legion in the Sahara, 1960-62; traveling around the world by working as seaman, copper miner, laborer, actor, and at various other jobs, 1962—.

WRITINGS—All historical novels: *Young Jethro,* Heinemann, 1975, published as *The Valiant and the Damned,* Dutton, 1976; *The King's Bounty,* Heinemann, 1976; *The Drums of War,* Heinemann, in press.

WORK IN PROGRESS: Research on rural life in England at the close of the Napoleonic wars, for a novel dealing with returning soldiers and sailors.

SIDELIGHTS: Clews writes: "I have spent twelve years of my life travelling the world, and doing it the hard way since for most of my life I have only known comparative poverty, and for extended periods utter poverty.... I have ... served as a merchant seaman on ships of many registrations. I've been in military and civil prisons in many countries normally for brawling and drunkeness, and have in fact been in some sort of trouble or other for most of my years. This type of life is a good education, it taught me to ... survive, in deserts, mountains, cities and across the seas. Life's been rough and at times very unpleasant, but never dull. In most aspects of life I am a hard-liner. I believe that those who offer violence must be met and mastered by violence.

"I write about an age when England was still a nation that was not afraid to win, and was led by patriots who no matter what their personal defects were, at least put the English nation above all others. I passionately believe that the British could again become a great nation. Equally passionately, I despise the politicians who have dragged my country down for the last sixty years, and who ensure that their own personal mediocrity is injected into every aspect of Britain's performance on the world stage." *Avocational interests:* Scuba diving, playing chess, collecting medieval and traditional folk music.

BIOGRAPHICAL/CRITICAL SOURCES: Scottish Sunday Post, six-week serial in Sunday editions, March-April, 1963; *Birmingham Post,* July 1, 1975; *Sunday Express,* August 31, 1975; *Worcestershire and Warwickshire Life,* June, 1976.

* * *

CLINE, Linda 1941-

PERSONAL: Born February 11, 1941, in New York, N.Y.; daughter of Eleanor Fellers; married C. Terry Cline, Jr. (a writer), October 23, 1959; children: Cabeth, Blaise, Trey, Marc. *Education:* Educated in public high school in Thomasville, Ga. *Politics:* "An angry Republican-conservative." *Religion:* "Catholic (also angry)." *Home and office:* 66 Hannon Ave., Mobile, Ala. 36604. *Agent:* Jay Garon, Jay Garon-Brooke Associates, 415 Central Park W., Suite 17D, New York, N.Y. 10025.

CAREER: Land Alive Foundation, Inc., Thomasville, Ga., began as vice-president and member of board of directors, became president and owner of Land Alive of America.

WRITINGS—Juvenile: Weakfoot, Lothrop, 1975; *Miracle Season,* Berkely Publishing, 1976. Co-author, with Wesley C. Ellis, of "Switchwitch," a children's musical drama, first produced in Mobile, Ala., at Mobile Theatre Guild, February 20, 1974. Editor, *Land Alive* of Land Alive Foundation, 1969-70.

WORK IN PROGRESS: A juvenile, *Taylor's Raiders,* for Lothrop; a book about animals for children, similar to *Miracle Season.*

SIDELIGHTS: Linda Cline writes that she "would like to produce quality, factual fiction for all-age appeal, sell to Disney repeatedly, and thereby teach about living things as an extension of my sixteen years work with animals."

* * *

CLINE, Victor (Bailey) 1925-

PERSONAL: Born January 23, 1925, in Seattle, Wash.; son of George E. (an electrical engineer) and Betty Cline; married Lois Lowe; children: Russell, Janice, Robyn, Christopher, Richard, Constance, Paul, Julie, Becky. *Education:* University of California, Berkeley, B.A., 1949, Ph.D., 1953. *Politics:* Independent. *Religion:* Church of Jesus Christ of Latter-day Saints (Mormons). *Home:* 2087 Millstream Lane,

Salt Lake City, Utah 84109. *Office:* 717 Behavioral Science Building, University of Utah, Salt Lake City, Utah 84112.

CAREER: George Washington University, Washington, D.C., research scientist in Human Resources Research office, 1953-58; University of Utah, Salt Lake City, 1958—, began as assistant professor, became professor of psychology. Director of Southern Utah Guidance Clinic, 1965-73. *Military service:* U.S. Army, Infantry, 1942-45; served in Europe; became sergeant. *Member:* American Psychological Association, Phi Beta Kappa, Sigma Xi.

WRITINGS: Where Do You Draw the Line?: Explorations in Media Violence, Pornography, and Censorship, Brigham Young University Press, 1974. Contributor of about one hundred articles to scientific journals and popular magazines.

WORK IN PROGRESS: A book on marriage adjustment.

* * *

CLOETE, Stuart 1897-1976

July 23, 1897—March 20, 1976; South African novelist, essayist, and author of short stories. Obituaries: *New York Times,* March 21, 1976; *Washington Post,* March 23, 1976; *Time,* April 5, 1976; *AB Bookman's Weekly,* April 26, 1976. (See index for previous *CA* sketch)

* * *

CLOTHIER, Peter (Dean) 1936-

PERSONAL: Born August 1, 1936, in England; came to the United States in 1964; son of Harry (a clergyman) and Peggy Clothier; married Elizabeth Foot, 1964 (divorced, 1969); married Ellen Blankfort (an art dealer), November 11, 1972; children: (first marriage) Matthew, Jason; (second marriage) Sarah. *Education:* Gonville & Caius College, Cambridge, B.A., 1957, M.A., 1962; University of Iowa, Ph.D., 1969. *Home:* 2341 Ronda Vista Dr., Los Angeles, Calif. 90027.

CAREER: Teacher of English, French, and German literature and language in grammar schools in London, England, 1957-61, and Halifax, Nova Scotia, 1962-64; University of Iowa, Iowa City, instructor in comparative literature and creative writing, 1964-68; University of Southern California, Los Angeles, assistant professor of comparative literature, 1968-76, director of "Semester of the Arts" program, 1971-76; Otis Art Institute, Los Angeles, Calif., dean of the college, 1976—. *Member:* American Association of University Professors. *Awards, honors:* Art critics fellowship from National Education Association, 1976.

WRITINGS: Aspley Guise (poems), Red Hill Press, 1971; (with Gary Lloyd) *Bob Went Home,* Ellie Blankfort Gallery Publishers, 1972; *The Long Thin* (stories), Ellie Blankfort Gallery Publishers, 1974; *Parapoems,* Horizon Press, 1975. Contributor of articles, stories, and poems to art journals and literary magazines, including *South and West, Northeast,* and *Micromegas.*

WORK IN PROGRESS: Studies in art and literature; research on the use of words and literary forms in contemporary art.

BIOGRAPHICAL/CRITICAL SOURCES: Margins, summer, 1974; *Art News,* March, 1975.

* * *

CLOUTIER, Cecile 1930-
(Cecile de Lantagne)

PERSONAL: Born June 13, 1930, in Quebec City, Quebec,

Canada; daughter of Adrien (a civil servant) and Maria (de Lantagne) Cloutier; married Jerzy Wojciechowski (a university professor), December 27, 1966; children: Marie-Berenice, Eve-Moira. *Education:* Laval University, B.A., 1951, M.A., 1953, L.esL., 1953, D.E.S., 1954; Sorbonne, University of Paris, D.deL.U., 1961. *Home:* 20 Highbourne St., Toronto, Ontario, Canada. *Office:* Department of French, University of Toronto, Toronto, Ontario, Canada.

CAREER: University of Ottawa, Ottawa, Ontario, assistant professor of French literature and aesthetics, 1958-64; University of Toronto, Toronto, Ontario, associate professor of French and Quebec literatures and aesthetics, 1964—. Lecturer, Royal Ontario Museum, 1966, New York University, 1966, and at learned societies in Ottawa, 1967; consultant to Canadian Council of the Arts and Canadian Humanities Council. *Member:* Modern Language Association of America, Association of Teachers of French, Association Canadienne des professeurs de francais, Societe des ecrivains, Societe des poetes, P.E.N. Club, Societe d'Esthetique, American Society of Aesthetics, Le Societe des gens de Lettres de France, Societe des ecrivains de France et d'outre-mer. *Awards, honors:* Silver medal from Societe des ecrivains de France, 1960, for *Mains de sable;* Canada Council scholar, 1964-65 and 1967-68; Cocteau prize from Center for Continuing Education, 1964; prizes for poetry from the Canadian Centennial Commission, 1968.

WRITINGS—Poetry: Mains de sable, Editions de L'Arc (Quebec), 1960; *Cuivre et soies, suivi de Mains de sable,* Editions du Jour (Montreal), 1964; *Cannelles et craies,* J. Grassin (Paris), 1969; *Paupieres,* Librairie Deom (Montreal), 1970; *Cablogrammes,* G. Chambelland (Paris), 1972. Contributor of articles, sometimes under pseudonym Cecile de Lantagne, and of poetry to French and French-Canadian journals.

WORK IN PROGRESS: Four books of poetry, *L'Echangeur, Pain, Vin d'ombre et de lumiere,* and *Bagues;* two volumes of essays, *De Poesia quebecence* and *Au pied du courant.*

AVOCATIONAL INTERESTS: Crafts, travel, languages (Cecile Cloutier has studied Polish, German, Russian, Spanish, Chinese, Sanskrit, Eskimo, Latin, and Greek).

*   *   *

CLUFF, Charles E.   1937-

PERSONAL: Born February 4, 1937, in Pomona, Calif.; son of Harold E. (an engineer) and Thelma (a registered nurse; maiden name, McCoy) Cluff; married Betty Faulkner (a teacher), May 24, 1958; children: Mark E., Carrie Lyne. *Education:* California Baptist College, B.A., 1958; American Baptist Seminary of the West, M.Div., 1961; San Francisco Theological Seminary, D.Min., 1975. *Home and office:* 140 East 21st, Merced, Calif. 95340.

CAREER: Pastor of American Baptist churches in Norwalk, Calif., 1960-65, Lemoore, Calif., 1965-68, and Merced, Calif., 1968-72; private practice in marriage, family, and child counseling, 1972—. Lecturer. Counselor for local probation department; president of local mental health association, 1972-74; member of local ministers' council. *Member:* National Alliance for Family Life, Academy of Parapsychology and Medicine, Institute of Noetic Sciences, California Association of Marriage and Family Counselors, Rotary International.

WRITINGS: Parapsychology and the Christian Faith, Judson, 1976; *Premarital Experience Workbook,* with instructor's manual, privately printed, 1977.

WORK IN PROGRESS: A Holistic View for a Whole Person, completion expected in 1978.

SIDELIGHTS: Cluff writes that his books are based on the suppositions that "the world is opening up—this is friendly, not threatening! In life people are seeking intimacy—the most natural setting for this is within the framework of marriage and the family! People are looking for a complete understanding of their life journey."

*   *   *

COALE, Samuel Chase   1943-

PERSONAL: Born July 26, 1943, in Hartford, Conn.; son of Samuel Chase (a photographer) and Harriet (Kimberly) Coale; married Gray Emory, June 24, 1972. *Education:* Trinity College, Hartford, Conn., B.A., 1965; Brown University, M.A. and Ph.D., both 1970. *Office:* Wheaton College, Norton, Mass. 02766.

CAREER: Wheaton College, Norton, Mass., instructor, 1968-71, assistant professor, 1971-76, associate professor of American literature, 1976—. Member of board of directors of Trinity Square Repertory Theatre, Looking Glass Theatre, and Rhode Island Dane Repertory Theatre. Member of Rhode Island Bicentennial Commission. *Member:* Modern Language Association of America, English-Speaking Union (president, 1975—), Phi Beta Kappa. *Awards, honors:* Ford Foundation summer grants, 1970 and 1971; grants for study in England, 1970, 1972; Fulbright fellowship in Greece, 1976-77.

WRITINGS: (Contributor) Committee on the Frost Centennial of University of Southern Mississippi English Department, editors, *Frost: Centennial Essays,* University Press of Mississippi, 1975; *John Cheever,* Ungar, 1977. Contributor of articles and reviews to literature journals.

WORK IN PROGRESS: A mystery novel, tentatively titled *October Light;* a novel set in Greece, tentatively titled *Open Spaces;* research on Robert Frost, Jerzy Kosinski, William Faulkner, Lawrence Durrell, and Edgar Allan Poe.

SIDELIGHTS: Coale writes: "The American sees motion and fails to reflect on the invisible. Maybe I'm trying to get at some essence, aesthetic or moral, I think we're missing, in all things, critical as well as creative work. Pretentious? It is, yet baldly stated, it could be it." He adds that he has been "nurtured by strong traditional New England values." *Avocational interests:* Film, piano composition, European travel.

*   *   *

COBURN, Karen Levin   1941-

PERSONAL: Born July 20, 1941, in New Jersey; daughter of Alfred Phillip (a businessman) and Helen (Smarak) Levin; married A. Stephen Coburn (a university administrator), July 12, 1964; children: Andrew Arthur, Alison Joy. *Education:* Skidmore College, B.A., 1963; Harvard University, M.A.T., 1964; graduate study at University of Michigan, 1970-71; Washington University, St. Louis, Mo., M.A.Ed., 1973. *Home:* 7010 Washington Ave., St. Louis, Mo. 63130. *Office:* Fontbonne College, 6800 Wydown, Clayton, Mo. 63105.

CAREER: High school librarian in Weston, Mass., 1964-65; high school English teacher in Westwood, Mass., 1965-67; Cambridge School Volunteers Project, Cambridge, Mass., volunteer teacher of English as a second language, 1967-69; Lasell Junior College, Newton, Mass., instructor in English, 1969-70; Fontbonne College, Clayton, Mo., counselor-intern, 1972-73, director of counseling, 1973—. Instructor at University of Missouri-St. Louis Extension Division, 1973-75, and Washington University, St. Louis, Mo., 1976; founding member and staff member of St. Louis Women's Counseling Center, 1973—; member of women's council and higher education coordinating council for St. Louis Area Colleges and Universities, 1973—. Counselor for Planned Parenthood, Ann Arbor, Mich., 1970-71. Has appeared on local and national television and radio programs. *Member:* American Personnel and Guidance Association, American College Personnel Association, Phi Beta Kappa.

WRITINGS: (With Lynn Z. Bloom and Joan Pearlman) *The New Assertive Women* (selection of Woman Today Book Club, Modern Psychology Book Club, Psychology Today Book Club, and Nurses' Book Club), Delacorte, 1975. Co-author and director of script for "Assertive Training for Women: A Stimulus Film," and co-author of film guide, Parts I and II, American Personnel and Guidance Association, 1973. Contributor to *Cosmopolitan* and *Family Circle.*

SIDELIGHTS: Karen Coburn writes: "My main professional interest is in working with women of all ages. I find it exciting to help them to explore options, learn skills, and to gain more control over their lives." *Avocational interests:* "Beach sitting," snorkeling, biking, travel.

* * *

COE, Richard L(ivingston) 1916-

PERSONAL: Born November 8, 1916, in New York, N.Y.; son of Elmer J. S. (a banker) and Lillie (a writer; maiden name, Musgrave) Coe; married Christine Sadler (a writer), May 4, 1946. *Education:* Attended George Washington University, 1934. *Religion:* Episcopalian. *Home:* 2713 Dumbarton Ave. N.W., Washington, D.C. 20007. *Office: Washington Post,* 1150 15th St. N.W., Washington, D.C. 20011.

CAREER/WRITINGS: Washington Post, Washington, D.C., journalist, 1938—, author of "One on the Aisle" column syndicated by Washington Post-Los Angeles Times Syndicate, 1946-68, drama critic, 1946—. Commentator for NBC-Television. Contributor to magazines and newspapers in the United States, London, Cairo, and Palestine, including *Smithsonian, Shakespeare Quarterly, Ambassador,* and *Washingtonian. Military service:* U.S. Army, Middle East editor, *Stars and Stripes,* 1942-46. *Member:* National Press Club, Prayers Club (New York, N.Y.). *Awards, honors:* Newspaper Guild award, 1949; awards from Washington Board of Trade, 1957, General Federation of Women's Clubs, 1957, and American Theater Association, 1975; named critic of the year by Directors Guild of America, 1963.

SIDELIGHTS: Coe writes that he believes in "the drama critic as activist. In 1950 Washington had been reduced to *no professional theater* in this capital city. By highlighting this situation, by writing about its absurdity, by appearing on lecture platforms and at Congressional hearings, this trend has been reversed in twenty-five years. We now have the Kennedy Center, Arena Stage; Ford's Theater reconstructed. Washington now is recognized as a major American theater city. By taking an activist role as critic, I have had a leadership role in the city's turnabout. The critic also has a constructivist role to play in a city which presents an increasing number of new works on their way to New York's still important but no longer entirely decisive role."

COFFEY, Robert E(dward) 1931-

PERSONAL: Born May 1, 1931, in Brookings, S.D.; son of Robert E. (an Army officer) and Kathryn (Bonesteel) Coffey; married Helen Clark (a teacher), July 10, 1954. *Education:* Principia College, B.A. (honors), 1953; Northwestern University, M.B.A. (with distinction), 1958; University of Illinois, Ph.D., 1963. *Home:* 6828 Vallon Dr., Rancho Palos Verdes, Calif. 90274. *Office:* School of Business Administration, University of Southern California, Los Angeles, Calif. 90007.

CAREER: University of Southern California, Los Angeles, assistant professor, 1963-68, associate professor, 1968-76, professor of management, 1976—, director of master of business administration program, 1968-71, chairman of department of business administration, 1971-73, director of entrepreneur and venture management program, 1974—. Regional consultant to State Farm Insurance Co. *Member:* Academy of Management (secretary-treasurer, 1973-76).

WRITINGS: (With Anthony Athos) *Behavior in Organizations: A Multi-Dimensional View,* Prentice-Hall, 1968, 2nd edition (with Athos and Peter A. Raynolds), 1975.

* * *

COGLEY, John 1916-1976

March 16, 1916—March 29, 1976; American religious news editor, journalist, and author of books in his field. Obituaries: *New York Times,* March 30, 1976; *Washington Post,* April 1, 1976; *Newsweek,* April 12, 1976; *Time,* April 12, 1976. (See index for previous *CA* sketch)

* * *

COHEN, Joseph 1926-

PERSONAL: Born April 27, 1926, in Central City, Ky.; son of Louis Aaron and Hattie (Klein) Cohen; married Gloria Ann Plitman (assistant executive director of New Orleans Jewish Community Center), July 20, 1952; children: Susan Emily, Cynthia Gail, Jeffrey Daniel. *Education:* Austin Peay State College, junior college diploma, 1945; University of Minnesota, student, 1946; Vanderbilt University, A.B., 1949, M.A., 1951; University of Texas, Ph.D., 1955. *Politics:* Democrat. *Religion:* Jewish. *Home:* 7029 Freret St., New Orleans, La. 70118. *Office:* Department of English, Newcomb College, Tulane University, New Orleans, La. 70118.

CAREER: University of Texas, Austin, instructor in English, 1953-55; Tulane University, New Orleans, La., instructor, 1955-58, assistant professor, 1958-63, associate professor, 1963-75, professor of English, 1975—, assistant dean of College of Arts and Sciences, 1957-58, associate dean of Newcomb College, 1967-76, associate director of Scholars and Fellows Program, 1964-65, director of program, 1965-67, co-director, 1968—. Secretary of area clinic on Great Britain, of National Conference on Undergraduate Study Abroad, 1960; member of executive committee of National Collegiate Honors Council, 1966-71, vice-president, 1969-70, president, 1970-71; member of national advisory committee on Jewish college youth for National Jewish Welfare Board, 1969-71. Chairman of regional selection committee for Woodrow Wilson National Fellowship Foundation, 1970—. Member of board of governors of I. Newman School, 1969-71. Vice-president of board of governors of local Jewish Community Center, 1968-70. Rare book consultant for New Orleans Philharmonic Symphony Association, 1965—. *Military service:* U.S. Army, 1945-46.

MEMBER: Modern Language Association of America, National Council of Teachers of English, Bibliographical Society of America, Modern Humanities Research Association, American Association of University Professors, South Central Modern Language Association (business manager, 1956-59; member of executive committee, 1956-59), Kappa Delta Pi, Alpha Epsilon Delta, Phi Eta Sigma, Omicron Delta Kappa.

WRITINGS: (Editor and contributor) *Proceedings of the Southern Honors Symposium,* Tulane University, 1968; *Journey to the Trenches: The Life of Isaac Rosenberg, 1890-1918,* Basic Books, 1975. Contributor of about thirty-five articles and reviews to literature journals. Contributing editor of *Journal of Higher Education,* 1968-71; member of editorial board of *English Literature in Transition,* 1964-70.

WORK IN PROGRESS: Books on twentieth century war poets and on as yet unexplored motifs in modern anti-war writing; research for books on the "Jewish princess syndrome" and the characteristics and lifestyles of contemporary southern Jews; research on British and American literature from 1880 to the present.

SIDELIGHTS: Cohen writes: "It was always my intention to write and write well. However, if there was one thing I knew when my Ph.D. was awarded it was that I couldn't write at all. This was certainly no bar to publication, but it meant spending some years striving for articulation." *Avocational interests:* Rare book hunting.

* * *

COHEN, Lawrence Jonathan 1923-

PERSONAL: Born May 7, 1923, in London, England; son of Israel and Theresa Cohen; married Gillian Mary Slee, 1953; children: Stephen Benedict, Daniel Charles, Robin John, Juliet Rose. *Education:* Balliol College, Oxford, M.A., 1947. *Home:* Sturt House, East End, North Leigh, Oxfordshire, England. *Office:* Queen's College, Oxford University, Oxford, England.

CAREER: University of Edinburgh, Edinburgh, Scotland, assistant in logic and metaphysics, 1947-50; St. Andrews University, Dundee, Scotland, lecturer in philosophy, 1950-57; Oxford University, Queen's College, Oxford, England, praelector in philosophy and fellow of the college, 1957—. Visiting lecturer at Hebrew University of Jerusalem, 1952; visiting professor at Columbia University, 1967, and Yale University, 1972. *Military service:* British Naval Intelligence, 1942-45. Royal Naval Volunteer Reserve, 1945; became lieutenant. *Member:* British Academy (fellow). *Awards, honors:* Commonwealth Fund fellow at Princeton and Harvard Universities, 1952-53.

WRITINGS: The Principles of World Citizenship, Basil Blackwell, 1954, Transatlantic, 1954; *The Diversity of Meaning,* Methuen, 1962, 2nd edition, 1966, Herder & Herder, 1963; *The Implications of Induction,* Barnes & Noble, 1970; *The Probable and the Provable,* Oxford University Press, in press. Contributor to British, Belgian, Dutch, French, Israeli, and American philosophy journals.

AVOCATIONAL INTERESTS: Gardening, working for the Council for the Protection of Rural England.

* * *

COHEN, Stewart 1940-

PERSONAL: Born December 30, 1940, in New York, N.Y.; son of Louis and Betty (Wood) Cohen; married Muriel Berkman (a counselor), September 2, 1961; children:

Joseph, Michelle, David. *Education:* City College of the City University of New York, B.A., 1961; University of Oklahoma, M.S., 1963; Purdue University, Ph.D., 1967. *Religion:* Jewish. *Office:* Department of Child Development and Family Relations, Quinn Hall, University of Rhode Island, Kingston, R.I. 02881.

CAREER: University of Illinois, Urbana, assistant professor of educational psychology, 1967-72; University of Rhode Island, Kingston, associate professor of child development and family relations, 1972—. President of Champaign Council on Adoptable Children, 1969-70. *Member:* Association for Childhood Education International, Society for Research in Child Development, American Association of University Professors, American Home Economics Association.

WRITINGS: Child Development: A Study of Growth Processes, F. E. Peacock, 1971; *Social and Personality Development in Childhood,* Macmillan, 1976; *Child Development: Contemporary Perspectives,* F. E. Peacock, in press.

* * *

COHN, Victor (Edward) 1919-

PERSONAL: Born August 4, 1919, in Minneapolis, Minn.; son of Lewis (a salesman) and Lillian (Bessler) Cohn; married Marcella Rigler (an accountant), August 30, 1941; children: Jeffrey, Deborah (Mrs. Lee Runkle), Phyllis. *Education:* University of Minnesota, B.A. (honors), 1941. *Religion:* Jewish. *Home:* 4701 Willard Ave., Apt. 1603, Chevy Chase, Md. 20015. *Office: Washington Post,* 1150 15th St. N.W., Washington, D.C. 20071.

CAREER: Minnesota Daily (at University of Minnesota), Minneapolis, Minn., editor, 1940-41; *Minneapolis Star,* Minneapolis, desk man, 1941-42; *Minneapolis Tribune,* Minneapolis, copy reader, 1946, reporter, 1946-47, science reporter, 1947-67; *Washington Post,* Washington, D.C., science editor, 1968-72, science-medicine reporter, 1972—. Visiting lecturer at University of Minnesota, 1966-67; lecturer at Weizmann Institute of Science (Israel), 1967. Incorporator and director of Council for the Advancement of Science Writing, 1960—, vice-president, 1967-68; co-organizer of International Science Writers Tour of Israeli Universities, 1974. *Military service:* U.S. Naval Reserve, active duty, 1942-45; became lieutenant.

MEMBER: American Association for the Advancement of Science (fellow), National Association of Science Writers (president, 1961-62), Newspaper Guild, Phi Beta Kappa. *Awards, honors:* George Westinghouse Award from American Association for the Advancement of Science, 1951, 1959; distinguished reporting award from Sigma Delta Chi, 1952, 1956, 1959; citations from Minnesota Medical Association, 1955, and Minnesota Public Health Association, 1966; Albert Lasker medical journalism award from Albert and Mary Lasker Foundation, 1958; National Headliner Club awards, 1959, 1962; Howard W. Blakeslee Award from American Heart Association, 1963; distinguished citizen award from Phi Beta Kappa Association of Minnesota, 1966; James T. Grady Award from American Chemical Society, 1971; Science-in-Society Award from National Association of Science Writers, 1973; nine Page One Awards from Twin Cities Newspaper Guild.

WRITINGS: 1999: Our Hopeful Future, Bobbs-Merrill, 1956; (author of epilogue) Keith Bill, *Plug in for Life,* Thomas Nelson, 1971; *Sister Kenny: The Woman Who Challenged the Doctors,* University of Minnesota Press, 1976.

Contributor: Jerome Beatty, Jr. and others, editors, *Saturday Review Gallery*, Simon & Schuster, 1959; Robert T. Holt and John E. Turner, editors, *Soviet Union: Paradox and Change*, Holt, 1962; Bryce W. Rucker, editor, *Twentieth Century Reporting at Its Best*, Iowa State University Press, 1964; Clifford Simak, editor, *From Atoms to Infinity: Readings in Modern Science*, Harper, 1965; John Hohenberg, editor, *The New Front Page*, Columbia University Press, 1966; Donn Byrne and Marshall Hamilton, editors, *Personality Research*, Prentice-Hall, 1966; Ira Goodwin, editor, *Paying for America's Health Care*, Washington Journalism Center, 1973.

Author of Washington column in Massachusetts Institute of Technology's *Technology Review*, 1968-75. Contributor to scientific journals and to popular magazines, including *Reader's Digest, Ladies' Home Journal,* and *Smithsonian.* Member of editorial advisory board of *Technology Review.*

SIDELIGHTS: Cohn writes on man, the atom, health, disease, youth, aging, the environment, space, and the stars. His efforts have helped establish better care for mentally ill children and voluntary (rather than compulsory) screening for sickle cell testing. One of his awards was for his discovery and disclosure of wasteful hospital building that was leading directly to sharply rising hospital rates. He was also one of the first American reporters to tour Soviet science centers.

BIOGRAPHICAL/CRITICAL SOURCES: David Botter, *News Reporters and What They Do*, Watts, 1959; David Warren Burkett, *Writing Science News for the Mass Media*, Gulf Publishing, 1965; Hillier Krieghbaum, *Science and the Mass Media*, New York University Press, 1967.

*   *   *

COLE, Ann   1937-

PERSONAL: Born January 6, 1937, in Ohio; daughter of Daniel (a businessman) and Clementine (Flesheim) Sherby; married Roger Bruce Cole (a physician), March 23, 1958; children: Gary, Laurie, Danny, Nancy. *Education:* Student at Wellesley College, 1955-57, and Western Reserve University (now Case Western Reserve University), 1957-58; California State University, San Francisco (now San Francisco State University), B.A., 1960. *Politics:* Independent. *Home:* 576 Hill Ter., Winnetka, Ill. 60093. *Agent:* Curtis Brown Ltd., 60 East 56th St., New York, N.Y. 10022. *Office:* Parents as Resources (PAR) Project, 464 Central, Northfield, Ill. 60093.

CAREER: Bedside teacher and tutor in Evanston, Ill., 1962-65, and Winnetka, Ill., 1965-68; Parents as Resources Project, Northfield, Ill., consultant, 1968—. Substitute teacher in public schools in Winnetka, 1965-68. Member of board of directors of Winnetka Human Relations Committee and International Visitors Center, 1962-67. *Member:* Chicago Association for the Education of Young Children, Chicago Round Table of Children's Authors.

WRITINGS: (With Carolyn Buhai Haas and Betty Kiralfy Weinberger) *Recipes for Fun* (juvenile), six volumes, Parents as Resources Project, 1970-76; (with Haas, Weinberger, and Faith Phillips Bushnell) *I Saw a Purple Cow* (juvenile), Little, Brown, 1972; (with Haas, Weinberger, and Elizabeth Henkel Heller) *A Pumpkin in a Pear Tree* (juvenile), Little, Brown, 1976; (with Haas) *Children are Children are Children*, Little, Brown, in press. Co-author of "Recipes for Fun," a syndicated column, 1970—. Contributor to education journals, *Parent's Magazine, Daycare and Early Education,* and *McCall's.* Consultant to television series, "Look at Me!" on WWTW-Television, Chicago, 1975-76.

SIDELIGHTS: Ann Cole writes: "The PAR Project has concentrated on assisting parents in working more creatively and effectively with their young children. As one of the founding partners of this program, I have long seen the importance of helping parents to see themselves as the primary resources in their children's lives. Now, with so many mothers and fathers of pre-school children working, the need is even greater to assist these parents in making what little time they do have with children more meaningful and more enjoyable for both themselves and for the children. The purpose of all our published writings to date has been to facilitate positive child/parent interactions."

*   *   *

COLE, Arthur C(harles)   1886-1976

April 22, 1886—February 26, 1976; American historian, educator, and author of books in his field. Obituaries: *New York Times,* February 28, 1976.

*   *   *

COLE, Bruce   1938-

PERSONAL: Born August 2, 1938, in Cleveland, Ohio; son of Jerome (a salesman) and Selma (Kaufman) Cole; married Doreen Luff (a student), 1962; children: Stephanie, Ryan. *Education:* Western Reserve University (now Case Western Reserve University), B.A., 1962; Oberlin College, M.A., 1964; Bryn Mawr College, Ph.D., 1969. *Home:* 1908 Viva Dr., Bloomington, Ind. *Office:* Department of Fine Arts, Indiana University, Bloomington, Ind. 47401.

CAREER: University of Rochester, Rochester, N.Y., assistant professor of art history, 1969-73; Indiana University, Bloomington, associate professor of art history, 1973—. *Awards, honors:* National Endowment for the Humanities fellowship, 1972-73; Guggenheim fellowship, 1975-76.

WRITINGS: Giotto and Florentine Painting, 1280-1375, Harper, 1976; *Agnolo Gaddi,* Clarendon Press, 1976. Contributor to art journals.

WORK IN PROGRESS: Masaccio and Florentine Painting, 1375-1430; a collection of essays on Florentine art of the early Renaissance.

*   *   *

COLE, C(harles) Robert   1939-

PERSONAL: Born August 24, 1939, in Harper, Kan.; son of Charles Edward (a farmer) and Olive (a teacher; maiden name, Collumber) Cole; married Glenda White (an instructor), August 9, 1963; children: Teresa Anne. *Education:* Ottawa University, B.A., 1961; Kansas State University, M.A., 1966; Claremont Graduate School, Ph.D., 1971. *Politics:* Democrat. *Religion:* Episcopal. *Home:* 1695 East 1400 North, Logan, Utah 84321. *Office:* Department of History, Utah State University, Logan, Utah 84321.

CAREER: Utah State University, Logan, assistant professor, 1970-76, associate professor of history, 1976—. *Member:* American Historical Association, Conference on British Studies (member of national executive committee, and president of Rocky Mountain branch, 1974-76).

WRITINGS: (Contributor) E. M. Robertson, editor, *The Origins of the Second World War*, Macmillan, 1971; (editor with Michel E. Moody) *The Dissenting Tradition: Essays for Leland H. Carlson,* Ohio University Press, 1975. Contributor of essays and reviews to journals, including *Rocky Mountain Social Science Journal, American Historical Review,* and *Journal of Modern History.*

WORK IN PROGRESS: A short analytical study of British historian A.J.P. Taylor; research on the British Ministry of Information in World War II.

SIDELIGHTS: Cole told *CA:* "As with most in my profession I am motivated mostly by a love of the subject and a passion, almost, for finding out 'what happened.' This certainly is the case with my present efforts to untangle the complex and provocative career of A.J.P. Taylor."

* * *

COLE, Cannon
See COOK, Arlene Ethel

* * *

COLE, Eddie-Lou 1909-

PERSONAL: Born February 9, 1909, in Ridgefield, Wash.; daughter of James Raymond (a boat builder) and E. Pearl (a teacher; maiden name, White) Neill; married Laurence A. Cole, 1928 (died, 1945); married Ray Wehrner Howard, December 8, 1966; children: (first marriage) David Laurence, Donna Ruth (Mrs. David Stallings). *Education:* Attended Sacramento City College, Heald Business College, and University of California, Berkeley. *Home:* 1841 Garden Highway, Sacramento, Calif. 95833. *Office:* 801 Portola Dr., Suite 211, San Francisco, Calif. 94127.

CAREER: State of California, 1934-70, began as file clerk in department of motor vehicles, transferred to department of social welfare, worked in several other departments, became bookkeeper in department of education. *Member:* World Poetry Society International, National Federation of State Poetry Societies, Major Poets, California Writer's Club (Sacramento chapter), California State Poetry Society, Florida Poetry Society, New York Poetry Forum, El Camino Poets, California Federation of Chaparral Poets, Ina Coolbrith Circle (Berkeley, Calif.). *Awards, honors:* One hundred thirty-five poetry awards, including Gordon W. Norris Poet Laureate Memorial Award from *Chaparral,* 1975.

WRITINGS—Poetry: Of Winter, Little Gem Books, 1962; *Pinions to the Sun,* Portfolio Poet's Press, 1963, reissued in two volumes, JTC Books, 1965; *Shadows on Sundials,* JTC Books, 1966; *The Great Wall,* Aldine Society of California, 1968; *Strange,* Pleiad, 1972; (with Kay Larsen) *Ballads and Story Poems,* Mellon Books (San Francisco), 1976. Contributor to poetry magazines. Former editor of *California State Employee's Magazine;* poetry editor of Harlequin Press, 1966-68, and of *World of Poetry,* 1975—.

WORK IN PROGRESS: Travelogue, a book-length poem; a textbook on workshop technique.

AVOCATIONAL INTERESTS: Travel.

* * *

COLE, George F(raser) 1935-

PERSONAL: Born March 18, 1935, in Attleboro, Mass.; son of Stanley G. (a refrigerator mechanic) and Rubena (Fraser) Cole; married Joan L. Washburn (an artist), August 10, 1957; children: David A., Jonathan W. *Education:* University of Massachusetts, B.A., 1956, M.A., 1962; University of Washington, Seattle, Ph.D., 1968. *Home:* 546 Wormwood Hill Rd., Mansfield Center, Conn. 06250. *Office:* Department of Political Science, University of Connecticut, Storrs, Conn. 06268.

CAREER: Allegheny College, Meadville, Pa., assistant professor of political science, 1965-69; University of Connecticut, Storrs, associate professor of political science, 1969—. *Military service:* U.S. Air Force, 1956-61. *Member:* American Political Science Association, Academy of Criminal Justice Sciences.

WRITINGS: (Editor with John Kessell and Robert Seddig) *Micropolitics,* Holt, 1970; *Criminal Justice: Law and Politics,* Duxbury Press, 1972, 2nd edition, 1976; *Politics and the Administration of Justice,* Sage Publications, 1973; *American System of Criminal Justice,* Duxbury Press, 1976; (editor with Albert Cohen and Robert Bailey) *Prison Violence,* Lexington Books, 1976.

* * *

COLEN, B. D. 1946-

PERSONAL: Born August 23, 1946, in New York, N.Y.; son of Donald J. (a public relations director) and Marcia (a writer; maiden name, Sufrin) Colen; married Sara Hannan (an artist), December 11, 1971; children: Benjamin Donald. *Education:* George Washington University, B.A., 1973. *Politics:* "Liberal conservative/conservative liberal." *Home:* 3900 Cathedral Ave., Washington, D.C. 20016. *Agent:* Edward J. Acton, 288 West 12th St., New York, N.Y. *Office: Washington Post,* 1150 15th St. N.W., Washington, D.C. 20071.

CAREER: Washington Post, Washington, D.C., staff writer, specializing in medicine, health, and medical ethics, 1970—. Lecturer in journalism at George Washington University.

WRITINGS: Karen Ann Quinlan: Dying in the Age of Eternal Life, Nash Publishing, 1976. Health and medicine columnist for *Gentlemen's Quarterly.*

* * *

COLLIER, Ethel 1903-

PERSONAL: Born July 24, 1903, in Toledo, Ohio; daughter of Henry Eberhard (an artist and artisan) and Pauline (Hoffman) Kuhlman; married Joseph Collier, November 9, 1929; children: Rachel (Mrs. Heinrich Bosch). *Education:* University of Toledo, student, 1921-23; University of Michigan, B.A., 1928. *Politics:* Independent. *Residence:* Chagrin Falls, Ohio.

CAREER: Toledo News-Bee, Toledo, Ohio, reporter, 1923-25 and 1928-33; *Toledo Times,* Toledo, reporter, 1928-33. *Member:* Authors Guild of Authors League of America.

WRITINGS—For children: I Know a Farm, William R. Scott, 1960; *The Birthday Tree,* William R. Scott, 1961; *Who Goes There in My Garden?,* William R. Scott, 1963; *The Gypsy Tree,* William R. Scott, 1966; *Hundreds and Hundreds of Strawberries,* William R. Scott, 1969.

WORK IN PROGRESS: Children's fiction; an adult story.

* * *

COLLIER, John 1901-

PERSONAL: Born May 3, 1901, in London, England; son of John George Collier; married Shirley Lee Palmer, 1936 (divorced, 1943); married Margaret Elizabeth Eke, 1945. *Education:* Educated privately. *Residence:* London, England. *Agent:* A. D. Peters & Co., 10 Buckingham St., London WC2N 6BU, England.

CAREER: Poetry editor of *Time and Tide* during 1920's and 1930's; novelist, writer of history and short stories, poet, and playwright. *Awards, honors:* Four awards from *This Quarter,* all in 1922, for poems.

WRITINGS: *His Monkey Wife; or, Married to a Chimp* (novel), P. Davies, 1930, Appleton, 1931; *Epistle to a Friend* (short stories), Ulysses Bookshop, 1931; *No Traveller Returns* (stories), White Owl Press, 1931; *Gemini: Poems*, Harmsworth, 1931; (editor) John Aubrey, *Scandals and Incredulities*, Appleton, 1931; (with Iain Lang) *Just the Other Day: An Informal History of Britain since the War*, Harper, 1932; *Green Thoughts* (short stories), Joiner & Steele, 1932; *Full Circle: A Tale* (novel), Appleton, 1933 (published in England as *Tom's A-Cold: A Tale*, Macmillan, 1933); *Defy the Foul Fiend; or, The Misadventures of a Heart* (novel), Knopf, 1934; *The Devil and All* (stories), Nonesuch Press, 1934; *Variation on a Theme* (stories), Grayson, 1935; *Witch's Money*, Viking, 1940; *Presenting Moonshine: Stories*, Viking, 1941; *A Touch of Nutmeg and More Unlikely Stories* (foreword by Clifton Fadiman), Heritage Press, 1943; *Fancies and Goodnights* (stories), Doubleday, 1951; *Pictures in the Fire* (stories), Hart-Davis, 1958; *Of Demons and Darkness*, Transworld Publications, 1965; *The John Collier Reader* (anthology), Knopf, 1972; *Milton's Paradise Lost: Screenplay for Cinema of the Mind*, Knopf, 1973. Also author of one-act play, "Wet Saturday," first produced in New York City.

SIDELIGHTS: Collier's great-grandfather was physician to King William IV. Although Collier began as a poet, he is perhaps best known for fantastic short stories combining satire, the grotesque, and the supernatural. He lived for a time in Virginia, and around 1942 in Los Angeles, later in France, and is now living in London. *Avocational interests:* Gardening, sailing, tennis.

BIOGRAPHICAL/CRITICAL SOURCES: *New York Herald Tribune*, October 7, 1951.*

* * *

COLLIER, Peter 1939-

PERSONAL: Born June 2, 1939, in Hollywood, Calif.; son of Donovan L. and Doris Y. Collier; married Mary Giachino (a toymaker), September 27, 1967; children: Andrew, Caitlin, Nicholas. *Education:* University of California, Berkeley, A.B. (cum laude), 1961, M.A., 1963. *Home and office:* 6107 Harwood Ave., Oakland, Calif. 94618. *Agent:* Georges Borchardt, Inc., 145 East 52nd St., New York, N.Y. 10022.

CAREER: University of California, Berkeley, instructor in English, 1964-69; *Ramparts* (magazine), San Francisco, Calif., staff writer, 1967-68, executive editor, 1968-69, editor, 1969-73; free-lance writer, 1973—.

WRITINGS: (Editor) *Crisis: A Contemporary Reader*, Harcourt, 1969; (editor) *Justice Denied: The Black Man in White America*, Harcourt, 1970; *When Shall They Rest: The Cherokees' Long Struggle*, Holt, 1973; *The Rockefellers: An American Dynasty* (Book-of-the-Month Club main selection), Holt, 1976. General editor of a Harcourt series on contemporary American problems. Contributor to popular magazines, including *Ramparts, Progressive, Esquire*, and *Mademoiselle*.

WORK IN PROGRESS: A book on Henry A. Wallace and the origins of the Cold War; a novel, tentatively titled *Downriver*.

SIDELIGHTS: Collier writes: "I came to writing as a natural outgrowth of my involvement in new politics and still consider myself, to some degree, an 'advocacy journalist.' My outlook regarding this profession was formed by my years at *Ramparts* magazine, which in its heyday pioneered the renaissance of muckraking and investigative journalism later to be taken up by the *New York Times, Washington Post*, and other journalistic giants. Writers must create, it seems to me, out of conscience and commitment, yet not in the service of orthodoxies."

BIOGRAPHICAL/CRITICAL SOURCES: *Book-of-the-Month Club News*, February, 1976; *New York Post*, April 2, 1976.

* * *

COLLINS, Alice H(esslein) 1907-

PERSONAL: Born January 24, 1907, in New York, N.Y.; daughter of Max (a stock broker) and Alice (Rosenblatt) Hesslein; married Harry Wilson Collins (a social worker), January 18, 1932 (deceased); children: John B., Elizabeth C. (Mrs. U. C. Wells). *Education:* Smith College, B.A. (cum laude), 1928; Columbia University, M.S.W., 1931. *Politics:* Democrat. *Home and office:* 2680 Southwest Ravensview Dr., Portland, Ore. 97201.

CAREER: Madison House, New York City, director of girl's program, 1931-33; New York State Training School, Warwick, N.Y., resident, 1933-47; Springfield Child Guidance Clinic, Springfield, Mass., psychiatric social worker, 1947-49; Area Mental Health Clinic, Holyoke, Mass., chief social worker, 1949-54; Massachusetts Youth Service Board, Boston, Mass., deputy director, 1954-59; Community Council, Portland, Ore., consultant, 1959-72; social worker in Portland, Ore., 1972—. Director of "day care neighbor project" in Portland, Ore., 1964-72. Visiting lecturer at Portland State University, 1972—. *Member:* National Association of Social Workers, Oregon Foundation for Psychoanalysis (member of board of directors).

WRITINGS: *The Lonely and Afraid: Counseling the Hard to Reach*, Odyssey, 1969; *The Human Services: An Introduction*, Bobbs-Merrill, 1972; (with Eunice L. Watson) *Family Day Care*, Beacon Press, 1976; (with Diane L. Pancoast) *Natural Helping Networks*, National Association of Social Workers Press, 1976. Contributor to psychiatry and social work journals.

WORK IN PROGRESS: *Casebook in Consultation*, with Diane L. Pancoast and June Dunn, for Portland State University; *At This Time*, a book for children.

SIDELIGHTS: Alice Collins writes: "I always expected to be both a writer and a social worker though I intended to write great novels, not professional books. I wrote them—and much else—but did not get them published and now find professional writing exciting and rewarding. . . ." *Avocational interests:* "Growing things (including small children)," reading, needlework, sculpture.

* * *

COLLINS, Larry 1929-

PERSONAL: Born September 14, 1929, in Hartford, Conn.; son of John Lawrence and Helen (Cannon) Collins; married Nadia Hoda Sultan, September 17, 1966; children: John Lawrence III, Michael Kevin. *Education:* Yale University, B.A., 1951. *Home:* La Biche Niche, Valderian, Ramatvelle Var, France.

CAREER: United Press International (UPI), Paris correspondent, 1956, news editor in Rome, 1957, Middle East correspondent, 1957-59; *Newsweek* (magazine), New York, N.Y., Middle East editor, 1959-61, chief of Paris Bureau, 1961—. *Military service:* U.S. Army, 1953-55.

WRITINGS—All with Dominique Lapierre: *Is Paris Burning?*, Simon & Schuster, 1965; *Or I'll Dress You in Mourning,* Simon & Schuster, 1968; *O Jerusalem,* Simon & Schuster, 1972; *Freedom at Midnight,* Simon & Schuster, 1975.

AVOCATIONAL INTERESTS: Tennis.

BIOGRAPHICAL/CRITICAL SOURCES: Life, July 14, 1972.

* * *

COLLINS, Marjorie A(nn)   1930-

PERSONAL: Born December 29, 1930, in Attleboro, Mass.; daughter of Harry M. (a gladiola grower) and Muriel (Bessom) Collins. *Education;* Barrington College, B.A., 1952; University of Miami, Coral Gables, Fla., graduate study, 1967-68. *Religion:* Protestant. *Home:* 5004 Fairforest Dr., Stone Mountain, Ga. 30088.

CAREER: International Christian Fellowship, Pakistan, missionary, 1954-58; Barrington College, Barrington, R.I., secretary of department of education, 1959-60; Bethlehem Baptist Church, Springfield, Mass., secretary and director of Christian education, 1960-61; World Radio Missionary Fellowship, Inc., Miami, Fla., administrative assistant and personnel secretary, 1961-68; Boston University, School of Nursing, Boston, Mass., executive secretary to dean, 1968-69; Children's Hospital Medical Center, Boston, Mass., executive secretary to chief of endocrine division, 1969-70; University of Miami, School of Medicine, Coral Gables, Fla., administrative supervisor in department of otolaryngology, 1970-71; free-lance Christian writer in Stone Mountain, Ga., 1971—; Ocean, Inc. (Organization of Continuing Education for American Nurses), Pine Lake, Ga., executive secretary, 1975—. Visiting professor at Columbia Bible College, 1975.

WRITINGS: Manual for Missionaries on Furlough, William Carey Library, 1972; *Manual for Accepted Missionary Candidates,* William Carey Library, 1972; *Search the Bible Quizzes,* Moody, 1974; *Search the Gospels and Acts,* Moody, 1974; *Who Cares about the Missionary?,* Moody, 1974; *Dedication: What It's All About,* Bethany Fellowship, 1976; *Search the Books of Poetry,* Moody, 1976; *Search the Old Testament Law and History,* Moody, 1976. Contributor of weekly devotional column to *Laconia News,* 1973-75. Contributor of more than three hundred articles to religious periodicals.

WORK IN PROGRESS: Revising *Manual for Accepted Missionary Candidates* and *Manual for Missionaries on Furlough;* a novel, *Darkest Before Dawn;* a nonfiction book on aspects of loneliness.

AVOCATIONAL INTERESTS: Stamp collecting, travel (North, Central, and South America, Europe, Asia, and Africa).

* * *

COLTER, Cyrus (J.)   1910-

PERSONAL: Born January 8, 1910, in Noblesville, Ind.; married, wife's name, Imogene. *Education:* Attended Youngstown University and Ohio State University; Chicago-Kent College of Law, LL.B., 1940. *Home:* 601 East 32nd St., #PH-2, Chicago, Ill. 60616.

CAREER: Worked for Young Men's Christian Association (YMCA) in Youngstown, Ohio, 1932-34, and in Chicago, Ill., 1934-40; deputy collector of internal revenue, 1940-42; attorney in Chicago, Ill., 1946—. Assistant commissioner for Illinois Commerce Commission, 1950, commissioner, 1951—. Chairman of Illinois Emergency Transport Board; member of Administrative Conference of the United States. Member of board of trustees of Chicago Symphony Orchestra; vice-chairman of citizens committee of Chicago Public Library. *Military service:* U.S. Army, 1942-46; became captain.

MEMBER: National Association of Regulatory Utility Commissioners (member of Commission on Railroads), National Association for the Advancement of Colored People, Chicago Urban League, Chicago Bar Association, Commercial Club, Cliff Dwellers Club, Kappa Alpha Psi. *Awards, honors:* Fiction prize from University of Iowa for book *The Beach Umbrella.*

WRITINGS: The Beach Umbrella (stories), University of Iowa Press, 1970; *The River of Eros* (novel), Swallow Press, 1972; *The Hippodrome* (novel), Swallow Press, 1973.

Work represented in anthologies. Contributor of stories to magazines.

BIOGRAPHICAL/CRITICAL SOURCES: Negro Digest, January, 1968; *National Observer,* July 8, 1972.*

* * *

COLYER, Penrose   1940-

PERSONAL: Born September 12, 1940, in Kettering, Northamptonshire, England; daughter of Cecil Frederick (a designer and craftsman) and Ruth (Reddaway) Colyer. *Education:* St. Clare's Hall, London, B.A., 1961. *Home:* Flat 3, 1 Mandeville Pl., London W1M 5LB, England.

CAREER: Teacher of Spanish in private school, and of English to foreign students, 1961-62; teacher of English and French in Beirut, Lebanon, 1962-63; Mary Glasgow Publications, Ltd., London, England, head of French department and secretary of advisory panel, 1963-67; free-lance writer and editor, 1967-68; assistant head of publishing division, Linguaphone Institute, Ltd., 1968-69; Macdonald Educational, London, arts editor, 1969-70; free-lance writer and editor, 1970-72; Brooking School of Ballet and General Education, London, headmistress, 1972—. *Member:* Society of Authors, National Trust, National Union of Teachers, Youth Hostels Association, Players Theatre, Mensa, League of Friends of Middlesex Hospital.

WRITINGS: Les Cahiers rouges (title means "The Little Red Books"), Mary Glasgow Publications, 1965; *Les Cahiers verts* (title means "The Little Green Books"), Mary Glasgow Publications, 1967; *Les Aventures d'Auguste* (comic strips; title means "The Adventures of Augustus"), Mary Glasgow Publications, c.1967; *French for Fun!*, Sonodisc, 1968; *Le Voyage du Jericho* (title means "The Journey of the Jericho"), Longmans, Green, 1969; *I Can Read French,* Peter Lowe, 1972, F. Watts, 1974; (translator) Jane Carruth, *Parlez Francais avec Dougal* (title means "Speak French with Dougal"), Hamlyn, 1973; *Book of Numbers,* Mary Glasgow Publications, 1973; *Famous and Fabulous Animals,* Peter Lowe, 1973; *Catherine Verneuil: Danseuse* (title means "Catherine Verneuil: Dancer"), Longman, 1973; (with C. Roe) *One Europe: France,* Longman, 1975; *Who Works Here?,* Hamlyn, 1975; *Who Plays Here?,* Hamlyn, 1975; *Who Lives Here?,* Hamlyn, 1975; *Who Was Here?,* Hamlyn, 1975; *Lost in London,* European Schoolbooks, 1976.

Also author of books for Longman, *Pierre Leroy: Sous-chef de Gare* (title means "Pierre Leroy: Assistant Station-Master''), *Marius Masse: Forestier* (title means ''Marius Masse: Forester''), *Monique et Marie-Claire: Infirmieres* (title means ''Monique and Marie-Claire: Nurses''), and *Robert: Boulanger* (title means ''Robert: Baker'').

Also writer of French teaching materials for Mary Glasgow Publications, 1963-65, including ''Bon Voyage,'' and for Longman, 1973-75, including ''Histoire de France'' (title means ''French History''), ''La Vie en France'' (title means ''Life in France''), and ''Le Pays de France'' (title means ''The Land of France'').

Contributor of articles to *Cherwell, Dundee Evening Courier, Guardian,* and *Punch,* and of book reviews to *New Era.*

WORK IN PROGRESS: An educational French reader, *Voyage en Normandie;* a novel; a French comic book; a historical biography.

SIDELIGHTS: Penrose Colyer told *CA:* ''When teaching, I find all too often that published material is difficult, condescending, and distinctly unfunny. To teach via material which is comprehensible, entertaining, and interesting is the aim of my educational writing.'' *Avocational interests:* Dress-making, theatre, flower arranging, cooking, jewelry-making, swimming, riding, brass-rubbing, tennis, international travel.

*   *   *

COMEY, James Hugh   1947-

PERSONAL: Born December 18, 1947, in Philadelphia, Pa.; son of John Joseph (a field engineer) and Mary (a medical records supervisor; maiden name Waters) Comey; married Patricia Ann Borda, December 20, 1969; children: Jennifer Tricia, Colleen Patricia (deceased). *Education:* West Chester State College, B.S., 1969, M.Ed., 1972; University of Pennsylvania, Ed.D. candidate, 1975-78. *Home:* 105 Treaty Road, Drexel Hill P.O., Haverford, Pa. 19026. *Office:* Upper Darby School District, Lansdowne Ave. and School Lane, Upper Darby, Pa. 19084.

CAREER: Teacher of high school English in Kennett Square, Pa., 1969-74; Upper Darby High School, Upper Darby, Pa., teacher of English, 1974—. Coadjutant lecturer in English, Delaware County Community College, Media, Pa., 1975—. *Member:* National Education Association, National Writers Club, Political Action Committee for Education, Pennsylvania State Education Association.

WRITINGS: Death of the Poet King, Branden Press, 1975.

WORK IN PROGRESS: A doctoral dissertation considering violence in American education; a science fiction short story; a children's story.

SIDELIGHTS: Comey says of *Death of the Poet King:* ''The style is unusual for it blends the harsh realities of a city with the highly imaginative and impressionable narrative of a boy trying to retain his sanity and follow his conscience.'' *Avocational interests:* Directing and acting in amateur theatre.

*   *   *

COMINS, Jeremy   1933-

PERSONAL: Born May 8, 1933, in Ohio; son of Harry L. (a writer) and Edith (a psychologist) Comins; married Eleanor Fishman (a teacher), February 11, 1959; children: Aaron, Daniel. *Education:* New York University, B.S., 1954, M.A., 1956. *Home:* 1776 East 19th St., Brooklyn, N.Y. 11229.

CAREER: Sculptor and artist (one-man exhibitions in New

York area and group exhibitions at galleries and museums, including Museum of Modern Art, Cooper Union Museum, and Philadelphia Museum). Art teacher in public schools in New York, N.Y., 1955—. *Awards, honors:* Photography prizes, 1971-72, for color slide transparencies.

WRITINGS—All self-illustrated with drawings and photographs: *Getting Started in African Crafts,* Bruce Books, 1971; *Latin American Crafts and Their Cultural Backgrounds,* Lothrop, 1974; *Art from Found Objects,* Lothrop, 1974; *Eskimo Crafts and Their Cultural Backgrounds,* Lothrop, 1975; *Totems, Decoys, and Covered Wagons,* Lothrop, 1976. Contributor to *School Arts.*

WORK IN PROGRESS: Slotted Sculpture and *Far Eastern Crafts,* both for Lothrop.

*   *   *

COMMITTE, Thomas C.   1922-

PERSONAL: Born August 3, 1922, in Wheeling, W.Va.; son of Thomas Farrel (an attorney) and Anna Mae (Carney) Committe; married wife, Rosemary (in real estate sales); children: Thomas C., Bruce E., Frank, Patrick. *Education:* Bethany College, Bethany, W.Va., B.A., 1943; West Virginia University, LL.B., 1949; Texas Christian University, M.A., 1964; University of Alabama, Ph.D., 1966. *Home:* 8870 Thunderbird Dr., Pensacola, Fla. 32504. *Office:* Department of Finance and Accounting, University of West Florida, Pensacola, Fla. 32504.

CAREER: Attorney, 1949—; University of Texas, Arlington, assistant professor, 1960-61; Birmingham-Southern College, Birmingham, Ala., associate professor, 1963-64; University of Texas, Arlington, assistant professor, 1964-67; University of West Florida, Pensacola, professor of finance and accounting, 1967—, chairman of department. Certified public accountant; engaged in public utility rate regulation work as attorney and consultant; has worked on state regulatory commissions. Member of Pensacola revenue study committee. *Military service:* U.S. Naval Reserve, active duty, 1943-46; became lieutenant junior grade.

MEMBER: American Economic Association, National Council for Small Business Management, American Bar Association, American Institute of Certified Public Accountants, American Cancer Society (member of board of directors), Southeastern Economic Association, Southeastern Finance Association, Southeastern Accounting Association, Florida Institute of Certified Public Accountants, West Virginia Bar Association.

WRITINGS: Managerial Finance for the Seventies, McGraw, 1972. Contributor to *Managerial Planning,* edited by Ralph W. Estes and Lee H. Smith, 1974. Also contributor to economics, public utilities, and law journals.

WORK IN PROGRESS: Revising *Managerial Finance for the Seventies.*

*   *   *

COMMONER, Barry   1917-

PERSONAL: Born May 28, 1917, in New York, N.Y.; son of Isidore (a tailor) and Goldie (Yarmolinsky) Commoner; married Gloria C. Gordon (a psychologist), December 1, 1946; children: Lucy Alison, Fredric Gordon. *Education:* Columbia University, A.B., 1937; Harvard University, M.A., 1938, Ph.D., 1941. *Religion:* Humanist. *Home:* 25 Crestwood Dr., Clayton, Mo. 63104. *Office:* Center for Biology of Natural Systems, Washington University, St. Louis, Mo. 63130.

CAREER: Queens College (now of the City University of New York), Flushing, N.Y., instructor in biology, 1940-42; *Science Illustrated* magazine, New York, N.Y., associate editor, 1946-47; Washington University, St. Louis, Mo., associate professor, 1947-53, professor of plant physiology, 1953—, chairman of department of botany, 1965-69, director of Center for the Biology of Natural Systems, 1965—. St. Louis Committee for Environmental Information (formerly St. Louis Committee for Nuclear Information), co-founder, member of board of directors, 1958—, vice-president, 1958-65, president, 1965-66; Scientists Institute for Public Information, member of board of directors, 1963—, chairman, 1969—; member of board of directors, Universities National Anti-War Fund; member of board of consulting experts, Rachel Carson Trust for Living Environment, 1967—; member of advisory board or council, University of Oklahoma Law Center Committee, 1967-70, U.S. Department of the Interior study group on sonic boom, 1967-68, and Office of Education council on environmental education, 1971—. *Military service:* U.S. Naval Reserve, 1942-54; served in Naval Air Force and as liaison officer with Senate Committee on Military Affairs; became lieutenant.

MEMBER: American Association for the Advancement of Science (fellow; member of board of directors, 1967—), American Institute of Biological Sciences (member of governing board, 1965-67), Society of General Physiologists (member of council, 1961), American Society of Plant Physiologists, American Society of Biological Chemists, American Association of University Professors, National Parks Association (member of board of directors, 1968—), American Chemical Society, American School Health Association, Ecological Society of America, British Soil Association (honorary life vice-president, 1968—), Sigma Xi, Phi Beta Kappa. *Awards, honors:* Newcomb Cleveland Prize from American Association for the Advancement of Science, 1953; LL.D. from University of California, 1967; First International Humanist Award from International Humanist and Ethical Union, 1970; Phi Beta Kappa Award, 1972, and International Prize for Safeguarding the Environment, 1973, from the City of Cervia, Italy, both for *The Closing Circle;* D.Sc. from Hahnemann Medical College, 1963, Grinnell College, 1968, Lehigh University, 1969, Williams College, 1970, Ripon College, 1971, Colgate University, 1972, and Clark University, 1974.

WRITINGS: Science and Survival, Viking, 1966; *The Closing Circle: Nature, Man, and Technology,* Knopf, 1971; (editor) Virginia Brodine, *Air Pollution,* Harcourt, 1973; (editor) Julian McCaull and Janice Crossland, *Water Pollution,* Harcourt, 1974; *The Poverty of Power,* Knopf, 1976. Writer of ninety minute phonotape, "The Human Meaning of the Environmental Crisis," Big Sur Recordings, 1973. Contributor of more than two hundred articles to journals in his field. Member of editorial board, *International Review of Cytology,* 1957-65, *Problems of Virology,* 1956-60, *American Naturalist,* 1959-63, *Theoretical Biology,* 1960-64, *Science Year,* 1967-72, *World Book Encyclopedia,* 1968-73, *Environmental Pollution,* 1969—, and *National Wildlife,* 1970—; honorary member of editorial advisory board, *Chemosphere,* 1972—.

WORK IN PROGRESS: Research on the origins and significance of the environmental and energy crises, and other technical studies.

SIDELIGHTS: In a review of Commoner's *The Closing Circle,* Christopher Lehmann-Haupt wrote: "Dr. Commoner's is not a Doomsday book at all. . . . Dr. Commoner presents as lucid a description of ecology and its laws as I have yet come across. In between, he illustrates how those laws have been broken with disastrous consequences. . . . He weighs the impacts on the environment of our population explosion and in particular our shockingly high per capita consumption of natural resources."

Commoner explains, "Human beings have broken out of the circle of life, driven not by biological need, but by the social organization which they have devised to 'conquer' nature; means of gaining wealth that are governed by requirements conflicting with those which govern nature. The end result is the environmental crisis, a crisis of survival. Once more, to survive, we must close the circle. We must learn how to restore to nature the wealth that we borrow from it."

BIOGRAPHICAL/CRITICAL SOURCES: Time, February 2, 1970; *New York Times,* April 22, 1970; Anne Chisholm, *Philosophers of the Earth,* Dutton, 1972.

* * *

CONKLE, E(llsworth) P(routy) 1899-

PERSONAL: Born July 10, 1899, in Peru, Neb.; son of Elza Green and Mary Estella (Prouty) Conkle; married Virginia Carroll McNeal; children: Ellsworth Prouty Conkle II, Alice Elena Conkle Cogdell. *Education:* University of Nebraska, A.B., 1921, A.M., 1923, additional study, 1931-32; Yale University, graduate study, 1926-28; University of Iowa, Ph.D., 1936. *Home:* 510 Cater Dr., Austin, Tex. 78704.

CAREER: High school principal in Comstock, Neb., 1921-22; University of North Dakota, Grand Forks, instructor in English, 1923-26; University of Delaware, Newark, assistant professor of English, 1928-30; University of Iowa, Iowa City, assistant professor of speech, 1936-39; University of Texas, Austin, associate professor, 1939-45, professor of drama, 1945-73, professor emeritus, 1973—. Guest professor of playwriting, University of Alberta, beginning 1945. *Member:* Sigma Tau Delta, Purple Mask (University of Iowa). *Awards, honors:* Guggenheim fellowship, 1930; Rockefeller fellowships, 1935-36 and 1945; University of Texas graduate school research grant, 1966; D.Litt. from University of Nebraska, 1970.

WRITINGS—All plays; all published by Samuel French, except as noted: *Crick Bottom Plays: Five Mid-Western Sketches* (includes one-act plays: "Minnie Field," produced in New Haven, Conn., at Yale University, 1928; "Things Is That-A-Way," produced at Yale University, 1930; "Sparkin'"; "Warter-Wucks"; and "'Lection"), 1928; *The Owl and the Two Young People: A One Act Play for Two Boys,* 1934; *Loolie and Other Short Plays* (includes one-act plays: "P'taters in the Spring," produced in Iowa City, Iowa, at University of Iowa, 1933; "Little Granny Graver," produced at University of Iowa, 1936; "Loolie"; "The Owl and the Young Men"; "Lace"; and "Madge"), 1935; *The Juber-Bird: A Small Play for Small Boys,* 1936; *In the Shadow of a Rock: A Drama in Three Acts* (produced at University of Iowa, 1933), 1937; *200 Were Chosen: A Play in Three Acts* (produced in New York at 48th Street Theatre, 1937), 1937; *Prologue to Glory: A Play in Eight Scenes Based on the New Salem Years of Abraham Lincoln* (produced at Maxine Elliott Theatre, 1938), 1938; *We'd Be Happy Otherwise* (one-act), Dramatists Play Service, 1939.

Five Plays (includes "Paul and the Blue Ox," produced at University of Iowa, 1939; "Johnny Appleseed," produced in Austin, Tex., at University of Texas, 1940; "Bill and the Widow Maker," produced at University of Texas, 1942; "The Delectable Judge," produced in Washington at Arena

Theatre, 1951; and "49 Dogs in the Meathouse"), 1947; *A China-Handled Knife: A One Act Play about Abe Lincoln,* 1949; *Son-of-a-Biscuit Eater: Comedy in One Act,* 1958; *Granny's Little Cheery Room: A Comedy in One Act,* 1960; *Kitten in the Elm Tree: A Comedy in One Act,* 1962; *Lots of Old People Are Really Good for Something: A Comedy in One Act,* 1964.

Unpublished plays: "Oxygenerator," produced at Pasadena Playhouse, 1931; "The Mayor of Sherm Center," produced at University of Iowa, 1932; "The Lovings," produced at University of Iowa, 1933; "The 'Nitiated," produced at University of Iowa, 1933; "Gold Is Where You Don't Find It," produced at University of Texas, 1939; "What D'You Call It?," produced at Provincetown Playhouse, 1940; "They Die for Peace," produced at University of Texas for Office of Civilian Defense, 1943; "Afternoon Storm," produced at Maxine Elliott Theatre, 1948; "Don't Lose Your Head," produced in London at Saville Theatre, 1950; "No More Wars But the Moon," produced at University of Texas, 1956; "No Time for Heaven," produced at University of Texas, 1961; "Quest for an Answer," produced at University of Texas, 1963; "Way Down in the Paw-Paw Patch," produced in Arlington, N.J., by Producing Actors' Co., 1963.

Author of radio drama series, "Honest Abe," fifty two episodes, Columbia Broadcasting System (CBS), 1942. Co-author, with Ray Middleton, of television drama, "Day's End," National Broadcasting Co. (NBC-TV), 1952.

Also author of play, "Fraeulein Klauber," privately printed, and of other unpublished plays, "Th' Young Feller from Omaha," "Chief Sittum Bull," "Chickadee," "If You Can't Eat Fish without Tenderloin," "Papa Never Done Nothing . . . Much," "Incident at Eureka Bumps," "Muletail Prime," "The Least One," "Arbie, the Bug Boy," "Poor Old Bongo," "A Bauble for the Baby," "The Reticent One," "Heaven Is Such a Long Time to Wait," "Lavender Gloves," and "Day's End."

Work represented in many anthologies, including *Twenty-Five Best Plays of the Modern American Theatre: Early Series,* edited by John Gassner, Crown, 1949; *Best Short Plays of 1958-1959,* edited by Margaret Mayorga, Beacon Press, 1959; and *Plays as Experience: One Act Plays for the Secondary School,* edited by Irwin J. Zachar, Odyssey, 1962.

Contributor of articles, essays, and short stories to periodicals, including *English Journal, Players Magazine,* and *Theatre Arts.*

SIDELIGHTS: Conkle's play, "Prologue to Glory," has been adapted for television.

*   *   *

CONLEY, Enid Mary   1917-

PERSONAL: Born January 30, 1917, in New South Wales, Australia; daughter of Robert (a builder) and Minna (a seamstress; maiden name, Clauss) Cooper; married Kelvin Allan Conley (a quantity surveyor), June 21, 1946 (deceased); children: Kenneth Allan, Jeffrey Robert, Maxwell David, Douglas James. *Education:* Attended Brighton College and Williams Business College. *Politics:* Liberal. *Religion:* Methodist. *Home:* 148 Cammeray Rd., Cammeray, New South Wales, Australia 2062.

CAREER: Has worked as a secretary and a teacher; Technical College, Hornsby, Sydney, Australia, part-time teacher of secretarial studies, 1976—. Member of National

Book Council and Children's Book Council of Australia. *Military service:* Women's Royal Australian Naval Services, in Communications Branch, 1942-46. *Member:* International P.E.N., Society of Women Writers (Australia; president, 1974), Australian Society of Authors, Fellowship of Australian Writers, Society of Children's Book Writers (United States).

WRITINGS: The Dangerous Bombora, Coolarlie, 1968; *Gecko Gully,* Thomas Nelson (Australia), 1975.

Work has been anthologized in *The Bad Deeds Gang and Other Stories,* Australian Association for the Teaching of English, 1971. Contributor of articles and stories to women's magazines and education journals.

WORK IN PROGRESS—For children: *Glowworm Gully,* a sequel to *Gecko Gully; Lucas and the Kiteman.*

AVOCATIONAL INTERESTS: Travel.

*   *   *

CONNER, Berenice Gillete   1908-

PERSONAL: Born December 29, 1908, in Baltimore, Md.; daughter of Troy (a surgeon) and Berenice (a musician; maiden name, Patterson) Gillette; married James Conner (a clergyman), 1943 (died, 1950); children: William, Gillette (Mrs. Richard Tarbox), Berenice (Mrs. John Hooten). *Education:* University of Pittsburgh, student, 1929-32; University of Miami, Coral Gables, Fla., B.A., 1955, M.A., 1957; Oxford University, graduate study, 1958. *Religion:* Episcopalian. *Home:* 8960 Southwest 192nd Dr., Miami, Fla. 33157.

CAREER: Worked with Girl Scouts of America, 1940-55, executive director of overseas unit in Canal Zone, 1945; teacher of English literature in public and private schools in Miami, Fla., 1955-59; teacher of English literature at University of Miami, Coral Gables, Fla., 1959-69; Killian Senior High School, Miami, Fla., English teacher and chairman of department, 1969-74; writer. Teacher of hand loom weaving and spinning, 1936—; owner of Weaving Studio, 1950—; has also worked as a professional photographer; lecturer on crafts, travel, and literature. *Member:* National League of American Pen Women (president), Handweavers Guild of America (state representative), Delta Kappa Gamma, Theta Sigma Phi.

WRITINGS: Dyes from Your Garden, E. A. Seeman, 1976. Author of teaching handbooks. Contributor to *Travel* and *Ideal Crafts.*

WORK IN PROGRESS: Writing about weaving, spinning, and dyeing.

*   *   *

CONNOLLY, Paul
See WICKER, Thomas Grey

*   *   *

CONNOR, Joyce Mary
See MARLOW, Joyce

*   *   *

CONRAN, Anthony   1931-

PERSONAL: Born April 7, 1931, in Kharghpur, India; son of Denzil Arthur Stewart and Clarinda Wynne (Jones) Conran. *Education:* University of Wales, University College of North Wales, Bangor, B.A. (honors), 1953, M.A., 1956. *Home:* 1 Frondirion, Bangor, Gwynedd, Wales.

Agent: A. D. Peters, 10 Buckingham St., London WC2N 6BU, England. *Office:* Department of English, University College of North Wales, Bangor, Gwynedd, Wales.

CAREER: University of Wales, University College of North Wales, Bangor, research assistant, 1957-66, tutor in English, 1966—. *Member:* Yr Academi Gynreig (English section). *Awards, honors:* Prize from Welsh Arts Council, 1960, for *Formal Poems.*

WRITINGS—Poetry: *Formal Poems,* Christopher Davies, 1960; *Metamorphoses,* Dock Leaves Press, 1961; *Icons: Opus 6,* privately printed, 1963; *Asymptotes: Opus 7,* privately printed, 1963; *A String of Blethers: Opus 8,* privately printed, 1963; *Sequence of the Blue Flower,* privately printed, 1963; *The Mountain,* privately printed, 1963; *For the Marriage of Gerard and Linda,* privately printed, 1963; *Stelae and Other Poems, Opus 9,* Clive Allison, 1965; *Guernica,* Gee & Son, 1966; *Collected Poems,* Volume I, Clive Allison, 1966, Volumes II-IV, Gee & Son, 1966-68; (editor and translator) *The Penguin Book of Welsh Verse,* Penguin, 1967; *Claim, Claim, Claim: A Book of Poems,* Circle Press, 1969; *Spirit Level,* Christopher Davies, 1974; *Poems, 1951-1967,* Deiniol Press, 1974; (translator) *Eighteen Poems by Dante Alighieri,* Tern Press, 1975.

WORK IN PROGRESS: Essays on Anglo-Welsh Poetry; poems; research on folksongs.

SIDELIGHTS: Born in India and at first alien to Wales, Conran has become deeply involved in Welsh culture and custom, and is well-known for his translations from the Welsh.

BIOGRAPHICAL/CRITICAL SOURCES: Poetry Wales, spring, 1967.

*   *   *

CONSTABLE, W(illiam) G(eorge)   1887-1976

October 27, 1887—February 3, 1976; British-born art historian, museum administrator, and author of books in his field. Obituaries: *New York Times,* February 7, 1976; *AB Bookman's Weekly,* March 1, 1976. (See index for previous *CA* sketch)

*   *   *

COOK, Arlene Ethel   1936-
(Cannon Cole)

PERSONAL: Born July 1, 1936, in Escondido, Calif.; daughter of Oscar E. and Leona (Wells) Knappe; married Richard H. Cook (a stock broker); children: Alan Jason, Alyse Jennifer, Jon Andrews. *Education:* Palomar College, A.A., 1955; San Diego State University, B.A., 1958. *Politics:* Republican. *Religion:* Lutheran. *Residence:* Escondido, Calif. *Agent:* Johnson/Johnson, P.O. Box 1044, Wheaton, Ill. 60187. *Office address:* P.O. Box 184, Escondido, Calif. 92025.

CAREER: Party Plastics, San Diego, Calif., Tupperware dealer and unit manager, 1958-62; junior high school teacher in Poway, Calif., 1962-67; free-lance writer, 1967—; Shustek Oil & Chemical, Escondido, Calif., part-time bookkeeper, 1969—. Substitute teacher in Escondido, Calif., 1961-62; organizer and adviser to women's stock investment clubs, 1970-73; member of local mayor's first Blue Ribbon Committee, 1973.

MEMBER: International Platform Association, National League of American Pen Women (president of local branch, 1970-72), National Writers Club, National Association of Investment Clubs (vice-president of San Diego chapter, 1970-73), Society of Children's Book Writers, Scribblers (president, 1974-76), California Federation of Poets, Southern California Writers Guild.

WRITINGS: (With Robert F. Kontz and Lynn C. Mohr) *The World of Long Ago: The Testimony of the Fossils,* Creation Science Research Center, 1971; (under pseudonym Cannon Cole) *From the Ashes of Hell* (novel), Creation House, 1973. Contributor to a variety of periodicals, including such literary magazines as *American Haiku, Haiku Highlights, Bitterroot, Bardic Echoes,* and *American Bard.*

WORK IN PROGRESS: A second "true experience" novel; magazine articles.

SIDELIGHTS: Arlene Cook writes: "Most important is what we do with our ideas, as writers. Every manuscript must better or enrich the reader in some way. For me, it is not enough to enrich the reader's mind when it is his spirit that needs feeding. Therefore I lean heavily toward Christian writing, of taking the reader where he is and moving him, through others' examples, to a closer relationship with our Saviour, Jesus Christ. *From the Ashes of Hell* is that kind of novel. It begins where so many are today and moves the reader from search to everlasting security."

*   *   *

COOK, David T.   1946-

PERSONAL: Born December 28, 1946, in Boston, Mass.; son of Theodore (a church executive) and Charlotte Margret Cook; married Laurie Knights, July 28, 1973. *Education:* Principia College, Elsah, Ill., B.A., 1969; Columbia University, graduate study, 1976-77. *Home:* 917 Oronoco St., Alexandria, Va. 22314. *Office: Christian Science Monitor,* 910 16th St. N.W., Washington, D.C. 20006.

CAREER/WRITINGS: Christian Science Monitor, Washington, D.C., Washington correspondent, 1969—, editor of business-financial page, 1975—. *Military service:* U.S. Army, 1969-71.

*   *   *

COOK, Reginald L.   1903-

PERSONAL: Born November 5, 1903, in Mendon, Mass.; son of Lyman (a farmer) and Wilhelmina (Rittmann) Cook; married L. Juanita Pritchard, August 24, 1929. *Education:* Middlebury College, A.B., 1924, A.M., 1926; Oxford University, B.A., 1929. *Politics:* Independent liberal. *Religion:* Protestant. *Home:* Pulp Mill Bridge Road, Middlebury, Vt. 05753.

CAREER: Wyoming Seminary, Kingston, Pa., teacher of English literature and language, 1924-25; Middlebury College, Middlebury, Vt., instructor, 1929-31, associate professor, 1931-32, professor, 1932-55, Abernethy Professor of American Literature, 1955-67, Charles Dana Professor of American Literature, 1967-69, Charles Dana Professor Emeritus, 1969—. Director of Bread Loaf School of English, 1946-64. *Member:* Thoreau Society (president, 1967-68), Vermont Academy of Arts and Sciences (trustee, 1970-75), Phi Beta Kappa, Kappa Delta Rho. *Awards, honors:* Rhodes scholar, 1926-29, Doctor of Letters, Middlebury College, 1960, L.H.D., St. Michael's College, Winooski, Vt., 1972.

WRITINGS: Passage to Walden, Houghton, 1949; *Selected Prose and Poetry of Emerson,* Rinehart, 1950, revised edition, 1969; *The Dimensions of Robert Frost,* Rinehart, 1958; *Themes, Tones and Motifs in the American Renais-*

sance, Transcendental Books, 1969; (contributor) Jackson R. Pryer, editor, *Sixteen Modern American Authors,* Norton, 1973; *Robert Frost: A Living Voice,* University of Massachusetts Press, 1974.

WORK IN PROGRESS: Learn of the Green World: A Reading of American Nature Writings; Changing Subjects: A Series of Mini Essays.

SIDELIGHTS: Professor Cook told *CA:* "Before World War II, I triangulated the American West, hopping like a nomadic Morman cricket from desert to mesa, and from canyon to butte throughout the Rocky Mountain states and clear to 'continent's end.' I have stayed for periods of three months or more in six different places in California, two in Colorado, and three in New Mexico. The Indian Pueblos of the Rio Grande and the desert country of the Navajos are my familiar. And so, too, is Mexico—from Nogales to Oaxaca, and from Matamoras to Merida—a magnetic country to me.

"My roothold is in New England, where, a solo daily walker, I have the Green Mountains always within sight and shouting distance. My deepest intellectual satisfaction has been teaching American literature. My most exacting responsibility was directing the Bread Loaf School of English for nineteen years, and my greatest social satisfaction has been the Middlebury-Breadloaf connections. I am reading-oriented, nature-magnetized, sports-minded, and, as an amateur, I write for fun."

Cook's latest book, *Robert Frost: A Living Voice,* recounts the author's personal encounters with Frost and includes twelve of the poet's talks at the Bread Loaf School. Patricia Beer calls the book "fascinating", and goes on to say that the "talk ambles and wanders, shying away from any question that the audience may ask, but it is funny and it is shrewd: the wit and wisdom of Robert Frost as it were. The wisdom, it is true, is neither sustained nor systematic and tends to express itself in gnomic sideswipes at the great figures of our age: for example, 'Marx didn't know what capital was'—which may be true but needs expanding. The wit rarely flags."

AVOCATIONAL INTERESTS: American native culture, history of the American Indian, personal contacts with nature, travel in the United States and Mexico.

BIOGRAPHICAL/CRITICAL SOURCES: Times Literary Supplement, October 31, 1975.

*   *   *

COOKE, Joseph R(obinson)   1926-

PERSONAL: Born April 29, 1926, in Muchengpo, Yunan, China; son of Allyn Bushnell (a missionary) and Leila Adelaide (a missionary; maiden name, Robinson) Cooke; married Laura M. Hopping, March 18, 1951. *Education:* Hartnell College, student, 1944; Biola College, Th.B., 1949, B.A., 1952; University of California, Berkeley, B.A., 1961, Ph.D., 1965. *Home:* 8178 23rd Ave. N.E., Seattle, Wash. 98115. *Office:* Department of Asian Languages and Literature, University of Washington, Seattle, Wash. 98195.

CAREER: Pastor of community church in Seeley, Calif., 1952-53; Overseas Missionary Fellowship, Chiengmai, Thailand, missionary, 1954-57; Northern Illinois University, DeKalb, assistant professor of English, linguistics, and Thai, 1965-67; University of Washington, Seattle, assistant professor, 1967-69, associate professor of Thai, 1969—. Lecturer at Chulalongkorn University, 1973.

WRITINGS: Pronominal Reference in Thai, Burmese, and

Vietnamese, University of California Press, 1968; *Free for the Taking: The Life-Changing Power of Grace,* Revell, 1975.

WORK IN PROGRESS: A study guide for *Free for the Taking; Thai Sentence-Final Particles;* research on cross-cultural aspects of "grace" and applications of "grace" to real-life situations.

SIDELIGHTS: Cooke writes: "The turning point in my life was an emotional breakdown that terminated my missionary career in Thailand in 1957. Little by little I came to realize the crucial importance of the concept of grace as a key to one's relationship with God, self, and others. Slowly I worked my way from squirrel-cage Christianity to a new life of increasing freedom and productiveness."

*   *   *

COOPER, Dominic (Xavier)   1944-

PERSONAL: Born February 25, 1944, in Winchester, England; son of Martin Du Pre (a writer) and Mary (an artist; maiden name, Stewart) Cooper. *Education:* Attended Magdalen College, Oxford, 1963-65. *Religion:* Christian. *Home:* 7 Well Court, Edinburgh EH4 3BE, Scotland. *Agent:* Andrew Hewson, John Johnson, 12/13 Henrietta St., London WC2E 8LF, England.

CAREER: Wallace Collection, London, England, catalogue stall assistant, 1965-67; Decca Record Co., London, promotional assistant, 1967-69; Fabbri & Partners, London, editor, 1969-70; Malaskolinn Mimir, Reykjavik, Iceland, teacher, 1970-71; Argyll County Council, Isle of Mull, Scotland, roadworker, 1972; free-lance writer, 1972-74; self-employed clockmaker in Edinburgh, Scotland, 1974—. *Awards, honors:* Somerset Maugham Award from Society of Authors, 1976, for *The Dead of Winter.*

WRITINGS—Novels: The Dead of Winter, Chatto & Windus, 1975; *Sunrise,* Chatto & Windus, in press.

WORK IN PROGRESS: A novel, set in Iceland.

SIDELIGHTS: Cooper writes: "I have a passionate interest in the Scottish West Coast countryside and a fascination with the solitude of individuals as reflected in such terrain." *Avocational interests:* Hill walking, birdwatching.

*   *   *

COOPER, Parley J(oseph)   1937-

PERSONAL: Born June 8, 1937, in Glendale, Ore.; son of Howard (a lumberman) and Dorothy (McKinney) Cooper. *Education:* Attended Santa Monica City College, 1956-57, University of Hawaii, 1959-60, and University of California, Berkeley, 1961-63. *Religion:* Christian. *Residence:* Santa Clara, Calif. *Agent:* Jay Garon, Jay Garon-Brooke Associates, Inc., 415 Central Park W., #17D, New York, N.Y. 10025.

CAREER: Worked in New York City and Washington, D.C., 1963-65; associate editor and business manager of *Diplomat* (magazine), 1965-67; David L. Wolper Productions, Hollywood, Calif., business manager, 1967-68; writer, 1968—. *Military service:* U.S. Navy, 1955-56.

WRITINGS—Novels: The Feminists, Pinnacle Books, 1971; *The Devil's Child,* Pocket Books, 1972; *Marianne's Kingdom,* Pocket Books, 1972; *The Inheritance,* Popular Library, 1972; *A Reunion of Strangers,* Berkley, 1973; *My Lady Evil,* Simon & Schuster, 1974; *The Shuddering Fair One,* Pocket Books, 1974; *Moonblood,* Pocket Books, 1975; *The Studio,* Ace Books, 1975; *The Scapegraces,* Pyramid,

1975; *Reverend Mama,* Pocket Books, 1975; *Dark Desires,* Pocket Books, 1976; *Wreck!,* Ace Books, 1977; *San Francisco,* Pocket Books, 1977. Contributor of stories to magazines.

WORK IN PROGRESS: Golden Passions (tentative title), a sequel to *Dark Desires,* for Pocket Books; *Club Caribe* (tentative title); *The Crop,* a collection of short stories previously published in popular magazines.

SIDELIGHTS: Cooper writes: "At a very young age after reading my first novel, *The Wizard of Oz,* I knew I must become a writer—and my determination never varied or waned. I'm still happiest when I'm sitting at the typewriter creating characters and stories."

* * *

COPELAND, Carolyn Faunce 1930-

PERSONAL: Born September 30, 1930; daughter of James Philips (a journalist) and Florence (a music teacher; maiden name, Palmer) Copeland. *Education:* University of California, Berkeley, B.A., 1955; Southern Connecticut State College, M.S., 1960; University of Iowa, Ph.D., 1973. *Politics:* "The betterment of humanity." *Home:* 405 Crestview Ave., Iowa City, Iowa 52240.

CAREER: Elementary school teacher in Chester, Conn., 1956-57, Milford, Conn., 1958-59, Long Beach, Calif., 1959-61, and Agha Jari, Iran, 1961-64; University of Iowa, Iowa City, part-time instructor in English, 1964-69; junior high school teacher in Abadan, Iran, 1970-72; writer, 1972—. Study skills consultant for University of Iowa Extension. *Member:* Modern Language Association of America, Women in Communications.

WRITINGS: Language and Time and Gertrude Stein, University of Iowa Press, 1976.

WORK IN PROGRESS: And the Guilts Go Round and Round (tentative title), with Sally Osborne.

SIDELIGHTS: Carolyn Copeland writes: "My life has been a series of shocks that have prevented me from closing my mind comfortably. I set out to be a quiet school teacher, and in one of my first jobs I was in a devastating copper mine explosion in the Andes Mountains in Chile. I was thousands of miles from home, standing there in the raining sand wondering what had hit the world and why I was still in it. A few years later I stood on a dirt floor in a mud hut in the Middle East trying to help a young girl who was struggling to give birth to a baby on her knees in the filth. The baby wouldn't come. When I finally returned home to live in the United States again, my first novel was destroyed in a fire that razed the building I worked in. The fire had been set by demonstrators against the war in Cambodia. I have decided that life is a human mind that never stops expanding."

BIOGRAPHICAL/CRITICAL SOURCES: Iowa City Press Citizen, February 25, 1976; *Cedar Rapids Gazette,* April 11, 1976.

* * *

CORBETT, James A(rthur) 1908-

PERSONAL: Born April 17, 1908, in New Haven, Conn.; son of Thomas William and Rose (Clark) Corbett; married Suzanne Langlais, 1938; children: Mary R. Kerby, Philip J., Jennifer. *Education:* Georgetown University, A.B., 1929; Ecole Nationale des Chartes, Paris, France, Archiviste-Paleograph, 1935. *Address:* Box 135, Notre Dame, Ind. 46556.

CAREER: University of Notre Dame, Notre Dame, Ind.,

1935—, began as instructor, became professor of medieval history, professor emeritus, 1973—.

WRITINGS: (Editor with P. S. Moore) *Petri Pictaviensis Allegoriae super tabernaculum Moysi,* University of Notre Dame Press, 1938; *Catalogue des manuscrits alchimiques des bibliotheques publiques de Paris anterieurs au XVII siecle,* Union Academique Internationale (Brussels), 1939; *Catalogue des manuscrits alchimiques des bibliotheques publiques des departments francais anterieurs au XVII siecle,* Union Academique Internationale, 1951; (editor) *The De instructione Puerorum of William of Tournai, O.P.,* Medieval Institute, University of Notre Dame Press, 1955; *The Papacy: A Brief History,* Van Nostrand, 1956; (editor with J. N. Garvin) *The Summa contra haereticos Ascribed to Praepositinus of Cremona,* University of Notre Dame Press, 1958; (editor) *Praepositini Cremonensis Tractatus de officiis,* University of Notre Dame Press, 1969; (with Joseph Bobik) *The Commentary of Conrad of Prussia on the De ente et essentia of St. Thomas Aquinas,* Nijhoff, 1974. Contributor to journals.

WORK IN PROGRESS: A Catalogue of the Medieval and Renaissance Manuscripts in the University of Notre Dame Libraries; with Joseph Bobik, *Conrad of Prussia's Commentary on the De unitate et uno of Dominicus Gundissalinus,* for Nijhoff.

* * *

CORBISHLEY, Thomas 1903-1976

May 30, 1903—March 11, 1976; British Roman Catholic ecumenist and author of books in his field. Obituaries: *New York Times,* March 12, 1976; *AB Bookman's Weekly,* April 5, 1976. (See index for previous *CA* sketch)

* * *

CORMACK, Alexander James Ross 1942-
(Sandy Cormack)

PERSONAL: Born April 2, 1942, in Edinburgh, Scotland; son of Alastair J. (a company director), and D. I. (Ross) Cormack; married Jill Mary Taylor (a nurse), October 30, 1971; children: Alastair L. R. *Education:* Attended school in Edinburgh, Scotland. *Religion:* Church of Scotland. *Home and office:* Flodden Lodge, 65 Morningside Rd., Edinburgh EH10 4AZ, Scotland.

CAREER: James Ross & Sons, Ltd., Edinburgh, Scotland, managing director, 1975-76. Consultant firearms designer.

WRITINGS: Gun Lore, Profile Publications, 1977. Editor of "Small Arms Series," Profile Publications, 1973-75. Contributor to magazines. Small arms editor of *Brassey's Military Annual.*

WORK IN PROGRESS: A History of the Browning Brothers; A History of German Small Arms—WW II; A History of Sporting Weapons.

* * *

CORMACK, Sandy
See CORMACK, Alexander James Ross

* * *

CORREY, Lee
See STINE, G(eorge) Harry 1928-

* * *

CORRIGAN, John Thomas 1936-

PERSONAL: Born February 28, 1936, in Brooklyn, N.Y.;

son of William Michael (an engineer) and Ann Elizabeth (a teacher; maiden name, Rafter) Corrigan. *Education:* Catholic University of America, B.A., 1960; St. John's University, Jamaica, N.Y., M.S.L.S., 1967. *Home:* 22-5 Valley Rd., Drexel Hill, Pa. 19026. *Office:* 461 West Lancaster Ave., Haverford, Pa. 19041.

CAREER: Entered Congregatio Fratrum Sancti Francisci Xaverii (C.F.X.; Brothers of St. Francis Xavier), 1954; media center director at high school in Brooklyn, N.Y., 1963-71; Spalding College, Louisville, Ky., media center director, 1971-73; *Catholic Library World,* Haverford, Pa., editor, 1973—. Director of new projects for Roman Catholic schools in Brooklyn, N.Y., 1968-71; lecturer at St. John's University, Spalding College, and Villanova University. *Member:* American Library Association, Library Public Relations Association (vice-president of Philadelphia chapter, 1976), Association for Educational Communications and Technology, National Council of Library Associations (vice-president), National Catholic Educational Association, Catholic Library Association. *Awards, honors:* Named librarian of the year by Catholic Library Association, 1970, and outstanding librarian, 1971.

WRITINGS: Guide for Religious Education Resource Centers and Parish Libraries, Catholic Library Association, 1976.

SIDELIGHTS: Corrigan writes that he is "motivated by a sense of service to humanity and a love of recorded literature. The library profession offers an individual an opportunity to serve the public with vital information that is indispensable to living in our complex society. Thus, as a librarian, I have found not only a fulfilling role that serves people, but also a role in helping to shape the future for a better society that will respond responsibly to the wants and demands of a constantly changing world."

*   *   *

CORTESE, A(nthony) James   1917-

PERSONAL: Born August 11, 1917, in Canada; naturalized U.S. citizen, 1943; son of Angelo (a concert harpist) and Lorienne (Mann) Cortese; married Anne Slagle, July 16, 1951; children: Angelo Ted, W. James, Richard, Michael. *Education:* Louisiana State University, B.A., 1940. *Religion:* Roman Catholic. *Home:* 4383 Castle, Memphis, Tenn. 38122. *Office: Commercial Appeal,* Memphis, Tenn.

CAREER: Iberville South (weekly newspaper), Plaquemine, La., editor, 1941; *Ruston Daily Leader,* Ruston, La., managing editor, 1942; *Duncan Daily Banner,* Duncan, Okla., sports editor and columnist, 1948; *Commercial Appeal,* Memphis, Tenn., Sunday editor, 1949-63; Pemiscot Publishing Co., Caruthersville, Mo., publisher, 1963-72; *Commercial Appeal,* columnist, 1972—. *Military service:* U.S. Army Air Forces, 1942-45; became sergeant. *Awards, honors:* Press award for best column, 1965, 1966, and 1967, all for column "Cortese Says."

WRITINGS: P. K. Seidman: The Man Who Likes Memphis, Carnation Press, 1975; *Rambling Southern Roads with James Cortese,* Memphis State University Press, in press. Columnist, "Sittin' and Thinkin'" column in *Duncan Daily Banner,* 1948, "Cortese Says" column, 1963-72, and "Rambling" column in *Commercial Appeal,* 1972—.

WORK IN PROGRESS: Another book, *Monks, News, and Rollerskates.*

COTLER, Sherwin B(arry)   1941-

PERSONAL: Born March 2, 1941, in Chicago, Ill.; son of Leo and Bessie (Lustig) Cotler; married Susan J. Morgan (a college teacher), January 24, 1965; children: Stacy R., Lisa M. *Education:* California State University, Long Beach, B.A., 1964, M.A., 1966; Washington State University, Ph.D., 1970. *Residence:* Seal Beach, Calif. *Office:* 16152 Beach Blvd., No. 250E, Huntington Beach, Calif. 92647.

CAREER: Long Beach Recreation Department, Long Beach, Calif., assistant park director, 1961-65; Los Angeles Suicide Prevention Center, Los Angeles, Calif., trainee, 1967; Veterans Administration Hospital, Long Beach, psychology trainee, 1968; Camarillo State Hospital, Camarillo, Calif., clinical psychology intern, 1969-70; California State University, Long Beach, assistant professor of psychology, 1970—, adjunct clinical assistant professor of psychology, 1970-71. Private practice as psychologist and consultant, 1971—. Community mental health psychologist for County of Los Angeles Department of Health Services, 1970-75; therapist at Los Angeles Free Clinic, 1971-72; child psychologist at North Orange County Child Guidance Center, 1975—.

MEMBER: American Psychological Association, Association for the Advancement of the Behavioral Therapies, Council for the Advancement of the Psychology Professions and Science, Western Psychological Association, Long Beach Psychological Association, Harbor Society of Clinical Hypnosis, Sigma Xi, Phi Kappa Phi.

WRITINGS: (With Julio Guerra) *Assertion Training: A Humanistic-Behavioral Guide to Self-Dignity,* Research Press, 1976. Contributor to psychology and mental health journals.

WORK IN PROGRESS: Research on assertion training, anxiety reduction, and parenting skills.

SIDELIGHTS: Cotler writes: "One of my main interests at this time is in the broad area of behavior therapy as it applies to the establishment of appropriate behaviors and the prevention and/or elimination of disruptive behaviors. Coupled with my interest in child development, I would like to become more involved in community programs aimed at making the school and home more of a 'success experience' for students, teachers, and parents. I am also interested in various aspects of experimental-clinical psychology and the application of clinical psychology to areas such as: therapist-client interactions; parent-child interactions; physiological, cognitive, and behavioral changes in psychotherapy; comparisons of various therapeutic approaches (for children and adults) in terms of process and outcome variables; and assessing the effectiveness of community mental health programs."

*   *   *

COTLOW, Lewis N(athaniel)   1898-

PERSONAL: Born February 5, 1898, in Brooklyn, N.Y.; son of Nathaniel and Lena (Greene) Cotlow; married Charlotte Faith Messenheimer, December 18, 1966. *Education:* Attended George Washington University and New York University. *Home:* 480 Park Ave., New York, N.Y. 10022. *Office:* 540 Madison Ave., New York, N.Y. 10022.

CAREER: Worked as insurance broker in New York City; visited and reported on harbors for U.S. Shipping Board in the Far East, Near East, and South America, 1919-21; explorer, writer, and lecturer, 1921—. *Military service:* U.S. Army, during World War I. U.S. Navy, Naval Intelligence, during World War II. *Member:* Ends of the Earth Club, Explorers Club, Adventurers Club (past president), Dutch Treat Club, Salmagundi Club, Overseas Press Club (New York chapter), Circumnavigators Club (past president), Royal Geographical Society (fellow), Bohemian Club (San Francisco). *Awards, honors:* Gold medal from Adventurers Club, 1937.

WRITINGS: Passport to Adventure, Bobbs-Merrill, 1942; *Amazon Head-Hunters,* Holt, 1953; *Zanzabuku* (title means "Dangerous Safari"), Rinehart, 1956; *In Search of the Primitive,* Little, Brown, 1966; (contributor) Bruce Price, editor, *Into the Unknown,* Platt, 1968; *The Twilight of the Primitive,* Macmillan, 1971.

Films: "Adventures in South America," 1945; "Savage Splendor," 1947; "Jungle Headhunters," 1949; "Zanzabuku," 1955; "Primitive Paradise," 1959; "High Arctic," 1962.

SIDELIGHTS: Cotlow has conducted numerous expeditions to the Upper Amazon and other parts of South America, and to Africa, New Guinea, and Ellesmere Island. His particular interest is in primitive people. He made a collection of ethnological specimens for the American Museum of Natural History in 1949.*

*　　*　　*

COTTON, John   1925-

PERSONAL: Born March 7, 1925, in London, England; son of Arthur Edmund (a structural engineer) and Florence (Mandy) Cotton; married Peggy Midson (a secretary), December, 1948; children: Toby, Bevis. *Education:* University of London, B.A. (honors), 1956. *Home:* 37 Lombardy Dr., Berkhamsted, Hertfordshire HP4 2LQ, England.

CAREER: Middlesex Education Authority, England, teacher of English, 1947-57; Southall Grammar Technical School, England, head of English department, 1957-63; Highfield Comprehensive School, Hemel Hempstead, England, headmaster, 1963—. *Military service:* Royal Naval Commandos, 1942-46; served in the Far East. *Member:* National Poetry Society (member of council; chairman of council, 1973-75). *Awards, honors:* Publication award from Arts Council of Great Britain, 1971, for *Old Movies and Other Poems;* Page scholarship from English Speaking Union, 1975.

WRITINGS—Poetry: *Fourteen Poems,* Priapus, 1967; *Outside the Gates of Eden and Other Poems,* Taurus Press, 1969; *Ampurias,* Priapus, 1969; *Old Movies and Other Poems,* Chatto & Windus, 1971; *The Wilderness,* Priapus, 1971; *Columbus on St. Dominica,* Sceptre Press, 1972; *Photographs,* Sycamore Press, 1973; *A Sycamore Press Broadsheet,* Sycamore Press, 1973; *British Poetry Since 1965: A Selected List,* National Book League, 1973; *Kilroy Was Here* (Poetry Book Society selection), Chatto & Windus, 1974; *Places,* Priapus, 1975.

Poetry represented in anthologies, including *Holding Your Eight Hands,* edited by Edward Lucie-Smith, Doubleday, 1969; *Children of Albion,* edited by Michael Horovitz, Penguin, 1969; *Best Science Fiction, 1972,* edited by Harry Harrison and Brian Aldiss, Putnam, 1972; P.E.N. poetry annuals, 1965, 1967, 1974, and 1975, and others.

Editor of *Priapus,* 1962-72, and *Private Library,* 1970—; advisory editor for *Contemporary Poets of the English Language.*

WORK IN PROGRESS: Tom Deakin, Lunacy Collector, a novel; a book of poems.

BIOGRAPHICAL/CRITICAL SOURCES: Poetry Book Society Bulletin 69, summer, 1971; *Stand,* Volume XIV, number 1, 1972; *Teacher,* May, 1973; *Hertfordshire Countryside,* July, 1973; *Poetry Book Society Bulletin 84,* spring, 1975.

*　　*　　*

COTTRELL, Alan (Howard)   1919-

PERSONAL: Born July 17, 1919, in Birmingham, England; son of Albert and Elizabeth Cottrell; married Jean Elizabeth Harber, 1944; children: Geoffrey Alan. *Education:* University of Birmingham, B.Sc., 1939, Ph.D., 1942. *Office:* Master's Lodge, Jesus College, Cambridge University, Cambridge, England.

CAREER: University of Birmingham, Birmingham, England, lecturer, 1943-49, professor of metallurgy, 1949-55; Atomic Energy Research Establishment, Harwell, Berkshire, England, deputy head of metallurgy division, 1955-58; Cambridge University, Cambridge, England, Goldsmiths' Professor of Metallurgy, 1958-65; Ministry of Defense, London, England, deputy chief scientific adviser, 1965-67, chief adviser, 1967; Her Majesty's Government, London, deputy chief scientific adviser, 1968-71, chief scientific adviser, 1971-74; Cambridge University, master of Jesus College, 1974—. Part-time member of United Kingdom Atomic Energy Authority, 1962-65; member of Advisory Council on Scientific Policy, 1963-64, and Central Advisory Council for Science and Technology, 1967—.

MEMBER: Royal Society (fellow, 1955; vice-president, 1964, 1976), Royal Swedish Academy of Sciences (fellow), American Academy of Arts and Sciences (foreign honorary member), National Academy of Sciences (foreign associate), National Academy of Engineering (foreign associate), American Society for Metals (fellow; honorary member), Athenaeum Club. *Awards, honors:* Christ's College, Cambridge, fellow, 1958-70, honorary fellow, 1970; Institute of Metals Rosenhain medal, 1961, platinum medal, 1965; Royal Society Hughes medal, 1961, Rumford medal, 1974; Reamur medal from Societe Francaise de Metallurgie, 1964; James Alfred Ewing medal from Institution of Civil Engineers, 1967; Holweck medal from Societe Francaise de Physique, 1969; Albert Sauveur achievement award from American Society for Metals, 1969; knighted in 1971; James Douglas gold medal from American Institute of Mining, Metallurgy, and Petroleum Engineers, 1974; Harvey prize from Technion-Israel Institute of Technology, 1974; Acta Metallurgica gold medal, 1976; honorary degrees from Columbia University, 1965, University of Newcastle, 1967, University of Liverpool, 1969, University of Manchester, 1970, University of Warwick, 1971, University of Sussex, 1972, University of Bath, 1973, and University of Strathclyde, Cranfield Institute of Technology, and University of Aston in Birmingham, all 1975; Sc.D., Cambridge University, 1976.

WRITINGS: Portrait of Nature, Scribner, 1975.

Technical works: *Theoretical Structural Metallurgy,* Edward Arnold, 1948, 2nd edition, 1955; *Dislocations and Plastic Flow in Crystals,* Oxford University Press, 1953; *The Mechanical Properties of Matter,* Wiley, 1964; *Theory of Crystal Dislocations,* Gordon & Breach, 1964; *An Introduction to Metallurgy,* Edward Arnold, 1967. Contributor to scientific journals.

AVOCATIONAL INTERESTS: Music.

COUGHLAN, (John) Robert 1914-

PERSONAL: Born July 7, 1914, in Kokomo, Ind.; son of William Henry (a teacher) and Lucile (a teacher; maiden name, DeNevers) Coughlan; married Patricia Ann Collins (a photographer), June 30, 1939; children: John Robert, Jr., Brian Christopher, Kevin Brooks, Cynthia Davis (Mrs. William Paul Rogers, Jr.). *Education:* Northwestern University, B.S., 1936. *Politics:* Eclectic. *Religion:* Agnostic. *Home and office:* 52 Prescott Ave., Bronxville, N.Y. 10708. *Agent:* Perry Knowlton, Curtis Brown Ltd., 60 East 56 St., New York, N.Y. 10022.

CAREER: Coughlan told *CA:* "I became a professional writer within months after graduating from university." *Fortune* magazine, member of staff, 1937-43, associate editor, 1938-43; *Life* magazine, text editor, 1943-49, writer-editor, 1943-70; editorial associate of Kennedy Foundation, 1971-73. *Member:* The Century Association. *Awards, honors*—for articles: Benjamin Franklin magazine awards, 1953 and 1954; Lasker medical journalism awards, 1954 and 1959; Sigma Delta Chi distinguished service award and Overseas Press Club citation, both 1957; Education Writers Association citation, 1962; American Newspaper Guild honorable mention in Heywood Broun memorial award, 1963. For Books: National Association of Independent Schools annual book award, 1967, for *The World of Michelangelo;* Putnam award, 1974, for *Elizabeth and Catherine.* Other: Achievement award, 1961, from Northwestern University Class of 1936.

WRITINGS: (Contributor) *The Aspirin Age, 1919-1941,* Simon & Schuster, 1949; *The Wine of Genius: A Life of Maurice Utrillo,* Harper, 1951; *The Private World of William Faulkner,* Harper, 1954, revised edition, 1972; *Tropical Africa,* Time-Life, 1962, revised edition, 1966; *The World of Michelangelo,* Time-Life, 1966; *Elizabeth and Catherine, Empresses of Russia,* Putnam, 1974; (collaborator) Rose F. Kennedy, *Times to Remember,* Doubleday, 1974.

WORK IN PROGRESS: An encompassing book on the Kennedy family and its extensions; a biography of Czar Alexander I; his memoirs.

* * *

COULETTE, Henri Anthony 1927-

PERSONAL: Born November 11, 1927, in Los Angeles, Calif.; son of Robert Roger and Genevieve (O'Reilly) Coulette; married Jacqueline Meredith, December 27, 1950. *Education:* Los Angeles State College, B.A., 1952; University of Iowa, M.F.A., 1954, Ph.D., 1959. *Politics:* Democrat. *Home:* 485 Madeline Dr., Pasadena, Calif. 91105. *Office:* California State University, 5151 State College Dr., Los Angeles, Calif. 90032.

CAREER: Former high school teacher of English; University of Iowa, Iowa City, instructor at writer's workshop, 1957-59; currently professor of English at California State University, Los Angeles. Has given poetry readings at universities and museums. *Military service:* U.S. Army, 1945-46. *Member:* International P.E.N., American Federation of Teachers. *Awards, honors:* Lamont Poetry Award from Academy of American Poets, 1965; James D. Phelan Award for Poetry, 1966.

WRITINGS: The War of the Secret Agents and Other Poems, Scribner, 1966; (editor with Philip Levine) *Character and Crisis: A Contemporary Reader,* McGraw, 1966; *The Family Goldschmitt* (poems), Scribner, 1971. Also author of *The Unstrung Lyre* (poems), 1971.*

COULTER, N(orman) Arthur, Jr. 1920-

PERSONAL: Born January 9, 1920, in Atlanta, Ga.; son of Norman Arthur (a salesman) and Clarabelle (Clark) Coulter; married Elizabeth Harwell Jackson (a professor), June 23, 1951; children: Robert Jackson. *Education:* Virginia Polytechnic Institute and University, B.S., 1941; Harvard University, M.D., 1950; Johns Hopkins University, postdoctoral study, 1950-52. *Home:* 1825 North Lake Shore Dr., Chapel Hill, N.C. 27514. *Office:* Department of Surgery, University of North Carolina, 123 Clinical Sciences Building, Chapel Hill, N.C. 27514.

CAREER: Virginia Polytechnic Institute and University, Blacksburg, instructor in mathematics, 1946; Ohio State University, Columbus, assistant professor, 1952-59, associate professor of physiology and biophysics, 1959-65, director of Biophysics Division, 1962-65; University of North Carolina, Chapel Hill, associate professor, 1965-67, professor of bioengineering, 1967—, chairman of biomedical engineering and mathematics curriculum, 1969—. *Military service:* U.S. Army, 1941-46; became major.

MEMBER: International Society of Biorheology, Institute of Electrical and Electronics Engineers, Biophysical Society, Biomedical Engineering Society, Association for Computing Machinery, Society for General Systems Research, Synergetic Society, American Society for Cybernetics, Society for Neuroscience, Sigma Xi.

WRITINGS: Synergetics: An Adventure in Human Development, Prentice-Hall, 1976. Contributor of about sixty articles to scientific journals.

WORK IN PROGRESS: A book on group synergetics, research on synergetics, hemodynamics, and teleogenic system theory.

SIDELIGHTS: Coulter writes: "The work on synergetics began August 6, 1945, with Hiroshima. . . . The only way to prevent a nuclear holocaust would be to abolish war itself. The United Nations clearly could not do this, and conventional diplomacy has never worked in the past. And a limited world government—the logical step—simply was not feasible. . . . Thirty years of study and research led to the development of a new science—synergetics. Techniques have been developed which enable individuals to turn on a new state of mind, characterized by a high degree of synergy, or working togetherness, of mental functions. There is an expanded awareness, an enhancement of rationality, and think-feel synergy. More important, a person operating in the synergic mode acts naturally not only to achieve his own goals, but also to promote the goals and interests of others affected by his actions. Techniques have also been developed which enable small groups to operate as synergic teams. . . . It is hoped that synergetics, in synergic alignment with other efforts, will contribute to the abolition of war. If enough people learn synergetics and use it, I believe that some day war will be as unthinkable as cannibalism and slavery are today."

* * *

COUSTEAU, Jacques-Yves 1910-

PERSONAL: Born June 11, 1910, in St. Andre-de-Cubzac, France; son of Daniel P. (a lawyer) and Elizabeth (Duranthon) Cousteau; married Simone Melchoir, July 12, 1937; children: Jean-Michel, Philippe. *Education:* French Naval Academy, graduate, 1933. *Residence:* Monaco. *Office:* Cousteau Society, 777 Third Ave., New York, N.Y. 10017.

CAREER: Undersea explorer, photographer, inventor, and

writer. Entered French Navy in 1930; became interested in diving in 1936; began working on underwater breathing apparatus, and with Emile Gagnan developed the Aqualung in 1942; founder and head, with Philipe Taillez, of Groupe d'Etudes et Recherches Sous-Marines (Undersea Research Group) of French Navy, 1946-56; Campagnes Oceanographiques Francaises, Marseilles, France, founder, president, and chairman, 1950—; Centre d'Etudes Marines Advancees, Marseilles, founder, president, and chairman, 1952—; Institute Oceanographique et Musee (Oceanographic Institute and Museum), Monaco, director, 1957—; US Divers Co., Santa Ana, Calif., chairman, 1957—. After World War II founded various marketing, manufacturing, engineering, and research organizations that were incorporated as Cousteau Group in 1973; director of Conshelf Saturation Dive program, 1962—; general secretary of International Commission for the Scientific Exploration of the Mediterranean, 1966—; chairman of Eurocean, 1971-76; founder and president, Cousteau Society, 1975—. Inventor of numerous undersea devices, including diving saucers, the Bathygraf cinecamera, deepsea camera sleds, and mini-submarines. Leader of oceanographic research expeditions throughout the world in cooperation with many research institutes and universities, including National Geographic Society, French National Research Center, National Aeronautics and Space Administration, and Texas A & M University. *Military service:* French Navy, 1930-57; resigned with rank of lieutenant commander; member of French underground during World War II; received Croix de Guerre with palm; named Commander, Legion of Honor. *Member:* National Academy of Sciences (United States).

AWARDS, HONORS: Gold Medal, National Geographic Society, 1961; Bradford Prize, Boston Museum of Science, 1965; Potts Medal, Franklin Institute, 1970; D.Sc., Brandeis University, 1970, University of California, Berkeley, 1970; Gold Medal, Grand Prix d'Oceanographie Albert Ier, 1971; Grande Medaille d'Or (Gold Medal), Societe d'Encouragement au Progres, 1973; New England Aquarium award, 1973; Prix de la Couronne d'Or, 1973; Gold Medal, New York Zoological Society; named Officier des Arts et Letters, Officier du Merite Maritime, Officier du Merite Agricole, Commandeur du Merite Sportif. Film awards include: Cannes Film Festival awards, 1946 for "Epaves," and 1956 for "Le Monde du silence"; Motion Picture Academy of Arts and Sciences (Oscar) Awards, 1957 for "The Silent World," 1960 for "Golden Fish," and 1964 for "World Without Sun." Television awards include eight National Academy of Television Arts and Sciences (Emmy) Awards with over forty-five nominations.

WRITINGS—All illustrated with own photography: (With Philippe Taillez and Frederic Dumas) *Par dix-huit metres de fond: Histoire d'un film* (title means "Sixty Feet Down: The Story of a Film"), Durel, 1946; *La Plongee en schaphandre* (title means "SCUBA Diving"), Elzevir, 1950; (with Dumas) *The Silent World* (Reader's Digest Book Club selection; Book-of-the-Month Club selection), Harper, 1953; (with Jacques Bourcart) *Le Mer* (title means "The Sea"), Larousse, 1953; (contributor) John Oliver LaGorce, editor, *Book of Fishes,* National Geographic Society, 1958; (editor with James Dugan) *Captain Cousteau's Underwater Treasury,* Harper, 1959.

(With Dugan) *The Living Sea,* Harper, 1963; (compiler) *Bibliographie de la sismique marine* (title means "Bibliography of Marine Seismology"), Oceanographic Institute (Monaco), 1964; *Le Monde sans soleil,* Hachette, 1964, English-

language version edited by Dugan, published as *World Without Sun,* Harper, 1965.

"Undersea Discovery" series; all published by Doubleday, except as noted: (With son, Philippe Cousteau) *Les Requins,* Flammarion, 1970, translation by Francis Price published as *The Shark: Splendid Savage of the Sea,* 1970; (with Philippe Diole) *Un Tresor englouti,* Flammarion, 1971, translation by J. F. Bernard published as *Diving for Sunken Treasure,* 1971; *La Vie et mort des coraux,* Flammarion, 1971, translation by Bernard published as *Life and Death in a Coral Sea,* 1971; (with Diole) *Nos Amies les baleines,* Flammarion, 1972, translation by Bernard published as *The Whale: Mighty Monarch of the Sea,* 1972; (with Diole) *Pieuvres: La Fin d'un malentendu,* Flammarion, 1973, translation by Bernard published as *Octopus and Squid: The Soft Intelligence,* 1973; (with Diole) *Trois Aventures de la Calypso,* Flammarion, 1973, translation by Bernard published as *Three Adventures: Galapagos, Titicaca, the Blue Holes,* 1973; (with Diole) *Compagnons de plongee,* Flammarion, 1974, translation by Bernard published as *Diving Companions: Sea Lion, Elephant Seal, Walrus,* 1974; (with Diole) *Les Dauphins et la liberte,* Flammarion, 1975, translation by Bernard published as *Dolphins,* 1975.

"The Ocean World" encyclopedia series: Volume I: *Oasis in Space,* World Publishing, 1972; Volume II: *The Act of Life,* World Publishing, 1972; Volume III: *Quest for Food,* World Publishing, 1973; Volume IV: *Window in the Sea,* World Publishing, 1973; Volume V: *The Art of Motion,* World Publishing, 1973; Volume VI: *Attack and Defense,* World Publishing, 1973; Volume VII: *Invisible Messages,* World Publishing, 1973; Volume VIII: *Instinct and Intelligence,* Abrams, 1975; Volume IX: *Pharoahs of the Sea,* Abrams, 1975; Volume X: *Mammals of the Sea,* Abrams, 1975; Volume XI: *Provinces of the Sea,* Abrams, 1975; Volume XII: *Man Reenters the Sea,* Abrams, 1975; Volume XIII: *A Sea of Legends: Inspiration from the Sea,* Abrams, 1975; Volume XIV: *The Adventure of Life,* Abrams, 1975; Volume XV: *Outer and Inner Space,* Abrams, 1975; Volume XVI: *The White Caps,* Abrams, 1975; Volume XVII: *Riches of the Sea,* Abrams, 1975; Volume XVIII: *Challenges of the Sea,* Abrams, 1975; Volume XIX: *The Sea in Danger,* Abrams, 1975; Volume XX: *Guide to the Sea and Index,* Abrams, 1975.

Films: "Par Dix-huit Metres de fond," 1942; "Epaves," 1945, released in U.S. as "Danger Under the Sea," 1952; "Paysages du silence," 1947; "Autour d'un recif," 1948, released in U.S. as "Rhythm on the Reef," 1952; "Carnets de plongees," 1949; "Une Plongee de rubis," 1949; "Le Monde du silence," 1956, released in U.S. as "The Silent World"; (and producer) "Histoire d'un poisson rouge," 1960, released in U.S. as "Golden Fish"; "Le Monde sans soleil," 1964, released in U.S. as "World Without Sun"; "The Undersea World of Jacques-Yves Cousteau," 1967.

A series of 36 films based on Cousteau's expeditions around the world were braodcast quarterly by ABC-TV, 1968-76.

Writer of "Pulse of the Sea" monthly column, *Saturday Review,* 1976—; contributor to magazines, including *National Geographic.*

WORK IN PROGRESS: "Voyage To the Edge of the World."

SIDELIGHTS: "Never before has the marine environment been as raped and poisoned as it is today," claims Jacques Cousteau. All the urban and industrial effluents of 500 million Europeans and Africans flow freely—practically without treatment—into the Mediterranean, a near-closed sea that was once the cradle of civilization. Millions of tons of toxic chemicals are either dumped directly into the ocean or find their way there indirectly by way of river pollution or rain. . . .

"Meanwhile," he continues, "swamps are filled. Coastline development ruins the natural and only breeding grounds of thousands of species of marine creatures. Multinational corporations are starting to build their plants in those developing countries that have no environmental-protection regulations. Overfishing is such that the catch of most commercial fish has dropped, on average, 40 percent in the past ten years, in spite of an increase in fishing-fleet tonnage and the use of scientific data and technological aids. An estimated two miles of coral reef are destroyed with crowbars each day to supply souvenior shops—often those of scientific institutions—with shells and coral fragments! Spearfishermen perforate the last groupers and lobsters of the reefs or scare them away from their spawning grounds."

Since 1943, when he co-invented the Aqualung in the midst of Nazi occupied France, the accumulation of seven years spent underwater has had a radical influence on the pioneer. "During that time I have observed and studied closely," he said, "and with my own two eyes I have seen the oceans sicken."

Cousteau doesn't see an easy answer nor is he optimistic. He believes: "There is no possibility of improving the situation without a worldwide agreement and the consideration of all nations. Especially new ones are very jealous about their national sovereignty, independence, do what they want, even if it is not in the general interest. And it is difficult for us (established nations) to criticize them because that's how we have been behaving, of course, for two or three centuries. It is a matter of emergency. If we do not unite behind a certain number of rules, then we will be wiped out. . . .

"I'm counting on public opinion to help bring that about. I believe in the power of public opinion—that people can force their governments into positive action. So I want to open the eyes of the public to the problems of today—to convince them that if they want to, they can change the world. . . . Write your congressman, your newspaper, take out advertising space," Cousteau urges. "Public opinion is stronger than people think, and public opinion must react strongly, because there is no time."

It was in order to foster public opinion that Cousteau founded, in 1975, the society that bears his name. The list of organizations he headed was already long—the Oceanographic Institute and Museum in Monaco, Eurocean (a European consortium of twenty-three countries)—yet he still finds much time and energy to devote to the New York based society. So much energy in fact that people are always amazed when they learn his age.

The discovery of a submerged, ancient harbor off the coast of the Greek island Dia in the Aegean Sea is one of Cousteau's recent archaeological discoveries. It may be the commercial harbor of the Minoan city, Knossos. Experiments were recently completed in the Caribbean, under the auspices of NASA and Texas A & M University, for the use of satellites in marine cartography. A Eurocean project has begun building a man-made industrial island in the North Sea and a floating recreational island is proposed for the Mediterranean. A very active man, Cousteau may one day give speech in Washington, race to a business meeting on the West Coast the next, and then finish the week aboard the Calypso at sea. His obligations hardly ever allow him to be in one place for longer than two days. The unique structure of the Cousteau Group offers its chief executive the special freedom and funding he needs for his many activities. Unprofitable organizations engaged in marine research are financed by the lucrative businesses that manufacture industrial gases and sport diving equipment. As an expression of the responsibility Cousteau feels, profits taken indirectly from the sea are returned in efforts to study and preserve. Dave Schulz said: "He is continuously studying the sea, for he feels—no, seriously believes—that the ocean is the last frontier for mankind. This frontier must not be abused the way a number of land areas have been, worldwide, where forests were cleared and wildlife reduced without sufficient consideration of the ecological consequences. If the ocean frontier is tamed with the same wantoness that has marked other pioneering efforts of man, then mankind will be lost, for there is no recovering a dead sea."

Cousteau personally attends the Involvement Days sponsored by the Cousteau Society throughout the United States. With other environmentalists, he meets members and discusses his observations, ideas, and goals. He gives numerous speeches, directs films, and he writes books. The sea in his estimation is terribly misunderstood by most people. "As long as writers are going to go on distorting facts in novels," he said, "they contribute to the anti-education of the public. Certainly 'Jaws,' for example, is completely fake, has no reality, no correlation with the behavior of sharks at all. No sharks behave like that. It is a myth, and, unfortunately, it is not specified in the introduction that it is a complete myth. There are a lot of people I have met who consider this a reference book on sharks, which is a disaster. It is a tissue of mistakes. . . . However well-written and advertised it was, it is a bad book."

In his books, Cousteau maintains an envious balance between scientific accuracy and entertainment. Joe Evans said his book on sharks, written with his son Phillipe, "concerns their preparation and voyage on the *Calypso* to seek, study, research, and photograph the activities and habitual movements of sharks. There are vivid, exciting narratives of encounters with sharks—sharks of different species and size, from the large whale shark to the hammerhead and dogfish. Experiences with the beautiful, agile, graceful vultures of the sea are told in a very special way proper only to one who has encountered them face to face or has watched them from within the protective cages that were used to study these 'killers of the deep.'"

The educational aim of Cousteau's work never detracts from its excitement and adventure. Desmond Young said: "Whether Captain Cousteau is describing the recovery of artifacts from a Greek galley sunk more than two centuries before Christ, or his battle to prevent the dumping of radio-active waste into the Mediterranean, he is unfailingly interesting. His descriptions gracefully combine literary style and scientific nomenclature." Lewis Gannet admires his writing because "its special tang is the sheer joy of living which shines from almost every page."

Cousteau's work is sometimes criticized by academic oceanographers for being too little science and too much adventure. "I am not a scientist," counters Cousteau. "I am an impresario of scientists, perhaps. I can speak their jargon, but more important I can make it accessible to the layman." R. C. Cowen commented that "the years of effort that have been compressed into the pages of this book [*The Living Sea*] speak for themselves of the great contribution Captain Cousteau has made to oceanographic science." More importantly, adds Cowen, this book "conveys the sense of adventure and the vision that continue to inspire his work."

BIOGRAPHICAL/CRITICAL SOURCES—Books: James Dugan, *Undersea Explorer: The Story of Captain Cousteau* (juvenile), Harper, 1957; Philip Dunaway and George De Kay, editors, *Turning Point*, Random House, 1958; Frederick Wagner, *Famous Underwater Adventurers*, Dodd, 1962; Muriel Guberlet, *Explorers of the Sea*, Ronald, 1964; Terry Shannon, *Saucer in the Sea* (juvenile), Golden Gate, 1965; John Canning, editor, *100 Great Adventures*, Taplinger, 1969; Ross R. Olney, *Men against the Sea*, Grosset, 1969; Robert Elliot, *Banners of Courage* (juvenile), Platt & Munk, 1972.

Articles: *Science Illustrated*, December, 1948; *Life*, November 27, 1950; *New York Herald Tribune Book Review*, February 22, 1953; *New York Times Book Review*, February 22, 1953, April 28, 1963; *Holiday*, September, 1955; *Nature*, January 12, 1957; *Time*, March 28, 1960; *Cosmopolitan*, January, 1960; *New York Times Magazine*, April 21, 1963; *Christian Science Monitor*, April 25, 1963; *New York Herald Tribune*, April 28, 1963; *l'Express*, August 4-10, 1969; *Best Sellers*, November 15, 1970; *Detroit Free Press*, December 16, 1973, May 26, 1976; *The American Way*, August, 1974; *Pittsburgh Press*, March 2, 1975; *Parade Magazine*, March 16, 1975; *People*, September 15, 1975; *Saturday Review*, July 10, 1976.

*   *   *

COWAN, Gregory M(ac)   1935-

PERSONAL: Born August 17, 1935, in Seattle, Wash.; son of Walter G. (a physician) and Pearl (Ramsey) Cowan; married Elizabeth Wooten (a college professor), 1975. *Education:* Whitman College, B.A., 1957; University of Washington, Seattle, M.A., 1960; graduate study at Washington State University, 1957-60, Portland State University, 1960-61, and New School for Social Research, 1974-76. *Home:* 2608 Melba Cir., Bryan, Tex. 77801. *Office:* Department of English, Texas A & M University, College Station, Tex. 77843.

CAREER: Clark College, Vancouver, Wash., 1960-67, began as instructor, became assistant professor of English; Forest Park Community College, St. Louis, Mo., assistant professor, 1967-69, associate professor, 1969-71, professor of English, 1971-74; State University of New York, associate professor, 1975-76; Texas A & M University, College Station, associate professor, 1976—. National Junior College Committee, representative, 1969-75, chairman, 1972-74.

MEMBER: American Association of University Professors, Association of Humanistic Psychology, Conference on College Composition and Communication (member of executive committee, 1969-75; chairman of Committee to Develop Guidelines for Junior College English Teacher Training Programs, 1969-70), Modern Language Association of America, National Council of Teachers of English, Midwest Regional Conference on English in the Two-Year College (member of executive committee, 1969-75), Pacific Northwest Regional Conference on English in the Two-Year College, Southeast Regional Conference on English in the Two-Year College.

WRITINGS: (With Elisabeth McPherson) *Plain English Please*, Random House, 1966, 3rd edition, 1975; (with McPherson) *Background for Writing*, Random House, 1967; (with McPherson) *Exercising Plain English*, Random House, 1970; (with McPherson) *Plain English Rhetoric and Reader*, Random House, 1970, 2nd edition, 1976; (with McPherson) *English in Plain Words*, five volumes, Random House, 1971; *Guidelines for Junior College English Teacher*

Training Programs (monograph), National Council of Teachers of English, 1971; *Three for Show: A Visual Approach to the Short Story*, Random House, 1973. Contributor to journals in his field. Consulting editor to Random House junior and community college texts, 1969-74.

AVOCATIONAL INTERESTS: Cooking, sailing, jogging, carpentry, folk music, politics of issue campaigning, democratization of education, traveling.

*   *   *

COWLES, Virginia (Spencer)   1912-

PERSONAL: Born August 24, 1912, in Brattleboro, Vt.; daughter of Edward Spencer (a physician and psychiatrist) and Florence Wolcott (Jaquith) Cowles; married Aidan M. Crawley, 1945; children: two sons, one daughter. *Education:* Educated privately. *Home:* 19 Chester Sq., London S.W. 1, England.

CAREER: Columnist for the Boston (Mass.) *Breeze* in the early 1930's; then fashion magazine and free-lance writer in New York City; free-lance newspaper correspondent, 1937-41 and 1943-45, traveling during that time to Europe and the Far East and covering the Spanish Civil War; roving correspondent for *The London Sunday Times* at the beginning of World War II. Special assistant to the American Ambassador, American Embassy, London, England, 1942-43. *Awards, honors:* Order of the British Empire, 1947.

WRITINGS—All nonfiction: *Looking for Trouble* (journalistic experiences), Harper, 1941; *How America Is Governed*, Lutterworth, 1944; *No Cause for Alarm*, Harper, 1949 (published in England as *No Cause for Alarm: A Study of Trends in England Today*, Hamish Hamilton, 1949); *Winston Churchill: The Era and the Man*, Harper, 1953; *Gay Monarch: The Life and Pleasures of Edward VII*, Harper, 1956 (published in England as *Edward VII and His Circle*, Hamish Hamilton, 1956); *The Phantom Major: The Story of David Stirling and His Desert Command*, Harper, 1958 (published in England as *The Phantom Major: The Story of David Stirling and the S.A.S. Regiment*, Collins, 1958, junior edition, 1962).

The Great Swindle: The Story of the South Sea Bubble, Harper, 1960; *The Kaiser*, Harper, 1963; *1913: The Defiant Swan Song*, Weidenfeld & Nicolson, 1967, published as *1913: An End and a Beginning*, Harper, 1968; *The Russian Dagger: Cold War in the Days of the Czars*, Harper, 1969; *The Romanovs*, Harper, 1971; *The Rothschilds: A Family of Fortune*, Knopf, 1973.

Contributor of articles to various magazines, including *Vogue* and *Harper's.**

*   *   *

CRABB, Lawrence J(ames), Jr.   1944-

PERSONAL: Born July 13, 1944, in Evanston, Ill.; son of Lawrence J. (in sales) and Isabel (an occupational therapist; maiden name, Craigmile) Crabb; married Rachel Lankford, June 18, 1966; children: Keplen, Kenton. *Education:* Ursinus College, B.A., 1965; University of Illinois, M.A., 1969, Ph.D., 1970. *Religion:* "Conservative Evangelical Protestant." *Office:* 891 East Palmetto Park Rd., Boca Raton, Fla. 33432.

CAREER: University of Illinois, Urbana, assistant professor of psychology, and staff psychologist at Psychological Counseling Center, 1970-71; Florida Atlantic University, Boca Raton, director of Psychological Counseling Center, 1971-73; private practice of clinical psychology in Boca Raton, Fla., 1973-76. *Member:* American Psychological Association.

WRITINGS: Basic Principles of Biblical Counseling, Zondervan, 1975; *Effective Counseling: A Model for Helping Caring Christians Become Capable Counselors,* Zondervan, in press. Contributor of articles and reviews to religious magazines and psychology journals.

SIDELIGHTS: Crabb writes: "Motivated by a desire to see a clearly and thorough Biblical view of counseling developed, I have written and intend to continue writing books which integrate conservative evangelical Christianity with psychological concern and to think through the role of the local church in meeting the needs of the people. I am committed to a theistic world view in which an infinite personal God is the Supreme Being and has revealed Himself in Scripture and in His Son, Jesus Christ. To the best of my awareness, I endeavor to . . . reflect this world view in my writings."

* * *

CRAFT, Maurice 1932-

PERSONAL: Born May 4, 1932, in London, England; son of Jack (an upholsterer) and Polly (Lewis) Craft; married Alma Sampson (a university research officer), May 19, 1957; children: Anna, Naomi. *Education:* University of London, B.Sc.Econ., 1953, Academic Diploma in Education, 1959; University of Dublin, H.Dip.Ed., 1956; University of Liverpool, Ph.D., 1972. *Office:* Goldsmith's College, University of London, London SE14 6NW, England.

CAREER: High school teacher in London, England, 1956-60; Edge Hill College of Education, Ormskirk, Lancashire, England, principal lecturer in sociology and head of department, 1960-67; University of Exeter, Exeter, Devonshire, England, senior lecturer in School of Education, 1967-73; La Trobe University, Melbourne, Australia, professor of education and chairman of Centre for the Study of Urban Education, 1973-75; University of London, London, England, Goldsmiths' Professor of Education at Institute of Education, 1976—. *Military service:* British Army, Royal Army Ordnance Corps, 1953-55; served in Suez Canal Zone; became second lieutenant.

MEMBER: British Sociological Association, Association of Teachers in Colleges and Departments of Education (past member of national executive committee; founder and chairman of sociology section, 1967-69). *Awards, honors:* Research grants from Social Science Research Council, 1966-72, 1974-76, Government of the Commonwealth of Australia, 1974-75, and Japan Foundation, 1975.

WRITINGS: (Chief editor) *Linking Home and School,* Longmans, Green, 1967, revised edition, 1972; (editor with H. Lytton) *Guidance and Counselling in British Schools,* Edward Arnold, 1969, revised edition, 1974; (editor) *Family Class and Education: A Reader,* Longmans, Green, 1970.

Contributor: W. H. Pealey, editor, *Education and Social Work,* Pergamon, 1967; W. Taylor, editor, *Towards a Policy for the Education of Teachers,* Butterworth, 1969; J. W. Tibble, editor, *The Future of Teacher Education,* Routledge & Kegan Paul, 1971; R. Jackson, editor, *Careers Guidance: Practice and Problems,* Edward Arnold, 1973; S. J. Eggleston, editor, *Contemporary Research in the Sociology of Education,* Methuen, 1974; J. Raynor, editor, *The Urban Context,* Open University Press, 1974.

Joint general editor of "Aspects of Modern Sociology" series, Longmans, Green, 1965—. Contributor to professional journals. Member of management committee of *Sociology of Education Abstracts.*

WORK IN PROGRESS: A major study of family values in Melbourne, with particular reference to educability; a study of guidance, counseling, school social work support, and school health provision in Australia; continuing research on school-leaving in Dublin.

AVOCATIONAL INTERESTS: Music, walking.

* * *

CRAWFORD, John R. 1915(?)-1976

1915(?)—February 14, 1976; American bridge master and author. Obituaries: *Washington Post,* February 17, 1976.

* * *

CRAWFORD, Linda 1938-

PERSONAL: Born August 2, 1938, in Detroit, Mich.; daughter of Arthur R. (a foundry owner) and Mary E. (a weaver; maiden name, Forshar) Crawford. *Education:* University of Michigan, B.A., 1960, M.A., 1961. *Home:* 149 Sixth St., Greenport, N.Y. 11944. *Agent:* Warren Bayless, 156 East 52nd St., New York, N.Y. 10022.

CAREER: Chicago Tribune, New York Bureau, New York, N.Y., feature writer, 1961-67. Writer. *Awards, honors:* Grant from Ludwig Vogelstein Foundation, 1975.

WRITINGS: In a Class By Herself (novel), Scribner, 1976.

WORK IN PROGRESS: A novel, for Simon & Schuster, publication expected spring, 1978.

SIDELIGHTS: Crawford told *CA:* "I am a recovered alcoholic. The time from 1967-71 included the worst of my alcoholic drinking, and pill addiction, and I did little during that period except feed my addictions. I began writing in 1972 after being sober for more than a year. I had always wanted, and intended, to write but for years my drinking interfered with that desire. Mercifully, that is no longer the case." Crawford lives with Sandra Scoppettone.

* * *

CRONNE, H(enry) A(lfred) 1904-

PERSONAL: Born October 17, 1904, in Ulster, Ireland (now Northern Ireland); son of James Kennedy (a clergyman) and Elizabeth Jane (Sloane) Cronne; married Lilian Mey Seckler, 1936; children: one daughter. *Education:* Queen's University, Belfast, B.A., 1925, M.A., 1931; Balliol College, Oxford, B.A., 1927, M.A., 1931; additional study at King's College, London, and Institute of Historical Research, 1927-28. *Home:* Winswood Cottage, Cheldon, Chumleigh, North Devon EX18 7JB, England.

CAREER: Queen's University of Belfast, Belfast, Northern Ireland, assistant to the professor of history, 1928-31; University of London, King's College, London, England, 1931-45, began as lecturer in medieval history, became lecturer in paleography, reader in medieval history, 1945; University of Birmingham, Birmingham, England, professor of medieval history, 1946-70, professor emeritus, 1970—, dean of faculty, 1952-55. *Military service:* Served in Home Guard from its beginning as Local Defence Volunteers until 1941; transferred to Somerset Special Constabulary until 1943; Fire Guard duties in London until 1945. *Awards, honors:* M.A., University of Birmingham, 1947.

WRITINGS: Bristol Charters, 1378-1499, Bristol Record Society Publications, 1946; (editor with T. W. Moody and D. B. Quinn) *Essays in British and Irish History in Honour* of James Eadie Todd, Frederick Muller, 1949; The Borough of Warwick in the Middle Ages, Dugdale Society, 1951; (editor with Charles Johnson) Regesta regum Anglo-Normannorum (title means "Acts of the Anglo-Norman Kings"; a collection of all their charters and writs), Clarendon Press, Volume II (Cronne not associated with Volume I): 1100-1135, 1956; Volume III (with R. H. Davis): Regesta Regis Stephani Ad Mathildis Imperatricis Ac Gaufridi et Henriciducum Normannorum, 1135-1154 (title means "Acts of King Stephen, Empress Mathilda, and Geoffrey and Henry, Dukes of Normandy"), 1968, Volume IV (with Davis): Facsimiles of Original Charters and Writs of King Stephen, the Empress Mathilda, and Dukes Geoffrey and Henry, 1135-1154, 1969; The Reign of Stephen, 1135-1154: Anarchy in England, Beekman, 1970.

Contributor to Chamber's Encyclopaedia, and to history journals, including English Historical Review, Scottish Historical Review, History, and University of Birmingham Historical Journal.

AVOCATIONAL INTERESTS: Drawing, writing.

BIOGRAPHICAL/CRITICAL SOURCES: Spectator, May 16, 1970; Bookseller, September 12, 1970; Observer, September 20, 1970; Irish Historical Studies, September, 1972.

* * *

CROSS, Frank Moore, Jr. 1921-

PERSONAL: Born July 13, 1921, in Ross, Calif.; son of Frank Moore and Mary (Ellison) Cross; married Elizabeth A. Showalter, June 20, 1947; children: Susan E., Ellen M., Priscilla Rachel. Education: Maryville College, Maryville, Tenn., A.B., 1942; McCormick Theological Seminary, B.D., 1946; Johns Hopkins University, Ph.D., 1950. Home: 31 Woodland Rd., Lexington, Mass. 02173. Office: Harvard Semitic Museum 102, Harvard University, Cambridge, Mass. 02138.

CAREER: McCormick Theological Seminary, Chicago, Ill., visiting instructor in Old Testament, 1948-49; Wellesley College, Wellesley, Mass., instructor in Biblical history, 1950-51; McCormick Theological Seminary, instructor, 1951-53, assistant professor, 1954-55, associate professor of Old Testament, 1955-57; Harvard University, Cambridge, Mass., associate professor of Old Testament, 1957-58, Hancock Professor of Hebrew and Other Oriental Languages, 1957—, chairman of department of Near Eastern languages, 1958-65, Semitic Museum, curator, 1958-61, director, 1975—. Annual professor at American Schools of Oriental Research (Jerusalem), 1953-54; Haskell lecturer at Oberlin College, 1957; visiting scholar at University Center (Georgia), 1957; Jeffrey lecturer at Goucher College, 1958; Zwerdling lecturer at University of Michigan, 1960; Rushton lecturer at Samford University, 1967; Mary Farnum Brown lecturer, Haverford College, 1974. Co-director of archaeological expedition to Judean Buqei'ah, 1955; archaeological director of Hebrew Union College (Jerusalem), 1963-64. Member: American Oriental Society, American Schools of Oriental Research (trustee, 1973—; president, 1974-76; principal investigator of expedition to Carthage, 1975-76), American Academy of Arts and Sciences (fellow), American Philosophical Society, Society of Biblical Literature (president, 1973-74), Biblical Colloquium (president, 1966-68), Phi Beta Kappa. Awards, honors: M.A. from Harvard University, 1957; Litt.D. from Maryville College, 1968.

WRITINGS: (With David N. Freedman) Early Hebrew Orthography, American Oriental Society, 1952; The An-

cient Library of Qumran and Modern Biblical Studies, Doubleday, 1958, 2nd edition, 1961; (contributor) C. Ernest Wright, editor, The Bible and the Ancient Near East, Doubleday, 1961; (editor) Scrolls from the Wilderness of the Dead Sea: A Guide to the Exhibition, the Dead Sea Scrolls of Jordan, American Schools of Oriental Research, 1965; The Origin and Early Evolution of Alphabet, Eretz Israel, 1967; Freedman and Jonas C. Greenfield, editors, New Directions in Biblical Archaeology, Doubleday, 1969; (editor with Freedman, James A. Sanders, and John C. Trever) Scrolls from Qumran Cave I, Albright Institute of Archaeological Research, 1972; Canaanite Myth and Hebrew Epic: Essays in the History of the Religion of Israel, Harvard University Press, 1973; (contributor) Paul W. Lapp and Nancy L. Lapp, editors, Discoveries in the Wadi ed-Daliyeh, American Schools of Oriental Research, 1974; (with Freedman) Studies in Ancient Yahwistic Poetry, Scholars' Press, 1975; (editor with Shemaryahu Talmon, and contributor) Qumran and the History of the Biblical Text, Harvard University Press, 1975; (editor with Werner E. Lemke and Patrick D. Miller, Jr., and contributor) Magnalia Dei: In Memoriam G. Ernest Wright, Doubleday, 1976. Contributor to professional journals. Biblical Archaeologist, co-editor, 1952-59, member of editorial board, 1959—; associate editor of Harvard Theological Review, 1963-74; Bulletin of the American Schools of Oriental Research, associate editor, 1969—, member of editorial board; member of international staff for editing Dead Sea Scrolls, 1953—.

* * *

CROSS, Leslie (Frank) 1909-

PERSONAL: Born May 12, 1909, in Milwaukee, Wis.; son of James L. (an engineer) and Zoe S. (Windfelder) Cross; married Helene Catherine O'Keefe, March 9, 1929 (died, 1975); children: Dion Leslie, James O'Keefe. Education: Attended Beloit College, 1927-28. Home: 400 East Belle Ave., Milwaukee, Wis. 53217. Office: Milwaukee Journal, Journal Sq., Milwaukee, Wis. 53201.

CAREER: Chicago Tribune, Chicago, Ill., reporter with Milwaukee Bureau, 1929; Milwaukee Leader, Milwaukee, Wis., reporter and copy editor, 1929-38; New Milwaukee Leader, Milwaukee, Wis., copy editor, 1938-39; Milwaukee Post, Milwaukee, Wis., copy editor, news editor, assistant to the editor-in-chief, and author of column "Inasmuch," 1939-41; Milwaukee Journal, Milwaukee, Wis., reporter and copy editor, 1941-46, exchange editor and writer, 1946-51, book editor and author of column "Reading Glass," 1951-53, "Reading and Writing," 1953-75, "Between the Lines," 1975—. Director of Wisconsin Guardian Publishing Co., 1940-41. Guest lecturer at University of Wisconsin, Madison, University of Wisconsin, Milwaukee, and Marquette University.

MEMBER: National Book Critics Circle, Council for Wisconsin Writers, Society of Midland Authors, Milwaukee Press Club, Sigma Delta Chi. Awards, honors: Awards from Milwaukee Press Club, 1964-65, Bookfellows of Milwaukee, 1966, Wisconsin Committee for National Library Week, 1967, Society of Midland Authors, 1969, Council for Wisconsin Writers, 1974, and Friends of Literature, 1976.

WRITINGS: Written in Wisconsin, Journal Co. (Milwaukee, Wis.), 1972.

Anthologized in New Poetry Out of Wisconsin, edited by August Derleth, Stanton & Lee, 1969.

Contributor of articles and poems to magazines, including American Mercury, Nation, Two Worlds, Poetry, and Wisconsin Magazine of History.

SIDELIGHTS: Cross has written on American publishing and on the literary scene abroad; in the course of his career he has interviewed several hundred authors in the United States, London, Paris, and Ireland. He writes: "Having done a good deal of 'creative' writing in addition to journalism, I am keenly interested in books and other arts both from the point of view of their form and as sources or conveyors of ideas and new intellectual perspectives. I've done some translation from the French and from the Italian, which I read, but don't speak well."

*   *   *

CROW, William Bernard   1895-1976

September 11, 1895—June 28, 1976; British biologist, educator, and author of books on a variety of subjects. Obituaries: *AB Bookman's Weekly*, July 19, 1976. (*CAP*-1; earlier sketch in *CA*-13/14)

*   *   *

CROWE, Philip Kingsland   1908-

PERSONAL: Born January 7, 1908, in New York, N.Y.; son of Earle Rosman and Kathleen McMullin (Higgins) Crowe; married Irene Pettus, June 31, 1937; children: Phillippa, Irene, Mary. *Education:* University of Virginia, B.A., 1932. *Office:* American Embassy, Dag Hammarskjolds Alle 24, Copenhagen, Denmark.

CAREER: New York Evening Post, New York, N.Y., 1929-32, began as reporter, became assistant financial editor; Milmine Bodman & Co. (brokers), New York, N.Y., chief of customers' department, 1932-35; explorer and big game hunter in French Indo-China, 1935-37; *Life* (magazine), New York, N.Y., director of travel advertising, 1937-38; *Fortune* (magazine), New York, N.Y., member of advertising staff, 1938-41, 1944-48; Economic Cooperation Administration, special representative of economic cooperation mission to China, 1948-49; farmer and writer, 1949-53; U.S. ambassador to Ceylon, 1953-57; special assistant to U.S. Secretary of State in Washington, D.C., 1957-59; ambassador to Union of South Africa in Pretoria, 1959-61, and Republic of South Africa, 1961; led wildlife conservation expeditions to fifty-seven countries in Asia, South America, Africa, and Australia, 1962-68; ambassador to Norway in Oslo, 1969-73, and to Denmark in Copenhagen, 1973—. U.S. delegate to Economic Commission on Asia and the Far East, 1954, U.S. representative at United Nations Economic Commission on East Asia. Director of World Wildlife Fund (international), World Wildlife Fund (United States), African Wildlife Leadership Foundation, and American Committee for International Wildlife Protection. Trustee of Foreign Service Educational Foundation and Johns Hopkins University's School of Advanced International Studies. Member of board of advisers of Tufts University's Fletcher School of Law and Diplomacy. Member of New York Council on Foreign Relations. *Military service:* U.S. Army Air Forces, 1941-45, chief of intelligence for Office of Strategic Services (OSS); became lieutenant colonel; served in China, Burma, and India; received Bronze Star Medal.

MEMBER: Society of Cincinnati, Society of Colonial Wars, Huguenot Society, St. Nicholas Society, Royal Geographical Society (fellow), Royal Asiatic Society (life member), Ceylon Wildlife Protection Society (life member), One Thousand One (of World Wildlife Fund), Racquet and Tennis Club, Boodle's Club, White's Club, Flyfishers Club, Brook Club, Century Club, Explorers Club, Anglers Club, Boone and Crocket Club (New York, N.Y.), Metropolitan Club, Dacor Club (Washington, D.C.), Harvard Travellers (Boston, Mass.), Chesapeake Bay Yacht Club, Lakota Club, Royal Danish Yacht Club (Copenhagen), Round Table (Woodstock, Vt.), Rand Club (Johannesburg, South Africa), Hill Club (Ceylon), Norske Selskab, Royal Norwegian Yacht Club, Linge Club (Oslo). *Awards, honors:* Officer of French Legion of Honor, 1959; grand official first class of Portugal's Military Order of Christ, 1960; Yun Hui first class of Republic of China's Cloud and Banner, 1961; grand cross of Norway's Order of St. Olav, 1973.

WRITINGS: Sport Is Where You Find It, Van Nostrand, 1953; *Diversions of a Diplomat in Ceylon*, Van Nostrand, 1956; *Sporting Journeys in Asia and Africa*, Barre, 1966; *The Empty Ark* (on wildlife conservation), Scribner, 1967; *Out of the Mainstream* (on fishing), Scribner, 1970; *World Wildlife: The Last Stand*, Scribner, 1970; (with E. M. Blaiklock) *Adam to Esau: The God Who Speaks* (on Bible characters and doctrines), Eerdmans, 1972.

AVOCATIONAL INTERESTS: Fishing, shooting, hunting.*

*   *   *

CROWTHER, (Francis) Bosley   1905-

PERSONAL: Born July 13, 1905, in Lutherville, Md.; son of Francis Bosley (a merchant) and Eliza (Leisenring) Crowther; married Florence Ellinger Marks (a literary agent), January 20, 1933; children: F. Bosley III, John M., Jefferson H. *Education:* Princeton University, B.A., 1928. *Home:* 17 Murchison Pl., White Plains, N.Y. 10605.

CAREER: New York Times, New York City, cub reporter covering police news and rewrite man, 1928-32, assistant drama editor, 1932-37, assistant screen editor, 1937-40, screen editor and film critic, 1940-68; Columbia Pictures Industries, Inc., New York City, creative consultant, 1968-73; independent consultant and writer, 1973—. Lecturer. *Member:* New York Film Critics (chairman, 1944, 1951-67), Century Club (New York City). *Awards, honors: New York Times* intercollegiate current events winner, 1928; Critics award from Screen Directors Guild of America, 1953; New York Film Critics honorary special award, 1968.

WRITINGS: (With William Du Bois) "East of the Sun" (three-act play), produced in Philadelphia at Broad St. Theatre, 1935; (contributor) Jack Goodman, editor, *While You Were Gone*, Simon & Schuster, 1946; *The Lion's Share: The Story of an Entertainment Empire* (history of Metro-Goldwyn-Mayer), Dutton, 1957; *Hollywood Rajah: The Life and Times of Louis B. Mayer*, Holt, 1960; *The Great Films: Fifty Golden Years of Motion Pictures*, Putnam, 1967; *Vintage Films*, Putnam, 1976. Contributor to magazines.

WORK IN PROGRESS: More Vintage Films, for Putnam.

SIDELIGHTS: "Throughout my career as a film critic," Crowther told *CA*, "I was a persistent opponent of film censorship and thus an ardent advocate of freedom of the screen, and I strongly urged and applauded the distribution of worthy foreign-language films in the United States." He further remarked, "I openly condemned the attempted restraints on filmmakers by the congressional committees, and I early deplored excessive violence in films."

AVOCATIONAL INTERESTS: Sailing, wood carving, gardening.

BIOGRAPHICAL/CRITICAL SOURCES: Time, December 1, 1967; *Films in Review*, January, 1968; Frank E. Beaver, editor, *Bosley Crowther: Social Critic of the Film*, University of Michigan, 1970.

CRUMM, Lloyd C(arlton), Jr. 1927-

PERSONAL: Born September 19, 1927, in Joliet, Ill.; son of Lloyd Carlton (a shoemaker and used car salesman) and Johanna (a souvenir shopkeeper; maiden name Solej) Crumm; married Vera Mutter (a professional Canasta player), June 15, 1945 (divorced, 1968); living with Melody (a beautician and poet); children: (first marriage) Cookie, Lloyd III, Clint; Serenity Jean. *Education:* Cicero Heights Community College, A.A. (communications), 1968; attended Dale Carnegie Institute. *Politics:* "Not my bag, but was active in the '60's." *Religion:* "Into Zen and Yoga." *Home and office:* 16673 Hubbell, Detroit, Mich. 48235.

CAREER: Has worked as pet shop laborer, beauty shop sweeper, and pin setter in various bowling alleys in Joliet, Ill., 1948-53; free-lance vacuum cleaner salesman in Ashtabula, Ohio, 1953-60; Dyno-Plast Inc., Sonoma, Calif., screw technician, 1960-68; Oh Wow Inc. (a poster and paraphernalia shop), San Francisco, Calif., part owner, 1968-73; freelance marriage counselor and sex therapist in Detroit, Mich., 1973—. Member of board of directors, Roc-Starr Tee-Shirt Co., 1970—; treasurer, Haight-Ashbury Neighborhood Association, 1971-72. *Military service:* U.S. Marine Corps, 1945-48; became sergeant; received bleeding heart. *Member:* Sanpoku Society International, Horatio Alger Society, Self-Realization Fellowship (fellow), West Side Saturday Love Club. *Awards, honors:* Herb Hoover Statuette from Sweeper Society, 1957, for Swedish Massage Attachment Sales; Bay Area Beauticians Literary Award, 1969, for *Get That Tonette and Change Your Life;* B.S. from Cleeter Counard College, 1974.

WRITINGS: (With covivant, Melody) *Babs and Suzette* (a case study in verse), privately printed, 1968; *You Can Improve Your Awareness on Your Lunch Hour—Here's How,* New You Press, 1969; *Get That Tonette and Change Your Life,* Peale Press, 1969; *How to Get the Most Out of Your Computer Dates,* Growth House, 1971; *Let's Go With That* (autobiography), Cicero Heights Community College Press, 1973. Also author of play scripts for Living Theatre groups, as yet neither published nor produced. Editor, *Crumm's Confidential* (newsletter), 1972—.

WORK IN PROGRESS: Come Here Often?, a book of tips for the "suddenly single" on how to get back into circulation; *Meet Your Mate: A Guide to Swingin' Singles Cruises,* publication by New You Press expected, 1978.

SIDELIGHTS: Crumm writes: "My experience as a vacuum cleaner salesman shaped what was to become my new lifestyle. You see, most of life, well, all of life, really, is contingent upon cleanliness—of house, mind and body. When I was truly certain all of the houses in Ashtabula were cleaned, I felt my mission in life was to make things even cleaner—I wanted to try cleaning minds, but Harvard told me I needed a BS before I could go be a top-notch brain surgeon. So I decided to devote myself to cleaning up other people's acts, as it were. I am currently working on a new theory in which all of the important questions of life will be simply answered (which also may, incidentally, be released as a 45 r.p.m. disco hit soon). I call this theory 'Primal Scrub.'"

* * *

CRUSO, Thalassa 1909-

PERSONAL: Born January 7, 1909, in London, England; came to the United States in 1935, naturalized citizen, 1947; daughter of Henry Anthony and Mildred (Robinson) Cruso; married Hugh O'Neill Hencken, October 12, 1935; children: Ala Mary (Mrs. William S. Reid), Sophia (Mrs. David L. Stone), Thalassa (Mrs. Asghar Ali). *Education:* Attended schools in London. *Religion:* Episcopalian. *Home:* 329 Hammond St., Chestnut Hill, Mass. 02167. *Office:* WGBH-Television, Western Ave., Boston, Mass. 02134.

CAREER: London Museum, London, England, assistant keeper, 1933-35; worked for British Consulate in Boston, Mass., 1938-46; WGBH-Television, Boston, Mass., and National Educational Television network, hostess of series "Making Things Grow," and "Making Things Work." *Member:* Society of Antiquaries (London; fellow), English-Speaking Union, Chilton Club, Chestnut Hill Garden Club (president, 1962-64). *Awards, honors:* Citation from New York Horticultural Society, 1970; distinguished service medal from Garden Club of America, 1970.

WRITINGS: Costume, London Museum, 1934; *Making Things Grow: A Practical Guide for the Indoor Gardener,* Knopf, 1969; *Making Things Grow Outdoors,* Knopf, 1971; *To Everything There Is a Season: The Gardening Year with Thalassa Cruso,* Knopf, 1973; *Making Vegetables Grow,* Knopf, 1975. Contributor to archaeology journals.

SIDELIGHTS: Thalassa Cruso is an archaeologist as well as a television performer. She excavated Bredon Hill in Worcestershire, England, 1934-36.

* * *

CRUZ, Victor Hernandez 1949-

PERSONAL: Born February 6, 1949, in Aguas Buenas, P.R.; son of Severo and Rosa Cruz; children: Ajani. *Education:* Attended high school in New York, N.Y. *Home address:* P.O. Box 40148, San Francisco, Calif. 94140.

CAREER: Poet. Guest lecturer at University of California, Berkeley, 1969. *Awards, honors:* Creative Artists public service award, 1974, for *Tropicalization.*

WRITINGS: Snaps (poems), Random House, 1969; *Mainland* (poems), Random House, 1973; *Tropicalization* (poems and prose), Reed, Cannon, 1976.

WORK IN PROGRESS: A novel for Random House.

SIDELIGHTS: Cruz writes: "My family life was full of music, guitars and conga drums, maracas and songs. My mother sang songs. Even when it was five below zero in New York she sang warm tropical ballads."

BIOGRAPHICAL/CRITICAL SOURCES: Bilingual Review, September-December, 1974.

* * *

CULLIFORD, Stanley George 1920-

PERSONAL: Born March 18, 1920, in Napier, New Zealand; son of Arthur Frank (a draper) and May (Dingwall) Culliford; married June Neale, May 11, 1946; children: Graham, John, Neil, David. *Education:* Victoria University of Wellington, M.A., 1940, diploma in education, 1947; University of London, Ph.D., 1950. *Home:* 39 Ayton St., Gisborne, New Zealand.

CAREER: Victoria University of Wellington, Wellington, New Zealand, lecturer, 1950-56, senior lecturer in English, 1957-60, assistant to vice-chancellor, 1964-64, assistant principal, 1964—. *Military service:* Royal New Zealand Air Force, 1941-45; became flight lieutenant; received Distinguished Service Order and Virtuti Militari. *Member:* Returned Services Association, Wellington Rugby Football Union (president, 1976). *Awards, honors:* Polonia Restituta, from Government of Poland, 1968.

WRITINGS: *Scouting in New Zealand*, Boy Scouts Association, 1959; *William Strachey, 1572-1621*, University Press of Virginia, 1966.

WORK IN PROGRESS: *Piracy Off the Indian Coast, 1690-1700; Air Operations in World War II.*

* * *

CULLINEY, John L. 1942-

PERSONAL: Born August 7, 1942, in New York, N.Y.; son of Lawrence J. (a bank examiner) and Catherine (a teacher; maiden name, Gillen) Culliney; married Barbara Symroski (a teacher and marine bioligist), November 27, 1968; children: Aaron. *Education:* Yale University, B.A., 1964; Duke University, Ph.D., 1969. *Home:* 41-049 Ehukai St., Waimanalo, Hawaii 96795.

CAREER: Harvard University, Cambridge, Mass., research fellow at Museum of Comparative Zoology, 1970-75; Marine Biological Laboratory, Woods Hole, Mass., researcher on the development of marine invertebrates, 1972-76. *Member:* American Association for the Advancement of Science, National Audubon Society, Sanibel-Captiva Conservation Foundation.

WRITINGS: *The Forests of the Sea*, Sierra Club, 1976. Contributor to scientific journals.

WORK IN PROGRESS: *The New Underwater Explorer* (tentative title), on techniques and evocations of diving in several areas surrounding North America; *The Sherpas of Summer*, a novel about backpacking in New England; books about New England and the sea and Hawaii and the sea, "a blending of ancient and modern natural and human history."

SIDELIGHTS: Culliney, as consultant to the Seacoast Anti-Pollution League of New Hampshire and the Society for the Protection of New Hampshire Forests, has spent the last four years involved in legal battles against the siting of a twenty-two hundred megawatt nuclear power plant in that area. He writes: "The environment turns me on. The invironment is the sine qua non. Beside environmental quality, the short-range issues are child's play: silly ideological disputes, war games, the plight of the cities—we are busy shoring up sand castles after the tsunami warning has sounded. Perhaps the cities will make interesting fossils for someone or something to ponder, but they better be quick. Will the Big Apple remain identifiable as long as Brontosaurus has? I doubt it. My misanthropic moods are getting worse. Do I love mankind less or the miraculous evolution which produced us more? Perhaps there will be another go-round. Somewhere some small intelligence will survive (porpoise or squid?), and will grow in wisdom through the eons. But why take a chance?"

* * *

CUNNINGHAM, Imogen 1883-1976

April 12, 1883—June 24, 1976; American photographer. Obituaries: *New York Times*, June 26, 1976; *Washington Post*, June 26, 1976; *Time*, July 5, 1976.

* * *

CURE, Karen 1949-

PERSONAL: Born June 17, 1949, in Chicago, Ill.; daughter of Charles William (a physician) and Eloise (Greer) Cure. *Education:* Brown University, A.B., 1971; Columbia University, graduate study, 1976—. *Home and office:* 365 West End Ave., New York, N.Y. 10024.

CAREER: *Holiday* (magazine), Indianapolis, Ind., associate editor, 1971-73; free-lance writer, 1973—.

WRITINGS: *Mini-Vacations U.S.A.*, Follett, 1976. Contributor to magazines and newspapers, including *Better Homes and Gardens, Apartment Life, Diversion, Travel and Leisure, Vista U.S.A., Newsday, American Home*, and *Vacation Ideas.*

WORK IN PROGRESS: A travel catalog of the United States, Canada, and the Caribbean, for Holt.

SIDELIGHTS: Karen Cure writes: "For the most part I have done service-oriented travel pieces; my aim has always been to motivate people to go out and explore the places that I've enjoyed, and to give them enough information to keep from running down too many blind alleys. I also want to make sure that they don't miss anything they ought to see."

* * *

CURRY, Windell
See SUJATA, Anagarika

* * *

CURTIS, Lewis Perry 1900-1976

November 30, 1900—April 8, 1976; American historian, educator, and author of books in his field. Obituaries: *New York Times*, April 9, 1976; *AB Bookman's Weekly*, May 31, 1976. (*CAP*-2; earlier sketch in *CA*-23/24)

* * *

CUTLER, Charles L(ocke, Jr.) 1930-

PERSONAL: Born September 8, 1930, in Springfield, Mass.; son of Charles L. (a manufacturer) and Annie (Harris) Cutler; married Katharine Church, July 7, 1962; children: Charles L. III, Pamela. *Education:* Harvard University, student, 1948-53; University of California, Berkeley, B.A., 1954; University of Edinburgh, graduate study, 1954-55; Springfield College, M.Ed., 1956. *Politics:* Republican. *Religion:* Christian. *Home address:* Cider Mill Rd., Rockfall, Conn. 06481. *Office:* Xerox Education Publications, 245 Long Hill Rd., Middletown, Conn. 06457.

CAREER: Prentice-Hall, Inc., Englewood Cliffs, N.J., production editor, 1956-58; Xerox Education Publications, Middletown, Conn., editor, 1959—. Member of board of directors of Levi E. Coe Library. *Member:* Mensa, Middletown Judo Club.

WRITINGS: *Connecticut's Revolutionary Press*, Pequot Press, 1975. Contributor to *American Heritage* and *American History Illustrated.*

WORK IN PROGRESS: A book on "dynamic centenarians, dealing with the persistence of skills and ability into extreme old age."

SIDELIGHTS: Cutler writes: "For more than twelve years I've been preoccupied with people who continue to be vital and active though extremely old. I shall soon produce a manuscript—complete with numerous case studies—examining these people, their achievements, and the sources of their vitality." *Avocational interests:* Writing haiku.

* * *

CUTRIGHT, Paul Russell 1897-

PERSONAL: Born March 18, 1897, in Lorentz, W.Va.; son of Dennis Monroe (a physician) and Harriet Eva (a teacher; maiden name, Brooks) Cutright; married Gladys Marshall

Pennington, December 25, 1922; children: Paul Russell, Jr. *Education:* West Virginia University, A.B., 1921, A.M., 1923; University of Pittsburgh, Ph.D., 1932. *Politics:* Republican. *Religion:* Presbyterian. *Home:* 312 Summit Ave., Jenkintown, Pa. 19046.

CAREER: Geneva College, Beaver Falls, Pa., professor of biology and chairman of department, 1923-29; University of Pittsburgh, Pittsburgh, Pa., instructor in zoology, 1929-33; Beaver College, Glenside, Pa., professor of biology and chairman of department, 1933-64; writer, 1964—. Has conducted research on the Dry Tortugas Islands and in the Canal Zone. *Military service:* U.S. Army, Corps of Engineers, served with American Expeditionary Force, 1918.

MEMBER: American Association for the Advancement of Science (fellow), Sigma Xi, Phi Sigma Kappa Alpha. *Awards, honors:* Teaching award from Lindback Foundation, 1962; achievement award from Lewis and Clark Trail Heritage Foundation, 1974.

WRITINGS: The Great Naturalists Explore South America, Macmillan, 1940; *Theodore Roosevelt the Naturalist,* Harper, 1956; *Meriwether Lewis: Naturalist,* Oregon Historical Society, 1968; *Lewis and Clark: Pioneering Naturalists,* University of Illinois Press, 1969; *A History of the Lewis and Clark Journals,* University of Oklahoma Press, 1976. Contributor to history journals and to *American Heritage.*

WORK IN PROGRESS: A biography of Elliott Coues, with Michael J. Brodhead.

*   *   *

CZERNY, Peter G(erd) 1941-

PERSONAL: Born May 14, 1941, in Guben, Germany; came to the United States in 1953, naturalized citizen, 1960; son of Walter (a carpenter) and Helene (Platzke) Czerny. *Education:* University of Utah, B.A., 1970. *Religion:* Church of Jesus Christ of Latter-day Saints (Mormons). *Home:* 951 Wilson Ave., Salt Lake City, Utah 84105. *Office address:* P.O. Box 1307, Provo, Utah 84601.

CAREER: Church of Jesus Christ of Latter-day Saints, missionary in Austria, 1961-63; Brigham Young University, Provo, Utah, supervising film editor at Motion Picture Studio, 1970-76, part-time faculty member in department of communications, 1974-75. Has worked as radio broadcaster. *Military service:* U.S. Army, 1963-65. *Member:* Utah State Historical Society, Beethoven-House Society (Bonn, Germany). *Awards, honors:* Cine Golden Eagle award, 1974, for educational film "Cipher in the Snow," and Cindy Blue Ribbon award, 1975, for educational film "A Different Drum," both of which he edited.

WRITINGS: The great Great Salt Lake, Brigham Young University Press, 1976. Contributor to *Ensign.*

WORK IN PROGRESS: Research for *Johnston's Army and the Utah War;* research on music of Beethoven that is unperformed or only rarely performed.

SIDELIGHTS: Czerny was a child when his parents escaped from East Germany and emigrated to the United States.

*   *   *

DABKIN, Edwin Franden 1898(?)-1976

1898(?)—March 26, 1976; American magazine editor, public relations executive, and author. Obituaries: *New York Times,* March 29, 1976; *AB Bookman's Weekly,* June 28, 1976.

DAHL, Nils A(lstrup) 1911-

PERSONAL: Born June 25, 1911, in Oslo, Norway; resident alien in United States; son of Theodor (a minister) and Sigrid (Aars) Dahl; married Birgit Rosencrantz, June 26, 1939; children: Eva. *Education:* University of Oslo, student, 1929-34, Dr.theol., 1941; graduate study at universities of Tuebingen and Marburg, 1935-36, and universities of Leipzig, Strasbourg, and Lund, 1937-38. *Religion:* Lutheran (Church of Norway). *Home:* 38 Broadfield Rd., Hamden, Conn. 06517. *Office:* Yale University Divinity School, New Haven, Conn. 06520.

CAREER: University of Oslo, Oslo, Norway, lecturer, 1938-43, 1945-46, professor of New Testament, 1946-65, dean of faculty of theology, 1954-59; Yale University, Divinity School, New Haven, Conn., professor, 1965-75, Buckingham Professor of New Testament Criticism and Interpretation, 1974—. Chairman, Norwegian Student Christian Movement, 1946-53; member, Lutheran World Federation Commission on Theology, 1957-69. *Member:* American Academy of Religion, Society of Biblical Literature, Studiorum Novi Testamenti Societas, Det Norske Videnskaps-Akademi i Oslo, Norwegian Bible Society (board member and consultant, 1950-65). *Awards, honors:* Dr.theol. from University of Heidelberg, 1963, and University of Lund, 1968.

WRITINGS: Apostelen Paulus' hoisang om kjaerligheten (title means "The Apostle Paul's Canticle of Love, I Corinthians 13"), Groendahl (Oslo), 1936; *Das Volk Gottes: Eine Untersuchung zum Kirchenbewusstsein der Urchristentums* (title means "The People of God: A Study of Church Consciousness in Early Christianity"), Det Norske Videnskaps-Akademi (Oslo), 1941, reprinted with new preface, Wissenschaftliche Buchgesellschaft (Darmstadt), 1963; *Matteusevangeliet* (lecture notes; title means "The Gospel of Matthew"), two volumes, Universitetsforlaget, 1949; *Rett laere og kjetterske meninger* (essays; title means "Right Doctrine and Heretical Opinions"), Land og kirke, 1953; (editor with A. S. Kapelrud) *Interpretationes ad Vetus Testamentum pertinentes* (title means "Interpretations Pertaining to the Old Testament"), S. Mowickel missae, Fabritius (Oslo), 1955; (with H. Dietzfelbinger and others) *Kurze Auslegung des Epheserbriefes* (title means "Short Exposition of the Epistle to the Ephesians"), Vandenhoeck & Ruprecht, 1965, revised edition published as *Et kall: Bibelstudium over Efeserbrevet* (title means "A Call: Bible Study on the Epistle to the Ephesians"), Land og kirke, 1966; *The Crucified Messiah and Other Essays,* Augsburg, 1974; *Jesus in the Memory of the Early Church* (essays), Augsburg, 1976.

Contributor of articles to journals and festschriften. Editor and contributor, *Norsk Kirkeblad,* 1954-57.

SIDELIGHTS: Dahl is a Norwegian citizen who returns to Scandinavia every year. *Avocational interests:* Travel (has visited Western Europe, Estonia, Poland, Greece, U.S.S.R., Israel, Tanzania, and Virgin Islands).

*   *   *

DAHL, Robert Alan 1915-

PERSONAL: Born December 17, 1915, in Inwood, Iowa; son of Peter Ivor and Vera (Lewis) Dahl; married Mary Louise Bartlett, June 20, 1940 (died June, 1970); married Ann Sale Barber, May 26, 1973; children: (first marriage) Ellen Kirsten, Peter Bartlett, Eric Lewis, Christopher Robert. *Education:* University of Washington, Seattle, A.B., 1936; Yale University, Ph.D., 1940. *Home:* 17

Cooper Rd., North Haven, Conn. 06473. *Office:* Department of Political Science, Yale University, New Haven, Conn. 06473.

CAREER: Management analyst in Office of the Secretary, U.S. Department of Agriculture, 1940; economist in Office of Production Management, 1941, and on War Production Board, 1942; Yale University, New Haven, Conn., instructor, 1946-47, assistant professor, 1948-52, associate professor, 1953-57, Ford Research Professor, 1957, Eugene Meyer Professor of Political Science, 1957-63, Sterling Professor of Political Science, 1963—, chairman of department, 1957-62. Walgreen lecturer at University of Chicago, 1954; lecturer in Chile, 1967. Fellow of Center for the Advanced Study of the Behavioral Sciences, 1955-56, 1967. Member of U.S. Group Control Council in Germany, 1945; consultant to U.S. Department of State. *Military service:* U.S. Army, 1943-45; became first lieutenant; received Bronze Star Medal with oak leaf cluster.

MEMBER: American Civil Liberties Union, American Academy of Arts and Sciences (fellow), American Philosophical Society (fellow), National Academy of Sciences (fellow), American Political Science Association (president, 1966-67), Center for Studies in Advanced Behavioral Sciences (member of board of trustees), British Academy of Arts and Sciences (corresponding member), Southern Political Science Association, New England Political Science Association (president, 1951), Phi Beta Kappa.

AWARDS, HONORS: Guggenheim fellowship, 1950-51; Woodrow Wilson prize from American Political Science Association, 1961, Talcott Parsons Prize for Social Science from the American Academy of Arts and Sciences, 1977.

WRITINGS: Congress and Foreign Policy, Harcourt, 1950; (with Ralph S. Brown, Jr.) *Domestic Control of Atomic Energy* (pamphlet), Social Science Research Council, 1951; (editor) *The Impact of Atomic Energy,* American Academy of Political and Social Science, 1953; (with Charles E. Lindblom) *Politics, Economics, and Welfare: Planning and Politico-Economic Systems Resolved into Basic Social Processes,* Harper, 1953; *A Preface to Democratic Theory,* University of Chicago Press, 1956; *A Critique of the Ruling Elite Model,* Bobbs-Merrill, 1958; (with Mason Haire and Paul F. Lazarsfeld) *Social Science Research on Business: Product and Potential,* Columbia University Press, 1959.

Who Governs?: Democracy and Power in an American City, Yale University Press, 1961; *Modern Political Analysis,* Prentice-Hall, 1963, 3rd edition, 1976; (editor) *Political Oppositions in Western Democracies,* Yale University Press, 1966; *Pluralist Democracy in the United States: Conflict and Consent,* Rand McNally, 1967, 2nd edition published as *Democracy in the United States: Promise and Performance,* 1972, 3rd edition, 1976; *After the Revolution?: Authority in a Good Society,* Yale University Press, 1970; *Polyarchy: Participation and Opposition,* Yale University Press, 1971; *Regimes and Opposition,* Rand McNally, 1971; (with Edward R. Tufte) *Size and Democracy,* Stanford University Press, 1973; *Regimes and Oppositions,* Yale University Press, 1974.

WORK IN PROGRESS: Research on essential conditions, characteristics, and consequences of democratic political orders.

SIDELIGHTS: Dahl's books have been published in French, Italian, Portuguese, Spanish, Japanese, German, and Norwegian.

DALLAS, Ruth 1919-

PERSONAL: Born September 29, 1919, in Invercargill, New Zealand; daughter of Francis Sydney (a businessman) and Minnie Jane (Johnson) Mumford; *Education:* Attended Southland Technical College, Invercargill, New Zealand. *Home:* 448 Leith St., Dunedin, New Zealand.

CAREER: Poet and children's writer. Began to write as a child for the children's page of the *Southland Daily News* (now *Southland Times*), 1932. *Member:* P.E.N. (New Zealand). *Awards, honors:* New Zealand Literary Fund achievement award, 1963, for *The Turning Wheel;* Robert Burns fellow at Otago University, 1968.

WRITINGS—Poetry; published by Caxton Press: *Country Road and Other Poems,* 1953; *The Turning Wheel,* 1961; *Day Book: Poems of a Year,* 1966; *Shadow Show,* 1968; *Walking on the Snow,* 1976.

Children's fiction: *Ragamuffin Scarecrow,* Bibliography Room, Otago University, 1969; *The Children in the Bush,* Methuen, 1969; *A Dog Called Wig,* Methuen, 1970; *The Wild Boy in the Bush,* Methuen, 1971; *The Big Flood in the Bush,* Methuen, 1972; *The House on the Cliffs,* Methuen, 1975.

Poems included in anthology, *Ten Modern New Zealand Poets,* Longman, 1974. Contributor to literary quarterlies, including *Landfall,* 1947—, *Meanjin,* 1964—, *Islands,* 1973—, and to school journals.

WORK IN PROGRESS: Song for a Guitar, poems, for publication by Otago University Press; a children's historical novel set in New Zealand; and short stories for use in schools.

SIDELIGHTS: Ruth Dallas' great-grandparents and grandparents were early settlers in New Zealand, landing at Lyttelton from England in 1851 and 1959, and at Port Chalmers from Scotland and Sweden in 1873. All stayed in the new country and Ruth Dallas grew up in the extreme south of the South Island, where, she says, "we enjoyed the ancient solitary peace of the earth, and where the sheer magnitude of the sky and sea seemed to dwarf human beings to insignificance." As a child she could not find any books about New Zealand children and vowed that when she grew up she would write some; but in writing about New Zealand children she found she had written for children everywhere as her books have been translated into other languages, such as German, Danish, and Swedish, and widely distributed in the English speaking world.

She is deeply rooted in her own country, writes about it and the people who live in it, and is also interested in the culture of Asia as well as Europe. She has been much influenced by Chinese and Japanese poetry and the philosophy of the East. In an autobiographical essay in *Landfall 76* she states, "although we had inherited a European culture, in the antipodes, I could not see why we should not be at liberty to explore others, especially when, to return to the roots of our own, we had to go past our nearer neighbours geographically."

BIOGRAPHICAL/CRITICAL SOURCES: Landfall 76, December, 1965; *Ten Modern New Zealand Poets,* Longman, 1974; *Review* (annual of Otago University), 1975.

*   *   *

DANIELS, Les(lie Noel III) 1943-

PERSONAL: Born October 27, 1943, in Danbury, Conn.; son of Leslie Noel, Jr. (a copywriter) and Eva (Ruppaner)

Daniels. *Education:* Brown University, B.A., 1965, M.A., 1968. *Residence:* Providence, R.I. *Agent:* Max Gartenberg, 331 Madison Ave., New York, N.Y. 10017.

CAREER: Musician, composer, and writer. Formerly associated with the musical group "Soop."

WRITINGS: Comix: A History of Comic Books in America, Outerbridge & Dienstfrey, 1971; *Living in Fear: A History of Horror in the Mass Media,* Scribner, 1975; (editor) *Dying of Fright: Masterpieces of the Macabre,* Scribner, 1976; (editor) *Thirteen Tales of Terror* (textbook), Scribner, 1976.

WORK IN PROGRESS: A Castle in Spain (tentative title), a novel with a supernatural theme and a medieval setting.

*   *   *

DANZIG, Fred P(aul) 1925-

PERSONAL: Born September 17, 1925, in Springfield, Mass.; son of Philip (a businessman) and Sylvia (Levine) Danzig; married Edith S. Goret (a credit manager), March 16, 1952; children: Steven, Ellen Kay. *Education:* New York University, B.A., 1949. *Agent:* McIntosh & Otis, 475 Fifth Ave., New York, N.Y. 10017. *Office: Advertising Age,* 708 Third Ave., New York, N.Y. 10017.

CAREER: Evening Telegram, Herkimer, N.Y., reporter, 1949-50; *Daily Item,* Port Chester, N.Y., reporter, 1950-51; United Press International, New York, N.Y., feature writer and author of columns, "Time Out" and "Television in Review," 1951-62; *Advertising Age,* New York City, executive editor, 1962—. Lecturer at New York University and Fairfield University. Chairman of Eastchester United Civic Organization; trustee of Huntley Civic Association. *Military service:* U.S. Army, Infantry, 1943-46; served in European theater; received Bronze Star, Purple Heart, Presidential Unit Citation with oak-leaf cluster, five battle stars.

WRITINGS: (With Ted Klein) *How to Be Heard: Making the Media Work for You,* Macmillan, 1974.

WORK IN PROGRESS: A book on the American news media and economic growth; research on the dynamics of the news/entertainment media.

SIDELIGHTS: Danzig told *CA:* "I am turned on by the unique dynamics of gathering news, writing (and rewriting), editing, and disseminating it, and following community responses and actions. This is the process that elevates the free press to its essential role in our nation's maturation. And it is a process that must keep the lines of communication open to all, not just the leadership elite.

I would be on guard always against those who, in the name of imposing 'order,' would lay heavy hands on our sometimes disorderly newsgathering process. Such efforts to 'regulate' a free press only upset the fragile balance that exists between the fourth estate and the community. By definition, the free press is going to be less than perfect. And this is why the compact requires the professionals within the fourth estate to be sensitive to their shortcomings and to strive to improve their performance without yielding that rare, self-correcting quality known as independence."

*   *   *

DARDIS, Tom 1926-

PERSONAL: Born August 19, 1926, in New York, N.Y.; son of Michael Gregory (an accountant) and Josephine Coletta (O'Hara) Dardis; married Jane Buckelew (a nurse), October 25, 1947; children: Anthony, Anne, Francis. *Edu-*

cation: New York University, A.B., 1949; Columbia University, M.A., 1952. *Agent:* John Cushman Associates, 25 West 43rd St., New York, N.Y. 10036.

CAREER: Avon Books, New York, N.Y., associate editor, 1952-55; Berkley Publishing Corp., New York City, executive editor, 1955-60, editor-in-chief, 1960-72; free-lance writer, 1972-74; Adelphi University, Garden City, N.Y., adjunct professor of English, 1974—. *Military service:* U.S. Army, 1943-46; became sergeant.

WRITINGS: Some Time in the Sun (nonfiction), Scribner, 1976.

Editor: *Daughters of Eve,* Berkeley Publishing, 1958; *Banned!,* Berkeley Publishing, 1961; *Banned #2,* Berkeley Publishing, 1962.

WORK IN PROGRESS: Keaton, a biography of Buster Keaton, publication by Sribners expected in 1978.

*   *   *

DAREFF, Hal 1920-
(Scott Foley)

PERSONAL: Born May 8, 1920, in Brooklyn, N.Y.; son of Barnett and Bessie (Littman) Dareff; married Gladys Wilkowitz, September 12, 1944; children: Scott, Brooks. *Education:* Attended New School for Social Research and Washington and Lee University. *Home:* 3 Colony Rd., Weston, Conn. 06880. *Office:* 45 Riverside Ave., Westport, Conn. 06880.

CAREER: Free-lance writer and editor, 1946-52; Parents' Magazine Enterprises, Inc., New York, N.Y., editor of *Children's Digest,* 1952-67; Grosset & Dunlap, Inc., New York, N.Y., editor-in-chief of juvenile and young books, 1967-69; Greenwood Press, Inc., and its affiliate Negro Universities Press, both Westport, Conn., vice-president and publisher, 1969-70; New American Library, Inc., New York, N.Y., publisher's consultant, 1970—; Hyperion Press, Inc., Westport, Conn., president and publisher, 1972—. Editorial consultant and general editor of Dell Seal Books, Dell Publishing Co., 1963-65; contributing editor to *Parents' Magazine* and *Better Family Living,* 1965-66. Critic and reviewer. *Military service:* U.S. Army, 1941-45.

MEMBER: Author's Guild, Author's League of America. *Awards, honors:* Book of the Year, Child Study Association of America, 1962, for *The First Microscope,* and 1966, for *The Story of Vietnam: A Background Book for Young People;* best books of the year list of *New York Times,* 1966, for *The Story of Vietnam: A Background Book for Young People;* best books of the year list of *Library Journal,* 1971, for *From Vietnam to Cambodia: A Background Book about the Struggle in Southeast Asia.*

WRITINGS—All juveniles; all published by Parents' Magazine Press: *The First Microscope,* 1962; (under pseudonym Scott Foley) *Man in Orbit,* 1962; *Jacqueline Kennedy: A Portrait in Courage,* 1965; *Fun with ABC and 1-2-3: An Alphabet and Counting Book in Rhyme,* 1965; *The Story of Vietnam: A Background Book for Young People,* 1966, revised edition published as *The Story of Vietnam: A Background Book on the War in Southeast Asia,* 1971; *From Vietnam to Cambodia: A Background Book about the Struggle in Southeast Asia,* 1971.*

*   *   *

DART, John 1936-

PERSONAL: Born August 4, 1936, in Peekskill, N.Y.; son

of Seward H. (an engineer) and Vella (Haverstock) Dart; married Gloria J. Walker, August 31, 1957; children: Kim, John, Randall, Christoper. *Education:* University of Colorado, B.A., 1958; Stanford University, graduate study, 1973-74. *Office: Los Angeles Times,* Times-Mirror Sq., Los Angeles, Calif. 90053.

CAREER: United Press International, Los Angeles, Calif., staff writer, 1962-65; Caltech News Bureau, Pasadena, Calif., science writer, 1966-67; *Los Angeles Times,* Los Angeles, Calif., religion writer, 1967—. Assistant professor at California State University, Northridge, autumn, 1975. *Military service:* U.S. Army, Security Agency, 1958-62. *Member:* Society of Professional Journalists (member of board of directors of Los Angeles chapter, 1975-77; president, 1976). *Awards, honors:* Professional journalism fellowship from the National Endowment for the Humanities, 1973-74.

WRITINGS: The Laughing Savior, Harper, 1976. Contributor of articles to *National Catholic Reporter;* translator of Russian sports news for magazines, including *World Tennis* and *Swimming World.*

SIDELIGHTS: Dart told *CA:* "While covering religion news for the *Los Angeles Times,* I did a few stories on the discovery of Gnostic religious manuscripts in Egypt. While comparable in importance to the Dead Sea Scrolls, the Nag Hammadi Gnostic library was not described in any updated, popular book for the layman. With the aid of a professional journalism fellowship at Stanford, I was able to do the needed research for my first book, *The Laughing Savior.* If I have a special interest worth noting, it would be the strange interplay between religion and laughter."

* * *

DARVEAUX, Terry A(lan) 1943-

PERSONAL: Born May 23, 1943, in Buffalo, N.Y.; son of Francis V. (employed by General Motors) and Mona (Schmelzel) Darveaux; married Joyce E. Rumsey, August 3, 1963 (deceased); children: Cheri, Thomas, Jacquilyn. *Education:* State University of New York College at Geneseo, B.S., 1965, M.S., 1967. *Politics:* Republican. *Residence:* Henrietta, N.Y. *Office:* Manufacturers Hanover Trust—Central New York, 183 Main St. E., Rochester, N.Y. 14603.

CAREER: Public school teacher in Rochester, N.Y., 1965-66; Lincoln First Bank of Rochester, Rochester, N.Y., training officer, 1967-74; Manufacturers Hanover Trust—Central New York, Rochester, N.Y., vice-president, 1974—. *Member:* American Institute of Banking, National Society for Programmed Instruction, American Society for Training and Development, Genesee Region Council on Economic Education (treasurer), Genesee Valley Programming Society (chapter president), Phi Delta Kappa, Kappa Delta Pi.

WRITINGS: The Economics of Consumer Education (of "Gale Information Guide Library"), Gale, 1976.

* * *

DAUER, Rosamond 1934-

PERSONAL: Born June 29, 1934, in New York, N.Y.; daughter of R. Sterling Mueller (a surgeon) and Edith Louise (a businesswoman; maiden name, Welleck) Greenman; married John A. Dauer, Jr. (in leather business), December 8, 1962; children: Christian John, Matthew John. *Education:* Middlebury College, B.A., 1956; Columbia University,

M.A., 1957. *Home and office:* 90 Olmstead Lane, Ridgefield, Conn. 06877. *Agent:* A. Watkins, Inc., 77 Park Ave., New York, N.Y. 10016.

CAREER: Colby-Sawyer College, New London, N.H., member of staff in English department, 1957-61; *Encyclopedia Americana,* New York, N.Y., editor, 1961-62; Staten Island Institute of Arts and Sciences, Staten Island, N.Y., curator of education, 1962-63; poet and writer, 1963—. Vice-president of Staten Island Council on the Arts, 1973-75.

WRITINGS—For children: *Bullfrog Grows Up,* Greenwillow Books, 1976; *Mrs. Piggery Snout,* Harper, 1977; *Bullfrog Builds a House,* Greenwillow Books, in press; *My Friend, Jasper Jones,* Parents' Magazine Press, in press. Contributor of poems to national periodicals.

WORK IN PROGRESS: An adult book of poems.

* * *

DAVEY, Frank
  See DAVEY, Frankland Wilmot

* * *

DAVEY, Frankland Wilmot 1940-
  (Frank Davey)

PERSONAL: Born April 19, 1940, in Vancouver, British Columbia, Canada; married Helen Simmons, 1962 (divorced, 1969). *Education:* University of British Columbia, B.A. (honours), 1961, M.A., 1963; University of Southern California, Los Angeles, Ph.D., 1968.

CAREER: Sir George Williams University, Montreal, Quebec, writer-in-residence, 1969-70; assistant professor at Royal Roads Military College, Victoria, British Columbia. *Awards, honors:* Macmillan prize for poetry, 1962; Canada Council fellowship, 1966.

WRITINGS—All poetry: *D-Day and After,* Rattlesnake Press for Tishbooks, c. 1962; *City of the Gulls and Sea,* privately printed, 1964; (under name Frank Davey) *Bridge Force,* Contact Press, 1965; *The Scarred Hull,* Imago, 1966; (contributor) L. Dudek and M. Gnarowski, editors, *The Making of Modern Poetry in Canada,* Ryerson Press, 1967; (contributor) *Black Mountain College: A Book of Documents,* M.I.T. Press, 1969; *Four Myths from Sam Perry,* Talonbooks, 1969; (contributor) John Robert Colombo, editor, *How Do I Love Thee: Sixty Poets of Canada (and Quebec) Select and Introduce Their Favourite Poems from Their Own Work,* M. G. Hurtig, 1970; (under name Frank Davey) *King of Swords,* Talonbooks, 1972.

Represented in anthologies, including *Poesie/Poetry 64,* Ryerson Press, 1963; *Fifteen Winds,* edited by A. W. Purdy, Ryerson Press, 1969; *New Generation of Poets,* Black Sun Press, 1969. Contributor of poetry to *Tish* and *Evidence;* contributor of articles to *Tamarack Review.*

* * *

DAVIDSON, Harold G(ordon) 1912-

PERSONAL: Burn July 22, 1912, in Winnipeg, Manitoba, Canada; son of William James (a builder) and Ethyl (Strachan) Davidson; married Annette Nita Nautiv (an executive secretary), July 15, 1939; children: Carol Joan (Mrs. Sanford C. Williams). *Education:* Attended technical high school in Winnipeg, Manitoba. *Home and office:* 4573 Nueces Dr., Santa Barbara, Calif. 93110.

CAREER: Richardson Brothers Art Gallery, Winnipeg, Manitoba, fine art salesman, 1929-41; International Business

Machines (IBM), Toronto, Ontario, field engineer, 1941-42, field engineer in Ottawa, Ontario, 1942-48; Santa Barbara Medical Clinic, Santa Barbara, Calif., data processing manager, 1949-68; Santa Barbara City College, Santa Barbara, Calif., instructor and assistant to head of computer science department, 1968-71; writer, 1971—. Owner and operator of Western Art Gallery, Santa Barbara, Calif., 1962—. *Member:* Santa Barbara Corral of the Westerners. *Awards, honors:* Co-founders award from Westerners International, 1974, Western Heritage award from National Cowboy Hall of Fame and gold medal from National Academy of Western Art, both 1975, all for *Edward Borein, Cowboy Artist.*

WRITINGS: (Assistant compiler with Warren R. Howell) John Galvin, *The Etchings of Edward Borein,* John Howell, 1971; *Edward Borein, Cowboy Artist,* Doubleday, 1974. Also author of biography, *Jimmy Swinnerton, Lover of the Desert,* as yet unpublished.

SIDELIGHTS: Davidson has spent several years and several thousand dollars restoring, with his own hands, a dilapidated old tented circus wagon, originally built in 1915, last used in 1936. His interest in circuses consumes much of his time, and he has a large collection of books and memorabilia on the American circus, which, one day, will become part of the library at Santa Barbara City College. He also has an extensive collection of Western American art, paintings, etchings, and memorabilia. *Avocational interests:* Western history, hockey and football (in 1939 he played football on Canada's Grey Cup championship team).

BIOGRAPHICAL/CRITICAL SOURCES: Santa Barbara News Press, October 8, 1972, July 24, 1975.

*   *   *

DAVIES, Stan Gebler   1943-

PERSONAL: Born July 16, 1943, near Dublin, Ireland; son of Max (an entrepreneur) and Olive (Gebler) Davies; married Jan Collins, June 11, 1966 (divorced); children: Clancey (daughter). *Education:* Educated in Ireland and Canada. *Politics:* "Conservative libertarian." *Religion:* "Mozart." *Agent:* Stephanie Bennett, 140 West 30th St., New York, N.Y. 10001.

CAREER: Free-lance journalist in London, 1964-74. Worked as diarist on *London Evening Standard,* and as theater critic and feature writer for British newspapers and magazines. Writer, 1974—. *Member:* National Union of Journalists.

WRITINGS: (With Zsuzsi Roboz) *Chichester Ten,* Davis-Poynter, 1975; *James Joyce: A Portrait of the Artist,* Davis-Poynter, 1975, Stein & Day, 1976; (with Robin Moore) *The Kaufmann Snatch,* Concord Books, 1976. Also author of two plays as yet unpublished and unproduced. Contributor of articles to *Harper's, Queen,* and *Punch.*

WORK IN PROGRESS: Ballet Mecanique, a novel set in Paris, 1923; research on American composer George Antheil.

SIDELIGHTS: Stan Davies described himself for *CA:* "Motivation: money. Have expensive tastes—like pretty women, drink, food, travel. Wish to buy Georgian mansion in south-west of Ireland. Wish to be produced on stage, in films, for all the usual reasons. Stagestruck, music-struck. Bitterly regret that I did not write Die Meistersinger and Die Zauberflote . . . have taken up writing thrillers for fun and profit."

DAVIS, Daphne

OFFICE: American Home, 641 Lexington Ave., New York, N.Y. 10022.

CAREER: Rags (magazine), New York, N.Y., co-founder and editor, 1970-71; *Women's Wear Daily,* New York City, reporter and movie-music reviewer, 1971-74; *New York,* New York City, consulting editor, 1973; *American Home,* New York City, contributing editor and movie reviewer, 1976—. Lecturer at Radcliffe College, 1971-72.

WRITINGS: (With Kimbal Drake) *The New York In/Out Book,* Random House, 1966; *Twenty Minute Fandangoes,* Random House, 1972; *The Passionate Shopper,* New York Magazine Press, 1974.

Co-author of teleplays "Seventh Avenue: Coming Apart at the Seams," for Public Broadcasting System, 1971, "News Front," National Educational Television, 1971, "Behind the Lines," National Educational Television, 1971, "New York Magazine Live," Manhattan Cable Television, 1973, "Good Morning New York," WABC-TV, 1973.

Contributor to magazines and newspapers, including *New York, Viva, Playgirl, Gallery, New York Times, Los Angeles Times, Village Voice* and *W.*

SIDELIGHTS: Among Daphne Davis' innovations in the publishing field are the creation of the first anti-fashion magazine (*Rags*) and editing the first "couples" issue of *New York.*

*   *   *

DAVIS, Earle (Rosco)   1905-

PERSONAL: Born January 3, 1905, in Coin, Iowa; son of David Milton and Mary Isabel (Watterson) Davis; married Kathrine K. Laurie, August 4, 1938; children: Nina Virginia, Joseph Scott L., Earle Rosco, Sallie K., Charles W. *Education:* Monmouth College, A.B. and B.Mus., 1927; University of Illinois, M.A., 1928; Princeton University, Ph.D., 1935. *Religion:* Episcopal. *Home:* 1711 Fairchild St., Manhattan, Kan. 66502. *Office:* Department of English, Kansas State University, Manhattan, Kan. 66504.

CAREER: Monmouth College, Monmouth, Ill., instructor in English, 1928-33; Wichita State University, Wichita, Kan., professor of English and chairman of department, 1935-49; Kansas State University, Manhattan, professor of English, 1949—, head of department, 1950—. Fulbright lecturer at University of Adelaide, 1962, and at University College of National University of Ireland, 1969-70. *Member:* Modern Language Association of America.

WRITINGS: An American in Sicily (poetry), Margent Press, 1944; (editor with William C. Hummel) *Readings for Opinion: From Literary Ideas and Attitudes,* Prentice-Hall, 1952, 2nd edition, 1960; (editor with Hummel) *Readings for Enjoyment,* Prentice-Hall, 1959; *The Flint and the Flame: The Artistry of Charles Dickens,* University of Missouri Press, 1963; *Vision Fugitive: Ezra Pound and Economics,* University Press of Kansas, 1969. Author of articles published in University of Wichita bulletins; contributor of poems and articles to magazines.

WORK IN PROGRESS: Collected poetry; studies of Jane Austen, Emily Bronte, George Eliot, Joseph Conrad, and Anthony Burgess.

*   *   *

DAVIS, Flora   1934-

PERSONAL: Born December 21, 1934, in New Jersey;

daughter of Ralph H. (an executive of a chemical company) and Marion (Smith) Ball; children: Rebecca, Jeffrey. *Education:* McGill University, B.A., 1956. *Home and office:* 620 East 20th St., Apt. 1F, New York, N.Y. 10009. *Agent:* Emilie Jacobson, Curtis Brown Ltd., 575 Madison Ave., New York, N.Y. 10022.

CAREER: Eaton's (department store), Montreal, Quebec, advertising copywriter, 1956-58; *Vogue,* London, England, assistant travel editor, 1958-59; *Vogue,* New York City, fashion copywriter, 1959-63; *Glamour,* New York City, feature writer and editor, 1963-67; free-lance writer, 1967-71; *Glamour,* feature writer and editor, 1971-74; free-lance writer, 1974—. *Member:* American Society of Journalists and Authors.

WRITINGS: Inside Intuition: What We Know About Nonverbal Communication, McGraw, 1973. Contributor to popular magazines, including *Woman's Day, Redbook, Family Health, Mademoiselle,* and *Reader's Digest.*

WORK IN PROGRESS: A book on animal communication.

SIDELIGHTS: Flora Davis writes: "Perhaps because I've been over-endowed with curiosity, I find free-lance writing a highly satisfactory way to live. It gives me the chance to pick a subject that interests me and really dig into it. I began with an interest in psychology, curious about people and the different ways they lead their lives. This has pulled me in all kinds of directions—into articles about obstetrics and meditation, about time management and biofeedback. A good subject unfolds and unfolds. However, writing also entails responsibilities. Accuracy is overwhelmingly important, but by itself it's not enough. Since in many cases objective reporting is virtually impossible, I believe it's part of the writer's responsibility to spell out her or his own prejudices and preconceptions, so that the reader can take them into account."

* * *

DAVIS, Genevieve 1928-

PERSONAL: Born April 12, 1928, in Philadelphia, Pa.; daughter of Aaron S. (a lawyer) and Sylvia (Levine) Rosenthal; married Murray B. Davis (in the import business), August 16, 1948; children: Caroline, Catherine. *Education:* Attended International School, Geneva, Switzerland, and Sorbonne, University of Paris. *Religion:* Jewish. *Home:* 2411 Briarcrest Rd., Beverly Hills, Calif. 90210. *Agent:* Jay-Garon-Brooke Associates, 415 Central Park W., #17D, New York, N.Y. 10025.

CAREER: Writer.

WRITINGS: A Passion in the Blood (novel), Simon & Schuster, 1977.

WORK IN PROGRESS: The Orsinis, a romantic historical novel; *The Transference,* a contemporary novel.

SIDELIGHTS: Genevieve Davis writes: "I write because I must. It makes me feel complete and together. I have completed two romantic novels which take place in Italy in the fifteenth and sixteenth centuries because that period fascinates me. I have the feeling of deja-vu, of having been there, almost. I made my third novel contemporary because I was afraid of being so locked in another time that I would have difficulty emerging into the here and now. I don't know why, but I feel that almost any other century is more exciting than my own."

DAVIS, George 1939-

PERSONAL: Born November 29, 1939, in West Virginia; son of Clarence, Sr. (a clergyman) and Winnie Davis; married Mary Cornelius (a secretary), August 31, 1963; children: Pamela, George. *Education:* Colgate University, B.A., 1961; Columbia University, M.F.A., 1971. *Home and office:* 40 East Sidney Ave., Mount Vernon, N.Y. 10550.

CAREER: Served in U.S. Air Force, 1961-68, leaving service as captain; *Washington Post,* Washington, D.C., staff writer, 1968-69; *New York Times,* New York, N.Y., deskman, 1969-70; Bronx Community College of the City University of New York, Bronx, N.Y., assistant professor, 1974—; president of Black Swan Enterprises (marketing firm). *Member:* Authors Guild of Authors League of America. *Awards, honors*—Military: Air Medal. Other: Awards from New York State Council on the Arts, America the Beautiful Fund, and National Endowment for the Humanities.

WRITINGS: Coming Home (novel), Random House, 1972. Contributor of articles and stories to popular magazines and newspapers, including *Black World, Essence, National Observer, Smithsonian,* and *Beauty Trade.*

WORK IN PROGRESS: A book on love, for Doubleday; a novel.

* * *

DAVIS, Horance G(ibbs), Jr. 1924-

PERSONAL: Born July 14, 1924, in Manchester, Ga.; son of Horance G. and Florence Gray (Beavers) Davis; married Marjorie Lucile Davis, June 23, 1948; children: Gregory Rawson, Jennifer Diane. *Education:* University of Florida, B.A. (high honors), 1948, M.A., 1952. *Religion:* Episcopalian. *Home and office:* 3290 Northwest 37th St., Gainesville, Fla. 32605.

CAREER/WRITINGS: Florida Times-Union, Jacksonville, reporter, 1949-50, state capitol correspondent, 1950-54; University of Florida, Gainesville, instructor, 1954-57, assistant professor, 1957-61, associate professor, 1961-65; professor of journalism, 1965—. Notable assignments include interviews with Alf Landon, Albert Sabin, Mrs. Mary Hemingway, Jim Farley, President Jimmy Carter, and Hubert Humphrey. Reporter for *Atlanta Constitution,* summers, 1959-60, and *Miami Herald,* summers, 1961, 1966. Member of editorial advisory board of *Quill;* editorial consultant for New York Times Media, Inc., 1962—. Has lectured at the Pentagon. *Military service:* U.S. Army Air Forces, 1943-46; served in Pacific theater; became first lieutenant; received Air Medal.

MEMBER: Society of Professional Journalists, National Conference of Editorial Writers, Sigma Delta Chi (former national vice-president), Kappa Tau Alpha. *Awards, honors:* National award from Sigma Delta Chi, 1963, for editorials; Sidney Hillman Award from Amalgamated Clothing Workers, 1963, for editorials; Pulitzer Prize for editorial writing, 1971; merit certificates from American Bar Association, 1972 and 1976, for editorials.

* * *

DAVIS, James Richard 1936-

PERSONAL: Born November 21, 1936, in Cleveland, Ohio; son of John Willis (a business manager) and Marion (Davidson) Davis; married Nancilee Rogos (a physical fitness instructor), June 7, 1958; children: Julianne, Annalise. *Education:* Oberlin College, A.B., 1958; Yale University, B.D.,

1961; Michigan State University, Ph.D., 1969. *Politics:* Democrat. *Home:* 10918 West 30th Pl., Lakewood, Calif. 90215. *Office:* School of Education, University of Denver, Denver, Colo. 80208.

CAREER: Pastor of United Church of Christ in Springfield, Ohio, 1961-63; Wilberforce University, Wilberforce, Ohio, instructor in religion, 1963-68, academic dean, 1965-68; University of Denver, Denver, Colo., associate professor of higher education, 1969—, associate vice-chancellor, 1975—. Visiting lecturer at Yale University, 1968-69. *Member:* American Association for Higher Education.

WRITINGS: Teaching Strategies for the College Classroom, Westview Press, 1976; *Going to College: The Study of Students and the Student Experience,* Westview Press, 1977.

* * *

DAVIS, Morton D(avid) 1930-

PERSONAL: Born May 31, 1930, in New York, N.Y.; son of Harry and Fannie (Sobol) Davis; married Gloria Steinman (a psychologist), August 18, 1963; children: Jeanne, Joshua. *Education:* Attended Illinois Institute of Technology, 1948-51; University of Colorado, A.B. (magna cum laude), 1952; University of California, Berkeley, M.A., 1956, Ph.D., 1961. *Home:* 25 Brinkerhoff Ave., Teaneck, N.J. 07666. *Office:* Department of Mathematics, City College of the City University of New York, 138th St. and Convent Ave., New York, N.Y. 10031.

CAREER: Princeton University, Princeton, N.J., research associate, 1961-63, assistant professor of mathematics, 1963-65; Rutgers University, New Brunswick, N.J., assistant professor of mathematics, 1963-65; City College of the City University of New York, New York, N.Y., associate professor of mathematics, 1965—. *Military service:* U.S. Navy, 1952-55; became lieutenant junior grade.

WRITINGS: Game Theory: A Non-Technical Introduction, Basic Books, 1970. Contributor to journals in his field. Consultant to *Mathematica,* 1962-65.

* * *

DAVIS, Suzanne
See SUGAR, Bert Randolph

* * *

DAVIS, William 1933-

PERSONAL: Born March 6, 1933, in Hanover, Germany; married Sylvette Jouclas, April 8, 1967. *Education:* Attended City of London College. *Office:* 23 Tudor St., London EC4Y OHR, England.

CAREER: London Financial Times, London, staff member, 1954-59; *Investor's Guide,* London, editor, 1959-60; *London Evening Standard,* London, financial editor, 1960-65; *Manchester Guardian,* Manchester, financial editor, 1965-68; *Punch,* London, editor, 1968—; *High Life* (in-flight magazine of British Airways), editor, 1973—. Director of City Arts Trust; broadcaster and lecturer. *Member:* Hurlingham Club (London).

WRITINGS: Three Years Hard Labour: The Road to Devaluation, Deutsch, 1968, published with a foreword by Eliot Janeway, Houghton, 1970; *Merger Mania,* Constable, 1970; *Money Talks—William Davis Translates: A Glossary of Money,* published as *The Language of Money: An Irreverent Dictionary of Business and Finance,* Houghton, 1973;

Have Expenses, Will Travel, Deutsch, 1975; *It's No Sin to Be Rich,* Osprey, 1976.

Editor of annual *Pick of "Punch,"* Hutchinson, 1969—; editor of "Punch" series, published by Hutchinson and others, including *"Punch" Book of Golf, Bedside Book,* and *Good Living Book.*

SIDELIGHTS: Davis told *CA:* "People always ask what made an economist and leading financial editor become editor-in-chief of *Punch,* the world's best-known humorous weekly. Natural progression, I tell them. I have always believed in exposing pomposity and pretence, and the business world has more than its share of it. My five books are all on various aspects of economics and business, and I write a weekly essay in *Punch* on a wide range of subjects—politics, business and the social scene. An American magazine once called me 'the poor man's Galbraith.'" Eliot Janeway, in a foreword to his first book, said that "Davis is an individualist in the great tradition of British and American reporters whose careers have personified society's defences against presumptions which are unworkable."

AVOCATIONAL INTERESTS: Drinking wine, traveling, thinking about retirement, tennis.

* * *

DAVISON, Jean 1937-

PERSONAL: Born May 25, 1937, in Spanish Fort, Miss.; daughter of Walter Leon (a heavy equipment worker) and Eva (state civil service employee; maiden name, Pettus) Jeffries; married John A. Davison (a professor of zoology), June 16, 1965; children: Jennifer Suzanne. *Education:* Louisiana College, B.A., 1959; Louisiana State University, M.A., 1963. *Residence:* Burlington, Vt. *Agent:* Emilie Jacobson, Curtis Brown Ltd., 575 Madison Ave., New York, N.Y. 10022.

CAREER: University of Georgia, Athens, instructor in English, 1963-65; free-lance writer, 1965—. *Awards, honors:* First prize in a gothic novel contest sponsored jointly by Lancer Books and *Writer's Digest,* 1972, for *The Devil's Horseman.*

WRITINGS: The Devil's Horseman (romantic suspense novel), Doubleday, 1976. Contributor of articles, stories, and crossword puzzles to magazines and newspapers, including *Good Housekeeping, TV Guide,* and *National Review.*

WORK IN PROGRESS: A romantic suspense novel, for Doubleday; a "telepathic gothic" novel, for Berkley.

SIDELIGHTS: Jean Davison told *CA:* "I have done considerable research on the assassination of President Kennedy and would like to write a book on the subject someday."

* * *

DAY, Dorothy 1897-

PERSONAL: Born November 8, 1897, in Brooklyn, N.Y.; daughter of John J. (a journalist and editor) and Grace (Satterlee) Day; married Forster Batterham, 1925 (marriage dissolved); children: Tamar Teresa. *Education:* University of Illinois, student, 1914-16. *Religion:* Roman Catholic. *Home address:* Box 33, Tivoli, N.Y. 12583. *Office: The Catholic Worker,* 36 East First St., New York, N.Y. 10003.

CAREER: Joined the International Workers of the World and began career as reporter and columnist with the Socialist *Call,* in New York in 1916-17; later worked briefly for the

Anti-Conscription League at Columbia University, then for the *Masses;* was jailed for thirty days for picketing the White House with the suffragists; worked for the *Liberator,* and for a year as a probationary nurse in Kings County Hospital, Brooklyn, N.Y., during the World War I flu epidemic; traveled to Europe and remained for a year; after returning to the United States, worked for Robert Minor, editor of the *Liberator* in Chicago, then as a writer for the New Orleans *Item;* converted to Roman Catholicism in 1927; employed for three months as a scriptwriter in Hollywood, spent six months in Mexico, and wrote for *Commonweal;* founded *Catholic Worker* with Peter Maurin, 1933, as well as the first of the "houses of hospitality" for the poor and unemployed; has continued as publisher of *Catholic Worker,* living in voluntary poverty as a pacifist leader involved with worker movement. *Awards, honors:* Laetare medal, University of Notre Dame, 1971; Melcher Book award, 1972.

WRITINGS: From Union Square to Rome, Preservation of the Faith Press, 1938; *House of Hospitality,* Sheed, 1939; *On Pilgrimage,* Catholic Worker Books, 1948; *The Long Loneliness: The Autobiography of Dorothy Day,* Harper, 1952; *Therese,* Fides, 1960; *Loaves and Fishes,* Harper, 1963; *Meditations,* selected and arranged by Stanley Vishnewski, Newman, 1970; *On Pilgrimage: The Sixties,* Curtis Books, 1972. Author of a booklet about Peter Maurin, cofounder of the *Catholic Worker,* published by the American Friends Service Committee.

SIDELIGHTS: According to John Cogley, Dorothy Day, ". . . daughter of an agnostic newspaperman, . . . was destined to become the most influential lay person in the history of American Catholicism, and it is just possible that she will be numbered among the outstanding Christians of the twentieth century, an era that for all its vaunted secularism has not lacked for saints. Whether she will finally be found in that small company the church formally recognizes as models for others, no one can yet say. But it is already clear that the Demil's Advocate has his work cut out for him. . . . She has proven her devotion to the poor by being poor herself. She has demonstrated her dedication to peace, time and time again, by going to jail. She has strengthened the cause of women, not by haranguing men but by actually leading them, in that most rigid of male monopolies, the Roman Catholic Church."

"I never considered myself a liberal—I considered myself a radical," Miss Day has said. She is an avowed pacifist and has spent time in the New York Women's House of Detention for helping lead demonstrations against an annual New York City compulsory civil defense drill. Although willing to break the law when necessary to support pacifist beliefs, Miss Day, like Gandhi, does not believe in avoiding prosecution. "Gandhi emphasized that everything should be in the open—it should be on open terms with the authorities. You should accept the penalties."

The Reverend Theodore Hesburgh has described Miss Day's role in life as "comforting the afflicted and afflicting the commfortable." Discussing her faith, Miss Day has said, "All the way to heaven is heaven. Hell is not to love anymore."

BIOGRAPHICAL/CRITICAL SOURCES: Pat Ross, editor, *Young and Female,* Random House, 1972; *New York Times,* November 8, 1976.

*   *   *

DAY, J(ohn) Laurence 1934-

PERSONAL: Born October 27, 1934, in Preston, Idaho; son of William Franklin (a telephoneman) and Edna (a writer; maiden name, Hickman) Day; married Margaret Christensen (a teacher), December 17, 1960; children: Stephanie, David. *Education:* Brigham Young University, B.A., 1959, M.A., 1963; University of Minnesota, Ph.D., 1966. *Politics:* Independent. *Religion:* Church of Jesus Christ of Latter-day Saints (Mormons). *Home:* 1017 Holiday Dr., Lawrence, Kan. 66044. *Office:* 222 Flint Hall, University of Kansas, Lawrence, Kan. 66045.

CAREER: United Press International (UPI), Buenos Aires, Argentina, foreign correspondent, 1961-62; *Minneapolis Tribune,* Minneapolis, Minn., copy editor, 1965-66; University of Kansas, Lawrence, assistant professor, 1966-70, associate professor of journalism, 1970—. Fulbright lecturer in Argentina, 1974-75; lecturer at University of Honduras, 1973, 1975. Notable assignments include, the overthrow of the Argentine Government in 1962, and the rise and fall of Isabel Peron in that country between 1974 and 1976. *Member:* Association for Education in Journalism (International Communications Division), Sigma Delta Chi, Kappa Tau Alpha. *Awards, honors:* Stephen A. Freeman Award from Northeast Conference on the Teaching of Foreign Languages, 1973, for an article on foreign language pedagogy.

WRITINGS: (With H. Ned Seelye) *The Newspaper: Mini-Culture Unit,* National Textbook Co., 1973; *The Sports Page: Mini-Culture Unit,* National Textbook Co., 1977.

Editor—All published by National Textbook Co., 1976: Renate Schulz, *The Newspaper: French Mini-Culture Unit;* Anke Culver, *The Magazine: German Mini-Culture Unit;* Helen Jorstad, *The Magazine: French Mini-Culture Unit.*

SIDELIGHTS: When asked to comment on motivation and circumstances important to his writing, Day told *CA:* "One cold July morning in Artigas, Uruguay (1956), they sent a lad to tell me that Don Ernesto was dead. I shivered as I walked down the cobblestone streets. Don Ernesto lay in the bed with a white rag tied around his head to hold his jaw closed. Dona Maria, who was eighty, was sitting up in her bed in the other room, rocking back and forth. I embraced her. 'Se fue papa, hermano,' she kept saying, 'Se fue papa.' Her son went out on the patio and picked a pomegranate and gave it to me.

In Choloma, Honduras in 1975 on a hot day in July, I stood in a thatched roof hut and watched five or six barefoot kids watch me. Hurricane Fifi had been through—literally—the previous September. 'The hurricane took everything we had,' the children's father said. He meant that the hurricane blew away their fourteen chickens and drowned their four-month old pig.

It's a cold December day in 1976 and my brain can't deal with 'your comments on motivation, circumstances, etc., important to your career,' any more than it can deal with 'Journalism 350, Reporting I Spring Semester Outline,' so I get up and go to the water fountain down the hall, and go down the stairs and check the mail for the fourth time this afternoon, and keep hoping that the garage will call and tell me my car heater's been fixed so I'll have an excuse to kill some more time walking down to pick it up.

Are those personal data illuminating enough?"

*   *   *

DEAN, Nancy 1930-

PERSONAL: Born July 19, 1930, in New York, N.Y.; daughter of Archie Leigh (a physician) and Ella (Lang)

Dean. *Education:* Vassar College, B.A., 1952; Radcliffe College, M.A., 1953; New York University, Ph.D., 1963. *Residence:* City Island, N.Y. *Office:* Department of English, Hunter College of the City University of New York, 695 Park Ave., New York, N.Y. 10021.

CAREER: Teacher of English literature and composition in high schools in Greenway, Va., 1953-55, and Arlington, Va., 1955-56; American College for Girls, Istanbul, Turkey, instructor in English, 1956-59; Vassar College, Poughkeepsie, N.Y., instructor in English, 1962; Hunter College of the City University of New York, New York, N.Y., lecturer, 1963, instructor, 1963-67, assistant professor, 1967-73, associate professor of medieval English literature and composition, 1973—.

MEMBER: International Courtly Literature Society, Mediaeval Academy of America, Modern Language Association of America, National Council of Teachers of English, American Association of University Professors, Medieval Club of New York. *Awards, honors:* Woodrow Wilson fellowship, 1962-63.

WRITINGS: In the Mind of the Writer, Canfield Press, 1973; (editor with Myra Stark) *In the Looking Glass: Contemporary Short Fiction by Women,* Putnam, 1976. Contributor to literature journals.

WORK IN PROGRESS: Short stories; a book on the structural organization of Chaucer's poetry.

* * *

DEAN, Winton Basil 1916-

PERSONAL: Born March 18, 1916, in Birkenhead, England; son of Basil (an actor and theater director) and Esther (Van Gruisen) Dean; married Thalia Mary Shaw, 1939; children: one son, two daughters (both deceased), one adopted daughter. *Education:* King's College, Cambridge, B.A., 1938, M.A., 1940. *Home:* Hambledon Hurst, Godalming, Surrey, England.

CAREER: Free-lance musicologist, 1945—. Ernest Bloch Professor of Music, University of California, Berkeley, 1965-66. *Military service:* British Navy, Naval Intelligence, 1944-45.

MEMBER: International Musicological Society, British Academy (fellow), Royal Musical Association (member of council, 1965—; vice-president, 1970—), Royal Academy of Music (honorary member), Handel Opera Society, British Arts Council (member of music panel, 1957-60), English Speaking Union.

WRITINGS: The Frogs of Aristophanes (translation of choruses to music by Walter Leigh), Oxford University Press, 1937; *Bizet,* Dent, 1948, Collier Books, 1962, 3rd edition, revised and enlarged, Dent, 1975; (with Prosper Merimee) *Carmen,* Folio Society, 1949; *Introduction to the Music of Bizet,* Dobson, 1950; *Franck,* Novello, 1951; *Hambledon versus Feathercombe, 1928-1950: The Story of a Village Cricket Match,* Metcalfe, 1951; *Puccini,* Oxford University Press, 1951; (contributor) Hubert Foss, editor, *The Heritage of Music,* Oxford University Press, 1951; *Handel's Dramatic Oratorios and Masques,* Oxford University Press, 1959; (contributor) Phyllis May Hartnoll, editor, *Shakespeare in Music,* Macmillan, 1964; *Georges Bizet: His Life and Work,* Dent, 1965; *Handel and the Opera Seria,* University of California Press, 1969; (contributor) Denis Arnold and Nigel Fortune, editors, *The Beethoven Companion,* Faber, 1971; (editor) G. F. Handel, *Three Ornamental Arias,* Oxford University Press, 1976.

Contributor to *Grove's Dictionary of Music and Musicians.* Contributor to encyclopedias, journals, and festschriften.

AVOCATIONAL INTERESTS: Cricket, shooting, naval history.

* * *

DE BONA, Maurice, Jr. 1926-

PERSONAL: Born July 25, 1926, in Chicago, Ill.; son of Maurice (a builder) and Marguerite (Reuter) De Bona. *Education:* University of California, Los Angeles, B.A., 1952. *Politics:* "Non-Partisan." *Religion:* Atheist. *Home address:* P.O. Box 8071, Mammoth Lakes, Calif. 93546. *Office address:* P.O. Box 2433, Culver City, Calif. 90230.

CAREER: U.S. Geological Survey, Sacramento, Calif., cartographer, 1952-54; design consultant in engineering, 1955—. *Military service:* U.S. Navy, hospital apprentice, 1945-46.

WRITINGS: God Rejected, Desserco Publishing, 1976.

WORK IN PROGRESS: Continuing research on differing atheistic philosophies.

SIDELIGHTS: De Bona writes that he "was prompted to write *God Rejected* after failing to find a comprehensive coverage of atheistic thought. The book . . . condenses an amazing number of aspects of atheism. Formerly one was required to read thousands of pages, many of which were not available to the general public. . . ."

* * *

de BRUYN, Monica (Jean) G(rembowicz) 1952-

PERSONAL: Surname is pronounced de-Brian; born May 12, 1952, in Chicago, Ill.; daughter of Eugene T. and Theodora A. (Pawelski) Grembowicz; married Randall K. de Bruyn, June 10, 1972. *Education:* University of Illinois, B.A., 1973. *Religion:* Roman Catholic. *Home:* 4904 Southeast Brooklyn, Portland, Ore. 97206.

CAREER: Writer and artist.

WRITINGS—Self-illustrated picture books: *Six Special Places,* Albert Whitman, 1975; *The Beaver Who Wouldn't Die,* Follett, 1975.

* * *

DECKER, Robert Owen 1927-

PERSONAL: Born November 6, 1927, in Lafayette, Ind.; son of Owen (a county employee) and Helen Dale (licensed practical nurse; maiden name, Noble) Decker; married Margaret Ann Harris (a businesswoman), May 30, 1948; children: Terry Lynn (Mrs. Marcello DeIulis). *Education:* Butler University, A.B., 1953; Indiana University, A.M., 1958; graduate study at Ripon College and University of Wyoming, both 1959; University of Connecticut, Ph.D., 1970; postdoctoral study at Changehi University, 1971. *Politics:* Republican. *Religion:* Congregationalist. *Home:* 2623 Main St., Rocky Hill, Conn. 06067. *Office:* Department of History, Central Connecticut State College, New Britain, Conn. 06050.

CAREER: History teacher in public school in LaPorte, Ind., 1956-59; Central Connecticut State College, New Britain, instructor, 1959-63, assistant professor, 1963-73, associate professor of history, 1973—. Adviser to National Endowment for the Humanities; member of Connecticut State Planning and Advisory Council. Delegate to National Conference for Social Action, 1963, 1964; founder and director of local Operation Involvement, 1967-76. Director of Inner-

City Exchange, 1970—. *Military service:* U.S. Army, 1946-48, 1950-51; became sergeant.

MEMBER: American Historical Association, Organization of American Historians, American Association of University Professors, Association for the Study of Connecticut History, New England Historical Association, Connecticut Historical Association, New London County Historical Association.

WRITINGS: The Whaling Industry of New London, Shumway, 1973; *The Whaling City: A History of New London*, Pequot Press, 1976. Contributor of articles and reviews to local magazines and newspapers.

WORK IN PROGRESS: Nathaniel Shaw, Jr.: Merchant Patriot of the American Revolution, publication expected in 1981; a history of the missionary work of the Congregational church in Hartford, Conn., 1851-1976, for Christian Activities Council, publication expected in 1978.

SIDELIGHTS: Decker writes: "I spend a great deal of my time in the inner city areas and schools. . . . Why? Because I grew up in a midwestern inner city situation in the Great Depression and feel fortunate that I was able to successfully move into a more affluent life style. I want others to know it can be done if they are willing to work and are determined to make it in our Great Society. . . . My interests in writing and history are much the same—the history of people who have overcome whatever obstacles they faced to achieve their respective goals in life. No greater challenge appears to have faced any group of Americans than that of the sea. As a result this is why my writing began with relating the story of people, especially the crewmen, during the 'age of wooden ships and iron men.'"

BIOGRAPHICAL/CRITICAL SOURCES: Hartford Times, April 25, 1971; *Accent*, April 14, 1974.

*   *   *

DEDINI, Eldon   1921-

PERSONAL: Born June 29, 1921, in King City, Calif.; son of Grutly S. (a rancher) and Oleta (a school teacher; maiden name, Loeber) Dedini; married Virginia Conroy (a painter), July 15, 1944; children: Giulio. *Education:* Hartnell College, A.A., 1942; Chouinard Art Institute, graduated, 1944. *Religion:* Episcopalian. *Home and office address:* P.O. Box 1630, Monterey, Calif. 93940.

CAREER: Salinas Index Journal and *Salinas Morning Post*, both in Salinas, Calif., staff cartoonist, 1940-41; Walt Disney Studios, Burbank, Calif., cartoonist in story department, 1944-46; *Esquire*, Chicago, Ill., staff cartoonist, 1946-50; *New Yorker*, New York, N.Y., cartoonist, 1950—. Cartoonist for *Playboy*, 1960—. *Member:* National Cartoonists Society, Cartoonists Guild (second vice-president, 1970). *Awards, honors:* Best cartoonist award from National Cartoonists Society, 1958-61, 1964.

WRITINGS: The Dedini Gallery (cartoon collection), Holt, 1961; (with Yvette de Petra) *La Clef* (self-illustrated; title means "The Key"), Holt, 1970.

Work has been represented in many anthologies, including *The Great American Cartoon Album*, edited by Bob Abel, Dodd, 1974; *The Twentieth Anniversary Playboy Cartoon Album*, Playboy Press, 1974; *The New Yorker Album of Drawings 1925-75*, Viking, 1975. Contributor to a wide variety of popular magazines, including *Punch, Collier's, Saturday Evening Post, Judge, Sports Illustrated, True, Holiday*, and *Art in America*.

WORK IN PROGRESS: Experimenting with the "be-all, end-all" cartoon concept.

SIDELIGHTS: Dedini writes: "I try first of all for a good laugh, but my main concern is the thoughts the reader is left with after the laugh. Thoughts on the inconsistencies of our lives. This edge between laughter and tragedy is where I get my satisfaction. Sometimes I can pull this off. . . . Three trips to Western Europe visiting museums and the sites and sources of it all has been and is my greatest joy."

AVOCATIONAL INTERESTS: "My vocational and avocational interests are almost identical. Cartooning first, but studying the history of painting and graphic art past and present is my daily diet."

BIOGRAPHICAL/CRITICAL SOURCES: Cartoonist Profiles, June, 1973.

*   *   *

DE GRAZIA, Sebastian   1917-

PERSONAL: Born August 11, 1917, in Chicago, Ill.; son of Alfred Joseph and Catherine Cardinale (Lupo) De Grazia; married Miriam Lund Carlson (divorced); married Anna Maria d'Annunzio di Montenevoso (divorced, 1967); children: (first marriage) Alfred Joseph III, Margherita, Sebastian, Jr.; (second marriage) Marco, Tancredi. *Education:* University of Chicago, A.B., 1938, Ph.D., 1947. *Home:* 12 Chestnut St., Princeton, N.J. 08540. *Office:* Eagleton Institute, Rutgers University, New Brunswick, N.J. 08903.

CAREER: Federal Communication Commission, Washington, D.C., member of research staff, 1941-43; University of Chicago, Chicago, Ill., assistant professor of political philosophy, 1945-50; University of Florence, Florence, Italy, visiting professor of political philosophy, 1950-52; George Washington University, Washington, D.C., senior research scientist, 1952-55; director of Metron, Inc., 1955-57; Twentieth Century Fund, New York, N.Y., director of research, 1957-62; Rutgers University, New Brunswick, N.J., professor of political philosophy at Eagleton Institute, 1962—. Visiting professor at Princeton University, 1957, University of Madrid, 1963, and John Jay College of Criminal Justice of the City University of New York, 1967-73. *Military service:* U.S. Army, Office of Strategic Services (OSS), 1943-45.

MEMBER: Institut International de Philosophie Politique, Association Internationale de Science Politique, American Political Science Association, American Society for Political and Legal Philosophy, Quadrangle Club (Chicago), Nassau Club (Princeton). *Awards, honors:* Research grants from American Philosophical Society, Social Science Research Council, and American Council of Learned Societies.

WRITINGS: The Political Community: A Study of Anomie, University of Chicago Press, 1948; *Errors of Psychotherapy*, Doubleday, 1952; *Of Time, Work, and Leisure*, Twentieth Century Fund, 1962; *Time and the Machine*, Pratt Adlib Press, 1963; (with Livio C. Stecchini) *The Coup d'Etat: Past Significance and Modern Technique*, U.S. Naval Ordnance Test Station, 1965; (editor) *Masters of Chinese Political Thought: From the Beginnings to the Han Dynasty*, Viking, 1973. Also author of *Shostakovich's Seventh Symphony: Reactivity-Speed and Adaptiveness in Musical Symbols*, 1943.

*   *   *

DEIKMAN, Arthur J(oseph)   1929-

PERSONAL: Born September 27, 1929, in New York,

N.Y. *Education:* Harvard University, B.A., 1951, M.D., 1955. *Office:* 649 Irving St., San Francisco, Calif. 94122.

CAREER: Brandeis University, Waltham, Mass., instructor in biology, 1954; Philadelphia Hospital, Philadelphia, Pa., rotating intern, 1955-56; West Haven Veterans Administration Hospital, West Haven, Conn., resident in neuropsychiatry, 1956-57; Amarillo Air Force Base, Amarillo, Tex., chief of psychiatry, 1957-58; Andrews Air Force Base Hospital, Washington, D.C., staff psychiatrist, 1958-59; Austen Riggs Center, Stockbridge, Mass., fellow in psychiatry, 1959-61, special research fellow for U.S. Public Health Service, 1961-63, associate member of research staff, 1963-68; University of Colorado, Denver, associate professor of psychiatry, 1968-71; San Francisco Community Mental Health Services, Bureau of Alcoholism, San Francisco, Calif., senior physician specialist, 1971-73, supervising physician specialist, 1973—. Instructor at University of Massachusetts, 1960; associate clinical professor at University of California, San Francisco, 1972—. Diplomate of American Board of Psychiatry and Neurology; associate member of staff at Pittsfield General Hospital (Pittsfield, Mass.), 1961-68; candidate for Western New England Institute for Psychoanalysis, 1961-68. Member of board of directors of Institute for the Study of Human Consciousness.

WRITINGS: (Contributor) Charles T. Tart, editor, *Altered States of Consciousness*, Wiley, 1969; (contributor) Robert Ornstein, editor, *The Nature of Human Consciousness*, W. H. Freeman, 1973; *Personal Freedom*, Grossman, 1976; *A Guide to Implementing the Receptive Mode*, Division of Interpretation, National Park Service, U.S. Department of the Interior, 1976. Contributor of about twenty articles and reviews to professional journals.

WORK IN PROGRESS: Psychiatry and Eastern Thought, completion expected in 1978; research on Sufism and psychiatry.

SIDELIGHTS: Deikman comments: "I am interested in making use of our rational ('scientific') skills to help develop our intuitive ('mystical') capacities. My writings attempt to make understandable the aims and procedures of mystical traditions through our knowledge of developmental psychology and our growing awareness of the severe limitations of scientific materialism. The possibility of a new alliance between East and West is emerging and needs to be facilitated."

* * *

DELANEY, Ned 1951-

PERSONAL: Born July 6, 1951, in Glenridge, N.J.; son of Nicholas Thomas (a stockbroker) and Antoinette (an artist and writer; maiden name, Barret) Delaney. *Education:* Tufts University, B.F.A., 1974; also studied at Boston Museum School and Art Institute of Boston. *Politics:* "Liberally Independent." *Home and office:* 31 Woodberry St., South Hamilton, Mass. 01982.

CAREER: Artist and writer.

WRITINGS—For children; self-illustrated: *One Dragon to Another*, Houghton, 1976; *Two Strikes Four Eyes*, Houghton, 1976; *A Worm for Dinner*, Houghton, 1977.

SIDELIGHTS: Delaney writes: "As far as writing and illustrating children's books goes—if the morals or the emotions of a character in a particular book subconsciously, or consiously, influences someone, or helps someone through some sort of crisis sometime in their life, then I feel I have done my job." *Avocational interests:* European travel,

"trying to outwit the squirrels at the birdfeeder, and battling the slugs in the garden."

* * *

DELANO, Hugh 1933-

PERSONAL: Born December 14, 1933, in Cranford, N.J.; son of Philip Ingalls (a mechanical engineer) and Margaret (Hawks) Delano; married Marylou Lyons (a registered nurse), April 9, 1958; children: Hugh P., Jonathan, Peter, Craig. *Education:* Attended Washington College, Chestertown, Md. *Home:* 6 Manor Ave., Cranford, N.J. 07016. *Office: New York Post*, 210 South St., New York, N.Y. 10002.

CAREER: Plainfield Courier-News, Plainfield, N.J., news writer, sports writer, and author of column "Sports Slants," 1956-64; *Newark News*, Newark, N.J., sports writer and author of columns "Over the Blue Line" and "College Chatter," 1964-71; *New York Post*, New York, N.Y., sports writer and author of columns "Working Press" and "Hockey Beat," 1971—. His sports writing concentrates on major league baseball, professional hockey, and college sports; he has appeared on television and radio programs. Member of National Football Foundation and National Football Hall of Fame. Selector for National Hockey League All-Star teams; former member of Heisman Football Trophy selection committee. *Military service:* U.S. Marine Corps, 1953-56; served in Philippines; became sergeant.

MEMBER: Professional Hockey Writers Association (president of New York chapter; member of board of directors of national association), Baseball Writers Association of America, National Sportscasters and Sports Writers Association, Overseas Press Club of America, Sigma Delta Chi. *Awards, honors:* Sports reporting award from New Jersey Sports Writers Association, 1965; sports column award from New Jersey Press Association, 1971, for "College Sports Chatter."

WRITINGS: (With Ken Hodge and Don Awrey) *Power Hockey*, Atheneum, 1975; *Eddie: A Goalie's Story* (biography of Eddie Giacomin), Atheneum, 1976. Contributor to *Complete Handbook of Pro Hockey* and to sports magazines and newspapers.

BIOGRAPHICAL/CRITICAL SOURCES: Stan Fischler, *Slashing!* Crowell, 1974.

* * *

de LANTAGNE, Cecile
See CLOUTIER, Cecile

* * *

DELL, Christopher 1927-

PERSONAL: Born September 26, 1927, in New York, N.Y.; son of Floyd (a novelist and poet) and B. Marie (a librarian; maiden name, Gage) Dell; married Barbara Widutis, August, 1959 (divorced August, 1967); married Kathleen Kane, November 22, 1967. children: Jerri, Kathryn, Millie Marie. *Education:* Goddard College, B.A., 1951; University of Maryland, M.A., 1956. *Politics:* Republican. *Religion:* None. *Home:* 15 Circle, Washington Grove, Md. 20880. *Office:* Congressional Research Service, Library of Congress, Washington, D.C. 20540.

CAREER: Elementary and junior high school teacher at public schools in Vermont and Massachusetts, 1951-53; Foster Associates (economic research), Washington, D.C., assistant librarian, 1957-58; Library of Congress, Congressional Research Service, Washington, D.C., analyst in history and public affairs, 1958—. *Military service:* U.S. Army, 1946-47. *Member:* Civil War Round Table of Washington, D.C., Lincoln Club of Washington, D.C., Black Employees of the Library of Congress, Ethnic Employees of the Library of Congress (treasurer).

WRITINGS: Lincoln and the War Democrats: The Grand Erosion of Conservative Tradition, Fairleigh Dickinson University Press, 1975. Contributor of articles and book reviews to *Nation* and *Washington Star-News.*

WORK IN PROGRESS: Republican Roots of the New Deal: The Grand Expansion of Liberal Tradition.

*　　*　　*

DELLINGER, David (T.) 1915-

PERSONAL: Born August 22, 1915, in Wakefield, Mass.; son of Raymond Pennington and Marie E. (Fiske) Dellinger; married Elizabeth Peterson, February 4, 1942; children: Patchen, Ray, Natasha (Mrs. Val Burd), Daniel, Michele. *Education:* Yale University, B.A. (magna cum laude), 1936; graduate study at New College, Oxford, 1936-37; Union Theological Seminary, New York, N.Y., student, 1939-40. *Office: Seven Days,* 206 Fifth Ave., New York, N.Y.

CAREER: Jube Memorial Church, Newark, N.J., associate minister, 1939-40; Libertarian Press, Glen Gardner, N.J., partner, 1946-67; *Liberation,* New York, N.Y., editor and publisher, 1956-72; writer. Coordinator, Fifth Avenue Vietnam Peace Parade Committee, 1965-72; member, Bertrand Russell War Crimes Tribunal, 1966-67; chairman, National Mobilization Commission to End the War in Vietnam, 1967-70. *Member:* International Association of Sociology Cooperatives (member of board of directors), Berzelius and The Colony Foundation, Phi Beta Kappa. *Awards, honors:* Henry fellow, 1936-37; Poynter fellow in journalism, 1969; Thomas Paine Award from Emergency Civil Liberties Union, 1970, and New Jersey American Civil Liberties Union, 1971; War Resisters League Peace Award, 1975.

WRITINGS: (Editor, and author of introduction) *In the Teeth of War: Photographic Documentary of the March 26th, 1966, New York City Demonstration against the War in Vietnam,* OAK Publications, 1966; *Revolutionary Nonviolence: Essays by Dave Dellinger,* Bobbs-Merrill, 1970; *More Power than We Know: The People's Movement toward Democracy,* Doubleday, 1976.

Contributor: Paul Goodman, editor, *Seeds of Liberation,* Braziller, 1965; Staughton Lynd, editor, *Nonviolence in America: A Documentary History,* Bobbs-Merrill, 1966; John Duffett, editor, *Against the Crime of Silence: International War Crimes Tribunal, 1967,* O'Hare Books, 1969; Walter Schneir, editor, *Telling It Like It Was: The Chicago Riots,* New American Library, 1969; Peter Babcock, editor, *Conspiracy,* Bantam, 1970; Frederick J. Streng and others, editors, *Ways of Being Religious: Readings for a New Approach to Religion,* Prentice-Hall, 1973. Contributor of articles to *Liberation, Peace News, Village Voice, Skeptic, Seven Days,* and *Humanist.*

WORK IN PROGRESS: An autobiography, *Notes from My New Childhood.*

SIDELIGHTS: Mr. Dellinger served two prison terms as a draft resistor in World War II. According to R. R. Harris, "Many will oppose Dellinger's politics, but they would do well to emulate his honesty and concern for humanity." Dellinger once said about his own motivations: "There are no comforts, no luxuries, no honors, nothing that can compare with having a sense of one's own integrity." Bruce Wasser-

stein capsulized the history of Dellinger's draft resistance this way: "Although as a minister he was eligible for an automatic exemption, Dellinger refused to register for the draft, and later spurned service in a c.o. camp. He opposed the war because he thought all war is 'evil and useless'; but he also questioned the allies' motives because they supported some fascist regimes, restricted immigration, had business deals with the Axis Powers. Massive resistance in countries like Holland were to him more meaningful than any victories won by force of arms."

"Dave Dellinger catapulted into national prominence . . ., as a member of the much publicized 'Chicago 7,'" said Stephen Clark, "but his service to the American left as editor of *Liberation* magazine and as an energetic leader of the movement for social and political revolution extends back 30 years. . . . In Dellinger's scenario of the contemporary world it is not difficult to single out the villain. Capitalism, he contends, dialectically results in and is supported by sexism, racism, war, pollution, imperialism and gross inequities of wealth and power. In spite of this strident critique of American society, Dellinger consistently strives to avoid dogma. . . . Unlike many pacifists, Dellinger unabashedly rejects reform politics, in keeping with his conviction that 'moderate (ineffective) dissent encourages the illusion that the country's goals are proper and its 'shortcomings' are being taken care of. . . .'" According to the *New Republic,* "he believes his ideas won't work without American willingness to renounce special privileges: 'Would you be willing for your son to share a standard of living somewhere between the one he is 'entitled to,' and that of an impoverished Gautemalan peasant?' Unwillingness of American liberals to face this kind of challenge is, to him, the root of their failure."

*　　*　　*

DELMAR, Vina (Croter) 1905-

PERSONAL: Born January 29, 1905, in New York, N.Y.; daughter of Charles (an actor) and Jean (Guran) Croter; married Eugene Delmar, May 10, 1921; children: Gray. *Education:* Attended public schools in New York, N.Y.

CAREER: Author. Had first short story published in 1922; worked variously as typist, switchboard operator, usher, actress, and as assistant manager of a movie theater in Harlem, N.Y.

WRITINGS—All published by Harcourt, except as indicated: *Bad Girl* (novel; Literary Guild selection), 1928; *Kept Woman* (novel), 1929; *Loose Ladies* (short stories), 1929; *Women Live Too Long,* 1932, published as *The Restless Passion,* Avon, 1947; *The Marriage Racket,* 1933; *Mystery at Little Heaven,* Times-Mirror Press, 1933; *The End of the World,* International Magazine Co., 1934; *The Love Trap* (originally titled "Yellow Rose Farm"), Avon, 1949; *New Orlean's Lady,* Avon, 1949; *About Mrs. Leslie* (novel), 1950; *Strangers in Love,* Dell, 1951; *The Marcaboth Women* (novel), 1951; *The Laughing Stranger* (novel), 1953; *Ruby,* Pocket Books, 1953; *Beloved,* 1956; *The Breeze from Camelot,* 1959; *The Big Family,* 1961; *The Enchanted,* 1965; *Grandmere* (novel), 1967; *The Becker Scandal: A Time Remembered* (autobiography), 1968; *The Freeways,* 1971; *A Time for Titans,* 1974.

Plays: *The Rich, Full Life: A Play in Three Acts,* Samuel French, 1946; *Midsummer: A Comedy in Three Acts,* Samuel French, 1954; *Warm Wednesday: A Comedy in Three Acts,* Samuel French (London), 1959, (New York), 1960. Also author of play "Make Way for Tomorrow."

Contributor of serials to magazines; author of short stories and film scripts.

SIDELIGHTS: Mrs. Delmar's novel *Bad Girl* was dramatized in 1930; her play "Make Way for Tomorrow" was produced as "The Rest Is Silence" in Moscow in 1970. Several of her stories have been filmed, and *Midsummer: A Comedy in Three Acts* was adapted for a 1958 television presentation.*

* * *

del REY, Lester 1915-
(John Alvarez, Marion Henry, Philip James, Wade Kaempfert, Henry Marion, Edson McCann, Philip St. John, Erik van Lhin, Kenneth Wright)

PERSONAL: Name originally Ramon Felipe San Juan Mario Silvio Enrico Alvarez-del Rey; born June 2, 1915, in Clydesdale, Minn.; son of Franc (a carpenter and farmer) and Jane (Sidway) del Rey; married Judy-Lynn Benjamin (a writer and science fiction editor), March 21, 1971. *Education:* Attended George Washington University, 1931-33. *Politics:* Democrat. *Home:* 160 West End Ave., New York, N.Y. 10023. *Agent:* Scott Meredith Literary Agency, 845 Third Ave., New York, N.Y. 10022.

CAREER: Writer, 1937—; McDonnell Aircraft Corp., St. Louis, Mo., sheet metal worker, 1942-44; Scott Meredith Literary Agency, New York, N.Y., author's agent, 1947-50; *Science Fiction Adventures* magazine, editor under pseudonym Philip St. John, 1952-53; *Space Science Fiction* magazine, editor, 1952-53; *Fantasy Fiction* magazine, editor, 1953; *Rocket Stories* magazine, editor under pseudonym Wade Kaempfert, 1953; *Worlds of Fantasy* magazine, editor, 1968-70; *Galaxy* magazine and *If* magazine, New York, N.Y., managing editor, 1968-69, feature editor, 1969-74; Ballantine Books, New York, N.Y., fantasy editor, 1975—. Teacher of fantasy fiction at New York University, 1972-73. *Member:* Authors Guild, Trap Door Spiders Club. *Awards, honors:* Boy's Clubs of America Science Fiction Award, 1953, for *Marooned on Mars;* Guest of Honor, World Science Fiction Convention, 1967.

WRITINGS: ... And Some Were Human, Prime Press, 1948, abridged edition, Ballantine, 1961; *It's Your Atomic Age: An Exploration in Simple Everyday Terms of the Meaning of Atomic Energy to the Average Person,* Abelard Press, 1951; (under pseudonym Edson McCann with Frederik Pohl) *Preferred Risk,* Simon & Schuster, 1955; *Nerves,* Ballantine, 1956, revised edition, 1976; (under pseudonym Erik van Lhin) *Police Your Planet,* Avalon, 1956, enlarged edition under name Lester del Rey with Erik van Lhin, Ballantine, 1975; *Robots and Changelings: Eleven Science Fiction Stories,* Ballantine, 1957; *Day of the Giants,* Avalon, 1959; *The Mysterious Earth,* Chilton, 1960.

The Mysterious Sea, Chilton, 1961; *The Eleventh Commandment,* Regency Books, 1962, revised edition, 1970; *Two Complete Novels: The Sky is Falling and Badge of Infamy,* Galaxy, reissued as *The Sky is Falling and Badge of Infamy,* Ace, 1973; *The Mysterious Sky,* Chilton, 1964; *Mortals and Monsters: Twelve Science Fiction Stories,* Ballantine, 1965; (with Paul Fairman) *The Scheme of Things,* Belmont, 1966; (with Paul Fairman) *Siege Perilous,* Lancer, 1966, published under name Lester del Rey as *The Man Without a Planet,* Lancer, 1970; *Pstalemate,* Putnam, 1971; *Gods and Golems: Five Short Novels of Science Fiction,* Ballantine, 1973; *Early del Rey,* Doubleday, 1975.

Editor and author of introduction: (With Cecile Matschat and Carl Carmer) *The Year After Tomorrow: An Anthology of Science Fiction Stories,* Winston, 1954; (with Isaac Asimov) *John W. Campbell Anthology,* Doubleday, 1973; *The Best of Frederik Pohl,* Ballantine, 1975; *The Best of C. L. Moore,* Ballantine, 1975; *Fantastic Science Fiction Art,* Ballantine, 1975; *The Best of John W. Campbell,* Ballantine, 1976.

For young readers: *A Pirate Flag for Monterey,* Winston, 1952; *Marooned on Mars,* Winston, 1952; (under pseudonym Philip St. John) *Rocket Jockey,* Winston, 1952 (published in England as *Rocket Pilot,* Hutchinson, 1955); *Attack from Atlantis,* Winston, 1953; (under pseudonym Erik van Lhin) *Battle on Mercury,* Winston, 1953; (under pseudonym Kenneth Wright) *The Mysterious Planet,* Winston, 1953; *Step to the Stars,* Winston, 1954; (under pseudonym Philip St. John) *Rockets to Nowhere,* Winston, 1954; *Mission to the Moon,* Winston, 1956; *Rockets Through Space: The Story of Man's Preparations to Explore the Universe,* Winston, 1957, revised edition, 1960; *The Cave of Spears,* Knopf, 1957; *Space Flight,* Golden Press, 1959; *Moon of Mutiny,* Holt, 1961; *Rocks and What They Tell Us,* Whitman, 1961; *Outpost of Jupiter,* Holt, 1963.

With Paul Fairman: *The Runaway Robot,* Westminster, 1965; *Tunnel Through Time,* Westminster, 1966; *Prisoners of Space,* Westminster, 1966; *Rocket From Infinity,* Holt, 1966; *The Infinite Worlds of Maybe,* Holt, 1966.

Contributor of short fiction, sometimes under pseudonyms John Alvarez, Marion Henry, Philip James, Wade Kaempfert, and Henry Marion to *Galaxy, Analog, Amazing Stories, Fantastic Universe, Fantasy and Science Fiction,* and to other periodicals. Editor, *Best Science Fiction Stories of the Year,* Dutton, 1972-76.

WORK IN PROGRESS: Science Fiction: 1926-1976, for Garland; several novels.

SIDELIGHTS: Lester del Rey told *CA:* "Professionally, I love finding a story that is well crafted and is a real story. I detest the substitution of symbolism (so-called) and pseudo-relevance for plot; and I despise the bad writing that is substituted for good under the term 'experimental writing.' I believe in telling a good story, with genuine consistency, and I consider myself rather good at helping younger writers develop the necessary skills. Above all, I like to see characters that seem to take real life—even if that life is fantastic, as in robots and mermen!"

In conjunction with his extensive background and expertise in fantasy and science fiction, del Rey says [I am] "fascinated by real science, and try to keep up with all the fields. (I bless the man who developed the calculator with functions, logs, and powers built in, so tables don't have to be consulted.)" He is also extremely interested in electronics, at which he is by his own admission, "very, very good."

Mr. del Rey went on to further describe himself and his feelings. "I've been active in politics (running a club, etc., not running for office) off and on. I love what politics could be [but] I'm not too happy with what the slackers among the voting citizens have let it become.... I guess above all I hate needless stupidity. If a man is ignorant but trying to learn, I bless him; and if he is not very bright, but is using all of his potential, I bless him doubly."

AVOCATIONAL INTERESTS: Cooking, typewriters ("including repair and modification of.... I use my own keyboard, so I have to be able to make major modifications).

DE LUNA, Frederick Adolph 1928-

PERSONAL: Born June 22, 1928, in New York, N.Y.; son of Carlos M. and Ruth (Oyer) de Luna; married Barbara L. Nielson, 1952 (divorced, 1973); married Phyllis R. Komarek Lombard, 1973; children: (stepdaughters), Cindy, Christine, Susan. *Education:* State University of Iowa, B.A., 1954, M.A., 1955, Ph.D., 1962. *Home:* 54 Hearthstone, Edmonton, Alberta, Canada T6H 5E5. *Office:* Department of History, University of Alberta, Edmonton, Alberta, Canada.

CAREER: University of Oregon, Eugene, instructor in history, 1960-62; State University of Iowa, Iowa City, visiting assistant professor of history, 1962-63; University of Alberta, Edmonton, assistant professor, 1963-68, associate professor, 1968-73, professor of English, 1973—. *Military service:* U.S. Marine Corps, 1950-52; U.S. Marine Corps Reserve, 1952-58; became sergeant. *Member:* American Historical Association, Society for French Historical Studies, Societe d'Histoire moderne. *Awards, honors:* Fulbright fellow, 1958-59.

WRITINGS: The French Republic under Cavaignac, 1848, Princeton University Press, 1969.

AVOCATIONAL INTERESTS: Tennis.

*   *   *

deMAUSE, Lloyd 1931-

PERSONAL: Born September 19, 1931, in Detroit, Mich.; son of Leon (an engineer) and Martha (a teacher; maiden name, Koren) deMause; married Gladys Brown (a teacher of dance), December 15, 1963; children: Neil. *Education:* Attended General Motors Institute, 1948-52; Columbia University, B.A., 1957, graduate study, 1957-61; National Psychological Association for Psychoanalysis, graduate study, 1957-60. *Politics:* Democrat. *Religion:* None. *Home:* 140 Riverside Dr., New York, N.Y. 10024. *Office:* Institute for Psychohistory, 2315 Broadway, New York, N.Y. 10024.

CAREER: Atcom, Inc. (publishers), New York, N.Y., founder and chairman of board, 1959—; Institute for Psychohistory, New York, N.Y., founder and director, 1974—. Instructor at New York Center for Psychoanalytic Training, 1975—. Consultant to Boston State College Center of Family Studies. *Military service:* U.S. Army, 1952-54. *Member:* International Psychohistorical Association (founder and chairman, 1976—), American Historical Association, American Anthropological Association, Association for Applied Psychoanalysis (executive-secretary, 1970-72), Mediaeval Academy of America, Phi Beta Kappa.

WRITINGS: (Editor and contributor) *The History of Childhood,* Psychohistory Press, 1974; (editor and contributor) *A Bibliography of Psychohistory,* Garland Publishing, 1975; (editor and contributor) *The New Psychohistory,* Psychohistory Press, 1975. Contributor to *Journal of Psychohistory. History of Childhood Quarterly,* founder and editor, 1973—.

WORK IN PROGRESS: The Psychogenic Theory of History.

*   *   *

DEMETZ, Peter 1922-

PERSONAL: Born October 21, 1922, in Prague, Czechoslovakia; came to United States in 1952, naturalized in 1958; son of Hans and Anna (Brod) Demetz; married Hana Mueller, April 21, 1950; children: Anne-Marie Bettina. *Education:* Charles University, Dr.Phil., 1948; Columbia University, M.A., 1954; Yale University, Ph.D., 1956. *Home:* 126 Ridgewood Ave., North Haven, Conn. 06517.

CAREER: Radio Free Europe editor, 1950-52; Yale University, New Haven, Conn., instructor, 1956-58, assistant professor, 1958-60, associate professor of German, 1960-62, professor of German and comparative literature, 1962—, chairman of department, 1963-69. *Member:* Modern Language Association of America, American Association of Teachers of German, P.E.N., Berliner Akademie der Kuenste. *Awards, honors:* Yale Morse fellow, 1959-60; Guggenheim fellow, 1965-66; Golden Goethe Medal (Germany).

WRITINGS: Goethes "Die Aufgeregten": Zur Frage der Politischen Dichtung in Deutschland, F. Nowack, 1952; *Rene Rilkes Prager Jahre,* E. Diederichs, 1953; (compiler) *Neviditelny domov: Verse exulantu, 1948-53,* Sokolova, c. 1954; *Marx, Engels und die Dichter: Zur Grundlagenforschung des Marxismus,* Deutsche Verlags-Anstalt, 1959, translation of revised and enlarged edition by Jeffrey L. Sammons published as *Marx, Engels, and the Poets: Origins of Marxist Literary Criticism,* University of Chicago Press, 1967.

(Editor and author of introduction) *Brecht: A Collection of Critical Essays,* Prentice-Hall, 1962; *Formen des Realismus: Theodor Fontane, Kritische Untersuchungen,* C. Hanser, 1964; (editor and author of documentation) Gotthold Ephraim Lessing, *Nathan der Weise,* Ullstein, 1966; (editor with W. T. H. Jackson) *An Anthology of German Literature, 800-1750,* Prentice-Hall, 1968; (editor with Thomas Greene and Lowry Nelson, Jr.) *The Disciplines of Criticism: Essays in Literary Theory, Interpretation, and History,* Yale University Press, 1968.

Kitsch, Belletristik, Kunst: Theodor Fontane, Akademie der Kuenste, 1970; *Postwar German Lieterature: A Critical Introduction,* Pegasus, 1970. Contributor of articles to professional journals.

SIDELIGHTS: Marx, Engels, und die Dichter has been translated into Spanish and Japanese.*

*   *   *

de MILLE, Agnes
See PRUDE, Agnes George

*   *   *

DENISON, Norman 1925-

PERSONAL: Born, 1925; married, 1950; children: one son, one daughter. *Education:* Cambridge University, B.A., 1949, M.A., 1952, Ph.D., 1955. *Office:* Department of Language Studies, London School of Economics and Political Science, Houghton St., Aldwych, W.C.2, England.

CAREER: University of Helsinki, Helsinki, Finland, lecturer, 1951-54; University of Wales, University College of Wales, Aberystwyth, assistant lecturer, 1954-56, lecturer, 1956; University of Glasgow, Glasgow, Scotland, lecturer, 1956-58; University of the Punjab, Lahore, Pakistan, professor, 1958-60; University of Glasgow, lecturer, 1960-63; university lecturer in Moscow, U.S.S.R., 1963-64; University of London, London School of Economics and Political Science, London, England, department of language studies, director, 1964—. *Member:* Council for National Academic Awards (chairman, Languages Board, 1971).

WRITINGS: The Partitive in Finnish, Kirjakauppa (Helsinki), 1957; (contributor) Edwin Ardener, editor, *Social Anthropology and Language,* Barnes & Noble, 1971. Contributor of articles to professional journals and collections.*

DENNIS, Charles 1946-

PERSONAL: Born December 16, 1946, in Toronto, Ontario, Canada; came to the United States in 1972; son of Samuel (a manufacturer) and Sade (Iscove) Dennis; married Catherine Grace Brendan Hickey (a designer), September 20, 1975. *Education:* University of Toronto, B.A., 1968. *Residence:* Los Angeles, Calif. *Agent:* Richard Heckenkamp, Paul Brandon & Associates, 9046 Sunset Blvd., Los Angeles, Calif. 90069.

CAREER: Toronto Telegram, Toronto, Ontario, theater and film critic, 1964-67; Colonnade Theatre, Toronto, producer and performer in his own play "Everyone Except Mr. Fontana," 1968; full-time novelist, playwright, and screenwriter, 1969—; Rangeloff-Century, Inc. (production company), Los Angeles, Calif., president, 1975—. *Member:* Authors Guild, Writers Guild of America, West.

WRITINGS: Stoned Cold Soldier (novel), Bachman & Turner, 1973; *The Next-to-Last Train Ride* (novel), Macmillan (England), 1974, St. Martin's, 1975; *The Broken Sabre Quartet* (novel series), Volume I: *This War Is Closed Until Spring,* Futura Publishing, 1975; *Somebody Just Grabbed Annie!* (political thriller), St. Martin's, 1976.

Plays: "Everyone Except Mr. Fontana" (three one-act comedies), first produced in Toronto, Ontario, at Colonnade Theatre, November 12, 1968; "Bonfire" (three-act), first broadcast on BBC-Radio, June 18, 1973; "The Alchemist of Cecil Street" (three-act comedy), first broadcast on CBC-TV, October, 1976.

Created "Marked Personal" series for Thames Television, 1973.

WORK IN PROGRESS: A Divine Case of Murder, a novel; *Kashmar,* a novel; *The Broken Sabre Quartet,* Volume II: *The Periwinkle Assault; Nikki Ever After,* a novella.

SIDELIGHTS: Dennis writes: "People used to remark of my writing when I first ventured into the area of the novel that I was weird, my mind was bent, things like 'that' didn't happen. Perhaps they were referring to my first novel *Stoned Cold Soldier* in which an all-American boy in Viet Nam wiped out his entire platoon and how a cover-up extending to the White House was attempted. I wrote that book in 1970. Lieutenant Calley and Watergate were yet to happen. . . . I like to use the basic structure of the thriller or adventure story to develop and present the bizarre and larger-than-life characters that I encounter and/or create. Characters from all the novels (and plays) spill over throughout the body of work whose chronological time encompasses 1914 to the present."

*   *   *

DENNIS, Landt 1937-

PERSONAL: Born February 7, 1937, in Oklahoma City, Okla.; son of Frank Landt (an editor for *Washington Post*) and Katherine (Wright) Dennis; married Elizabeth Jones (a photographer), September 19, 1970. *Education:* Harvard University, B.A., 1959; University of Pennsylvania, M.B.A., 1963. *Home and office:* 135 East 39th St., New York, N.Y. 10016. *Agent:* Roslyn Targ, 250 West 57th St., New York, N.Y. 10019.

CAREER: Correspondent for *Christian Science Monitor* in Boston, Mass., and New York, N.Y., 1968-71; Photo Features International, New York City, writer of column, "Travel Facts," 1972—. *Member:* Society of American Travel Writers, New York Travel Writers.

WRITINGS: Catch the Wind (nonfiction), Four Winds Press, 1976; *Collecting Photographs: A Guide to Investing in the New Art Boom,* Dutton, 1977. Contributor to *Reader's Digest, Family Circle, Essence, Signature, Travel,* and other magazines. Contributing travel editor of *Apartment Life.*

*   *   *

DENNIS, Wayne 1905-1976

September 1, 1905—July 21, 1976; American child psychologist, anthropologist, educator, and author of books in his field. Obituaries: *New York Times,* July 24, 1976. (See index for previous *CA* sketch)

*   *   *

DENNISTON, Lyle (William) 1931-

PERSONAL: Born March 16, 1931, in Nebraska; son of Earl Wilson (a grocer) and Grace (Browne) Denniston; married Elizabeth Claire Rohwer (a public relations director), January 16, 1954; children: Clark, Stuart, Alan. *Education:* University of Nebraska, B.A. (honors), 1955; Georgetown University, M.A., 1957. *Religion:* Protestant. *Home:* 5070 Fulton St. N.W., Washington, D.C. 20016. *Office: Washington Star,* 225 Virginia Ave. S.E., Washington, D.C. 20061.

CAREER: Nebraska City News-Press, Nebraska City, Neb., reporter, 1948-51; *Lincoln Journal,* Lincoln, Neb., reporter, 1951-55; *Wall Street Journal,* New York, N.Y., reporter with Washington bureau, 1957-60; Prentice-Hall, Inc., Washington, D.C., editor of newsletter, 1960-63; *Washington Star,* Washington, D.C., reporter, 1963—. Lecturer at colleges and universities. Member of executive committee of Reporters Committee for Freedom of the Press. Has appeared on television panel programs and at seminars; specialist on the law, especially the activities of the U.S. Supreme Court.

WRITINGS: The Reporter and the Law, American Bar Association-American Newspaper Publishers Association, 1977.

*   *   *

DENNY, Brian
See DOUGHTY, Bradford

*   *   *

DENZER, Ann
See WISEMAN, Ann (Sayre)

*   *   *

DERMAN, Lou 1914(?)-1976

1914(?)—February 15, 1976; American television comedy writer. Obituaries: *New York Times,* February 17, 1976; *Washington Post,* February 18, 1976.

*   *   *

DeROIN, Nancy 1934-
(Nancy Ross)

PERSONAL: Born February 11, 1934, in Washington, D.C.; daughter of John Rae (an architect) and Jane (Cupples) Ross; married Gene DeRoin (an advertising manager), September 13, 1954; children: Martin, Julie, John. *Education:* American University, B.S., 1954. *Religion:* Buddhist. *Home:* 440 West Oakdale, Chicago, Ill. 60657.

CAREER: Washington Times-Herald, Washington, D.C., reporter, 1952-54; free-lance writer and editor. Teacher at Buddhist Educational Center, Chicago, Ill., 1970-76.

WRITINGS: (Editor) Gyomay M. Kubose, *Zen Koans,* Regnery, 1973; *Jataka Tales,* Houghton, 1975. Contributor of feature articles, sometimes under name Nancy Ross, to popular magazines.

WORK IN PROGRESS: Translating with Kubose *Sukhavati-Vuyha* (title means "The Great Eternal Life Sutra"); editing Kubose's other work.

*   *   *

de ROTHSCHILD, Pauline (Fairfax-Potter)   1908(?)-1976

1908(?)—March 8, 1976; American-born designer, museum co-founder, and author. Obituaries: *New York Times,* March 9, 1976.

*   *   *

DESCHLER, Lewis   1905-1976

March 3, 1905—July 12, 1976; American parliamentarian and author. Obituaries: *Washington Post,* July 13, 1976.

*   *   *

DES GAGNIERS, Jean   1929-

PERSONAL: Born February 4, 1929, in St. Joseph de-la-Rive, Quebec, Canada. *Education:* University of Montreal, B.A., 1949; College Jean de Brebeuf, graduate study, 1951-53; Laval University, Licencie en philosophie, 1953; Ecole du Louvre, diploma in art history and archaeology, 1956. *Religion:* Roman Catholic. *Office:* Department of Greek Archaeology, Laval University, Quebec 10, Quebec, Canada.

CAREER: Laval University, Quebec, Quebec, assistant professor, 1952-62, professor of archaeology, 1962—, director of classics department, 1967—, director of excavations in Laodikeia, Turkey, 1961-64, and in Soli, Cyprus, 1964—. Member of Art Council of Canadian Scholars, 1956—; consultant to Musee du Quebec, 1966—; member of board of trustees of National Museums of Canada, 1972-76; lecturer on Greek art. *Member:* Canadian Classical Association.

WRITINGS: (Author of text) *Objects d'art grec du Louvre,* Musee du Quebec, Ministere des affaires culturelles, 1967; (with others) *Laodicee du Lycos: Le Nymphee, campagnes 1961-63,* Presses de l'Universite Laval, 1969; *L'Ile-aux-Courdes,* Lemeac, 1969; *L'Acropole d'Athenes,* Presses de l'Universite Laval, 1971; *J. M. Morrice,* Pelican, 1971.

WORK IN PROGRESS: The Pictorial Style in Cypriot Vase Painting, with V. Karageorghis, for Edizioni dell'Ateneo in Rome.

*   *   *

DESSI, Giuseppe   1909-

PERSONAL: Surname is accented on last syllable; born August 7, 1909, in Cagliari, Italy; son of Francesco and Mariacristina (Pinna) Dessi-Fugheri; married Raffaella Baraldi, December 21, 1939 (divorced, 1971); married Luisa Babini (a social worker), April 27, 1972; children: Francesco. *Education:* University of Pisa, degree in arts and philosophy, 1936. *Home:* Via Prisiano, 75, Rome, Italy 00136.

CAREER: Writer. Italian Ministry of Public Instruction,

manager of studies in Sassari, Ravenna, Teramo, and Grosseto, 1941-70, central inspector in Rome, 1970-73, general director in Rome, 1973. *Member:* P.E.N. (Italy), Sindicato Nazionale Scrittori. *Awards, honors:* Premio Salento, 1955, for *I Passeri;* Premio Puccini-Senigallia, 1957, for *Isola dell'Angelo;* Premio St. Vincent per il Teatro, 1959, for "La Giustizia"; Premio Bagutta, 1962, for *Il disertore;* Premio Strega, 1972, for *Paese d'ombre.*

WRITINGS: La sposa in citta, Guanda, 1939; *San Silvano* (novel), Le Monnier, 1939, translation by Isabel Quigley published as *The House at San Silvano,* Harvill Press, 1966.

Michele Boschino, Mondadori, 1942; *Racconti vecchi e nuovi,* Einaudi, 1945; *Storia del principe Lui* (novel), Mondadori, 1949.

I passeri (novel), Nistri-Lischi, 1955; *Isola dell'Angelo ed altri racconti,* Salvatore Sciascia, 1957; *La ballerini di carta,* Capelli, 1957; (translator) Rafael Sabatini, *La congiura di Scaramouche* (title means "Scaramouche the Kingmaker"), Sonzogno, 1958; *Introduzione alla vita di Giacomo Scarbo* (novel), Sodalizio del Libro, 1959.

(With Franco Pinna and Antonio Pigliaru) *Sardegna, una civilta di pietra,* LEA (Rome), 1961; *Il disertore* (novel), Feltrinelli, 1961, translation by Virginia Hathaway Moriconi published as *The Deserter,* Harcourt, 1962; (editor with Nicola Tanda, and author of introduction and notes) *Narratori di Sardegna,* 2nd edition (Dessi not associated with earlier edition), Edizioni Mursia, 1965; (editor and author of introduction) *Scoperta della Sardegna: Antologia di testi di autori italiani e stranieri,* Il Prolifilo, 1965; *Lei era l'acqua,* Mondadori, 1966.

Paese d'ombre (novel), Mondadori, 1972, translation by Frances Frenaye published as *The Forests of Norbio,* Harcourt, 1975.

Plays: *Racconti drammatici* (includes "La giustizia," produced in Torino, Italy, at Teatro Stabile, January, 1959; and "Qui non c'e' guerra," produced in Torino at Teatro Stabile, March, 1960), Feltrinelli, 1959; "Il grido" (one-act), produced in Rome at Teatro Quirino, March, 1959.

Screenplays: "La trincea," 1961; "La frana," 1963; *Eleonora d'Arborea: Racconto drammatico in quattro atti,* produced on Radiotelevision Italia [RAI], April, 1964), Mondadori, 1964; "Una giornata di sole," RAI, 1964.

WORK IN PROGRESS: Short stories and a novel.

SIDELIGHTS: Dessi is interested in the cultural, social, and economic problems of Sardinia, and the connection of Sardinia with Italy and the rest of the world. A television adaptation of *Isola dell'Angelo* was broadcast on March 5, 1965.

*   *   *

DETHIER, Vincent Gaston   1915-

PERSONAL: Born February 20, 1915, in Boston, Mass.; son of Jean Vincent and Marguerite Frances (Lally) Dethier; married Lois Evelyn Check, January 23, 1960; children: Jehan Vincent, Paul. *Education:* Harvard University, A.B. (cum laude), 1936, A.M., 1937, Ph.D., 1939. *Home:* 331 Strong St., Amherst, Mass. 01002. *Office:* Department of Zoology, University of Massachusetts, Amherst, Mass. 01002.

CAREER: Clark University, Worcester, Mass., fellow in biology, 1937; G. W. Pierce Laboratory, Franklin, N.H., entomologist, 1937-38; John Carroll University, Cleveland, Ohio, instructor, 1939-41, assistant professor of biology,

1941-42; Ohio State University, Columbus, professor of zoology and entomology, 1946-47; Johns Hopkins University, Baltimore, Md., associate professor, 1947-51, professor of biology, 1952-58; University of Pennsylvania, Philadelphia, professor of zoology and psychology and associate of Neurological Institute, all 1959-67; Princeton University, Princeton, N.J., professor of biology, 1967-75; University of Massachusetts, Amherst, professor of zoology, 1975—. Harvard fellow at Atkins Institute of Arnold Arboretum (Soledad, Cuba), 1939-40; Hixon Lecturer at California Institute of Technology, 1949. Director of research at International Centre for Insect Physiology and Ecology (Kenya). President of board of trustees of Chapin School, 1971-74. Consultant to Canadian Defence Board and Office of the U.S. Surgeon General. *Military service:* U.S. Army Air Forces, research physiologist in Chemical Corps, 1942-45. U.S. Army Reserve, Office of the Surgeon General, 1948-62; became lieutenant colonel.

MEMBER: Entomological Society of America (fellow), National Academy of Science (fellow), American Academy of Arts and Sciences (fellow), American Association for the Advancement of Science (fellow), American Society of Zoologists (president, 1967), Society of General Physiologists, American Society of Naturalists, Royal Entomological Society (fellow; honorary member), Royal Society of Arts (fellow), Southern California Academy of Sciences (fellow). *Awards, honors:* Belgian-American Educational Foundation fellow in the Belgian Congo, 1952; Fulbright senior research scholar at London School of Hygiene and Tropical Medicine, 1954; Sc.D. from Providence College, 1964, and Ohio State University, 1970; Guggenheim fellow in the Netherlands, 1964-65, and at University of Sussex, 1972-73.

WRITINGS: Chemical Insect Attractants and Repellents, Blakiston, 1947; (contributor) K. D. Roeder, editor, *Insect Physiology,* Wiley, 1953; (with Eliot Stellar) *Animal Behavior: Its Evolutionary and Neurological Basis,* Prentice-Hall, 1961, 3rd edition, 1970; *To Know a Fly* (partially self-illustrated), Holden-Day, 1962; *The Physiology of Insect Senses,* Wiley, 1963; *Fairweather Duck* (juvenile; self-illustrated), Walker & Co., 1970; *Topics in the Study of Life: The BIO Source Book,* Harper, 1971; (with Claude Alvin Villee) *Biological Principles and Processes,* Saunders, 1971, 2nd edition, 1976; *Buy Me a Volcano,* Vantage, 1972; *The Hungry Fly,* Harvard University Press, 1976; *Man's Plague,* Darwin Press, 1976.

Short stories anthologized in *Best of Kenyon Review.* Contributor to scientific journals, and of short stories to periodicals, including *Kenyon Review* and *Texas Quarterly.* Member of editorial board of *Journal of Comparative Physiology* and *Journal of Experimental Biology.*

AVOCATIONAL INTERESTS: Boating, skiing.

* * *

DEUTSCH, Eliot (Sandler) 1931-

PERSONAL: Born January 8, 1931, in Gary, Ind.; son of Adolph E. and Pearl (Sandler) Deutsch; married Sanna Saks, July 15, 1957; children: Adley. *Education:* University of Wisconsin, B.S., 1952; graduate study, Harvard University, 1952-53; Columbia University, Ph.D., 1960. *Home:* 4837 Kolohala St., Honolulu, Hawaii 96816. *Office:* Department of Philosophy, University of Hawaii, Manoa Campus, Honolulu, Hawaii 96822.

CAREER: Rensselaer Polytechnic Institute, Troy, N.Y., professor of philosophy and chairman of department, 1960-67; University of Hawaii, Honolulu, professor of philoso-phy, 1967—. Director of East-West Philosophers' Conference program; faculty fellow of American Institute of Indian Studies, 1963-64; senior fellow on National Endowment for the Humanities, 1973-74. *Military service:* U.S. Army, 1953-55. *Member:* Society for Asian and Comparative Philosophy (secretary-treasurer, 1968—), Institute for Religion and Social Change (board of directors, 1968—), American Philosophical Association, Association for Asian Studies, Metaphysical Society of America, American Society for Aesthetics.

WRITINGS: (Translator and author of introduction and critical essays) *The Bhagavad Gita,* Holt, 1968; *Advaita Vedanta: A Philosophical Reconstruction,* East-West Center, 1969; *Humanity and Divinity: An Essay in Comparative Metaphysics,* University Press of Hawaii, 1970; (with J.A.B. van Buitenen) *A Source Book of Advaita Vedanta,* University Press of Hawaii, 1971; *Studies in Comparative Aesthetics,* University Press of Hawaii, 1975. Editor, *Philosophy East and West,* 1967—.

* * *

DE VEAUX, Alexis 1948-

PERSONAL: Born September 24, 1948, in New York, N.Y.; daughter of Richard Hill and Mae De Veaux. *Education:* State University of New York Empire State College, B.A., 1976. *Residence:* West Haven, Conn. *Office:* Coeur de l'Unicorne Gallery, P.O. Box 328, New Haven, Conn. 06510.

CAREER: New York Urban League, New York, N.Y., assistant instructor in English for WIN Program, 1969-71; Frederick Douglass Creative Arts Center, New York City, instructor in creative writing, 1971-72; Bronx Office of Probations, New York City, community worker, 1972-73; Project Create, New York City, instructor in reading and creative writing, 1973-74; free-lance writer, 1974—. Free-lance illustrator, 1974. Intern for Roundabout Theatre/Stage One, 1974; cultural coordinator of Black Expo for the Black Coalition of Greater New Haven, 1975. Has given readings at colleges, churches, and theaters; has appeared on radio and television programs in New York City, Washington, D.C., and New Haven, Conn. Artist and co-founder of Coeur de l'Unicorne Gallery, 1975—.

MEMBER: Screen Writers Guild of America (East), Poets and Writers, Inc., American Theatre Association, Black Theatre Alliance, Afro-American Cultural Center (Yale University). *Awards, honors:* First prize from Black Creation, 1972, for short story; best production award from Westchester Community College Drama Festival, 1973, for "Circles"; Art Books for Children awards from Brooklyn Museum, 1974 and 1975, for *Na-ni.*

WRITINGS: Na-ni (juvenile), Harper, 1973; *Spirits in the Street* (novel), Doubleday, 1973; *Li Chen/Second Daughter First Son* (prose poem), Ba Tone Press, 1975.

Plays: "Circles" (one-act), first produced in New York, N.Y., at Frederick Douglass Creative Arts Center, March, 1973; "The Tapestry," first broadcast on KCET-TV (PBS), March, 1976, produced in New York at Harlem Performance Center, May, 1976. Contributor of poems and stories to *Sunbury II, Encore, Black Creation,* and *New Haven Advocate.*

WORK IN PROGRESS: This Handed/That Handed (tentative title), for children; "Fox Street War" (tentative title), a play; research on the life of Lorraine Hansberry.

AVOCATIONAL INTERESTS: Studying Egyptian mythology and ancient culture, astrology, art history, "development of a new language composed of musical sounds and derived from African, Haitian, American Black, and neo-sexual sources."

* * *

DEVLIN, Harry 1918-

PERSONAL: Born March 22, 1918, in Jersey City, N.J.; son of Harry George (general manager of Savarin Co.) and Amelia (Crawford) Devlin; married Dorothy Wende (an artist and writer), August 30, 1941; children: Harry Noel, Wende Elizabeth (Mrs. Geoffrey Gates), Jeffrey Anthony, Alexandra Gail (Mrs. James Eldridge), Brion Phillip, Nicholas Kirk, David Matthew. *Education:* Syracuse University, B.F.A., 1939. *Religion:* Congregationalist. *Home:* 443 Hillside Ave., Mountainside, N.J. 07092.

CAREER: Artist, 1939—. Lecturer at Union College (Cranford, N.J.), 1966, chairman of Tomasulo Art Gallery; New Jersey State Council on the Arts, member, 1970—, chairman of grants committee, 1976—; member of Rutgers University's advisory council on children's literature; president of board of trustees of Mountainside Library, 1968-70. *Military service:* U.S. Naval Reserve, artist for Office of Naval Intelligence, active duty, 1942-46; became lieutenant.

MEMBER: Society of Illustrators, National Cartoonists Society (past president; honorary president), Artists' Equity Association (New Jersey), Authors Guild of Authors League of America, Dutch Treat Club. *Awards, honors:* New Jersey Teachers of English award, 1970, for *How Fletcher Was Hatched!;* award of excellence from Chicago Book Fair, 1974, for *Old Witch Rescues Halloween;* New Jersey Institute of Technology award, 1976, for *Tales of Thunder and Lightning.*

WRITINGS: Self-illustrated books for children: *To Grandfather's House We Go,* Parents' Magazine Press, 1967; *The Walloping Window Blind,* Van Nostrand, 1968; *What Kind of House Is That?,* Parents' Magazine Press, 1969; *Tales of Thunder and Lightning,* Parents' Magazine Press, 1975.

Self-illustrated children's books, with wife, Wende Devlin: *Old Black Witch,* Encyclopaedia Britannica Press, 1963; *The Knobby Boys to the Rescue,* Parents' Magazine Press, 1965; *Aunt Agatha, There's a Lion Under the Couch,* Van Nostrand, 1968; *How Fletcher Was Hatched!,* Parents' Magazine Press, 1969; *A Kiss for a Warthog,* Van Nostrand, 1970; *Old Witch and the Polka Dot Ribbon,* Parents' Magazine Press, 1970; *Cranberry Thanksgiving,* Parents' Magazine Press, 1971; *Old Witch Rescues Halloween,* Parents' Magazine Press, 1973.

Author and host of films, "Fare You Well Old House" and "Houses of the Hackensack," both for New Jersey Public Broadcasting, 1976.

WORK IN PROGRESS: A book of American domestic architecture, 1776-1876, *Made in America;* illustrating *Cranberry Christmas,* by wife, Wende Devlin.

SIDELIGHTS: The Devlins' first book sold over a million copies, "which beguiled us," wrote Devlin, "into the belief that we could write. Wende writes more and better than I can. I write only about those things that I think may fascinate, and pay no heed to trends or styles."

Old Black Witch was adapted by Gerald Herman as the film, "The Winter of the Witch," Parents' Magazine Films, 1972.

DeWEESE, (Thomas Eu)Gene 1934-
(Jean DeWeese; Thomas Stratton, joint pseudonym)

PERSONAL: Born January 31, 1934, in Rochester, Ind.; son of Thomas Jacob and Alfreda (a print shop worker; maiden name, Henning) DeWeese; married Beverly Joanne Amers (a librarian), May, 1955. *Education:* Valparaiso Technical Institute, associate degree in electronics, 1953; also studied at University of Wisconsin, Milwaukee, Indiana University, and Marquette University. *Politics:* Independent. *Religion:* None. *Home and office:* 2718 North Prospect, Milwaukee, Wis. 53211. *Agent:* Larry Sternig, 742 Robertson, Milwaukee, Wis. 53213.

CAREER: Delco Radio, Kokomo, Ind., technician, 1954-59; Delco Electronics, Milwaukee, Wis., technical writer, 1959-74; free-lance writer, 1974—. *Member:* Science Fiction Writers of America, Mystery Writers of America.

WRITINGS—Under name Gene DeWeese: (With Gini Rogowski) *Making American Folk Art Dolls,* Chilton, 1975; (with Robert Coulson) *Gates of the Universe* (science fiction), Laser Books, 1975; (with Coulson) *Now You See It/Him/Them* (science fiction), Doubleday, 1975; *Jeremy Case* (science fiction), Laser Books, 1976.

Under pseudonym Jean DeWeese: *The Reimann Curse* (Gothic fantasy), Ballantine, 1975; *The Moonstone Spirit* (Gothic fantasy), Ballantine, 1975; *The Carnelian Cat* (Gothic fantasy), Ballantine, 1975; *Web of Guilt* (Gothic novel), Ballantine, 1976; *Cave of the Moaning Wind* (Gothic fantasy), Ballantine, 1976; *The Doll with Opal Eyes* (romantic suspense), Doubleday, 1976.

Science fiction; under pseudonym Thomas Stratton (joint pseudonym with Robert Coulson): *The Invisibility Affair,* Ace Books, 1967; *The Mind Twisters Affair,* Ace Books, 1967. Contributor to science fiction magazines and to *Milwaukee Journal* and *Yandro.*

WORK IN PROGRESS: Romantic suspense and science fiction novels, for Doubleday.

* * *

DeWEESE, Jean
See DeWEESE, (Thomas Eu)Gene

* * *

DEXTER, (Norman) Colin 1930-

PERSONAL: Born September 29, 1930, in Stamford, Lincolnshire, England; son of Alfred (a taxi driver) and Dorothy (Towns) Dexter; married Dorothy Cooper (a physiotherapist), March 31, 1956; children: Sally, Jeremy. *Education:* Christ's College, Cambridge, B.A., 1953, M.A., 1958. *Politics:* Socialist (lapsed). *Religion:* Methodist (lapsed). *Home:* 456 Banbury Rd., Oxford, England. *Office:* Oxford Local Examinations, Summertown, Oxford, England.

CAREER: Assistant classics master in Leicester, England, 1954-57; sixth form classics master in Loughborough, England, 1957-59; senior classics master in Corby, England, 1959-66; Oxford Local Examination Board, Oxford, England, assistant secretary, 1966—. Reader of English and classics texts for Oxford University Press and Macmillan Publishers Ltd. *Military service:* National Service, 1949-50. *Member:* Association of Assistant Masters. *Awards, honors:* M.A., Oxford University, 1966.

WRITINGS: (With E. G. Rayner) *Liberal Studies: An Outline Course,* two volumes, Pergamon, 1964, revised edition, 1966; (with Rayner) *Guide to Contemporary Politics,* Pergamon, 1966; *Last Bus to Woodstock* (mystery), Macmillan, 1975; *Last Seen Wearing* (mystery), Macmillan, 1976; *The Silent World of Nicholas Quinn* (mystery), Macmillan, 1977. Short story represented in anthology, *Winter's Crimes,* edited by Lord Hardinge, Macmillan, in press. Contributor of articles to *Didaskalos* and *Latin Teaching.*

WORK IN PROGRESS: A fourth mystery.

SIDELIGHTS: Dexter told *CA:* "I suppose the main 'sidelight' in my life has been crossword puzzles. For three or four years I was the national champion in the (famous!) Ximenes competitions. I suppose, too, that this interest has influenced my style in the writing of whodunnits; indeed, in my own desultory reading of the genre I much prefer the 'puzzle' to the thriller/psychological approaches."

* * *

DEYRUP, Astrith Johnson 1923-

PERSONAL: Born April 22, 1923, in Englewood, N.J.; daughter of Alvin S. (an educator) and Edith (Henry) Johnson. *Education:* Barnard College, A.B., 1944; Columbia University, M.A., 1947. *Religion:* Protestant. *Home:* 395 Riverside Dr., New York, N.Y. 10025. *Office:* The New School for Social Research, New York, N.Y. 10011.

CAREER: The New School for Social Research, New York, N.Y., art faculty member, 1960—. Member of summer faculty, College of New Rochelle; visual arts coordinator, the Children's Arts and Science Workshops. *Member:* The Society of Batik Artists (president, 1969, 1975).

WRITINGS: Getting Started in Batik, Bruce Books, 1971; *The Complete Book of Tie-Dyeing,* Lancer Books, 1972; *Tie Dye and Batik,* Doubleday, 1974.

WORK IN PROGRESS: Research on life styles in the middle years.

SIDELIGHTS: Astrith Deyrup, who was educated by her mother until her entrance into college, told *CA:* "Home education made me believe deeply in my personal worth as a craftswoman—I wanted to hand on my knowledge to others."

AVOCATIONAL INTERESTS: Travel, volunteer work, playing the flute.

* * *

DIAMOND, Jay 1934-

PERSONAL: Born January 25, 1934, in New York; son of Charles (a retailer) and Helen (a retailer; maiden name, Klar) Diamond; married Ellen Clements (an artist), June 1, 1958; children: Sheri, Caryn, David. *Education:* City College (now of the City University of New York), B.B.A., 1955; New York University, M.A., 1965. *Home:* 3780 Greentree Dr., Oceanside, N.Y. 11572. *Office:* Department of Marketing-Retailing, Nassau Community College, Stewart Ave., Garden City, N.Y. 11530.

CAREER: Helen Diamond (retail chain), Brooklyn, N.Y., partner and buyer, 1955-64; New York Community College, Brooklyn, instructor in retailing and marketing, 1964-65; Nassau Community College, Garden City, N.Y., assistant professor, 1965-67, associate professor, 1967-70, professor of marketing and retailing, 1970—, chairman of department, 1969—. Adjunct instructor at City College of the City University of New York and Pratt Institute, 1955-64. *Member:* National Retail Merchants Association (associate member).

WRITINGS—All with Gerald Pintel: *The Mathematics of Business,* with workbook, Prentice-Hall, 1970; *Retailing,* with workbook, Prentice-Hall, 1971, 2nd edition, in press; *Principles of Marketing,* with study guide, Prentice-Hall, 1972; *Basic Mathematics of Business,* Prentice-Hall, 1972; *Introduction to Contemporary Business,* with study guide, Prentice-Hall, 1975; *Retail Buying,* Prentice-Hall, 1976.

WORK IN PROGRESS—Both with Gerald Pintel: *Basic Mathematics of Business,* 2nd edition, for Prentice-Hall; *Salesmanship.*

AVOCATIONAL INTERESTS: Tennis, travel.

* * *

DIAMOND, William 1917-

PERSONAL: Born December 20, 1917, in Baltimore, Md.; son of Isidore and Yetta (Mirtenbaum) Diamond; married Lois Marie Wilhelm, October 28, 1946. *Education:* Johns Hopkins University, A.B., 1937, Ph.D., 1942. *Home:* 3315 Garfield St. N.W., Washington, D.C. 20008. *Office:* 1818 H St. N.W., Washington, D.C. 20433.

CAREER: With U.S. Board of Economic Warfare and U.S. Foreign Economic Administration, both Washington, D.C., 1942-46; with United Nations Relief and Rehabilitation Administration, Prague, Czechoslovakia, and London, England, 1946-47; World Bank, 1947-62, deputy director of Foreign Trade Administration in Greece, 1947-48, member of staff of Economic Development Institute, 1956-58; director of development finance companies department, International Finance Corp., 1962-68; World Bank, director of development finance companies department, 1968-72, director of South Asia department, 1972-75, special assistant to vice-president of finance, 1975—. *Member:* Phi Beta Kappa, Cosmos Club.

WRITINGS: Economic Thought of Woodrow Wilson, Johns Hopkins Press, 1943; *Czechoslovakia Between East and West,* London Institute of World Affairs, 1947; *Development Banks,* Johns Hopkins Press, 1957; (editor) *Development Finance Companies: Aspects of Policy and Operation,* Johns Hopkins Press, 1968.

* * *

DIARA, Agadem Lumumba 1947-

PERSONAL: Born August 2, 1947, in Inkster, Mich.; stepson of Howard White and son of Annabell (Anderson) White; married Schavi M. Ross (an instructor in English), July 25, 1969. *Education:* Wayne State University, Ph.B., 1972; University of Detroit, graduate study, 1973—. *Politics:* Pan-African Congress. *Religion:* Islam. *Residence:* Detroit, Mich. *Office:* Office of Admissions, University of Michigan, Ann Arbor, Mich. 48104.

CAREER: Substitute teacher of mathematics in public schools in Detroit, Mich., 1969-70; Agascha Productions, Detroit, co-founder and president, 1970—; Wayne State University, Detroit, admissions counselor, 1973-74; University of Michigan, Ann Arbor, admissions counselor, 1974—.

WRITINGS: Islam and Pan-Africanism, Agascha Productions, 1973.

WORK IN PROGRESS: Three books, *The Final Revolution; Anthropological Considerations from a Black Perspective; The African Ancestry of the Holy Prophet Mohamed.*

BIOGRAPHICAL/CRITICAL SOURCES: Black World, March, 1975.

DICKENS, Roy S(elman), Jr. 1938-

PERSONAL: Born March 16, 1938, in Atlanta, Ga.; son of Roy Selman (a government worker) and Edith (Metcalf) Dickens; married Carol McClendon (a historian), August 13, 1961; children: David. *Education:* Georgia State University, B.A., 1963; University of Alabama, M.A., 1966; University of North Carolina, Ph.D., 1970. *Office:* Department of Anthropology, Georgia State University, University Plaza, Atlanta, Ga. 30303.

CAREER: University of North Carolina, Chapel Hill, assistant state archaeologist, 1968-70; California State College, San Bernardino, assistant professor of anthropology, 1970-71; Georgia State University, Atlanta, assistant professor, 1971-76, associate professor of anthropology, 1976—. *Member:* American Anthropological Association, Society for American Archaeology, American Association for the Advancement of Science, Sigma Xi.

WRITINGS: Cherokee Prehistory: The Pisgah Phase in the Appalachian Summit Region, University of Tennessee Press, 1976; (contributor) *The Cherokees in Historical Perspective,* University of Tennessee Press, in press. Contributor of articles to *American Antiquity,* and various regional journals.

WORK IN PROGRESS: Research for a study of American urban culture and Southeastern cultures through archaeology.

*   *   *

DICKENSON, James R. 1931-

PERSONAL: Born December 31, 1931, in Kansas; son of Richard Doak (a businessman) and Anna Avis (a teacher; maiden name, Phipps) Dickenson; married Mollie Anne McCauley, March 2, 1963; children: (stepchildren) Elizabeth Anne Lerch, John Hunt Lerch. *Education:* San Diego State College (now University), A.B., 1953; University of Iowa, M.A., 1959. *Home:* 4101 Glenrose St., Kensington, Md. 20795. *Office: Washington Star,* 225 Virginia Ave. S.E., Washington, D.C. 20061.

CAREER/WRITINGS: Huntington Park Daily Signal, Huntington Park, Calif., reporter, 1959-60; United Press International (UPI), San Francisco, Calif., reporter, 1960; *National Observer,* Silver Spring, Md., rewrite man, sports writer, and political reporter, 1962-74; *Washington Star,* Washington, D.C., author of column "Politics Today" (also syndicated by Washington Star-New York Times News Service to about four hundred newspapers), 1974—. Notable assignments include the 1964 and 1965 World Series, the 1967 Newark and Detroit urban riots, and political primary elections and national conventions. Guest lecturer at American University. *Military service:* U.S. Marine Corps, 1954-58; became first lieutenant. *Member:* White House Correspondents Association, U.S. Senate Press Gallery, U.S. House Press Gallery.

*   *   *

DICKER, Ralph Leslie 1914-

PERSONAL: Born February 3, 1914, in New Jersey; son of Maxwell (a businessman) and Freda (Neuman) Dicker; married Shirley C. Banks, March, 1942; children: Jo-Ellen Dicker Malen, Dennis. *Education:* Johns Hopkins University, B.A., 1934; St. Louis University, M.D., 1938. *Residence:* Dover, N.J. *Agent:* Helmut Meyer, 330 East 79th St., New York, N.Y. *Office:* 245 East 63rd St., New York, N.Y. 10021.

CAREER: Completed medical and surgical internships; physician in private practice, 1938-42; did surgical residency training at Flower-Fifth Ave. Hospital, New York City, 1946-49; returned to private practice, 1950—; New York Facial Plastic and Reconstructive Surgery Group, New York City, director, 1972—. Has lectured to professionals in Japan, the Soviet Union, Kenya, Ethiopia, Iran, South Africa, Southeast Asia, Singapore, and Poland. *Military service:* U.S. Army Medical Corps, 1942-46; became major.

MEMBER: International Academy of Cosmetic Surgery, International College of Surgeons, Pan-American Medical Association, American Medical Association, American Academy of Facial Plastic and Reconstructive Surgery, American Society of Cosmetic Surgery, French Society of Cosmetic Surgery.

WRITINGS: Consultation with a Plastic Surgeon, Nelson-Hall, 1975.

*   *   *

DICKINSON, Eleanor 1931-

PERSONAL: Born February 7, 1931, in Knoxville, Tenn.; daughter of Robert Elmond (a lawyer) and Evelyn (a poet; maiden name, Van Gilder) Creekmore; married Ben Wade Oakes Dickinson (a physicist), June 12, 1952; children: Mark Wade, Katherine Van Gilder, Peter Somers. *Education:* University of Tennessee, B.A., 1952; also attended San Francisco Art Institute, 1961-63. *Politics:* Democrat. *Religion:* Episcopalian. *Home:* 2125 Broderick St., San Francisco, Calif. 94115. *Agent:* Russell & Volkening, Inc., 551 Fifth Ave., New York, N.Y. 10017. *Office:* California College of Arts and Crafts, Oakland, Calif. 94618.

CAREER: Artist in San Francisco, Calif., 1952—; associate professor at California College of Arts and Crafts, 1971—. Trustee and member of board of directors of San Francisco Art Institute; member of board of directors of International Child Art Center and Westminster Community Center (1956-59); vice-president of board of directors of local Young Women's Christian Association (YWCA), 1957-63. Has had more than a dozen solo exhibitions at museums and galleries; paintings are in fifteen permanent collections, including those at National Collection of Fine Arts, Corcoran Gallery of Art, Smithsonian Institution, and Library of Congress.

MEMBER: American Association of University Professors, College Art Association, Women's Art Caucus, Artists Equity Association (member of board of directors and vice-president, 1958-76), San Francisco Art Association (member of board of directors), San Francisco Women Artists (member of board of directors), Junior League. *Awards, honors:* Purchase award from Butler Institute of American Art; awards from San Francisco Museum and Oakland Museum; three awards from San Francisco Art Festival.

WRITINGS—Self-illustrated: (With Ann Chandonnet) *The Complete Fruit Cookbook,* 101 Productions, 1972; (with Barbara Benziger) *Revival!,* Harper, 1974; (with Benziger) *That Old Time Religion,* Harper, 1975. Author of catalogs for art exhibitions. Writer of column in *Visual Dialogue.* Art critic for *San Francisco Review of Books.*

WORK IN PROGRESS: Young Lovers, Old Lovers.

BIOGRAPHICAL/CRITICAL SOURCES—Films: "Artist's Studio Too: A Face in the Mirror, Eleanor Dickinson," KQED-Television, 1966; "The Corcoran Gallery of Art, 1970," WETA-Television, 1970; "Revival at the Corcoran," on "The Today Show," National Broadcasting Corp.,

1970; "Eleanor Dickinson," on "On the Square," KTVU-Television, 1974.

Tapes, by Fine Arts Museum of San Francisco in 1975: "Eleanor Dickinson, Drawing Life," and "Eleanor Dickinson and Lovers."

Other: *La Revue Moderne,* December 1, 1960; *Art Forum,* May, 1963; *San Francisco Examiner,* May, 1965; *Newsweek,* October 26, 1971; *San Francisco Chronicle,* November 29, 1971; *Art Week,* December 4, 1971; *New York Times,* March 4, 1972; *Art News,* April, 1972; *Arts,* April, 1972; *Art International,* April 20, 1972.

*   *   *

DIENSTAG, Eleanor 1938-

PERSONAL: Born April 13, 1938, in Naples, Italy; daughter of Bruno (an economist) and Lisa (Haimann) Foa; married Jerome Dienstag (an attorney), June 29, 1958 (separated); children: Joshua, Jesse. *Education:* Smith College, B.A., 1959. *Home:* 10 Manhattan Sq., Rochester, N.Y. 14607. *Agent:* Betty Anne Clarke, International Creative Management, 40 West 57th St., New York, N.Y. 10019.

CAREER: Reader and assistant editor for major publishing firms, including Harper and Random House, in New York, N.Y., 1959-61; *Monocle* (magazine of political satire), New York City, editor, 1961-65; free-lance writer, 1965—. Television book critic in Rochester, N.Y., 1976—. *Member:* Women in Communications.

WRITINGS: Whither Thou Goest: The Story of an Uprooted Wife (nonfiction), Dutton, 1976. Author of a column on book publishing in *New York Herald Tribune,* and cultural columnist for Genesee Valley Newspapers, 1970-72. Contributor of articles and reviews to a variety of national magazines, including *New Republic, Ms., Travel and Leisure,* and *Upstate,* and newspapers, including *New York Times* and *Village Voice.*

WORK IN PROGRESS: Co-author with Renee Richards of her autobiography.

SIDELIGHTS: Eleanor Dienstag writes: "As a magazine and newspaper feature writer I have found myself increasingly focusing on cultural, marital, and women's issues, ranging from the controversy over radical mastectomies to a roundup of books on divorce. My latest venture, as co-author of the autobiography of a transsexual, should pose fascinating questions for men and women who are reevaluating the meaning of sexual roles and sexual identity."

*   *   *

DIETZ, Marjorie (Priscilla) J(ohnson) 1918-

PERSONAL: Born May 15, 1918, in New Haven, Conn.; daughter of George M. (a teacher and writer) and Marjorie (Thatcher) Johnson; married William E. Dietz, March 1, 1956 (deceased). *Education:* Attended Temple University, 1939-40. *Home:* 240 West 98th St., New York, N.Y. 10025; and East Hampton, N.Y.

CAREER: Flower Grower, New York City, editor, 1961-67; *Home Garden,* New York City, editor, 1967; *Plants and Gardens,* Brooklyn, N.Y., associate editor, 1968—.

WRITINGS: Concise Encyclopedia of Favorite Flowering Shrubs, Doubleday, 1963; *Concise Encyclopedia of Favorite Wildflowers,* Doubleday, 1965; (editor) Roy E. Biles, *Complete Illustrated Book of Garden Magic,* J. G. Ferguson, 1969; *Landscaping and the Small Garden,* Doubleday, 1973; (editor) *Ten Thousand Garden Questions Answered,*

3rd edition (Marjorie Dietz was not associated with earlier editions), Doubleday, 1974. Contributor to magazines.

*   *   *

DIKSHIT, R(amesh) D(utta) 1939-

PERSONAL: Born November 3, 1939, in Varanasi, India; son of Baldeo (a farmer) and Roopkali (Chaube) Dikshit; married Krishna Dubey, February 16, 1960; children: Jaya, Ashutosh, Ila. *Education:* Allahabad University, B.A., 1956, M.A., 1958; Australian National University, Ph.D., 1971. *Religion:* Hindu. *Home:* Punjabi University Campus, Patiala, Panjab, India. *Office:* Department of Geography, Punjabi University, Patiala, Panjab, India.

CAREER: Gorakhpur University, Gorakhpur, Uttar Pradesh, India, lecturer in geography, 1960-74; Punjabi University, Patiala, Panjab, India, reader in geography and head of department, 1974—.

WRITINGS: The Political Geography of Federalism: An Inquiry into Origins and Stability, Halsted, 1975. Contributor to geography and political science journals.

WORK IN PROGRESS: Research on nation-building in federal societies and on spatial concomitants of politics in India.

*   *   *

DILLON, Millicent 1925-

PERSONAL: Born May 24, 1925, in New York, N.Y.; daughter of Ephraim (a salesman) and Clara (a nurse; maiden name, Millman) Gerson; married Murray L. Lesser, June 1, 1948 (divorced, 1959); married David F. Dillon, January 18, 1964 (divorced, 1966); children: (first marriage) Wendy, Janna. *Education:* Hunter College (now of the City University of New York), A.B., 1944; San Francisco State University, M.A., 1966. *Religion:* Jewish. *Home:* 4062 Ben Lomond Dr., Palo Alto, Calif. 94306. *Agent:* Maxine Groffsky, 2 Fifth Ave., New York, N.Y. 10011. *Office:* News and Publications, Stanford University, Stanford, Calif. 94305.

CAREER: Assistant physicist on government projects at Princeton University, 1944-45, and Oak Ridge, Tenn., 1947; Standard Oil Co., Kettleman Hills Oil Field, technical assistant, 1946; Los Angeles County, Hawthorne, Calif., case worker in social services department, 1949-52; Foothill College, Los Altos Hills, Calif., instructor in English, 1968-71, part-time instructor, 1971-74; Stanford University, Stanford, Calif., writer for news and publications office, 1974—. *Member:* Authors Guild of Authors League of America.

WRITINGS: Baby Perpetua and Other Stories, Viking, 1971; *The One in the Back in Medea* (novel), Viking, 1973. Contributor to *Nation.*

WORK IN PROGRESS: Second Present, a novel; a critical biography of Jane Bowles; a collection of short stories.

*   *   *

DILTZ, Bert Case 1894-

PERSONAL: Born February 10, 1894, in Port Credit, Ontario, Canada; son of Charles Elisha and Martha Jane (Case) Diltz; married Agnes Marcella Brown, August 7, 1926; children: Charles Herbert, David Alexander, Douglas Graden. *Education:* Queen's University, B.A. (with honors), 1921, M.A. (with gold medal in English), 1922; University of Toronto, specialist's teaching certificate, 1923; also studied at Columbia University, summers, 1923-25. *Religion:* Presbyterian. *Home:* 92 Colin Ave., Toronto, Ontario, Canada.

CAREER: Lindsay Collegiate Institute (secondary school), Ontario, teacher of English, 1923-28, head of department, 1923-28, vice-principal, 1926-28; University of Toronto, Toronto, Ontario, instructor, 1928-31, professor of methods in English and history, 1931-58, dean of college, 1958-63; writer, 1963—. *Military service:* Canadian Expeditionary Forces, Signal Section of Infantry Brigade, 1916-19; served in France and Belgium. *Awards, honors:* LL.D. from Queen's University, 1960.

WRITINGS: Models and Projects for English Composition, Clarke, Irwin (Toronto), 1932; (with Honora M. Cochrane) *Sense and Structure in English Composition,* Clarke, Irwin, 1933; (with Cochrane) *Aim and Order in English Composition,* Clarke, Irwin, 1934; (with H. E. Cavell) *Living English,* Clarke, Irwin, 1939; *Poetic Pilgrimage: An Essay in Education,* Clarke, Irwin, 1942; *Pierian Spring: Reflections on Education and the Teaching of English,* Clarke, Irwin, 1946; *New Models and Projects for Creative Writing,* three parts, Clarke, Irwin, 1949-51; *The Sense of Wonder,* McClelland & Stewart (Toronto), 1953; (editor) *New Horizons: An Anthology of Short Poems for Senior Students,* McClelland & Stewart, 1954; *Poetic Experience,* McClelland & Stewart, 1955; (editor) *Word Magic: An Anthology of Poems for Grades Nine and Ten,* McClelland & Stewart, 1957; *Patterns of Surmise,* Clarke, Irwin, 1962; (editor with R. J. McMaster) *Many Minds: An Anthology of Prose,* McClelland & Stewart, Book 1, 1963, Book 2, 1965; (editor) *Frontiers of Wonder: Prose and Poetry for the Intermediate Levels,* Books 1 and 2, McClelland & Stewart, 1968; *Stranger Than Fiction,* McClelland & Stewart, 1969; *Sense or Nonsense: Contemporary Education at the Crossroads,* McClelland & Stewart, 1972.

WORK IN PROGRESS: A novel, *The Plights of Nils Lapraik and His Melody Pipe;* a collection of original stories, *Postscripts on Life; The Joys of Retirement; A Teacher's Diary of Life and Literature.*

AVOCATIONAL INTERESTS: Reading, writing, gardening.

* * *

DISNEY, Doris Miles 1907-1976

December 22, 1907—March 8, 1976; American mystery novelist. Obituaries: *New York Times,* March 10, 1976; *Washington Post,* March 11, 1976; *Publishers Weekly,* March 22, 1976; *AB Bookman's Weekly,* May 17, 1976; (See index for previous *CA* sketch)

* * *

DITSKY, John (Michael) 1938-

PERSONAL: Born March 9, 1938, in Detroit, Mich.; son of John George (an automotive worker) and Elizabeth (a bookseller and buyer; maiden name, Brestovansky) Ditsky; married Claire Suzette Ponka (a graduate student), June 16, 1962; children: Katherine. *Education:* University of Detroit, Ph.B., 1958, M.A., 1961; New York University, Ph.D., 1967. *Home:* 18235 Oak Dr., Detroit, Mich. 48221. *Office:* Department of English, University of Windsor, Windsor, Ontario, Canada.

CAREER: University of Detroit, Detroit, Michigan, instructor in English, 1964-66; Wayne State University, Detroit, instructor in English, 1966-67; University of Windsor, Windsor, Ontario, assistant professor, 1967-71, associate professor, 1971-75, professor of English, 1975—. Writer. *Member:* Modern Language Association of America, Stein-

beck Society, Canadian Association for American Studies, Kyushu American Literature Society.

WRITINGS: The Katherine Poems, Killaly Press (London, Ontario), 1975. Work represented in anthologies: *Soundings,* edited by Andy Wainright and Jack Ludwig, Anansi Press (Toronto), 1970; *Windsor Salt,* edited by Marty Gerudis, Black Moss Press (Toronto), 1970; *Contraverse: Nine Poets,* edited by Dorothy Farmiloe, Concorde Press (Windsor), 1971. Contributor of over six hundred poems, reviews, and articles to over three hundred journals and periodicals, including *Modern Poetry Studies, Southern Humanities Review, Ariel, Canadian Forum, North American Review, Georgia Review,* and *Epoch.* Member of the editorial board of *Steinbeck Quarterly.*

WORK IN PROGRESS: A critical study of John Steinbeck; poems; articles.

SIDELIGHTS: "I have old-fashioned motivations," Ditsky told *CA,* "I enjoy trying to say things well; lust after print. It all helps in the classroom."

* * *

DIXON, Bernard 1938-

PERSONAL: Born July 17, 1938, in Darlington, England; son of Ronald and Grace (Peirson) Dixon; married Margaret Helena Charlton, 1963; children: two sons, one daughter. *Education:* King's College, University of Durham, B.Sc., 1961; University of Newcastle-upon-Tyne, Ph.D., 1964. *Home:* 81 Falmouth Rd., Chelmsford, Essex, England. *Office: New Scientist,* King's Read Tower, Stamford St., London SE1 9LS, England.

CAREER: University of Newcastle-upon-Tyne, Newcastle-upon-Tyne, England, research microbiologist, 1961-65; *World Medicine,* London, England, assistant editor, 1965-66, deputy editor, 1966-68; *New Scientist,* London, deputy editor, 1968-69, editor, 1969—. *Member:* British Association for the Advancement of Science (council member), Association of British Science Writers (member of committee, 1969—; chairman, 1971-72), Society for General Microbiology, Institute of Biology. *Awards, honors:* Luccock Research Fund fellowship, 1961-64; Frank Schon fellowship from Maschon Products, 1964-65.

WRITINGS: (Editor) *Journeys in Belief,* Allen & Unwin, 1968; *What Is Science For?,* Harper, 1973; *Magnificent Microbes,* Atheneum, 1976; *Invisible Allies,* Temple Smith, 1976. Correspondent for *World Medicine,* 1968—; science correspondent for *Spectator,* 1971—. Contributor to scientific and popular journals.

AVOCATIONAL INTERESTS: Playing Scottish country dance music.

* * *

DIXON, Jeane 1918-

PERSONAL: Born January 5, 1918, in Medford, Wis.; daughter of Frank (a lumber businessman) and Emma (Von Graffee) Pinckert; married James L. Dixon (a realtor), 1939. *Education:* Attended college in Los Angeles, Calif. *Religion:* Roman Catholic. *Home:* 1312 19th St. N.W., Washington, D.C. 20036. *Office:* 1765 N St. N.W., Washington, D.C. 20036.

CAREER: Author, lecturer, humanitarian. Secretary-treasurer and director of residential properties section of James L. Dixon & Co. (a real estate brokerage firm), Washington, D.C. Founder and president, Children to Children, Inc.,

1964—; chairwoman of Christmas Seal Campaign, Washington, D.C., 1968. *Wartime service:* Served on Home Hospitality Committee, Washington, D.C., during World War II; entertained servicemen by giving prophetic readings. *Member:* International Platform Association (member of board of governors), International Club (Washington, D.C.), National League of American Pen Women, American Society of Composers, Authors, and Publishers. *Awards, honors:* Named Woman of the Year by International Orphans, 1968; named first Anglo Honorary Navajo Princess, 1968; International L'Enfant Award of Holy Family Adoption League, 1969; Loreto International Award, 1969.

WRITINGS: (Co-author) *Jeane Dixon, My Life and Prophecies: Her Own Story as Told to Rene Noorbergen,* Morrow, 1969; *Reincarnation and Prayers to Live By,* Morrow, 1970; *The Call to Glory: Jeane Dixon Speaks of Jesus,* Morrow, 1972; *Yesterday, Today, and Forever,* Morrow, 1976. Writer of daily newspaper column, "Jeane Dixon," syndicated by Chicago Tribune-New York News Syndicate, Inc.

WORK IN PROGRESS: Astrological Cook Book.

SIDELIGHTS: Jeane Dixon's parents were German immigrants, and she learned to speak German before English. She had already begun to predict the future by the time she was eight years old. During World War II, she began to prophesy for legislators and diplomats in Washington, D.C.

BIOGRAPHICAL/CRITICAL SOURCES: Ruth Montgomery, *A Gift of Prophecy: The Phenomenal Jeane Dixon,* Morrow, 1965; *Holiday,* July, 1973; *Saturday Evening Post,* September, 1973.

* * *

DOAK, (Dearle) Donn(ell) 1930-

PERSONAL: Born October 28, 1930, in Canyon, Tex.; son of Robert Alvin (a tradesman) and Thelma Emma (Crawford) Doak; married Shirley Esther Saari (in public service radio traffic), September 7, 1957; children: Daryn (daughter), Robin (son), Galen (son). *Education:* University of Oregon, B.A., 1952; Syracuse University, M.A., 1957. *Religion:* Protestant. *Home:* 325 Bayberry Lane, Westport, Conn. 06880. *Office:* National Broadcasting Co.—Radio, 30 Rockefeller Plaza, New York, N.Y. 10020.

CAREER: National Broadcasting Co. (NBC), New York, N.Y., television news anchor man in Eugene, Ore., 1957-61, television news anchor man in Baltimore, Md., 1961-62, television news anchor man in Washington, D.C., 1962-73, radio news anchor man, 1962-73, radio news anchor man in New York City, 1973—. Adviser to WWPT-FM Radio (high school station). Has covered national events, including the 1963 Martin Luther King, Jr. march on Washington and the funeral of President John F. Kennedy. *Military service:* U.S. Air Force, linguist in Intelligence Division, 1952-56; served in Europe; became staff sergeant. *Member:* Sigma Delta Chi. *Awards, honors:* George F. Peabody Award from University of Georgia, 1972, for "Crime in the Cities."

WRITINGS: Author of material for "Crime in the Cities," broadcast on NBC-Radio, 1972.

* * *

DOBBS, Greg 1946-

PERSONAL: Born October 9, 1946, in San Francisco, Calif.; son of Harold S. (an attorney) and Annette (a fundraiser; maiden name, Lehrer) Dobbs; married Carol Walker (a special education teacher), November 25, 1973. *Educa-tion:* University of California, Berkeley, B.A., 1968; Northwestern University, M.S.J., 1969. *Residence:* Evanston, Ill. *Office:* American Broadcasting Co. News, 190 North State St., Chicago, Ill. 60601.

CAREER/WRITINGS: American Broadcasting Co. (ABC) Radio, Chicago, Ill., editor, 1969-71; WLS-Television, Chicago, Ill., assignment editor, 1971; American Broadcasting Co. News, Chicago, Ill., television producer, 1971-73, radio and television correspondent, 1973—. Notable assignments include U.S. Senate Watergate hearings, the Indian occupation of Wounded Knee, the Gary Gilmore execution, as well as presidential campaigns and conventions. Teacher at Northwestern University, 1976.

* * *

DOBRINER, William M(ann) 1922-

PERSONAL: Born October 28, 1922, in Springfield, Mass.; son of J. E. (a salesman) and Marion (Mann) Dobriner; married Eileen Phypers, September 2, 1950; children: Gail Evans, Jill Hampton, Scott Blackwell. *Education:* Hofstra College, A.B., 1948; Columbia University, M.A., 1950, Ph.D., 1956. *Home:* 152 Pennsylvania Ave., Easton, Pa. 18042. *Office:* Department of Sociology, Lafayette College, Easton, Pa. 18042.

CAREER: Hofstra University, Hempstead, N.Y., assistant professor, 1956-60, associate professor, 1960-64, professor of sociology, 1964-71; Lafayette College, Easton, Pa., Charles A. Dana Professor of Sociology, 1971—. Visiting professor at University of Vermont, 1969-70. *Military service:* U.S. Army Air Forces, 1942-45.

WRITINGS: The Suburban Community, Putnam, 1958; *Class in Suburbia,* Prentice-Hall, 1963; *Social Structures and Systems,* Goodyear Publishing, 1969.

* * *

DOBROWOLSKI, Tomasz B. 1914(?)-1976

1914(?)—February 1, 1976; Polish-born American radio writer, journalist, and author. Obituaries: *Washington Post,* February 4, 1976.

* * *

DODGE, David (Francis) 1910-

PERSONAL: Born in August, 1910, in Berkeley, Calif.; son of George (an architect) and Maude (Bennett) Dodge; married Elva Keith, July 17, 1936; children: Kendal (daughter). *Education:* Attended high school in Los Angeles. *Politics:* Democrat. *Home:* 706 Kingston Rd., Princeton, N.J.

CAREER: Worked as bank clerk, ship's fireman, and as a social service worker in San Francisco; public accountant in California, 1935-42; author, 1940—. *Military service:* U.S. Naval Reserve, 1941-45.

WRITINGS—Suspense novels: Death and Taxes, Macmillan, 1941; *Shear the Black Sheep,* Macmillan, 1942; *Bullets for the Bridegroom,* Macmillan, 1944; *It Ain't Hay,* Simon & Schuster, 1946; *The Long Escape,* Random House, 1948; *Plunder of the Sun,* Random House, 1949; *The Red Tassel,* Random House, 1950; *To Catch a Thief,* Random House, 1952; *The Lights of Skaro,* Random House, 1954; *Angel's Ransom,* Random House, 1956 (published in England as *Ransom of the "Angel,"* Penguin, 1961); *Loo Loo's Legacy,* M. Joseph, 1960, Little, Brown, 1961; *Carambola,* Little, Brown, 1961; *High Corniche,* M. Joseph, 1961; *Hooligan,* Macmillan, 1969 (published in England as *Hatchetman,* M. Joseph, 1970); *Troubleshooter,* Macmillan, 1970.

Travel books: *How Green Was My Father: A Sort of Travel Diary*, Simon & Schuster, 1947; *How Lost Was My Weekend: A Greenhorn in Guatemala*, Random House, 1948; *The Crazy Glasspecker; or, High Life in the Andes*, Random House, 1949 (published in England as *High Life in the Andes*, A. Barker, 1951); *20,000 Leagues Behind the 8 Ball*, Random House, 1951; *The Poor Man's Guide to Europe*, Random House, 1953, revised edition, 1956; *Time Out for Turkey*, Random House, 1955; *The Rich Man's Guide to the Riviera*, Little, Brown, 1962; *The Poor Man's Guide to the Orient*, Simon & Schuster, 1965; *Special Guide to the XIX Olympic Games*, Macmillan, 1968; *Fly Down, Drive Mexico: A Practical Motorists' Handbook for Travel South of the Border*, Macmillan, 1968, revised edition published as *The Best of Mexico by Car: A Selective Guide to Motor Travel South of the Border*, 1969.*

* * *

DODGE, Nicholas A. 1933-

PERSONAL: Born May 26, 1933, in Seattle, Wash.; son of Alexander (an engineer) and Natalie (Balakshin) Dodge; married Kathryn Kaser (a teacher), August 14, 1962. *Education:* Oregon State University, B.Sc., 1954; graduate study at University of Washington, Seattle, 1957; Washington State University, M.Sc., 1960; graduate study at Portland State University, 1962-64. *Home:* 4609 S.W. 29 Pl., Portland, Ore. 97201. *Office:* U.S. Army Corps of Engineers, Custom House, Portland, Ore. 97209.

CAREER: Alaska Road Commission, office worker, 1954; Boeing Airplane Co., Seattle, Wash., engineer, 1957; Collins Construction Co., Port Lavaca, Tex., engineer, 1958; Pacific Power & Light Co., Portland, Ore., engineer, 1959; U.S. Army Corps of Engineers, North Pacific Division, engineer, 1960-65, instructor in engineering, 1965-68, supervisor, 1968—. *Military service:* U.S. Army, 1955-56. *Member:* American Alpine Club, American Society of Civil Engineers, Oregon Historical Society, Portland Art Museum, Mazamas.

WRITINGS: A Climber's Guide to Oregon, Touchstone, 1968. Contributor to *Off Belay, Summit, Canadian Alpine Journal, Mazama, Oregon Journal*, and to engineering journals.

WORK IN PROGRESS: Mexico's Frontiers.

AVOCATIONAL INTERESTS: Mountaineering.

* * *

DODGE, Wendell P(hillips) 1883-1976

August 12, 1883—May 26, 1976; American explorer, theatrical producer, and author. Obituaries: *New York Times*, May 28, 1976.

* * *

DODSON, Owen 1914-

PERSONAL: Born November 28, 1914, in Brooklyn, N.Y.; son of Nathaniel and Sarah Elizabeth (Goode) Dodson. *Education:* Bates College, B.A., 1936; Yale University, M.F.A., 1939. *Residence:* New York, N.Y. 10024.

CAREER: Director of drama at Spelman College, 1938-41; instructor and drama director at Atlanta University, summers, 1938-39, full-time, 1939-42, and at Hampton Institute, 1942-43; professor of drama at Howard University, Washington, D.C. Lecturer at Vassar College, Kenyon College, and Cornell University; director of theatre at Theatre Lobby

(Washington, D.C.) and Lincoln University; poet-in-residence at Ruth Stephen Poetry Center of University of Arizona, 1969. Has conducted seminars in theatre and playwriting.

MEMBER: American Film Center (executive secretary; member of executive committee for mass education in race relations), American Negro Theatre (director), Phi Beta Kappa. *Awards, honors:* General Education Board fellowship, 1937; Rosenwald fellowship, 1945; Guggenheim fellowship, 1953; *Paris Review* prize, 1956; D.Litt. from Bates College, 1967; Rockefeller Foundation fellowship, 1968.

WRITINGS: Powerful Long Ladder (poems), Farrar, Straus, 1946; *Boy at the Window* (novel), Farrar, Straus, 1951, paper edition published as *When Trees Were Green*, Popular Library, 1951; *The Confession Stone: A Song Cycle Sung by Mary About Jesus*, P. Bremen, 1970, 2nd edition, 1971; *Come Home Early, Child*, Popular Library, 1977. Also author of play "Divine Comedy," produced in New York at New Federal Theatre, January, 1977. Work has been included in anthologies.

WORK IN PROGRESS: The Morning Duke Ellington Praised the Lord and Seven Little Black Davids Tap Danced Unto (a libretto).

SIDELIGHTS: Owen Dodson has been praised by many critics for his work. He has been called the "poet laureate now that Langston Hughes is dead," as well as a peer of Sandburg and Frost. His collected work was performed as a dramatic collage entitled "Owen's Song." It has been staged in Washington, D.C., by the D.C. Black Repertory Company in November, 1974, and later in New York. It was most recently presented at the John F. Kennedy Center for the Performing Arts.

* * *

DOHERTY, Catherine de Hueck 1900-

PERSONAL: Born August 15, 1900, in Nijni-Novgorod, Russia; immigrated to Canada, 1921; became Canadian citizen; daughter of Theodore (a diplomat) and Emma (a concert pianist; maiden name, Thompson) de Kolyschkine; married Boris de Hueck, January 25, 1915 (deceased); married Edward Doherty, June 25, 1943 (deceased); children: (first marriage) George Theodore. *Education:* Attended University of Petrograd (now Leningrad). *Religion:* Roman Catholic. *Home and office:* Madonna House Apostolate, Combermere, Ontario, Canada K0J 1L0.

CAREER: After leaving Russia, worked as waitress, salesclerk, and factory girl; Leigh Emmerich Lecture Bureau, New York, N.Y., 1925-30, started as lecturer, became lecture manager; member and director general of Lay Apostolate of Catholic Action (organization which establishes religious study centers called Madonna Houses), in Toronto, 1930-38, in New York City, 1938-48, in Combermere, Ontario, 1948—. *Awards, honors:* Member of Order of Canada, 1976.

WRITINGS: Friendship House, Sheed, 1947; *Dear Bishop*, Sheed, 1947; *Dear Seminarian*, Bruce Publishing (Milwaukee), 1950; *My Russian Yesterdays*, Bruce Publishing, 1951; *Dear Sister*, Bruce Publishing, 1953; *Where Love Is God Is*, Bruce Publishing, 1953; *Poustinia*, Ave Maria Press, 1975; *The Gospel Without Compromise*, Ave Maria Press, 1976; *Not Without Parables*, Ave Maria Press, 1976. Editor of monthly religious newspapers, *Social Forum*, 1934-38, *Friendship House News*, 1938-48, and *Restoration*, 1948—.

WORK IN PROGRESS: I Live on an Island.

DOHERTY, Eddie
   See DOHERTY, Edward J(oseph)

* * *

DOHERTY, Edward J(oseph) 1890-1975
   (Eddie Doherty)

PERSONAL: Born October 30, 1890, in Chicago, Ill.; son of James E. and Ellen (Rogers) Doherty; married Marie Ryan, December 15, 1914 (died in October, 1918); married Mildred Frisby (an actress and film reviewer), July 16, 1919 (died in March, 1939); married Catherine de Hueck (a founder of Chicago's Friendship House), June 25, 1943; children: (first marriage) Edward Joseph, Jr.; (second marriage) Jack Jim. *Education:* Educated in public, parochial, and private schools in Chicago, Ill., and Granville, Wis. *Home:* Madonna House, Combermere, Ontario, Canada; and Madonna House, Winslow, Ariz. 86047.

CAREER: Newspaper journalist in Chicago, Ill. (with brief periods in Mexico and California), 1906-24; worked in the 1930's as a scriptwriter in Hollywood, Calif.; worked as staff member of *New York Daily News* and city editor of *New York American* until World War II; worked as staff writer for *Liberty* (magazine) and as their war correspondent from England, France, and Finland, during World War II; *Chicago Sun,* Chicago, editorial writer, 1941-46; retired from journalism after the war to establish Madonna House (a lay church for international charity work) in Combermere, Ontario, and Winslow, Ariz.; ordained priest of the Byzantine Catholic Church of the Melchite rite, 1969, served as priest, 1969-75.

WRITINGS: The Saint of Paralytics (biography of Milton H. Berry), Los Angeles Times-Mirror Press, 1923; *The Broadway Murders: A Night Club Mystery,* Doubleday, 1929.

The Rain Girl: The Tragic Story of Jeanne Eagels, Macrae, 1930; *Shackled Cinderella,* Covici, Friede, 1932.

Gall and Honey: The Story of a Newspaperman (autobiographical anecdotes), Sheed, 1941; (under name Eddie Doherty) *Splendor of Sorrow: For Sinners Only* (on the Virgin Mary), Sheed, 1943; *The Corpse Who Wouldn't Die* (mystery novel), Mystery House, 1945; *Martin* (biography of Martin de Porres), Sheed, 1948; *Tumbleweed: A Biography* (of his wife, Catherine de Hueck), Bruce Publishing, 1948.

(Editor, under name Eddie Doherty) Nicholas Patrick Stephen Wiseman, *Fabiola,* Kenedy, 1951; (with Louis Bennett Davidson) *Captain Marooner,* Crowell, 1952; *My Hay Ain't In* (on Catholic action), Bruce Publishing, 1952; *Blessed Martin de Porres,* Blessed Martin Guild, 1953; *The Conquering March of Don John Bosco,* Volume I: *Lambs in Wolfskins,* Scribner, 1953, Volume II: *Bold Shepherds,* bound with Volume III: *God's Sheep Dog,* Salesiana, 1957; *Matt Talbot* (biography), Bruce Publishing, 1953; (with Davidson) *Strange Crimes at Sea,* Grosset, 1954; (adaptor, under name Eddie Doherty) Louis Marie Grignon de Montfort, *True Devotion to Mary,* translated by Francoise de Castro, Montfort, 1956.

A Nun with a Gun: Sister Stanislaus, a Biography, Bruce Publishing, 1960; *I Cover God,* Bruce Publishing, 1962; *King of Sinners* (fiction based on the life of Jesus Christ), Bruce Publishing, 1964.

Former editor of *Restoration* (publication of Madonna House).

SIDELIGHTS: Doherty's career as a newspaperman was a colorful one. Refusing to accept a life behind a desk, he traveled all over the world, covering stories on Prohibition and the Lindbergh flight to Paris, as well as on leading criminal figures of his time (he covered the Pancho Villa insurrection in Mexico). The death of his second wife turned him toward a contemplative life, and after his third marriage, he devoted himself to charitable work, and eventually to the priesthood, as a member of an order that recognizes the Roman Catholic pope, but would permit him to remain married.

OBITUARIES: New York Times, May 5, 1975; *Washington Post,* May 8, 1975.*

   (Died May 4, 1975, in Renfrew, Ontario, Canada.)

* * *

DOLBIER, Maurice (Wyman) 1912-

PERSONAL: Born May 5, 1912, in Skowhegan, Me.; son of Elmer and Melissa (Jones) Dolbier; married Mary Helen Brown; children: Cordelia, Stephanie, Mary Melissa. *Education:* Attended Whitehouse Academy of Dramatic Arts. *Office: Providence Journal,* 75 Fountain St., Providence, R.I. 02902.

CAREER: Toured as an actor with Shakespearean companies and appeared in the Groucho Marx production of "Twentieth Century"; former program director of WABI-Radio, Bangor, Me.; former news editor and announcer, WPJB-Radio, Providence, R.I.; *Providence Journal,* Providence, literary editor, 1951-56; *New York Herald Tribune,* New York, N.Y., author of "Books and Authors" column and member of book review staff, 1956-66; *New York World Journal Tribune,* New York, N.Y., daily book critic, 1966-67; *Providence Journal,* Providence, R.I., literary editor, 1967—. *Member:* Players Club.

WRITINGS—Juveniles: Jenny, the Bus that Nobody Loved (written from play; also see below), Random House, 1944, published as *The Magic Bus,* Wonder Books, 1948; *The Magic Shop,* Random House, 1946; *The Half-Pint Jinni and Other Stories,* Random House, 1948; *Torten's Christmas Secret,* Little, Brown, 1951; *A Lion in The Woods,* Little, Brown, 1955; *Paul Bunyan,* Random House, 1959.

Adult: *Nowhere Near Everest* (humor), Knopf, 1955; *All Wrong on the Night: A Comedy of Theatrical Errors,* Frank R. Walker, 1966; *Benjy Boone: A Novel,* Dial, 1967; *The Mortal Gods* (novel), Dial, 1971.

Plays: "Word to the Wise," first produced in Bar Harbor, Me., at Bar Harbor Playhouse; "Pastime," first produced in Providence, R.I., at Providence Playhouse; "Jenny, the Bus that Nobody Loved" (television play), first broadcast on "Columbia Workshop."

Contributor to *Saturday Review* and *Publisher's Weekly.*

AVOCATIONAL INTERESTS: Reading books and acting.*

* * *

DONLEY, Marshall O(wen), Jr. 1932-

PERSONAL: Born March 20, 1932, in Christiana, Pa.; son of Marshall Owen (a radio-television shop owner) and Edna (Detwiler) Donley; married Margaret T. Reagan, September 18, 1971; children: Marshall Owen III, Susan Reagan. *Education:* Pennsylvania State University, B.A., 1954; University of Southern California, graduate study, 1954-55; American University, M.A., 1965, Ph.D., 1971. *Politics:* Democrat. *Religion:* Protestant. *Home:* 10365 May Wind

Court, Columbia, Md. 21044. *Office:* National Education Association, 1201 16th St. N.W., Washington, D.C. 20036.

CAREER: Lancaster Intelligencer Journal, Lancaster, Pa., reporter, 1950-52; writer for WGAL-Radio and Television, in Lancaster, Pa., 1953; National Education Association, Washington, D.C., assistant editor of *Today's Education,* 1958-70, editor of *NEA Reporter,* 1970—. Instructor at State University of New York at Buffalo, summers, 1964-65. Has worked as a free-lance musician. *Military service:* U.S. Naval Reserve, 1949-54; U.S. Army, linguist for Security Agency, 1955-58.

MEMBER: Educational Press Association (president of local chapter, 1962), National Education Association (staff organization president, 1961; management organization board member, 1976-77), Phi Kappa Phi, Phi Delta Kappa, Phi Sigma Kappa, Sigma Delta Chi. *Awards, honors:* More than twenty national awards from Educational Press Association.

WRITINGS: Handbook for Education Editors, World Confederation of Organizations of the Teaching Profession, 1969; *NEA Launches a New Decade of Action,* National Education Association, 1970; *NEA: Vital Force for Action,* National Education Association, 1971; *Power to the Teacher,* Indiana University Press, 1976. Contributor to professional journals and newspapers.

WORK IN PROGRESS: Should Teachers Strike? and *Why Teachers Organize,* for Phi Delta Kappa, publication expected in 1978; *A History of American Public Employees.*

SIDELIGHTS: Donley writes: "Most of my writing has been related to my interest in the history of education, specifically the history of the organization of teachers in the United States into teacher unions and associations. My trips to other countries, e.g., the Soviet Union, have been tied to an interest in the teaching profession in those nations. As a linguist, I have been interested in Korean, French, and Russian. . . ."

AVOCATIONAL INTERESTS: Classical music (has played oboe), eighteenth-century British fiction, contemporary science fiction.

*   *   *

DORN, William S. 1928-
(Ian Malcolm Earlson)

PERSONAL: Born July 12, 1928, in Pittsburgh, Pa.; son of Earl Stanley (a steelworker) and Emma Margaret (a bank teller; maiden name, Schroeder) Dorn; married Nancy Lou Wootton, November 15, 1952; children: Julia Ellen, Philip John Earl, Abigail Margaret. *Education:* Carnegie Institute of Technology (now Carnegie-Mellon University), B.S., 1951, Ph.D., 1955. *Home:* 2120 South Monroe St., Denver, Colo. 80210. *Office:* Department of Mathematics, University of Denver, Denver, Colo. 80208.

CAREER: General Electric Co., Cincinnati, Ohio, mathematician and manager of system analysis, 1955-56; New York University, New York, N.Y., research scientist, 1956-59; International Business Machines Corp. (IBM), Research Center, Yorktown Heights, N.Y., member of research staff, 1959-68; University of Denver, Denver, Colo., professor of mathematics, 1968—, chairman of department, 1974—. Consultant to National Science Foundation. *Military service:* U.S. Army, 1946-47, 1952-53; became second lieutenant.

MEMBER: American Association for the Advancement of Science (fellow), Mathematical Association of America, National Council of Teachers of Mathematics, Association

for Computing Machinery, Society for Industrial and Applied Mathematics. *Awards, honors:* Fulbright-Hays senior scholar, Open University (England), 1972-73.

WRITINGS: Numerical Methods with Fortran Programming, Wiley, 1964; *Mathematics and Computing,* Wiley, 1972; *Numerical Methods with Fortran IV Case Studies,* Wiley, 1974; *Computer Applications for Calculus,* Prindle, 1974; *Who Runs the Computer?,* Westview Press, 1976; *Introductory Finite Mathematics with Computing,* Wiley, 1976. Contributor of fiction, under pseudonym Ian Malcolm Earlson, to *Creative Computing.* Editor-in-chief of *Computer Surveys,* 1968-72.

WORK IN PROGRESS: Research on the use of computers in education, university administration, and the teaching of mathematics.

*   *   *

DORSONVILLE, Max 1943-

PERSONAL: Born January 30, 1943, in Port-au-Prince, Haiti; son of Max H. (a diplomat) and Fernande (Derenoncourt) Dorsinville; married Marielle d'Auteuil (a copywriter), August 22, 1964; children: Hans. *Education:* University of Sherbrooke, B.A., 1966, M.A., 1968; City University of New York, Ph.D., 1972. *Home:* 3434 Harvard Ave., Montreal, Quebec, Canada H4A 2W3. *Agent:* Dave Godfrey, 70 Main St., Erin, Ontario, Canada. *Office:* Department of English, McGill University, Montreal, Quebec, Canada.

CAREER: McGill University, Montreal, Quebec, lecturer, 1970-72, assistant professor, 1972-75, associate professor of English, 1976—, director of French Canada studies, 1975—. *Member:* Canadian Comparative Literature Association, Association of Canadian University Teachers of English.

WRITINGS: Caliban without Prospero: Essay on Quebec and Black Literature, Press Porcepic, 1974; (with Leopold Senghor, Jean-Ethier Blais, and others) *Litteratures Ultramarines de Langue Francaise* (title means "French Literature Overseas"), Naaman, 1974.

Contributor: W. H. New, editor, *Dramatists in Canada,* University of British Columbia Press, 1972; Rowland Smith, editor, *Exile and Tradition,* Longman, 1976; Richard Kostelanetz, editor, *The Younger Critics of North American,* Assembly Press, 1976. Contributor to language and literature journals in the United States and Canada and to *Contemporary Poets.*

WORK IN PROGRESS: The "Outsider" in Quebec and African Novels, 1915-1975; research on Quebec nationalism.

SIDELIGHTS: Dorsinville writes: "Born in Haiti, raised in Canada and the United States, trained in comparative literature, I am at ease in a number of cultures, speak French, English, Creole, read Spanish. This cultural, literary, and linguistic mix influences . . . my research in the fields of Quebec, American, Canadian, and African literatures."

*   *   *

DORWART, Reinhold August 1911-

PERSONAL: Born August 12, 1911, in Holyoke, Mass.; son of George and Katherine (Pfeiffer) Dorwart; married Juanita Deauvais, March 1, 1934; children: Jeffery M., David A. *Education:* Amherst College, A.B., 1931; Harvard University, A.M., 1932, Ph.D., 1935. *Politics:* Democrat. *Religion:* Christian. *Home:* 187 Wormwood Hill Rd., Mansfield Center, Conn. 06250.

CAREER: University of Connecticut, Storrs, instructor, 1935-38, assistant professor, 1938-42, associate professor, 1942-48, professor of history, 1948-73, professor emeritus, 1973—. *Military service:* U.S. Navy, 1942-46; became captain. *Member:* American Historical Association, U.S. Naval Institute, New England Historical Association (president, 1967-68), Connecticut Academy of Arts and Sciences, Phi Beta Kappa.

WRITINGS: The Administrative Reforms of Frederick William I of Prussia, Harvard University Press, 1953; *The Prussian Welfare State Before 1740,* Harvard University Press, 1971. Contributor to history journals. Editorial adviser and contributor to *Collier's Encyclopedia.*

WORK IN PROGRESS: Christian Wolff's Politics; research on the Prussian Cameralists.

* * *

DOTY, C(harles) Stewart 1928-

PERSONAL: Born September 8, 1928, in Fredonia, Kan.; son of Charles M. (a clerk) and Ethel (Stewart) Doty; married Jean Schmechel (a librarian), June 5, 1954; children: David C., Theodore R., Peter S. *Education:* Washburn University of Topeka, B.A., 1950; University of Kansas, M.A., 1955; Ohio State University, Ph.D., 1964. *Home:* 18 Sunrise Ter., Orono, Me. 04473. *Office:* 145 Stevens Hall, University of Maine, Orono, Me. 04473.

CAREER: Kent State University, Kent, Ohio, instructor in history, 1961-64; University of Maine, Orono, assistant professor, 1964-67, associate professor, 1967-76, professor of history, 1976—. *Military service:* U.S. Army, 1955-56. *Member:* American Historical Association, Society for French Historical Studies, New England Historical Association.

WRITINGS: The Industrial Revolution, Holt, 1969; *Western Civilization: Recent Interpretations,* Volume II (Doty was not associated with Volume I), Crowell, 1973; *From Cultural Rebellion to Counterrevolution: The Politics of Maurice Barres,* Ohio University Press, 1976.

* * *

DOUGHTY, Bradford 1921-
(Brian Denny)

PERSONAL: Born July 9, 1921, in Stevens Point, Wis.; married wife, Christine; children: Stephanie. *Politics:* None. *Religion:* None. *Home:* 1400 Sawyerwood Ave., Orlando, Fla. 32809. *Agent:* Austin Wahl Agency, 21 East Van Buren St., Chicago, Ill. 60605.

CAREER: Uncle John's Restaurants, Santa Barbara, Calif., regular supervisor, 1960-68; K-Mart, Orlando, Fla., food department manager, 1974—. Novelist. *Military service:* U.S. Marine Corps, 1941-46; served in Pacific theatre.

WRITINGS—Novels: *Marine Raiders,* Challenge Books, 1967; (under pseudonym Brian Denny) *The Love Connection,* Lancer Books, 1972; *The Tree,* Venice, 1972; *Stalking Killer,* Greenleaf Books, 1972; *Girl on Ice,* Greenleaf Books, 1972; *Family Will,* Midwood, 1972.

WORK IN PROGRESS: Five Bloody Stars; Hell-Bent Leatherneck; Cry Not for Spring.

SIDELIGHTS: Doughty writes: "Have been writing for about 20 years, off and on. Have had numerous short stories published. At present still have some 15 manuscripts out to publishers for consideration with hopes of returning to writing full time once market conditions improve. Unfortunately, I must continually return to restaurant work between

highs of selling material. Own a country home to which I will go when and if I realize the success I had earlier where, amongst the huge cypress trees and peace and quiet of the woods, I will turn out some of the more serious work of my beginning years."

* * *

DOVLOS, Jay
See JOYCE, Jon L(oyd)

* * *

DOWD, Maxine
See JENSEN, Maxine Dowd

* * *

DOWLING, Eddie 1894-1976

December 9, 1894—February 18, 1976; American theatrical performer, producer, director, playwright, and author. Obituaries: *New York Times,* February 19, 1976; *Newsweek,* March 1, 1976; *Time,* March 1, 1976; *Current Biography,* April, 1976.

* * *

DOXEY, William S(anford, Jr.) 1935-

PERSONAL: Born January 20, 1935, in Miami, Fla.; son of William S. (a pilot) and Elizabeth (a teacher; maiden name, Latham) Doxey; married Lyndall Blackburn, August 22, 1959; children: William S. III, Beth, Charles Latham. *Education:* Florida State University, A.B., 1961, M.A., 1963; University of North Carolina, Ph.D., 1970. *Politics:* Democrat. *Religion:* Baptist. *Home and office:* 550 North White, Carrollton, Ga. 30117. *Agent:* Julie Fallowfield, McIntosh & Otis, 475 Fifth Ave., New York, N.Y. 10017.

CAREER: West Georgia College, Carrollton, assistant professor, 1968-70, associate professor, 1971-75, professor of English, 1976—. Has also worked as a lifeguard, roofer, and land surveyor. *Military service:* U.S. Army, 1957-58.

WRITINGS: A Winter in the Woods (poems), Windless Orchard Press, 1975. Contributor of stories and poems to literary journals and magazines, including *Carolina Quarterly, Southern Review, Descant, Quartet, Four Quarters, Esquire, Galaxy, Amazing Stories,* and *Alfred Hitchcock Mystery Magazine.* Founder and co-editor of *Notes on Contemporary Literature.*

WORK IN PROGRESS: The Other Side, a novel, for Geis; *M'Clu,* a novel; *Madness Is a State of Mind,* poems; *A Primer of Ludistic Thought,* nonfiction.

SIDELIGHTS: Doxey writes that he is "... perhaps best known as Father of Ludistic Philosophy (based on idea that if God exists He is a comedy writer); am devoted to LSD (long slow distance) running, and manage to cover eight to ten miles a day; have competence in the language of dreams; love a good fight; hate fatness and professional patriots; believe S. Dali is best artist of the century ..." and adds: "If I had known at fifteen what I know now, I would've killed myself."

* * *

DOYLE, Richard J(ames) 1923-

PERSONAL: Born March 10, 1923, in Toronto, Ontario, Canada; son of James A. (a salesman) and Lillian (Hilts) Doyle; married Florence Chandra, January, 1952; children: Kathleen Judith, Sean Gibson. *Education:* Attended Chatham Collegiate Institute. *Home:* 36 Long Cres., Toronto, Ontario, Canada. *Office: Toronto Globe & Mail,* 444 Front St., Toronto, Ontario, Canada.

CAREER: Chatham Daily News, Chatham, Ontario, city editor, 1940-51; *Toronto Globe & Mail,* Toronto, Ontario, copy editor, 1951-54, night city editor, 1954-57, weekly editor, 1957-59, managing editor, 1959-63, editor, 1963—. *Military service:* Royal Canadian Air Force, in Bomber Squadron, 1942-45; became flying officer.

WRITINGS: The Royal Story (history), McGraw, 1951.

* * *

DOYLE, Robert V(aughn)   1916-

PERSONAL: Born June 5, 1916, in Madison, Wis.; son of William V. (a textile merchant) and Frances E. (White) Doyle; married Margaret Serdahely (a registered nurse), March 15, 1941; children: Kathleen M. (Mrs. Paul Mayer). *Education:* Studied at University of Wisconsin, Milwaukee. *Politics:* "Registered Democrat, independent philosophy." *Home:* 1209 Fairweather Dr., Sacramento, Calif. 95833.

CAREER: Worked in home furnishing industry in Wisconsin, 1936-39; Sears Roebuck, New Orleans, La., salesman, 1940-42; Cutler-Hammer, Milwaukee, Wis., supervisor, 1942-44; interior designer for Barker Brothers department stores in California, 1944-54; R. V. Doyle Interiors, Bakersfield, Calif., owner, 1954-57; John Breuner Co., Sacramento, Calif., interior designer, 1957-72. Educational consultant in interior design, 1951-72; teacher of interior design, Bakersfield College (now California State University, Bakersfield), 1952-55. Free-lance writer of radio drama, 1945-52, of magazine articles, 1957—; author, 1967—. *Military service:* 1939-40.

WRITINGS: Your Career in Interior Design, Simon & Schuster, 1969, 2nd edition, 1975; *Careers in Elective Government,* Simon & Schuster, 1976.

WORK IN PROGRESS: Appropriate Technology and Your Future; research for a novel set in 1793; a contemporary novel dealing with politics; a book on the restoration of Tudor mansions; and a book of poems, self-illustrated with black-and-white photographs, all expected to be complete about 1980.

SIDELIGHTS: Doyle writes briefly: "Complete happiness is found in research, in writing, in photography. . . . There is so much about which to write, and so little time remaining. . . ." *Avocational interests:* Gardening.

* * *

DRAGONWAGON, Crescent   1952-

PERSONAL: Born November 25, 1952, in New York, N.Y.; daughter of Maurice (a biographer) and Charlotte (a children's book writer; maiden name, Shapiro) Zolotow; married Crispin Dragonwagon (an archaeologist), March 20, 1970 (divorced August 10, 1975). *Education:* Educated in Hastings-on-Hudson, N.Y. and Stockbridge, Mass. *Religion:* Buddhist. *Home address:* Dairy Hollow, Eureka Springs, Ark. 72632.

CAREER: Cook and writer. *Member:* Authors Guild of Authors League of America, Association of Journalists and Authors.

WRITINGS: Rainy Day Together, Harper, 1970; *The Commune Cookbook,* Simon & Schuster, 1971; *The Bean Book,* Workman Publishing, 1972; *Putting Up Stuff for the Cold Time,* Workman Publishing, 1973; *Strawberry Dress Escape,* Scribner, 1975; *When Light Turns into Night,* Harper, 1975; *Wind Rose,* Harper, in press. Contributor to popular magazines, including *Cosmopolitan, Seventeen, Organic Gardening, New Ingenue,* and *Aphra.*

WORK IN PROGRESS: A Seeker's Calendar, completion expected in 1977; poems, drawings, keeping a journal.

SIDELIGHTS: Crescent Dragonwagon writes: "My personal favorite of the books I've done would have to be *When Light Turns into Night.* To me, the big dilemma in life has to do with balancing the need to be with other people with the need to be alone, which is what 'light' is about. It seems to me that one without the other goes nowhere. I think there are many 'different' children—kids who seem out of step with their contemporaries, kids who are often lonely, kids who are asking questions of themselves that most people don't ask until later on in life. I wish someone had told me that if you change yourself, the world changes. This is very important, and many people never get it. To change the world, change yourself."

AVOCATIONAL INTERESTS: Practicing yoga and meditation, drawing, gardening, reading.

* * *

DRAKE, (John Gibbs) St. Clair (Jr.)   1911-

PERSONAL: Born January 2, 1911, in Suffolk, Va.; son of John Gibbs St. Clair (a Baptist minister and African civil rights organizer) and Bessie Lee (Bowles) Drake; married Elizabeth Dewey Johns (a sociologist), June, 1942; children: Sandra, Kail. *Education:* Hampton Institute, B.Sc. (with honors), 1931; University of Chicago, Ph.D., 1954. *Home:* 245 Leland Ave., Palo Alto, Calif. *Office:* African and Afro-American Studies Program, Stanford University, Stanford, Calif. 94305.

CAREER: High school teacher and soccer coach in boarding school in Cambria, Va., 1932-35; Dillard University, New Orleans, La., research assistant in anthropology, 1935, instructor in social anthropology, 1936-37; Works Progress Administration, Chicago, Ill., supervisor of research project, 1937-40; Illinois State Commission on Conditions of the Urban Colored Population, associate director, 1940-41; Dillard University, assistant professor of social anthropology, 1941-42; Roosevelt College, Chicago, Ill., assistant professor, 1946-48, associate professor, 1948-54, professor of sociology and anthropology, 1954-69; Stanford University, Stanford, Calif., professor of sociology and anthropology and director of Afro-American studies program, 1969—. Visiting lecturer at Boston University, 1953; visiting professor at University of Liberia, 1954; professor and head of sociology department at University of Ghana, 1958-61; visiting professor at Stanford University, 1963 and 1965, University of Ghana, 1965, and Columbia University, 1967. Research associate of Twentieth Century Fund's Survey of Tropical Africa, 1953-54. Member of Ghana Peace Corps Training Program teaching staff, 1961, 1962, and 1964, member of staff for Sierra Leone, 1966; U.S. State Department representative to World Festival of Negro Arts (Dakar), 1966. Former speaker for Race Relations Committee of Society of Friends, and worker at American Friends Service Committee's summer camps. *Military service:* U.S. Merchant Marine, pharmacist's mate and statistician, 1943-46.

MEMBER: International Society for the Study of Race Relations, African Studies Association, American Anthropological Association (fellow), American Society of African Culture, Phi Beta Sigma. *Awards, honors:* Anisfeld Wolf Award, 1945, for *Black Metropolis;* Ford Foundation fellowship for West African study, 1954-55; Social Science Research Council fellowship, 1965.

WRITINGS: Churches and Voluntary Associations in the

Chicago Negro Community, Works Progress Administration, 1940; (with Horace R. Cayton) *Black Metropolis: A Study of Negro Life in a Northern City* (introduction by Richard Wright), two volumes, Harcourt, 1945, revised edition, 1970; *Representative Government and the Traditional Cultures and Institutions of West African Societies,* [Ibadan, Nigeria], 1959; (with Peter Omari) *Seminar on Social Work in West Africa,* University of Ghana, 1962; *The American Dream and the Negro: One Hundred Years of Freedom?* (three lectures), Division of Continuing Education and Extension, Roosevelt University, 1963; (contributor) *The United States and Africa,* Praeger, 1963; *Race Relations in a Time of Rapid Social Change: Report of a Survey,* National Federation of Settlements and Neighborhood Centers, 1966; *Our Urban Poor: Promises to Keep and Miles to Go,* introduction by Bayard Rustin, A. Philip Randolph Educational Foundation, 1967; *The Redemption of Africa and Black Religion,* Third World Press, 1970. Contributor of poems and articles to professional journals and religious magazines.

AVOCATIONAL INTERESTS: Tennis.*

* * *

DRATH, Viola Herms 1926-

PERSONAL: Born February 8, 1926, in Duesseldorf, Germany; came to the United States in 1947, naturalized citizen, 1949; daughter of Ernst (a jurist and banker) and Annemarie Herms; married Francis S. Drath (a professor), February 5, 1947; children: Constance Drath Dwyer, Francesca. *Education:* Attended Leipzig Art Academy; University of Nebraska, M.A., 1952. *Politics:* Independent. *Religion:* "In favor, but not practising." *Home and office:* 3206 Q St. N.W., Washington, D.C. 20007.

CAREER: Peter Publications, editor, 1952-65; free-lance contributor to national magazines, 1965-70; *Vorwaerts,* Bonn, Germany, White House correspondent, 1970-75; free-lance writer for German and U.S. periodicals, 1975—. Guest lecturer at University of Southern California, University of Nebraska, American University, and Washington College, Chestertown, Md. Moderator of television programs for University of Nebraska educational television network and for National Education Television Council for Higher Education. *Member:* International P.E.N., State Department Correspondents Association, National Press Club, Altrusa, Lincoln Artists' Guild (president, 1958-60), Young Women's Christian Association (Lincoln; member of board of directors, 1963-67).

WRITINGS: Leb Wohl, Isabell (three-act play; title means "Farewell, Isabel"; first produced in Straubing, Germany at Municipal Theatre, February, 1946), Desch, 1947; *Kein Verlass auf eine Frau* (three-act play; title means "No Reliance Upon a Woman"; first produced in Munich, Germany at Junge Buehne, April, 1948), Menge, 1948; (with Harold von Hofe) *Kultur und Alltag* (title means "Culture and Everyday"), Scribner, 1973; *Willy Brandt: Prisoner of His Past* (biography), Chilton, 1975.

Textbooks: *Reporter in Deutschland,* Holt, 1959; *Typisch deutsch?* (title means "Typically German?"), Holt, 1961, 2nd edition, 1969; *The Complicated Germans,* Ginn, 1967; (editor) Kurt Hoffman, Heinz Pauck and Guenter Neumann, *Wir Wunderkinder* (filmscript; title means "Aren't We Wonderful"), Ginn, 1969; *Was Wollen die Deutschen?* (title means "What Do the German's Want?"), Macmillan, 1970; *Engagement und Provokation* (anthology; title means "Commitment and Provocation"), Macmillan, 1973. Con-

tributor of articles and reviews to journals in the United States and abroad, including *Commentary, Harper's, National Observer, Prairie Schooner,* and *Chicago Tribune.*

WORK IN PROGRESS: Hollywood East (tentative title), a novel about the power structure of Washington, D.C.

SIDELIGHTS: Viola Drath writes: "Being born in Germany and married to an American my interests focus basically on German-American relations, their political and cultural ramifications."

BIOGRAPHICAL/CRITICAL SOURCES: Lincoln Journal, September 17, 1965, February 23, 1976; *Women's Wear Daily,* December 11, 1975; *Philadelphia Bulletin,* February 9, 1976.

* * *

DRAWBELL, James Wedgwood 1899-

PERSONAL: Born April 15, 1899. *Address:* c/o Midland Bank, 70 St. Martins Lane, London W.C.2, England. *Agent:* Curtis Brown Group Ltd., 1 Craven Hill, London W2 3EW, England.

CAREER: Worked for *Edinburgh Evening Dispatch,* Edinburgh, Scotland, 1921, for *Montreal Star,* Montreal, Quebec, 1922, and for *New York World,* New York, N.Y., 1922-23; *People,* London, England, assistant editor, 1924-25; *Sunday Chronicle,* London, editor, 1925-46; *Woman's Own* (weekly magazine), managing editor and editorial consultant, 1946-64; Edinburgh Civic Theatre, Edinburgh, Scotland, press consultant, 1965-66; *Evening News,* Edinburgh, book critic, 1966—. Free-lance editorial adviser to publishers, 1964—. *Military service:* Royal Scots Fusiliers, 1914-18. *Member:* Scottish Liberal Club, Kilspindie Golf Club.

WRITINGS: This Year Next Year, Laurie, 1929; (with Reginald Simpson) *Who Goes Next?: A Play in Three Acts,* Samuel French, 1931; *Film Lady,* Collins, 1932; *Good Time!,* Dial, 1932; *A Gallery of Women* (nonfiction), Collins, 1933; *Innocents of Chicago,* Collins, 1933; *Love and Forget,* Collins, 1934; *Experiment in Adoption,* Gollancz, 1935; *Dorothy Thompson's English Journey: The Record of an Anglo-American Partnership,* Collins, 1942; *All Change Here* (nonfiction), Hutchinson, 1943; *Night and Day,* Hutchinson, 1945; *Drifts My Boat* (reminiscences), Hutchinson, 1947; *The Long Year* (1939-40; diary of first year of World War II), Wingate, 1958; *The Bright Lights,* Mills & Boon, 1962; *The Sun Within Us,* Collins, 1963, published as *James Drawbell: An Autobiography,* Pantheon Books, 1964; *The Lonely One,* Mills & Boon, 1963; *Lady in the Dark,* Mills & Boon, 1964; *Time on My Hands* (autobiography), Macdonald & Co., 1968; *A Garden: The Story of a Creative Experience,* Macdonald & Co., 1970; *Scotland Bitter-Sweet* (nonfiction), Macdonald & Co., 1972.

WORK IN PROGRESS: A nonfiction book, *Scot-Free in U.S.A.*

* * *

DREISS-TARASOVIC, Marcia M(argaret) 1943-

PERSONAL: Born July 8, 1943, in Bridgeport, Conn.; daughter of Thomas Joseph (a physician) and Mary Louise (Foytho) Tarasovic; married Joseph E. Dreiss, March 4, 1967 (divorced, August, 1976); children: Kristin Bishop, Ingrid Ross. *Education:* Attended Sacred Heart University, 1964-65, Duquesne University, 1965-67, and University of Pittsburgh, 1972-76. *Home:* 5644 #7 Forbes, Pittsburgh, Pa. 15217.

CAREER: Private practice in transactional analysis, 1975—. Teacher of transactional analysis and laborer for U.S. Steel Corp., Duquesne, Pa., 1976—. Member of board of directors of Oakland Children's Center, 1973-74. Has had solo shows of paintings and sculpture. *Member:* International Transactional Analysis Association (clinical member in training), United SteelWorkers of America (Local 1256), Pennsylvania Art Association. *Awards, honors:* First prize from Pennsylvania Art Association, 1973, second prize, 1974.

WRITINGS: *Ownings* (poems), V Mark Press, 1977.

WORK IN PROGRESS: Another book of poems.

SIDELIGHTS: Marcia Dreiss-Tarasovic writes: "With my background in TA and my abilities as a woman in the labor force I have a unique vantage on my world. It is my belief as a poet that my insights broaden the experience of those who read my work. I deal with very real issues in a cognitive way.... Words are a way of touching and allowing another's world to become more human. In using all of my skills I then enable someone else the option of using his or hers.

* * *

DREYFACK, Raymond 1919-

PERSONAL: Born 1919, in New York, N.Y.; son of Marcus (a manufacturer) and Frances (Wagner) Dreyfack; married Tess Karlitz (a special assistant to a psychiatrist); children: Kenneth, Madeleine. *Education:* Attended City College of New York (now City College of the City University of New York), Columbia University, and New York University, 1945-55. *Home:* 0-57 Pine Ave., Fair Lawn, N.J. 07410.

CAREER: Henry Kelly Importing and Distributing Co., New York, N.Y., data processing manager, 1947-52; Faberge Perfumes, Inc., Ridgefield, N.J., systems director, 1953-63; free-lance writer and public relations consultant, 1963—. Former lecturer at New York University. *Member:* American Society of Journalists and Authors.

WRITINGS: *Twelve Psychic Selling Strategies That Will Multiply Your Income,* Parker Publishing, 1975; *Sure Fail: The Art of Mismanagement,* Morrow, 1976; *How to Boost Company Productivity and Profits,* Dartnell Corp., 1976; *The Image Makers* (novel), Major Books, 1976; *Zero-Base Budgeting: Pros and Cons,* Dartnell Corp., 1977.

Ghost writer of books and articles. Contributor of chapters of books and articles to business and management journals. Special projects editor of *Plant Engineering;* contributing editor of *Supervision* and *American Salesman;* former editor and co-publisher of *Profit Improvement News.*

WORK IN PROGRESS: *Marital Misguidance; A Dark and Ominous Silence,* a novel.

* * *

DREYFUSS, Larry 1928-

PERSONAL: Born June 2, 1928, in New York, N.Y.; son of Robert (an engineer) and Pauline (Friede) Dreyfuss; married wife, Marilyn (a teacher), June 20, 1948; children: Nancy, Joanne. *Education:* Attended City College (now of the City University of New York). *Religion:* Jewish. *Office:* 112 John St., New York, N.Y. 10038.

CAREER: N. D. Construction Co., New York, N.Y., owner, 1946—; Owners Adjustment Bureau, New York, N.Y., owner, 1963—. *Military service:* U.S. Army, 1942-46.

WRITINGS: *My Life with Xaviera,* Warner, 1974; *Beyond Xaviera,* Pinnacle Books, 1975.

WORK IN PROGRESS: Two books, *Hooker Happy* and *Age Is Just Numbers.*

AVOCATIONAL INTERESTS: Piloting own plane, watching and participating in sports, travel.

* * *

DRIBERG, Thomas Edward Neil 1905-
(Tom Driberg)

PERSONAL: Born May 22, 1905, in Crowborough, Sussex, England; son of John James Street and Amy Mary Irving (Bell) Driberg; married Ena Mary Binfield, 1951. *Education:* Attended Christ Church College, Oxford. *Address:* Higham Associates Ltd., 5-8 Lower John St., Golden Sq., London W1R 4HA, England.

CAREER: *Daily Express,* London, England, member of editorial staff, 1928-43; House of Commons, London, England, independent member from Maldon Division of Essex, 1942-45, Labour member, 1945-55, 1956—, Labour member from Barking, 1959—, chairman of Select Committee on Publications and Debates Reports, 1964-65, chairman of Communications, 1965-67, chairman of Select Committee on Broadcasting of Proceedings in Parliament, 1965-67, member of delegation to Buchenwald Camp, 1950, leader of delegation to Sabah and Sarawak, 1966. Member of national executive committee of Labour Party, 1949-72, chairman, 1957-58, chairman of Commonwealth and Colonies Group, 1965-68. Select preacher at Oxford University, 1965. Member of Churches' Commission on International Affairs, 1968-75; member of Historic Buildings Council for England, 1966—. *Awards, honors:* Bronze Medal from First National Crossword Championship, 1970.

WRITINGS—All under name Tom Driberg: *Mosley? No!,* W. H. Allen, 1948; *Colonnade, 1937-1947* (essays), Pilot Press, 1949; *The Best of Both Worlds: A Personal Diary,* Phoenix House, 1953; *Beaverbrook: A Study in Power and Frustration,* Macmillan, 1956; *Guy Burgess: A Portrait with Background,* Weidenfeld & Nicolson, 1956; *MRA: A Critical Examination,* Shenval Press, 1962; *The Mystery of Moral Re-Armament: A Study of Frank Buchman and His Movement,* Secker & Warburg, 1964, Knopf, 1965; *"Swaff": The Life and Times of Hannen Swaffer,* Macdonald & Jane's, 1974. War correspondent during World War II, 1944-45, and from Korea, 1950. Television and radio critic for *New Statesman,* 1955-61. Contributor to newspapers.*

* * *

DRIBERG, Tom
See DRIBERG, Thomas Edward Neil

* * *

DRINAN, Adam
See MACLEOD, Joseph (Todd Gordon)

* * *

DRURY, Roger W(olcott) 1914-

PERSONAL: Born March 3, 1914, in Boston, Mass.; son of Samuel S. (a schoolmaster) and Cornelia F. (Wolcott) Drury; married Virginia Jenney (a sculptor), September 13, 1941; children: Tom, Geoffrey, Daniel, Julia. *Education:* Harvard University, A.B., 1936. *Politics:* Independent. *Religion:* Episcopalian. *Home and office address:* Barnum St., Sheffield, Mass. 01257.

CAREER: *New York Herald Tribune*, New York, N.Y., cub reporter, 1936-37; Macmillan Co. (publishers), New York City, worked in advertising department, 1937-39; worked as assistant director of alternative service camp, as a forester, and in mental hospitals, all for alternative service as a conscientious objector from military service, 1939-46; dairy farmer in Sheffield, Mass., 1946-60; writer, 1960—. Member of Sheffield Planning Board.

WRITINGS—Juvenile: (With father, Samuel S. Drury) *In Pursuit of Pelicans*, privately printed, 1931; *Drury and St. Paul's*, Little, Brown, 1964; *The Finches' Fabulous Furnace*, Little, Brown, 1971; *The Champion of Merrimack County*, Little, Brown, 1976. Editor of *Alumnae Horae*, 1966—.

WORK IN PROGRESS: More children's books.

AVOCATIONAL INTERESTS: Photography, archaeology, travel (Greece, the Middle East, mountaineering in the Yukon Territory), carpentry and cabinet making.

* * *

DUBAY, Robert W. 1943-

PERSONAL: Born April 29, 1943, in Detroit, Mich.; son of John Francis Gordon and Alvina (Engel) Dubay; married Linda Gail Shuff (a high school teacher), November 20, 1965. *Education:* University of South Florida, B.A., 1964; University of Southern Mississippi, M.S., 1967, Ph.D., 1971. *Politics:* Republican. *Religion:* Lutheran. *Home:* 1501 Twin Lake Dr., Bainbridge, Ga. 31717. *Office:* Bainbridge Junior College, Bainbridge, Ga. 31717.

CAREER: University of Southern Mississippi, Hattiesburg, instructor in history, 1967-68; Dalton Junior College, Dalton, Ga., assistant professor, 1968-71, associate professor of history and chairman of Division of Social Sciences, 1971-73; Bainbridge Junior College, Bainbridge, Ga., associate professor of history and academic dean, 1973—. *Member:* Society for History Education, Community College Social Science Association, Southern Historical Association, Mississippi Historical Society, Mississippi Folklore Society, Phi Alpha Theta, Omicron Delta Kappa.

WRITINGS: *John Jones Bettus, Mississippi Fire-Eater: His Life and Times, 1813-1867*, University Press of Mississippi, 1975. Contributor of articles and reviews to literature, history, and social science journals, and to newspapers. Editor of *Dug Gap Review*, 1969-71; member of editorial board of *Southern Historian*, 1967.

WORK IN PROGRESS: A biography of former Georgia governor S. Marvin Griffin.

SIDELIGHTS: Dubay writes: "I have long been interested in Southern history and politics, especially from the period 1850 to 1960. Often, by examining the careers of lesser-known personalities at the state level, considerable insight into the broader spectrum of regional and national affairs is achieved. State chief executives clearly illustrate the dimensions of events and issues. This, in turn, sheds light on the average person."

* * *

DUBE, Pierre Herbert 1943-

PERSONAL: Surname is pronounced Du-*bay*; born August 23, 1943, in Toronto, Ontario, Canada; son of Herbert (an importer) and Raymonde Helene Dube; married Carol Ann Rutherford (a teacher), August 26, 1968; children: Jean-Pierre, Diane Elizabeth. *Education:* University of Toronto,

B.A., 1967, M.A., 1968; Ohio State University, Ph.D., 1972. *Home:* 583 Rolling Hills Dr., Waterloo, Ontario, Canada N2L 5A1. *Office:* Department of Classics and Romance Languages, University of Waterloo, Waterloo, Ontario, Canada N2L 3G1.

CAREER: University of Waterloo, Waterloo, Ontario, assistant professor of French, 1972—.

WRITINGS: *A Concordance of Pascal's "Pensees"*, Cornell University Press, 1975.

WORK IN PROGRESS: Concordances of the Complete Works of Flaubert.

* * *

DU BOIS, David G(raham) 1925-

PERSONAL: Born September, 1925, in Seattle, Wash.; son of William Edward Burghardt (stepfather; a writer and scholar) and Shirley (Graham) Du Bois; divorced. *Education:* Attended Oberlin Conservatory of Music, 1942-43; Hunter College (now of the City University of New York), B.A., 1950; New York University, M.A., 1972. *Politics:* Independent. *Residence:* Oakland, Calif. *Office:* 8501 East 14th St., Oakland, Calif. 94621.

CAREER: First National City Bank of New York, New York, N.Y., clerk-typist, 1950-59; *Arab Observer*, Cairo, Egypt, editor/reporter, 1960-72. In public relations for Ghana government, Cairo, 1965-66; official spokesperson for Black Panther Party. *Military service:* U.S. Army Air Forces, Infantry, 1942-46; became second lieutenant.

WRITINGS: *And Bid Him Sing*, Ramparts, 1975. Contributor to *Black Scholar*. Editor of *Black Panther*, 1973—.

WORK IN PROGRESS: *The Bald Eagle: U.S. Racism, War, and Revolution.*

SIDELIGHTS: Du Bois wrote: "I write to share ideas and feelings which move me to serve humankind. Thirteen years outside the U.S.A. (in China and Africa) opened up new worlds of experience. As a Black American and revolutionary Marxist-Leninist, I am committed to radical change toward liberating the human spirit. I am committed to revolutionary suicide."

* * *

DUBOUT, C(harles) A(lbert) 1905-1976

May 15, 1905—June 27, 1976; French cartoonist and book illustrator. Obituaries: *New York Times*, June 28, 1976; *AB Bookman's Weekly*, July 26, 1976.

* * *

DUCKER, Bruce 1938-

PERSONAL: Born August 10, 1938, in New York, N.Y.; son of Allen (a lawyer) and Lillian (Goldner) Ducker; married Jaren Jones; children: Foster, Penelope, John. *Education:* Dartmouth College, A.B., 1960; Columbia University, M.A., 1963, LL.B., 1964. *Home:* 359 Marion St., Denver, Colo. 80218. *Office:* 1420 Larimer Sq., Denver, Colo. 80202.

CAREER: Lawyer in private practice, 1964—. Instructor at University of Colorado. General counsel to Great Western United Corp., 1972-74; president and chairman of board of directors of Great Western Cities, 1974; member of board of directors of Great Western Sugar Co., Shakey's, Inc., National Demographics Ltd., and Management Development Foundation.

WRITINGS: Rule by Proxy (novel), Crown, 1977. Contributor to legal journals and law reviews.

SIDELIGHTS: Ducker writes: "My single novel reflects an interest in how the individual fares in the structure of commerce and middle-class life. It's up to the same business—if not the same standards—as the work of Marquand, Sinclair Lewis, and Auchincloss."

*   *   *

DUDA, Margaret B(arbalich)   1941-

PERSONAL: Born January 17, 1941, in Bridgeport, Conn.; daughter of Andrew Stephen (a small businessman) and Margaret (Labai) Barbalich; married John L. Duda (a professor of chemical engineering), January 27, 1962; children: John, David (twins), Paul, Laura. Education: University of Delaware, B.A., 1963. Politics: Democrat. Religion: Roman Catholic. Home and office: 602 North Holmes St., State College, Pa. 16801. Agent: Ann Elmo, 52 Vanderbilt Ave., New York, N.Y. 10017.

CAREER: Delaware State News, Dover, Del., feature writer, 1959 and 1960 (summers); Saginaw Valley College, Saginaw, Mich., part-time instructor in English, 1970. Member: Detroit Women Writers. Awards, honors: First prize in Michigan regional play competition, 1970, for "Thirty Pieces of Copper."

WRITINGS: "Thirty Pieces of Copper" (play), first produced in Midland, Mich., at Little Theatre Guild, 1970; Dollhouse Accessories: How to Design and Make Them, A. S. Barnes, 1975; Miniature Shops for the Making, A. S. Barnes, in press.

WORK IN PROGRESS: A novel, The Passing of a Shadow; short stories and articles; a children's biography of Robert Rillieux, the inventor.

AVOCATIONAL INTERESTS: Travel, photography, illustration of own articles and books.

*   *   *

DUDLEY, Barbara Hudson   1921-
(Barbara Hudson Powers)

PERSONAL: Born February 2, 1921, in St. James, Minn.; daughter of Lloyd Edwin and Lois (Hardin) Hudson; married Jessee Wilbert Powers, October 27, 1946 (divorced May 8, 1970); married Lawrence Kneeland Dudley (a sales manager), December 5, 1971; children: (first marriage) Jean Lois (Mrs. Daniel Christian Cross), Cathy Colleen. Education: University of Iowa, A.B., 1942; University of Southern California, M.A., 1951. Politics: "May the best man win." Religion: Christian. Home: 1851 Village Ct., Thousand Oaks, Calif. 91360.

CAREER: High school teacher of speech and drama in South Gate, Calif., 1944-45; youth director for Presbyterian church in Hollywood, Calif., 1945-47; principal of Isabelle Buckley elementary schools in Beverly Hills, Calif., 1948-50; Bob Jones University, Greenville, S.C., assistant professor of drama, 1950-51; Litton Industries, Canoga Park, Calif., technical writer, 1959-60; California Lutheran College, Thousand Oaks, assistant professor, 1961-68, associate professor of drama, 1968-76. Free-lance writer, producer, and actress for about one thousand religious radio, television, and film presentations since 1946; has appeared in Off-Broadway stage productions and on television. Member of Conejo Community Players. Military service: U.S. Marine Corps Women's Reserve, 1943-45; became first lieutenant.

MEMBER: American Theatre Association, American Association of University Women, National Collegiate Players, Conejo Valley Historical Society, Pi Kappa Delta, Zeta Phi Eta, Gamma Phi Delta.

WRITINGS: (Under name Barbara Hudson Powers) The Henrietta Mears Story, Revell, 1957; (under name Barbara Hudson Powers) Going with God, World Vision, 1957; Where is God?: Three Church Dramas, Augsburg, 1963; The Teacher as a Human Being, Resource, 1971; (contributor) Carl Linder, editor, Drama for Heaven's Sake, American Lutheran Church, 1973; The Bridge of Nothing Less (three dramas), Augsburg, 1975; God's Power in Your Life: Lentendramas, Augsburg, 1975. Author of one thousand radio scripts, religious pageants, plays, and films.

WORK IN PROGRESS: Pogo, Nogo, and Thrump, three church dramas; Sailing with Bogey; The Stone, a novel of the Holy Land.

*   *   *

DUFTY, William   1916-

PERSONAL: Born February 2, 1916, in Merrill, Mich.; son of John R. (a banker) and Grace (Doyle) Dufty; married Maely Daniele, August 5, 1953 (divorced, 1967); married Gloria Swanson, February 2, 1976; children: (first marriage) Bevan Doyle. Education: Attended Wayne State University, 1935-37, and University of Southern California, 1937. Residence: Colares, Portugal. Office: Globill, Inc., 2 East 73rd St., New York, N.Y. 10021.

CAREER: United Automobile Workers International, Detroit, Mich., speechwriter, counter-intelligence operative, editor, and writer, 1937-42; Congress of Industrial Organizations, Detroit, Mich., editor, 1946; Americans for Democratic Action, Washington, D.C., editor, 1947-48; American Jewish Committee, New York City, consultant, 1949; Brotherhood of Sleeping Car Porters, New York City, consultant, 1950; New York Post, New York City, assistant to the editor, 1951-60; writer, 1955—. Editor, University Books, Secaucus, N.J., 1965-66. Consultant, Centro Europeo di Bio-Fisica Applicata, Rome, Italy, 1974-75. Military service: U.S. Army, 1942-46; served with First French Army in North Africa, France, Germany, and Austria; became sergeant.

MEMBER: East West Foundation (vice-president). Awards, honors: Page One Award from Newspaper Guild and George Polk Award for investigative journalism from New York Post, both 1958.

WRITINGS: (With Billie Holliday) Lady Sings the Blues, Doubleday, 1956; (with Edward G. Robinson, Jr.) My Father, My Son, Fell, 1957; (translator and author of introduction) Georges Ohsawa, You Are All Sanpaku, University Books, 1965; Sugar Blues (macrobiography), Chilton, 1975.

Screenplays: "Ni Temps Passe, Ni Amour" (title means "Neither Time Gone By, nor Love Ever Returns"), 1966; "To Be Continued," 1969. Contributing editor of East West Journal, 1975—.

WORK IN PROGRESS: Get Me Somebody Else, with James R. Fletcher; W: A History of Waxey Gordon and the United States; Cowboys and Bullgirls, a study of the role of animal milk in human biological degeneration; a musical version of Sugar Blues.

SIDELIGHTS: Dufty writes: "After rediscovering the hard way, through pain and suffering, that illness can be the doorway to health, I hope to encourage rediscovery in the West of the ancient Eastern principles underlying the relation between food and spiritual development, with a primary emphasis on embryological education."

BIOGRAPHICAL/CRITICAL SOURCES: People, February 9, 1976; Paris Match, February 28, 1976; Chicago Tribune, April 11, 1976.

* * *

DUKE, James T(aylor) 1933-

PERSONAL: Born October 8, 1933, in Salt Lake City, Utah; son of Otto (an engineer) and Beatrice (Taylor) Duke; married Ruth Stella Sidwell, August 22, 1958; children: James B., Sharon, David, Steven, Richard, Kathleen, Angela, Jeffrey. Education: University of Utah, B.A., 1957, M.A., 1958; University of California, Los Angeles, Ph.D., 1963. Religion: Church of Jesus Christ of Latter-day Saints (Mormons). Home: 475 South 450th E., Orem, Utah 84057. Office: Department of Sociology, Brigham Young University, Provo, Utah 84602.

CAREER: Idaho State University, Pocatello, assistant professor of sociology, 1962-63; Brigham Young University, Provo, Utah, assistant professor, 1963-66, associate professor, 1966-71, professor of sociology, 1971—. Member: American Sociological Association, American Association of University Professors. Awards, honors: National Institute of Mental Health grant, 1967-68.

WRITINGS: (Contributor) Wendell Bell, editor, Democratic Revolution in the West Indies, Schenkman, 1967; Issues in Sociological Theory, Brigham Young University, Department of Sociology, 1972; Conflict and Power in Social Life, Brigham Young University Press, 1976. Contributor to sociology journals.

WORK IN PROGRESS: A textbook on sociological theory.

* * *

DUMOND, Dwight Lowell 1895-1976

August 27, 1895—May 30, 1976; American historian, educator, and author of books in his field. Obituaries: New York Times, June 2, 1976; AB Bookman's Weekly, July 5, 1975.

* * *

DUNHAM, Katherine 1910-
(Kaye Dunn)

PERSONAL: Born June 22, 1910, in Chicago, Ill.; daughter of Albert Millard (an operator of a cleaning and dyeing establishment, a musician, and a singer) and Annette (a teacher; maiden name, Poindexter) Dunham; married John Thomas Pratt (a theatre designer), July 10, 1941; children: Marie Christine. Education: University of Chicago, Ph.B.; also attended Northwestern University. Home: 338 West 88th St., New York, N.Y. 10024; and Residence Leclerc, Port au Prince, Haiti, West Indies. Agent: Lee Mosell, 608 Fifth Ave., New York, N.Y. 10020. Office: Performing Arts Training Center, Southern Illinois University, East St. Louis, Ill. 62201.

CAREER: Director and teacher of own schools of dance, theatre, and cultural arts in Chicago, New York, Haiti, Stockholm, and Paris, 1931—; professional dancer, 1934—, with theatre experience beginning with performances in Chicago Opera, Chicago World's Fair, and eventually including world-wide tours; choreographer for theatre, opera, motion pictures, and television nationally and internationally. Lecturer nationally and internationally, 1937—; Southern Illinois University, artist-in-residence at Carbondale and Edwardsville campuses, 1967, cultural counselor and director of Performing Arts Training Center at East St. Louis campus, 1967—, university professor at Edwardsville campus, 1968—. Member of Chicago Opera Co., 1935-36; supervisor of Chicago City Theater Project on cultural studies, 1939; dance director of Labor Stage, 1939-40; producer and director for Katherine Dunham Dance Co., 1945; established school in Port-au-Prince, Hatiti, 1961. U.S. State Department adviser to First World Festival on Negro Art, 1966; artistic and technical adviser to president of Senegal, 1966-67. Productions for her own dance companies include "Bal Negre," 1946, "New Tropical Revue," 1948, "Caribbean Rhapsody," 1948, and "Bamboche," 1963. Appearances in motion pictures include "Star Spangled Rhythm," Paramount Pictures, 1943; "Stormy Weather," Twentieth Century-Fox, 1943; "Casbah," Universal-International, 1949; "Mambo," Paramount Pictures, 1966; and "The Bible," Twentieth Century-Fox, 1966. President, Dunham Fund for Research and Development of Cultural Arts, Inc.; vice-president, Foundation for the Development and Preservation of Cultural Arts, inc.; board member, National Institute on Aging and Illinois Arts Council; member, Illinois committee of J. F. Kennedy Center-Alliance Arts Education. Consultant, Interamerican Institute for Ethnomusicology and Folklore (Caracas, Venezuela), National Endowment for the Humanities review committee, and Organization of American States; advisory board member, Modern Organization for Dance Evolvement.

MEMBER: American Council for the Arts in Education, American Guild of Variety Artists, American Society of Composers, Authors, and Publishers (ASCAP), American Guild of Music Artists (member of board of governors, 1943-49), American Federation of Radio Artists, National Council on the Aging (board member), Screen Actors Guild, Writers Guild, Actors' Equity Association, Black Academy of Arts and Letters, Institute of the Black World (board member), Negro Actors Guild, Arts/Worth Project, Foundation for the Study of Arts and Sciences of the Vodun (founder), Royal Anthropological Society, Lincoln Academy, Sigma Epsilon.

AWARDS, HONORS: Julius Rosenwald travel fellowship to West Indies, 1936-37; Haitian Legion of Honor and Merit Chevalier, 1950, Commander, 1958, Grand Officer, 1968; Dance Magazine award, 1969; Eight Lively Arts award, 1969; Southern Illinois University distinguished service award, 1969; St. Louis Argus Award, 1970; American Association for Health, Physical Education, and Recreation dance division heritage award, 1972; National Center of Afro-American Artists award, 1972; L.H.D., MacMurray College, Jacksonville, Ill., 1972; Black Merit Academy award, 1972; Mather scholar, Case Western Reserve University, 1973; Black Filmmakers Hall of Fame, 1974; State Department of International Education Fulbright fellow.

WRITINGS: Katherine Dunham's Journey to Accompong, Holt, 1946, Greenwood Press, 1972; A Touch of Innocence (autobiography), Harcourt, 1959; Island Possessed, Doubleday, 1969; (author of foreword) Lynne F. Emery, Black Dance in the United States from 1619 to 1970, Mayfield, 1972; Kasamance: A Fantasy, Third Press, 1974.

Author of television scripts, produced in Mexico, Australia, France, England, and Italy. Contributor of short stories, sometimes under pseudonym Kaye Dunn, to popular magazines, including Esquire, Mademoiselle, Show, Realities, and to anthropology, travel, and dance magazines. Consulting editor, Dance Scope.

AVOCATIONAL INTERESTS: Steam baths, horseback riding, cooking, painting (her work has been shown in Australia, Italy, and England), reading, walking after midnight.

BIOGRAPHICAL/CRITICAL SOURCES: Solomon Hurok and Ruth Goode, *Impresario: A Memoir,* Random House, 1946; Richard Buckle, editor, *Katherine Dunham: Her Dancers, Singers, and Musicians,* Ballet Publications, 1949; Madeleine E. Cluzel, *Glimpses of the Theatre and Dance,* Kamin, 1953; Hurok, *Solomon Hurok Presents,* Hermitage, 1953; Fletcher Martin, editor, *Our Great Americans,* Gamma Corp., 1953; *Vogue,* November 15, 1953; Jane McConnell, *Famous Ballet Dancers* (juvenile), Crowell, 1955; Margaret Crosland, *Ballet Carnival,* Arco, 1955; Ben Albert Richardson, *Great American Negroes,* Crowell, 1956; *Dance,* autumn, 1956, April, 1969; Katherine Dunham, *A Touch of Innocence,* Harcourt, 1959; Russell L. Adams, *Great Negroes, Past and Present,* Afro-American Publishing, 1963, 3rd edition, 1969; Ruth Biemiller, *Dance: The Story of Katherine Dunham,* Doubleday, 1969; Edgar A. Toppin, *A Biographical History of Blacks in America Since 1528,* McKay, 1971.

*   *   *

DUNLAP, Jan

PERSONAL: Born in Merced, Calif.; daughter of Andrew Jackson and Belle (La Mar) Dunlap. *Education:* University of California, Berkeley, B.S., 1945; New York University, M.S., 1947; graduate study at University of Paris, summer, 1954; North Carolina State University, doctoral student, 1976—. *Office:* Center for Contemporary Management and Education, 2447 New Bern Ave., Raleigh, N.C. 27610.

CAREER: Assistant advertising manager and fashion coordinator, Nelly Gaffney Retail, 1947-48; *Sunset* (magazine), Menlo Park, Calif., editor of food trade journal, 1948-50; owner of Dunlap Merchandising (food merchandising and research firm), 1950-58; escrow officer, Veterans Administration-Federal Housing Administration (VA/FHA), 1960-65; Keystone Mortgage Co., Inc., manager of commercial and industrial loan closing departments, 1966-74, advertising manager, 1973-74; owner, manufacturer, and importer, 1970-73; Self-Management Institute, Santa Monica, Calif. (now Center for Contemporary Management and Education, Raleigh, N.C.), management consultant, specializing in management training for women, 1970—. Visiting lecturer at Drake University, 1972. Member of plans board of American Industrial Real Estate Brokers Conference, 1972.

MEMBER: American Society of Training and Development, Personnel and Industrial Relations Association, Adult Educators of Greater Los Angeles, Los Angeles Chamber of Commerce (Women's Division). *Awards, honors:* Lulu Award in Commercial Art Design from Los Angeles Advertising Women, Inc., 1958.

WRITINGS: Personal and Professional Success for Women, Prentice-Hall, 1972. Contributor to real estate journals and to *American Home* and *Cosmopolitan.*

WORK IN PROGRESS: Writing a ten-volume work, *Management Series for Women,* completion expected in 1977.

*   *   *

DUNN, Kaye
See DUNHAM, Katherine

*   *   *

DUNNETT, Alastair M(acTavish)   1908-
PERSONAL: Born December 26, 1908, in Kilmalcolm, Scotland; son of David Sinclair and Isabella Crawford (MacTavish) Dunnett; married Dorothy Halliday (an author and artist), 1946; children: Ninian, Mungo (sons). *Education:* Educated in Glasgow, Scotland. *Home:* 87 Colinton Rd., Edinburgh, Scotland. *Office:* Thomson Scottish Petroleum Ltd., 17 Charlotte Sq., Edinburgh EH2 4DJ, Scotland.

CAREER: Worked for various newspapers in Scotland during 1930's; chief press officer for secretary of state of Scotland, 1940-46; *Daily Record,* Glasgow, Scotland, editor, 1946-55; *The Scotsman,* Edinburgh, Scotland, editor, 1956-72; Scotsman Publications Ltd., Edinburgh, managing director, 1962-70, chairman, 1970-74; Thomson Scottish Petroleum Ltd., Edinburgh, executive chairman, 1972—; Thomson Organisation Ltd., Edinburgh, member of executive board, 1973—. Governor of Pitlochry Theatre. *Member:* Council of Commonwealth Press Union, Scottish International Education Trust, Scottish Ballet Committee, Scottish Opera Committee, Edinburgh Festival Society. *Awards, honors:* Smith-Mundt scholarship, 1951.

WRITINGS: Treasure at Sonnach, Nelson, 1935; *Heard Tell,* Albyn Press (Edinburgh), 1946; *Quest by Canoe, Glasgow to Skye,* G. Bell, 1950; *Highlands and Islands of Scotland,* Collins, 1951; (editor) *Alistair Maclean Introduces Scotland,* McGraw, 1972.

Plays: "The Original John Mackay," first produced in Glasgow at Citizen's Theatre, 1956; "Fit to Print," first produced in London at Duke of York's Theatre, 1962.

Also author of genealogy, *The Donaldson Line: A Century of Shipping, 1854-1954,* Jackson (Glasgow), 1960.

*   *   *

DURKA, Gloria   1939-
PERSONAL: Born October 12, 1939, in Buffalo, N.Y.; married Paul Bumbar. *Education:* Medaille College, B.A., 1968; Fordham University, M.A., 1969; New York University, Ph.D., 1973. *Religion:* Roman Catholic. *Home:* 432 Great Elm Way, Acton, Mass. 01718. *Office:* Department of Theology, Boston College, Chestnut Hill, Mass. 02167.

CAREER: W. H. Sadlier, Inc., New York, N.Y., consultant to Seminar Service, 1971-73; Boston College, Chestnut Hill, Mass., assistant professor of theology, 1973—, academic director of Institute for the Study of Religious Education and Service, 1973-76. Chairperson of religious education committee at Boston Theological Institute. *Member:* Religious Education Association, Association of Professors and Researchers in Religious Education (member of executive committee), American Academy of Religion, Religious Research Association, Association of Directors of Graduate Religious Education (chairperson), Pi Lambda Theta.

WRITINGS: Sexuality: Suggested Guidelines for a Four-Year High School Catechesis, Fordham University, 1968; (editor with Joanmarie Smith) *Emerging Issues in Religious Education,* Paulist/Newman, 1976; (with Smith) *Modeling God: Religious Education for Tomorrow,* Paulist/Newman, 1976; (with Smith) *Re-Imaging the Faith,* Paulist/Newman, in press. Co-author of "Media, Morality and Youth: A Teacher Training Kit." Contributor to theology journals. Member of editorial board of *Living Light* and *Religious Education.*

WORK IN PROGRESS: Several articles and two chapters for books; research for U.S. Catholic Conference on Teaching and Learning Processes.

SIDELIGHTS: Gloria Durka writes: "I am interested in exploring the ramifications of process philosophy and theology for the educational enterprise as a whole.'' She has made a cassette tape series, ''Basic Guidelines for Creative Religious Education.''

* * *

DUSHKIN, Alexander M(ordecai) 1890-1976

August 21, 1890—June 2, 1976; Polish-born Israeli educator, college administrator, and author of books in his field. Obituaries: *New York Times*, June 4, 1976.

* * *

DUTOURD, Jean Hubert 1920-

PERSONAL: Born January 14, 1920, in Paris, France; son of Francois and Andree (Haas) Dutourd; married Camille Lemercier, May 22, 1942; children: Frederic, Clara. *Education:* Sorbonne, University of Paris, Ph.D., 1940. *Home:* 63 Avenue Kleber, Paris 16, France.

CAREER: Journalist for the daily newspapers, *Liberation, Franc-Tireur,* and *L'Aurore,* all in Paris, France, 1944-47; British Broadcasting Corp. (BBC), London, England, program assistant, 1947-50; Editions Gallimard (publishing house), Paris, editor, 1950-66; film critic for *Carrefour* (weekly film and theatre review), 1954-62; columnist for *La Tribune de Geneve* (daily newspaper), 1955-65; *Candide* (weekly newspaper), television critic, 1962-63, columnist, 1966-67; *France-Soir* (daily newspaper), drama critic, 1963-70, columnist, 1970—. *Military service:* French Army, 1940; fought with French Resistance, 1940-44; twice captured by the Germans and escaped both times; received commander of Merite, Legion d'honneur. *Member:* French Writers Union (president, 1958-59). *Awards, honors:* Prix Stendahl, 1946, for *Le Complexe de Cesar;* Prix Courteline, 1951, for *Une tete de chien;* Prix Interallie, 1952, for *Au Bon Beurre;* Prix de Monaco, 1961, for the body of his work.

WRITINGS: Le Complexe de Cesar (essays), Laffont, 1945, 10th edition, 1946; *Le Dejeuner du lundi* (novel), Laffont, 1947; *L'Arbre, piece en trois journees* (three-act play; first produced in Paris at Marigny Theatre, 1956), Gallimard, 1948; *Une tete de chien* (novel), Gallimard, 1950, translation by Robin Chancellor published as *A Dog's Head,* Lehmann, 1951, Simon & Schuster, 1953; *Le Petit Don Juan: Traite de la seduction* (essays), Laffont, 1950; *Au Bon Beurre; ou, Scenes de la vie sous l'occupation* (novel), Gallimard, 1952, translation by Chancellor published as *The Best Butter,* Simon & Schuster, 1955 (published in England as *The Milky Way,* Museum Press, 1955); *Doucin, confession* (novel), Gallimard, 1955, translation by Chancellor published as *Five A.M.,* Simon & Schuster, 1956; *Les Taxis de la Marne* (autobiographical essays), Gallimard, 1956, translation by Harold King published as *The Taxis of the Marne,* Simon & Schuster, 1957; *Le Fond et la forme: Essai alphabetique sue le morale et sur le style* (essays), three volumes, Gallimard, 1958-65; *L'Ame sensible* (novel), Gallimard, 1959, translation by Chancellor published as *The Man of Sensibility,* Simon & Schuster, 1961; *Les Dupes* (short stories; includes ''Definition de la dupe,'' ''Baba; ou, L'Existence,'' ''Ludwig Schnorr; ou, La Marche de l'histoire,'' ''Emile Tronche; ou, Le Diable et l'athee,'' and ''Andre Breton; ou, L'Anatheme''), Gallimard, 1959.

Les Horreurs de l'amour (novel), Gallimard, 1963, translation by Chancellor published as *The Horrors of Love,* Doubleday, 1967; *La Fin des Peaux-Rouges* (stories), Gallimard, 1964, translation by Grace T. Mayes published as *The Last of the Redskins,* Doubleday, 1965; *Le Demi-Solde* (memoirs), Gallimard, 1965; *Pluche ou l'Amour de l'art* (novel), Flammarion, 1967, translation by Chancellor published as *Pluche or the Love of Art,* Doubleday, 1970; *Petit journal, 1965-1966* (diary), Julliard, 1969; *L'Ecole des jocrisses* (essays), Flammarion, 1970; *Le Paradoxe du critique* (critical essay), Flammarion, 1971; *Le Crepuscule des loups* (short stories), Flammarion, 1971; *Le Printemps de la vie* (novel), Flammarion, 1972, translation by Denver and Helen Lindley published as *The Springtime of Life,* Doubleday, 1974; *Sept saisons* (critical essays; includes ''Le Paradoxe du critique'' and ''Impressions de theatre''), Flammarion, 1972; *Carnet d'un emigre* (essays), Flammarion, 1973; *2024* (novel), Gallimard, 1975.

Editor: *Stendahl,* Hachette, 1961; Marie Henri Beyle, *Les Plus belles Lettres,* Calmann-Levy, 1962; Antoine Rivarol, *Rivarol,* Mercure de France, 1963.

Also author of privately printed critical essays, *La Mort du Chasseur, Hemingway,* 1961, *''Papa'' Hemingway,* 1961, and of a pamphlet, *Rivarol, un oracle pour notre epoque,* 1961. Author of columns, ''La Tribune de Jean Dutourd,'' in *La Tribune de Geneve,* 1955-65; ''Le Petit Journal de Jean Dutourd,'' in *Candide,* 1966-67; and ''Le Semaine de Jean Dutourd,'' in *France-Soir,* 1970—. Contributor to numerous French and foreign newspapers, journals, and magazines.

WORK IN PROGRESS: Cinq ans chez les sauvages, for Flammarion; the fourth volume of *Le Fond et la forme,* for Gallimard.

AVOCATIONAL INTERESTS: Painting, fencing (former champion of Paris).

* * *

DUVERGER, Maurice 1917-

PERSONAL: Born June 5, 1917, in Angouleme, France; son of Georges (a businessman) and Anna (Gobert) Duverger; married Odile Batt, June 3, 1949. *Education:* University of Bordeaux, Agrege des Facultes de Droit, 1942. *Home:* 24, rue des Fosses Saint Jacques, 75005 Paris, France.

CAREER: University of Poitiers, Poitiers, France, professor of law, 1942; University of Bordeaux, Bordeaux, France, professor of law, 1943-55; University of Paris I, Paris, France, professor of political sociology and economics, 1955—. Director of Institute for Political Studies, Bordeaux; director of studies of National Foundation of Political Science, Paris. *Member:* American Academy of Arts and Sciences. *Awards, honors:* Chevalier de la Legion d'honneur.

WRITINGS—In English or in English translation: *Les Partis politiques,* Librairie Armand Colin, 1951, translation by Barbara North and Robert North published as *Political Parties: Their Organization and Activity in the Modern State,* Wiley, 1954, 3rd edition, 1969, 8th French edition, 1973; *The Political Role of Women,* UNESCO (Paris), 1955; *The French Political System,* translation by Barbara North and Robert North, University of Chicago Press, 1958; *Methodes de la science politique,* Presses universitaires de France, 1959, 2nd edition, 1961, translation by Malcolm Anderson published as *An Introduction to the Social Sciences, with Special Reference to Their Methods,* Praeger, 1964; *Introduction a la politique,* Gallimard, 1964, translation by Robert North and Ruth Murphy published as *The Idea of Politics: The Uses of Power in Society,* Regnery, 1966; *Sociologie politique,* Presses universitaires de France, 1966, 3rd edition, 1968, translation by Robert Wagoner published as *The Study of Politics,* Crowell, 1972;

Party Politics and Pressure Groups: A Comparative Introduction, Crowell, 1972; *Modern Democratic Institutions,* Holt, 1973; *Modern Democracies: Economic Power vs. Political Power,* Holt, 1974.

Other writings: *Cours de droit constitutionnel,* Recueil Sirey, c. 1946, 5th edition published as *Manuel de droit constitutionnel et de science politique,* Presses universitaires de France, 1948; *L'Affectation des immeubles domaniaux aux services publics: Traite theorique et practique,* Librairie generale de droit et de jurisprudence, 1941; *La Situation des fonctionnaires depuis la revolution de 1940,* Librairie generale de droit et de jurisprudence, 1941; *Les Constitutions de la France,* Presses universitaires de France, 1944, 9th edition, 1971; *Les Regimes politiques,* Presses universitaires de France, 1948, 4th edition, 1958.

Les Finances publiques, Presses universitaires de France, 1950, 4th edition, 1967; (with Francois Goguel and others) *L'Influence des systemes electoraux sur la vie politique,* Librairie Armand Colin, 1950; *Amme maliyesi,* [Ankara], 1955; *Droit constitutionnel et institutions politiques,* two volumes, Presses universitaires de France, 1955, 5th edition published as *Institutions politiques et droit constitutionnel,* 1960, 13th edition, 1973; *Institutions financieres,* Presses universitaires de France, 1956, 4th edition published as *Finances publiques,* 1963; *Constitutions et documents politiques,* Presses universitaires de France, 1957, 6th edition, 1971; *Cours de vie politique en France et a l'entranger,* Cours de droit, 1957; (with Goguel and Jean Touchard) *Les Elections du 2 janvier 1956,* Librairie Armand Colin, 1957; *Demain, la Republique,* Editions Rene Julliard, 1958; *La Cinquieme Republique,* Presses universitaires de France, 1959, 5th edition, 1969; *Cours de science politique,* Cours de droit, 1959; (with Pierre Lalumiere) *Droit public,* Presses universitaires de France, 1959, 6th edition published as *Elements de droit public,* 1970.

Cours de sociologie politique, Cours de droit, 1960, 3rd semi-annual edition published as *Sociologie politique: Licence 1re annee, 1964-1965,* 1965; *De la dictature,* Editions Rene Julliard, 1961; *La Sixieme Republique et la regime presidentiel,* Librairie Artheme Fayard, 1961; *Les Institutions francaises,* Presses universitaires de France, 1962; (with Manuel Bridier) *Evolution des structures de l'etat,* Centre d'etudes socialistes (Paris), 1963; *Introduction a la sociologie politique,* Cours de droit, 1963, 2nd edition, 1964; *La Democratie sans le peuple,* Editions du Seuil, 1967, new edition, 1971.

Janus: Les deux faces de l'Occident, Librairie Artheme Fayard, 1972; *Sociologie de la politique: Elements de science politique,* Presses universitaires de France, 1973; *La Monarchie republicaine: Comment les democraties se donnent des rois,* Laffont, 1974.

Daily writer for *La Monde,* 1946—, *Express,* 1954-65, and *Nouvel Observateur,* 1966—.

*   *   *

DYGERT, James H(erbert)   1934-
PERSONAL: Born December 19, 1934, in Detroit, Mich.; son of James J. (a businessman) and Ida V. (Hoover) Dygert; married Mabel Ann Lewis, August 17, 1957; children: Sally Ann, Susan Elizabeth, David Lewis. *Education:* University of Michigan, B.B.A., 1956. *Home:* 183 Woodbury Dr., Dayton, Ohio 45415. *Office: Dayton Daily News,* Fourth and Ludlow, Dayton, Ohio 45402.

CAREER: Associated Newspapers, Inc., Wayne, Mich.,

editor of weekly newspapers in Belleville and Garden City, Mich., 1956-57; Jim Robbins Co., Royal Oak, Mich., executive assistant, 1960-62; *Pontiac Press,* Pontiac, Mich., reporter, 1962-64; Oakland Enterprises, Inc., Troy, Mich., co-publisher and editor of weekly newspapers in Rochester and Troy, Mich., 1964; *Detroit Free Press,* Detroit, Mich., entertainment editor, 1965-68; *Scope,* Detroit, publisher and editor, 1968-69; WJR Radio, Detroit, state capital correspondent, 1970-72; *Dayton Daily News,* Dayton, Ohio, city editor, 1972—. President, Media Ventures, Inc., Dayton, 1976—. Lecturer at Michigan State University, 1970-71. *Military service:* U.S. Army, Corps of Engineers, 1957-59. *Member:* Evans Scholars Alumni Association.

WRITINGS: The Investigative Journalist: Folk Heroes of a New Era, Prentice-Hall, 1976; *Land Investment: Guide to a Second Income Fortune,* Prentice-Hall, 1976; *Big Story High* (novel), Prentice-Hall, 1977; *Massacre at Fort Pillow* (nonfiction), Prentice-Hall, 1977. Contributor to *Esquire, Parade, Reader's Digest, Playboy, True,* and other magazines.

WORK IN PROGRESS: How to Start with Nothing and Get Rich in Real Estate, completion expected in 1978.

AVOCATIONAL INTERESTS: Magazine publishing, real estate investment, golf, travel.

*   *   *

EARLSON, Ian Malcolm
    See DORN, William S.

*   *   *

EASSON, William M(cAlpine)   1931-
PERSONAL: Born 1931, in Evanston, Ill.; son of Alexander and Anne Meldrum (Watson) Easson; married Gwendolyn Bowen, May 30, 1958; children: Anne, Jane, David, Michael. *Education:* University of Aberdeen, M.B. and Ch.B. (honors), 1954, M.D. (commendation), 1967. *Office:* Department of Psychiatry, Louisiana State University, School of Medicine, 1542 Tulane Ave., New Orleans, La. 70112.

CAREER: Certified by American Board of General Psychiatry, 1963, American Board of Child Psychiatry, 1966, and Medical Research Council of Psychiatry, London, 1972; Aberdeen Royal Infirmary, Aberdeen, Scotland, house physician (intern), 1954-55; Western General Hospital, Edinburgh, Scotland, house surgeon (intern), 1955; General Hospital, West Hartlepool, England, senior house officer, 1955; Mayo Clinic, Rochester, Minn., fellow in internal medicine, 1956-57, fellow in psychiatry, 1957-59; University Hospital, Saskatoon, Saskatchewan, resident in psychiatry, 1959-60; University of Saskatchewan, Saskatoon, instructor in psychiatry, 1959-61; Menninger Foundation, Topeka, Kan., fellow in child psychiatry, 1961-63, Children's Division staff psychiatrist, 1963-67; Medical College of Ohio, Toledo, professor of psychiatry, 1967-72, head of department, 1967-72; University of Minnesota, Minneapolis, professor of child and adolescent psychiatry, 1972-74; Louisiana State University Medical Center, New Orleans, professor of psychiatry and head of department, 1974—.

MEMBER: American Psychiatric Association (fellow), American Orthopsychiatric Association (fellow), American College of Psychiatrists (fellow), Royal College of Psychiatry (London), Louisiana Psychiatric Association, Orleans Parish Medical Association, New Orleans Area Psychiatric Association.

WRITINGS: The Severely Disturbed Adolescent, International Universities Press, 1969; *The Dying Child,* C. C Thomas, 1970; (contributor) H. D. Werner, editor, *New Understanding of Human Behavior,* Association Press, 1970; (contributor) S. J. Shamsie, editor, *Youth: Problems and Approaches,* Lea & Febiger, 1972; (with L. G. Gerber and M. E. Gottlieb) *Continuing Education in Psychiatry,* Medical Examination Publishing, 1973; *Psychiatry Examination Review,* Arco, 1974; (contributor) Maurice Freehill, editor, *Disturbed and Troubled Children,* Spectrum, 1974; (contributor) J. G. Howells, editor, *Modern Perspectives in the Psychiatric Aspects of Surgery,* Brunner, in press; (contributor) E. M. Pattison and S. H. Gruber, editors, *Death Throughout the Life Cycle,* Prentice-Hall, in press; *Psychiatry: Patient Management Review,* Arco, in press. Contributor to proceedings and professional journals.

WORK IN PROGRESS: Second editions of *Psychiatry Continuing Education Review, The Dying Child,* and *Textbook of Adolescent Psychiatry,* completion of the first two expected in 1977.

*   *   *

EASTON, Carol 1933-

PERSONAL: Born September 27, 1933, in San Francisco, Calif.; daughter of Jack Osborne (a talent agent) and Jean (Miller) Easton; married Jerry Kinnon, October 18, 1956 (divorced, 1967); children: Elizabeth, Kelly, Andy. *Education:* Los Angeles Valley College, A.A., 1954; University of California, Los Angeles, further study, 1954-56. *Politics:* "Sometimes." *Religion:* "Never." *Home:* 210 Calle de Madrid, Redondo Beach, Calif. 90277.

CAREER: Copywriter, book and record reviewer, researcher, political speechwriter, and free-lance journalist, 1970—. *Member:* Authors Guild of Authors League of America.

WRITINGS: Champagne Sec (one-act play; first produced in Los Angeles at University of California, Los Angeles, 1956), Samuel French, 1956; *Straight Ahead: The Story of Stan Kenton,* Morrow, 1973; *The Search for Sam Goldwyn,* Morrow, 1976; (contributor) George T. Simon, editor, *The Music Makers,* Vineyard Books, in press. Contributor to *People's Almanac.*

WORK IN PROGRESS: Are You Waiting for Someone?: Coming to Terms with Living Alone; a book on contemporary small town America and one on the history of classified advertisements.

SIDELIGHTS: Carol Easton writes: "Until quite recently, the motivation for my writing was, alas, food on the table. My education is haphazard in all but three areas: people, Southern California, and writing. Other than that, I am a generalist in the Age of Specialization. My hobby is eavesdropping."

*   *   *

EBENSTEIN, William 1910-1976

May 11, 1910—April 28, 1976; Austrian-born educator and author of books on political science. Obituaries: *New York Times,* April 30, 1976; *AB Bookman's Weekly,* July 5, 1976. (See index for previous *CA* sketch)

*   *   *

ECCLES, John Carew 1903-

PERSONAL: Born January 27, 1903, in Melbourne, Australia; son of William James (a teacher) and Mary (a teacher; maiden name, Carew) Eccles; married Irene Frances Miller, July 3, 1928 (divorced April 10, 1968); married Helena Taborikova (a medical scientist), April 27, 1968; children: (first marriage) Rosamund Margaret (Mrs. Richard Mason), Peter James, Alice Catherine, William, Mary Rose (Mrs. Brian Mennis), John Mark, Judith Clare, Frances Joan, Richard Aquinas. *Education:* University of Melbourne, M.B. (first class honors) and B.S., both 1925; Magdalen College, Oxford, graduate study, 1925-27; Exeter College, Oxford, M.A. and D.Phil., both 1929. *Religion:* Unaffiliated theist. *Home:* Ca' a la Gra', CH 6611 Contra (Ticino), Switzerland.

CAREER: Oxford University, Magdalen College, Oxford, England, tutorial fellow and demonstrator in physiology, 1934-37; Sydney Hospital, Sydney, Australia, director of Kanematsu Memorial Institute of Pathology, 1937-43; University of Otago, Dunedin, New Zealand, professor of physiology, 1944-51; Australian National University, Canberra, professor of physiology, 1952-66; American Medical Association, Institute for Biomedical Research, Chicago, Ill., head of research laboratory group, 1966-68; State University of New York at Buffalo, distinguished professor of physiology and biophysics and Dr. Henry C. and Bertha H. Buswell Research Fellow, both 1968-75. Waynflete Lecturer at Magdalen College, Oxford, 1952; Herter Lecturer at Johns Hopkins University, 1955; Ferrier Lecturer at Royal Society of London, 1959; Sherrington Lecturer at University of Liverpool, 1966; Patten Lecturer at Indiana University, 1972. Chairman of committees on vision, hearing, and airsickness for Australian Armed Forces Organization, 1941-43.

MEMBER: Muscular Dystrophy Association of America (member of advisory board, 1966-71), American Philosophical Society (honorary member), National Academy of Science (foreign associate), American Physiological Society (foreign honorary member), American Academy of Arts and Sciences (foreign honorary member), American College of Physicians (honorary member), American Neurological Association, Electroencephalographic Society (honorary member), Australian Academy of Sciences (fellow; president, 1957-61), Physiological Society of Great Britain (honorary member), Royal Society of London (fellow), Accademia Nazionale dei Lincei (foreign honorary member), Indian Academy of Sciences (foreign associate), Royal Belgian Academy, Deutsche Akademie der Naturforschung, Leopoldina, Royal Society of New Zealand (fellow), Pontifical Academy of Science, New York Academy of Science (honorary life member). *Awards, honors:* Rhodes scholar, 1925; junior research fellow at Exeter College, Oxford, 1927-32, Staines medical fellowship, 1932-34; Rolleston Memorial Prize from Oxford University, 1932; named knight bachelor, 1958; honorary degrees include Sc.D. from Cambridge University, 1960, University of Tasmania, 1964, University of British Columbia, 1966, Gustavus Adolphus College, 1967, Marquette University, 1967, and Loyola University of Chicago, 1969; LL.D. from University of Melbourne, 1965; M.D. from Charles University, Prague, 1969, Yeshiva University, 1969, and Oxford University, 1974; Baly Medal from Royal College of Physicians, 1961; Royal Medal from Royal Society of London, 1962; joint winner of Nobel Prize for Medicine and Physiology, 1963; Cothenius Medal from Deutsche Akademie der Naturforschung Leopoldina, 1963; honorary fellow of Exeter College, Oxford, 1961, and Magdalen College, Oxford, 1964; special award from Parkinson's Disease Foundation, 1972.

WRITINGS: (With Charles Sherrington and others) Reflex Activity of the Spinal Chord, Clarendon Press, 1932; The Neurophysiological Basis of Mind: The Principles of Neurophysiology, Clarendon Press, 1953; The Physiology of Nerve Cells, Johns Hopkins Press, 1957; The Physiology of Synapses, Academic Press, 1964; The Brain and the Unity of Conscious Experience, Cambridge University Press, 1965; The Brain and the Person, Australian Broadcasting Commission , 1965; (editor) Brain and Conscious Experience, Springer-Verlag, 1966; (with Masao Ito and Janos Szentagothai) The Cerebellum as a Neuronal Machine, Springer-Verlag, 1967; The Inhibitory Pathways of the Central Nervous System, C. C Thomas, 1969; Facing Reality: Philosophical Adventures by a Brain Scientist, Springer-Verlag, 1970; (editor with A. G. Karczmar) The Brain and Human Behavior, Springer-Verlag, 1972; The Understanding of the Brain, McGraw, 1973, 2nd edition, 1976; (with K. R. Popper) The Self and Its Brain, Springer-Verlag, 1976. Contributor of more than four hundred papers to scientific journals.

SIDELIGHTS: Eccles received the Nobel Prize in 1963 for establishing a relationship between inhibition of nerve cells and repolarization of a cell's membrane. Avocational interests: Walking, European travel, art, archaeology, classical music.

BIOGRAPHICAL/CRITICAL SOURCES: Sarah R. Riedman and Elton T. Gustafson, Portraits of Nobel Laureates in Medicine and Physiology, Abelard, 1963; Donald Robinson, One Hundred Most Important People in the World Today, Putnam, 1970; Newsweek, June 21, 1971.

* * *

EDARI, Ronald S(amuel) 1943-

PERSONAL: Born December 12, 1943, in Nairobi, Kenya; came to the United States in 1966, naturalized citizen; son of Jonah S. (a housing superintendent and farmer) and Syovata (a farmer; maiden name, Kimanzi) Bechitsao; married Julie Kailin, June 12, 1970; children: Kimanzi (son), Syovata. Education: University of Waterloo, B.A. (first class honors), 1966; Northwestern University, M.A., 1967, Ph.D., 1971. Home: 3327 North Hackett, Milwaukee, Wis. 53211. Office: Department of Sociology, University of Wisconsin, Milwaukee, Wis. 53201.

CAREER: California State University, Northridge, assistant professor of sociology, 1970-71; Purdue University, Hammond, Ind., assistant professor of sociology, autumn, 1971; Northwestern University, Evanston, Ill., visiting professor of sociology, winter, 1972; University of Wisconsin, Milwaukee, assistant professor of sociology, 1972—. Research associate at Black Strategy Center (Chicago), 1970. Member: American Sociological Association, Midwest Sociological Society.

WRITINGS: (Contributor) John N. Paden, editor, National Integration in Africa, Northwestern University Press, 1974; Social Change, W. C. Brown, 1976; (contributor) Louis Masotti and John Walton, editors, The City in Comparative Perspective, Sage Publications, Inc., 1976. Contributor to Milwaukee Journal.

WORK IN PROGRESS: Research on third-world urbanization, on neighborhood change and urban crisis in the United States, and on African economic development.

* * *

EDELMAN, Maurice 1911-1975

PERSONAL: Born March 2, 1911, in Cardiff, Wales; son of Joshua (an artist) and Ester (Solomon) Edelman; married Matilda Yager, 1932; children: Sonia, Natasha. Education: Trinity College, Cambridge, B.A., 1932, M.A., 1941. Politics: Labour. Religion: Jewish.

CAREER: Supervisor of research development of plastics and timber in aircraft industry, 1932-41; Picture Post, London, England, war correspondent in North Africa and France, 1943-45; member of Parliament, representing Coventry West, 1945-50, representing Coventry North, 1950-74. Delegate to the Anglo-French Parliamentary Relations Committee, 1948; Council of Europe, House of Commons delegate to consultative assembly and member of economic committee, 1949, parliamentary delegate, 1950, United Kingdom delegate, 1951 and 1965-70; Franco-British Parliamentary Relations Committee, vice-chairman, 1950-53, chairman, 1953; vice-chairman of British Council, 1951-67; leader of parliamentary delegation to Hungary, 1965; special representative of Colonial Section to Cayman Islands and Turks and Caicos Islands, 1965; member of Air League Council, 1966-67; chairman, Socialist Group of Western European Union, 1968-70; president, Federation Britannique de Comites de l'Alliance Francaise, 1973.

MEMBER: P.E.N., Hurlingham Club and Queen's Club (both London). Awards, honors: Coronation medal, 1953; Legion of Honor (France), Chevalier, 1954, Officier, 1960.

WRITINGS—Novels: A Trial of Love, Wingate, 1951; Who Goes Home (Book Society and Book-of-the-Month Club selections), Lippincott, 1953; A Dream of Treason, Wingate, 1954, Lippincott, 1955; The Happy Ones, Wingate, 1957; A Call on Kuprin, Lippincott, 1959; The Minister, Hamish Hamilton, 1961, published as Minister of State, Lippincott, 1962; The Fratricides, Random House, 1963; The Prime Minister's Daughter, Hamish Hamilton, 1964, Random House, 1965; Shark Island, Random House, 1967; All on a Summer's Night, Hamish Hamilton, 1969, Random House, 1970; Disraeli in Love (Literary Guild and Doubleday Book Club selections), Stein & Day, 1972; Disraeli Rising, Stein & Day, 1975.

Other: (With H.A.N. Cole) Duet (poems), E. Goldstein, 1933; G.P.U. Justice (political writing), Allen & Unwin, 1938; Production for Victory, Not Profit (excerpts of speeches), Gollancz, 1941; How Russia Prepared: The U.S.S.R. Beyond the Urals, Penguin, 1942; France: The Birth of the Fourth Republic (war experiences), Penguin, 1944; Herbert Morrison: A Pictorial Biography, Lincolns-Prager, 1948; Ben Gurion: A Political Biography, Hodder & Stoughton, 1964, published as David: The Story of Ben Gurion, Putnam, 1965; The 'Mirror': A Political History, London House, 1966. Author of television scripts, including "The Trial of Admiral Byrd," 1958, "A Distant Thunder," 1970, and adaptations of novels. Contributor of articles to political journals and magazines.

AVOCATIONAL INTERESTS: Tennis and painting.

BIOGRAPHICAL/CRITICAL SOURCES: New York Herald Tribune Book Review, October 11, 1953; New York Times Book Review, June 16, 1963; Roy Newquist, Counterpoint, Simon & Schuster, 1964; National Observer, January 5, 1970.*

(Died December 14, 1975)

* * *

EDELSTEIN, Arthur 1923-

PERSONAL: Born June 20, 1923, in Brooklyn, N.Y.; son of Harry (a trumpeter) and Miriam (Stewart) Edelstein; married Eleanor Frances Steiner, September 10, 1957 (divorced September 1, 1963); children: Michael Stewart. *Education:* Brooklyn College (now of the City University of New York), B.A., 1956; graduate study, Columbia University, 1956-57; Stanford University, M.A., 1962, Ph.D., 1976. *Home:* 2 Dale St., Wellesley, Mass. 02181. *Office:* Department of English, Brandeis University, Waltham, Mass. 02154.

CAREER: Ford Instrument Co., New York City, machine operator, 1941-43, 1947-55; Fernandez Bilingual Institute, New York City, instructor in English, 1956-57; Stanford University, Stanford, Calif., instructor in creative writing, 1962-63; Hunter College of the City University of New York, New York City, lecturer in literature, 1963-66; Brandeis University, Waltham, Mass., visiting assistant professor, 1966-71, assistant professor of English, 1971—, director of writing program, 1971-74. Has lectured at major U.S. universities. *Military service:* U.S. Army, 1942-46; served in Pacific theater; became sergeant. *Member:* Modern Language Association of America. *Awards, honors:* National Endowment for the Humanities fellowship, 1972-73.

WRITINGS: (Editor) Theodore Dreiser, *Sister Carrie,* Harper, 1965; (editor with Jonathan Baumbach) *Moderns and Contemporaries* (anthology of short stories), Random House, 1968, revised edition, in press; (editor) Stephen Crane, *Three Great Novels,* Fawcett, 1970; *Contemporary World Literature,* Brandeis National Women's Committee, 1975; (editor) *Philip Rahn Memorial Essays in Contemporary Culture,* Brandeis University Press, in press. Contributor of articles and stories to professional and popular journals, including *Southern Review, Commentary, Modern Occasions, Saturday Review, New Leader,* and *National Observer,* and to newspapers. East Coast editor of *Per Se: An International Quarterly,* 1964-67.

WORK IN PROGRESS: The Sense of the Past: Social and Literary Perceptions of America, completion expected about 1978.

SIDELIGHTS: Edelstein writes: "During my years as a factory worker, I came to literature through the works of American literary realists (Dreiser, Crane, Howells, et al). Since they wrote mainly of workers and the poor, I saw my childhood and youth in their writings." *Avocational interests:* American politics.

* * *

EDMISTON, Susan 1940-

PERSONAL: Born March 30, 1940, in New York, N.Y.; daughter of Frank (a police detective) and Julia (a legal secretary; maiden name, Klessics) Szekely; married Peter H. Edmiston, February, 1968 (divorced, January, 1975). *Education:* Bryn Mawr College, B.A., 1961. *Home:* 35 West Ninth St., New York, N.Y. 10011. *Agent:* Wendy Weil, Julian Bach Agency, 3 East 48th St., New York, N.Y. 10017.

CAREER: Tucson Daily Citizen, Tucson, Ariz., reporter for the women's page, 1961-63; *New York Post,* New York, N.Y., reporter and author of column "Teen Talk," 1963-67; *Eye* (magazine), New York City, editor-in-chief, 1967-68; free-lance writer, 1968—. President and editor of Pentacle Press, 1968-69. *Member:* International P.E.N., Authors Guild of Authors League of America. *Awards, honors:* Missouri-Penney magazine awards, 1973, for "How to Write Your Own Marriage Contract," and 1975, for "Out from Under: A Major Report on the Women's Movement;" Clarion Award from Women in Communications, 1975, for "Out from Under."

WRITINGS: (contributor) *The New York Woman's Directory,* Workman Publishing, 1974; (with Linda D. Cirino) *Literary New York: A History and a Guide,* Houghton, 1976. Contributor to popular magazines, including *Esquire, Ms., Redbook, Mademoiselle, Glamour,* and *Woman's Day,* and to *Village Voice.*

WORK IN PROGRESS: A novel.

BIOGRAPHICAL/CRITICAL SOURCES: Joyce Teitz, *What's a Nice Girl Like You Doing in a Place Like This?,* Coward-McCann, 1972.

* * *

EDMONDS, Helen G(rey) 1911-

PERSONAL: Born December 3, 1911, in Lawrenceville, Va.; daughter of John Edward and Ann (Williams) Edmonds. *Education:* Morgan State College, A.B., 1933; Ohio State University, M.A., 1938, Ph.D., 1946; University of Heidelberg, postdoctoral study, 1954-55. *Religion:* Episcopalian. *Home:* 118 Nelson St., Durham, N.C. 27707. *Office:* Graduate School, North Carolina Central University, Durham, N.C. 27707.

CAREER: Virginia Seminary and College, Lynchburg, professor of Greek, Latin, and history, and dean of women, 1933-35; St. Paul's College, Lawrenceville, Va., instructor in history, 1935-40; social science consultant, Virginia State Department of Education, summer, 1940; North Carolina Central University, Durham, professor of history, 1941-71, distinguished professor of history, 1971—, chairman of department of history and social science, 1963-64, dean of Graduate School of Arts and Sciences, 1964-71. Participated in U.S. State Department exchange program with Austria, Denmark, France, Germany, and Sweden; delegate to UNESCO Conference, 1961; U.S. alternate delegate to United Nations General Assembly, 1970. Trustee of St. Paul's College; member of advisory council to U.S. Peace Corps; member of board of directors of Southern Fellowships Fund.

MEMBER: American Historical Association, Association of Social Science Teachers, American Teachers Association, Association for the Study of Negro Life and History (member of executive council), National Links (president, 1970), National Association of College Deans and Registrars, National Education Association, Organization of American Historians, National Council of Negro Women, National Council of Women, Council of Graduate Deans, Southern Historical Association, Virginia Society for Research, North Carolina Association of Academic Deans, Phi Alpha Theta, Pi Gamma Mu, Alpha Phi Gamma, Alpha Kappa Delta, Kappa Delta Pi, Delta Sigma Theta. *Awards, honors:* Carnegie Foundation grant, 1949; Fund for the Advancement of Education grant, 1954-55; LL.D. from Morgan State College, 1958; named "Woman of the year in the South" by National Links, 1965; Southern Fellowships Fund research grant, 1948, 1969-70; National Foundation for the Humanities senior fellowship, 1970-71; L.H.D. from Shaw College at Detroit, 1975.

WRITINGS: The Negro and Fusion Politics in North Carolina, 1894-1901, University of North Carolina Press, 1951, Russell, 1973; (editor with Horace Dawson) *Appropriate Directions for the Liberal Arts College,* Seeman Printery (Durham), 1962; *Black Faces in High Places: Negroes in Government,* Harcourt, 1971. Contributor to academic journals.

EDWARDS, Donald (Isaac) 1904-

PERSONAL: Born September 27, 1904, in Bolton, Lancashire, England; son of Isaac (a Methodist preacher) and Mary (Donaldson) Edwards; married Enid Bent, 1930; children: Anthony, Julian. *Education:* Emmanuel College, Cambridge, M.A., 1930. *Home:* Spindles, Miles Lane, Cobham, Surrey, England.

CAREER: Bolton Evening News, Bolton, England, editorial assistant, 1926-28; sub-editor, *Daily News,* Manchester, England, 1928-30, Allied Newspapers, Manchester, 1930-33, and *Daily Telegraph,* London, England, 1933-39; British Broadcasting Corp., London, assistant European news editor, 1940-42, European news editor, 1942-45, correspondent in India, 1946, director of European news, 1946-48, head of external services news department, 1948-58, news editor, 1958-60, editor for news and current affairs, 1960-67, general manager of local radio development, 1967-68; Independent Television News, London, managing director, 1968-71. *Awards, honors:* Order of the British Empire, 1958; Commander of the British Empire, 1965.

WRITINGS: The Two Worlds of Donald Edwards (autobiography), Hutchinson, 1970.

*   *   *

EDWARDS, Hilton 1903-

PERSONAL: Born February 2, 1903, in London, England; son of Thomas George and Emily (Murphy) Edwards. *Education:* St. Aloysius School, Highgate, England. *Home:* 4 Harcourt Terrace, Dublin, Ireland.

CAREER: Actor, stage director and producer. Member of Charles Doran's Shakespearean Company, 1920-21, and Old Vic Shakespearean Company, 1922-26; founder and life director, with Micheal Mac Liammoir, of Dublin Gate Theatre and Edwards-Mac Liammoir Productions Ltd., 1928—; director of over 360 plays, including the works of Shakespeare, Arthur Miller, O'Neill, Anderson, Sartre, Anouilh, Brecht, Chekhov, and Wilde; director and actor in theatre productions in Cairo, Malta, Athens, Belgrade, Bucharest, Paris, London, New York, and other cities in North America and Europe. Head of drama, Telefis Eireann (Irish Television), 1961-63; producer and director of 3 films in Ireland and actor in over 10 films; director of several sound recordings for Spoken Arts and Spoken Word; producer of television drama in England. *Awards, honors:* Named Freeman of City of Dublin, 1973; LL.D., National University of Ireland, 1974; D.Lit., Trinity College, Dublin, 1974.

WRITINGS: (Contributor) George Freedley and John A. Reeves, editors, *A History of the Theatre,* Crown, 1940, 3rd edition, 1968; *The Mantle of Harlequin,* Progress House (Dublin), 1958; *Elephant in Flight,* Dufour, 1968.

*   *   *

EDWARDS, Mark U(lin), Jr. 1946-

PERSONAL: Born June 2, 1946, in Oakland, Calif.; son of Mark Ulin (an attorney) and Margaret (a librarian; maiden name, Newsom) Edwards; married Linda Johnson (in health care management), March 23, 1968; children: Teon Elizabeth. *Education:* Stanford University, A.B., 1968; M.A., 1969, Ph.D., 1974. *Home:* 18 Lovewell Rd., Wellesley, Mass. 02181. *Office:* Department of History, Wellesley College, Wellesley, Mass. 02181.

CAREER: Wellesley College, Wellesley, Mass., assistant professor of history, 1974—. *Member:* American Society for

Reformation Research, American Church History Society, American Historical Association, Luther-Gesellschaft.

WRITINGS: (Editor and translator, with H. C. Erik Midelfort) Bernd Moeller, *Imperial Cities and the Reformation,* Fortress, 1972; *Luther and the False Brethren,* Stanford University Press, 1975.

WORK IN PROGRESS: Luther's Last Years, 1531-1546, completion expected in 1981.

*   *   *

EHRENBERG, Victor (Leopold) 1891-1976

November 22, 1891—January, 1976; German-born British educator, scholar, and author of books on ancient Greece. Obituaries: *AB Bookman's Weekly,* March 1, 1976. (See index for previous *CA* sketch)

*   *   *

EHRLICH, Paul R(alph) 1932-

PERSONAL: Born May 29, 1932, in Philadelphia, Pa.; son of William (a salesman) and Ruth (a Latin teacher; maiden name Rosenberg) Ehrlich; married Anne Fitzhugh Howland (a biological research assistant), December 18, 1954; children: Lisa Marie. *Education:* University of Pennsylvania, B.A., 1953; University of Kansas, M.A., 1955, Ph.D., 1957. *Politics:* Independent. *Home:* Pine Hill, Stanford, Calif. 94305. *Office:* Department of Biological Sciences, Stanford University, Stanford, Calif. 94305.

CAREER: Field officer on Northern Insect Survey, summers, 1951-52; associate investigator on USAF research project in Alaska, 1956-57; research associate at Chicago Academy of Science, Chicago, Ill., 1957-58, and at University of Kansas, Lawrence, 1958-59; Stanford University, Stanford, Calif., assistant professor, 1959-62, associate professor, 1962-66, professor of biological sciences, 1966—. Has conducted field work in Africa, Latin America, Antarctica, Australia, and in Southeast Asia. Associate of Center for the Study of Democratic Institutions; editor and consultant to McGraw-Hill.

MEMBER: International Association for Ecology, Zero Population Growth (founder; president, 1969-70), Society for the Study of Evolution (vice-president, 1970), American Institute of Biological Science, Society of Systematic Zoology, American Society of Naturalists, Lepidopterists Society (secretary, 1957-63), American Museum of Natural History (honorary life member), American Association of University Professors, National Pilots Association, Airplane Owners and Pilots Association, California Academy of Sciences (fellow), Sigma Xi, Royal Aero Club of New South Wales. *Awards, honors:* National Science Foundation fellow at University of Sydney, 1965-66.

WRITINGS: (With wife, Anne H. Ehrlich and others) *How to Know the Butterflies,* W. C. Brown, 1961; (with Richard W. Holm) *The Process of Evolution,* McGraw, 1963; (compiler with Holm and Peter H. Raven) *Papers on Evolution,* Little, Brown, 1968; *The Population Bomb,* Ballantine, 1968, revised edition, 1971.

(With A. H. Ehrlich) *Population, Resources, Environment: Issues in Human Ecology,* W. H. Freeman, 1970, 2nd edition, 1972; (compiler with John P. Holdren) *Global Ecology: Readings toward a Rational Strategy for Man,* Harcourt, 1971; (compiler with Holdren and Holm) *Man and the Ecosphere: Readings from Scientific American,* W. H. Freeman, 1971; (with Richard L. Harriman) *How To Be a Survivor,* Ballantine, 1971; (with A. H. Ehrlich and Holdren)

Human Ecology: Problems and Solutions, W. H. Freeman, 1973; (with Holm and Michael E. Soule) *Introductory Biology,* McGraw, 1973; (with A. H. Ehrlich) *The End of Affluence,* Ballantine, 1974; (with Holm and I. L. Brown) *Biology and Society,* McGraw, 1976.

Contributor: Garrett DeBell, editor, *The Environmental Handbook,* Ballantine, 1970; Harold W. Helfrich, Jr., editor, *The Environmental Crisis,* Yale University Press, 1970. Contributor of articles to publications. Member of editorial board, *Systematic Zoology,* 1964-67, and *International Journal of Environmental Science,* 1969—.

SIDELIGHTS: MGM purchased documentary film rights to *The Population Bomb.*

BIOGRAPHICAL/CRITICAL SOURCES: Donald W. Cox, *Pioneers of Ecology,* Hammond, 1971.

* * *

EHRLICHMAN, John Daniel 1925-

PERSONAL: Born March 20, 1935, in Tacoma, Wash.; son of Rudolph I. and Lillian (Danielson) Ehrlichman; married Jeanne Fisher, August 21, 1949; children: Peter, Jan, Tom, Jody, Robert. *Education:* University of California at Los Angeles, A.B., 1948; Stanford University, LL.B., 1951. *Politics:* "Retired." *Religion:* "Renewed." *Home:* Federal Prison Camp, Safford, Ariz. 85546. *Agent:* Morton Janklow, 375 Park Ave., New York, N.Y. 10022.

CAREER: Worked as a milk truck driver, store clerk, and mailman; Hullin, Ehrlichman, Roberts and Hodge (law firm), Seattle, Wash., founding partner, 1952-68; counsel to the president, Washington, D.C., 1968-69; assistant to the president for domestic affairs, Washington, D.C., 1969-73; resigned as chief presidential adviser in midst of Watergate investigation and related probes, April, 1973; convicted of conspiracy, obstruction of justice, and two counts of perjury, January, 1975; involved in public-spirited work with American Indians, Chicanos, church and community groups, 1975-76; began serving thirty month sentence at Federal Prison Camp, Safford, Ariz., October, 1976 (expected date of release, April, 1979); writer. Instructor in law, University of Washington, 1967; director of convention activities, Republican National Convention, 1968; tour manager, Republican presidential campaign, 1968; executive director, Domestic Council, 1970-73. *Military service:* U.S. Army Air Corps, 1943-45; became first lieutenant; received Distinguished Flying Cross, Air Medal with clusters. *Member:* Kappa Sigma, Phi Delta Phi.

WRITINGS: The Company, Simon & Schuster, 1976.

WORK IN PROGRESS: A novel for Simon & Schuster; a chapter, "The Effect of Elections on Doing the Business of Government," for Sage Electoral Series.

SIDELIGHTS: Ehrlichman told Norman Mailer in an interview: "All right, the two juries in those two cases said: that guy that you thought you were is not believable to us; we find no credibility. We disapprove. Okay, at the same time the papers, magazines, television were full of an image of me that I didn't accept as my sense of myself in most particulars, most important particulars, anyway. So, there came a time when I was walking along the beach down in Oregon, thinking about all of this, when it became obvious to me for the first time really, and probably it should have come a lot sooner, that I had nothing to hold me to the sense of myself that was shared by virtually the whole world outside me. There was nothing there to defend, nothing there to fight, bleed and die for. Moreover, I was powerless to affect it. It was there, that view other people had of me, sunk in stainless steel and concrete. It would be there forever as far as I could see. If my old personality was the most relevant, important thing in my life, then my life was over."

Following his 1975 conviction and disbarment, Ehrlichman's life was strikingly altered. Once the second most powerful administrator in Washington, Ehrlichman moved to an adobe house in Santa Fe. Susan Diamond described the house as: "four rustic rooms up a dirt road hill, with his VW 'Thing' parked outside, and inside, nubby fabrics and earthenware, a fire lit against morning chill, a window flat of kale and corn seedlings for the little vegetable bed out back." He began to draw pen and ink drawings of churches, write about twenty five pages of his first novel each morning, and freely offer his special knowledge to anyone seeking it: "from a student confronting a particularly bewildering array of academic applications," wrote Diamond, "to a mountain village considering the possibilities of private or government aid in restoring their colonial ruins." His motivation, he told Diamond, is not "penitence, which implies some self-flagellation. Probably the more correct theological word is atonement, with a very precise meaning to me rather than the vulgar meaning—not a question of self-punishment or self-doubt, but self-clarification and improvement for my own sake, on my own terms, and by myself."

The Company, a roman a clef novel for which Ehrlichman received a $50,000 advance from Simon & Schuster and an estimated $75,000 from Paramount Pictures for movie rights, is reviewed by Mailer: "the restraint of the novel, its intricate clockwork of plot, and its lack of overt rage, speak a full volume of the passions Ehrlichman chose to contain within himself." Mailer observed that to lose power because one was set up "is to be marooned in obsession, paranoia and inpotent fury. The absence of passion and the lucidity of Ehrlichman's novel offers therefore a spiritual credential—it is a virtuoso if ironic act to write sympathetically, even intimately, about the problems of one's enemies as they are plotting to destroy your power. *The Company,* as a result, has to be one of the most curious novels ever published in America." *New York Times* columnist William Safire offered a pre-publication opinion of Ehrlichman's character, Monckton: "Ehrlichman's 'President Richard Monckton' reflects only the dark side of the leader he followed all his life. In presenting a self-deluded, hate-filled moralizer as President, the author settles his score with the man he feels led him into crimes, abandoned his defense, and denied his pardon." How closely the characters parallel their real life counterparts, however, remains to the reader's discretion. "I wrote a novel," Ehrlichman insists.

Ehrlichman petitioned Federal Judge John J. Sirica to allow him to serve an alternative sentence working with the Pueblo Indians in the New Mexico mountains. Though Sirica turned down the petition and Ehrlichman began serving his thirty month sentence in October, 1976, Ehrlichman still maintains his interest in alternative sentencing: "There are hundreds in Federal prisons," he told *CA,* "who could be useful and valuable in local communities if judges would wake up to their waste of human resource and sentence them to such work. It could be done at no public risk."

BIOGRAPHICAL/CRITICAL SOURCES: Time, August 11, 1975; *Newsweek,* December 1, 1975; *Time,* December 1, 1975, March 1, 1976; *Village Voice,* June 7, 1976; *Esquire,* July, 1976; *Chic,* December, 1976 (and, according to Ehrlichman, "many inaccurate accounts, the most egregiously erroneous being Dan Rather's *Palace Guard* and John Dean's *Blind Ambition.*").

EID, Leif 1908(?)-1976

1908(?)—March 28, 1976; American journalist and writer. Obituaries: *Washington Post*, March 31, 1976.

* * *

EINSTEIN, Charles 1926-

PERSONAL: Born August 2, 1926, in Boston, Mass.; son of Harry (radio comedian "Parkyakarkas") and Lillian (Anshen) Einstein; married Corrine Pendlebury, April 18, 1947; children: David, Michael, Jeffrey, Laurie. *Education:* University of Chicago, Ph.B., 1945. *Home:* 29 Midway, Mill Valley, Calif. 94941.

CAREER: International News Service, New York City and Chicago, Ill., reporter, sports and feature writer, 1945-53; *San Francisco Examiner*, San Francisco, Calif., general columnist, entertainment editor, and baseball writer, 1958-61; *San Francisco Chronicle*, San Francisco, baseball columnist, 1965-70; *Sport*, New York City, columnist, 1968-70. Editor of first wire-service news report specifically designed for television, New York City, 1950; chief writer, Goddard-for-governor, Arizona, 1964 and 1966; Northern California campaign director, Unruh-for-governor, 1970. Writer. *Member:* Authors League of America, Writers Guild of America, American Newspaper Guild, Baseball Writers Association of America. *Awards, honors:* Benjamin Franklin Award citation from University of Illinois for short story, 1957; American Cancer Society journalism citation, 1957; Junior Book Award from Boys' Clubs of America, 1964.

WRITINGS—Novels: *The Bloody Spur*, Dell, 1953; *The Only Game in Town*, Dell, 1955; *Wiretap!*, Dell, 1955; *The Last Laugh*, Dell, 1956; *No Time at All*, Simon & Schuster, 1957; *The Day New York Went Dry*, Fawcett, 1965; *The Blackjack Hijack*, Random House, 1976.

Non-fiction: (With Willie Mays) *Born to Play Ball*, Putnam, 1955; (editor) *The Fireside Book of Baseball*, Simon & Schuster, 1956; (editor) *The Second Fireside Book of Baseball*, Simon & Schuster, 1958; *A Flag for San Francisco*, Simon & Schuster, 1962; *Willie Mays: Coast to Coast Giant*, Putnam, 1963; (with Willie Mays) *My Life In and Out of Baseball*, Dutton, 1966; (with Juan Marichal) *A Pitcher's Story*, Doubleday, 1967; (with Orlando Cepeda) *My Ups and Downs in Baseball*, Putnam, 1968; (editor) *The Third Fireside Book of Baseball*, Simon & Schuster, 1968; *How to Coach, Manage, and Play Little League Baseball*, Simon & Schuster, 1968; *How to Win at Blackjack*, Cornerstone Library, 1968; (with Art Fisher and Neal Marshall) *Garden of Innocents*, Dutton, 1972; (with Mary Ann Harbert) *Captivity*, Delacorte, 1973; *The San Francisco Forty-Niners*, Macmillan, 1974.

Adaptations: *Naked City* (from television series), Dell, 1958; *Woman Times Seven* (from motion picture), Fawcett, 1967.

Plays: "Key Location," first produced in Phoenix, Ariz., by Arizona Repertory Theatre, 1958; "No Time at All," teleplay based on own novel, 1957. Also author of three hundred radio scripts.

Contributor to *Playboy, Sport, True, Argosy, Atlantic, Colliers, Esquire, Saturday Evening Post*, and other periodicals.

SIDELIGHTS: Einstein's first novel, *The Bloody Spur*,

was the basis for the R.K.O. Screenplay, "While the City Sleeps," by Casey Robinson.

* * *

EISENHOWER, Dwight D(avid) 1890-1969

PERSONAL: Born October 14, 1890, in Denison, Tex.; son of David and Ida Elizabeth (Stover) Eisenhower; married Mamie Geneva Doud, July 1, 1916; children: Doud Dwight (deceased), John Sheldon Doud. *Education:* West Point Military Academy, graduate, 1915; Command and General Staff College, graduate, 1926; attended Army War College and Army Industrial College. *Politics:* Republican. *Religion:* Presbyterian. *Home:* R.D. 2, Gettysburg, Pa. 17325. *Office:* 300 Carlisle St., Gettysburg, Pa. 17325.

CAREER: Thirty-fourth president of the United States. U.S. Army, commissioned 2nd lieutenant, 1915, executive officer at Camp Gaillard, Canal Zone, 1922-24, member of American Battle Monuments Commission, 1927-29, assistant executive to assistant secretary of war, 1929-33; American Military Mission to Philippine Islands, assistant to General Douglas MacArthur, 1935-39, chief-of-staff of U.S. Third Army, 1941, appointed commanding general of European theater of operations, 1942, commander in chief of Allied forces, North Africa, 1942-43, supreme commander of Allied Expeditionary Force, 1943-45, Army Chief of Staff, 1945-48; Columbia University, New York, N.Y., president, 1948-52, on leave, 1950-51; Joint Chiefs of Staff, Washington, D.C., chairman ex-officio, 1950-51; NATO commander of Allied powers in Europe, 1951-52; Republican candidate for U.S. presidency, 1952, elected to office with 442 of total 531 electoral votes; re-elected for second term, 1956, with 457 electoral votes; retired, 1961.

WRITINGS: Eisenhower's Own Story of The War: The Complete Report by the Supreme Commander, General Dwight D. Eisenhower, on the War in Europe from the Day of Invasion to the Day of Victory, Arco, 1946, also published as *Report by the Supreme Commander to the Combined Chiefs of Staff on the Operations in Europe of the Allied Expeditionary Force, 6 June 1944 to 8 May 1945*, U.S. Government Printing Office, 1946; *Crusade in Europe* (Book of the Month Club selection), Doubleday, 1948; *The White House Years*, Doubleday, Volume I: *Mandate for Change, 1953-56*, 1963, Volume II: *Waging Peace, 1956-61*, 1965; *At Ease: Stories I Tell to Friends*, Doubleday, 1967; *In Review, Pictures I've Kept: A Concise Pictorial Autobiography*, Doubleday, 1969.

Collections: *Eisenhower Speaks: Excerpts from the General's Speeches, with a Biographical Sketch*, edited by H. S. Bagger, Interallied, 1946; *Eisenhower Speaks: Dwight D. Eisenhower in His Messages and Speeches*, selected and edited by Rudolph Treuenfels, Farrar, Straus, 1948; *Peace with Justice: Selected Addresses*, Columbia University Press, 1961; *The Quotable Dwight D. Eisenhower*, compiled and edited by Elsie Gollagher and others, Droke, 1967; *The Papers of Dwight David Eisenhower, the War Years*, edited by Alfred D. Chandler, Jr. with others, five volumes, Johns Hopkins Press, 1970; *Selected Speeches of Dwight David Eisenhower, 34th President of the United States, Selected from Three Principal Periods of His Life: As Supreme Allied Commander in Europe During the War Years, as Supreme NATO Commander, and as President*, U.S. Government Printing Office, 1970; *Dear General: Eisenhower's Wartime Letters to Marshall*, edited by Joseph Hobbs, Johns Hopkins Press, 1971.

Author of speeches, addresses, government papers, and military reports published by U.S. Government Printing Office and other government and public organizations. Contributor of articles to *Reader's Digest, Saturday Evening Post,* and other magazines.

AVOCATIONAL INTERESTS: Golf, swimming, fishing, painting, playing bridge, watching western films, Civil War literature.

BIOGRAPHICAL/CRITICAL SOURCES: Kenneth Davis, *Soldier of Democracy,* Doubleday, 1945; John Gunther, *Eisenhower, the Man and the Symbol,* Harper, 1952; Alden Hatch, *General Ike,* Holt, 1952; Wilson Hicks, *This Is Ike,* Holt, 1952; Allan Taylor, editor and author of interpretations, *What Eisenhower Thinks,* Crowell, 1952; Hatch, *Young Ike,* Messner, 1953; Robert Donovan, *Eisenhower: The Inside Story,* Harper, 1956; D. W. Lovelace, *Ike Eisenhower, Statesman and Soldier of Peace,* Crowell, 1956; Merlo Pusey, *Eisenhower, the President,* Macmillan, 1956; Richard Rovere, *The Eisenhower Years: Affairs of State,* Farrar, Straus, 1956; Walter Smith, *Eisenhower's Six Great Decisions: Europe, 1944-45,* Longmans, Green, 1956; Marquis W. Childs, *Eisenhower, Captive Hero: A Critical Study of the General and the President,* Harcourt, 1958; Grayson Kirk, *Peace With Justice,* Columbia University Press, 1961; Ezra Benson, *Cross-Fire: The Eight Years With Eisenhower,* Doubleday, 1962; Robert Vexler, editor, *Dwight D. Eisenhower, 1890-1969: Chronology, Documents, Bibliographical Aids,* Oceana, 1970; John S. D. Eisenhower, *Strictly Personal,* Doubleday, 1974.

OBITUARIES: New York Times, March 29, 1969; *Life,* April 4, 1969; *Time,* April 4, 1969; *New Yorker,* April 5, 1969; *U.S. News and World Report,* April 7, 1969; *Newsweek,* April 7, 1969; *National Review,* April 22, 1969.

(Died March 28, 1969)

[Sketch verified by John S. D. Eisenhower]

* * *

EISMAN, Hy 1927-

PERSONAL: Born March 27, 1927, in Paterson, N.J.; son of Harry (a weaver) and Hilda (Sadovsky) Eisman; married Adrienne Ames, December 4, 1955; children: Merle (daughter), Mindy. *Education:* Attended Art Career School, 1947-50. *Residence:* Glen Rock, N.J. *Office:* King Features Syndicate, 235 East 45th St., New York, N.Y. 10017.

CAREER/WRITINGS: Free-lance cartoonist, 1950-75. Author of "It Happened in New Jersey," column in *Newark Sunday News,* 1954-57, and comic strip "Little Iodine," syndicated by King Features Syndicate to about three hundred twenty-five newspapers, 1956—. Lecturer at northern New Jersey schools and at Joe Kubert School of Cartoon and Graphic Art. Member of Glen Rock's Community Resource Program. Art work has been displayed at the Museum of Cartoon Art and in the Smithsonian Institution's Collection of Comic Art. *Military service:* U.S. Army, Infantry and Signal Corps, 1945-47. *Member:* National Cartoonists Society, Newspaper Comics Council, New Jersey Cartoonists Luncheon Club. *Awards, honors:* Silver plaque from National Cartoonists Society, 1975, for best humor from a comic book artist.

SIDELIGHTS: Eisman writes: "I am still fascinated by the comic strip where all the roles of creation are employed by a single individual. In addition to script writer, the cartoonist operates as producer, director, set designer, costume designer, casting director, make-up department, and cameraman. He makes the illusions magically appear with only a bottle of ink, pen, and a sheet of bristol. The comics have

entertained more people, all over the world, longer than any other graphic media. They continue to be the single most important feature in attracting and holding newspaper readers."

* * *

ELBOW, Peter (Henry) 1935-

PERSONAL: Born April 14, 1935, in New York, N.Y.; son of William C. and Helen (Platt) Elbow; married Linda Smickle, September 1, 1964 (divorced, March, 1968); married Cami Pelz (a therapist), July 8, 1972; children: (second marriage) Abigail Lockwood. *Education:* Williams College, B.A. (magna cum laude), 1957; Exeter College, Oxford, B.A., 1959, M.A., 1963; graduate study at Harvard University, 1959-60; Brandeis University, Ph.D., 1969. *Home:* 222 North Sherman, Olympia, Wash. 98502. *Office:* Evergreen State College, Olympia, Wash. 98505.

CAREER: Massachusetts Institute of Technology, Cambridge, instructor in humanities, 1960-63; Franconia College, Franconia, N.H., member of English faculty and chairman of core curriculum, 1963-65, associate dean of faculty, 1964-65; Massachusetts Institute of Technology, lecturer, 1968-69, assistant professor of literature, 1969-72; Evergreen State College, Olympia, Wash., member of faculty, 1972—. *Member:* National Council of Teachers of English, Society for Values in Higher Education, Phi Beta Kappa. *Awards, honors:* Honorary Woodrow Wilson fellowship, 1957; Danforth fellowship, 1957; essay prize from English Institute, 1966.

WRITINGS: Thoughts on Writing Essays (student handbook), Franconia College, 1965; *Writing Without Teachers,* Oxford University Press, 1973; *Oppositions in Chaucer,* Wesleyan University Press, 1975.

Contributor: Philip Damon, editor, *Literary Criticism and Historical Understanding,* Columbia University Press, 1967; Don Flourney, editor, *The New Teachers,* Jossey-Bass, 1971; Henry B. Maloney, editor, *Goal-Making for English Teaching,* National Council of Teachers of English, 1973.

Contributor to education and literature journals, and to *Christian Century.*

SIDELIGHTS: Elbow writes: "I had to get interested in writing twice. First in school when a couple of teachers encouraged me and it seemed to come naturally. Then again in my late twenties after I had grown completely frightened and blocked about writing in college and graduate school."

* * *

ELIADE, Mircea 1907-

PERSONAL: Born March 9, 1907, in Bucharest, Romania; came to United States, 1956; son of Gheorghe and Ioana (Stoenescu) Eliade; married Georgette Christinel Cottescu, January 9, 1950. *Education:* University of Bucharest, M.A., 1928, Ph.D., 1933; graduate study at University of Calcutta, 1928-32. *Office:* Swift Hall, University of Chicago, 1025-35 East 58th St., Chicago, Ill. 60637.

CAREER: University of Bucharest, Bucharest, Romania, assistant professor of philosophy, 1933-39; Romanian legation, cultural attache in London, England, 1940-41, cultural adviser in Lisbon, Portugal, 1941-45; University of Paris, Sorbonne, Paris, France, visiting professor of history of religion, 1946-48; lecturer at universities in Rome, Lund, Marburg, Munich, Frankfurt, Uppsala, Strasbourg, and Padua, 1948-56; University of Chicago, Chicago, Ill., Haskell Lecturer, 1956, professor of history of religions, 1957-62, Sewell L. Avery Distinguished Service Professor, 1962—.

MEMBER: American Academy of Arts and Sciences, American Society for Study of Religion (president, 1963-67), British Academy, Centre Roumain de Recherches (Paris; president, 1950-55), Societe Asiatique, Romanian Writers Society (secretary, 1939), Frobenius Institut, Academie Royale de Belgique, Osterreichische Akademie der Wissenschaften. *Awards, honors:* Honorary doctorates from Yale University, 1966, Universidad Nacional de la Plata, 1969, Universidad del Salvador, 1969, Ripon College, 1969, Loyola University, 1970, Boston College, 1971, La Salle College, 1972, Oberlin College, 1972, University of Lancaster, 1975, and Sorbonne, University of Paris, 1976.

WRITINGS—In English: *Traite d'histoire des religions,* Payot, 1948, translation by Rosemary Sheed published as *Patterns in Comparative Religion,* Sheed, 1958, 7th French edition, Payot, 1968; *Le Mythe de l'eternel retour: Archetypes et repetition,* Gallimard, 1949, translation by Willard R. Trask published as *The Myth of the Eternal Return; or, Cosmos and History,* Pantheon, 1955, published as *Cosmos and History: The Myth of the Eternal Return,* Harper, 1959.

Le Chamanisme et les techniques archaiques de l'extase, Payot, 1951, translation by Trask published as *Shamanism: Archaic Techniques of Ecstasy,* Pantheon, 1964, 2nd French edition, Payot, 1968, 2nd English edition, Princeton University Press, 1970; *Images et symboles: Essais sur le symbolisme magicoreligieux,* Gallimard, 1952, translation by Philip Mairet published as *Images and Symbols: Studies in Religious Symbolism,* Harvill Press, 1961; *Le Yoga: Immortalite et liberte,* Payot, 1954, translation by Trask published as *Yoga: Immortality and Freedom,* Pantheon, 1958; *Forgerons et alchemistes,* Flammarion, 1956, translation by Stephen Corrin published as *The Forge and the Crucible,* Harper, 1962; *The Sacred and the Profane: The Nature of Religion,* translated by Trask, Harcourt, 1959; *Mythes, reves, et mysteres,* Gallimard, 1957, translation by Mairet published as *Myths, Dreams, and Mysteries: The Encounter between Contemporary Faiths and Archaic Realities,* Harvill Press, 1960; *Birth and Rebirth: The Religious Meanings of Initiation in Human Culture,* translated by Trask, Harper, 1958, published as *Rites and Symbols of Initiation: The Mysteries of Birth and Rebirth,* 1965; (editor with Joseph M. Kitagawa) *The History of Religions: Essays in Methodology,* University of Chicago Press, 1959.

Patanjali et le Yoga, Editions du Seuil, 1962, translation by Charles Lam Markmann published as *Patanjali and Yoga,* Funk, 1969; *Mephistopheles et l'Androgyne,* Gallimard, 1962, translation by J. M. Cohen published as *Mephistopheles and the Androgyne: Studies in Religious Myth and Symbol,* Sheed, 1965 (published in England as *The Two and the One,* Harvill Press, 1965); *Myth and Reality,* translated by Trask, Harper, 1963; (editor) *From Primitives to Zen: A Thematic Sourcebook of the History of Religions,* Collins, 1967; (editor with Kitagawa and Charles H. Long, and contributor) *The History of Religions: Essays on the Problem of Understanding,* University of Chicago Press, 1967; *The Quest: History and Meaning in Religion,* University of Chicago Press, 1969; (with Mihai Niculescu) *Fantastic Tales,* translated and edited by Eric Tappe, Dillon's University Bookshop, 1969.

De Zalmoxis a Genghis Khan: Etudes comparatives sur les religions et le folklore de la Dacie et de l'Europe orientale, Payot, 1970, translation by Trask published as *Zalmoxis, the Vanishing God: Comparative Studies in the Religions and*

Folklore of Dacia and Eastern Europe, University of Chicago Press, 1972; *Two Tales of the Occult,* translated from the Romanian by William Ames Coates, Herder & Herder, 1970; *Religions australiennes* (translation of lectures originally given in English), translated by L. Jospin, Payot, 1972, published as *Australian Religions: An Introduction,* Cornell University Press, 1973; *Fragments d'un journal,* translated from the Romanian by Luc Badesco, Gallimard, 1973, translation by Fred H. Johnson, Jr., published as *No Souvenirs: Journal, 1957-1969,* Harper, 1977.

Contributor: K. Bharatha Iyer, editor, *Art and Thought,* Luzac & Co., 1947; V.T.A. Ferm, editor, *Forgotten Religions, including Some Living Primitive Religions,* Philosophical Library, 1950; P. A. Sorokin, editor, *Forms and Techniques of Altruistic and Spiritual Growth: A Symposium,* Beacon Press, 1954; Joseph Campbell, editor, *Man and Time,* Pantheon, 1957; Carl H. Kraeling and R. M. Adams, editors, *City Invincible,* University of Chicago Press, 1960; Henry A. Murray, editor, *Myth and Mythmaking,* Braziller, 1960; Sylvia L. Thrupp, editor, *Millenial Dreams in Action: Essays in Comparative Study,* Mouton, 1962; Campbell, editor, *Man and Transformation,* Pantheon, 1964; Francis Lee Utley, Lynn Z. Bloom, and Arthur F. Kinney, editors, *Bear, Man, and God: Seven Approaches to William Faulkner's "The Bear,"* Random House, 1964; Frank E. Manuel, editor, *Utopias and Utopian thought,* Houghton, 1966; Paul Tillich, *The Future of Religions,* edited by Jerald C. Brauer, Harper, 1966; Walter J. Ong, editor, *Knowledge and the Future of Man: An International Symposium,* Holt, 1968; Joseph M. Kitagawa and Charles H. Long, editors, *Myths and Symbols: Studies in Honor of Mircea Eliade,* University of Chicago Press, 1969; Eric J. Sharpe and John R. Hinnells, editors, *Man and His Salvation,* Manchester University Press, 1973.

Other writings: *Isabel si Apele Diavolului* (novel; title means "Isabel and the Devil's Waters"), Editura Nationale Ciornei (Bucharest), 1930; *Maitreyi* (novel), Editura Nationale Ciornei, 1933; *Intoarcerea din Rai* (novel; first and second part of trilogy; title means "The Return from Paradise"), Editura Nationala Ciornei, 1934-54; *Yoga: Essai sur les origines de la mystique indienne* (title means "Yoga: Essays on the Origins of Indian Mystic Techniques"), Librairie Orientaliste Paul Geuthner, 1936; *Sarpele* (novel; title means "The Serpent"), Editura Nationale Ciornei, 1937; *Nunta in Cer* (novel; title means "Marriage in Heaven"), Editura Cugetarea, 1938; *Os Romenos latinos do Oriente,* Livraria Classica Editora, 1943; *Techniques du yoga* (title means "Techniques of Yoga"), Gallimard, 1948, new edition, 1975; *Foret interdite* (novel; title means "Forbidden Forest"), translated from the Romanian by Alain Guillormou, Gallimard, 1955; *Minuit a Serampore, Suivi de Le Secret du Docteur Honigberger* (title means "Midnight at Serampore" and "The Secret of Dr. Honigberger"), translated from the Romanian by Albert Marie Schmidt, Stock, 1956; (contributor) Giuseppe Tucci, editor, *Le Symbolisme cosmique des monuments religieux* (title means "The Cosmic Symbolism of Religious Monuments"), Istituto Italiano per il Medio e Estremo Oriente (Rome), 1957; *Nuvele* (novellas; includes "La Tiganci," "O fotografie veche de 14 ani," "Ghicitor in pietre," "Un om mare," "Feta capitanului," and "Douasprezece mil de capete de vite"), Destin (Madrid), 1963; *Amintiri: I. Mansarda* (title means "An Autobiography: I. The Attic"), Destin, 1966; *Pe strada Mantuleasa* (title means "On the Mantuleasa Street"), Caietele Inorugului, 1968; *Histoire des croyances et des idees religieuses,* Volume I, Payot, 1976.

Also author of some twenty volumes published in Romanian, 1933-45. Founder and editor, *Zalmoxis* (an international journal for history of religions), 1938-42; founder and senior editor, *History of Religions,* 1961—. Contributor to journals in his field.

WORK IN PROGRESS: An autobiography and a journal, written in Romanian; a multi-volume history of religions, in French.

SIDELIGHTS: Eliade's second novel, *Maitreyi,* published in 1933, became a best seller immediately after its publication. Eliade found this popularity annoying, and turned instead to publishing only rather difficult novels and scholarly works. While his novels were well received by the public and the critics, Eliade personally preferred his critical and philosophical work on Indian religions, Asiatic alchemy, and mythical thought. He says that he has continued to write novels and short stories because "sometimes my ideas on myth, time, or religious symbolism can be presented in more cogent form in fiction that in scientific treatises." Eliade feels, nevertheless, that history, philosophy, and fiction are complementary as instruments of expression. His writing, since his work at the Sorbonne, has been about the problems for which he is internationally known, and which he claims have obsessed him from his youth, including the history of religions, the structure of myths, and religious symbolism.

For Eliade, religion "does not necessarily imply belief in God, gods, or ghosts, but refers to the experience of the sacred." The function of religion is "that of maintaining an 'opening' toward a world which is superhuman . . . to awaken and sustain . . . [in man] the consciousness of another world, of a 'beyond' . . . This experience of the sacred, that is, the meeting with a transhuman reality, . . . generates the idea . . . that there are absolute, intangible values which confer a meaning upon human existence."

The difference between religious and nonreligious man, Eliade observes, is that "the nonreligious man refuses transcendence, . . . accepts no model for humanity outside the human condition," and "desacralizes himself and the world." Yet beyond that, the tragedy of modern nonreligious man is that his "camouflaged myths and degenerated rituals" show that he can never completely desacralize himself and should not try: "Do what he will he is an inheritor. He cannot utterly abolish his past, since he is himself the product of his past."

If the sacred experience is seen to give meaning to man's existence, then Eliade contends it is worthwhile to examine the nature of that experience. This historian of religions has criticized early ethnologists and philologists for having too little patience trying to understand what a religion meant for its believer. He insists that the historian of religions must respect the character of religious experience and grasp religious phenomena "on their own plane of reference." Further, Eliade insists he attempt to understand it as it is for the person who has had that experience, and in order to do that, one needs to participate. For the historian of religions, that means dealing with religious facts, the experience of time and space.

Central to the patterns of Eliade's thought on the history of religions are sacred time and space, problems to which he has returned frequently and about which he has contributed much research. The three books that Jonathan Z. Smith claims have established Eliade's reputation in the United States—*The Myth of the Eternal Return, Patterns in Comparative Religion,* and *The Sacred and the Profane*—are centrally concerned with sacred time and space. These are experienced by religious man as a breakthrough, a manifestation of "something that does not belong to this world," a point of communication which is value-laden, "indefinitely recoverable, indefinitely repeatable," and which revivifies and strengthens the cosmos, society, and the individual.

Smith notes that man has been defined, since Kant, as a world-creating being. His creativity, involved in "undertaking the creation of the world one has chosen to inhabit," is actually a participation in or repetition of the original archetypal acts of creation. Man can not receive his inheritance only passively, Eliade contends; rather, he must actively engage in the original creative process through a repetition of it.

Eliade would join with Old Testament scholar Sigmund Mowinckel in saying that for religious man, participating in cult "means salvation from that death and destruction which would befall, if life were not renewed."

BIOGRAPHICAL/CRITICAL SOURCES: Thomas J. J. Altizer, *Mircea Eliade and the Dialectic of the Sacred,* Westminster Press, 1963; *Journal of Bible and Religion,* July, 1965; *Time,* February 11, 1966; *New York Review of Books,* October 20, 1966; *Religion in Life,* Spring, 1967; Joseph M. Kitagawa and Charles H. Long, editors, *Myths and Symbols: Studies in Honor of Mircea Eliade,* University of Chicago Press, 1969; *Union Seminary Quarterly Review,* winter, 1970, summer, 1970; *Journal of Religion,* April, 1972; *Religious Studies,* 1972, 1974; *Religion: Journal of Religion and Religions,* spring, 1973.

* * *

ELLIOTT, William Douglas 1938-

PERSONAL: Born January 13, 1938, in Bemidji, Minn.; son of Alfred M. (a zoologist) and Lulu (a school teacher; maiden name, Maynard) Elliott; married Gwendolyn Warren (a librarian), July 19, 1960; children: Sharon Elizabeth, Douglas Warren. *Education:* Miami University, Oxford, Ohio, B.A., 1960; University of Michigan, M.A., 1961, Ed.D., 1967; University of Iowa, M.F.A., 1962. *Home:* 3308 Cedar Lane, Bemidji, Minn. 56601. *Agent:* Ann Elmo Literary Agency, Inc., 52 Vanderbilt Ave., New York, N.Y. 10017. *Office:* Department of English, Hagg-Sauer 393, Bemidji State University, Bemidji, Minn. 56601.

CAREER: Ohio University, Zanesville, instructor in English, 1964-65; Washtenaw Community College, Ann Arbor, Mich., instructor in English, 1966-67; Bemidji State College, Bemidji, Minn., assistant professor, 1967-68, associate professor of English, 1968—. Instructor at Muskingum College, 1964-65. Co-founding director of Upper Midwest Writers' Conference, 1969, 1970; founding director of Minnesota State College Poets' Exchange Program, 1973—; panelist on Minnesota State Arts Board. Has given readings from his poetry.

MEMBER: Modern Language Association of America, Midwest Modern Language Association, Minnesota Council of Teachers of English, Phi Kappa Phi. *Awards, honors:* Jule and Avery Hopwood Awards in Creative Writing from University of Michigan, 1959, 1961, and 1962; scholarship from Breadloaf Writers' Conference, 1961; humanities award in shorter fiction from McKnight Foundation, 1968, for novella "Stopping Off in Switzerland;" Pulitzer Prize nomination for poetry, 1974; American Philosophical Society travel grant to England and Australia, spring, 1974; fellowship from Minnesota State Arts Council, 1975.

WRITINGS: *European Sketches and Other Poems* (chapbook), New Concord Press, 1964; *Pine and Jack Pine* (poetry chapbook), Northwoods Press, 1973; *Winter in the Rex* (poetry chapbook), Kendall Press, 1973; *Eco-Catastrophe* (poetry chapbook), Bemidji State University Press, 1973; *Flood* (broadsheet), Sceptre Press, 1973; *Minnesota* (broadsheet), Smith-Park Poets, 1975; *Henry Handel Richardson,* Twayne, 1975. Also author of two short story collections, *Ascent,* 1970, and *Moving Out,* 1972, as yet unpublished.

Work has been anthologized in *The New Generation of Poets Anthology,* edited by Frederick Wolven, Ann Arbor Review Press, 1971; *1972 Minnesota Poetry Anthology,* edited by William Meissner, 1972; *Mid-America,* edited by David Anderson, Michigan State University Press, 1975.

Plays: "This Night in Sleep" (one-act), first produced in Bemidji, Minn. at Community Arts Council, May 31, 1968; "The Replacement" (one-act), first produced in Bemidji, Minn. at Community Arts Council, May 31, 1968.

Contributor of hundreds of articles, plays, poems, stories, and reviews to literary journals, including *Poetry Review, Epoch, Shore Review, Encore, Sou'wester, Snowy Egret,* and *Wisconsin Review.* Founding editor of *Northern Minnesota Review;* poetry editor of *Leatherleaf; North Country,* editor, 1971-72, presently advisory editor; literature editor of *North Country Anvil,* 1971-72.

WORK IN PROGRESS: Novels include *Catastrophe* (science fiction), *Stopping Off in Switzerland, Community College, Moving Out, Charlene, Charlene,* and *Big Birch;* books of poetry include *Crossing the Borders, Late March Blizzard, By the Mississippi, The Eastern Bird Wars,* and *Traveling in the Sun;* non-fiction includes *Genre into Form,* a text, and *This Summer, the Frail Sea,* on the ecological crisis; research on Australian literature, especially poetry of contemporary living authors.

*   *   *

ELLIS, Audrey

PERSONAL: Born in Leinster Corner House, London, England; daughter of Bertram (an engineer) and Dorothy (de Pappe) Marians; married second husband, Frederick Gelhar (a civil servant in customs and excise); children: (first marriage) Christopher John Ellis. *Education:* St. Mary's College of Domestic Science, diploma, 1939; also attended Institut Britannique (Paris). *Home and office:* Hermitage, Petersham Rd., Richmond, Surrey TW10 7AW, England. *Agent:* Winant, Towers, Ltd., 14 Clifford's Inn, London EC4A 1DA, England.

CAREER: *Home Chat* (national women's weekly magazine), London, England, secretary in charge of readers' letters, 1950; Incorporated Press of Great Britain, London, staff writer, 1951-54; *Modern Woman* (national magazine), London, cookery editor, 1954-65; editor and author for *Woman's Own* magazine, 1965-67; Hamlyn Publishing Group, London, managing editor of cookery and home management books, 1967-70; writer, 1970—. Frequently broadcasts on British Broadcasting Corp. (BBC) "Woman's Hour"; gives cookery demonstrations throughout British Isles. Cookery adviser for "Magpie," a children's program for Thames Television.

WRITINGS: *Modern Cake Decorating,* George Newnes, 1965; *The Woman's Own Book of Cake Making and Cake Decorating,* George Newnes, 1966; *Casserole Cookery,* George Newnes, 1967; *The Woman's Own Book of Casserole Cookery,* George Newnes, 1967; *A Hundred and One*

Quick and Easy Cookery Hints, Dickens, 1968; *Home Guide to Deep Freezing,* P. Hamlyn, 1968, Transatlantic, 1971; *Meals to Enjoy from Your Freezer,* Hamlyn Publishing Group, 1969, Transatlantic, 1971; *All About Home Freezing,* Hamlyn Publishing Group, 1969, Transatlantic, 1971.

(With Mary Berry and Ann Body) *The Hamlyn All Colour Cook Book,* Hamlyn Publishing Group, 1970; *Cooking for Your Freezer,* Transatlantic, 1970; (with Mabel Cavaiani) *Farmhouse Kitchen,* Stanley Paul, 1971, Regnery, 1973; *Step by Step Guide to Home Freezing,* Hamlyn Publishing Group, 1971; *Kitchen Garden Cook Book: Honey, Herbs, Flowers and Fruit, Vegetables,* Stanley Paul, 1972; *Entertaining from Your Freezer,* Hamlyn Publishing Group, 1972; *The Step by Step Guide to Meat Cookery,* Hamlyn Publishing Group, 1973; *Easy Freeze Cooking,* Gorgi, 1973; *French Family Cooking,* Hamlyn Publishing Group, 1973; *The Complete Book of Home Freezing,* Hamlyn Publishing Group, 1973; *Home Guide to Food Freezing,* Transatlantic, 1974; *Wine Lovers Cookbook,* Hutchinson, 1975, Grove, 1976; *The Kid Slimming Book,* Regnery, 1975; *Colourful Entertaining,* Hamlyn Publishing Group, 1975; *Home Freezing Through the Year,* Hamlyn Publishing Group, 1975; *Cooking to Make Kids Slim,* Stanley Paul, 1976.

Author of "Four Seasons" series, Sampson, Marston & Co., 1975-76, Two Continents Publishing, 1976. Cooking adviser for *Cooking in Britain Through the Ages.*

SIDELIGHTS: Audrey Ellis has appeared on Scottish, Irish, and British television programs. She was born in the same house where James Barrie wrote *Peter Pan.*

*   *   *

ELLIS, Brooks (Fleming) 1897-1976

August 2, 1897—July 11, 1976; American geologist, micropaleontologist, educator, museum administrator, and author of books in his field. Obituaries: *Washington Post,* July 14, 1976.

*   *   *

ELLIS, (J.) Frank(lyn) 1904(?)-1976

1904(?)—March 1, 1976; American operator of ski information service and author. Obituaries: *New York Times,* March 3, 1976.

*   *   *

ELSASSER, Glen Robert 1935-

PERSONAL: Surname is accented on first syllable; born October 18, 1935, in Marion, Ohio; son of Glen (a pharmacist) and Mary (a teacher; maiden name, Hogan) Elsasser; married Katharine Kersting (a librarian), September 8, 1973. *Education:* Ohio State University, B.A. (with distinction), 1957; Columbia University, M.S., 1961. *Home:* 319 C St. N.E., Washington, D.C. 20002. *Office:* Chicago Tribune, 1707 H St. N.W., Washington, D.C. 20006.

CAREER/WRITINGS: United Press International (UPI), Louisville, Ky., reporter, 1957-58; *Indianapolis Star,* Indianapolis, Ind., reporter, 1961-62; *Chicago Tribune,* Chicago, Ill., reporter in Chicago, New York City, and Washington, D.C., 1963—. Notable assignments include coverage of the resignation of Vice-President Spiro Agnew, the Watergate hearings, and the U.S. Supreme Court and the Justice Department. *Military service:* U.S. Army, staff member of Home Town News Center, 1959-60.

ELSOM, John Edward 1934-

PERSONAL: Born October 31, 1934, in Leigh, Essex, England; son of Leonard Ernest (an engineer) and Marjorie Louis (Dines) Elsom; married Sally Mays (a concert pianist), December 3, 1955; children: Simon Mays, Jonathan Mark. *Education:* Magdalene College, Cambridge, B.A. (honors), 1957. *Politics:* Liberal. *Home:* 39 Elsham Rd., Kensington, London W14 8HB, England. *Agent:* John McLaughlin, Campbell, Thomson & McLaughlin, 31 Newington Green, London N16 9PV, England.

CAREER: Writer, 1957—. Part-time employment includes substitute teaching in Essex, 1957-60, scriptreader for Paramount Pictures, 1960-69, adult education college instructor for Inner London Education Authority, 1960-71, and theatre critic for *Listener,* 1972—. Chairman of board of directors of Bush Theatre. *Member:* Critics Circle.

WRITINGS: Theatre Outside London, Macmillan, 1971; *Erotic Theatre,* Secker & Warburg, 1973; *Post-War British Theatre,* Routledge & Kegan Paul, 1976; (with Nicholas Tomalin) *The History of the National Theatre,* J. Cape, in press.

Plays: (With Sally Mays) "Peacemaker," first produced in Cambridge, England, at ADC Theatre, August 8, 1957; "One More Bull" (three-act), first produced in London at Cockpit Theatre, November 3, 1970; "The Well-Intentioned Builder" (one-act), first produced at Cockpit Theatre, November 3, 1970; "Scenes from National Life" (documentary drama), first produced in London at National Theatre Restaurant/Foyer, March, 1976. Also author of three musicals prior to 1955, and the libretto to Barry Anderson's opera, "Maui."

SIDELIGHTS: Elsom told *CA:* "I started as a historian with a strong interest in the theatre, music and literature; and became actively involved in the theatre partly through education, through my work as a teacher, as well as through working in the script department of Paramount Pictures. Before going to university, I had written three musicals, which had been performed by local amateurs in my home town of Brentwood, Essex, and had received some local and national publicity. These musicals I would prefer to forget. As time passed, I also became particularly interested in trying to change the stage relationship between works and music—away from set songs towards a system using the rhythmic stresses of words within a musical context. The chief example of this was "Peacemaker," written with Sally Mays.

"Trying to define what kind of writer I am is still a source of puzzlement to me. My particular delight was in writing plays, but I knew by some strange instinct when there was a play in me to write, and when there was not. It never seemed possible to trap this instinct into some clear professional working system. Central to my concerns (in whatever area I chose to write—books, criticism, plays) was the feeling that there was an organising muscle in the mind, responding and trying to coordinate many impressions. Thus, on one level, this muscle might wish to exercise itself on the surroundings in which one lived—an obvious example would be decorating a flat or improving a sound system. On another level, it would be concerned with trying to understand the changing transactions, taking place in the friendships around me. On another level again, it might be the consideration of different political, aesthetic or indeed religious approaches.

"Political and social ideas became of importance to me, when, after being a lame socialist, I started to read and come into contact with the works and attitudes of British liberals.

The theories of Liberalism fascinated me, as they still do, creating a yearning to see them in action." But Elsom added that politics were not a pre-eminent concern. "It was just one of the ways in which this organising muscle could exercise itself."

* * *

ELSTAR, Dow
See GALLUN, Raymond Z(inke) 1911-

* * *

EMERY, Fred 1933-

PERSONAL: Born October 19, 1933, in England; married E. Marianne Nyberg; children: two sons. *Education:* St. John's College, Cambridge, B.A., 1958. *Office: Times,* 541 National Press Building, Washington, D.C. 20045.

CAREER/WRITINGS: Times, London, England, reporter, 1958-61, correspondent from Paris, France, 1961-64, Tokyo, Japan, 1964-67, and Singapore, 1967-70, chief Washington correspondent, 1970-77, political editor, London, 1977—. In the United States, Emery covered the Watergate hearings; his assignments abroad include the Algerian War, and events in Vietnam and Indochina. *Military service:* Royal Air Force, 1951-53. *Member:* National Press Club, Overseas Writers.

* * *

EMMERSON, Donald K(enneth) 1940-

PERSONAL: Born June 10, 1940, in Tokyo, Japan; son of John Kenneth (a writer and diplomat) and Dorothy (McLaughlin) Emmerson; married Carolyn Holm (a teacher), December 27, 1965; children: Kirsten Holm, Katrina Louise. *Education:* Princeton University, B.A., 1961; Yale University, M.A., 1966, Ph.D., 1972. *Home:* 19-D University Houses, Madison, Wis. 53705. *Office:* Department of Political Science, University of Wisconsin, 306 North Hall, Madison, Wis. 53706.

CAREER: University of Wisconsin, Madison, instructor, 1970-72, assistant professor, 1972-76, associate professor of political science, 1976—. Visiting fellow at Australian National University, 1975. Has conducted field research in Indonesia, 1967-69, 1974-75. *Member:* American Political Science Association. *Awards, honors:* Fulbright-Hays grant and Ford Foundation Southeast Asia fellowship, both 1973-74.

WRITINGS: (Editor and contributor) *Students and Politics in Developing Nations,* Praeger, 1968; (contributor) R. William Liddle, editor, *Political Participation in Modern Indonesia,* Yale University Press, 1973; (contributor) W. Howard Wriggins and James F. Guyot, editors, *Population, Politics, and the Future of Southern Asia,* Columbia University Press, 1973; *Indonesia's Elite: Political Culture and Cultural Politics,* Cornell University Press, 1976; *Myths as Mirrors: The Ramayana and the Mahabharata in Contemporary Indonesia,* University Press of Hawaii, in press. Contributor to political science and Asian studies journals.

WORK IN PROGRESS: Research on growth, equality, and technology in poor countries, and on the politics of meaning (space, time, and language).

SIDELIGHTS: Emmerson writes: "Growing up in the Foreign Service meant changing countries every two years. So much of my life has been spent overseas and on the move that living in any one place now seems unnatural. My background probably also accounts for my anthropological bent.

In my pantheon, empathy is a prime god. I enjoy meeting strangers and trying to understand their ways of seeing and doing. I am amazed and grateful that scholar-authors actually get paid for what amounts to intellectual fun. The cup of my luck runneth over.''

AVOCATIONAL INTERESTS: California beach-jogging, Balinese sunset-watching, ''the company of my family.''

BIOGRAPHICAL/CRITICAL SOURCES: Walter Bedell Smith, *My Three Years in Moscow,* Lippincott, 1949; *Foreign Service Journal,* November, 1955, August, 1960.

* * *

ENDO, Mitsuko 1942-

PERSONAL: Born February 6, 1942, in Sapporo, Japan; came to the United States in 1970; daughter of Takahisa (a physician) and Takako (Sawamura) Fuwa; married Takashi Endo (employed at the United Nations), November 10, 1963; children: Taketo (son), Yoko (daughter). *Education:* Fuji Joshi College, diploma, 1962. *Home:* 144 Nelson Rd., Scarsdale, N.Y. 10583.

CAREER: Writer.

WRITINGS: (With Elisabeth Ortiz) *The Complete Book of Japanese Cooking,* M. Evans, 1976.

WORK IN PROGRESS: Collecting recipes from around the world.

SIDELIGHTS: Mitsuko Endo has traveled in Europe and has a special interest in European Recipes. *Avocational interests:* Playing the piano, tennis, golf, painting.

* * *

ENGEN, Rodney K(ent) 1948-

PERSONAL: Born September 14, 1948, in Sioux Falls, S.D.; son of Lee Emerson (a banker) and Elizabeth (Eaton) Engen. *Education:* International Academie fur Bildende Kunst, degree (with honors), 1969; University of Missouri, B.A. (with honors), 1970; attended University of Minnesota, 1972-73. *Home:* 13 Belsize Park Gardens, London NW3, England.

CAREER: Artist; University of Minnesota, Minneapolis, lecturer in art history, 1972-73; free-lance writer, 1973-76; London Art Bookshop, London, England, assistant to manager, 1975—. Organizer of Randolph Caldecott exhibition for Manchester City Art Gallery, 1977. *Member:* Society of British Authors.

WRITINGS: Walter Crane as a Book Illustrator, St. Martin's, 1975; *Victorian Engravings,* St. Martin's, 1975; *Kate Greenaway,* Crown Press, 1976; *Randolph Caldecott,* Oresko Books, 1976. Author of exhibition catalogue for Bolton Art Gallery, Bolton, England, 1975, and of catalogues for Chatwyck-Healey, Ltd. Contributor of articles on antiques to periodicals.

SIDELIGHTS: Engen's work has been exhibited in various galleries in United States, in Salzburg, Austria, and in Venice, Italy.

* * *

ENGSTROM, Ted W(ilhelm) 1916-

PERSONAL: Born March 1, 1916, in Cleveland, Ohio; son of David W. (an engineer) and Ellen E. (Olson) Engstrom; married Dorothy E. Weaver, November 3, 1939; children: Gordon, Donald, Jo Ann (Mrs. Michael Bengel). *Education:* Taylor University, A.B., 1938. *Politics:* Republican.

Religion: Congregationalist. *Home:* 3205 La Encina Way, Pasadena, Calif. 91107. *Office:* World Vision International, 919 West Huntington Dr., Monrovia, Calif. 91016.

CAREER: Zondervan Publishing House, Grand Rapids, Mich., editorial director, 1940-51; Youth for Christ International, Wheaton, Ill., president, 1951-63; World Vision International, Monrovia, Calif., executive vice-president and chairman of hunger task force, 1963—. Member of board of directors of World Union International, Tom Skinner Associates, American Institute of Church Growth, World Vision (Canada; Australia; Korea), African Enterprise, and George Fox College; former chairman of board of directors of Taylor University and honorary lifetime trustee; co-director of ''Managing Your Time,'' a management seminar series. *Military service:* U.S. Army, 1943-45; became sargeant.

MEMBER: Arcadia Rotary Club. *Awards, honors:* D.H.L. from Taylor University, 1955; named evangelical layman of the year by National Association of Evangelicals, 1970; Order of Civil Merit (Korea), 1973.

WRITINGS: (Editor) *Victorious and Fruitful Living, and Other Sermons: A Compilation of Sermons Written by Leading Teachers, Preachers and Evangelists in the Holiness Movement,* Zondervan, 1942; (editor) *Sermon Outlines and Illustrations,* Zondervan, 1942; (editor) *Great Sermons by Great American Preachers,* Zondervan, 1943; (editor) *Golden Nuggets,* Volume IV: *The Gospels,* Zondervan, 1944; (editor) *Treasury of Gospel Gems,* five volumes (Volume IV originally published as *Golden Nuggets,* Volume IV), Zondervan, 1944; *Bible Stories for Boys and Girls,* Zondervan, 1948; (editor) *Two Hundred Twenty-Seven Heart-Reaching Illustrations,* Zondervan, 1949; (editor) Frederic William Farrar, *Life of Christ* (condensed edition), Zondervan, 1949.

Fifty-Two Workable Young People's Programs, Zondervan, 1950; *One Hundred Eighty-Eight Heart-Reaching Outlines* (sermons), Zondervan, 1950; (editor) *Bedtime Stories for Boys and Girls,* Zondervan, 1951; (editor) *Great Sermons from Master Preachers of All Ages,* First Series, Zondervan, 1951; (editor) *One Hundred Thirty-Two Heart-Reaching Poems,* Zondervan, 1952; *Workable Prayer Meeting Programs,* Zondervan, 1955.

(With Warren M. Wiersbe) *Fifty-Two Workable Junior High Programs,* Zondervan, 1960; (with R. Alec Mackenzie) *Managing Your Time: Practical Guidelines on the Effective Use of Time,* Zondervan, 1967.

The Making of a Christian Leader, Zondervan, 1976; (with Ed Dayton) *Strategy for Living,* Regal Books, 1976; (with Dayton) *The Art of Management for Christian Leaders,* Word, 1976. Contributor of several hundred articles to religious magazines. Publisher of *World Vision;* editor of *Christian Digest,* 1941-53.

WORK IN PROGRESS: A book on world missions.

SIDELIGHTS: Engstrom has made more than seventy trips abroad, to seventy-five different countries, in the interest of his mission work. World Vision International, with which he is presently associated, was founded mainly to work in Korea, but now is actively involved in ministries in more than forty countries. In addition to childcare, emergency relief, and community development, the organization supports evangelistic activities of national churches and carries on a program of mission education in the United States.

AVOCATIONAL INTERESTS: Golf, music, reading.

ENKE, Stephen 1916-1974

PERSONAL: Surname is pronounced *En*-ka; born July 15, 1916, in Victoria, British Columbia, Canada; came to United States from Europe, 1933; naturalized U.S. citizen, 1942; son of Max (a manufacturer) and Marion (Lejeune) Enke; children: Max, Karen (Mrs. Nicholas Kallay). *Education:* Stanford University, A.B., 1937, A.M., 1939; Harvard University, M.P.A., 1940, Ph.D., 1943. *Religion:* Episcopalian. *Home:* Apt. 502, 1026 16th St. N.W., Washington, D.C. 20036. *Office:* Suite 500, 777 14th St. N.W., Washington, D.C. 20005.

CAREER: University of California, Los Angeles, instructor, then assistant professor of economics, 1942-46, research associate, Institute of Industrial Relations, 1946-47, visiting lecturer, Business School, 1948-51; RAND Corp., Santa Monica, Calif., research scientist, 1948-53, head of logistics department, 1953-58; visiting professor at Yale University, New Haven, Conn., 1959-60, and University of Cape Town, Cape Town, South Africa, 1961; Duke University, Durham, N.C., professor of economics, 1961-62; Institute for Defense Analyses, Arlington, Va., assistant to president, 1962-65; U.S. Department of Defense, Washington, D.C., deputy assistant secretary (economics), 1965-66; General Electric Co.-TEMPO, Santa Barbara, Calif., consulting economist, 1967-74. Consultant at various times to Ford Foundation, Agency for International Development, National Security Council, Bureau of the Budget, and Hudson Institute. *Member:* American Economic Association, Royal Economic Society, Phi Beta Kappa, Cosmos Club (Washington, D.C.). *Awards, honors:* Guggenheim fellow, 1955-56.

WRITINGS: (With Virgil Salera) *International Economics,* Prentice-Hall, 1947, 3rd edition, 1957; *Intermediate Economic Theory,* Prentice-Hall, 1950; *Economics for Development,* Prentice-Hall, 1963; (editor) *Defense Management,* Prentice-Hall, 1967. Contributor of about eighty articles and reviews to economic, political science, and other journals.

SIDELIGHTS: Enke lived in England, Belgium, and Switzerland, spending (including travels) a total of about twenty years abroad. He sailed more than 32,000 miles on ocean cruising trips in small sailboats and was a member of alpine, cruising, yacht, tennis, and flying clubs.*

(Died September 21, 1974)

* * *

EPHRON, Nora 1941-

PERSONAL: Born May 19, 1941, in New York, N.Y.; daughter of Henry (a writer) and Phoebe (a writer; maiden name, Wolkind) Ephron; married second husband, Carl Bernstein (a journalist), April 14, 1976. *Education:* Wellesley College, B.A., 1962. *Agent:* Lynn Nesbit, International Creative Management, 40 West 57th St., New York, N.Y. *Office:* Esquire Magazine, 488 Madison Ave., New York, N.Y. 10022.

CAREER: New York Post, New York City, reporter, 1963-68; free-lance journalist, 1968-72; *Esquire* magazine, New York City, columnist and contributing editor, 1972-73; *New York* magazine, New York City, contributing editor, 1973-74; *Esquire,* senior editor and columnist, 1974—. *Awards, honors:* Penney-Missouri award from University of Missouri Journalism School and J. C. Penney & Co., 1973; D.H.L. from Briarcliff College, 1974.

WRITINGS: Wallflower at the Orgy, Viking, 1970; *Crazy Salad,* Knopf, 1975. Writer of "Women" column, in *Es-quire,* 1972-73; in *New York,* 1973-74; of "Media" column in *Esquire,* 1974—. Contributor of articles to *Esquire, New York, Oui, McCall's,* and *Cosmopolitan.*

SIDELIGHTS: Critics have had a hard time pinning down Nora Ephron. One critic finds her writing best "when probing and exposing the masscult sensibility," another prefers it "when she brings a great deal of herself to her writing," and a third recommends the talent at its best when interviewing "the phonies and cherubs alike, sniffing them out like a hungry tiger." It has been suggested that her journalistic success springs from a "particular sensibility which infuses her pieces with a freely acknowledged moral bias or ambivalence"; and someone else turns around to counter: "It is her balanced perspective (neither too gamey nor too wise), her pointed style" that makes her "irresistible reading."

Nora Ephron's working routine is just as unpredictable. She told Michael Lasky: "I go through periods where I work a great deal at all hours of the day whenever I am around the typewriter, and then I go through spells where I don't do anything. I just sort of have lunch—*all day.* I never have been able to stick to a schedule. I work when something is due or when I am really excited about a piece.

"The way I write," she continued, "is that I keep writing over and over again. What will happen is I will write the first three pages and I'll have to get this transition that stumps me, and rather than think too hard about it, I will retype the first three pages in the hopes that the speed of my typing will leap me over this transition. And if it doesn't, I will begin again. And what results is that the beginnings of my pieces are always better written than the ends of them. A piece that I turn in is probably in its twelfth draft—every section has been through the typewriter many times.... By the time I get to the last page, the whole work is almost in final draft except for the end."

Both her books may best be described as collections on popular culture. In *Crazy Salad* Ephron collected twenty-five pieces written on or about women (her former columns were both simply entitled "Women"). "Her feminist consciousness," said Barbara Zelenko, "is evident throughout, but Ephron is a far too perceptive and original writer to take the usual movement line on every occasion...." This individual feminist consciousness has also helped Ephron shape her approach to her work. "Interview subjects do tend to underrate women interviewers," she explained, "and it seems to me the best approach to this is not to be helpless and feminine but to work terribly hard at the beginning to prove yourself, to show them that you *know* what you are talking about—that you've read up and that you are not there cold."

The daughter of two Hollywood filmwriters, Ephron always wanted to be a writer; a "woman who made her living by her wits." Of her childhood, she said: "Other children grow up loving the smell of fresh-cut grass and raked leaves; I grew up in Beverly Hills loving the smell of mink, the smell of the pavement after it rained, and the smell of dollar bills. A few years ago, I went back to Beverly Hills and all I could smell was jasmine, and I realized that that smell had always been there and I had never known it."

In her current column Ephron's talent ranges over a wide choice of techniques—from straight reporting, interviews, and personal narratives to offbeat stories and fables. Her virtuosity in each type of story, leading to the critical debate over which is her finest, was probably best noted by a reviewer looking over the variety offered in *Crazy Salad:*

"The short, clipped introduction (which dismisses the collection as 'just some things I wanted to write about') is the only disappointing part of the book."

BIOGRAPHICAL/CRITICAL SOURCES: Saturday Review, November 21, 1970; *Writer's Digest,* April, 1974; *New York Times Book Review,* July 13, 1975; *Library Journal,* August, 1975; *Best Sellers,* September, 1975; *Esquire,* December, 1975; *Newsweek,* April 26, 1976.

* * *

EPSTEIN, Perle S(herry) 1938-

PERSONAL: Born August 21, 1938, in New York; daughter of Jacob A. and Lillian (a volunteer worker with children; maiden name, Tobachnick) Besserman; married Gerald Epstein (a psychiatrist), June 7, 1958. *Education:* Brooklyn College (now of the City University of New York), B.A., 1959; Columbia University, M.A., 1961, Ph.D., 1967. *Agent:* Elizabeth Darhansoff, 52 East 91st St., New York, N.Y. 10028.

CAREER: Assistant to ambassador of Korean mission to United Nations, summers, 1961-62; Kingsborough Community College, Brooklyn, N.Y., instructor in English, 1963-64; Jersey City State College, Jersey City, N.J., assistant professor of English, 1964-66; New York University, Washington Square College, New York, N.Y., lecturer in humanities and Eastern philosophy, 1966—. Assistant professor at Briarcliff College, 1970-72, 1976-77.

WRITINGS: The Private Labyrinth of Malcolm Lowry, Holt, 1969; *The Yoga of the Jews,* Doubleday, in press.

For children: *Individuals All,* Macmillan, 1972; *The Way of Witches,* Doubleday, 1973; *Monsters: Their Histories, Homes, and Habits,* Doubleday, 1974; *Oriental Mystics and Magicians,* Doubleday, 1975. Contributor to *Encyclopedia Americana* and to literary journals, including *Transatlantic Review, Present Tense,* and *University of British Columbia Literary Review.*

SIDELIGHTS: Perle Epstein writes: "My parents revered the written word—my brother and I started to read when we were two, were members of the local library at age four. It was always taken for granted that we'd go the academic route—but there is also a strong mystical and spiritual family tradition that kept life—which was frequently, materially speaking, hard—from becoming a grind. . . . We're all a bit eccentric—even other-worldly sometimes. But we laugh a lot."

AVOCATIONAL INTERESTS: Travel.

* * *

ERICSSON, Emily (Alice) 1904-1976

April 6, 1904—March 16, 1976; American international economist, educator, diplomat, and author of books in her field. Obituaries: *Washington Post,* March 20, 1976.

* * *

ERNST, Barbara 1945-

PERSONAL: Born August 14, 1945, in Tampa, Fla.; daughter of Richard W. and Beatrice (Kemmler) Ernst; married Corrado DiGennaro, February 15, 1975. *Education:* Brandeis University, A.B., 1967, teaching certificate, 1969. *Religion:* Unitarian-Universalist. *Address:* c/o DiGennaro, PMB 1143, Benin City, Nigeria.

CAREER: Selective Educational Equipment, Newton, Mass., administrative assistant, 1967-69; elementary school teacher in Brookline, Mass., 1969-72, Kampala, Uganda, 1972, and Nairobi, Kenya, 1973; Brookline Public Schools, Brookline, Mass., elementary school teacher, 1974-76.

WRITINGS: (With Jim Blake) *The Great Perpetual Learning Machine,* Little, Brown, 1976.

WORK IN PROGRESS: Studying teacher training methods and elementary education in a developing African country; research for a photographic essay on African children and/or African life.

SIDELIGHTS: Barbara Ernst writes: "Since graduation from college, I've spent my professional energy in helping to make children's elementary classroom experiences exciting and relevant to their lives. I strongly believe in the concepts of 'open education' and that children, if encouraged to explore their many interests in the world around them, will delight in learning. . . . I love teaching and I consider it one of the most valuable professions . . ." Ms. Ernst has traveled in the Soviet Union, England, and several parts of Africa. She will spend the next two years in Nigeria, where her husband supervises building sites.

* * *

ERNST, Max 1891-1976

April 2, 1891—April 1, 1976; German-born surrealist painter, sculptor, collagist, and writer. Obituaries: *New York Times,* April 2, 1976; *Newsweek,* April 12, 1976; *Time,* April 12, 1976; *Current Biography,* May, 1976.

* * *

ERNST, Morris L(eopold) 1888-1976

August 23, 1888—May 21, 1976; American lawyer, civil libertarian, and author of books on a variety of topics. Obituaries: *New York Times,* May 23, 1976; *Washington Post,* May 23, 1976; *Newsweek,* May 31, 1976; *Time,* May 31, 1976; *Publishers Weekly,* June 7, 1976; *Current Biography,* July, 1976. (See index for previous *CA* sketch)

* * *

ERSKINE, Thomas L(eonard) 1939-

PERSONAL: Born June 2, 1939, in Waterville, Me.; son of Chauncey Lee (in personnel) and Florence (a teacher; maiden name, Hapworth) Erskine: married Suzanne Fourcade (a teacher), August 19, 1961; children: Harden Peter, Jeffrey Louis. *Education:* Bowdoin College, B.A., 1961; University of Kansas, M.A., 1963; Emory University, Ph.D., 1969. *Religion:* Presbyterian. *Home:* 420 Elberta Ave., Salisbury, Md. 21801. *Office:* Department of English, Salisbury State College, Salisbury, Md. 21801.

CAREER: University of Delaware, Newark, instructor, 1965-69, assistant professor of English, 1969-71; Salisbury State College, Salisbury, Md., associate professor, 1971-72, professor of English, 1972—, chairman of department, 1971-72, academic dean, 1972-76. Secretary of Ice World, Inc. Mid-Delmarva Young Men's Christian Association, president, 1976-77, former member of board of directors.

MEMBER: Modern Language Association of America, National Council of Teachers of English, Society for Cinema Studies, American Association for Higher Education, South Atlantic Modern Language Association, Maryland Association for Higher Education, Academic Affairs for Administrators, Rotary International.

WRITINGS: (Editor with Elaine Safer) *John Milton: "L'Allegro" and "Il Penseroso,"* C. E. Merrill, 1970; (editor with W. Bruce Finnie) *Words on Words: A Language Reader,* Random House, 1971; (editor with Gerald R. Barrett) *From Fiction to Film: Conrad Aiken's "Silent Snow, Secret Snow,"* Dickenson, 1972; (editor with Barrett) *From Fiction to Film: Ambrose Bierce's "An Occurrence at Owl Creek Bridge,"* Dickenson, 1973; (editor) *From Fiction to Film: D. H. Lawrence's "Rocking-Horse Winner,"* Dickenson, 1974. Founder and editor of *Literature/Film Quarterly,* 1973—.

WORK IN PROGRESS: Introduction to Literature and Film.

* * *

ESCOTT, Jonathan 1922-
(Jack S. Scott)

PERSONAL: Born June 16, 1922, in London, England; son of William (an actor) and Mabel (Terry) Escott; married Dorothy Oates; children: Nicola Jane. *Education:* Educated in England and Australia. *Politics:* "None. Too ingrained contempt for politicians." *Religion:* "There is a God, and a special Hell for parsons." *Home:* 4 Holly Mount, High Grove, Halifax, Yorkshire, England. *Agent:* Mary Irvine, 4 Coombe Gardens, Wimbledon, London SW20 OQU, England.

CAREER: Began as semi-professional vocalist for dance bands in London, England; vaudeville actor in London, 1938-41; worked as comedian, actor, and singer-guitarist in England and France, 1946-68; writer, 1971—. Has been broadcast on radio and television; has worked in repertory and in pantomimes; director of entertainment on Canadian Pacific ocean liners, 1968-71. *Military service:* British Army, 1941-46; served in North Africa, Italy, and Austria.

WRITINGS: Landfall in Sefton Carey (mystery), R. Hale, 1976; *The Shadow of Katie* (romantic drama), R. Hale, in press.

Under pseudonym Jack S. Scott: *The Poor Old Lady's Dead* (suspense novel), Harper, 1976; *The Bastard's Name Was Bristow* (suspense novel), Harper, in press.

Author of "Oh Dear" (three-act comedy), first produced in Bournemouth, England, February, 1965. Contributor of more than one hundred stories to magazines in England and Europe, as well as South Africa.

WORK IN PROGRESS: A book on the effects of a murder upon a family; a comedy, built around the family of an old street-market seller of flowers and fruit.

SIDELIGHTS: Escott writes that, primarily, he "seeks to entertain. Believes that the best things are said by people not mounted on soap boxes. Tends to emphasize the comedy element, even in serious themes . . . because tragi-comedy is the normal condition of mankind—a fact that is overlooked by too many grave and ponderous writers. Better be a sad clown deliberately than a pompous clown and not know it."

* * *

ESHERICK, Joseph W(harton) 1942-

PERSONAL: Born August 14, 1942, in Ross, Calif.; son of Joseph (an architect) and Rebecca Wood (an architect; maiden name, Watkin) Esherick; married Judy Teng, July 4, 1965 (divorced, 1976); children: Joseph Scott, Christopher Michael. *Education:* Harvard University, B.A. (summa cum laude), 1964; University of California, Berkeley, M.A., 1966, Ph.D., 1971. *Politics:* "Radical." *Home:* 2635 Onyx St., Eugene, Ore. 97403. *Office:* Department of History, University of Oregon, Eugene, Ore. 97403.

CAREER: University of Michigan, Ann Arbor, research associate in Chinese studies, 1970-71; University of Oregon, Eugene, assistant professor, 1971-76, associate professor of history, 1976—, chairman of Asian studies, 1975-77. Chairman of standing committee for Asian Studies on the Pacific Coast, 1976-77. *Member:* Association for Asian Studies, Committee of Concerned Asian Scholars, Phi Beta Kappa.

WRITINGS: (With Orville Schell) *Modern China: The Story of a Revolution,* Knopf, 1972; (editor) *Lost Chance in China: The World War Two Despatches of John S. Service,* Random House, 1974; *Reform and Revolution in China: The 1911 Revolution in Hunan and Hubei,* University of California Press, 1976. Contributor to Asian studies journals.

WORK IN PROGRESS: A book on social change and rural revolution in China; research on the Chinese conception of the "restoration of capitalism" and its Marxist context.

SIDELIGHTS: Esherick writes: "I consider myself a radical China scholar: seeking a sympathetic understanding of the Chinese revolution and the historical process which produced it. I learned during the 1960's that all scholarship is inextricably related to politics, and that this fact must always be recognized and admitted. At the same time I feel no sacrifice of 'objectivity' in my commitment to radical scholarship—for history is itself the study of a changing human experience whose nature is such that good history will always be radical history."

* * *

ESSAME, Hubert 1896-1976

December 2, 1896—March 2, 1976; British military officer, historian, educator, and author. Obituaries: *AB Bookman's Weekly,* April 26, 1976. (See index for previous *CA* sketch)

* * *

ESSLINGER, Pat M.
See CARR, Pat M(oore)

* * *

ETTINGHAUSEN, Richard 1906-

PERSONAL: Born February 5, 1906, in Frankfurt-on-Main, Germany; came to the United States in 1934, naturalized in 1938; son of Edmund S. and Selma (Stern) Ettinghausen; married Basia Gruliow, 1934 (died, 1935); married Elizabeth Sgalitzer, September 22, 1945; children: (second marriage) Stephen Edmund, Thomas Andrew David. *Education:* University of Frankfurt, Ph.D., 1931; postdoctoral study at University of Munich and Cambridge University. *Home:* 24 Armour Rd., Princeton, N.J. 08540. *Office:* 1 East 78th St., New York, N.Y. 10021.

CAREER: American Institute of Persian Art and Archaeology, research associate, 1934-37; Institute of Advanced Study, Princeton, N.J., member, 1937-38; University of Michigan, Ann Arbor, associate professor of Islamic art, 1938-44; Smithsonian Institution, Freer Gallery of Art, Washington, D.C., associate in Near Eastern art, 1944-58, curator, 1958-61, head curator, 1961-67; Los Angeles County Museum of Art, Los Angeles, Calif., adjunct curator, 1967-69; Metropolitan Museum of Art, New York, N.Y., consultive chairman of Islamic Department, 1969—. Research professor, University of Michigan, 1949—; New York University, Institute of Fine Arts, adjunct professor, 1961-67, professor, 1967—. Trustee of Phillips Gallery,

Washington, D.C.; trustee, member of the executive committee, and chairman of the accessions committee of the Textile Museum, Washington, D.C.

MEMBER: College Art Association of America, American Oriental Society, Asia House, American Research Center in Egypt, International Society of Oriental Research, Archaeological Institute of America (president, 1960-61, 1963-64), Institut d'Egypte (associate), German Archeological Institute (honorary member), French Academie des Inscriptions et Belles Lettres, British Academy (honorary member).

WRITINGS: The Unicorn, Smithsonian Institution Press, 1950; (editor) *A Selected and Annotated Bibliography of Books and Periodicals in Western Languages Dealing with the Near and Middle East, with Special Emphasis on Mediaeval and Modern Times,* Middle East Institute, 1952, with supplement, 1954; *Early Realism in Islamic Art,* Instituto per l'oriente (Rome), 1956; *The "Wade Cup" in the Cleveland Museum of Art: Its Origins and Decorations,* [Washington], 1957; (editor) *Aus der Welt der Islamaischen Kunst: Festschrift fur Ernst Kuehuel zum 75 Geburtstag am 26.10.1957,* Gebr. Mann (Berlin), 1959.

Medieval Near Eastern Ceramics in the Freer Gallery of Art, Smithsonian Institution Press, 1960; *Persian Miniatures in the Bernard Berenson Collection,* Officine Grafiche Ricordi (Milan), 1961; (with Grace Dunham Guest) *The Iconography of a Kashan Luster Plate,* [Washington], 1961; *Paintings of the Sultans and Emperors of India in American Collections,* William Heinman, 1961; *Arab Painting,* World Publishing, 1962; *Ancient Glass in the Freer Gallery of Art,* Smithsonian Institution Press, 1962; *Turkish Miniatures from the Thirteenth to the Eighteenth Century,* New American Library, 1965; *Masterpieces from Turkey,* Skira (Geneva), c. 1966; (with Ekrem Akurgal and Cyril Mango) *Treasures of Turkey,* Skira, 1966.

(Editor) Leo Ary Mayer, *Mamluk Playing Cards,* Brill, 1971; (editor) *Islamic Art in the Metropolitan Museum of Art,* [New York], 1972. Editor, *Ars Islamica,* 1938-50; Near Eastern editor, *Ars Orientalis,* 1954-57, and member of editorial board, 1957-61; member of editorial board, *Artibus Asiae,* 1971—, and *Art Bulletin;* co-editor, *Kunst des Orients,* 1968—.

*   *   *

EVANG, Karl   1902-

PERSONAL: Born October 19, 1902, in Oslo, Norway; son of Jens Ingolf (a bureau chief) and Anna Beate (a teacher; maiden name, Wexelsen) Evang; married Gerda Sophie Landmark Moe (a physician), December 4, 1929; children: Anders, Turid Sofie, Kari Bente, Anne Cecile. *Education:* University of Oslo, M.D., 1929; additional study at University of Berlin, 1937, and in England and France, 1938. *Politics:* Socialist. *Religion:* None. *Home:* Maltrostveien 11B, Oslo 3, Norway. *Office:* Helsedircktoratet, Oslo, Norway.

CAREER: Physician in private practice in Oslo, Norway, 1929-39; Oslo Municipal Hospital, Oslo, member of staff, 1932-34; State Factory Inspection Office, Oslo, medical officer, 1937-39; director-general of Norwegian Health Services, 1939-72. Representative to League of Nations conference on nutrition, 1937; member of standing advisory committee on nutrition for Food and Agriculture Organization of the United Nations, 1945-47; chairman of Norwegian Nutritional Council and Food and Agriculture Organization Committee, 1946. World Health Organization, member of technical preparation commission, 1946, member of interim commission, 1946-48, chairman of Norwegian delegations to world assemblies, 1948—, president of second assembly in Rome, 1949, vice-chairman of expert missions to Israel, 1950, and India, 1952, chairman of executive committee on Public Health Administration, 1952, currently chairman of World Health Organization executive committee. Vice-chairman of Norwegian Foundation for Assistance to Underdeveloped Countries, 1952—.

MEMBER: Norwegian Medical Association, Norwegian Society of Hygiene, Norwegian Dental Association, Royal Society of Medicine (fellow), American Public Health Association (fellow). *Awards, honors:* Chevalier Legion d'Honneur, 1949; Leon Bernard Foundation Prize, 1966; Bronfman Prize, 1970; Commander with Star of Royal Order of St. Olav.

WRITINGS: Fodselsregulering (title means "Birth Control"), Fram (Oslo), 1931; (editor) *Norsk medisinsk ordbok* (title means "Norwegian Medical Dictionary"), Sem & Stenersen (Oslo), 1933, 7th edition (with wife, Gerda Evang, and daughter, Turid S. Evang) published as *Norsk medisinsk ordbok og Dan Internasjonale sykdomsog doedsarsaksnomenklatur* (title means "Norwegian Medical Dictionary and International Morbidity and Mortality Nomenclature"), 1968; *Rasepolitikk og reaksjon* (title means "Race Policy and Reaction"), Fram, 1934; (with Otto Galtung Hansen) *An Inquiry into the Diet of 301 Poorly Situated Families in Norway,* Mercators trycheri (Helsinki), 1939.

Gjenreising av folkehelsa i Norge (title means "The Rehabilitation of Public Health in Norway"), Fabritius (Oslo), 1947; (editor) *Seksuell opplysning* (title means "Sexual Education"), two volumes, Tiden (Oslo), 1947, revised edition, 1951; *Det offentlige helsearbeid* (title means "The Public Health Services"), Sem & Stenersen, 1948; *Oppdraglse til fred* (title means "Education to Peace"), Tiden, 1948; *Mere frimodighet; om utenrikspolitikk, konflikten i Oesten og miligheten for avspenning* (title means "More Outspokenness about Foreign Policy, the Conflict in the East, and the Possibility of Detente"), Tiden, 1951; *Health Services in Norway,* translated by Dorothy Burton Skardal, Norwegian Joint Committee on International Social Policy, 1957, 4th edition, Universitetforlaget, 1976.

Health Service, Society and Medicine: Present Day Services in their Relation to Medical Science and Social Structure, Oxford University Press, 1960; (editor with others) *Familiens store legebok* (title means "Popular Health Education for the Family"), Tiden, 1960; *Report on a General Evaluation of the Health Services in Israel,* World Health Organization, 1960; (with D. S. Murray and W. J. Lear) *Medical Care and Family Security,* Prentice-Hall, 1963; *Fred er aa skape: Artilker og taler* (title means "Peace Is to Create"), Pax bokene (Oslo), 1964; *Bruk og misbruk av legimidler en almenfatteling fremstilling* (title means "Use and Misuse of Medicines"), Tiden, 1965; (editor) *Physical Activity in Health and Disease,* Williams & Wilkins, 1966; *Aktuelle narkotiksproblemer* (title means "Current Narcotics Problems"), Tiden, 1967.

Narkotika, generasjonene og samfunnet (title means "Narcotics, the Generations, and Society"), Tiden, 1972; *Helse og samfunn* (title means "Health and Society"), Gyldendal (Oslo), 1972.

Contributor of articles to international periodicals and newspapers.

WORK IN PROGRESS: Memoirs.

SIDELIGHTS: Evang became interested in international health problems while spending five years in exile with the government of Norway, during World War II.

BIOGRAPHICAL/CRITICAL SOURCES: Festschrift for Karl Evang on His 60th Birthday, Gylendal, 1962.

* * *

EVANS, M(edford) Stanton 1934-

PERSONAL: Born July 20, 1934, in Kingsville, Tex.; son of Medford Bryan and Alice Josephine (Stanton) Evans. Education: Yale University, B.A., 1955; graduate study, New York University, 1955. Politics: Republican. Religion: Methodist. Office: 422 First St. S.E., Washington, D.C. 20003.

CAREER: Freeman, Irvington-on-Hudson, N.Y., assistant editor, 1955; National Review, New York, N.Y., editorial staff member, 1955-56; Human Events, Washington, D.C., managing editor, 1956-59; Indianapolis News, Indianapolis, Ind., chief editorial writer, 1959-60, editor, 1960-74; syndicated columnist, Los Angeles Times Syndicate, 1974—; columnist, National Review, 1976—. Intercollegiate Society of Individualists, publications director, 1956-59, trustee, 1960—; broadcaster on the C.B.S. Radio "Spectrum" series, 1971—. Member: American Society of Newspaper Editors, National Headliners Club, American Conservative Union (chairman, 1971-77), Phi Beta Kappa, Sigma Delta Chi, Capitol Hill Club (Washington, D.C.), Elizabethan Club (Yale). Awards, honors: Freedoms Foundation awards for editorial writing, 1959, 1960, 1965, 1966; National Headliners Club award for outstanding editorial pages, 1960.

WRITINGS: Revolt on the Campus, Regnery, 1961; The Liberal Establishment, Devin-Adair, 1965; The Politics of Surrender, Devin-Adair, 1966; The Lawbreakers: America's Number One Domestic Problem, Arlington House, 1968; The Future of Conservatism: From Taft to Reagan and Beyond, Holt, 1968, revised edition, Anchor Books, 1969; Clear and Present Dangers, Harcourt, 1975. Associate editor, National Review, 1960-73; contributing editor, Human Events, 1968—.

* * *

EVANS, Mark

PERSONAL: Born in St. Louis, Mo.; son of Yale (an accountant) and Rea Evans. Education: California Institute of the Arts, B.Mus. (summa cum laude), 1966; Claremont Graduate School, M.A., 1968, Ph.D., 1970; has studied composition with Mario Castelnuovo-Tedesco and Roy Harris, conducting with Fritz Zweig and Joseph Wagner, and piano with Helena Lewyn. Home: 8560 West Olympic Blvd., Los Angeles, Calif. 90035.

CAREER: Writer and professional musician (composer, conductor, pianist, and organist). Creator and host of series "Mark My Words!" for National Public Radio, 1974—. Member: International P.E.N., American Musicological Society, American Guild of Organists, Academy of Science Fiction, Fantasy, and Horror Films (chairman of music committee), California Writers Guild, Phi Mu Alpha Sinfonia. Awards, honors: Recipient of Ford Foundation fellowship, Disney Foundation fellowship, California State graduate fellowship, Smith-Hobson music fellowship, and Aubrey Douglass Award.

WRITINGS: Will the Real Young America Please Stand Up?, Stackpole, 1973; Soundtrack: The Music of the Movies, Hopkinson & Blake, 1975; The Spectacular Stunt Book, Grosset, 1976; Scott Joplin and the Ragtime Years, Dodd, 1976; The Morality Gap, Alba, 1976. Author of book and lyrics, and composer of musical revue "Going Around in

Academic Circles," based on the writings of Richard Armour, first performed in Claremont, Calif., at Balch Auditorium, March 12, 1976, as yet unpublished.

WORK IN PROGRESS: Satirical fiction and plays for stage and screen; writing for the musical theater.

SIDELIGHTS: Evans writes: "As both writer and composer with a sense of dedication to the stage, I hope to participate in a renaissance of creative work which provokes an emotional rather than cerebral response. Laughter, love, tears, and human values are rewarding for both the writer and his reader, regardless of how unfashionable these sentiments may seem to the commercial mind. Elegance, style, and ironic wit are infinitely more entertaining than superficial indulgences in vulgarity or intellectual exercises masquerading as reality. All of the writers, composers, and playwrights I admire exhibit the former qualities, and these are my artistic goals as well."

AVOCATIONAL INTERESTS: Collecting books, records, and tapes (especially those relating to film music, jazz, musical theater, and classical music), spectator sports (baseball, football, basketball, wrestling, and roller derby), ballroom dancing, collecting menus, gourmet cooking, travel, classic film scores, swashbuckling adventures, Sherlock Holmes, and Oxford accents; he particularly dislikes "television commercials, musicians who use the electric guitar as a deadly weapon, battleaxe secretaries, small dogs that make large noises, forms of any kind, and writers who take themselves too seriously."

* * *

EVANS-PRITCHARD, Edward Evan 1902-1973

PERSONAL: Born September 21, 1902, in Crowborough, Sussex, England; son of Thomas John (a minister) and Dorthea Annie (Edwards) Evans-Pritchard; married Ioma Heaton Nicholls, 1939 (died, 1959); children: three sons, two daughters. Education: Attended Winchester College, Oxford; Exeter College, Oxford, M.A.; University of London, Ph.D. Home: The Ark, Jack Straws Lane, Headington, Oxford, England.

CAREER: Has made six major and several minor anthropological expeditions to Central, East, and North Africa, 1926-39; Egyptian University, Cairo, Egypt, professor of sociology, 1930-33; Oxford University, Oxford, England, research lecturer, 1935-40; Cambridge University, Cambridge, England, reader, 1945-46; Oxford University, professor of social anthropology, 1946-70, fellow of All Souls College, 1946-70, sub-warden of All Souls College, 1963-65. Honorary fellow, School of Oriental and African Studies, University of London, 1963; honorary professor, University of Wales, 1971. Military service: In active service, 1940-45; mentioned in dispatches.

MEMBER: British Academy (fellow), Royal Anthropological Institute (president, 1949-51), Association of Social Anthropologists (life president), American Academy of Arts and Sciences (honorary member), American Philosophical Society, Institute Francaise de Socologie (honorary member). Awards, honors: D.Sc. from University of Chicago, 1967, and University of Bristol, 1968; D.Litt from University of Manchester, 1969; named knight Buchela, 1971; received chevalier of Legion of Honor, 1971.

WRITINGS: (Co-editor) Essays Presented to C. G. Seligmann, Kegan Paul, 1934, Negro Universities Press, 1970; Witchcraft, Oracles, and Magic Among the Azande, Clarendon Press, 1937, revised edition, 1958; (editor with Meyer

Fortes) *African Political Systems,* Oxford University Press, 1940, 3rd edition, 1970; *The Nuer: A Description of the Modes of Livelihood and Political Institutions of a Nilotic People,* Clarendon Press, 1940, 3rd edition, 1968; *The Political System of the Anuak of the Anglo-Egyptian Sudan,* Lund, Humphries, 1940; *Cyrenaican Tribes—Habitat and Way of Life: Handbook of Cyrenaica, Part 7,* H.M.S.O., 1944; *Tribes and their Divisions: Handbook of Cyrenaica, Part 8,* H.M.S.O., 1944; *Some Aspects of Marriage and the Family Among the Nuer,* Rhodes-Livingstone Institute, 1945; *The Divine Kingship of the Shilluk of the Nilotic Sudan,* Cambridge University Press, 1948; *Social Anthropology* (lecture), Clarendon Press, 1948; *The Sanusi of Cyrenaica,* Clarendon Press, 1949, revised edition, 1963; *Kinship and Marriage Among the Nuer,* Clarendon Press, 1951, 3rd edition, 1966; *Social Anthropology* (broadcast talks), Cohen & West, 1951, Free Press, 1952, revised edition, 1956; (with others) *The Institutions of Primitive Society* (broadcast talks), Blackwell, 1954, revised edition, 1961, Free Press, 1956; *Nuer Religion,* Clarendon Press, 1956.

Anthropology and History (lecture), Manchester University Press, 1961; *Essays in Social Anthropology,* Faber, 1962, Free Press of Glencoe, 1963; *The Comparative Method in Social Anthropology* (lecture), Athlone Press, 1963; *Zande Texts,* Oxford University Press, 1963; *The Zande State: The Huxley Memorial Lectures, 1963,* Royal Anthropological Institute, 1963; *Social Anthropology and Other Essays,* Free Press, 1964; *The Position of Women in Primitive Societies and Other Essays in Social Anthropology,* Free Press, 1965; *Theories of Primitive Religion,* Oxford University Press, 1965; (editor) *The Zande Trickster* (collection of folktales), Oxford University Press, 1967; *The Sociology of Comte: An Appreciation* (lecture), Manchester University Press, 1970; *The Azande: History and Political Institutions,* Clarendon Press, 1971; (editor) *Peoples of the World,* three volumes, Danbury Press, 1972; *Man and Woman Among the Azande,* Free Press, 1974. Contributor to *Encyclopaedia Britannica,* and to scholarly journals.

AVOCATIONAL INTERESTS: Gardening, bird watching.*

(Died September 11, 1973)

*   *   *

EVERITT, C(harles) W(illiam) F(rancis)   1934-

PERSONAL: Born March 8, 1934, in Sevenoaks, England; came to the United States in 1960; son of Robert Arthur (a patent attorney) and Grace Beryl Fanny (Milner) Everitt. *Education:* University of London, B.Sc. and A.R.C.S., both 1955, D.I.C., 1958, Ph.D., 1959. *Religion:* Episcopalian. *Home:* 28081 Natoma Rd., Los Altos Hills, Calif. 94022. *Office:* Department of Physics, Stanford University, Stanford, Calif. 94022.

CAREER: University of London, London, England, research associate, 1959-60; University of Pennsylvania, Philadelphia, research associate, 1960-62; Stanford University, Stanford, Calif., senior research physicist, 1962-74, adjunct professor of physics, 1974—. Member of International Academy of Astronautics Space Relativity Committee and National Aeronautics and Space Administration Shuttle Astronomy Working Group. *Member:* American Physical Society, Sigma Xi.

WRITINGS: James Clerk Maxwell, Physicist and Natural Philosopher, Scribner, 1975. Contributor of about forty articles to scientific journals.

WORK IN PROGRESS: A full-length biography, *James Clerk Maxwell;* editing, with S. E. Brush and E. W. Garber, *The Unpublished Papers on Kinetic Theory of Gases,* for Reidel.

*   *   *

EYRE, Annette
See WORBOYS, Anne(tte) Isobel

*   *   *

EZEKIEL, Mordecai J(oseph) B(rill)   1899-1974

PERSONAL: Born May 10, 1899, in Richmond, Va.; son of Jacob and Rachel (Brill) Ezekiel; married Lucille Finsterwald, December 24, 1927; children: David, Jonathan, Margaret. *Education:* University of Maryland, B.S., 1918; University of Minnesota, M.S., 1923; Robert Brookings Graduate School of Economics and Government, Ph.D., 1966. *Residence:* Washington, D.C.

CAREER: Employed as statistical assistant in agriculture by U.S. Census Bureau, 1920-22; U.S. Department of Agriculture, Washington, D.C., agricultural economist for Bureau of Agricultural Economics, 1922-27, senior agricultural economist, 1927-29; Federal Farm Board, Washington, D.C., assistant chief economist, 1930-33; U.S. Department of Agriculture, economic adviser to secretary of agriculture, 1933-46; United Nations, Food and Agriculture Organization, New York, N.Y., deputy director of Economic Division, 1946-58, head of economics department, 1959-60, assistant director general, 1961, special assistant to director general, 1961-62, also member of missions to Poland and Greece; Agency for International Development, Washington, D.C., chief of United Nations Division of U.S.-United Nations Relations, 1962-65, member of Agricultural Division for International Agricultural Development in Sectorial Analysis Office, 1965-67; economic consultant, 1967-69. Executive assistant to vice-chairman of War Production Board, 1942-43; former member of board of directors of Overseas School of Rome. *Military service:* U.S. Army, 1918-19; became lieutenant.

MEMBER: International Conference on Agricultural Economics (fellow), American Economic Association, Econometric Society (fellow), American Agricultural Economics Association (fellow), American Statistical Association (fellow), American Farm Economic Association (fellow). *Awards, honors:* Guggenheim fellowship, Europe, 1930-31; D.Agr. from University of Maryland, 1963.

WRITINGS: Factors Affecting Farmers' Earnings in Southeastern Pennsylvania, U.S. Government Printing Office, 1926; *Methods of Correlation An'alysis,* Wiley, 1930, 3rd edition (with Karl A. Fox) published as *Methods of Correlation and Regression Analysis, Linear and Curvilinear,* 1959; *The Interest of Agriculture in Reciprocal Trade Agreements,* U.S. Government Printing Office, 1935; *Twenty-Five Hundred Dollars a Year: From Scarcity to Abundance,* Harcourt, 1936, Da Capo Press, 1973; *Jobs for All Through Industrial Expansion,* Knopf, 1939; *Economic Relations Between the Americas,* Division of Intercourse and Education, Carnegie Endowment for International Peace, 1941; (with D'Alton B. Myers, John J. Quigley, and Aaron J. Blumberg) *Will Making Concrete Block Pay in Your Community?,* U.S. Government Printing Office, 1945; (editor) *Towards World Prosperity, Through Industrial and Agricultural Development and Expansion,* Harper, 1947; (with Lawrence William Witt) *The Farm and the City,* Food and Agriculture Organization, United Nations, 1953.

Also author of *The Use of Agricultural Surplus to Finance Economic Development in Underdeveloped Countries,* 1955, and *Preisvoraussage bei landwirtschaftlichen erzeugnissen,* K. Schroeder, 1930. Contributor to professional journals.

OBITUARIES: *New York Times,* November 2, 1974.

(Died October 31, 1974, in Washington, D.C.)

* * *

FABER, Nancy W(eingarten) 1909-1976

June 13, 1909—March 8, 1976; American educator, novelist, and author of books on mental retardation. Obituaries: *New York Times,* March 10, 1976. (See index for previous *CA* sketch)

* * *

FALCK, (Adrian) Colin 1934-

PERSONAL: Born July 14, 1934, in London, England; son of Frederick Walter and Jessie Dorothy (Edmonds) Falck. *Education:* Magdalen College, Oxford, B.A. (philosophy, politics, and economics), 1957, B.A. (philosophy and psychology), 1959. *Politics:* Labour. *Religion:* None. *Home:* 16 St. Augustine's Rd., London NW1 9RN, England. *Agent:* John Johnson, 51-54 Goschen Buildings, 12-13 Henrietta St., London WC2E 8LF, England. *Office:* Chelsea College, University of London, Manresa Rd., London SW3 6LX, England.

CAREER: University of London, London School of Economics and Political Science, London, England, lecturer in sociology, 1961-62; University of Maryland, European Division, London, part-time lecturer in philosophy, 1962-64; University of London, Chelsea College, lecturer in humanities, 1964—. *Military service:* British Army, Royal Artillery, 1952-54. Royal Air Force Volunteer Reserve, 1954-56.

WRITINGS—Poetry: *The Garden in the Evening: Poems from the Spanish of Antonio Machado* (pamphlet), Review, 1964; *Promises* (pamphlet), Review, 1969; *Backwards into the Smoke,* Carcanet, 1973; (editor) *Poems Since 1900,* Macdonald & Janes, 1975. *Review* (poetry magazine), co-founder, 1962, co-editor, 1965-72; poetry critic of *New Review,* 1974—.

WORK IN PROGRESS: A book of critical essays on twentieth-century English and American poetry.

SIDELIGHTS: Falck writes: "My main literary interest is in poetry and is divided between 1/ writing it, 2/ criticising it, and 3/ trying to explain why almost no one reads it except people who i/ write it, ii/ criticise it, or iii/ (etc. etc.)."

* * *

FALCOFF, Mark 1941-

PERSONAL: Born September 14, 1941, in St. Louis, Mo.; son of Michael M. (a sales executive) and Dell Joyce (Denison) Falcoff. *Education:* University of Missouri, B.A. (honors), 1963; Columbia University, graduate study, 1965-66; Princeton University, M.A., 1969, Ph.D., 1970. *Home:* 2208 Fairmount Blvd., Eugene, Ore. 97403. *Office:* 175 Prince Lucien Campbell Hall, University of Oregon, Eugene, Ore. 97403.

CAREER: University of Illinois, Urbana, assistant professor of history, 1969-71; University of Oregon, Eugene, assistant professor, 1971-75, associate professor of history, 1976—.

WRITINGS: (With Ronald H. Dolkart) *Prologue to Peron:*

Argentina in Depression and War, 1930-1943, University of California Press, 1975. Contributor to *Commentary, New Republic,* and journals in his field.

WORK IN PROGRESS: A biography of Mexican revolutionary intellectual Jose Vasconcelos; a study of Latin America and the Spanish Civil War with Frederick B. Pike.

SIDELIGHTS: Falcoff told *CA:* "In general I find a curious childishness about North American and European attitudes towards Latin America. Formerly there was much patronizing of 'our little brown brothers to the south'; now, however, we insist upon turning them into bloodthirsty revolutionaries ten feet tall—all 200 million of them! The role of the United States in determining Latin American events has been vastly overblown in the public prints; the European press does this, of course, for reasons of its own. One of the obstacles to understanding is the fact that the articulate Latin Americans whose views get a hearing in English translation are a small, and frequently quite unrepresentative minority of deracinated intellectuals. I think that my scholarship (on Latin American intellectual history) and my public interest concerns mesh very nicely by trying to elucidate the point at which Latin American illusions part company with Latin American reality."

Falcoff's interests in Latin America include the intellectual history; the historiography; and the mythologies about Latin America held by the developed world, especially as manifested in literature and film. Since 1966, he has regularly traveled throughout Latin and South America.

* * *

FALK, Roger (Salis) 1910-

PERSONAL: Born June 22, 1910; son of Lionel David Falk; married Margaret Helen Stroud, 1938 (died, 1958); children: one son, two daughters. *Education:* Attended Haileybury and Imperial Service College; and University of Geneva. *Home:* 603 Beatty House, Dolphin Square, London S.W.1, England; Old Barn Cottage, Little Marlow, Buckinghamshire, England.

CAREER: Rhodesia Railways, Bulawayo, Rhodesia, in general manager's office, 1931; D. J. Keymer & Co., London, manager in Bombay and Calcutta, India, 1932-35, director, 1935-49, managing director, 1945-49, vice-chairman, 1950; British Export Trade Research Organisation, London, director-general, beginning 1949. Director and deputy chairman of P. E. International Ltd.; director of Gordon and Gotch Holdings; director and chairman of the London Board of Provincial Insurance. Member of Shoreditch Borough Council, 1937-45; Parliamentary candidate for Southeastern Southwark, 1938, resigned, 1939. Member of Council of Industrial Design, 1958-67; chairman of Furniture Development Council, 1963—; member of Monopolies Commission, 1965—; chairman of Central Council for Agricultural and Horticultural Cooperation, 1967. *Military service:* Royal Air Force Volunteer Reserve, 1939-45; became wing commander.

MEMBER: Royal Society of Arts (council member, 1968—), Institute of Management Consultants (president, 1971-72), Garrick Club, Marylebone Cricket Club. *Awards, honors:* Order of the British Empire, 1945; knighted by Queen Elizabeth II, 1969.

WRITINGS: The Business of Management: Art or Craft?, Penguin, 1961, 4th edition, 1970.

AVOCATIONAL INTERESTS: Writing, music, and reading.*

FARAGO, Ladislas 1906-

PERSONAL: Born September 21, 1906, in Csurgo, Hungary; came to United States, 1937; son of Arthur and Irma (Lang) Farago; married Liesel Mroz, March 22, 1934; children: John Michael Arthur. *Education:* Academy of Commerce and Consular Affairs, Budapest, Hungary, graduated, 1926. *Home address:* 1225 Park Ave., New York, N.Y. 10028; and Skyline Ridge, Bridgewater, Conn. 06752.

CAREER: Worked as journalist in Hungary, 1924-28; New York Times-Wide World Bureau, Berlin, Germany, journalist, 1928-35; Associated Press, Ethiopia, special correspondent in 1930's; *Sunday Chronicle,* London, England, foreign editor, 1935; Committee for National Morale, New York, N.Y., director of research, 1940-42; U.S. Office of Naval Intelligence, staff member, 1942-46; *Corps Diplomatique,* editor, 1946; *UN World,* senior editor, 1947-50; Radio Free Europe, chief desk X, 1950-53; writer, 1952—. *Member:* Authors Guild, P.E.N. (American center). *Awards, honors:* Order of St. George (Ethiopia), 1935; World War Officers special award; Overseas Press Club award, 1972, for *The Game of the Foxes.*

WRITINGS: Abyssinia on the Eve, Putnam, 1935; (editor and contributor) *Abyssinia Stop Press,* R. Hale, 1936; *Palestine on the Eve,* Putnam, 1936, published as *Palestine at the Crossroads,* Putnam, 1937; *Arabian Antic,* Sheridan House, 1938 (published in England as *The Riddle of Arabia,* R. Hale, 1939); (editor with Lewis F. Gittler) *German Psychological Warfare,* Committee for National Morale, 1941, Putnam, 1942, reprinted, Arno Press, 1972; (editor and compiler) *The Axis Grand Strategy: Blueprints for the Total War,* Farrar & Rinehart, 1942; (with Ellis M. Zacharias) *Behind Closed Doors,* Putnam, 1950.

War of Wits: The Anatomy of Espionage and Intelligence, Funk, 1954 (published in England as *War of Wits: Secrets of Espionage and Intelligence,* Hutchinson, 1956); *Burn after Reading: The Espionage History of World War II,* Walker, 1961; *Strictly from Hungary,* Walker, 1962; *The Tenth Fleet,* Obolensky, 1962; *Patton: Ordeal and Triumph,* Obolensky, 1964; *It's Your Money: Waste and Mismanagement in Government Spending,* Random House, 1964; *The Broken Seal: The Story of Operation Magic and the Pearl Harbor Disaster,* Random House, 1967.

The Game of the Foxes: The Untold Story of German Espionage in the United States and Great Britain during World War II, McKay, 1972; *Aftermath: Martin Bormann and the Fourth Reich,* Simon & Schuster, 1974; *The Secret American: The Political Biography of J. Edgar Hoover,* Doubleday, in press. Also author of screenplays "Patton" (based on his novel), Twentieth Century-Fox, 1970; and "Tora, Tora, Tora" (based on his novel, *The Broken Seal*), 1972. Author of radio and television programs.

WORK IN PROGRESS: The Dreamers and the Plotters: The Secret History of Germany from Bismarck to Brandt, publication by Doubleday expected, 1978; two original screenplays; a screenplay based on *The Secret American* for Twentieth Century-Fox.

SIDELIGHTS: Much new information about World War II secret intelligence was revealed by Farago in *The Game of the Foxes.* While doing research for the book he happened upon a metal footlocker in an attic of the U.S. National Archives. The footlocker contained extensive microfilm records of Nazi intelligence in the United States and Great Britain.

In his book, *Aftermath,* Farago gives his evidence to further support his assertion made in earlier newspaper articles that Martin Bormann and several other Nazi war criminals are still alive. On one of his trips to South America, Farago reportedly saw Bormann in an infirmary near Tupiza, Bolivia. Farago said of the meeting: "The agreement was that I would not speak to him unless he spoke to me. I was there about five minutes when he told me to get the hell out of there, so I left." Mapping Bormann's escape aided by a Vatican passport, Farago contends Juan Peron granted Argentine asylum in exchange for three-quarters of the Nazi war booty Bormann secreted out of Germany via submarine.

* * *

FARLEY, James A(loysius) 1888-1976

May 30, 1888—June 9, 1976; American political party organizer and author. Obituaries: *New York Times,* June 10, 1976, June 11, 1976, June 13, 1976; *Current Biography,* August, 1976.

* * *

FARLIE, Barbara L(eitzow) 1936-

PERSONAL: Born June 11, 1936, in St. Paul, Minn.; daughter of Herman W. (a pharmaceutical executive) and Blanche R. Leitzow; married William Newman Farlie, Jr. (an advertising executive), January 30, 1960; children: Elisabeth Anne, William Newman III, Craig L., Matthew B. *Education:* Smith College, B.A. (cum laude), 1958. *Address:* c/o Bobbs-Merrill Co., Inc., 4 West 58th St., New York, N.Y. 10019.

CAREER: J. Walter Thompson, New York, N.Y., assistant editor, 1958-60; craft instructor and designer, 1960-67; designer for boutiques, 1967-68; writer, 1969—. Co-hostess of nationally syndicated television program "All About Crafts," 1973, and lecturer on crafts. Member of Arts Council, University of California, Los Angeles, 1967-68. Consultant on architecture and interior design.

WRITINGS: Beading: Basic and Boutique, Meredith Corp., 1971; *Pennywise Boutique,* Meredith Corp., 1974; (with Charlotte L. Clarke) *All About Doll Houses,* Bobbs-Merrill, 1975; *Your House in Needlepoint,* Bobbs-Merrill, 1976. Contributor to craft magazines, including *Creative Crafts, Better Homes and Gardens Christmas Ideas,* and *Teaching.*

WORK IN PROGRESS: A book on creating artificial flowers, with Vivian Abell; a book on making decorative accessories, with Dorothy Brockel.

AVOCATIONAL INTERESTS: Antiques.

* * *

FARMER, Don 1938-

PERSONAL: Born September 27, 1938, in St. Louis, Mo.; son of William S. (a chemist) and Doris K. (Stephenson) Farmer; married De Ann Niedfeldt, June 3, 1962 (divorced, 1970); married Chris Curle (a television news commentator), February 28, 1972; children: Laurie Lynn, Justin James. *Education:* University of Missouri, B.J., 1960, graduate study, 1961-62. *Residence:* Washington, D.C. *Office:* American Broadcasting Co.—News, 1124 Connecticut Ave. N.W., Washington, D.C. 20007.

CAREER/WRITINGS: St. Louis Globe-Democrat, St. Louis, Mo., reporter, 1960-61; WRCV-Television, Philadelphia, Pa., reporter, 1962-65; American Broadcasting Co. (ABC) News, New York City, correspondent or bureau chief in New York City, 1965-66, Chicago, Ill., 1966-68, Atlanta, Ga., 1968-72, London, England, 1972-73, Bonn, Germany, 1973-75, congressional correspondent in Washington, D.C., 1975—. Notable assignments include events in Vietnam, the Yom Kippur War, the Dominican Revolution, U.S. Presidential campaigns and elections, and the civil rights movement in the 1960's.

* * *

FARMER, Kathleen 1946-

PERSONAL: Born November 21, 1946, in Cincinnati, Ohio; daughter of John Robert (a postal supervisor) and Alice (an accountant; maiden name, Young) Usher; married Charles J. Farmer (a writer and photographer), June 6, 1972; children: Brittany Ann. *Education:* University of Dayton, B.A., 1967, M.A., 1969. *Religion:* Roman Catholic. *Home and office:* 2909½ Ocean Front Walk, Marina Del Rey, Calif. 90291. *Agent:* Jane Jordan Browne, 170 Beverly Dr., Beverly Hills, Calif. 90212.

CAREER: Dayton State Hospital, Dayton, Ohio, psychology trainee, 1967-69; Southeast Wyoming Mental Health Center, Cheyenne, family counselor, 1970-72; writer and photographer, 1972—. Public relations consultant, 1976—. *Member:* National Federation of Press Women, Outdoor Women (member of founding board of directors, 1976—). *Awards, honors:* Third place in Wyoming Press Women's state writing contest, 1975, for feature article "The Psychology of the Solitary Backpacker."

WRITINGS: (Editor with husband, Charles J. Farmer) *Campground Cooking,* Digest Books, 1974; *Woman in the Woods,* Stackpole, 1976. Contributor to *Camping Journal, Sports Afield, Outdoor Photographer's Digest,* and *Trout Fisherman's Digest.*

WORK IN PROGRESS: The Female Outdoor Spirit, "an in-depth analysis of the lives and motivation of outstanding outdoorswomen who have pioneered advances in their respective fields of backpacking, river running, mountain climbing, hunting, and fishing."

SIDELIGHTS: Working with her husband, Kathleen Farmer has participated in a wide variety of outdoor activities in the United States, Canada, Mexico, and South America, as well as Japan and several of the Hawaiian islands. She spent a six-year period in a log cabin in the high country of Wyoming, where she developed her technique and philosophy of outdoor living. Now she lives on a California beach, and is preparing new ideas for living outdoors in what she calls a "more civilized" kind of wilderness. She writes: "I believe that helping a woman gain confidence and expertise in outdoor skills will also increase self-confidence and a new outlook on life for her."

* * *

FARMER, Laurence 1895(?)-1976

1895(?)—May 5, 1976; American physician, expert on allergies, and author of books in his field. Obituaries: *New York Times,* May 6, 1976; *AB Bookman's Weekly,* July 5, 1976.

* * *

FARNY, Michael H(olt) 1934-

PERSONAL: Born December 23, 1934, in Geneva, Ill.; son of Cyril (a businessman) and Phyllis (Holt) Farny; married Ethel Hooper (a flutist), June 9, 1968; children: Suzannah, Natasha, Nathaniel. *Education:* Princeton University, A.B., 1956; Harvard University, M.B.A., 1968. *Politics:* Republican. *Religion:* Episcopalian. *Home address:* Lincoln Rd., Lincoln, Mass. 01773. *Office:* Lincoln Guide Service, Lincoln Rd., Lincoln, Mass. 01773.

CAREER: History teacher in private school in Pomfret, Conn., 1961-64; Princeton University, Princeton, N.J., deputy director of admissions and financial aid, 1965-66; Lincoln Guide Service, Lincoln, Mass., president, 1969—. President of Charles River Canoe Service, 1973—, and Weston Ski Track, 1974—. Member of New England River Basins Commission, 1968-72; chairman of Lincoln Recreation Committee, 1969-71. *Military Service:* U.S. Marine Corps, 1957-61; became captain. *Member:* Eastern Professional Ski Touring Instructors (vice-president of board of directors, 1972—), Harvard Club of Boston.

WRITINGS: Priorities, 1971-1976, U.S. Government Printing Office, 1969; *Maine Coastal Planning,* U.S. Government Printing Office, 1971; *New England Over the Handlebars,* Little, Brown, 1975.

SIDELIGHTS: Farny writes: "My writing and my commercial and civic work are devoted to promoting physical fitness, teaching techniques of bicycling, canoeing, and cross-country skiing, and heightening appreciation of the local natural environment. Adventure is available as near as one's back yard; adventure is very important for citizens of a space age society."

* * *

FARRAR, John C(hipman) 1896-1974
(John Prosper, joint pseudonym)

PERSONAL: Born February 25, 1896, in Burlington, Vt.; son of Edward Donaldson (in advertising) and Sally (a teacher and librarian; maiden name, Wright) Farrar; married Margaret Petherbridge (a writer and crossword editor of the *New York Times*), May 28, 1926; children: John Curtis, Alison (Mrs. George W. Wilson), Janice Farrar Thaddeus. *Education:* Yale University, A.B., 1919. *Politics:* Republican. *Religion:* Episcopalian. *Residence:* New York, N.Y.

CAREER: New York World, New York, N.Y., reporter for Sunday magazine section and feature writer, 1919-21; George H. Doran Co., New York City, editor of *Bookman,* 1921-27, editor of publishing company, 1925-27; Doubleday, Doran & Co., New York City, editor and member of board of directors, 1927-29; Farrar & Rinehart, Inc., New York City, founder, editor, vice-president, and chairman of board of directors, 1929-44; Farrar, Straus & Giroux (formerly Farrar, Straus & Co., Farrar, Straus & Young, and Farrar, Straus & Cudahy), New York City, founder, editor, and chairman of board of directors, 1946-74. Lecturer at Columbia University, 1945-47; faculty member at New York University in the early 1920's. Founder and first director of Breadloaf Writers' Conference at Middlebury College, 1926-29; director of Marlboro Fiction Writers' Conference, 1949-51. Directed the plays "The Fall of the City," "They Burned the Books," and "Listen to the People," on National Broadcasting Co. (NBC)-Radio, 1937; conducted interview series with authors on WEVD-Radio. *Military service:* U.S. Aviation Service, 1917-19; became first lieutenant. Office of War Information, editor of *Die Amerikanische Rundschau* for Psychological Warfare Branch, 1943-45; served in North Africa.

MEMBER: International P.E.N. (president of New York Center, 1951-54), National Conference of Christians and Jews, Federal Grand Jury Association (member of executive committee, 1949), Poetry Society of America (member of executive board, 1959-74), Writers' Board for World

Government, Phi Beta Kappa, Alpha Delta Phi, Century Club, Yale Club, Elizabethan Club (New Haven, Conn.).

WRITINGS: A Pageant, privately printed, 1910; *Fire Water: An Abnaki Indian Allegory* (play), privately printed, 1912; *Dreams of Boyhood,* privately printed, 1914; *Portraits* (poems), Yale University Press, 1916; *Forgotten Shrines* (poems), Yale University Press, 1919, AMS Press, 1971; (editor with John Andrews, Stephen Vincent Benet, and Pierson Underwood) *The Yale Book of Student Verse, 1910-1919,* Yale University Press, 1919.

Songs for Parents (memoirs of childhood), Yale University Press, 1921; *Timothy Tubby's Journal* (published anonymously), Doran, 1922; (with Prosper Buranelli, under joint pseudonym John Prosper) *Gold-Killer: A Mystery of the New Underworld,* Doran, 1922; (editor) *The Bookman Anthology of Verse,* Doran, 1st series, 1922, 2nd series, 1927; (editor) *The Bookman Anthology of Essays,* Doran, 1923; *The Magic Seashell and Other Plays for Children* (seven one-act plays), Doran, 1923, reissued as *Indoor and Outdoor Plays for Children, Including The Magic Sea Shell,* Noble & Noble, 1933; *The Middle Twenties* (poems), Doran, 1924; "That Awful Mrs. Eaton" (historical play), first produced in New York, N.Y. at Morosco Theatre, September 29, 1924; (editor) *The Literary Spotlight* (essays), Doran, 1924, Books for Libraries, 1970.

Nerves (one-act play; first produced in New Haven, Conn. by Yale University Dramatic Association, 1919; produced later on Broadway, September, 1924), Samuel French, 1930; *Songs for Johnny-Jump-Up* (juvenile poems), R. R. Smith, 1930; *Jack* (play), Samuel French, 1935.

For the Record (his memoirs of Stephen Vincent Benet; bound with *Stephen Vincent Benet: My Brother Steve,* by William Rose Benet), Farrar & Rinehart, 1943, Folcroft, 1970.

(Translator) Carlo Levi, *The Watch* (novel), Farrar, Straus, 1951.

(Editor with Melville Cane and Louise Townsend Nicholl) *The Golden Year: The Poetry Society of America Anthology, 1910-1960,* Poetry Society of America, 1960, reissued by Books for Libraries, 1969.

Work has been anthologized in *Atlantic Book of Junior Plays,* Little, Brown, 1924; *One-Act Plays for Young Folks,* edited by M. A. Jagendorf, Brentano's, 1924; *C'est la Guerre!: The Best Stories of the World War,* edited by James G. Dunton, Stratford, 1927; *Short Narratives,* edited by Paul M. Fulcher, Century, 1928.

Co-author of book column in *Time,* 1923-24. Contributor of stories, plays, articles, and reviews to popular magazines, including *Saturday Review of Literature* and *Collier's.* Drama critic for *Charm,* 1924-25; film critic for *Ladies' Home Journal,* 1925-26.

SIDELIGHTS: Farrar liked to read "a good story" and during his publishing career, took an active and outspoken interest in a wide range of literary works, especially encouraging new writers. His publishing firms, over the years, were responsible for many best-selling books, in which Farrar took a special interest.

OBITUARIES: New York Times, November 7, 1974; *Washington Post,* November 8, 1974.*

(Died November 5, 1974, in New York, N.Y.)

* * *

FARRAR, Richard B(artlett), Jr. 1939-

PERSONAL: Born April 25, 1939, in Penn Yan, N.Y.; son of Richard B. (a food broker) and Margaret (Stevenson) Farrar; married Gay Green (an education specialist), August 23, 1963; children: Michelle, Marc. *Education:* Cornell University, student, 1956-58; Houghton College, B.S., 1960; graduate study at Western Michigan University, 1964-65, and University of Chicago, 1965-68. *Residence:* Franklin Lakes, N.J. 07417. *Office:* New Jersey Audubon Society, 790 Ewing Ave., Franklin Lakes, N.J. 17417.

CAREER: High school teacher of biology and geology in Hinkley, Maine, 1960-61, and Concord, Mass., 1961-64; Massachusettes Audubon Society headquarters, Lincoln, program directory for sanctuaty, 1964-65; University of Illinois at Chicago Circle, Chicago, instructor in biology, 1965-68; science teacher and chairman of department at a private school in Woodstock, Vt., 1968-71; Vermont Institute of Natural Science, Woodstock, executive director, 1971-74; New Jersey Audubon Society, Franklin Lakes, executive director, 1975—. Program administrator at Environmental Centers, Inc., 1974; member of steering committee of New Jersey Alliance for Environmental Education.

MEMBER: American Association for the Advancement of Science, American Association of Interpretive Naturalists, American Ornithologists Union, American Nature Study Society, National Wildlife Federation, Wildlife Society. Northeastern Bird-Banding Association, Skylands Association (member of board of directors). *Awards, honors:* Conservation award from Connecticut River Watershed Council, 1971; teaching award from National Association of Biology Teachers, 1972; science book award from Children's Book Council, 1975, for *The Hungry Snowbird.*

WRITINGS: Birds of East Central Vermont, Vermont Institute of Natural Science, 1973; *The Hungry Snowbird* (children's book), Coward, 1975; *The Birds' Woodland* (children's book), Coward, 1976. Contributor to scientific natural history journals. Editor of *New Jersey Audubon.*

WORK IN PROGRESS: Manuscripts on leaf color, field succession, and the behavior of bird flocks at winter feeding stations.

SIDELIGHTS: Farrar writes that he began watching birds at the age of three and was writing in a natural history journal by the age of five. His wildlife research was intended for adults and older students until, realizing that it sometimes took as long as ten years for "fun-type discoveries made by curious researchers" to filter from the graduate student level down to the elementary school level, he wrote *The Hungry Snowbird.*

* * *

FARRELL, Cliff 1899-

PERSONAL: Born November 20, 1899, in Zanesville, Ohio; son of Charles Alfonso and Laura (Hess) Farrell; married Mildred K. Raddon, June 1, 1927; children: Clifford R., Mildred (Mrs. Herbert Hueg). *Education:* Attended public schools in Zanesville, Ohio. *Address:* P.O. Box F, Crestline, Calif. 92325.

CAREER: Los Angeles Examiner, Los Angeles, Calif., telegraph editor, night news editor, and sports news editor, 1925-56; full-time author, 1956—. *Member:* Western Writers of America. *Awards, honors:* Golden Spur Award from Western Writers of America, 1970.

WRITINGS—Western novels, published by Doubleday, except as noted: *Follow the New Grass,* Random House, 1954; *West with the Missouri,* Random House, 1955; *Santa Fe Wagon Boss,* 1958; *Ride the Wild Trail,* 1959; *The Lean*

Rider, 1960; *Fort Deception,* 1960; *Trail of the Tattered Star: A Historical Novel of the West,* 1961; *The Walking Hills,* 1962; *Ride the Wild Country,* 1963 (published in England as *The Wild Country,* Ward, Lock, 1964); *Return of the Long Riders,* 1964; *Cross-fire,* 1965; *Bucko,* 1965; *Comanch',* 1966; *The Guns of Judgment Day,* 1967; *Death Trap on the Platte,* 1968; *Treachery Trail,* 1969; *The Renegade,* 1970; *Owlhoot Trail,* 1971; *Patchsaddle Drive,* 1972; *Shoot-out at Sioux Wells,* 1973; *The Mighty Land* (history), 1975; *Terror in Eagle Basin,* 1976; *The Devil's Playground,* 1976. Author of more than 600 short stories and novellettes appearing in U.S. fiction magazines.

* * *

FARREN, David
   See McFERRAN, Douglass David

* * *

FARRER, Claire R(afferty)   1936-

PERSONAL: Born December 26, 1936, in New York, N.Y.; daughter of Francis Michael (a welder) and Clara Anna (a nurse; maiden name, Guerra) Rafferty; married Donald Nathanael Farrer (a psychologist), February 2, 1957 (divorced, 1973); children: Suzanne Claire. *Education:* University of California, B.A., 1970; University of Texas, M.A., 1974, Ph.D., 1977. *Politics:* Democrat. *Religion:* Unitarian. *Home:* 4701 Connecticut Ave., N.W. #209, Washington, D.C. 20008. *Office:* National Endowment for the Arts, Folk Arts Program, Washington, D.C., 20506.

CAREER: San Jose State University, San Jose, Calif., worked in personnel office, 1956; International Business Machines (IBM), San Jose, Calif., statistical analyst, 1956-57; Jennings Radio Manufacturing Co., San Jose, Calif., statistical consultant, executive secretary, 1957-58; Washington State University, Pullman, clerk, 1958-59, executive secretary, 1959-61; *Otero County Star,* Alamogordo, N.M., columnist, 1963-65; Unitarian-Universalist Fellowship, Alamogordo, N.M., founder, administrator, 1964-71; curriculum consultant and teacher, Zia School, Alamogordo, N.M., 1966-68, 1970-71; Otero County Child Care Center, Alamogordo, N.M., fund raiser, 1967-71; Smithsonian Institution, Washington, D.C., conducted survey, 1973-74; Joint Senate-House Committee on prison reform, Texas, ethnographic analyst, 1974; Mescalero Apache Indian Reservation, ethnographic researcher, 1974-75; National Endowment for the Arts, Washington, D.C., administrator of Folk Arts program, 1976—.

MEMBER: American Anthropological Association, American Association for the Advancement of Science, American Ethnological Society, American Folklore Society, British Folklore Society, Council on Anthropology and Education (charter member), Society for the Anthropology of Visual Communication, Society for Historical Archaeology (charter member), Association for the Anthropological study of Play (charter member). California Scholastic Federation, Phi Kappa Phi.

WRITINGS: (Editor) *Women and Folklore,* University of Texas Press, 1976; (contributor) David F. Lancy and B. Allan Tindall, editors, *The Anthropological Study of Play: Problems and Prospects,* Cornwall, 1976. Also author of "Graded Supplementary Reading Materials for the Children of the Bent-Mescalero School" (twenty-four stories concerning Mescalero Apache history). Co-founder and co-editor of first issue, *Folklore Feminists Communication;* editor of *Women and Folklore,* special issue of *Journal of Amer-*

ican Folklore. Contributor of articles to professional journals.

WORK IN PROGRESS: Further research on Mescalero Apache society and culture; folklore of women and children; cross-cultural aesthetics.

* * *

FARRINGTON, Benjamin   1891-1974

PERSONAL: Born July 10, 1891, in Cork, Ireland; son of Thomas and Mary Emily (Foreman) Farrington; married Ruth Hedwig Schechter, 1935 (died, 1942); married Cecily Barbara Sell, 1943; children: one daughter. *Education:* Educated at University College, Cork, and Trinity College, Dublin. *Home:* 8 Daniell's Walk, Lymington, Hantshire, England.

CAREER: Queen's University, Belfast, Northern Ireland, assistant in classics, 1916-20; University of Cape Town, Cape Town, South Africa, lecturer in Greek, 1920-22, senior lecturer in classics, 1920-30, professor of Latin, 1930-35; University of Bristol, Bristol, England, lecturer in classics, 1935-36; University of Wales, University College of Swansea, Swansea, Wales, professor of classics, 1936-56, professor emeritus, 1956-74.

WRITINGS: (Author of introduction and commentary) *Primum Graius Homo: An Anthology of Latin Translations from the Greek, from Ennius to Livy,* Cambridge University Press, 1927; *Samuel Butler and the Odyssey,* J. Cape, 1929; (translator with Isaac Schapera) Schapera, editor, *The Early Cape Hottentots, Described in the Writings of Olfert Dapper (1668), Willem Ten Rhyne (1686), and Johannes Gulielmus de Grevenbroek (1695),* Publications of the Van Riebeeck Society, 1933, reprint, Negro Universities Press, 1970; *Science in Antiquity,* Butterworth, 1936, 2nd edition, Oxford University Press, 1969; *The Civilisation of Greece and Rome,* Gollancz, 1938; *Science and Politics in the Ancient World,* Allen & Unwin, 1939, 2nd edition, 1965, Barnes & Noble, 1966.

Greek Science: Its Meaning for Us, Penguin, volume one, 1944, volume two, 1949, revised one volume edition, 1961; *Head and Hand in Ancient Greece: Four Studies in the Social Relations of Thought,* C. A. Watts, 1947; *Francis Bacon, Philosopher of Industrial Science,* H. Schuman, 1949, Collier, 1961, revised edition, Haskell House, 1973; *Has History a Meaning?* (lecture), South Place Ethical Society, 1950; *Francis Bacon, Pioneer of Planned Science,* Weidenfeld & Nicolson, 1963, Praeger, 1969; *The Philosophy of Francis Bacon: An Essay on Its Development from 1603 to 1609, with New Translations of Fundamental Texts,* University of Liverpool Press, 1964, University of Chicago Press, 1966; *The 'New Atlantis' of Francis Bacon* (lecture), New Atlantis Foundation, 1965; *Aristotle, Founder of Scientific Philosophy,* Weidenfeld & Nicolson, 1965, Praeger, 1969; *What Darwin Really Said,* Schocken, 1966; *The Faith of Epicurus,* Basic Books, 1967.

Editor, "Marxism Today Series," Lawrence & Wishart, beginning 1943; general editor, "Past and Present: Studies in the History of Civilisation" series, Cobbett Press, beginning 1946. Contributor of articles to professional journals.*

(Died November 17, 1974)

* * *

FAULKNER, Elsie   1905-

PERSONAL: Born January 5, 1905, in Eastern Kentucky; daughter of James Monroe (a farmer) and Dora Jane (Allen)

Witt; married Jesse Faulkner, February 25, 1926 (died December 22, 1961); children: Sallie Faulkner McGuffey, Susan Faulkner Gooch. *Education:* Earned B.S. at Eastern Kentucky University. *Politics:* Democrat. *Religion:* Methodist Episcopal. *Home:* 311 West Main St., Stanford, Ky. 40484. *Office: Lincoln County Post,* Main St., Stanford, Ky. 40484.

CAREER: Elementary school teacher in Lincoln and Harlan County, Ky., 1922-71; *Lincoln County Post,* Stanford, Ky., co-editor and feature writer, 1972—. Active in local social and civic affairs.

WRITINGS: Bounce: A Trail Blazing Dog (juvenile), Denison, 1975. Author of the play "Out of the Wilderness," broadcast on WHIR-Radio. *Danville Advocate,* feature writer, 1965-72. Contributor of poems to newspapers.

WORK IN PROGRESS: Topsy, a juvenile book.

SIDELIGHTS: Elsie Faulkner writes: "I always enjoyed writing and seemed to be a 'natural' for it. School children enjoyed my 'covered wagon' story so much I decided to write it down. They are now asking for a horse story. I am not interest in profit. I want books at a price children can enjoy and afford."

*   *   *

FAULKNER, Virginia (Louise)   1913-

PERSONAL: Born March 1, 1913, in Lincoln, Neb.; daughter of Edwin Jerome and Leah (Meyer) Faulkner. *Education:* Attended University of Nebraska, 1928-30, Moxley School, 1930-31, and Radcliffe College, 1932-33. *Politics:* Republican. *Religion:* Presbyterian. *Home:* 721 South 14th St., Lincoln, Neb. 68508. *Office:* University of Nebraska Press, 901 North 17th St., Lincoln, Neb. 68588.

CAREER: Washington Post, Washington, D.C., special writer, 1933-34; *Town and Country,* New York, N.Y., assistant editor, 1934-35; Metro-Goldwyn-Mayer, Culver City, Calif., screenwriter, 1935-38; free-lance writer, 1938-56; University of Nebraska Press, Lincoln, assistant editor, 1956-59, editor-in-chief, 1959—; professor of English at University of Nebraska, 1970—.

WRITINGS: Friends and Romans, Simon & Schuster, 1934; *The Barbarians,* Simon & Schuster, 1935; *My Heyday,* Duell, Sloan & Pearce, 1940; (compiler and editor) *Roundup: A Nebraska Reader,* University of Nebraska Press, 1957; (editor) *Hostiles and Friendlies: Mari Sandoz's Selected Short Writings,* University of Nebraska Press, 1959; (editor) *Willa Cather's Collected Short Fiction, 1892-1912,* University of Nebraska Press, 1965, revised edition, 1970; (editor) *Sandhill Sundays and Other Recollections by Mari Sandoz,* University of Nebraska Press, 1970; (editor with Bernice Slote) *The Art of Willa Cather,* University of Nebraska Press, 1974. Co-author of "Maiden Voyage," a screenplay produced by Metro-Goldwyn-Mayer, 1938. Contributor of sketches and lyrics to review "All in Fun" (two-act), first produced in New York at Majestic Theatre, December 26, 1939, and with Dana Suesse "It Takes Two" (three-act), first produced in New York at Biltmore Theater, February 3, 1946. Contributor to national magazines and scholarly publications, including *Saturday Evening Post, College English,* and *Cosmopolitan.* Associate editor, *Prairie Schooner,* 1959—.

*   *   *

FEINBLOOM, Deborah Heller   1940-

PERSONAL: Born August 19, 1940, in Brooklyn, N.Y.;

children: Joshua, Sarah, David. *Education:* Smith College, A.B. (honors), 1961; Boston College, M.A., 1972, Ph.D., 1977. *Home:* 37 Corey Rd., Brookline, Mass. 02146. *Office:* Gender Identity Service, Boston, Mass.

CAREER: U.S. Peace Corps, Washington, D.C., staff member in San Juan, P.R., 1962-63; Children's Hospital Medical Center, Boston, Mass., research assistant in health education, 1966-67; Newbury Junior College, Boston, instructor in sociology and psychology and counselor, 1967-71; Gender Identity Service, Boston, Mass., organizer and director, 1973-76, coordinator of counseling for Women's Health Clinic, 1976—. Faculty associate at Goddard College, 1973-76. Volunteer counselor for Boston's Pregnancy counseling Service; volunteer coordinator of Putney, Vt.'s Experiment in International Living; member of advisory board of local Community Sex Information. *Member:* American Sociological Association, Society for the Study of Social Problems, Society for the Scientific Study of Sex, Eastern Sociological Association, Massachusetts Sociological Association.

WRITINGS: The Transvestite and Transsexual: Mixed Views, Delacorte, 1976. Contributor to professional journals.

*   *   *

FEINMAN, Jeffrey   1943-

PERSONAL: Born November 21, 1943, in New York, N.Y.; son of Max L. (a physician) and Sylvia (Mann) Feinman. *Education:* New York University, B.A., 1965. *Religion:* Jewish. *Home:* 301 East 62nd St., New York, N.Y. 10021. *Office:* Ventura Associates, 40 East 49th St., New York, N.Y. 10017.

CAREER: D. L. Blair Corp. (in sales promotion), New York, N.Y., executive vice-president, 1967-72; Ventura Associates (in sales promotion), New York City, president, 1972—. Corporate director and faculty member at New School for Social Research, 1974—.

WRITINGS: Catalog of Kits, Morrow, 1975; *One Hundred Sure Fire Businesses You Can Start Part Time,* Playboy Press, 1975; *The T-Shirt Book,* Doubleday, 1976; *How to Win Sweepstakes,* Playboy Press, 1976; *Inflation Fighter Guidebook,* Award, 1976.

WORK IN PROGRESS: Business books; "how-to" books.

*   *   *

FEITEL, Donald G.   1925(?)-1976

1925(?)—June 3, 1976; American editorial director, journalist, and author. Obituaries: *New York Times,* June 4, 1976.

*   *   *

FELLINI, Federico   1920-

PERSONAL: Born January 20, 1920, in Rimini, Italy; son of Urbano (a businessman) and Ida (Barbiani) Fellini; married Giulietta Masina, October 30, 1943. *Religion:* Roman Catholic. *Home:* Via Margutta 110, Rome, Italy.

CAREER: Contributor of cartoons to periodicals and tourist caricaturist in Rome, Italy, 1936-37; *Marc'Aurelio* (weekly magazine), Rome, story editor, 1937; scriptwriter for radio and writer of skits and dialogue for Macario and other traveling comedians, 1938-39; became interested in writing screenplays and began working in various production capacities for the Italian director, Mario Mattoli, in 1939; collaborated on screenplays and continued production work with Roberto Rossellini and Alberto Lattuada, 1940-50; co-director with Lattuada of original screenplay, "Luci del varieta," 1950; director of collaborated screenplays, 1952—. Acting roles include the part of the Stranger in "Il Miracolo," 1948, and the part of himself in "Alex in Wonderland," 1970.

AWARDS, HONORS: First prizes in Rome, Venice, Zurich, and Cannes Film Festivals, awards for best foreign film from New York Film Critics and National Board of Review of Motion Pictures (United States), all 1946, all for "Roma citta aperta"; grand prize from World Film Festival, 1947, and awards for best foreign film from New York Film Critics and National Board of Review of Motion Pictures, 1948, for "Paisa"; Nastro d'Argento (Italy's highest film award), 1948, for "Senza pieta," 1950, for "Luci del varieta," and 1951, for "Europa '51"; New York Film Critics award, 1950, for "L'Amore"; grand prize from Venice Film Festival, 1954, New York Film Critics award, 1956, Screen Directors Guild award for best direction of foreign film, 1956, and Academy Award for best foreign film (Oscar) from American Academy of Motion Picture Arts and Sciences, 1956, all for "La Strada"; Academy Award, 1957, for "Le Notti di Cabiria"; first prize at Cannes Film Festival, 1960, and New York Film Critics award, 1961, both for "La Dolce Vita"; Academy Award, 1963, for "8½"; Golden Globe Award from Hollywood Foreign Press Association, 1965, for "Giulietta degli spiriti"; Academy Award and New York Film Critics award, both 1974, both for "Amarcord"; and countless other film awards. Honorary doctor of humane letters, Columbia University, 1970.

WRITINGS—Collaborator on screenplays: "Avanti c'e posto," 1942; "Roma citta aperta" (released in U.S. as "Paisan"), 1946; "Campo dei fiori" (released in U.S. as "The Path of Hope"), 1947; "Il Delitto di Giovanni Episcopo" (released in U.S. as "Without Pity"), 1948; "In nome della legge" (released in U.S. as "Mafia"), 1949; "Il Mulino del Po" (released in U.S. as "Flowers of St. Francis"), 1950; "Europa '51," 1951; "La Citta si difende," 1951; "Fortunella," 1958.

Screenplays; all as director: (With Ennio Flaiano, Alberto Lattuada, and Tullio Pinelli; directed with Alberto Lattuada) "Luci del varieta" (released in U.S. as "Variety Lights"; also see collected screenplays), released in 1950; (with Michelangelo Antonioni and Pinelli) "Lo Sceicco Bianco" (relased in U.S. as "The White Sheik"; also see collected screenplays), 1952; (with Flaiano and Pinelli) "I Vitelloni" (released in U.S. as "The Young and the Passionate"; also see collected screenplays), 1953; (with Pinelli) *La Strada* (film released in 1954), Bianco e nero (Rome), 1955; (with Flaiano and Pinelli) *Il Bidone* (released in 1955; released in U.S. as "The Swindler"; also see collected screenplays), translation from the Italian into French by Dominique Delouche, published under same title, Flammarion (Paris), 1956; (with Flaiano and Pinelli) *Le Notti di Cabiria* (released in 1956; released in U.S. as "Nights of Cabiria"), edited by Lino del Fra, Cappelli (Bologna), 1957.

(With Flaiano, Pinelli, and Brunello Rondi) *La Dolce Vita* (released in 1959), edited by Tullio Kezich, Cappelli, 1961; (with Flaiano, Pinelli, and Rondi) *8½* (released in 1963), Cappelli, 1963; (with Flaiano, Pinelli, and Rondi) *Gulietta degli spiriti* (released in 1965), edited by Kezich, Cappelli, 1965, translation by Howard Greenfeld published as *Juliet of the Spirits,* Orion Press, 1965, new edition with transcription of final screenplay by John Cohen, translated by Cecilia Perrault, Ballantine, 1966; "A Director's Notebook" (televi-

sion film), first broadcast by National Broadcasting Corp., April 11, 1969; (with Bernardino Zapponi) *Fellini Satyricon* (released in 1969), edited by Dario Zanelli with preface by Fellini, includes critical essays and conversations, Cappelli, 1969, translation by Eugene Walter and John Matthews published under same title, Ballantine, 1970; (with Zapponi) *I Clowns* (first broadcast on Italian television, 1970), edited by Renzo Renzi, Cappelli, 1970, published with block notes as *Fellini TV,* 1972; (with Zapponi) *Roma* (released in 1972), edited by Zapponi, Cappelli, 1972; (with Tonio Guerra) *Amarcord* (released in 1973; released in U.S. with subtitle "I Remember"), Rizzoli (Milan), 1973; (with Zapponi) "Casanova," released in 1976.

Contributor to films: (Screenwriter of Italian script, "Il Miracolo") "L'Amore" (film trilogy), 1947; (screenwriter and director of "Una Agenzia Matrimoniale" section) "Amore in citta," 1952; (author of screenstory) "Il Brigante di Tacca del Lupo," 1953; (screenwriter and director of act two, "Le Tentazioni del dottor Antonio"; also see collected screenplays) "Boccaccio '70," 1961; (screenwriter and director of "Toby Dammit" episode) "Histoires Extraordinaires," 1967.

Collected screenplays *8½* (includes "Le Tentazoni del dottor Antonio"), edited by Camilla Cederna, Cappelli, 1965; *Il Primo Fellini* (includes "Lo Sceicco Bianco," "I Vitelloni," "La Strada," and "Il Bidone"), edited by Liliana Betti and Eschilo Tarquini, Cappelli, 1969; *Three Screenplays* (includes "The Young and the Passionate," "The Swindler," and "The Temptations of Doctor Antonio"), translated by Judith Green, Orion Press, 1970; *Early Screenplays* (includes "Variety Lights" and "The White Sheik"), translated by Green, Grossman, 1971; *Quattro Film* (includes "I Vitelloni," "La Dolce Vita," "8½," and "Giulietta degli spiriti"), Einaudi (Turin), 1974.

Other: (With Dominique Delouche) *Entretiens avec Federico Fellini* (excerpts of interview appearing on Belgian television), Radiodiffusion television belge, 1962; (author of text with Francoise Sagan, photographs by Wingate Paine) *Mirror of Venus,* Random House, 1966; (contributor) Renzo Renzi, editor, *La mia Rimini* (memories and descriptions of Rimini), Cappelli, 1967; (contributor) Liliana Betti, Ornella Valta, and Bernardino Zapponi, editors, *Tre passi nel delirio* (filmscript anthology; all scripts based on short stories by Edgar Allan Poe), Cappelli, 1968; *Fellini,* L'Arc (Aix-en-Provence), 1971; *Fellini on Fellini,* translated by Isabel Quigley, Delacorte, 1976.

WORK IN PROGRESS: Another picture.

SIDELIGHTS: "It seemed to me I would never be a movie director," Fellini once said. But, he added: "Within one hour after I began directing, I suddenly knew all about the mechanics of filmmaking. Believe me, I had no preparation for this knowledge. I only know that it happened." With that unexplainable start Fellini has become one of the most successful directors in film history. Critical and popular acclaim greeted his second screenplay collaboration in 1945 and has followed ever since. "La Strada" was said to contain the unmistakable touch of an artist. "La Dolce Vita" was called awesome, moral, and vastly sophisticated in attitude. Roger Greenspun reported his viewing of "Roma" was constantly interrupted by audience applause. "Satyricon" was said to be the work of a master and nothing less than the creation of a new world—a kind of subterranean Oz. "Juliet of the Spirits" was called a cinematographic miracle. "8½" was described as a masterpiece, the film world's best work about an artist's desperation as artist, and the directorial landmark of the sixties. "Pure enchantment" was one critic's response to "The Clowns."

It has been said that Fellini works in truly an Italian temperament. He shouts, screams, coaxes, and flatters his actors as he vocally choreographs every move. Leo Janos called him a latter day D. W. Griffith because while watching him one would think the talkies have yet to be invented. But the sound track is not ignored and, of course, Fellini's absolute control extends there. He examines all the voices and replaces any that do not suit his idea of the character. Every device available is used to re-create the characters of his imagination on film.

In casting, the face means everything. Louis Giannetti pointed out: "In accordance with the director's celebrated instinct for the 'right' face and body type, the performers playing the school 'children' [in 'Amarcord'] range in ages from about twelve to thirty! Fellini is obviously not concerned with considerations of plausibility, but with the spiritual essence of each performer." Casting is the first important part of any film's production, but "for me," Fellini says, "to choose—to cast a picture, to choose faces—is really the most fascinating and heavy and—the moment in which I feel the difficulty of the picture." Style of direction and the practice of voicing-over the sound track allow him to choose potential actors from any continent, speaking any language, without acting experience. During production, extras are cast by Fellini sketching out the face he desires, using the skills he developed as a young cartoonist and tourist caricaturist in Rome, and sending assistants out to run up and down the streets until they find a match. After a few touches by make-up artists, the result is a remarkable likeness of the original sketch. 500 of these sought after extras were used in "Casanova."

There are numerous anecdotes about Fellini at work. For example, during the filming of "Casanova" he suddenly stopped the cameras in a scene which included 200 rats, when he noticed that half the rats were white. "Paint them brown!" he ordered. . . . Mario De Vecchi tells another story. It occurred during the filming of the ocean liner episode in "Amarcord": "We had this incredible movement of people, of props. All the extras. All the boats. Et cetera. Et cetera. David Lean said 'The guy is crazy. He'll never get it.' . . . David Lean lives in Rome. He came to watch. Everybody came to watch. So there we are. Two hundred extras. All the little boats. Fellini says 'Lights. Action. Camera.' Bam! He gets it! Just like that! Beautiful! Then. Listen to this. You wouldn't believe it. He with his eye. His eye for detail. Incredible! He notices. He saw, way up, on the top deck, they forgot to swing the string of lights! So he does a retake. David Lean says, 'He'll never get it.' But he does it again, and this time, with the string of lights swinging on the top deck, again he gets it!"

This eye for detail can be extremely expensive. Producer Alberto Grimaldi claimed extravagance when he halted production of "Casanova" in December, 1975. Already the equivalent of seven million dollars had been spent. Fellini had to go through the courts before Grimaldi would yield and he could continue. Although he has a reputation for being temperamental, Fellini would be more accurately described a perfectionist. His sets, which often spread larger than football fields, are constructed whenever possible. "I'm not interested in looking at reality or reproducing it," he explains. "And moreover I believe that film should be like a painting rather than literature. The thing I care about most is light, I'm interested only in the results I can get working with light. Therefore, since I don't rely on sunlight,

because I can't regulate it the way I'd like, I have to reconstruct everything, absolutely everything, perhaps at the studio, where I can get all the non-realistic effects I want with artificial lighting."

When "Nights of Cabiria" appeared in New York during October of 1957 Bosley Crowther observed: "Like 'La Strada' and several other of the post-war Italian neo-realistic films, this one is aimed more surely toward the development of a theme than a plot. Its interest is not so much the conflicts that occur in the life of the heroine as the deep, underlying implications of human pathos that the pattern of her life shows." When approached with this idea that his films attempt patterns, he admitted: "If I considered my pictures like the seasons of my life, I have to say that they are enchained strictly one to each other." Stanley Kauffman also noticed the underlying relationship in the early films. He picked it up as early as 1956 while he was dubbing some of the voices in "Il Bidone." Kauffman reported: "Disjunctive though my introduction [to Fellini's film] was, I became aware of a style: the then prevalent gritty Italian neorealism tempered with something else—a love of the sheerly theatrical. Soon afterward, I saw 'I Vitelloni' and other Fellini films, had my sense of the style confirmed, and became addicted only to the first Fellini. A different one was to come. Within four years the grit had been outweighed by the theatrical, and I had to alter the terms of my addiction, though I certainly did not lose it." The first product of this new theatrical style was "8½." Most critics, Kauffman among them, consider this to be the pivotal film of Fellini's career.

"Since '8½,'" Jay Cocks believes, "his work has been piecemeal and ruminative. The spiritual and artistic crisis at the core of '8½' was as much truth as drama, and the movies that followed it showed Fellini searching for some new form, like a diary ('The Clowns,' 'A Director's Notebook') or a primitive pageant ('Satyricon'). What began to emerge in 'Roma' was a synthesis of direct reminiscence and archetype. 'Roma' was unsteady and uncertain, but 'Amarcord' marks a triumphant consolidation. It represents some of the finest work Fellini has ever done—which also means that it stands with the best that anyone in films has ever achieved."

All of Fellini's films draw heavily from reminiscence, but the point where autobiography ends and fantasy begins is hard to define. Fellini himself coyly expressed a difficulty in sorting out the sources of his work. "I don't know if my memories are true or false, I suspect, however, that they are in a great part invented." Even "Satyricon," the movie based on Petronius' novel about ancient Rome, ultimately becomes Fellini's own. "Paradoxically, it is his most original film," observed the *New York Times* reviewer. And Arthur Schlesinger, Jr. described it as "a dazzling rendition of private fantasy, an unconstrained release of all the things Fellini sees or imagines or wants or fears."

Cocks described "Amarcord" as "the exhilaration of an artist re-exploring old territory with heightened powers. In a real sense, it seems that much of Fellini's work over the past decade has been a preparation for 'Amarcord,' a masterly film in which half-formed jottings and free flights of fancy merge together and are exalted into art." "Amarcord" is an excellent example of this autobiographical-fanciful, grit-outweighed-by-theatrical style. It takes place in the Rimini of Fellini's youth. Of this film, Fellini said: "They say that I have made a political movie. Actually, 'Amarcord' conveys mostly the emotive, psychological part of being fascist—fascism as a mental sluggishness, as a loss of imagination. But the movie is also nostalgic. Nostalgia for the past is just as valuable for us as rejection of its mistakes. In order to change, we have to assimilate the past and de-mystify it.''

Most critical discussion of Fellini's films center on his contradictions—his love of the theatrical and his genuineness; the apparent aimlessness of his work and his strong desire for order; the simplicity of his visual image and the complex arrangement of these images; the desire for satisfaction of both spirit and flesh. Much of Fellini's success may lie in his ability to accept these contradictions. ''I do everything I can to make a film. But there is something I do not understand that does the best part of my work. It is always difficult for an author to judge his own work. This is particularly true for me, since I emerge from my movies, once they are finished, like a sleeper awaking from a dream.'' He also added: ''I am not someone who can say every time the same things. And I don't want to define things. I don't want to make things very clear. I don't want to understand the world. Why does the world have to be understood by me? I refuse to make clear ideas about life.''

Robert E. Lauder proposes: ''Though both Ingmar Bergman and Michelangelo Antonioni seem to have a better eye, a greater ability to construct a frame of film with shades of lighting and levels of meaning, Fellini is the most popular and ultimately may be judged the most significant of cinema's triumvirate. For many viewers, Bergman's endless probing of man's failure in faith and refusal to love and Antonioni's nihilistic vision of human relations fade in appeal and relevance before Fellini's hopeful humanism. What emerges clearly from all of Fellini's films is the Italian director's love for his characters.'' Schlesinger added: ''No director sees more deeply into human faces, evokes more vividly feelings of degradation and despair, searches more poignantly for traces of compassion and love, converts emotion more wonderfully into cinematic image, better understands and commands the medium.''

Of that medium he commands so well, Fellini has said: ''Cinema is neither new nor art. Cinema is an old whore, like circus and variety, who knows how to give many kinds of pleasure. Oh, they've been trying to wash her face and make her respectable, but it can't be done. They've brought her in off the street and propped her up in the parlor with a thick volume of philosophy in one hand, and an *Introduction to Freud* in the other, but she's still an old whore. Once a whore always a whore. Besides, you can't teach old fleas new dogs. . . . Fiction imposes order and invents a manner to contain life, but cinema just picks up her muddy skirts and chooses a path through chaos. She just wants to give pleasure. She solicits memory or association as easily as she does daily reality.''

Two of Fellini's screenplays have been made into musicals. ''Nights of Cabiria'' appeared as ''Sweet Charity'' in 1965 and ''La Strada'' was adapted in 1969.

AVOCATIONAL INTERESTS: Dining with friends.

BIOGRAPHICAL/ CRITICAL SOURCES—Books: Angelo Solmi, *Fellini*, translated by Elizabeth Greenwood, Humanities, 1968; Gilbert Salachas, *Federico Fellini*, translated by Rosalie Siegel, Crown, 1969; Eileen L. Hughes, *On the Set of Fellini Satyricon: A Behind-the-Scenes Diary*, Morrow, 1970; *Fellini Satyricon*, Ballantine, 1970; James M. Wall, editor, *Three European Directors: Bunuel, Fellini, Truffaut*, Eerdmans, 1973; Stuart Rosenthal, *The Cinema of Federico Fellini*, A. S. Barnes, 1974; Albert Benderson, *Critical Approaches to Federico Fellini's ''8½''*, Arno, 1974; Edward Murray, *Fellini the Artist*, Unger, 1976; *Fellini on Fellini*, translated by Isabel Quigley, Delacorte, 1976; Charles B. Ketchan, *Federico Fellini*, Paulist Press, 1976.

Articles: *New York Times*, April 20, 1961, November 4, 1965, May 10, 1970, June 14, 1971, July 4, 1971, May 1, 1972, October 19, 1972; *Vogue*, April 15, 1970; *New York*, March 16, 1970; *Holiday*, January/February, 1974; *New Yorker*, October 7, 1974; *Time*, October 7, 1974, May 17, 1976; *Sacramento Bee*, October 26, 1974; *Horizon*, spring, 1976; *Western Humanities Review*, spring, 1976.

* * *

FELTON, Bruce 1946-

PERSONAL: Born September 27, 1946, in New York, N.Y.; son of Alfred (a postal worker) and Dorothy (Sharashoff) Felton; married Judith Stolowitz (a psychotherapist), June 13, 1971. *Education:* Brooklyn College of the City University of New York, B.A., 1967; Case Western Reserve University, M.A., 1968. *Home:* 215 West 90th St., New York, N.Y. 10024. *Agent:* Edward J. Acton, 288 West 12th St., New York, N.Y. 10014. *Office:* Communicate, RCA Corp., 30 Rockefeller Plaza, New York, N.Y. 10020.

CAREER: U.S. Peace Corps, Washington, D.C., volunteer teacher in Malaysia, 1968-70; *Herald* (weekly newspaper), New York, N.Y., reporter, 1971-72; Texaco, Inc., New York City, writer in Publications Division, 1972-74; RCA Corp., New York City, managing editor of *Communicate*, 1974—. Consultant with Skills/Services/Resources Bank, of the Arts and Business Council.

WRITINGS: (With Mark Fowler) *Felton and Fowler's Best, Worst, and Most Unusual*, Crowell, 1975; (with Fowler) *Felton and Fowler's More Best, Worst, and Most Unusual*, Crowell, 1976. Contributor to magazines, including *Cosmopolitan* and *Signature*.

WORK IN PROGRESS: A book about ''inventions, innovations, and sundry brainchildren,'' with emphasis on ''the absurd and the incongruous,'' with Mark Fowler.

SIDELIGHTS: Felton writes: ''Neither of the two . . . books I wrote in collaboration with Mark Fowler can really be considered derivative, ideologically based, or worthy of scholarly analysis. Rather, the most meaningful thing that can be said of them is that they grew out of the 'Bridge Mix' School of American literature, which includes those books that can be consumed easily in discrete bite-sized chunks. . . . They were fun to research and write, but I don't plan to go on doing this sort of thing forever. I've been writing short stories for a long time, and while they remain fragmentary and unpublished, I've been devoting more and more time to them in recent months. They tend toward the absurd and the satirical.''

AVOCATIONAL INTERESTS: Playing the piano.

* * *

FERGUSON, Ted 1936-

PERSONAL: Born January 1, 1936, in Victoria, British Columbia, Canada; son of Robert (a shipyard worker) and Janet (Taylor) Ferguson; married Jessica Simpson (a weaver), August 1, 1964; children: Alexander Russell. *Education:* Attended school in Victoria, British Columbia. *Politics:* None. *Religion:* Protestant. *Home address:* P.O. Box 1406, Westlock, Alberta, Canada.

CAREER: Montreal Gazette, Montreal, Quebec, sports writer, 1958-62; free-lance writer, 1962-64; *Montreal Star*, Montreal, Quebec, general reporter, 1964-66; free-lance writer, 1966-71; *Vancouver Sun*, Vancouver, British Columbia, television critic, 1971—. Has worked as a journalist and scriptwriter in Europe and Quebec. *Awards, honors:* Canada Council writing grant, 1976.

WRITINGS: *A White Man's Country,* Doubleday, 1976.

Author of radio play "The Boy in the Rain" (mystery drama), first produced on CBC-Radio, Montreal, April, 1964. Contributor to Canadian magazines, including *Maclean's, En Route,* and *Canadian.*

WORK IN PROGRESS: A book on Kit Watkins, "Canada's first love-lorn columnist, and the first lady war correspondent in history;" a book on the seige of Hong Kong in 1941.

SIDELIGHTS: Ferguson writes: "I'm specializing in dramatic people and events in Canadian history. I'm not interested in things that are already in the school textbooks but in exciting characters or incidents that require a good deal of research to fully uncover. My first book, for instance, took two years' research and unearthed letters, documents, etc., that have remained buried in government files since 1914.... *A White Man's Country* is a tale of racial conflict and murder that developed in Vancouver, British Columbia, in 1914.... I came across the story—which was all but completely forgotten—purposely, because the white community acted shamefully—when anti-East Indian incidents began taking place again in 1972."

Ferguson's drama "The Boy in the Rain" has been performed on radio and television in West Germany, Switzerland, France, and South Africa.

* * *

FERNANDEZ, John P(eter) 1941-

PERSONAL: Born October 22, 1941, in Boston, Mass.; son of Domingo P. and Julia E. (Fernandes) Fernandez; children: Michele, Eleni, Sevgi. *Education:* Harvard University, A.B. (magna cum laude), 1969; University of California, Berkeley, M.A., 1971, Ph.D., 1974, M.B.A., 1975. *Politics:* None. *Religion:* None. *Home:* 488 Crow's Nest Rd., Forest Lakes, N.J. 07821. *Agent:* Jerry Galbo, 605 Third Ave., New York, N.Y. 10016. *Office:* American Telephone & Telegraph, 195 Broadway, New York, N.Y. 10007.

CAREER: Young Men's Christian Association (YMCA), Dorchester, Mass., teacher and program director, 1965-69; Harvard University, Cambridge, Mass., historian and researcher, 1969; Urban Institute, Washington, D.C., research intern, 1970, consultant, 1970-73; American Telephone & Telegraph, New York, N.Y., personnel supervisor and researcher, 1973-74; Yale University, New Haven, Conn., assistant professor of sociology, 1974-75; American Telephone & Telegraph, manager of management education and development, 1975—. Self-employed management consultant, 1972—. Vice-president of American Telephone & Telegraph Alliance for Women, 1974; member of board of directors of Ulysses S. Grant Foundation of Yale University, 1974—. *Military service:* U.S. Navy, electronics technician, 1960-64. *Member:* American Association of Affirmative Action, Council for Concerned Black Executives, American Sociological Association.

WRITINGS: *Black Managers in White Corporations,* Wiley, 1975.

WORK IN PROGRESS: *Universities/Corporations: Which Institution Is More Likely to Provide Minorities and Women Equal Opportunities More Rapidly?;* articles on university bureaucracy versus corporate bureaucracy and on oppressor and oppressee psychoses.

SIDELIGHTS: Fernandez writes: "I am primarily concerned about the oppression of minorities and women in America. I am very concerned also about the environment and the sick ... double standard attitudes of American leaders." *Avocational interests:* Sports, music, dancing, cooking.

* * *

FERRIL, Thomas Hornsby 1896-

PERSONAL: Born February 25, 1896, in Denver, Colo.; son of Will C. and Alice Lawton (MacHarg) Ferril; married Helen Drury Ray, October 5, 1921; children: Anne Milroy. *Education:* Colorado College, A.B., 1918. *Home:* 2123 Downing St., Denver, Colo. 80205.

CAREER: *Denver Times* and *Rocky Mountain News,* both Denver, Colo., reporter and drama critic, 1919-21; employed in motion picture advertising in Denver, 1921-26; Great Western Sugar Co., Denver, editor of *Through the Leaves* and *Sugar Press* (company publications), 1926-68; *Rocky Mountain Herald* (weekly newspaper), editor, 1939—. Poet. Lecturer and member of council of regional authors, University of Colorado, Writers Conference in the Rocky Mountains, in the 1930's and 1940's; lecturer, Colorado Institute of Humanistic Studies, 1951. *Military service:* U.S. Army, Signal Corps, 1918; became 2nd lieutenant in aviation section. *Member:* American Historical Trails Association, The Westerns, Phi Beta Kappa, Sigma Delta Chi, Phi Delta Theta, Cactus Club, Mile High Club, Denver Press Club. *Awards, honors:* Yale Competition for Younger Poets award, 1926; *Nation* poetry prize, 1927; Oscar Blumenthal prize from *Poetry,* 1937; prize from Academy of American Poets, 1939; national competition first prize of $10,000 from *Denver Post* and Central City Opera House, 1958, for " ... and Perhaps Happiness"; Robert Frost award from Poetry Society of America, 1960; Ridgely Torrence award, 1963; and other awards for poetry, including Mitchell Kennerly award, *Forum* award, Borestone Mountain awards, and Colorado Authors League awards. Honorary degrees from University of Colorado, Boulder, 1934 and 1960, University of Denver, 1947, and Colorado College, 1949. Named Colorado Centennial-Bicentennial Poet, 1975.

WRITINGS–Poetry: *High Passage,* Yale University Press, 1926, reprinted, AMS Press, 1971; *Westering,* Yale University Press, 1934; *Trial by Time,* Harper, 1944; *New and Selected Poems,* Harper, 1952, reprinted, Greenwood Press, 1970; *Words for Denver and Other Poems,* Morrow, 1966.

Other: *I Hate Thursday* (essays), Harper, 1946; " ... and Perhaps Happiness" (verse play), first produced in Central City, Colo., at Opera House, 1958; (editor with wife, Helen Ferril) *The Rocky Mountain Herald Reader,* Morrow, 1966. Columnist, "Ideas and Comment," in *Rocky Mountain Herald,* 1939-72, and "Western Half-Acre," in *Harper's,* 1945-47. Contributor of numerous poems and articles to periodicals and poetry journals. Contributing editor, *Rocky Mountain Herald,* 1918-39.

WORK IN PROGRESS: *A Range of Poems.*

SIDELIGHTS: Ferril's poetry has been presented on a one-hour television program by the Third Eye Theatre, musically interpreted in a symphony by Cecil Effinger, and recorded by the poet on tape records for the Library of Congress. In addition to being printed on paper, his poetry is printed on stone beside the murals in the rotunda of the Colorado State Capitol Building and was engraved in crystal for the Steuben Glass Company's exhibition in New York in 1963, and in 1976, a bronze plaque, inscribed with Ferril's poem "Two

Rivers,'' was dedicated at the junction of Platte River and Cherry Creek, the origin point of the city of Denver. In recognition of Ferril's strong regional ties the Denver City Council designated his home as a Landmark for Preservation in 1973 and the Denver Public Library houses his manuscript collection.

* * *

FIELD, Daniel 1938-

PERSONAL: Born July 26, 1938, in Boston, Mass.; son of Richard H. (a lawyer and professor) and Caroline (Crosby) Field; married Harriet Beecher (a teacher), June 25, 1959; children: Richard Henry, Jonathan Beecher. *Education:* Harvard University, B.A., 1959, M.A., 1962, Ph.D., 1969. *Home address:* R.D. 2, South Royalton, Vt. 05068. *Office:* Department of History, Syracuse University, Syracuse, N.Y. 13210.

CAREER: Moscow University, Moscow, Soviet Union, research fellow, 1964-65; Harvard University, Cambridge, Mass., lecturer in history, 1968-70; Barnard College, New York, N.Y., assistant professor of history, 1970-76; Syracuse University, Syracuse, N.Y., associate professor of history, 1976—. Research fellow at Russian Research Center of Harvard University, 1972-73, and Russian Institute of Columbia University, 1972-73. *Member:* American Historical Association, American Association for the Advancement of Slavic Studies; Russian Research Center (associate).

WRITINGS: Rebels in the Name of the Tsar, Houghton, 1976; *The End of Serfdom: Nobility and Bureaucracy in Russia, 1855-1861,* Harvard University Press, 1976. Contributor of articles and reviews to history and Russian studies journals. Corresponding editor of *Russian History,* 1975—.

WORK IN PROGRESS: Research on Russian radicalism in the 1870's and on comparative studies in serfdom in Russia and slavery in the United States.

* * *

FIELDS, Rick 1942-

PERSONAL: Born May 16, 1942, in Manhattan, N.Y.; son of Allen D. (in public relations) and Reva (Freed) Fields. *Education:* Attended Harvard University, 1960-62, 1963-64, and University of New Mexico, 1965. *Politics:* "Interdependence of all sentient beings." *Religion:* Buddhist. *Home:* 200 West 16th St., Apt. 3K, New York, N.Y. 10011.

CAREER: Has worked as an English teacher for Berlitz in Guadalajara, Mexico, as an apple picker, a street theatre writer and actor, a warehouse worker, a reporter, an editor, and a teacher at University of Colorado, Naropa Institute, and at Loretto College. Member of Center for Book Arts.

WRITINGS: Oriental Love (novel), Cybertype, 1971; *Act Like Lettuce* (poems), privately printed, 1972; *Loka: A Journal from Naropa Institute,* Doubleday, 1974; *Loka II,* Doubleday, 1975. Contributing editor of *New Age Journal;* former editor of *Art Direction Book Arts,* and *Rallying Point;* former religion editor of *Co-Evolution Quarterly.*

WORK IN PROGRESS: North American Buddhism, Lineage and Practice, for Shambhala; *Crooked Clouds,* poems.

* * *

FIESTER, Mark (Lafayette) 1907-

PERSONAL: Born June 12, 1907, in Williamsport, Pa.; son of Daniel Alonza (a merchant) and Maude Alice (Olmstead) Fiester; married Roberta Dexheimer (a teacher and writer), June 12, 1937; children: Pamille (Mrs. Robert F. LaMarche), Kenneth Mark. *Education:* Albright College, B.A., 1934; Evangelical Theological Seminary, Naperville, Ill., B.D., 1937. *Politics:* Republican. *Home and office address:* P.O. Box 156, Frisco, Colo. 80443.

CAREER: Pastor of Evangelical church in Jersey City, N.J., 1937-48, and of Evangelical United Brethren in Ordway, Colo., 1948-53, and Denver, Colo., 1953-65; Father Dyer United Methodist Church, Breckenridge, Colo., pastor, 1965-72, pastor emeritus, 1972—.

WRITINGS: Blasted Beloved Breckenridge, Pruett, 1973.

WORK IN PROGRESS: A biography of John Lewis Dyer.

SIDELIGHTS: Fiester's interest in the early history of Breckenridge, once a gold mining town, now a ski resort, led to his first book. He writes that his second book "will cover the life-time of the beloved, old-fashioned Methodist preacher, John Lewis Dyer, who carried mail and gospel over the highest snow-packed Rocky Mountains, earning for himself the sobriquet 'Snow-Shoe Itinerant'—memorialized in his autobiography of the same title and with his likeness in a stained glass window in the dome of Colorado's Capitol Building, Denver, as one of the sixteen founders of Colorado. . . .''

* * *

FIGUEROA, John L(ewis) 1936-

PERSONAL: Born September 1, 1936, in New York, N.Y.; son of Luis and Lucy (Rosario) Figueroa; married Alba Griselda De Leon, March 27, 1970; children: Juan Carlos, Rima Griselda, Luis Enrique. *Education:* East Los Angeles College, A.A., 1969; attended University of California, Los Angeles, 1969. *Home and office:* 7910 East Alpaca St., San Gabriel, Calif. 91777.

CAREER: U.S. State Department Foreign Service, administrative assistant in U.S. Embassy in La Paz, Bolivia, 1959-61; U.S. Merchant Marine, San Francisco, Calif., engine yeoman, 1961-65; playground director and public information officer for Los Angeles City schools, 1967; KCET-TV, Los Angeles, scriptwriter, 1968; Centro Joaquin Murrietta, Los Angeles, director and counselor of educational program, 1968-71; Economic and Youth Opportunities Agency, Los Angeles, public information specialist, 1971; Los Angeles Model Cities Program, project director of youth coordinated services, 1971-72; free-lance writer and producer in Los Angeles, 1973—. Co-producer and co-director of stage play, "My Brother's Shoes," 1973; producer of filmstrips for language arts series, 1974-75. *Member:* Writers Guild of America. *Awards, honors: Milestone* magazine (of East Los Angeles College) first prizes for fiction, 1968 and 1969; National Story Award honorable mention, 1969.

WRITINGS: Antonio's World (juvenile short stories), Hill & Wang, 1971; (with others) "My Brother's Shoes" (two-act play), first produced in Hollywood at Aquarius Theatre, June, 1973.

Short story and play included in anthology, *The American Disinherited,* edited by Abe C. Ravitz, Random House, 1973. Writer of television script, "Seek No More My Lady," for CBS-TV, 1970, and of screenplay, television documentary, and scripts for children's programs. Contributor to *Elan* and *Milestone.* Fiction editor, *Con Safos* magazine, 1968-73.

WORK IN PROGRESS: A screenplay about two ex-policemen (a Puerto Rican and a Chicano) who break up an Anglo dominated drug connection; an outline for a historical/fictional novel about the Puerto Rican.

SIDELIGHTS: Figueroa told *CA:* "Writing has been my abiding interest from childhood. I am primarily interested in developing a body of literature about Puerto Rican experience. I have traveled all over the world as a merchant marine and with the U.S. State Department Foreign Service. I am bilingual in English and Spanish."

*   *   *

FILOSA, Gary Fairmont Randolph de Marco II 1931-

PERSONAL: Born February 22, 1931, in Wilder, Vt.; son of Gary F. R. (a publisher) and Roseline (a columnist; maiden name, Falzarano) Filosa; married Edith Wilson du Motier Schonberg (a writer and editor), November 24, 1953; children: Marc Christian Bazire de Villodon III, Gary Fairmont Randolph de Marco III. *Education:* University of Chicago, Ph.B., 1954; University of the Americas, B.A., 1967; California Western University, M.A., 1968; U.S. International University, Ph.D., 1970. *Politics:* Democrat. *Religion:* Episcopal. *Home:* 711 Ocean Dr., Huntington Beach, Calif. 92648. *Agent:* Shirley Burke, 370 East 76th St., New York, N.Y. 10021. *Office:* 1303 Avocado Ave., Newport Beach, Calif. 92660.

CAREER: Sports reporter for *Claremont Daily Eagle,* Claremont, N.H., *Rutland Herald,* Rutland, Vt., and *Vermont Informer,* White River Junction, Vt., all 1946-50; *Clay Pipe News,* Chicago, Ill., editor, 1953-54; Fuller, Smith & Ross, New York City, copywriter, 1954-55; *Esquire,* New York City, associate editor, 1955-56; *Teenage,* New York City, editor, 1957-61; *Science Digest,* New York City, associate editor, 1961-62; American Association of Social Directories, Los Angeles, Calif., editor, 1969-75; writer, 1975—. Associate editor of *Apparel Arts,* 1955-56; editor of *Teen Life,* 1957-61. President of U.S. Surfing Foundation. *Military service:* U.S. Army, 1954-55.

MEMBER: International Surfing Federation (president), American Surfing Association (president), Authors Guild, Authors League of America, Sierra Club, Chapultapec Club (Mexico City), Embajadores (Puebla, Mexico), Los Angeles Athletic Club, Town Hall Club, Commonwealth Club, Kona Kai Club.

WRITINGS: Technology Enters the Twenty-First Century, Columbia University Press, 1964; *No Public Funds for Nonpublic Schools,* privately printed, 1968; *Creative Function of the College President,* University of Michigan Press, 1969; "Feather Light" (musical drama; music composed by Peter Duchin), first produced in London at Devonshire Theatre, January, 1969; *The Surfers Almanac,* Dutton, in press. Ghostwriter of one book.

WORK IN PROGRESS: The Olympic Almanac, a quadrennial publication; *Bibliotherapy,* "the first book on my longstanding theory of bringing psychological counseling (through reading) to those who cannot obtain it otherwise"; a biography and a screenplay on Duke Paoa Kahanamoku, "father of modern surfing."

SIDELIGHTS: Filosa's ancestors came to Mexico with Cortes and to California with De Anza in 1776. He speaks Spanish, Italian, and French. He writes that presently he is "devoting all my extracurricular time to the worldwide effort to make our oldest American sport, surfing, an Olympic event."

FINKE, Blythe Foote   1922-

PERSONAL: Born December 24, 1922, in Pasadena, Calif.; daughter of Robert Ordway and Blythe Crawford (Mendenhall) Foote; married John Georg Wilhelm Finke (an army officer), November 15, 1958; children: Ann Reiff, Detmar (stepchildren). *Education:* Woodbury College, B.B., 1944; University of California, Berkeley, B.A., 1946. *Residence:* Sneden's Landing, Palisades, N.Y. *Office:* U.S. Information Agency/United Nations, First Ave. at 42nd St., New York, N.Y. 10017.

CAREER: Union Oil Co., Los Angeles, Calif., administrative assistant, 1941-44; American Embassy in Vienna, Austria, administrative assistant, 1947-49; Shell Oil Co., Wilmington, Calif., editor of house organ, 1950-51; U.S. Information Agency/United Nations, New York City, information officer and U.N. correspondent in Turkey, Germany, and Washington, D.C., 1951-58; Brooklyn Public Library System, Brooklyn, N.Y., director of public relations, 1959-60; Voice of U.N. Command, radio news commentary writer for U.S. Broadcasting/Visual Activity, Tokyo, Japan, 1960-61; U.S. Department of State, assistant to general manager of International Cultural Exchange Program, New York City, 1961-62; U.S. Information Agency, information officer and news feature writer, 1962—. Notable assignments include interviews of many world leaders and Washington personalities. *Member:* Overseas Press Club of America, Public Relations Society of America, United Nations Correspondent Association, Women in Communications.

WRITINGS—All juveniles; all edited by D. Steve Rahmas; all published by SamHar Press: *John Foster Dulles: Master of Brinksmanship and Diplomacy,* 1971; *Angela Davis: Traitor or Martyr of the Freedom of Expression?,* 1972; *Bernard M. Baruch: Speculator and Statesman,* 1972; *Charlie Chaplin: Famous Silent Movie Actor and Comic,* 1972; *General Patton: Fearless Military Leader,* 1972; *George Meany: Modern Leader of the American Federation of Labor,* 1972; *Konrad Adenauer: Architect of the New Germany,* 1972; *W. C. Fields: Renowned Comedian of the Early Motion Picture Industry,* 1972; *Aleksandr Solzhenitsyn: Beleaguered Literary Giant of the U.S.S.R.,* 1973; *Berlin: The Divided City,* 1973; *China Joins the United Nations,* 1973; *Howard R. Hughes: Twentieth Century Multi-Millionaire and Recluse,* 1974; *Our Beseiged Environment: The Pollution Problem,* 1975. Contributor to newspapers and magazines.

*   *   *

FIRTH, Raymond (William)   1901-

PERSONAL: Born March 25, 1901, in Auckland, New Zealand; son of Wesley Hugh Bourne and Marie Elizabeth Jane (Cartmill) Firth; married Rosemary Upcott, 1936; children: Hugh William Bourne. *Education:* Auckland University College, B.A., 1921, M.A., 1922, diploma in social science, 1923; London School of Economics and Political Science, Ph.D., 1927. *Home:* 33 Southwood Ave., London N.6, England.

CAREER: Conducted anthropological field research in the British Solomon Islands, 1928-29; and Kelantan, Malaysia, 1939-40; University of Sydney, Sydney, New South Wales, Australia, lecturer, 1930-31, acting professor of anthropology, 1931-32; University of London, London School of Economics and Political Science, London, England, lecturer, 1933-35, reader, 1935-44, professor of anthropology, 1944-68, professor emeritus, 1968—; writer, 1968—. Visiting professor at University of Chicago, 1955 and 1971, University of Hawaii, 1968-69, University of British Columbia, 1969, Cornell University, 1970, City University of New York, 1971, University of California, Davis, 1974, University of California, Berkeley, 1977. Fellow of Center for Advanced Studies in the Behavioral Sciences (Stanford, Calif.), 1958-59. Secretary of Colonial Social Science Research Council, 1944-45. Conducted social research surveys in West Africa, 1945, Malaya, 1947, 1963, New Guinea, 1951, and among Tikopia, 1952, 1966, and 1973. *Military service:* Royal Navy, Naval Intelligence Division of the Admiralty, 1941-44.

MEMBER: British Academy (fellow), American Academy of Arts and Sciences (foreign honorary member), American Philosophical Society (foreign member), Royal Society of New South Wales (foreign honorary member), Royal Society of New Zealand (honorary member), Royal Danish Academy of Sciences and Letters. *Awards, honors:* Leverhulme research fellowship, 1939-40; Viking Fund medal, 1959; Huxley memorial medal from Royal Anthropological Institute, 1959; honorary degrees include D.Ph. from University of Oslo, 1965; LL.D. from University of Michigan, 1967; Litt.D. from University of East Anglia, 1968; D.H.L. from University of Chicago, 1968; D.Letters from Australian National University, 1969; D.Sc. from University of British Columbia, 1970, and D.Litt. from University of Exeter, 1972; knighted by Queen Elizabeth II in 1973.

WRITINGS: The Kauri-Gum Industry: Some Economic Aspects, W.A.G. Skinner, 1924; *Primitive Economics of the New Zealand Maori,* Dutton, 1929, 2nd edition published as *Economics of the New Zealand Maori,* Humanities, 1959.

(Editor with E. E. Evans-Pritchard and others) *Essays Presented to C. G. Seligman,* Kegan Paul, 1934; *Art and Life in New Guinea,* Studio Publications, 1936; *We, the Tikopia: A Sociological Study of Kinship in Primitive Polynesia* (preface by Bronislaw Malinowski), Allen & Unwin, 1936, 2nd edition, 1957, Barnes & Noble, 1961, abridged edition, Beacon Press, 1963; *Human Types: An Introduction to Social Anthropology,* Thomas Nelson, 1938, 2nd edition, 1956, New American Library, 1958, revised edition, Sphere Books, 1975; *Primitive Polynesian Economy,* Routledge & Sons, 1939, 2nd edition, Archon Books, 1965.

The Work of the Gods in Tikopia, two volumes, Lund, Humphries, 1940, 2nd edition in one volume, Humanities, 1967; *Malay Fishermen: Their Peasant Economy,* Kegan Paul, French, Trubner & Co., 1946, 2nd edition, Archon Books, 1966.

Elements of Social Organization, C. A. Watts, 1951, Beacon Press, 1963, 4th edition, Tavistock, 1971; *The Fate of the Soul: An Interpretation of Some Primitive Concepts,* Cambridge University Press, 1955; (editor and contributor) *Two Studies of Kinship in London,* Athlone Press, 1956; (editor and contributor) *Man and Culture: An Evaluation of the Work of Bronislaw Malinowski,* Humanities, 1957; *Social Anthropology as Science and as Art,* University of Otago, 1958; *Social Change in Tikopia: A Re-Study of a Polynesian Community After a Generation,* Macmillan, 1959.

History and Traditions of Tikopia, Polynesian Society (New Zealand), 1961; (with James Spillius) *A Study in Ritual Modification: The Work of the Gods in Tikopia in 1929 and 1952,* Royal Anthropological Institute of Great Britain and Ireland, 1963; *Essays on Social Organization and Values,* Athlone Press, 1964, Humanities, 1969; (editor with B. S. Yamey, and contributor) *Capital, Saving, and Credit in*

Peasant Societies: Studies from Asia, Oceania, the Caribbean, and Middle America, Aldine, 1964; *Tikopia Ritual and Belief,* Beacon Press, 1967; (editor and contributor) *Themes in Economic Anthropology,* Tavistock, 1967, Barnes & Noble, 1970; (editor and commentator) William Halse Rivers, *Kinship and Social Organization,* Humanities, 1968; (editor with Jane Hubert and Anthony Forge) *Families and Their Relatives: Kinship in a Middle-Class Sector of London—An Anthropological Study,* Humanities, 1969.

Rank and Religion in Tikopia, Beacon Press, 1970; *The Sceptical Anthropologist?: Social Anthropology and Marxist Views on Society,* Oxford University Press, 1972; *Symbols: Public and Private,* Cornell University Press, 1973. Contibutor to *International Encyclopedia of the Social Sciences* and to anthropological periodicals.

AVOCATIONAL INTERESTS: Romanesque art, fifteenth- to eighteenth-century music.

* * *

FISCHER, Fritz 1908-

PERSONAL: Born March 5, 1908, in Ludwigsstadt, Germany; son of Max (a railroad inspector) and Emilie (Schreider) Fischer; married Margarete Lauth, March 25, 1942; children: Anke (Mrs. Kersten Hochbaum), Jan-Hinrich. *Education:* Attended University of Erlangen, 1926-28; University of Berlin, Dr.theol., 1934, Dr.phil., 1937. *Politics:* "Sympathizing with Social Democrats." *Religion:* Lutheran. *Home:* Frenssenstrasse 19 a, 2 Hamburg 55 (Blankenese), West Germany. *Office:* Historisches Seminar der Universitaet, Von-Melle-Park 6 IX, 2 Hamburg 13, West Germany.

CAREER: University of Berlin, Berlin, Germany, assistant professor of church history, 1934-39, assistant professor of history, 1939-42; University of Hamburg, Hamburg, Germany, associate professor, 1942-48, professor of history, 1948-73, professor emeritus, 1973—, director of history seminars, 1948-73. Visiting professor at universities in United States, 1952-53, 1964; guest professor, University of Notre Dame, 1954, St. Antony's College, Oxford, 1969-70; lecturer at universities in Austria, Belgium, Canada, Denmark, England, France, Holland, Japan, Poland, and Switzerland, 1961—; participant in history symposium in London and Oxford, 1950. *Military service:* German Air Force, 1939-45; became first lieutenant; prisoner of war with American army, 1945-47. *Member:* P.E.N., Mitarbeiter des Internationalen Schulbuchinstituts (Brunswick, West Germany), British Academy (corresponding member), Verband der Historiker Deutschlands, Kommission fuer Geschichte der politischen Parteien und des Parlamentarismus (Bonn), Mitarbeiter der Friedrich Ebert-Stiftung (Bonn). *Awards, honors:* Fellow, Institute for Advanced Study, 1964-65; D.Litt., University of Sussex, 1974; Bundesverdienstkreuz der Bundesrepublik Deutschland, 1974.

WRITINGS: Moritz August von Bethmann-Hollweg und der Protestantismus: Religion, Rechts- und Staatsgedanke (title means "Moritz August von Bethmann-Hollweg and Protestantism: His Religion and His Ideas of State and Law"), Verlag dr. Emil Ebering (Berlin), 1938, Kraus Reprint, 1965; *Ludwig Nicolovius: Rokoko, Reform, Restauration* (biography of Ludwig Nicolovius), Verlag W. Kohlhammer (Stuttgart), 1939; (contributor) Alfred Herrmann, editor, *Festschrift Ludwig Bergstraesser,* Droste Verlag, 1954; *Deutsche Kriegsziele Revolutionierung und Separatfrieden im Osten, 1914-1918,* R. Oldenbourg Verlag, 1959;

Griff nach der Weltmacht: Die Kriegszielpolitik des kaiserlichen Deutschland, 1914/18, Droste Verlag, 1961, 4th edition, 1970, translation published as *Germany's Aims in the First World War*, Norton, 1967; *Weltmacht oder Niedergang*, Europaeische Verlagsanstalt (Frankfurt), 1965, translation by Lancelot L. Farrar, Robert Kimber, and Rita Kimber published as *World Power or Decline: The Controversy over Germany's Aims in the First World War*, Norton, 1974; *Krieg der Illusionen: Die deutsche Politik von 1911 bis 1914*, Droste Verlag, 1969, 2nd edition, 1970, translation by Marion Jackson published as *War of Illusions: German Policies from 1911 to 1914*, Norton, 1975.

Contributor to *Historische Zeitschrift*. Editor, *Hamburger Studien zur neueren Geschichte*, 1965-68; co-editor, *Studien zur modernen Geschichte*, 1971—.

WORK IN PROGRESS: Research on problems of continuity in German policies, 1890-1945, to be published in a third volume on the time following 1919.

SIDELIGHTS: Fischer told *CA:* "After World War II historical research was, naturally enough, mostly concentrated on this war and on the dark characteristics of Nazi Germany. Looking back critically at the events which led up to the Third Reich, I felt it was impossible for me to accept the assumption that this was an isolated phenomenon but rather that there were conditions—spiritual, psychological, economic, social, and constitutional—which made the seizure of power by Hitler possible. This consideration led me back to the spirit and aims of Wilhelminian Germany and thus to the elements of continuity in German history from 1890 to 1945."

The resulting book caused a resounding scandal. "When the German edition of [*Germany's Aims in the First World War*] first appeared in 1961," wrote Bernard D. Williams, "it naturally caused a bitter reaction within Germany since Professor Fischer has uncovered many unpublished documents from various archives that reveal how the industrial and intellectual circles, as well as the military, supported the aggressive policy of making Germany a great world power." Describing the book as "a blow of almost lethal destructiveness," Geoffrey Barraclough reasoned that "no wonder that Fischer's book . . . has been the subject of violent controversy. . . . His arguments were too destructive of orthodox German mythology, his documentation too solid simply to be brushed aside. It is good that there should be controversy, because the questions Fischer raises transcend the normal disputes of academic history. What is at issue is not simply the validity of the specific evidence he cites, or of the conclusions he draws from it, but the character of an epoch. . . . Fischer shows beyond all reasonable doubt that the so-called 'war-guilt clause' which attributed 'responsibility' to Germany was essentially correct. This is why his book produced such an uproar in the Federal Republic."

Since the appearance of Fischer's book in Germany, historians have digested its contents and followed up with a number of new books. Barraclough contended that "it may be said of all this work . . . that its effect has been to confirm, rather than impair, the 'Fischer thesis.' It is possible that Fischer overshoots his mark at certain points; but few, if any, foreign historians have rejected his interpretation, and even in Germany it is remarkable how closely Fischer's leading opponent, Gerhard Ritter, came to adopting Fischer's views in the last volume of *Staatskunst und Kriegshandwerk* which appeared before his death."

George L. Mosse feels that "Fischer has . . . written a prophetic book about the ambitions of nations—the 'Great Power complex,' as it might be called. . . . The Germany example shows how self-confidence led to a quest for domination, war and ultimate destruction through an excessive faith in the nation's power and might. This seems to be the moral of this important book, and as such it is relevant far beyond that period with which it deals and that nation whose particular war aims it analyzes."

BIOGRAPHICAL/CRITICAL SOURCES: Ernst W. Graf Lynar, editor, *Deutsche Kriegsziele, 1914-1918: Eine Diskussion*, Ullstein Buecher (Frankfurt), 1964; *Best Sellers*, December 1, 1967; *New York Times Book Review*, December 24, 1967; *Times Literary Supplement*, February 22, 1968; *New York Review of Books*, March 14, 1968; John A. Moses, *The War Aims of Imperial Germany: Professor Fritz Fischer and His Critics*, University of Queensland Papers, 1968; George W. Hallgarten, *Deutsche Selbstschau nach 50 Jahren: Fritz Fischer, seine Gegner und Vorlaeufer*, Europaeische Verlagsanstalt, 1969; Imanuel Geiss, *Studien ueber Geschichte und Geschichtswissenschaft*, Suhrkamp Verlag, 1972; Geiss and B. J. Wendt, editors, *Festschrift fuer Fritz Fischer*, Bertelsmann Universitaetsverlag, 1973; Moses, *The Politics of Illusion: The Fischer Controversy in German Historiography*, Harper, 1975.

* * *

FISHER, Clavin C(argill) 1912-

PERSONAL: Born July 12, 1912, in Arlington, N.J.; son of Charles V. and Pearl (Burroughs) Fisher; married Elizabeth Stuart Murray, September 17, 1938; children: Wendy (Mrs. Charles Kirchofer), Peter. *Education:* Bucknell University, B.S., 1934; New York University, M.B.A., 1937. *Home:* 26 Nimrod Rd., West Simsbury, Conn. 06092. *Agent:* McIntosh & Otis, Inc., 475 Fifth Ave., New York, N.Y. 10017.

CAREER: Aetna Life & Casualty, Hartford, Conn., 1937-75, became administrator of employee benefits; writer, 1975—. Director of American Revolution bicentennial project to build an Indian village in Simsbury, Conn. *Military service:* U.S. Naval Reserve, communications liaison officer on U.S. Army transports, active duty, 1943-46; served in Atlantic and Pacific theaters, and in the Mediterranean; became lieutenant, senior grade. *Member:* Life Office Management Association (fellow), Connecticut Writers League, Simsbury Historical Society (member of board of directors, 1970—), Simsbury Civitan Club (past president), Friends of the Simsbury Public Library (member of board of directors, 1973—).

WRITINGS: A Spy at Ticonderoga (juvenile novel), Berkshire Traveller Press, 1975. Contributor of stories to *Boys' Life* and *Our Navy*.

WORK IN PROGRESS: Three Spies for General Washington and *The King's Sword*, both juvenile novels.

SIDELIGHTS: Fisher writes that his long association with young people, coupled with his intense interest in American history, inspired him to write *A Spy at Ticonderoga* as fiction for young people. In writing adventure and mystery stories, he attempts to provide the reader with a historical background, or an unusual setting. *Avocational interests:* Foreign travel.

* * *

FISHER, Rhoda Lee 1924-

PERSONAL: Born October 10, 1924, in Chicago, Ill.; daughter of Isadore Mordecae (a retailer) and Mary (a retailer; maiden name, Margolis) Feinberg; married Seymour

Fisher (a professor), March 22, 1947; children: Jerid M., Eve Phyllis. *Education:* De Paul University, B.Mu.Ed., 1946; University of Chicago, Ph.D., 1956. *Home:* 4855 Armstrong Rd., Manlius, N.Y. 13104. *Office:* Kinlock Plaza, Manlius, N.Y. 13104.

CAREER: Private practice in clinical psychology in Houston, Tex., 1951-61; Syracuse University, Syracuse, N.Y., lecturer in psychology, 1961—. Private practice in clinical psychology in Manlius, N.Y., 1968—. Research associate of State University of New York Upstate Medical School, 1961-64. *Member:* American Psychological Association.

WRITINGS: The Family, Basic Books, 1964; *The Female Orgasm,* Basic Books, 1976; *What We Really Know About Childrearing,* Basic Books, 1976.

WORK IN PROGRESS: Research on the nature of humor.

* * *

FISHER, William Bayne   1916-

PERSONAL: Born September 24, 1916, in Darwen, Lancashire, England; son of George and Martha (Bayne) Fisher. *Education:* Attended University of Manchester, 1933-37, University of Louvain, 1936, and University of Caen, 1939; University of Paris, docteur de l'universite, 1940. *Home:* 42 South St., Durham, England. *Office:* 34 Old Elvet, Durham, England; and Department of Geography, University of Durham, South Rd., Durham, England.

CAREER: University of Manchester, Manchester, England, assistant lecturer in geography, 1945; University of Aberdeen, Aberdeen, Scotland, lecturer in geography, 1946-53; University of Durham, Durham, England, reader, 1954-56, professor of geography, 1956—, head of department, 1954—, principal of graduate society, 1965—; director of Centre for Middle Eastern and Islamic Studies, 1962-65, leader of expedition to Libya, 1951. Visiting professor at University of Malta, 1966, Harvard University, 1967, University of Libya, 1969, and University of Ottawa, 1971. Consultant to Government of Libya. *Military service:* Royal Air Force, 1940-45, liaison officer in Syria and Lebanon, 1944-45. *Awards, honors:* Carnegie fellowship, 1951; Murchison Award from Royal Geographical Society, 1973.

WRITINGS: Les Mouvements de population en Normandie (title means "Population Movements in Normandy"), University of Paris, 1940; *The Middle East: A Physical, Social, and Regional Geography,* Dutton, 1950, 6th edition, Barnes & Noble, 1971; *The Middle East: Then and Now,* University of Durham, 1958; (with Howard Bowen-Jones and J. C. Dewdney) *Spain: A Geographical Background,* Christophers (London), 1958, published as *Spain: An Introductory Geography,* Praeger, 1966; (with Paul Dickinson) *The Mediaeval Land Surveys of County Durham,* King's College, University of Newcastle-upon-Tyne, 1959; (with Bowen-Jones) *Malta: Base for Development,* University of Durham, 1960, published as *Malta: Background for Development,* 1962; *Soil Survey of Wadi Ziqlab, Jordan,* Department of Geology, University of Durham, 1966; *Geography and the Middle East,* Department of Geology, University of Durham, 1967; (editor) *The Cambridge History of Iran,* Volume I: *The Land of Iran,* Cambridge University Press, 1968; (with John Innes Clark) *Populations of the Middle East and North Africa,* Africana Publishing, 1972. Contributor to professional journals.

AVOCATIONAL INTERESTS: Travel, music, gastronomy.

FISK, Nicholas   1923-

PERSONAL: Born October 14, 1923, in London, England; married Dorothy Antoinette, 1949; children Moyra and Nicole (twins), Steven, Christopher. *Education:* Educated in private secondary school in Sussex, England. *Home:* 59 Elstree Rd., Bushey Heath, Hertfordshire, England. *Agent:* A. M. Heath & Co., 35 Dover St., London W.1, England. *Office:* Percy Lund, Humphries & Co., 12 Bedford Sq., London W.C.1, England.

CAREER: Writer and illustrator. Percy Lund, Humphries & Co. (publishers), London, England, head of creative group. Has worked as actor, publisher, and musician. *Military service:* Royal Air Force. *Member:* Savile Club.

WRITINGS: Look at Cars (self-illustrated juvenile), Hamish Hamilton, 1959, revised edition, Panther, 1970; *Look at Newspapers* (juvenile), Hamish Hamilton, 1962; *Cars,* Parrish, 1963; *The Young Man's Guide to Advertising,* Hamish Hamilton, 1963; *The Bouncers* (self-illustrated), Hamish Hamilton, 1964; *The Fast Green Car,* Hamish Hamilton, 1965; *There's Something on the Roof,* Hamish Hamilton, 1966; *Making Music,* Crescendo Publishing Co., 1966; *Space Hostages* (juvenile), Hamish Hamilton, 1967, Macmillan, 1969; *Richthofen the Red Baron,* Coward, 1968; *Lindbergh the Lone Flier* (juvenile), Coward, 1968; *Making Music,* M. Joseph, 1969.

Trillions (juvenile), Hamish Hamilton, 1971, Pantheon, 1973; *High Way Home,* Hamish Hamilton, 1973; *Grinny* (juvenile science fiction), Heinemann, 1973, Thomas Nelson, 1974; (with Carol Barker) *Emma Borrows a Cup of Sugar* (juvenile), Heinemann, 1974; *Little Green Spacemen,* Heinemann, 1974; (contributor) Edward Blishen, editor, *The Thorny Paradise* (juvenile anthology), Pelham Books, 1975; *The Witches of Wimmering,* Pelham Books, 1976.

Illustrator: *Look at Aircraft,* Hamish Hamilton, 1960; (contributor of photographs) Eric Fenby, *Menuhin's House of Music,* Praeger, 1970; W. Mayne, *Skiffy,* Hamish Hamilton, 1973. General editor of "Hamish Hamilton Monographs," Hamish Hamilton, 1964. Contributor to *Pears Junior Encyclopaedia.* Contributor of articles and science fiction stories to magazines.

WORK IN PROGRESS: A children's novel, for Pelham Books; self-illustrated short stories for Penguin.

SIDELIGHTS: Fisk writes: "I cannot escape the word 'communication,' which is my metier. I am principally a writer; but also an illustrator, designer, and photographer. I am an impresario of printed things in my office job—I head a creative team that may produce anything from more or less learned works to advertising brochures. I write for children because children have generous, wide minds; today, they are separated from the adult race only by size, power, and experience. Children are not, as formerly, a distinctive tribe because today they live among adults. My mind is set in the past or the future, not the present. I admire human products rather more than I admire humans—the arts more than the artist. . . ."

BIOGRAPHICAL/CRITICAL SOURCES: Edward Blishen, editor, *The Thorny Paradise,* Pelham Books, 1975.

* * *

FITTER, Richard Sidney Richmond   1913-

PERSONAL: Born March 1, 1913, in London, England; son of Sidney Harry and Dorothy (Isacke) Fitter; married Alice Mary Stewart Park, 1938; children: Jenny Elizabeth, Julian Richmond, Alastair Hugh. *Education:* London School of

Economics and Political Science, London, B.Sc., 1933. *Home:* Drifts, Chinnor Hill, Oxford OX9 4BS, England.

CAREER: Member of research staff, Political and Economic Planning, 1936-40, Mass-Observation, 1940-42; member of operational research section, Coastal Command, 1942-45; secretary of Wildlife Conservation Special Committee, Hobhouse Committee on National Parks, 1945-46; assistant editor, *Countryman,* 1946-59; Council for Nature, director of intelligence unit, 1959-63, presently honorary treasurer; editor of *Kingfisher,* 1965-72. *Member:* International Union for the Conservation of Nature (member of Survival Service Commission, 1963), Fauna Preservation Society (honorary secretary, 1964—), British Trust for Ornithology, Royal Society for the Protection of Birds, Berkshire, Buckinghamshire, and Oxfordshire Naturalists' Trust, Zoological Society of London (fellow), Athenaeum Club.

WRITINGS: The Starling Roosts of the London Area, London Naturalist, 1943; (with E. R. Parrinder) *A Check-List of the Birds of the London Area,* London Naturalist, 1944; *London's Natural History: The New Naturalist, a Survey of British Natural History,* Collins, 1945; *Bird-Watching in London,* Royal Society for the Protection of Birds, 1948; *London's Birds,* Collins, 1949.

(Editor) *British Birds in Colour,* Odhams, 1951; *Home Counties,* Collins, 1951; *The Pocket Guide to British Birds,* Collins, 1952, Dodd, 1953, revised edition published as *Collins Pocket Guide to British Birds,* Collins, 1966, 3rd edition, 1970; (with Job Edward Lousley) *The Natural History of the City,* Corporation of London, 1953; *Birds of Town and Village,* Collins, 1953; *The Starling,* School-Aid Department, Daily Mail, 1953; (with Guy Charteris) *The Pocket Guide to Nests and Eggs,* Collins, 1954, revised edition published as *The Collins Pocket Guide to Nests and Eggs,* 1968; (with David McClintock) *The Pocket Guide to Wild Flowers,* Collins, 1956; *Fontana Bird Guide,* Collins, 1956; *Fontana Wild Flower Guide,* Collins, 1957; (editor with H. N. Southern) Marie N. Stephens, *The Natural History of the Otter,* University Federation for Animal Welfare (London), 1957; *Your Book of Bird Watching* (juvenile), Transatlantic, 1958; *The Ark in Our Midst: The Story of the Introduced Animals of Britain: Birds, Beasts, Reptiles, Amphibians, Fishes,* Collins, 1959; *Six Great Naturalists: White, Linnaeus, Waterton, Audubon, Fabre, Huxley,* Hamish Hamilton, 1959.

(Editor) *The Countryman Nature Book: An Anthology from the Countryman,* Brockhampton Press, 1960; *Your Book About Wild Flowers* (juvenile), Faber, 1960; *Collins Guide to Birdwatching,* Collins, 1963, 2nd edition, 1970; *Fitter's Rural Rides: The Observer Illustrated Map-Guide to the Countryside,* Observer, 1963; *Wildlife in Britain,* Gannon, 1963; *Wildlife and Death,* Newman Neame, 1964; *British Wildlife: Rarities and Introductions,* Kay, 1966; (with wife, Maisie Fitter) *The Penguin Dictionary of British Natural History,* Penguin, 1967, Barnes & Noble, 1968, revised edition, A. & C. Black, 1968; *Vanishing Wild Animals of the World,* F. Watts, 1968.

(With Hermann Heinzel and J.L.F. Parslow) *The Birds of Britain and Europe with North Africa and the Middle East,* Lippincott, 1972, 2nd edition, Collins, 1974; *Finding Wild Flowers,* Collins, 1972; (author of introduction) *BBONT: The First Ten Years, 1959-1969,* Berkshire, Buckinghamshire, and Oxfordshire Naturalists' Trust, 1973; (contributor) Alan Aldridge, *The Butterfly Ball and the Grasshopper's Feast,* J. Cape, 1973; (with son, Alastair Fitter) *The*

Wild Flowers of Britain and Northern Europe, Scribner, 1974. Open air correspondent for *Observer,* 1958-66. Editor of *London Naturalist,* 1942-46.

AVOCATIONAL INTERESTS: Observing wild life and human life, exploring new habitats, reading.

* * *

FITZGIBBON, Russell H(umke) 1902-

PERSONAL: Born June 29, 1902, in Columbus, Ind.; son of Thomas Francis and Frances A. (Moore) Fitzgibbon; married Irene Cory, July 6, 1929; children: Alan Lee, Katherine Irene (Mrs. David G. Lilly). *Education:* Hanover College, A.B., 1924; Indiana University, A.M., 1928; University of Wisconsin, Ph.D., 1933. *Religion:* Presbyterian. *Home:* 9729 Pinecrest Dr., Sun City, Ariz. 85351.

CAREER: Hanover College, Hanover, Ind., instructor, 1924-27, assistant professor, 1927-29, associate professor, 1929-32, professor of history and political science, 1932-36; University of California, Los Angeles, assistant professor, 1936-42, associate professor, 1942-48, professor of political science, 1948-64, chairman of department, 1942-43 and 1948-50, director of Center for Latin American Studies, 1959-62, academic assistant to the state-wide university president, 1962-64 and 1967-68; University of California, Santa Barbara, professor of political science, 1964-72. Senior political analyst, Office of Inter-American Affairs, 1944-45; visiting summer professor, Ohio State University, 1952, University of Nebraska, 1954, University of Illinois, 1956, Indiana University, 1960, Georgetown University, 1963 and 1964, Arizona State University, 1972-73. *Member:* American Political Science Association, Western Political Science Association (member of executive council, 1951-53 and 1957-58; president, 1956-57), Phi Delta Theta (national editor, 1931-36), Pi Sigma Alpha (member of executive council, 1948-50), Pi Gamma Mu, Alpha Phi Gamma. *Awards, honors:* Del Amo Foundation fellowships, 1943-44 and 1959; Doherty Foundation and Social Science Research Council fellowship, 1951; LL.D., Hanover College, 1952; Fulbright research grant, 1958-59; Order of Don Cristobal Colon (Dominican Republic), 1962.

WRITINGS: Cuba and the United States, 1900-1935, G. Banta, 1935; *Visual Outline of Latin American History,* Longmans, Green, 1938; (editor and contributor) *Global Politics,* University of California Press, 1944; (with Flaud C. Wooton) *Latin America, Past and Present,* Heath, 1946; (editor-in-chief) *The Constitutions of the Americas, as of January 1, 1948,* University of Chicago Press, 1948; *Uruguay: Portrait of a Democracy,* Rutgers University Press, 1954; *Latin America: A Panorama of Contemporary Politics,* Appleton, 1971; (editor) Jesus de Galindez, *The Era of Trujillo,* University of Arizona Press, 1973.

* * *

FITZPATRICK, James K(evin) 1942-

PERSONAL: Born September 25, 1942, in Flushing, N.Y.; son of Cornelius M. (a construction worker) and Margaret (a teacher; maiden name, Burke) Fitzpatrick; married Evalyn A. Mangan, June 17, 1967; children: Brendan, Eileen. *Education:* Fordham College (now University), B.A., 1964; St. John's University, Jamaica, N.Y., M.A., 1968. *Politics:* Conservative. *Religion:* Roman Catholic. *Home:* 69 Bass Rd., R.D. 4, Mahopac, N.Y. 10541.

CAREER: High school teacher of history in Bronx, N.Y., 1965-69; Lakeland High School, Shrub Oak, N.Y., history teacher, 1969——. Member of board of directors of Walter Bagehot Research Council on National Sovereignty, 1973——.

WRITINGS: How to Survive in Your Liberal School, Arlington House, 1975; *Jesus Christ Before He Became a Superstar*, Arlington House, 1976; *Builders of the American Dream*, Arlington House, in press. Contributor to magazines, including *National Review, Wanderer, Academic Reviewer*, and *State of the Nation*, and to newspapers. Assistant editor of *Irish People*, 1975; contributing editor of *Triumph*, 1976.

WORK IN PROGRESS: A study of key issues in American history which have shaped political, economic, and cultural development, publication expected, 1978.

SIDELIGHTS: Fitzpatrick told *CA:* "Most of my scholarly work examines the drift, in the United States, from the original understanding of society held by the Founding Fathers.... [This drift is] a result of the work of 20th century secular, internationalist, and liberal ideologues. The hope has been to revivify the American confidence in our cultural heritage."

AVOCATIONAL INTERESTS: Baseball, fishing, gardening, big band jazz.

* * *

FLANNER, Janet 1892-
(Genet)

PERSONAL: Born March 13, 1892, in Indianapolis, Ind.; daughter of Francis (a businessman) and Mary Ellen (Hockett) Flanner. *Education:* Attended University of Chicago, 1912-13. *Politics:* "Democrat now—on principle a mugwump." *Home:* 785 Park Ave., New York, N.Y. 10028; and Ritz Hotel, Place Vendome, Paris, France. *Office:* c/o *New Yorker* Magazine, 25 West 43rd St., New York, N.Y. 10036.

CAREER: Indianapolis Star, Indianapolis, Ind., cinema critic, 1916-17; writer in New York City, worked in reform school in Philadelphia, Pa., and traveled in Greece, Crete, Constantinople (now Istanbul), Turkey, and Vienna, Austria, 1918-22; writer in Paris, France, 1922-39, 1944——; *New Yorker* magazine, New York City, foreign correspondent under pseudonym Genet, 1925——, writer of "Letter from Paris," beginning 1925, political profiles, beginning 1935, and "Letter from London," 1934-39. War-time broadcaster and free-lance writer. *Member:* American Academy of Arts and Letters, Lucy Stone League (co-founder, 1921). *Awards, honors:* French Legion of Honor, 1947, for "Letter from Paris" column; Litt.D. from Smith College, 1958; National Book Award, 1966, for *Paris Journal, 1944-1965*.

WRITINGS: The Cubical City (novel), Putnam, 1926; *Cheri*, A. & C. Boni, 1929; (translator) Georgette Leblanc, *Maeterlinck and I*, Methuen, 1932; *An American in Paris: Profile of an Interlude between Two Wars*, Simon & Schuster, 1940; *Petain: The Old Man of France*, Simon & Schuster, 1944; *Men and Monuments*, Harper, 1957; *Paris Journal* (selection of letters first published in *New Yorker* magazine), edited by William Shawn, Atheneum, Volume I: *1944-1965*, 1965, Volume II: *1965-1971*, 1971; (author of introduction) Colette, *The Pure and the Impure*, Farrar, Straus, 1967; (author of introduction) Jane Grant, *Ross, The New Yorker, and Me*, Morrow, 1968; *Paris Was Yesterday, 1925-1939*, edited by Irving Drutman, Viking, 1972; *London Was Yesterday, 1934-39*, edited by Irving Drutman, Viking, 1975. Also author of *Master*, profile of Georges Braque, 1956, and *The Surprise of the Century*, profile of Pablo Ruiz Picasso, 1957; also translator of *Claudine at School* by Colette.

SIDELIGHTS: While a child, Janet Flanner had always wanted to be a fiction writer, but criticism of her first book, a novel, made it clear to her that nonfiction would be her metier. "I had some rather good reviews," she related to Mary McCarthy, "and they said, if she would work a little harder, she might be able to write as well as Rose Macaulay. That's what determined me. I knew that I had no talent for fiction. I certainly knew I couldn't write like Henry James and at that time I was a little stuck on Henry James. So Ross offered me this job, and more and more I began doing reporting, straight reporting. But the news of the world was assuming the character of the most terrifying fiction. And that has always been my control. I had to write within those terms. There has to be a certain amount of fiction, fictional quality, in the kind of reporting I do."

The only instructions Miss Flanner received from Harold Ross, founding editor of *New Yorker* magazine, were: "Don't write about France. Write about the French." She reported that "because I was easily intimidated by and distrustful of French officialdom and because, as at first a fortnightly correspondent, I was in no condition to compete with daily cable New York newspapers, in my helplessness I invented for my *New Yorker* 'Letters' a formula which dealt not with political news itself, but with the effect public political news had on private lives."

Donald Keene said that "Genet's letters have always struck exactly the right note . . . crisp, detached, informative," and having a distaste for extremism in politics, but he added that it was precisely these virtues that caused him to be disappointed in Miss Flanner's letters. "Like all journalism, . . . Miss Flanner's letters contain material of only ephemeral interest . . . not in sufficient depth for us. . . . Yet," he continued, "by the time we reach the final letter, portraying a France young and confident, respected politically and intellectually, prosperous and well-governed, we have only to remember the France described in the letters of 1946 and 1947 for our scattered experiences to fall into place. The lasting impression . . . is of an extraordinary drama."

AVOCATIONAL INTERESTS: Conversation, croquet, card games, chess, harmonica.

BIOGRAPHICAL/CRITICAL SOURCES: New Republic, December 25, 1965; *New York Herald Tribune*, March 18, 1966.

* * *

FLATH, Arnold W(illiam), J. 1929-

PERSONAL: Born August 19, 1929; son of Arnold and Elsie (Frasse) Flath; married Reita Ramage, December 26, 1951; children: Deneva, Douglas, Robin, Andrew, Rachel. *Education:* North Dakota State Teachers College, B.S., 1951; University of North Dakota, M.Ed., 1958; University of Michigan, Ph.D., 1963. *Office:* Department of Health and Physical Education, Oregon State University, Corvallis, Ore. 97331.

CAREER: High school teacher of physical education, English, and social science, and football, baseball, and basketball coach in the public schools of La Moure, N.D., 1951-52, and Casselton, N.D., 1954-57; Valley City State Teachers College, Valley City, N.D., assistant football coach, 1957-60; Central Connecticut State College, New Britain, associate professor of physical education, head of department, and freshman basketball coach, 1963-64; University of Illinois, Urbana, assistant professor of physical education, 1964-67; Oregon State University, Corvallis, associate professor, and head of department, 1967-71, professor of physical education and assistant dean, 1971—, *Military service:* U.S. Army, Signal Corps, 1952-54.

MEMBER: North American Society for Sport History, American Affiliation of Health, Physical Education and Recreation, National College of Physical Education for Men, American Association of University Professors, Philosophic Society for the Study of Sport, Western States College Physical Education Association, Oregon Association for Health, Physical Education and Recreation, Oregon Historical Society, Phi Epsilon Kappa, Alpha Phi Gamma.

WRITINGS: A History of Relations Between the National Collegiate Athletic Association and the Amateur Athletic Union, 1906-63, Stipes, 1964; (editor) *Athletics in America,* Oregon State University Press, 1972; (contributor) Earle Zeigler, editor, *A History of Sport and Physical Education in the United States,* Stipes, 1975. Contributor to physical education journals.

AVOCATIONAL INTERESTS: Reading, playing badminton and paddle racquetball, fishing, hiking.

*   *   *

FLATTAU, Edward   1937-

PERSONAL: Born May 18, 1937, in New York, N.Y.; son of Henry (a lawyer) and Mary (Mass) Flattau. *Education:* Brown University, B.A., 1958; Columbia University, graduate study, 1959-60. *Residence:* Washington, D.C. *Office:* 1330 New Hampshire Ave. N.W., Washington, D.C. 20036.

CAREER/WRITINGS: United Press International (UPI), reporter in the state of New York, 1962-66, and Washington, D.C., 1966-69; legislative assistant to Democratic Congressman Ben Rosenthal in Washington, D.C., 1969-70 (dealt with foreign affairs and the environment); European Communities, Washington, D.C., director of information, 1970-71; Los Angeles Times Syndicate, Los Angeles, Calif., author of column "Our Environment," 1972—. Notable assignments include pre-Olympic student riots in Mexico City, 1968, race riots in Washington, D.C., following the assassination of Martin Luther King, Jr., and the march on the Pentagon. Host of environmental commentary program for National Public Radio. Contributor to popular magazines, including *Washington Monthly, Parents' Magazine, Science Digest, National Observer, Audobon, New Republic, Saturday Review,* and *Vista. Military service:* U.S. Army Reserve. *Awards, honors:* Grant from European Common Market, 1975.

AVOCATIONAL INTERESTS: Tennis (has worked as a professional tennis player).

*   *   *

FLEISHER, Wilfried   1897(?)-1976

1897(?)—July 13, 1976; American journalist, radio correspondent, and author of books on Japan and Sweden. Obituaries: *Washington Post,* July 21, 1976.

*   *   *

FLESCHER, Joachim   1906(?)-1976

1906(?)—July 3, 1976; Polish-born psychiatrist, educator, and author. Obituaries: *New York Times,* July 5, 1976.

*   *   *

FLETCHER, Basil Alais   1900-

PERSONAL: Born April 10, 1900, in London, England; son of Walter Henry and Julia Fletcher; married Gerrardine

Mary Daly, 1928; children: John Alais, Julia Mary. *Education:* University of London, M.A., 1922, B.Sc., 1935. *Home:* Camerton Lodge, Camerton, Bath, Somerset, England.

CAREER: Physics master at private school in Holt, Norfolk, England, 1922-26; Cambridge University, Sidney Sussex College, Cambridge, England, fellow commoner, 1926-27; senior science master at private school in Holt, Norfolk, England, 1927-30; Albert Kahn Fellow for Great Britain, 1930-31; headmaster of school in Chippenham, England, 1932-35; Dalhousie University, Halifax, Nova Scotia, O. E. Smith Professor of Education, 1935-39; University of Southampton, Southampton, England, professor of education, 1939-41; University of Bristol, Bristol, England, professor of education, 1942-55; University College of Rhodesia and Nyasaland, Salisbury, vice-principal, 1956-60; University of Leeds, Leeds, England, professor of education, 1961-64, professor emeritus, 1968—. Research fellow at University of Bristol, 1940-45.

WRITINGS: (With Hugh W. Heckstall-Smith) *Laboratory Physics,* Oxford University Press, 1928; *Youth Looks at the World,* Methuen, 1932, F. A. Stokes, 1933; *Religion and the Younger Generation,* Lutterworth, 1933; *Education and Colonial Development,* Methuen, 1936; *Child Psychology for Parents,* Ryerson, 1938; *An Educational Survey of Antigonish County, Nova Scotia,* Imperial Publishing Co., 1938; *The Next Step in Canadian Education: An Account of the Larger Unit of School Administration,* Macmillan, 1939.

Education and Crisis: Educational Issues of Today, University of London Press, 1946; *Our Children's Future,* Littlebury & Co., 1946; *The Educated Man,* Oxford University Press, 1956; *The Training of Teachers in Central Africa,* Edinburgh University Press, 1958; *A Short Report on the Background of Educational Development in the Federation,* University College of Rhodesia and Nyasaland, 1958; *The Works of an Institute of Education in Central Africa,* University College of Rhodesia and Nyasaland, 1960; *The Importance of the Humanities and Creative Arts in the Modern World,* University of Natal, 1960; *A Philosophy for the Teacher: A Study of the Child and Human Knowledge,* Oxford University Press, 1961; *The Building of a University in Central Africa,* Leeds University Press, 1962; *The Planning of Education,* Institute of Education, University of Leeds, 1963; *The Aramaic Sayings of Jesus,* Hodder & Stoughton, 1967; *Universities in the Modern World,* Pergamon, 1968; *The Freedom and Autonomy of Universities,* S.C.M. Press, 1968; *Outward Bound: Students of Outward Bound Schools in Great Britain; A Follow-Up Study,* School of Education, University of Bristol, 1970; *The Challenge of Outward Bound,* Heinemann, 1972.

*   *   *

FLORES, Janis   1946-

PERSONAL: Born January 12, 1946, in Fort Benton, Mont.; daughter of J. Eldon (an airline dispatcher) and Dorothea (a legal secretary; maiden name, Dickens) Overholser; married Raynaldo G. Flores (a horseshoer), January 13, 1968. *Education:* Immaculate Heart College, Los Angeles, Calif., B.A., 1967; St. Luke Hospital, Pasadena, Calif., license in medical technology, 1969. *Residence:* Sebastopol, Calif. *Agent:* Albert Zuckerman, Writer's House, 132 West 31st St., New York, N.Y. 10001.

CAREER: Live Oak Laboratory, Arcadia, Calif., medical technologist, 1969-72; Biskind Laboratory, Santa Rosa, Calif., supervisor, 1972-76; Empire Laboratory, Santa Rosa,

Calif., supervisor, 1976—. *Member:* American Society of Clinical Pathologists, National Mustang Association, Defenders of Wildlife, Fund for Animals, California Writers Club, Redwood Writers Club.

WRITINGS: Hawkshead (novel), Doubleday, 1976; *Peregrine House* (novel), Doubleday, in press.

WORK IN PROGRESS: Gyrfalcon Hall, a romantic suspense novel.

AVOCATIONAL INTERESTS: Animals (especially horses—she owns three—and endangered species); piano, gardening, needlework.

* * *

FLOWERS, Betty S(ue) 1947-

PERSONAL: Born February 2, 1947, in Waco, Tex.; daughter of Paul Davis (in banking) and Betty (Lewis) Marable; married John Garland Flowers (a rehabilitation counselor), July 14, 1967. *Education:* University of Texas, B.A. (honors), 1969, M.A., 1970; Queen Mary College, London, Ph.D., 1973. *Home:* 2607 Fiset, Austin, Tex. 78731. *Office:* Department of English, University of Texas, Austin, Tex. 78712.

CAREER: Beaver College, London, England, lecturer in drama, 1971-72; University of Texas, Austin, assistant professor of English, 1973—. Has given poetry readings and judged poetry contests. *Member:* Modern Language Association of America, Browning Society of London, Texas Association of College Teachers, Texas Association of Creative Writing Teachers, Phi Beta Kappa, Mortar Board. *Awards, honors:* Andrew W. Mellon fellowship, 1975-76.

WRITINGS: (contributor) Janice White, editor, *Fiction and Poetry by Texas Women,* Texas Center for Writers Press, 1975; *Browning and the Modern Tradition,* Macmillan, 1976. Contributor to *Critique.*

WORK IN PROGRESS: A novel exploring the male-female relationships in a twenty-first century society; research on dreams and creativity, on Browning's later poetry, on Christina Rossetti, and on women poets and Victorian poetic theory.

SIDELIGHTS: "I suppose, in all of my work," Betty Flowers wrote, "I'm motivated by a central curiosity: how things are related. How are dreams related to creativity (psychological work), how is twentieth-century poetry related to that of the nineteenth century (critical work), how are words related to experiences (my own poetry), how is a woman's concept of herself as a female related to her concept of herself as an artist (work in progress)."

* * *

FLYNN, George L. 1931-

PERSONAL: Born November 2, 1931, in Chicago, Ill.; son of Clifford Joseph (a traffic manager) and Louise (Maloney) Flynn; married Jill Gilbert, October 12, 1957; children: Kathleen, George Thomas, William Clifford. *Education:* University of Detroit, B.S., 1953. *Politics:* Independent. *Religion:* Roman Catholic. *Home:* 97 Minnehaha Blvd., Oakland, N.J. 07436. *Office:* 175 Rock Rd., Glen Rock, N.J. 07452.

CAREER: Prentice-Hall, Inc., Englewood Cliffs, N.J., 1957-67, began as field representative, became editor; Simon & Flynn, Inc., New York, N.Y., vice-president, 1967-71; free-lance writer, editor, and film producer, 1971—. *Military service:* U.S. Air Force, 1954-56; became first lieutenant.

Awards, honors: Award from Council on International Nontheatrical Events and Ohio State award, both 1971, for television documentary "A Man Named Lombardi."

WRITINGS: Vince Lombardi on Football, two volumes, New York Graphic Society, 1973; *The Vince Lombardi Scrapbook,* Grosset, 1976.

WORK IN PROGRESS: A Parents' Guide to Their Young Athlete, with E. Vandeweghe, for Crown; *The Black Squadron,* and a screenplay with the same title, completion expected in 1978; a book and a television series on the history of boxing.

SIDELIGHTS: Flynn played varsity basketball in college; as a publisher, he worked with Red Smith, W. C. Heinz, Bob Cousy, and Bart Starr. In films, he worked with Vince Lombardi to produce a series of thirteen films on football, syndicated for television.

* * *

FODOR, Ronald V(ictor) 1944-

PERSONAL: Born June 10, 1944, in Cleveland, Ohio; son of Alex V. (a laborer) and Helen (Majoros) Fodor; married Marilyn Komarc (a public school teacher), August 20, 1966; children: Germaine Victoria, John Victor. *Education:* Ohio University, B.S., 1966; Arizona State University, M.S., 1968; University of New Mexico, Ph.D., 1971. *Home:* 3313 Wilway N.E., Albuquerque, N.M. 87106. *Office:* Department of Geology, University of New Mexico, Albuquerque, N.M. 87131.

CAREER: University of New Mexico, Albuquerque, research scientist in geology, 1971—. *Member:* Geological Society of America, Meteorological Society, American Geophysical Union.

WRITINGS: Meteorites: Stones from the Sky (juvenile), Dodd, 1976; *What Does a Geologist Do?* (juvenile), Dodd, in press; *The Complete Handbook on Auto Repair and Maintenance: With the Repair-O-Matic Guide,* Parker Publishing, in press.

WORK IN PROGRESS: Earth in Motion: The Concept of Plate Tectonics, for children; *Competitive Weightlifting.*

SIDELIGHTS: Fodor writes: "I am writing science on a popular level as a scientist—that is, as a specialist on the subject—as opposed to most books of similar subject matter being written by professional writers who have only an interest in science." His current scientific work involves "the mineralogy, geochemistry, and petrology of volcanic rocks and meteorites." This research has taken him to South America, Africa, Europe, and Hawaii.

* * *

FOGARTY, Robert S(tephen) 1938-

PERSONAL: Born August 30, 1938, in Brooklyn, N.Y.; son of Michael and Gretta Fogarty; married Geraldine Wolpman, December 30, 1961; children: David, Suzanne. *Education:* Fordham University, B.S.S., 1960; University of Denver, M.A., 1962, Ph.D., 1968. *Home:* 216 Fairfield Pike, Yellow Springs, Ohio 45387. *Office:* Department of History, Antioch College, Yellow Springs, Ohio 45387.

CAREER: Michigan State University, East Lansing, assistant professor of American studies, 1963-68; Antioch College, Yellow Springs, Ohio, associate professor of history, 1968—. *Member:* Organization of American Historians, American Studies Association, American Association of University Professors.

WRITINGS: (Editor) *American Utopianism*, F. T. Peacock, 1972, 2nd edition, 1974; (editor with Lawrence Grauman) *Letters from a Self-Made Merchant to His Son*, Outerbridge & Dientsfrey, 1974. Consulting editor for nineteen-volume "American Utopian Adventure," Porcupine Press, 1975. Contributor to history and American studies journals. Associate editor of *Antioch Review*.

WORK IN PROGRESS: *Righteous Remnant: The House of David; American Communes, 1865-1914.*

* * *

FOLEY, Scott
    See DAREFF, Hal

* * *

FONTAINE, Andre   1910-

PERSONAL: Born March 14, 1910, in Brooklyn, N.Y.; son of Andre Camille (a teacher) and Mildred (a camp director; maiden name, Arey) Fontaine; married Dorothy Roselius (a social worker), April 6, 1935; children: Deborah (Mrs. D. A. McCormick), Mark, Andree (Mrs. David Lauterbach). *Education:* Amherst College, student, 1927-30; Columbia University, A.B., 1931, further study, 1931-32. *Home:* 124 Remington Ave., Syracuse, N.Y. 13210. *Agent:* Sterling Lord Agency, 660 Madison Ave., New York, N.Y. 10021. *Office:* School of Public Communications, Syracuse University, Syracuse, N.Y. 13210.

CAREER: *Collier's,* New York, N.Y., associate editor, 1944-48; free-lance writer, 1948-54; *Bluebook*, New York City, editor, 1954-56; *Redbook*, New York City, roving editor, 1956-59; free-lance writer, 1959-65; Syracuse University, Syracuse, N.Y., professor of communications, 1965—. *Member:* Society of Magazine Writers. *Awards, honors:* Benjamin Franklin magazine citation, 1954, from University of Illinois; brotherhood citation from National Conference of Christians and Jews, 1959; School Bell Award from National Education Association, 1962.

WRITINGS: *The Art of Writing Nonfiction*, Crowell, 1974. Contributor to *Reader's Digest, Saturday Evening post, McCall's, Look, Sports Illustrated, Good Housekeeping, Better Homes and Gardens, Nation's Business, True, Yachting,* and other periodicals.

WORK IN PROGRESS: A biography of William Ellery Channing; research projects in newspaper and magazine editing.

SIDELIGHTS: Fontaine spent 1961 in India on assignment from *Reader's Digest*. He was editorial consultant to *Ford Times* in 1948 and 1961.

* * *

FONZI, Bruno   1913(?)-1976

1913(?)—June 5, 1976; Italian scholar, translator, novelist, and author. Obituaries: *Washington Post,* June 7, 1976.

* * *

FORBES, Eric Gray   1933-

PERSONAL: Born March 30, 1933, in St. Andrews, Scotland; son of Robert James (a clerk) and Christina (Gray) Forbes; married Martha Maria Sibilla Luerken (a translator), March 25, 1966; children: Edgar William, Andrea Christine. *Education:* University of St. Andrews, B.Sc. (first class honors), 1954, Ph.D. (astrophysics), 1961; University of London, M.Sc., 1965, Ph.D. (history and philos-

ophy of science), 1972; University of Edinburgh, M.Litt., 1975; also studied at Royal Aircraft Establishment and Royal Greenwich Observatory. *Home:* 23 Carfrae Rd., Edinburgh EH4 3QG, Scotland. *Office:* Department of History, University of Edinburgh, 50 George Sq., Edinburgh EH8 9JY, England.

CAREER: Guest observer and research assistant at Osservatorio Astrofisico di Arcetri, Florence, Italy, and University of Goettingen, Goettingen, Germany, 1957-60; teacher of science in junior secondary school in St. Andrews, Scotland, 1960-61; British Council, London, England, regional officer, 1961; St. Mary's College, Twickenham, England, lecturer in physics, 1961-63, senior lecturer in mathematics, 1963-65; University of Edinburgh, Edinburgh, Scotland, lecturer in the history of science, 1965-72, senior lecturer, 1972, reader in history, 1973—. Member of National Committee on the History of Science, Medicine, and Technology, 1973-82; secretary of Fifteenth International Congress of the History of Science, 1977.

MEMBER: International Astronomical Union, Academie International d'Histoire des Sciences (corresponding member), Royal Astronomical Society (fellow), British Society for the History of Science (member of council, 1967-69 and 1974-76), Deutsche Gesellschaft fuer die Geschichte der Medezin, Naturwissenschaften und Technik. *Awards, honors:* Alexander von Humboldt research fellowship from von Humboldt Stiftung, 1973-74; British Academy European exchange fellowship, 1973-74.

WRITINGS: (Editor and translator) Georg Christoph Lichtenberg, *Opera Inedita Tobiae Mayeri* (title means "Unpublished Works of Tobias Mayer"), Macmillan (England), 1971, American Elsevier, 1972; (editor and translator) *The Euler-Mayer Correspondence, 1751-1755: A New Perspective on Eighteenth Century Advances in Lunar Theory,* Macmillan (England), 1971, American Elsevier, 1972; (editor) *The Unpublished Writings of Tobias Meyer,* Volume I: *Astronomy and Geography,* Volume II: *Artillery and Mechanics,* Volume III: *Theory of the Magnet and Its Application to Terrestrial Magnetism,* Vandenhoeck & Ruprecht, 1972; *The Birth of Scientific Navigation,* H.M.S.O., 1974; *Greenwich Observatory,* Volume I: *Origins and Early History, 1675-1835,* Taylor & Francis, 1975; (editor and author of introduction) *The Gresham Lectures of John Flamsteed,* International Scholastic Book Service, 1975.

Contributor: A. W. Haslett and John St. John, editors, *Science Survey,* Longacre Press, 1962; J. Stradins, editor, *Contributions to the History of Natural Sciences and Technology in the Baltics,* Zinatne Publishing House, 1971; Paul Fritz and David Williams, editors, *City and Society in the Nineteenth Century,* Association for Eighteenth Century Studies, 1973; Arthur Beer, editor, *Vistas in Astronomy,* Volume 19, Pergamon, 1976. Contributor of more than fifty articles to scientific journals. Sub-editor of *Journal for the History of Astronomy,* 1970-75.

WORK IN PROGRESS: Editing *The Correspondence of John Flamsteed, 1646-1719,* in three volumes, for Mansell; editing William Black's *Aberdeen Lectures in Natural Philosophy, 1690,* with Christine M. Shepherd; editing Colin Maclaurin's *Student Notebook, 1713, 1915,* with C. M. Shepherd; research on Gauss's contributions to astronomical science and Cook's contributions to oceanic navigation.

AVOCATIONAL INTERESTS: Sports (cricket, rugby, badminton, tennis).

FOREMAN, Richard 1937-

PERSONAL: Born June 10, 1937, in New York, N.Y.; son of Albert (an attorney) and Claire (Levine) Foreman. *Education:* Brown University, B.A. (magna cum laude), 1959; Yale University, M.F.A., 1962. *Religion:* Jewish. *Home and office:* 152 Wooster St., New York, N.Y. 10012. *Agent:* Artservices, 463 West St., New York, N.Y. 10014.

CAREER: Actors Studio, New York, N.Y., member of playwrights' group, 1962-68; Ontological-Hysteric Theater, New York, N.Y., founder and director, 1968—. Director of "Three-Penny Opera" at Lincoln Center, 1976. Member of board of directors of Anthology Film Archives. *Awards, honors:* Obie awards from *Village Voice,* 1970, for "Elephant Steps," and 1973, for work with Ontological-Hysteric Theater; grants from Creative Artists Public Service Program; Rockefeller Foundation grant, 1974; Guggenheim play-writing fellowship, 1975.

WRITINGS: Plays and Manifestos of Richard Foreman, New York University Press, 1976.

Plays: "Angelface," first produced in New York, N.Y. at Cinematheque, April, 1968; "Elephant Steps," first produced in Lenox, Mass., at Tanglewood, July, 1968; "Ida-Eyed," first produced in New York City at New Dramatists Workshop, May, 1969; "Real Magic in New York" (concert), first produced in New York at Cinematheque, May, 1970; "Total Recall" ("Sophia-(Wisdom): Part II"), first produced in New York at Cinematheque, December, 1970; "Dream Tantras for Western Massachusetts," first produced in Lenox, Mass., at Lenox Arts Center, August, 1971; "Hotel China," first produced in New York at Cinematheque, December, 1971; "Evidence," first produced in New York at Theatre for the New City, April, 1972; "Dr. Selavy's Magic Theatre," first produced in Lenox, Mass., at Lenox Arts Center, July, 1972; "Sophia-(Wisdom): Part III—The Cliffs," first produced in New York at Cinematheque, December, 1972; "Particle Theory," first produced in New York at Theatre for the New City, April, 1973; "Daily Life," first produced (in part) in New York at Cubiculo Theatre, May, 1973; "Classical Therapy or a Week under the Influence," first produced in Paris, France, at Festival d'Automne, September, 1973; "Vertical Mobility" ("Sophia-(Wisdom): Part IV"), and "Pain(t)," both first produced in New York at Ontological-Hysteric Theatre, April, 1974; "Sophia-(Wisdom): Part I," first produced in New York at Theatre for the New City, November, 1974; "Hotels for Criminals," first produced in New York at Exchange Theatre, January, 1975; "Pandering to the Masses: A Misrepresentation," first produced in New York at Ontological-Hysteric Theatre, January, 1975; "Thinking (One Kind)," first produced in San Diego, Calif., at University of California, March, 1975; "Out of the Body Travel," first produced in New London, Conn., at American Dance Festival, July, 1975; "Rhoda in Potatoland (Her Fall-Starts)," first produced in New York at Ontological-Hysteric Theatre, December, 1975; "Livre des Splendeurs," first produced in Paris, France, at Festival d'Automne, October, 1976.

Plays—Unpublished and not yet produced: "Rhoda—Returning," 1969; "Maudlin Notations," 1970; "Forest: Depth," 1970; "Two Vacations," 1970; "Holy Moly," 1970; "Lines of Vision," 1970; "Op/Ra: An Isomorphic Representation of the Gradual Dismemberment from Within of Western Art in Which a New Unity That of Consciousness Itself Emerges," 1972; "Africa," 1972; "The Rem(ar)kable Cabin-Cruiser: Depth," 1972; "Inspirational Analy-sis," 1973; "Walled Garden (Language)," 1973; "Life of the Bee (I've Goet der Shakes)," 1973; "Africanns-Instructis," 1973; "Seance," 1975; "Place plus Target," 1975; "End of a Beautiful Friendship," 1975; "Radiant City," 1975.

WORK IN PROGRESS: "Work," a play.

SIDELIGHTS: The Ontological-Hysteric Theater has been incorporated since 1972 as a non-profit organization. It is this company that has produced most of Foreman's plays, usually under his direction and with his designs. Some of his work (a libretto and four music-theater pieces) have had the help of composer Sidney Silverman.

*   *   *

FORM, William H. 1917-

PERSONAL: Born June 2, 1917, in Rochester, N.Y.; son of Anthony (a cabinet maker) and Mary (Conet) Form; married Joan Huber (a professor); children: Helen Form Land, Catherine Form Sternberg. *Education:* University of Rochester, A.B. (cum laude), 1938, M.A., 1939; University of Maryland, Ph.D., 1944. *Residence:* Champaign, Ill. *Office:* Department of Sociology, University of Illinois, Urbana, Ill. 61801.

CAREER: University of Maryland, College Park, instructor in sociology, 1943; American University, Washington, D.C., instructor in sociology, 1944; Stephens College, Columbia, Mo., instructor in sociology, 1944-45; Kent State University, Kent, Ohio, assistant professor of sociology, 1945-47; Michigan State University, East Lansing, began as assistant professor, became professor of sociology, 1947-71, research professor, 1962-71, acting director of School of Labor and Industrial Relations, 1963-64, chairman of department of sociology, 1965-68; University of Illinois, Urbana, professor of sociology and labor and industrial relations, 1971—. Member of research advisory committee of U.S. Department of Labor's Manpower Commission, 1971—. Consultant to National Science Foundation, U.S. Department of Labor, and U.S. Department of Health, Education & Welfare.

MEMBER: International Sociological Association, American Sociological Association (member of council, 1968—), Industrial Relations Research Association, American Association of University Professors, North Central Sociological Association (president, 1953). *Awards, honors:* National Research Council fellowship, 1953-54; Fulbright research fellowship at University of Turin, 1961-62; National Science Foundation fellowship, 1962-64; distinguished professor award from Michigan State University, 1965; Ford Foundation fellowship, 1965-66.

WRITINGS: Industrial Sociology, Harper, 1951, new edition, 1965; *Community in Disaster,* Harper, 1958; (with others) *Industry, Labor, and Community,* Harper, 1960; (editor with others) *Man, Work, and Society,* Basic Books, 1962; (with others) *Influentials in Two Border Cities,* Notre Dame University Press, 1965; *Industrial Relations and Social Change in Latin America,* University of Florida Press, 1965; *Comparative Perspectives on Industrial Society,* Little, Brown, 1969; *Income and Ideology,* Free Press, 1974; *Blue Collar Stratification,* Princeton University Press, 1976. Contributor to professional journals.

WORK IN PROGRESS: The Stratification of the Working Class.

SIDELIGHTS: Form has studied the automobile industry in the United States and abroad. *Avocational interests:* Opera, cabinet making.

FORTE, Dan 1935-
  (Donato Fortebraccia)

PERSONAL: Born June 7, 1935, in Haverhill, Mass.; son of John J. and Mary (Coppola) Forte; married Arlene Orenstein (a reading consultant); children: Daniel F., Jr., David Mark. *Education:* Lowell State College, B.S.Ed., 1957; Salem State College, M.Ed., 1959; University of Palm Beach, D.Ed., 1968. *Religion:* Roman Catholic. *Residence:* Boca Raton, Fla.; and Rye Beach, N.H. *Office:* Department of Management, New Hampshire College, Alumni Dr., Portsmouth, N.H. 03801.

CAREER: Member of faculty and judiciary board of appeals at New Hampshire College, Portsmouth. *Member:* Benevolent Protective Order of Elks, Catholic Order of Foresters. *Awards, honors:* D.H.L., University of Aruba.

WRITINGS: (Under pseudonym Donato Fortebraccia) *My Godfather's Recipe Book,* New Hampshire Publishing Co., 1973; *Field Trips in New Hampshire,* JOAR Corp., 1975; *Project Cooking,* JOAR Corp., 1975.

WORK IN PROGRESS: Tap the Resources in Town.

*   *   *

FORTEBRACCIA, Donato
  See FORTE, Dan

*   *   *

FOSTER, Catharine Osgood 1907-

PERSONAL: Born April 26, 1907, in Newton Highlands, Mass.; daughter of George Laurie (an executive) and Hannah C. (Webb) Osgood; married Thomas H. Foster (a writer), June 19, 1937. *Education:* Mount Holyoke College, B.A., 1930, M.A., 1931. *Home and office address:* Monument Rd., P.O. Box 397, Bennington, Vt. 05201.

CAREER: Sophie Newcomb College, New Orleans, La., instructor in English, 1931-34; Bennington College, Bennington, Vt., teacher of English and American literature, 1934-68; writer, 1968—. *Member:* Nature Conservancy (Vermont chapter), American Horticultural Society, Wilderness Society, New England Wild Flower Society, Vermont Natural Resources Council (former member of board of directors), Vermont Natural Foods and Farming Association, Massachusetts Horticultural Society, Conservation Society of Southern Vermont (member of board of directors), Bennington Garden Club, Bennington League of Women Voters (chairman for environmental quality). *Awards, honors:* Conservation award from Zone 1 of the Garden Club of America, 1968; Vermont Governor's Award for Conservation, 1973.

WRITINGS: The Organic Gardener, Knopf, 1972; (editor) *Terrific Tomatoes,* Rodale Press, 1974; *Organic Flower Gardening,* Rodale Press, 1975; *Plant Propagation Guide,* Rodale Press, in press. Author of "Around the Corner," weekly column in *Bennington Banner,* 1966—, and "Garden Away!," bi-weekly column in *Boston Globe.* Contributor to gardening and country magazines and to newspapers.

SIDELIGHTS: Catharine Foster writes: "I have had a life-long interest in gardening. I found . . . [writing] on gardening, specifically on organic gardening . . . an appealing occupation for someone just retired from teaching."

*   *   *

FOULKE, Adrienne 1915-

PERSONAL: Born May 28, 1915, in Strasburg, Pa.; daughter of Charles P. (a building contractor) and Nanette (a teacher; maiden name, Whitaker) Foulke. *Education:* Attended Smith College, 1932-34; Barnard College, B.A., 1936; Universita per Stranieri, certificate, 1937; additional study at Columbia University, 1952, 1953. *Home:* 218 East 12th St., New York, N.Y. 10003. *Office: New Yorker,* 25 West 43rd St., New York, N.Y. 10036.

CAREER: Ferragamo, Inc., Florence, Italy, worked on publicity, 1937-39; Montgomery Ward, New York City, worked on publicity, 1940-41; Coordinator of Information (COI), New York City, editor, 1941-43; Office of War Information, New York City, editor, 1943-45; U.S. Information Service, NewYork City, editor, 1943-52; *Life,* New York City, researcher for book program, 1953; *Time,* New York City, copy editor, 1954; *New Yorker,* New York City, copy editor, 1955—. *Member:* International P.E.N.

WRITINGS: English for Everyone, Pocket Books, 1964.

Translator: Silvia Lombroso, *No Time for Silence,* Roy, 1945; Francesco Jovine, *Seeds in the Wind,* Roy, 1946; Elsa Morante, *House of Liars,* Harcourt, 1951; Dante Arfelli, *Fifth Generation,* Scribner, 1953; Giovanni Papini, *The Devil,* Dutton, 1954; Georges Simenon, *Inspector Maigret in the New York Underworld,* Doubleday, 1955.

Maurice Percheron, *Marvellous Life of the Buddha,* St. Martin's, 1960; Francois Mauriac, *Second Thoughts,* World Publishing, 1961; Indro Montanello, *General Della Rovere,* Doubleday, 1961; Ado Kyrou, *Luis Bunuel,* Simon & Schuster, 1963; Jean Guitton, *Handbook for Intellectual Work,* [Notre Dame], 1964; Antoine de Saint-Exupery, *Sense of Life,* Funk, 1965; Leonardo Sciascia, *Council of Egypt,* Knopf, 1966; Guitton, *Man in Time,* [Notre Dame], 1966; Andre Maurois, *Collected Short Stories,* Washington Square Press, 1967; Francois Nourissier, *The French,* Knopf, 1968; Sciascia, *A Man's Blessing,* Harper, 1968; Boris Kochno, *Diaghilev and the Ballets Russes,* Harper, 1970; Suzanne Prou, *Mlle. Savelli?,* Harper, 1971; Prou, *The Yellow Summer,* Harper, 1972; Sciascia, *Equal Danger,* Harper, 1973; Prou, *The Paperhanger,* Harper, 1974; Prou, *The Terrace of the Bernardini,* Harper, 1976.

Contributor of translations to anthologies, and to magazines, including *Vogue, Dissent, Hudson Review, Chelsea,* and *Poet Lore.*

WORK IN PROGRESS: Translating *One Way or Another* by Leonardo Sciascia, for Harper, and *We Ate the Stone Forest Goo* by Georges Condominas, for Hill & Wang.

SIDELIGHTS: Adrienne Foulke has studied, worked, and traveled in England, France, Italy, Germany, the Middle East, India, and Pakistan.

*   *   *

FOWLER, Mark 1949-

PERSONAL: Born May 1, 1949, in Akron, Ohio; son of Floyd J. (a physician) and Marion (a social worker; maiden name, Holoman) Fowler; married Jessica Kaplan (a teacher), September 18, 1975. *Education:* Brandeis University, A.B., 1971; also attended Columbia University, 1973. *Politics:* "Yes." *Home and office:* 15 Purchase St., Rye, N.Y. 10580. *Agent:* Edward J. Acton, 288 West 12th St., New York, N.Y. 10014.

CAREER: Free-lance writer.

WRITINGS: (With Bruce Felton) *Felton and Fowler's Best, Worst, and Most Unusual,* Crowell, 1975; (with Felton) *More Best, Worst, and Most Unusual,* Crowell,

1976; (contributor) Stephen Rosen, editor, *Future Facts,* Simon & Schuster, 1976. Contributor of articles, stories, and poems to magazines, including *Penthouse* and *Carleton Miscellany.*

WORK IN PROGRESS: Eureka! (tentative title), with Bruce Felton, a book dealing with inventors and their inventions; a mystery novel.

SIDELIGHTS: Fowler writes: "Bertrand Russell once said that the useless fact has a 'peculiar savor' all its own, that 'it is well worth knowing simply because it is odd.' In our first two books Bruce Felton and I have prepared a salmagundi of useless information—achievements, blunders, oddities, and curiosities in fields ranging from astronomy to taxidermy, from music to muktuk. Our latest joint extravaganza is a homage to eccentric geniuses: inventors, gadgeteers, and visionaries whose ideas have changed the world.

"Looking ahead, here is a short inventory of my wildest dreams and ambitions: to write a *feuilleton* as funny as Perelman's 'Eine Kleine Mothmusik'; to write a poem as haunting as Dickey's 'Heaven of Animals'; to write a mystery as entertaining as Burgess' *Tremor of Intent;* and to write a children's book that begs to be read aloud. Obviously I have my work cut out for me."

*   *   *

FOWLER, Roger 1938-

PERSONAL: Born August 23, 1938, in Worcestershire, England. *Residence:* Norwich, England. *Agent:* Curtis Brown Academic, 1 Craven Hill, London W2 3EP, England. *Office:* School of English and American Studies, University of East Anglia, Norwich NR4 7TJ, England.

CAREER: University of Hull, Hull, England, lecturer in English, 1960-64; University of East Anglia, Norwich, England, lecturer, 1964-69. Senior lecturer in English and linguistics, 1969—. Visiting lecturer, University of California, Berkeley, 1966-67, 1969; visiting professor, Brown University, 1972-73.

WRITINGS: Essays on Style and Language: Linguistic and Cultural Approaches to Literary Style, Routledge & Kegan Paul, 1966, Humanities Press, 1970; *Old English Prose and Verse: An Annotated Selection,* Humanities Press, 1966, revised edition, Routledge & Kegan Paul, 1974; *The Languages of Literature,* Routledge & Kegan Paul, 1971; *Introduction to Transformational Syntax,* Routledge & Kegan Paul, 1971; (editor) Wulfstan, *Canons of Edgar,* Oxford University Press, 1972; (editor) *A Dictionary of Modern Critical Terms,* Routledge & Kegan Paul, 1973; *Understanding Language: An Introduction to Linguistics,* Routledge & Kegan Paul, 1974; *Style and structure in Literature: Essays in the New Stylistics,* Cornell University Press, 1975; *Linguistics and the Novel,* Methuen, 1977. Contributor of articles on linguistics and literature to journals.

WORK IN PROGRESS: Continuing research in linguistic criticism, in point of view in narrative, and in history.

*   *   *

FOX-GENOVESE, Elizabeth 1941-

PERSONAL: Born May 28, 1941, in Boston, Mass.; daughter of Edward Whiting (a professor of history) and Elizabeth (Simon) Fox; married Eugene Dominick Genovese (a professor of history), June 6, 1969. *Education:* Bryn Mawr College, A.B., 1963; Harvard University, A.M., 1966, Ph.D., 1974. *Home:* 54 Corwin Rd., Rochester, N.Y.

14610. *Office:* Department of History, University of Rochester, Rochester, N.Y. 14627.

CAREER: University of Rochester, Rochester, N.Y., assistant professor of history and liberal arts, 1973-76, associate professor of history, 1976—. *Member:* American Historical Association, Society for French Historical Studies, Societe des Etudes Robespierristes, Berkshire Conference of Women Historians.

WRITINGS: The Origins of Physiocracy: Economic Revolution and Social Order in Eighteenth-Century France, Cornell University Press, 1976.

WORK IN PROGRESS: The Consolidation of an Urban Mentality: Bordeaux, 1760-1830; research on the social creation of woman in the eighteenth and nineteenth centuries.

*   *   *

FRANCIS, Frank Chalton 1901-

PERSONAL: Born October 5, 1901, in Liverpool, England; son of Frank William and Elizabeth (Chalton) Francis; married Katrina Florence McClennon, April 20, 1927; children: Jane, Jeremy, Guy. *Education:* University of Liverpool, B.A., 1923; Emmanuel College, Cambridge, M.A., 1925. *Home:* The Vine, Nether Winchendon, Aylesbury, Buckinghamshire, England.

CAREER: Assistant master of classics in a school in Holyhead County, England, 1925-26; British Museum, London, England, assistant keeper, 1926-46, secretary, 1946-47, keeper of department of printed books, 1948-59, director and principal librarian, 1959-68; writer, 1968—. Lecturer at University of London, 1945-59; David Murray Lecturer at University of Glasgow, 1957. Chairman of the trustees of National Central Library; trustee of Imperial War Museum. Member of Council of British National Bibliography, 1949-59; member of national committee for International Council of Museums; member of Library Advisory Council of England. Governor of Birkbeck College. Chairman of United Nations International Committee of Library Experts, 1948; vice-president of UNESCO international advisory committee on bibliography, 1954-60; chairman of International Conference on Cataloging Principles, 1961.

MEMBER: International Federation of Library Associations (president, 1963-69), Society of Antiquaries (fellow), Museums Association (fellow; member of council, 1960—; vice-president, 1964-65; president, 1965-66), Bibliographical Society (president, 1964-66), Library Association (honorary fellow; member of council, 1948-59; chairman of executive committee, 1954-57; president, 1965), Association of Special Libraries and Information Bureaus (president, 1957-58), Anglo-Swedish Society (chairman, 1964-68), Circle of State Librarians (chairman, 1947-50), Bibliographical Society of America, American Academy of Arts and Sciences (foreign honorary member), Institut de France (corresponding member), Kungliga Gustav Adolfs Akademien (honorary member), Academie des Beaux Arts (corresponding member), Oxford Bibliographical Society, Cambridge Bibliographical Society, Edinburgh Bibliographical Society, Massachusetts Historical Society (corresponding member), Worshipful Company of Clockmakers (master, 1974), Athenaeum Club, Royal Commonwealth Society, Grolier Club.

AWARDS, HONORS: Named companion of the Bath, 1958, and knight commander, 1960; honorary fellow of Emmanuel College, Cambridge, and Pierpont Library (New York, N.Y.); honorary degrees include D.Litt. from University of British Columbia, 1960, Trinity College, Dublin,

1962, University of Exeter, 1966, University of New Brunswick, 1967, University of Leeds, 1967, Oxford University, 1968, and University of Wales, 1968, Litt.D. from University of Liverpool, 1963, and Cambridge University, 1968.

WRITINGS: Historical Bibliography in a Year's Work in Librarianship, 1927-38, Library Association, 1928-39; (translator from the German) William Cohn, *Chinese Art*, Studio Books, 1930; *Three Unrecorded English Books of the Sixteenth Century*, Cleveland Public Library for U.S. Library of Congress, 1938; *A List of the Writings of Ronald Brunless McKerrow*, Cleveland Public Library for U.S. Library of Congress, 1941; *Recent Bibliographical Work*, Cleveland Public Library for U.S. Library of Congress, 1942; *A. W. Pollard, 1859-1944*, Cleveland Public Library for U.S. Library of Congress, 1944; *A List of Dr. Greg's Writings*, Cleveland Public Library for U.S. Library of Congress, 1945; (editor) *The Bibliographical Society, 1892-1942: Studies in Retrospect*, Bibliographical Society, 1945; *The Catalogues of the British Museum*, British Museum, Volume I: *Printed Books*, 1948, Volume III (Francis was not associated with Volume II.)

Oriental Printed Books and Manuscripts, 1951, revised edition, 1959; (author of introduction) *Narcissus Luttrell's Popish Plot Catalogues*, Blackwell, 1956; *Robart Copland: Sixteenth-Century Printer and Translator*, University of Glasgow Press, 1961; *Many Cultures: One World*, Graduate School of Librarianship, University of Denver, 1970; (editor and author of introduction) *Treasures of the British Museum*, Thames & Hudson, 1971, Transatlantic, 1972, revised edition, 1975; *Bibliographical Information in Manuscript Collections*, Graduate School of Library Service, Rutgers University, 1972; *A Bibliographical Ghost Revisits His Old Haunts*, University of Texas Press, 1973.

Also author of *The Shakespeare Collection in the British Museum*, 1950, and editor of *Facsimile of "The Compleat Catalogue," 1680*, 1956. Contributor to the proceedings of the British Academy, 1973; contributor of articles and reviews to library journals and newspapers. Editor of *Library*, 1936-53; joint editor of *Journal of Documentation*, 1947-68; associate editor of *Libri*; advisory editor of *Library Quarterly*.

AVOCATIONAL INTERESTS: Walking, gardening, golf.

* * *

FRANK, Florence Kiper 1885(?)-1976

1885(?)—June 27, 1976; American poet, playwright, and author. Obituaries: *New York Times*, June 29, 1976.

* * *

FRANK, Robert J(oseph) 1939-

PERSONAL: Born July 4, 1939, in Dickinson, N.D.; son of Ralph (a grocer) and Rose (a grocer; maiden name, Schoch) Frank; married Arva Utter (a teacher), August 15, 1964; children: Kirsten, Andrew. *Education:* St. John's University, Collegeville, Minn., B.A. (cum laude), 1962; University of Minnesota, M.A., 1968, Ph.D., 1969. *Home:* 403 Northwest 13th, Corvallis, Ore. 97330. *Office:* Department of English, Oregon State University, Corvallis, Ore. 97331.

CAREER: High school teacher of English in Abad, Puerto Rico, 1962-63; Oregon State University, Corvallis, assistant professor of English, 1969-70; Eastern Michigan University, Ypsilanti, assistant professor of English, 1970-71; Oregon State University, assistant professor, 1971-75, associate professor of English, 1975—, vice-chairman of department, 1975—. *Member:* Modern Language Association of America, Philological Association Pacific Coast, Rocky Mountain Modern Language Association.

WRITINGS: Don't Call Me Gentle Charles!: An Essay on Lamb's "Essays of Elia", Oregon State University Press, 1976.

WORK IN PROGRESS: Research on Blake, Byron, Shelley, "Romantic Tradition," and the literature of the Northwest.

AVOCATIONAL INTERESTS: The Northwest, music, gardening, "celebrating with family and friends."

* * *

FRANKEL, Max 1930-

PERSONAL: Born April 3, 1930, in Gera, Germany; came to U.S., 1940, naturalized citizen, 1948; son of Jacob A. and Mary (Katz) Frankel; married Tobia Brown (an editor), June 19, 1956; children: David, Margot, Jonathan. *Education:* Columbia University, A.B., 1952, M.A., 1953. *Religion:* Jewish. *Residence:* Riverdale, N.Y. *Office: New York Times*, Times Square, New York, N.Y. 10036.

CAREER/WRITINGS: New York Times, New York City, reporter, 1952-63, diplomatic correspondent, 1963-66, White House correspondent, 1966-68, Washington bureau chief, 1968-72, Sunday editor, 1973-76, editorial page editor, 1977—. *Military service:* U.S. Army, 1935-55, became corporal. *Member:* Council on Foreign Relations, Century Association. *Awards, honors:* Pulitzer Prize, 1973, for international reporting.

* * *

FRANKENTHAL, Kate 1889-1976

January 30, 1889—April 21, 1976; German-born American psychiatrist and author. Obituaries: *New York Times*, April 24, 1976.

* * *

FRANKL, Viktor E(mil) 1905-

PERSONAL: Born March 26, 1905, in Vienna, Austria; son of Gabriel (a government employee) and Elsa (Lion) Frankl; married Mathilde Grosser, December, 1941 (died, 1945); married Eleonore Katharina Schwindt, July 18, 1947; children: (second marriage) Gabrielle (Mrs. Franz Josef Vesely). *Education:* University of Vienna, M.D., 1930, Ph.D., 1949. *Home:* 1 Mariannengasse, Vienna 1090, Austria.

CAREER: Rothschild Hospital, Vienna, Austria, director of department of neurology, 1940-42; University of Vienna, Vienna, professor of neurology and psychiatry, 1947—. Director of department of neurology at Poliklinik Hospital, 1946-70; distinguished professor of logotherapy at U.S. International University, 1970—; visiting professor at Harvard University, 1961, Southern Methodist University, 1966, Stanford University, 1971-72, and Duquesne University, 1972; guest lecturer at more than a hundred colleges and universities in the United States; has also lectured in Australia, Asia, and Africa.

MEMBER: International Federation of Medical Psychotherapy (member of executive board), Austrian Medical Society of Psychotherapy (president, 1950—), National Character Laboratory (honorary life member), Brazilian Society of Integral Psychoanalysis (honorary president), Argentine Society of Medical Anthropology (honorary member), Peruvian Society of Neuropsychiatry and Legal Medicine (honorary member), Peruvian Society of Geriatrics (honorary member), Spanish Society of Clinical and

Experimental Hypnosis (honorary member), Peruvian Society of Neurology, Psychiatry, and Neurosurgery (honorary member), Medical Society of Vienna (honorary member). *Awards, honors:* Austrian State Prize for Public Education, 1956; citations from Religion in Education Foundation, 1960, and Indianapolis Pastoral Counseling Center; founders award from West Virginia Wesleyan College, 1968; Austrian Cross of Honor, first class, for science and art, 1969; distinguished lecturer award from Washington College, 1970; prize for scientific achievement from City of Vienna, 1970; named honorary citizen of Austin, Tex., 1976; Quest Medal from St. Edward's University, 1976; plaque of appreciation from University of the Philippines and University of Santo Tomas, 1976; honorary degrees include LL.D. from Loyola University, Chicago, Ill. and Edgecliff College, both 1970; L.H.D. from Rockford College, 1972.

WRITINGS: In English: *Aerztliche Seelsorge,* 4th edition, Deuticke, 1947, translation by Richard Winston and Clara Winston published as *The Doctor and the Soul: An Introduction to Logotherapy,* Knopf, 1955, 2nd expanded edition published as *The Doctor and the Soul: From Psychotherapy to Logotherapy,* 1965, 8th German edition, Deuticke, 1971; *Ein Psycholog erlebt das Konzentrationslager,* Jugend & Volk, 1946, translation by Ilse Lasch published as *From Death-Camp to Existentialism: A Psychiatrist's Path to a New Therapy,* Beacon Press, 1959, revised and enlarged edition published as *Man's Search for Meaning: An Introduction to Logotherapy,* 1963; *Der umbewusste Gott,* Wissenschaftliche Buchgesellschaft, 1966, 3rd edition, Koesel, 1974, translation published as *The Unconscious God: Psychotherapy and Theology,* Simon & Schuster, 1975; (with James C. Crumbaugh, Hans O. Gerz, and Leonard T. Maholick) *Psychotherapy and Existentialism: Selected Papers on Logotherapy,* Washington Square Press, 1967, revised edition, 1973; *The Will to Meaning: Foundations and Applications to Logotherapy,* World Publishing, 1969, revised edition, 1976; *Meaninglessness: Today's Dilemma* (phonotape), Creative Resources, 1971.

Other works: *Trotzdem Ja zum Leben sagen,* 2nd edition, Deuticke, 1947; *Zeit und Verantwortung,* Deuticke, 1947; *Logos und Existenz,* Amandus, 1951; *Theorie und Therapie der Neurosen: Einfuehrung in Logotherapie und Existenzanalyse,* Urban & Schwarzenberg, 1956, 2nd edition, E. Reinhardt, 1968; *Das Menschenbild der Seelenheilkunde,* Hippokrates Verlag, 1959; *Die Psychotherapie in der Praxis,* 2nd edition, Deuticke, 1961; *Psychotherapie fuer jedermann,* Herder, 1971; *Der Wille zum Sinn: Ausgewaehlte Vortraeger ueber Logotherapie,* Huber, 1972.

Contributor to professional journals.

SIDELIGHTS: Frankl is the originator of the school of logotherapy, which is often referred to as the "third Viennese school of psychotherapy," following Freud's psychoanalysis and Adler's individual psychology. His books have been translated into fourteen languages, including Chinese and Japanese, and the U.S. edition of *Man's Search for Meaning* has, by itself, sold more than a million and a half copies.

BIOGRAPHICAL/CRITICAL SOURCES: Donald F. Tweedie, *Logotherapy and the Christian Faith: An Evaluation of Frankl's Existential Approach to Psychotherapy,* Baker Book, 1961; Tweedie, *The Christian and the Couch: An Introduction to Christian Logotherapy,* Baker Book, 1963; Robert C. Leslie, *Jesus and Logotherapy: The Ministry of Jesus as Interpreted through the Psychotherapy of Viktor Frankl,* Abingdon, 1965; Joseph B. Fabry, *The Pur-

suit of Meaning: A Guide to the Theory and Application of Viktor E. Frankl's Logotherapy,* Beacon Press, 1968, revised edition, 1975; *Orientamenti Pedagogici,* Volume 17, number 3, 1970.

* * *

FRANKLAND, (Anthony) Noble 1922-

PERSONAL: Born July 4, 1922, in Ravenstonedale, England; son of Edward Percy and Maud (Metcalfe Gibson) Frankland; married Diana Madeline Fovargue Tavernor, February 28, 1944; children: Roger, Linda. *Education:* Trinity College, Oxford, M.A., 1947, D.Phil., 1951. *Home:* Thames House, Eynsham, Oxford, England. *Office:* Imperial War Museum, Lambeth Rd., London S.E.1, England.

CAREER: Air Ministry, London, England, Air Historical Branch, narrator, 1948-51, Cabinet Office, official military historian, 1951-60; Royal Institute of International Affairs, London, deputy director of studies, 1956-60; Imperial War Museum, London, England, director, 1960—. Lees Knowles Lecturer at Trinity College, Cambridge, 1963. Member of council of Morley College, 1962-66; trustee of Military Archives Center at King's College, University of London, 1963—, and Her Majesty's Ship Belfast Trust, 1971— (vice-chairman, 1972—). *Military service:* Royal Air Force, 1941-45, Bomber Command, 1943-45; decorated, Distinguished Flying Cross. *Member:* Society of Antiquaries (fellow), Royal United Services Institution. *Awards, honors:* Rockefeller Foundation fellowship, 1953.

WRITINGS: (Editor with Vera King) *Documents on International Affairs,* Oxford University Press, Volume I: *1955,* 1958, Volume II: *1956,* 1959, Volume III: *1957,* 1960; *Crown of Tragedy: Nicholas II,* W. Kimber, 1960, published as *Imperial Tragedy: Nicholas II, Last of the Tsars,* Coward, 1961; (with Charles Kingsley Webster) *The Strategic Air Offensive against Germany, 1939-1945,* four volumes, H.M.S.O., 1961; *The Bombing Offensive against Germany: Outlines and Perspectives,* Faber, 1965; *Bomber Offensive: The Devastation of Europe,* Macdonald & Co., 1969. Contributor to *Manual of Air Force Law* and other professional journals.

* * *

FRANKLIN, Sidney 1903-1976

July 11, 1903—April 26, 1976; American bullfighter, Hispanophile, and writer. Obituaries: *New York Times,* May 2, 1976; *Washington Post,* May 3, 1976; *Newsweek,* May 17, 1976.

* * *

**FRASER, Anthea
(Vanessa Graham)**

PERSONAL: Born in Lancashire, England; daughter of William Wallace (a director) and Mary Adelaide (a writer) Roby; married Ian Mackintosh Fraser, March 22, 1956; children: Fiona, Rosalind. *Education:* Attended private girls' school in Cheltenham, England. *Politics:* Conservative. *Religion:* Church of England. *Home:* 26 Celtic Ave., Shortlands, Bromley, Kent, England. *Agent:* Laurence Pollinger, 18 Maddox St., Mayfair, London W.1, England.

CAREER: Writer. Has worked as a private secretary. *Member:* Society of Women Writers and Journalists.

WRITINGS—Novels: Designs of Annabelle, Mills & Boon, 1971; *In the Balance,* Mills & Boon, 1973; *Laura Possessed* (ghost story), Dodd, 1974; *Home through the Dark (thriller), Milton House Books, 1974, Dodd, 1976; *Whistler's Lane* (ghost story), Dodd, 1975; *Breath of Brimstone,* Dodd, in press. Also author of two gothic novels, under pseudonym Vanessa Graham, *Bright Face of Danger* and *Such Men Are Dangerous.* Contributor of stories to magazines in England, Australia, South America, South Africa, and in the United States, including *Homes and Gardens, Woman's Own,* and *Cosmopolitan.*

WORK IN PROGRESS: Presence of Mind, a novel, for Corgi; *Time Will Tell,* a novel on the nature of time.

SIDELIGHTS: Fraser's books have also been published in Denmark, Germany, Holland, Italy, and Sweden.

* * *

FREDERICK, Carl Louis 1942-

PERSONAL: Born June 26, 1942, in Latrobe, Pa.; son of Thomas James (a sales manager) and Margaret (Depetris) Frederick; married Shirlee Benjamin, June 18, 1965 (divorced, January, 1973); children: Kirsten, Kendall. *Education:* Pennsylvania State University, B.S. (honors), 1964; University of Illinois, graduate study, 1964-65. *Home and office address:* P.O. Box 46060, Los Angeles, Calif. 90046. *Agent:* Ron Bernstein Agency, 200 West 58th St., New York, N.Y. 10019.

CAREER: Procter & Gamble, Cincinnati, Ohio, brand manager, 1965-69; Heublein, Hartford, Conn., acquisitions manager, 1969-72; Mattel, Los Angeles, Calif., director of marketing, 1972-73; Marketing Center West, Los Angeles, Calif., president, 1973-75. Writer.

WRITINGS: Playing the Game the New Way, Delacorte, 1976.

WORK IN PROGRESS: Evolutionary Notions.

SIDELIGHTS: Frederick is "actively interested [in] pursuing the subject of human awareness, with an eye toward a breakthrough idea which could transform the reality of the free world."

* * *

FREEBORN, Brian (James) 1939-

PERSONAL: Born November 18, 1939, in Sussex, England; son of Harry James (a plumber) and Gladys (Ovenden) Freeborn; married Clo Hack (a market researcher), June 14, 1973. *Education:* University of Cape Town, B.Arch., 1963. *Politics:* "Free fall leaning left." *Religion:* "Considered and ignored." *Residence:* London, England. *Agent:* John Farquharson Ltd., 15 Red Lion Sq., London WC1R 4QW, England.

CAREER: Worked as architectural assistant and bank clerk in Rhodesia, 1956-58; Marius J. Vonk, Cape Town, South Africa, architect, 1963-64; architect in London, England, for George Wimpey, 1964-65, Gerald Shenstone & Partners, 1965-66, and Briscoe & Stanton, 1966-72; Wigley, Fox Partnership, London, architect, 1972—. *Member:* Royal Institute of British Architects, Architects' Registration Council of the United Kingdom.

WRITINGS: Good Luck, Mister Cain (thriller), Secker & Warburg, 1976, St. Martin's, 1977; *Ten Days, Mister Cain?* (thriller), Secker & Warburg, 1977.

Plays: "The Master" (comedy), first produced in Cape Town, South Africa, at University of Cape Town, June, 1964; "Anouecket" (one-act comedy), first produced in Cape Town, South Africa, at University of Cape Town, June, 1966; "Hall of Mirrors" (one-act drama), first pro-

duced at Fish Hoek Festival, June, 1967. Also author of "Who Precisely Will be Supplying the Bits and Pieces?" and "The Master Department," as yet neither published or produced. Contributor to magazines.

WORK IN PROGRESS: An untitled thriller, completion expected in 1977.

SIDELIGHTS: Freeborn told *CA:* "I am spurred on by a need to entertain, a head stuffed full of old movies, a love of London, and an earful of London speech. I am fascinated by conspiracy and cunning—through inept myself. I have a hatred of racialism bred by my Rhodesian and South African childhood. I regularly attend serious theatre and *any* kind of cinema."

AVOCATIONAL INTERESTS: Travel (most of Western Europe, U.S.S.R., Israel, South Africa, and Rhodesia).

* * *

FREEDLAND, Michael 1934-

PERSONAL: Born December 18, 1934, in London, England; son of David (a sales manager) and Lily (Mindel) Freedland; married Sara Hockerman (a secretary), July 3, 1960; children: Fiona Anne, Danielle Ruth, Jonathan Saul. *Education:* National Council for Training of Journalists, proficiency certificate, 1955. *Religion:* Jewish. *Home and office:* 35 Hartfield Ave., Elstree, Hertfordshire WD6 3JB, England.

CAREER: Luton News, Luton, England, journalist, 1951-60; *Daily Sketch,* London, England, journalist, 1960-61; British Broadcasting Corp., London, executive producer and presenter of radio show "You Don't Have to Be Jewish", 1971—. Member of board of deputies of British Jews, 1969-72.

WRITINGS: Jolson, Stein & Day, 1972; *Irving Berlin,* Stein & Day, 1974; *Cagney,* Stein & Day, 1975; *Fred Astaire,* W. H. Allen, 1976. Contributor to *London Times, London Evening Standard,* and national magazines.

WORK IN PROGRESS: Two biographies and a study of the Jewish contribution to show business.

* * *

FREEDLAND, Nat(haniel) 1936-
(Paul Kenyon)

PERSONAL: Legal surname is Friedland; born August 20, 1936, in New York, N.Y.; son of David (an engineer) and Luba (Chudnovsky) Friedland; married second wife, Norma Harms, November 28, 1975. *Education:* Hunter College (now of the City University of New York), B.A., 1958; Iowa State University, M.A., 1959; Columbia University, M.S., 1960. *Politics:* Democrat (Ultra-Liberal). *Religion:* Jewish (non-practicing). *Residence:* Glendale, Calif. *Office: Billboard,* 9000 Sunset Blvd., Los Angeles, Calif. 90069.

CAREER: Long Island Daily Press, New York, N.Y., journalist, 1963-66; *Huntington Hartford's Entertainment World Magazine,* Los Angeles, Calif., journalist, 1969-70; *Billboard* (magazine), Los Angeles, Calif., journalist, 1971—. *Military service:* U.S. Army, 1961-63. *Member:* Recording Academy, Authors Guild, Rock Writers of the World, Sierra Club, Count Dracula Society.

WRITINGS: The Occult Explosion, Putnam, 1972; *Mexico (Diana),* Michael Joseph, 1972; (editor) Andrew H. Meyer, *Dancing on the Seats,* Billboard, 1972. Contributor of about fifty articles to *TV Guide, Cavalier,* and other magazines. Author of column "Wailing," *Los Angeles Free Press,* 1967-68.

WORK IN PROGRESS: The Minstrel Machine (tentative title), a novel about the record industry; a paperback suspense series novel under pseudonym, Paul Kenyon.

SIDELIGHTS: Freedland told CA: "On moving from New York City to Los Angeles in 1967-68, for the first time I came in contact with rational people well-versed in the occult and psychic phenomena. Through magazine assignments my interest grew into a book. I examined the contemporary occult as a part of Pop Culture—which is my general specialty as a journalist and entertainment reporter."

* * *

FREEMAN, Roger A(nthony Wilson) 1928-

PERSONAL: Born May 11, 1928, in Ipswich, England; married Jean Margaret Blain; children: Sarah, Emma, Daniel. Education: Educated in secondary school in Colchester, England. Religion: Church of England. Home: Mayes Barn, Dedham, Colchester, Essex, England.

CAREER: Farmer; partner in family concern, F.F.C. Freeman & Sons, Colchester, Essex, England, 1959—.

WRITINGS—All nonfiction: The Mighty Eighth, Doubleday, 1970; Republic Thunderbolt, Ducimus, 1970; (with M.J.F. Bowyer and P. Berry) U.S. Army and Air Force Fighters, Harley Ford, 1972; American Bombers, Volume I, Profile Publications, 1972; Mustang at War, Doubleday, 1974; The U.S. Strategic Bomber, Macdonald & Jane's, 1975; Camouflage and Markings: U.S.A.A.F., Ducimus, 1975.

Monographs: Consolidated B-24 H & J Liberator, Profile, 1969; Boeing B-17G Fortress, Profile, 1972; Republic P-47N Thunderbolt, Profile, 1974. Also author of twelve monographs on U.S. Army Air Force aircraft markings during World War II, Ducimus, 1971-73.

Author of television documentaries. Contributor to magazines.

WORK IN PROGRESS: Fortress At War; More of the Mighty Eighth; three other books.

* * *

FREEMANTLE, Brian Harry 1936-

PERSONAL: Born June 10, 1936, in Southampton, England; son of Harold (a seaman) and Violet (Street) Freemantle; married Maureen Tipney (a television make-up artist), December 8, 1957; children: Victoria, Emma, Charlotte. Education: Educated in secondary school in Southampton, England. Politics: Liberal. Religion: Church of England. Home and office address: Pine Walk, Southampton, Hampshire, England. Agent: Jonathan Clewes, Jeffrey's Place, London, England.

CAREER: Evening News, London, England, reporter, 1959-61; Daily Express, London, assistant foreign editor, 1961-69; Daily Sketch, London, foreign editor, 1969-70; Daily Mail, London, foreign editor, 1971-75; writer, 1975—.

WRITINGS: Goodbye to an Old Friend (thriller), Putnam, 1973; Face Me When You Walk Away (novel), Putnam, 1974; The Man Who Wanted Tomorrow (thriller), Stein & Day, 1975; The November Man (thriller), J. Cape, 1976; Charlie Muffin (thriller), J. Cape, in press.

WORK IN PROGRESS: Clap Hands, Here Comes Charlie, a sequel to Charlie Muffin.

SIDELIGHTS: Freemantle has worked and traveled in twenty-six countries, including the Soviet Union, the United States, and Vietnam, where he was "ambushed on Viet-nam's Highway One at the moment peace was supposed to come into being."

* * *

FRENCH, Ashley
See ROBINS, Denise (Naomi)

* * *

FRIEBERT, Stuart (Alyn) 1931-

PERSONAL: Born July 12, 1931, in Milwaukee, Wis.; son of Edward (a pharmacist) and Gertrude (a pianist; maiden name, Garber) Friebert; married Diane Vreuls (a writer); children: Sarah, Stephen. Education: University of Wisconsin, Milwaukee, B.A., 1952; University of Wisconsin, Madison, M.A., 1953, Ph.D., 1957. Home: 172 Elm, Oberlin, Ohio 44074. Office: Creative Writing Program, Oberlin College, Oberlin, Ohio 44074.

CAREER: Mt. Holyoke College, South Hadley, Mass., professor of German, 1957-59; Harvard University, Cambridge, Mass., professor of German, 1959-61; Oberlin College, Oberlin, Ohio, professor of German and director of creative writing program, 1961—. Military service: U.S. Army, Military Intelligence, 1954-57. Member: Die Kogge (International German Writers Association). Awards, honors: Many poetry awards from magazines.

WRITINGS—Books of poems: Dreaming of Floods, Vanderbilt University Press, 1969; Kein Trinkwasser, Ateleier Verlag, 1969; Calming Down, Triskelion Press, 1970; Die Prokuristen kommen, Lenos Presse, 1972; Der gast und sei er noch so schlecht, Gilles & Francke, 1973; Up in Bed, Cleveland State University, 1974; Nicht Hinaus-lennen, Delp Verlag, 1975. Co-editor of Field.

WORK IN PROGRESS: Straw, a book of poems.

AVOCATIONAL INTERESTS: Higher mathematics, reading mythology, reading Guenter Eich.

* * *

FRIEDAN, Betty (Naomi) 1921-

PERSONAL: Born February 4, 1921, in Peoria, Ill.; daughter of Harry (a jeweler) and Miriam (Horowitz) Goldstein; married Carl Friedan, June, 1947 (divorced May, 1969); children: Daniel, Jonathan, Emily. Education: Smith College, A.B. (summa cum laude), 1942; further study at University of California, Berkeley, University of Iowa, and Esalen Institute. Politics: Democrat. Residence: New York, N.Y. Office: One Lincoln Plaza, New York, N.Y. 10023.

CAREER: Feminist organizer, writer, and lecturer at more than fifty universities, institutes, and professional associations world-wide, including Harvard Law School, University of Chicago, Vassar College, Smithsonian Institution, New York Bar Association, U.S. Embassy in Bogata, Columbia, and in Sweden, the Netherlands, Brazil, Israel, and Italy, 1960's—; New York University, New York City, teacher of non-fiction creative writing, 1965-70; New School for Social Research, New York City, teacher of non-fiction creative writing, 1965-70; teacher of course on women and urban problems, 1972-73; First Women's Bank & Trust Co., New York City, organizer and director, 1974—. Consultant to President's Commission on the Status of Women, 1964-65, Rockefeller Foundation project on education of women, 1965, University of California at Los Angeles project on continuing education for women, 1965, Philadelphia Psychiatric Center, 1972, and Harvard University, Kennedy Institute of Political Science, 1972; organizer of Women's Strike for Equality, 1970, International Feminist Congress, 1973, and Economic Think Tank for Women, 1974; visiting professor, Temple University, 1972, Yale University, 1974, and Queens College of the City University of New York, 1975.

MEMBER: National Organization for Women (NOW; founding president, 1966-70; member of board of directors of legal defense and education fund), National Women's Political Caucus (founder; member of national policy council, 1971-73), National Association to Repeal Abortion Laws (vice-president, 1972-74), National Conference of Public Service Employment (member of board of directors), Girl Scouts of the U.S.A. (member of national board), Women's Forum, American Sociological Association, Association for Humanistic Psychology, P.E.N., American Federation of Television and Radio Artists (AFTRA), American Society of Journalists and Authors, Phi Beta Kappa. *Awards, honors:* New World Foundation—New York State Education Department grant, 1958-62; Wilhelmina Drucker prize for contribution to emancipation of men and women, 1971; Humanist of the Year award, 1975; American Public Health Association citation, 1975.

WRITINGS: The Feminine Mystique, Norton, 1963, new edition, 1974; *It Changed My Life,* Random House, 1976; (contributor) Mary Lou Thompson, editor, *Voices of the New Feminism,* Beacon Press, 1970. Work represented in anthologies, including *Anatomy of Reading,* edited by L. L. Hackett and R. Williamson, McGraw, 1966; *Gentlemen, Scholars, and Scoundrels: Best of Harper's 1850 to the Present,* and *A College Treasury.* Writer of column, "Betty Friedan's Notebook," for *McCall's.* Contributor of articles to *Saturday Review, New York Times Magazine, Harper's, Redbook, Mademoiselle, Ladies Home Journal, Social Policy, Good Housekeeping, New York, Newsday, Working Woman,* and other periodicals. Contributing editor, *McCall's,* 1971-74; member of editorial board, *Present Tense.*

SIDELIGHTS: Speaking in her characteristically straightforward manner, Betty Friedan says of herself: "I'm nasty and I get mad but, my God, I'm absorbed in what I'm doing." Her role in the women's movement has been, and is, unquestionably vital. Jean Sprain Wilson observes, "For sheer impact on the lives of American women, no book written in the sixties compares with Betty Friedan's *Feminine Mystique,* sometimes called the *Uncle Tom's Cabin* of the women's liberation movement." Ms. Friedan has been called a revolutionary (a designation generally suggestive, to some people, of violence and irrationality). She is non-violent and highly rational. *Kirkus Reviews* says of Ms. Friedan's latest book, *It Changed My Life:* "it establishes her beyond question as an American revolutionary in the best tradition of impassioned reasonableness." Ms. Friedan's concept of revolution is constructive rather than destructive. She readily admits: "I *am* a revolutionary. This revolution is not what anyone else ever meant by revolution, but it will transform society in ways more radical and more life-enhancing than any other. I also happen to be an American pragmatist, a 'middle American' if you will, since I did grow up in Peoria, Illinois. And I think we have the power to make this revolution happen now, the power of fifty-five percent of us who are women, along with the growing number of men who support us."

Ms. Friedan presumes that the changes which will be sparked by the women's movement will be more easily accepted by the young, but she does not believe that revolution can be accomplished without the efforts of people of all ages. "For women in their thirties and forties, women who have patterned their entire lives on the idea that fulfillment can only come as wives and mothers, it has been painful, sometimes too painful, to change all that now. It's easier for the young to take a chance. But it's also easier for the young to fall into traps of pseudo-radical rhetoric, because they haven't experienced enough of the realities of life as women. The revolution will be carried by the young, but if left to the young alone, it might never be more than just rhetoric."

While some have argued that the scope and vision of the women's movement is too limited and its goals too self contained, Betty Friedan does not separate the problems of the world into problems of men and problems of women. "I would be bored to write only about women's liberation," she maintains. "Women are as involved with the life-and-death questions of war and peace, the crisis of the planet and our cities, the unknowns of theology and art and space, as they are with food and children and the home. I believe the women's liberation movement cannot remain isolated from everything else that's happening in America today; the liberation of women is germane to the agony of our whole nation: Until we free ourselves and men from the obsolete sex roles that imprison us both, the hostility between the sexes will continue to inflame the violence we're perpetrating in the world."

Friedan has traveled extensively throughout Europe, on a lecture tour. In 1971, she compared the U.S. with England: "If in liberating American women, we also liberate our men from that blustering world power machismo that keeps us courting death in Vietnam, perhaps we could make our cities green and beautiful and human, like London. Perhaps we could make our blood banks and medical care, abortion and marriage laws human. We might even begin to have human sex—and really human politics. England is an older nation, but it doesn't seem about to die. In fact, they seem less afraid of life and changes than we do."

Ms. Friedan feels it is unfortunate that the term "women's lib" has become a catch-all phrase. Some equate it with "gay liberation", or call it anti-male or anti-family. She has said: "I have always been uneasy about the pseudo-radical talk that includes the elimination of men, sex, and children among the aims of women's liberation. This makes for kickier headlines than do child-care centers or abortion reform, but it's just a way of dismissing the whole movement as a dirty joke. I don't believe homosexuals should be oppressed; people's sex lives are their own concern if they don't hurt anyone else . . . but it isn't the point of *this* movement." When asked if she felt that the promotion of such misconceptions are part of a maneuver to ruin the movement, Ms. Friedan replied: "To some extent there are genuine ideological differences. Some women in the movement genuinely feel—and I might disagree with them—that this is a class warfare against men, that childbearing, motherhood, and sex are the enemies. But it is my feeling that an overfocus on sexual issues, on sexual politics, as opposed to the condition of women in society in general, may have been accentuated by those who wish to immobilize the movement politically. According to the Gallup and Harris polls, the majority of American women, and even a majority of men support the basic goals of equality for women in society. But when it is made to seem that women must renounce the love of men or children, you alienate the majority of women . . ."

Ms. Friedan remains optimistic despite opposition. A strong sense of herself and of her strength makes her confident for the future. Commenting on her fiftieth birthday, she celebrates the extent to which she has grown personally, and looks forward to whatever is to follow. "I suddenly remember what day it was and can't help laughing. I have gotten over my fiftieth birthday. I'm fifty, on this magic day, in this age of Aquarius. I'm my age and I feel glorious. What's the point of making it if you can't celebrate being fifty? I celebrate putting it all together finally, this half century that's me, all of it . . . the net I've cast for 'herstory'—and what I am today: my body as it is, is me. . . . I have no dread now, of what opens ahead." Through all, Ms. Friedan appears to have kept her determination and her sense of humor. "When I realize what has to be done next, it seems impossibly big. Still, it is a lot of fun making a revolution happen."

The Schlesinger Library of Radcliff College maintains a collection of Ms. Friedan's personal papers.

BIOGRAPHICAL/CRITICAL SOURCES: Detroit News, August 17, 1966; *Senior Scholastic,* November 9, 1970; *McCall's,* June, 1971, August, 1971, February, 1974; *Ladies Home Journal,* June, 1975; *Saturday Review,* June, 1975; *Harper's Bazaar,* July, 1976; *Kirkus Reviews,* April 15, 1976.

* * *

FRIEDENBERG, Edgar Zodiag 1921-

PERSONAL: Born March 18, 1921, in New York, N.Y.; son of Edgar M. and Arline (Zodiag) Friedenberg. *Education:* Centenary College, B.S., 1938; Stanford University, M.A., 1939; University of Chicago, Ph.D., 1946. *Home address:* Conrad Rd., Hubbards, Nova Scotia, Canada. *Office:* Department of Education, Dalhousie University, Halifax, Nova Scotia, Canada.

CAREER: University of Chicago, Chicago, Ill., instructor, 1946-49, assistant professor of education, 1949-53; Brooklyn College (now of the City University of New York), Brooklyn, N.Y., assistant professor, 1953-60, associate professor of education, 1960-64; University of California, Davis, professor of sociology, 1964-67; State University of New York at Buffalo, professor of sociology and education, 1967-70; Dalhousie University, Halifax, Nova Scotia, professor of education, 1970—. *Member:* American Sociological Association, American Civil Liberties Union, Phi Delta Kappa.

WRITINGS: A Technique for Developing Courses in Physical Science Adapted to the Needs of Students at the Junior College Level, University of Chicago Press, 1946; (with Julius A. Roth) *Self-Perception in the University: A Study of Successful and Unsuccessful Graduate Students,* University of Chicago Press, 1954; *The Vanishing Adolescent,* Beacon Press, 1959; (with Carl Nordstrom) *Why Successful Students of the Natural Sciences Abandon Careers in Science,* Brooklyn College of the City University of New York, 1961; (with Nordstrom) *Influence of Resentment on Student Experience in Secondary School,* Brooklyn College of the City University of New York, 1965; *Coming of Age in America: Growth and Acquiescence,* Random House, 1965; *The Dignity of Youth and Other Atavisms,* Beacon Press, 1965; (with Nordstrom and A. Hilary Gold) *Society's Children,* Random House, 1967; (editor) *The Anti-American Generation,* Aldine, 1971, 2nd edition, Transaction Books, 1972; *Laing,* Fontana, 1973, published as *R. D. Laing,* Viking, 1974; *The Disposal of Liberty and Other Industrial Wastes,* Doubleday, 1975.

* * *

FRIEDMAN, Judi 1935-

PERSONAL: Born November 13, 1935, in Milwaukee,

Wis.; daughter of Roland Spuhler (a physician) and Florence (Schroeder) Cron; married Louis A. Friedman (a headmaster), December 28, 1957; children: Kimberly, Dana, Seth. *Education:* Vassar College, B.S., 1957; also attended St. Joseph's College, New York University, and Stanford University. *Home and office address:* 101 Lawton Rd., Canton, Conn. 06019.

CAREER: Writer. Elementary school teacher in Canton, Conn., 1958-63. President of Canton Educational Research Committee; member of board of directors of Canton Community Kindergarten and Trinity Episcopal Church Nursery School. Vice-president of Canton Land Trust; volunteer worker for Republican Party Minorities Division and Day Care Center for Minority Working Mothers; founder of Farmington Valley Chapter of People's Action for Clean Energy.

WRITINGS: The Story of Connecticut, privately printed, 1960; (editor with L. K. Porritt) *Tales of Early Life in Connecticut,* privately printed, 1960; *Jelly Jam, the People Preserver* (self-illustrated elementary school text), with teacher's guide, Educational Methods, 1972; *The ABC of a Summer Pond* (juvenile), Johnny Reads, 1975; *The Biting Book* (juvenile), Prentice-Hall, 1975; *The Eel's Strange Journey* (juvenile), Crowell, 1975. Author of environmental television commercials, for Communications Specialists; author of environmental articles.

SIDELIGHTS: Judi Friedman writes that her concern for the environment focuses on "alternate energy (sun, wind, wood)" and that she is "violently opposed to nuclear energy." She adds that she believes in "racial equality, children's rights. I want to further understanding of each other, of earth, and of all creatures who inhabit the earth." *Avocational interests:* The outdoors, sports, animals, European and Caribbean travel.

* * *

FRIEDMAN, Ken(neth Scott)

PERSONAL: Born in New London, Conn.; son of Abraham Morris and Ruth (Shifreen) Friedman. *Education:* Attended California Western University, 1965, Shimer College, 1965-66; San Francisco State University, B.A., 1971, M.A., 1971; United States International University, Ph.D., 1976. *Home and office:* 6361 Elmhurst Dr., San Diego, Calif. 92120.

CAREER: Artist and writer. Work has been exhibited in one-man shows throughout Europe, North and South America; has been included in group exhibitions in museums, art galleries around the world; visiting artist and critic at universities, including University of South Carolina, University of Nevada, University of Colorado, University of Tennessee, and University of California. Instructor, San Francisco State College Experimental College, 1966-69, San Francisco State College (now University), 1967-68, and Free University of Berkeley, 1970-71; adjunct professor, Eastern Washington State College, 1974; visiting professor, East Tennessee State University, 1975; member of faculty, Starr King School for the Ministry, summer, 1976. Executive director and editor-in-chief, Fluxus West, 1966-76; general manager, Something Else Press, 1971; executive director, Institute for Advanced Studies in Contemporary Art, 1975—. Lecturer.

MEMBER: College Art Association, American Anthropological Association, American Sociological Association, American Association of Museums, Society for Esthetic Research, Society for the Anthropology and Sociology of

Art, American Society for Aesthetics, Aktual, Western Association of Art Museums. *Awards, honors:* F. G. Fischer Award, 1966, for essay; Governor's Award, State of Idaho, 1975; work and projects have been supported under grants from the National Endowment for the Arts and other public and private agencies.

WRITINGS: This Breathing Miracle, Series Point Seventy (Berkeley, Calif.), 1969; *The Stone Forest: An Existential Approach to Education* (limited edition), privately printed, 1971; *The Aesthetics,* Beau Geste Press (Devon, England), 1973; *Notes: A Ready Hand Novel,* Edition After Hand (Skraldhede, Denmark), 1974; *A Conversation with Arman,* The Henry Gallery, University of Washington, 1974; *James Edwards* (catalogue), Grossmont College Art Gallery, La Mamelle Art Center, and the Everson Museum, 1976.

Editor: *Art Folio,* Religious Arts Guild (Boston, Mass.), 1971; *International Contact List of the Arts,* Fluxus West and Image Bank, 1972; *International Sources,* Source Magazine and Composer/Performer Editions, 1974.

Contributor: J. F. Bory, editor, *Once Again,* New Directions, 1968; John Cage, editor, *Notations,* Something Else Press, 1968; Wolfgang Feelich, editor, *Sammlung Feelich,* Museum am Ostwall, 1970; Harold Szeemann and Hanns Sohm, editors, *Fluxus and Happenings,* Kolnischer Kunstverein, 1970; Jorge Glusberg, editor, *Arte de Sistemas,* Museum of Modern Art (Buenos Aires), 1971; Joseph Beuys, editor, *Joseph Beuys Multiples,* Edition Jorg Schellmann, 1972; Jean-Marc Poinsot, editor, *Mail Art: Communications a Distance,* Editions C.E.D.I.C. (Paris, France), 1972; Richard Kostelanetz, editor, *Breakthrough Fictioneers,* Something Else Press, 1972; Lucy Lippard, editor, *Six Years: The Dematerialization of Art,* Praeger, 1973; Nam June Paik, editor, *Videa and Videology,* Everson Museum of Art, 1974; Terry Reid and G. Kerr, editors, *Inch Art Issue,* University of Auckland, 1975.

Also illustrator of *Thomas Onetwo,* Something Else Press, 1971. Author of booklets, pamphlets and monographs. Contributor to magazines and journals, including *Artweek, FlashArt, Art and Artists, Coda, La Mamelle, Ben, Front, Intermedia, Open Process, International Times, Tout* and *Approches.* Founder, *Contemporary Art/Southeast;* consultant to *Who's Who in American Art* and *The American Art,* 1973—.

WORK IN PROGRESS: Society, Art and Knowledge, a collection of essays and papers on the sociology of art.

SIDELIGHTS: Ken Friedman told *CA:* "I have given my concern to the arts of the new mentality which critic Dick Higgins termed the *intermedia.* I am concerned not only with form as an issue in art and literature, but with content. A multi-disciplinary approach to the arts emerges when one seeks forms sufficient to the expression of contemporary content. In the early days of the century, it became evident that word or picture or sound alone would not always suffice.

"My background in the social and behaviorial sciences naturally led me to actions and roles as a participant in my culture, and in the social world of the arts. This leads to the form of critical studies which embraces not only art and literature theory and criticism, but the history and sociology of art. As much of my work has taken place as a critic and writer as it has as a producing artist and creative writer. The forms seem to work together, giving balance and perspective to full field of thought and action."

Henry Hunt commented of Friedman's wide range of con-

cerns with art. He wrote: "Friedman's work continually seeks to involve the viewer and to extend the audience it reaches. Whether his physical materials are steel, paper or a whisper, his work is firmly rooted in fundamental service to a comprehensive art idea. His art is as portable as thought, as substantial as the total physical environment in which he works."

Peter Frank also commented of Friedman's embracing of disciplines in the service of his art. "It is not easy," says Frank, "for a critic to deal with someone who, in his art and his career, so bluntly ignores all distinctions between aesthetic and social disciplines, no matter how intermedial current art and literature have become. Friedman produces many art objects, but, when he visits one of the regions so far from New York where he spends much of his time, he serves also as a sociologist, philosopher, anthropologist, art historian, theologian and poet. He has written extensively on ethical and philosophical problems, has authored much verse (which at its best is delicate and plangent), and maintains extensive critical contacts with artists around the world about whose work he writes and lectures as much as his own."

Friedman himself explains rather simply his comprehensive approach to art. He states: "The world changes too rapidly to afford any human being the luxury of an overly specialized career. I see a world around us which demands that we be broadly-educated humanists and scholars—an attitude which is once again attaining currency even in the scientific community. The world demands of us activism, advocacy in service of duties imposed on us by our culture and in the human race. I feel that I am to some degree responsible for the conduct of that discourse which collectively comprises our world."

In 1968, the University of California at San Diego established in its Mandeville Department of Special Collections a unit entitled The Ken Friedman Collection, which houses his manuscripts, writings, and a large selection of materials on modern literature and art. In 1975, the Archives of American Art of the Smithsonian Institution began to collect Friedman's papers as an artist and critic, as well as photographs and documents.

BIOGRAPHICAL/CRITICAL SOURCES: Thomas Albright, *A Dialogue with Ken Friedman,* Joslyn Art Museum, 1973; Henry Hunt, editor, *Ken Friedman,* Gallery of Visual Art, University of Montana; Radford Thomas, editor, *Ken Friedman: Sightings,* Department of Art, Eastern Washington State College, 1974, revised edition, Department of Art, East Tennessee State University, 1975; John M. Armleder, editor, *Ken Friedman at Ecart,* Ecart Publications (Geneva, Switzerland), 1975; Allen Dodworth, editor, *Ken Friedman,* Boise Gallery of Art, 1975; Marilyn Ravicz, *Ken Friedman,* edited by George Moldovan, Slocumb Gallery, East Tennessee State University, 1975; *Kunstforum,* February-April, 1975.

*   *   *

FRIESS, Horace L(eland) 1900-1975

PERSONAL: Born March 4, 1900, in New York, N.Y.; son of Louis G. and Louise S. (Jagle) Friess; married Ruth Adler, June 25, 1923; children: Anne Friess Kirschner. *Education:* Columbia University, A.B., 1918, Ph.D., 1926. *Residence:* New York, N.Y.

CAREER: Columbia University, New York, N.Y., instructor, 1921-26, assistant professor, 1926-36, associate professor, 1936-46, professor of philosophy, 1946-64, Joseph L.

Buttenwieser Professor of Human Relations, 1964-66, professor emeritus, 1966-75, chairman of department of religion, 1962-65. Executive officer of department of religion at Barnard College, 1940-47; faculty member at Elliott Institute; chairman of committee on the history of religion for American Council of Learned Societies.

MEMBER: American Philosophical Association, American Ethical Association, Society for the Scientific Study of Religion (past president), New York Society for Ethical Culture (member of board of directors, 1950-75), Phi Beta Kappa. *Awards, honors:* Cutting traveling fellowship, University of Heidelberg, 1924-25; Guggenheim fellowship, 1942-43.

WRITINGS: (With Herbert W. Schneider) *Religion in Various Cultures,* Holt, 1932, Johnson Reprint, 1965; *Reconstruction of Ethical Ideals,* American Ethical Union, 1951; (translator, editor, and author of introduction) Friedrich Ernst Daniel Schleiermacher, *Soliloquies,* Open Court, 1957; (editor) Helmuth von Glasenapp, *Non-Christian Religions A to Z,* Grosset, 1963. Also editor of Felix Adler, *Our Part in This World,* 1946. Contributor to scholarly journals. Editor of *Review of Religion,* 1942-58.

OBITUARIES: New York Times, October 13, 1975.*

(Died October 12, 1975, in New York, N.Y.)

* * *

FRIIS, Harald T(rap) 1893-1976

February 22, 1893—June 15, 1976; Danish-born American electrical engineer, pioneer in radio communications, and author of an autobiography. Obituaries: *New York Times,* June 17, 1976.

* * *

FRISBY, Terence (Peter Michael) 1932-

PERSONAL: Born November 28, 1932, in London, England; son of William Alfred (a railway supervisor) and Kathleen (a cashier; maiden name Casely) Frisby; married Christine Vecchione, August 28, 1963 (divorced 1970); children: Dominic. *Education:* Attended Central School of Speech Training and Dramatic Art (London), 1955-57. *Politics:* "Left of centre." *Religion:* Athiest. *Home:* 52 Cloncurry St., London SW6, England. *Agent:* Harvey Unna, 14 Beaumont Mews, Marylebone High Street, London W1, England.

CAREER: Worked as a salesman, laborer, lathe operator, and waiter; acted and directed in United Kingdom under name Terence Holland, 1957-69; professional actor, director, 1957—. Writer. *Member:* Wentworth Golf Club. *Awards, honors:* Best British Screenplay award from Writers Guild of Great Britain, 1970, for "There's a Girl in My Soup."

WRITINGS—Plays: *The Subtopians* (3-act; first produced in London at Guildford Theatre, March, 1962), Samuel French, 1964; *There's a Girl in My Soup* (3-act; first produced in London at Globe Theatre, June, 1966), Samuel French, 1968; *The Bandwagon* (2-act; first produced in London at Mermaid Theatre, November, 1969), Samuel French, 1973; "It's All Right if I Do It," first produced in Leicestershire at Haymarket Theatre, January, 1977. Also author of screenplay, "There Is a Girl in My Soup," 1970. Author of several teleplays for B.B.C., including "Guilty," 1964; "Public Eye" series, 1964; "Take Care of Madam," 1965; "Adam Adamant" series, 1966; "More Deadly Than the Sword," 1966; "Don't Forget the Basics," 1967; "Lucky Feller" series, 1976.

WORK IN PROGRESS: An autobiography.

* * *

FROST, Everett L(loyd) 1942-

PERSONAL: Born October 17, 1942, in Salt Lake City, Utah; son of Henry H. (a sociologist) and Ruth S. (a university administrator) Frost; married Janet Owens (an anthropologist), March 26, 1967; children: Noreen Karyn. *Education:* University of Utah, B.A., 1965; University of Oregon, Ph.D., 1970. *Politics:* Democrat. *Religion:* Protestant. *Home:* 208 Oklahoma Dr., Portales, N.M. 88130. *Office address:* P.O. Box 2213, Eastern New Mexico University, Portales, N.M. 88130.

CAREER: Eastern New Mexico University, Portales, assistant professor, 1970-74, associate professor of anthropology, 1974-75; University of Hawaii, Honolulu, visiting associate professor of anthropology, 1975-76; Eastern New Mexico University, associate professor of anthropology, 1976—. Has conducted field research in Utah, Wyoming, California, Fiji, Hawaii, and Samoa. *Member:* American Anthropological Association (fellow), Current Anthropology (associate), School of American Research, Society of American Archaeology, Polynesian Society, Anthropological Society of Washington, Phi Kappa Phi. *Awards, honors:* National Science Foundation grant for work in Fiji, 1968-69.

WRITINGS: Archaeological Excavations of Fortified Sites on Taveuni, Fiji, University Press of Hawaii, 1974; (with E. Adamson Hoebel) *Cultural and Social Anthropology,* McGraw, 1976. Co-author of study guide and instructor's manual, Hoebel, *Anthropology: The Study of Man,* McGraw, 1972.

* * *

FRY, E(dwin) Maxwell 1899-
(Maxwell Fry)

PERSONAL: Born August 2, 1899, in Wallasey, Cheshire, England; son of Ambrose and Lydia (Thompson) Fry; married Ethel Speakman, 1927 (divorced); married Jane Beverly Drew, 1942; children: (first marriage) one daughter; (second marriage) two stepdaughters. *Education:* University of Liverpool, B.Arch., 1923. *Home:* 63 Gloucester Pl., London W1H 4DJ, England; and The Lake House, Rowfont, Worthing, Sussex, England.

CAREER: Architect; partner of Adams, Thompson & Fry, 1927-34, Gropis & Fry, 1934-46; in private practice, 1936-39; town planning adviser to Resident Minister for West Africa, 1943-45; partner of Maxwell Fry & Jane Drew, 1945-50, Fry, Drew & Lasdun, 1951-58, Fry, Drew & Partners, beginning 1958; now partner of Fry, Drew, Knight & Creamer. Professor of architecture, Royal Academy of Arts. Senior architect to New Capital, Chandigarh, India, 1951-54. Former member of Royal Fine Art Commission. *Military service:* British Army, King's Liverpool Regiment, 1917-19, Royal Engineers, 1939-44. *Member:* Royal Institute of British Architects (fellow; vice-president, 1961-62), Royal Academy, American Institute of Architects (honorary fellow), Town Planning Institute (fellow), Academie Flamande (corresponding member), Garrick Club. *Awards, honors:* Commander of the Order of the British Empire, 1953; Royal Gold Medal for Architecture, 1964; LL.D. from Ibadan University, 1966.

WRITINGS: (With Thomas Adams) *Recent Advances in Town Planning,* Macmillan, 1932; *Fine Building,* Faber, 1944; (with wife, Jane B. Drew) *Architecture for Children,*

Allen & Unwin, 1944; (with J. B. Drew) *Village Housing in the Tropics,* Lund Humphries, 1947, U.S. Department of Housing and Development, 1967; (with J. B. Drew) *Tropical Architecture in the Humid Zone,* Reinhold, 1956; (with J. B. Drew) *Tropical Architecture in the Dry and Humid Zones,* Reinhold, 1964; *Art in a Machine Age: A Critique of Contemporary Life Through the Medium of Architecture,* Methuen, 1969, distributed in United States by Barnes & Noble; *Tapestry and Architecture,* Keepsake Press, 1970; (under name Maxwell Fry) *Autobiographical Sketches,* Technical Impex, 1975. Also author, with Kenneth William Farms, of *Town Planning Scheme for Freetown,* 1945. Contributor to architecture journals.

AVOCATIONAL INTERESTS: Reading, drawing, gardening.

BIOGRAPHICAL/CRITICAL SOURCES: London, January, 1970; Maxwell Fry, *Autobiographical Sketches,* Technical Impex, 1975.

*   *   *

FRY, Maxwell
   See FRY, E(dwin) Maxwell

*   *   *

FRYD, Norbert   1913-1976

April 21, 1913—March 18(?), 1976; Czechoslovakian journalist, novelist, and author of books on Mexico and Latin America. Obituaries: *New York Times,* March 19, 1976.

*   *   *

FUCHIDA, Mitsuo   1902(?)-1976

1902(?)—May 30, 1976; Japanese navy pilot and author of religious tracts and war histories. Obituaries: *New York Times,* May 31, 1976; *Time,* June 14, 1976.

*   *   *

FULFORD, Roger (Thomas Baldwin)   1902-

PERSONAL: Born November 24, 1902, in Flaxley, Gloucestershire, England; son of Frederick John and Emily Constance (Ellis) Fulford; married Sibell Adeane Lyttelton, 1937. *Education:* Worcester College, Oxford, M.A., 1941. *Politics:* Liberal. *Home:* Barbon Manor, Carnforth, Lancashire, England.

CAREER: Called to the Bar, 1931; free-lance writer, 1931—. Member of editorial staff, *London Times,* London, England, 1933-39; War Office, London, assistant censor, 1939-40, civil assistant, 1940-42; assistant private secretary, Office of Secretary of State for Air, London, 1942-45. Lecturer in English, King's College, University of London, 1937-48. Liberal candidate for Woodbridge, England, 1929, for Holderness, England, 1945, and Rochdale, England, 1950; president of Liberal party, 1964-65. *Member:* Boodle's Club. *Awards, honors: Evening Standard* book prize, 1959, for *The Liberal Case;* Commander of Royal Victorian Order, 1970.

WRITINGS: The Wicked Uncles: The Father of Queen Victoria and His Brothers, Putnam, 1933 (published in England as *Royal Dukes: The Father and Uncles of Queen Victoria,* Duckworth, 1933), revised edition, Collins, 1973; *George the Fourth,* Putnam, 1935, revised edition, Duckworth, 1949, Capricorn Books, 1963; (editor with Lytton Strachey) Charles C. F. Greville, *The Greville Memoirs, 1814-1860,* eight volumes, Macmillan, 1938.

The Right Honourable Gentleman: A Satire, J. Murray, 1945; *Five Decades of the British Electric Traction Company,* privately printed, 1946; *The Prince Consort,* Macmillan, 1949, St. Martin's, 1966.

Queen Victoria, Collins, 1951; *The Pictorial Life Story of King George the Sixth: The Story of the Beloved Monarch,* Pitkin Pictorials for *Daily Graphic,* 1952; *Glyn's, 1753-1953: Six Generations in Lombard Street,* St. Martin's, 1953; *The Sixth Decade, 1946-1956* (British Electric Traction Co.), privately printed, 1956; *Votes for Women: The Story of a Struggle,* Faber, 1957; *The Liberal Case,* Penguin, 1959.

Hanover to Windsor, Macmillan, 1960; (editor) Ellis Cornelia Knight, *The Autobiography of Miss Knight, Lady Companion to Princess Charlotte,* Kimber & Co., 1960; (editor) *Dearest Child: Letters between Queen Victoria and the Princess Royal, 1858-1861,* Evans Brothers, 1964, Holt, 1965; (contributor) C. H. Wilkinson, *C. H. Wilkinson, 1888-1960,* Oxford University Press, 1965; *Samuel Whitbread, 1764-1815: A Study in Opposition,* Macmillan, 1967; *The Trial of Queen Caroline,* Batsford, 1967, Stein & Day, 1968; (editor) *Dearest Mama: Letters between Queen Victoria and the Crown Princess of Prussia, 1861-1864,* Evans Brothers, 1968, Holt, 1969; (author of introduction and text) Harold Town, *Drawings,* McClelland & Stewart, 1969.

(Editor) *Your Dear Letter: Private Correspondence of Queen Victoria and the Crown Princess of Prussia, 1865-1871,* Scribner, 1971; (editor) *Darling Child: Private Correspondence of Queen Victoria and the Crown Prince of Prussia, 1871-1878,* Evans, 1976. Author of pamphlets, *Osbert Sitwell,* British Council, 1951, and *The Member of His Constituency,* Ramsay Muir Educational Trust (Surrey, England), 1957.

*   *   *

FULLER, Harold   1940-

PERSONAL: Born September 9, 1940, in Pekin, Ill.; son of Harold Fray (in U.S. Army) and Frances (Turk) Fuller. *Education:* Kansas State University, student, 1961-62; Southern Illinois University, B.S., 1965. *Home address:* Route 1, Bigfork, Mont. 59911. *Agent:* Charles Neighbors, 240 Waverly Pl., New York, N.Y. 10014. *Office:* Fuller Enterprises, 1737 York Ave., New York, N.Y. 10028.

CAREER/WRITINGS: Pekin Daily Times, Pekin, Ill., police reporter, 1965-68; *Sporting News,* St. Louis, Mo., associate editor, 1968-70; *Suburban Newspapers,* St. Louis, Mo., sports editor and columnist, 1970-71; *Virginian-Pilot,* Norfolk, Va., copy editor and columnist, 1971-73; Fuller Enterprises, New York, N.Y., author of columns (syndicated to more than one hundred newspapers) "The Music Box," "In Your Ear," and "Spin Off," all 1971—. Member of Yorkville Community Football Board of Directors and St. Louis County American Legion baseball program. *Military service:* U.S. Army, radio broadcast specialist, 1960-63. *Member:* American Newspaper Guild, Overseas Press Club.

SIDELIGHTS: Fuller has interviewed sports figures and entertainers including Bob Gibson, Bobby Orr, and Albert King. He comments: "I am interested in the entertainment industry and feel strongly that we need a diversion from the confusions of everyday life. I am also interested in history and like to research same. I think I could be happy as a historian."

FUNABASHI, Seiichi 1904(?)-1976

1904(?)—January, 1976; Japanese best-selling novelist and playwright. Obituaries: *AB Bookman's Weekly,* March 1, 1976.

* * *

FUNIGIELLO, Philip J. 1939-

PERSONAL: Born June 28, 1939, in New York; son of Pasquale R. (a laborer) and Frances (Petruzzelli) Funigiello. *Education:* Hunter College of the City University of New York, A.B., 1961; University of California, Berkeley, M.A., 1962; New York University, Ph.D., 1966. *Home:* 101 Lawnes Cir., Williamsburg, Va. 23185. *Office:* College of William & Mary, 334 Morton Hall, Williamsburg, Va. 23185.

CAREER: College of William & Mary, Williamsburg, Va., assistant professor, 1966-71, associate professor of history, 1971—. Fulbright lecturer, University of Genoa, 1977. *Member:* American Historical Association, Organization of American Historians, Urban History Group, Phi Beta Kappa, Delta Kappa Pi. *Awards, honors:* Fellowship from National Endowment for the Humanities, 1968.

WRITINGS: Toward a National Power Policy: The New Deal and the Electric Utility Industry, 1933-1941, University of Pittsburgh Press, 1973. Contributor to journals, including *Social Science Quarterly.*

WORK IN PROGRESS: Federal-Urban Relations in World War Two, for University of Tennessee Press.

* * *

GABEL, Medard 1946-

PERSONAL: Born January 24, 1946, in Evanston, Ill.; son of Medard Anthony (a banker) and Dorothy (a teacher; maiden name, Wenthe) Gabel. *Education:* University of Illinois, student, 1965-66; Southern Illinois University, B.A., 1972; International College, Los Angeles, Calif., Ph.D., 1977. *Home:* Colonial Pennsylvania Plantation, Ridley Creek State Park, Edgement, Pa. 19028. *Office:* R. Buckminster Fuller, 3500 Market St., Philadelphia, Pa. 19104.

CAREER: R. Buckminster Fuller, Philadelphia, Pa., research associate and archivist, 1969—. Co-director of Earth Metabolic Design, Inc., 1972—; member of board of directors of Upland Hills Ecological Awareness Center, 1975—. *Member:* American Association for the Advancement of Science, World Future Society, Society for International Development.

WRITINGS: Energy, Earth, and Everyone, Straight Arrow Books, 1975; (with Howard Brown and Robert Cook) *Environmental Design Science Primer,* Earth Metabolic Design, Inc., 1975.

WORK IN PROGRESS: Ho-Ping: Food for Everyone, a book on world food problems and prospects, to accompany *Energy, Earth, and Everyone.*

SIDELIGHTS: Gabel writes: "The world has more than four billion people. At least half of these people have inadequate food, shelter, clothing, health care, education, employment, and recreational opportunities and access to decision making that affects their lives. Often times the world is a great place to visit but not to live in. It can be greatly improved. There are enough resources on the earth for everyone. We know how to take care of everyone on earth at a standard of living higher than anyone currently enjoys. My books (so far) have shown how this could come about."

GABRIEL, Mabel McAfee 1884(?)-1976

1884(?)—February 5, 1976; British-born artist, philanthropist, and author. Obituaries: *New York Times,* February 7, 1976; *AB Bookman's Weekly,* March 1, 1976.

* * *

GAEDEKE, Ralph M(ortimer) 1941-

PERSONAL: Born May 25, 1941, in East Prussia; son of Horst F. and Margot (Boltz) Gaedeke; married Johanna V. House (an administrative assistant), June 19, 1965; children: one. *Education:* University of Washington, Seattle, B.A., 1964, M.A., 1965, Ph.D., 1969. *Home:* 237 Hartnell Pl., Sacramento, Calif. 95825. *Office:* School of Business and Public Administration, California State University at Sacramento, 6000 J. St., Sacramento, Calif. 95819.

CAREER: University of Saskatchewan, Saskatoon, instructor in business administration, 1965-66; California State University, Sacramento, associate professor of marketing and international business, 1969-71; University of Alaska, Anchorage, associate professor of business administration, 1971-73; California State University, Sacramento, associate professor, 1973-74, professor of marketing and international business, 1974—. Summer professor at University of Alaska, 1974. Consultant to Small Business Administration and private corporations in Anchorage, 1971-72 and 1974-75, and Sacramento, 1973-74 and 1974-75; consultant to Community Economic Development Corp., Anchorage, 1974-75. *Member:* American Marketing Association, Academy of International Business, American Council on Consumer Interests, Beta Gamma Sigma, Delta Sigma Pi.

WRITINGS: (With Guy Gordon, John Wheatley, John Hallag, and D. McNabb) *The Impact of a Consumer Credit Limitation Law—Washington State: Initiative 245* (monograph), University of Washington Press, 1970; (with Warren W. Etcheson) *Consumerism: Viewpoints from Business, Government and the Consumer Interest,* Canfield Press, 1972; (with Dean F. Olson and Jack W. Peterson) *A Study of the Impact of Ten Rural Consumer Cooperative Stores* (monograph), Office of Economic Opportunity, 1973; (with Eugene Eaton) *Dimensions of Relevant Markets: The Case of Urethane Building Insultation in Alaska* (monograph), Upjohn, 1975; *Village Development Alternatives for Old Chitina* (monograph), AHTNA Regional Corp., 1975; *Marketing in Private and Public Nonprofit Organizations,* Goodyear Publishing, in press. Contributor of book reviews to professional journals.

WORK IN PROGRESS: Small Business Management: Operations and Profiles.

* * *

GAGNIER, Ed 1936-

PERSONAL: Surname is pronounced Gone-yae; born February 1, 1936, in Canada; son of Rene and Alphonsine (Riviat) Gagnier; married Carolyn Calvin, August 9, 1958; children: Bonnie, Becky. *Education:* University of Michigan, B.S., 1958, M.A., 1959. *Office:* Department of Physical Education, Iowa State University, Ames, Iowa 50011.

CAREER: High school coach and teacher of physical education in the public schools of Brown Deer, Wis., 1959-60; Iowa State University, Ames, assistant professor, 1964-67, associate professor of physical education, 1967—, head gymnastics coach, 1961—. Chairman of National Collegiate Athletic Association Gymnastics rules committee, 1968-75; member, Olympic Gymnastics Committee, 1970-74.

WRITINGS: Inside Gymnastics, Regnery, 1974.

WORK IN PROGRESS: Philosophy of Coaching: Gymnastics.

SIDELIGHTS: Gagnier was a member of the 1956 Canadian Olympic gymnastics team.

*   *   *

GALINSKY, Ellen   1942-

PERSONAL: Born April 24, 1942, in Pittsburgh, Pa.; daughter of Melvin H. (a businessman) and Leora (a businesswoman; maiden name, Osgood) May; married Norman Galinsky (an artist), August 15, 1965; children: Philip Andrew, Lara Elizabeth. *Education:* Vassar College, A.B., 1964; Bank Street College of Education, M.S.Ed., 1970. *Home address:* Lawrence Lane, Palisades, N.Y. 10964. *Agent:* Virginia Barber, 44 Greenwich Ave., New York, N.Y. 10011. *Office:* Bank Street College of Education, 610 West 112th St., New York, N.Y. 10025.

CAREER: Teacher in private elementary school in New York, N.Y., 1964-68; Bank Street College of Education, New York, N.Y., film maker, writer, and photographer, 1968—. Founder of Family Center at Bank Street; free-lance photographer. *Member:* Authors Guild of Authors League of America.

WRITINGS: Catbird (juvenile; with own photographs), Coward, 1971; *Beginnings* (nonfiction), Houghton, 1976. Contributor to magazines, including *Parents' Magazine* and *Redbook.*

WORK IN PROGRESS: A book on child care in the United States, with William H. Hooks, including her own photographs, for Houghton; a photographic book for children, for Putnam.

SIDELIGHTS: Ellen Galinsky writes: "I am interested in nature, in how natural forces wear away at and shape each other; I am interested in how the natural world relates to the human ones; I am interested in people and how they change; I am interested in how institutions affect people; and I am interested in myths and realities. I write and photograph to probe the dualities that lie at the end of every search."

*   *   *

GALLAGHER, Buell Gordon   1904-

PERSONAL: Born February 4, 1904, in Rankin, Ill.; son of Elmer David (a clergyman) and Elma Maryel (Poole) Gallagher; married June Lucille Sampson, September 1, 1927; children: Helen Maryel (Mrs. Sidney S. Herman), Barbara Lucille (Mrs. F. Tomasson Jannuzi). *Education:* Carleton College, B.A., 1925; Union Theological Seminary, New York, N.Y., B.D., 1929; London School of Economics and Political Science, further graduate study, 1929-30; Columbia University, Ph.D., 1939. *Residence:* Granite Springs, N.Y. 10527.

CAREER: Doane College, Crete, Neb., instructor in economics, 1925-26; ordained Congregational minister, 1929; National Interseminary Movement, student division of Young Men's Christian Association (YMCA), national secretary, 1930-31; pastor of Congregational church in Passaic, N.J., 1931-33; Talladega College, Talladega, Ala., president, 1933-43; Pacific School of Religion, Berkeley, Calif., professor of Christian ethics, 1944-49; U.S. Office of Education, Washington, D.C., consultant, 1950-51, assistant commissioner, 1951-52; College of the City of New York (now City College of the City University of New York), New York, N.Y., president, 1952-61; chancellor, California State Colleges, 1961-62; City College of the City University

of New York, president, 1962-69, president emeritus, 1970—; writer, 1969—. Chairman of U.S. general committee of World University Service, 1953-66, chairman of international assembly, 1962-66; member of Permanent Panel on Educational and Corporate Relations, 1956—; member of Commission on Religion and Race of National Council of Churches, 1962—. Member of board of directors of Manhattanville Community Centers, Herman Muehlstein Foundation, and Union Theological Seminary, New York, N.Y. Democratic nominee for U.S. Congress, 8th district, Calif. 1948.

MEMBER: National Association for the Advancement of Colored People (member of board of directors, 1934—, vice-chairman of board, 1971—), Phi Beta Kappa, Delta Sigma Rho. *Awards, honors:* Honorary degrees include LL.D. from Doane College, 1953, Columbia University, Lincoln University, and Brandeis University, all 1954, Carleton College, 1959, Hebrew Union University, 1961, and Tuskegee Institute, 1963; L.H.D. from Wagner College, 1954, Moravian College, 1958, Adelphi College, 1966, Alfred University and Iona College, both 1967, Akron University, 1970, City College of the City University of New York, 1972, and Talladega College, 1973; Litt.D. from University of Cincinnati, 1957; D.D. from Oberlin College, 1943, Pacific School of Religion, 1970; chevalier of Legion of Honor; outstanding civilian service medal from U.S. Army, 1961; John H. Finley Medal from City College of the City University of New York Alumni Association, 1962; gold medal from *San Francisco Chronicle,* 1961, Amistad Medal, 1968; Martin Luther King, Jr. Medal from City College of the City University of New York, 1969.

WRITINGS: American Caste and the Negro College, Columbia University Press, 1938, Gordian, 1966; *Portrait of a Pilgrim: A Search for the Christian Way in Race Relations,* Friendship Press, 1946; *Color and Conscience: The Irrepressible Conflict,* Harper, 1946; *A Preface to the Study of Utopias,* Antioch College Press, 1960, Folcroft, 1970; *Controversy: Eristic and Heuristic* (pamphlet), American Association of University Professors, 1965; *A Clear and Compelling Vision* (pamphlet), American Association of University Professors, 1966; *The Continuing Revolution* (pamphlet), City College of the City University of New York, 1968; (editor and contributor) *College and the Black Student: National Association for the Advancement of Colored People Tract for the Times,* Committee on Campus Troubles, National Association for the Advancement of Colored People, 1971; *Campus in Crisis,* Harper, 1974.

BIOGRAPHICAL/CRITICAL SOURCES: New York Post, June 22, 1952; *New York Herald Tribune,* February 15, 1953, March 23, 1953; *Newsweek,* March 2, 1953.

*   *   *

GALLAGHER, Dorothy   1935-

PERSONAL: Born April 28, 1935, in New York, N.Y.; daughter of Isidor and Bella (Rendar) Rosen. *Education:* Hunter College (now of the City University of New York), student, 1952-54. *Home:* 215 Bowery, New York, N.Y. 10002. *Agent:* Jay Acton, 288 West 12th St., New York, N.Y. 10014.

CAREER: Screen Stars, New York, N.Y., editor, 1960-64; *Redbook,* New York City, associate editor, 1966-70; writer, 1970—.

WRITINGS: Hannah's Daughters (social history), Crowell, 1976. Contributor of articles and reviews to national magazines and newspapers, including *Harper's, Glamour, Money, Playboy, New York Times,* and *Village Voice.*

SIDELIGHTS: Dorothy Gallagher writes: "I am interested in the connections, often hidden, between personal life and the workings of society, and that is what I most often write about." Avocational interests: Photography.

* * *

GALLAGHER, Patricia

PERSONAL: Born in Lockhart, Tex.; daughter of Frank (in construction business) and Martha (Rhody) Bienek; married James D. Gallagher (a television engineer; died, 1966); children: James C. Education: Attended Trinity University, San Antonio, Tex., 1951. Residence: San Antonio, Tex. Agent: Scott Meredith Literary Agency, Inc., 845 Third Ave., New York, N.Y. 10019.

CAREER: Writer, 1949—. Limited operator for KTSA-Radio, 1950-51; has appeared on television and radio programs in Texas.

WRITINGS—Novels: The Sons and the Daughters, Messner, 1961; Answer to Heaven, Avon, 1964; The Fires of Brimstone, Avon, 1966; Shannon, Avon, 1967; Shadows of Passion, Avon, 1971; Summer of Sighs, Avon, 1971; The Thicket, Avon, 1974; Castles in the Air (historical novel), Avon, 1976.

WORK IN PROGRESS: Two historical novels.

SIDELIGHTS: Patricia Gallagher writes: "I've been interested in writing since childhood, wrote short stories in high school, and walked three miles each way to the Public Library. 'Making it' was a long hard struggle, writing on a small portable on my kitchen table between the chores of housewife and mother, and often late at night when my family was asleep, and the kitchen was the quietest place in the house." Her books have been published in French, German, Spanish, Portuguese, Dutch, Danish, Swedish, and Norwegian.

AVOCATIONAL INTERESTS: Travel, reading.

BIOGRAPHICAL/CRITICAL SOURCES: San Antonio News, March 11, 1961; Dallas News, April 16, 1961, May 27, 1976; Houston Post, April 1, 1962, June 1, 1976; Dallas-Times-Herald, March 25, 1962; San Antonio Light, May 23, 1976; San Antonio Magazine, October, 1976.

* * *

GALLICO, Paul (William) 1897-1976

July 26, 1897—July 15, 1976; American sportswriter, columnist, bon vivant, screenwriter, short story writer, novelist, and children's author. Obituaries: New York Times, July 17, 1976; Washington Post, July 17, 1976; Newsweek, July 26, 1976; Publishers Weekly, July 26, 1976; Current Biography, September, 1976. (See index for previous CA sketch)

* * *

GALLIMORE, Ronald 1938-

PERSONAL: Born May 17, 1938, in Madison County, Ohio; son of Ross (a farmer) and Marjorie Vaughn Douglass Gallimore; married Sharon Lee McGill, January 26, 1963; children: Christine Margery, Andrea Laura. Education: University of Arizona, B.A., 1960; Northwestern University, M.A., 1963, Ph.D., 1964. Office: Department of Psychiatry, University of California at Los Angeles, Los Angeles, Calif. 90024.

CAREER: California State University, Long Beach, assistant professor of psychology, 1964-66; Bernice P. Bishop Museum, Honolulu, Hawaii, research psychologist, 1966-68; University of Hawaii, Honolulu, associate professor of psychology and anthropology, 1968-71; University of California at Los Angeles, associate professor of psychology, 1971—. Chairman, Hawaii Education Council, 1970-71. Military service; U.S. Army National Guard, 1956-60. Member: American Psychological Association.

WRITINGS: Studies in a Hawaiian Community, Bishop Museum Press, 1968; Battle in the Classroom, Intext Press, 1971; Culture Behavior and Education, Sage Publications, 1974. Contributor to professional journals.

WORK IN PROGRESS: Educational research and development concerning minority culture children; a study of the placebo phenomena; naturalistic studies of the mentally retarded.

* * *

GALLOP, David 1928-

PERSONAL: Born March 9, 1928, in London, England; son of Constantine (a barrister) and Irene (Klaber) Gallop; married Catharine Mary Trist (a teacher), August 1, 1956; children: Frances, Paul, Martin, Timothy. Education: Magdalen College, Oxford, B.A., 1950, M.A., 1955. Home: 1595 Rockland Rd., Peterborough, Ontario, Canada K9J 6R8. Office: Department of Philosophy, Trent University, Peterborough, Ontario, Canada K9J 7B8.

CAREER: University of Toronto, Toronto, Ontario, lecturer, 1955-60, assistant professor, 1960-64, associate professor, 1964-66, professor of philosophy, 1966-69; Trent University, Peterborough, Ontario, professor of philosophy, 1969—. Military service: Royal Air Force, Education Branch, 1950-52. Member: Canadian Philosophical Association, Society for Ancient Greek Philosophy.

WRITINGS: (Translator and author of notes) Plato, Phaedo, Clarendon Press, 1975. Contributor to philosophy journals.

WORK IN PROGRESS: Continuing research on Plato, especially "the thought of his 'middle period'" and on the Eleatics, especially Parmenides.

* * *

GALLUN, Raymond Z(inke) 1911-
(John Callahan; Dow Elstar; E. V. Raymond)

PERSONAL: Surname is accented on last syllable; born March 22, 1911, in Beaver Dam, Wis.; son of Adolph and Martha (Zinke) Gallun; married Frieda Ernestine Talmey (a high-school foreign language teacher), December 26, 1959 (died May 19, 1974). Education: Attended University of Wisconsin, Madison, 1929-30, Alliance Francaise, Paris, France, 1938-39, and San Marcos University, Lima, Peru, 1960. Politics: "No party affiliation." Religion: Agnostic. Home: 110-20 71st Ave., Forest Hills, N.Y. 11375. Agent: Robert P. Mills, 156 East 52nd St., New York, N.Y. 10022.

CAREER: Science fiction writer. Construction worker for U.S. Army Corps of Engineers, 1942-43; marine blacksmith at Pearl Harbor Navy Yard, 1944; technical writer on sonar equipment for EDO Corp., College Point, N.Y., 1964-75. Member: Science Fiction Writers of America.

WRITINGS—Science fiction: People Minus X, Simon & Schuster, 1957; The Planet Strappers, Pyramid Press, 1961; The Eden Cycle, Ballantine, 1974; The Best of Raymond Z. Gallun, edited by Frederik Pohl, Ballantine, in press.

Work has been represented in anthologies, including The Best of Scinece Fiction, edited by Groff Conklin, Crown,

1946; *Adventures in Time and Space,* edited by J. Healy and J. Francis McComas, Random House, 1946, published as *Famous Science-Fiction Stories,* Modern Library, 1957; *Imagination Unlimited,* edited by Everett F. Bleiler and T. E. Dikty, Farrar, Straus & Young, 1951; *Space Service,* edited by Andre Norton, World Publishing, 1953; *Space Pioneers,* edited by Norton, World Publishing, 1954; *Thinking Machines,* edited by Conklin, Vanguard Press, 1954; *Escales dans l'infini,* edited by Georges Gallet, Hachette, 1954.

Possible Worlds of Science Fiction, edited by Conklin, Vanguard Press, 1951; *Coming of the Robots,* edited by Sam Moscowitz, Collier, 1963; *Five Unearthly Visions,* edited by Conklin, Gold Medal Books, 1965; *Tomorrow's Worlds,* edited by Robert Silverberg, Meredith Press, 1969; *The Astounding-Analog Reader,* edited by Harry Harrison and Brian W. Aldiss, Doubleday, 1972; *Jupiter,* edited by Carol Pohl and Frederik Pohl, Ballantine, 1973; *Before the Golden Age,* edited by Isaac Asimov, Doubleday, 1974; *History of the Science-Fiction Magazine,* edited by Michael Ashley, Pitman Press, 1974; *The Best of Planet Stories,* edited by Leigh Brackett, Ballantine, 1975. Contributor of several hundred stories, sometimes under pseudonyms John Callahan, Dow Elstar, and E. V. Raymond, to science fiction magazines and other popular periodicals, including *Astounding Stories, Collier's,* and *Family Circle.*

WORK IN PROGRESS: Gemi the Finder, a novel about "perhaps the first scientist," in ancient Egypt; *Ormund House,* a novel, largely autobiographical.

SIDELIGHTS: Most of Gallun's stories were published in the thirties, a period of science-fiction writing presently being revived and gaining considerable popularity among fans of the genre. He writes of himself: "Have strong but scattered work ethic—like physical labor, no interest in rat races or mutual admiration cliques. Have traveled in a large portion of the world—shoestring style mostly—still love it!" *Avocational interests:* Egyptology, languages.

BIOGRAPHICAL/CRITICAL SOURCES: Michael Ashley, *The History of the Science Fiction Magazine,* Part I: *1926-1935,* Pitman, 1974.

* * *

GAMER, Robert E(manuel) 1938-

PERSONAL: Born April 26, 1938, in Urbana, Ill.; son of Carl Wesley (a professor) and Alice Clara (a sculptress; maiden name, Michael) Gamer. *Education:* Monmouth College, B.A., 1960; Brown University, Ph.D., 1965. *Home:* 5605 Kenwood, Kansas City, Mo. 64110. *Office:* Department of Political Science, University of Missouri, Kansas City, Mo. 64110.

CAREER: University of Singapore, Singapore, assistant lecturer, 1964-65, lecturer in political science, 1965-68; University of Missouri, Kansas City, assistant professor, 1968-72, associate professor of political science, 1972—. Interpretive archaeological ranger at Mesa Verde National Park, 1959-61; owner of Temple Slug (retail store), 1970—. *Member:* American Political Science Association, American Association of University Professors, Phi Beta Kappa.

WRITINGS: (Contributor) Chiang Hai Ding and Ooi Jin Bee, editors, *Modern Singapore,* University of Malaya Press, 1969; *The Politics of Urban Development in Singapore,* Cornell University Press, 1972; *The Developing Nations: A Comparative Perspective,* Allyn & Bacon, 1976. Contributor of articles and reviews to law and political science journals.

WORK IN PROGRESS: A book, *The Prosperity Trap.*

SIDELIGHTS: Gamer writes: "My writing explores relationships between political systems and personal environments. As I progress, I hope to bring this subject increasingly down to earth. . . . I have . . . traveled widely in Asia and Europe, meeting peasants and Cabinet Ministers." His forthcoming book, *The Prosperity Trap* deals with "why prosperity eventually replaces efficacy and options, and what we can do about it." *Avocational interests:* Jogging.

* * *

GANS-RUEDIN, E(rwin) 1915-

PERSONAL: Born May 8, 1915, in Zurich, Switzerland. *Education:* Attended secondary schools in Wiesbaden, Germany; The Hague, Holland; and Neuchatel, Switzerland. *Home:* Goutte d'Or,11, 2014 Bole, Neuchatel, Switzerland. *Agent:* Office du Livre S.A., 1700 Fribourg, Switzerland. *Office:* E. Gans-Ruedin S.A., Grand Rue 2, 2001 Neuchatel, Switzerland.

CAREER: Carpet seller, 1936-40; E. Gans-Rudein (oriental carpet wholesalers), Neuchatel, Switzerland, owner and manager, 1940—. Expert on Tibetan refugees for Swiss Government in Nepal, 1963-65.

WRITINGS: Tapis d'Orient, Payot Lausanne, 1953, translation published as *Oriental Carpets,* Hippocrene Books, 1975; *The Connoisseur's Guide to Oriental Carpets,* translated from the French by Valerie Howard, Tuttle, 1971 (published in England as *Modern Oriental Carpets,* Thames & Hudson, 1971); *Antique Oriental Carpets: From the Seventeenth to the Early Twentieth Century,* Kodansha International, 1975.

SIDELIGHTS: Gans-Ruedin's business interests have taken him to Turkey, Iran, Pakistan, India, China, and the Soviet Union.

* * *

GANTOS, John (Bryan), Jr. 1951-
(Jack Gantos)

PERSONAL: Born July 2, 1951, in Mount Pleasant, Pa.; son of John (a construction superintendant) and Elizabeth (Weaver) Gantos. *Education:* Emerson College, B.F.A., 1976. *Home:* 304 Marlborough St., Boston, Mass. 02116.

CAREER: Has held a variety of jobs, including apprentice electrician, construction foreman, electric saw-blade sharpener, shortorder cook, beach sweeper, and x-ray technician; full-time writer, 1976—.

*WRITINGS—*All published by Houghton: *Rotten Ralph,* 1976; *Sleepy Ronald,* 1976; *Fair Weather Friends,* 1977.

WORK IN PROGRESS: An adult novel.

* * *

GARDNER, Howard 1943-

PERSONAL: Born July 11, 1943, in Scranton, Pa.; son of Ralph (a businessman) and Hilde (Weilheimer) Gardner; married Judith Krieger (a psychologist), June 9, 1966; children: Kerith, Jay, Andrew. *Education:* Harvard University, A.B. (summa cum laude), 1965, Ph.D., 1971; London School of Economics and Political Science, graduate study, 1966. *Home:* 48 Prentiss Lane, Belmont, Mass. 02178.

CAREER: Harvard University, Cambridge, Mass., research associate, 1971—. Research psychologist at Boston Veterans Administration Hospital, 1972—. *Member:* Society for Research in Child Development, Academy of Aphasia, Phi Beta Kappa. *Awards, honors:* Claude Bernard Journalism Award from National Society for Medical Research, 1975, for "Brain Damage: Gateway to the Mind."

WRITINGS: (With Martin Grossack) *Man and Men*, Intext, 1970; *The Quest for Mind*, Knopf, 1973; *The Arts and Human Development*, Wiley, 1973; *The Shattered Mind* (selection of *Psychology Today* Book Club and Quality Paperback Book Club), Knopf, 1973. Editor of "Classics in Psychology" and "Classics in Child Development," both for Arno. Contributor to professional journals.

WORK IN PROGRESS: A textbook on developmental psychology, publication by Little, Brown expected in 1978.

SIDELIGHTS: Gardner writes: "I am trained as a developmental psychologist. At present I conduct basic research on the development and breakdown of the capacity to use various kinds of symbols (words, pictures, gestures, and the like). I work with normal and gifted children and with once normal adults who have suffered brain damage. . . . I enjoy the challenge of trying to make my research, and that of other social scientists, accessible to the interested layman."

* * *

GARDNER, John Champlin, Jr. 1933-

PERSONAL: Born July 21, 1933, in Batavia, N.Y.; son of John Champlin and Priscilla (Jones) Gardner; married Joan Louise Patterson, June 6, 1953; children: Joel, Lucy. *Education:* De Pauw University, student, 1951-53; Washington University, St. Louis, A.B., 1955; State University of Iowa, M.A., 1956, Ph.D., 1958. *Address:* c/o Boskydell Artists Ltd., 72 Monument Ave., Bennington, Vt. 05201.

CAREER: Oberlin College, Oberlin, Ohio, instructor, 1958-59; Chico State College (now California State University), Chico, Calif., instructor, 1959-62; San Francisco State College (now San Francisco State University), San Francisco, Calif., assistant professor of English, 1962-65; Southern Illinois University, Carbondale, professor of English, 1965-76; author, 1976—. Distinguished visiting professor, University of Detroit, 1970-71; visiting professor, Northwestern University, 1973, and Bennington College, 1975. *Member:* Modern Language Association of America, American Association of University Professors. *Awards, honors:* Woodrow Wilson fellowship, 1955-56; Danforth fellowship, 1970-73; Guggenheim fellowship, 1973-74; National Education Association award, 1972; *Grendel* named one of 1971's best fiction books by *Time* and *Newsweek; October Light* named one of the ten best books of 1976 by *Time* and *New York Times;* National Book Critic's Circle award for fiction, 1976, for *October Light.*

WRITINGS: (Editor with Lennis Dunlap) *The Forms of Fiction*, Random House, 1961; (editor and author of introduction) *The Complete Works of the Gawain-Poet* (modern English version), University of Chicago Press, 1965; *The Resurrection* (novel), New American Library, 1966; (editor with Nicholas Joost) *Papers on the Art and Age of Geoffrey Chaucer*, Southern Illinois University Press, 1967; (editor and author of notes) *The Gawain-Poet*, Cliff's Notes, 1967.

The Wreckage of Agathon (novel), Harper, 1970; *Grendel* (novel), Knopf, 1971; (editor and author of notes) *The Alliterative Morte Arthure, The Owl and the Nightingale and Five Other Middle English Poems* (modern English version), Southern Illinois University Press, 1971; *The Sunlight Dialogues* (novel), Knopf, 1972; *Jason and Medeia* (epic poem), Knopf, 1973; *Nickel Mountain: A Pastoral Novel*,

Knopf, 1973; *The Construction of the Wakefield Cycle*, Southern Illinois University Press, 1974; *The King's Indian and Other Fireside Tales*, Knopf, 1974; *The Construction of Christian Poetry in Old English*, Southern Illinois University Press, 1975; *Dragon, Dragon and Other Tales*, Knopf, 1975; *Gudgekin the Thistle Girl and Other Tales*, Knopf, 1976; *October Light* (novel), Knopf, 1976; (contributor) Matthew Bruccoli and C. E. Frazer Clark, Jr., editors, *Pages*, Volume I, Gale, 1976; *The Poetry of Chaucer*, Southern Illinois University Press, in press; *The Life and Times of Chaucer*, Knopf, in press.

Contributor of short stories to *Southern Review, Quarterly Review of Literature*, and *Perspective;* of poetry to *Kenyon Review, Hudson Review*, and other literary quarterlies; and of articles to *Esquire, Saturday Evening Post*, and other magazines.

WORK IN PROGRESS: Three opera libretti; a "book of rant" regarding modern fiction; more tales for children; a novel.

SIDELIGHTS: Gardner is referred to by Timothy Foote as "bulging with genius and philosophy." Thomas R. Edwards said: "Gardner is that rare creature, a philosophical novelist, concerned with conflicts of mind within a physical world that in itself is, as Grendel says, 'nothing: a mechanical chaos of casual, brute enmity on which we stupidly impose our hopes and fears.'"

Gardner lives near Bennington, Vermont, and claims that this environment offers "isolation" and a sense of balance. He is quoted in *Newsweek* as saying that "people are again realizing it is telling a story that really is important. Most of the hand wringing over the death of the novel went on in New York and an awful lot of people didn't pay much attention. . . . There is despair on both coasts, really a preoccupation with the darker things."

As Barton Midwood points out, some confusion exists about Gardner. "There are two other John Gardners known to the public, one who writes satiric mystery novels and the other who was once the head of the Department of Health, Education and Welfare, and [this] author ought not to be confused with them."

BIOGRAPHICAL/CRITICAL SOURCES: Esquire, January, 1971; *Book World*, December 24, 1972; *Time*, January 1, 1973, December 20, 1976; *Newsweek*, December 24, 1973; Joe David Bellamy, editor, *The New Fiction: Interviews With Innovative American Writers*, University of Illinois Press, 1974; *Contemporary Literary Criticism*, Gale, Volume II, 1974, Volume III, 1975, Volume V, 1976; *New York Times*, November 14, 1976, December 26, 1976, January 2, 1977.

* * *

GARDNER, Lewis 1943-

PERSONAL: Born January 29, 1943, in Chelsea, Mass.; son of Philip (a merchant) and Goldie (Stepansky) Gardner; married Sandra Jane Shindell (a writer and editor), February 16, 1969; children: Barbara and Brenda Platek (stepdaughters); Jonathan Alexander. *Education:* Columbia University, A.B., 1964; University of Chicago, M.A., 1966. *Home:* 448 Palmer Ave., Teaneck, N.J. 07666. *Office:* Scholastic Magazines, Inc., 50 West 44th St., New York, N.Y. 10036.

CAREER: Peace Corps, Washington, D.C., English teacher in Monrovia, Liberia, 1964-65; high school teacher of English in Wilmington, Mass., 1966-70; Scholastic Magazines, Inc., New York, N.Y., managing editor of *Scope* and textbook editor, 1970—. Member of poet-in-residence program of New Jersey State Council on the Arts; has given poetry readings. Former member of Wilmington Human Rights Committee. Has acted in stage productions, a film, and a television play.

MEMBER: Dramatists Guild, Poets and Writers of New Jersey (founding member; member of board of directors, 1975-76), Brooklyn Ferry Poets Cooperative. *Awards, honors:* Winner of William Carlos Williams Poetry Center competition, 1975.

WRITINGS: (Editor) *English Teacher's Companion,* Scholastic Book Services, 1974; (editor with wife, Sandra Gardner) *English Teacher's Companion #2,* Scholastic Book Services, 1975.

Plays: "Falstaff and Hal" (adapted from Shakespeare), first produced on tour in eastern United States, 1968; "The Chariot of the Sun" (musical; music by Oscar Brand), first produced in eastern U.S., 1969; "Hadleyburg" (musical in two acts), first produced in New York City at Columbia University, February, 1971.

Work has been represented in anthologies, including *Search the Silence,* edited by Betsy Ryan, Scholastic Book Services, 1974; *The Adventures of the Speckled Band and Other Plays,* edited by Katharine Robinson, Scholastic Book Services, 1975; *Brooklyn Ferry,* edited by Jay McDonnell, Howard Ostwind, and Fran Richetti, Brooklyn Ferry Poets Cooperative, 1975; *Juggernaut,* edited by Dan Georgakas, Smyrna Press, 1976; and in *Within You/Without You,* edited by Ryan, 1973.

Contributor of poems to magazines, including *Jeopardy* and *Fireweed.*

WORK IN PROGRESS: Rat's Choice, a book of poems; *Children of the Wild,* nonfiction for teenagers, with John R. Burger; "Hot Dimes," a play.

SIDELIGHTS: Gardner writes: "I started acting at the age of eight; my interest in the stage has continued through acting—including readings of my poems—and the writing of plays and lyrics for musicals. I began writing poems when I suffered a temporary loss of the stamina needed for working in longer forms. In periods when I have been unable to write at all, I have done paintings and drawings.

"Because of interest in young people and education, I have been involved in Poets-in-the-Schools programs and in educational publishing.

"The themes of my work come from my attempts to understand the individual's place in and relation to the world of others, from bizarre extremes (werewolves, creeps) to the everyday (being a father, a son, a husband)."

*   *   *

GARDNER, Wynelle B.   1918-

PERSONAL: Born September 12, 1918, in Granite, Okla.; daughter of Ben Cabell (a farmer) and Annie (Gaines) Bennett; married John Stevenson Gardner (a manufacturer's representative), December 20, 1950; children: William, Tammy (Mrs. Bruce Beiderman), John. *Education:* Attended Rutherford Business College. *Politics:* "Republican mostly." *Religion:* "Charismatic Presbyterian." *Home:* 183 Pleasant Ave., Fanwood, N.J. 07023.

CAREER: Manager of photo studio in Southwest, 1936-44; Delta Air Lines, Dallas, Tex., ticket agent, operations agent, and ticket office manager, 1944-50; writer, 1962—.

WRITINGS: The Mouse That Glowed, Logos Interna-

tional, 1976. Contributor to church magazines, *Delta Digest,* and local newspapers.

WORK IN PROGRESS: The Mouse of the Promise and *The Mouse in the House of Knowledge,* sequels to *The Mouse That Glowed;* a biography of a Black friend, mother of eighteen children, "whose life has been a series of miracles."

SIDELIGHTS: Wynelle Gardner writes: "Until 1972, I wrote bright, clever, rather frothy articles and stories, more witty than wise, containing scores of problems but no solutions. In 1972, with children quite grown, a new life opened up for our family, beginning with a spiritual experience that enriched and revitalized our lives. Priorities were rearranged, new goals appeared and writing took on a different tone. The churchmouse story came to me in a dream.... Traveling in company with a family of imaginary, allegorical mice has been far more exciting than our travels in England, France, Holland, Scotland, Canada and Nova Scotia. In those countries our visits always came to an end. On this new journey it appears that only the sky is the limit!"

AVOCATIONAL INTERESTS: Music, the theater, making personalized infant greeting cards.

BIOGRAPHICAL/CRITICAL SOURCES: Plainfield Courier News, July 10, 1976; *Blair Enterprise,* October 21, 1976.

*   *   *

GARRISON, Christian (Bascom)   1942-

PERSONAL: Born February 14, 1942, in Monroe, La.; son of Robert Allen (a postal inspector) and Olivette (a civil servant; maiden name, Benson) Garrison; married Martha Frances Taylor, July 20, 1965; children: Anne Walton. *Education:* Millsaps College, student, 1960-61; University of Mississippi, B.A., 1965, graduate study, 1969-71. *Politics:* Democrat. *Religion:* Presbyterian. *Home:* 912 Belhaven St., Jackson, Miss. 39202. *Office:* Mississippi Agricultural and Industrial Board, P.O. Box 849, Jackson, Miss. 39205.

CAREER: Peekskill Military Academy, Peekskill, N.Y., teacher of English, 1965-67; University of Mississippi, Oxford, director of educational film production at Extension, 1967-71; Power and Communications (film company), Jackson, Miss., screenwriter and producer, 1971-72; Mississippi Educational Television, Jackson, producer-director, 1973-74; University of Georgia, Georgia Center for Continuing Education, Athens, film production manager, 1974-76; Mississippi Agricultural and Industrial Board, Jackson, special projects director, 1976—. Judge for Mississippi Arts Festival and Southern Literary Festival.

MEMBER: Society of Children's Book Writers. *Awards, honors:* Won Mississippi Educational Television script writing competition, 1970, with teleplay "Too Soon Passing"; CINE Golden Eagle from Council on International Non-theatrical Events, 1970, for writing, directing, and cinematography of film "Bluesmaker"; won Mississippi Arts Festival writing-for-children competition, 1973; Golden Image Award from Long Island International Film Festival, 1975, for directing and cinematography of film "Benjamin E. Mays: Born to Rebel."

WRITINGS: The Calico Tiger (play for children), Performance Publishing, 1973; *Little Pieces of the West Wind* (picture book), Bradbury, 1975; *Flim and Flam and the Big Cheese* (picture book), Bradbury, 1976.

Films: Author of more than two dozen educational films, including "Theatre and Your Community," University of

Mississippi, 1969; "It All Begins With One," University of Mississippi, 1970; "Shadow-Light," Power and Communications, 1971; "Mississippi Government—Executive Branch," Mississippi Educational Television, 1973; and "Poor Academia, Or Who Goosed, Juiced, and Seduced Big Money?," University of Georgia, 1975.

Plays: "Too Soon Passing" (teleplay), Mississippi Educational Television, 1971. Also author of "The Brain Machine" (feature-length screenplay), and "A Rhyme in Time Saves Nine" (one-act). Author of several short film scripts for children.

SIDELIGHTS: Garrison writes: "I've been very lucky: I grew up in the South where people still carry on conversations with each other and have a certain love for language; I've had associations with other writers who've encouraged me in my own work; I've found publishers who believed enough in my works to have published them. . . . I realized that I want to concentrate most of my writing energies on things for children. . . . I like making films. I like traveling. I just wish I had more money so I could do more of both."

* * *

GARVEY, John 1944-

PERSONAL: Born May 8, 1944, in Decatur, Ill.; son of Hugh Michael (a publisher) and Jane (Driscoll) Garvey; married Regina Carbonell (a musician), June 10, 1967; children: Maria, Hugh Daniel. *Education:* University of Notre Dame, A.B., 1967. *Politics:* "I'm against it." *Religion:* Catholic. *Home:* 1600 Holmes, Springfield, Ill. 62704.

CAREER: Teacher of English, creative writing, and religion in high school in Mishawaka, Ind., 1967-68; Templegate Publishing Co., Springfield, Ill., writer and editor, 1968-71; draft counselor in Springfield, Ill., 1969-73; Sangamon State University, Springfield, publications editor, 1971-73; Templegate Publishing Co., editor, 1973—.

WRITINGS: A Contemporary Meditation on Saints, Thomas More Press, 1975; *Saints for Confused Times,* Thomas More Press, 1976. Columnist for *Commonweal,* 1975—. Work represented in anthology, *On the Run,* edited by Michael F. McCauley, Thomas More Press, 1974. Contributor of articles to *Critic, Concilium, Katallagete/Be Reconciled, U.S. Catholic,* and *Illinois Times,* and of poems to *Apple* and *Ohio Review.* Editor, *University Today,* 1968-71.

WORK IN PROGRESS: A book, *Hard Questions,* about the problems facing contemporary institutional religion—"the real problems, not the ones the leaders of the churches imagine"—publication by Thomas More Press expected in 1978; research on the relationship between Christianity and other religions, particularly between Christianity and Judaism and the phenomenon of Christian anti-Semitism.

SIDELIGHTS: Garvey writes: "I am especially interested in the intersection of religion and great social change, and am lucky to be alive at a time when there is plenty to look at in this area; interesting things may happen when tradition encounters the myths of a new age. (I suspect this interest may have come about as a result of a life-long fascination with mythology, fantasy, and science fiction.) The recent interest on the part of a lot of people in Jung, in the fantasies of Lewis and Tolkien, and in eastern religion shows that I am not alone—it is all evidence of a search for living symbols, and the need to express, in a new way, realities which are as old as the race. In our time there has been a shift away from a purely intellectual, exteriorized attitude toward dogma to one which emphasizes a personal experience of religious truth, an approach which allows growth and change to reflect the reality of the symbol, while drawing deeper levels of meaning from it.

When tradition encounters something new it seems awkward—its past is so obvious, like the shell of a tortoise. Traditional religion confronts one set of myths (the most recent ones, perhaps, being a fierce belief in the possibility of personal autonomy, and the belief that one creates one's life in an indifferent universe) with another set, which teach a kind of mythological ecology: there are true and false things, and choices which align you with or against the universe.

It is not a case of the new myths being false. They are simply limited. They may take on depth in the encounter with tradition, if tradition can work as a living language, a genuinely informative one. Nor is it a matter of traditional religion being simply true: when it is not living, but has become a smug consolation, tradition can be the most dangerous and limiting myth of all."

* * *

GASCOYNE, David Emery 1916-

PERSONAL: Born October 10, 1916, in Harrow, England; son of Leslie Noel (a bank manager); and Winnifred Isobel Gascoyne; married Judy Lewis, May 17, 1975. *Education:* Attended Regent Street Polytechnic. *Home:* 48 Oxford St., Northwood, Cowes, Isle of Wight, England. *Agent:* Alan Clodd, 22 Huntington Road, London N29 DV, England.

CAREER: Writer. *Member:* Royal Society of Literature (fellow). *Awards, honors:* Rockefeller-Atlantic Award, 1949.

WRITINGS—Poems: *Roman Balcony and Other Poems,* Lincoln Williams, 1932; *Man's Life Is This Meat,* Parton Press, 1936; *Holderlin's Madness,* Dent, 1938; *Poems 1937-1942,* Editions Poetry, 1943; *A Vagrant and Other Poems,* Lehmann, 1950; *Night Thoughts,* Grove, 1956; *Collected Poems,* edited by Robin Skelton, Oxford University Press, 1965; (with Kathleen Raine and W. S. Graham) *Penguin Modern Poets 17,* Penguin, 1970; *The Sun at Midnight: Notes on the Story of Civilisation Seen as the History of the Great Experimental Work of the Supreme Scientist,* Enitharmon Press, 1970; (with Skelton and Alan Clodd) *Collected Verse Translations,* Oxford University Press, 1970.

Other: *Opening Day* (novel), Cobden Sanderson, 1933; *A Short Survey of Surrealism,* Cobden Sanderson, 1935, International Scholastic Book Service, 1971; (translator with Humphrey Jennings) Benjamin Peret, *A Bunch of Carrots: Twenty Poems,* Roger Roughton, 1936, revised edition published as *Remove Your Hat,* 1936; (translator) Andre Breton, *What Is Surrealism?,* Faber, 1936; (editor) Kenneth Patchen, *Outlaw of the Lowest Planet,* Grey Walls Press, 1946; *Thomas Carlyle,* Longmans, Green, 1952.

Author of "The Hole in the Fourth Wall: or, Talk Talk Talk" (one-act play), first produced in London at Watergate Theatre, 1950.

SIDELIGHTS: Gascoyne's first novel and volume of poetry were published when he was sixteen years old. Noted as a Thirties Surrealist poet, Gascoyne explained the relationship between the surrealist attitude and poetry: "Surrealism, profiting from the discoveries of Freud and a few other scientific explorers of the unconscious, has conceived poetry as being, on the one hand, a perpetual functioning of the *psyche,* a perpetual flow of irrational thought *in the form of images,* taking place in every human mind and needing only a certain predisposition and discipline in order to be brought to light in the form of written words (or plastic images), and on the other hand a universally valid attitude to experience, a possible mode of living." During the war, Gascoyne's themes shifted to include an awareness of a world overwhelmed by war, an existential expression of personal anguish, and deep interest in Christian myth and symbol. In the 1950's Gascoyne lived in France and wrote quasi-dramatic works. Kathleen Raine wrote of Gascoyne's remarkable imagination: "There is nothing, in David Gascoyne's kind and quality of imagination, which is typical of, expressive of, suburban values or modes of thought; he is no more of the world into which he was born than the angel Tolstoi's cobbler found naked in the snow behind a church, and brought into his house to learn shoemaking."

BIOGRAPHICAL/CRITICAL SOURCES: Observer, December, 1950; *London,* July, 1957, November, 1965; Kathleen Raine, *Every Changing Shape,* Deutsch, 1961; Raine, *Defending Ancient Springs,* Oxford University Press, 1967; *Sewanee Review,* spring, 1967.

*   *   *

GASKIN, Catherine 1929-

PERSONAL: Born April 2, 1929, in Dundalk, Ireland; daughter of James (an engineer) and Mary (Harrington) Gaskin; married Sol Cornberg, 1955. *Education:* Educated at Holy Cross College, Sydney, Australia. *Home:* Ballymacahara, Wicklow, County Wicklow, Ireland.

CAREER: Novelist.

WRITINGS: This Other Eden, Collins, 1947; *With Every Year,* Collins, 1949; *Dust in the Sunlight,* Collins, 1950; *All Else Is Folly,* Harper, 1951; *Daughter of the House,* Harper, 1952; *Sara Dane,* Lippincott, 1955; *Blake's Reach,* Lippincott, 1958; *Corporation Wife,* Doubleday, 1960; *I Know My Love,* Doubleday, 1962; *The Tilsit Inheritance,* Doubleday, 1963; *The File on Devlin,* Doubleday, 1965; *Edge of Glass,* Doubleday, 1967; *Fiona,* Doubleday, 1970; *A Falcon for a Queen,* Doubleday, 1972; *The Property of a Gentleman,* Doubleday, 1974; The *Lynmara Legacy,* Doubleday, 1976; *The Summer of the Spanish Woman,* Doubleday, in press.

SIDELIGHTS: The File on Devlin was adapted for dramatic presentation on NBC-Television's "Hall of Fame," November 21, 1969. Catherine Gaskin's novels have been issued in eleven languages, including Hebrew, Turkish, and Japanese.

WORK IN PROGRESS: Novels.

AVOCATIONAL INTERESTS: Music, cinema.

*   *   *

GASQUE, W(oodrow) Ward 1939-

PERSONAL: Born October 7, 1939, in Conway, S.C.; naturalized Canadian citizen; son of Claude Jackson (a hotelier) and Catherine (a businesswoman; maiden name, Ward) Gasque; married Laurel Sandfor (an art historian), August 25, 1961; children: Catherine Michelle. *Education:* Wheaton College, Wheaton, Ill., B.A., 1960; Fuller Theological Seminary, B.D., 1964, M.Th., 1965; University of Manchester, Ph.D., 1969; also studied at University of Basel, 1966-67, Cambridge University, and University of Lausanne, 1975-76. *Religion:* Evangelical Protestant. *Home:* 2516 Courtenay St., Vancouver, British Columbia, Canada V6R 3X3.

CAREER: University of British Columbia, Regent College, Vancouver, lecturer, 1969-70, assistant professor, 1970-72, associate professor of New Testament, 1972—, registrar, 1970—, member of board of governors, 1976—. Vice-president of Vancouver chapter of Evangelical Fellowship of Canada, 1972-75, member of council, 1973—, national vice-president, 1973-75; member of Vancouver Council of Churches.

MEMBER: Canadian Society of Biblical Studies, Canadian Bible Society (member of board of directors of British Columbia chapter, 1976—), Society of Biblical Literature (Pacific Northwest vice-president, 1971-72; president, 1972-73; executive secretary, 1976—), American Academy of Religion (Pacific Northwest vice-president, 1971-72; president, 1972-73; executive secretary, 1976—), Studiorum Novi Testamenti Societas, Evangelical Theological Society, Institute for Biblical Research, Tyndale Fellowship for Biblical Research.

WRITINGS: Sir William M. Ramsay: Archaeologist and New Testament Scholar, Baker Book, 1966; (editor with Ralph P. Martin) *Apostolic History and the Gospel: Biblical and Historical Studies Presented to F. F. Bruce on the Occasion of His Sixtieth Birthday,* Paternoster Press, 1970; (contributor) Richard N. Longenecker and Merrill C. Tenney, editors, *New Dimensions in New Testament Study,* Zondervan, 1974; *A History of the Criticism of the Acts of the Apostles,* J.C.B. Mohr, 1975, Eerdmans, 1976; (editor with Carl Edwin Armstrong) *Dreams, Visions and Oracles: The Layman's Guide to Biblical Prophecy,* Baker Book, 1976.

Contributor to *Baker's Dictionary of Christian Ethics, New International Dictionary of the Christian Church, Zondervan Pictorial Encyclopedia of the Bible, The New International Standard Bible Encyclopedia, Eerdmans Handbook to Christian History,* and *The Interpreter's Dictionary of the Bible.* Contributor to theology journals. Book review editor and member of editorial committee of *Journal of the Evangelical Theological Society,* 1975—; editor-at-large of *Christianity Today,* 1972—.

WORK IN PROGRESS: Editing "The New International Greek Testament," a series of about twenty volumes, with I. Howard Marshall, for Eerdmans, completion expected in 1996; editing *The Church and Its Ministry: Studies in Honour of G.C.D. Howley,* with David J. Ellis, for Pickering & Inglis; editing *Scripture, Tradition and Interpretation: Festschrift for E. F. Harrison,* with William Sanford LaSor, for Eerdmans; editing *The Oxford Companion to the Bible and Literature* (tentative title), with David Lyle Jeffrey.

SIDELIGHTS: Gasque has conducted independent study in Europe and the Near East.

*   *   *

GATTI, Arthur Gerard 1942-
(Andrew Gerard, Basho Katz, Charles Lane)

PERSONAL: Born September 5, 1942, New York, N.Y.; son of Anthony Carmelo (a tailor) and Anntoinette (a publisher's assistant; maiden name, Giannone) Gatti; lives with Constance MacNamee; children: Eileen, Jennifer; stepchildren: Eden Harvest, Rainbow Harvest. *Education:* Hofstra College, student, 1961-62; Queens College of the City University of New York, B.A., 1965. *Politics:* "Enlightened anarchy; participatory democracy; benevolent despotism—in that order." *Religion:* "Aumni." *Home:* 121 Bank St., New York, N.Y. 10014. *Agent:* Susan Ann Protter, 156

E. 52nd St., New York, N.Y. 10022. *Office:* Cosmic Publications, 521 Fifth Ave., New York, N.Y. 10017.

CAREER: Sybil Leek's Astrology, New York City, features editor, 1970-72; *Astrology Guide,* New York City, managing editor, 1973-75; *Your Personal Astrology,* New York City, managing editor, 1973-75; *Cosmic Frontiers,* New York City, editor-in-chief, 1976—. Consulting astrologer. Caseworker, Welfare board, Essex Co., N.J., 1966-69. *Member:* American Federation of Astrologers, National Council for Geocosmic Research. *Awards, honors:* Dwight Durling Award, 1963-64, for poetry manuscript; Queens College service award, 1964.

WRITINGS: The Kennedy Curse, Regnery, 1976. Contributor of astrology articles and columns to periodicals, including *East Village Other, Gambler's World,* and *High Times.*

* * *

GAUNT, Michael
See ROBERTSHAW, (James) Denis

* * *

GAVRONSKY, Serge 1932-

PERSONAL: Born August 16, 1932, in Paris, France; came to United States in 1940, naturalized citizen, 1956; son of Victor and Anne (Minor) Gavronsky; married, 1960; children: Adriane. *Education:* Columbia University, B.A., 1954, M.A., 1955, Ph.D., 1965. *Home:* 525 West End Ave., New York, N.Y. 10024. *Office:* Department of French, Barnard College, Columbia University, 606 West 120th St., New York, N.Y. 10027.

CAREER: Columbia University, Barnard College, New York, N.Y., lecturer, 1960-63, instructor, 1963-65, assistant professor, 1965-69, associate professor, 1969-74, professor of French, 1974—, chairman of department, 1975—. Lecturer at Ecole Libre des Hautes Etudes, 1966. *Awards, honors:* Fulbright travel grant, 1958-59; French Government fellow, 1958-59, 1970-71, summer, 1975.

WRITINGS: The French Liberal Opposition and the American Civil War, Humanities, 1968; (editor and translator) *Poems and Texts: Eight Contemporary French Poets,* October House, 1969; *Lectures et compte-rendu, poemes* (title means "Readings and Accounts"), Flammarion, 1973; *Le Moyen Age* (title means "The Middle Ages"), Macmillan, 1974; (editor with Patricia Terry, and translator) *Modern French Poetry: A Bilingual Anthology,* Columbia University Press, 1975; *Francis Ponge: The Sun and Other Texts,* Sun Books, 1976. Contributor to scholarly journals. Co-founder and American editor of *Two Cities,* 1960-65; New York representative of *El Corno Emplumado,* 1965-68.

* * *

GELFMAN, Judith S(chlein) 1937-
(Judy Starr)

PERSONAL: Born May 26, 1937, in New York, N.Y.; daughter of Samuel R. (a production manager) and Rose (Friedman) Schlein; married Stanley Gelfman (an engineer), July 14, 1957; children: Debra Dawn, Sari Susanne. *Education:* Columbia University, B.F.A. (cum laude), 1958, M.A., 1962, D.Ed., 1974. *Politics:* Democrat. *Religion:* Jewish. *Home:* 4455 Douglas Ave., Riverdale, N.Y. 10471. *Office:* JSG Productions, 521 Fifth Ave., New York, N.Y. 10017.

CAREER: WNET-Television, New York City, producer,

broadcaster, and script writer, 1962-66; free-lance television writer and consultant, 1966-71; JSG Productions (television production company), New York City, founder and president, 1974—. Professional ballet dancer and actress, performing under name Judy Starr; television and film appearances include "The Ed Sullivan Show," "The Defenders," "Love of Life," and "North by Northwest." Has also appeared in summer stock and in television commercials. Lecturer at Columbia University's Teacher College. Member of board of directors of Justonics Corp.

MEMBER: International Radio and Television Society, National Academy of Television Arts and Sciences, American Federation of Television and Radio Artists, Actors Equity Association, Screen Actors Guild, Kappa Delta Pi, Pi Lambda Theta.

WRITINGS: Women in Television News, Columbia University Press, 1976. Author of scripts for television series and programs, including "Adventures in Language," a WNET-Television program for children, "Jobs for Tomorrow," "Volunteer: A Bridge to Paid Employment," and "Frankly Female."

WORK IN PROGRESS: Research for "Performing Arts Parade" (tentative title), a public affairs television series to introduce children to the performing arts.

SIDELIGHTS: Judith Gelfman writes: "Through my unique combination of academic and professional credentials I hope to bring to the television medium programs of interest and value that will entertain while educating. I subscribe to Moss Hart's adage 'If it's good it's educational.' Television is the most powerful medium of communication ever devised and it is deserving of the best efforts by men and women working together in the public interest."

AVOCATIONAL INTERESTS: Tennis, swimming, travel.

* * *

GEMMING, Elizabeth 1932-

PERSONAL: Born December 27, 1932, in Glen Cove, N.Y.; daughter of Alexander Henry (a teacher and school principal) and Ruth (a secretary; maiden name, Smith) Prinz; married Klaus Gemming (a book designer), July 3, 1957; children: Marianne, Christina. *Education:* Wellesley College, B.A., 1954; University of Munich, graduate study, 1954-55. *Home:* 49 Autumn St., New Haven, Conn. 06511.

CAREER: Teacher of English in secondary schools in Munich, Germany, 1954-55; Pantheon Books, Inc., New York, N.Y., assistant editor and member of promotion staff, 1955-57; free-lance writer, editor, and translator, 1957—. *Member:* Phi Beta Kappa. *Awards, honors:* Fulbright scholarship, University of Munich, 1954-55.

WRITINGS—Juveniles, except as indicated: *Huckleberry Hill: Child Life in Old New England,* Crowell, 1968; (with husband, Klaus Gemming) *Learning through Stamps,* Barre Publishers, Volume I: *The World of Art,* 1968, Volume II: *Around the World,* 1968, Volume III: *Portraits of Greatness,* 1969; *Getting to Know New England,* Coward, 1970; *Blow Ye Winds Westerly: The Seaports and Sailing Ships of Old New England,* Crowell, 1972; *Block Island Summer* (adult book; photographs by Klaus Gemming), Chatham Press, 1972; *Getting to Know the Connecticut River,* Coward, 1974; *Born in a Barn: Farm Animals and Their Young* (photographs by Klaus Gemming), Coward, 1974; *Maple Harvest: The Story of Maple Sugaring,* Coward, 1976.

Translator from the German; all juveniles: Renato Rascel, *Piccoletto: The Story of the Little Chimney Sweep,* Pantheon, 1958; Max Bolliger, *Sandy at the Children's Zoo*, Crowell, 1967; Alfons Weber, *Elizabeth Gets Well*, Crowell, 1970.

WORK IN PROGRESS: A juvenile, *Squirrel Wood*, with photographs.

AVOCATIONAL INTERESTS: Travel (Europe, especially France and Austria), American cultural history, medieval history and art, knitting (especially the Icelandic style), family history (is descended from Mayflower pilgrims), visiting old graveyards in rural New England.

* * *

GENET
  See FLANNER, Janet

* * *

GENSZLER, G(eorge) William II   1915-
PERSONAL: Born November 2, 1915, in Columbia, Pa.; son of George W. (a clergyman) and Stella K. (Hunsicker) Genszler; married Dorothy Helen Mezinis, June 15, 1940; children: Sandra Joy (Mrs. John Knutson), George William III, David Garrett. *Education:* Carthage College, B.A., 1937; Northwestern Lutheran Theological Seminary, M.Div., 1940. *Home:* 705 South 26th St., Sheboygan, Wis. 53081. *Office:* First United Lutheran Church, 2401 Kohler Memorial Dr., Sheboygan, Wis. 53081.

CAREER: Ordained Lutheran minister, 1940; pastor in Killdeer, N.D., 1940-44, and in Wisconsin Dells, Wis., 1944-51; First United Lutheran Church, Sheboygan, Wis., pastor, 1951—. President of Ecumenical Dialogue Society, 1966-68, Sheboygan Human Rights Committee, 1967, and Sheboygan Ministerial Association, 1969; member of board of directors of Sheboygan Family Service Association, 1954-62, Sheboygan Boy Scouts, 1958-62, Sheboygan United Way, 1969-77, and Sheboygan Red Cross, 1975-79; member of Wisconsin Council of Church Broadcast Ministry, 1968-78. State chairman of Lutheran World Relief, 1968-78; member of executive board of Wisconsin-Upper Michigan Synod of Lutheran Church in America, 1969-76; and of Board of Publication of Lutheran Church in America. *Awards, honors:* D.D., Carthage College, 1967; twenty-five years service citation from Lutheran World Federation, 1976, for service through Lutheran World Relief.

WRITINGS: Don't Fall Flat on Your Faith, CSS Publishing, 1973; *Hay, Harmony, Hallelujah*, CSS Publishing, 1974.

WORK IN PROGRESS: A stewardship book, *Pay or Burn,* completion expected in 1977.

SIDELIGHTS: Genszler told *CA:* "One of the glories of the Christian ministry is that I have found an outlet for every creative talent I possess from sign painting, architecture, carpentry, building, together with the joy of preaching, writing (poems, plays, articles and books) and lecturing across the country and abroad."

* * *

GENTRY, Peter
  See NEWCOMB, Kerry and SCHAEFER, Frank

* * *

GEOFFREY, Theodate
  See WAYMAN, Dorothy G(odfrey)

GEORGE, Sara   1947-
PERSONAL: Born June 26, 1947, in England; daughter of Peter (a writer) and Margaret (a teacher; maiden name, Brennan) George. *Education:* University of East Anglia, B.A. (honors), 1968. *Politics:* Socialist. *Religion:* None. *Home:* 150 Cannon Street Rd., London E.1, England. *Agent:* Patricia Falk Feeley, 52 Vanderbilt Ave., New York, N.Y. 10017.

CAREER: Teacher of English at St. Catherine's School in Guildford, Surrey, England, 1968-71; and at Lady Margaret School, London, England, 1971-73—. *Awards, honors:* John Creasey Award from Crime Writers Association, "best first crime novel of 1975," for *Acid Drop.*

WRITINGS: Acid Drop (crime novel), Atheneum, 1975; *The Psi Kick* (crime novel), Putnam, 1976.

WORK IN PROGRESS: A third novel.

AVOCATIONAL INTERESTS: Film, music, art, reading.

* * *

GERLER, William R(obert)   1917-
PERSONAL: Born February 16, 1917, in Forest Park, Ill.; son of William C. and Elizabeth (Brunke) Gerler; married Frances M. Brunner, August 19, 1942; children: Barbara (Mrs. Gary Sorensen), Mary Frances (Mrs. James Murray), Janet Louis, S. Lauretta (Mrs. James Minnie). *Education:* University of Illinois, B.S., 1939; graduate study at University of Minnesota and University of Wisconsin, Milwaukee. *Religion:* Protestant. *Home and office:* 1315 Valley View Dr., Racine, Wis. 53405.

CAREER: Young & Rubicam, Chicago, Ill., worked in new business department, 1939-40; Investors Diversified Services, Minneapolis, Minn., advertising and public relations director, 1940-42 and 1946; S. C. Johnson & Son, Inc., Racine, Wis., public relations administrator, 1947-60; Healy, Baker, Bowden & Gerler (public relations agency), Chicago, partner, 1960-66; Lennen & Newell Advertising Agency, Racine, account executive and public relations director, 1966-71; Engineers & Scientists of Milwaukee, Milwaukee, Wis., managing director, 1972—. President of General Communications, 1960—. Instructor at University of Wisconsin extensions, Racine and Kanosha, 1968-73. *Military service:* U.S. Naval Reserve, active duty, 1942-46; served in Atlantic and Pacific theater; commander of Naval Air Intelligence Training units #721 and #723, 1960-63.

MEMBER: International Council of Industrial Editors (past president), International Council of Business and Publication Editors (president, 1952), American Society of Association Executives, Western Society of Engineers (executive director, 1971—), Wisconsin Society of Association Executives, Council of Engineering and Scientific Society Executives, Chicago Press Club, Chicago Society of Association Executives, Union League Club of Chicago, Elks (exalted ruler, 1960). *Awards, honors:* Awards from International Council of Industrial Editors, 1947, 1948; award from Wisconsin Manufacturers Association, 1952; awards from Council of Engineering and Scientific Society Executives, 1970, 1971, and 1976.

WRITINGS: Air Group Six, Air Group Six, 1947; *Executives Treasury of Humor for Every Occasion,* Parker & Son, 1965; *Educators' Treasury of Humor for All Occasions,* Parker & Son, 1972; *A Pack of Riddles,* Dutton, 1975; *Riddles, Jokes, and Other Funny Things,* Golden Press, 1975. Contributor to professional and trade journals, and to *Popular Science.* Publisher, *Midwest Engineer;* editor, *Milwaukee Engineering.*

WORK IN PROGRESS: The Medical Laugh Book; Golf-ers' Treasury of Wit and Humor.

* * *

GERMANY, (Vera) Jo(sephine)

PERSONAL: Born in Cambridge, England; daughter of Arthur (a warehouse foreman) and Jessie (a postmistress; maiden name, Garner) Savidge; married Leslie Germany (a chartered electrical engineer), October 28, 1944. Education: Attended secondary schools and technical college in England. Religion: Agnostic. Residence: Cambridge, England.

CAREER: Writer. Has worked as office clerk and concert party artist. Past chairman of St. John's Players; member of local Arts Theatre Club. Member: Society of Women Writers and Journalists, Society of Authors, Romantic Novelists Association, English Folklore Society, Pye Dramatic Society. Awards, honors: Special merit award from Romantic Novelists Association, 1974, for Bride for a Tiger.

WRITINGS—Gothic novels: Bride for a Tiger, Hurst & Blackett, 1973, Pocket Books, 1975; Candles Never Lie, Hurst & Blackett, 1974; Black Moonlight, Hurst & Blackett, 1975; Devil Child, Hurst & Blackett, in press. Contributor of articles on English folklore to periodicals.

WORK IN PROGRESS: A book for Hurst & Blackett; City of Golden Cages (tentative title); a modern suspense novel; research on the French Revolution for another novel.

SIDELIGHTS: Jo Germany writes: "I am insatiably curious about the way people lived and behaved during the eighteenth and nineteenth centuries and I also find their customs and beliefs fascinating. Therefore all my published works have historical backgrounds."

BIOGRAPHICAL/CRITICAL SOURCES: Cambridge Evening News, May 11, 1973; Pye World, August, 1973; Cambridge Independent Press, May 15, 1975; Writer, December, 1975.

* * *

GETTY, J(ean) Paul 1892-1976

December 15, 1892—June 6, 1976; American oil billionaire and author. Obituaries: Washington Post, June 7, 1976; New York Times, June 9, 1976, June 11, 1976; Newsweek, June 14, 1976; Time, June 14, 1976.

* * *

GHOSE, Zulfikar 1935-

PERSONAL: Born, 1935, in Sialkot, Pakistan; came to United States in 1969. Agent: Harold Matson Co., Inc., 22 East 40th St., New York, N.Y. 10016.

WRITINGS: The Loss of India (poems), Routledge & Kegan Paul, 1964; (with B. S. Johnson) Statement Against Corpses (stories), Constable, 1964; Confessions of a Native-Alien (autobiography), Routledge & Kegan Paul, 1965; The Contradictions (novel), Macmillan, 1966; Jets from Orange (poems), Dufour, 1967; The Murder of Aziz Khan (novel), Macmillan (London), 1967, John Day, 1969; The Violent West (poems), Macmillan, 1972; The Incredible Brazilian (fiction), Holt, 1972; The Beautiful Empire, Macmillan, 1975; (with Gavin Ewart and Johnson) Penguin Modern Poets Twenty-Five, Penguin, 1975; Crump's Terms (fiction), Macmillan, 1976.

BIOGRAPHICAL/CRITICAL SOURCES: Zulfikar Ghose, Confessions of a Native-Alien, Routledge & Kegan Paul, 1965.

GIBSON, Robert (Donald Davidson) 1927-

PERSONAL: Born August 21, 1927, in London, England; son of Nicol Aitken (a policeman) and Ann (Campbell) Gibson; married Sheila Elaine Goldsworthy (a teacher), December 21, 1953; children: Ian, Graham, Robin. Education: King's College, London, B.A. (1st class honors), 1948; Magdalen College, Cambridge, Ph.D., 1953; additional study at Ecole Normale Superieure, Paris, France, 1953-54. Politics: "None (confirmed skeptic)." Religion: "None (see politics)." Home: 97A St. Stephens Rd., Canterbury, Kent CT2 7JT, England. Office: Rutherford College, University of Kent at Canterbury, Canterbury, Kent, England.

CAREER: University of St. Andrews, St. Andrews, Scotland, assistant lecturer in French, 1954-55; University of Dundee, Dundee, Scotland, lecturer in French, 1955-58; University of Aberdeen, Aberdeen, Scotland, lecturer in French, 1958-61; Queen's University, Belfast, Northern Ireland, professor of French and chairman of department, 1961-65; University of Kent at Canterbury, Canterbury, Kent, England, professor of French and chairman of department, 1965—, deputy master of Rutherford College, 1966-71, sub-dean of faculty of humanities, 1967-72. Military service: Royal Air Force, 1948-50; became flying officer. Member: Society for French Studies.

WRITINGS: The Quest of Alain-Fournier, Hamish Hamilton, 1953, Yale University Press, 1954; Roger Martin du Gard, Hillary, 1961; (author of introduction and notes) Alain-Fournier, Le Grand Meaulnes (title means "Big Meaulnes"), Harrap, 1968; The Land without a Name, St. Martin's, 1975.

Editor: Modern French Poets on Poetry: An Anthology, Cambridge University Press, 1961; (and author of introduction and notes) Claude Aveline, Le bestiaire inattendu (title means "The Unlikely Beast Book"), Harrap, 1961; (and author of introduction and notes) Claude Aveline, Brouart et le desordre (title means "Brouart and Disorder"), Harrap, 1964; (and author of introduction and notes) Jean Giraudoux, Provinciales (title means "Country Sketches"), Oxford University Press, 1965.

Also co-author of phonotape, "French Romantic Poetry," for Holt Information Systems, 1972.

Contributor to Encyclopaedia Britannica and Collier's Encyclopedia, and of reviews to French Studies, Modern Language Review, and Times Literary Supplement.

WORK IN PROGRESS: The Secret Village, an evocation of an English village through archive material, photographs, and interviews; an autobiography; research on Anglo-French relations, the critical reception of the works of Marcel Proust, and on Valery Larbaud.

SIDELIGHTS: Gibson writes: "Much of my literary activity has focused on the work of Alain-Fournier: I first read his only novel, Le Grand Meaulnes, in the summer of 1944. At that same period in time, I was first introduced to a remote English village which has enriched my imaginative life for 30 years in much the same way as the Fournier novel. Book and village have, indeed, become intricately interwoven." He adds: "I'm an erstwhile athlete and an occasional humorist."

* * *

GIFFORD, Barry 1946-

PERSONAL: Born October 18, 1946, in Chicago, Ill.; son of Adolph Edward (a pharmacist) and Dorothy (a model; maiden name, Colby) Stein; married Mary Lou Nelson; children: Phoebe Lou, Asa Colby. *Education:* Attended University of Missouri, 1964, University of London, 1965, and Cambridge University, 1966. *Politics:* "Anti-organizationalist." *Religion:* None. *Address:* 1213 Peralta Ave., Berkeley, Calif. 94706.

CAREER: Poet and novelist. Visiting lecturer at State University of New York at Buffalo, 1974. Has worked as a seaman, dance hall operator, high school baseball coach, choker setter, carpenter, laborer, post office clerk, rock and roll musician, freight handler, and truck driver. *Awards, honors:* Silverthorne Award for Poetry from Silverthorne Press, 1967, for *The Blood of the Parade.*

WRITINGS: The Blood of the Parade (poems), Silverthorne Press, 1967; *Coyote Tantras and Other Poems,* Silverthorne Press, 1968; *A Boy's Novel,* Christopher Books, 1973; *Kerouac's Town* (nonfiction), Capra, 1973; *Coyote Tantras,* Books 1-4, Christopher Books, 1974; *From Persimmons* (poems), Blackberry Books, 1974; *Persimmons: Poems for Paintings,* Shaman Drum Press, 1976; *The Boy You Have Always Loved* (poems), Talonbooks, 1976; *Letters to Proust* (poems), White Pine Press, 1976; (translator) *Selected Poems of Francis Jammes,* Utah State University Press, 1976; *My Mother's People* (novel), Creative Arts Book Co., 1976; (editor) *Selected Writings of Edward S. Curtis: The Portable Curtis,* Creative Arts Book Co., 1976; *Living in Advance* (songs), Open Reading Books, 1976; *Horse Hauling Timber Out of Hokkaido Forest* (poems), Jordan Davies Press, in press. Contributor of stories, poems, articles, and reviews to literary and music journals, including *Chicago Review, Rolling Stone, Jazz and Pop, Beloit Poetry Journal, California Quarterly, Wisconsin Review,* and *Poetry Japan.*

WORK IN PROGRESS: Ghosts No Horse Can Carry, a novel, for Houghton; *Delacroix's White Horse,* poems; translating plays by Francis Jammes.

SIDELIGHTS: Gifford writes: "I grew up in Chicago where my father's friends were gangsters; he ran an all-night drugstore on the corner of Chicago and Rush; I stayed up late listening to their talk and dunking doughnuts with the organ-grinder's monkey; afternoons I spent watching showgirls rehearse at the Club Alabam. I was always interested in language; I always listened. After my father died (I was twelve) there was no money, my mother and I went to work. I began to read everything: early influences were Jack London, Thomas Wolfe; later Jack Kerouac, Ezra Pound, B. Traven." Gifford has traveled in Europe, South America, Japan, and North Africa.

BIOGRAPHICAL/CRITICAL SOURCES: Western American Literature, February, 1975.

*   *   *

GILBERT, Edmund W(illiam)   1900-1973

PERSONAL: Born October 16, 1900, in Hemsworth, Yorkshire, England; son of Robert Gilbert; married Barbara M. Dundas, 1926. *Education:* Educated in England. *Home:* Old Cottage, Appleton, Abingdon, Oxfordshire, England.

CAREER: Oxford University, Hertford College, Oxford, England, lecturer in human geography, 1936-43, reader, 1943-53, professor of geography, 1953-67, professor emeritus, 1967-73.

WRITINGS: The Exploration of Western America, 1800-1850: An Historical Geography, Cambridge University Press, 1933, Cooper Square, 1966; (editor with John Frederick Unstead) *A Systematic Regional Geography,* Vol-

umes VI-IX, University of London Press, 1935-60; *How the Map Has Changed, 1938-1940,* G. Philip, 1941; *Brighton: Old Ocean's Bauble,* Methuen, 1954, International Publications Service, 1975; *Geography as a Humane Study,* Clarendon Press, 1955; *The University Town in England and West Germany: Marburg, Goettingen, Heidelberg, and Tuebingen, Viewed Comparatively with Oxford and Cambridge,* Department of Geography, University of Chicago, 1961; *Sir Halford Mackinder, 1861-1947: An Appreciation of His Life and Work,* G. Bell, 1961; *University Towns,* University of Sussex, 1962; *Vaughan Cornish, 1862-1948, and the Advancement of Knowledge Relating to the Beauty of Scenery in Town and Country,* Oxford Preservation Trust, 1965; *Urbanization and Its Problems,* Barnes & Noble, 1968; *British Pioneers in Geography,* Barnes & Noble, 1972. Also author of *Spain and Portugal,* four volumes, with R. P. Beckinsale and S. DeSa, 1941-45; also editor and author of introduction of *The Scope and Methods of Geography and the Geographical Pivot of History,* by Halford J. Mackinder, 1951.

(Died October 2, 1973)

*   *   *

GILBERT, (Lerman) Zack   1925-

PERSONAL: Born April 21, 1925, in McMullin, Mo.; son of Van Luther (a clergyman) and Cora (Allen) Gilbert; married Edna Sneed (a teacher), October 7, 1950; children: Marsha Leverne. *Education:* Attended Peters Business College of Chicago. *Politics:* "Independent. A workable socialism, with equal economic opportunity for all." *Religion:* "Universal." *Home:* 350 West 97th St., Chicago, Ill. 60628. *Office:* Chessie System Railroads, 2250 West 79th St., Chicago, Ill.

CAREER: Employed in defense plant in Chicago, Ill., 1943-45; insurance agent in Chicago, 1946-48; postal clerk in Chicago, 1948-53; shipping clerk in Chicago, 1953-57; insurance agent and broker in Chicago, 1957-66; Chessie System Railroads, Chicago, clerk, 1967—. Has given poetry readings in schools, churches, and clubs.

WRITINGS: "Black Mother of Soul" (one-act play), first performed in Chicago public school system, 1969; *My Own Hallelujahs* (poems), Third World Press, 1971.

Work has been anthologized in *Ebony Rhythm,* edited by Beatrice Murphy, Exposition Press, 1948; *For Malcolm,* edited by Dudley Randall and Margaret G. Burroughs, Broadside Press, 1967; *Projection in Literature,* edited by Robert C. Pooley, Edythe Daniel, Edmund J. Farrell, and others, Scott, Foresman, 1967; *The Poetry of the Negro,* edited by Langston Hughes and Arna Bontemps, Doubleday, 1970; *Richard Wright's Native Son,* edited by Richard Abcarian, Wadsworth, 1970; *To Gwen with Love,* edited by Patricia L. Brown, Don L. Lee, and Francis Ward, Johnson Publishing (Chicago), 1971; *Explorations in Literature,* edited by Philip McFarland, Linda Konicher, Jeanne King, and others, Houghton, 1972; and *The Poetry of Black America,* edited by Arnold Adoff, Harper, 1973.

Author of column "A Broader View," in *Chicago Bulletin,* 1965. Contributor of poems to periodicals, including *Voices, Negro Digest/Black World,* and *Liberator.*

WORK IN PROGRESS: A novel, *The Pergatories of Benjamin Todd;* a book of poems, *Up North Big City Street;* a play, "An Evening at Sally's Pad."

SIDELIGHTS: Gilbert writes; "Being black in America, my work naturally reflects the essence of that blackness in all of its many dimensions. I try to explore the many facets of these troubled contemporary times and attempt to point out a direction for the youths of today that will make their travels a little less difficult. I advocate or believe in no utopian world, but I do sincerely believe that there could be a more equitable distribution of wealth and power for all.''

BIOGRAPHICAL/CRITICAL SOURCES: Leaonead Pack Bailey, editor, *Broadside Authors and Artists,* Broadside Press, 1974.

* * *

GILCHRIST, Agnes A(ddison) 1907-1976

December 25, 1907—July 3, 1976; American architectural historian, educator, and author of books in her field. Obituaries: *New York Times,* July 10, 1976.

* * *

GILLESPIE, I(ris) S(ylvia) 1923-
    (Iris Andreski)

PERSONAL: Born December 20, 1923, in England; daughter of James (a contractor) and Ethel (a nurse; maiden name, Thyer) Gillespie; married Stanislaw Andreski, May 20, 1952 (divorced March 1, 1974); children: Deborah Felicity, Lucretia Consuelo, Adam Theophilus, Lukas Casimir, Sophia Carmen. *Education:* University of Manchester, student, 1942, 1975—. *Politics:* Socialist. *Religion:* Protestant. *Office:* University of Manchester, Manchester, Lancashire, England.

CAREER: Writer. Conducted research at University of Ibadan, 1963-64.

WRITINGS: (Under name Iris Andreski) *Old Wives' Tales: Life-Stories of African Women,* Schocken, 1970 (published in England as *Old Wives' Tales: Lives of Ibibio Women,* Routledge & Kegan Paul, 1970). Contributor of articles to *New Society, Book of Life, Marxism Today,* and *New Behaviour.*

WORK IN PROGRESS: A Theory of Social Evolution; Plato and the Intellectual Eros; The Collorg and the Isolate; The Soul of Eva Braun; A Manifesto for Free Women.

SIDELIGHTS: Iris Gillespie writes: "Man has frequently been described as a 'social animal.' He is, in fact, so much more social than other animals that he might with justice be described as a 'communist animal,' were it not for his tendency to exploit his social gifts for anti-social ends, using the sociability of his follow humans to captivate, coerce, or enslave them. It is possible that a great deal of our sociability is based on innate mechanisms. Apart from the basic survival instincts, which we share with bugs and plants, it seems fair to say that if other human instincts exist, they are mainly concerned with social interaction.''

* * *

GILLIE, Oliver (John) 1937-

PERSONAL: Born October 31, 1937, in North Shields, England; son of John Calder (an optician) and Ann (an artist; maiden name, Philipson) Gillie; married Louise Panton (a television producer), 1970; children: Lucinda, Juliet. *Education:* University of Edinburgh, B.Sc., 1960, Ph.D., 1966; Stanford University, graduate study, 1960-61. *Residence:* London, England. *Agent:* Harold Matson Co., Inc., 22 East 40th St., New York, N.Y. 10016. *Office: Sunday Times,* 200 Gray's Inn Rd., London W.C.1, England.

CAREER: University of Edinburgh, Edinburgh, Scotland,

assistant lecturer in genetics, 1961-65; Medical Research Council, London, England, researcher, 1965-68; *Science Journal,* London, England, biological sciences editor, 1968-69; *General Practitioner,* London, England, editor, 1970-71; *Sunday Times,* London, England, medical correspondent, 1971—.

MEMBER: Royal Society of Medicine (fellow), Genetical Society, National Union of Journalists, Association of Science Writers, Medical Journalists Association. *Awards, honors:* Co-winner with wife of Glaxo science writers' prize, 1975, for articles on childbirth; Order of the Bifurcated Needle from World Health Organization, 1976, for services in eradication of smallpox.

WRITINGS: The Living Cell, Thames & Hudson, 1970; *Who Do You Think You Are?* Saturday Review Press, 1976.

* * *

GILMAN, William H(enry) 1911-1976

August 9, 1911—February 16, 1976; American Emerson and Melville scholar, educator, and author of books in his field. Obituaries: *AB Bookman's Weekly,* April 5, 1976. (See index for previous *CA* sketch)

* * *

GILMORE, Daniel F(rancis) 1922-

PERSONAL: Born March 24, 1922, in New York; son of Patrick (an engineer) and Elizabeth (a teacher) Gilmore; married Clare L. Brubaker (an accountant), March 22, 1952. *Education:* Attended New York University. *Religion:* Roman Catholic. *Home:* 3850 Tunlaw Rd. N.W., Washington, D.C. 20007. *Office:* United Press International, 315 National Press Building, Washington, D.C. 20045.

CAREER/WRITINGS: United Press International (UPI), foreign correspondent in Asia, Europe, the Middle East, and Africa, 1941-48, bureau manager in London, England, Rome, Italy, Frankfurt, Germany, and Vienna, Austria, 1948-65, general European editor, based in London, 1965-71, general Asian editor, 1970-73, editor of national security affairs in Washington, D.C., 1973—. Notable assignments include covering the aftermath of the Arab-Israeli war in 1949, conflicts in Cyprus in 1950, American intervention in Lebanon in 1958, the Iraqi revolt in Baghdad in 1958, the Czech revolt in Prague and its aftermath in the 1960's, as well as activities in Moscow, Vietnam, and Cambodia. *Military service:* U.S. Army Air Forces, 1942-45. *Member:* White House Correspondents Association, State Department Correspondents Association, Overseas Writers, Air Force Association.

* * *

GILNER, Elias 1888(?)-1976

1888(?)—February 2, 1976; Russian-born American playwright, novelist, and author of nonfiction works. Obituaries: *New York Times,* February 4, 1976.

* * *

GINDER, Richard 1914-
    (Christopher McGlynn; Michael Monday)

PERSONAL: Born May 5, 1914, in Pennsylvania; son of William H. H. (a chemist and metallurgist) and Florence V. (a musician; maiden name, Stanton) Ginder. *Education:* Attended Duquesne University and Carnegie-Mellon University, both 1931-33; Catholic University of America,

A.B., 1935, M.A., 1936; graduate study at Peabody Institute, 1942-43; St. Mary's University, Baltimore, Md., S.T.L., 1947. *Home address:* P.O. Box 42273, Pittsburgh, Pa. 15203. *Agent:* Foley Agency, 34 East 38th St., New York, N.Y. 10036.

CAREER: Ordained Roman Catholic priest, 1940; assistant pastor in Zelienople, Pa., 1940-42; high school English teacher in Baltimore, Md., 1942-45; St. Mary's University, Baltimore, Md., instructor in homiletics English, 1942-45; *Priest* (monthly review), founder and editor, 1945-68; writer, 1968—. Parish priest of Roman Catholic churches in Blairsville, Pa., New Castle, Pa., Pittsburgh, Pa., and chaplain at parochial schools, 1946-67. Speaker for National Broadcasting Corp., Columbia Broadcasting System, and American Broadcasting Co., 1942-50. Censor librorum for Diocese of Pittsburgh, 1951-62. *Member:* American Guild of Organists (fellow). *Awards, honors:* First prize for original composition, from Pittsburgh Musical Arts Society, 1940.

WRITINGS: Everything To Gain, Our Sunday Visitor, 1942; *With Ink and Crozier: A Biography of Archbishop John F. Noll,* Our Sunday Visitor, 1950; *Thou Art the Rock,* Catholic Laymen of America, 1968; *Binding with Briars: Sex and Sin in the Catholic Church,* Prentice-Hall, 1975.

Musical compositions: *Missa Dominicalis,* McLaughlin & Reilly, 1936; *Mass in Honor of the Paraclete,* G. Schirmer, 1942; *Missa Marialis,* J. Fischer, 1945; also composer of six Marian hymns for four male voices, published by McLaughlin & Reilly, 1953-54.

Author of "Right or Wrong," column in *Our Sunday Visitor,* 1942-64, and "Father Jim," for Pflaum Publications, 1955-59; weekly columnist for *Pittsburgh Catholic,* 1955-61, and for *The Wanderer,* 1967-69. Contributor to church publications. Associate editor of *Our Sunday Visitor,* 1942-68; editor of *Catholic Choirmaster,* 1952-64. Consulting editor of Catholic Information Society, 1942-69, John Crawley Publications, 1955-65, and Catholic Viewpoint Publications, 1974—.

WORK IN PROGRESS: Two books, *A Testament of Faith: Problems in Belief,* and *Crazy About Sex: The Sexual Mania of the Catholic Church.*

AVOCATIONAL INTERESTS: Music, philosophy, English literature, languages (Greek, Latin, German, French, Italian), detective stories.

* * *

GINGRICH, Arnold 1903-1976

December 5, 1903—July 9, 1976; American men's magazine founding editor and author or editor of books on a variety of subjects. Obituaries: *New York Times,* July 10, 1976; *Washington Post,* July 11, 1976; *Newsweek,* July 19, 1976; *Time,* July 19, 1976; *AB Bookman's Weekly,* July 26, 1976; *Publishers Weekly,* July 26, 1976; *Current Biography,* September, 1976. (See index for previous *CA* sketch)

* * *

GINSBERG, Louis 1895-1976

October 1, 1895—July 8, 1976; American poet, educator, and author. Obituaries: *New York Times,* July 9, 1976. (See index for previous *CA* sketch)

* * *

GIRDLESTONE, Cuthbert Morton 1895-1975

September 17, 1895—December, 1975; British educator, scholar, musicologist, and author of books on French classicism and on other topics. Obituaries: *AB Bookman's Weekly,* March 8, 1976. (See index for previous *CA* sketch)

* * *

GITTLEMAN, Sol 1934-

PERSONAL: Born June 5, 1934, in Hoboken, N.J.; son of Frank and Edna Gittleman; married Robyn Singer (an educator), September 9, 1956; children: Julia, Peter, Thomas. *Education:* Drew University, B.A., 1955; Columbia University, M.A., 1956; University of Michigan, Ph.D., 1962. *Home:* 32 Fletcher St., Winchester, Mass. 01890. *Office:* Department of German, Tufts University, Medford, Mass. 02155.

CAREER: Mt. Holyoke College, South Hadley, Mass., assistant professor of German, 1962-64; Tufts University, Medford, Mass., associate professor, 1964-70, professor of German, 1970—, chairman of department, 1964—. *Member:* Modern Language Association of America, American Association of Teachers of German, American Association of Teachers of Yiddish, American Association of University Professors, Massachusetts Modern Language Association.

WRITINGS: Frank Wedekind, Twayne, 1969; *Sholom Aleichem,* Mouton & Co., 1974. Contributor to drama and language journals.

WORK IN PROGRESS: Fascism and the European Intellectuals.

* * *

GLASS, Andrew J(ames) 1935-

PERSONAL: Born November 30, 1935, in Warsaw, Poland; came to the United States in 1941, naturalized citizen, 1948; son of Martin A. and Wanda M. Glass; married Eleanor Sorrentino (a psychoanalyst), June 3, 1962. *Education:* Yale University, B.A., 1957. *Home:* 2901 Brandywine St. N.W., Washington, D.C. 20008. *Office:* Cox Newspapers, 1901 Pennsylvania Ave. N.W., Washington, D.C. 20006.

CAREER: New Haven Journal-Courier, New Haven, Conn., editor, 1957-60; *New York Herald Tribune,* New York, N.Y., reporter, 1960-66; *Washington Post,* Washington, D.C., staff reporter, 1966-68; *National Journal,* Washington, D.C., editor, 1970-74; Cox Newspapers, Washington, D.C., correspondent in Washington Bureau, 1974—.

WRITINGS: (Contributor) Judith G. Smith, editor, *Political Brokers: People, Organizations, Money, and Power,* Liveright, 1972.

* * *

GLASSTONE, Victor 1924-

PERSONAL: Born February 8, 1924, in Belgian Congo (now Zaire); son of Reuben and Gertrude (Hermann) Glasstone. *Education:* University of Cape Town, diploma in architecture, 1948. *Home:* Castello, 55040 Montemagno, Lucca, Italy. *Office:* 62 Westbourne Ter., London W.2, England.

CAREER: Architect, critic, and consultant in theater architecture. Member of central executive committee of Theatre's Advisory Council and British Centre of the International Theatre Institute. Delegate to theater congresses all over the world. Lecturer at many British universities in Tufts University London Program, University of Cape Town, University of Johannesburg, Glasgow School of Art, and other schools and institutions of art, architecture, and theatre. Has appeared on television and radio programs in England, Scotland, South Africa, the Soviet Union, Norway, and Northern Ireland. Consultant to Arts Council of Great Britain and Ireland and National Theatre. *Member:* Royal Institute of British Architects (associate), Institute of Architects (South Africa), Society for Theatre Research (member of central executive committee), Association of Theatre Technicians.

WRITINGS: Victorian and Edwardian Theatres, Harvard University Press, 1975; (with Charles Osborne) *Opera House Album,* Latimer New Dimensions, 1977. Contributor to *The Oxford Companion to the Theatre* and *Enciclopedia dello Spettacolo.* Contributor of articles, photographs, and drawings to architecture and theater journals; to popular magazines, including *Harper's Bazaar, Vogue, Queen, Fair Lady;* and to newspapers.

WORK IN PROGRESS: Theatre Architecture, a worldwide history of theatre building; *Nineteenth Century Theatres.*

SIDELIGHTS: Glasstone's photographs and drawings have been exhibited in London, Cape Town, and Belfast.

* * *

GLEASNER, Diana (Cottle) 1936-

PERSONAL: Born April 26, 1936, in New Jersey; daughter of Delmar Leroy (a research chemist) and Elizabeth (Stanton) Cottle; married G. William Gleasner (a free-lance photographer), July 12, 1958; children: Stephan William, Suzanne Lynn. *Education:* Ohio Wesleyan University, B.A. (cum laude), 1958; University of Buffalo, M.A., 1964. *Home and office:* 268 Hopkins Rd., Williamsville, N.Y. 14221.

CAREER: High school teacher of English and physical education in Kenmore, N.Y., 1958-64; free-lance photojournalist, 1964—. Instructor at State University of New York at Buffalo, 1973-76. *Member:* American Society of Journalists and Authors, Outdoor Writers of America, National League of American Pen Women (president of western New York branch), New York State Outdoor Writers Association, Women in Boating (president).

WRITINGS: The Plaid Mouse, Daughters of St. Paul, 1966; *Pete Polar Bear's Trip down the Erie Canal,* University of Buffalo Press, 1969; *Women in Swimming,* Harvey House, 1976; (with husband William Gleasner) *The Garden of Kauii: Hawaii's Garden Isle,* Oriental, 1977; *Women in Track and Field,* Harvey House, in press. Contributor of more than two hundred articles to magazines, including *Better Homes and Gardens, Field and Stream, Good Housekeeping, Travel, Argosy, Rotarian, Boating, Camping Journal,* and *Science Digest.* Eastern editor of *Great Lakes Cruise Guide.*

SIDELIGHTS: Diana Gleasner writes: "My husband and I are a full time free-lance photojournalism team. He handles the photography. I do the writing. We're currently spending a year on the island of Kauii, Hawaii, researching, writing, and photographing. We both enjoy capturing the beauty of the outdoor world and conveying it to our readers."

* * *

GLEASON, Ralph J(oseph) 1917-1975

PERSONAL: Born March 1, 1917, in New York, N.Y.; son of Ralph A. and Mary (Quinlisk) Gleason; married Jean Rayburn, October 12, 1940; children: Bridget, Stacy, Toby. *Education:* Attended Columbia University, 1934-38. *Residence:* Berkeley, Calif.

CAREER: Journalist; co-founder and editor of *Jazz Information,* 1939-41; music reviewer for *San Francisco Chronicle,* 1950-53, author of daily music column after 1953; editor and publisher of *Jazz: A Quarterly of American Music,* 1957-59; radio disc jockey in San Francisco, Calif., during the 1960's; co-founder of *Rolling Stone* in 1967, also editor, critic, and author of column "Perspectives." Became vice-president of Fantasy-Prestige Milestone Records, 1970. Executive producer of feature film "Payday"; producer and host of television program "Jazz Casual," for National Educational Television, 1962, and of a documentary program on Duke Ellington. Lecturer at University of California, Extension Division, 1960-63, and Sonoma State College (now California State College, Sonoma), 1965-67; member of advisory board of Lenox School of Jazz and Institute of Jazz. Adviser to University of California Jazz Festival, 1967-68. *Wartime service:* Worked with Office of War Information, 1942-44.

AWARDS, HONORS: Two nominations for Emmy awards from National Academy of Television Arts and Sciences, for television documentary program on Duke Ellington; Deems Taylor Award from American Society of Composers, Authors and Publishers, 1967, for "Jazz: Black Art, Black Music," and 1973, for a tribute to Louis Armstrong; awards from Screen Writers Guild and National Film Critics Board for feature film "Payday."

WRITINGS: (Editor) *Jam Session: An Anthology of Jazz,* Putnam, 1958; *The Jefferson Airplane and the San Francisco Sound,* Ballantine, 1969; *Celebrating the Duke: And Louis, Bessie, Billie, Bird, Carmen, Miles, Dizzy, and Other Heroes,* Atlantic, 1975. Author of the first syndicated newspaper column on jazz. Contributor to popular magazines, including *New Statesman, American Scholar, Esquire, Show Business Illustrated,* and *Saturday Review.* Former editor of *Ramparts;* associate editor, columnist, and critic for *Downbeat,* 1948-60; contributing editor of *Hi/Fi Stereo Review* and *Scholastic Roto.*

SIDELIGHTS: Gleason discovered jazz music in high school and spent the rest of his life writing about it. His first column came about following mixed criticism and praise for his reviews of folk music, popular music, and jazz, appearing in a column previously devoted only to classical music.

OBITUARIES: New York Times, June 4, 1975; *Washington Post,* June 6, 1976.*

(Died June 3, 1975, in Berkeley, Calif.)

* * *

GLOAG, John (Edwards) 1896-

PERSONAL: Born August 10, 1896, in London, England; son of Robert McCowan and Lillian (Morgan) Gloag; married Gertrude Mary Ward, 1922; children: Frances Joy Custance, Julian. *Education:* Attended technical high school in London, England. *Home:* 3 Mall, East Sheen, London SW14 7EN, England. *Agent:* A. D. Peters & Co. Ltd., 10 Buckingham St., Adelphi, London WC2N 6BU, England; and Georges Borchardt, Inc., 145 East 52nd St., New York, N.Y. 10022.

CAREER: Employed at studio of Thornton-Smith Ltd., 1913-16, and in advertising department of Lever Organisation, 1920-22; *Cabinet Maker,* technical and art editor, 1922-27, editor, 1927; director of Pritchard, Wood & Partners Ltd., 1928-61; full-time writer, 1961—. Director of public relations for Timber Development Association, 1936-38. Member of utility furniture and advisory committee of Board of Trade, 1943-47; chairman of International Conference on Industrial Design, 1951. Member of board of trustees of Sir John Soane's Museum, 1960-70. Has broadcast lectures and stories since 1933 and appeared on television programs. *Military service:* British Army, 1916-18; served in Essex Regiment, 1916-17, and Welsh Guards, 1917-19; became 2nd lieutenant; invalided home, 1918.

MEMBER: Society of Arts (fellow), Royal Institute of British Architects (fellow), Society of Industrial Artists and Designers (fellow), Society of Antiquaries (London; fellow), Council of Industrial Design, Royal Society of Arts (member of council, 1948-56, 1958-63; vice-president, 1952-54), Society of Architectural Historians of Great Britain (president, 1960-64), Arts Club, Garrick Club. *Awards, honors:* Royal Society of Arts silver medal, 1943, bicentenary gold medal, 1958.

WRITINGS—Non-fiction: *Simple Schemes for Decoration,* Duckworth, 1922; (with Leslie Mansfield) *The House We Ought to Live In,* Duckworth, 1923; *Colour and Comfort,* Duckworth, 1924, Frederick A. Stokes, 1925; *Time, Taste, and Furniture,* G. Richards, 1925; *Artifex, or the Future of Craftsmanship,* Dutton, 1926; (with C. Thompson Walker) *Home Life in History: Social Life and Manners in Britain, 200 B.C.-A.D. 1926,* Ernest Benn, 1927; *Men and Buildings,* Scribner, 1931, illustrated edition, Chantry Publications, 1950; *English Furniture,* A. & C. Black, 1934, 6th edition, 1973; (editor) *Design in Modern Life,* Allen & Unwin, 1934; *Industrial Art Explained,* Allen & Unwin, 1934, enlarged edition, 1946; *Word Warfare: Some Aspects of German Propaganda and English Liberty,* Nicolson & Watson, 1939.

The American Nation: A Short History of the United States, Cassell, 1942, revised edition (with son, Julian Gloag), 1955; (editor) *The Place of Glass in Building,* Allen & Unwin, 1942; *What About Business?,* Penguin, 1942, revised edition published as *What About Enterprise?,* Allen & Unwin, 1948; *The Missing Technician in Industrial Production,* Allen & Unwin, 1944; *The Englishman's Castle: A History of Houses, Large and Small, in Town and Country, from A.D. 100 to the Present Day,* Eyre & Spottiswoode, 1944, 2nd edition, 1949; *Plastics and Industrial Design,* Allen & Unwin, 1945; *British Furniture Makers,* Collins, 1945; (with Grey Wornum) *House Out of Factory,* Allen & Unwin, 1946; *Good Design, Good Business,* H.M.S.O., 1947; *Self-Training for Industrial Designers,* Allen & Unwin, 1947; *The English Tradition in Design,* King Penguin, 1947, revised edition, A. & C. Black, 1959, Macmillan, 1960; (with D. L. Bridgewater) *A History of Cast Iron in Architecture,* Allen & Unwin, 1948; (contributor) Richard Herbert Sheppard, editor, *Building for Daylight,* Allen & Unwin, 1948; *How to Write Technical Books,* Allen & Unwin, 1950; *Two Thousand Years of England,* Cassell, 1952; *A Short Dictionary of Furniture,* Allen & Unwin, 1952, abridged edition, 1966, 3rd edition, revised, 1969; *Georgian Grace: A Social History of Design from 1660 to 1830,* Macmillan, 1956, revised edition, Spring Books, 1967; *Guide to Western Architecture,* Grove, 1958, revised edition, Spring Books, 1969; (author of introduction) Irwin Untermyer, *Catalogue of a Collection of English Furniture,* Metropolitan Museum of Art, 1958; *Advertising in Modern Life,* Heinemann, 1959.

Victorian Comfort: A Social History of Design from 1830-1900, Macmillan, 1961, revised edition, St. Martin's, 1973; *Victorian Taste: Some Social Aspects of Architecture and Industrial Design from 1820-1900,* Macmillan, 1962, revised edition, 1972; *The English Tradition in Architecture,* Barnes & Noble, 1963; *Architecture,* Cassell, 1963, Hawthorn,

1964; *The Englishman's Chair: Origins, Design, and Social History of Seat Furniture in England,* Allen & Unwin, 1964, published as *The Chair: Its Origins, Design, and Social History,* A. S. Barnes, 1967; *Enjoying Architecture,* Oriel Press, 1965; (editor) *Early English Decorative Detail from Contemporary Source Books,* A. Tiranti, 1965; (editor) *Introduction to Early English Decorative Detail,* Academy Editions, 1965; *A Social History of Furniture Design from B.C. 1300 to A.D. 1960,* Crown, 1966; (author of introduction) Dora Ware, *A Short Dictionary of British Architects,* Allen & Unwin, 1967; *Mr. Loudon's England: The Life and Work of John Claudius Loudon, and His Influence on Architecture and Furniture Design,* Oriel Press, 1970; (with Maureen Stafford) *Guide to Furniture Styles: English and French, 1450-1850,* A. & C. Black, 1972. Also author of *The Architectural Interpretation of History,* 1975.

Fiction: *Tomorrow's Yesterday* (film drama), Allen & Unwin, 1932; *The New Pleasure,* Allen & Unwin, 1933; *Winter's Youth,* Allen & Unwin, 1934; *Sweet Racket,* Cassell, 1936; *Ripe for Development,* Cassell, 1936; *Sacred Edifice,* Cassell, 1937, revised edition, 1954; *It Makes a Nice Change* (stories), Nicolson & Watson, 1938; *Documents Marked Secret,* Cassell, 1938, Penguin, 1945; *Manna,* Cassell, 1940; *Unwilling Adventurer,* Cassell, 1940; *I Want an Audience,* Cassell, 1941; *Mr. Buckby Is Not at Home,* Cassell, 1942; *Ninety-Nine Percent,* Cassell, 1944; *In Camera,* Cassell, 1945; *First One and Twenty* (includes "Tomorrow's Yesterday" and twenty short stories), Allen & Unwin, 1946; *Kind Uncle Buckby,* Cassell, 1947; *All England at Home,* Cassell, 1949; *Take One a Week: An Omnibus Volume of 52 Short Stories,* Chantry Publications, 1950; *Not in the Newspapers,* Cassell, 1953; *Slow,* Cassell, 1954; *Unlawful Justice,* Cassell, 1962; *Rising Suns,* Cassell, 1964; *Caesar of the Narrow Seas,* Cassell, 1969; *The Eagles Depart,* St. Martin's, 1973.

Poems: *Board Room Ballads, and Other Verses,* Allen & Unwin, 1933.

AVOCATIONAL INTERESTS: Reading.

*   *   *

GLOAG, Julian   1930-

PERSONAL: Born July 2, 1930, in London, England; son of John Edwards (a writer) and Mary Gertrude (Ward) Gloag; married Danielle J. H. Haase-Dubosc (a university professor), September 4, 1968; children: Oliver Toby Jacques, Vanessa Agnes Judith. *Education:* Magdalene College, Cambridge, B.A., 1953, M.A., 1958. *Home:* 4 place du 18 juin 1940, 75006 Paris, France. *Agent:* Georges Borchardt, Inc., 145 East 52nd St., New York, N.Y. 10022.

CAREER: Chamber's Encyclopaedia, London, England, researcher, 1954-56; Ronald Press, New York, N.Y., assistant editor, 1956-59; free-lance writer, 1959-61; Hawthorn Books, New York, N.Y., editor, 1961-63; free-lance writer, 1963—. *Military service:* British Army, rifleman, 1949-50. *Member:* Royal Society of Literature (fellow), Royal Society of Arts (fellow), Authors Guild of Authors League of America, Garrick Club.

WRITINGS: Our Mother's House (novel), Simon & Schuster, 1963; *A Sentence of Life* (novel), Simon & Schuster, 1966; *Maundy* (novel), Simon & Schuster, 1969; *A Woman of Character* (novel), Random House, 1973.

*   *   *

GODECHOT, Jacques Leon   1907-

PERSONAL: Born January 3, 1907, in Luneville, France;

son of Georges and Therese (Lazard) Godechot; married Lambert Arlette, September 13, 1933; children: Didier, Thierry, Yves, Eveline (Mrs. Dominique Mouries). *Education:* University of Nancy, licence es lettres, 1927; Sorbonne, University of Paris, Doctorat, 1938. *Home:* 17 rue A Mercie, Toulouse 31000, France. *Office:* Universite de Toulouse-Le Mirail, Toulouse 31081, France.

CAREER: Lycee Kleber, Strasbourg, France, history teacher, 1933-35; Ecole Navale, Brest, France, professor of maritime history, 1935-40; University of Toulouse, Toulouse, France, professor of contemporary history, 1945-74, director of history department, 1956-76, dean of School of Literature and Humanities, 1961-71. *Military service:* French Army, 1929-30 and 1939-45; served in infantry; became captain. *Member:* International Committee on the French Revolution (president, 1975—), Societe des etudes robespierristes (president, 1926—), Societe d'Histoire Moderne (president, 1974-75), Societa di Storia del Risorgimento (honorary member), American Historical Association, Societe d'histoire de la Revolution de 1848 (president, 1961—), French Committee on Economic and Social History of the French Revolution (president, 1975—). *Awards, honors:* Chevalier de la Legion d'honneur, 1962; chevalier del Merite italien, 1963.

WRITINGS: La Propagande royaliste aux armees sous le directoire, Mellottee (Paris), 1933; *Les Commissaires aux armees sous le Directoire: Contribution a l'etude des rapports entre les pouvoirs civils et militaires,* Fustier (Paris), 1937; *Histoire de l'Atlantique,* Bordas (Paris), 1947; (editor) *La Revolution de 1848 a Toulouse et dans la Haute-Garonne,* Prefecture de la Haute-Garonne (Toulouse), 1949; *Les Institutions de la France sous la Revolution et l'Empire,* Presses Universitaires de France (Paris), 1951, 2nd edition, 1968; *Histoire de Malte,* Presses Universitaires de France, 1952, 2nd edition, 1970; *La Grande Nation: L'Expansion revolutionnaire de la France dans le monde de 1789 a 1799,* Aubier (Paris), 1956.

La Contre-revolution: Doctrine et action, 1789-1804, Presses Universitaires de France, 1961, translation by Salvator Attanasio published as *The Counter-Revolution: Doctrine and Action, 1789-1804,* Fertig, 1971; (with others) *Babeuf [et] Buonarroti: Pour le deuxieme centenaire de leur naissance* (Societe des etudes robespierristes), Thomas (Nancy), 1961; *Les Revolutions, 1770-1799,* Presses Universitaires de France, 1963, 3rd edition, 1970, translation by Herbert H. Rowen published as *France and the Atlantic Revolution of the Eighteenth Century, 1770-1799,* Free Press, 1965; (editor and author of introduction) *La Pensee revolutionnaire en France et en Europe, 1780-1799,* A. Colin (Paris), 1964; *La Prise de la Bastille, 14 juillet 1789,* Gallimard, 1965, translation by Jean Stewart published as *The Taking of the Bastille, July 14th, 1789,* Scribner, 1970; (with Suzanne Moncassin) *Demographie et subsistances en Languedoc [du XVIII au debut du XIXe–siecle],* Bibliotheque Nationale, 1965; (author of introduction) *La Presse ouvriere, 1819-1850: Angleterre, Etats-Unis, France, Belgique, Italie, Allemagne, Tchecoslovaquie, Hongrie,* Societe d'histoire de la Revolution de 1848 (Bures-sur-Yvette), 1966; *L'Europe et l'Amerique a l'epoque napoleonienne, 1800-1815,* Presses Universitaires de France, 1967, translation with Beatrice Hyslop and David Dowd published as *The Napoleonic Era in Europe,* Holt, 1971; (contributor) *L'-Abolition du regime feodal dans le monde occidental,* Societe des etudes robespierristes (Paris), 1969; *Napoleon,* A. Michel (Paris), 1969; *L'epoca delle rivoluzioni,* Unione tipografico-editrice torinese, 1969; (with Claude Bellanger,

Claude Levy and others) *Histoire General de la presse francaise,* five volumes, Presses Universitaires de France, 1969-76.

(Editor) *Les Constitutions de la France depuis 1789,* Garnier-Flammarion (Paris), 1970; (contributor) *L'Abolition de la feodalite dans le monde occidental,* two volumes, Editions du Centre national de la recherche scientifique (Paris), 1971; *Les Revolutions de 1848,* A. Michel (Paris), 1971; (with M. Vaussard) *Histoire de l'Italie moderne,* two volumes, Hachette (Paris), 1972; *Un Jury pour la Revolution,* R. Laffont (Paris), 1974; (with Philippe Wolff and others) *Histoire de Toulouse,* Edouard Privat (Toulouse), 1974.

WORK IN PROGRESS: La vie quotidienne en France sous le Directoire, publication expected in 1977; a study of "Jacobin Europe"; a study of the origins of democracy in France.

* * *

GODOLPHIN, Francis R(ichard) B(orroum) 1903-1974

PERSONAL: Born April 8, 1903, in Del Rio, Tex.; son of Francis Richard and Alma (Borroum) Godolphin; married Isabelle Simmons, July 25, 1925 (died December, 1964); married Catherine Vanderpoel Clark, June 19, 1965; children: (first marriage) Jeane (Mrs. Stephen C. Kurtz), Thomas (deceased). *Education:* Princeton University, A.B., 1924, Ph.D., 1929; New York University, M.A., 1926. *Politics:* Democrat. *Residence:* Princeton, N.J.

CAREER: New York University, New York, N.Y., instructor in classics, 1924-26; New Jersey College for Women, instructor in classics, 1926-27; Princeton University, Princeton, N.J., instructor, 1927-30, assistant professor, 1930-40, associate professor, 1940-45, professor of classics, 1946-70, acting chairman of department, 1941-42, chairman, 1942-45, dean of College of Arts and Sciences, 1945-55. *Military service:* U.S. Marine Corps Reserve, active duty, 1942-45; served in Pacific theater; became captain; received Bronze Star Medal. *Member:* American Philological Association, Classical Association of the Atlantic States, American Association of University Professors, Eastern Association of Deans and Advisers of Men (past vice-president).

WRITINGS: (Editor and author of introduction) *The Greek Historians,* Random House, 1942; (editor) *The Latin Poets,* Modern Library, 1949; (editor) *The Great Classical Myths,* Modern Library, 1964. Contributor to journals in the classics.

OBITUARIES: New York Times, December 30, 1974; *Washington Post,* December 30, 1974.*

(Died December 29, 1974, in Tucson, Ariz.)

* * *

GOEBEL, Dorothy (Burne) 1898-1976

August 24, 1898—March 12, 1976; American historian, educator, and author of books in her field. Obituaries: *New York Times,* March 14, 1976; *AB Bookman's Weekly,* April 5, 1976.

* * *

GOFFIN, Raymond C. 1890(?)-1976

1890(?)—June 23, 1976; British Chaucerian scholar, publisher, and editor of books in the field of English literature. Obituaries: *AB Bookman's Weekly,* July 26, 1976.

GOFMAN, John W(illiam) 1918-

PERSONAL: Born September 21, 1918, in Cleveland, Ohio; son of David M. (a merchant) and Sarah (Kaplan) Gofman; married Helen Fahl (a professor and physician), August 10, 1940; children: John David. *Education:* Oberlin College, A.B., 1939; University of California, Berkeley, Ph.D., 1943; University of California, San Francisco, M.D., 1946. *Home:* 1045 Clayton St., San Francisco, Calif. 94117.

CAREER: University of California, Berkeley, intern at university hospital, 1946-47, assistant professor, 1947-51, associate professor, 1951-54, professor of medical physics, 1954-73, professor emeritus, 1973—. Chairman of Committee for Nuclear Responsibility, 1971—. *Awards, honors:* Stouffer prize, 1972, for research on heart disease.

WRITINGS: Coronary Heart Disease, C. C Thomas, 1958; (with Alex Nichols and Virginia Dobbin) *Dietary Prevention and Treatment of Heart Disease,* Putnam, 1958; *What We Do Know About Heart Attacks,* Putnam, 1958; (with Arthur Tamplin) *Population Control through Nuclear Pollution,* Rodale Books, 1970; (with Tamplin) *Personal Power: The Case Against Nuclear Power Plants,* Rodale Books, 1971.

WORK IN PROGRESS: Research on plutonium toxicity.

*   *   *

GOLANT, William 1937-

PERSONAL: Born May 10, 1937, in Chicago, Ill.; son of Samuel and Evelyn (Stock) Golant; married Alexandra Adam (a city councillor), July 1, 1963; children: Benjamin, Rebecca. *Education:* University of California, Los Angeles, B.A., 1958, M.A., 1960; Queen's College, Oxford, B.Litt., 1967. *Politics:* "Humanity's advance." *Religion:* "Wandered Jew-ish." *Home:* 38 Lower North St., Exeter, Devonshire, England. *Agent:* David Higham Associates, 76 Dean St., London W.1, England. *Office:* Department of History, University of Exeter, Exeter, Devonshire EX4 4QJ, England.

CAREER: University of Exeter, Exeter, Devonshire, England, lecturer in history, 1964—.

WRITINGS: The Long Afternoon (non-fiction), St. Martin's 1975.

WORK IN PROGRESS: Images of the Empire, photographs of the Imperial Institute in London, from about 1900 to 1940.

SIDELIGHTS: Golant writes: "I acquired the wish to be a writer with venturing outwards: as a bicycle-rider voyaging through the metropolis, tourist in Mexico, and woman's companion at tea. Only in a few writing sessions have I felt a writer, times when there was the confidence to let sensibility mould knowledge, attaining what Jackson Pollack called a 'controlled accident.'"

*   *   *

GOLDBERG, Arthur J(oseph) 1908-

PERSONAL: Born August 8, 1908, in Chicago, Ill.; son of Joseph and Rebecca (Perlstein) Goldberg; married Dorothy Kurgans (an artist), July 18, 1931; children: Barbara Goldberg Cramer, Robert Michael. *Education:* Attended Crane Junior College, Chicago; Northwestern University, B.S.L., 1929, J.D. (summa cum laude), 1930. *Home:* 2801 New Mexico Ave. N.W., Washington, D.C. 20007. *Office:* 1101 17th St. N.W., Suite 1100, Washington, D.C. 20036.

CAREER: Admitted to Illinois State Bar, 1929, U.S. Supreme Court Bar, 1937; practiced law privately in Chicago,

Ill., 1929-41; partner of Goldberg, Devoe, Shadur & Mikva, Chicago, 1945-61; U.S. secretary of labor, 1961-62; associate justice of Supreme Court, 1962-65; U.S. ambassador to United Nations, 1965-68; Princeton University, Princeton, N.J., Charles Evans Hughes Professor, 1968-69; Columbia University, New York, N.Y., distinguished professor, 1969-70; American University, Washington, D.C., University Professor of Law and Diplomacy, 1971-73; Hastings College of the Law, San Francisco, Calif., visiting distinguished professor, 1974—. General counsel, Congress of Industrial Organizations, 1945-61, United Steel Workers of America, 1948-61; special counsel and general counsel of industrial union department, American Federation of Labor-Congress of Industrial Organizations (AFL-CIO), 1955-61. Chairman, Truman Center for the Advancement of Peace, 1968—. *Military service:* U.S. Army, Office of Strategic Services, 1942-44; became major. *Member:* National Legal Aid Association (director), American Bar Association, American Jewish Committee (former president; now honorary president), Illinois Bar Association, D.C. Bar Association, Association of the Bar of the City of New York, Chicago Bar Association, Order of the Coif, Literary Club, City Club of Chicago. *Awards, honors:* Voted outstanding labor personality of the year by New York Newspaper Guild, 1961; awarded Herbert H. Lehman Medal from Jewish Theology Seminary; recipient of honorary degrees from colleges and universities, including Boston College, Brown University, Catholic University, University of Denver, Fordham University, Hebrew University, and Tel Aviv University.

WRITINGS: AFL-CIO: Labor United, McGraw, 1956; *The Defenses of Freedom: The Public Papers of Arthur J. Goldberg,* edited by Daniel Patrick Moynihan, Harper, 1966; *Equal Justice: The Warren Era of the Supreme Court,* Northwestern University Press, 1971. Also author of legal papers and of speeches and addresses published by governmental and legal organizations.

*   *   *

GOLDEN, Robert Edward 1945-

PERSONAL: Born March 2, 1945, in St. Louis, Mo.; son of Robert Edward (a businessman) and Marian (O'Brien) Golden; married Barbara Masana (a teacher), October 7, 1967. *Education:* University of Michigan, A.B., 1967; University of Rochester, M.A., 1970, Ph.D., 1972. *Home:* 261 Antlers Dr., Rochester, N.Y. 14619. *Office:* Department of Language and Literature, Rochester Institute of Technology, 1 Lamb Memorial Dr., Rochester, N.Y. 14623.

CAREER: Rochester Institute of Technology, Rochester, N.Y., assistant professor of language and literature, 1971—. *Member:* Modern Language Association of America, American Association of University Professors, Northeast Modern Language Association, Phi Beta Kappa, Phi Kappa Phi.

WRITINGS: (Editor with J. Albert Robbins) *American Literary Manuscripts,* University of Georgia Press, 1977; *Flannery O'Connor: A Reference Guide,* G. K. Hall, 1977. Contributor to *Critique.*

WORK IN PROGRESS: Research on contemporary American fiction writers.

*   *   *

GOLDGAR, Bertrand A(lvin) 1927-

PERSONAL: Born November 17, 1927, in Macon, Ga.; son of Benjamin Meyer (an accountant) and Annie (Shapiro)

Goldgar; married Corinne Hartman (an executive assistant), April 6, 1950; children: Arnold Benjamin, Anne Hartman. *Education:* Vanderbilt University, B.A., 1948, M.A., 1949; Princeton University, M.A., 1957, Ph.D., 1958. *Home:* 914 East Eldorado St., Appleton, Wis. 54911. *Office:* Department of English, Lawrence University, Appleton, Wis. 54911.

CAREER: Clemson University, Clemson, S.C., instructor, 1948-50, assistant professor of English, 1951-52; Lawrence University, Appleton, Wis., instructor, 1957-61, assistant professor, 1961-65, associate professor, 1965-71, professor of English, 1971—. *Military service:* U.S. Army, 1952-54. *Member:* Modern Language Association of America, American Society of Eighteenth Century Studies. *Awards, honors:* American Council of Learned Societies fellowship, 1973-74.

WRITINGS: The Curse of Party: Swift's Relations with Addison and Steele, University of Nebraska Press, 1961; (editor) *The Literary Criticism of Alexander Pope,* University of Nebraska Press, 1965; (contributor) *The Augustan Milieux,* Clarendon Press, 1970; *Walpole and the Wits: The Relation of Politics to Literature, 1722-1742,* University of Nebraska Press, 1976. Contributor to literature and philology journals.

WORK IN PROGRESS: An annotated edition of *The Grub-Street Journal, 1730-1737.*

* * *

GOLDMAN, Susan 1939-

PERSONAL: Born March 14, 1939, in New York, N.Y.; daughter of Abraham (a manufacturing jeweler) and Julia (Berlin) Moldof; married Hubert M. Goldman (a physician), June 7, 1959 (separated); children: Katherine, John, Peter. *Education:* Attended Art Students League of New York, 1951-55, 1959; Oberlin College, B.A. (honors), 1959; University of California, Los Angeles, graduate study, 1962. *Politics:* Democrat. *Religion:* Jewish. *Home and office:* 19431 Romar St., Northridge, Calif. 91324.

CAREER: Artist and writer. Lecturer at California State University, Northridge, 1977—. Art work has been shown in California since 1968. *Member:* Society of Children's Book Writers, Southern California Council on Literature for Children and Young People, Los Angeles County Museum of Art, Center of Films for Children (University of Southern California), University of California Los Angeles Art Council.

WRITINGS: Grandma Is Somebody Special (juvenile), Albert Whitman, 1976.

Filmstrips: "How We Grow," for Windmills Ltd.; "What Is a Handicap," Windmills Ltd.; "The Retarded Child: Answers to Questions Parents Ask," Windmills Ltd.; "First Aid Rescue," Alan Burks Associates.

Author of film "The Neighborhood Store," for television, Avatar Learning.

Contributor to *Highlights for Children.*

WORK IN PROGRESS: I'm Dancing, a juvenile picture book; a humorous novel for children; a series of filmstrips on maps and globes, for elementary school children.

SIDELIGHTS: Susan Goldman writes: "Books have always been vitally important to me. My dream was to illustrate children's books, but I never imagined I'd be able to write them as well. I want to make books and filmstrips that are meaningful to children. I want to entertain and delight

but I also want to express the feelings and problems of children so that they will recognize themselves in books and gain understanding."

* * *

GOLDSTEIN, Stewart 1941-

PERSONAL: Born June 26, 1941, in New York; son of Irving C. and Tillie A. (Alpern) Goldstein; married Rosalind Merritt (an interior designer), March 6, 1976; children: Jennifer Lynn, Robyn Faye. *Education:* Attended University of Miami, Coral Gables, Fla., 1959-60, and Pasadena Playhouse, 1960-62. *Religion:* Jewish. *Home:* 11537 Southwest 64th St., Miami, Fla. 33173.

CAREER: Real estate salesman, 1964—; construction coordinator, 1965—; Carol Housing Corp., Miami, Fla., sales manager, 1975—.

WRITINGS: Oldies But Goodies: The Rock and Roll Years, Mason/Charter, 1977. Author of about thirty songs.

WORK IN PROGRESS: Another book dealing with nostalgia.

SIDELIGHTS: Goldstein writes: "As a teen of the fifties, I had a more than casual interest in the music of those times. My show business aspirations included music. The combination of attending acting school, writing songs and acting and singing professionally, led to the book. The primary motivation was love of the subject." *Avocational interests:* Playing the guitar, singing, playing Jai Alai.

* * *

GOLDSTONE, Aline L(ewis) 1878(?)-1976

1878(?)—May 3, 1976; American poet, lecturer, and author. Obituaries: *New York Times,* May 6, 1976.

* * *

GONZALEZ, Gloria 1940-

PERSONAL: Born January 10, 1940, in New York, N.Y.; daughter of Angel and Mary (Cabrera) Gonzalez; children: Arleen, Kelly, Troy. *Education:* Studied playwrighting at the New School with Harold Callen and Jean-Claude van Itallie, playwrighting and directing with Lee Strasberg, and acting with Anthony Mannino. *Residence:* West New York, N.J. *Agent:* Robert Freedman, Brandt & Brandt, 101 Park Ave., New York, N.Y. 10017.

CAREER: Investigative reporter for various New Jersey daily newspapers; free-lance writer; now full-time playwright. *Member:* Dramatists Guild, Authors League of America, Drama Desk. *Awards, honors:* First prize in Jacksonville University College of Fine Arts national playwriting contest, 1975, for "Curtains"; finalist for Stanley Drama Award, 1975; Webster Groves Russell B. Sharp Annual Playwriting Award, 1976, for "Lights."

WRITINGS—Plays: Moving On! (all one-act; includes "Moving On!," first produced in New York City at Playbox Theatre, October, 1972; "Cuba: Economy Class!"; and "The New America"), Samuel French, 1971; *The Glad Man,* Knopf, 1975; *Curtains* (produced in New York City at Hudson Guild Theatre, October, 1975), published by Dramatists Play Service.

Unpublished plays: (With Edna Schappert) "Celebrate Me," first produced in New York City at Playbox Theatre, April, 1971; "Love Is a Tuna Casserole," produced by New York Theatre Ensemble, September, 1971; "Waiting Room," produced in New York City at Theatre at Noon,

January, 1974; "A Sanctuary in the City," produced in Altadena, Calif., at Theatre Americana, March, 1975; "Let's Hear It for Miss America," produced in St. Petersburg, Fla., at Country Dinner Playhouse, August, 1976; "Lights," produced in St. Louis, August, 1976.

Television drama: "Gaucho," first broadcast on Columbia Broadcasting System, Inc. (CBS-TV), June 2, 1970.

Also author of play, *Checkmate of a Queen,* published by Performance Publishing.

Plays included in anthologies, *One-Act Plays for Our Times,* edited by Frances Griffith and others, Popular Library, 1973; and *Best Short Plays of 1976,* edited by Stanley Richards, Dodd, 1976. Contributor of articles to *New York Times* and *New York Daily News;* regular contributor to *Dramatists Quarterly.*

WORK IN PROGRESS: Gaucho, a juvenile novel for Knopf, based on her own television drama; a comedy and another play.

SIDELIGHTS: Gloria Gonzalez told *CA:* "Despite the inherent pain, frustrations and anguish—the theatre, for me, remains the only arena worth writing for. I require the excitement and challenge of an instant reaction from a friendly or hostile audience as opposed to book reviews months, even a year after the book is written."

*   *   *

GOODMAN, Emily Jane   1940-

PERSONAL: Born March 30, 1940, in Brooklyn, N.Y.; daughter of Martin and Sally (Sirota) Goodman. *Education:* Brooklyn College of the City University of New York, B.A., 1961; Brooklyn Law School, J.D., 1968. *Home:* 50 Riverside Dr., New York, N.Y. 10024. *Office:* 1414 Avenue of the Americas, New York, N.Y. 10019.

CAREER: Admitted to the Bar of New York State, 1968; attorney in private practice, 1971—. Teacher, Long Island University, 1968, and City University of New York at Staten Island, 1974. Director, Women's Law Center, 1972—; New York counsel to National Council of Negro Women, 1975. Lecturer. *Member:* National Lawyers' Guild (member of New York Board of directors), Women's Bar Association, New York City Bar Association, Women's Forum, New York County Lawyers.

WRITINGS: The Tenant Survival Book, Bobbs-Merrill, 1972; (with Phyllis Chesler) *Women, Money and Power,* Morrow, 1976. Contributor of articles to periodicals, including *New York Times, McCall's, Village Voice,* and to professional journals.

*   *   *

GOODWIN, Donald W(illiam)   1931-

PERSONAL: Born September 25, 1931, in Parsons, Kan.; son of William Wesley (a publisher) and Georgia Mae (Coad) Goodwin; married Sarah Hovorka, January 5, 1957; children: Caitlin, Mary, Sarah, William. *Education:* Baker University, B.A., 1953; graduate study at Columbia University, 1955-56, and Pittsburg State College, Pittsburg, Kansas, 1959-60; University of Kansas, M.D., 1964. *Home:* 6130 Morningside Dr., Kansas City, Kan. 64113. *Office:* Medical Center, University of Kansas, 39th & Rainbow, Kansas City, Kan. 66103.

CAREER: Licensed to practice medicine in Missouri and Kansas; diplomate in psychiatry, American Board of Psychiatry and Neurology. St. Luke's Hospital, Kansas City,

Mo., intern, 1964-65; Washington University, St. Louis, Mo., department of psychiatry, resident, 1965-67, research fellow, 1967-68, instructor, 1968-69, assistant professor, 1969-72, associate professor, 1972-74, professor of psychiatry, 1974-76, director of addiction research center, 1973-76; University of Kansas, Kansas City, Kan., professor of psychiatry and chairman of department, 1976—. Assistant psychiatrist, Barnes Hospital, 1968-76, Renard Hospital, 1968-76; consulting psychiatrist, Malcolm Bliss Mental Health Center, 1968-76, Kansas City Veterans Administration Hospital, 1976—; visiting professor, Menninger School of Psychiatry, 1976—. Investigator and consultant in alcohol and drug abuse for universities, associations, and private industry. *Military service:* U.S. Army, 1953-55.

MEMBER: American Medical Association, American Psychiatric Association (fellow; president of Eastern Missouri branch, 1975-76), Psychiatric Research Society, American Psychopathological Association, Association for Psychophysiological Study of Sleep, North American Association of Alcoholism Programs, Society for Life History Research in Psychopathology, Association for Research in Nervous and Mental Disease, American Medical Society on Alcoholism (chairman of research committee), Society of Biological Psychiatry, Royal College of Psychiatry, Sigma Xi, Alpha Omega Alpha. *Awards, honors:* Hoffheimer Award from American Psychiatric Association, 1970; career development award from National Institute of Mental Health, 1970-76; Jellinek Memorial Award for research in alcoholism, 1974.

WRITINGS: (With Robert Woodruff and Samuel B. Guze) *Psychiatric Diagnosis,* Oxford University Press, 1973; *Is Alcoholism Hereditary?,* Oxford University Press, 1976.

Contributor: M. J. Bruccoli, editor, *Profile of F. Scott Fitzgerald,* Merrill, 1971; *Life History Research in Psychopathology,* Volume II, University of Minnesota Press, 1972; D. W. Matheson, editor, *The Behavioral Effects of Drugs,* Holt, 1972; P. J. Woods and F. J. McGuigan, editors, *Contemporary Studies in Psychology,* Appleton, 1972; B. Kissin and H. Begleiter, editors, *Biology of Alcoholism,* Plenum, 1974; *Genetics, Environment, and Psychopathology,* North Holland, 1974; E. Majchrowicz, editor, *Biochemical Pharmacology of Ethanol,* Plenum, 1975; M. M. Gross, editor, *Alcohol Intoxication and Withdrawal,* Plenum, 1975.

R. E. Tarter and A. A. Sugerman, editors, *Alcoholism: Interdisciplinary Approaches to an Enduring Problem,* Addison-Wesley, 1976; *Alcohol, Other Drugs, and Addiction,* Psychological Dimensions, in press; M. E. Jarvik, editor, *Psychopharmacology for Nonpsychiatric Physicians and Psychologists,* Appleton, in press; S. Medwick, editor, *Biology and Asocial Problems,* Gardiner Press, in press; D. S. Segal, editor, *Biochemical Basis of Psychiatry,* Butterworth, in press.

Author of syndicated column "Male Polish," 1955-60. Contributor to studies published by American and foreign foundations, research centers, and academies, and to medical journals. Member of editorial boards and publications consultant to journals in his field.

WORK IN PROGRESS: Continuing research on drug and alcohol abuse.

*   *   *

GORDON, Kermit   1916-1976

July 3, 1916—June 21, 1976; American economist, educator, institution administrator, presidential adviser, and author.

Obituaries: *New York Times,* June 23, 1976; *Washington Post,* June 23, 1976; *Current Biography,* August, 1976.

*   *   *

GORDON, Kurtz
   See KURTZ, C(larence) Gordon

*   *   *

GORDON, (Irene) Linda   1940-

PERSONAL: Born January 19, 1940, in Chicago, Ill.; daughter of William (a social worker) and Helen (a nursery school teacher; maiden name, Appelman) Gordon; children: Rosie Gordon Hunter. *Education:* Swarthmore College, B.A., 1961; Yale University, M.A. (Russian studies), 1962, M.A. (history), 1963, Ph.D., 1970. *Residence:* Somerville, Mass. *Office:* Department of History, University of Massachusetts, Boston, Mass. 02125.

CAREER: University of Massachusetts, Boston, instructor, 1968-69, assistant professor, 1970-75, associate professor of history, 1975—.

WRITINGS: (Contributor) Leslie Tanner, editor, *Voices from Women's Liberation,* Signet, 1970; *Families* (pamphlet), New England Free Press, 1970; (contributor) Joseph Boskin and Robert A. Rosenstone, editors, *Seasons of Rebellion,* Free Press, 1972; (contributor) Richard C. Edwards, Michael Reich, and Thomas E. Weisskopf, editors, *The Capitalist System,* Prentice-Hall, 1972; *The Fourth Mountain: Women in China* (pamphlet), New England Free Press, 1973; (contributor) Mary Hartmann and Lois W. Banner, editors, *Clio's Consciousness Raised,* Harper, 1974; *Woman's Body, Woman's Right: A Social History of Birth Control in America,* Grossman, 1976; (with Rosalyn Baxandall and Susan Reverby) *America's Working Women: A Documentary History,* Random House, 1976,; (contributor) Bernice A. Carroll, editor, *Liberating Women's History,* University of Illinois Press, 1976. Contributor to academic journals. Editor of *Radical America* and *Signs.*

WORK IN PROGRESS: Revolutionary Banditry: The Origins of the Cossacks; a history of feminist theory.

SIDELIGHTS: Gordon told *CA* that she "trained as a historian of Russia, and that her early interest in women's history focused on women in revolutionary countries. She traveled in the Soviet Union, China, and Cuba and wrote on women's situation in those countries. Gordon is active in the women's liberation movement and is the author of theoretical articles on feminism.

*   *   *

GOTS, Ronald E(ric)   1943-

PERSONAL: Born October 10, 1943, in Tampa, Fla.; son of Joseph Simon (a scientist) and Selma (a counselor; maiden name, Shienbeck) Gots; married Barbara Ann Manis (a physician), August 14, 1965; children: Jason Andrew, Meredith Tiffany. *Education:* University of Pennsylvania, A.B., 1964, M.D., 1968; University of Southern California, Ph.D., 1973. *Home:* 7707 Cindy Lane, Bethesda, Md. 20034. *Agent:* Sheri Safran, 860 United Nations Plaza, New York, N.Y. 10017. *Office:* National Medical Advisory Service, 7315 Wisconsin Ave., Washington, D.C. 20014.

CAREER: Johns Hopkins University Hospital, Baltimore, Md., intern, 1968-69; Harbor General Hospital, Torrance, Calif., resident in general surgery, 1969-70; Westminster Community Hospital, Westminster, Calif., emergency physician, 1970-73; Prince George's County Hospital, Prince George County, Md., emergency physician, 1973; Walter Reed Army Institute of Research, Washington, D.C., senior investigator, 1973-74, chief of department of gastroenterology, 1974-75; National Medical Advisory Service, Washington, D.C., director, 1975—. Licensed to practice medicine in California, District of Columbia, Maryland, and Virginia; emergency physician at Northern Virginia Doctor's Hospital, 1975—; medical officer for National Aeronautics and Space Administration, 1975. Guest member of faculty of American College of Physicians, 1975. *Military service:* U.S. Army Reserve, Medical Corps, 1973-75; became major.

MEMBER: American Association for the Advancement of Science, American Federation for Clinical Research, American Medical Association, American Society for Law and Medicine, New York Academy of Sciences, District of Columbia Medical Society, Sigma Xi, Alpha Omega Alpha. *Awards, honors:* National Institutes of Health fellowship, 1971-73.

WRITINGS: The Truth About Medical Malpractice: Patients' Rights, Doctors' Rights, Stein & Day, 1975. Contributor to medical journals.

WORK IN PROGRESS: Caring for Your Unborn Child.

SIDELIGHTS: Gots writes: "My goal is to translate information from the laboratory, the medical sciences and clinical medicine into meaningful terms and form for the laymen. Science and medicine is unnecessarily aloof and removed from the common man. People need to be involved in those matters that so critically affect their well-being."

*   *   *

GOULD, John (Thomas)   1908-

PERSONAL: Born October 22, 1908, in Boston, Mass.; son of Franklin Farrar (a railway postal clerk) and Hilda Dobson (Jenkins) Gould; married Dorothy Florence Wells, October 22, 1932; children: John Thomas, Jr., Kathryn MacLeod Gould Christy. *Education:* Bowdoin College, B.A., 1931. *Home and office address:* Star Route, Friendship, Me. 04547.

CAREER: Brunswick Record, Brunswick, Me., member of staff, 1931-39; writer of nonfiction and humor, 1939—. Author of column "Dispatch from the Farm," in *Christian Science Monitor* 1942—; feature writer for *Boston Sunday Post,* 1924-54, and *Baltimore Evening Sun,* 1975—. Co-owner of Lisbon Enterprise, 1945-51. *Member:* New England Veteran Journalists Association (president, 1961-62), Grange, Masons. *Awards, honors:* Litt.D. from Bowdoin College, 1968; and from University of Maine, 1976.

WRITINGS: New England Town Meeting, Stephen Daye, 1940; *Pre-Natal Care for Fathers,* Stephen Daye, 1941; *Farmer Takes a Wife,* Morrow, 1945; *The House That Jacob Built,* Morrow, 1947; *And One to Grow On,* Morrow, 1949; *Neither Hay Nor Grass,* Morrow, 1951; (with F. Wenderoth Saunders) *The Fastest Hound Dog in the State of Maine,* Morrow, 1953; *Monstrous Depravity,* Morrow, 1963; *The Parables of Peter Partout,* Little, Brown, 1964; *You Should Start Sooner,* Little, Brown, 1965; *Last One In,* Little, Brown, 1966; *Europe on Saturday Night,* Little, Brown, 1968; *The Jonesport Raffle,* Little, Brown, 1969; *Twelve Grindstones,* Little, Brown, 1970; *The Shag Bag,* Little, Brown, 1972; (with Lillian Ross) *Maine Lingo,* Down East, 1975; *Glass Eyes by the Bottle,* Little, Brown, 1975.

WORK IN PROGRESS: More humor books for Little, Brown.

GOULDING, Dorothy Jane 1923-

PERSONAL: Born November 26, 1923, in Toronto, Ontario, Canada; daughter of Arthur (a doctor) and Dorothy (a children's theatre founder; maiden name, Massey) Goulding; married William Needles (an actor), February 5, 1945; children: Jane, Arthur, Dan, Reed, Laura. *Education:* Attended Royal Academy of Dance, 1940, East York College, 1942, and Toronto Teachers College, 1942; Royal Conservatory of Music, associate, 1942. *Home:* 234 Cortleigh Blvd., Toronto, Ontario, Canada M5N 1P7. *Office:* Curriculum Branch, Etobicoke Board of Education, Etobicoke, Ontario, Canada.

CAREER: Worked as teacher, radio artist, musician, farmer, theatre producer, director, and stage manager; youth editor, Canadian *Audubon* magazine, 1951-66; consultant, Etobicoke (Ontario) Board of Education. Owner and part manager, Globe Hotel Restaurant, Rosemont, Ontario.

WRITINGS: Dorothy Jane's Book: Songs and Stories from Kindergarten of the Air, Dent, 1949; *Dorothy Jane's Other Book: Songs and Stories from Kindergarten of the Air,* Dent, 1953; *Master Cat and Other Plays,* Coach House Press, 1955; *Margaret* (juvenile fiction), McGraw, 1966; (author of text) *Boris Spremo and His Camera Look at Toronto,* McGraw, 1967; *We're Doing a Play,* Ryerson, 1969; *Play-Acting in the Schools,* Ryerson, 1970. Also author of *Toronto* and *Play Acting in the Language Program.*

WORK IN PROGRESS: Writing and directing a film (an experience in three-dimensional education); two detective stories; a juvenile novel; a costume textbook.

* * *

GRAHAM, Vanessa
See FRASER, Anthea

* * *

GRANT, Robert M(cQueen) 1917-

PERSONAL: Born November 25, 1917, in Evanston, Ill.; son of Frederick Clifton and Helen McQueen (Hardie) Grant; married Margaret Huntington Horton, December 21, 1940; children: Douglas McQueen, Peter Williams, Susan Hardie, James Frederick. *Education:* Northwestern University, A.B., 1938; graduate study at Episcopal Theological School, 1938-39, and Columbia University, 1939-40; Union Theological Seminary, New York, N.Y., B.D., 1941; Harvard University, S.T.M., 1942, Th.D., 1944. *Home:* 5728 Harper Ave., Chicago, Ill. 60637. *Office:* Swift Hall, University of Chicago, Chicago, Ill. 60637.

CAREER: Ordained Episcopal minister, 1942; pastor of Episcopal church in South Groveland, Mass., 1942-44; University of the South, Sewanee, Tenn., instructor, 1944-45, assistant professor, 1945-46, associate professor, 1946-49, professor of New Testament, 1949-53, acting dean, 1947; University of Chicago, Chicago, Ill., associate professor, 1953-58, professor of New Testament, 1958—, Carl Darling Buck Professor of Humanities, 1973—. University of Chicago, visiting lecturer, 1945, research associate, 1952-53; visiting lecturer, Vanderbilt University, 1945-47, and Seabury-Western Theological Seminary, 1954-55; Fulbright research professor at University of Leiden, 1950-51; lecturer for American Council of Learned Societies, 1957-58; visiting professor at Yale University, 1964-65.

MEMBER: Society of Biblical Literature (president, 1959), American Society of Church History (president, 1970), Chicago Society for Biblical Research (president, 1963-64), Phi Beta Kappa, Alpha Delta Phi, Quadrangle Club (Chicago). *Awards, honors:* Guggenheim fellowships, 1950, 1954, 1959; D.D. from Seabury-Western Theological Seminary, 1969.

WRITINGS: (Editor) *Second Century Christianity: A Collection of Fragments,* Allenson, 1946; *The Bible in the Church: A Short History of Interpretation,* Macmillan, 1948, revised edition published as *A Short History of the Interpretation of the Bible,* 1963; *Miracle and Natural Law in Graeco-Roman and Early Christian Thought,* North-Holland Publishing, 1952; *The Sword and the Cross,* Macmillan, 1955; *The Letter and the Spirit,* Macmillan, 1957; *Gnosticism and Early Christianity,* Columbia University Press, 1959, 2nd edition, 1966.

(With David Noel Freedman) *The Secret Sayings of Jesus,* Doubleday, 1960; (editor) *Gnosticism: A Source Book of Heretical Writings from the Early Christian Period,* Harper, 1961; *The Earliest Lives of Jesus,* Harper, 1961; *A Historical Introduction to the New Testament,* Harper, 1963; (editor) *The Apostolic Fathers,* Thomas Nelson, Volume I: *An Introduction,* 1964, Volume II (with Holt H. Graham): *First and Second Clement,* 1965, Volume IV: *Ignatius of Antioch,* 1966; *U-Boats Destroyed: The Effect of Anti-Submarine Warfare, 1914-1918,* Putnam, 1964; *The Formation of the New Testament,* Harper, 1965; *A History of Early Christian Literature,* revised edition (Grant not associated with earlier edition), University of Chicago Press, 1966; *The Early Christian Doctrine of God,* University Press of Virginia, 1966; *After the New Testament,* Fortress, 1967; *U-Boat Intelligence, 1914-1918,* Archon Books, 1969; (editor and translator) St. Theophilus, Bishop of Antioch, *Ad Autolycum* (title means "To Autolycus"), Clarendon Press, 1970; *Augustus to Constantine: The Thrust of the Christian Movement into the Roman World,* Harper, 1970.

Director of *Anglican Theological Review;* co-editor of *Church History;* associate editor of *Vigiliae Christianae.*

* * *

GRANVILLE, Joseph E(nsign) 1923-

PERSONAL: Born August 20, 1923, in Yonkers, N.Y.; son of W. Irving and Dorothy D. (Crehore) Granville; married Katherine Reese, May 5, 1945 (divorced, October, 1947); married Paulina Delp (a music teacher), July 11, 1950; children: Leslie, Blanchard, Leona, Sara, Paul, Mary, Johanna, John. *Education:* Duke University, B.A., 1948. *Politics:* Republican. *Religion:* Episcopal. *Agent:* Ruth Aley, 135 East 35th St., New York, N.Y. 10016. *Office:* P.O. Box 2614, Ormond Beach, Fla. 32074.

CAREER: Will, Folsom & Smith, New York City, statistician, 1946-47; Granville Stamp Corp., New York City, president, 1949; *Philatelic Investment Letter,* New York City, publisher, 1950-57; E. F. Hutton & Co., New York City, writer for *Market Letter,* 1957-63; *Granville Market Letter,* Ormond Beach, Fla., publisher and writer, 1963—. President of Granville Productions, 1949. *Military service:* U.S. Navy, 1942-46. *Member:* Veterans of Foreign Wars, New York Speakers Club (president, 1949).

WRITINGS: A Schoolboy's Faith (poems), Revell, 1941; *Price Predictions,* privately printed, 1945, 4th edition, 1957; *Everybody's Guide to Stamp Investment,* Hermitage House, 1952; *A Strategy of Daily Stock Market Timing for Maximum Profit,* Prentice-Hall, 1960; *Granville's New Key to Stock Market Profits,* Prentice-Hall, 1963; *Granville's New Strategy of Daily Stock Market Timing for Maximum Profit,* Prentice-Hall, 1976; *How to Win at Bingo: An Adventure in Probability,* Parker Publishing, in press.

Author of "Hot Tropics" (three-act comedy), first produced in Durham, N.C., at Duke University, 1946.

Contributor to financial journals.

WORK IN PROGRESS: Why?, a "major work in philosophy dealing with the ten most basic philosophical questions."

SIDELIGHTS: Granville writes that he has traveled extensively in Europe. He is "interested in all games of chance as background for later contemplated mathematical works on probability . . . particularly . . . chess and bingo." Among his current plans are attempts to introduce the game of bingo to the Soviet Union at the International Book Fair in Moscow, and another plan to legislate a balanced national budget, based on a national lottery to raise more than fifteen billion dollars annually as a fund to support a balanced federal budget.

BIOGRAPHICAL/CRITICAL SOURCES: Collier's, April 2, 1949.

* * *

GRATHWOHL, Larry D(avid) 1947-

PERSONAL: Born October 13, 1947, in Cincinnati, Ohio; son of Earl and Mary (Huff) Grathwohl; married Donna Riestenberg, September 24, 1966 (divorced January, 1974); married Sandi Araujo (a model), April 27, 1974; children: Denise Jane, Lisa Diane. *Education:* Attended University of Cincinnati, 1968-69. *Politics:* Independent. *Residence:* Hayward, Calif.

CAREER: Federal Bureau of Investigation (FBI), Cincinnati, Ohio, informant, 1968-69; laborer, 1969—. Consultant on terrorist tactics to law enforcement agencies, 1969—. *Military service:* U.S. Army, 1964-68; served with 101st Airborne Division in Vietnam; became sergeant.

WRITINGS: Bringing Down America, Arlington House, 1976.

SIDELIGHTS: As a result of a chance meeting in 1969, Grathwohl infiltrated the revolutionary Weather Underground, an organization with ostensibly one purpose, "the overthrow of the U.S. government and the American way of life." He informed the FBI of its activities and simultaneously disrupted many of their violent plans. A premature arrest of one of the group's members inadvertently caused the revelation of Grathwohl's identity, and his underground affiliation abruptly ended.

"When the Weathermen tell me they're going to destroy my country and my way of life, I don't like that," contends Grathwohl. "I don't think any group, whether the Weathermen, John Birch Society or Ku Klux Klan has the right to impose its will upon us without us having any say. . . . Politically, I tend to set right in the middle. If it helps the majority of the people, then that's the way it should be."

BIOGRAPHICAL/CRITICAL SOURCES: Cincinnati Post, February 15, 1975; *Cincinnati Enquirer,* February 16, 1975, February 18, 1975, March 19, 1975, March 20, 1975; *Hayward Daily Review,* February 16, 1975, February 18, 1975, February 19, 1975; *Time,* October 6, 1975.

* * *

GRAU, Joseph A(ugust) 1921-

PERSONAL: Born March 24, 1921, in Milwaukee, Wis.; son of Phil A. (a news commentator) and Gertrude (Ziegler) Grau; married Lois Ackermann (a doctoral student), March, 1970; children: Chris, Kate. *Education:* St. Louis Univer-

sity, A.B. (honors), 1943, Ph.L., 1947, S.T.L. (honors), 1955; Marquette University, M.A., 1967; Catholic University of America, S.T.D. (honors), 1973. *Politics:* Liberal Independent. *Religion:* Roman Catholic. *Home:* 3710 North Prospect, Shorewood, Wis. 53211. *Office:* Justice and Peace Center, 3900 North Third, Milwaukee, Wis. 53212.

CAREER: Marquette University High School, Milwaukee, Wis., teacher of Latin and religion, 1954-64, chairman of religious studies department, 1964, Marquette University, Milwaukee, instructor in religious studies, 1964-68; St. Mary's College of Maryland, St. Mary's City, assistant professor of social ethics, director of student activities, 1970-71; director of religious education at a Roman Catholic church in Franklin, Wis., 1974-76; Justice and Peace Center, Milwaukee, Wis., executive director, 1976—. Member of Wisconsin governor's committee on children and youth, 1963-66; member of board of directors of Campaign for Human Development, 1976-77. *Member:* American Society for Christian Ethics, American Teilhard de Chardin Association for the Future of Man, Alpha Sigma Nu.

WRITINGS: Morality and the Human Future in the Thought of Teilhard de Chardin, Fairleigh Dickinson University Press, 1976. Contributor to *Review of Social Economy.*

WORK IN PROGRESS: Exploring the possibilities of a "Teilhard-based 'liberation theology' for North Americans"; exploring ecumenical dialogue and action collaboration for social justice.

SIDELIGHTS: Grau writes that he has a "long-standing concern about the practical connection between religious values (including Marxist and other secular humanists) and the social process," and "the importance of experiential field learning education for social justice." *Avocational interests:* St. Bernard dogs, Triumph Spitfires ("when they run"), tennis, mountains, drama, film, loud stereo music (especially classical music).

* * *

GRAVES, Richard Perceval 1945-

PERSONAL: Born December 21, 1945, in Brighton, England; son of John Tiarks Ranke (a teacher) and Mary (a teacher; maiden name, Wickens) Graves; married Anne Katharine Fortescue, April 4, 1970; children: David John Perceval, Philip Macartney. *Education:* St. John's College, Oxford, B.A., 1968, M.A., 1972. *Politics:* "Liberal/Conservative." *Religion:* Church of England. *Home:* Pen-Y-Bryn House, Boot St., Whittington, Oswestry, Shropshire SY11 4DG, England. *Agent:* Andrew Best, Curtis Brown Academic Ltd., 1 Craven Hill, London W2 3EP, England.

CAREER: Teacher of English, history, and Latin at private schools in England, 1968-73; writer, 1973—. Whittington parish councillor, 1973-76; chairman of Whittington Youth Club, 1974—. *Member:* United Oxford and Cambridge University Club.

WRITINGS: Lawrence of Arabia and His World, Scribner, 1976. Editor of *Housman Society Journal.*

WORK IN PROGRESS: A biography of A. E. Housman, for Routledge & Kegan Paul.

SIDELIGHTS: Graves is the nephew of poet Robert Graves and the grandson of Irish writer Alfred Perceval Graves.

GRAY, Anne 1931-

PERSONAL: Born October 26, 1931, in London, England; came to the United States in 1947, naturalized citizen, 1948; daughter of Joseph (a jeweler) and Clara (an accountant; maiden name, Laub) Gray; married, August 7, 1966; children: two sons. Education: Hunter College (now of the City University of New York), B.A. (cum laude), 1953; San Diego State University, M.A., 1968. Politics: Conservative. Religion: Protestant. Residence: La Jolla, Calif.

CAREER: Elementary school teacher in San Diego, Calif., 1960-64, high school teacher of music, speech, and drama, 1964-68; teacher of English at junior college in San Diego, Calif., 1968-69; presently gives private piano lessons. Passenger service agent for American Airlines, 1955-56. Member: La Jolla Penwomen, La Jolla Republican Women's League.

WRITINGS: The Wonderful World of San Diego, Pelican, 1975, 2nd edition, 1975; Donald Duck, Television Star, Western Publishing, 1974. Has written material for "Walt Disney Foreign Comics."

WORK IN PROGRESS: The Mystery of Cragmoor Manor, a Gothic novel; The Kitten Without a Tail and Other Children's Stories; The Castle of Mystery, a children's book; Natural Childbirth? Bah! Humbug!, based on her personal experiences.

AVOCATIONAL INTERESTS: International travel (New Zealand, Australia, Cambodia, Kuala Lumpur, Singapore, Hong Kong, Japan, Fiji, Mexico, Europe, Scandinavia).

*   *   *

GRAY, Darrell 1945-

PERSONAL: Born April 20, 1945, in Sacramento, Calif.; son of Horace W. and Virgie (Wilson) Gray. Education: University of California, Hayward, B.A., 1967; University of Iowa, M.F.A., 1969. Home: 9828 Lawlor St., Oakland, Calif. 94708.

CAREER: Actualist Institute, Iowa City, Iowa, director, 1967-68; editor, Suction: A Magazine of Actualist Poetry, and co-editor, Journal of Pre-Verbal Behavior, both 1968-74; Center for Public Art, Berkeley, Calif., director, 1974; connected with Institute for Actualist Studies, Berkeley, 1975—. Director of Center for Actual Public Art. Member: American Actualist Institute (president, 1974-75), Institute of Conceptual Actualists. Awards, honors: Award for poetry from California Writer's Conference, 1964; American Poetry Society award, 1969; Blue Wind Press poetry award, 1974; Margorie Holmes Award for Poetry, 1975; received Gum magazine poetry award; received Puncyual Actual Weekly Award for short prose, "The Man Who Glowed in the Dark."

WRITINGS: The Beauties of Travel (poems), Doones Press, 1965; Something Swims Out (poems), Blue Wind Press, 1972; Scattered Brains (poems), Toothpaste Press, 1974; The Mathematics of the Nervous System (pamphlet), Institute for Future Studies, c.1974; Essays and Dissolutions (essays), Abraxas Press, 1976; The Plain That Became a Mountain (poems), Tendon Press, 1976; The Cloud Feast (novel), Simon & Schuster, in press; Some Chickens (stories), Houghton, in press. Contributor to literary journals, including Northstone Review, Ahim, and Partisan Review, and to newspapers.

SIDELIGHTS: Gray writes: "In prose, I write what seems most actual to me: I am most directly interested in character formation over an extended period of time. I use prose as a vehicle for understanding what would remain otherwise incomprehensible."

*   *   *

GRAY, Harriet
See ROBINS, Denise (Naomi)

*   *   *

GRAY, John E(dmund) 1922-

PERSONAL: Born April 13, 1922, in Woonsocket, R.I.; son of John Joseph and Alice (Naylor) Gray; married Mary Lightbody, December 3, 1944; children: Jane Elizabeth (Mrs. Peter W. Redmond), John Carlton, Jeffrey Naylor. Education: University of Rhode Island, B.S., 1943. Home and office: 2007 Windsor Rd., Alexandria, Va. 22307.

CAREER: Westinghouse Electric Corp., Bloomfield, N.J., research engineer, 1943-46; General Electric Co., Hanford, Wash., senior design engineer in engineering division, 1946-47; General Engineering and Consulting Laboratory, Schenectady, N.Y., head of materials section in atomic power department, 1948-49; Atomic Energy Commission and U.S. Navy, Washington, D.C., materials administrator in naval reactors branch, 1949-50; Atomic Energy Commission, Savannah River Operations Office, S.C., director of technical and production division, 1950-54; Duquesne Light Co., Pittsburgh, Pa., project manager for Shippingport Atomic Power Station, 1954-60; NUS Corp., Rockville, Md., president and chief executive officer, 1969-72; energy consultant, 1972—; International Energy Associates Ltd., Washington, D.C., president, 1976—.

Chairman of board of directors, Neutron Products, Inc., 1962-72, and Consultec, Inc., 1967-72; member of board of directors, Institute of Public Transportation, 1972—, Aviation Values Corp., 1972-74, Abacus Controls, 1974—, GEOMET Exploration, Inc., 1975—; Atlantic Council of the United States, member of energy committee, 1974—, member of board, 1976—; member of nuclear energy subcommittee, Committee for Economic Development, 1976—. Military service: U.S. Army, 1945-46. Member: American Institute of Chemical Engineers, American Association for the Advancement of Science, American Nuclear Society, Atomic Industrial Forum, University Club (Washington, D.C.), Belle Haven Country Club.

WRITINGS: Energy Policy: Industry Perspectives, Ballinger, 1975; (with J. Herbert Hollomon and others) Energy Research and Development, Ballinger, 1975; Financing Free World Energy Supply, Atlantic Council of the United States, 1975; (with others) Nuclear Fuels Policy (report of Atlantic Council Nuclear Fuels Policy Working Group), Heath, 1976. Contributor to Mark's Standard Handbook for Engineers and to Public Utilities Fortnightly.

*   *   *

GRAY, (Lucy) Noel (Clervaux)

PERSONAL: Born February 24, 1898, in Kidderminster, Worcestershire, England; daughter of Reginald Seymour (a carpet manufacturer) and Margaret Anne (Clarke) Brinton; married James Gray, September 4, 1937 (died August 4, 1951); children: Robert, Wendy-Ann. Education: Somerville College, Oxford, B.A. (with honors), 1921; London Day Training College, Cambridge, teachers certificate, 1928. Home: 5 Parliament Hill, London NW3 2S4, England. Office: Anglo-Chinese Educational Institute, 152 Camden High St., London N.W.1, England.

CAREER: Ecole Normale de Jeunes Filles, Laval, France, English teacher, 1921-22; Girls' Collegiate School, Leicester, England, French teacher, 1922-24; Raines Foundation, London, England, French teacher, 1924; English teacher in Moscow, U.S.S.R., 1928-29; Girls Public Day School Trust, Sutton, England, teacher of handicapped, 1930-35; English teacher for Chinese trade delegation in London, 1955-67; Anglo-Chinese Educational Institution, London, library research and information assistant, 1968—.

WRITINGS: (With F. L. Clark) *Men, Medicine, and Food in the U.S.S.R.,* Lawrence & Wishart, 1936; (translator) K. Bazilevich, *The Russian Art of War,* Soviet War News, 1945; *Looking at China,* Lippincott, 1974. Contributor of articles to *Women Today* and to *China Now* (of Society for Anglo-Chinese Understanding).

* * *

GREEN, Celia (Elizabeth) 1935-

PERSONAL: Born November 26, 1935, in London, England; daughter of William Alfred (a school headmaster and writer) and Dorothy E. (Cleare) Green. *Education:* Somerville College, Oxford, B.A., 1957, B.Litt. and M.A., both 1960. *Office:* Institute of Psychophysical Research, 118 Banbury Rd., Oxford OX2 6JU, England.

CAREER: Institute of Psychophysical Research, Oxford, England, founder and director, 1961—.

WRITINGS: Lucid Dreams, Hamish Hamilton, 1968; *Out-of-the-Body Experiences,* Hamish Hamilton, 1968, Ballantine, 1973; *The Human Evasion,* Hamish Hamilton, 1969; (with Charles McCreery) *Apparitions,* Hamish Hamilton, 1975, St. Martin's, 1976; *The Decline and Fall of Science,* Hamish Hamilton, 1976. Contributor of articles to *Punch; New Knowledge; Man, Myth, and Magic;* and other periodicals.

WORK IN PROGRESS: An autobiography up to the age of 21, *Myself and the Universe,* publication by Hamish Hamilton expected in 1978.

SIDELIGHTS: Celia Green told *CA:* "I have in Oxford a place in which it is possible to carry on the struggle for survival, and I am looking for young people to join me. There are at present too few of us, and this makes the struggle for survival even more difficult. The Institute of Psychophysical Research exists to carry out research in hitherto unexplored areas. What is needed is for some far-sighted individual to recognise the revolutionary potential of the Institute's work, and to endow its research on a scale commensurate with its importance."

* * *

GREEN, Robert L(ee) 1933-

PERSONAL: Born November 23, 1933, in Detroit, Mich. son of Thomas and Alberta (Vinson) Green; married Lettie Cornelius, August 10, 1956; children: Robert, Melvin, Kurt. *Education:* San Francisco State College (now University), B.A., 1958, M.A., 1960; Michigan State University, Ph.D., 1963. *Home:* 1170 Dryant Dr., East Lansing, Mich. 48823. *Office:* College of Urban Development, Michigan State University, East Lansing, Mich. 48824.

CAREER: University of California, San Francisco, research assistant at Langley Porter Research Institute, 1959-60; psychology intern in public schools of Oakland, Calif., 1959-60; Juvenile Court, San Francisco, group counselor, 1960; Michigan State University, East Lansing, instructor, 1960-62, assistant professor of education, 1963-65; Southern

Christian Leadership Conference, Atlanta, Ga., education director, 1965-66, director of adult education project, 1967; Michigan State University, professor of educational psychology, 1968—, assistant provost, 1968-72, director of Center for Urban Affairs, 1968-74, College of Urban Development, acting dean, 1972-73, dean, 1973—. Visiting lecturer, Hebrew University of Jerusalem and University of Nairobi, both 1971-72. Psychologist at Lansing Child Guidance Clinic, 1961-62; former member of the President's Youth Opportunity Commission. Member of board of directors, Center for National Policy Review, Washington, D.C.; trustee, Martin Luther King, Jr. Center for Social Change. *Member:* Association of Black Psychologists (co-chairman), American Psychological Association, American Educational Research Association, Society for the Psychological Study of Social Issues.

WRITINGS: (With Louis J. Hofmann, Richard J. Morse, and Marilyn E. Hayes) *The Educational Status of Children in a District without Public Schools,* College of Education, Michigan State University, 1964; (Hofmann, Morse, and Robert F. Morgan) *The Educational Status of Children during the First School Year Following Four Years of Little or No Schooling,* College of Education, Michigan State University, 1966; (editor) *Racial Crisis in American Education,* Follett, 1969; (with Nicholas Peter Georgiady) *American Negro Musicians,* Franklin (Milwaukee, Wis.), 1969. Editor of "Famous Negro American Series," 1968. Contributor to scholarly journals.

* * *

GREENBERG, Judith Anne 1938-

PERSONAL: Born July 28, 1938, in Baltimore, Md.; daughter of Maurice (a businessman) and Chapel Azrael; married Herbert Greenberg, December 20, 1959 (divorced, 1976); children: Denise, Jeffrey. *Education:* University of Wisconsin, Madison, B.A., 1959; University of Oregon, M.F.A. (honors), 1972. *Home address:* P.O. Box 565, Mendocino, Calif. 95460.

CAREER: Mendocino Art Center, Mendocino, Calif., teacher of creative writing, 1969-71; College of the Redwoods, Mendocino, instructor at creative writing workshops, 1974—. *Awards, honors:* Writing grant from Helene Wurlitzer Foundation, 1973-74.

WRITINGS—Poetry: Fire in August, Zeitgeist, 1969; *Fields of Light,* Casseopeia Press, 1975.

Work represented in anthologies, including *Intro Five,* edited by Walton Beacham and George Garrett, University Press of Virginia, 1974; and *Luckiamute,* edited by Phillip Gregory Hope and Gary L. Lark, 1972, *Sequoia,* edited by Douglas Musella and Michael Waters, 1973, and *Country Women Fiction Anthology,* edited by Sharon Dubiago and Loretta Manill. Contributor of poems and stories to national periodicals, including *Nation,* and to literary journals, including *Western Humanities Review, Southern Poetry Review, December, Lillabulero, Wormwood Review, Sunstone Review,* and *Stonecloud.*

WORK IN PROGRESS: Poetry, *Twenty-Eight for the Small Green Horse; Migration;* and *Prayers to the Moon.*

SIDELIGHTS: Judith Greenberg writes: "My poetry explores the inner landscape . . . of dream. Dreams not of sleep but of wide eyed waking . . . those images of myth and memory and landscape that come from a vision within me (within all of us) that we can sometimes reach."

GREIF, Martin 1938-

PERSONAL: Born February 4, 1938, in New York, N.Y.; son of Louis and Lillian (Perlmutter) Greif. *Education:* Hunter College (now of the City University of New York), B.A. (cum laude), 1959; Princeton University, M.A. (honors), 1961. *Home address:* Pinegrove, Pittstown, N.J. 08867. *Office:* Main Street Press, 42 Main St., Clinton, N.J. 08809.

CAREER: New York University, New York, N.Y., instructor in English, 1962-65; Queens College of the City University of New York, New York, N.Y., instructor in English, 1965-68; Time Incorporated Book Clubs, New York, N.Y., managing editor, 1969-73; Main Street Press, Clinton, N.J., co-founder and editorial director, 1974—. *Member:* Phi Beta Kappa. *Awards, honors:* Woodrow Wilson fellow, 1959; Danforth Foundation associate, 1963.

WRITINGS: (Editor) *Aunt Sammy's Radio Recipes: The Great Depression Cookbook,* Universe Books, 1975; *Depression Modern: The Thirties Style in America,* Universe Books, 1975; *The St. Nicholas Book,* Universe Books, 1976. Contributor to *Modern Maturity.* Compiler of an annual "Historic Preservation" calendar, 1975, and other engagement calendars.

* * *

GRIEST, Guinevere L(indley) 1924-

PERSONAL: Born January 14, 1924, in Chicago, Ill.; daughter of Euclid Eugene (a businessman) and Marianna (Lindley) Griest. *Education:* Cornell University, A.B., 1944; University of Chicago, A.M., 1947, Ph.D., 1961. *Office:* Division of Fellowships, National Endowment for the Humanities, 806 15th St. N.W., Washington, D.C. 20506.

CAREER: University of Illinois at Chicago Circle, instructor, 1947-53, 1955-61, assistant professor, 1961-66, associate professor of English, 1966-73; National Endowment for the Humanities, Washington, D.C., program officer, 1969-73, deputy director of Division of Fellowships, 1973—. *Member:* Modern Language Association of America, National Council of Teachers of English, Phi Beta Kappa, Phi Kappa Phi. *Awards, honors:* Fulbright fellowship, Cambridge University, 1953-55.

WRITINGS: Mudie's Circulating Library and the Victorian Novel, Indiana University Press, 1970. Contributor of articles and reviews to literature journals.

* * *

GRIFFIN, Charles C(arroll) 1902-1976

May 24, 1902—June 13, 1976; American historian, educator, and author of books on Latin American history. Obituaries: *New York Times,* June 14, 1976.

* * *

GRILL, Nannette L. 1935-
(Louise Christian)

PERSONAL: Born March 26, 1935, in Los Angeles, Calif. *Education:* Stanford University, student, 1952-55; Immaculate Heart College, Los Angeles, Calif., B.A., 1956; University of California, Los Angeles, M.A., 1969. *Home:* 11516 Moorpark St., No. 10, North Hollywood, Calif. 91602. *Office:* Department of English, Pasadena City College, 1570 East Colorado Blvd., Pasadena, Calif.

CAREER: Entered Sisters of Immaculate Heart of California, 1956, Roman Catholic nun, 1968; Pasadena City College, Pasadena, Calif., assistant professor of English,

1969—. Owner of Scarecrow Publications, 1971-73. Member of Westside Kidney Foundation, 1970—, and Cerebral Palsy Guild (Coastline, Calif.), 1975—. Member of Los Angeles Chamber of Commerce, 1975—, Los Angeles County Museum Service Council, 1975-76. Has appeared on national television programs.

MEMBER: Marina del Rey Chamber (vice-president of Women's Division, 1975—), Reading Is Fundamental (Southern California chapter; member of board of directors, 1972-73), Westside Club (Stanford University and University of California, Los Angeles), University of California, Los Angeles Alumni Association (life member). *Awards, honors:* National Endowment for the Humanities fellowship, 1974.

WRITINGS: (With Charonne Wali) *Mister Abracadabra* (juvenile), Scarecrow Publications, 1971. Contributor, under name Louise Christian, of articles to magazines, 1970-74.

WORK IN PROGRESS: The Perfect Murder, a detective mystery, with Charonne Wali; *Fragments, Bits, and Pieces of Manchild's Story,* a philosophical essay on the meaning of existence; juveniles, *Dear Bear* and *Winifred Goes West.*

SIDELIGHTS: Nannette Grill told *CA:* "No one is writing in layman's language about philosophy or modern man's plight with the cosmic consciousness of this brave new world. My dilemma is not writing but getting to the publisher who wants to take a gamble with a new writer and not impose on him or her what should be written. Young people need books to read, shorter in length, less jargony and yet with some meat to them in the ideas they pose. Perhaps we all want that. I am interested in the mental prisons we make for ourselves in all areas of life."

AVOCATIONAL INTERESTS: Visiting museums, "think tanks," scientists, factories, art, travel.

* * *

GRIMSHAW, Allen Day 1929-

PERSONAL: Born December 16, 1929, in New York, N.Y.; son of Austin (a professor) and Elizabeth (Thompson) Grimshaw; married Polly Ann Swift (a librarian), June 3, 1952; children: Gail Elizabeth (deceased), Andrew Swift, Adam Thompson. *Education:* Attended Purdue University, 1946-48; University of Missouri, A.B., 1950, M.A., 1952; University of Pennsylvania, Ph.D., 1959. *Home:* 4001 Morningside Dr., Bloomington, Ind. 47401. *Office:* Department of Sociology, Indiana University, Bloomington, Ind. 47401.

CAREER: Indiana University, Bloomington, instructor, 1959-61, assistant professor, 1961-65, associate professor, 1965-69, professor of sociology, 1969—, director of Institute for Comparative Sociology, 1966-69. Visiting associate professor at University of California, Berkeley, 1968-69. Consultant to American Council of Learned Societies, National Endowment for the Humanities, National Institute for Mental Health, National Institute for Child Health and Development, National Science Foundation, Social Science Research Council, Social Science Research Council of Britain, International Cooperative Study on Social Values and Public Policy at University of Pennsylvania, 1964-67, Disaster Research Center at Ohio State University, 1964, National Advisory Commission on Civil Disorders, 1967, National Commission on the Causes and Prevention of Violence, Task Force on Collective Protest, 1968, and to Educational Testing Service, 1969. *Military service:* U.S. Air Force Reserve, 1952-54.

MEMBER: American Sociological Association (fellow),

American Anthropological Association (fellow), Association for Asian Studies (life member), Linguistic Society of America, American Association for the Advancement of Science (fellow), Peace Research Society, American Association of University Professors (president of Indiana University, Bloomington chapter, 1970-71), North Central Sociological Association, Phi Beta Kappa, Alpha Pi Zeta, Alpha Kappa Delta. *Awards, honors:* American Institute of Indian Studies faculty research fellow, 1962-63; National Institute of Mental Health research grant, 1964-66; National Science Foundation research grant, 1975.

WRITINGS: (Editor) *Racial Violence in the United States,* Aldine, 1969; (editor with J. Michael Armer, and contributor) *Comparative Social Research: Methodological Problems and Strategies,* Wiley, 1973.

Contributor: Raymond J. Murphy and Howard Elison, editors, *Problems and Prospects of the Negro Movement,* Wadsworth Publishing, 1961; Kimball Young and Ray Mack, editors, *Principles of Sociology: A Reader in Theory and Research,* 3rd edition (Grimshaw was not associated with earlier editions), American Book Co., 1965; Stanley Lieberson, editor, *Explorations in Sociolinguistics,* Indiana University Research Center in Anthropology, Folklore, and Linguistics, 1966; Louis H. Massotti and Don R. Bowen, editors, *Riots and Rebellion: Civil Violence in the Urban Community,* Sage Publications, 1968; Simon Dinitz and others, editors, *Deviance: Studies in the Process of Stigmatization and Social Reaction,* Oxford University Press, 1969; Doris Y. Wilkinson, editor, *Black Revolt: Strategies of Protest,* McCutchan, 1969.

Dell Hymes, editor, *Pidginization and Creolization of Languages,* Cambridge University Press, 1971; Joshua A. Fishman, editor, *Advances in the Sociology of Language,* Mouton & Co., 1971; James F. Short and Marvin E. Wolfgang, editors, *Collective Violence,* Aldine, 1972; Bernhard Badura and Klaus Gloy, editors, *Soziologie der Kommunikation* (title means "Sociology of Communication"), F. F. Verlag Gunther Holzboog, 1972; Roger W Shuy, editor, *Twenty-Third Annual Round Table, Monograph Series on Language and Linguistics,* Georgetown University Press, 1973; Wilbur Schramm, Ithiel Pool, Nathan Maccoby, Edwin Parker, Frederick Frey, and Leonard Fein, editors, *Handbook of Communication,* Rand McNally, 1973; Richard A. Bauman and Joel Sherzer, editors, *Explorations in the Ethnography of Speaking,* Cambridge University Press, 1974.

Contributor of more than fifty articles and reviews to professional journals. Editor, *American Sociologist,* 1976-78; associate editor, *Journal of Conflict Resolution,* 1967-71, *American Sociological Review,* 1970-73, *Language in Society,* 1971—, and *Sociometry,* 1974—.

WORK IN PROGRESS: Sociolinguistics: An Introduction; research on theories of social organization, on conflict theories, on continuing language socialization, and on analytic frames for verbal interaction.

AVOCATIONAL INTERESTS: Squash.

* * *

GRINDEL, John Anthony 1937-

PERSONAL: Born September 14, 1937, in Kansas City, Mo.; son of Edward Anthony (an electronics engineer) and Inez (a hospital administrator; maiden name, Weber) Grindel. *Education:* St. Mary's Seminary, Perryville, Mo., B.A., 1960; Catholic University of America, S.T.L., 1965,

M.A., 1966; Pontifical Biblical Institute, S.S.L., 1967. *Home and office:* St. John's Seminary, 5012 East Seminary Rd., Camarillo, Calif. 93010.

CAREER: Roman Catholic priest of Congregation of the Mission, ordained, 1964; American School of Oriental Research, Jerusalem, Israel, research associate, 1967-68; St. John's Seminary, Camarillo, Calif., associate professor, 1968-73, professor of scripture and rector, 1973—. *Member:* Society of Biblical Literature, Catholic Biblical Association of America.

WRITINGS: (With Charles E. Miller) *Repentance and Renewal,* Alba, 1970; (with Miller) *Until He Comes,* Alba, 1971; *I and II Chronicles,* Paulist/Newman, 1973. Contributor to religious journals.

WORK IN PROGRESS: Research on the validity of criteria for E strata in the Pentateuch.

* * *

GROSS, Sarah Chokla 1906-1976

October 13, 1906—July 20, 1976; American educator, translator, children's book reviewer and editor, and author. Obituaries: *New York Times,* July 21, 1976. (See index for previous *CA* sketch)

* * *

GROSSMAN, Lawrence 1945-

PERSONAL: Born July 29, 1945, in New York, N.Y.; son of Hyman (a rabbi) and Anne (a college professor; maiden name, Wertheimer) Grossman; married Barbara Pineles, January, 1977. *Education:* Yeshiva University, B.A., 1966, M.H.L. and rabbi, 1969; Columbia University, M.A., 1967; City University of New York, Ph.D., 1973. *Politics:* Democrat. *Home:* 137-01 70 Rd., Kew Garden Hills, N.Y. 11367. *Office:* Department of History, Yeshiva University, 245 Lexington Ave., New York, N.Y. 10016.

CAREER: Congregation Beth Tefilla, Paramus, N.J., rabbi, 1969-70; Yeshiva University, New York, N.Y., instructor, 1972-73, assistant professor of history, 1973—. Adjunct assistant professor at Herbert H. Lehman College of the City University of New York, 1973—.

MEMBER: Organization of American Historians, American Jewish Historical Society, Society for Values in Higher Education, Rabbinical Council of America, Southern Historical Association. *Awards, honors:* Danforth fellowship, 1966-73; award from Colonial Dames Society, 1970-71.

WRITINGS: The Democratic Party and the Negro: Northern and National Politics, 1868-1892, University of Illinois Press, 1976. Contributor of articles and reviews to history and Jewish studies journals.

WORK IN PROGRESS: Research on several specific aspects of Black life in the North in the nineteenth century; research on the development of Judaism in nineteenth-century America.

SIDELIGHTS: Grossman writes: "I am fascinated by the way American ethnic minorities deal with their dual identities—that is, Americanism, and their own ethnicity—and also how others perceive and treat their dilemmas. The history of blacks and Jews in America are the most interesting in this respect."

* * *

GRYLLS, Rosalie Glynn

PERSONAL: Born in London, England; daughter of A. C.

and Hilda (Viner) Grylls; married Geoffrey Mander (member of Parliament), 1930 (died, 1962); children: one son, one daughter. *Education:* Lady Margaret Hall, Oxford, M.A., 1927. *Home:* Wightwick Manor, Wolverhampton, Staffordshire, England. *Office:* 35 Buckingham Gate, London S.W.1, England.

CAREER: Honorary curator for National Trust, Wightwick Manor, Wolverhampton, England. Lecturer in United States. *Member:* Byron Society, Keats-Shelley Association.

WRITINGS: Mary Shelley: A Biography, Oxford University Press, 1938, Haskell House, 1969, Folcroft, 1973; *Claire Clairmont, Mother of Byron's Allegra,* J. Murray, 1939; *Queen's College, 1848-1948, Founded by Frederick Denison Maurice,* Routledge, 1948; *Trelawny,* Richard West, 1950; *William Godwin and His World,* Richard West, 1953, Folcroft, 1973; *Portrait of Rossetti,* Macdonald & Co., 1964, Southern Illinois University Press, 1970; *I. Compton-Burnett,* Longman, 1971; (editor) Mary Kingsley, *Travels in West Africa,* C. Knight, 1972. Contributor to periodicals.

* * *

GUENTHER, (Robert) Wallace 1929-

PERSONAL: Born August 30, 1929, in Van Nuys, Calif.; son of Earl L. (a government worker) and Maurie (Angel) Guenther; married Jolene Fitz, April 14, 1954. *Education:* California State College, Los Angeles, B.A., 1954. *Office: House Beautiful,* 717 Fifth Ave., New York, N.Y. 10022.

CAREER/WRITINGS: Los Angeles Daily News, Los Angeles, Calif., reporter and copy editor, 1948-53; *Los Angeles Times,* Los Angeles, Calif., writer and editor of *Home* (the Sunday magazine), 1954-69; *House Beautiful,* New York, N.Y., editor-in-chief, 1969—. *Military service:* U.S. Army, 1950-51. *Member:* American Society of Interior Design, Sigma Delta Chi.

* * *

GUEST, Harry
See GUEST, Henry Bayly

* * *

GUEST, Henry Bayly 1932-
(Harry Guest)

PERSONAL: Born October 6, 1932, in Penarth, Wales; son of Walter Howard and Elsie (Matthews) Guest; married Lynn Doremus Dunbar (a writer and translator), December 28, 1963; children: Natalie Doremus, Nicholas Bayly Dunbar. *Education:* Trinity Hall, Cambridge, B.A., 1954; Sorbonne, University of Paris, D.E.S., 1955. *Religion:* Church of England. *Home:* 1 Alexandra Ter., Exeter, Devonshire EX4 6SY, England.

CAREER: Teacher of French, German, and English literature at private schools in Essex, England, 1955-61, and Sussex, England, 1961-66; Yokohama National University, Yokohama, Japan, lecturer in English literature, 1966-72; Exeter School, Exeter, England, teacher of French and head of department, 1972—. *Member:* Poetry Society (member of general council, 1972-75).

WRITINGS—Under name Harry Guest: *Arrangements* (poems), Anvil Press, 1968; *The Cutting-Room* (poems), Anvil Press, 1970; *Another Island Country* (textbook), Eikosha, 1970; (with wife, Lynn Guest, and Kajima Shozo) *Post-War Japanese Poetry,* Penguin, 1972; *The Achievements of Memory* (visual poem), Sceptre, 1974; *The Enchanted Acres* (poems), Sceptre, 1975; *Mountain Journal* (poem), Rivelin,

1975; *A House Against the Night* (poems), Anvil Press, 1976; *English Poems,* Words Press, 1976, in press. Author of "The Emperor of Outer Space," a poem for four voices, first broadcast on British Broadcasting Corp. (BBC) Radio 3, February, 1976.

WORK IN PROGRESS: A novel.

AVOCATIONAL INTERESTS: Playing the piano, "going for long walks in remote areas, particularly to visit Stone Age sites."

* * *

GUETT, Dieter 1924-

PERSONAL: Born February 24, 1924, in Marienbad, Czechoslovakia; son of Arthur (a physician) and Countess Jenny (Henrard) Guett; married wife Erika, November 11, 1963 (died October 25, 1976); children: Astrid, Annette. *Education:* Attended University of Berlin and University of Kiel; University of Cologne, M.D., 1949. *Home:* 1 Fifth Ave., New York, N.Y. 10003. *Office:* 58 West 58th St., New York, N.Y. 10019.

CAREER: Weltbuehne, Berlin, Germany, editor, 1946-49; free-lance writer for German daily newspapers, 1949-59; ARD-Television, Cologne, Germany, editor-in-chief, 1959-72; free-lance correspondent from New York, N.Y., 1973—. Professor at Eidgenoessische Hochschule (Zurich). *Military service:* German Army, 1942-45; received Iron Cross. *Member:* National Academy of Television Arts and Sciences, Cavendish Club. *Awards, honors:* Adolf-Grimme Prize, 1969; Carl V. Ossietzky Prize, 1970.

WRITINGS: Es Spricht Dieter Guett, Desch, 1969; *Verlorene Geschichte,* Desch, 1971.

SIDELIGHTS: Guett writes that he reports on "liberal and radical engagement." He comments that he has covered all major wars and international conferences since 1950.

* * *

GUIDO, (Cecily) Margaret 1912-
(C. M. Piggott)

PERSONAL: Born May 8, 1912, in West Wickham, Kent, England; daughter of Arthur Gurney and E. M. (Fidgeon) Preston; married Luigi Guido (divorced). *Education:* University College, London, post-graduate diploma, 1936. *Politics:* Liberal. *Home:* 3 Brock St., Bath BA1 2LN, England.

CAREER: Archaeologist. *Member:* Prehistoric Society, Royal Archaeological Institute, Society of Antiquaries of London (fellow), Society of Antiquaries of Scotland, Wiltshire Archaeological Society (member of council), Dorset Archaeological Society, Bath Anglo-Italian Society. *Awards, honors:* Leverhulme research award, 1954; British Academy research award, 1975.

WRITINGS: Syracuse: A Handbook to Its History and Principal Monuments, Parrish, 1958; *Sardinia,* Thames & Hudson, 1963; *Sicily: An Archaeological Guide,* Faber, 1968; *Southern Italy: An Archaeological Guide,* Faber, 1972; *The Prehistoric and Roman Glass Beads of the British Isles,* Society of Antiquaries of London, 1977. Contributor of articles under pseudonym of C. M. Piggott, to proceedings of *Prehistoric Society* and *Society of Antiquaries of Scotland,* and to journals, including *Antiquity* and *Antiquaries Journal.*

WORK IN PROGRESS: With K. Annable and P. Robinson, a catalog of Devizes Museum Iron Age collections; a study of glass beads of the post-Roman period in Britain, completion expected in 1985.

SIDELIGHTS: Margaret Guido lived for several years in Sicily. Most of her excavations have been in England and Scotland, however, where her work was carried out under the auspices of the Royal Commission on Ancient and Historical Monuments of Scotland. During and after World War II she conducted work on sites that had been threatened by the war or post-war development.

* * *

GUINNESS, (Ian) Os(wald) 1941-

PERSONAL: Born September 30, 1941, in Hsiang Cheng, China; son of Henry W. (a Christian missionary) and Mary (a surgeon; maiden name, Taylor) Guinness; married Jenny Macdonald (a fashion model, under the name Windsor Elliott). *Education:* University of London, B.D. (honors), 1966; Oxford University, B.Phil., 1968. *Religion:* Christian. *Home:* 5 Plantation Rd., Oxford, England.

CAREER: Writer.

WRITINGS: The Dust of Death: A Critique of the Counter-Culture, Inter-Varsity Press, 1973; *In Two Minds: The Dilemma of Doubt and How to Resolve It,* Inter-Varsity Press, 1976.

* * *

GULKER, Virgil G. 1947-

PERSONAL: Born September 17, 1947, in Pipestone, Minn.; son of Johann and Nellie (Sas) Gulker. *Education:* Grand Valley State College, B.A., 1969; University of Michigan, M.A., 1971, D.A., 1973; attended Western Theological Seminary, 1975-76. *Religion:* Protestant. *Home:* 486 Harrison Ave., Holland, Mich. 49423.

CAREER: Washtenaw Community College, Milan Federal Correctional Institute, Milan, Mich., instructor in English, 1971, librarian, 1971-72; Miami-Dade Community College, Miami, Fla., designer/coordinator of county jails educational programs and libraries, 1972-73; University of Michigan, Ann Arbor, lecturer in prison library science, 1973-74; Genesee Community College, Attica Correctional Facility, Batavia, N.Y., education program officer, 1974-75; writer, 1975—. Member of field faculty for graduate program, Goddard College, 1976—. Prison education and library services consultant, 1975—.

WRITINGS: Books Behind Bars, Scarecrow, 1973. Contributor to *Catholic Library World.*

WORK IN PROGRESS: The Prison Experience: Three Perspectives.

* * *

GUNGWU, Wang
See WANG Gungwu

* * *

GUNNING, Monica Olwen 1930-

PERSONAL: Born January 5, 1930, in Jamaica, West Indies; daughter of Reginald (a produce dealer) and Gwen (an infant nurse; maiden name, Spence) Morgan; married Elon Gunning (in real estate), February 2, 1957; children: Michael Anthony, Mark Elon. *Education:* City College (now of the City University of New York), B.A., 1957; University of Guadalajara, graduate study, 1971; Mount St. Mary's College, Los Angeles, Calif., M.S.Ed., 1971. *Politics:* Democrat. *Religion:* Methodist. *Home:* 7604 Willow Glen Rd., Los Angeles, Calif. 90046. *Office:* Los Angeles Board of Education, Los Angeles, Calif.

CAREER: Bilingual elementary teacher in Los Angeles, Calif., 1959-72; Union Avenue Elementary School, Los Angeles, Calif., teacher of English as a second language, 1973—. Training teacher for University of California, Los Angeles, and University of Southern California. Chairperson of Parent Volunteer Program, Union Avenue School, 1975-76. *Member:* International Students Association, Society of Children's Book Writers, Southern California Council on Literature for Children and Young People, Association of Friends of the Library (Los Angeles).

WRITINGS—Bilingual books in Spanish and English for children: *Perico Bonito* (title means "Pretty Parrot"), Blaine-Ethridge, 1976; *Los Dos Jorges* (title means "The Two Georges"), Blaine-Ethridge, 1976.

WORK IN PROGRESS: Folk Tales of the West Indies; The Use of Cognates in Teaching a New Language.

SIDELIGHTS: Monica Gunning writes: "Mexico is one of my favorite countries. I am affiliated with an inter-cultural exchange program for elementary students between Mexico and the United States. In 1973 I chaperoned a group of students into Mexico and spent Christmas there.

"I am also a member of the International Students Association. The purpose of this organization is to entertain foreign students in American homes for better understanding among peoples. Through this organization I have had the opportunity to be the hostess for students from all over the world, and establish friendships among many races."

AVOCATIONAL INTERESTS: Interior decorating ("especially refinishing inexpensive items from thrift shops"), cooking her native West Indian foods, playing the guitar, singing calypsos.

* * *

GUTHRIE, Hunter 1901-1974

PERSONAL: Born January 8, 1901, in New York, N.Y.; son of Jacob Francis and Mary (Ross) Guthrie. *Education:* Woodstock College, A.B., 1923, A.M., 1924; Gregorian University, S.T.D., 1931; postdoctoral study at universities in Belgium and Germany, 1931-37; Sorbonne, University of Paris, Dr. de l'U. (highest honors), 1937. *Residence:* Philadelphia, Pa.

CAREER: Entered Society of Jesus (Jesuits), 1917, ordained Roman Catholic priest, 1930; Virgan Seminary, the Philippines, instructor in English and Latin, 1924-25; Ateneo de Manila, Manila, the Philippines, instructor in English, Latin, and economics, 1925-27; Woodstock College, Woodstock, Md., professor of history and philosophy, 1937-40; Fordham University, Bronx, N.Y., professor of philosophy, 1940-43; Georgetown University, Washington, D.C., professor of philosophy, head of department, and dean of Graduate School, 1949-52, president of university, 1949-52; St. Joseph's College, Philadelphia, Pa., professor of philosophy and head of department, 1952-72, professor emeritus, 1972-74. Guest professor at Jewish Theological Seminary, 1941. Member of U.S. Commission on Reconstruction of Education and National Fund for Medical Education; U.S. State Department specialist on Latin America, 1954, 1958.

MEMBER: American Philosophical Association, American Catholic Philosophical Association, American Academy of Political and Social Science, Mediaeval Academy of America, Association of American Colleges, National Catholic Education Association, Catholic Commission for Intellectual and Cultural Affairs (co-founder), Institute of Religion Studies. *Awards, honors:* Grand Cross of Alfonso X el Sa-bio, Spain; officer of the Legion of Honor and Merit, Haiti; Freedom Award from the Freedoms Foundation, 1950; award from Air University, 1958.

WRITINGS: Introduction au probleme de l'histoire de la philosophie: La metaphysique de l'individualite a priori de la pensee, F. Alcan, 1937. Also: *Modern Trends in American Culture,* 1923; (editor) *Symposium on American Catholic Education,* 1941; (translator) *History of Theology,* 1968. Assistant editor of *Dictionary of Philosophy* and of *Thought.*

OBITUARIES: Washington Post, November 13, 1974.*

(Died November 11, 1974, in Wernersville, Pa.)

*   *   *

GUTHRIE, William Keith Chambers   1906-

PERSONAL: Born August 1, 1906, in London, England; son of Charles Jameson and Catherine Guthrie; married Adele Marion Ogilvy, June 10, 1933; children: Robert, Anne. *Education:* Trinity College, Cambridge, B.A., 1928, M.A., 1931. *Home:* 3 Roman Hill, Barton, Cambridge CB3 7AX, England.

CAREER: Member of research expeditions of the American Society for Archaeological Research in Asia Minor, 1929, 1930, 1932; Cambridge University, Cambridge, England, fellow of Peterhouse, 1930, 1932-57, university proctor, 1936-37, public orator of the university, 1939-57, P. M. Laurence Reader in Classics, 1947-53, Laurence Professor of Ancient Philosophy, 1957-73, master of Downing College, 1957-72. Messenger Lecturer at Cornell University, 1957; James B. Duke Visiting Professor of Philosophy at Duke University, 1966; Raymond Visiting Professor of Classics at State University of New York, Buffalo, 1974. *Military service:* British Army, Intelligence Corps, 1941-45; became temporary major.

MEMBER: Classical Association (president, 1967-68), British Academy (fellow). *Awards, honors:* Honorary fellow of Peterhouse, Cambridge, 1957, and Downing College, Cambridge, 1972; D.Litt. from University of Melbourne, 1957, and University of Sheffield, 1967; Litt.D. from Cambridge University, 1959.

WRITINGS: (With William Calder and W. H. Buckler) *Monumenta Asiae Minoris Antiqua,* Volume IV, Manchester University Press, 1933; *Orpheus and Greek Religion: A Study of the Orhpic Movement,* Methuen, 1935, revised edition, Methuen, 1957, Norton, 1967; (editor and translator) *Aristotle De Caelo,* Harvard University Press, 1939.

The Greeks and Their Gods, Methuen, 1950, Beacon Press, 1951; *The Greek Philosophers from Thales to Aristotle,* Methuen, 1950, Barnes & Noble, 1967; (editor and contributor) F. M. Cornford, *The Unwritten Philosophy and Other Essays,* Cambridge University Press, 1950; *Greek Philosophy: The Hub and the Spokes,* Cambridge University Press, 1953; *Myth and Reason,* London School of Economics and Political Science, University of London, 1953; *In the Beginning: Some Greek Views on the Origins of Life and the Early State of Man,* Cornell University Press, 1956; (translator) Plato, *Protagoras and Meno,* Penguin, 1956; (contributor) *Recherches sur la tradition platonicienne* (title means "Investigation of the Platonic Tradition"), Entretiens Hardt, 1957; *Socrates and Plato,* University of Queensland Press, 1958.

(With B. A. Van Gronigen) *Tradition and Personal Achievement in Classical Antiquity,* Athlone Press, 1960; *A History*

of Greek Philosophy, Cambridge University Press, Volume I: *The Early Presocratics and the Pythagoreans,* 1962, Volume II: *The Presocratic Tradition from Parmenides to Democritus,* 1965, Volume III: *The Fifth Century Enlightenment,* 1969 (also published separately; see below), Volume IV: *Plato, Earlier Period,* 1975; *Twentieth Century Approaches to Plato,* Princeton University Press for University of Cincinnati, 1967.

Socrates (first half of *The Fifth Century Enlightenment*), Cambridge University Press, 1971; *The Sophists* (second half of *The Fifth Century Enlightenment*), Cambridge University Press, 1971; (translator) Malcolm Brown, *Plato's Meno, with Essays,* Bobbs-Merrill, 1971.

Contributor to *Cambridge Ancient History.* Contributor to professional journals.

*   *   *

GUTMAN, Herbert G(eorge)   1928-

PERSONAL: Born March 18, 1928, in New York, N.Y.; son of Joseph and Anna Gutman; married Judith Mara Markowitz (a writer), June 16, 1950; children: Marta Ruth, Nell Lisa. *Education:* Queens College (now of the City University of New York), B.A., 1949; Columbia University, M.A., 1950; University of Wisconsin, Madison, Ph.D., 1959. *Home:* 97 Sixth Ave., Nyack, N.Y. 10960. *Agent:* Sterling Lord Agency, 660 Madison Ave., New York, N.Y. 10021. *Office:* Department of History, Graduate Center, City University of New York, 33 West 42nd St., New York, N.Y.

CAREER: Fairleigh Dickinson University, Rutherford, N.J., 1956-63, began as instructor, became assistant professor of history; State University of New York, Buffalo, associate professor, 1963-66, professor of history, 1966; University of Rochester, Rochester, N.Y., professor of history, 1966-72; City University of New York, New York, N.Y., professor of history at City College and Graduate Center, 1972—, chairman of department at City College, 1972-75. Fellow of Center for the Advanced Study of the Behavioral Sciences (Palo Alto, Calif.), 1966-67; Harrison visiting professor at College of William and Mary, 1976-77. Member of National Historical Publications and Records Commission, 1974-78; director of New York Council for the Humanities, 1976-80.

MEMBER: Organization of American Historians (member of executive board, 1975-78), American Historical Association. *Awards, honors:* Social Science Research Council fellowship, 1970-71; National Endowment for the Humanities fellowship, 1975-76; fellow of Princeton University's Shelby Cullom Davis Center for Historical Studies, 1975-76.

WRITINGS: (Editor with Gregory Kealey) *Many Pasts: Readings in American Social History,* Prentice-Hall, 1973; *Slavery and the Numbers Game: A Critique of Time on the Cross,* University of Illinois Press, 1975; *Work, Culture, and Society in Industrializing America,* Knopf, 1976; (with Paul A. David and others) *Reckoning with Slavery,* Oxford University Press, 1976; *The Black Family in Slavery and Freedom, 1750-1925,* Pantheon, 1976. Contributor to history and social science journals.

WORK IN PROGRESS: A study of slaves and ex-slaves during the Civil War and up to 1868, with emphasis on familial and related social beliefs and practices, for Pantheon; a social history of American industrialization, 1840-1920, for Knopf; a study of the first American working class; a study of migrants and immigrants to New York City.

GUTT, Dieter
    See GUETT, Dieter

* * *

GUTTERIDGE, Don(ald George) 1937-

PERSONAL: Born September 30, 1937, in Point Edward, Ontario, Canada; son of William (a railroad employee) and Margaret Grace (a civil servant; maiden name, McWatters) Gutteridge; married Anne Barnett (a teacher), June 30, 1961; children: John, Catherine. *Education:* University of Western Ontario, B.A. (honors), 1962. *Home:* 114 Victoria St., London, Ontario, Canada N6A 2B5. *Office:* Faculty of Education, University of Western Ontario, 1137 Western Rd., London, Ontario, Canada.

CAREER: English teacher at a school in Elmira, Ontario, 1960-62; teacher and head of English department in Ingersoll, Ontario, 1963-64, and London, Ontario, 1964-68; University of Western Ontario, London, assistant professor, 1968-74, associate professor of English, 1975—. *Member:* League of Canadian Poets, Canadian Association of University Teachers. *Awards, honors:* President's Medal from University of Western Ontario, 1972, for the poem "Death at Quebec"; Canada Council travel grant, 1973.

WRITINGS: Riel: A Poem for Voices, Fiddlehead, 1968, revised edition, Van Nostrand, 1972; *The Village Within: Poems toward a Biography,* Fiddlehead, 1970; *Death at Quebec and Other Poems,* Fiddlehead, 1971; *Perspectives* (poems), Pennywise Press, 1971; *Language and Expression: A Modern Approach,* McClelland & Stewart, 1971; *Saying Grace: An Elegy* (poems), Fiddlehead, 1972; *Coppermine: The Quest for North* (poems) Oberon, 1973; *Bus-Ride* (novel), Nairn Publications, 1974; *Borderlands* (poems), Oberon, 1975; *Tecumseh: Dreams and Visions* (poems), Oberon, 1976.

WORK IN PROGRESS: A True History of Lambton County (tentative title), poetry.

SIDELIGHTS: Gutteridge's poetry reaches into Canada's past, to help establish for Canadians a sense of time and place, to give them roots which he feels are presently lacking. *Coppermine* and *Borderlands* have been dramatized for radio by Canadian Broadcasting Corp.

BIOGRAPHICAL/CRITICAL SOURCES: Edge Nine, summer, 1969; Margaret Atwood, *Survival: Themes in Canadian Literature,* House of Anansi, 1971.

* * *

HAAS, Carolyn Buhai 1926-

PERSONAL: Born January 1, 1926, in Chicago, Ill.; daughter of Michael (a manufacturer) and Tillie (a social worker; maiden name, Weiss) Buhai; married Robert G. Haas (an advertising executive), June 29, 1947; children: Andrew, Mari, Betsy, Thomas, Karen. *Education:* Smith College, B.Ed., 1947; also attended National College of Education and Chicago Art Institute. *Politics:* Democrat. *Religion:* Jewish. *Home:* 280 Sylvan Rd., Glencoe, Ill. 60022. *Agent:* Marilyn Marlow, Curtis Brown Ltd., 60 East 56th St., New York, N.Y. 10022. *Office:* Parents As Resources Project, 464 Central, Northfield, Ill. 60022.

CAREER: Elementary school teacher in Chicago, Ill., 1947-49; art teacher in public schools of Glencoe, Ill., 1969-70; Parents As Resources Project, Northfield, Ill., co-founder and partner, 1970—. Member of board of directors of Glencoe Family Counseling Service and Glencoe Human Relations Committee. *Member:* American Jewish Committee (member of national board), Scholarship and Guidance Association (Chicago; president), Chicago Reading Roundtable, Smith College Club (president; member of board).

WRITINGS: (With Ann Cole and Betty Kiralfy Weinberger) *Recipes for Fun* (juvenile), six volumes, Parents As Resources Project, 1970-76; (with Faith Bushnell, Cole, and Weinberger) *I Saw a Purple Cow* (juvenile), Little, Brown, 1972; (with Elizabeth Heller, Cole, and Weinberger) *A Pumpkin in a Pear Tree* (juvenile), Little, Brown, 1976. Coauthor of "Recipes for Fun," a newspaper column in *Des Moines Register and Tribune,* 1970—. Contributor to education journals and magazines for parents. Consultant to WWTW-Television's series "Look at Me!," 1974-76.

WORK IN PROGRESS: Parenting.

* * *

HAAS, Lynne 1939-

PERSONAL: Born November 3, 1939, in Philadelphia, Pa.; daughter of James (a transit worker) and Helen (Clinch) Flannery; married James Haas (a religious education consultant), March 22, 1969; children: James, Jr., Daniel. *Education:* Presently attending Chestnut Hill College. *Religion:* Roman Catholic. *Residence:* Annapolis, Md.

CAREER: Elementary school teacher in the public schools of Philadelphia, Pa., 1960-64, and Baltimore, Md., 1964-68; parochial high school teacher of religion in Annapolis, Md., 1975—.

WRITINGS: (With husband, Jim Haas) *Make a Joyful Noise,* Morehouse, 1973.

AVOCATIONAL INTERESTS: Women's movement, especially in church-related activities.

* * *

HABER, Joyce 1932-

PERSONAL: Born December 28, 1932, in New York, N.Y.; daughter of John Sanford (a business executive) and Lucille (Buckmaster) Haber; married Douglas S. Cramer, Jr. (a producer), September 25, 1966 (divorced); children: Douglas Schoolfield III, Courtney Sanford. *Education:* Attended Bryn Mawr College, 1949-50; Barnard College, B.A., 1953. *Residence:* Beverly Hills, Calif. *Agent:* Irving Lazar, 211 South Beverly Dr., Beverly Hills, Calif. 90212.

CAREER: Time, New York, N.Y., researcher, 1953-63, Hollywood reporter, 1963-66; *Los Angeles Times,* Los Angeles, Calif., columnist, 1967-75; writer, 1975—. Has appeared in films and on television and radio. *Member:* American Federation of Television and Radio Artists, Screen Actors Guild, American Civil Liberties Union, Actors and Others for Animals (honorary member of board of directors), Hollywood Women's Press Club. *Awards, honors:* Award from Variety Clubs of Southern California.

WRITINGS: Caroline's Doll Book, Putnam, 1962; *The Users* (novel), Delacorte, 1976. Columnist, "Joyce Haber" Hollywood column, syndicated by Los Angeles Times News Syndicate, 1967-75. Contributor to magazines, including *Esquire, Harper's Bazaar, New York, Town and Country.* Contributing editor, *Los Angeles,* magazine, 1977—.

AVOCATIONAL INTERESTS: Politics, show business, reading, the theater, filmmaking.

HABERER, Joseph 1929-

PERSONAL: Born January 31, 1929, in Villingen, Germany; came to United States, 1946, naturalized citizen, 1952; son of Berthold (a government official) and Georgine (a seamstress; maiden name, Seckels) Haberer; married Beverly Young, April 20, 1960 (divorced, August, 1970); married Rose Weiss (an anthropologist), November, 1970; children: (first marriage) Eugene, Robert; (second marriage) Leila, Nina. Education: San Francisco State College (now University), B.A., 1950; Columbia University, M.A., 1954; University of California, Berkeley, Ph.D., 1965. Politics: Democrat. Religion: Jewish. Home: 129 East Navajo St., West Lafayette, Ind. 47906. Office: Department of Political Science, Purdue University, West Lafayette, Ind. 47907.

CAREER: WQXR-Radio, New York, N.Y., staff member, 1952-55; New York Welfare Department, New York City, social worker, 1956-57; San Francisco Welfare Department, San Francisco, Calif., social worker, 1958-60; University of California, Berkeley, instructor in political science, 1965-66; Rutgers University, New Brunswick, N.J., assistant professor of political science, 1966-71; Purdue University, West Lafayette, Ind., associate professor of political science, 1971—, director of science and public policy, 1971—. Member of board of directors of Science and Public Policy Studies Group, 1971—; member of West Lafayette Environmental Commission. Military service: California National Guard, 1948-51. Member: American Political Science Association, American Association for the Advancement of Science, Policy Studies Association. Awards, honors: Woodrow Wilson fellowship, 1963-65.

WRITINGS: Politics and the Community of Science, Van Nostrand, 1969. Contributor to scientific journals. Editor of STPP [Science, Technology, and Public Policy] News, 1973—.

WORK IN PROGRESS: Ethical and Human Value Dimensions of Science and Technology; research on political perceptions and involvement of American scientists.

SIDELIGHTS: Haberer writes that he is "concerned with the social, cultural, political impacts of science with sensitizing emerging cadres of professionals (engineering, science, medicine) to the implications of the products of their work." He adds that he is "opposed to narrow pragmatism that infuses so much decision-making."

*   *   *

HADER, Berta (Hoerner) 1890(?)-1976

1890(?)—February 6, 1976; American author and illustrator of books for children. Obituaries: AB Bookman's Weekly, May 17, 1976.

*   *   *

HAFEN, LeRoy R(euben) 1893-

PERSONAL: Born December 8, 1893, in Bunkerville, Nev.; son of John George and Mary Ann (Stucki) Hafen; married Ann Woodbury, September 3, 1915 (died, 1970); married Mary Woodbury Adams, 1971; children: (first marriage) Norma (deceased), Karl LeRoy. Education: Brigham Young University, A.B., 1916; University of Utah, M.A., 1919; University of California, Ph.D., 1924. Home: 1102 Fir Ave., Provo, Utah 84601.

CAREER: High school teacher of history in Bunkerville, Nev., 1916-18, principal, 1918-20; teacher in private school in Berkeley, Calif., 1923-24; State Historical Society of Colorado, Denver, executive director and state historian, 1924-

54; Brigham Young University, Provo, Utah, professor of history, 1954-71, professor emeritus, 1971—; writer, 1971—. Associate professor at University of Denver, 1933-39, professor, 1939-52; visiting professor at University of Glasgow, 1947-48.

MEMBER: International Institute of Arts and Letters (fellow), American Historical Association, Organization of American Historians, Western Historical Association, Utah Writers League, Colorado Authors League, Utah Westerners, Denver Westerners, Riverside Country Club. Awards, honors: Fellow of Huntington Library, 1950-51; Litt.D. from University of Colorado, 1935, and from University of Zurich.

WRITINGS: The Overland Mail, 1849-1869: Promoter of Settlement, Precursor of Railroads, Arthur H. Clark, 1926, reprinted, AMS Press, 1969; (editor with J. H. Baker) History of Colorado, three volumes, Linderman, 1927.

(With W. J. Ghent) Broken Hand: The Life Story of Thomas Fitzpatrick, Chief of the Mountain Men, Old West, 1931, revised edition, 1973; (editor) Henry Villard, The Past and the Present of the Pike's Peak Gold Region, Princeton University Press, 1932; Colorado: The Story of a Western Commonwealth, Peerless Publishing Co., 1933, reprinted, AMS Press, 1970; (with Francis Marion Young) Fort Laramie and the Pageant of the West, 1834-1890, Arthur H. Clark, 1938.

(Editor) Colorado Gold Rush: Contemporary Letters and Reports, 1858-1859, Arthur H. Clark, 1941, reprinted, Porcupine Press, 1974; (editor) Pike's Peak Gold Rush Guidebooks of 1859, Arthur H. Clark, 1941; (with Carl Coke Rister) Western America: The Exploration, Settlement, and Development of the Region Beyond the Mississippi, Prentice-Hall, 1941, 3rd edition with W. Eugene Hollon, 1950; (editor) Overland Routes to the Gold Fields, 1859, from Contemporary Diaries, Arthur H. Clark, 1942, reprinted, Porcupine Press, 1974; (with wife, Ann W. Hafen) Colorado: A Story of the State and Its People, Old West, 1943, revised edition published as The Colorado Story: A History of Your State and Mine, 1953, 2nd revised edition published as Our State: Colorado, a History of Progress, 1966; (editor) Colorado and Its People: A Narrative and Topical History of the Centennial State, four volumes, Lewis Historical Publishing Co., 1948.

(Editor) Ruxton of the Rockies, University of Oklahoma, 1950; (editor) Life in the Far West, University of Oklahoma, 1951; (editor with A. W. Hafen) Journals of Forty-Niners: Salt Lake to Los Angeles, Arthur H. Clark, 1954; (with A. W. Hafen) Old Spanish Trail: Santa Fe to Los Angeles, Arthur H. Clark, 1954; (editor with A. W. Hafen) To the Rockies and Oregon, 1839-1842, Arthur H. Clark, 1955; (editor with A. W. Hafen) The Utah Expedition, 1857-1858, Arthur H. Clark, 1958; (editor with A. W. Hafen) Relations with the Indians of the Plains, 1857-1861, Arthur H. Clark, 1959.

(Editor with A. W. Hafen) Fremont's Fourth Expedition: A Documentary Account of the Disaster of 1848-1849, Arthur H. Clark, 1960; (with A. W. Hafen) Handcarts to Zion: The Story of a Unique Western Migration, 1856-1860, Arthur H. Clark, 1960; (editor with A. W. Hafen) Powder River Campaigns and Sawyers Expedition of 1865, Arthur H. Clark, 1961; (editor with A. W. Hafen) Reports from Colorado: The Wildman Letters, 1859-1865, Arthur H. Clark, 1961; (editor with A. W. Hafen) The Far West and Rockies: General Analytical Index to the Fifteen Volume Series, Arthur H. Clark, 1961; The Hafen Families of Utah, privately printed, 1962; *LeRoy R. and Ann W. Hafen: Their Writings and Their Notable Collection of Americana Given to Brigham Young University Library,* Brigham Young University, 1962; (editor) *The Mountain Men and the Fur Trade of the Far West,* ten volumes, Arthur H. Clark, 1965-72; *The Mormons on the Frontier,* Columbia Records Legacy Collection, 1965.

The Joyous Journey of LeRoy R. and Ann W. Hafen: An Autobiography, Arthur H. Clark, 1973; *Arapaho-Cheyenne Land Area: Historical Background and Development,* Clearwater Publishing, 1974; *Ute Indians and the San Juan Mining Region: Historical Summary,* Clearwater Publishing, 1974. Editor of "The Far West and the Rockies Historical Series," Arthur H. Clark, 1954-61. Contributor to *World Book Encyclopedia, Encyclopaedia Britannica, Encyclopedia Americana, Dictionary of American History,* and *Atlas of American History.* Contributor to history journals. Editor of *Colorado Magazine,* 1925-54.

* * *

HAGER, Robert M. 1938-

PERSONAL: Born October 8, 1938, in New York, N.Y.; son of V. Mitchell (an artist) and Florence (an artist; maiden name, Burke) Hager; married Honore Vargas, August 29, 1959; children: Gabrielle, Jennifer, Christina. *Education:* Dartmouth College, B.A., 1960. *Office:* National Broadcasting Co. News, 30 Rockefeller Plaza, New York, N.Y. 10020.

CAREER/WRITINGS: WBUY-Radio, Lexington, N.C., news and sports director, 1960-62; WTPF-Radio, Raleigh, N.C., reporter and newscaster, 1962-63; WBT-Television, Charlotte, N.C., political reporter, 1963-65; WRC-Television, Washington, D.C., reporter and co-anchor man of late news program, 1965-69; National Broadcasting Co. (NBC) News, New York, N.Y., correspondent in Vietnam, 1969, West Germany and Moscow, 1970-72, and New York City, 1972—. Notable assignments include the first troop pull-outs from Vietnam, the Moscow summit meeting of 1972, the massacre of the Israeli Olympic team, the Mitchell-Stans trial, and labor leader James Hoffa's disappearance.

* * *

HAILE, H(arry) G(erald) 1931-

PERSONAL: Born July 31, 1931, in Brownwood, Tex.; son of Frank and Nell (Goodson) Haile; married Mary Elizabeth Huff, September 1, 1952; children: Jonathan, Christian, Constance. *Education:* University of Arkansas, B.A., 1952, M.A., 1954; graduate study at University of Cologne, 1955-56; University of Illinois, Ph.D., 1957. *Home:* 1001 West White, Champaign, Ill. 61820. *Office:* Department of Germanic Languages, University of Illinois, Urbana, Ill. 61801.

CAREER: University of Pennsylvania, Philadelphia, instructor in German, 1956-57; University of Houston, Houston, Tex., assistant professor, 1957-60, associate professor of German, 1960-63; University of Illinois, Urbana, associate professor, 1963-65, professor of German, 1965—, head of department, 1964-73, associate member of Center for Advanced Study, 1969-70. *Member:* Modern Language Association of America, American Association of Teachers of German, Goethe Society. *Awards, honors:* Fulbright grant, 1955; American Council of Learned Societies grant, 1960; Deutsche Forschungsgemeinschaft grant, 1962-63; has also received a number of research grants from University of Illinois.

WRITINGS: (Editor) *Das Faustbuch nach der Wolfenbuettel Handschrift* (title means "The Faustbook Edited from the Wolfenbuettel Manuscript"), Erich Schmidt, 1961; *The History of Doctor John Faustus, Recovered from the German,* University of Illinois Press, 1965; *Artist in Chrysalis: A Biographical Study of Wolfgang Goethe,* University of Illinois Press, 1973; *Invitation to Goethe's "Faust,"* University of Alabama Press, 1975; *Goethe's Roman Elegies,* University of Alabama Press, in press. Contributor to journals in his field.

WORK IN PROGRESS: Old Man, Death, and the Devil, a study of the elder Martin Luther.

SIDELIGHTS: Haile told *CA:* "Although I started out as professor of German, I have come more and more to think of myself as a biographer. The attempt to appreciate and sympathize with the interests of a distant fellow human helps writer and reader to detach themselves from themselves and from the arrogance of the present."

* * *

HAINES, Charles G(rove) 1906-1976

December 10, 1906—May 25, 1976; American educator, university administrator, diplomat, and author of books on American diplomacy. Obituaries: *Washington Post,* May 28, 1976.

* * *

HAKIM, Seymour 1933-

PERSONAL: Born January 23, 1933, in New York, N.Y.; son of Sol (an industrial chemist) and Renee (Greenblat) Hakim; married Odetta Roverso (a librarian), August 18, 1970. *Education:* Eastern New Mexico University, A.B., 1957; New York University, M.A., 1960; graduate study at University of Southern California. *Home:* Piazza Scamozzi #1, Vicenza, Italy.

CAREER: Teacher of English in New York, N.Y., 1957; teacher and traveler in New York, California, and Europe, 1960-70; London Central School, London, England, instructor in creative writing and painting, 1971-72; Vicenza American School, Vicenza, Italy, instructor in literature and creative writing, 1972—; exhibiting artist and poet. *Military service:* U.S. Army, 1952-54.

WRITINGS—All published by Poet Gallery Press: *Manhattan Goodbye,* 1970; *Under Moon,* 1970; *The Sacred Family* (play), 1970; *In the Museum of the Mind,* 1971; *Wine Theorem,* 1972; *Substituting Memories,* 1975.

WORK IN PROGRESS: Paintings for an exhibition in Italy; a collection of poetry.

SIDELIGHTS: Hakim told *CA:* "Living and traveling in Europe for the past fifteen years has made me aware that I am both a human, an American, and share all men's alienation. I live with joy and zest and sun for the search that can only end."

* * *

HALBERSTAM, Michael 1932-

PERSONAL: Born August 9, 1932, in Bronx, N.Y.; son of Charles (a physician) and Blanche (a teacher; maiden name, Levy) Halberstam; married Linda Brackett, 1958 (divorced); married Elliott Jones (a journalist), June 1, 1976; children: Charles, Eben. *Education:* Harvard University, A.B., 1953; Boston University, M.D., 1957. *Politics:* Democrat. *Religion:* Jewish. *Residence:* Washington, D.C. *Agent:* Wendy

Weil, Julian Bach Literary Agency, 3 East 48th St., New York, N.Y. 10017. *Office:* 2520 L St. N.W., Washington, D.C.

CAREER: Mary Fletcher Hospital, Burlington, Vt., resident in medicine, 1960-62; George Washington University Hospital, Washington, D.C., fellow in cardiology, 1962-64; private practice of medicine and cardiology in Washington, D.C., 1964—. Assistant clinical professor at George Washington University; member of American Board of Internal Medicine and National Academy of Science's Institute of Medicine. *Military service:* U.S. Public Health Service, physician for Division of Indian Health, 1958-60.

WRITINGS: The Pills in Your Life, Grosset, 1972; (with Stephan Lesher) *A Coronary Event,* Lippincott, 1976. Contributor to magazines. Editor, *Modern Medicine,* 1977—.

WORK IN PROGRESS: A book on the medical and social aspects of competitive sports for adults; a political novel, publication expected in 1978.

* * *

HALE, Frank (Wilbur), Jr. 1927-

PERSONAL: Born March 24, 1927, in Kansas City, Mo.; son of Frank Wilbur and Novella Hale; married Ruth Colleen Saddler, June 16, 1947; children: Ruth Hale Carey, Frank W. III, Sherilyn Renene. *Education:* University of Nebraska, A.B., 1950, M.A., 1951; Ohio State University, Ph.D., 1955; University of London, postdoctoral study, summer, 1960. *Office:* Oakwood College, Huntsville, Ala. 35806.

CAREER: Oakwood College, Huntsville, Ala., instructor in English and speech, 1951-53, director of public relations, 1952-53; Ohio State University, Columbus, assistant instructor in speech, 1954-55; Oakwood College, associate professor of speech and head of department, 1955-59; Central State College, Wilberforce, Ohio, professor of English and chairman of department, 1959-66; Oakwood College, president, 1966-71; Ohio State University, Columbus, associate dean of Graduate School, 1971—. Visiting professor, Andrews University, summer, 1957. Member of board of directors of Riverside Hospital, 1966—, and Alabama Center for Higher Education, 1967.

MEMBER: American Association of Colleges and Universities, Association for the Study of Negro Life and History, American Association of School Administrators, National Council of Teachers of English, Modern Language Association of America, Speech Association of America, Ohio Speech Association, Ohio English Association. *Awards, honors:* British Council award, 1960.

WRITINGS: A Manual of Public Speaking, Brown Publishers, 1964; (editor) *Cry for Freedom: An Anthology of the Best That Has Been Said and Written on Civil Rights Since 1954,* A. S. Barnes, 1970; *They Came . . . And They Conquered,* Ohio State University, 1973. Contributor to magazines. Book consultant for *Choice.*

* * *

HALE, Richard W(alden) 1909-1976

August 5, 1909—February 25, 1976; American archivist, educator, and author of history books. Obituaries: *AB Bookman's Weekly,* April 5, 1976.

* * *

HALL, Edward Twitchell (Jr.) 1914-

PERSONAL: Born May 16, 1914, in Webster Groves, Mo.; son of Edward Twitchell and Jessie Gilroy (Warneke) Hall; married Mildred Ellis Reed, December 16, 1946; children: Ellen McCoy, Eric Reed. *Education:* Pomona College, student, 1929-30; University of Denver, A.B., 1936; University of Arizona, M.A., 1938; Columbia University, Ph.D., 1942. *Home:* 642 Camino Lejo, Santa Fe, N.M. 87501. *Office:* Department of Anthropology, Northwestern University, Evanston, Ill. 60201.

CAREER: Laboratory of Anthropology, Santa Fe, N.M., assistant staff archaeologist, 1937; Peabody Museum, Cambridge, Mass., staff dendroconologist on Awatovi expedition, 1937-39; Columbia University, New York, N.Y., director of Governador expedition, 1941; University of Denver, Denver, Colo., associate professor of anthropology, 1946-48, chairman of department, 1948; Bennington College, Bennington, Vt., member of faculty of social studies, 1948-51; U.S. Department of State, Washington, D.C., professor of anthropology and director of training program at Foreign Service Institute, 1950-55; Overseas Training & Research, Inc., Washington, D.C., president, 1955-60; Washington School of Psychiatry, Washington, D.C., director of communications research project, 1959-63, also member of executive committee and member of council of fellows; Illinois Institute of Technology, Chicago, professor of anthropology, 1963-67; Northwestern University, Evanston, Ill., professor of anthropology, 1967—. Staff member of Washington School of Psychiatry, 1952-56; Leatherbee Lecturer at Harvard University, 1962. Director of research and deputy director of Washington Office of Human Relations Area Files, 1955-57. Has conducted anthropological field research in Micronesia, the southwestern United States, and Europe. Former member of Northeast Illinois Planning Commission, small grants committee of National Institute of Mental Health, and building research advisory board of National Research Council-National Academy of Science. Director of Ansul Corp. *Military service:* U.S. Army, Corps of Engineers, 1942-46; served in European and Pacific theaters; became captain.

MEMBER: American Anthropological Association (fellow), American Association for the Advancement of Science (fellow), Society for Applied Anthropology, American Ethnological Association, Society for American Archaeology, Tree Ring Society. *Awards, honors:* National Institute of Mental Health grants, 1960-67, 1971-74; Wenner-Gren Foundation grants, 1961, 1962, 1965, 1971; Human Ecology Fund grant, 1964.

WRITINGS: Archaeological Survey of Walhalla Glades, Northern Arizona Society of Science and Art, 1942; *Early Stockaded Settlements in the Governador, New Mexico: A Marginal Anasazi Development from Basket Maker III to Pueblo I Times,* Columbia University Press, 1944; *The Silent Language,* Doubleday, 1959; (with William Foote White) *Intercultural Communication: A Guide to Men of Action,* New York State School of Industrial and Labor Relations, Cornell University, 1960; *Sensitivity and Empathy at Home and Abroad,* Graduate School of Business Administration, Harvard University, 1962; *The Hidden Dimension,* Doubleday, 1966; *The Manpower Potential in Our Ethnic Groups,* Department of Labor, Manpower Administration, 1967; *Handbook for Proxemic Research,* Society for the Anthropology of Visual Communication, 1974; (with Mildred Hall) *The Fourth Dimension in Architecture: The Impact of Building on Man's Behavior,* Sunstone Press, 1975; *Beyond Culture,* Doubleday, 1976.

Contributor to professional journals.

HALL, Elizabeth 1929-

PERSONAL: Born September 17, 1929, in Bakersfield, Calif.; daughter of Edward Earl (an accountant) and Ethel Mae (Butner) Hall. *Education:* Bakersfield College, A.A., 1947; Fresno State College (now California State University, Fresno), B.A., 1964. *Residence:* Waccabuc, N.Y. *Agent:* McIntosh & Otis, Inc., 475 Fifth Ave., New York, N.Y. 10017. *Office: Human Nature,* Harcourt Brace Jovanovich, Inc., 757 Third Ave., New York, N.Y. 10017.

CAREER: Kern County Free Library, Shafter, Calif., librarian, 1958-66; University of California, Irvine, librarian, 1966-67; *Psychology Today,* Del Mar, Calif., associate editor, 1967-68, assistant managing editor, 1968-72, managing editor, 1972-75, managing editor in New York City, 1975-76; *Human Nature,* New York City, editor, 1976—. *Member:* Authors Guild, Jean Piaget Society. *Awards, honors:* National Media Award honorable mention from American Psychological Foundation, 1974, for *Why We Do What We Do,* and 1976, for *From Pigeons to People.*

WRITINGS: Voltaire's Micromegas, Golden Gate, 1967; *Phoebe Snow,* Houghton, 1968; *Stand Up, Lucy!,* Houghton, 1971; *Why We Do What We Do,* Houghton, 1973; *From Pigeons to People,* Houghton, 1975; (editor) *Developmental Psychology Today,* 2nd edition (Hall was not associated with earlier edition), CRM Books, 1975; *Possible Impossibilities,* Houghton, in press. Also editor, with Peter Drucker, of nine films released by Bureau of National Affairs, and with B. F. Skinner, of three films released by CRM Films.

WORK IN PROGRESS: A third edition of *Developmental Psychology Today,* for Random House.

* * *

HALL, H(essel) Duncan 1891-1976

March 8, 1891—July 12, 1976; Australian-born educator, historian, and author of books on the British Commonwealth. Obituaries: *Washington Post,* July 7, 1976. (See index for previous *CA* sketch)

* * *

HALL, (Frederick) Leonard 1899-

PERSONAL: Born October 30, 1899, in Seneca, Mo.; son of Frederick Bagby (a physician) and Corinne (a poet; maiden name, Steele) Hall; married Frances Mabley, April 19, 1924 (deceased); married Virginia Watson (a creative assistant in film making), May 28, 1941; children: (first marriage) Frederick Leonard, Jr. *Education:* Attended Washington University, St. Louis, Mo., 1921-22, and University of Wisconsin, Madison, 1923. *Politics:* Democrat. *Religion:* Congregationalist. *Home and office:* Possum Trot Farm, Caledonia, Mo. 63631.

CAREER: Worked for National Oats Company, 1926-29, and R. R. Donnelley & Sons Co., Chicago, Ill., 1929-44; *St. Louis Post Dispatch,* St. Louis, Mo., columnist, 1940-50; *St. Louis Globe-Democrat,* St. Louis, Mo., columnist, 1951-76; writer, 1976—. Lecturer for National Audubon Society, 1950-65, and wildlife photographer; member of Cornell Laboratory of Ornithology. Chairman of advisory commission for Ozark National Scenic Railways, 1965-69. *Military service:* U.S. Naval Reserve, active duty, 1918-19.

MEMBER: Wilderness Society, Nature Conservancy, National Audubon Society, National Parks and Conservation Association (member of board of trustees), American Forestry Association, Defenders of Wildlife (past member of board of directors), Humane Society of the United States (past member of board of directors), Sierra Club, Missouri Conservation Federation, Sigma Delta Chi. *Awards, honors:* Named master conservationist by Missouri Department of Conservation, 1948, 1970; Thomas Stokes Award from Nieman Fellows of Harvard University, 1959; named state conservationist by the governor of Missouri, 1966; appointed to the Governors Academy of Missouri Squires, 1967; honorary degrees include LL.D. from Westminster College, 1950, and Washington University, St. Louis, Mo., 1970.

WRITINGS: Possum Trot Farm: An Ozark Journal, Caledonia Press, 1949; *Country Year: A Journal of the Seasons at Possum Trot Farm,* Harper, 1957; *Stars Upstream: Life Along an Ozark River,* University of Chicago Press, 1958, revised edition, University of Missouri Press, 1969; *Ozark Wildflowers,* Sayers, 1969. Contributor to national magazines.

SIDELIGHTS: Hall has produced the films "An Ozark Anthology," "Audubon's Wilderness," "Birds Over Florida," and, for National Park Service, "Forever Yours."

* * *

HALLER, Robin Meredith 1944-

PERSONAL: Born September 27, 1944, in Atlanta, Ga.; daughter of Joseph Clay (a hospital administrator) and Dorothy Louise (Meador) Gillespie; married John Samuel Haller, Jr. (a professor of history), February 3, 1968; children: Peter Nolan. *Education:* University of Maryland, A.B., 1968; University of Chicago, M.A., 1969. *Home and office:* 1127 Ripley St., Gary, Ind. 46403.

CAREER: Writer. Part-time lecturer at Indiana University, 1975-76. Member of staff of U.S. Representative James McClure, 1968. *Member:* North American Guild of Change Ringers.

WRITINGS: (With husband, John S. Haller, Jr.) *The Physician and Sexuality in Victorian America,* University of Illinois Press, 1974.

WORK IN PROGRESS: A novel.

AVOCATIONAL INTERESTS: Changeringing at Mitchell Tower in Chicago, Ill.

* * *

HALLGARTEN, George W(olfgang) F(elix) 1901-1975

PERSONAL: Born January 3, 1901, in Munich, Germany; came to United States, 1937; son of Robert and Constance (Wolff-Arndt) Hallgarten; married Katherine MacArthur Drew, February 15, 1941. *Education:* University of Munich, Ph.D., 1925. *Home:* 4200 Cathedral Ave. N.W., Washington, D.C. 20016.

CAREER: Institute for Foreign Politics, Hamburg, Germany, assistant, 1925; engaged in private research, 1926-34; Ecole des Hautes Etudes Sociales et Internationales, Paris, France, lecturer, 1935; Brooklyn College (now of the City University of New York), Brooklyn, N.Y., lecturer, 1938; University of California, Berkeley, research assistant, 1940-41; U.S. Department of State and Department of Army, Washington, D.C., research analyst, 1945-46, senior research analyst, 1947-49; author in Washington, D.C., 1951-75. Visiting professor, University of Munich, 1950, University of New Mexico, 1968-69; Robert Lee Baily Professor of History, University of North Carolina, Charlotte, 1972; lecturer at universities in India, Japan, and Germany, and at

University of Rome. Co-founder of war documents committee of American Historical Association, 1955. *Military service:* U.S. Army, 1942-45; served in combat intelligence. *Member:* American Historical Association, Societe d'-Histoire Moderne, Authors Guild. *Awards, honors:* American Philosophical Society grant, 1940-41; President's Scholar at University of Dayton, 1970-71.

WRITINGS: Studien ueber die deutsche Polenfreundschaft in der Periode der Maerzrevolution, Oldenbourg (Munich), 1925; *Vorkriegs Imperialismus,* privately printed, 1933, published as *Vorkriegs Imperialismus: Die soziologischen Grundlagen der Aussenpolitik europaeischen Grossmaechte bis 1914,* Editions Meteore (Paris), 1935, published in two volumes as *Imperialismus vor 1914,* Volume I: *Theoretisches, soziologische Skizzen der aussenpolitischen Entwicklung in England und Frankreich,* Volume II: *Soziologische Darstellung der deutschen Aussenpolitik bis zum Ersten Weltkrieg,* C. H. Beck (Munich), 1951; *Hitler, Reichswehr und Industrie: Zur Geschichte der Jahre, 1918-1933,* Europaeishe Verlag (Frankfurt), 1954; *Why Dictator? The Causes and Forms of Tyrannical Rule Since 600 B.C.,* Macmillan, 1954; *Daemonen oder Retter? Eine kurze Geschichte der Diktatur seit 600 vor Christus,* Europaeische Verlagsanstalt (Frankfurt), 1957, translation by Gavin Gibbons published as *Devils or Saviors: A History of Dictatorship Since 600 B.C.,* Humanities, 1960; *Das Wettruesten: Seine Geschichte bis zur Gegenwart,* Europaeische Verlagsanstalt, 1967; *Das Schicksal des Imperialismus im 20. Jahrhundert: Drei Abhandlungen ueber Kriegsursachen in Vergangenheit und Gegenwart,* Europaeische Verlagsanstalt, 1969; *Als die Schatten fielen: Erinnerungen vom Jahrhundertbeginn zur Jahrtausendwende,* Ullstein (Berlin), 1969; (with Joachim Radkau) *Deutsche Industrie und Politik von Bismarck bis heute,* Europaeische Verlagsanstalt, 1974.

SIDELIGHTS: Hallgarten was fluent in German, French, Russian, Italian, Greek, and Latin.*

(Died May 22, 1975, in Washington, D.C.)

*   *   *

HALLIWELL, David (William) 1936-
(Johnson Arms)

PERSONAL: Born July 31, 1936, in Brighouse, Yorkshire, England; son of Herbert (a managing director of a textile firm) and Ethel (Spencer) Halliwell. *Education:* Attended Huddersfield College of Art, 1953-59; Royal Academy of Dramatic Art, diploma, 1961. *Politics:* Socialist. *Home:* 28 Chepstow Court, Chepstow Crescent, London W11 3ED, England. *Agent:* Sheila Lemon, Spokesmen Ltd., 1 Craven Hill, London W2 3EW, England.

CAREER: Actor in Nottingham, England, 1962, Stoke-on-Trent, England, 1962-63, and London, England, 1963-67; Quipu Productions, London, co-founder and director, 1966-71, member of committee, 1971—, directed plays in London at New Arts Theatre, 1966-67, at Little Theatre, 1971-73, at Bankside Globe Theatre, 1974, and at New End Theatre, 1975. Director for productions of other managements, in Edinburgh, Scotland, at Traverse Theatre, 1971, and in London for National Theatre at Young Vic Theatre, 1975, and at Royal Court, 1976-77. Visiting fellow, University of Reading, 1970; resident dramatist, Royal Court, 1976-77. Interviewer for Thames Television "Question '68" show, 1968. *Member:* Dramatists Club, Buckston Club. *Awards, honors:* Named most promising playwright by *Evening Standard,* 1966, for *Little Malcolm.*

WRITINGS—Plays: *Hail Scrawdyke* (produced in New

York, 1966), Grove, 1966 (published in England as *Little Malcolm and His Struggle against the Eunuchs* [produced in London at Unity Theatre, March 30, 1965], Samuel French, 1966); *K. D. Dufford Hears K. D. Dufford Ask K. D. Dufford How K. D. Dufford'll Make K. D. Dufford* (first produced in London at Lambda Theatre, 1969), Faber, 1970; *A Who's Who of Flapland and Other Plays,* Faber, 1971. Also author, under pseudonym Johnson Arms, of *They Travelled by Tube* (biographies of notable people who moved by means of London's Underground), Butterworth.

Unpublished plays: (With David Calderisi) "The Experiment," first produced in London at New Arts Theatre, January 16, 1967; "The Girl Who Didn't Like Answers," first produced in London at Mercury Theatre, June 29, 1971; "A Last Belch for the Great Auk," first produced at Mercury Theatre, 1971; "An Amour, and a Feast" (sketches), first produced in London at Little Theatre, January, 1972; "Bleats from a Brighouse Pleasureground," first produced at Little Theatre, 1972; "Janitress Thrilled by a Prehensile Penis," first produced at Little Theatre, 1972.

Television plays: "A Plastic Mac in Winter," 1963; "Cock, Hen and Courting Pit," 1966; "Triptych of Bathroom Users," 1972; "Blur and Blank via Checkheaton," 1972; "Triple Exposure," 1972; "Steps Back," 1972; "Daft Mam Blues," 1976; "Pigmented Patter," 1976; "Meriel the Ghost Girl," 1976; "Treewomen of Jagden Crag," 1976.

WORK IN PROGRESS: A stage play commissioned by the Royal Court Theatre; "Blood Relations," working title of a serial for British Broadcasting Corp. (BBC)-TV.

SIDELIGHTS: Halliwell has directed his own plays at various theatres, as well as plays by Harold Pinter, George Bernard Shaw, and others; he has performed in his own plays and those by other playwrights, including Shakespeare, Shaw, Anouilh, Beckett, and Robert Bolt. Several plays have been broadcast in England. *Hail Scrawdyke* was used as the basis for the film "The Movement" in 1970.

BIOGRAPHICAL/CRITICAL SOURCES: New Statesman, September 26, 1969; *Plays and Players,* October, 1970.

*   *   *

HALPERIN, Mark (Warren) 1940-

PERSONAL: Born February 19, 1940, in New York, N.Y.; son of George W. (a dentist) and Minna (Scherzer) Halperin; married Barbara Scott (a painter), July 15, 1966; children: Noah. *Education:* Bard College, B.A., 1960; New School for Social Research, graduate study, 1962-64; University of Iowa, M.F.A., 1966. *Home address:* Route 4, Box 279A, Ellensburg, Wash. 98926. *Office:* Department of English, Central Washington State College, Ellensburg, Wash. 98926.

CAREER: Machlett Laboratories, Inc., Stanford, Conn., junior physicist, 1960-62; Rockefeller Institute, New York, N.Y., electron microscope technician, 1963; University of Iowa, Iowa City, electron microscope technician, 1964-66; Central Washington State College, Ellensburg, assistant professor of English, 1966—. *Member:* Yakima River Conservancy (president, 1969-74), Alpine Lakes Protection Society (trustee, 1968-71). *Awards, honors:* U.S. Award from International Poetry Forum, 1975, for *Backroads.*

WRITINGS: Backroads (poems), University of Pittsburgh Press, 1976. Contributor to literary magazines, including *Iowa Review, North American Review, Yale Review,* and *Poetry Northwest.*

WORK IN PROGRESS: A second book of poems.

SIDELIGHTS: Halperin writes: "There's a decidedly traditional element to my poems. I have my version of meter and rhyme that I use with some regularity. It surprises me, but less and less. I'm a devoted five-string banjo player, mostly of traditional, old-time styles. I love to listen to and play early, finger-picking style blues on the guitar. Even in my fishing, which I do avidly, I quickly gravitated to fly-fishing, to tying my own flies and using real feathers and fur. But my father never took me wading in streams; I grew up in a city and never heard a banjo except on a stage. So whatever feeling I have for things traditional comes largely from the outside, in an 'unnatural' way. Perhaps what all this indicates most is that I'm reluctant to talk about what's in the poems, how I go about them or why. That's basic mystery-territory to me and I'd just as soon leave it that way.''

* * *

HALSEY, Elizabeth Tower 1903(?)-1976

1903(?)—April 7, 1976; American association executive and author of books on home furnishing. Obituaries: *New York Times*, April 9, 1976.

* * *

HALWARD, Leslie G. 1904(?)-1976

1904(?)—April 2, 1976; British radio dramatist and author. Obituaries: *AB Bookman's Weekly*, May 31, 1976.

* * *

HAMILTON, Dave
See TROYER, Byron L(eRoy)

* * *

HAMM, Marie Roberson 1917-
(Marie Roberson)

PERSONAL: Born May 16, 1917, in Minneapolis, Minn.; daughter of Gustave J. (an engineer) and Marie (a singer; maiden name, Anderson) Norstrom; married John Roberson (divorced); married Frederick Hamm (deceased); married Stanley Ryan Ketcham (a chartered financial analyst), November 24, 1970. *Education:* Barnard College, student, 1935-36. *Politics:* "As I please." *Religion:* Protestant. *Home and office:* 360 East 72nd St., New York, N.Y. 10021.

CAREER: Best & Co., New York City, accessory buyer, 1937-43; *Harper's Bazaar*, New York City, associate editor, 1943-45; Gourmet Accessory Shops, New York, N.Y. and Greenwich, Conn., founder, owner, and manager, 1946-52; Robinson Hannagan, New York, N.Y., public relations account executive, 1953-54; Batten, Barton, Durstin & Osborn, New York City, public relations account executive, 1954-70; writer, 1970—. *Member:* American Women in Radio and Television, National Home Fashion League. *Awards, honors:* Gold medal, 1970, for *Fondue Cookbook*, and 1971, for *The Blender Cookbook*.

WRITINGS: The Second Chafing Dish Cookbook, Prentice-Hall, 1963; *Money-in-the-Bank Cookbook*, Macmillan, 1968; *The Gold Medal Fondue Cookbook*, Fawcett, 1970; *The Gold Medal Blender Cookbook*, Fawcett, 1971; *The Gold Medal Italian Cookbook*, Fawcett, 1973; *Gifts from Your Kitchen*, Fawcett, 1974; (editor) *Woman's Day Encyclopedia of Cooking*, twenty-three volumes, Fawcett, 1974; *Crockery Cookbook*, Fawcett, 1976; (with James Beard and others) *Garden to Table Cookbook*, McGraw, 1976.

Under name Marie Roberson; all with John Roberson: *The*

Chafing Dish Cookbook, Prentice-Hall, 1949, revised edition, 1959; *The Casserole Cook Book*, Prentice-Hall, 1951; *The Complete Barbecue Book*, Prentice-Hall, 1952; *The Complete Small Appliance Cook Book*, A. A. Wyn, 1952; *The Meat Cookbook*, Holt, 1953; *The Poultry Cookbook*, Fawcett, 1954; *The Buffet Cookbook*, Fawcett, 1954; *The Famous American Recipes Cook Book*, Prentice-Hall, 1955.

Contributor to boating and women's magazines, and to newspapers.

WORK IN PROGRESS: A travel book; a book on the environment.

AVOCATIONAL INTERESTS: Gardening, sailing, travel, entertaining, ecology, nature studies.

* * *

HAMMOND, Mason 1903-

PERSONAL: Born February 14, 1903, in Boston, Mass.; son of Samuel (a trustee) and Grace (Learoyd) Mason; married Florence Hobson Pierson, August 27, 1935; children: Florence (Mrs. John C. Phillips), Anstiss (Mrs. William Drake), Elizabeth. *Education:* Harvard University, A.B., 1925; Balliol College, Oxford, B.A., 1928, B.Litt., 1930. *Religion:* Episcopal. *Home:* 153 Brattle St., Cambridge, Mass. 02138. *Office:* Widener Library, Harvard University, Cambridge, Mass. 02138.

CAREER: Harvard University, Cambridge, Mass., instructor, 1928-34, assistant professor, 1934-39, associate professor, 1939-46, professor of Greek, Latin, and history, 1946-50, Pope Professor of Latin Language and Literature, 1950-73, tutor in Division of Ancient Languages, 1928-73, master of Kirkland House, 1945-55. Radcliffe College, Cambridge, instructor, 1928-34, assistant professor, 1934-39, associate professor, 1939-42; American Academy in Rome, professor in charge of classical studies, 1937-39, 1955-57, summer professor, 1949, Fulbright professor, 1951-52, 1963; acting director, Villa I Tatti, Florence, Italy, 1972, 1973; visiting professor at University of Wisconsin, 1973. Trustee, American Academy in Rome, 1946—, St. Mark's School, 1946-75, and Isabella Stewart Gardner Museum, Boston, Mass., 1966—. *Military service:* U.S. Army Air Forces, 1942-45; served in military government in European theater; became lieutenant colonel; received Bronze Star, Legion of Honor, and Order of Orange and Nassau.

MEMBER: American Philological Association, American Archaeological Institute, American Historical Association, American Academy of Arts and Sciences (fellow), Association of American Rhodes Scholars, English Speaking Union, Classical Association of New England, Massachusetts Historical Society, German Archaeological Institute, Phi Beta Kappa, Somerset Club, Tavern Club. *Awards, honors:* Rhodes scholar at Oxford University, 1925-28; L.H.D., St. Bonaventure University, 1945; Legion of Merit towards the Republic from the Italian Government, 1959; medal for distinguished service from American Academy in Rome, 1971.

WRITINGS: The Augustan Principate, Harvard University Press, 1933, enlarged edition, 1968; (editor with Nicholas Moseley) Plautus, *Menaechmi*, Harvard University Press, 1933; *City State and World State in Greek and Roman Political Thought to Augustus*, Harvard University Press, 1951; *The Antonine Monarchy*, American Academy in Rome, 1959; (editor with Anne Amory) *Aeneas to Augustus: A Beginning Latin Reader for College Students*, Harvard University Press, 1962; (editor with Arthur M. Mack and Walter Moskaley) Plautus, *Miles Gloriosus*, Harvard University Press, 1963, 2nd edition, 1970; *The City in the Ancient World,* Harvard University Press, 1972; *Latin: A Historical and Linguistic Handbook for Students and Teachers of Beginning Latin,* Harvard University Press, 1976.

*   *   *

HANAGHAN, Jonathan   1887-1967

PERSONAL: Born 1887, in Birkenhead, Cheshire, England; came to Ireland, c. 1917; married Rhoda Taylor; children: two sons, five daughters. *Education:* Attended schools in England. *Home:* 2 Belgrave Tce., Monkstown, Dublin, Ireland. *Office:* Runa Press, Monkstown, Dublin, Ireland.

CAREER: Poet. Editor of "Poetry Quartos" series, Runa Press, Dublin, Ireland. *Member:* Irish Psychoanalytic Association (founder; past president).

WRITINGS—All published by Runa Press, except as noted: *By Mortal and Immortal Seas* (verse), Talbot Press (Dublin), 1931; (editor) *Earth Fire* (poetry anthology), 1943; *Poems to Mary,* 1945; *Eve's Moods Unveiled* (poems), 1957; *Society, Evolution and Revelation: An Original Insight into Man's Place in Creation,* 1957; (with others) *Tidings* (verse), 1958; *Sayings* (Irish aphorisms), 1960; *Christian Leadership: A Psychoanalytic Study,* 1965; *Freud and Jesus,* 1966; *The Wisdom of Jonty: A Notebook of Aphorisms and Discourses, Spoken by Jonathan Hanaghan,* edited by Richard Cameron, 1970; *The Courage to Be Married* (lectures), edited by Brendan McCann, Abbey Press, 1974. Contributor to *Focus.**

(Died, 1967)

*   *   *

HANDLIN, Mary (Flug)   1913-1976

September 14, 1913—May 24, 1976; American historian and co-author of books in her field. Obituaries: *New York Times,* May 25, 1976; *Washington Post,* May 26, 1976; *Time,* June 7, 1976. (See index for previous *CA* sketch)

*   *   *

HANKE, Lewis (Ulysses)   1905-

PERSONAL: Born January 2, 1905, in Oregon City, Ore.; son of William U. and Mamie E. (Stevenson) Hanke; married Kate Gilbert, August 12, 1926; children: Jonathan, Peter, Susan, Joanne. *Education:* Northwestern University, B.S., 1924, M.A., 1925; Harvard University, Ph.D., 1936. *Home:* 65 Echo Hill Rd., Amherst, Mass. 01002. *Office:* Department of History, University of Massachusetts, Amherst, Mass. 01002.

CAREER: University of Hawaii, Honolulu, instructor in history, 1926-27; American University of Beirut, Beirut, Lebanon, adjunct professor of history, 1927-30; Harvard University, Cambridge, Mass., instructor in history, 1934-39; Library of Congress, Washington, D.C., director, 1939-51; University of Texas, Austin, professor of Latin American history, 1951-61, director of Institute of Latin American Studies, 1951-58; Columbia University, New York, N.Y., professor of Latin American history, 1961-67; University of California, Irvine, professor of Latin American history, 1967-69; University of Massachusetts, Amherst, Clarence and Helen Haring Professor of Latin American History, 1969-75, professor emeritus, 1975—. Carnegie lecturer in Brazil, 1938; James W. Richard lecturer, University of Virginia, 1948; Phi Beta Kappa Society visiting lecturer, 1961. Member of U.S. national committee for UNESCO, 1952-54.

MEMBER: American Historical Association (president, 1974), Hispanic Society of America (trustee, 1961-67), Real Academia de la Historia (Madrid), Academia Nacional de la Historia (Buenos Aires), Sociedad Peruana de Historia, Sociedad de Historia Argentina (Buenos Aires), Academia Colombiana de Historia (Bogota), Sociedad de Historia y Geografia de Guatemala, Instituto Historico y Geografico de Uruguay. *Awards, honors:* Social Science Research Council fellowship, 1937-38, grant, 1961; Albert Beveridge Memorial fellowship from American Historical Association, 1947; A.S.W. Rosenbach fellowship in bibliography, 1951; Doctor Honoris Causa, Universidade de Bahia (Brazil), 1959, Universidad Tomas Frias (Potosi, Bolivia), 1965, and Universidad de Sevilla (Spain), 1966; book award from Texas Institute of Letters, 1960, for *Aristotle and the American Indians;* Order of the Condor of the Andes, Bolivia, 1965; honorary citizen of Municipality of Potosi, Bolivia, 1965.

WRITINGS: The First Social Experiments in America: A Study in the Development of Spanish Indian Policy in the Sixteenth Century (monograph), Harvard University Press, 1935; *Las teorias politicas de Bartolome de las Casas* (title means "The Political Theories of Bartolome de las Casas"), Casa J. Peuser, 1935; (co-editor) *Handbook of Latin American Studies,* Harvard University Press, 1935-39; *Cuerpo de documentos del siglo XVI sobre los derechos de Espana en las Indias y las Filipinas* (title means "Sixteenth-Century Documents on the Rights of Spain in the Indies and the Philippines"), edited by Agustin Millares Carlo, Fondo de Cultura Economica, 1943; *The Spanish Struggle for Justice in the Conquest of America,* University of Pennsylvania Press, 1949.

Bartolome de las Casas: An Interpretation of His Life and Writings, Nijhoff, 1951; (editor with Carlo and Agustin Millares; author of introduction) *Historia de las Indias* (title means "History of the Indies"), three volumes, Fondo de Cultura Economica, 1951, 2nd edition, 1965; *Bartolome de las Casas: Bookman, Scholar, and Propagandist,* University of Pennsylvania Press, 1952; *Bartolome de las Casas, Historian: An Essay in Spanish Historiography,* University of Florida Press, 1952; (with Manuel Gimenez Fernandez) *Bartolome de las Casas, 1474-1566: Bibliografia critica y cuerpo de materiales para el estudio de su vida, escritos, actuacion y polemicas que suscitaron durante cuatro siglos* (title means "Bibliography of the Writings on the Life of and the Writings of Bartolome de las Casas"), Fondo Historico y Bibliografico Jose Toribio Medina (Santiago de Chile), 1954; *The Imperial City of Potosi: An Unwritten Chapter in the History of Spanish America,* Nijhoff, 1956; *Aristotle and the American Indians: A Study of Race Prejudice in the Modern World,* Regnery, 1959; *Modern Latin America: Continent in Ferment,* Volume I: *Mexico and the Caribbean,* Volume II: *South America,* Van Nostrand, 1959, revised edition, 1967; (editor) Luis Capoche, *Relaciones historico-literarias de la America meridional: Relacion general de la villa imperial de Potosi,* Atlas, 1959.

Do the Americans Have a Common History?: A Critique of the Bolton Theory, Knopf, 1964; *Bartolome Arzans de Orsua y Vela's History of Potosi,* Brown University Press, 1965; (editor with Gunnar Mendoza) *Historia de la villa imperial de Potosi* (title means "History of Potosi"), three volumes, Brown University Press, 1965; (editor) *Readings in Latin American History: Selected Articles from the Hispanic American Historical Review,* Volume I: *To 1810,* Volume II: *Since 1810,* Crowell, 1966; (compiler) *History of Latin American Civilization: Sources and Interpretations,*

Volume I: *The Colonial Experience,* Volume II: *The Modern Age,* Little, Brown, 1967, 2nd edition, 1973, abridged edition published as *Latin America: A Historical Reader,* 1974; *Contemporary Latin America: A Short History; Text and Readings,* Van Nostrand, 1968; *Estudios sobre fray Bartolome de las Casas y sobre la lucha por la justicia en la conquista espanola de America* (essays; title means "Studies on Las Casas and on the Struggle for Justice in the Conquest of America"), Ediciones de la Biblioteca, 1968; *All Mankind Is One,* Northern Illinois University Press, 1974.

Contributor to proceedings of American Philosophical Society and to journals in his field.

WORK IN PROGRESS: Various studies on the history of Spanish viceroys in Mexico and Peru up to 1700.

* * *

HANLEY, Michael F. IV 1941-
(Mike Hanley)

PERSONAL: Born June 25, 1941, in Medford, Ore.; son of Michael F. (a rancher) and Hazel (McEwen) Hanley; married Judi Terry, August 28, 1965; children: Mary Martha, Michael F. V. *Education:* Eastern Oregon College, B.S., 1963. *Politics:* Republican. *Religion:* Protestant. *Address:* Jordan Valley, Ore. 97910.

CAREER: Rancher. Member of Bureau of Land Management advisory board, Vale District, Ore., 1975-77. *Military service:* Idaho National Guard, 1963-69. *Member:* American National Cattlemen's Association, Oregon Cattlemen's Association, Oregon Trailwriters Historical Society, Oregon Historical Society, Idaho Cattlemen's Association, Hudson's Bay Record Society, Macheur Country Historical Society, Owyhee County Historical Society, Harney County Historical Society, Owyhee County Cattlemen's Association, Jordan Valley Commercial Club, Lions Club, Masonic Lodge. *Awards, honors:* Wrangler award from Western Heritage Foundation for *Owyee Trails: The West's Forgotten Corner.*

WRITINGS—All under name Mike Hanley: (With Ellis Lucia) *Owyee Trails: The West's Forgotten Corner,* Caxton, 1973; *Sage Brush and Axle Grease,* Shorb Printing (Caldwell, Idaho), 1976.

WORK IN PROGRESS: A book of short stories on western folk lore.

SIDELIGHTS: Hanley told *CA,* "Writing is like the cattle business, you have to be dedicated; success is measured by accomplishment not money." *Avocational interests:* Breaking work horses, rebuilding wagons, collecting horse-drawn vehicles, illustrating own stories.

BIOGRAPHICAL/CRITICAL SOURCES: E. R. Jackman and John Scharff, *Steen's Mountain in Oregon's High Desert Country,* Caxton, 1967; Lambert F. Florin, *Western Wagon Wheels,* Superior, 1970; Ralph Friedman, *Oregon for the Curious,* Caxton, 1972; Robert O. Beatty, *Idaho: A Pictorial Overview,* Idaho First National Bank, 1975.

* * *

HANLEY, Mike
See HANLEY, Michael F. IV

* * *

HANNUM, Alberta Pierson 1906-

PERSONAL: Born August 3, 1906, in Condit, Ohio; daughter of James Ellsworth and Caroline Adelle (Evans) Pierson; married Robert Fulton Hannum (a businessman), January 7, 1929 (deceased); children: Kay (Mrs. Miner Jurgens), Sara Lee (Mrs. John Terry Chase). *Education:* Ohio State University, B.A., 1927; graduate study at Columbia University, 1928. *Politics:* Republican. *Religion:* Episcopalian. *Home:* Howard Place, Wheeling, W.Va. 26003.

CAREER: Writer. *Member:* League of American Pen Women, Author's Guild, Delta Gamma, Mortar Board, Wheeling Country Club, Wheeling Garden Club. *Awards, honors:* L.H.D. from West Virginia University, 1968; annual book award from Columbus, Ohio, branch of American Association of University Women, 1971; community service award from American Association of University Professors, 1974.

WRITINGS: Thursday April, Harper, 1931; *The Hills Step Lightly,* Morrow, 1934; *The Gods and One,* Duell, Sloan & Pearce, 1941; *The Mountain People,* Vanguard, 1943; *Spin a Silver Dollar: The Story of a Desert Trading Post,* Viking, 1945 (published in England as *Spin a Silver Coin: The Story of a Desert Trading Post,* M. Joseph, 1947), published as *The Blue House,* U.S. Information Agency for Peace through Understanding for Indo-China, 1970; *Roseanna McCoy* (novel), Holt, 1947; *Paint the Wind* (on the Navajo Indians), Viking, 1958; *Look Back with Love: A Recollection of the Blue Ridge,* Vanguard, 1969. Author of radio play, "Spin a Silver Dollar," 1946, and screenplay, "Roseanna McCoy," released by RKO General, 1949. Contributor to magazines both in United States and abroad.

SIDELIGHTS: Hannum's books have appeared in Italian, Korean, Laotian, Russian, and Yugoslavian editions. Her collection of Navajo artifacts and paintings pertinent to *Spin a Silver Dollar* and *Paint the Wind* were exhibited in Wheeling, W.Va., in October, 1975.

* * *

HANSON, Harvey 1941-

PERSONAL: Born August 25, 1941, in Chicago, Ill.; son of Harvey Lee (a laborer) and Evelyn (a dietician; maiden name, Gill) Hanson; married Noreen O. Baldi. *Home:* 1130 South Michigan, Chicago, Ill. 60605. *Agent:* Knox Burger Literary Agency, 39½ Washington Square S., New York, N.Y. 10012.

CAREER: Worked at Chicago Post Office, Bee Bindery Co., and General Finance and Loan Co., 1962-65; Harris Bank, Chicago, Ill., securities analyst, 1965-70; Albion Shoes-High Arch Shoe Bazaar, New York, N.Y., shoe designer, 1970-73; Tom Jackson Studios, New York City, photographer's representative, 1972—.

WRITINGS: Game Time (novel), F. Watts, 1975. Ghost writer for books adapted from Broadway plays.

WORK IN PROGRESS: A second novel; a screenplay; a record album.

* * *

HARARI, Ehud 1935-

PERSONAL: Born July 27, 1935, in Ramat-Gan, Israel; married; children: two. *Education:* University of California, Berkeley, Ph.D., 1968. *Politics:* Zionist. *Religion:* Jewish. *Office:* Department of Political Science, Hebrew University of Jerusalem, Jerusalem, Israel.

CAREER: Formerly taught at University of California, Berkeley, and University of Tel-Aviv; Hebrew University of Jerusalem, Jerusalem, Israel, senior lecturer in political science, 1975—. *Awards, honors:* Grants from Ford Foundation, 1973-74, and Center for Japanese and Korean Studies, 1974-75.

WRITINGS: The Politics of Labor Legislation in Japan: National-International Interaction, University of California Press, 1973. Contributor to journals.

WORK IN PROGRESS: Research on public policy-making in Japan, on the system of advisory commissions, on organizational behavior and employee attitudes in non-Japanese multinational corporations operating in Japan, and on management development in multinational corporations.

* * *

HARBAGE, Alfred (Bennett)   1901-1976

July 18, 1901—May 2, 1976; American educator, scholar, and editor of Shakespeare collections. Obituaries: *New York Times,* May 4, 1976; *Washington Post,* May 7, 1976; *Time,* May 17, 1976; *AB Bookman's Weekly,* July 5, 1976. (See index for previous *CA* sketch)

* * *

HARBISON, Frederick Harris   1912-1976

December 18, 1912—April 5, 1976; American economist, industrial relations specialist, educator, and author. Obituaries: *New York Times,* April 6, 1976; *AB Bookman's Weekly,* May 17, 1976.

* * *

HARBISON, Peter   1939-

PERSONAL: Born January 14, 1939, in Dublin, Ireland; son of J. A. (a physician) and Sheelagh (MacSherry) Harbison; married Edelgard Soergel (a paleozoologist), December 6, 1969; children: Jean-Philippe, Maurice. *Education:* B.A. and M.A. from University College, Dublin, National University of Ireland; D.Phil. from University of Marburg; also attended University of Freiburg and University of Kiel. *Religion:* Roman Catholic. *Home:* 1A Castleview Park, Malahide, County Dublin, Ireland. *Office:* Bord Failte, Baggot Street Bridge, Dublin 2, Ireland.

CAREER: Bord Failte (Irish Tourist Board), Dublin, Ireland, archaeologist, 1966-76. Director of School of Irish Studies, 1975—. *Member:* Royal Society of Antiquaries of Ireland (past member of council), Association of Irish Art Historians, Association of Professional Irish Archaeologists (vice-chairman), Friends of the National Collections of Ireland (member of council), Kildare and University Club (Dublin). *Awards, honors:* German Academic Exchange scholarship, 1959-63; traveling scholarship from German Archaeological Institute, 1965.

WRITINGS: The Axes of the Early Bronze Age in Ireland, Beck, 1969; *The Daggers and the Halberds of the Early Bronze Age in Ireland,* Beck, 1969; *Guide to the National Monuments in the Republic of Ireland,* Macmillan, 1970; *The Archaeology of Ireland,* Scribner, 1976. Contributor of articles and reviews to professional journals in Ireland, England, France, the Netherlands, Germany, Spain, Portugal, and the United States.

WORK IN PROGRESS: Research for a book on C. W. Harrison, an architectural sculptor; research on archaeological, art-historical, and architectural subjects of Irish interest, publication expected by 1978.

AVOCATIONAL INTERESTS: Music, travel.

HARDY, Peter   1931-

PERSONAL: Born July 17, 1931, in Wath upon Dearne, Yorkshire, England; son of Lawrence (a miner) and Ivy Hardy; married Margaret Ann Brookes, July 28, 1954; children: Christopher, Martin. *Education:* Attended Westminster College, University of London, 1951-53, College of Preceptors, Associateship Diploma, 1958, Licentiateship Diploma, 1962; attended University of Sheffield, 1966-67. *Office:* House of Commons, London S.W.1, England.

CAREER: Mexborough County Secondary School, South Yorkshire, England, schoolmaster, 1953-70, head of department, 1960-70; House of Commons, London, England, Labour member of Parliament from Rother Valley, 1970—, and secretary of state for the environment. President of Wath upon Dearne Labour Party, 1960-68; Wath upon Dearne District Council, member, 1960-70, chairman, 1968-69; Wath Grammar School, member of governing body, chairman of governors, 1969-70. *Military service:* Royal Air Force, 1949-51. *Member:* National Union of Public Employees, Yorkshire Naturalists Trust, Rawmarsh Trades and Labour Club, Kennel Club.

WRITINGS: (Contributor) Frank Whitehead, editor, *Creative Writing,* Chatto & Windus, 1968; *A Lifetime of Badgers,* David & Charles, 1975. Contributor to country magazines and to newspapers.

WORK IN PROGRESS: One Man's Nature (tentative title), on nature conservation and the individual.

SIDELIGHTS: Hardy's major programs in the House of Commons have been aimed at conservation legislation; he promoted the Badgers Act in 1973 and the Wild Creatures and Wild Plants Act in 1976.

* * *

HAREL, Isser   1912-

PERSONAL: Born 1912, in Vitebsk, Russia; son of Nathan and Yoheveth (Levin) Halperin; married Rivka Borovick, 1932; children: Miriam. *Education:* Educated in Dvinsk, Latvia. *Religion:* Jewish. *Residence:* Tel Aviv, Israel.

CAREER: Security Service (Shin Bet) of the State of Israel, head, 1948-52; Central Bureau of Intelligence and Security of the State of Israel, head, 1952-63; member of Knesset (Israel Parliament), 1969-74. Lecturer and writer. *Military service:* Hagana, 1930-48; Israel Defense Force, 1948-50, became lieutenant colonel. *Awards, honors:* Honorary member of Mark Twain Society and recipient of the Edgar Allan Poe award of Mystery Writers of America for *The House on Garibaldi Street,* 1976.

WRITINGS: The Great Ruse (novel), Shikmona Publishing, 1971; *Jihad* (novel), Carel, 1972, translation by author into English under same title, Transowrld Publishers, 1977; *The House on Garibaldi Street,* Viking, 1975.

SIDELIGHTS: Harel told *CA* of his initial feelings about the discovery of Eichmann in Argentina: "We searched for Eichmann for years, but without result. But when the first promising scraps of information reached us from Argentina I put everything else aside and oblivious to everything around me I immersed myself in the nightmare subject of Adolph Eichmann." With passages quoted from *The House on Garibaldi Street,* Harel described the night he resolved to capture Eichmann: "I sat for hours reading the Eichmann dossier, and in my mind's eye an image took shape, the image of an archfiend whose vicious crimes were unprecedented in the annals of humanity, a man on whose shoulders rested the direct responsibility for the butchery of millions . . . I knew when I rose from my desk at dawn that in everything pertaining to the Jews he was the paramount authority and his were the hands that pulled the strings controlling manhunt and massacre . . . I knew that the blood-drenched earth which held the remains of his millions of victims was crying out for vengeance, but no agency in the entire world, no government, no police were looking for him to answer for his crimes . . . That night I resolved that if Eichmann were alive, come hell or high water he'd be caught.'' On May 22, 1960, Harel and Israeli Secret Service members successfully landed Eichmann in Israel. "While the operation lasted," Harel told *CA*, "I was utterly absorbed, mentally and physically, in its planning and command and had no time to give thought to its deeper significance. But the moment we landed safely in Israel and I was able to hand Eichmann over to the lawful authorities I felt as if I had been relieved of a vast burden of historic responsibility.''

Harel's reasons for writing, he told *CA*, include "dedication to the security, integrity and survival of Israel; to focus public attention on the moral values inherent in activities it had been my privilege to direct—for the sake of historic justice which could only have been achieved by the sovereignty of the Jewish people attained at the establishment of the State of Israel; to portray the uniqueness and true nature of the Israeli Secret Service; and to grapple with the intricate issues—moral and pragmatic—involved in the preservation of national security in a democratic state, in Israel and elsewhere.''

* * *

HARPER, Michael 1931-

PERSONAL: Born March 12, 1931, in London, England; son of Claude Reginald (a businessman) and Dorothy (Handley) Harper; married Jeanne Underwood (a musical director), September 1, 1956. *Education:* Emmanuel College, Cambridge, M.A. (with honors), 1953; graduate study at Ridley Hall, Cambridge, 1953-55. *Politics;* Christian Socialist. *Home and office:* Holy Trinity Church, High St., Hounslow, Middlesex, England. *Agent:* Curtis Brown Ltd., 60 East 56th St., New York, N.Y. 10022.

CAREER: Ordained priest of Anglican Church, 1955; curate in London, England, 1955-58; industrial chaplain in London, 1958-64; Fountain Trust, London, director, 1964—; Holy Trinity Church, Hounslow, Middlesex, England, curate, 1975—. Examining chaplain to Bishop of Guilford

WRITINGS: Power for the Body of Christ, Logos International, 1964; *As at the Beginning*, Logos International, 1965; *Walk in the Spirit*, Logos International, 1968; *Spiritual Warfare*, Logos International, 1970; *None Can Guess* (autobiography), Logos International, 1971; *A New Way of Living*, Logos International, 1973; *Glory in the Church*, Hodder & Stoughton, 1974. Editor of *Renewal*, 1966-75.

WORK IN PROGRESS: "Lots, but very hush-hush."

* * *

HARRAH, David Fletcher 1949-

PERSONAL: Born June 21, 1949, in Toledo, Ohio; son of Dale Fletcher (a businessman) and Rosanna (a teacher; maiden name, Crow) Harrah; married Barbara Koch (a writer), August 25, 1971. *Education:* Columbia University, B.A., 1971, M.A., 1973. *Home:* 83 Morgan St., Apt. 6A, Stamford, Conn. 06905. *Office:* Rye Country Day School, Cedar St., Rye, N.Y. 10580.

CAREER: Rye Country Day School, Rye, N.Y., history

teacher, 1973—. *Member:* Civil War Roundtable of New York.

WRITINGS—All with wife, Barbara K. Harrah: *Conservation/Ecology: Resources for Environmental Education*, Scarecrow, 1975; *Alternate Sources of Energy: A Bibliography of Solar, Geothermal, Wind, and Tidal Energy, and Environmental Architecture*, Scarecrow, 1975; *Funeral Service: A Bibliography*, Scarecrow, in press.

WORK IN PROGRESS: Sports Books for Children: A Guide, with wife, Barbara K. Harrah; a reference book on historic preservation, with B. K. Harrah; research on the Civil War.

* * *

HARRINGTON, Charles (Christopher) 1942-

PERSONAL: Born January 14, 1942, in New York, N.Y.; son of William Treanor and Lucette (Van Limbeek) Harrington; married Giselle Nemeth (a college teacher), June 3, 1962; children: Christopher, Jonathan. *Education:* Syracuse University, A.B., 1962; Harvard University, Ph.D., 1968. *Religion:* Unitarian Universalist. *Home address:* Ancram, N.Y. 12502. *Office address:* Box 95, Columbia University, Teachers College, New York, N.Y. 10027.

CAREER: Columbia University, Teachers College, New York, N.Y., assistant professor, 1967-71, associate professor of anthropology and education, 1971—, associate director of Institute for Urban and Minority Education, 1975—. *Member:* American Anthropological Association (fellow), Society for Applied Anthropology (fellow), Council on Anthropology and Education, American Sociological Association.

WRITINGS: Errors in Sex Role Behavior, Teachers College Press, 1970; (co-author) *The Learning of Political Behavior*, Scott, Foresman, 1970; (editor) *Readings in Anthropology and Education*, Mss Information, 1971; (editor) *Cross-Cultural Approaches to Learning*, Mss Information, 1973. Contributor of reviews to *American Record Guide*.

WRITINGS: Psychological Anthropology and Education; Political Socialization.

* * *

HARRIS, Edward Arnold 1910-1976

October 20, 1910—March 14, 1976; American news correspondent, columnist, and author. Obituaries: *Washington Post*, March 16, 1976.

* * *

HARRIS, John S(terling) 1929-

PERSONAL: Born October 29, 1929, in Salt Lake City, Utah; son of Sterling R. (a school superintendent) and Viola (Green) Harris; married Sue Spencer (a professor of nursing), March 1, 1954; children: Steven, Scott, Polly. *Education:* University of Utah, student, 1947-49, 1952; Brigham Young University, B.A., 1953, M.A., 1958; University of Texas, further graduate study, 1958-62. *Religion:* Church of Jesus Christ of Latter-day Saints (Mormons). *Home:* 243 South 400 E., Springville, Utah 84663. *Office:* Department of English, Brigham Young University, A246 JKB, Provo, Utah 84602.

CAREER: Brigham Young University, Provo, Utah, assistant professor, 1962-72, associate professor of English, 1972—. Visiting professor at Bowling Green State University, 1974. Consultant to government and industry. *Military service:* U.S. Army, 1953-55. U.S. Army Reserve, 1955-67. *Member:* National Council of Teachers of English, Conference on College Composition and Communication, Society for Technical Communication, Association of Teachers of Technical Writing (national president, 1973-77), Sigma Xi, Phi Kappa Phi, Delta Tau Kappa.

WRITINGS: Barbed Wire (poems), Brigham Young University Press, 1974; (with Reed H. Blake) *Technical Writing for Social Scientists,* Nelson-Hall, 1976.

WORK IN PROGRESS: Books on technical writing and on teaching technical writing.

*   *   *

HARRIS, Kathryn (Beatrice) Gibbs 1930-
(Wilson Hayes)

PERSONAL: Born July 7, 1930, in Havre de Grace, Md.; daughter of F. Lee (a clergyman) and Margaret E. (a teacher; maiden name, Wilson) Gibbs; married Robert F. Gibbons (a novelist; divorced, 1960); married Kerry Francis Harris (a scientist), July 7, 1965. *Education:* University of Pittsburgh, B.A., 1954, M.A., 1957; Michigan State University, Ph.D., 1976. *Religion:* Anglican. *Home:* 1814 Wilde Oak Circle, Bryan, Tex. 77801.

CAREER: Grove City College, Grove City, Pa., instructor in English, 1958-59; University of New Orleans, New Orleans, La., instructor in English, 1959-65; Michigan State University, East Lansing, instructor in English, 1967-68; Lansing Community College, Lansing, Mich., instructor in humanities, autumn, 1968; writer, 1968—. Co-founder and editor for East Lansing Arts Workshop.

MEMBER: American Association of University Women (member-at-large), Modern Language Association of America, Society for the Study of Midwestern Literature (patron member), South-Central Modern Language Association, National Association for Psychoanalytic Criticism (member of advisory board), Thoreau Fellowship, Midwest Modern Language Association, Brazos Valley Arts Council, New Orleans Poetry Forum. *Awards, honors:* Grant to attend Bread Loaf Writers' Conference, 1975.

WRITINGS: (Under pseudonym Wilson Hayes) *Ironwood* (poems), Old Marble Press, 1973; (editor, under name Kathryn Gibbs Harris, and contributor, under pseudonym Wilson Hayes) *Marrow* (anthology of women's poetry), Old Marble Press, 1975; (under pseudonym Wilson Hayes) *Ironwood II: Poems of Place,* Old Marble Press, 1975.

Work under pseudonym Wilson Hayes, has been anthologized in *Fadge: An East Lansing Anthology,* edited by Terry Henry, Old Marble Press, 1974. Contributor of articles, poems (under pseudonym Wilson Hayes), and reviews to magazines, including *Human Dimensions, Thoreau Journal, Mississippi Quarterly, South Carolina Review,* and *Visvabharati Quarterly.* Assistant editorial adviser for *Driftwood,* 1959-63; book review editor of *Literature and Psychology,* 1975.

WORK IN PROGRESS: A book on Robert Frost; a novel, set in Harford County, Md.; poems; essays on contemporary poets.

SIDELIGHTS: Kathryn Harris writes: "Although study has taught the manner of contemporary poetry, the principal motivating source for my verse and much other writing was time spent at the farm of my maternal grandparents near Aberdeen, Maryland. Childhood Christmases and summers remain in the dream, a pastoral dream essentially, against which the actuality of contemporary adult life strikes dissonant, iron chords. I celebrate both the irony and the dream.

I have written verse and other related literary forms steadily since the age of twelve and have gathered poets around me in reading groups since age fourteen. I have found as many persons devoted to the elusive lyric when I was driving a truck or working for an insurance company as when teaching literature."

*   *   *

HARRIS, Leonard 1929-

PERSONAL: Born September 27, 1929, in New York, N.Y.; son of Saul B. (a businessman) and Frances (Paley) Harris; children: Sally, David. *Education:* City College (now of the City University of New York), B.S.S., 1950; Yale University, graduate study, 1950-52. *Agent:* Morton Janklow, 375 Park Ave., New York, N.Y. 10022. *Office:* Goodson-Todman, 375 Park Ave., New York, N.Y. 10022.

CAREER: Writer, actor, and critic. *Hartford Courant,* Hartford, Conn., reporter, editor, and rewrite man, 1958-60; *New York World-Telegram and Sun,* New York, N.Y., critic, feature writer, and reporter, 1960-66; WCBS-Television, New York, N.Y., arts editor, critic, and correspondent, host of talk show "Gateway," and producer and writer for documentary series "Eye on New York," 1966-74; free-lance writer and actor, 1974—. Adjunct associate professor at Fordham University, 1969-74, and Hunter College of the City University of New York, 1975. Film and theater critic for WCBS-Radio, 1972—; host of "In Conversation," a live interview series produced at 92nd St. Y, intermittently, 1972-74; co-host of magazine news program, "The Fifty-First State," January-August, 1975; television appearances include guest host of "Midday Live" and panelist on "What's My Line?" and "To Tell the Truth." Co-star of the feature film "Taxi Driver," 1976. Member of theater advisory panel of New York State Arts Council. *Member:* Phi Beta Kappa.

WRITINGS: The Masada Plan (suspense novel), Crown, 1976. Contributor to theater journals.

WORK IN PROGRESS: A novel.

SIDELIGHTS: Leonard Harris wrote: "I began *The Masada Plan* as a Doomsday story, an adventure, and it still is that, I hope. But in writing it, I began to experience startling, exhilarating revelations. Expansions of my awareness. Deep excavations into my memories. Tough battles with the unresolved theses and antitheses which play tennis in my conscious mind. None of this ever happened to me before, not as a newspaperman, TV critic, radio interviewer, communications teacher, dabbling actor, or any of the other things I've done."

AVOCATIONAL INTERESTS: Long-distance running, hiking, and mountain walking.

*   *   *

HARRIS, R(obert) J(ohn) C(ecil) 1922-

PERSONAL: Born March 14, 1922, in Maidstone, Kent, England; son of John Henry (a superintendent of nurses) and Susannah (Campling) Harris; married Annette Constance Daphne Brading (a school librarian), March 2, 1946; children: Suzanne, Timothy. *Education:* University of London, B.Sc., 1943, Ph.D., 1945. *Religion:* Church of England. *Home:* 24 Harnwood Rd., Salisbury, Wiltshire, England. *Office:* Microbiological Research Establishment, Porton Down, Wiltshire, England.

CAREER: University of London, London, England, research fellow at Chester Beatty Research Institute, 1943-58;

Imperial Cancer Research Fund Laboratory, London, head of Division of Experimental Biology and Virology, 1958-68, head of department of environmental carcinogenesis, 1968-71; Microbiological Research Establishment, Porton Down, England, director, 1970—. *Member:* Royal Institute of Chemistry (fellow), Institute of Biology (fellow), Royal College of Pathologists (fellow), Athenaeum Club. *Awards, honors:* D.Tech. from Brunel University, 1973.

WRITINGS: Cancer: The Nature of the Problem, Penguin, 1962, 3rd edition, 1976; (editor) *What We Know about Cancer,* Allen & Unwin, 1970, St. Martin's, 1972. Contributor to scientific journals.

WORK IN PROGRESS: Research on microbes and their products, including vaccines, therapeutic enzymes, continuous culture, and environmental aspects.

SIDELIGHTS: Harris told *CA* that "with some thirty years' experience of research into the causation of cancer, I took Schrodinger's dictum to heart, namely: 'Never lose sight of the role your particular subject has within the great performance of the tragi-comedy of human life.... If you cannot—in the long run—tell everyone what you have been doing, your doing has been worthless.' The media prefer to highlight the new advances. I wanted to give a more balanced account with stress on the nature of the problems to be solved."

* * *

HARRIS, Radie

PERSONAL: Born in New York, N.Y. *Education:* Educated in New York City elementary and high schools. *Politics:* Democrat. *Office: Hollywood Reporter,* Paramount Building, 1501 Broadway, New York, N.Y.

CAREER: Hollywood Reporter, New York, N.Y., author of column "Broadway Ballyhoo." Member of executive board of American Theatre Wing; member of Tony Awards board of League of New York Theatres. *Member:* American Federation of Television and Radio Artists.

WRITINGS: Radie's World (career memoirs), Putnam, 1975. Contributor to popular magazines, including *Woman's Day.*

SIDELIGHTS: Radie Harris has covered motion picture news all over Europe and the United States.

* * *

HARRIS, S(eymour) E(dwin) 1897-1974

PERSONAL: Born September 8, 1897, in New York, N.Y.; son of Henry and Augusta (Kulick) Harris; married Ruth Black, September 3, 1923 (deceased); married Dorothy Marshall, 1968. *Education:* Harvard University, A.B., 1920, Ph.D., 1926. *Politics:* Liberal Democrat. *Residence:* La Jolla, Calif.

CAREER: Princeton University, Princeton, N.J., instructor in economics, 1920-22; Harvard University, Cambridge, Mass., instructor, 1922-27, lecturer, 1927-33, assistant professor, 1933-36, associate professor, 1936-45, professor of economics, 1945-57, Lucius N. Littauer Professor of Political Economy, 1957-64, professor emeritus, 1964-74, chairman of department, 1955-59; University of California (now San Diego State University), La Jolla, professor of economics and chairman of department, 1964-67, professor emeritus, 1967-74. Member of U.S. Board of Economic Warfare, 1942; director of export-import price control in Office of Price Administration, 1942-43; member of U.S.

Secretary of State's committee on postwar commercial economy, 1943; adviser to vice-chairman of War Production Board, 1944-45, National Security Resources Board, 1946-47, and Commodity Credit Corp., 1949-52; member of Agricultural Mobilization Policy Board, 1951-53. Chairman of New England Governors' Textile Committee, 1955-60. Member of President's Council of Economic Advisers, 1950-51; economic adviser to Adlai Stevenson, 1954-56, John F. Kennedy, 1960 (later member of task force on the economy), Secretary of the Treasury Douglas Dillon, 1961, and Democratic National Committee. Visiting professor at University of California, San Diego (now San Diego State University), 1948. Trustee of John F. Kennedy Library. *Military service:* U.S. Army, 1918.

MEMBER: American Economic Association (past member of executive committee; vice-president, 1945-48), American Academy of Arts and Sciences, Harvard Club. *Awards, honors:* Co-winner of Greater Boston Metropolitan Contest, 1944; gold medal from Northern Textile Association, 1954, for service to the New England economy; LL.D. from Monmouth College, 1961, and University of Massachusetts, 1963; Carnegie Commission grant, 1968-72; Alexander Hamilton Prize from U.S. Department of the Treasury, 1968.

WRITINGS: The Assignats, Harvard University Press, 1930, AMS Press, 1969; *Monetary Problems of the British Empire,* Macmillan, 1931; *Twenty Years of Federal Reserve Policy, Including an Extended Discussion of the Monetary Crisis, 1927-1933,* Harvard University Press, 1933; *Exchange Depreciation: Its Theory and Its History, 1931-1935, with Some Consideration of Related Domestic Policies,* Harvard University Press, 1936.

The Economics of American Defense, Norton, 1941; *The Economics of Social Security: The Relation of the American Program to Consumption, Savings, Output, and Finance,* McGraw, 1941, Greenwood Press, 1970; *The Economics of America at War,* Norton, 1943; (editor) *Postwar Problems,* McGraw, 1943, Books for Libraries, 1972; (editor) *Economic Problems of Latin America,* McGraw, 1944, Books for Libraries, 1972; (editor) *Economic Reconstruction,* McGraw, 1945; *Inflation and the American Economy,* McGraw, 1945; *Price and Related Controls in the United States,* McGraw, 1945; *The National Debt and the New Economics,* McGraw, 1947; (editor) *The New Economics: Keynes' Influence on Theory and Public Policy,* Knopf, 1947, Augustus Kelley, 1965; *The European Recovery Program,* Harvard University Press, 1948; (editor) *Foreign Economic Policy for the United States,* Harvard University Press, 1948, Greenwood Press, 1968; *How Shall We Pay for Education?: Approaches to the Economics of Education,* Harper, 1948; (editor) *Saving American Capitalism: A Liberal Economic Program,* Knopf, 1948; *The Market for College Graduates and Related Aspects of Education and Income,* Harvard University Press, 1949, Greenwood Press, 1969; *ERP: Progress and Prospects,* Foreign Policy Association, 1949; *Economic Planning: The Plans of Fourteen Countries with Analyses of the Plans,* Knopf, 1949.

Foreign Aid and Our Economy, Public Affairs Institute, 1950; *The Economics of Mobilization and Inflation,* Norton, 1951, Greenwood Press, 1968; (editor) *Schumpeter: Social Scientist,* Harvard University Press, 1951, Books for Libraries, 1969; *The Economics of New England: Case Study of an Older Area,* Harvard University Press, 1952; *National Health Insurance and Alternative Plans for Financing Health,* League for Industrial Democracy, 1953; *John Maynard Keynes: Economist and Policy Maker,* Scribner, 1955;

New England Textiles and the New England Economy, Littauer Center, Harvard University, 1956; *International and Interregional Economics,* McGraw, 1957; *An Economist Looks at Medicine,* privately printed, 1958; *Taxation and Revenue: Current Tax Problems,* U.S. Industrial College of the Armed Forces, 1958; *The Incidence of Inflation; or, Who Gets Hurt?,* U.S. Government Printing Office, 1959.

(Editor) *Higher Education in the United States: The Economic Problems,* Harvard University Press, 1960; *More Resources for Education,* Harper, 1960; *American Economic Policy,* McGraw, 1961; (editor) *The Dollar in Crisis,* Harcourt, 1961; *The Economics of the Political Parties: With Special Attention to Presidents Eisenhower and Kennedy,* Macmillan, 1962; *Higher Education: Resources and Finance,* McGraw, 1962; *Economics of the Kennedy Years and a Look Ahead,* Harper, 1964; *The Economics of American Medicine,* Macmillan, 1964; *Challenge and Change in American Education,* McCutchan, 1965; (editor with Alan Levensohn) *Education and Public Policy,* McCutchan, 1965; *My Wife Ruth,* privately printed, 1966.

The Economics of Harvard, McGraw, 1970; *Academic Activist, 1920-1970,* privately printed, 1972; *A Statistical Portrait of Higher Education,* McGraw, 1972.

Also author of *Stabilization Subsidies,* 1948; *Inflation and Anti-Inflationary Policies of American States,* 1950; *Economic Aspects of Higher Education,* 1964. Editor of *Review of Economics and Statistics,* 1943-64; associate editor of *Quarterly Journal of Economics,* 1947-74.

OBITUARIES: Washington Post, October 29, 1974; *New York Times,* October 29, 1974; *Time,* November 11, 1974.*

(Died October 27, 1974, in San Diego, Calif.)

*   *   *

HARRIS, (Theodore) Wilson 1921-

PERSONAL: Born March 24, 1921, in New Amsterdam, Guyana (formerly British Guiana); emigrated to England, 1959; son of Theodore Wilson (an insurer and underwriter) and Millicent Josephine (Glasford) Harris; married Margaret Nimmo Burns (a writer), April 2, 1959. *Education:* Queen's College, Georgetown, Guyana, 1934-39; studied land surveying and geomorphology under government auspices, 1939-42. *Residence:* London, England. *Address:* c/o Faber and Faber, 3 Queen Square, London W.C. 1, England.

CAREER: British Guiana Government, government surveyor, 1942-54, senior surveyor, 1955-58; full-time writer in London, England, 1959—. Visiting lecturer, State University of New York, Buffalo, 1970; writer-in-residence, University of West Indies, 1970, and University of Toronto, 1970; visiting professor, University of Texas, Austin, 1972, University of Aarhus, 1973. Delegate, UNESCO Symposium on Caribbean Literature in Cuba, 1968, National Identity Conference in Australia, 1968. *Awards, honors:* English Arts Council grants, 1968 and 1970; Commonwealth fellow at University of Leeds, 1971; Guggenheim fellow, 1972-73; Henfield writing fellow at University of East Anglia, 1974.

WRITINGS—Novels; all published by Faber: *Palace of the Peacock* (Book I of the "Guiana Quartet"), 1960; *The Far Journey of Oudin* (Book II of the "Guiana Quartet"), 1961; *The Whole Armour* (Book III of the "Guiana Quartet"), 1962; *The Secret Ladder* (Book IV of the "Guiana Quartet"), 1963; *Heartland,* 1964; *The Eye of the Scarecrow,* 1965; *The Waiting Room,* 1967; *Tumatumari,* 1968; *Ascent to Omai,* 1970; *Black Marsden,* 1972; *Companions of the*

Day and Night, 1975; *Da Silva da Silva's Cultivated Wilderness and Genesis of the Clowns,* in press.

Poetry: *Fetish,* privately printed (Georgetown, Guyana), 1951; *Eternity to Season,* privately printed (Georgetown, Guyana), 1954.

Nonfiction: *Tradition and the West Indian Novel,* New Beacon, 1965; *Tradition, the Writer and Society,* New Beacon, 1967.

Short stories: *The Sleepers of Roraima,* Faber, 1970; *The Age of the Rainmakers,* Faber, 1971.

Short story anthologized in *Caribbean Rhythms: The Emerging English Literature of the West Indies,* edited by J. T. Livingston, Washington Square Press, 1974. Excerpt from *Genesis of the Clowns* appeared in *Review* (of the Center for Inter-American Relations), winter, 1975.

SIDELIGHTS: Harris told *CA:* "A summary of motivations by a writer is inevitably an unfinished statement since with each imaginative work a new discovery arises that alerts one to intuitive and implicit dimensions, in previous novels, that acquire a new significance and bearing on future work. It is as if each novel is another step in a drama of consciousness or unpredictable creative potential in the past and in the future.

"I think all this bears on a vision of community as a capacity for evolving insight and deepseated change. The nature of freedom is complex, subtle, and demanding of unceasing responsibility to that still unfathomable 'muse' (however apparently archaic that expression may sound) in a world that is susceptible to polarisations, tyrannies and monoliths that are as frightful and dangerous today as they have ever been in the history of cultures and civilisations."

Harris' manuscripts are collected at the University of the West Indies, the University of Texas, Austin, and the University of Indiana, Bloomington.

BIOGRAPHICAL/CRITICAL SOURCES: Louis James, editor, *The Islands In Between,* Oxford University Press, 1968; Gerald Moore, *Chosen Tongue,* Longman, 1969; *Journal of Commonwealth Literature,* July, 1969, June, 1971, April, 1975; *Language and Literature,* autumn, 1971; *Literary Half-Yearly,* January, 1972; Ivan Van Sertima, *Enigma of Values,* Dangaroo Press (Aarhus, Denmark), 1975; John Fletcher, *Commonwealth Literature and the Modern World,* Didier (Brussels), 1975; Michael Gilkes, *Wilson Harris and the Caribbean Novel,* Longman, 1975; Hena Maes-Jelinek, *The Naked Design,* Dangaroo Press, 1976.

*   *   *

HARRISON, Tony 1937-

PERSONAL: Born April 30, 1937, in Leeds, Yorkshire, England; son of Harry Ashton (a baker) and Florence (Horner) Harrison; married Rosemarie Crossfield Dietzsch (an artist), January 16, 1960; children: Jane, Max. *Education:* University of Leeds, B.A., 1958. *Religion:* None. *Home:* 9 Grove, Gosforth, Newcastle-upon-Tyne NE3 1NE, England. *Agent:* Kenneth Ewing, Fraser & Dunlop, 91 Regent St., London, England.

CAREER: Poet. Lecturer at Ahmadu Bello University (Nigeria), 1962-66, and Charles University (Prague), 1966-67. Northern Arts fellow in poetry at Universities of Newcastle and Durham, 1967-68, and 1976-77; UNESCO traveling fellow in poetry, 1969; Gregynog Arts Fellow at University of Wales, 1973-74. *Member:* Writers' Action Group.

Awards, honors: Cholmondeley Award for Poetry from Society of Authors, 1969; Geoffrey Faber Memorial Prize, 1972, for *The Loiners.*

WRITINGS—Poetry: *Earthworks,* Northern House, 1964; *Aikin Mata,* Oxford University Press, 1966; *Newcastle Is Peru,* Eagle Press, 1969; *The Loiners,* London Magazine Editions, 1970; *The Misanthrope,* Rex Collings, 1973; *Phaedra Britannica,* Rex Collings, 1975; *The Poems of Palladas,* Anvil Press, 1975. Poems have been included in *Rex Collings Christmas Book,* Rex Collings, 1976. Author of the lyrics for the film ''Bluebird,'' 1976. Contributor to British magazines and newspapers.

WORK IN PROGRESS: The School of Eloquence, poems; a new version of Aeschylus' *Oresteia,* for London's National Theatre; a new libretto for Smetana's ''Bartered Bride,'' for New York City's Metropolitan Opera.

SIDELIGHTS: Harrison has traveled all over the world, including Cuba, the Soviet Union and much of Africa.

BIOGRAPHICAL/CRITICAL SOURCES: Honest Ulsterman, September-October, 1970.

* * *

HART, Carol 1944-

PERSONAL: Born August 2, 1944, in Norfolk, Va.; daughter of Rollin E. (a boat builder) and Ruth (a secretary; maiden name, Shreve) Grant; married Daniel Hart (director of Massachusetts Audubon Drumlin Farm), October 16, 1968. *Education:* College of William and Mary, B.A., 1967; also attended Wooster Community Art Center, Brookfield Craft Center, College of Marin, and Academy of Advertising Art. *Home and office address:* Salmon-Kill Gallery, Route 112, Lime Rock, Lakeville, Conn. 06039.

CAREER: Craftswoman and teacher; has studied basketry of England, New England, the Pennsylvania Dutch, and the Hopi Indians. Elementary school teacher in New Milford, Conn., 1969-70; nature and Indian studies teacher at Pratt Education Center, 1968-75; and basketry teacher at Museum of American Folk Art, Brookfield Craft Center, and Worcester Craft Center; has had exhibitions of her work in the New York-New England area and in Arizona.

WRITINGS: (With husband, Dan Hart) *Natural Basketry,* Watson-Guptill, 1976. Author of film ''Basketry,'' released by ACI, 1975. Contributor to *Nature Study* and *Sphere.*

WORK IN PROGRESS: Researching basketry materials and techniques of American Indian tribes and exploring use of local plants.

SIDELIGHTS: Hart told *CA* that ''a close relationship with the land and feeling a need to process materials from nature as well as create useful forms with them has led to my experimentation in basketry.''

* * *

HART, John 1948-

PERSONAL: Born June 18, 1948, in Berkeley, Calif.; son of Lawrence (a teacher and writer) and Jeanne (a writer, under pseudonym Jeanne McGahey; maiden name, Brown) Hart. *Education:* Princeton University, A.B., 1970. *Politics:* Independent. *Religion:* None. *Home and office:* 13 Jefferson Ave., San Rafael, Calif. 94903.

CAREER: Pacific Sun, Mill Valley, Calif., writer on environment and planning, 1970-73; free-lance writer, 1973—. *Member:* Sierra Club, Wilderness Society, Friends of the Earth, California Tomorrow. *Awards, honors:* James D.

Phelan Award from San Francisco Foundation, 1970, for an unpublished manuscript of poetry; merit award from California chapter of American Institute of Planners, 1972, for articles on planning.

WRITINGS: (Contributor) David Walker and Rowan Roundtree, editors, *Tomales Bay Environmental Study,* Conservation Foundation, 1973; *Hiking the Bigfoot Country: The Wildlands of Northern California and Southern Oregon,* Sierra Club, 1975; (contributor) Randall W. Scott, editor, *Management and Control of Growth,* Urban Land Institute, 1975.

Work has been anthologized in *Accent on Barlow,* edited by Lawrence Hart, privately printed, 1962; *Mark in Time,* edited by Nick Harvey, Glide Publications, 1971; *Poems One Line and Longer,* edited by William Cole, Grossman, 1973. Contributor of articles, poems, and translations to *Cry California, Works, Ishmael, Pacific Sun,* and *Sierra Club Bulletin.* Associate editor of *California Land,* 1975; script consultant for television documentary film, ''The Wild Places.''

WORK IN PROGRESS: The Climbers, poems; *Walking Softly in the Wilderness* (tentative title), a book on low-impact methods of wilderness travel, for Sierra Club; research for a book on the poetry of the Wagner librettos.

SIDELIGHTS: Hart writes: ''Although I make my living writing expository prose, I regard myself first of all as a poet. I am a member of the nationally-known Activist Group of poets, professionals who work, or have worked, in seminars conducted since 1935 by Lawrence Hart.

''I find this an odd time in which to be writing poetry. The condition of that art, in America in the 1970's, can hardly fail to distress anyone anxious to do good and disciplined work. To be sure, poetry is popular as never before; more than that, it is subsidized as never before. But this climate, apparently so favorable, actually seems to promote a poetry so slack and trivial that it scarcely counts as poetry at all.

''Thirty years ago there were at least five major American poets alive. Today there is not one. Historians will, I think, look back on this period as one of drought in poetry—a period in which the growth of the art progressed, as it were, underground, while work of little importance commanded the chief rewards and set the admired style.

''If such unfavorable climates had not been recorded before, in the literature of other languages and in the other arts, the present situation would be even more disheartening than it is.''

AVOCATIONAL INTERESTS: Wilderness travel and climbing, winter mountaineering, European travel, opera and theatre, the politics of wilderness preservation.

* * *

HARTMAN, Jan 1938-

PERSONAL: Born May 23, 1938, in Stockholm, Sweden; came to United States, 1938, naturalized citizen, 1948; son of Robert Schirokauer (a philosopher) and Rita (Emanuel) Hartman; married Lorie Selz (a writer), June 9, 1960; children: Katherine Emanuel, Tanya Elizabeth. *Education:* Harvard University, B.A., 1960. *Residence:* New York, N.Y. *Agent:* Robert Freedman, Brandt & Brandt, 101 Park Ave., New York, N.Y. 10017.

CAREER: Playwright and television and film scriptwriter. Resident playwright at Theatre of the Living Arts, Philadelphia, Pa., 1964-65; director and founder of Playwrights Theatre Project, Circle in the Square, New York City, 1967-

69; instructor in theatre at New School, New York City, 1969; resident dramatist at Performance Center Theatre and Academy, New York City, 1976—; founder and director, Muckrakers, 1977.

MEMBER: Eugene O'Neill Memorial Theatre Foundation, Writers Guild of America, American National Theatre and Academy, Dramatists Guild, American Educational Theatre Association. *Awards, honors:* Writer Guild nomination for best anthology script, 1966-67, for "The Alchemists" and "The Terezin Requiem"; Freedom's Foundation award, 1971, for play, *Flatboatman;* New York International Film Festival, first prize for best religious film, 1970, for "If Salt Has Lost Its Savor," silver medal, 1976, for "Choose Life"; Virgin Islands Film Festival bronze medal, 1976, for "Choose Life." Fellowships from Guggenheim Foundation, 1964, and New York Council of the Arts, 1976.

WRITINGS: Joshua (novel), Popular Library, 1970; *Elements of Film Writing,* Crowell, 1976.

Published plays: *The Shadow of the Valley* (includes "The Shadow of the Valley" and other plays, first produced in Le Mars, Iowa, 1964), Paulist Press, 1965; *Samuel Hoopes Reading from His Own Works: A Play for One Actor* (first produced in Wichita, Kan., at Wichita State University Theatre, 1966), Dramatists Play Service, 1968; *Every Year at Carnival* (first produced as "Fragment of a Last Judgement" in New York at Eugene O'Neill Memorial Theatre, 1967), Dramatists Play Service, 1970; *Flatboatman* (first produced by American Broadcasting Corp. Television, 1971), Dramatists Play Service, 1970.

Other plays: "Legend of Daniel Boone," first produced in Harrodsburg, Kentucky, at outdoor festival, 1965; "Antique Masks," first produced in Villanova, Pa., at Villanova University Theatre, 1966; "Freeman! Freeman!," first produced in Cleveland, Ohio, at Karamu House, 1970; "Final Solutions," first produced in New York City at Madison Square Garden, Felt Forum, 1968; "The American War Crimes Trial," first produced in New Haven, Conn., at Long Wharf Theatre, 1973. Also author of plays, "Ministrel War," "A Temporary Madness," and "Winter Visitor," as yet neither published nor produced.

Screenplays: "Hail to the Chief" (rewrite), Twentieth Century-Fox, 1972; "The Cursed Medallion," Italian-International, 1974. Also author of over thirty scripts for public and private institutions, including IBM, National Park Service, U.S. Information Agency, American Cancer Society, Monsanto Chemical Co., and American Telephone and Telegraph.

Television scripts include such specials as "Bound for Freedom," "All Deliberate Speed," "Song of Myself," and "Journeys in Place," all broadcast by national television networks in 1976. Writer of over seventy other dramas, biographical profiles, and documentaries for network television broadcast.

WORK IN PROGRESS: The Tradition of the American Theatre, a discussion of the coherent American tradition in theatre; two novels, *Ashes* and *Dear Lysette;* research for a third novel, *The Atomic Age.*

SIDELIGHTS: Hartman told *CA:* "Though I began my writing career fresh out of college with an aim toward working as a playwright in the theatre, necessity and opportunity compelled me to work in television. I've been lucky to carve a niche for myself in the areas of so-called 'quality' where I've been able to buck a pervasive commercialism with dramas of some power and dramatic value. Overall, however, television remains a merchants' medium. Theatre is a first love. As the years move on I find myself drawn to book writing. Fiction now has the same power over my heart and imagination as theatre—as it did when I was a child. . . .

"The effect of literature (and I include drama in that word) on public thought and the collective mind of a society intrigues and puzzles me. How effective *is* a work of art in influencing thought? Do works of art change minds? Direct them? Or do we live in such transient times that only journalism is taken seriously day-to-day? These are questions that can not be definitively answered but should engage any writer who is interested in more than entertainment. Solzhenitsyn says that a country with a great writer has an alternate government—this may be true inside totalitarian regimes where truth is a threat. In a culture such as ours, awash in media, where truth is just another medium—the artist may be just another baying hound.

"I would like to become one of those writers who casts strong hard light on corners of society and human beings revealing all the eccentricities, vagaries, ironies, and forces that are at work there. Then, finally, I would like to fulfill this dictum of the artist that Solzhenitsyn sets forth in his Nobel Prize acceptance speech: 'The task of the artist is to sense more keenly than others the harmony of the world, the beauty and the outrage of what man has done to it, and poignantly to *let people know!*' My italics."

Jan Hartman won critical acclaim for his television special on Walt Whitman. The script attempted to shed light on the dark corners of the poet's eccentricities—one, a dark corner not often seen on television. Martin Duberman said: " 'Song of Myself' marks out a path angels have not been allowed to see and Whitman scholars have refused to tread. That's right: the script deals with Whitman's homosexuality. Indeed, centers on it. Apparently, the more the creators of his dramatization researched Whitman's life, the more convinced they became that homoeroticism was at its core. Having decided that, they went ahead and did the program accordingly. . . . Gutsiness, of course, is hardly a guarantee of art. Fortunately, 'Song of Myself' has a lot more to recommend it than its willingness to break a taboo. The text (some of it Whitman's own poetry) and the visual images are beautifully interwoven, the subtleties of one complimenting and highlighting the other."

AVOCATIONAL INTERESTS: Reading history, studying languages (Hartman knows French and Spanish and has an understanding of German).

BIOGRAPHICAL/CRITICAL SOURCES: New York Times, January 11, 1976.

*   *   *

HARVEY, David Dow   1931-

PERSONAL: Born October 30, 1931, in Colorado; son of Lashley G. and Ernestine (Dow) Harvey; married Mary Ann Sedgwick, June, 1955 (divorced, 1965); married Jocelyn Gilbertson (an editor), September 3, 1966; children: (first marriage) Christopher; (second marriage) Kerridwen, John. *Education:* Harvard University, A.B. (cum laude), 1955; Columbia University, M.A., 1958, Ph.D., 1962. *Home address:* General Delivery, Barry's Bay, Ontario, Canada. *Office address:* Mine Rd., R.R. 1, Chelsea, Quebec, Canada.

CAREER: Vassar College, Poughkeepsie, N.Y., instructor in English, 1959-60; University of Washington, Seattle, assistant professor of English, 1961-66; State University of New York at Albany, associate professor of English, 1966-69; free-lance writer and editor, 1968—. *Military service:* U.S. Army, 1955-57; became sergeant. *Awards, honors:* Fulbright grant, University of London, 1960-61; Canada Council explorations grant, 1974.

WRITINGS: Ford Madox Ford, 1873-1939, Princeton University Press, 1962.

WORK IN PROGRESS: Americans in Canada, a social history from 1840 to the present, publication expected in 1978.

SIDELIGHTS: When Harvey moved to Canada, to a "new country and way of living" in the Madawaska Valley, he built an octagonal log cabin, which is still his primary residence, although he has been conducting research in Ottawa since 1974.

* * *

HARVEY, Nancy Lenz 1935-

PERSONAL: Born November 3, 1935, in Newport News, Va.; daughter of George W., Jr. (a merchant) and Grace (Adams) Lenz; divorced. *Education:* Longwood College, B.A., 1957; University of Richmond, M.A., 1965; University of North Carolina, Ph.D., 1969. *Residence:* Cincinnati, Ohio. *Office:* Department of English, University of Cincinnati, Cincinnati, Ohio 45221.

CAREER: High school English teacher in Williamsburg, Va., 1957-64; University of Richmond, Richmond, Va., instructor in English, 1965; University of North Carolina, Chapel Hill, part-time instructor, 1965-68, instructor in English, 1968-69; University of Cincinnati, Cincinnati, Ohio, assistant professor, 1969-73, associate professor, 1973-76, professor of English, 1976—, director of undergraduate studies in English, 1976—.

MEMBER: Modern Language Association of America, Mediaeval Academy of America, Renaissance Society of America, Southeastern Institute of Medieval and Renaissance Studies (fellow). *Awards, honors:* American Philological Society grant, 1974; National Endowment for the Humanities fellowship, summer, 1975; fellow of the Folger Shakespeare Library, 1976; Ohioana Award from Marjorie Kinney Cooper Library Association of Ohio and Indiana, 1976, for *The Rose and the Thorn.*

WRITINGS: (Contributor) Richard H. Rupp, editor, *Critics on Emily Dickinson,* University of Miami Press, 1971; *Medieval and Tudor Drama: 1954-1969,* Nether Press, 1971; *Elizabeth of York: The Mother of Henry VIII,* Macmillan, 1973; *The Rose and the Thorn: The Lives of Mary and Margaret Tudor,* Macmillan, 1975. Contributor of articles and reviews to literature journals.

* * *

HATCH, Alden 1898-1975

PERSONAL: Born September 26, 1898, in New York, N.Y.; son of Frederic Horace and May Palmer (Daly) Hatch; married Ruth Brown, December 28, 1932; married second wife, Allene Pomeroy Gaty, September 9, 1950; children: (first marriage) Alden Denison. *Education:* Attended University of Chicago Extension, 1918-20, and Blackstone Institute, 1919-21. *Politics:* Republican. *Religion:* Episcopalian. *Home:* 1312 South Orange Ave., Sarasota, Fla. 33579.

CAREER: Biographer and historian. *Member:* P.E.N., Overseas Press Club, Rockaway Hunting Club (Cedarhurst, Long Island).

WRITINGS: Gaming Lady (novel), Farrar & Rinehart, 1931; *Glass Walls* (novel), Dial, 1933; (with Foxhall P. Keene) *Full Tilt: the Sporting Memoirs of Foxhall Keene,* Derrydale Press, 1938.

(With Nutchuk, pseudonym of Simeon Oliver) *Son of the Smoky Sea,* Messner, 1941; (editor) Caroline Bell and Edward Bell, *Thank You Twice; or, How We Like America,* Harcourt, 1941; *Bridle-Wise* (novel), Messner, 1942; *Glenn Curtiss: Pioneer of Naval Aviation,* Messner, 1942; *Heroes of Annapolis,* Messner, 1943; *General Ike: A Biography of Dwight D. Eisenhower,* Holt, 1944, revised and enlarged edition, 1952 (published in England as *General Eisenhower: A Biography of Dwight D. Eisenhower,* Skeffington, 1946); *Young Wilkie,* Harcourt, 1944; (with Nutchuk, pseudonym of Simeon Oliver) *Back to the Smoky Sea,* Messner, 1946; *Franklin D. Roosevelt: An Informal Biography,* Holt, 1947 (published in England as *Citizen of the World, Franklin D. Roosevelt: An Informal Biography,* Skeffington, 1948); *Woodrow Wilson: A Biography for Young People,* Holt, 1947.

American Express: A Century of Service (history), Doubleday, 1950; *George Patton: General in Spurs,* Messner, 1950; *Young Ike* (juvenile), Messner, 1953; *Red Carpet for Mamie* [Eisenhower], Holt, 1954; *Remington Arms in American History* (history), Rinehart, 1956, revised edition, 1972; *Ambassador Extraordinary Clare Booth Luce,* Holt, 1956; (with Seamus Walshe) *Crown of Glory: The Life of Pope Pius XII,* Hawthorn, 1957, revised and enlarged edition, 1958; (with Robert Briscoe) *For the Life of Me,* Little, Brown, 1958; *The Wadsworths of the Genessee,* Coward, 1959; *The Miracle of the Mountain: The Story of Brother Andre and the Shrine on Mount Royal,* Hawthorn, 1959.

The De Gaulle Nobody Knows: An Intimate Biography of Charles de Gaulle, Hawthorn, 1960; (with Henry Ringling North) *The Circus Kings: Our Ringling Family Story,* Doubleday, 1960; *Edith Bolling Wilson: First Lady Extraordinary,* Dodd, 1961; *Bernhard, Prince of the Netherlands,* Doubleday, 1962 (published in England as *H.R.H. Bernhard, Prince of the Netherlands,* Harrap, 1962); *A Man Named John: Pope John XXIII,* Hawthorn, 1963 (published in England as *His Name Was John: A Life of Pope John,* Harrap, 1963); *The Mountbattens: The Last Royal Success Story,* Random House, 1965; *Apostle of Peace: The Story of Pope Pius XII* (juvenile), Hawthorn, 1965; *Pope Paul VI,* Random House, 1966 (published in England as *Pope Paul VI, Apostle on the Move,* W. H. Allen, 1966); (with Krishna Nehru Hertheesing) *We Nehrus,* Holt, 1967; *The Byrds of Virginia: An American Dynasty, 1670 to the Present,* Holt, 1969.

The Lodges of Massachusetts, Hawthorn, 1973; *Buckminster Fuller: At Home in the Universe,* Crown, 1974.

Contributor of numerous articles to national magazines.

WORK IN PROGRESS: Research for a biography of Marjorie Merriweather Post, for Regnery.

SIDELIGHTS: Hatch's books have been published in Spanish, Polish, and French.*

(Died February 1, 1975, in Sarasota, Fla.)

* * *

HATFIELD, Henry Caraway 1912-

PERSONAL: Born June 3, 1912, in Evanston, Ill.; son of James Taft and Estelle (Caraway) Hatfield; married Jane Stauff, March 15, 1937; children: Robert, Allan, Barbara. *Education:* Harvard University, A.B., 1933; graduate study at Oxford University, 1933-34, and University of Berlin, 1934-35; Columbia University, A.M., 1938, Ph.D., 1942. *Home:* 7 Avon St., Cambridge, Mass. 02138. *Office:* Widener Library, Harvard University, Cambridge, Mass. 02138.

CAREER: Williams College, Williamstown, Mass., instructor, 1928-42, assistant professor of German, 1942-46; Columbia University, New York, N.Y., assistant professor, 1946-48, associate professor of German, 1948-54; Harvard University, Cambridge, Mass., associate professor, 1954-56, professor of German, 1956-67, Kuno Francke Professor of German Literature, 1967—, chairman of department of Germanic language and literature, 1957-59. Visiting professor at Free University of Berlin, 1961; broadcaster and interviewer with Office of War Information, London, England, 1944-45. *Member:* Modern Language Association of America (member of executive committee, 1956-59), American Academy of Arts and Sciences, American Association of Teachers of German, American Civil Liberties Union, Americans for Democratic Action. *Awards, honors:* Guggenheim and Fulbright fellowships, both 1952-53; American Council of Learned Societies awards, 1962, 1967, 1975; National Endowment for the Humanities grant, 1975.

WRITINGS: Winckelmann and His German Critics, 1755-1781: A Prelude to the Classical Age, King's Crown Press, 1943; *Thomas Mann: A Critical Guidebook,* New Directions, 1951, revised edition, 1962; *Thomas Mann: An Introduction to His Fiction,* P. Owen, 1952; (editor with Jack M. Stein) *Schnitzler, Kafka, Mann,* Houghton, 1953; (editor with F. H. Mautner) *The Lichtenberg Reader,* Beacon Press, 1959; *Goethe: A Critical Handbook,* New Directions, 1963; (editor) *Thomas Mann: A Collection of Critical Essays,* Prentice-Hall, 1964; *Aesthetic Paganism in German Literature: From Winckelmann to the Death of Goethe,* Harvard University Press, 1964; *Modern German Literature: The Major Figures in Context,* Edward Arnold, 1966, St. Martin's, 1967; (editor) *Lichtenberg: Aphorisms and Letters,* J. Cape, 1969; *Crisis and Continuity in Modern German Fiction: Ten Essays,* Cornell University Press, 1969; *Clashing Myths in German Literature: From Heine to Rilke,* Harvard University Press, 1974.

General editor of *Germanic Review,* 1947-53; member of editorial board of *PMLA,* 1951-56.

*   *   *

HATTAWAY, Herman (Morell)   1938-

PERSONAL: Born December 26, 1938, in New Orleans, La.; son of Samuel Morell and Mary Amelia (Cook) Hattaway; married Margaret Ann Troth, August 19, 1961. *Education:* Nicholls State College, student, 1961; Louisiana State University, B.A., 1961, M.A., 1963, Ph.D., 1969. *Religion:* Episcopalian. *Home:* 605 East 66th St., Kansas City, Mo. 64131. *Office:* Department of History, University of Missouri, 5212 Rockhill Rd., Kansas City, Mo. 64110.

CAREER: University of Missouri, Kansas City, assistant professor, 1969-73, associate professor of history, 1973—. Visiting assistant professor at Louisiana State University, 1972. *Military service:* U.S. Army, Infantry, 1961-65; became first lieutenant. *Member:* Organization of American Historians, American Military Institute, Southern Historical Association.

WRITINGS: General Stephen D. Lee, University Press of Mississippi, 1976. Contributor to *Encyclopedia of Southern History* and to military and history journals.

WORK IN PROGRESS: The Civil War: An Interpretive Military History, with Archer Jones; *The United Confederate Veterans; The U.S. Military Code of Conduct; Jefferson Davis.*

*   *   *

HAURY, Emil W(alter)   1904-

PERSONAL: Born May 2, 1904, in Newton, Kan.; son of Gustav A. (a professor) and Clara K. (Ruth) Haury; married Hulda E. Penner, June 7, 1928; children: Allan Gene, Loren Richard. *Education:* Bethel College, Newton, Kan., student, 1923-25; University of Arizona, A.B., 1927, M.A., 1928; Harvard University, Ph.D., 1934. *Home:* 2749 East Fourth St., Tucson, Ariz. 85717. *Office:* P.O. Box 4366, Tucson, Ariz. 85717; and Department of Anthropology, University of Arizona, Tucson, Ariz. 85721.

CAREER: University of Arizona, Tucson, instructor, 1928-29, research assistant, 1929-30, associate professor, 1937-38, head of department, 1937-64, professor of anthropology, 1938-70, Fred A. Riecker Distinguished Professor of Anthropology, 1970—; Gila Pueblo, Globe, Ariz., assistant director, 1930-37. Director of Arizona State Museum, 1938-64. Faculty adviser at University of Bogota, 1958. Chairman of National Research Council's Division of Anthropology and Psychology, 1960-62; chairman of National Academy of Science's Section on Anthropology, 1960-63. Advisory Board on National Parks, Historic Sites, Buildings, and Monuments, member, 1964-70, chairman, 1968-70; National Council on the Humanities, member, 1966-68.

MEMBER: American Anthropological Association (vice-president, 1947; president, 1956), Society for American Archaeology (president, 1944), American Association for the Advancement of Science, American Academy of Arts and Sciences, National Academy of Sciences, American Philosophical Society, Tree-Ring Society, National Speleological Society (honorary life member), Phi Beta Kappa, Sigma Xi, Phi Kappa Phi. *Awards, honors:* Viking Fund medal for anthropology, from Wenner-Gren Foundation for Anthropological Research, 1950; LL.D. from University of New Mexico, 1959; Salgo-Noren Foundation award, 1967, for excellence in teaching; conservation service award, 1976, from U.S. Department of the Interior.

WRITINGS: (With Lyndon L. Hargrave) *Recently Dated Pueblo Ruins in Arizona,* Smithsonian Institution, 1931; *Kivas of the Tusayan Ruin, Grand Canyon, Arizona,* privately printed, 1931; *Roosevelt:9:6, a Hohokam Site of the Colonial Period,* privately printed, 1932; *The Canyon Creek Ruin and the Cliff Dwellings of the Sierra Ancha,* privately printed, 1934; *The Mogollon Culture of Southwestern New Mexico,* privately printed, 1936; *Excavations in the Forestdale Valley, East-Central Arizona,* University of Arizona, 1941; *The Excavation of Los Muertos and Neighboring Ruins in the Slat River Valley, Southern Arizona: Based on the Work of the Hemenway Southwestern Archaeological Expedition of 1887-1888,* Peabody Museum of Archaeology & Ethnology, Harvard University, 1945, reprinted, Kraus Reprint, 1968; (with E. B. Sayles) *An Early Pit House Village of the Mogollon Culture, Forestdale Valley, Arizona,* University of Arizona, 1947; (with Kirk Bryan and others) *The Stratigraphy and Archaeology of Ventana Cave, Arizona,* University of Arizona Press, 1950, 2nd edition, 1975; (contributor) G. R. Willey, editor, *Prehistoric Settlement Patterns in the New World,* Wenner-Gren Foundation, 1956; (contributor) Thomas Weaver, editor, *Indians of Arizona: A Contemporary Perspective,* University of Arizona

Press, 1974; *The Hohokam, Desert Farmers and Craftsmen: Excavations at Snaketown, 1964-1965,* University of Arizona Press, 1976. Contributor to scholarly journals.

WORK IN PROGRESS: Reports on fieldwork at Forestdale and Point of Pines, both in the White Mountain region of east-central Arizona.

SIDELIGHTS: Haury told *CA:* "A chance introduction to archaeology on the National Geographic Society project in the Valley of Mexico convinced me that archaeology was what I wanted to pursue. I perceive archaeology to be a humanistic subject employing scientific procedures wherever applicable in developing an understanding of how man saw himself, how he behaved, and especially how he adjusted his life style to his natural setting."

* * *

HAWKE, Nancy
  See NUGENT, Nancy

* * *

HAWKINS, (Alec) Desmond 1908-

PERSONAL: Born October 20, 1908, in East Sheen, Surrey, England; married Barbara Skidmore; children: two sons, two daughters. *Home:* 2 Stanton Close, Blandford Forum, Dorset DT11 7RT, England. *Agent:* David Higham Associates Ltd., 5-8 Lower John St., Golden Sq., London W1R 4HA, England.

CAREER: Free-lance writer, critic, and broadcaster, 1935-45; British Broadcasting Corp. (BBC), Bristol, England, features producer of West region, 1945-55, program director, 1955-66, founder of natural history unit, 1959, regional controller, 1966-69; free-lance writer, critic, and broadcaster, 1970—. London correspondent, *Partisan Review,* prior to 1940. *Member:* BBC Club. *Awards, honors:* Silver medal from Royal Society for the Protection of Birds, 1959; Officer of the Order of the British Empire, 1963; LL.D., Bristol University, 1974.

WRITINGS: Hawk among the Sparrows (novel), Knopf, 1939; *Lighter than Day* (novel), Longmans, Green, 1940; *Thomas Hardy,* Alan Swallow, 1950, new edition published as *Hardy the Novelist,* David & Charles, 1966; *Sedgemoor and Avalon: A Portrait of Lowland Somerset,* R. Hale, 1954; *Wildlife of the New Forest,* Russell & Co., 1972; *Avalon and Sedgemoor,* David & Charles, 1973; *Hardy: Novelist and Poet,* Barnes & Noble, 1976.

Editor: (Under name A. Desmond Hawkins, and author of introduction) *Poetry and Prose of John Donne,* Thomas Nelson, 1938; (and author of introduction) D. H. Lawrence, *Stories, Essays, and Poems,* Dent, 1939; (with Donald Boyd, Frank Gillard, and Chester Wilmot) *War Report: A Record of Dispatches Broadcast by the BBC's War Correspondents with the Allied Expeditionary Force, 6 June 1944—5 May 1945,* Oxford University Press, 1946; *BBC Naturalist Book,* Rathbone Books, 1957; *The Second BBC Naturalist,* Adprint, 1960.

Literary editor, *New English Weekly,* 1935-40, and *Purpose* (quarterly), 1936-40; fiction critic, *Criterion,* 1936-39.

* * *

HAWLEY, Donald Thomas 1923-

PERSONAL: Born March 13, 1923, in St. Paul, Minn.; son of Donald Dewey and Ruth Lucille (Thomas) Hawley; mar-

ried Helen Weston Beasley, July 9, 1946; children: Cassandra June, Craig Scott, Shareen Renee. *Education:* Union College, Lincoln, Neb., B.A., 1950. *Home:* 1405 Colesberg St., Silver Spring, Md. 20904. *Office: Life and Health,* 6856 Eastern Ave. N.W., Washington, D.C. 20012.

CAREER: Ordained Seventh-day Adventist minister, 1955; Nebraska Book and Bible House, Lincoln, assistant manager, 1950-51; pastor of Seventh-day Adventist churches in Nebraska, 1951-56; Seventh-day Adventist Hospital, Karachi, Pakistan, chaplain, 1956-61; Hinsdale Sanitarium and Hospital, Hinsdale, Ill., director of public relations, 1961-63; Michigan Conference of Seventh-day Adventists, Lansing, director of communications, 1963-66; Greater New York Conference of Seventh-day Adventists, New York, N.Y., director of communications, 1966-71; *Life and Health,* Washington, D.C., managing editor, 1972-75, editor, 1975—. *Military service:* U.S. Navy, 1943-46; served in the South Pacific. *Member:* Rotary International.

WRITINGS: Pakistan Zindabad!, Pacific Press Publishing Association, 1960; *From Gangs to God,* Review & Herald, 1973; *Getting It All Together,* Review & Herald, 1974; *Come Alive!,* Review & Herald, 1975. Contributor to magazines.

WORK IN PROGRESS: Keeping It All Together.

AVOCATIONAL INTERESTS: Ham radio, caving.

* * *

HAY, John 1915-

PERSONAL: Born August 31, 1915, in Ipswich, Mass.; son of Clarence Leonard and Alice (Appleton) Hay; married Kristi Putnam, February 14, 1942; children: Susan, Katherine, Rebecca (deceased), Charles. *Education:* Harvard University, A.B., 1938. *Religion:* Episcopalian. *Residence:* Brewster, Mass. 02631.

CAREER: Charleston News & Courier, Charleston, S.C., Washington correspondent, 1939-40; writer, 1946—. Visiting professor at Dartmouth College, 1972, 1973, 1974, 1975, and 1976. President of board of directors of Cape Cod Museum of Natural History, 1956—; chairman of Brewster Conservation Commission, 1964-71. *Military service:* U.S. Army, 1940-45. *Member:* Phi Beta Kappa. *Awards, honors:* John Burroughs Medal, 1964, for *The Great Beach;* named conservationist of the year by Massachusetts Wildlife Federation, 1970.

WRITINGS: A Private History (poems), Duell, Sloan & Pearce, 1947; *The Run,* Doubleday, 1959, revised edition, 1965; *Nature's Year: The Seasons of Cape Cod,* Doubleday, 1961; (with Arline Strong) *A Sense of Nature,* Doubleday, 1962; *The Great Beach,* Doubleday, 1963; (with Peter Farb) *The Atlantic Shore: Human and Natural History from Long Island to Labrador,* Harper, 1966; *Sandy Shore,* Chatham Press, 1968; *Six Poems,* privately printed, 1969; *In Defense of Nature,* Little, Brown, 1970; *Spirit of Survival: A Natural and Personal History of Terns,* Dutton, 1974; (with Richard Kauffman) *The Primal Alliance: Earth and Ocean,* edited by Kenneth Brower, Friends of the Earth, 1974. Contributor of poems, articles, and reviews to magazines.

* * *

HAYDEN, Dolores 1945-

PERSONAL: Born March 15, 1945, in New York, N.Y.; daughter of J. Francis (an attorney) and Katharine (a social work administrator; maiden name, McCabe) Hayden; married James Campen (an economist), February 4, 1968 (divorced, 1971); married Peter Marris (a sociologist), April 18, 1975. *Education:* Mount Holyoke College, B.A. (magna cum laude), 1966; Girton College, Cambridge, diploma, 1967; Harvard University, M.Arch., 1972. *Office:* Department of Architecture, Massachusetts Institute of Technology, Cambridge, Mass. 02139.

CAREER: University of California, Berkeley, lecturer in architecture, 1973; Massachusetts Institute of Technology, Cambridge, assistant professor, 1973-76, associate professor, 1977—. *Awards, honors:* Farrand fellow, 1972; National Endowment for the Humanities fellow, 1976-77; Radcliffe Institute fellow, 1976-77.

WRITINGS: Seven American Utopias: The Architecture of Communitarian Socialism, 1790-1975, M.I.T. Press, 1976.

WORK IN PROGRESS: A history of feminist housing reform, 1840—; essays on architecture and politics in America; a study of the influence of Charles Fourier on American planning and design.

*   *   *

HAYES, Geoffrey   1947-

PERSONAL: Born December 3, 1947, in Pasadena, Calif.; son of Philip Dutton (a waiter) and Juliette (a secretary; maiden name, Dante) Hayes. *Education:* Attended John O'Connell Institute, San Francisco Academy of Art, and New York School of Visual Arts. *Home:* 316 East 83rd St., New York, N.Y. 10028. *Office:* Harper & Row Publishers, Inc., 10 East 53rd St., New York, N.Y. 10022.

CAREER: Harcourt, Brace, Jovanovich, Inc., New York City, clerk, 1966-69; Dun & Bradstreet, New York City, clerk, 1969-72; Merling, Marx & Seidman (advertising agency), New York City, in art department, 1972-73; Kajima International, New York City, interior designer, 1973-75; Harper & Row Publishers, Inc., New York City, artist and designer, 1975—.

WRITINGS: Bear by Himself (juvenile; self-illustrated), Harper, 1976; *The Alligator and His Uncle Tooth* (juvenile; self-illustrated), Harper, in press.

WORK IN PROGRESS: Illustrating *Seventeen Cats and One Kitten,* by Margaret Wise Brown, for Harper.

SIDELIGHTS: Hayes comments: "Writing and drawing have always come naturally to me. My brother and I, being only two years apart, channeled our creative energies into stories and books which we gave to one another. All the writing I do now is an extension and development of those early works. Many authors relive their past in their fiction, but while some (such as Proust) do so in autobiographical novels, I find fantasy not only the best form for expressing my feelings, but as viable as any literary genre."

*   *   *

HAYES, Wilson
See HARRIS, Kathryn (Beatrice) Gibbs

*   *   *

HAYN, Annette   1922-

PERSONAL: Born February 4, 1922, in Breslau, Germany; came to United States, 1940; naturalized citizen, 1946; daughter of Salo (a lawyer) and Susanne (a laboratory assistant; maiden name, Gottstein) Lewyn; married Gerald A. Hayn (a high school teacher), September 15, 1946 (deceased); children: Katherine Janet, Robert Charles, Deborah Leslie. *Education:* Brooklyn Jewish Hospital, R.N.,

1943; Teachers College, B.S., 1948; also attended New School of Social Research. *Home:* 228-18 Stronghurst Ave., Queens Village, N.Y. 11427.

CAREER: Registered nurse with Presbyterian Hospital Medical Center, 1944-45, and part-time nurse, 1946-47, both in New York City; public school creative-writing volunteer teacher, Harlem, N.Y., 1963-72; participant in New York State Poets-in-the-Schools Program, 1974—. *Awards, honors:* Bernice Kavinsky Isacson award from New School of Social Research, 1969, for poem, "City Street."

WRITINGS: Rapunzel, Fiddlehead Poetry Books, 1971; *One Armed Flyer,* Poet's Press, 1976.

Play: "Incident on Madison Avenue" (one act), first performed in Jamaica, N.Y., at St. Mary Magdalene Church, March 5, 1973. Also author of "The Destruction of Delilah" (two act), 1969, and "Plastic Daisies" (one act), 1973, both as yet neither published nor produced.

WORK IN PROGRESS: Carousel Poems, a book of poems dealing mostly with circles, or things coming back to where they began.

SIDELIGHTS: Annette Hayn told *CA:* "I became completely obsessed with writing rather late, when my children were almost grown. I was influenced by Kenneth Koch, William Carlos Williams, and lately by the Swedish poet Tomas Transtromer. I have also helped children to write and perform their own plays, and some of these plays have been published. . . ."

AVOCATIONAL INTERESTS: Directing and acting.

*   *   *

HAYNES, Glynn W(alker)   1936-

PERSONAL: Born September 6, 1936, in Shongaloo, La.; son of Curtis L. (a construction supervisor) and Valorie (McEachern) Haynes; married Dolores Ann Kramel (a secretary), August 15, 1964. *Education:* Northeast Louisiana University, B.S., 1971. *Religion:* Baptist. *Home:* 212 Quail Lane, Wake Village, Tex. 75501. *Office:* International Paper Co., Texarkana Mill, Texarkana, Tex. 75501.

CAREER: J. E. Sirrine Co., Greenville, N.C., quality control engineer, 1971-72; Red Lobster Inns of America, Orlando, Fla., project manager, 1972-73; International Paper Co., Texarkana, Tex., construction superintendent, 1973—. *Military service:* U.S. Air Force, 1959-62. *Member:* American Paint Horse Association, Louisiana Paint Horse Association (director).

WRITINGS: The American Paint Horse, University of Oklahoma Press, 1976. Contributor to horsemen's journals.

WORK IN PROGRESS: Early Paint Racing Horses; Paint Horse Foundation Sires.

SIDELIGHTS: Haynes writes that he was born on a farm where raising and riding horses was a very big part of his life. During high school he participated in Louisiana rodeos, until he was injured when thrown from a bucking horse. His book began as a leisure-time project, and eventually took six years to write. *Avocational interests:* Collecting books and magazines on western horses.

*   *   *

HEAD, (Joanne) Lee   1931-

PERSONAL: Born March 3, 1931, in Bartlesville, Okla.; daughter of G. W. and Frances (Aurandt) Price; married John V. Head, March 28, 1953 (terminated, November, 1971); children: Stephanie (Mrs. Dave Hargrove), Tracy

(Mrs. Bill Nichols), Cynthia. *Education:* Rockford College, student, 1949-50; University of Oklahoma, B.A., 1953; Oklahoma State University, M.A. (cum laude), 1961. *Residence:* Santa Fe, N.M. *Agent:* Roberta Kent, W. B. Agency, 155 East 56th St., New York, N.Y. 10022. *Office:* Investment Realty, 504 Jose, Santa Fe, N.M. 87501.

CAREER: Writer. Instructor at Oklahoma State University, 1954-58 and 1960-62; chairman of legal research for Oklahoma Commission on the Status of Women, 1963-64; worked for Russian countess, 1973-74; Investment Realty, Santa Fe, N.M., secretary and agent, 1976—. *Member:* Mystery Writers of America.

WRITINGS—Novels: *The First of January,* Putnam, 1974; *The Terrarium,* Putnam, 1976; *The Crystal Clear Case,* Putnam, in press. Creator of the ballets "Tapestries," produced by New York City ballet in Oklahoma City, 1975, and "White Moon, Blue Sun," 1976, to be produced in Oklahoma City. Contributor to magazines, including *Ladies' Home Journal.*

* * *

HEAD, Sydney W(arren) 1913-

PERSONAL: Born October 9, 1913, in England; came to the United States in 1920, naturalized citizen; married Dorothy Mack. *Education:* Stanford University, A.B., 1936, M.A., 1937; New York University, Ph.D., 1952. *Office:* Department of Radio-Television-Film, Temple University, Philadelphia, Pa. 19122.

CAREER: University of Miami, Coral Gables, Fla., 1938-61, began as instructor, became professor of radio-television-film; African American Institute, Addis Ababa, Ethiopia, regional representative and media consultant, 1962-64; RTV International, Addis Ababa, Ethiopia, chief of government media advisory team, 1964-69; Temple University, Philadelphia, Pa., professor of communications, 1970—. Fulbright Professor at University of Ghana, 1976-77. Broadcasting consultant in Ethiopia and the Sudan. *Military service:* U.S. Army, 1942-45. *Member:* International Broadcast Institute, National Association of Educational Broadcasters, Association for Education in Journalism, Broadcasting Education Association.

WRITINGS: Broadcasting in America, Houghton, 1952, 3rd revised edition, 1976; *Broadcasting in Africa,* Temple University Press, 1974.

WORK IN PROGRESS: Research on British colonial broadcasting policies, and on broadcasting as a patron of indigenous culture in developing countries.

* * *

HEARN, Janice W. 1938-

PERSONAL: Born March 19, 1938, in Warren, Ohio; daughter of Myron J. (an electrician) and Gertrude (Heintz) Walter; married Neal E. Hearn (an industrial engineering manager), September 12, 1959; children: Steven, Diane, Sharon. *Education:* Mount Union College, B.S., 1960; also studied at University of Oklahoma and San Diego State University. *Politics:* "Basically Republican." *Religion:* Presbyterian. *Home:* 5633 Carnegie St., San Diego, Calif. 92122.

CAREER: Timken Mercy Hospital, Canton, Ohio, medical technologist, 1961-66; Pathology Laboratory, Canton, Ohio, medical technologist, 1966-68; Palmer Laboratory, La Jolla, Calif., medical technologist, 1969; Scripps Memorial Hospital, La Jolla, Calif., medical technologist, 1973—. *Member:* National League of American Pen Women.

WRITINGS: Peace with the Restless Me, Word Books, 1976. Work represented in anthologies. Contributor of articles and poems to church magazines, and to *Hyacinths and Biscuits* and *Tennis U.S.A.* Former editor of local church publication, *Presbyterian.*

WORK IN PROGRESS: A book on community in the church.

SIDELIGHTS: Janice Hearn writes: "Probably most interesting is that I was not a writer, and had no idea that I *could* write, until I became a Christian in 1969. My first article was written in the middle of the night, and sold to *Today's Christian Mother.* I see my writing as part of the potential I'm discovering in being God's person. . . . I enjoy writing humor articles, mostly about my children. So far, I've only collected rejection slips on these articles! Most of my poetry is written for fun, also. I like playing with words."

AVOCATIONAL INTERESTS: Cooking, sewing, needlepoint, decorating, playing tennis, bicycling for exercise, reading.

BIOGRAPHICAL/CRITICAL SOURCES: Bookstore Journal, May, 1976.

* * *

HEARNDEN, Arthur (George) 1931-

PERSONAL: Born December 15, 1931, in Belfast, Northern Ireland; son of Hugh William (a manager of an insurance company) and Violet (Frazer) Hearnden; married Josephine Honor McNeill (a teacher), August 25, 1962; children: Barney, Louise, Anna. *Education:* Christ's College, Cambridge, B.A., 1952, M.A., 1956; Wadham College, Oxford, D.Phil., 1970. *Home:* Courtyard House, Oakley Park, Frilord Heath Oxford OX13 6QW, England. *Office:* Standing Conference on University Entrance, 29 Tavistock Sq., London WC1H 9EZ, England.

CAREER: Foreign language teacher in secondary schools in Northern Ireland, England, France, and Germany, 1952-68; Oxford University, Oxford, England, research officer in department of education, 1968-70; University of London, London, England, lecturer at Institute of Education, 1971-73; Standing Conference on University Entrance, London, secretary, 1973—. *Military service:* British Army, Royal Signal Corps, 1955-57; became second lieutenant.

WRITINGS: Paths to the University: Preparation, Assessment, Selection, Macmillan, 1973; *Bildungspolitik in der BRD und DDR,* Schwann, 1973, translation published as *Education in the Two Germanies,* Basil Blackwell, 1974, Westview Press, 1976; (contributor) P. R. Cox, H. B. Miles, and John Peel, editors *Equalities and Inequalities in Education,* Academic Press, 1975; *Education, Culture, and Politics in West Germany,* Pergamon, 1976; (editor) *The British in Germany: Educational Reconstruction after 1945,* Hamish Hamilton, in press; (contributor) Brian Holmes and Ray Jackson, editors, *Education in Europe,* Wiley, in press; (contributor) Edmund King, editor, *Reorganizing Education,* Sage Publications, Inc., in press. Contributor to education journals.

* * *

HEDDEN, Walter Page 1898(?)-1976

1898(?)—July 24, 1976; American port authority director, transportation consultant, and author. Obituaries: *New York Times,* July 26, 1976.

HEGARTY, Walter 1922-

PERSONAL: Born November 10, 1922, in Derry, Northern Ireland; son of George Joseph (a company secretary) and Teresa (Gillespie) Hegarty; married Mollie Dickson, January 27, 1947 (deceased); children: Maura, Denise, Marese, Walter, Patricia, Vera. *Education:* Attended secondary school in Derry, Northern Ireland. *Politics:* "Left of centre, liberal." *Religion:* Roman Catholic. *Home:* Inishowen, Evora Park, Howth, County Dublin, Ireland. *Agent:* London Management, Regent St., London W1A 2J7, England. *Office:* Walter Hegarty & Associates, 79 Upper Dorset St., Dublin 1, Ireland.

CAREER: Worked at Bank of Ireland, 1942-70; *Northern Standard,* Monaghan, Ireland, columnist, 1968—; Walter Hegarty & Associates, Dublin, Ireland, property and finance consultant, 1970—. *Member:* International P.E.N., National Library of Scotland.

WRITINGS: The Price of Chips, Davis-Poynter, 1973; *You Can't Get There from Here,* Davis-Poynter, 1975. Author of a financial advice series in *Irish Press.* Contributor to Irish newspapers.

WORK IN PROGRESS: An Age for Fortunes, a novel, for Coward; the first of four long historical novels in a family series, set in Derry, Northern Ireland, 1840-1900.

SIDELIGHTS: Hegarty comments that his main reason for writing is "anger at injustices enforced either by law or custom," especially as they apply to the under-privileged. *Avocational interests:* Theater, bridge, chess, swimming, languages.

*   *   *

HEIDEGGER, Martin 1889-1976

September 26, 1889—May 26, 1976; German philosopher, ontologist, theologian, educator, and writer. Obituaries: *New York Times,* May 27, 1976; *Washington Post,* May 27, 1976; *Detroit Free Press,* May 27, 1976; *Time,* June 7, 1976; *Newsweek,* June 7, 1976; *Current Biography,* July, 1976.

*   *   *

HEIMAN, Marcel 1909-1976

August 17, 1909—June 14, 1976; Austrian-born American psychiatrist, neurologist, educator, and author of books in his field. Obituaries: *New York Times,* June 16, 1976.

*   *   *

HEISENBERG, Werner 1901-1976

December 5, 1901—February 1, 1976; German physicist, educator, research institute director, and author. Obituaries: *New York Times,* February 2, 1976.

*   *   *

HELLER, Bernard 1896-1976

1896—May 6, 1976; Ukrainian-born American theologian, educator, and author. Obituaries: *New York Times,* May 7, 1976.

*   *   *

HELMERING, Doris Wild 1942-

PERSONAL: Born October 22, 1942, in St. Louis, Mo.; daughter of Wilmar John (a machinist) and Doris (Stuckey) Wild; married Raymond Joseph Helmering (a scientist), June 13, 1964; children: John William, Paul Frederick. *Edu-*

cation: St. Louis University, B.S., 1964, M.S.W., 1968. *Religion:* Roman Catholic. *Office:* 200 South Hanley, Suite 512, St. Louis, Mo. 63105.

CAREER: Family Service Agency, West Lafayette, Indiana, caseworker, 1968-70; psychotherapist in private practice in St. Louis, Mo., 1970—. Practicum instructor at Washington University, St. Louis, Mo., 1972—. *Member:* International Transactional Analysis Association (clinical member).

WRITINGS: Group Therapy: Who Needs It, Celestial Arts, 1976; (contributor) Muriel James, editor, *Techniques and Transactional Analysis for Psychotherapists and Counselors,* Addison-Wesley, 1976.

WORK IN PROGRESS: We Are Going to Have a Baby, a juvenile, for Abingdon; a book on raising children; a series of three books for Spanish-American children.

AVOCATIONAL INTERESTS: Remodeling a large old home.

*   *   *

HELMREICH, Robert Louis 1937-

PERSONAL: Born April 29, 1937, in Kansas City, Kan.; son of Ralph Louis (an American Telephone and Telegraph executive) and Caroline (Shertz) Helmreich. *Education:* Yale University, B.A., 1959, M.S., 1965, Ph.D., 1966. *Home:* 3811 West Lake Dr., Austin, Tex. 78746. *Office:* Department of Psychology, University of Texas, Austin, Tex. 78712.

CAREER: University of Texas, Austin, assistant professor, 1966-69, associate professor, 1969-73, professor of psychology, 1973—. President, Robert Helmreich, Inc. (psychological consulting), Austin, Tex., 1973—. *Military service:* U.S. Navy, 1959-63; became lieutenant. *Member:* American Psychological Association, American Association for the Advancement of Science, Phi Beta Kappa, Sigma Xi, Yale Club of Austin, Austin Yacht Club. *Awards, honors:* Woodrow Wilson fellow, 1959; National Aeronautics and Space Administration grant, 1972-73.

WRITINGS: (With Roland Radloff) *Groups under Stress: Psychological Research in Sealab II,* Appleton, 1968; (contributor) J. W. Miller, J. Vanderwalker, and R. Waller, editors, *Tektite 2: Scientists in the Sea,* U.S. Government Printing Office, 1971; (contributor) Bert King and Elliot McGinnies, editors, *Attitudes, Conflict and Social Change,* Academic Press, 1972; (editor with Elliot Aronson) *Social Psychology,* Van Nostrand, 1973. Contributor to psychological journals.

WORK IN PROGRESS: Studies on group behavior, sex-roles and their acquisition, physical attractiveness, and creativity.

*   *   *

HENDERSON, C(harles) William 1925-

PERSONAL: Born July 20, 1925, in San Francisco, Calif.; son of Charles William (a physician) and Vivien (Hart) Henderson. *Education:* University of California, Berkeley, B.A. (architecture), 1949, M.A., 1950; University of California, Santa Cruz, B.A. (psychology; honors), 1975. *Home:* 24764 Soquel Rd., Los Gatos, Calif. 95030.

CAREER: Staff architect in Macon, Ga., and Los Angeles, Calif., 1950-59; Douglas Aircraft Co., Santa Monica, Calif., advance systems engineer, 1959-63; National Aeronautics and Space Administration (NASA) Headquarters, Washington, D.C., head of lunar base planning, 1963-66; Lockheed Missiles and Space Co., Sunnyvale, Calif., lunar systems engineer, 1966-68; self-employed, 1968—. *Military service:* U.S. Navy, 1944-46. *Member:* Association of Humanistic Psychology, Association of Transpersonal Psychology, American Mensa Ltd., Kappa Alpha Order.

WRITINGS: Awakening: Ways to Psycho-Spiritual Growth, Prentice-Hall, 1975. Contributor to aerospace journals.

WORK IN PROGRESS: Contributing a chapter on meditation to *New Ways of Growth,* edited by Herbert Otto and Roberta Otto.

AVOCATIONAL INTERESTS: Painting, traveling.

* * *

HENDERSON, Vivian (Wilson) 1923-1976

PERSONAL: Born February 10, 1923, in Bristol, Tenn.; son of William Thomas and Sallie (Richmond) Henderson; married Anna Powell, September 8, 1949; children: Wyonella Marie, Dwight Cedric, David Wayne, Kimberly Ann. *Education:* North Carolina Central University, B.S., 1947; University of Iowa, M.A., 1948, Ph.D., 1952. *Religion:* United Methodist. *Residence:* Atlanta, Ga.

CAREER: Prairie View College, Prairie View, Tex., instructor in economics, 1948-49; Fisk University, Nashville, Tenn., professor of economics and chairman of department, 1952-65; Clark College, Atlanta, Ga., president, 1965-76. Visiting professor at North Carolina State University, Raleigh, 1962-64; lectured in Brazil. Director of Citizens and Southern Bank, 1972-76. Former member of U.S. National Commission to UNESCO, Southern Regional Council (past president), and National Urban Coalition. Former trustee of National Bureau of Economic Research, Ford Foundation, and Teachers Insurance and Annuity Association. *Military service:* U.S. Army, 1943-46.

MEMBER: American Economic Association, American Academy of Arts and Sciences, Black Academy of Arts and Letters, National Association for the Advancement of Colored People, Urban League, Alpha Kappa Mu, Omicron Delta Epsilon, Kappa Alpha Psi. *Awards, honors:* Distinguished service award from Teachers College, at Columbia University, 1970.

WRITINGS: The Economic Status of Negroes: In the Nation and in the South, Southern Regional Council, 1963; (with Herman Hodge Long) *Negro Employment in Tennessee State Government: A Report from Nashville Community Conference on Employment Opportunity,* Tennessee Council on Human Relations, 1962. Also author of *The Economic Imbalance; Economic Dimensions in Race Relations; Economic Opportunity and Negro Education; The Economic Status of Negroes; The Advancing South; Employment, Race, and Poverty;* and *Negro Colleges Face the Future.*

SIDELIGHTS: Henderson devoted his career to the study of economics as it applied to blacks in the United States and the impact of economics on the poor in general.

OBITUARIES: New York Times, January 29, 1976; *Washington Post,* January 30, 1976; *Time,* February 9, 1976.*

(Died January 28, 1976, in Atlanta, Ga.)

* * *

HENLEY, Wallace (Boynton) 1941-

PERSONAL: Born December 5, 1941, in Birmingham,

Ala.; son of Wallace Boynton and Wilfred (Vassar) Henley; married Mary Irene Lambert, September 4, 1961; children: Mary Lauri, Travis Wallace. *Education:* Samford University, B.A., 1964; Southwestern Baptist Theological Seminary, graduate study, 1964-65. *Home:* 7 Cavalry Charge, Spanish Fort, Ala.

CAREER: Ordained Baptist minister, 1962; associate pastor of Baptist church in Birmingham, Ala., 1963, minister of youth education in Fort Worth, Tex., 1964-66, pastor in Nuremberg, West Germany, 1966; Mobile College, Mobile, Ala., director of public relations, 1966-68; *Birmingham News,* Birmingham, Ala., religion editor and editorial writer, 1968-70; Cabinet Committee on Education, Washington, D.C., assistant director, 1970-71; staff assistant to the President of the United States, in Washington, D.C., 1971-73; Old Spanish Fort Baptist Church, Mobile, Ala., pastor, 1973—. Host of "Know Your News," on Alabama Educational Television Network, 1968-69.

MEMBER: Birmingham Press Club, Sigma Delta Chi. *Awards, honors:* R. S. Reynolds Award from the Presbyterian Church in the United States, 1969, for excellence in religion journalism; Green Eyeshade Award from Atlanta chapter of Sigma Delta Chi, 1970, for writing on the evolution of Birmingham's race relations; award from Alabama Associated Press, 1973, for a study of a changing suburb of Birmingham.

WRITINGS: Enter at Your Own Risk, Revell, 1974; *The White House Mystique,* Revell, 1976; (contributor) Frank Mead, editor, *Tarbell's Teacher's Guide,* Revell, 1976; *Missionaries To the Almighty,* Good News, in press. Contributor to church magazines.

WORK IN PROGRESS: A study of Christians and the mass media.

SIDELIGHTS: Religious work has taken Henley to Central America, Europe, and Asia. He is also one of the people who helped to organize the White House prayer breakfast.

* * *

HENSLEY, (Malcolm) Stewart 1914(?)-1976

1914(?)—February 15, 1976; American news correspondent and editor. Obituaries: *Washington Post,* February 16, 1976.

* * *

HERBERT, Theodore T(erence) 1942-

PERSONAL: Born September 10, 1942, in Kinston, N.C.; son of Frank Ellis (in the U.S. Marine Corps) and Jeanne (Chmielewski) Herbert; married Janice Summers (an owner of oriental rug business), December 14, 1968; children: Russell Allen. *Education:* Georgia State University, B.B.A., 1967, M.B.A., 1968, D.B.A., 1971. *Politics:* Republican. *Religion:* Episcopal. *Home:* 3121 Athens Rd., Silver Lake, Cuyahoga Falls, Ohio 44224. *Office:* Department of Management, University of Akron, Akron, Ohio 44325.

CAREER: University of Texas, Arlington, assistant professor of management, 1970-73; University of Akron, Akron, Ohio, associate professor of management, 1973—. Program analyst at George C. Marshall Space Flight Center, 1971. *Member:* American Institute of Decision Sciences, National Association of Management Educators, Academy of Management (chairman of Management Education and Development Division, 1977-78), Southern Management Association, Beta Gamma Sigma, Sigma Iota Epsilon. *Awards, honors:* Apollo Eleven Medallion from National Aeronautics and Space Administration, 1971.

WRITINGS: Exploring the New Management, Macmillan, 1974, revised edition, in press; *Dimensions of Organizational Behavior,* Macmillan, 1976; (editor) *Organizational Behavior: Readings and Cases,* Macmillan, 1976; (with E. B. Yost) *The ATWAM Scale* (monograph), University of Akron, 1976; *Management Education and Development,* Blue Hill Publishing, in press.

Contributor to business and management journals. Editor of *Newsletter* of Management Education and Development Division of the Academy of Management; associate editor of *Akron Business and Economic Review.*

WORK IN PROGRESS: Management Foundations, publication expected in 1978; research on barriers to women as effective managers, group decision-making effectiveness, leadership correlates, educational innovations, and effectiveness of graduate business education.

SIDELIGHTS: Herbert writes: "My wife is writing a book on oriental rugs, and I've been privileged to help her and learn about a most interesting and complex subject; a trip to Iran is in the offing to further explore her interests."

* * *

HERMAN, A(rthur) L(udwig) 1930-

PERSONAL: Born November 16, 1930, in Minneapolis, Minn.; son of Arthur L. (a surgeon) and Helen (Sorlie) Herman; married Barbara Flaaten (a teacher), May 12, 1956; children: Arthur L., Helen A. *Education:* University of Minnesota, B.A., 1952, M.A., 1958, Ph.D., 1970; also attended Stanford University, 1960-61, and Harvard University, 1961-63. *Office:* Department of Philosophy, University of Wisconsin, Stevens Point, Wis. 54481.

CAREER: University of Florida, Gainesville, instructor in philosophy, 1957-60; Hamilton College, Clinton, N.Y., instructor in philosophy, 1963-65; University of Wisconsin, Stevens Point, assistant professor, 1965-71, associate professor, 1971-72, professor of philosophy, 1973—. St. Thomas Aquinas lecturer at Mount Mary College, Milwaukee, Wis., 1975; visiting professor at University of Minnesota, 1976; lecturer at Clarke College, 1976. *Wartime service:* Alternative service as psychiatric aide, 1953-55. *Awards, honors:* Ford Foundation overseas training fellowship, 1962-63.

WRITINGS: (Editor and translator from Sanskrit) *Indian Folk Tales,* Peter Pauper, 1968; *The Bhagavad Gita: A Translation and Critical Commentary,* C. C Thomas, 1973; (editor with Russell T. Blackwood) *Problems in Philosophy: East and West,* Prentice-Hall, 1975; *The Problem of Evil and Indian Thought,* Motilal Banarsidass, 1976; *An Introduction to Indian Thought,* Prentice-Hall, 1976. Author of three tape recordings on Indian Yoga, for Center for Cassette Studies, 1973. Contributor of more than thirty-five articles and reviews to scholarly journals.

WORK IN PROGRESS: An Introduction to Buddhist Thought.

* * *

HERZBERG, Joseph Gabriel 1907-1976

January 1, 1907—February 12, 1976; American news editor, correspondent, and educator. Obituaries: *New York Times,* February 14, 1976.

* * *

HESS, Beth B(owman)

PERSONAL: Born in Buffalo, N.Y.; daughter of Albert A. (an advertising executive) and Yetta (a social worker; maiden name, Lurie) Bowman; married Richard C. Hess (a businessman), April 26, 1953; children: Laurence Albert, Emily Frances. *Education:* Radcliffe College, B.A. (magna cum laude), 1950; Rutgers University, M.A., 1966, Ph.D., 1970. *Politics:* Democrat. *Religion:* Jewish. *Home:* 17 Pepperidge Rd., Morristown, N.J. *Office:* Department of Social Science, County College of Morris, Dover, N.J.

CAREER: County College of Morris, Dover, N.J., assistant professor, 1969-73 associate professor of social science, 1973—. *Member:* American Sociological Association, Sociologists for Women in Society, National Council on Family Relations, Society for the Study of Social Problems, Gerontological Society, Gerontological Society of New Jersey.

WRITINGS: (With Matilda White Riley and Anne Foner) *Aging and Society,* Volume I, Russell Sage Foundation, 1968; (contributor) Riley, Foner, and Marilyn Johnson, editors, *Aging and Society,* Volume III, Russell Sage Foundation, 1971; (editor) *Growing Old in America,* Transaction Books, 1976. Contributor to *Handbook of Socialization Theory and Research,* and to communications and social studies journals.

WORK IN PROGRESS: Research on parent-child relationships in later life, and on friendship patterns of middle-aged women.

SIDELIGHTS: Dr. Hess writes: "It seems that the theme which best describes my adulthood, as is probably the case for most achieving women today, is 'balance'; that is, managing the demands of scholarship, teaching, parenthood and marriage. This has been a richly rewarding mix; one which I hope will increasingly characterize the lives of both men and women.

I have also sought to balance my commitment to sociology with an obligation to social activism. My biography in this respect is no doubt similar to that of most academics my age: active involvement at the community level in the major movements of the last two decades: civil liberties, civil rights, antiwar, and the feminist movement.

Admittedly, this balancing act can strain one's abilities and energies; to achieve all one wishes in all these roles is perhaps impossible. So, while there is much that I regret not doing better, there is little to which I would not commit myself again."

* * *

HEYWARD, Carter 1945-

PERSONAL: Born August 22, 1945, in Charlotte, N.C.; daughter of Robert C., Jr. (a salesman for an oil company) and Mary Ann (Carter) Heyward. *Education:* Randolph-Macon Women's College, A.B., 1967; Union Theological Seminary, M.Div., 1968, further graduate study, 1970-74; Columbia University, M.A., 1971. *Politics:* Democrat. *Religion:* Episcopal. *Office:* Episcopal Divinity School, 99 Brattle St., Cambridge, Mass. 02138.

CAREER: Parish assistant at Episcopal church in Charlotte, N.C., 1968-70; educational resources teacher in Charlotte, N.C., 1970; Emergency Shelter, New York, N.Y., psycho-therapist, 1971-72; Union Theological Seminary, New York, N.Y., lecturer in Practical Theology, 1973-75; Episcopal Divinity School, Cambridge, Mass., assistant professor of theology, 1975—.

WRITINGS: A Priest Forever: The Formation of a Woman and a Priest, Harper, 1976.

WORK IN PROGRESS: A television film script based on A Priest Forever; research on images of God, human sexuality, and women in mythology and religion.

SIDELIGHTS: Carter Heyward writes: "I believe contemporary Western religion, especially Judaeo-Christian, to be in throes of rebirth; and I believe this rebirth is being brought about by the *feminism* emerging in the midst of institutional religion. It is to this movement—feminism in Christianity—that I am fully and radically committed—and to the probing of the various tangential 'issues': family and lifestyle; human sexuality (including homosexuality); abortion; economic distribution to the benefit of *all* humankind; creation of deep-flowing religion."

* * *

HEYWORTH, Peter (Lawrence Frederick) 1921-

PERSONAL: Born June 3, 1921, in New York, N.Y.; son of Lawrence Ormerod and Ellie (Stern) Heyworth. *Education:* Balliol College, Oxford, B.A. (honors), 1950; attended University of Goettingen, 1950. *Home:* 32 Bryanston Sq., London W1H 7LS, England. *Office: Observer,* London, England.

CAREER: *Times Educational Supplement,* London, England, music critic, 1950-55; *Observer,* London, music critic, 1955—. *Military service:* British Army, Royal Artillery, 1940-46. *Awards, honors:* Guest of the Ford Foundation in Berlin, Germany, 1964-65.

WRITINGS: (Editor) *Berlioz, Romantic and Classic: Writings by Ernest Newman,* Gollancz, 1972, Humanities, 1974; (editor) *Conversations with Klemperer,* Gollancz, 1973, International Publications Service, 1974. Contributor to music magazines and newspapers. Record critic for *New Statesman,* 1956-59.

SIDELIGHTS: Heyworth writes that he has a "special interest in the borderline between music and politics" with a "subordinate interest in the difference between the nations of Europe." He has traveled extensively in Europe, including Poland and the Soviet Union. *Avocational interests:* Wine.

* * *

HIBBS, Ben 1901-

PERSONAL: Born July 23, 1901, in Fontana, Kan.; son of Russell (a retail lumber merchant) and Elizabeth (Smith) Hibbs; married Edith Kathleen Doty (a teacher), June 3, 1930; children: Stephen Doty. *Education:* University of Kansas, A.B., 1923. *Politics:* Republican. *Religion:* Methodist. *Home:* 737 Braeburn Lane, Penn Valley, Narberth, Pa. 19072.

CAREER: *Fort Morgan Times,* Fort Morgan, Colo., news editor, 1923; *Pratt Tribune,* Pratt, Kan., news editor, 1924; Hays State College, Hays, Kan., professor of journalism, 1924-26; *Goodland News-Republic,* Goodland, Kan., editor and manager, 1926-27; *Arkansas City Traveler,* Arkansas City, Kan., managing editor, 1927-29; Curtis Publishing Co., Philadelphia, Pa., associate editor of *Country Gentleman,* 1929-40, editor, 1940-42, editor of *Saturday Evening Post,* 1942-61, senior editor, 1962, member of executive committee of publishing company, 1940-61; *Reader's Digest,* Pleasantville, N.Y., senior editor, 1963-72. Member of U.S. Advisory Commission on Information, 1951-54.

MEMBER: Phi Beta Kappa, Sigma Delta Chi, Sigma Phi Epsilon, Merion Cricket Club. *Awards, honors:* D.Litt., Northwestern University, 1947, Temple University, 1948,

Southwestern College, 1964; journalism award from University of Pennsylvania, 1947; national award for journalistic merit from William Allen White Foundation, 1959; George Washington Medal from Freedoms Foundation, 1963; School Bell Award from National Education Association, 1964.

WRITINGS: *Two Men on a Job: A Behind-the-Scenes Story of a Rowdy Genius and His Mentor,* Curtis Publishing Co., 1938; (author of foreword) *Post Stories, 1942-45,* Random House, 1946; (editor) *Great Stories from the Saturday Evening Post, 1947,* Bantam, 1948; *Some Thoughts on Magazine Editing,* William Allen White Foundation, 1959; *White House Sermons* (introduction by Richard M. Nixon), Harper, 1972; (editor) *A Michener Miscellany, 1950-1970,* Random House, 1973. Contributor to popular magazines.

* * *

HICKMAN, Janet 1940-

PERSONAL: Born July 8, 1940, in Kilbourne, Ohio; daughter of Bernard Franklin (a plumber) and Pauline (Williams) Gephart; married John D. Hickman (a teacher), January 14, 1961; children: John H., Holly. *Education:* Ohio State University, B.Sc., 1960, M.A.Ed., 1964, currently enrolled in doctoral program. *Religion:* Presbyterian. *Home:* 356 Gudrun Rd., Columbus, Ohio 43202.

CAREER: Junior high school teacher in public schools of Whitehall, Ohio, 1961-64; Ohio State University, Columbus, part time instructor in children's literature, 1968-73; researcher for textbook authors.

WRITINGS—Juveniles: *The Valley of the Shadow,* Macmillan, 1974; *The Stones,* Macmillan, 1976. Contributor to *Ohio Reading Teacher,* and to *Ingenue* and *Teen* magazine.

WORK IN PROGRESS: A juvenile novel, tentatively titled *Zoar Blue;* research on the history of the German Separatists settlement at Zoar Village, Ohio, and other Ohio historical facts.

* * *

HICKMAN, Martin B(erkeley) 1925-

PERSONAL: Born May 16, 1925, in Utah; married JoAnn Emmett; children: Allison, Patricia, Heather, Betsy, Melissa, Ann. *Education:* University of Utah, B.S. (honors), 1951, M.A., 1952, Ph.D., 1954; Harvard University, M. Public Administration, 1960. *Religion:* Church of Jesus Christ of Latter-day Saints (Mormons). *Office:* College of Social Sciences, 164 F.O.B., Brigham Young University, Provo, Utah 84601.

CAREER: Missionary of the Church of Jesus Christ of Latter-day Saints in France, 1947-49; U.S. Department of State, Washington, D.C., consular and economic officer in Hamburg, Germany, 1954-56, consul and economic officer in Hong Kong, 1956-59, German area specialist at Harvard University, 1959-60, economic officer in Eastern affairs section of U.S. Mission to Berlin, Germany, 1960-61; University of Southern California, Los Angeles, associate professor of international relations, 1961-67, coordinator of International Public Administration Program, 1961-65, resident professor in London Program, 1966; Brigham Young University, Provo, Utah, professor of political science, 1967—, dean of College of Social Sciences, 1970—. Participated in National Strategy Conference, 1970; visiting professor at University of Southern California, summers, 1970 and 1973, and spring, 1973; chairman of Utah County Local Government Study Commission, 1974-76; consultant to

U.S. Agency for International Development and Systems Development Corp. *Military service:* U.S. Army, Infantry, 1944-46; served in European theater.

MEMBER: International Studies Association (member of executive committee of West section, 1967-68), American Political Science Association, Western Political Science Association, Utah Academy of Letters, Arts and Sciences, Phi Kappa Phi.

WRITINGS: Problems of American Foreign Policy, Glencoe Press, 1968, 2nd edition, 1975; *The Military and American Society,* Glencoe Press, 1971; (contributor) Truman Madsen, editor, *For the Glory of God,* Deseret, 1972. Contributor to academic journals.

WORK IN PROGRESS: Research on Constitutional law.

* * *

HICKS, George L(eon) 1935-

PERSONAL: Born May 4, 1935, in Panama City, Fla.; son of George L. (a carpenter) and Lillian (Roberts) Hicks; married Linne Hall, April 23, 1954; children: Martha Elizabeth (Mrs. William S. Coleman, Jr.), Leslie Douglas. *Education:* Florida State University, B.A., 1960; University of California, Berkeley, M.A., 1961; University of Illinois, Ph.D., 1969. *Politics:* Democrat. *Religion:* "Heathen." *Home:* 48 Montague St., Providence, R.I. 02906. *Office:* Department of Anthropology, Brown University, Providence, R.I. 02912.

CAREER: University of North Carolina, Chapel Hill, archaeologist's assistant at Research Laboratories for Anthropology, 1961-62; Brown University, Providence, R.I., assistant professor, 1967-72, associate professor of anthropology, 1972—. *Military service:* U.S. Army, 1954-57; served in Germany. *Member:* American Anthropological Association (fellow), American Ethnological Society, Southern Anthropological Society. *Awards, honors:* Woodrow Wilson fellowship, 1960-61; National Endowment for the Humanities fellowship, 1975; National Science Foundation faculty fellowship, 1976.

WRITINGS: (Contributor) David W. Plath, editor, *Aware of Utopia,* University of Illinois, 1971; *Appalachian Valley,* Holt, 1976; (editor with Philip E. Leis, and contributor) *Ethnic Encounters,* Duxbury, 1977.

WORK IN PROGRESS: Research on sex roles and family structure among immigrants from the Azore Islands to the United States and Canada and on the relationship of utopianism and ethnicity.

* * *

HICKS, John (Richard) 1904-

PERSONAL: Born in 1904; son of Edward and Dorothy Catharine Hicks; married Ursula K. Webb, 1935; *Education:* Balliol College, Oxford, student, 1922-26, B.A., 1925; University of London, D.Sc., 1932. *Office:* All Souls College, Oxford University, Oxford OX1 4AL, England.

CAREER: University of London, London School of Economics and Political Science, London, England, lecturer in economics, 1926-35; Cambridge University, Cambridge, England, fellow of Gonville & Caius College, 1935-38; University of Manchester, Manchester, England, professor of political economy, 1938-46; Oxford University, Oxford, England, official fellow of Nuffield College, 1946-52, Drummond Professor of Political Economy, 1952-65, fellow of All Souls College, 1952—. Member of Nigeria Revenue Alloca-

tion Committee, 1950, and Royal Commission on the Taxation of Profits and Income, 1951.

MEMBER: British Academy (fellow), Royal Economic Society (president, 1962), Swedish Academy, Italian Academy, American Academy. *Awards, honors:* Knighted in 1964; honorary fellow of London School of Economics and Political Science, 1969, and Gonville & Caius College, Cambridge, 1971; Nobel Prize for Economics, 1972, for contributions to General Equilibrium theory and welfare economics.

WRITINGS: The Theory of Wages, Macmillan, 1932, 2nd edition, 1963, St. Martin's, 1964; *Value and Capital: An Inquiry into Some Fundamental Principles of Economic Theory,* Clarendon Press, 1939, 2nd edition, 1946; (with wife, Ursula K. Hicks, and L. Rostas) *The Taxation of War Wealth,* Clarendon Press, 1941, 2nd edition, 1942; *The Social Framework: An Introduction to Economics,* Clarendon Press, 1942, published as *The Social Framework of the American Economy: An Introduction to Economics* (with Albert Gailord Hart), Oxford University Press (New York City), 1945, 4th British edition, 1971; (with U. K. Hicks) *Standards of Local Expenditure: A Problem of the Inequality of Incomes,* Cambridge University Press, 1943; (with U. K. Hicks and C.E.V. Leser) *The Problem of Valuation for Rating,* Cambridge University Press, 1944; (with U. K. Hicks) *The Incidence of Local Rates in Great Britain,* Cambridge University Press, 1945; *The Problems of Budgetary Reform,* Clarendon Press, 1948.

A Contribution to the Theory of the Trade Cycle, Clarendon Press, 1950; (with U. K. Hicks) *Report on Finance and Taxation in Jamaica,* Government Printer (Jamaica), 1955; *A Revision of Demand Theory,* Clarendon Press, 1956; *Essays in World Economics,* Clarendon Press, 1959; *International Trade: The Long View,* Central Bank of Egypt, 1963; *Capital and Growth,* Oxford University Press, 1965; *After the Boom: Thoughts on the 1966 Economic Crisis,* Transatlantic, 1966; *Critical Essays in Monetary Theory,* Clarendon Press, 1967; *Theory of Economic History,* Oxford University Press, 1969; (editor) *Carl Menger and the Austrian School of Economics,* Clarendon Press, 1973; *Capital and Time: A Neo-Austrian Theory,* Clarendon Press, 1973; *The Crisis in Keynesian Economics,* Basil Blackwell, 1974, Basic Books, 1975.

* * *

HIEBEL, Friedrich 1903-

PERSONAL: Given name listed in some sources as Frederick; born February 10, 1903, in Vienna, Austria; naturalized U.S. citizen, 1945; son of Gustav and Adele (von Goldberger-Buda) Hiebel; married Beulah Emmet, June 24, 1945; children: Benedict Thomas, Margaret Sophia. *Education:* Attended University of Jena, 1924-25, and University of Goettingen, 1925-26; University of Vienna, Ph.D., 1928. *Religion:* Catholic. *Home:* Luzernestrasse 14, CH 4143 Dornach, Switzerland. *Office:* Goetheanum College, Freie Hochschule fuer Geisteswissenschaft, CH 4143 Dornach, Switzerland.

CAREER: Teacher at Waldorfschool, Stuttgart, Germany; Princeton University, Princeton, N.J., instructor in German literature, 1945-46; Upsala College, East Orange, N.J., associate professor of German and chairman of department, 1946-47; Rutgers University, New Brunswick, N.J., assistant professor of German, 1947-53; Wagner College, Staten Island, N.Y., associate professor, 1953-56, professor of German, 1956-63; Goetheanum College, Dornach, Switzerland, professor, head of literature section, and dean of College, 1963—, publisher and editor of weekly periodical, *Das Goetheanum*, 1966—. Wayne State University, resident director of junior year at University of Freiberg, 1961-62. *Member:* Modern Language Association of America, P.E.N. (Switzerland), Schweizerischer Schriftsteller Verein.

WRITINGS: Paulus und die Erkenntnislehre der Freiheit (title means "St. Paul and the Philosophy of Freedom"), Rudolf Geering Verlag, 1946, 2nd edition, Goetheanum Buecherei, 1959; *The Gospel of Hellas: The Mission of Ancient Greece and the Advent of Christ,* Anthroposophic Press (New York), 1948; *Novalis: Der Dichter der blauen Blume* (title means "Novalis: The Poet of the Blue Flower"), Francke Verlag, 1951, revised edition published as *Novalis: Deutscher Dichter, europaeischer Denker, christlicher Seher,* 1972, translation published as *Novalis: German Poet, European Thinker, Christian Mystic,* University of North Carolina Press, 1954, revised edition, 1959; *Goethe,* Francke Verlag, 1951; *Die Botschaft von Hellas: Von der griechischen Seele zum christlichen Geist* (title means "The Gospel of Hellas"), Francke Verlag, 1953, 2nd edition, 1963; *Christian Morgenstern: Wende und Aufbruch unseres Jahrhunderts* (title means "Christian Morgenstern: Turning Point of Our Century"), Francke Verlag, 1957; *Bibelfunde und Zeitgewissen: Die Schiftrollen vom Toten Meer im Lichte der Christologie Rudolf Steiners* (title means "The Qumran Texts"), Rudolf Geering Verlag, 1959.

Albert Steffen: Die Dichtung als schoene Wissenschaft (title means "Albert Steffen: Poetry and Belles Lettres"), Francke Verlag, 1960; *Goethe: Die Erhoehung des Menschen; Perspektiven einer morphologischen Lebensschau* (title means "Goethe: Perspectives of a Morphological Biography"), Francke Verlag, 1961; (editor with others) *Alpha und Omega: Sprachbetrachtungen* (title means "Alpha and Omega: Reflections about Language"), Philosophisch-Anthroposophischer Verlag, 1963; (editor with others) *Himmelskind und Adamsbotschaft: Kunstgeschichtliche Menschheitsmotive im besonderen Zusammenhang mit Michelangelos Sixtinischer Decke* (title means "Heavenly Childhood and Adam's Message: In Connection with Michelangelo's Sistine Ceiling"), Philosophisch-Anthroposophischer Verlag, 1964; *Rudolf Steiner in Geistesgang des Abendlandes* (title means "Rudolf Steiner in the Evolution of the Occident"), Francke Verlag, 1965.

Biographik und Essayistik (title means "Biography and Essay"), Francke Verlag, 1970; *Campanella: Der Sucher nach dem Sonnenstaat; Geschichte eines Schicksals* (novel; title means "Campanella: The Seeker for the Sun"), Verlag Freies Geistesleben, 1972; *Seneca: Drama,* [Stuttgart], 1974.

*   *   *

HIGHBERGER, Ruth 1917-

PERSONAL: Born June 28, 1917, in Pennsylvania; daughter of Joseph M. (a teacher) and Mary W. (Boyd) Highberger. *Education:* Western College, Oxford, Ohio, A.B., 1938; Cornell University, M.S., 1944; University of Iowa, Ph.D., 1953. *Politics:* Democrat. *Home:* 8000 Livingston Dr., Knoxville, Tenn. 37919. *Office:* College of Home Economics, University of Tennessee, Knoxville, Tenn. 37916.

CAREER: Home economics teacher in public schools of Youngwood, Pa., 1939-43; Cornell University, Ithaca, N.Y., part-time instructor in home economics, 1943-44; Paul

Revere Center, Cleveland, Ohio, director of nursery school, 1944-45; Michigan State University, East Lansing, instructor in child development, 1945-49; University of Iowa, Iowa City, instructor in pre-school education, 1949-50; University of Cincinnati, Cincinnati, Ohio, associate professor of child development and family life, and director of nursery school, 1953-57; University of Tennessee, Knoxville, associate professor, 1957-58, professor of child development and family relations, 1959-69, professor of child and family studies, 1969—, head of department and director of nursery school, 1959-69. Has directed workshops for pre-school education since 1960.

MEMBER: American Psychological Association, American Home Economics Association, American Association of University Professors, National Association for the Education of Young Children, Society for Research in Child Development, Southern Association for Children Under Six, Tennessee Association for Children Under Six (president, 1963-65), Sigma Xi, Omicron Nu (national vice-president, 1956-58), Pi Lambda Theta, Alpha Delta Epsilon. *Awards, honors:* Effie I. Raitt fellowship from American Home Economics Association, 1951; annual award from Tennessee Association for Children Under Six, 1973, for outstanding service to teachers and young children; award from Child Development Association of Tennessee, 1975, for service to Head Start programs.

WRITINGS: (Contributor) Ada D. Stephens, editor, *Toward the Development of Creativity in Early Childhood,* University of Toledo College of Education, 1963; (with Carol Schramm) *Child Development for Day Care Workers,* Houghton, 1976. Contributor to *Early Childhood Education Handbook* and to home economics and child development journals. Member of editorial board of *Child Development,* 1969-71.

WORK IN PROGRESS: Research on the etiology of children's eating behavior, and on training of staff members for day care programs.

AVOCATIONAL INTERESTS: Travel, camping in Europe, hiking, gourmet cooking.

*   *   *

HIGHWATER, Jamake
(J Marks)

PERSONAL: Given name is pronounced Ja-*mah*-key; son of Blackfeet and Cherokee Indians. *Education:* Has earned B.A., M.A., and Ph.D. *Residence:* New York, N.Y. *Agent:* Alfred Hart, Fox Chase Agency, 419 East 57th St., New York, N.Y. 10022.

CAREER: Writer and lecturer on the American Indian. Consultant on American Indians to New York Council on the Arts. *Member:* White Buffalo Council of American Indians, Authors League of America, Dramatists Guild, American Federation of Television and Radio Artists, Business Music, Inc. *Awards, honors:* Named honorary citizen of Oklahoma; named colonel on staff of governor of New Mexico.

WRITINGS: (under pseudonym, J Marks) *Rock and Other Four Letter Words,* Bantam, 1969; (under J Marks) *Mick Jagger: The Singer Not the Song,* Curtis Books, 1973; *Europe Under Twenty-Five: A Young Person's Guide,* Fodor's, 1971; *Indian America: A Cultural Guide,* McKay, 1975; *Song from the Earth: Indian Painting* (Literary Book Club selection), Little, Brown, 1976; *Anpao: An American Indian Odyssey,* Lippincott, in press. Senior editor of

"Fodor Travel Guides," 1970—. Writer of radio and television scripts. Contributor to popular magazines, sometimes under pseudonym J Marks, including *Smithsonian, Diversion, Esquire, Look, Saturday Review, Vogue, Horizon, American Heritage, Harper's Bazaar,* and *Dance,* and to newspapers. Contributing editor of *Stereo Review,* 1969—; classical music editor of *Soho Weekly News,* 1975—.

WORK IN PROGRESS: The Dance: From Ritual to Romance, for A & W Visual Books; *Ritual of the Wind: American Indian Ceremonies and Dances,* Studio Books; *Journey to the Sky: The Discovery of the Maya by John L. Stephens and Frederick Catherwood,* Crowell.

SIDELIGHTS: Highwater's book on Mick Jagger has been translated into French, Dutch, German, Italian, and Portuguese.

*　　*　　*

HIGONNET, Patrice Louis-Rene 1938-

PERSONAL: Born February 3, 1938, in Paris, France; son of Rene (an engineer) and Marie-Therese (David) Higonnet; married Ethel Parmele Cardwell, June 3, 1970 (deceased); married Margaret Randolph Cardwell (a professor), August 13, 1974; children: Anne, Philippe. *Education:* Harvard University, A.B., 1958, graduate study, 1960-63; Oxford University, graduate study, 1958-60.

CAREER: Writer. *Awards, honors:* Grants from Social Science Research Council and American Philosophical Society.

WRITINGS: Pont de Montvert, Harvard University Press, 1971. Contributor to history journals in the United States and France.

*　　*　　*

HILL, Herbert 1924-

PERSONAL: Born January 24, 1924, in New York, N.Y.; son of Jack (a musician) and Mary (Ziebeck) Hill. *Education:* New York University, B.A., 1945; New School for Social Research, graduate study, 1946-47. *Home:* 160 Riverside Dr., New York, N.Y. 10024.

CAREER: United Steelworkers of America, Newark, N.J., researcher and organizer, 1947-48; National Association for the Advancement of Colored People (NAACP), New York, N.Y., special assistant to the executive director, 1948-52, national labor secretary, 1952-60, national labor director, 1961—. Member of faculty at New School for Social Research, 1963-68; distinguished visiting professor at California State University, Northridge, 1968-69; Danforth visiting professor at Immaculate Heart College, Los Angeles, Calif., 1969-70; regents lecturer at University of California, Irvine, 1969-70, and University of California, Santa Cruz, 1974; distinguished visitor-in-residence at Kenyon College, 1970; visiting professor at Princeton University, 1972-73, and University of Wisconsin, Madison, 1973-75; has lectured at universities all over the United States and in England. Has testified before U.S. Congress; consultant to State of Israel and United Nations.

MEMBER: American Historical Association, Association for the Study of Afro-American Life and History, Industrial Relations Research Association, Organization of American Historians, Society for the Study of Social Problems, Southern Historical Association.

WRITINGS: (With Jack Greenberg) *Citizen's Guide to Desegregation: A Study of Social and Legal Change in*

American Life, Beacon Press, 1955; *No Harvest for the Reaper: The Story of the Migratory Agricultural Worker in the United States,* NAACP, 1960; (editor and author of introduction) *Soon One Morning: New Writing by American Negroes,* Knopf, 1963, published in England as *Black Voices,* Elek, 1964; (editor and author of introduction) *Anger and Beyond: The Negro Writer in the United States,* Harper, 1966; (editor with Arthur M. Ross) *Employment, Race, and Poverty,* Harcourt, 1967; *Black Labor and the American Legal System,* Volume I: *Race, Work, and the Law,* Volume II: *Development of the Law of Equal Employment Opportunity,* Bureau of National Affairs, in press.

Contributor of chapters or essays to over 26 books, including: Louis Ferman with others, editors, *Negroes and Jobs: A Book of Readings,* University of Michigan Press, 1968; Louis Ferman with others, editors, *Poverty in America: A Book of Readings,* revised edition, University of Michigan Press, 1968; Julius Jacobson, editor, *The Negro and the American Labor Movement,* Doubleday, 1968; Jerold Auerbach, editor, *American Labor: The Twentieth Century,* Bobbs-Merrill, 1969; John Kain, editor, *Race and Poverty: The Economics of Discrimination,* Prentice-Hall, 1969; Patrica Romero, *In Black America, 1968: The Year of Awakening,* United Publishing, 1969.

Richard Sherman, editor, *The Negro and the City,* Prentice-Hall, 1970; John Bracey with others, editors, *The Rise of the Ghetto,* Wadsworth, 1971; Gary Marx, editor, *Racial Conflict: Tension and Change in American Society,* Little, Brown, 1971; Richard Rowan, editor, *Readings in Labor Economics and Labor Relations,* revised edition, Irwin, 1972; Arnold Rose and Caroline Rose, editors, *Minority Problems,* 2nd edition, Harper, 1972; Orley Ashenfelter and Albert Rees, editors, *Discrimination in Labor Markets,* Princeton University Press, 1974.

General editor of "New Perspectives on Black America" series, six volumes, Putnam, 1972—; advisory editor of *Studies in Black Literature.* Contributor to *Annals of American Academy of Political and Social Science* and to academic journals and popular magazines, including *Nation, Journal of Negro Education, Harvard Civil Rights-Civil Liberties Law Review,* and *Industrial Relations Law Journal.*

*　　*　　*

HILL, I(saac) William 1908-

PERSONAL: Born August 8, 1908, in Opelika, Ala.; son of Isaac W. (an educator) and Laura (Jones) Hill; married Catherine H. Dawson, June 25, 1932 (died September 5, 1974); children: Catherine Roxane (Mrs. Martin C. Hughes), Joyce Elizabeth (Mrs. W. Patrick Stoner). *Education:* George Washington University, student, 1925-26; Washington & Lee University, A.B., 1929. *Politics:* Independent. *Religion:* Presbyterian. *Home:* 3203 Leland St., Chevy Chase, Md. 20015. *Office:* Editor and Publisher, 1295 National Press Building, Washington, D.C. 20045.

CAREER: Mobile Press, Mobile, Ala., reporter and editor, 1929-30; *Washington Evening Star,* Washington, D.C., deskman, 1930-37, city editor, 1937-49, news editor, 1949-54, assistant managing editor, 1954-62, managing editor, 1962-68, associate editor, 1968-73; *Editor and Publisher,* New York, N.Y., Washington correspondent, 1974—. Lecturer at Columbia University, 1955-73; Kilgore journalism counselor at DePauw University, 1970. Chairperson of Newspaper Comics Council, 1960-61; director of Maryland Media, Inc., 1970-73.

MEMBER: International Press Club, National Press Club, American Society of Newspaper Editors (member of board of directors, 1972-73), Associated Press Managing Editors Association (president, 1966-67), Chevy Chase Club, P. T. Barnum Tent, Circus, Saints and Sinners Club (vice-president, 1973—), Sigma Delta Chi, Pi Delta Epsilon, Lambda Chi Alpha.

WRITINGS: (With John W. Stepp) *Mirror of War,* Prentice-Hall, 1961. Contributor of articles and stories to popular magazines, including *Cosmopolitan.*

SIDELIGHTS: Hill's views on education in journalism are that "every reporter should be trained as an investigator, every journalism student should take part in undergraduate public speaking, theater, and should become an expert typist." He visited the People's Republic of China in 1972, and has traveled extensively in Europe.

AVOCATIONAL INTERESTS: Playing the banjo.

*   *   *

HILL, R. Lance   1943-

PERSONAL: Born May 1, 1943, in Toronto, Ontario, Canada; married Darlene Moroz, December 29, 1971. *Education:* Educated in technical secondary school in Toronto, Ontario. *Politics:* "Non-political." *Religion:* None. *Office:* Bart Levy Associates, Beverly Hills, Calif.

CAREER: Full-time writer. Formerly a professional automobile race driver and engine builder. *Member:* Authors Guild of Authors League of America. *Awards, honors:* Hill was U.S. champion four times in his racing class.

WRITINGS: Nails, Lester & Orpen, 1974; *King of White Lady,* Putnam, 1975. Author of screenplay adaptation of *King of White Lady* for Hal Roach Studios.

WORK IN PROGRESS: "The Doctor," a screenplay, with a novel of the same title.

*   *   *

HILLS, Denis (Cecil)   1913-

PERSONAL: Born November 8, 1913, in Birmingham, England; son of Henry (a bank manager) and Caroline (Oldham) Hills; married Ingrid Jahn (a university lecturer), June, 1955; children: Hansen, John Rupert. *Education:* Lincoln College, Oxford, B.A. (honors), 1935. *Politics:* Liberal Conservative. *Religion:* Church of England. *Home:* 28 St. Mary's Crescent, Leamington Spa, Warwickshire, England. *Office address:* Teacher Training College, P.O. Box 9055, Gwelo, Rhodesia.

CAREER: Free-lance journalist in central Europe for *Birmingham Post,* 1935-36; employed by Polish Foreign Office to edit anti-Nazi publications at Institut Baltycki in Gdynia, Poland, 1937-39; University of Mainz, Germersheim, Germany, lecturer in English and economic history, 1951-53; teacher and lecturer in English, in Turkey, at Ankara College (Ankara), Zonguldak College (Zonguldak), and Middle East Technical University (Ankara), 1955-63; lecturer in English literature at Makarere University and National Teachers' College, Kampala, Uganda, 1964-75; Teacher Training College of African Division of Education, Gwelo, Rhodesia, lecturer in English and environmental studies, 1976—. Journalist for British press, 1964-76; overseas contributor on countries, including Turkey, Iran, and East Africa. Broadcaster for Ankara radio, 1960, British Broadcasting Corp. (BBC) radio and television, 1975-76, Frankfurt radio, 1975-76, Canadian radio and television, 1975, U.S. radio and television, 1976, and Rhodesian radio, 1976—. *Military service:* British Army, 1940-50; served in Middle East, Italy, Austria, and Germany; served on control commission in Germany, 1949-50; became major; mentioned in dispatches. *Member:* Royal Central Asian Society.

WRITINGS: My Travels in Turkey, Allen & Unwin, 1964; *Man with a Lobelia Flute,* Allen & Unwin, 1971; *The White Pumpkin,* Allen & Unwin, 1975, Grove, 1976. Contributor to newspapers, including *London Times, Washington Post, New York Review of Books, New York Times,* and *Glasgow Herald.*

WORK IN PROGRESS: A fourth book, on Africa.

SIDELIGHTS: "I attracted some publicity in 1975 (April—August) as prisoner of Amin in Uganda," Hills told *CA.* "On the basis of a paragraph in the manuscript [of *The White Pumpkin*], in which I accused Amin of 'governing like a village tyrant, by fear,' I was charged with sedition and detained at Luzira Prison. On May 9, the sedition charge was withdrawn, and I was charged instead with treason and told I would have to appear before a military tribunal."

The secret military tribunal subsequently ordered Hills executed, yet even before the tribunal had reached its verdict, Uganda President General Idi Amin offered to trade Hills's life for certain political concessions from the British Government. It was Amin's desire to use Hills as a political pawn to force his nation's former colonial rulers to "kneel at [his] feet." Two British envoys, bearing Queen Elizabeth's appeal to spare the life of the British citizen, were required to crawl on their knees in order to pass through the very low entrance to the thatched hut where Amin awaited them. These first negotiations resulted in a short stay of execution; his reprieve, however, required the mediating presence of British Foreign Secretary James Callaghan.

Prior to Hills's imprisonment, he had noted the accelerated degree of change in Uganda since its liberation under Amin, as well as concomitant serious setbacks in many areas of achievement. "In education," Hills explained, "a gradual phasing-out of foreign teachers had been accepted; hence the expansion of teacher-training colleges to produce African replacements. But the loss of 90 per cent of the old expatriate teaching staff in Uganda has been disastrous. Outside the class and lecture room, fear and apathy have clouded the once gay and extroverted student life. At the National Teachers' College I had helped to build up a library of 20,000 books. Scarcely a new book has been added for more than two years. 'We are walking through a dark valley,' one student told me, 'and we dare not stumble.'"

In Hills's estimation, Amin's most radical act since seizing power in 1971 was to evict the Asians, and "though his methods of eviction were inhumane, he was entitled to tell the Asians to go. For no one denies the right of native Ugandans to be the masters in their own house; and clearly the overwhelming Asian presence was inhibiting the growth of an African middle class." The resident Europeans, especially the British, were Amin's next subjects of harassment, "to the point where thousands of them decided, in Amin's phrase, 'to run away.' From about 7,000 the number of British in Uganda has dropped to 700. Since the Israeli commando raid on Entebbe and Britain's diplomatic rupture with Uganda (28 July 1976), only 2-300 British are now left, and of these many have had to kneel before Amin as the price of his protection."

Amin's actions clearly caused his country to lose much. In Hills's analysis, "Uganda has not only lost the business acumen and technical skills of the Asians. The native Ugandans who have stepped into their shoes have been unable satisfactorily to replace them. The result, worsened by world inflationary trends, has been economic chaos and disaster to public services. The new class of African shopkeepers and businessmen who inherited the Asian (as well as British) assets and property . . . have been accused by ordinary Ugandans of hoarding, smuggling, cheating and overcharging on a scale hitherto unknown.''

Why did Hills remain in Uganda when he began to see the direction in which the country was heading? "One of my own motives for staying was curiosity," he reported early in Amin's regime. "Uganda was going through an exciting phase. How would it turn out? Though, to Africans, Amin's 'revolution' looked to be a grandiose affair attracting world attention, it was but a tiny moment in history. The upheavals and the pressures could not last." Hills also observed, "hot tempered yet ponderous, driven by urges whose origins must partly lie in the obscurity of his childhood, Amin is a man in a hurry. . . . It is widely believed in Uganda that a counter *coup* within his own army will one day finish Amin. This is not to say that Ugandans are looking forward to such an event with its inevitable reprisals and bloodshed." "Some say," wrote Hills latter in *New York Review of Books,* "that Amin's successor might even be worse. But no replacement is likely to be so formidable as Amin or so difficult to dislodge.''

Asked what he feels about Amin now that his imprisonment is part of his past, Hills replied, "I bear no special resentment against him for my recent arrest and death sentence. When my writings were discovered, I knew what to expect, and I was prepared to take my medicine. I do not know if my critical remarks about the President genuinely hurt him or not. After all, he is used to being attacked by writers, and when, for instance, German journalists criticize him, he does not react by threatening them. It is clear that he used me as a pawn, in order to wring concession from the British Government, which turned out to be a message from the Queen, a visit by the Foreign Minister, and perhaps some improvements in relations with London." Moreover, he contended that "Amin is not mad. But absolute power has gone to his head. He has emerged from an army barracks to find . . . a whole country, with every person and every stick and stone within it, under his command." Amin can not be dismissed as a buffoon or murderer, because, as his apologists say, "he is an African reality. He has realized an African dream, the creation of a truly black African state. He has called into being a new, crude but vigorous Ugandan middle class of technicians and businessmen, who must learn through their mistakes. Yet others stress that he has destroyed souls, and like a rogue elephant trampled and torn up what was a relatively stable and happy piece of Africa. For us, Amin's unforgiveable crime ought to be not that he has seized British and Asian assets and maltreated their owners, but that he has murdered his own black subjects, terrified and corrupted them. Abject and spiritless, people wait for *Mungo* (God) to remove their tormentor.''

Hills felt that in another sense, he was a pawn on which Amin could take out his wrath against the press. He recalled that on December 12, 1972, "Amin had threatened . . . to put David Martin, the *London Observer* correspondent, in army custody for criticizing him. In this sense, I was a second-rate substitute for Martin. But teachers, even poor teachers, are respected by Ugandans. In jailing and threatening me with public execution, Amin has discredited himself with many of his own people—and advertised my book.''

A *New Yorker* reviewer of *The White Pumpkin* noted that,

until Amin made them an issue, Ugandan politics were not as important in the book as Hills's interest in Ugandan customs and African writing, and that, in fact, the author was "more sympathetic to the dictator than many other commentators have been." Wrote Paul Theroux, "It is obvious for most of the way that Mr Hills assumed what he was writing was inoffensive.''

Hills told *CA* that "while in the army, I wrote what Solzhenitsyn described in *Gulag Archipelago* as that 'one random little document'—a British Army protest report on the forcible repatriation of Russians from Italy in 1947—which caught Solzhenitsyn's eye and for him disclosed 'the last secret, or one of the last, of the Second World War.' '' Hills wrote on this incident in his article in the *Washington Post,* August 1, 1976, and Nicholas Bethell discussed it in his book, *The Last Secret.*

AVOCATIONAL INTERESTS: Foreign travel and languages, mountain climbing, exploration.

BIOGRAPHICAL/CRITICAL SOURCES: Newsweek, June 30, 1975; *Time,* July 7, 1975; *New York Times Magazine,* September 7, 1975; *New Statesman,* December 12, 1975; *New Yorker,* April 5, 1976; *Washington Post,* August 1, 1976; *New York Review of Books,* September 16, 1976; Denis Hills, *The White Pumpkin,* Grove, 1976; Nicholas Bethell, *The Last Secret,* revised edition, Futura Publications, 1976.

*   *   *

HILT, Douglas Richard   1932-

PERSONAL: Born October 3, 1932, in London, England; naturalized U.S. citizen in 1976; son of Eugene Henry (an engineer) and Margrit (Lobig) Hilt; married Marquita Lee Farris, July 11, 1968. *Education:* University of Bristol, B.A. (with honors), 1954; University of the Americas, M.A., 1965; University of Arizona, Ph.D., 1967. *Home:* 4338 Huerfano Ave., San Diego, Calif. 92117. *Office:* Department of Languages, U.S. International University, San Diego, Calif. 92101.

CAREER: U.S. International University, San Diego, Calif., assistant professor, 1967-72, associate professor of languages, 1972—. *Member:* United Nations Association, American Association of University Professors, Modern Language Association of America.

WRITINGS: Ten Against Napoleon (history), Nelson-Hall, 1975. Contributor to professional journals.

WORK IN PROGRESS: Manuel Godoy: Prince of the Peace, a full-length biography on the effective ruler of Spain from 1792-1808, the court favorite, and Napoleon's opponent, completion expected in 1977.

SIDELIGHTS: Hilt told *CA:* "I am interested in modern languages and literatures, history, and the interaction of these cultural forces. My background is European, and no doubt having taught in several countries on two continents has been the genesis of this interest. I firmly believe that the fruits of research should be accessible to a wide audience in coherent form."

*   *   *

HINES, William H.   1909(?)-1976

1909(?)—March 14, 1976; American author and educator. Obituaries: *New York Times,* March 17, 1976; *AB Bookman's Weekly,* April 5, 1976.

HINTZ, (Loren) Martin 1945-

PERSONAL: Born June 1, 1945, in New Hampton, Iowa; son of Loren (a flier) and Gertrude (an office manager; maiden name, Russell) Hintz; married: Sandra Lee Wright (a literary agent), May 1, 1971; children: Daniel, Stephen. *Education:* College of St. Thomas, St. Paul, Minn., B.A., 1967; Northwestern University, M.A., 1968. *Politics:* Liberal. *Religion:* Roman Catholic. *Home and office:* 4572 North 39th St., Milwaukee, Wis. 53209. *Agent:* Ray Puechner, 2625 North 36th St., Milwaukee, Wis. 53209.

CAREER: Milwaukee Sentinel, Milwaukee, Wis., reporter and editor, 1968-75; *Group Travel,* New York, N.Y., contributing editor (Midwest), 1976; free-lance writer and photographer, 1976—; writer of travel scripts. Has covered World Cup Soccer Championships, 1970, 1974, and Expo '74; worked as a case worker for American Red Cross, 1968-71. Associate member of School of the Sisters of St. Francis.

MEMBER: Society of American Travel Writers, Society of Professional Journalists, Caledonian Society, Circus Model Builders of America, Northwest Territorial Alliance (public relations officer), Midwest Travel Writers' Association, Wisconsin News Photographers Association, Wisconsin Soccer Press and Radio Association, Milwaukee Kickers (soccer club; member of board of directors, 1972-74), Milwaukee Press Club, Clan Donald (Midwest district), Sigma Delta Chi (member of board of directors of Milwaukee chapter, 1972-74; president-elect, 1975-76; president, 1976). *Awards, honors:* Kicker of the year award from Milwaukee Kickers, 1970; school bell award from Wisconsin Education Association, 1971, for educational news coverage; community service award from Inland Daily Press Association, 1974.

WRITINGS: (With wife, Sandra Hintz) *We Can't Afford It,* Raintree, 1976. Contributor to magazines and newspapers, including *Friends, Americana, Easy Living, Billboard,* and *Amusement Business.*

WORK IN PROGRESS: Jason's Window; Pals; The Hunters; book on American invasion of Canada during Revolutionary period; a teenage adventure story; articles for periodicals.

SIDELIGHTS: Hintz has played soccer and coached for the Milwaukee Kickers. During his college years he worked for Royal American Shows, the United States' largest carnival, and has used that experience as a basis for several stories. He writes that his broadening travel experience enlarges his view of the world and his "competence to comment on the changing social scene."

*   *   *

HINZ, Evelyn J. 1938-

PERSONAL: Born December 7, 1938, in Humboldt, Saskatchewan, Canada; daughter of Andrew Bruno (a farmer) and Alyosia (Nenzel) Hinz. *Education:* University of Saskatchewan, B.A. (cum laude), M.A., 1967; University of Massachusetts, Ph.D., 1973. *Home:* 19—3000 Pembina Hwy., Winnipeg, Manitoba, Canada R3T 3Z2. *Office:* Department of English, University of Manitoba, Winnipeg, Manitoba, Canada R3T 2N2.

CAREER: Department of Northern Affairs, Pelican Narrows, Saskatchewan, teacher; Province of Saskatchewan, Regina, social worker, 1961-63; CFQC-TV, Saskatoon, Saskatchewan, writer and producer, 1963-65; University of Saskatchewan, Saskatoon, teacher of English, 1966-68; University of Manitoba, Winnipeg, lecturer in English,

1973—; free-lance writer. *Member:* Association of Canadian University Teachers of English, Modern Language Association of America, Humanities Association of Canada, Poe Studies Association, Otto Rank Association. *Awards, honors:* Governor-General's Medal, 1957; Killam postdoctoral research scholarship, 1973-75; University of Manitoba postdoctoral fellowship, 1975-76.

WRITINGS: The Mirror and the Garden: Realism and Reality in the Writings of Anais Nin, Ohio State University Libraries, 1971, revised edition, Harcourt, 1973; (editor and author of introduction, notes, and commentary with John J. Teunissen) Roger Williams, *A Key into the Language of America,* Wayne State University Press, 1973; (editor and author of introduction) *A Woman Speaks: The Lectures, Seminars, and Interviews of Anais Nin,* Swallow Press, 1975; (with Teunissen) *Dream the Myth Onward: Key Texts in Archetypal Criticism,* Swallow Press, in press. Contributor of more than thirty articles to journals in her field, including *Journal of Modern Literature, PMLA, Contemporary Literature, Nineteenth-Century Fiction,* and *Journal of Aesthetics and Art Criticism.* Member of editorial board, *Mosaic.*

WORK IN PROGRESS: The authorized biography of Anais Nin, completion expected in 1980; books on the art of Canadian literature and mythic literature; articles for literary journals; a novel.

SIDELIGHTS: The first woman to receive Canada's prestigious Killam grant and one of the initiators of a women's studies program at the University of Manitoba, Evelyn Hinz has always been interested in the relationships of women with society. While writing an undergraduate paper on D. H. Lawrence's presentation of women in literature, she discovered a similar study done by Anais Nin. This first encounter prompted Hinz into doing further research resulting in *The Mirror and the Garden,* the first complete critical study of Nin's work. She explains: "Nin's strength makes you recognize within yourself things you'd never think about. . . . She does a marvelous job of exploring character types."

Hinz believes "women should find their own language and powers which are different from men's," and is particularly interested in Anais Nin's approach to the problem. In her words: "Language is by definition masculine in its orientation, and women who write must accept this situation; they can modify and adapt the uses to which language can be put, but they cannot change the nature of language in itself. The so-called attempts to do so, in turn, really reflect a masculine approach to the problem—a 'logos' rather than an 'eros' attitude—and hence are self-defeating. My interest in the work of Anais Nin stems in great part from the way she positively exemplifies this principle: her persistent struggle has been to translate the non-verbal idiom of the emotions into a verbal medium, or to translate, as she puts it, 'woman to man.'"

Speaking of her own literary career, Dr. Hinz recalls that her inspirations and motivations "have changed throughout the years and I expect will in some ways continue to change. On the humorous or humanistic side, I can recall my grade school teacher having charged me with plagiarism for an essay I wrote for her, and my vowing that I would prove her wrong by becoming a literary celebrity. Later it was my Aunt, the principal of the convent school I attended, who somehow insinuated that I had to do what circumstances prevented her from doing. Still later it was my dissatisfaction or lack of sense of fulfillment in other occupations I attempted, coupled with the encouragement of the man who has subsequently become my collaborator in numerous projects. At present, I think my motivation has largely to do with the 'Canadian' and 'Feminist' issues, in the sense that I am appalled by much of what is published under these sanctions, and am determined, accordingly, to prove that one can rise above such petty advantages and make it in spite of them.''

In addition to teaching and writing non-fiction, Hinz told *CA* that she is presently concerned with "preparing for a career in creative writing. (Incidently, I think, and I believe the history of literary criticism supports me here, that all aspiring artists should be prevented from publishing until they have reached 'maturity' and have demonstrated critical ability. They should write, yes; and if they should die before 'maturity' and have written great works these will be discovered certainly by their executors. They themselves will not experience recognition, of course, but where recognition becomes a primary concern, art tends to suffer).''

AVOCATIONAL INTERESTS: Painting and doing pastel portraits of friends and literary personalities, writing parodies and satire.

BIOGRAPHICAL/CRITICAL SOURCES: Winnipeg *Free Press*, August 29, 1975.

* * *

HIPPLE, Theodore W(allace) 1935-

PERSONAL: Born July 2, 1935, in Galesburg, Ill.; son of Bruce M. (a salesman) and Erma (Williams) Hipple; married Marjorie Levy (a professor), August 18, 1956; children: Kathryn, Bruce, Betsy. *Education:* Northern Illinois University, B.S.Ed., 1957; University of Illinois, M.Ed., 1960, Ph.D., 1968. *Home:* 3957 Northwest Ninth Ct., Gainesville, Fla. 32605. *Office:* College of Education, University of Florida, Gainesville, Fla. 32611.

CAREER: University of Florida, Gainesville, assistant professor, 1968-70, associate professor, 1970-72, professor of education, 1972—. *Member:* National Council of Teachers of English, Conference on English Education, Phi Delta Kappa.

WRITINGS: Secondary School Teaching: Problems and Methods, Goodyear Publishing, 1970; *Teaching English in Secondary Schools,* Macmillan, 1973; *Readings for Teaching English in Secondary Schools,* edited by Lloyd C. Chilton, Macmillan, 1973; *The Future of Education: 1975-2000,* Goodyear Publishing, 1974; *Crucial Issues in Contemporary Education,* Goodyear Publishing, 1974.

Editor, "Goodyear Series in Education," Goodyear Publishing, 1969—.

WORK IN PROGRESS: Editing four short story collections for Allyn & Bacon.

* * *

HIRST, Paul H(eywood) 1927-

PERSONAL: Born November 10, 1927, in Huddersfield, England; son of Herbert (a foreign correspondent) and Winifred (Michelbacher) Hirst. *Education:* Trinity College, Cambridge, B.A., 1948, M.A. and certificate in education, 1952; University of London, diploma in education, 1955; Christ Church, Oxford, M.A., 1955. *Residence:* Cambridge, England. *Office:* Department of Education, Wolfson College, Cambridge University, 17 Trumpington St., Cambridge CR2 1JG, England.

CAREER: William Hulme's Grammar School, Manchester, England, assistant master, 1948-50; Eastbourne College,

Eastbourne, England, mathematics master, 1950-55; Oxford University, Oxford, England, lecturer and tutor in department of education, 1955-59; University of London, Institute of Education, London, England, lecturer in philosophy, 1959-65, King's College, professor of education, 1965-71; Cambridge University, Wolfson College, Cambridge, England, professor of education, 1971—. Visiting professor at University of British Columbia, 1964, 1967, and at University of Malawi, 1969. Governor of Chestnut School, 1969-74; member, council of Gordonstoun School, 1969—. *Member:* Philosophy of Education Society of Great Britain (chairman, 1975—), Universities Council for the Education of Teachers (vice-chairman, 1974—), Royal Institute of Philosophy (member of council, 1973—), Athenaeum Club.

WRITINGS: (With R. S. Peters) *The Logic of Education,* Routledge & Kegan Paul, 1970, Humanities, 1971; (with R. F. Dearden and Peters) *Education and the Development of Reason,* Routledge & Kegan Paul, 1971; *Moral Education in a Secular Society,* Methuen, 1974; *Knowledge and the Curriculum,* Routledge & Kegan Paul, 1974.

Contributor: R. D. Archambault, editor, *Philosophical Analysis and Education,* Humanities, 1965; J. W. Tibble, editor, *The Study of Education,* Humanities, 1965; Peters, editor, *The Concept of Education,* Humanities, 1966; C. Macy, editor, *Let's Teach Them Right,* Pemberton Publishing, 1969. Contributor to education journals.

WORK IN PROGRESS: Research on curriculum theory, epistemology, moral education, and Marxism and education.

AVOCATIONAL INTERESTS: Music, opera, painting, antiques.

* * *

HIVNOR, Robert 1916-
(Jack Askew, Osbert Pismire)

PERSONAL: Born May 19, 1916, in Zanesville, Ohio; son of Harry Franklin and Glovina (Jones) Hivnor; married Mary Otis, August, 1947; children: James, Margaret, Henry. *Education:* University of Akron, A.B., 1936; Yale University, M.F.A., 1946; Columbia University, further graduate study, 1952-54; studied painting privately. *Politics:* Democrat. *Religion:* "Raised as a Presbyterian." *Home:* 420 East 84th St., New York, N.Y. 10028.

CAREER: Political cartoonist and commercial artist, 1934-38; Craftsman Press, Akron, Ohio, office manager, 1936-37; University of Minnesota, Minneapolis, instructor in English, 1946-48; Reed College, Portland, Ore., instructor in humanities, 1954-55; Bard College, Annandale-on-Hudson, N.Y., assistant professor of literature, 1956-59. Member of the President's Committee on the Teaching of English, 1966. *Military service:* U.S. Army, cryptanalyst, 1942-45. *Member:* Dramatists Guild. *Awards, honors:* Rockefeller Foundation grants, 1951, 1968.

WRITINGS—Plays: "Martha Goodwin" (comedy; adapted from a story by Katherine Anne Porter), first produced in New Haven, Conn., at Yale University, 1942; *Too Many Thumbs* (comedy; first produced in Minneapolis, Minn., at University of Minnesota, 1948; produced in New York, N.Y., at Cherry Lane Theatre, 1949), University of Minnesota Press, 1949; (under pseudonyms Osbert Pismire and Jack Askew) "DMZ" (three plays), first produced in New York at DMZ Cafe, 1969.

Plays have been anthologized in *Playbook: Five Plays for a New Theatre,* New Directions, 1956; *Plays for a New Theatre: Playbook Two,* New Directions, 1966; *Breakout!:*

In Search of New Theatrical Environments, edited by James Schevill, Swallow Press, 1973. Contributor of plays to *Anon* and poems to literary journals.

WORK IN PROGRESS: Plays; a comic novel; a novel set during World War Two, completion expected in 1978.

BIOGRAPHICAL/CRITICAL SOURCES: Martin Esslen, *The Theatre of the Absurd,* Methuen, 1961; Gerald Weales, *American Drama Since World War II,* Harcourt, 1962; Richard Kostelanetz, *The New American Arts,* Horizon Press, 1965; *Southern Review,* summer, 1970.

* * *

HIXSON, Joseph R(andolph) 1927-

PERSONAL: Born January 15, 1927, in New York, N.Y.; son of Joseph Randolph (a stock broker) and Ella (a knitting teacher; maiden name, Nelson) Hixson; married wife, Briggs (divorced, 1955); married wife, Betty (divorced, 1965); children: (first marriage) Judith, John, Catherine, Edward; (second marriage) Justin, Sarah, Mark. *Education:* Attended Princeton University, 1944-47. *Politics:* "Stevenson-Johnson-Humphrey-McGovern-Kennedy." *Religion:* Protestant Episcopalian. *Home and office address:* Box 310, R.D. 2, Red Hook, N.Y. 12571.

CAREER: Assistant editor at Topics Publishing Co., 1948-50, and Medical and Pharmaceutical Information Bureau, 1951-54 and 1958-60; public relations manager at Pfizer Inc. (pharmaceuticals firm), 1956-57; *New York Herald Tribune,* New York City, science reporter, 1962-66; *Chemical Week,* New York City, assistant editor, 1966-68; *Medical World News,* New York City, assistant editor, 1968-70; Memorial Sloan-Kettering Cancer Center, New York City, public affairs director, 1971-72; free-lance writer, 1972—.

WRITINGS: The History of the Human Body, Cooper Square, 1965; (with Warren Young) *LSD on Campus,* Dell, 1966; *The Patchwork Mouse* (politics and intrigue in cancer research), Doubleday, 1976.

WORK IN PROGRESS: A book about the results of genetic engineering.

SIDELIGHTS: Hixson writes that his "major interest is in the interface of technology and human lifestyle as an impact of hallucinogenics and other psychoactive drugs on the young, fear of cancer and heart disease on the old and the results of such impact on politics, economics, religious attitudes." Of his writing, he adds: "Writing is an arduous discipline requiring minimal physical activity and sensorimotor coordination i.e. can be accomplished in debilitated states and for relatively short periods of three to four hours. The idea is to combine physically active endeavors that either produce modest income or reduce outgo with such writing projects as satisfy the integrated ego, thus reducing dependence on quirky editors, commercial entrepreneurs, agents, promoters, and other riff-raff. My attempt is to make 'less is better' work while taking advantage of certain acceptable and, in terms of hourly remuneration, highly profitable 'creative labors.' The goal, in short, is survival with minimal compromise for writing projects best left undone."

* * *

HOARE, Wilber W., Jr. 1921-1976

December 22, 1921—February 29, 1976; American historian and author. Obituaries: *Washington Post,* March 7, 1976.

HOCH, Paul L(awrence) 1942-

PERSONAL: Born October 16, 1942, in London, England; came to the United States in 1950; naturalized citizen. *Home:* 2599 Le Conte Ave., Berkeley, Calif. 94709.

CAREER: Writer.

WRITINGS: (Editor with Peter Dale Scott and Russell Stetler) *The Assassinations: Dallas and Beyond,* Random House, 1976.

* * *

HODGE, William H(oward) 1932-

PERSONAL: Born June 21, 1932, in Coffeyville, Kan.; son of Howard G. (a chemical engineer) and Wenonah (Lambe) Hodge; married Doris Keller, September 14, 1957; children: Susan, Matthew, Peter. *Education:* Washington University, St. Louis, Mo., A.B., 1953, M.A., 1954; Brandeis University, Ph.D., 1966. *Office:* Department of Sociology-Anthropology, University of Wisconsin, Oshkosh, Wis. 54901.

CAREER: Valparaiso University, Valparaiso, Ind., instructor in sociology, 1958-59; University of Wyoming, Laramie, assistant professor of anthropology, 1965-67; Prescott College, Prescott, Ariz., associate professor of anthropology, 1967-68; University of Wisconsin, Milwaukee, assistant professor of anthropology, 1968-72; University of Wisconsin, Oshkosh, associate professor of anthropology, 1972—. *Military service:* U.S. Naval Reserve, 1951-55.

MEMBER: Society for Applied Anthropology (fellow), American Anthropological Association (fellow), Current Anthropology (associate member), Gypsy Lore Society, American Ethnological Society, Polynesian Society, Royal Anthropological Institute of Great Britain and Ireland (fellow).

WRITINGS: The Albuquerque Navahos, University of Arizona Press, 1969; *A Bibliography of Contemporary North American Indians: Selected and Partially Annotated with Study Guide,* Interland, 1976; *North American Indians: Persistence and Change,* St. Martin's, in press. Contributor of chapters on North American Indians to anthologies and of articles to anthropology journals.

WORK IN PROGRESS: "Relocation and Urban Experiences," for inclusion in *The Handbook of North American Indians,* edited by D'arcy McNicol and E. Spicer, for Smithsonian Institution.

SIDELIGHTS: Hodge writes: "I am an anthropologist because I have to be. I enjoy writing about modern American Indians at both professional and popular levels. I am also interested in popular white American culture." *Avocational interests:* The history of World War I, tropical fish.

* * *

HOFFER, William 1943-

PERSONAL: Born June 11, 1943, in Cleveland, Ohio; son of Frank and Lucile (Koeblitz) Hoffer; married Edie Bauer, June 12, 1966; children: Jennifer, Amanda. *Education:* Columbia Union College, B.A., 1969. *Address:* P.O. Box 6, Damascus, Md. 20750. *Agent:* Julian Bach, 3 East 48th St., New York, N.Y. 10017.

CAREER: PHC Business Magazine, Washington, D.C., associate editor, 1968-69; *Life Association News,* Washington, D.C., associate editor, 1969-70; free-lance writer, 1970—. *Member:* American Society of Journalists and Authors (director-at-large, 1976-78), Authors Guild.

WRITINGS: (With William W. Pearce) *Caught in the Act* (nonfiction), Stein & Day, 1976; (with Billy Hayes) *Midnight Express* (nonfiction), Dutton, 1977. Contributor to *True, Popular Science, House Beautiful, Mechanix Illustrated, Today's Health, Saga, Family Health, Modern Medicine,* and other magazines.

WORK IN PROGRESS: A book with record-holding balloonist, Ed Yost.

* * *

HOFFMAN, Joseph G(ilbert) 1909-1974

PERSONAL: Born August 19, 1909, in Buffalo, N.Y.; son of Joseph (a barber) and Helene (Seyler) Hoffman; married Ruth A. Buckland (a teacher and librarian), August 17, 1940; children: Joseph H., Paul G. *Education:* Cornell University, B.A. (honors), 1935, Ph.D., 1939. *Politics:* Independent. *Religion:* Unitarian-Universalist.

CAREER: Roswell Park Memorial Institute, Buffalo, N.Y., x-ray assistant, 1939-41, assistant radiophysicist, 1941; Carnegie Institution, Washington, D.C., physicist in department of terrestrial magnetism, 1941; National Bureau of Standards, Washington, D.C., associate physicist, 1941-43, assistant chief of Electronic Engineering Division, 1943-44; Los Alamos Manhattan Project (developing the atomic bomb), staff assistant, 1944, group leader, 1944-45; Roswell Park Memorial Institute, director of cancer research, beginning 1946. Research professor at University of Buffalo, beginning 1947. Consultant to Los Alamos Scientific Laboratory and U.S. Atomic Energy Commission.

MEMBER: American Cancer Research Society, Federation of American Scientists, American Physical Society (fellow), New York Academy of Science, Sigma Xi, Phi Kappa Phi. *Awards, honors:* Naval ordnance development achievement award; service award from Office of Scientific Research and Development; Manhattan District Service Award for work at Los Alamos.

WRITINGS: The Size and Growth of Tissue Cells, C. C Thomas, 1953; *The Life and Death of Cells,* Hanover House, 1957. Contributor to scientific journals.

SIDELIGHTS: While Hoffman was associated with the Manhattan Project, he witnessed two deaths resulting from the atomic testing, and was able to conduct extensive research on the effects of radiation on living cells. He spent the rest of his life engaged in cancer research. *Avocational interests:* Enjoyed mountain hiking and fishing, playing the piano and clarinet, photography.*

(Died December 9, 1974, in Buffalo, N.Y.)

* * *

HOFFMAN, Ross John Swartz 1902-

PERSONAL: Born February 2, 1902, in Harrisburg, Pa.; son of Edgar Grant and Mary (Hargest) Hoffman; married Hannah Elizabeth McCruden, 1926; children: one. *Education:* Lafayette College, A.B., 1923; University of Pennsylvania, A.M., 1926, Ph.D., 1932. *Home address:* Helen Ave., Rye, N.Y. 10580.

CAREER: New York University, New York, N.Y., instructor, 1926-33, assistant professor of history, 1933-38; Fordham University, Bronx, N.Y., associate professor, 1938-44, professor of history, 1944-67, professor emeritus, 1967—, Richard Lecturer, 1950.

MEMBER: American Historical Association, American Catholic Historical Association (president, 1938-39), Con-

ference on British Studies. *Awards, honors:* D.Litt. from Villanova College, 1936; LL.D. from Marquette University, 1937, Fordham University, 1947, and St. John's University, 1970; L.H.D. from University of Detroit, 1950; Litt.D. from National University of Ireland, 1957; Beer Prize from American Historical Association, 1934; King Award from U.S. Catholic Historical Society, 1975.

WRITINGS: Great Britain and the German Trade Rivalry, 1875-1914, University of Pennsylvania Press, 1933, Russell & Russell, 1964; *Visual Outline of Medieval History,* Longmans, Green, 1933; *Restoration,* Sheed, 1934; *The Will to Freedom,* Sheed, 1935; *Tradition and Progress, and Other Historical Essays in Culture, Religion, and Politics,* Bruce Books, 1938, Kennikat, 1968; *The Organic State: An Historical View of Contemporary Politics,* Sheed, 1939; *The Great Republic: A Historical View of the International,* Sheed, 1942; (with C. G. Haines) *Origin and Background of the Second World War,* Oxford University Press, 1943; *Durable Peace: A Study in American National Policy,* Oxford University Press, 1944; (with A. P. Lecak) *Burke's Politics: Selected Writings and Speeches on Reform, Revolution, and War,* Knopf, 1949.

The Spirit of Politics and the Future of Freedom, Bruce Books, 1951; *Edmund Burke, New York Agent, with His Letters to the New York Assembly and Intimate Correspondence with Charles O'Hara, 1761-1776,* American Philosophical Society, 1956; (with Gaetano L. Vincitorio and Morrison V. Swift) *Man and His History: World History and Western Civilization,* Doubleday, 1958, revised edition, 1963; (with Peter J. Stanlis and others) *The Relevance of Edmund Burke,* Kenedy, 1964; *The Marquis: A Study of Lord Rockingham, 1730-1782,* Fordham University Press, 1973.

Editor of "Christendom Series," Macmillan, 1940-42, and "Christian Democracy Series," Doubleday, 1955-56.

SIDELIGHTS: Hoffman told *CA:* "As an historian I have ever been most interested in *homo politicus,* man as a political creature; and in the principles that underly and preserve civil society. Of all political thinkers I esteem Edmund Burke as the wisest."

* * *

HOFFMANN, Malcolm A(rthur) 1912-

PERSONAL: Born November 26, 1912, in Brooklyn, N.Y.; son of Abraham Albert (a lawyer) and Minna (Newmark) Hoffmann; married Anna Frances Luciano (a director of a private school), April 13, 1939; children: Gertrude Nina (Mrs. William Bolter), Jessica Ann (Mrs. William Davis). *Education:* Harvard University, A.B. (magna cum laude), 1934, LL.B., 1937 (later converted to J.D.). *Home:* 5440 Independence Ave., Riverdale, N.Y. 10471. *Office:* 12 East 41st St., New York, N.Y. 10017.

CAREER: Performed various law functions for U.S. Government; Department of Justice, Antitrust Division, special assistant to attorney general, 1944-55; Malcolm A. Hoffman (law firm), New York City, senior partner, 1955—. Chairman of the board and vice-president of Hoffmann School, Inc., 1960—. Lecturer at Practicing Law Institute, 1957—, and for American Bar Association antitrust and litigation sections.

WRITINGS: Government Lawyer, Federal Legal Publications, 1956; *Hoffmann's Antitrust Laws and Techniques,* three volumes, Matthew Bender, 1963; (contributor) Morris L. Ernst, editor, *The Teacher,* Prentice-Hall, 1967; *Back and Forth* (essays), Peter Pauper, 1969.

Work anthologized in *Novel and Story,* edited by Ellory Sedgwick, Little, Brown, 1939. Contributor of stories and articles to magazines.

WORK IN PROGRESS: A chronicle of the private school operated by his wife; a comparison of the conduct of British and American Bars.

* * *

HOFSOMMER, Donovan Lowell 1938-

PERSONAL: Born April 10, 1938, in Fort Dodge, Iowa; son of Vernie G. (an insurance agent) and Helma J. (a clerk; maiden name, Schager) Hofsommer; married Sandra L. Rusch (a high school teacher), June 13, 1964; children: Kathryn Anne, Kristine Beret. *Education:* University of Northern Iowa, B.A., 1960, M.A., 1966; Oklahoma State University, Ph.D., 1973. *Religion:* Presbyterian. *Home:* 808 Vernon, Plainview, Tex. 79072. *Office:* Department of History, Wayland College, Plainview, Tex. 79072.

CAREER: High school history teacher in Fairfield, Iowa, 1961-65; Lea College, Albert Lea, Minn., instructor in history, 1966-70; Wayland College, Plainview, Tex., associate professor of history, 1973—. *Military service:* Iowa National Guard, 1960-66.

MEMBER: Organization of American Historians, Western History Association, Railway and Locomotive Historical Association, National Railway Historical Association, Lexington Group, State Historical Society of Iowa, Texas Historical Society, Phi Alpha Theta, Phi Delta Kappa. *Awards, honors:* Award from American Association for State and Local History, 1976, for *Prairie Oasis.*

WRITINGS: Prairie Oasis: The Railroads, Steamboats, and Resorts of Iowa's Spirit Lake Country, Waukon & Mississippi Press, 1975; (editor) *Railroads of the Trans-Mississippi West: A Selected Bibliography of Books,* Llano Estacado Museum, 1976; *Katy Northwest: The Story of a Branch Line Railroad,* Pruett, 1976. Contributor of more than twenty articles to history and railroad journals and to newspapers. Editor of *Lexington Newsletter;* member of editorial board of *Railroad History.*

WORK IN PROGRESS: Quit Arguing and Push: A History of the Quanah, Acme & Pacific Railway, for Pruett; *Steel Trails Through Hawkeye-Land: The Railroads of Iowa,* for Pruett; *"The Louie": An Illustrated History of the Minneapolis & St. Louis Railway,* for Pruett; editing *The Iron Horse in Oklahoma,* for Oklahoma Historical Society.

* * *

HOIJER, Harry 1904-1976

September 6, 1904—March 11, 1976; American anthropologist, linguist, educator, and author. Obituaries: *New York Times,* March 6, 1976; *AB Bookman's Weekly,* May 17, 1976.

* * *

HOLDEN, Paul E. 1894(?)-1976

1894(?)—April 9, 1976; American economist, management educator, and author. Obituaries: *Washington Post,* April 14, 1976.

* * *

HOLENSTEIN, Elmar 1937-

PERSONAL: Born January 7, 1937, in St. Gallen, Switzerland; son of Adolf and Johanna (Fuerer) Holenstein; married

Daniela Varvazovska (an architect), November 25, 1970. *Education:* University of Louvain, Belgium, student, 1964-67, Ph.D., 1970; University of Heidelberg, student, 1967-69; University of Zurich, student, 1969-71. *Home:* Schuetzenstrasse 19, Zollikon, Switzerland CH 8702. *Office:* Philosophisches Seminar, Universitaet, Zurich, Switzerland CH 8702.

CAREER: Husserl Archives, Louvain, Belgium, scientific collaborator, 1971-73; University of Cologne, Cologne, Germany, scientific collaborator, 1975—; University of Zurich, Zurich, Switzerland, lecturer, 1976—. *Member:* Allgemeine Gesellschaft fuer Philosophie in Deutschland, Deutsche Gesellschaft fuer Phaenomenologische Forschung, Philosophische Gesellschaft der Schweiz. *Awards, honors:* Bourse Burrus from Swiss National Foundation for Scientific Research, 1974.

WRITINGS—In English translation: *Roman Jakobsons phaenomenologischer Strukturalismus,* Suhrkamp (Frankfurt), 1975, translation by Cathrine Schelbert and Tarcisius Schelbert published as *Roman Jakobson's Approach to Language,* Indiana University Press, 1976.

Other work: *Phaenomenologie der Assoziation* (title means "Phenomenology of Association"), Nijhoff (The Hague), 1972; (editor) *Edmund Husserl: Logische Untersuchungen I* (title means "Logical Investigations I"), Nijhoff, 1975; (editor) *Roman Jakobson: Hoelderlin–Klee–Brecht,* Suhrkamp, 1976.

WORK IN PROGRESS: Research in universal elements in language and their functional explanations, semiotics, and the phenomenological foundations of ethics.

* * *

HOLLANDER, Zander 1923-
(Alexander Peters)

PERSONAL: Born March 24, 1923, in New York, N.Y.; son of Herman and Tobye (Karesh) Hollander; married Phyllis Rosen (a writer and editor), December 31, 1951; children: Susan, Peter. *Education:* Attended City College (now of the City University of New York), and Queens College (now of the City University of New York). *Religion:* Jewish. *Residence:* New York, N.Y.; and Millertown, N.Y. *Office:* Associated Features Inc., 370 Lexington Ave., New York, N.Y. 10017.

CAREER: United Press International, New York, N.Y., staff member on foreign desk; New York *World Telegram,* New York, N.Y., sports writer; Associated Features Inc. (publisher), New York, N.Y., president. *Military service:* U.S. Army; served as correspondent for *Brief* magazine.

WRITINGS: (With Joe Carrieri) *Yankee Bat Boy,* Prentice-Hall, 1955; (with Larry Fox) *The Home Run Story,* Norton, 1966; (with Paul Zimmerman) *Football Lingo,* Norton, 1967; (with Sandy Padwe) *Basketball Lingo,* Grosset, 1971. Also author of *Street Hockey* (with Steve Clark), Hawthorn; and (under pseudonym Alexander Peters) *Heroes of the Major Leagues,* Random House.

Editor: *Great American Athletes of the Twentieth Century,* Random House, 1966, revised edition, 1972; *Baseball Lingo,* Norton, 1967; *Strange but True Football Stories,* Random House, 1967; *The Modern Encyclopedia of Basketball,* Four Winds Press, 1969, revised edition, 1973; *Great Moments in Pro Football,* Random House, 1969; *Great Rookies of Pro Basketball,* Random House, 1969; (with Hal Bock) *The Complete Encyclopedia of Ice Hockey,* Prentice-Hall, 1970, revised edition, 1974; *Pro Basketball: Its Super-*

stars and History, Scholastic Book Services, 1971; *Basketball's Greatest Games,* Prentice-Hall, 1971; (with wife, Phyllis Hollander) *They Dared to Lead,* Grosset, 1972; *The Complete Handbook of Pro Hockey,* Lancer, 1972; *The Complete Handbook of Baseball,* Lancer, 1973; *The Complete Handbook of Basketball,* Lancer, 1973; *Madison Square Garden: A Century of Sport and Spectacle on the World's Most Versatile Stage,* Hawthorn, 1973; *More Strange but True Football Stories,* Random House, 1973.

Also editor of: (With Phyllis Hollander) *It's the Final Score that Counts,* Grosset; *Improve Your Sport,* Popular Library; *Ballantine Beer Pro Football TV Manual,* Popular Library; *The Complete Handbook of Pro Football,* New American Library; (with Dave Schulz) *The Sports Quiz Book,* New American Library; *The Nostalgia Sports Record Book,* New American Library.

*   *   *

HOLMES, Efner Tudor   1949-

PERSONAL: Born February 11, 1949, in Boston, Mass.; daughter of Thomas L. (a farmer) and Tasha (a writer and illustrator; maiden name, Tudor) McCready; married Peter Holmes (in construction), July 31, 1971; children: Nathan, Jason. *Education:* Attended private schools in New England. *Religion:* Episcopalian. *Home address:* Route 1, Concord, N.H. 03301.

CAREER: Writer.

WRITINGS: The Christmas Cat (juvenile), Crowell, 1976.

WORK IN PROGRESS: Amy's Goose, a juvenile book; a third book.

SIDELIGHTS: Efner Holmes writes: "My writing is purposely about animals and country living as I have great empathy for those." *Avocational interests:* Farming, music, travel (Europe), crafts.

*   *   *

HOLZ, Loretta (Marie)   1943-

PERSONAL: Born June 4, 1943, in Holden, Mass.; daughter of Joseph Ciro and Loretta (Crump) Celle; married George Ernest Holz (an electronics engineer and inventor), August 22, 1965; children: G. Andrew, Matthew J. *Education:* Emmanual College, Boston, Mass., B.A., 1965; Rutgers University, M.Ed., 1972. *Home and office:* 97 Grandview Ave., North Plainfield, N.J. 07060.

CAREER: German teacher in junior high school in Bergenfield, N.J., 1965-66; German and English teacher in Warren, N.J., 1966-69; writer and crafts demonstrator, 1969—. *Member:* International Guild of Craft Journalists, Authors, and Photographers, Embroiderers' Guild of America.

WRITINGS: Teach Yourself Stitchery, Lothrop, 1974; *Mobiles You Can Make,* Lothrop, 1975; *How to Sell Your Arts and Crafts,* Scribner, in press. Has designed original material for craft and women's magazines. Author of "Your Crafts" column in *Creative Crafts.* Contributor of more than one hundred articles to craft journals and other magazines, including *Golden Hands Monthly, Prevue, Modern Maturity, Highlights for Children,* and *Art and Craft in Education.* Contributing editor of *Lady's Circle Home Crafts.*

WORK IN PROGRESS: Crafts Together: A Handbook for Children and Their Parents or Grandparents; A World of Stitchery Techniques and How to Do Them; How to Make and Use Puppets and Marionettes; Yarn Painting: A Mex- *ican Craft with Contemporary Applications; A World of Dolls to Make; Make Your Own Greeting Cards; The Crafts of the Ukraine.*

SIDELIGHTS: Loretta Holz writes: "While to date my articles and books have been mainly in the area of crafts for adults and children I hope to branch out to other areas while continuing to write about crafts. I have a great diversity of interests in addition to crafts: religion, computers, the elderly . . . to name a few. I hope soon to get time to write fiction, both short stories and perhaps novels for young adults."

AVOCATIONAL INTERESTS: Gardening, Oriental cooking, puppets and marionettes.

*   *   *

HOMER, Frederic D(onald)   1939-

PERSONAL: Born June 9, 1939, in Oceanside, N.Y.; son of Kip (an accountant) and Mildred (Rubenstein) Homer; married Carole G. Krane (a social worker), June 10, 1961; children: Scott, Marc, Laurie. *Education:* Rutgers University, A.B., 1961; Indiana University, Ph.D., 1970. *Home:* 1315 Curtis, Laramie, Wyo. 82070. *Office:* Department of Political Science, University of Wyoming, Laramie, Wyo. 82070.

CAREER: University of Wyoming, Laramie, director of administration of justice program, 1974—, associate professor of political science, 1976—, head of department, 1976—. *Military service:* U.S. Army, 1961-63; became second lieutenant.

WRITINGS: Guns and Garlic: Myths and Realities of Organized Crime, Purdue University Press, 1974.

WORK IN PROGRESS: Perspectives on Criminal Justice; a contribution for a book to be edited by Michael Stohl.

*   *   *

HONE, Joseph   1937-

PERSONAL: Born February 25, 1937, in London, England; son of Nathaniel and Bridget Hone; married Jacqueline Mary Yeend, March, 1963; children: Lucy, William. *Education:* Attended University of London, 1953-54. *Home:* Manor Cottage, Shutford, near Banbury, Oxfordshire, England. *Agent:* Deborah Rogers, 29 Goodge St., London W.1, England.

CAREER: English teacher in grammar school in Drogheda, Ireland, 1956; third assistant director to film-makers John Ford ("The Rising of the Moon"), Mark Robson ("The Little Hut"), John Gilling ("Interpol"), Joseph Losey ("The Gypsy and the Gentleman"), and Denys de la Patelleire ("Retour de Manivelle"), 1956-57; Egyptian Ministry of Education, Cairo, English teacher in Heliopolis and Suez, 1957-58; Rupert Hart-Davis (publishers), London, England, editorial assistant, 1958-59; Envoy Productions (play producers), Dublin, Ireland, co-founder and co-producer of plays and musicals, 1960-62; British Broadcasting Corp. (BBC)—Radio, London, England, producer in talks and current affairs department, 1963-66; United Nations, Secretariat, New York, N.Y., radio and television officer for Office of Public Information, 1967-68; World Bank, Washington, D.C., producer of radio programs dealing with the bank's various projects in India and Southeast Asia, 1968-69; free-lance writer and broadcaster (mainly for BBC), 1969—.

WRITINGS: The Private Sector (novel), Hamish Hamilton, 1971, Dutton, 1972; *The Sixth Directorate* (novel), Dutton, 1975; *The Dancing Waiters* (travel memoirs), Hamish

Hamilton, 1975. Contributor to screenplay, "King and Country"; author of radio scripts for BBC. Contributor of articles and reviews to magazines and newspapers, including *New Statesman*. Radio and television critic for *Listener*.

WORK IN PROGRESS: The Paris Trap, a novel.

SIDELIGHTS: Hone's books have appeared in French, Dutch, Swedish, and Spanish editions. His novel, *The Sixth Directorate,* has been adapted as a screenplay for Tony Richardson, 1976.

* * *

HONEYMAN, Brenda
See CLARKE, Brenda Margaret Lilian

* * *

HOOPES, James 1944-

PERSONAL: Born May 16, 1944, in Pittsburgh, Pa.; son of Edgar Martin (a teacher) and Ruth (a teacher; maiden name, Pelton) Hoopes; married Carol Aberbach (a health administrator), April 12, 1975. *Education:* Bowling Green State University, B.A., 1965; University of Wisconsin, Madison, M.A., 1969; Johns Hopkins University, M.A., 1971, Ph.D., 1973. *Politics:* "Interested in social justice." *Home:* 1031 Bailard Ave., #3, Carpenteria, Calif. 93013. *Office:* Department of English, University of California, Santa Barbara, Calif. 93106.

CAREER: U.S. Peace Corps, Washington, D.C., volunteer English teacher in Malaysian Borneo, 1966-67; Brown University, Providence, R.I., lecturer, 1973-75, assistant professor of American civilization, 1975-76; University of California, Santa Barbara, visiting assistant professor of English, 1976—. *Member:* American Historical Association, American Studies Association, Modern Language Association of America.

WRITINGS: Van Wyck Brooks: In Search of American Culture, University of Massachusetts Press, 1977.

WORK IN PROGRESS: Consciousness in New England (tentative title), a history of psychological theory from the time of the Puritans to Freud's visit to Clark University.

SIDELIGHTS: Hoopes comments that he is "appalled" at the "contemporary scholarly trend away from culture and ideas. [I] believe in precision but abhor the false claims of 'cliometricians' and some practitioners of the 'new social history.'"

* * *

HOPPER, Robert 1945-

PERSONAL: Born November 2, 1945, in Schenectady, N.Y.; son of Jack Hicks (an engineer) and Olga (a teacher and psychologist; maiden name, Butler) Hopper; married Kathryn Quammen, June 10, 1967; children: Brian, Christine. *Education:* Bowling Green State University, B.A., 1966, M.A., 1967; University of Wisconsin, Madison, Ph.D., 1970. *Home:* 2601 Bend Cove, Austin, Tex. 78704. *Office:* Department of Speech Communication, University of Texas, Austin, Tex. 78712.

CAREER: University of Texas, Austin, assistant professor, 1970-75, associate professor of speech, 1975—, senior staff research associate at Center for Communication Research, 1973—. *Member:* International Communication Association, Speech Communication Association.

WRITINGS: (With Rita C. Naremore) *Children's Speech: A Practical Introduction to Communication Development,*

Harper, 1973; *Human Message Systems,* Harper, 1976; (with Frederick Williams and Diana Natalicio) *The Sounds of Children,* Prentice-Hall, in press. Contributor to speech journals.

WORK IN PROGRESS: Human Communication Concepts and Skills, with Jack Whitehead; *Communication in Law Enforcement,* with D. F. Gundersen.

SIDELIGHTS: Hopper writes: "I write because it acts as a tonic for depression. I find writing about myself quite spooky, though in reality I write about nothing else—I usually veil it some." *Avocational interests:* Gardening, songwriting, hiking.

* * *

HORN, Edward Newman 1903(?)-1976

1903(?)—July 18, 1976; American novelist and poet. Obituaries: *New York Times,* July 19, 1976.

* * *

HORNBLOW, Arthur, Jr. 1893-1976

March 15, 1893—July 17, 1976; American stage and film producer, lawyer, and author of children's books. Obituaries: *New York Times,* July 18, 1976.

* * *

HOROWITZ, Morris A(aron) 1919-

PERSONAL: Born November 19, 1919, in Newark, N.J.; son of Samuel and Ann (Litwin) Horowitz; married Jean Ginsburg, July 12, 1941; children: Ruth, Joel. *Education:* New York University, B.A., 1940; Harvard University, Ph.D., 1954. *Home:* 5 Riedesel Ave., Cambridge, Mass. 02138. *Office:* Department of Economics, Northeastern University, Boston, Mass. 02115.

CAREER: U.S. Department of Labor, Washington, D.C., labor economist, 1941-42; Office of Defense Transportation, Washington, D.C., labor economist, 1942-44; National War Labor Board, Washington, D.C., labor economist and director of Shipbuilding Commission's Case Analysis Division, 1944-46; University of Illinois, Urbana, research assistant professor of economics at Institute of Labor and Industrial Relations, 1947-51; Wage Stabilization Board, Washington, D.C., director of Office of Case Analysis, 1951-52, vice-chairman of review and appeals committee, 1952-53; Harvard University, Cambridge, Mass., research associate in law, 1953-54, research associate in labor economics, 1954-56; Northeastern University, Boston, Mass., associate professor, 1956-59, professor of economics, 1959—, chairman of department, 1959—, research associate in Bureau of Business and Economic Research, 1956-59. Lecturer at Northeastern University, 1953-56; visiting professor at Massachusetts Institute of Technology, 1968-69, 1973. Ford Foundation manpower specialist for Argentina, 1961-62; member of arbitrators' panel of Federal Mediation and Conciliation Service; consultant to government and private business.

MEMBER: American Economic Association, Industrial Relations Research Association, American Arbitration Association (member of labor panel), Latin American Studies Association, Association of Evolutionary Economics, National Academy of Arbitrators, Phi Beta Kappa, Phi Kappa Phi, Pi Mu Epsilon.

WRITINGS: (Contributor) Joseph S. Rancek, editor, *The Challenge of Science Education,* Philosophical Library,

1959; *The New York Hotel Industry: A Labor Relations Study*, Harvard University Press, 1960; *Structure and Government of the Carpenters' Union*, Wiley, 1962; (with Miguel A. Almada and Eduardo A. Zalduendo) *Los Recursos Humanos de Nivel Universitario y Tecnico en La Republica Argentina* (title means "High Level Manpower in the Republic of Argentina"), Instituto Torcuato di Tella, 1963; (contributor) Frederick Harbison and Charles A. Myers, editors, *Manpower and Education*, McGraw, 1964; (contributor) *Employment Impact of Technological Change*, Appendix Volume II, National Commission on Technology, Automation, and Economic Progress, 1966; (contributor) G. L. Mangum and R. T. Robson, editors, *Metropolitan Impact of Manpower Programs: A Four City Comparison*, Olympus, 1973; *Manpower and Education in Franco Spain*, Archon, 1974.

Author of about thirty research reports for Institute of Labor and Industrial Relations at University of Illinois, Bureau of Business and Economic Research at Northeastern University, and other private and government institutions. Contributor to professional journals.

WORK IN PROGRESS: Research on health manpower and on manpower planning in Italy.

*   *   *

HOSKINS, Katharine Bail 1924-

PERSONAL: Born March 28, 1924, in Albuquerque, N.M.; daughter of Ernest Benjamin (a civil engineer) and Effie (a teacher; maiden name, Barron) Bail; married Herbert Wilson Hoskins, Jr. (a professor of English), October 19, 1950; children: Janet Alison, Susan Miranda and Judith Ann (twins). *Education:* University of New Mexico, B.A. (honors), 1944; Columbia University, M.A., 1947, Ph.D., 1965. *Politics:* "Democratic, more or less." *Religion:* Unaffiliated. *Home:* 1687 Shaw Pl., Claremont, Calif. 91711. *Office:* Department of Communication Arts, La Verne College, La Verne, Calif. 91750.

CAREER: Columbia University Press, New York City, editorial assistant, 1947-48; *World Labor Forum* (English-Italian magazine), New York City, editorial assistant, 1948-49; Rutgers University, New Brunswick, N.J., instructor in English at Douglass College, 1949-53; Harvey Mudd College, Claremont, Calif., part-time instructor in English, 1961-64; Upland College, Upland, Calif., associate professor of English, 1964-65; La Verne College, La Verne, Calif., associate professor, 1965-71, professor of English, 1971—, chairman of English department, 1968-73, chairman of humanities division, 1969-72. Member of Claremont Motion Picture Council. *Military service:* U.S. Naval Reserve, Women Accepted for Volunteer Emergency Service, instructor in radio navigation with naval aviation, 1944-46. *Member:* Modern Language Association of America, American Association of University Professors. *Awards, honors:* American Council of Learned Societies travel and study grant, 1974.

WRITINGS: Today the Struggle: Literature and Politics in England during the Spanish Civil War, University of Texas Press, 1969.

SIDELIGHTS: Katharine Hoskins writes: "I am primarily a teacher, by taste and choice. I write when it is necessary, and I enjoy trying to do it well, but writing is not my vocation. When I know enough, I may write another book, but only if I feel I have something important to say. I disapprove of most scholarly writing on the grounds that it is done for the wrong reasons, and so far I have not felt impelled to do any other kind of writing."

HOSTETLER, Marian 1932-

PERSONAL: Born February 9, 1932, in Ohio; daughter of M. Harry (a grocer; in insurance) and Esther (Hostetler) Hostetler. *Education:* Goshen College, B.A., 1954; Goshen Biblical Seminary, graduate study, 1957-58; Indiana University, M.S., 1973. *Religion:* Mennonite. *Home:* 1910 Morton, Elkhart, Ind. 46514.

CAREER: Mennonite Board of Missions, Elkhart, Ind., editorial assistant, 1958-60, teacher in Algeria, 1960-70; Concord Community Schools, Elkhart, Ind., elementary teacher, 1971—. Member of Mennonite Publication Board. *Member:* National Education Association, Indiana State Teachers Association.

WRITINGS: African Adventure, Herald Press, 1976; *Foundation Series Curriculum*, Grade 3, Quarter 2, Herald Press, in press.

WORK IN PROGRESS: Nightmare Awakening, a suspense novel; a juvenile book on the people of Palestine.

SIDELIGHTS: Marian Hostetler writes: "The years I spent in North Africa were important in giving me the occasion to begin writing as well as giving me background useful in most of what I've written. A summer spent working in Chad gave me the inspiration and background for *African Adventure*. A Christian perspective is also an integral part of most of what I write."

AVOCATIONAL INTERESTS: Painting, reading.

*   *   *

HOUGHTON, (Charles) Norris 1909-

PERSONAL: Born December 26, 1909, in Indianapolis, Ind.; son of Charles D. M. (a businessman) and Grace Houghton. *Education:* Princeton University, A.B. (summa cum laude), 1931. *Office:* Division of Theatre Arts, State University of New York College at Purchase, Purchase, N.Y.

CAREER: Stage manager, designer, and director of Broadway productions in New York, N.Y., 1932-56; Phoenix Theatre, New York City, founder and co-managing director, 1953-64; Vassar College, Poughkeepsie, N.Y., professor of drama and director of experimental theatre, 1962-67; State University of New York College at Purchase, professor of theater arts, 1967—, dean of division of theatre arts, 1967-75. Art director of St. Louis Municipal Opera, 1939-40; director of Elitch's Garden Theatre, 1947-48. Lecturer at Princeton University, 1941-42, Smith College, 1947, Columbia University, 1948-54, Union Theological Seminary, 1954, and Yale University, 1970-72; adjunct professor at Barnard College, 1954-58, and Vassar College, 1959-60; visiting professor at Harvard University, 1954. President of National Theatre Conference, 1969-73; member of advisory council of Institute for Advanced Studies in Theatre Arts; member of Rockefeller Brothers Fund panel on the performing arts, 1962-64. *Military service:* U.S. Naval Reserve, active duty, 1943-45; became lieutenant.

MEMBER: American Council for the Arts in Education (president, 1973-75), American Academy of Arts and Sciences (fellow), Phi Beta Kappa. *Awards, honors:* Guggenheim fellowships, 1934-35, 1960-61; D.F.A. from Denison University, 1959.

WRITINGS: Moscow Rehearsals, Harcourt, 1936, reprinted, Octagon, 1975; *Advance from Broadway*, Harcourt, 1941, reprinted, Greenwood Press, 1971; *But Not Forgotten*, Sloane, 1951; *Return Engagement*, Holt, 1962; *The Exploding Stage*, Weybright, 1970.

Editor: *Great Russian Short Stories,* Dell, 1958; *Great Russian Plays,* Dell, 1960; *Masterpieces of Continental Drama,* three volumes, Dell, 1964. Associate editor of *Theatre Arts,* 1945-48.

AVOCATIONAL INTERESTS: Travel (three times around the world; special interest in the Soviet Union).

* * *

HOUGHTON, Samuel G(ilbert) 1902-1975

PERSONAL: Born January 24, 1902, in Boston, Mass.; son of Clement Stevens (an investor) and Martha Gilbert (Colt) Houghton; married Sally White, 1935 (divorced, 1936); married Edda Kreiner, June 20, 1939; children: John Greenleaf, Catherine, Linda, Monica Topliff. *Education:* Attended U.S. Naval Academy, 1919, and Harvard University, 1920-23. *Politics:* Republican.

CAREER: Stone & Webster, engineer in Boston, Mass., and Columbus, Ga., 1923-25; Walworth Co., Buffalo, N.Y., sales engineer, 1926-30; *Writer,* Boston, Mass., editor and publisher, 1933-36; in mining in Nevada, 1940-41, 1946-48; Double-O Timber and Mining Co., Calif., mine operator and vice-president, 1948-51; Nevada State Legislature, Carson City, assemblyman, 1953-54; investor and writer, 1954-75. Member of Nevada State Committee on Federal Land Laws, 1965-70; member of Reno War Price and Rationing Board during World War Two. Director of Nevada Art Gallery Board, 1958-72 (president, 1964-69); director of civil defense for Washoe County, 1950-53; chairman of Lake Tahoe Park Committee, 1964; former trustee of Washoe County Library and Northern Nevada Land Foundation; former member of board of directors of Sierra Arts Foundation and local Community Concert Association. Performed with Reno Little Theater and Reno Men's Chorus. *Military service:* U.S. Naval Reserve, active duty with Construction Battalion (Seabees), 1943-45; served in South Pacific; received three battle stars.

WRITINGS: The Writer's Handbook, Writer, Inc., 1936; *The Music Album,* Morrow, 1938; *Seventy-Fourth Construction Battalion Review,* U.S. Navy, 1945; *A Trace of Desert Waters: The Great Basin Story,* Arthur H. Clark, 1976. Contributor to regional magazines and newspapers.

SIDELIGHTS: Houghton enjoyed extensive travel in Europe and the Far East, including Bali, and lived in Peking. One time he worked his passage to Europe on a cattle boat. *Avocational interests:* Skiing, hiking, photography.

(Died October 14, 1975, in Reno, Nev.)

* * *

HOUSTON, James A(rchibald) 1921-

PERSONAL: Born June 12, 1921, in Toronto, Ontario, Canada; came to the United States in 1962; son of James Donald and Gladys Maud (Barbour) Houston; married Alice Daggett Watson, December 9, 1967; children: John James, Samuel Douglas. *Education:* Attended Ontario College of Art, 1938-40, Ecole Grand Chaumiere, 1947-48, Unichi-Hiratsuka, 1958-59, and Atelier 17, 1961. *Residence:* Escoheag, R.I.

CAREER: Government of Canada, West Baffin, Northwest Territories, first civil administrator, 1952-62; Steuben Glass, New York, N.Y., associate director of design, 1962-72. Visiting lecturer at Wye Institute and Rhode Island School of Design. Chairman of board of directors of Canadian Arctic Producers, 1976-77, and American Indian Art Center; member of board of directors of Canadian Eskimo Arts Council; president of Indian and Eskimo Art of the Americas; vice-president of West Baffin Eskimo Cooperative and Eskimo Art, Inc. Member of primitive art committee of Metropolitan Museum of Art. *Military service:* Canadian Army, 1940-45. *Member:* Explorers Club, Century Association, Grolier Club, Leash.

AWARDS, HONORS: Decorated officer of Order of Canada; award from American Indian and Eskimo Cultural Foundation, 1966; Canadian Library Association Book of the Year awards, 1966, for *Tikta'Liktak,* and 1968, for *The White Archer;* American Library Association Notable Books awards, 1967, for *The White Archer,* 1968, for *Akavak,* and 1971, for *The White Dawn;* Chicago Book Clinic award for design, 1970, for *America Was Beautiful;* D.Litt., Carleton University, 1972; D.H.L., Rhode Island College, Providence, 1975.

WRITINGS: Canadian Eskimo Art, Queen's Printer, 1955; *Eskimo Graphic Art,* Queen's Printer, 1960; *Eskimo Prints,* Barre Publishing, 1967, 2nd edition, 1971; (author of introduction) G. F. Lyon, *The Private Journal of Captain G. F. Lyon,* Barre Publishing, 1970; *The White Dawn: An Eskimo Saga* (Book-of-the-Month Club Selection), Harcourt, 1971; *Ojibwa Summer,* Barre Publishing, 1972; (editor) *Songs of the Dream People: Chants and Images from the Indians and Eskimos of North America* (self-illustrated), Atheneum, 1972; *Ghost Fox,* Harcourt, 1977.

Juvenile books; all self-illustrated: *Tikta'liktak: An Eskimo Legend,* Harcourt, 1965; *Eagle Mask: A West Coast Indian Tale,* Harcourt, 1966; *The White Archer: An Eskimo Legend,* Harcourt, 1967; *Akavak: An Eskimo Journey,* Harcourt, 1968; *Wolf Run: A Caribou Eskimo Tale,* Harcourt, 1971; *Ghost Paddle: A Northwest Coast Indian Tale,* Harcourt, 1972; *Kiviok's Magic Journey: An Eskimo Legend,* Atheneum, 1973.

Screenplays: "The White Dawn," Paramount Pictures, 1973; "The Mask and the Drum," Swannsway Productions, 1975; "So Sings the Wolf," Devonian Group, 1976; "Kalvak," Devonian Group, 1976.

Also illustrator of books for other authors.

SIDELIGHTS: "In the autumn of 1948," Houston told *CA,* "after finishing life drawing classes in Paris, I returned to Canada, looking for suitable people to draw, and happened to visit an Eskimo settlement called Inukjuak. It was on the northeast coast of Hudson Bay, a gateway to the Eskimo world. About three hundred Eskimos traded into Inukjuak from their hunting area which extended over roughly sixty thousand square miles. They spoke only Eskimo, lived in domed snow igloos, and hunted for a living in whaleboats and sealskin kayaks. I was excited at the prospect of making drawings of these short, vital, oriental-looking people, and decided to camp with them for a few weeks. I stayed in the Arctic for fourteen years!

"Eskimos . . . have always been keenly aware of theatrics and were conducting spectacular performances thousands of years before the written word existed. Theater, it seems to me, is the most total of all art experiences. Theater alone combines the art of storytelling with fanciful costumes, singing, dancing, musical instruments, the play of light and dark, laughter, weeping, all the drama and excitement necessary to retell the dreams and legends of this and other worlds for future generations.

"When I lived with the Eskimos, I knew their songs and dancing. I knew, as well, those of the Nascopi and the Cree who danced in the east, the Zuni and Hopi dancing in the south, and the Kwakiutl and Tlingat in the far west. Each group has different songs and deities and vastly different art styles that seem to have grown out of their environment, their special way of life.

"When I hear their singing, when I read the words of their songs and see their masks and other art objects moving in the winter firelight or the desert sun, I have an unshakable feeling that we are all of us everywhere celebrating the same someone, though he or she has a thousand different forms and wears a different mask for each of us.

"Kiakshuk, a famous Eskimo carver who had grown old on Baffin Island and had seen his whole world change, said to me, 'When I was young, shaman still had magic power. They could fly out of the dance house and ride the drum into the other world. In those days we were people ruled by dreams.'"

* * *

HOWARD, Dorothy (Arlynne) 1912-

PERSONAL: Born February 8, 1912, in Danbury, Conn.; daughter of Friend (a researcher and developer) and Edith (a teacher; maiden name, Patterson) Sherwood; divorced, 1951; children: Priscilla, Deborah (Mrs. Peter Hansen). *Education:* New England Conservatory of Music, B.Mus., 1938; also attended Berkshire College, Clark University, and New York University. *Religion:* Protestant. *Home:* 11 Riverside Dr., Apt. 15-O-W, New York, N.Y. 10023. *Office:* Mutual of New York, 1740 Broadway, New York, N.Y. 10017.

CAREER: Assistant auditor for an electrical engineering company, Boston, Mass., 1944-48; assistant treasurer of an oils and lubricants company, Worcester, Mass., 1950-59; *Faith at Work,* New York City, business manager, 1959-63; Mutual of New York, New York City, insurance analyst, 1963—. Concert pianist and organist in the New England area, 1932-62; associate organist for Boston and Worcester churches. *Member:* National Association of Accountants, American Management Association, National Office Management Association, National Organists Guild, Christian Business and Professional Women of America.

WRITINGS: No Longer Alone, David Cook, 1976. Contributor to business journals and religious magazines.

WORK IN PROGRESS: The Challenging World of Singles; Cathie, a novel; research for a book on alcoholism.

AVOCATIONAL INTERESTS: Travel, reading.

* * *

HOWARD, Edwin 1924-
(Monroe Lott)

PERSONAL: Born July 26, 1924, in Florida; son of John Zollie (a newspaper editor) and Jessie (Magill) Howard; married Olivia LeMaster, July 11, 1946 (divorced, May, 1975); married Corinne Hanover (an art gallery manager), August 25, 1975; children: Meg, Heather. *Education:* Attended Southwestern at Memphis, 1946-48. *Home:* 196 Cherry Circle, Memphis, Tenn. 38117. *Office: Memphis Press-Scimitar,* 495 Union Ave., Memphis, Tenn. 38101.

CAREER: Memphis Press-Scimitar, Memphis, Tenn., amusements editor and film and drama critic, both 1946—, book review editor, 1955—, and author of daily column, "The Front Row," 1961—. "Lively arts" critic for WMC-Television, 1968-76, guest commentator, 1972-76, writer-producer-narrator of documentary film "Film Is a Four-

Letter Word," 1975; his television special presentations include interviews with Arthur Rubinstein and Johnny Cash; produced a newspaper series on the Cold War for Newspaper Enterprise Association Service, 1946-47; co-founder and member of board of directors of Memphis Shakespeare Festival. *Military service:* U.S. Army, Armored Infantry, 1942-45; served in European theater; received four battle stars. *Member:* Summit Club. *Awards, honors:* Boyd Martin Motion Picture Page Award, 1964.

WRITINGS: (Editor and author of introduction) *The Editorial We: A Posthumous Autobiography of Edward J. Meeman,* Memphis State University, 1977. Contributor to motion picture fan magazines, under pseudonym Monroe Lott, and to theater journals. Contributing editor of *Delta Review,* 1965-69.

WORK IN PROGRESS: A novel, *The Day When I Must Die;* a play to be adapted from a novel by Joan Williams.

SIDELIGHTS: Howard writes that he was "born writing, reviewing; decided to be newspaperman at three; wrote first review, *Pierre Pons,* children's book, for father's *Knoxville News-Sentinel* Book Page, at six. Consider both easier than working." During his career, he has conducted numerous interviews with well-known performers, including Clark Gable, Cary Grant, Patricia Neal, Bing Crosby, Paul Newman, Joanne Woodward, Elvis Presley, James Earl Jones, and Doris Day.

* * *

HOWARD, Philip 1933-

PERSONAL: Born November 2, 1933, in London, England; son of Peter D. (a writer and farmer) and Doris (Metaxas) Howard; married Myrtle Houldsworth, October 7, 1959; children: Juliette, John Henry. *Education:* Trinity College, Oxford, B.A., 1956. *Religion:* Church of England. *Home:* 47 Ladbroke Grove, Flat 1, London W.11, England. *Office: Times,* New Printing House Sq., Gray's Inn Rd., London W.C.1, England.

CAREER: Glasgow Herald, Glasgow, Scotland, Parliamentary correspondent, 1959-64; *Times,* London, England, reporter and feature writer, 1964—. *Military service:* British Army, Black Watch, 1956-58. *Awards, honors:* Press award for descriptive writing from International Publishing Corp., 1971.

WRITINGS: The Black Watch (history), Hamish Hamilton, 1968; *The Royal Palaces* (nonfiction), Gambit, 1970; *London's River* (nonfiction), Hamish Hamilton, 1975; *The British Royal Family in the Past Century,* Hamish Hamilton, 1976; *New Words for Old,* Oxford University Press, 1976.

* * *

HOWATCH, Joseph 1935-

PERSONAL: Born December 4, 1935, in Pennsylvania; son of John and Helen (Kovac) Howatch; married Susan Sturt, August 15, 1964 (legally separated); children: Antonia. *Education:* King's College, Wilkes-Barre, Pa., B.A., 1958. *Residence:* Sparta, N.J. *Agent:* Claire Smith, Harold Ober Associates, 40 East 49th St., New York, N.Y. 10017.

CAREER: Owner and manager of a lumbering and construction business, 1958-64; American Heart Association, New York, N.Y., analyst, 1964-68; Research and Information Services for Education, King of Prussia, Pa., director of information services, 1968-69; American Heart Association, assistant director of research, 1969-70; free-lance writer, 1970—.

WRITINGS: *Antonio, Antonia* (novel), Houghton, 1976.

WORK IN PROGRESS: *Modern Persons,* a novel; *Engaging Lies,* a novel.

AVOCATIONAL INTERESTS: Sculpture, painting, architecture, music.

* * *

HOWE, William Hugh 1928-

PERSONAL: Born June 18, 1928, in Stockton, Calif.; son of Edwin Walter and Eugenia Ursula (Mercante) Howe. *Education:* Ottawa University, Ottawa, Kan., A.B., 1951. *Politics:* None. *Religion:* Roman Catholic. *Home:* 822 East 11th St., Ottawa, Kan. 66067.

CAREER: Merchandise Mart, Kansas City, Mo., artist, 1952-55; U.S. Army, Corps of Engineers, Kansas City, Mo., civilian artist, 1959-65; Howard Needles Tammen & Bergendoff (consulting engineers and architects), artist in urban and regional planning section, 1965-70. Paintings of butterflies are in many permanent collections, including those of Denver Museum of Natural History, Cranbrook Institutions, San Diego Museum of Fine Arts, Smithsonian Institution, Carnegie Museum, and Los Angeles County Museum.

WRITINGS: *Our Butterflies and Moths,* True Color Publishing Co., 1964; *The Butterflies of North America,* Doubleday, 1975. Contributor of articles on butterflies to magazines and newspapers.

WORK IN PROGRESS: Painting Mexican butterflies in their natural habitats, including migratory flights, for an exhibit at Museum of Anthropology in Mexico City.

SIDELIGHTS: Howe has written: "The purpose of butterflies will not be found . . . in the few flowers they may inadvertently pollinate . . . nor in the numbers of parasitic wasps they may support. And to peer beneath a microscope at their dissected fragments will in no way elucidate the reason for their being. Their purpose is their beauty and the beauty they bring into the lives of those of us who have paused long enough from the cares of the world to listen to their fascinating story. . . ."

* * *

HOWELL, Benjamin Franklin 1890-1976

September 30, 1890—May 28, 1976; American paleontologist, geologist, and editor. Obituaries: *New York Times,* June 3, 1976.

* * *

HOWKINS, John 1945-

PERSONAL: Born August 3, 1945, in Northampton, England; son of Walter and Lesley (Stops) Howkins. *Education:* Keele University, B.A., 1968; Architectural Association, diploma in town planning, 1972. *Home:* Honeysuckle Cottage, London, Suffolk, England. *Office:* 9e Transept St., London N.W.1, England.

CAREER: Free-lance journalist. International Institute of Communications, London, England, editor of *InterMedia* magazine, 1975—; British Academy of Film and Television Arts, London, England, editor of *Vision* magazine, 1977—. Director of Whittet Books; member of executive committee of British Standing Conference on Broadcasting, 1975—. *Member:* National Union of Journalists, Critics Circle, Guild of Broadcasting Journalists.

WRITINGS: *Understanding Television,* Sundial, 1976; (editor) *Vision and Hindsight: The Future of Communications,* International Institute of Communications, 1976. Contributor to *Encyclopaedia Britannica,* and to periodicals, including *Sunday Times* (London) and *Time Out.*

WORK IN PROGRESS: A book, *TV Is Only the Beginning.*

* * *

HUBBARD, Frank T. 1921(?)-1976

1921(?)—February 4, 1976; American musical-instrument maker and author. Obituaries: *AB Bookman's Weekly,* March 22, 1976.

* * *

HUBBELL, John G(erard) 1927-

PERSONAL: Born July 14, 1927, in New York, N.Y.; son of Lester Sprague (a salesman) and Margaret (Malia) Hubbell; married Katherine Hartigan, June 2, 1956; children: Charles W., John Paul, Mary Louise, Joseph, Mary Margaret, William, Andrew, Mary Katherine. *Education:* University of Minnesota, B.A., 1950. *Religion:* Roman Catholic. *Home:* 4004 Queen Ave. S., Minneapolis, Minn. 55410. *Office: Reader's Digest,* Pleasantville, N.Y. 10570.

CAREER: Honeywell, Inc., Minneapolis, Minn., member of public relations staff in aeronautical division, 1949-55; *Reader's Digest* magazine, Pleasantville, N.Y., staff writer, 1955-60, roving editor, 1960—. Member of board of directors, Operation H.O.P.E.; editorial consultant to President's Blue Ribbon Defense Panel, 1970-72. *Military service:* U.S. Navy, 1945-46. *Member:* National Press Club, Delta Kappa Epsilon, Minneapolis Golf Club. *Awards, honors:* International Conference of Industrial Writers award, and Northwest Industrial Editors Association writing award, both 1952; Sigma Delta Chi Distinguished Service award, 1966, for magazine article, "The Case of the Missing H-Bomb."

WRITINGS: *Strike in the West: The Complete Story of the Cuban Missile Crisis,* Holt, 1963; *P.O.W.: A Definitive History of the American Prisoner of War Experience in Vietnam, 1964-1973,* Reader's Digest Press, 1976. Contributor to *Saturday Evening Post, True, Flying, Catholic Digest, Popular Mechanics,* and other magazines and newspapers.

WORK IN PROGRESS: Adventure, human interest, military and foreign affairs articles for *Reader's Digest.*

SIDELIGHTS: Hubbell told *CA* that his writing of *P.O.W.* "was motivated by a desire to learn how Americans had fared in the prisoner of war camps in Vietnam during the longest of American wars. There had never been a deep study of the American prisoner of war experience following any war. The American P.O.W.'s had remained in captivity longer than any other Americans in our history. What had it been like? What had been the nature of their war? What of their captors' strategy and tactics, and how had the P.O.W.s countered them? How had they endured? The effort was made to make a significant contribution to the body of American history; to provide Americans with knowledge of this aspect of their heritage."

AVOCATIONAL INTERESTS: Golf, raquetball, sailing, cycling.

BIOGRAPHICAL/CRITICAL SOURCES: *Minneapolis Star,* November 6, 1953, September 9, 1966.

HUDSON, Richard (McLain, Jr.) 1925-

PERSONAL: Born June 18, 1925, in Los Angeles, Calif.; son of Richard McLain (a businessman) and Helen (Grant) Hudson; married Helen Lundstrom, December 6, 1958; children: Lucinda Ellen, Anne Linnea. *Education:* University of Minnesota, B.S. (cum laude), 1946; University of Southern California, graduate study, 1947. *Home:* 150 West 80th St., New York, N.Y. 10024. *Office:* Center for War/Peace Studies, 218 East 18th St., New York, N.Y. 10003.

CAREER: University of Southern California, Los Angeles, assistant in department of economics, 1946-47; *Monrovia Daily News-Post,* Monrovia, Calif., reporter and desk man, 1948-50; *Pasadena Star-News,* Pasadena, Calif., reporter and desk man, 1950-52; *Stars & Stripes,* European edition, Darmstadt, West Germany, reporter and desk man, covering stories in Germany and France, 1952-53; Texaco, New York, N.Y., staff writer in public relations department, 1953-56; *Picture News* (of Sinclair Oil Co.), New York City, editor, 1956-58; *Daily Journal,* Caracas, Venezuela, managing editor, 1958-60; *War/Peace Report,* New York City, founder and editor, 1960-75; free-lance writer, 1976—. Reorganizer of Center for War/Peace Studies, 1976—. Accredited United Nations correspondent, 1961—; free-lance writer and photographer in Europe and North Africa, 1952-53, and South America, 1958-60. Radio-television commentator for Canadian Broadcasting Corp., 1964-70; moderator of "World Affairs Forum," a monthly radio program on WEVD-New York City, 1955-57. *Military service:* U.S. Navy, 1944-46; became ensign. *Member:* Overseas Press Club (founding president of Caracas chapter), United Nations Correspondents Association.

WRITINGS: (With Ben Shahn) *Kuboyama: The Saga of the Lucky Dragon* (on the first victim of the hydrogen bomb), Yoseloff, 1965. Contributor of articles and photographs to a wide variety of national publications, including *Saturday Review* and *Cosmopolitan,* and newspapers, including *Christian Science Monitor, New York Times,* and *Chicago Tribune.*

WORK IN PROGRESS: Writing on the Law of the Sea Conference, for the United Nations Food and Agriculture Organization; writing and editing material for United Nations Association, World Federalist Political Education Committee, and Council on Religion and International Affairs.

SIDELIGHTS: Richard Hudson told *CA:* "While I have done many kinds of writing, world affairs has always been my special interest. My viewpoint might best be termed globalist. Although I favor the maximum individual freedom compatible with a system of law and order, I feel at the same time that some world problems, and especially war, urgently require the building of new global institutions able to provide humanity a world of peace with justice. I include within the concept of justice a decent material well-being for everyone as well as political and spiritual freedom. What's more, I believe it is possible for the world to achieve this goal within 25 to 50 years.

My travels reflect this interest. In 1962 I went to Geneva to cover the opening of the U.N. Conference of the Committee on Disarmament. In October 1963 I published in *War/Peace Report* my first editorial condemning U.S. involvement in Vietnam, and I made trips to Paris in 1969 and 1972 to interview the North Vietnamese and Viet Cong delegations. In 1964 I went to Cuba on a junket with a large number of leading U.S. journalists at a time when I think Fidel Castro was making his first tentative feeler for a reconciliation with the U.S.

In 1965 I spent a month in the Soviet Union, where I gave a seminar on disarmament issues—but found myself spending much more time discussing the bombing which had recently begun in Vietnam and the U.S. invasion of the Dominican Republic, which took place while I was there.

In 1970 I spent a month in the Middle East, visiting Israel and the four contiguous Arab countries. From this, I did a special issue of *War/Peace Report* entitled, "Peace in the Middle East Is Just, Maybe, Barely Possible."

In 1973 I went to Panama to cover the unique meeting there on the Panama Canal of the United Nations Security Council. In addition to my coverage for *War/Peace Report,* I subsequently wrote articles on the Panama Canal for *The New York Times Magazine* in 1974 and 1976.

In 1974 I went to Caracas, Venezuela, for the first substantive session of the Third United Nations Law of the Sea Conference, and I have also covered the two Law of the Sea sessions at the U.N. in New York this year. I am now making a study of how the international community can go about mining the seabed for copper- and nickel-rich nodules, which is the issue that may cause the conference to fail. This is expected to be the first study of the newly-reorganized Center for War/Peace Studies.

Other high priority studies which the Center, which I will head, intends to make include the following: What procedures and what terms for an overall Middle East peace settlement? How to reverse the arms race? How to make development really work in poor countries? How to make the United Nations power structure more functional?"

*   *   *

HUEY, Lynda 1947-

PERSONAL: Born May 13, 1947, in Vallejo, Calif.; daughter of Robert Walter (a real estate broker) and Glenn Margaret (a dental assistant; maiden name, Bryant) Huey. *Education:* San Jose State University, B.A., 1969, M.A., 1971. *Residence:* Los Angeles, Calif. *Agent:* Mike Hamilburg, 292 La Cienega, Suite 212, Los Angeles, Calif. 90211.

CAREER: Federal City College, Washington, D.C., instructor in health, physical education, and recreation, 1971-72; California Polytechnic State University, San Luis Obispo, assistant professor of physical education and coach of women's intercollegiate track and field team, 1972-73; Oberlin College, Oberlin, Ohio, women's sports coordinator and coach of women's intercollegiate basketball team, 1973-74; Mira Costa College, Oceanside, Calif., volleyball coach, 1974-75; free-lance writer, 1975—. Represented the United States at International Olympic Academy, 1973; visited People's Republic of China on sports tour, 1976. Has participated in sports as member of women's amateur track, volleyball, field hockey, and football teams.

MEMBER: American Association for Health, Physical Education and Recreation, U.S. Women's Track Coaches Association, National Association of Physical Education College Women (Western Society), U.S. Volleyball Association, U.S. Field Hockey Association, National Women's Football League, Amateur Athletic Union, National Organization of Women, California Association for Health, Physical Education and Recreation, Tau Gamma.

WRITINGS: A Running Start: A Woman, an Athlete, Quadrangle, 1976. Contributor to sports magazines. Contributing editor of *Volleyball.*

WORK IN PROGRESS: Television filmscripts; an article on volleyball in China; an article for *Sport* magazine.

SIDELIGHTS: Lynda Huey would like to begin broadcasting on the sports in which she is most interested. Presently she works as a cocktail waitress at a local club in order to listen to the jazz musicians who perform there. *Avocational interests:* Bicycling, swimming, beach volleyball, racquetball, dancing, scuba diving, travel, piano.

BIOGRAPHICAL/CRITICAL SOURCES: San Diego Union, March 2, 1975; *Pasadena Guardian,* October 18, 1975; *Seattle Times,* January 5, 1976; *Coast Dispatch,* January 16, 1976; *San Jose Mercury,* April 5, 1976.

* * *

HUFF, Afton (A.) W(alker) 1928-

PERSONAL: Born February 12, 1928, in Manchester, England; came to United States in 1928, naturalized citizen, 1969; daughter of Harry James (a diamond broker) and Jessie (a physical therapist; maiden name, Carter) Walker; married Paschel M. Huff (a medical social analyst), March 13, 1944; children: Patricia Mary Huff Olesen. *Education:* Brigham Young University, student, 1943-44; Hill's Business University, degree in accounting, 1962; University of Oklahoma, degree in writing, 1967. *Religion:* Church of Jesus Christ of Latter-day Saints (Mormons). *Residence:* Midwest City, Okla. *Agent:* Robert P. Mills, 156 East 52nd St., New York, N.Y. 10022. *Office:* Harr Drive Co., 401 Harr Dr., Midwest City, Okla. 73110.

CAREER: Free-lance lecturer and book reviewer, 1946-51; self-employed in field of dance and eurythmics, 1949-60; partner in Pro Writing Help (correspondent teaching aid for writers), 1962—; Harr Drive Co., Midwest City, Okla., property manager, 1962—. Teacher of creative writing at Oklahoma University, 1969-70, and at Oscar Rose Junior College, 1972. *Member:* National League of American Pen Women, Authors Guild of Authors League of America, Beta Sigma Phi (past president of Sigma Rho chapter).

WRITINGS: The Silent Message (juvenile mystery novel), Steck, 1969; *The Key to Hawthorn Heath* (adult mystery novel), Berkley, 1973.

WORK IN PROGRESS: Thursday's Child, an adult mystery novel; *Phantom of Rodondo,* a sequel to *Silent Message;* a cookbook for people with impaired vision; a security training manual for prisons and corrections departments.

SIDELIGHTS: Afton Huff writes: "I am a handicapped (their words) person, being legally deaf. Few realize I do not hear as I have seventeen years of speech therapy, and lip read exceptionally well. The overcoming of all physical handicaps is something I feel strongly about, as the only real handicap is the inability to learn and so help others. I love music, and made a fair living as a teen in U.S.O. musicals. I danced barefoot (to feel music beat)." Huff has taught dancing to people impaired by blindness, polio, and other handicaps.

AVOCATIONAL INTERESTS: Travel (both foreign and domestic).

* * *

HUGHES, J(ohnson) Donald 1932-

PERSONAL: Born June 5, 1932, in Santa Monica, Calif.; son of Johnson (an architect) and Vannelia Anna (a teacher; maiden name, Blanchfield) Hughes; married Pamela Louise Peters (a guitar teacher), 1964; children: Peter Jay, Melissa

Jane. *Education:* Attended Oregon State University, 1950-52; University of California, Los Angeles, A.B., 1954; Boston University, S.T.B., 1957, Ph.D., 1960; also studied at Cambridge University, 1958-59, and American School of Classical Studies at Athens, 1966-67. *Politics:* Democrat. *Religion:* Methodist. *Office:* Department of History, University of Denver, Denver, Colo. 80210.

CAREER: San Diego State College (now University), San Diego, Calif., director of Wesley Foundation, 1960-62; California Western University, San Diego, assistant professor of history, 1961-66; Pierce College, Athens, Greece, professor of history, 1966-67; University of Denver, Denver, Colo., assistant professor, 1967-72, associate professor of history, 1972—. National Park Service ranger at Yosemite National Park, summers, 1952, 1957-58; ranger-naturalist at Grand Canyon National Park, summers, 1960-68.

MEMBER: American Historical Association, Association of Ancient Historians, American Society for Environmental History, American Indian Historical Society, National Parks and Conservation Association, Sierra Club, Classical Association of the Midwest and South, Colorado Mountain Club, Phi Beta Kappa. *Awards, honors:* Danforth associate, 1965—.

WRITINGS: The Story of Man at Grand Canyon, Grand Canyon Natural History Association, 1967; *Ecology in Ancient Civilization,* University of New Mexico Press, 1975; *American Indians in Colorado,* Pruett, 1976. Also author of *Ecology and the American Indians.* Contributor to history, folklore, and conservation magazines.

WORK IN PROGRESS: Theophrastus: The Father of Ecology in Greece.

SIDELIGHTS: Hughes writes: "I have traveled in Europe, the Mediterranean, the Near East, and Latin America. A recent trip to archaeological sites in Peru has made me decide to do some research into the possibility that the Incas had the only truly balanced civilization in terms of their relationship to the natural environment."

* * *

HUGHES, Richard (Arthur Warren) 1900-1976

April 19, 1900—April 28, 1976; British author and playwright. Obituaries: *New York Times,* April 30, 1976; *Washington Post,* April 30, 1976; *Time,* May 10, 1976; *Newsweek,* May 10, 1976; *Publishers Weekly,* May 24, 1976; *AB Bookman's Weekly,* May 31, 1976. (See index for previous *CA* sketch)

* * *

HUGHES, Terry A. 1933-

PERSONAL: Born February 28, 1933, in Brighton, England; son of William Cyril (a hotelier) and Ivy (Jennings) Hughes; married Iris Eleanor Park (a social worker), July 14, 1956; children: Richard William, Christopher Rene, Sarah Frances. *Education:* Pembroke College, Oxford, B.A., 1957. *Religion:* Church of England. *Home:* 19 Coalecroft Rd., London S.W.15, England. *Agent:* John Hawkins, Paul R. Reynolds, Inc., 12 East 41st St., New York, N.Y. 10017.

CAREER: British Broadcasting Corp. (BBC)-Television, London, England, executive, 1958-60, producer, 1960-65, senior producer and editor of political and economic affairs, 1965-69; London Weekend Television, London, England, executive producer of features, 1969-71; *Sunday Times,* London, England, correspondent on communications, 1972-

74; Director of Nautic Presentations and Atlantic Communications. Member of audio visual committee of the European Economic Community and International Broadcast Institute. *Military service:* Royal Air Force, 1951. *Member:* British Academy of Film and Television Artists, Greater London Arts Association.

WRITINGS—All with John Costello: *The Battle for Concorde,* Julian Berry, 1970; *D-Day,* Macmillan, 1974; *The Concorde Conspiracy,* Scribner, 1976; *Jutland 1916,* Holt, 1976; *Battle of the Atlantic,* Dial, 1977. Contributor to *Punch* and *Sunday Times.* Editor of *Intermedia* (of International Broadcast Institute).

WORK IN PROGRESS: A series of films for television; several contemporary history projects.

SIDELIGHTS: Hughes writes: "Writing can be more satisfying intellectual occupation than television or film, although they have other rewards. My major interest is to explain and involve people in the major formative events which have influenced our present world. Also I strongly believe that people should be *entertained* as well as *educated.*"

* * *

HUGHES, Thomas M(ears) 1927-

PERSONAL: Born November 18, 1927, in Forrest City, Ark.; son of Thomas M. (a farmer) and Lucille (Carter) Hughes; married Kendall Sechler (a biology teacher), December 18, 1950; children: Thomas Patrick. *Education:* Memphis State University, B.S., 1953, M.A., 1959; University of Tennessee, Ed.D., 1967. *Home:* 990 Brower Rd., Memphis, Tenn. 38111. *Office:* Department of Foundations of Education, Memphis State University, Memphis, Tenn. 38152.

CAREER: Elementary school teacher in Shelby County, Tenn., 1953; high school teacher of social sciences in Shelby County, 1954-55; Memphis Veterans Administration Hospital, Memphis, Tenn., chief of educational and speech therapy, 1955-64; Arlington Hospital and School for the Mentally Retarded, Arlington, Tenn., director of human development, 1969; Memphis State University, Memphis, Tenn., associate professor of educational psychology, 1970—. School psychologist for public schools of Memphis, Tenn., 1968-69. *Military service:* U.S. Marine Corps, 1945-49; served in Pacific theater and China; became staff sergeant. *Member:* American Psychological Association, National Society for the Study of Education, Mid-South Educational Research Association, Tennessee Psychological Association, Tennessee Education Association, Mississippi Psychological Association.

WRITINGS: MENSA: A Study of High Intelligence, Bureau of Educational Research, Memphis State University, 1974; *Teaching for Independence: The New Psychological Foundations,* Interstate, 1975. Author of scripts for videotape films "Jean Piaget" and "Robert Sears," for Memphis State University College of Education, 1972. Contributor of nearly twenty articles and reviews to education and psychology journals.

WORK IN PROGRESS: A Casebook for Special Education and Elementary Education, for Interstate; a textbook on educational psychology; a novel "on the metamorphosis of a young man."

SIDELIGHTS: Hughes writes: "My text, *Teaching for Independence,* is a highlight of my writing career. It brought together some approaches to solving the main problem of schools—teaching kids to be independent."

HUNSINGER, George 1945-

PERSONAL: Born April 7, 1945, in Pittsburgh, Pa.; son of George O. (an electrical engineer) and Edith M. Hunsinger; married Susan Kent, December 29, 1968 (divorced, June 15, 1975); married Deborah van Deusen, September 21, 1976; children: (first marriage) Amy Lynn. *Education:* Stanford University, A.B. (honors), 1967; Harvard University, B.D. (cum laude), 1971; University of Tuebingen, further graduate study, 1971-72; Yale University, M.A., 1977, M.Phil., 1977, Ph.D., 1977. *Politics:* "Democratic socialist." *Home:* 32 High St., Apt. 504, New Haven, Conn. 06511.

CAREER: Writer. Teacher in a storefront school, for New York Urban League, 1967-68. *Awards, honors:* First prize in Richard Fletcher Essay Contest in Religion at Dartmouth College, 1973.

WRITINGS: (Editor, translator, and contributor) *Karl Barth and Radical Politics,* Westminster, 1976.

WORK IN PROGRESS: Theology and Politics in the Third Reich: How Various Theologians Responded to the Rise of Hitler, completion expected in 1979.

SIDELIGHTS: Hunsinger writes: "I am primarily a constructive theologian, with strong philosophical, historical, and political interests. My current project is an exercise in 'political theology,' which involves learning to read politics theologically and theology politically. In the future I hope to do work in relating theology and philosophy (Marxist and analytic) as well as in constructive theology per se. The thinkers whom I have found most compelling are Karl Barth, Carl Jung, Karl Marx, and Ludwig Wittgenstein." Hunsinger is presently a candidate for the ministry in the United Presbyterian Church.

* * *

HUNT, James Gerald 1932-

PERSONAL: Born February 2, 1932, in Denver, Colo.; son of Newell M. and Rosalind G. Hunt; married, 1956; children: three. *Education:* Michigan Technological University, B.S., 1954; University of Illinois, M.A., 1957, Ph.D., 1966. *Office:* Department of Administrative Sciences, Southern Illinois University, Carbondale, Ill. 62901.

CAREER: General Motors Corp., Pontiac, Mich., project engineer in power development section of Pontiac Motor Division, 1954-56; U.S. Steel Corp., Detroit, Mich., personnel assistant at Michigan Limestone Division, 1957-58; West Virginia Institute of Technology, Montgomery, instructor in business administration, 1958-61; University of Illinois, Urbana-Champaign, instructor in industrial administration, 1963-66, research associate, 1965-66; Southern Illinois University, Carbondale, assistant professor, 1966-69, associate professor, 1969-72, professor of administrative sciences, 1972—. Instructor, Millikan University, 1962-63; management development consultant.

MEMBER: Academy of Management (vice-president of Midwest Division, 1974-75; president, 1976-77), American Institute for Decision Sciences, Midwest Business Administration Association. *Awards, honors:* Ford Foundation grant, summer, 1968; National Institute of Mental Health grant, 1970-73; grant from Office of Naval Research and Smithsonian Institution, 1973-76.

WRITINGS: (Editor with E. A. Fleishman, and contributor) *Current Developments in the Study of Leadership,* Southern Illinois University Press, 1973; (editor with L. L. Larson) *Contingency Approaches to Leadership,* Southern Illinois University Press, 1974; (editor with L. L. Larson)

Leadership Frontiers, Comparative Administration Research Institute, 1975; (with R. N. Osborn) *A Contingency Approach to Organization Theory,* Wiley, in press.

Contributor: M. S. Wortman and Fred Luthans, editors, *Emerging Concepts in Management,* Macmillan, 1969; Gene Dalton, editor, *Motivation and Control in Organizations,* Irwin-Dorsey, 1970; S. Chilton, editor, *Readings in Educational Administration,* MSS Educational Publishing, 1970; W. K. Graham and Karlene Roberts, editors, *Comparative Studies in Organizational Behavior,* Holt, 1972; J. L. Gibson, J. M. Ivancevich, and J. H. Donnelly, editors, *Readings in Organization: Structure, Processes, and Behavior,* Business Publications, 1973, 2nd edition, in press; R. H. Kilmann, L. R. Pondy, and D. P. Slevin, editors, *The Management of Organizational Design Research and Methodology,* Volume II, American Elsevier, in press.

Contributor to proceedings and to professional journals. Guest editor of *Organization and Administrative Sciences,* June, 1975; member of editorial review board of *Journal of Business Research,* 1973—, and *Academy of Management Review,* 1975—; manuscript reviewer for *Business Perspectives,* 1967-73, *Organization and Administrative Sciences, Journal of Applied Social Psychology,* and *Journal of Applied Psychology,* all 1973—; manuscript reviewer for Dryden Press and Scott, Foresman, 1973—, and for Irwin, West Publishing, and Science Research Associates, all 1975—.

* * *

HUNT, Leon (Gibson) 1931-

PERSONAL: Born October 25, 1931, in Dallas, Tex.; son of Leonidas Greene (an engraver) and Clarice (Gibson) Hunt; married Lois M. Kelso (an actress and politician), February 6, 1954; children: Lucille Kelso, Rachel Gibson, Nathaniel Hammerlund, Charles Webster. *Education:* Louisiana State University, B.S., 1952; attended Columbia University, 1953-54; University of Denver, M.A., 1964. *Home:* 310 Park Rd., Alexandria, Va. 22301. *Office:* 1800 M St. N.W., Washington, D.C. 20036.

CAREER: Marathon Oil Co., Terre Haute, Ind., geologist, 1954-62; Martin-Marietta Corp., Denver, Colo., senior engineer, 1962-64; Center for Naval Analysis, Arlington, Va., member of professional staff, 1964-66; Office of the Assistant Secretary of Defense, Washington, D.C., director of anti-submarine warfare studies, 1966-67; Planning Research Corp., Washington, D.C., manager of marine systems department, 1967-68; Systems Research Corp., Washington, D.C., director of corporate development, 1968-69; Analytic Sciences Corp., Washington, D.C., chief scientist and vice-president of research, 1971-73; Federal Energy Administration, Office of Energy Statistics, Washington, D.C., director, 1974-75; Antioch College, James Dixon Institute for Public Health Research, Columbia, Md., senior research professor, 1976—. Consultant to Drug Abuse Council, 1972—, Executive Office of the President, 1973—, World Health Organization, 1974-75, governments of Venezuela, the Netherlands, and Indonesia, 1974—, National Institute on Durg Abuse, 1975—, and to U.S. Department of State, 1975—. Adviser, President's Commission on Federal Statistics, 1970-71, and U.S. Commission on Railroad Retirement, 1972-73; member of advisory council, Citizens Conference on State Legislation, 1975—. *Military service:* U.S. Navy, 1954-58; became lieutenant. *Member:* New York Academy of Sciences. *Awards, honors:* Distinguished service award from Executive Office of the President, 1975;

award from National Academy of Medicine of Venezuela, 1976.

WRITINGS: Drug Incidence Analysis (monograph), U.S. Government Printing Office, 1974; *Recent Spread of Heroin Use in the United States* (monograph), Drug Abuse Council (Washington, D.C.), 1974; (with Carl Chambers) *The Heroin Epidemics,* Spectrum, 1976; *Assessment of Local Drug Abuse,* Heath, 1977. Also author of more than one hundred technical reports, monographs, and pamphlets on applied mathematics, operations research, epidemiology, and statistics.

Contributor: D. Wesson, editor, *Polydrug Use and Abuse in the United States,* Academic Press, 1977; S. N. Pradhan, editor, *Drug Abuse: Clinical and Basic Aspects,* C. V. Mosby, 1977; J. L. Rementaria, editor, *Drug Use in Pregnancy and the Neonate,* C. V. Mosby, 1977; *Manual of Drug Abuse Epidemiology,* National Institute on Drug Abuse, 1977. Contributor to *American Journal of Public Health* and *Journal of Addictive Diseases.*

WORK IN PROGRESS: Evolution of Addictive States, a comparison of alcoholism, drug addiction, and nicotine dependence; *Theory of Drug Epidemics,* concerning the underlying dynamics of contagious drug use; *Voyages of Discovery,* science fiction.

SIDELIGHTS: Hunt told *CA:* "Since 1968, I have worked mainly as a free-lance researcher applying mathematical techniques to the study of public health problems such as drug abuse, environmental and occupational diseases. I am particularly interested in seeing that research results are used as a basis for federal health policy, since they have often been ignored in the past. This is the motivation behind my writing: that policy makers need to understand a problem before they can solve it."

BIOGRAPHICAL/CRITICAL SOURCES: Washington Post, July 5, 1973, September 15, 1974; *Scientific American,* February, 1975; *Commentary,* April, 1975; *New Republic,* February 7, 1976.

* * *

HURD, Michael John 1928-

PERSONAL: Born December 19, 1928, in Gloucester, England; son of John Edwin George and Amy Florence (Hatton) Hurd. *Education:* Pembroke College, Oxford, M.A., 1953. *Home:* 4 Church St., West Liss, Hampshire, England.

CAREER: Royal Marine School of Music, professor of music theory, 1953-59; free-lance composer, writer, and lecturer, 1959—. Conductor of Alton Choral Society and Petersfield Operatic Society. *Military service:* British Intelligence Corps, 1947-49.

WRITINGS: Immortal Hour: The Life and Period of Rutland Boughton, Routledge & Kegan Paul, 1962; *Young Person's Guide to Concerts,* Routledge & Kegan Paul, 1962, Roy, 1965; *Young Person's Guide to Opera,* Routledge & Kegan Paul, 1963, Roy, 1965; *Sailors' Songs and Shanties,* Walck, 1965; *Young Person's Guide to English Music,* Roy, 1965; *Soldiers' Songs and Marches,* Walck, 1966; *Benjamin Britten,* Novello, 1966; *The Composer,* Oxford University Press, 1968; *An Outline History of European Music,* Novello, 1968; *Elgar,* Crowell, 1969; *Mendelssohn,* Faber, 1970, Crowell, 1971; *Vaughan Williams,* Crowell, 1970. Composer of choral, orchestral, and chamber music, songs, and operas, all published by Novello.

WORK IN PROGRESS: The Ordeal of Ivor Gurney; rewriting and updating Percy Scholes' *Junior Companion to Music* for Oxford University Press; musical compositions.

SIDELIGHTS: In spite of his considerable output as an author, Hurd told *CA* he would mainly like to be considered a composer.

* * *

HURWITZ, Johanna 1937-

PERSONAL: Born October 9, 1937, in New York, N.Y.; daughter of Nelson (a journalist and book seller) and Tillie (a library assistant; maiden name, Miller) Frank; married Uri Levi Hurwitz (a college teacher and author), February 19, 1962; children: Nomi, Beni. *Education:* Queens College (now of the City University of New York), B.A., 1958; Columbia University, M.L.S., 1959. *Home:* 10 Spruce Pl., Great Neck, N.Y. 11021. *Office:* Manor Oaks School, New Hyde Park, N.Y.

CAREER: New York Public Library, New York, N.Y., children's librarian, 1959-63; Queens College of the City University of New York, Flushing, N.Y., lecturer on children's literature, 1965-68; Calhoun School, New York City, children's librarian, 1968-75; Manor Oaks School, New Hyde Park, N.Y., children's librarian, 1975—. *Member:* American Library Association, Amnesty International, Beta Phi Mu.

WRITINGS: Busybody Nora (juvenile), Morrow, 1976; *Nora and Mrs. Mind-Your-Own-Business* (juvenile), Morrow, 1977.

WORK IN PROGRESS: More Nora stories; a book about an older girl.

SIDELIGHTS: Johanna Hurwitz told *CA:* "Memories of my childhood and those of my children fill me with ideas, adventures, and emotions to be shared with others. Books have always been an important part of my life, both professionally and recreationally. I knew that I would be a writer even when I was a young child."

* * *

HUTCHENS, John Kennedy 1905-

PERSONAL: Born August 9, 1905, in Chicago, Ill.; son of Martin Jay and Leila (Kennedy) Hutchens; married Katherine Regan Morris (deceased); married Marjorie Kohl Brophy (deceased); children: (first marriage) Anne, Timothy; (second marriage) Janice and Peter (stepchildren). *Education:* Hamilton College, A.B., 1926. *Politics:* Democrat. *Home:* 306 Milton Rd., Rye, N.Y. 10580. *Office:* Book-of-the-Month Club, 280 Park Ave., New York, N.Y. 10017.

CAREER: Daily Missoulian & Sentinel, Missoula, Mont., reporter, 1926-27; *New York Evening Post,* New York, N.Y., reporter, film critic, and assistant drama editor, 1927-28; *Theatre Arts,* New York City, assistant editor, 1928-29, drama critic, 1929-32; *New York Times,* New York City, on drama staff, 1929-38; *Boston Evening Transcript,* Boston, Mass., drama critic, 1938-41; *New York Times,* radio editor, 1941-44; *New York Times Book Review,* New York City, assistant editor, 1944-46, editor, 1946-48; *New York Herald Tribune,* New York City, author of book news column, 1948-56, daily book reviewer, 1956-63; Book-of-the-Month Club, New York, N.Y., member of editorial board, 1963—.

MEMBER: International P.E.N. (American Center), Authors Guild of Authors League of America (member of council), Sigma Phi, Dutch Treat Club, Players Club (New

York City), Shenorock Club. *Awards, honors:* Litt.D. from Hamilton College, 1951.

WRITINGS: (Editor) *The American Twenties: A Literary Panorama,* Lippincott, 1952, Cooper Square, 1972; *One Man's Montana: An Informal Portrait of a State,* Lippincott, 1964; (editor with George Oppenheimer) *The Best in the World: A Selection of News and Feature Stories, Editorials, Poems, and Reviews, 1921-1928,* Viking, 1973.

* * *

HYDE, Janet Shibley 1948-

PERSONAL: Born August 17, 1948, in Akron, Ohio; daughter of Grant O. (a safety engineer) and Dorothy (a housemother; maiden name, Reavy) Shibley; married Clark Hyde (an Episcopal priest), June 2, 1969. *Education:* Oberlin College, B.A., 1969; University of California, Berkeley, Ph.D., 1972. *Religion:* Episcopalian. *Home:* 917 Westmont, Napoleon, Ohio 43545. *Office:* Department of Psychology, Bowling Green State University, Bowling Green, Ohio 43403.

CAREER: Bowling Green State University, Bowling Green, Ohio, assistant professor, 1972-76, associate professor of psychology, 1976—. *Member:* American Psychological Association, Behavior Genetics Association, Psychometric Society, Sigma Xi.

WRITINGS: (With B. G. Rosenberg) *Half the Human Experience: The Psychology of Women,* Heath, 1976. Contributor to *Behavior Genetics.*

WORK IN PROGRESS: Understanding Human Sexuality, a textbook, for McGraw.

SIDELIGHTS: Janet Hyde writes: "I have dual identities as a feminist and a scientific psychologist. I hope to make some contributions by integrating feminist perspectives into the mainstream of psychology."

* * *

INGSTAD, Helge Marcus 1899-

PERSONAL: Born December 30, 1899, in Meraker, Norway; son of Olav (an engineer) and Olga Marie (Quam) Ingstad; married Anne Stine Moe (an archaeologist), May 21, 1941; children: Benedicte. *Education:* University of Oslo, J.D., 1922. *Religion:* Protestant. *Home:* Vettalivei 24, Oslo, Norway. *Agent:* Harold Matson Co., Inc., 22 East 40th St., New York, N.Y. 10016.

CAREER: Barrister in Levanger, Norway, 1922-25; animal trapper northwest of Great Slave Lake, in Arctic Canada, 1926-30; writer and lecturer, 1930-32; Norwegian governor of northeast Greenland, 1932-33, and Svalbard, in Spitzbergen, 1933-35; conducted research on Apache Indians in Arizona and the Sierra Madre Mountains in Mexico, 1936-38; writer and lecturer, 1939-40; leader of relief action in Norway, later participant in underground movement, 1940-45; writer and lecturer, 1945-49; studied inland Nunamiut Eskimo group in northern Alaska, 1949-50; conducted expedition to study old Norse settlements in southwestern Greenland, 1953; writer, 1953-60; conducted eight archaeological expeditions to Norse pre-Columbian site in L'Anse aux Meadows, Newfoundland, 1960-68; writer, 1968—. *Military service:* Norwegian Army, 1920. *Member:* Explorers Club (corresponding member), Norwegian Polar Club (president; honorary member), Norwegian Geographical Society (honorary member). *Awards, honors:* Franklin L. Burr Award from National Geographic Society, 1964; Fridtjof Nansen Award from University of Oslo, 1965; D.Sc. from St. Olaf

College, 1965, Memorial University, St. John's, Newfoundland, 1969, McGill University, 1975, and University of Oslo, 1976; Wahlberg Award from Swedish Society for Anthropology and Geography, 1968; named commander of Norwegian Order of St. Olav, 1970.

WRITINGS: Pelsjegerliv blant Nord-Kanadas Indianere, Gyldendal, 1931, translation by Eugene Gay-Tifft published as *The Land of Feast and Famine,* Knopf, 1933; *Oest for den store bre,* Gyldendal, 1935, translation by Gay-Tifft published as *East of the Great Glacier,* Knopf, 1937; *Apache-indianerne: Jakten paa den tapte stamme* (title means "The Apache Indians: The Search for the Lost Tribe"), Gyldendal, 1939; *Klondyke Bill: Roman* (in Norwegian), Gyldendal, 1941; *Siste baat: Skuespill, fem akter* (play; title means "Last Boat"; first performed in Oslo at Det Nye Teater, 1948), Gyldendal, 1946; *Landet med de kalde kyster* (title means "The Land with the Cold Coasts"), Gyldendal, 1948.

Nunamiut: Blant Alaskas innlands-eskimoer, Gyldendal, 1951, translation by F. H. Lyon published as *Nunamiut: Among Alaska's Inland Eskimos,* Norton, 1954; *Landet under leidarstjernen: En ferd til Groenlands norroene bygder,* Gyldendal, 1959, translation by Naomi Walford published as *Land Under the Pole Star: A Voyage to the Norse Settlements of Greenland and the Saga of the People That Vanished,* St. Martin's, 1966; *Vesterveg til Vinland: Oppdagelsen av norroene boplasser: Nord-America,* Gyldendal, 1965, translation by Erik J. Friis published as *Westward to Vinland: The Discovery of Pre-Columbian Norse House-Sites in North America,* St. Martin's, 1969, Harper, 1972.

(With Geoffrey Ashe and others) *The Quest for America,* Praeger, 1971. Contributor to *National Geographic.*

WORK IN PROGRESS: The Problem of Vinland, a historical assessment referring to his discovery of a Norse settlement from about the year 1000 in Newfoundland, for Yale University Press.

SIDELIGHTS: Ingstad began by studying Eskimos and Indians in North America and Mexico, and is currently engaged in study of early Norse settlements in Arctic and sub-Arctic areas, especially in Greenland and Newfoundland. Ingstad is credited with the discovery of the first known Norse settlement in Newfoundland. His books have been published in German, Danish, Russian, Swedish, and French, and in Eskimo language as well. *Avocational interests:* Chess.

* * *

IRION, Ruth (Hershey) 1921-

PERSONAL: Born October 28, 1921, in Hamburg, Pa.; daughter of Hiram Frey (a fruit grower) and Adele (an art teacher; maiden name, Hostetter) Hershey; married Louis A. Irion, Jr. (a cabinetmaker), June 22, 1946; children: Christoper, Louis III, Lenore, Jennifer. *Education:* Kutztown State College, B.S., 1944; attended University of Pennsylvania, 1945-47, and Pennsylvania Academy of Fine Arts, 1947-49. *Home:* 114 Runnymede Ave., Wayne, Pa. 19087. *Office:* Berwyn Furniture Shop, Berwyn, Pa. 19312.

CAREER: Art teacher in public primary and secondary school in Marple-Newtown, Pa., 1944-45, and public elementary school in Upper Darby, Pa., 1945-47; Berwyn Furniture Shop, Berwyn, Pa., interior designer, 1958—.

WRITINGS: The Christmas Cookie Tree (self-illustrated), Westminster, 1976.

SIDELIGHTS: Irion told *CA:* "Because I have always

loved Frakturs—the illuminated manuscripts of the early Pennsylvania Dutch—I have illustrated this book in the manner of the Fraktur artist. The design motifs I have used are authentic. I felt children would enjoy the feeling of these folk artists whose work can now be seen mostly in museums. In the way my main character Eva paints cookies, my own family has painted cookies for twenty-some years. It' been a great tradition."

* * *

IRISH, Richard K. 1932-

PERSONAL: Born June 26, 1932, in Salt Lake City, Utah; son of Wynot Rush (an army officer) and Juliet (Wilken) Irish; married Sally Goldsmith (a day care center director), April 4, 1959. *Education:* Georgetown University, B.S., 1954. *Politics:* Independent. *Religion:* Episcopalian. *Home:* RR 2, Box 172-A, Marshall, Va. 22115. *Agent:* Don Cutler, Sterling Lord Agency, 660 Madison Ave., New York, N.Y. 10021. *Office:* TransCentury Corp., 1789 Columbia Rd., N.W., Washington, D.C. 20009.

CAREER: Peace Corps, Washington, D.C., volunteer and staff member, 1962-66; Council for a Livable World, Washington, D.C., executive secretary, 1966-67; TransCentury Corp., Washington, D.C., vice president, 1967—. Lecturer. *Military Service:* U.S. Army, Corps of Engineers, 1954-56.

WRITINGS: Go Hire Yourself an Employer, Doubleday, 1973; *If Things Don't Improve Soon, I May Ask You to Fire Me,* Doubleday, 1975.

WORK IN PROGRESS: Revision and update of *Go Hire Yourself an Employer;* magazine articles on management.

SIDELIGHTS: Aside from his interest in trying to reform current placement philosophy, Irish is keenly interested in historical subjects, particularly North Pole expeditions. Writing is a sideline to his regular work as a management consultant.

* * *

IRSFELD, John H(enry) 1937-

PERSONAL: Born December 2, 1937, in Bemidji, Minn.; son of Hubert L. and Mary Lillian (McKee) Irsfeld; married Margaret Elizabeth Drushel (a systems analyst), August 29, 1965; children: Hannah Christine. *Education:* University of Texas, B.A., 1959, M.A., 1966, Ph.D., 1969. *Agent:* Rhoda A. Weyr, William Morris Agency, 1350 Avenue of the Americas, New York, N.Y. 10019. *Office:* Department of English, University of Nevada, Las Vegas, Nev. 89154.

CAREER: High school teacher of Spanish and English in Calallen, Tex., 1959-60; University of Nevada, Las Vegas, assistant professor, 1969-73, associate professor of English, 1973—. *Military service:* U.S. Army, Infantry, 1961-64; became sergeant.

WRITINGS: Little Kingdoms (novel), Putnam, 1976.

Contributor of more than fifteen poems, articles, and reviews to journals, including *Western American Literature, Redneck Review, Sparrow, Kansas Quarterly,* and *Creative Review.*

WORK IN PROGRESS: Essays in English and American Studies, for Whitston Publishing; *starting at Ø,* a novel; *A Handbook for Teaching Assistants in the Humanities;* rewriting a novel.

SIDELIGHTS: Irsfeld writes: "If I weren't doing this, I'd be doing something else. I finally got it: The world is a playground and it is always recess."

IRWIN, Theodore 1907-

PERSONAL: Born September 7, 1907, in New York, N.Y.; son of Ira (in real estate) and Rebecca (Arlow) Irwin; married Rita Reisman, May 7, 1935 (died, 1962); married Helen R. Ross, April 13, 1964; children: Jed, Kenneth. *Education:* New York University, B.S., 1928. *Agent:* Joan Stewart, William Morris Agency, 1350 Avenue of the Americas, New York, N.Y. 10019.

CAREER: Free-lance magazine writer and novelist, 1931-39; *Cue* magazine, New York City, managing editor, 1939-41; *Look* magazine, New York City, associate director and war correspondent, 1941-45; Digest Group, New York City, editorial director, 1945-62; *Real,* New York City, editor, 1962-64; *Mediguide,* New York City, editor, 1972-73; writer. *Member:* American Society of Journalists and Authors (president, 1969-70), National Association of Science Writers.

WRITINGS: Collusion (novel), Godwin, 1933; *Strange Passage* (novel), Smith & Haas, 1935; (with editors of *Fortune*) *The Accident of Birth,* Farrar & Rinehart, 1938; (Robert Mallory) *Modern Birth Control,* Paperback Library, 1961; *Better Health after Fifty,* Harper, 1964; *Let's Travel in Holland,* Children's Press, 1964; (editor) *What the Executive Should Know about Tension,* American Research Council, 1965; (with James A. Brussel) *Instant Shrink,* Cowles, 1971; (with Brussel) *Understanding and Overcoming Depression,* Hawthorn, 1973.

WORK IN PROGRESS: Two novels and a nonfiction book on crime.

*   *   *

IRWIN, W(illiam) R(obert) 1915-

PERSONAL: Born September 17, 1915, in Shenandoah, Iowa; son of William Edward (a merchant) and Nellie (Coffman) Irwin; married Patricia Beesley, June 7, 1939 (deceased); married Constance H. Frick (a writer), June 15, 1954; children: William Andrew. *Education:* Grinnell College, B.A., 1936; Columbia University, M.A., 1937, Ph.D., 1941. *Home:* 415 Lee St., Iowa City, Iowa 52240. *Office:* Department of English, University of Iowa, Iowa City, Iowa 52242.

CAREER: Long Island University, Brooklyn, N.Y., instructor in English, 1938-42; Cornell University, Ithaca, N.Y., instructor in English, 1942-47; University of Iowa, Iowa City, assistant professor, 1947-54, associate professor, 1954-62, professor of English, 1962—. Fulbright professor of University of Tuebingen, 1958-60. *Member:* International Association of University Professors of English, Modern Language Association of America, Deutsche Gesellschaft fuer Amerikastudien, Midwest Modern Language Association, Phi Beta Kappa.

WRITINGS: The Making of Jonathan Wild, Columbia University Press, 1941; (editor) *Challenge: An Anthology of the Literature of Mountaineering,* Columbia University Press, 1950; (with J. B. Ratermanis) *The Comic Style of Beaumarchais,* University of Washington Press, 1961; *The Game of the Impossible: A Rhetoric of Fantasy,* University of Illinois Press, 1976.

WORK IN PROGRESS: Work toward a study of a change in basic popular ethics, from the rejection of an inherited heroic ideal to an ideal of common decency and goodness, as this is found in English and French literature of the seventeenth and eighteenth centuries.

IVERSON, Genie 1942-

PERSONAL: Born November 10, 1942, in Newport News, Va.; daughter of Elmer Victor (a naval officer) and Willa (an author and journalist; maiden name, Okker) Iverson. *Education:* Attended New York University, 1964-65; University of California, Berkeley, B.A., 1966. *Address:* P.O. Box 405, San Mateo, Calif. 94401.

CAREER: Contra Costa Times, Walnut Creek, Calif., staff reporter and youth editor, 1968-71; Lesher News Bureau, Martinez, Calif., reporter, 1971-72; Iverson Game Bird Calls, San Mateo, Calif., promotion director, 1971—.

WRITINGS: Jacques Cousteau (juvenile biography), Putnam, 1976; *Louis Armstrong* (juvenile biography), Crowell, 1976.

WORK IN PROGRESS: Researching a biography and a history for children.

SIDELIGHTS: Genie Iverson told *CA:* "I write because I must. So far I have worked on profiles and biography because I am interested in people, human behavior, and history interpreted through individual lives."

*   *   *

JACKSON, Allan 1905(?)-1976

1905(?)—April 26, 1976; American news correspondent and radio broadcaster. Obituaries: *New York Times,* April 28, 1976.

*   *   *

JACKSON, Laura (Riding) 1901-

PERSONAL: Born January 16, 1901, in New York, N.Y.; daughter of Nathaniel S. and Sarah (Edersheim) Reichenthal; married Louis Gottschalk (a professor of history), 1920 (divorced, 1925); married Schuyler B. Jackson (a poet, critic, and former poetry editor of *Time* magazine, 1941 (died, 1968). *Education:* Attended Cornell University, 1918-21. *Home address:* Box 35, Wabasso, Fla. 32970. *Agent:* A. P. Watt & Son, 26/28 Bedford Row, London WC1R 4HL, England.

CAREER: Poet, critic, and author in various fields "with progressive concern with language as the natural human truth-system." Regular member of The Fugitives, a group of Southern poets of the 1920s; lived abroad 1926-39, mainly in England and Spain; worked at "furthering sensitivity of writer-associates, poets especially, to the importance of linguistic integrity as the basis of literary integrity;" her activities expanded to publishing, as managerial partner in the Seizin Press, and the editing of *Epilogue* (a series of volumes in which new principles of general criticism were explored); returned to United States in 1939, has lived in Florida, 1943—, working with her husband at growing and shipping citrus fruit, and working "towards the enlargement of the knowledge of words and capability of using them in truthfully exact consciousness of their meanings—towards the initiating of a new lexicography." After her husband's death in 1968, she continued the linguistic work alone, completing in 1974 the book-result of it, *Rational Meaning: A New Foundation for the Defining of Words,* which she is currently engaged in revising and perfecting. In recent years she has continued to publish articles on poetry and language.

AWARDS, HONORS: Received prize and honorary membership in Fugitives Group, 1924; Mark Rothko award, 1972; Guggenheim fellowship, 1973.

WRITINGS—All under name Laura Riding, except as indicated: (Under name Laura Riding Gottchalk) *The Close Chaplet* (poems), Hogarth Press, Adelphi Press, 1926; (Robert Graves second author) *A Survey of Modernist Poetry*, Heineman, 1927, Doubleday, Doran, 1928; *Voltaire: A Biographical Fantasy* (long poem), Hogarth Press, 1927; *Love as Love, Death as Death* (poems), Seizin Press, 1928; *Contemporaries and Snobs*, J. Cape, 1928; *Anarchism Is Not Enough*, J. Cape, Doubleday, Doran, 1928; (Robert Graves second author) *A Pamphlet Against Anthologies*, J. Cape, Doubleday, Doran, 1928.

Though Gently, Seizin Press, 1930; *Poems: A Joking Word*, J. Cape, 1930; *Experts Are Puzzled* (essays and stories), J. Cape, 1930; *Twenty Poems Less*, Hours Press (Paris), 1930; *Four Unposted Letters to Catherine*, Hours Press, 1930; *Laura and Francisca* (poem), Seizin Press, 1931; *Life of the Dead*, Barker, 1933; *Poet: A Lying Word*, Barker, 1933; (editor) *Everybody's Letters*, Barker, 1933; (George Ellidge second author) *14A*, Barker, 1934; *Americans* (poem), Primavera, 1934; *Progress of Stories*, Seizin Press, Constable, 1935; (editor) *Epilogue: A Critical Summary*, three volumes, Seizin Press, Constable, 1935-37; (under pseudonym Madeleine Vara) *Convalescent Conversations*, Seizin Press, Constable, 1936; (Robert Graves second translator) Georg Schwarz, *Almost Forgotten Germany*, Seizin Press, Constable, 1936; *A Trojan Ending* (historical novel), Seizin Press, Constable, 1937; (editor and author of commentary) *The World and Ourselves* (symposium), Chatto & Windus, 1938; *Collected Poems*, Cassell, Random House, 1938; *Lives of Wives* (stories), Cassell, Random House, 1939; (Harry Kemp first author) *The Left Heresy*, Methuen, 1939.

Selected Poems: In Five Sets, Faber, 1970, Norton, 1973; (under name Laura (Riding) Jackson) *The Telling*, Athlone Press, 1972, Harper, 1973. Work represented in numerous anthologies. Contributor to periodicals, including *Wilson Library Bulletin, Art and Literature, Civilta Delle Macchine, Denver Quarterly, Ms., Anteaus, Stand,* and *Chelsea* (entire issue #35, 1977 devoted to her writings). [Mrs. Jackson used the name Laura Riding Gottschalk for early contributions to periodicals.]

WORK IN PROGRESS: Rational Meaning: A New Foundation for the Definition of Words, currently in final revision; another book, *The Failure of Poetry;* a book of personal narrative and comment on things literary, tentatively titled *Praeterita: The Authorial Experiences;* a book on the English poet Charles M. Doughty, embracing her husband's work on this subject.

SIDELIGHTS: Mrs. Jackson wrote the following summary for *CA:* "At the beginning of the 'forties, Laura (Riding) Jackson made the drastic decision that she must renounce poetry, as imposing irremovable obstacles to the realizing of the full potential afforded by language, when words are used faithfully, as they mean, of general human speaking, writing, in what she called, in an introduction to a reading of her poems in 1962 on a British Broadcasting programme, 'the style of truth.' Her work on language was accompanied by a long look at not only poetry and literature but the entire human scene, historical and contemporary, with clarifying perception of the so far largely unfulfilled responsibility that human beings have of telling the 'one story' of their being, and the world—the central theme of all her earlier work. She came to think that this story required a personal truth exceeding literary, poetic, and all other categorically professionalized intellectual points of view, and linguistic styles. Her book, *The Telling*, which sets forth this 'personal gospel,' as she calls it, has, she says, been received in some quarters with devoted excitement, but with almost total 'pat-

ently deliberate avoidance of notice' in the literary press of both countries in which I was published.''

* * *

JACOB, Margaret Candee 1943-

PERSONAL: Born June 9, 1943, in New York; daughter of Thomas W. (a mechanic) and Margaret (a maid; maiden name, O'Reilly) Candee; married James R. Jacob (a historian), November 3, 1967. *Education:* St. Joseph's College, Brooklyn, N.Y., B.A., 1964; Cornell University, M.A., 1966, Ph.D., 1969. *Home:* 520 La Guardia Pl., New York, N.Y. 10012. *Office:* Department of History, Bernard M. Baruch College of the City University of New York, 17 Lexington Ave., New York, N.Y. 10010.

CAREER: University of South Florida, Tampa, assistant professor of history, 1968-69; University of East Anglia, Norwich, England, lecturer in European studies, 1969-71; Bernard M. Baruch College of the City University of New York, New York, N.Y., assistant professor, 1971-76, associate professor of history, 1976—. Co-chairwoman of Coordinating Committee on Women in the Historical Profession, 1973-74; assistant director of Institute for Research in History. *Member:* American Historical Association, Past and Present Society. *Awards, honors:* American Council of Learned Societies summer grants, 1973, 1976; National Endowment for the Humanities summer grant, 1975; American Philosophical Society grant, 1976.

WRITINGS: (Editor with husband, J. R. Jacob) *Seventeenth Century Peace Proposals*, Garland Publishing, 1973; (editor) *Eighteenth Century Peace Proposals*, Garland Publishing, 1974; *The Newtonians and the English Revolution, 1689-1720*, Cornell University Press, 1976; (with Marvin Perry, Theodore Von Laue, and Andrew Whiteside) *The West: A Conceptual Approach*, Houghton, in press. Contributor of articles and reviews to history journals. History of science editor of *The Eighteenth Century: A Current Bibliography*, 1974-76.

WORK IN PROGRESS: Irrational Modes of Enlightenment, for Allen & Unwin, completion expected in 1979; "Astronomy and Society from the Renaissance to the French Revolution," to be included in *The General History of Astronomy*, edited by Michael Hoskin, for Cambridge University Press.

SIDELIGHTS: Margaret Jacobs writes: "My vision of history has been shaped profoundly by my opposition to the Vietnam war and by my long periods of residency in England. At all times I seek to show the relationship between ideas and interests, philosophical perspective and social reality."

* * *

JACOBS, Howard 1908-
(Bard of Avondale)

PERSONAL: Born June 23, 1908, in Lake Charles, La.; son of Joseph (in manufacturing) and Bessie (Straus) Jacobs; married Harryette Katz, 1950 (divorced April 30, 1954); married Sheila Craig (a physical therapist), December 28, 1965; children: Diane, Kenneth Stephen. *Education:* Attended Tulane University. *Home:* 2441 Nashville Ave., New Orleans, La. 70115. *Office: New Orleans Times-Picayune*, 3800 Howard Ave., New Orleans, La. 70140.

CAREER: New Orleans Times-Picayune, New Orleans, La., reporter and feature writer, 1938-48, author of column "Remoulade," 1948—; correspondent for *Newsweek*, 1952-

74. *Military service:* U.S. Army, 1942-46; became sergeant. *Member:* Press Club of New Orleans (president, 1962-63). *Awards, honors:* Thirty-one awards from Press Club of New Orleans, 1958—.

WRITINGS: Charlie the Mole and Other Droll Souls, Pelican, 1973; (with Justin Wilson) *Justin Wilson's Cajun Humor,* Pelican, 1974; *Once Upon a Bayou,* privately printed, 1976. Contributor of poems, under pseudonym Bard of Avondale, to literary magazines.

WORK IN PROGRESS: The Jocular Vein, a collection of columns, publication expected in 1977; *Erotic Viands and Hot Pinches,* about problems encountered by newsmen.

SIDELIGHTS: Jacobs writes that he is considered an authority on Acadian patois.

* * *

JACOBSON, Sibyl C(hafer) 1942-

PERSONAL: Born September 30, 1942, in Waukon, Iowa; daughter of Arthur H. (an attorney) and Isabel (Chafer) Jacobson. *Education:* Attended University of Vienna, 1963; St. Olaf College, B.A. (cum laude), 1964; Northwestern University, M.A.T., 1965; University of Wisconsin, Madison, Ph.D., 1972. *Home:* 1433 East Johnson St., Madison, Wis. 53703; and 22 Fourth Ave. N.W., Waukon, Wis. 52172.

CAREER: Iowa Wesleyan College, Mt. Pleasant, instructor in English, 1965-66; Quinsigamond Community College, Worcester, Mass., instructor in English, 1966-68; University of Wisconsin, Madison, administrative assistant, 1968-70; University of Wisconsin, Whitewater, instructor, 1970-71, assistant professor of English, 1972—. Fulbright senior lecturer at University of Jyvaskyla, University of Turku, and Abo Akademi, 1973-74. *Member:* Modern Language Association of America, Phi Beta Kappa, Phi Kappa Delta.

WRITINGS: (With Robert J. Dilligan and Todd K. Bender) *Concordance to Joseph Conrad's Heart of Darkness,* Southern Illinois University Press, 1973. Contributor of articles and reviews to literature journals.

* * *

JAFFIN, David 1937-

PERSONAL: Born September 14, 1937, in New York, N.Y.; son of George Monroe (a lawyer) and Janet (Guzy) Jaffin; married Rosemarie Kraft-Lange (a language teacher), September 14, 1961; children: Raphael, Andreas. *Education:* Attended University of Michigan, 1955-56; New York University, B.A., 1959, M.A., 1961, Ph.D., 1966; additional study at University of Tuebingen, 1971-74. *Home:* Moerikestrasse 12, Magstadt 7031, West Germany. *Office:* Evangelische Pfarramt, Pfarrstrasse 3, Magstadt 7031, West Germany.

CAREER: University of Maryland, European Division in Munich and Augsburg, Germany, lecturer in European history, 1966-71; vicar of Lutheran church in Tuebingen, Germany, 1974-75; ordained Lutheran clergyman, 1975; Evangelische Kirche, Magstadt, Germany, Lutheran minister, 1975—. *Member:* Phi Beta Kappa. *Awards, honors:* Oreon E. Scott Award from University of Michigan, 1956; Avery Hopwood Award in Poetry, 1956; Founders Day awards from New York University, 1959 and 1966.

WRITINGS—Poetry: *Conformed to Stone,* Abelard, 1968; *Emptied Spaces,* Abelard, 1972; *Objects,* Headlands Publications, 1973; *Late March,* Sceptre Press, 1973; *Of,* Sceptre Press, 1974; *As One,* Elizabeth Press, 1975; *In the Glass of Winter,* Abelard, 1975; *The Half of a Circle,* Elizabeth Press, in press. Contributor of poems to more than one hundred fifty periodicals in United States and abroad, and articles to *International Journal for Offender Therapy and Comparative Criminology* and *European Judaism.*

WORK IN PROGRESS: Poems, Space Of, publication by Elizabeth Press expected in 1978, and *Pre-ceptions,* Elizabeth Press, 1980.

SIDELIGHTS: Jaffin writes: "My poetry is concerned with deriving a new aesthetic, one in which every word, every sound, every image is reduced to its ultimate function. Everything must count, just as the slightest inflection in speech, even the non-stated (silence) speaks. It is an art of reduction and abstraction, an art of still life and reflection. The reason why I am a poet is the same reason why I was an historian and became a minister, because the concept 'reality' is of central importance to me. What is the relation between perception and object? Do objects (including inanimate ones) have a meaning of their own detached from our perceptions? My art then attempts to refine, to clarify until external appearance is cleansed and thereby nearer to the truth which is God. The artists I most admire such as Haydn and Schuetz, Duccio, Bellini (later phase), Vermeer and Guardi were also concerned with the interior of reality."

BIOGRAPHICAL/CRITICAL SOURCES: Yorkshire Post, September 9, 1972; *Bristol Evening Post,* November 9, 1972; *Workshop New Poetry Eighteen,* 1973; *Poet Lore,* summer, 1974; *Samphire,* spring, 1976.

* * *

JAKUBOWSKI, Patricia (Ann) 1941-

PERSONAL: Born October 10, 1941, in Milwaukee, Wis.; daughter of John Adam (a bookbinder) and Frances (a sales clerk; maiden name, Orzechowski) Jakubowski. *Education:* Wisconsin State University, Oshkosh, B.S., 1963; University of Illinois, Ed.M., 1965, Ed.D., 1968. *Office:* Department of Behavioral Studies, University of Missouri, St. Louis, Mo. 63121.

CAREER: Washington University, St. Louis, Mo., counseling psychologist, 1967-73, assistant professor of counselor education, 1968-73; University of Missouri, St. Louis, associate professor of counselor education, 1973—. Co-director of film "Assertive Training for Women." *Member:* Association for the Advancement of Behavior Therapy, American Personnel and Guidance Association (senator, 1976-79), American Psychological Association, Association for Counselor Education and Supervision, Kappa Delta Phi. *Awards, honors:* Service awards from Association of Counselor Education and Supervision and from St. Louis Administrative Management Society, both 1975.

WRITINGS: (Contributor) Carleton Beck, editor, *Guidelines for Guidance,* Brown Publishing, 1971; *An Introduction to Assertive Training for Women,* American Personnel and Guidance Association, 1973; (with Joan Pearlman and Karen Coburn) *A Leader's Guide to Assertive Training for Women,* American Personnel and Guidance Association, 1973; (with Arthur Lange) *Responsible Assertive Behavior: Cognitive-Behavioral Procedures for Trainers,* Research Press, 1976. Contributor to education journals. Associate editor of *Counselor Education and Supervision* and for American Personnel and Guidance Association.

WORK IN PROGRESS: Developing Responsible Assertive Skills, for Research Press; research toward developing a scale to measure assertive behavior.

SIDELIGHTS: Patricia Jakubowski writes: "My interest in assertion training stems from my former difficulties in asserting myself as an adolescent and young adult. Also, as a psychologist I found that nonassertion was the underlying cause of many people's problems." *Avocational interests:* Chess, horse-back riding, reading, "being with friends and giving myself permission to have fun."

* * *

JAMES, Philip
See del REY, Lester 1915-

* * *

JANTSCH, Erich 1929-

PERSONAL: Born January 8, 1929, in Vienna, Austria; son of Hans (a grocer) and Olga (Kantor) Jantsch. *Education:* University of Vienna, Ph.D., 1951; Indiana University, postdoctoral study, 1951-52. *Address:* 1962 University Ave., No. 4, Berkeley, Calif. 94704; and 111 Gentzpasse, A-1180 Vienna, Austria. *Office:* Center for Research in Management Science, University of California, Berkeley, Calif. 94720.

CAREER: Astronomer, 1940-45; Indukont, Vienna, Austria, manager, 1953-56; employed by Eternit, Vienna, 1957; Brown, Boveri, Baden, Switzerland, engineer and physicist, 1957-62; Organization for Economic Cooperation and Development (OECD), Paris, France, consultant with Scientific Directorate, 1962-68; University of Genoa, Genoa, Italy, conducted seminar, 1968; Massachusetts Institute of Technology, Cambridge, director of special project at Sloan School of Management, 1969; Technical University of Hannover, Hannover, Germany, visiting professor-at-large, 1970; University of California, Berkeley, worked in department of city and regional planning, and in Institute of International Studies, 1971, in School of Public Health, 1972, in program of conservation of natural resources, 1973, and in Center for Research in Management Science, 1974—. Visiting professor, Portland State University, 1972, University of Bielefeld, 1972-73, Technical University of Denmark, 1973-74, Institute of Advanced Studies, Vienna, 1974, University of Paris, 1974, University of Lund, 1975-76, and St. Gall Graduate School of Economics, Business and Public Administration, 1976. Lecturer at universities all over the world. Co-founder and member of executive committee of Club of Rome, 1968-70. Member of program board of International Management Symposium, St. Gall, Switzerland. Consultant to government and business in the United States and abroad.

WRITINGS: Die Verantwortung des Interpreten, [Vienna], 1950; Technological Forecasting in Perspective, Organization for Economic Cooperation and Development, 1967; (editor) Perspectives of Planning, Organization for Economic Cooperation and Development, 1969; Technological Forecasting in Corporate Planning (in Japanese), Japan Techno-Economics Society, 1970; Technological Planning and Social Futures, Wiley, 1972; Design for Evolution: Selforganization and Planning in the Life of Human Systems, Braziller, 1975; (editor with Conrad H. Waddington) Evolution and Consciousness: Human Systems in Transition, Addison-Wesley, 1976.

Contributor: James Reiser Bright, editor, Technological Forecasting for Industry and Government: Methods and Applications, Prentice-Hall, 1968; Alvin Toffler, editor, The Futurists, Random House, 1972; Bright, editor, A Practical Guide to Technological Forecasting, Prentice-Hall, 1972;

Interdisciplinarity, Organization for Economic Cooperation and Development (Paris), 1972; Bernard Hentsch and Fredmund Malik, editors, Systemorientiertes Management, Paul Haupt, 1973; Georg Baur, Gitti Hug, and Claus Loewe, editors, Unternehmensstrategie im Wandel, Paul Haupt, 1976; C. West Churchman and Richard O. Mason, editors, World Modeling: A Dialogue, American Elsevier, 1976.

Contributor of about sixty articles to scientific journals. Music and theater critic for *Musical America, Neues Oesterreich, Express,* and other periodicals, 1948-65. Founding co-editor of *Technological Forecasting and Social Futures,* 1968-71; associate editor of *Management Science,* 1974—; member of advisory board of *Policy Sciences,* 1969-74.

WORK IN PROGRESS: Research on theory of evolution, systems theory and philosophy, the role of humanity in evolution, process thinking, and the non-dualistic attitude.

SIDELIGHTS: Jantsch's aims are toward "providing a perspective of hope for young people, understanding how open systems, including human systems, live and evolve, and bringing together science and the humanities in a unified view."

* * *

JARVIS, Ana C(ortesi) 1936-

PERSONAL: Born September 6, 1936, in Asuncion, Paraguay; came to the United States in 1962, naturalized citizen, 1966; daughter of Santiago (a musician) and Dolores (Bures) Cortesi; married Bill Jarvis (a systems analyst), February 1, 1963; children: Ronald, Michelle. *Education:* California State College, San Bernardino, B.A., 1968; University of California, Riverside, M.A., 1970, Ph.D., 1973. *Home and office:* 1128 East 26th St., San Bernardino, Calif. 92404.

CAREER: University of California, Riverside, instructor in Spanish, 1968-72; San Bernardino Valley College, San Bernardino, Calif., instructor in Spanish, 1973-75; Riverside City College, Riverside Calif., instructor of Spanish, 1975—. Interpreter for "Point Four," an American government program in Paraguay.

WRITINGS: Por los senderos de lo hispanico (title means "Along the Hispanic Path"), Wiley, 1967; Career Education and Foreign Languages, Houghton, 1975; Como se dice . . .? (title means "How Does One Say . . .?"), Heath, 1977.

WORK IN PROGRESS: A novel in Spanish; Come se dice . . .?, second level; a book of poems.

SIDELIGHTS: Ana Jarvis comments briefly: "I firmly believe that Americans *need* to study foreign languages and cultures. I will continue to work toward fulfilling my dream: to see the day when *all* Californians are bilingual."

* * *

JASON
See STANNUS, (James) Gordon (Dawson)

* * *

JAY, Douglas (Patrick Thomas) 1907-

PERSONAL: Born March 23, 1907, in Woolwich, England; son of Edward Aubrey Hastings (a barrister) and Isobel (Craigie) Jay; married M. C. Garnett, September 30, 1933 (divorced, 1972); married Mary Lavinia Thomas (an administrator), May 27, 1972; children: Peter, Martin, Catherine (Mrs. Stewart Boyd), Helen (Mrs. David Kennard). *Education:* Attended Winchester College, 1920-26; New College, Oxford, B.A., 1929, M.A., 1930. *Politics:* Labour. *Religion:*

None. *Agent:* David Higham, 5-8 Lower John St., London W1R 4HA, England. *Office:* House of Commons, London SW1A 0AA, England.

CAREER: Oxford University, Oxford, England, fellow of All Souls College, 1930-37, 1968—. Labour member of British Parliament, 1945—; economic secretary to the Treasury, 1947-50, financial secretary to the Treasury, 1950-51, president of the Board of Trade, 1967-70.

WRITINGS: The Socialist Case, Faber, 1937; *Who is to Pay for the War and the Peace,* Routledge & Kegan Paul, 1940; (with others) *The Road to Recovery,* Fabian Society, 1948; *Socialism in the New Society,* Longmans, Green, 1962, St. Martin's, 1963; *After the Common Market,* Penguin, 1968.

*   *   *

JAYNES, Richard A(ndrus) 1935-

PERSONAL: Born May 27, 1935, in New Iberia, La.; son of Harold Andrus (an entomologist) and Virginia (Bier) Jaynes; married Sarah Humphrey, July 25, 1959; children: Burton, Linda, Bingham Scott. *Education:* Wesleyan University, Middletown, Conn., B.A., 1957; Yale University, M.S., 1959, Ph.D., 1961. *Religion:* Protestant. *Home address:* Broken Arrow Rd., Hamden, Conn. 06518. *Office:* Connecticut Agricultural Experiment Station, P.O. Box 1106, New Haven, Conn. 06504.

CAREER: Connecticut Agricultural Experiment Station, New Haven, assistant geneticist, 1961-65, associate geneticist, 1965-75, geneticist, 1975—. *Member:* International Plant Propagators Society, American Association for the Advancement of Science, American Horticulture Society, American Rhododendron Society, American Rock Garden Society, American Society of Horticultural Science, Northern Nut Growers Association. *Awards, honors:* James R. Jewett Award from Arnold Arboretum, 1972; bronze medal from local chapter of American Rhododendron Society, 1974; Evelyn Moody certificate for creative horticultural achievement from National Council of State Garden Clubs, 1974; scientific citation from American Horticulture Society, 1976; Jackson Dawson Award from Massachusetts Horticulture Society, 1976.

WRITINGS: (Editor) *Handbook of North American Nut Trees,* Northern Nut Growers Association, 1969; *The Laurel Book,* Hafner, 1975. Contributor of more than eighty-five articles to scientific and popular journals. Editor for Northern Nut Growers Association, 1963—.

WORK IN PROGRESS: Editing *American Nut Tree Culture,* completion expected in 1978.

SIDELIGHTS: Jaynes writes: "My professional interest is primarily breeding and selection of new plants. Gratification for years of experiments comes, in part at least, from communicating results to scientists and especially laymen. The acceptance of new ideas and products that evolve from research is the ultimate justification of the research."

*   *   *

JEFFERS, Lance 1919-

PERSONAL: Born November 28, 1919, in Fremont, Neb.; son of Henry Nelson (a messenger) and Dorothy Jeffers; married Trellie James (a college professor), May 22, 1958; children: Lance, Valjeanne, Sidonie, Honoree. *Education:* Columbia University, B.S. (cum laude), 1951. *Politics:* Democrat. *Religion:* African Methodist Episcopal. *Home:* 2608 East Weaver St., Durham, N.C. 27707. *Office:* Department of English, North Carolina State University, Raleigh, N.C.

CAREER: Florida A & M University, Tallahassee, assistant professor of English, 1964-65; Indiana University, Kokomo, instructor in English, 1966-68; California State University, Long Beach, assistant professor of English, 1968-73; North Carolina State University, Raleigh, associate professor of English, 1973—. Visiting professor, Duke University, 1976-77. Has lectured at Shaw University, Federal City College, Bowie State College, and Tuskegee Institute. *Military service:* U.S. Army, 1942-46. *Member:* International P.E.N., College Language Association.

WRITINGS: My Blackness Is the Beauty of This Land, Broadside Press, 1970; *When I Know the Power of My Black Hand,* Broadside Press, 1974.

Poems have been included in about thirty anthologies, including *New Black Voices,* edited by Abraham Chapman, New American Library, 1971; *A Broadside Treasury,* edited by Gwendolyn Brooks, Broadside Press, 1971; *You Better Believe It: The Penguin Book of Black Verse,* edited by Paul Bremen, Penguin, 1973; and *Vietnam and Black America,* edited by Clyde Taylor, Doubleday, 1973. Contributor of about thirty-five poems, articles, and stories to literary magazines, including *Confrontation, Mainstream, Black Scholar, Blackstage, Hyperion, Southern Poetry Review,* and *Negro Digest.*

WORK IN PROGRESS: Two books of poetry, tentatively titled *Whales* and *The Janitor's Wife,* both for Dark Harbingers Press.

SIDELIGHTS: Jeffers writes: "I look at the unrealized potentialities of humanity—not in technological development, but in tenderness, empathy, and wisdom—and I write, in essence, of the potential grandeur that lies undeveloped in the genes of man, of the obstacles that frequently defeat him, of his tenacity and vision. This is the motive force behind my writing: the passion to help create an environment that will allow humanity to move into an unlived-in region of its personality. I dredge up from my own personal seabed everything that I can and move it into poetry, for what is in me and innumerable others is what is most basic in human experience and character: the defeat, the oppression, the sorrow, the strength, the struggle, the movement forward, the vision forged from empathy, and the empathy wrenched, in my own personal experience, from the oppression as a Black person in America, which is, simultaneously the experience of a people."

*   *   *

JENKINS, John H(olmes III) 1940-

PERSONAL: Born March 22, 1940, in Beaumont, Tex.; son of J. Holmes (an artist) and Sue (Chalmers) Jenkins; married Maureen Vera Mooney, June 5, 1962; children: John Holmes IV. *Education:* Graduated from University of Texas, 1962, graduate study, 1962-63. *Politics:* Liberal Democrat. *Religion:* Agnostic. *Home:* 8 Cromwell Hill, Austin, Tex. 78703. *Agent:* Bertha Klausner, 71 Park Ave., New York, N.Y. 10016. *Office:* P.O. Box 2085, Austin, Tex. 78767.

CAREER: Pemberton Press, Austin, Tex., publisher, 1962—. President of Jenkins Co. (rare book dealers), 1962—, and Country Store Gallery, 1963—. Founding member and member of board of directors of Collectors Institute; member of board of directors of North Austin Bank. *Military service:* U.S. Army, Counterintelligence, 1966; became sergeant.

MEMBER: Antiquarian Booksellers Association of America (member of board of governors), Antiquarian Booksellers Association of the Southwest (president), Texas State Historical Association (life fellow; member of executive council), Texas Institute of Letters, Texas Philosophical Society, Delta Tau Delta. *Awards, honors:* Outstanding author award from Theta Sigma Thi, 1959, for *Recollections of Early Texas;* award from American Association for State and Local History, 1966. for *Cracker Barrel Chronicles;* Summerfield G. Roberts Award from Sons of the Republic of Texas, 1973, for *Papers of the Texas Revolution;* D.Litt. from Union College, Schenectady, N.Y., 1976.

WRITINGS: (Editor) *Recollections of Early Texas: The Memoirs of John Holland Jenkins,* University of Texas Press, 1958; *Neither the Fanatics nor the Fainthearted* (personal recollections of the assassination of John F. Kennedy), Pemberton Press, 1963; (editor) Robert M. Coleman, *Houston Displayed: Or, Who Won the Battle of San Jacinto,* Brick Row Book Shop, 1964; *Honest Bob and the Texas Congress,* Pemberton Press, 1964; *A Catalogue of the Writings of J. Frank Dobie: Comprising the Largest Selection Ever Offered for Sale, and Further Contributing to a Bibliography,* privately printed, 1964; *Cracker Barrel Chronicles: A Bibliography of Texas Town and County Histories,* Pemberton Press, 1965; *Audubon and Texas,* Pemberton Press, 1965; *Patriotic Songs and Poems of Early Texas, 1836-1848,* Pemberton Press, 1966; *A Catalogue of Over Fourteen Hundred County and Town Histories of Texas,* Jenkins Co., 1967; (editor) *Bluebonnets and Cactus,* Fine Arts Corporation Press, 1967; (with H. Gordon Frost) *I'm Frank Hamer: The Life of a Texas Peace Officer,* Pemberton Press, 1968; (editor) *Along the Early Trails of the Southwest,* Fine Arts Corporation Press, 1968; (with Stephen B. Oates and others) *The Republic of Texas,* American West, 1968.

Texas Delineated: Some Disconnected Views from the Past, Pemberton Press, 1971; *Thrill All the Modern Kinds,* Pemberton Press, 1972; *The Notting Bough, the Signal Tower, and the Fixing of Oscar,* Pemberton Press, 1973; (editor and author of notes) *Western Travel Books from Wagner-Camp,* Jenkins Co., 1973; (editor) *The Papers of the Texas Revolution, 1835-1836: Military Papers of Texas,* ten volumes, Presidial Press, 1973; *A Valentine in a Rough Winter,* Pemberton Press, 1974; *Works of Genius: A Catalogue and a Commentary,* Jenkins Publishing, 1974; *The Eberstadt Caper,* Pemberton Press, 1975; *Audubon, and Other Capers: Confessions of a Texas Bookmaker,* Pemberton Press, 1976; *American Celebration: The Creation and Evolution of the United States as Reflected in the Printed and Written Word,* Pemberton Press, 1976. Contributor to a wide variety of magazines, including *Argosy, American Mercury, Mad, Southwestern Art Journal, Cattleman, Antiquarian Bookman, Union, Texas Libraries,* and history journals.

WORK IN PROGRESS: Editing *The Letters of Thomas Jefferson to Charles Wilson Peale; Basic Texas Books: A Bibliography,* completion expected in 1978; a novel about Colonel Anthony Butler, 1978; the last three volumes of *Works of Genius: A Catalogue and a Commentary,* publication by Pemberton Press expected in 1979; research for *A History of the Texas Revolution,* completion expected in 1980.

SIDELIGHTS: In 1950, when he was ten years old, Jenkins received the money from a hundred-dollar bond. With that, he started a mail order rare book and coin business, Southwestern Investment Co., which earned him more than thirty-five thousand dollars before he entered college. His first book was begun at the age of fourteen and released by its publisher on the day he graduated from high school; Jenkins probably became one of the first people to enter college and take a course which used his own book as a text. In addition to his publishing company, he now owns the largest art gallery in the Southwest and a rare book company which he claims is the largest in the world. One of his purchases was of such a magnitude that the removal of the books involved was labeled in the media as a major cultural shift from New York. In 1971, Jenkins was instrumental in recovering some lost Audubon works and other national treasures. He was cited by the Federal Bureau of Investigation for bravery, and the story of his adventure was an episode on the television series, "Kojac."

BIOGRAPHICAL/CRITICAL SOURCES: "A Corner Forever Texas: Johnny Jenkins," American Broadcasting Co.—Radio, 1961; Otho Plummer, *John H. Jenkins: Author, Publisher, Bookseller,* Texian Press, 1965; J. Frank Dobie, *Prefaces,* Little, Brown, 1975; Al Lowman, *Printing Arts in Texas,* Roger Beacham, 1975; *Texas Monthly,* May, 1975; *New York Times,* August 21, 1975; *Zest,* September, 1975, *Antiquarian Bookman,* September, 1975; "The Diogenes Syndrome," on "Kojac," Columbia Broadcasting System—Television, 1976; *Discovery,* September, 1976; *Southern Living,* October, 1976.

* * *

JENKINS, Reese V(almer) 1938-

PERSONAL: Born June 28, 1938, in Muncie, Ind.; son of John Thomas (an engineer) and Vada (a social worker; maiden name, Fraze) Jenkins; married Alyce Mitchem (a teacher and writer), December 27, 1962; children: David W., Elizabeth A. *Education:* University of Rochester, B.A. (with distinction), 1960; University of Wisconsin, Madison, M.S., 1963, Ph.D., 1966. *Religion:* Protestant. *Home:* 1051 Pennfield Rd., Cleveland Heights, Ohio 44121. *Office:* Crawford Hall, Case Western Reserve University, Cleveland, Ohio 44106.

CAREER: High school teacher of mathematics and history in Madison, Wis., 1963-64; Northern Illinois University, DeKalb, assistant professor of the history of science, 1966-67; Case Western Reserve University, Cleveland, Ohio, assistant professor, 1967-74, associate professor of the history of science and technology, 1974—. Visiting associate professor at University of Rochester, 1976-77.

MEMBER: International Museum of Photography (associate), Society for the History of Technology, History of Science Society, American Historical Association, Economic History Association, Mid-West Junto of History of Science (council officer, 1973-75). *Awards, honors:* National Science Foundation grant, 1967-69; Harvard-Newcomen business history fellowship, 1969-70.

WRITINGS: (With John Neu and Fred Ives) *Chemical, Medical, and Pharmaceutical Books at Wisconsin Published before 1800,* University of Wisconsin Press, 1965; *Images and Enterprise: Technology and the American Photographic Industry, 1839-1925,* Johns Hopkins Press, 1975. Contributor to *Dictionary of American History* and to academic journals.

WORK IN PROGRESS: A biography of Marion B. Folsom, completion expected in 1978; a biography of George Eastman, 1981; research on relations between technology and culture and on German Naturphilosophie.

SIDELIGHTS: Jenkins writes: "My approach to the history of science and technology is strongly non-positivistic, with emphasis on cultural and intellectual ideas as well as on social and economic forces. I am particularly anxious to show the conceptual congruence between technology and its contemporary culture and values as reflected in the fine arts, literature, and philosophy." *Avocational interests:* Tennis, music, literature, art.

* * *

JENSEN, Maxine Dowd   1919-
(Maxine E. Dowd)

PERSONAL: Born April 7, 1919, in Sedalia, Mo.; daughter of Luther Clare (a blacksmith) and I. Emaline (Taylor) Dowd; married Clifford Jensen (a communications consultant), September 26, 1959 (deceased); children: (stepdaughters) Joyce (Mrs. A. J. Williams), Lorraine (Mrs. Roy Swanson). *Education:* Wright Junior College, certificate, 1938; also attended Northwestern University. *Politics:* "Never vote a straight ticket." *Religion:* Methodist. *Home:* Rte. 7, Mountain Home, Ark. 72653.

CAREER: Follett Book Co., Chicago, Ill., pricer, 1940-41; worked for American Mutual Liability Insurance Co., 1941-46; Illinois Bell Telephone Co., Chicago, representative, 1946-58, benefit administrative assistant, 1958-66, division staff assistant, 1966-72; writer, 1972—. Soloist; former member of Swedish Choral Club and Bell Telephone Chorus. *Member:* Telephone Pioneers of America.

WRITINGS: The Warming of Winter (inspirational), Abingdon, 1977. Columnist, "Sing No Sad Song," syndicated by Trans-World News Service, 1976—. Contributor, sometimes under maiden name, Maxine E. Dowd, to church and popular magazines, including *Women's World, Sunshine, Guideposts,* and *Evangelical Beacon,* and newspapers.

WORK IN PROGRESS: The Little People; Heavy Heavy Hangs over Thy Head; Victory Is Jesus; Commandment with Promise.

SIDELIGHTS: Maxine Jensen writes: "Since first I remember, at about age eight, I have wanted to write, sing, and travel. Until 1973 family responsibilities, then marriage, kept me from all but a haphazard following of my first love. In writing my goal is to learn to write with such excellence that I can convincingly present the faith I believe through any media I choose. I believe in facing life, and its problems, with optimism, confidence, and joy. More than anything I would like to help people love life and live it to its fullest experiencing real peace and happiness."

AVOCATIONAL INTERESTS: World-wide travel.

BIOGRAPHICAL/CRITICAL SOURCES: Baxter Bulletin, January 15, 1976.

* * *

JOHNS, Glover S., Jr.   1911(?)-1976

American military officer and author. Obituaries: *Time,* June 7, 1976.

* * *

JOHNSON, Bea   ?-1976

?—April 29, 1976; American journalist, columnist, radio and television broadcaster and administrator, and author. Obituaries: *Washington Post,* May 1, 1976.

JOHNSON, Charles R.   1925-
(Chuck Johnson)

PERSONAL: Born September 16, 1925, in Williston, N.D.; son of Charles A. (a grain elevator manager) and Lena (Quick) Johnson; married Lillian Hilmo, August 21, 1949; children: Linda, Eric, Paul, Thomas. *Education:* Attended Mississippi College, 1944, Massachusetts Institute of Technology, 1944-45; University of North Dakota, Ph.B., 1948. *Religion:* Lutheran. *Home:* 1722 North 58th St., Milwaukee, Wis. 53208. *Agent:* Larry Sternig, 742 Robertson, Milwaukee, Wis. 53213. *Office: Milwaukee Journal,* Milwaukee, Wis. 53201.

CAREER: Fargo Forum, Fargo, N.D., assistant sports editor, 1948-52; *Milwaukee Journal,* Milwaukee, Wis., sports writer, 1952-58, assistant sports editor, 1958-68, sports editor, 1968-75, assistant news editor, 1975—. *Member:* Milwaukee Press Club (president, 1972-74), Sigma Delta Chi, Wisconsin Associated Press Sports Writers (president, 1971-72).

WRITINGS—Under name Chuck Johnson: *The Green Bay Packers: Pro Football's Pioneer Team,* Nelson, 1961; *The Greatest Packers of Them All,* Putnam, 1968.

WORK IN PROGRESS: Another sports book for Putnam; a textbook on sports writing.

* * *

JOHNSON, La Verne B(ravo)   1925-

PERSONAL: Born May 23, 1925, in Stockton, Calif.; daughter of Edward E. (a men's clothier) and Gertrude O'Neil Bravo; married Frank T. Johnson (a men's clothier), October 21, 1945; children: Thomas E., William P., James D., Lanette M. *Education:* Stanford University, B.A., 1948. *Residence:* Stockton, Calif. *Office:* P.O. Box 2088, Stockton, Calif., 95201.

CAREER: Writer.

WRITINGS: Night Noises (juvenile), Parents' Magazine Press, 1968.

WORK IN PROGRESS: A juvenile novel, about the Yokuts Indians; adult short stories.

SIDELIGHTS: La Verne Johnson comments: "I believe children need the reassuring feeling of security and their own worth. Come to think of it, that is also the message of my short stories for adults." Her book has appeared in Japanese and in a Swedish anthology.

* * *

JOHNSON, Malcolm (Malone)   1904-1976

September 27, 1904—June 18, 1976; American journalist, public relations executive, and author. Obituaries: *Washington Post,* June 18, 1976; *New York Times,* June 19, 1976; *Current Biography,* August, 1976.

* * *

JOHNSON, Peter   1930-

PERSONAL: Born March 26, 1930, in London, England; son of John (a British Army officer) and Carol (Haas) Johnson; married Caroline Hodsoll; children: one son, two daughters. *Education:* Shrivenham College of Science, B.Sc., 1953. *Home:* Dene End, Buckland Dr., Lymington SO4 9DT, England. *Office:* Nautical Publishing, Lymington SO4 9BA, England.

CAREER: British Army, in Royal Artillery, served in

Egypt, Cyprus, and on Mediterranean staff, 1948-61, left service as captain; employed by Bordon Chemical Co., 1961-64; director of Yacht equipment company, 1965-70; Nautical Publishing, Lymington, England, director and editor, 1970—.

WRITINGS: Passage Racing: Cruising and Racing Offshore, Newnes, 1969; *Ocean Racing and Offside Yachts,* Dodd, 1970, 2nd edition, 1972; (editor) *Yachting World Handbook,* St. Martin's, 1971, revised and enlarged edition, 1973; (with others) *Yachtsman's Guide to Rating Rule,* Quadrangle, 1972; *Boating Britain,* Nautical Publishing, 1973; *The Guinness Book of Yachting Facts and Feats,* Sterling, 1975, published as *Boating Facts and Feats,* 1976. Author of "In the Offing," a monthly column in *Yachting World,* 1971—.

SIDELIGHTS: Sir Peter Johnson, the seventh baronet of New York (a title first conferred in 1755), is associated with the Offshore Rating Council, an international yachting organization.

* * *

JOHNSON, Ray DeForest 1926-

PERSONAL: Born December 27, 1926, in New York, N.Y.; son of Albert (a farmer) and Doris (Mortaugh) Johnson; married Sallie L. Bratten, November 4, 1968 (divorced October, 1974); married Sandy Stokes (director of SHARE), December 27, 1974. *Education:* Took extension courses from the University of California, 1956-66. *Politics:* Independent. *Religion:* None. *Home and office:* 1150 Silverado St., La Jolla, Calif. 92037.

CAREER: Folsom Prison, Folsom, Calif., secretary to Catholic chaplain, 1960-64; California Department of Corrections, research assistant, 1964-67; California Medical Facility, Vacaville, Calif., coordinator of psychotherapy study program, 1967, assistant investigator for study of stress assessment, 1967; San Diego State University, San Diego, Calif., co-director of Study of the Protective Service Agency for Older People, 1968—; Ex-Offender Resources, Inc., San Diego, Calif., vice-president, 1970—. Chairman, Inmate Council, Folsom Prison, 1962-63; co-director, San Diego Department of Honor Camps Volunteer Drug Program, 1970-71; research member, Urban Observatory, San Diego State University, 1970-71; coordinator-instructor, Criminal Justice Conference Series, University of California at San Diego, 1971-74; instructor at San Diego State University, 1971-74; Western Behavioral Sciences Institute, research assistant, 1971-72, assistant project director, 1972-75, research associate, 1972—. *Member:* Association for Criminal Justice Research.

WRITINGS: (With Mona McCormick) *Too Dangerous to Be at Large,* Quadrangle, 1975.

WORK IN PROGRESS: Obsolescent Crime, a book dealing with crime careers that have been displaced by technology.

* * *

JOHNSON, W(alter) R(alph) 1933-

PERSONAL: Born July 9, 1933, in Trinidad, Colo.; son of William Ralph (a barber) and Thelma (Bushnell) Johnson; married Sabina Thorne (a writer), March 2, 1962; children: Nicholas, Leatrice. *Education:* Attended San Diego State College (now San Diego State University), 1951-53; University of California, Berkeley, B.A., 1961, M.A., 1963, Ph.D., 1966. *Residence:* Ithaca, N.Y. *Office:* Department of Classics, Cornell University, Ithaca, N.Y. 14853.

CAREER: University of California, Berkeley, assistant professor, 1966-72, associate professor of classics and comparative literature, 1972-74; Cornell University, Ithaca, N.Y., associate professor, 1974-76, professor of classics, 1976—. *Military service:* U.S. Army, 1953-58. *Member:* American Philological Association.

WRITINGS: A Messenger of Satan, Janus Press, 1957; *Luxuriance and Economy: Cicero and the Alien Style,* University of California Press, 1971; (author of foreword) Horace, *Selected Odes, Epodes, Satires, Epistles,* translated by Burton Raffel, New American Library, 1973; (author of afterword) Horace, *The Art of Poetry,* translated by Raffel, State University of New York Press, 1974; *Darkness Visible: A Study of Vergil's Aeneid,* University of California Press, 1976. Contributor of essays to journals in his field.

WORK IN PROGRESS: A translation of Seneca's *Thyestes;* a book on ancient and modern lyric.

* * *

JOHNSTON, Brian 1932-

PERSONAL: Born April 14, 1932, in Cranwell, Lincolnshire, England; came to United States in 1964; son of Edward Thomas and Florence (Anderson) Johnston. *Education:* Attended Fircroft College, 1956-57; Gonville & Caius College, Cambridge, M.A., 1964. *Politics:* Radical. *Religion:* Humanist. *Home:* 1740 Loma St., Santa Barbara, Calif. 93103.

CAREER: Norges Laererhoegskolen, Trondheim, Norway, instructor, 1962-64; Northwestern University, Evanston, Ill., instructor in English literature, 1964-68; University of California, Berkeley, lecturer in comparative literature, 1968-70; University of California, Santa Barbara, assistant professor of dramatic art, 1970-76; free-lance writer. *Military service:* Royal Air Force, 1950-53. *Member:* American Theatre Association.

WRITINGS: The Ibsen Cycle, Twayne, 1975. Contributor to professional journals.

WORK IN PROGRESS: The Argument of Romantic Drama, emphasizing Kant, Schiller, Hegel, Nietzsche, and Ibsen.

* * *

JOHNSTON, Ellen Turlington 1929-

PERSONAL: Born October 31, 1929, in Washington, D.C.; daughter of Edgar (a lawyer) and Catherine (a writer; maiden name, Hackett) Turlington; married Eugene Reed Johnston, 1952 (divorced, 1971); children: Barbara Elizabeth, Reed, Patricia Turlington. *Education:* Mt. Holyoke College, student, 1947-49; University of North Carolina at Chapel Hill, A.B., 1951; University of North Carolina at Charlotte, teacher's certificate, 1962-63.

CAREER: Junior high school English teacher in Statesville, N.C., 1964-65, and in Charlotte, N.C., 1966-68; North Mecklenburg High School, N.C., teacher of English and director of actor's workshop, 1969—. *Member:* North Carolina Poetry Society, North Carolina Writers Club. *Awards, honors:* Award from Carolina Dramatic Association, 1963, for musical drama "Listen to Your Heart."

WRITINGS: So What Happened to You? (stories in verse), Moore Publishing, 1974. Also author of "Listen to Your Heart," a musical drama.

WORK IN PROGRESS: We Don't Do Nothin' in Here, a book of poems, for Moore Publishing.

SIDELIGHTS: Ellen Johnston writes: "My book . . . contains true stories in verse about my experiences in the classroom. It is a story of frustration, futility, failure, and disillusionment. It is a story, also, of faith, friendship, forgiveness, and warm moments. And it is a story of hope—always hope. . . . This is my eleventh year of teaching, nine of these having been in the Charlotte Mecklenburg school system. I have watched Black-White relationships gradually mellow from bitter anger and hostility to a mutual understanding and appreciation. The best news I have to report is that we can, and do, laugh at ourselves and our differences now."

*　　*　　*

JONAS, Gerald 1935-

PERSONAL: Born October 4, 1935, in New York, N.Y.; son of Myron and Margaret (Wurmfeld) Jonas; married second wife, Susan Krieger (a correspondent), December 4, 1966; children: (second marriage) Sarah, Phoebe. *Education:* Yale University, B.A., 1957; Pembroke College, Cambridge, graduate study, 1957-58. *Politics:* Liberal Democrat. *Religion:* Jewish. *Home:* 450 West End Ave., New York, N.Y. 10024. *Agent:* Lyn Nesbit, 40 West 57th St., New York, N.Y. 10019. *Office: New Yorker,* 25 West 43rd St., New York, N.Y. 10036.

CAREER: Boston Herald, Boston, Mass., reporter and education writer, 1959-61; *New Yorker,* New York, N.Y., staff writer, 1961—. *Military service:* U.S. Army Reserve, active duty, 1959-61. *Awards, honors:* Henry fellowship, 1957-58; national media award from American Psychological Association, 1973, for a series of *New Yorker* articles, "Visceral Learning"; Guggenheim fellowship, 1974-75.

WRITINGS: On Doing Good: The Quaker Experiment, Scribner, 1971; *Visceral Learning: Toward a Science of Self-Control,* Viking, 1973. Author of book review columns "Of Things to Come," in *New York Times Book Review,* and "Browsing," in *Present Tense.* Contributor of poems and articles to popular magazines.

WORK IN PROGRESS: A book on the brain, for the layman.

SIDELIGHTS: Jonas writes: "I am primarily a writer on scientific subjects, especially psychology, physiology, and biology. Unless the non-scientifically trained person understands what is happening in these fields, he cannot consider himself educated, and he runs the risk of losing control of his own affairs. In its own way, science fiction also helps people grasp the spirit of the scientific enterprise."

*　　*　　*

JONES, Dan Burne 1908-

PERSONAL: Born August 16, 1908, in Dalzell, Ill.; son of Aaron and Mary (Griffin) Jones; married Lucille Clery (an office manager), 1943; children: Daniel A. D. *Education:* Art Institute of Chicago, B.Art Education, 1931; also attended University of Chicago, University of Illinois, and State Teacher College, DeKalb, Ill. *Politics:* Republican. *Religion:* Baptist. *Home:* 816 North Blvd., Oak Park, Ill. 60301.

CAREER: Art Institute of Chicago, Chicago, Ill., teacher in Saturday School, 1928-30; teacher and playground director at public school in Ladd, Ill., 1933-37; Lee Art Academy, Memphis, Tenn., instructor and head of department of design, 1937-39; Art Institute of Chicago, assistant instructor in lithography and etching, 1940-42; U.S. Coast and Geodetic Survey, Washington, D.C., lithographic draftsman of

aeronautical charts, 1942-43; B. Brookema Co. (commercial insert and display packagers), Oak Park, Ill., package and display machine instructor, also involved in fine art, 1945-73; writer and lecturer, 1973—. Summer instructor at State Teachers College, Kirksville, Mo., 1932, 1937; teacher at Peninsula Art School, Ephraim, Wis., 1940, 1941. Draft board examiner in Memphis, 1941-42. Has judged art work at national and local exhibitions. His own work has been exhibited all over the United States, including the 1938 New York World's Fair, and in French Morocco and Denmark. *Military service:* U.S. Army Air Forces, Air Transport Command, 1943-45; served in Italy and French Morocco, and in India-China-Burma theater.

MEMBER: Genuine Indian Relic Society, Arctic Circle Club, National Emergency Civil Liberties Committee, Americans United, National Wildlife Federation (world associate member), Monhegan Associates, American Museum of Natural History (associate), Smithsonian Associates, Illinois State Archaeological Society, Indiana Archaeological Society, Foundation for Illinois Archaeology, Greater St. Louis Archaeological Society, Friends of the Libraries of Columbia University, Princeton University, Philadelphia Museum of Art, and Bowdoin College Library and Museum of Art, Delta Phi Delta (Zeta chapter). *Awards, honors:* Travel grant from Smithsonian Institution, 1971; awards from Art Libraries Society of North America, American Institute of Graphic Arts, and Association of American University Presses, all 1976, all for *The Prints of Rockwell Kent;* Chicago Book Clinic award, 1976.

WRITINGS: Eldorado (poems; self-illustrated), privately printed, 1935; *The Least of These* (stories), Black Cat Press, 1937; (editor and illustrator) *History of the Village of Ladd,* privately printed, 1946; *The Prints of Rockwell Kent,* University of Chicago Press, 1975; (contributor) *1976 Bicentennial Year Book,* American Bookplate Society for Collectors and Designers, 1976.

Illustrator: Frank Ankenbrand, Jr., *Poems of Li Po,* translated by John A. Dixon, privately printed, 1941. Contributor to art, hobby, and book collectors' journals and to little literary magazines. Art editor of *Imprimatur,* 1948; special editor of *American Book Collector,* summer, 1964.

WORK IN PROGRESS: Lynd Ward: A Chronological Bibliography; Rockwell Kent: A Descriptive Bibliography.

SIDELIGHTS: Jones has traveled extensively in the United States and abroad. He owns large collections of prints and written and illustrated works of Rockwell Kent and Lynd Ward, Robinson Jeffers, Walt Whitman, and Thomas Wolfe, as well as smaller collections of Melville and Hemingway, and works on North and South American archaeology.

BIOGRAPHICAL/CRITICAL SOURCES: Audrey Arellanes, editor, *Bookplates: A Selected Bibliography of the Periodical Literature,* Gale, 1971.

*　　*　　*

JONES, Marvin 1886-1976

February 26, 1886—March 4, 1976; American federal magistrate, government administrator, and author. Obituaries: *New York Times,* March 6, 1976.

*　　*　　*

JORDAN, Donald A. 1936-

PERSONAL: Born June 6, 1936, in Chicago, Ill.; son of Frank William (in management) and Mildred (Work) Jordan;

married Mary Katherine Steltzer (a linguist and teacher), August 17, 1963; children: Benjamin William, Matthew Frank, Nathan John. *Education:* Allegheny College, B.A., 1958; University of Pittsburgh, M.A., 1963; University of Wisconsin, Madison, Ph.D., 1967. *Politics:* Independent. *Religion:* Presbyterian. *Home:* 8 North Shannon Ave., Athens, Ohio 45701. *Office:* Department of History, Ohio University, Athens, Ohio 45701.

CAREER: Ohio University, Athens, assistant professor, 1967-74, associate professor of history, 1974—. Industrial consultant on Taiwan. *Military service:* U.S. Naval Reserve, active duty, 1959-62; served in Taiwan; became lieutenant. *Member:* Association of Asian Studies, Ohio Asianists (member of board of directors), Ohio Education Association. *Awards, honors:* Fulbright fellowship, Taiwan, 1965-66; National Defense Foreign Language fellowship, 1966-67.

WRITINGS: The Northern Expedition: China's National Revolution of 1926-1928, University Press of Hawaii, 1976; (contributor) Gilbert Chan, editor, *China in the 1920's,* New Viewpoints, 1976.

WORK IN PROGRESS: The Shanghai Incident of 1932: Japan's Response to Chinese Nationalism.

SIDELIGHTS: Jordan writes that his current work involves "research in Chinese materials which require a continuing study of an extremely difficult language."

* * *

JORDAN, Robin 1947-

PERSONAL: Born March 5, 1947. *Office:* P.O. Box 5025, Washington Station, Reno, Nev. 89513.

CAREER: Writer.

WRITINGS: (With Gene Damon and Jan Watson) *The Lesbian in Literature: A Bibliography,* Ladder, 1975; *Speak Out, My Heart* (novel), Naiad Press, 1976.

WORK IN PROGRESS: The Rekindling, a novel concerning integrated attitudes toward life and death, completion expected in 1978; poems; research on all branches of metaphysics.

SIDELIGHTS: Robin Jordan writes that she has a "growing interest in reclaiming our lesbian heritage as well as documenting contemporary lesbian writings. Beyond that, my energies go toward supporting all those who are working to build a better, more humane world for everyone."

* * *

JORGENS, Jack J(ohnstone) 1943-

PERSONAL: Born January 4, 1943, in Minneapolis, Minn.; son of Jack J. (a salesman) and Valerie (a teacher; maiden name, Litchke) Jorgens; married Elise Bickford (a musicologist), June 12, 1965; children: Elisabeth and Catherine (twins). *Education:* Carleton College, B.A., 1965; City College of the City University of New York, M.A., 1967; New York University, Ph.D., 1970. *Office:* Department of Literature, American University, Washington, D.C. 20760.

CAREER: University of Connecticut, Storrs, assistant professor of English, 1970-71; University of Massachusetts, Amherst, assistant professor of English, 1971-75; American University, Washington, D.C., associate professor of literature, 1975—, director of cinema studies, 1976—. Visiting professor at Clark University and University of Bridgeport. *Member:* Modern Language Association of America, Na-

tional Council of Teachers of English, Shakespeare Association of America, American Film Institute. *Awards, honors:* Andiron Club Prize, 1970.

WRITINGS: Shakespeare on Film, Indiana University Press, 1976. Contributor of articles and reviews to literature and film journals.

WORK IN PROGRESS: Shakespeare on Stage and Screen: A Checklist of Criticism, publication by Indiana University Press expected in 1978.

SIDELIGHTS: Jorgens writes that he is the "unlikely product of specialized training as a Shakespearean, a father who worked for MGM, and a continuing love for the theatre."

* * *

JOUDRY, Patricia 1921-

PERSONAL: Born October 18, 1921, in Spirit River, Alberta, Canada; daughter of Clifford G. (a magazine editor) and Beth (a potter; maiden name, Gilbart) Joudry; married Delmar Dinsdale (divorced, 1952); married John Steele (divorced); children: Gay (Mrs. Paul Gilbaud), Sharon (Mrs. Michael Martin), Stephanie, Melanie, Felicity. *Education:* Attended high school in Montreal. *Politics:* None. *Religion:* "Every possible kind." *Home:* Ste. Agnes de Dundee, Quebec, Canada.

CAREER: Playwright. *Awards, honors:* Named Canadian Woman of the Year by Toronto Press, 1955; best play award from Dominion Drama Festival, 1956, for "Teach Me How to Cry"; prizes from Stratford-Globe playwriting competition for "Walk Alone Together," and National Playwriting Seminar, for "Don the Dinted Armour".

WRITINGS: Teach Me How to Cry (three-act play; first produced in New York City, Off-Broadway, 1955), Dramatists' Play Service, 1955; *The Song of Louise in the Morning* (one-act play), Dramatists' Play Service, 1960; *The Dweller on the Threshold* (novel), McClelland & Stewart, 1973; *And the Children Played* (nonfiction), Tundra Books, 1975; *Spirit River to Angels' Roost* (nonfiction), Tundra Books, 1977.

Unpublished plays: "The Sand Castle"; "Three Rings for Michelle"; "Stranger in My House"; "Walk Alone Together" (comedy); "Semi-Detached"; "Valerie" (comedy); "Don the Dinted Armour" (comedy); "The Man with the Perfect Wife" (comedy); "God Goes Heathen"; "Think Again" (comedy); "Now" (science-fiction multi-media play); "I Ching."

Author of radio scripts for "The Henry Aldrich Show," 1946-49, and for "Penney's Diary," and of several hundred radio and television plays.

WORK IN PROGRESS: A novel; "O Listen!," a three-act play.

SIDELIGHTS: Patricia Joudry comments that she "finished high school, and the least said about that whole subject the better. I obtained my revenge in my book, *And the Children Played,* which relates how I kept my own children out of school and properly educated, at home—with all their faculties and gifts preserved." She adds that her most recently published book, *Spirit River to Angels' Roost,* is a discussion of her religious beliefs.

* * *

JOURNET, Charles 1891-1975

PERSONAL: Born January 26, 1891, in Switzerland. *Address:* Grand Seminaire, Fribourg, Switzerland.

CAREER: Ordained Roman Catholic priest; professor of theology at Grand Seminaire, Fribourg, Switzerland; consecrated archbishop and created cardinal, both 1965.

WRITINGS—In English: *Our Lady of Sorrows,* translated by F. J. Sheed, Sheed, 1938; *L'Eglise du Verbe incarne: Essai de theologie speculative,* Desclee de Brouwer, 1941, translation by A. H. C. Downes published as *The Church of the Word Incarnate: An Essay in Speculative Theology,* Sheed, 1955, abridged French edition published as *Theologie de l'eglise,* Desclee de Brouwer, 1958, 3rd French edition, 1962; *Introduction a la theologie,* Desclee de Brouwer, 1947, translation by R. F. Smith published as *The Wisdom of Faith: An Introduction to Theology,* Newman Press, 1952; *Primaute de Pierre dans la perspective protestante et dans la perspective catholique,* Alsatia, 1953, translation by John Chapin published as *The Primacy of Peter from the Protestant and from the Catholic Point of View,* Newman Press, 1954; *Entretiens sur la grace,* Desclee de Brouwer, 1959, translation by A. V. Littledale published as *The Meaning of Grace,* Kenedy, 1960; *Le Mal: Essai theologique,* Desclee de Brouwer, 1960, translation by Michael Barry published as *The Meaning of Evil,* Kenedy, 1963; *Le Dogme: Chemin de la foi,* Fayard, 1963, translation by Mark Pontifex published as *What Is Dogma?,* Hawthorn, 1964.

Other works: *L'Esprit du protestantisme en Suisse,* Nouvelle Librairie Nationale, 1925; *L'Union des eglises et le christianisme practique,* Grasset, 1927; *La Juridiction de l'eglise sur la cite,* Desclee de Brouwer, 1931; *Vues chretiennes sur la politiques,* Beauchemin, 1942; *Destinees d'Israel, a propos du Salut par les Juifs,* Egloff, 1945; *Exigenees chretiennes en politique,* Egloff, 1945; (translator) Adam Mickiewicz, *Le Livre des pelerins polonais,* Egloff, 1947; (with others) *Trouble et lumiere,* Desclee de Brouwer, 1949; *Les Septs Paroles du Christ en croix,* Editions du Seuil, 1952; *Esquisse du developpement du dogme marial,* Alsatia, 1954; *Notre-Dame des septs douleurs,* L'Oeuvre St. Augustin, 1955; *La Messe: Presence du sacrifice de la croix,* Desclee de Brouwer, 1957, 3rd edition, 1961; (author of preface) *Sendung der Stille: Kartaeuserschriften fuer Christen von heute,* Benziger, 1957; *La Volonte divine salvifique sur les petits enfants,* Desclee de Brouwer, 1958; *L'Eglise et la Bible,* Editions St. Augustin, 1960; (with Jacques Maritain and Philippe de la Trinite) *Le Peche de l'ange: Peccabilite, nature et surnature,* Beauchesne, 1961; (translator) Girolamo Maria Francesco Matteo Savonarola, *Derniere meditation,* Desclee de Brouwer, 1961; *Le Message revele: Sa transmission, son developpement, ses dependances,* Desclee de Brouwer, 1964; *Teologia delle indugenze,* Ancora (Milan), 1966; *Saint Nicolas de Flue,* 3rd edition, Editions du Seuil, 1966; *Le Mariage indissoluble,* Editions St. Augustin, 1968; *La Riforma protestante,* Ares, 1968; *Sur le pardon du peche et la part laissee aux indulgences,* Editions St. Augustin, 1968; *Connaissance et inconnaissance de Dieu,* Desclee de Brouwer, 1969.

Contributor to *Twentieth Century Encyclopedia of Catholicism.* Former director of *Nova et Vetera.**

(Died April 15, 1975, in Fribourg, Switzerland)

*　　*　　*

JOUVE, Pierre Jean   1887-1976

October 11, 1887—February(?), 1976; French poet, novelist, and author of nonfiction. Obituaries: *AB Bookman's Weekly,* March 1, 1976.

JOWETT, Garth Samuel   1940-

PERSONAL: Born March 2, 1940, in Cape Town, South Africa; son of William George and Ada (Landman) Jowett; married Miriam Ruth McEwen (a teacher), July 20, 1963; children: Adam. *Education:* York University, B.A., 1968; University of Pennsylvania, M.A., 1971, Ph.D., 1972. *Home:* 3300 Randolph Ave., Windsor, Ontario, Canada N9E 3E7. *Office:* Department of Communication Studies, University of Windsor, Windsor, Ontario, Canada N9B 3P4.

CAREER: Marketing executive for advertising agencies in Toronto, Ontario, 1958-68; Temple University, Philadelphia, Pa., instructor in American studies, summer, 1970; University of Pennsylvania, Philadelphia, instructor in history, 1970-71; Carleton University, Ottawa, Ontario, assistant professor of journalism, 1971-74; University of Windsor, Windsor, Ontario, associate professor of communication studies, 1974—. Director of social research and program development for Department of Communication (Ottawa), 1972-74.

MEMBER: International Communications Association, Society for Cinema Studies, Popular Culture Association, University Film Association, Association for Education in Journalism. *Awards, honors:* Newcomen Society award for contributions to the cause of material history, 1971, for research on the acceptance pattern of the early motion picture industry in the United States; Canada Council grant, 1975-76; research grant from Department of Communications (Ottawa), 1975-76; two grants from Ontario Royal Commission on Violence in the Communications Industry.

WRITINGS: (Contributor) Benjamin Singer, editor, *Communications in Canadian Society,* Copp Clark, 2nd edition (Jowett was not included in 1st edition), 1975; *Film, the Democratic Art: A Social History of Movie-Going in America,* Little, Brown, 1976; (contributor) Seth Feldman and Joyce Nelson, editors, *Canadian Cinema Studies,* Peter Martin Associates, in press. Contributor of about thirty articles and reviews to film and history journals. Advisory editor for series "Cinema Reprints," Arno; "Motion Pictures: Their Impact on Society," Jerome S. Ozer; "Film Dissertations," Arno.

WORK IN PROGRESS: A Social History of Communications, for Macmillan; *Communications: A Canadian Perspective,* publication by Fitzhenry & Whiteside expected in 1978; *Popular Culture and Mass Society,* Prentice-Hall, 1978.

SIDELIGHTS: Jowett writes: "I am a historian by training, but combining this with my interest in communication, I have attempted to make some sense out of the history of various forms of communication, and their impact on human development."

*　　*　　*

JOYCE, J(ames) Avery   1902-

PERSONAL: Born May 24, 1902, in London, England; married Barbara Escombe (died, 1971). *Education:* Attended Geneva School of International Studies, 1935-38; London School of Economics and Political Science, B.Sc., 1942; University of London, Bar-at-Law, 1943, Ph.D., 1953. *Politics:* Labour Party. *Religion:* Methodist. *Home:* 7 rue de Courvoisier, Versoix, Geneva 1290, Switzerland. *Office:* Palais des Nations, Geneva, Switzerland; and, 3 King's Bench Walk, Temple, London, England. *Agent:* Anne Harrel, Bolt & Watson, 8 Sterling's Gate, London S.W.1, England.

CAREER: Practice of international law, primarily in London, 1943—. Special correspondent, League of Nations Assemblies, Geneva, Switzerland, 1935-38, and at the United Nations in New York and Geneva, 1948—; secretary, International Association for Social Progress in London, 1937-38; consultant, United Nations Economics Security Council, 1953-56; staff member, International Labour Office, Geneva, Switzerland, 1956-63. Senior research associate, Fletcher School of Law and Diplomacy, Tufts University, 1968-71; visiting professor at Morningside College; former lecturer, University of London; visiting lecturer at University of Chicago, Columbia University, New York University, Cornell University, Vanderbilt University, University of California, and others. *Member:* Royal Geographic Society (fellow), American Association of University Professors. *Awards, honors:* LL.D., Morningside College, 1970.

WRITINGS: Youth Faces the New World, Pelican Press, 1931; *Peacemaking for Beginners,* H. Joseph, 1938; *The Phantom Broadcast,* H. Joseph, 1939; (editor) *Three Peace Classics,* H. Joseph, 1940; *Bring Me My Bow,* privately printed, 1942; (editor) *World Unity Booklets,* World Unity Movement (London), 1944-49; *World Organisation: Federal or Functional?,* Watts, 1945; *Chicago Commentary: Case for World Airways,* World Citizenship Movement (London), 1946; *Education for a World Society,* World Citizenship Movement, 1947; (with Ithel Davies) *World Law,* World Citizenship Movement, 1949.

Now is the Time, World Calendar Association (London), 1951; *Justice at Work,* Chapman & Hall, 1952; *World in the Making,* Schuman, 1953; *Economic and Social Advantages of Calendar Reform,* World Calendar Association (Geneva), 1954; *Studies in Charter Revision,* Council for United Nations Review (London), 1955; *Revolution on East River,* Abelard, 1956; *Red Cross International,* Oceana, 1959.

The Right to Life, Gollancz, 1961; *Capital Punishment: A World View,* Nelson, 1961; *Human Rights: The Dignity of Man,* Oceana, 1963; *Education and Training,* United Nations (Geneva), 1963; *The Story of International Co-Operation,* Watts, 1964; *World of Promise,* Oceana, 1965; *Labour Faces the New Age,* International Labor Office (Geneva), 1965; *Decade of Development,* Coward, 1966; *End of an Illusion,* Bobbs-Merrill, 1968; *Broken Star: Story of the League of Nations,* Grosset, 1976.

Contributor to *Contemporary Review, Saturday Review, Nation, Christian Century, Labor's Daily, Vista, Churchman,* and *British Weekly.*

WORK IN PROGRESS: Fourth World Perspectives, an analysis of the 1970's.

* * *

JOYCE, Jon L(oyd) 1937-
(Jay Dovlos)

PERSONAL: Born March 26, 1937, in Akron, Ohio; son of H. Loyd and Murriel (Spikerman) Joyce; married Anne Johnson (a teacher), June 9, 1959; children: Jeffrey J., Jan M., David G. *Education:* Wittenberg University, B.A., 1959; Lutheran Theological Seminary at Philadelphia, M.Div., 1962. *Home:* 824 Shrine Rd., Springfield, Ohio 45504. *Office:* CSS Publishing Co., 1628 Main St., Lima, Ohio 45504.

CAREER: Ordained Lutheran minister, 1962; pastor in Norristown, Pa., 1962-64, Englewood, Ohio, 1964-67, Orchard Lake, Mich., 1967-68, and in Springfield, Ohio, 1968-

72; free-lance writer in Springfield, 1972-75; CSS Publishing Co., Lima, Ohio, editor and public relations director, 1975-76; free-lance writer, editor, and member of management personnel of Field Enterprises Educational Corp., 1976—.

WRITINGS—All published by CSS Publishing, except as indicated: *The Acts of the Apostles* (Bible study), 1972; *The Seven Deadly Sins* (one-act play), 1972; *Arise, Shine!* (nonfiction), Augsburg, 1973; *Reaching Out in Love* (manual), Augsburg, 1973; *Unlikely Conversations about Jesus* (minidrama), 1973; *Sunday School Stewardship* (manual), 1973; *Stewardship Emphasis* (manual), 1973; *Nuggets* (short stories), 1973; *A Family Decides* (skits), 1973; (editor) *Select Stewardship Sermons,* 1973; (editor) *Laymen on Stewardship,* 1973; *Splinters and Collars and Checkbooks and Things* (sermons), 1973; *The Path to Commitment* (devotions), 1973; (under pseudonym Jay Dovlos) *Sandy and Ed and Kim and Jim and Others* (interviews), 1973; *More Conversations about Jesus* (mini-dramas), 1974; *The Pastor and Grief,* 1974; *From Word of Mouth to Scratches and Papyrus to Us* (skit), 1974; *Rejoice! Resources for the Easter Season,* 1975; *Scripture Notes—Series B* (background to Bible lessons), 1975; *Watermelons from Pumpkin Seeds? and Other Dramas on the Parables,* 1975; (with wife, Anne Joyce) *Church Graffiti* (vignettes), 1975; *Tell It on the Mountain,* Augsburg, 1975.

WORK IN PROGRESS: Research on two suspense novels.

* * *

JUPP, Kenneth 1939-

PERSONAL: Born December 5, 1938, in London, England; son of Alfred George and Ethel May (Jessop) Jupp; married Deborah Condon, March 27, 1962 (divorced, 1971); children: Jemma. *Education:* Attended University of London, 1955-57. *Home:* 58 Oakwood Court, London W.1.4, England. *Agent:* Douglas Rae Management, 28 Charing Cross Rd., London W.C.2, England.

CAREER: Writer; has held various jobs, including one on a coffee plantation in Brazil. *Awards, honors:* Award from Arts Council of Great Britain, 1958, for play "The Buskers."

WRITINGS—Plays: "The Buskers," first produced in London at Arts Theatre, March, 1959, produced in New York City at Cricket Theatre, October, 1961; "The Socialites," produced in England, 1959, produced in New Haven, Conn., at Yale University, 1961; *A Chelsea Trilogy* (three plays; includes "The Photographer," first produced at Cambridge Arts Theatre, 1964; "The Explorer," first produced on British television, 1965; "The Tycoon," first produced on British television, 1966), Calder & Boyars, 1969.

Television plays; all produced on British television: "My Representative," 1960; "Strangers in the Room," 1960; "Blue and White," 1962.

Work represented in anthology, *Satan, Socialites, and Solly Gold: Three New Plays from England,* Coward, 1961.

WORK IN PROGRESS: Working with Robert Bolt in Los Angeles, Calif., on production of his original screenplay, as yet untitled, based on the life of George Sand.

* * *

KAEMPFERT, Wade
See del REY, Lester 1915-

KAHN, E(ly) J(acques), Jr. 1916-

PERSONAL: Born December 4, 1916, in New York, N.Y.; son of Ely Jacques (an architect) and Elsie (a writer; maiden name, Plaut) Kahn; married Virginia C. Rice, February 14, 1945 (divorced, 1969); married Eleanor Munro Frankfurter (a writer), June 30, 1969; children: Ely Jacques III, Joseph Plaut, Hamilton Rice; David T. Frankfurter, Alexander M. Frankfurter (stepsons). *Education:* Harvard University, B.A., 1937. *Home:* 1095 Park Ave., New York, N.Y. 10028. *Agent:* Monica McCall, International Creative Management, 1301 Avenue of the Americas, New York, N.Y. 10019. *Office: New Yorker,* 25 West 43rd St., New York, N.Y. 10036.

CAREER: New Yorker magazine, New York, N.Y., staff writer, 1937—; Columbia University, New York, N.Y., adjunct professor of writing, 1974-75. Chairman of board of trustees, Scarborough School, 1959-69; director, Associated Harvard Alumni, 1969-72. *Military service:* U.S. Army, 1941-45; awarded Legion of Merit, and Commendation Ribbon. *Member:* Authors Guild of America, Authors League of America, Phi Beta Kappa, Kappa Alpha Tau, Harvard Club (New York City), Century Association. *Awards, honors:* Sidney Hillman Foundation prize, 1975.

WRITINGS: The Army Life, Simon & Schuster, 1942; *G.I. Jungle,* Simon & Schuster, 1943; *McNair: Educator of An Army,* Infantry Journal Press, 1945; *The Voice,* Harper, 1947; *Who, Me?,* Harper, 1948; *The Peculiar War,* Random House, 1952; *The Merry Partners,* Random House, 1955.

The Big Drink, Random House, 1960; *A Reporter Here and Here,* Random House, 1961; *The Stragglers,* Random House, 1962; *The World of Swope,* Simon & Schuster, 1964; *A Reporter in Micronesia,* Norton, 1966; *The Separated People: A Look at Contemporary South Africa,* Norton, 1968; *Harvard: Through Change and Through Storm,* Norton, 1969.

(With son, Joseph P. Kahn) *The Boston Underground Gourmet,* Simon & Schuster, 1972; *Fraud: The United States Postal Inspection Service and Some of the Fools and Knaves It Has Known,* Harper, 1973; *The American People: A Noted Journalist Explores the Findings of the 1970 Census,* Weybright & Talley, 1974, published as *The American People: The Findings of the 1970 Census,* Penguin, 1975; *The China Hands: America's Foreign Service Officers and What Befell Them,* Viking, 1975. Contributor to national magazines.

*   *   *

KAHN, Herman 1922-

PERSONAL: Born February 15, 1922, in Bayonne, N.J.; son of Abraham and Yetta (Koslowsky) Kahn; married R. Jane Heilner (a mathematician at time of marriage), March 21, 1953; children: Deborah Yetta, David Joshua. *Education:* University of California, Los Angeles, B.A., 1945; California Institute of Technology, M.A., 1948. *Home:* 19 Birch Lane, Chappaqua, N.Y. 10514. *Office:* Hudson Institute, Quaker Ridge Rd., Croton-on-Hudson, N.Y. 10520.

CAREER: Rand Corp., Santa Monica, Calif., mathematician, 1948-60; Hudson Institute, Croton-on-Hudson, N.Y., director, 1961—. Member of the board of Hudson Institute, Hudson Research Services, Advanced Computer Techniques, and of Hudson of Canada. *Military service:* U.S. Army, 1943-45. *Member:* Council on Foreign Relations, Center for Inter-American Relations, American Political Science Association, Phi Beta Kappa, Phi Mu Epsilon.

Awards, honors: Honorary Ph.D., University of Puget Sound and Worcester Polytechnic Institute, both 1976.

WRITINGS: On Thermonuclear War, Princeton University Press, 1962; *Thinking about the Unthinkable,* Horizon Press, 1962; *On Escalation,* Praeger, 1965; *The Year 2,000,* Macmillan, 1967; *Can We Win in Vietnam?,* Praeger, 1968; *Why ABM?,* Pergamon, 1969; *The Emerging Japanese Superstate,* Prentice-Hall, 1970; (with B. Bruce-Briggs) *Things to Come,* Macmillan, 1972; (editor) *The Future of the Corporation,* Mason & Lipscomb, 1974; (with Leen Martel and William M. Brown) *The Next 200 Years: A Scenario for America and the World,* Morrow, 1976.

BIOGRAPHICAL/CRITICAL SOURCES: Esquire, September, 1962; *New York Herald Tribune Magazine,* July 4, 1965; *Der Spiegel,* April 3, 1967; *Life,* December 6, 1968; *U.S. News & World Report,* February 8, 1971, March 12, 1973; *Readers Digest,* April, 1973; *Nations Business,* July, 1973; *Futurist,* December, 1975; *Newsweek,* July 4, 1976; *New York,* August 9, 1976; *Dun's Review,* December, 1976.

*   *   *

KAISER, Robert G(reeley) 1943-

PERSONAL: Born April 7, 1943, in Washington, D.C.; son of Philip M. (a government official and diplomat) and Hannah (Greeley) Kaiser; married Hannah Jopling (a translator), April 14, 1965; children: Charlotte Jerome, Emily Eli. *Education:* Yale University, B.A., 1964; London School of Economics and Political Science, M.Sc., 1967. *Home:* 1711 S St. N.W., Washington, D.C. 20009. *Agent:* Julian Bach, 3 East 48th St., New York, N.Y. 10017. *Office: Washington Post,* Washington, D.C. 20071.

CAREER: Washington Post, Washington, D.C., reporter, 1963—, correspondent in Saigon, 1969-70, bureau chief in Moscow, 1971-74, member of national staff, 1975—. Visiting professor at Duke University, Durham, N.C. *Member:* Elihu Club. *Awards, honors:* Washington-Baltimore Newspaper Guild Front Page award, 1973; Overseas Press Club award for best foreign correspondence, 1974.

WRITINGS: Cold Winter, Cold War, Stein & Day, 1974; *Russia: The People and the Power,* Antheneum, 1976. Contributor of articles to periodicals, including *Esquire, New York, The Observer of London.*

SIDELIGHTS: On Kaiser's most recent book, *Russia,* Erwin Canham makes this comment "This is a perfectly fascinating tour d'horizon of the Soviet Union. Not a page is dull. It is crammed with first-hand precise reporting: episodes, anecdotes, events, observations.... Kaiser's account of the dead hand of bureaucratic mediocrity, bearing down on nearly everything, is persuasive." Phillip Knightley observes: "For the first time, I now know something about today's Russians as a people. And there are certain realities about the Russian people we will need to face squarely."

BIOGRAPHICAL/CRITICAL SOURCES: New York Times Book Review, January 25, 1976; *Christian Science Monitor,* February 10, 1976; *Harper's,* March, 1976; *New Republic,* May 1, 1976.

*   *   *

KALICKI, Jan H(enryk) 1948-

PERSONAL: Born August 5, 1948, in London, England; came to United States, 1951; naturalized citizen, 1956; son of Jan (a professor) and Mireya (a professor; maiden name, Jaimes-Freyre) Kalicki; married Anne Cleveland (a photographer), June 1, 1968; children: Jan Harlan. *Education:* Columbia University, A.B., 1968; London School of Economics and Political Science, University of London, Ph.D., 1971. *Home:* 6 Bay View Rd., Harwich Port, Mass. 02646. *Office:* Policy Planning Staff, U.S. Department of State, Washington, D.C. 20520.

CAREER: Princeton University, Princeton, N.J., research associate and lecturer in politics, 1971-72; Harvard University, Cambridge, Mass., visiting assistant professor of government, 1972; U.S. Arms Control & Disarmament Agency, Washington, D.C., foreign affairs officer, 1972-74; U.S. Department of State, Washington, D.C., member of policy planning staff, 1974—. *Member:* International Institute for Strategic Studies, International Studies Association, Association for Asian Studies, Council on Foreign Relations, Royal Institute of International Affairs. *Awards, honors:* International affairs fellowship from Council on Foreign Relations, 1974-75.

WRITINGS: The Pattern of Sino-American Crises, Cambridge University Press, 1975. Contributor to current affairs journals.

WORK IN PROGRESS: Studies in nuclear and regional arms control, and on Sino-American relations.

* * *

KAMERMAN, Sheila B(rody) 1928-

PERSONAL: Born January 7, 1928; daughter of S. Lawrence (an executive) and Helen (Golding) Brody; married Morton Kamerman (an attorney), September 11, 1947; children: Nathan Brody, Eliot Herbert, Laura Kamerman Barouch. *Education:* New York University, B.A. (honors), 1946; Hunter College of the City University of New York, M.S.W., 1966; Columbia University, D.S.W., 1973. *Home:* 1125 Park Ave., New York, N.Y. 10028. *Office:* School of Social Work, Columbia University, 622 West 113th St., New York, N.Y. 10025.

CAREER: New York University, New York, N.Y., social work supervisor at Medical Center, 1966-69; Columbia University, New York City, research associate, 1971-73, senior research associate in social policy research, 1973—. *Member:* National Association of Social Workers, American Society for Public Administration, American Public Welfare Association, Gerontological Society, Phi Beta Kappa.

WRITINGS: (With Alfred J. Kahn and Brenda McGowan) *Child Advocacy,* U.S. Government Printing Office, 1973; (with Kahn) *Not for the Poor Alone,* Temple University Press, 1975; *Child Care Programs in Nine Countries,* Office of Child Development, U.S. Department of Health, Education & Welfare, 1975; (with Kahn) *Social Services in the United States,* Temple University Press, 1976. Contributor to professional journals.

WORK IN PROGRESS: Social Services in International Perspectives, with Alfred J. Kahn; directing a study of working mothers; co-directing long-range projects on family policy in the United States and Europe.

* * *

KAMINSKY, Melvin
See BROOKS, Mel

* * *

KANE, Julia
See ROBINS, Denise (Naomi)

KAPLAN, Martin (Harold) 1950-

PERSONAL: Born August 21, 1950, in Newark, N.J.; son of William (an accountant) and Fay (Katz) Kaplan. *Education:* Harvard University, A.B., 1971; St. John's College, Cambridge, B.A., 1973; Stanford University, Ph.D., 1975. *Politics:* Quasi-Socialist. *Religion:* "A capital question." *Residence:* New York, N.Y. *Office:* Aspen Institute, 717 Fifth Ave., New York, N.Y. 10022.

CAREER: Aspen Institute, New York, N.Y. and Aspen, Colo., program officer in education and pluralism programs, 1973—; writer. *Awards, honors:* Woodrow Wilson fellow, 1971; Marshall scholar, 1971-73; Danforth Foundation fellow, 1973-75.

WRITINGS: (Editor) *The Harvard Lampoon Centennial Celebration, 1876-1973,* Atlantic-Little, Brown, 1973; (editor) *The Monday Morning Imagination,* Aspen Institute, 1976; *Why Bother with Poetry?,* Lyceum Press, in press. Contributor to *Change* magazine.

WORK IN PROGRESS: A play, "The United States of America vs. Alger Hiss"; editing *What Is an Educated Person?; Collage Itself,* on the farce tradition in ethics.

SIDELIGHTS: Kaplan notes that he has worked in molecular biology, public policy, higher and non-traditional education, philosophy, literature, magazine editing, and publishing, and hopes "the list will continue to continue." He adds, "I make exquisite food, hold a tan well, and articulate clearly. I love to teach. Some people call me an intellectual."

* * *

KAPLAN, Milton 1910-

PERSONAL: Born March 6, 1910, in New York, N.Y.; son of Israel (a clothing worker) and Rebecca Kaplan; married Marion Wall, August 24, 1939 (died, June, 1967); married Marie Grimaldi, July 29, 1973; children: (first marriage) Joan (Mrs. Edwin Allaire, Jr.), Jonathan. *Education:* City College (now of the City University of New York), B.S.S., 1929, M.S., 1934; Columbia University, M.A., 1937, Ph.D., 1946. *Home:* 554 Summit Ave., Oradell, N.J. 07649. *Agent:* John Schaffner, 425 East 51st St., New York, N.Y. 10022.

CAREER: High school English teacher, 1934-54; George Washington High School, New York City, chairman of English department, 1954-64; Columbia University, Teachers College, New York City, associate professor, 1964-67, professor of English, 1967-75; writer, 1975—. *Member:* Poetry Society of America (member of executive committee, 1968-70). *Awards, honors:* Christopher Morley Memorial Award from Poetry Society of America, 1974.

WRITINGS: Radio and Poetry, Columbia University Press, 1949; (editor with Murray Rockowitz) *World of Poetry,* Globe Book Co., 1965; *In a Time Between Wars* (poems), Norton, 1973. Contributor of poems, stories, and essays to periodicals, including *New Yorker, Harper's, Harper's Bazaar, Nation, New Republic, Saturday Review, Poetry: A Magazine of Verse,* and *American Scholar.*

WORK IN PROGRESS: A second book of poems.

* * *

KAPP, K(arl) William 1910-1976

October 27, 1910—April 10, 1976; German-born economist and author. Obituaries: *New York Times,* April 26, 1976. (See index for previous *CA* sketch)

KARNAD, Girish 1938-

PERSONAL: Born May 19, 1938, in Matheran, India; son of Raghunath (a doctor) and Krishnabai (Mankikar) Karnad. Education: Karnatak University, B.A., 1958; Oxford University, B.A., 1963. Home: 18 Saraswatpur, Dharwar 580002, India.

CAREER: Oxford University Press, Madras, India, assistant manager, 1963-69, manager, 1969-70; Film and Television Institute of India, Poona, director, 1974—. Member: Sangeet Natak Akademi, Children's Film Society (member of executive council), Oxford Union Society (president, 1963). Awards, honors: Homi Bhabha fellowship for creative writing, 1970-72; Kamaladevi Chattopadhyayo award for best Indian play of the year, 1971, for Hayavadana; Sangeet Natak Akademi award for best Indian playwright of the year, 1971; Indian president's gold medal for best film, 1971, for "Samskara"; Indian president's award for excellence in direction, 1972, for "Vamsha Vriksha"; Indian president's silver medal, 1974, for "Kaadu"; "Kaadu" named official Indian entry to Fifth International Film Festival, 1974; awarded Padma Shri, 1974.

WRITINGS—Plays: Yayati (four-act; first produced in Bombay at Indian National Theatre, August, 1967), Manohara Grantha Mala (Dharwar, India), 1961; Tughlaq (thirteen-scene; first produced at Indian National Theatre, December, 1965), Manohara Grantha Mala, 1964, translation by author published under same title (first produced in Bombay at Bhulabhai Auditorium, August, 1970), Oxford University Press, 1973; Hayavadana (two-act; first produced in New Delhi at AIFACS Theatre, May, 1972), Manohara Grantha Mala, 1971, translation by author published under same title (produced in Madras at Museum Theatre, December, 1972), Oxford University Press, 1975; (translator) Badal Sircar, Evam Indrajit (first produced at Museum Theatre, April, 1970), Oxford University Press, 1974.

Author of motion picture scripts, "Samskara," 1970, "Vamsha Vriksha," 1971, and "Kaadu," 1973. Art critic for Indian Express, Madras, 1968-70.

WORK IN PROGRESS: A couple of plays; ideas for several filmscripts.

*   *   *

KARPEL, Craig S. 1944-

PERSONAL: Born in Midland, Tex. Education: Columbia University, A.B., 1965. Agent: Don Congdon, Harold Matson Co., Inc., 22 East 40th St., New York, N.Y. 10016. Office: 350 West 57th St., New York, N.Y. 10019.

MEMBER: Overseas Press Club.

WRITINGS: Author and contributor of numerous articles to Playboy, Esquire, Penthouse, Oui, Harper's, Village Voice, New York Times Book Review, and other publications.

*   *   *

KAUL, Donald 1934-

PERSONAL: Born December 25, 1934, in Detroit, Mich.; son of Alexander Edward and Nettie (Zwick) Kaul; married Suzanne Dutil, August 24, 1957; children: Leslie, Christopher, Rachel. Education: Attended Wayne State University, 1951-53; University of Michigan, A.B., 1958, M.A., 1960. Politics: "Agnostic." Religion: Agnostic. Office: Des Moines Register, Des Moines, Iowa.

CAREER: Des Moines Register, Des Moines, Iowa, reporter, 1960-65, author of daily column "Over the Coffee," 1965—. Awards, honors: Jule and Avery Hopwood Award for Drama from University of Michigan, 1959.

WRITINGS: How to Light a Water Heater and Other War Stories, Iowa State University Press, 1970. Also author of play, "Man on a Tiger," first produced at University of Michigan, Ann Arbor, 1959.

SIDELIGHTS: Kaul writes: "I am a bicycle rider and one of my proudest accomplishments is to lead the Register's Annual Bicycle Ride across Iowa with a colleague. I write four times a week about any foolishness I can think of. When I'm good, I'm funny. My career goal is to become as good as Finley Peter Dunne. I believe in keeping goals well out of reach."

*   *   *

KAY, E(lizabeth) Alison 1928-

PERSONAL: Born September 27, 1928, in Kauai, Hawaii; daughter of Robert (an engineer) and Jessie (McConnachie) Kay. Education: Mills College, B.A., 1950; Cambridge University, B.A., 1952, M.A., 1956; University of Hawaii, Ph.D., 1957. Home: 2642 Halelena Pl., Honolulu, Hawaii 96822. Office: Graduate Division, University of Hawaii, Honolulu, Hawaii 96822.

CAREER: University of Hawaii, Honolulu, assistant professor, 1957-62, associate professor, 1962-67, professor of general science, 1967—, associate dean of Graduate Division, 1975—. Honorary malacologist at Bernice P. Bishop Museum, 1960—; president of Conservation Council of Hawaii, 1968-70.

MEMBER: American Association for the Advancement of Science (fellow), Systematic Zoology, Challenger Society, Marine Biological Association of the United Kingdom, Linnaean Society of London (fellow), Malacological Society of London, Western Society of Naturalists, Hawaii Historical Society (president, 1974-76), Save Diamond Head Association (vice-president, 1968—), Phi Beta Kappa.

WRITINGS: (Editor) A Natural History of the Hawaiian Islands: Selected Readings, University Press of Hawaii, 1972. Contributor of about fifty articles to scientific journals. Editor-in-chief of Pacific Science.

WORK IN PROGRESS: Research on the natural history of the Pacific islands.

*   *   *

KAZZIHA, Walid W. 1941-

PERSONAL: Born January 1, 1941, in Damascus; son of Rafia A. Kahhala and Wassel K. Kazziha; married Mona Abdel Aziz Atcek, 1966; children: Khaled, Basil. Education: American University of Beirut, B.A., 1965; University of Edinburgh, M.Sc., 1967; School of Oriental and African Studies, University of London, Ph.D., 1970. Office: Department of Economics, Political Science, and Mass Communication, American University in Cairo, 113 Sharia Kasr el Aini, Cairo, Egypt.

CAREER: Beirut Arab University, Beirut, Lebanon, lecturer in comparative government and political theory, 1970-71; American University in Cairo, Cairo, Egypt, assistant professor, 1972-74, associate professor of political science, 1974—, chairman of faculty, 1974-75, chairman of department of economics, political science, and mass communication, 1975-76. Research associate at American University of

Beirut, 1970-71. *Awards, honors:* Ford Foundation award for Middle East social science research, 1971-72.

WRITINGS: (Assistant editor, with Walid Khadduri) *International Documents on Palestine,* 1969, Kuwait University and Institute of Palestine Studies, 1972; *The Social History of Southern Syria in the Nineteenth and Early Twentieth Century* (monograph), Beirut Arab University Press, 1972; *Revolutionary Transformation in the Arab World,* St. Martin's, 1975. Contributor to Middle East studies journals.

WORK IN PROGRESS: Research on Middle East politics, political and economic development, theories of imperialism, the "New Left" in the Middle East, comparative government, and political sociology.

* * *

KEARNEY, Jean Nylander 1923-

PERSONAL: Born March 2, 1923, in Loomis, Neb.; daughter of John Bror (a farmer) and Mable (McAfee) Mylander; married John A. Kearney (a plant manager), February 17, 1945; children: Kathryn Ann Kearney Stevens, James Alan, Kevin Jean. *Education:* Attended Nebraska Wesleyan University. *Home:* 2509 South Glendale Ave., Sioux Falls, S.D. 57105. *Office:* Sioux Falls School District #49-5, 201 East 38th St., Sioux Falls, S.D. 57102.

CAREER: U.S. Air Force Base, Kearney, Neb., vehicle dispatcher, 1942-45; Sioux Falls School District #49-5, secretary and administrative assistant, 1961—. Shipping clerk, U.S. Army, medical/surgical overseas supply, 1942-43; Served as president of local Parent/Teacher Associations, 1951-52, 1955-58, and chairperson of State Executive Board, 1958-62.

WRITINGS: Pickle Packin' Grandma's Recipes, Brevet Press, 1976.

WORK IN PROGRESS: Research on recipes.

SIDELIGHTS: Jean Kearney writes: "I had long wanted a book devoted only to pickle packing. I looked for a book which would relate to me the rigors to which our forebears were subjected; a book which would encourage and entice the novice to begin an exciting new adventure; a book which would read as well in the living room as in the kitchen. Long searching yielded nothing and it became apparent that it was my obligation to meet my own needs. Thus began the study of old books—my own and others'—and the contents of my own recipe box." *Avocational interests:* Sewing, macramé, plants, travel.

* * *

KEAY, John (Stanley Melville) 1941-

PERSONAL: Surname is pronounced Kay; born September 18, 1941, in Devon, England; son of S. W. (a master mariner) and F. J. (Keeping) Keay; married Julia Margaret Atkins, April 22, 1972; children: Alexander John Melville, Anna Julia. *Education:* Magdalen College, Oxford, B.A. (honors), 1963. *Home and office:* Succoth, Dalmally, Argyll, Scotland.

CAREER: During his early career worked in advertising, journalism, printing, selling, engineering, and plumbing, and traveled widely in Europe, Asia, Australia, and United States; special correspondent to *Economist,* 1965-71; freelance writer, journalist, and editor, 1972—. *Member:* Royal Geographical Society (fellow).

WRITINGS: Into India, John Murray, 1973, Scribner, 1975. Contributor to *London Sunday Telegraph.*

WORK IN PROGRESS: When Men and Mountains Meet: Explorers of the Western Himalayas, 1820-1875; The Gilgit Game: Explorers of the Western Himalayas, 1865-1895, publication expected in 1978.

SIDELIGHTS: Keay writes: "The two works on the Western Himalayas will represent five years of largely original research and more than four years of experience of what is the most formidable mountain complex in the world. This will be the first full-length account of its exploration."

* * *

KEELY, Harry Harris 1904-

PERSONAL: Born March 13, 1904, in Burma; son of Thomas Harris and Ngway (Nyun) Keely; married Vanessa Bradley, January 26, 1928; children: Vernon, Vanessa June Keely Calamvokis. *Education:* University College, Rangoon, Burma, B.Sc. (honors), 1927. *Religion:* Church of England. *Home:* 220 High Street, Burbage, Wiltshire 5N8 3AR, England.

CAREER: Burma Civil Service, under training, 1928-30, superintendent of ruby mines, Mogok, 1931-34, subdivisional officer, Mowlaik, 1935-37, special officer of jade mines, Myitkyina District, 1938, treasury officer and headquarters magistrate, Kalewa District, 1939, jade mines officer, 1940-42, deputy comissioner of Kyaukse District, 1947-48, deputy commissioner of Tavoy District, 1948-50, commissioner of Arakan Division, 1950-53, secretary in the Ministry of Social Welfare, Government of the Union of Burma, 1953-56. *Military service:* British Army, 1942-45; became acting brigadier. *Awards, honors:* Order of the British Empire, 1945, for military services.

WRITINGS: City of the Dagger, Frederick Warne, 1971.

WORK IN PROGRESS: Who Owned the Jade Mines; an autobiography, tentatively titled *The Land of My Birth.*

* * *

KEEP, Carolyn 1940-

PERSONAL: Born August 1, 1940, in Sutton Coldfield, England; daughter of Leslie (an insurance surveyor) and Dorothy Edna (Cadby) Herbert; married David John Keep (a lecturer), August 1, 1962; children: Nicholas Herbert, Philippa Ruth. *Education:* St. Hughs College, Oxford, M.A. (honors), 1962; University of Zurich, graduate study, 1962-63. *Religion:* Methodist. *Home:* Heatherdene, Woodbury, Exeter EX5 1NR, England.

CAREER: Chemistry teacher in county school in Coalville, Leicester, England, 1963-64; supply teacher of science and sports in schools in Derbyshire and Bedford, England, 1964-73; Rolle College of Education, Exmouth, Devonshire, England, supply lecturer in science education, 1974-75; high school teacher of chemistry in Exeter, England, 1974-75; Exmouth School, Devonshire, England, teacher of chemistry, 1976—. Former treasurer of local play group. *Member:* National Trust, Association for Science Education, Devon Nature Trust, Woodbury Garden Club.

WRITINGS: The Family Garden, John Bartholomew, 1976.

SIDELIGHTS: Carolyn Keep writes: "My book arose from a life-long love of plants together with the need to entertain small children in a tiny town plot in Bedford." *Avocational interests:* Travel in France and Switzerland.

KEITH, Sam 1921-

PERSONAL: Born September 14, 1921, in Plainfield, N.H.; son of Merle Vivian (a wildlife artist) and Florence (a cook; maiden name, Holmes) Keith; married Jane Marie Saltamacchia, May 11, 1958; children: Laurel Marie. *Education:* Cornell University, B.A., 1950; Bridgewater State College, Bridgewater, Mass., M.E., 1961. *Politics:* Independent. *Religion:* Deist. *Home:* 306 Keene St., Duxbury, Mass. 02332. *Office:* Silver Lake Regional High School, Route 27, Kingston, Mass. 02360.

CAREER: Civilian Conservation Corps, Elgin, Ore., forest worker, 1940; Bay State Tap and Die Co., Mansfield, Mass., thread grinder, 1951-52; U.S. Naval Station, Kodiak, Alaska, laborer, 1952-54; U.S. Fish and Wildlife Service, Kodiak and Kenai, Alaska, enforcement agent, 1955; junior high and high school English teacher in Kingston, Mass., 1958-61, head of department, 1961-63; assistant principal in Pembroke, Mass., 1964-73; high school English teacher in Kingston, 1973—. *Military service:* U.S. Marine Corps, 1942-45; became staff sergeant; served in South Pacific theater. *Member:* National Education Association, Massachusetts Teachers Association.

WRITINGS: One Man's Wilderness: An Alaskan Odyssey, From the Journals and Photograph Collection of Richard Proenneke, Alaska Northwest Publishing, 1973. Contributor to *Alaska Magazine, Field and Stream, Massachusetts Wildlife, Massachusetts Out-of-Doors, New England Outdoors, New Hampshire Outdoorsman, Good Old Days,* and *Herald American Book Review.*

WORK IN PROGRESS: A novel, *Bay of the Giant.*

AVOCATIONAL INTERESTS: Hunting, fresh-water fishing, gardening, enjoying the green earth.

* * *

KEKES, John 1936-

PERSONAL: Born November 22, 1936, in Hungary; came to the United States in 1965. married wife, Jean, 1967. *Education:* Queen's University, Kingston, Ontario, B.A., 1961, M.A., 1962; Australian National University, Ph.D., 1967. *Home:* 114 South Pine Ave., Albany, N.Y. 12208. *Office:* Department of Philosophy, State University of New York at Albany, Albany, N.Y. 12222.

CAREER: California State University, Northridge, instructor, 1965-67, assistant professor, 1967-69, associate professor of philosophy, 1969-71; University of Saskatchewan, Regina, professor of philosophy, 1971-74; State University of New York at Albany, professor of philosophy, 1974—, chairman of department, 1974—. *Member:* American Philosophical Association, Mind Association, Royal Institute of Philosophy, Creighton Club (of New York State Philosophical Association). *Awards, honors:* Woodrow Wilson fellowship, 1961; Canada Council grant, 1973.

WRITINGS: A Justification of Rationality, State University of New York Press, 1976. Contributor of nearly thirty articles to philosophy journals.

WORK IN PROGRESS: The Common Pursuit: Philosophy; research on rationality, the nature of philosophy, and the concept of culture.

* * *

KELLER, Franklin J. 1887(?)-1976

1887(?)—April 19, 1976; American educator, natural historian, pianist, and author of books on vocational education. Obituaries: *New York Times,* April 21, 1976.

KELLER, Suzanne 1930-

PERSONAL: Born April 16, 1930, in Vienna, Austria; came to United States in 1939, naturalized citizen, 1944. *Education:* Hunter College (now of the City University of New York), A.B., 1948; Columbia University, M.A., 1950, Ph.D., 1953. *Office:* Department of Sociology, Princeton University, Princeton, N.J. 08540.

CAREER: Interpreter and translator in Paris, France, 1952-53; Massachusetts Institute of Technology, Center for International Studies, Cambridge, research associate in international relations, 1954-57; Brandeis University, Waltham, Mass., assistant professor of sociology, 1957-60; New York Medical College, New York, N.Y., research associate in psychiatry, 1961-62; Vassar College, Poughkeepsie, N.Y., associate professor of sociology, 1962-63; Fulbright lecturer in Athens, Greece, 1963-65; Athens Center of Ekistics, Athens, Greece, lecturer and research analyst, 1965-67; Princeton University, Princeton, N.J., professor of sociology, 1968—. Visiting professor at Princeton University, 1966. *Member:* World Society for Ekistics, World Future Society, American Sociological Association (vice-president, 1975-77). *Awards, honors:* Guggenheim Foundation fellow, 1972.

WRITING: Beyond the Ruling Class, Random House, 1963; *The Urban Neighborhood,* Random House, 1968; (with Donald Light, Jr.) *Sociology,* Random House, 1975. Contributor to sociology and other journals.

WORK IN PROGRESS: Studies on the evaluation of a new town, the family, sex roles, and futurism.

AVOCATIONAL INTERESTS: Travel.

* * *

KELLY, Alfred H. 1907-1976

June 23, 1907—February 14, 1976; American historian, educator, and author of books in his field. Obituaries: *AB Bookman's Weekly,* April 26, 1976. (See index for previous *CA* sketch)

* * *

KELLY, George W. 1894-

PERSONAL: Born May 8, 1894, in Scotch Ridge, Ohio; son of Alfred Nathan (an evangelist) and Flora (a teacher; maiden name, Lepard) Kelly; married Jane Cleveland (deceased); married Augusta Zientara, May 16, 1952; children: Winston. *Education:* Attended Valparaiso University, 1910; attended Dickson College, 1911. *Politics:* "The best man." *Religion:* "My own philosophy." *Home:* McElmo Route, Cortez, Colo. 81321.

CAREER: Grew up in Ohio and wilderness highlands of Tennessee; worked for Union Pacific railroad for five years; worked as a grower, orchardist and landscape architect, 1919-30; established Arapahoe Acres Nursery in Littleton, Colo., 1930; director of Horticulture House in Denver, Colo., 1944-55; conducted radio and television programs entitled "Green Thumb," 1951-56; operated Cottonwood Garden Shop, Littleton, 1955-66; designed Denver Garden Show, 1964-70; bought 100 acres of desert in McElmo Canyon, Colo., and experiments with landscape materials and native plants, 1966—. Writer. *Member:* American Horticultural Council (founding member), Colorado Forestry and Horticulture Association. *Awards, Honors:* American Horticultural Council award, 1957; American Horticulture Society award, 1959; National Council of State Garden Clubs award, 1959; American Rose Society award, 1975.

WRITINGS: *Rocky Mountain Horticulture Is Different,* privately printed, 1950, expanded edition published as *How to Have Good Gardens in the Sunshine States,* Pruett, 1967, published as *Rocky Mountain Horticulture,* Pruett, 1967; *Sort Guide to the Perennial Garden Flowers,* Crown, 1964; *A Guide to the Woody Plants of Colorado,* Pruett, 1970; *A Way to Beauty,* Pruett, 1976; *Trees for the Rocky Mountains,* privately printed, 1976. Contributor of several hundred short stories to magazines and newspapers. Editor, *Green Thumb* magazine, 1944-55.

WORK IN PROGRESS: *Shrubs for the Rocky Mountains;* a simplified study of Colorado wildflowers; a program for beautifying communities.

SIDELIGHTS: "For thirty years or so," Kelly told *CA,* "my whole effort and ambition has been to furnish horticultural literature fitted for this arid alkaline area of the Rocky Mountains which has been almost completely neglected by the garden writers of the East and California."

* * *

KELLY, Marguerite (Lelong) 1932-

PERSONAL: Born June 26, 1932, in New Orleans, La.; daughter of Charles Andre and Alice (Richardson) Lelong; married Thomas V. Kelly (a free-lance writer), September 6, 1952; children: Katherine Anne, Michael Thomas, Marguerite Mary, Helen Alice. *Education:* Attended Tulane University. *Politics:* Democrat. *Religion:* Roman Catholic. *Home and office:* 420 Constitution Ave. N.E., Washington, D.C. 20002. *Agent:* Paul R. Reynolds, Inc., 12 East 41st St., New York, N.Y. 10017.

CAREER: *New Orleans Item,* New Orleans, La., reporter, 1950-53, assistant women's editor, 1952-53; writer, 1967—. Member of board of directors of Washington Friendship House, 1959-69; member of Democratic Central Committee (District of Columbia), 1968, active in precinct and ward politics, 1964-68. Moderator of talk show on WJMR-Radio, 1951. *Member:* Washington Independent Writers.

WRITINGS: (Editor with Bette Glickert, and contributor) *Finishing Touches* (on refinishing furniture), Friendship House, 1963; (editor with Lorna McCarthy, and contributor) *Small Fryers* (juvenile cookbook), Friendship House (Washington, D.C.), 1964; (with Elia S. Parsons) *The Mother's Almanac* (Doubleday Book Club selection), Doubleday, 1975. Writer of column, "Li'l Lagniappe," *New Orleans Item,* 1950-53. Contributor to local periodicals and to popular magazines, including *Harper's Bazaar* and *Canada Today/D'Aujourd'hui.*

WORK IN PROGRESS: Magazine articles on child care.

* * *

KEMERER, Frank R(obert) 1940-

PERSONAL: Born October 22, 1940, in Minneapolis, Minn.; son of Robert W. (a business executive) and Marion (Nordin) Kemerer; married Barbara Kellner, 1971; children: Ann Elizabeth. *Education:* Stanford University, A.B. (history) and A.B. (political science), both 1963, M.A., 1968, Ph.D., 1974; graduate study at University of Minnesota, 1963-64. *Politics:* Democrat. *Home:* 2 Kimberly Dr., Geneseo, N.Y. 14454. *Office:* Office of the President, State University of New York College at Geneseo, Geneseo, N.Y. 14454.

CAREER: High school teacher of history, speech, and journalism, and counselor in Minneapolis, Minn., 1964-67; Stanford University, Stanford, Calif., admissions officer, 1967-68; high school teacher and counselor in Minneapolis, 1968-69; assistant headmaster at a private school in Chicago, Ill., 1969-72; director of a private school in San Francisco, Calif., 1973-75; State University of New York College at Geneseo, College of Arts and Science, assistant to president and lecturer in political science, 1975—. Guest lecturer at State University of New York College at Brockport, at Indiana University of Pennsylvania, and other colleges. *Member:* American Association of School Administrators, American Association of University Administrators, American Association of Higher Education, Phi Delta Kappa.

WRITINGS: (With J. Victor Baldridge) *Unions on Campus: A National Study of the Consequences of Faculty Bargaining,* Jossey-Bass, 1975; *Understanding Faculty Unions and Collective Bargaining* (monograph), National Association of Independent Schools, 1976; (with Ronald P. Satryb) *Facing Financial Exigency: Strategies for Educational Administrators,* Lexington Books, in press. Contributor to education journals.

WORK IN PROGRESS: *Civil Liberties and Student Life: Casebook and Commentaries,* with Kenneth L. Deutsch; *Mr. Justice Hugo Black: A Study in Judicial Activism Or Restraint?,* a monograph; *Adjusting to Hard Times: A Guide for Educational Administrators,* a monograph.

SIDELIGHTS: Kemerer writes that he is "distressed by the lack of knowledge about how students learn and what the curriculum at all levels of schooling should be. I am also distressed by the haphazard manner of educational administration in general and the lack of knowledge by administrators about the law as it applies to the world of education. I hope through research, teaching, and writing to promote a better understanding of these subjects and a more rational approach in general to assisting professionals conduct educational activities."

* * *

KENNEDY, Ludovic Henry Coverley 1919-

PERSONAL: Born November 3, 1919, in Edinburgh, Scotland; son of E. C. (a naval officer) and Rosalind (Grant) Kennedy; married Moira Shearer King (a ballerina), 1950; children: three daughters, one son. *Education:* Christ Church, Oxford, M.A. *Politics:* Liberal. *Address:* c/o A. D. Peters, 10 Buckingham St., London W.C.2, England.

CAREER: Private secretary and aide-de-camp to governor of Newfoundland (Canada), 1943-44; Ashridge College, England, librarian, 1949; British Broadcasting Corp., London, England, feature editor, 1953-54; lecturer for British Council in Denmark, Finland and Sweden, 1955; Associated Television Ltd., England, introducer of feature "Profile," on "Sunday Afternoon" program, 1955-56; lecturer for British Council in Belgium and Luxembourg, 1956; Independent Television News, England, newscaster, 1956-58; Associated Rediffusion (television) England, introducer of "This Week" program, 1958-59; British Broadcasting Corp., London, England, commentator, introducer, or chairman of features, 1960—, including "Panorama," 1960-63, "Time Out," 1964-65, Liberal Party General Election broadcasts, 1966, "24 Hours," 1969-72, and "Ad Lib," 1970-72. Member, Liberal Party Council, 1965-67. *Military service:* Royal Navy Volunteer Reserve, 1939-46; became lieutenant.

MEMBER: Navy Records Society (member of council, 1957-60), National League of Young Liberals (president, 1959-61), Sir Walter Scott Club (Edinburgh; president, 1968-69), St. James' Club, Marylebone Cricket Club. *Awards, honors:* Rockefeller Foundation Atlantic award for literature, 1950; English Festival of Spoken Poetry prize, 1953.

WRITINGS: Sub-Lieutenant: A Personal Record of the War at Sea, Batsford, 1942; *Nelson's Band of Brothers,* Odham's Press, 1951, published as *Nelson's Captains,* Norton, 1951; *One Man's Meat* (autobiography), Longmans, Green, 1953; *Murder Story: A Play in Three Acts with an Epilogue on Legal Killing* (produced as "Murder Story" at Cambridge Theatre, 1954), Gollancz, 1956; *Ten Rillington Place,* Simon & Schuster, 1961; *The Trial of Stephen Ward,* Gollancz, 1964, Simon & Schuster, 1965; *Very Lovely People: A Personal Report on Some Americans Abroad,* Hamilton, 1969, Simon & Schuster, 1970; *Pursuit: The Chase and Sinking of the Bismarck,* Viking, 1974.

Also author of screenplays, including "The Sleeping Ballerina", "The Singers and the Songs", "Scapa Flow", "Battleship Bismarck", "Life and Death of the Scharnorst."

SIDELIGHTS: Ludovic Kennedy's book *Very Lovely People* is, as the subtitle implies, an account of his interviews with Americans abroad. He gathered the information during extensive travels in Europe, Latin America, the Near, Middle, and Far East, and Africa, interviewing and observing American businesspeople, missionaries, students, tourists, and government representatives. On the occasion of the U.S. publication of *Very Lovely People,* a reviewer for the *National Observer* noted: "In his fifteen years of English television, Mr. Kennedy has learned to use implication and understatement to make his points without causing undue pain or annoyance. He knows what he is saying and takes care to say it rightly, and this happy combination has made him one of the best-appreciated reporters and talkmen on English television today. It has also permitted him to say some rather nasty things in a nice way about the American character."

When asked if his television experience had influenced his narrative style in the book, Kennedy told Bruce Cook, "a book simply couldn't have been written in this style in 1939, but television has opened things up so in journalism. And readers expect more now. They expect not to be bored."

AVOCATIONAL INTERESTS: Fishing, golf, shooting.*

*   *   *

KENNEDY, Paul Michael   1945-

PERSONAL: Born June 17, 1945, in Wallsend, England; married; children: two. *Education:* University of Newcastle-upon-Tyne, M.A. (first class honors), 1966; Oxford University, D.Phil., 1970. *Politics:* "Wobbly." *Religion:* Roman Catholic. *Office:* School of English and American Studies, University of East Anglia, Norwich NR2 2AH, England.

CAREER: University of East Anglia, Norwich, lecturer, 1970-75, reader in history, 1975—. *Member:* Royal Historical Society (fellow). *Awards, honors:* Fellow of Alexander von Humboldt Foundation, 1972.

WRITINGS: Pacific Onslaught, Ballantine, 1972; *Pacific Victory,* Ballantine, 1973; *The Samoan Tangle,* Barnes & Noble, 1974; *The Rise and Fall of British Naval Mastery,* Scribner, 1976. Contributor to history journals in England, Germany, Australia, Canada, and the United States.

WORK IN PROGRESS: Editing *Germany in the Pacific and Far East,* with J. A. Moses, for University of Queensland Press; *The Origins of the Anglo-German Antagonism, 1864-1914,* completion expected in 1978; *The Realities Behind Diplomacy,* publication by Fontana expected in 1980.

KENT, Harold W(infield)   1900-

PERSONAL: Born March 29, 1900, in Oskaloosa, Iowa; son of Charles Almet (an educator) and Lena (Brown) Kent; married Ethel Ida Elmer, December 24, 1929; children: Thomas Richard. *Education:* Northwestern University, B.A., 1921, M.S.Ed., 1936. *Politics:* Republican. *Religion:* Congregationalist. *Home:* 1451 Ohialoke St., Honolulu, Hawaii 96821. *Office:* Bernice P. Bishop Estate, P.O. Box 346, Honolulu, Hawaii 96801.

CAREER: Elementary school teacher in Chicago, Ill., 1921-23, high school teacher of science and social studies, 1923-25; principal of elementary school in Chicago, Ill., 1925-37, and of technical high school, 1938; Chicago Public Schools, Chicago, Ill., director of radio council, 1938-41; U.S. Department of War, Washington, D.C., educational director of radio bureau and bureau of public relations, 1941-42; Kamehameha Schools, Honolulu, Hawaii, president, 1946-62, president emeritus, 1962—; Bernice P. Bishop Estate, Honolulu, Hawaii, consultant to the trustees, 1962—. Director of Prussing Community Center, 1932-37; principal of Camp Roosevelt High School Camp, 1925-30. Incorporator and director of Lahalna Restoration Foundation; member of board of governors of Honolulu Shriners Hospital; founder and president of Masonic Public Library; member of executive committee of Arcadia Retirement Residence. *Military service:* U.S. Army Reserve, 1921-60, active duty, 1942-46; became colonel; received Legion of Merit.

MEMBER: National Congress of Parents and Teachers (honorary life member), National Education Association, Reserve Officers Association, Sons of the American Revolution, Association for Education by Radio (president, 1941-44), Hawaiian Historical Society (president, 1960-64), Hawaii Society for Crippled Children and Adults (president), Social Science Association of Honolulu (secretary, 1957—), Lambda Chi Alpha, Phi Delta Kappa, Rotary International, Masons, Shriners (potentate of Aloha Temple), Red Cross of Constantine (grand sovereign), Northwestern University (life regent).

WRITINGS: Album of Likenesses: Charles Reed and Bernice Pauahi Bishop, Kamehameha Schools Press, 1962, 2nd edition, Bishop Museum, 1972; *Charles Reed Bishop: Man of Hawaii,* Pacific Books, 1965; *Charles Reed Bishop: Letter File,* Edwards Brothers, 1972; *Dr. Hyde and Mr. Stevenson,* Tuttle, 1973; *Centennial of the Honolulu Scottish Rite,* Edwards Brothers, 1974; *Kamehameha Schools: 1942-1962,* Edwards Brothers, 1976.

WORK IN PROGRESS: Dr. Hyde and the Hawaiian Language, publication expected in 1978.

*   *   *

KENYON, Paul
See FREEDLAND, Nat(haniel)

*   *   *

KERBY, Susan Alice
See BURTON, (Alice) Elizabeth

*   *   *

KERMAN, Joseph Wilfred   1924-

PERSONAL: Born April 3, 1924, in London, England; U.S. citizen; married Vivian Shaviro, September 12, 1945; children: Jonathan, Peter, Lucy. *Education:* New York University, A.B., 1943; Princeton University, Ph.D., 1950. *Office:* Department of Music, University of California, Berkeley, Calif. 94720.

CAREER: Westminster Choir College, Princeton, N.J., director of graduate studies, 1949-51; University of California, Berkeley, assistant professor, 1951-56, associate professor, 1956-60, professor of music, 1960—, chairman of department, 1961-64. Visiting fellow, All Souls College, Oxford, 1966-67, and Clare Hall, Cambridge, 1971; Heather Professor of Music, Oxford University, 1971-74. *Military service:* U.S. Naval Reserve, 1946. *Member:* American Musicological Society, American Academy of Arts and Sciences (fellow). *Awards, honors:* National Institute of Arts and Letters grant, 1956; Hodder junior fellowship, 1957-58; Guggenheim fellowship, 1960; Fulbright fellowship, 1966-67; L.H.D. from Fairfield University, 1970.

WRITINGS: *Opera as Drama,* Knopf, 1956; *The Elizabethan Madrigal,* American Musicological Society, 1962; *The Beethoven Quartets,* Knopf, 1967; (with Horst W. Janson) *History of Art and Music,* Abrams, 1968; *Ludwig von Beethoven: Autograph Miscellany, 1786-99,* two volumes, British Museum, 1970; *Listen,* Worth, 1972; (editor with Alan Tyson) *Beethoven Studies,* Norton, 1973. Contributor of articles and reviews to journals in his field, and to newspapers.

WORK IN PROGRESS: A study of the Latin sacred music of William Boyd.

* * *

KERN, Gary 1938-

PERSONAL: Born October 4, 1938, in Washington, D.C.; son of Charles Elsworth (a zoo keeper) and Elizabeth (Mills) Kern; married Jean Marie Bryant, December 30, 1960; children: Kira Maria, Lara Alexandra. *Education:* George Washington University, A.A., 1961, B.A., 1963; Manchester University, M.A., 1965; Princeton University, M.A., 1967, Ph.D., 1969; summer postdoctoral study at Moscow State University, 1972. *Politics:* Independent. *Religion:* Omism. *Office:* Department of German and Russian, University of California, Riverside, Calif. 92502.

CAREER: University of Rochester, Rochester, N.Y., assistant professor of Russian literature, 1969-76; University of California, Riverside, lecturer in Russian, 1976—.

WRITINGS: (Editor and translator) Boris Eikhenbaum, *The Young Tolstoi,* Ardis, 1972; (editor and translator) Mikhail Zoshchenko, *Before Sunrise,* Ardis, 1974; (editor with Christopher Collins) *The Serapion Brothers: Stories and Essays,* Ardis, 1975; (editor and translator) Velimir Khlebnikov, *Snake Train: Poetry and Prose,* Ardis, 1976. Contributor to literary journals.

WORK IN PROGRESS: *The Art of Solzhenitsyn; Voices,* a novel in dialogue.

* * *

KERNODLE, George R(iley) 1907-

PERSONAL: Born March 17, 1907, in Camp Hill, Ala.; son of Julius Arthur and Anne (Slaughter) Kernodle; married Portia Baker. *Education:* St. Lawrence University, B.S., 1926; graduate study at Carnegie Institute of Technology (now Carnegie-Mellon University), 1926-28, and Columbia University, 1928-29; University of Chicago, M.A., 1930, additional graduate study, 1932-34, Yale University, Ph.D., 1937. *Home:* 420 Rebecca St., Fayetteville, Ark. 72701. *Office:* Department of Speech and Dramatic Arts, University of Arkansas, Fayetteville, Ark. 72701.

CAREER: Ball State Teachers College (now Ball State University), Muncie, Ind., instructor in English and dramat-

ics, 1930-32; Western Reserve University (now Case Western Reserve University), Cleveland, Ohio, assistant professor of English and director of dramatics, 1936-45; University of Iowa, Iowa City, associate professor of dramatic arts, 1945-50; University of Tulsa, Tulsa, Okla., associate professor of speech, 1950-52; University of Arkansas, Fayetteville, professor of dramatic arts, 1952—. Lecturer at Shakespeare Institute (England), 1956; visiting professor at University of California, Los Angeles, summer, 1947, University of Colorado, summer, 1951, Michigan State University, summer, 1952, San Francisco State College, summer, 1959, University of Iowa, spring, 1962, University of British Columbia, summer, 1963, and University of Hawaii, summer, 1967.

MEMBER: American Theatre Association, American Society for Theatre Research. *Awards, honors:* Sterling fellow in Europe, 1938-39; Rockefeller Foundation fellowship, 1939; Arkansas Alumni Association award, 1973.

WRITINGS: *From Art to Theatre,* University of Chicago Press, 1944; (with Allardyce Nicoll and John McDowell) *The Renaissance Stage,* University of Miami Press, 1958; *Invitation to the Theatre,* Harcourt, 1967, abridged edition, 1971. Contributor to professional journals.

WORK IN PROGRESS: A third edition of *Invitation to the Theatre,* completion expected in 1978; *The Theatre in History,* a study of theatre as it relates to human culture.

SIDELIGHTS: Kernodle has directed more than one hundred plays, twenty-five of them Shakespeare's, and has translated and produced eight Moliere plays.

* * *

KESS, Joseph Francis 1942-

PERSONAL: Born February 27, 1942, in Cleveland, Ohio; son of Joseph (a factory worker) and Sophie (a factory worker maiden name, Blatnik) Kess; married Cathleen Ann Converse (a college teacher), June 13, 1966. *Education:* University of Dayton, student, 1958-61; Georgetown University, B.Sc. (cum laude), 1962; University of Hawaii, M.A., 1965, Ph.D., 1967; also attended Keio University, 1963, Indiana University, summer, 1964, and Universities of Ljubljana and Zagreb, summer, 1969. *Office:* Department of Linguistics, University of Victoria, Victoria, British Columbia, Canada.

CAREER: University of Victoria, Victoria, British Columbia, associate professor of psycholinguistics, 1967—. Language coordinator for U.S. Peace Corps Philippine project. Victoria chairman of Canadian University Service Overseas, 1968-69. *Member:* International Linguistics Association, Canadian Linguistic Association, Canadian Slavic Association, Linguistic Society of America, American Anthropological Association. *Awards, honors:* Phillips Fund Award from American Philosophical Society, 1967-68; Canada Council fellowship, 1973-74.

WRITINGS: (Contributor) M. H. Scargill, editor, *Essays in Linguistics,* Department of Linguistics, University of Victoria, 1974; *Psycholinguistics: Introductory Perspectives,* Academic Press, 1976; (contributor) G. E. Gobetz, editor, *Anthology of Slovenian American Literature,* in press. Contributor of more than twenty-five articles to professional journals.

WORK IN PROGRESS: Psycholinguistic studies in ambiguity in Japanese and Tagalog; studies on respectful address in South Slavic and on Slavic ethnicity in North America.

SIDELIGHTS: Kess writes that he has "varying degrees of

competence in Slovene, Croation, Japanese, Tagalog, Spanish, French; can read Russian, Latin; have done analytical work on Haida, an American Indian language, Tolai, a language of New Guinea, and Hiligaynon, a language of the Philippines. My travels are commensurate with my linguistic interests and research."

*   *   *

KESSLER, Gail 1937-

PERSONAL: Born July 5, 1937, in New York, N.Y.; daughter of Edgar and Minnie (Kessler) Shapiro; married Donald Kmetz (a writer), October 24, 1959; children: Seth, Kira. *Education:* Bard College, B.A., 1960; Fairleigh Dickinson University, M.A., 1968; Columbia Universtiy, Ph.D., 1973; also attended University of Paris, 1958-59. *Residence:* Tenafly, N.J. *Agent:* Emilie Jacobson, Curtis Brown Ltd., 575 Madison Ave., New York, N.Y. 10022.

CAREER: French teacher in private school in Washington Township, N.J., 1965-67; English teacher in private schools in Englewood, N.J., 1967-68, and Paramus, N.J., 1968-69; William Paterson College, Wayne, N.J., instructor in English, 1970-72; Bergen Community College, Paramus, N.J., instructor in English, 1972-73; writer, 1973—. Director of Teaneck, N.J. Women's Rights Information Center, 1975-76.

WRITINGS: Judgment: A Case of Medical Malpractice, Mason/Charter, 1976. Contributor of articles to magazines, including *Ms., New Dawn, Cosmopolitan, Working Woman, Glamour,* and *Woman's Day.*

WORK IN PROGRESS: A biographical novel about Mary Shelley.

SIDELIGHTS: Gail Kessler writes: "I learned of the medical malpractice case in *Judgment* through my uncle, who was the lawyer for the plaintiff. My major interest is in writing historical/biographical novels. . . . I am strongly motivated to make a living as a writer because I enjoy writing and like being my own boss. Literature is my greatest passion—love to read novels, and the poetry of Donne, Vaughan, Blake, Keats, Tennyson, Christina Rossetti, and others."

*   *   *

KIDD, Virginia 1921-

PERSONAL: Born June 2, 1921, in Philadelphia, Pa.; daughter of Charles Lemuel (a printer) and Zetta Daisy (Whorley) Kidd; married Jack Emden (an operatic singer), April 17, 1943 (divorced, 1947); married James Blish (a writer), May 23, 1947 (divorced, 1963); children: (first marriage) Karen Anne; (second marriage) Asa Benjamin (deceased), Elisabeth, Benjamin. *Education:* Attended public schools in Catonsville, Md.; studied languages privately. *Politics:* Independent (but registered as Democrat). *Religion:* "Raised Episcopalian." *Home:* 538 East Harford St., Milford, Pa. *Agent:* James Allen of Virginia Kidd with James Allen Literary Agents, Box 278, Milford, Pa. 18337. *Office address:* Box 278, Milford, Pa. 18337.

CAREER: Worked in book store in Baltimore, Md., as a Spanish-speaking receptionist for four doctors in Tucson, Ariz., as a music librarian for radio station WFBC in Greenville, S.C., and as a free-lance proofreader, translator, editor, and ghost writer. Virginia Kidd with James Allen Literary Agents, Milford, Pa., founder and literary agent, 1965—. *Member:* Science Fiction Writers of America, Authors Guild, Vanguard Amateur Press Association (official tyrant, 1948).

WRITINGS: (Editor with Roger Elwood) *Saving Worlds,* Doubleday, 1973, published as *The Wounded Planet,* Bantam, 1974; (editor) *The Best of Judith Merrill,* Warner, 1976; (editor with Ursula K. Le Guin) *Nebula Award Stories Eleven,* Harper, 1976. Contributor of poetry to *Accent, Kirgo's, Mad River Review* and to other periodicals and anthologies. Contributor of stories to *Galaxy, Quark, Venus,* and to magazines and anthologies, including *Orbit I,* and *Dark Stars.*

WORK IN PROGRESS: Editing a feminist anthology of original fiction, *Millennial Women;* co-editing with Ursula K. Le Guin, *Aegis,* an anthology of original science fiction, publication expected in 1977; editing a reprint anthology titled *Hell;* writing a novelization of "Kangaroo Court" for Doubleday, titled *A Lien on Earth.*

*   *   *

KIKER, Douglas 1930-

PERSONAL: Born January 7, 1930, in Griffin, Ga.; son of Ralph Douglas (a builder) and Nora (Bunn) Kiker; married Ruth Rusling, December 18, 1954 (divorced, 1969); married Diana Simpson, May 30, 1974; children: Ann, James, Craig, Douglas. *Education:* Presbyterian College, A.B., 1952. *Religion:* Episcopal. *Office:* 4001 Nebraska Ave. N.W., Washington, D.C. 20016.

CAREER: Atlanta Journal, Atlanta, Ga., Washington correspondent, 1960-62; *New York Herald Tribune,* New York City, White House correspondent, 1963-66; National Broadcasting Co. (NBC) News, New York City, Washington correspondent, 1966—. Notable assignments include Kennedy assassination, Nasser funeral, both Democratic and Republican conventions of 1972, and Watergate investigation. *Military service:* U.S. Naval Reserve, 1951-54; became lieutenant. *Awards, honors:* Peabody award, 1970; D.Lit., Presbyterian College, 1971.

WRITINGS—Novels: *The Southerner,* Rinehart, 1956; *Strangers on the Shore,* Random House, 1959. Contributor to periodicals, including *Harper's, Atlantic, New York, Yale Review, Playboy,* and others.

*   *   *

KILBOURN, Jonathan 1916(?)-1976

1916(?)—March 11, 1976; American magazine and newspaper editor, and author. Obituaries: *New York Times,* March 12, 1976.

*   *   *

KILLIAN, Ida F(aith) 1910-

PERSONAL: Born August 25, 1910, in Camden, N.J.; daughter of Paul David and Maggie (Link) Faith; married F. Earl Killian (a public accountant), June 18, 1937; children: Ruth (Mrs. Reynold Stuart). *Education:* Attended Glassboro State Normal School (now Glassboro State College), 1928-30. *Religion:* Baptist. *Home:* 1310-A Virginia Ave., Cape May, N.J. 08204.

CAREER: Elementary school teacher in the public schools of Camden, N.J., 1931-41. Writer.

WRITINGS: Message of the Shells, Warner Press, 1973. Contributor to *Link, Grade Teacher, Creative Crafts, Jack and Jill, Venture,* and religious periodicals.

AVOCATIONAL INTERESTS: Swimming, walking, sewing, reading, developing art projects.

KILLINGSWORTH, Frank R. 1873(?)-1976

1873(?)—April 20, 1976; American evangelical church elder, educator, and author of books on catechism and other religious topics. Obituaries: *Washington Post,* May 25, 1976.

* * *

KINCAID, James R(ussell) 1937-

PERSONAL: Born August 31, 1937, in East Liverpool, Ohio; son of Robert E. and Ruth E. (Todd) Kincaid; married, December 28, 1962; children: Anne Meredith, Elizabeth Holly. *Education:* Case Institute of Technology (now Case Western Reserve University), B.S.E.E., 1959; Western Reserve University (now Case Western Reserve University), M.A., 1962, Ph.D., 1965. *Home:* 59 West Schreyer Pl., Columbus, Ohio 43214. *Office:* Department of English, Ohio State University, 164 West 17th Ave., Columbus, Ohio 43210.

CAREER: Union Carbide Corp., Bennington, Vt., project engineer, 1959-61; Western Reserve University (now Case Western Reserve University), Cleveland, Ohio, lecturer in English, 1961-65; Ohio State University, Columbus, assistant professor, 1965-69, associate professor, 1969-71, professor of English, 1971—. Member of executive committee of National Endowment for the Humanities' Ohio committee for public programs in the humanities.

MEMBER: Modern Language Association of America, Dickens Society (trustee; chairman of executive committee), Tennyson Society, Midwest Modern Language Association. *Awards, honors:* National Endowment for the Humanities Younger Humanist fellowship, 1971; Guggenheim fellowship, 1973-74.

WRITINGS: (Contributor) Robert B. Partlow, Jr., editor, *Dickens the Craftsman: Strategies of Presentation,* Southern Illinois University Press, 1970; *Dickens and the Rhetoric of Laughter,* Clarendon Press, 1972; *Tennyson's Major Poems: The Comic and Ironic Patterns,* Yale University Press, 1975; *The Novels of Anthony Trollope,* Clarendon Press, 1977. Contributor of about twenty-five articles and reviews to literature journals, including *English Literary History, PMLA, Nineteenth Century Fiction,* and *Victorian Poetry.* Member of advisory committee of *PMLA,* 1973-77.

* * *

KINES, Pat Decker 1937-
(Pat Decker Tapio)

PERSONAL: Born December 22, 1937, in Grangeville, Idaho; daughter of Floyd E. (a farmer) and Minette (Foster) Decker; married William Robertson, August 20, 1960 (divorced, August, 1965); married Einar Tapio, February 16, 1968 (divorced, February, 1975); married Clifford Kines (a personnel officer for a fire department), July 12, 1975; children: (first marriage) Diana Rose Robertson, Katherine A. Robertson; (second marriage) E. Markus Tapio. *Education:* University of Idaho, B.S.Ed. (with high honors), 1959; graduate study at University of Washington, Seattle, University of Alaska, and De Anza College. *Religion:* Protestant. *Residence:* San Jose, Calif.

CAREER: Teacher, 1959-61 and 1968-73; composition reader in public schools in Santa Clara County, Calif., 1973—.

WRITINGS: (Under name Pat Decker Tapio) *The Lady Who Saw the Good Side of Everything* (juvenile), Seabury, 1975. Contributor to children's magazines.

WORK IN PROGRESS: Three books similar to one already published; a juvenile book on California riverboats, illustrated by husband, Clifford Kines.

AVOCATIONAL INTERESTS: Square dancing, sewing, travel.

* * *

KINROSS, Patrick 1904-1976
(Patrick Balfour)

June 25, 1904—June 5, 1976; British journalist, travel writer, and author. Obituaries: *Publishers Weekly,* June 28, 1976. (See index for previous *CA* sketch)

* * *

KIRBY, F(rank) E(ugene) 1928-

PERSONAL: Born April 6, 1928, in New York, N.Y.; son of Russell Thorpe and Dorothy (Clement) Kirby; married Emily Baruch (an educational psychologist), August 17, 1952; children: Russell Steven, Nicholas Quentin, Paula Rachel, Nathaniel Benedict. *Education:* Colorado College, B.A., 1950; Yale University, Ph.D., 1957; studied abroad at University of Hamburg and University of Zurich. *Religion:* Unitarian-Universalist. *Residence:* Riverwoods, Ill. *Office:* Department of Music, Lake Forest College, Lake Forest, Ill. 60045.

CAREER: Peabody Institute Library, Baltimore, Md., music cataloger, 1957-58; University of Virginia, Charlottesville, visiting assistant professor of music, 1958-59; University of Texas, Austin, guest assistant professor of music, 1959-60; West Virginia University, Morgantown, assistant professor of music, 1961-63; Lake Forest College, Lake Forest, Ill., assistant professor, 1963-66, associate professor of music, 1967—. Lecturer at DePaul University, autumn, 1972, spring, 1975; visiting associate professor at Washington University (St. Louis, Mo.), 1973-74. Member of board of directors of North Shore Ecology Center.

MEMBER: International Musicological Society, German Society for Research in Music, College Music Society, American Musicological Society (member of national council, 1962-65), American Association of University Professors, Audubon Society, Appalachian Mountain Club, Chicago Council on Foreign Relations. *Awards, honors:* Ford Foundation internship, Williams College, 1957; Alexander von Humboldt-Stiftung grant, 1966.

WRITINGS: (Translator) Hanns Neupert, *Harpsichord Manual,* Kassel, 1960; (contributor) John Glowacki, editor, *Paul Pisk: Essays in His Honor,* University of Texas, College of Fine Arts, 1966; *A Short History of Keyboard Music,* Free Press, 1966; *An Introduction to Western Music: Bach, Beethoven, Wagner, Stravinsky,* Free Press, 1970; (contributor) Paul Henry Lang, editor, *The Creative World of Beethoven,* Norton, 1971; (contributor) Edgar Lohner, editor, *Interpretationen zum West-oestlichen Divan Goethes,* Wissenschaftliche Buchgesellschaft, 1973. Author of "Quarterly Review of Records" for Piano Quarterly. Contributor to *Encyclopaedia Britannica* and *Grove's Dictionary of Music and Musicians.* Contributor of articles and reviews to music journals. Contributing editor to *Piano Quarterly,* 1967—.

WORK IN PROGRESS: Editing *Music of the Classical Period: An Anthology with Commentary* for Schirmer Books.

AVOCATIONAL INTERESTS: Hiking in the mountains, canoeing, foreign travel, cookery, goal-judge at hockey games at Lake Forest College.

KIRTLAND, Kathleen 1945-

PERSONAL: Born August 3, 1945, in New York, N.Y.; daughter of Edward Clement (an engineer) and Mary Patricia (Flannery) Nilsson; married Robert Hackney Kirtland, April 15, 1965 (divorced, 1974). Education: Attended University of Southern California Dental School. Office: Marketing/Media Group, 9581 West Pico Blvd., Los Angeles, Calif. 90035.

CAREER: California Fashion Publications, Los Angeles, creative director for advertising for trade journals California Apparel News and Mensnews, 1975—. Owner, Marketing/Media Group (advertising agency).

WRITINGS—All with Ferne Kadish: London on $500 a Day, Macmillan, 1975; Los Angeles on $500 a Day, Macmillan, 1976; Paris on $500 a Day, Macmillan, 1976. Contributor to Holiday, Newsday, and other periodicals.

WORK IN PROGRESS: New York on $500 a Day, completion expected in 1977.

SIDELIGHTS: Kathleen Kirtland told CA that she was "motivated to write a series of travel guides that were readable, as personal as a friend sitting down to discuss his latest trip with you, and oriented toward finding the best in a city rather than the cheapest way to bet by. It is our feeling that people who live well at home will want to live well while traveling, and that people who live more modestly at home will want to do a few special things while traveling to indulge themselves."

* * *

KIZER, Carolyn (Ashley) 1925-

PERSONAL: Born December 10, 1925, in Spokane, Wash.; daughter of Benjamin Hamilton (a lawyer and planner) and M. (a biologist and professor; maiden name, Ashley) Kizer; married Charles Stimson Bullitt, January 16, 1948 (divorced, 1954); married John Marshall Woodbridge (an architect and planner), April 11, 1975; children: (first marriage) Ashley Ann, Scott, Jill Hamilton. Education: Sarah Lawrence College, B.A., 1945; graduate study at Columbia University, 1945-46, and University of Washington, Seattle, 1946-47. Politics: Radical Socialist. Religion: Episcopalian.

CAREER: Poetry Northwest, Seattle, Wash., founder and editor, 1959-65; National Endowment for the Arts, Washington, D.C., director of literary programs, 1966-70; University of North Carolina, Chapel Hill, poet-in-residence, 1970-74; Ohio University, Athens, McGuffey Lecturer and poet-in-residence, 1975; Iowa Writers Workshop, Iowa City, professor of poetry, 1976. Hurst Professor at Washington University, St. Louis, Mo., 1971; lecturer at Barnard College, spring, 1972; acting director of graduate writing program at Columbia University, 1972. Volunteer worker for American Friends Service Committee, 1960; U.S. State Department specialist in Pakistan, 1964-65. Member of founding board of directors of Seattle Community Psychiatric Clinic. Has participated in international literary festivals. International P.E.N., Association of Literary Magazines of America (founding member), Poetry Society of America, Poets and Writers, Academy of American Poets, American Civil Liberties Union.

WRITINGS—Poems: The Ungrateful Garden, Indiana University Press, 1960; Knock Upon Silence, Doubleday, 1965; Midnight Was My Cry: New and Selected Poems, Doubleday, 1971. Contributor to New Republic and to literary reviews, including Poetry, St. Andrews Review, and Hudson Review.

WORK IN PROGRESS: A book of poems.

SIDELIGHTS: While working in Pakistan, Carolyn Kizer made friends with as many Pakistani writers as she could find, and with them translated poetry from Urdu into English. She made arrangements for further translation into English of Ghalib, an early Urdu poet. She taught at a distinguished women's college, Kinnaird College for Women, and found that her upper-class students did not speak their own language, so she introduced them to some modern Urdu classics in translation. She tape-recorded the poetry of leading Bengali poets, many of whom are now missing or dead. Her visit was terminated early at her own request following a decision from the United States to bomb North Vietnam in 1965. After attending an international meeting in Pakistan in 1969, she joined a Smithsonian Institution archaeological tour through the hill state of Swat, through the Khyber Pass to Kabul, then to archaeological sites in Afghanistan and Iran.

* * *

KLARSFELD, Beate 1939-

PERSONAL: Born February 13, 1931, in Berlin, Germany; daughter of Kurt (a clerk) and Helene (Scholz) Kuenzel; married Serge Klarsfeld (a lawyer), November 7, 1963; children: Arno David, Lida Myriam. Education: Attended schools in Germany. Religion: Lutheran. Home: 230 Avenue de Versailles, Paris 16, France 75016.

CAREER: Typist in West Germany, 1957-60; French-West German Youth Service, Paris, France, secretary, 1963-68; active against impunity of Nazi criminals and for support of Jewish people and Israel, 1968—. Member, Central Committee of International League against Racism and Antisemitism, Paris, France, 1971—. Member: B'nai B'rith (Tel Aviv). Awards, honors: Medal Lambrakis from World Council of Peace, Berlin, 1969; Medal of Courage of the Revolt of the Ghetto from Israel Government, Jerusalem, 1974.

WRITINGS: The German Girls in Paris, Voggenreiter Verlag, 1964; Kiesinger: A Documentation, foreword by Heinrich Boell, Melzer Verlag, 1969; (with Joseph Billing) Kiesinger ou le facisme subtil (title means "The Subtle Fascism"), [Paris], 1969; Partout ou ils seront, Editions Jean-Claude Lattes, 1972, translation published as Wherever They May Be, Vanguard, 1975.

SIDELIGHTS: Beate Klarsfeld, a crusader to track down and bring to trial former Nazi war criminals still at large, perceives that her mission in part is to "try to revive and rehabilitate the German people morally." She feels strongly that in Germany today, the old people want to forget and the young are ignorant, and that "every German, even those of the younger generation, must take responsibility for the awful crimes of its people." Mrs. Klarsfeld encourages the younger Germans "to be opposed, to act, to take stands, to take moral positions."

Her own public acts of defiance were initiated in November, 1968, when she walked into a session of the National Congress of the Christian Democratic Union and slapped the face of West German Chancellor Kurt-Georg Keisinger. The act was intended "to tell the German people, look who is your Chancellor, a man who has been a Nazi Party member, and is a former official of the radiophonic hitlerian propaganda during World War II."

Since that time, researching, writing and publishing, badgering the press and haranguing officials, traveling, and speaking to mass rallies, have been her daily way of life. Acting for the Jewish people, Beate Klarsfeld was arrested for her protests in Warsaw, 1970, and in Prague, 1971. Acting for Israeli prisoners of war, she protested in Damascus in January of 1974 and in October of 1975, she was arrested at Arab States Summit in Rabat. "Wherever Jews happen to be persecuted, it is our German duty to intervene on their side," Mrs. Klarsfeld has said.

Her task of assembling and releasing information on former Nazis, as she defines it, is "to try to build a fire under legal means for bringing criminals to trial so that public opinion would be aroused. What counts is doing something concrete." She has added, however, that "perhaps justice will never be given by the courts, perhaps [it] never can be." The January, 1975 ratification of the Franco-German accord on the retrial of war criminals is a product of Mrs. Klarsfeld's work, and paves the way for what she says will probably be the last big trials of twenty to twenty-five such men now living openly in Germany.

Golda Meier has praised her, noting that Beate Klarsfeld "has a fierceless unmatched integrity [whose] passionate humanity has led her to identify herself in the most personal sense with Jews everywhere.... To Israel and the Jewish people Mrs. Klarsfeld is a 'Woman of Valor'—a title in Jewish tradition that has no peer. Her personal example serves as one woman's assertion of the supremacy of Right and Justice."

BIOGRAPHICAL/CRITICAL SOURCES: Le Monde, February 5, 1972, July 11, 1974; *Sunday Times* (London), March 5, 1972; *Jewish Chronicle,* March 12, 1972, July 12, 1974, January 24, 1975; *Chicago Daily News,* February 12, 1973; *Time,* March 10, 1973, July 22, 1974; *Philadelphia Jewish Exponent,* November 23, 1973, February 28, 1975, October 24, 1975; *Newsweek,* July 22, 1974; *Pioneer Women,* October-November, 1975; *National Jewish Monthly,* November, 1975; *National Observer,* November, 1975.

* * *

KLASS, Allan Arnold 1907-

PERSONAL: Born August 13, 1907, in Russia; came to Canada in 1913, naturalized citizen, 1920; son of William (a tailor) and Bertha (Dolgin) Klass; married Helen Jacob, November 5, 1939; children: Baillie (Mrs. Christopher Tolkien), Daniel. *Education:* University of Manitoba, B.A., 1927, M.D., 1932; Royal College of Surgeons (Edinburgh), F.R.C.S. (Edin.) 1937; Royal College of Surgeons (Canada), F.R.C.S.(C), 1942. *Religion:* Hebrew. *Home:* 594 Oak St., Winnipeg, Manitoba, Canada. *Office:* Mall Medical Group, 280 Memorial Building, Winnipeg, Manitoba, Canada R3C 1V2.

CAREER: British Indian Ship Line, ship surgeon on voyages to India and the east African coast, 1936; University of Manitoba, Winnipeg, assistant professor, 1945-65, associate professor of surgery and anatomy, 1965—. Surgeon, practicing with Mall Medical Group, 1948—; associate surgeon at Winnipeg General Hospital and Misericordia General Hospital. Chairman of Manitoba Government Commission on Procurement and Distribution of Prescription Drugs; chairman of medical advisory board of Manitoba Cancer Treatment and Research Foundation; main-line examiner in clinical surgery for Medical Council of Canada; member of Rhodes scholarship selection committee for Manitoba. *Military service:* Royal Canadian Army, Medical Corps, surgeon specialist, 1940-46; became major.

MEMBER: International College of Surgeons (fellow), Canadian Institute of International Affairs (president, 1951-52), College of Physicians and Surgeons of Manitoba (presi-

dent and member of council), Medico-Legal Society of Manitoba (president, 1963, 1964, 1965), Alumni Association of University of Manitoba (president, 1958-59), Sigma Alpha Mu, Rotary International (Winnipeg; president of Model United Nations Assembly, 1960, 1961, 1965), Masons, Glendale Country Club. *Awards, honors:* University of Manitoba, named honorary fellow of University College, 1965, LL.D., 1974.

WRITINGS: There's Gold in Them Thar Pills, Penguin, 1975. Contributor to medical and legal periodicals and to Winnipeg newspapers. Member of editorial board of University of Manitoba literary periodical, *Mosaic.*

WORK IN PROGRESS: Translating the meaning of homeostasis, Circadian rhythms, biofeedback, and normality from professional jargon to language for the layman, with a book expected to result.

AVOCATIONAL INTERESTS: Current history, restoring old automobiles.

BIOGRAPHICAL/CRITICAL SOURCES: British Columbia Colonist, December 28, 1975; *Washington Evening Star,* February 14, 1976.

* * *

KLEIN, Holger Michael 1938-

PERSONAL: Born March 4, 1938, in Dresden, Germany; son of Gerhard (a clergyman and writer) and Elisabeth (a teacher and writer for children; maiden name, Von Staudt) Klein; married Dorothea Souchay, May 8, 1967; children: Anna Daniela, Rosa Bettina, Marie Jeanette. *Education:* Attended University of Saarbruecken, 1959-60, University of Freiburg, 1960-62, and University of Nottingham, 1962-63; University of Munich, M.A., 1966, D.Phil., 1970. *Politics:* Liberal. *Religion:* "Christian Community." *Home:* The Old Rectory, Taverham, Norwich, England. *Agent:* Andrew Best, Curtis Brown Ltd., 1 Craven Hill, London, England. *Office:* School of European Studies, University of East Anglia, Norwich, England.

CAREER: University of East Anglia, Norwich, England, lecturer in comparative literature, 1970—. *Military service:* Federal German Air Force Reserve, active duty, 1958-59; became first lieutenant. *Member:* British Society for Eighteenth-Century Studies, British Society for Renaissance Studies, Modern Humanities Research Association, Modern Language Association of America. *Awards, honors:* M.A. from University of East Anglia, 1974.

WRITINGS: Das Weibliche Portrait in der Versdichtung der Englischen Renaissance (title means "The Portrait of the Lady in English Renaissance Poetry"), two volumes, Wienand (Cologne), 1970; (editor and translator) William Wycherly, *The Country Wife* (dual-language edition), Reclam, 1972; (editor) *The First World War in Fiction,* Macmillan, 1976. Contributor of articles and reviews to European and Australian studies journals.

WORK IN PROGRESS: Editing *Hamlet: A Dual-Language Edition,* publication by Reclam expected in 1978; *English Eighteenth-Century Comedy,* for Athenaion; editing *The Golden Age of the Sonnet: An Anthology of European Sonnets, Thirteenth to Seventeenth Century,* for Olms; two crime novels.

AVOCATIONAL INTERESTS: Verse translation, detective fiction, tennis, chess, language barriers, "the problems of enthusiastic, determined education versus neutral conveyance of information."

KLEUSER, Louise C(aroline) 1889(?)-1976

1889(?)—March 3, 1976; German-born educator, church administrator, and author or editor of books on a variety of subjects. Obituaries: *Washington Post,* March 5, 1976.

* * *

KLINGHOFFER, Arthur Jay 1941-

PERSONAL: Born July 30, 1941, in New York; son of Sidney and Libby Klinghoffer; married Judith Apter (a teacher), May 18, 1969; children: Joella. *Education:* University of Michigan, B.A., 1962; Columbia University, M.A., 1964, Ph.D., 1966. *Home:* 103 Wayside Dr., Cherry Hill, N.J. 08034. *Office:* Department of Political Science, Rutgers University, Camden, N.J. 08102.

CAREER: University of Waterloo, Waterloo, Ontario, lecturer in political science, 1965-66; Fairleigh Dickinson University, Rutherford, N.J., assistant professor of political science, 1966-70; Rutgers University, Camden, N.J., associate professor of political science, 1970—. Faculty adviser for National Model United Nations, 1967-69; project director for Volunteers in Government, 1967. *Member:* American Political Science Association, African Studies Association, American Association for the Advancement of Slavic Studies, American Association of University Professors, American Professors for Peace in the Middle East, New Jersey Political Science Association, Phi Beta Kappa, Phi Kappa Phi, Phi Eta Sigma.

WRITINGS: Soviet Perspectives on African Socialism, Fairleigh Dickinson University Press, 1969; *The Soviet Union and International Oil Politics,* Columbia University Press, in press. Contributor to political science journals and to *New Leader.*

* * *

KLOPPENBURG, Boaventura 1919-

PERSONAL: Born November 2, 1919, in Molbergen, Germany; son of Franz Bernard and Josephine (Westerkamp) Kloppenburg. *Education:* Attended Seminario Menor and Seminario Maior, Sao Leopoldo, Brazil, 1931-42, Instituto Teologico, Petropolis, Brazil, 1943-47; Antonianum, Rome, Italy, Doctor Theologiae, 1950. *Home:* Apartado Aereo 1931, Medellin, Colombia.

CAREER: Entered Ordo Fratrum Minorum (Order of Friars Minor; Franciscans; O.F.M.), 1941; ordained Roman Catholic priest, 1946; Instituto Teologico, Petropolis, Brazil, full professor of theology, 1951-72; Secretariat for Christian Union, Rome, Italy, 1973; director of Instituto Pastoral, 1974—. Member of International Theological Commission; 1974—; peritus at Vatican Council II.

WRITINGS—In English translation: *A Eclesiologia do Vaticano II,* Editora Vozes, 1971, translation from Portuguese by Matthew J. O'Connell, published as *The Ecclesiology of Vatican II,* Franciscan Herald, 1974; *The Priest: Living Instrument and Minister of Christ the Eternal Priest,* translated by Matthew J. O'Connell, Franciscan Herald, 1974; *Temptations for Liberation Theology,* translated by Matthew J. O'Connell, Franciscan Herald, 1974.

Untranslated work—In Latin: *De alterius Arausicanae Synodi (529) canone secundo,* Herder (Rome), 1951; *De relatione inter peccatum et morten,* Herder, 1951.

In Portuguese; all published by Editora Vozes (Petropolis, Brasil): *O Espiritismo no Brasil* (title means "Spiritualism in Brazil"), 1960; *A Umbanda no Brasil* (title means "The Umbanda in Brazil"), 1961; *O Reencarnacionismo no Brasil* (title means "The Reincarnation in Brazil"), 1961; *A Maconaria no Brasil* (title means "The Masonry in Brazil"), 1961; *Acao Pastoral perante o Espiritismo* (title means "Pastoral Action with Spiritualists"), 1961; *Concilio Vaticano II* (title means "The Vatican II Council"), five volumes, 1962-65; *Vaticano II: Uma Igreja diferente* (title means "Vatican II: A Different Church"), 1968; *O Cristao Secularizado* (title means "The Secularized Christian"), 1970.

Contributor of more than one hundred articles to theological reviews.

* * *

KLOSINSKI, Emil 1922-

PERSONAL: Born January 31, 1922, in South Bend, Ind.; son of John T. (a professional football player, carpenter, and automobile mechanic) and Mary (Sasadek) Klosinski; married Sheila Berchan (in real estate), December 27, 1947; children: Sheril Marie (Mrs. Julius Charba), Denise Helen, Marc Emil. *Education:* American Extension School of Law, LL.B., 1953; South Bend College of Commerce, real estate certificate, 1957; also studied at University of Notre Dame, University of California, Los Angeles, DePauw University, Marquette University, and University of Iowa. *Politics:* Independent Republican. *Home:* 3149 Raiders Run, Winter Park, Fla. 32792.

CAREER: Chicago Motor Club, La Porte, Ind., assistant district manager, 1957; Walker & Lee Realty, Long Beach and Anaheim, Calif., salesman, 1959-65. Has also worked in social services and insurance, as a football coach and scout, and as an automotive worker. Has directed plays for Catholic Theater Guild. Member of board of directors of Sports Immortals Museum. *Military service:* U.S. Navy Air Force, 1943-46. *Member:* National High School Coaches Association.

WRITINGS: Pro Football in the Days of Rockne, Carlton, 1970; *Notre Dame, Chicago Bears, and Hunk,* Florida Sun Gator Publishing Co., 1976. Author of radio scripts for Catholic Theater Guild, aired on WHOT-Radio, 1949. Contributor to magazines and newspapers.

WORK IN PROGRESS: A novel, "about a world revolution against taxes, regulations, politicians, and bureaucracies," publication expected in 1978.

SIDELIGHTS: Klosinski played college football for University of Iowa, DePauw University, and University of California, Los Angeles.

BIOGRAPHICAL/CRITICAL SOURCES: South Bend Tribune, January 17, 1971.

* * *

KLOSS, Robert Marsh 1938-

PERSONAL: Born November 20, 1938, in Erie, Pa.; son of Marsh Charles (a locomotive assembler) and Anna Elizabeth (Sowa) Klosieski. *Education:* Pennsylvania State University, B.S., 1963; Louisiana State University, M.A., 1967, Ph.D., 1969. *Residence:* Sacramento, Calif. *Office:* Department of Sociology, California State University, Sacramento, Calif. 95819.

CAREER: California State University, Sacramento, assistant professor, 1969-73, associate professor of sociology, 1973—. Visiting assistant professor at Louisiana State University, 1970, University of Northern Iowa, 1972-73, and

Iowa State University, 1974. Regional board member of labor education union; delegate to Sacramento Area Counties Public Employees Council; member of Democratic Socialist Organizing Committee. *Military service:* U.S. Air Force, 1957-60. *Member:* American Civil Liberties Union, Mine Lamp Collectors Society of America, United Professors of California.

WRITINGS: (With Ron E. Roberts) *Social Movements: Between the Balcony and the Barricade,* Mosby, 1974; (with Roberts and Dean S. Dorn) *Sociology with a Human Face,* Mosby, 1976. Contributor to *Encyclopedia of Sociology.* Consulting editor of *American Sociological Review.*

WORK IN PROGRESS: Introduction to Labor Sociology (tentative title), a critique of labor history and labor economics, with a definition of labor sociology; *Mobility for What?: Restratification versus Destratification* (tentative title), a critique of political sociology and social stratification theory in the United States.

SIDELIGHTS: Kloss writes: "As a young boy [I] observed differences between groups: between the East side and West side of my home town . . .; in the military between enlisted and officers; between the educated and the uneducated as a university student; and now, as a political sociologist, between the powerful and the powerless—those who make a difference (those who make decisions which make differences). . . . These observations and understandings convince me that changing the ratio of the haves to the have-nots is a matter of political education and action. The Democratic question of the nineteenth century and the Socialist question of the twentieth must be brought together in the twenty-first so that democratic socialism might be possible for all."

AVOCATIONAL INTERESTS: Collecting antique lamps.

* * *

KNECHTGES, David R(ichard) 1942-

PERSONAL: Born October 23, 1942, in Great Falls, Mont.; son of Carl Jacob (a boilermaker) and Gertrude (a registered nurse; maiden name, Clauson) Knechtges. *Education:* University of Washington, Seattle, B.A., 1964, Ph.D., 1968; Harvard University, A.M., 1965. *Religion:* None. *Home:* 18126 94th Ave. N.E., Bothell, Wash. 98011. *Office:* Department of Asian Languages and Literature, University of Washington, Seattle, Wash. 98195.

CAREER: Yale University, New Haven, Conn., instructor, 1968-70, assistant professor of Chinese literature, 1970-1971; University of Wisconsin, Madison, assistant professor of Chinese literature, 1971-72; University of Washington, Seattle, assistant professor, 1972-74, associate professor of Asian languages and literature, 1974—. *Member:* American Oriental Society, Association for Asian Studies, Society for the Study of Early China, Phi Beta Kappa. *Awards, honors:* Woodrow Wilson fellowship, 1965; Fulbright-Hayes fellowship, Taiwan, 1971; American Council of Learned Societies fellowship, 1975.

WRITINGS: (Contributor) David Buxbaum and Frederick Mote, editors, *Transition and Permanence: Chinese History and Culture,* Cathay Press, 1972; *The Han Rhapsody: A Study of the fu of Yang Hsiung, 53 B.C.–A.D. 18,* Cambridge University Press, 1975; (contributor) David T. Roy and Tsuen-hsiun Tsien, editors, *Ancient China: Studies in Early Civilization,* Chinese University of Hong Kong Press, 1977; (contributor) Chow Tse-tsung, editor, *Wen-lin: Studies in the Chinese Humanities II,* University of Wisconsin Press, in press. Contributor to *McGraw Encyclo-*

pedia of World Biography. Contributor of articles and reviews to professional journals. Associate editor of *Journal of the American Oriental Society,* 1972-75.

WORK IN PROGRESS: A Source Book of Han Literature, with Hellmut Wilhelm; *The Rhapsody in China from the Third Century B.C. to the Sixth Century A.D.,* completion expected in 1978; *A History of Old Chinese Prose,* 1980; editing an eleven-volume history of Chinese literature, for Yale University Press, with Stephen Owne.

SIDELIGHTS: Knechtges writes: "I was first introduced to Chinese literature by . . . Hellmut Wilhelm. . . . Wilhelm had a strong interest in the Chinese rhapsody as well as other genres of early Chinese literature. My work on this subject is essentially a continuation of his studies. I began my study of the Chinese language at the age of eighteen, and I have traveled and lived in Taiwan and Hong Kong. In addition to Chinese, I also have studied Japanese, French, and German. My primary purpose in studying Chinese literature is to make one of the world's greatest and largest literatures accessible to the Western reader in accurate, authoritative translations accompanied by commentary and analysis that help the non-initiated reader better understand the works. My main interest has been Chinese literary history."

* * *

KNIGHT, Wallace E(dward) 1926-

PERSONAL: Born February 4, 1926, in Charleston, W.Va.; son of Clarence H. and Ednah (Thomas) Knight; married Betty Howery, August 16, 1950; children: John Sydney, Stephen Howery, Leslie Harriett, Stuart Edward. *Education:* West Virginia Wesleyan College, A.B., 1949; Ohio University, M.A., 1950. *Politics:* Democrat. *Religion:* Protestant. *Home:* 121 Mount Savage Dr., Ashland, Ky. 41101. *Office:* Ashland Oil, Inc., 1409 Winchester Ave., Ashland, Ky. 41101.

CAREER: Charleston Gazette, Charleston, W.Va., reporter and business editor, 1950-55; Ashland Oil, Inc., Ashland, Ky., held various public relations posts, 1955-72, communications manager, 1972—. *Military service:* U.S. Army, Third Armored Division, 1944-46; served in Europe; became sergeant. *Member:* Association of Petroleum Writers, Ashland Area Chamber of Commerce, Rotary Club (Russell, Ky.).

WRITINGS: The Way We Went (fiction), Great Books Foundation, 1976.

Work has been anthologized in *Best American Short Stories of 1973,* edited by Martha Foley, Houghton, 1973. Contributor of articles, stories, and poems to *Atlantic Monthly* and regional magazines.

WORK IN PROGRESS: A novel; "Out of Wilderness," a narrative poem.

SIDELIGHTS: Knight told *CA:* "My employment as an oil company public relations manager involves responsibility for an extensive publications program as well as press relations and related public relations services; this leaves very little time for writing 'for fun.' However, beginning in 1972 I decided to write one evening a week. Most of the short stories I've written have sold."

* * *

KNOCK, Warren 1932-

PERSONAL: Born November 27, 1932, in London, England; son of Sidney (a naval blacksmith) and Edith (Ralph)

Knock; married Judy Oliver (an educational psychologist), March 29, 1956; children: Vivien Philippa, Jenefer Caroline, Daniel Alexander. *Education:* Christ's College, Cambridge, M.A. (honors), 1954. *Home:* 47 Magdalen Rd., London S.W.18, England. *Office:* Cassell & Co. Ltd., 35 Red Lion Sq., London WC1R 4SG, England.

CAREER: Former retailer with Simpson of Piccadilly; worked as editor and in promotion at Thomas Nelson & Sons Publishers, Edinburgh, for ten years; marketing director of Geoffrey Chapman Publishers until 1972; Cassell & Co. Ltd., London, England, publisher, 1972—. *Military service:* British Army, National Service and Intelligence Corps, 1954-56. British Army Reserve (TAVR), Royal Pioneer Corps, 1959—; current rank major. *Member:* Prehistoric Society, African Studies Association, Round Table (Great Britain and Ireland; president of Wimbeldon Table, 1973-74).

WRITINGS: Beers of Britain, Johnston & Bacon, 1975. Contributor to *In Britain* and *Penthouse.*

WORK IN PROGRESS: Magazine articles.

SIDELIGHTS: Knock told *CA* that while his writing to date has been on leisure topics—touring, beer and wine, and topography, his particular interests are in African history and development. For the past ten years, for up to ten weeks each year, he has traveled in Africa, especially Nigeria, Ghana, Sierra Leone, and Kenya, as well as in the Caribbean, the United States, and in Europe.

* * *

KNOKE, David (Harmon) 1947-

PERSONAL: Born March 4, 1947, in Philadelphia, Pa.; son of Donald Glenn (a carpenter) and Frances (a school teacher; maiden name, Dunn) Knoke; married Joann Margaret Robar, August 29, 1970; children: Margaret Frances. *Education:* University of Michigan, B.A., 1969, M.S.W., 1971, Ph.D., 1972; University of Chicago, M.A., 1970. *Politics:* "Passive observer of the parade." *Religion:* Unitarian-Universalist. *Home:* 525 Cabot Court, Bloomington, Ind. 47401. *Office:* Department of Sociology, Indiana University, Bloomington, Ind. 47401.

CAREER: Indiana University, Bloomington, assistant professor, 1972-75, associate professor of sociology, 1975—. Member of advisory committee of National Opinion Research Center's general social survey, 1976—. *Member:* American Sociological Association, American Political Science Association, Association of Voluntary Action Scholars, Phi Beta Kappa. *Awards, honors:* National Science Foundation fellowship, 1969-70.

WRITINGS: Change and Continuity in American Politics, Johns Hopkins Press, 1976. Contributor to social science journals.

WORK IN PROGRESS: Research on voluntary associations engaged in social change in Indianapolis, with a monograph expected to result.

SIDELIGHTS: Knoke writes: "The study of American political behavior has been my continuing intellectual interest since undergraduate days. For the last decade I have conducted a series of secondary analyses of survey data on political party affiliation and voting data. Most recently, my attention has switched to studying how citizens try to work through voluntary associations to achieve social changes in a variety of areas." *Avocational interests:* Gardening.

KOBLER, (Albert) John (Jr.) 1910-

PERSONAL: Born January 7, 1910, in Mount Vernon, N.Y.; son of Albert John and Mignon (Sommers) Kobler; married Adele Palmer, January 7, 1932 (divorced, 1945); married Ruth Margaret Low, April 5, 1945 (divorced, 1963); married Evelyn Cummins, February 10, 1966; children: Albert John III, Lynn (Mrs. James Hannon, Jr.), Karen, Andrea. *Education:* Williams College, B.A., 1931. *Home:* 165 West 66th St., New York, N.Y. 10023.

CAREER: Has worked as a foreign correspondent for Hearst Newspapers, 1931-39; worked as a foreign correspondent for International News Service (now United Press International) and Universal Syndicate; worked for *Time,* 1939; *New York Daily Mirror,* New York City, reporter and feature writer, 1940-42; crime editor of *PM* (magazine), 1940-42; served as a civilian intelligence officer in North Africa, Italy, and France, 1943-44; employed by the American Embassy, Paris, France, 1943-46; *Life,* New York City, associate editor, 1946-47; free-lance writer, 1947-57; *Saturday Evening Post,* contributing editor, 1957-64, editor-at-large, 1965-69, writer, 1969—.

WRITINGS: Some Like It Gory: A Post-Graduate Course in the Art of Murder, Dodd, 1940; *Afternoon in the Attic,* Dodd, 1950; (editor) *Adventures of the Mind,* Knopf, 1959; *The Reluctant Surgeon: A Biography of John Hunter,* Doubleday, 1960; *Luce: His Time, Life, and Fortune,* Doubleday, 1968; *The Rockefeller University Story,* Rockefeller University Press, 1970; *Capone: The Life and World of Al Capone,* Putnam, 1971; *Ardent Spirits: The Rise and Fall of Prohibition,* Putnam, 1973. Also author of the *Trial of Ruth Snyder and Judd Gray,* 1938. Contributor to popular magazines, including *New Yorker* and *Collier's.*

WORK IN PROGRESS: A biography of John Barrymore.

* * *

KOBRE, Sidney 1907-

PERSONAL: Born September 7, 1907, in Winston-Salem, N.C.; son of Max (a manufacturer) and Sadie (Harris) Kobre; married Reva Hoppenstein, March 4, 1939; children: Ellen Sue (Mrs. Henry Katz), Kenneth Robert. *Education:* John Hopkins University, A.B., 1927; Columbia University, M.A., 1934, Ph.D., 1944. *Politics:* Democrat. *Religion:* Jewish. *Home:* 8215 Scotts Level Rd., Baltimore, Md. 21208. *Office:* Department of Journalism, Community College of Baltimore, 2901 Liberty Heights Ave., Baltimore, Md. 21215.

CAREER: Newark Star Eagle, Newark, N.J., reporter and business editor, 1928-31; *Newark Ledger,* Newark, N.J., reporter and editorial writer, 1931-38; *Baltimore Home News,* Baltimore, Md., reporter and editor, 1938-39; managing editor in *Guide* newspaper chain, Baltimore, 1939-41, 1946-49; *Suburban Times,* Baltimore, owner and publisher, 1941-42; National Labor Relations Board, Washington, D.C., field examiner in Pittsburgh, Baltimore, and Philadelphia, 1942-46; Florida State University, Tallahassee, associate professor and director of graduate work, 1949-50, professor of journalism, 1950-64, director of Bureau of Media Research, 1955-64; Community College of Baltimore, Baltimore, professor of journalism, 1964—, director of News Bureau, 1964—. Information specialist for U.S. Department of Labor, 1940. Publicity director for Maryland Committee for Educational Television and of local community organizations. *Member:* Association for Education in Journalism, Maryland Association of Community Colleges (Public Relations Division), Junior/Community College Journalism Association.

WRITINGS: Backgrounding the News, Twentieth Century Press, 1939, Greenwood Press, 1974; *The Development of the Colonial Newspaper,* Colonial Press, 1944, Peter Smith, 1960; (with Juanita Parks) *Psychology and the News,* Florida State University, Bureau of Media Research, 1955; *News Behind the Headlines,* Florida State University, Bureau of Media Research, 1955; *Behind the Shocking Crime Headlines,* Florida State University, Bureau of Media Research, 1957; *The Press and Contemporary Affairs,* Florida State University, Bureau of Media Research, 1957, Greenwood Press, 1969; *Foundations of American Journalism,* Florida State University, Bureau of Media Research, 1958, Greenwood Press, 1970; *Modern American Journalism,* Florida State University, Bureau of Media Research, 1959; *The Yellow Press and the Gilded Age of Journalism,* Florida State University, Bureau of Media Research, 1964; *The Development of the American Newspaper,* W. C. Brown, 1969; *Successful Public Relations for Colleges and Universities,* Hastings House, 1974. Author of about a dozen monographs on journalism since 1953.

WORK IN PROGRESS: Books on reporting, journalism history, and public relations.

SIDELIGHTS: Kobre writes: "My histories of journalism have a sociological approach showing interaction between the newspaper, a social institution, and changing environment of people and technology. In my reporting books and research, I sought to combine journalistic techniques with social sciences to background and give depth to spot news."

* * *

KOCHER, Paul H(arold) 1907-

PERSONAL: Born April 23, 1907, in Trinidad, British West Indies; came to the United States in 1919, naturalized citizen, 1926; son of Paul William and Frieda (Schwabe) Kocker; married Annis Cox (a Montessori teacher), August 31, 1936; children: Paul Dana, Carl Alvin. *Education:* Columbia University, A.B., 1926; Stanford University, J.D., 1929, M.A., 1932, Ph.D., 1936. *Residence:* San Luis Obispo, Calif.

CAREER: Attorney, 1929-31; Stanford University, Calif., instructor in English, 1936-38; University of Washington, Seattle, assistant professor of English literature, 1938-46; University of Nebraska, Lincoln, professor of English literature, 1948-49; Claremont Graduate School, Claremont, Calif., professor of English literature, 1949-58; Stanford University, Stanford, Calif., professor of English and humanities, 1960-70, professor emeritus, 1971—.

MEMBER: Modern Language Association of America, Authors Guild of Authors League of America, Renaissance Society of America, Catholic Historical Society, San Luis Obispo Historical Scoiety, Order of the Coif. *Awards, honors:* Fellow of Folger Shakespeare Library, 1939-40; Guggenheim fellowships, 1946-47, 1955-56; Huntington Library fellowship, 1952-53.

WRITINGS: Christopher Marlowe: A Study of His Thought, Learning, and Character, University of North Carolina Press, 1946; (editor) Christopher Marlowe, *The Tragical History of Doctor Faustus,* Appleton, 1950; *Science and Religion in Elizabethan England,* Huntington Library, 1953; *Master of Middle-Earth: The Fiction of J.R.R. Tolkien,* Houghton, 1972 (published in England as *Master of Middle-Earth: The Achievement of J.R.R. Tolkien,* Thames

& Hudson, 1973); *Mission San Luis Obispo de Tolosa, 1772-1972: A Historical Sketch,* Blake Printing & Publishing, 1972; *California's Old Missions,* Franciscan Herald, 1976. Contributor of about twenty-five articles to language and literature journals. Assistant editor of *Huntington Library Quarterly,* 1952-53; member of editorial board of *Journal of the History of Ideas,* 1951-59.

WORK IN PROGRESS: A historical novel "set in the California Mission period."

SIDELIGHTS: Kocher writes briefly: "Consider modern public education a pitiful failure. Will there be a reading public for . . . writers?" *Avocational interests:* "Tolkien and his friends," reading (especially fiction), raising fruits and vegetables, rock collecting and polishing.

* * *

KOERTGE, Ronald 1940-

PERSONAL: Surname is pronounced *Kur*-chee; born April 22, 1940, in Olney, Ill.; son of William Henry and Bulis Olive (Fiscus) Koertge; married Cheryl Vasconcellos (a teacher). *Education:* University of Illinois, B.A., 1962; University of Arizona, M.A., 1965. *Home:* 1121 Grevelia, South Pasadena, Calif. 91030. *Agent:* William Reiss, Paul R. Reynolds, Inc., 21 East 41st St., New York, N.Y. 10017. *Office:* Department of English, Pasadena City College, 1560 Colorado Blvd., Pasadena, Calif. 91106.

CAREER: Pasadena City College, Pasadena, Calif., assistant professor of English, 1965—.

WRITINGS: Meat: Cherry's Market Diary, Mag Press, 1973; *The Father Poems,* Sumac Press, 1974; *The Hired Nose,* Mag Press, 1974; *My Summer Vacation,* Venice Poetry Co., 1975; *Men Under Fire,* Duck Down Press, 1976; *Twelve Photographs of Yellowstone,* Red Hill Press, 1976; *How to Live on Five Dollars a Day,* Venice Poetry Co., 1976.

* * *

KOGAN, Leonard S(aul) 1919-1976

April 22, 1919—June 28, 1976; American psychologist, educator, and author. Obituaries: *New York Times,* June 30, 1976.

* * *

KOHL, Herbert 1937-

PERSONAL: Born August 22, 1937, in Bronx, New York; son of Samuel (a building contractor) and Marion Kohl; married Judy Murdock (a teacher and weaver), 1963; children: Antonia, Erica, Joshua. *Education:* Harvard University, A.B. (magna cum laude), 1958; graduate study, University College, Oxford, 1958-59; Columbia University Teachers College, M.A., 1962; additional graduate study, 1965-66. *Home:* 178 Tamalpais, Berkeley, Calif. 94708. *Agent:* Robert Lescher, 155 East 71st St., N.Y. 10021.

CAREER: Elementary school teacher in New York, N.Y., 1962-66; Horace Mann-Lincoln Institute, New York City, research associate, 1966-1967; Teachers and Writers Collaborative, New York City, director, 1966-67; University of California, Berkeley, visiting associate professor of English education, 1967-68; Other Ways (public alternative high school), Berkeley, Calif., teacher and director, 1968-71; Berkeley Unified School District, Berkeley, consultant on public alternative schools, 1971-72; Center for Open Learning and Teaching, Berkeley, co-director, 1972—. Educational consultant to University of Minnesota, Des Moines Community Corporation, University of California, San Mateo County Schools, Stockton Unified School District, and other public and private institutions, 1967-73. *Member:* Phi Beta Kappa. *Awards, honors:* Henry fellowship, 1958-59; Woodrow Wilson fellowship, 1959-60; National Endowment for the Arts award for non-fiction article, 1968.

WRITINGS: The Age of Complexity, Mentor, 1965; *The Language and Education of the Deaf,* Center for Urban Education, 1966; *36 Children,* New American Library, 1967; *Teaching the Unteachable,* New York Review of Books, 1967; *The Open Classroom: A Practical Guide to a New Way of Teaching,* Vintage, 1969; *Fables: A Curriculum Unit,* Teachers and Writers Collaborative, 1969; *A University for Our Time,* Other Ways, 1970; (editor with Victor Hernandez Cruz) *Stuff: A Collection of Poems, Visions and Imaginative Happenings from Young Writers in Schools—Open and Closed,* World Publishing, 1970; (author of introduction) Sata Repo, editor, *This Book is About Schools,* Pantheon, 1970; *Golden Boy as Anthony Cool: A Photo Essay on Names and Graffiti,* Dial, 1972; (editor) *An Anthology of Fables,* Houghton, Volume I, 1972, Volume II, 1973; *Reading: How to—A People's Guide to Alternative Ways of Teaching and Testing Reading,* Dutton, 1973; (editor) *Stories of Sport and Society,* Houghton, 1973; *Games, Math and Writing in the Open Classroom,* Random House, 1973; *Half the House,* Dutton, 1974; *On Teaching,* Schocken, 1976.

Author of column, "Insight," in *Grade Teacher* (now *Teacher*) magazine, 1968—. Contributor of articles and reviews to *New York Review of Books, New York Times, London Times Educational Supplement, Harvard Educational Review, This Magazine is About Schools, Cultural Affairs, New School Education Journal* and other publications.

WORK IN PROGRESS: A book on being a parent, tentatively entitled *Taking Care of Children.*

SIDELIGHTS: Herbert Kohl is one of the most persistant voices in the call for re-evaluation and reformation of the American educational system. He has taught in ghetto schools, alternative schools, and the university, and his writings on the subject of education have been generally well received. *36 Children* appeared in 1967 and was the first of his books to be widely read. The book grew out of his experiences as a teacher in a ghetto elementary school. Nat Hentoff, in a review in the *New Yorker* wrote of *36 Children,* "Kohl shows how a sixth-grade class of wary Negro children in East Harlem learned to trust him as a teacher and trust themselves and thereby beat the system. Temporarily. After their one year with Kohl, most of them, too, were mutilated, but they demonstrated in that one year what they could have become—poor as they were, black as they were, and without a head start. In this book, they are trenchant proof that their defeat is the fault not of themselves or their families but of the system."

A *New York Times Book Review* writer describes Kohl's success in the classroom as a "time of intense creative collaboration.... Following the children's needs, he let his students sit where they wished, take 10-minute talk periods between subjects, dance once a week in class, and visit his apartment regularly." Amid what would seem like pandemonium by conventional classroom standards of decorum, the reviewer goes on to note that "they began to write, and this sometimes heartbreaking book is as much by the chil-

dren as by the author. Starting with simple descriptions of their surroundings, some progressed to the perceptive stories, fables and poems that comprise about half the text." Some readers and reviewers have suggested that Kohl included so much of the children's work as a final act of educational encouragement.

In his own writing about *36 Children* Kohl said that he was "able to take children who had experienced failure and self-hatred in school and enable them to flower emotionally and intellectually. This involved my throwing out the standard curriculum, reworking the schedule of the day, and most of all, listening and learning from my students and building a curriculum that used the strengths in their lives."

While still vitally concerned with the strategy of "infiltrating" the existing school systems with the now well known "open classroom" concept, Kohl focused his attention on the most discouraging example of the failure of the schools to meet the educational needs of the students—the inability to read. A reviewer for the *Christian Science Monitor* writing about *Reading: How To* said, "Kohl has never met a child who didn't want to learn to read. But this young educational reformer has met many adults who make children afraid they can't learn to read. It is the spirit in which reading is taught that needs to be changed." Lisa Hammel reports that Kohl "thinks the major reason for the increasing problem of semi-illiteracy is 'because teachers are more and more demoralized and have given up. Respecting the kids seems to be one of the keys to success . . . and giving them a chance to make choices.' Many teachers, he believes, expect some children—particularly from minority groups—to fail and help this self-fulfilling prophecy along by maintaining that there is only one correct way to learn."

Half the House says Kohl, "is an attempt to answer, or at least wrestle with two questions: Is it possible to live a healthy life in an unhealthy society? and is it possible to change oneself in midlife despite one's education and the practical pressures to survive? I've been teaching for twelve years now. Five years ago I taught at a public alternative high school in Berkeley, California. At the school we tried to develop a multiracial, open, nonsexist, congenial learning community. We failed after three years of struggle not because of the students, but because the adults were not able to live their ideas. We could claim to be free of racism or sexism, but our daily practice proved the opposite. Moreover, we were under constant political and economic pressure from the school district. Over those years I learned about myself, about the need to center one's existence, and about the need to relate one's work to other people's struggles. *Half the House* is an account of an adult struggling to define relevant work and a fulfilling life in this unhappy culture."

BIOGRAPHICAL/CRITICAL SOURCES: New Yorker, March 16, 1968; *Carleton Miscelany,* Winter, 1969; *New Republic,* November 7, 1970, November 21, 1970; *Saturday Review,* May 27, 1972; *New York Times,* July 9, 1973; *American Libraries,* March, 1975.

*   *   *

KOLB, David A(llen) 1939-

PERSONAL: Born December 12, 1939, in Moline, Ill.; son of John A. and Ethel M. (Petherbridge) Kolb. *Education:* Knox College, A.B., (cum laude), 1961; Harvard University, M.A., 1964, Ph.D., 1967. *Home:* 283 Lowell Ave., Newton, Mass. 02160. *Office:* Development Research Associates, 16 Ashton Ave., Newton, Mass. 02159.

CAREER: Massachusetts Institute of Technology, Cambridge, assistant professor, 1965-70, associate professor of organizational psychology and management, 1970-75; Development Research Associates, Newton, Mass., senior associate, 1966—; Institute for Development Research, Newton, Mass., president, 1974—. Senior associate at Behavioral Science Center, 1969-70. Visiting professor at University of London, Graduate School of Business Studies, 1971. Consultant to business, governmental, and private organizations, including International Achievement Motivation Project, Australian Institute of Management, Island of Curacao, Netherland Antilles, General Foods, Bundy Corp., Department of Health, Education and Welfare, Office of Economic Opportunity, U.S. Peace Corps, American Management Association, Streetcorner Research, Sun Oil Co., U.S. Navy, Microwave Associates, American Telephone and Telegraph Massachusetts Youth Service Board, Outward Bound, Massachusetts Correctional Institution at Concord, and Bellewood Home for Children.

MEMBER: International Association of Applied Social Scientists (charter member), American Psychological Association, Society for Intercultural Learning and Research (charter member). *Awards, honors:* Woodrow Wilson fellow, 1961-62.

WRITINGS: (Contributor) Richard Saxe, editor, *Opening the Schools: Alternative Ways of Learning,* McCutchan, 1965; (editor with Irwin Rubin and James McIntyre) *Organizational Psychology: A Book of Readings,* Prentice-Hall, 1971, 2nd edition, 1974; (with Rubin and McIntyre) *Organizational Psychology: An Experiential Approach,* Prentice-Hall, 1971, 2nd edition, 1974; (contributor) Warren Bennis, David Berlow, Fred Schein, and Edgar Steele, editors, *Interpersonal Dynamics,* Dorsey, 1973; (with Ralph Schwitzgebel) *Changing Human Behavior: Principles of Planned Intervention,* McGraw, 1974; (contributor) Cary Cooper, editor, *Theories of Group Processes,* Wiley, 1975. Contributor to journals in his field.

* * *

KOPP, William LaMarr 1930-

PERSONAL: Born May 6, 1930, in Ephrata, Pa.; son of Lehman L. and Ella (Kurtz) Kopp; married Nel Boon (a physician), January 3, 1959; children: Kristine Ann, Erik LaMarr, Ingrid Marie. *Education:* Goshen College, B.A., 1952; University of Minnesota, M.A., 1954; University of Pennsylvania, further graduate study, 1959-60; Pennsylvania State University, Ph.D., 1965. *Home:* 230 Ronan Dr., State College, Pa. 16801. *Office:* 136 Sparks Building, Pennsylvania State University, University Park, Pa. 16802.

CAREER: Augsburg College, Minneapolis, Minn., instructor in German, 1953-54; Mennonite Voluntary Service, Basel, Switzerland, executive secretary, 1954-57; Goshen College, Goshen, Ind., assistant professor of German, 1957-59; Pennsylvania State University, University Park, instructor, 1963-65, assistant professor, 1965-70, associate professor, 1970-74, professor of German, 1974—, director of language laboratory, 1963-65, resident director of Junior-Year-in-Marburg Program, 1966-67, assistant dean for resident instruction, 1969, associate dean of undergraduate studies, 1973—. Member of board of directors of Pennsylvania State University United Campus Ministry, 1969-72; member of Mennonite Student Services Committee, 1971—. Member of board of trustees of Eastern Mennonite College, 1971—.

MEMBER: Modern Language Association of America, American Association of Teachers of German (national treasurer and member of executive council, 1968-75), Na-

tional Association of Self-Instructional Language Programs (member of board of directors, 1974—), American Council on German Studies (member of board of directors, 1974-76), National Carl Schurz Association (member of board of directors, 1976—), Council of Colleges of Arts and Sciences (national treasurer and member of executive board, 1975—), Pennsylvania State Modern Language Association.

WRITINGS: German Literature in the United States, 1945-1960, University of North Carolina Press, 1967.

WORK IN PROGRESS: Research on German-American literary relations; German drama on the American stage.

* * *

KORY, Robert B(ruce) 1950-

PERSONAL: Born May 23, 1950, in Nashville, Tenn.; son of Ross C. (a physician) and Virginia (Highsmith) Kory; married Robin Ann Bierman (a transcendental-meditation instructor), February 14, 1976. *Education:* Yale University, B.A. (summa cum laude), 1973. *Agent:* Peter McWilliams, 46 Morton St., New York, N.Y. 10014. *Office:* American Foundation for the Science of Creative Intelligence, 133 East 58th St., New York, N.Y. 10023.

CAREER: American Foundation for the Science of Creative Intelligence (transcendental-meditation organization), New York, N.Y., vice-president for expansion, 1973—. *Member:* Phi Beta Kappa.

WRITINGS: (With H. H. Bloomfield, M. P. Cain, and P. T. Jaffe) *TM: Discovering Inner Energy and Overcoming Stress,* Delacorte, 1975; (with Bloomfield) *Happiness: The TM Program, Psychiatry and Enlightenment,* Simon & Schuster, 1976; *The Transcendental Meditation rogram for Business People,* American Management Association, 1976; *The Science of Creative Intelligence,* Simon & Schuster, in press.

WORK IN PROGRESS: TM: Working and Wealth.

* * *

KOSTASH, Myrna 1944-

PERSONAL: Born September 2, 1944, in Edmonton, Alberta, Canada; daughter of William (a teacher) and Mary (a teacher; maiden name, Maksymiuk) Kostash. *Education:* University of Alberta, B.A., 1965; University of Washington, Seattle, graduate study, 1965-66; University of Toronto, M.A., 1968. *Politics:* "Socialist feminist." *Home:* 8726 117th St., Edmonton, Alberta, Canada.

CAREER: Free-lance journalist, 1968—. Instructor in women's studies at University of Toronto, Toronto, Ontario, 1972-74; associate producer for Canadian National Film Board, 1975. *Member:* Professional Writers Association of Canada (Prairie representative).

WRITINGS: (With Erna Paris, Valerie Miner, Heather Robertson, and Melinda McCracken) *Her Own Woman* (essays), Macmillan, 1975. Author of dramatic and documentary scripts for Canadian National Film Board. Also author of column "Women," for *Maclean's Magazine,* 1974-75. Contributor of articles and reviews to Canadian journals.

WORK IN PROGRESS: It's a Long Long Way from Bukovina, on the experiences of Ukrainian-Canadians in Two Hills, Alberta.

SIDELIGHTS: Myrna Kostash writes: "Two ambitions impel my writing: to provide a socialist feminist perspective on sociological and existential events; and to convince Canadian literary critics that journalism is a form of creative writing."

KOT, Stanislaw 1886(?)-1976

1886(?)—December 26, 1976; Polish-born author of books on political and cultural history of Poland. Obituaries: *AB Bookman's Weekly*, March 8, 1976.

* * *

KRAF, Elaine

PERSONAL: Born in New York; daughter of Harry (a judge) and Lena (a teacher; maiden name, Rosenfeld) Kraf. *Education:* Hunter College of the City University of New York, A.B., 1965, currently engaged in graduate study; also attended Pennsylvania Academy of Fine Arts. *Religion:* Jewish. *Home:* 116 West 72nd St., New York, N.Y. 10025.

CAREER: Preschool and kindergarten teacher in New York City, 1965-67, substitute teacher of retarded and handicapped children, 1968; Research and Rehabilitation Center for Retarded Adults, New York City, teacher, 1970; writer. Has taught art classes. *Member:* International P.E.N. *Awards, honors:* Award from National Endowment for the Arts, 1970, for story "Westward and Up a Mountain"; Yaddo Colony fellowships, 1971, 1973, 1976; Breadloaf Conference fellowship, 1971; MacDowell Colony fellowship, 1972.

WRITINGS: I Am Clarence (novel), Doubleday, 1969; *The House of Madelaine* (novel), Doubleday, 1971.

Work has been anthologized in *The American Literary Anthology,* edited by George Plimpton and Peter Ardery, Viking, 1970; *The Stonewall Book of Short Fictions,* edited by Kent Dixon and Robert Coover, Stone Wall Press, 1973; *Bitches and Sad Ladies,* edited by Pat Rotter, Harper, 1975; and *New Directions 31,* edited by James Laughlin, New Directions, 1975. Contributor to *Quarterly Review* and *Fiction* magazine.

WORK IN PROGRESS: A novel, *The Princess of 72nd Street;* a book of stories about men; the journal of a twelve-year-old girl.

SIDELIGHTS: Elaine Kraf writes: "I am interested in many arts—study dance, have exhibited my art. My writing reflects interest in color, music, new form. I am not interested in the old form of the novel. My writing is influenced by musical composition, choreography, and painting—not by reading."

* * *

KRAFFT, Maurice 1946-

PERSONAL: Born March 25, 1946, in Mulhouse, France; son of Raymond (a physician) and Elisabeth (a physician; maiden name, Dopff) Krafft; married Katia Conrad (a volcanologist), August 18, 1970. *Education:* University of Strasbourg, M.Geology, 1971, specialized volcanologist, 1974. *Religion:* Roman Catholic. *Home:* 15 Rue de la Reine de Pres, Ensisheim 68190, France. *Office:* B.P. 14, Ensisheim 68190, France.

CAREER: Geological Institute, Strasbourg, France, geologist, 1970-72; Center of Volcanological Research, Ensisheim, France, director, 1972—. Consultant to Government of Indonesia. *Member:* French Geological Society, Explorers Club, Volcanological Association, American Geophysical Union, Smithsonian Institution Center of Short-Lived Phenomena. *Awards, honors:* Prize from Vocation Foundation, 1969; explorer's prize from the President of the French Republic, 1975.

WRITINGS: Volcans et tremblements de Terre (title means "Volcanos and Earthquakes"), Deux Cog d'Or, 1971; *Guide des Volcans d'Europe* (title means "Guidebook of European Volcanos"), Delachaux et Niestle, 1974; *Les Volcans* (title means "Volcanos"), Draeger, 1975; *Volcano* (translated into English by John Shepley), Abrams, 1975; *Climbing Volcanos,* Presses de la Cite, 1976. Author of television scripts dealing with geology, for French, Swiss, Belgian, and Canadian television.

WORK IN PROGRESS: A book on continental drift; a book of his experiences on volcanos; a book on African volcanos; research on geophysical methods and volcanos.

SIDELIGHTS: Krafft saw his first volcano at age seven, and began his studies at that time. He has visited sites of eruptions in Italy, Iceland, Indonesia, Africa, and Central America, and reports that his wife is the only woman volcanologist in the world.

* * *

KRAHN, Fernando 1935-

PERSONAL: Born January 4, 1935, in Santiago, Chile; son of Otto (a lawyer) and Laura (a singer; maiden name, Parada) Krahn; married Maria de la Luz Uribe (a writer), February, 1966; children: Fernanda, Santiago, Matias. *Education:* Attended Catholic University, Santiago, 1952-55, and University of Chile, 1954-62. *Home:* San Guadencio 23, Sitges, Spain. *Agent:* Harriet Wasserman, Russell & Volkening, Inc., 551 Fifth Ave., New York, N.Y. 10017.

CAREER: Cartoonist for American magazines and writer-illustrator of children's books, 1962—. *Awards, honors:* Guggenheim fellowship for film animation experiments, 1972-73.

WRITINGS: The Possible Worlds of Fernando Krahn (collection of (cartoons), Dutton, 1965.

Children's books; all self-illustrated: *Journeys of Sebastian,* Delacorte, 1968; *Gustavus and Stop,* Dutton, 1968; *Hildegarde and Maximilian,* Delacorte, 1970; *The Flying Saucer Full of Spaghetti,* Dutton, 1970; *How Santa Claus Had a Long and Difficult Journey Delivering His Presents,* Delacorte, 1971; *What Is a Man?,* Delacorte, 1972; *April Fools,* Dutton, 1974; *The Self Made Snowman,* Lippincott, 1975; *Who's Seen the Scissors?,* Dutton, 1975; *Sebastian and the Mushroom,* Delacorte, 1976; *Little Love Story,* Lippincott, 1976. Illustrator and co-author: (With Carol Newman) *Strella's Children,* Atheneum, 1967; (with Alastair Reid) *Uncle Timothy's Traviata,* Delacorte, 1967; (with wife, Maria Krahn) *The First Peko-Neko Bird,* Simon & Schuster, 1969; (with Maria Krahn) *The Life of Numbers,* Simon & Schuster, 1971.

Illustrator: Jan Wahl, *The Furious Flycycle,* Delacorte, 1968; Fred Gardner, *The Lioness Who Made Deals,* Norton, 1969; Wahl, *Abe Lincoln's Beard,* Delacorte, 1972; Wahl, *Lorenzo Bear and Co.,* Delacorte, 1972; Wahl, *S.O.S. Bobomobile,* Delacorte, 1973; Miriam Chaikin, *Hardlucky,* Lippincott, 1975; Walt Whitman, *I Hear America Singing,* Delacorte, 1975.

Contributor to magazines and newspapers in the United States, France, Germany, and England, including *Esquire, Horizon, New Yorker, Reporter, Show, Evergreen, Atlantic Monthly, Gourmet, Sky, National Lampoon,* and *Playboy.*

SIDELIGHTS: Krahn's books for children have been translated and published in German, Norwegian, Swedish, and Danish.

KRAJEWSKI, Frank R. 1938-

PERSONAL: Born December 31, 1938, in Milford, Mass.; son of Frank C. and Theresa (Ruscitti) Krajewski; divorced; children: James F., Lisa M., Tanya (deceased), Peter D. *Education:* Providence College, A.B., 1960; Michigan State University, M.A., 1964, Ph.D., 1969. *Home:* 1560 Geary, Reno, Nev. 89503. *Office:* College of Education, University of Nevada, Reno, Nev. 89507.

CAREER: Junior high and high school teacher and coach in the public schools of Woonsocket, R.I., 1960-61; U.S. Peace Corps, teacher's aide, 1961-63; Colegio Panamericano, Bucaramanga, Colombia, director, 1966-68; Michigan State University, East Lansing, instructor in social science, 1968-69; University of Nevada, Reno, assistant professor of educational foundations, 1969—. *Member:* International Council on Education for Teaching, American Educational Studies Association, Comparative and International Education Scoiety.

WRITINGS: (With G. L. Peltier) *Education: Where It's Been, Where It's At, Where It's Going,* C. E. Merrill, 1973; (with E. E. Loveless) *The Teacher and School Law,* Interstate Printers and Publishers, 1974.

WORK IN PROGRESS: Compiling an anthology of past and current court decisions and federal legislation that have had an impact on teachers' and students' rights.

AVOCATIONAL INTERESTS: Traveller, sports car mechanic, driver, and enthusiast.

*   *   *

KRATOS
See POWER, Norman S(andiford)

*   *   *

KREUSLER, Abraham A(rthur) 1897-

PERSONAL: Born October 1, 1897, in Gologory, Ukraine; son of Lazarus (a businessman) and Bertha (Drettel) Kreusler; married Esther Srebrnik (a teacher), July 5, 1927; children: Lucy Kreusler Carey. *Education:* Yaghellonian University of Cracow, M.A., 1928, Ph.D., 1929, M.A., 1933. *Home:* 210 Cleveland Ave., Lynchburg, Va. 24503. *Office:* Department of Languages, Randolph Macon Woman's College, Lynchburg, Va. 24503.

CAREER: Gymnasiums Lyceum, Wloclawek, Poland, teacher of modern languages, 1925-36, director, 1936-39; Stanislav Teachers College, Stanislav, Ukrainian S.S.R., assistant professor of modern languages, 1940-41; Frunze Teachers College, Frunze, Kirghiz S.S.R., associate professor of modern languages, 1944-46; Randolph Macon Woman's College, Lynchburg, Va., professor of Russian studies, 1948-69. *Member:* American Association of Teachers of Slavic and East European Languages (president of Virginia branch, 1968-69).

WRITINGS: (Author of commentary) H. G. Wells, *The Country of the Blind and Other Stories,* Ksiaznica Atlas (Warsaw), 1932; (author of commentary) Frances Burnett, *Little Lord Fauntleroy,* Ksiaznica Atlas, 1933; (author of commentary) Alfred Tennyson, *Enoch Arden,* State Publishing House (Lvov, Poland), 1938; (author of commentary) Anton Chekhov, *The Three Sisters,* privately printed, 1954; *The Teaching of Modern Foreign Languages in the Soviet Union,* E. J. Brill, 1963; *A Teacher's Experiences in the Soviet Union,* E. J. Brill, 1965; *Perspectives on World Education,* W. C. Brown, 1970. Editor, "English Library" series, State Publishing House, 1935-38.

WORK IN PROGRESS: Contemporary Education and Moral Upbringing in the Soviet Union.

*   *   *

KRISTIAN, Hans
See NEERSKOV, Hans Kristian

*   *   *

KROLL, Judith 1943-

PERSONAL: Born October 16, 1943, in Brooklyn, N.Y.; daughter of Jerry R. and Marian (Cohen) Kroll; married Syed A. R. Zaidi. *Education:* Attended Ithaca College, 1960-61; Smith College, B.A., 1964; Yale University, M.A., 1966, M.Phil., 1967, Ph.D., 1974. *Home:* 1 Kensington Gate, Great Neck, New York 11021.

CAREER: Vassar College, Poughkeepsie, N.Y., instructor, 1968-73, assistant professor of English, 1973-75; Indian Institute of Advanced Study, Simla, visiting fellow in literature, 1976—. *Awards, honors:* Poetry fellowship from National Endowment for the Arts, 1974-75.

WRITINGS: In the Temperate Zone (poems), Scribner, 1973; *Chapters in a Mythology: The Poetry of Sylvia Plath,* Harper, 1976. Contributor to literary journals, including *Antioch Review, Sewanee Review,* and *Poetry,* and to *Mademoiselle.*

WORK IN PROGRESS: A critical book on contemporary American poetry; poems; translating Kannada bhakti devotional poems, with U. R. Anantha Murthy.

*   *   *

KROLL, Steven 1941-

PERSONAL: Born August 11, 1941, in New York, N.Y.; son of Julius (a diamond merchant) and Anita (a business executive; maiden name, Berger) Kroll; married Edite Niedringhaus (a children's book editor), April 18, 1964. *Education:* Harvard University, B.A., 1962. *Politics:* "Committed to change." *Religion:* Jewish. *Home and office:* 64 West 11th St., New York, N.Y. 10011. *Agent:* Elaine Markson, 44 Greenwich Ave., New York, N.Y. 10011.

CAREER: Transatlantic Review, London, England, associate editor, 1962-65; Chatto & Windus Ltd., London, England, reader and editor, 1962-65; Holt, Rinehart & Winston, New York, N.Y., acquiring editor in trade department, 1965-69; full-time writer, 1969—. University of Maine, Augusta, instructor in English, 1970-71. *Member:* Harvard Club.

WRITINGS—All juvenile: *Is Milton Missing?,* Holiday House, 1975; *The Tyrannosaurus Game,* Holiday House, 1976; *That Makes Me Mad!,* Pantheon, 1976. Contributor of book reviews to *New York Times Book Review, Book World, Commonweal, Village Voice, Listener, Spectator, Times Literary Supplement,* and *London Magazine.*

WORK IN PROGRESS: Sleepy Ida and Other Nonsense Poems, publication by Pantheon expected in 1977; three juvenile books, *Gobbledygook,* Holiday House, 1977, *Santa's Crash-Bang Christmas,* Holiday House, 1977, and a sequel to *That Makes Me Mad!,* Pantheon, 1978; an adult novel, *Spread the Goodness.*

SIDELIGHTS: Kroll told *CA:* "Language—what we say and what we write—defines us. But no one is taught that truth in school, and through the mass media language has been everywhere debased. If we are to escape our current confusion, we must regain some sense of our use of language. I have always felt this way, was drawn to writing for that reason as well as by the need to tell stories. I also play a lot of tennis and squash, walk all over New York, and travel wherever I can. Sometimes I think languid thoughts about cruising down the Mississippi on a riverboat.

* * *

KROPF, Richard W(illiam Bartlett) 1932-

PERSONAL: Born January 9, 1932, in Milwaukee, Wis.; son of Richard Bartlett (a metallurgist) and Aileen Katherine (a teacher; maiden name, Foley) Kropf. *Education:* Attended Xavier University and St. Gregory Seminary, both in Cincinnati, Ohio; Sacred Heart Seminary, Detroit, Mich., B.A., 1954; St. John's Provincial Seminary, Plymouth, Mich., S.T.B., 1958; St. Paul University, Ottawa, Ontario, S.T.L., 1969, S.T.D., 1977; University of Ottawa, M.Th., 1969, Ph.D., 1973; also studied at Universidad Ibero-Americana, 1955, and Michigan State University, 1965-66. *Home and office:* 666 Lakeview Ave., Birmingham, Mich. 48009.

CAREER: Ordained Roman Catholic priest, 1958; associate pastor of Roman Catholic churches in Flint, Battle Creek, Grand Ledge, and Kalamazoo, Mich., 1958-67; Spiritual Life Institute of America, Sedona, Ariz., resident associate, 1967-68; Lansing Community College, Lansing, Mich., part-time instructor in philosophy and religion, 1972-76; Olivet College, Olivet, Mich., part-time associate professor of religion, 1974-75; Mercy College, Detroit, Mich., chaplain for Christian Ministries, 1975-76, adjunct associate professor of religion, 1976—. Adjunct instructor at Madonna College, 1976—; teacher of religion at Roman Catholic high schools in Burton, Mich., 1958-60, Lansing, Mich., 1962-66, and Kalamazoo, Mich., 1966-67; part-time teacher at private school in Sedona, Ariz., 1968. Associate priest of Madonna House Apostolate (Ontario). Member of Fellowship of St. Augustine (Oxford, Mich.).

MEMBER: American Academy of Religion, American Teilhard de Chardin Society for the Future of Man, Societe des amis de Teilhard de Chardin (Paris), Michigan Academy of Science, Arts, and Letters.

WRITINGS: Teilhard, Scripture, and Revelation, Fairleigh Dickinson University Press, 1976. Contributor to theology and philosophy journals.

WORK IN PROGRESS: Writing on faith development and dynamics "particularly as derived from the 'logotherapeutic' ideas of Viktor Frankl," and on science and religion, especially evolution, process philosophy, and theology.

SIDELIGHTS: Fr. Kropf has traveled extensively in Europe and Mexico. In 1970, he spent a summer in research at the Foundation Teilhard de Chardin in Paris, and the archives of the Paris Provence of the Society of Jesus. He writes: "I see my own thinking as dominated by a general 'convergent' view of human knowledge, that is, I am convinced that all areas of research, whether in the natural sciences, social sciences, medicine, psychology, or whatever else, together with the speculative disciplines of philosophy and theology, (including the study of the sacred writings of all religions) will combine, when respectful of each discipline's area and method of discovery, to reveal an ultimate truth which as of yet is only partially grasped by human consciousness. If I have concentrated on the problems posed by general evolutionary theory and Christian theology, it has been because, at least for me, that these two areas have presented the sharpest point of conflict and, for Western thought, the greatest stimulant to and promise of fruitful synthesis for the future of human thought."

AVOCATIONAL INTERESTS: Geological and archaeological studies, nature and scenic photography, the out-of-doors.

* * *

KUCHARSKY, David (Eugene) 1931-

PERSONAL: Born August 3, 1931, in Pittsburgh, Pa.; son of Leon (a tailor) and Marie (Dachko) Kucharsky; married Patricia Eleanor Patterson, August 31, 1957; children: Brenda, Deborah, Sandra, David John. *Education:* Attended Pennsylvania State Center, 1949-50; Duquesne University, B.A., 1953; American University, M.A., 1961. *Religion:* Christian and Missionary Alliance. *Home:* 400 North Livingston St., Arlington, Va. 22203. *Office: Christianity Today,* 1014 Washington Bldg., Washington, D.C. 20005.

CAREER: United Press International (UPI), Pittsburgh, Pa., staff correspondent, 1955-57; *Christianity Today,* Washington, D.C., news editor, 1957-67, associate editor, 1967-71, managing editor, 1971-76, senior editor, 1976—. Notable assignments include coverage of the coronation of Pope Paul, the launch of Apollo 11, and Richard Nixon's visit to Moscow in 1972; toured the United States with Nikita Khrushchev in 1959. *Military service:* U.S. Air Force, 1953-55; became lieutenant. *Member:* National Press Club, Associated Church Press (member of board of directors, 1971—), American Citizens Concerned for Life (member of advisory board, 1974—), Sigma Delta Chi.

WRITINGS: The Man from Plains: The Mind and Spirit of Jimmy Carter, Harper, 1976. Contributor to magazines.

SIDELIGHTS: Kucharsky comments: "I am concerned that the American people realize their need for a greater consensus on moral values, and that they begin setting some priorities accordingly. I am a born-again evangelical Christian. That does not give me all the answers, but it does enable me to ask some of the right questions about the concerns that should be pre-eminent in our society." He has traveled extensively abroad and made two trips to the Soviet Union.

AVOCATIONAL INTERESTS: Ice skating, tennis, gardening, building radio-control model airplanes.

* * *

KUHLMAN, Kathryn 1910(?)-1976

1910(?)—February 20, 1976; American evangelist, faith healer, and author. Obituaries: *New York Times,* February 22, 1976; *Newsweek,* March 1, 1976. (See index for previous *CA* sketch)

* * *

KUHN, Karl F(rancis) 1939-

PERSONAL: Born October 25, 1939, in Louisville, Ky.; son of Fred L. (a pharmacist) and Mary Francis (a teacher; maiden name, Walsh) Kuhn; married Mary Sharon Roos, November 24, 1960; children: Karyn, Kimberly, Karl, Jr., Keith, Kevin. *Education:* Bellarmine College, B.A., 1961; University of Kentucky, M.S., 1964, Ph.D., 1973. *Religion:* Roman Catholic. *Home:* 264 Sunset Ave., Richmond, Ky. 40475. *Office:* Department of Physics, Eastern Kentucky University, Richmond, Ky. 40475.

CAREER: Eastern Kentucky University, Richmond, instructor, 1963-68, assistant professor, 1969-72, associate professor of physics, 1973—. Development engineer for Sylvania Electric Co., 1965-66. *Member:* American Association of Physics Teachers, Astronomical Society of the Pacific, Kentucky Association of Physics Teachers, Kentucky Association for Progress in Science.

WRITINGS: (With Jerry Faughn) *Physics for People Who Think They Don't Like Physics,* Saunders, 1976. Contributor to *Physics Teacher.*

WORK IN PROGRESS: Your Basic Physics, for Wiley.

SIDELIGHTS: Kuhn writes: "My primary professional interest is in teaching elementary physics and astronomy. I try not to take myself too seriously, and I hope that this attitude is reflected in *Physics for People Who Think They Don't Like Physics.* Nonprofessionally, I am working in the Cursillo movement to share what I have found in my church."

* * *

KURTZ, C(larence) Gordon   1902-
(Kurtz Gordon)

PERSONAL: Born June 12, 1902, in Highland, N.Y.; son of Daniel Harding (a plumber) and Daisy (Rose) Kurtz. *Education:* Columbia University, student, 1928-29. *Religion:* Protestant. *Home and office:* 4 Spray Ave., Ocean Grove, N.J. 07756. *Agent:* Samuel French, Inc., 25 W. 45th St., New York, N.Y. 10036.

CAREER: Title Guarantee Co. (insurance company), New York, N.Y., head of plant department in Mineola, N.Y., 1921-67. *Military service:* U.S. Army, 1942-45.

WRITINGS—All plays; all three-act comedies, except as indicated: *Training a Butler* (two-act), School Publishing, 1921; *Suitors Three* (one-act), Frank J. Stanton, 1921; *Heedless Sex* (one-act), Frank J. Stanton, 1922; *Haunted* (mystery), Willis N. Bugbee, 1928.

Under pseudonym, Kurtz Gordon: *Strictly Improper* (one-act), Willis N. Bugbee, 1931; *The Black Ace* (mystery), Fitzgerald, 1934; *The Sky's the Limit,* Fitzgerald, 1934; *F Is for Family,* Fitzgerald, 1934; *Treasure Trove,* Fitzgerald, 1935; *Murder Sails at Midnight* (mystery; produced on Broadway at President Theatre, December 13, 1937), Baker's Plays, 1938; *The Mad Hatters,* Baker's Plays, 1939; *Tricking Tricksters,* Baker's Plays, 1939. *Senior Prom,* Baker's Plays, 1940; *Double Date,* Baker's Plays, 1941; *Come to Dinner,* Baker's Plays, 1941; *Happy is the Bride,* Baker's Plays, 1942; *Hit with a Horseshoe,* Baker's Plays, 1946; *Doctor's Orders,* Baker's Plays, 1946; *Henrietta the Eighth,* Dramatists Play Service, 1947; *The Overnight Ghost* (mystery), Baker's Plays, 1948; *Ladies Lounge,* Baker's Plays, 1948; *Dressed to Kill* (mystery), Baker's Plays, 1949.

Not for Sale, Baker's Plays, 1950; *Paperplates for Papa,* Baker's Plays, 1951; *Money Mad,* Dramatists Play Service, 1954; *The Babbling Brooks,* Samuel French, 1955; *That's My Cousin,* Dramatists Play Service, 1957; (with Robert Emmett) *The Broom and the Groom,* Samuel French, 1958; *Fair Exchange,* Dramatists Play Service, 1959. *Helpful Henry,* Baker's Plays, 1962; *Utopia, Inc.,* Dramatists Play Service, 1964; *The Bride's Bouquet* (mystery), Dramatists Play Service, 1968; *New Beat on an Old Drum,* Dramatists Play Service, 1976.

WORK IN PROGRESS: Two plays, *Dead and Delighted* and *the Twenty Wills of William Wild,* to be published in 1978 by Dramatists Play Service.

SIDELIGHTS: Gordon Kurtz writes: "I am strongly interested in the rapid development and growth of the amateur and semi-professional theatre in America. It is most heart-

ening to view the great progress of these two important couriers of the American theatre into the vast regions of the United States." Several of Gordon's plays have been translated and published in Holland.

* * *

KYLE, Duncan
See BROXHOLME, John Franklin

* * *

LABER, Jeri   1931-

PERSONAL: Born May 19, 1931, in New York, N.Y.; daughter of Louis (an engineer) and Mae (Zias) Lidsky; married Austin Laber (an attorney), October 3, 1954; children: Abigail, Pamela, Emily. *Education:* New York University, B.A., 1952; Columbia University, M.A., 1954. *Home:* 257 W. 86th St., New York, N.Y. 10024.

CAREER: Current Digest of Soviet Press, New York City, foreign editor, 1954-56; Institute for study of U.S.S.R., New York City, publications director, 1961-70. Freelance writer and editor. *Member:* Amnesty International, Index on Censorship (board member).

WRITINGS: Czechoslovakia: Some Soviet People Protest, Radio Liberty Committee, 1968; (with Molly Finn) *Cooking for Carefree Weekends,* Simon & Schuster, 1974. Contributor of articles to *Commentary, Newsday, New Republic, House and Garden, New York Times Book Review, Commonweal,* and other periodicals.

WORK IN PROGRESS: A major revision of *Fannie Farmer Cook Book,* publication by Knopf expected in 1978.

SIDELIGHTS: "In recent years," Laber told *CA,* "I have combined my interest in Russian affairs and human rights with an interest in cooking and cookbooks. Each of the subjects can be demanding, although in very different ways. And each provides satisfaction, depending on the project. Russian affairs and human rights are often combined in articles I write—but cooking so far has remained separate. Together they provide good counterpoint in my working life."

* * *

LAFAYETTE, Carlos
See BOILES, Charles Lafayette (Jr.)

* * *

LaHAYE, Tim   1926-

PERSONAL: Born April 27, 1926, in Detroit, Mich.; son of Francis T. (an electrician) and Margaret (a fellowship director; maiden name, Palmer) LaHaye; married Beverly Jean Ratcliffe (a writer and lecturer), July 5, 1947; children: Linda (Mrs. Gareld Murphy), Larry, Lee, Lori. *Education:* Bob Jones University, B.A., 1950; Western Conservative Baptist Seminary, D.Min., 1977. *Religion:* Baptist. *Home:* 2447 Camino Monte Sombra, El Cajon, Calif. 92021. *Office:* 2100 Greenfield Dr., El Cajon, Calif. 92021.

CAREER: Pastor of Baptist churches in Pickens, S.C., 1948-50, and in Minneapolis, Minn., 1950-56; Scott Memorial Baptist Church, El Cajon, Calif., senior pastor, 1956—. President of Christian Heritage College, 1970—; lecturer for Family Life Seminars, 1972—. *Military service:* U.S. Army Air Forces, 1944-46; became sergeant. *Awards, honors:* D.D. from Bob Jones University, 1962.

WRITINGS: Spirit-Controlled Temperaments, Tyndale House, 1966; *How to Be Happy Though Married,* Tyndale

House, 1968; *Transformed Temperaments*, Tyndale House, 1971; *The Beginning of the End*, Tyndale House, 1972; *How to Win Over Depression*, Zondervan, 1973; *Revelation Illustrated and Made Plain*, Zondervan, 1973; *The Act of Marriage*, Zondervan, 1976; *How to Study the Bible for Yourself*, Harvest House, 1976; *The Bible's Influence on American History*, Creation-Life Publishers, 1976.

WORK IN PROGRESS: Understanding the Male Temperament, for Revell.

SIDELIGHTS: From 1976 to 1977 LaHaye and his wife will be traveling with their Family Life Seminar to more than fifty population centers around the world. LaHaye also served on committees to help elect conservative Christians to public office. *Avocational interests:* Flying his own twin-engine plane, skiing, football.

* * *

LAING, Alexander (Kinnan) 1903-1976

August 7, 1903—April 23, 1976; American educator, librarian, poet, novelist, and author of non-fiction books. Obituaries: *New York Times*, April 24, 1976; *Washington Post*, April 25, 1976. (See index for previous *CA* sketch)

* * *

LAIRD, Melvin R(obert) 1922-

PERSONAL: Born September 1, 1922, in Omaha, Neb.; son of Melvin R. and Helen (Connor) Laird; married Barbara Masters, October 15, 1945; children: John Osborne, Alison, David Malcolm. *Education:* Carleton College, B.A., 1943. *Politics:* Republican. *Religion:* Presbyterian. *Home address:* P.O. Box 279, Marshfield, Wis. 54449. *Office:* Reader's Digest Association, Inc., 1730 Rhode Island Ave. N.W., Washington, D.C. 20036.

CAREER: Wisconsin State Senator, 1946-52, served as chairman of state legislative council; U.S. House of Representatives, Washington, D.C., congressman from 7th District, 1953-69, served on House Appropriations Committee, on Defense Appropriations Subcommittee, as ranking member of Labor and Health, Education, and Welfare Appropriations Subcommittee, and as chairman of Joint House-Senate Committee on Republican Principle and Policy; secretary of defense, 1969-73; domestic advisor to President Nixon, 1973-74; Reader's Digest, Pleasantville, N.Y., senior counsellor for national and international affairs, 1974—. Chairman of U.S. delegation to World Health Organization, 1953, 1963, and 1965; Republican National Convention platform committee, vice-chairman, 1960, chairman, 1964; chairman of Republican Congressional Conference, 1968-69. Member of board of directors, Chicago Pneumatic Tool Co., Metropolitan Life Insurance Co., Northwest Airlines, Communications Satellite Corp., Purolator Inc., Investors Group of Companies, and Phillips Petroleum Co.; trustee, George Washington University, Kennedy Center for the Performing Arts; chairman of the American Enterprise Institute National Defense Project. Elder of Presbyterian Church.

MILITARY SERVICE: U.S. Navy, 1942-46; became lieutenant (junior grade). Received Purple Heart, Asiatic-Pacific Ribbon with five battle stars, Philippine Liberation Medal with one battle star. *Member:* Disabled American Veterans, Veterans of Foreign Wars, American Legion, 40 et 8, Junior Chamber of Commerce, Masons, Elks. *Awards, honors:* Over 100 awards, including Albert Lasker award, Medal of Freedom (U.S.), Order of Merit—First Class (west Germany), and Commander, National Order of the Legion of Honor (France).

WRITINGS: A House Divided: America's Strategy Gap, Regnery, 1962; (author of introduction) *Conservative Papers*, Books for Libraries, 1964; (author of introduction) *Republican Papers*, Books for Libraries, 1968; (with others) *The Nixon Doctrine: Town Hall Meeting*, American Enterprise Publications, 1972. Contributor to periodicals.

* * *

LAKE, David J. 1929-

PERSONAL: Born March 26, 1929, in Bangalore, India; naturalized Australian citizen; son of William George (a merchant) and Norah (Babington) Lake; married Marguerite Ferris, December 30, 1964; children: Sarah; (stepchildren) Margarita, Anne, David. *Education:* Cambridge University, B.A., 1952, M.A., 1956; University College of North Wales, diploma in linguistics, 1965; University of Queensland, Ph.D., 1974. *Politics:* "Liberal/pragmatic." *Religion:* Ex-Catholic agnostic." *Home:* 7 Eighth Ave., St. Lucia, Brisbane, Queensland 4067, Australia. *Agent:* E. J. Carnell Agency, 17 Burwash Rd., London SE18 7QY, England. *Office:* Department of English, University of Queensland, St. Lucia, Brisbane, Queensland 4067, Australia.

CAREER: Teacher of English in Saigon, Vietnam, 1959-61, and in Bangkok, Thailand, 1961-63; university teacher in Calcutta, India, 1965-67; University of Queensland, Brisbane, Australia, lecturer, 1967-72, senior lecturer, 1973-76, reader in English, 1977—. *Military service:* British Army, gunner in Royal Artillery, 1948-49. *Member:* Queensland Council for Civil Liberties, Anti-Slavery and Aboriginals Protection Society (London; life member).

WRITINGS: John Milton: Paradise Lost, Mukhopadhyay, 1967; *Greek Tragedy*, Excelsus Academy, 1969; *Hornpipes and Funerals* (poems), University of Queensland Press, 1973; *The Canon of Thomas Middleton's Plays*, Cambridge University Press, 1975; *Walkers on the Sky* (science fiction novel), Daw Books, 1976; *The Right Hand of Dextra* (science fiction novel), Daw Books, in press; *The Wildings of Westron* (science fiction novel), Daw Books, in press; *The Gods of Xuma* (science fiction novel), Daw Books, in press. Contributor to *Notes and Queries*.

WORK IN PROGRESS: A science fiction novel; research on slavery and the status of women in the ancient world and in medieval Islam.

SIDELIGHTS: Lake writes that the most important influences on his writing are "my early life in India as the son of an imperialist family and a victim of the Christian sexual ethic; also, the writings of C. S. Lewis. In my novels my main preoccupations are beauty, sex, and religion, and in general the predicament of being a rational animal."

* * *

LAMBERG, Robert F(elix) 1929-

PERSONAL: Born October 23, 1929, in Reichenberg, Czechoslovakia; son of Axel L. (a professor) and Margit (Springer) Lamberg; married: Vera Bohac, April 10, 1954. *Education:* Charles University, Dr.Iur., 1952. *Home:* Avenida Atlantica, 1800, Copacabana, Rio de Janeiro, Brazil. *Office: Neue Zuercher Zeitung*, Zurich, Switzerland.

CAREER: Researcher and journalist in Western Europe and Latin America, 1957-69; Colegio de Mexico, Guanajuato, guest professor of Latin American politics and contemporary history, 1969-71; *Neue Zuercher Zeitung*, Zurich, Switzerland, foreign correspondent, 1971—, covering the American economic and financial situation, the United Nations, and the northern part of Latin America. *Member:* Foreign Correspondents Association (vice-president, 1975-76), United Nations Correspondents Association.

WRITINGS: Den Oekonomiske Intgrasjon i Oest-Europa (title means "Economic Integration in Eastern Europe"), Libertas (Oslo), 1963; *Prag und die Dritte Welt* (title means "Prague and the Third World"), Verlag fuer Literatur und Zeitgeschehen, 1965; *Die Guerilla in Lateinamerika* (title means "The Guerilla in Latin America"), Deutscher Taschenbuch Verlag, 1972.

WORK IN PROGRESS: A book, *Social Democracy and Latin America: A History of Continental "Aprismo,"* to be published in German.

*   *   *

LANCE, James Waldo 1926-

PERSONAL: Born October 29, 1926, in Wollongong, New South Wales, Australia; son of Waldo Garland (a company director) and Jessie (Forsyth) Lance; married Judith Lilian Logan, July 6, 1957; children: Fiona, Sarah, Jennifer, Robert, Sophie. *Education:* University of Sydney, M.B. and B.S., both 1950, M.D., 1955. *Home:* 15 Coolong Rd., Vaucluse, New South Wales 2030, Australia. *Office:* University of New South Wales, P.O. Box 1, Kensington, New South Wales 2033, Australia.

CAREER: Royal Prince Alfred Hospital, Sydney, Australia, resident medical officer, 1950-51; University of Sydney, Sydney, research fellow, 1952-53; Hammersmith Hospital, London, England, house physician, 1954; National Hospital for Nervous Diseases, London, assistant house physician, 1955; Sydney Hospital, Sydney, honorary house physician, 1956-60; Massachusetts General Hospital, Boston, research fellow, 1960-61; University of New South Wales, Kensington, Australia, senior lecturer in medicine, 1961-63, associate professor of medicine, 1964-75, professor of neurology, 1975—. Chairman of neurology division at Prince Henry Hospital, Sydney, 1961—. *Member:* World Federation of Neurology, Australian Association of Neurologists (member of council), American Association for the Study of Headache. *Awards, honors:* Harold G. Wolff Award from American Association for the Study of Headache, 1967; gold medal from British Migraine Association, 1975.

WRITINGS: The Mechanism and Management of Headache, Butterworth & Co., 1969, 2nd edition, 1973; *A Physiological Approach to Clinical Neurology,* Butterworth & Co., 1970, 2nd edition, 1975; *Headache,* Scribner, 1975; *The Golden Trout* (juvenile), Thomas Nelson, 1977.

WORK IN PROGRESS: The Mechanism and Management of Headache, third edition.

*   *   *

LANGER, Lawrence L(ee) 1929-

PERSONAL: Born June 20, 1929, in New York, N.Y.; son of Irving and Esther (Strauss) Langer; married Sondra Weinstein (an educator), February 21, 1951; children: Andrew, Ellen. *Education:* City College (now of the City University of New York), B.A., 1951; Harvard University, A.M., 1952, Ph.D., 1961. *Home:* 249 Adams Ave., West Newton, Mass. 02165. *Office:* Department of English, Simmons College, 300 Fenway, Boston, Mass. 02115.

CAREER: University of Connecticut, Storrs, instructor in

English, 1957-58; Simmons College, Boston, Mass., instructor, 1958-61, assistant professor, 1961-66, associate professor, 1966-72, professor of English, 1972—. Fulbright lecturer at University of Graz, 1963-64. Program associate in interdisciplinary studies at Institute for Services to Education. *Member:* Modern Language Association of America, American Association of University Professors, Phi Beta Kappa. *Awards, honors:* Pro Meritus medal from University of Graz, 1964.

WRITINGS: The Holocaust and the Literary Imagination, Yale University Press, 1975; *Beyond Atrocity: Perspectives on Death in Modern Literature,* Yale University Press, in press.

WORK IN PROGRESS: Research for *Children of the Holocaust* and *The Holocaust: Guilt and Survival.*

*   *   *

LANKFORD, T(homas) Randall 1942-

PERSONAL: Born August 7, 1942, in Texarkana, Tex.; son of Thomas Wilbur (a salesman) and Jeanette (a bank bookkeeper; maiden name, Farringer) Lankford; married Billie Jo Haynes (a biochemistry researcher), August 21, 1971. *Education:* Texas A & I University, B.S., 1965; Sam Houston State University, M.S., 1968; East Texas State University, graduate study. *Home:* 5071 Winding Way, Dickinson, Tex. 77539. *Office:* Department of Biology, Galveston College, 4015 Ave. Q, Galveston, Tex. 77551.

CAREER: Galveston College, Galveston, Tex., instructor in biology, 1968—. Chairman of Galveston County Environmental Coalition. *Member:* American Institute of Biological Sciences, American Association of University Professors, National Science Teachers Association, Texas Junior College Teachers Association.

WRITINGS: Integrated Science for Health Students, with laboratory manual and study guide (with Paige Dinn), Reston, 1976.

WORK IN PROGRESS: Integrated Science for Health Students, 2nd edition, completion expected in 1980.

*   *   *

LARSON, Cedric Arthur 1908-

PERSONAL: Born May 5, 1908, in Fond du Lac, Wis.; son of John J. and Augusta C. (Peterson) Larson; married Mildred June Vandenbergh (a church organist and choir director), May 6, 1944; children: Sandra (Mrs. Lynn F. Stiles), Judith Esther (Mrs. Steven Pipia), Peter. *Education:* Stanford University, A.B. (cum laude), 1935; George Washington University, A.M., 1938; graduate study, Columbia University, 1948-49, New York University, 1950-56, and City College of the City University of New York. *Politics:* Republican. *Religion:* Protestant. *Home:* 53 Arch Lane, Hicksville, N.Y. 11801.

CAREER: Library of Congress, Washington, D.C., accessions worker, 1935-37; high school teacher of history and band in Alexandria, Va., 1938-39; National Archives, Washington, D.C., worked in historical reference division, 1938-40; Home Owners Loan Corp., Washington, D.C. and New York City, personnel officer, 1941-42; U.S. Veterans Administration, personnel officer in Buffalo, N.Y., 1946-47, training officer in New York City, 1947-58; Rutgers University, Newark, N.J., university college instructor in psychology, 1955-74. Writer, 1948—. High school guidance director, 1958-60; school psychologist for New York State Board of Cooperative Educational Services, 1960-75. *Military ser-*

vice: U.S. Naval Reserve, personnel officer, on active duty, 1942-45.

MEMBER: Cheiron: International Society for the History of Behavioral and Social Sciences, Association for the Advancement of Behavior Therapy, American Psychological Association, Eastern Psychological Association, New York State Psychological Association, Nassau County Psychological Association, Suffolk County Psychological Association, Phi Beta Kappa, Kappa Delta Pi, Phi Delta Kappa. *Awards, honors:* American Philosophical Society grants, 1954 and 1974.

WRITINGS: (With James Mock) *Words That Won the War,* Princeton University Press, 1939; (contributor) G. H. Lundbeck, compiler, *The Will to Succeed: Stories of Swedish Pioneers,* Albert Bonnier, 1948; *Who: Sixty Years of American Eminence—The Story of Who's Who in America,* McDowell-Obolensky, 1958; (contributor) William Daugherty and Morris Janowitz, editors, *Psychological Warfare Casebook,* Johns Hopkins University Press, 1958; (contributor) H. Van Slooten and J. C. Bushman, editors, *Read and Write: Studies in Current Prose,* Harper, 1961; (contributor) V. S. Sexton and H. Misiak, editors, *Historical Perspectives in Psychology: Readings,* Wadsworth, 1971. Contributor to Scribner's *Dictionary of American Biography,* to journals in the behavioral and social sciences, and to national magazines, including *American Scholar, American Heritage,* and *Saturday Review.*

WORK IN PROGRESS: Research for a biography of John Broadus Watson, founder of behaviorism.

*   *   *

LARSON, George C(harles) 1942-

PERSONAL: Born March 31, 1942, in New Jersey; son of George Lester (an architect) and Mildred (Frehner) Larson; married Valerie Thompson, July 7, 1971. *Education:* Harvard University, A.B., 1964. *Residence:* Thousand Oaks, Calif. *Office: Flying,* 1 Park Pl., New York, N.Y. 10016.

CAREER: Medical World News, New York City, junior editor, beginning, 1966; *Scholastic,* New York City, staff writer, beginning, 1971; *Flying,* New York City, author of column "Westerlies," 1971—. Covered the 1976 Aerobatic Championships in Kiev. Has worked as a musician. *Military service:* U.S. Army, 1966-70; became captain; received Bronze Star. *Member:* Aerospace Writers Association.

WRITINGS: I Learned About Flying from That, Delacorte, 1976.

SIDELIGHTS: Larson is rated as a commercial single- and multi-engine instrument pilot.

*   *   *

LASKA, P. J. 1938-

PERSONAL: Born December 4, 1938, in Farmington, W.Va.; son of Lewis Olshewski (a miner) and Nellie (a store clerk; maiden name, Moshanko) Laska; married Ann Williams Yellott (divorced July 1, 1973); married Warene Jo Hobson (an artist) August 4, 1974; children: Stephen, Saro-Jane. *Education:* University of Maryland, B.A., 1964; graduate study University of Cincinnati, 1964-65; University of Rochester, Ph.D., 1968. *Home address:* Box 53, Prince, W.Va. 25907. *Office:* Antioch College/Appalachia, 107 Earwood St., Beckley, W.Va. 25801.

CAREER: York University, Toronto, Ontario, lecturer, 1968-69, assistant professor of humanities and philosophy,

1969-71; University of Arizona, Tuscon, assistant professor of philosophy, 1972-74; Antioch College/Appalachia, Beckley, W.Va., assistant professor of humanities and social sciences, 1974—. *Military service:* U.S. Air Force, 1956-60. *Member:* Hegel Society of America, West Virginia Labor History Association. *Awards, honors:* Younger Humanist fellow, 1971-72; National Book Award nominee, 1975, for *D.C. Images and Other Poems.*

WRITINGS: D.C. Images and Other Poems, Mountain Union Books, 1975; *Songs for a Severed Ear/Revolutionary Dances,* Mountain Union Books, 1977. Also editor, with Micael Rigsby, of a book of poems, *What's a Nice Hillbilly Like You . . .?,* 1975.

Work represented in *New Ground: Contemporary Writings from Southern Appalachia,* Southern Appalachian Writers Cooperative, 1976; and *Soupbean: An Anthology of Contemporary Appalachian Literature,* Moutain Union Books, 1977.

WORK IN PROGRESS: A novel, set in Appalachia and Washington, D.C., in the early sixties.

SIDELIGHTS: Laska told *CA:* "My early work was schooled by what Roger Taus has called 'William Carlos Williams' materialist poetics.' The imagist movement, of which Williams' work was the strongest part, was the starting point for a new American poetry. For me, the discipline of imagism is the starting point of poetic development. What follows is the development of extended forms that do not compromise the clarity and precision of this discipline. Again, it is a problem of poetric development, and it is one that has occupied me in writing *Songs for a Severed Ear/Revolutionary Dances.* Our fragmented forms are the reflection of our privatized, fragmented lives as a nation and a people. Now the pressures of our system are forcing change. We are discovering heritage and class, new forms of unity. The new movement in poetry is a movement toward revolutionary art:

> The dance of life and the dance of death
> are danced together
> with the sun and the moon
> in timeless movement
> through eternity.
> The dances of history are danced in darkness
> and the last dances before dawn
> are revolutionary dances.

*   *   *

LATHAM, Lorraine 1948-

PERSONAL: Born September 30, 1948, in Eta Jima, Japan; daughter of Peter Greig (an Australian Army officer) and Mary Ballantyne (Sanderson) Latham; married Norman Bogner (a writer), June 6, 1975. *Education:* Attended high school in Melbourne, Australia. *Politics:* Republican. *Religion:* Church of England. *Home:* 484 South Roxbury Dr., Beverly Hills, Calif. 90212. *Agent:* Paul Gitlin, 7 West 51st St., New York, N.Y. 10019.

CAREER: Hughes, Satchwell & Asso. (advertising agency), Melbourne, Australia, copywriter, 1967; Berry, Curry & Asso. (advertising agency), Melbourne, copywriter, 1968; Foote, Cone & Belding (advertising agency), Sydney, Australia, copywriter, 1968-69; Leo Burnett-L. P. E. (advertising agency), London, England, copywriter, 1969-70; Dorland Advertising, London, copywriter, 1969-70; free-lance consultant to advertising agencies in London, England, 1971-73; writer.

WRITINGS: *Identity Crisis* (a suspense novel), Morrow, 1975.

WORK IN PROGRESS: Filmscripts; novels.

SIDELIGHTS: Lorraine Latham is competent in Japanese, French, German, Italian, Malay, and Spanish.

* * *

LATNER, Pat Wallace
 See WALLACE, Pat

* * *

LATORRE, Dolores L(aguarta Blasco) 1903-

PERSONAL: Born May 2, 1903, in Huesca, Spain; came to United States in 1908, naturalized citizen, 1939; daughter of Praxedes Daniel Laguarta Laguarta and Dolores Blasco Morro de Laguarta; married Elza Marion Perry, June 21, 1927 (died May 21, 1941); married Felipe Augusto Latorre (a writer; former general in Chilean Air Force), August 26, 1944; children: (first marriage) Richard, Dolores Maria (Mrs. Ben Neubauer). Education: University of Texas, B.A., 1953; also studied at Columbia University, Universidad Nacional Autonoma de Mexico, University of San Marcos, and Southern Methodist University. Home: 3506 West Ave., Austin, Tex. 78705.

CAREER: Teacher of Spanish in high school in Galveston, Tex., 1923-27; worked for naval and army intelligence, 1941-42; writer, 1960—.

WRITINGS: (With husband, Felipe Latorre) *The Mexican Kickapoo Indians,* University of Texas Press, 1976; *Cooking and Curing with Herbs of Mexico,* Encino Press, in press. Contributor to anthropology journals.

WORK IN PROGRESS: *Myths, Stories, and Anecdotes of the Mexican Kickapoo Indians,* with husband, Felipe Latorre; *Ethnobotany of the Mexican Kickapoo Indians.*

SIDELIGHTS: Dolores Latorre spent twelve years studying Kickapoo Indians in Coahuila, Mexico. She has also traveled extensively throughout the world, and has visited archaeological sites from Caracas, Venezuela, to Rio de Janeiro, Brazil.

* * *

LATORRE, Felipe A(ugusto) 1907-

PERSONAL: Born December 16, 1907, in Linares, Chile; came to the United States in 1950; son of Santiago Y. (a physician) and Matilde E. (an educator; maiden name, Espinosa) Latorre; married Dolores Laguarta (an anthropologist), August 26, 1944; children: (stepchildren) Richard Perry, Dolores Maria (Mrs. Ben Neubauer). Education: Attended Columbia University, 1951; University of Texas, B.A., 1953; graduate study at University of Texas, 1954-56, and Universidad Nacional Autonoma de Mexico, 1957. Home: 3506 West Ave., Austin, Tex. 78705.

CAREER: Career officer in Chilean Air Force, 1926-50; conducted study of aeronautical organizations in United States and Europe, 1931, study of Chilean airline, 1934-39, and study of problems of Magallanes, Chile, 1942; named chief of crews at Kelly Field, 1943; secretary to commander in chief, 1945; director of aviation school, 1946; commander of air bases, 1948; professor at National Defence Academy, Santiago, Chile, 1949; director of services, 1950; retired as general, 1950. Writer, 1960—. Conducted field work on Kickapoo Islands in Coahuila, Mexico, 1960-72. *Member:* Sociedad Mexicana de Antropologia, Austin Committee on Foreign Relations, Heritage Society of Austin.

WRITINGS: (With wife, Dolores L. Latorre) *The Mexican Kickapoo Indians,* University of Texas Press, 1976. Contributor to anthropology journals.

WORK IN PROGRESS: *Myths, Stories, and Anecdotes of the Mexican Kickapoo Indians,* with wife, Dolores L. Latorre; research on the ethnobotany of the Mexican Kickapoo Indians.

SIDELIGHTS: Latorre has traveled all over the world, including the Orient, Europe, and the Iron Curtain countries.

* * *

LATZER, Beth Good 1911-

PERSONAL: Born April 30, 1911, in Brantford, Ontario, Canada; daughter of William Charles (a farmer and writer) and Jean (McCormick) Good; married Thomas F. Latzer (a business executive), January 1, 1938; children: Robert, Elizabeth, Margaret (Mrs. Bruce Grindley), Louis. *Education:* University of Toronto, B.A. (honors), 1936; Radcliffe College, A.M., 1937. *Politics:* Independent. *Religion:* Episcopalian. *Home:* 641 West Polo Dr., St. Louis, Mo. 63105.

CAREER: Writer. Has done local volunteer work.

WRITINGS: *Myrtleville: A Canadian Farm and Family, 1837-1967,* Southern Illinois University Press, 1976.

WORK IN PROGRESS: Research on a series of diaries kept by a young lawyer in London, England, during the 1830's.

SIDELIGHTS: Beth Latzer writes: "My first book may be called a retirement project which grew out of discovering many old letters and diaries in the houses of several elderly relatives. With time now available, I used my academic training and my life-long interest in history to research and write the story of *Myrtleville.* I was particularly well-equipped to do this because I lived at Myrtleville until I was grown, and have been there much of most summers since."

* * *

LAVELLE, Mike 1933-

PERSONAL: Born June 20, 1933, in New York; divorced; children: Lora, Danny. *Education:* Attended elementary school in Brooklyn, N.Y. *Politics:* "Classical liberal as opposed to modern." *Religion:* "Pantheist." *Home:* 919 West Altgeld, Chicago, Ill. 60614. *Office: Chicago Tribune,* 435 North Michigan Ave., Chicago, Ill. 60611.

CAREER: Traveled around United States and worked at odd jobs on farms and in factories; columnist for *Chicago Tribune,* Chicago, Ill. Member of local learning exchange. *Military service:* U.S. Navy, 1950-54.

WRITINGS: *Red, White and Blue Collar Views,* Saturday Review Press, 1976.

SIDELIGHTS: Lavelle writes that he builds his own furniture, explaining that "events can make writings look dumb in retrospect, whereas furniture's beauty can last forever barring fire and flood. History books are screwed up because not enough historians have ever been furniture makers, painters, sculptors, etc. Beard was a Marxist, Welles an atheist, and too many current historians are revisionists copping out to a liberal left zeitgeist that will not stand the test of time. Ideology and objective history are mutually exclusive. The passion of things belongs in novels."

* * *

LAVENDER, William 1921-

PERSONAL: Born December 23, 1921, in Elrod, Ala.; son

of Claude B. (a physician) and Maggie Mae (Neel) Lavender; married Mary Bridget Kanitz (a research assistant), June 4, 1949; children: Debra (Mrs. John Zaller), Lawrence, Randall. *Education:* Birmingham-Southern College, B.Mus., 1946; University of Southern California, M.Mus., 1949. *Politics:* Democrat. *Religion:* None. *Home:* 4210 Carney Court, Riverside, Calif. 92507. *Agent:* Mary Dolan, Gloria Safier Agency, 667 Madison Ave., New York, N.Y. 10021.

CAREER: Norton Air Force Base, Aerospace Audiovisual Service, San Bernardino, Calif., staff composer and supervisor of sound track recording for documentary film production center, 1950—. *Military service:* U.S. Army Air Forces, 1943-46; became sergeant. *Member:* American Federation of Musicians.

WRITINGS: Chinaberry (novel), Pyramid Publications, 1975; *Flight of the Seabird* (novel), Simon & Schuster, in press.

Musical plays: "The Invisible People," first produced in California at Northridge Theatre Guild, June 26, 1967; "Changing Times," first produced in Thousand Oaks, Calif., at California Lutheran College, March, 1971.

WORK IN PROGRESS: The Hargrave Journal, a three-volume historical novel, dealing with early America, Volume I: *Children of the River.*

SIDELIGHTS: Lavender writes that he has experienced, in the last ten years, a "gradual transition of creative energies from music to letters." He is presently interested in writing novels and books on American history.

*   *   *

LAVOIX, Jean
   See SAUVAGEAU, Juan

*   *   *

LAW, Janice
   See TRECKER, Janice Law

*   *   *

LAWLOR, Florine   1925-

PERSONAL: Born August 25, 1925, in Las Vegas, Nev.; daughter of Keith W. (a song writer) and Eileen (a legal secretary; maiden name, Morley) Erickson; married James Lawlor (a casino boxman), June 13, 1950; children: Jim, Jeff. *Education:* Attended Santa Monica City College, 1949, and Terrell's School of Prospecting and Minerals, 1965-66. *Residence:* Las Vegas, Nev. *Office address:* P.O. Box 5574, Las Vegas, Nev. 89102.

CAREER: Las Vegas Sun, Las Vegas, Nev., columnist, "Out From Las Vegas," 1967—; Indian exhibition promoter, 1971—; free-lance writer.

WRITINGS: Out From Las Vegas, La Siesta Press, 1969; *Indian Trails of Southern Nevada,* privately printed, in press. Contributor to *National Parks, Sunset, Desert, Nevada Outdoors, Eastern Sierra News,* and other magazines.

WORK IN PROGRESS: Two books, *Out From Las Vegas Again* and *Follow the Trails.*

AVOCATIONAL INTERESTS: The Mojave Desert—its people, animals, birds, plants.

*   *   *

LAWRENCE, John A.   1908-1976

August 24, 1908—April 9, 1976; Scottish-born American civil servant, jazz musician, and writer on music. Obituaries: *Washington Post,* April 13, 1976.

*   *   *

LAWRENCE, R(onald) D(ouglas)   1921-

PERSONAL: Born September 12, 1921, in Vigo. Spain; son of Thomas Edward and Esther (Rodriguez) Lawrence; married Joan Frances Gray, September 18, 1962 (died June 7, 1969); married Sharon Janet Frise (a teacher), December 16, 1973. *Education:* Educated at private school in Madrid, Spain, and by a private tutor. *Politics:* None. *Religion:* None. *Home and office:* 8 Lomond St., Suite 2003, Toronto, Ontario, Canada. *Agent:* Paul Reynolds, Inc., 12 East 41st St., New York, N.Y. 10017.

CAREER: Daily Mirror, London, England, journalist, 1945-54; trapper, logger, and cattle farmer on homestead in northern Ontario, 1954-57; *Free Press,* Winnipeg, Manitoba, night editor, 1957-61; *Telegram,* Toronto, Ontario, worked as reporter, entertainment and financial editor, and publisher of affiliate suburban weekly newspaper, 1960-70. *Military service:* British Army, Military Intelligence, Tank Corps, 1939-44. *Awards, honors:* Frank H. Kortright awards from Toronto Sportsman's Show, 1967 and 1968, for writing on conservation.

WRITINGS: Wildlife in Canada, M. Joseph, 1966; *The Place in the Forest,* M. Joseph, 1967; *Where the Water Lilies Grow,* M. Joseph, 1968; *The Poison Makers,* Thomas Nelson, 1968; *Maple Syrup,* Thomas Nelson, 1970; *Cry Wild,* Thomas Nelson, 1970; *Wildlife in North America: Mammals,* Chilton, 1974; *Wildlife in North America: Birds,* Chilton, 1974; *Orphan of the Wild,* Knopf, 1976. Contributor to education pamphlets and magazines.

WORK IN PROGRESS: Research on man and his environment, ecology, biology, conservation, and animals.

SIDELIGHTS: Lawrence writes: "The single most potent motive force is my consuming interest in living things, from mouse to man, and it was on this subject that I wrote a diary of wildlife seen which I later expanded into my first book. . . . I have travelled on expedition extensively in Canada and the U.S.A. in hinterland, usually northern areas, also in Central America and Africa."

*   *   *

LAWRENCE, Sharon   1945-

PERSONAL: Born July 31, 1945, in Los Angeles, Calif.; daughter of Jean Castle (a sportswriter) and Margaret (a model; maiden name, Lennartz). *Education:* Attended University of California at Los Angeles, 1961-63. *Politics:* Democrat. *Religion:* Protestant. *Home:* 3177 Lindo St., Hollywood, Calif. 90068. *Agent:* Dorothy Pittman, John Cushman & Associates, 25 West 43rd St., New York, N.Y. 10036.

CAREER: United Press International, Los Angeles, Calif., feature writer, 1965-70; public relations and management consultant to musical groups including Rolling Stones, Beatles, Lynyrd Skynyrd, Elton John, and others, 1970—; writer.

WRITINGS: So You Want to Be a Rock and Roll Star, Dell, 1976. Contributor of articles to *Los Angeles Free Press, Sounds,* and *Ladies Home Journal.*

WORK IN PROGRESS: Telling Secrets, a book about the growth of contemporary American record industry and the rise and fall of artists and executives therein.

SIDELIGHTS: "I am primarily writing," Lawrence told CA, "about the emotions, goals, creativity and handicaps of everyone involved in the music world, including the influence of and on the audience."

* * *

LAWSON, James 1938-

PERSONAL: Born December 8, 1938, in New York, N.Y.; son of Marcel James (an advertising executive) and Renata May (an interior decorator; maiden name, Hyams) Eysler; married Katharine Frances Rieke (a Ph.D. candidate in biopsychology), December 28, 1968. Education: Attended Sorbonne, University of Paris, 1959-60; Boston University, B.A., 1961. Home: 756 Greenwich St., New York, N.Y. 10014. Agent: John Schaffner, 425 East 51st St., New York, N.Y. 10022. Office: Doyle Dane Bernbach, 437 Madison Ave., New York, N.Y. 10022.

CAREER: McCann-Marschalk, New York, N.Y., advertising copywriter, 1962-63; J. Walter Thompson, New York City, advertising copywriter, 1963-64; Al Paul Lefton, Philadelphia, Pa., advertising copywriter, 1964-65; Doyle Dane Bernbach, New York City, vice-president, 1966—. Reporter for Aspen Times, 1963. Awards, honors: About seventy advertising awards from organizations and publications, including New York Art Director's Club, Cannes and Venice Festivals. Received Cleo Awards.

WRITINGS: The Girl Watcher (novel), Putnam, 1976.

WORK IN PROGRESS: The Golden Days Conspiracy, a novel, publication by Putnam expected in 1978; Eleventh Street, a novel set in Greenwich Village; a novel, as yet untitled, about "three generations of a weird family"; Among the Tyuu, "an anthropological hoax."

SIDELIGHTS: Lawson writes: "I had started a dozen books and finished five before I got one published. Some were pure therapy, dealing with whatever I was afraid of the most, others pure fun, some fantasies, others stories I had to tell." Avocational interests: Classical music, ballet, travel, playing squash.

* * *

LAYBOURNE, Lawrence E. 1914(?)-1976

1914(?)—February 12, 1976; American newsman, editor, and magazine executive. Obituaries: Washington Post, April 13, 1976.

* * *

LAYMAN, Richard 1947-

PERSONAL: Born September 7, 1947, in Louisville, Ky.; son of Lewis L. (a production supervisor) and Mary A. (a systems analyst) Layman; married Nancy Staats (a teacher), May 12, 1973. Education: Indiana University, student, 1965-68; University of Louisville, B.A., 1971, M.A., 1972; University of South Carolina, Ph.D., 1975. Politics: None. Religion: None. Home: 3943 Live Oak St., Columbia, S.C. 29205. Office: Department of English, University of South Carolina, Columbus, S.C. 29208.

CAREER: University of South Carolina, Columbus, assistant to the director of the Center for Editions of American Authors, 1975—. Member: Modern Language Association of America, South Atlantic Modern Language Association.

WRITINGS: (Contributor and volume editor) Matthew J. Bruccoli, C. E. Frazer Clark, Jr., and others, editors, First Printings of American Authors, Volume I, Gale, 1975; (with Bruccoli) Ring Lardner: A Descriptive Bibliography, University of Pittsburgh Press, 1976; (editor with Bruccoli) Some Champions: Previously Uncollected Fiction and Autobiographical Non-Fiction by Ring Lardner, Scribner, 1976. Associate editor, Fitzgerald/Hemingway Annual, 1976—. Contributor to literary journals.

WORK IN PROGRESS: Editing a book of criticism on Ring Lardner; compiling a descriptive bibliography of Dashiell Hammett.

SIDELIGHTS: Layman wrote: "Bibliography is the basis of all literary criticism. It is impossible to discuss an author's career unless you know what he wrote."

* * *

LAZELL, James Draper, Jr. 1939-

PERSONAL: Born September 5, 1939, in New York, N.Y.; son of James Draper (a businessman) and Katee (in porcelain restoration; maiden name, Quin) Lazell; children: Bonny. Education: University of the South, B.A., 1961; University of Illinois, M.S., 1963; Harvard University, M.A., 1966; University of Rhode Island, Ph.D., 1970. Politics: Libertarian. Religion: Atheist. Home: Drumlin Farm, Lincoln, Mass. 01773. Office: Massachusetts Audubon Society, Lincoln, Mass. 01773.

CAREER: Massachusetts Audubon Society, member of scientific staff, 1966—. Science teacher and head of department at Palfrey Street School in Watertown, Mass., 1966-74; collaborator with National Park Service, 1969—. Member: American Society of Ichthyologists and Herpetologists, American Society of Mammalogists, American Society of Zoologists, American Association for the Advancement of Science, Federation of American Scientists, Sierra Club, Zero Population Growth, Philadelphia Zoological Society.

WRITINGS: The Anoles (Sauria: Iquaridae) of the Lesser Antilles, Harvard University, Museum of Comparative Zoology, 1972; Reptiles and Amphibians in Massachusetts (pamphlet), Massachusetts Audubon Society, 1972, revised edition, 1974; This Broken Archipelago, Quadrangle, 1976. Contributor of about forty articles to scientific periodicals.

WORK IN PROGRESS: Raccoons; New England Conservation; Island Biogeography; Ecological Effects of Acid Precipitation.

SIDELIGHTS: Lazell began as a field biologist, ecologist, and herpetologist. It is only recently that he has turned to mammalogy. He writes: "I am a biological conservationist primarily concerned with preserving endangered species and habitats. I believe human overpopulation is the root cause of all the Earth's problems, and that all other issues are near-trivial side effects of overpopulation. I believe in eugenics and would like to live in a laissez-faire meritocracy."

* * *

LAZENBY, Walter S(ylvester), Jr. 1930-

PERSONAL: Born October 8, 1930, in Del Rio, Tex.; son of Walter Sylvester (an accountant) and Ruby Inez (Coleman) Lazenby; married Sharon Pearson, April 8, 1958 (divorced, 1974); children: Brenda, Keith, Allison. Education: Southwestern at Memphis, B.A., 1951; Yale University, M.A., 1953; Indiana University, Ph.D., 1962. Politics: Democrat. Religion: Unitarian-Universalist. Home: 1527 Second St., Charleston, Ill. 61920. Office: Department of English, Eastern Illinois University, Charleston, Ill. 61920.

CAREER: Kentucky Wesleyan College, Owensboro, instructor, 1954-55, assistant professor, 1955-56; Kinkaid School, Houston, Tex., instructor, 1956-57; North Texas State University, Denton, assistant professor, 1957-61, associate professor, 1961-67, professor, 1967-69; Eastern Illinois University, Charleston, professor of English, 1969—. *Military service:* U.S. Navy, 1952-54. *Member:* Phi Beta Kappa.

WRITINGS: Paul Green (monograph pamphlet), Steck, 1970; *Arthur Wing Pinero,* Twayne, 1972. Contributor to *Modern Drama* and *Quarterly Journal of Speech.* Theater reviewer for *Times-Courier,* Charleston, Ill., 1974—.

*   *   *

LEADER, Charles
   See SMITH, Robert Charles

*   *   *

LEAMER, Laurence Allen   1941-

PERSONAL: Born October 30, 1941, in Chicago, Ill.; son of Laurence E. (a professor) and Helen (a librarian; maiden name, Burkey) Leamer; married Eliana Robitschek (an educator), September 12, 1968; children: Daniela. *Education:* University of Besancon, diploma, 1962; Antioch College, B.A., 1964; University of Oregon, M.A., 1968; Columbia University, M.S., 1969. *Home and office:* 5301 Bangor Dr., Kensington, Md. 20795. *Agent:* Ann Buchwald.

CAREER: U.S. Peace Corps, volunteer worker in Nepal, 1964-66; Columbia University, New York, N.Y., international fellow, 1968-69; *Newsweek,* New York, N.Y., associate editor, 1969-70; free-lance writer, 1970—. Consultant to National Committee for an Effective Congress. *Awards, honors:* Ford Foundation fellowship, 1966-68; Pulitzer travel fellow, 1969; Citation from Overseas Press Club, 1973, for article "Bangladesh in Morning"; new contributor award (2nd place) from *Playboy,* 1973, for "Last of the Coal Barons".

WRITINGS: The Paper Revolutionaries: The Rise of the Underground Press, Simon & Schuster, 1972; *Playing for Keeps in Washington,* Dial, 1977. Contributor to magazines, including *Playboy, New York Times Magazine, Harper's, New Times, New Republic,* and *New Leader,* and to newspapers. Contributing editor of *Washingtonian,* 1975—.

*   *   *

LEAVITT, Harvey R(obert)   1934-

PERSONAL: Born July 8, 1934, in St. Paul, Minn.; son of Edward E. (a merchant) and Pearl (Makiesky) Leavitt; married Carol Beaulieu, August 31, 1962; children: David Edward, Robin Sue. *Education:* Attended State University of Iowa, 1952-56; Municipal University of Omaha (now University of Nebraska at Omaha), B.G.E., 1966, M.A., 1968; graduate study at University of Nebraska, Lincoln, 1968-72. *Home:* 822 South 59th St., Omaha, Neb. 68106. *Office:* Department of English, University of Nebraska at Omaha, 60th and Dodge, Omaha, Neb. 68106.

CAREER: Self-employed as stockbroker and automotive supplies salesman in Fort Dodge, Iowa, 1956-64; Wisconsin State University, Eau Claire, instructor in English, 1966-68; University of Nebraska at Omaha, assistant professor of English, 1968-75, ombudsman, 1975—. Lecturer. President of Interracial Commission, Fort Dodge, 1963; citizen advisory board member of Metro Area Planning Agency, 1974—; task force member of Develop Growth and Development Alternatives for five-county region, 1976, and of Cit-

izens Committee to Review Urban Development Policy, 1976. *Member:* Sigma Tau Delta. *Awards, honors:* Named regional humanist by Nebraska Committee for the Humanities, 1976.

WRITINGS: (Editor and author of introduction) *Riverfront: The Humanist Speaks,* University of Nebraska at Omaha, 1976. Contributor to *Critique.*

WORK IN PROGRESS: Research on current critical modes for reevaluating literature in terms of contemporary assumptions; models of idealism research in an effort to discover useful humanistic models and explain them to a pragmatic society.

SIDELIGHTS: Leavitt told *CA:* "I am essentially motivated by the failure of the humanities to have a significant impact on contemporary American life. I am attempting to reach wider audiences than the humanities have traditionally sought in an effort to help establish different criteria for measuring the quality of life. I am both a pragmatist in that I am willing to communicate with the decision-makers and to help with the decision processes, and an idealist who holds up models of humanistic achievement as a device to measure contemporary achievement. It is often a lonely task because my overview of the aesthetic, socio-psychological ambience of the region and nation makes me suspect in the eyes of more traditional scholars in the humanities, and my penchant for holding up idealistic models before the pragmatists often creates discomfort for them as they measure their view of the possible against a humanistic standard. I don't know if I am perceived as a kind of gentle crackpot or an idealist, but I continue to be called upon to make my contribution. Human dignity and life are enhanced or diminished in a variety of ways, and I have found my current interest in the land and setting an area of genuine humanistic concern."

*   *   *

LEDERER, Charles   1910-1976

December 31, 1910—March 5, 1976; American stage and film producer, and author of screenplays. Obituaries: *New York Times,* March 7, 1976; *Washington Post,* March 10, 1976.

*   *   *

LEE, George J.   1920(?)-1976

1920(?)—March 10, 1976; American museum curator, expert on Oriental art, and author. Obituaries: *New York Times,* March 15, 1976.

*   *   *

LEE, Malka   1905(?)-1976

1905(?)—March 22, 1976; American author of stories and poems in Yiddish. Obituaries: *New York Times,* March 24, 1976.

*   *   *

LEE, Norma E.   1924-

PERSONAL: Born August 28, 1924, in Ross County, Ohio; daughter of John Edward (a farmer) and Geraldine (Gates) Hardy; married Bruce Emery Lee (an accountant), May 22, 1948; children: Rhonda Carol, Randall Dale, Janice Elaine. *Education:* Educated in public high school in Frankfort, Ohio. *Politics:* Republican. *Religion:* Presbyterian. *Home and office:* 192 Cherokee Way, Boulder, Colo. 80303. *Agent:* Ruth Cantor, 156 Fifth Ave., New York, N.Y. 10010.

CAREER: U.S. Government, Wright Field, Dayton, Ohio, stenographer, 1943-45; National Fireworks, Inc., Chillicothe, Ohio, secretary, 1945; *Welding Engineer*, Chicago, Ill., secretary, 1946-48; free-lance writer, 1963—. *Member:* Society of Children's Book Authors, Colorado Authors League. *Awards, honors:* Top Hand Award from Colorado Authors League, 1972, for article "Only a Hill."

WRITINGS: *Chewing Gum* (picture book), Prentice-Hall, 1976. Contributor of about fifty articles and stories to children's and education magazines, religious periodicals, and national magazines, including *National Observer*.

WORK IN PROGRESS: Research for *The Great Cleanup* (tentative title), a book about soap; a juvenile novel.

SIDELIGHTS: Norma Lee writes: "In this age of world tensions, moral decline, silly philosophy, people take themselves too seriously. We worry too much. I'd like to help people to laugh, even when they don't want to. I find humor very difficult to sell, possibly because editors can't laugh, either." *Avocational interests:* Flower gardening, sewing, nature study, "trying to coax music from my guitar," "dabbling in pastels."

* * *

LEE, Patrick C(ornelius) 1936-

PERSONAL: Born May 20, 1936, in Marion, Ind.; son of Dennis R. (a salesman) and Mary (a secretary; maiden name, Hickey) Lee. *Education:* St. Peter's College, A.B., 1958; Syracuse University, Ph.D., 1966. *Agent:* Berenice Hoffman, 215 West 75th St., New York, N.Y. 10023. *Office:* Department of Early Childhood Education, Teachers College, Columbia University, New York, N.Y. 10027.

CAREER: Harvard University, Cambridge, Mass., research associate, 1966-68; Columbia University, New York, N.Y., assistant professor, 1968-72, associate professor of early childhood education, 1972—. Consultant to children's television program, "Captain Kangaroo," 1971-73. *Military service:* U.S. Army, 1959-60; became lieutenant. *Member:* National Association for the Education of Young Children, Society for Research in Child Development.

WRITINGS: (Contributor) Shirley Cohen and Nancy Koehler, editors, *Implications of Recent Research in Early Child Development for Special Education,* Division for Handicapped Children, New York State Department of Education, 1974; (contributor) H. D. Lindgren, editor, *Children's Behavior: An Introduction to Research Studies,* Mayfield, 1975; (editor with R. S. Stewart) *Sex Differences: Cultural and Developmental Dimensions,* Urizen Books, 1976; (contributor) R. D. Parke and E. M. Hetherington, editors, *Child Psychology: Contemporary Readings,* McGraw, 1976. Contributor of articles and reviews to education journals.

WORK IN PROGRESS: Research on children's perceptions of their rights and on the economic socialization of children; *Prosocial Development in Children.*

AVOCATIONAL INTERESTS: Hiking, climbing, camping, outdoor living, travel.

* * *

LEE, Tom(my L.) 1950-

PERSONAL: Born March 7, 1950, in Grand Rapids, Mich.; son of Howard (a factory supervisor) and Yvonne (Sperry) Lee; married, wife's name, Benita. *Education:* Attended Grand Rapids Junior College, 1968, Grand Valley State Col-

lege, 1972. *Home:* 2472 Abbington Dr. S.E., Grand Rapids, Mich. 49506.

CAREER: Writer and independent communications and public relations consultant actively involved in the development, funding, and execution of major art products, 1971—. *Member:* The Author's Guild, Author's League of America. *Awards, honors:* Mead Book Award, 1971, for *Black Portrait of an African Journey.*

WRITINGS: *Black Portrait of an African Journey,* Eerdmans, 1971; *Le Senegal: Perspective d'un artiste* (title means "Senegal: An Artist's Perspective"), U.S. Information Service, 1971; (with Paul Collins) *Other Voices,* Native American Education Committee, 1975. Also author of motion picture scripts, "Guru of Vindhya" and "The President." Contributor of articles to periodicals, including *La Revue Moderne, Dakar-Matin, African Progress,* and *Soleil.*

WORK IN PROGRESS: A book, *Great Kings of Africa;* a novel, *The African;* a book about Americans at work.

SIDELIGHTS: Lee told *CA:*"In my fiction and non-fiction, I want to show—and perhaps reassure myself—that people, of every culture and language, share sorrow, anguish and the problems of survival, and yet are able to live and grow and retain their essential humaneness. Harsh circumstances do not necessarily create harsh spirits. I write only of people, people of simplicity, people who are born and who die but who try to do some good—something of value for others—in between. It's that simple. Or complex. Depending upon your point of view."

Mr. Lee lived in West Africa for two years, a venture that he says resulted in *Black Portrait of an African Journey.* His experiences among the Oglala Sioux, he writes, "are largely responsible for my contributions to *Other Voices,* a simple, direct artistic and literary view of a remarkable people."

BIOGRAPHICAL/CRITICAL SOURCES: *La Revue Moderne,* April 1, 1971; *Ebony,* October, 1971.

* * *

LEEMING, Owen (Alfred) 1930-

PERSONAL: Born August 1, 1930, in Christchurch, New Zealand; son of Ernest (a pictorial artist) and Ida (Collings) Leeming. *Education:* University of Canterbury, B.A., 1951, M.A., 1952, further graduate study in Paris, 1954-55. *Home:* 21 Rue de la Liberte, 13980 Alleins, France.

CAREER: New Zealand Broadcasting Service, Christchurch, announcer, 1953-54; worked as a salesman, television gossip-column writer, and box-office clerk, 1955-56; British Broadcasting Corp. (BBC), London, producer of talks and documentary presentations, 1956-59, worked on "Third Programme" (on literary and poetry output), 1959-62; New Zealand Broadcasting Corp., Wellington, producer of television documentary programs and dramas, 1963-64; UNESCO, Paris, France, expert on educational television project in Senegal, 1965-66; free-lance writer in France, 1967-71; UNESCO, expert on population control and the media in Malaysia, 1971-72; writer and real estate salesman in France, 1973—. Has worked as theatrical director since 1952. *Awards, honors:* Katherine Mansfield Menton Memorial Fellowship, 1970.

WRITINGS: *Venus Is Setting* (poems), Caxton Press, 1972.

Plays: "White Gardenia" (biography), New Zealand Broadcasting Corp. Television, 1968; "Order" (radio Play),

British Broadcasting Corp., 1969; "The Quarry Game" (two-act), first produced in Wellington, New Zealand, at Downstage Theatre, November 30, 1969; "Yellow" (radio play), New Zealand Broadcasting Corp., 1970; "Reefer's Boys" (radio play), British Broadcasting Corp., 1971; "The Sanctum" (radio play), New Zealand Broadcasting Corp., 1975.

Work represented in anthologies, including *Recent Poetry in New Zealand*, edited by Charles Doyle, Collins, 1965; *An Anthology of Twentieth Century New Zealand Poetry*, edited by Vincent O'Sullivan, Oxford University Press, 1970, 2nd edition, 1976; and *London Magazine Stories, 1970*, edited by Alan Ross, London Magazine Editions. Contributor of articles, stories, and poems to *London Magazine, Landfall*, and *Islands*.

WORK IN PROGRESS: "Les Visages Detruits" (title means "Broken Faces"), a television play.

SIDELIGHTS: Leeming told *CA:* "It is probably the early example of my father, a battling, sense-loving, amazingly inventive man, which propelled me towards a life of trying to produce more than I consume. Otherwise, there have been few exceptional tensions to drive me towards the writing-desk. True, between a stable childhood in the 'perfect' country and my present peaceful existence in a French village, I have lived fairly unconventionally, what with exotic travel, and all the years spent in theatres, television and radio studios on different sides of the planet. Rather as UNESCO picked on me, on up-till-now bachelor, to work on family planning problems in Asia, so couples, families, politics, and various forms of alienation turn up regularly as the subjects of my plays and fiction.

"My impression is that I have a very transparent, immediate view of the world. As a result, my writing no doubt tends to be straight, direct, or even 'earnest,' as one London *Times Literary Supplement* reviewer recently condescended. Still, the world I think I see is a complex place, and I should be wary of confusing directness with simple-mindedness. My goal, one of them anyway, is to give solid dramatic shape to some of the manifestations of human vitality. No message in this—although it would be pleasant to hint at an underlying neo-pagan morality. So far, I feel I have turned out some worthwhile stuff, but the best is hopefully to come, as I suspect I am 'a late developer.'"

AVOCATIONAL INTERESTS: Playing tennis, bridge, piano, and chamber music.

BIOGRAPHICAL/CRITICAL SOURCES: Kendrick Smithyman, *A Way of Saying*, Whitcombe & Tombs, 1965.

*   *   *

LEES, Francis A(nthony)   1931-

PERSONAL: Born January 19, 1931, in Brooklyn, N.Y.; son of Roy A. (a banker) and Mary A. (Oszuscowitz) Lees; married Kathryn Veronica Murphy, June 6, 1959; children: Veronica, Francis, Daniel, Jeanette Marie. *Education:* Brooklyn College (now of the City University of New York), B.A., 1952; St. Louis University, M.A., 1953; New York University, Ph.D., 1961. *Religion:* Roman Catholic. *Home:* 192 Coolidge Dr., East Meadow, N.Y. 11554.

CAREER: Fordham University, New York, N.Y., instructor in economics and finance, 1956-60; St. John's University, Jamaica, N.Y., assistant professor, 1960-61, associate professor, 1962-65, professor of economics and finance, 1965—. *Military service:* U.S. Army, 1953-56. *Member:* American Association of University Professors,

American Finance Association, Academy of International Business, Eastern Finance Association.

WRITINGS: (With Nicholas K. Bruck) *Foreign Investment, Capital Controls, and the Balance of Payments* (monograph), Institute of Finance, New York University, 1968; *International Banking and Finance*, Macmillan, 1974; (with Maximo Eng) *International Financial Markets*, Praeger, 1975; *Foreign Banking and Investments in the United States*, Macmillan, 1976; (with Hugh Brooks) *Economics and Political Development of the Sudan*, Macmillan, in press. Contributor to economics, business, and banking journals.

WORK IN PROGRESS: Research on petrodollar competition in international financial markets; a case study on foreign investment in the United States.

SIDELIGHTS: In addition to the professional interests indicated by the titles of his books, Lees is concerned with the place of the United States in world politics. He has traveled in the Sudan, Egypt, and Europe.

*   *   *

LEGEZA, (Ireneus) Laszlo   1934-

PERSONAL: Born June 25, 1934, in Debrecen, Hungary; son of Ireneus (a doctor of political science) and Gizella (Kovesi) Legeza; married Ilona Iren Levai, February 18, 1957. *Education:* Eoetvoes Lorand Tudomanyegyetem, B.A. (honors), 1956; University of London, B.A. (honors), 1960. *Religion:* Taoist. *Home:* 52 Ashdown Ave., Durham DH1 1DD, England. *Office:* Gulbenkian Museum of Oriental Art and Archaeology, University of Durham, Durham, England.

CAREER: University of Durham, Durham, England, assistant librarian and Chinese cataloger, 1963-67, deputy curator of Gulbenkian Museum of Oriental Art and Archaeology, 1967—. *Member:* Oriental Ceramic Society (London; member of council, 1973—). *Awards, honors:* Ford scholar at University of London, 1960-63.

WRITINGS: Guide to Transliterated Chinese in the Modern Peking Dialect, two volumes, E. J. Brill, 1968-69; *A Descriptive and Illustrated Catalogue of the Malcolm MacDonald Collection of Chinese Ceramics*, Oxford University Press, 1972; (with Philip Rawson) *Tao: The Chinese Philosophy of Time and Change*, Avon, 1973; *Tao Magic*, Pantheon, 1975. General editor of "Oxford in Asia in Ceramics," Oxford University Press (Kuala Lumpur), 1973—. Contributor to art magazines.

WORK IN PROGRESS: Chinese Taoist Art; Chinese ceramic studies.

SIDELIGHTS: Legeza's books on Tao have been published in French, German, and Dutch. *Avocational interests:* Foreign travel, languages, cooking.

*   *   *

LEGGITT, (Samuel) Hunter (Jr.)   1935-

PERSONAL: Born December 24, 1935, in Marshall, Mich.; son of Samuel Hunter (civil engineer) and Mildred E. (a teacher; maiden name, Pace) Leggitt; married Carol McClurg, 1957 (divorced, 1964); married Mary Goodrich Curran, 1965 (divorced, 1972); married Darla Kesler Passwaters, 1975; children: (second marriage) Richard Ives, Margaret Goodrich. *Education:* University of Texas, B.A., 1957; Starr King School for the Ministry, M.Div., 1960; currently attending Gestalt Institute of Chicago. *Politics:* Democrat. *Home:* 3163 North Pine Grove Ave., Chicago, Ill. 60657.

CAREER: Ordained Unitarian-Universalist clergyman, 1960; pastor of churches in Oneonta, N.Y., 1960-64, and Chicago, Ill., 1964-70; Trust, Inc. (To Reshape Urban Systems Together), Chicago, Ill., administrative assistant, 1970-76; free-lance writer, 1976—. Director, Southwest Chicago Draft Counseling Center, 1965-69, and of Chicago Committee to Defend the Bill of Rights, 1966-69. *Member:* Unitarian-Universalist Ministers Association, Amnesty International, American Association of Sex Educators, Counselors, and Therapists.

WRITINGS: (With Lonny Myers) *Adultery and Other Private Matters,* Nelson-Hall, 1975; (editor) *Managing Chicago's Urban Dollar,* Trust, Inc., 1976. Contributor to *Sexual Behavior.* Editor of booklets for Trust, Inc.

SIDELIGHTS: Leggitt told *CA* he is continuing his education in the fields of human sexuality and gestalt approaches to human problem solving.

* * *

LEHR, Paul E(dwin) 1918-

PERSONAL: Born January 26, 1918, in Boston, Mass.; son of Joseph (a sign painter) and Pearl (Crown) Lehr; married Adele Fred (a teacher), April 7, 1946; children: Janet, Carol. *Education:* Empire State College of the State University of New York, B.S., 1973. *Residence:* Silver Spring, Md. *Office:* Environmental Data Service, National Oceanic and Atmospheric Agency, Washington, D.C. 20235.

CAREER: U.S. Air Force, civilian airways weather forecaster, 1940-48, civilian instructor in meteorology and mathematics, 1948-52, meteorologist and analyst in Washington, D.C., 1952-58, meteorological researcher in Belleville, Ill., 1958-61; National Environmental Satellite Service, Washington, D.C., meteorologist, 1961-70; Environmental Data Service of National Oceanic and Atmospheric Administration, Washington, D.C., scientific review editor, 1970—. Instructor at U.S. Department of Agriculture Graduate School, 1963—. *Military service:* U.S. Army Air Forces, 1937-46; became warrant officer. *Member:* American Meteorological Society, National Weather Association.

WRITINGS: (With R. Will Burnett and Herbert S. Zim) *Weather,* Golden Press, 1957, 3rd edition, 1975; *Storms,* Golden Press, 1966, 2nd edition, 1969; (with Lester F. Hubert) *Weather Satellites,* Blaisdell, 1967. Contributor to meteorology journals. Editor of World Meteorological Organization *Technical Note.*

WORK IN PROGRESS: A general text on weather and climate.

SIDELIGHTS: Lehr writes: "My major interest in writing is to bring scientific subjects of considerable complexity to the general reader in a form understandable to those with little or no scientific background. *Weather* has been translated into six European languages."

* * *

LEIBY, Adrian C(oulter) 1904-1976

December 16, 1904—February 16, 1976; American attorney, historian, and author of books in his field. Obituaries: *New York Times,* February 18, 1976; *AB Bookman's Weekly,* April 12, 1976. (*CAP*-1; earlier sketch in *CA*-9/10)

LEIKIND, Morris C. 1906(?)-1976

1906(?)—March 15, 1976; American educator, archivist, medical historian, and writer on scientific subjects. Obituaries: *New York Times,* March 20, 1976; *AB Bookman's Weekly,* July 5, 1976.

* * *

LEISTER, Mary 1917-

PERSONAL: Surname is pronounced *Lye*-ster; born October 4, 1917, in Brackenridge, Pa.; daughter of W. Clare and Martha (Nolf) McFarland; married Robert E. Leister (an electronics engineer), June 4, 1942. *Education:* Attended Johns Hopkins University. *Residence:* Sykesville, Md.

CAREER: Writer. Has worked as a stenographer and volunteer elementary school teacher. *Member:* International Wildlife Association, National Wildlife Association, National Audubon Society, Natural History Association, Environmental Defense Fund, Maryland Ornithological Society.

WRITINGS: The Silent Concert (juvenile), Bobbs-Merrill, 1970; *Wildlings* (adult nonfiction), Stemmer House, 1976; *Flying Fur, Fins, and Scales: Strange Animals that Swoop and Soar,* Stemmer House, 1977. Author of columns in *Baltimore Sunday Sun,* 1972—, and "Read Aloud Nature Story," in *Humpty Dumpty,* 1976—. Contributor of stories, articles, and poems to nature and children's magazines, including *Ranger Rick, Boys' Life, Jack and Jill, National Wildlife,* and *American Forests.*

WORK IN PROGRESS: Children's books, mainly concerned with nature and wildlife; an adult book about India.

SIDELIGHTS: Mary Leister writes: "With a deep belief in the inter-relatedness, the oneness, of all life—and believing that, possibly, everything is alive—I write of animals, and plants, and weather, and water, and earth that others may learn to love all those things that share our small planet, and accord them the right to grow and to be. I realize that this is a closed system, that one species must prey upon another, that all life lives upon life, but it should be done respectfully and not wantonly. However, mostly my writing is light and happy and makes creatures interesting to humans because of the out-of-the-ordinary observations I have been permitted to make."

AVOCATIONAL INTERESTS: Camping, hiking, traveling, reading, gardening, dogs, cats, public speaking, good conversation.

BIOGRAPHICAL/CRITICAL SOURCES: Baltimore Sunday Sun, June 20, 1976; *Valley News Dispatch,* July 27, 1976; *New York Times,* August 7, 1976; *National Wildlife Federation Conservation News,* September 15, 1976; *Detroit Free Press,* October 24, 1976.

* * *

LEMMON, Kenneth 1911-

PERSONAL: Born May 13, 1911, in York, England; son of Rowland (a businessman) and Margaret (Dodsworth) Lemmon; married Madge Clough, June 10, 1936; children: Frank Stuart, Margaret Elizabeth Diane. *Education:* Attended Leeds School of Commerce. *Religion:* Methodist. *Home:* 21 Winterbourne Ave., Morley, Yorkshire, England. *Agent:* Curtis Brown Ltd., 13 King St., Covent Garden, London W.C.2, England. *Office: Yorkshire Evening Post,* Wellington St., Leeds, Yorkshire, England.

CAREER: Yorkshire Evening Post, Leeds, England, gardening correspondent, 1960-67, assistant news editor, 1967-

74. Lecturer at Grantley Hall Residential College; chairman of West Riding Newspaper Press Fund; proprietor of Leeds Library; member of council of Swarthmore Educational Centre. *Military service:* Royal Air Force, 1939-45; became flight sergeant. *Member:* National Union of Journalists (past chairman of Leeds branch), Royal Horticultural Society, Garden History Society (member of executive committee).

WRITINGS: The Covered Garden, Museum Press, 1962, Dufour, 1963; *The Shell Garden Book,* Phoenix House, 1964; *Gardening in the North,* Pan Books, 1965, revised edition, Arthur Barker, 1966; *Cool Greenhouse Plants,* Studio Vista, 1967; *Indoor Plants,* Corgi, 1967; *The Botanical Travellers,* Phoenix House, 1968; *The Golden Age of Plant Hunters,* Phoenix House, 1968, A. S. Barnes, 1969; (with August Guese) *House Plants,* Wakefield Educational Productions, 1969. Contributor to magazines. Editor, *Royal National Race Society Annual;* honorary editor, *Northern Gardener* of Northern Horticultural Society.

WORK IN PROGRESS: Travels of Early Plant Hunters; research on orangeries.

* * *

LEMONT, George 1927-

PERSONAL: Born March 5, 1927, in Santa Barbara, Calif.; son of George William (a musician) and Lauretta (Duff) Lemont; married Tosca Amati (in television sales), May 12, 1958. *Education:* Heald Engineering College, student, 1947-50. *Religion:* Roman Catholic. *Home and office:* 108 Palm Ave., San Francisco, Calif. 94118.

CAREER: KRON-Television, San Francisco, Calif., actor on juvenile program "Fireman Prank," 1950-59; Newspaper Enterprise Association, writer for "Station Break," a daily syndicated television panel show, 1961-73; Unived Feature Syndicate, New York, N.Y., author of "Doctor Smock" comic strip, appearing daily in more than one hundred-sixty newspapers in the United States and abroad, 1973—. Host of radio and television programs in San Francisco, KPIX-Television, 1951, KGO-Television, 1951-59, KGO-Radio, 1952-54, KNBC-Radio, 1958-60; host of "Comedy Capers," KRCA-Television, Hollywood, Calif., 1952. Creative consultant for San Francisco area advertising agencies, 1960-67. *Military service:* U.S. Air Force, 1944-47; became technical sergeant.

MEMBER: National Cartoonists Society. *Awards, honors:* Emmy Awards from Northern California Academy of Television Arts and Sciences, 1951, for best children's show, and 1954.

WRITINGS: Il letale ospedale del dr. Smock (title means "The Lethal Hospital of Dr. Smock"; cartoons), Mondadori, 1976. Author of columns in *San Francisco Chronicle,* 1958-60, *San Francisco Examiner,* 1958-60, *San Francisco Fault,* 1971, "Bay Fill," in *San Francisco Progress,* 1972-73; author of "George Lemont," a daily column for ABC-TV. Ghost writer for daily syndicated comic strips. Contributor to *San Francisco.*

WORK IN PROGRESS: A comic strip for syndication.

SIDELIGHTS: In addition to his writing and broadcasting, Lemont has worked as a stand-up comic performer at San Francisco nightclubs, including The Purple Onion, hungry i, Outside at the Inside, and Club Neve.

* * *

LEONARD, George H. 1921-

PERSONAL: Born December 24, 1921, in Malden, Mass.; son of George and Dorothy (Hill) Cooper; married Phyllis Bachner (a school media specialist), July 29, 1949; children: Jeffrey, Jonathan, Elissa. *Education:* Harvard University, A.B., 1949; Littauer School of Public Administration, graduate study, 1949-50. *Home:* 812 Burdette Rd., Rockville, Md. 20851. *Agent:* Dominick Abel, 529 South Wabash, Chicago, Ill. 60605.

CAREER: U.S. Public Health Service, Washington, D.C., health planner and administrator, 1950-65, field director of Equal Health Opportunity, 1966-67, regional director of Comprehensive Health Planning in Boston, 1967-69, director of policy for Comprehensive Health Planning, 1970-73; writer, 1973—. *Military service:* U.S. Army, Armored Infantry, 1942-45; received Bronze Star, three battle stars, Purple Heart.

WRITINGS: Somebody Else Is on the Moon (nonfiction), McKay, 1976; *Alien* (novel), Playboy Press, 1977.

WORK IN PROGRESS: The Happy Family, a novel; *Somebody Else Controls Our World,* nonfiction.

SIDELIGHTS: Leonard writes: "I left the Public Health Service . . . in order to write full time. It was a gamble. . . . My only regret is that I wish I had done it sooner."

* * *

LERNET-HOLENIA, Alexander 1898(?)-1976

1898(?)—July 6, 1976; Austrian novelist and historical dramatist. Obituaries: *Washington Post,* July 7, 1976; *New York Times,* July 7, 1976.

* * *

LesSTRANG, Jacques 1926-

PERSONAL: Born June 13, 1926, in Pittsburgh, Pa.; son of Jacques E. and Ada (Mehaffey) LesStrang; married Barbara Hills; children: Michelle LesStrang Cortwright, Diane LesStrang McAllister, Paul, David, Christian; (stepchildren) Steven Marcks, Linda Marcks. *Education:* George Washington University, A.A., 1949; University of Michigan, A.B., 1951. *Office address:* Harbor Island, Maple City Postal Station, Mich. 49664.

CAREER: LesStrang Advertising, Inc., Ann Arbor, Mich. and London, England, president and creative director, 1952-68; *Seaway Review,* Ann Arbor, senior editor and publisher, 1969—. Consultant to Great Lakes Commission. *Military service:* U.S. Army Air Forces, 1945-47. *Member:* National Press Club.

WRITINGS: Seaway, Superior, 1976; *The Lake Carriers,* Superior, 1977. Contributor to magazines.

WORK IN PROGRESS: A novel set in Jamaica; two more maritime volumes for Superior, publication expected in 1978.

* * *

LE TORD, Bijou 1945-

PERSONAL: Born January 15, 1945, in St. Raphael, France; came to the United States in 1966; daughter of Jacques (an artist) and Paule (Pigoury) Le Tord. *Education:* Attended Ecole des Beaux Arts, Lyon, France. *Politics:* None. *Religion:* Protestant. *Home:* 140 Riverside Dr., New York, N.Y. 10024.

CAREER: Onondaga Silks, New York City, textile stylist, 1963-64; Robaix Corp., New York City, textile stylist, 1964-68; Dan River, Inc., New York City, textile stylist, 1968-74; textile stylist, 1974—. *Member:* Society of Illustrators.

WRITINGS: *A Perfect Place to Be* (self-illustrated juvenile), Parents' Magazine Press, 1976; *The Generous Cow* (self-illustrated juvenile), Parents' Magazine Press, 1977.

WORK IN PROGRESS: *The Little Dreamer,* self-illustrated juvenile, publication by Parents' Magazine Press expected in 1978.

AVOCATIONAL INTERESTS: European travel.

* * *

LEVENSON, Sam(uel) 1911-

PERSONAL: Born December 28, 1911, in New York, N.Y.; son of Hyman (a tailor) and Rebecca (Fishelman) Levenson; married Esther Levine, December 27, 1936; children: Conrad Lee, Emily Sue. *Education:* Brooklyn College (now of the City University of New York), B.A., 1934; Columbia University, M.A., 1938. *Religion:* Jewish. *Agent:* Peter Matson, Harold Matson Co., Inc., 22 East 40th St., New York, N.Y. 10016. *Office:* 156 Beach 147 St., New York, N.Y. 11694.

CAREER: Teacher of Spanish at public high schools in Brooklyn, N.Y., 1934-46; worked as part-time entertainer, master of ceremonies, and folk-humorist, 1940-46; became full-time entertainer and appeared on radio and television programs, including "Cavalcade of Stars" and "The Milton Berle Show," 1949, "Toast of the Town," 1949-50; regular panelist on "This is Show Business," 1951-54; host of C.B.S. program "The Sam Levenson Show," 1951-52; appeared on "Two for the Money," 1955-56; lecturer and night club performer, 1957-58; regular panelist on "Masquerade Party," 1959-60, "To Tell the Truth," 1961-63, and "The Match Game," 1965; has made guest appearances on "The Jack Paar Show," "The Ed Sullivan Show," and other television and radio programs. Member of board of directors, League School for Seriously Disturbed Children, and New York Clinic for Mental Health; honorary president, Citizen's Scholarship Program; president, Rockaway Music and Arts Council.

MEMBER: American Federation of Television and Radio Artists, American Guild of Variety Artists, Actors Equity Association, Screen Actors Guild, B'nai Brith—Anti-Defamation League (member of district board of governors), Friends of Music of New York City, Brooklyn College Alumni Association. *Awards, honors:* Brooklyn College Alumnus Award, 1956; D.Lett., St. Francis College, 1973; D.Humane Letters, Brooklyn College of the City University of New York, 1976.

WRITINGS: *Meet the Folks: A Session of American-Jewish Humor,* Citadel Press, 1948; *Everything But Money,* Simon & Schuster, 1966; *Sex and the Single Child,* Simon & Schuster, 1969; *In One Era and Out the Other,* Simon & Schuster, 1973; *You Can Say That Again Sam,* Simon & Schuster, 1975. Contributor of articles to magazines, including *Ladies' Home Journal, McCall's,* and other popular periodicals.

WORK IN PROGRESS: Another book, *American Folk Humor.*

SIDELIGHTS: Humorist Sam Levenson, actually a serious man like most humorists, wants to bring his perspectives on life to the reader through humor. While everyone wants to be happy, he recalls that "the Founding Fathers guaranteed only the pursuit of happiness, not happiness itself. Lots of kids today seem to want the happiness without bothering about the pursuit."

He admits, "Making a child unhappy today in the interest of a better tomorrow requires a stout heart. Happiness, if it comes at all, comes after the solution of problems, after the conquest of obstacles. We must all serve time at hard labor before we become free. Celebration comes after victory, not before. There are too many children celebrating without cause." Levenson remarks, "I guess I shall never get used to the sight of children out on the streets late at night. To this day, when I find myself out late, I expect to see my mother turning the corner to greet me with 'Hey, bum, you looking for trouble? Come on home and I'll give you some.'"

The principles for upright living and resulting happiness which Levenson gleaned from his upbringing are still valid, he feels, and he passes them along to his children: "Do not 'play it cool.' Get involved. Now is the time for all good men to come to. Men of good will are inclined to take freedom for granted. They believe that freedom, like the sun, will rise every morning. History has proved that it can be blacked out for decades.... In dealing with the world, ask yourself: 'What would a good father, a good mother, a good brother or sister, a good family do in such a case?' Perhaps Grandma's approach to settling an argument among her children might work: It is not a question of who is right, but what is right, not who pushed whom first, but why must we push each other at all. Like Grandma, consider the possibility that both may be right or both wrong, and that a third premise may be needed, the premise of sacrifice in order to keep peace in the family.

"Do not look upon the conquest of space as the beginning of the Messianic era. Like Grandma who cleaned the old apartment before she moved, before you leave this earth and move into outer space, take a hand in cleaning up some of the dirty spaces down here—the spaces between nations, religions, races." He reminds his children, "We are now in the 'Live and help live' era of democracy. Like your immigrant grandparents who sent for those left behind, you will have to help others to cross over into freedom."

AVOCATIONAL INTERESTS: Music (second violinist), books.

* * *

LEVENTHAL, Albert Rice 1907-1976
(Albert Rice)

PERSONAL: Born October 30, 1907, in New York, N.Y.; son of Philip and Ida F. (Rice) Leventhal; married Janis H. Hilpp, March 14, 1934; children: Barbara Leventhal Crosby, Jane Leventhal Quinson, John Philip. *Education:* University of Michigan, A.B., 1928. *Residence:* Mamaroneck, N.Y.

CAREER: *Brooklyn Times-Union,* Brooklyn, N.Y., reporter, 1928-30, Sunday editor, 1930-32; Simon & Schuster, Inc., New York, N.Y., promotion manager, 1933-38, sales manager, 1938-44, vice-president, 1945-52, executive vice-president, 1952-57; Western Printing & Lithographing Co., president of Artists & Writers Press Division, 1958-68; American Heritage Press, New York, N.Y., president, 1968-70; McGraw-Hill Book Co., New York City, group vice-president, 1970-72, senior consultant, 1973; Vineyard Books, Inc., New York, N.Y., founder and president, 1973-76. Partner of Sandpiper Press, 1945; president of Golden Press, Inc., 1958-68.

MEMBER: American Book Publishers Council (member of board of directors), Phi Beta Kappa, Phi Kappa Phi, Zeta Beta Tau, Regency Club.

WRITINGS: (Editor) Louis Allen, *Japan: The Years of*

Triumph, new edition, McGraw, 1972; (editor) W. P. Cumming and others, *The Discovery of North America,* McGraw, 1972; (editor) A. E. Campbell, *America Comes of Age: The Era of Theodore Roosevelt,* new edition, McGraw, 1972; *War: A Photographic History,* Playboy Press, 1973; *War: The Camera's Battlefield View of Man's Most Terrible Adventure, from the First Photographer in the Crimea to Vietnam* (edited by Jerry Mason and Adolph Suehsdorf), A. & W. Visual Library, 1975. Also: (Under pseudonym Albert Rice) *I Wish I'd Said That,* 1934; *False Colors,* 1941; *Book Publishing in America,* 1973. Contributor to popular magazines.

SIDELIGHTS: Leventhal was responsible for many of the "Little Golden Books" that children have treasured for years. These books have been translated into nearly thirty languages. Another of his interests was adapting certain adult books for juvenile readers. *Avocational interests:* Played bridge, studied the Civil War.

OBITUARIES: New York Times, January 8, 1976; *Publishers Weekly,* January 19, 1976.*

(Died January 6, 1976, in New York, N.Y.)

* * *

LEVI, Carlo 1902-1975

PERSONAL: Born November 29, 1902, in Turin, Italy; son of Ercole (a merchant and painter) and Annetta (Treves) Levi. *Education:* University of Turin, M.D., 1924.

CAREER: University of Turin, Turin, Italy, medical assistant, 1924; painter (portraits, landscapes, still life), 1925-75. Writer, 1939-75. Practiced medicine while exiled in Southern Italy, 1935; founder of Italian Action Party (anti-Fascist movement), 1930; independent Communist member of Italian Senate, 1963-72. Had numerous one-man exhibits of his art work all over Europe and in the United States. *Military service:* Served in Italy, 1925-26. *Awards, honors:* Arianna Mondadori del Corriere Lombardo Prize, 1945, for *Christ Stopped at Eboli.*

WRITINGS: Cristo si e fermato a Eboli, Einaudi, 1945, 1963, English translation by Frances Frenaye published as *Christ Stopped at Eboli: The Story of a Year* (memoirs of exile in Lucania), Farrar, Straus, 1947, 1963; *L'Orologio,* Einaudi, 1948, English translation by John C. Farrar published as *The Watch* (novel), Farrar, Straus, 1951; *Paura della liberta,* Einaudi, 1948, expanded version, translated by Adolphe Gourevitch, published in the United States as *Of Fear and Freedom* (essays), Farrar, Straus, 1950; *Le parole sono pietre: Tre giornate in Sicilia,* Einaudi, 1956, English translation by Angus Davidson published as *Words Are Stones: Impressions of Sicily,* Farrar, Straus, 1958; *La doppia notte dei tigli,* Einaudi, 1959, 4th edition, 1962, English translation by Joseph M. Bernstein published as *The Linden Trees* (travel book on Germany), Knopf, 1962, published in England as *The Two-Fold Night: A Narrative of Travel in Germany,* Cresset, 1962; *Italien: Alles ist gewessen, alles ist Gegenwart,* C. Belser, 1959, English translation by Frances Frenaye published as *Eternal Italy,* Viking, 1960.

Books not translated into English: *Carlo Levi: Con Testo Critico di Carlo L. Ragghianti e un Saggio Inedito,* Edizioni U., 1948; *Oedipus: Soggetto Cinemato grafico,* Tip. S.A.I.G., 1948; (author of introduction) Giuseppe Santomaso, *Sei litografie a colori,* C. Bestetti, 1950; *Il futuro ha un cuore antico: Viaggio nell' Unione Sovietica* (travel book on the Soviet Union), Einaudi, 1956; (co-author of introduction) Charles de Brosses, *Viaggio in Italia,* three volumes (originally published in French), Parenti, 1957; (co-author) *Un volto che ci somiglia: Ritratto dell' Italia,* Einaudi, 1960; *Venti Pitture di Carlo Levi, 1929-1935* (edited by Antonio del Guercio), Editori riuniti, 1962; *Tutto il miele e finito* (travel book on Sardinia), Einaudi, 1964. Contributor of articles and drawings to Italian and American magazines and newspapers. Co-founder and director of *Giustizia e Liberta* (title means "Justice and Liberty"), 1931-33; editor of *Nazione del Popolo* (title means "The People's Nation"), 1944-45; chief editor of *Italia Libera* (title means "Free Italy"), 1945-46.

SIDELIGHTS: A colorful and popular figure in Italy, Levi was best known as an artist and sculptor whose paintings have been increasing in value. An outspoken anti-Fascist since the 1920's, he spent the World War Two years in and out of Italian prisons and often in exile or in hiding. Levi formally practiced medicine only during his year of exile in Lucania; there the peasants protected him and he treated them in secret, although ordered by the Fascists to desist. He traveled all over Europe and made two visits to the United States, exhibiting his paintings and remaining politically active. Much of his writing (including *Christ Stopped at Eboli*) and some of his best paintings came out of his exile in Lucania. His books have been translated into Spanish, French, Russian, Polish, and Finnish.

BIOGRAPHICAL/CRITICAL SOURCES: Domenico Javarone, Alberto Moravia, Pablo Neruda, and others, *Carlo Levi,* Carte Segrete, 1970.

OBITUARIES: New York Times, January 5, 1975; *Publishers Weekly,* January 15, 1975, *AB Bookman's Weekly,* January 20, 1975.*

(Died January 4, 1975, in Rome, Italy)

* * *

LEVIN, Betty 1927-

PERSONAL: Born September 10, 1927, in New York, N.Y.; daughter of Max (a lawyer) and Eleanor (a musician; maiden name, Mack) Lowenthal; married Alvin Levin (a lawyer), 1947; children: Katherine, Bara, Jennifer. *Education:* University of Rochester, A.B., 1949; Radcliffe College, M.A., 1951; Harvard University, A.M.T., 1951. *Home:* Old Winter St., Lincoln, Mass. 01773.

CAREER: Museum of Fine Arts, Boston, Mass., assistant in research, 1952; Pine Manor Open College, Chestnut Hill, Mont., instructor in literature, 1970—. Instructor at Emmanuel College, 1975, and Radcliffe College, 1976—. *Member:* Authors Guild of Authors League of America. *Awards, honors:* Fellowship in creative writing at Radcliffe Institute, 1968-70.

WRITINGS: The Zoo Conspiracy (juvenile fiction), Hastings House, 1973; *The Sword of Culann* (young adult fiction), Macmillan, 1973; *A Griffon's Nest* (young adult historical fiction), Macmillan, 1975; *The Forespoken* (young adult historical fiction), Macmillan, 1976. Contributor of articles to education journals and to *Horn Book.*

WORK IN PROGRESS: A biography; a children's novel; a novel for young adults.

* * *

LEVIN, Kristine Cox 1944-

PERSONAL: Born September 5, 1944, in Brunswick, Maine; daughter of John Jennings (in U.S. Food and Drug

Administration) and Margaret (Svedlund) Cox; married Edward David Levin, 1967 (divorced, 1974). *Education:* University of Colorado, B.A., 1966; Bank Street College of Education, M.S., 1973. *Politics:* Liberal. *Address:* Box 325, Eldorado Springs, Colo. 80025.

CAREER: Elementary school teacher in alternative education program in Lakewood, Colo., 1968-74, resource teacher and staff developer in Boulder, Colo., 1974-76; Jefferson County Public Schools, Lakewood, Colo., elementary teacher, 1976—. *Member:* Colorado Association for the Education of Young Children, Boulder Resources for the Education of Young Children.

WRITINGS: Silent Wings: Experimenting with Paper Airplanes and Balsa Gliders, Pruett, 1977.

WORK IN PROGRESS: The Alpen-Wing, a children's story book.

SIDELIGHTS: Kristine Levin writes: "I believe that the education of young children needs to include curriculum that is developmentally appropriate and personal interaction with adults (all adults teach children something!) that is humanly sensitive and fosters intellectual development, divergent thinking, and personal growth."

*   *   *

LEVIN, Marlin 1921-

PERSONAL: Born October 21, 1921, in Harrisburg, Pa.; son of Isadore R. and Rose (Hoffman) Levin; married Betty Florence Schoffman (a teacher); children: Sara, Oren, Don. *Education:* Temple University, B.Sc. (honors). *Office:* Time-Life News Service, 2285 Prudential Center, Boston, Mass. 02199.

CAREER: Worked for *Women's Wear Daily,* New York, N.Y., 1947; *Jerusalem Post,* Jerusalem, Israel, diplomatic correspondent and news editor, 1947-59; Time-Life News Service, Jerusalem correspondent for *Time* and *Life,* 1958-76, Boston correspondent for *Time,* 1976—. Jerusalem correspondent for United Press International, 1949-51, and for ABC-TV and Radio, 1952-67; Israel correspondent for London *Daily Mail,* 1956-62. Former instructor in journalism at Hebrew University of Jerusalem. *Military service:* U.S. Army, cryptographer in Signal Corps, 1943-46; served in European and Pacific theaters; became sergeant. *Member:* Overseas Press Club, Israel Foreign Press Association (chairman, 1973).

WRITINGS: Balm in Gilead, Schocken, 1973. Levin's bylines have appeared in magazines and newspapers in England and the United States, including *Fortune* and *Sports Illustrated.*

SIDELIGHTS: Levin has covered Israel from its founding to the "Kissinger Shuttle and Disengagement Pacts in the Mid-East," including the Palestine War, Sinai Campaign, Eichmann trial, Six-Day War, Yom Kippur War, and the Cyprus Civil War.

*   *   *

LEVIN, Robert J. 1921(?)-1976

1921(?)—May 5, 1976; American social scientist, sexologist, and author of works in his field. Obituaries: *New York Times,* May 7, 1976.

*   *   *

LEVINE, Andrew 1944-

PERSONAL: Born November 28, 1944, in Philadelphia,

Pa.; son of Arnold S. (a physician) and Libby (Zibelman) Levine. *Education:* Columbia University, A.B., 1966, Ph.D., 1971. *Politics:* "Yes." *Religion:* "No." *Home:* 2113 Keyes Ave., Madison, Wis. 53711. *Office:* Department of Philosophy, University of Wisconsin, Madison, Wis. 53706.

CAREER: Teacher at University of British Columbia, Vancouver, 1971-74; University of Wisconsin, Madison, assistant professor of philosophy, 1974—.

WRITINGS: The Politics of Autonomy: A Kantian Reading of Rousseau's "Social Contract", University of Massachusetts Press, 1976. Contributor to philosophy and political journals.

WORK IN PROGRESS: Research on social and political philosophy.

*   *   *

LEVYTSKJY, Borys 1915-

PERSONAL: Listed in some sources as Boris Levyts'kyi or Borys Lewytzkyj; born May 19, 1915, in Vienna Austria; son of Bazilius and Maria (Sonevytska) Levytskyj; married Oxana Koverko, 1939 (died June, 1967). *Education:* University of Lemberg, M. Phil, 1939. *Home:* Albert Rosshaupter Strasse, 3-B, Munich 70, Germany.

CAREER: Political and economic analyst, specializing in study of the Soviet Union. *Awards, honors:* D.Phil. from University of Lemberg, 1971.

WRITINGS: Vom roten Terror zur sozialistischen Gesetzlichkeit, Nymphenburger Verlagshandlung, 1961, 2nd edition published as *Die rote Inquisition: Die Geschichte der sowjetischen Sicherheitsdienste,* Societaets-Verlag, 1967, translation by H. A. Piehler published as *The Uses of Terror: The Soviet Secret Police, 1917-1970,* Sidgwick & Jackson, 1971, Coward, 1972; (with Kurt Mueller) *Sowjetische Kurzbiographen,* Verlag fuer Literatur und Zeitgeschehen, 1964; *Die Sowjetukraine 1944-1963* (Cologne), Kiepenheuer & Witsch, 1964; *Terror i Rewolucja* (Paris), Kultura, 1965; *Polityka Narodowoscoiowa Z.S.S.R.* (Paris) Instytut Literacki, 1966. *Die Kommunistische Partei der Sowjetunion* (stuttgart), Klett, 1967; *Die Gewerkschaften in der Sowjetunion,* Europaeische Verlagsanst, 1970; *Die Sowjetische Nationalitaetenpolitik nach Stalins Tod* (Munich), Ukrainishe Freie Universitat, 1970; *Die Marschaelle und die Politik* (Cologne), Markus Verlag, 1971; *Politische Opposition in der Sowjetunion* (Munich), DTV, 1972; *Die linke Opposition in der Sowjetunion* (Hamburg), Hoffmann und Campe, 1974; *Sowjetische Entspannungspolitik heute* (Stuttgart), Seewald, 1975; *Who Is Who in the Socialist Countries* (Munich), Verlag Dokumentation, 1976.

Compiler: *The Stalinist Terror in the Thirties: Documentation from the Soviet Press,* Hoover Institution, 1967; *The Soviet Political Elite: Brief Biographies,* Hoover Institution, 1970.

Also author of *Die Ukrainische Sozialistische Sowjetrepublik* series, Bundesinstitut fuer Ostwissenschaftliche und Internationale Studien, annually, 1969-71; and of booklets and pamphlets in his field.

*   *   *

LEWIN, Bertram D(avid) 1896-1971

PERSONAL: Born November 30, 1896, in Victoria, Tex.; son of Samuel and Justine (Levy) Lewin; married Alice J. Benjamin, February 5, 1926 (died, 19); children: Barbara (Mrs. Kessel Schwartz), David Benjamin. *Education:* University of Texas, A.B., 1916; Johns Hopkins University, M.D., 1920. *Home:* 32 East 64th St., New York, N.Y.

CAREER: Licensed psychiatrist in New York and Maryland. Johns Hopkins Hospital, Baltimore, Md., intern in Phipps Psychiatric Clinic, 1920-21, resident psychiatrist, 1921-22; New York Psychiatric Institute, New York City, assistant in neuropathology, 1922-24, senior assistant physician, 1924-25; Neurologic and Psychoanalytic Institute, Berlin, Germany, medical trainee, 1926-27; New York Psychoanalytic Institute, New York City, member of faculty, 1931-56; American Psychoanalytic Association, New York City, director of survey for psychoanalytic education, 1956-60, consultant, 1960-71. Clinical instructor of medicine in department of psychiatry, Cornell University, 1922-25; consulting psychiatrist, Society for Psychosomatic Research; lecturer on psychoanalysis at psychoanalytic societies and at universities. *Member:* American Psychoanalytic Association (past president), American Psychiatric Association (fellow), American Medical Association (fellow), American Orthopsychiatric Association (fellow), New York Psychoanalytic Society (past president, vice-president, secretary, and treasurer), New York Academy of Medicine, New York State Medical Society, New Jersey State Psychoanalytic Society (honorary member), Pittsburgh Psychoanalytic Society (honorary member), Philadelphia Psychoanalytic Society (honorary member).

WRITINGS: (Translator with B. Glueck) Franz Alexander. *The Psychoanalysis of the Total Personality,* Nervous & Mental Diseases Publishing, 1930; (translator with G. Zilboorg) Otto Fenichel, *Outline of Clinical Psychoanalysis,* Norton, 1934; (with W. C. Langer and E. Kris) *A Psychological Analysis of Adolf Hitler,* U.S. Office of Strategic Services, 1944; *The Psychoanalysis of Elation,* Norton, 1950; *Dreams and the Uses of Regression: Freud Anniversary Lecture,* International Universities Press, 1958; (with Helen Ross) *Psychoanalytic Education in the United States,* Norton, 1960; (editor and author of introduction) *On Character and Libido Development: Six Essays by Karl Abraham,* Norton, 1966; *The Image and the Past,* International Universities Press, 1969.

Author of introduction or foreword: Otto Fenichel, *Collected Papers,* Norton, 1953; R. Ekstein and R. S. Wallerstein, editors, *The Teaching and Learning of Psychotherapy,* Basic Books, 1958; A. Garma, *The Psychoanalysis of Dreams,* Quadrangle, 1966; Samuel Novey, *The Second Look,* Johns Hopkins Press, 1968.

Contributor: S. Lorand, editor, *Psychoanalysis Today,* Covici-Friede, 1933, 2nd edition, International Universities Press, 1944; F. Dunbar, editor, *Synopsis of Psychosomatic Diagnosis and Treatment,* Mosby, 1948; *Drives, Affects, Behavior,* International Universities Press, Volume I, 1953, Volume II, 1965; I. Hendrick, editor, *The Birth of an Institute,* Wheelwright, 1961; M. Wangh, editor, *Fruitation of an Idea: Fifty Years of Psychoanalysis in New York,* International Universities Press, 1962. Also contributor to various volumes of *The Psychoanalytic Study of the Child* and other symposia, to *International Encyclopedia of the Social Sciences,* and to *Encyclopaedia Britannica.* Contributor of about one hundred thirty articles and reviews to professional journals and to *Saturday Review* and *New York Post.* Assistant editor and later editor, *Psychoanalytic Quarterly,* 1932-71.

BIOGRAPHICAL SOURCES: Psychoanalytic Quarterly (a tribute on Lewin's 70th birthday and bibliography), Volume XXXV, 1966.*

LEWIS, James 1935-

PERSONAL: Born October 1, 1935, in Baltimore, Md.; son of Earl R. (a businessman) and Sara (Selfe) Lewis; married Judith Graham, June 14, 1958; children: Stephen, Elizabeth, Deborah, Katherine. *Education:* Washington & Lee University, B.A., 1958; Virginia Theological Seminary, M.Div., 1964. *Politics:* Democrat. *Home:* 512 Linden Rd., Charleston, W.Va. 25314. *Office:* St. John's Episcopal Church, 1105 Quarrier St., Charleston, W.Va. 25301.

CAREER: Ordained priest of the Episcopal Church. Assistant for college work at Episcopal church in Annapolis, Md., 1964-68; rector in Martinsburg, W.Va., 1968-74; St. John's Episcopal Church, Charleston, W.Va., rector, 1974—. Member of West Virginia governor's task force on day care, 1973; president of Norborne Day Care Center, 1969-74; chairman of legislative affairs committee of West Virginia Council of Churches, 1974-76; member of board of directors of Kanawha Pastoral Counseling Center, 1975-76. *Military service:* U.S. Marine Corps, 1958-61; became first lieutenant.

WRITINGS: West Virginia Pilgrim, Seabury, 1976. Contributor to *Los Angeles Times.*

WORK IN PROGRESS: A book on modern saints, *Some Were Slain by a Fierce Wild Beast;* a book on his role in the Kanawha County textbook crisis of 1974-75.

SIDELIGHTS: "I am eager to write a novel," Lewis told *CA.* "The basis of my experience is the parish ministry and I am challenged by the idea of doing metaphysical writings in a fictional setting." Lewis was an all-American lacrosse player in 1958, and was assistant lacrosse coach at the U.S. Naval Academy, 1964-68.

*   *   *

LEWIS, John D(onald) 1905-

PERSONAL: Born October 6, 1905, in Paterson, N.J.; son of John T. (a bookkeeper) and Mary (Jones) Lewis: married Ewart R. Kellogg, June 20, 1933 (died December, 1968); married Mary Jane Miller (a teacher), January 20, 1972; children: David K., Donald E., Ellen; stepchildren: David Miller, Leslie Miller. *Education:* Oberlin College, A.B., 1928; University of Wisconsin, M.A., 1929, Ph.D., 1934; University of Berlin, graduate study, 1932-33. *Home:* 255 East College St., Oberlin, Ohio 44074. *Office:* Department of Government, Oberlin College, Oberlin, Ohio 44074.

CAREER: University of Wisconsin, Madison, instructor, 1930-32, 1933-35; Oberlin College, Oberlin, Ohio, assistant professor, 1935-42, associate professor, 1942-48, professor of government, 1948-72, professor emeritus, 1972—, head of department, 1953-70. Visiting professor at University of Michigan, 1949 (summer), Wesleyan University, 1950-51, University of Minnesota, 1951 (summer), Columbia University, 1954 (summer), University of California, Berkeley, 1957 (summer), Western Reserve University (now Case Western Reserve University), 1966-67, and Colorado College, 1972. Fulbright senior scholar at Oxford University, 1959-60. *Member:* American Political Science Association (vice-president, 1962-63; representative in American Council of Learned Societies, 1970-73), American Association of University Professors, American Academy of Political and Social Science, American Society of Legal and Political Philosophy (vice-president, 1967-69), Midwest Political Science Association (president, 1967-68), Phi Beta Kappa. *Awards, honors:* Social Science Research Council fellowship, 1939-40; Guggenheim Foundation fellowship, 1943-44.

WRITINGS: The Genossenschaft-Theory of Otto von Gierke, University of Wisconsin Press, 1935; (editor with Carl Wittke) *Democracy Is Different,* Harper, 1941; (editor with Jasper Shannon) *The Study of Comparative Government,* Appleton, 1949; (with Oscar Jaszi) *Against the Tyrant,* Free Press, 1957; (editor) *Anti-Federalists Versus Federalists: Selected Documents,* Chandler Publishing, 1967. Contributor to *American Political Science Review, International Journal of Ethics, Journal of Politics,* and *International Encyclopedia of the Social Sciences. American Political Science Review,* book review editor, 1956-59, member of editorial board, 1960-64; member of editorial board of *Midwest Journal of Political Science,* 1959-62.

WORK IN PROGRESS: Research on seventeenth and eighteenth century English and American political theory and theories of modern constitutional governments.

* * *

LEWIS, Wilmarth Sheldon 1895-

PERSONAL: Born November 14, 1895, in Alameda, Calif.; son of Azro Nathaniel (a dentist and oil executive) and Miranda Wilmarth (Sheldon) Lewis; married Annie Burr Auchincloss, January 25, 1928 (died, 1959). *Education:* Yale University, B.A., 1920. *Address:* Main St., Farmington, Conn. 06032.

CAREER: Worked at Yale University Press, New Haven, Conn., 1920-22; bibliophile, 1922—; Yale University Press, research associate, 1933-38, writer and editor, 1938—. Yale University, fellow of Calhoun College, 1933-64, chairman of Yale Library Associates, 1933-45, trustee of university, 1938-64. Sandars Reader in Bibliography, Cambridge University, 1957; Mellon lecturer, U.S. National Gallery of Art, 1960. Member of Winterthur Museum, 1955—, and American Heritage Foundation, 1962—. Founding chairman of librarians' council of Library of Congress, 1942-46; member of Smithsonian Institution's National Portrait Gallery Commission, 1964, and Art Commission of National Collection of Fine Arts. Has served as trustee of private schools and libraries, Avon Old Farms, Heritage Foundation, and Henry Francis Dupont Museum. *Military service:* U.S. Army, Field Artillery, 1917-19; served in France; became second lieutenant. Office of Strategic Services, chief of Central Information Division, 1941-43.

MEMBER: American Philosophical Society (fellow), American Academy of Arts and Sciences (fellow), Society of Colonial Wars, Royal Society of Literature (fellow), Society of Antiquaries (fellow), Royal Society of Arts (fellow), Society of Cincinnati (honorary member), Phi Beta Kappa (honorary member), Beta Theta Pi, Yale Club (New York), Scroll and Key, Pacific Union Club (San Francisco), Tavern Club (Boston), Metropolitan Club (Washington, D.C.), Century Club (New York City), Athenaeum Club (London).

AWARDS, HONORS: Yale University, M.A., 1937, LL.D., 1965; Litt.D., Brown University, 1945, University of Rochester, 1946, National University of Ireland, 1957, University of Delaware, 1961, Cambridge University, 1962; L.H.D., Trinity College, Hartford, Conn., 1950, Bucknell University, 1958, University of Melbourne, 1972; Yale Medal, 1965; Donald F. Hyde Award of Princeton University, 1968; LL.D., University of Hartford, 1972.

WRITINGS: Tutor's Lane (novel), Knopf, 1922; (editor) *Selected Letters of Horace Walpole,* Harper, 1926, Yale University Press, 1973.

A Library Dedicated to the Life and Works of Horace Walpole, privately printed, 1930; *The Forlorn Printer: Being Notes on Horace Walpole's Alleged Neglect of Thomas Kirgate,* privately printed, 1931; *Horace Walpole's Fugitive Verses,* Oxford University Press, 1931; (editor) *Horace Walpole's Letters from Madame de Sevigne,* privately printed, 1933; *The Genesis of Strawberry Hill* (monograph), Metropolitan Museum of Art, 1934; *Le triomphe de l'amitie: Ou l'histoire de Jacqueline et de Jeanneton* (title means "The Triumph of Friendship"), privately printed, 1935; *Bentley's Designs for Walpole's Fugitive Pieces,* privately printed, 1936; (senior editor, with R. S. Brown, Jr., Robert A. Smith, Warren H. Smith, A. Dayle Wallace, and others) *Horace Walpole's Correspondence,* thirty-nine volumes, Yale University Press, 1937-74; (with Ralph M. Williams) *Private Charity in England, 1747-1757,* Yale University Press, 1938.

Three Tours Through London in the Years 1748, 1776, 1797, Yale University Press, 1941, Greenwood Press, 1971; (author of preface) Allen Tracy Hazen, *A Bibliography of the Strawberry Hill Press, with a Record of the Prices at Which Copies Have Been Sold,* Yale University Press, 1942, new edition, Dawsons of Pall Mall, 1973; *The Yale Collections,* Yale University Press, 1946; (editor with Hazen) *A Bibliography of Horace Walpole,* Yale University Press, 1948.

Collector's Progress, Knopf, 1951, Greenwood Press, 1974; *The Layman and the Libraries,* Friends of the Dartmouth Library, 1956; *Horace Walpole's Library,* Cambridge University Press, 1958.

Horace Walpole, Pantheon, 1960; (editor with Philip Hofer) William Hogarth and William Blake, *Beggar's Opera by Hogarth and Blake: A Portfolio,* Harvard University Press, 1965; *One Man's Education* (autobiography), Knopf, 1967; (editor) Horace Walpole, *The Castle of Otranto: A Gothic Story,* Oxford University Press, 1964, revised edition, 1969; (contributor) Hazen, *A Catalogue of Horace Walpole's Library,* Yale University Press, 1969.

See for Yourself (on his favorite works of art), Harper, 1971; *Thomas Gray, 1716-1771,* Pembroke College, Cambridge University, 1971; *A Guide to the Life of Horace Walpole (1717-1797), Fourth Earl of Orford, as Illustrated by an Exhibition Based on the Yale Edition of His Correspondence,* Yale University Press, 1973.

Author of play, with Winchell Smith, "The Tadpole" first produced in Jackson Heights, Conn., 1931. Contributor to professional and popular magazines, including *Atlantic Monthly, Virginia Quarterly Review, Yale Review,* and *American Scholar.* Past editor of *Yale Literary Magazine.*

WORK IN PROGRESS: Editing further volumes of Horace Walpole's correspondence, with complete series to contain about fifty volumes, for Yale University Press, completion expected about 1980.

SIDELIGHTS: Over the years, Lewis has compiled an extensive collection of books and memorabilia of Horace Walpole and some of his associates. This library, and the Farmington estate, which also houses a collection of more than six thousand eighteenth century British political and satirical prints said to be second only to that of the British Museum, is bequeathed to Yale University, with provisions made for maintenance and new acquisitions.

AVOCATIONAL INTERESTS: Art.

BIOGRAPHICAL/CRITICAL SOURCES: New Yorker, August 6, 1949, August 13, 1949, October 31, 1959; *New York Post Magazine,* January 21, 1962; Wilmarth Sheldon Lewis, *One Man's Education,* Knopf, 1967; *New York Times Book Review,* October 8, 1967.

LHAMON, W(illiam) T(aylor), Jr. 1945-

PERSONAL: Born January 3, 1945, in Washington, D.C.; son of William Taylor (a physician and teacher) and Elizabeth (a psychologist; maiden name, Kearton) Lhamon; married Judith Clay; children: William Taylor III, Catherine Elizabeth. *Education:* Johns Hopkins University, B.A., 1966; Indiana University, Ph.D., 1973. *Politics:* "Homeless Left." *Home:* 2412 Willow Ave., Tallahassee, Fla. 32303. *Agent:* Donald Cutler, Sterling Lord Agency, 660 Madison Ave., New York, N.Y. 10021. *Office:* Department of English, Florida State University, Tallahassee, Fla. 32306.

CAREER: Fresno State College (now California State University, Fresno), assistant professor of English, 1970-71; Florida State University, Tallahassee, assistant professor, 1971-75, associate professor of English, 1975—. *Member:* College English Association, Modern Language Association of America, Popular Culture Association. *Awards, honors:* Amoco Foundation award, 1975.

WRITINGS: (Editor with Kenneth R. Johnston) *The Rhetoric of Conflict,* Bobbs-Merrill, 1969; (contributor) George L. Levine and David Leverenz, editors, *Selected Essays on Thomas Pynchon,* Little, Brown, 1975. Author of jazz and rock music column, "Record Review," in *New Republic.* Contributor of about thirty articles and reviews to popular magazines and literary journals, including *Western Humanities Review, Studies in Black Literature,* and *American Studies.*

WORK IN PROGRESS: Surviving Doom, a book of sociocultural criticism dealing with "the idea of apocalypse in contemporary fiction and music and television."

SIDELIGHTS: Lhamon writes: "What this country needs along with justice and a modicum of dignity is a magazine that takes popular culture seriously. That pays attention to the same things that *Rolling Stone* does, but at the level that *New York Review* attends to books."

* * *

LIEB, Michael 1940-

PERSONAL: Born October 21, 1940, in Newark, N.J.; son of Saul (a physician) and Adele (Kraemer) Lieb; married Roslyn Corenzwit (an attorney), August 18, 1963; children: Larry, Mark. *Education:* Rutgers University, A.B., 1962, A.M., 1964, Ph.D., 1967. *Office:* Department of English, University of Illinois at Chicago Circle, Chicago, Ill. 60680.

CAREER: College of William and Mary, Williamsburg, Va., assistant professor of English, 1967-70; University of Illinois at Chicago Circle, associate professor, 1970-75, professor of English, 1975—. President of Oak Park Housing Center, 1972—, member of board of directors, 1975—. *Member:* Milton Society of America (treasurer, 1973—), Modern Language Association of America, American Academy of Religion, Friends of Bemerton Society, University of Chicago Renaissance Seminar. *Awards, honors:* Fellowships from Folger Shakespeare Library, 1970 and 1976, Huntington Library, 1975; and National Endowment for the Humanities, 1975-76.

WRITINGS: The Dialectics of Creation: Patterns of Birth and Regeneration in Paradise Lost, University of Massachusetts Press, 1970; (editor with John T. Shawcross) *Achievements of the Left Hand: Essays on the Prose of John Milton,* University of Massachusetts Press, 1974; (editor with Albert Labriola) *"Eyes Fast Fixt": Current Perspectives in Milton Methodology,* University of Pittsburgh Press, 1975. Contributor to professional journals.

WORK IN PROGRESS: 'The Holy': A Reading of Paradise Lost, completion expected in 1977.

* * *

LILLIE, Helen 1915-

PERSONAL: Born September 13, 1915, in Scotland; came to the United States in 1939; daughter of Thomas (a banker) and Helen Barbara (Lillie) Lillie; married Charles S. Marwick (a journalist). *Education:* University of Glasgow, M.A., 1938; Yale University, graduate study, 1938-40. *Home and office:* 3219 Volta Pl. N.W., Washington, D.C. 20007. *Agent:* John Cushman Associates, 25 West 43rd St., New York, N.Y. 10036.

CAREER: Manila Times, Manila, Philippines, assistant U.S. manager, 1947-54; *Family Circle,* New York, N.Y., in advertising sales, 1954-56; *Glasgow Herald,* Glasgow, Scotland, U.S. correspondent and author of column "Inside the U.S.A.," 1956—. Teacher at Washington Saturday College. *Member:* Society of Women Geographers, American Newspaper Women's Club (District of Columbia), Cosmopolitan Business and Professional Womens Club (District of Columbia), Advertising Women of New York, Glasgow University Club of America (past president).

WRITINGS: The Listening Silence *(novel),* Hurst & Blackett, 1970, Hawthorn, 1974; Call Down the Sky *(novel),* Hurst & Blackett, 1972; (with husband, Charles S. Marwick) *Living with Alcohol, Walker & Co., in press.* Contributor to medical journals in England, Australia, and West Germany.

WORK IN PROGRESS: A novel.

SIDELIGHTS: Helen Lillie lists her professional interest as "the U.S.A. and Scotland, in particular trying to interpret America to the Scots, the position of women in today's society, writing about medicine, in particular for doctor-publications." She adds: "My special love is writing gothic suspense stories but this doesn't pay enough to live on." *Avocational interests:* Cooking, cats, sailing, traveling on freighters, "all forms of escape literature such as detective stories and gothics."

BIOGRAPHICAL/CRITICAL SOURCES: Washington Post, November 26, 1972.

* * *

LIN, Robert K(wan-Hwan) 1937-

PERSONAL: Born July 7, 1937, in Canton, China; came to United States in 1963, naturalized citizen, 1969; son of Chuan Foo (an educator) and Huey-jen (Chen) Lin; married Deborah Shieh, February 22, 1964; children: Hsia-Pin, Hsia-Lynn, Hsia-Min. *Education:* National Taiwan University, B.A., 1960; University of Oklahoma, M.L.S., 1965; University of Michigan, M.A., 1971. *Politics:* Independent. *Religion:* Agnostic. *Home:* 506 North Seventh St., Canton, Mo. 63435. *Office:* Department of History and Political Science, Culver-Stockton College, College Hill, Canton, Mo. 63435.

CAREER: High school English teacher in Chungli, Taiwan, 1960-63; Woodbury College, Los Angeles, Calif., librarian and instructor in library science, 1966; Culver-Stockton College, Canton, Mo., assistant professor of Asian history, 1966—. Member of Canton Public Library Board. *Member:* Canton Roundtable Club.

WRITINGS: Common Expressions in Chinese and English: A Comparative Study, Meiya Publications, 1975. Contributor of articles and translations to professional journals and to *Christian Science Monitor.*

WORK IN PROGRESS: Chinese Mind and Manners (tentative title); research on "the idea of naturalness in Taoism and Zen."

* * *

LIN Yu T'ang 1895-1976

October 10, 1895—March 26, 1976; Chinese novelist, translator, university president, and author of books on China. Obituaries: *Washington Post,* March 28, 1976; *Newsweek,* April 5, 1976; *Current Biography,* May, 1976.

* * *

LINDBERG, Gary H(ans) 1941-

PERSONAL: Born June 16, 1941, in Minneapolis, Minn.; son of Sigurd (a mechanic) and Alice (Olson) Lindberg; married Judith Halvorsen (a librarian), September 9, 1961; children: Peter. *Education:* Harvard University, B.A. (magna cum laude), 1963; Stanford University, M.A., 1966, Ph.D., 1967. *Home:* 5 Elm St., Dover, N.H. 03820. *Office:* Department of English, University of New Hampshire, Durham, N.H. 03824.

CAREER: University of Virginia, Charlottesville, assistant professor of English, 1967-73; Rhode Island College, Providence, assistant professor of English, 1973-74; University of New Hampshire, Durham, associate professor of English, 1974—.

WRITINGS: Edith Wharton and the Novel of Manners, University Press of Virginia, 1975.

WORK IN PROGRESS: The Confidence Man in America, completion expected in 1978.

* * *

LINDEN, George William 1938-

PERSONAL: Born August 18, 1938, in Virginia, Minn.; married, 1952; children: four. *Education:* University of Missouri, A.B., 1951; University of Illinois, M.A., 1954, Ph.D., 1956. *Office:* Department of Philosophical Studies, Southern Illinois University, Edwardsville, Ill. 62025.

CAREER: North Texas State College, Denton, assistant professor, 1956-58, associate professor of philosophy, 1958-62; Southern Illinois University, Edwardsville, associate professor, 1962-68, professor of philosophy, 1968—, chairman of department, 1964—, dean of humanities, 1969-70. *Military service:* U.S. Army, 1946-48. *Member:* American Association of University Professors, American Philosophical Association, American Association for Aesthetics, Southwestern Philosophical Society, Illinois Philosophical Association.

WRITINGS: Reflections on the Screen, Wadsworth, 1970; (contributor) Richard Tursman, editor, *Studies in Philosophy and the History of Science: Essays in Honor of Max Fisch,* Coronado Press, 1970; (contributor) James C. Austin and Donald A. Koch, editors, *Popular Literature in America,* Bowling Green University Popular Press, 1972. Contributor of articles, poems, and reviews to professional journals and to popular magazines and literary journals, including *Saturday Review, Scimitar and Song, Personalist, Sou'wester,* and *Back Door.*

WORK IN PROGRESS: Editing an anthology to be called *Film and the Fine Arts.*

* * *

LINDLEY, Betty G(rimes) 1900(?)-1976

1900(?)—March 18, 1976; American businesswoman, civic

leader, and writer on political subjects. Obituaries: *Washington Post,* March 19, 1976.

* * *

LINDQUIST, Donald 1930-

PERSONAL: Born September 28, 1930, in Rockford, Ill.; son of Roy George and Martha (Rieth) Lindquist; married Christine Rosenkranz, January 29, 1966; children: Kirsten, Emily, Martha. *Education:* Yale University, B.A., 1952; Columbia University, Ed.D., 1960. *Home:* 5118 Thackeray Court, Fairfax, Va. 22050. *Agent:* Manuscripts Unlimited, 229 East 79th St., New York, N.Y. 10021.

CAREER: Rockford Morning Star, Rockford, Ill., reporter, 1955-57; New York Stock Exchange, New York, N.Y., executive, 1960-69; Conomikes Associates, Los Angeles, Calif., vice-president of training company, 1969-72; Securities Investor Protection Corp., Washington, D.C., executive, 1972—. Public school teacher in Rockford, Ill., 1956-57. *Military service:* U.S. Army, Corps of Engineers, 1952-54; became second lieutenant. *Member:* American Association of School Administrators (life member). *Awards, honors:* Short story award from *Yale Literary Magazine,* 1952.

WRITINGS: A Moment's Surrender (novel), Holt, 1976.

WORK IN PROGRESS: A novel.

SIDELIGHTS: Lindquist writes: "I began writing when I was fourteen—I sent a short-short story about my scoutmaster to *Collier's.* It was rejected—too bad—it was pretty good, and I've been writing nonfiction in various occupational roles ever since and plugging away at fiction on my own time, confident that some day I would be published. I was, and I believe in the eleventh commandment: Thou shalt not quit!"

* * *

LINDSEY, George R(oy) 1920-

PERSONAL: Born June 2, 1920, in Toronto, Ontario, Canada; son of Charles Bethune (a civil servant) and Wanda (Gzowski) Lindsey; married June Broomhead (a university demonstrator), August 20, 1951; children: Charles Robin, Jane Casimira. *Education:* University of Toronto, B.A., 1942; Queen's University, M.A., 1946; Cambridge University, Ph.D., 1950. *Home:* 55 Westward Way, Ottawa, Ontario, Canada K1L 5A8. *Office:* Operational Research & Analysis Establishment, Department of National Defence, Ottawa, Ontario, Canada K1A 0K2.

CAREER: Worked on Defence Research Board in Canadian Department of National Defence, Ottawa, Ontario, 1950-53, and on Air Defence Command of Royal Canadian Air Force in St. Hubert, Quebec, 1954-59; Defence Analysis Group, Ottawa, director, 1959-61; employed by Supreme Allied Commander, Atlantic (SACLANT) Antisubmarine Research Centre, La Spezia, Italy, 1961-64, and by Operational Research Establishment, Ottawa, 1964-67; Operational Research & Analysis Establishment, Ottawa, chief, 1967—. Consultant to Institute for Research on Public Policy. *Military service:* Canadian Army, Royal Canadian Artillery, 1942-45; became captain. *Member:* International Institute for Strategic Studies, Canadian Operational Research Society (national president, 1961), Royal Canadian Astronomical Society, Operational Research Society of America, U.S. Naval Institute, American Statistical Association, U.S. Strategic Institute, Society for American Baseball Research.

WRITINGS: (With Albert Legault) *Le Feu Nucleaire* (title means "The Nuclear Conflagration"), Seuil, 1973; (contributor) A.M.J. Hyatt, editor, *Dreadnought to Polaris,* Copp Clark, 1973; (with Legault) *The Dynamics of the Nuclear Balance,* Cornell University Press, 1974. Contributor to technical and military journals and to *Behind the Headlines.*

WORK IN PROGRESS: "The future of Antisubmarine Warfare and Its Impact on Naval Activities in the North Atlantic and Arctic Regions," to be included in *New Strategic Factors in the North Atlantic,* edited by Johan Holst, for Norwegian Institute of International Affairs; "A Scientific Approach to Strategy in Baseball," to be included in a book, *Optimal Strategies in Sports,* edited by Robert E. Machol, for North-Holland Publishing.

SIDELIGHTS: Lindsey writes: "Thirty years of scientific work on defence problems have persuaded me of the existence of several needs and opportunities awaiting physical or political scientists able and willing to write for non-specialist readers. Most people who take an intelligent interest in the terribly important questions of defence come from one of the 'Two Cultures' identified by C. P. Snow. They are likely to be seriously uninformed about the engineering and military aspect which determine what it is physically possible to do with modern or foreseeable weapon systems, or else they have a very incomplete acquaintance with the political and economic aspects of international relations. But a mature understanding of the real strategic issues demands comprehension of both of these disparate areas.

"Stemming from the problems of defence, although detached from them, two other subjects offer opportunities for useful writing. One concerns the impact of technological developments on society, especially in terms of planning alternative futures for Western society. The other subject concerns human competition. It is, of course, at the root of the defence questions. In the area of sporting competition one finds very well defined conditions and a surfeit of data. Although the subject may not have much significance for the future of humanity, it is instructive and amusing, and could sharpen the tools of analysis that could be important for problems of greater import."

* * *

LINDSEY, Jim 1957-

PERSONAL: Born August 19, 1957, in Bogota, Tex.; son of Jim Luke (a farmer) and Moja Yvonne (a postmistress; maiden name Birdwell) Lindsey; married Estrella Reina (a potter), December 15, 1974; children: Ja. *Education:* Austin College, B.A., 1975; Boston University, M.A., 1976. *Religion:* "Gnostick." *Home:* P.O. Box 915, Texarkana, Tex. 75501. *Agent: Office:* Provincetown Fine Arts Work Center, Provincetown, Mass. 02657.

CAREER: Wing Rodeo, Bogota, Tex., stockhandler, 1967-69; Telluride Mountaineering, Telluride, Colo., guide, 1969-71; Chemaax (nightclub), Tegucigalpa, Honduras, owner and musician, 1973; Trans-Cold Express, Dallas, Tex., night watchman, 1976.

WRITINGS: *In Lieu of Mecca* (long poem), University of Pittsburgh Press, 1976.

WORK IN PROGRESS: Translations of Latin American contemporary poets, and Scotch poets before 1100; "Pictures Out of Doors," a long poem.

SIDELIGHTS: Boston poet George Starbuck reviewed *In Lieu of Mecca* for *CA:* "I like this book. It's an adventure in style, and it also gives me a *life* to look at. Romantic vaga-

bondage in the seventies takes young Americans to places like Honduras, but it's a rare wanderer who can conjure up the dreamy power of exotic landscape, proclaim his right to be lovesick and damn sad, and yet *place* himself and his life with a comedian's precision. It's finally the comicset-pieces of American expatriates in Honduras and American expatriates in New Orleans, that persuade me Lindsey will do even grander things. He's all there, on stage."

Lindsey wrote to *CA:* "I tried learning what was necessary without benefit of the university. In Central America I was writing and managing a nightclub, both of which went bankrupt. A friend of mine at Austin College wangled me money there, and I have since discovered that if there is nothing to be learned in the institution, at least there is support to be had."

* * *

LINDSKOOG, Kathryn (Ann) 1934-

PERSONAL: Born December 27, 1934, in Petaluma, Calif.; daughter of John Welby (a Navy bandmaster) and Margarete (Zimmerman) Stillwell; married John Samuel Lindskoog (a social studies teacher), August 15, 1959; children: Jonathan, Peter. *Education:* University of Redlands, B.A. (magna cum laude), 1956; University of London, graduate study, 1956; California State University, Long Beach, M.A. (high honors), 1957. *Politics:* "Common Cause." *Religion:* Christian. *Home:* 1344 East Mayfair Ave., Orange, Calif. 92667.

CAREER: High school teacher of English in Orange, Calif., 1957-63; writer, 1965—. *Member:* Conference on Christianity and Literature, Evangelical Women's Caucus, Mythopoeic Society, Western Association of Christians for Psychological Studies, New York C. S. Lewis Society, Southern California C. S. Lewis Society, Portland C. S. Lewis Society. *Awards, honors:* Mythopoeic Society scholarship award, 1974; first prize in national essay contest sponsored by Norman Vincent Peale, 1975; award from Evangelical Press Association, 1976, for article, "Reactions from a Partial Woman."

WRITINGS: *C. S. Lewis: Mere Christian,* Regal Books (Glendale), 1973; *The Lion of Judah in Never-Never Land,* Eerdmans, 1973; *Up from Eden,* David Cook, 1976; *Loving Touches,* Regal Books (Glendale), 1976. Contributor to theology journals; contributing editor of *Wittenburg Door* and *Other Side.*

WORK IN PROGRESS: Continuing research on C. S. Lewis.

SIDELIGHTS: Kathryn Lindskoog writes: "I am a C. S. Lewis scholar. I met him in 1956. He heartily endorsed my study of his work in 1957. I am a Christian feminist. (That is the basis of my book *Up from Eden*). . . . I am extremely interested in many areas including psychology, medicine, parapsychology and metaphysics. An extreme Anglophile."

AVOCATIONAL INTERESTS: International travel (Europe and the Soviet Union).

* * *

LINKE, Maria (Zeitner) 1908-

PERSONAL: Born August 13, 1908, in Russia; came to the United States in 1957, naturalized citizen, 1963; daughter of Max and Maria (Schmidt) Zeitner; married Fred Linke (an engineer), 1956 (deceased). *Religion:* "Born again Christian." *Home address:* Main St., Emlenton, Pa. 16373.

CAREER: Maid and cook, 1957-58; housekeeping supervisor in a hospital, 1958-60; executive housekeeper in Cleveland, Ohio and Pittsburgh, Pa., 1960-70; lecturer and writer.

WRITINGS: Eastwind (autobiography), Zondervan, 1976.

SIDELIGHTS: Maria Linke worked as a translator in a German labor camp, and later was herself imprisoned by Russian Communists. She writes of the religious faith that sustained her through those times and accompanied her to a new land and a new life.

BIOGRAPHICAL/CRITICAL SOURCES: New Herald, Franklin, Pa., August 10, 1976.

* * *

LINTHICUM, Robert Charles 1936-

PERSONAL: Born December 25, 1936, in Philadelphia, Pa.; son of Dabney O. and Nellie (Capper) Linthicum; married Karen Marlene Kimmons (a secretary), June 9, 1959; children: Susan Christine, Robert Charles, Jr. *Education:* Wheaton College, Wheaton, Ill., A.B., 1959, M.A., 1963; McCormick Theological Seminary, M.Div., 1963; San Francisco Theological Seminary, D.Min., 1975. *Home:* 1866 Littlestone, Grosse Pointe Woods, Mich. 48236. *Office:* Grosse Pointe Woods Presbyterian Church, 19950 Mack Ave., Grosse Pointe Woods, Mich. 48236.

CAREER: Ordained minister of United Presbyterian Church, 1963; pastor in Milwaukee, Wis., 1963-65, assistant pastor in Rockford, Ill., 1965-69, senior pastor in Chicago, Ill., 1969-75, and Grosse Pointe Woods, Mich., 1975—. Instructor at McCormick Theological Seminary, 1970-75. Chairman of board of directors, Edgewater Community Council, 1970-72; member of board of directors, Edgewater-Uptown Mental Health Council, 1972, and Organization of the North East, 1972-75; president of Edgewater-Uptown Consortium of Religious Institutions, 1973-75.

WRITINGS: Christian Revolution for Church Renewal, Westminster, 1972; (contributor) Russell Q. Chilcote and others, editors, *Upper Room Disciplines,* Upper Room Press, 1973; *Choose You This Day: A Handbook on Creating the Future for Your Congregation,* Presbytery of Chicago, 1975. Contributor to religious journals.

WORK IN PROGRESS: Strategies for Living in a Dying World; The Story of the People Who Knew God, completion expected in 1977; *The Story of the New Covenant,* 1978; *God's New People* (tentative title), 1979.

SIDELIGHTS: "I am concerned about our world, and particularly western society," Linthicum wrote. "Our commitment to technological development and consumerism is leading us to collapse or, at the least, to an inversion of our mode of living. . . . I am exploring the development of a lifestyle which is not committed to acquisition or technological development, but . . . to living within limits, the practice of asceticism, the development of human relationships, the creation of a just society. . . ."

* * *

LIPMAN, Ira A 1940-

PERSONAL: Born November 15, 1940; son of Mark (a private investigator) and Belle (Ackerman) Lipman; married Barbara Couch, July 5, 1970; children: Gustave Keith, Joshua S. *Education:* Attended Ohio Wesleyan University, 1960. *Politics:* Republican. *Religion:* Jewish. *Home:* 4490 Park Ave., Memphis, Tenn. 38117. *Office:* Guardsmark, Inc., 22 South Second St., Memphis, Tenn. 38101.

CAREER: Guardsmark, Inc., Memphis, Tenn., president

and chairman of board of directors, 1963—. Member of Young Leadership Cabinet of United Jewish Appeal; member of president's council of Memphis State University; member of board of directors of National Council on Crime and Delinquency. *Member:* International Association of Chiefs of Police, National Alliance of Businessmen (Metro chairman in Memphis, 1970-71), American Society of Industrial Security, Economic Club. *Awards, honors:* LL.D. from John Marshall University.

WRITINGS: How to Protect Yourself from Crime, Atheneum, 1975.

* * *

LIPSON, Milton 1913-

PERSONAL: Born February 3, 1913, in New York, N.Y.; son of Aaron (a manufacturer) and Anna (Newman) Lipson; married Esther Brooks Davidson (a researcher), May 14, 1941; children: Eden Ross, Merek Evan. *Education:* Columbia University, student, 1930-33; St. Lawrence University, LL.B., 1936. *Home:* 9 Circle Way, Sea Cliff, N.Y. 11579. *Office:* District Attorney's Office, Nassau County Court House, Mineola, N.Y. 11501.

CAREER: Office of Fiorello H. La Guardia, New York, N.Y., researcher, 1933; Corporation Counsel of the City of New York, New York, N.Y., special investigator, 1933-38; U.S. Secret Service, Washington, D.C., agent, 1938-46; private practice of law in New York City, 1946-62; commissioner of accounts (investigations) for Nassau County in Mineola, N.Y., 1962-66; American Express Co., New York City, vice-president of corporate security, 1966-74; District Attorney's Office, Mineola, N.Y., assistant district attorney and deputy chief of Corruption Bureau, 1975—. *Member:* International Association of Chiefs of Police, Society of Professional Investigators, Association of Former Agents of the U.S. Secret Service, New York County Lawyers Association, Nassau County Bar Association.

WRITINGS: On Guard: The Business of Private Security, Quadrangle, 1975. Contributor to magazines.

WORK IN PROGRESS: Research on "official" or "political" corruption.

* * *

LITTLE, Jack
See LITTLE, John D(utton)

* * *

LITTLE, John D(utton) 1894-
(Jack Little)

PERSONAL: Born October 12, 1894, in Malden, Mass.; son of John William and Cora (Dutton) Little; married Margaret Jones, 1920; married second wife, Grace Smith, 1947; children: John Dutton Conant, Margaret (Mrs. John R. Dice), Frances (Mrs. John J. Schonenberg, Jr.). *Education:* Attended Dartmouth College, 1912-15. *Residence:* Boulder, Colo.

CAREER: Boston Herald, Boston, Mass., reporter and rewrite man, 1917-18; *United Business Service,* Washington, D.C., editor, 1919-22; Harris Forbes, Boston, bonds salesman, 1922-33; Estabrook & Co., Boston, bonds salesman, 1933-42; *Labor Management News,* Washington, D.C., associate editor, 1942-47; Federal Power Commission, Washington, D.C., editorial assistant, 1947; has worked as a credit manager in Buffalo, N.Y., 1947-55, a Social Security interviewer in San Jose, Calif., 1955-57, and a credit manager in Sacramento, Calif., 1957-58; writer, 1958—. *Military service:* American Field Service, 1916. U.S. Army, American Expeditionary Forces, chauffeur in Signal Corps, 1917-19. *Member:* National Press Club, Authors Guild of Authors League of America.

WRITINGS: Complete Credit and Collection Letter Book, Prentice-Hall, 1953, 2nd edition, 1964; (under name Jack Little) *Moon of Isis* (juvenile fiction), Altair Press, 1976. Washington correspondent for *New York Journal of Commerce,* 1942-47.

WORK IN PROGRESS: Fiction for young adults.

*   *   *

LLOYD-THOMAS, Catherine   1917-
(Thomas Muschamp)

PERSONAL: Born May 27, 1917, in London, England; daughter of Thomas A. (an aircraft engineer) and Ethel (a philatelist; maiden name, Barber) Muschamp; divorced. *Education:* Educated in London, England, and privately in India. *Politics:* None. *Religion:* Agnostic. *Home:* 9 Damon Close, Lansdown Rd., Sidcup, Kent DA14 4HP, England. *Agent:* Eric Glass Ltd., 28 Berkeley Sq., London W1X 6HD, England.

CAREER: Director and stage manager in theatres in London and New York City. Producer, CKGB, Timmons, Ontario, 1965; associate producer, WTOP-TV, Washington, D.C., 1965-66; assistant in film operations, Columbia Broadcasting System (CBS), New York City, 1966-67; manager of film operations, Granada TV Network, Manchester, England, 1967-68; director, Associated Rediffusion, London, 1968-69. *Member:* Dramatists Guild, British Actors Equity. *Awards, honors:* Foyle award, 1959-60, for "The Bridge of Sighs."

WRITINGS—Plays; all under pseudonym Thomas Muschamp: *Bridge of Sighs* (three-act; produced in Coventry, England, at Belgrade Theatre, September 20, 1959), Samuel French, 1960; (translator) Jeannine Worms, *Archiflore* (two-act), Davis-Poynter, 1973; *The Beheading* (two-act; produced in West End at Apollo Theatre, February 24, 1972), Samuel French, 1975.

Unpublished: "Stranger in Manhattan" (two-act), produced in Leamington at Talisman Theatre, April, 1959; "Nothing to Declare" (three-act), produced in Liverpool at Royal Court Theatre, November 18, 1959; "Belle Vista" (two-act), produced at Pitlochry Festival Theatre, June 20, 1960; "Out of Season" (two-act), produced in West End at Queen's Theatre, March 12, 1961; "A Girl for George" (two-act), produced in West End at Cambridge Theatre, September 18, 1961; "Tie the Noose Tighter" (two-act), produced at The Chelmsford New Play Festival, June 10, 1963; "I Dreamt I Dwelt in Marble Halls" (two-act), produced at The Chelmsford New Play Festival, July 12, 1963; "The Brass Hat" (two-act), produced in Guildford, England, at Yvonne Arnaud Theatre, July 4, 1972; "The Game of Kings" (two-act), produced in Cape Town, September 8, 1975.

Also author of "Seekers," a two-act play, and "The Tarnished Cage," two-act, both as yet neither published nor produced.

WORK IN PROGRESS: A two-act play, "The Flycatchers."

SIDELIGHTS: Catherine Lloyd-Thomas believes that she is "Britain's most neglected playwright," and writes that she uses a pseudonym "since the theatre seldom takes female playwrights seriously." She adds that she has "now turned to the cruelty within us and our isolations."

Her plays have been produced in United States, South Africa, Germany, Singapore, Malta, and Australia. "A Girl for George" and "Bridge of Sighs" have been adapted and produced on television in the United Kingdom, and "I Dreamt I Dwelt in Marble Halls" has been translated and adapted for German television, produced under the title "Gwendoline."

*   *   *

LOBB, Charlotte   1935-

PERSONAL: Born August 28, 1935, in Oakland, Calif.; daughter of Edwin M. (an accountant) and Valrie (Moore) Carter; married Charles W. Lobb (an engineering manager), August 9, 1961; children: Carolyn Jane, Patricia Ann. *Education:* University of Southern California, B.S. (cum laude), 1956. *Home:* 1843 West 244th St., Lomita, Calif. 90717.

CAREER: Employed in the aerospace industry in Los Angeles, Calif., as an employment interviewer and supervisor, 1956-61; *Daily Breeze,* Torrance, Calif., columnist, 1969—. Member of board of directors of South-Bay Harbor Voluntary Action Center; vice-chairman of Torrance Manpower Council; member of Torrance League of Women Voters.

WRITINGS: Exploring Careers through Volunteerism, Richards Rosen, 1976; *Exploring Careers through Part-Time and Summer Employment,* Richards Rosen, in press. Columnist, "Can You Help?" and "A Child Is Waiting," *Daily Breeze,* 1969—.

WORK IN PROGRESS: Exploring Apprenticeship Careers, publication by Richards Rosen expected in 1978; research on career guidance for teenagers.

SIDELIGHTS: Charlotte Lobb writes: "It should make a difference that we are here. Each one of us should make some contribution to our community, no matter how small or how large that contribution might be."

*   *   *

LOCHNER, Louis P(aul)   1887-1975

PERSONAL: Born February 22, 1887, in Springfield, Ill.; son of Frederick (a clergyman) and Maria (von Haugwitz) Lochner; married Emmy Hoyer, September 7, 1910 (died, 1920); married Hilde De Terra Steinberger, April 4, 1922; children: (first marriage) Elsbeth Lochner Sailer, Robert H.; (second marriage) Rosemarie (deceased). *Education:* Wisconsin Conservatory of Music, graduated, 1905; University of Wisconsin, A.B. (honors), 1909. *Residence:* West Germany.

CAREER: Journalist. Between 1909 and 1914, edited *Wisconsin Alumni,* then *Cosmopolitan Student;* secretary to Henry Ford (and press agent for "Ford Peace Ship"), 1915-16, and to Neutral Conference for Continuous Mediation, 1916; editor for International Labor News Service, beginning in 1918; *Milwaukee Free Press,* Milwaukee, Wis., reporter, until 1924; employed by Associated Press, 1924-42, chief of Berlin Bureau, in Germany, 1928-42; news analyst and commentator for National Broadcasting Corp. (NBC), 1942-44; Associated Press, war correspondent with U.S. Army in England, France, and Belgium, 1944-46; journalist in Germany, 1946-52; German affairs consultant for U.S. Department of State, 1952-58, and United Nations, 1958-60; worked as radio commentator, 1960-63; writer, 1963-75. Lecturer at University of Wisconsin Extension. Former member of board of directors of American Council on Germany; president of American Chamber of Commerce in Berlin, 1935-41. Vice-president and trustee of Correspondents Fund of America; chairman of Edward R. Murrow Memorial Library and trustee of its Foundation.

MEMBER: International P.E.N., Rotary International, Overseas Rotary Fellowship, American Academy of Political and Social Science, American Peace Society (past director of Central-West department), Association of Foreign Correspondents in Germany (president, 1928-31, 1934-37), Lutheran Academy for Scholarship, Lutheran Human Relations Association, Overseas Press Club (vice-president, 1949; president, 1950, 1955), Milwaukee Press Club, Lansing Press Club, Phi Beta Kappa, Sigma Delta Chi. *Awards, honors:* Pulitzer Prize for general foreign correspondence, 1939; Litt.D. from Muhlenberg College, 1942, and University of Wisconsin, 1961.

WRITINGS: The Cosmopolitan Club Movement, American Association for International Conciliation, 1912; *Internationalism among Universities* (pamphlet), World Peace Foundation, 1913; *La conference des neutres pour une mediation continue,* Neutral Conference for Continuous Mediation, 1916; *America's Don Quixote: Henry Ford's Attempt to Save Europe* (preface by Maxim Gorkı), K. Paul, 1924, published in the United States as *Henry Ford: America's Don Quixote,* International Publishers, 1925; *What About Germany?,* Hodder & Stoughton, 1943; (editor and translator) *The Goebbels Diaries, 1942-1943,* Doubleday, 1948, Universal Publishing and Distributing, 1973; *Fritz Kreisler,* Macmillan, 1950; *Tycoons and Tyrant: German Industry from Hitler to Adenauer,* Regnery, 1954; *Always the Unexpected: A Book of Reminiscences,* Macmillan, 1956; *Herbert Hoover and Germany,* Macmillan, 1960. Author of columns in *Lutheran Layman* and *Lutheran Witness Reporter.* Contributor to magazines. Former member of board of editors of *Lutheran Witness.*

SIDELIGHTS: Some of Lochner's assignments, while in Berlin, were the Amsterdam Olympics, interviews with Adolph Hitler and other leaders, and the first appearance of the dirigible "Hindenburg." In 1941, he was taken to a Gestapo prison with several other correspondents and remained there, with his notes intact, until 1942. He was returned to the United States, but spent the rest of the war covering stories in Europe, and after the war returned at once to Germany, where he spent most of his life.

OBITUARIES: New York Times, January 9, 1975; *Washington Post,* January 12, 1975, *AB Bookman's Weekly,* February 3, 1975; *Current Biography,* February, 1975.*

(Died January 8, 1975, in Wiesbaden, West Germany)

* * *

LOCKWOOD, Guy C. 1943-

PERSONAL: Born January 7, 1943, in Columbus, Ohio; son of Thomas Lewin (an equine trainer and husbandryman) and Margaret Mary (an executive secretary; maiden name, Weir) Lockwood; married Vicki Ruth Kemper, September 21, 1964; children: Matthew Thomas, Todd Kemper. *Education:* Ohio State University, D.V.M., 1967. *Politics:* Independent. *Home:* 3530 East Hatcher Rd., Phoenix, Ariz. 85028. *Office:* Sugarloaf Animal Clinic, Phoenix, Ariz. 85022.

CAREER: McDowell Animal Hospital, Phoenix, Ariz., associate, 1972-74; Sugarloaf Animal Clinic, Phoenix, Ariz., director and veterinarian, treating both pets and farm animals, 1974—. *Military service:* U.S. Army, Veterinary

Corps, 1967-71, veterinarian to President Lyndon B. Johnson, 1967-68; became captain. *Member:* American Veterinary Medical Association, American Association of Equine Practitioners, National Wildlife Health Foundation, National Geographic Society, Arizona Veterinary Medical Association, Central Arizona Veterinary Medical Association, Omega Tau Sigma, Kiwanis Club. *Awards, honors:* Award for oil painting.

WRITINGS: Animal Husbandry and Veterinary Care for Self-Sufficient Living, White Mountain Publishing, 1977.

WORK IN PROGRESS: Training the Young Horse, with father, Thomas L. Lockwood; research on the humane care of livestock.

SIDELIGHTS: Lockwood writes: "The motivation for the current book developed over a period of time as I saw ever larger numbers of people 'returning to the land' in the form of family farms, small farms and ranches, and back-yard animal raising projects. Most of these 'new farmers' who were my clients had little background or experience in farming, ranching, or raising livestock. I found that most of their problems could be prevented or helped by teaching them basic principles.

"I feel that the current U.S. population movement trends toward rural and farming areas are a reflection of the conflict and direction of life in America. I feel that many people are seeking to return to self-sufficiency, or at least partial self-sufficiency, on their own land, so that they are not so vulnerable to the whims of labor strife, urban crime, and big government."

AVOCATIONAL INTERESTS: Aviation (pilot, with commercial and instrument ratings in land planes and sea planes; especially bush flying for camping and fishing), oil painting (animals and landscapes).

* * *

LOENING, Grover C. 1889(?)-1976

1889(?)—1976; American pioneer aviator, businessman, and author of books in his field. Obituaries: *Time,* March 15, 1976.

* * *

LOEWENSTEIN, Rudolph M(aurice) 1898-1976

January 17, 1898—April 14, 1976; Polish-born American physician and psychoanalyst, authority on psychology of anti-semitism, and author of books in his field. Obituaries: *New York Times,* April 15, 1976; *AB Bookman's Weekly,* May 31, 1976. (*CAP*-2; earlier sketch in *CA*-21-22)

* * *

LONDON, Artur 1915-

PERSONAL: Born February 1, 1915, in Ostrava, Czechoslovakia; moved to France, 1963; naturalized French citizen, 1971; son of Emil and Berta (Lippe) London; married Elizabeth Ricol, 1946; children: Francoise, Gerard, Michel. *Education:* Attended public schools. *Politics:* Socialist. *Religion:* None. *Home:* 22-26 rue du Sergent Bauchat, Paris 12, France.

CAREER: French Army, 1939—; became commandant; received Legion d'honneur, Croix de guerre avec palmes, and Medaille de la Resistance. Vice-minister of Czechoslovakian foreign affairs, 1949-51. *Awards, honors:* Prix d'Aujour d'hui, 1969.

WRITINGS: Spanelsko, Spanelsko, Editions Politique

(Prague), 1963; *L'Aveu,* Gallimard (Paris), 1968, translation by Alastair Hamilton published as *Confession,* Morrow, 1970.

*   *   *

LONG, Charles 1938-

PERSONAL: Born January 19, 1938, in Norman, Okla. son of James Franklin (a businessman) and Katherine (Nemeck) Long; married Joan Hampton, September 16, 1961; children: Charles, David, Andrew. *Education:* Attended Michigan State University, summer, 1959; University of Oklahoma, B.A., 1961. *Religion:* United Methodist. *Home:* 539 East Hawthorne Blvd., Wheaton, Ill. 60187. *Office:* The *Quill,* Magazine, 35 East Wacker Dr., Chicago, Ill. 60601.

CAREER: San Angelo Standard-Times, San Angelo, Tex., sports reporter, 1961-62; *Norman Transcript,* Norman, Okla., reporter, 1962-63; University of Oklahoma, Norman, associate editor of *Sooner* magazine, 1963-67; Sigma Delta Chi (Society of Professional Journalists), Chicago, Ill., executive assistant, 1967-71; *Quill* magazine, Chicago, editor, 1971—. Free-lance writer. Consultant to *Letterman* (high school sports magazine), 1971-72, and the *Journalist* (journalism publication), 1976—. *Member:* American Society of Business Press Editors, Association for Education in Journalism (associate member), Radio-Television News Directors Association (associate member), Sigma Delta Chi, Beta Theta Pi. *Awards, honors:* Society of Publication Designers merit award, 1975.

WRITINGS: With Optimism for the Morrow (history of University of Oklahoma), University of Oklahoma Press, 1965. Writer of column, "Editor's Notes," *Quill,* 1971—.

SIDELIGHTS: "My parents, through gentle persuasion and by their own example, taught their sons to be curious and conscientious," writes Long. "Without any particular career goals in mind while growing up, I suppose it was those principles which eventually led me into a career in journalism—and to come to realize that the supreme test of any good journalism is the measure of its public service. Journalism is an endeavor we seek to cultivate through monthly publication of *Quill,* a national magazine for professional and college newsmen and women. A journalist's duty is to serve the truth, to subscribe to ethical standards which steadfastly support the public's right to know and constantly alert him or her to the meaning of fair play in the gathering and dissemination of information. Directly or indirectly through our efforts in *Quill,* we hope to better enlighten the general public as to the nature and meaning of journalistic pursuits—especially in how those efforts support the American people's stake in *their* First Amendment to the Constitution."

*   *   *

LONG, Judith Elaine 1953-
(Judy Long)

PERSONAL: Born April 20, 1953, in Norfolk, Va.; daughter of David Pershing (a state employee) and Mildred Maxene Taylor. *Education:* DePauw University, B.A., 1975. *Residence:* New York, N.Y.

CAREER: Atheneum Publishers, New York, N.Y., executive secretary, 1975—.

WRITINGS: (Under name Judy Long) *Volunteer Spring* (novel for young adults), Dodd, 1976.

WORK IN PROGRESS: Another novel for young adults.

LONG, Judy
See LONG, Judith Elaine

*   *   *

LOOKER, (Reginald) Earle 1895-1976

February 11, 1895—May 22, 1976; American newspaperman, presidential aide, speechwriter, and biographer. Obituaries: *New York Times,* May 26, 1976; *Washington Post,* May 26, 1976. (See index for previous *CA* sketch)

*   *   *

LOPEZ, Barry Holstun 1945-

PERSONAL: Born January 6, 1945, in Port Chester, N.Y.; son of Adrian Bernard (a publisher) and Mary (Holstun) Lopez; married Sandra Landers (an archivist), June 10, 1967. *Education:* University of Notre Dame, A.B., 1966, M.A.T., 1968; University of Oregon, graduate study, 1969-70. *Residence:* Finn Rock, Ore. 97401.

CAREER: Full-time writer and free-lance photographer, 1970—.

WRITINGS: Desert Notes: Reflections in the Eye of a Raven (book I of proposed trilogy), Sheed, 1976; *Coyote: A Collection of American Indian Trickster Tales,* Sheed, in press; *The Book of the Wolf* (self-illustrated with photographs), Scribner, in press. Contributor of numerous articles to literary magazines, travel and natural history journals, including *Harper's, North American Review,* and *Audubon.*

WORK IN PROGRESS: River Notes and *Animal Notes,* books II and III of proposed trilogy (also see above); writing for magazines.

*   *   *

LORD, George deF(orest) 1919-

PERSONAL: Born December 2, 1919, in New York, N.Y.; son of George deForest (a lawyer) and Hazen (Symington) Lord; married Ruth duPont (a research associate), March 22, 1947; children: Pauline, George deForest, Jr., Henry. *Education:* Yale University, B.A., 1942, Ph.D., 1951. *Politics:* Democrat. *Religion:* Episcopalian. *Home:* 11J Crown Towers, 123 York St., New Haven, Conn. 06520. *Office:* Department of English, Yale University, 2055 Yale Station, New Haven, Conn. 06520.

CAREER: Yale University, New Haven, Conn., instructor, 1948-66, professor of English, 1966—. Member of board of directors of Fiduciary Trust Co. of New York, Fair Haven Housing, Outward Bound, Inc., Winterthur Museum, and Mary Holmes College. *Military service:* U.S. Marine Corps Reserve, command pilot, active duty, 1942-45; became captain; received Air Medal with four gold stars and Distinguished Flying Cross. *Member:* Modern Language Association of America, English Institute, Century Association.

WRITINGS: Homeric Renaissance: The "Odyssey" of George Chapman, Yale University Press, 1956; *Heroic Mockery: Variations on Epic Themes from Homer to Joyce,* University of Delaware Press, 1977.

Editor: *Poems on Affairs of State: Augustan Satirical Verse, 1660-1678,* Yale University Press, 1963; *Andrew Marvell: Complete Poetry,* Random House, 1968; *Andrew Marvell: A Collection of Modern Essays,* Prentice-Hall, 1968; *Anthology of Poems on Affairs of State,* Yale University Press, 1975.

Contributor to journals in his field.

WORK IN PROGRESS: Research on the myth of Knossos, the labyrinth motif in literature, and the role of play in literary creativity.

SIDELIGHTS: Lord told *CA:* "Ultimately, the most important intellectual influence has been Homer, whom I've been reading for thirty years. After Homer, Milton and Joyce. I am greatly influenced by twentieth-century revelations on how to read myth."

* * *

LORD, Jess R. 1911-

PERSONAL: Born December 28, 1911, in Silverdale, Kan.; son of Rollin S. Lord (a contractor); married Josephine Pollard, 1938 (marriage ended, 1968); married Nancy Roberts, 1969; children: Rollin, Richard P., Michael, Stephen, Gary; (stepson) Richard R. *Education:* Texas Wesleyan College, B.S., 1959; Texas Christian University, M.A., 1960; University of Texas at Austin, Ph.D., 1964. *Home:* 2016 Rockcreek Dr., Arlington, Tex. 76010. *Office:* Department of Social Sciences, University of Texas, Arlington, Tex. 76019.

CAREER: American Airlines, New York, N.Y., pilot, 1943-49; Lord & Rean Production Co., Fort Worth, Tex., president and chairman of the board, 1954-63; Texas Wesleyan College, Fort Worth, assistant professor, 1963, associate professor, 1964, professor of sociology, 1964-68, head of department, 1963-70; University of Texas, Arlington, associate professor of sociology, 1970—. Consultant to National Aeronautics and Space Administration (NASA), 1964-65. *Member:* American Sociological Association, Southwestern Sociological Association.

WRITINGS: Marijuana and Personality Change, Heath-Lexington, 1971. Columnist for *Fort Worth Star-Telegram,* 1968-69.

WORK IN PROGRESS: Research on the exchange theory and marital satisfaction, on corporate merger and management integration, and on social organization in prolonged stress situations.

AVOCATIONAL INTERESTS: Travel, potting and ceramic murals.

* * *

LORD, Shirley
See ANDERSON, Shirley Lord

* * *

LOSS, Richard (Archibald John) 1938-

PERSONAL: Born July 18, 1938, in Boston, Mass.; son of Alexander Archibald (a manufacturers' representative) and Helen (O'Connor) Loss. *Education:* Pennsylvania State University, B.A., 1960, M.A. (philosophy), 1962; University of Chicago, M.A. (political science), 1965; Cornell University, Ph.D., 1971. *Home:* 855 Hinman Ave., No. 314, Evanston, Ill. 60202.

CAREER: University of Rhode Island, Kingston, visiting assistant professor of political science, summer, 1968; Ohio Wesleyan University, Delaware, instructor in political science, 1968-71; Loyola University of Chicago, Chicago, Ill., assistant professor of political science, 1971-76. *Member:* American Political Science Association, Center for the Study of the Presidency.

WRITINGS: (Editor and author of introduction) Edward S. Corwin, *Presidential Power and the Constitution: Essays,*

Cornell University Press, 1976; (editor and author of introduction) *The Letters of Pacificus and Helvidius on the Proclamation of Neutrality of 1793,* Scholar's Facsimiles & Reprints, in press. Contributor to political science journals, including *Political Science Reviewer, Presidential Studies Quarterly,* and *Public Administration Review.*

WORK IN PROGRESS: A book on Dean Acheson; editing a book on the presidency, *The President's War Power and the Constitution.*

* * *

LOTT, Monroe
See HOWARD, Edwin

* * *

LOUIS, Ray Baldwin 1949-
(Razor Saltboy)

PERSONAL: Born June 25, 1949, in Sanders, Ariz.; son of John Baldwin (a horse trainer) and Eleanor (a cook; maiden name, Francisco) Louis; married Sarah Brown (a teacher), August 20, 1971; children: Shane Baldwin, Hondo Baldwin, Tasha Koa. *Education:* Brigham Young University, student, 1970-74. *Politics:* Democrat. *Religion:* Church of Jesus Christ of Latter-day Saints (Mormons). *Home address:* P.O. Box 255, Navajo, N.M. 87328. *Office:* Navajo Film and Media Commission, P.O. Box 308, Window Rock, Ariz. 86515.

CAREER: Vegetable picker in Bountiful, Utah, 1966-67; Mormon missionary in Arizona and New Mexico, 1968-70; Brigham Young University, Provo, Utah, activities coordinator, 1973-74; Navajo Film and Media Commission, Window Rock, Ariz., public relations representative, 1974—. Actor, playwright, producer, and director of plays in Arizona, New Mexico, and Utah, especially at Brigham Young University; producer, director, and host of "The Razor Saltboy Show," 1973-76; reporter for *Daily Universe* and *Provo Daily Herald,* 1973-74.

WRITINGS: Child of the Hogan, Brigham Young University Press, 1975.

Films: "Navajo: Wisdom of the First Americans," KBYU-Television, 1974; "Indian," distributed by Keith Merrill, 1976.

Plays: "The Real American Christmas" (musical/dialogue presentation), first produced in Salt Lake City, Utah, at Utah State Prison, December 8, 1971; "The Song of the People" (reader's theatre), first produced in Provo, Utah, at Brigham Young University, November 15, 1972; "From Where the Sun Now Stands" (multi-media presentation), first produced at Brigham Young University, February 22, 1973; "Soul of the Eagle" (musical), first produced in Orem, Utah, April 18, 1974; "I Did Not Beg Like a Dog" (three-act drama), first produced in Brigham, Utah, at the Indian School, February 27, 1974.

Author of "25 Razor's Strip," a column in *Davis County Clipper,* 1967-68. Reporter and managing editor for Eagle's Eye' 1973-74. Contributor to Utah newspapers.

WORK IN PROGRESS: Cowboy Blue, an autobiography, completion expected in 1978; *The Great American Indian,* adapted from his film; "Night Arrows," a screenplay on contemporary Indian warriors; "Dark Thunder Hogan," a screenplay on modern Indian conflicts.

SIDELIGHTS: Louis writes: "I know that there are many errors and misconceptions that have to be corrected about the American Indians, more specifically, the Navajo people. Also there are contemporary events in the lives of the Indians that are not elevated as they should be. It is these things that I try to convey in my present writings. Too many people dwell on the Indian of yesterday; it is time we bring the Indians from the past to the present.''

* * *

LOVEMAN, Samuel 1885(?)-1976

1885(?)—May 14, 1976; American book dealer and publisher, poet, translator, and magazine editor. Obituaries: *New York Times,* May 18, 1976; *AB Bookman's Weekly,* July 5, 1976.

* * *

LOVETT, Gabriel H(arry) 1921-

PERSONAL: Born August 11, 1921, in Berlin, Germany; came to the United States in 1939, naturalized citizen, 1944; name legally changed, 1946; son of David (an executive) and Cornelia (an art lecturer; maiden name, Mandel) Lvovitch; married Patricia Ann Coleman, August 24, 1952; children: David, Richard, Andrew, Deborah. *Education:* New York University, B.A., 1942, M.A., 1946, Ph.D., 1951. *Office:* Department of Spanish, Wellesley College, Wellesley, Mass. 02181.

CAREER: New York University, Washington Square College, New York, N.Y., instructor, 1944-52, assistant professor of Spanish, 1952-57; Monmouth College, West Long Branch, N.J., instructor in Spanish and German, 1957-60; New York University, Washington Square College, New York City, visiting associate professor, 1960-61, associate professor, 1961-65, professor of Spanish, 1966-69, resident director of New York University in Spain, 1960-65; Wellesley College, Wellesley, Mass., professor of Spanish, 1969—. *Military service:* U.S. Army, 1942-43.

MEMBER: Modern Language Association of America, American Association of Teachers of Spanish and Portuguese, Society for Spanish and Portuguese Historical Studies. *Awards, honors:* Author's award from New Jersey Association of Teachers of English, 1966, for *Napoleon and the Birth of Modern Spain;* National Endowment for the Humanities summer grant, 1974.

WRITINGS: (With Michael Martin) *An Encyclopedia of Latin-American History,* Abelard, 1956, 2nd edition, Bobbs-Merrill, 1968; (with Zenia Da Silva) *Al buen hablador* (title means ''Toward Better Speech''), Norton, 1958; (with Da Silva) *A Concept Approach to Spanish,* Harper, 1959, 2nd edition, 1965; *Napoleon and the Birth of Modern Spain,* two volumes, New York University Press, 1965; *The Duke of Rivas,* Twayne, in press. Contributor to language journals.

SIDELIGHTS: Lovett has traveled widely in Europe and Latin America. In addition to German, Spanish, and French, he speaks Russian and reads Italian and Portuguese.

* * *

LOWDER, Jerry 1932-

PERSONAL: Born June 3, 1932, in North Carolina; son of E. Paul (a textile mill worker) and Vitus (a private music teacher) Lowder; married Harriett Talley (a secretary), October 6, 1956; children: Jay, Suzanne, Marcia. *Education:* Elon College, A.B., 1955; Columbia University, M.A., 1956; Indiana University, D.M.E., 1970. *Politics:* Independent. *Religion:* Methodist. *Home:* 2362 Edgevale Rd.,

Columbus, Ohio 43221. *Office:* School of Music, Ohio State University, 1899 College Rd., Columbus, Ohio 43210.

CAREER: Samford University, Birmingham, Ala., instructor in music, 1961-64; University of Illinois, Champaign, instructor in music, 1964-68; Indiana University, Bloomington, teaching assistant in music, 1968-70; Ohio State University, Columbus, assistant professor, 1970-75, associate professor of music, 1976—. Church organist in Columbus, Ohio; former clinician for National Piano Foundation. *Military service:* U.S. Army, 1957-59. U.S. Army Reserve, 1959-63. *Member:* American Association of University Professors, Music Educators National Conference, Music Teachers National Association, Ohio Music Educators Association, Ohio Music Teachers Association (membership chairman), Columbus Music Teachers Association (member of board of management), Pi Kappa Lambda, Phi Delta Kappa.

WRITINGS: Basic Piano Skills, Charles A. Jones Publishing, 1975. Contributor to music and music education journals.

WORK IN PROGRESS: Group Piano Pedagogy, completion expected about 1978; compiling previously published articles on piano pedagogy.

SIDELIGHTS: Lowder reports that he is ''vitally interested in continuing education, teaching numerous courses for non-music majors and offering workshops for teachers and pre-college students.''

BIOGRAPHICAL/CRITICAL SOURCES: Clavier, January, 1976; *Music Educators Journal,* March, 1976; *Canadian Music Educator,* April, 1976.

* * *

LOWENFELS, Walter 1897-1976

May 10, 1897—July 8, 1976; American newspaper editor, anthologist, Marxist social critic, and poet. Obituaries: *New York Times,* July 8, 1976; *AB Bookman's Weekly,* July 26, 1976. (See index for previous *CA* sketch)

* * *

LUCAS, Lawrence E(dward) 1933-

PERSONAL: Born July 8, 1933, in New York, N.Y.; son of George Alvin (a storeowner) and Miriam (Grant) Lucas. *Education:* Cathedral College, student, 1947-53; St. Joseph's College and Seminary, New York, N.Y., B.A., 1955, graduate study, 1955-59; further graduate study at Union Theological Seminary, Indiana University, Butler University, Christian Theological Seminary, and School of Modern Photography. *Home and office:* Church of the Resurrection, 276 West 151st St., New York, N.Y. 10039. *Agent:* Scott Meredith Literary Agency, Inc., 845 Third Ave., New York, N.Y. 10036.

CAREER: Ordained Roman Catholic priest, 1959; assistant pastor of Roman Catholic churches in Croton Falls, N.Y., summer, 1959, and New York, N.Y., 1959-69; Church of the Resurrection, New York, N.Y., pastor, 1969—. Member of Black Economic Development Council; mediator for Institute of Mediation and Conflict Resolutions; member of advisory board of Malcolm-King Community College; lecturer. *Member:* Catholic Biblical Association, National Alliance Against Racist and Political Oppression, Center for Democratic Institutions, National Conference of Black Churchmen (member of board of directors), National Black Catholic Clergy Caucus (co-founder; president, 1972-74), National Rifle Association, Fifteenth Infantry Rifle and Pistol Club.

WRITINGS: *Black Priest/White Church: Catholics and Racism,* Random House, 1970. Author of "The Black Voice," a column syndicated by Universal Press Syndicate, 1968-75. Contributor to religious periodicals and New York area newspapers. Member of editorial board of *Amsterdam News and Renewal* and of advisory board of *Clergy Report.*

WORK IN PROGRESS: A book on the Black church; a book comparing the teachings of Malcolm X to those of the New Testament.

SIDELIGHTS: Lucas' goals are aimed toward "a serious understanding of the Christian commitment and relating it to the present world, especially in terms of racial injustice and exploitation, unequal distribution of and access to resources, with an emphasis on the American scene and its relation to the world scene." *Avocational interests:* Sports, photography, amateur radio.

* * *

LUCE, William (Aubert) 1931-

PERSONAL: Born October 16, 1931, in Portland, Ore.; son of Darrel (a merchant) and Elenora (a Christian Science practitioner; maiden name, Kuul) Luce. *Education:* Attended Boston University, University of Washington, Seattle, and Lewis and Clark College. *Home:* 3200 West La Rotonda Dr., Rancho Palos Verdes, Calif. 90274. *Agent:* Ed Bondy, William Morris Agency, 151 El Camino, Beverly Hills, Calif. 90212.

CAREER: Church organist and composer of church music, 1948-66; playwright, 1966—. Christian Science practitioner, 1954-66. Singer; has performed with Norman Luboff Choir, Ray Charles Singers, Roger Wagner Chorale, Gregg Smith Singers, and on the "Julie London Show"; has also performed with national singing tours, and on television programs and recordings. *Member:* American Society of Composers, Authors and Publishers, National Federation of Poets, California State Poetry Society. *Awards, honors:* Award from Chicago Poets' Club, 1973, for "Odyssey Sonnets."

WRITINGS: *Catalogue of Sacred Songs,* Carl Fischer, 1962; *Spring Song and Other Poems,* Ritchie, 1963; *Catalogue of Sacred Songs,* Guerison Music Co., 1969; *The Belle of Amherst* (one-woman two-act play; first produced in Seattle, Wash., at Moore Theatre, February 25, 1976; produced in New York City on Broadway at Longacre Theatre, April 28, 1976), Houghton, 1976. Contributor to literary journals, including *California State Poetry Quarterly,* and to newspapers.

WORK IN PROGRESS: *The Odyssey Sonnets,* a book of poems.

SIDELIGHTS: Luce writes: "*The Belle of Amherst* is my first play. It is the culmination of years of interest in poetry—first motivated by the influence of a high school English teacher." Julie Harris has appeared both on Broadway and on tour in *The Belle of Amherst,* based on the life of Emily Dickinson, and won the Sarah Siddons Award of 1976 for her performance.

Several songs composed by Luce have been recorded by Doris Day, including "Let No Walls Divide," "Be a Child at Christmas Time," "Be Still and Know," and "The Prodigal Son."

AVOCATIONAL INTERESTS: Piano, genealogy.

BIOGRAPHICAL/CRITICAL SOURCES: *Oregonian,* February 25, 1976; *Rocky Mountain News,* March 5, 1976; *Christian Science Monitor,* April 22, 1976; *Washington Post,* September 24, 1976.

* * *

LUNDQUIST, James (Carl) 1941-

PERSONAL: Born September 24, 1941, in Duluth, Minn.; son of Philip (an engineer) and Florence (Nelson) Lundquist; married Virginia Cody (a medical technologist), November 21, 1961; children: Kurt, Karen, Kirsten. *Education:* Westminster College, Fulton, Mo., B.A., 1964; University of Florida, Ph.D., 1967. *Home:* 325 Riverside N., Sartell, Minn. 56377. *Agent:* William Morris Agency, 1350 Avenue of the Americas, New York, N.Y. 10019. *Office:* Department of English, St. Cloud State University, St. Cloud, Minn. 56301.

CAREER: *Fulton Daily Sun-Gazette,* Fulton, Mo., reporter, 1963; *Skagit Valley Daily Herald,* Mt. Vernon, Wash., sports editor, 1964; St. Cloud State University, St. Cloud, Minn., assistant professor, 1967-72, associate professor of English, 1972—. *Member:* Modern Language Association of America, National Council of Teachers of English, Midwest Modern Language Association, Minnesota Council of Teachers of English, Minnesota Historical Society, Phi Beta Kappa. *Awards, honors:* Named honorary director of Sinclair Lewis Foundation, 1972.

WRITINGS: *A Guide to Sinclair Lewis,* C. E. Merrill, 1970; *A Sinclair Lewis Checklist,* C. E. Merrill, 1970; *Sinclair Lewis,* Ungar, 1972; *Theodore Dreiser,* Ungar, 1974; *Chester Himes,* Ungar, 1976; *Kurt Vonnegut,* Ungar, 1977. Scriptwriter for "Sinclair Lewis's Minnesota: A State of Mind," a radio series for Corp. for Public Broadcasting, 1970. Contributor to literature journals. Editor of *Sinclair Lewis Newsletter,* 1968—.

WORK IN PROGRESS: *Lewis and Dreiser in Hollywood;* a novel, *The Bicycle Ride of Dr. Alagash.*

SIDELIGHTS: Lundquist told *CA:* "When I reach forty I hope I have some vital insights. Right now, I'm still searching for a critical vocabulary that works and someone to publish *The Bicycle Ride of Dr. Alagash.*"

* * *

LUTZ, John (Thomas) 1939-

PERSONAL: Born September 11, 1939, in Dallas, Tex.; son of John Peter and Jane (Gundelfinger) Lutz; married Barbara Jean Bradley, March 25, 1958; children: Steven, Jennifer, Wendy. *Education:* Attended Meramec Community College, 1965. *Politics:* "Reasonable." *Home and office:* 880 Providence Ave., Webster Groves, Mo. 63119. *Agent:* Richard Curtis, 156 East 52nd St., New York, N.Y. 10022.

CAREER: Writer. Has worked in construction and as a truck driver. *Member:* Mystery Writers of America.

WRITINGS—Mystery novels: *The Truth of the Matter,* Pocket Books, 1971; *Buyer Beware,* Putnam, 1976; *Bonegrinder,* Putnam, in press.

Anthologized in *Ellery Queen's Mystery Bay,* edited by Ellery Queen, World Publishing, 1972; *Ellery Queen's Murdercade,* edited by Queen, Random House, 1975; *Best Detective Stories,* edited by E. Hoch, Dutton, 1976; *Tricks and Treats,* edited by J. Gores and B. Pronzini, Doubleday, 1976; *Dark Sins, Dark Dreams,* edited by Barry N. Malzberg, Doubleday, in press; *Midnight Specials,* edited by Bill Prozini, Bobbs-Merrill, in press. Contributor of about one hundred stories to magazines.

WORK IN PROGRESS: Short stories; a novel.

SIDELIGHTS: Lutz writes: "It would be difficult for me to say exactly what motivated me to begin writing; it's possible that the original motivation is gone, much as a match that starts a forest fire is consumed in the early moments of the fire. I continue writing for selfish reasons. I thoroughly enjoy it."

* * *

LUZWICK, Dierdre 1945-

PERSONAL: Born September 13, 1945, in Oak Park, Ill.; daughter of Edward G. (a judge) and Geene (Gallagher) Schultz; married Roger A. Luzwick (a musician), December 30, 1967. *Education:* Attended Ripon College, 1963-64. *Politics:* Conservative. *Religion:* "Entrepreneur." *Home and office:* 900 Ainslie, Chicago, Ill. 60640.

CAREER: Artist and writer. Has worked as a typist in Chicago, Ill., since 1966.

WRITINGS: The Surrealist's Bible, Jonathan David, 1976.

WORK IN PROGRESS: The Babies, a collection of "poetry in charcoal," publication expected in 1978; classical poetry; original art.

SIDELIGHTS: Dierdre Luzwick states her goal: "To draw the picture I would myself most like to see at any given moment in time and space—with fondest regards to Jerome David Salinger."

* * *

LYMAN, Helen (Lucille) Huguenor 1910-

PERSONAL: Born March 16, 1910, in Hornell, N.Y.; daughter of Leon C. (a farmer) and Lora M. (Hamilton) Huguenor; married Vreelandt B. Lyman, Jr. (an artist), April 29, 1939 (died February 7, 1946); married Samray Smith (an editor), June 17, 1953 (divorced, February, 1959). *Education:* University of Buffalo (now State University of New York at Buffalo), B.A., 1932, B.S.L.S., 1940; graduate study at University of Chicago, 1955-56. *Politics:* Democrat. *Religion:* Episcopal. *Home:* 1306 Whenona Dr., Madison, Wis. 53711; and S4528 Freeman Rd., Orchard Park, N.Y. 14127 (summer). *Office:* Library School, University of Wisconsin-Madison, Helen C. White Hall, 600 North Park, Madison, Wis. 53706.

CAREER: Buffalo Public Library, Buffalo, N.Y., circulation assistant, 1932-35, co-head of readers' bureau, 1935-42, administrative assistant, 1943-44, head of adult education department, 1944-52; American Library Association, Chicago, Ill., director of adult education survey, 1952-53; Chicago Public Library, Chicago, adult services librarian, 1957-59; consultant to the libraries of Wisconsin, 1959-63; State University of New York at Buffalo, associate professor and director of reference department at Lockwood Memorial Library, 1964-65; University of Wisconsin-Madison, assistant professor and principal investigator and director of library materials research project, 1966-73, associate professor, 1973-76, professor of library science, 1976—, director of Institute for Training in Librarianship, 1969. University of Buffalo (now State University of New York at Buffalo), instructor, 1950-51, visiting lecturer, summer, 1967; special lecturer at State University of New York College at Geneseo, summer, 1964. Public library specialist for U.S. Department of Health, Education & Welfare, 1965-67. Member of board of directors of Buffalo Council on World Affairs, 1949-52, Council on Adult Education, 1950-52, and Great Books Foundation, 1950-54; Wisconsin Arts Foundation and Council, member, 1959-63, director, 1961-63, Madison Adult Education Group, 1961-63, and Albright-Knox Art Gallery, 1964-67; member of board of trustees of Madison University Book Store, 1973-77.

MEMBER: American Library Association (council member-at-large, 1962-65, 1968-70; president of adult services division), Adult Education Association of the United States, American Association of University Professors, American Association of Library Schools, National Reading Conference, Wisconsin Library Association, Altrusa Club of Madison.

WRITINGS: Adult Education Activities in Public Libraries, American Library Association, 1954; (editor) *Proceedings of the Ninth Institute on Public Library Management: Public Library Service to Adults,* Wisconsin Free Library Commission, 1963; *Library Materials in Service to the Adult New Reader,* American Library Association, 1973; *Reading and the Adult New Reader,* American Library Association, 1976; *Literacy and the Nation's Libraries,* American Library Association, in press. Author of pamphlets for the American Library Association. Contributor to *Dictionary of American Library Biography.* Contributor of about forty articles to library journals, including *Library Trends. Wisconsin Library Bulletin,* special editor, September-October, 1960, consulting editor, 1961-63.

WORK IN PROGRESS: Literacy and Public Libraries in the United Kingdom and Selected Countries; Reading Materials for the Adult New Reader: An Annotated Selective Bibliography; MAC Checklist: Materials Analysis Criteria and Guide.

SIDELIGHTS: Helen Lyman writes: "My earliest memories are of my mother reading to my brothers and sisters and me. My father read every evening undisturbed by an active family swirling around him. Books and reading have been an important part of personal and professional life. Motion pictures, records, television have been added and have extended this interest. The conviction of this importance of the various media in bringing facts, ideas, and pleasure into people's lives is strengthened by the importance of the communication network of today.

"I feel that librarians have a significant role in providing educational and recreational materials that can have meaning in the daily lives of people of all ages. They have a great social responsibility for developing literacy and learning programs. Library services should be dynamic and geared to the needs and interests of a community."

AVOCATIONAL INTERESTS: European travel, gardening, walking, cooking, antiques, art, collecting books (including herbals and herbs, gardening, art, poetry, fiction, classics, library science, rare books, and first editions), reading (English and American poets, Shakespeare, D. H. Lawrence, Lawrence Durrell, Gertrude Stein, Colette, Anais Nin, Virginia Woolf, and Freya Stark).

* * *

LYNDE, Stan 1931-

PERSONAL: Surname rhymes with mind; born September 23, 1931, in Billings, Mont.; son of Myron Wayne (a rancher) and Eleanor (Graf) Lynde; married Sandra J. Dunning, February, 1952 (divorced, 1956); married Jane P. Quinn, June, 1958 (divorced, 1967); married Sidne Henderson, April 13, 1968; children: Shannon Kathleen, Michael Casey, Mark Arnold, Richard Lewis, Matthew Stephan, Taylor Justaad. *Education:* University of Montana, student, 1949-51. *Poli-*

tics: Democrat. *Religion:* Protestant. *Home address:* P.O. Drawer H, Red Lodge, Mont. 59068. *Agent:* Edward J. Keating, Keating Management Agency, Inc., Investment Plaza, Suite 909, Cleveland, Ohio 44114. *Office:* 202 South Houser, Red Lodge, Mont. 59068.

CAREER: Wall Street Journal, New York, N.Y., reporter, 1956-58; Chicago Tribune-New York News Syndicate, New York, N.Y., creator and author of comic strip "Rick O'Shay" (syndicated to about a hundred twenty-five newspapers), 1958—. Lecturer at colleges. Painter of landscapes, wildlife, and western scenes. Deputy U.S. marshal, 1969-76. Director of Carbon County Art Guild, 1976—. *Military service:* U.S. Navy, 1951-55. *Member:* Red Lodge Rodeo Association (member of board of directors, 1971—), Sigma Chi.

WRITINGS: Rick O'Shay and Hipshot: The Great Sunday Pages (cartoons), Grosset, 1976.

SIDELIGHTS: Lynde writes: "Christianity is the motivating force of my life—and I try to live the tenets of the religion in every aspect of my life (with varying degrees of success). I believe that love of country, family, and my fellow man are supremely important—the reason we're here, in fact—and that service to others is our reason for being. My own family and my obligations to them come before other obligations, but I feel a strong obligation to my readers and to those who read my strip or who buy my paintings. I'm strongly ecology-minded, have a deep interest in history, politics, and religion, and am deeply content with my life-style and area of residence. I feel at home only in the mountains. . . .''

AVOCATIONAL INTERESTS: The outdoors, horses, hunting, camping in the high country.

* * *

LYSTAD, Mary (Hanemann) 1928-

PERSONAL: Born April 11, 1928, in New Orleans, La.; daughter of James and Mary (Douglass) Hanemann; married Robert Lystad, June 20, 1953; children: Lisa Douglass, Anne Hanemann, Mary Lunde, Robert Douglass, James Hanemann. *Education:* Newcomb College, A.B. (cum laude), 1949; Columbia University, M.A., 1951; Tulane University, Ph.D., 1955. *Home:* 4900 Scarsdale Rd., Washington, D.C. 20016. *Office:* National Institute of Mental Health, 5600 Fishers Lane, Rockville, Md. 20852.

CAREER: Southeast Louisiana Hospital, Mandeville, fellow in social psychology, 1955-57; conducted field research in social psychology in Ghana, 1957-58; Charity Hospital of Louisiana, New Orleans, chief psychologist on collaborative child development project, 1958-61; American University, Washington, D.C., consultant to special operations research office, 1962; Voice of America, Washington, D.C., feature writer for African division, 1964-73; National Institute of Mental Health, Rockville, Md., special assistant to director of special mental health programs, 1973—. Consultant to White House national goals research staff on youth, 1969-70.

MEMBER: American Sociological Society (fellow). *Awards, honors: Millicent the Monster* was chosen as one of the children's books of the year, 1968, by Child Study Association of America, *James the Jaguar* was chosen in 1972, and *Halloween Parade* in 1973.

WRITINGS: Social Aspects of Alienation, U.S. Public Health Service, 1969; *As They See It: Changing Values of College Youth,* Schenkman, 1973; *A Child's World As Seen in His Stories and Drawings,* U.S. Department of Health,

Education and Welfare, 1974; *Violence at Home,* U.S. Department of Health, Education and Welfare, 1974.

Juveniles—All with social psychological themes: *Millicent the Monster,* Harlin Quist, 1968; *Jennifer Takes Over P.S. 94,* Putnam, 1972; *James the Jaguar* (Weekly Reader Book Club selection), Putnam, 1972; *That New Boy,* Crown, 1973; *The Halloween Parade,* Putnam, 1973. Contributor to academic journals.

SIDELIGHTS: Millicent the Monster has had editions in French, German, and Danish.

* * *

LYUDVINSKAYA, Tatyana 1885(?)-1976

1885(?)—1976; Russian Bolshevik revolutionary figure, Soviet political leader, and author of political literature. Obituaries: *New York Times,* February 6, 1976.

* * *

MA, Nancy Chih 1919-

PERSONAL: Name originally Po-Chang Chih; name legally changed in 1973; born November 18, 1919, in Harbin North, China; daughter of Shi Foo and Foo-Chien (Teng) Chih; married Paul Ma (a businessman), October 12, 1941; children: Mary (Mrs. H. Stavonhagen), Tomy, John, Helen (Mrs. Makoto Yamawaki). *Education:* Attended Giyu Gakuten College. *Religion:* Christian. *Home:* 208 Chateau Mita Mita 2-7-1, Minatoku, Tokyo 108, Japan. *Office:* 165 Chateau Mita Mita 2-7-1, Minataku, Tokyo 108, Japan.

CAREER: Nancy Chih Ma's Chinese Restaurant, Tokyo and Osaka, Japan, and Honolulu, Hawaii, owner and president, 1965—. President of Chang Hung Development Co. Conducts Chinese cooking school in Tokyo; has lectured all over the world, most notably on television programs in the United States. Consultant to Mashin Co. *Member:* International Ladies Benevolent Society, Asian Friendship Society, Nancy Ma's Gourmet Club. *Awards, honors:* Bronze Medal from Gastronomic Academy of Germany, 1968, for *Cook Chinese.*

WRITINGS—In English: Mrs. Ma's Chinese Cook Book, Tuttle, 1960; *Cook Chinese,* Kodansha International, 1964; *Mrs. Ma's Favorite Chinese Recipes,* Kodansha International, 1968 (published in England as *Favourite Chinese Recipes,* Ward Lock, 1968); (with daughters, Mary Ma Stavonhagen and Helen Ma Yamawaki, and daughter-in-law, Irene Tsoi Ma) *Don't Lick the Chopsticks: The Creative, Harmonious Ma Family Chinese Cookbook,* Kodansha International, 1973; *Chinese Cookbook,* Associated Book Publishers, 1970. Also author of cookbooks in Japanese language. Contributor to Japanese magazines and newspapers.

WORK IN PROGRESS: Chinese Cooking that Is Absolutely Delicious; a biography.

SIDELIGHTS: When her family moved to Tokyo after World War II, Mrs. Ma was unable to find a Chinese cook with enough talent and expertise to prepare the kind of receptions she had in mind, so she went to Hong Kong and learned Chinese cooking from the masters of the art. After her return to Tokyo, dinner guests spread the news about her cooking ability, and before long, Mrs. Ma was asked to contribute a series of recipes to a Japanese magazine, and to give lessons to the imperial princesses of Japan. Since then, she has been recognized as an authority in her art. She teaches in her own cooking school, through books, which have also appeared in French and Dutch editions, and through articles, public lectures, and demonstrations.

During annual visits to family in the United States, Mrs. Ma conducts lectures and makes television appearances. She would like to open a cooking school or a Chinese or international restaurant in the United States. She told *CA:* "I think that is the fast way to make friends. I believe cooking is a universal friendship maker."

BIOGRAPHICAL/CRITICAL SOURCES: San Francisco Chronicle, August 14, 1964; *South China Morning Post,* January 4, 1965; *Los Angeles Valley Times,* July 7, 1965; *San Diego Evening Tribune,* July 30, 1965; *Los Angeles Times,* August 19, 1965; *Japan Times,* January 28, 1967, April 24, 1968, January 28, 1969; *Guam Pacific Journal,* November 27, 1967; *New York Times,* December 12, 1968; *Guam Pacific Sunday News,* July 25, 1971; *Santa Cruz Sentinel,* September 28, 1972, October 8, 1972; *Orlando Sentinel,* October 5, 1972.

*   *   *

MACDONALD, Elisabeth 1926-

PERSONAL: Born September 22, 1926, in Vernal, Utah; daughter of John Rex and Edna (Peterson) Spendlove; married Lamont G. Macdonald, August 15, 1948; children: Brian D., Karen M. *Education:* Attended College of Southern Utah, 1944-46, and Utah State University, 1946-47; additional study through University of California extension courses, 1950-54. *Residence:* Fresno, Calif. *Agent:* McIntosh & Otis, Inc., 475 Fifth Ave., New York, N.Y. 10017.

CAREER: U.S. Steel Co., San Francisco, Calif., marketing research assistant, 1948-56; Foremost Foods, Fresno, Calif., member of staff, 1958-62; free-lance writer. *Member:* Authors Guild of Authors League of America.

WRITINGS: The House at Gray Eagle (novel), Scribner, 1976.

WORK IN PROGRESS: A long novel, set in the pioneer era of Utah territory; other novels.

SIDELIGHTS: Elisabeth Macdonald told *CA:* "Writing has always been my chosen profession, but until I declared independence of house and garden at the age of forty I was unable to devote full time to it. Even with at least four hours a day at the typewriter I may never write all the stories waiting inside my head.

"History is my passion, especially western United States history, and I am an avid collector of books on the subject. One must have a special affinity for the past in order to write authentic historical novels.

"Most of my summers are spent in the mountains of Utah, where we are restoring the 100 year old ranch house Grandfather Macdonald built for his bride. This place has provided many of the settings, climate, flora and fauna, sounds and smells for my novels."

*   *   *

MACDONALD, Gordon A. 1911-

PERSONAL: Born October 15, 1911, in Boston, Mass.; son of John A. (a hotel manager) and Grace (Griffin) Macdonald; married Ruth Binkley, May 22, 1938 (died May 17, 1972); married Virginia Stoffel (a planner), December 27, 1975; children: (first marriage) John Alan, James Gordon, Duncan Edwin, William Andrew. *Education:* University of California, Los Angeles, B.A., 1933, M.A., 1934; University of California, Berkeley, Ph.D., 1938. *Home:* 326 Lanipo Dr., Kailua, Hawaii 96734. *Office:* Hawaii Institute of Geophysics, 2525 Correa Rd., Honolulu, Hawaii 96822.

CAREER: U.S. Geological Survey, Honolulu, Hawaii, assistant geologist, 1939-45, geologist, 1945-47; University of Southern California, Los Angeles, assistant professor of geology, 1947-48; U.S. Geological Survey, Denver, Colo., geologist, 1948-58; University of Hawaii, Honolulu, senior professor of geology, 1958—. Volcanologist at Hawaii Institute of Geophysics, 1958—.

MEMBER: International Association of Volcanology and Chemistry of the Earth's Interior (past president), Geological Society of America (fellow), American Geophysical Union (past president of petrology and geochemistry section), American Association for the Advancement of Science (fellow).

WRITINGS: (With A. T. Abbott) *Volcanoes in the Sea: The Geology of the Hawaiian Islands,* University Press of Hawaii, 1970; *Volcanoes,* Prentice-Hall, 1972; (with B. A. Bolt, W. L. Horn, and R. F. Scott) *Geological Hazards,* Springer-Verlag, 1975. Contributor of more than one hundred fifty articles to scientific journals.

WORK IN PROGRESS: Research on volcanoes, especially their activity and structure, and alleviation of damage from eruptions, on igneous petrology and petrogenesis, and on geothermal energy.

*   *   *

MACDONALD, Malcolm
See ROSS-MACDONALD, Malcolm J(ohn)

*   *   *

MacINNES, Colin 1914-1976

1914—April 22, 1976; British novelist and journalist. Obituaries: *Washington Post,* April 25, 1976.

*   *   *

MACK, J. A. 1906-

PERSONAL: Born January 21, 1906, in Glasgow, Scotland; son of John Anderson (a boiler maker) and Jean (Aitken) Mack; married Beatrice Agnes McDonald, January 1, 1932; children: Donald, Alistair, Alison (Mrs. J. A. Sharp). *Education:* University of Glasgow, M.A. (first class honors), 1928; Balliol College, Oxford, B.A. (first class honors) and M.A., both 1930; University of Edinburgh, further graduate study, 1937-38. *Home:* Stroul Lodge, Clynder, Helensburgh, Dunbartonshire G84 0QA, Scotland. *Office:* School of Social Study, University of Glasgow, Glasgow G12, Scotland.

CAREER: University of Glasgow, Glasgow, Scotland, Stevenson Lecturer in Citizenship, 1947-60, director of School of Social Study, 1960-71, senior research fellow in criminology, 1971—. Head of modern studies at Army College (Newbattle Abbey); also works as industrial consultant. *Member:* Various sociological and criminological associations.

WRITINGS: (With H. J. Kerner) *The Crime Industry,* Heath, 1975. Author of television play on Joseph Conrad. Contributor to professional journals.

WORK IN PROGRESS: The Able Criminal; Bank Robbery.

*   *   *

MacKAY, Joy 1918-

PERSONAL: Born July 27, 1918, in Philadelphia, Pa.; daughter of John Wesley and Anna (Ankins) MacKay. *Edu-*

cation: Attended Philadelphia College of Bible, 1936-39, and University of Pennsylvania, 1949-50; Wheaton College, Wheaton, Ill., A.B. (summa cum laude), 1958, M.A., 1962; graduate study at Ohio State University, 1965. *Home address:* Box 289, Cedarville, Ohio 45314. *Office:* Department of Education, Central State University, Wilberforce, Ohio 45384.

CAREER: With Pioneer Girls, 1949-61, served as executive director, 1951-61; Cedarville College, Cedarville, Ohio, assistant professor, 1962-70, associate professor of Christian education, 1970-71; Central State University, Wilberforce, Ohio, associate professor of education, 1972—, supervisor of student-teaching, 1972-76. Campcraft instructor with American Camping Association, 1958; instructor at Summer Institute of Camping, 1960-76; instructor in first aid, water safety, and small craft with Red Cross. *Member:* Christian Camping International, American Camping Association, National Association of Christian College Professors, National Association of Professors of Christian Education, Ohio Association of Teacher Educators.

WRITINGS: Creative Counseling for Christian Camps, Scripture Press, 1966; *Raindrops Keep Falling on My Tent,* Victor, 1972; *Ecology Is for the Birds—And All God's Outdoors,* Victor, 1974. Contributor of articles and book reviews to *Moody Monthly Magazine, Camping Journal,* and *Ohio High School Athlete.*

WORK IN PROGRESS: Contributing to a college textbook on camping for Moody; a book for Scripture Press.

SIDELIGHTS: Joy MacKay has spent forty-one summers as camp counselor, director, program staff member, arts and crafts head, member of waterfront staff, counselor trainer, and camp consultant.

* * *

MacKENZIE, John P(ettibone) 1930-

PERSONAL: Born July 19, 1930, in Glen Ellyn, Ill.; son of John P. and Elizabeth (Andersen) MacKenzie; married Amanda Fisk, October 24, 1959; children: Bradley John, Alice Fisk, Douglas Bain. *Education:* Amherst College, B.A. (cum laude), 1952; Harvard University, graduate study, 1964-65. *Home:* 4200 Cathedral Ave. N.W., Apt. 417, Washington, D.C. 20016. *Office: Washington Post,* Washington, D.C. 20071.

CAREER: Washington Post, Washington, D.C., staff writer, 1956—, Supreme Court reporter, 1965-77; writer, 1977—. *Military service:* U.S. Navy, engineer officer on destroyer escort, 1952-55; became lieutenant junior grade. *Awards, honors:* Gavel award from American Bar Association, 1967, for Supreme Court coverage, and 1975, for *The Appearance of Justice.*

WRITINGS: (Contributor) Leon Friedmann and Fred L. Israel, editors, *Justices of the U.S. Supreme Court,* Bowker, 1969; *The Appearance of Justice,* Scribner, 1974; (contributor) Charles Peters and James Fallows, editors, *The System,* Praeger, 1976; (contributor) Ralph Nader and Mark Green, editors, *Verdicts on Lawyers,* Crowell, 1976. Contributor to law journals and *Civil Liberties Review.*

WORK IN PROGRESS: A book about clients of legal services offices.

* * *

MACKENZIE, Manfred 1934-

PERSONAL: Born October 30, 1934, in Ceylon; son of Wil-

liam Fraser (an engineer) and Constance (Clarke) Mackenzie; married Janet Sculfer (a social worker), 1959; children: Conrad, Gabriel. *Education:* University of Sydney, B.A. (honors), 1958; Oxford University, B.Litt., 1961; Brown University, A.M., 1964. *Office:* School of English, Macquarie University, Sydney, New South Wales, Australia.

CAREER: Brown University, Providence, R.I., instructor in English, 1962-64; University of Adelaide, Adelaide, Australia, began as lecturer, became senior lecturer in English, 1964-69; Macquarie University, Sydney, Australia, began as senior lecturer, became associate professor of English, 1970—. *Awards, honors:* William Wentworth traveling fellowship, Oxford University, 1958-60; English-Speaking Union fellowship, Brown University, 1961-62; American Council of Learned Societies fellowship, New York University, 1967-68.

WRITINGS: Communities of Honor and Love in Henry James, Harvard University Press, 1976. Contributor to literary journals, including *Yale Review, Modern Fiction Studies, Southern Review, Novel,* and *Essays in Criticism.*

WORK IN PROGRESS: Literature of Place, covering English Renaissance, Romantic, and modern writers.

* * *

MACKEY, J(ames) P(atrick) 1934-

PERSONAL: Born February 9, 1934, in Dungarvan, County Waterford, Ireland; son of Peter (an estate agent) and Esther (Morrissey) Mackey; married Noelle Quinlan, August 25, 1973; children: Ciara, James. *Education:* National University of Ireland, B.A. (first class honors), 1954; Pontifical University, Maynooth, Ireland, B.Ph., 1955, B.D. (first place), 1957, S.T.L., 1959, D.D., 1960; Queen's University, Belfast, Ph.D., 1965; also studied at University of London, Oxford University, University of Strasbourg, Institut Catholique, University of Heidelberg, and University of Vienna. *Office:* Department of Theology and Religious Studies, University of San Francisco, San Francisco, Calif.

CAREER: Pontifical University, Maynooth, Ireland, assistant lecturer in Hebrew and Old Testament, 1959; Queen's University, Belfast, Northern Ireland, assistant lecturer, 1960-63; lecturer in philosophy, 1963-66; St. John's College, Waterford, Ireland, lecturer in philosophical theology and theology, 1966-69; University of San Francisco, San Francisco, Calif., associate professor, 1969-73, professor of philosophy of religion and theology, 1973—. Visiting professor at Catholic University of America, summer, 1968, and University of California, Berkeley, autumn, 1974; lecturer at Belmont Abbey College, summer, 1970; has lectured in South Africa. Member of Center for Hermeneutical Studies, 1974—. *Member:* Irish Theological Association, College Theology Society. *Awards, honors:* British Academy research scholarship, 1964-65.

WRITINGS: The Modern Theology of Tradition, Darton, Longman & Todd, 1962, Herder, 1963; *Life and Grace,* Gill, 1966, published as *The Grace of God: The Response of Man,* Magi Books, 1967; (contributor) Donal Flanagan, editor, *The Meaning of the Church,* Gill, 1966; (contributor) Denis O'Callaghan, editor, *Sin and Repentance,* Gill, 1967; *Tradition and Change in the Church,* Pflaum, 1968; *Contemporary Philosophy of Religion,* Magi Books, 1968; (editor) *Morals, Law, and Authority: Sources and Attitudes in the Church,* Pflaum, 1969; *The Church: Its Credibility Today,* Bruce Books, 1970; *The Problems of Religious Faith,*

Franciscan Herald, 1972; (contributor) Paul Surlis, editor, *Faith: Its Nature and Meaning,* Macmillan, 1973; (contributor) Patrick Corcoran, editor, *Looking at Lonergan's Method,* Talbot Press, 1975. Contributor to *Encyclopedic Dictionary of Christian Doctrine.* Contributor of articles and reviews to theology journals.

WORK IN PROGRESS: Jesus: The Man and the Myth.

SIDELIGHTS: Mackey's books have been published in Spanish, French, Polish, and Italian.

* * *

MACKSEY, (Catherine Angela) Joan 1925-

PERSONAL: Born November 9, 1925, in Cheltenham, England; daughter of Thomas Henry (a garage proprietor) and Margaret Eleanor (Chick) Little; married Kenneth Macksey (a military historian and writer), June 22, 1946; children: Susan (Mrs. Michael Williams), Andrew. *Education:* Attended school in Cheltenham, England. *Politics:* Liberal. *Religion:* "Church of England (nonconformist at heart)." *Home:* Whatley Mill, Beaminster, Dorset DT8 3EN, England. *Agent:* Sheila Watson, Bolt & Watson, 8 Storey's Gate, London S.W.1, England.

CAREER: Writer. *Wartime service:* U.S. Services of Supply, civilian employee of adjutant general's department, 1942-45. *Member:* Fawcett Society, Beaminster and District Gardens and Allotments Society.

WRITINGS: (With husband, Kenneth Macksey) *The Guinness Guide to Feminine Achievements,* Guinness Superlatives, 1975, published in the United States as *The Book of Women's Achievements,* Stein & Day, 1976.

WORK IN PROGRESS: Show Fever, a novel set in a present-day Dorset village.

SIDELIGHTS: Joan Macksey writes: "Widely travelled, I found an international outlook easy when tackling the women's book. The three years research involved uncovered for me the undoubted disadvantages and anomalies of law inflicted on women in the past. It also showed that education and politics, rather than militancy, plus women's self-confidence in their ability, are the real keys to equality."

* * *

MACLEOD, Joseph (Todd Gordon) 1903-
(Adam Drinan)

PERSONAL: Born April 24, 1903, in Ealing, Middlesex, England; son of James Gordon (a company director) and Helen (Todd) Macleod; married Kathleen Macgregor Davis (a lecturer and district councillor), 1928 (died, 1953); married Maria Teresa Foschini (a sculptor); children: Alessandra, Iain Anthony. *Education:* Balliol College, Oxford, B.A., 1925, M.A., 1945. *Politics:* Labour. *Home:* Via delle Ballodole 9/7, Trespiano, Florence, Italy 50139.

CAREER: Called to Bar, Inner Temple, 1928; Festival Theatre, Cambridge, England, director and lessee, 1933-36; Huntingdonshire Divisional Labour Party, Huntingdonshire, England, secretary and parliamentary candidate, 1937-38; British Broadcasting Corp. (BBC), London, England, newsreader and announcer, 1938-45; Scottish National Film Studios, Glasgow, Scotland, managing director, 1946-47; free-lance theatrical director in London, Edinburgh, and Aberdeen, 1948-52; free-lance announcer and broadcaster in Edinburgh, 1950-63; poet, playwright, and writer. Toured Holland as guest of Dutch Ministry of Education, 1945; toured Soviet Union as guest of Soviet Government, 1947.

Member: British Actors' Equity (honorary life member), Society for Theatre Research, World Wildlife Fund, Italiana per la Protezione degli Uccelli. *Awards, honors:* Silver Medal of the Royal Society of Arts, 1944; Scottish Arts Council prize for drama for play "Leap in September," and prize for poetry, 1972, for *An Old Olive Tree.*

WRITINGS: Beauty and the Beast, Chatto & Windus, 1927; *Overture to Cambridge* (novel; first produced as play in Cambridge, England, 1934), Allen & Unwin, 1934; *The New Soviet Theatre,* Allen & Unwin, 1943; *Actors Cross Volga,* Allen & Unwin, 1946; *A Job at the BBC* (autobiography), Maclellan (Glasgow), 1947; *A Soviet Theatre Sketch-Book,* Allen & Unwin, 1951; *Piccola Storia del Teatro Britannico* (title means "A Short History of the British Theatre"), Sansoni (Florence), 1958; *People of Florence,* Allen & Unwin, 1968; *The Sisters d'Aranyi* (biography), Allen & Unwin, 1969.

Poetry: *The Ecliptic,* Faber, 1930; *Foray of Centaurs,* This Quarter (Paris), 1931; *The Passage of the Torch,* Oliver & Boyd, 1948; *An Old Olive Tree,* Macdonald, 1971.

Poetry under pseudonym Adam Drinan: *The Cove: A Sequence of Poems,* privately printed, 1940; *The Men of the Rocks,* Fortune Press, 1942; *Women of the Happy Island,* Maclellan, 1944; *Script from Norway* (also printed under name Joseph Macleod), Maclellan, 1953.

Plays: "The Suppliants of Aeschylus with a Verse Sequel," first produced in Cambridge, England, 1933; "A Woman Turned to Stone," first produced in Cambridge, 1934; "Miracle for St. George," first produced in Cambridge, 1935; (under pseudonym Adam Drinan) *The Ghosts of the Strath,* Fortune Press, 1943; "Leap in September," first produced in Perth, Scotland, 1952. Also author of music, "The Kid from the City," Dix, 1941; and of screenplay, "Someone Wasn't Thinking," 1947. Contributor of articles and stories to periodicals.

WORK IN PROGRESS: Harriet Siddons and the Edinburgh Theatre; The Planets, a long satirically narrative poem.

SIDELIGHTS: Joseph Macleod wrote: "I started writing as a highbrow, and somewhat too learnedly trying to interpret the world of the 1920s as the Diaghilev Ballet did on the stage and Pound did in verse and Virginia Woolf in fiction. Eight years as a professional actor or play-director reduced exaggeration of self. Similarly, living in Huntingdonshire turned me from being a theoretical socialist into an active worker for the agricultural labourers. My first wife (who was on the local district council) and I were partly responsible for starting the Left Book Club and local branches throughout Britain.

"The years I chattered professionally on the air emasculated my prose for a time; but I did succeed in getting it again as accurate as verse. Broadcasting also kept me in constant close touch with public events and real people. I got more and more involved with meaning, even metaphysical (not religious) meaning; both of the world and its governments and of words themselves. I often find it necessary to break up the ambiguity of popular grammar to reveal or define real meaning. For this reason, I think I have practically no channels left to reach the reading public; but I go on writing.

"I am married to an Italian wife and have been living in Italy for 20 years. I have some ability in Italian; perhaps more than I had in French or Spanish. Latin, Greek and Russian are still to some extent in my head as written languages, but I am a poor linguist."

AVOCATIONAL INTERESTS: Driving cars, listening to music, cats and dogs, pruning trees, making olive oil.

* * *

MACNAB, Roy 1923-

PERSONAL: Born September 17, 1923, in Durban, South Africa; son of Andrew M. (a director) and Ethel Helen (Griffith) Macnab; married Rachel Heron-Maxwell, December 6, 1947; children: Celia, Simon. *Education:* Jesus College, Oxford, M.A., 1955. *Religion:* Protestant. *Office:* South Africa Foundation, 7 Buckingham Gate, London S.W.1, England.

CAREER: South African High Commission, London, England, cultural attache, 1955-59; South African Embassy, Paris, France, counselor, 1959-67; South Africa Foundation, London, director, 1968—. *Military service:* South African Navy, 1942-45, serving with Royal Navy. *Member:* Royal Society of Arts. *Awards, honors:* Silver medal from Royal Society of Arts, 1957.

WRITINGS: (Editor with Martin Starkie) *Oxford Poetry, 1947,* Basil Blackwell, 1947; *Testament of a South African and Other Poems,* Fortune Press, 1947; (editor with Charles Gulston) *South African Poetry: A New Anthology,* Collins, 1948; (editor) *Poets in South Africa,* Maskew Miller, 1958; *The Man of Grass and Other Poems,* St. Catherine Press, 1960; *Journey into Yesterday* (historical), Howard Timmins, 1962; *The French Colonel: Villebois-Mareuil and the Boers, 1899-1900* (historical biography), Oxford University Press, 1975.

Work has been anthologized in *The Oxford Book of South African Verse,* edited by Guy Butler, Oxford University Press, 1959; and *The Penguin Book of South African Verse,* edited by Jack Cope and Uys Krige, Penguin, 1969.

* * *

MACRORIE, Ken(neth) 1918-

PERSONAL: Born September 8, 1918, in Moline, Ill.; married, 1952 (divorced); married second wife, 1965. *Education:* Oberlin College, A.B., 1940; University of North Carolina, M.A., 1948; Columbia University, Ph.D., 1955. *Home:* 1030 West Main, Kalamazoo, Mich. 49007. *Office:* Department of English, Western Michigan University, Kalamazoo, Mich. 49001.

CAREER: University of North Carolina, Chapel Hill, instructor in English, 1946-48; Michigan State University, East Lansing, instructor, 1948-55, assistant professor of communication skills, 1955-60; San Francisco State College (now University), San Francisco, Calif., associate professor of English, 1960-61; Western Michigan University, Kalamazoo, associate professor, 1961-66, professor of English, 1966—. *Military service:* U.S. Army, 1942-46. *Member:* National Council of Teachers of English, Conference on College Composition and Communication.

WRITINGS: The Perceptive Writer, Reader, and Speaker, Harcourt, 1959; (editor) *Four in Depth,* Houghton, 1963; *Writing to Be Read* (high school text), Hayden, 1968; *Telling Writing,* Hayden, 1970; *Uptaught,* Hayden, 1970; *A Vulnerable Teacher,* Hayden, 1974. Writer of column, "A Room with Class," in *Media & Methods* magazine, 1975—. Contributor to literature journals, including *Reporter* and *Antioch Review.* Editor of *Journal of the Conference on College Composition and Communication,* 1962-64.

MacVANE, John (Franklin) 1912-

PERSONAL: Born April 29, 1912, in Portland, Me.; son of William Leslie and Bertha (Achorn) MacVane; married Lucy Maxwell, December 19, 1937 (divorced, 1967); married Henriette Butler Kidder (a bus tour designer), May 27, 1969; children: Ian (deceased), Myles Angus, Sara Ann Andrew, Mathew Chattan, Fiona Ellen (Mrs. Reginald Phipps). *Education:* Williams College, B.A., 1933; Exeter College, Oxford, B.Litt., 1936. *Residence:* Westport, Conn. *Office:* ABC Bureau, Room C-321, United Nations, New York, N.Y. 10017.

CAREER: Brooklyn Daily Eagle, Brooklyn, N.Y., reporter and ship news columnist, 1935-36; *New York Sun,* New York City, reporter, 1937-38; *Daily Express,* London, England, sub-editor, 1938-39; International News Service, Paris, France, correspondent covering fall of France, 1939-40; National Broadcasting Co. (NBC), New York City, war correspondent, 1940-45, assigned to British Army, London, 1940-42, to North African campaign in Morocco, Algeria, and Tunisia, 1942-43, to British and U.S. armies covering Casablanca conference, 1943, to U.S. Army, 1944-45, covering Normandy on D-Day, United Nations correspondent, 1946-50, assignments including coverage of UN Security Council, 1946, Berlin air lift, 1948, and UN General Assembly in Paris, 1948, adviser to U.S. mission to UN, 1950-52; American Broadcasting Co. (ABC), New York City, UN bureau chief, 1953—. Notable assignments include wartime coverage of Dieppe raid and liberation of Paris, and the meeting of U.S. and Russian armies on the Elbe river.

MEMBER: United Nations Correspondents Association (president, 1964), Association France-Etats Unis, American Federation of Television and Radio Artists, Association of Radio-Television News Analysts (president, 1948-49, 1955-56), Pilgrims of the United States, Society of the Silurians, Deadline Club, St. Andrew's Society of the State of New York, Press Club of London, Gargoyle Society, Sigma Delta Chi, Sigma Phi (trustee of Williams College chapter, 1968-73), Fairfield County Hunt Club, Williams Club. *Awards, honors:* National Headliners award, 1947, for UN coverage, Chevalier of Legion of Honor, 1947; Medaille de la France liberee, 1948; American Association for the United Nations award, 1960, for UN coverage; received Purple Heart and European medals.

WRITINGS: Journey into War: War and Diplomacy in North Africa, Appleton, 1942 (published in England as *War and Diplomacy in North Africa,* R. Hale, 1944). Also author of pamphlets for Public Affairs Committee (New York): *Embassy Extraordinary: The U.S. Mission to the United Nations,* 1961; *The House that People Built: The United Nations,* 1964; *This House Divided: Issues Before the United Nations,* 1964. Author and commentator of six-program series, "Alaska: The Last Frontier," National Education Television (NET), 1960. Writer of column, "A Line on Liners," *Brooklyn Daily Eagle,* 1935-36.

SIDELIGHTS: MacVane writes, "I started covering the United Nations because I had seen so much death and destruction during World War II that I wanted to see how humanity would learn, however slowly, to work together to construct and consolidate peace through the postwar years."

* * *

MADDEN, Daniel Michael 1916-

PERSONAL: Born October 30, 1916, in New York, N.Y.; son of Thomas P. and Anna Elizabeth (Hanlon) Madden;

married Huan Wilson (in public relations), October 18, 1941. *Education:* City College (now of the City University of New York), B.A., 1939. *Politics:* Independent. *Religion:* Roman Catholic. *Home:* 4750 North Central, Phoenix, Ariz. 85012. *Office:* Via G. Mercalli 6, Rome 00197, Italy.

CAREER: Free-lance writer in New York, 1939-42; *Phoenix Gazette,* Phoenix, Ariz., general reporter, 1945-48, legislative correspondent, 1954-57; U.S. Foreign Service, Washington, D.C., foreign service officer in Paris, Brussels, Copenhagen, and Vienna, 1948-54; free-lance writer from Europe (especially for *New York Times*), 1957—. *Military service:* U.S. Naval Reserve, active duty, 1942-45; served in Pacific theater. *Member:* Foreign Press Club of Italy. *Awards, honors: Operation Escape* was named "book for brotherhood" by B'nai B'rith and among one hundred best books for young people by *New York Times,* both 1962.

WRITINGS: Operation Escape (juvenile), Hawthorn, 1962; *Monuments to Glory* (juvenile), Hawthorn, 1964; (with James F. Cunningham) *American Pastor in Rome,* Doubleday, 1966; (with Kay Sullivan) *Journey of Love,* Appleton, 1966; *Spain and Portugal: Iberian Portrait,* Thomas Nelson, 1969; *A Religious Guide to Europe,* Macmillan, 1975. Contributor to popular magazines and to newspapers.

SIDELIGHTS: Madden writes that he has an "interest in foreign languages, including classical Latin and Greek; and non-verbal means of communication." He believes that "the development of the United States is linked to an understanding of other civilizations, especially the European."

* * *

MADISON, Joyce
  See MINTZ, Joyce Lois

* * *

MAGNUSSEN, Daniel Osar   1919-

PERSONAL: Born April 4, 1919, in Sturgeon Bay, Wis.; son of Daniel Ingebert (a warrant officer in the U.S. Coast Guard) and Tillie Dorothea (Engleson) Magnussen; married Lucille Marie Gordon, August 18, 1942. *Education:* University of Montana, B.A., 1963, M.A., 1964, Ph.D., 1972. *Politics:* "Apolitical." *Religion:* None. *Home:* 736 River Heights Rd., Menomonie, Wis. 54751. *Office:* Department of Social Sciences, University of Wisconsin-Stout, Menomonie, Wis. 54751.

CAREER: Green Bay & Western Railroad, Green Bay, Wis., secretary to superintendent of motive power, 1939-41; Amity Leather Products Co., West Bend, Wis., assistant to sales manager, 1946-47; Robert A. Johnston Co., Milwaukee, Wis., assistant to sales manager, 1948-50; U.S. Postal Service, Carmel, Calif., dispatcher, 1957-61; University of Wisconsin-Stout, Menomonie, Wis., assistant professor, 1965-68, associate professor, 1969-74, professor of history, 1975—. *Military service:* U.S. Army, 1941-46, 1950-56; received Silver Star, Bronze Star, and Belgian Fouragerre; U.S. Army Reserve, 1946-50, 1956-67; became lieutenant colonel. *Member:* National Historical Society, Montana Historical Society, Third Armored Division Association, Retired Officers Association, University of Montana Alumni Association, Phi Alpha Theta.

WRITINGS: Peter Thompson's Narrative of the Little Bighorn Campaign, 1876, Arthur H. Clark, 1974.

WORK IN PROGRESS: Fiction.

SIDELIGHTS: Magnussen entered college as a freshman at the age of forty-two and received his bachelor's degree in nineteen months.

* * *

MAHER, James T(homas)   1917-

PERSONAL: Surname is pronounced Mar; born January 27, 1917, in Cleveland, Ohio; son of James T. (a city construction inspector) and Anna Marie (a lawyer) Maher; married Virginia M. Maddocks, May 28, 1948 (divorced July 2, 1954); married Barbara Joan Judd, February 9, 1962; children: (second marriage) Frederick James. *Education:* Attended Ohio State University. *Residence:* New York, N.Y. *Agent:* Donald K. Congdon, Harold Matson Co., Inc., 22 East 40th St., New York, N.Y. 10016.

CAREER: Cleveland Plain Dealer, Cleveland, Ohio, sports reporter, 1934-35; Ohio State University, Columbus, publicity assistant in athletics department, 1937-40; United Press Associations, Columbus, Ohio, regional sports editor, 1940; Intercollegiate Conference of Faculty Representatives (Western Conference, or "Big Ten"), Chicago, Ill., public relations director, 1942-43; Texas Co. (now Texaco, Inc.), New York City, in public relations department, 1945-50; Cunningham & Walsh, Inc. (advertising agency), New York City, in public relations department, 1950-54; Texaco, Inc., in public relations department 1954-58; writer, 1958—. *Military service:* U.S. Army, 1943-45; served in England and Northern Ireland. *Awards, honors: American Popular Song* was nominated for National Book Award in 1972, and won Deems Taylor Award from American Society of Composers, Authors, and Publishers, 1975.

WRITINGS: (Editor and author of introduction) Alec Wilder, *American Popular Song: The Great Innovators, 1900 to 1950,* Oxford University Press, 1972, revised edition, 1975; *Chronicles of the Age of the American Palaces,* Little, Brown, Volume I: *The Twilight of Splendor,* 1975, Volume II: *A Season of Splendor,* in press. Author of television script for "Omnibus," Columbia Broadcasting System, 1954. Author of record album liner notes. Contributor of articles to industrial and corporate publications and of articles and stories to music journals and popular magazines, including *Saturday Evening Post, Ladies' Home Journal,* and *Holiday.*

WORK IN PROGRESS: Let's Dance: Music on the Air, nonfiction; *The Distant Music of Summer,* a novel; a novella; "Seascape, with Lovers," a libretto for a musical comedy, with Will Lorin.

* * *

MAISKY, Ivan (Mikhailovich)   1884-1975

PERSONAL: Original name Ivan Mikhailovich Lyakhovetsky; born January 19, 1884, in Kiriloff (Siberia), Russia; son of a Russian Army physician; married Agnes Alexandrovna Skippin, 1922. *Education:* Attended University of St. Petersburg and University of Munich.

CAREER: Began as a journalist in England in 1912; entered Soviet Diplomatic Service after the Revolution of 1917; headed government-sponsored expedition to explore Mongolia and establish the Mongolian Republic, 1919; president of Siberian State Planning Commission, 1921; Moscow Foreign Office, Moscow, Soviet Union, chief of press department, 1922; Soviet Embassy, London, England, counselor, 1925-27; Soviet Embassy, Tokyo, Japan, counselor, 1927-29; minister to Finland, 1929-32; Soviet Embassy, London, England, ambassador, 1933-43; assistant People's Commissar for Foreign Affairs of the Soviet Union, 1943-46; academician and writer, 1946-75. *Member:* Academy of Sciences of the Union of Soviet Socialist Republics. *Awards, honors:* Order of Lenin, 1942; Order of the Red Banner of Labor, 1944, 1945, 1964.

WRITINGS: Before the Storm: Recollections (in Russian), State Publishing House of Art and Literature, 1944, English translation by Gerard Shelley, Hutchinson & Co., 1944; *Journey into the Past: Reminiscences of a Russian Political Emigrant in London, 1912-1917* (in Russian), Academy of Sciences of the Union of Soviet Socialist Republics, 1960, English translation by Frederick Holt published as *Journey into the Past*, Hutchinson, 1962; *Who Helped Hitler: From the Recollections of a Soviet Ambassador* (in Russian), [Moscow], 1962, English translation by Andrew Rothstein published as *Who Helped Hitler?*, Hutchinson, 1964; *Spanish Notebooks* (in Russian), [Moscow], 1962, English translation by Ruth Kisch, Hutchinson, 1966; *Memoirs of a Soviet Ambassador: The War, 1939-1943* (in Russian), [Moscow], 1964, English translation by Rothstein, Hutchinson, 1967, Scribner, 1968.

Books not published in English: *Marxism and the Questions of War and Peace*, [St. Petersburg], 1916; *On the Origins of the German Professional Movement*, [Petrograd], 1917; *Contemporary Mongolia: Account of the Mongolian Expedition Equipped by the Irkutsk Bureau All-Russian Central Union Consumers' Society*, [Irkutsk], 1921; *Soviet Russia and the Capitalist World*, [Moscow], 1922; *Democratic Counter-Revolution*, [Moscow], 1923; *Spain, 1808-1917: A Historical Essay*, Academy of Sciences of the Union of Soviet Socialist Republics, 1957; *Mongolia on the Eve of Revolution*, [Moscow], 1959; (editor) *On the History of the Freedom Fighters of the Spanish People*, Academy of Sciences of the Union of Soviet Socialist Republics, 1959; *Recollections of a Soviet Ambassador in England*, [Moscow], 1960; (editor) *Problems of the Working-Class Anti-Fascist Movement in Spain*, Academy of Sciences of the Union of Soviet Socialist Republics, 1960; (editor) *The Spanish People against Fascism*, Academy of Sciences of the Union of Soviet Socialist Republics, 1963; *Memoirs of a Soviet Ambassador*, two volumes, [Moscow], 1964; *War Or Peace*, Nauka, 1964; (editor) *International Relations*, Academy of Sciences of the Union of Soviet Socialist Republics, 1964; (editor) *Under the Banner of the Spanish Republic*, Soviet Committee of War Veterans, 1965; (editor) *The Workers' Movement in the Scandinavian Countries*, Academy of Sciences of the Union of Soviet Socialist Republics, 1965; *Bernard Shaw and the Others: Reminiscences*, Iskusstvo, 1967; *Recollections of a Soviet Diplomat, 1925-1945*, Nauka, 1971.

Other untranslated works: *Germany and the War*, 1916; *Political Germany*, 1917; *Foreign Policy of R.S.F.S.R., 1917-1922*, 1922; *So Near and Yet So Far* (novel), 1958; (editor) *Problems of Spanish History*, 1971; *Trade Union Movement in the West*.

SIDELIGHTS: Jailed and later exiled from Russia for his revolutionary activities, Lyakhovetsky went to Germany in 1908 and became a Social Democrat. After the Revolution of 1917, he returned to the Soviet Union, changed his name to Maisky, and became a Communist. During his diplomatic career, his signature accompanied many important international agreements involving the Soviet Union. His books have appeared in Italian, French, and German.

OBITUARIES: Washington Post, September 5, 1975.*

(Died in 1975, in Moscow, Soviet Union)

MAJERUS, Janet 1936-

PERSONAL: Born March 30, 1936, in Illinois; daughter of I. L. (a teacher) and Gertrude (a librarian; maiden name, Duncan) Brakensiek; married Philip W. Majerus (a college professor), December 28, 1957; children: Suzanne, David, Julie, Karen. *Education:* University of Illinois, B.S., 1958. *Residence:* University City, Mo. 63130.

CAREER: C. V. Mosby Co. (publishers), St. Louis, Mo., book editor, 1958-60; free-lance editor and writer, 1960—. *Member:* Authors Guild of Authors League of America.

WRITINGS: Grandpa and Frank (novel), Lippincott, 1976.

WORK IN PROGRESS: Benediction, a novel.

SIDELIGHTS: Janet Majerus writes: "I am a product of small town, middle America. Even though I have lived in large metropolitan areas in the East (Boston and Washington), I find my writing keeps returning to the Midwest and, in particular, to the people who live in its small towns and rural areas." *Avocational interests:* Organic gardening, wilderness backpacking.

* * *

MAJOR, Mark Imre 1923-

PERSONAL: Born March 26, 1923, in Budapest, Hungary; naturalized U.S. citizen, 1974; son of John M. (a farmer) and Agnes (Handrick) Major. *Education:* Cistercian Academy, Zirc, Hungary, B.A. (philosophy and religion), 1949; Peter Pazmany University, B.A. (history and literature), 1950; Texas Christian University, M.A., 1971, Ph.D., 1972. *Religion:* Roman Catholic. *Home address:* Route 2, Box 1, Irving, Tex. 75062. *Office:* Cisterian Preparatory School, Route 2, Box 1, Irving, Tex. 75062.

CAREER: High school teacher in Hungary, 1951-56; Cisterian Preparatory School for Gifted Children, Irving, Tex., teacher, 1972—. Associate professor of history and chairperson of department, University of Plano, 1973-76. *Member:* American Historical Association, Academy of Political Science, American Association for the Study of Hungarian History, Southern Conference on Slavic Studies.

WRITINGS: American-Hungarian Relations, 1918-1945, Danubian Press, 1974; (translator) John Zinner, *Noteworthy Letters and Writings by Famous Generals in America With Their Biographies Appended*, Alpha, 1977. Contributor to history and political science journals.

WORK IN PROGRESS: Daniel Webster and Louis Kossuth: The Impact of the Hungarian Revolution in 1848 upon American Foreign Policies, publication expected in 1978.

SIDELIGHTS: Major writes: "The English colonists who landed at Massachusetts Bay colony carry with themselves not only the memories of the past but the visions of the future, too. I am interested in tracing the fulfillment of this vision: how the American idea of liberty and democracy influenced and challenged faraway countries and peoples in Europe.

"Being born and brought up in Europe I witnessed wars, dictatorships, and revolutions. I also witnessed the yearning of nations and peoples for freedom, liberty, and democracy. I met many people; scholars, statesmen, and ordinary common men of the present, as well as of the past through my research, who looked upon America as a spearhead of those great ideas in an oppressed world. The attraction of American history and thought is the main theme of my writings."

BIOGRAPHICAL/CRITICAL SOURCES: Hungarian Studies Newsletter, autumn, 1975.

MAKOWER, Addie (Gertrude Leonaura) 1906-

PERSONAL: Born January 8, 1906, in London, England; daughter of Sir Leonard (a member of Parliament) and Laura (Ladborough) Franklin; married John Makower, July 8, 1926; children: Rachel Nugee, Frances, Oliver, Prudence Ingham Clark, Prudence Monck. *Education:* Attended University College, London. *Politics:* Liberal. *Religion:* Jewish. *Home:* Holmwood Shiplake, Henley, Oxford, England.

CAREER: Worked as rural district councillor in England. Free-lance writer. Member, Women's Voluntary Services; president, Women's Institute. *Member:* Writers Circle (chairwoman). *Awards, honors: Observer* short story prize.

WRITINGS—All children's books: *Little Black Spillikins,* Pitman, 1938; *Daffy Down Dilly* (play), Pitman, 1938; *Little Mr. Huffy-Puffy,* Collins, 1946; *Smuggler's Gold,* Dennis Dobson, 1968. Also author of play "Jennifer Walks In Springtime," 1938, and of scripts for children's radio series, 1972.

WORK IN PROGRESS: A television series for children.

* * *

MALABRE, Alfred L(eopold, Jr.) 1931-

PERSONAL: Surname is pronounced Ma-*larb;* born April 23, 1931, in New York, N.Y.; son of Alfred L. and Marie (Cassidy) Malabre; married Mary Patricia Wardropper; children: Richard, Ann, John. *Education:* Yale University, B.A., 1952; Columbia University, M.S., 1953. *Politics:* Independent. *Home:* 320 East 72nd St., New York, N.Y. 10021. *Office: Wall Street Journal,* 22 Cortlandt St., New York, N.Y. 10007.

CAREER: U.S. Navy, career officer, 1953-56, retiring as lieutenant; worked as rewrite man on *Hartford Courant,* 1957-58; *Wall Street Journal,* New York City, worked on Midwest edition in Chicago, Ill., 1958-60, transferred to London bureau, 1960-61, Bonn bureau chief, 1961-62, joined New York City bureau as economics reporter, 1962-68, news editor for economics, 1968-72, news editor, 1972—. *Member:* Pilgrims Society of the United States. *Awards, honors:* Poynter fellow at Yale University, 1976.

WRITINGS: Understanding the Economy: For People Who Can't Stand Economics, Dodd, 1976.

Work represented in anthologies, including *Here Comes Tomorrow* and *The World of the Wall Street Journal.* Columnist, "Outlook" in *Wall Street Journal.* Contributor to *Encyclopaedia Britannica* and *Dow Jones Investors Handbook,* and to popular magazines, including *Harper's, Money, Saturday Review, Reporter,* and *Science Digest.*

SIDELIGHTS: Malabre feels "that understanding of our economic system and the forces that move our economy is vital to country's well-being." He adds that "economics need not be a dismally dull and hard-to-grasp subject—which unfortunately seems to be the case at many schools and universities."

* * *

MALLET-JORIS, Francoise 1930-

PERSONAL: Born July 6, 1930, in Antwerp, Belgium; became French citizen; daughter of Albert (Belgian Minister of Justice) and Suzanne (a dramatist; maiden name, Verbist) Lilar; married Robert Amadou (divorced); married Alain Joxe (marriage ended); married Jacques Delfau (a painter); children: Daniel, Vincent, Alberte, Pauline. *Education:* Attended Bryn Mawr College, and Sorbonne, University of Paris. *Religion:* Roman Catholic. *Home:* 7 rue Jacob, 75006 Paris, France. *Office:* Editions Grasset, 61 rue des Saints-Peres, Paris 6eme, France.

CAREER: Novelist, 1950—; Editions Julliard (publishers), Paris, France, director of "Nouvelle" collection, 1960-65; Editions Grasset (publishers), Paris, member of reading committee, 1965—. Member of jury for Prix Femina, 1969-70; Goncourt Academy, member of prize jury, 1970-73, vice-president, 1973—. *Awards, honors:* Prix Femina, 1958, for *L'Empire Celeste;* Grand Prix Litteraire de Monaco, 1965.

WRITINGS: Poemes du dimanche (title means "Sunday Poems"), 1947; *Le Rempart des Beguines* (novel), Julliard, 1951, translation by Herma Briffault published as *The Illusionist,* Farrar, Straus, 1952 (published in England as *Into the Labyrinth,* W. H. Allen, 1953); *La Chambre rouge* (novel), Julliard, 1955, translation by Briffault published as *The Red Room,* Farrar, Straus, 1956; *Cordelia* (short novels), Julliard, 1956, translation by Peter Green published as *Cordelia and Other Stories,* Farrar, Straus, 1965; *Les Mensonges* (novel), Julliard, 1956, translation by Briffault published as *House of Lies,* Farrar, Straus, 1957; (editor) *Nouvelles* (stories), Julliard, 1957; *L'Empire Celeste* (novel), Julliard, 1958, translation by Briffault published as *Cafe Celeste,* Farrar, Straus, 1959.

Les Personnages (novel), Julliard, 1961, translation by Briffault published as *The Favourite,* Farrar, Straus, 1962; (compiler) *Le Rendez-vous donne par Francoise Mallet-Joris a quelques jeunes ecrivans,* Julliard, 1962; *Lettre a moi-meme* (memoir), Julliard, 1963, translation by Patrick O'Brian published as *A Letter to Myself,* Farrar, Straus, 1964; *Marie Mancini: Le Premier amour de Louis XIV* (historical novel), translation by O'Brian published as *The Uncompromising Heart: A Life of Marie Mancini, Louis XIV's First Love,* Farrar, Straus, 1966; *Les Signes et les prodigies* (novel), B. Grasset, 1966, translation by Briffault published as *Signs and Wonders,* Farrar, Straus, 1966; *Enfance, ton regard,* Hachette, 1966; *Trois ages de la nuit, histories de sorcellerie* (novel), B. Grasset, translation by Briffault published as *The Witches: Three Tales of Sorcery,* Farrar, Straus, 1969; (editor) *Lettres de Madame de Sevigne,* Club des classiques, 1969.

La Maison de papier (memoir), B. Grasset, 1970, translation by Derek Coltman published as *The Paper House,* Farrar, Straus, 1971; *Le Roi qui aimait trop les fleurs,* Casterman, 1971; *Le Jeu du souterrain,* B. Grasset, 1973; *Les Feuilles mortes d'un bel ete,* B. Grasset, 1974. Also author of screenplays, "Le Gigolo," 1962, and "Le Rempart des Beguines" (an adaptation of her novel), 1972.

SIDELIGHTS: Francoise Mallet-Joris' first novel, *Le Rempart des Beguines,* was written while the author was still a teenager. The book, published in the United States as *The Illusionist* was a *succes de scandale,* as it dealt with the seduction of a fifteen year old girl by her father's mistress. Mallet-Joris was compared to Sagan and Laclos as a result of the novel, but those designations have been generally dropped, and the novel remains as a successful deliniation of adolescent trauma as recorded by a writer barely out of adolescence herself.

In the years following the publication of *The Illusionist,* Mallet-Joris became something of a celebrity in France. Although her work is widely read and admired in some circles, it is largely ignored in others. Regardless, she is interviewed by the press frequently. A writer for the *Times Literary Supplement* reports that "even people who have never read any of her books know that she has four children, that her husband is a painter, that she is a devout Catholic convert, and that she gets up very early in the morning to go to a cafe to do her writing."

Mallet-Joris' intense Catholicism is felt by many critics to be an important force in her writing. Her sixth novel, published in English as *Signs and Wonders* is a love story set against the French-Algerian conflict. The novel deals with questions relative to war in general and with the kinds of personal compromises which must be made as a result of war. Her protagonist, Nicolas Leclusier, is traced through his attempt and final failure to come to terms with himself and with compromise. The character Nicolas says, "Everything becomes transformed beneath my eyes, becomes polluted in my hands; God is my malady."

Charles Managhan compares her not to Sagan, but to Proust and recognizes the Catholic influence in her work. "Francoise Mallet-Joris is the sort of novelist who makes young French intellectuals apoplectic," he writes. "*Signs and Wonders,* a beautifully constructed novel abrim with wisdom is a good indication why. Mallet-Joris is the master of an art that walks in the footsteps of Proust, an art that is one generation old. That is both her strength and her weakness.

"Her art lives in awe of Proust's incredible demonstration that unraveling a love affair can reveal all a writer would want to reveal: passion, venality, fun, stupidity, class antagonisms, tenderness. But it is also a Roman Catholic's art—a very contemporary Roman Catholic, that is, working within a philosophical framework close to those of Graham Greene and Muriel Spark, reacting against the soppy tide of uplift that dominated Catholic writing in the '20's and '30's. For Mrs. Mallet-Joris, the hallmark of the seriously religious man is continuous reappraisal, not G. K. Chesterton's *joie de vivre.*"

In a turn away from the reflective love story motif employed in *Signs and Wonders,* Mallet-Joris produced a historical novel. *The Witches,* as it appeared in English, deals with three documented witch trials in the age of the Renaissance. Mallet-Joris presents the women's life histories and the events leading up their eventual denunciations as witches and consequent trials. In her preface to the novel Mallet-Joris stated that while the women she chose to portray were actual historical figures, she departed from strict adherence to the available facts regarding them and their trials in order to explore the "spirit" of the witch trial phenomenon.

Pierre Courtines comments: "Since the author's intention was mainly to recapture the spirit of the times in which her heroines lived, she has not hesitated to change historical facts. . . . Each of the three short stories could be called a case history in abnormal psychology with emphasis on the struggle between good and evil, and the religious obsessions of her characters, their families, and relations. In doing so, she involves the reader, for the three heroines, in spite of their personal demons, are very close to the norm in their reactions to their environment, their families, and townsfolk. What is particularly fascinating is the intuitive knowledge of psychology revealed by the three women, who seem to manipulate those around them in a manner not unworthy of today's most subtle hidden persuaders."

A reviewer for *Time* praised Mallet-Joris' gift for historic imagination. He said "statistics and dry records are unlikely to convey . . . any idea of the atmosphere that hangs for days, according to the author, in a town square after a witch has been burned. Is the smell, for instance reassuring, since it signifies that evil has been expunged? Or is it unsettling, because it calls to mind a dreadful spectacle too heartily enjoyed? Such questions elude the historian.

"Novelist Mallet-Joris, however, seems imaginatively sure of the answers. . . . It is not frivolous to say that she learned the feel of the late 16th and early 17th centuries by writing these novels, and that she wrote them in order to learn. . . . What clay and fire make a witch? Write a novel, watch, and find out."

BIOGRAPHICAL/CRITICAL SOURCES: Saturday Review, April 28, 1962, May 23, 1964; *New Yorker,* July 11, 1964, July 31, 1971; Francoise Mallet-Joris, *Letter to Myself,* translated by Patrick O'Brian, Farrar, Straus, 1964; *New Statesman,* August 27, 1965; *National Observer,* October 9, 1967; Dorothy Nyren Curley and Arthur Curley, *Modern Romance Literatures,* Ungar, 1967; *Commonweal,* December 27, 1968, January 16, 1970; *Books Abroad,* Spring, 1969; *Atlantic,* September, 1969; *Newsweek,* September 22, 1969; *Time* October 31, 1969; Francoise Mallet-Joris, *The Paper House,* translated by Derek Coltman, Farrar, Straus, 1971; *New York Times Book Review,* May 29, 1971; *Times Literary Supplement,* May 4, 1973.*

*   *   *

MALONE, Bill C(harles) 1934-

PERSONAL: Born August 25, 1934, in Smith County, Tex.; son of Cleburne and Maude (Owins) Malone. *Education:* University of Texas, B.A., 1956, M.A., 1958, Ph.D., 1965. *Politics:* Democrat. *Religion:* Unaffiliated. *Home:* 2030 Jefferson Ave., New Orleans, La. 70115. *Office:* Department of History, Tulane University, New Orleans, La. 70118.

CAREER: Southwest Texas State University, San Marcos, instructor, 1962-64, assistant professor of history, 1964-67; Murray State University, Murray, Kan., associate professor of history, 1967-69; Wisconsin State University, Whitewater, associate professor of history, 1969-71; Tulane University, New Orleans, La., associate professor of history, 1971—. *Member:* Organization of American Historians, American Folklore Society, Popular Culture Association, Country Music Association, Southern Historical Association, Louisiana Historical Association.

WRITINGS: Country Music, U.S.A.: A Fifty-Year History, University of Texas Press, 1968; (editor with Judith McCulloh) *Stars of Country Music: Uncle Dave Macon to Jonny Rodriguez,* University of Illinois Press, 1975. Contributor to *Encyclopedia of Southern History* and *Grove's Dictionary of Music and Musicians.* Contributor to folklore and country music magazines.

WORK IN PROGRESS: The Lingering South: Country Music in an Urban Society; History of Texas Country Music, completion expected in 1978.

SIDELIGHTS: Malone is himself a musician; he has a bluegrass band, "The Hill Country Ramblers," which performs regularly in the New Orleans area and at music festivals.

*   *   *

MALTZ, Maxwell 1899-1975

PERSONAL: Born March 10, 1899, in New York, N.Y.; son of Joseph and Tobey (Ellsweig) Maltz; married Anne Harabin, February 10, 1966. *Education:* Columbia University, B.S., 1919, M.D., 1923; graduate study of plastic surgery in Europe, 1924-25. *Home:* 300 East 56th St., New York, N.Y. 10022.

CAREER: Plastic surgeon in New York City at Beth Israel Hospital, 1925-35, and Metropolitan Hospital, 1930-36; plastic reconstructive surgeon at Beth David Hospital, 1930-39; also served as director of department of plastic reconstructive surgery at West Side Hospital; free-lance writer. Honorary professor at University of Santo Domingo, University of Nicaragua, University of Honduras, University of El Salvador, University of Guatemala, and University of Athens; lecturer in Cuba, Panama, and Costa Rica; professor and director of Fort Lauderdale University's Institute of Cybernetics, 1972. President of Tobey Maltz Foundation for Research in Tissue Growth, Degeneration, and Repair.

MEMBER: International College of Surgeons (fellow), Latin-American Society of Plastic Surgeons (fellow), Brazilian College of Surgeons (honorary fellow), Mexican College of Military Surgeons (honorary fellow), Mexican Association of Plastic Surgeons (fellow), University of Santo Domingo Academy of Medicine (honorary fellow), American Physicians Literary Guild (fellow), American Association for the Advancement of Science (fellow), American Medical Association, New York Academy of Sciences (fellow), New York State Medical Society, New York County Medical Society. *Awards, honors:* Sc.D. from University of Guatemala.

WRITINGS: New Faces, New Futures: Rebuilding Character with Plastic Surgery, R. R. Smith, 1936; *The Evolution of Plastic Surgery,* Froben Press, 1946; *Doctor Pygmalion: The Autobiography of a Plastic Surgeon,* Crowell, 1953; *Adventures in Staying Young* (memoirs), Crowell, 1955 (published in England as *Prescription for Youth,* Museum Press, 1956); *Psycho-Cybernetics: A New Way to Get More Living Out of Life,* Prentice-Hall, 1960; *Five Minutes to Happiness,* Obolensky, 1962; *The Magic Power of Self-Image Psychology: The New Way to a Bright, Full Life,* Prentice-Hall, 1964; *Creative Living for Today,* Trident, 1967; (with Raymond Charles Barker) *The Conquest of Frustration,* Constellation International, 1969; *Power Psycho-Cybernetics for Youth: A New Dimension in Personal Freedom,* Grosset, 1971; *The Search for Self-Respect,* Grosset, 1973; *Psycho-Cybernetics and Self-Fulfillment,* Bantam, 1973; *Psycho-Cybernetics Principles for Creative Living,* Pocket Books, 1974; *Thoughts to Live By,* Pocket Books, 1975; *The Time Is Now* (novel), Simon & Schuster, 1975; (with Charles Schreiber) *A New Way to Live and Be Free,* O'Sullivan Woodside, 1975.

Plays: "The Unseen Scar," 1945; "Galatea," 1957; "Doctor Pygmalion's Mirror," 1958; "The Other Door," 1959; "The Sound of the Ram's Horn," 1960; "Juliet's Daughter," 1961; "The Four of Us," 1961; "The Fountain of Youth," 1961; "Somewhere to Go," 1963; "Emma," 1964; "Dorothy," 1964; "Cracks in the Wall," 1965.

Also author of *They Challenged Fate,* 1940, *The Long and Short of It,* 1943, *Cyrano's Dream: The Evolution of Plastic Surgery,* 1956, *The Goddess with the Golden Eye* (novel), 1956, *The Miracle of Doctor Fleming* (novel), 1957, *The Private Life of Doctor Pygmalion,* 1958, *The Face of Love,* 1959, *Fifty-Two Prescriptions,* 1960, *The Open Window,* 1963, *The Quest for Success and Happiness,* 1964; and of *Doctor Psycho-Cybernetics* published by Wilshire. Author of textbooks on rhino-plastic surgery. Contributor to professional journals.

SIDELIGHTS: Maltz produced "Secrets: Cassettes for Children Six to Twelve," 1970, and "The Maltz Cassette System for Self-Fulfillment," 1971.

(Died April 7, 1975, in New York, N.Y.)

MANNERS, William 1907-

PERSONAL: Born April 3, 1907, in Butler, Pa.; son of Harris (a rabbi) and Bertha (Schildhaus) Rosenberg; married Ande Miller (a writer), September 7, 1947 (died May 17, 1975); children: Julie, Jane, Tracy. *Education:* University of Cincinnati, B.A., 1932; Hebrew Union College (now Hebrew Union College—Jewish Institute of Religion), B.H.L., 1933. *Politics:* Independent. *Religion:* Jewish. *Home:* 239 East Rocks Road, Norwalk, Conn. 06851. *Agent:* Roberta Pryor, International Creative Management, 40 West 57th Street, New York, N.Y. 10019.

CAREER: Professional boxer, 1926-34; Hillman Periodicals, New York, N.Y., editor of reprints, 1943-50; *Alfred Hitchcock's Mystery Magazine,* New York City, editorial director, 1956-62; Famous Writers School, Westport, Conn., instructor, 1965-72. Writer of nonfiction works and novels.

WRITINGS: Father and the Angels, Dutton, 1947; (with Ted Cott and David X. Manners) *Isn't It a Crime?,* Arc Books, 1947; *One Is a Lonesome Number,* Dutton, 1950; *The Big Lure,* Lion Books, 1953; *Wharf Girl,* Lion Books, 1954; *The Do-It-Yourself Gadget Hunters Guide,* Bantam, 1955; *You Call That a House?,* John Day, 1956; *Wake Up and Write,* Arc Books, 1962; *The Barking Cat Case,* P. Collier, 1963; *The Crying Schoolhouse Case,* P. Collier, 1963; *The Fifty-pound Giant Case,* P. Collier, 1963; *The Talking Pigeon Case,* P. Collier, 1963; *The Frightened Dr. Pfanstock,* Putnam, 1965; *One, Two, Three, Go,* Four Winds Press, 1967; *TR and Will,* Harcourt, 1969; *Patience and Fortitude: Fiorello LaGuardia,* Harcourt, 1976.

WORK IN PROGRESS: Three non-fiction books.

SIDELIGHTS: Manners told *CA:* "I've been a vegetarian since I was a child—long before it became an in thing. As a pro boxer I did road work. Now I manage a 26 mile marathon every thirteen days, at the rate of two miles per day. Jogging is the present word for this sort of thing, but I insist on calling what I do running. I like to alternate between fiction and non-fiction; the former is my favorite."

*   *   *

MANNING, Michael 1940-

PERSONAL: Born December 31, 1940, in Muncie, Ind.; son of William John (a meatpacker) and Myrtle (a pianist; maiden name, Green) Manning. *Education:* State University of New York at Albany, B.A., 1965; Catholic University of America, S.T.B., 1969, M.F.A., 1971. *Home and office:* Divine Word Missionaries, 11316 Cypress Ave., Riverside, Calif. 92505.

CAREER: Roman Catholic priest of order of Divine Word; high school teacher of religion and English in Watts neighborhood of Los Angeles, Calif., 1969-71; Divine Word Missionaries, Riverside, Calif., recruiter for Divine Word College (Epworth, Iowa), 1971—. Pastor in Las Vegas, Nev. Host and producer of television show, "Run for Daylight," 1972-73; has worked as marriage counselor and vocation director; toured with Evangelist Morris Cerullo, 1974-75. *Member:* Society of the Divine Word (vice-provincial of Western Province).

WRITINGS: Pardon My Lenten Smile (Scripture meditations), Alba House, 1976. Author of "Stick Man," a television play on abortion, 1973.

WORK IN PROGRESS: Proclaimed from the Rooftops, a book of meditations on scripture, moving from the Easter experience to that of Pentecost; a musical on the life of Saint Paul, for television or the stage.

SIDELIGHTS: Fr. Manning writes: "I am very interested in the study of the Bible and the experience of Jesus Christ. I want to express this through the writing of meditations on scripture and then writing creatively for the media to convey the Jesus reality." *Avocational interests:* Sculpting, riding his motorcycle, taking photographs.

* * *

MANSFIELD, Peter 1928-

PERSONAL: Born September 2, 1928, in Ranchi, India; son of Philip Theodore (a civil servant in India) and Helen (Aked) Mansfield. *Education:* Pembroke College, Cambridge, B.A., 1952, M.A., 1957; studied at Middle East Center for Arabic Studies in Lebanon, 1955-56. *Politics:* Democratic Socialist. *Religion:* Christian. *Home and office:* 10 Wetherby Gardens, London S.W.5, England. *Agent:* Michael Sissons, A. D. Peters & Co., 10 Buckingham St., London W.C.2, England.

CAREER: Taught English in Paris, France, 1953-54; administrative assistant for U.S. Education Commission in United Kingdom, 1954-55; editor of *Middle East Economic Survey,* 1956-58; editor of *Middle East Forum,* 1958-60; *London Sunday Times,* London, England, correspondent in Middle East, 1961-67; free-lance writer, 1967—. *Military service:* British Army, 1947-49; became sergeant. *Member:* Royal Institute of International Affairs, British Middle East Studies Association (member of council, 1975-77), Middle East Studies Association of North America.

WRITINGS: Nasser's Egypt, Penguin, 1965, revised edition, 1969; *Nasser: A Political Biography,* Methuen, 1969; *The British in Egypt,* Weidenfeld & Nicolson, 1971; *The Ottoman Empire and Its Successors,* Macmillan, 1973; (editor and contributor) *The Middle East: A Political and Economic Survey,* Oxford University Press, 1973; *The Arabs,* Crowell, 1976.

WORK IN PROGRESS: Editing *Who's Who of the Arab World.*

* * *

MARCHAND, Leslie A(lexis) 1900-

PERSONAL: Born February 13, 1900, in Bridgeport, Wash.; son of Alexis (an inventor) and Clara (Buckingham) Marchand; married Marion Knill Hendrix (an artist and writer), July 8, 1950. *Education:* University of Washington, Seattle, B.A. 1922, M.A., 1923; Columbia University, Ph.D., 1940; attended Sorbonne, University of Paris, 1927-28, and University of Munich, summer, 1932. *Home:* 97 Lakeview Lane, Englewood, Fla. 33533.

CAREER: Alaska Agricultural College and School of Mines (now University of Alaska), Fairbanks, professor of English and French, 1923-27, 1934-35; Columbia University, lecturer in English, 1936-37; Rutgers University, New Brunswick, N.J., instructor, 1937-42, assistant professor, 1942-46, associate professor, 1946-53, professor of English, 1953-66, professor emeritus, 1966—. Instructor at University of Washington, Seattle, summer, 1924, visiting professor, summers, 1925, 1958; instructor at Columbia University, summers, 1929-31, visiting professor, summers, 1945-46, 1965; visiting professor at University of California, Los Angeles, summer, 1949, University of Illinois, summer, 1954, Arizona State University, 1966-67, and Harvard University, summer, 1969; Fulbright professor at University of Athens, 1958-59; professorial lecturer at Hunter College of the City University of New York, 1960-62; Berg Visiting

Professor at New York University, 1962-63; John Cranford Adams Professor of English at Hofstra University, 1967-68.

MEMBER: International P.E.N., Modern Language Association of America, Keats-Shelley Association of America (member of board of directors), Byron Society (vice-president), Phi Beta Kappa. *Awards, honors:* Book of the year award from New Jersey Association of Teachers of English, 1958, for *Byron: A Biography;* grants from American Council of Learned Societies, 1964, 1971, Carl and Lily Pdorzheimer Foundation, 1970, American Philosophical Society, 1970, and National Endowment for the Humanities, 1972-73, 1974-75, 1976-79; Guggenheim fellowship, 1968-69; James Russell Lowell Prize from Modern Language Association of America, 1974, for *Byron's Letters and Journals;* D.H.L. from University of Alaska, 1976.

WRITINGS: The Athenaeum: A Mirror of Victorian Culture, University of North Carolina Press, 1941; (editor and author of introduction) *Letters of Thomas Hood from the Dilke Papers in the British Museum,* Rutgers University Press, 1945; (editor and author of introduction) *Selected Poetry of Lord Byron,* Random House, 1951, revised edition, 1967; (contributor) Klaus W. Jones, editor, *The Maugham Enigma,* Citadel, 1954; *Byron: A Biography,* three volumes, Knopf, 1957; (editor and author of introduction) *Lord Byron: "Don Juan",* Houghton, 1958.

(Contributor) Rudolf Kirk and C. F. Main, editors, *Essays in Literary History,* Rutgers University Press, 1960; *Byron's Poetry: A Critical Introduction,* Houghton, 1965; *Byron: A Portrait,* Knopf, 1971; (editor) *Byron's Letters and Journals,* six volumes, Harvard University Press, Volume I: *In My Hot Youth,* 1973, Volume II: *Famous in My Time,* 1973, Volume III: *Alas! the Love of Women,* 1974, Volume IV: *Wedlock's the Devil,* 1975, Volume V: *So Late into the Night,* 1976, Volume VI: *The Flesh Is Frail,* 1976.

Reporter and city editor of *Fairbanks Daily News-Miner,* summer, 1926; night wire filing editor for Associated Press (Newark Bureau), 1943-44; author of "The Once Over," a column in *MS: A Magazine for Writers,* 1930. Contributor to *Encyclopedia Americana, Collier's Encyclopedia,* and *Encyclopaedia Britannica.* Contributor of about eighty articles and reviews to scholarly journals and to magazines and newspapers, including *Spectator, Christian Science Monitor, New York Times,* and *Saturday Review.*

WORK IN PROGRESS: Editing *Byron's Letters and Journals,* Volumes VII-XI, for Harvard University Press, completion expected in 1979.

SIDELIGHTS: In 1936, Marchand conducted tourists through Scotland, England, Belgium, the Netherlands, France, Germany, Switzerland, and Italy, for Intercollegiate Travel Bureau. Of his work, he writes: "I have spent thirty years in studying the life and work of the English poet Lord Byron. With all his peccadillos Byron had a sane and humane view of the world. He was a champion of liberty and a foe of cant and hypocrisy and pretension. And he is never dull."

BIOGRAPHICAL/CRITICAL SOURCES: Richard D. Altick, *The Scholar Adventurers,* Macmillan, 1950.

* * *

MARCHI, Giacomo
See BASSANI, Giorgio

* * *

MARCUS, Joe 1933-

PERSONAL: Born November 30, 1933, in New York,

N.Y.; son of David (a restaurant owner) and Celia (Halpern) Marcus; married Margaret Alberle, January 25, 1958; children: Bruce, Arthur. *Education:* City College (now of the City University of New York), B.A., 1955. *Religion:* Jewish. *Home:* 8 Hudson St., Hicksville, N.Y. 11801. *Agent:* Arthur Pine, 1780 Broadway, New York, N.Y. 10016. *Office: New York Post,* 220 South St., New York, N.Y. 10002.

CAREER: New York Post, New York, N.Y., sports writer, 1955—. Member of soccer board of U.S. committee of Sports for Israel; manager of U.S. team participating in Israel's Maccabiah Games, 1973; coach for soccer clubs in New York City. Part-owner of *Billiard Review.*

MEMBER: Soccer Writers and Broadcasters Association of America (president), North Shore Soccer Club (president), Glen Cove Soccer Club (vice-president), Hicksville Baseball Association (manager), B'nai B'rith (vice-president). *Awards, honors:* Humanitarian award from United Jewish Appeal, 1962; outstanding soccer writer awards from International Soccer League, 1965, 1966.

WRITINGS: Total Soccer, Popular Library, 1976; *The World of Pele,* Mason/Charter, 1976; *Tablesports,* Popular Library, 1976; *The Encyclopedia of Soccer,* Ritchie, in press. Contributor to *Encyclopedia Americana* and *Collier's Yearbook.* Contributing editor of *Soccer America, Black Sports, Kick,* and "Soccer on the Air" broadcasts.

* * *

MARGOLIES, Edward 1925-

PERSONAL: Born December 19, 1925, in Boston, Mass.; son of Jacob and Bessie (Freidson) Margolies; married Claire Norman (a researcher and high school language teacher), June 30, 1958; children: Jacob, Peter, William. *Education:* Brown University, B.A., 1950; New York University, M.A., 1959, Ph.D., 1964. *Home:* 141 East Third St., New York, N.Y. 10009. *Agent:* Gunther Stuhlmann, 65 Irving Pl., New York, N.Y. 10003. *Office:* Department of English, Staten Island College, 715 Ocean Terr., Staten Island, N.Y. 10301.

CAREER: Elementary and high school teacher of English in the public and private schools of New York, N.Y. 1952-59; College of Staten Island, Staten Island, N.Y., 1959—, began as assistant professor, became professor of English and American studies, 1968. *Military service:* U.S. Army, 1944-46. *Member:* Modern Language Association of America, American Studies Association, Popular Culture Association, American Civil Liberties Union, Phi Beta Kappa. *Awards, honors:* American Council of Learned Societies fellow, 1965.

WRITINGS: Native Sons: A Critical Study of Twentieth-Century Negro-American Authors, Lippincott, 1968; *The Art of Richard Wright,* Southern Illinois University Press, 1969; (editor) *A Native Sons Reader,* Lippincott, 1970; (with others) *The Black Writer in Africa and the Americas,* Hennessey & Ingalls, 1973; (with others) *Dimensions of Detective Fiction,* Popular Press, 1976. Also author of a pamphlet, *Antebellum Slave Narratives: Their Place in American Literary History,* Harper, 1975. Contributor to journals in his field. Advisory editor, Studies in Black Literature, 1971—.

WORK IN PROGRESS: Co-editing *The Letters of Richard Wright;* research in popular culture emphasizing hardboiled detective fiction and film, and antebellum slave narratives and the literary history and influence; a bibliography for Gale, *Afro-American Fiction;* a novel.

MARGOLIES, Marjorie 1942-

PERSONAL: Born June 21, 1942, in Philadelphia, Pa.; daughter of Herbert Edward (a purchasing agent) and Mildred (an artist; maiden name, Harrison) Margolies; married Ed Mezvinsky (Democratic congressman from Iowa), October 5, 1975; children: (adopted children) Lee Heh, Holly; (stepchildren) Margo, Vera, Elsa, Eve. *Education:* Attended Skidmore College, and Syracuse University in Italy, 1962; University of Pennsylvania, B.A., 1963; attended Columbia University, 1970. *Residence:* Washington, D.C. *Agent:* Bill Adler, Playboy Press, 747 Third Ave., New York, N.Y. 10017. *Office:* 4001 Nebraska Ave. N.W., Washington, D.C.

CAREER: High school teacher of Spanish and social studies in Cherry Hill, N.J., 1963-65; WUHY-FM Radio, Philadelphia, Pa., producer and reporter, 1966-68; WCAU-Television, Philadelphia, Pa., reporter, 1968-71; WNBC-Television, New York, N.Y., reporter, 1971-75; WRC-Television, Washington, D.C., reporter, 1975—. Led youth hostel groups on summer bicycle tours of the Near East, Europe, Mexico, and the United States, summers, 1963-65. Coordinator and counselor for Philadelphia Neighborhood Youth Corps, 1966.

MEMBER: American Federation of Television and Radio Artists, Congressional Wives Club, National Democratic Women's Club. *Awards, honors:* Sigma Delta Chi awards for television documentary programs, 1968, for "Foster Care in Philadelphia," and 1970, for "Abortion: A Woman's Choice?"; named woman of the year by Professional and Business Women of the City of Philadelphia, 1969; Columbia Broadcasting System (CBS) Foundation fellowship, 1969-70; Women in Communications Award from American Women in Radio and Television, 1971.

WRITINGS: They Came to Stay (on her experiences as a single mother of adopted children), Coward, 1976. Contributor to women's magazines.

SIDELIGHTS: Marjorie Margolies was the first unmarried U.S. citizen to be permitted to adopt a foreign child. She adopted a Korean, then a Vietnamese daughter. Her other four children are from her husband's previous marriage. Most of her television reporting in recent years has involved special reports on children. Her education and career have given her extensive opportunities to travel abroad.

BIOGRAPHICAL/CRITICAL SOURCES: Mademoiselle, December, 1972, December, 1973; *Ladies' Home Journal,* February, 1974; *Family Circle,* October, 1974; *People,* December 15, 1975; *American Home,* December, 1975.

* * *

MARGOLIN, Victor 1941-

PERSONAL: Born June 3, 1941, in New York, N.Y.; son of Benjamin (a lawyer) and Olya (Washington representative for National Council of Jewish Women; maiden name, Feinstein) Margolin; married Sylvia Samuels (a teacher), August 23, 1975. *Education:* Columbia University, B.A., 1963; Institute of Higher Cinema Studies, Paris, France, graduate study, 1963-64. *Religion:* Jewish. *Home:* 2209 West Arthur, Chicago, Ill. 60625.

CAREER: National Broadcasting Co. (NBC), Washington, D.C., film editing assistant, 1964-65; free-lance writer, 1966-67; Library of Congress, Washington, D.C., editor, research associate, and bibliographer, working on *A Guide to a Study of the United States of America,* 1968-69; White House Conference on Children, Washington, D.C., media adviser, 1969-70; WETA-Television, Washington, D.C., associate producer, 1971; free-lance writer and communications and education consultant in New York City and Washington, D.C., 1972-74; Chicago Metropolitan Higher Education Council, Chicago, Ill., executive director, 1975—. Member of planning advisory board of Interversitas: A World Network of Experimenters in Higher Education; member of internship task force of Northeastern Illinois Planning Commission. *Member:* American Association for Higher Education. *Awards, honors:* Fulbright scholarship, 1963-64.

WRITINGS: (Editor) *The Little Pun Book,* Peter Pauper, 1960; (editor) *Peter Pauper's Pun Book,* Peter Pauper, 1962; *The World of Children: A Guide to Films for, by, and about Children,* U.S. Government Printing Office, 1970; *American Poster Renaissance,* Watson-Guptill, 1975; (editor and contributor) *Propaganda: The Art of Persuasion, World War Two,* Chelsea House, 1976. Contributor to film journals. Editor-in-chief of *Columbia Jester,* 1962-63.

SIDELIGHTS: Margolin has lived in Germany and traveled in Western Europe and Indonesia.

* * *

MARINE, Gene 1926-

PERSONAL: Born December 31, 1926, in San Francisco, Calif.; son of Fred (a tractor driver) and Gloria (a housekeeper; maiden name, Rodrigues) Marine; married three times (now divorced); children: April, Craig, Shelia, Kevin. *Education:* Attended San Francisco State College, 1948-49. *Politics:* "More or less Left, but increasingly cranky." *Religion:* "Reared as Roman Catholic; now mostly amused." *Home and office:* 1740 Rose St., Berkeley, Calif. 94703.

CAREER: KPFA-radio, Berkeley, Calif., news analyst, 1951-57; *Frontier* magazine, Los Angeles, Calif., associate editor, 1957-59; KPFK-radio, Los Angeles, Calif., public affairs and program director, 1959-60; KPFA-radio, Berkeley, news director, 1960-62; political campaign manager in California, 1962-63; Columbia Broadcasting System (CBS), New York, N.Y., member California election news staff, 1964; *Ramparts* magazine, San Francisco, Calif., senior editor, 1966-69; free-lance editor and writer, 1969—. West coast correspondent for *Nation,* 1954-64; *Military service:* U.S. Marine Corps, 1943-46. *Member:* Author's Guild of America. *Awards, honors:* Radio-TV Newswriting award from Sigma Delta Chi, 1960; California Associated Press Radio-TV Association award from broadcast news, 1961.

WRITINGS: America the Raped, Simon & Schuster, 1969; *The Black Panthers,* New American Library, 1969; (co-author with Judith Van Allen) *Food Pollution,* Holt, 1972; *A Male Guide to Women's Liberation,* Holt, 1972. Contributor of several hundred articles to magazines; contributing editor of *Pacific Scene,* 1964-65.

WORK IN PROGRESS: Research on energy, a possible novel.

SIDELIGHTS: Marine told *CA:* "The principal influence on my career was Carey McWilliams, then editor of *Nation,* who took me in hand when I was a punk and taught me professionalism. I have tried over the years to repay him by retaining a respect for the truth, however unpopular or widely disbelieved the truth may be. Mostly I look for subjects in regard to which stereotypes are widely held (the idea being to examine stereotypes, dismiss them, and substitute the facts—which sounds as pompous as it probably is).

"I am probably thought of most often as an 'investigative reporter,' a currently fashionable term, with some overtones of 'social critic.' I would rather be the latter; I am tired of digging in musty basements, and I think it is time to share the results of a career spent in such digging.

"I am most concerned about power that is wielded in the pursuit of private profit—even when, as is sometimes the case, those who wield the power don't understand what they're doing—and especially in the manipulation of popular thinking that accompanies that pursuit. For example: Major networks, newspapers, and magazines often discuss serious issues, but most always confine their discussions within acceptable ideological boundries—depriving Americans of the chance to hear other approaches. This doesn't make Walter Cronkite venal; he is merely conventional. I like books because they give me freedom to tell the truth, which I try to do in a language as clear as is within my command, avoiding political jargon that is as stereotyped as the ideas it would combat.

"I would someday like to write about the change in some Americans that comes when they become aware of mortality; about the importance to my and to the next generation of the history and content of popular music; about jazz in all of its manifestations; about the importance of a sense of history, in general; and about how nice it would be if, after I die, there will be someone left on earth who has heard of Catullus. I am also playing with a mystery novel, as another possible way to comment on America without setting up an advance defensiveness in readers (and reviewers)."

* * *

MARINO, Trentino J(oseph) 1917-

PERSONAL: Born August 13, 1917, in Franklin, Mass.; son of Guiseppe (a railroad fireman) and Ernestine (D'Orazio) Marino; married Gladys Sanatass, September 7, 1941; children: Richard, John, Patricia, Susan, Donna. *Education:* Studied with private tutors. *Politics:* "Erratic-variable." *Religion:* Roman Catholic. *Home and office:* 29 51st St., Weehawken, N.J. 07087.

CAREER: Court stenographer in New York, N.Y., 1940-43; Cutler-Hammer, Inc., New York, N.Y., in special apparatus design, 1946-58; X-Ray Institute Corp., New York, N.Y., x-ray manufacturer and designer, 1959-65; New York Institute of Photography, New York, N.Y., chief instructor, 1966-72, general manager, 1972-75; free-lance photographer and writer. Photographer and researcher for Center for Migration Studies, New York, N.Y., 1971—; consultant and teacher at Floating Foundation of Photography, 1973—; teacher of advanced photography, Napanoch Correctional Facility, 1974-75. Member of board of directors of Bottega (drug-related, self-help organization), New York, N.Y., 1969. *Military service:* U.S. Army, 1943-45; became sergeant. *Member:* American Society of Picture Professionals, American-Italian Historical Society, Photographic Historical Society of New York.

WRITINGS: Pictures Without a Camera, Sterling, 1974.

WORK IN PROGRESS: A pictorial documentary, *The Italian in America: One-Hundred Years, 1875-1975.*

SIDELIGHTS: Marino's photographs appear in the collections of Betmann Archives, New York Public Library, and Bibliotheque Nationale. His one-man shows include Brookdale College, Rhode Island School of Design, and Floating Foundation of Photography.

BIOGRAPHICAL/CRITICAL SOURCES: Popular Photography, April, 1972.

MARION, Henry
See del REY, Lester 1915-

* * *

MARKS, J
See HIGHWATER, Jamake

* * *

MARKUS, R(obert) A(ustin) 1924-

PERSONAL: Born October 8, 1924, in Budapest, Hungary; son of Victor (an engineer) and Helene M. (a potter; maiden name, Elek) Markus; married Margaret Catherine Bullen (a teacher), August 15, 1955; children: Stephen Austin, Jean Cecilia, Francis John. *Education:* University of Manchester, B.Sc., 1945, M.A., 1948, Ph.D., 1950. *Politics:* Labour. *Religion:* "Catholic (anti-Roman)." *Home:* 15 Devonshire Ave., Beeston, Nottingham NG9 1BS, England. *Office:* Department of History, University of Nottingham, Nottingham NG7 2RD, England.

CAREER: University of Liverpool, Liverpool, England, lecturer, 1955-64, senior lecturer, 1964-69, reader in medieval history, 1970-72; University of Nottingham, Nottingham, England, professor of medieval history, 1973—. *Member:* Royal Historical Society, Historical Association, Society for the Promotion of Roman Studies, Ecclesiastical History Society.

WRITINGS: (With A. H. Armstrong) *Christian Faith and Greek Philosophy,* Darton, Longman & Todd, 1964; (with Eric John) *Papacy and Hierarchy,* Sheed, 1969; *Saeculum: History and Society in the Theology of Saint Augustine,* Cambridge University Press, 1970; (editor) *Augustine: A Collection of Critical Essays,* Doubleday, 1972; *Christianity in the Roman World,* Scribner, 1975.

Contributor: D. J. O'Connor, editor, *Critical History of Western Philosophy,* Macmillan, 1964; Armstrong, editor, *Cambridge History of Later Greek and Early Medieval Philosophy,* Cambridge University Press, 1967; J. W. Binns, editor, *Latin Literature of the Fourth Century,* Routledge & Kegan Paul, 1974. Contributor of articles and reviews to scholarly journals.

WORK IN PROGRESS: Research on late antiquity and the early Middle Ages, especially the church and culture, with extra emphasis on Gregory the Great and his times.

SIDELIGHTS: Markus states that his motivation is "to discover the truth on matters that interest me and to communicate it to others similarly interested. Especially on questions concerned with cultural continuity, transformation and break. Attempting to understand a mind or a culture in its own terms, and in its widest sense, including its artistic, literary and ideological expressions."

* * *

MARLOW, Joyce 1929-
(Joyce Mary Connor)

PERSONAL: Legal name Joyce Mary Connor; professional name Joyce Marlow; born December 27, 1929, in Manchester, England; daughter of William (a decorator) and Mary Thorpe (Smethurst) Lees; married Patrick Albert John Connor (an actor), July 25, 1955; children: Nicholas John, Julian Michael. *Education:* Attended Bradford Civic Theatre School, Bradford, England, 1947-49. *Politics:* Socialist. *Religion:* Agnostic. *Home:* Magnolia Cottage, East Lane, Bedmond, Watford WD5 0QG, England. *Agent:* Anthony Sheil Associates, 52 Floral St., Covent Garden, London WC2E 9DA, England.

CAREER: Professional actress in theatre, films, and television, 1949-66; writer, 1966—. Governor, Leavesden School for the Mentally Handicapped, 1974—. *Member:* Writers Guild of Great Britain (executive councillor, 1975—).

WRITINGS: The Man with the Glove (juvenile), Dobson Books, 1964; *A Time to Die* (novel), R. Whiting & Wheaton, 1966; *Billy Goes to War* (juvenile), R. Whiting & Wheating, 1967; *The House on the Cliffs* (juvenile), Dobson Books, 1968; *The Peterloo Massacre* (history), Rapp & Whiting, 1969, Transatlantic, 1971.

The Tolpuddle Martyrs (history), Transatlantic, 1972; *Captain Boycott and the Irish* (history), Saturday Review Press, 1973; *The Life and Times of George I* (biographical series), Weidenfeld & Nicolson, 1973; *The Prime Ministers* (essay on Spencer Perceval), Allen & Unwin, 1974; *The Uncrowned Queen of Ireland: The Life of 'kitty' O'shea,* Saturday Review Press, 1975.

WORK IN PROGRESS: A dual biography of Mr. and Mrs. William Ewart Gladstone, for Doubleday.

AVOCATIONAL INTERESTS: Reading, watching cricket.

* * *

MARRANCA, Bonnie 1947-

PERSONAL: Born April 28, 1947, in Elizabeth, N.J.; daughter of Angelo Joseph (a small businessman) and Evelyn (Mirabelli) Marranca; married Gautam Dasgupta (a critic), August 1, 1975. *Education:* Montclair State College, B.A., 1969; attended University of Copenhagen, 1969; graduate study at University Center of the City University of New York, 1973—; Hunter College of the City University of New York, M.A., 1976. *Politics:* Independent. *Religion:* Roman Catholic. *Home:* 92 St. Marks Pl., Apt. 4, New York, N.Y. 10009. *Office: Performing Arts Journal,* P.O. Box 858, Peter Stuyvesant Station, New York, N.Y. 10009.

CAREER: Assistant to Broadway press agent Max Eisen in New York City, 1968; Theatre in Education, New York City, administrative assistant, 1970; assistant to playwright-producer Irv Bauer in New York City, 1970-71; New York City Department of Cultural Affairs, New York City, assistant in Street Theatre Division, 1973; Herbert H. Lehman College of the City University of New York, Bronx, N.Y., instructor in theater, spring, 1974; *Soho Weekly News,* New York City, theatre critic, 1975—. Instructor in theatre, Richmond College of the City University of New York, summer, 1976. *Member:* American Theatre Critics Association, National Society of Literature and the Arts.

WRITINGS: (Editor) *The Theatre of Images,* Drama Book Specialists, 1976. Contributor of essays and reviews to journals and magazines, including *Nation, Art in Society, Educational Theatre Journal, Margins, Village Voice, Viva, Rolling Stone,* and *Changes.* Co-editor of *Performing Arts Journal,* 1975—.

WORK IN PROGRESS: Research on American avant-garde theater; essays on contemporary European theatre.

SIDELIGHTS: Bonnie Marranca writes: "Whenever I am dealing with American theatre I try to emphasize its American roots, not out of patriotic feelings, but because I feel that critics have too often overlooked our American artistic heritage in favor of praising European influences. Over the last dozen years American experiments in art, dance, film, and theatre have synthesized in a truly American aesthetic that now makes New York the most exciting, innovative center of the arts in the world. It's time American institutions and the government realized this and started supporting the arts and our artists. *Performing Arts Journal* is a special project of my husband and mine. We started the publication simply because there was no public forum for good, solid, analytical writings on the performing arts." *Avocational interests:* Travel, visiting museums, browsing in book stores.

* * *

MARRINGTON, Pauline 1921-

PERSONAL: Born December 13, 1921, in Montreal, Quebec, Canada; daughter of Francis Stephen (an officer in the Royal Canadian Flying Corps) and Milly (Mainwaring) Miller; married John Frederick Marrington (a medical practitioner), October 14, 1944; children: Christine Marrington Hartgill, Peter. *Education:* Attended National Art School, Sydney, Australia, 1938. *Office address:* P.O. Box 103, Beecroft, New South Wales 2119, Australia.

CAREER: Copy writer and free-lance artist, 1958-61; art teacher, 1962—. *Member:* Australian Society of Authors, Society of Women Writers. *Awards, honors:* First prize from City of Sydney Waratah Festival Contest, 1973, for story, "Let Your Song Be Delicate"; first prize from *Australian,* 1975, for mystery story, "The Hair of Madeleine Clichy"; research grant from Literature Board of the Government of Australia, 1975.

WRITINGS: The October Horse (period novel; Australian Literary Guild selection), St. Martin's 1975, paperback edition published as *The Lindseys,* New American Library, in press.

WORK IN PROGRESS: A novel based on the life of one of the commandants of the second penal settlement of Norfolk Island; research on Norfolk Island aimed at a biographical reconstruction.

SIDELIGHTS: Pauline Marrington writes: "The ambition to write was fostered when, in 1968, I was one of fifteen 'Emergent Writers' chosen to attend a Writers' Retreat at the University of New England, Armidale, New South Wales, sponsored by the Commonwealth Literary Fund and the Myer Foundation. The fact that I was born in Canada and mainly educated in England meant that I brought an alien viewpoint to Australia. There is a harsh and arid quality about the landscape, even the wild flowers seem spiked for resistance. I sensed its indifference and was afraid. I write about Australia and have spent most of my adult life here but I have never lost the sense of rejection. The beauty of this land is not for touching. My writing is concerned with the inter-dependence of the early settlers—both free and bonded—played out against an unfamiliar background."

BIOGRAPHICAL/CRITICAL SOURCES: Brisbane Telegraph, May 28, 1975; *Melbourne Herald,* June 6, 1975; *Northern District Times,* January 1, 1976.

* * *

MARSHALL, Bill 1937-

PERSONAL: Born May 16, 1937, in Mampong Akwapim, Ghana; son of Albert Obiri and Hilda Marshall; married Clara Jackson-Davies; children: Beulah, Bill, Jr., Aida. *Education:* Guildhall School of Music and Drama, L.G.S.M., 1964; City Literary Institute, London, England, A.D.B., 1964; School of Television Production, London, certificate, 1965. *Religion:* Christian. *Home:* Pen Lodge, Achimota, Accra, Ghana. *Office address:* P.O. Box 449, Accra, Ghana.

CAREER: Television producer and director, and writer. *Awards, honors:* Best drama award from Hollywood Festival of World Television, 1972; best television producer award from Ghana Broadcasting Corp., 1973.

WRITINGS—All plays: *Stranger to Innocence and Shadow of an Eagle* (two plays), Ghana Publishing Corp., 1969, Panther House, 1970; *The Son of Umbele* (three-act), Ghana Publishing Corp., 1973.

Television dramas: "Midnight Strangers," Ghana Broadcasting Corp. (GBC-TV), 1968; "A Matter of Class," GBC-TV, 1972; "Naki," GBC-TV, 1976.

Radio plays: "Trial by Dice," GBC-Radio, 1968.

Also author of three plays, *The Queue, No Time for Tears,* and *Strange Neighbours,* all published by Ghana Publishing Corp.

WORK IN PROGRESS: A novel, *Bukom,* for Sedco; a play, "Goat Street."

SIDELIGHTS: Marshall writes: "I write as I please. And what pleases me is the mind, for I think it is that which belies man's behaviour. I do not, ever, attempt to impose my personal 'mind' in any of my works. Any form of philosophy or 'mind' that may emerge or be observed in my writing is not subjective but that of the people or the situations I write about. In this respect, I think a writer should be wickedly fair. He must be an impartial observer of Society and present it as a discussion, a debate and without drawing conclusions. I pray that freedom for creative expression be preserved for all times throughout the world. I also pray that the writer recognizes the need for some form of ethics and to resist the temptation to abuse this freedom or to indulge in dirt-splashing simply for the sake of art."

* * *

MARSHALL, D(onald) Bruce 1931-

PERSONAL: Born April 15, 1931, in Portland, Maine; son of John T. and Olive (Schultz) Marshall; married Susan Dunn. *Education:* Yale University, A.B., 1952, M.A., 1953, Ph.D., 1968; University of Paris, certificate in American studies, 1955. *Office:* Institute of International Studies, University of South Carolina, Columbia, S.C. 29208.

CAREER: Ohio State University, Columbus, instructor in political science, 1956-64; Smith College, Northampton, Mass., lecturer in government, 1964-67; University of South Carolina, Columbia, assistant professor, 1967-71, associate professor of government and international studies, 1971—, associate director for research and publications at Institute of International Studies, 1972—.

MEMBER: International Studies Association, American Political Science Association, Conference Group on French Politics (chairman, 1974—), Southern Political Science Association. *Awards, honors:* Fulbright fellowship in France, 1954-55; grant from Hoover Institution on War, Revolution and Peace, summer, 1970, national fellowship, 1971-72.

WRITINGS: (Contributor) Prosser Gifford and William Roger Louis, editors, *France and Britain in America,* Yale University Press, 1971; *The French Colonial Myth and Constitution-Making in the Fourth Republic,* Yale University Press, 1973. Contributor to political science journals and to *Orbis.*

WORK IN PROGRESS: Editing and writing material to be included in *France and the Future of Atlantic Security.*

*   *   *

MARTIN, Allie Beth   1914-1976

June 28, 1914—June 13, 1976; American librarian, association executive, and author of books in her field. Obituaries: *New York Times,* June 14, 1976; *Current Biography,* June 1976.

*   *   *

MARTIN, David Grant   1939-

PERSONAL: Born June 15, 1939, in Mt. Pleasant, Mich.; son of Kerswell Payne (a merchant) and Sylva (a teacher; maiden name, MacNellis) Martin; married Nona Ann Roush, August 27, 1960; children: Joel David, Laura Ann, Kathy Lynn, Mark Colin, Kristen Lee. *Education:* Albion College, B.A. (magna cum laude), 1961; University of Chicago, M.A. and Ph.D., both 1965. *Home:* 94 Macalester Bay, Winnipeg, Manitoba, Canada R3T 2X5. *Office:* Department of Psychology, University of Manitoba, Winnipeg, Manitoba, Canada R3T 2N2.

CAREER: Institute for Juvenile Research, Chicago, Ill., psychology intern, 1964-65; University of Iowa, Iowa City, assistant professor of psychology and staff psychologist, 1965-69; University of Manitoba, Winnipeg, assistant professor, 1969-70, associate professor of psychology, 1970—, staff psychologist, 1969—. *Member:* American Psychological Association, Phi Beta Kappa, Sigma Xi. *Awards, honors:* National Institute of Mental Health award, 1966-68; Canada Council grant, 1973-74, fellowship, 1975-76.

WRITINGS: Introduction to Psychotherapy, Brooks/Cole, 1971; *Learning Based Client Centered Therapy,* Brooks/Cole, 1972; *Personality: Effective and Ineffective,* Brooks/Cole, 1976. Contributor to psychology journals. Editorial consultant to *Journal of Abnormal Psychology.*

WORK IN PROGRESS: Feminine and Masculine: Social Learning and Sex Roles, with Cynthia Jordan; research on unconscious influences on behavior.

SIDELIGHTS: Martin comments: "The theme of my career is to 'think like a learning theorist and live like a humanist.' My writing and research are aimed at bringing scientifically valid methods and data to the exploration of complex human phenomena." *Avocational interests:* The outdoors, guitar.

*   *   *

MARTIN, Donald Franklin   1944-

PERSONAL: Born September 22, 1944, in Baltimore, Md.; son of Sidney (a mechanic) and Mytle (Tillman) Martin; married Geraldine Farrington (an educator), July 11, 1969; children: Nichole Frances. *Education:* North Carolina Agricultural and Technical State University, B.S., 1969; University of Akron, M.A., 1971; Ohio State University, Ph.D., 1973. *Home:* 101 Warren Way Rd., Chapel Hill, N.C. 27514.

CAREER: University of North Carolina, Chapel Hill, assistant professor of higher and adult education and assistant director of Extension, 1974—. *Military service:* U.S. Navy, 1964-66. *Member:* Adult Education Association of the United States of America, North Carolina Adult Education Association (member of executive committee).

WRITINGS: Quiz Book on Black America, Houghton, 1976. Contributor to *Adult Leadership* and *Spectator.*

WORK IN PROGRESS: A comparative analysis of adult and child learning methodologies.

SIDELIGHTS: Martin writes: "The conception of this book grew out of a need to have learning materials that were informative, fun, and easily shared. Not enough attention has been given to the contributions Blacks have made for the good of the American society. The basic audience for this book is the secondary school student. Those not related to academia may find great enjoyment reading and sharing this book."

*   *   *

MARTIN, Lynne   1923-

PERSONAL: Born August 8, 1923, in Flushing, N.Y.; daughter of Charles J. (a carpenter) and Lee (Steurer) Svec; married Joseph B. Martin (an engineer), September 11, 1948; children: Peter, Priscilla, Laura, Joe, Jim, Ursula, Pamela. *Education:* Educated in public high school in Flushing, N.Y. *Residence:* Roslyn Heights, N.Y.

CAREER: Publicity writer for advertising agencies and public relations firms, 1942-50; free-lance writer, 1950—.

WRITINGS—Juvenile: *Amazing Animal Appetites,* Criterion, 1966; *Museum Menagerie,* Criterion, 1971; *The Giant Panda* (Junior Literary Guild selection), Addison-Wesley, 1972; *The Orchid Family,* Morrow, 1974; *Peacocks,* Morrow, 1975; *Bird of the Open Seas,* Puffin, 1976. Author of monthly column "Diary of a Mother," in *Modern Baby,* 1950-55. Contributor of articles to popular magazines and to *Science Digest* and *International Wildlife.*

SIDELIGHTS: Lynne Martin writes that she spends her time "introducing our children to the world."

*   *   *

MARTIN, M(arilynn) Kay   1942-

PERSONAL: Born October 19, 1942, in Niagara Falls, N.Y.; daughter of Russell and May (Coombs) Martin. *Education:* State University of New York College at Buffalo, B.A., 1964, M.A., 1966, Ph.D., 1970. *Residence:* Santa Barbara, Calif. *Office:* Department of Anthropology, University of California, Santa Barbara, Calif. 93106.

CAREER: University of California, Santa Barbara, assistant professor of anthropology, 1969—. *Member:* American Anthropological Association (fellow), American Ethnological Association (fellow), Current Anthropology (associate), Sigma Xi.

WRITINGS: (With Barbara Voorhies) *Female of the Species,* Columbia University Press, 1975.

WORK IN PROGRESS: The Economics of Kinship, completion expected in 1977; research on the ecological adaptations of nonliterate or primitive societies, with special emphasis on the effects of economic institutions on kinship, social organization, and human sex roles.

*   *   *

MARTIN, Ralph P(hilip)

PERSONAL: Born in Liverpool, England; came to United States in 1969; married Lily Nelson; children: Patricia Martin Losie, Elizabeth. *Education:* Attended Manchester Baptist College; University of Manchester, B.A. and M.A.; King's College, University of London, Ph.D. *Office:* Fuller Theological Seminary, 135 North Oakland Ave., Pasadena, Calif. 91101.

CAREER: Ordained Baptist minister, 1949; pastor of Baptist churches in Gloucester, England, 1949-53, and Dunstable, England, 1953-59; London Bible College, London, England, lecturer in theology, 1959-65; University of Manchester, Manchester, England, lecturer in New Testament, 1965-69; Fuller Theological Seminary, Pasadena, Calif., professor of New Testament, 1969—. Visiting professor at Bethel College and Seminary, St. Paul, Minn., 1964-65; and Fuller Theological Seminary, 1968. *Member:* Society of Biblical Literature, Institute for Biblical Research, Studiorum Novi Testamenti Societas.

WRITINGS: The Epistle of Paul to the Philippians: An Introduction and Commentary, Eerdmans, 1959; *An Early Christian Confession: Philippians II, 5-11 in Recent Interpretation,* Tyndale Press, 1960; (editor) *Vox Evangelica: Biblical and Historical Essays,* Epworth, Volume I, 1962, Volume II, 1963; *Worship in the Early Church,* Revell, 1964, revised edition, Eerdmans, 1975; *Acts,* Scripture Union, 1967, Eerdmans, 1968; *Carmen Christi: Philippians II, 5-11 in Recent Interpretation and in the Setting of Early Christian Worship,* Cambridge University Press, 1967; *First and Second Corinthians, Galatians,* Eerdmans, 1968; (editor with W. Ward Gasque) *Apostolic History and the Gospel: Biblical and Historical Essays,* Eerdmans, 1970; *Colossians, the Church's Lord and the Christian's Liberty: An Expository Commentary with a Present-Day Application,* Paternoster Press, 1972, Zondervan, 1973; *Mark, Evangelist and Theologian,* Paternoster Press, 1972; *Colossians and Philemon,* Attic Press, 1974; *New Testament Foundations: A Guide for Christian Students,* Volume I, Eerdmans, 1975; *Philippians,* Attic Press, 1976; *Where the Action Is: Mark's Gospel Today,* Regal Books, in press.

Contributor: Carl F. H. Henry, editor, *Jesus of Nazareth, Saviour and Lord,* Eerdmans, 1965; C. A. Joyce, editor, *My Call to Preach,* Marshall, Morgan & Scott, 1966; F. L. Cross, editor, *Studia Evangelica,* Volume II, Akademie Verlag, 1964; Cross, editor, *Studia Patristica,* Volume VI, Akademie Verlag, 1966; Clifford J. Allen, editor, *Commentary on Ephesians,* Broadman, 1971.

Contributor to *New Bible Dictionary, New Bible Commentary, Baker's Dictionary of Christian Ethics, New International Dictionary of the Christian Church,* and *Zondervan Pictorial Bible Dictionary.* Contributor to theology journals.

WORK IN PROGRESS: New Testment Foundations: A Guide for Christian Students, Volume II, for Eerdmans.

*   *   *

MARWICK, Helen
   See LILLIE, Helen

*   *   *

MASON, Carola
   See ZENTNER, Carola

*   *   *

MASSANARI, Jared (Dean)   1943-
PERSONAL: Born May 28, 1943, in Champaign, Ill.; son of Karl L. (an educator) and Christine (Yoder) Massanari; married Alice J. Eicher; children: Caleb (deceased), Adrienne. *Education:* Goshen College, B.A. (honors), 1965, graduate study, 1965-66; Florida State University, M.S., 1967; Syracuse University, Ph.D., 1973. *Home:* 2058 Clematis, Sarasota, Fla. 33579.

CAREER: Administrator of a private school in New Orleans, La., 1967-69; substitute high school teacher in Syra-

cuse, N.Y., 1971-72; Syracuse University, Syracuse, N.Y., adjunct instructor, 1973-74, assistant professor of religion, 1974-75; Keuka College, Keuka Park, N.Y., instructor in philosophy and religion, 1975-76; writer, 1976—. *Member:* American Academy of Religion, Society for Arts, Religion, and Culture, Theta Chi Beta.

WRITINGS: Our Life with Caleb, Fortress, 1976.

WORK IN PROGRESS: Working with Anna Neagoe on her autobiography; stories; poems.

SIDELIGHTS: Massanari's main interest is "mythologies of American life and their psychological-social implications."

*   *   *

MASSEY, Floyd, Jr.   1915-
PERSONAL: Born July 25, 1915, in Rock Hill, S.C.; son of Floyd (a butler) and Alice Massey; married Ethel Hurley (a high school teacher), August 28, 1944; children: Floyd III, Ronald Bruce, Thomas Rickie. *Education:* Johnson C. Smith University, A.B., 1936; Colgate Rochester Divinity School, B.D., 1944; Colgate Rochester Divinity School, M.Div., 1972; and D.Min., from Colgate Rochester/Bexley Hall/Crozer Seminary, 1975. *Home:* 1526 West 124th St., Los Angeles, Calif. 90047. *Office:* Macedonia Baptist Church, 1751 East 114th St., Los Angeles, Calif. 90059.

CAREER: High school teacher of history, sociology, and economics in Columbia, S.C., 1936-41; pastor of Baptist church in St. Paul, Minn., 1944-65; Macedonia Baptist Church, Los Angeles, Calif., pastor, 1965—. Past member of board of directors of National Baptist Church; vice-president of American Baptist Church, 1974-75 and member of executive committee of its General Board; president of Foreign Mission Societies. Member of board of trustees of American Baptist Theological Seminary and American Baptist Seminary of the West. Member of board of directors of Western Baptist State Convention of California; president of American Baptist Churches of the Pacific Southwest. Member of St. Paul (Minn.) Planning Board, 1955-65; former vice-chairman of Minnesota governor's Commission on Human Rights, St. Paul Urban League Board, and Minnesota Council of Churches; past president of Minnesota Pastors Conference.

MEMBER: National Association for the Advancement of Colored People (life member), Masons, Omega Psi Phi. *Awards, honors:* D.D. from Johnson C. Smith University, 1955.

WRITINGS: (With Samuel McKinney) *Church Administration in Black Perspective,* Judson, 1976.

AVOCATIONAL INTERESTS: Travel (Europe, the Soviet Union, India, Burma, Thailand, the Philippines, Hong Kong, Japan, West Africa, Greece, Israel, Jamaica, Haiti, Mexico).

*   *   *

MASSINGHAM, Harold William   1932-
PERSONAL: Born October 25, 1932, in Mexborough, Yorkshire, England; son of Harold Winfield (a collier) and Gwendoline (Adams) Massingham; married Patricia Audrey Moran (a teacher), May 24, 1958; children: Stephen Lawrence, Ian David, Frances Ingrid, Richard Harold. *Education:* University of Manchester, B.A., 1954. *Home:* 29 Moorland Rd., Manchester, Lancashire M20 0BB, England.
CAREER: Teacher of English in secondary schools in Man-

chester, England, 1955-70; free-lance writer, 1970-74; Wright Robinson High School, Manchester, English teacher and head of department, 1974-75; free-lance writer, 1975—. Part-time tutor at University of Manchester, 1971—. Has given poetry readings at Hollins College and University of Tennessee at Chattanooga. *Member:* Poetry Society. *Awards, honors:* Guinness Poetry Prize from Cheltenham Festival, 1962, for poem "Graveside"; award from Arts Council of Great Britain, 1965; Cholmondeley Poetry Award from Society of Authors, 1968, for *Black Bull Guarding Apples.*

WRITINGS—Poetry: *Black Bull Guarding Apples,* Longmans, Green, 1965; *The Magician,* Phoenix, 1969; *Frost-Gods,* Macmillan, 1971; *The Pennine Way,* British Broadcasting Corp., 1971; *The Magician's Chameleon,* privately printed, 1976.

Work represented in anthologies, including *The Penguin Book of Animal Verse,* edited by George Macbeth, Penguin, 1965; *Breakthrough,* edited by R. B. Heath, Hamish Hamilton, 1970; *The House that Jack Built,* edited by Brian Peters and Pat Krett, Shelter Organization, 1973; and *New Poetry,* edited by Charles Osborne and Peter Porter, Arts Council of Great Britain, 1975.

Contributor to literary magazines and journals of the arts, including *Encounter, Listener, London Magazine, New Statesman, New Yorker,* and *Times Literary Supplement.* Co-founder of *Manchester University Poetry,* 1953; editor of *Poetry Workshop,* 1973, 1974, 1976.

WORK IN PROGRESS: The Feast of Thawian, a juvenile novel; *Beowulf* and *Havelok,* both nonfiction; *Dust on the Street,* an autobiography; poetry, including *The Nero Sonata* (tentative title), *The Phoenix* (from an old English poem), and *From the Alps to Zanzibar.*

SIDELIGHTS: Massingham writes: "I have been committed to existence, as opposed to the mentors called doctrines, since boyhood. Such mentors are too intent on teaching what to think instead of how, and I eschew them heartily.

"During boyhood and the post-puberty decade my environment sickened and thrilled me: in part of England's industrial-pastoral dichotomy I lived a galling and golden age. Though God still haunts me, more than quasars and bleepings, I have a happier rapport with Pan—who has given meaning to music, sexual urge, and a mysticism that has one foot on the ground. Shakespeare and Beethoven became my other gods; Milton and Keats showed up; I was agog at my first Van Goghs; I discovered the Englands of Hardy, Kenneth Grahame and Housman and the instinctual side of Wordsworth and D. H. Lawrence, helped by John Fisher, English teacher—and true mentor, a 'man of transmission and evocation,' if I may quote myself; and eventually I found in Anglo-Saxon poetry a sense of literary roots homely and keen as horse-radish.

"In music I like national lyricism—Sibelius, Debussy, Grieg, Wagner, Copland, Vaughan Williams etc.; in fact I respond to rooted awareness in all the arts. I like chess, trees, credit where it's due, Virginia, carols, and the enthralling word-tasks of *Azed* and *Listener* crosswords; I like nostalgia, craftsmanship, the peaceable kingdom, crown-green bowling, board-games, beauty, beer, herbs, snuff, all sensuous experience; I like my family, singularity, solitude, and people of goodwill.

"I have worked as a painter and decorator, and still do; also, as farm laborer, strawberry farmer, ice cream vendor, hotel kitchen-hand, dairy worker, milkroundsman and window-cleaner."

BIOGRAPHICAL/CRITICAL SOURCES: London Magazine, April, 1969.

* * *

MASUR, Jenny 1948-

PERSONAL: Born December 7, 1948, in Washington, D.C.; daughter of Jack (a physician) and Barbara (Forsch) Masur. *Education:* Mount Holyoke College, A.B., 1971; University of Chicago, M.A., 1974, further graduate study, 1974—. *Religion:* Jewish. *Home:* 3710 Davenport St. N.W., Washington, D.C. 20016.

CAREER: Anthropologist.

WRITINGS: Jewish Grandmothers (oral history), Beacon Press, 1976.

WORK IN PROGRESS: Field work in Andalusia on rural women and internal and external migration of Spanish workers.

SIDELIGHTS: Jenny Masur writes: "*Jewish Grandmothers* reflects my interest in the lives of people often neglected in conventional histories or macro-accounts of a society. By using the women's own words in my book, the object has been to present the point of view of the women themselves and not that of a third party."

* * *

MATHERS, Michael 1945-

PERSONAL: Born February 3, 1945, in Washington, D.C.; son of William Harris (a lawyer) and Myra (Martin) Mathers; married Andrea Carlisle (a writer), February 29, 1976. *Education:* Harvard University, B.A., 1968. *Home address:* Cove Neck Rd., Oyster Bay, N.Y. 11771. *Office address:* Route 2, Box 83, Hillsboro, Ore. 97123.

CAREER: Photographer and writer.

WRITINGS: Riding the Rails, Gambit, 1973; *Sheepherders: Men Alone,* Houghton, 1975.

* * *

MATHIEU, Beatrice 1904-1976

November 7, 1904—July 12, 1976; American fashion writer. Obituaries: *Washington Post,* July 16, 1976.

* * *

MATSCHAT, Cecile H. 1895(?)-1976

1895(?)—March 4, 1976; American artist, botanist, author of historical novels and horticulture books. Obituaries: *New York Times,* March 10, 1976; *AB Bookman's Weekly,* May 17, 1976.

* * *

MATTE, Robert G., Jr. 1948-

PERSONAL: Born May 10, 1948, in Paris, France; son of Robert G. (an army officer) and Beverly (Ewald) Matte; married Mary Beth Squillace (a teacher), November 11, 1970. *Education:* University of Florida, B.A., 1970, M.Ed., 1972. *Religion:* "Soandsoistic." *Home:* 2540 College Ave. #212, Berkeley, Calif. 94704.

CAREER: Worked as a laborer, security guard, taco vendor, soil sampler, actor, cook, steel worker, drug counselor, teacher; director of Poet's Gallery at the Oakland (Calif.) Upstairs Art Association, 1976—; Reralta College, Berkeley, Calif., instructor in creative writing, 1976—; participant in Poetry in the Schools Program, Oakland, Calif., 1976—;

poet and editor. *Military service:* U.S. Army Reserve, 1970—; currently first lieutenant. *Member:* Coordinating Council of Literary Magazines, Committee of Small Magazine Editors and Publishers, Bay Area Poets' Coalition.

WRITINGS: Starkissing, Vagabond, 1975; *Eating the English Army,* Windless Orchard Press, 1975. Founder and coeditor of *Yellow Brick Road* (literary magazine).

WORK IN PROGRESS: Three volumes of poetry entitled *Rasdale, The Cloud Racers,* and *Asylum Picnic.*

SIDELIGHTS: "I write," Matte told *CA,* "because there is a fire inside which nothing will put out but placing words on paper keeps it under control. If I follow any sort of creed it is that, 'In the absurd lurks reality.' My writings have been influenced by Kenneth Patchen, W. S. Merwin, Edward Field, and Ronald Koertge among others."

* * *

MATTHEWS, Robert J(ames) 1926-

PERSONAL: Born September 12, 1926, in Evanston, Wyo.; son of Roland J. (a farmer) and Elsie (Gulliver) Matthews; married Shirley Neves, May 28, 1954; children: Camille, Daniel, Robert D., Tricia. *Education:* Brigham Young University, Ph.D., 1968. *Religion:* Church of Jesus Christ of Latter-day Saints (Mormons). *Office:* Joseph Smith Building, Brigham Young University, Provo, Utah 84602.

CAREER: An educator.

WRITINGS: A Burning Light (biography of John the Baptist), Brigham Young University Press, 1972; *Joseph Smith's Translation of the Bible,* Brigham Young University Press, 1975; *Who's Who in the Book of Mormon,* Deseret, 1976.

* * *

MATURA, Mustapha 1939-

PERSONAL: Born December 17, 1939, in Trinidad, West Indies; son of Chandra (a salesman) and Violet (Rivers) Mathura; married Marian Walsh (a health visitor), October 5, 1961; children: Ann Simone, Dominic. *Education:* Educated in Roman Catholic intermediate school. *Religion:* Muslim. *Home and office:* 5 Mayberry Pl., Surbiton, Surrey, England. *Agent:* Peggy Ramsey, 14A Goodwins Court, London W.C.2, England.

CAREER: In Trinidad, worked as office boy, stock clerk, insurance salesman, and tally clerk, 1954-61; in England worked as hospital porter, cosmetic display assistant, and stockroom assistant, 1961-68; full-time writer, 1968—. *Member:* Theatre Writers Group. *Awards, honors:* John Withing Award from Arts Council of Great Britain, 1970; George Devine Award from English Stage Co., 1972, for "As Time Goes By"; named most promising writer by *Evening Standard,* 1975, for "Play MAS."

WRITINGS—Plays: *As Time Goes By and Black Pieces* (six plays), Calder & Boyars, 1972; *Play MAS* (three-act; first produced in London at Royal Court Theatre, 1974), Calder & Boyars, 1976.

Unpublished plays: "Bakerloo Line" (one-act), first produced in London at Almost Free Theatre, 1972; "Nice" (one-act), first produced at Almost Free Theatre, 1973; "Black Slaves—White Chains" (one-act), first produced in London at Theatre Upstairs, 1975; "Bread" (three-act), first produced in London at Young Vic Theatre, 1976.

Author of screenplay "Murders of Boysie Singh," 1972.

SIDELIGHTS: Matura writes that his motivations are "to increase the awareness of human beings to their present realities and thereby cause a change or movement toward a new reality."

* * *

MAXA, Rudolph Joseph, Jr. 1949-
(Rudy Maxa)

PERSONAL: Born September 25, 1949, in Cleveland, Ohio; son of Rudolph (an army officer) and Christine (a stockbroker; maiden name, Kimpel) Maxa; married Kathleen Zolciak (a journalist), June 19, 1971; children: Sarah. *Education:* Ohio University, B.S.J., 1971. *Politics:* Independent. *Home:* 2841 29th St., N.W., Washington, D.C. 20008. *Agent:* David Obst, Rm. 1614, 527 Madison Ave., New York, N.Y. 10022. *Office: Washington Post,* 1150 15th St., N.W., Washington, D.C. 20071.

CAREER: Washington Post, Washington, D.C., reporter, 1971—. Lecturer. *Member:* Sigma Delta Chi. *Awards, honors:* John Hancock Award for Journalism, 1972; Associated Press Managing Editor's Award, 1976.

WRITINGS—Under name Rudy Maxa: *Dare to Be Great,* Morrow, 1977; (with Marion Clark) *Public Trust, Private Lust,* Morrow, 1977.

SIDELIGHTS: Maxa told *CA:* "I won't hesitate to say that I have always wanted to be a journalist. A natural curiosity and a desire to write have been with me since I was very young, when I issued hand-written newspapers and satire magazines on the various Army posts where I lived." He says that although "magazine writing is my first love, and I can satisfy my penchant for lengthy feature and investigative writing in the *Post's* magazine section, I appreciate having access to the news columns, should a story arise that would be applicable to that kind of treatment."

BIOGRAPHICAL/CRITICAL SOURCES: New York, June 21, 1976; *Esquire,* October, 1976.

* * *

MAXA, Rudy
See MAXA, Rudolph Joseph, Jr. 1949-

* * *

MAXWELL, Vicky
See WORBOYS, Anne(tte) Isobel

* * *

MAY, George S(mith) 1924-

PERSONAL: Born November 17, 1924, in Ironwood, Mich.; son of Eslie William (a chemist) and Louise (Smith) May; married Frances Gerber Sharp (a secretary), May 11, 1957; children: (stepdaughter) Sally Ann Sharp (Mrs. Donald Stinedurf). *Education:* Attended Gogebic Community College, 1943-44, and Michigan Technological University, 1944; University of Michigan, A.B., 1947, A.M., 1948, Ph.D., 1954. *Politics:* Democrat. *Religion:* Episcopal. *Home:* 1480 Collegewood, Ypsilanti, Mich. 48197. *Office:* Department of History, Eastern Michigan University, Ypsilanti, Mich. 48197.

CAREER: Allegheny College, Meadville, Pa., instructor in history, 1948-50; State Historical Society of Iowa, Iowa City, research associate, 1954-56; Michigan Historical Commission, Lansing, historic sites specialist, 1956-58, research archivist and editor, 1958-66; Eastern Michigan University, Ypsilanti, associate professor, 1966-68, professor of history, 1968—. Member of advisory council of Regional Archives, of National Archives. *Member:* Historical Society of Michigan, Michigan Academy of Science, Arts, and Letters. *Awards, honors:* Award of merit from American Association of State and Local History, 1970, for *Pictorial History of Michigan.*

WRITINGS: History Along Michigan's Highways: A Report on Michigan's New State Historical Marking Program (pamphlet), Michigan Historical Commission, 1957; *Historic Michigan: A Guide to Michigan's Official State Markers* (pamphlet), Michigan Historical Commission, 1958; (editor) *James Strang's Ancient and Modern Michilimackinac, Including an Account of the Controversy Between Mackinac and the Mormons,* W. S. Woodfill, 1959.

(Editor) *The Doctor's Secret Journal,* Fort Mackinac Division Press, 1960; (editor) *Michigan Civil War History: An Annotated Bibliography,* Wayne State University Press, 1961; *The Forts of Mackinac* (pamphlet), Mackinac Island State Park Commission, 1962; *War 1812!* (pamphlet), Mackinac Island State Park Commission, 1962; *Historic Guidebook: Mackinac Island* (pamphlet), Mackinac Island State Park Commission, 1962; *Michigan and the Civil War Years, 1860-1866: A Wartime Chronicle,* Michigan Civil War Centennial Observance Commission, 1964; *A Guide to Michigan's Historical Attractions* (map and guide), Michigan Historical Commission, 1965; *Let Their Memories Be Cherished: Michigan's Civil War Monuments,* Michigan Civil War Centennial Observance Commission, 1965; *Pictorial History of Michigan,* two volumes, Eerdmans, Volume I: *The Early Years,* 1967, Volume II: *The Later Years,* 1969.

(Editor with Herbert Brinks) *A Michigan Reader: 11,000 B.C. to A.D. 1865,* Eerdmans, 1974; *A Most Unique Machine: The Michigan Origins of the American Automobile Industry,* Eerdmans, 1975; *R. E. Olds: Auto Industry Pioneer,* Eerdmans, in press.

Author of "Historic Michigan" (illustrated map), Historical Society of Michigan, 1963. Contributor of about forty articles to history journals, *Michigan State Bar Journal, New Leader, Michigan Christian Advocate,* and *Palimpsest.* Editor of *Michigan History,* 1965-66.

WORK IN PROGRESS: Research on the automotive industry.

AVOCATIONAL INTERESTS: Building a summer home on Lake Michigan.

*   *   *

MAYNARD, John (Rogers)   1941-

PERSONAL: Born October 6, 1941, in Buffalo, N.Y.; son of A. Rogers (a business executive) and Olive (Fisher) Maynard; married Florence Michelson (an artist), July 1, 1967; children: Alex Stevens. *Education:* Harvard University, B.A. (summa cum laude), 1963, Ph.D., 1970. *Home:* 287 Henry St., Brooklyn, N.Y. 11201. *Office:* Department of English, New York University, 19 University Pl., Room 200, New York, N.Y. 10003.

CAREER: Harvard University, Cambridge, Mass., assistant professor of English, history, and literature, 1969-74; New York University, New York, N.Y., assistant professor, 1974-76, associate professor of English, 1976—. Sponsor of Concord Housing, a Boston community development project. *Member:* Modern Language Association of America, Phi Beta Kappa. *Awards, honors:* Frederick Sheldon traveling fellowship, 1963-64; Woodrow Wilson fel-

lowship, 1964-65; American Philosophical Society grant, 1972-73; National Endowment for the Humanities grant, 1972-73; Thomas J. Wilson Prize from Harvard University Press, 1975, for *Browning's Youth.*

WRITINGS: Browning's Youth, Harvard University Press, 1976. Contributor of articles and reviews to literature journals.

WORK IN PROGRESS: Articles on poetry and literary tradition; courses on the literature of England, 1880-1920.

SIDELIGHTS: Maynard writes: "Literary biography can be much more than the usual day by day record of things done, people seen, meals eaten, with occasional stops for discussion of major texts; and it can be more than the imposition of one or a few key explanations, psychological or pathological, that we find in Strachey's lesser followers. The challenge is to understand that complex thing, the emergence of genius. Biography is a meaningful nexus in our world of necessarily fragmented ways of looking at reality. It is not a gimcrack for making complexity into one simplicity of explanation. It is the human center that demands focus and appropriate integration of perspectives—a matter of judgment, imagination, and good sense. It is where the last new view must take its place among the rest, establish its claim to space as best it can in the full portrait. It is one way for my generation to put its badly traversed and centrifugal mind together."

AVOCATIONAL INTERESTS: Fixing up old city houses, relaxing in the Massachusetts woods.

*   *   *

MAYOR, Alfred Hyatt   1934-

PERSONAL: Born June 4, 1934, in Boston, Mass.; son of A. Hyatt (a museum curator) and Virginia S. Mayor; married: Bruni Hillmann (a translator). *Education:* Harvard University, A.B., 1956, M.A., 1957, Ph.D., 1961. *Office:* Straight Enterprises, 551 Fifth Ave., New York, N.Y. 10017.

CAREER: Newsweek, New York, N.Y., researcher, 1961-62; Reuters Ltd., London, England, sub-editor, 1962-63; *Herald Tribune,* Paris, France, rewrite man, 1963-64; *Holiday,* New York, N.Y., senior editor, 1964-68; Corinthian Editions, New York City, managing editor, 1968, worked at American Heritage Press, New York City, 1969-72; now at Straight Enterprises, New York City, 1972—. *Member:* Century Association.

WRITINGS: Parliament's Passport to London, Renaissance Editions, 1968. Contributor to magazines, including *Amerika, Atlantic Monthly,* and *Municipal Journal.*

*   *   *

McALEAVEY, David   1946-

PERSONAL: Born March 27, 1946, in Wichita, Kan.; son of F. L. (an architect) and J. (Ayers) McAleavey; married Christina Dickson, January 24, 1970 (divorced, June, 1972); married Katherine Perry, 1977. *Education:* Cornell University, B.A. (summa cum laude), 1968, M.F.A., 1972, Ph.D., 1975. *Home:* 2623 Woodley P. N.W., Washington, D.C. 20008. *Office:* Department of English, George Washington University, Washington, D.C. 20052.

CAREER: George Washington University, Washington, D.C., instructor, 1974-75, assistant professor of English, 1975—. *Member:* Modern Language Association of America, Phi Beta Kappa.

WRITINGS: Sterling 403 (poems), Ithaca House, 1971; The Forty Days (poems), Ithaca House, 1975.

WORK IN PROGRESS: Poems; research on objectivism in modern American poetry.

*　　*　　*

McBRIDE, Katharine 1904-1976

May 14, 1904—June 3, 1976; American educator, college president, and author of books on psychology. Obituaries: New York Times, June 4, 1976; Current Biography, July, 1976.

*　　*　　*

McBRIDE, Mary Margaret 1899-1976

November 16, 1899—April 7, 1976; American radio talk-show hostess, journalist, and author of travel books and memoirs. Obituaries: New York Times, April 8, 1976; Washington Post, April 8, 1976; Newsweek, April 19, 1976; Time, April 19, 1976; Current Biography, June, 1976.

*　　*　　*

McCANDLISH, George E(dward) 1914-1975

PERSONAL: Born May 31, 1914, in Seattle, Wash.; married, 1950; children: Joan, Brooks, David. Education: Swarthmore College, student; University of Washington, Seattle, graduated; Harvard University, Ph.D., 1962; also studied at University of Marburg. Religion: Society of Friends (Quakers).

CAREER: University of Delaware, Newark, member of English faculty, 1951-52; Harvard University Press, Cambridge, Mass., editorial assistant, 1956-65; Brown University, Providence, R.I., fellow, 1965; George Washington University, Washington, D.C., member of English faculty, 1965-70, professor of English and chairman of department, 1970-75. Former executive director of United Nations Relief and Rehabilitation Administration in the French Zone. Wartime service: American Field Service, ambulance driver in World War II; received French Croix de Guerre.

WRITINGS: (Editor) The Puritans; (editor) Cotton Mather, Magnalia Christi Americana, Harvard University Press, in press.

OBITUARIES: Washington Post, May 21, 1975.

(Died May 19, 1975, in Perugia, Italy)

*　　*　　*

McCANN, Edson
See del REY, Lester 1915-

*　　*　　*

McCARTY, Doran Chester 1931-

PERSONAL: Born February 3, 1931, in Bolivar, Mo.; son of Bartie Lee (a tool and die setter) and Donta (an inventory controller; maiden name, Russell) McCarty; married Gloria Laffoon (a teacher), June 14, 1952; children: Gaye, Rise, Marletta, Beth. Education: Southwest Baptist College, A.A., 1950; William Jewell College, A.B., 1952; New Orleans Baptist Theological Seminary, graduate study, 1952-53; Southern Baptist Theological Seminary, B.D., 1956, Ph.D., 1963; also attended Indiana University. Office: Department of Theology and Christian Philosophy, Midwestern Baptist Theological Seminary, 5001 North Oak St. & Trafficway, Kansas City, Mo. 64118.

CAREER: Pastor of Baptist churches in Springfield, Mo., 1949-50, Jameson, Mo., 1951-52, Elliston, Ky., 1953-56, Switz City, Ind., 1956-62, Pleasant Hill, Mo., 1962-65, and Independence, Mo., 1965-67; Midwestern Baptist Theological Seminary, Kansas City, Mo., associate professor, 1967-71, professor of theology and Christian philosophy, 1971—, director of supervised ministry, 1971—. Instructor at William Jewell College, 1966-67, Metropolitan Junior College (Kansas City, Mo.), 1969, and Penn Valley Community College, 1969-74. Chairman of Missouri Baptist Historical Commission; member of executive committee of Indiana Baptist Convention.

MEMBER: American Academy of Religion, American Philosophical Association, Association of Baptist Professors of Religion, American Teilhard Association, Association for Theological Field Education (member of executive committee), Association for Professional Education for Ministry, Hegel Society of America, Association for Theological Education, Society of Biblical Literature, Southern Baptist Historical Society, Southern Baptist Social Work Association, Kansas City Society for Theological Study, William Jewell College Alumni Association (vice-president of board of governors), Optimist Club (member of executive committee), Ministerial Association (past president), Blue River Baptist Association (chairman of executive committee), Linton Baptist Association (moderator).

WRITINGS: (Co-author) Invitation to Dialogue: The Professional World, Broadman, 1970; (co-author) These Missouri Baptists, Missouri Baptist Press, 1970; (co-author) Encyclopedia of Southern Baptists, Volume III, Broadman, 1971; Rightly Dividing the Word, Broadman, 1973; The Marks of a Christian, Sunday School Board, 1974; Social Implications for Churches with the Mobile American, Home Mission Board, 1975; Sociological Aspects of Rural Urban Life in America Today, Home Mission Board, 1975; (co-author Adult Life and Work Annual Lessons, Convention Press, 1974, 1975; (co-author) The Mobile American in Multi-Family Housing, Home Mission Board, 1975; Teilhard de Chardin, Word Publications, 1976. Contributor to church periodicals. Co-editor of Journal of Missouri Baptist History.

WORK IN PROGRESS: Growing a Church in a Changing Community; Supervision in the Education of Ministers.

*　　*　　*

McCLAIN, Alva J. 1888-?

PERSONAL: Born April 11, 1888, in Aurelia, Iowa; son of Walter Scott and Mary Ellen (Gnagey) McClain; married Josephine Gingrich, June 7, 1911. Education: Attended University of Washington, Seattle, 1908-09, and Antioch College, 1915-16; Xenia Theological Seminary, diploma in theology, 1917, Th.M., 1925; Occidental College, A.B., 1925; Bible Institute, Los Angeles, Calif., D.D., 1940. Home address: P.O. Box 586, Winona Lake, Ind.

CAREER: Ordained minister of the Brethren Church, 1917; pastor of Brethren church in Philadelphia, Pa., 1919-23; Ashland College, Ashland, Ohio, professor of Old Testament theology, 1925-27; taught at Bible Institute, Los Angeles, Calif., 1927-29; Ashland Theological Seminary, Ashland, professor of Christian theology and apologetics, 1930-37, associate dean, 1930-33, dean, 1934-37; Grace Theological Seminary, Winona Lake, Ind., founder and professor of Christian theology, 1937-62, president of Grace College, 1953-62, president of seminary, until 1962. Lectured at Philadelphia School of the Bible, 1919-23; W.H.G. Thomas

Memorial Lecturer at Dallas Theological Seminary, 1954; Frederick Bueerman and John B. Champion Lecturer at Western Conservative Baptist Theological Seminary, 1956; Lyman Steward memorial lecturer at Talbot Theological Seminary, 1958. Winona Lake Christian Assembly, Inc., member of board of directors, beginning 1942, secretary, 1947-56. Moderator of General Conference of the Brethren Church, 1930, 1934.

MEMBER: Foreign Missionary Society (of the Brethren Church; member of board of directors, beginning, 1918), Evangelical Theological Society (charter member), Phi Beta Kappa. *Awards, honors:* LL.D. from Bob Jones College (now University), 1945.

WRITINGS: Bible Truths, [Ashland, Ohio], 1935; *Daniel's Prophecy of the Seventy Weeks,* Zondervan, 1940; *The Greatness of the Kingdom: An Inductive Study of the Kingdom of God as Set Forth in the Scriptures,* Zondervan, 1959; *Romans: The Gospel of God's Grace,* edited by Herman A. Hoyt, Moody, 1973. Also author of *The Outline and Argument of St. Paul's Epistle to the Romans,* 1928, and *Law and the Christian in Relation to the Doctrine for Grace,* 1954. Contributor to religious journals. Member of *Scofield Reference Bible* Revision Committee of Oxford University Press.*

(Deceased)

* * *

McCLINTON, Leon 1933-

PERSONAL: Born January 29, 1933, in Des Moines, Iowa; son of John Keith (an engineer) and Leona (Stamp) McClinton; married Joan Elinor Cox, February 23, 1957; children: Cheryl Lee, Mark James, Scott Eugene. *Education:* Arkansas Polytechnic College, student, 1952-53, 1956; University of Central Arkansas, B.S.Ed., 1959; Wisconsin State University—Stevens Point, M.A.Ed., 1968. *Religion:* Methodist. *Home:* 413 Lincoln St., Antigo, Wis. 54409. *Office:* Antigo High School, Antigo, Wis. 54409.

CAREER: Professional baseball player with Cleveland Indians, 1951-52, and St. Louis Cardinals, 1953-57; high school English teacher and athletic coach in Osceola, Ark., 1959-60, and Winnipeg, Manitoba, 1960-65; Antigo High School, Antigo, Wis., English teacher and athletic coach, 1965—. Has pitched for minor league baseball teams in Green Bay, Wis., Winnipeg, Manitoba, Fort Smith, Ark., Peoria, Ill., Lynchburg, Va., and Hazelhurst, Ga. *Military service:* U.S. Army, 1953-55, member of Ninth Corps battalion rifle team in Korean Far East championships; served in Korea and Japan. *Member:* Council for Wisconsin Writers. *Awards, honors: Cross-Country Runner* was named "top juvenile book" by Wisconsin Writers Council, 1974, and "outstanding juvenile book" by *World Book Encyclopedia,* 1975.

WRITINGS: Cross-Country Runner (juvenile), Dutton, 1974.

WORK IN PROGRESS: A juvenile novel based on legends and old stories of baseball.

SIDELIGHTS: McClinton told *CA:* "Both as an athlete and a coach, I have been interested in the talent and motivation which go into the making of a successful athlete, particularly the individual drive necessary to produce a long-distance runner."

* * *

McCLURE, Arthur F(rederick) II 1936-

PERSONAL: Born January 24, 1936, in Leavenworth, Kan.; son of Arthur F. (a chemical engineer) and Dorothy (Davis) McClure; married Judith A. Hallaux (a special education teacher), January 20, 1959; children: Allison, Arthur Kyle, Amy Louise, Steven Anderson. *Education:* University of Kansas, B.A., 1958, Ph.D., 1966; University of Colorado, M.A., 1960. *Politics:* Republican. *Religion:* Episcopalian. *Home:* 304 Jones Ave., Warrensburg, Mo. 64093. *Office:* Department of History, Central Missouri State University, Warrensburg, Mo. 64093.

CAREER: Central Missouri State University, Warrensburg, assistant professor, 1965-69, associate professor, 1969-72, professor of history, 1972—, chairman of department, 1971—. Member of film advisory committee for Missouri State Council on the Arts, 1972-73. *Military service:* U.S. Army Reserve, 1958-64, active duty, 1958. *Member:* Society of American Archivists, Phi Alpha Theta. *Awards, honors:* Grants from Kansas City Regional Council for Higher Education, 1969-70, and Harry S. Truman Library Institute, 1971; honorary commissioner for Missouri American Revolution Bicentennial Commission, 1975.

WRITINGS: (With Alfred E. Twomey) *The Versatiles: A Study of Supporting Players in the American Motion Picture, 1930-1955,* A. S. Barnes, 1969; *The Truman Administration and the Problems of Postwar Labor,* Fairleigh Dickinson University Press, 1970; (with Twomey and Ken D. Jones) *The Films of James Stewart,* A. S. Barnes, 1970; (editor) *The Movies: An American Idiom; Readings in the Social History of the American Motion Picture,* Fairleigh Dickinson University Press, 1971; (with Jones) *Heroes, Heavies, and Sagebrush: A Pictorial History of the "B" Western Player,* A. S. Barnes, 1973; (with Jones) *Hollywood at War: The American Motion Picture and World War Two, 1939-1945,* A. S. Barnes, 1973; (with Naomi B. Lynn) *The Fulbright Premise: Senator J. William Fulbright's Views on Presidential Power,* Bucknell University Press, 1973; (with Jones) *Star Quality: Screen Actors from the Golden Age of Films,* A. S. Barnes, 1974; (with Jones and Twomey) *Character People: Supporting Players in the American Motion Picture,* A. S. Barnes, 1976; (with James V. Young) *Remembering Their Glory: Sports Heroes of the 1940's,* A. S. Barnes, 1976. Contributor to history magazines, film journals, and local area publications.

WORK IN PROGRESS: The World of William Inge; a biographical study of William Allen White; a history of distributive education in America; editing memoirs of President Truman's military aide, Harry Vaughan; a social and legal history of motion picture censorship in America, 1900-75.

* * *

McCONNELL, Grant 1915-

PERSONAL: Born June 27, 1915, in Portland, Ore.; son of Leslie Grant (a banker) and Nellie Maud (a teacher: maiden name, Nelson) McConnell; married Jane Foster (a public health nurse), October 7, 1939; children: Ann Katherine, James Andrew. *Education:* Reed College, B.A., 1957; graduate study at Oxford University, 1938-39, and Harvard University, 1939-40; University of California, Berkeley, Ph.D., 1951. *Politics:* Democrat. *Religion:* "Druid." *Home:* 4825 Bonny Doon Rd., Santa Cruz, Calif. 95060. *Agent:* Alan Ravage Associates, 789 West End Ave., New York, N.Y. 10025. *Office:* University of California, Santa Cruz, Calif. 95064.

CAREER: Mount Holyoke College, South Hadley, Mass., instructor in economics, 1939-40; worked for U.S. Department of Agriculture and Office of Price Administration,

1940-42; University of California, Berkeley, lecturer, 1951-53, assistant professor of political science, 1953-57; University of Chicago, Chicago, Ill., associate professor, 1957-65, professor of political science, 1965-69, chairman of department, 1967-69, director of exchange program with Makerere College, 1961-17; University of California, Santa Cruz, professor of government, 1969—, executive vice-chancellor, 1970-71. *Military service:* U.S. Naval Reserve, active duty, 1943-46; served in Pacific theater; became lieutenant.

MEMBER: American Political Science Association (vice-president, 1970-71), National Parks Association, Sierra Club, Wilderness Society, Friends of the Earth, North Cascades Conservation Council (member of board of directors). *Awards, honors:* Rhodes scholarship, 1938.

WRITINGS: The Decline of Agrarian Democracy, University of California Press, 1953; *The Steel Seizure of 1952,* Inter-University Case Program, 1960; *Steel and the Presidency,* Norton, 1963; *Private Power and American Democracy,* Knopf, 1966; *The Modern Presidency,* St. Martin's, 1967, revised edition, 1976. Contributor to political science journals and popular magazines, including *Nation* and *Saturday Evening Post.*

WORK IN PROGRESS: A book on wilderness life; a book on the changing pattern of American politics.

* * *

McCOY, Charles A(llan) 1920-

PERSONAL: Born May 19, 1920, in Chicago, Ill.; son of Charles Richard (a businessman) and Maria (Peterson) McCoy; married Noreen Webb, March 20, 1946 (deceased); married Elaine Langan, April 7, 1969; children: (first marriage) Bruce A., Craig R.; (second marriage) Sarah L., C. Ian, C. Graeme. *Education:* Illinois State University, B.S., 1948; Colgate University, M.A. (with distinction), 1950; Boston University, Ph.D., 1958. *Politics:* "Independent Marxist." *Religion:* Roman Catholic. *Home:* 389 12th St., Atlantic Beach, Fla. 32233. *Office:* Department of Political Science and Sociology, University of North Florida, Jacksonville, Fla. 32211.

CAREER: Worcester Polytechnic Institute, Worcester, Mass., assistant professor of government and business, 1950-53; University of Virginia, Charlottesville, research assistant at Bureau of Public Administration, 1953-56; Temple University, Philadelphia, Pa., instructor, 1956-58, assistant professor, 1958-62, associate professor, 1962-66, professor of political science, 1966-68; Lehigh University, Bethlehem, Pa., professor of government and chairman of department, 1968-76; University of North Florida, Jacksonville, professor of political science and chairman of department, 1976—. Visiting professor at California State University, Los Angeles, summer, 1968; visiting lecturer at University of Leeds, 1961-62; Fulbright professor at Monash University, 1966, and University of Hong Kong, 1971-72. Founding officer and vice-chairman of Caucus for a New Political Science, 1967-69. *Military service:* U.S. Army Air Forces, navigator with Troop Carrier Command, 1941-46; became first lieutenant; received Air Medal with two oak leaf clusters.

MEMBER: International Political Science Association, American Political Science Association, American Association of University Professors, American Academy of Political and Social Science, International Studies Association. *Awards, honors:* Faculty fellowship from National Aeronautics and Space Administration and American Society for Engineering Education, summer, 1973.

WRITINGS: Polk and the Presidency, University of Texas Press, 1960; (editor with John Playford) *Apolitical Politics: A Critique of Behavioralism,* Crowell, 1967; (with Alan Wolfe) *Political Analysis: An Unorthodox Approach,* Crowell, 1972; (with Benjamin Cooper, M. D. Devine, and others) *The Energy Dilemma and Its Impact on Air Transportation,* Langley Research Center, National Aeronautics and Space Administration, 1973. Contributor to political science journals.

WORK IN PROGRESS: Research on political economy and on democratic theory.

SIDELIGHTS: McCoy told *CA* that the Caucus for a New Political Science is an organization of radical political scientists interested in changing the nature of the political dialogue in the United States. "It has a critical perspective," he wrote. "Some members, myself included, advocate a socialist economy and greater democratic participation."

* * *

McCOY, F(lorence) N(ina) 1925-

PERSONAL: Born July 22, 1925, in Philadelphia, Pa. *Education:* Hunter College (now of the City University of New York), B.A., 1954; Sacramento State University, M.A., 1963; University of California, Berkeley, M.L.S., 1972; University of Oregon, Ph.D., 1972. *Residence:* Berkeley, Calif. *Office:* Armstrong College, Berkeley, Calif. 94704.

CAREER: Armstrong College, Berkeley, Calif., assistant professor of English and history 1972—. *Member:* American Historical Association, American Society for Legal History, West Coast Association of Women Historians, California Writers' Club. *Awards, honors:* American Council of Learned Societies research fellowship, 1973-74.

WRITINGS: Robert Baillie and the Second Scots Reformation, University of California Press, 1974; *Researching and Writing in History,* University of California Press, 1974. Contributor to *California Librarian.*

WORK IN PROGRESS: A historical novel, set in Sacramento during the gold rush; a novel about the academic world.

* * *

McDANIEL, Elsiebeth

PERSONAL: Born in Evanston, Ill.; daughter of Moses S. and Amy Louise (Schults) McDaniel. *Education:* Wheaton College, Wheaton, Ill., B.A., M.A., 1971. *Religion:* Protestant. *Home:* 812 East Liberty Dr., Wheaton, Ill. 60187. *Office:* SP Publications, 1825 College Ave., Wheaton, Ill. 60187.

CAREER: Encyclopaedia Britannica, Chicago, Ill., copy controller, 1943-48; Hitchcock Publishing Co., Wheaton, Ill., managing editor, 1948-60; SP Publications, Inc., Wheaton, director of Early Childhood Publications, 1960—. *Member:* Association of Childhood Education, Beta Sigma Phi.

WRITINGS: Stories of Jesus, Scripture Press, 1965; *Early Heroes of the Bible,* Scripture Press, 1965; *You and Children,* Moody, 1973; *You and Preschoolers,* Moody, 1975.

WORK IN PROGRESS: Research on church-oriented day care centers, on religious education for the mentally-retarded child, and on the Christian day school.

* * *

McDANIEL, Eugene B(arker) 1931-

PERSONAL: Born September 27, 1931, in New Bern,

N.C.; son of Willard G. (a farmer) and Helen (Griffen) McDaniel; married Dorothy Howard, June 23, 1956; children: Michael H., David E., Leslie A. (daughter). *Education:* Campbell Junior College, A.A., 1952; Elon College, B.A., 1954. *Religion:* Baptist. *Home:* 100 San Pedro Rd., Alameda, Calif. 94501. *Office:* U.S. Navy, "U.S.S. Niagara Falls," AFS-3, F.P.O. San Francisco, Calif. 96601.

CAREER: U.S. Navy, 1955—, present rank, captain. Designated naval aviator, 1956, member of naval air attack squadron, 1956-60, replacement air wing instructor, 1960-63, carrier controlled approach officer, 1963-65, maintenance officer, 1965-67, prisoner of war in North Vietnam, 1967-73, joint warfare plans officer for Commander of the Atlantic Staff, 1973-75, commander of "U.S.S. Niagara Falls," 1975—. Has appeared on nationally broadcast television programs, including American Broadcasting Corp.'s "Issues and Answers," and in a documentary film "P.O.W."

AWARDS, HONORS—Military: Navy Cross, two Silver Stars, Legion of Merit, Distinguished Flying Cross, three Bronze Stars, five air medals, seven strike flight air medals, two Purple Hearts, two Navy Commendation Medals.

WRITINGS: (With James L. Johnson) *Before Honor* (on experiences as a prisoner of war), A. J. Holman, 1975.

SIDELIGHTS: McDaniel told *CA* he was a brutally tortured prisoner of war during the Vietnam conflict as a result of his active role in camp communications during an organized escape attempt by fellow prisoners in 1969.

*   *   *

McDERMOTT, Beverly Brodsky   1941-

PERSONAL: Born August 16, 1941, in Brooklyn, N.Y.; married Gerald McDermott (a graphic artist and filmmaker). *Education:* Brooklyn College of the City University of New York, B.A., 1965; attended School of Visual Arts, New York City, one year. *Address:* c/o J. B. Lippincott Co., East Washington Sq., Philadelphia, Pa. 19105.

CAREER: Author and illustrator of children's books; textile designer and colorist. Teacher for three years.

WRITINGS—Self-illustrated: *The Crystal Apple: A Russian Tale,* Viking, 1974; *Sedna: An Eskimo Myth,* Viking, 1975; *The Golem,* Lippincott, 1976.

Illustrator: John R. Townsend, *Forest of the Night,* Lippincott, 1975. Work has appeared in *New York Times Book Review, Print Magazine, Horn Book, Booklist, Library Journal,* and as the cover illustration of the *Wilson Library Bulletin,* January, 1976.

SIDELIGHTS: Mrs. McDermott writes: "While living in the south of France several years ago, I saw the German version of the film "The Golem" which was made in the 1920's. It was then that I decided to do my own adaptation for a picture book. Research for the story and its development took two years, during which time I studied the symbols of the Hebrew alphabet and their corresponding magical qualities."

*   *   *

McDONALD, Hugh C(hisholm)   1913-

PERSONAL: Born May 6, 1913, in Hopkins, Minn.; son of John Harold (in U.S. Army) and Jennie Marie (Dessert) McDonald; married Theodora Coony, 1935; children: Hugh, John, Mary, Patricia, Edmond, Theresa. *Education:* Attended University of Southern California, University of Michigan, and Stanford University. *Residence:* Playa Del Ray, Calif.

CAREER: Los Angeles County Sheriff's Department, Los Angeles, Calif., 1940-1967, began as sheriff's deputy, became chief of detectives, 1960; World Associates (security company), president, 1968-73; Hollywood Turf Club, Hollywood, Calif., director of security, 1973—; writer. Employed part-time by Central Intelligence Agency, 1947-70. *Military service:* U.S. Army, Military Intelligence, 1942-46; became major.

WRITINGS: The Auditorium Affair (mystery novel), John Hale, 1973; *Hour of the Blue Fox* (documentary novel), Pyramid Publications, 1975; *Appointment in Dallas* (documentary novel), Zebra Publications, 1975; *Five Signs from Ruby* (documentary novel), Pyramid Publications, 1976; *Two Words from Kiev* (documentary novel), Pyramid publications, in press.

WORK IN PROGRESS: The Conspirators, a documentary novel; *Five on Five,* a mystery.

*   *   *

McDONALD, Jill (Masefield)   1927-

PERSONAL: Born October 30, 1927, in New Zealand; daughter of Reginald Bedford (an architect) and Cecily Sutherland (Chambers) Hammond; married Alec McDonald, March 27, 1948 (divorced September 21, 1960); children: Glen Rohan (Mrs. Philip Spicer), Murray James. *Education:* Attended University of Auckland, 1946-48. *Home and office:* 43 Blackheath Rd., London S.E.10, England.

CAREER: Free-lance illustrator, 1953-57; Department of Education, Wellington, New Zealand, art editor for School Publications Branch, 1957-65; free-lance illustrator and writer, 1965—.

WRITINGS—For children: *Counting on an Elephant,* Penguin, 1975; *Maggy Scraggle Loves the Beautiful Ice-Cream Man,* Penguin, in press.

WORK IN PROGRESS—For children: *The Terrible Happy-Helper Engine; The Hermit and the Mouse-House Boat; Song of Snake; Mr. Rory Dog; The Exploding Feather Rhinoceros; The Hair Pill; Pretty Kitty Fisher; Mighty Moth,* all self-illustrated picture books.

SIDELIGHTS: Jill McDonald writes that "motivation for getting anything actually finished is usually that I need the money. I don't really know what makes me start in the first place. Probably best not to think too much about this—I feel chaotic and dispersed if I don't and at my very best if I do. I very much like the freshness and wonder with which little kids view the world and so like to write and draw for them. On the other hand I have a steadily growing list of unborn pictures and stories which noway fit within a child's-eye view and which are becoming more and more strident in their demand to see themselves on paper."

*   *   *

McELRATH, Joseph R(ichard), Jr.   1945-

PERSONAL: Born June 10, 1945, in Jesup, Ga.; son of Joseph R. (a business executive) and Marguerite (Hodges) McElrath; married Sharon Morrison, August 27, 1966; children: Gregory Mark, Christopher Matthew. *Education:* LeMoyne College, B.A., 1967; Duquesne University, M.A., 1969; University of South Carolina, Ph.D., 1973. *Home:* 2412 Shalley Dr., Tallahassee, Fla. 32303. *Office:* Department of English, Florida State University, Tallahassee, Fla. 32306.

CAREER: Florida State University, Tallahassee, assistant professor of English, 1974—. *Member:* Modern Language Association of America, South Atlantic Modern Language Association, New York Historical Society.

WRITINGS: *Frank Norris: A Reference Guide*, G. K. Hall, 1975; *The Complete Works of Anne Bradstreet*, Faust, 1976. Contributor to literature journals. Editor of *Editorial Quarterly*.

WORK IN PROGRESS: *Frank Norris: The Critical Reception*, publication by Burt Franklin expected in 1978; *Richard Harding Davis: A Reference Guide*, for G. K. Hall, 1979.

* * *

McFARLAN, Donald M(aitland) 1915-

PERSONAL: Born October 20, 1915, in Aberdeen, Scotland; son of Donald (a clergyman) and Mary Proudfoot (Maitland) McFarlan; married Elspeth G. McQueen, December 1, 1942; children: Donald R. McQueen. *Education:* University of Glasgow, M.A. (honors), 1937, diploma in divinity (with distinction), 1940, Ph.D., 1957. *Home:* 94 Southbrae Dr., Glasgow G13 1TZ, Scotland. *Office:* Jordanhill College of Education, 76 Southbrae Dr., Glasgow G13 1TZ, Scotland.

CAREER: Ordained Church of Scotland clergyman, 1940; educational missionary in Calabar, Nigeria, 1940-51; Jordanhill College of Education, Glasgow, Scotland, lecturer, 1951-65, senior lecturer, 1965-67, principal lecturer in religious education, 1967—. External lecturer at University of Ibadan and University of Ife. Convener of business committee of general council of University of Glasgow, 1974-77. Host of "Fireside Sunday School," a children's program on British Broadcasting Corp. (BBC)—Scotland, 1959-70. *Member:* Field Society of Nigeria, Royal Scottish Automobile Club.

WRITINGS—Juveniles: *The Greatest Book in the World*, Sheldon Press, 1944; *Write Good English*, Sheldon Press, 1946; *World Travellers*, Sheldon Press, 1946; *Calabar: The Church of Scotland Mission*, Thomas Nelson, 1946, 2nd edition, 1957; *The Story of Trade*, Sheldon Press, 1947; *Saint Columba*, Sheldon Press, 1947; *The Story of Writing*, Sheldon Press, 1948; *A Book of Bible Prayers*, Sheldon Press, 1948; *Elephant's Birthday Party*, Thomas Nelson, 1948; *Stumpy Sings on Wednesdays, Too*, Thomas Nelson, 1948; *The Secret of the Drum*, Thomas Nelson, 1948; *Timothy Wins a Medal*, Thomas Nelson, 1948; *Pioneers of Health*, Thomas Nelson, 1948; *Trading through the Ages*, Thomas Nelson, 1948; *The Story of Healing*, Sheldon Press, 1949; *The Story of Education*, Sheldon Press, 1949.

Cross River Tales, two volumes, Thomas Nelson, 1950; *Jacob and Esau*, Thomas Nelson, 1950; *Moses the Leader*, Thomas Nelson, 1950; *Joseph and His Brothers*, Thomas Nelson, 1950; *The Story of Joshua*, Thomas Nelson, 1950; *David the Shepherd Boy*, Thomas Nelson, 1950; *Elijah the Prophet*, Thomas Nelson, 1950; *Four Great Leaders*, Thomas Nelson, 1950; *The Pilgrim's Progress*, Thomas Nelson, 1950; *The Countryside Bible Book*, Stirling Tract Enterprise, 1954; *Countryside Bible Prayers*, Stirling Tract Enterprise, 1957; *White Queen: The Story of Mary Slessor*, Lutterworth, 1957; *Mackay of Uganda*, Lutterworth, 1958; *The Lively Oracles: The Story of the National Bible Society of Scotland*, Thomas Nelson, 1959.

Highway to the Bible, Books 1-4, Blackie & Son, 1962; *A Bible Reference Book*, Blackie & Son, 1973; *Who and What and Where in the Bible*, John Knox, 1974; *The Nazarene File*, Blackie & Son, in press.

WORK IN PROGRESS: *Stepping Westward*, a book of Scottish literary interest; research on world religions.

McFERRAN, Douglass David 1934-
(David Farren)

PERSONAL: Born July 16, 1934, in Los Angeles, Calif. *Education:* Gonzaga University, A.B., 1958, M.A., 1959; University of California, Los Angeles, further graduate study, 1964-68. *Home:* 24704 Sand Wedge Lane, Valencia, Calif. 91355. *Agent:* Ned Brown Associated, P.O. Box 5020, Beverly Hills, Calif. 90210.

CAREER: High school teacher in San Francisco, Calif., 1959-62, and in Los Angeles, Calif., 1962-66; Los Angeles Pierce College, Woodland Hills, Calif., instructor, 1966-69, assistant professor, 1969-73, associate professor of philosophy, 1973—.

WRITINGS—Under pseudonym David Farren: *The Return of Magic*, Harper, 1972; *Living with Magic*, Simon & Schuster, 1974; *Sex and Magic*, Simon & Schuster, 1975. Contributor to church magazines, and to *American Teacher*, *Commonweal*, *America*, and *Listening Studies*.

WORK IN PROGRESS—Novels: *Believers; Mendaga's Morning; Station Break*.

SIDELIGHTS: McFerran writes: "From 1952 to 1962 I was a Jesuit seminarian. After I began my college teaching in 1966 I found myself unable to retain the belief system in which I was raised. For a while I referred to myself as a Marxian existentialist, then I became involved in the study of the Western occult tradition. In a way all my writing, which has focussed on the history of ideas, has been an effort to comprehend the psychology and sociology of both belief and unbelief."

* * *

McGILLIGAN, Patrick (Michael) 1951-

PERSONAL: Born April 22, 1951, in Madison, Wis.; son of William A. (in upholstery) and Marion (a secretary; maiden name, Schubert) McGilligan. *Education:* University of Wisconsin, Madison, B.A., 1974. *Home:* 1564 Massachusetts Ave., Apt. 4, Cambridge, Mass. 02138; and c/o McGilligans, 1107 Buena Vista, San Clemente, Calif. 92672. *Office:* Boston Globe, Boston, Mass. 02107.

CAREER: Writer; *Boston Globe*, Boston, Mass., film writer, back-up critic, book reviewer, 1973—. Correspondent for *Quixote* and *Take-Over*.

WRITINGS: *Cagney: The Actor as Auteur*, A. S. Barnes, 1975; *Ginger Rogers*, Pyramid Publications, 1975; *I Aim for the Stars*, Quixote Press, 1975; *Eddie Elson: Ten Years Sluggin' on the State Street Front*, Quixote Press, 1976. Regular contributor to *American Film*, *Take One*, *Focus on Film*, and *Velvet Light Trap*.

WORK IN PROGRESS: A novel about Wisconsin.

* * *

McGINNIS, Thomas C(harles) 1925-

PERSONAL: Born June 2, 1925, in Monroe, N.C., son of Robert Ashe (a textile supervisor) and Mamie (Warlick) McGinnis; married Mary Yorke Kluttz (a librarian), February 15, 1947; children: Thomas Charles, Jr., Karen Yorke McGinnis Mercantino, John Richard. *Education:* Davidson College, student, 1942; Catawba College, B.A., 1946; University of North Carolina, M.S.S.W., 1949; William Alanson White Institute of Psychiatry, Psychoanalysis, and Psychology, certificate, 1957; Columbia University, Ed.D., 1962. *Home:* 346 Owen Ave., Fair Lawn, N.J. 07410. *Office:* Counseling and Psychotherapy Center, 0-100 27th St., Fair Lawn, N.J. 07410.

CAREER: Cartaret County Department of Public Welfare, Beaufort, N.C., superintendent, 1949-51; private practice in clinical psychology, 1952—. Civilian director of Mental Hygiene Consultation Service (Fort Dix, N.J.), 1952-53; executive director of Clinic for Mental Health Services of Passaic County (N.J.), 1953-59; executive director of Counseling and Psychotherapy Center, 1959—; co-director of Human Services Center for Education and Research, 1972—. Instructor at Fairleigh Dickinson University, 1963-65; assistant professor at New York University, 1965-68, associate professor, 1969-73, 1976. Member of board of directors of New Jersey League for Emotionally Disturbed Children, 1955-56; chairman of New Jersey Welfare Council, 1956-57, and New Jersey Community Mental Health Advisory Council, 1958-59; member of New Jersey Board of Marriage Counselor Examiners, 1969—. Member of U.S. national committee of International Union of Family Organizations, 1968—, member of executive board of International organization, 1969-73, member of board of directors, 1970—. Member of grant review board of National Institute of Mental Health, 1969-70. President of Yorktom Corp., 1971—. Consultant to major league baseball teams, Swedish Air Force, and Music Corp. of America. Military service: U.S. Merchant Marine Cadet Corps, 1945-46. U.S. Naval Reserve, active duty as supply and dispersing officer and treasury agent, 1946-47; served in Pacific theater; became lieutenant junior grade. U.S. Army, directior of Mental Hygiene Consultation Service at Fort Dix, 1948-51; became first lieutenant.

MEMBER: American Association of Marriage and Family Counselors (fellow; president, 1970-71), American Psychological Association, American Association of Sex Educators and Counselors (member of advisory board, 1968—; vicepresident, 1969-70), American Academy of Psychotherapists, Academy of Psychologists in Marital Counseling, National Association of Social Workers (charter member), National Council on Family Relations, Society for the Scientific Study of Sex, Association of Couples for Marriage Enrichment, Authors Guild of Authors League of America, New Jersey Psychological Association, New Jersey Association of Marriage Counselors (president, 1963-68), New Jersey Association of Mental Hygiene Clinics (presidentelect, 1959), Rotary International. Awards, honors: Citations from American Association of Sex Educators and Counselors Board of Marriage Counselor Examiners; Whitner Medal from Catawba College, 1956.

WRITINGS: Your First Year of Marriage, Doubleday, 1967; A Girl's Guide to Dating and Going Steady, Doubleday, 1968; (with Dana G. Finnegan) Open Family and Marriage, Mosby, 1976; (with John U. Ayres) Open Family Living, Doubleday, 1976. Contributor to professional and popular magazines. Member of editorial board of Sexual Behavior, 1971-74, and Journal of Divorce, 1976.

WORK IN PROGRESS: Crises in the Middle Years of Marriage; The Dynamics of Human Interaction.

SIDELIGHTS: McGinnis' books have been published in French, Spanish, Japanese, German, and Dutch.

* * *

McGLYNN, Christopher
See GINDER, Richard 1914-

* * *

McHANEY, Thomas L(afayette) 1936-

PERSONAL: Born October 17, 1936, in Paragould, Ark.; son of Thomas L. (a lawyer) and Maxine (Brown) McHaney; married Karen Honigmann (a cartographer), May 30, 1962; children: Sudie Ann, Jessie Wynne, Molly Josephine. Education: Christian Brothers College, student, 1954-56; Mississippi State University, B.A., 1959; University of North Carolina, Chapel Hill, M.A., 1963; University of South Carolina, Ph.D., 1968. Politics: Democrat. Home: 985 Courtenay Dr., Atlanta, Ga. 30306. Office: Department of English, Georgia State University, University Plaza, Atlanta, Ga. 30303.

CAREER: University of Mississippi, Oxford, instructor in English, 1963-65; Georgia State University, Atlanta, assistant professor, 1968-73, associate professor of English, 1973—. Fulbright lecturer, University of Bonn, 1976. Member: Modern Language Association of America, American Association of University Professors, Southern Humanities Conference, South Atlantic Modern Language Association. Awards, honors: Woodrow Wilson fellowship, 1960; special award for fiction from Henry Bellaman Foundation, 1970, for short stories; fiction award from Prairie Schooner, 1973.

WRITINGS: (Contributor) Matthew J. Bruccoli, editor, The Chief Glory of Every People, Southern Illinois University Press, 1973; William Faulkner's The Wild Palms: A Study, University Press of Mississippi, 1975; William Faulkner: A Reference Guide, G. K. Hall, 1976. Contributor to literary journals, including PMLA and Mississippi Quarterly. Member of editorial board of Costerus: A Journal of English and American Literature, 1972—.

* * *

McHUGH, Roland 1945-

PERSONAL: Born October 13, 1945, in Brighton, Sussex, England; son of Leslie (a harbor pilot) and Ingeborg (Jensen) McHugh. Education: Imperial College of Science and Technology, University of London, B.Sc., 1967; Institute of Acoustic Physiology (France), graduate study, 1968; City of London Polytechnic, Ph.D., 1971. Politics: "Vaguely leftist." Religion: None. Home: c/o 75 Hill Crest Rd., Newhaven, Sussex BN9 9EG, England. Office: James Joyce Tower, Sandycove, County Dublin, Ireland.

CAREER: University of Dundee, Dundee, Scotland, research assistant in entomology, 1972-73; Lilmar Pharmaceuticals, Dublin, Ireland, quality control chemist, 1973-74; biology teacher in technical college in Dublin, Ireland, 1974-76; James Joyce Tower, Sandycove, Ireland, curator, 1976—. Member of council of James Joyce Institute of Ireland.

WRITINGS: (Contributor) Michael H. Begnal and Fritz Senn, editors, A Conceptual Guide to "Finnegans Wake", Pennsylvania State University Press, 1974; The Sigla of "Finnegans Wake", University of Texas Press, 1976. Contributor to Wake Newsletter.

WORK IN PROGRESS: Annotations for "Finnegans Wake" ("the pages could be interleaved with those of Finnegans Wake, providing an instant gloss on the facing page").

AVOCATIONAL INTERESTS: Extremely amplified music.

* * *

McKIBBIN, Frank L(owell) 1917-

PERSONAL: Born January 30, 1917, in Kansas City, Mo.; son of Frank L. and Mayme (Spitzer) McKibbin; married

Jean Halmond Richey (an author), November 24, 1961; children: Michael, Mitchel; stepdaughter: Mary Lynn (Mrs. Donald Lowry). *Education:* University of Missouri, B.A., 1938; graduate study at University of California at Los Angeles, 1966. *Home:* 6020 Wright Terr., Culver City, Calif. 90230; and 1175 Barbara Dr., Vista, Calif. 92083. *Office:* 3810 Wilshire Blvd., Los Angeles, Calif. 90010.

CAREER: Folger Coffee Co., Kansas City, Mo., clerk in advertising and sales departments, 1938-42; Ben Hur Products, Inc. (coffee, tea, and spices manufacturer), Los Angeles, Calif., personal assistant to vice-president of sales, 1946-47; Honig-Cooper/Hal Stebbins (advertising agency), Los Angeles, Calif., vice-president and account supervisor, 1947-50; McCann-Erickson (advertising agency), Los Angeles, Calif., account executive, 1950-55; Dan B. Miner Co. (advertising agency), Los Angeles, account executive, 1955-56; Stromberger, LaVene & McKenzie (advertising agency), Los Angeles, vice-president and account supervisor, 1956-60; Fuller & Smith & Ross (advertising agency), Los Angeles and San Francisco, Calif., West Coast manager, 1960-65; self-syndicated newspaper columnist, 1965-66; Davis, Johnson, Mogul & Colombatto (advertising agency), Los Angeles, executive vice-president and general manager, 1967—; Franje, Inc., Culver City, Calif., president, 1972—. Consultant and manager, Mastec Method, 1975—. Owner of commercial greenhouses. *Military service:* U.S. Coast Guard, 1942-45. *Member:* Natural History Museum Alliance, Smithsonian Institution, Cousteau Society (founding member).

WRITINGS: (With wife, Jean McKibbin) *Cookbook of Foods from Bible Days,* privately printed, 1971, Whitaker Books, 1973. Contributor to business magazines.

WORK IN PROGRESS: A book on creative problem solving techniques; research on morphological analysis applied to business.

AVOCATIONAL INTERESTS: Woodworking, gardening, and hydrophonics.

* * *

McKIBBIN, Jean 1919-

PERSONAL: Born August 3, 1919, in Michigan; daughter of George Andrew and Grace E. (McKercher) Halmond; married John W. Rickey, January 3, 1941 (died 1942); married Frank L. McKibbin (in advertising and marketing), November 24, 1961; children: Mary Lynn (Mrs. Donald Lowry); stepsons: Michael McKibbin, Mitchel McKibbin. *Education:* Purdue University, B.S., 1941; graduate study at University of Southern California, 1962-63, and University of California at Los Angeles, 1966-67. *Home:* 6020 Wright Terr., Culver City, Calif. 90230; and 1175 Barbara Dr., Vista, Calif. 92083.

CAREER: Franje, Inc. (research and publishing), Culver City, Calif., executive vice-president, 1972—. Volunteer preparer of exhibitions, Los Angeles County Museum of Natural History, 1968-76. *Member:* Natural History Museum Alliance, Smithsonian Institution, Cousteau Society (founding member).

WRITINGS—Self-illustrated: (With husband, Frank L. McKibbin) *Cookbook of Foods from Bible Days,* privately printed, 1971, Whitaker Books, 1973; *Frugal Colonial Housewife,* Doubleday, 1976.

WORK IN PROGRESS: Other Ma, a collection of short stories, completion expected in 1980.

McLAUGHLIN, Bethany J.
See STRONG, Bethany J(une)

* * *

McLAUGHLIN, Emma Maude 1901-
(Alice M. Weir)

PERSONAL: Born July 14, 1901, in Somerville, Mass.; daughter of William Henry (a tinsmith) and Alice (Weir) Lantz; married John Joseph McLaughlin (an accountant and U.S. Post Office employee), December 1, 1944 (died December 1, 1968). *Education:* Attended high school in Arlington, Mass. *Politics:* Independent. *Religion:* Baptist. *Residence:* Tucson, Ariz. *Agent:* Phyllis W. Heald, 351 East Smoot Pl., Tucson, Ariz. 85705. *Office:* Research Associates, 535 South Irving Ave., Tucson, Ariz. 85711.

CAREER: Bookkeeper, U.S. Post Office employee, and office manager, 1918-46; Research Associates, Tucson, Ariz., associate member, 1950—. Member of board of trustees of Tucson General Hospital, 1954-56. *Wartime service:* U.S. Coast Guard, volunteer worker, 1944-46. *Member:* National Association of Retired Civil Employees (charter member of Tucson branch), American Education Association, Defenders of American Education (chairwoman, 1954—), Disabled Veterans Auxiliary (adjutant, 1949-51), Friends of the Library (Tucson; charter member; executive secretary, 1949-50). *Awards, honors:* Liberty award from Congress of Freedoms, 1976.

WRITINGS: (Under name Alice M. Weir) *And There's Tomorrow* (novel; Christian Book Club of America selection), Omni, 1975. Contributor to periodicals.

WORK IN PROGRESS: The Establishments, on James Earl Carter, Jr.; *Colton Incident,* fiction.

SIDELIGHTS: Emma McLaughlin writes: "Steeped in the intrigue and subversion of the movement to change Moral Order based on the Natural Laws to a social order (socialism) based on Naturalism by my mother ..., I spent many years delving into the background of individuals and organizations particularly those involved in religion and education. Realizing I had been cheated of American Education I devised the novel ... to extend my documentation of the subversion hoping to attract young readers. The novel is interwoven with documentation exposing the evil. I intend to continue to document and expose the movements and those individuals destroying civil governments and attempting to destroy all religion. ... My deepest wish is to return American education to the schools of the nation. For it is only with American education that we can create responsible citizens and hold fast to the principles of the American Dream of Our Founding Fathers."

AVOCATIONAL INTERESTS: Gardening (especially raising prize-winning roses).

* * *

McLAURIN, R(onald) D(e) 1944-

PERSONAL: Born October 8, 1944, in Oakland, Calif.; son of Lauchlin De and Marie (Friedman) McLaurin; married Joan Adcock (a nurse), June 11, 1966; children: Leila, Cara. *Education:* attended Universite de Tunis, 1964-65; University of Southern California, B.A., 1965; Fletcher School of Law and Diplomacy, A.M., 1966, M.A.L.D., 1967, Ph.D., 1973. *Politics:* Independent. *Home:* 18405 Cabin Rd., Triangle, Va. 22172. *Office:* Abbott Associates, Inc., 300 North Washington St., Alexandria, Va. 22314.

CAREER: Merrimack College, North Andover, Mass., instructor in political science, 1966-67; Office of Assistant Secretary of Defense, Washington, D.C., management assistant, 1967-68, assistant for Africa, 1968-69; American Institutes for Research, Washington, D.C., research scientist in social science, 1969-75; Abbott Associates, Inc., (social science researchers), Alexandria, Va., research scientist, 1975—. Member of Triangle Civic Association, 1975—; consultant to University of Miami Center for Advanced International Studies, 1973, A. R. Wagner & Co., 1975—, and American Institutes for Research, 1975. *Member:* International Political Science Association, International Studies Association, American Political Science Association, American Academy of Political and Social Science, American Civil Liberties Union, American Philatelic Society, National Capital Area Political Science Association.

WRITINGS: (Contributor) D. M. Condit and Bert H. Cooper, Jr., editors, *United States Military Response to Overseas Insurgencies,* American Institutes for Research, 1970; (contributor) Condit and Cooper, editors, *Population Protection and Resources Management in Internal Defense Operations,* American Institutes for Research, 1971; (with Arnold E. Dahlke, Jane Meyer, Richard H. Orth, and Carl F. Rosenthal) *Dissent in the Military,* American Institutes for Research, 1971; (with Mohammed Mughisuddin) *The Soviet Union and the Middle East,* American Institutes for Research, 1974; *The Middle East in Soviet Policy,* Heath, 1975; (with Mughisuddin) *Cooperation and Conflict: Egyptian, Iraqi, and Syrian Objectives and U.S. Policy,* American Institutes for Research, 1975; (with Edward E. Azar, Thomas Havener, Craig Murphy, Thomas Sloan, and Charles Wagner) *Early Warning of Strategic Crisis in the Middle East,* American Institues for Research, 1975; (with Jon Cozean, Suhaila Haddad, Phillip P. Katz, and Charles Wagner) *The Arab Elite Worldview,* American Institutes for Research, 1975; (editor with Daniel C. Pollock, Rosenthal, and Sarah A. Skillings) *The Art and Science of Psychological Operations,* U.S. Government Printing Office, 1976; (with Mughisuddin and Abraham R. Wagner) *War and Foreign Policy: Issues and Policy Making in Four Middle Eastern States,* Praeger, in press; (contributor) Mughisuddin, editor, *Conflict and Cooperation in the Persian Gulf,* Praeger, in press; (contributor) Norman Palmer and Gulam Chadhury, editors, *Forecasting in International Relations,* Foreign Policy Research Institute and Center for International Affairs, in press. Contributor to *Maghreb Digest* and to newspapers. Member of board of consulting editors of *Asia-Pacific Defense Forum.*

WORK IN PROGRESS: "The Soviet-American Strategic Balance: Arab Elite Views," for inclusion in a book edited by Edward E. Azar, publication by University of Pittsburgh expected in 1977; *The Political Impact of U.S. Military Force in the Middle East,* with Suhaila Haddad; research on psychological operations, lessons learned from the conflict in Southeast Asia, on contact analysis of Arabic language newspapers, and on political-military developments in the Middle East since the 1973 war.

*   *   *

McLEAN, Hugh   1925-

PERSONAL: Surname is pronounced Mc-*Lane;* born February 5, 1925, in Denver, Colo.; son of Hugh (a banker and lawyer) and Rosamond (Denison) McLean; married Katharine Hoag, February 2, 1957; children: Anna Scattergood, Clara Denison, Gregory Hugh. *Education:* Yale University,

A.B., 1947; Columbia University, A.M., 1949; Harvard University, Ph.D., 1956. *Home:* 827 Indian Rock Ave., Berkeley, Calif. 94707. *Office:* Department of Slavic Languages and Literatures, University of California, Berkeley, Calif. 94720.

CAREER: Harvard University, Cambridge, Mass., instructor, 1953-56, assistant professor of Slavic languages and literatures, 1956-59; University of Chicago, Chicago, Ill., associate professor, 1959-62, professor of Russian literature, 1962-68, chairman of department of Slavic languages and literatures, 1961-67; University of California, Berkeley, professor of Slavic languages and literatures, 1968—, chairman of department, 1970-72 and 1974-76, divisional dean of humanities in College of Letters and Science, 1976—. *Military service:* U.S. Naval Reserve, active duty, 1943-46. *Member:* American Association of Teachers of Slavic and East European Languages, American Association for the Advancement of Slavic Studies. *Awards, honors:* American Council of Learned Societies fellowship to England, 1958-59; Fulbright fellowship to England, 1958-59; Guggenheim fellowship, 1965-66.

WRITINGS: (Editor with Morris Halle, Horace G. Lunt, and Cornelius H. van Schoonefeld) *For Roman Jakobson,* Mouton, 1956; (editor with Martin E. Malia and George Fischer) *Russian Thought and Politics,* Harvard University Press, 1957; (editor and translator, with Walter N. Vickery) *The Year of Protest, 1956: An Anthology of Soviet Literary Materials,* Vintage Books, 1961; (translator with Maria Gordon, and editor) Mikhail Zoshchenko, *Nervous People and Other Satires,* Pantheon, 1963; *Nikolai Leskov: The Man and His Art,* Harvard University Press, in press.

Contributor: Lunt, editor, *Harvard Slavic Studies,* Volume I, Harvard University Press, 1953; Paul L. Horecky, editor, *Basic Russian Publications,* University of Chicago Press, 1962; Donald W. Treadgold, editor, *The Development of the U.S.S.R.: An Exchange of Views,* University of Washington Press, 1964; Horecky, editor, *Basic Russian Publications in Western Languages,* University of Chicago Press, 1965; *To Honor Roman Jakobson,* Mouton, 1967; W. B. Edgerton, editor, *Satirical Stories of Nikolai Leskov,* Pegasus, 1969; Lyman H. Letgers, editor, *Russia: Essays in History and Literature,* Humanities, 1972. Contributor to *Encyclopedia Americana.* Contributor of about forty articles and reviews to professional journals.

*   *   *

McNEILL, John J.   1925-

PERSONAL: Born September 2, 1925. *Education:* Canisius College, A.B. (magna cum laude), 1948; Bellarmine College, M.A. and Ph.L., both 1954; Woodstock College, Woodstock, Md., S.T.L., 1960; Catholic University of Louvain, Ph.D. (with great distinction), 1964; Institutes of Religion and Health, postdoctoral study, 1975—.

CAREER: Entered Society of Jesus (Jesuits), and ordained Roman Catholic priest; served as pastor of Roman Catholic churches; teacher of Latin, English, and communications, and director of educational training at Roman Catholic high school in Buffalo, N.Y., 1954-57; Fordham University, Bronx, N.Y., adjunct professor of philosophy, summer, 1964; Le Moyne College, Syracuse, N.Y., assistant professor, 1964-68, associate professor of philosophy, 1968-69; Woodstock College, New York, N.Y., associate professor of pastoral theology, 1970-75. Lecturer at Union Theological Seminary, 1970-75; adjunct professor at Fordham University at Lincoln Center, 1974-75; lecturer at Colgate University, State University of New York at Albany and College at Oswego, Clarke College, Duke University, and Georgetown University. Director of Community of Christian Life (religious community for laymen); organized Dignity (for homosexuals in New York and New Jersey). Has appeared on television panel programs. *Military service:* U.S. Army, Infantry, 1942-44.

MEMBER: American Association of University Professors, American Catholic Philosophical Association, Jesuit Philosophical Association, American Council of Learned Societies, Metaphysical Society of America, Hegel Society of America, American Society of Christian Ethics. *Awards, honors:* Grant from American Council of Learned Societies for European study, 1965.

WRITINGS: The Blondelian Synthesis: A Study of the Influence of German Philosophical Sources on Blondel's Method and Thought, E. J. Brill, 1966; (contributor) W. C. Bier, editor, *Conscience: Its Freedom and Limitation,* Fordham University Press, 1971; *The Church and the Homosexual,* new edition, Sheed, 1976. Contributor to *Philosophical Dictionary* and to theology and philosophy journals.

WORK IN PROGRESS: The New Christian Sexual Ethics, completion expected in 1978; a book "dealing from a philosophical and theological perspective with the concept of conscience, its freedom and formation, and its social dimensions."

SIDELIGHTS: Fr. McNeill writes: "I am presently in training at the Institutes of Religion and Health as a psychotherapist. I'd hope to be able to add a psychotherapeutic dimension to my moral studies in the field of human sexuality."

*   *   *

McNEILL, Stuart   1942-

PERSONAL: Born September 3, 1942, in Letchworth, England; son of Donald S. (an engineer) and Dorothy L. McNeill; married Jean M. Sinclair, September, 1967; children: Shona, Louise. *Education:* University of Aberdeen, B.Sc. (honors), 1964; Imperial College of Science and Technology, University of London, Ph.D., 1964. *Home:* 56 Northumberland Ave., Reading, Berkshire, England. *Office:* Imperial College Field Station, Silwood Park, Ascot, Berkshire, England.

CAREER: University of London, Imperial College of Science and Technology, Field Station, Ascot, Berkshire, England, assistant lecturer, 1967-70, lecturer in animal ecology, 1970—. Visiting professor at University of California, Santa Barbara, 1972. *Member:* British Ecological Society, Royal Entomological Society (fellow), Institute of Biology.

WRITINGS: (With M. P. Hassell) *Ecologists at Work,* Aldus Books, 1976. Contributor to animal ecology and nature journals.

SIDELIGHTS: McNeill writes: "Although there are many excellent natural history books coming out at the moment, popular books on ecology as a science are very few and far between despite the flood of material on 'environment.' This is a field, I feel, that could be expanded, especially as our understanding of how populations and communities work has greatly increased in the last two-three years."

AVOCATIONAL INTERESTS: Gardening, photography.

*   *   *

McNULTY, Edward N.   1936-

PERSONAL: Born June 6, 1936, in Indianapolis, Ind.; son of Bernard R. (an electrical technician) and Thelma (an office worker; maiden name, White) McNulty; married Sandra H. Meredith (an editor), February 14, 1959; children: Nevin, Ellen, Rebecca, Paul, Daniel. *Education:* Butler University, B.A., 1958; McCormick Theological Seminary, B.D., 1963. *Politics:* "Democrat—most of the time." *Home:* 703 Frank St., Pittsburgh, Pa. 15227. *Office:* Bethel Presbyterian Church, 2999 Bethel Church Rd., Bethel Park, Pa. 15102.

CAREER: Pastor of Presbyterian churches in Bottineau, Omemee, and Souris, N.D., 1963-68; minister of education at Presbyterian church in Parkersburg, W.Va., 1968-72, and Methodist church in Morgantown, W.Va., 1972-74; Bethel Presbyterian Church, Bethel Park, Pa., minister of education, 1974—. President of Parkersburg chapter of Brotherhood of Christians and Jews, 1971-72; member of Presbyterian Appalachian Broadcasting Council (chairman). *Member:* World Association of Christian Communicators.

WRITINGS: Television: A Guide for Christians, Abingdon, 1976; *Gadgets, Gimmicks and Grace: Multimedia in Church and School,* Abbey Press, 1976.

Multi-media kits, from Visual Parables: "Signs Along the Way," "Celebration for Bridge Builders," "Promises, Promises, Promises, Promises," "To Live Is to Dance," "Share the Dream," "Emmanuel," "*Almost* Heaven— West Virginia?," "Daughters of Eve," "Alternative to Violence," "The Greatest Week," "Like a Mighty *What*?," "What Does It Profit?," "Joy," and "Child of the Universe."

Slide shows and films: "Children," "Lord of the Dance," "Look, Love Is Here," "T-V Commercials," "God on Prime Time," and "Electronic Learning Environment." Author of a media column in *Marriage and Family Life,* 1977—. Contributor to church periodicals.

WORK IN PROGRESS: A novel; a "satirical polemic against the church's misuses of time, people, and resources," with wife, Sandra McNulty.

SIDELIGHTS: McNulty writes: "I have a longstanding interest in the relationship of the arts and theology. I see them as allies frequently and sometimes in the case of the popular arts as adversaries, at least when the media fall prey to commercial interests. My TV book grew out of a concern that most people watch TV when their guard is down (they think they're 'only being entertained'); thus this book and many of my shorter pieces were written to raise awareness to the effects of media and to suggest defenses." He adds that he has been deeply affected by working in Mississippi in 1964 toward voter registration and by a visit in 1970 to a conference on the arts and architecture in Belgium. "The setting was broadening, but even more so were the theologians, artists, and European radical students whom I met. I especially became more aware of the relationship of the arts, theology, and the social revolutions of our time."

AVOCATIONAL INTERESTS: Camping and hiking, photography, reading (novels and history), "dabbling in the arts."

*   *   *

McPHEE, John   1931-

PERSONAL: Born March 8, 1931, in Princeton, N.J.; son of Harry Roemer (a doctor) and Mary (Ziegler) McPhee; married Yolanda Whitman (a horticulturist), March 8, 1972; children: Laura, Sarah, Jenny, Martha. *Education:* Princeton University, A.B., 1953; graduate study at Cambridge University, 1953-54. *Home:* Drake's Corner Rd., Princeton, N.J. 08540.

CAREER: Playwright for "Robert Montgomery Presents" television show, 1955-57; *Time,* New York City, associate editor, 1957-64; *New Yorker,* New York City, staff writer, 1964—.

WRITINGS: All published by Farrar, Straus, except as noted: *A Sense of Where You Are,* 1965; *The Headmaster,* (biographical profile of Frank L. Boyden of Deerfield Academy), 1966; *Oranges,* (historical, geographical, botanical, and anecdotal study of the fruit), 1967; *The Pine Barrens,* 1968; *A Roomful of Hovings and Other Profiles* (profiles of Thomas Hoving, Euell Gibbons, Carroll Brewster, Robert Twynam, and Temple Fielding), 1969; *The Crofter and the Laird,* 1969; *Levels of the Game,* 1970; *Encounters with the Archdruid* (portraits of David Brower and three others), 1972; *Wimbledon: A Celebration,* with photographs by Alfred Eisenstaedt, Viking, 1972; *The Deltoid Pumpkin Seed* (story of the development of an experimental aircraft), 1973; *The Curve of Binding Energy* (profile of Theodore Taylor and the world's nuclear-materials safeguards problem), 1974; *Pieces of the Frame* (collected pieces of writing), 1975; *The Survival of the Bark Canoe,* 1975; *The John McPhee Reader,* edited by William Howarth, 1977.

Contributor to numerous popular magazines, including *Holiday, National Geographic, Playboy, Atlantic,* and, primarily, *New Yorker.*

WORK IN PROGRESS: Writing on Alaska.

SIDELIGHTS: A *New Republic* reviewer wrote: "John McPhee can make almost any subject interesting, as he has proven with books on the New Jersey Pine Barrens, the Hebridean island of Colonsay, fellow Princetonian Bill Bradley and oranges." This wide diversity may not seem out of the ordinary for a magazine staff writer whose books are basically collections of his articles, but the reoccurring critical acclaim of his style is. Richard Horwich commented: "Sometimes it seems that McPhee deliberately chooses unpromising subjects, just to show what he can do with them." Whatever the subject, reviewers are inevitably drawn towards the underlying unity of constantly precise and highly descriptive prose. Horwich said, "McPhee's powers of description are such that we often feel the shock of recognition even when what is being described is totally outside our experience.... McPhee penetrates the surface of things and makes his way toward what is essential and unchanging." A *Time* magazine reviewer has said, "he combines the fastidious appetite for detail of a Sherlock Holmes with the snails-pace anecdotal style of a Dr. Watson."

BIOGRAPHICAL/CRITICAL SOURCES: Time, January 13, 1969; *New Republic,* September 1, 1973, July 5, 1975.

*　　　*　　　*

McQUADE, Donald A(nthony)　1941-

PERSONAL: Born December 26, 1941, in New York, N.Y.; son of Francis C. and Adelina (in insurance; maiden name, Pisano) McQuade; married Susanne Batschelet (an educator), July 14, 1968; children: Christine Alexandra. *Education:* Saint Francis College, Brooklyn, N.Y., B.A., 1963; Rutgers University, M.A., 1964, Ph.D., 1971. *Home:* 425 Riverside Dr., New York, N.Y. 10025. *Agent:* Francis Greenburger, 201 East 50th St., New York, N.Y. 10022. *Office:* Department of English, Queens College of the City University of New York, Flushing, N.Y. 11367.

CAREER: New Jersey Institute of Technology, Newark, N.J., instructor, 1967-70; Queens College of the City Uni-

versity of New York, Flushing, N.Y., instructor, 1970-72, assistant professor, 1972-75, associate professor of English, 1975—, assistant head of department, 1971-74, director of writing program, 1975—. Editorial consultant to Random House, Oxford University Press, and Houghton-Mifflin. *Member:* International Society of General Semantics, Modern Language Association of America, National Council of Teachers of English, Conference on College Composition and Communication, College English Association, Popular Culture Association, American Studies Association, Common Concerns of English Educators, New York State English Council, City University of New York Association of Writing Supervisors.

WRITINGS: (Editor with Robert Atwan) *Popular Writing in America,* Oxford University Press, 1974; (with Atwan and John Wright) *The History of American Advertising: Images of a Changing Society,* Doubleday, 1977. Contributor to professional journals.

WORK IN PROGRESS: Editor with Atwan and John J. McDermott, *American Writing,* two volumes, publication by Houghton-Mifflin expected in 1978; *Borzoi College Rhetoric,* publication by Knopf expected in 1979.

AVOCATIONAL INTERESTS: Playing water polo (former U.S. and North American champion).

*　　　*　　　*

McTAGGART, Fred　1939-

PERSONAL: Born March 30, 1939, in Pawnee, Ill.; son of Ray Terry (a railroad car inspector) and Etheline (Verry) McTaggart; married Patricia Finney, September 9, 1962 (divorced, March, 1972); married Donna M. Carroll, March 10, 1973; children: (first marriage) Duncan Alexander, Brendan Blake. *Education:* Millikin University, A.B., 1961; University of Illinois, M.A., 1962; University of Iowa, Ph.D., 1973. *Home:* 435 Park Pl., Kalamazoo, Mich. 49001. *Agent:* Arthur F. Gould, 1234 Sherman, Evanston, Ill. 60201. *Office:* Department of English, Western Michigan University, Kalamazoo, Mich. 49001.

CAREER: Decatur Herald, Decatur, Ill., sports reporter, 1956-62; University of Missouri, Columbia, instructor in English, 1962-64; United Automobile Workers, International Union, St. Louis, Mo., editor and writer, 1964-67; Western Michigan University, Kalamazoo, assistant professor of English, 1974—. *Member:* Modern Language Association of America, American Association of University Professors, Midwest Modern Language Association. *Awards, honors:* Post-doctoral fellowship from Newberry Library Center for the History of the American Indian, 1973-74.

WRITINGS: Wolf That I Am: In Search of the Red Earth People, Houghton, 1976.

WORK IN PROGRESS: A historical and autobiographical account of the breakdown of traditional Highland Scottish culture and the attempts of the author's ancestors to establish new roots on the land in North America.

SIDELIGHTS: McTaggert writes: "*Wolf That I Am* is an autobiographical narrative of my experiences trying to understand the stories and the culture of the Mesquakie Indians who live on a settlement near Tama, Iowa. I traveled to the settlement in 1971 and 1972 in an attempt to study the oral literature of the Mesquakies for my Ph.D. dissertation in English from the University of Iowa. I did not collect large numbers of stories, as I had expected, but I did learn something about the way stories function in the Mesquakies' vital oral culture. And I learned a great deal about myself and the relation between my own literature and the land on which we live.

"*Wolf That I Am* is written as a story—the story of my attempt to learn Mesquakie stories. Within my story are the stories told me by the Mesquakies—to be understood in context as the teaching of the Mesquakies to the naive newcomer on their shores. I use many techniques of fiction but try to remain meticulously faithful to the factual truth of my experience. As I discovered from the Mesquakies, there need be no distinction between history and poetry. Within the factual experience are artistic truths.

"I am now working on a second book, written in a similar manner. Following the advice given my by the Mesquakies, I am trying to learn the stories of my own people—the Scottish people who were uprooted from their Highland soil in the late eighteenth century and who finally emigrated to Illinois in 1854. The book concerns two hundred years of history, seen from a personal and autobiographical perspective. From the stories of my ancestors and relatives, I hope to find meaning for the present and future."

*   *   *

MEAD, D(onald) Eugene   1934-

PERSONAL: Born September 30, 1934, in Mansfield, Ohio; son of Stanley Lewis (a businessman) and Mildred (Painter) Mead; married Sherrill Dean Leavitt (an educator), September 11, 1954; children: Stanley Lester, Marcia Renee, Christine Lynne. *Education:* University of Oregon, B.A., 1956, Ed.D., 1967; San Jose State College (now University), M.A., 1963. *Religion:* Church of Jesus Christ of Latter-day Saints (Mormons). *Office:* Department of Child Development and Family Relationships, Brigham Young University, Provo, Utah 84602.

CAREER: Wenatchee Valley College, Wenatchee, Wash., instructor in psychology, 1963-65; Parent-Teacher Education Center, Eugene, Ore., assistant director, 1966-67; Brigham Young University, Provo, Utah, assistant professor, 1967, associate professor of child development and family relationships, 1970—. *Military service:* U.S. Air Force, 1957-61; became first lieutenant. *Member:* American Psychological Association, American Association of Marriage and Family Counselors, National Council on Family Relations, Phi Delta Kappa, Psi Chi.

WRITINGS: Six Approaches to Child Rearing, Brigham Young University Press, 1976. Contributor to journals in psychology and family studies.

WORK IN PROGRESS: Modifying Family Behavior: An Empirical Approach to Family Counseling; Winning Parenthood (tentative title); research on methods for teaching better problem-solving techniques and methods for improving the probability that family members will actually put such techniques into practice.

SIDELIGHTS: "While modern technology has harnessed the power of nature," Mead told *CA,* "we are still the same biological beings that captured fire and painted upon cave walls. We are still giving birth to stone age babies. More study, more research, more teaching is needed to help us better socialize the next generation of adults. I am dedicated to assisting in the development of better family life for each family member, that each family member may learn to contribute fully to his culture."

MEDVED, Michael   1948-

PERSONAL: Born October 3, 1948, in Philadelphia, Pa.; son of David Bernard (a physicist) and Renate (a chemist; maiden name, Hirsch) Medved; married Nancy Herman (a writer and researcher), August 5, 1972. *Education:* Yale University, B.A., 1969, graduate study, 1969-70; San Francisco State University, M.A., 1974. *Politics:* "A fan of *Commentary* magazine." *Religion:* "Traditional Judaism." *Home and office:* 228 Third Ave., Venice, Calif. 90291. *Agent:* Arthur Pine Associates, 1780 Broadway, New York, N.Y. 10019.

CAREER: Teacher in Hebrew day school in New Haven, Conn., 1969-70; speechwriter for congressional and presidential campaigns, 1970-72; Anrick, Inc. (advertising agency), Oakland Calif., creative director and advertising copywriter, 1972-74; free-lance writer and lecturer, 1974—.

WRITINGS: (With David Wallechinsky) *What Really Happened to the Class of '65?,* Random House, 1976. Contributor to *Growing Up in America,* Doubleday, 1969, and *The People's Almanac,* 1975.

WORK IN PROGRESS: The Unofficial Presidents, about White House aides, for Reader's Digest Press.

SIDELIGHTS: Medved writes: "I will freely admit that I am a frustrated writer of fiction. I have two youthful unpublished novels sitting at the top of my closet, and after rereading them recently I've decided it's best that they should stay there. Undoubtedly, I'll give fiction another try in the future, and this time I hope it's more successful.

"Though I was not raised in an Orthodox background, a commitment to traditional Judaism has become a central feature of my life. Living as part of a community, together with other Jews of all ages, gives me enormous joy." *Avocational interests:* Music (especially the music of Handel, Haydn, and Prokofiev).

*   *   *

MEEKER, Oden   1919(?)-1976

1919(?)—January 1, 1976; American international organization official, and travel writer. Obituaries: *AB Bookman's Weekly,* April 5, 1976.

*   *   *

MELAS, Evi   1930-

PERSONAL: Born February 23, 1930, in Athens, Greece; daughter of Alexander (a lawyer) and Maria (Kanellopoulou) Zissis; married Victor Melas (a lawyer), July 14, 1951 (divorced, 1970). *Education:* Attended University of Athens, 1948-51. *Religion:* Greek Orthodox. *Home and office:* Phokylidduq, Athens, Greece.

CAREER: Political correspondent in Athens for *Die Welt, Stuttgarter Zeitung,* and *Muenchner Merkur,* all German newspapers, 1959-67; free-lance writer, 1967—. *Member:* International Press Institute.

WRITINGS: (Editor, contributor, and translator from the Greek into German) *Tempel und Staetten der Goetter Griechenlands: Ein Begleiter zu den antiken Kultzentren der Griechen,* DuMont Schauberg (Cologne), 1970, translation from the German by F. Maxwell Brownjohn published as *Temples and Sanctuaries of Ancient Greece: A Companion Guide,* Thames and Hudson, 1973, also published as *The Greek Experience: A Companion Guide to the Major Architectural Sites and an Introduction to Ancient History and Myth,* Dutton, 1974; (editor, contributor, and translator from the Greek into German) *Alte Kirchen und Kloester Griechenlands: Ein Begleiter zu die byzantinische Staetten,* DuMont Schauberg, 1972; (editor, contributor, and translator from the Greek into German) *Griechische Inseln,* DuMont Schauberg, 1973, 2nd edition, 1974; *Athen,* DuMont Schauberg, 1975.

Co-author of *Merian Heft,* published in Greece. Co-author of "Zwei Tage in . . ." and "Zwei Wochen auf . . ." series, both published by Piper (Munich). Short stories represented in anthologies, including *Liebe 1963,* Desch (Munich), 1963. Contributor of articles to *Die Zeit* newspaper (Hamburg), 1974-75.

WORK IN PROGRESS: Third edition, in two volumes, of *Griechische Inseln;* a book on Rumania for DuMont Schauberg.

*   *   *

MELLEN, Joan 1941-

PERSONAL: Born September 7, 1941, in New York, N.Y.; daughter of Louis (a lawyer) and Norma (Wieder) Spivack. *Education:* Hunter College of the City University of New York, B.A., 1962; City University of New York Graduate Center, M.A., 1964, Ph.D., 1968. *Home:* Elm Ridge Road, Pennington, N.J. 08534. *Agent:* Berenice Hoffman, Hoffman-Sheedy Literary Agency, 145 W. 86th Street, New York, N.Y. 11417. *Office:* Department of English, Temple University, Philadelphia, Pa. 19122.

CAREER: Temple University, Philadelphia, Pa., assistant professor, 1967-73, associate professor, 1973-76, professor of English, 1977—. Lecturer. *Member:* Phi Beta Kappa. *Awards, honors:* Mainichi Shimbun award and study tour of Japan, 1972; National Endowment for the Humanities summer stipend, 1976.

WRITINGS: A Film Guide to the Battle of Algiers, Indiana University Press, 1973; *Marilyn Monroe,* Pyramid Publications, 1973; *Women and Their Sexuality in the New Film,* Horizon Press, 1974; *Voices from the Japanese Cinema,* Liveright, 1975; *The Waves at Genji's Door: Japan through Its Cinema,* Pantheon, 1976.

Contributor: *Japan and the Japanese,* Japan Publications, 1973; Gerald R. Barrett and Thomas L. Erskine, editors, *From Fiction to Film: The Rocking-Horse Winner,* Dickenson, 1974; E. Bradford Burns, editor, *Latin American Cinema: Film and History,* University of California at Los Angeles Latin American Center, 1975; Stuart M. Kaminsky, editor, *Ingmar Bergman: Essays in Criticism,* Oxford University Press, 1975.

Member of editorial board, *Quarterly Review of Film Studies,* 1975—; consultant to *Antioch Review,* Oxford University Press, and Pantheon Books.

WORK IN PROGRESS: Big Bad Wolves: Hollywood's Depiction of Men, publication by Pantheon in 1977; *Luis Bunuel,* publication by Oxford University Press expected in 1977; two chapters for *The Films of Akira Kurosawa,* edited by Donald Richie for University of California Press.

*   *   *

MELLORS, John (Parkin) 1920-

PERSONAL: Born June 30, 1920, in Wakefield, England; son of Claude Horsley (a colliery representative) and Nora (Parkin) Mellors; married second wife, Norah Millicent Pye (a school matron), June 26, 1976; children: Ruth Elizabeth Clarke, Catherine Mary Mirabel. *Education:* Queen's College, Oxford, B.A. (with honors), 1947. *Home and office:* 18 A Egliston Rd., Putney, London SW15, England.

CAREER: S. H. Benson, Ltd. (advertising agency), London, England, director and copywriter, 1947-70; reviewer for *Listener* and *London Magazine,* 1972—. *Military service:* British Army, 1940-45, became captain.

WRITINGS—Autobiographical: *Shots in the Dark,* London Magazine Editions, 1974; *Memoirs of an Advertising Man,* London Magazine Editions, 1976. Translator of *Cherie* by Edmond de Goncourt. Contributor to *Listener* and *London Magazine.*

WORK IN PROGRESS: A novel.

SIDELIGHTS: Mellors told *CA,* "I write mostly for pleasure and partly for 'beer money.' I'm interested in India and France; I speak bad French with a Provencal accent, and I used to speak Urdu with a Yorkshire accent. My main interests are my wife, my cats, and my books."

*   *   *

MELOON, Marion 1921-

PERSONAL: Born March 30, 1921, in Ossipee, N.H.; daughter of Calvin A. (a builder, seller, and racer of boats) and Bernice N. (White) Meloon. *Education:* Northwood Bible School, diploma, 1943.

CAREER: Bookkeeper, nurse; Bible school teacher in Northwood, N.H., 1944-53; New England Bible Institute, Framingham, Mass., teacher, 1953-55; church worker for Assemblies of God Church in Lancaster, N.H., 1955-64, and Newport, Vt., 1964-66; Elim Bible Institute, Lima, N.Y., teacher, 1966—, in charge of publications, 1968—.

WRITINGS: Ivan Spencer: Willow in the Wind, Logos International, 1975. Contributor of short stories and articles to magazines.

WORK IN PROGRESS: Three books; one on the life of Alex Manzewitsch in Paraguay and Argentina; another on Nellie Meloon in the Congo; and the third, a sequel to *Ivan Spencer,* about the Elim story in East Africa.

*   *   *

MENAKER, Daniel 1941-

PERSONAL: Born September 17, 1941, in New York, N.Y.; son of Robert Owen (a businessman) and Mary (an editor; maiden name, Grace) Menaker. *Education:* Swarthmore College, B.A. (high honors), 1963; Johns Hopkins University, M.A., 1965. *Office: New Yorker,* 25 West 43rd St., New York, N.Y. 10036.

CAREER: Teacher of English at private schools in Newtown, Pa., 1965-66, and New York, N.Y., 1966-68; *New Yorker,* New York City, researcher, 1969-71, copy editor, 1972-76, fiction and fact editor, 1976—. *Member:* International P.E.N.

WRITINGS: Friends and Relations (short stories), Doubleday, 1976. Contributor to popular magazines, including *Harper's,* and to newspapers, including *Village Voice.*

WORK IN PROGRESS: A novel.

SIDELIGHTS: "I believe writing requires more discipline and concentration than virtually anything else," Menaker wrote. "I take immense pride in my craftsmanship as a writer. I believe that every word counts. I admire most writers who combine control and imagination." *Avocational interests:* Country music, athletics, playing the guitar and autoharp.

MENDELSON, Edward 1946-

PERSONAL: Born March 15, 1946, in New York; son of Ralph (a lawyer and teacher) and Grace (a teacher; maiden name, Stein) Mendelson. *Education:* University of Rochester, B.A., 1966; Johns Hopkins University, Ph.D., 1969. *Home:* 123 York St., #14C, New Haven, Conn. 06511. *Office:* Department of English, Yale University, New Haven, Conn. 06520.

CAREER: Yale University, New Haven, Conn., assistant professor, 1969-75, associate professor of English, 1975—. Visiting associate professor at Harvard University, 1977-78.

WRITINGS: (With B. C. Bloomfield) *W. H. Auden: A Bibliography,* University Press of Virginia, 1972; (editor) W. H. Auden, *Collected Poems,* Random House, 1976; (editor with Michael Seidel) *Homer to Brecht: The European Epic and Dramatic Traditions,* Yale University Press, 1977; (editor) *The English Auden,* Random House, in press; (editor) *Thomas Pynchon: A Collection of Critical Essays,* Prentice-Hall, in press.

Contributor: Robert Shaw, editor, *American Poetry Since 1960,* Carcanet, 1973; Kenneth Baldwin and David Kirby, editors, *Individual and Community,* Duke University Press, 1975; Stephen Spender, editor, *W. H. Auden: A Tribute,* Macmillan, 1975; George Levine and David Leverenz, editors, *Mindful Pleasures: Essays on Thomas Pynchon,* Little, Brown, 1976. Contributor to magazines, including *New Statesman, Yale Review,* and *Times Literary Supplement, New Republic,* and to professional journals in his field.

WORK IN PROGRESS: Auden's Landscape, a critical study; a critical study of Thomas Pynchon.

* * *

MENDENHALL, Ruth Dyar 1912-

PERSONAL: Born August 16, 1912, in Kiesling, Wash.; daughter of Ralph Emerson (a newspaperman, playwright, and historian) and Else (Kiesling) Dyar; married John D. Mendenhall (a structural engineer), September 22, 1939; children: Vivian Margaret, Valerie Patricia (Mrs. Michael Peter Cohen). *Education:* University of Washington, Seattle, B.A. (cum laude), 1934. *Home:* 335 Sequoia Dr., Pasadena, Calif. 91105.

CAREER: Worked as a secretary in various cities in California, 1934-39; free-lance writer, 1939—. Instructor in rock climbing, mountaineering, backpacking, snow camping and various other outdoor activities for the Sierra Club, Boy Scouts of America, Long Beach State College (now California State University, Long Beach), and others, 1939-76; director, American Alpine Club, 1974-77. *Member:* Sierra Club (life member), American Alpine Club (chairman of membership committee), Rendez-vous Hautes Montagnes, Theta Sigma Phi.

WRITINGS: (Contributor) Hervey Voge, editor, *A Climber's Guide to the High Sierra,* Sierra Club, 1941, 2nd revised edition, 1965; (editor) Bob Kamps, *A Climber's Guide to the Needles of the Black Hills of South Dakota,* American Alpine Club, 1971; *Backpack Cookery,* La Siesta Press, 1966, revised edition, 1974; *Backpack Techniques,* La Siesta Press, 1967, revised edition, 1973; (with husband, John D. Mendenhall) *Introduction to Rock and Mountain Climbing,* Stackpole, 1969, revised edition issued as *Beginner's Guide to Rock and Mountain Climbing,* 1975. Contributor to historical and mountaineering journals and outdoor magazines, including *Summit, Desert, National Park, Mountain Gazette, Off Belay,* and *Climbing.* Editor, *Mugelnoos,* 1938-76; member of editorial board of Sierra Club, 1939-55.

WORK IN PROGRESS: Climbing memoirs.

SIDELIGHTS: Mrs. Mendenhall has been an avid mountain climber since 1938. Her mountain ascents include all of the 14,000-foot peaks on the Pacific Coast, the Wildspitz, Eiger, and Matterhorn in the Alps, first ascents of Mt. Confederation and Aiguille Peak in the Canadian Rockies, and numerous new routes, first ascents, and other technical climbs in the Sierra Nevada and elsewhere.

AVOCATIONAL INTERESTS: Traveling, fishing, reading, photography, handcrafts.

* * *

MENKITI, Ifeanyi 1940-

PERSONAL: Born August 24, 1940, in Onitsha, Nigeria; came to United States in 1961; son of Charles N. (an agronomist) and Nwamgbaa (Olieh) Menkiti; married Carol Josephine Bowers (a teacher), February 11, 1971; children: Nneka (daughter). *Education:* Pomona College, B.A., 1964; Columbia University, M.S., 1965; New York University, M.A., 1968; Harvard University, Ph.D., 1974. *Home:* 8 Grant St., Cambridge, Mass. 02138. *Office:* Department of Philosophy, Wellesley College, Wellesley, Mass. 02181.

CAREER: Wellesley College, Wellesley, Mass., assistant professor of philosophy, 1973—. Has given readings of his poetry at East Coast universities, in New York schools, and on New York City and Boston radio programs. *Member:* American Association of University Professors. *Awards, honors:* Creative arts fellowship award in poetry from Massachusetts Art and Humanities Foundation, 1975.

WRITINGS: Affirmations (poems), Third World Press, 1971.

Work has been anthologized in *Contemporary African Literature,* edited by Edris Makward and Leslie Lacy, Random House, 1972; *Open Poetry,* edited by Ronald Gross and George Quasha, Simon & Schuster, 1973; *The Word Is Here,* edited by Keorapetse Kgositsile, Doubleday, 1973; and *Poems of Black Africa,* edited by Wole Soyinka, Hill & Wang, 1975. Contributor to literary journals, including *Sewanee Review, Southwest Review, Evergreen Review, Bitterroot, New Letters, Journal of Black Poetry, Liberator, Pan African Journal, Transition, Massachusetts Review, Chelsea, Sumac,* and *Boston Review of the Arts.*

WORK IN PROGRESS: Two books of poems.

SIDELIGHTS: Menkiti writes: "I consider myself a poet of people and events. In the words of one of the poems, my theme, very often, is 'of collectivities in deep dance / the human constellations heavy / with historical act.' And yet there are also poems of a very personal nature and others of outright political anger provoked by problems of racial oppression and abuse."

BIOGRAPHICAL/CRITICAL SOURCES: Theresa Rush and Carol Myers, editors, *Black American Writers Past and Present,* Scarecrow, 1975.

* * *

MENON, R(amakrishna) Rabindranath 1927-

PERSONAL: Born June 13, 1927, in Perumpavoor, India; son of K. Ramakrishna (a lawyer) and Seetha (Radha Devi) Menon; married wife, Syamala, December 14, 1950; children: Surendra and Balachandra (sons), Latha (daughter). *Education:* University of Kerala, B.Sc. (first class honors), 1947; Indian Institute of Science, Bangalore, D.I.I.Sc., 1950. *Politics:* None. *Home:* Eanchakkal House, Vallakkadavoo, Trivandrum-8, Kerala, India. *Office:* Coir Board, Coir House, M.G.Road, Cochin-682016, India.

CAREER: Indian Government, Administrative Service, served as income tax officer, 1951-58, district magistrate and collector in Bihar, 1959-61, director of evaluation in Bihar, 1961-63, deputy commissioner in South Kanara, 1963-64, managing director of Board of Mineral Development in Bangalore, 1964-66, director of treasuries in Karnataka, 1966, managing director of sugar factory in Hiriyoor, 1966, controller of civil supplies in Mysore, 1966-67, managing director of Government Electirc Factory in Bangalore, 1967-68, joint secretary in departments of public works and finance, 1968-70, chairman of Marine Products Export Promotion Council, 1970-71, chairman of Coir Board, 1970—. Member of governing body, All India Shippers Council, 1971—, Indian Council of Arbitration, 1972—; chairman of experts panel, Export Inspection Council of India, 1973—. *Member:* Indian Society of Auditors and Accountants (fellow), Indian Institute of Metals, World Poetry Society (regent), Poetry Society of England. *Awards, honors:* Gold medal and poet laureate crown from United Poet Laureate International of the Philippines, 1971; Litt.D., University of Asia, 1973; D.Litt., Academicia Pax Mundi, 1975.

WRITINGS—All poetry: *Ode to Parted Love and Other Poems,* Jaico (Bombay), 1958; *Dasavatara and Other Poems,* Writers Workshop (Calcutta), 1967; *Seventy-Seven,* Writers Workshop, 1971; *Straws in the Wind,* Writers Workship, 1974; *Gananjali* (Malayalam poetry), National Book Stall (Kottayam, India), 1974; *Shadows in the Sun,* Writers Workshop, 1975. Poetry editor, *Adam and Eve* magazine, 1972—.

WORK IN PROGRESS: Poems, 1976.

SIDELIGHTS: Menon told *CA:* "Poetry is my hobby, not any laboured attempt, yet I consider that every piece must pass through a process of careful polishing. As a matter of fact, I don't publish any poem until at least six months have elapsed since its original birth, and during that interval I come to it again and again working on it and improving upon it. There is no motivation of profit. I don't seek fame either. Not that I am against either, but true poetry should have no motivation except that of pure pleasure, 'pleasure' in its enlarged sense, and this includes the enjoyment of others also.

"I can't remember any particular circumstance as having been the cause of my becoming a poet. My father taught me Sanscrit at an early age, and this gave me a wonderful reservoir of words with which to express in my own mother-tongue, which is related to Sanscrit. But later I veered round to English in which I find even a greater facility to express. I believe that a poet should use the language which he can wield with the maximum facility, and this need not be his mother-tongue, as in my case. I am a bilingual poet, but I don't believe in translation for poetry, for poetry is untranslatable expression."

*   *   *

MERBAUM, Michael 1933-

PERSONAL: Born November 6, 1933, in New York, N.Y.; son of Max J. (a lawyer) and Molly (Rubin) Merbaum; married Marta Ettinger, November 18, 1962; children: Marc, Tal. *Education:* Drake University, B.A., 1956; University of Missouri, Kansas City, M.A., 1957; University of North Carolina, Ph.D., 1961. *Religion:* Jewish. *Home:* 127 Einstein St., Haifa, Israel. *Office: Department of Psychology, University of Haifa, Haifa, Israel.*

CAREER: Diplomate in clinical psychology of American Board of Professional Examiners in Psychology; certified clinical psychologist in state of New York; University of Chicago, Chicago, Ill., instructor for Psychiatric Inpatient Service, 1961-64, lecturer in psychology, 1962-64; Bowling Green State University, Bowling Green, Ohio, assistant professor of psychology and director of Psychology Clinic, 1964-66; Adelphi University, Garden City, N.Y., associate professor of psychology at Institute of Advanced Psychological Studies, 1966-72; University of Haifa, Haifa, Israel, professor of psychology and director of Psychological Counseling Center, 1972—. Private practice in psychology, 1966—. Clinical assistant professor at Cornell University, 1966-68.

MEMBER: American Psychological Association, American Association for the Advancement of Behavior Therapy, American Association of University Professors, Society for Projective Techniques and Personality Assessment (fellow), Israel Psychological Association, Sigma Xi.

WRITINGS: (Editor with Eugene Southwell) *Personality: Readings in Theory and Research,* Wadsworth, 1964, revised edition, 1971; (editor with George Stricker, and contributor) *Search for Human Understanding,* Holt, 1971, revised edition, 1975; (contributor) Donald Milman and George Goldman, editors, *Innovations in Psychotherapy,* C. C Thomas, 1972; (editor with Marvin Goldfried, and contributor) *The Modification of Behavior Through Self-Control,* Holt, 1973; (with Stricker) *Growth of Personal Awareness,* Holt, 1973; (contributor) Milman and Goldman, editors, *The Marathon Group,* C. C Thomas, 1975. Contributor to journals in the behavioral sciences.

WORK IN PROGRESS: Research on behavior modification, and on applications of biofeedback training to epilepsy.

SIDELIGHTS: Merbaum writes: "As a clinical psychologist and teacher my main interest is in helping people approach personal problems more successfully, more creatively, and with greater personal satisfaction."

Avocational Interests: Playing tennis and basketball, cooking and eating Chinese food.

*   *   *

MERCER, Johnny 1906-1976

November 18, 1906—June 25, 1976; American composer and singer of popular songs. Obituaries: *Washington Post,* June 26, 1976; *New York Times,* June 26, 1976.

*   *   *

METCALF, E(ugene) W(esley) 1945-

PERSONAL: Born May 18, 1945, in Pasadena, Calif.; son of Eugene Wesley (a businessman) and Margaret (Grimsley) Metcalf; married Carolyn Belknap; children: Justin Ames. *Education:* DePauw University, B.A., 1967; University of California, Irvine, Ph.D., 1973. *Home:* 10 East Collins St., Oxford, Ohio 45056. *Office:* Peabody Hall, Western College, Miami University, Oxford, Ohio 45056.

CAREER: San Diego State University, San Diego, Calif., assistant professor of American literature and studies, 1973-74; Miami University, Oxford, Ohio, assistant professor of interdisciplinary studies, 1974—. *Member:* Modern Language Association of America, American Studies Association.

WRITINGS: Paul Laurence Dunbar: An Annotated Bibliography, Scarecrow, 1975; *William Wells Brown, Martin*

Delany, and Charles Chestnutt: An Annotated Bibliography, G. K. Hall, 1976.

WORK IN PROGRESS: Editing *The Letters of Paul Laurence Dunbar;* a book on utopian communities of Ohio; general research on American utopian communities.

* * *

METWALLY, M(okhtar) M(ohamed) 1939-

PERSONAL: Born February 7, 1939, in El-Minya, Egypt. *Education:* University of Cairo, B.Com., 1959; University of Leeds, M.A., 1962, Ph.D., 1965. *Office:* Department of Economics, University of Queensland, St. Lucia, Brisbane, Queensland, Australia 4067.

CAREER: University of Cairo, Cairo, Egypt, lecturer in economics, 1965-66; University of Baghdad, Baghdad, Iraq, lecturer in economics, 1966-67; University of Mosul, Mosul, Iraq, lecturer in economics, 1967-68; University of Waikato, Hamilton, New Zealand, senior lecturer in economics, 1968-70; Victoria University of Wellington, Wellington, New Zealand, senior lecturer in economics, 1970-71; University of Queensland, Brisbane, Queensland, Australia, senior lecturer, 1971-75, reader in economics, 1976—. *Member:* American Economic Association, Royal Economic Society, Egyptian Society of Economics, Statistics, and Legislation, Economic Society of Australia and New Zealand (Queensland branch; honorary secretary, 1974-76).

WRITINGS: A Research in the Economics of the Arab World (in Arabic language), El Resala Press (Cairo), 1965; *Models of Arab Economic Co-operation* (in Arabic), El Resala Press, 1966; *Mathematical Formulation of Microeconomics,* Asia Publishing House, 1975; *Price and Non-Price Competition: Dynamics of Marketing,* Asia Publishing House, 1976. Editor, *Economic Analysis and Policy* (journal of Economic Society of Australia and New Zealand), 1974—.

WORK IN PROGRESS: Mathematical Theories of Development and Growth; Economic Performance of Small Economies: The Maltese Case; Preface to Operations Research; Introduction to Business Economics.

AVOCATIONAL INTERESTS: Travel.

* * *

MEYER, David R. 1943-

PERSONAL: Born September 15, 1943, in Lansing, Mich.; son of Kermit C. (a school superintendent) and Ruth K. (Rau) Meyer; married Judith Wangerin (a professor), August 28, 1965; children: Kimberly, Joel. *Education:* Concordia Teachers College, B.A., 1965; Southern Illinois University, M.S., 1967; University of Chicago, Ph.D., 1970. *Residence:* Willimantic, Conn. *Office:* Morrill Science Center, University of Massachusetts, Amherst, Mass. 01002.

CAREER: University of Massachusetts, Amherst, assistant professor, 1970-76, associate professor of geography, 1976—. *Member:* American Geographical Society, Association of American Geographers, Real Estate and Urban Economics Association, Regional Science Association, New England—St. Lawrence Valley Geographical Society.

WRITINGS: (Contributor) Brian J. L. Berry, editor, *City Classification Handbook: Methods and Applications,* Wiley, 1972; (contributor) Harold M. Rose, editor, *Geography of the Ghetto: Perceptions, Problems, and Alternatives,* Northern Illinois University Press, 1972; *From Farm to Factory to Urban Pastoralism: Urban Change in Central*

Connecticut, Ballinger, 1976; (contributor) John S. Adams, editor, *Contemporary Metropolitan America: Twenty Geographical Vignettes,* Ballinger, in press; (contributor) Ronald Abler, editor, *A Comparative Atlas of America's Great Cities: Twenty Metropolitan Regions,* University of Minnesota Press, in press. Contributor of about fifteen articles and reviews to geography, anthropology, and Black studies journals.

WORK IN PROGRESS: Studying the evolution of the American system of cities.

AVOCATIONAL INTERESTS: Travel, hiking, backpacking, cooking.

* * *

MEYER, Philip (Edward) 1930-

PERSONAL: Born October 27, 1930, in Deshler, Neb.; son of Elmer Edward (a salesman) and Hilda (Morrison) Meyer; married Sue Quail, August 5, 1956; children: Caroline, Kathy, Melissa, Sarah. *Education:* Kansas State University, B.S., 1952; University of North Carolina, M.A., 1963; Harvard University, further graduate study, 1966-67. *Religion:* Episcopal. *Home:* 11650 Mediterranean Court, Reston, Va. 22090. *Office:* 11600 Sunrise Valley Dr., Reston, Va. 22070.

CAREER: Topeka Daily Capital, Topeka, Kan., assistant state editor, 1954-56; *Miami Herald,* Miami, Fla., reporter, 1958-62; Knight-Ridder Newspapers, Washington, D.C., correspondent, 1962—. *Military service:* U.S. Naval Reserve, active duty, 1952-54. *Member:* Council for the Advancement of Science Writing (president, 1976—), American Association for Public Opinion Research, American Political Science Association. *Awards, honors:* Nieman fellow at Harvard University, 1966-67; Pulitzer Prize for general local reporting, 1968, for covering the Detroit riots of 1967, as a member of the *Detroit Free Press* staff.

WRITINGS: Precision Journalism, Indiana University Press, 1973; (with David Olson) *To Keep the Republic,* McGraw, 1975. Contributor to journalism magazines, and to *Public Opinion Quarterly, Esquire,* and *Playboy.*

BIOGRAPHICAL/CRITICAL SOURCES: Newsweek, August, 1968; William L. Rivers and Everette Dennis, *Other Voices,* Canfield, 1974.

* * *

MEYERS, Michael Jay 1946-

PERSONAL: Born February 7, 1946, in New York, N.Y.; son of Norman M. and Marilyn Meyers; married Patricia Kanner (an artist), August 12, 1973. *Education:* Lafayette College, A.B., 1968; New Jersey College of Medicine, M.D., 1972. *Home:* 1747 Bryn Mawr Ave., Santa Monica, Calif. 90405. *Agent:* I.R.U. Schechter Co., 404 North Roxbury, Beverly Hills, Calif. *Office:* Medical Center, Santa Monica Hospital, 1225 15th St., Santa Monica, Calif.

CAREER: Intern in Martland, N.J., 1972-73; Mt. Sinai Hospital, New York, N.Y., psychiatry resident, 1974-75; Holy Name Hospital, Teaneck, N.J., emergency room physician, 1976; Santa Monica Hospital, Medical Center, Santa Monica, Calif., resident in family practice, 1976—. Has appeared on television talk shows. *Member:* American Academy of Family Physicians.

WRITINGS: Goodbye, Columbus, Hello, Medicine (novel), Morrow, 1976.

WORK IN PROGRESS: A novel.

SIDELIGHTS: Meyers' main professional interests are the role of the physician in society, health care, and the social aspects of medicine.

*   *   *

MIDDLEBROOK, Jonathan 1940-

PERSONAL: Born October 6, 1940, in New York, N.Y.; son of Samuel M. (a professor) and Leah Ruth (a professor; maiden name, Rudman) Middlebrook; married Helen Diane Wood Shough, June 15, 1963 (divorced, June, 1972); married Eugenia Margaret DiSabatino, November 24, 1973; children: (first marriage) Leah Wood; (second marriage) Sophia Carmody. *Education:* Harvard University, A.B., 1961; Yale University, M.A., 1963, Ph.D., 1965. *Politics:* "Ad hoc, occasionally ad hominem." *Religion:* "Literary christian." *Home:* 3733 Sacramento St., San Francisco, Calif. 94118. *Agent:* Clair Peterson, 3665 Clay St., San Francisco, Calif. 94118.

CAREER: University of California, Berkeley, assistant professor of English Victorian literature, 1965-69; San Francisco State University, San Francisco, Calif., associate professor of English and American literature, 1969—. Lecturer and research fellow at Reading University, 1971. Chairman of Nonce Carpentry Associates. *Member:* Melville Society, Philological Association of the Pacific Coast, San Francisco Maritime Association, Phi Beta Kappa.

WRITINGS: (Editor) Matthew Arnold, *Dover Beach,* C. E. Merrill, 1971; *Mailer and the Times of His Time,* Bay Books, 1976. Contributor to literature journals and popular magazines, including *New Republic, Ramparts, Berkshire Eagle, Victorian Poetry,* and *College English.*

WORK IN PROGRESS: Leave Her to Heaven (tentative title), a novel; "Generativity and American Literature," an extended essay which reexamines classic American authors and their purportedly infantile fantasies.

*   *   *

MIELZINER, Jo 1901-1976

March 19, 1901—March 15, 1976; American set and lighting designer for musical comedies, dramas, operas and ballets, and author of books in his field. Obituaries: *New York Times,* March 16, 1976; *Washington Post,* March 17, 1976; *Newsweek,* March 19, 1976; *Time,* March 29, 1976; *Current Biography,* May, 1976.

*   *   *

MILES, Judith Mary (Huhta) 1937-

PERSONAL: Born January 18, 1937, in Hancock, Mich.; daughter of John Michael (a civil servant) and Sylvia (a civil servant; maiden name, Tikkanen) Huhta; married Donald Gene Miles (a mental health administrator), December 25, 1956; children: Kristin, Paul, Jonathan. *Education:* University of Colorado, B.A. (with distinction), 1964, M.A., 1968; University of Denver, further graduate study, 1967-69. *Religion:* Lutheran. *Residence:* 305 Elaine Dr., Roswell, Ga. 30075.

CAREER: Writer. *Member:* Phi Beta Kappa.

WRITINGS: The Feminine Principle, Bethany Fellowship, 1975; *Mind Games and Hobby Horses,* Bethany Fellowship, 1976.

WORK IN PROGRESS: Speak Me a House (tentative title), a book on language.

SIDELIGHTS: Judith Miles writes: "After some years of floundering about in intellectual waters, I am totally caught, convinced, and sold out to orthodox Christianity.... The spiritual dimension gives the motivation, meaning, and direction to my life as well as to my writing. *The Feminine Principle* discusses the impact of real Christianity on my women's liberation tendencies and exposes some of the thorny emotional and intellectual issues that prick a thoughtful woman. The warfare in the mind between the Word of God and his opposition is the subject analyzed in *Mind Games and Hobby Horses.*"

*   *   *

MILLER, Al 1936-

PERSONAL: Born December 17, 1936, in Pennsylvania; son of Albert S. (a president of a trucking company) and Edna (Speck) Miller; married Patricia Smith, August 28, 1954; children: Karen Joy, Kathy Elizabeth, John Ian. *Education:* East Stroudsburg State College, B.S., 1960. *Religion:* Protestant. *Home:* 2940 Forest Hills Lane, Richardson, Tex. *Office:* Dallas Tornado Soccer Club, 6116 North Central Expressway, Dallas, Tex. 75206.

CAREER: Albright College, Reading, Pa., golf coach, 1961; State University of New York College at New Paltz, soccer coach, 1961-66; Hartwick College, Oneonta, N.Y., soccer coach, 1967-73; Philadelphia Atoms, Philadelphia, Pa., head coach, 1973-75; Dallas Tornado Soccer Club, Dallas, Tex., head coach, 1975—. U.S. national soccer team, assistant to coach, 1974, head coach, 1975. *Member:* National Soccer Coaches Association of America. *Awards, honors:* Named All-American soccer player, 1958, 1959; named coach of the year by North American Soccer League, 1973.

WRITINGS: (with Norm Wingert) *Winning Soccer,* Regnery, 1975.

SIDELIGHTS: Miller's twelve-year college coaching record was 105-22-4, for a remarkable .802 winning percentage.

*   *   *

MILLER, Martin A. 1938-

PERSONAL: Born May 23, 1938, in Baltimore, Md.; son of Leon (a businessman) and Sophie (Long) Miller; married Ylana Feiler (a professor), December 26, 1964; children: Joshua Leon. *Education:* University of Maryland, B.A., 1960; University of Chicago, M.A., 1962, Ph.D., 1967. *Office:* Department of History, Duke University, Durham, N.C. 27708.

CAREER: Stanford University, Stanford, Calif., instructor in history, 1967-70; Duke University, Durham, N.C., assistant professor, 1970-73, associate professor of history, 1974—. *Member:* American Association for the Advancement of Slavic Studies, American Historical Association, Study Group on European Labor and Working Class History, Group for the Study of Psychology and History, Conference Group for Social and Administrative History. *Awards, honors:* Grants from American Philosophical Society, summer, 1972; younger humanist fellowship from National Endowment for the Humanities, 1972-73; senior research fellowship from Russian Institute of Columbia University, 1975-76; award from International Research and Exchanges Board, in the Soviet Union, 1976.

WRITINGS: (Editor, author of introductory essay, and co-translator) P. A. Kropotkin, *Selected Writings on Anarchism and Revolution,* M.I.T. Press, 1970; (editor and author of introduction) D. D. Akhsharumov, *Iz moikh vos-*

pominanii (title means "From My Reminiscences"), Oriental Research Partners, 1974; *Kropotkin,* University of Chicago Press, 1976. Contributor to history and Slavic studies journals.

WORK IN PROGRESS: Research on social origins of Russian revolutionaries during the 1870's and on the politics and culture of the Russian emigre community before 1917.

SIDELIGHTS: Miller has conducted research in Moscow and Leningrad, in Paris, London, Amsterdam, and Bern, and at Hoover Institution.

* * *

MILLER, R(ay Stephans) June 1923-

PERSONAL: Born July 8, 1923, in Tennessee; daughter of William Right (a baker) and Mabel (Coffman) Stephens; married Hal Miller (a collector and trader of Indian and Oriental art), September 8, 1940; children: Ray, Mark, Michael, Jeffrey, Joy Lynn (Mrs. Richard P. Engle). *Education:* Attended Moody Bible Institute. *Politics:* Republican. *Religion:* Baptist. *Home address:* P.O. Box 6068, Santa Barbara, Calif. 93111.

CAREER: Director of youth and Christian education at Baptist church in Torrance, Calif., 1959-61; Universal Schools, San Diego, Calif., enrollment counselor, 1964-66; Norton's Christian Supplies, Seattle, Wash., Christian education consultant, 1966-68; worked for Baptist church in Seattle, Wash., 1968-71. Writer and guest speaker. Broadcaster for "Something Special for Women," on KGDN-Radio, 1970-71; has appeared on several radio and television shows.

WRITINGS: Why Sink When You Can Swim?, Zondervan, 1973, study guide, 1975; *The God of the Impossible,* Zondervan, 1976; *Running Free,* Zondervan, in press.

WORK IN PROGRESS: Land of the Fires; a novel, based on the legendary survivors of Masada and their descendants; "Inside the Mask," a tape cassette dealing with rape victims and their families.

SIDELIGHTS: June Miller's writing draws upon extensive study in Israel, Turkey, and the Middle East (including Iraq). Her books have been published in Spanish and German. She has also made tape cassettes for Magnemedia, including "Why Sink When You Can Swim?," "Treasures of Darkness," "Conquering the New LSD," "Christmas Specials," and "The Secret You."

She writes: "My motivation for writing and speaking is to be of value to people in becoming free of all that limits them from achieving their highest potential. I have used many personal experiences such as our actual accidental wedding, my bout with cancer, overcoming fears of flying, the freeing forgiveness of a drunken woman who was responsible for our debilitating auto accident, and amny such potentially damaging experiences to discover that through these and other happenings in our lives God has brought triumph out of every tragedy. All people focus on and develop losses or gains. And it is the result of this choice that influences much of physical and emotional illness. As we understand the fascinating interworking of the inner self, and the impact on the physical body, we recognize the value of coping with guilt and resentment and the root of all our fears—that of personal inadequacy. The book *Running Free* opens the door of understanding of these things as well as recognizing our unique blend of temperaments, natural talents, and super-natural gifts."

MILLER, Ruby 1890(?)-1976

1890(?)—April 2, 1976; British music hall star and author of autobiography. Obituaries: *New York Times,* April 3, 1976.

* * *

MILLINGTON, Roger 1939-

PERSONAL: Born January 11, 1939, in Liverpool, England; son of George (a compositor) and Lilian (Murray) Millington; married Anne Rimmer; children: Matthew, Daniel, Benjamin. *Education:* University of Manchester, B.Sc., 1962. *Home:* 25 Alexandra Rd., Kingston, Surrey, England. *Office:* Ogilvy, Benson & Mather, Brettenham House, Lancaster Pl., London W.C.2, England.

CAREER: Girling Ltd., Birmingham, England, automobile development engineer, 1962-63; Stanley Dickson Advertising, Sheffield, England, copy chief, 1963-65; International Business Machines (IBM), Winchester, England, senior editor, 1965-66; Maxwell Clarke Advertising, London, England, copy chief, 1966-68; Notley Advertising, London, copywriter, 1968-69; Burford Design Group, London, creative director, 1969-72; General Advertising, Weybridge, England, creative director, 1972-74; Wasey-Campbell Ewald Advertising, London, copywriter, 1974-76; Ogilvy, Benson & Mather, London, copywriter, 1976—. *Member:* Royal Society of Arts (fellow), Design and Art Directors Association.

WRITINGS: The Birth of the Computer, 3-M Co., 1971; *The Strange World of the Crossword,* M. Joseph, 1974, published in the United States as *The Crossword and Its Cult,* Thomas Nelson, 1975. Contributor to professional journals.

WORK IN PROGRESS: The Other Jack the Ripper (tentative title), a biography of a Victorian English murderer.

SIDELIGHTS: Millington writes to *CA:* "As an inveterate collector of useless and offbeat information, I have a vast file of ideas for books and articles—enough to keep me going for many years if only I could find the time. Dealing strictly with non-fiction topics, my criterion is that my material should be entertaining as well as informative."

* * *

MILLWARD, Eric (Geoffrey William) 1935-

PERSONAL: Born March 12, 1935, in Longnor, Staffordshire, England; son of Kenneth (a farmer) and Jane (Lomas) Millward; married Anne Craig, December 30, 1961 (divorced, 1975); married Rosemary Anne Stevenson Wood (a nurse), May 16, 1975; children: Julian Craig, Roderic Neil. *Education:* Educated in Buxton, Derbyshire, England. *Politics:* "No formal politics." *Home:* 4 King's Rd., Horsham, Sussex, England.

CAREER: British Airways Ltd., London, England, chief steward, 1961—; poet, 1963—. *Military service:* Royal Air Force, 1954-56. *Member:* International Poetry Society (fellow), Conservation Society (founder-member; secretary of Sussex branch, 1971-74). *Awards, honors:* Borestone Mountain Poetry award, 1974.

WRITINGS: A Child in the Park (poems), Outposts Publications, 1969; *Dead Letters,* Peterloo Poets, in press.

Poems represented in anthologies, including *Active Anthologies IV,* edited by A. W. Rowe, Blond, 1968; *The Golden Bird,* edited by Frank Whitehead, Oliver & Boyd, 1969; and *The Poet's Sphere,* edited by C. F. Bricknell Smith, Wheaton, 1970. Also included in P.E.N. *New Poems,* Hutchinson, 1965, 1975, 1976, and other anthologies. Contributor of poems to periodicals, including *Poetry Review, Listener, Outposts, Orbis,* and *Tribune,* and of stories to *Storyteller.* Poetry editor, *Towards Survival,* 1973-75.

WORK IN PROGRESS: Earthwords, poems on the care of environment; *Cynic Songs,* light verse.

SIDELIGHTS: Millward told *CA* that he is motivated "to write good poems, making statements (as memorably as possible) about what I consider important/happy/sad/beautiful/ugly/kind/cruel. At fourteen I decided to be a Great Poet, and I continue to work downward towards the truth.

"I live with the frustration of knowing my head will constantly be filled with poems I shall never write. My output is relatively small because I believe a poem should be a 'finished' creation. I often wonder how some prolific and illustrious poets can bear to see their every hiccup in print!

"I am a reluctant convert to pessimism, and though my work gives evidence of my new faith, I hope I will not become too negative. That is not my intention. I have many likes/loves, but am becoming more widely known for my dislikes, of which a short list follows: 'Trendies'—and the sycophantism of critics who, to justify their own existence, claim to understand the incomprehensible; any system that grants gratuitous honours in recognition of outstanding work in the cause of the perpetuation of a bureaucracy; the 'closed shop' cliques that constitute the 'Arts Industry'; the alienation of 'leaders' from 'led'; the sacrifice of all recognisable standards in the desire to touch the garments of Mammon....

"As a founder-member of the Conservation Society, I have been credited with the invention of all our current environmental problems—though I feel others deserve to share that honour. Like so many Pawns, I have no great love for our Grand Masters, among whom must be listed so many 'expert' professionals that it would be invidious to single out Lawyers....''

*   *   *

MINDSZENTY, Jozsef   1892-1975

PERSONAL: Surname originally Pehm; changed surname, 1940; born March 29, 1892, in Mindszent, Hungary; son of Janos (a farmer) and Borbala (Kovacs) Pehm. *Education:* Attended Roman Catholic seminary in Szombathely, Hungary, 1911-15, and University of Vienna. *Home:* Pazmaneum Bldg., Vienna, Austria.

CAREER: Ordained Roman Catholic priest, 1915; chaplain in Felsoepaty, Hungary, 1915-17; high school religion teacher in Zalaegerszeg, Hungary, 1917-19, school administrator, 1919-22, parish priest and rural dean, 1922-44, named Abbe of Porno, 1924, appointed papal prelate, 1937; consecrated bishop of Veszprem, 1944; served as archbishop of Esztergom, Hungary, and prince primate of church in Hungary, 1945-74; created cardinal, 1946. Political prisoner, 1948-56, incarcerated in various prisons in Hungary, including Budapest, Vacz, and Puespoekszentlaszlo; political refugee in American Embassy in Budapest, 1956-71; resident in Vienna, Austria, and lecturer in United States and Europe, 1971-75. Member, Sacred Congregations of Sacraments, of Ceremonies, and of Seminaries and Universities of Study.

WRITINGS: Cardinal Mindszenty Speaks: Authorized White Book, Longmans, Green, 1949; *Four Years of Struggle of the Church in Hungary,* translated by Walter C. Breitenfeld, Longmans, Green, 1949; *Le Forcat accuse,* edited by Bela Just, Bloud & Gay (Paris), 1949; *Die Mutter* (translation of original Hungarian text, *Az edesanya*), Rex Verlag, Volume I, 1949, Volume II: *Mutter in Gottes Augen,* 1950, translation by Benedict P. Lenz of Volume I published as *The Mother,* Radio Replies Press (St. Paul), 1949, translation by Charles Donahue of Volume II published as *The Face of the Heavenly Mother,* Philosophical Library, 1951; *Kardinal Mindszenty: Beitraege zu seinem siebzigsten Geburtstag,* edited by Josef Vecsey, Donau Verlag, 1962; "... *The World's Most Orphaned Nation,"* J. Tarlo, 1962; *Memoirs: Jozsef Cardinal Mindszenty,* translated by Richard Winston and Clara Winston, documents translated by Jan van Heurck, Macmillan, 1974. Also author of books in Hungarian, "Motherhood," 1917, "Zala Cries Out for Help," 1927, and "The Life and Times of Martin Padanyi Biro," two volumes, 1934.

SIDELIGHTS: In his analysis of the background of Cardinal Mindszenty's show trial of 1949, Stephen Kertesz wrote that "the Soviet mentality has no sympathy for the cornerstones of Western Civilization, because liberty and dignity of human individuals are incompatible with their system. Since both the Catholic and Protestant religions are exponents of these ideologies, their existence cannot be tolerated in Soviet-dominated countries." Kertesz notes that in Hungary, nearly two-thirds of the population at that time was Catholic, and furthermore, that Moscow considered the Catholic Church to be one of the most serious obstacles to complete Communist domination.

In a statement made on February 16, 1949, Pope Pius XII defined the general ideological and moral nature of the issue between Communism and Western civilization brought out by the Mindszenty stand. He pointed out that "this conflict opposes the defenders of a totalitarian regime against the champions of a conception of the state and society founded upon the dignity and the liberty of man." On this same point, Kertesz emphasized that "Communist totalitarian dictatorship ... demands from each individual total allegiance and establishes total control over all human relationships. This ideology cannot tolerate independent Churches, the only remaining free institutions in East Europe." The Church as an organization became synonymous with individual freedom and human dignity, and Mindszenty's actions in these matters corresponded to official Church policy.

Before Mindszenty's arrest, priests were being placed in custody on the charge of anti-democratic incitement, while anti-Mindszenty and anti-Catholic demonstrations were permitted whenever desired. Mindszenty therefore refused to negotiate on the question of nationalization of Church schools since his "opinion was that mere government statements were insufficient guaranties. What the Communists might be prepared to yield today [Church retention of a few upper class high schools] they would take back later."

After the passage of the school nationalization act of June 16, 1948, Mindszenty excommunicated every Catholic deputy who voted for the bill, an act for which he was severely criticized. As recorded in the *New York Times,* Mindszenty countered: "Abroad my position is said to be mediaeval. But if the parochial schools of the United States were taken away and in their places were substituted schools for the inculcation of Marxism, what would they say? In his book *Religion and Marxism,* ... Lenin says 'We desire the true Communist education of children. We must teach youth Communist ethics and morals, including denial of the Ten Commandments. We do not believe in eternal moral values.' ... I do not want the Middle Ages; I want the rights of man.... The rights I demand were expressed long before the Middle Ages, and I notice that they have been incorporated in the charters drawn up since. . . . The church will continue the struggle against the nationalization of the schools with every legal means." Kertesz pointed out that "Cardinal Mindszenty, refusing to cooperate . . . thus sealed his fate. He knew that he would be a victim of his uncompromising attitude and was prepared for the supreme sacrifice."

Mindszenty was arrested after he led demonstrations against Hungary's Communist government in 1948, tortured, tried on trumped-up treason charges, and given a death sentence that was commuted to life imprisonment. Hungarian insurrectionists freed him in 1956 and he was given asylum in the American Embassy in Budapest. Since he felt that the proper place for the primate of Hungary was in Hungary, he refused repeated efforts of the Vatican to acquire his safe passage to Rome; however, in a 1971 letter from President Nixon, Mindszenty was assured that his continuing presence under the American wing was not in the best interests of the American Government. Militant anti-Communism ironically had given way to detente in world affairs, and the official no-compromise Church policy, in effect at the time of Mindszenty's arrest, had been modified to one seeking modus vivendi with the Soviet bloc. The man described as a symbol of inflexible resistance to Communism turned to attacking the Vatican regarding its new policy of detente with Communist regimes, claiming that it weakened the Church. In his later years he had become an obstacle to Church-State relations in Hungary. "This is how I arrived at complete and total exile," Mindszenty said in his *Memoirs*.

Perhaps Mindszenty's words at the time of his 1948 arrest were full of prophetic irony: "I am sacrificing my life for the Hungarian people. . . . A dead Cardinal may be worth more to the cause of freedom than a live one." Execution after his trial might easily have made him a martyr.

BIOGRAPHICAL/CRITICAL SOURCES—Books: *Documents on the Mindszenty Case*, Athenaeum, 1949; Bela Fabian, *Cardinal Mindszenty: The Story of a Modern Martyr*, Scribner, 1949; Jozsef Mindszenty, *The Trial of Jozsef Mindszenty* (transcript of Mindszenty's testimony), Hungarian State Publishing House, 1949; A. W. Sheppard, *Mindszenty and the Protestant Pastors*, Free Citizen Press (Sydney), 1949; Stephen K. Swift, *Cardinal's Story: The Life and Work of Joseph, Cardinal Mindszenty, Archbishop of Esztergom, Primate of Hungary*, Macmillan, 1949; Helen Homan, *Letters to the Martyrs*, McKay, 1951; George N. Shuster, *In Silence I Speak: The Story of Cardinal Mindszenty Today and of Hungary's New Order*, Farrar, Straus, 1956; *Britannica Book of the Year*, 1957, 1972; Brandt Aymar and Edward Sagarin, *Pictorial History of the World's Great Trials from Socrates to Eichmann*, Crown, 1967; Joseph Vecsey and Phyllis Schlafly, *Mindszenty the Man*, Pere Marquette Press, 1972; Jozsef Mindszenty, *Memoirs: Jozsef Cardinal Mindszenty*, Macmillan, 1974.

Periodicals: *Review of Politics*, April, 1949; *Nation*, August 6, 1949; *New York Herald Tribune*, July 6, 1950, November 26, 1956; *Newsweek*, July 17, 1950, December 27, 1954, July 25, 1955, August 27, 1956, April 29, 1963, October 30, 1967, October 11, 1971, December 2, 1974; *Time*, December 27, 1954, July 25, 1955, November 12, 1956, November 26, 1956, December 17, 1956, April 12, 1963, October 27, 1967, October 11, 1971, July 30, 1973, February 18, 1974, May 19, 1975; *New York Times*, June 29, 1948, July 17, 1955, October 31, 1956, November 3, 1956; *U.S. News & World Report*, July 29, 1955; *American Weekly*, November 20, 1955, November 27, 1955; *Collier's*, April 13, 1956; *New York World-Telegram Magazine*, October 13, 1956; *America*, November 10, 1956, November 17, 1956, November 24,

1956, May 4, 1963; *Life*, November 12, 1956; *Commonweal*, November 16, 1956; *Look*, December 25, 1956; *Reporter*, November 24, 1960; *National Review*, July 18, 1963, March 1, 1974, May 23, 1975; *Commonwealth*, January 17, 1964; *Economist*, February 9, 1974; *New Yorker*, May 19, 1975.*

(Died May 6, 1975, in Vienna, Austria)

* * *

MINICK, Michael 1945-

PERSONAL: Born March 26, 1945, in Albany, N.Y.; son of Jason (a real estate entrepreneur) and Ruth (Solomon) Minick. *Education:* Attended University of Virginia, 1963-66; Long Island University, B.A., 1969. *Home and office:* 107 MacDougal St., New York, N.Y. 10012. *Agent:* Erica Spellman, International Creative Management, 40 West 57th St., New York, N.Y. 10019.

CAREER: Magazine Management, New York City, editorial director of *Man's World* and *Action for Men*, 1969-73; Genesis Publications, Inc., New York City, managing editor of *Genesis*, 1975; Esquire, Inc., New York City, managing editor of *Gentleman's Quarterly*, 1975—.

WRITINGS: *The Kung Fu Exercise Book*, Simon & Schuster, 1973; *The Wisdom of Kung Fu*, Morrow, 1974; *The Kung Fu Avengers*, Bantam, 1975. Contributor to men's magazines.

WORK IN PROGRESS: Research for a novel and for nonfiction projects.

SIDELIGHTS: Minick writes: "I published dozens of stories and articles before I felt good enough about my skills to put my name on anything. To this day much of my writing is still done under a variety of nom de plumes. I gain enormous satisfaction editing magazines and will one day try to publish one of my own. Despite my publishing interests, I'll continue to write books in a wide variety of areas."

AVOCATIONAL INTERESTS: Art, motorcycles, music, dance.

* * *

MINTZ, Joyce Lois 1933-
(Joyce Madison)

PERSONAL: Born January 13, 1933, in Hollywood, Calif.; daughter of Arthur C. (a transportation engineer) and Frances (a registered nurse; maiden name, Cantor) Jenkins; married Charles P. Mintz (a writer and comedian), February 1, 1959. *Education:* Attended University of California at Los Angeles, 1953; University of California, Berkeley, A.B. and elementary teacher credentials, 1955; University of Southern California, M.A., 1958. *Politics:* Republican. *Religion:* Jewish. *Home and office:* 14600 Saticoy St., No. 204, Van Nuys, Calif. 91405. *Agent:* Carolyn McCoy & Associates, 6144 West Sixth St., Los Angeles, Calif. 90048.

CAREER: Elementary and junior high school teacher in the public schools of Lafayette, Calif., 1955-57, Los Angeles, Calif, 1958-59, and Hayward, Calif., 1960-62; nightclub comedy writer, 1958-69; Nash Publishing Co., Los Angeles, free-lance editor, 1971-73; *Human Behavior*, Los Angeles, copy editor and writer, 1973—. Television and motion picture comedienne, model for television commercials, and stage actress. Media director and speakers' bureau director of National Organization for Non-Parents, Greater Los Angeles chapter, 1974-75. *Member:* University of California Alumni Association, Pi Alpha Sigma. *Awards, honors:* West Coast Non-Parents of the Year Award from National Organization for Non-Parents, 1975-76.

WRITINGS: (Under pseudonym Joyce Madison) *Off the Beaten Track in San Francisco,* Nash Publishing, 1973. Editor of *National Organization for Non-Parents Newsletter* for Greater Los Angeles chapter, 1974-75; free-lance editor, *Silver Foxes* magazine.

WORK IN PROGRESS: With husband, Charles Mintz, a book on nonparenthood; a book on obesity; a movie-for-television script "Run If You Can," and a television comedy script "It's in the Bag".

SIDELIGHTS: Joyce Mintz told *CA* that she wrote her first play in French at the age of twelve, and produced and starred in it at school. *Avocational interests:* Travel, painting (acrylics), playing piano.

*   *   *

MITCHELL, Joyce Slayton   1933-

PERSONAL: Born August 13, 1933, in Hardwick, Vt.; daughter of George Dix (an automobile dealer) and Sarah (Arkin) Slayton; married William E. Mitchell (an anthropologist), July 4, 1959; children: Ned Slayton, Elizabeth Dix. *Education:* Denison University, A.B., 1955; University of Bridgeport, M.S., 1958; Columbia University, further graduate study, 1960-62. *Home and office address:* Wolcott, Vt. 05680.

CAREER: Junior high school teacher of physical education in Norwalk, Conn., 1955-58; high school counselor in Greenwich, Conn., 1959-62; consultant, 1962—. Visiting lecturer at Johnson State College, 1975. Member of advisory council of Harvard University's Divinity School, 1974-75. *Member:* American Personnel and Guidance Association (member of board of directors of Women's Caucus, 1976), National Vocational Guidance Association (professional member), American School Counselor Association, National Association of College Admissions Counselors, National Organization for Women (founder and coordinator of Vermont chapter, 1973-74), Vermont Guidance Association.

WRITINGS: The Guide to College Life, Prentice-Hall, 1968; *The Guide to Canadian Universities,* Simon & Schuster, 1970; (contributor) Mordica Pollack, editor, *N.O.W. Anthology,* Know, Inc., 1973; (editor) *Other Choices for Becoming a Woman,* Know, Inc., 1974, revised edition, Dell, 1975; *I Can Be Anything: Careers and Colleges for Young Women,* College Entrance Examination Board, 1975; (editor) *Free to Choose: Decision Making for Young Men,* Dell, 1976; *Tokenism: The Opiate of the Oppressed,* Know, Inc., 1976. Contributor to education, counseling, and feminist journals, and to *Seventeen.* Member of editorial board of *School Counselor,* 1975-78.

WORK IN PROGRESS: The Work Book, a non-sexist, non-racist guide to trade, technical, and business careers; a male version of *I Can Be Anything,* careers for college level students.

SIDELIGHTS: Joyce Mitchell writes: "As a feminist and an educator my work all reflects the importance of decision-making on the basis of a student's abilities and interests rather than from a stereotypic expectation of what 'girls should do' or what 'boys should do.' My books are designed to help high school students understand the many choices open in developing all facets of their lives, so that they are not bound by traditional views of women and men."

*   *   *

MITRANY, David   1888-1975

PERSONAL: Born January 1, 1888, in Bucharest, Romania; son of Moscu and Jeannette Mitrany; married Ena Victoria Limebeer, 1923. *Education:* London School of Economics and Political Science, University of London, Ph.D. and D.Sc. *Residence:* Oxford, England.

CAREER: Guardian, Manchester, England, member of editorial staff, 1919-22; Carnegie Endowment for International Peace, assistant European editor of *Economic and Social History of the World War,* 1922-29; Princeton University, Princeton, N.J., professor of economics at Institute for Advanced Study since 1933. Visiting professor at Harvard University, 1931-33; Dodge lecturer at Yale University, 1932; Nielsen Research Professor at Smith College, 1951. International affairs adviser to Unilever and Lever Brothers, 1943-75. Member of British Coordinating Committee for International Studies, 1927-30.

WRITINGS: Rumania, Her History and Politics, Oxford University Press, 1915; *Greater Rumania: A Study in International Ideals,* Hodder & Stoughton, 1917; *The London School of Economics and Political Science* (pamphlet), Students' Union, London School of Economics and Political Science, University of London, 1919; *The Problem of International Sanctions,* Oxford University Press, 1925; *The Land and the Peasant in Rumania: The War and Agrarian Reform, 1917-1921,* Yale University Press, 1930, Greenwood Press, 1968; *The Progress of International Government,* Yale University Press, 1933; *The Effect of the War in Southeastern Europe,* Yale University Press, 1936, Fertig, 1973; *A Working Peace System: An Argument for the Functional Development of International Organization,* Oxford University Press, 1943, 4th edition, National Peace Council, 1946, Quadrangle, 1966; *The Road to Security* (pamphlet), National Peace Council, 1944; *American Interpretations: Four Political Essays,* Contact Publications, 1946; (with Maxwell Garnett) *World Unity and the Nations* (pamphlet), privately printed, 1950; *Marx against the Peasant: A Study in Social Dogmatism,* University of North Carolina Press, 1951, Collier Books, 1961; *Food and Freedom,* Batchworth Press, 1954; *The Making of the Functional Theory,* Martin Robertson, 1975.

Also author of *O Cauza Dreapta,* 1915; *Marx versus the Peasant,* 1927; *American Policy and Opinion: A Survey of International Affairs,* 1940; *The Progress of International Government,* 1943; translator of *Correspondenta relativa la Criza Europeana,* 1914; contributor to *The United Nations Charter: The Text and a Commentary,* 1945. Contributor to *Encyclopaedia Brittannica* and *Encyclopedia of the Social Sciences.* Contributor to academic journals.

SIDELIGHTS: Mitrany's books have been translated into Italian, Danish, Norwegian, German, Portuguese, Chinese, Japanese, and French.

OBITUARIES: AB Bookman's Weekly, September 22-29, 1975.*

(Died in 1975, in London, England)

*   *   *

MOCSY, Andras   1929-

PERSONAL: Born May 15, 1929, in Budapest, Hungary; son of Janos (a university professor) and Erzsebet (Szabady) Mocsy; married Eva Kabay (a literary adviser), June 22, 1957. *Education:* Eoetvoes Lorand Tudomanyegyetem, Ph.D., 1959. *Home:* Sajto utca 6, Budapest H-1161, Hungary. *Agent:* Artisjus Agency, Hungarian Bureau for Copyright Protection, Voeroesmarty ter 1, 1051 Budapest, Hungary. *Office:* Eoetvoes Lorand Tudomanyegyetem, Pesti Barnabas utca 1, Budapest H-1364 Pf.1o7, Hungary.

CAREER: Hungarian National Museum, Budapest, conservator, 1951-59; Eoetvoes Lorand Tudomanyegyetem, Budapest, lecturer, 1959-64, senior lecturer, 1964-69, professor of archaeology of the Roman Empire, 1969—, vice-rector of the university, 1974-76. Member of Hungarian Academy's Institute of Archaeology, 1958-64. *Member:* Hungarian Archaeological Society (member of board of directors), Society of Classical Studies (member of board of directors), Hungarian Academy of Science, German Institute of Archaeology, Archaeological Institute of Austria. *Awards, honors:* Medals from Hungarian Archaeological Society, 1961, 1975; prize from Hungarian Academy of Science, 1971; medal from Society of Classical Studies, 1975.

WRITINGS: *Die Bevoelkerung von Pannonien* (title means "The Population of Pannonia"), Hungarian Academy of Science, 1959; *Pannonia,* Druckenmueller, 1962; *Gesellschaft und Romanisation der roemischen Provinz Moesia Superior* (title means "Society and Romanization in the Roman Province Moesia Superior"), Hungarian Academy of Science, 1970; *Pannonia and Upper Moesia,* Routledge & Kegan Paul, 1974. Co-editor of *The Roman Inscriptions of Hungary,* 1971—.

WORK IN PROGRESS: Research on personal names in the Roman Empire.

* * *

MOERI, Louise 1924-

PERSONAL: Surname rhymes with "story"; born November 30, 1924, in Klamath Falls, Ore.; daughter of Clyde (a farmer) and Hazel (Simpson) Healy; married Edwin Albert Moeri (a civil servant), December 15, 1946; children: Neal Edwin, Rodger Scott, Patricia Jo Ann. *Education:* Stockton Junior College, A.A., 1944; University of California, Berkeley, B.A., 1946. *Religion:* Protestant. *Home:* 18262 South Austin Rd., Manteca, Calif. 95336.

CAREER: Manteca Branch Library, Manteca, Calif., library assistant, 1961—.

WRITINGS: *Star Mother's Youngest Child,* Houghton, 1975; *A Horse for XYZ,* Dutton, 1977; *How the Rabbit Stole the Moon,* Houghton, 1977.

WORK IN PROGRESS: An adult novel, *Or the Horse May Talk.*

SIDELIGHTS: "I began writing poetry as a very small child," Louise Moeri wrote, "and continued over a long period of time to struggle to get something down on paper. I have received innumerable rejection slips. The thing that kept me going is a picture I have in my mind. I see myself as a very old lady in a rest home with a blanket over my knees with a choice of two statements to make: 'I tried very hard to write—gave it everything I had' and 'how I wish I had tried harder'."

* * *

MOGLEN, Helene 1936-

PERSONAL: Born March 22, 1936, in New York; daughter of Edward L. (an insurance agent) and Edythe (Levin) Rosenbaum; married Sig Moglen (an editor), 1957; children: Eben, Damon, Seth. *Education:* Bryn Mawr College, B.A., 1957; Yale University, M.A., 1958, Ph.D., 1965. *Home:* 7 Cabin Ridge, Cappaqua, N.Y. 10514. *Office:* Department of Humanities, State University of New York College at Purchase, Purchase, N.Y.

CAREER: New York University, New York, N.Y., instructor, 1965-66, assistant professor of English, 1966-71; State University of New York College at Purchase, associate professor, 1971-76, professor of English, 1976—. *Member:* Modern Language Association of America. *Awards, honors:* American Council of Learned Societies fellowship, 1973-74.

WRITINGS: *The Philosophical Irony of Laurence Sterne,* University of Florida Press, 1975; *Charlotte Bronte, The Self Conceived,* Norton, 1976. Member of editorial board of *Literature and Psychology.*

WORK IN PROGRESS: *A Critical Psychobiography of Lewis Carroll.*

* * *

MOLEN, Ronald Lowry 1929-

PERSONAL: Born August 7, 1929, in Hammond, Ind.; son of Ronald Lowry and Ann Rose (Kloch) Molen; married Norma Lowe, June 10, 1955; children: Mark Wilson, Jill, Lee, Steven Lowe. *Education:* Attended Indiana University, 1948-50; University of Utah, B.Arch., 1958. *Religion:* Church of Jesus Christ of Latter-day Saints. *Home:* 906 East Capitol Blvd., Salt Lake City, Utah 84103. *Office:* Ronald Lowry Molen & Associates, 165 South West Temple, Salt Lake City, Utah 84101.

CAREER: Ronald Lowry Molen & Associates, Salt Lake City, Utah, architect, 1964—. Chairman of Environmental Design Committee of Utah Division of Fine Arts, 1972-76; chairman of Utah State Trees Committee Bicentennial Program; member of Capitol Hill Neighborhood Council, 1970-76. *Military service:* U.S. Army, 1955-57. *Member:* American Institute of Architects.

WRITINGS: *House Plus Environment,* Olympus, 1974.

WORK IN PROGRESS: *The Survival Community.*

* * *

MOLLO, Andrew 1940-

PERSONAL: Born May 15, 1940, in Epsom, England; son of Eugene (a historian) and Ella (a photographer and portrait painter; maiden name, Cockell) Mollo; married Maria del Carmen Diez, August 13, 1966; children: Alexander, Nicholas. *Education:* Attended Regent Street Polytechnic. *Religion:* Russian Orthodox. *Home:* 23 Stanhope Gardens, London S.W.7, England.

CAREER: Writer, film director, historical consultant, and scriptwriter.

WRITINGS: *Uniforms of the S.S.,* Volumes I-VII, Historical Research Unit, 1968-76; *Army Uniforms of World War Two,* Macmillan, 1973; *Naval, Marine, and Air Force Uniforms of World War Two,* Macmillan, 1975; *German Uniforms of World War Two,* Hipocrene Books, 1975; *Pictorial History of the S.S.,* Stein & Day, 1976. Co-author and director of feature films "It Happened Here," Woodfall Film Productions, 1964, and "Winstanley," British Film Institute, 1976.

WORK IN PROGRESS: *Pictorial History of the Soviet Army, 1917-1945.*

SIDELIGHTS: Mollo writes: "From an early interest in toy soldiers has grown a consuming passion for the external appearance of past societies and civilisations. The knowledge acquired over the years—coupled with an artistic and cosmopolitan upbringing—has enabled me to work not only on books, but on both documentary and feature films, and other forms of historical reconstruction." He has been a historical consultant on several films, including "Doctor Zhivago," "Night of the Generals," "Great Catherine," and "The Eagle Has Landed."

*   *   *

MONACO, Richard   1940-
(Dwight Robhs)

PERSONAL: Born April 23, 1940, in New York, N.Y.; son of Vincent G. (a musician) and Mae (a dancer; maiden name, Bottinelli) Monaco; married Judy Jacobs (a poet), August 15, 1967. Education: Attended Columbia University, 1966-70. Home: 270 Roundhill Dr., Yonkers, N.Y. 10701. Agent: Peter Lampack, William Morris Agency, 1350 Avenue of the Americas, New York, N.Y. 10019.

CAREER: Columbia University, New York City, assistant to directors of Group for Contemporary Music, 1966-68, curator of music, 1967-68; WBAI-FM, New York City, co-host of "New York Poetry" series, 1968-69; editor of New York Poetry, 1969-70; New School for Social Research, New York City, member of faculty, 1973—; Mercy College, Westchester, N.Y., member of faculty, 1975—. Co-director, The Contemporary Concert: Composition and Improvisation (music group), 1974—. Visiting lecturer at New York University, 1974; lecturer at Regenesis (experimental school for adults), Westchester, N.Y., 1977—. Co-host of "The Logic of Poetry" series and "Poetry P.M.," WNYC-FM, New York City, 1975—. Member: International Poetry Society, Writer's Guild of America, American Society of Composers, Authors, and Publishers.

WRITINGS: New American Poetry, McGraw, 1973; (with John Briggs) The Logic of Poetry, McGraw, 1974. Author of screenplays for Warner Brothers, MGM, and other film companies. Author of a libretto for opera, "The Politics of Harmony," 1968. Work represented in anthologies, including Ipso Facto, edited by Rubin Gregory, Hub Publication, 1975. Contributor of poetry, articles, and reviews to magazines, including Saturday Review. Founding editor, Contemporary Music Newsletter, 1967; poetry and fiction editor, University Review, 1969-70.

WORK IN PROGRESS: Two books, A Knight's Tale and its sequel.

*   *   *

MONAD, Jacques   1910-1976

February 9, 1910—May 31, 1976; French biologist and author of book on philosophy. Obituaries: New York Times, June 1, 1976; Washington Post, June 1, 1976; Current Biography, July, 1976.

*   *   *

MONDADORI, Alberto   1914(?)-1976

1914(?)—February 14, 1976; Italian publisher of poetry, essays, and social science. Obituaries: Publishers Weekly, March 22, 1976.

*   *   *

MONDALE, Walter F(rederick)   1928-

PERSONAL: Born January 5, 1928, in Ceylon, Minn.; son of Theodore Seigvaard (a Methodist minister) and Claribel Hope (Cowan) Mondale; married Joan Adams, December 27, 1955; children: Theodore Adams, Eleanor Jane, William Hall. Education: Attended Macalester College, 1946-49; University of Minnesota, B.A. (cum laude), 1951, LL.B.,

1956. Politics: Democratic Farm Labor. Religion: Presbyterian. Home: 3421 Lowell St. N.W., Washington, D.C. 20016. Office: 443 Russell, Senate Office Bldg., Washington, D.C. 20510.

CAREER: Admitted to Minnesota State Bar, 1956; Larson, Loevinger, Lindquist, Freeman & Fraser (law firm), Minneapolis, Minn., lawyer, 1956-60; Minnesota State Government, Minneapolis, special assistant to attorney general, 1958-60, attorney general, 1960-64; U.S. senator from Minnesota, 1964-76, appointed by Minnesota governor to vacant seat, 1964, re-elected, 1966 and 1972, served on Finance Committee, Labor and Public Welfare Committee, Nutrition and Human Needs Select Committee, Special Committee on Aging, and Select Committee on Intelligence Activities; vice-president of United States, 1977—, elected in Democratic campaign with Jimmy Carter, received 297 electoral votes. Member of executive board and chairman of Midwest region, National Association of Attorneys General, 1960-64; member of President's Consumer Advisory Council, 1962-64. Military service: U.S. Army, 1951-53. Member: American Bar Association, American Association for the United Nations, Minnesota Bar Association, Hennepin County Bar Association, Hennepin County Citizen's League, Sons of Norway, American Legion, Loyal Order of Moose, Fraternal Order of Eagles.

WRITINGS: East-West Trade: A Congressional Perspective, New York University Center for International Studies, 1970; Justice for Children, U.S. Government Printing Office, 1972; (with others) Is the Energy Crisis Contrived?, American Enterprise, 1974; The Accountability of Power: Toward a Responsible Presidency, McKay, 1976.

*   *   *

MONDAY, Michael
See GINDER, Richard   1914-

*   *   *

MONET, Jacques   1930-

PERSONAL: Born January 26, 1930, in Saint-Jean, Quebec, Canada. Education: Loyola College, Montreal, Quebec, B.A., 1954; College de l'Immaculee Conception, Ph.L., 1956, Th.L., 1967; University of Toronto, M.A., 1961, Ph.D., 1964. Office: Department of History, University of Ottawa, Ottawa, Ontario, Canada K1N 6N5.

CAREER: Entered Society of Jesus (Jesuits; S.J.), 1949, ordained Roman Catholic priest, 1966; Loyola College, Montreal, Quebec, sessional lecturer in history, 1965-68; University of Toronto, Toronto, Ontario, visiting professor of history, 1968-69; University of Ottawa, Ottawa, Ontario, associate professor of history, 1969—, chairman of department, 1972—. Member: Canadian Historical Association (president, 1975-76).

WRITINGS: The Last Cannon Shot, University of Toronto Press, 1969. Contributor to journals.

WORK IN PROGRESS: Research on the role of the Crown in Canada.

*   *   *

MONOD, (Andre) Theodore   1902-

PERSONAL: Born April 9, 1902, in Rouen, France; son of Wilfred (a pastor) and Dorina (Monod) Monod; married Olga Pickova, March 22, 1930; children: Beatrice (Mme. Jean-Claude Morlot), Cyrille, Ambroise. Education: University of Paris, docteur-es-sciences, 1921; Ecole nationale des langues orientales vivantes, diploma, 1938. *Home:* 14 Quai d'Orleans, Paris 4eme, France. *Office:* Museum national d'Histoire naturelle, 57 rue Cuvier, 75005 Paris, France.

CAREER: Museum national d'Histoire naturelle, Paris, France, assistant, 1922-42, professor, 1942-73. Director of Institut Francais d'Afrique Noire, Dakar, Senegal, 1938-65; dean of faculty of sciences, University of Dakar, 1957-58. *Member:* Institut de France (Academie des Sciences), Academie des Sciences d'Outre-mer, Academie de Marine. *Awards, honors:* Officer of Legion of Honor; Commander, Order of Christ; Commandeur de Merite Saharien; Gold Medal of the Royal Geographic Society, 1960; Charles P. Daly Medal of the American Geographical Society, 1961; Haile Selassie Prize for African Research.

WRITINGS: Contribution a l'etude de la faune du Cameroun (title means "Contribution to the Study of the Fauna of the Cameroons"), Societe d'Editions Geographiques, Maritimes et Coloniales, 1927; *Thermosboena mirabilis Monod,* Societe d'Editions Geographiques, Maritimes et Coloniales, 1927; *Inventaire des manuscrits de Risso conserves a la Bibliotheque du Museum d'histoire naturelle* (title means "Inventory of the Risso Manuscripts Kept in the Library of the Museum d'Histoire naturelle"), Archives of the Museum d'Histoire naturelle, Paris, 1931; *L'Adrar Ahnet* (title means "The Adrar Ahnet"), Institut d'Ethnologie, Paris, 1932; *Missions A. Gruvel dans le canal de Suez* (title means "The A. Gruvel Missions in the Suez Canal"), Institut Francais d'Archaeologie Orientale, 1937; (editorial director) *Contributions a l'etude du Sahara occidental* (title means "Contributions to the Study of the Western Sahara"), Larose, 1938.

L'hippopotame et le philosophe (title means "The Hippopotamus and the Philosopher"), Julliard, 1946; *Sur la presence du genre Acanthocarpus dans l'Atlantique oriental* (title means "On the Presence of the Genus Acanthocarpus in the Western Atlantic"), Braga (Portugal), 1946; *Meharees, explorations au vrai Sahara* (title means "Dromedary Rides, Explorations in the True Sahara"), Editions "Je Sers," 1937, 2nd edition, 1947; *Le phoque moine dans l'Atlantique* (title means "The Monk Seal in the Atlantic"), Porto (Portugal), 1948; (with R. Maire) *Etudes sur le flore et la vegetation du Tibesti* (title means "Studies on the Flora and the Vegetation of Tibesti"), Larose, 1950; (translator) Valentim Fernandes, *Description de la cote occidentale d'Afrique* (title means "Description of the West Coast of Africa"), Bissau, 1951; (with R. Schnell) *Melanges botaniques* (title means "Botanical Miscellanea"), Institut Francais d'Afrique Noire, 1952; (with others) *Xylophages et petricoles ouest africains* (title means "West African Xylophages and Stone-Boring Mollusks"), Institut Francais d'Afrique Noire, 1952; *Bathyfolages: plongees profondes, 1948-1954* (title means "Having Fun in the Bathysphere: Deep Dives, 1948-1954"), Julliard, 1954; *Hippidea et Brachyura ouest-africains* (title means "West African Hippidea and Brachyura"), Institut Francais d'Afrique Noire, 1956; *Les grandes divisions chorologiques de l'Afrique* (title means "The Great Biogeographical Divisions of Africa"), Scientific Council for Africa South of the Sahara, 1957; *Majabat al-Koubra: contribution a l'etude de l'Empty Quarter ouest-saharien* (title means "Majabat al-Koubra: Contribution to the Study of the West Saharan Empty Quarter"), Institut Francais d'Afrique Noire, 1958; (editor) Diogo Gomes, *De la premiere decouverte de la Guinee* (title means "Of the First Discovery of Guinea"), Bissau, 1959.

International West African Atlas, U.S. Joint Publications

Research Service, 1962; *Notice sur la vie et l'oeuvre de Gaston Ramon (1886-1963),* l'Institut, Paris, 1964; *Contribution a l'etablissement d'une liste d'accidents circulaires d'origine meteoritique (reconnue, possible ou supposee), cryptoexplosive, etc.,* (title means "Contribution to the Establishment of a List of Circular Accidents of Meteoric Origin [Recognized, Possible, or Supposed], Cryptoexplosive, etc."), Institut Francais d'Afrique Noire, 1965; *Rapport sur une mission executee dans le nord-est du Tchad en decembre 1966 et janvier 1967* (title means "Report of a Mission Undertaken in the North-East of Chad in December 1966 and January 1967"), Fort-Lamy, 1968; *Le complexe urophore des poissons teleosteens* (title means "The Urophorous Complex of Teleostean Fishes"), Institut Francais d'Afrique Noire, 1968; *John Cranch, zoologiste de l'expedition du Congo (1816),* Trustees of the British Museum, 1970; *Les deserts,* [Paris], 1973.

Contributor of almost six hundred articles to scientific journals.

WORK IN PROGRESS: Historical research on George Glas and on Alexander Gordon Laing; further research on scientific topics.

SIDELIGHTS: A member of a family that has repeatedly won intellectual distinctions both in France and in the international academic world, Theodore Monod is recognized as the world's leading expert on the Sahara. *Avocational interests:* Botany.

* * *

MONSKY, Mark 1941-

PERSONAL: Born August 28, 1941, in New York, N.Y.; son of Leo (a journalist) and Irma (a publicist; maiden name, Reinhold) Monsky; married Beverly Du Bose (a travel consultant), May 2, 1965; children: Alexander, Eric. *Education:* Attended University of Miami, Coral Gables, Fla., 1959-60, and Columbia University, 1960-62. *Politics:* Independent. *Religion:* Non-denominational. *Residence:* New York, N.Y. *Agent:* Oliver Swan, 18 East 48th St., Room 903, New York, N.Y. 10017. *Office:* Metromedia Television, 205 East 67th St., New York, N.Y. 10021.

CAREER: Employed by Hearst Newspapers, New York City, 1962-64; Newshouse Newspapers, New York City, reporter, 1964-65; Columbia Broadcasting System, New York City, reporter and producer, 1965-70; Metromedia Television, New York City, manager and editor, 1970-74, vice-president in news, 1974—. *Member:* Independent Television News Association (vice-president and member of board of directors). *Awards, honors:* Feature award from Newspaper Reporters Association, 1964, for column on night life in New York; Gold Shield from New York Press Club, 1974, for best breaking news coverage.

WRITINGS: Looking Out for Number One (novel), Simon & Schuster, 1975.

WORK IN PROGRESS: Mad Dash (tentative title), fiction on the emotional breakdown of a deep cover agent; *Soldier in a Silent War,* a book and screenplay on an assassin; *Chrysalis,* a novel of life, mid-life crises, love, and death.

BIOGRAPHICAL/CRITICAL SOURCES: New York, January 12, 1976.

* * *

MONTAIGNE, Sanford H(oward) 1935-

PERSONAL: Born December 23, 1935, in Philadelphia,

Pa.; married Genevieve Bialczak (a reading specialist), January 1, 1967; children: Hugh Scott, David Sanford, Lauren Fern. *Education:* Temple University, B.S., 1957, Ed.M., 1962, M.A., 1967; University of Sarasota, Ed.D., 1976. *Politics:* Conservative. *Home:* 24 Overlook Ave., Willow Grove, Pa. 19090.

CAREER: School District of Philadelphia, Philadelphia, Pa., social studies and Spanish teacher, 1957—. Executive board member, Upper Moreland Homeowners Association, 1975. *Member:* Organization of American Historians, Western Writers of America, Texas State Historical Association, Texas Numismatic Association, University of Sarasota Alumni Association.

WRITINGS: Blood Over Texas: The Truth About Mexico's War with the United States, Arlington House, 1976. Author of "Republican," column in *Temple News,* 1968-69. Contributor to *Cattleman* of Fort Worth, Tex.

WORK IN PROGRESS: Research on gold and paper money.

SIDELIGHTS: Montaigne's special interests are the history of Texas and "the entire question of gold versus paper money. On the latter, I'm a definite gold bug. Have an abiding distrust of fiat paper money. I hold strong views, backed by primary research, that Mexico was responsible for the 1846 war with the U.S. This is contrary to the traditional view." He has traveled in Europe and the Near East.

* * *

MONTGOMERY, Bernard Law 1887-1976

November 17, 1887—March 24, 1976; British soldier and author of books in his field. Obituaries: *Washington Post,* March 25, 1976; *Time,* April 5, 1976.

* * *

MOODY, Anne 1940-

PERSONAL: Born September 15, 1940, in Mississippi; daughter of Fred and Elmire (Williams) Moody; married Austin Straus, March 9, 1967 (divorced); children: Sascha. *Education:* Tougaloo College, B.S., 1964. *Residence:* New York, N.Y.

CAREER: Congress of Racial Equality (CORE), Washington, D.C., organizer, 1961-63, fundraiser, 1964; Cornell University, Ithaca, N.Y., civil rights project coordinator, 1964-65; artist-in-residence in Berlin, Germany, 1972. Counsel for New York City's poverty program, 1967. *Member:* International P.E.N. *Awards, honors:* Gold medal from National Council of Christians and Jews, 1969; silver medal from *Mademoiselle,* 1970, for "New Hopes for the Seventies"; German Academic Exchange Service grant, 1972.

WRITINGS: Coming of Age in Mississippi (autobiography), Dial, 1969; *Mr. Death* (short stories), Harper, 1975. Contributor to *Ms.* and *Mademoiselle.*

WORK IN PROGRESS: Variations on a Dream of Death, short stories; *Black Womans Book; The Clay Gully,* a novel.

SIDELIGHTS: Anne Moody writes: "In the beginning I never really saw myself as a writer. I was first and foremost an activist in the Civil Rights Movement in Mississippi. When I could no longer see that anything was being accomplished by our work there, I left and went North. I came to see through my writing that no matter how hard we in the Movement worked, nothing seemed to change; that we made a few visible little gains, yet at the root, things always remained the same; and that the Movement was not in control of its destiny—nor did we have any means of gaining control of it. We were like an angry dog on a leash who had turned on its master. It could bark and howl and snap, and sometimes even bite, but the master was always in control. I realized that the universal fight for human rights, dignity, justice, equality and freedom is not and should not be just the fight of the American Negro or the Indians or the Chicanos, it's the fight of every ethnic and racial minority, every suppressed and exploited person, every one of the millions who daily suffer one or another of the indignities of the powerless and voiceless masses. And this trend of thinking is what finally brought about an end to my involvement in the Civil Rights Movement, especially as it began to splinter and get more narrowly nationalistic in its thinking."

BIOGRAPHICAL/CRITICAL SOURCES: Anne Moody, *Coming of Age in Mississippi,* Dial, 1969.

* * *

MOONEY, Michael Macdonald 1930-

PERSONAL: Born May 14, 1930, in New York, N.Y.; son of James David (an executive) and Ida May (a designer; maiden name, Macdonald) Mooney; married Nancy Loomis, September 4, 1950 (divorced, 1965); married Anne Sears (an editor), October 18, 1975; children: Michael, Jr., Laird, Christopher. *Education:* Georgetown University, B.S.F.S., 1955. *Home:* Main St., Wainscott, N.Y., 11975. *Agent:* Roberta Pryor, International Creative Management, 40 W. 57th St., New York, N.Y. 10019.

CAREER: National Review, New York City, editor, writer, advertising manager, 1957-63; *Saturday Evening Post,* New York City, senior editor, 1963-68; Macmillan Co., New York City, director of school and library division, 1968-69; full-time writer, 1969—.

Executive director, Committee for a Better New York, 1957-62. Historian, William M. Tweed Regular Democratic Club, 1974—. Professor of English at Southhampton College, Long Island University, 1976. *Military service:* U.S. Army, Corps of Engineers, 1951-55; became first lieutenant. *Member:* The Coffee House.

WRITINGS: (With Mort Gerberg) *The Handwriting Is on the Wall,* Hirsch Organization, 1967; *The Hindenburg,* Dodd, 1972; *George Catlin,* C. N. Potter, 1975; *Evelyn Nesbit and Sanford White,* Morrow, 1976. Writer and producer of television shows, including "Post-Time" and "Sunday in New York." Contributor to periodicals, including *Atlantic, Harper's, Travel and Leisure.*

WORK IN PROGRESS: Memento, publication by Crowell expected in 1978.

BIOGRAPHICAL/CRITICAL SOURCES: Otto Friedrich, *Decline and Fall,* Harper, 1970.

* * *

MOORE, Edward J(ames) 1935-

PERSONAL: Born June 2, 1935, in Chicago, Ill.; son of Irwin James (a truck driver) and Mary (Kase) Moore. *Education:* Attended Goodman Theatre and School of Drama, 1959-63, and Uta Hagen School of Acting, 1967-70. *Residence:* New York, N.Y. *Agent:* Earl Graham, 317 West 45th St., New York, N.Y. 10036.

CAREER: Professional actor and playwright. Founder, New York Playwrights' Workshop of Greenwich Village.

Military service: U.S. Navy, 1954-58. *Member:* American Federation of Television and Radio Artists, Actors Equity Association, Screen Actors Guild, Dramatists Guild. *Awards, honors:* Vernon Rice Drama Desk Award for outstanding new playwright, 1974, for "The Sea Horse".

WRITINGS: The Sea Horse (two-act play; first produced in New York at Westside Theatre, April 15, 1974), James T. White, 1974.

WORK IN PROGRESS: "Everything Together," a play.

* * *

MOORE, J(ohn) Preston 1906-

PERSONAL: Born November 1, 1906, in Lexington, Va.; son of Frank (a lawyer) and Lois (Thorn) Moore; married Anna Dart, September 18, 1942; children: John Preston (deceased), Frank Laird. *Education:* Washington and Lee University, B.A., 1927; Harvard University, M.A., 1930; Northwestern University, Ph.D., 1942. *Religion:* Episcopalian. *Home:* 17 Jordan St., Lexington, Va.

CAREER: University of Arkansas, Fayetteville, instructor in history, 1934-36; Citadel, Charleston, S.C., assistant professor of history, 1938-42; Louisiana State University, Baton Rouge, associate professor, 1946-50, professor of history, 1950-72, professor emeritus of colonial history, 1972—. *Military service:* U.S. Naval Reserve, active duty, 1942-45; became lieutenant commander. *Member:* American Historical Association, Southern Historical Association, Louisiana Historical Association (president, 1966), Phi Beta Kappa. *Awards, honors:* Guggenheim fellowship, 1967, honorable mention from American History Association, 1967, for best study in Latin American history.

WRITINGS: The Cabildo in Peru Under the Hapsburgs, Duke University Press, 1954; *My Ever Dearest Friend: Letters to Jefferson Davis,* Confederate Press, 1960; *The Cabildo in Peru Under the Bourbons,* Duke University Press, 1967; (contributor) John Frank McDermott, editor, *The Spanish in the Mississippi Valley, 1762-1804,* University of Illinois Press, 1974; *Revolt in Louisiana: The Spanish Occupation, 1766-1770,* Louisiana State University Press, 1976.

WORK IN PROGRESS: A biography of Antonio de Ulloa, eighteenth-century Spanish scientist and colonial administrator.

SIDELIGHTS: Moore told *CA:* "My father and grandfather were both lawyers. So, logically, I should have followed the legal tradition. But, as far back as I can remember, I've had an impelling interest in history; I find history more enthralling than fiction. I have long believed that Americans have failed to realize the contributions of the Spanish and French to our national heritage. To give this balance to our understanding of the past has certainly been a major purpose of my historical writings."

* * *

MORAND, Paul 1888-1976

March 13, 1888—July 23, 1976; French poet, novelist, diplomat, and author of travel books. Obituaries: *Washington Post,* July 24, 1976; *New York Times,* July 24, 1976.

* * *

MORE, Daphne (pseudonym) 1929-

PERSONAL: Born August 25, 1929, in Kent, England; daughter of an Irish-born businessman; divorced; children: Jonathan. *Education:* Educated at private girls' schools in England. *Politics:* "Confused." *Religion:* Church of England. *Residence:* Hampshire, England.

CAREER: Writer and artist (ink drawings for books). Has worked as a horse breeder, yacht hand, teacher, and broadcaster in England and East Africa. *Member:* International Bee Research Association, British Beekeepers Association.

WRITINGS: Ideas for Interesting Gardens, David & Charles, 1974; *The Bee Book: The History and Natural History of the Honeybee,* Universe Publishers, 1976. Contributor to magazines.

WORK IN PROGRESS: A novel; research on the mythology of bees.

SIDELIGHTS: Daphne More, who prefers to maintain her privacy with a pseudonym, writes that she is a "passionate lover of the countryside and its life, and ardent conservationist; I think mankind is suicidal in the way he pollutes the land, sea, and air, and his own body." *Avocational interests:* History, natural history, riding horses, beekeeping, gardening.

* * *

MORGAN, Clifford T(homas) 1915-1976

July 21, 1915—February 11, 1976; American psychologist, educator, and author of books in his field. Obituaries: *New York Times,* February 17, 1976. (See index for previous *CA* sketch)

* * *

MORGAN, Fred Bruce, Jr. 1919-1975

PERSONAL: Born March 12, 1919, in Charleston, W.Va.; son of Fred Bruce and Helen (Pidcock) Morgan; married Ruth Marian McNamee, May 27, 1942; children: Dorothy Jill (Mrs. G. Ian Marshall), Timothy Bruce, Rebecca Anne. *Education:* Maryville College, Maryville, Tenn., A.B., 1939; Princeton Theological Seminary, Th.B., 1942, Ph.D. 1958; graduate study at Western Theological Seminary, 1944-45, Yale University, 1946-47, and College of Chinese Studies, Peking, 1948. *Politics:* Democrat. *Residence:* Northfield, Minn.

CAREER: Ordained Presbyterian minister, 1942; pastor of Presbyterian church in Pennsylvania, 1942-46; Church of Christ, church food and relief administrator in China, 1947-49; consultant in Hong Kong, 1949-50; McGilvary Theological Seminary, Chiengmai, Thailand, professor of New Testament and homiletics, 1950-51; Presbyterian university pastor at Princeton University, Princeton, N.J., 1952-54; Wilson College, Chambersburg, Pa., assistant professor, 1954-58, associate professor of Bible and religion, 1958-59; Syracuse University, Syracuse, N.Y., associate professor of religion, 1959-60; Amherst College, Amherst, Mass., associate professor, 1960-63; professor of religion and American studies, 1963-72, acting dean of faculty, 1970-71; Carleton College, Northfield, Minn., professor of American studies and religion, and dean of college, 1972-75. Member of general council of United Presbyterian Church in the United States, 1968-71.

MEMBER: American Association of University Professors, Association for Asian Studies, Society for the Scientific Study of Religion, American Society for Christian Ethics, Church Service Society. *Awards, honors:* Danforth Foundation Grant, 1957-58; M.A. from Amherst College, 1963; Lilly Endowment fellowship, 1965-66.

WRITINGS: Called in Revolution, Stud. Vol. Movement,

1956; *Christians, the Church, and Property,* Westminster, 1963; *Here and Now: An Approach to Writing through Perception,* with instructor's manual, Harcourt, 1968, Book II, 1972; *Experiences,* with instructor's manual, Harcourt, 1975. Also author of *Thai Buddhism and American Protestantism,* 1966, and contributor to *Sons of the Prophets: Leaders of Protestantism from Princeton Seminary,* 1963. Contributor to academic journals.

OBITUARIES: New York Times, October 4, 1975.*

(Died October 2, 1975, in Northfield, Minn.)

* * *

MORGAN, Janet 1945-

PERSONAL: Born December 5, 1945, in Montreal, Quebec, Canada; daughter of Frank (a scientist) and Shiela (Sadler) Morgan. *Education:* St. Hugh's College, Oxford, M.A. (first class honors), 1967; University of Sussex, M.A., 1968; Nuffield College, Oxford, D.Phil., 1971. *Politics:* None. *Religion:* None. *Agent:* Hilary Rubinstein, 26-8 Bedford Row, London W.C.1., England. *Office:* Department of Political Science, Exeter College, University of Oxford, Oxford, England.

CAREER: Oxford University, Oxford, England, lecturer in politics at Exeter College, 1974-76, and St. Hugh's College, 1976—.

WRITINGS: The House of Lords and the Labour Government, 1964-1970, Clarendon Press, 1975; (editor) *Diaries of a Cabinet Minister, Richard Crossman,* Hamish Hamilton, Volume I, 1975, Volume II, 1976, Volume III, in press; *Reinforcing Parliament,* Political and Economic Planning, 1976.

* * *

MORGENSTERN, Soma 1891(?)-1976

1891(?)—April 17, 1976; Polish-born American novelist and journalist. Obituaries: *New York Times,* April 19, 1976; *AB Bookman's Weekly,* July 5, 1976.

* * *

MORISON, Samuel Eliot 1887-1976

July 9, 1887—May 15, 1976; American educator and author of books on naval and early American history. Obituaries: *New York Times,* May 16, 1976; *Washington Post,* May 16, 1976; *Newsweek,* May 24, 1976; *Time,* May 24, 1976; *Publishers Weekly,* May 31, 1976; *Current Biography,* July, 1976. (See index for previous *CA* sketch)

* * *

MORRIS, Ivan Ira Esme 1925-1976

November 29, 1925—July 19, 1976; British linguist, educator, translator, and author of books on Japan. Obituaries: *New York Times,* July 21, 1976; *Publishers Weekly,* August 16, 1976.

* * *

MORRIS, Joe A(lex) 1904-

PERSONAL: Born March 5, 1904, in Lancaster, Mo.; son of Alexander D. and Clare (Rippey) Morris; married Maxine Pooler, September 16, 1926; children: Joe Alex, Jr., Clare Morris Peckham. *Education:* University of Missouri, B.J., 1925. *Home:* Little Meadow Rd., Guilford, Conn. *Agent:* William Morris Agency, 1350 Avenue of the Americas, New York, N.Y. 10019.

CAREER: United Press Association, New York City, foreign editor, 1938-44; *New York Herald Tribune,* foreign editor, 1944; *Collier's Weekly,* managing editor, 1945-50. *Member:* Sigma Delta Chi, Overseas Press Club, National Press Club, Dutch Treat Club.

WRITINGS: The Private Papers of Senator Vandenberg, Houghton, 1952; *Those Rockefeller Brothers,* Harper, 1953; *What a Year,* Harper, 1956; *Deadline Every Minute: The Story of the United Press,* Doubleday, 1957; *Nelson Rockefeller* (biography), Harper, 1960; *Bird Watcher,* Popular Library, 1968. Contributor to national magazines.

* * *

MORRISON, Robert S(tanley) 1909-

PERSONAL: Born November 19, 1909, in Ashtabula, Ohio; son of Fred Root (a merchant) and Edith (Root) Morrison; married Helen Scott, July 22, 1939; children: Louise (Mrs. Thomas Raffa), Robert D., Nancy S. (Mrs. Glen Warner), Richard S. *Education:* Oberlin College, B.A., 1930; Harvard University, graduate study, 1930-31. *Politics:* Independent. *Religion:* Protestant. *Home:* 2982 Brown Rd., Ashtabula, Ohio 44004. *Office:* Molded Fiber Glass Companies, 1315 West 47th St., Ashtabula, Ohio 44004.

CAREER: Self-employed, 1933-36; Morrison Motors, Inc., Ashtabula, Ohio, owner, 1938-48; Molded Fiber Glass Companies, Ashtabula, chairman and chief executive officer, 1948—. Founder and president of Ashtabula Industrial Corp. *Member:* Society of the Plastics Industry (director), Ohio Manufacturers Association (trustee). *Awards, honors:* Charter member of Plastics Hall of Fame.

WRITINGS: The Contax Plan, privately printed, 1970; *Inflation Can Be Stopped,* Western Reserve Press, 1973; *Handbook for Manufacturing Entrepreneurs,* Western Reserve Press, 1973, 2nd edition, 1974. Author of weekly newspaper column in 1974 and daily newspaper column in 1975. Contributor to trade magazines.

WORK IN PROGRESS: A book on inflation and national economic problems.

SIDELIGHTS: Morrison feels that "Those of us who have lived through the period from 1909 to 1976 have a much different view of our national economic and social problems than those born much later."

BIOGRAPHICAL/CRITICAL SOURCES: Christian Science Monitor, August 7, 1974; *Oberlin Alumni,* March-April, 1975; *National Observer,* June 21, 1975; *Iron Age,* July 7, 1975; *In the Know,* December, 1975.

* * *

MORRISS, Mack 1920(?)-1976

1920(?)—February 18, 1976; American war correspondent, magazine writer, and novelist. Obituaries: *New York Times,* February 20, 1976.

* * *

MORSE, J(osiah) Mitchell 1912-

PERSONAL: Born January 14, 1912, in Columbia, S.C.; son of Josiah (a professor) and Etta (Ferguson) Morse; married Frances Belkin, June 30, 1936; children: Jonathan, Carolyn. *Education:* University of South Carolina, A.B., 1932, M.A., 1933; Pennsylvania State University, Ph.D., 1952. *Home:* 115 Morris Rd., Ambler, Pa. 19002. *Office:* Department of English, Temple University, Philadelphia, Pa. 19122.

CAREER: Columbia Record, Columbia, S.C., reporter, 1934; American Banker, New York, N.Y., news editor, 1935-42; Nation, New York, N.Y., assistant editor, 1943-45; Free Press of India, New York, N.Y., United Nations correspondent, 1945-47; Pennsylvania State University, University Park, 1948-67, began as instructor, became professor of English; Temple University, Philadelphia, Pa., professor of English, 1967—. Fulbright lecturer in France, 1964-65. Member: International Comparative Literature Association, International Federation for Modern Languages and Literatures, International Association of University Professors of English, Modern Language Association of America, Modern Humanities Research Association, College English Association, National Council of Teachers of English, American Association of University Professors. Awards, honors: American Council of Learned Societies fellow, 1952.

WRITINGS: The Sympathetic Alien: James Joyce and Catholicism, New York University Press, 1959; Matters of Style, Bobbs-Merrill, 1967; The Irrelevant English Teacher, Temple University Press, 1972; Prejudice and Literature, Temple University Press, 1976. Contributor to Nation, New Republic, and professional journals. Book review editor of Journal of General Education, 1960-67; member of editorial advisory committee of PMLA, 1970-74.

SIDELIGHTS: Morse told CA that to the extent that the establishment depends on the inarticulacy of the governed, good writing is inherently subversive, which is why many students never learn to write well.

* * *

MORTON, Louis 1913-1976

December 30, 1913—February 12, 1976; American military historian, editor, and educator. Obituaries: New York Times, February 14, 1976; Washington Post, February 15, 1976; AB Bookman's Weekly, April 12, 1976.

* * *

MOSCOTTI, Albert D(ennis) 1920-

PERSONAL: Born September 14, 1920, in Atlantic City, N.J.; son of Anthony Denis (in the hotel business) and Amy (Wilson) Moscotti. Education: New Jersey State Teachers College, Montclair (now Montclair State College), B.A. (cum laude), 1942; University of Michigan, M.A., 1947; Yale University, Ph.D., 1950. Home: 4237 Pahoa Ave., Honolulu, Hawaii 96816. Office: Asian Studies Program, University of Hawaii, Honolulu, Hawaii 96822.

CAREER: U.S. Department of State, Washington, D.C., foreign service officer in Washington, D.C., 1949-52, Bangkok, 1952-54, 1955, 1957, Karachi, 1957-59, Madras, 1960-62, Washington, D.C., 1962-66, Kuala Lumpur, 1966-68, and Washington, D.C., 1968-70; University of Hawaii, Honolulu, associate professor of Asian studies, 1970—, associate director of Overseas Career Program, 1970-73, director of Language and Area Center for Asian Studies, 1971-73. Military service: U.S. Army Air Forces, 1942-46; served in India-Burma theater; became captain.

MEMBER: Association for Asian Studies, American Association of University Professors, Honolulu Academy of Arts, Friends of the East West Center. Awards, honors: Rowec Award from Montclair State College, 1969.

WRITINGS: British Policy and the Nationalist Movement in Burma, 1917-1937, University Press of Hawaii, 1974. Contributor to Michigan Library News.

WORK IN PROGRESS: Research on the constitution of the Socialist Republic of the Union of Burma.

SIDELIGHTS: Moscotti has traveled in Japan, South Korea, Taiwan, Sri Lanka, Indonesia, the Philippines, Cambodia, South Vietnam, and Laos.

* * *

MOSES, Joel C(harles) 1944-

PERSONAL: Born January 23, 1944, in Toledo, Ohio; son of David and Rose (a secretary; maiden name, Levinson) Moses. Education: Beloit College, B.A. (cum laude), 1966; University of Wisconsin, Madison, M.A., 1968, Ph.D., 1972. Politics: "Liberal-radical." Religion: Jewish. Home: 263 North Hyland, No. 1, Ames, Iowa 50010. Office: Department of Political Science, 503 Ross Hall, Iowa State University, Ames, Iowa 50010.

CAREER: Iowa State University, Ames, instructor, 1971-72, assistant professor, 1973-76, associate professor of political science, 1976—. Member: American Political Science Association.

WRITINGS: Regional Party Leadership and Policy-Making in the U.S.S.R., Praeger, 1974; (contributor) Dorothy Atkinson, Alex Dallin, and Gail Lapidus, editors, Women in Russia, Stanford University Press, 1976; (contributor) George Breslauer and Paul Cocks, editors, The Communist Party and Soviet Society, Stanford University Press, 1976. Contributor to political science journals.

WORK IN PROGRESS: A study of the changing political role of women in the Soviet Union.

SIDELIGHTS: Moses conducted research in the Soviet Union in 1970 and 1976. He writes: "Following a well-established tradition in Western scholarship, I have been concerned as a political scientist with the sources of continuity and change in the Soviet political system. My research has primarily focused upon the Soviet Communist Party as the pivotal agent of change and adaptation to newly emerging demands for political participation in the Soviet Union."

AVOCATIONAL INTERESTS: Tennis, basketball, classical music.

BIOGRAPHICAL/CRITICAL SOURCES: Perspective, March, 1975; Soviet Studies, January, 1976; Western Political Quarterly, March, 1976.

* * *

MOSS, Cynthia J(ane) 1940-

PERSONAL: Born July 24, 1940, in Ossining, N.Y.; daughter of Julian B. (a newspaper publisher) and Lillian (Drion) Moss. Education: Smith College, B.A., 1962. Home and office address: P.O. Box 48177, Nairobi, Kenya. Agent: Wendy Weil, Julian Bach Literary Agency, 3 East 48th St., New York, N.Y. 10017.

CAREER: Newsweek, New York, N.Y., reporter and researcher, 1964-68; full-time research assistant studying elephant behavior and ecology in Manyara, East Africa, 1968; assistant to veterinary researchers in Nairobi, Kenya, 1969; research assistant to environmental physiologist on the Athi Plains, Kenya, 1970, and in Tsavo National Park, Kenya, 1970; free-lance journalist, 1970-71; Wildlife News, Washington, D.C., editor, 1971—. Research assistant in Amboseli, Kenya, 1972-75. Member: East African Natural History Society. Awards, honors: African Wildlife Leadership Foundation grant, 1975.

WRITINGS: Portraits in the Wild: Behaviour Studies of

East African Mammals, Houghton, 1975. Author of research report used in making the film "The African Elephant," for Cinema Center Films, 1969. Contributor to popular magazines, including *Smithsonian* and *Ms.*

WORK IN PROGRESS: Research on the social behavior of elephants in Amboseli National Park, Kenya, with publications expected to result.

AVOCATIONAL INTERESTS: Camping in wild parts of East Africa; horseback riding on the Athi plains.

* * *

MOSS, Walter (Gerald) 1938-

PERSONAL: Born April 20, 1938, in Cincinnati, Ohio; son of Walter Benjamin (a press mechanic) and Alvina (Meibers) Moss; married Nancy Pierce, September 7, 1963; children: Jennifer, Thomas, Daniel. *Education:* Xavier University, Cincinnati, Ohio, B.S. (honors), 1960; Georgetown University, Ph.D., 1968. *Home:* 208 Doty, Ann Arbor, Mich. 48103. *Office:* Department of History and Philosophy, Eastern Michigan University, Ypsilanti, Mich. 48197.

CAREER: Wheeling College, Wheeling, W.Va., instructor, 1967-68, assistant professor of history, 1968-70; Eastern Michigan University, Ypsilanti, assistant professor, 1970-74, associate professor of history, 1974—, executive director of Presidential Commission on the Future of Eastern Michigan University, 1975-76. Research associate at Case Western Reserve University, 1975-76; project director of Southeastern Michigan Consortium on Gerontology and the Humanities, 1973-75; evaluator for National Endowment for the Humanities, 1973—. Member of board of directors of Greater Wheeling Community Development Council, 1968-70. Consultant to National Council on Aging, 1975-76. *Military service:* U.S. Army, 1960-62; became first lieutenant.

MEMBER: American Historical Association, American Association for the Advancement of Slavic Studies, American Association of University Professors, Common Cause, Alpha Sigma Nu. *Awards, honors:* National Endowment for the Humanities grants, 1973-75.

WRITINGS: (Editor with Gordon Moss, and contributor) *Growing Old,* Pocket Books, 1975; *Aging in Humanistic Perspective* (booklet), Eastern Michigan University, 1975, revised edition published as *Humanistic Perspectives on Aging,* Institute of Gerontology, Wayne State University and University of Michigan, 1976.

Author of script, "Aging and the American Experience," for television presentation in United States and abroad. Contributor of articles and reviews to Slavic studies journals and to *Choice.*

WORK IN PROGRESS: Research for *Death and Immortality in Russian Thought, 1825-1929;* a biography of Vladimir Soloviev, nineteenth-century Russian philosopher, poet, religious thinker, and social critic; an essay on aging and death in the thought of Turgenev and Chekhov.

SIDELIGHTS: Moss writes: "One of my principal motivations has been the belief that individually and socially we are presented with continuing opportunities for humanistic growth and development, and that we are obliged to foster such growth. I therefore have a positive view of aging, for it can be synonymous with growing." *Avocational interests:* Playing sports (especially basketball and tennis) and music (guitar and harmonica), reading.

MOWRER, Lilian Thomson

PERSONAL: Born in London, England; daughter of Octavious Leopold and Elizabeth Jane (Green) Thomson; married Edgar Ansel Mowrer (a journalist), February 8, 1916; children: Diana Jane (Mrs. Jean Beliard). *Education:* Attended Sorbonne, University of Paris, 1907-08, University of Liverpool, 1911-13, and Sapienza, Rome, 1920-22. *Home:* Wonalancet, N.H. 03897. *Agent:* Herbert von Thal, London Management, 235-241 Regent St., London W1A 2JT, England.

CAREER: Writer on world affairs and drama critic. Chairman of Women's Action Committee for Lasting Peace, Washington, D.C. chapter, 1943-49. *Member:* Pen and Brush, English-Speaking Union, American Newspaper Women's Club, Women in Communications, Institute of Contemporary Arts, Washington Art Centre Association (vice-chairman and board member, 1942—), Marquis Biographical Library Society (board member and trustee, 1968-70). *Awards, honors:* Decorated by Italian Government, 1918, for Red Cross activities.

WRITINGS: Journalist's Wife, Morrow, 1937; *Arrest and Exile,* Morrow, 1940; *Rip Tide of Aggression,* Morrow, 1942; *Concerning France,* Union for Democratic Action Educational Fund, 1944; *The United States and World Relations,* Harper, 1950; *The Indomitable John Scott,* Farrar, Straus, 1960; *I've Seen It Happen Twice,* Devin-Adair, 1969; (with husband, Edgar A. Mowrer) *Umano and the Price of Lasting Peace,* Philosophical Library, 1973. Contributor of numerous articles to popular magazines.

SIDELIGHTS: Lilian Mowrer married foreign correspondent Edgar Ansel Mowrer in 1916 and left England immediately for Rome, where they lived for eight years. Assignments following in Germany, France, Russia, and Central Europe during the late 1920's and the 1930's allowed her and her husband to watch the turbulent era between the wars firsthand. In 1940 they left Paris just two days before the Germans marched in. Her first book, a best seller, was translated into four languages, and *Rip Tide of Aggression,* an outline of World War II, was required reading in freshman courses at Harvard University. She lectures frequently and appears on various radio and television programs. She spent part of the summer of 1972 in Italy gathering material for newspaper feature articles on music festivals and for research on *Umano.*

AVOCATIONAL INTERESTS: Music, art, skiing, swimming, walking.

* * *

MOYLES, R(obert) Gordon 1939-

PERSONAL: Born June 5, 1939, in Newfoundland, Canada; married Ada K. Brown; children: Robert, Kathy, Susan. *Education:* Memorial University of Newfoundland, B.A. (education), 1962, B.A. (honors), 1965, M.A., 1967; University of London, Ph.D., 1969. *Home:* 16011 103rd Ave., Edmonton, Alberta, Canada T5P OP7. *Office:* Department of English, University of Alberta, Edmonton, Alberta, Canada.

CAREER: University of Alberta, Edmonton, associate professor of English literature, 1969—, associate chairman of department of English, 1975—. *Member:* Canadian Association of University Teachers, Association of Canadian University Teachers of English. *Awards, honors:* Canada Council awards, 1967-69, 1974-75.

WRITINGS: (Contributor) Carl F. Klinck, editor, *Literary*

History of Canada, University of Toronto Press, 1965, revised edition, 1976; *English-Canadian Literature: A Student Guide and Annotated Bibliography,* Athabascan Publishing, 1972; *"Complaints Is Many and Various, But the Odd Divil Likes It": Nineteenth-Century Views of Newfoundland,* Peter Martin Associates, 1975; *English-Canadian Literature to 1900,* Gale, 1976. Associate editor of *Modernist Studies.*

WORKS IN PROGRESS: An official history of the Salvation Army in Canada; a book on Edward Capell, the nineteenth-century editor of works by Shakespeare and Milton; editing Eben McAdam's diary of a trip to the Klondike, 1898-99.

AVOCATIONAL INTERESTS: "Fly-fishing with a Silver Doctor appetizingly skimming the surface of an inland British Columbia Lake."

* * *

MUELLER, Claus 1941-

PERSONAL: Born July 23, 1941, in Berlin, Germany; came to the United States in 1964; son of Wilhelm (a secret service agent) and Dorothea (Milsch) Mueller; married second wife, Martha A. Link (a flight attendant), June 5, 1976. *Education:* University of Cologne, B.A., 1964; New School for Social Research, M.A., 1966, Ph.D., 1970; also studied at Institut d'Etudes Politiques, 1966-67, and Ecole Pratique des Hautes Etudes, 1968-69. *Home:* 420 East 64th St., No. W2H, New York, N.Y. 10021. *Office:* Department of Sociology, Hunter College of the City University of New York, 695 Park Ave., New York, N.Y. 10021.

CAREER: City College of the City University of New York, New York City, adjunct lecturer in sociology, summer, 1968; Hunter College of the City University of New York, New York City, adjunct assistant professor, 1970-71, assistant professor, 1971-74, associate professor of sociology, 1974—. Has been interviewed on Canadian Broadcasting Corp. and "Voice of America." Has had group shows of videotapes at Artists' Space.

MEMBER: Institut International de Sociologie, International Beaux Arts Society (honorary member), American Sociological Association, Association of Independent Video and Filmmakers, Center for Inter-American Relations, Experimental Television Cooperative, Special Citizens Futures Unlimited (honorary board member). *Awards, honors:* French Government fellowship, 1966-67.

WRITINGS: (Contributor) Peter Dreitzel, editor, *Recent Sociology II,* Macmillan, 1970; (contributor) Dorothy Flapan, editor, *American Social Institutions,* Behavioral Publications, 1972; (contributor) C. C. Conway and Nelson Foote, editors, *Social Institutions,* Kendall/Hunt, 1973; *The Politics of Communication: A Study in the Political Sociology of Language, Socialization, and Legitimation,* Oxford University Press, 1973. Author of scripts for Manhattan Television broadcasts, 1974—; producer of videotapes. Reviewer for Random House, 1974-75; consultant to Herder & Herder, 1971-72.

WORK IN PROGRESS: Temporary Man, on identity problems in contemporary society, for Oxford University Press; *Crosscurrent,* a historical novel about Berlin and Paris in the late 1930's and early 1940's; research on the psychopathology of the family and the impact of children's television.

SIDELIGHTS: Mueller writes: "Underlying my academic and fictional writing is a strong biographical concern. I hope to explore and clarify the world in and around me."

BIOGRAPHICAL/CRITICAL SOURCES: Cable TV World, September 27, 1975; *Psychology Today,* July, 1976.

* * *

MUELLER, Virginia 1924-

PERSONAL: Born March 22, 1924, in Sheboygan, Wis.; daughter of Arno and Cora (Hoogstra) Kernen; married Walter A. Mueller (a teacher), July 20, 1946; children: Linda (Mrs. Jerome Medlin), Christine (Mrs. Reed Simon), Walter David, David John. *Education:* Attended Rhinelander School of Art (University of Wisconsin Extension); additional study through Institute of Children's Literature. *Home address:* Route 1, Glenbeulah, Wis. 53023.

CAREER: State of Wisconsin, stenographer in Sheboygan, 1967-70, typist in Plymouth, 1970-75; writer, 1975—. *Member:* Society of Children's Book Writers.

WRITINGS—Juveniles: *Noises and Sounds,* Columbia Broadcasting System, 1968; *The King's Invitation,* Concordia, 1968; *The Secret Journey,* Concordia, 1968; *What Is Faith?,* Standard Publishing, 1969; *The Silly Skyscraper,* Concordia, 1970; *Who Is Your Neighbor?,* Standard Publishing, 1973; *Clem, the Clumsy Camel,* Concordia, 1974.

WORK IN PROGRESS: Jenny's Bargain, a juvenile.

AVOCATIONAL INTERESTS: Collecting antiques, flower and vegetable gardening, visiting historical sites, quilting, reading.

* * *

MUKHERJEE, Meenakshi 1937-

PERSONAL: Born August 3, 1937, in Calcutta, India; daughter of Basanta K. (a lawyer) and Parul (Chakrabarty) Banerjee; married Sujit Mukherjee (a writer), January 15, 1959; children: Rukmini, Rohini (daughters). *Education:* Patna University, B.A., 1956, M.A., 1958; University of Pennsylvania, M.A., 1962; Poona University, Ph.D., 1969. *Home:* C-123 Greater Kailash, New Delhi 110048, India. *Office:* Department of English, Lady Shri Ram College, University of Delhi, Lajpatnagar, New Delhi 110024, India.

CAREER: Patna University, Patna, India, lecturer in English literature, 1958-60; State University of New York College at Geneseo, lecturer in English literature, 1962-63; Ferguson College, Poona, India, lecturer in English literature, 1967-70; University of Delhi, Lady Shri Ram College, New Delhi, India, lecturer in English literature, 1971—.

WRITINGS: The Twice Born Fiction: Themes and Techniques in Indian Writing in English, Heinemann, 1971, 2nd edition, 1974; (translator from Bengali) Lokehath Bhattachenya, *The Virgin Fish of Babughat* (novel), Arnold-Heinemann, 1975; (translator from Bengali, with husband, Sujit Mukherjee) Nirendranath Chakrabarti, *The Naked King and Other Poems,* Writers Workshop (Calcutta, India), 1975; (editor) *Let's Go Home and Other Stories,* Orient Longman, 1976; (editor) *Considerations,* Allied Publishers (Delhi, India), 1976. Contributor of translations and articles to magazines. Editor of *Vagartha* (literary journal), 1973—.

WORK IN PROGRESS: A book, in English, on the Indian novel from 1850 to the present, with a sociological approach.

* * *

MULHEARN, John 1932-

PERSONAL: Born March 16, 1932, in England; came to the United States in 1967, naturalized citizen, 1974; son of John Gerard (an engineer) and Evelyn (Black) Mulhearn; married

Josephine Weaver (an artist), November 22, 1970. *Education:* Liverpool College of Technology, diploma, 1954; Heythrop College, Oxford, B.A., 1960; University of Chicago, M.A., 1969. *Politics:* Democrat. *Religion:* Roman Catholic. *Home:* 4615 North Park Ave., #819, Chevy Chase, Md. 20015. *Office:* Central Office, Veterans Administration, Washington, D.C. 20420.

CAREER: Joint Commission on Accreditation of Hospitals, Chicago, Ill., director of research, 1970-75; Veterans Administration, Central Office, Washington, D.C., acting director of Health Care Review Service, 1976—.

WRITINGS: (With Gayle Momeny) *The Psychiatric Hospital Today: A Quality Profile,* Ballinger, 1976.

WORK IN PROGRESS: Health Care: The Limits of Quality (tentative title); *The Fringe* (possible title), a novel.

SIDELIGHTS: Mulhearn writes: "My present interests are in working toward a reorganization of the nation's health care resources to effect a more efficient distribution of these resources and easier accessibility in areas where there is a major problem. My work with the Veterans Administration enables me to experiment with various models of delivery systems for health care." *Avocational interests:* Reading and writing poetry, music, ballet, books, visual arts.

*   *   *

MULLIGAN, Robert S(mith)   1941-

PERSONAL: Born July 17, 1941, in La Porte, Ind.; son of Robert H. and Almira (a teacher; maiden name, Smith) Mulligan. *Education:* Indiana University, B.S., 1963, M.S., 1968. *Politics:* Independent. *Religion:* "Undecided (but devout)." *Home:* 208 South Main St., Knox, Ind. 46534. *Office:* John Glenn High School, Walkerton, Ind. 46574.

CAREER: Teacher of English and director of drama at high school in Knox, Ind., 1963-67; John Glenn High School, Walkerton, Ind., English teacher, drama director, and chairman of department of English, 1968—. Instructor at Ancilla College, 1973-76. Area representative for American Institute for Foreign Study. Chairman of local mental health association, 1963-65. *Member:* International Thespian Society, National Education Association, National Council of Teachers of English, National Society of Literature and the Arts, Indiana State Teachers Association, Indiana Speech Association, Polk-Lincoln-Johnson Education Association (vice-president, 1974-75).

WRITINGS: (With John W. Pulver) *A Time for Madness* (three-act play; first produced in Walkerton, Ind., 1966), Samuel French, 1975. Also author of "Mary Queen of Scots" (three-act play).

WORK IN PROGRESS—Plays: "The Strauss Phase," a comedy of modern youth; "Sun Stain," on the early adult years of Shakespeare; "Wind Song," on the fall of Troy.

SIDELIGHTS: Mulligan writes: "I have spent the past eight summers supervising groups of area high school students on six-week study and travel programs at major campuses throughout Europe and the Soviet Union. During these tours, as well as in additional foreign travel of my own, I have developed a great love for Ireland, Scotland, England, and in the antiquities of Ancient Greece, Rome, and Egypt. My play, 'Mary, Queen of Scots,' was researched and written during two summers spent at the University of St. Andrews and University of Aberdeen in Scotland, and 'Wind Song' was conceived and written during two summers spent studying 'Classical Civilizations' with the Hellenic-American Union in Rome, Egypt, Greece, and the nearby

islands. 'Sun Stain' has grown from my great interest in Shakespearean literature and from a dozen trips to England, one of which was spent studying 'The Performing Arts' at Goldsmith College in London. Still ahead are plays on modern Irish and Russian themes which have been 'growing' as a result of experiences in those countries.

"The opportunity to teach and travel with today's teenagers has provided me with certain insights into what makes this very special group of people 'tick,' and they encouraged me to attempt to demonstrate this dramatically by creating humorous examinations of the adolescent society in such plays as 'A Time for Madness' and 'The Strauss Phase.'"

*   *   *

MULLINS, Carolyn J(ohns)   1940-

PERSONAL: Born April 29, 1940, in Worcester, Mass.; daughter of Corydon Thayer and Elizabeth (Eddy) Johns; married Nicholas Creed Mullins (a professor), June 21, 1962; children: Nicholas Johns, Robert Corydon, Nancy Carolyn. *Education:* Emory University, student, 1958-59; Cornell University, A.B., 1962; Vanderbilt University, graduate study, 1966; Andover Newton Theological School, M.R.E. (cum laude), 1967. *Politics:* Democrat. *Religion:* Methodist. *Home and office:* 2006 Sussex Dr., Bloomington, Ind. 47401.

CAREER: Secretary, 1962-66; free-lance manuscript editor and ghostwriter in the social and behavioral sciences, 1967—. Editorial consultant to Indiana University's Institute of Social Research, 1972—.

WRITINGS: Writing and Publishing in the Behavioral Sciences, Wiley, 1977.

Editor: Charles A. Dailey, *Entrepreneurial Management,* McGraw, 1971; Dailey, *The Assessment of Lives,* Jossey-Bass, 1971; Nicholas C. Mullins, *The Art of Theory,* Harper, 1971; N. C. Mullins, *Science: Some Sociological Perspectives,* Bobbs-Merrill, 1973; (and contributor) N. C. Mullins, *Theories and Theory Groups in Contemporary American Sociology,* Harper, 1973; Whitney Pope, *Suicide: A Classic Analyzed,* University of Chicago Press, 1976; Corydon T. Johns, *Taking Statements,* National Association of Independent Insurance Adjustors, in press; Dailey and Ann Madsen, *Good Judgment: The Compassionate Science,* McGraw, in press. Contributor to social and behavioral science journals, including *Sociological Quarterly.*

WORK IN PROGRESS: A Manual for Typists of Scholarly Manuscripts.

*   *   *

MURDOCK, Kenneth Ballard   1895-1975

PERSONAL: Born June 22, 1895, in Boston, Mass.; son of Harold and Mary (Lawson) Murdock; married Laurette Eustis Potts, June 24, 1922; married second wife, Eleanor Eckhart McLaughlin, January 1, 1942; children: (first marriage) Mary Laurette, Sara; (second marriage—stepsons) Charles C. McLaughlin, Donald H. McLaughlin, Jr. *Education:* Harvard University, A.B., 1916, A.M., 1921, Ph.D., 1923. *Religion:* Episcopalian. *Residence:* Boston, Mass.

CAREER: Harvard University, Cambridge, Mass., instructor, 1923-26, assistant professor, 1926-30, associate professor, 1930-32, professor of English and Francis Lee Higginson Professor of English Literature, 1932-64, professor emeritus, 1964-75, director of Center for Italian Renaissance Culture, 1961-64, dean of faculty of arts and sciences, 1931-36, master of Leverett House, 1931-41. Lecturer at Scandinavian universities, 1946; visiting professor at University of Oslo and University of Uppsala, 1949, and University of Copenhagen, 1953; Lord Northcliffe lecturer in London, 1951. Trustee of American Scandinavian Foundation. *Military service:* U.S. Navy, 1918-19; became ensign.

MEMBER: American Academy of Arts and Sciences, American Antiquarian Society, Modern Language Association of America, Modern Humanities Research Association, American Historical Association, Society of Mayflower Descendants, American Philosophical Society, Societas Scientiarum Finnica, Colonial Society of Massachusetts (president, 1938-45), Massachusetts Historical Society, Century Club, Somerset Club, Harvard Club, Odd Volumes Club, Tavern Club. *Awards, honors:* Honorary degrees include Litt.D. from Middlebury College, 1930, L.H.D. from Trinity College, 1932, and University of Vermont, 1938, LL.D. from Bucknell University, 1933, Fil.D. from University of Uppsala, 1950, and D.Litt. from Harvard University, 1960; decorated Knight of Order of the North Star, 1950.

WRITINGS: The Portraits of Increase Mather, with Some Notes on Thomas Johnson, an English Mezzotinter, privately printed, 1924; *Increase Mather: The Foremost American Puritan,* Harvard University Press, 1925, Russell, 1966; (editor) *Handkerchiefs from Paul: Being Pious and Consolatory Verses of Puritan Massachusetts,* Harvard University Press, 1927, Garrett Publications, 1970; *The Sun at Noon: Three Biographical Sketches,* Macmillan, 1939; *Literature and Theology in Colonial New England,* Harvard University Press, 1949, Greenwood Press, 1970; (editor) Michael Wigglesworth, *The Day of Doom,* Russell, 1966; (editor) Cotton Mather, *Great Works of Christ in America,* Volume I, Harvard University Press, in press.

Editor of *Selections from Cotton Mather,* 1926; *A Leaf of Grass from Shady Hill,* 1928; Cotton Mather, *Manuductio ad Ministerium,* 1938; (with F. O. Matthiessen) *The Notebooks of Henry James,* 1947; *Ett Kvinnoportraett,* 1947; *The Literature of the American People,* Part I, (edited by A. H. Quinn), 1951. Contributor to *Commonwealth History of Massachusetts* and *Encyclopaedia Britannica.* Publisher and editor of *New England Quarterly,* 1928-38, 1939-62, *American Literature,* 1929-38, 1939-49, and *Harvard Gazette,* 1929-31.

OBITUARIES: Publishers Weekly, December 1, 1975; *AB Bookman's Weekly,* December 8, 1975.*

(Died November 14, 1975, in Newton, Mass.)

* * *

MURO, Diane Patricia 1940-

PERSONAL: Born November 10, 1940, in Tylertown, Miss.; daughter of Fain Patton (a contractor) and Louise (a real estate broker; maiden name, Brumfield) Cochran; married A. L. Muro (a clergyman), May 22, 1959; children: David, Stephen, Mark, Matthew. *Education:* Attended San Diego State University, 1958, and California State University, Sacramento, 1974—. *Politics:* Democrat. *Religion:* American Baptist. *Home:* 2570 Warrego Way, Sacramento, Calif. 95826.

CAREER: Police officer in Davis, Calif., 1964-66; deputy sheriff in Santa Ana, Calif., 1966-70; Pacifica Police Department, Pacifica, Calif., police officer, 1972-74; writer, 1974—. *Member:* California Writers Club.

WRITINGS: Woman on Patrol, Judson, 1976. Contributor to magazines, including *Lady's Circle, True West, California Highway Patrolman,* and to *National Enquirer.*

WORK IN PROGRESS: Police Careers for Women; A New Marriage Lifestyle, with husband, Al Muro, "a Christian marriage book . . . using the idea of androgyny."

SIDELIGHTS: Diane Muro writes: "I am particularly interested in the changing roles of men and women and how these changes can help them to better relate to one another and experience personal growth. For example, a successfl police officer must have the masculine qualities of aggressiveness and objectivity as well as the feminine qualities of compassion and tenderness. Men and women working together or sharing together as husband and wife help each other to develop both sides of their natures and become whole persons."

* * *

MURRAY, Jim 1919-

PERSONAL: Born December 29, 1919, in Hartford, Conn.; son of James Patrick (a pharmacist) and Mary (O'Connell) Murray; married Geraldine Norma Brown, October 20, 1945; children: Theodore, Anthony, Pamela, Eric. *Education:* Trinity College, Hartford, Conn., B.A. *Politics:* "Monarchist." *Residence:* Los Angeles, Calif. *Office:* Los Angeles Times Syndicate, Times-Mirror Sq., Los Angeles, Calif. 90053.

CAREER: New Haven Register, New Haven, Conn., reporter, 1943; *Los Angeles Examiner,* Los Angeles, Calif., reporter, 1944-48; *Time,* New York, N.Y., reporter, 1948-61; *Sports Illustrated,* New York City, co-founder and writer, 1954-61; Los Angeles Times Syndicate, Los Angeles, Calif., author of "Jim Murry" column, syndicated to about one hundred-eighty newspapers, 1961—.

WRITINGS: The Best of Jim Murray, Doubleday, 1965; *The Sporting World of Jim Murray,* Doubleday, 1968.

* * *

MURRAY, Philip 1924-

PERSONAL: Born September 8, 1924, in Philadelphia, Pa.; son of Philip J. (a salesman) and Margaret V. (Boyle) Murray. *Education:* St. Joseph's College, Overbrook, Pa., B.A., 1947; Columbia University, M.A., 1955. *Religion:* Roman Catholic. *Home:* 375 Riverside Dr., New York, N.Y. 10025.

CAREER: City College of the City University of New York, New York, N.Y., lecturer in English, 1955-56; Brooklyn College of the City University of New York, Brooklyn, N.Y., lecturer in English, 1956-57; Hofstra University, Hempstead, N.Y., instructor in English, 1957-61; poet, 1961—. *Awards, honors:* Approach prize, 1965, for poem "Marcus Aurelius"; Union League prize from *Poetry,* 1971, for set of poems, "T'ang"; Star Award from *Kansas City Times,* 1972, for poem "Adolescence."

WRITINGS: Poems after Martial, Wesleyan University Press, 1967.

Work has been anthologized in *Columbia University Forum Anthology,* edited by Peter Spackman and Lee Ambrose, Atheneum, 1968; *Lyric Poems,* edited by Coralie Howard, F. Watts, 1968; *A Book of Animal Poems,* edited by William Cole, Viking, 1973.

Contributor of poems and translations to literary journals, including *Modern Poetry Studies, American Poetry Review, Andover Review, American Scholar, Poetry, North Stone Review,* and *Hudson Review.*

WORK IN PROGRESS: A book of poems; *Late Latin Lyrics; A Garland of Troubador Lyrics.*

SIDELIGHTS: Murray writes: "With Scotch and Irish forebears, loyal and imaginative parents, an exemplary education, extensive travel abroad, and generous leisure time, I feel I have had uncommon advantages in leading a poet's life, and although I have rarely known just where my next peach melba was coming from, I have managed to get a great number of poems and Latin translations written and published in a wide variety of magazines over several decades. In my view, the aesthetic model for poems is Apollo, not Dionysus. But the matter is still under dispute.

"The influence of the classics on my work as a poet has grown steadily over the years. The root of the matter lies in my Catholic education at the capable, knowledgeable and dedicated hands of Christian Brothers and Jesuit fathers. Underlying every subject, from biology to rhetoric, there was a reverence for excellence and harmony, for diligence and patience that developed for me in literary channels, upon deeper acquaintance with life, to enjoyment, admiration, and finally as a poet, to emulation."

AVOCATIONAL INTERESTS: Travel, book-hunting, "watching the Nativity scene on my Russian icon."

*   *   *

MURRAY, Sonia Bennett   1936-

PERSONAL: Born May 15, 1936, in Norfolk, England; came to the United States in 1957, naturalized citizen, 1961; daughter of Marcus Warburton (a theatrical producer) and Ruth Lillian (a variety artiste; maiden name, Clarke) Bennett; married Gilbert Lafayette Murray (a landlord), June 25, 1955; children: Gilbert Lafayette III, Keith David, Kathryn Sonia. *Education:* Attended Carlton College and University of Mississippi. *Politics:* Republican. *Religion:* Agnostic. *Home:* 1609 Oaklawn Pl., Biloxi, Miss. 39530.

CAREER: Airway Apartments and Trailer Court, Biloxi, Miss., manager, 1959-65, co-owner, 1965—.

WRITINGS: Shell Life and Shell Collecting, Sterling, 1969; *Seashell Collectors' Handbook and Identifier,* Sterling, 1975.

WORK IN PROGRESS: Season of Growth, a novel.

SIDELIGHTS: Sonia Murray writes: "My interest in mollusks was whetted as a child on English beaches and honed through years of travel in Europe, making possible collecting from the North Sea to Morocco and the Bosphorus." Her husband took the macrophotographs which illustrate her books.

*   *   *

MUSCHAMP, Thomas
See LLOYD-THOMAS, Catherine

*   *   *

MUSGRAVES, Don   1935-

PERSONAL: Born August 20, 1935, in Ducor, Calif.; son of Claude Everett (a salesman) and Ruby (Ogletree) Musgraves; married Loris Isaacs (a dietetic aide), August 31, 1957; children: Michael, Lynne, Tracy. *Education:* Attended Santa Ana College, 1956; Oklahoma State University, B.S., 1960; Southern California College, B.D., 1967. *Religion:* Christian. *Home:* 835 North Mallard St., #3, Orange, Calif. 92667. *Office:* Hollywood Lifeline, 1760 North Gower St., Hollywood, Calif. 90028.

CAREER: Melodyland Christian Center Church, Anaheim, Calif., youth counselor, 1967-69, director of Hotline Center,

1969-70; Action Center (for prevention of drug abuse), San Diego, Calif., director, 1971; M-2 Program (to help prison parolees), Hayward, Calif., field representative, 1971-72; Hollywood Lifeline, Hollywood, Calif., director, 1972—. *Military service:* U.S. Army, paratrooper, 1953-55.

WRITINGS: One More Time (spiritual), Bethany Fellowship, 1973.

WORK IN PROGRESS: Research for *Keys to Calming a Person in a Crisis—Without Drugs.*

*   *   *

MUSGROVE, Margaret Wynkoop   1943-

PERSONAL: Born November 19, 1943, in New Britain, Conn.; daughter of John T. (an electrician) and Margaret (Holden) Wynkoop; married George Gilbert (a coordinator of human resources), August 28, 1971; children: Taura Johnene, George Derek. *Education:* University of Connecticut, B.A., 1966; Central Connecticut State College, M.S., 1970; University of Massachusetts, doctoral study, 1972—. *Politics:* Democrat. *Religion:* Christian. *Home and office:* 130 Roger White Dr., New Haven, Conn. 06515.

CAREER: High school English teacher in Hartford, Conn., 1967-69, 1970; South Central Community College, New Haven, Conn., a counselor and teacher of English composition, 1971-72. English teacher at community school in Accra, Ghana, 1970. *Member:* Society of Children's Book Writers, League of Women Voters.

WRITINGS: Ashanti to Zulu: African Traditions (juvenile), Dial, 1976.

WORK IN PROGRESS: Tobacco Girl, on "growing up Negro in Plainville, U.S.A."

SIDELIGHTS: Margaret Musgrove writes: "The overt and covert racism in children's literature are insidious forces that must be overcome for the good of all children."

*   *   *

MUSKE, Carol   1945-

PERSONAL: Born December 17, 1945, in St. Paul, Minn.; daughter of William Howard (in real estate) and Elizabeth (Kuchera) Muske; married. *Education:* San Francisco State College (now University), M.A., 1970. *Home and office:* 211 East 18th St., New York, N.Y. 10003.

CAREER: Free Space (a writing program for women prisoners), New York, N.Y., director, 1973—. Instructor at New School for Social Research and New York University. *Awards, honors:* Dylan Thomas Poetry Award from New School for Social Research, 1973, for poem, "Swansong."

WRITINGS: Camouflage, University of Pittsburgh Press, 1975. Poems anthologized in *Eating the Menu,* edited by B. E. Taylor, W. C. Brown, 1974, and *The American Poetry Anthology,* edited by Daniel Halpern, Avon, 1975. Contributor of articles and reviews to *Ms., Oui,* and *Village Voice.* Assistant editor of *Antaeus,* 1972—.

WORK IN PROGRESS: A novel, *The Honey-Producers;* a travel guide for women.

AVOCATIONAL INTERESTS: Travel.

*   *   *

MYERS, Bernard S(amuel)   1908-

PERSONAL: Born May 4, 1908, in New York, N.Y.; son of Louis (a businessman) and Dora (Waxenberg) Myers; married Shirley Levene (an editor of art books), August 11,

1938; children: Peter Lewis, Lucie Ellen. *Education:* New York University, Sc.B. (cum laude), 1928, M.A., 1929, Ph.D., 1933; also attended the Sorbonne, University of Paris, summer, 1931. *Home:* 82 Willow St., Brooklyn Heights, N.Y. 11201. *Office:* Rizzoli International Publications, 712 Fifth Ave., New York, N.Y. 10019.

CAREER: New York University, New York City, lecturer in architecture, 1930-33, lecturer in education, 1930-43, 1945-48, instructor in fine arts, 1933-43; Rutgers University, New Brunswick, N.J., assistant professor of art history, 1946-47; University of Texas, Austin, guest professor of art history, 1948-50; New York University, lecturer in fine arts, 1951; City College of New York (now City College of the City University of New York), New York City, lecturer in fine arts, 1952-58; McGraw-Hill Book Co., New York City, editor-in-chief and manager of art books department, 1958-70, consultant, 1970-75; Rizzoli International Publications, New York City, publishing consultant, 1976—. Lecturer at Art Students League (New York City), 1946-48; visiting associate professor at University of Southern California, summer, 1948; visiting professor at University of Colorado, summer, 1951. Education director of National Committee for Art Appreciation, 1937-39; member of executive committee of Citizens' Committee for the Arts, 1940-43; member of New York City's National Art Week Committee, 1940-41; member of an advisory committee of Princeton University, 1969-75, and of art advisory committee of New York Health and Hospitals Corp., 1971—. Led summer art tours through Europe, 1934-36, 1947. *Member:* National Association of Museums, Institute of Fine Arts Alumni Association (New York University; president, 1974—), Phi Beta Kappa. *Awards, honors:* Bollingen Foundation grant, 1950-51; Rockefeller Foundation grant, 1953-56.

WRITINGS: (editor with H. E. Barnes and others, and contributor) *An Intellectual and Cultural History of the Western World,* Cordon, 1937, revised edition in three volumes, Dover, 1965; (editor and contributor) *Forty-Eight Famous Paintings* (portfolio with text), National Committee for Art Appreciation, 1938; (editor and contributor) *American Art Today* (portfolio with text), New York World's Fair, 1939; *The Pageant of Art* (listener's guide to accompany National Broadcasting Corp. program), Columbia University Press, 1940; (editor and contributor) *Roubillac, Eighteenth-Century Printmaker* (portfolio with text), Fischer, 1942; *Modern Art in the Making* (college text), McGraw, 1950, 2nd edition, 1959; *Fifty Great Artists,* Bantam, 1953; (editor and contributor) *Encyclopedia of Painting,* Crown, 1955, 3rd edition, 1970; *Mexican Painting in Our Time,* Oxford University Press, 1956; *Problems of the Younger American Artist,* City College Press, 1957; *Art and Civilization* (college text), McGraw, 1957, revised edition, 1967; *The German Expressionists,* Praeger, 1957; *Understanding the Arts* (college text), Holt, 1958, 3rd edition, 1977; (co-editor) *Dictionary of Twentieth Century Art,* McGraw, 1974.

Editor and contributor to portfolios for *Scribner's* (magazine) "American Painter's Series," 1938; general editor, with S. D. Myers, *McGraw-Hill Dictionary of Art,* five volumes, 1969. Contributor of articles and reviews to art magazines, to *Saturday Review,* and to newspapers. Consulting editor and contributor to *Encyclopedia of World Art,* 1959-69.

WORK IN PROGRESS: The Gifted Hand: A Selective History of Art.

SIDELIGHTS: Myers has traveled extensively throughout the world; his books have been published in Germany, Italy, France, Spain, and Yugoslavia. He writes that he is 'very much concerned by the tendency of younger people to forget that they were not the first to inhabit this planet—some feel that everything that came before them is not worth bothering with. Both as teacher and writer I am very much concerned with the backgrounds of culture, with the importance of tradition as it affects the present-day cultural world and, finally, with the possibility of our judging art as good or bad, effective or ineffective, a decent work of art or a failure.'

* * *

MYERS, Lonny 1922-

PERSONAL: Born November 9, 1922, in Hartford, Conn.; daughter of Rawdon Wright (an insurance executive) and Emily (Rulon-Miller) Myers; married Shu-Yung Wang (a plastic surgeon), October 23, 1949; children: Sharon, Susie, Sheila, Sherwood, Sandra. *Education:* Vassar College, B.A., 1944; University of Michigan, M.D., 1948. *Politics:* Liberal. *Home:* 333 East Ontario St., Chicago, Ill. 60611. *Office:* Midwest Population Center, 100 East Ohio St., Chicago, Ill. 60611.

CAREER: Anesthesiologist in private practice in Chicago, Ill., 1951-69; Midwest Population Center, Chicago, clinician and director of medical education, 1971—. Active in human rights campaigns, including Illinois Citizens for the Extension of Birth Control Services, 1961-65, and Illinois Citizens for the Medical Control of Abortion, beginning 1966. Instigator and active participant in national conferences and congresses on population control, sexual behavior, and related topics. *Member:* American Association of Sex Educators, Counselors and Therapists (chair-person of Midwest region). *Awards, honors:* Volunteer-of-the-year award from Chicago Planned Parenthood, 1963; Clarence Darrow Humanitarian Award, 1965; Hannah G. Soloman Award from National Council of Jewish Women, 1971.

WRITINGS: (With Hunter Leggitt) *Adultery and Other Private Matters,* Nelson-Hall, 1975.

SIDELIGHTS: Lonny Myers writes that her motivation is a "belief in responsible sex for recreation as opposed to sex for procreation as essential to human joy and environmental ecology."

* * *

NABHOLTZ, John R(obert) 1931-

PERSONAL: Born January 6, 1931, in Cleveland, Ohio; son of Lawrence N. (a golf professional) and Marguerite (Warman) Nabholtz. *Education:* Loyola University, Chicago, Ill., A.B., 1951; University of Chicago, M.A., 1952, Ph.D., 1961. *Politics:* Independent. *Religion:* Roman Catholic. *Home:* 6157 North Sheridan Rd., Chicago, Ill. 60660. *Office:* Department of English, Loyola University, Chicago, Ill. 60626.

CAREER: Cornell University, Ithaca, N.Y., instructor in English, 1959-63; University of Rochester, Rochester, N.Y., assistant professor of English, 1963-69; Loyola University, Chicago, Ill., associate professor of English, 1969—. *Member:* Modern Language Association of America, American Association of University Professors, Independent Voters of Illinois, Charles Lamb Society, Byron Society. *Awards, honors:* Fulbright fellow to United Kingdom, 1954-55.

WRITING—Editor: *Charles Lamb: Selected Essays,* AHM Publishing, 1967; *William Hazlitt: Selected Essays,* AHM Publishing, 1970; *William Hazlitt: Essay on the Prin-*

ciples of Human Action, Scholars Facsimiles & Reprints, 1969; *Prose of the British Romantic Movement,* Macmillan, 1974. Contributor to English journals.

WORK IN PROGRESS: A study of the rhetorical design of English Romantic prose.

*   *   *

NACHMAN, Gerald 1938-

PERSONAL: Born January 13, 1938, in Oakland, Calif.; son of Leonard C. (a salesman) and Isabel (Weil) Nachman; married Mary McGeachy (a film critic), September 3, 1966. *Education:* Merritt College, A.A., 1958; San Jose State University, B.A., 1960. *Politics:* Independent. *Religion:* Jewish. *Home:* 411 East 53rd St., New York, N.Y. 10022. *Agent:* Scott Meredith, 845 Third Ave., New York, N.Y. *Office: New York Daily News,* 220 East 42nd St., New York, N.Y. 10017.

CAREER: San Jose Mercury, San Jose, Calif., humor columnist and television critic, 1960-63; *New York Post,* New York City, feature writer, 1964-66; *Oakland Tribune,* Oakland, Calif., drama and film critic and columnist, 1966-71; *New York Daily News,* New York City, feature writer and television critic, 1972-73; humor columnist, 1973—. Adjunct professor of journalism, New York University, spring, 1976. *Awards, honors:* Page One Award, 1965, for humor piece in *New York Post;* Associated Press feature-writing award, 1974, for series, "The Partygoers."

WRITINGS: Playing House, Doubleday, 1977. Writer of thrice-weekly humor column appearing in *New York Daily News* and syndicated by Tribune-News syndicate. Contributor of articles to *Esquire, Newsweek, Penthouse, Saturday Review, TV Guide, Travel and Leisure,* and many other magazines and newspapers.

SIDELIGHTS: Nachman's fast rising popularity as a humor columnist is due, a great deal, to his versatility. Unlike most other humor columnists, he is as equally successful writing about politics as he is writing about social fashion. His column, roaming over a wide choice of targets, doesn't compete for the faithful of other columns but cultivates a readership of its own.

Nachman created the mythical Trendy family—Elsie and Fenton. They appeared among the marijuana set (without quite getting the slang right), celebrated their divorce with a reception at a massage parlor, and have remolded their lives through self-awareness sessions. His other creations include a home for pregnant wives who feel guilty defying zero population growth—its chief therapy is the film "Cheaper by the Dozen"—and Ye Olde Nostalgia Shoppe, which found so large a market that its inventory has dropped to back issues of *People* magazine. In order to come up with enough ideas like this to feed a thrice-weekly column, Nachman spends his days reading numerous magazines and newspapers, or harvesting ideas from the conversation at a cocktail party. The freedom to cover a wider range of topics puts pressure on Nachman because of the larger number of sources that must be scanned for ideas.

Nachman's style is as various as his subject matter. He may run one column as an interview with a fictious expert, another as a coy confession in the first person, and the third as if it were straight reporting. The alter ego of the reporter, however, is his greatest problem. Nachman muses, "sometimes I worry that half my readers don't know whether I'm being serious or not."

BIOGRAPHICAL/CRITICAL SOURCES: Newsweek, June 9, 1975; *Time,* August 23, 1976.

NAISMITH, Grace 1904-

PERSONAL: Born November 20, 1904, in Fort Collins, Colo.; daughter of A. I. and Nellie (Taylor) Akin; married John E. Naismith, 1922 (divorced); married Edward T. Pierce, 1943 (divorced); married John C. Devlin (a journalist), November 23, 1960; children: (first marriage) James Akin, Stuart D. *Education:* Attended William Woods College, University of Colorado, American University, and University of Denver. *Politics:* Independent. *Religion:* Presbyterian. *Home address:* Westview Lane, South Norwalk, Conn. 06854. *Office:* 51 East 42nd St., New York, N.Y. 10017.

CAREER: Reporter for *Rocky Mountain News,* 1929-30; U.S. Department of Agriculture, Washington, D.C., information and education specialist, 1936; *Reader's Digest,* Pleasantville, N.Y., associate editor, 1938-69, consulting editor, 1969-76; writer, 1976—. *Member:* National Association of Science Writers, American Society of Journalists and Authors (vice-president), Overseas Press Club (past governor), Woman Pays Club (president, 1975-77). *Awards, honors:* D.Sc. from William Woods College, 1969; award for health journalism from International Health Foundation, 1973.

WRITINGS: Hagar's Child, Macauley, 1934; *Private and Personal,* McKay, 1966. Author of column in *Overseas Press Club Bulletin.* Contributor to several dozen national magazines, including *Today's Health* and *New York Times Magazine,* and to newspapers. Editor of newsletter of American Society of Journalists and Writers.

WORK IN PROGRESS: A biography of Roger Tory Peterson (with husband, John C. Devlin), for Quadrangle.

SIDELIGHTS: Grace Naismith writes that she sold her first prize story to *Youth's Companion* at the age of ten. It was her first *Reader's Digest* article, on abortion, that led to her many medical pieces on birth control, infertility, venereal disease, feminine hygiene, menopause, and male and female sex problems, marriage, nervous breakdown, blindness, and emphysema, all topics of current widespread concern.

*   *   *

NAM, Charles B(enjamin) 1926-

PERSONAL: Born March 25, 1926, in Lynbrook, N.Y.; son of Samuel (a shopkeeper) and Yetta (a shopkeeper; maiden name, Huff) Nam; married Marjorie Lee Tallant (a college instructor), January 1, 1956; children: David Wallace, Rebecca Jane. *Education:* New York University, B.A., 1950; University of North Carolina, M.S., 1957, Ph.D., 1959. *Politics:* Independent Democrat. *Religion:* "Freethinker." *Home:* 820 Live Oak Plantation Rd., Tallahassee, Fla. 32303. *Office:* Center for the Study of Population, Institute for Social Research, Florida State University, Tallahassee, Fla. 32306.

CAREER: U.S. Bureau of the Census, Washington, D.C., statistician in Population Division, 1950-53; U.S. Air Force, Human Resources Research Institute, Montgomery, Ala., analytical statistician for manpower branch, 1953-54; U.S. Bureau of the Census, head of education statistics unit of Population Division, 1957-62, chief of education and social stratification branch, 1962-64; Florida State University, Tallahassee, professor of sociology and demography, 1964—, chairman of department of sociology, 1968-71, director of Center for the Study of Population, 1967—. Member-at-large of National Academy of Science's Division of Behavioral Science, 1968-70; member of grants panel of National Science Foundation, 1970-72, and research panel of National Institute of Child Health and Human Development's Center for Population Research, 1971—. Consultant to National Institutes of Health and to Organization for Economic Co-operation and Development. *Military service:* U.S. Army, 1943-46; became sergeant.

MEMBER: International Union for the Scientific Study of Population, Population Association of America (second vice-president), American Sociological Association, American Statistical Association, Southern Sociological Society (vice-president).

WRITINGS: (With John Folger) *Education of the American Population,* U.S. Government Printing Office, 1967; (editor and contributor) *Population and Society,* Houghton, 1968; (contributor) Henry S. Shryock and Jacob S. Siegel, editors, *Methods and Materials of Demography,* U.S. Government Printing Office, 1972; (with Susan Gustavus) *Population: The Dynamics of Demographic Change,* Houghton, 1976. Contributor to sociology journals. Editor of *Demography,* 1973-75.

WORK IN PROGRESS: A book integrating research on how children and youth develop ideas about population conditions; research on the effects of socioeconomic status on life expectancy, and research on population factors related to changes in occupational status.

SIDELIGHTS: Nam writes: "The general public still lacks good comprehension of the causes and consequences of population changes. Writing which is perceived as scientific turns many people off. I have toyed with the idea of writing a mystery novel in which one of the key figures is a demographer who keeps injecting demographic insights into his conversations." *Avocational interests:* Travel.

* * *

NANDY, Pritish 1947-

PERSONAL: Born January 15, 1947, in Bhagalpur, Bihar, India; son of Satish Chandra (a schoolteacher) and Prafulla Nandy; married Rina Mumtaz, January 17, 1966 (divorced); children: Teesta, Kushan. *Education:* Educated in Calcutta. *Politics:* None. *Religion:* None. *Home:* 5 Pearl Rd., Park Circus, Calcutta 700017, India.

CAREER: Guest Keen Williams Ltd., Calcutta, India, publicity and public relations manager, 1969—. Communications specialist and photojournalist; industrial writer; poet.

WRITINGS—Poetry: Of Gods and Olives, Writers Workshop (Calcutta), 1967; *On Either Side of Arrogance,* Writers Workshop (Calcutta), 1968; *I Hand You in Turn My Nebbuk Wreath,* Dialogue Publications, 1968; *From the Outer Bank of the Brahmaputra,* New Rivers Press, 1969; *Masks to Be Interpreted in Terms of Messages,* Writers Workshop (Calcutta), 1970; *Madness Is the Second Stroke,* Dialogue Publications, 1971; *The Poetry of Pritish Nandy,* Oxford (Calcutta), 1973; *Dhritarashtra Downtown: Zero,* Dialogue Publications, 1974; *Riding the Midnight River,* Arnold Heinemann, 1975; *Lonesong Street,* Poets Press, 1975.

Editor of anthologies: *Indian Poetry in English: 1947-1972,* Oxford (Calcutta), 1972; *Indian Poetry in English Today,* Sterling, 1973; *Modern Indian Poetry,* Heinemann, 1974; *Bengali Poetry Today,* Michigan State University, 1974.

Translator: *The Complete Poems of Samar Sen,* Writers Workshop (Calcutta), 1970; *Subhas Mukhopadhyay: Poet of the People,* Dialogue Publications, 1970; *Poems from Bangladesh,* Perspective Publications, 1971; *The Prose Poems of Lokenath Bhattacharya,* Dialogue Publications, 1971; *Bangladesh: Voice of a New Nation,* Lyrebird, 1972; *Shesh Lekha: The Last Poems of Rabindranath Tagore,* Dialogue Publications, 1973; *The Songs of Mirabai,* Arnold Heinemann, 1975; *The Poetry of Kaifi Azmi,* Poets Press, 1975; *The Flaming Giraffe: Poems by Sunil Gangopadhyay,* Poets Press, 1975.

Also author of "Rites for a Plebeian Statue," a verse play, Writers Workshop (Calcutta), 1969. Editor of *Dialogue India;* poetry editor of *Illustrated Weekly of India.*

* * *

NAPIER, Mary
See WRIGHT, (Mary) Patricia

* * *

NATHAN, Andrew J(ames) 1943-

PERSONAL: Born April 3, 1943, in New York, N.Y. *Education:* Harvard University, B.A. (summa cum laude), 1963, M.A., 1965, Ph.D., 1971. *Home:* 560 Riverside Dr., Apt. 5-P, New York, N.Y. 10027. *Office:* East Asian Institute, Columbia University, New York, N.Y. 10027.

CAREER: University of Michigan, Ann Arbor, lecturer in history, winter, 1971; Columbia University, New York, N.Y., assistant professor, 1971-75, associate professor of political science, 1975—. *Awards, honors:* Guggenheim fellowship, 1973-74; fellowship from joint committee on contemporary China of American Council of Learned Societies and Social Science Research Council, 1973-74.

WRITINGS: A History of the China International Famine Relief Commission (monograph), Harvard University East Asian Research Center, 1965; *Modern China, 1840-1972: An Introduction to Sources and Research Aids,* Michigan Center for Chinese Studies, 1973; *Peking Politics, 1918-1923: Factionalism and the Failure of Constitutionalism,* University of California Press, 1976. Contributor to *China Quarterly.*

WORK IN PROGRESS: The Rise of Public Opinion in China, 1895-1920.

* * *

NAU, Erika S(chwager) 1918-

PERSONAL: Born September 30, 1918, in Heidelberg, Germany; came to the United States in 1927, naturalized citizen, 1945; daughter of Leonard Frederick (a manufacturer) and Frieda (Bretzer) Schwager; married Paul Samuel Nau (vice-president and real estate appraiser), June, 1944; children: Philip, Greg, Stephen, Tracy Joanne, Christopher. *Education:* Attended University of California, San Diego. *Politics:* Republican. *Religion:* Independent. *Home and office:* 4973 Academy St., San Diego, Calif. 92109.

CAREER: Prudential Insurance Co., Newark, N.J., general clerical worker, 1938-43; free-lance writer, 1943—. *Military service:* U.S. Marine Corps (Women's Reserves), 1943-45. *Member:* U.S. Marine Corps Combat Correspondents, Women Marine Association (president of local chapter).

WRITINGS: Angel in the Rigging, Putnam, 1976. Contributor of articles and stories to magazines and newspapers. Woman Marine editor of *Chevron,* 1944-45.

WORK IN PROGRESS: Native Daughter, a historical novel from the point of view of the Cherokee Indians; two books on the female point of view on World War II; a biblical novel; a novel dealing with reincarnation; a fictional account of Huna ("an ancient Polynesian psycho-religious way of life"), with a modern setting.

SIDELIGHTS: Erika Nau, a certified psychic counselor and healer under California law, comments on the subject of her writings: "Since I am an avowed psychic, I admit freely much of my information comes from these sources, though I try always to get some sort of creditable feedback already in print, however obscure." She adds: "I believe the world is long overdue in giving women just due credit, and removing the veil, so to speak. Everyone of my books has a female protagonist, be she a Marine, an Indian medicine woman, a Kahuna, an intelligence officer or a Temple Initiate. Women read most of the books in America. Why not let them identify with the characters?"

*   *   *

NAUGLE, John E(arl)   1923-

PERSONAL: Born February 9, 1923, in Belle Fourche, S.D.; son of John E. and Delphia (Hall) Naugle; married Ethel Hale, December 7, 1945; children: Leleta K., Merridy, Scott. *Education:* University of Minnesota, B.S., 1949, M.S., 1950, Ph.D., 1953. *Home:* 7211 Rollingwood Dr., Chevy Chase, Md. 20015. *Office:* National Aeronautics & Space Administration, 400 Maryland Ave. S.W., Washington, D.C. 20546.

CAREER: University of Minnesota, Minneapolis, researcher on cosmic radiation, 1953-56; Convair Scientific Research Laboratory, San Diego, Calif. senior staff scientist, 1956-59; National Aeronautics and Space Administration, Washington, D.C., head of Nuclear Emulsion Section at Goddard Space Flight Center, 1959-61, chief of physics in Washington, D.C., 1961, director of physics and astronomy programs for Office of Space Science and Applications, 1962-66, deputy associate administrator in sciences, 1966-67, associate administrator of space science and applications, 1967-74, deputy associate administration of entire organization, 1974—, acting associate administrator, 1975—. *Military service:* U.S. Army, Infantry, 1943-45.

MEMBER: Physical Review Society, American Geophysical Union, American Rocket Society, American Institute of Aeronautics and Astronautics, Sigma Xi. *Awards, honors:* Space science award from American Institute of Aeronautics and Astronautics, 1969; distinguished service medal from National Aeronautics and Space Administration, 1969; career service award for sustained excellence from National Civil Service League, 1974.

WRITINGS: Unmanned Space Flight, Holt, 1965. Contributor to scientific journals.

*   *   *

NAUMANN, Rose   1919-

PERSONAL: Born November 22, 1919, in Darmstadt, Germany; daughter of George Wilhelm (a lawyer) and Gerda (Wizemann) Gauss; married Dieter Naumann (divorced, 1972); children: Andreas, Cornelius. *Education:* Attended Vancouver School of Art, 1964-68, and S. Miguel de Allende Instituto, 1968-69. *Home:* 2329 Lawson Ave., West Vancouver, British Columbia, Canada. *Agent:* Barthold Fles, 507 Fifth Ave., New York, N.Y. 10017. *Office:* Department of Art, Capilano College, North Vancouver, British Columbia, Canada.

CAREER: Capilano College, North Vancouver, British Columbia, instructor in weaving, 1971—.

WRITINGS: (With Raymond Hull) *The Off-Loom Weaving Book,* Scribner, 1973.

WORK IN PROGRESS: Research on weaving.

SIDELIGHTS: Rose Naumann has travelled to Korea, Japan, and Hawaii.

*   *   *

NEALE, John E(rnest)   1890-1975

PERSONAL: Born December 7, 1890, in Liverpool, England; married Elfreda Skelton, October 10, 1932; children: Stella. *Education:* University of Liverpool, M.A., 1915; attended University of London, 1914-19. *Residence:* Buckinghamshire, England.

CAREER: University of London, London, England, assistant lecturer in history, 1919-25; University of Manchester, Manchester, England, professor of modern history, 1925-27; University of London, Astor Professor of English History, 1925-56, professor emeritus, 1956-75, Neale Lecturer in English History, 1970. Ford's Lecturer at Oxford University, 1941-42; Raleigh Lecturer at British Academy, 1948; Creighton Lecturer at University of Manchester, 1950; also lectured in the United States. Trustee of London Museum, 1945-70. Member of treasury committee for House of Commons Records.

MEMBER: British Academy (fellow), Royal Historical Society (honorary vice-president, 1935), American Academy of Arts and Sciences (foreign honorary member), American Historical Association (honorary member). *Awards, honors:* D.Litt. from University of Wales, University of Birmingham, University of Leeds, and University of London; Litt.D. from University of Liverpool and Cambridge University; L.H.D. from Amherst College; James Tait Black Memorial Prize, 1934, for *Queen Elizabeth;* created knight, 1955.

WRITINGS: Queen Elizabeth, Harcourt, 1934, reissued as *Queen Elizabeth I: A Biography,* Doubleday, 1957 (published in England as *Queen Elizabeth I,* J. Cape, 1959, Penguin, 1971); *The Age of Catherine de Medici,* J. Cape, 1943, Barnes & Noble, 1959; *The Elizabethan House of Commons,* J. Cape, 1949, Yale University Press, 1950, revised edition, Penguin, 1963; *The Elizabethan Political Scene,* G. Cumberlege, 1949; *The Elizabethan Age,* University of London, 1951; *Elizabeth I and Her Parliaments, 1559-1581,* two volumes, St. Martin's, 1953-57; *England's Elizabeth,* Folger Shakespeare Library, 1958; *Essays in Elizabethan History,* J. Cape, 1958, St. Martin's, 1959. Contributor to history journals. Member of editorial board of *History of Parliament Trust,* 1951-71.

OBITUARIES: New York Times, September 4, 1975; *Washington Post,* September 6, 1975; *Publishers Weekly,* September 15, 1975.*

(Died September 2, 1975, in London, England)

*   *   *

NEERSKOV, Hans Kristian   1932-
(Hans Kristian)

PERSONAL: Born May 12, 1932, in Copenhagen, Denmark; son of Alfred E. (in wholesale business) and Astrid (Kloch) Neerskov; married Ninna Green, November 11, 1961; children: Peter, Marianne, Henning, Carsten. *Education:* Attended Danmarks Handelsskole, 1951-53, and Theological Seminary, 1955-59. *Home address:* P.O. Box 60, 2880 Bagsvaerd, Denmark. *Office address:* P.O. Box 2014, Denton, Tex. 76201.

CAREER: Moeller & Mammen, Copenhagen, Denmark, department manager, 1959-63; ordained clergyman, 1963; pastor of Pentecostal church in Blaahoej, Denmark, 1963-67, and of Tabor-Church, 1967-69; Danish European Mission, Bagsvaerd, founder and president of mission and of program "Mission Possible," 1969—. *Military service:* Danish Army, telegrapher, 1952-53.

WRITINGS—Under name Hans Kristian; all published by Danish European Mission, except as noted: *Liv og Kraft ved Helliganden* (title means "Life and Power through the Holy Spirit"), 1961; *Er Bibelen trovaerdig* (title means "Is the Bible Believable?"), 1962; *Oikumene* (title means "Ecumenical"), 1966; *De lukkede kirkers land,* 1967, translation by the author published as *Land of Closed Churches,* 1974; *En Martyrs Sejr,* 1972, translation by the author published as *A Russian Martyr,* 1974; (with Dave Hunt) *Mission: Possible,* Revell, 1975.

WORK IN PROGRESS: The Secret of the Martyr Church.

SIDELIGHTS: Neerskov has traveled in the Soviet Union, Poland, Czechoslovakia, Hungary, Rumania, Bulgaria, Yugoslavia, and most of the Far East and the Philippines.

* * *

NEIDHARDT, W(ilfried) S(teffen) 1941-

PERSONAL: Born May 7, 1941, in West Germany; came to Canada in 1953, naturalized citizen, 1959; son of Willy and Sofie (Kohut) Neidhardt; married Anne Kay, August 10, 1968; children: Catherine. *Education:* University of Toronto, B.A., 1965; University of Western Ontario, M.A., 1967; Ontario College of Education, certificate, 1967. *Home:* 60 Donbrook Pl., Downsview, Ontario, Canada M3H 4P4.

CAREER: Northview Heights Secondary School, Willowdale, Ontario, teacher of history, 1967—. *Member:* Canadian Historical Association.

WRITINGS: Struggle for the Fourteenth Colony, Clarke, Irwin, 1971; *Canadian-American Relations,* Clarke, Irwin, 1975; *Feminism in North America,* Pennsylvania State University Press, 1975. Author of scripts for educational filmstrips. Contributor to professional and popular history magazines.

WORK IN PROGRESS: Classroom-related learning materials, including audio-visual material.

* * *

NELL, Edward John 1935-

PERSONAL: Born July 16, 1935, in Chicago, Ill.; son of Edward John (a teacher, editor, and journalist) and Marcella E. (an administrator and professor; maiden name, Roach) Nell; married Onora O'Neill (a professor of philosophy), January 19, 1963; children: Adam, Jacob, Miranda, Guinivere. *Education:* Princeton University, A.B., 1957; Oxford University, B.A. (first class honors) 1959; B.Litt., 1964. *Politics:* Socialist. *Religion:* None. *Home:* 173 Warren St., Brooklyn, N.Y. 11201. *Office:* Graduate Faculty, New School for Social Research, 66 West 12th St., New York, N.Y. 10011.

CAREER: Wesleyan University, Middletown, Conn., assistant professor, 1962-67; University of East Anglia, Norwich, England, senior lecturer in economics, 1967-69; New School for Social Research, New York, N.Y., graduate professor of economics, 1969—, chairman of department, 1973-75. Vice-chairman, Connecticut Americans for Democratic

Action, 1966-67. *Member:* American Association of University Professors (secretary of Wesleyan University branch, 1964-67, American Economic Association, Union for Radical Political Economics, Phi Beta Kappa. *Awards, honors:* Rhodes scholar, 1957-60.

WRITINGS: (With Martin Hollis) *Rational Economic Man,* Cambridge University Press, 1975; (editor) *Growth Profits and Property,* Cambridge University Press, in press.

WORK IN PROGRESS: A collection of essays tentatively titled *An Introduction to Political Economy;* a novel on social issues; research on economic and social theory, social philosophy, and Marxian economics.

SIDELIGHTS: Nell described himself for *CA* as being antiwar, egalitarian, and a critic of "individualist philosophy" and capitalism. He "hopes for a better world." More specifically, he would like to see a "reunification of reason and passion, reconstruction of the economy on a basis of common responsibility and common ownership, and the development of non-hierarchical social order." Nell also keeps in contact with groups of left-wing economists connected with Labour parties or other socialist parties in Germany, Brazill, Australia, England, Scotland, Ireland, and India. He has visited all of these countries professionally.

* * *

NEUBAUER, David William 1944-

PERSONAL: Born February 25, 1944, in Chicago, Ill.; son of Fred (a sales engineer) and Katherine (Anderson) Neubauer; married Carole Roselle Barclay, August 20, 1966; children: Jeffrey Mark, Kristen Lynn. *Education:* Augustana College, Rock Island, Ill., B.A., 1966; University of Illinois, M.A., 1969, Ph.D., 1972. *Home:* 7416 Dogwood Dr., New Orleans, La. 70126. *Office:* Department of Political Science, University of New Orleans, New Orleans, La. 70122.

CAREER: University of Florida, Gainesville, assistant professor of political science, 1970-73; University of New Orleans, New Orleans, La., assistant professor of political science, 1973—. Visiting assistant professor at Washington University, St. Louis, Mo., 1972-73. *Member:* American Political Science Association, Law and Society Association, Midwest Political Science Association, Phi Beta Kappa, Omicron Delta Kappa, Pi Kappa Delta.

WRITINGS: Criminal Justice in Middle America, General Learning Corp., 1974; (contributor) John Gardiner and Michael Mulkey, editors, *Crime and Criminal Justice: Issues in Public Policy Analysis,* Lexington Books, 1975; (contributor) Russell Wheeler and Howard Whitcomb, editors, *Perspective on Court Administration,* Prentice-Hall, in press. Contributor of articles and book reviews to journals in his field.

WORK IN PROGRESS: Research on criminal justice.

* * *

NEWCOMB, Kerry 1946-
(Shana Carrol, Peter Gentry, Christina Savage, joint pseudonyms)

PERSONAL: Born December 7, 1946, in Milford, Conn.; son of Paul Guy (a tool designer) and Anne Marie (Reno) Newcomb; married Patricia Blackwell (a potter), June 14, 1976. *Education:* University of Texas, Arlington, B.A., 1969; Trinity University, San Antonio, Tex., M.F.A., 1973. *Politics:* "Populist." *Religion:* Roman Catholic. *Agent:* Aaron Priest, 150 East 35th St., Suite 620, New York, N.Y.

10016. *Office:* Shanew Writes, 3419 Hall, #4, Dallas, Tex. 75219.

CAREER: Teacher in American Indian school in Ashland, Mont., 1973-74; writer, 1974—. Has worked as a singer, entertainer, and director of plays. *Awards, honors:* Greer Garson Award for Achievement in the Theatre from Dallas Theatre Centre, 1972.

WRITINGS—Novels; all with Frank Schaefer: (Under joint pseudonym Shana Carrol) *Paxton Pride,* Pyramid Publications, 1976; (under joint pseudonym Peter Gentry) *Rafe,* Fawcett, 1976; (under joint pseudonym Peter Gentry) *Titus Gamble,* Fawcett, in press.

Plays: "Dear Luger" (comedy), first produced in Dallas, Tex., at Dallas Theatre Center, January 12, 1973; "Feathers" (one-act), first produced at Dallas Theatre Center, March 10, 1972. Contributor to theater magazines.

WORK IN PROGRESS—All with Frank Schaefer: *Raven,* a novel under joint pseudonym Shana Carrol; *Gladwyn's Lady,* a novel under joint pseudonym Christina Savage.

* * *

NEWELL, Edythe W(eatherford) 1910-

PERSONAL: Born October 28, 1910, in Arlington, Ore.; daughter of Marion Earl (a farmer) and Minnie Clara (a teacher; maiden name, Snell) Weatherford; married George L. Newell (an electronics engineer), September 2, 1931; children: Lora Joan (Mrs. David P. Moller), Susan Clara (Mrs. Ben L. Bachulis). *Education:* Attended University of Maryland, Overseas Extension, and University of Alaska. *Religion:* Protestant. *Residence:* Prineville, Ore.

CAREER: University of Alaska, Fairbanks, technical librarian in periodicals, 1964-67; librarian in public elementary school in Fairbanks, 1967-69; writer, 1969—. Trustee of Crook County Library, 1971-74.

WRITINGS: Rescue of the Sun and Other Tales from the Far North, Albert Whitman, 1970.

WORK IN PROGRESS: A series of nature tales for first readers, set in the desert; a tenth-century legend for teenagers.

SIDELIGHTS: Edythe Newell writes: "I've been a full-time wife and mother, following my husband as he pursued his career in electronics. This has forced me to develop many interests while allowing me to discover for myself the richness and variety of many cultures, both old world and primitive. I was fascinated most by the Indian and Eskimo peoples, the lore and legends of the far north. I have more of their tales to tell."

AVOCATIONAL INTERESTS: Travel, art, music.

* * *

NEWMAN, Harold 1899-

PERSONAL: Born December 22, 1899, in New Orleans, La.; son of Harold W. (an investment banker) and Bellagie (Israel) Newman; married Gwynneth Orme, December 2, 1952. *Education:* Tulane University, B.A., 1920; Harvard University, LL.B., 1923. *Residence:* (Winter) 54 Cadogan Sq., London, England; (summer) Maser (Treviso), Italy.

CAREER: Private practice of law in New York, N.Y., 1923-32; Reconstruction Finance Corp., Washington, D.C., assistant general counsel, 1932-36; Metropolitan Casualty Insurance Co., Newark, N.J., vice-president and general counsel, 1936-39; private practice of law in New York, N.Y., 1939-41; Office of Civilian Defense, Washington,

D.C., general counsel, 1941-43; writer. *Member:* English Ceramic Circle, Phi Beta Kappa.

WRITINGS: Newman's European Travel Guide, Holt, 1951, 11th revised edition, 1968, *Veilleuses,* A. S. Barnes, 1967; (with George Savage) *Illustrated Dictionary of Ceramics,* Thames & Hudson, 1974, 2nd edition, 1975; *Illustrated Dictionary of Glass,* Thames & Hudson, in press. Contributor to *Antiques, Apollo, Antique Collector, Connoisseur,* and *Collectors Guide.*

WORK IN PROGRESS: Genealogical Chart of Greek Mythology.

AVOCATIONAL INTERESTS: Collecting veilleuses.

* * *

NEWMAN, Jay Hartley 1951-

PERSONAL: Born December 20, 1951, in New York, N.Y.; son of Jack (a businessman) and Thelma (an author and educator; maiden name, Siegel) Newman. *Education:* Attended London School of Economics and Political Science, University of London, 1971-72; Yale University, B.A., 1973; Columbia University, J.D., 1976. *Home:* 1101 Prospect St., Westfield, N.J. 07090.

CAREER: Law clerk to Francis L. Van Dusen, U.S. circuit judge, Philadelphia, Pa., 1976—; writer. *Member:* Phi Delta Phi.

WRITINGS—All published by Crown: (With brother, Lee Scott Newman) *Plastics for the Craftsman,* 1972; (with L. S. Newman and mother, Thelma R. Newman) *Paper as Art and Craft,* 1973; (with L. S. Newman and T. R. Newman) *The Frame Book,* 1974; (with L. S. Newman) *Kite Craft,* 1974; (with L. S. Newman) *Wire Art,* 1975; (with L. S. Newman and T. R. Newman) *The Lamp and Lighting Book,* 1976; (with T. R. Newman) *The Container Book,* in press; (with T. R. Newman) *The Mirror Book,* in press. Notes and comments editor, *Columbia Law Review,* 1974-76.

AVOCATIONAL INTERESTS: Traveling.

* * *

NEWMAN, Lee Scott 1953-

PERSONAL: Born November 9, 1953, in New York, N.Y.; son of Jack (a businessman) and Thelma (an author and artist; maiden name, Siegel) Newman. *Education:* Amherst College, B.A. (magna cum laude), 1975; Cornell University, M.A., 1976; now attending Vanderbilt University. *Home and office:* 1101 Prospect St., Westfield, N.J. 07090.

CAREER: Courier-News, Somerville, N.J., reporter, 1970-73; Poly-Dec Co., Inc., Bayonne, N.J., designer, 1970—. *Member:* Advisory for a Healthy Reality, Sigma Xi.

WRITINGS: (With brother, Jay Hartley Newman) *Plastics for the Craftsman,* Crown, 1972; (with mother, Thelma R. Newman and J. H. Newman) *Paper as Art and Craft,* Crown, 1973; (with T. R. Newman and J. H. Newman) *The Frame Book,* Crown, 1974; (with J. H. Newman) *Kite Craft,* Crown, 1974; (with J. H. Newman) *Wire Art,* Crown, 1975; (with T. R. Newman and J. H. Newman) *The Lamp and Lighting Book,* Crown, 1976. Contributor to *Woman's Day* and *Journal of Personality and Social Psychology.*

WORK IN PROGRESS: The Mirror Book, with Thelma R. Newman and Jay H. Newman.

AVOCATIONAL INTERESTS: Playing percussion instruments, playing tennis and squash, gardening, protecting the ecology, photography, traveling, studying psychology.

NEWMAN, Robert S. 1935-

PERSONAL: Born April 27, 1935, in Utica, N.Y.; son of Edward I. (a teacher) and Anna (Shindler) Newman; married Milda Norkunas, February 5, 1965; children: Richard, Eric, Ruth. *Education:* University of California at Los Angeles, B.A., 1956, M.A., 1957, Ph.D., 1965. *Politics:* Democrat. *Home:* 190 Minnesota, Buffalo, N.Y. 14214. *Agent:* Gary Goss, 17 Center Shore Rd., Centerport, N.Y. *Office:* Department of English, State University of New York at Buffalo, Buffalo, N.Y. 14214.

CAREER: San Fernando Valley State College, San Fernando, Calif., assistant professor of English, 1964-67; State University of New York at Buffalo, assistant professor, 1967-72, associate professor of English, 1972—. *Member:* Northeast Modern Language Association.

WRITINGS: Language and Writing, Dickenson, 1967. Contributor to *Studies in English Literature.*

* * *

NICKELSBURG, Janet 1893-

PERSONAL: Born March 1, 1893, in San Francisco, Calif.; daughter of Jacob Jackson (a merchant) and Edith (Brandenstein) Jacobi; married Melvil S. Nickelsburg, December 9, 1917 (deceased); children: Stephen L., Ruth Denmark, Edith Parker. *Education:* Attended University of California, Stanford, and San Francisco State College (now University). *Home and office:* 2585 Union St., San Francisco, Calif. 94123.

CAREER: Curator of science room in Josephine Randall Junior Museum for five years; head teacher at child care center during World War II; conducted television and radio programs in San Francisco, Calif., area, including "Signposts for Young Scientists," 1947-52, "Stop, Look and Listen," released by National Broadcasting Co. (NBC-TV) and KQED-Television, and "Children's Forum," broadcast on KPFA-Radio, Berkeley, Calif.; director of nature services in children's camps during the 1950's; teacher at Presidio Open Air School for eight years; now elementary school science teacher in San Francisco public schools. Docent of California Academy of Sciences, 1970—; past extension lecturer at San Francisco State College (now University), and Sonoma State College (now California State College, Sonoma); now volunteer science teacher in elementary schools in California cities. Feature speaker at nursery school, child care, and recreation and camp conferences. Former education chairman at Audubon Canyon Ranch. Chairman of local committee on recreation for the handicapped. *Member:* Golden Gate Audubon Society (education chairman), Hearing Society for the San Francisco Bay Area (past president; member of executive committee). *Awards, honors:* Gulick award from National Camp Fire Girls, 1927; National award from Chicago School Broadcast Council, 1948, for radio program "Signposts for Young Scientists"; award from California Conservation Society, 1955; received award from California Camping Association, 1975.

WRITINGS: The Nature Program at Camp, Burgess, 1960; *Stargazing: A Group Leader's Guide,* Burgess, 1964; *California from the Mountains to the Sea* (juvenile), Volume I: *California Climates,* Volume II: *California's Mountains,* Volume III: *California: Water and Land,* Volume IV: *California's Natural Resources,* Lippincott, 1964; *Field Trips: Ecology for Youth Leaders,* Burgess, 1966; *Ecology: Habitats, Niches, and Food Chains,* Lippincott, 1969; *Nature Activities for Early Childhood,* Addison-Wesley, 1976.

Author of a series of about two hundred fifty radio scripts and of scripts for a ten-record album series for Educational Activities, Inc., 1964, both titled "Signposts for Young Scientists." Frequent contributor to magazines, including *Camping* and *Children Today.* Editor of *Cygnet* (children's leaflet from local Audubon Society), 1965-68.

WORK IN PROGRESS: Fiction; her memoirs.

SIDELIGHTS: Janet Nickelsburg continues her education at California Academy of Sciences, most recently having studied spiders and fish. She writes: "I am interested in seeing that children become once more in tune with the outdoors, with an ecological and conservational outlook."

* * *

NICOLL, (John Ramsay) Allardyce 1894-1976

June 28, 1894—April 17, 1976; Scottish educator and historian of English drama. Obituaries: *Publishers Weekly,* May 24, 1976; *AB Bookman's Weekly,* June 7, 1976. (See index for previous *CA* sketch)

* * *

NICOLSON, James R(obert) 1934-

PERSONAL: Born July 10, 1934, in Shetland Islands, Scotland; son of Frank Huggins (a customs officer) and Helen (Tait) Nicolson; married Violet Sinclair, September 6, 1965; children: Eileen, Margaret, Robert. *Education:* University of Aberdeen, M.A., 1956, B.Sc., 1961. *Home:* Fairhaven, Castle St., Scalloway, Shetland Islands ZE1 0TP, Scotland. *Agent:* John Austin, Passatempo, Welcomes Rd., Kenley, Surrey, England.

CAREER: Mining geologist for Sierra Leone Development Co., Marampa mine, 1961-67; fisherman in the Shetland Islands, Scotland, 1969-72; Member of Blacksness Pier Trust, 1973-76. *Member:* Royal Geographical Society, Geological Society of London.

WRITINGS: Shetland, David & Charles, 1972, revised edition, 1975; *The Tent and the Simbek* (nonfiction), William Luscombe, 1974; *Beyond the Great Glen* (nonfiction), William Luscombe, 1975; *Shetland and Oil,* William Luscombe, 1975; *Lerwick Harbour,* Lerwick Harbour Trust, in press. Author of "Scalloway Notes," in *Shetland0Times,* 1976. Contributor to Scottish magazines and newspapers.

WORK IN PROGRESS: Shetland Traditional Life; research on the Scottish herring industry.

SIDELIGHTS: Nicolson writes that his special interests are working people "such as West African peasants, Scottish crofters and fisherman" and life in the north of Scotland, especially the Shetland Islands.

* * *

NIDEFFER, Robert M(orse) 1942-

PERSONAL: Born February 6, 1942, in Oxnard, Calif.; son of Richard G. (a farmer) and Mary (executive director of Campfire Girls; maiden name, Morse) Nideffer; married Lilly Dauenhauer, July, 1963 (divorced, 1970); married Peggy Johnson (a psychiatric nurse), May 29, 1971; children: Robert F., James A. *Education:* Lewis and Clark College, B.S., 1967; Vanderbilt University, M.A., 1969, Ph.D., 1971. *Home:* 17 Stuyvesant Rd., Pittsford, N.Y. 14534. *Office:* Department of Psychology, University of Rochester, Rochester, N.Y. 14627.

CAREER: University of Oregon, Eugene, intern in medical psychology, 1971; University of Rochester, Rochester,

N.Y., assistant professor, 1971-75, associate professor of psychology and psychiatry, 1976—, director of Biofeedback Laboratory, 1975—. Senior clinical psychology associate at Strong Memorial Hospital, 1975—; faculty member of National Academy of Professional Psychologists, 1975—; member of advisory board of Pretrial Services and of executive board of Monroe County Sports Medicine Committee. *Military service:* U.S. Army, Security Agency, 1959-62; served in Japan.

MEMBER: American Psychological Association, Society for Psychophysiological Research, Society for Clinical and Experimental Hypnosis, National Register of Health Services Providers in Psychology.

WRITINGS: The Inner Athlete, Crowell, 1976. Contributor to psychology journals and to *Coach and Athlete, Redbook, Gentleman's Quarterly,* and *Sundancer.*

WORK IN PROGRESS: The I of the Storm: Strategies for Reduction of Stress; Attentional and Interpersonal Style: The Prediction of Human Behavior.

SIDELIGHTS: Nideffer comments: "A combination of the study of Aikido and the Martial Arts in Japan and the study of psychology and the disorganization associated with psychotic processes led to the development of a theory of human performance. Research in both areas (athletics and schizophrenia) seemed to support the theory and led to application of techniques designed to help individuals function under stress. In addition a test was developed to be used as a diagnostic and selection tool to identify individuals who function effectively under stress."

* * *

NIE, Norman H.   1943-

PERSONAL: Born April 1, 1943, in St. Louis, Mo.; son of Ben Phillip and Lucille Rose (Blaker) Nie; married, 1964; children: two. *Education:* Washington University, St. Louis, Mo., B.A., 1964; Stanford University, M.A., 1966, Ph.D., 1970. *Home:* 5659 South Woodlawn Ave., Chicago, Ill. 60637. *Office:* National Opinion Research Center, University of Chicago, 6030 South Ellis Ave., Chicago, Ill. 60637.

CAREER: Stanford University, Institute of Political Studies, Stanford, Calif., lecturer in Political science, 1967-68; University of Chicago, Chicago, Ill., assistant professor, 1968-72, associate professor of political science, 1972—, senior study director of National Opinion Research Center, 1968—. Visiting professor at University of Leiden, autumn, 1972. President of Statistical Programs for the Social Sciences, Inc., 1975—. Member of council of Inter-University Consortium for Political Research (chairman, 1975—).

MEMBER: American Political Science Association. *Awards, honors:* Woodrow Wilson fellowship, 1964-65; National Science Foundation grant, 1970—; senior Fulbright fellowship, 1971-72; Gladys M. Kammerer Award from American Political Science Association and Woodrow Wilson Foundation Award, both 1972, for *Participation in America;* Twentieth Century Fund grant, 1973-75.

WRITINGS: (With Sidney Verba and John R. Petrocik) *The Changing American Voter,* Harvard University Press, 1966; (with others) *SPSS: The Statistical Package for the Social Sciences,* McGraw, 1970, new edition, 1975; (editor with Harold Sackman, and contributor) *The Information Utility and Social Change,* AFIPS Press, 1970; (with Verba and Jae-On Kim) *The Modes of Democratic Participation: A Cross-National Comparison,* Sage Publications, Inc.,

1971; (with Verba) *Participation in America: Political Democracy and Social Equality,* Harper, 1972; (contributor) Andrew M. Greeley, editor, *Ethnicity in the United States: A Preliminary Reconnaissance,* Wiley, 1974; (contributor) Albert Somit, editor, *Political Science and the Study of the Future,* Dryden, 1974; (with William R. Klecka and C. Hadlai Hull) *SPSS Primer,* McGraw, 1975; (contributor) Freed Greenstein and Nelson Polsby, editors *Handbook of Political Science,* Addison-Wesley, 1975; (with Verba and Kim) *Social Stratification and Political Stratification: A Multi-National Perspective,* Cambridge University Press, in press. Contributor to political science and social science journals. Member of board of editors of *American Journal of Political Science,* 1973-75, and *Comparative Political Sociology,* 1974—.

* * *

NIVEN, John   1921-

PERSONAL: Born October 26, 1921, in Brooklyn, N.Y.; son of William John, Sr. (an engineer) and Marion (Fredericks) Niven; married Elizabeth Pope Thompson (a school psychologist), September, 1948; children: John Drake, Katherine Pope. *Education:* University of Connecticut, B.A., 1943; Columbia University, M.A., 1947, Ph.D., 1954. *Office:* Department of History, Claremont Graduate School, Claremont, Calif. 91711.

CAREER: Mitchell College, New London, Conn., instructor in history, 1949-51; General Dynamics Corp., New York, N.Y., supervisor of employee relations in Electric Boat Division, 1951-54, assistant to vice-president of communications, 1954-55, assistant to chairman of the board and chief executive officer, 1955-57, director of publications, 1955-60; Claremont Graduate School, Claremont, Calif., associate professor, 1960-65, professor of American history, 1965—, head of department, 1964-66, 1969-70, 1973-74. Senior research associate, Smithsonian Institution, 1966-67. Consultant to National Endowment for the Humanities and Educational Testing Service. *Military Service:* U.S. Naval Reserve, active duty, 1942-46; became lieutenant.

MEMBER: American Historical Association, Organization of American Historians, Society of American Historians (fellow), Southern Historical Association, Association for the Study of Connecticut History. *Awards, honors:* American Philosophical Society grant, 1962; American Council of Learned Societies grant, 1962; Pacific Coast Branch of American Historical Association Award, 1966, for the best work in history; award of merit from National Association of State and Local History, 1966; New Haven Civil War Round Table Award, 1966; silver medal from Commonwealth Club of California, 1974, for non-fiction by a California author.

WRITINGS: (Editor with Eliot Janeway) *Struggle for Survival,* Yale University Press, 1952; (with Courtlandt Canby and Vernon Welsh) *Dynamic America,* Doubleday, 1960; *Connecticut for the Union,* Yale University Press, 1965; (editor) *Years of Turmoil: The Civil War and Reconstruction,* Addison-Wesley, 1969; *Gideon Welles,* Oxford University Press, 1973; (contributor) James Mohr, editor, *The Northern States During Reconstruction* (monograph), Johns Hopkins Press, 1976; (contributor) Marcus Cunliffe, editor, *Brother Against Brother,* Orbis, in press; (contributor) Paolo Coletta, editor, *American Secretaries of the Navy,* U.S. Naval Institute, in press; *Israel Putnam,* Connecticut Bicentennial Commission, in press. Contributor to history journals.

WORK IN PROGRESS: A study of Israel and Rufus Putnam, and Manasseh Cutler.

* * *

NKOSI, Lewis 1936-

PERSONAL: Born December 5, 1936, in Natal, South Africa; son of Samson and Christine Margaret (Makathini) Knosi; married Bronwy Ollerenshaw; children: Louise, Joy (twins). Education: Attended M. L. Sultan Technical College, 1954-55, and Harvard University, 1961-62; University of London, diploma in English literature, 1974; University of Sussex, 1977. Agent: Deborah Rogers Ltd., 29 Goodge St., London W.C.1, England.

CAREER: Worked at Ilanga lase Natal (title means "Natal Sun," Zulu-English weekly newspaper), 1955, and Drum (magazine), 1955-56, Johannesburg, South Africa; Golden City Post, Johannesburg, chief reporter, 1956-60; The New African, London, England, literary editor, 1965-68. Producer of British Broadcasting Company (BBC) radio series "Africa Abroad," 1962-65, interviewer of leading African writers for National Education Television (NET) series "African Writers of Today"; visiting Regents Professor of African Literature, University of California, Irvine, 1970.

WRITINGS: The Rhythm of Violence (play), Oxford University Press, 1964; Home and Exile (essays), Longmans, Green, 1965. Also author of radio play, "We Can't All Be Martin Luther King," broadcast by BBC, 1971, and of a Libretto for "The Chameleon and the Lizard," produced in London at Queen Elizabeth Hall, 1971. Work represented in anthologies, African Writing Today, edited by Ezekiel Mphalele, Penguin, 1967, and Plays From Black Africa, edited by Frederic N. Litto, Hill & Wang, 1968. Contributor to periodicals and journals in his field, including Guardian, New Statesman, Observer, Transition, Black Orpheus, Spectator, and New Yorker.

WORK IN PROGRESS: A study of African literature, in English and French, for Longman; a novel; a libretto for the King's Singers.

SIDELIGHTS: When Nkosi left his homeland to study in the United States, he was given an exit permit, but no passport, making it impossible for him to return. He has settled in England.

* * *

NOAKES, Vivien 1937-

PERSONAL: Born February 16, 1937, in Twickenham, England; daughter of Marcus (an aeronautical engineer) and Helen (Box) Langley; married Michael Noakes (a portrait painter) July 9, 1960; children: Anya, Jonathan, Benedict. Education: Educated in Reigate, Surrey, England. Home: 146 Hamilton Terr., St. John's Wood, London N.W.8, England. Agent: Bolt & Watson, 8 Storey's Gate, London S.W.1, England.

CAREER: Biographer. Member: Writers' Action Group.

WRITINGS: Edward Lear: The Life of a Wanderer, Collins, 1968, Houghton, 1969. Contributor to Harvard Magazine and Times Literary Supplement.

WORK IN PROGRESS: A novel about World War I, The Wild Honey; a complete nonsense of Edward Lear.

* * *

NOBLE, Elizabeth Marian 1945-

PERSONAL: Born January 2, 1945, in Australia; came to the United States in 1973; daughter of Richard Neetlee (a civil servant) and Phyllis (Heggaton) Bagot; married Geoffrey Noble (a businessman), December 19, 1970. Education: University of Adelaide, diploma, 1965; University of Western Australia, B.A., 1972. Politics: "Member of no political party." Religion: None. Home and office: 162 Summer St., #41, Somerville, Mass. 02143.

CAREER: Private physical therapy practitioner and childbirth educator in Singapore, and Adelaide, Australia, 1966-70, Perth, Australia, 1971-73, and Somerville, Mass., 1974—. Teacher of prepared childbirth at Malden Hospital; medical liaison for Homebirth, Inc., 1976-77. Member: American Physical Therapy Association (founder of obstetrics-gynecology special interest group, 1976), American Society for Psychoprophylaxis in Obstetrics, International Childbirth Education Association, National Association for Parents and Professionals for Safe Alternatives in Childbirth, Australian Physiotherapy Association. Awards, honors: American Field Service exchange scholarship, 1961-62.

WRITINGS: Essential Exercises for the Childbearing Year, Houghton, 1976.

WORK IN PROGRESS: A research project "involving female pelvic floor function evaluation through the childbearing year, objectively measured with Kegel's perineometer with attention to women instructed in exercise and who do not have an episiotomy"; research on separation of the abdominal muscles (diastis recti) and the value of early exercise in this regard.

SIDELIGHTS: Elizabeth Noble writes: "Women in the USA do very little preparation and rehabilitation for childbearing other than preparation for labor and delivery—physical therapists are little involved. . . . While I am actively trying to upgrade the P.T. input—I wrote my book for the laywoman as resources are so limited—I am very interested in the philosophical/sociological aspects of childbearing." Avocational interests: Travel to Europe ("lived two years in the Netherlands and speak Dutch") and to the Middle East, Asia, and North and South America.

* * *

NOLIN, Bertil 1926-

PERSONAL: Born December 6, 1926, in Tingsryd, Sweden; son of C. O. (a member of the Riksdag) and Hulda (Carlsson) Nolin; married Elly Hjertonsson, 1955; children: Bo, Jan. Education: University of Uppsala, M.A., 1954; University of Stockholm, Ph.D., 1966. Home: Ljungbackenvaegen 52, Lerum 44300, Sweden. Office: Department of Drama, University of Gothenburg, Viktoriagatan 13, Goeteborg 41125, Sweden.

CAREER: Teachers College of Bothenburg, Goeteborg, Sweden, assistant professor of literature, 1965-67; University of Gothenburg, Goeteborg, Sweden, assistant professor of literature, 1967-68; University of Chicago, Chicago, Ill., visiting professor of literature, 1968-70; University of Gothenburg, associate professor of drama, 1970—, head of department.

WRITINGS: Den gode europen Svenski Bokfoerlaget, 1965; Georg Brandes, Twayne, 1976.

WORK IN PROGRESS: The Modes of Expression of Modern Drama.

* * *

NOON, William T(homas) 1912-1975

PERSONAL: Born May 17, 1912, in Utica, N.Y.; son of

William Matthew (a salesman) and Lucy Mary (Shaughnessy) Noon. *Education:* Hamilton College, A.B., 1934; Loyola University, Chicago, Ill., M.A., 1943; West Baden College, Ph.L., 1943; Woodstock College, S.T.L., 1950; Yale University, Ph.D., 1954. *Politics:* "Varies." *Religion:* Catholic. *Home and office:* Loyola Hall, Le Moyne College, Syracuse, N.Y. 13214.

CAREER: Ordained priest, 1949. High school teacher in New York public schools, 1934-37, in private schools, 1943-46; Canisius College, Buffalo, N.Y., assistant professor of English, 1954-59, graduate dean, 1954-55; Fordham University, New York, N.Y., associate professor of English, 1959-64; Le Moyne College, Syracuse, N.Y., professor of English, 1964-75. *Member:* Modern Language Association of America, American Association of University Professors, English Institute, Society of Jesus, College English Association, Catholic Renascence Society, Hamilton College Alumni.

WRITINGS: Immortal Diamond, Sheed, 1949; *Joyce and Aquinas,* Yale University Press, 1957, reprinted, Shoe String, 1970; *Poetry and Prayer,* Rutgers University Press, 1967. Contributor of over fifty articles to American and foreign scholarly journals. Member of editorial board, *James Joyce Quarterly* and *PMLA.*

WORK IN PROGRESS: Comparative comment on *Ulysses* and *The Waste Land.*

AVOCATIONAL INTERESTS: Music and its various interactions with poetry.*

(Died January 17, 1975)

*   *   *

NOREN, Catherine (Hanf)   1938-

PERSONAL: Born April 5, 1938, in Germany; came to the United States in 1946, naturalized citizen, 1955; daughter of Eric (an importer) and Lotte (Wallach) Hanf; married Andrew Noren, December 27, 1963 (divorced, 1970). *Education:* Bennington College, B.A., 1959; graduate study at Boston University and Harvard University, 1961-63; studied photography privately, 1969-72. *Residence:* New York, N.Y. *Agent:* Anne Borchardt, Georges Borchardt, Inc., 145 East 52nd St., New York, N.Y. 10022.

CAREER: High school teacher of drama and English in Massachusetts, 1960-63; television quiz program writer, 1964-69; free-lance editor and translator, 1969-71; photographer and writer, 1971—. Has had group shows (for photographs) in major U.S. cities, and solo exhibitions in New York City and Milan, Italy. *Awards, honors:* Grant from International Fund for Concerned Photography, 1972.

WRITINGS: (Translator from the German) Jo Imog, *The Demon Flower,* Maurice Girodias Associates, 1973; *Photography: How to Improve Your Technique,* F. Watts, 1973; *The Camera of My Family,* Knopf, 1976. Contributor of articles and photographs to magazines.

WORK IN PROGRESS: U.S. Male (tentative title), a photographic essay "on the nature of maleness as seen through my (female) viewfinder."

SIDELIGHTS: Catherine Noren writes: "I like to take pictures—photographs freeze time, they give the illusion of stopping change, they are mysterious and magic. I am interested, always, in the disclosure of secrets and the revelation of our ongoing identification with each other. For me, this is the way the hierarchy and mythology of power will be recognized as a mistaken notion, one that dissatisfies and despiritizes us."

AVOCATIONAL INTERESTS: Humor, music, mime.

*   *   *

NORMAN, Joyce Ann   1937-

PERSONAL: Born May 1, 1937, in Fort Worth, Tex.; daughter of William Calvin and Daisy (Gardner) Norman. *Education:* Texas Wesleyan College, B.S., 1956. *Religion:* Christian. *Home and office:* 653-A Idlewild Circle, Birmingham, Ala. 35205.

CAREER: "Cartoon Clubhouse" and "Cartoon Wonderland", WBAP-TV, Fort Worth, Tex., hostess, 1958-60; high school English teacher in public schools in Birmingham, Ala., 1961-68; *Birmingham News,* Birmingham, Ala., women's state editor, 1968-74; Southeastern Bible College, Birmingham, professor of English, 1975; writer and photographer. *Member:* National Journalism Society, National Music Sorority, Alabama Press Photographers Association, Beta Sigma Phi, Sigma Alpha Iota, Birmingham Business and Professional Women's Club, Birmingham Aero Club. *Awards, honors:* Cameo Award I (honorary member of 20th Special Forces) from Green Berets, 1973; Big "N" Award from *Birmingham News,* 1973, for creative enterprise in the field of journalism.

WRITINGS: Personal Assignment (autobiography), Revell, 1973; (editor) *Above All Else,* Revell, 1975; (with Jane Hunt) *Come and See* (biography), Word Books, 1976. Author of movie and television scripts; author of column "Norman's Conquest," *Alabama Educational Association Journal,* 1966-68.

WORK IN PROGRESS: How Do You Hug a Sandwich; Follow Me Close; researching a novel about Mangrove Cay, Andros Island, Bahamas.

AVOCATIONAL INTERESTS: Traveling, flying.

BIOGRAPHICAL/CRITICAL SOURCES: Birmingham News, November 22, 1973; *Fort Worth Press,* December 8, 1973; *Fort Worth Star Telegram,* January 10, 1974.

*   *   *

NORRIS, Nigel (Harold)   1943-

PERSONAL: Born February 25, 1943, in Manchester, England; son of Harold (an accountant) and Bessie (an opthalmologist; maiden name, Hopley) Norris; married Caroline Margaret de Spon (a secretary), November 9, 1974; children: Richard James Ivatt. *Education:* University of Bristol, B.V.Sc., 1965. *Politics:* "Right Wing." *Religion:* Agnostic. *Home and office:* 496 Hornsey Rd., London N19 4EF, England. *Agent:* Anthony Shields, 52 Floral St., London W.C.2, England.

CAREER: Blue Cross (animal hospital), London, England, intern, 1965-67; in private practice of veterinary medicine, 1967—. Managing director of Sugar Mountain Enterprises, 1976—. Has appeared on British television and radio programs as a regular contributor and adviser. *Member:* Royal College of Veterinary Surgeons, Rolls Royce Enthusiasts Club, Rolls Royce Owners Club of America.

WRITINGS: A to Z of Dog and Cat Care, Collins, 1975; *Complete Home Medical Guide for Dogs,* Stein & Day, 1976; *Complete Home Medical Guide for Cats,* Stein & Day, 1976.

WORK IN PROGRESS: A Children's Guide to Pet Care; Behaviour of Domestic Animals; City Vet, a semi-autobiographical novel.

AVOCATIONAL INTERESTS: Motor racing, riding, collecting antique automobiles.

BIOGRAPHICAL/CRITICAL SOURCES: Kirkus, February-March, 1976.

* * *

NORTH, Gary 1942-

PERSONAL: Born February 11, 1942, in San Pedro, Calif.; son of Sam W. and Peggy K. (Kilgore) North; married Sharon Rushdoony, February 23, 1972; children: Darcy. *Education:* University of California, Riverside, B.A., 1963, M.A., 1966, Ph.D., 1972; attended Westminster Theological Seminary, 1963-64. *Politics:* "Neo-Puritan." *Religion:* Presbyterian. *Office:* Institute for Christian Economics, P.O. Box 1608, Springfield, Va. 22151.

CAREER: Foundation for Economic Education, Irvington, N.Y., director of seminars, 1971-73; Chalcedon Foundation, Vallecito, Calif., vice-president, 1973—. Congressional assistant in Washington, D.C., 1976—; president of Institute for Christian Economics, 1977. *Member:* Committee on Monetary Research and Education (member of board of directors, 1973—), Philadelphia Society (member of board of directors, 1973-76). *Awards, honors:* George Washington Medal from Freedoms Foundation, 1974.

WRITINGS: Marx's Religion of Revolution, Craig Press, 1968; *An Introduction to Christian Economics,* Craig Press, 1973; *None Dare Call It Witchcraft,* Arlington House, 1976; (editor) *Foundations of Christian Scholarship,* Ross House, 1976. Contributor to a wide variety of magazines, including *Wall Street Journal, Journal of Political Economy, The Freeman, National Review, Human Events, Schism, Coin Mart, California Farmer, Alternative,* and *Applied Christianity.* Editor of *Remnant Review,* 1974—, and *Journal of Christian Reconstruction,* 1974—.

WORK IN PROGRESS: Christian Survival on a Secular Campus; How You Can Profit from the Coming Price Controls; Creation: Implications and Applications, completion expected in 1979.

SIDELIGHTS: North writes: "I write from the perspective of Protestant Christianity in the fields of history, economics, and the social sciences generally."

* * *

NOVOTNY, Fritz 1903-

PERSONAL: Born February 10, 1903, in Vienna, Austria; son of Franz (a mechanic) and Josefine (Bartosch) Novotny. *Education:* University of Vienna, Dr.phil., 1938. *Religion:* Roman Catholic. *Home:* Linke Wienzeile 168/22, 1060 Vienna, Austria. *Office:* Kunsthistorisches Institut d. Universitaet Wien, Universitaetsstrasse 7, 1010 Vienna, Austria.

CAREER: University of Vienna, Institute of Art History, Vienna, Austria, assistant professor of art history, 1938—; Oesterreichische Galerie, Vienna, Austria, 1960-68, began as curator, became director; retired, 1968. *Member:* Association Internationale des Critiques d'Art (president of Austrian section, 1962-68), Adalbert Stifter-Institut des Landes Oberoesterreich, Adalbert Stifter-Gesellschaft (Vienna; member of board of directors), Wilhelm Busch-Gesellschaft (Hannover; adviser). *Awards, honors:* Prize of the City of Vienna for the Arts, 1956; gold medal of the City of Vienna, 1968; first class Austrian Cross for Knowledge and Art, 1968.

WRITINGS—In English: *Painting and Sculpture in Europe, 1780 to 1880,* Penguin, 1960, 2nd edition, 1970; (with Johannes Dobai) *Gustav Klimt,* Verlag Galerie Welz (Salzburg), 1967, translation by Karen Olga Philippson published as *Gustav Klimt: With a Catalogue Raisonne of His Paintings,* Praeger, 1968; *Toulouse-Lautrec,* translated by Michael Glenney, Phaidon, 1969.

Works in German: *Romanische Bauplastik in Oesterreich* (title means "Architectural Sculpture of the Romanesque Period in Austria"), privately printed, 1930; *Cezanne und das Ende der wissenschaftlichen Perspektive* (title means "Cezanne and the End of Mathematical Perspective"), Anton Schroll, 1938, reprinted, 1970; *Adalbert Stifter als Maler* (title means "Adalbert Stifter as a Painter"), Anton Schroll, 1941, 3rd edition, 1947; *Der Maler Anton Romako, 1832-1889* (title means "The Painter Anton Romako, 1882-1889"), Anton Schroll, 1954; *Die Grossen franzoesischen Impressionsten: Ihre Vorlaeufer und ihre Nachfolger* (title means "The Great French Impressionists: Their Predecessors and Their Followers"), Anton Schroll, 1952; *Ueber das "Elementare" in der Kunstgeschichte und andere Aufsaetze* (title means "The Phenomenon of the 'Elementary' in Art, and Other Selected Essays"), Brueder Rosenbaum, 1968.

Author of catalogues and text, *Cezanne,* Phaidon, 1937; *Wilhelm Busch als zeichner und Maler,* Anton Schroll, 1949; *Die Monatsbilder Pieter,* F. Deuticke Verlag, 1954; and *Gerhart Frankl,* Verlag Galerie Welz, 1973. Also author or co-author of other catalogues, including *Franz Zuelow, Egon Schiele, Oskar Kokoschka,* and *Max Kurzweil.*

* * *

NUGENT, Nancy 1938-
(Nancy Hawke)

PERSONAL: Born July 13, 1938, in Chicago, Ill.; daughter of Wheeler (a publisher) and Jeanne (an antique dealer; maiden name, East) Sammons; married Walter R. Nugent (an artist), July 2, 1975; children: Ralph Richard Manis, Christopher Alan Manis. *Education:* Attended University of Chicago, 1955-56, 1961-62, and Art Institute of Chicago, 1961. *Politics:* Republican. *Religion:* None. *Residence:* New York, N.Y. *Agent:* Mike Hamilburg, 292 La Cienega Blvd., Beverly Hills, Calif. 90211.

CAREER: Held miscellaneous clerical positions in Minneapolis, Minn., 1956-58; Modern Medicine Publications, Minneapolis, proofreader and editor, 1958-60; *Journal of the American Medical Association,* Chicago, Ill., editor, photographer, and writer, 1960-64; free-lance writer and photographer in Chicago and New York City, 1964-66; *Roche Medical Image,* New York City, staff writer, 1966-69; *Medical World News,* New York City, staff writer, 1970-71; free-lance writer and photographer, 1971—. *Member:* Bar Point House of Backgammon (charter member).

WRITINGS: (Contributor, under pseudonym Nancy Hawke) Norman Hill, editor, *Free Sex: A Delusion,* Popular Library, 1971; *Hysterectomy,* Doubleday, 1976; *The Nervous Stomach,* Little, Brown, in press. Contributor to medical journals.

WORK IN PROGRESS: Love from a Greenwich Village Kitchen, a cook book; *The Covered Wagon,* a novel; research for a book of baseball nostalgia; research for *Paramedic's Guide to Emergency Medical Techniques.*

AVOCATIONAL INTERESTS: Sports, theatre, travel, animals, backgammon, crocheting.

* * *

NULL, Gary 1945-

PERSONAL: Born January 6, 1945, in Parkersburg, W.V.; son of Robert C. and Blandenia J. (Whitehead) Null; children: Shelly Dawn. *Politics:* None. *Religion:* None. *Address:* 200 West 86th St., New York, N.Y. 10024.

CAREER: Director of nutritional science, New Jersey Hypoglycemia Foundation, 1974—; director of Nutrition Institute of America, 1976—. *Member:* Authors Guild, Overseas Press Club, Institute of Applied Biology (fellow), French Academy of Applied Science, Italian Academy of Science.

WRITINGS—On nutrition: (With Steve Null) *The Complete Handbook of Nutrition,* Speller, 1972; (with others) *The Complete Question and Answer Book of General Nutrition,* Speller, 1972; (with others) *The Complete Question and Answer Book on Natural Therapy,* Speller, 1972; *Grow Your Own Food Organically,* Speller, 1972; (with Steve Null) *Herbs for the 'Seventies,* Speller, 1972; *The Natural Organic Beauty Book,* Speller, 1972; *Body Pollution,* edited by James Dawson, Arco, 1973; *Protein for Vegetarians,* Pyramid Publications, 1974; *Foodcombing Handbook,* Pyramid Publications, 1974; *Biofeedback, Fasting, and Meditation,* Pyramid Publications, 1975; *Alcohol and Nutrition,* Pyramid Publications, 1976; *Whole Body Health and Nutrition Book,* Pinnacle Books, 1976; *Successful Pregnancy,* Pyramid Publications, 1976; *Handbook of Skin and Hair,* Pyramid Publications, 1976.

General Interest: (With Richard Simonson) *How to Turn Ideas into Dollars,* Pilot Books, 1969; *The Conspirator Who Saved the Romanovs,* Prentice-Hall, 1971; *Profitable Part-Time Home Based Businesses: How You Can Make Up to $150 a Week Extra Income,* Pilot Books, 1971; *Surviving and Settling in New York on a Shoestring,* Pilot Books, 1971; *Black Hollywood: The Negro in Motion Pictures,* Citadel, 1975; *Italio-Americans,* Stackpole, 1976; *Man and His Whole Earth,* Stackpole, 1976.

WORK IN PROGRESS: Nine books will be coming out in the next two years.

* * *

NURCOMBE, Barry 1933-

PERSONAL: Born January 11, 1933, in Brisbane, Queensland, Australia; son of Arthur Cyril (a cotton classer) and Alice (a teacher; maiden name, O'Gorman) Nurcombe; married Alison Thatcher, December 7, 1956; children: Victor, Stephen, Lisa. *Education:* University of Queensland, M.D.B.S., 1956, M.D., 1974; University of Melbourne, D.P.M., 1959; Harvard University, graduate study, 1963-64. *Religion:* Agnostic *Home:* 106 DeForest Heights, Burlington, Vt. 05401. *Office:* College of Medicine, University of Vermont, Burlington, Vt. 05401.

CAREER: University of New South Wales, Sydney, Australia, began as lecturer, became associate professor of child psychiatry, 1967-76; University of Vermont, Burlington, professor of child psychiatry and director of program, 1976—. *Member:* Australian and New Zealand College of Psychiatrists (fellow), Australian Psychological Society, Australian Pediatric Society, American Psychiatric Association, Royal College of Psychiatrists.

WRITINGS: An Outline of Child Psychiatry, University of New South Wales Press, 1972, 2nd edition, 1976; *Children of the Dispossessed,* University Press of Hawaii, 1976. Author of script and narration for "Children on the Fringe," a film for Tertiary Education Research Section of University of New South Wales, 1973.

WORK IN PROGRESS: The Clinical Process in Child Psychiatry.

SIDELIGHTS: Nurcombe writes: "My main area is research, while in Australia, in transcultural child psychiatry and also in the intellectual development of culturally different and disadvantaged Australian Aboriginal children. My recent research interest has changed to a consideration of the strategies used by psychiatric diagnosticians from the outset of a diagnostic encounter with a new patient."

* * *

NWANKWO, Nkem 1936-

PERSONAL: Born June 12, 1936, in Nawfia, Nigeria; came to United States, 1972; married Ifeoma Azuka Ejindu (a nurse); children: Ikenna (son), Adora (daughter). *Education:* University of Ibadan, B.A. (honors), 1962; Indiana University, M.A., 1976, further graduate study, 1976—. *Religion:* Roman Catholic. *Home:* 4921 College Ave., San Diego, Calif.

CAREER: High school English teacher in Ibadan, Nigeria, 1962-64; Nigerian Broadcasting Corp., Lagos, writer and producer of radio programs, 1964-70; *Daily Times,* Lagos, Nigeria, deputy editor, 1970-71; *African Impact* (weekly news magazine), Benin, Nigeria, editor-in-chief, 1971-72; Michigan State University, East Lansing, writer-in-residence and specialist at African Studies Center, 1972-73; San Diego State University, San Diego, Calif., visiting professor, 1976—. *Member:* National Society of Literature and the Arts (United States). *Awards, honors:* National short story prize from Nigerian Arts Council, 1960, for story, "The Gambler"; international drama prize from *Encounter,* 1960, for "The Two Sisters."

WRITINGS: Danda (novel), Deutsch, 1964; *Tales Out of School,* African Universities Press, 1965; *More Tales Out of School,* African Universities Press, 1966; *My Mercedes Is Bigger than Yours,* Harper, 1975.

Plays: "Eroya," first produced in Ibadan, Nigeria, at Arts Theatre of University of Ibadan, April, 1964; "Danda" (dramatized version of his novel by the same title), produced in Dakar, Senegal, at First World Festival of Negro Arts, 1966.

Radio plays; all produced by Nigeria Broadcasting Corp.: "The Inheritors," 1964; "Fire and Brimstone," 1965; "In My Father's House," 1965; "Full Circle," 1965; "The Two Sisters," 1966; "Who Gave Monkey Banana?" (satire for radio), 1966; "The Serpent in the Garden," 1966.

Contributor of stories and poems to magazines, including *Black Orpheus* and *Nigeria.*

WORK IN PROGRESS: The Scapegoat, a novel; *When Beggars Die,* an account of the Nigerian civil war.

SIDELIGHTS: Nwankwo told *CA:* "I came of age at the highpoint of Nigerian nationalism, with the achievement of self-government. We were the inheritors of a brave new world rescued from the West. My first book responded to the mood of euphoria. My subsequent books have reflected the inevitable disillusionment with the gap between idyll and reality. The Nigerian civil war caused a three year gap in my literary activities. I fought with the Biafrans who lost the war. Afterwards, feeling myself spiritually out of tune with post-war Nigeria, I came to the United States as a spiritual exile, and have been [here] ever since. My writing from now [on] is going to be progressively picaresque; it is the point of view of the rogue. It is my way of paying life back for having conspired with events to alienate me from most of the human race."

NYGAARD, Anita 1934-

PERSONAL: Born October 4, 1934, in Salem, Ore.; daughter of Earl W. and Esther (Farrell) Strickland. *Education:* Willamette University, B.A. (magna cum laude), 1957; University of Washington, Seattle, M.A., 1965. *Home:* 316 North Sixth, Lompoc, Calif. 93436. *Office:* Lompoc Museum, 200 South H, Lompoc, Calif. 93436.

CAREER: National Bank of Commerce, Seattle, Wash., librarian, 1973-74; Lompoc Museum, Lompoc, Calif., director, 1974—. Librarian for Mountaineers, Inc. *Member:* American Association of Museums (Western Regional Conference), American Association for State and Local History, Sierra Club, Santa Barbara County Archaeological Society (librarian), Lompoc Creative Writers (president).

WRITINGS: Earthclock: A Narrative Calendar of Nature's Seasons, Stackpole, 1976. Contributor to regional history journals. Group editor for *Condor Call.*

WORK IN PROGRESS: Another book on nature, based on her exploring and mountain climbing experience, and on domestic and European travel.

SIDELIGHTS: Anita Nygaard writes: "To climb a mountain—or to write a book—are both struggles of creation. The physical world of nature: the enduring mountains, the eternal oceans, are all we can see or seize of the processes of the life within us. Human relationships crumble; we build sand castles on a dying lonely planet spinning in an unguessable universe of scattered worlds; our dreams are nothing more than the passing sighs of the wind. Yet, to clasp a tree, or to see our reflection in a wolf's eye is to catch glimpses of ourselves and perhaps to guess what ultimately we may be, for nature is the dizzying changing continual spectacle of love."

* * *

OBERMAYER, Herman J. 1924-

PERSONAL: Born September 19, 1924, in Philadelphia, Pa.; son of Leon J. (a lawyer) and Julia (Sinsheimer) Obermayer; married Betty Nan Levy, June 28, 1955; children: Helen Julia, Veronica Levy, Adele Beatrice, Elizabeth Rose. *Education:* Attended University of Geneva, 1946; Dartmouth College, A.B. (cum laude), 1948. *Religion:* Jewish. *Home:* 4114 North Ridgeview Rd., Arlington, Va. 22207. *Office: Northern Virginia Sun,* 1227 North Ivy St., Arlington, Va 22210.

CAREER/WRITINGS: Long Island Daily Press, Jamaica, N.Y., reporter, 1950-53; *New Orleans Item,* New Orleans, La., classified advertising manager, 1953-55; *Standard-Times,* New Bedford, Mass. and Hyannis, Mass., promotion director, 1955-56; *Long Branch Daily Record,* Long Branch, N.J., editor and publisher, 1957-71; *Northern Virginia Sun,* Arlington, editor and publisher, and author of column "Editor's Viewpoint," 1963—. Contributor to journalism magazines and to popular journals, including *Saturday Evening Post, This Week, Pageant, Everybody's Digest, Pic, Travel, Ebony,* and *Japan Economic Journal.* Editor of *Editor's Viewpoint* (annual publication), 1971—. Director of Moleculon Research Corp. Member of Virginia Alcoholic Beverage Control Study Commission, 1972-74. Boy Scouts of America, 1st vice-president of National Capital Council, 1975—, member of National Jewish Committee, 1976—. Trustee of Friends of the Long Branch Libraries, 1958-71, of regional advisory committee of the Anti-Defamation League, 1962-71, Twin Lights Historical Museum, 1962-71, and Monmouth Art Museum, 1968-71. *Mili-*

tary service: U.S. Army, 1943-46, served in European theater, became staff sergeant.

MEMBER: National Press Club, American Society of Newspaper Editors, American Newspaper Publishers Association, Sigma Delta Chi, Sigma Chi, Rotary International, Ocean Beach Club.

* * *

O'BRIEN, Conor Cruise 1917-
(Donat O'Donnell)

PERSONAL: Surname listed in some sources as Cruise O'Brien; born November 3, 1917, in Dublin, Ireland; son of Francis Cruise (a journalist and literary critic) and Katherine (Sheehy) O'Brien; married Christine Foster, September, 1939 (divorced, 1962); married Maire MacEntee, January 9, 1962; children: Donal, Fedelma (Mrs. Nicholas Simms), Kathleen (Mrs. Joseph Kearney), Sean Patrick, Margaret. *Education:* Trinity College, Dublin, B.A. (modern literature), 1940, B.A. (modern history), 1941, Ph.D., 1953. *Home:* Whitewater, Howth Summit, Dublin, Ireland. *Office:* Dail Eireann, Leinster House, Kildare St., Dublin 2, Ireland.

CAREER: Entered Irish Civil Service, 1942, served with Department of Finance, 1942-44; Department of External Affairs, member of staff, 1944-61, served as head of Information and Cultural Section, and managing director of Irish News Agency, 1948-55, counsellor in Irish Embassy in Paris, France, 1955-56, delegate and head of United Nations Irish section, 1955-61, assistant secretary of Department of External Affairs, 1960, named member of executive staff of United Nations secretariat, 1961, and served as representative of the Secretary General in Katanga (now Shaba, Zaire), 1961; University of Ghana, Legon, vice-chancellor, 1962-65; New York University, New York, N.Y., Albert Schweitzer Professor of Humanities, 1965-69; Labour Party Member of the Dail representing Dublin North-East, 1969—; Minister for Posts and Telegraphs, 1973—; University of Dublin, Dublin, Ireland, pro-chancellor, 1973—. Visiting fellow, Nuffield College, Oxford, 1973. *Member:* Royal Irish Academy. *Awards, honors:* D.Litt. from University of Bradford, 1971, University of Ghana, 1974, and University of Edinburgh, 1976.

WRITINGS: (Under pseudonym Donat O'Donnell) *Maria Cross: Imaginative Patterns in a Group of Modern Catholic Writers,* Oxford University Press, 1952; *Parnell and His Party: 1880-90,* Oxford University Press, 1957; (editor) *The Shaping of Modern Ireland,* Routledge & Kegan Paul, 1960; *To Katanga and Back: A UN Case,* Hutchinson, 1962, Simon & Schuster, 1963; *Writers and Politics* (essays), Pantheon, 1965.

(With Northrop Frye and Stuart Hampshire) *The Morality of Scholarship,* edited by Max Black, Cornell University Press, 1967; (contributor) Irving Howe, editor, *The Idea of the Modern in Literature and the Arts,* Horizon, 1968; *The United Nations: Sacred Drama,* illustrated by Feliks Topolski, Simon & Schuster, 1968; (contributor) Arthur I. Blaustein and R. R. Woock, editors, *Man Against Poverty: World War III,* introduction by John W. Gardner, Random House, 1968; (editor) Edmund Burke, *Reflections on the Revolution in France,* Penguin, 1969; *Conor Cruise O'Brien Introduces Ireland,* edited by Owen Dudley Edwards, Deutsch, 1969, McGraw, 1970; (editor with William Dean Vanech) *Power and Consciousness,* New York University Press, 1969.

Albert Camus of Europe and Africa, Viking, 1970 (published in England as *Camus,* Fontana, 1970); (with wife, Maire MacEntee O'Brien) *The Story of Ireland,* Viking, 1972 (published in England as *A Concise History of Ireland,* Thames & Hudson, 1972); *The Suspecting Glance,* Faber, 1972; (contributor) George A. White and C. H. Newman, editors, *Literature in Revolution,* Holt, 1972; *States of Ireland,* Pantheon, 1972; (contributor) *Teilhard de Chardin: In Quest of the Perfection of Man,* Fairleigh Dickinson University Press, 1973.

Plays: "King Herod Explains," first produced in Dublin at Gate Theatre, October 7, 1969; *Murderous Angels: A Political Tragedy and Comedy in Black and White* (first produced in Los Angeles at Mark Taper Forum, February 5, 1970; produced in New York at American National Theatre and Academy, March 20, 1970), Little, Brown, 1968. Contributor of articles to *New Statesman, Nation, Saturday Review, Atlantic* and other publications.

WORK IN PROGRESS: A life of Edmund Burke.

SIDELIGHTS: Conor Cruise O'Brien has spent his life to date distinguishing himself as a literary critic, diplomat, dramatist, professor and politician. He rose to world prominence as Irish delegate to the United Nations and as special representative of Dag Hammarskjöld. It has been suggested that Hammarskjöld's knowledge of and admiration for *Maria Cross,* a volume of critical essays, was influential in his decision to ask O'Brien to serve on his executive staff. In this capacity O'Brien was assigned, in 1961, to oversee U.N. operations at Katanga in the Congo. Later that year, at O'Brien's request, he was relieved of his duties in the Congo, and at the same time, resigned from the foreign service altogether.

O'Brien announced his intention to write a book about the difficulties he had encountered in the service of the U.N. in the Congo. Shortly following this announcement, O'Brien received a letter from then acting Secretary General U Thant advising him that unauthorized disclosure of United Nations affairs was prohibited by regulation. Thant's letter serves as the preface of *To Katanga and Back,* published in 1963. Of O'Brien's book, Russell Howe wrote: "[It] helps to explain why this sensitive, slightly swashbuckling Irishman, the antithesis of the classical U.N. official, inspired respect in those who knew him. O'Brien failed in his job of 'settling Katanga,' but the way in which he failed helped to shape a new attitude to the problem; it was partly thanks to O'Brien that the U.N. finally wrote a page of victory in the dust of the high plateau."

Although he had officially ended his diplomatic career with the United Nations, O'Brien was still concerned with the intricate workings of the organization. His continued interest resulted in another book, *The United Nations: Sacred Drama.* In it O'Brien perceives the U.N. as both temple and stage. John Osborne interprets O'Brien's concept of the U.N. He wrote: "If the United Nations is in its useful essence a temple of last resort to which men go for salvation, a theatre in which they act out the means of salvation, it follows that the Secretary General of the United Nations must be 'the high priest of the shrine'—or be nothing. His real authority, like that of the organization he serves, is moral, spiritual, *religious.* A profanation occurs, the Secretary General's authority and usefulness are impaired and may be destroyed, when he 'steps down from the religious level of politics, to the level of applied politics.' And this is all but certain to happen when the Secretary General becomes responsible for the UN's 'peace-keeping' operations. However necessary these missions may be in themselves, they are military and therefore sordid and not 'always such that the chief priest of peace can with any propriety carry responsibility for them.'" Albert Bremel commented on O'Brien's conception of the dramatic aspects of the United Nations. "Theater is an art. If it is to be good theater, it requires the exercise of imagination. That is what Mr. O'Brien is really concerned with. Imaginative participants will recognize (some have already recognized) the U.N. as a superb arena for dramatizing the threats to survival. Like most countries, the U.S. 'wants to cut a good figure on the world stage (and especially to play on the domestic stage the part of one who is cutting a good figure on the world stage).'

"At present the U.N. drama 'swings from tragedy to farce and back again; neither pathos or buffoonery is alien to it.' Yet the performances are also sacred, passion plays of a sort, since the U.N. constitutes 'humanity's prayer to itself to be saved from itself.' Its spectacles should be acknowledged as rituals akin to the Greek myths or to . . . African tribal rites. . . .''

Seemingly a logical extension of O'Brien's concept of the U.N. as drama, he culled his experiences in Katanga to produce his first play, *Murderous Angels.* Controversial critical opinion and interpretation appeared even before the drama was staged. The play was not intended to be viewed as a documentary drama or as 'theatre of fact,' but rather as a tragedy, as the subtitle implies. O'Brien stated: "As long as I have Aristotle on my side, I don't care who's against me." Since the point of tragical drama is to mirror the events of life, Harold Clurman points out that if "its details should be found inaccurate or misleading, O'Brien's purpose still would not be invalidated." He goes on to say that the "play mirrors a real historical situation. . . . The murderous angels of the title are 'the great and noble abstractions . . . of Peace in the case of Hammarskjöld, Freedom in the case of Lumumba.'

"It is not of first importance whether O'Brien's theory is correct in this instance; it is important that what he suggests is in general more than probable. Statesmen are the gods of the machine, a mechanism in which we are enmeshed and too often destroyed. The mechanism is so vast and complicated that we commonly fear ourselves impotent to master it. And that is tragic."

A *New Statesman* portrait of O'Brien contends that "In so far as a civil servant can, he became a minor national hero; the Irish independent, asserting his country's independence along with his own." It goes on to say: "Hero-worshippers have always accumulated around O'Brien. . . . He is a hero to many American radicals, particularly the group clustered around the *New York Review of Books.* But the American avant-garde can rarely have found a stranger champion. There is no mind-blowing, no anti-thought, no Godardian fragmented sensibility in O'Brien. He belongs to the alcohol generation not the drugs generation; speaks slowly—to American ears, exactly like an Englishman—and with old-fashioned, graceful, leisurely wit. His idea of a good evening is a few friends and a few drinks and intelligent conversation. It is too Ivy League by far for the disciples who nevertheless recognize in him a man who may sell, but will never sell out. He is a modern version of that 19th-century radical phenomenon, the Only White Man the Natives Trust."

AVOCATIONAL INTERESTS: Travel.

BIOGRAPHICAL/CRITICAL SOURCES: New York Times, September 15, 1961; *Commentary,* September, 1965; *Newsweek,* October 17, 1966; *Listener,* May 30, 1968; *New York Times Book Review,* August 4, 1968; *New Statesman,*

December 6, 1968; *The Observer*, January 26, 1969; *Nation*, February 23, 1970, March 27, 1972; John Weightman, *The Concept of the Avant-Garde*, Open Court, 1973; Catherine Hughes, *Plays, Politics, and Polemics*, Specialist Publications, 1973.

* * *

OCHS, Phil 1940-1976

December 19, 1940—April 9, 1976; American folk song composer, singer, and guitarist. Obituaries: *New York Times*, April 10, 1976; *Washington Post*, April 11, 1976; *Newsweek*, April 19, 1976.

* * *

O'CONNOR, Mark 1945-

PERSONAL: Born March 19, 1945, in Melbourne, Australia; son of Kevin J. (a magistrate) and Elaine (a journalist; maiden name, Riordan) O'Connor. *Education:* University of Melbourne, B.A. (first class honors), 1965. *Politics:* "Humanist." *Religion:* "Biologist." *Home address:* c/o 8 Ailsa Ave., East Malvern, Victoria 3145, Australia. *Agent:* Howard Nicholson, 87 Jersey Rd., Woollahra, Sydney, Australia.

CAREER: University of Western Australia, Perth, lecturer in English, 1966; Australian National University, Canberra, lecturer in English, 1967-68; writer, 1968—. *Member:* Australian Society of Authors (Australian Capital Territory state vice-president), Australian Capital Territory Fellowship of Australian Authors (vice-president, 1973-74). *Awards, honors:* International prize from *Poetry Australia*, 1973, for "Flight Poem," and 1975, for "Turtle Hatching"; Marten Bequest Travelling Scholarship for poetry, 1976.

WRITINGS: Reef Poems, University of Queensland Press, 1976.

Plays: "Cure of the Ring" (one-act), first produced in Canberra, Australia, at Street Theatre Locations, March, 1973; "Reft" (one-act), first produced in Canberra at Act IV Festival, August, 1974; "Dillion" (four-act), first produced in Melbourne, Australia, at Melbourne Theatre, August, 1974; "Scenes" (four-act), first produced in Canberra at Australian National University, September, 1976. Contributor of articles and stories to periodicals.

WORK IN PROGRESS: The Illiteracy Conspiracy, "on the spelling reform issue."

SIDELIGHTS: O'Connor writes that he has "a particular interest in biology, ecology, conservation, and islands. A strong anti-populationist. (Two children is *not* zero population growth. Having three is a crime.) Have spent much time on the Great Barrier Reef, am about to . . . spend two years traveling around Mediterranean islands."

AVOCATIONAL INTERESTS: Diving, gardening.

* * *

ODDO, Sandra (Schmidt) 1937-
(Sandra Schmidt)

PERSONAL: Surname is pronounced Oh-dough; born July 8, 1937, in Chicago, Ill.; daughter of Ernest F. and Mildred (Weaver) Schmidt; married Jasper Oddo (a playwright), April 27, 1969. *Education:* Wilson College, B.A. (cum laude), 1959; New York University, M.A., 1962. *Home:* 340 West 88th St., New York, N.Y. 10024. *Agent:* Julie Fallowfield, McIntosh & Otis, 18 East 41st St., New York, N.Y. 10017.

CAREER: Berkeley Daily Gazette, Berkeley, Calif., copy girl and drama critic, 1959-60; New York University, New York, N.Y., editor of faculty magazine, 1960-62; *Village Voice*, New York, N.Y., contributing drama critic, 1960-64; *Life*, New York, N.Y., reporter, 1963-65; *Newsweek*, New York, N.Y., by-line book critic and associate editor, 1965-67; *Los Angeles Times*, Los Angeles, Calif., New York theater reviewer, 1967-70; free-lance writer, 1967-73; *House & Garden*, New York, N.Y., staff writer, 1973-76; *Solar Age* magazine, New York, N.Y., managing editor, 1975—. Member of Margo Jones Award judging panel. *Member:* Phi Beta Kappa. *Awards, honors:* Ford Foundation travel grant, 1964; National Endowment for the Arts grant, 1967, to visit and make a critical evaluation of every U.S. professional regional theater.

WRITINGS: Home Made: An Alternative to Supermarket Living (Book-of-the Month Club selection), Atheneum, 1972. Contributor to *New York Times Sunday Book Review, Christian Science Monitor, Drama Review, World Theatre, Washington Post, Houston Chronicle, Newsday, National Observer, Purple Thumb*, and *Mother Earth News*.

* * *

ODEN, Clifford 1916-

PERSONAL: Original name, Clifford Oder, legally changed in 1939; born June 21, 1916, in Texas; son of Alonzo (a clergyman) and Belle (Embree) Oder; married Louise Lightfoot, May 21, 1940; children: Virginia (Mrs. John Collier), James, John, Michael. *Education:* Howard Payne College, B.A., 1940; East Texas Baptist College, M.S., 1951. *Politics:* Independent. *Religion:* Baptist. *Home:* 3225 Sheridan Dr., Garland, Tex. 75041. *Office:* Jupiter Road Baptist Church, Garland, Tex. 75042.

CAREER: U.S. Navy, Corpus Christi, Tex., civilian employee in engineering department, 1940-46; Le Tourneau College, Longview, Tex., instructor in Bible, mathematics, and chemistry, 1946-55; pastor of several Baptist churches in Dallas, Tex., 1955-59, Garland, Tex., 1959-69, Dallas, 1969-72; Jupiter Road Baptist Church, Garland, Tex., associate pastor, 1972—. Dean, and instructor in psychology and Bible, Garland College, 1961-68. *Awards, honors:* LL.D. from Garland College, 1964.

WRITINGS: The Return of the Lord, Zondervan, 1951; *Thank God I Have Cancer*, Arlington House, 1976; *Man, Woman, and God*, Fellowship Publications, 1976.

WORK IN PROGRESS: Cleansing the Temple, publication expected in 1978.

SIDELIGHTS: Oden's book, *Man, Woman, and God*, claims, through "historical, Biblical, psychological, and sociological evidence that human sexuality can reach full expression only in the framework of the Christian faith. The myth that Christianity is ascetic is thoroughly exploded. Asceticism is shown to have its origins in paganism, not in Christianity."

* * *

O'DONNELL, Donat
See O'BRIEN, Conor C(ruise)

* * *

O'DONNELL, Thomas J(oseph) 1918-

PERSONAL: Born March 8, 1918, in Baltimore, Md.; son of Thomas Joseph (a physician) and Anna May (Brophy) O'Donnell. *Education:* Attended St. Charles College,

Catonsville, Md., 1937, and College of St. Isaac Jogues, 1938-41; Georgetown University, A.B., 1943, Ph.L., 1944, M.A., 1954; Woodstock College, S.T.B., 1951. *Office:* Seminary of Pius X, Erlanger, Ky. 41018.

CAREER: Entered Society of Jesus (Jesuits), 1938, ordained Roman Catholic priest, 1950; Georgetown University, Washington, D.C., professor of medical ethics, 1952-62, regent, 1953-60, dean of students, 1956-60; Woodstock Theological Seminary, Woodstock, Md., lecturer in medical morals and spiritual director, 1962-65; lecturer, writer, and consultant to North Carolina Apostolate, 1966-76; Seminary of St. Pius X, Erlanger, Ky., lecturer in general and special ethics, 1976—. Director of National Kidney Disease Foundation, 1963-68; consultant to U.S. Catholic Conference. *Member:* American Medical Association, National Society for Medical Research (vice-president, 1959), National Transplant Council.

WRITINGS: Morals in Medicine, Paulist/Newman, 1956, revised edition, 1960; (contributor) Frank J. Ayd, Jr., editor, *Medical Moral and Legal Issues in Mental Health Care,* Williams & Wilkins, 1974; *Medicine and Christian Morality,* Alba House, 1976.

Contributor to *New Catholic Encyclopedia,* McGraw, 1966. Contributor of articles and reviews to theology and medical journals.

* * *

OEHMKE, T(homas) H(arold) 1947-
(Warren Plain)

PERSONAL: Surname is pronounced *Em*-kee; born November 13, 1947, in Detroit, Mich.; son of Harold Warren (an attorney) and Elizabeth (a legal assistant; maiden name, Ryerse) Oehmke; married Carol Bukrey, June 14, 1968 (divorced March 25, 1975); children: Theodore, Jason. *Education:* Attended University of Madrid, summer, 1965; Wayne State University, Ph.B., 1969, J.D., 1973. *Politics:* Independent. *Religion:* Agnostic. *Home:* 13548 Tacoma Ave., Detroit, Mich. 48205. *Office:* 1010 Commonwealth Bldg., Detroit, Mich. 48226.

CAREER: Elementary school teacher in Detroit, Mich., 1967-69; high school teacher of English and Spanish in Stephenson, Mich., 1969-70; Employers Association of Detroit, Detroit, Mich., research analyst, 1970-73; New Detroit, Inc., Detroit, Mich., political economist, 1973—. Private practice of law in Detroit, 1973—; instructor at Macomb County Community College, 1973-74. Advisor to Michigan governor's Advisory Commission on Workmen's Compensation, 1974-75, and Michigan Economic Action Council, 1975-76; member of Wayne County Advisory Council on Business and Commercial Development, 1975-76; member of Detroit mayor's Economic Development Planning Advisory Council, 1975-76. Member of advisory council of Detroit Central City Community Mental Health, Inc., 1975—. Member of State Bar of Michigan and American Arbitration Association's Commercial Panel of Arbitrators.

MEMBER: American Bar Association, American Arbitration Association, Society of Professionals in Dispute Resolution, Industrial Relations Research Association, American Judicature Society, Detroit Bar Association, Council on Urban Economic Development.

WRITINGS: Compulsory Arbitration of Police and Fire Disputes, Employers Association of Detroit, 1971; *Complete Guide to the Affirmative Action Program,* Employers Association of Detroit, 1973; *Sex Discrimination in Employ-*

ment, Trends Publishing, 1974; *Michigan Incorporation Manual,* Michigan Law Research Institute, 1976. Contributor to *Menominee County Journal.*

WORK IN PROGRESS—Nonfiction: *The Second War Between the States: Competitive Economic Development.* Fiction, to appear under pseudonym Warren Plain: *The Labyrinth,* poems; "Coming of Age," a three-act play; "The Squirrel Who Stayed for Dinner," a children's short story.

SIDELIGHTS: Oehmke writes: "*Sex Discrimination in Employment* treated a subject that was topical in 1974 when it was published. From a socio-economic standpoint, women were eliminated, systematically and institutionally, from full participation in the American workplace; more specifically, the tool of their liberation, namely economic independence, was being kept from them. In order to liberate the employment opportunities from which women were excluded, they had to identify those discriminatory and illegal employment practices and then confront and eliminate them. Power often derives from knowledge applied and this book was written to offer such knowledge, hoping that it would lead, in some small measure, to the elimination of sex discrimination in employment. But, most important was the style of writing: this book took a very technical subject of law and expressed that subject in terms that a high school graduate could understand; an achievement, moreover, was that the substance of the book was accurate and could also be relied upon by a lawyer in a court proceeding. Such was the literary challenge.

"My second book further advances the principal of simplicity in expressing the law. The *Michigan Incorporation Manual* is a 'cookbook' for attorneys. It is a recipe for concocting a corporation. This handbook takes a lengthy and complex process, that even few attorneys can perform well, and translates that process into a step-by-step procedure that minimizes the mistakes which often are made when practicing law in an area that you know little about. The feeling of achievement in having written that book comes from knowing that it explains a technical legal process in terms that even an attorney can understand.

"Writing non-fiction, business-oriented books is a drain on one's time; though the royalties are surely greater, the intrinsic psychic income is less than one might receive from writing good fiction or poetry. Thus, my writing plans in the future include a balance between producing saleable business publications which provide the economic cushion against which I can compose plays, poetry, short stories and, eventually, novels. Hopefully, the same economy of words used to address the business-reader will be helpful in communicating more complex human emotions and experience to readers of fiction." *Avocational interests:* Jogging, handball, skiing, reading, playing guitar.

* * *

OERUM, Poul (Erik) 1919-

PERSONAL: Born December 23, 1919, in Nykoebing, Denmark; son of Lauritz (a boiler attendant) and Constance (Noerholm) Oerum; married Signe Andersen, May 27, 1944; children: Bente, Jan, Eva. *Education:* High school graduate. *Religion:* Danish Official Church. *Home:* 6720 Nordby, Fanoe, Denmark.

CAREER: Worked as laborer, farmer, sailor, and as a journalist (during the later years of this period as a crime reporter in Copenhagen), 1944-57; author, 1957—. *Member:* Danish Writers' Association. *Awards, honors:* Danish Writers'

Association award, 1957, for *Slet dine spor;* Danish Literary Critics' award, 1958, for *Lyksalighedens oe;* Author of the Year golden laurels from Danish Booktrade, 1963, for *Natten i ventesalen;* Johannes Ewald award, 1964; Henry Nathansen award, 1966; Otto Rung award, 1969; Henrik Pontoppidan award, 1970; Soeren Gyldendal prize, 1973; Edgar Allan Poe awards, 1974, for *Kun sandheden,* and 1975, for *De uforsonlige;* Hans Christian Andersen prize, 1976.

WRITINGS—All published by Forlaget Fremad, except as noted—Novels in English translation: *Syndebuk,* 1972, translation by Kenneth Barclay published as *Scapegoat: A Mystery,* Pantheon, 1975; *Kun sandheden,* 1974, translation by Barclay published as *Nothing But the Truth,* Pantheon, 1976.

Novels in the original Danish: *Dansen med de fire vinde* (title means "The Dance with the Four Winds"), E. Wangel, 1953; *Ulveleg* (title means "Wolf's Playing"), E. Wangel, 1954; *Sidste flugt* (title means "Last Escape"), 1955; *Slet dine spor* (title means "Cover Your Tracks"), 1956; *Det gyldne rav* (title means "The Golden Amber"), 1957; *Raeven og jomfruen* (title means "The Fox and the Virgin"), 1957; *Lyksalighedens oe* (title means "The Island of Happiness"), 1958; *Skyggen ved din hoejre haand* (title means "The Shadow at Your Right Hand"), 1959; *Komedie i Florens* (title means "Comedy in Florence"), 1960; *Natten i ventesalen* (title means "The Night in the Waiting Room"), *Rundt om en enebaerbusk* (title means "Round the Mulberry Bush"), 1963; *Hanegal* (title means "Cockcrow"), Gyldendal, 1965; *Romance for Selma,* Gyldendal, 1966; *Ukendt offer* (title means "Unknown Victim"), Gyldendal, 1967; *Spionen ud af den blaa luft* (title means "The Spy Out of the Blue Air"), Gyldendal, 1968; *Et andet ansigt* (title means "Another Face"), 1970; *Hjemkomst til drab* (title means "Homecoming to Homicide"), 1970; *Den stjaalne ild* (title means "The Stolen Fire"), 1971; *Det 11. bud* (title means "Scapegoat"), 1972; *De uforsonlige* (title means "The Irreconcilables"), 1975; *Tavse vidner* (title means "The Silent Witnesses"), 1976.

Short story collections: *Det lille lys* (title means "The Small Light"), 1959; *I vandenes dyb* (title means "In the Depth of the Waters"), 1961; *Tagdryp* (title means "Dripping from the Eaves"), 1962; *Uskylds frugt* (title means "Fruit of Innocence"), 1964; *Nattens gaester* (title means "Guests of the Night"), Gyldendal, 1969. Story included in anthology, *Tre danske noveller* (title means "Three Danish Stories"), compiled by Erik Mertz, Gjellerup, 1970.

Poetry: *Sommerens genfaerd* (title means "The Ghost of the Summer"), 1956; (with Tom Kristensen) *Groenlandsskibet* (title means "The Greenland Ship"), Thejls bogtryk., 1959; *Et udvalg af Poul Oerums digte* (title means "A Selection of Poul Oerum's Poems"), Kilding Tekniske Skole, 1967.

Autobiography: *Tilbagerejsen* (title means "The Return Journey"), 1973. Also author of radio plays, television plays and motion picture scripts.

SIDELIGHTS: Groenlandsskibet was originally the title of a poem by Oerum written on the occasion of the tragic wreck of a Danish ship bound for Greenland. The ship was on its maiden voyage and the entire crew was lost. The poem, first published in a Danish newspaper, was later combined with the work of Tom Kristensen and published under the name *Groenlandsskibet.* The proceeds of the sale of the book were donated to the bereaved families of the lost crewmen.

O'FLAHERTY, Wendy Doniger 1940-

PERSONAL: Born November 20, 1940, in New York, N.Y.; daughter of Lester L. (a publisher) and Rita (Roth) Doniger; married Dennis M. O'Flaherty (a lawyer), March 31, 1964; children: Michael Lester. *Education:* Radcliffe College, B.A. (summa cum laude), 1962; Harvard University, M.A., 1963, Ph.D., 1968; Oxford University, D.Phil., 1973. *Home:* 1101 Hillview Rd., Berkeley, Calif. 94708. *Office:* Graduate Theological Union, 2465 Le Conte Ave., Berkeley, Calif. 94709.

CAREER: University of London, London, England, lecturer in Indian studies and comparative religion, 1968-75; University of California, Berkeley, lecturer in South and Southeast Asian studies, 1975—. Lecturer at Graduate Theological Union, 1976—. *Member:* American Oriental Society, Association of Asian Studies, American Academy of Religion, California Dressage Society, Phi Beta Kappa.

WRITINGS: (With R. Gordon Wasson) *Soma: Divine Mushroom of Immortality,* Harcourt, 1968; *Asceticism and Eroticism in the Mythology of Siva,* Oxford University Press, 1973; *Hindu Myths,* Penguin, 1975; *The Origins of Evil in Hindu Mythology,* University of California Press, 1976. Contributor to Asian and Oriental studies, theology, and literary journals.

WORK IN PROGRESS: Ancient Indian Horsemanship; a translation, with J. F. Staal, of 100 hymns from the Rig Veda.

* * *

OGLETREE, Earl Joseph 1930-

PERSONAL: Born June 26, 1930, in Philadelphia, Pa.; son of Earl L. (a barber) and Helen (Conway) Ogletree; married Gerda Sebauer (a teacher). *Education:* Chicago Teachers College, B.Ed., 1961; University of Chicago, M.A., 1962; Wayne State University, Ed.D., 1967. *Politics:* Independent. *Religion:* Christian. *Office:* Department of Curriculum and Instruction, Chicago State University, 95th and King Dr., Chicago, Ill. 60628.

CAREER: Radio Corp. of America, Chicago, Ill., radio and television serviceman, 1957-61; Chicago State University, Chicago, Ill., assistant professor, 1968-73, associate professor of education, 1974—. Founder and director of Esperanza School for Retarded Children, 1968-72; trustee of Christian Community, 1969-72. *Military service:* U.S. Army, Signal Corps, 1951-53; served in Korea.

MEMBER: American Educational Research Association, American Association of Special Educators (member of board of directors), American Association of Parapsychology and Medicine, Waldorf School Association of Chicago (president, 1962-72), Esperanza School Association (president of board of directors), Westside Parents of Retarded Children, Anthroposophical Society of Chicago (trustee, 1968-72), Phi Delta Kappa.

WRITINGS: Understanding Readiness: A Rationale (A Rejoinder to Jenses), ERIC Clearinghouse on Early Childhood Education, 1973; (with Maxine Hawkins) *Writing Instructional Objectives and Activities for the Modern Curriculum: A Programmed Approach,* MSS Educational Publishing, 1973; (editor with David Garcia, and contributor) *The Socially Disadvantaged: The Physiological and Psychological Aspects of Deprivation,* two volumes, MSS Information Corp., 1974; (with Garcia) *Schooling and the Spanish Speaking Urban Child,* C. C Thomas, 1975; (with Patricia Gebauer) *Unit Planning for the Modern Curricu-*

lum, C. C Thomas, 1975; (editor) *Issues in Urban Education,* MSS Information Corp., 1976. Contributor of more than one hundred articles and reviews to education journals and newspapers, particularly *Times Educational Supplement.* Member of editorial board of *Journal for Special Educators of the Mentally Retarded.*

WORK IN PROGRESS: A novel; books on teaching mathematics in the elementary grades; a book on Waldorf education; research on bioplasmic forces and human development.

*   *   *

O'KEEFE, Paul   1900(?)-1976

1900(?)—February 5, 1976; American politician, real estate executive, and author of books in his field. Obituaries: *New York Times,* February 8, 1976.

*   *   *

OLSON, Donald   1938-

PERSONAL: Born November 28, 1938, in Jamestown, N.Y.; son of Ernest Theodore (a carpenter and house builder) and Ava (Smith) Olson. *Education:* Attended New York University. *Politics:* "Eclectic." *Religion:* "Eclectic." *Home:* 216 Baker St., Jamestown, N.Y. 14701. *Agent:* Blanche C. Gregory, Inc., 2 Tudor City Pl., New York, N.Y. 10017.

CAREER: Writer. Has worked as railroad construction worker, proprietor of a book store, treasure hunter, antique appraiser, and house builder. *Member:* Mystery Writers of America. *Awards, honors:* Award from Mystery Writers of America, 1975, for story "Screams and Echoes."

WRITINGS: The Truth About Mrs. G. (novella), Signet, 1970; *The Sky Children* (novella), Avon, 1975; *If I Don't Tell* (suspense novel), Putnam, 1976; *Beware, Sweet Maggie* (novella), Pyramid Press, 1977. Contributor of stories to mystery magazines.

WORK IN PROGRESS: Another suspense novel.

SIDELIGHTS: Olson writes: "I have been writing from a very early age indeed, inspired by those great authors whose works were deeply infused with elements of mystery and suspense: the Dickens of *Edwin Drood* and *Bleak House,* the Henry James of *Aspern Papers,* the Trollope of *Eustace Diamonds,* all 'mystery stories' which at the same time seek to explore that alienation of the human spirit—call it loneliness, call it lovelessness—which in one way or another excites those acts of desperation or despair from which their plots evolve. The novel of suspense, as it's been recently developed by its better practitioners, is usually an examination of those aberrant human drives that weave a complex of tension involving at least two opposing characters. It is much more than the traditional 'mystery story' inasmuch as it reflects so tellingly the violent forces governing so much of what is happening in real life today.

"When I was very young my uncle loaned me a copy of *The Hound of the Baskervilles,* imparting to me at the same time the astonishing news that he himself was a black sheep younger brother of the famous sleuth. Being a credulous and romantic youth, I was inclined to amuse myself by believing this secret to be rooted in truth. After all, my uncle's name was Holmes, and he did live on Baker Street. Eventually I inherited his house and his library, a very old house and a very fine library. I write my stories at an old rolltop desk which once belonged to this Mr. Holmes of Baker Street. Before settling down at this desk to compose my stories, I did a great deal of roaming about the continent, working at

more jobs than I can easily remember, but always obsessed by that game Arthur Machen called 'the chase of the phrase.' I brought home with me to this old house in Baker Street remembrances of those myriad characters who, transfigured by art, explore their far more romantic destinies in my stories and novels."

*   *   *

OLSON, Merle Theodore
See OLSON, Toby

*   *   *

OLSON, Toby   1937-

PERSONAL: Birth-given name, Merle Theodore Olson; born August 17, 1937, in Berwyn, Ill.; son of Merle T. Olson and Elizabeth (Skowbo) Olson Potokar (a telephone company supervisor); married Ann Yeomans, September 10, 1963 (divorced, 1965); married Miriam Meltzer (a social worker), November 27, 1966. *Education:* Occidental College, B.A., 1965; Long Island University, M.A., 1967. *Home:* 2126 Cypress St., Philadelphia, Pa. 19103.

CAREER: Long Island University, Brooklyn, N.Y., assistant professor of English, 1966-74; Friends Seminary, New York, N.Y., writer-in-residence, 1974-75; Temple University, Ambler, Pa., instructor in English, 1975—. Member of faculty at New School for Social Research, 1967-75; poet-in-residence at State University of New York College at Cortland, 1972. Associate director and instructor at Aspen Writers' Workshop, 1964-67; has given poetry readings all over the United States. *Military service:* U.S. Navy, surgical technician, 1957-61. *Member:* Coordinating Council of Literary Magazines. *Awards, honors:* Award from Creative Artists Public Service Program of New York State Council on the Arts, 1975.

WRITINGS: The Hawk-Foot Poems, Abraxas Press, 1968; *Maps* (poems), Perishable Press, 1969; *Worms Into Nails* (poems), Perishable Press, 1969; *The Brand* (poems), Perishable Press, 1969; *Pig's Book* (poems), Dr. Generosity Press, 1969; *Cold House* (poetry broadside), Perishable Press, 1970; *Tools* (poetry broadside), Dr. Generosity Press, 1970; *Shooting Pigeons* (poetry broadside), Perishable Press, 1972; *Vectors* (poems), Membrane Press, 1972; *From Home* (poetry broadside), Wine Press, 1972; (author of introduction) Carl Thayler, *Goodrich,* Capricorn Books, 1972; *Fishing* (poems), Perishable Press, 1974; *The Wrestlers and Other Poems,* Barlenmir House, 1974; *City* (poems), Membrane Press, 1974; (author of introduction) Helen Saslow, *Arctic Summer,* Barlenmir House, 1974; *Changing Appearance: Poems 1965-1970,* Membrane Press, 1975; *The Life of Jesus* (fiction), New Directions, 1976; *Home* (poems), Membrane Press, 1976; (author of introduction) Annette Hayn, *One Armed Flyer,* Poets Press, 1976; *Four Poems,* Perishable Press, 1976. Also editor of *Margins* 1976.

Poems and stories represented in anthologies, including *Inside Outer Space,* edited by Robert Vas Dias, Doubleday, 1970; *New Directions-25,* edited by J. Laughlin, New Directions, 1972; *Loves, Etc.,* edited by Marguerite Harris, Doubleday, 1973; and *Active Anthology,* edited by George Quasha, Sumac Press, 1974.

Contributor of articles, stories, poems, and reviews to more than one hundred journals, including *Nation, New York Quarterly, Choice, Confrontation, Ohio Review, American Poetry Review,* and *Poetry Now.*

WORK IN PROGRESS—Poetry: *Country*, for Perishable Press; *Doctor Miriam*, Perishable Press; *Birdsongs*, Broadway Boogie Press.

SIDELIGHTS: Olson writes: "I attended six grade schools, five high schools, the United States Navy, and six colleges; I moved a lot, living in eight states. I think the fact of this movement—which, in my young years, was a literal search for a 'healthy' place for my sick father to live—has a lot to do with what I write. I tend to see my writing (both poetry and prose) as a kind of salvage—a way of validating my past, of making something meaningful out of the places and experiences I have lived in. I don't mean to suggest that my writing is strictly autobiographical, only that the source of it is. I think that autobiography is another kind of fiction, the one that we call our past."

* * *

O'MALLEY, Mary Dolling (Sanders) 1889-1974 (Ann Bridge)

PERSONAL: Born September 11, 1889, in Shenley, Hertfordshire, England; daughter of James Harris and Marie (Day) Sanders; married Owen St. Clair O'Malley (a British Foreign Office official), October 25, 1913; children: Jane, John Patrick, Kate (Mrs. Paul Willert). *Education:* London School of Economics and Political Science, diploma, 1913. *Religion:* Roman Catholic. *Home:* 27 Charlbury Rd., Oxford, England.

CAREER: Author, 1932-74. Member of prize committee, Prix Femina-Vie Heureuse, 1935-39; British Red Cross representative in Hungary, 1940-41; worked with Polish Red Cross, 1944-45; did relief work in France after World War II. *Member:* Society of Antiquaries of Scotland (fellow), Royal Horticulture Society (fellow), Wine and Food Society (fellow), Charity Organization Society (London; secretary, 1911-13), Wives Fellowship (central president, 1923-25). *Awards, honors:* *Atlantic Monthly* prize, 1932, for *Peking Picnic*.

WRITINGS—All novels, except as noted: *Peking Picnic*, Little, Brown, 1932; *The Ginger Griffin* (British Book Society selection), Little, Brown, 1934; *Illyrian Spring* (British Book Society selection), Little, Brown, 1935; *The Song in the House* (short stories), Chatto & Windus, 1936; *Enchanter's Nightshade* (British Book Society selection), Little, Brown, 1937; *Four-Part Setting*, Little, Brown, 1939.

Frontier Passage, Little, Brown, 1942; *Singing Waters* (British Book Society and Literary Guild selection), Chatto & Windus, 1945, Macmillan, 1946; *And Then You Came*, Chatto & Windus, 1948, Macmillan, 1949; (with Susan Lowndes) *The Selective Traveller in Portugal* (nonfiction), Evans Brothers, 1949, Knopf, 1952, revised edition, McGraw, 1961.

The House at Kilmartin (juvenile), Evans Brothers, 1951; *The Dark Moment* (Literary Guild selection), Macmillan, 1952; *A Place to Stand*, Macmillan, 1953; *Portrait of My Mother* (autobiography), Chatto & Windus, 1955, published as *A Family of Two Worlds: A Portrait of Her Mother*, Macmillan, 1955; *The Lighthearted Quest* (also see below), Macmillan, 1956; *The Portuguese Escape* (Literary Guild selection; also see below), Macmillan, 1958.

The Numbered Account (also see below), McGraw, 1960; *Julia Involved: Three Julia Probyn Novels* (includes *The Lighthearted Quest*, *The Portuguese Escape*, and *The Numbered Account*), McGraw, 1962; *The Tightening String*, McGraw, 1962; *The Dangerous Islands*, McGraw, 1963; *Emergency in the Pyrenees*, McGraw, 1965; *The Episode at Toledo*, McGraw, 1966; *Facts and Fictions*, (autobiography) Chatto & Windus, 1968; *The Malady in Madeira*, McGraw, 1969.

Moments of Knowing: Some Personal Experiences Beyond Normal Knowledge (autobiography), Hodder & Stoughton, 1970, published as *Moments of Knowing: Personal Experiences in the Realm of Extra-Sensory Perception*, McGraw, 1970; *Permission To Resign: Goings-On in the Corridors of Power* (autobiography), Sidgwick & Jackson, 1971; *Julia In Ireland*, McGraw, 1973.

(Died March 9, 1974)

[Sketch verified by daughter, Kate Willert]

* * *

OPPITZ, Rene 1905(?)-1976

1905(?)—1976; French writer of poetry and prose under pseudonym J. J. Marine. Obituaries: *AB Bookman's Weekly*, March 1, 1976.

* * *

ORBACH, Ruth Gary 1941-

PERSONAL: Born January 16, 1941, in New York, N.Y.; daughter of Joseph and Francis (Lahn) Gary; married Laurence Orbach (a historian); children: Shannah. *Education:* Attended Antioch College; City University of New York, B.A., 1972. *Home:* 21 Hartham Rd., London N.7, England.

CAREER: Weaver and fabric designer in New York, N.Y., 1962-63; art teacher and painter in New York City, 1963-67; free-lance designer in New York City and London, England, 1967-70; illustrator of children's books in London, England, 1970—.

WRITINGS—All self-illustrated children's books: *One Eighth of a Muffin and That Was That*, J. Cape, 1972; *Acorns and Stew*, Collins, 1973, Collins World, 1976; *Apple Pigs*, Collins, 1976, Collins World, in press.

WORK IN PROGRESS: Three children's books.

SIDELIGHTS: Ruth Orbach writes briefly: "I write so that I can illustrate—this fact is often overlooked because reviewers tend to be literary people and look only at the words. For young children however pictures always come first."

* * *

OREN, Uri 1931-

PERSONAL: Born September 28, 1931, in Tel Aviv, Israel; son of Yosef (a farmer) and Chaya (a farmer; maiden name, Diskin) Oren; married Aliza Rousso (a teacher), September 14, 1967; children: Tamar, Etai, Karin. *Education:* Hebrew University of Jerusalem, B.A., 1957, M.A., 1973. *Religion:* Jewish. *Home:* 1 Rabina, Tel Aviv, Israel. *Agent:* Joan Daves, 515 Madison Ave., New York, N.Y. 10022. *Office:* 66 Harakevet, Tel Aviv, Israel.

CAREER: Journalist in Tel Aviv, Israel, 1951-57; assistant to Israel's minister of education and culture in charge of public relations, 1957-65; journalist in Tel Aviv, 1965—. *Military service:* Israel Air Force, 1948-51; became sergeant. *Awards, honors:* Two short story awards and four feature reporting awards from Israel Association of Journalists.

WRITINGS: *Eshet Ha-M'Faked* (short stories; title means "The Commandant's Wife"), Bitan, 1968; *Ir U-v'liba Homah* (short stories; title means "A Wall Within the

City"), Yavneh, 1970; *Ninety-Nine Days in Damascus* (nonfiction), Weidenfeld & Nicolson, 1971; *A Town Called Monastir* (nonfiction), Naor, 1972; *B'Tsohorey Lailah* (travel stories; title means "At Midnight"), Bustan, 1973; *Loving Strangers* (novel), Bitan, 1975. Contributor of about one hundred-fifty stories to magazines and newspapers in Israel and the United States.

WORK IN PROGRESS: Two novels, *Childhood and Farm Life in Israel* and *An Israeli in New York*, completion expected in 1978; a short story collection, 1978.

SIDELIGHTS: Oren writes: "Most of my writing, fiction and nonfiction, deals with Arab-Israel relations, motivated by the fact that my twin sister, Tamar, was murdered by Arab terrorists on our farm in 1950—Yarkona."

* * *

ORENSTEIN, Gloria Feman 1938-

PERSONAL: Born March 8, 1938, in New York, N.Y.; daughter of Louis G. (an international consultant in the shoe industry) and Gertrude (Appel) Feman; divorced; children: Nadine Monica, Claudia Danielle. *Education:* Brandeis University, B.A. (magna cum laude), 1959; Radcliffe College, M.A., 1961; Northwestern University, further graduate study, 1962; New York University, Ph.D., 1971; also studied at Middlebury college, summer, 1956, and Sorbonne, University of Paris, and Ecole du Louvre, both 1957-58. *Religion:* Jewish. *Home:* 711 Amsterdam Ave., New York, N.Y. 10025. *Office:* Department of English, Douglass College, New Brunswick, N.J. 08903

CAREER: High school French teacher in Lexington, Mass., 1963-64; University of Paris, Paris, France, *charge de cours* on English language and American literature, 1971-72; Douglass College, New Brunswick, N.J., assistant professor of English, 1974—, acting chairperson of women's studies department. Lecturer on women and art history; co-founder of Woman's Salon (New York, N.Y.). *Member:* Association Internationale pour l'Etude de Dada et du Surrealisme, Modern Language Association of America, Society for Religion in Higher Education, Society for Values in Higher Education.

WRITINGS: The Theatre of the Marvelous: Surrealism on the Contemporary Stage, New York University Press, 1975; (author of introduction) Leonora Carrington, *La Dama Oval* (title means "The Oval Lady"), Capra, 1975. Contributor to journals in the arts and to feminist publications including *Ms., Feminist Art Journal,* and *Woman Art.* Associate editor of *Shantih: A Quarterly of International Writings;* contributing editor of *Feminist Art Journal;* member of staff of *Woman Art.*

WORK IN PROGRESS: "My Frienship with Betty Bargonetti," to be included in *Interracial Bonds,* edited by Rhoda Goldstein.

SIDELIGHTS: Gloria Orenstein writes: "I am very interested in the relationship between consciousness and creativity. I am also interested in the female tradition in the arts and its contribution to intellectual and cultural history." She has traveled in Mexico and Europe, and lived in Italy. She is doing research on the salon tradition.

* * *

ORLOW, Dietrich 1937-

PERSONAL: Born June 2, 1937, in Hamburg, Germany; naturalized U.S. citizen in 1958; son of Otto Hinrich and Wihelmine (Haack) Orlow; married Maria Wimmersparg (a reading specialist), April 4, 1958; children: Ingrid. *Education: Ohio University, A.B., 1958; Univerisity of Michigan, A.M., 1959, Ph.D., 1962; Boston University, postdoctoral study, summers, 1971, 1973.* Home: *39 Nickerson Rd., Chestnut Hill, Mass. 02167.* Office: *Department of History, Boston University, 226 Bay State Rd., Boston, Mass. 02215.*

CAREER: College of William and Mary, Williamsburg, Va., instuctor, 1962-63, assistant professor of history, 1963-67; Syracuse University, Syracuse, N.Y., associate professor of history, 1967-71; Boston University, Boston, Mass., professor of history, 1971—. Visiting professor at University of Hamburg, spring, 1975. *Member:* American Historical Association, Conference Group on Central European History. *Awards, honors:* American Philosophical Society grants, summers, 1966, 1967; Social Science Research Council grants, summers, 1968, 1969, spring, 1970; National Endowment for the Humanities stipend for younger scholars, summer, 1972; Alexander von Humboldt-Stiftung senior research fellowship, 1974-75, summers, 1976, 1977, 1978-79.

WRITINGS: The Nazis and the Balkans, University of Pittsburgh Press, 1968; *The History of the Nazi Party, 1919-1933,* University of Pittsburgh Press, 1969; *The Hostory of the Nazi Party, 1933-1945,* University of Pittsburgh Press, 1973. Contibutor of articles and reviews to history journals. Member of board of editors of *Central European History,* 1974-76.

WORK IN PROGRESS: Research for a political history of Prussia in the Weimar Republic, 1918-1933.

* * *

ORMOND, John 1923-

PERSONAL: Born April 3, 1923, in Dunvant, Glamorgan, Wales; son of Arthur Thomas (a shoemaker) and Elsie Ormond; married Glenys Roderick, September 21, 1946; children: Eirianedd Evans, Garan Thomas, Branwen. *Education:* University of Wales, B.A., 1945. *Home:* 15 Conway Rd., Cardiff, Wales. *Office:* Broadcasting House, British Broadcasting Corp., Llandaff, Cardiff, Wales.

CAREER: Picture Post, London, England, writer, 1945-49; *South Wales Evening Post,* Swansea, sub-editor, 1949-55; British Broadcasting Corp., Cardiff, Wales, television news assistant, 1955-57, producer, director, and documentary film maker, 1957—. Has lectured at British and American universities. Chariman of Cardiff's Civic Trust Organization, 1973-77. *Awards, honors:* Literature prizes from Welsh Arts Council, 1970 and 1974; Cholmondeley Award, 1975.

WRITINGS—Poetry: (With James Kirkup and John Bayliss) *Indications,* Grey Walls Press, 1942; *Requiem and Celebration,* Christopher Davies, 1969; *Definition of a Waterfall,* Oxford University Press, 1973.

Work has been anthologized in *Corgi Modern Poets in Focus 5,* edited by Dannie Abse, Corgi, 1971.

Television documentary films for British Broadcasting Corp. include "Under a Bright Heaven," 1966; "A Bronze Mask," 1968, "The Fragile Universe," 1969, and "R. S. Thomas: Priest and Poet," 1971.

WORK IN PROGRESS: In Certain Lights, an autobiography; a book of poems.

SIDELIGHTS: With Raymond Garlick, Ormond made the record album "Poets of Wales."

BIOGRAPHICAL/CRITICAL SOURCES: Poetry Wales, winter, 1969, summer, 1973; *Poetry,* November, 1970; *Anglo-Welsh Review,* Volume XXIII, number 51, 1974.

OSBORN, Eric (Francis) 1922-

PERSONAL: Born December 9, 1922, in Melbourne, Australia; son of William Francis (an accountant) and Hilda (Gamlen) Osborn; married Lorna Grace Grierson (a teacher), December 20, 1946; children: Robert Stanley, Eric Peter. *Education:* University of Melbourne, B.A., 1946, M.A., 1948, B.D., 1949; Cambridge University, Ph.D., 1954, B.D., 1970. *Home and office:* 3 Queen's College, University of Melbourne, Melbourne, Victoria 3052, Australia.

CAREER: Ordained Methodist minister, 1950; pastor of Methodist churches in Victoria, Australia, 1948-58; University of Melbourne, Queen's College, Melbourne, Australia, professor of Biblical studies, 1958-73, professor of New Testament and early church history, 1973—. *Military service:* Australian Army, bombardier, 1942-44. *Member:* Australian Academy of the Humanities (fellow), Studiorum Novi Testamenti Societas.

WRITINGS: The Philosophy of Clement of Alexandria, Cambridge University Press, 1957; *Word and History,* University of Western Australia Press, 1967; *Justin Martyr,* J.C.B. Mohr, 1973; *Ethical Patterns in Early Christian Thought,* Cambridge University Press, 1976. Editor of *Australian Biblical Review,* 1960—, and *Colloquium,* 1967—.

WORK IN PROGRESS: Research on second-century Christian thought, the relationship of Christianity to Platonism, the influence of Paul on the early church, and the application of Wittgensteinian philosophy to the history of ideas.

*   *   *

OSBORNE, Linda Barrett 1949-

PERSONAL: Born February 1, 1949, in New York, N.Y.; daughter of James (in systems management) and Josephine (Valeri) Barrett; married Robert Osborne (an architect), September 23, 1972. *Education:* Swarthmore College, B.A. (honors), 1971. *Residence:* Houston, Tex.

CAREER: Teacher in Navajo demonstration school in Chinle, Ariz., 1971; Franklin Mint, Franklin Center, Pa., and Franklin Mint International, London, England, researcher and writer, 1972-74; Museum of Fine Arts, Houston, Tex., assistant librarian, 1975-76; editor and writer, R. Douglass Associates, 1976—. Has conducted writing workshops. Member of Houston Rape Crisis Coalition, 1974-75. *Member:* Associated Authors of Children's Literature (Houston). *Awards, honors:* Writers-in-the-Schools grant from Texas Commission on the Arts and Humanities, 1976-77.

WRITINGS: Son of the Harp (stories for children), Christopher Davies, 1975. Contributor of articles and reviews to magazines and newspapers.

WORK IN PROGRESS: A novel; *Twice As Good,* children's stories on living in bicultural settings.

SIDELIGHTS: Linda Osborne writes: "I am interested in writing children's books which reflect my experiences in specific, unusual settings such as a small Welsh town or the Navajo reservation in northeast Arizona, but which also focus on common feelings, perceptions and responses. Background and research are important; I wrote *Song of the Harp* . . . while living in Wales."

AVOCATIONAL INTERESTS: Dance, theatre, jogging, embroidery, travel (Europe and Mexico).

OSEN, Lynn M(oses) 1920-

PERSONAL: Born November 13, 1920, in Alabama; daughter of William Benjamin and Portia (Bailey) Moses; married Donald Shotwell Osen (a real estate developer), May 20, 1950; children: Frank Sanford. *Education:* University of California, Irvine, B.A., 1967; California State University, Fullerton, M.A., 1969. *Politics:* "Wavering Democrat." *Home and office:* 1091 Castlegate Lane, Santa Ana, Calif. 92705.

CAREER: U.S. Navy Department, Industrial Relations, Alameda, Calif., statistician, 1945-50; Osen-Ojeda Development Corp., Santa Ana, Calif., vice-president, 1961-65; University of California, Irvine, lecturer in women's studies, 1969—, board member of University of California at Irvine Foundation, 1976. Member of board of directors, Democratic State Central Committee, California, 1957. *Member:* Author's Guild, Association for Women in Mathematics, National Organization for Women, American Civil Liberties Union, League of Women Voters. *Awards, honors:* Received civilian service award from U.S. Navy Department for original work in systems analysis.

WRITINGS: Biographical Citations, Ann Arbor Publishers, 1970; *The Feminine Math-tique,* Know, Inc., 1971; *Women in Mathematics,* M.I.T. Press, 1974. Also author of *Women Pirates* 1975. Contributor to *Psychonomic Science.*

AVOCATIONAL INTERESTS: Travel, including Russia, Scandinavia, and People's Republic of China.

BIOGRAPHICAL/CRITICAL SOURCES: Santa Ana Register, September 3, 1969, August 17, 1971; *Los Angeles Times,* September 11, 1969, November 28, 1975, January 6, 1976; *Daily Pilot,* October 14, 1976; *Orange County Illustrated,* November, 1976.

*   *   *

OSOFSKY, Gilbert 1935-1974

PERSONAL: Born March 14, 1935, in Brooklyn, N.Y.; married, 1961; children: two. *Education:* Brooklyn College (now of the City University of New York), B.A., 1956; New York University, M.A., 1958; Columbia University, Ph.D., 1963. *Residence:* Chicago, Ill.

CAREER: University of Illinois, Chicago Circle, assistant professor, 1963-65, associate professor, 1965-68, professor of history, 1968-75. Fellow of Institute for Advanced Study at University of Illinois, 1966-67. *Military service:* U.S. Army, 1959-66. *Awards, honors:* American Council of Learned Societies fellowship, 1971-72.

WRITINGS: Harlem: The Making of a Ghetto—Negro New York, 1890-1930, Harper, 1966, 2nd edition, 1971; *The Burden of Race: A Documentary History of Negro-White Relations in America,* Harper, 1967; (editor) *Puttin' on Ole Massa: The Slave Narratives of Henry Bibb, William Wells Brown, and Solomon Northrup,* Harper, 1969. Also author of introduction to *Preface to Peasantry,* Atheneum, 1968. Contributor to academic journals.

BIOGRAPHICAL/CRITICAL SOURCES: Book World, October 22, 1967, September 7, 1969; *New York Times Book Review,* December 10, 1967; *Nation,* June 3, 1968. *Obituaries: AB Bookman's Weekly,* October 7, 1974.*

(Died in 1974, in Washington, D.C.)

*   *   *

OSTEN, Gar 1923-

PERSONAL: Born August 20, 1923, in Newton, Iowa; son

of Alva Daniel (a farmer-electrician) and Louise (Hilde-brand) Osten. *Education:* Attended Kansas City Art Institute, 1946-48; Parsons School of Design, graduated, 1950. *Religion:* "Cosmic consciousness." *Home and office:* 315 South Third Ave. E., Newton, Iowa 50208.

CAREER: Astrologer, 1963—. Drapery designer in New York, N.Y., 1950-70; has also worked as theatrical costume designer. *Military service:* U.S. Army, 1943-46; became staff sergeant.

WRITINGS: The Astrological Chart of the United States, 1776-2141, Stein & Day, 1976.

WORK IN PROGRESS: The Dark Side of the Moon, "an astrological study of noted kidnapping, murder and disappearance cases of this century."

SIDELIGHTS: Osten writes that he "became interested in astrology because I felt that it was a valuable tool to self knowledge and because I felt that there is much yet to be discovered in this area, and in the area of psychic phenomena. While living in New York [I] did research with psychic Shawn Robbins and with Hans Holzer, parapsychologist. The motivation for the U.S. chart was the challenge . . . that it had never been done at depth previously. It was an attempt to not only establish that history does repeat itself, but that it will repeat itself in the future under similar past configurations, and in the nature of the past events. This is already confirmed by my predictions for 1976."

BIOGRAPHICAL/CRITICAL SOURCES: Hans Holzer, *The Dictionary of the Occult,* Regnery, 1974; Holzer, *The Alchemist,* Stein & Day, 1974; Holzer, *Astrology: What It Can Do for You,* Regnery, 1975.

* * *

OSTRANDER, Gilman Marston 1923-

PERSONAL: Born August 2, 1923, in San Francisco, Calif.; son of Frank Sidney and Katherine (Burnham) Ostrander; married Katherine Hill, July 7, 1946; married second wife, Jean Frappier, July 3, 1963; children: David, Robert, Sara. *Education:* Columbia University, A.B., 1946; University of California, Berkeley, Ph.D., 1954. *Office:* Department of History, University of Waterloo, Waterloo, Ontario, Canada.

CAREER: Ohio State University, Columbus, instructor in history, 1954-57; University of Missouri, Columbia, assistant professor of history, 1957-59; Michigan State University, East Lansing, 1959-67, began as associate professor, became professor of history; University of Missouri, St. Louis, professor of history, 1968-71; University of Waterloo, Waterloo, Ontario, professor of history, 1971—. Fulbright lecturer in Tokyo, 1967-68. *Military service:* U.S. Army, 1943-45.

WRITINGS: The Prohibition Movement in California, 1848-1933, University of California Press, 1957; *The Rights of Man in America, 1606-1861,* University of Missouri Press, 1960, 2nd edition, 1969; *A Profile History of the United States,* McGraw, 1964, 2nd edition, 1972; *Nevada: The Great Rotten Borough, 1859-1964,* Knopf, 1966; *American Civilization in the First Machine Age, 1890-1940,* Harper, 1970; (editor) *The American Enlightenment,* Marston, 1970; (editor) *Early Colonial Thought,* Marston, 1970; (editor) *The Romantic Democracy, 1835-1855,* Marston, 1971.

* * *

PACKER, Bernard J(ules) 1934-

PERSONAL: Born July 7, 1934, in Philadelphia, Pa.; son of Samuel (a farmer) and Eve (Devine) Packer; married Lili Skibsted (an interpreter), December 20, 1960; children: Tatiana Consuelo, Jessica Lisa. *Education:* Attended West Point Military Academy, 1953-54, University of California at Los Angeles, 1954-55, 1956-58, and National University of Mexico, 1955-56. *Politics:* Apolitical. *Religion:* Jewish. *Home:* 2126 Connecticut Ave. N.W., Washington, D.C. 20008. *Agent:* Carl Brandt, 101 Park Ave., New York, N.Y. 10016. *Office:* American Institute for Free Labor Development, 1015 20th St. N.W., Washington, D.C. 20008.

CAREER: Merchant seaman, 1958-59; U.S. State Department, Washington, D.C., contract interpreter and translator, 1960-67, interpreter for American Institute for Free Labor Development, 1967—. *Military service:* U.S. Air Force, 1952-53.

WRITINGS: Caro (novel), Dutton, 1975.

WORK IN PROGRESS: Zackmanville.

AVOCATIONAL INTERESTS: Playing classical guitar, studying history.

* * *

PACKER, Nancy Huddleston 1925-

PERSONAL: Born May 2, 1925, in Washington, D.C.; daughter of George (a U.S. Congressman) and Bertha (Baxley) Huddleston; married Herbert L. Packer (a professor of law), March 15, 1958 (died December 6, 1972); children: Ann, George. *Education:* Birmingham-Southern College, A.B., 1945; University of Chicago, M.A., 1947; Stanford University, further graduate study, 1959-60. *Politics:* Democrat. *Religion:* None. *Home:* 807 San Francisco Ter., Stanford, Calif. 94305. *Office:* Department of English, Stanford University, Stanford, Calif. 94305.

CAREER: Birmingham Chamber of Commerce, Birmingham, Ala., staff writer, 1952-54; Stanford University, Stanford, Calif., assistant professor, 1968-74, associate professor of English, 1974—. *Member:* American Association of University Professors.

WRITINGS: (Editor with Wilfred Stone and Robert Hoopes) *The Short Story: An Introduction,* McGraw, 1976; *Small Moments and Other Stories,* University of Illinois Press, 1976. Contributor of stories to literary journals and popular magazines, including *Harper's, Kenyon Review, Yale Review, Reporter,* and *Southwest Review.*

WORK IN PROGRESS: Short stories, including "The Women Who Walk."

SIDELIGHTS: Nancy Packer told *CA:* "The youngest of five children, I grew up in a political environment. Knowing motivations in all their complexity always seemed important. Working with and becoming friends with Wallace Stegner and Richard Scowcroft, at Stanford, opened up a career in teaching for me. I like students more all the time, and I find this university a sufficiently complex institution, and yet a small town."

* * *

PAINE, Roger W(arde) III 1942-

PERSONAL: Born February 27, 1942, in Hawaii; son of Roger W., Jr. (a U.S. Navy admiral) and Isla Rea (Vaile) Paine; divorced; children: Catherine Anne. *Education:* Washington and Lee University, B.A., 1964; Yale University, M.Div., 1967. *Politics:* Independent. *Home:* 1015 Arapahoe, Boulder, Colo. 80302. *Agent:* Tim Seldes, 551 Fifth Ave., New York, N.Y. 10017.

CAREER: Ordained Congregationalist minister, 1969; assistant pastor of Congregationalist church in Minneapolis, Minn., 1967-70; Relate (family counseling service), Minneapolis, Minn., director, 1970-73; Attention, Inc. (operates homes for troubled teenagers), Boulder, Colo., executive director, 1974—.

WRITINGS: We Never Had Any Trouble Before, Stein & Day, 1975.

WORK IN PROGRESS: A novel.

* * *

PAINTER, Nell Irvin 1942-

PERSONAL: Born August 2, 1942, in Houston, Tex.; daughter of Frank Edward (a chemist) and Dona Lolita (a personnel officer; maiden name, McGruder) Irvin. Education: University of California, Berkeley, B.A., 1964; University of California, Los Angeles, M.A., 1967; Harvard University, Ph.D., 1974; also attended University of Bordeaux, 1962-63, and University of Ghana, 1965-66. Politics: Democrat. Religion: None. Residence: Philadelphia, Pa. Office: Department of History, University of Pennsylvania, Philadelphia, Pa. 19174.

CAREER: University of Pennsylvania, Philadelphia, assistant professor of American and Afro-American history, 1974—. Member: Organization of American Historians, Association for the Study of Afro-American Life and History, Berkshire Conference. Awards, honors: Coretta Scott King Award from American Association of University Women, 1969; American Council of Learned Societies fellowship, 1976-77; fellow of the Charles Warren Center for Studies in American History, Harvard University, 1976-77; Radcliffe Institute fellowship, 1976-77.

WRITINGS: Exodusters: Black Migration to Kansas after Reconstruction, Knopf, 1977.

WORK IN PROGRESS: "Hosea Hudson: The Personal Account of a Black Communist in the Deep South," an oral history, 1925-55; "Mixed Blood and Pure Blood in the Minds of Americans, 1890-1920," an intellectual history.

* * *

PALMER, B. C.
See SCHMIDT, Laura M(arie)

* * *

PALMER, Laura
See SCHMIDT, Laura M(arie)

* * *

PALMER, Winthrop Bushnell 1899-

PERSONAL: Born September 14, 1899, in New York, N.Y.; daughter of Ericsson Foote and Bertha Tudor (Thompson) Bushnell; married Carleton Humphreys Palmer, October 2, 1919 (died, 1970); children: Winthrop (Mrs. James O. Boswell), Rosalind (Mrs. Henry Walter, Jr.), Carleton H., Jr. (deceased), Lowell M. II (deceased). Education: Attended Columbia University, 1917 and 1924-28, New York University, 1930-38, and Jacques Maritain University in Exile, New York City, 1943-45. Home: 435 East 52nd St., New York, N.Y. 10022; and, Centre Island, Oyster Bay, N.Y.

CAREER: National Association Junior Leagues of America, New York, N.Y., president 1926-28; worked on political and government commissions, 1928-38; Long Island

University, C. W. Post College, Brookville, N.Y., member of executive committee, 1955, professor of literature and fine arts, 1956-74, trustee, 1969-75, board chairman, 1974-75, chairman emeritus, 1975—. Member: P.E.N., Poetry Society of America (member of New York City executive council, 1974—), Academy of American Poets, Joyce Society, Alliance Francaise (New York), Poets and Writers, New York Public Library (member of women's advisory council), Piping Rock Club, Metropolitan Club, Seawanhaka Corinthian Yacht Club (all New York). Awards, honors: Litt.D., Long Island University, 1956.

WRITINGS—Poetry: The Invisible Wife and Other Poems, Fine Editions Press, 1945; The New Barbarian, Farrar, Straus, 1951; Fables and Ceremonies, Peter Pauper, 1956; A L'Envers (title means "The Other Side of the Picture"), bilingual edition, Jean Grassin (Paris, France), 1961; Like a Passing Shadow, Steamboat Press, 1968.

Plays: "Rosemary and the Planet" (musical play), music by Sol Berkowitz, first produced in New York City at Le Marquis Theatre, 1958; "Beat the Wind" (verse play), first produced in New York City at Provincetown Playhouse, 1960; (with Maurice Edwards and Jean Reavey) "A Place for Chance" (American chronicle), first produced in New York City at Stage Theatre, 1961, published as American Kaleidoscope, Dramatic Publishing, 1972. Also author of ballet libretto, "The Man from Midian," 1942, and contributor of one-act play, "Our Belle," to Express magazine of Long Island, 1969.

Nonfiction: Theatrical Dancing in America, A. S. Barnes, 1945.

Contributor of poetry to newspapers and journals, including Commonweal, Poetry, New York Times, New York Herald Tribune. Associate editor, Dance News, 1935-50, Confrontation, 1973—.

WORK IN PROGRESS: An updated edition of Theatrical Dancing in America.

* * *

PANNABECKER, Samuel Floyd 1896-

PERSONAL: Born April 15, 1896, in Petoskey, Mich.; son of Jacob Nelson (a clergyman) and Luna May (Plowman) Pannabecker; married Sylvia Tschantz, August 3, 1921; children: Richard F., Robert T., Alice Ruth (Mrs. Robert L. Ramseyer). Education: Bluffton College, A.B., 1917; Witmarsum Theological Seminary, A.M., 1918; Garrett Theological Seminary, B.D., 1933; Yale University, Ph.D., 1944. Office: Mennonite Biblical Seminary, 3003 Benham Ave., Elkhart, Ind. 46514.

CAREER: Bluffton College, Bluffton, Ohio, instructor in physics and chemistry, 1918-23; General Conference of the Mennonite Church, Board of Missions, Kai Chow, Hopei, China, high school teacher and administrator, 1923-31, 1935-41; Bluffton College, Bluffton, Ohio, researcher and teacher, 1941-44; relief supervisor in Honan, China, under Mennonite Central Committee, 1944-46; Mennonite Biblical Seminary, Elkhart, Ind., dean, 1946-48, president, 1948-58, professor of missions, 1958-66, and dean, 1958-64, archivist, 1966—. Member: Midwest Fellowship of Professors of Missions, American Professors of Missions, Mennonite Historical Society. Awards, honors: D.D. from Bethel College, Newton, Kan., 1950, and Bethany Theological Seminary, Oakbrook, Ill., 1958; D.H.L. from Bluffton College, 1958.

WRITINGS: (Editor) The Christian Mission of the General Conference Mennonite Church, Faith & Life, 1960, revised edition, 1961; *Faith in Ferment: A History of the Central District Conference,* Faith & Life, 1968; *Open Doors: History of the General Conference Mennonite Church,* Faith & Life, 1975; *Ventures of Faith: The Story of Mennonite Biblical Seminary,* Mennonite Biblical Seminary, 1975.

WORK IN PROGRESS: Christian Missions in China and National Development in the Twentieth Century.

* * *

PANOS, Chris(tos) 1935-

PERSONAL: Born August 25, 1935, in Galveston, Tex.; son of George and Katherine Panos; married Earnestine Gardner; children: Georganna, Chris. *Education:* Attended Massey Business College and Texas Christian University. *Religion:* Greek Orthodox. *Home:* 14822 Dogwood Tree, Houston, Tex. 77037. *Office:* Release the World for Christ, 600 Jefferson Building, Houston, Tex. 77002.

CAREER: Business executive with Mansion Home and 3-16 Building, Inc., 1956-62; President of Release the World for Christ, 1962—, and Auxosia Books, 1972—; *Far East Reporter,* Houston, Tex., publisher, editor, and contributor, 1967—. Host of "The Chris Panos Show," a Christian talk show for television, 1973—.

WRITINGS: He Called, I Followed, Auxosia Books, 1970; *Faith Under Fire,* Whitaker House, 1974; *God's Spy* (autobiography), Logos International, 1976; *How to Have a Miracle Ministry,* Logos International, 1976. Author of scripts for his television series.

WORK IN PROGRESS: Books on angels, marriage, money, prayer, and power.

SIDELIGHTS: Panos was once a successful businessman mainly involved in real estate. A near-fatal automobile accident was followed by a profound religious experience after which he sold his business interests and turned to spreading the word of God. Described as "a real-life Christian version of James Bond," he travels throughout the world, speaking to large audiences on his "Miracle Life Crusades" and smuggling Bibles into places where free expression of religious faith is proscribed. He has addressed heads of state as well as crowds, particularly in India. He writes: "I love the country of India, but conditions there are heartbreaking to me. That is why I feel I must go back again and again. It is bad enough for people to have to endure the many trials that they go through here: the heat, the pain, the sickness, the hunger. But there is a hunger that is worse than physical hunger, and that is spiritual hunger."

BIOGRAPHICAL/CRITICAL SOURCES: Far East Reporter, June, 1976.

* * *

PAPIN, Joseph 1914-

PERSONAL: Born October 2, 1914, in Parchoviany, Slovakia; son of United States citizens, George and Helen (Velcko) Papin. *Education:* University of Berchmanianum, Ph.L., 1937, Ph.D., 1939; University of Nijmegen, S.T.D., 1946; University of Louvain, postdoctoral study, 1946. *Home:* 1030 Lancaster, Chetwynd 117, Rosemont, Pa. 19085. *Office:* Department of Theology, Villanova University, Villanova, Pa. 19085.

CAREER: Roman Catholic priest; Lafranconi Institute, Bratislava, Slovakia, director, 1943-44; University of Nijmegen, Nijmegen, Netherlands, docent in philosophy and Russian literature, 1945-47; St. Andrew's Abbey, St. Procopius College, Lisle, Ill., professor of philosophy, classics, biblical Greek, and scientific German, 1947-50; De Paul University, Chicago, Ill., professor of contemporary politics, philosophy, and theology, and acting chairman of the department, 1950-53; University of Notre Dame, Notre Dame, Ind., professor of theology, political science, and history of Russian philosophy, 1953-63; Villanova University, Villanova, Pa., professor of theology, 1963—, chairman of graduate studies, 1963—, director of Theology Institute, 1966—. Visiting professor at Loyola University, Chicago, Ill., 1952, University of Valparaiso, 1962, and Rosemont College, 1964. Member of Vatican delegation for refugees of Holland, Luxembourg, and Belgium, 1945-47; member of parliament, United World Federation; president, International Mariological Congress at Lourdes, France, 1958; member of screening committee, Fulbright-Hays fellowship program; member of Concillium of Holland and Germany, 1969; lecturer in United States and Europe; speaker on radio and television.

MEMBER: American Philosophical Association, Theological Society of America, Academy of Political Sciences, American Association of University Professors, American Catholic Philosophical Association, Catholic Theological Society of America, Mariological Society of America, International Mariological Academy (Rome), Polish Institute of Arts and Sciences in America, Slovak Institute, Middle European Federal Academic Club (Vienna; president), Intercontinental Biographical Association (fellow). *Awards, honors:* Gold medal for Byzantine studies from Imperial University of Madrid, 1952; Bene Merenti from Pope Pius XII, for academic contributions to the international congress, 1958.

WRITINGS: Doctrina de Bono Perfecto, E. J. Brill, 1946; *Christus by Dostoyevsky,* Dekker & Van de Vegt, 1946; (contributor) Mikulas Sprinc, editor, *Bergson's Philosophy,* Obrama Press, 1947; *History of Diocese Gary,* Benedictine Press, 1957; (contributor) Sprinc, editor, *Bukovec Manuscript,* Slovak Institute, 1958; (contributor) E. D. O'Connor. editor, *The Dogma of Immaculate Conception,* University of Notre Dame Press, 1958; *Bratislava: Center of Scholars in the XIX Century,* Slovak Institute, 1958; *Jozrf Jurek: Slovak Educator,* Slovak Institute, 1959; *The Holy Land Pilgrimage of Daniel Igumen Palomnik in the Bukovec Manuscript,* Slovak Institute, 1959.

Christian Inroots into the Territory of Present Slovakia Prior to the Cyrilo-Methodian Era, Slovak Institute, 1965; (editor) *The Dynamic in Christian Thought,* Villanova University Press, Volume I, 1968, Volume II, 1969; *Openness to the World,* Villanova University Press, 1970; *The Pilgrim People: A Vision with Hope,* Villanova University Press, 1971; *The Eschaton: A Community of Love,* Vallanova University Press, 1972; *The Church and Human Society at the Threshold of the Third Millenium,* Villanova University Press, 1972; *Man's Religious Quest,* Villanova University Press, 1973; *Perspectives,* Abbey Press, 1973; *Christian Encounter,* Abbey Press, 1974.

Monographs—All published by Slovak Editions: *Legal Process of Leningrad,* 1970; *An Unknown Slovak Prayer Book,* 1970; *King of Madagascar,* 1970; *Christmas Reflections at the Threshold of the Third Millennium,* 1970; *An Unknown Picture of Bratislava,* 1971; *New Year's Reflections,* 1971; *Slovak World Congress,* 1971. Contributor to *New Catholic Encyclopedia,* and to symposia and journals in his field. Editor, Villanova University Theological Folia Series, 1973-74.

BIOGRAPHICAL/CRITICAL SOURCES: Jan Okal and

Marian Yankovsky, editors, *Papin: Life and Work,* Slovak Editions, 1971; J. E. Bors, editor, *Festschrift for Joseph Papin,* Lanus Oeste, 1972; Joseph Armenti, editor, *Festschrift in Honour of Joseph Papin,* Abbey Press, 1972, Volume I: *Transcendence and Immanence: Reconstruction in the Light of Process Thinking,* Volume II: *Wisdom and Knowledge.*

* * *

PARHAM, Joseph Byars 1919-

PERSONAL: Born May 17, 1919, in Winder, Ga.; son of Joseph B. (a printer) and Katherine (Thornton) Parham; married Wendell Rider, April 14, 1943 (died June 28, 1966); married Hazel Rogers, June 24, 1969; children: Richard, Martin, Joseph B. III, Kinsey. *Education:* Attended schools in Canton, Ga. *Home:* 1837 Flintwood Dr., Macon, Ga. 31201. *Office: Macon News,* Box 4167, Macon, Ga. 31208.

CAREER: Macon News, Macon, Ga., reporter, 1941-49, editor and columnist, 1949—, regularly covering Georgia legislature, 1950-56. Notable assignments include coverage of national political conventions, 1952, 1956, and 1966. Member of board of directors, Macon Area Transportation Agency, Macon Bibb County Board of Health, and Booker T. Washington Community Center. *Military service:* U.S. Army Air Corps, 1942-46; became staff sergeant. *Member:* American Society of Newspaper Editors, March of Dimes, Young Men's Christian Association (YMCA; board member, 1958-60), Georgia Press Association (board member, 1950-53, 1976—), Georgia Easter Seal Society (member of board of directors, 1972-75), Lions Club (member of board of directors, 1960-61). *Awards, honors:* Associated Press awards, 1954, for feature writing, 1959, for general excellence; Georgia Press Association best daily column awards, 1956, 1971, 1972, 1973, 1974; American Legion award, 1973, for column; Epilepsy Association award, 1973, for column.

WRITINGS: (Contributor) Donald Cleavenger Shoemaker, editor, *With All Deliberate Speed: Segregation-Desegregation in Southern Schools,* Harper, 1958. Writer of daily column for *Macon News,* 1949—.

AVOCATIONAL INTERESTS: Travel (including Central and South America and western Europe, especially England.)

* * *

PARKER, Donn B(lanchard) 1929-

PERSONAL: Born October 9, 1929, in San Jose, Calif.; son of Donald W. (a salesman) and Miriam (Blanchard) Parker; married Lorna Schroeder, August 16, 1952; children: Diane, David. *Education:* University of California, Berkeley, B.A., 1952, M.A., 1954. *Religion:* Lutheran. *Home:* 265 Vernal Court, Los Altos, Calif. 94022. *Office:* Stanford Research Institute, Menlo Park, Calif. 94025.

CAREER: General Dynamics Corp., San Diego, Calif., senior research engineer, 1954-62; Control Data Corp., Palo Alto, Calif., manager, 1962-69; Stanford Research Institute, Menlo Park, Calif., researcher, 1969—. Instructor, University of California, San Diego, 1955. *Member:* Association for Computing Machinery (member of board of directors, 1957—), American Federation of Information Processing Societies (member of board of directors and chairman of professional standards, 1970-75). *Awards, honors:* National Science Foundation reserach grant, 1973.

WRITINGS: Crime by Computer, Scribner, 1976. Contributor to *Encyclopedia of Computer Science* and of articles to *Datamation, New York Times,* and journals in his field.

WORK IN PROGRESS: Research on computer abuse and security.

SIDELIGHTS: Parker states that his interests are "in the impact of computer technology on society, including privacy issues, crime, and public attitudes toward being served by computers."

* * *

PARKER, Rowland 1912-

PERSONAL: Born October 5, 1912, in Lincolnshire, England; son of William (a farmer) and Clara (Bond) Parker; married Madge Hulbert, March 24, 1940; children: Jane (adopted). *Education:* University of Nottingham, B.A. (honors), 1934. *Politics:* "I detest all politics." *Religion:* "Live and let live." *Home:* Cottage on the Green, Foxton, Cambridgeshire, England. *Agent:* A. P. Watt, 26-28 Bedford Row, London WC1R 4HL, England.

CAREER: Cambridge Crammar School, Cambridge, England, teacher of French, 1935-72; writer, 1972—. *Military service:* British Army, Royal Artillery, 1940-46; served in North Africa, Italy, Yugoslavia, Egypt, Palestine, and Syria; became lieutenant.

WRITINGS: Cottage on the Green, Research Publications, 1973; *The Common Stream* (History Book Club selection), Holt, 1975; *On the Road,* Papworth Industries, 1976.

WORK IN PROGRESS: A historical novel set in Dunwich, "a sea-port which has almost disappeared due to erosion by the sea."

SIDELIGHTS: Parker writes: "Condemned by circumstances to teach a foreign language to unwilling learners within four walls, I almost welcomed the advent of World War II. It presented me with the opportunity to teach myself two more languages, and took me to places where history and archaeology were crying out for my interest. Then, satiated with travel, I wanted a 'home' where I could live the rest of my life and grow tomatoes. The home I found by sheer fluke was a sixteenth-century thatched cottage in a quiet Cambridgeshire village.... I set about unearthing, unravelling, deciphering, transcribing, interpreting, and at times guessing the history of my cottage; and, of more importance, the history of the people who had lived in it.... *Cottage on the Green,* published at my own expense, [was] as eagerly sought after as were my top-quality tomatoes.

"From the pile of information collected in ten years of research I knocked out a history of the village.... *The History of Foxton* . . . became *The Common Stream,* and everybody liked it—even Angus Wilson.

"Now retired from teaching, I tried to write the history of a British tribe called the Iceni, believing that their descendants are still living in the Fenland.... But they must have changed in the meantime.... My current venture is. . .a story of Dunwich, once a thriving seaport and now a hamlet slowly disappearing into the North Sea. I want to resurrect it as it was around the year 1300, with a background of 100% fact, on which I hope to weave a story wholly fictional." *The Common Stream* has been issued in a Braille edition.

* * *

PARKS, Robert James 1940-

PERSONAL: Born March 23, 1940, in Kalamazoo, Mich.; son of Robert Jay and Hazel May (a saleswoman; maiden name, Hobbs) Parks; married Mary Kathleen Stelson (a college professor), June 13, 1965; children: Robert Joseph,

Alan Michael. *Education:* Western Michigan University, B.A., 1962; Michigan State University, M.A., 1963, Ph.D., 1967; currently attending law school. *Home:* 1713 Downey St., Laramie, Wyo. 82070. *Office:* Department of History, University of Wyoming, Box 3334, University Station, Laramie, Wyo. 82071.

CAREER: University of Wyoming, Laramie, assistant professor, 1970-73, associate professor of history, 1973-76. *Military service:* U.S. Army, historical unit of Medical Department, 1968-70. *Member:* American Historical Association, Organization of American Historians, Economic History Association.

WRITINGS: The Democracy's Railroads: Public Enterprise in Jacksonian Michigan, 1825-1846, Kennikat, 1972; (contributor) William S. Mullins and Rose C. Engelman, editors, *A Decade of Medical Progress in the U.S. Army Medical Department, 1959-1969,* U.S. Government Printing Office, 1972; *History of Training in World War Two,* Medical Department, U.S. Army, 1975. Contributor to history, social science, and military journals.

WORK IN PROGRESS: Research on public enterprise and economic development in the old Northwest, 1790-1860.

*   *   *

PARKS, Stephen Robert   1940-

PERSONAL: Born July 18, 1940, in Columbus, Ohio; son of Robert E. (a businessman) and Hilda (Easton) Parks. *Education:* Yale University, B.A., 1961; Cambridge University, Ph.D., 1965. *Home:* 248 Bradley St., New Haven, Conn. 06510. *Office:* Beinecke Library, Yale University, 1630A Yale Station, New Haven, Conn. 06520.

CAREER: University of Edinburgh, Edinburgh, Scotland, post-doctoral fellow in English, 1964-67; Yale University, New Haven, Conn., curator of Osborn Collection at Beinecke Library, 1967—. *Member:* Wrexham Foundation, Elizabethan Club (Yale University), Johnsonians, Metropolitan Club (New York City), Grolier Club, Yale Club (New York City), Graduates' Club (New Haven), United Oxford and Cambridge University Club.

WRITINGS: (Editor and author of introductions) *Sale Catalogues of Libraries of Eminent Persons,* Volume V, Mansell, 1972; (editor of reprint and author of notes) *The English Book Trade, 1660-1853,* thirty-eight volumes, Garland Publishing, 1974-75; *John Dunton and the English Book Trade: A Study of His Career with a Checklist of His Publications,* Garland Publishing, 1976. Contributor to journals.

WORK IN PROGRESS: Research on Charles Cotton, and the Edinburgh book trade in the late eighteenth century.

*   *   *

PARMAN, Donald L(ee)   1932-

PERSONAL: Born October 10, 1932, in New Point, Mo.; son of Dennis W. (a farmer) and Carrie (Abplanalp) Parman; married Nadyne Crockett (a secretary), July 20, 1953; children: Vince Robert, Steven Ryan. *Education:* Central Missouri State College, B.S.Ed. (high honors), 1958; Ohio University, M.A., 1963; University of Oklahoma, Ph.D., 1967. *Politics:* Democrat. *Religion:* United Methodist. *Home:* 614 Rose St., West Lafayette, Ind. 47906. *Office:* Department of History, Purdue University, West Lafayette, Inc. 47907.

CAREER: High school social studies teacher in Sedalia, Mo., 1959-62; Central Missouri State College, Warrensburg, laboratory school supervisor, 1962-63; Purdue University,

West Lafayette, Ind., assistant professor, 1966-75, associate professor of American history, 1975—. *Military service:* U.S. Army, 1953-55. *Member:* Organization of American Historians, Agricultural History Society, Western History Association, Phi Alpha Theta. *Awards, honors:* Grants from American Philosophical Society, summers, 1971, 1973, and National Endowment for the Humanities, 1972-73.

WRITINGS: (Editor) *The American Search,* Volume I (with F. J. Fithian, H. G. Waltmann, and W. E. Stickle): *Readings in American History to 1877,* Volume II (with Stickle, Waltmann, and J. R. Riggs): *Readings in American History Since 1877,* Forum Press, 1974; (contributor) Norris Hundley, editor, *The American Indian,* Clio Books, 1974; *The Navajo and the New Deal,* Yale University Press, 1976. Contributor to academic journals.

WORK IN PROGRESS: Indians of the Twentieth Century, completion expected in 1980; research on Indian affairs during the Progressive Era.

SIDELIGHTS: Parman writes that he "became interested in the book on the Navajos while doing interviews in New Mexico in the summer of 1970 and attempted to evaluate how well government policy and philosophy of Indian affairs in the 1930's worked out on the reservation."

*   *   *

PARRINO, Michael   1915(?)-1976

1915(?)—March 2, 1976; American lawyer and author. Obituaries: *New York Times,* March 4, 1976.

*   *   *

PARSONS, William T(homas)   1923-

PERSONAL: Born January 5, 1923, in Palmerton, Pa.; son of Walter Alvin (a foreman) and Florence (Greene) Parsons; married Phyllis J. Vibbard (a borough secretary), December 8, 1945. *Education:* Ursinus College, B.A., 1947; attended University of Pittsburgh, 1943, and Middlebury College, summers, 1947, 1949; University of Pennsylvania, M.A., 1949, Ph.D., 1955. *Politics:* Republican. *Religion:* United Church of Christ (Old German Reformed). *Home:* 712 Chestnut St., Collegeville, Pa. 19426. *Office:* Institute of Pennsylvania Dutch Studies, Ursinus College, Collegeville, Pa. 19426.

CAREER: Ursinus College, Collegeville, Pa., instructor in French, 1947-53, assistant professor of history, 1953-65, associate professor, 1965-70, professor, 1970—, director of Pennsylvania Dutch Studies Program and Institute of Pennsylvania Dutch Studies, 1974—. Visiting professor at Eastern Baptist College, summer, 1964. Member of Borough council of Schwenksville, Pa., 1953-59; member of Collegeville-Trappe Municipal Authority, 1970-74. Organizer and member of "Die Sivva Schwowe," a group of dialect folksingers. *Military service:* U.S. Army, 1943-45; served in European theater; received five battle stars.

MEMBER: American Historical Association, Friends Historical Association, Swiss-American Historical Society, Evangelical and Reformed Historical Society, National Trust for Historic Preservation, Goschenhoppen Historians, Historical Society of Pennsylvania, German Society of Pennsylvania, Pennsylvania German Society (member of board of directors, 1974—), Pennsylvania Historical Association, Pennsylvania Genealogical Society, New York State Historical Association, Historical Society of Montgomery County (member of board of trustees, 1973—). *Awards, honors:* Research grant from Evangelical and Reformed Historical Society, 1974.

WRITINGS: (Editor) Benjamin Rush, *An Account of the Manners of the German Inhabitants of Pennsylvania,* Institute on Pennsylvania Dutch Studies, Ursinus college, 1974; *Ethnic Tradition: The Legacy of the Pennsylvania Dutch,* Institute on Pennsylvania Dutch Studies, Ursinus College, 1975; *The Preachers' Appeal of 1775,* Pennsylvania Southeast Conference, United Church of Christ, 1975; *The Pennsylvania Dutch: A Persistent Minority,* Twayne, 1976; *Another Rung Up the Ladder: German Reformed People in American Struggles, 1754-1783,* Institute on Pennsylvania Dutch Studies, Ursinus College, 1976; *German Reformed Experience in Colonial America,* United Church Press, 1976. Editor of Pennsylvania Dutch study series, for Institute on Pennsylvania Dutch Studies at Ursinus College, 1974—. Contributor of about fifteen articles to regional history magazines. Editor of *Bulletin* of the Historical Society of Montgomery County, 1961-65; assistant editor of *Pennsylvania Folklife,* 1975—.

WORK IN PROGRESS: Folklife and Folklore of the Pennsylvania Dutch; Pfarrer Abraham Blumer, 1736-1822; "Proclaim Liberty": The life of Isaac Norris II, 1701-1766; Minutes and Records of Old First Reformed Church, Philadelphia, completion expected in 1979.

SIDELIGHTS: Parsons comments that he uses a "biographical approach to history and folkculture, so as to make both more real." He has traveled to the places, both in the United States and abroad, where his ancestors have lived and where the events in his books have taken place, and has conducted genealogical research on his own family. *Avocational interests:* Rockhound.

* * *

PARTRIDGE, Edward B(ellamy) 1916-

PERSONAL: Born March 21, 1916, in Phelps, N.Y.; son of Leonard Scott (a businessman) and Clarissa (Hammond) Partridge; married Viola Ahlborn (a teacher), May 16, 1943; children: Eric, Scott, Rosemary. *Education:* Hobart and William Smith Colleges, A.B., 1938; University of Rochester, M.A., 1939; Harvard University, further graduate study, 1940-41; Columbia University, Ph.D., 1950. *Politics:* Democrat. *Religion:* Episcopalian. *Home:* 1801 Octavia St., New Orleans, La. 70115. *Office:* Newcomb College, Tulane University, New Orleans, La. 70118.

CAREER: Hobart and William Smith Colleges, Geneva, N.Y., instructor in English, 1939-40; University of Rochester, Rochester, N.Y., instructor in English, 1942-46; Columbia University, New York, N.Y., instructor in English, 1946-47; Cornell University, Ithaca, N.Y., instructor, 1949-53, assistant professor of English, 1953-57; Bucknell University, Lewisburg, Pa., assistant professor, 1957-59, associate professor of English, 1959-65; Tulane University, New Orleans, La., professor of English, 1965-67; University of Iowa, Iowa City, professor of English, 1967-68; Tulane University, professor of English, 1968—. Visiting professor at California State College, Los Angeles, 1964-65.

MEMBER: Modern Language Association of America, College English Association, Renaissance Society of America, Malone Society, Phi Beta Kappa.

WRITINGS: The Broken Compass: A Study of the Major Comedies of Ben Jonson, Columbia University Press, 1958; (editor) Ben Jonson, *Bartholomew Fair,* University of Nebraska Press, 1964; (editor) Jonson, *Epicoene,* Yale University Press, 1971. Contributor to literature journals.

WORK IN PROGRESS: A book on Oscar Wilde.

PASS, Gail 1940-

PERSONAL: Born June 15, 1940, in Toledo, Ohio; daughter of Arthur R. (a manufacturer) and Helen (Miller) Pass. *Education:* Attended Smith College, 1958-60; University of California, Berkeley, B.A., 1962. *Politics:* "Voter." *Religion:* Jewish. *Home and office:* 19 Whidden St., Portsmouth, N.H. 03801. *Agent:* Ellen Levine, Curtis Brown Ltd., 575 Madison Ave., New York, N.Y. 10022.

CAREER: Has been an advertising receptionist, employment counselor, Kelly Girl, personnel assistant, typist, advertising assistant, census taker, library assistant and motel maid in San Francisco, Mendocino, and San Mateo County, Calif., 1962-75; writer, 1975—.

WRITINGS: Zoe's Book (novel), Houghton, 1976.

WORK IN PROGRESS: A novel that is a contemporary vision of Antigone's sister, completion expected in 1977.

SIDELIGHTS: Gail Pass told *CA:* "The main concern of *Zoe's Book* was the nature of the fictional experience. I am increasingly interested in the possibilities of a female aesthetic.

I believe the relationships between author and reader, and critic and author, are fruitful when based on respect and the desire to explore together. I think the function of fiction is to illuminate; that story-telling is an art form which must be richly textured if it is to do more than entertain; that the structure and content of a novel have to reflect one another; that reading should not be a passive pasttime.

"I hope to continue sharing my life with a loving woman, living near the sea, seeing my dogs as muses sometimes, enjoying puzzles, keeping friends, and being a vegetarian."

* * *

PATRICK, Claudia
See WALLACE, Pat

* * *

PATTERSON, David S(ands) 1937-

PERSONAL: Born April 26, 1937, in Bridgeport, Conn.; son of James Tyler (a lawyer) and Sarah (Sands) Patterson; married Mary Margaret Sharp (a journalist), June 15, 1968. *Education:* Yale University, B.A., 1959; University of California, Berkeley, M.A., 1962, Ph.D., 1968. *Residence:* Clinton, N.Y. *Office:* Department of History, Colgate University, Hamilton, N.Y. 13346.

CAREER: Teacher of history in Lakeville, Conn., 1959-61; San Jose State College (now University), San Jose, Calif., instructor in history, 1965; California State College (now University), Hayward, instructor in history, 1965; Ohio State University, Columbus, instructor in history, 1965-69; University of Illinois at Chicago Circle, Chicago, assistant professor of history, 1969-71; Rice University, Houston, Tex., assistant professor of history, 1971-76; Colgate University, Hamilton, N.Y., visiting associate professor of history, 1976—. *Member:* American Historical Association, Organization of American Historians, Society for Historians of American Foreign Relations, American Studies Association, Conference on Peace Research in History (member of executive council, 1972—). *Awards, honors:* National Endowment for the Humanities grant, 1971.

WRITINGS: (Author of introduction) Frederick Lynch, *Through Europe on the Eve of War: A Record of Personal Experiences, including an Account of the First World Conference of the Churches for International Peace,* new edition, Garland Publishing, 1971; (author of introduction) Lucia Ames Mead, *Law or War?*, new edition, Garland Publishing, 1971; (contributor) Charles Chatfield, editor, *Peace Movements in America*, Schocken, 1973; *Toward a Warless World: The Travail of the American Peace Movement, 1887-1914*, Indiana University Press, 1976. Contributor to *Proceedings of the American Philosophical Society*, and to journals, including *Historian, Political Science Quarterly*, and *Wisconsin Magazine of History*.

WORK IN PROGRESS: A monograph, *Pacifists' Search for a Negotiated Peace: An Adventure in Private Diplomacy, 1914-1917*; an interpretive history, *The United States and the Problem of Armaments in the Twentieth Century*.

SIDELIGHTS: Patterson told *CA:* "I believe I am most motivated by intellectual curiosity and a desire for self-actualization, and I perceive my career as a historian as a process of intellectual growth. I am constantly searching for new ideas to broaden my historical understanding. My research began in the area of peace research. I have continued to work in this area but have moved from analytic-narrative history to a greater interest in new perspectives brought to these issues by scholars in other disciplines in the humanities and social sciences. I am also concerned about the future of higher education and have begun to research and write in this area."

*   *   *

PATTERSON, K(arl) David   1941-

PERSONAL: Born April 6, 1941, in Newport News, Va.; son of Karl Dana (an office manager) and Elizabeth (Carlson) Patterson; married Carolyn L. Durdle, 1963; children: three. *Education:* Syracuse University, B.S., 1963, M.A., 1967; Stanford University, Ph.D., 1971. *Home:* 6910 Linda Lake Dr., Charlotte, N.C. 28215. *Office:* Department of History, University of North Carolina, Charlotte, N.C. 28223.

CAREER: State University of New York Upstate Medical Center, Syracuse, research assistant, 1964-67; University of North Carolina, Charlotte, assistant professor of history, 1971—. *Member:* American Historical Association, African Studies Association, Southern Association of Africanists. *Awards, honors:* Grants from National Library of Medicine, 1975 and 1976.

WRITINGS: The Northern Gabon Coast to 1875, Clarendon Press, 1975. Contributor of articles and reviews to history journals.

WORK IN PROGRESS: Research on western Africa in the nineteenth and twentieth centuries, and on medical and demographic developments in the colonial period, particularly on colonial medicine and health problems in the Gold Coast.

*   *   *

PATTERSON, (Horace) Orlando (Lloyd)   1940-

PERSONAL: Born June 5, 1940, in Jamaica, West Indies; came to the U.S., 1970, domiciled, 1972; son of Charles A. and Almina (Morris) Patterson; married Nerys Wyn Thomas, September 5, 1965; children: Rhiannon, Barbara. *Education:* University of the West Indies, B.Sc., 1962; London School of Economics, Ph.D., 1965. *Home:* 15 Shepard St., Cambridge, Mass., and Red Hills P.O., Jamaica (January, June-September). *Office:* 520 James Hall, Harvard University, Cambridge, Mass. 02138.

CAREER: University of London, London School of Eco-

nomics and Political Science, London, England, assistant lecturer, 1965-67; University of the West Indies, Kingston, Jamaica, lecturer, 1967-70; Harvard University, Cambridge, Mass., visiting lecturer, 1970-71, Allston Burr senior tutor, 1971-73, professor of sociology, 1972-73. Visiting member, Institute for Advanced Study, Princeton, N.J., 1975-76. Member of technical advisory committee to prime minister and government of Jamaica, 1972—, special adviser to prime minister for social policy and development, 1973—. *Member:* American Sociological Association. *Awards, honors:* M.A., Harvard University, 1971.

WRITINGS: The Children of Sisyphus (novel), Hutchinson, 1964; *The Sociology of Slavery: An Analysis of the Origins, Development, and Structure of Negro Slave Society in Jamaica*, MacGibbon & Kee, 1967, Farleigh Dickinson University Press, 1969; *An Absence of Ruins* (novel), Hutchinson, 1967; *Die the Long Day* (novel), Morrow, 1972; *The Tribal Tradition: A Critical Study of Ethnicity*, Stein & Day, 1977. Contributor of articles to journals.

WORK IN PROGRESS: The Theory of Slavery and Slave Societies: A Comparative Analysis; Harvard Square, a novel.

SIDELIGHTS: Patterson told *CA:* "I am a chronic cosmopolite, having lived all my adult life in other cultures. I presently keep homes in two totally different societies and enjoy them both. I have loved the women of every race and none of the men. My abiding conviction is the psychic unity of the human race, and my only passionate hatred is tradition and those obsessed with it."

BIOGRAPHICAL/CRITICAL SOURCES: Books and Bookmen, June, 1967; *Times Literary Supplement*, July 13, 1967; Kenneth Ramchand, *The West Indian Novel and Its Background*, Humanities, 1970.

*   *   *

PATTERSON, W. Morgan   1925-

PERSONAL: Born October 1, 1925, in New Orleans, La.; son of E. Palmer (an auditor) and Jess (Wood) Patterson; married Ernestine North, June 10, 1948; children: W. Morgan II, Jay North. *Education:* Stetson University, A.B., 1950; New Orleans Baptist Theological Seminary, M.Div., 1953, Th.D., 1956. *Office:* Golden Gate Baptist Seminary, Strawberry Point, Mill Valley, Calif. 94941.

CAREER: Ordained Southern Baptist clergyman, 1952; pastor of Baptist churches in Alabama, 1952-54, Mississippi, 1954-56; New Orleans Baptist Theological Seminary, New Orleans, La., assistant professor of church history, 1956-59; Southern Baptist Theological Seminary, Louisville, Ky., associate professor, 1959-69, David T. Porter professor of church history, 1959-76, director of graduate studies, 1970-76; Golden Gate Baptist Seminary, Mill Valley, Calif., professor of church history and academic dean, 1976. Chairman of Historical Commission of Southern Baptist Convention, 1969-72. *Military service:* U.S. Army Air Forces, flight officer, bombardier, and radar observer, 1943-46.

MEMBER: American Society of Church History, Southern Baptist Historical Society, Conference on Faith and History, Filson Club. *Awards, honors:* American Association of Theological Schools fellowship, 1965-66.

WRITINGS: (Editor) *Professor in the Pulpit*, Broadman, 1963; *Baptist Successionism: A Critical View*, Judson, 1969; (contributor) *Baptists in Kentucky, 1776-1976: A Bicentennial Volume*, Kentucky Baptist Convention, 1975; (contributor) *Baptists and the American Experience*, Judson, 1976. Book review editor of *Review & Expositor*, 1965-70.

PAULSTON, Christina Bratt

PERSONAL: Born in Stockholm, Sweden; came to the United States in 1951, naturalized citizen, 1959; daughter of Lennart and Elsa (Facht) Bratt; married Rolland Paulston (a professor), July 26, 1963; children: Christopher-Rolland, Ian Rollandsson. *Education:* Carleton College, B.A., 1953; University of Minnesota, M.A., 1955; Columbia University, Ed.D., 1966. *Office:* English Language Institute, University of Pittsburgh, 121 Meyran Ave., Pittsburgh, Pa. 15260.

CAREER: High school teacher of English and French in Clara City, Minn., 1955-56, and Pine Island, Minn., 1956-60; American School of Tangier, Tangier, Morocco, grade school teacher, 1960-62; Katrineholm Allmanna Laroverk, Katrineholm, Sweden, teacher of French, English, and Swedish, 1962-63; Columbia University, New York, N.Y., circulation librarian at East Asian Library, 1963-64, instructor in English as a second language at Teachers College, 1964-66; University of Punjab, Chandgarh, India, instructor in methodology of teaching English as a second language, summer, 1966; Pontificia Universidad Catolica del Peru, Lima, teacher of English as a second language, 1966-67; Instituto Linguistico de Verano, Lima, Peru, consultant, 1967-68; University of Pittsburgh, Pittsburgh, Pa., assistant professor, 1969-73, associate professor of linguistics, 1973—, assistant director of English Language Institute, 1969-70, director, 1970—, chairman of department of general linguistics, 1975—.

MEMBER: International Association of Teachers of English as a Foreign Language, National Association of Foreign Student Advisers, Linguistic Society of America, Modern Language Association of America, American Council on the Teaching of Foreign Languages, Association of Teachers of English to Speakers of Other Languages (member of executive committee, 1972-75; chairman of research committee, 1973-75; president, 1976—).

WRITINGS: (Translator with Robert Bly) Gunnar Ekeloef, *Late Arrival on Earth* (poems), Rapp & Carrol, 1967; *Course in Oral Spanish for the Bilingual Schools, First Year* (in Spanish), Summer Institute of Linguistics, Pucallpa, Peru, revised edition (Paulston was not associated with original edition), 1968; (translator with Bly) Ekeloef, *I Do Best Alone at Night* (poems), Charioteer Press, 1968; (with Gerald Dykstra) *Controlled Composition*, Regents Publishing, 1973; (with Dale Britton, Barry Brunetti, and John Hoover) *Developing Communicative Competence: Roleplays in English as a Second Language*, English Language Institute and University Center for International Studies, University of Pittsburgh, 1974; (with Mary Bruder) *From Substitution to Substance: A Handbook of Structural Pattern Drills*, Newbury House, 1975; *Implications of Language Learning Theory for Language Planning*, Center for Applied Linguistics, 1975; (with William Slager and William Norris) *English Today*, Books IV and V, McGraw, 1975; (with Bruder) *Procedures and Techniques in Teaching English as a Second Language*, Winthrop Publishing, 1976; (with Robert Henderson, Mary Call and Patricia Furey) *Write On: A Program in Controlled Composition*, Barron's, 1976; *Teaching English to Speakers of Other Languages in the United States, 1976: A Dipstick Paper*, Center for Applied Linguistics, 1976; (with Francis Johnson) *Individualizing the Language Classroom*, Jacaranda Press, 1976.

Contributor: Harold Allen and Russell Campbell, editors, *Teaching English as a Second Language*, McGraw, 1972; Kenneth Croft, editor, *Readings on English as a Second Language*, Winthrop Publishing, 1972; James Alatis, editor, *ESL in Bilingual Education*, Teachers of English to Speakers of Other Languages, 1976. Contributor of articles and reviews to language and education journals, and of translations of Swedish poems to *Nation, Hudson, Sixties,* and other periodicals.

WORK IN PROGRESS: Research on language acquisition and bilingual education.

AVOCATIONAL INTERESTS: Indoor and outdoor gardening, horses.

* * *

PAYNE, Ben Iden   1881-1976

September 5, 1881—April 6, 1976; American actor, drama instructor, director, and author of autobiography and books in his field. Obituaries: *New York Times,* April 7, 1976; *Time,* April 19, 1976.

* * *

PEARS, David Francis   1921-

PERSONAL: Born August 8, 1921, in Bedfont, Middlesex, England; son of Robert and Gladys (Meyers) Pears; married Anne Drew, 1963; children: Rosalind Jane, Julian Conrad. *Education:* Balliol College, Oxford, B.A., 1947, M.A., 1948. *Home:* 31 Northmoor Row, Oxford, England.

CAREER: Oxford University, Oxford, England, Christ Church, research lecturer, 1948-50, student, 1960—, curator of pictures, 1975, Corpus Christi College, fellow and tutor, 1950-59, university lecturer, 1950-72, reader in philosophy, 1972—, delegate to university press, 1976. Visiting professor at Harvard University, 1959, University of California, Berkeley, 1964, Rockefeller University, 1967; Humanities Council Research fellow, Princeton University, 1966; Hill Professor, University of Minnesota, 1970. Governor, Westminster School, 1975. *Member:* British Academy (fellow).

WRITINGS: (Editor) *The Nature of Metaphysics,* St. Martin's, 1957; (translator from the German with B. F. McGuinness) Ludwig Wittgenstein, *Tractatus Logico-Philosophicus,* Humanities Press, 1961, 2nd edition, 1974; (editor) Stuart Hampshire and others, *David Hume: A Symposium,* St. Martin's, 1963; (editor) *Freedom and the Will,* St. Martin's, 1963; (with J. F. Thomson) *Is Existence a Predicate?,* Aquinas Press, 1963; *Predicting and Deciding,* Oxford University Press, 1965; *Bertrand Russell and the British Tradition in Philosophy,* Random House, 1967, 2nd edition, Fontana, 1972; *Ludwig Wittgenstein,* Viking, 1970, published as *Wittgenstein,* Fontana, 1971; *What Is Knowledge?,* Harper, 1971; (translator from the German with McGuinness) Wittgenstein, *Prototractatus: An Early Version of Tractatus Logico-Philosophicus,* Cornell University Press, 1971; (editor) *Bertrand Russell: A Collection of Critical Essays,* Anchor Books, 1972; (editor and author of introduction) *Russell's Logical Atomism,* Fontana, 1972; *Questions in the Philosophy of Mind,* Duckworth, 1974; *The Naturalism of Book I of Hume's Treatise,* Oxford University Press, 1977.

* * *

PEARSON, B(enjamin) H(arold)   1893-

PERSONAL: Born April 25, 1893, in Los Angeles, Calif.; son of Benjamin F. (an engineer) and Florence L. (Wyatt) Pearson; married Emma Iola Corson, April 15, 1926 (died April 17, 1973); children: Esther Elizabeth (Mrs. Wayne V. Houser). *Education:* University of Southern California, B.A., 1924, M.Th., 1929. *Politics:* Conservative. *Home:* 13341 Twin Hills Dr. #57C, Seal Beach, Calif. 90740. *Of-*

fice: World Gospel Crusades, P.O. Box 3, Upland, Calif. 91786.

CAREER: Ordained Free Methodist minister, 1921; Free Methodist Mexican Missions, superintendent, 1919-35; Free Methodist Youth, general superintendent, 1935-43; Oriental Missionary Society International (now OMS-International), director of missions in Colombia, 1943-48, and Brazil, 1949-55; World Gospel Crusades, Upland, Calif., executive director, 1955-60, president, 1960-75, president emeritus, 1975—; writer, 1975—. Founding president of United Biblical Seminary of Colombia, 1945-48, and Londrina Seminary and Bible Institute of Brazil, 1950-55. *Military service:* U.S. Army, 1918; became sergeant major. *Member:* Phi Delta Kappa, Alpha Kappa Delta.

WRITINGS: Mexican Missions, Free Methodist Missions, 1925; (with Harry O. Harper) *Wings to Aztec Lands* (juvenile), Laverne Bell Davis, 1930; *Off to Panama!,* Free Tract Society, 1935; *Adventures in Christlike Living,* Free Tract Society, 1936; *The Lost Generation Returns,* Light & Life Press, 1937.

The Monk Who Lived Again, Light & Life Press, 1940; *Next!: Our Sunday School Adventure in South America,* Young People's Missionary Society, 1941; *Don Pedro,* Cowman Publications, 1950; *The Headhunter's Bride,* Cowan Publications, 1951.

The Vision Lives, Cowman Publications, 1961; *Memlo, the Persian Stable Boy* (juvenile), Good News Publishers, 1965; *Men Plus God,* Men for Missions International, 1967; *But If It Dies,* Christian Literature Crusade, 1970; (with Muriel Dennis) *Apprentice to the King,* Good News Publishers, 1972; *My God Just Went By,* Moody, 1972; *Still Flowing,* Oriental Missionary Society International, 1975.

Author of booklets and church school materials. Co-editor and contributor to "Sunday Evenings with Jesus," a youth series, Light & Life Press, 1935. Author of "Home Mission Echoes" and "Youth in Action," columns in *Free Methodist.* Contributor to religious periodicals. Editor of *Light and Life Evangel,* 1939-43.

WORK IN PROGRESS: Seeing the Glory!

SIDELIGHTS: Pearson writes: "My first real 'nudge' towards writing was an ex-convict, Whitey Marston, a member of the 'Jigger' Leary Gang, who told me at thirteen years of age, 'If you want to write, look out the window and write a hundred pages on what you see!'

"The Monk Who Lived Again, my most successful book, was an attempt to portray the soul and genius of Latin America. In it I sought to portray the religious life of Latin lands at its best. In *Don Pedro,* after living in 'la violencia' of Colombia, South America, amidst the political violence that took some three hundred thousand lives, and released every type of vendetta, including unholy alliances between political and religious leaders, I looked at the other side of the coin." Pearson's books have been published in Spanish, French, Portuguese, Afrikaans, Italian, and Norwegian.

*   *   *

PEARSON, (Edith) Linnea   1942-

PERSONAL: Born February 25, 1942, in Oak Park, Ill.; daughter of Per Oscar and Edith (a dean of women at a university; maiden name, Bengtson) Pearson; married former spouse, Rudolph C. Schoppe (a banker), June 23, 1962. *Education:* University of Illinois, B.S., M.A., and Ph.D., Harvard University, M.Th., 1971; also studied at Graduate Theological Union, 1973-75. *Politics:* Independent. *Home:*

D26, 1101 Northwest 39th Ave., Gainesville, Fla. 32601. *Office:* Unitarian Fellowship, P.O. Box 13309, Gainesville, Fla. 32604.

CAREER: WTTW-Television, Chicago, Ill., writer, 1965; Virginia State College, Norfolk, associate professor, 1967-70; Evergreen State College, Olympia, Wash., professor, 1972-74; Unitarian Fellowship, Gainesville, Fla., Unitarian-Universalist minister, 1975—. *Member:* American Civil Liberties Union (member of board of directors), National Organization for Women (founder and president in Norfolk, Va., 1965), Theta Sigma Phi (local president, 1960).

WRITINGS: Separate Paths: Why People End Their Lives, Harper, 1977. Contributor of articles and poems to *Etai* and to newspapers.

WORK IN PROGRESS: Sermons in Search: The First Year of A Woman's Ministry; Palckf: Life Is a Spiral.

SIDELIGHTS: Linnea Pearson writes: "I write primarily out of my experience, as a woman-person. At this point in time it has become clear, as perhaps never before, how different it is to be 'woman' than 'man.' "

*   *   *

PEARSON, Richard Joseph   1938-

PERSONAL: Born May 2, 1938, in Kitchener, Ontario, Canada; son of John Cecil (a businessman) and H. Anne Pearson; married Kazue Miyazaki (a researcher), December 12, 1964; children: Sarina Riye. *Education:* University of Toronto, B.A. (honors), 1960; University of Hawaii, graduate study, 1960-61; Yale University, Ph.D., 1966. *Office:* Department of Anthropology, University of British Columbia, Vancouver, British Columbia, Canada V6T 1W5.

CAREER: University of Hawaii, Honolulu, assistant professor, 1966-69, associate professor of archaeology, 1969-71; University of British Columbia, Vancouver, associate professor, 1971-74, professor of archaeology, 1974—. *Member:* American Anthropological Association, American Association for the Advancement of Science, Current Anthropology.

WRITINGS: (Editor) *Archaeology on the Island of Hawaii,* University Press of Hawaii, 1968; *Archaeology of the Ryukyu Islands,* University Press of Hawaii, 1969; (editor) *Traditional Society and Culture of Korea: Prehistory,* University Press of Hawaii, 1975.

WORK IN PROGRESS: Translating Kim Jeong-hak's *Prehistory of Korea* from the original Japanese, with wife Kazue Pearson; research on Korean, Japanese, and Chinese prehistory.

AVOCATIONAL INTERESTS: Horticulture, landscape architecture, plant propagation.

*   *   *

PEARSON, Robert Paul   1938-

PERSONAL: Born August 20, 1938, in Newark, N.J.; son of Oscar Paul (a statistician) and Ethelwyn (a teacher; maiden name, Martz) Pearson; married Rosalind Pace (a painter and poet), June 5, 1961; children: Erik Paul, Timothy Pace. *Education:* Brown University, A.B., 1960; University of Michigan, M.A., 1961; University of Massachusetts, Ed.D., 1973. *Politics:* Democrat. *Religion:* None. *Home:* 252 Taylor, Easton, Pa. 18042. *Office:* Department of Education, Lafayette College, Easton, Pa. 18042.

CAREER: U.S. Peace Corps, Washington, D.C., desk officer for Afghanistan and Libya and volunteer in Afghanistan, 1966-68, regional director in Libya, 1968-69; Swarthmore College, Swarthmore, Pa., assistant professor of education, 1972-73; Lafayette College, Easton, Pa., assistant professor of education, 1973—.

WRITINGS: Through Middle Eastern Eyes, Praeger, 1975.

WORK IN PROGRESS: Research on cross-cultural and inter-cultural communication and on the dynamics of cross-cultural interaction.

SIDELIGHTS: Pearson comments: "I am concerned with making communication across cultures easier and helping people see the degree to which they are products of their cultures and the degree to which cultural values are arbitrary and relative."

*   *   *

PEARSON, Susan 1946-

PERSONAL: Born December 21, 1946, in Boston, Mass.; daughter of Allen M. and Chloris (Horsman) Pearson. *Education:* St. Olaf College, B.A., 1968. *Residence:* New York, N.Y. *Office:* Dial Press, 1 Dag Hammarskjold Plaza, New York, N.Y. 10017.

CAREER: Volunteers in Service to America (VISTA), Columbia, S.C., volunteer worker, 1968-69; Quaker Oats Co., Minneapolis, Minn., sales representative, 1969-71; Viking Press, New York, N.Y., assistant, 1971-72; Dial Press, New York City, assistant editor, 1972-75, associate editor, 1976—. *Awards, honors: Izzie* was named *New York Times* outstanding book of the year and Child Study Association children's book of the year, 1975.

WRITINGS—For children: *Izzie,* Dial, 1975; *Monnie Hates Lydia,* Dial, 1975; *Monday I Was an Alligator,* Lippincott, in press.

WORK IN PROGRESS: Two picture books for Dial; *The Attic* and *Music Without Dirge,* both juvenile novels.

*   *   *

PEDOE, Daniel 1910-

PERSONAL: Born November 29, 1910, in London, England; married Mary Tunstall; children: Dan Tunstall, Hugh Tunstall. *Education:* Magdalene College, Cambridge, B.A., 1930, Ph.D., 1937; Institute for Advanced Study, postdoctoral study, 1935-36. *Home:* 1956 East River Terrace, Minneapolis, Minn. 55414. *Office:* Department of Mathematics, University of Minnesota, Minneapolis, Minn. 55455.

CAREER: University of London, London, England, reader in mathematics, 1948-52; University of Khartoum, Khartoum, Sudan, professor of mathematics, 1952-59; University of Singapore, Singapore, professor of mathematics, 1959-62; University of Minnesota, Minneapolis, professor of mathematics, 1964—. *Member:* Royal Commonwealth Society, American Mathematical Society, American Mathematics Association. *Awards, honors:* Leverhulme fellowship, 1947; Lester Ford prize from American Mathematics Association, 1968; Fulbright-Hays travelling fellowship from U.S. Department of State, 1973.

WRITINGS: (With William Hodge) *Methods of Algebraic Geometry,* Cambridge University Press, Volume I, 1947, Volume II, 1952, Volume III, 1954; *Circles* (textbook), Pergamon, 1957; *The Gentle Art of Mathematics,* English Universities Press, 1958, Dover, 1974; *Geometry and the Liberal Arts,* Penguin Books, 1976. Contributor to *Encyclopaedia Britannica.*

WORK IN PROGRESS: Methods of Elementary Geometry for Teachers and Students.

SIDELIGHTS: Pedoe is dedicated to spreading an enjoyment of geometry. *Geometry and the Liberal Arts* deals with the fascination that subject held for Albrecht Dùrer, Leonardo da Vinci, and other great men. He writes that since the 1960's a popular book on algebra or calculus could make an author rich. "Geometry was forced out by the 'new math,' which has done much harm to mathematics education. The Austrian Mathematical Society has just issued a report describing the damage the 'new math' has done in the German-speaking countries, and no doubt this will encourage the less sheeplike educators here to follow suit."

*   *   *

PENDERGAST, Charles 1950-
(Chuck Pendergast)

PERSONAL: Born September 2, 1950, in Superior, Wis.; son of Raymond and Marion Pendergast. *Education:* University of California, Los Angeles, B.A., 1973. *Home:* 4048B Via Zorro, Santa Barbara, Calif. 93110. *Office:* Wiley/Hamilton, 1129 State St., Santa Barbara, Calif. 93101.

CAREER: Currently production manager at Wiley/Hamilton (publishing group), Santa Barbara, Calif.

WRITINGS: (Under name Chuck Pendergast) *Introduction to Organic Gardening,* Nash Publishing, 1970. Contributor of articles to airline inflight magazines. Associate editor, *Motor Trend* magazine, 1969-1972.

WORK IN PROGRESS: Research on Wilhelm Reich and Orgone energy.

*   *   *

PENDERGAST, Chuck
See PENDERGAST, Charles

*   *   *

PENDLETON, Mary

PERSONAL: Born in Rochester, Ind.; daughter of Oren Edward (in civil service) and Augusta Marie (Knoll) Reddick; married Arthur Frederick Pendleton (a woodworker), July 18, 1943. *Education:* Attended Dayton Art Institute and Cranbrook Academy of Art. *Home and office:* 407 Jordon Rd., Sedona, Ariz. 86336.

CAREER: The Pendleton Shop (a handweaving-knitting studio), Sedona, Ariz., co-owner, 1947—; Mary Pendleton Handweavers (a retail craft shop), Sedona, Ariz., co-owner, 1960—; Pendleton Fabric Craft School, Sedona, Ariz., co-owner and instructor, 1960—. *Member:* American Crafts Council, Arizona Designer Craftsmen (charter member), Soroptimist International.

WRITINGS: Navajo and Hopi Weaving Techniques, Macmillan, 1974; *Double Weave Series* (pamphlet), privately printed, 1975. Editor and publisher of *Looming Arts,* 1966—.

WORK IN PROGRESS: A book, *Basic Handweaving;* an enlarged edition of *Navajo and Hopi Weaving Techniques.*

*   *   *

PENDO, Stephen 1947-

PERSONAL: Born November 8, 1947, in Hanover, N.H.; son of Anatole George (a school principal) and Eleanor (a teacher; maiden name, Thompson) Pendo. *Education:* University of Vermont, B.A., 1972, M.A., 1975. *Home:* 128 Colchester Ave., Burlington, Vt. 05401. *Agent:* Bertha Klausner, 71 Park Ave., New York, N.Y. 10016.

CAREER: Writer. *Member:* Society for Cinema Studies, Writers Guild of America (West).

WRITINGS: *Raymond Chandler on Film: His Novels into Films,* Scarecrow, 1976. Author of story and screenplay "A History of the Catholic Church in Vermont," 1976. Contributor to *Films in Review.*

WORK IN PROGRESS: *Aviation in the Cinema.*

SIDELIGHTS: Pendo writes: "I enjoy studying the history of motion pictures because effective film criticism only comes through a thorough knowledge of film's past. I like writing films because of the challenge involved in creating characters and plot in a filmic context. Film is probably the most important art form of the Twentieth Century, and it is important to educate the public in the intricacies. . . ."

*   *   *

PENFIELD, Wilder (Graves) 1891-1976

January 26, 1891—April 5, 1976; American-born Canadian neurosurgeon and author of novels and books in his field. Obituaries: *Time,* April 19, 1976; *Current Biography,* June, 1976. (See index for previous *CA* sketch)

*   *   *

PENROSE, Boies 1902-1976

November 20, 1902—February 27, 1976; American travel historian and author of books in his field. Obituaries: *New York Times,* March 1, 1976; *AB Bookman's Weekly,* May 17, 1976.

*   *   *

PEPPIN, Brigid (Mary) 1941-

PERSONAL: Born May 22, 1941, in Oxford, England; daughter of Gerald Sydenham John and Helen (Carleton) Peppin; married David Robert Malseed Curtis (an artist and writer), summer, 1967; children: Daniel, Robert. *Education:* University College, University of London, D.F.A., 1965. *Home:* 126 Long Acre, London W.C.2, England.

CAREER: Lecturer and writer in London, England, 1965—. Helped organize and operate London Arts Laboratory and New Arts Laboratory, 1967-71.

WRITINGS: *Fantasy* (non-fiction), Watson-Guptill, 1975.

WORK IN PROGRESS: Continuing research on book illustration.

AVOCATIONAL INTERESTS: Book illustrating, painting, making clothes, viewing architecture and landscapes, visiting art exhibitions.

BIOGRAPHICAL/CRITICAL SOURCES: *Art and Artists,* August, 1967.

*   *   *

PERCY, Charles H(arting) 1919-

PERSONAL: Born September 27, 1919, in Pensacola, Fla.; son of Edward H. and Elisabeth (Harting) Percy; married Jeanne Valerie Dickerson, June 12, 1943 (died, 1947); married Loraine Diane Guyer, August 7, 1950; children: (first marriage) Valerie (died September 18, 1966) and Sharon Lee (twins), Roger; (second marriage) Gail, Mark. *Education:* University of Chicago, A.B., 1941. *Religion:* Christian Scientist. *Residence:* Willamette, Ill. 60091. *Office:* U.S. Senate Office Building, Washington, D.C. 20510.

CAREER: Bell & Howell, Chicago, Ill., sales trainee and apprentice, 1938, manager of war coordinating department, 1941-43, assistant secretary, 1943-46, corporation secretary, 1946-49, president, 1949-61, chief executive officer, 1951-63, chairman of board of directors, 1961-66; U.S. Congress, Washington, D.C., Republican senator from Illinois, 1967—. Member of Senate Committee on Investigations, Joint Economic Committee, Special Committee on Aging, Foreign Relations Committee, and several subcommittees. President of United Republican Fund of Illinois, 1955-58; vice-chairman of Republican National Finance Committee, 1955-59; chairman of Republican platform committee, 1960; Republican candidate for governor of Illinois, 1964; chairman of New Illinois Committee, 1965-69. Speical U.S. ambassador in Peru and Bolivia, 1956; member of U.S. delegation to United Nations General Assembly, 1974. In sales promotion for Crowell-Collier Publishing Co., 1939. Past director of Harris Trust and Savings Bank and Outboard Marine Corp.; trustee of Illinois Institute of Technology, 1950-54, and University of Chicago; past trustee of California Institute of Technology. Chairman of adult education fund of Ford Foundation, 1958-61. *Military service:* U.S. Naval Reserve, active duty, 1943-45; became lieutenant senior grade.

MEMBER: American Management Association (past director), National Photographic Manufacturers Association, Photographic Society of America, Chicago Association of Commerce, Phi Delta Phi, Alpha Delta Phi, Chicago Club, Economic Club (past director), Executives Club (past director), Commercial Club, Commonwealth Club. *Awards, honors:* World Trade Award from World Trade Award Committee, 1955; management award from National Sales Executives, 1956; decorated officer of French Legion of Honor; honorary degrees include LL.D. from Illinois College, 1961, Roosevelt University, 1961, and Lake Forest College, 1962; H.H.D. from Willamette University, 1962.

WRITINGS: *Growing Old in the Country of the Young,* McGraw, 1974; *I Want to Know About the U.S. Senate* (juvenile), Doubleday, 1976.

SIDELIGHTS: Senator Percy was reelected to his second term in the U.S. Senate in November, 1972 by 1,146,000 votes, the largest plurality ever amassed by a candidate for president, governor, or senator in Illinois history. He was the only candidate in Illinois history to carry all 102 of the state counties. An early critic of U.S. military involvement in Vietnam, Percy's major domestic interests have been in the fields of the elderly, consumer protection, and the economy.

Growing Old in the Country of the Young is an outgrowth of Senator Percy's experience as a member of the Senate Special Committee on Aging. Gary Thatcher comments that the book is a "disturbing account of growing old [which] raises the gnawing feeling that, unless government acts, many of us face the loneliness and poverty that some senior citizens now endure."

AVOCATIONAL INTERESTS: Outdoor photography, hunting, fishing, skiing, tennis.

BIOGRAPHICAL/CRITICAL SOURCES: *Christian Science Monitor,* December 4, 1974.

*   *   *

PERRY, Robin 1917-

PERSONAL: Born December 27, 1917, in New York, N.Y.; son of Clinton McKesson and Natalie (Forbes) Perry; divorced. *Education:* Attended and graduated from at least four colleges and universities, including the Army Command

and General Staff college and the Industrial College of the Armed Services. *Home and office:* 820 Hartford Rd., Waterford, Conn. 06385.

CAREER: Eastman Kodak Co., Rochester, N.Y., executive trainee, 1946-48; free-lance photographer, 1949—, work has appeared in almost every national magazine and been exhibited in Antwerp, Brussels, London, Munich, Copenhagen, Paris, New York, and many other cities in the United States, recent work selected for the U.S. Information Agency's "Photography—USA" exhibit now touring Eastern Europe; free-lance writer, 1950—. Professional pilot. Organizer and teacher of creative photography and writing workshops; lecturer in the United States, Canada, and Europe. *Military service:* U.S. Army and U.S. Navy; served as a commissioned officer, photographic officer, intelligence officer, and officer in charge of teaching at Army Reserve Command and General Staff College. *Member:* Authors Guild, American Society of Journalists and Authors, American Society of Magazine Photographers, American Society of Photographers, Europhot, Institute of Incorporated Photographers (England; fellow), Professional Photographers of America (master photographer), Royal Photographic Society of Great Britain (associate member).

WRITINGS: The Woods Rider (motorcycling), Crown, 1973; *The Road Rider* (motorcycling), Crown, 1974; *The Trials Motorcyclist,* Crown, 1975; *The Creative Color Photography of Robin Perry,* Amphoto, 1975; *Welcome for a Hero* (novel), Livingston Press, 1975; *Photography for the Professionals,* Livingston Press, 1976. Author of column in *Dexter Bulletin,* 1964—. Contributor of over 200 articles and short stories to photography and popular magazines.

WORK IN PROGRESS: A novel, *Shadows of the Mind;* editing a book with sections by three other famous photographers to be called *The American Contemporary Color Photographer.*

SIDELIGHTS: Perry told *CA* how he started on his own in photography, and said: "It was during this time that I wrote a story and sold it to *Flying* magazine for 115 dollars, and my appetite was whetted as they say. So started my nefarious career as a writer. Photography held me together financially and was my mainstay. Writing was purely a hobby and I wrote mostly articles. Fame came and I was honored all over the world and have lectured almost everywhere. Articles and stories were published from time to time but it was not until I had reached the age of 54 that I wrote my first book. It came about because the local library had nothing on woods riding of motorcycles and I had ridden for some forty years. So, I wrote the *Woods Rider* and my editor encouraged me to write more.

"I did. Within four years, I wrote six books and found a ready market for all of them, but I also discovered much chicanery and decided that I could do a better job than some of the publishers. So I formed the Livingston Press (my middle name is Livingston) and luckily got back my novel from two different publishers. Each had eagerly purchased it with a photographic book: a double book contract. I knew the novel would be buried so I formed my own publishing company. I had visions of publishing many great works by unknown authors—until I started to pay some of the bills and found out that 40% went to the bookstore, 10% to the author, 25% of the remainder went to the distributor and his salesmen and warehouse, billing, credit and collection. Then the printer came in for his 18% and quite suddenly, I was working for 7% and I had to handle advertising, promotion and all the other production expenses. So much for my adventure in publishing."

Despite the unanticipated expense and hard work involved in his publishing experiment, Perry maintains, "The knowledge I gained was enormous. All my books for the next twenty or thirty years, God willing, will be well produced. My last two books are cited for their style and quality of production. All new contracts for books will include me in the production. Getting published was never a problem; writing a book that meets my critical standards is."

"I have been writing all my life and never cease to thrill at the simple task of placing one word after another on the typed page. This isn't to say that I don't have to agonize over the Thesaurus, checking for that precise word; annoyed at being delayed—learning grammar and punctuation over and over again. Rewriting and revising (I draw a distinction here; I revise with different thought direction, I rewrite phrases by recasting). Even the chores of editing and retyping are fun to do—and sometimes, just sometimes, on someone else's manuscript."

"I often bemoan the fact that I never wrote seriously (whatever that means) until I was in my fifties. Yet I'm aware that the vicissitudes of life have molded me into perceptions that I did not have as a young man. I've had to learn that my writing is never going to be great literature but that in those fields I choose to plow, I shall reap a harvest of readers; readers who will be touched with the clarity of words, transmuted into understandable thoughts. Perhaps this is enough."

In addition to being an avid motorcyclist, Perry is also a professional pilot with commercial, instructor, and multi-engine land and sea ratings. He has owned aircraft for over twenty-five years, and holds patents on pilots' navigational computers and plotters. At one time he had an aviation talk show on television.

AVOCATIONAL INTERESTS: Flying, motorcycling, photography, writing, inventing, "I've given up skydiving—too time consuming."

* * *

PERRY, Will 1933-

PERSONAL: Born May 11, 1933, in Morris, Ill.; son of Wilbur and Mary Perry; married Patricia C. Pezet (an advertising director), May 26, 1956; children: Stephen, Karen, Susan. *Education:* University of Michigan, B.A., 1955. *Home:* 1540 King George Court, Ann Arbor, Mich. 48104. *Office:* University of Michigan, 1000 South State St., Ann Arbor, Mich. 48109.

CAREER: Belvidere, Ill., reporter and staff writer, 1958-60; *Grand Rapids Press,* Grand Rapids, Mich., assistant sports editor, 1960-68; University of Michigan, Ann Arbor, sports information director, 1968—.

WRITINGS: The Wolverines: A Story of Michigan Football, Strode, 1974. Contributor to National Collegiate Athletic Association programs and to magazines, including *Argosy* and *Coach and Athlete.*

* * *

PETERS, Ludovic
See BRENT, Peter (Ludwig)

* * *

PETERSEN, Arnold 1885-1976

April 16, 1885—February 5, 1976; Danish-born American politician and author of books and pamphlets in his field. Obituaries: *New York Times,* February 7, 1976.

PETRIE, Rhona
See BUCHANAN, Marie

* * *

PETTERSSON, Karl-Henrik 1937-

PERSONAL: Born September 13, 1937, in Linkoeping, Sweden; son of Timar and Saga (Andersson) Pettersson; married Anita Klintsell, July, 1974. *Education:* Stockholm University, M.A., 1963; Royal Institute of Technology, Stockholm, Ph.D., 1966. *Office:* Ministry of Industry, Storkyrkobrinken 7, 10310 Stockholm, Sweden.

CAREER: Sundsvallsbanken (a commercial bank), Stockholm, Sweden, assistant to general manager, 1967-70; Swedish Government, Ministry of Industry, Stockholm, special advisor, 1970-72, head of department of sectorial policy work, 1973-75, undersecretary of planning, 1975—. Visiting scholar, Stanford University, 1967.

WRITINGS: (With Jan Erik Berglund) *Produktionens omvaerld* (title means "Industrial Production and the 'World' Around"), Aldus, 1969; *Det herreuloesa industrisamhaellet* (title means "Industrial Society Out of Control"), Forum, 1973; *Reap the Whirlwind,* Atheneum, 1975. Contributor to periodicals.

SIDELIGHTS: Pettersson writes: "The root of evil, and of course all the good things, in our society . . . is the uncontrolled research and development work which gives us a technology we are not able to master. Competition forces industry to produce what is technically possible to produce. Whether we want it or not, whether it draws on our already reduced natural resources or not, whether it leads to a monstrous waste of capital or not."

* * *

PETTIT, Clyde Edwin 1932-

PERSONAL: Born December 29, 1932, in Chicago, Ill.; son of Clyde Edwin, Sr. and Minnie (Oberly) Pettit. *Education:* Attended Yale University; University of Arkansas, Juris Doctor, 1959. *Politics:* Democrat. *Home and office:* 120 Third St. N.E., Washington, D.C. 20002.

CAREER: Self-employed in investments, 1959-63; member of U.S. Senate staff in Washington, D.C., 1963-64; Democratic National Committee, Washington, D.C., member of campaign staff and radio producer, 1964; special assistant to president pro tempore of U.S. Senate, 1964-69; WTOP-Television, Washington, D.C., producer and director of special effects, 1969-71; writer, 1971—. *Military service:* U.S. Army, 1954-56.

WRITINGS: The Experts, Lyle Stuart, 1975.

WORK IN PROGRESS: The Iconoclasts; a history of the armaments industry and its effect on international affairs.

SIDELIGHTS: The Experts, a chronological history of U.S. involvment in the Vietnam war, is an outgrowth of radio broadcasts made as a foreign correspondent in Vietnam in the mid-1960's. During his career, he has made hundreds of broadcasts from all over the world, including Europe, the Middle East, and Asia.

BIOGRAPHICAL/CRITICAL SOURCES: Long Island Newsday, April 20, 1975; *Washington Times,* April 25, 1975; *New York Times,* May 6, 1975.

* * *

PETTY, Mary 1899-1976

April 29, 1899—March 6, 1976; American magazine cartoonist. Obituaries: *New York Times,* March 11, 1976; *Newsweek,* March 22, 1976.

* * *

PETTY, William Henry 1921-

PERSONAL: Born September 7, 1921, in Bradford, England; son of Henry (a manager) and Eveline Ann (a teacher; maiden name, Downs) Petty; married Margaret Elaine Bastow, March 31, 1948; children: Christine Margaret, Rowena Anne, Stephen William. *Education:* Peterhouse College, Cambridge, B.A., 1946, M.A., 1950; University of London, B.Sc., 1953. *Religion:* Church of England. *Home:* Godfrey House, Hollingbourne, Maidstone, Kent, England.

CAREER: London County Council, Education Department, London, England, senior assistant, 1946-47; Borough of Doncaster, Yorkshire, England, administrative assistant, technical school English master, and youth service worker, 1947-51; North Riding County Council, Yorkshire, assistant education officer, 1951-57; West Riding County Council, Yorkshire, assistant education officer, 1957-64; Kent County Council, England, deputy education officer, 1964-73, county education officer, 1973—. *Military service:* British Army, Royal Artillery, 1941-45.

MEMBER: Society of Education Officers (member of executive committee), English Association, Poetry Society. *Awards, honors:* Prizes from Cheltenham Festival of Literature, 1968, and Camden Festival of Music and the Arts, 1969.

WRITINGS—Poetry: *No Bold Comfort,* Outposts, 1957; *Conquest,* Outposts, 1967.

Work anthologized in *New Poems,* edited by Rex Warner, Christopher Hassall, and Laurie Lee, Methuen, 1954; *New Poems,* edited by C. V. Wedgwood, Harold Pinter, and others, J. Cape, 1965, 1967, 1970.

Contributor of articles and poems to newspapers, education and literature journals, and to literary magazines, including *Transatlantic Review, Ambit, Twentieth Century, Delta,* and *York Poetry.*

WORK IN PROGRESS: A new collection of poems.

BIOGRAPHICAL/CRITICAL SOURCES: Times Literary Supplement, July, 1957; *Outposts,* summer, 1957; *Poetry Review,* winter, 1958; *Times Educational Supplement,* July, 1967.

* * *

PEYREFITTE, (Pierre) Roger 1907-

PERSONAL: Born August 17, 1907, in Castres, France; son of Jean (a landowner) and Eugenie (Jamme) Peyrefitte. *Education:* University of Toulouse, diplome d'etudes lange et de litterature francaise, 1925; School of Political Studies, Paris, diplome, 1930. *Religion:* Catholic. *Home:* 9 avenue du Marechal-Maunoury, Paris 75016, France.

CAREER: French Ministry of Foreign Affairs, attache in Paris, 1931-33, 3rd secretary in French Embassy in Athens, 1933-38, attache in Paris, 1938-40 and 1943-45. Author, 1944—. *Awards, honors:* Theophraste Renaudot prize, 1945, for *Les Amities particulieres;* prize from the city of Palermo, Italy, 1953, for *Du Vesuve a l'Etna.*

WRITINGS—Novels in English translation: *Les Amities particulieres,* J. Vigneau, 1945, translation by Felix Giovanelli published as *Special Friendships,* Vanguard, 1950, translation by Edward Hyams published under same title, Secker & Warburg, 1958; *Les Ambassades,* Flammarion,

1951, translation by James FitzMaurice published as *Diplomatic Diversions,* Thames & Hudson, 1953; *La Fin des Ambassades,* Flammarion, 1953, translation by Edward Hyams published as *Diplomatic Conclusions,* Thames & Hudson, 1954; *Les Cles de Saint Pierre,* Flammarion, 1955, translation by Edward Hyams published as *The Keys of St. Peter,* Criterion, 1957; *Chevaliers de Malte,* Flammarion, 1957, translation by Edward Hyams published as *Knights of Malta,* Criterion, 1959; *L'Exile de Capri,* forward by Jean Cocteau, Flammarion, 1959, translation by Edward Hyams published as *The Exile of Capri,* Secker & Warburg, 1961, Fleet Publishing Corp., 1965; *La Nature du Prince,* Flammarion, 1963, translation by Peter Fryer published as *The Prince's Person,* Secker & Warburg, 1964, Farrar, Straus, 1965; *Les Juifs,* Flammarion, 1965, new edition, 1968, translation by Bruce Lowery published as *The Jews: A Fictional Venture Into the Follies of Antisemitism,* Bobbs-Merrill, 1967.

Other fiction: *Mademoiselle de Murville* (novel), J. Vigneau, 1947; *L'Oracle* (novel; title means "The Oracle"), Flammarion, 1947; *Les Amours Singulieres* (short stories; title means "Strange Loves"), Flammarion, 1949; *La Mort d'une mere* (autobiography; title means "The Death of a Mother"), Flammarion, 1950; *Jeunes Proies* (short stories; title means "Young Preys"), Flammarion, 1956; *Les Fils de la lumiere* (novel; title means "The Sons of Light"), Flammarion, 1961; *Notre amour* (auto-confession; title means "Our Love"), Flammarion, 1967; *Les Americains* (novel; title means "The Americans"), Flammarion, 1968; *Des Francais* (satire; title means "Frenchmen"), Flammarion, 1970; *La Coloquinte* (novel; title means "The Colocynth"), Flammarion, 1971.

Plays: *Le Prince des neiges* (three act; first produced in Paris at Hebertot Theatre, 1946), Flammarion, 1947; *Le Spectateur Nocturne* (three act), Flammarion, 1960.

Nonfiction: *Du Vesuve a l'Etna,* Flammarion, 1952, translation by J.H.F. McEwen published as *South From Naples,* Thames & Hudson, 1954; *Les Secrets des conclaves* (title means "Secrets of the Conclaves"), Flammarion, 1964; *Lettre ouverte a Monsieur Francois Mauriac* (title means "Open Letter to Mr. Francois Mauriac"), Editions Dynamo, 1964; *L'Enfant amour* (title means "Child and Love"), Flammarion, 1969; (conversations with Paul Xavier Giannoli) *Roger Peyrefitte; ou, les cles du scandale* (title means "Roger Peyrefitte; or, The Keys to Scandal"), Fayard, 1970; *Manouche* (biography of Germaine Germain), Flammarion, 1972, translation by Derek Coltman published under same title, Hart-Davis, 1973, translation by Sam Flores published under same title, Grove, 1974; *Tableaux de halle; ou, la vie extraordinaire de Fernand Legros* (biography; title means "The Painting Racket; or, The Extraordinary Life of Fernand Legros"), Albin Michel, 1976.

Editor: *Un Musee de l'amour,* Editions du Rocher (Monaco), 1972; (and translator) Straton of Sardis and Lucian of Samosata, *La Muse garconniere et Les Amours,* Flammarion, 1973.

WORK IN PROGRESS: A comprehensive work about Alexander the Great, of which the first part will appear in 1977 under the title *Alexander's Youth.*

SIDELIGHTS: Peyrefitte has been denounced as a "mere scandalmonger and sly pornographer" and vindicated as a "moralist of genuine indignation" for his satirical parodies of European society. The author has been involved in five legal suits because of his writings. In 1958, he accepted amnesty from a suit filed by the Italian Government in response to an article about Pope Pius XII. Another suit was filed involving the *Exile of Capri* in 1959. In 1965, he defeated an attempt by members of the Rothschild family to stop the sale of *Les Juifs,* although a few lines of the book had to be changed in later printings. In 1970, Marlene Dietrich sued over *Des Francais.* The latest case is currently pending in Italy. But the sensation spread far beyond the borders of that country, when Peyrefitte wrote a magazine article accusing Pope Paul VI of having had a homosexual relationship before he rose to the papacy. Out of court his work has sparked confrontation between artists and other writers. During the filming of *Les Amities particulieres* in 1964 a protest occurred which divided the Paris literary world nineteen years after the book's original appearance.

Critics have been equally divided in their opinions of Peyrefitte's books. Panning *The Jews,* Renee Winegarten concluded: "Peyrefitte, who has been called an industrialist of scandal, has merely seized yet another opportunity to exercise his talent as backbiter and mischief-maker royal." Other critics have pointed out his elegant style and claimed his right as an artist to choose subject matter without having to anticipate reader prejudice. In a review of *The Prince's Person,* a book heavily impugning the Catholic Church during the Renaissance, Laurent LeSage asserted: "To tell a tale so bawdy Peyrefitte deploys all the graces of his style. Nuance, delicate thrust, allusion, humorous understatement, and the strictest propriety of language keep the story from foundering in its offensiveness. He is an artist, not a pornographer. A historian, too, if you will, of impressive erudition—but still an artist, who makes fact and document cast their own spell within a most terse narration." LeSage's only regret is "that such art is not put to nobler uses."

In the biography of Germaine Germain, the famous paramour of Mistinguett and Paul-Bonaventure Carbone, *Newsweek* observed the apt parallel of the woman to the times. "As Roger Peyrefitte implies in his book, a best seller in Europe, she was symptomatic both of France's frenetic gaiety during the early 1930s and of the nation's moral deterioration during the Nazi occupation. . . . If this book is nominally a biography of a colorful, raunchy personality, it is equally an evocation of France's most ignominious era." In this book, he evokes bitter memories of occupied France and revives some accusations of alleged collaboration. Peyrefitte's latest biography was the best-seller of 1976 in France.

In addition to the filming of *Les Amities particulieres,* another work has been adapted to a different medium. Andre Paul Antoine put *Les Ambassades* on the stage in 1961.

AVOCATIONAL INTERESTS: Antiques (the sale of his Greek and Roman coin collection in 1974 was the largest auction of its kind ever held in France), erotic art, rare books.

BIOGRAPHICAL/CRITICAL SOURCES: Kenyon Review, summer, 1962; *Saturday Review,* May 8, 1965; *Time,* July 16, 1965; *Newsweek,* July 19, 1965; September 30, 1974; *New York Times Book Review,* October 14, 1965; *Commentary,* January, 1968.

* * *

PFEIFFER, Charles F. 1919-1976

May 23, 1919—July 18, 1976; American educator and author of books on biblical history and archaeology. Obituaries: *Publishers Weekly,* August 2, 1976. (See index for previous CA sketch)

PFORDRESHER, John 1943-

PERSONAL: Born October 15, 1943, in Chicago, Ill.; son of Albert G. (a dentist) and Virginia (Rausch) Pfordresher; married Karen Floody, June 15, 1968; children: Peter, Rebecca. Education: Georgetown University, B.A., 1965; University of Minnesota, Ph.D., 1970. Religion: Roman Catholic. Office: Department of English, Georgetown University, Washington, D.C. 20057.

CAREER: University of New Hampshire, Durham, assistant professor of English, 1970-73; Georgetown University, Washington, D.C., assistant professor, 1973-76, associate professor of English, 1976—. Member: Modern Language Association of America, National Council of Teachers of English, Research Society for Victorian Periodicals, Tennyson Society, Northeast Modern Language Association, Phi Beta Kappa.

WRITINGS: (Editor) Variorum Edition of Tennyson's Idylls of the King, Columbia University Press, 1973; (with Edmund Farrell, Thomas Gage, and Raymond Rodriguez) Exploring Life Through Literature, Scott, Foresman, 1973; (with Farrell, Gage, and Rodriguez) Science Fiction/Fact, Scott, Foresman, 1974; (with Farrell, Gage, and Rodriguez) Fantasy: Shape of Things Unknown, Scott, Foresman, 1974; (with Farrell, Gage, and Rodriguez) Myth, Mind, and Moment, Scott, Foresman, 1976; (with Farrell, Gage, and Rodriguez) I/We—You/They, Scott, Foresman, 1976; (with Farrell, Gage, and Rodriguez) Reality in Conflict, Scott, Foresman, 1976; (with Carl Dawson) Matthew Arnold: The Prose, Routledge & Kegan Paul, 1976.

WORK IN PROGRESS: Research on Dickens.

*   *   *

PHILLIPS, Irv(ing W.) 1908-

PERSONAL: Born October 29, 1908, in Wilton, Wis.; married Lucille D. Defnet, October 2, 1910; children: Arden (Mrs. Able Bomberault). Education: Attended Chicago Academy of Fine Arts and Columbia Music College. Home: 2807 East Sylvia Street, Phoenix, Ariz. 85032.

CAREER: Cartoonist, illustrator, writer. Esquire Magazine, New York, N.Y., cartoon humor editor, 1937-39; Chicago Sun-Times Syndicate, Chicago, Ill., cartoon staff, 1940-52; Phoenix College, Phoenix, Ariz., instructor. Has had motion picture assignments with Warner Brothers, RKO, Charles Rodgers Productions, and United Artists. Work has been exhibited at National Cartoonist Society Exhibits; Arizona State University (one-man show), "Comedy in Art"; New York Worlds Fair Exhibits; Cartoon Council traveling exhibits; Smithsonian Institute, permanent collection; El Prado Gallery, Sedona, Ariz.; Phoenix College Gallery, Phoenix, Ariz.; Studio Gallery, Southbury, Conn. Awards, honors: Salone dell'Umorismo of Bordighera, Italy, international first prize and cup, 1969.

MEMBER: Writers Guild, Dramatists Guild, National Cartoonists Society, Magazine Cartoonists Guild, Newspaper Cartoon Council, American Society of Composers, Authors and Publishers.

WRITINGS: (Self-illustrated) The Strange World of Mr. Mum, Putnam, 1965; The Twin Witches of Fingle Fu, Random House, 1969; No Comment by Mr. Mum, Popular Library, 1971. Author-illustrator of syndicated cartoon strip appearing in one hundred eighty papers in twenty-two countries, The Strange World of Bordighera. Author or co-author of two hundred sixty television scripts; contributor of scripts and animation to ABC television children's program,

Curiosity Shop; contributor to Saturday Evening Post and others.

SIDELIGHTS: Phillips paints under the name of Sabuso.

*   *   *

PHILLIPS, Jill (Meta) 1952-

PERSONAL: Born October 22, 1952, in Detroit, Mich.; daughter of Leyson Kirk (a writer and editor) and Leona A. (a writer and researcher; maiden name, Rasmussen) Phillips. Education: Attended high school in Covina, Calif. Politics: Conservative Republican ("avidly Anti-Communist"). Religion: "Existentialist Christian." Home: 851 North Garsden Ave., Covina, Calif. 91724. Office: P.O. Box 4213, Covina, Calif. 91723.

CAREER: Book Builders, Charter Oak, Calif., ghost writer, literary critic, and counselor, 1968-74; writer, 1974—. Member: Young Americans for Freedom.

WRITINGS: (Editor with mother, Leona Phillips, and contributor) A Directory of American Film Scholars, Gordon Press, 1975, revised edition, in press; The Good Morning Cookbook, Pelican, 1976; George Bernard Shaw, Volume I: A Review of the Literature–An Annotated Bibliography, Gordon Press, 1976; (author of introduction) Leona Phillips, D. W. Griffith: Titan of the Film Art–A Critical Study, Gordon Press, 1976; T. E. Lawrence: Portrait of the Artist as Hero–Controversy and Caricature in the Biographies of "Lawrence of Arabia", Gordon Press, 1977; (with Leona Phillips) The Occult: An Annotated Bibliography, Gordon Press, in press; The Archaeology of the Collective East: An Annotated Bibliography, Gordon Press, in press; (contributor of notes) Leona Phillips, Hitler and the Third Reich: An Annotated Bibliography, Gordon Press, in press. Contributor of articles, poems, and reviews to New Guard and San Gabriel Valley Tribune.

WORK IN PROGRESS—All for Gordon Press: The Films of Montgomery Clift; D. H. Lawrence: A Review of the Novels, Biographies, and Criticism; Music and the Cinema; George Bernard Shaw, Volume II: A Review of the Dramas, Volume III: A Review of the Films and Filmed Plays; The Black Death and Peasants Revolt, completion expected in 1978; The Liberated Mind: Conservatives, Communists, and Women in Twentieth-Century Society, 1978; The Trinity of Evil: Hitler, Himmler, and Heydrich; The Art of David Lean; The Operas of Gian-Carlo Menotti; Geoffrey Plantagenet; Isabel of Hainault; The Apple Cookbook; The Holiday Cookbook; The Wet Priest, a novel; Sarah, a novel; Everywhere, Christmas, a novel; books on Medieval society and history.

SIDELIGHTS: Jill Phillips writes: "I feel as though my work shows constantly my strong political and religious focus: the value of individuality in a world rapidly acquiesing to the evils of Big-Brotherism; the sanctity of a world indifferent to honor and spirituality. . . . I may disagree violently with liberals and opponents of Christianity but if they are speaking and writing their consciences, I have more respect for them than pseudo-Christians who believe that going to church is the answer to salvation, or Conservatives who are too timid or too politically motivated to act according to their own beliefs. . . . I can only hope that my writing, whatever the subject, will influence people away from materialism, pleasure-seeking, and a collective society—while enlightening them to the spirituality of the Ruskin ethic of beauty, humility; all the while acknowledging the continual struggle between Good and Evil, of which we are all, perhaps unwittingly, a part. I hope to enlighten indifferent readers to the worth of the Middle Ages; being, as it was, a time 'truer,' more spiritual, than our own."

AVOCATIONAL INTERESTS: Writing music for the flute, sculpting miniature Sumerian heads in clay, collecting books, researching the "Holy Grail" legend.

* * *

PHILLIPS, Kevin Price 1940-

PERSONAL: Born November 30, 1940, in New York, N.Y.; son of William Edward (a state administrator) and Dorothy (Price) Phillips; married Martha Henderson (director of U.S. House Republican Policy Committee), September 23, 1968; children: Elizabeth Russell, Andrew Douglas, Alexander Evan. *Education:* Colgate University, A.B., 1961; Harvard University, LL.B., 1964; also attended University of Edinburgh, 1959-60. *Politics:* Republican. *Religion:* Protestant. *Home:* 5115 Moorland Lane, Bethesda, Md. 20014. *Office:* American Political Research Corp., 4720 Montgomery Ave., Bethesda, Md. 20014.

CAREER: Administrative assistant to Congressman Paul Fino, 1964-68; special assistant to campaign manager of Nixon for President committee, 1968-69; special assistant to U.S. Attorney General, 1969-70; American Political Research Corp., Bethesda, Md., president, 1971—. Consultant to Media Institute. *Member:* New York Bar Association, Washington D.C. Bar Association, Phi Beta Kappa, Pi Sigma Alpha.

WRITINGS: The Emerging Republican Majority, Arlington House, 1969; *Electoral Reform and Voter Participation,* American Enterprise Institute for Public Policy Research, 1975; *Mediacracy,* Doubleday, 1975. Author of columns for King Features Syndicate, 1970—, and *TV Guide,* 1974—. Editor of *American Political Report.*

* * *

PHILLIPS, Leona Rasmussen 1925-

PERSONAL: Born November 11, 1925, in Powellsville, Ohio; daughter of Niels (a Lutheran clergyman) and Clara (Potratz) Rasmussen; married Leyson Kirk Phillips (a writer and editor), November 6, 1948; children: Jill, Glen, Sally, Donna, Dorothy. *Education:* Attended University of Michigan. *Politics:* Conservative Republican. *Religion:* Lutheran. *Home:* 851 North Garsden Ave., Covina, Calif. 91724. *Office:* P.O. Box 4213, Covina, Calif. 91723.

CAREER: Has worked as stenographer and switchboard operator; *Tracks,* Cleveland, Ohio, correspondent, 1943-47; writer, 1950—.

WRITINGS: You Can Write, Book Builders, 1966; (editor with daughter, Jill Phillips, and contributor) *A Directory of American Film Scholars,* Gordon Press, 1975, revised edition, in press; *D. W. Griffith: Titan of the Film Art—A Critical Study,* Gordon Press, 1976; *Americana: Colonial Days and Revolutionary War—An Annotated Bibliography,* Gordon Press, 1976; *Hitler and the Third Reich: An Annotated Bibliography,* Gordon Press, 1977; *The Romance of Food: Two Hundred Years of Food Usage in America,* Pelican, in press; (with Jill Phillips) *The Occult: An Annotated Bibliography,* Gordon Press, in press. Contributor of stories and poems to *Bible Storytime.*

WORK IN PROGRESS—All for Gordon Press: *Christmas Literature: An Annotated Bibliography; History of the Celtic Peoples,* two volumes, completion expected in 1978; *The Treatment of Nazis in American Cinema,* 1978; books on film, with daughter, Jill Phillips.

SIDELIGHTS: Leona Phillips writes: "In the fifties I began writing in the field of fiction and since then have written twenty-seven full-length novels; the subject backgrounds involve: biographical, historical, political, religious, romance, sports, occult, musical, cinema, and every-day life. I have published no fiction, but some day they will all be in print. I have written hundreds of poems (the rhyming kind), lyrics to some of my fictional books and about fifteen plays and screenplays. There is one important truth a writer must realize. Anytime the written word reaches out, it influences. The farther it reaches, the greater the influence. It is necessary that the writer be factual without being pedantic; and that he write with sincerity without undue bias. Nevertheless, I feel that if it is acceptable for other writers to inflict their un-Christian and un-American beliefs and ideas on me and my children, then I am at liberty to try and convince them with my own Christian and patriotic ideas. We can only hope that the day never dawns when moral ideas are considered harmful."

* * *

PHILLIPS, Richard C(laybourne) 1934-

PERSONAL: Born December 21, 1934, in Wilkes County, N.C.; son of Walter W. (a salesman) and Carrie B. (Hart) Phillips; married Sara Jo Hennis (a dental hygienist), August 23, 1958. *Education:* University of North Carolina, A.B., 1956, M.Ed., 1958; Northwestern University, Ph.D., 1962. *Politics:* Democrat. *Religion:* Baptist. *Home address:* P.O. Box 2351, Chapel Hill, N.C. 27514. *Office:* 201-D Peabody Hall, University of North Carolina, Chapel Hill, N.C. 27514.

CAREER: Social studies teacher in public schools in Winston-Salem, N.C., 1957-60; University of North Carolina, Chapel Hill, assistant professor, 1962-65, associate professor, 1965-70, professor of education, 1970—. Consultant to Prentice-Hall and Random House, both publishers. *Member:* National Society for the Study of Education, John Dewey Society, National Council for the Social Studies, History of Education Society, Phi Beta Kappa.

WRITINGS: Teaching for Thinking in High School Social Studies, Addison-Wesley, 1974. Contributor to social studies and education journals. Editor of *High School Journal,* 1964-69.

WORK IN PROGRESS: A book on values in the social studies, completion expected in 1978; a book on future trends in society, 1981.

SIDELIGHTS: Phillips writes: "I have been greatly influenced by the writings of John Dewey and the reflective thinking paradigm of Alan Griffin, Lawrence Metcalf, Joe Park, and James Shaver." *Avocational interests:* International travel.

* * *

PHILP, Kenneth R(oy) 1941-

PERSONAL: Born December 6, 1941, in Pontiac, Mich.; son of Harold M. and Alberta Philp; married Marjory Kay Donovan (a teacher), June 13, 1968. *Education:* Michigan State University, B.A., 1963, Ph.D., 1968; University of Michigan, M.A., 1964. *Politics:* Democrat. *Home:* 2801 Greenbrook Dr., Arlington, Tex. 76016. *Office:* Department of History, University of Texas, Arlington, Tex. 76019.

CAREER: University of Texas, Arlington, assistant professor, 1968-73, associate professor of history, 1973—.

Member: American Historical Association, Organization of American Historians, Western Historical Association.

WRITINGS: John Collier's Crusade for Indian Reform, 1920-1954, University of Arizona Press, 1976; (editor with Elliott West) *Essays on Walter Prescott Webb,* University of Texas Press, 1976; (editor) *Walter Prescott Webb Memorial Lectures,* University of Texas Press, in press. Contributor to history and social science journals.

WORK IN PROGRESS: A Return to the Century of Dishonor: Indian Policy During the Truman and Eisenhower Years, completion expected in 1980.

*   *   *

PICCARD, Betty
    See PICCARD, Elizabeth J(ane)

*   *   *

PICCARD, Elizabeth J(ane)   1925-
    (Betty Piccard)

PERSONAL: Born January 10, 1925, in St. Paul, Minn.; daughter of James J. (a carpenter) and Mary (a teacher; maiden name, Breman) Koalska; married Paul J. Piccard (a professor), August 1, 1947; children: Robert, Jane, John, Mary, Ann. *Education:* University of Minnesota, B.A., 1945, M.A., 1948. *Politics:* Democrat. *Religion:* Roman Catholic. *Home:* 404 Terrace St., Tallahassee, Fla. 32303. *Office:* School of Social Work, Florida State University, Tallahassee, Fla. 32306.

CAREER: Florida State University, School of Social Work, Tallahassee, assistant professor of sociology, 1969-75, director of undergraduate program, 1975—. *Military service:* Women Accepted for Voluntary Emergency Service, 1945-46. *Member:* National Association of Social Workers, American Council of Social Workers, Council on Social Workers Education.

WRITINGS—Under name Betty Piccard: *Introduction to Social Work: A Primer,* Dorsey, 1975.

WORK IN PROGRESS: The Settlement Movement Ninety Years Later: A Case in Point.

AVOCATIONAL INTERESTS: The history of British social services.

*   *   *

PICCARD, Jacques   1922-

PERSONAL: Born July 28, 1922, in Brussels, Belgium. *Education:* University of Geneva, Licence es Sciences economiques et sociales, 1946; Graduate Institute of International Studies, Geneva, Switzerland, diploma, 1947. *Home:* 19 Avenue De L'Avenir, Lausanne, Switzerland 1012.

CAREER: University of Geneva, Geneva, Switzerland, assistant professor, 1946-48; teacher in private home, 1948-51; deep sea researcher and writer, 1951—. Visiting professor at Stevens Institute of Technology, 1967. Creator of Foundation for the Study and Preservation of Seas and Lakes, 1966, and International Institute of Ecology, 1971. *Military service:* French Army, mountain infantry, 1944-45.

MEMBER: National Geographic Society (life member), Societe Academique Vaudoise (honorary member), Explorers Club (corresponding member). *Awards, honors:* War Cross, 1945; Theodore Roosevelt Distinguished Service Award, 1960; Distinguished Public Service Award from President Eisenhower, 1960; Giant of Adventure Award

from *Argosy,* 1961, for scientific research; Dr.Sc. from American International College, 1962, and Hofstra University, 1970; gold medal from French Society of Arts, Sciences, and Letters, 1970, and Royal Geographic Society (Belgium), 1971; named officer of Order of Leopold (Belgium), 1972; Commander of Miranda Order (Venezuela), 1974; Officer of the Golden Ark (Netherlands), 1976; named honorary citizen of San Diego, Calif., Trieste and Ponza, Italy, and St. Augustine, Fla.

WRITINGS: Le Bathyscaphe et les Plongers effectuees avec le Trieste (title means "The Bathyscaphe Trieste and its Dives"), 1957; *De la Stratosphere aux Abysses* (title means "From the Stratosphere down to the Deepest Depth"), Connaissance du Monde, 1957; (with R. S. Dietz) *Seven Miles Down,* Putnam, 1961; *Un Univers mysterieux* (title means "A Mysterious Universe"), Harmonies Universelles, 1962; *Le Mesoscaphe Auguste Piccard,* Spes, 1968; *Voyages au fond des oceans* (title means "Traveling in the Ocean Depth"), Le Grand Livre de la Mer, 1970; *The Sun Beneath the Sea,* Scribner, 1971; *Logbuch aus der Meerestiefe* (title means "Deep Sea Log Book"), Deutsche Verlags-Anstalt, 1975.

SIDELIGHTS: In 1968, Piccard was a member of the expedition of the bathyscaphe "FNRS2" in Dakar. From 1952 to 1960 he collaborated on the construction and participated in the diving of the "Trieste" which made several dives, one in the Marianas Trench reaching a depth of 35,800 feet. Between 1963 and 1964 he constructed the mesoscaph "Auguste Piccard" which carried about thirty-three thousand passengers in 1964 and 1965. Between 1966 and 1968 he constructed the mesoscaph "Ben Franklin" with Grumman Aerospace Corp and worked on the "Gulf Stream Drift Mission," 1969.

*   *   *

PIENKOWSKI, Jan   1936-

PERSONAL: Born August 8, 1936, in Warsaw, Poland; son of Jerzy Dominik and Wanda (a chemist; maiden name, Garlicka) Pienkowski. *Education:* King's College, Cambridge, B.A., 1957, M.A., 1961. *Politics:* None. *Religion:* Catholic. *Home:* 45 Lonsdale Rd., Barnes, London S.W.13, England. *Office:* Gallery Five, 14 Ogle St., London W1P 7LG, England.

CAREER: J. Walter Thompson (advertising agency), London, England, art director, 1957-59; William Collins Sons & Co. (publisher), London, England, art director in publicity, 1959-60; *Time and Tide,* London, England, art editor, 1960-61; Gallery Five, London, England, art director, 1961—. *Member:* Society of Authors. *Awards, honors:* Kate Greenaway Award, 1971, for illustrating *The Kingdom Under the Sea.*

WRITINGS—Self-illustrated children's books: (With Helen Nicoll) *Meg and Mog,* Heinemann, 1972, Atheneum, 1973; (with Nicoll) *Meg's Eggs,* Heinemann, 1972, Atheneum, 1973; (with Nicoll) *Meg on the Moon,* Heinemann, 1973; (with Nicoll) *Meg at Sea,* Heinemann, 1973; (with Nicoll) *Meg's Car,* Heinemann, 1975; (with Nicoll) *Meg's Castle,* Heinemann, 1975; *Numbers,* Harvey House, 1975; *Colours,* Harvey House, 1975; *Shapes,* Harvey House, 1975; *Sizes,* Harvey House, 1975.

Illustrator: *Run Along Josie,* Harcourt, 1970; Jessie Gertrude Townsend, *Annie, Bridget and Charlie: An A.B.C. for Children of Rhymes,* Pantheon, 1967; Joan Aiken, *A Necklace of Raindrops and Other Stories,* Doubleday, 1967; Edith Brill, *The Golden Bird,* F. Watts, 1970; Aiken, *The*

Kingdom Under the Sea and Other Stories, J. Cape, 1971; Agnes Szndek, *The Amber Mountain,* Hutchinson, 1976. Made the graphic illustrations for "Watch!," a British Broadcasting Corp. television series, 1969-71.

WORK IN PROGRESS: Six miniature books, illuminated and hand-lettered; *Tale of a One-Way Street,* with Joan Aiken; *Mog's Mumps; Meg's Veg.*

SIDELIGHTS: Pienkowski writes: "I had no formal art school training but went to Cambridge University to read classics and English literature. It was there that I began designing: plays, posters, and greeting cards for friends which led to the formation of Gallery Five. . . . Book illustration came later. The silhouette technique evolved out of my first book with Joan Aiken. . . . I began to experiment with 'marble' backgrounds sometimes producing marvellously unexpected results. It may be that my work harks back to Polish background; the two-dimensional approach I use is characteristic of that part of the world. The 'Meg and Mog' books are in a completely different style, with bold black line on vibrant flat colour, again rooted in the Polish ethnic artistic tradition. What I particularly enjoy about them is the opportunity to use the devices of the strip cartoon, with its merits of impact and economy. Words and pictures are completely integrated, and the kids seem to enjoy them."

* * *

PIERRE, Clara 1939-

PERSONAL: Born December 29, 1939, in Philadelphia, Pa.; daughter of Louis I. (a dental surgeon) and Emma (a teacher; maiden name, MacIntyre) Grossman; married Andre Jules Marie Pierre (a staff member of Council on Foreign Relations), July 5, 1969. *Education:* Sarah Lawrence College, B.A., 1961; Columbia University, M.A., 1967. *Politics:* Democrat. *Religion:* Society of Friends (Quakers). *Home:* 697 West End Ave., New York, N.Y. 10025. *Agent:* Hy Cohen, 111 West 57th St., New York, N.Y. 10019.

CAREER: Museum of Contemporary Crafts, New York, N.Y., teacher with Headstart Project, 1961-67; World Law Fund, New York City, writer, editor, and research associate on World Order Models Project, 1967-70; Fund for Peace, New York City, writer and researcher for Student Forum for International Order, 1970-71; free-lance writer, 1971—. Writer for United Nations Secretariat, 1962—, and World Affairs Council of Philadelphia, 1965—. Member of faculty at New School for Social Research, 1976—. *Awards, honors:* Marshall Scholarship from British Marshall Foundation, 1961, to study at Lady Margaret Hall, Oxford.

WRITINGS: Looking Good: The Liberation of Fashion, Crowell, 1976.

Work has been anthologized in *The Passionate Shopper,* edited by *New York Magazine* staff, Dutton, 1972. Author of "Booked Ahead," a column in *World,* 1972-73. Contributor of about thirty articles and reviews to national magazines, including *New York, Saturday Review, House and Garden, Wisdom's Child, Bride's,* and *Craft Horizons,* and to newspapers.

WORK IN PROGRESS: Another nonfiction book.

SIDELIGHTS: To discover how the fashion and beauty business is responding to the challenge of a looser and more individual attitude toward what women wear, Clara Pierre has interviewed trend setters and image makers, including designers Yves St. Laurent and Andre Courreges, and Diana Vreeland, Nicholas Kounovsky, as well as dietitians,

plastic surgeons, and cosmeticians; she has inspected beauty farms, and "the vats and cauldrons of Charles of the Ritz's New Jersey factory," and worked in Valentino's first Manhattan boutique. She discovered that "chic is no longer simply a matter of dress: it encompasses health, exercise, beauty care—and one's own personal environment as well."

AVOCATIONAL INTERESTS: Skiing, skating, playing tennis, hiking, jogging, bicycling, horseback riding, international travel, reading.

BIOGRAPHICAL/CRITICAL SOURCES: Elle, August 30, 1976; *International Herald Tribune,* September 1, 1976.

* * *

PIGGOTT, C. M.
See GUIDO, (Cecily) Margaret

* * *

PILPEL, Robert H(arry) 1943-

PERSONAL: Born February 16, 1943, in New York, N.Y.; son of Robert Cecil (a lawyer) and Harriet (a lawyer; maiden name, Fleischl) Pilpel. *Education:* Stanford University, B.A. (with great distinction), 1963; Yale University, J.D., 1966; University of Rome, further study, 1970-72. *Home:* 70 East 96th St., New York, N.Y. 10028. *Agent:* Timothy Seldes, Russell & Volkening, Inc., 551 Fifth Ave., New York, N.Y. 10017. *Office:* Vicolo del Puttarello 25, Rome 00187, Italy.

CAREER: U.S. Air Force Reserve, Rome, Italy, judge advocate, 1972—. *Military service:* U.S. Air Force, lawyer, 1967-70; became captain. *Member:* Phi Beta Kappa. *Awards, honors:* Fulbright fellowship, 1970-71.

WRITINGS: (With Joel Rosenman and John Roberts) *Young Men with Unlimited Capital,* Harcourt, 1974; *Churchill in America,* Harcourt, 1976. Contributor to *Harper's, Harper's Bookletter,* and *New York Sunday Times.*

WORK IN PROGRESS: To the Honor of the Fleet, a historical novel, publication by Atheneum expected in 1978.

AVOCTIONAL INTERESTS: Bicycling ("have bicycled from Italy to Frankfurt, around Corsica, around Sardinia, and from Italy to Hungary"), flying (holds commercial pilot license with instrument rating).

* * *

PIMSLEUR, Paul 1927-1976

October 17, 1927—June 22, 1976; American educator and author of books in his field. Obituaries: *New York Times,* June 29, 1976. (See index for previous *CA* sketch)

* * *

PIRES, Joe
See STOUT, Robert Joe

* * *

PISMIRE, Osbert
See HIVNOR, Robert

* * *

PITTS, Denis 1930-

PERSONAL: Born January 6, 1930 in Harwich, England; son of Charles (a sailor) and Margaret (a teacher; maiden name, Crotty) Pitts. *Education:* Attended schools in Devanshire and Wiltshire, England. *Politics:* Radical liberal. *Home:* Rookery Cottage, Lockeridge, Marlborough, Wiltshire, England. *Agent:* Curtis Brown Ltd., 1 Craven Hill, London W2 3EW, England. *Office:* Wyvern Authors (Jersey) Ltd., Kirkella House, St. Helier, Jersey, United Kingdom.

CAREER: London Daily Herald, London, England, feature writer and foreign correspondent based in Cyrprus, 1955-58; *Lilliput* magazine, writer, 1958, editor, 1959-60; *London Daily Express,* London, feature writer and foreign correspondent based in Moscow, 1960-61; free-lance journalist, 1961-63; Independent Television (ITV)-News, London, reporter, 1963; Granada Television, Manchester, England, interviewer and producer, 1963-68; British Broadcasting Corp. (BBC)-TV, London, producer and director, 1967-71; Independent Television, producer, 1971-74; novelist and free-lance scriptwriter, 1974—. Has produced more than one hundred network programs for Granada TV and BBC-TV, including "World in Action," "What the Papers Say," "The World of Bob Hope," and "What the Hell Ever Happens in Marlborough?"

WRITINGS—Novels, except as noted: *Clem Attlee* (interview), Panther Books, 1967; *This City Is Ours,* Mason/Charter, 1975; *The Predator,* Mason/Charter, 1976; *The Pariahs,* Hodder & Stoughton, 1977.

Television scripts: "No Peace on the Western Front," for British Broadcasting Corp. (BBC)-TV, 1970; "Crown Court," Granada TV, 1973; "Mycroft Ferguson (Genius)," BBC-TV, 1974. Also author of "Sorry, We've Only One Bath," HTV (Bristol).

Contributor to journals and magazines, including *New Statesman, Life, Look, Spectator,* and to *London Sunday Times.*

WORK IN PROGRESS: A stage play, "The Bailiff"; a television play, "The Hammering"; a novel, as yet untitled.

SIDELIGHTS: "While a resident of New York," Pitts told *CA,* "I chose to add to the ever increasing number of disaster novels with *This City Is Ours,* a gutsy adventure in which the American Activist Movement threatened Manhattan with a (super-charged super-tanker. The book was generally well reviewed. Having unsuccessfully hi-jacked New York, I set myself the task of taking over Europe in my second book, *The Predator.* Someone (King Features) has actually raved about *The Predator.* Eclipses George Orwell, they say. My third book, *Juliet Is Doomed,* is an adventure story about gunrunning into Rhodesia.

"Like so many other contemporary writers," he continued, "I am forced to write commercial books in order to survive in a country which has got into such an inflationary mess. On the other hand, they are not bad commercial books. I am lucky that I can draw from several hundred locations around the world in which I have worked. Indeed, I suppose that the first twenty or so years of my working life would be counted as research for the present set of novels. I think the next book is likely to be that much more serious, although more than anything else I'd like to write a truly funny novel. The trouble about my present books, as I see it, is that the men are particularly strong and the women are weak. I do not understand women. They worry and bewilder me and it shows."

AVOCATIONAL INTERESTS: Racing a fast trimaran dinghy, backing slow racehorses.

* * *

PLAIN, Warren
    See OEHMKE, T(homas) H(arold)

PLENDELLO, Leo
    See SAINT, Andrew (John)

* * *

POLANYI, Michael   1892(?)-1976

1892(?)—February 22, 1976; Hungarian-born British scientist, philosopher, and author of books in his field. Obituaries: *Newsweek,* March 8, 1976; *Time,* March 8, 1976; *AB Bookman's Weekly,* March 22, 1976.

* * *

POLESE, Marcia Ann   1949-

PERSONAL: Born March 23, 1949, in Brooklyn, N.Y.; daughter of Albert Lawrence (a research chemist) and Ida (Arena) Polese. *Education:* Wheaton College, Norton, Mass., B.A. (magna cum laude), 1970. *Home address:* Oakland Shores, Spencer, Mass. 01562. *Office:* Creative Communication Group, Beacon Hill Press, 43 Charles St., Boston, Mass. 02114.

CAREER: Clark University, Worcester, Mass., assistant director of public relations, 1973-74, director, 1974-75; Beacon Hill Press, Boston, Mass., copywriter, 1975—, editorial director of Creative Communication Group, 1975—. Advertising copywriter for Sunergy Co., 1976—. Writer for Massachusetts Polytechnic Institute.

MEMBER: Council for the Advancement and Support of Education, Phi Beta Kappa. *Awards, honors:* Time-Life achievement award, 1973, for improvement in magazine publishing; student recruitment and promotion award from Nations Schools and Colleges, 1975; exceptional achievement award for educational promotion and award of merit for excellence in student recruitment publications, both from Council for the Advancement and Support of Education, 1975.

WRITINGS: (With Dorothy Wender) *Frankie and the Fawn* (juvenile), Abingdon, 1975. Editor of *Wheaton College Alumni,* 1971-73.

WORK IN PROGRESS: Cry Like a Man, a children's book on divorce; *To Reach the Sky,* an adult novel; a notebook of poems.

AVOCATIONAL INTERESTS: Acting and writing for the theater, European travel (to attend theater festivals), yoga, meditation, mountaineering, psychic research.

* * *

POLUNIN, Nicholas (Vladimir)   1909-

PERSONAL: Born June 26, 1909, at Checkendon, Oxfordshire, England; son of Vladimir (an artist) and Elizabeth Violet (an artist; maiden name, Hart) Polunin; married Helen Lovat Fraser, 1939 (divorced, 1945); married Helen Eugenie Campbell, January 3, 1948; children: (first marriage) Michael; (second marriage) April Xenia, Nicholas V. C., Douglas H. H. *Education:* Christ Church, Oxford, B.A. (first class honors), 1932, M.A., 1935, D.Phil., 1935, D.Sc., 1942; Yale University, M.S., 1934. *Politics:* None. *Religion:* "None, but I believe in the Christian way of life." *Home:* 15 chemin F.-Lehmann, 1218 Grand-Saconnex, Geneva, Switzerland.

CAREER: Participant or leader of numerous scientific expeditions, primarily in arctic and subarctic regions, and in Middle East and West Africa, 1930-65; Oxford University, Oxford, England, Fielding Curator and keeper of university herbaria, and university demonstrator and lecturer in botany, 1939-47, university moderator, 1941-45, lecturer and later senior research fellow in New College, 1942-47; McGill University, Montreal, Quebec, Macdonald Professor of Botany, 1947-52; director of U.S. Air Force botanical research project in North Polar Basin, and consultant to U.S. Army Corps of Engineers, 1953-55; University of Baghdad, Baghdad, Iraq, professor of plant ecology and taxonomy, head of department of botany, and director of botanical garden and university herbarium, 1955-58; University of Geneva, Geneva, Switzerland, guest professor, 1959-61; University of Ife, Ibadan and Ile-Ife, Nigeria, professor of botany, founding head of department, and founding dean of faculty of science, 1962-66; International Conferences on Environmental Future, Finland, editor and secretary-general, 1971—; Foundation for Environmental Conservation, Geneva, founding chairman, 1973, constituted life president. Curator, tutor, demonstrator, or lecturer at various institutions, 1932-47; visiting professor of botany, McGill University, 1946-47; Haley Lecturer, Acadia University, 1950; lecturer at Yale University and Brandeis University, 1953-55. Research associate, Harvard University, 1936-37, foreign research associate, 1973—. *Wartime service:* Home Guard, 1942-45; served as intelligence officer.

MEMBER: International Association for Ecology (INTE-COL), International Union for Conservation of Nature and Natural Resources (former councillor), Arctic Institute of North America (fellow), Botanical Society of America (life member), American Association for the Advancement of Science (fellow), American Fern Society (life member), Botanical Society of the British Isles (life member; formerly member of council), British Ecological Society, Royal Geographical Society (life fellow), Royal Horticultural Society (life fellow), British Association for the Advancement of Science (life member), Canadian Field Naturalists' Club (life member), Biological Society of Iraq (first honorary member), Linnean Society of London (life fellow), Systematics Association (life member), New England Botanical Club, Torrey Botanical Club (New York City; life member), Sigma Xi, Explorers' Club, Harvard Club of New York City (life member), Lake Placid Club (New York), Reform Club (London; life member).

AWARDS, HONORS: Senior research award from Department of Scientific and Industrial Research (England), 1935-38; Rolleston Memorial prize, 1938; Leverhulme research award, 1941-43; Arctic Institute of North America research fellow, 1946-47; Guggenheim Memorial fellow, 1950-52; Harvard University research fellow, 1950-53; Ford Foundation award, 1966-67; Marie-Victorin medal for services to Canadian botany, 1969; U.S. Order of Polaris, 1948; decorated Commander of the British Empire, 1976.

WRITINGS: Russian Waters, Edward Arnold, 1931; *The Isle of Auks* (diary), Edward Arnold, 1932; *Botany of the Canadian Eastern Arctic,* National Museum, Ottawa, Volume I: *Pteridophyta and Spermatophyta,* 1940, Volume II: *Thallophyta and Bryophyta,* 1947, Volume III: *Vegetation and Ecology,* 1948; *Arctic Unfolding: Experiences and Observations during a Canadian Airborne Expedition in Northern Ungava, the Northwest Territories, and the Arctic Archipelago,* Hutchinson, 1949; *Circumpolar Arctic Flora,* Clarendon Press, 1959; *Introduction to Plant Geography, and Some Related Sciences,* McGraw, 1960; *Elements de Geographie botanique,* Gauthier-Villars (Paris), 1967 (editor) *The Environmental Future,* Barnes & Noble, 1972; Founding editor, "World Crops Books" series, Leonard Hill Books, 1954-74 and "Plant Science Monographs" series, Leonard Hill Books, 1954—. Contributor of some 200

articles and reviews to journals in his field. Founding editor, *International Industry,* 1943-46, and *Environmental Conservation,* 1974—; *Biological Conservation,* founding editor, 1967-74, editor, 1974—; associate editor, *Environmental Pollution,* 1969—.

WORK IN PROGRESS: Plant Sciences in the Arctic and Subarctic, four companion volumes to *Circumpolar Arctic Flora;* plans for a major environmental encyclopedia; a new edition of *Introduction to Plant Geography,* with Askell Loeve; preparation of another International Conference on Environmental Future; plant science monographs; a series of small books on environmental topics.

SIDELIGHTS: Polunin told *CA* that during his study in Scandinavia and U.S.S.R. he "realized the deteriorating state of the world." He decided to leave the academic life in an effort to do something "to warn against mounting human population pressures and their drastic effects on the biosphere."

Polunin has made nearly twenty expeditions resulting in various scientific and geographical observations and discoveries, including visits to the vicinity of the north magnetic pole and early flights over the geographic north pole. On his own expedition to southwest Greenland in 1937, Polunin discovered plants introduced from America by the Vikings, and found large new islands during his Canadian Eastern Arctic airborne expedition in 1946. The islands turned out to be, by far, the largest areas of land to to added to the map in recent decades.

Collections of Polunin's work are housed in the British Museum, the Canadian National Museum in Ottawa, the U.S. National Herbarium in Washington, D.C., the Gray Herbarium of Harvard University, and the Fielding Herbarium of Oxford University.

*   *   *

POMERANTZ, Edward 1934-

PERSONAL: Born June 24, 1934, in Montclair, N.J.; son of Alexander (a fish dealer) and Gertrude (Projan) Pomerantz; married Sandra Kazan (an actress and teacher), March 17, 1957; children: Francesca, Alexandra. *Education:* City College (now of the City University of New York), B.A., 1956; Yale University, M.F.A., 1960. *Agent:* Lynn Nesbit, International Creative Management, 40 West 57th St., New York, N.Y. 10019.

CAREER: Lotte Kaliski School for Exceptional Children, New York, N.Y., dramatics teacher, 1960-61; Long Island University, Brooklyn, N.Y., began as instructor, became assistant professor, 1961-64, associate professor of English, 1964-73. Associate director of Aspen Writers' Workshop and Theatre, 1965-67; lecturer at New York University, 1968. *Awards, honors:* John Golden Foundation awards, 1955, 1956, and 1970; first prize in Samuel French national playwriting contest, 1956, for "The Garden" (three-act); Theatre Guild Foundation prize, 1958; Ford Foundation grant, 1965; American Broadcasting Corp./Yale University playwright-in-residence grant, 1966-67; Creative Artists Public Service grant, 1974-75.

WRITINGS—Plays: The Garden (one-act; first produced in New York City at City College of the City University of New York, 1953), Samuel French, 1952; *Only a Game* (one-act), Samuel French, 1954; "The Garden" (three-act), first produced in New Haven, Conn., at Yale Drama School Theatre, 1956; "Kid" (full-length), first produced in New York City at Chelsea Theatre Center, 1965; "What You

Don't Know Can't Hurt You'' (one-act), first produced in East Hampton, N.Y., at the Moon, 1972; "Teddy and Tommy" (one-act), first produced in East Hampton, N.Y., at the Moon, 1972; "Nothing Personal" (one-act), first produced in Aspen, Colo., at Aspen Institute for Humanistic Studies, 1973; "Brisburial" (full-length), first produced in New York City at New Federal Theatre, 1974. Also author of "A Change of Pace" (one-act) published, with "Nothing Personal," in *Ms.* magazine, October, 1974.

Novels: *Into It,* Dial, 1972.

Screenplays: (With Robert M. Young) "Man Running," 1975; (with Adam Holender) "The Kiss," 1975; "Mo's Movie," 1976; "Into It" (adaptation of author's novel), 1976.

Writer of television drama documentary, "First Allegiance," broadcast on Columbia Broadcasting System's "American Parade" series, 1975. Contributor of two novellas to *Contact,* of articles to *Holiday* and *Esquire,* and of short story to *Ms.*

WORK IN PROGRESS: "A novel, based on plays, journals, diaries, screenplays, suicide notes, pre-Columbian legends, dreams, visions, and works-in-progress of various fictional characters."

SIDELIGHTS: Pomerantz writes: "I want to tell a good story—in equal to my vision and amibiton for it . . . to make essential connections and go beyond where I've been before."

Thomas Lask said Pomerantz's novel, *Into It,* "is full of shrewd and breath-taking insights. What remains is not Edward Pomerantz's cleverness but his ability to transmute it into good narrative. *Into It* is like a certain kind of cosmic matter: its size is no indication of its density." Pomerantz recently sold his own screen adaptation of his novel to Filmhaus, Inc.

BIOGRAPHICAL/CRITICAL SOURCES: New York Times, July 14, 1972; *New Leader,* April 1, 1974.

*　　*　　*

POMEROY, Sarah B(erman)   1938-

PERSONAL: Born March 13, 1938, in New York, N.Y.; daughter of Jack (a real estate investor) and Rae (an elementary school teacher; maiden name, Ginsberg) Berman; married Lee Harris Pomeroy (an architect); children: Jordana, Jeremy, Alexandra. *Education:* Barnard College, A.B., 1957; Columbia University, M.A., 1960, Ph.D., 1961. *Office:* Department of Classics, Hunter College of the City University of New York, 695 Park Ave., New York, N.Y. 10021.

CAREER: University of Texas, Austin, instructor in classics, 1961-62; Hunter College of the City University of New York, New York, N.Y., lecturer, 1964-70, assistant professor, 1970-75, associate professor of classics, 1975—. *Member:* American Philological Association, American Society of Papyrologists, American Historical Association, Association of Ancient Historians, American Institute of Archaeology, Women's Classical Caucus (chairwoman, 1973—). *Awards, honors:* Grants from American Council of Learned Societies, 1973-74; National Endowment for the Humanities, 1973; Ford Foundation grant, 1974; faculty research award from City University of New York, 1975-77.

WRITINGS: Goddesses, Whores, Wives, and Slaves: Women in Classical Antiquity, Schocken, 1975. Contributor to scholarly journals.

WORK IN PROGRESS: Research on women in the Hellenistic period and on children in antiquity.

*　　*　　*

POSTMA, Magdalena Jacomina   1908-
(Minnie Postma)

PERSONAL: Born August 18, 1908, in Ficksburg, South Africa; daughter of Jacobus (a farmer) and Martha (van der Walt) Wille; married Philippus Postma, December 19, 1933 (died, 1962); children: Wille (Mrs. Earl Martin), Philmi (deceased), Kumi, Okulis, Werda (Mrs. Lukas Visagie), Yda (Mrs. Berend J. Krygsman). *Education:* Attended high school in Ficksburg, South Africa. *Religion:* Protestant, Reformed Church. *Home:* 28 Du Preez St., Heidelberg, Transvaal 2400, South Africa.

CAREER: Free-lance writer, 1948-68; Technical College, East London, South Africa, instructor in weaving, 1967; tutor, 1968—. *Member:* South Africa Writer's Association (honorary member).

WRITINGS—All under name Minnie Postma: *Toe Ma nog Meintjie was* (title means "When Mother Was Meintjie"), Van Schaik, 1948; (compiler) *Legendes uit die Misrook* (title means "Tales Round the Dungfire"), Perskor Publishers, 1950; *Meintjie betaal skoolgeld* (title means "Meintjie Pays to Learn"), Van Schaik, 1950; *Meintjie raak verlief* (title means "Meintjie Falls in Love"), Van Schaik, 1952; *Bulane,* Van Schaik, 1953; *Meintjie kry haar deel* (title means "Meintjie Gets Her Partner"), Van Schaik, 1953; (compiler) *Legendes uit Lesotho* (title means "Tales from Lesotho"), Perskor Publishers, 1954; *Ek en my bediendes* (title means "My Servants and I"), A. A. Balkema, 1955; *Meintjie word Mevron* (title means "Meintjie Married"), Van Schaik, 1955; *Lettie Bock kom kuier* (title means "Lettie Bock Comes to Visit"), A. A. Balkema, 1956; *Hoe ek n skryfster geword het* (title means "How I Became an Authoress"), Naweekpos, 1957; *Toon Prens,* Perskor Publishers, 1958; *Totsiens Talettie* (title means "Goodbye, Aunt Lettie"), A. A. Balkema, 1957; *Alweer my bediendes* (title means "My Servants Once More"), Van Schaik, 1959.

Oom Pop gooi dium (title means "Uncle Pop Hitchhikes"), Perskor Publishers, 1961; *Onder een kombers* (title means "When the Children Were Small"), Human & Rousseau Publishers, 1961; *Brug oor die see* (title means "Bridge Over the Sea"), Afrikaanse Pers-Boekhandel, 1963; *Raaisel van die kruithoring* (title means "Mystery of the Gunpowder Horn"), Tafelberg-uitgewers, 1963, 3rd edition, Nasionale Boekhandel, 1970; *Uit die skadeweekant van die straat* (title means "From the Shady Side of the Street"), Nasionale Boekhandel, 1963; (compiler) *Litsomo* (fairy tales), Afrikaanse Pers-Boekhandel, 1964, translation by Susie McDermid published as *Tales from the Basotho,* University of Texas Press, for American Folklore Society, 1974; *Bobbie van der Jaan* (title means "Baboon"), Perskor Publishers, 1966; *Die Vrygesel van Lowergroen* (title means "The Bachelor from Lowergroen"), Tafelberg-uitgewers, 1967; *Kabouter Kapot* (title means "A Gnome Called Kapot"), Perskor Publishers, 1967.

Bart Minnaar die huiskat, Tafelberg-uitgewers, 1970; *Bartjie Minnaar* (title means "Bartjie (Lover), a Tomcat, Tells about His People"), Tafelberg-uitgewers, 1972. Also translator of *Aan moeder se knie* (title means "Mary Schoolands Bible Stories"), by Mary Schooland, published by Van Schaik.

Collaborator, with C. F. Albertyn, of "Kinders van die wereld" series, published by Albertyn Kaapstad, 1962.

Author of radio series for South African Broadcasting Corp. Writer of regular column, "Rooi Rose: The Woman Alone," *Heidelberg News,* 1968-69. Contributor to South African periodicals, including *Huisgenoot, Brandwag,* and many others.

SIDELIGHTS: Minnie Postma points out that her "Meintjie" books are autobiographical.

* * *

POSTMA, Minnie
See POSTMA, Magdalena Jacomina

* * *

POSTON, Richard W(averly) 1914-

PERSONAL: Born December 31, 1914, in Farmington, Mo.; son of Felix O. (an attorney) and Blanche (Thomas) Poston; married Marjorie Atkinson, May 16, 1941; children: Gregory R., Stephanie. *Education:* University of Montana, B.A., 1940. *Religion:* Methodist. *Home:* 35 Hillcrest Dr., Carbondale, Ill. 62901. *Office:* Southern Illinois Power Cooperative, Route 4, Box 560, Marion, Ill. 62959.

CAREER: U.S. Civil Service Commission, investigator in Washington, D.C., Boston, Mass., Bangor, Maine, and New Haven, Conn., 1940-54; free-lance writer, 1945-47; War Assets Administration, Seattle, Wash., special agent for Compliance Enforcement Division, 1947-48; public relations consultant and free-lance writer in Seattle, 1948-50; University of Washington, Seattle, organizer and director of Bureau of Community Development, 1950-53; Southern Illinois University, Carbondale, organizer and director of Community Development Service, 1953-60, professor of community development, 1960-74, professor emeritus, 1975—; Southern Illinois Power Cooperative, Marion, director of area development, 1974—. *Member:* Community Development Society of America (past president). *Awards, honors:* Newberry Library fellowship, 1948-49.

WRITINGS: Small Town Renaissance, Harper, 1950, Greenwood Press, 1971; *Democracy Is You,* Harper, 1953; *Democracy Speaks Many Tongues,* Harper, 1961; *Experiment in North Carolina,* University of North Carolina, School of Social Work, 1967; *The Gang and the Establishment,* Harper, 1971; *Action Now!: A Citizens Guide to Better Communities,* Southern Illinois University Press, 1976. Contributor to professional journals.

* * *

POWER, Norman S(andiford) 1916-
(Kratos)

PERSONAL: Born October 31, 1916, in Birmingham, England; son of Walter S. (a clergyman) and May (Dixon) Power; married Jean Edwards, April 17, 1944; children: Michael, Diana (Mrs. John Frew), Althea (Mrs. Michael Draper), Angela. *Education:* Worcester College, Oxford, B.A. (history), 1938, M.A. (history), 1942; Ripon Hall, Oxford, B.A. (theology), 1940. *Politics:* Liberal. *Home and office:* Ladywood Vicarage, Birmingham 16, England. *Agent:* Virginia Kidd, P.O. Box 278, Milford, Pa. 18337.

CAREER: Ordained priest of Anglican Church, 1940; Christ Church, Summerfield, Birmingham, England, curate, 1940-43; All Saints Mental Hospital and parish, Birmingham, chaplain-in-charge, 1943-45; vicar of Highter's Heath, Birmingham, 1945-52; vicar of Ladywood, Birmingham, 1952—, canon of Birmingham, 1965—. Lecturer on pastoral psychology; teacher of creative writing; community service volunteer worker. *Member:* East Birmingham Chess Club (president, 1964—).

WRITINGS: The Technique of Hypnosis, Ellisdon's, 1953; *The Forgotten People: A Challenge to a Caring Community,* A. James, 1965; *The Firland Saga,* Halmer, 1970, published as *The Forgotten Kingdom,* Blackie, 1973, Volume II: *Fear in Firland,* Blackie, 1974; *Ends of Verse,* Mowbray, 1972. Volume III of *The Firland Saga* has been published in Scandinavia as *Firland i Flammer* (title means "Fire in Firland") and is not yet published in English. Writer of weekly column in Birmingham *Evening Mail,* 1953—. Contributor of articles, stories, and verse, sometimes under pseudonym Kratos, to *Argosy, Punch, Observer, Guardian, Birmingham Post,* and other periodicals.

WORK IN PROGRESS: With daughter, Althea Power Draper, *The Edge of Darkness,* a study of the Old Testament, and *More Ends of Verse.*

SIDELIGHTS: Power told *CA:* "I write, I suppose, for the love of it—because of some secret creative spring which bubbles up . . . in childhood it produced a flow of jingles and rhymes. But AFTER writing, one takes the trouble to revise, type, retype, and to submit to editors out of need, even from desperation, as the children's needs become more clamant and the bills pour in.

"I wrote *The Forgotten People* in passionate protest against what the bulldozers did to old people and poor but loving communities in 'slum clearance.' This protest of the destruction of living communities against their will (only the developers, speculators, and demolition firms benefited) typifies my views. I believe in freedom with obsessional love. I want people to live in freedom from interference with community life and the family ties of centuries. I love deep roots in community, in nature, in life's source. Hence, I love any place that has grown slowly and naturally down through the centuries—and old trees. I loath the community killers, the tree destroyers, the desecrators of the past.

"*The Firland Saga* grew out of stories told to my children as good-night tales. Also, because at the same time, we were all addicted to Tolkien and Lewis. I love fantasy—it is so much more real than 'kitchen sink.' I was entranced by Middle-Earth and Narnia. I felt that if Tolkien could create a world and Lewis a planet, I'd create an island or bust!

"In his last years, Tolkien wrote several times to me. His treasured letters are and were a great encouragement. The coincidence of his boyhood home being near where I live began his correspondence. He wanted to know what had happened to it. Later he was gracious and encouraging about my writing.

"I admire excellence—the combination of the Divine Fire and enormous application to cherish the gift. Hence I am obsessed with Keats, craftsman par-excellence, and against appalling odds. I have an entire section of my library dedicated to Keats. I have little use for poetry by new craftsmen who couldn't write a limerick!"

AVOCATIONAL INTERESTS: Travel (Israel, Jordan, France, Italy), cricket, swimming, sailing, chess, France (French language, literature, history, culture).

* * *

POWERS, Barbara Hudson
See DUDLEY, Barbara Hudson

* * *

PRABHAVANANDA, Swami 1893-1976

December 26, 1893—July 4, 1976; Indian author of religious

books and translator of Indian scriptures. Obituaries: *Publishers Weekly,* August 2, 1976. (See index for previous *CA* sketch)

* * *

PRATT, Charles 1926(?)-1976

1926(?)—May 25, 1976; American photographer and author. Obituaries: *New York Times,* May 26, 1976; *AB Bookman's Weekly,* July 5, 1976.

* * *

PRESTERA, Hector A(nthony) 1932-

PERSONAL: Born May 7, 1932, in Brooklyn, N.Y.; son of Antonio (a tailor) and Madallena (Zitarosa) Prestera; divorced; children: Tory, Derek. *Education:* Brooklyn College (now of the City University of New York), B.A., 1953; University of Naples, M.D. (magna cum laude), 1959; Chinese College of Acupuncture of the United Kingdom, Lic.Ac., 1975, B.A.Acup., 1976. *Home:* 27401 Schulte Rd., Carmel, Calif. 93940. *Office:* 880 Cass St., Monterey, Calif. 93940.

CAREER: King's County Hospital, New York City, intern, 1959-60; resident in internal medicine, St. Agnes Hospital, Baltimore, Md., 1960-61, Queens General Hospital, New York City, 1961-62, and Veterans Administration Hospital, Brooklyn, N.Y., 1962-63; in private practice in Yorktown Heights, N.Y., 1964-69; Esalen Institute, Big Sur, Calif., group leader in Gestalt body-oriented therapy, 1969-72; private practice of medicine in California, 1972—. *Member:* North American College of Manipulative Medicine (fellow), American Medical Association, Cranial Academy of Osteopathic Medicine (associate), California Medical Society, Monterey County Medical Society. *Awards, honors:* National Heart Institute fellow, 1963-64.

WRITINGS: The Body Reveals, Harper, 1976.

WORK IN PROGRESS: Holistic Medicine, on integrating Chinese medicine with Western medicine.

SIDELIGHTS: Prestera writes: "My current work is in the fields of medicine and psychology. The emphasis of my work is to integrate so-called esoteric knowledge—i.e., acupuncture, Sufi teachings—and data accumulated through the Human Potential Movement into the contemporary stream of Western medicine.

"It is becoming increasingly clear that the body, in its form, represents a template upon which all our emotional and physical states of being are superimposed. By discovering the ways in which imbalance is produced in our actual physical being, changes ranging from biochemical through emotional and even psychic/spiritual orders can be produced. When unity is accomplished in the physical, emotional, and spiritual being then a jump, often of a quantum nature, is made in consciousness. Medicine of the future will be, and is beginning to be involved with such necessary changes."

* * *

PRIBICHEVICH, Stoyan 1905(?)-1976

1905(?)—May 15, 1976; Yugoslavian-born American journalist and author of a book on Central Europe. Obituaries: *New York Times,* May 17, 1976; *Current Biography,* July, 1976.

* * *

PRIESAND, Sally J(ane) 1946-

PERSONAL: Born June 27, 1946, in Cleveland, Ohio; daughter of Irving Theodore and Rosetta Elizabeth (Welch) Priesand. *Education:* University of Cincinnati, B.A., 1968; Hebrew Union College, B.H.L., 1971, M.A.H.L., 1972, rabbi, 1972. *Office:* Stephen Wise Free Synagogue, 30 West 68th St., New York, N.Y. 10023.

CAREER: Interim rabbi of Jewish congregation in Champaign, Ill., 1968, student rabbi in Hattiesburg, Miss., 1969-70, and Jackson, Mich., 1970-71, rabbinic intern in Cincinnati, Ohio, 1971-72; Stephen Wise Free Synagogue, New York, N.Y., assistant rabbi, 1972—. Associated with Cincinnati Housing Opportunities Made Equal, 1971—, Jewish Family Service, 1972—, Federation of Jewish Philanthropies of New York, 1972—, and its Commission on Synagogue Relations and task force on Jewish singles, and with sex crimes analysis unit of the New York Police Department, 1974—. Member of task force on equality of women in Judaism, of New York Federation of Reform Synagogues, 1972—; member of New York Board of Rabbis, 1975—. Associate of Kirkland College, 1973—.

MEMBER: National Federation of Temple Sisterhoods, Institute for Creative Judaism, American Jewish Congress, National Council of Jewish Women, United Jewish Appeal and Federation (member of Synagogue Advisory Council, 1975—), Jewish Peace Fellowship, B'nai B'rith Women, Central Conference of American Rabbis, American Civil Liberties Union, Common Cause, Hadassah (life member of New York chapter), Women's League for Israel (life member). *Awards, honors:* D.H.L. from Florida International University, 1973.

WRITINGS: Judaism and the New Woman, Behrman, 1975. Contributor to religious publications.

SIDELIGHTS: Sally Priesand was the first female rabbi ordained by a theological seminary.

* * *

PRINGLE, Mia Kellmer

PERSONAL: Born in Vienna, Austria; daughter of Samuel (a forestry adviser) and Sophie (Sobel) Kellmar; married W.J.S. Pringle (a biochemist), April 18, 1946 (died, 1962); married W. L. Hooper (assistant director general of Greater London Council), April 5, 1969. *Education:* Birkbeck College, University of London, B.A. (honors), 1944, diploma in educational psychology, 1949, Ph.D., 1950. *Home:* 68 Wimpole St., London W.1, England. *Office:* National Children's Bureau, 8 Wakley St., London EC1V 7QE, England.

CAREER: Teacher in nursery and elementary schools in Hertfordshire, England, 1940-45; Child Guidance and School Psychological Service of Hertfordshire County Council, Hertfordshire, England, senior educational and clinical psychologist, 1945-50; University of Birmingham, Birmingham, England, lecturer, 1950-52, senior lecturer in educational psychology, 1956-63, deputy head of department of child study, 1954-63; National Children's Bureau, London, England, founding director, 1963—. Governor of London Hospital for Sick Children, 1970—. Member of Secretary of State's Advisory Council for Handicapped Children, 1969-73, and Personal Social Services Council, 1971—; member of London Borough of Islington Social Services Committee, 1971—.

MEMBER: Royal Society of Medicine (fellow), Royal Society of Arts (fellow), British Psychological Society (fellow), Association of Child Psychology and Psychiatry (chairperson, 1966-67). *Awards, honors:* Henrietta Szold Award for Services to Children, 1970; Doctor of Science from University of Bradford, 1972; named honorary fellow of Manchester Polytechnic, 1972; named commander of the Order of the British Empire, 1975.

WRITINGS: The Emotional and Social Adjustment of Physically Handicapped Children, National Foundation for Educational Research in England and Wales, 1964; *The Emotional and Social Adjustment of Blind Children,* National Foundation for Educational Research in England and Wales, 1964; (editor) *Investment in Children,* Longmans, Green, 1965; *Deprivation and Education,* Longmans, Green, 1965, 2nd edition, 1971; *Social Learning and Its Measurement,* Longmans, Green, 1966; *Adoption: Facts and Fallacies–A Review of Research in the United States, Canada, and Great Britain Between 1948 and 1965,* Longmans, Green, 1966, Humanities, 1967; (with Stan Gooch) *Four Years On,* Longmans, Green, 1966, Humanities, 1967; (with N. R. Butler and Ronald Davie) *Eleven Thousand Seven Year Olds,* Longmans, Green, 1966, Humanities, 1967; (with Rosemary Dinnage) *Residential Child Care: Facts and Fallacies,* Humanities, 1967; (with Dinnage) *Foster Home Care: Facts and Fallacies,* Humanities, 1967; (editor) *Caring for Children,* Longmans, Green, 1968, Humanities, 1969; (with Davie and L. E. Hancock) *A Directory of Voluntary Organisations Concerned with Children,* Longmans, Green, 1969.

Able Misfits: A Study of Educational and Behaviour Difficulties of 103 Very Intelligent Children, Longman, 1970; (with D. O. Fiddes) *The Challenge of Thalidomide: A Pilot Study of the Educational Needs of Children in Scotland Affected by the Drug,* Longman, 1970; (with Eileen Younghusband, Dorothy Birchall, and Davie) *Living with Handicap,* National Children's Bureau, 1971; (with Eileen Crellin and Patrick West) *Born Illegitimate,* N.F.E.R., 1971; (with Jean Seglow and Peter Wedge) *Growing Up Adopted,* N.F.E.R., 1972; (with V. P. Varma) *Advances in Educational Psychology,* Volume II (Pringle was not associated with Volume I), London University Press, 1974; (with Davie, Elsa Ferri, and others) *The Parental Role,* National Children's Bureau, 1972; *The Needs of Children,* Schocken, 1975; (with Shonda Naidoo) *Early Child-Care in Britain,* Gordon & Breach, 1975. Contributor to national and international journals and newspapers. Co-editor of *Concern,* 1968—.

SIDELIGHTS: Mia Pringle comments: "My over-riding professional interest is to bring the needs of children to the forefront of public debate and, hopefully, priority; as well as to increase our basic knowledge about their development." *Avocational interests:* Theater, poetry, travel, cooking, walking, tennis.

*   *   *

PRIOR, Allan 1922

PERSONAL: Born January 13, 1922, in Newcastle on Tyne, England; son of Percy (an army officer) and Martha (Henderson) Prior; married Edith Playford, July 13, 1944; children: Michael, Maddy. *Education:* Educated in Blackpool, England. *Home:* Summerhill, Waverly Road, St. Albans, Hertfordshire, England.

CAREER: Novelist, freelance writer. *Military service:* Royal Air Force, 1942-45. *Member:* Savage Club, P.E.N. *Awards, honors:* Critics Award of Crime Writers Association for *One Away;* Screenwriters Guild Award for "Z Cars."

WRITINGS—Novels: A Flame in the Air, M. Joseph, 1951; *The Joy Ride,* M. Joseph, 1952; *The One-Eyed Monster,* Bodley Head, 1958; *One Away,* Eyre & Spottiswoode,

1962; *The Interrogators,* Simon & Schuster, 1965; *The Operators,* Simon & Schuster, 1967; *The Loving Cup,* Simon & Schuster, 1970; *The Contract,* Simon & Schuster, 1971; *Pasadiso,* Simon & Schuster, 1974; *Affair,* Simon & Schuster, 1976.

Author of screenplays and of television scripts for British Broadcasting Corp.'s "Armchair Theatre."

SIDELIGHTS: "I began to write," Prior told *CA,* "while serving in the Royal Air Force. Won a competition. Subsequently wrote for many little reviews and became a full-time author at 26, been one ever since. Keep winning awards, both for television plays and books, but don't take it too seriously!"

*   *   *

PRITCHARD, William H(arrison) 1932-

PERSONAL: Born November 12, 1932, in Binghamton, N.Y.; son of William (a lawyer) and Marion (a teacher; maiden name, La Grange) Pritchard; married Marietta Perl (a teacher), August 24, 1957; children: David, Michael, William. *Education:* Amherst College, BA., 1953; Harvard University, M.A., 1956, Ph.D., 1960. *Politics:* Democrat. *Religion:* Protestant. *Home:* 86 Northampton Rd., Amherst, Mass. 01002. *Office:* Department of English, Amherst College, Amherst, Mass. 01002.

CAREER: Amherst College, Amherst, Mass., instructor, 1958-61, assistant professor, 1961-65, associate professor, 1965-70, professor of English, 1970—. *Awards, honors:* Guggenheim fellowship, 1973-74.

WRITINGS: Wyndham Lewis, Twayne, 1968; *Wyndham Lewis: Profile in Literature,* Routledge & Kegan Paul, 1972; (editor) *Penguin Critical Anthology: Yeats,* Penguin, 1972; *Seeing Through Everything: English Writers, 1918-1940,* Oxford University Press, in press. Contributor to magazines, including *Hudson Review, Bookletter, Times Literary Supplement,* and *Poetry.* Advisory editor of *Hudson Review.*

WORK IN PROGRESS: Lives of the Modern Poets, completion expected in 1978.

*   *   *

PROBST, Leonard 1921-

PERSONAL: Born June 10, 1921, in Brooklyn, N.Y.; son of Alexander (a pharmacist) and Edith (Weichert) Probst; married Bethami Gitlin (a mayoral assistant), May 10, 1944; children: Kenneth, Katherine. *Education:* Attended Los Angeles City College, 1939-41; University of California, Berkeley, 1942; University of California, Los Angeles, B.A., 1943. *Religion:* Jewish. *Home:* 266 Henry St., Brooklyn, N.Y. 11201. *Office:* NBC News, 30 Rockefeller Plaza, New York, N.Y. 10020.

CAREER: United Press, Hollywood, Calif., reporter, 1945-48; *Los Angeles Mirror,* Los Angeles, Calif., assistant drama critic, 1948-49; Cooperative for American Relief Everywhere (CARE), New York City, roving press chief in Europe, 1949-51; United Nations High Commisioner for Refugees, Geneva, Switzerland, chief press officer, 1951-52; United Press International, bureau chief in Geneva, and Dublin, Ireland, assistant European news editor, and ballet and theatre critic in London, England, 1952-57; National Broadcasting Co. (NBC), New York City, staff writer, 1958-63, radio drama critic, 1959—, television drama critic, 1963-74, television arts editor, 1963-74. Occasional "Bylines" reporter for NBC's "Today Show," 1970-76; faculty member, New School For Social Research, New York City, 1972—; lecturer at 92nd Street Young Men's Hebrew Association (YMHA). *Military service:* U.S. Navy, 1941-45. *Member:* American Theatre Critics—New Dramatists Forum, American Federation of Television and Radio Artists (AFTRA), National Association of Broadcast Employees and Technicians.

WRITINGS: Off Camera, Stein & Day, 1976. Contributor of articles to periodicals, including *Village Voice, New York Times, TV Guide, Atlantic, House Beautiful, Saturday Review, Reader's Digest,* and *Brooklyn Heights Press.*

WORK IN PROGRESS: Two articles, "Brother Can You Spare Nine Cents," about postcards, and one concerning the reason why some men stay married.

SIDELIGHTS: Probst has been named "Dean of Television Drama Critics," by Jack Gould, for being the first television critic to review plays on opening nights. Besides his fine reputation as newsperson and drama critic, Probst is known for this prowess on the tennis courts of Brooklyn and Martha's Vineyard: the "Probstian Hoist," which he describes as "a lob of lofty proportions," has been named in his honor. Probst is also a connoisseur of wine and has served as a wine taster for books and serious wine functions.

*   *   *

PROCTOR, Priscilla 1945-

PERSONAL: Born January 24, 1945, in Mineola, N.Y.; daughter of John A. (an optician) and Florence (a dental assistant; maiden name, Russell) Moore; married William G. Proctor, Jr. (a writer), June 17, 1967. *Education:* Mount Holyoke College, B.A., 1967; Claremont Graduate School, M.A., 1970. *Religion:* Methodist. *Home:* 7 Peter Cooper Rd., #1F, New York, N.Y. 10010. *Office: Parade,* 733 Third Ave., New York, N.Y. 10017.

CAREER: Radio Japan, Tokyo, script writer and broadcaster, 1969; Greenwich House Settlement, New York, N.Y., public relations director, 1970-71; National Jewish Hospital, Denver, Colo., East Coast public relations director, 1971-74; *Parade,* New York, N.Y., associate editor, 1974—. Chairperson of Vietnamese Friends Committee. *Member:* Japan Society, Mount Holyoke Club of New York.

WRITINGS: (with husband, William Proctor) *Women in the Pulpit: Is God an Equal Opportunity Employer?,* Doubleday, 1976.

*   *   *

PROSPER, John (joint pseudonym)
See FARRAR, John C(hipman)

*   *   *

PRUDE, Agnes George 1905-
(Agnes de Mille)

PERSONAL: Born, 1905, in New York, N.Y.; daughter of William C. (a film producer) and Anna (George) de Mille; married Walter Foy Prude, June 14, 1943; children: Jonathan. *Education:* University of California, Los Angeles, A.B. (cum laude); studied dancing under Koslov, Marie Rambert, Antony Tudor, and Tamara Karsavina in London, 1922-38. *Home:* 25 East Ninth St., New York, N.Y. 10009. *Agent:* Harold Ober Associates Inc., 40 East 49th St., New York, N.Y. 10017.

CAREER: Choreographer, director, dancer, author. First

appeared in New York as a dancer in MacKlin Marrow's production of "La Finta Giardiniera," by Mozart, in 1927; in 1928, made her concert debut at the Republic Theatre, New York, N.Y.; toured the United States, England, France, and Denmark as a dance recitalist and choreographer from 1930-42; joined the Ballet Theatre, New York, N.Y., as choreographer in 1939, and directed and danced in her own compositions; on tour with American Ballet Theater at Royal Opera House, Covent Garden, London, dancing in her own compositions "Three Virgins and the Devil" and "Rodeo," 1956; headed the Agnes de Mille Dance Theatre, during tour of 126 cities, 1953-54; appeared on "Omnibus" television shows as lecturer and dancer, 1956-57; head of Agnes de Mille Heritage Dance Theatre, 1973—. Choreographed the films, "Romeo and Juliet," 1936, "Oklahoma!," 1955; choreographed over fourteen musicals including "Oklahoma," 1943, "Bloomer Girl," 1944, "Carousel," 1945, "Brigadoon," 1947, and "Paint Your Wagon," 1951; directed "Rape of Lucrecia," 1949, "Out of this World," 1950; choreographed numerous ballets for companies including Ballet Russe de Monte Carlo, 1942, and the Royal Winnipeg Ballet, 1972; danced with the Royal Winnipeg Ballet in "The Rehearsal," her own composition. Member of National Advisory Council of the Performing Arts, 1965-66.

MEMBER: Society for Stage Directors and Choreographers (vice-president, 1965-66; president, 1965-67), Merriewold Country Club (New York). *Awards, honors:* Donaldson awards, 1943, 1945, and 1947; Madamoiselle merit award, 1944; New York Critics awards, 1945 and 1947; Woman of the Year, American Newspaper Woman's Guild, 1946; Antoinette Perry award for best choreographer, 1947 and 1962; Lord and Taylor award, 1947; Dancing Masters award of merit, 1950; *Dance* Magazine award, 1957; Woman of the Year, American National Theatre and Academy, 1962; Capezio award, 1966. Litt.D. from Mills College, 1952, Russell Sage College, 1953, Clark University, 1962, Franklin and Marshall College, 1965, Western Michigan University, 1967, and Nasson College, 1970; D.H.L. from Smith College, 1954, Western College, 1955, Hood College, 1957, and Goucher College, 1961; D.F.A. from Northwestern University, 1960, and University of California, Los Angeles, 1964.

WRITINGS—All under name Agnes de Mille: *Dance to the Piper: Memoirs of the Ballet* (autobiography), Hamish Hamilton, 1951, published as *Dance to the Piper,* Little, Brown, 1952; *And Promenade Home* (autobiography), Little, Brown, 1958; (contributor) Jack D. Summerfield and Lorlyn Thatcher, editors, *The Creative Mind and Method: Exploring the Nature of Creativeness in American Arts, Sciences, and Professions,* University of Texas Press, 1960; *To a Young Dancer: A Handbook,* Little, Brown, 1962 (published in England as *To a Young Dancer: A Handbook for Dance Students, Parents, and Teachers,* Putnam, 1963); *The Book of the Dance,* Golden Press, 1963; *Lizzie Borden: A Dance of Death,* Little, Brown, 1968; *Russian Journals,* Dance Perspectives Foundation, 1970; (contributor) Walter Terry, *The Dance in America,* revised edition, Harper, 1971; *Speak to Me, Dance with Me,* Little, Brown, 1973. Contributor to *Atlantic Monthly, Theatre Arts, Good Housekeeping, Esquire, Horizon, Vogue, McCalls, New York Times.*

WORK IN PROGRESS: A book, for Doubleday.

AVOCATIONAL INTERESTS: Tennis and gardening.

BIOGRAPHICAL/CRITICAL SOURCES: Edwin Cole,

editor, *Dance Memoranda,* Duell, 1947; Alice Isabel Hazeltine, compiler, *We Grew Up in America,* Abingdon, 1954; Jane McConnell, *Famous Ballet Dancers,* Crowell, 1955; Hope Stoddard, *Famous American Women,* Crowell, 1970; *Dance,* October, 1971; *Time,* February 25, 1974.

* * *

PUNCH, Maurice 1941-

PERSONAL: Born June 21, 1941, in London, England; son of David (a turner) and Margaret (a clerk; maiden name, Sexton) Punch; married Cornelia Venneman, September 29, 1969; children: Julio, Maria. *Education:* University of Exeter, B.A. (honors), 1963; University of London, graduate study, 1963-64; University of Essex, M.A., 1966, Ph.D., 1972. *Politics:* "Vague socialist." *Religion:* None. *Home:* 49 Camminghalaan, Bunnik, Utrecht 2767, Netherlands. *Office:* Department of Sociology, State University of Utrecht, Heidelberglaan, Utrecht 2506, Netherlands.

CAREER: University of Essex, Colchester, Essex, England, lecturer in sociology, 1970-75; State University of Utrecht, Utrecht, Netherlands, senior lecturer in sociology, 1975—. *Member:* British Sociological Association.

WRITINGS: Fout is fout: Gesprekken met de politie in de binnenstad van Amsterdam, Boom, 1976; *Progressive Retreat: A Sociological Study of Dartington Hall School and Some of Its Former Pupils,* Cambridge University Press, 1977. Contributor to education and sociology journals, and to *New Society, New Era,* and *Universities Quarterly.*

WORK IN PROGRESS: Front-Line Amsterdam: Police Work in a Cosmopolitan City-Centre, based on field work with police in a red-light district of Amsterdam.

SIDELIGHTS: Punch writes: "I have moved from studying English progressive education to researching the Dutch police. Perhaps the connection is a concern with authority and social control. My work favours qualitative methods, broadly-based reporting, and readable 'human' data. On completion of a monograph on the patrolmen in the red-light district of Amsterdam I hope to turn my attention to detective work in Dutch society."

* * *

PURDY, Alexander 1890-1976

May 6, 1890—April 10, 1976; American educator, biblical scholar, and author of books in his field. Obituaries: *New York Times,* April 15, 1976.

* * *

PUTNAM, Carleton 1901-

PERSONAL: Born December 19, 1901, in New York, N.Y.; son of Israel and Louise (Carleton) Putnam; married Elizabeth Marshall Perrow, 1934 (divorced, 1941); married Lucy A. Chapman, September 12, 1944 (divorced, 1956); married Esther Willcox, 1956; children: (third marriage) Esther Louise. *Education:* Princeton University, B.S., 1924; Columbia University, LL.B., 1932. *Politics:* Republican. *Religion:* Presbyterian. *Home:* 1465 Kirby Rd., McLean, Va. 22101.

CAREER: Chicago & Southern Air Lines, Memphis, Tenn., founder and president, 1933-48, chairman of board of directors, 1948-53; Delta C & S Airlines, Atlanta, Ga., chairman of board of directors, 1953-54; Delta Airlines, Atlanta, Ga., director, 1954—. Member of national labor-management manpower policy committee of Office of Defense

Mobilization, 1953-61. *Member:* National Aeronautic Association (past governor for Missouri), Air Transport Association of America (past director), Theodore Roosevelt Society (trustee), Cosmos Club, Chevy Chase Club, Princeton Club (New York City).

WRITINGS: High Journey: A Decade in the Pilgrimage of an Air Line Pioneer, Scribner, 1945; *Theodore Roosevelt: A Biography,* Volume I: *The Formative Years,* Scribner, 1958; *Race and Reason: A Yankee View,* Public Affairs Press, 1961; *Race and Reality: A Search for Solutions,* Public Affairs Press, 1967.

Also author of published speeches, addresses, and letters on race relations and free enterprise.

* * *

PUTNAM, Robert D(avid) 1941-

PERSONAL: Born January 9, 1941, in Rochester, N.Y.; son of Frank (a businessman) and Ruth (a teacher and librarian; maiden name Swank) Putnam; married Rosemary Werner (a teacher), June 15, 1963; children: Jonathon, Lara. *Education:* Swarthmore College, B.A. (summa cum laude), 1963; Balliol College, Oxford, graduate study, 1963-64; Yale University, M.A., 1965, Ph.D. (with distinction), 1970. *Office:* Department of Political Science, University of Michigan, Ann Arbor, Mich. 48104.

CAREER: University of Michigan, Ann Arbor, lecturer, 1968-70, assistant professor, 1970-72, associate professor, 1972-75, professor of political science, 1975—, research associate at Institute of Public Policy Studies, 1972-75, research scientist at Institute, 1975—, research associate at Center for Political Studies, 1973. Visitng professor at Stockholm University, 1974; Philips Distinguished Visitor at Haverford College, 1975. Fellow of Center for Advanced Study in the Behavioral Sciences, 1974-75.

MEMBER: American Political Science Association, British Politics Group (member of executive committee, 1974-76), Midwest Political Science Association, Conference Group on Italian Politics, Phi Beta Kappa. *Awards, honors:* Fulbright fellowship at Oxford University, 1963-64; Woodrow Wilson fellowship, 1964-65; James K. Pollock research fellowship in West Germany, 1970; National Science Foundation grant, 1972-73, 1976-77.

WRITINGS: (Contributor) Betty H. Zisk, editor, *American Political Interest Groups: Readings in Theory and Research,* Wadsworth, 1969; (contributor) Jason Finkle and Richard W. Gable, editors, *Political Development and Social Change,* revised edition, Wiley, 1971; (contributor) Giuseppe Di Palma, editor, *Politics in Industrialized Societies,* Markham, 1972; *The Beliefs of Politicians: Ideology, Conflict, and Democracy in Britain and Italy,* Yale University Press, 1973; (contributor) Mattei Dogan, editor, *The Political Role of Top Civil Servants: The New Mandarins,* Sage Publications, 1975; (contributor) Donald L. M. Blackmer and Sidney Tarrow, editors, *Communism in Italy and France,* Princeton University Press, 1975; *The Comparative Study of Political Elites,* Prentice-Hall, 1976. Contributor of articles and reviews to political science reviews. Member of editorial board of *American Political Science Review,* 1971-75, and *British Journal of Political Science,* 1975—.

WORK IN PROGRESS: Research includes a comparative study of political and bureaucratic elites in England, Italy, and West Germany, a study of regional government in Italy, and a project on comparative policy analysis.

PUTTER, Irving 1917-

PERSONAL: Born December 3, 1917, in New York, N.Y.; son of Joseph P. and Anna (Schrank) Putter; married Martha Lemaire, 1941; married Kim Xuyen Nguyen (a teacher), 1970; children: (first marriage) Paul Stephen, Candace Anne Putter Newlin. Education: Yale University, Ph.D., 1949. Home: 115 St. James Dr., Piedmont, Calif. 94611. Office: Department of French, University of California, Berkeley, Calif. 94720.

CAREER: State University of Iowa, Iowa City, instructor in French, 1939-43; Stephens College, Columbia, Mo., instructor in French, 1943-44; University of California, Berkeley, lecturer, 1947-49, instructor, 1949-50, assistant professor, 1950-55, associate professor, 1955-61, professor of French, 1961—, chairman of department, 1968-71.

MEMBER: International Association for French Studies, Modern Language Association of America, Philological Association of the Pacific Coast. Awards, honors: French Government fellowship, 1946; Guggenheim fellowship, 1955-56; Fulbright fellowship, 1955-56; Humanities Research fellowship from University of California, 1971-72.

WRITINGS: Leconte de Lisle and His Contemporaries, University of California Press, 1951; (editor and translator) Chateaubriand's "Atala" and "Rene", University of California Press, 1952; The Pessimism of Leconte de Lisle: Sources of Evolution, University of California Press, 1954; The Pessimism of Leconte de Lisle: The Work and the Time, University of California Press, 1961; Le Derniere Illusion de Leconte de Lisle: Letters Inedites a Emilie Leforestier (title means "The Last Illusion of Leconte de Lisle: Unpublished Letters to Emilie Leforestier"), University of California Press, 1968. Contributor to language journals, including Revue d'Histoire Litteraire de la France.

*   *   *

PUZO, Mario 1920-

PERSONAL: Born October 15, 1920, in New York, N.Y.; son of Antonio (a railroad trackman) and Maria (Le Conti) Puzo; married Erika Lina Broske, 1946; children: Anthony, Joey, Dorothy, Virginia, Eugene. Education: Attended New School for Social Research and Columbia University. Residence: Long Island, N.Y. Agent: Candida Donadio & Associates, Inc., 111 West 57th St., New York, N.Y. 10019.

CAREER: Novelist. Worked briefly for New York Central Railroad, New York, N.Y., as messenger; following World War II, served as public relations administrator for U.S. Air Force in Europe, and later as administrative assistant in U.S. Civil Service in New York, N.Y.; sometime editor of Male magazine during 1960's; free-lance book reviewer and writer. Military service: U.S. Air Force, served in Germany during World War II. Awards, honors: Academy Awards for best screenplay based on material from another medium, 1973, for "The Godfather," and 1975, for "The Godfather: Part II."

WRITINGS: The Dark Arena (novel), Random House, 1955; The Fortunate Pilgrim (novel), Atheneum, 1965; The Runaway Summer of Davie Shaw (juvenile), Platt & Munk, 1966; The Godfather (novel; Literary Guild and Book-of-the-Month Club selections), Putnam, 1969; (contributor) Thomas C. Wheeler, editor, The Immigrant Experience: The Anguish of Becoming an American, Dial, 1971; The Godfather Papers and Other Confessions, Putnam, 1972.

Screenplays: (With Francis Ford Coppola) "The Godfather," Paramount, 1972; (with Coppola) "The Godfather: Part II," Paramount, 1974; "Earthquake," Universal, 1974. Contributor of articles, reviews and stories to American Vanguard, New York, Redbook, Holiday, New York Times Magazine and other publications.

WORK IN PROGRESS: A non-fiction book about Las Vegas for Grosset, publication expected in 1977; Fools Die, a novel, publication by Putnam expected in 1977.

SIDELIGHTS: Mario Puzo's third novel, The Godfather, seemed to catapult him from out of nowhere onto the contemporary literary scene. However, the phenomenal success of The Godfather was preceded by two highly praised, but little read novels. The Godfather attracted the opposite attention from many critics and the reading public. A writer for the London Times Literary Supplement wrote: "[Puzo] was clearly a writer of unusual talent and one looked forward to what he might come up with next. . . . The Godfather is a brutal disappointment. It is quite simply, a package for bestsellerdom: huge, vulgar and sensational, it has all the formula requirements."

Gerald Walker responded to Puzo's detractors in New York magazine. He wrote: "Never mind that they ought to know better by now. They're reviewing the money again and not the book. This time it's . . . a knowing, muscular, many charactered, and—what's worse—absolutely readable New York folktale about the Mafia. Granted, The Godfather does ask for it in a way, with almost $500,000 in advance from hardcover, paperback and movie rights; consider what book reviews usually pay and you'll see why a book like this so easily brings out the worst sort of moral indignation in so many critics. . . . He's got to be just another literary crapshooter who's made the Big Killing overnight." Walker went on to note that Puzo's "overnight" success was actually the result of twenty years of steady writing, including, it might be mentioned, reviewing books. Walker added, ". . . he painstakingly set his wit to mastering about as much as a man needs to know about the craft of writing fiction. With his second novel The Fortunate Pilgrim, he had in fact, nailed down a solid name for himself as a good but little known (and therefore uncorrupted, right?) chronicler of Italian-American life.

"Now Puzo is making money from his writing. So naturally he's only writing in order to make money. You don't have to be Sicilian to enjoy a vendetta."

A writer for the Washington Post characterized Puzo as "not the best novelist in the world, nor the most sensitive, nor certainly the most realistic. But he is without a doubt one of the most ambitious. In The Godfather, Puzo set himself two excruciatingly difficult tasks: to humanize the Mafia and to make a fortune. He succeeds on both counts. . . . It was all done with mirrors—and some of the most readable writing since the well plotted novel went out of style."

In 1970, The Godfather had had the largest first printing in the history of paperback books. The movie, adapted from the novel was extremely successful and received three Academy Awards. The sequel film, "The Godfather: Part II," also was awarded three Oscars.

AVOCATIONAL INTERESTS: Gambling, tennis, Italian cuisine and dieting.

BIOGRAPHICAL/CRITICAL SOURCES: New York, March 31, 1969; Washington Post, March 12, 1970; Life, July 10, 1970; McCall's, May, 1971; Time, March 13, 1971; Thomas C. Wheeler, editor, The Immigrant Experience: The Anguish of Becoming an American, Dial, 1971; Mario Puzo, The Godfather Papers and Other Confessions, Putnam, 1972; David Madden, editor, *Rediscoveries*, Crown, 1972; Carolyn Riley, editor, *Contemporary Literary Criticism*, Gale, Volume I, 1973, Volume II, 1974, Volume VI, 1976; Rose B. Green, *The Italian-American Novel*, Fairleigh Dickinson University Press, 1974.

* * *

QUARLES, John R(hodes), Jr. 1935-

PERSONAL: Born April 26, 1935, in Boston, Mass.; son of John Rhodes (a lawyer) and Josephine (Franklin) Quarels; married Barbara Harris, June 21, 1961; children: Laura Willis, Nancy Franklin, John Rhodes III. *Education:* Yale University, B.A., 1957; Harvard University, LL.D. (magna cum laude), 1961. *Home:* 726 Lawton St., McLean, Va. 22101. *Office:* Environmental Protection Agency, Waterside Mall, 401 M St. S.W., Washington, D.C. 20460.

CAREER: U.S. Court of Appeals for the Fifth Circuit, New Orleans, La., attorney, 1961-62; Herrick, Smith, Donald, Farley & Ketchum, Boston, Mass., attorney, 1962-69; U.S. Department of the Interior, Washington, D.C., assistant to undersecretary and later to secretary of the interior, 1969-70; U.S. Environmental Protection Agency, Washington, D.C., assistant administrator for enforcement and general counsel, 1970-73, deputy administrator, 1973—. Instructor at Harvard University, 1964. *Military service:* U.S. Army, 1961. *Member:* Boston Bar Association, Phi Beta Kappa.

WRITINGS: Cleaning Up America, Houghton, 1976. Contributor to magazines.

* * *

QUINN, Sally 1941-

PERSONAL: Born July 1, 1941, in Savannah, Ga.; daughter of William Wilson (an army officer) and Bette (Williams) Quinn. *Education:* Smith College, B.A. *Religion:* None. *Home:* 1712 21st St. N.W., Washington, D.C. 20009. *Agent:* Sterling Lord, 660 Madison Ave., New York, N.Y. 10021. *Office:* 1150 15th St. N.W., Washington, D.C. 20071.

CAREER: Worked as translator, librarian, secretary, public relations agent, and dancer; *Washington Post*, Washington, D.C., profile writer, 1969-73; Columbia Broadcasting System (CBS) News, New York City, anchorwoman on "Morning News," 1972-73; *Washington Post*, general assignments writer, 1974—. Notable assignments include political conventions and Presidential campaigns in 1968, 1972, and 1976, Iran's [Persia] 2,500th anniversary celebration, and profiles of many famous personalities. Lecturer.

WRITINGS: We're Going to Make You a Star, Simon & Schuster, 1975. Contributor of articles to *Esquire, Redbook, Family Circle, Cosmopolitan, New York, Vogue,* and *Harper's Bazaar.*

SIDELIGHTS: Sally Quinn writes: "The most important thing to me is the challenge of the newness of each day and every assignment; the learning and growing; the trying out of different types of stories. There is never a moment in daily journalism when I have been bored—when I have not looked forward to the next day."

* * *

QUOIST, Michel 1921-

PERSONAL: Born June 18, 1921, in Havre, France; son of Claude and Helene (Pollet) Quoist; *Education:* Attended Grande Seminaire de Rouen, 1943; Institute Catholique de Paris, received doctorate, 1951. *Address:* 10 rue Docteur-Fauvel, 76600, Le Havre, France.

CAREER: Ordained Roman Catholic priest, July, 1947. Served as vicar of parish in Havre, 1947-50; and as head of Catholic Action youth movement, 1950-53; secretary general of French Episcopal Committee for Latin America, 1953-63; named curate of Sainte-Marie, 1970—, and Saint-Leon, 1975—; writer and lecturer. Participant, Commission Nationale de Sociologie Religieuse. *Awards, honors:* Societe de Geographie a Paris Prix Jansen, 1954, for *La Ville et l'homme.*

WRITINGS—in English translation: *Prieres,* Editions ouvrieres, 1954, translation by Agnes M. Forsyth and Marie de Commaille published as *Prayers,* Sheed & Ward, 1963, revised edition, 1974 (published in England as *Prayers of Life,* Gill, 1967); *Reussir,* Editions ouvrieres, 1960, translation by Donald P. Gray published as *The Meaning of Success,* Fides Press, 1963 (published in England as *The Christian Response,* Gill, 1963); *Donner; ou, Le Journal d'Anne-Marie,* Editions Ouvrieres, 1962, translation by Charles Davenport published as *With Love, Ann Marie: Letters for Growing Up,* Newman Press, 1968; *Le Christ est vivant,* Editions ouvrieres, 1970, translation by J. F. Bernard published as *Christ is Alive!,* Doubleday, 1971; *Jesus-Christ m'a donne rendez-vous,* Editions Ouvrieres, 1971, translation by Bernard published as *I've Met Jesus Christ,* Doubleday, 1972 (published in England as *Meet Jesus Christ and Live!,* Gill, 1973).

Writings in French: *La Ville et l'homme: Rouen, etude sociologique d'un secteur proletarian suivi de conclusions pour l'action,* Editions ouvrieres, 1952; (with L. J. Lebret, R. Bride and others) *L'Enquete Urbaine,* Presses Universitaires de France, c.1955; *Aimer, ou, Le Journal de Dany,* Editions ouvrieres, 1956. Also author of journals, letters, and Christian testimonies in French, and contributor to *L'Equipe d'enquette et d'action,* published in France.

WORK IN PROGRESS: More books.

* * *

RAAB, Lawrence 1946-

PERSONAL: Born May 8, 1946, in Pittsfield, Mass.; married Judith Michaels, 1968. *Education:* Middlebury College, B.A., 1968; Syracuse University, M.A., 1972. *Home:* 39 Ann Dr., Pittsfield, Mass. 01201. *Office:* Department of English, Williams College, Williamstown, Mass. 01267.

CAREER: American University, Washington, D.C., instructor in English, 1970-71; New York State Council for the Arts, Syracuse, instructor at poetry workshop for children, 1972; University of Michigan, Ann Arbor, lecturer in English, autumn, 1974; Bread Loaf Writer's Conference, Middlebury, Vt., staff assistant, 1974-76; Williams College, Wiliamstown, Mass., lecturer in English, 1976—. Has given poetry readings at colleges and universities throughout the United States. *Member:* Phi Beta Kappa, Blue Key. *Awards, honors:* Woodrow Wilson fellowship, 1968; CINE Eagle from Council on International Non-theatrical Events, 1968, for film "Or I'll Come to You;" Academy of American Poets prize, 1972, for "The Wolf's Journey"; creative writing grant from National Endowment for the Arts, 1972-73; Robert Frost fellow at Bread Loaf Writers' Conference, 1973; junior fellow of University of Michigan Society of Fellows, 1973-76.

WRITINGS: Mysteries of the Horizon (poems), Doubleday, 1972; *The Collector of Cold Weather* (poems), Ecco Press, 1976.

Work anthologized in *Borestone Mountain Awards An-*

thology: *Best Poems of 1969*, Pacific Books, 1970; *The Berkshire Anthology*, edited by Gerald Houseman and David Silverstein, Bookstore Press, 1972; *Academy of American Poets: University and College Poetry Prizes, 1967-72*, edited by Daniel Hoffman, Academy of American Poets, 1974; *The American Poetry Anthology*, edited by Daniel Halpern, Avon, 1975.

Author of film scripts "The Distances," 1967, and "Or I'll Come to You," 1968. Also author of "The Birds" (adaptation of a play by Aristophanes), first produced in Ann Arbor, Mich., at Power Center, April, 1975. Also author of "Dracula" (libretto for an opera adapted from the novel by Bram Stoker), as yet unpublished and unproduced.

Contributor of poems, essays, reviews, and translations from the French, to literary journals, including *Poetry, Paris Review, Kayak, Antioch Review, Shenandoah,* and *Prairie Schooner,* to popular magazines, including *New Yorker, Atlantic Monthly,* and *American Scholar,* and also to *Fantasy and Science Fiction.* Editor of *Frontiers,* 1967 and 1968; member of editorial board of *Alkahest,* 1968.

* * *

RAE, Gwynedd 1892-

PERSONAL: Born July 23, 1892, in London, England; daughter of George Bentham (a stock broker) and Mary Victorine (Thompson) Rae. *Education:* Attended Manor House School, Brondesbury, London, 1907-09, and Villa St. George's School, Paris, France, 1909-10. *Politics:* Conservative. *Religion:* Anglican. *Home:* Tott Close, Burwash, Sussex, England. *Agent:* Lawrence Pollinger Ltd., 18 Maddox St., London, England.

CAREER: Social worker for Girls Diocesan Association, Invalid Children's Association, and East End clergy, in London, England. Author, 1930—. *Wartime service:* Member of Voluntary Aid Detactment in Kent during World War I. *Member:* National Book League, Voluntary Aid Detactment Club.

WRITINGS—"Mary Plain" series of children's books: *Mostly Mary,* E. Mathews & Marrot, 1930, Morrow, 1931, reprinted, Avon, 1972; *All Mary,* E. Mathews & Marrot, 1931, Avon, 1972; *Mary Plain in Town,* Cobden-Sanderson, 1935; *. . . on Holiday,* Cobden-Sanderson, 1937; *. . . in Trouble,* G. Routledge & Sons, 1940; *. . . in Wartime,* G. Routledge & Sons, 1942, published as *Mary Plain Lends a Paw,* 1949; *Mary Plain's Big Adventure,* G. Routledge & Sons, 1944; *Mary Plain Home Again,* Routledge & Kegan Paul, 1949; *. . . to the Rescue,* Routledge & Kegan Paul, 1950; *. . . and the Twins,* Routledge & Kegan Paul, 1952; *. . . Goes Bob-a-Jobbing,* Routledge & Kegan Paul, 1957; *. . . Goes to America,* Routledge & Kegan Paul, 1957; *. . ., V.I.P.,* Routledge & Kegan Paul, 1961; *Mary Plain's "Whodunit,"* Routledge & Kegan Paul, 1965.

Adult novels: *And Timothy Too,* Blackie & Son, 1934; *Leap Year Born,* Blackie & Son, 1935. Also author of *Lovely Heritage* (family history), privately printed.

WORK IN PROGRESS: An autobiography; an omnibus volume of "Mary Plain" books.

SIDELIGHTS: Gwynedd Rae's ever popular series, "Mary Plain," is about a bear who lives in the famous pit in Bern, Switzerland. In a letter to *CA* Miss Rae explained the inspiration for the series: "In the 30's I had to spend two years at Dr. Kocher's Clinic in Bern for a thyroid treatment and while there I visited the bear pit, which has been in existence since 1513, almost daily. . . ." Many critics believe the success of her series is in large part due to her accurate observations of both animal and human behavior. Miss Rae commented: "All the children in my books are either my own nieces and nephews or those of my friends, and the Owl Man [Mary Plain's human friend who wears glasses] is my brother. This fact, and that of Mary being a real bear has, I think, greatly contributed to the success of the books through 45 years." "I was immensely lucky," she continued, "in being one of the few juvenile writers whose books survived World War II. Considering the rising costs and the general climate of affairs, both hardbacks and paperbacks are still doing quite well and I continue to receive a fair amount of fan mail, which is very heartening."

Miss Rae told *CA* of the "Teddy Bears Picnic," held on June 19, 1976, at Hartfield, Sussex, England to commemorate the fiftieth anniversary of the death of A. A. Milne, author of the "Winnie the Pooh" series of books.

Miss Rae wrote: "I myself have a lovely Teddy Bear, given to me by my nieces and nephews when I dedicated *All Mary* to them. I took her with me, with her name "Mary Plain," and address "The Bear Pits, Bern, Switzerland," printed on a placard fixed on her back. We had, alas, the first rain for months, which fell heartily all the afternoon and spoilt all the plans made for entertainments, but bears from all over the world were there.

"I was sitting in my car when there came a tap on the window and a lady said, 'I have come from America with Christopher Robin's original bear and we fly back tomorrow, but he wants to shake Mary Plain's paw, please.' So the two bears solemnly did this."

Twelve of the original fourteen books are still in print, including the books written in the 1930's. The first five books in the series have been read on the "Children's Hour" BBC-Radio program and they, with others, have recently appeared on the childrens television program "Jackanory" in England.

Miss Rae has traveled extensively in Europe; "in Italy, France, Holland, Germany, Austria, and Belgium but, best of all I loved the winter skating holidays in Switzerland whose mountains and scenery I adore." In 1955 she made her first visit to the United States to do research in Pennsylvania and California for her family genealogy.

* * *

RAGAN, David 1925-

PERSONAL: Born August 26, 1925, in Jackson, Tenn.; son of Amos and Esther Lee (Tacker) Ragan; married Claire Sills (a college instructor), December 27, 1948; children: David Nathaniel, Sarah Sills, Jennifer Leigh. *Education:* Union University, Jackson, Tenn., B.A., 1947; California School of the Theatre, M.T.A., 1950. *Politics:* Republican. *Religion:* Presbyterian. *Home:* 1230 Park Ave., New York, N.Y. 10028.

CAREER: Motion picture actor in Hollywood, Calif., 1947-50; General Features Syndicate, New York, N.Y., author of syndicated column "Hollywood South Side," 1950-52; free-lance magazine writer, 1952-57; *TV and Movie Screen,* New York, N.Y., editor-in-chief, 1957-61; *Motion Picture,* New York City, managing editor, 1961-65; *TV Radio Mirror,* New York City, editor-in-chief, 1965-71; Warner Communications, New York City, publisher and editorial director of *Movie Digest, Words and Music,* and *Planet,* 1971-72, editorial director of all the firm's motion picture and television magazines, 1972-74; writer and researcher,

1974—. Managing editor of *Tele-Views*, 1950-52. *Military service:* U.S. Army, 1952-54; became sergeant.

WRITINGS: Who's Who in Hollywood, 1900-1976, two volumes, Arlington House, 1976. Author of radio scripts for Columbia Broadcasting System, 1950-54. Author of monthly column "Stars of the Late Show" in *TV Radio Mirror*, 1969-74. Contributor to magazines, including *Guideposts, Sir, Fate, Holiday, Physical Culture*, and *This Week*, and to newspapers.

WORK IN PROGRESS: A book on Howard Hughes' Hollywood years.

SIDELIGHTS: Ragan writes that his book "is the first reference to endeavor to chronicle the achievements of all who have appeared on the screen from the beginning—stars, characters, supporting players, bit actors. . . ." He remains fondest of the character actors, writing: "I have always found them more colorful and substantial, as well as interesting, than the stars. . . . I personally celebrate them and scores more like them, people who have enriched my life and the lives of all who ever entered a movie theater. . . ." About actors in general, he writes: "I have always been most interested in the 'why' behind an actor's career—why he chose to act, why his career took flight (or failed to) at one point instead of another, why he could—or could not—sustain its momentum, and why he remained a performer to the end or, as happens more often in motion pictures, eventually withdrew from the fray."

*   *   *

RAKOVE, Milton L(eon)   1918-

PERSONAL: Born October 30, 1918, in Buhl, Minn.; son of Jacob and Rose (Rovel) Rakove; married Shirley Bloom, May 24, 1942; children: Jack, Roberta. *Education:* Attended Chicago City Junior College, 1941-43; Roosevelt University, B.A., 1948; University of Chicago, M.A., 1949, Ph.D., 1956. *Religion:* Jewish. *Home:* 141 Hibbard Rd., Wilmette, Ill. 60091. *Office:* Department of Political Science, University of Illinois, Chicago Circle, Chicago, Ill.

CAREER: Chicago City Junior College, Herzl Branch, Chicago, Ill., instructor in political science, 1954; Indiana University, East Chicago, lecturer, 1954-55; instructor in political science, 1955-56; University of Florida, Gainesville, assistant professor of political science, 1956-57; University of Illinois, Chicago Circle, assistant professor, 1958-63, associate professor, 1963-67, professor of political science, 1968—. Lecturer at University of Chicago and Roosevelt University, both 1957-60, and at Barat College of the Sacred Heart, 1960; associate professor at Loyola University, Chicago, Ill., 1965-66; member of faculty at Lincoln Academy of Illinois, 1966—; professor at Northeastern Illinois State University, 1967-68; visting profesor at California State College, Los Angeles, summers, 1968-69. Field research associate and director of American Foundation for Political Education's Chicago World Politics Program, 1957-60. Democratic candidate for Cook County Board of Commissioners, 1970, member of Home Rule Commission, 1973-74. Has appeared on television and radio programs; commentator for WBBM-Radio. Member of Illinois advisory committee to U.S. Civil Rights Commission, 1965—; political consultant and speechwriter; consultant to Oak Ridge Institute for Nuclear Studies, Brookings Institution, and Boeing Co. *Military service:* U.S. Army, 1943-46.

MEMBER: American Political Science Association, American Foundation for World Youth Understanding (member of board of directors, 1962-64), American Civil Liberties

Union (member of board of directors of Illinois Division, 1964-65), United Nations Association (member of board of directors of Illinois Division, 1968—; vice-president, 1971-72), Chicago Area Lay Movement (member of board of directors, 1963—), Chicago Council on Foreign Relations, Pi Sigma Alpha. *Awards, honors:* Invited by West German Government to study politics in Germany, 1963.

WRITINGS: The Changing Patterns of Suburban Politics in Cook County, Illinois (monograph), Loyola University Press, 1965; (contributor) William A. Robson, editor, *Great Cities of the World: Their Government, Politics, and Planning*, Allen & Unwin, 1972; (editor) *Arms and Foreign Policy in the Nuclear Age*, Oxford University Press, 1972; *Don't Make No Waves, Don't Back No Losers: The Dynamics of the Chicago Machine*, Indiana University Press, 1975. Contributor of about twenty-five articles to professional journals, and to popular magazines, including *Harper's*, and to newspapers.

WORK IN PROGRESS: The Governance of Chicago (tentative title), for Indiana University Press; an international relations textbook.

*   *   *

RAMAGE, Edwin S(tephen)   1929-

PERSONAL: Born July 19, 1929, in Vancouver, British Columbia, Canada; came to the United States in 1953; son of Edwin Havelock and Mary (Cardinell) Ramage; married Shirley Sue LaRue, June 16, 1956; children: Bruce Edwin, Victoria Sue. *Education:* University of British Columbia, B.A., 1951, M.A., 1952; University of Illinois, further graduate study, 1953-54; University of Cincinnati, Ph.D., 1957. *Home:* 1935 Montclair Ave., Bloomington, Ind. 47401. *Office:* Department of Classics, Ballantine 547, Indiana University, Bloomington, Ind. 47401.

CAREER: Indiana University, Bloomington, instructor, 1957-60, assistant professor, 1960-64, associate professor, 1964-68, professor of classics, 1968—, chairman of department, 1971-75, assistant dean of College of Arts and Sciences, 1962, co-director of joint excavations (with University of Chicago) at Kenchreai, Greece, 1963-66. *Member:* American Philological Association, Archaeological Institute of America, Classical Association of Canada, Classical Association of the Middle West and South.

WRITINGS: Roman Urbanitas: Ancient Sophistication and Refinement, University of Oklahoma Press, 1973; (with D. L. Sigsbee and S. C. Fredericks) *Roman Satirists and Their Satire*, Noyes, 1974; (translator) Ulrich Knoche, *Roman Satire*, Indiana University Press, 1975. Contributor to philology and classical studies journals.

WORK IN PROGRESS: New Perspectives on Atlantis, with J. R. Fears, S. C. Fredericks, J. V. Luce, D. B. Vitaliano, and H. E. Wright, Jr.; continuing research on urban problems in ancient Rome and on Roman satire (especially the work of Persius).

*   *   *

RAMSEY, Roy S.   1920(?)-1976

1920(?)—June 26, 1976; American journalist. Obituaries: *Washington Post*, July 1, 1976.

*   *   *

RANDALL, John E(rnest, Jr.)   1924-

PERSONAL: Born May 22, 1924, in Los Angeles, Calif.;

son of John Ernest (a builder) and Mildred (McKibben) Randall; married Helen Lai Sinn Au (an administrative assistant), November 9, 1951; children: Loreen Ann, Rodney Dean. *Education:* University of California, Los Angeles, B.A., 1950; University of Hawaii, Ph.D. (honors), 1955. *Residence:* Kaneohe, Hawaii. *Office:* Bernice P. Bishop Museum, 1355 Kalihi St., Honolulu, Hawaii 96819.

CAREER: Yale University, New Haven, Conn., research fellow, 1955-57; University of Miami, Coral Gables, research assistant professor of marine biology at Marine Laboratory, 1957-61; University of Puerto Rico, Mayaguez, professor of biology, 1961-65, director of Institute of Marine Biology, 1962-65; Oceanic Institute, Waimanolo, Hawaii, director, 1965-66; University of Hawaii, Honolulu, marine biologist at Hawaii Institute of Marine Biology, 1967-69; Bernice P. Bishop Museum, Honolulu, Hawaii, ichthyologist, 1969—. Research fellow at Bernice P. Bishop Museum, 1955-57, part-time ichthyologist, 1965-69; member of zoology department graduate faculty at University of Hawaii, 1966-75. Founding member of Bahamas National Trust; member of Gulf and Caribbean Fisheries Institute. Member of International Biological Program's subcommittee on conservation of ecosystems; member of Hawaii advisory committee on invertebrates and aquatic vertebrates; member of Great Barrier Reef Committee. Has conducted expeditions throughout the Pacific, Caribbean, Red Sea, South America, Indonesia, India, and Ceylon. *Military service:* U.S. Army, Medical Administrative Corps, 1943-46; became second lieutenant.

MEMBER: Association of Island Marine Laboratories (president, 1962-63), American Society of Ichthyologists and Herpetologists, American Association of Museums, Hawaiian Academy of Sciences, Phi Beta Kappa, Sigma Xi, Phi Sigma Kappa. *Awards, honors:* Expeditions have been supported by Office of Naval Research, National Science Foundation, Bureau of Sport Fisheries and Wildlife, National Park Service, National Geographic Society, Oceanic Foundation, Smithsonian Institution, American Philosophical Society, and United States-Israel Binational Science Foundation.

WRITINGS: (Contributor) W. A. Gosline and V. E. Brock, editors, *Handbook of Hawaiian Fishes,* University Press of Hawaii, 1960; (with Perry W. Gilbert and others) *Sharks and Survival,* Heath, 1963; *Caribbean Reef Fishes,* T.F.H. Publications, 1968. Contributor to proceedings and transactions and to professional and popular journals in his field. Contributing editor of *Sea Frontiers;* member of board of editors of *Caribbean Journal of Sciences,* 1962-63.

WORK IN PROGRESS: Hawaiian Reef Fishes, to be printed on waterproof paper; *Fishes of the Antilles.*

AVOCATIONAL INTERESTS: Scuba and skin diving.

BIOGRAPHICAL/CRITICAL SOURCES: Robert E. Schroeder, *Something Rich and Strange,* Harper, 1965; Wade Doak, *Sharks and Other Adventures,* Hodder & Stoughton, 1975.

*   *   *

RANDLES, Anthony V(ictor), Jr.   1942-
    (Slim Randles)

PERSONAL: Born July 27, 1942, in Los Angeles, Calif.; son of Anthony Victor (an attorney) and Lavanche (a consultant; maiden name, Post) Randles; married Verna Lee, 1961 (divorced); married Meredith Johnson, 1965 (divorced); married Kathleen Daugherty, 1967 (divorced); married

Pamela T. Himsworth (a journalist), April 29, 1972; children: (first marriage) Gail Elizabeth; (third marriage) Kyra Lynette, Scott Anthony; (fourth marriage) Amanda Lois. *Education:* Attended Coalinga College, 1960-62, and Antelope Valley College, 1962-64. *Politics:* Democrat. *Religion:* Protestant. *Home:* Mile 239.5 Alaska Railroad, Talkeetna, Alaska 99676. *Office:* Raven House Publishing, P.O. Box 128, Talkeetna, Alaska 99676.

CAREER: Itinerant reporter and newspaper editor in California, 1964-69; *Anchorage Daily News,* Anchorage, Alaska, feature writer, 1969-70, columnist, 1970—. Owner of Raven House Publishing. Member of Alaska Fish and Game Advisory Committee; licensed big game guide. Democratic candidate for Alaska State Senate, 1972. *Member:* Alaska Professional Hunters Association, Alaska Society for the Prevention of Cruelty to Animals (honorary life member), Alaska Press Club, Montana Creek Dog Mushers Association, Save Talkeetna Committee. *Awards, honors:* Best column award from Alaska Press Club, 1974, for "Slim's Column."

WRITINGS: Dogsled: A True Tale of the North, Winchester Press, 1976. Author of "Slim's Column," a column in *Anchorage Daily News* (syndicated to six other regional newspapers), 1970—.

WORK IN PROGRESS: A book about his eight years as a High Sierra packer.

SIDELIGHTS: Randles writes: "I have had more fun than anyone deserves, and feel it would be a sin to keep it all to myself. . . . The outdoors has been a great part of my life, as a cowboy, horse trainer, rodeo hand, packer, dog musher, and now hunting guide. It would be obscene for someone to have that much fun and not share it. Good Lord willing, I'll continue to do my best."

*   *   *

RANDLES, Slim
    See RANDLES, Anthony V(ictor), Jr.

*   *   *

RAPHAELSON, Samson   1896-

PERSONAL: Born March 30, 1896, in New York, N.Y.; son of Ralph and Anna (Marks) Raphaelson; married Dorothy Wegman, December 24, 1927; children: Joel, Naomi. *Education:* University of Illinois, A.B., 1917. *Office:* Film Division, Columbia University, New York, N.Y. 10027.

CAREER: Reporter for City News Service, 1917-18; worked in various advertising agencies in Chicago, Ill., 1918-20; University of Illinois, Urbana, instructor in English, 1920-21; short story writer, 1918—, playwright, 1925—, screenwriter, 1930—; stage director, 1933— (has directed "Jason," "Skylark," "Accent on Youth," "The Wooden Slipper," and "The Perfect Marriage"); photographer, 1951—. Visiting professor at University of Illinois, 1948; adjunct professor at Columbia University, 1976—. *Member:* Dramatists Guild, Screen Writers Guild, Authors Guild of Authors League of America.

WRITINGS: The Human Nature of Playwriting, Macmillan, 1949.

Plays: *The Jazz Singer* (three-act; first produced in New York City at Fulton Theatre, September 15, 1925), Brentano's, 1925; *Young Love* (three-act comedy; first produced in New York City at Theatre Masque, October 30, 1928), Brentano's, 1928; "The Magnificent Heel" (three-act; first produced in Stamford, Conn., 1929), *The Wooden Slipper* (three-act comedy; first produced in New York City at Ritz Theatre, January 3, 1934), Row, Peterson, 1934; *Accent on Youth* (three-act; first produced in New York City at Plymouth Theatre, December 25, 1934), Samuel French, 1935; *Accent on Youth and White Man* (two plays), Samuel French, 1935; *Skylark* (three-act comedy; first serialized as "Streamlined Heart" in *Saturday Evening Post;* first produced in New York City at Morosco Theatre, October 11, 1939), Random House, 1939. *Jason* (three-act: first produced in New York City at Hudson Theatre, January 21, 1942), Random House, 1942; *The Perfect Marriage* (three-act play; first produced in New York City at Ethel Barrymore Theatre, October 26, 1944), Dramatists Play Service, 1945; *Hilda Crane* (three-act; first produced in New York City at Coronet Theatre, November 1, 1950), Random House, 1951.

Also author of two plays, "The Store" (three-act), 1926, and "The Peanut Bag," 1967, both as yet neither published nor produced.

Screenplays include: "That Lady in Ermine," "Green Dolphin Street," "Heaven Can Wait," "Suspicion," "The Shop Around the Corner," "Trouble in Paradise," "The Smiling Lieutenant," "Broken Lullaby," "One Hour with You," "Angel," and "The Merry Widow."

A radio play and stories are anthologized in *Free World Theatre,* edited by Thomas Mann, Random House, 1944; *Best American Stories,* edited by Martha Foley, 1947; *Editor's Choice,* edited by Herbert Mayes, Random House, 1956. Contributor of stories and articles to film journals and to popular magazines, including *Esquire, Saturday Evening Post, Nation, Century,* and *Good Housekeeping.*

WORK IN PROGRESS: A series of essays on cinema; a series of short stories set in the Hollywood of the 1930's and 1940's; a book of memoirs; a play about Israel.

* * *

RAPOPORT, Amos 1929-

PERSONAL: Born March 28, 1929, in Warsaw, Poland; Australian citizen; son of Joshua (a writer) and Mala (a teacher; maiden name, Miodownik) Rapoport; married Dorothy Hassin, September 2, 1967; children: Micah David. *Education:* University of Melbourne, B.Arch., 1954, diploma in town and regional planning, 1966; Rice University, M.Arch., 1957. *Religion:* Jewish. *Home:* 2925 North Summit, Milwaukee, Wis. 53211. *Office:* Department of Anthropology, University of Wisconsin, Milwaukee, Wis. 53201.

CAREER: Registered architect in Victoria and New South Wales, Australia. International Basic Economy Corporation, New York, N.Y., planning and housing advisor to developing countries, 1957-58; Bates, Smart & McCutcheon, Melbourne, Australia, architect, 1959-60; University of Melbourne, Melbourne, Australia, lecturer in architecture, 1962; University of California, Berkeley, assistant professor of architecture and assistant research architect, 1963-67; University of London, Bartlett School of Architecture, London, England, lecturer in architecture, 1967-69; University of Sydney, Sydney, Australia, senior lecturer in architecture, 1969-72; University of Wisconsin, Milwaukee, associate professor, 1972-74, professor of architecture and anthropology, 1974—. Visiting professor at University of Wisconsin, Milwaukee, 1970-71, and at Technion-Israel Institute of Technology, 1976; research professor at University of Wisconsin, Milwaukee, 1974-77. Has lectured at colleges and universities all over Europe, Australia, and the United States, and appeared on Australian television.

Member of planning committee for several international conferences.

MEMBER: International Society for the Study of Symbols, World Society for Ekistics (member of executive committee, 1973—), Association for the Study of Man-Environment Relations, Architectural Association, Environmental Design Research Association (member of board of directors, 1972-74), Royal Australian Institute of Architects (fellow), Royal Institute of British Architects (associate). *Awards, honors:* Fulbright fellowship from Australia to the United States, 1956-58; technical cooperation fellowship from the French Government, 1961; research awards from Central Research Fund of University of London and from Royal Institute of British Architects, both in 1968.

WRITINGS: (With H. Sanoff and T. Porter) *Low Cost Housing Demonstration* (monograph), Department of Architecture, University of California, Berkeley, 1965; (with Sanoff) *Evaluation of Three Case Study Dwellings* (monograph), Department of Architecture, University of California, Berkeley, 1966; *House, Form, and Culture,* Prentice-Hall, 1969; (editor with B. Davis) *Proceedings of Man-Environment Studies Seminar,* Royal Australian Institute of Architects, 1971; (editor and contributor) *Australia as Human Setting: Approaches to the Designed Environment,* Angus & Robertson, 1972; *Aspectos de la Calidad Del Entorno* (title means "Aspects of Environmental Quality"), Colegio oficial de arquitectos, de cataluna y baleares, 1975; (editor and contributor) *The Mutual Interaction of People and Their Built Environment: A Cross-Cultural Perspective,* Mouton & Co., in press; *Human Aspects of Urban Form: Toward a Man-Environment Approach to Urban Form and Design,* Pergamon, in press.

Contributor: G. Broadbent and A. Ward, editors, *Design Methods in Architecture,* Lund Humphries, 1969; P. Oliver, editor, *Shelter and Society,* Barrie & Rockliffe, 1969; G.J.R. Linge and P. J. Skinner, editors, *Government Influence and the Location of Economic Activity,* Department of Human Geography, Australian National University, 1971; Wolfgang F. E. Preiser, editor, *Environmental Design Perspectives,* United Press International, 1972; W. Mitchell, editor, *Environmental Design: Research and Practice,* University of California, Los Angeles, 1972; R. Gutman, editor, *People and Buildings,* Basic Books, 1972; Preiser, editor, *Environmental Design Research,* Dowden, Hutchinson & Ross, 1973; Thomas O. Byerts, editor, *Environmental Research and Aging,* Gerontological Society, 1974; P. W. Windley, Byerts, and others, editors, *Theory Development and Aging,* Gerontological Society, 1975; Basil Honikman, editor, *Responding to Social Change,* Dowden, Hutchinson & Ross, 1975; Oliver, editor, *Shelter, Sign, and Symbol,* Barrie & Jenkins, 1975; G. Moore and R. G. Golledge, editors, *Environmental Knowing,* Dowden, Hutchinson & Ross, in press.

Also author of monograph, *Applied Design Sciences,* with E. R. Alexander and R. M. Beckley for U.S. Department of Commerce.

Author of "Environment," a weekly column in *Australian,* 1970-72. Contributor to *Encyclopedia of Anthropology.* Contributor of articles and reviews to architecture, planning, and anthropology journals. Member of managing committee of *Australian Journal of Social Issues,* 1970-72; member of editorial board of *Environment and Behavior,* 1974—, Urban *Ecology,* and *Urbanism: Past and Present.*

SIDELIGHTS: Rapoport's writings have been translated into several languages. He writes: "I am one of the founders of the new field of man-environment studies, which deals with how people and environments interact. In this field my special interests are theory-synthesis, cross-cultural studies, socio-cultural variables, meaning and symbolism. An important additional interest in vernacular architecture.''

AVOCATIONAL INTERESTS: Travel, archaeology.

* * *

RATLIFF, Richard C(harles) 1922-

PERSONAL: Born May 26, 1922, in Oklahoma City, Okla.; son of Edgar Samuel (an attorney) and Katherine Lee (Underwood) Ratliff; married first wife, Mary Jane, December 23, 1947 (divorced, 1965); married Nan Elizabeth Lee (a college teacher), December 19, 1972; children: Richard Charles, Jr., Janis Lynn. *Education:* University of Oklahoma, B.A., 1948, M.A., 1950, Ph.D., 1971. *Politics:* Democrat. *Religion:* Unitarian-Universalist. *Home:* 14004 North Everest, Edmond, Okla. 73034. *Office:* Department of Humanities, Oscar Rose Junior College, Midwest City, Okla. 73110.

CAREER: Daily Oklahoman, Oklahoma City, news reporter, 1945; *Shawnee News-Star,* Shawnee, Okla., news editor, 1948; Southern State College, Magnolia, Ark., instructor in journalism, 1949-55; Northwestern State College, Alva, Okla., instructor in journalism, 1955-59; Midwestern University, Wichita Falls, Tex., assistant professor of government and journalism, 1960-65; Central Missouri State College, Warrensburg, assistant professor of political science, 1965-67; Oklahoma Baptist University, Shawnee, assistant professor of government, 1968-69; Sul Ross State University, Alpine, Tex., associate professor of government and chairman of department, 1969-71; University of Wisconsin, Stevens Point, associate professor of political science, 1971-72; writer, 1972-74; Oscar Rose Junior College, Midwest City, Okla., instructor in journalism, 1974—. *Military service:* U.S. National Guard Medical Corps, 1938-41.

MEMBER: American Political Science Association, American Academy of Social Science, American Association of University Professors, Sigma Delta Chi, Pi Sigma Alpha. *Awards, honors:* Sigma Delta Chi citation for editorial work from University of Oklahoma, 1949.

WRITINGS: Constitutional Rights of College Students: A Study in Case Law, Scarecrow, 1972; *American Government,* Cliff's Notes, 1972. Domestic correspondent for *Christian Science Monitor,* 1944-58. Contributor of several dozen articles and reviews to lithography, education, and social science journals.

WORK IN PROGRESS: Damn the Academy, a memoir of higher education in America; "The Five Fool Factors," a play about college life.

AVOCATIONAL INTERESTS: Propaganda analysis, archaeology.

* * *

RAUP, Robert 1888(?)-1976

1888(?)—April 13, 1976; American educator and author of books in his field. Obituaries: *New York Times,* April 15, 1976.

* * *

RAYMOND, E. V.
See GALUN, Raymond Z(inke)

RAZOR SALTBOY
See LOUIS, Ray Baldwin

* * *

REARDEN, Jim 1925-

PERSONAL: Born April 22, 1925, in Petaluma, Calif.; son of Barton B. (a teacher) and Grace (Miller) Rearden; married: Ursula Budde, 1943 (divorced, 1965); married Audrey Roberts (an editorial assistant), January 25, 1966; children: Kathleen Rearden Prevost, Mary, Michael, Nancy, Jim K.; (stepchildren) Terry Sagmoen, Tamara Sagmoen, Michael Sagmoen. *Education:* Oregon State University, B.S., 1948; University of Maine, M.S., 1950. *Politics:* Independent. *Religion:* Protestant. *Home and office address:* P.O. Box 313, Homer, Alaska 99603.

CAREER: University of Alaska, Fairbanks, assistant professor, 1950-51, professor of wildlife and fishery, 1952-54, head of department of wildlife management, 1950-54; Alaska Department of Fish and Game, Homer, area biologist, 1959-69; *Alaska* (magazine), Homer, Alaska, outdoors editor, 1970—. Alaska field editor for *Outdoor Life,* 1976—. Member of Alaska Board of Fish and Game, 1970, 1973-75; member of Alaska Board of Game, 1975—; member of National Advisory Committee on Oceans and Atmosphere, 1976—. *Member:* American Society of Journalists and Authors.

WRITINGS: Wonders of Caribou (juvenile), Dodd, 1976. Contributor of more than two hundred articles to national magazines, including *Outdoor Life, Field and Stream, Sports Afield, National Wildlife, International Wildlife,* and *National Geographic.*

WORK IN PROGRESS: A novel about bush flying in Alaska; editing a collection of magazine articles, dating from the early 1950's, that illustrate the changes that have occurred in Alaska in the last quarter of a century; *The Wolf Man,* a biography of Frank Glaser, who was a federal predator control agent in Alaska for many years.

SIDELIGHTS: Rearden writes that his "major interest is Alaska's natural history" and adds that he has "made a career of reporting on the ups and downs of wildlife populations, of recreational pursuits in Alaska's wilderness regions. People and places of Alaska are of secondary interest. Recent winter travels to New Zealand sparked an interest in the natural history of that area, and I expect to continue to report on both Alaska and New Zealand natural history subjects.''

* * *

RED FOX, William 1871(?)-1976

1871(?)—March 1, 1976; American actor and author. Obituaries: *Time,* March 15, 1976; *AB Bookman's Weekly,* May 17, 1976.

* * *

REDINGER, Ruby V(irginia) 1915-

PERSONAL: Born April 3, 1915, in Cleveland, Ohio; daughter of Elber E. (a railroad engineer) and Maud (Dawson) Redinger. *Education:* Fenn College (now Cleveland State University), B.A., 1936; Western Reserve University (now Case Western Reserve University), M.A., 1937, Ph.D., 1940. *Home:* 138 Edgewood Dr., Berea, Ohio 44017. *Office:* Marting Hall, Baldwin-Wallace College, Berea, Ohio 44017.

CAREER: Case Western Reserve University, Cleveland, Ohio, lecturer, 1939-40, instructor in English, 1940-41; Fenn College (now Cleveland State University), Cleveland, Ohio, instructor, 1941-45, assistant professor, 1945-47, associate professor of English, 1947-49, associate professor of philosophy and chairman of department, 1949-51; tutor, researcher, and writer, 1951-57; Baldwin-Wallace College, Berea, Ohio, lecturer, 1957-58, assistant professor, 1958-64, associate professor, 1964-69, professor of English, 1969—. *Member:* Modern Language Association of America, American Association of University Professors, Writers Guild of America.

WRITINGS: (With W. H. Rogers and Hiram C. Haydn) *Explorations in Living,* Reynal, 1941; *The Golden Net* (novel), Crown, 1948; *George Eliot: The Emergent Self,* Knopf, 1975. Contributor to *Encyclopedia Americana* and to *American Scholar.*

WORK IN PROGRESS: A novel; notes toward a philosophy of language.

SIDELIGHTS: Ruby Redinger told *CA:* "I feel that a revitalized and critical curiosity about language (its nature, its functions, its dynamics, and especially its role as master and/or servant to the human mind) is very much in the air today."

* * *

REED, John P(lume) 1921-

PERSONAL: Born July 4, 1921, in New Orleans, La.; son of Theodore John and Sophia (Pastor) Reed; married Robin Smith (a psychologist), November 24, 1969; children: David Langdon, Jan Patricia, Kevin Michael, Ryan Morgan. *Education:* Louisiana State University, student, 1940-42, Ph.D., 1964; Tulane University, B.A., 1947; University of Illinois, M.A., 1949, J.D., 1953. *Politics:* Independent. *Home:* 6560 Hounds Run, Mobile, Ala. 36608. *Office:* Department of Sociology, University of South Alabama, Mobile, Ala. 36688.

CAREER: University of Nevada, Reno, instructor and lecturer in sociology, business law, and economics, 1953-57; Clemson University, Clemson, S.C., assistant professor of sociology and business law, 1957-58; Southeastern Louisiana State College, Hammond, assistant professor of sociology, 1958-60; Louisiana State University, New Orleans, lecturer in sociology, 1960-61, research assistant at Institute of Population, 1961-62; Northern Arizona University, Flagstaff, assistant professor of sociology, 1962-63; University of North Carolina, Chapel Hill, assistant professor of sociology and research analyst at Institute of Government, 1963-65; Jacksonville University, Jacksonville, Fla., associate professor of sociology, 1965-68; Western Kentucky University, Bowling Green, professor of sociology, 1968-72; University of South Alabama, Mobile, professor of sociology, 1972—, chairman of department, 1972—. Member of Jacksonville Crime Commission, 1966-68. *Military service:* U.S. Army Air Forces, 1942-46.

MEMBER: American Sociological Association, Law and Society Association, American Society of Criminology, Southern Sociological Association, Southwestern Sociological Association, Alabama-Mississippi Sociological Society (president, 1974—), Alpha Kappa Delta, Delta Theta Phi.

WRITINGS: (Contributor) Robert M. Carter and Leslie T. Wilkins, editors, *Probation and Parole,* Wiley, 1970; (with Fuad Baali) *Faces of Delinquency,* Prentice-Hall, 1972; (contributor) Clifton D. Bryant, editor, *Work and Its Social*

Dimensions, Prentice-Hall, 1972; (contributor) Terrence P. Thornberry and Edward Sagarin, editors, *Images of Crime: Offenders and Victims,* Praeger, 1974. Contributor to behavioral science journals.

WORK IN PROGRESS: *The Affected, the Afflicted, and the Agitated Criminal Perspectives of Our Times;* research on decision-making in six different politico-legal groups, using the Eysenck-Nagel Liberalism-Conservatism Scale; other research on criminals, social distance, and choice of sanctions, on liberalism-conservatism, jury service, and voting outcome, on class and racial images of the white-collar criminal, on criminal thresholds, and on law, morality, and social expectation.

* * *

REED, Robert C(arroll) 1937-

PERSONAL: Born July 26, 1937, in Toledo, Ohio; son of John Frederick (an executive) and Alyce Reed. *Education:* Miami University, Oxford, Ohio, B.A., 1959; Bowling Green State University, M.A., 1968; also studied at University of Maryland, 1962-64. *Religion:* Episcopal. *Home:* 3307 Cleveland Ave. N.W., Washington, D.C. 20008. *Office:* Department of English, St. Stephens School, Alexandria, Va.

CAREER: St. Stephens School, Alexandria, Va., teacher of writing and American literature, 1964—. Teacher at U.S. Department of Agriculture Graduate School, 1960—. *Member:* Cleveland Park Literary Society.

WRITINGS: *Train Wrecks,* Superior, 1960; *The Streamline Era,* Golden West, 1975.

WORK IN PROGRESS: *The New York Elevated Railway, 1868-1955.*

* * *

REESE, Francesca Gardner 1940-

PERSONAL: Born August 17, 1940, in New Haven, Conn.; daughter of John W. and Aida (Marroquin) Gardner; married John Robert Reese (an attorney), September 5, 1964; children: Jennifer, Justine. *Education:* Stanford University, B.S., 1962, LL.B., 1965. *Home and office:* 3970 Clay St., San Francisco, Calif. 94118.

CAREER: Admitted to California State Bar, 1965; Crist, Peters, Donegan, & Brenner, Palo Alto, Calif., attorney, 1965-66; Covington & Burling, Washington, D.C., attorney, 1967; Heller, Ehrman, White, & McAuliffe, San Francisco, Calif., attorney, 1969-71.

WRITINGS: (Editor with father, John W. Gardner) *Know or Listen to Those Who Know,* W. W. Norton, 1975.

BIOGRAPHICAL/CRITICAL SOURCES: *San Francisco Examiner,* November 2, 1975.

* * *

REEVES, Martha Emilie 1941-

PERSONAL: Born November 9, 1941, in Kansas City, Mo.; daughter of Albert Lee, Jr. (an attorney) and Louise (Glasner) Reeves; married Loyal Martin Griffin, Jr. (a physician, winemaker, and rancher), April 26, 1975. *Education:* Skidmore College, student, 1959-61; Stanford University, A.B. (with distinction), 1963. *Politics:* "We must learn to live within our resources or perish." *Religion:* Anglican. *Home and office:* 6050 Westside Rd., Healdsburg, Calif. 95448.

CAREER: Editor at various presses in New York City, including, Seabury, Dial, Crown, and Scribners, 1966-73; grower of wine grapes for family winery in California, 1974—. Chamber musician in New York City, 1967-74. Co-founder of Wildlife Preservation Trust International. *Member:* Authors Guild of Authors League of America.

WRITINGS: The Total Turtle, Crowell, 1975. Contributor of poems and reviews to local magazines and newspapers.

WORK IN PROGRESS: A book on grapes and wine, for young people; a book of essays; a book of Chinese fables, with a friend from the People's Republic of China.

SIDELIGHTS: Martha Reeves writes: "Although I have been fortunate enough to crowd many unforgettable experiences in my thirty-three years up to 1974, they are part of a dream from another lifetime. My whole existence now is caught up in the mystical cycle of vine and grape, death and resurrection of the vines and the wine that pours from the press. The past, my past, is part of it, of course, but there is so much now that seems unimportant, and yet the whole, the joys and agonies, the nations and upheavals, the wailing and laughter of individual people, seem a harmonious reticulum sounding in an everbuilding, never-ending chord, of which we can but dimly be aware."

* * *

REID, Victor Stafford 1913-

PERSONAL: Born May 1, 1913, in Kingston, Jamaica; son of Alexander Burbridge (a businessman) and Margaret (Campbell) Reid; married Monica Jacobs, August 10, 1935; children: Shirley June (Mrs. Carlton Davis), Victor Stafford, Jr., Fran Elaine (Mrs. Giles Endicott), Peter Johnathan. *Education:* Educated in Jamaica. *Home address:* Valley Hill Farm, Rock Hall, Jamaica.

CAREER: Novelist and journalist; has edited newspapers and newsmagazines in Jamaica. Chairman, National Trust Commission of Jamaica, 1973—. *Member:* International P.E.N. *Awards, honors:* Canada Council fellowship, 1958-60; Guggenheim fellowship, 1961.

WRITINGS—All novels: *New Day,* Knopf, 1948; *The Leopard,* Viking, 1958; *Sixty-Five,* Collins, 1963; *The Young Warriors,* Longmans Canada, 1968; *Peter of Mount Ephraim,* Jamaica Publishing House, 1970; *The Jamaicans,* Institute Jamaica, 1975. Also author of short stories.

WORK IN PROGRESS: A biography of Norman Manley, former premier of Jamaica.

* * *

REIFSNYDER, William E(dward) 1924-

PERSONAL: Born March 29, 1924, in Ridgway, Pa.; son of Howard W. and Madolin (Boyer) Reifsnyder; married Marylou Bishop (a writer and illustrator), December 19, 1954; children: Rita Hall (stepdaughter), Cheryl (Mrs. Reynaldo Cantu), Gawain A. *Education:* New York University, B.S., 1944; University of California, Berkeley, M.F., 1949; Yale University, Ph.D., 1954. *Home address:* Stantack Rd., Middletown, Conn. 06457. *Office:* School of Forestry and Environmental Studies, Yale University, 360 Prospect St., New Haven, Conn. 06511.

CAREER: Pacific Southwest Forest and Range Experiment Station, Berkeley, Calif., meteorologist, 1950-54; Yale University, New Haven, Conn., assistant professor, 1955-60, associate professor, 1960-65, professor of forest meteorology, 1965—, professor of public health, 1967—. Visiting professor at University of Munich, 1968. Chairman of advisory committee on climate to U.S. Weather Bureau, National Academy of Sciences, and National Research Council, 1957-63; visiting scientist for Society of American Foresters and National Science Foundation, 1961—. Member of board of directors of American Youth Hostels, Inc. Consultant to World Meteorological Organization of the United Nations. *Military service:* U.S. Army Air Forces, 1943-47; became first lieutenant.

MEMBER: International Society of Biometeorology, American Association for the Advancement of Science (fellow), American Meteorological Society, Society of American Foresters, Solar Energy Society.

WRITINGS: Hut Hopping in the Austrian Alps, Sierra Club Books, 1974; *Footloose in the Swiss Alps,* Sierra Club Books, 1975; *High Mountain Huts: A Planning Guide,* Colorado Mountain Trails Foundation, 1976. Regional editor of *Agricultural Meteorology.*

WORK IN PROGRESS: A book of essays on forestry practices and the environment.

SIDELIGHTS: Reifsnyder writes that he "became interested in problems of protecting the wildland environment by virtue of long experience as a forester and a backpacker and hiker. During a half-year stay in Munich, [I] became aware that despite heavy recreational use of the Alps, the Alpine landscape has not suffered that degradation that the American wilderness has. Furthermore, it was apparent that few Americans hiked in the Alps and utilized the facilities of the Alpine Club huts. This led [me] to . . . a variety of projects concerning recreational use of the wilderness."

* * *

REIGELMAN, Milton Monroe 1942-

PERSONAL: Born April 28, 1942, in Washington, D.C.; son of Milton Sievers (a machinist foreman for the Bureau of Engraving) and Ethel Virginia (a real estate broker; maiden name, Fairbanks) Reigelman; married Sandra Elizabeth Dail (a teacher), June 19, 1965; children: Carrie Linda and Jennie Elizabeth (twins), Jon Milton. *Education:* College of William and Mary, A.B., 1964; University of Pennsylvania, M.A. (communications), 1965; Johns Hopkins University, further graduate study, 1966-67; University of Iowa, M.A. (English), 1970, Ph.D., 1973; Yale University, postdoctoral study, 1976. *Politics:* Independent. *Religion:* "Agnostic Christian Humanist." *Home:* 513 Seminole Trail, Danville, Ky. 40422. *Office:* Department of English, Centre College, Walnut St., Danville, Ky. 40422.

CAREER: Washington Post, Washington, D.C., employed in special projects, 1964; Centre College, Danville, Ky., assistant professor of English, 1971—. *Military service:* U.S. Army, Intelligence, 1965-67; became captain. *Member:* Modern Language Association of America, American Association of University Professors, Kentucky Philological Association. *Awards, honors:* National Endowment for the Humanities fellowship, 1976; prize from Kentucky Philological Association, 1976, for an essay on George Eliot.

WRITINGS: The Midland: A Venture in Literary Regionalism, University of Iowa Press, 1975. Contributor to magazines. Editor of *Danville Quarterly.*

WORK IN PROGRESS: A monograph on the function of whiskey in the fiction of William Faulkner; a collection of poems about children.

SIDELIGHTS: Reigelman writes that he became interested in the magazine *Midland* "after meeting its founder and editor, John T. Frederick. When I met him he was almost eighty, but still railing against the literary domination of New York. He interested me as an example of what a single, dedicated individual can accomplish in spurring a regional consciousness—which is what he did with his magazine fifty years ago.

"Nietzsche was right in thinking that philology was not only the most fascinating and compelling subject, but the key to all knowledge, if there is one. It is the shape of inidividual words and their ability to play tricks on us that keeps me interested in writing and in teaching literature."

* * *

REINHARZ, Jehuda 1944-

PERSONAL: Born August 1, 1944, in Haifa, Israel; came to the United States in 1961, naturalized citizen, 1966; son of Fred and Anita (Weigler) Reinharz; married Shulamit (a lecturer; maiden name, Rothschild). Education: Columbia University, B.S., 1967; Harvard University, M.A., 1968; Brandeis University, Ph.D., 1972. Office: Department of History, University of Michigan, Ann Arbor, Mich. 48104.

CAREER: Hebrew College, Brookline, Mass., instructor in Jewish history, 1969-70; Brandeis University, Hiatt Institute, Jerusalem, Israel, instructor in Jewish history, autumn, 1970; University of Michigan, Ann Arbor, assistant professor, 1972-76, associate professor of history, 1976—, staff member of Center for Near Eastern and North African studies, 1972—. Instructor at Boston University, 1969-70, and Clark University, spring, 1972; visiting professor at Hiatt Institute, of Brandeis University, 1973; member of Leo Baeck Institute, 1968—.

MEMBER: Association for Jewish Studies (member of board of governors, 1974-77), Conference on Jewish Social Studies, World Union of Jewish Studies, American Historical Association. Awards, honors: Woodrow Wilson fellowship for research in Germany and Israel, 1970-71, 1973, 1975-76.

WRITINGS: (Contributor) Herbert A. Strauss, editor, Conference on Intellectual Policies in American Jewry, American Federation of Jews from Central Europe, 1972; (contributor) Geoffrey Wigoder, editor, Zionism, Keter Publishing House, 1973; (contributor) Michael A. Fishbane and Paul R. Flohr, editors, Texts and Studies: Essays in Honor of Nahum N. Glatzer, E. J. Brill, 1975; Fatherland or Promised Land?: The Dilemma of the German Jew, 1893-1914, University of Michigan Press, 1975; (editor) Letters and Papers of Chaim Weizmann, Volume IX (Reinharz is not associated with other volumes), Oxford University Press, in press. Contributor to Encyclopaedia Judaica. Contributor of articles and reviews to scholarly journals. Judaic editor of Choice, 1972—.

WORK IN PROGRESS: Editing and translating diaries of FranzRosenzweig; editor of volume in honor of Alexander Altmann, wtih Kalman Bland and Daniel Swetschinski, for Duke University Press; editing Passage to Modernity: A Documentary Study Guide to Modern Jewish History, with Paul Mendes-Flohr; editing A Documentary History of German Zionism, for Leo Baeck Institute; editing documents on Zionism in German-speaking countries for Documentary History of Zionism, edited by Israel Kolatt, Michael Heymann, and Gedalia Yogev; co-author of "From Relativism to Religious Faith: The Testimony of Franz Rosenzweig's Unpublished Diaries," to be included in Yearbook of the Leo Baeck Institute XXII, edited by Robert Weltsch and Arnold Paucker.

SIDELIGHTS: Reinharz is proficient in Hebrew, German, French, Yiddish, and Aramaic.

* * *

RENDLEMAN, Danny L(ee) 1945-

PERSONAL: Born November 25, 1945, in Flint, Mich.; son of William F. (a laborer) and Beatrice (Winn) Rendleman; married Alice M. Sanford (an elementary school teacher), January 26, 1970; children: Eliot Franklin. Education: Central Michigan University, student, 1963-67; University of Michigan, Flint, B.G.S., 1974; Goddard College, graduate study, 1976—. Home: 4382 Carrie St., Burton, Mich. 48509. Office: Department of English, University of Michigan, 1321 East Court St., Flint, Mich. 48503.

CAREER: University of Michigan, Flint, assistant to the director of the "Right to Read Project," 1974-75, instructional associate in English, 1975—. Member: National Council of Teachers of English, Rhetoric Society of America, Sigma Chi, Sigma Tau Delta. Awards, honors: Awards from International P.E.N., 1974, 1975.

WRITINGS—Poetry: Signals to the Blind, Ithaca House, 1972; The Winter Rooms, Ithaca House, 1975; Asylum, Red Hill Press, 1976.

Work anthologized in Unexpected, edited by Nadra Ballentine, Ballentine Press, 1976; The Third Coast: Contemporary Michigan Poetry, edited by Conrad Hilberry, Herbert Scott, and James Tipton, Wayne State University Press, 1976. Contributor of almost two hundred poems and of reviews to literary magazines, including Wormwood Review, Wisconsin Review, West Coast Poetry Review, Shore Review, and Rolling Stone.

WORK IN PROGRESS: Playing Dead, Desire, Camus, and Exchanging Breath, four books of poems.

* * *

RENFROE, Martha Kay 1938-
(M. K. Wren)

PERSONAL: Born June 5, 1938, in Amarillo, Tex.; daughter of Charles Albert (a geologist) and Katharyn (Miller) Renfroe. Education: Attended Amarillo Junior College, 1955, and Oklahoma City University, 1956; University of Oklahoma, B.F.A., 1961; additional study at Kansas City Art Institute, 1962, and University of Washington, Seattle, 1963. Residence: Otis, Ore.

CAREER: Hallmark Cards, Inc., Kansas City, Mo., designer, 1961-62; Cascade Artists Gallery, Lincoln City, Ore., permanent exhibitor, 1964—; novelist. Member: Authors Guild, Pacific Northwest Writers' Conference, Portland Art Museum, Willamette Writers.

WRITINGS—All novels; under pseudonym M. K. Wren: Curiosity Didn't Kill the Cat, Doubleday, 1973; A Multitude of Sins, Doubleday, 1975; Oh, Bury Me Not (mystery), Doubleday, 1976.

WORK IN PROGRESS: The Phoenix, a science fiction novel.

SIDELIGHTS: Martha Kay Renfroe writes that she is "an artist for whom writing was a sideline that got out of hand. Began studying painting at age ten, bachelor's degree in fine arts with major in sculpture (too expensive to pursue outside an institution) and painting, by which I still make part of my living. Interest in writing paralleled art, beginning about twelve." Her work has been exhibited at museums, galleries, and in private collections in Kansas, Missouri, Oklahoma, Texas, Oregon, and Washington.

RENO, Marie R(oth)

PERSONAL: Born in Sewickley, Pa.; daughter of John Linford (an engineer) and Marie (a teacher; maiden name, Roth) Reno. Education: University of Illinois, B.S. Home: 520 East 81st St., New York, N.Y. 10028. Agent: Claire Smith, Harold Ober Associates, Inc., 40 East 49th St., New York, N.Y. 10017. Office: Pyramid Books, Harcourt, Brace, Jovanovich, Inc., 757 Third Ave., New York, N.Y. 10017.

CAREER: Literary Guild, Garden City, N.Y., began as associate editor, 1959, editor of Mystery Guild, 1966-72, managing editor, 1970-72, executive editor of Literary Guild, 1972-74; full time writer, 1974-76; Pyramid Books, New York, N.Y., editor-in-chief, 1976—. Member: Mystery Writers of America.

WRITINGS: (Editor) Treasury of Modern Mysteries, Doubleday, 1973; Final Proof (mystery novel), Harper, 1976.

WORK IN PROGRESS: From Manuscript to Murder (tentative title), a sequel to Final Proof.

*   *   *

RESHEVSKY, Samuel Herman 1911-

PERSONAL: Born November 29, 1911, in Ozarkow, Poland; came to United States, October, 1920; son of Jacob and Shaindel (Eibeschitz) Reshevsky; married Norma Mindick, June 24, 1941; children: Sylvia, Joel, Marcia. Education: University of Chicago, Ph.B., 1933. Home: 5 Hadassah Lane, Spring Valley, N.Y. 10977.

CAREER: Became International Grand Master and first professional chess player in United States, 1935—; worked as accountant during 1940's; investment analyst, 1957-74; television broadcaster and performer, 1972-74; writer on chess. Participant in Olympic games, 1950. Awards, honors: U.S. chess champion, 1936, 1938, 1940, 1942, 1946, 1970-71, tie, 1972; winner of National Chess Congress and Western Chess Federation titles, 1931; winner of numerous international tournaments, including eastern congress of Kent County Chess Association in Margate, 1935, British Chess Federation title, 1935, Pan American Chess Masters, 1945, Havana title, 1951, Stardust First National Open, 1967, Buenos Aires open, 1968.

WRITINGS: Learn Chess Fast!, McKay, 1947; Reshevsky on Chess, Chess Review, 1948, published as Reshevsky's Best Games of Chess, Dover, 1960; How Chess Games Are Won, Pitman, 1962; (annotator with others) Isaac Kashdan, editor, First Piatigorsky Cup, Ritchie, 1965; Reshevsky on the Fischer-Spassky Games, Arco, 1972; Reshevsky Teaches Chess, Arco, 1973; The Great Chess Upsets, Arco, 1975; The Art of Positional Play, McKay, 1976. Contributor of articles on chess to New York Herald Tribune, New York Times, Chess Review, Chess Life, and other periodicals.

SIDELIGHTS: Reshevsky learned chess moves at age four, and at five was a recognized prodigy. At age eight he drew a game with noted chess player Curt von Bardeleben, both playing blindfolded. A week after arriving in the United States, nine year old Reshevsky startled the chess world by defeating nineteen of West Point's best chess players in simultaneous exhibition. The same year Reshevsky played in New York, Philadelphia, Chicago, St. Louis and Los Angeles exhibitions. He attended the University of Chicago with financial help from philanthropist Julius Rosenwald.

In 1935 Reshevsky defeated former world champion Jose Capablanca at Margate. The following year he defeated fifteen opponents and won the United States Chess Championship which had been held by Frank Marhsall since 1909. Reshevsky later wrote: "Chess was, for me, a natural function, like breathing. It required no conscious effort."

Aside from chess, Reshevsky enjoys reading, ice skating, classical music, and singing. A former high school pitcher, he still avidly follows baseball and basketball.

*   *   *

RESTON, James (Barrett) 1909-

PERSONAL: Born November 3, 1909, in Scotland; came to the United States in 1920, naturalized citizen, 1927; son of James (a machinist) and Johanna (Irving) Reston; married Sarah Fulton (a journalist), December 24, 1935; children: Richard Fulton, James Barrett, Jr., Thomas Busey. Education: University of Illinois, B.A., 1932. Residence: Washington, D.C. Office: New York Times, 1920 L St. N.W., Washington, D.C. 20036.

CAREER: Associated Press (AP), sports writer in New York, N.Y., 1934-37, and London, England, 1937-39; New York Times, New York, N.Y., reporter in London, England, 1939-45, diplomatic correspondent in Washington, D.C., 1945-53, Washington bureau chief, 1953-64, associate editor in Washington, 1964-68, executive editor in New York City, 1968-69, vice-president in Washington, 1969-73, director of company, 1973—. Columnist, 1945-68, 1969—, and author of column "Washington," 1974—. Co-publisher of Vineyard Gazette.

AWARDS, HONORS: Pulitzer Prize, 1945, 1957, both for national reporting; awards from Overseas Press Club, 1949, 1951, 1955; George Polk Memorial Award from Long Island University, 1953; medal from University of Missouri, 1961; John Peter Zenger Award from University of Arizona, 1964; Elijah Parish Lovejoy fellowship from Colby College, 1974; chevalier of the Legion d'Honneur (France); Order of St. Olav (Norway); Order of Merit (Chile); Order of Leopold (Belgium); honorary degrees from Boston College, Brandeis University, Colgate University, Columbia University, Dartmouth College, Harvard University, University of Illinois, Kenyon College, University of Maryland, University of Michigan, New York University, Northeastern University, Oberlin College, Rutgers University, and University of Utah.

WRITINGS: Prelude to Victory, Knopf, 1942; Sketches in the Sand, Knopf, 1967; Artillery of the Press, Council on Foreign Relations, 1967.

*   *   *

REYNOLDS, David K(ent) 1940-

PERSONAL: Born September 28, 1940, in Dayton, Ohio; son of Charles K. (a security guard) and Marguerite (a secretary; maiden name, Worrell) Reynolds. Education: University of California, Los Angeles, B.A., 1964, M.A., 1965, Ph.D., 1969. Home: 11411 Venice Blvd., Los Angeles, Calif. 90066. Office: Department of Human Behavior, School of Medicine, University of Southern California, Los Angeles, Calif. 90033.

CAREER: University of California, Los Angeles, assistant professor of public health, 1970-71; University of Southern California, Los Angeles, assistant professor of human behavior, 1974—. Research anthropologist for Veterans Administration Central Research Unit, 1969-75; chief of Behavioral Analysis Division for Deputy Coroner's Branch of Los Angeles County Coroner's Office, 1971-73. Military service: U.S. Navy, radioman, 1958-61; served in Pacific Fleet.

MEMBER: American Anthropological Association, American Association of Suicidology, Society for Medical Anthropology, Sigma Xi. *Awards, honors:* National Science Foundation grant, 1969; Fulbright-Hays grant, 1973; National Institute of Mental Health grant, 1972-73.

WRITINGS: Morita Psychotherapy, University of California Press, 1976; (with Norman L. Farberow) *Suicide: Inside and Out,* University of California Press, 1976; (with Richard A. Kalish) *Death and Ethnicity: A Psychocultural Study,* University of Southern Califormia Gerontology Press, 1976; (with Farberow) *Endangered Hope,* University of California Press, in press.

WORK IN PROGRESS: The Quiet Therapies, for University of California Press; *From Discharge to Readmission: A Lifeway,* with Norman L. Farberow.

SIDELIGHTS: Reynolds writes: "I see man as much more rational (although not necessarily with awareness), flexible, and situationally responsive than he appears to be in many personality texts. On the mental hospital wards where I have done research this perspective of human nature more closely approximates that which is implicitly held by the nursing assistants rather than that held by the psychiatrists. I think this is because the nursing assistants' perspective is grounded firmly in continuous observation of everyday human behavior.

"My research has been both stimulating and personally rewarding. It has had practical impact on the individuals and institutions that opened themselves to study, and it can be said to have theoretical significance, as well. Although I enjoy the spontaneity and feedback of teaching (and my students seem to, as well), I find teaching most fruitful when sustained by ongoing research interests and activities."

* * *

REYNOLDS, Jonathan 1942-

PERSONAL: Born February 13, 1942, in Fort Smith, Ark.; son of Donald W. (a publisher) and Edith (Remick) Reynolds. *Education:* Denison University, B.F.A., 1965; London Academy of Music and Dramatic Art, graduate study, 1965-69. *Residence:* New York, N.Y. *Agent:* Flora Roberts, Inc., 65 East 55th St., New York, N.Y. 10022.

CAREER: Farm worker in Waitsfield, Vt., 1960; professional actor in New York, N.Y. and London, England, 1961-67; political organizer, 1968-69; writer, 1969—. *Awards, honors:* Rockefeller grant for play writing, 1976.

WRITINGS: Yanks 3 Detroit 0 Top of the Seventh (one-act play; first produced Off-Broadway at American Place Theatre, May 30, 1975), Dramatists Play Service, 1976; *Rubbers* (one-act play; first produced Off-Broadway at American Place Theatre, May 30, 1975), Dramatists Play Service, 1976.

Author of screenplays "Scramble Scramble," 1976, and "Nose Candy," 1976.

WORK IN PROGRESS: A play about opera; a play about a movie; a play about labor unions; a play about television news.

SIDELIGHTS: Reynolds told *CA:* "I'm lucky because I've always had just barely enough money not to have to write for television, which to me is analagous to an artist taking up house painting. I did write for television for a while, and the dedicated second-rateness of the people in the medium—producers, performers, writers, agents—makes me feel very comfortable and privileged to be in the theater. This may all change, but right now, the theatre is home."

REYNOLDS, Michael Shane 1937-

PERSONAL: Born April 1, 1937, in Kansas City, Mo.; son of Raymond (a geologist) and Theresa (Donnici) Reynolds; married Ann Eubanks (a college teacher), December 30, 1960; children: Dierdre Alisoun, Shauna Iseult. *Education:* Rice University, B.A., 1959; Universtiy of North Carolina, M.A., 1960; Duke University, Ph.D., 1970. *Home:* 909 Vance St., Raleigh, N.C. 27608. *Office:* Department of English, North Carolina State University, Raleigh, N.C. 27607.

CAREER: North Carolina State University, Raleigh, instructor, 1965-71, assistant professor, 1971-73, associate professor of English, 1974—. Member of board of directors, Theatre in the Park, 1972-75, and Raleigh Little Theatre, 1973-75. *Military service:* U.S. Navy, 1961-65; became lieutenant. *Member:* Modern Language Association of America. *Awards, honors:* National Endowment for the Humanities grants, 1974 and 1975.

WRITINGS: Hemingway's First War: The Making of A Farewell to Arms, Princeton University Press, 1976. Author of television script, "Nobody's Listening," for UNC-TV. Contributor of poetry to *Southern Poetry Review, Georgia Review, Poet Lore,* and *Carolina Quarterly.*

WORK IN PROGRESS: A literary biography of Hemingway, completion expected in 1981; *Something's Burning,* a book length set of poems studying the disintegration of a marriage which parallels the disintegration of the country; "Hemingway: The Cuban Years," a television script.

SIDELIGHTS: Reynolds told *CA* that important events in his life have included "flunking calculus in 1956, which assured I would not be a chemical engineer, and the Democratic convention in 1968, which broke my conservative mold. Important people: Radoslav Tsanoff and Alan D. McKillop—they made me think; my children—they set me free. Sailing and bass fishing are the only activities I would rather do than write. What I do best is research. It is the doing that is important, not the thing done. Hemingway was right: pursuit is happiness."

* * *

RHODES, Clifford Oswald 1911-

PERSONAL: Born April 12, 1911, in Leeds, England; son of Edward (a clergyman) and Clarice Evelyn (Ware) Rhodes; married Irene Betty Bowden, March 8, 1941; children: Susan Elizabeth Court, Juliet Diana, Helen Sylvia, Keith Oliver. *Education:* St. Peter's College, Oxford, M.A. (second class honors), 1934; Wycliffe Hall, Oxford, further study, 1937-38. *Home:* Rectory, Somerton, Oxfordshire OX5 4NF, England.

CAREER: Norfolk and Suffolk Journal, South Norfolk, England, editorial assistant, 1934-35; *East Anglian Daily Times,* Ipswich, England, editorial assistant, 1935-37; ordained clergyman of the Church of England, 1938; curate of Church of England in Wythenshawe, Manchester, England, 1938-40; *Record,* London, England, editor, 1946-49; *Church of England Newspaper,* London, editor, 1949-59; St. James's Church, Somerton, Oxfordshire, England, rector, 1958—. Director and secretary of Modern Churchmen's Union, 1954-60. Lecturer at St. Margaret's Church, Lothbury, 1954—. Licensed to preach by Oxford University, 1957. Account executive for Gilbert McAllister & Partners (public relations consultants), 1963-65. *Military service:* British Army, chaplain, 1940-45. *Awards, honors:* Named honorary chaplain of St. Bride's Church, 1952.

WRITINGS: The New Church in the New Age, Jenkins, 1958; Mass Communications and the Spirit of Man, Lindsey Press, 1959; The Awful Boss's Book, Wolfe, 1968; Let's Look at Musical Instruments and the Orchestra, Albert Whitman, 1968; (editor) Authority in a Changing Society, Constable, 1969, International Publications Service, 1971. Also author of The Necessity for Love: The History of Interpersonal Relations, 1972. Contributor to learned journals and to newspapers. Editor of Business, 1960-63; editorial director for Harcourt Kitchin & Partners, 1964.

AVOCATIONAL INTERESTS: The arts, country life.

* * *

RICE, Albert
See LEVENTHAL, Albert Rice

* * *

RICE, Anne 1941-

PERSONAL: Born October 4, 1941, in New Orleans, La.; daughter of Howard (a sculptor) and Katherine (Allen) O'Brien; married Stan Rice (a poet), October 14, 1961; children: Michele (deceased). Education: Texas Woman's University, student, 1959-60; San Francisco State College (now University), B.A., 1964, M.A., 1971; graduate study at University of California, Berkeley, 1969-70. Home: 2800 Claremont Blvd., Berkeley, Calif., 94705.

CAREER: Held a variety of jobs, sometimes two at a time, including waitress, cook, and insurance claims examiner. Member: Authors Guild. Awards, honors: Joseph Henry Jackson Fund, honorable mention, 1970.

WRITINGS: Interview with the Vampire, Knopf, 1976.

WORK IN PROGRESS: Research on the history of New Orleans for two novels, one concerning the gens de coleur libre and one concerning Irish immigrants who settled in New Orleans; a collection of surrealistic short stories.

SIDELIGHTS: Anne Rice told CA: "I was brought up a Catholic in New Orleans and the religion, atmosphere, and history of New Orleans have profoundly influenced my writing. Though Interview with the Vampire was a novel which included the supernatural as fact, I doubt that I will deal with the supernatural again in my fiction. My present interests are much connected with people and times in the 19th century. However I do not see myself as an historical novelist. I am concerned with character, with the soul, with the search in all ages for a rich and meaningful life. Though I do not consciously think of it as an intention, I know that much of my writing is concerned with the problems of sexual identity.

"For me writing is the grand passion, the activity which makes my life worthwhile. For fifteen years I have been married to Stan Rice who is a poet . . . and I know that I have been deeply influenced by Stan's writing and his attitudes. We live perpetually in the atmosphere of our work, a world of clicking typewriters, booklined walls, passionate conversation about this person, that idea, this theme. It is a rich and marvelous life."

AVOCATIONAL INTERESTS: Traveling, ancient Greek history, archaeology, social history since the beginning of recorded time, old movies on television, and she adds, "I enjoy going to boxing matches—am fascinated by performers of all kinds, and by sports which involve one man against another or against a force."

RICE, Charles L(ynvel) 1936-

PERSONAL: Born December 12, 1936, in Chandler, Okla. Education: Baylor University, B.A., 1959; Southern Baptist Theological Seminary, B.D., 1962; Union Theological Seminary, S.T.M., 1963; Duke University, Ph.D., 1967. Office: Theological School, Drew University, Madison, N.J. 07940.

CAREER: Minister of the United Church of Christ; pastor of churches in Chapel Hill, N.C., 1967-68, and Durham, N.C., 1970; Duke University, Durham, N.C., instructor in Homiletics, 1963-67; Salem College, Winston-Salem, N.C., visiting assistant professor of religion and chaplain, 1967-68; Federal Theological Seminary, Alice, South Africa, tutor in theology, 1968; Duke University, visiting assistant professor of American Christianity, 1969-70; Drew University, Madison, N.J., associate professor of homiletics and lecturer in theology and literature, 1970—. Voight Lecturer at McKendree College, 1976; adjunct professor at Princeton Theological Seminary and Union Theological Seminary, 1975-76. Member: American Academy of Religion, American Academy of Homiletics, American Association of University Professors.

WRITINGS: Interpretation and Imagination, Fortress, 1970; (with J. Louis Martyn) Proclamation: Aids for Interpreting the Lessons of the Church Year, Fortress, 1975. Editor of Word and Witness.

WORK IN PROGRESS: A textbook on homiletics, with Edmund A. Steimle and Morris Niedenthal.

* * *

RICHARDS, Alun 1929-

PERSONAL: Born October 27, 1929, in Pontypridd, Wales; married Barbara Helen Howden; children: three sons, one daughter. Education: Earned Diploma in Social Science and Diploma in Education at University College of Wales. Home: 326 Mumbles Rd., Swansea, Wales. Agent: Curtis Brown Ltd., 1 Craven Hill, London, England.

CAREER: Probation officer in London, England, 1954-55; schoolmaster in Cardiff, Wales, 1955-66; writer, 1966—. Military service: Royal Navy, instructor, 1949-53; became lieutenant. Member: Writers Guild of Great Britain (chairman in Wales), Savage Club.

WRITINGS: The Elephant You Gave Me (novel), M. Joseph, 1963; The Home Patch, M. Joseph, 1966; A Woman of Experience, Dent, 1969; Dai Country (stories), M. Joseph, 1973; Home to an Empty House, Gomer Press, 1974; (editor) Penguin Welsh Short Stories, Penguin, 1975; The Former Miss Merthyr Tydfil: Stories, M. Joseph, 1976; (editor) Collected Plays, Gomer Press, 1976; Ennal's Point (novel), M. Joseph, 1977; (editor) Penguin Sea Stories, Penguin, 1977.

Plays: "The Big Breaker" (three-act), first produced in Coventry, England, at Belgrade Theatre, 1963; "The Victualler's Ball" (three-act), first produced in Leatherhead, England, at Leatherhead Repertory Theatre, 1967; "The Snow Dropper" (two-act), first produced at Hampstead Theatre, 1973.

Also author of television plays, including "Ready for the Glory," "Albinos in Black," and "The Straight and Narrow." Work represented in anthology, Pick of Today's Stories, edited by John Pudney, Putnam, 1962.

WORK IN PROGRESS: Television scripts, "The Onedin Line," "Orson Welles Great Mysteries," and "Henry VII," for British Broadcasting Corp. (BBC)-Television;

adaptations of work by Simenon, Wells, and Somerset Maugham.

AVOCATIONAL INTERESTS: Angling, oceanography, travel.

* * *

RICHARDS, Arlene Kramer 1935-

PERSONAL: Born June 24, 1935, in New York, N.Y.; daughter of Emanuel and Edith (Burstein) Kramer; married Arnold David Richards (a psychoanalyst), March 21, 1953; children: Stephen Louis, Rebecca Dawn, Tamar Beth. *Education:* University of Chicago, A.B., 1953; graduate study at Brooklyn College (now of the City University of New York), 1955-56, and Washburn University, 1960-61; Columbia University, M.A., 1965, Ed.D., 1969. *Home:* 50 East 89th St., New York, N.Y. 10028. *Office:* 40 East 89th St., New York, N.Y. 10028.

CAREER: Substitute teacher in public schools in New York City, 1956-60; Washburn University, Topeka, Kan., instructor in reading and study skills, 1961-63; College of William and Mary (branch), Petersburg, Va., instructor in reading and study skills at Richard Bland College, 1963-64; Columbia University, New York City, assistant supervisor of Reading Clinic at Teachers College, 1965-67; Center for Urban Education, New York City, tester, 1967; Centenary College for Women, Hackettstown, N.J., instructor in reading and study skills, 1967-68; Columbia University, Teachers College, associate project director at Center for Research and Education in American Liberties, 1968-70, instructor in educational psychology, 1969-70; New York University, New York City, adjunct assistant professor, 1970-71, associate professor of psychology, 1970-71; psychologist with private practice in New York City, 1971—. Remedial therapist at Northside Center for Child Development, 1967-70; educational therapist at Mount Sinai Hospital, 1971-72; consultant to White House Conference on Children and Youth.

MEMBER: International Reading Association, American Psychological Association, American Educational Research Association, National Council on Measurement in Education, New York State Psychological Association, Pi Lambda Theta, Alpha Omega Alpha.

WRITINGS: Learning to Participate by Taking Part in Learning, Center for Research and Education in American Liberties, Teachers College, Columbia University, 1969; *A Cross-Sectional Study of Schools in Four Communities,* Center for Research and Education in American Liberties, Teachers College, Columbia University, 1969; *Moral Development in Adolescence,* Center for Research and Education in American Liberties, Teachers College, Columbia University, 1970; *Civic Education: Urban and Suburban,* Center for Research and Education in American Liberties, Teachers College, Columbia University, 1970; *Schools with Black Students,* Center for Research and Education in American Liberties, Teachers College, Columbia University, 1970; (contributor) John P. DeCecco, editor, *The New Educational Psychology: A Book of Readings,* Holt, 1970; (contributor) DeCecco, editor, *Introduction to Educational Psychology,* CRM Books, 1972; (contributor) John P. DeCecco, editor, *The Regeneration of the School,* Holt, 1972; (with DeCecco) *Growing Pains: Uses of High School Conflict,* Aberdeen Press, 1974; (with Irene Willis) *How to Get It Together When Your Parents Are Coming Apart,* McKay, 1976. Contributor to *Standard Reference Encyclopedia* and to psychology, psychiatry, and sociology journals.

WORK IN PROGRESS: A psychological study of friendship; a study of identity formation in adolescence among Jewish youth.

SIDELIGHTS: Dr. Richards told *CA:* "I am interested in the interaction between cognition and affects; between thought and feeling. While my most current research and thinking has to do with adolescents and their development, I have always been interested in how people of all ages work out their views of the world to correspond with their feelings. The despondent person picks out sombre interests, pursues difficult or impossible tasks, chooses to do what can give little satisfaction. The optimistic one finds easier jobs, more fun, more friends. In my current writing, I am attempting to help adolescents find ways of coping with their world. In my practise as a psychologist, I try to help patients shed their guilt and shame so that they are no longer despondent and can allow themselves satisfaction."

AVOCATIONAL INTERESTS: Bicycling, poetry, cooking, travel.

* * *

RICHARDSON, Don(ald MacNaughton) 1935-

PERSONAL: Born June 23, 1935, in Prince Edward Island, Canada; son of Henry George and Harriet Ruth Richardson; married Carol Joy Soderstrom (a registered nurse), August 20, 1960; children: Stephen Laird, Shannon Douglas, Paul Andrew, Valerie Ruth. *Education:* Prairie Bible Institute, diploma, 1957; University of Washington, Seattle, student, summer, 1961. *Home address:* c/o Mrs. Henry Richardson, 1148 Union Rd., Victoria, British Columbia, Canada V8P 2J3. *Office:* Regions Beyond Missionary Union, 8102 Elberon Ave., Philadelphia, Pa. 19111.

CAREER: Pastor in Langford, British Columbia, 1957-60; Regions Beyond Missionary Union, Philadelphia, Pa., Protestant missionary, 1960—. Lecturer in Stone Age cultures of Irian Jaya, and on methods of cross-cultural communication with them.

WRITINGS: Peace Child, Regal Books (Glendale, Calif.), 1974. Also author of privately printed books, *A Short Biography of Henry Martyn,* 1957, *A Dictionary of the Sawi Language,* 1974, and *The New Testament in Sawi,* 1974. Contributor to *Reader's Digest.*

WORK IN PROGRESS: Lords of the Earth, a study of the cannibal Yali tribe of Irian Jaya; *The Seven Thunders of Truth; Skulls for Their Pillows,* translations of pre-Christian legends of the Sawi tribe of Irian Jaya.

SIDELIGHTS: Richardson writes: "My fascination is with the diversity of human cultures, and particularly with solutions to problems of cross-cultural communication. I am especially intrigued by 'redemptive analogies'—elements of pagan cultures which seem to anticipate Christian truth, and if appropriated, facilitate its entrance. On a larger scale, I am fascinated by the way Christian truth, pagan religions, and modern man's scientific discoveries anticipate the existence of a philosophical unified field. I believe I have discovered that unified field. That is what *The Seven Thunders of Truth* is about." Richardson assisted in the script preparation and direction of the film "Peace Child," based on his book, and performed in it as well.

Following a major earthquake (late summer, 1976) in Irian Jaya, the former Dutch New Guinea, unsympathetic criticism by the press of missionary activity occasioned Richardson's defense in an open letter to the *Washington Post.* The following is an excerpt.

"There were other reasons why the missionaries had to go in as soon as they could. History has taught them that even the most isolated minority cultures must eventually be overwhelmed by the commercial and political expansion of majority peoples. Naive academics . . . may protest that the world's remaining miners, hunters, military leaders, roadbuilders, art collectors, tourists, and drug peddlers aren't listening. They are going in anyway. Often to destroy. Cheat. Exploit. Victimize. Corrupt. Taking, and giving little other than diseases for which primitives have no immunity. And no medical help. That is why, since the turn of the century, more than ninety tribes have become extinct in Brazil alone. Many other Latin American, African, and Asian countries also show a similar high extinction rate for their primitive minorities. Primitives are, in fact, vanishing more quickly than the world's endangered animal species. A grim toll of five or six tribes per year is probably a conservative worldwide estimate.

"We missionaries don't want the same fate to befall these magnificent tribes in Irian Jaya. So we risk our lives to get to them first. Because we believe we are more sympathetic agents of change than profit-hungry commercialists. Like our predecessor John Sargent, who in 1796 launched a program which saved the Mohican tribe from extinction, and like our colleagues in Brazil who saved the WaiWai from a similar fate just one generation ago, we believe we know how to precondition tribes in Irian Jaya for survival in the modern world.

"The question 'Should anyone go in?' is obsolete, because obviously someone *will*. It has been replaced by a more practical question: 'Will the most sympathetic persons get there first?' To make the shock of coming out of the Stone Age as easy as possible. To see that tribals gain new ideals to replace those they must lose in order to survive. To teach them the national language so they can defend themselves in civil disputes with 'civilizados.' And yet produce literature in their own language so it will not be forgotten. To teach them the value of money, so that unscrupulous traders cannot easily cheat them. And better yet, set some of them up in business, so that commerce in their areas will not fall entirely into the hands of outsiders. To care for them when epidemics sweep through, or when earthquakes strike. And better yet, train some of them as nurses and doctors to carry on when we are gone.

"We do not go in as parasites. We go in as paracletes. Ombudsmen who help clashing cultures understand each other. Advocates, not only of spiritual truth, but also of physical survival."

BIOGRAPHICAL/CRITICAL SOURCES: Christian Herald, March, 1976.

*   *   *

RICHARDSON, Midge Turk   1930-

PERSONAL; Born March 26, 1930, in Los Angeles, Calif.; daughter of Charles A. (in law and contract division of Los Angeles city school system) and Marie (Lindekin) Turk; married Hamilton F. Richardson (in investments), February 8, 1974. *Education:* Immaculate Heart College, Los Angeles, Calif., M.A., 1956; also attended University of Pittsburgh and University of California, Santa Barbara. *Politics:* Democrat. *Religion:* Roman Catholic. *Home:* 920 Park Ave., PH-B, New York, N.Y. 10028. *Agent:* Sterling Lord Agency, 660 Madison Ave., New York, N.Y. 10021. *Office:* *Seventeen,* 850 Third Ave., New York, N.Y. 10022.

CAREER: Member of Roman Catholic women's religious

order, Sisters of the Immaculate Heart of Mary (I.H.M.), Los Angeles, Calif., 1948-66; high school principal in California, 1959-66; New York University, New York City, assistant dean, School of the Arts, 1966-67; *Glamour,* New York City, college editor, 1967-74; *Coed,* New York City, editor-in-chief, 1974-75; *Seventeen,* New York City, executive editor, 1975—.

WRITINGS: The Buried Life: A Nun's Journey, World Publishing, 1971; *Gordon Parks: A Biography for Children,* Crowell, 1971. Author of "Our Young People," a film for NBC-Television.

BIOGRAPHICAL/CRITICAL SOURCES: New York Times, Februray 5, 1970; *New York Post,* July 29, 1972; *New York News,* June 2, 1974.

*   *   *

RICHLER, Mordecai   1931-

PERSONAL: Born January 27, 1931, in Montreal, Quebec, Canada; son of Moses Isaac and Lily (Rosenberg) Richler; married Florence Wood, 1960; children: Daniel, Noah, Emma, Martha, Jacob. *Education:* Attended Sir George Williams University, 1949-51. *Religion:* Jewish. *Home and office:* 218 Edgehill Rd., Westmount, Quebec, Canada. *Agent:* Monica McCall, International Creative Management, 40 West 57th St., New York, N.Y. 10019; (for films) William Morris Agency, 1350 Avenue of the Americas, New York, N.Y. 10019.

CAREER: Author and screenwriter. Left Canada in 1951; free-lance writer in Paris, France, 1952-53, and in London, England, 1954-72; returned to Canada, 1972—. Writer in residence, Sir George Williams University, 1968-69; visiting professor, Carleton University, 1972-74. Member of editorial board, Book of the Month Club, 1972—. *Awards, honors:* President's medal for nonfiction, University of Western Ontario, 1959; Canadian Council junior art fellowships, 1959 and 1960, senior arts fellowship, 1967; Guggenheim Foundation creative writing fellowship, 1961; *Paris Review* humor prize, 1967, for section from *Cocksure;* Canadian Governor-General's award for literature, 1969, for *Cocksure;* Canadian Governor-General's award and London Jewish Chronicle literature award, both 1972, both for *St. Urbain's Horseman;* Berlin Film Festival Golden Bear, Academy Award nomination, and Screenwriters Guild of America award for best comedy, all 1974, all for the screenplay, "The Apprenticeship of Duddy Kravitz"; Canadian Bookseller's award for best children's book and Canadian Librarian's medal, both 1976, both for *Jacob Two-Two Meets the Hooded Fang.*

WRITINGS—Novels: The Acrobats, Putnam, 1954; *Son of a Smaller Hero,* Collins (Toronto), 1955, Paperback Library, 1965; *A Choice of Enemies,* Collins, 1957; *The Apprenticeship of Duddy Kravitz,* Little, Brown, 1959; *The Incomparable Atuk,* McClelland & Stewart, 1963, published as *Stick Your Neck Out,* Simon & Schuster, 1963; *Cocksure,* Simon & Schuster, 1968; *St. Urbain's Horseman* (Literary Guild featured alternate), Knopf, 1971.

Other: *Hunting Tigers under Glass: Essays and Reports,* McClelland & Stewart, 1969; *The Street: Stories,* McClelland & Stewart, 1969, New Republic, 1975; (editor) *Canadian Writing Today* (anthology), Peter Smith, 1970; *Shoveling Trouble* (essays), McClelland & Stewart, 1973; *Notes on an Endangered Species and Others* (essays), Knopf, 1974; *Jacob Two-Two Meets the Hooded Fang* (juvenile), Knopf, 1975.

Screenplays: (With Nicholas Phipps) "No Love for Johnnie," Embassy, 1962; "Life at the Top," Royal International, 1965; (with Nicholas Phipps) "Young and Willing," Universal, 1965 (released in England as "The Wild and the Willing"); "The Apprenticeship of Duddy Kravitz" (adapted from own novel), Paramount, 1974.

Contributor to Canadian, U.S., and British periodicals.

WORK IN PROGRESS: A novel, *Gursky Was Here.*

SIDELIGHTS: "*St. Urbain's Horseman* is a delight," wrote Peter Corodimas. "It moves at breakneck speed with nothing slowing it down, and it contains a wild assortment of characters who all miraculously contribute to the momentum of the book. Characters come and go; scenes shift and explode into other scenes, and all the time the novel holds together. A remarkable job of writing. At times the obscenity and the scatological images really seem too much, but Richler has an amazing ability to transform sordid material into first-rate satire."

Mordecai Richler is a rare case in literary criticism. Critics all agree that he is an extremely talented writer. Anthony Burgess said *Cocksure* was so good, he wished he'd written it himself. Jonathan Yardley called Richler one of the finest writers around anywhere—and yet amazingly, Yardley reported a local bookstore had none of Richler's books, and what's more, the proprietor's response to a query was—"Mordecai *Who?*" Yardley explained: "The trouble is, Richler exists in a peculiar literary limbo: He is a Canadian. As he has pointed out in some of his essays, his fellow countrymen either take their native writers too seriously (especially, it seems, the bad ones) or not seriously at all. Readers in other countries, the United States in particular, seem persuaded that nothing of value can issue from a nation that appears condemned to occupy a perpetual (and distant) second place on the North American continent." Richler characteristically sees this as basically a Canadian problem: "I've never felt there's any stigma attached to Canadian work per se—but a lot of artists there with chips on their shoulders will assume that if it's Canadian, it's not going to sell. Canadians seem to prefer failure to success—failure is somehow more reassuring."

Richler grew up in Montreal on St. Urbain Street, a Jewish no-man's-land between the French Canadians on the east and the English on the west. Neil Compton, who spent part of his youth on that west side, commented: "Understandably, the residents of St. Urbain St. felt little urge to identify with either of our 'two founding cultures.' The intellectual and cultural capital to which they looked was not Ottawa, Quebec, Moscow, London or Tel Aviv, but New York. Unlike Canada, the United States seemed to offer Jews the possibility of social and political advancement with little apparent risk of lost identity." This conflict with Canadian culture and the stifling creative atmosphere caused Richler to leave Canada in 1951, "foolishly convinced that merely by quitting the country, I could put my picayune past behind me." Many other Canadian writers have done likewise, so many in fact that when Richler's anthology of Canadian writing appeared in 1970, Phyllis Grosskurth remarked: "If *Canadian Writing Today* makes good reading it is because a surprising amount of good work is being turned out by Canadians—even if it is being written somewhere else."

Instead of going to New York, where Compton pointed out the young Canadian Jew felt his affinities, Richler went to England. "Unpublished, but hopeful, I sailed for England, fabled England, all my possessions fitting neatly into one cabin trunk and, in my breast pocket, a letter from the managing editor of the now defunct *Montreal Herald,* saying I had been loyal, industrious and (the clincher, this) a sober employe." He spent two years of his expatriation in Paris and the next eighteen in London, writing for such magazines as the *New Statesman, Spectator, Observer, Punch,* and occasionally doing a film or television script.

The labyrinthine influences of Richler's origins and working environments were surveyed by the *Times Literary Supplement.* In a review of *Hunting Tigers Under Glass,* he was called a writer from numerous wry angles, "some of them coming from Mr. Richler's intelligently common sense radical view of two forms of provincialism he knows very well indeed, the Jewish and the Canadian; and some from the fact that for a Jewish novelist he has taken the unpredictable tack of finding his cosmopolis not in New York but in London. More still come from the fact that the pieces address heterodox reading-publics; some were directed at American general audiences (*Holiday*), some for American intellectual audiences (*New York Review of Books*), some for Jewish-American intellectual audiences (*Commentary*), some for Anglo-American intellectual audiences (*Encounter*), and some for English readers (*London Magazine*). Experts in tone will be interested in determining the differences and the complexity of Mr. Richler's consequent culture."

In a review of that same collection, which appeared while Richler still lived in England, the *New Statesman* said: "Mordecai Richler is an exile twice over. A stranger in Canada because he's a Jew, he's now a stranger in Britain because he's Canadian; and both personae seem capable of irritating him to the point of sneering glibness, a matter of naming writers with funny names or reprinting silly quotes from unimportant Canadian magazines. This collection of bits and pieces is best when he uses his sharp mind rather than his sharp tongue; which he does, particularly, in a delicate, sensitive record of a trip to Israel. Richler the novelist can be heard here, a better man than Richler the witty journalist."

Although he was an exile twice over, the *Times Literary Supplement* went on to discover the remnant of a provincialism, lingering along after Richler left Canada. "Mr. Richler is a writer of ironies, detachments and comic involvements rather than a voice of exile or anomie; but one can see in his writings why the Jewish writer or intellectual might have gone a good deal deeper into self-doubt. In a critically sharp review of Malamud's *The Fixer,* he points out the way in which the Jewish writer tends, his modern experience being now pretty well on file in the Jewish-American efflorescence of the 1950s, to hark back to origins, to the *shtetl* or the archetypal pogrom. Mr. Richler himself holds to the fascination of ordinary origins, and comes out as a grand supraprovincial. That, perhaps, is why he takes as the real clue to the meaning of the *Superman* comic strip—which turns Clark Kent, the provincial square, into an invincible hero—the fact that it was invented by a Canadian Jew."

That perhaps, may also be why, as Marian Engel said: "His first two books, *The Acrobats* and *Son of a Smaller Hero,* were serious, and important to Canada. It was he who first told us how it was to be a Jew here, how there were signs on Montreal Island, 'No dogs or Jews allowed,' He was our angry young man and a good one."

Canadians may like Mordecai Richler just to spite him. He makes no attempt to hide any of his dislike of many things Canadian. In his essays and articles he has taken on Canadian nationalism, Canadian publishing and filmmaking, the new National Arts Center in Ottawa, even the Governor-

General, as well as the United States and the Jewish religion. For example, here is what he says of Canada's only newsmagazine: "A supernationalist bore, the sort of booster's publication that could happily be issued by a national chamber of commerce. What with its endlessly lyrical color photographs of Canadian riverbanks, wheat fields, and barns, there is little in it but patriotism to detain any demanding reader." Of religious intermarriage: "Look at it this way: there can be no equal opportunity in Canada so long as one group raises Einsteins like rabbits and another still has to count on its fingers." Of Canadian nationalists and American corporations: "The pity is that the nationalists, if they would only stay clear of cultural matters, obviously beyond them, do, indeed, have a strong case. We are too much subject to the whims of multinational corporations, largely American-owned. It would be simply spiffy if we owned more of Canada, say, half." Of a former Governor-General's wife: "A case of life improving on the art of Grant Wood. She was born to chaperone the dance in the small-town high-school gym." As David Pryce-Jones has said: "Mr. Richler can hold his own against anybody. A stuntman with language, a master of the tiny illuminating but embarrassing moment."

Though Canadians may have ambiguous feelings about his nonfiction, they don't question the quality of his fiction. *The Apprenticeship of Duddy Kravitz* has been called a coming-of-age classic and is taught in many Canadian schools. The screen adaptation has become the highest grossing film in Canadian history and has been very important in giving the industry an international face. However, Richler remains skeptical. "Just wait—if 'Duddy Kravitz' continues to do business, particularly in the United States, the Canadian critics will start doing 'reexaminations' and get all huffy because there are no Canadian actors in it."

Some Canadian critics are puzzled by the motives behind his fiction. They ask why Richler, claiming allegiance to a country so unsure of itself, works with satire and parody?. . . Why, in a country struggling to gain acceptance in world literature, does he deliberately choose to work in a currently unappreciated genre? Some critics propose that traditional forms of fiction are possible only in a society with a long established national identity. Therefore, Canadian authors, like Richler, who are seriously searching for a truly individual identity, should naturally be unable to use these traditional forms. Phyllis Grosskuth on the other hand points out, it is not inability but rather choice. She believes the Canadians are suspicious of traditional forms. "Here," she says, "we may be approaching one of the basic strengths of Canadian writers—a wry, skeptical view of life. In this regard, Neil Compton in 'Broadcasting and Canadian Culture' makes some pertinent comments on the irony and parody which he believes is the closest we come to a native popular art. 'Though Canadians may lack a strong identity,' he writes, 'they do not allow this to inhibit them in deflating fraud or pomposity.' The sustaining humour of all Richler's work is directed at the self-important and the humourless." Grosskuth goes on to predict: "Sensing that they are out of the mainstream, still pursuing an elusive identity, our writers may turn increasingly to the study of marginal men, figures who hover on the outskirts of society. The lost, the damned and the hopeless. . . ."

With the exception of Jake in *St. Urbain's Horseman*, Richler's main characters are damned. Some critics find the uncomfortable feeling of this satire ultimately threatening. They contend Richler becomes obscene when his work builds nothing more than self-disgust, because positive solu-

tions or actions are not advanced. Philip Toynbee suggests this criticism may be a natural result of critics sensing indecision on the author's part. "A general weakness of this funny and memorable book [*Cocksure*] is that it is quite impossible to detect the moral platform on which Mr. Richler is standing and from which his darts are launched. Nobody wants a satirist to make a solemn declaration of faith, but that declaration is implied by the best satirists in everything they write. . . . The weakness is a serious one, and before Mr. Richler writes a really good satire he will have to learn not only what he hates but where he hates it from." After reading *St. Urbain's Horseman*, Pryce-Jones agreed, and added: "Mr. Richler sees how the bad old days have become the bright and shiny present, and he is not sure whether to laugh or cry about it. The novel in which eventually he decides will be one worth waiting for."

Neil Compton proposes these critics miss the unique point of view in Richler's writing. He believes that the value in Richler's satire "is revealed in the moral conservation which distinguishes his handling of the immigrant ghetto myth from the ethically more reckless versions of such American writers as Paul Goodman, Bernard Malamud, Leslie Fiedler and Philip Roth. (Interestingly enough, the Montreal-born Saul Bellow resembles Richler in this respect.) Never having been taken in by the dangerous promises of the American Dream, Richler has not been tempted by any of the modish extremisms which the current wave of disillusion is producing. His black and savage humour stems from a thoroughly traditional sense of outrage. A Jewish Diogenes, he is still unsuccessfully looking for honest men, but remains an acute encyclopedist of hypocrisy and self-deception (including his own)."

Richler would probably resent the plea for a larger moral conscience in his work. During the politically active sixties he rejected a similar plea. "I do resent any proposition that presupposes a larger conscience for writers or artists. We are only writers or artists when we work at it, and the rest of the time we're citizens (husbands, fathers, tax-payers), no less boring or worthy than other middle- and working-class people. As such, we should be expected to protest in proportion to our political conscience, unevenly spread among artists as it is among miners, dentists and shoe salesmen. . . . About instinct and integrity. Alas, these qualities are more commonplace among artists than talent. Those Hollywood screenwriters who said no to McCarthy, for instance, had decidely more integrity than Faulkner, more honour than Hemingway and others who remained conspicuously silent in a shameful era, but they were also a clearly untalented lot. If I continue to respect the *political* integrity of the Hollywood Ten and others, I still cannot read them with pleasure as I do Faulkner and Hemingway."

When a reviewer for *Newsweek* asked, "How shall we judge 'pornography' when it is bright, authentically witty and imaginative and knocks you cockeyed sprawling in the aisles?," it became obvious Richler had created a definite dilemma for many critics who saw and admired the creative ability in *Cocksure,* but couldn't go along with some of the coarse nature of the satire. Anthony Burgess protested that Richler was only mirroring the society about which he was writing: "But nothing is dwelt on with depraved fascination: we are conducted so rapidly through the contemporary sewers that the trip seems positively bracing. Anyway, the obscenity belongs not to the book but to the world it lacerates. But, please remember, it's a funny book, gorgeously so."

Ironically, Richler returned to Canada in 1972, because he

felt his experience in England was becoming provincial. "Everyone I knew was in the arts, and I was closing myself off into a very dry and sheltered existence. I just don't have the kind of imagination to propel myself from one novel to the next without refueling with new and different experiences." He also added, "I worry about being away so long from—well, the roots of my discontent."

In addition to *The Apprenticeship of Duddy Kravitz,* Richler's book for children, *Jacob Two-Two Meets the Hooded Fang* has been filmed. Film rights have been sold for both *Stick Your Neck Out* and *Cocksure.*

BIOGRAPHICAL/CRITICAL SOURCES—Articles: *Life,* March 15, 1968, July 9, 1971; *London Magazine,* May, 1968, August, 1968; *Saturday Night,* May, 1968, July, 1969, October, 1970; *New York Times Book Review,* May 5, 1968; *Times Literary Supplement,* January 23, 1969; *New Statesman,* January 31, 1969; *Best Sellers,* August 1, 1971; *Washington Star-News,* August 13, 1974; *Miami Herald,* September 22, 1974; *Harper's,* June, 1975.

Books: George Woodcock, *Mordecai Richler,* McClelland & Stewart, 1970; G. David Sheps, *Mordecai Richler,* Ryerson, 1970; Robert Fulford, *Mordecai Richler,* Coles, 1971; *Contemporary Literary Criticism,* Gale, Volume 3, 1975, Volume 5, 1976.

*   *   *

RICHTER, Hans 1888-1976

1888—February 1, 1976; German-born American painter, film director, and author of a book on the Dada movement. Obituaries: *New York Times,* February 3, 1976; *Newsweek,* February 16, 1976; *Time,* February 16, 1976.

*   *   *

RICKEY, George Warren 1907-

PERSONAL: Born June 6, 1907, in South Bend, Ind.; son of Walter J. and Grace (Landon) Rickey; married Edith Leighton, May 24, 1947; children: Stuart Ross, Philip J. L. *Education:* Balliol College, Oxford, B.A., 1929, M.A. (honors), 1941; also attended Ruskin School of Drawing and Fine Art, Oxford, 1928-29, Academie Andre L'hote and Academie Moderne, 1929-30, New York University, 1945-46, State University of Iowa, 1947, and Chicago Institute of Design, 1948-49; also studied privately. *Religion:* Episcopal. *Home address:* Route 2, East Chatham, N.Y. 12060.

CAREER: Groton School, Groton, Conn., instructor in European history, 1930-33; *Newsweek,* New York, N.Y., copy reader in editorial department, 1936; Olivet College, Olivet, Mich., artist-in-residence commissioned for mural, 1937-39; Kalamazoo Institute of Arts, Kalamazoo, Mich., director, 1939-40; Knox College, Galesburg, Ill., artist-in-residence, 1940-41; Muhlenberg College, Allentown, Pa., professor of art, 1941-48, and head of department, 1941, 1946-48; Indiana University, Bloomington, associate professor of design, 1949-55; Tulane University, New Orleans, La., professor of art, 1955-62, head of department, 1955-59; Rensselaer Polytechnic Institute, Troy, N.Y., professor of art, 1961-65; became full-time sculptor, 1965—. Visiting professor at University of California, Santa Barbara, 1960, regents lecturer, 1967; visiting artist at Dartmouth College, 1966. Has had solo exhibitions all over the world; work is represented in permanent collections in the United States and abroad, including Museum of Modern Art, Tate Gallery, Corcoran Gallery of Art, and National Collection of Fine Arts, and in private collections; much of his work in the

United States and Europe has been commissioned; also commissioned to do sculpture for Expo in Osaka, Japan, 1970.

MEMBER: College Art Association, National Institute of Arts and Letters. *Awards, honors:* Guggenheim fellowship, 1960-62; American Institute of Architects fine arts medal, 1972; sculpture award from Indiana Arts Commission, 1975; received honorary degrees from Knox College, Williams College, and Union College.

WRITINGS: (Contributor) *Art and Artist,* University of California Press, 1956; *Constructivism: Origins and Evolution,* Braziller, 1967; (contributor) Gyorgy Kepes, editor, *Contempory Art, 1942-1972,* Praeger, 1973. Contributor to art journals.

BIOGRAPHICAL/CRITICAL SOURCES: New Yorker, October 21, 1961; *Time,* November 4, 1966.

*   *   *

RIES, Lawrence R(obert) 1940-

PERSONAL: Born October 6, 1940, in Newport, Ky.; son of Daniel E. (a bartender) and Mary (a city clerk; maiden name, Barker) Ries; married Madelaine Ice (an education administrator), December 30, 1965; children: Christopher, Jessica. *Education:* St. Michael's College, Conesus, N.Y., A.A., 1961; Villa Madonna College, B.A., 1963; Southern Illinois University, M.A., 1965, Ph.D., 1971. *Home:* 179 Whitehall Rd., Albany, N.Y. 12209. *Office:* Department of English, State University of New York at Albany, 1400 Western, Albany, N.Y. 12222.

CAREER: Notre Dame International School, Rome, Italy, lecturer in literature, 1965-67; State University of New York at Albany, assistant professor of English, 1970—. News reporter in the Vatican, 1965-67, translator for Vatican Council, 1965-66.

WRITINGS: Wolf Masks: Violence in Contemporary Poetry, Kennikat, 1977.

WORK IN PROGRESS: A book on the use of the primitive in contemporary literature; studying "the philosophical underpinnings of such authors as John Gardner, Ted Hughes."

SIDELIGHTS: Ries writes: "My writing tries to trace the connections between what is happening in the world at large and what is being produced by our contemporary artists. We are all both the victims and benefactors of recent historical events. . . . The Humanities are in a period of decline within our institutions, but not in our society."

*   *   *

RIGBY, Ida Katherine 1944-

PERSONAL: Born May 10, 1944, in Los Angeles, Calif.; daughter of George A. (in public administration) and Edith S. (a teacher; maiden name, Hausler) Rigby. *Education:* Stanford University, B.A. (cum laude), 1965, M.A. (education), 1966; University of California, Berkeley, M.A. (art history), 1969, Ph.D., 1974. *Residence:* La Mesa, Calif. *Office:* Department of Art, San Diego State University, San Diego, Calif. 92182.

CAREER: University of Montana, Missoula, assistant professor of art history, spring, 1972; Tulane University, New Orleans, La., instructor of art history, 1972-74; University of Victoria, Victoria, British Columbia, assistant professor of art history, 1974-76; San Diego State University, San Diego, Calif., lecturer in art history, 1976—.

Member: College Art Association of America, American

Association of University Professors, American Society of Aesthetics, Universities Art Association (Canada), Art Historians of the Pacific Northwest, Art Historians of Southern California. *Awards, honors:* Research grant from Deutscher Akademischer Austauschdienst, summer, 1975.

WRITINGS: (Contributor) Herschel B. Chipp, editor, *Friedrich Hundertwasser,* University of California Press, 1969; *Karl Hofer,* Garland Publishing, 1976; (contributor) O. P. Reed, editor, *German Expressionist Prints and Illustrated Books from the Collection of Robert Gore Rifkind* (exhibition catalog), University of California, Los Angeles, 1977; *Karl Hofer: Sein Leben und Schaffen* (title means "Karl Hoffer: His Life and Work") translated into German by Elisabeth Furler, in press; Contributor to *SECAC Review and Newsletter.*

SIDELIGHTS: Ida Rigby writes that she has "lectured on nineteenth century German romantic art and on the painting and official sculpture during the Nazi period." The latter interests her "for what it indicates about a regime and those who support it." She has lived in Germany and France. *Avocational interests:* History of architecture, art of the ancient Near East.

*   *   *

RINDFLEISCH, Norval (William)   1930-

PERSONAL: Born April 2, 1930, in Los Angeles, Calif.; son of Adolph Caspar (an accountant) and Lillian Mary (Nolan) Rindfleisch; married Carol Lucille Olson (a librarian), April 24, 1954; children: Mary, Julie, Kate, Joe. *Education:* University of Minnesota, student, 1948-49; Long Beach City College, A.A., 1955; University of Chicago, A.B., 1957, A.M., 1958. *Politics:* Democrat. *Religion:* Roman Catholic. *Office:* Phillips Exeter Academy, Exeter, N.H. 03833.

CAREER: English teacher in a private school in Pomfret, Conn., 1958-68; Phillips Exeter Academy, Exeter, N.H., teacher of English, 1968—. *Military service:* U.S. Coast Guard Reserve, active duty, 1950-53; served in Korea. *Member:* New England Small Press Association, Phi Beta Kappa. *Awards, honors:* Woodrow Wilson fellowship, 1957-58; O. Henry Award from Doubleday, 1970, for "Cliff of Fall."

WRITINGS: In Loveless Clarity and Other Stories, Ithaca House, 1972. Contributor of stories to literary journals, including *Epoch, Literary Review, Yale Literary Magazine,* and *Northern New England Review.*

WORK IN PROGRESS: The Partnership, a book of stories.

*   *   *

RISENHOOVER, Morris   1940-

PERSONAL; Born November 6, 1940, in Dallas, Tex.; son of William Jordan (a barber) and Lorene (Walker) Risenhoover; children: M. Steven. *Education:* Southern Methodist University, B.Mus., 1964; University of Michigan, M.Mus., 1965, Ph.D., 1972. *Office:* School of Music, University of Michigan, Ann Arbor, Mich. 48109.

CAREER: Youngstown University, Youngstown, Ohio, instructor in music, 1965-67; University of Michigan, Ann Arbor, assistant to the dean of School of Music, 1971—. *Member:* Phi Mu Alpha, Pi Kappa Lambda.

WRITINGS: Artists as Professors, University of Illinois Press, 1976.

RIST ARNOLD, Elisabeth   1950-

PERSONAL: Born November 21, 1950, in England. *Education:* St. George Williams University, B.F.A., 1974. *Home:* 1539 Wrexham Ave., Montreal, Quebec, Canada H3J 1B2.

CAREER: Concordia University, Montreal, Quebec, secretary in audio-visual department, 1972—.

WRITINGS: I Like Birds (juvenile; self illustrated), Tundra Books, 1977.

WORK IN PROGRESS: I Like Cats, self illustrated children's book; *The Escape,* self illustrated children's book; research on sculpture and photography.

SIDELIGHTS: "At the moment I write and paint for my own satisfaction," Rist Arnold told *CA.* "Within the next two or three years I hope to give up my job to do this full time. By that time I will be living in the country and have more time.

"I find it very difficult to illustrate another author's work, that is why I prefer to write my own stories. I usually draw or paint first and then write around these illustrations and add to them if necessary. When I work I never aim at any particular audience, children or adult, because I feel it is too easy to find oneself talking down to children. Even if they don't understand all of the words they can still appreciate the sounds.

"My photography is useful in my drawing and painting and I use it primarily for research into plants and animals."

*   *   *

RITZ, Charles   1891-1976

August 1, 1891—July 11, 1976; Swiss-born French hotel director, magazine editor, and author of a book on fly fishing. Obituaries: *New York Times,* July 14, 1976.

*   *   *

RIVKIN, Allen (Erwin)   1903-

PERSONAL: Born November 20, 1903, in Hayward, Wis.; son of Samuel Richard (a merchant) and Rose (Rosenberg) Rivkin; married Laura Hornickel (a writer, under pseudonym Laura Kerr), November 8, 1952; children: Caroline (Mrs. Philip Saltzman). *Education:* University of Minnesota, B.A., 1925. *Residence:* Los Angeles, Calif. *Agent:* Phyllis Jackson, International Creative Management, 1301 Avenue of the Americas, New York, N.Y. 10019. *Office:* P.O. Box 1644, Beverly Hills, Calif. 90213.

CAREER: Writer, 1925—. Has also worked as a newspaper man, publicity man, and advertising man. Television producer (produced the series "Troubleshooters," 1958-59); founder and president of Motion Picture Industry Council, 1951-52; secretary of Writers-Producers Pension Fund, 1965-66; treasurer of Writers Guild Foundation, 1966—. Chairman of U.S. delegation to Cannes Film Festival, 1962; vice-president of Hollywood Guilds Festival Committee, 1962-63; national director of Jewish Film Advisory Committee, 1963-76. National director of Democratic National Committee (performing arts division), 1948-52; public relations director of Democratic National Convention, 1960. *Wartime service:* U.S. War Department, head motion picture officer in Special Services Division, 1942-44.

MEMBER: International Writers Guild (co-founder, 1963), Dramatists Guild, Academy of Motion Picture Arts and Sciences, Writers Guild of America (founder of West branch; vice-president, 1954; director of public relations, 1962—), Screen Writers Guild (founder; member of board of directors; president, 1960-62), West Side Riding and Asthma Club, Sigma Alpha Mu. *Awards, honors:* Valentine Davies Award from Writers Guild of America, 1963, for community service; Morgan Cox Award from Writers Guild of America, 1972, for guild service.

WRITINGS: (With Leonard Spigelgass) *I Wasn't Born Yesterday: An Anonymous Autobiography,* Macauley, 1935; (with wife, Laura Kerr) *Hello, Hollywood: A Book About the Movies by the People Who Make Them,* Doubleday, 1962; (editor) *Who Wrote the Movie . . . And What Else Did He Write?,* Academy of Motion Picture Arts and Sciences, 1970.

Author of the play "Knock on Wood" (three-act), first produced on Broadway at Cort Theatre, May 28, 1935. Author of eighty-five screenplays and sixty television scripts since 1931, including "Battle Circus," "Prisoner of War," "Joe Smith, American," "Eternal Sea," and "Big Operator." Editor of *Writers Guild Newsletter,* 1965—.

WORK IN PROGRESS: Hollywood Is No Laughing Matter.

* * *

ROBANA, Abderrahman 1938-

PERSONAL: Born January 29, 1938, in Tunis, Tunisia; came to the United States in 1960, became permanent resident, 1974; son of Ayad ben Ali and Amna (Koutino) Robana; married Zakia M'rabet; children: Ramzi. *Education:* Washington University, St. Louis, Mo., B.S.B.A., 1962, M.B.A., 1964; New York University, Ph.D., 1971. *Religion:* Islam. *Home:* 36 High St., Alfred, N.Y. 14802. *Office:* Department of Business Administration, Alfred University, Alfred, N.Y. 14802.

CAREER: Center for Industrial Studies, Tunis, Tunisia, researcher, 1969; Adelphi University, Garden City, N.Y., instructor in economics, 1970-71; Alfred University, Alfred, N.Y., assistant professor, 1971—. Lecturer at Rutgers University and Hofstra University, both 1971-72. *Member:* American Finance Association, Financial Management Association, American Economic Association, Phi Kappa Phi, Omicron Delta Epsilon, Beta Gamma Sigma, Delta Mu Delta.

WRITINGS: The Prospects for an Economic Community in North Africa, Praeger, 1973.

WORK IN PROGRESS: Research on mergers and acquisitions and on small business.

BIOGRAPHICAL/CRITICAL SOURCES: American Political Science Review, March, 1976.

* * *

Robbins, Roy M(arvin) 1904-

PERSONAL: Born July 26, 1904, in Richmond, Ind.; son of William J. (a politician) and Lydia Josephine (McMath) Robbins; married Felicia Joyce Gowen, August 24, 1929; children: Marvin Edward, Philip Jerome. *Education:* Earlham College, A.B., 1925; University of Washington, Seattle, M.A., 1926; University of Wisconsin, Madison, Ph.D., 1929. *Politics:* Independent. *Religion:* Episcopalian. *Home:* 617B Midway Dr., Silver Springs Shores, Ocala, Fla. 32670.

CAREER: University of Washington, Seattle, assistant professor of history, 1928-29; Western Reserve University (now Case Western Reserve University), Cleveland, Ohio, assistant professor of history, 1929-38; Butler University, Indi-

anapolis, Ind., associate professor, 1938-42, professor of history and head of department, 1942-54, director of Graduate Division, 1941-48; University of Nebraska, Omaha, professor of history, 1954-71, professor emeritus, 1971—, director of Graduate Division, 1954-59. Summer professor at University of Washington, Seattle, University of Montana, and University of Cincinnati; member of Indiana Constitutional Convention Centennial Commission, 1950. *Wartime service:* Civilian Defense Service, head of departments of history and geography for U.S. Army Air Forces at Butler University, 1942-45.

MEMBER: American Historical Association, Organization of American Historians (member of executive board, 1965-68), Indiana Academy of Social Sciences (president, 1942), Nebraska Historical Society, Douglas County Historical Society (Nebraska; founder, 1956), Phi Alpha Theta, Phi Kappa Phi, Alpha Kappa Lambda. *Awards, honors:* Social Science Research Council research awards, 1937 and 1946; J. I. Holcomb Distinguished Professor Award from Butler University, 1951; D.H.L. from University of Nebraska at Omaha, 1974.

WRITINGS: Bibliography of American Periodicals in Libraries of Cleveland and Oberlin, Ohio, Graduate School, Western Reserve University, 1936; *Our Landed Heritage: The Public Domain, 1776-1936,* Princeton University Press, 1942, revised edition published as *Our Landed Heritage: The Public Domain, 1776-1970,* University of Nebraska Press, 1976; (contributor) Joseph T. Lambie and Richard V. Clemence, editors, *Economic Change in America: Readings in the Economic History of the United States,* Stackpole, 1954; (contributor) Stephen Salzbury, editor, *Essays on the History of the West,* Holt, 1975. Contributor to *The Book of Knowledge* and *New Century Cyclopedia of Names,* and to history journals. Member of editorial board of *Journal of American History,* 1954-58.

WORK IN PROGRESS: Continuing research on public lands, the history of farm and irrigation lands, conservation, national forests and parks, and grazing and mineral lands.

SIDELIGHTS: Robbins writes: "The distribution of the public lands of the Republic to citizens and corporations has been of greatest significance to the success of our democracy. One-third of the area of the United States, rich in natural resources, is still owned by the federal government. This vast patrimony has been and continues to be a great treasure chest of our natural wealth. The preservation and intelligent use of this vast patrimony needs the constant vigilance of every citizen—lest we lose our heritage—and maybe our democracy."

AVOCATIONAL INTERESTS: Gardening, fishing, shortwave radio, reading.

* * *

ROBERSON, Marie
See HAMM, Marie Roberson

* * *

ROBERTS, Denys Kilham 1904(?)-1976

1904(?)—March 15, 1976; British association official and author. Obituaries: *AB Bookman's Weekly,* April 12, 1976.

* * *

ROBERTS, Evelyn Lutman 1917-

PERSONAL: Born April 22, 1917, in Warsaw, Mo.; daughter of Edgar (a merchandizer) and Edna (Wingate)

Lutman; married Granville Oral Roberts (a minister), December 25, 1938; children: Rebecca, Ronald, Richard, Roberta. *Education:* Northeastern State College, Tahlequah, Okla., student, 1935-37; Texas College of Arts and Industries, student, 1937-38. *Religion:* Methodist. *Address:* Box 7706, Tulsa, Okla. 74105. *Office:* Oral Roberts University, Tulsa, Okla. 74135.

CAREER: Elementary school teacher in rural Oklahoma and Texas, 1935-38; assistant to husband's radio and television ministry, 1965—. Lecturer. *Member:* Phi Sigma Alpha, Delta Kappa Gamma, Rotary Anns (secretary, 1966-67).

WRITINGS: His Darling Wife, Evelyn, Dial, 1976. Also author of booklets, *I Married Oral Roberts,* 1956, and *Whither Thou Goest,* 1960.

WORK IN PROGRESS: A book based on counseling sessions with married couples.

SIDELIGHTS: Mrs. Roberts writes: "Too many families are breaking up. I'm interested in helping young couples to see beyond the wedding day and to try to help older couples learn how to love each other and communicate."

* * *

ROBERTS, Florence Bright   1941-

PERSONAL: Born February 20, 1941, in Bryan, Tex.; daughter of Gordon Stanley (a chemist) and Harriet Alice (a teacher; maiden name, Raymer) Bright; married Paul Benjamin Roberts (an Episcopal priest), November 28, 1968; children: Laura Kathleen, Nancy Alice. *Education:* Lon Morris College, A.A., 1960; University of Texas at Galveston, B.S.N., 1963; Emory University, M.N., 1964; University of Tennessee, further graduate study, 1976—. *Religion:* Episcopalian. *Home:* 3711 Frostwood Rd., Knoxville, Tenn. 37921.

CAREER: John Sealy Hospital, Galveston, Tex., staff nurse, summer, 1963; University of Tennessee, Memphis, instructor, 1964-68, assistant professor of pediatrics, 1968-69, 1971; Summer County Guidance Center, Gallatin, Tenn., part-time pediatric nurse/child therapist, 1972-74; University of Tennessee, Knoxville, clinical instructor in psychosocial nursing, winter, 1975; writer, 1975—. Member of board of directors of Tyson House (Episcopal student center). *Member:* Sigma Theta Tau.

WRITINGS: A Review of Pediatric Nursing, Mosby, 1974; (contributor) Gladys M. Scipien, Marilyn A. Chard, and others, editors, *The Child in the Family: Comprehensive Nursing Care,* McGraw, 1975; *Perinatal Nursing: Care of Newborns and Their Families,* McGraw, 1977. Contributor to nursing journals.

WORK IN PROGRESS: Children's books on feelings; children's stories; research on the mental health implications of the transition to parenthood, maternal attachment, play therapy as an adjustment tool for school children, and metnal hygiene for young mothers.

SIDELIGHTS: Florence Roberts writes: "My major professional interest is in the area of preventive mental health, particularly as it relates to young families. I am vitally interested in the needs of mothers of young children and the needs of children as they approach major milestones, such as entering school. I am especially interested in the immediate newborn period as one that is vital to the development of good mental health and one that is often overlooked in terms of active intervention by health professionals."

ROBERTS, Mervin F(rancis)   1922-

PERSONAL: Born June 7, 1922, in New York, N.Y.; son of Gus R. (an inventor) and Esther N. (a school teacher) Roberts; married Edith May Foster, June, 1949; children: Edith, Robin (deceased), Martha, Nancy, Neel, William. *Education:* Alfred University, B.S., 1944. *Politics:* Republican. *Religion:* Congregationalist. *Home and office address:* Duck River Lane, Old Lyme, Conn. 06371.

CAREER: Writer; photographer of animal movements; consultant on animal behavior; consultant on fish behavior to Northeast Utilities, 1970—; councillor for marine resources to governor of Connecticut, 1971-72. Chaplain of Old Lyme Fire Department, 1970—. *Military service:* U.S. Naval Reserve, active duty, 1942-46; became lieutenant junior grade. *Member:* National Rifle Association (life member), American Society of Ichthyologists and Herpetologists, Connecticut Association of Conservation Commissioners (president).

WRITINGS: Turtles as Pets, T.F.H. Publications, 1953; *Beginning Your Aquarium,* T.F.H. Publications, 1955; *Chameleons,* T.F.H. Publications, 1956; *Parakeets in Your Home,* Sterling, 1956; *How to Raise Hamsters,* T.F.H. Publications, 1957; *Guinea Pigs,* T.F.H. Publications, 1957; *Snakes,* T.F.H. Publications, 1958, reissued under title *All about Boas and Other Snakes,* 1975.

A Camera Is Thrust Upon You (manual), U.S. Navy, 1961; *Pigeons,* T.F.H. Publications, 1962.

Tidal Marsh Plants of Connecticut, Connecticut Arboretum, 1970; *Your Terrarium,* T.F.H. Publications, 1972; *Teddy Bear Hamsters,* T.F.H. Publications, 1974. Associate editor of *Factory,* 1959.

WORK IN PROGRESS: Iguanas; Newts and other Salamanders; Chameleons; Anoles.

AVOCATIONAL INTERESTS: Duck hunting, trapshooting, working as a gunsmith, inventing (has invented glass bottle color sorter for the recycling industry and heaters and pumps for aquariums).

* * *

ROBERTSHAW, (James) Denis   1911-
(Michael Gaunt)

PERSONAL: Born March 26, 1911, in Leeds, England; son of James William (a rating officer) and Mary Helen (Gaunt) Robertshaw; married Margaret Winn Pollard, June 3, 1939; children: Hazel Winn (Mrs. A. Chigwell), Roland Peter, Mary Frances. *Education:* Attended school in Yorkshire, England. *Religion:* Church of England. *Home:* 97 Hazelwood Rd., Oxted, Surrey RH8 0JA, England. *Agent:* Mark Hamilton, A. M. Heath & Co., 35 Dover St., London W.1, England.

CAREER: Has worked as member of staff of *London Times,* London, England; and as free-lance writer. *Member:* International P.E.N., Society of Authors, Limpsfield Chart Golf Club.

WRITINGS—All under pseudonym Michael Gaunt: *Belle Isle* (historical novel), Hodder & Stoughton, 1957; *The Invaders* (historical novel), Hodder & Stoughton, 1969; *The Queen's Hour* (historical novel), Hodder & Stoughton, 1961; *Brim's Boat* (juvenile), J. Cape, 1964, Coward, 1966; *Brim Sails Out* (juvenile), J. Cape, 1965, Coward, 1967; *Brim's Valley* (juvenile), Coward, 1967.

WORK IN PROGRESS: A contemporary novel.

AVOCATIONAL INTERESTS: Painting (including portraiture), walking, golf.

ROBESON, Gerald B(yron) 1938-

PERSONAL: Born December 1, 1938, in Blue Earth, Minn.; son of Byron Berniel (a minister) and Winnifred (Gennow) Robeson; married Carol Hansen (a teacher), August 26, 1960; children: Suzanne Dianne, Deborah Kay. *Education:* Northwest College, B.A., 1961; further study with Famous Writers Course, 1965-69, and at Spanish Language Institute, San Jose, Costa Rica, 1967-68. *Home:* 251 Olive Ave., Woodburn, Ore. 97071. *Office:* Apartado 840, San Jose, Costa Rica.

CAREER: Ordained minister of Assemblies of God Church, 1965. Free-lance writer in Woodburn, Ore., 1965-69; Assemblies of God Church representative in Managua, Nicaragua, 1969-72, and in San Jose, Costa Rica, 1973—. Producer and director of two hundred live television programs in Nicaragua, 1969-71, and in Costa Rica, 1973—; recording artist for Northwest Recording Co., Seattle, Wash.

WRITINGS: Faith in Eruption, Banner Press-Whitaker House, 1973. Contributor to religious periodicals.

WORK IN PROGRESS: Supernatural Faith, for Banner Press-Whitaker House.

SIDELIGHTS: Robeson told *CA:* "Missionary life in Central America has been an exciting adventure. From erupting volcanos, to life in Managua, Nicaragua shortly before the devastating earthquake of 1972, to television studios for our program each week, to Crusades with thousands of people in attendance, there has never been a dull moment. Writing, however, has given me the opportunity to enlarge my sphere of influence to an even greater degree. In the past two years here in San Jose, Costa Rica, we have built two large church buildings complete with congregations of two thousand people each.

"Music has always been an important part of my life. In the past fifteen years I have made four long-playing records with trumpet and vocal arrangements. In our religious services, which we have every night of the year in the new churches, I also keep things lively with my electric bass. My dream is to be free from some of these obligations to write full-time, but for the moment it must remain in the future because I am having a ball doing just what I am doing."

* * *

ROBHS, Dwight
See MONACO, Richard

* * *

ROBIN, Ralph 1914-

PERSONAL: Born September 7, 1914, in Pittsburgh, Pa.,; son of Peter (a pharmacist) and Bessie (an artist; maiden name, Silverberg) Robin; married Irene Hebard, December 14, 1951 (died April 19, 1968). *Education:* University of Pittsburgh, B.S., 1936; graduate study at Washington School of Psychiatry, 1959-64, and University of Maryland, 1964-66. *Home:* 5432 Connecticut Ave. N.W., Apt. 706, Washington, D.C. 20015.

CAREER: Pennsylvania Highways Department, Pittsburgh, Pa., chemist, 1936-38; City of Pittsburgh Bureau of Tests, Pittsburgh, chemist, 1938-40; U.S. Navy Yard, Philadelphia, Pa., chemist, 1940-42; National Housing Agency, Washington, D.C., chemist, 1946-47; National Bureau of Standards, Washington, D.C., chemist, 1947-50; poet and fiction writer, 1950-56; American University, Washington, D.C., lecturer, 1956-59, professorial lecturer, 1959-60, ad-

junct professor of English, 1960-71; poet, fiction writer, and playwright, 1971—. Fellow of Virginia Center for the Creative Arts, 1974, and Ossabaw Island Project, 1974 and 1975. *Military service:* U.S. Army, Chemical Warfare Service, 1942-46; became captain.

MEMBER: Poetry Society of America, American Chemical Society. *Awards, honors:* MacDowell Colony fellowships, 1958, 1969, 1971, 1972-73, 1974; poetry recorded for Library of Congress, 1970; Christopher Morley Memorial Award from Poetry Society of America, 1976, for "Shakespeare's Muse."

WRITINGS: Cities of Speech (poems), Byron Press, 1971. Also author of play, "Another Island" (three-act), as yet neither published nor produced.

Work included in science fiction anthologies and literary collections, including *The Best American Short Stories of 1958,* edited by Martha Foley and David Burnett, Houghton, 1958; *The New York Times Book of Verse,* edited by Thomas Lask, Macmillan, 1970; *Accent: An Anthology, 1940-1960,* edited by Daniel Curley, George Scouffas, and Charles Shattuck, University of Illinois Press, 1973; *Best Poems of 1974: Borestone Mountain Poetry Awards 1975,* Pacific Books, 1975. Contributor of more than 170 poems and stories to popular magazines, including *Saturday Review, New Republic, Magazine of Fantasy and Science Fiction,* and *Reporter,* and to literary journals, including *Encounter, Prairie Schooner, Southwest Review, Chelsea, Canadian Forum,* and *Poetry Northwest.*

WORK IN PROGRESS: A Comedy of Time, an historical novel; fiction, poetry, and drama.

SIDELIGHTS: Robin writes: "In 1965 . . . I said: 'Showmanship is too influential in the current literary scene. I would like to see more works conspicuous for their inherent artistry and intelligence. Ideally, they would be infused with a strongly humane quality. Poetry, without readopting poetic diction, should strengthen its identity as an unique art. Fiction should transcend its origin in fact and pseudo fact. Poetry and fiction should increase their power to organize contemporary knowledge and experience—and knowledge as experience. What I am proposing is a movement beyond a rather shallow avant-garde to an avant-avant-garde—at once original, lively, intelligent, and humane.' I cannot say it better now."

* * *

ROBINS, Denise (Naomi) 1897-
(Ashley French, Harriet Gray, Julia Kane, Francesca Wright)

PERSONAL: Born February 1, 1897, in London, England; daughter of Herman (a music critic and singing teacher) and Denise (a writer; maiden name, Cornwell) Klein; married Arthur Robins, June 18, 1918 (divorced, 1938); married O'Neill Pearson (an army officer), October 30, 1939; children: (first marriage) Eve Louise, Patricia Denise, Anne Eleanor. *Education:* Attended schools in Staten Island, N.Y., San Diego, Calif., and London, England. *Politics:* Conservative. *Home:* 15 Oathall Rd., Haywards Heath, Sussex RH16 3EG, England.

CAREER: Dundee Courier, Dundee, Scotland, journalist, 1914-15; free-lance journalist, broadcaster, and novelist, 1915—. Has made many appearances on British Broadcasting Corp. (BBC)-TV. *Member:* Romantic Novelists Association (co-founder, 1960; president, 1960-66), Men and Women of Today Club (past vice-president).

WRITINGS—All romantic novels: *The Marriage Bond*, Hodder & Stoughton, 1924; *Sealed Lips*, Hodder & Stoughton, 1924; *The Forbidden Bride*, Newnes' Pocket Novels, 1926; *The Man Between*, Newnes' Pocket Novels, 1926; *The Passionate Awakening*, Newnes' Pocket Novels, 1926; *The Inevitable End*, Mills & Boon, 1927; *Jonquil*, Mills & Boon, 1927; *The Triumph of the Rat*, P. Allan & Co., 1927; *Desire Is Blind*, Mills & Boon, 1928; *The Passionate Flame*, Mills & Boon, 1928; *White Jade*, Mills & Boon, 1928; *Women Who Seek*, Mills & Boon, 1928; *The Dark Death*, Mills & Boon, 1929; *The Enduring Flame*, Mills & Boon, 1929; *Heavy Clay*, Mills & Boon, 1929; *Love Was a Jest*, Mills & Boon, 1929.

(With Roland Pertwee) *Heat Wave* (play; first produced in London at St. James's Theatre, 1929), Dial Press, 1930; *And All Because . . .*, Mills & Boon, 1930, published as *Love's Victory*, G. H. Watts, 1933; *It Wasn't Love*, Mills & Boon, 1930; *Love Poems, and Others*, Mills & Boon, 1930; *Swing of Youth*, Mills & Boon, 1930; *Crowns, Pounds, and Guineas*, Mills & Boon, 1931; *Fever of Love*, Mills & Boon, 1931; *Lovers of Janine*, Mills & Boon, 1931; *One Night in Ceylon, and Others*, Mills & Boon, 1931; *Second Best*, Mills & Boon, 1931, G. H. Watt, 1933; *Blaze of Love*, Mills & Boon, 1932; *The Boundary Line*, G. H. Watt, 1932; *The Secret Hour*, Mills & Boon, 1932; *There Are Limits*, Mills & Boon, 1932; *The Wild Bird*, G. H. Watt, 1932; *Gay Defeat*, Mills & Boon, 1933; *Life's a Game*, Mills & Boon, 1933; *Men Are Only Human*, Macaulay, 1933; *Shatter the Sky*, Mills & Boon, 1933; *Strange Rapture*, Mills & Boon, 1933; *Brief Ecstasy*, Mills & Boon, 1934; *Never Give All*, Macaulay, 1934; *No Sacrifice*, G. H. Watt, 1934; *Slave-Woman*, Mills & Boon, 1934, Macaulay, 1935; *Sweet Love*, Mills & Boon, 1934; *All This for Love*, Mills & Boon, 1935; *Climb to the Stars*, Nicholson & Watson, 1935; *How Great the Price*, Mills & Boon, 1935; *Life and Love*, Nicholson & Watson, 1935; (author of novelized version) *Ivor Novello's Murder in Mayfair*, Mills & Boon, 1935; *Love Game*, Nicholson & Watson, 1936; *Those Who Love*, Nicholson & Watson, 1936; *Were I Thy Bride*, Nicholson & Watson, 1936; *Kiss of Youth*, Nicholson & Watson, 1937; *Set Me Free*, Nicholson & Watson, 1937; *The Tiger in Men*, Nicholson & Watson, 1937; *The Woman's Side of It*, Nicholson & Watson, 1937; *Restless Heart*, Nicholson & Watson, 1938, Arcadia House, 1940; *Since We Love*, Nicholson & Watson, 1938, Arcadia House, 1941; *You Have Chosen*, Nicholson & Watson, 1938; *Dear Loyalty*, Nicholson & Watson, 1939; *Gypsy Lover*, Nicholson & Watson, 1939; *I, Too, Have Loved*, Nicholson & Watson, 1939; *Officer's Wife*, Nicholson & Watson, 1939.

Forget That I Remember, Arcadia House, 1940; *Island of Flowers*, Nicholson & Watson, 1940; *Little We Know*, Hutchinson, 1940; *Sweet Sorrow*, Nicholson & Watson, 1940; *To Love Is to Live*, Hutchinson, 1940; *If This Be Destiny*, Hutchinson, 1941; *Set the Stars Alight*, Hutchinson, 1941, new edition, Arrow Books, 1971; *Winged Love*, Hutchinson, 1941; *This One Night*, Hutchinson, 1942; *War Marriage*, Hutchinson, 1942; *What Matters Most*, Hutchinson, 1942; *The Changing Years*, Hutchinson, 1943; *Daughter Knows Best*, Hutchinson, 1943; *Dust of Dreams*, Hutchinson, 1943; *Escape to Love*, Hutchinson, 1943; *This Spring of Love*, Hutchinson, 1943; *War Changes Everything*, Todd Publishing, 1943; *Give Me Back My Heart*, Hutchinson, 1944, new edition, Arrow Books, 1971; *How to Forget*, Hutchinson, 1944; *Never Look Back*, Hutchinson, 1944; *Desert Rapture*, Hutchinson, 1945; *Love So Young*, Hutchinson, 1945; *All for You*, Hutchinson, 1946; *Heart's Desire*, William Foster, 1946; *Separation*, William Foster, 1946; *The Story of Veronica*, Hutchinson, 1946; *Forgive Me, My Love*, Docker Hanley, 1947; *More than Love*, Hutchinson, 1947; *Could I Forget*, Hutchinson, 1948; *Khamsin*, Hutchinson, 1948; *Love Me No More!*, Hutchinson, 1948, new edition, Arrow Books, 1971; *The Hard Way*, Hutchinson, 1949; *To Love Again*, Hutchinson, 1949; *The Uncertain Heart*, Hutchinson, 1949.

The Feast Is Finished, Hutchinson, 1950; *Love Hath an Island*, Hutchinson, 1950; *Heart of Paris*, Hutchinson, 1951; *Infatuation*, Hutchinson, 1951; *Only My Dreams*, Hutchinson, 1951; *Second Marriage*, Hutchinson, 1951; *Something to Love*, Hutchinson, 1951; *The Other Love*, Hutchinson, 1952; *Strange Meeting*, Hutchinson, 1952; *The First Long Kiss*, Hutchinson, 1953; *My True Love*, Hutchinson, 1953; *The Long Shadow*, Hutchinson, 1954; *Venetian Rhapsody*, Hutchinson, 1954; *Bitter Sweet*, Hutchinson, 1955; *The Unshaken Loyalty*, Hutchinson, 1955; *All that Matters*, Hutchinson, 1956; *The Enchanted Island*, Hutchinson, 1956; *Arrow in the Heart*, Hodder & Stoughton, 1957; (with Michael Pertwee) *Light the Candles: A Play in One-Act* (adapted from Robins' short story of the same title), English Theatre Guild, 1957; *The Noble One*, Hodder & Stoughton, 1957; *The Seagull's Cry*, Hutchinson, 1957, new edition, Arrow Books, 1971; *Chateau of Flowers*, Hodder & Stoughton, 1958; *The Untrodden Snow*, Hodder & Stoughton, 1958; *Do Not Go, My Love*, Hodder & Stoughton, 1959; *Light the Candles* (stories), Hurst & Blackett, 1959; *We Two Together*, Hodder & Stoughton, 1959.

The Unlit Fire, Hodder & Stoughton, 1960; *I Should Have Known*, Hodder & Stoughton, 1961; *A Promise Is for Ever*, Hodder & Stoughton, 1961; *Ce jour-la a Torremolinos* (title means "That Day in Torremolinos"), translation by O. L. Debont-Jodoche, Editions de Trevise, 1962; *Put Back the Clock*, Hodder & Stoughton, 1962; *Mad Is the Heart*, Hodder & Stoughton, 1963; *Nightingale's Song*, Hodder & Stoughton, 1963; *Reputation*, Hodder & Stoughton, 1963; *Meet Me in Monte Carlo*, Arrow Books, 1964; *Moment of Love*, Hodder & Stoughton, 1964; (editor) *The World of Romance* (stories), New English Library, 1964; *Loving and Giving*, Hodder & Stoughton, 1965; *Stranger than Fiction: Denise Robins Tells Her Life Story*, Hodder & Stoughton, 1965; *The Strong Heart*, Hodder & Stoughton, 1965; *Lightning Strikes Twice*, Hodder & Stoughton, 1966; *Love Is Enough*, Arrow Books, 1966; *Dark Secret Love* (earlier edition published under pseudonym Julia Kane), Mayflower Books, 1967; *The Sin Was Mine* (earlier edition published under pseudonym Julia Kane), Mayflower Books, 1967; *Wait for Tomorrow*, Hodder & Stoughton, 1967; *House by the Watch Tower*, Arcadia House, 1968; *Laurence, My Love*, Hodder & Stoughton, 1968; *Love and Desire and Hate*, Hodder & Stoughton, 1969; *A Love Like Ours*, Hodder & Stoughton, 1969.

Forbidden, Hodder & Stoughton, 1971; *House of the Seventh Cross*, Coronet, 1973; *The Other Side of Love*, Hodder & Stoughton, 1973; *Twice Have I Loved*, Hodder & Stoughton, 1973; *Dark Corridor*, Hodder & Stoughton, 1974; *The Snow Must Return*, Coronet Books, 1974; *Come Back, Yesterday*, Hodder & Stoughton, 1976.

Under pseudonym Ashley French: *Once Is Enough*, Hutchinson, 1953, reprinted under name Denise Robins, Panther Books, 1963; *The Bitter Core*, Hutchinson, 1954, reprinted under name Denise Robins, Panther Books, 1965; *The Breaking Point*, Hutchinson, 1956, reprinted under name Denise Robins, Panther Books, 1965.

Under pseudonym Harriet Gray: *Gold for the Gay Masters*, Rich & Cowan, 1954, reprinted under name Denise Robins, Arrow Books, 1965; *Bride of Doom*, Rich & Cowan, 1956, reprinted under name Denise Robins, Mayflower Books, 1966; *The Flame and the Frost*, Rich & Cowan, 1957; *Dance in the Dust*, R. Hale, 1959, reprinted under name Denise Robins, Mayflower Books, 1973; *My Lady Destiny*, R. Hale, 1961.

Under pseudonym Julia Kane: *Time Runs Out*, Hodder & Stoughton, 1965.

Under pseudonym Francesca Wright: *The Loves of Lucrezia*, Rich & Cowan, 1953. Also author of *She Devil*, Corgi Books.

Contributor to *Nash's Magazine, Ideal Home, She, Woman's Weekly*, and to *Daily Express* and *Evening Standard*. Editor of correspondence page, *She* magazine, 1954—.

WORK IN PROGRESS: More novels.

SIDELIGHTS: Denise Robins wrote: "With a few exceptions it is inevitable that a novelist who begins to write when young, and continues through a long literary career, must necessarily produce a change in his work when he is older. . . . I know that my own novels show this clearly. As a young writer my style was purely romantic and sentimental. That sort of book may still interest a few faithful readers but might well bore those who no longer understand romantic love in its purest form." She observed, "I myself, have matured. The writer of today is no longer the young girl who published her first book in 1924. I think my latest novels are indicative of my maturity. My writing has improved. It is certainly more serious. I am still incurably romantic but I have also become more of a realist. I would find it impossible today to write only about innocence, humility, self-sacrifice, etc., and all the 'lilies and languors' of the almost impossible love of forty years ago. I am interested in modern youth. They give me their views, and I like to write about them. Their new world moves at a terrific pace so I find that I also like to write about it."

In Ms. Robins' opinion, "their attitude to life has changed mainly because of the new freedom allowed by parents and teachers—freedom of thought as well as movement. The things the girls in my original books used not to know about until they were at least 17 or 18, they now start learning in junior classes." She concluded, "I find that I enjoy writing about the modern girl. I can admire her, and the liking has increased over the years."

AVOCATIONAL INTERESTS: Travel, music, collecting antiques and books, gardening, dogs (present pet a Yorkshire terrier).

BIOGRAPHICAL/CRITICAL SOURCES: Denise Robins, *Stranger than Fiction: Denise Robins Tells Her Life Story*, Hodder & Stoughton, 1965; *Books and Bookmen*, July, 1968.

*   *   *

ROBINSON, Spider 1948-
(B. D. Wyatt)

PERSONAL: Born November 24, 1948, in New York, N.Y.; son of Charles Vincent (a salesman) and Evelyn (a secretary; maiden name, Meade) Robinson; married Jeanne Rubbicco (a dancer, dance teacher, and writer), July, 1975; children: Luanna Mountainborne. *Education:* State University of New York at Stony Brook, B.A., 1972; also attended State University of New York College at Plattsburgh and Le Moyne College. *Politics:* "None whatever." *Religion:*

"Pantheist/Humanist." *Home and office:* Red Palace, R.R.1, Hampton, Nova Scotia, Canada BOS 1LO. *Agent:* Kirby McCauley, 220 East 26th St., New York, N.Y. 10010.

CAREER: Long Island Commercial Review, Syosset, N.Y., realty editor, 1972-73; science fiction writer, 1973—. *Member:* Writers Federation of Nova Scotia (member of council, 1975—). *Awards, honors:* Tied for John W. Campbell Award for the best new science fiction writer, from Conde Nast Publications, 1974, for story "The Guy With the Eyes".

WRITINGS—Science fiction: *Telempath* (novel), Putnam, 1976; *Callahan's Crosstime Saloon* (stories), Ace Books, 1977.

Anthologized in *Analog Annual*, edited by Ben Bova, Pyramid Publications, 1976; *The Best of Galaxy*, Volume III, edited by Jim Bain, Award, 1976. Contributing editor and writer of "Galaxy Bookshelf" column in *Galaxy*, 1975—. Contributor of stories and novelettes to science fiction magazines (sometimes under pseudonym B. D. Wyatt), including *Analog, Vertex, Fantastic, Cosmos*, and *Galaxy*.

WORK IN PROGRESS: The Magnificent Conspiracy (tentative title), a science fiction novel; *And Call Her Blessed* (tentative title), a science fiction novel; *Stardance*, a short novel, with wife, Jeanne Robinson.

SIDELIGHTS: Robinson writes: "Many SF writers have eloquently indicted mankind. I intend to spend my life presenting the case for the defense. I believe that shared pain is lessened, shared joy increased; I further maintain that to be a specific formula for saving the world. I find doom-crying (like all forms of despair) to be a cop-out, a personal irresponsibility the world can no longer afford."

BIOGRAPHICAL/CRITICAL SOURCES: Fourth Estate, June 16, 1976.

*   *   *

ROBSON, E(manuel) W(alter) 1897-

PERSONAL: Born June 12, 1897, in London, England; married Mary Major (died, 1967); children: Elizabeth Mary Geddes. *Education:* Educated in public schools of London, England. *Politics:* "Any policy conducive to public good. Opposed to dialectical materialism." *Religion:* "Creation and Evolution both true versions of same sequence of events. One poeticized, the other more detailed." *Home and office:* 2890 Point Grey Rd., No. 213, Vancouver, British Columbia, Canada V6K 1A9.

CAREER: Associated British Picture Corp., London, England, in publicity, 1938-46, script consultant, 1945; engaged in broadcasting and free-lance publicity activities in Canada, 1948—.

WRITINGS—All with wife, Mary M. Robson: *The Film Answers Back: An Historical Appreciation of the Cinema*, John Lane, 1939, Arno, 1972; *In Defense of Moovie* (transcribed from Sir Philip Sidney's *In Defense of Poesie*), H. J. Pillans & Wilson (Edinburgh), 1940; *Dear Joe: Letters from Bill Smith to Joseph Stalin*, Secker & Warburg, 1942; *The Shame and Disgrace of Colonel Blimp*, Sydneyan Society (London), 1944; *Bernard Shaw Among the Innocents*, Sydneyan Society, 1945; *The World Is My Cinema*, Sydneyan Society, 1947; *Termites in the Shape of Men: Commonsense Versus Pierre Berton*, North Star Books, 1966.

(Sole author of book and lyrics; music by Kathleen la Marche) "The Dunmow Flitch" (musical drama), first produced in White Rock, British Columbia, at Theatre Playhouse, April, 1976.

Contributor to journals.

WORK IN PROGRESS: A book urging "elimination of certain negative influences in our lives that most of us are unaware are negative."

* * *

ROCKLAND, Mae Shafter 1937-

PERSONAL: Born December 18, 1937, in Bronx, N.Y.; daughter of Joseph (a glazier) and Bella (Dunsky) Shafter; married Michael Aaron Rockland (a professor), September 4, 1955; children: David, Jeffrey, Keren. *Education:* Attended Hunter College (now of the City University of New York), 1954-55, and Alfred College of Ceramic Design, 1955-56; University of Minnesota, B.A. (cum laude), 1962. *Politics:* "Not important to me." *Religion:* Jewish. *Home and studio:* 8 Madison St., Princeton, N.J. 08540.

CAREER: Free-lance graphic artist, 1960—, textile designer, 1970—, and writer, 1972—. Member of Craft Council of America. *Member:* Authors Guild of Authors League of America, Phi Beta Kappa.

WRITINGS: (Self-illustrated) *The Work of Our Hands: Jewish Needlecraft for Today,* Schocken, 1973; (self-illustrated) *The Hanukkah Book,* Schocken, 1975; *The Jewish Yellow Pages,* Schocken, 1976.

WORK IN PROGRESS: A contemporary and folkloric guide to Jewish hospitality, publication by Schocken expected in 1978; *The Expanded Jewish Yellow Pages,* for Schocken; a Jewish science fiction novel.

SIDELIGHTS: Mae Rockland writes that she "lived for six years in the Hispanic world (Argentina and Spain), lived in Japan for a year and traveled in Central and North America as well as Europe. My vocational and avocational interests overlap. I'm fascinated by the various forms of folkloric expression, including costume, food, music and dance. I'm a folkdance addict and dance at least twice a week, favorites are Greek and Balkan. My writing is an attempt to form a bridge between the Jewish traditions and philosophical beliefs and a contemporary American life style. To this end I am continually searching for new examples of Jewish-American foods, crafts, music, literature, dance, theatre, etc. If I can't find what I want and have the skills at hand I'll make it. I'd like the archaeologists who dig us up in a few hundred years to conclude that there was a vibrant, creative, and productive Jewish-American community here in the 1970's, so I make as much stuff as I can for them to find."

* * *

ROCKWELL, Jane 1929-

PERSONAL: Born December 27, 1929, in Chicago, Ill.; daughter of John G. (a professor) and Eugenia (a social worker; maiden name, Madsen) Rockwell; divorced. *Education:* University of Nebraska, B.A., 1951; also attended University of Chicago, New York University, New School for Social Research, and Fairfield University. *Home:* 19 Mountain Rd., Ridgefield, Conn. 06877.

CAREER: Lincoln Star, Lincoln, Neb., reporter and feature writer, 1947-50; *Torrington Telegram,* Torrington, Wyo., 1951-52; J. C. Penney Co., New York City, assistant editor of *Pay Day,* 1952-53; Field Museum of Natural History, Chicago, Ill., associate editor of *Bulletin,* and associate public relations counsel, 1954-58; *Science World,* New York City, staff writer, 1958-59; National Association for Retarded Children, New York City, editor of *Children Limited,* 1959-63; New York University, New York City, writer in department of development, 1963-64; Sleepy Hollow Restorations, Tarrytown, N.Y., public relations writer, 1965-67; *Drug Trade News* and *Drug Topics,* New York City, associate editor, 1970-71; The National Foundation-March of Dimes, White Plains, N.Y., science writer and administrative assistant, 1971-72; children's book author, 1972—.

*WRITINGS—*For children: *Cats and Kittens,* F. Watts, 1974; *Dogs and Puppies,* F. Watts, 1976; *Wolves,* F. Watts, in press.

WORK IN PROGRESS: A children's fiction book, the first in a series of stories about a non-conformist nine-year old.

SIDELIGHTS: Jane Rockwell writes: "Children's books finally are emerging from their cocoon of constriction. Writers are addressing themselves to real emotions and problems facing children and adolescents—and they are being published. And happily, whimsy, fantasy, and imagination are very much in evidence. Writing for children has become an exciting occupation for both the reader and the writer."

AVOCATIONAL INTERESTS: Social problems, politics, drama, art, ecology and the preservation of natural resources and wildlife, gardening, golf, tennis.

* * *

RODEWYK, Adolf 1894-

PERSONAL: Born December 4, 1894, in Cologne, Germany; son of Wilhelm and Anna (Kirch) Rodewyk. *Education:* Educated at University of Bonn and University of Innsbruck. *Home and office:* St. Georgen Philos.-Theol Hochschule, 224 Offenbacher Landstrasse, 6 Frankfurt am Main 70, West Germany.

CAREER: Ordained Roman Catholic priest of the Society of Jesus (Jesuit), 1925, at Volkenburg, Holland; served as night school and college administrator in Bonn and Hamburg, Germany; has done pastoral work with religious communities and in hospitals in Trier and Frankfurt am Main, Germany; became professor of Biblical languages, currently at St. Georgen Philos.-Theol Hochschule, Frankfurt am Main, Germany. *Military service:* German Army, 1917; served in artillery; became lieutenant.

WRITINGS: Zwei Menschen fuer ein ander (title means "Two People Dedicated to Each Other," [Paderborn, Germany], 1932; *Unser Geld und gut* (title means "Our Money and Propriety," [Paderborn], 1933; (with Konrad Kirch) *Helden des Christentums* (title means "Heroes of Christianity"), Bonifacius Drucherei (Paderborn), 1954; *Die daemonische Besessenheit in der Sicht des Rituale Romanum,* Pattloch, 1963, translation by Martin Ebon published as *Possessed by Satan: The Church's Teaching on the Devil, Possession, and Exorcism,* Doubleday, 1975; *Daemonische Besessenheit heute: Tatsachen und Deutungen* (title means "Demonic Possession Today: Facts and Interpretations"), Pattloch, 1966, 2nd edition, 1970.

* * *

ROE, Richard Lionel 1936-

PERSONAL: Born March 3, 1936, in Detroit, Mich.; son of Edgar Harold (a realtor) and Rose (Chapman) Roe; married Nancy Louise Quigley, August 1, 1958 (marriage ended 1969); married Margery Knoll (an associate publisher), July 1, 1971; children: Deborah Lynn. *Education:* University of Michigan, B.A., 1959. *Politics:* Independent. *Home:* 1128 Cuchara Drive, Del Mar, Calif. 92014. *Office:* Publisher's Inc., 243 12th Street, Del Mar, Calif. 92014.

CAREER: Prentice-Hall Inc., Englewood Cliffs, N.J., editor, 1959-67; Random House/Alfred Knopf, New York, N.Y., editor, 1967-68; CRM Books, Del Mar, Calif., founder and vice-president, 1968-72; Dushkin Publications Group, Guilford, Conn., publisher, 1973—; Publishers Inc., Del Mar, president, 1974—. Freelance writer and editor. Director, Omega Business Services; contractual consultant to Holt, Rinehart & Winston, and *Saturday Review.* *Member:* Southern California Bookbuilders, Sigma Alpha Epsilon, San Quintin Beach Club.

WRITINGS: (Editor with A. Lask) *This is a Sociology Reader,* Holt, 1973; (editor with R. Jones) *Valence and Vision: A Reader in Psychology,* Holt, 1974; (editor with Samuel Wilson) *Readings in the Life Sciences: Biology Anthology,* West Publishing, 1974; (editor with Wilson and Autry) *Readings in Human Sexuality,* West Publishing, 1975. Co-editor, *Grolier Encyclopedia Yearbook,* 1973.

WORK IN PROGRESS: Co-authoring a biology text for Holt; publication expected in 1977.

* * *

ROGERS, Barbara 1945-

PERSONAL: Born September 21, 1945, in Huddersfield, England; daughter of George Theodore (a government official) and Mary Katherine (a nurse; maiden name, Stedman) Rogers. *Education:* University of Sussex, B.A. (honors), 1968. *Politics:* Labour. *Home:* 10 Inner Park Rd., London S.W.19, England. *Office:* School of Development Studies, University of East Anglia, Norwich NR4 7JT, England.

CAREER: Progress Publishing House, Moscow, Soviet Union, translator and editor, 1968; Foreign and Commonwealth Office, London, England, third secretary, 1969-70; War on Want, London, England, Education officer, 1970-71; University of East Anglia, Norwich, England, research fellow, 1976—. Consultant to U.S. Congressman Charles C. Diggs and to the United Nations. *Member:* Anti-Apartheid Movement, Namibia Support Committee.

WRITINGS: South Africa's Stake in Britain, Africa Bureau (London, England), 1971; (contributor) Olav Stokke and Carl Widstrand, editors, *Southern Africa: The UN-OAU Conference,* Volume II, Scandinavian Institute of African Studies, 1973; (contributor) Mohamed El-Khawas and Francis Kornegay, editors, *American-South African Relations: Bibliographical Essays,* Greenwood Press, 1975; *Divide and Rule: South Africa's Bantustans,* International Defence and Aid, 1976; *White Wealth and Black Poverty: American Investments in Southern Africa,* Greenwood Press, 1976; (contributor) Hajo Hasenpflug and Karl Sauvant, editors, *The New International Economic Order: Analysis, Documents, Statistics,* Westview Press, 1977. Contributor to African studies journals in England and the United States, and to *Guardian.* Editor of *X-Ray,* 1970-71.

WORK IN PROGRESS: A book on South African and West German collaboration to produce nuclear weapons, with Zdenek Cervenka, for Julian Friedmann Publishers; research on the effect of sex discrimination on economic development, especially in the poorest countries.

SIDELIGHTS: Barbara Rogers writes: "While continuing to work on southern Africa, a major new topic of research is women in the poorest areas of the world. The two issues are quite different, but the principle is the same: liberty, equality and comradeship! Or, an end to 'home arrest.'"

ROGERS, Warren
See BRUCKER, Roger W(arren)

* * *

ROGIN, Gilbert 1929-

PERSONAL: Born November 14, 1929, in New York, N.Y.; son of Robert I. (a lawyer) and Lillian (Ruderman) Rogin; married Ruth Copes (a permissions editor for *New Yorker*), October 20, 1963 (separated); children: Ilona Nason, Ring Nason (stepchildren). *Education:* State University of Iowa, student, 1947-49; Columbia University, A.B., 1951. *Agent:* Liz Darhansoff, 52 East 91st St., New York, N.Y. *Office: Sports Illustrated,* Time & Life Building, New York, N.Y. 10020.

CAREER: Sports Illustrated, New York, N.Y., assistant managing editor, 1955—. *Military service:* U.S. Army, 1952-54; became sergeant. *Member:* Authors Guild of Authors League of America. *Awards, honors:* Best magazine sports story award from E. P. Dutton, 1964, for "Grown Man Playing a Child's Game"; award from American Academy/Institute of Arts and Letters, 1972.

WRITINGS: The Fencing Master and Other Stories, Random House, 1965; *What Happens Next?,* Random House, 1971. Contributor of stories and sports articles to national magazines, including *New Yorker, Sports Illustrated, Esquire, Vogue, Mademoiselle, Reporter,* and *Cosmopolitan.*

* * *

ROHWER, Juergen 1924-

PERSONAL: Born May 24, 1924, in Friedrichroda, Thuringia; son of Ernst (a surgeon) and Martha (Hundertmark) Rohwer; married Evi Katczor, July 14, 1955; children: Jochen, Jens. *Education:* University of Hamburg, Dr.Phil., 1954. *Home:* Am Sonnenhang 29, 7056 Weinstadt-Beutelsbach, West Germany. *Office:* Bibliothek fuer Zeitgeschichte, Konrad Adenauer Strasse 8, 7000 Stuttgart-1, West Germany.

CAREER: Arbeitskreis fuer Wehrforschung, Frankfurt am Main, West Germany, manager, 1954-59; Bibliothek fuer Zeitgeschichte, Stuttgart, West Germany, director, 1959—. Honorary professor of contemporary history, University of Stuttgart, 1971—. Chairman, Arbeitskreis fuer Wehrforschung, 1971—. *Military service:* German Navy, 1942-45; became sub-lieutenant; received Iron Cross, first and second class. *Member:* U.S. Naval Institute, Deutsche Gesellschaft fuer Wehrtechnik, Deutsche Gesellschaft fuer Marine-und Schiffahrtsgeschichte, Ranke-Gesellschaft, Verein deutscher Bibliothekare, Belgian Naval Research Association.

WRITINGS: Die Versenkung der juedischen Fluechtlingstransporter "Struma" und "Mefkure" im Schwarzen Meer (Februar 1942, August 1944) (title means "The Sinking of the Jewish Refugee Ships 'Struma' and 'Mefkure' in the Black Sea"), Bernard & Graefe, 1964; *66 Tage unter Wasser: Atom-U-Schiffe und Raketan* (title means "Sixty-six Days Submerged: Nuclear Submarines and Missiles"), Stalling, 1965; *Die U-Boot-Erfolge der Achsenmaechte, 1939-1945* (title means "Submarine Successes of Axis Powers 1939-45"), Lehmanns, 1968; (with Gerd Huemmelchen) *Chronik des Seekrieges, 1939-1945,* Stalling, 1968, translation published as *Chronology of the War at Sea, 1939-1945,* Ian Allan, Volume I: *1939-1942,* 1972, Volume II: *1943-1945,* 1974; *The Crucial Convoy Battles of March, 1943,* Ian Allan, 1975.

Editor: *Seemacht heute* (title means "Sea Power Today"), Stalling, 1957; (with Hans-Adolf Jacobsen) *Entscheidungsschlachten des zweiten Weltkrieges*, Bernard & Graefe, 1960, translation by Edward Fitzgerald published as *Decisive Battles of World War II: The German View*, Putnam, 1965; *U-Boote: Eine Chronik in Bildern* (title means "U-Boats: A Chronicle in Pictures"), Stalling, 1962; (and author of notes) N. A. Piterskij, *Kie Sowjet-Flotte im Zweiten Weltkrieg* (title means "The Soviet Navy in World War II"), Stalling, 1966; (with Elmer B. Potter and Chester W. Nimitz) *Seemacht* (title means "Sea Power"), 2nd edition (Rohwer was not associated with previous edition), Bernard & Graefe, 1974.

Contributor of articles to journals in his field. Editor, *Marine-Rundschau*, 1958—, *Jahresbibliographie der Bibliothek fuer Zeitgeschichte*, 1959—, and *Schriften der Bibliothek fuer Zeitgeschichte*, 1967—.

WORK IN PROGRESS: History of the Second World War; Sea Wars, 1850-1975; Political and Military Conflicts, 1945-1975; Battle of the Atlantic, 1939-1945; Military Technology, 1850-1975.

* * *

ROHWER, Jurgen
See ROHWER, Juergen

* * *

ROLFE, Sidney 1921-1976

June 20, 1921—March 10, 1976; American economist, educator, and author of books in his field. Obituaries: *New York Times*, March 11, 1976.

* * *

ROLFSRUD, Erling Nicolai 1912-

PERSONAL: Born September 3, 1912, in Keene, N.D.; son of Nils Halvorsen (a farmer) and Rebecca (Heide) Rolfsrud; married J. Beverly Brown (a singer and music teacher), September 6, 1941; children: Rebecca (Mrs. Allen Jerdee), Linda (Mrs. Ron Letnes), Stanley, Solveig (Mrs. William O. Shearer), Stephen, Virgil. *Education:* Concordia College, Moorhead, Minn., B.A., 1936; graduate study at State College of Education, Greeley, Colo., 1941. *Religion:* Lutheran. *Home address:* Route 2, Box 163, Alexandria, Minn. 56308.

CAREER: Rural school teacher in McKenzie County, N.D., 1930-33; Lockhart Consolidated School, Lockhart, Minn., principal, 1936-37; principal of experimental high school in Fargo, N.D., 1939-40; high school teacher of business education in Cottonwood, Minn., 1940-41; Concordia College, Moorhead, Minn., instructor, 1941-44, assistant professor of business education, 1944-46, head of department, 1941-46; free-lance writer, 1946—. High school English teacher in Evansville, Minn., 1957-59, and in Alexandria, Minn., 1959—. Teacher and writer for KFME-Television, 1967. *Awards, honors:* Ohio State award, 1969, for excellence in educational television; Pioneer Historian award from Red River Valley Historical Association, 1974; Concordia College Alumni Achievement award, 1974.

WRITINGS: Lanterns over the Prairies (juvenile), privately printed, 1949, Book II, 1949; *Church Etiquette for the Layman*, Fortress, 1950; *Gopher Tails for Papa* (juvenile), Augsburg, 1951; *White Angakok* (adult work), Augustana Book Concern, 1952; *Brother to the Eagle* (juvenile), privately printed, 1952; *Extraordinary North Dakotans* (young

adult), privately printed, 1954; *Boy from Johnny Butte* (juvenile), Augsburg, 1956; *Happy Acres* (juvenile), Augsburg, 1956; *The Family on Maple Street* (juvenile), Augsburg, 1958; *Ephphatha Missions History*, Ephphatha Missions, 1959.

One to One (adult), Augsburg, 1961; *The Story of North Dakota* (young adult), privately printed, 1963; *Cobber Chronicle* (adult), Concordia College (Moorhouse, Minn.) 1966, 2nd edition, 1976; *The Story of Red River Land* (juvenile), with teacher's manual, North Central Council for School Television, 1967; (with Patricia M. St. John, Robert Murfin, and Kenneth N. Taylor) *Great Stories for Children*, Tyndale, 1971; *Indians of the Upper Midwest* (juvenile), privately printed, 1971; (contributor) Wayne L. Brand and James G. Hector, editors, *North Dakota Decision Makers*, Analytical Statistics, 1972; *The Tiger-Lily Years* (juvenile), privately printed, 1975.

Author of "The Top Drawer," a column in *North Dakota Teacher*, 1937-51 and 1961-63. Contributor of articles and stories to children's magazines, education journals, and other periodicals. Associate editor of *North Dakota Teacher*, 1938-40.

BIOGRAPHICAL/CRITICAL SOURCES: Elwyn Robinson, *History of North Dakota*, University of Nebraska Press, 1966; Bernt Lloyd Wills, *North Dakota Geography and Early History*, privately printed, 1967; *Minnesota Journal of Education*, March, 1968; *North Dakota Horizons*, summer, 1976.

* * *

RONALD, David William 1937-
(D. Williams)

PERSONAL: Born December 30, 1937, in Edinburgh, Scotland; son of Archibald (a surgeon) and Florence E. (a teacher; maiden name, Driver) Ronald; married Mary Shephard (a teacher), December 22, 1964; children: Joanna M., Sarah E. *Education:* Attended Royal Military College of Science, 1968-70, Army Staff College, 1970, and National Defense College, 1975-76. *Religion:* Church of England. *Address:* c/o Midland Bank Ltd., Duke St., Barrow in Furness, Cumbria, England.

CAREER: British Army, career officer, 1960—; Royal Engineers, troop commander in Field Squadron in West Germany, 1960-63, troop commander in Ports Regiment in United Kingdom, 1963-65; Royal Corps of Transport, specialist in transport, 1965-66; became captain, served as operating officer of Railway Squadron in West Germany, 1966-67, elevated to second-in-command of Railway Squadron, 1967-68; became major; Ministry of Defense, member of Logistical Development staff in United Kingdom, 1970-73; Royal Corps of Transport, commanding officer of Railway Squadron, 1973-75; became lieutenant colonel; commanding officer of Transport Regiment in West Germany, 1976—. *Member:* Chartered Institute of Transport.

WRITINGS: (With R. J. Carter) *The Longmoor Military Railway*, David & Charles, 1973. Contributor, sometimes under name D. Williams, to railway technical and model engineering periodicals.

WORK IN PROGRESS: A history of the British military railways and transportation in World War I, completion expected in 1980; research on European secondary railways.

SIDELIGHTS: Ronald told *CA:* "The Longmoor history was prompted by the decision in 1969 to close Longmoor Camp. Having been trained there, as one of the last professional railwaymen in the British Army, I did not wish to see all records lost.''

* * *

ROOT, Judith C(arol)

PERSONAL: Born in Portland, Ore.; daughter of Bert Joseph (a restaurant operator) and Mary (Costanzo) Bechtold; children: Jennifer Lorca. *Education:* University of Oregon, B.A., 1961, M.A. (honors), 1963; University of North Carolina, Greensboro, M.F.A., 1972. *Home address:* P.O. Box 218, Boring, Ore. 97009.

CAREER: University of Washington, Seattle, instructor in English, 1963-65; University of North Carolina, Greensboro, instructor in English, 1965-66; Guilford Technical Institute, Jamestown, N.C., instructor in English, 1966-67; Multnomah County, Portland, Ore., researcher, 1973-75; Mt. Hood Community College, Gresham, Ore., part-time instructor in English, 1974-76; Southwest State University, Marshall, Minn., writer-in-residence, 1977—. Substitute teacher in elementary and secondary schools in California. Editorial consultant to Northwest Regional Education Laboratory, 1974—. *Awards, honors:* Honorable mention from Academy of American Poets international contest, 1972.

WRITINGS: Little Mysteries (poems), Stone Press, 1974.

Work anthologized in *Intro Five*, edited by Walton Beacham and George Garrett, University Press of Virginia, 1974; *Ten Oregon Poets*, edited by Vi Gale, Prescott Street Press, 1975; *Poetry Oregon '76*, edited by Winifred Haskell Layton, Ethel Fortner, and Sister Helena Brand. Pacific University Press, 1976. Contributor of articles, poems, and reviews to literary journals, including *Pacific Quarterly, Three Rivers Poetry Journal, Place, Northwest Review, Greensboro Review*, and *West Coast Review*, and to *New Republic*.

WORK IN PROGRESS: What Has Been Watching Us, poems; another book of poems.

SIDELIGHTS: Judith Root writes: ''Though I like writing fiction because it gives me room to 'explain' what I want to say, poetry, I think, gives a sudden, usually unexpected, glimpse of something that the reader, as he thinks about it, begins to explain to himself. The subject of my poetry is often animals and plants, but I am not at all a 'nature poet.' The relationship I suddenly realize I have with a turtle pulling himself slowly across my path, or my conflict with blackberry vines as I hack at them with a machete to keep them out of the vegetable garden, reveals something about myself, about someone I love, about life around me, something I already knew but never quite understood before. To me, most really important things are simple and I try to speak in simple but precise words and sharp images. I like poetry to confirm ideas and feelings I've always known but never quite understood.''

* * *

ROSCOE, George B(oggs) 1907-

PERSONAL: Born January 3, 1907, in Washington, Iowa; son of George C. and Marry (Boggs) Roscoe; married Anne Marie Johnson, April 7, 1944 (died, 1971); married May Lin (an accountant), February 1, 1972. *Education:* University of Kansas, A.B., 1928. *Politics:* Democrat. *Religion:* Methodist. *Home:* 7910 West Boulevard Dr., Alexandria, Va. 22308.

CAREER: Kansas City Post, Kansas City, Mo., editor, 1928; United Press, correspondent, Kansas City, Mo., 1928,

night bureau manager, Dallas, Tex., 1928-29, state bureau manager, Oklahoma City, Okla., 1928-33, divisional news editor, Kansas City, Mo., 1933-39, and New York, N.Y., 1936, day editor, Washington, D.C., 1939-41; National Association of Manufacturers, Washington, D.C., executive assistant, 1940-43; National Electrical Contractors Association, Washington, D.C., editor and publisher, 1945-72. Assistant to director, Smaller War Plants Corp., 1941-43; president, Columbia Pines Citizens Association, 1951-52; executive secretary, Mechanical Specialty Contracting Industries, 1952-61; member, President's Commission on the Employment of the Physically Handicapped, 1955—; member, Postmaster General's Technical Advisory Committee, 1962-72. *Military service:* U.S. Naval Reserve, 1943-45; became lieutenant. *Member:* Public Relations Society of America, Society of National Association Publications (founding president, 1963-65; life director), American Society of Association Executives, National Press Club, Jeffersons Island Club, Sigma Delta Chi.

WRITINGS: Enjoy and Build It Yourself, Acropolis Books, 1974. Editor, *Electrical Contractor*, 1945-72.

WORK IN PROGRESS: Here's the Dirt, a gardening book from the nutritional and ecological standpoints; a book on the place of mobile homes in the housing transition.

SIDELIGHTS: Roscoe writes that *Enjoy and Build It Yourself* was based on practical experience in building five houses for himself; *Here's the Dirt* is based on more than fifty years of experience in growing things in many parts of the country.

* * *

ROSE, Ada Campbell 1902(?)-1976

1902(?)—February 13, 1976; American magazine editor, reporter, and author of memoirs. Obituaries: *New York Times*, February 14, 1976.

* * *

ROSE, (Edward) Elliot 1928-

PERSONAL: Born February 10, 1928, in Romsey, Hampshire, England; son of Edward Snow (a physician) and Mabel (Rees-Davis) Rose. *Education:* Cambridge University, B.A., 1949, M.A., 1953. *Home:* 169 Howland Ave., Toronto, Ontario, Canada M5R BB7. *Office:* Department of History, University of Toronto, Toronto, Ontario, Canada M5S 1A1.

CAREER: University of Toronto, Toronto, Ontario, lecturer, 1955-62, assistant professor, 1962-66, associate professor, 1966-75, professor of British history, 1975—. *Member:* Canadian Society of Church History, American Historical Association, Catholic Historical Association, Victorian Studies Association of Ontario.

WRITINGS: A Razor for a Goat: Problems in the History of Witchcraft and Diabolism, University of Toronto Press, 1962; *Cases of Conscience: Alternatives Open to Recusants and Puritans Under Elizabeth I and James I*, Cambridge University Press, 1975.

WORK IN PROGRESS: Research on changing attitudes toward social rank and hierarchy in seventeenth-century England.

* * *

ROSE, Gerald Hembdon Seymour 1935-

PERSONAL: Born July 27, 1935, in Hongkong; son of

Henley Hembdon and Rachel Grace (Law) Rose; married Elizabeth Jane Pretty, July 28, 1955; children: Martin, Richard. *Education:* Attended Lowestoft School of Art; Royal Academy, national diploma in design (honors), 1955. *Home:* 19 Moorway, Poulton-le-Fylde, Lancashire, England.

CAREER: Writer and illustrator.

WRITINGS: (With wife, Elizabeth Rose; self-illustrated) *Alexander's Flycycle* (juvenile), Faber, 1967, Walker & Co., 1969.

Illustrator: E. Rose, *The Sorcerer's Apprentice* (juvenile), Walker & Co., 1966.*

*   *   *

ROSE, Lisle A(bbott)   1936-

PERSONAL: Born October 23, 1936, in Lake Linden, Mich.; son of Lisle A. (a professor) and Mildred Elizabeth (an editor; maiden name, Maddux) Rose; married Mary Elizabeth Lutz (a free-lance editor), August 13, 1960; children: Julie, Sheila, John. *Education:* University of Illinois, A.B., 1961; University of California, Berkeley, M.A., 1962, Ph.D., 1966. *Home:* 6661 Chestnut Ave., Falls Church, Va. 22042. *Office:* Historical Office, Bureau of Public Affairs, U.S. Department of State, Washington, D.C. 20520.

CAREER: University of Nebraska, Lincoln, assistant professor of American history, 1966-71; Carnegie-Mellon University, Pittsburgh, Pa., visiting associate professor of history, 1971-72; U.S. Department of State, Washington, D.C., foreign service historian, 1972—. Lecturer in American foreign relations at Johns Hopkins University, 1977—. *Military service:* U.S. Navy, 1954-57. *Member:* Authors Guild, Authors League. *Awards, honors:* Frederick Jackson Turner prize honorable mention from Organization of American Historians, 1966.

WRITINGS: Prologue to Democracy: The Federalists in the South, 1789-1800, University of Kentucky Press, 1968; *After Yalta: America and the Origins of the Cold War,* Scribner, 1973; *Dubious Victory: The United States and the End of World War II,* Kent State University Press, 1973; *Roots of Tragedy: The United States and the Struggle for Asia, 1945-53,* Greenwood Press, 1976. Contributor to *Encyclopedia of Southern History* and *Dictionary of American Biography.*

WORK IN PROGRESS: A book, *The Long Shadow: Essays on the Second World War Era;* research for a successor volume to *Dubious Victory,* and for a study on Antarctica, 1946-47.

SIDELIGHTS: Rose told *CA:* "In a time when language has been debased beyond measure, I try to write responsibly and well and to make sense of my own age so that I might leave behind a record of civility."

*   *   *

ROSEN, Joe   1937-

PERSONAL: Born October 20, 1937, in Kiev, Soviet Union; son of Nathan (a physicist) and Anna (Belkes) Rosen; married Dalia Musarov (a cell biologist), August 3, 1960; children: Laliv. *Education:* Technion—Israel Institute of Technology, B.S., 1960, M.S., 1962; Hebrew University of Jerusalem, Ph.D., 1967. *Home:* 40 Yehuda Hanasi St., Ramat-Aviv, Tel-Aviv, Israel. *Office:* Department of Physics and Astronomy, Tel-Aviv University, Tel-Aviv, Israel.

CAREER: Tel-Aviv University, Tel-Aviv, Israel, assistant, 1962-65, senior lecturer in theoretical physics, 1969—. Senior research associate at Boston University, 1965-66; research associate and assistant professor (research) at Brown University, 1966-69; visiting professor at University of North Carolina, 1976-77. *Military service:* Israel Defense Forces, 1960-62; became first lieutenant. *Member:* Israel Physical Society.

WRITINGS: Symmetry Discovered: Concepts and Applications in Nature and Science, Cambridge University Press, 1975; (editor with Giora Shaviv) *Proceedings of the Seventh International Conference on General Relativity and Gravitation GR7,* Wiley, 1975. Contributor to physics and mathematical physics journals.

WORK IN PROGRESS: An introductory textbook on the theory and application of symmetry; research on symmetry and conservation laws in theoretical physics.

AVOCATIONAL INTERESTS: Music (listening, playing, composing, conducting, and the physics of), linguistics, pistol shooting, "tinkering and repairing things," reading, travel.

*   *   *

ROSEN, Stephen   1934-

PERSONAL: Born May 3, 1934, in New York, N.Y.; son of Morris and Emma (Katzenelson) Rosen; married Miki Gold, 1959 (divorced, 1973); children: Lisa Jo, Daniel Marc. *Education:* Queens College (now of the City University of New York), B.S., 1955; Bryn Mawr College, M.A., 1966; Adelphi University, Ph.D., 1966. *Home and office:* 150 West End Ave., New York, N.Y. 10023. *Agent:* Peter Matson, Harold Matson Co., 22 East 40th St., New York, N.Y. 10016.

CAREER: International Business Machines (IBM), Owego, N.Y., research scientist, 1959-60; State University of New York Maritime College, Fort Schuyler, Bronx, N.Y., assistant professor of physics, 1960-67; General Research Corp., Bayonne, N.J., senior scientist, 1967-69; Hudson Institute, Croton-on-Hudson, N.Y., senior staff member, 1969-70; Marketing and Planning Group, New York, N.Y., consultant, 1970—. Research scientist at Centre d'Etudes Nucleaires de Saclay and at Institut d'Astrophysique, 1968. Consultant to Xerox Corp., American Telephone & Telegraph, General Telephone and Electronics, Twentieth Century Fund, and Carnegie Corp.

MEMBER: Institute for Management Sciences, Authors Guild of Authors League of America, New York Academy of Sciences. *Awards, honors:* U.S. Steel science writing award from American Institute of Physics, 1969.

WRITINGS: Cosmic Ray Origin Theories, Dover, 1970; *Future Facts,* Simon & Schuster, 1976. Contributor of articles on future research to science journals and to newspapers. Member of advisory board of *Technology Assessment.*

WORK IN PROGRESS: The Why-Not Project.

AVOCATIONAL INTERESTS: Skiing, jogging.

*   *   *

ROSENBERG, Wolfgang   1915-

PERSONAL: Born January 4, 1915, in Berlin, Germany; son of Curt (a solicitor) and Elsa (Stein) Rosenberg; married Ann Eichelbaum (a social worker), February 15, 1946; children: George, William, Vera. *Education:* University of New Zealand, M.Com., 1943, F.C.A., 1945. *Home:* 14 Sherwood

Lane, Christchurch, New Zealand. *Office:* Department of Economics, University of Canterbury, Christchurch, New Zealand.

CAREER: University of Canterbury, Christchurch, New Zealand, reader in economics, 1946—.

WRITINGS: Full Employment: Can New Zealand's Economic Miracle Last?, A. H. & A. W. Reed, 1960; *A Guideline to New Zealand's Future,* Caxton Press, 1968; *Money in New Zealand,* Reed Education, 1973; (contributor) Thomson and Trolin, editors, *Contemporary New Zealand,* Hicks, Smith & Wright, 1973.

WORK IN PROGRESS: Research on industrialization, on Korean development in north and south, and on economics of political independence.

SIDELIGHTS: Rosenberg writes: "My main interest is to throw light on the forces which move New Zealand society, a small homogeneous society which nonetheless is split into antagonistic interest groups and subject to the vagaries of the international trading system."

* * *

ROSENBLUM, Richard 1928-

PERSONAL: Born January 24, 1928, in Brooklyn, N.Y.; son of Archie (a retired tailor) and Anna Rosenblum; married Barbara Rhode (a secretary), May 5, 1959; children: Anne. *Education:* Attended Cooper Union, three years, received diploma. *Politics:* "Liberal/Democratic/Independent." *Religion:* Jewish. *Home:* 2 Grace Ct., Brooklyn, N.Y. 11201. *Office:* 370 Lexington Ave., New York, N.Y. 10017.

CAREER: Free-lance illustrator; *New York Herald Tribune,* New York, N.Y., art apprentice, 1950-51; CBS-TV News, New York, N.Y., staff artist, 1951-52, UPA Films, New York, N.Y., animation designer, 1955-57; teacher of illustration at Parsons School of Design. Has had exhibitions at Art Director Club and Society of Illustrators, both New York, N.Y. Member of executive board, Grace Court Association. *Military service:* U.S. Army, 1946.

WRITINGS: (Self illustrated) *Tugboats,* Holt, 1976.

Illustrator: Frank L. Baum, *Kidnapped Santa Claus,* Bobbs-Merrill, 1969; *Ecidujerp-Prejudice,* Watts, 1974.

SIDELIGHTS: "I work in pen and ink—water color and dye. Have a studio in Manhattan. Don't like to work home. Find I get more realistic as I get older."

* * *

ROSENFELD, Albert (Hyman) 1920-

PERSONAL: Born May 31, 1920, in Philadelphia, Pa.; son of Samuel and Annie (Zeiffert) Rosenfeld; married Lillian Elizabeth Snow (a librarian), August 24, 1948; children: Robert, Shana. *Education:* New Mexico State University, B.A., 1950. *Politics:* Democrat. *Religion:* Jewish. *Home:* 25 Davenport Ave., New Rochelle, N.Y. 10805. *Agent:* Ann Elmo, 52 Vanderbilt Ave., New York, N.Y. 10017. *Office: Saturday Review,* 488 Madison Ave., New York, N.Y. 10022.

CAREER: Acting bureau chief and correspondent for Time, Inc., based in Las Cruces, N.M., 1948-50, and Sante Fe, N.M., 1950-58; *Life* Magazine, New York City, worked on news desk, 1956-57, writer, 1957-58, science editor, 1958-69; *Family Health,* New York City, managing editor, 1970-71; *Saturday Review,* New York City, science editor, 1973—. Medical editor, Time-Life Video and Time-Life Broadcast,

1971-72. Senior research associate in contemporary ethics, Manhattanville College, 1972-73; adjunct professor of biophilosophy, Drexel University, 1971-74; adjunct assistant professor of human biological chemistry and genetics, University of Texas at Galveston, 1973—. Science interviewer for CBS's "Summer Semester", 1975; consultant, National Foundation-March of Dimes, 1973—. *Military service:* U.S. Army, European theater of operations, 1942-45.

MEMBER: Council for the Advancement of Science Writing (president 1968, 1970, 1974), National Association of Science Writers, American Medical Writers Association, American Society of Law and Medicine, Institute for Society, Ethics and the Life Sciences, Authors Guild, Smithsonian Associates, American Museum of Natural History, Sigma Delta Chi. *Awards, honors:* Aviation-Space Writers Association award, 1964; Distinguished Alumnus award from New Mexico State University, 1965; American Association for the Advancement of Science-Westinghouse writing award, 1966; Lasker Award, 1967; D.Lett. from New Mexico State University, 1970; Claude Bernard Science Journalism Award, 1975; Jesse H. Neal Award, 1976; National Magazine award, 1976.

WRITINGS: The Quintessence of Irving Langmuir, Pergamon, 1962, reissued as *Men of Physics: Irving Langmuir,* 1966; *The Second Genesis: The Coming Control of Life,* Prentice-Hall, 1969; *Prolongevity,* Knopf, 1976. Editorial consultant, Time-Life Books, 1972-73; consulting editor, *Physician's World,* 1972-74; consulting science editor, Knopf, 1972-74. Contributor of articles to over twenty periodicals and professional journals, including *Harper's, Commentary,* and *Smithsonian.*

WORK IN PROGRESS: Further research on scientific and biomedical subjects.

SIDELIGHTS: Rosenfeld writes that he is "increasingly concerned with the communication of science and science policy to the general public. I would especially like to make novelists and playwrights more aware of the scientific context in which they live." *Avocational interests:* Hiking, jogging, swimming, tennis, dancing, yoga.

* * *

ROSENFELD, Arnold (Solomon) 1933-

PERSONAL: Born April 18, 1933, in New York, N.Y.; son of William (a postman) and Sarah (Cohen) Rosenfeld; married Ruth Doris Lilly (a free-lance writer), September 30, 1956; children: William Bennett, Jonathan Andrew, Lauren Gay. *Education:* Attended University of Houston, 1951, and Stanford University, 1967. *Religion:* Jewish. *Home:* 563 East Dale Dr., Dayton, Ohio 45415. *Office: Dayton Daily News,* Dayton, Ohio 45401.

CAREER: Houston Post, Houston, Tex., staff writer, 1953-68, book editor, and editorial writer, 1965-68; *Detroit Free Press,* Detroit, Mich., associate editor of *Detroit* (weekly magazine), 1967, editor, 1968; *Dayton Daily News,* Dayton, Ohio, managing editor, 1968—. *Military service:* U.S. Army, 1951-53. *Member:* American Society of Newspaper Editors, Associated Press Managing Editors Association. *Awards, honors:* First place in editorial writing from Texas branch of Associated Press Managing Editors Association, 1967; awards from Texas chapter of Theta Sigma Phi, 1969, 1972.

WRITINGS: (Editor) *A Thomason Sketchbook,* University of Texas Press, 1969. Contributor to *Bulletin of the American Society of Newspaper Editors* and *AP Log.*

SIDELIGHTS: Rosenfeld writes: "I have been through a number of periods, a blue, a yellow, a rose. I suspect that right now I am mostly into discovering a daily journalism that deals with the life of people as if it were news, a journalism that is useful in the lives of its readers and in which they can recognize themselves. I think we have been doing elitist journalism for journalists in this country for too long, and even the youngest of us are bereft of the ability to sense something real happening in society that is not structured by the most conventional view of news. News is what's happening to people. We aren't reporting that."

*   *   *

ROSENOF, Theodore   1943-

PERSONAL: Born September 15, 1943, in Newark, N.J.; son of Irving and Josephine (Schmitt) Rosenof. *Education:* Rutgers University, B.A., 1965; University of Wisconsin, Madison, M.A., 1966, Ph.D., 1970. *Home:* 2715 Third St., #914, Lubbock, Tex. 79415. *Office:* Department of History, Texas Tech University, Lubbock, Tex. 79409.

CAREER: Texas Tech University, Lubbock, visiting instructor in history, 1975—. *Member:* American Historical Association, Organization of American Historians.

WRITINGS: Dogma, Depression, and the New Deal, Kennikat, 1975; (editor with E. David Cronon) *The Second World War and the Atomic Age,* AHM Publishing, 1975. Contributor to history and American studies journals.

*   *   *

ROSENTHAL, Harry F(rederick)   1927-

PERSONAL: Born February 21, 1927, in Germany; came to the United States in 1938, naturalized, 1945; son of Albert (a businessman) and Melani (Selig) Rosenthal; married Naidene Frank, May 13, 1956; children: David, Lesli. *Education:* University of Southern California, B.S., 1950; also studied photography. *Religion:* Jewish. *Home:* 14101 Blazer Lane, Silver Spring, Md. 20906. *Office:* Associated Press, 2021 K St., Washington, D.C. 20006.

CAREER: Evening Free-Lance, Hollister, Calif., reporter, 1950-51; Associated Press, San Francisco, Calif., reporter, 1951-52, based in Kansas City, Mo., 1952-67, member of major story task force, 1965-67, on special assignment team, 1967-69, Washington, D.C., general assignment reporter 1969—. Notable assignments include Watergate hearings and trials, Apollo space shots, My Lai trials, including Lieutenant Calley's, the trial of Sirhan Sirhan, civil rights events, and national political campaigns since 1968. *Military service:* U.S. Army, 1944-46; photographer and proofreader for *Pacific Stars and Stripes* (Tokyo), 1945-46; became technical sergeant.

MEMBER: Newspaper Guild. *Awards, honors:* Worth Bingham Prize for Investigative Journalism, 1968; top performance award from Associated Press Managing Editors Association, 1970, for covering Apollo Twelve space shot.

WRITINGS: (With Jules Loh, John Barbour, and Sid Moody) *Triumph and Tragedy: The Story of the Kennedys,* Morrow, 1968; (with Arthur Everett and Katherine Johnson) *Calley,* Dell, 1971.

*   *   *

ROSS, David   1896-1975

PERSONAL: Born July 7, 1896, in New York, N.Y.; son of Samuel and Fanny (Schmuller) Ross; married second wife, Beatrice Pons, October 14, 1937; children: (first marriage) David Andrews, Jr., Helen (Mrs. Banice Webber); (second marriage) Jonathan. *Education:* Attended Rutgers College (now University) and New York University. *Residence:* New York, N.Y.

CAREER: Radio announcer and commentator, 1926-58 (reader of poetry on "Poet's Gold," Columbia Broadcasting System-Radio, 1934-42, "Words in the Night," National Broadcasting Co.-Radio, 1953-58, and "A Rendezvous with David Ross"); writer and poet, 1958-75. Had worked as vaudeville actor, superintendent of an orphan asylum, and journalist; had appeared on television, narrated films, and made sound recordings; gave readings of his works at Library of Congress and at universities. *Member:* Poetry Society of America (past vice-president; member of board of directors, 1966-75), Academy of American Poets, Players Club. *Awards, honors:* Gold medal from American Academy of Arts and Letters, 1933; lyric poem award from Poetry Society of America, 1967; Christopher Morley Prize for light verse from Poetry Society of America, 1969, for "Elegy for an Overworked Undertaker."

WRITINGS: (Editor) *Poet's Gold: An Anthology of Poems to Be Read Aloud,* Macauley Co., 1933, 3rd edition, Devin-Adair, 1956; (editor) *The Illustrated Treasury of Poetry for Children,* Grosset, 1970. Also author of a book of poems, *Wintry Errand,* as yet unpublished. Contributor of poems to literary magazines.

OBITUARIES: New York Times, November 14, 1975.*

(Died November 12, 1975, in New York, N.Y.)

*   *   *

ROSS, Hal   1941-

PERSONAL: Born May 20, 1941, in Montreal, Quebec, Canada; son of Max and Grace (Hazenof) Ross; married Sheila Officer, August 31, 1961 (divorced, 1976); children: Steven, Michael. *Education:* Attended Sir George Williams University, 1970-72. *Home and office:* 2021 Atwater Ave., Apt. 415, Montreal, Quebec, Canada H3H2P2.

CAREER: CJQC radio, Quebec City, Quebec, announcer, 1959-60; Decca Records, Montreal, Quebec, promotion manager, 1960-63; London Records, Montreal, national field representative, 1963-66; Phonodisc Records, Montreal, Quebec, and Toronto, Ontario, national sales and promotion manager, 1966-69; MCA Records, New York, N.Y., sales and promotion manager, 1969; Irwin Toy Ltd., Montreal, Quebec, salesman, 1969—.

WRITINGS: The Fleur-de-Lys Affair (novel), Doubleday, 1975.

WORK IN PROGRESS: A novel based in New York City.

SIDELIGHTS: Ross writes that it wasn't until 1960 that he "discovered the value and importance of writing and began to devote every spare moment to learning the craft. My best work is done during the early morning (five to eight a.m.) and am regimented to a schedule six days a week."

*   *   *

ROSS, Nancy
See DeROIN, Nancy

*   *   *

ROSSI, William A(nthony)   1916-

PERSONAL: Born December 3, 1916, in Boston, Mass.; son of James (a shoe retailer) and Antoinette (Pellegrino)

Rossi; married Margaret Powers, August 20, 1942; children: Neil, Lynne, Marc, Dean. *Education:* New England School of Podiatry, D.S.P., 1937. *Home:* 84 Summer St., Hingham, Mass. 02043. *Agent:* David Otte, 9 Park St., Boston, Mass. 02108.

CAREER: Podiatrist in Boston, Mass., 1937-41; Rumpf Publishing Co., Chicago, Ill., editor, 1945-54; Chilton Co., Philadelphia, Pa., editor, 1955-65; William A. Rossi Associates, Boston, Mass., director, 1965—. Writer on podiatry and footware. *Military Service:* U.S. Navy, 1942-45; became chief pharmacist's mate. *Member:* Boston Museum of Science Advisory Board, Metropolitan Great Books Council (president), Norfolk Fellowship Foundation (vice-president). *Awards, honors:* Neal Award, 1963.

WRITINGS: Podometrics, Rumpf Publishing Co., 1947; *Your Feet and Their Care,* Emerson, 1955; *Starting and Managing a Small Shoe Store,* U.S. Small Business Administration, 1975; *The Sex Life of the Foot and Shoe,* Saturday Review Press, 1976. Contributor of articles on leather and footwear to *Encyclopaedia Britannica.*

WORK IN PROGRESS: Walk for a Better Sex Life; The 80-20 Law of Personal Power, expected date of publication, spring, 1978.

SIDELIGHTS: A former jazz pianist and music arranger for dance bands, Rossi has worked with volunteer rehabilitation programs for prison inmates since 1962. He has visited twenty four countries, including Russia and Eastern European countries, where he has studied footwear.

*   *   *

ROSS-MACDONALD, Malcolm J(ohn) 1932-
(Malcolm Macdonald)

PERSONAL: Name originally Malcolm John Ross Macdonald; name legally changed in 1947; born February 29, 1932, in Chipping Sodbury, England. Son of Alan Ross (an engineer) and Brenda (a secretary; maiden name, Edwards) Macdonald; married Ingrid Giehr, March 17, 1962; children: Petra Brigid, Candida Judith. *Education:* Attended Falmouth School of Art, 1950-54; University College London, Slade Diploma, 1958. *Politics:* "A sort-of far-right marxist—broad enough to offend all enthusiasts." *Religion:* "Atheist, humanist." *Residence:* Ireland. *Agent:* David Higham Associates, 7-9 Lower John St., Golden Sq., London W1R 4HA, England.

CAREER: Folkuniversitet, Umeaa, Sweden, lektor, 1959-61; Aldus Books Ltd., London, England, began as caption writer, became executive editor, 1961-65; free-lance writer, editor, and graphic designer, 1966—. Visiting lecturer, Hornsey College of Art, 1966-69. Consultant to publishing companies. *Military service:* British Army, 1954-56. *Member:* Society of Authors, Radio writers Association, Authors Guild.

WRITINGS: The Big Waves (novel), J. Cape, 1962; (with Donald Longmore) *Spare Part Surgery,* Doubleday, 1968; (with Longmore) *Machines in Medicine,* Doubleday, 1969; (with Longmore) *The Heart,* McGraw Hill, 1971; *The World Wildlife Guide,* Viking, 1971; *Beyond the Horizon* (history), Grolier, 1971; *Every Living Thing* (ecology), Danbury Press, 1974; *Doors Doors Doors* (closed circulation book for architects) Viking Aluminum, 1974; (under name Malcolm Macdonald) *The World from Rough Stones* (novel), Knopf, 1975; *The Origins of Johnny,* Knopf, 1975; *Life in the Future,* Danbury Press, 1976; (under name Malcolm Macdonald) *The Rich Are with You Always* (novel), Knopf, 1976.

Radio plays released by British Broadcasting Corporation (BBC): "Kristina's Winter," 1972; "Conditional People," 1973; (under name Malcolm Macdonald) "The World from Rough Stones" (trilogy), 1974. Also founding and consulting editor of the twenty volume "LIving World" series for Aldus Books, 1972.

WORK IN PROGRESS: a novel, *The Children of Fortune,* publication expected in 1978; seven or nine more novels tracing the rise and fall of Victorian-style capitalism and empire.

SIDELIGHTS: Ross-Macdonald told *CA:* "I set out to become the very opposite of what 'novelist' has come to mean—to become, instead, a simple storyteller." His stories are heavily influenced by his thirteen years as a nonfiction writer. Though his main characters and plots are all invented, he says he does not invent a "fact" if the truth will serve as well, and that his stories are made more vivid because of his obsession with history. He has collected an extensive library of Victorian source books, British and American guidebooks, lists of coach operators, textbooks, valuers' tables, topographies, and autobiographies, from which he draws material for his stories.

"I would like people to be, above all, entertained and enthralled by my stories," Ross-Macdonald writes. "I would like them to gain a new understanding of why we are where we are now—to see that the problems which beset us have not simply sprung up in the last few years. Indeed, those problems were often worse a hundred years ago, and I hope to dramatize that—but without making the difference merely sensational. We live in an age rich in communication, crammed with today's and even tomorrow's news. Perspective gets crowded out. Judgement gets warped in ways our forefathers would find ludicrously pessimistic. If one of the effects of my entertainments is to restore that perspective and straighten that judgement, I would be content."

AVOCATIONAL INTERESTS: "Reclaiming and restoring a decrepit house and fifteen acres of land."

*   *   *

ROTH, Eugen 1895-1976

January 24, 1895—April 29, 1976; German poet and author of books on Munich. Obituaries: *AB Bookman's Weekly,* June 14, 1976.

*   *   *

ROTH, Harry 1903(?)-1976

1903(?)—June 30, 1976; German-born American book illustrator and muralist. Obituaries: *New York Times,* July 3, 1976.

*   *   *

ROTH, Sol 1927-

PERSONAL: Born March 8, 1927, in Rzeszow, Poland; came to United States, 1934; naturalized citizen, 1939; son of Joseph (a businessman) and Miriam (Lamm) Roth; married Debra H. Stitskin, November 27, 1957; children: Steven D., Michael J., Sharon J. *Education:* Yeshiva College, B.A., 1948; Columbia University, M.A., 1953, Ph.D., 1966; Rabbi Isaac Elchanan Theological Seminary, Rabbi, 1950. *Home:* 99 Tioga Ave., Atlantic Beach, N.Y. 11509. *Office:* Jewish Center of Atlantic Beach, Park St. and Nassau Ave., Atlantic Beach, N.Y. 11509.

CAREER: Rabbi in Jeshurun, N.Y., 1950-51, 1954-56, and

in Cambridge, Mass., 1951-52; Jewish Center of Atlantic Beach, Atlantic Beach, N.Y., rabbi, 1956—. *Military service:* U.S. Army, chaplain, 1952-54; became first lieutenant. *Member:* Rabbinical Council of America (vice-president, 1974-75), American Philosophical Association, Philosophy of Science Association, New York Board of Rabbis (president, 1974-76).

WRITINGS: Science and Religion, Yeshiva University Press, 1967.

WORK IN PROGRESS: The Jewish Idea of Community.

* * *

ROTHEL, David 1936-

PERSONAL: Born December 23, 1936, in Berea, Ohio; son of Bert I. (a farmer) and Kate (Rogers) Rothel; married Ida Lorenzen, April 1, 1956 (divorced, 1966); married Nancy Chandler (an educator and administrator), December 18, 1966; children: (first marriage) David Michael, Loren Christopher; (second marriage) Laura Lynne. *Education:* Ashland College, B.S., 1959; Kent State University, graduate study, 1960-65. *Home:* 2751 Valencia Dr., Sarasota, Fla. 33579. *Office:* Sarasota Board of Public Instruction, Hatton St., Sarasota, Fla. 33579.

CAREER: Drama and speech teacher in public schools of North Royalton, Ohio, 1961-65, and Sarasota, Fla., 1966-68; Players Theatre, Sarasota, Fla., producer and director, 1968-71; Sarasota Board of Public Instruction, Sarasota, Fla., director of drug education program, 1972—. *Awards, honors:* Fulbright grant to teach in Iceland, 1965-66.

WRITING: Who Was That Masked Man: The Story of the Lone Ranger, A. S. Barnes, 1976.

WORK IN PROGRESS: The Singing Cowboys, "a nostalgic examination of the musical B Western films of the thirties, forties, and early fifties and the singing cowboy stars that made them so popular."

SIDELIGHTS: Rothel writes: "I have always been intrigued with the workings of show business—the career and business ups and downs; the audience's likes, dislikes and frequent fickleness; the human chemistry that results in stardom for one performer and failure for another. I am now enjoying the experience of researching and writing about particular show business personages and genres that have fascinated me over the years."

* * *

ROTHWEILER, Paul R(oger) 1931-
(James Paul Ruyerson)

PERSONAL: Born April 18, 1931, in Woodbridge, N.J.; son of George Frederick (a salesman) and Doris Eihleen (a church organist; maiden name, Dayer) Rothweiler; married Verna Jane Slutter (a nurse), August 30, 1952; children: Paul Roger, Jr., Dona Eihleen (Mrs. Richard L. Maynard), Judith Lynn, Edith Alison. *Education:* Educated in high school in Springfield, N.Y. *Politics:* Independent. *Religion:* Protestant. *Home and office address:* R.D. 1, Stewartsville, N.J. 08886. *Agent:* Patricia Falk Feeley, 52 Vanderbilt Ave., New York, N.Y. 10017.

CAREER: Courier-News, Somerville, N.J., sports and news reporter, 1948-57; Prudential Insurance Co., New Brunswick, N.J., special agent, 1957-68; Peoples Life Insurance Co., Metuchen, N.J., regional director, 1968-71; Prudential Insurance Co., Newark, N.J., brokerage manager, 1971-75, special agent, 1975—. *Military service:* U.S. Air

Force, 1951-55; became staff sergeant. *Member:* American Society of Chartered Life Underwriters (charter vice-president of Central Jersey chapter, 1966-67; president, 1968-69; educational vice-president, 1969—), Middlesex-Somerset Life Underwriters Association (member of board of directors, 1965-68), Authors League of America, Writers Association of New Jersey.

WRITINGS: The Sensuous Southpaw (sports novel), Putnam, 1976.

WORK IN PROGRESS: The New Olympians, a novel about the Winter Olympics at Lake Placid, N.Y., completion expected in 1980; revising the novel, *Corridor.*

SIDELIGHTS: Rothweiler writes: "I have always been a writer of sorts, though not until the last six years did I realize that fiction was my life's work. Although my lone published work is in the sports realm, my interests are diverse and I have completed manuscripts in a variety of different fields, including suspense and science fiction. *Corridor* is so radically different that it defies categorization. It contains elements of science fiction, the love story, the suspense story, yet is none of these. Having been a working life insurance man for almost twenty years I would dearly love to put together a simple encyclopedia covering the field for the average working man, though I am not presently engaged in the project I began years ago."

* * *

ROUDYBUSH, Alexandra (Brown) 1911-

PERSONAL: Born March 14, 1911, in Hyeres, Cote d'Azur, France; U.S. citizen; daughter of Constantine (a journalist) and Ethel (Wheeler) Brown; married Franklin Roudybush (a diplomat and school director), May 22, 1941. *Education:* London School of Economics and Political Science, B.A., 1929. *Politics:* Democrat. *Home:* 15 Avenue du President Wilson, Paris 16e, France. *Agent:* Harold Ober Associates, Inc., 40 East 49th St., New York, N.Y. 10017.

CAREER: London Evening Standard, London, England, Washington correspondent, 1931; news secretary with Drew Pearson, 1932; Agence Havas (French news agency), assistant in New York City, 1935; *Time* (magazine), New York City, research news analyst, 1936; Columbia Broadcasting System, Inc., New York City, staff member in news department, 1936; Mutual Broadcasting System, New York City, White House correspondent, 1940; National Academy of Science, Washington, D.C., staff member, 1940-57; Dewey, Ballantine, Bushby, Palmer & Wood, Paris, France, administrative secretary, 1965-70; author. *Member:* Writers Guild, Crime Writers of America, American Women's Club of Paris.

WRITINGS—All published by Doubleday; all crime novels: *Before the Ball Was Over,* 1965; *Death of a Moral Person,* 1967; *A Capital Crime,* 1969; *The House of the Cat,* 1970; *A Sybaritic Death,* 1972; *A Gastronomic Murder,* 1973; *Suddenly in Paris,* 1975; *The Female of the Species,* in press. Contributor to magazines.

WORK IN PROGRESS: Nebraska Gold, a story of early Nebraska; *Death in Darjeeling.*

SIDELIGHTS: Alexandra Roudybush has accompanied her husband on his various diplomatic posts, including Paris, Strasbourg, Saarland, Pakistan, and Dublin, Ireland. She speaks French, German, Italian, Portuguese, and some Turkish, and has studied Latin and Greek.

ROWELL, Galen 1940-

PERSONAL: Born August 23, 1940, in Berkeley, Calif.; son of Edward Z. (a professor) and Margaret (a music teacher and professor; maiden name, Avery) Rowell; married Carol Chevez, December 22, 1962; children: Nicole, Tony. *Education:* University of California, Berkeley, student, 1958-62. *Politics:* "As little as possible." *Religion:* "Less." *Home and office:* 913 Pomona Ave., Albany, Calif. 94706.

CAREER: Rowell Auto Service, Albany, Calif., owner, 1962-71; free-lance writer and photographer, 1971—. Instructor in mountaineering and its history at University of California, Berkeley, extension, 1972-73. *Member:* American Alpine Club (member of board of directors), Alpine Club of Canada.

WRITINGS: The Vertical World of Yosemite, Wilderness Press, 1974; *In the Throne Room of the Mountain Gods,* Sierra Club, 1977. Contributor of articles and photographs to magazines and newspapers, including *National Wildlife, Audubon, National Geographic, Sierra Club Bulletin, New York Times, Mountain Gazette, America Illustrated, Ascent, Backpacker,* and *Fortune.* Member of editorial board of *American Alpine Journal.*

WORK IN PROGRESS: A handbook of wilderness mountaineering; research and eleven thousand photographs for a book on the Owens Valley region of Eastern California.

SIDELIGHTS: Rowell writes that his work covers travel, conservation, mountaineering, ski touring, backpacking, and wildlife. His own mountain experiences began in the 1950's with Sierra Club pack trips. Since then he has made first ascents of more than a hundred routes in Yosemite, the High Sierra, Canada, and Alaska. He made several ascents of Yosemite's Half Dome and El Capitan and climbed on the 1975 American K2 Expedition, which attempted the second highest peak in the world on the Pakistan-China border.

* * *

ROWLEY, Peter 1934-

PERSONAL: Surname rhymes with "holy"; born July 20, 1934, in London, England; son of Owsley V. F. (an estate owner) and Winifred (Eyre) Rowley; married Terez de Tuboly (an assistant director of an art gallery), September 10, 1968. *Education:* Attended Princeton University, 1951-54. *Religion:* Roman Catholic. *Home and office:* 815 Park Ave., New York, N.Y. 10021. *Agent:* A. L. Hart, Fox Chase Agency, 419 East 57th St., New York, N.Y. 10022.

CAREER: Boston Post, Boston, Mass., reporter, 1956; *Gloucester Daily Times,* Gloucester, Mass., reporter, 1955-56; *Sunday Express,* London, England, reporter, 1958; *Newsweek,* New York, N.Y., stringer, 1958-60; independent investor, interested mainly in land, property, and the stock market (business plane and helicopter manufacturing industry, food industry, and medical equipment manufacturers), 1960—. Member of board of directors of Gilson's Hospital (for the elderly). *Military service:* U.S. Army Reserve, 1957-63. *Member:* Brooks's Club, Knickerbocker Club.

WRITINGS: New Gods in America, McKay, 1971; *Ken Rosewall: Twenty Years at the Top,* Putnam, 1976. Contributor of more than one hundred articles and reviews to magazines and newspapers, including *Nation, Economist, Catholic World, Mademoiselle, New Republic, New Statesman,* and *Spectator.*

WORK IN PROGRESS: Research on religion, tennis, fiction, and film.

ROY, Michael 1913-1976

July 18, 1913—June 26, 1976; American cooking show host, reporter, and author of books in his field. Obituaries: *New York Times,* June 28, 1976; *Washington Post,* June 28, 1976. (See index for previous *CA* sketch)

* * *

ROYSTER, Philip M. 1943-

PERSONAL: Born July 31, 1943, in Chicago, Ill.; married Sandra Howe (a poet; marriage terminated); children: Rebecca Suzanne, Francesca Therese. *Education:* Attended Roosevelt University and University of Illinois; De Paul University, B.A., 1965, M.A., 1967; Loyola University, Chicago, Ill., Ph.D., 1974. *Home:* 11 South Lake Ave., Albany, N.Y. 12203. *Office:* Department of African and Afro-American Studies, State University of New York at Albany, Albany, N.Y. 12222.

CAREER: Has worked as a clerk for Internal Revenue Service, 1962-63; has worked as a postal clerk for U.S. Postal Service, 1963-66; high school English teacher in Chicago, Ill., 1966-67; Loyola University, Chicago, Ill., instructor, 1969-70; Fisk University, Nashville, Tenn., instructor, 1970-74, assistant professor, 1974-75; State University of New York at Albany, assistant professor of African and Afro-American studies and director of Writers Workshop, 1975—. Instructor at Belmont College, 1972. Master drummer and percussionist with Burundi Dance Troupe, 1975—; member of Kuumba (Black theater company), 1969-70; has performed with groups for sound recordings and in concert; has given poetry readings and appeared on television and radio programs. *Member:* Modern Language Association of America, College Language Association, Organization of Black American Culture.

WRITINGS: (With Stanley A. Clayes) *Suggestions for Instructors to Accompany Clayes' and Spencer's Context for Composition,* Appleton, 1969; *The Back Door* (poems), Third World Press, 1971; *You'll Never Know How You Sound Till You Listen to Yourself* (poems), Third World Press, in press. Contributor of poems and reviews to literary journals, including *Journal of Black Poetry, Cadence, Liberator, Rap,* and *Black World.*

SIDELIGHTS: royster's sound recordings include "The Knack," "Backwoods Woman," "A White Sport Coat and a Pink Crustacean," "We Make Spirit," "Hangin' Around the Observatory" (album), and "Earth Blossom" (album).

* * *

RUBIN, Lillian Breslow 1924-

PERSONAL: Born January 13, 1924, in Philadelphia, Pa.; daughter of Sol and Rae (Vinin) Breslow; married Henry M. Rubin (a writer); children: Marcy R. *Education:* University of California, Berkeley, B.A. (with great distinction), 1967, M.A., 1968, Ph.D., 1971; postdoctoral study, 1971-72. *Religion:* Jewish. *Home and office:* 823 Craft Ave., El Cerrito, Calif. 94530. *Agent:* Rhoda Weyr, William Morris Agency, 1350 Avenue of the Americas, New York, N.Y. 10019.

CAREER: University of California, Cowell Memorial Hospital, Berkeley, research sociologist, 1971-72; Wright Institute, Berkeley, Calif., professor of sociology and psychology, 1972-76; licensed marriage, family, and child counselor in private practice, 1976—. Research sociologist, Institute for Scientific Analysis, 1972—; lecturer at Mills College, 1973.

MEMBER: American Sociological Association, Society for

the Study of Social Problems, Sociologists for Women in Society, Society for the Psychological Study of Social Issues, National Council on Family Relations, California Association of Marriage and Family Counselors, Phi Beta Kappa. *Awards, honors:* National Institute of Mental Health grants, 1974-76, 1976-79.

WRITINGS: Busing and Backlash: White Against White in an Urban School District, University of California Press, 1972; (contributor) Norene Harris and other editors, *The Integration of American Schools,* Allyn & Bacon, 1975; *Worlds of Pain: Life in the Working-Class Family,* Basic Books, 1976. Contributor to professional journals.

WORK IN PROGRESS: Women of a Certain Age (tentative title), publication by Basic Books expected in 1979; research for *Women in the Middle Years: Rejects from Life,* completion expected in 1979.

* * *

RUBY, Kathryn 1947-

PERSONAL: Born September 27, 1947, in Orange, N.J.; daughter of Myron (a stockbroker) and Leonore (Sacks) Ruby. *Education:* University of Wisconsin, Madison, student, 1965-67; New York University, B.A., 1969, M.A., 1972. *Home and office:* 535 Hudson St., No. 4F, New York, N.Y. 10014. *Agent:* Elaine Markson, 44 Greenwich Ave., New York, N.Y. 10014.

CAREER: Human Resources Administration, New York, N.Y., technical writer and management analyst, 1972-74; City College of the City University of New York, New York City, technical writer, 1974-75; free-lance technical writer, 1975—. *Member:* Modern Language Association of America. *Awards, honors:* MacDowell Colony fellowship, 1974; grant from International P.E.N., 1976.

WRITINGS: (Editor with Lucille Iverson) *We Become New: Poems by Contemporary American Women,* Bantam, 1975. Contributor of articles and reviews to *Ms., Metropolitan Review,* and *Margins.*

WORK IN PROGRESS: A book of poems.

* * *

RUCHAMES, Louis 1917-1976

May 25, 1917—June 2, 1976; American historian, educator, and author of books in his field. Obituaries: *New York Times,* June 3, 1976. (See index for previous *CA* sketch)

* * *

RUDDER, Virginia L. 1941-

PERSONAL: Born August 21, 1941, in Roxboro, N.C.; daughter of Byrd Jackson (a farmer) and Myrtle (Whitfield) Long; children: Michael, Shawn. *Education:* Attended Catawba College, 1958-61. *Politics:* "After Richard IV, I'm trying to quit." *Religion:* "Any other than Sunday Christian only." *Home:* Rt. 2, Box 54, Hurdle Mills, N.C. 27541.

CAREER: The Courier-Times, Roxboro, N.C., society editor and reporter, 1963-70; *The Chapel Hill Weekly,* Chapel Hill, N.C., typesetter, 1970-72; *The Courier-Times,* Roxboro, N.C., book page editor, columnist and reviewer, 1972-75; Piedmont Technical Institute, Roxboro, N.C., instructor in creative writing, 1976—. Poet. *Member:* North Carolina Poetry Society, Triangle Area Women Poets, The Byron Society. *Awards, honors:* Greensboro Writers' State Poetry Contest, first place award, 1964; North Carolina Poetry Contest, first place award, 1976.

WRITINGS: After the Ifaluk and Other Poems, Thorp Springs Press, 1976.

WORK IN PROGRESS: Five collections of poetry; *Augusta,* a novel based upon the relationship of Augusta Byron Leigh and her half brother, Lord Byron.

SIDELIGHTS: After the Ifaluk was conceived in "white hot rage after reading Dr. Sigmund Freud's lamentation, 'Despite my 30 years of research into the feminine soul, I have not yet been able to answer . . . the great question that has never been answered: What does a woman want?' " The thirteen blank verse dramatic monologues tracing woman's history attempt to answer Freud's question, "albeit belated." Rudder explains the significance of the book's title: "Ifaluk is an island in the South Pacific where they have a large body of love poetry written exclusively by women."

"I don't define poetry," says Rudder, "I just do it. Basically, I'm predominantly a bed poet with a permanent fascination for the intricacies of the male-female relationship, whether in a contemporary setting or a pre-history culture. I am convinced poetry possesses the power to illuminate, to instruct, to astound, to humble, to delight, to terrify, and to heal. A poet is a chameleon, an exorcist and a conductant, a vehicle for the poems to attain their own entities. Poetry is an addiction and I'm a mainliner. If I couldn't be a poet, I wouldn't want to be—period. Poets should write for people, *not* other poets, as poetry thrives and floursihes best when direct center of mainstream. To restrict poetry to the classroom is to deny it lifeblood and aïr. Poems abound, are waiting to be found and claimed everywhere—field and stream, freeways, locked wards, bedrooms, prisons, gas chambers, Mars. I live in mortal fear I might miss one. I find my best poems in my native environment: a remote section of the South on red clay which has been in my family for five generations now, a setting of hardwoods, pines, kudzu, catamounts and copperheads, with as little civilization as possible. My private collect of authors to admire tallies Christopher Marlowe, Lord Byron, Edgar Allan Poe and Anne Sexton. My avocations are simple: gin and sin, other poets, and a man who combines the roles of friend, lover, confessor and Eleventh Muse with an inborn grace and unfaltering warmth of spirit and heart."

* * *

RUEFF, Jacques (Leon) 1896-

PERSONAL: Born August 23, 1896, in Paris, France; son of Adolphe (a doctor) and Caroline (Levy) Rueff; married Christiane Vignat, April 13, 1937; children: Marie-Caroline, Passerose (daughter). *Education:* Attended Ecole polytechnique, diploma, 1921; further study at Ecole libre des sciences politiques, 1922-23. *Home:* 51 rue de Varenne, Paris 75007, France. *Office:* Institut de France, 23 Quai de Conti, Paris 75006, France.

CAREER: French government economic official. Served as inspector of finances, 1923-26; junior assistant to French premier and finance minister, Raymond Poincare, 1926-27; League of Nations Secretariat, member of economics and financial section, 1927-30, served on financial stabilization missions to Greece and Bulgaria, 1927, and Portugal, 1928; financial attache in French Embassy, London, 1930-31; Ecole Libre des Sciences Politiques, Paris, professor of economics, 1931-40; French Department of Treasury, Mouvement general des fonds, assistant director, 1934-36, director, 1936; special counselor of state, 1937-39; assistant governor of Bank of France, 1939-41; chairman of Military Mission for German and Austrian Affairs, 1944; chairman of

Paris Conference for German Reparations, 1945; French delegate to Reparations Commission in Moscow, 1945; president of Interallied Agency for Reparation, Brussels, 1946-52; European Community, judge in court of justice, 1952-62, member of social and economic council, 1962—; president of Institute de France, 1963—. Faculty member at University of Paris, Institut de statistique, 1923-30, and Institut d'etudes politiques, 1945-48. Economic advisor to Allied commander-in-chief of occupied Germany, 1945; alternate French delegate to first and second general assembly of United Nations; president of Committee for Reorganization of French Finances, 1958; vice-president of Committee for Suppression of Obstacles to Economic Expansion, 1959-60; chairman of European subsidiary of Lincoln National Life Insurance Co. *Military service:* French Army, 1915-18; served in artillery and with American Expeditionary Force; became lieutenant.

MEMBER: International Statistical Institute (vice-president), Conseil International de la Philosophie et des Sciences Humaines (UNESCO; president, 1949-53; now honorary president), Academie francaise, Academie des sciences morales et politiques, College des sciences sociales et economiques (president, 1960—), Compagnie de reassurances Nord-Atlantique (president, 1963—), Societe Elysees-Valeurs (president, 1967—), Academie royale des sciences, lettres et arts (Belgium; associate member), Academia Nazionale dei Lincei (Italy; associate member), Societe de statistique de Paris (honorary president), Societe d'economie politique de Paris (honorary president), Institut atlantique a Paris (vice-president, 1962—). *Awards, honors:* Croix de guerre, three citations; Commander, Palmes academiques; Grand Cross of Order of Chene (Luxembourg); Grand Officer of Order of Leopold (Belgium), Order of Orange Nassau (Holland), Order of Saint Charles (Monaco), and Polonia Restituta (Poland); Grand Prix Andre-Arnoux, 1967; Grand-Croix de la Legion d'honneur, 1968; grande medaille de vermeil from the city of Paris, 1970.

WRITINGS: Des Sciences physiques aux Sciences morales, Alcan, 1922, revised edition with additional commentary published as *Des Sciences physiques aux Sciences morales: Un Essai de 1922, reconsidere en 1969,* Payot, 1969, translation by Herman Green published as *From the Physical to the Social Sciences: Introduction to a Study of Economic and Ethical Theory,* Johns Hopkins Press, 1929; *Sur une theorie de l'inflation,* Berger-Levrault, 1925; *Theorie des phenomenes monetaires,* Payot, 1927; *Les Problemes actuels du credit,* Alcan, 1930; *L'Ordre Social,* two volumes, Librairie du Recueil Sirey, 1945, 3rd edition, revised with new preface, in one volume, M. T. Genin, 1967; *Il faut choisir: Monnaie saine on Etat totalitaire,* Editions SEDIF, 1947; *La Nouvelle Conception des relations economiques internationales,* Editions SPID du Comite d'Action Economique et douaniere, 1947; *Epitres aux dirigistes,* Gallimard, 1949.

Discours aux Independants, M. T. Genin, 1951; *La Regulation monetaire et le probleme institutionnel de la monnaie,* Recueil Sirey, 1953; *Un Instrument d'analyse economique: La Theorie des vrais et des faux droits,* College Libre des Sciences Sociales et Economiques, 1955; *Mission et responsabilite des elites dans une civilisation de masses,* Centre Economique et Social de Perfectionement des Cadres, 1956; *L'Age de l'inflation,* Payot, 1963, translation by A. H. Meeus and F. G. Clarke published as *The Age of Inflation,* Regnery, 1964; (with Fred Hirsch) *The Rose and the Rule of Gold: An Argument,* Department of Economics, Princeton University, 1965; *Discours de reception de Jacques Rueff a*

l'Academie francaise et response de M. Andre Maurois, Gallimard, 1965; *Le Lancinant probleme des Balances de Paiements,* Payot, 1965, translation by Jean Clement published as *Balance of Payments: Proposals for the Resolution of the Most Pressing World Economic Problem of Our Time,* Macmillan, 1967; *Les Dieux et les Rois: Regards sur le pouvoir createur,* Hachette, 1967, translation by George Robinson and Roger Glemet published as *The Gods and the King: A Glance at Creative Power,* Macmillan, 1973; *Les Fondements philosophiques des systemes economics,* Payot, 1967; *Le Peche monetaire de l'Occident,* Plon, 1971, translation by Roger Glemet published as *The Monetary Sin of the West,* Macmillan, 1972; *Combat pour l'ordre financier: Memoires et documents pour sevir a l'histoire du dernier demi-siecle,* Plon, 1972; *La Reforme du systeme monetaire international,* Plon, 1973; *La Creation du Monde: Comedie-Ballet en 5 journees,* Plon, 1974.

Contributor: (And editor) *Les Doctrines monetaires a l'epreuve des faits,* Alcan, 1932; *Monnaie d'hier et de demain,* Editions SPID du Comite d'Action Economique et Douaniere, 1952; *Enquete sur le liberte,* Hermann, 1953; M. H. Sennholz, editor, *On Freedom and Free Enterprise,* Van Nostrand, 1955.

Also author of economic pamphlets, reports, and research papers, including *Rapport sur la situation financiere de la France plan de stabilisation,* Imprimerie Nationale, 1958, and (with Louis Armand) *Rapport sur la suppression des obstacles a l'expansion economique,* two volumes, Imprimerie Nationale, 1960. Contributor to numerous conference proceedings and to English and French language journals in his field.

*   *   *

RUEGE, Klaus 1934-

PERSONAL: Surname is pronounced *Roo*-gy; born April 12, 1934, in Germany; came to the United States in 1952, naturalized citizen, 1955; son of Gerhard (an editor) and Maria (Becker) Ruege; married Marilyn Montgomery, February 23, 1955; children: Michael, Michele, Matthew. *Education:* Spencerian College, B.B.A., 1959. *Religion:* Lutheran. *Home:* 3555 Beach Lane, Northbrook, Ill. 60062. *Office:* Verbatim, 2970 Maria Ave., Northbrook, Ill. 60062.

CAREER: Milway Inc., Milwaukee, Wis., credit manager and assistant treasurer, 1955-62; Bell & Howell, Lincolnwood, Ill., president of Direct Marketing Group, 1962-69; Douglas Dunhill, Inc., Chicago, Ill., president, 1969-72; Plaza Group, Inc., Mount Prospect, Ill., president, 1972-74; Verbatim, Northbrook, Ill., president, 1974—. President and co-founder of Young Sportsmen's Soccer League. *Military service:* U.S. Military Police Corps, 1954-56. *Member:* International Society of Certified Consumer Credit Executives (charter member).

WRITINGS: Inside Soccer, Regnery, 1976. Contributor to direct marketing magazines in the United States and Europe.

WORK IN PROGRESS: Books on soccer, aimed at the novice coach, to assist in organizing effective practice sessions and in step-by-step application of modern tactics.

*   *   *

RUKEYSER, Louis 1933-

PERSONAL: Born January 30, 1933, in New York, N.Y.; son of Merryle Stanley (a financial columnist and lecturer) and Berenice (Simon) Rukeyser; married Alexandra Gill, March 3, 1962; children: Beverley Jane, Susan Athena,

Stacy Alexandra. *Education:* Princeton University, A.B., 1954. *Office:* 306 Taconic Rd., Greenwich, Conn. 06830.

CAREER: Baltimore Sun papers, Baltimore, Md., feature writer and political and foreign correspondent, 1954-57, chief political correspondent for *Evening Sun,* 1957-59, chief of London Bureau for *The Sun,* 1959-63, chief Asian correspondent for *The Sun,* 1963-65; American Broadcasting Co. (ABC), New York, New York, senior correspondent and commentator, 1965-73, Paris correspondent, 1965-66, chief of London Bureau, 1966-68, economic commentator, 1968-73, host of radio program "Rukeyser's World," 1971-73; Maryland Center for Public Broadcasting, Owings Mills, Md., host of national public television program "Wall Street Week," 1970—. *Military service:* U.S. Army, on editorial staff of European edition of *Stars and Stripes,* 1954-56.

AWARDS, HONORS: How to Make Money in Wall Street was named "best investment book of the year" by *Stock Traders Almanac,* 1974; Overseas Press Club awards for news interpretation, 1963 and 1964, for reporting on Vietnam and Asia; nominated for Emmy Award, 1970, and Peabody Broadcasting Awards, 1970, 1972, for ABC-TV and radio programs; received George Washington Honor Medal from Freedoms Foundation, 1973, for program "Rukeyser's World"; G. M. Loeb Award from University of Connecticut, 1973, for program "Wall Street Week"; D.L. from New Hampshire College, 1975; Janus Award from Mortgage Bankers Association of America, 1975, for program "Wall Street Week."

WRITINGS: How to Make Money in Wall Street (Literary Guild selection), Doubleday, 1974, revised edition, 1976. Author of a triweekly column of economic commentary for McNaught Syndicate, 1976—. Contributor to magazines and newspapers.

WORK IN PROGRESS: A book on investing, publication by Harper expected in 1978.

SIDELIGHTS: Rukeyser has said of his current television program: "This is not a stock-tip show. Its number one purpose is to give people a painless way of keeping up with the economy . . . and, if they are interested in investing, some knowledge of how to set about it. We're also trying to give outsiders some 'inside information'—what the pros are really thinking and doing. . . . When you say 'economics,' people's eyelids get heavy. But the minute you say 'money,' their eyes pop open and their nostrils flare, and you have their full attention. We've found that people are intensely interested in news about money, as long as you meet two requirements: First, that you put it to them in something resembling the English language, as opposed to polysyllabic jargon; second, that you do it with a certain amount of flair, because people want a little entertainment along with their information."

BIOGRAPHICAL/CRITICAL SOURCES: Christian Science Monitor, July 15, 1974; *New York,* December 22, 1975; *New York Times,* April 11, 1976.

* * *

RUMMEL, R(udolph) J(oseph) 1932-

PERSONAL: Born October 21, 1932, in Cleveland, Ohio; son of Rudolph Peter and Neilly Rummel; married Grace Sachiko, 1961; children: Dawn, Lei. *Education:* University of Hawaii, B.A., 1959, M.A., 1961; Northwestern University, Ph.D., 1963. *Home:* 46-393 Holopu Pl., Kaneohe, Hawaii 96744. *Office:* Department of Political Science, University of Hawaii, Honolulu, Hawaii 96822.

CAREER: Indiana University, Bloomington, assistant professor of government, 1963-64; Yale University, New Haven, Conn., assistant professor of political science, 1964-66; University of Hawaii, Honolulu, visiting assistant professor, 1966-67, associate professor, 1967-68, professor of political science, 1968—, research political scientist at Social Science Research Institute, 1966-68. Founder and director of PATH Institute of Research on International Problems, 1974—; cofounder and vice-president of Political-Economic Risk Consultants, 1976—.

MEMBER: Quantitative International Politics Society (chairman, 1969-70), American Political Science Association, Interpolimetrics Society (founder), Phi Beta Kappa, Phi Kappa Phi, Omicron Delta Kappa. *Awards, honors:* Grants from National Science Foundation, 1963-68, 1972-74, and Advanced Research Projects Agency, 1967-75.

WRITINGS: Applied Factor Analysis, Northwestern University Press, 1970; (contributor) Roull Naroll and Ronald Cohen, editors, *Handbook of Method in Cultural Anthropology,* Natural History Press, 1971; *Dimensions of Nations,* Sage Publications, 1972; (contributor) Bruce Russett, editor, *Peace, War, and Numbers,* Sage Publications, 1972; (contributor) Kevin Cox and other editors, *Locational Approaches to Power and Conflict,* Sage Publications, 1974; *The Dynamic Psychological Field,* Sage & Halsted, 1975; *Field Theory Evolving,* Sage Publications, 1976; *The Conflict Helix,* Sage & Halsted, 1976; *Peace Endangered: The Reality of Detente,* Sage Publications, 1976; *National Attributes and Behavior,* Sage Publications, 1976; *Conflict in Perspective,* Sage & Halsted, in press. Contributor to political science journals. Associate editor of *Journal of Conflict Resolution,* 1968-71; interim editor of *Interpolimetrics Newsletter,* 1970-72.

WORK IN PROGRESS: Analyzing Population Policy and Demographic Change; Understanding Correlation; Understanding Conflict and War.

SIDELIGHTS: Rummel writes: "My focal interest has been to eliminate or control social violence and war. . . . My major conclusions are: conflict is a bargaining process shaped by power and precipitated by a breakdown in expectations; the least violent social systems are those with the greatest individual freedom; and freedom is the essential element in peace, nonviolence and social justice."

* * *

RUSCO, Elmer R(itter) 1928-

PERSONAL: Born May 6, 1928, in Haviland, Kan.; son of William (a teacher) and Bertha (a teacher; maiden name, Weaver) Rusco; married Mary Kiehl (an archaeologist), June 17, 1955; children: Kathryn Ann Rusco Glaser, Franklin William. *Education:* University of Kansas, B.A., 1951, M.A., 1952; University of California, Berkeley, Ph.D., 1960. *Religion:* Unitarian-Universalist. *Home:* 117 West 10th St., Reno, Nev. 89503. *Office:* Department of Political Science, University of Nevada, Reno, Nev. 89507.

CAREER: San Diego State College (now University), San Diego, Calif., instructor in political science, 1957-58; University of Idaho, Moscow, instructor in political science, 1959-60; associate professor of political science at Parsons College, 1961-63; University of Nevada, Reno, assistant professor, 1963-67, associate professor, 1967-75, professor of political science, 1975—, director of Bureau of Governmental Research, 1966—. Chairman of board of directors of Reno's Race Relations Center, 1969-75. *Military service:* U.S. Army, 1952-54. *Member:* American Political Science

Association, American Civil Liberties Union (president of Nevada affiliate, 1971—), Western Political Science Association. *Awards, honors:* Annual award from Western Political Science Association, 1961; Thornton Peace Prize from University of Nevada, Reno, 1976.

WRITINGS: Voting Behavior in Nevada, University of Nevada Press, 1966; *Poverty in Washoe County,* Bureau of Governmental Research, University of Nevada, Reno, 1968; *Good Time Coming?: Black Nevadans in the Nineteenth Century,* Greenwood Press, 1975. Contributor to professional journals.

WORK IN PROGRESS: A history of Western Blacks in the nineteenth century, with Michael Coray; a history of American political ideas which takes into account the effects of racism.

SIDELIGHTS: Rusco writes: "I consider the study of politics to be concerned with the distribution of values, including how values are distributed and how they should be distributed. I have long felt that American patterns of race relations are central issues in our political life, have done writing which is relevant to this concern, and plan more."

* * *

RUSSELL, C(harles) Allyn 1920-

PERSONAL: Born September 3, 1920, in Bovina Center, N.Y.; son of Charles James (a businessman) and Hildreth (Tuttle) Russell; married Elizabeth Vigh (an office manager), June 9, 1947. *Education:* Houghton College, A.B., 1942; Eastern Baptist Theological Seminary, B.D., 1944, Th.M., 1946; University of Buffalo, M.A., 1955; Boston University, Ph.D., 1959. *Politics:* Independent. *Home address:* P.O. Box 39, Concord, Mass. 01742. *Office:* Department of Religion, Boston University, 745 Commonwealth Ave., Boston, Mass. 02215.

CAREER: Ordained Baptist minister, 1945; pastor of Baptist churches in Northampton, Mass., 1946-50, Fredonia, N.Y., 1950-56, and Pawtucket, R.I., 1959-60; Southern Baptist Theological Seminary, Louisville, Ky., assistant professor of church history, 1959; Boston University, Boston, Mass., lecturer, 1959-60, instructor, 1960-62, assistant professor, 1962-67, associate professor, 1967-73, professor of religion, 1973—.

MEMBER: American Association of University Professors, American Academy of Religion, American Society for Church History, American Baptist Historical Society, American Philatelic Society, Lincoln Philatelic Society, New York State Historical Association, Boston Philatelic Group, Lincoln Club of Boston. *Awards, honors:* Danforth associate, 1965—; Solon J. Buck Award from *Minnesota History,* 1972.

WRITINGS: A History of the Fredonia Baptist Church, McClenathan, 1955; *Voices of American Fundamentalism: Seven Biographical Studies,* Westminster, 1976. Contributor to history and theology journals.

WORK IN PROGRESS: A "bio-bibliography" of Fundamentalism, publication by G. K. Hall expected in 1979.

SIDELIGHTS: Russell writes: "My research and writing on Fundamentalism has been a literary offshoot of my academic interest in religion in America. Am interested in the possible relation of right-wing religion and right-wing politics." Russell has traveled widely abroad.

RUSSO, Sarett Rude 1918(?)-1976

1918(?)—June 13, 1976; Italian screen-writer and playwright. Obituaries: *New York Times,* June 18, 1976.

* * *

RUYERSON, James Paul
See ROTHWEILER, Paul R(oger)

* * *

SAAB, Edouard 1929-1976

1929—May, 1976; Lebanese journalist, editor, and author of books on the Middle East. Obituaries: *Time,* May 31, 1976.

* * *

SABOURIN, Leopold 1919-

PERSONAL: Born September 7, 1919, in St.-Jean-Baptiste, Manitoba, Canada; son of Omer (a farmer) and Mathilda (a farmer; maiden name, Clement) Sabourin. *Education:* University of Manitoba, B.A., 1939; University of Montreal, M.A., 1941; Pontifical Biblical Institute, Rome, Licentiate in Scripture, 1956; Jesuit Faculties, Montreal, Doctorate in Theology, 1959. *Home and office:* 25, via della Pilotta, Rome, Italy 00187.

CAREER: Ordained Roman Catholic priest of Society of Jesus (S.J.), 1945; University College of Addis Ababa, Addis Ababa, Ethiopia, teacher of philosophy, 1950-53; Theological Seminary, Port-au-Prince, Haiti, teacher of scripture, 1959-64; Biblical Institute, Jerusalem, Israel, teacher of scripture, 1964-67; Pontifical Biblical Institute, Rome, Italy, professor of psalms and synoptic gospels, 1967—. *Member:* Catholic Biblical Association of America. *Awards, honors:* Quebec Government award, 1962, for *Redemption sacrificielle.*

WRITINGS: Redemption sacrificielle: Une enquete exegetique, Desclee de Brouwer, 1961, partial translation included as Part 3 of *Sin, Redemption, and Sacrifice: A Biblical and Patristic Study* (with Stanislas Lyonnet), Biblical Institute (Rome), 1970; *Les Noms et les titres de Jesus: Themes de Theologie Biblique,* Desclee de Brouwer, 1963, translation by Maurice Carroll published as *The Names and Titles of Jesus: Themes of Biblical Theology,* Macmillan, 1967; *Un classement litteraire des Psaumes* (title means "Literary Classification of the Psalms"), Desclee de Brouwer, 1964; *The Psalms: Their Origin and Meaning,* Alba, 1969, 2nd edition, 1974; *Priesthood: A Comparative Study,* E. J. Brill, 1973; *Il Vangelo di Matteo* (title means "The Gospel of Matthew"), Edizioni Paoline, 1975, 2nd edition, 1976. Founder and editor, *Biblical Theology Bulletin,* 1971—.

WORK IN PROGRESS: An English edition of *Il Vangelo di Matteo;* an article for *Supplement au Dictionnaire de la Bible.*

SIDELIGHTS: Sabourin told *CA* that with his writings he "attempts to bridge the gap between specialized scholarship and the increasing demand for serious but not too technical exposition in exegesis and biblical theology."

* * *

SADLER, Julius Trousdale, Jr. 1923-

PERSONAL: Born April 12, 1923, in Henderson, N.C.; son of Julius Trousdale (an auditor) and Sue (Daly) Sadler; married Jacquelin Jones, October 1, 1955; children: Laura Kate, Jason, Garrett. *Education:* Attended College of William and Mary, 1940-41, and North Carolina State University, 1941-

43; University of Virginia, B.S.Arch., 1945. *Politics:* Republican. *Home and office address:* North St., Litchfield, Conn. 06759.

CAREER: Free-lance architectural designer; J. Sadler Designs, Litchfield, Conn., owner and architectural designer, 1958—. *Member:* Society of Architectural Historians, Victorian Society, National Trust for Historic Preservation.

WRITINGS: (With Desmond Guinness) *Mr. Jefferson, Architect,* Viking, 1973; (with Calder Loth) *The Only Proper Style,* New York Graphic Society, 1975; (with Guinness) *Palladio: A Western Progress,* Viking, 1976.

WORK IN PROGRESS: Portrait of Charleston; Architecture in Connecticut; articles for *Antique Monthly.*

*   *   *

SAGARRA, Eda   1933-

PERSONAL: Born August 15, 1933, in Dublin, Ireland; daughter of Kevin Roantree (a judge) and Cecil (Smiddy) O'Shiel; married Albert Sagarra (a professor of petrochemistry), April 4, 1961; children: Mireia. *Education:* National University of Ireland, B.A. (first class honors), 1954; University of Freibourg, M.A., 1955; further graduate study at University of Zurich, 1955-56; University of Vienna, Ph.D., 1958. *Religion:* Roman Catholic. *Politics:* Mild Conservative. *Home:* 30 Garville Ave., Rathgar, Dublin 6, Ireland. *Office:* Department of German, 35 Trinity College, Dublin, Ireland.

CAREER: University of Manchester, Manchester, England, assistant lecturer, 1958-61, lecturer in German, 1961-68, lecturer in German history, 1968-75; Trinity College, Dublin, Ireland, professor of German, 1975—. Tutor, 1969-75. Has lectured in German schools. *Member:* Association of German Teachers, Association of University Teachers, Irish Federation of University Teachers, Philological Club (University of Manchester).

WRITINGS: (Translator) *Zen Buddhism,* Ryder & Co., 1961; (translator) *Pain,* Hutchinson, 1963; *Tradition and Revolution: German Literature and Society, 1830-1890,* Basic Books, 1971. Also translator of book by M. Rodoreda, 1965. Contributor of articles and reviews to language and history journals.

WORK IN PROGRESS: Social History of Germany, 1648-1933; research on the changing image of Frederick II of Prussia.

*   *   *

SAINT, Andrew (John)   1946-
(Leo Plendello)

PERSONAL: Born November 30, 1946, in Shrewsbury, England; son of Arthur James Maxwell (a clergyman) and Elizabeth Yvetta (Butterfield) Saint; children: one daughter. *Education:* Balliol College, Oxford, B.A. (first class honors), 1969; Warburg Institute, University of London, M.Phil., 1971. *Religion:* None. *Home:* 28 Countess Rd., London N.W.5, England. *Office: Survey of London,* Greater London Council, County Hall, London S.E.1, England.

CAREER: University of Essex, Colchester, England, part-time lecturer in art history, 1971-74; *Survey of London,* London, England, architectural editor, 1974—. *Member:* Victorian Society (committee member).

WRITINGS: Richard Norman Shaw, Yale University Press, 1976. Contributor to magazines, sometimes under pseudonym Leo Plendello.

St. JOHN, Philip
See del REY, Lester, 1915-

*   *   *

SAKOIAN, Frances   1912-

PERSONAL: Born October 8, 1912, in Olmsted Falls, Ohio; daughter of Andrew (a greenhouse owner) and Sophia (Halster) Cherpic; married Thomas Aldred (a military commander), October 10, 1953 (died, 1964); married Vartkes Sakoian (a publisher), February 17, 1966; children: (first marriage) Brian Wilkin, Joan (Mrs. Aldo VanderMolen). *Education:* Attended high school in Olmsted Falls, Ohio. *Home and office:* 1 Monadnock Rd., Arlington, Mass. 02174.

CAREER: Astrologer and writer. Owner and operator of Dairy Mill, Inc. (ice cream company), 1942-53; director of New England School of Astrology, 1973—. Lecturer through American Program Bureau, 1971—. Presents "The Frances Sakoian Show" daily on WMEX-Radio, 1976, and "Beyond Reason" weekly for Canadian Broadcasting Corp. (Toronto), 1976—.

MEMBER: American Federation of Television and Radio Artists, American Federation of Astrologers (member of board of directors), National Council for Geocosmic Research (member of advisory board), Press Club of Boston, Women's Press Club of Boston.

WRITINGS: The Astrologer's Handbook, Harper, 1973; *The Astrology of Human Relationships,* Harper, 1976; *Transits: Key to the Psychology of Human Events,* Harper, in press.

Author of sixteen privately printed books on transits and other aspects of astrology. Contributor to American Federation of Astrologers *Bulletin,* 1950—.

WORK IN PROGRESS: A science fiction novel; a biography, to be adapted for a film script on astrology; continuing astrological research.

SIDELIGHTS: Frances Sakoian comments: "Personal involvement in the astrological profession over forty-eight years brought me, in the course of my review of astrological literature that has flooded the market in the past several years, to recognize the need for a more scientific approach to the subject—thus, . . . in the strictest sense, my avocation became my vocation."

*   *   *

SALES, Grover   1919-

PERSONAL: Born October 26, 1919, in Louisville, Ky.; son of Grover C. (an attorney) and Rosalind (Harris) Sales; married Enid Thompson, 1947 (divorced, 1956); married Georgia MacLeod (an architect and writer), December 30, 1972; children: (first marriage) Rachel. *Education:* Reed College, student, 1946-48; University of California, Berkeley, B.A. (highest honors), 1949, graduate study, 1949-51. *Politics:* Social Democrat. *Religion:* Jewish. *Home and office address:* P.O. Box 689, Belvedere, Calif. 94920. *Agent:* James Brown Associates, Inc., 22 East 60th St., New York, N.Y. 10022.

CAREER: Owner of public relations firm and publicist for notable people in the performing arts, San Francisco, Calif., 1956-68; KQED-Television, San Francisco, film and jazz critic on "Critics Circle," 1968-70, and "Newsroom," 1972-75; writer, 1975—. Instructor at University of California Extension, 1970—; faculty member at Eugene O'Neill

Memorial Theater, 1967-71. Conducted "The World of Duke Ellington," a weekly program on KHIP-FM Radio, 1962-64; producer and commentator for "Chevron School Broadcast," 1973—. Public relations representative for Monterey Jazz Festival, 1958-65; professional photographer, 1962-68, specializing in performing artists; founder of Third Stream Concerts, 1973-74. *Military service:* U.S. Army Air Forces, 1942-46; became sergeant.

MEMBER: American Federation of Television and Radio Artists, Phi Beta Kappa. *Awards, honors:* Honorable mention from Elsie and Philip D. Sang prize committee, Knox College, 1968, for drama criticism; George Foster Peabody Broadcasting Award, 1975, for radio presentation "Music Makers Series" on "Chevron School Broadcast."

WRITINGS: (With wife, Georgia MacLeod Sales) *The Clay-Pot Cookbook,* Atheneum, 1974; *John Maher of Delancey Street,* Norton, 1976. Contributor of articles and reviews to magazines, including *California Living, Jazz: A Quarterly of American Music, Saturday Review, Holiday,* and *Newsday.* Film and drama editor of *San Francisco,* 1964-74; book critic for *Official Bay Area Guide,* 1975—.

WORK IN PROGRESS: Soul and Camp: The Split in American Culture.

SIDELIGHTS: Sales writes: "I have written about, and taught, jazz music for over thirty years, and feel it to be the most vital, misunderstood and neglected of all contemporary art forms. Those who have influenced me most include: Shaw, Marx, Duke Ellington, Wright Mills, Mailer, Nelson Algren, Bach, Charlie Parker, Fitzgerald, Faulkner, Lew Welch, Matisse, Susan B. Anthony, and Professor Ernst Kantorowicz."

* * *

SALVATO, Sharon 1938-

PERSONAL: Born April 30, 1938, in Columbus, Ohio; daughter of Raymond Joseph (an owner of a hardware store) and Alice Virginia (Day) Zettler; married Guy J. Salvato (an owner of an art studio), October 14, 1961; children: Christopher Joseph, Gregory John, Stephen Andrew, Daniel Alexander. *Education:* University of Cincinnati, B.S.Ed., 1961. *Politics:* "Conservationistically Liberal." *Religion:* Roman Catholic. *Home:* 2465 East Broad St., Bexley, Ohio 43209. *Agent:* David Stewart Hull, 22 East 60th St., New York, N.Y. 10022.

CAREER: Worked in McClelland's Book Store, 1956-57, and in Wilde's Art Supply Store in Cincinnati, Ohio, 1957-58; art teacher in Findlay St. Neighborhood House, Cincinnati, 1958-59; teacher of slow learners in junior high school in Columbus, Ohio, 1961-62; writer, 1969—. *Member:* Authors Guild of Authors League of America, National League of American Pen Women, Ohioana Library.

WRITINGS: Briarcliff Manor (gothic novel), Stein & Day, 1974; *The Meredith Legacy* (gothic novel), Stein & Day, 1974; *Scarborough House* (historical romance), Stein & Day, 1975.

WORK IN PROGRESS: The Wormwood Cup, a historical romance; *The Black Swan,* a historical romance of the Civil War, with Cornelia Parkinson; *Caesar's Child,* a novel about an immigrant.

SIDELIGHTS: Sharon Salvato writes: "My motivation comes primarily from a nearly insatiable curiosity about practically everything. It seems that no matter what period of history one chooses to read or write about, the aims of politicians, powerful and lowly, change little. The problems and hopes of individuals remain very much the same. Consequently, I spend a good deal of my free time reading psychology and history books."

AVOCATIONAL INTERESTS: Raising tropical and semi-tropical plants in her greenhouse.

* * *

SANDBERG, (Karin) Inger 1930-

PERSONAL: Born August 2, 1930, in Karlstad, Sweden; daughter of Johan and Hanna (a teacher; maiden name, Carlstedt) Erikson; married Lasse Sandberg (an artist), April 27, 1950; children: Lena, Niklas, Mathias. *Education:* Swedish Training College for Teachers, teacher's certificate, 1954. *Home:* Vaestra Raden 16, 65227 Karlstad, Sweden.

CAREER: Teacher in Karlstad, Sweden public schools, 1957-63; writer of books and of television and radio productions for children, 1963—. *Member:* Swedish Writers Association. *Awards, honors:* Swedish Author's Fund award, 1963; Karlstad culture prize, 1965; Hans Christian Andersen honorable mention and International Board on Books for Young People (IBBY) honorable mention, both 1966, and Leipzig International Book Exhibit award, 1971, all for *Niklas roeda dag;* Heffaklump award from *Expressen* newspaper (Sweden), 1969, for *Pappa, kom ut!;* Nils Holgersson Medal, 1973; Astrid Lindgren Prize, 1974.

WRITINGS—All illustrated by husband, Lasse Sandberg; all first published by Raben & Sjoegren, except as noted: *Faaret Ullrik Faar medalj* (title means "Woolrik the Sheep Gets a Medal"), Eklund, 1953; *Jag maalar en . . .* (title means "I Paint a . . ."), Eklund, 1955; *Jonas bilen och aeventyret* (title means "Jonas the Car and the Adventure"), Geber, 1959.

Godnattsagor paa rullgardinen (title means "Bedtime Stories on the Blind"), Geber, 1960; *Filuren paa aeventyr* (title means "The Adventure of the Little Filur"), Geber, 1961; *Hemma hos mej* (title means "At My Place"), Geber, 1962; *Lena beraettar,* Geber, 1963, 3rd edition, 1971, translation by Patricia Crampton published as *Here's Lena,* Methuen, 1970; *Trollen i Lill-Skogen* (title means "The Trolls in the Little Wood"), Karlstad Town, 1963; *Niklas roeda dag,* Geber, 1964, 2nd edition, 1967, translation published as *Nicholas' Red Day,* Delacorte, 1967; *Barnens bildordlista* (title means "Children's Wordbook"), Skrivrit, 1965; *Den musikaliska myran* (title means "The Musical Ant"), Geber, 1965, 2nd edition, 1970; *En morgon i varuhuset* (title means "One Morning in the Department Store"), [Stockholm], 1965; *Lilla spoeket Laban,* Geber, 1965, 3rd edition, 1976, translation by Nancy S. Leupold published as *Little Ghost Godfrey,* Delacorte, 1968, translation by Kersti French published as *Little Spook,* Methuen, 1969; *Johan,* 1965, 3rd edition, 1970, translation by Patricia Crampton published as *Johan's Year,* Methuen, 1971.

Pojken med de Hundra bilarna, 1966, translation published as *The Boy With 100 Cars,* Delacorte, 1967; *Tomtens stadsresa* (title means "The Tomten Goes to Town"), General Post Office (Sweden), 1966; *En konstig foersta maj,* 1967; *Niklas oenskedjur,* 1967, translation by R. Sadler published as *Nicholas' Ideal Pet,* Sadler & Brown, 1968, published as *Nicholas' Favorite Pet,* Delacorte, 1969; *Pojken med de maanga husen,* 1968, translation published as *The Boy with Many Houses,* Delacorte, 1969; *Vi passar oss sjaelva* (title means "We Look after Ourselves"), Geber, 1968; *Pappa, kom ut!,* 1969, translation published as *Daddy Come Out!,* Sadler & Brown, 1970, published as *Come On Out, Daddy,* Delacorte, 1971; *Johan i 2:an,* 1969, 2nd edition, 1970, translation by Patricia Crampton published as *Johan at School,* Methuen, 1972; *Filurstjaernan* (title means "The Filurstar"), Geber, 1969.

Buffalo Bengt och indianerna, 1970, translation published as *Buffalo Bengt and the Indians,* Sadler & Brown, 1971; *Lena staar i koe* (title means "Lena Lines Up"), Geber, 1970; *Stora Tokboken* (title means "The Big Crazybook"), Geber, 1970; *Vad aer det som ryker?,* 1971, translation by Merloyd Lawrence published as *Where Does All That Smoke Come From?,* Delacorte, 1972; *Fred Strid krymper* (title means "Mr. Fred Strid Shrinks"), 1972; *Vi leker oeken, Froeken,* 1973, translation published as *The Desert Game,* Methuen, 1974, published as *Let's Play Desert,* Delacorte, 1974; *Hej, vaelkommen till mej!,* 1974, translation published as *Let's Be Friends,* Methuen, 1975; *Perry och osynlige Wrolf* (title means "Perry and the Invisible Wrolf"), 1975; *Var aer laanga farbrorns hatt?* (title means "Where's Tall Uncle's Hat?"), 1976.

Little Anna series: *Vad Anna fick se,* 1964, 4th edition, 1974, translation published as *What Anna Saw,* Lothrop, 1964; *Lilla Anna och trollerihatten,* 1965, 4th edition, 1976, translation published as *Anna and the Magic Hat,* Sadler & Brown, 1965, published as *Little Anna and the Magic Hat,* Lothrop, 1965; *Vad lilla Anna sparade paa,* 1965, 4th edition, 1974, translation published as *What Anna Saved,* Sadler & Brown, 1965, published as *What Little Anna Saved,* Lothrop, 1965; *Lilla Annas mama fyller aar,* 1966, 4th edition, 1974, translation published as *Little Anna's Mama Has a Birthday,* Sadler & Brown, 1965, published as *Little Anna's Mama Has a Birthday,* Lothrop, 1966; *Naer lilla Anna var foerkyld,* 1966, 4th edition, 1974, translation published as *When Anna Had a Cold,* Sadler & Brown, 1966, published as *When Little Anna Had a Cold,* Lothrop, 1966.

Lilla Anna och Laanga Farbrorn paa havet, 1971, translation published as *Little Anna and the Tall Uncle,* Methuen, 1973; *Var aer lilla Annas hund?,* 1972, translation published as *Where Is Little Anna's Dog?,* Methuen, 1974; *Lilla Annas julklapp,* 1972, 3rd edition, 1974, translation published as *Kate's Christmas Present,* A. & C. Black, 1974; *Lilla Anna flyttar saker,* 1972, 3rd edition, 1974, translation published as *Kate's Upside Down Day,* A. & C. Black, 1974; *Lilla Anna leker med bollar,* 1973, translation published as *Kate's Bouncy Ball,* A. & C. Black, 1974; *Lilla Anna kom och hjaelp!,* 1972, 2nd edition, 1974, translation published as *Kate, Kate Come and Help!,* A. & C. Black, 1974; *Lilla Anna i glada skolan* (title means "Little Anna in the Happy School"), 1975.

Mathias series: *Mathias bakar kakor,* 1968, 3rd edition, 1974, translation published as *Daniel and the Coconut Cakes,* A. & C. Black, 1973; *Mathias och trollet,* 1968, translation published as *Daniel's Mysterious Monster,* A. & C. Black, 1973; *Mathias maalar en . . .,* 1969, translation published as *Daniel Paints a Picture,* A. & C. Black, 1973; *Mathias hjaelper till,* 1969, 2nd edition, 1974, translation published as *Daniel's Helping Hand,* A. & C. Black, 1973.

Writer, with husband, of over 180 children's television and radio programs broadcast in Sweden. Contributor to Swedish journals and magazines.

WORK IN PROGRESS: A series of books about lilla spoeket Laban (the little spook) and his new sister, Labolina; two television series of five shows each; a film guide about open schools for television broadcast and use in a teacher's training program.

SIDELIGHTS: Mrs. Sandberg told *CA* that although she left teaching thirteen years ago she is still very interested in education. She recently went to study teaching programs for dyslexic children in England, and she and her husband both give lectures to teachers about open schools and children's books.

*   *   *

SANDE, Theodore Anton   1933-

PERSONAL: Born November 21, 1933, in New London, Conn.; son of Lars Anton and Viola (Edgecombe) Sande; married Solveig Inga-Maj Imselius, August 6, 1960; children: Susanne Ingrid, Lars Michael. *Education:* Rhode Island School of Design, B.Sc., 1956; Yale University, M.Arch., 1961; University of Pennsylvania, Ph.D., 1972. *Religion:* Episcopalian. *Home address:* Stetson Court, Williamstown, Mass. 01267.

CAREER: Hakon Ahlberg, Stockholm, Sweden, designer and architect, 1960; Washburn, Luther & Rowley, Attleboro, Mass., designer, 1961-62; Barker & Turoff Associates, Providence, R.I., designer, 1962-63; Turoff Associates, Providence, R.I., junior partner, 1964-67; Turoff & Sande, Providence, R.I., partner, 1968-70; self-employed architect and consultant in Cranston, R.I., 1970, Drexel Hill, Pa., 1970-72, and Williamstown, Mass., 1972—. Certified by National Council of Architectural Registration Boards; registered architect in Rhode Island and Massachusetts. Lecturer at Williams College, 1972-75; faculty member of Clark Art Institute, 1973—; visiting professor at Rensselaer Polytechnic Institute, 1973-74, and University of Pennsylvania, spring, 1976, 1977. Lecturer at University of Michigan, Brown University, Worcester Polytechnic Institute, University of Vermont, Rhode Island School of Design, and Williams College. Has exhibited drawings in Providence, R.I. Director of professional services for National Trust for Historic Preservation, 1975—; co-chairman of Smithsonian Institution's Conference on Industrial Archaeology, 1971; member of scientific committee of Ecomusee (Le Creusot, France), 1976—. Member of North Adams Historic District Study Commission, 1974; trustee of William H. Hall Free Library, 1970, and American Precision Museum. *Military service:* U.S. Naval Reserve, 1956-66, active duty as air intelligence officer, 1956-60; became lieutenant.

MEMBER: American Institute of Architects (member of executive committee of Rhode Island chapter, 1970), Society of Architectural Historians, Society for Industrial Archeology (founder; first president; member of board of directors, 1973-76), Providence Art Club. *Awards, honors:* George Frazer Award from Rhode Island chapter of American Institute of Architects, 1956, for excellence in architectural design.

WRITINGS: Industrial Archeology: A New Look at the American Heritage, Stephen Greene Press, 1976. Contributor to *Guidebook to Philadelphia Architecture.* Contributor of articles and reviews to history, technology, architecture, and archaeology journals.

*   *   *

SANDERS, Frederick K(irkland)   1936-

PERSONAL: Born December 30, 1936, in Charleston, S.C.; son of Paul Rupard (a college professor) and Eulalie (Kirkland) Sanders; married Donna Sherman (conference coordinator at Georgia Southern College), June 13, 1965; children: Karen, Sean. *Education:* Wofford College, B.A., 1958; Emory University, M.A., 1963; University of Georgia, Ph.D., 1971. *Religion:* Episcopal. *Home:* 606 Marvin

Ave., Statesboro, Ga. 30458. *Office:* Department of English, Georgia Southern College, Statesboro, Ga. 30458.

CAREER: Converse College, Spartanburg, S.C., instructor in English, 1962-65; Georgia Southern College, Statesboro, assistant professor, 1969-75, associate professor of English, 1975—. Member of board of trustees of Sherman College of Chiropractic, 1972—. *Awards, honors:* National Endowment for the Humanities summer research grant, 1974.

WRITINGS: John Adams Speaking: Pound's Sources for the Adams Cantos, University of Maine Press, 1975. Contributor to English journals.

WORK IN PROGRESS: A book-length commentary on Ezra Pound's Adams Cantos.

AVOCATIONAL INTERESTS: Gardening, bicycling.

* * *

SANDERS, Marlene 1931-

PERSONAL: Born January 10, 1931, in Cleveland, Ohio; married Jerome Toobin (a television executive), May 27, 1958; children: Jeff, Mark. *Education:* Attended Ohio State University. *Residence:* New York, N.Y. *Office:* ABC News, 7 West 66th St., New York, N.Y. 10024.

CAREER: WNEW-TV, New York City, producer, and writer, 1955-60; Westinghouse Broadcasting Corp., New York City, producer and writer for program "P.M.," 1961-62; WNEW-Radio, assistant director of news and public affairs, 1962-64; American Broadcasting Corp. (ABC) News, New York City, radio and television correspondent, 1964-72, documentary producer, 1972-76, vice-president and director of television documentaries, 1976—. Notable assignments as correspondent include funeral of President Kennedy and march on Washington, 1963, inauguration of President Johnson, 1965, tour in Vietnam, 1966, White House wedding of Lynda Bird Robb, 1967, Prime Minister Golda Meir's visit to United States, 1969.

AWARDS, HONORS: Robert E. Sherwood award, 1957, for work on "Night Beat"; brotherhood award from National Conference of Christians and Jews, 1962, for documentary "The Blockbuster"; Golden Mike award from *McCall's* magazine, 1964; Writers Guild of America radio award, 1964, for two-part program "The Battle of the Warsaw Ghetto"; National Headliner's award, 1971; communications award from Women in Communications, 1973; Golden Eagle certificate from Council on International Nontheatrical Events (CINE) and Clarion award, both 1973, both for hour-long television special "Woman's Place"; Ohio State University award, Front Page award, and Writers Guild of America award, all 1974, all for documentary "The Right to Die."

WRITINGS: Over 120 radio documentaries for WNEW Radio; various series for WNEW-TV and for ABC News and ABC's "Directions," "Now," and "News Closeup" series, 1964—, including such programs as "Children in Peril," broadcast, 1972, "Population: Boom or Doom" and "Woman's Place," 1973, "The Right to Die," 1974, and "Woman's Health: A Question of Survival," 1976. Scriptwriter for Westinghouse Broadcasting Corp. program "P.M.," 1961-62.

SIDELIGHTS: Marlene Sanders was the first woman to anchor an evening network newscast when, in 1964, she took over for the ailing ABC regular. She also anchored her own daytime television news program on ABC for four years and filled the same position for three months of the Saturday night edition of the "Weekend News" in 1971.

SANDERS, William B(rauns) 1944-

PERSONAL: Born June 7, 1944, in Taft, Calif.; son of Breeding William (a teacher) and Eleanore (a teacher; maiden name, Brauns) Sanders; married Elizabeth Griffith (an artist), August 8, 1968; children: Billy, David. *Education:* University of California, Santa Barbara, B.A., 1966, Ph.D., 1974; San Francisco State University, M.A., 1969. *Home:* 5515 Northwest 28th Ter., Gainesville, Fla. 32601. *Office:* Department of Sociology, University of Florida, Gainesville, Fla. 32611.

CAREER: California State College, Stanislaus, in Turlock, assistant professor of sociology, 1973-74; University of Florida, Gainesville, assistant professor of sociology, 1974—. *Member:* American Sociological Association, Society for the Study of Social Problems, Southern Sociological Society.

WRITINGS: The Sociologist as Detective, Praeger, 1974, 2nd edition, 1976; *Juvenile Delinquency,* Praeger, 1976; (with Howard Daudistel) *The Criminal Justice Process,* Praeger, 1976; *Detective Work,* Free Press, in press.

WORK IN PROGRESS: Criminal Justice, with Howard Daudistel and David Luckenbill, for Praeger, completion expected by 1978; a study of police on patrol in a Southern town.

SIDELIGHTS: Sanders writes: "I'm working with a couple of guys on the Presidential debates with a lie detector of sorts (spectrograph) to see if either or both of them were lying. Also, I'm trying to find out what causes crime, especially among the wealthier segment of society."

* * *

SANER, Reg(inald Anthony) 1931-

PERSONAL: Born December 30, 1931, in Jacksonville, Ill.; son of Reginald and Marie (Rexroat) Saner; married Anne Costigan (a teacher), August 16, 1958; children: Timothy, Nicholas. *Education:* St. Norbert College, B.A., 1950; University of Illinois, M.A., 1954, Ph.D., 1962. *Religion:* Atheist. *Home:* 1925 Vassar, Boulder, Colo. 80303. *Office:* Department of English, University of Colorado, Boulder, Colo. 80303.

CAREER: University of Illinois, Urbana, assistant instructor, 1956-60, instructor in English, 1961-62; University of Colorado, Boulder, assistant professor, 1962-67, associate professor, 1967-72, professor of English, 1972—. Free-lance photographer. *Military service:* U.S. Army, Infantry, 1951-53; became first lieutenant; received Bronze Star. *Member:* Shakespeare Association, Renaissance Society, Dante Society. *Awards, honors:* Fulbright grant for study at University of Florence, 1960; Borestone Mountain Poetry award, 1972; Walt Whitman award, 1975.

WRITINGS: Climbing into the Roots (poems), Harper, 1975. Editorial consultant, Montgomery Publishing Co. (Los Angeles), 1956—.

WORK IN PROGRESS: Another book of poems.

SIDELIGHTS: Saner writes: "As free-lance photographer I photographed celebrities, girdles, lawn sprinklers, and prize swine. My army service took me to Alaska, where I was trained in arctic survival and technical climbing. I continue semi-serious mountaineering, which has figured pervasively in my poetry. Presently, I'm collecting photographs for an eventual book in which alpine scenes complement poetry sprung from alpine sources."

SANFORD, Leda 1934-

PERSONAL: Born in 1934, in Tuscany, Italy; came to United States, 1939, naturalized citizen, 1939; daughter of Fausto Giovannetti (an artist) and Josephine (Lunardi) Giovannetti Cole; married Howard Sanford (divorced); children: Robert Wayne, Scott Howard. *Education:* Fashion Institute of Technology, New York City, A.A.S., 1953. *Home:* 160 East 65th St., New York, N.Y. 10021. *Office:* American Home Publishing Co., Inc., 641 Lexington Ave., New York, N.Y. 10022.

CAREER: Teens and Boys magazine, New York City, editor-in-chief, 1966-73; *Men's Wear* magazine, New York City, editor-in-chief, 1973-75; *American Home* magazine, New York City, editor and publisher, 1975—. Chairman of men's wear committee for COTY fashion awards, 1975. *Member:* Fashion Group, Fashion Institute of Technology Alumni Association, Manor Club (Pelham, N.Y.).

WRITINGS: Regular column in *American Home* magazine, entitled "For Your Information from the Desk of Leda Sanford," 1975—. Contributor of fashion articles to magazines.

SIDELIGHTS: Leda Sanford is the only woman publisher of a major magazine in the United States. From that position she directs her magazine on a course "more liberated than traditional 'shelter books' like *Better Homes and Gardens,* yet less radical than women's movement publications like *Ms.*" She told *CA:* "Our reader is a new traditionalist. She's a woman striving for self-fulfillment, a woman who has a career, a marriage and children, but who has ambivalent feelings about her priorities." Ms. Sanford believes that "this woman needs a supportive magazine, one that deals with living and reality. She needs a magazine that looks like 'today' and offers visual pleasure and information rather than more of the voyeurism that currently feeds the mass appetite for escape."

BIOGRAPHICAL/CRITICAL SOURCES: Chicago Daily News, January 14, 1976; *Philadelphia Inquirer,* February 23, 1976; *Detroit Free Press,* April 16, 1976; *Fort Lauderdale News,* May 18, 1976; *Miami Herald,* May 20, 1976; *New York Times,* June 15, 1976.

* * *

SANSOM, William 1912-1976

January 18, 1912—April 20, 1976; British novelist, biographer, screenwriter, and composer-lyricist. Obituaries: *New York Times,* April 21, 1976; *Washington Post,* April 24, 1976; *AB Bookman's Weekly,* June 14, 1976. (See index for previous *CA* sketch)

* * *

SARGANT, William (Walters) 1907-

PERSONAL: Born 1907, in London, England; son of Norman T. C. and Alice Rose Sargant; married Margaret Heriot Glen, 1940. *Education:* Attended St. John's College, Cambridge, and Royal College of Physicians; Royal College of Psychiatrists, D.P.M., 1937. *Agent:* A. P. Watt & Son, 26/28 Bedford Row, London WC1R 4HL, England. *Office:* 23 Harley St., London W1N 1DA, England.

CAREER: St. Mary's Hospital, London, England, assistant in medical professorial unit, 1932-34; Maudsley Hospital, London, physician, 1935-49; St. Thomas Hospital, London, physician in charge of department of psychological medicine, 1948-72, honorary consulting psychiatrist, 1972—. Assistant clinical director, Sutton Emergency Hospital, 1939-47; visiting professor, Duke University, 1947-48; examiner

in psychological medicine, Conjoint Board of England, 1960-63; acting dean of Royal College of Psychiatrists, 1971. Lecturer, American Society of Biological Psychiatry, 1964, New York College of Medicine, 1964, Royal College of Physicians, 1966, Royal Medico-Psychological Association, 1968, and University of Michigan, 1968.

Member: Royal Medico-Psychological Association (registrar, 1951-71), Royal Society of Medicine (president of psychiatry section, 1956-57), World Psychiatric Association (associate secretary, 1961-66; honorary member), Royal College of Psychiatrists (honorary fellow, 1974), Canadian Psychiatric Association (honorary fellow, 1962). *Awards, honors:* Rockefeller traveling and research fellowships to Harvard University, 1938-39; award from Taylor Manor Hospital, 1971; Starkey memorial prize from Royal Society of Health, 1973.

WRITINGS: (With Eliot Slater) *Introduction to Physical Methods of Treatment in Psychiatry,* E. & S. Livingstone, 1944, 5th edition, 1972; *Battle for the Mind: A Physiology of Conversion and Brain-Washing,* Heinemann, 1957; *The Unquiet Mind,* Heinemann, 1967; *The Mind Possessed: Physiology of Possession, Mysticism, and Faith Healing,* Heinemann, 1973. Contributor of articles to medical journals.

* * *

SASSOON, Beverly Adams

PERSONAL: Born in Alberta, Canada; daughter of Wayne and Tillie Adams; married Vidal Sassoon (a hair stylist and businessman); children: Catya, Eden, Elan, David. *Education:* Attended Valley State College, Santa Monica College; currently attending University of California at Los Angeles. *Residence:* California. *Office:* Vidal Sassoon, Inc., 1801 Century Park East, Los Angeles, Calif. 90067.

CAREER: Television and film actress; has appeared on popular television programs, including "Ozzie and Harriet," "Burke's Law," "Channing," "My Three Sons," and "Dr. Kildare," and in major motion pictures. Co-hostess of "The Beverly and Vidal Sassoon Show," on KCOP-Television, 1966—.

WRITINGS: (With husband, Vidal Sassoon, and Camille Duhe) *A Year of Beauty and Health,* Simon & Schuster, 1976.

AVOCATIONAL INTERESTS: Physical fitness, politics, sports, the arts.

* * *

SASSOON, Vidal 1928-

PERSONAL: Born January 17, 1928, in London, England; son of Jack and Betty (Kellin) Sassoon; married Beverly Gail Adams (an actress and writer), 1966; children: Catya, Eden, Elan, David. *Education:* Educated in London, England. *Residence:* California. *Office:* Vidal Sassoon, Inc., 803 Madison Ave., New York, N.Y. 10021.

CAREER: Chairman of board of directors, Vidal Sassoon, Inc. (salon with offices all over the world), New York, N.Y. Co-host of "The Beverly and Vidal Sassoon Show," on KCOP-Television; has also appeared on popular national television programs.

WRITINGS: (With wife, Beverly Adams Sassoon, and Camille Duhe) *A Year of Health and Beauty,* Simon & Schuster, 1976.

SIDELIGHTS: Sassoon's salons have spread all over the

world; he also trains hair stylists, styles wigs, produces and sells a complete line of hair appliances and hair care, treatment, and conditioning products. He has lectured and given demonstrations for professional and private groups all over the world. *Avocational interests:* Physical fitness, politics, sports, the arts.

* * *

SATTLER, Warren 1934-

PERSONAL: Born September 7, 1934, in Meriden, Conn.; son of Albert R. (a jockey) and Domenia (Marcellino) Sattler; married Margaret Ann Kopke, December 3, 1955; children: Steven, Marc, Craig, Casey, Cindy. *Education:* Attended technical high school in Meriden, Conn. *Politics:* Independent. *Home:* 269 Capitol Ave., Meriden, Conn. 06450.

CAREER: Famous Artists School, Westport, Conn., instructor, 1957-63; Al Smith Feature Service, Bomossen, Vt., author of syndicated cartoon strip "Grubby," 1965—. Author and writer of comic strips "Yang" and "Billy the Kid" for Charlton Publishing; artist of syndicated comic strip "Barnaby" for Hall Syndicate, and "Jackson Twins," for McNaught Syndicate. *Military service:* U.S. Air Force, 1953-57.

WRITINGS: (With P. Bernstein) *Great Moments in Hysteria,* Ace Books, 1969. Author and composer of about five hundred country-western songs. Contributor to *Playboy, New York Times Magazine, Cracked,* and *National Lampoon.*

SIDELIGHTS: Sattler comments that he has been "inspired by Milt Canife ("Steve Canyon" comic strip) to become a cartoonist. Studied art under Erst Lohrman—great German teacher who taught most of International Silver Co. and Wallace Silver Co. designers...." *Avocational interests:* Country-western singer (has made one record album and six single recordings).

* * *

SAUVAGEAU, Juan 1917-
(Jean Lavoix)

PERSONAL: Born December 26, 1917, in Sorel, Quebec, Canada; son of Charles (a ship builder) and Jeannette (Pro) Sauvageau; married Margarita Gonzalez Trevino (a university professor), December 28, 1971; children: Roger. *Education:* Attended University of Ottawa, 1937-41; Tulane University, M.A., 1963, Ph.D., 1967; Our Lady of the Lake College, M.Ed., 1970; St. Mary's University, M.A., 1972. *Home:* 2202 Louisiana, Kingsville, Tex. 78363. *Agent:* Publishing Services, Inc., 1800 Lovaca, Austin, Tex. 78701. *Office:* Department of Modern Languages, Texas A & I University, Kingsville, Tex. 78363.

CAREER: Pan American University, Edinburg, Tex., assistant professor, 1961-68; Our Lady of the Lake College, San Antonio, Tex., assistant professor of French and Spanish, 1968-71; Incarnate Word College, San Antonio, Tex., visiting professor, 1970-71; San Antonio Junior College, San Antonio, Tex., member of staff of Spanish department, 1971—; Texas A & I University, Kingsville, associate professor of French and Spanish, 1971—.

MEMBER: Modern Language Association of America, American Association of University Professors, Association of Professors of French, Association of Professors of Spanish, Texas Association of College Teachers. *Awards, honors:* First prize in Sigma Delta Pi poetry contest, 1975.

WRITINGS—Folklore studies: *Stories That Must Not Die,* Oasis Press, Volume I, 1975, Volume II, 1975, Volume III, 1976; *Cuentos de ayer para ninos de hoy* (title means "Tales of Yesterday for Today's Children"), Alice Press, 1975. Contributor, under the pseudonym Jean Lavoix, to *Le Samedi Litteraire.*

WORK IN PROGRESS: Le Portrait du pretre dans "La Comedie Humaine" d'Honore de Balzac (title means "The Portrait of the Priest in *La Comedie Humaine* of Balzac"); *The Wetback,* a bilingual novel studying Chicanos; a book of poems in Spanish, English, and French, for Oasis Press.

SIDELIGHTS: Sauvageau writes that his three books of folkloric studies are the result of a lifetime interest in the folklore of the region.

* * *

SAUVY, Jean (Maurice Paul) 1916-

PERSONAL: Born April 29, 1916, in Grasse, France; married Simonne Ragouilliaux (a writer); children: Olivier. *Education:* Ecole Nationale de Ponts et Chaussees, civil engineering diploma, 1940; Sorbonne, University of Paris, licence es lettres, 1949, diplome etudes superieures de philosophie, 1953. *Home:* 29 Avenue du Onze Novembre, Meudon 92190, France.

CAREER: Civil and economist engineer, and mathematics teacher.

WRITINGS: Le Katanga 50 ans decisifs (title means "Katanga during the Last Fifty Years"), Societe Cont d'Editions Modernes Illustrees, 1961; *Initiation a l'economie des pays en voie de developpement* (title means "Discovering the Economy of Developing Countries"), Institut International d'Administration Publique, 1968; (with wife, Simonne Sauvy) *L'Enfant a la decouverte de l'espace,* Casterman, 1972, translation by Pam Wells published as *The Child's Discovery of Space,* Penguin, 1974; (with S. Sauvy) *L'Enfant et les geometrie* (title means "The Child's Use of Geometry"), Casterman, 1974. Editor of *Activities Recherches Pedagogiques,* 1971-75.

SIDELIGHTS: Sauvy was a member of the French scientific expedition on the River Niger in 1947, traveling in a canoe from the springs to the ocean, a nine-month journey. *Avocational interests:* Anthropology, mathematics, language (semantics), painting, Norse skiing, soft technologies.

* * *

SAUVY, Simonne 1922-

PERSONAL: Born March 28, 1922, in Paris, France; married Jean Sauvy (a writer); children: Olivier. *Education:* Self-educated. *Home:* 29 Avenue du Onze Novembre, Meudon 92190, France.

CAREER: Free-lance educator.

WRITINGS: (With husband, Jean Sauvy) *L'Enfant a la decouverte de l'espace,* Casterman, 1972, translation by Pam Wells published as *The Child's Discovery of Space,* Penguin, 1974; (with J. Sauvy) *L'Enfant et les geometries* (title means "The Child's Use of Geometry"), Casterman, 1974; *L'Enfant a la decouverte de la langue maternelle* (title means "The Child's Discovery of His Maternal Language"), Casterman, 1976. Member of board of directors of *Activities et Recherches Pedagogiques,* 1971-75.

WORK IN PROGRESS: Translating *Science and Sanity* by Korzybski.

AVOCATIONAL INTERESTS: General semantics, pedagogy.

SAVAGE, Christina
See NEWCOMB, Kerry and SCHAEFER, Frank

*   *   *

SAVAGE, Marc 1945-

PERSONAL: Born July 23, 1945, in Kalamazoo, Mich.; son of George (a microbiologist) and Terry (a teacher; maiden name, Ender) Savage; married Sharon Wright (an insurance broker), February 22, 1975; children: Laura Jans. *Education:* University of Michigan, A.B. (cum laude), 1967; Columbia University, M.F.A., 1969. *Home and office:* 92 Horatio St., New York, N.Y. 10014. *Agent:* Carl Brandt, Brandt & Brandt, 101 Park Ave., New York, N.Y. 10017.

CAREER: Writer and editor. *Awards, honors:* Avery Hopwood Award from University of Michigan, 1967, for nonfiction "Impressions, 1965-66."

WRITINGS: The Light Outside (novel), Harper, 1976.

WORK IN PROGRESS: The Record Keeper (tentative title), a novel; *The Taste of Quinine,* a novella; short stories, songs, poems.

SIDELIGHTS: Savage writes: "What motivates a writer is perhaps no different from what prompts one man to go to the moon and another to go to a massage parlor. Craving comes in many forms, whether it be a craving to know a woman, a new world, or this old one with all its aches and mysteries. A writer goes only two thirds of the way with Caesar: I came, I saw. Where he goes after that, of course, is his own business.

"I find it more difficult, but more fruitful, to celebrate than to attack. Implication, not fulmination. Myths, their origin and power, fascinate. I am particularly interested in everything."

*   *   *

SCALI, John (Alfred) 1918-

PERSONAL: Born April 27, 1918, in Canton, Ohio; son of Paul M. and Lucia (Leone) Scali; married second wife, Denise St. Germaine, March 4, 1973; children: Donna, Paula (Mrs. Thomas M. Cronin), Carla. *Education:* Boston University, B.S., 1942. *Home:* 2801 New Mexico Ave. N.W., Washington, D.C. 20007. *Agent:* Gerald Dickler, Hall, Dickler, Lawler, Kent and Howley, 460 Park Ave., New York, N.Y. 10022.

CAREER/WRITINGS: Boston Herald, Boston, Mass., reporter, 1942; United Press, Boston, Mass., reporter, 1942-43; Associated Press, war correspondent in European theatre of operations, 1944, diplomatic and roving correspondent based in Washington, D.C., 1945-61; American Broadcasting Corp. (ABC) News, Washington, D.C., diplomatic correspondent, 1961-71; White House, Washington, D.C., special counsel for foreign affairs and communications, 1971-73; U.S. ambassador to United Nations, 1973-75; ABC News, Washington, D.C., senior correspondent, 1975—. Member of Council on Foreign Relations. Author of scripts for television and radio broadcast by ABC News. Contributor of articles to magazines and newspapers, including *Look, Saturday Evening Post,* and *Foreign Affairs.*

MEMBER: Tiro a Segno, Columbus Citizens Commission, Sigma Delta Chi, National Press Club, International Club (both Washington, D.C.), River Club (New York City). *Awards, honors:* University of Southern California journalism award, 1964; National Academy of Arts and Sciences special award from Washington chapter, 1964; Boston Uni-

versity public service award, 1965; Overseas Press Club award for distinguished reporting, 1965, for coverage of Cuban missile crisis.

SIDELIGHTS: In 1964, the American Federation of Television and Radio Artists created the John Scali award. It is presented to the person best exemplifying the example Scali set in service to the nation during the Cuban missile crisis. At the height of the crisis, Scali had been contacted by Alexandr Fomin, a KGB colonel and personal friend of Khrushchev. With President Kennedy's go-ahead, he met secretly with Fomin four times to work out the formula that averted war over Cuba. Afterwards, he held up the biggest story of his career when President Kennedy refused permission to release the information. A year later a State Department intelligence official broke the story of Scali's role in a book before he had a chance to publish his own account. Scali anchored the ABC News documentary of the events entitled "John Scali, ABC News."

Scali was the principal anchor of the ABC weekly 30 minute report on the Vietnam War, entitled "Scope—The Vietnam War," 1968-70. He also anchored numerous foreign policy documentaries for ABC News.

*   *   *

SCHACHTER, Oscar 1915-

PERSONAL: Born June 19, 1915, in New York, N.Y.; son of Max (a businessman) and Fannie (Javits) Schachter; married Mollie Miller, August 9, 1936; children: Judith (Mrs. John Modell), Ellen (Mrs. John P. Leventhal). *Education:* City College of New York (now City College of the City University of New York), B.S.S., 1936; Columbia University, J.D., 1939. *Home:* 36 Sutton Pl. S., New York, N.Y. 10022. *Office:* School of Law, Columbia University, New York, N.Y. 10027.

CAREER: Admitted to New York Bar, 1939; private practice of law in New York City, 1939-40; U.S. Department of Labor, Washington, D.C., attorney, 1940—; Federal Communications Commission, Washington, D.C., senior attorney, 1941-42; Board of War Communications, Washington, D.C., legal advisor on international communications, 1942; U.S. Department of State, Washington, D.C., adviser on international economic and financial affairs, 1942-43; United Nations, New York City, assistant general counsel for Relief and Rehabilitation Administration, 1944-46, senior legal counsellor for the Secretariat, 1946-47, deputy director of General Legal Division, 1947-52, director, 1953-66, deputy executive director and director of studies of Institute for Training and Research (UNITAR), 1966-75, adviser to UNESCO, 1948; Columbia University, New York City, professor of law, 1975—. Visiting lecturer at Yale University, 1955-71; visiting professor at University of Michigan, New York University, and Rutgers University; Carnegie Lecturer at Hague Academy of International Law, 1963. Member of advisory committees and councils for McGill University, York University, University of Sussex, University of Nice, University of Rhode Island, and Princeton University. Chairman of legal committee of United Nations Maritime Conference, 1948; executive secretary of International Arbitration Conference, 1958. Legal adviser of United Nations Atomic Energy Commission, 1946-47.

MEMBER: International Institute of Space Law, International Academy of Astronautics, International Law Association (member of executive committee of American branch), L'Institut de Droit International, World Academy of Art and Science, Fundacion Internacional Eloy Alfaro (honorary member), American Society of International Law (president, 1968-70; honorary vice-president, 1970—; member of executive council), Council on Foreign Relations, Commission for the Study of the Organization of Peace, Phi Beta Kappa.

WRITINGS: (Contributor) Cornelius Ryan, editor, *Across the Space Frontier,* Viking, 1952; (with Mahomed Nawaz and John H. Fried) *Toward the Wider Acceptance of Multilateral Treaties,* Arno, 1971; *The Role of the Institute of International Law and Its Methods of Work: Today and Tomorrow,* Geneva Tribune Press (Geneva, Switzerland), 1973; (contributor) J. N. Moore, editor, *Law and Civil War in the Modern World,* Johns Hopkins Press, 1974; *Sharing the World's Resources,* Columbia University Press, 1976. Contributor to law journals. Editor-in-chief of *Columbia Law Review,* 1938-39; member of board of editors of *American Journal of International Law* and *Journal of International and Comparative Environmental Law.*

* * *

SCHAEFER, Frank 1936-
(Shana Carrol, Peter Gentry, Christina Savage, joint pseudonyms with Kerry Newcomb)

PERSONAL: Born October 25, 1936, in Newburgh, N.Y.; son of Francis H., Jr. and Mary Elizabeth Schaefer; married Jerelyn Williams (a teacher), 1970; children: Clay, Matthew, Frankie. *Education:* Attended Cornell University and Del Mar Junior College; Texas Agricultural & Industrial University, B.A., 1963; Trinity University, San Antonio, Tex., M.A., 1968. *Politics:* "Cynic." *Religion:* None. *Agent:* Aaron Priest, 150 East 35th St., Suite 620, New York, N.Y. 10016. *Office:* Shanew Writes, 3419 Hall, #4, Dallas, Tex. 75219.

CAREER: Has worked as an actor, director, radio announcer, operating room technician, psychiatric technician, and film maker; U.S. Peace Corps worker in Costa Rica, 1977. *Military service:* U.S. Navy, hospital corpsman, 1958-60.

WRITINGS—All fiction with Kerry Newcomb: (Under joint pseudonym Peter Gentry) *Rafe,* Fawcett, 1976; (under joint pseudonym Shana Carrol) *Paxton Pride,* Pyramid Publications, 1976; (under joint pseudonym Peter Gentry) *Titus Gamble,* Fawcett, in press.

WORK IN PROGRESS: Two books with Kerry Newcomb: *Raven* (under joint pseudonym Shana Carrol), for Pyramid; *Gladwyn's Lady* (under joint pseudonym Christina Savage), for Dell.

* * *

SCHAETZEL, J(oseph) Robert 1917-

PERSONAL: Born January 28, 1917, in Holtville, Calif.; son of Arthur J. and Lois (Fahs) Schaetzel; married Imogen Hathaway Spencer, April 14, 1944; children: Ann, Wendy. *Education:* Pomona College, B.A., 1939; Harvard University, graduate study, 1940-42; attended National War College, 1954-55. *Address:* 2 Bay Tree Lane, Washington, D.C. 20016.

CAREER: U.S. Bureau of the Budget, Washington, D.C., administrative assistant, 1942-45; U.S. Department of State, Washington, D.C., special assistant to director of Office of International Trade Policy, 1945-50, special assistant to assistant secretary of state for economic affairs, 1950-54, officer in charge of peaceful uses of atomic energy in Office of the Special Assistant to the Secretary for Disarmament and Atomic Energy, 1955-59, directed task force on organization

and personnel policy of the State Department, 1960-61, special assistant to under-secretary of state, 1962-66, ambassador to European Communities in Brussels, Belgium, 1966-72; writer, lecturer, and consultant 1972—. Chairman of Task Force on Consultation for the Trilateral Commission; vice-chairman of Atlantic Institute (Paris); member of board of directors of Atlantic Council (Washington, D.C.). Member of board of visitors of Johns Hopkins University's Bologna Center; senior fellow of Woodrow Wilson Fellowship Foundation; member of board of directors of Honeywell, Inc. *Member:* Council on Foreign Relations, Atlantic Visitors Association (Brussels; vice-president). *Awards, honors:* Rockefeller Public Service Award from U.S. Department of State, 1959-60.

WRITINGS: The Unhinged Alliance: America and the European Community, Harper, 1975. Contributor to popular magazines, including *Fortune* and *Reader's Digest,* and to foreign affairs and political science journals.

* * *

SCHAKNE, Robert 1926-

PERSONAL: August 19, 1926, in New York, N.Y.; married; children: one. *Education:* Attended University of Chicago, 1947-50. *Residence:* Washington, D.C. *Office:* CBS News, 2020 M St. N.W., Washington, D.C. 20036.

CAREER/WRITINGS: International News Service, correspondent based in Chicago, New York, and Tokyo, 1949-55, war correspondent in Korea, 1950-53; Columbia Broadcasting System (CBS) News, 1955—, covered civil rights in the South during early 1960's, correspondent on West Coast, 1962-63, in Latin America, 1964-66, in Dominican Republic, 1965-66, in Vietnam, 1967-68, currently investigative correspondent in Washington, D.C. Notable assignments include small wars, coups, and riots worldwide. *Awards, honors:* Sigma Delta Chi award, 1971, for coverage of Attica prison uprising; Emmy Award, 197,, for story on Vice-President Agnew's resignation.

* * *

SCHAPIRO, Leonard (Bertram) 1908-

PERSONAL: Born April 22, 1908, in Glasgow, Scotland; son of Max and Leah (Levine) Schapiro. *Education:* Earned LL.B. from University College, London. *Office:* London School of Economics and Political Science, London, England.

CAREER: Called to the Bar, Gray's Inn, London, England, 1932; practiced law at the Bar, London, and on western circuit, 1932-39, at the Bar, 1946-55; University of London, London School of Economics and Political Science, professor of political science, 1962-75, professor emeritus, 1975—, University College, fellow, 1973—. Member of executive committee, Wiener Library. *Military service:* Served with British Broadcasting Corp. (BBC) monitoring service, 1940-42, War Office, 1942-45, and intelligence division of German Control Commission, 1945-46; became major. *Member:* American Academy of Arts and Sciences (foreign honorary member), British Academy (fellow), Institute for the Study of Conflict (council chairman, 1970—), Institute of Jewish Affairs (board member), Institute for Religion and Communism (council member), Reform Club.

WRITINGS: The Law: Servant or Master?, Batchworth Press, 1951; *How Strong Is Communism?,* Batchworth Press, 1954; *The Future of Russia,* Ampersand, 1955; *The Origin of the Communist Autocracy: Political Opposition in the Soviet State, First Phase, 1917-1922,* Harvard University Press, 1955, 2nd edition, 1976; *The Communist Party of the Soviet Union,* Random House, 1960, revised edition, 1971; (editor) *The U.S.S.R. and the Future: An Analysis of the New Programme of the Communist Party of the Soviet Union,* Institute for the Study of the U.S.S.R. (Munich), 1962, Praeger, 1963; *The Government and Politics of the Soviet Union,* Random House, 1965, 5th edition, 1973; (editor with Peter Reddaway) *Lenin, the Man, the Theorist, the Leader: A Reappraisal,* Praeger, 1967; *Rationalism and Nationalism in Russian Nineteenth-Century Political Thought,* Yale University Press, 1967; (compiler, contributor, and author of introduction) *Political Opposition in One-Party States,* Wiley, 1972; *Totalitarianism,* Praeger, 1972; (translator and contributor) Ivan Turgenev, *Spring Torrents,* Eyre Methune, 1972.

Contributor to *Encyclopaedia Britannica* and to professional journals and symposia. Chairman of editorial board, *Government and Opposition;* member of editorial board, *Soviet Survey* and *Soviet Jewish Affairs: A Journal on Jewish Problems in the U.S.S.R. and Eastern Europe.*

AVOCATIONAL INTERESTS: Music, travel, medieval art.

* * *

SCHARLEMANN, Dorothy Hoyer 1912-
(Donna Haye Sharon)

PERSONAL: Born December 6, 1912, in Denver, Colo.; daughter of Theodor (a clergyman) and Pauline (Aufdemberg) Hoyer; married Martin H. Scharlemann (a professor of theology), June 18, 1938; children: Edith (Mrs. David Rehbein), E. Theodor, Martin George, John Paul. *Education:* Attended St. John's College, Winfield, Kan., 1927-30, and Harris Teachers College, 1930-33; University of Illinois, B.S.Ed., 1942. *Politics:* Independent. *Religion:* Lutheran. *Home:* 17 Seminary Ter. N., St. Louis, Mo. 63105.

CAREER: Writer. Elementary school teacher in St. Louis, Mo., 1934-38. *Member:* Concordia Seminary Guild, Concordia Historical Society Auxiliary, Faculty Wives of Concordia Seminary, Chi Alpha Wives of St. Louis, Rotary Anns (Clayton, Mo.). *Awards, honors:* First prize from play contest sponsored by Lutheran Layman's League and Concordia Publishing House, 1954, for "Then Shall the Eyes."

WRITINGS: My Vineyard, Concordia, 1946; *Pearls for a King* (stories), Concordia, 1976.

Plays: "Then Shall the Eyes" (one-act), 1956; "Little Lord Jesus" (pageant, 1957; "By Love" (one-act), 1958.

Author of hymn "Christ Who Once Walked." Contributor of poems, stories (once under pseudonym Donna Haye Sharon), and reviews to church publications.

WORK IN PROGRESS: The Tenth Man, a novel based on the story of the healing of ten lepers; "The Eyes of the Blind," a modern adaptation of "Then Shall the Eyes."

SIDELIGHTS: Dorothy Scharlemann writes: "As a deeply committed Christian, my motivation in all my writings is to reinforce the message of Bible-based Christianity by whatever means opportunity offers. My favorite vehicle is fiction, usually based on minor Biblical characters. . . . A good deal of travel, as well as several months residence in Rome in 1966 and in Kenya in 1973 have given me insights into ancient civilizations and primitive societies that help, I think, to bring some authenticity into my fictional creations."

BIOGRAPHICAL/CRITICAL SOURCES: Concordia Commentator, summer, 1976.

SCHEIN, Clarence J(acob) 1918-

PERSONAL: Born January 15, 1918, in New York, N.Y.; son of Benjamin (a dentist) and Fannie (Feldman) Schein; married Ada Frenkel, September 1, 1960; children: Aviva Beth, Amy Hannah. *Education:* New York University, B.S. (cum laude), 1938, M.D., 1942. *Religion:* Jewish. *Home:* 113 Carthage Rd., Scarsdale, N.Y. 10583. *Agent:* Raines & Raines, 475 Fifth Ave., New York, N.Y. 10017. *Office:* 3355 Bainbridge Ave., Bronx, N.Y. 10467.

CAREER: Albert Einstein College of Medicine, New York, N.Y., instructor in surgery, 1955-57, assistant clinical professor, 1957-67, associate professor, 1967-71, professor of surgery, 1971—. Attending surgeon, Montefiore Hospital Medical Center, 1956—. Diplomate, American Board of Surgery, American Board of Thoracic Surgeons.

MEMBER: American Gastroenterological Association, Association for Academic Surgery, American Medical Writers Association, American Association for the Advancement of Science, American College of Surgeons (fellow), Society for Surgery of the Alimentary Tract, Digestive Disease Foundation, New York Academy of Science, New York Academy of Medicine, New York Society for Thoracic Surgery, Phi Beta Kappa. *Awards, honors:* Henry Moses Award from Montefiore Hospital and Albert Einstein College of Medicine, 1973, for *Acute Cholecystitis;* Honorable mention for best book for laymen, American Medical Writers Association, 1976, for *Surgeon at Work.*

WRITINGS: (With Harold Jacobson and William Stern) *The Common Bile Duct,* C. C Thomas, 1967; *Acute Cholecystitis,* Harper, 1972; *A Surgeon Answers,* Putnam, 1973; *Surgeon at Work,* Stein & Day, 1975; *Postcholecystectomy Syndromes,* Harper, in press.

WORK IN PROGRESS: Anthology of Dedications.

* * *

SCHEVITZ, Jeffrey M(orrie) 1941-

PERSONAL: Born January 11, 1941, in Wilmington, Del.; son of Mitchell and Sylvia (Sugarman) Schevitz; married Edita Harrott, May 24, 1962 (divorced, 1976); children: Andrei, Tanya. *Education:* Princeton University, A.B. (cum laude), 1962; University of California, Berkeley, M.A., 1966, Ph.D., 1974. *Office:* John F. Kennedy Institut fuer Amerikastudien, Freie Universitaet, Berlin, Germany.

CAREER: Washington University, St. Louis, Mo., instructor in sociology, 1969-72; State University of New York College at Cortland, instructor in sociology, 1972-74; State University of New York College at Buffalo, assistant professor of sociology, 1974-76; Freie Universitaet, Berlin, Germany, assistant professor of sociology, 1976—. Appeared weekly on "War/Peace Spotlight" on KDNA-FM and KFRH-FM Radio, 1971-72; panelist on "Eye on St. Louis" on KMCM-Television, 1971. *Awards, honors:* National Science Foundation grant for foreign study, 1961; Victor M. Rabinowitz Foundation grant, 1971-72.

WRITINGS: (Contributor) J. David Colfax and Jack Roach, editors, *Radical Sociology,* Basic Books, 1971; *The Weaponsmakers: The Scientific Estate and American Imperialism,* Schenkman, 1976.

Author of films, "But What Do We Do?," with Leonard Henny, 1968, "The Schizophrenia of Working for War," with Henny, 1969, and "The McDonnell Film," with members of the McDonnell Project, 1972.

Editor of "Schenkman Series in Radical Sociology." 1976.

Contributor to *Dushkin Encyclopedia of Sociology,* to sociology and scientific journals, and to *Ramparts. Berkeley Journal of Sociology,* member of editorial board, 1965-66, editor, 1966-67; editor of *Insurgent Sociologist,* 1969-70.

WORK IN PROGRESS: Work and Industry in Capitalist and Socialist Societies, for Schenkman; *Capitalism and the Development of Science in the United States.*

* * *

SCHIFF, Irwin A(llan)   1928-

PERSONAL: Born February 23, 1928, in New Haven, Conn.; son of Jacob (a cabinet maker) and Anna (Winnick) Schiff; married Ellen Wachsman, March 3, 1961 (divorced 1968); children: Peter, Andrew. *Education:* University of Connecticut, B.S., 1950. *Politics:* Libertarian. *Religion:* Jewish. *Home and office:* 2405 Whitney Ave., Hamden, Conn. 06518.

CAREER: Irwin A. Schiff, Inc., and Group Insurers, Inc., Hamden, Conn., president, 1960—. Writer and lecturer. *Military service:* U.S. Army Finance Corp, 1950-52.

WRITINGS: The Biggest Con: How the Government Is Fleecing You, Arlington House, 1976.

WORK IN PROGRESS: Articles on the status of the American economy.

SIDELIGHTS: Schiff told *CA* of his book and his refusal to pay taxes: "In my book, I explain how the government—by stealing through inflation, by counterfeiting U.S. currency, by operating a huge chain letter (Social Security), by illegally reporting only 10 percent of the national debt, by creating unnecessary financial pressures because of unnecessarily high taxes, and through pursuing policies that tax productivity while subsidizing idleness and waste—is undermining the nation's economic and social foundation.

In view of the criminal nature of so much of the government's activity, I decided in 1974 that I could no longer pay income taxes since that would make me a party to and an accessory to all the government crimes mentioned above.

I am, therefore, an enthusiastic supporter of the growing national tax revolt. I see in it the only effective antidote that might prevent us from traveling down the road to national oblivion—as is now being pursued by Great Britain and as traveled by other declining civilizations."

* * *

SCHLEGEL, Richard   1913-

PERSONAL: Born August 29, 1913, in Davenport, Iowa; son of Richard (a grocer) and Marie (Hansen) Schlegel; married Frances Sally McKee, June 26, 1946; children: Thomas Hansen, Catherine McKee. *Education:* University of Chicago, B.A., 1935, graduate study, 1937-38; University of Iowa, M.A., 1936; further graduate study, University of Colorado, 1940-41; University of Illinois, Ph.D., 1943. *Politics:* Independent. *Religion:* Christian. *Home:* 660 Stoddard Ave., East Lansing, Mich. 48823. *Office:* Department of Physics, Michigan State University, East Lansing, Mich. 48824.

CAREER: Museum of Science and Industry, Chicago, Ill., lecturer in physics, 1937-40; University of Chicago, Chicago, associate physicist in Metallurgical Laboratory, 1943-45; Princeton University, Princeton, N.J., instructor in physics, 1945-48; Michigan State University, East Lansing, assistant professor, 1948-54, associate professor, 1954-57, professor of physics, 1957—, acting head of department,

1955-56. Visitor at Cavendish Laboratory, Cambridge University, 1954-55, 1962, 1968-69, 1976; visiting professor at University of California, Berkeley, summer, 1959, University of Texas at Arlington, summer, 1964, 1965, and University of Minnesota, 1967. *Member:* American Physical Society (fellow), Philosophy of Science Association, American Association of Physics Teachers, American Association of University Professors, American Association for the Advancement of Science.

WRITINGS: Time and the Physical World, Michigan State University Press, 1961, revised edition, Dover, 1968; *Completeness in Science,* Appleton, 1967; *Steckbrief der Wissenschaft,* Deutsche Verlags-Anstalt, 1969, translation published as *Inquiry Into Science,* Doubleday, 1972.

Contributor: J. T. Fraser, editor, *Voices of Time,* Braziller, 1965; Milton K. Munitz, editor, *Contemporary Philosophic Thought,* Volume II, State University of New York Press, 1970; Jiri Zeman, editor, *Time in Science and Philosophy,* Elsevier, 1971; William B. Rolnick, editor, *Causality and Physical Theories,* American Institute of Physics, 1974; Libor Kubat and Zeman, editors, *Entropy and Information in Science and Philosophy,* Academia (Prague), 1975. Contributor of more than seventy articles and reviews to journals. Member of board of editors of *Zygon: Journal of Science and Religion.*

WORK IN PROGRESS: Superposition and Interaction (tentative title), a "presentation of the basic concepts of contemporary physics."

SIDELIGHTS: Schlegel writes: "Although I work professionally as a physicist, my research and writing are in philosophy of science as well as in physics proper. My interest is primarily in concepts of contemporary physics and how they relate to our answers to the basic philosophical questions. I feel myself to be thoroughly a mid-Western American; but, I have spent four years in Cambridge, England, and both my wife and I are admirers of English culture and devoted sight-see-ers there, especially of churches and cathedrals."

* * *

SCHLINK, Frederick John   1891-

PERSONAL: Born October 26, 1891, in Peoria, Ill.; son of Valentine L. and Margaret (Brutcher) Schlink; married Mary Catherine Phillips, 1932. *Education:* University of Illinois, B.S., 1912, M.E., 1917. *Office:* Consumers' Research, Inc., Washington, N.J. 07882.

CAREER: Licensed professional engineer; National Bureau of Standards, Washington, D.C., associate physicist, 1913-19; Firestone Tire & Rubber Co., Akron, Ohio, physicist in charge of Instruments-Control Department, 1919-20; Western Electric Co. (now Bell Telephone Laboratories), New York City, mechanical engineer-physicist, 1920-22; American Standards Association, New York City, assistant secretary, 1922-31; Consumers' Research, Inc., Washington, N.J., president and technical director, 1931—. Member of consumer advisory council of Underwriters' Laboratories, Inc., of U.S. standards committee on leakage current of electrical appliances, and U.S. national committee of International Commission on Rules for Approval of Electrical Equipment.

MEMBER: Scientific Research Society of North America, American Society of Mechanical Engineers (life fellow), Institute of Electrical and Electronics Engineers (life member), Society of Automotive Engineers, American Physical Society (fellow), American Institute of Physics, Franklin Institute (life fellow), American Association for the Advancement of Science (fellow), American Economic Association, Sigma Xi. *Awards, honors:* Edward Longstreth Medal from Franklin Institute, 1919, for design of a novel type of precision weighing scale; honor medals from University of Illinois, 1969 and 1971.

WRITINGS: Liquid-Measuring Pumps, U.S. Government Printing Office, 1916; *Stabilized-Platform Weighing Scale of Novel Design,* U.S. Government Printing Office, 1918; *Variance of Measuring Instruments and Its Relation to Accuracy and Sensitivity,* U.S. Government Printing Office, 1918; *Area Measurement of Leather,* U.S. Government Printing Office, 1920; (with Stuart Chase) *Your Money's Worth,* Macmillan, 1927; (with Arthur Kallet) *One Hundred Million Guinea Pigs,* Vanguard, 1932; *Eat, Drink, and Be Wary,* Covici, Friede, 1935; (with M. C. Phillips) *Meat Three Times a Day,* R. R. Smith, 1946; (with Phillips) *Don't You Believe It!,* Pyramid Publications, 1966. Contributor to encyclopedias and scientific journals in the United States and England.

SIDELIGHTS: Schlink has developed a number of specialized weighing and measuring instruments for which patents were assigned to the Bureau of Standards for public use without payment of royalty. He has been responsible for design of instruments and devices used for testing at Consumers' Research, Inc. (a non-profit consumer product testing agency); a number of these have been duplicated by industry for use in their laboratories, with Consumers' Research's permission, and without charge.

*   *   *

SCHMIDT, Alice M(ahany) 1925-

PERSONAL: Born February 19, 1925; in Coggon, Iowa; daughter of Alfred E. (a teacher) and Merlin (a teacher; maiden name, Sawyer) Mahany; married Donald T. Schmidt (a librarian and archivist), June 7, 1947; children: Donald A., Helen E., Rebecca G., David L., Kenneth H., Janet R. *Education:* Attended Morningside College, 1942-43; University of Iowa, B.S.N., 1947; Brigham Young University, M.S., 1964, currently a doctoral candidate, 1974—. *Religion:* Church of Jesus Christ of Latter-day Saints. *Home:* 1882 North 1500 East St., Provo, Utah 84602. *Office:* 2246 C SFLC, Brigham Young University, Provo, Utah 84602.

CAREER: Office nurse in Marion, Iowa, 1947-48; Tooele Valley Hospital, Tooele, Utah, staff nurse, 1954-56; Roosevelt Hospital, Roosevelt, Utah, head nurse and supervisor of nurses, 1956-58; Brigham Young University, Provo, Utah, assistant professor of nursing, 1958—. Red Cross instructor and trainer in home nursing and parent preparedness. *Member:* National League of Nurses, American Nurses Association, Utah State Nurses Association (chairperson of committee on by-laws), Sigma Theta Tau.

WRITINGS:—All published by Brigham Young University Press: *Exploring the Facts about Pregnancy, Labor, and Infant Care,* 1975; *A Short Course in Family Health and Home Nursing,* 1975; *Homemaker's Guide to Home Nursing,* 1976. Also author of "Relief Society Lessons" series, Brigham Young University Press, 1974-76.

WORK IN PROGRESS: Research for books on mother and baby care and on the cultural aspects of menopause.

SIDELIGHTS: "I am currently completing my doctoral dissertation," Schmidt told *CA,* "which involves a teaching syllabus for prenatal classes. My current teaching responsibilities involve teaching non-nursing majors about home nursing and parenting."

SCHMIDT, Laura M(arie) 1952-
(B. C. Palmer; Laura Palmer)

PERSONAL: Born July 7, 1952, in New York, N.Y.; daughter of Alexander and the Princess Francesca (Rospigliosi) Schmidt. *Education:* Marymount Manhattan College, B.A., 1976. *Home:* 115 East 86th St., New York, N.Y. 10028. *Office:* Tristar, 521 Fifth Ave., New York, N.Y. 10019.

CAREER: Booster, Schoharie, N.Y., stringer, 1968-69; *Seyfret,* New York, N.Y., poetry editor, 1974—. *Tristar,* New York, N.Y. member of public relations staff, 1976—. *Member:* International Society of Poets, International Platform Association, American Society of Poets, Authors Guild, Authors League of America, New York Poetry Forum.

WRITINGS: (Under pseudonym B. C. Palmer) *Winter's End* (poems), University of California Press, 1974; (under pseudonym Laura Palmer) *Golden Verses,* Golden Eagle Press, 1975. Feature writer for *Our Town* (newspaper), 1975—. Contributor of poetry under pseudonym B. C. Palmer to *Hartford Courant.*

WORK IN PROGRESS: A biography of the Stallo family of Cincinnati; *A Crying Rose,* a novel.

SIDELIGHTS: Laura Schmidt writes: "I began my career by reading and traveling widely in order to open my own small world. Although my world will never be big enough for me, my writing has added a new perspective. People do—and always will—fascinate me and it is this psychological interest in human nature that I seem to concentrate on the most in my work. *A Crying Rose* is the study of the family unit, one of the most intriguing psychological aspects of human existence."

*   *   *

SCHMIDT, Margaret Fox 1925-

PERSONAL: Born February 10, 1925, in Frankell, Tex.; daughter of Raymond E. (a lumberman) and Margaret (an accountant; maiden name, Kennedy) Fox; married Beverley V. Thompson, Jr., February 22, 1947 (divorced, June, 1957); married James Norman Schmidt (a university professor and writer), March 1, 1961; children: (first marriage) Melissa Margaret. *Education:* Texas Women's University, B.A., 1944; Ohio University, M.A., 1969. *Politics:* "Democratic liberal." *Religion:* Episcopalian. *Home:* 18 Second St., Athens, Ohio 45701; Apartado Postal #1, San Miguel de Allende, Mexico (summer). *Agent:* William Reiss, Paul R. Reynolds, Inc., 12 East 41st St., New York, N.Y. 10017.

CAREER: Albuquerque Tribune, Albuquerque, N.M., reporter, 1944-45; Civil Aeronautics Administration, air-traffic controller in Albuquerque, Fort Worth, Texas, and San Antonio, Texas, 1945-46; *Fort Worth Press,* Fort Worth, reporter and feature writer, 1946-60; free-lance writer, 1960—. Owner of an art gallery in San Miguel de Allende, Mexico, 1962-65. Member of board of directors of Fort Worth Family Service and Children's Museum, 1951-60. *Member:* League of American Voters (state vice-president, 1963), Fort Worth Junior League, Fort Worth Opera Association (member of board of directors, 1954-57), Fort Worth Art Association (member of board of directors, 1953-55), Theta Sigma Phi.

WRITINGS: (With husband, James Norman Schmidt), *A Shopper's Guide to Mexico,* Doubleday, 1973; *Passion's Child: The Extraordinary Life of Jane Digby* (Literary Guild selection), Harper, 1976. Contributor to *Ms.* and *New York Times.*

WORK IN PROGRESS: A gothic novel, set on Corfu; "a personal story of the adventures of writing a biography of Jane Digby."

AVOCATIONAL INTERESTS: Travel, collecting Mexican arts and crafts.

* * *

SCHMIDT, Sandra
See ODDO, Sandra Schmidt

* * *

SCHMITHALS, Walter 1923-

PERSONAL: Born December 14, 1923, in Wesel, Germany; son of Bernhard and Elisabeth (Indefrey) Schmithals; married Marlene Schubotz, May 19, 1953; children: Gesine, Elisabeth, Barbara, Kathrin, Doerte, Sixta. *Education:* Attended University of Muenster, 1949-50; University of Marburg, Dr.Theol., 1956. *Religion:* Evangelist. *Home:* Landauerstrasse 6, 1 Berlin 33, West Germany.

CAREER: Vicar in Minden, Germany, 1951-53; minister in Raumland, Germany, 1953-63; University of Marburg, Marburg, Germany, lecturer, 1963-68; University of Berlin, Berlin, Germany, professor of New Testament, 1968—.

WRITINGS: Die Gnosis in Korinth: Eine Untersuchung zu den Korintherbriefen, Vandenhoeck & Ruprecht (Goettingen), 1956, 3rd edition, 1969, translation by John Steely published as *Gnosticism in Corinth: An Investigation of the Letters to the Corinthians,* Abingdon, 1971; *Das Kirchliche Apostelamt: Eine historische Untersuchung,* Vandenhoeck & Ruprecht, 1961, translation by Steely published as *The Office of Apostle in the Early Church,* Abingdon, 1969; *Paulus and Jakobus,* Vandenhoeck & Ruprecht, 1963, translation by Dorothea Barton published as *Paul and James,* Allenson, 1965; *Paulus und die Gnostiker: Untersuchungen zu den kleinen Paulusbriefen,* Reich (Hamburg-Bergstedt), 1965, translation by Steely published as *Paul and the Gnostics,* Abingdon, 1972; *Die Theologie Rudolf Bultmanns: Eine Einfuehrung,* Mohr (Tuebingen), 1966, 2nd edition, 1967, translation by John Bowden published as *An Introduction to the Theology of Rudolf Bultmann,* Augsburg, 1968; *Wunder und Glaube: Eine Auslegung von Markus 4, 35-6, 6a,* Neukirchener (Neukirchen-Vluyn), 1970; *Das Christuszeugnis in der heutigen Gesellschaft: Zur gegenwaertigen Krise von Theologie und Kirche,* Reich, 1970; *Vernunft und Gehorsam: Zur Standortbestimmung der Theologie,* Reich, 1971; *Jesus Christus in der Verkuendigung der Kirche: Aktuelle Beitraege zum notwendigen Streit um Jesus,* Neukirchener, 1972; *Die Apokalyptik: Einfuehrung und Deutung,* Vandenhoeck & Ruprecht, 1973, translation by Steely published as *The Apocalyptic Movement: Introduction and Interpretation,* Abingdon, 1975; *Der Roemerbrief als historisches Problem,* Guetersloher Verlagshaus (Guetersloh), 1975. Contributor of more than three hundred articles to religious journals in Germany.

WORK IN PROGRESS: Kommentur zum Markusevangelium.

* * *

SCHNAUBELT, Franz Joseph 1914-
(Franz Joseph)

PERSONAL: Born June 29, 1914, in Chicago, Ill.; son of Frank (an engineer) and Marie Ann (a seamstress; maiden name Kenzler) Schnaubelt; married Hazel Van Kampen, November 27, 1945; children: Karen. *Education:* Educated in Cook County, Ill. *Politics:* Constitutionalist/Human Rights. *Religion:* Theist. *Office:* Franz Joseph Designs, 4137 Massachusetts Ave., La Mesa, Calif. 92041.

CAREER: Sanford Art Studios, Berwyn, Ill., manager and instructor, 1935-37; Exhibit Engineers, Chicago, Ill., chief designer, 1937-38; Display Engineers, Berwyn, Ill., co-owner and designer, 1939-40; General Dynamics Corp. (formerly Consolidated Aircraft Corp. and Consolidated Vultee), San Diego, Calif., design engineer, staff assistant to chief engineer, and engineering representative, 1941-70. Scoutmaster, assistant district commissioner, and program chairman for San Diego Area Council, Boy Scouts of America, 1928-50; director, Civic League of Vista La Mesa, La Mesa, Calif., 1948-54; director, United Taxpayers Association, San Diego, Calif., 1950-54; vice-chairman, Lemon Grove Planning Association, Lemon Grove, Calif., 1974-75; chairman, La Mesa Annexation, La Mesa, Calif., 1975-76. Freelance designer and writer. *Member:* American Association for the Advancement of Science, American Mensa, Institute of the Aeronautical Sciences-United States Navy A-1 Club.

WRITINGS—All under name Franz Joseph: *Booklet of General Plans for a Constitution Class Starship,* Franz Joseph Designs, 1974, Ballantine, 1975; *Star Fleet Technical Manual,* Ballantine, 1975.

WORK IN PROGRESS: Research into the interplanetary community of intelligent life forms and their security forces; "handedness" of the universe; and a graphics visual aid book on civil rights.

SIDELIGHTS: Both of Schnaubelt's works are permanent exhibits in the National Air and Space Museum, Washington, D.C. Schnaubelt is a firm believer in the existence of life throughout the universe, and that "it is very much like life here on the planet Earth.

"The 'reality'," Schnaubelt told *CA*, "I've created in the minds of 'earthmen' is most fascinating. The bulk of my 'fans' know the television series 'Star Trek' is Hollywood make-believe, but they are just as certain my work is 'real'. I've received at least a half-dozen applications from ex-servicemen on your planet who want to enter the Star Fleet Academy with the next regular class. They've given me their complete military records, etc., so you know that they're serious about this. With this kind of belief I don't want to be the one to destroy the illusion. Since the principles and purposes of the United Federation of Planets are admirable, it can't hurt earthmen to follow this belief—it might even cause some improvement in your 20th century society. Peace to the planet Earth."

As a Boy Scout leader, Schnaubelt helped introduce the seascout and cubscout programs in 1930-31.

* * *

SCHNEYDER, J. F.
See TAYLOR, (Frank Herbert) Griffin

* * *

SCHORR, Daniel (Louis) 1916-

PERSONAL: Born August 31, 1916, in New York, N.Y.; son of Louis and Tillie (Godiner) Schorr; married Lisbeth Bamberger (an economist), January 7, 1967; children: Jonathan, Lisa. *Education:* City College (now of the City University of New York), B.S., 1939. *Religion:* Jewish. *Home:* 3113 Woodley Rd. N.W., Washington, D.C. 20008. *Agent:* N. S. Bienstock Inc., 10 Columbus Cir., New York, N.Y. 10019.

CAREER: Jewish Telegraphic Agency, New York City, assistant editor, 1934-41; Aneta News Agency, news editor in New York City, 1941-43, head of European service in Netherlands, 1945-48; free-lance correspondent in Amsterdam for *Christian Science Monitor* and *London Daily Mail,* 1948-50, for *New York Times,* 1950-53; Columbia Broadcasting System (CBS) News, Moscow correspondent, 1955-57, and Washington general assignment correspondent, 1958-60, chief of bureau in Germany and Central Europe, 1960-66, Washington correspondent, 1966-76; University of California, Berkeley, Regents Professor of Journalism, spring, 1977. Notable assignments include the opening of the CBS news bureau in Moscow, Nikita Khrushchev's first American television interview, and the Watergate and Central Intelligence Agency congressional investigations. *Military service:* U.S. Army, Intelligence, 1943-45.

MEMBER: Council on Foreign Relations, American Federation of Radio and Television Artists, Radio and Television Analysts of New York. *Awards, honors:* William the Silent Award (Netherlands), 1950; Officer, Order of Orange-Nassau (Netherlands), 1955; Overseas Press Club citations, 1957, 1958, and 1963; Emmy Awards, 1972, 1974, and 1975; Ohio State University television award, 1972; American Medical Association award, 1973; American Bar Association award, 1974; four awards from American Civil Liberties Union, all 1976; National Headliners award, 1976; John F. Kennedy Profiles in Courage award, 1976; B'nai B'rith and Society of the Silurians awards, 1976.

WRITINGS—Books: *Don't Get Sick in America,* Aurora, 1970.

Television documentaries; all broadcast by CBS-TV: "See It Now: Poland, a Nation on a Tightrope," 1957; "Hungary Today," 1961; "East Germany: Land Beyond the Wall," 1962; "Germany: Red Spy Target," 1962; "Germany Since Hitler: Adenauer Sums Up," 1963; "The Plots Against Hitler," two parts, 1963-64; "Satellites Out of Orbit," 1964; "Who Killed Anne Frank?," 1964; "The Strange Case of Rudolph Hess," 1965; "The Day They Had to Close the Schools," 1970; "Don't Get Sick in America," 1970; "What Are We Doing to Our Children?," 1972; "A Boy Named Terry Egan," 1973. Writer of news scripts for television broadcast.

Contributor of articles to magazines, including *Newsweek.*

WORK IN PROGRESS: Final Assignment for Houghton, publication expected in fall, 1977. Schorr told *CA* the book will be the first full account of his experiences as a television reporter in Washington, culminating in his victorious confrontation with Congress and his resignation from CBS News. "The book will be personal but I will not be satisfied to have it simply personal," explained Schorr. "I want to try to illumine what goes on in government, what goes on in television, and what goes on between government and television."

SIDELIGHTS: In February of 1976, Dan Schorr gave the *Village Voice* a copy of the House intelligence committee's secret report on the CIA. That action lead to his suspension, later his resignation from CBS news; it sparked a House ethics committee investigation for the leak, with the possibility that Schorr could have been sent to jail for refusing to identify his source in testimony; and it caused a great deal of publicity.

In his analysis of the affair, I. F. Stone commended Schorr and the *Village Voice* for performing "a public service," and went on to explain: "A government cannot carry on lawless activity in public. If it is going to use assassination, burglary, bribery, corruption of elections, agents provocateurs, covert slander, it can only do so in secret. There is no way for Congress to 'oversee' such activities without revealing them and opposing them. To allow 'dirty tricks' is not only to make real oversight impossible but to make Congress an accomplice in lawlessness. That is the rock bottom issue which has to be faced in the debate over the intelligence agencies, and very few are facing it."

Dan Schorr was shocked to discover just how few of his colleagues were ready to face the issues. "With a *deja entendu* memory from the other side of the fence, I began muttering about reporters not caring for the big issues, just about gossip and trivia, preferably damaging," he said. He admitted making some errors in judgment but was totally unprepared for the subjects the press was to concern itself with. Instead of questions about government secrecy, a reporter's rights under the First Amendment, or why the House voted to keep the report secret; Schorr was asked: "Whether I was too abrasive, who in CBS didn't like me, how much I had been paid for the Pike report, and why I had chosen the *Village Voice.* (I cherish the question that I was asked only once—whether I had chosen the *Village Voice* because my daughter works there. My daughter, you see, is 6.)"

Some journalists, newspapers, and press organizations attacked Schorr; some CBS; some the House of Representatives. Much was made of Schorr's suggestion that any payment from the *Village Voice* be made in the form of a contribution to the Newspaperman's Committee for a Free Press. Many reporters found significance in Schorr's silence when another CBS correspondent was accused of being the source. The CBS Washington office was polled on Schorr's popularity. Schorr "wondered why these errors of detail dominated press discussion rather than the developing issue for the press—a confrontation with Congress that might parallel the 'prior restraint' confrontation with the Executive over the Pentagon papers."

He continued: "My problem, friends in the press advised, was that I had made the press establishment feel threatened by breaching several of its cardinal rules. I had made my own decision about publishing the Pike report, causing many editors to worry about the precedent for staff discipline. Though meeting all my employer's needs, I had disposed of a document that raised questions of property rights. (I had assumed it was the public's property.) I had involved television in an argument with Congress, when Congress was looking balefully at the broadcast industry anyway. And I had flaunted the idea of press disclosure when disclosure was retreating before a secrecy backlash, and the press was fretting about public hostility to the news media."

"There are two dangerous precedents for newsmen in the Schorr case," observed I. F. Stone. "The first lies in Schorr's suspension by CBS on the ground that he has put himself in an adversary position with the government. A newsman was *intended*—shades of Jefferson!—to be in an adversary position to government. . . . The other dangerous precedent lies in the sanctions which the House witch-hunters hope to apply. The House does not have a legal leg to stand on if it tries to prosecute Schorr. . . . The only way the House can punish Schorr is to take away his credentials as a correspondent and thus his job."

David Ignatius gloomily concluded: "It was a comic opera finale to the great era of investigation that had begun in 1973. Now Congress was attacking Congress, the press attacked the press, the Administration (and those charged with committing illegal acts) gloating, ever so slightly, from the sidelines.''

In contrast to that appraisal, Schorr's conclusions were drawn from the public's response to a lecture tour he took to explain the issues. ''And I found that while Americans were deeply, though vaguely, concerned about the power of the press, fearful of being manipulated by 'the media,' they valued the press when the chips were down. They trusted the government less than they trusted the press, and they wanted the press to watch the government vigilantly—including Congress.''

BIOGRAPHICAL/CRITICAL SOURCES: Washington Monthly, April, 1976; *New York Review of Books,* April 1, 1976; *Time,* October 11, 1976; *Newsweek,* October 11, 1976.

* * *

SCHREIBER, Jan 1941-

PERSONAL: Born July 31, 1941, in Wisconsin; son of Edward Everett (a storekeeper) and Lois (a teacher; maiden name, Colby) Schreiber; married Ruth Ann Bavry, December 8, 1961 (divorced October 28, 1975); children: Damon. *Education:* Stanford University, A.B., 1963; University of Toronto, M.A., 1969; Brandeis University, Ph.D., 1972. *Home:* 51 Cottage Farm Rd., Brookline, Mass. 02146. *Agent:* John Brockman, 241 Central Park W., New York, N.Y. 10024. *Office:* Center for Criminal Justice, Harvard University, Cambridge, Mass. 02138.

CAREER: University of Toronto Press, Toronto, Ontario, editor, 1965-70; Godine Press, Boston, Mass., editor-in-chief, 1972-73; Radcliffe Institute, Cambridge, Mass., director of research publications, 1974-75; Harvard University, Center for Criminal Justice, Cambridge, Mass., editor and writer, 1976—. Has broadcast on WGBH-FM; has given poetry readings in United States and Canada. Former chairman of board of directors and assistant executive director of Fathers United for Equal Justice. *Member:* Associated Writing Programs.

WRITINGS: Digressions (poems), Aliquando Press, 1970; *In the Course of Discovery: West Indian Immigrants in Toronto Schools,* Toronto Board of Education, 1970; (editor) *Godine Poetry Chapbooks,* David R. Godine, 1974; *Terrorism: The Basic Issues,* Law Enforcement Assistance Administration, 1976. Contributor of poems, articles, and reviews to literary journals, including *Far Point, Southern Review, Agenda, Chowder Review, Progressive, Hudson Review,* and *Modern Occasions.* Co-editor of *Canto: Review of the Arts.*

WORK IN PROGRESS: Schemes of Experience: Propositions in Twentieth Century Poetry; Therefore We Damned, poems; *The Terrorist,* non-fiction; a long poem based on the Orpheus legend; articles on Herman Melville, Louise Bogan, and John Berryman.

SIDELIGHTS: Schreiber writes: ''Touchstones: Passion with clarity. The beat of spoken language. Rhetorical dexterity in prose and in verse. Poetry is pain and logic made musical. I have worked to find a relation between formal structure and the rhythms of unselfconscious speech such that the form, though unnoticed, will be indelible.'' *Avocational interests:* Music of Bach, performances of Baroque music, work toward divorce reform.

* * *

SCHREINER, Samuel A(gnew), Jr. 1921-

PERSONAL: Born June 6, 1921, in Mt. Lebanon, Pa; son of Samuel Agnew (a lawyer) and Mary (Cort) Schreiner; married Doris Moon (an antique dealer and appraiser), September 22, 1945; children: Beverly Ann (Mrs. Jonathan S. Carroll), Carolyn Cort. *Education:* Princeton University, A.B., 1942. *Politics:* Republican. *Religion:* Presbyterian. *Home and office:* 111 Old Kings Highway S., Darien, Conn. 06820. *Agent:* Harold Ober, Inc., 40 East 49th St., New York, N.Y. 10017.

CAREER: McKeesport Daily News, McKeesport, Pa., reporter, 1946; *Pittsburgh Sun-Telegraph,* Pittsburgh, Pa., reporter, 1946-51; *Parade,* New York, N.Y., assistant managing editor, 1951-55; *Reader's Digest,* Pleasantville, N.Y., associate editor, 1955-68; senior editor, 1968-74; full time writer, 1974—. President of Schreiner Associates. Director of Darien Library; member of Darien Youth Advisory Commission. *Military service:* U.S. Army, Office of Strategic Services, 1942-45; served in China-Burma-India theater; became first lieutenant; received Bronze Star.

MEMBER: Authors Guild of Authors League of America, Overseas Press Club, Princeton Club of New York, Noroton Yacht Club.

WRITINGS: Urban Planning and Public Opinion, Bureau of Urban Research, Princeton University, 1942; *Thine Is the Glory* (novel), Arbor House, 1975; *Pleasant Places* (novel), Arbor House, 1976. Contributor of articles and stories to popular magazines, including *McCall's, Saturday Evening Post, Collier's, Redbook,* and *National Geographic.*

* * *

SCHULMAN, Grace

PERSONAL: Born in New York, N.Y.; daughter of Bernard Waldman (a president of an advertising agency) and Marcella (a writer; maiden name, Freiberger) Schulman. *Education:* American University, B.S., 1954; New York University, M.A., 1960, Ph.D., 1971. *Politics:* ''Eclectic.'' *Religion:* Jewish. *Home:* 1 University Pl., No. 14F, New York, N.Y. 10003.

CAREER: Bernard M. Baruch College of the City University of New York, New York, N.Y., assistant professor of English, 1973—. Director, Poetry Center, 92nd St. Young Men's-Young Women's Hebrew Association, 1974—. *Member:* International P.E.N., Poetry Society of America. *Awards, honors:* Yaddo fellowship, summer, 1973; fellowships from MacDowell Colony and Karolyi Foundation, both 1973; Lucille Medwick Memorial Award from International P.E.N., 1975.

WRITINGS: (Editor) *Ezra Pound: A Collection of Criticism,* McGraw, 1974; *Burn Down the Icons* (poems), Princeton University Press, 1976. Contributor of poems, articles, translations, and reviews to poetry journals and magazines, including *Hudson Review* and *Ms.,* and to newspapers. Poetry editor of *Nation,* 1972—.

WORK IN PROGRESS: A book of poems; a book of translations of Pablo Antonio Cuadra; a study of the poetry of Marianne Moore.

* * *

SCHULTHESS, Emil 1913-

PERSONAL: Born October 29, 1913, in Zurich, Switzerland; son of Emil Jakob (a gardener) and Marie (Leu) Schulthess; married Bruna Castellini, January 28, 1937; children: Alfred, Elisabeth (Mrs. Hanspeter Kamm). *Education:* Educated in public schools and photography schools in Zurich, Switzerland. *Religion:* Protestant. *Home and office:* 5 Langacher, 8127 Forch-Zurich, Switzerland. *Agent*— Photographs: Black Star, 450 Park Ave. S., New York, N.Y.

CAREER: Graphic artist apprentice, 1928-32; free-lance graphic artist, 1932-37; Conzett & Huber (printers and publishers), Zurich, Switzerland, graphic artist, 1937-41; *Du* (monthly magazine), Zurich, picture editor and photographer, 1941-57; free-lance photographer and art director producing pictorial books in Zurich, 1957—. *Awards, honors:* *U.S. Camera* award, 1950, for photographing the midnight sun in 24-hour panorama, and achievement award, 1967, for *Africa* and *China;* American Society of Magazine Photographers annual award, 1958, for projects, including *U.S.A.* and *Africa;* geographic point 84{ 47} southern latitude and 115{ 00} western longitude in Marie Byrd Land, Antarctica, named Schulthess Buttress by U.S. Board on Geographic Names, 1962; German Photographic Society culture prize, 1964, for photography.

WRITINGS—All with own photographs: (With others) *U.S.A.: Photos einer Reise durch die Vereinigten Staaten von Nordamerika,* Manesse Verlag, 1955; (with Otto Lehmann, Fritz Morgenthaler, and others) *Afrika,* Manesse Verlag, Volume I (with Lehmann and Morgenthaler): *Vom Mittelmeer zum Aequator* (title means "From the Mediterranean Sea to the Equator"), 1958, Volume II (with Lehmann and others): *Vom Aequator zum Kap der Guten Hoffnung* (title means "From the Equator to the Cape of Good Hope"), 1959, translation by Brian Battershaw published in single volume edition as *Africa* (with Emil Egli), Simon & Schuster, 1959; (with Raymond Priestley, George J. Dufek, and Henry M. Dater) *Antarctica,* translated by Peter George, Simon & Schuster, 1960; (with Egli) *The Amazon,* translated by H. A. Frey and C. Wayland, Simon & Schuster, 1962; (with Hans Keller, Egli, Edgar Snow, and Harry Hamm) *China,* translated by Michael Heron and Victor Andersen, Viking, 1966; (with Harrison Salisbury) *Soviet Union,* translated by T. Schelbert and K. Schelbert, Harper, 1971; (editor with Egli) *Switzerland: Air View,* Heinman, 1973.

SIDELIGHTS: Since 1949 Schulthess has traveled in Europe, the United States, Africa, the Far East, Antarctica, South America, China, and the Soviet Union. His books have also been published in French, Swedish, Norwegian, Finnish, Danish, Italian, Japanese, and Spanish editions.

* * *

SCHULTZ, Gwendolyn

PERSONAL: Born in Milwaukee, Wis.; daughter of Herbert (a judge) and Aurelia (an organist and teacher; maiden name, Nickel) Schultz. *Education:* University of Wisconsin, Madison, B.A. and M.A. *Religion:* Church member. *Home:* 111 West Wilson St., Madison, Wis. 53703. *Office:* University of Wisconsin, 1815 University Ave., Madison, Wis. 53706.

CAREER: University of Wisconsin, Madison, assistant professor, 1959-74, associate professor of geography, 1974—. *Member:* Arctic Institute of North America, National Writers Club, Authors Guild, American Association of University Professors, Association of American Geographers, American Quaternary Association, Council for Wisconsin Writers (member of board of directors, 1976—), Wisconsin Regional Writers, Wisconsin Academy of Sciences, Arts and Letters, Wisconsin Archaeological Society, Alaska Geographic Society, Friends of the Library. *Awards,*

honors: Council for Wisconsin Writers best nonfiction book by Wisconsin writer, 1975, for *Ice Age Lost,* best juvenile book by Wisconsin writer, 1976, for *Icebergs and Their Voyages.*

WRITINGS: Glaciers and the Ice Age, Holt, 1963; *The Blue Valentine* (juvenile fiction), Morrow, 1965; *Colorprint World Atlas,* Fawcett, 1966; *Ice Age Lost* (nonfiction), Doubleday, 1974; (compiler) *Atlas of Wisconsin,* University of Wisconsin Press, 1974; *Icebergs and Their Voyages* (juvenile), Morrow, 1975. Contributor of articles, reviews, and poems to periodicals.

WORK IN PROGRESS: Wisconsin's Geologic Foundations, publication by University of Wisconsin Press expected in 1978.

* * *

SCHULTZ, Terri 1946-

PERSONAL: Born April 9, 1946, in Reedsburg, Wis.; daughter of Sherman and Virginia (a bookkeeper; maiden name, Roloff) Zuehlke; married Ron Schultz, August, 1968 (divorced, 1973). *Education:* University of Wisconsin, Madison, B.A. (journalism) and B.A. (French), both 1968; also attended Universite d'Aix-en-Provence, 1966-67, and University of Chicago, 1971. *Home:* 320 West 11th St., New York, N.Y. 10014.

CAREER: Chicago Tribune, Chicago, Ill., reporter and copy editor on city desk, 1968-72; free-lance writer, 1972—.

WRITINGS: Bittersweet: Surviving and Growing from Loneliness, Crowell, 1976; (editor) Tom Sampson, *Cultivating the Presence,* Crowell, 1977. Columnist, "Our Town," *Chicago Tribune,* 1968-72. Contributor of more than thirty articles to popular magazines, including *Working Woman, Redbook, Playgirl, Viva, Science Digest, Today's Health, Penthouse,* and *Harper's,* and to newspapers, including *New York Times.* Contributing editor of *Chicago;* book review editor of *Genesis.*

WORK IN PROGRESS: A book on Wounded Knee, S.D., for Crowell; a novel.

* * *

SCHUYLER, Jane 1943-

PERSONAL: Born November 2, 1943, in Flushing, N.Y.; daughter of Frank J. (in real estate) and Helen (a social worker; maiden name, Oberhofer) Schuyler. *Education:* Queens College of the City University of New York, B.A., 1965; Hunter College of the City University of New York, M.A., 1967; Columbia University, Ph.D., 1972. *Politics:* Democrat. *Religion:* Roman Catholic. *Home:* 35-37 78th St., Jackson Heights, N.Y. 11372. *Office:* Department of Fine Arts, York College of the City University of New York, Jamaica, N.Y. 11451.

CAREER: Montclair State College, Upper Montclair, N.J., assistant professor of art history, spring, 1970; Long Island University, C. W. Post College, Greenvale, N.Y., adjunct assistant professor of art history, 1971-73; York College of the City University of New York, Jamaica, N.Y., assistant professor of art history, 1973—. Coordinator of college event information of the fine arts committee of International Women's Arts Festival, 1975. *Member:* College Art Association of America, American Association of University Professors, Renaissance Society of America, Women's Caucus for Art.

WRITINGS: Florentine Busts: Sculpted Portraiture in the Fifteenth Century, Garland Publishing, 1976.

WORK IN PROGRESS: A book on Renaissance artists and witchcraft, completion expected in 1978.

SIDELIGHTS: Jane Schuyler writes that she is "interested in the subject of witchcraft and in artists who dabbled in it. Many images with unusual iconography can be understood after being traced back to alchemy or superstitions of the Renaissance period." She has traveled in France, England, Greece, and Mexico, and in 1975, took a student group through Italy.

* * *

SCHWARTZ, Helene E(nid) 1941-

PERSONAL: Born October 25, 1941, in New York, N.Y.; daughter of Melvin C. (an attorney) and Ethel (national vice-president of Women's League for Conservative Judaism; maiden name, Weisenthal) Schwartz. *Education:* Brown University, A.B. (magna cum laude with distinction in religious studies), 1962; Columbia University, LL.B., 1965.

CAREER: Admitted to New York bar, 1965, District Court bars, 1967, U.S. Circuit Court bars, 1967 and 1970, and U.S. Supreme Court bar, 1971; private law practice in New York, 1965—. Member of faculty, Rutgers-Camden Law School, 1972—. Teacher of English to immigrant children in Israel, 1963; lecturer to university and community groups. Member of board of directors of Center for Constitutional Rights, 1973—. *Member:* Phi Beta Kappa. *Awards, honors:* Winner of *Saturday Review* photography contest, 1968, for photograph of Jerusalem after the six-day war; Brown University campus fellow, 1972; Columbia University visiting scholar, 1975-76.

WRITINGS: (With Arthur Kinoy and Doris Peterson) *Conspiracy on Appeal: Appellate Brief on Behalf of the Chicago Eight,* Center for Constitutional Rights, 1971; *Lawyering* (for laymen), Farrar, Straus, 1976; *Aspects of Jewish and American Criminal Law: An Introduction and Study Guide* (for laymen), Women's League for Conservative Judaism, 1976. Contributor to law journals, and to *Nation* and *National Review.*

SIDELIGHTS: Helene Schwartz writes: "Like most people who have had a traditional religious upbringing, I am sensitive to the need to seek social justice. I see my work as an attorney as an extension of that search. I wrote *Lawyering* (which describes some of my experiences as an attorney) because I was tired of hearing women complain about how they have been repressed. My attitudes about myself and my goals have changed because of the women's movement, but I prefer that women like me talk about their achievements rather than past repression."

AVOCATIONAL INTERESTS: Photography, travel.

BIOGRAPHICAL/CRITICAL SOURCES: Providence Journal, March 19, 1972; *Philadelphia Bulletin,* January 26, 1976; *Chicago Tribune,* February 2, 1976; *Philadelphia New Paper,* February 28, 1976.

* * *

SCHWARTZ, Ronald 1937-

PERSONAL: Born June 4, 1937 in Sea Gate, N.Y.; son of Irving (a retailer) and Marion (Rachlis) Schwartz; married Amelia Fletcher (a librarian), February 9, 1968; children: Jonathan Fletcher. *Education:* Attended Middlebury College, 1961, 1963; Brooklyn College (now of the City University of New York), B.A. (cum laude), 1959; University of Connecticut, M.A., 1961, Ph.D., 1967. *Politics:* "Registered Democrat but committed to intelligence." *Religion:*

Jewish. *Home:* 4024 Surf Avenue, Sea Gate, Brooklyn, N.Y. 11224. *Office:* Kingsborough Community College of the City University of New York, Brooklyn, N.Y. 11235.

CAREER: University of Massachusetts, Amherst, instructor in Spanish, 1963-64; Kingsborough Community College of the City University of New York, Brooklyn, N.Y., professor of romance languages, 1964—, chairman of department of foreign languages, 1969-71. Consultant for New York State Vocational Education Grant, 1973-75. *Member:* Association of Departments of Foreign Languages, Modern Language Association of America, Association of Teachers of Spanish and Portugese, Association of Teachers of French, Professional Staff Congress, Sea Gate Association, Community Council of Sea Gate.

WRITINGS: Jose Maria Gironella (biography and literary criticism), Twayne, 1972; *Spain's New Wave Novelists (1950-1974): Studies in Spanish Realism* (stylistics and literary criticism), Scarecrow, 1976. Contributor of reviews and articles to periodicals, including *Hispania.*

WORK IN PROGRESS: Spanish Cinema after Luis Bunuel; Latin America's New Wave Novelists, completion expected, 1978.

SIDELIGHTS: Schwartz told *CA* that he is interested in exploring the careers of lesser known Spanish and Latin American writers, "hoping to popularize their works in the United States and to encourage translations." These interests are reflected in Schwartz's teaching as well as in his writings. He has developed courses in Spanish and Latin American cinema and Spanish and Latin American literature in translation, and is "consciously proselytizing for interest and support in these two areas of scholarship."

AVOCATIONAL INTERESTS: The study of languages, films, water color and oil painting, classical ballet, year-round ice-skating, swimming, bicycling, and theatre.

* * *

SCHWARZ, Ted
See SCHWARZ, Theodore R., Jr.

* * *

SCHWARZ, Theodore R., Jr. 1945-
(Ted Schwarz)

PERSONAL: Born October 12, 1945, in Cleveland, Ohio; son of Theodore (a salesman) and Ruth (a home economist; maiden name, Stern) Schwarz; married Nancy Clark (a civil servant), December 17, 1966. *Education:* Attended Case Western Reserve University, 1964-66, and New York Institute of Photography, 1965. *Home and office address:* P.O. Box 1573, Tucson, Ariz., 85702. *Agent:* Dominick Abel, Dominick Abel Literary Services, 529 South Wabash Ave., Chicago, Ill. 60605.

CAREER: Akron Beacon Journal, Akron, Ohio, reporter, 1967-68; free-lance commercial photographer and writer, 1969—. Instructor at Pima College, 1976—. Radio writer, National Broadcasting Co., Inc. (NBC), 1966, Storer Broadcasting Co., 1966-74, and Westinghouse Broadcasting Co., 1967. *Wartime service:* Served as heart research technician in Akron, Ohio, as an alternative to military service, 1966-67. *Member:* Authors Guild, Numismatic Literary Guild.

*WRITINGS—*Under name Ted Schwarz: *The Business Side of Photography,* American Photographic Book Publishing, 1969; *How to Make Money with Your Camera,* H.P. Books, 1975; *Coins as Living History,* Arco, 1976; *How to Start a Professional Photography Business,* Regnery, 1976;

The Successful Promoter, Regnery, 1976; *How to Protect Your Home, Your Family, and Your Business*, H.P. Books, 1977; *The Fragments of My Mind*, Regnery, 1977. Columnist, "Tips by Ted", *Rangefinder*, 1970—, and "Civil War Postal History," *Linn's Stamp News*, 1976—. Contributor to *Free Enterprise* magazine. Contributing editor, *Physician's Management*, 1975—, and *Tucson*, 1976—.

WORK IN PROGRESS: Two books on multiple personality disorders; a book on choosing a psychiatrist; a book on the history of U.S. coinage; a book on the love affairs of the presidents.

SIDELIGHTS: In the fourth grade, after flunking history because the text was "too boring to read," Schwarz vowed that he would write history articles and books that people would enjoy reading. Schwarz told *CA* that although his main goal in writing has been "both to entertain and inform, my first book was written simply because I always wanted to see my name on a book jacket."

* * *

SCHWARZ, Wilhelm Johannes 1929-

PERSONAL: Born December 25, 1929, in Iba, Germany; son of Georg (a farmer) and Eliese (Stutzman) Schwarz. *Education:* University of Western Ontario, B.A., 1962, M.A., 1963; McGill University, Ph.D., 1965. *Residence:* Quebec, Canada. *Office:* Faculte des Lettres, Universite Laval, Quebec City, Quebec, Canada.

CAREER: Memorial University, St. John's, Newfoundland, assistant professor, 1965-67; Universite Laval, Quebec City, Quebec, assistant professor, 1967-69, associate professor, 1969-75, professor of German literature, 1975—. Visiting professor, University of Denver, 1976-77.

WRITINGS: Der Erzaehler Heinrich Boell, Francke Verlag, 1967, 3rd enlarged edition, 1973, English translation by Elizabeth Henderson and Alexander Henderson published as *Heinrich Boell, Teller of Tales,* Ungar, 1968; *War and the Mind of Germany,* Herbert Lang Verlag, 1975.

Untranslated works in German: *Der Erzaehler Guenter Grass* (title means "Guenter Grass, Teller of Tales"), Francke Verlag, 1969, 3rd enlarged edition, 1974; *Der Erzaehler Uwe Johnson* (title means "Uwe Johnson, Teller of Tales"), Francke Verlag, 1970, 2nd revised edition, 1973; *Mensch und Welt* (title means "Man and His World"), Blaisdell, 1970; *Der Erzaehler Martin Walser* (title means "Martin Walser, Teller of Tales"), Francke Verlag, 1971; *Der Erzaehler Siegfried Lenz* (title means "Siegfried Lenz, Teller of Tales"), Francke Verlag, 1974.

WORK IN PROGRESS: Der Protestsaenger Wolf Biermann (title means "The Protest Singer Wolf Biermann").

AVOCATIONAL INTERESTS: Hypnotism, parapsychological phenomena.

* * *

SCHWERIN, Doris H(alpern) 1922-

PERSONAL: Born June 24, 1922, in Peabody, Mass.; daughter of Harry (a physician) and Mary (a nurse; maiden name, Polivnick) Halpern; married Jules Victor Schwerin (a film director), March 2, 1946; children: Charles Norman. *Education:* Attended New England Conservatory of Music and Boston University, 1939-40; attended Juilliard School, 1941-44. *Home:* 317 West 83rd St., New York, N.Y. 10024.

CAREER: Musical composer. Member of Eugene O'Neill Memorial Theatre Center. *Member:* American Society of Composers, Authors, and Publishers, Dramatists Guild, Authors League of America. *Awards, honors:* Charles Sergel Drama Prize from University of Chicago, 1973, for "Daddy's in the Cold, Cold Ground."

WRITINGS: Diary of a Pigeon Watcher (memoirs), Morrow, 1976.

Plays: "Moxie Malone's Two Hundred Days" (two-act), produced at Eugene O'Neill Memorial Theatre Center, 1966; "The Drums Make Me Nervous" (one-act with music), produced at Eugene O'Neill Memorial Theatre Center, 1968; "Where Did You Put It . . . When You Had It?" (one-act with music), first performed in New York City at St. Clement's Church, 1971.

Composer of musical scores, "From Morning 'til Night" (for children), released by RCA Corp., 1962, and "O Oysters," 1961, "Marco's Millions," 1963, "Matty, the Moron, and Madonna," 1965, "Solomon and Ashmedi" (for children), 1968, "The Orchestra," 1969, "Kaboom," 1974, and "The Man Who Stole the Word," 1976. Also author of two-act play, "Daddy's in the Cold, Cold Ground."

WORK IN PROGRESS: An autobiography of a cat, *The Story of My Life;* a novel, *The Hippopotamus Triangle,* for Morrow.

* * *

SCOTT, Anthony Dalton 1923-

PERSONAL: Born August 2, 1923, in Vancouver, British Columbia, Canada; son of Sydney Dunn and Edith Evelyn Scott; married, December 13, 1952; children: two. *Education:* University of British Columbia, B.Comm., 1946, B.A., 1947; Harvard University, M.A., 1949; London School of Economics and Political Science, Ph.D., 1953. *Office:* Department of Economics, University of British Columbia, Vancouver, British Columbia, Canada.

CAREER: University of British Columbia, Vancouver, lecturer in economics, summer, 1949; Cambridge University, Cambridge, England, junior research worker in applied economics, 1949-50; University of London, London School of Economics and Political Science, London, England, assistant lecturer in economics, 1950-53; University of British Columbia, lecturer, 1953-54, instructor, 1954, assistant professor, 1954-57, associate professor, 1957-61, professor of economics, 1961—. Executive of British Columbia Natural Resources Conference, 1963; member of National Advisory Council on Water Resources, 1966-71; delegate to environmental directorate of Organization for Economic Cooperation and Development, 1971—.

MEMBER: Social Science Research Council of Canada, Canadian Political Science Association (member of executive committee, 1956-57; president, 1966-67), Royal Society of Canada (fellow), American Economic Association (member of executive committee, 1966-70), American Association for Environmental Economics. *Awards, honors:* Canada Council senior research fellow, 1959-60, 1971-72, Killam fellow, 1972, Killam senior research fellow, 1973-74; Lilly Faculty Fellow at University of Chicago, 1964-65; grants from Energy, Mines, and Resources Development and Environmental and Provincial Institute for Policy Analysis, Development and Environmental Fisheries, Canada Council, and Donner Foundation.

WRITINGS: (With William C. Hood) *Output: Labour and Capital in the Canadian Economy,* [Ottawa], 1958; (with T. N. Brewis, H. E. English, and Pauline Jewett) *Canadian Economic Policy,* Macmillan, 1961, revised edition, 1965;

(with W.R.D. Sewell, John Davis, and D. W. Ross) *Guide to Benefit-Cost Analysis,* Queen's Printer, 1962; (with F. T. Christy, Jr.) *The Common Wealth in Ocean Fisheries,* Johns Hopkins Press, 1966, 2nd edition, 1973; (editor) Paul A. Samuelson, *Economics* (Canadian edition), McGraw, 1966, 4th edition, 1975; (editor with J. D. Rae) Stefan Stykolt, *Efficiency in the Open Economy: Collected Writings on Canadian Economic Problems and Policies,* Oxford University Press, 1969; (editor and contributor) *Economics of Fisheries Management: A Symposium,* Institute of Animal Resource Ecology, University of British Columbia, 1970; *Government Policy and Self Sufficiency,* University of Calgary Press, 1976; (editor and contributor) *Who Should Get the Natural Resources Revenue?,* University of British Columbia Press, in press.

Contributor: *Natural Resources: The Economics of Conservation,* University of Toronto Press, 1955, revised edition, McClelland & Stewart, 1973; Ralph Turvey and Jack Wiseman, editors, *The Economics of Fisheries,* FAO (Rome), 1958; R. Goldsmith and C. Saunders, editors, *Income and Wealth,* Bowes & Bowes, 1959.

Wesley Ballaine, editor, *Taxation and Conservation of Privately Owned Timber,* University of Oregon Bureau of Business Research, 1960; R. M. Clark, editor, *Canadian Issues: Essays in Honour of Henry F. Angus,* University of Toronto Press, 1961; R. Hamlisch, editor, *Economic and Biologic Aspects of Fishery Regulation,* United Nations Food and Agriculture Organization, 1962; Marion Clawson, editor, *Natural Resources and International Development,* Johns Hopkins Press, 1964; D. B. Turner, editor, *Inventory of the Natural Resources of British Columbia,* Queen's Printer, 1964; Mason Gaffney, editor, *Extractive Resources and Taxation,* University of Wisconsin Press, 1967; M. Blaug, editor, *Economics of Education,* Penguin, 1969.

William J. McNeil, editor, *Marine Aquiculture,* Oregon State University Press, 1970; W. Lee Hansen, editor, *Education, Income, and Human Capital: Studies in Income and Wealth,* Columbia University Press, 1970; Charles Kindleberger and Andrew Shonfield, editors, *North American and Western European Economic Policies,* Macmillan, 1971; *Problems of Environmental Economics,* Organization for Economic Cooperation and Development (Paris), 1972; D. A. Auld, editor, *Economic Thinking and Pollution Problems,* University of Toronto Press, 1972; P. J. Crabbe and I. M. Spry, editors, *Natural Resource Development in Canada: A Multi-Disciplinary Seminar,* University of Ottawa Press, 1973; *Problems in Transfrontier Pollution,* Organization for Economic Cooperation and Development, 1973; P. H. Pearse, editor, *The Mackenzie Pipeline,* McClelland & Stewart, 1974; Ingo Walter, editor, *Studies in International Environmental Economics,* Wiley, 1976; Annette B. Fox and other editors, *Canada and the United States: Transnational and Transgovernmental Relations,* Columbia University Press, 1976; Emilio Gerelli and others, editors, *Economics of Transfrontier Pollution,* Organization for Economic Cooperation and Development, 1976; Neil Swainson, editor, *Managing the Water Environment,* University of British Columbia Press, 1976; Ingo Walter, editor, *Studies in International Environmental Economics,* New York University Press, 1976; Walter Meade, editor, *Forest Policy,* Institute for Economic Policy, University of British Columbia, 1976; Michael Crommelin, editor, *Minerals Leasing,* Institute for Economic Policy, University of British Columbia, 1976.

Contributor to *Encyclopedia Americana.* Contributor to proceedings and to professional journals. Special editor of *British Columbia Studies,* 1972; member of board of editors of *Western Economic Journal,* 1968-71, *Land Economics,* 1969—, and *Journal of Environmental Economics and Management,* 1973—.

WORK IN PROGRESS: Joint Selection and Optimization of Projects by Two Jurisdictions, with Robert Jones and P. H. Pearse; *Alberta Oil and Gas Policies,* with Pearse and Crommelin; *Federalism and Public Finance,* with Albert Breton; *Three-person Pareto-Optimal Redistribution,* with Breton; research on economics of high seas oil spills policies.

* * *

SCOTT, Jack S.
See ESCOTT, Jonathan

* * *

SCOTT, John M(artin) 1913-

PERSONAL: Born April 8, 1913, in Omaha, Neb.; son of Patrick John (a civil engineer) and Nettie (a clerk; maiden name, Martin) Scott. *Education:* St. Louis University, M.A., 1935, S.T.L., 1945, M.S., 1948. *Politics:* "Not bound to one party." *Home:* 305 East Campion St., Prairie du Chien, Wis. 53821. *Office:* Campion High School, Prairie du Chien, Wis. 53821.

CAREER: Entered Society of Jesus (Jesuits), 1931, ordained Roman Catholic priest, 1944; assigned to mission on Sioux Indian reservation in South Dakota, 1938-41; Campion High School, Prairie du Chien, Wis., physics teacher, 1948-75. Conducted science workshops at Creighton University, summers, 1949-75; regional chairman of Wisconsin Junior Academy of Science.

WRITINGS: Wonderland (juvenile), Loyola University Press, 1958; *Adventures in Science* (high school text), Loyola University Press, 1963; *Rain: Man's Greatest Gift,* Culligan, 1967; *Our Romance with Sun and Rain,* Culligan, 1968; *Adventure Awaits You,* Culligan, 1968; *The Everyday Living Approach to Teaching Elementary Science,* Parker Publishing, 1970; *What Is Science?* (juvenile), Parents' Magazine Press, 1972; *What Is Sound?* (juvenile), Parents' Magazine Press, 1973; *Heat and Fire* (juvenile), Parents' Magazine Press, 1973; *The Senses* (juvenile), Parents' Magazine Press, 1975; *To Touch the Face of God,* Our Sunday Visitor, 1975; *Phenomena of Our Universe,* Our Sunday Visitor, 1976.

Author of "Talking it over with Fr. John," a column in *Treasure Chest,* 1959-63. Author of about twenty pamphlets for adults and young people. Contributor to *Educators Guide.* Contributor of more than a hundred articles to magazines and newspapers. Science editor for *Queen's Work* and *Young Catholic Messenger,* 1949-63.

WORK IN PROGRESS: "Classroom Science Discovery Series," for Center for Applied Research in Education; *Fantastic You Are!*

AVOCATIONAL INTERESTS: Hiking, travel ("from the Arctic Circle to Australia and New Zealand, and from Hong Kong to Egypt").

* * *

SCULLY, Gerald William 1941-

PERSONAL: Born June 13, 1941, in New York, N.Y.; son of Francis Joseph (a banker) and Helen (Zimmerman) Scully; married Nancy Wuester, May 18, 1962 (marriage ended, 1974); children: Deirdre Koren, Audra Laine. *Education:* Fairleigh Dickinson University, B.A., 1962; graduate study at Columbia University, 1962-63; New School for Social Research, M.A., 1965; Rutgers University, Ph.D., 1968. *Office:* Institute for International Development, Harvard University, 1737 Cambridge St., Cambridge, Mass. 02138.

CAREER: Ohio University, Athens, assistant professor of economics, 1966-69; Southern Illinois University, Carbondale, associate professor of economics, 1969-72; Southern Methodist University, Dallas, Tex., professor of economics, 1972—. Economist, Harvard University, Institute for International Development, Cambridge, Mass. *Member:* American Economics Association, Econometrics Society.

WRITINGS: The Economics of Professional Sports, Schenkman, 1975; *Analytical Labor Economics,* Houghton, 1976. Contributor to economic journals.

AVOCATIONAL INTERESTS: Photography, travel.

* * *

SCUPHAM, John Peter 1933-

PERSONAL: Born February 24, 1933, in Liverpool, England; son of John (head of educational broadcasting for British Broadcasting Corp.) and Dorothy (Clark) Scupham; married Carola Nance Braunholtz (a teacher), August 10, 1957; children: Kate, Toby, Giles, Roger. *Education:* Emmanuel College, Cambridge, diploma (honors), 1957. *Home:* 2 Taylor's Hill, Hitchin, Hertfordshire, England. *Office:* St. Christopher School, Barrington Rd., Letchworth, Hertfordshire, England.

CAREER: Taught at grammar school in Lincolnshire, England, 1957-61; St. Christopher School, Letchworth, England, head of English department, 1961—. Co-founder and proprietor of Mandeville Press, 1974—.

WRITINGS—Poems: *The Small Containers* (pamphlet), H. Chambers, 1972; *The Snowing Globe,* E. J. Morten, 1972; *The Gift,* Keepsake Press, 1973; *Prehistories,* Oxford University Press, 1975.

WORK IN PROGRESS: Poems.

SIDELIGHTS: Scupham writes: "I like poetry of sense, sensibility, and formal elegance and try to write it." The small publishing business he operates prints by hand small editions of new poetry of quality.

* * *

SEALEY, (Bertram) Raphael (Izod) 1927-

PERSONAL: Born August 14, 1927, in Middlesbrough, England; came to the United States in 1963; son of Bertram I. (a teacher) and Gladys (a teacher; maiden name, Heath) Sealey; married Danguole Sadunaite, August 13, 1957 (divorced October 3, 1972); married Dagmar Schoelermann, December 19, 1972; children: Dorte. *Education:* Oxford University, B.A., 1947, M.A., 1951; further graduate study at University of Tuebingen, summer, 1952, and University of Hamburg, winter, 1952-53. *Politics:* "Confused." *Religion:* None. *Home:* 1206 Milvia St., Berkeley, Calif. 94709. *Office:* Department of History, University of California, Berkeley, Calif. 94720.

CAREER: University College of North Wales, Bangor, assistant lecturer in classics, 1954-58; University of London, London, England, lecturer in ancient history, 1958-63; State University of New York, Buffalo, associate professor, 1963-65, professor of ancient history, 1965-67; University of California, Berkeley, professor of ancient history, 1967—. *Military service:* British Army, 1947-49; became acting sergeant. *Member:* American Philological Association, Association of Ancient Historians, Societe des Etudes Grecques.

WRITINGS: (Translator from the Lithuanian) Ignas Seinius, *Ordeal of Assad Pasha,* Manyland Books, 1963; (translator from the Lithuanian) Vincas Kreve, *The Temptation,* Manyland Books, 1965; (contributor) Ernst Badian, editor, *Ancient Society and Institutions: Studies Presented to V. Ehrenberg,* Basil Blackwell, 1966; *Essays in Greek Politics,* Manyland Books, 1967; *A History of the Greek City States circa 700-338 B.C.,* University of California Press, 1976. Contributor of articles on Greek history and literature, Roman history, and Lithuanian studies to academic journals.

WORK IN PROGRESS: A study of the portrayal of women in ancient Greek literature.

AVOCATIONAL INTERESTS: Languages, "living in California."

* * *

SEDERBERG, Peter C(arl) 1943-

PERSONAL: Born August 8, 1943, in Minneapolis, Minn.; son of Carl E. (an accountant) and Gertrude (a government employee; maiden name, Pontius) Sederberg; married Nancy Belcher, September 1, 1966; children: Per Benjamin. *Education:* University of Minnesota, B.A. (summa cum laude), 1965; Johns Hopkins University, M.A., 1967, Ph.D., 1970. *Home:* 419 Edisto Ave., Columbia, S.C. 29205. *Office:* Department of Government and International Studies, University of South Carolina, Columbia, S.C. 29208.

CAREER: Wellesley College, Wellesley, Mass., instructor, 1969-70, assistant professor of political science, 1970-71; University of South Carolina, Columbia, assistant professor, 1971-74, associate professor of political science, 1974—. *Member:* American Political Science Association, World Future Society, Lindisfarne Association, Southern Political Science Association, Phi Beta Kappa. *Awards, honors:* Woodrow Wilson fellowship, 1968-69.

WRITINGS: (Editor with H. Jon Rosenbaum, and contributor) *Vigilante Politics,* University of Pennsylvania Press, 1976; *Interpreting Politics: An Introductory Analysis,* Chandler & Sharp, in press. Contributor to scholarly journals in the fields of politics and philosophy.

WORK IN PROGRESS: Research toward synthesizing artistic insight and scientific knowledge in the understanding of social violence.

* * *

SEGAL, Fred 1924(?)-1976

1924(?)—May 28, 1976; American author, playwright, and screenwriter. Obituaries: *New York Times,* May 30, 1976.

* * *

SEIBEL, Hans Dieter 1941-

PERSONAL: Born February 1, 1941, in Muelheim, Germany; permanent resident of United States; son of Peter (an administrative director) and Anna (Gross) Seibel; married Helga Renate Wolf (a sociologist), November 11, 1963; children: Saskia Tatjana, Tjark Errit. *Education:* University of Freiburg, Dr. phil., 1966; also attended University of London and University of Ibadan. *Home:* Rheinstrasse 18,

Urmitz-Rhein D-5401, Germany. *Office:* Paedagogische Hochschule Ruhr, Vogelpothsweg, Dortmund D-46, Germany.

CAREER: Arnold-Bergstraesser Institute, Freiburg, Germany, chairman of Africa department, 1966-67; University of Liberia, Monrovia, associate professor of sociology and chairman of department of sociology and anthropology, 1967-69; Princeton University, Princeton, N.J., visiting lecturer, 1969-72; Manhattanville College, Purchase, N.Y., associate professor of sociology and chairman of department, 1972-75; Paedagogische Hochschule Ruhr, Dortmund, Germany, professor of sociology, 1975—. Visiting professor, University of Muenster, 1971-72. *Member:* American Sociological Association, African Studies Association, Liberian Studies Association, Deutsche Gesellschaft fuer Soziologie. *Awards, honors:* German Academic Exchange Service fellowship, 1967-69; Tubman Center of African Culture grant, 1967-68; German Research Council grant, 1968-69, 1969-71; Thyssen Foundation grant, 1968-69; Dr. phil. habil., University of Muenster, 1972; Princeton University and Kraus-Thomson Organization grant, 1973; Volkswagen Foundation grant, 1974-75.

WRITINGS: Industriearbeit und Kulturwandel in Nigeria (title means "Industrial Labor and Cultural Change in Nigeria"), Westdeutscher Verlag, 1968; (with Michael Koll) *Einheimische Genossenschaften in Afrika: Formen wirtschaftlicher Zusammenarbeit bei westafrikanischen Staemmen* (title means "Indigenous Cooperatives in Africa: Types of Economic Cooperation among West African Tribes"), Bertelsmann Universitaetsverlag, 1968; (editor with Ukandi G. Damachi, and contributor) *Social Change and Economic Development in Nigeria,* Praeger, 1973; *Gesellschaft im Leistungskonflikt* (title means "The Dilemma of the Achieving Society"), Bertelsmann Universitaetsverlag, 1973; *The Dynamics of Achievement: A Radical Perspective,* Bobbs-Merrill, 1974; (with Andreas Massing) *Traditional Organizations and Economic Development: Studies of Indigenous Cooperatives in Liberia,* Praeger, 1974; (with Guenter Schroeder) *Ethnographic Survey of Southeastern Liberia: The Liberian Kran and the Sapo,* Liberian Studies Association in America (Newark, Del.), 1974.

Contributor: Dieter Oberndoerfer, editor, *Africana Collecta I* (title means "African Studies I"), Bertelsmann Universitaetsverlag, 1968; Dieter Oberndoerfer, editor, *Africana Collecta II* (title means "African Studies II"), Bertelsmann Universitaetsverlag, 1971; Robert A. Scott and Jack D. Douglas, editors, *Theoretical Perspectives on Deviance,* Basic Books, 1972.

Contributor of articles and book reviews to journals, including *American Journal of Sociology, Liberian Studies, Nigerian Journal of Social and Economic Research, Soziale Welt, Zeitschrift fuer Sozialpsychologie,* and *Internationales Afrikaforum.*

WORK IN PROGRESS: The Theory of Social Change; Business and Democracy: Self-Management in Yugoslavia.

AVOCATIONAL INTERESTS: International travel, mountaineering, tennis, skiing.

*   *   *

SELCHER, Wayne A(lan) 1942-

PERSONAL: Surname is pronounced *Sel*-ker; born July 18, 1942, in Harrisburg, Pa.; son of Charles Phillip and Sylvia Marie (Hoover) Selcher; married V. Susan George (a hospital administrator), August 24, 1963; children: Linda, Craig. *Education:* Lebanon Valley College, A.B. (magna cum laude), 1964; University of Florida, M.A., 1965, Ph.D., 1970. *Home:* 26 Elm Ave., Elizabethtown, Pa. 17022. *Office:* Department of Political Science, Elizabethtown College, Elizabethtown, Pa. 17022.

CAREER: Elizabethtown College, Elizabethtown, Pa., instructor, 1969-70, assistant professor, 1970-72, associate professor of political science, 1972—, chairman of department, 1970—. Consultant on Brazilian foreign relations to U.S. Government agencies. *Member:* International Studies Association, American Political Science Association, Latin American Studies Association, Pi Sigma Alpha, Phi Alpha Epsilon. *Awards, honors:* Fulbright scholar in Brazil, 1968.

WRITINGS: (Contributor) Daniel C. Matthews, editor, *Current Themes in African Historical Studies,* Negro Universities Press, 1970; *The Afro-Asian Dimension of Brazilian Foreign Policy, 1956-1972,* University of Florida Press, 1974. Contributor to journals.

WORK IN PROGRESS: A book on Brazil's foreign relations since 1964, *Security and Development: The Foreign Relations of the Brazilian Revolution.*

AVOCATIONAL INTEREST: Latin American folk music.

*   *   *

SELTZER, Alvin J(ay) 1939-

PERSONAL: Born April 10, 1939, in Philadelphia, Pa.; son of Joseph (a butcher) and Rose (Kushnir) Seltzer; married Madeline Liebman (a college teacher), September 1, 1968; children: Lara, Ryan. *Education:* Temple University, B.S., 1960; University of Michigan, M.A.; 1961; Pennsylvania State University, Ph.D., 1970. *Home:* 315 Ashbourne Rd., Elkins Park, Pa. 19117.

CAREER: University of Wisconsin, Milwaukee, acting instructor in English, 1961-63; Temple University, Philadelphia, Pa., instructor, 1968-70, assistant professor of English, 1970-75.

WRITINGS: Chaos in the Novel—The Novel in Chaos, Schocken, 1974. Contributor to *Contemporary Literature.*

*   *   *

SELWYN-CLARKE, Selwyn 1893-1976

December 17, 1893—March 13, 1976; British physician, politician, civil servant, and author of books on various subjects. Obituaries: *AB Bookman's Weekly,* April 26, 1976.

*   *   *

SELZER, Richard 1928-

PERSONAL: Born June 24, 1928, in Troy, N.Y.; son of Julius Louis (a family doctor) and Gertrude (Schneider) Selzer; married Janet White, February, 1955; children: Jonathan, Lawrence, Gretchen. *Education:* Union College, Schenectady, N.Y., B.S., 1948; Albany Medical College, M.D., 1953; postdoctoral study, Yale University, 1957-60. *Home:* 6 Saint Ronan Ter., New Haven, Conn. 06511. *Agent:* John Sterling, Paul R. Reynolds, Inc., 12 East 41st St., New York, N.Y. 10017. *Office:* 2 Church St. S., New Haven, Conn. 06510.

CAREER: Private practice in general surgery, 1960—. Yale University, associate professor of surgery in Medical School, fellow of Ezra Stiles College. *Military service:* U.S. Army, 1955-57. *Awards, honors:* National Magazine Award from Columbia University School of Journalism, 1975, for essays published in *Esquire.*

WRITINGS: *Rituals of Surgery* (short stories), Harper's Magazine Press, 1974; *Mortal Lessons* (collection of essays), Simon & Schuster, 1977. Contributor to popular magazines, including *Harper's, Esquire, Redbook, Mademoiselle, American Review,* and *Antaeus.*

WORK IN PROGRESS: A mythological treatment of the Civil War; a collection of essays, memoirs, and letters; short stories.

*   *   *

SENDLER, David A.   1938-

PERSONAL: Born December 12, 1938, in New York, N.Y.; son of Morris (a businessman) and Rose (Gaskin) Sendler; married Emily Shimm, October 17, 1965; children: Matthew, Karen. *Education:* Dartmouth College, B.A., 1960; Columbia University, M.S., 1961. *Home:* 369 Strathmore Rd., Rosemont, Pa. 19010. *Office: TV Guide,* 250 King of Prussia Rd., Radnor, Pa. 19010.

CAREER: *Sport,* New York, N.Y., associate editor, 1964-65; *Pageant,* New York City, executive editor, 1965-71; *Today's Health,* Chicago, Ill., editor, 1971-74; *Parade,* New York, N.Y., senior editor, 1974-75; *Ladies Home Journal,* New York City, articles editor, 1975-76; TV Guide, Radnor, Pa., managing editor, 1976—. *Military service:* U.S. Army, 1961-63. *Member:* Pennsylvania Society.

WRITINGS: (With Lou Sabin) *Stars of Pro Basketball,* Random House, 1970. Contributor to popular magazines, including *Boys' Life* and *Lithopincon.*

*   *   *

SENIOR, Clarence (Ollson)   1903-1974

PERSONAL: Born June 9, 1903, in Clinton, Mo.; son of Joseph Cressey (a paperhanger and painter) and Margaret (Ollson) Senior; married Ruth Louise Miller, January 24, 1934; children: Paul Norman. *Education:* Junior College of Kansas City, student, 1923-25; University of Kansas, A.B., 1927; attended University of Vienna, 1928, International People's College, Elsinore, Denmark, 1931, and University of Chicago, 1934; University of Missouri, A.M., 1941; Columbia University, Ph.D., 1955. *Politics:* Liberal. *Religion:* Unitarian-Universalist. *Residence:* Rio Grande, P.R.

CAREER: Employed by International City Managers Association and League of Kansas Municipalities in Kansas City, Mo., 1923-25; Adult Education Association, Cleveland, Ohio, field secretary, 1927, also organizer and secretary of Cleveland Labor College; national executive secretary of Socialist Party of the United States, 1929-36, campaign manager for the party's Presidential candidate, Norman Thomas, 1932, 1936; *Milwaukee Leader,* Milwaukee, Wis., labor editor, 1937; Information Center of the Americas, Mexico City, Mexico, Mexican representative, 1937-39; organizer of work camps for Mexican college students, 1939-41; University of Kansas City, Kansas City, Mo., faculty member and director of Inter-American Center, 1941-42; Board of Economic Welfare, Washington, D.C., worked on Mexican and Latin American economic affairs, 1942; National Planning Association, conducted field studies in Mexico, 1943-44; Foreign Economic Administration, Washington, D.C., researcher on Latin America, 1944-45; University of Puerto Rico, Rio Piedras, visiting professor and director of Social Science Research Center, 1945-48; Columbia University, New York, N.Y., director of field work for a study of Puerto Rican immigrants in New York City, 1948-49, lecturer in sociology, 1950-60; Brooklyn College of the City University of New York, Brooklyn, N.Y., professor of sociology, 1961-71, professor emeritus, 1971-74, director of Center for Migration Studies, 1965-71; most recently faculty member at Inter-American University in San Juan, P.R. Former faculty member at Chicago Labor College. Chief of Migration Division of New York office of Puerto Rican Department of Labor, 1951-60. U.S. delegate to Inter-American Congress on Indian Life, 1949. Member of housing advisory council of New York State Commission Against Discrimination. Conducted research for United Nations Economic Commission for Latin America, 1949-50, Twentieth Century Fund, 1950-51, Government of Jamaica, 1955, and American Society of Planning Officials, 1960; consultant to Ford Foundation and U.S. Secretary of Labor.

MEMBER: International Union for the Scientific Study of Population, International Planned Parenthood Federation, League for International Democracy, American Sociological Association, Rural Sociological Society, American Economic Association, Population Society of America, Citizens' Housing and Planning Council.

WRITINGS: *Mexico in Transition,* League for Industrial Democracy, 1939; *Democracy Comes to a Cotton Kingdom: The Story of Mexico's La Laguna,* Centro de Studios Pedagogicos e Hispanoamericanos, 1940; *Self-Determination for Puerto Rico,* Post War World Council, 1946; *Puerto Rican Emigration,* Social Science Research Center, University of Puerto Rico, 1947; *The Puerto Rican Migrant in St. Croix,* Social Science Research Center, University of Puerto Rico, 1947; (with Carmen Isales) *The Puerto Ricans of New York City,* New York Office of Employment and Migration Bureau, Puerto Rican Department of Labor, 1948.

(With Charles Wright Mills and Rose Kohn Goldsen) *The Puerto Rican Journey: New York's Newest Migrants,* Harper, 1950; (editor with Josefina de Roman) *A Selected Bibliography on Puerto Rico and the Puerto Ricans,* Migration Division, Department of Labor of Puerto Rico, 1951; *Strangers—and Neighbors: The Story of Our Puerto Rican Citizens,* Anti-Defamation League of B'nai B'rith, 1952, reissued as *Strangers—Then Neighbors: From Pilgrims to Puerto Ricans,* Freedom Books, 1961, reissued as *The Puerto Ricans: Strangers—Then Neighbors* (foreword by Hubert H. Humphrey), Quadrangle, 1965; (with Douglas Manley) *A Report on Jamaican Migration to Great Britain,* Government Printer, Kingston, Jamaica, 1955; (with Manley) *The West Indian in Britain* (edited by Norman Mackenzie), Fabian Colonial Bureau, 1956; *Land Reform and Democracy,* University of Florida Press, 1958, reprinted, Greenwood Press, 1974; *Bibliography on Puerto Ricans in the United States* (pamphlet), Migration Division, Department of Labor of Puerto Rico, 1959; *Our Citizens from the Caribbean,* McGraw, 1965; (with Don O. Watkins) *Toward a Balance Sheet of Puerto Rican Migration,* privately printed, 1966; (editor) *Toward Cultural Democracy,* Selected Academic Readings, 1968; *Santiago Iglesias: Labor Crusader* (edited by John Zebrowski; translated from Spanish by Jesus Benitez), Inter-American University Press, 1972.

Also: (With Kingsley Davis) *Immigracion procedent del Hemisferio Oeste,* Montevideo, 1951; (co-author) *One America,* 1951; *The Caribbean: Its Economy,* 1955; *Understanding Minority Groups,* 1956; *In a Strange Land,* 1961; *The School Dropout,* 1964; *Imperatives in Education,* 1965; *The Assault on Poverty,* 1966; *The Status of Puerto Rico,* 1966.

OBITUARIES: *New York Times,* September 10, 1974; *AB Bookman's Weekly,* November 18, 1974; *Current Biography,* November, 1974.*

(Died September 8, 1974, in San Juan, P.R.)

* * *

SERAGE, Nancy

PERSONAL: Born March 24, 1924, in Columbus, Ohio; daughter of Francis L. and Ophelia (Byers) Serage. *Education:* Ohio State University, B.F.A., 1945, M.A., 1946. *Home and office:* 3880 San Rafael Ave., Los Angeles, Calif. 90065.

CAREER: Toledo Museum of Art, Toledo, Ohio, docent, 1946-47; Cleveland Museum of Art, Cleveland, Ohio, docent, 1948-57; Self-Realization Fellowship, Los Angeles, Calif., monastic, 1958—.

WRITINGS: The Prince Who Gave Up a Throne: A Story of the Buddha, Crowell, 1966.

WORK IN PROGRESS: Children's biography of a great yogic master of this century.

SIDELIGHTS: Ms. Serage writes: "The story of the Buddha was for years an inspiration to me, also the story of St. Francis of Assisi. Both had all the world could offer but found it did not give happiness. Both had the strength to give up their material goods and way of life to seek the Giver of All Gifts. After telling the story of the Buddha to children in my work for about ten years, I found my own spiritual teacher and path and was able to take steps to turn my life Godward as I had always secretly longed to do.

"Because I suffered very deeply at one time not believing in the Divine, His love and power for good behind all life, I have always wanted to save others from similar suffering, to help them direct their thoughts, hearts and lives toward the one source of happiness."

* * *

SERLING, (Edward) Rod(man) 1924-1975

PERSONAL: Born December 25, 1924, in Syracuse, N.Y.; son of Samuel L. (a wholesale butcher) and Esther (Cooper) Serling; married Carolyn Kramer, July 31, 1948; children: Joyce, Ann. *Education:* Antioch College, B.A., 1950. *Home:* 1490 Monaco Dr., Pacific Palisades, Calif. 90272.

CAREER: WLW-Radio, Cincinnati, Ohio, network continuity writer, 1946-48; WKRC-TV, Cincinnati, television writer, 1948-53; free-lance television screenwriter, 1953-75. Writer and producer of television series, "The Twilight Zone," 1959-64; producer, narrator, and contributing writer of television series, "Rod Serling's Night Gallery," premier, 1969; free-lance television narrator. Taught dramatic writing at Antioch College during late 1950's, and at Ithaca College in the 1970's. *Military service:* U.S. Army, World War II; served with paratroopers in Pacific theater. *Member:* National Academy of Television Arts and Sciences (member of board of governors of New York City chapter, 1956-57, of California chapter, 1959; national president, 1965-66); Writers Guild of America, West (member of council, 1965-67). *Awards, honors:* National Academy of Television Arts and Sciences (Emmy) Awards, 1955, for "Patterns," 1957, for "Requiem for a Heavyweight," 1959, for "Twilight Zone," and three for "Playhouse 90" television dramas; Sylvania Awards, 1955, 1956; Christopher Awards, 1956, 1971; George Foster Peabody Award, 1957, for "Requiem for a Heavyweight"; Writers Guild nomina-

tion, 1964, for "Seven Days in May"; Golden Globe Award for Best Director, c.1965; D.H.L., Emerson College, 1971, Alfred University, 1972; Litt.D., Ithaca College, 1972.

WRITINGS: Patterns: Four Television Plays with the Author's Personal Commentaries (includes "Patterns," adapted as screenplay with same title, United Artists, 1956 [also see below]; "The Rack," adapted as screenplay with same title, Metro-Goldwyn-Mayer, 1956; "Requiem for a Heavyweight," adapted as screenplay with same title, Columbia, 1962 [also see below]; and "Old MacDonald Had a Curve"), Simon & Schuster, 1957; *Patterns: A Drama in Three Acts,* Samuel French, 1959.

Stories from The Twilight Zone, Bantam, 1960; *More Stories from The Twilight Zone,* Bantam, 1961; *New Stories from The Twilight Zone,* Bantam, 1962; *From The Twilight Zone,* Doubleday, 1962; *Requiem for a Heavyweight: A Reading Version of the Dramatic Script,* Bantam, 1962, new adaptation by James Olsen, McGraw, 1968; *Rod Serling's The Twilight Zone,* adapted by Walter B. Gibson, Grosset, 1963; (editor) *Rod Serling's Triple W: Witches, Warlocks, and Werewolves; A Collection,* Bantam, 1963; *Twilight Zone Revisited,* adapted by Gibson, Grosset, 1964; *The Season to Be Wary* (novellas; includes "The Escape Route," "Color Scheme," and "Eyes"), Little, Brown, 1967; (editor and author of introduction) *Devils and Demons: A Collection,* Bantam, 1967.

Night Gallery, Bantam, 1971; *Night Gallery 2,* Bantam, 1972.

Play: "The Killing Season," produced on Broadway, 1968.

Screenplays: "The Strike," United Artists, 1955; "The Rock," Metro-Goldwyn-Mayer, 1956; "Saddle the Wind," Metro-Goldwyn-Mayer, 1958; "Incident in an Alley" (based on author's own television drama, "Line of Duty"), United Artists, 1962; "The Yellow Canary" (based on novel, *Evil Come, Evil Go,* by Whit Masterson), Twentieth Century-Fox, 1963; "Seven Days in May" (based on a novel by Fletcher Knebel and Charles W. Bailey II), Paramount, 1964; "Assault on a Queen," Paramount, 1966; (with Michael Wilson) "Planet of the Apes" (based on *Monkey Planet* by Pierre Boulle), Twentieth Century-Fox, 1968; (with brother, Robert J. Serling) "The President's Plane Is Missing" (based on the novel by Robert J. Serling), Commonwealth-United, 1969; "R.P.M.," Columbia, 1969; "The Man" (adapted from television drama; based on the novel by Irving Wallace), Paramount, 1971; "A Time of Predators" (based on a novel by Joe Gores), Avco-Embassy, c. 1971.

Television dramas have been produced on "Kraft Theatre," "Studio One," "U.S. Steel Hour," "Playhouse 90," "Hallmark Hall of Fame," "Suspense," "Danger," and other major network series. Has also written radio plays.

SIDELIGHTS: Rod Serling, the man who in 1955 had become an overnight success in television writing with the airing of his drama "Patterns," decided only three years later to write less for television because of the censorship encountered by some of his scripts. By switching from controversial drama to the realm of fantasy, Serling was able to return to television writing in 1959 with his highly successful "Twilight Zone" series. At that time he explained that "I simply got tired of battling. You always have to compromise lest somebody—a sponsor, a pressure group, a network censor—gets upset. Result is that you settle for second best. It's a crime, but scripts with social significance can't get done on TV."

In fact, Serling continued to upbraid the television medium on this point throughout his career. In a 1974 lecture to Ithaca College School of Communications, he criticized the film and television industries for mediocrity, imitativeness, commercialism, and deadening and deadly lack of creativity and courage. "How do you put on a meaningful drama or documentary," he asked, "that is adult, incisive, probing, when every fifteen minutes the proceedings are interrupted by twelve dancing rabbits with toilet paper?" Television "is and always has been a director's medium," he said. "Sometimes that doesn't hurt the body of the writer's work. But after one year, I had no control with 'Gallery.' They don't want it good—they want it Thursday."

As a corollary to his complaints about the barriers to creative television writing set up by television executives, Serling added that scripts could not be developed with preconceptions about the actors who would be used. "You can't write with an eye for anyone. You write for Edward G. Robinson and you get Fabian. In 1972, I did 'A Storm in the Summer.' I wanted Zero Mostel for it and the director wanted Ernie Borgnine. We got Peter Ustinov and he won best dramatic show and I won 'most disappointed writer' for not being recognized—I gave that award to myself."

Though Serling thought that television forced the creative writer out of the medium by ridding itself of anthology dramas, he contended that the writer's place is where it always has been—as a social critic. Many of his stories, especially the "Twilight Zone" and "Night Gallery" episodes, attacked prejudice in all its forms; consequently, because of his controversial subjects, Serling spent much of his television career sparring with censors and network executives. He maintained nonetheless that "the writer's role is to be a menacer of [the] public's conscience." In a lecture at the Library of Congress, he attacked the medium for what he saw as its fear of taking on major issues in realistic terms. "Drama on television must walk tiptoe and in agony lest it offend some cereal buyer from a given state below the Mason Dixon [line]. Hence we find in this mass medium a kind of ritual track covering, in which we attack quite obliquely the business of minority problems."

Serling felt television could not afford to take the easy route to confronting social problems, that "when you invite prejudice out to joust with it, you display it in all its honest trappings. If it is deliberate withholding of homes to Negroes by virtue of color, now that is the nature of the opponent and that is what you attack, and this is the language that you use and the identification that you very clearly and overtly display."

While Serling's early sparring with the medium caused him to be known as the angry young man of television, the active campaigning in his later years had tapered off in favor of teaching at Ithaca College and lecturing at various universities. "There was a time," he said, "when I wanted to reform television. Now I accept it for what it is. So long as I don't write beneath myself or pander my work, I'm not doing anyone a disservice."

AVOCATIONAL INTERESTS: Building model airplanes, water skiing.

BIOGRAPHICAL/CRITICAL SOURCES: New York Times Magazine, December 2, 1956; *Cosmopolitan,* August, 1958; *Journal of Screen Producers Guild,* September, 1959, December, 1968; *Current Biography,* December, 1959; *Newsweek,* November 5, 1962; *Fort Lauderdale News,* January 28, 1975; *Miami Herald,* May 18, 1975; *New York Times,* June 29, 1975; *Washington Post,* June 29, 1975; *Advertising Age,* July 7, 1975; *Broadcasting,* July 7, 1975.*

(Died June 28, 1975, in Rochester, N.Y.)

*   *   *

SERVENTY, Vincent (Noel)

PERSONAL: Born in Armadale, Western Australia; son of Victor Vincent (a wine grower) and Annie (Gabelish) Serventy; married Caroline Darbyshire (a writer), September 1, 1955; children: Karen, Cathy, Matthew. *Education:* University of West Australia, B.Sc., 1945, B.Ed., 1950. *Home:* 8 Relby Rd., Hunters Hill, New South Wales 2110, Australia.

CAREER: Senior lecturer in science and mathematics at Claremont Teachers College, 1955-57; Education Department of Western Australia, Nature Advisory Service, Perth, instructor in science and head of department, 1958-61; writer; author and producer of documentary films; lecturer. Chairman, Nature Conservation Council of New South Wales, 1970-73, 1976—; member, National Parks and Wildlife Advisory Council of New South Wales, 1966—; trustee, National Photographic Index of Birds, Australian Museum, 1974—; councillor, Gould League of New South Wales, 1966—. Zoologist member of Australian Geographical Society expedition to the islands of the Recherche Archipelago, 1952; leader of first natural history expedition into the Great Victoria Desert of Australia, 1960; member of first party to make crossing of Lake Eyre by boat, 1975. *Member:* Society of Authors, Australian Heritage Commission, Western Australian Naturalists Society (honorary life member). *Awards, honors:* Natural History Medallion, 1974; Order of Australia, 1976.

WRITINGS: Australia's Great Barrier Reef, Georgian House, 1955, 2nd edition, 1966; *Australian Nature Trail,* Georgian House, 1965; *A Continent in Danger,* Andre Deutsch, 1966; *Nature Walkabout,* A. H. & A. W. Reed, 1967; *Landforms of Australia,* Angus & Robertson, 1967, 2nd edition, 1968; *Australian Wildlife Conservation,* Angus & Robertson, 1968; *Wildlife of Australia,* Nelson, 1968; *Australia's National Parks,* Angus & Robertson, 1969; *Southern Walkabout,* A. H. & A. W. Reed, 1969; *Turtle Bay Adventure,* Andre Deutsch, 1969; *Around the Bush,* Australian Broadcasting Commission, 1970; *Great Barrier Reef,* Golden Press, 1970; *Dryandra, the Story of an Australian Forest,* A. H. & A. W. Reed, 1970; (with John Warham and D. L. Serventy) *Handbook of Australian Sea-Birds,* A. H. & A. W. Reed, 1971; *The Singing Land,* Angus & Robertson, 1972; *Desert Walkabout,* Collins, 1973; (with A. H. Chisholm) *John Gould's The Birds of Australia,* Lansdowne, 1973; (with wife Carol Serventy) *The Koala,* Dutton, 1975. Contributor to *Emu* and *Western Australian Naturalist.* Editor, *Wildlife in Australia,* 1966—; editor-in-chief and contributor, *Australia's Wildlife Heritage,* 1973-76; member of editorial board, Collins Publishers, Australian Naturalist series, 1972—. Producer and author of "Nature Walkabout," twenty-six half-hour films on Australian natural history, and "Around the Bush," six quarter-hour films; advisor and co-producer of "The Australian Ark," thirteen one-hour films, 1972.

*   *   *

SERWER, Blanche L. 1910-

PERSONAL: Born July 13, 1910, in New York, N.Y.; daughter of Philip (a businessman) and Rebecca (Isaacson) Luria; married Zachary A. Serwer, May 15, 1938 (died May 15, 1961); married Nahum A. Bernstein (a lawyer), December 29, 1974; children: (first marriage) Philip, Daniel, Jeremy. *Education:* Barnard College, B.A., 1931; Teachers

Institute of Jewish Theological Seminary of America, New York, N.Y., B.H.L., 1931; City College (now of the City University of New York), M.S., 1960; New York University, Ph.D., 1966. *Religion:* Jewish. *Home and office:* 340 East 64th St., New York, N.Y. 10021.

CAREER: City College of the City University of New York, New York City, psychologist in counseling and testing, 1960-64; Queens College of the City University of New York, Queens, N.Y., psychologist in Speech and Hearing Center, 1960-64; City University of New York, New York City, research associate, 1964-66; Harvard University, Cambridge, Mass., research associate and visiting lecturer, 1966-69; Boston University, Boston, Mass., associate professor, 1969-73, professor, 1973-75; Charles River Counseling Center, Newton, Mass., senior psychologist, 1973-75. Consultant to SEEK at City College, Revere School Department in Massachusetts, and others. Member of board of Professional Affairs, Professional Advisory Committee of Cambridge Association for Children with Learning Disorders, Committee for Integrated Schools in New Rochelle (chairman), Board of Directors of Child Guidance Clinic of New Rochelle, New Rochelle Committee on Problems of the Aging, New Rochelle Committee on Character and Citizenship. *Member:* American Orthopsychiatric Association (fellow), American Psychological Association, American Association for Humanistic Psychology, Inter-American Society for Psychology, American Society for Group Psychotherapy and Psychodrama.

WRITINGS: Comparison of Reading Approaches in First-Grade Teaching with Disadvantaged Children Cooperative Research Project 2677, City University of New York, 1966; *Experimental Model School Program for Children with Specific Learning Disabilities* (Title VI-A), ESEA, 1970; *Let's Steal the Moon,* Little, Brown, 1970. Contributor to *Reading Research Quarterly, Exceptional Child, Elementary English, Journal of Special Education, Journal of Perceptual Motor Skills* and *Children's Digest.*

WORK IN PROGRESS: A book of Jewish folklore, with Professor DovNoy of Hebrew University in Jerusalem; research in psycho-social aspects of cleft-palate families.

SIDELIGHTS: Blanche Serwer writes: "I had two reasons for writing *Let's Steal the Moon* for children. The first is that the tales, some of which had not been written down before had been 'simmering' in my mind since I had heard them as a child. The second is that folktales and folklore have a marvelous way of zooming into the fantasy life of a child."

* * *

SETZEKORN, William David 1935-

PERSONAL: Born March 12, 1935, in Mount Vernon, Ill.; son of Merret Everett (a civil engineer) and Audrey (Ferguson) Setzekorn; married Georgia Sue Brown, February 4, 1958 (divorced, 1967); married Patricia Ann Paddock, June 4, 1970 (divorced, 1971); children: (first marriage) Jeffrey M., Randall M., Timothy M. *Education:* Kansas State University, B.Arch., 1953-57; Harvard University, certificate in architectural computer graphics, 1968. *Politics:* Republican. *Religion:* Unitarian-Universalist. *Home:* 37641 Murietta Terr., Fremont, Calif. 94536. *Office:* 1100 Alma, Menlo Park, Calif. 94025.

CAREER: William Setzekorn, A.I.A., Los Altos, Calif., and Seattle, Wash., principal architect, 1965-67; architectural coordinator for design and construction of Cal-Expo (state fair facility), Sacramento, Calif., 1967-69; Hagman Associates, Menlo Park, Calif., associate, 1969—; free-lance writer, 1970—. *Member:* American Institute of Architects, Author's Guild, National Writers Club, Aoudad Society, Pi Kappa Alpha, Heraldry Society (London), San Leandro Yacht Club.

WRITINGS: Origin and History of the Family Setzekorn, Goodway, 1970; *Looking Forward to a Career in Architecture,* Dillon, 1973; *Heraldry: The Ancient Art of Designing Coats of Arms,* Story House, 1974; *Formerly British Honduras: A Profile of the New Nation of Belize,* Dumbarton Press, 1976; *Tales of Old San Francisco Bay,* Spectator Books, 1977. Contributor to more than twenty magazines including *Woman's Circle, Art and Archaeology, Accent,* and *Pennant.*

WORK IN PROGRESS: Two biographies, one on the 1920's architect Louis Sullivan, and the other on bullfighter Carlos Arruza; research for a novel about the battle of St. George's Cay in Belize.

SIDELIGHTS: Setzekorn told *CA:* "I began writing as a hobby—an escape really. I use writing as a relief valve for the pressures from dealing with life's unreasonable demands. I write only on subjects that interest me at the time." *Avocational interests:* Yachting, travel.

* * *

SEWARD, James H(odson) 1928-

PERSONAL: Born September 14, 1928, in Washington, D.C.; son of Clarence Lee, Jr. (an aeronautical engineer) and Ethel Louise (Miller) Seward; married Marilyn Ann Rudzinski (a welfare worker), June 30, 1956; children: Jae, Julee, Jane, Christopher, James. *Education:* Princeton University, A.B., 1950; University of Michigan, M.A., 1957, Ph.D., 1968. *Home:* 341 Ben Avon St., Meadville, Pa. 16335. *Office:* Department of English, Edinboro State College, Edinboro, Pa. 16412.

CAREER: University of Michigan, Institute of Science and Technology, Willow Run, assistant editor, 1960-61; Laurentian University, Sudbury, Ontario, assistant professor of English, 1961-69; Edinboro State College, Edinboro, Pa., professor of English, 1969—. *Military service:* U.S. Air Force, 1950-53. *Member:* Shakespeare Association of America. Erie Zoological Society, Chesapeake Bay Maritime Museum, Neck District Association.

WRITINGS: Tragic Vision in Romeo and Juliet, Consortium, 1973; *Atlantis and Other Poems,* Libra, 1976.

WORK IN PROGRESS: A book of poems; a monograph on Hamlet.

SIDELIGHTS: Seward writes: "I have my roots on the Eastern Shore of Maryland, to which I return every summer. A goodly number of my poems are rooted in my memory of the Eastern Shore and consequently take their color from a quieter and somewhat more old-fashioned way of life than one is likely to find today. Even when the coloration is not regional, the poems tend to rely upon remembered experience."

Avocational interests: Walking in the woods, "puttering around the water."

* * *

SEXTON, A(da) Jeanette 1924-

PERSONAL: Born February 26, 1924, in Ohio; daughter of Charles Daniel and Mary Irene (McDevitt) Sexton. *Education:* Ohio State University, B.Sc., 1945, M.A., 1952; Michigan State University, Ph.D., 1963. *Home:* 1983 Jervis Rd.,

Columbus, Ohio 43221. *Office:* School of Music, Ohio State University, Columbus, Ohio 43210.

CAREER: Music teacher in public schools in Steubenville, Ohio, 1945-50; music consultant in public schools in Richmond, Va., 1950-52; Ohio State University, Columbus, instructor, 1952-56, assistant professor, 1956-68, associate professor, 1968-76, professor of music education, 1976—. *Member:* Music Educators National Conference, Ohio Music Education Association, Phi Kappa Lambda, Delta Omicron.

WRITINGS: (With Stephen Clark) *Fun, Folk, Frolic Songs,* Willis Music Co., 1962; *Musical Awareness Through Songs,* Appleton, 1971.

SIDELIGHTS: Both of Jeanette Sexton's books were originally designed to be used in college music classes.

*   *   *

SHAFER, Ronald G.   1939-

PERSONAL: Born April 22, 1939, in Columbus, Ohio, son of Glenn E. (a railroad engineer) and Mary (Kaelber) Shafer; married Barbara M. Lucas, January 6, 1968; children: Ryan Glen, Kathryn Darlene. *Education:* Ohio State University, B.A., 1962. *Home:* 1807 Baldwin Dr., McLean, Va. 22101. *Office: Wall Street Journal,* 245 National Press Building, Washington, D.C. 20045.

CAREER: Wall Street Journal, New York, N.Y., reporter in Chicago, Ill., 1963, Detroit, Mich., 1964-67, and Washington, D.C., 1968—. *Military service:* U.S. Army Reserve.

WRITINGS: (With Margaret B. Carlson) *How to Get Your Car Repaired Without Getting Gypped,* Harper, 1973; (editor) Joan McNamara, *The Adoption Adviser,* Hawthorn, 1975. Contributor of articles and humor to popular magazines, including *Reader's Digest, Sports Illustrated,* and *Harper's Bazaar.*

*   *   *

SHAFFER, Laurance Frederic   1903-1976

August 12, 1903—July 20, 1976; American psychologist, educator, college administrator, publisher, editor, and author. Obituaries: *New York Times,* July 22, 1976.

*   *   *

SHAHAR, David   1926-

PERSONAL: Born June 17, 1926, in Jerusalem, Israel; son of Meir Elkana (a teacher) and Sarah (Hurwitz) Shahar; married Shulamith Weinstock (a professor of medieval history), 1956; children: Meir, Dinah. *Education:* Attended Hebrew University of Jerusalem. *Religion:* Jewish. *Home:* 17 Hovevey Sion St., Jerusalem, Israel.

CAREER: Lecturer in Hebrew language, literature, and Bible at Kibbutz Shefaim, 1955, Teachers' Seminary, Petah-Tikva, Israel, 1957, Amal Vocational School, Jerusalem, Israel, 1959-69, and Ecole Nationale des Langues et Civilisations Orientales, Paris, France, 1972; Hebrew University of Jerusalem, Jerusalem, lecturer in Hebrew language, literature, and Bible, 1974—. Translator and editor from English and French into Hebrew, 1950-60. *Military service:* Israeli Defense Force, 1949 and 1951; served in infantry; became lieutenant. *Member:* P.E.N. (Israel; Israel's delegate to P.E.N. International congresses), Society of Hebrew Writers in Israel (chairman, 1972), Bet Ha-fer (founding member; board member, 1967). *Awards, honors:* Prime Minister's Award for Literature, 1969, for *Death of the Little*

God and *The Pope's Moustache;* Agnon Prize, 1973, for *The Palace of the Shattered Vessels* and *Ha-Masa' le-Ur-Kasdim.*

WRITINGS: Al-Hachalomot (title means "Concerning Dreams: Twelve Jerusalem Stories"), Am Oved, 1955; *Yerah Hadvash veHazahav* (novel; title means "Moon of Honey and Gold"), Hadar, 1959; *Kesar* (short stories; title means "Caesar"), Dvir, 1960; *Harpotkotav Shel Riki Maoz* (juvenile; title means "The Adventures of Riki Maoz"), Zionist Organization, 1961, 2nd edition, 1974; *Maggid Ha-Atidot* (short stories; title means "The Fortune Teller"), Massada Press, 1966; *Heichal haKelim haShvurim* (novel), Sifriat Poalim, 1969, translation published as *The Palace of the Shattered Vessels,* Houghton, 1975; *The Death of the Little God* (stories), Schocken, 1970; *Ha-Masa' le-Ur-Kasdim* (novel; title means "A Voyage to Ur of the Chaldees"), Sifriat Paolim, 1971; *The Pope's Moustache* (stories), Schocken, 1971; *La colombe et la lune: Nouvelles de Jerusalem* (title means "The Dove and the Moon"), translated by Madeleine Neige, Gallimard, 1971; *News from Jerusalem: Stories,* translated by Dalya Bilu and others, Houghton, 1974; *Yom Harozenet* (novel; title means "Day of the Countess"), Sifriat Poalim, 1976; *Stories from Jerusalem,* translated by Bilu and others, Elek, 1976.

WORK IN PROGRESS: A five-volume novel dealing with present-day Jerusalem, and the story of the Luria family, of which *The Palace of the Shattered Vessels* is the first volume.

SIDELIGHTS: Madeleine Neige writes: "David Shahar conveys in his work a sense of reality beyond the perceived reality in everyday life and portrays the city of Jerusalem and its inhabitants in a guise that reveals both their sacred and their profane purposes. His story of Luria interweaves beauty and mystery with a finite portrait of the social and religious crosscurrents in that most ancient and meaningful of cities." Shahar's works have been translated into several languages, including Danish, Norwegian, Italian, Spanish, and Arabic.

AVOCATIONAL INTERESTS: Painting.

*   *   *

SHAHEEN, Naseeb   1931-

PERSONAL: Surname and given name are accented on second syllable; born June 24, 1931, in Chicago, Ill.; son of Azeez and Saleemeh (Balluteen) Shaheen. *Education:* American University of Beirut, B.A. (with distinction), 1962; University of California, Los Angeles, M.A., 1966, Ph.D., 1969. *Home:* 3439 Southern Ave., Apt. 2, Memphis, Tenn. 38111. *Office:* Department of English, Memphis State University, Memphis, Tenn. 38152.

CAREER: Standard Textile Mills, Cartersville, Ga., plant manager, 1962-64; Memphis State University, Memphis, Tenn., assistant professor of English literature, 1969—. *Member:* Modern Language Association of America. *Awards, honors:* Woodrow Wilson fellowship, 1968-69.

WRITINGS: Biblical References in "The Faerie Queene", Memphis State University Press, 1976. Contributor to literature journals, including *Shakespeare Studies* and *Milton Quarterly.*

WORK IN PROGRESS: A book dealing with Shakespeare's use of the Bible.

*   *   *

SHAPIRO, Linda Gaye   1953-

PERSONAL: Born October 24, 1953, in Miami Beach, Fla.;

daughter of Lee (an editor) and Laurel (Rosenbaum) Shapiro; married Alan S. Richard, June 6, 1976. *Education:* Northwestern University, B.A. (honors), 1975. *Religion:* Jewish (Reform). *Home:* 6759 North Kendall Dr., #C-218, Miami, Fla. 33156; or 6471 Southwest 22nd St., Miami, Fla. 33155.

CAREER: Jewish Community Centers of South Florida, Miami, Fla., summer camp drama specialist, 1974-76; Teacher of drama, tap dancing, belly dancing, and puppetry to elementary and junior high school students, 1974—; drama teacher for senior citizens, 1975—; drama instructor for Community Schools of Dade County, 1976—. Reader. *Member:* Mortar Board, Temple Judea Sisterhood. *Awards, honors:* Award from South Florida Poetry Association, 1972, for "Appearances;" award from National Council of Teachers of English, 1971, for overall excellence in English.

WRITINGS: A Story of Chelm (one-act play; first produced in Chicago, Ill., at Northwestern University, December 7, 1973), Samuel French, 1975.

Work has been anthologized in *National High School Poetry Anthology,* edited by Dennis Hartman, National Poetry Press, 1968, 1971.

Unpublished plays: "The Third Answer" (one-act, with music), first produced in The Creative Arts Center at Jewish Community Centers of South Florida, August 11, 1975; "Leah, the Unicorn, and the Camp Counselor" (one-act) first produced in West Miami, Fla., at West Miami Junior High School, February 5, 1976. Book reviewer for *Miami Herald,* 1976—.

WORK IN PROGRESS: "The Rabbis of Chelm," a sequel to *A Story of Chelm;* a semi-autobiographical novel dealing with Hodgkins' Disease; children's stories; research on the demon Lilith, for a play.

SIDELIGHTS: Linda Shapiro writes: "I am Jewish, but I see Judaism as being important as a culture as much, if not more so, than as a religion. In order to preserve my culture, I take many of my themes from Jewish folklore. I also keep my writings comic because I feel people need a change from the violence and troubles of everyday living. It's not so much that my writing is escapist; rather I look for a happy ending to any problem. To me, a realistic ending need not be a tragic one.

My early training and continued involvement with the theater comes out in my work. I do not limit myself to plays, but I enjoy writing them more than anything else. However, unless you've experienced it, you cannot imagine how hard it is to sit in a theater watching someone else speak your words before a waiting audience. It is a feeling of overwhelming helplessness."

* * *

SHARON, Donna Haye
See SCHARLEMANN, Dorothy Hoyer

* * *

SHAW, Peter 1936-

PERSONAL: Born November 25, 1936, in New York, N.Y.; son of Arthur (a builder) and Margaret (a teacher; maiden name, Sandler) Shaw; married Penelope Pugliese (a modern dance teacher), January 12, 1958; children: Jennifer, Steven. *Education:* Cornell University, A.B., 1958; Columbia University, M.A., 1962, Ph.D., 1965. *Politics:* "Former liberal." *Home:* 106 West 69th St., New York, N.Y. 10023. *Agent:* Rick Balkin, 403 West 115th St., New

York, N.Y. 10025. *Office:* Department of English, State University of New York, Stony Brook, N.Y. 11794.

CAREER: State University of New York, Stony Brook, associate professor of English, 1965—. Visiting lecturer at New School for Social Research, 1967. Has appeared on television and radio programs. *Awards, honors:* American Council of Learned Societies grants, summers, 1972, 1976; National Endowment for the Humanities fellowship, 1973.

WRITINGS: The Character of John Adams, University of North Carolina Press, 1976. Author of brochures and study guides. Contributor of articles and reviews to scholarly journals, and to *Saturday Review.* Editor of *Reader's Encyclopedia of American Literature,* 1962-63; associate editor of *Commentary,* 1968-69.

WORK IN PROGRESS: A book on the psychology of patriot leaders and crowds in the American Revolution.

AVOCATIONAL INTERESTS: Playing table tennis, collecting antique typewriters.

BIOGRAPHICAL/CRITICAL SOURCES: Newsday, May 31, 1976.

* * *

SHEAHAN, Richard T(homas) 1942-

PERSONAL: Born May 17, 1942, in Rome, N.Y.; son of Richard David (an engineer) and Priscilla (Yasunas) Sheahan. *Education:* University of Notre Dame, B.S., 1964, M.S. (civil engineering), 1966; George Washington University, M.B.A., 1972. *Religion:* Catholic. *Home:* 4613 Sleaford Rd., Bethesda, Md. 20014. *Office:* Henningson, Durham & Richardson Inc., 5454 Wisconsin Ave., Washington, D.C. 20015.

CAREER: Registered professional engineer in Maryland; Ocean Science and Engineering Inc., Washington, D.C., project engineer, 1969-70; Engineering-Science Inc., Washington, D.C., assistant to vice-president, and project manager and engineer, 1970-73; Interdevelopment Inc., Arlington, Va., senior consultant to organizations concerned with environmental pollution equipment and nuclear and conventional energy systems, 1973-74; writer, 1974—. *Military service:* U.S. Coast and Geodetic Survey, 1966-68; became lieutenant. *Member:* Toastmasters International, Sigma Xi, Chi Epsilon.

WRITINGS: Fueling the Future: An Environmental and Energy Primer, St. Martin's, 1976. Contributor to *Public Utilities Fortnightly* magazine and to *Mass Transit.*

WORK IN PROGRESS: Research on new forms of mass transit systems for the future, on future energy sources, effects of population growth, and on possible social and institutional changes due to all of these areas.

SIDELIGHTS: Sheahan told *CA:* "I enjoy writing and speaking on energy and environmental subjects which are often perceived to be complex. My style is an easy-to-understand format addressed to the average layman, which I hope may educate people to understand and appreciate the importance of an area vital to all. My work and travels have taken me to over seventy countries and six continents, and has given me an appreciation of people's need for communications in all forms."

* * *

SHEED, Wilfrid (John Joseph) 1930-

PERSONAL: Born December 27, 1930, in London, England; came to the United States in 1940; son of Francis Joseph (an author and publisher) and Maisie (maiden name, Ward; an author and publisher) Sheed; married Miriam Ungerer; children: Elizabeth Carol, Francis, Marion. *Education:* Lincoln College, Oxford, B.A., 1954, M.A., 1957. *Religion:* Roman Catholic.

CAREER: Jubilee, New York, N.Y., movie reviewer, 1959-61, associate editor, 1959-66; *Commonweal,* New York, N.Y., drama critic and book editor, 1964-71; *Esquire,* New York, N.Y., movie critic, 1967-69; *New York Times,* New York, N.Y., columnist, 1971—. Visiting lecturer in creative arts, Princeton University, 1970-71; Book of the Month Club judge, 1972; free-lance reviewer for several publications. *Member:* P.E.N. Club. *Awards, honors:* National Book Award nominations, 1966, for *Office Politics* and 1971, for *Max Jamison; Max Jamison* selected by *Time* as one of best fiction books of 1970.

WRITINGS: Joseph (children's book), Sheed, 1958; (editor) G. K. Chesterton, *Essays and Poems,* Penguin, 1958; *A Middle Class Education: A Novel,* Houghton, 1960; *The Hack* (novel), Macmillan, 1963; *Square's Progress: A Novel,* Farrar, Straus, 1965; *Office Politics: A Novel,* Farrar, Straus, 1966; *The Blacking Factory & Pennsylvania Gothic: A Short Novel and a Long Story,* Farrar, Straus, 1968; *Max Jamison: A Novel,* Farrar, Straus, 1970 (published in England as *The Critic: A Novel,* Weidenfeld & Nicolson, 1970); *The Morning After: Selected Essays and Reviews,* Farrar, Straus, 1971; *People Will Always Be Kind,* Farrar, Straus, 1973; *Three Mobs: Labor, Church, and Mafia,* Sheed, 1974; *Muhammad Ali: A Picture Book,* Crowell, 1975. Contributor of articles to popular magazines.

WORK IN PROGRESS: A novel, provisionally titled *Transatlantic Blues,* publication expected by Farrar, Straus.

SIDELIGHTS: Sheed moved with his family to Pennsylvania in 1940 but returned to England to attend prep school. After Oxford, he spent a year in Sydney, Australia, before settling in New York City. In 1968 he worked in California on Senator Eugene McCarthy's presidential campaign.

Sheed is an erudite and witty critic whose fiction has been characterized by the same qualities of intelligence and humor. Jonathan Yardley has said: "Even at his darkest, he is a joy to read. His wit and perceptiveness are marvelous; he is a literary Buddy Rich, tossing off brilliant rimshots with off-hand abandon. It is a measure of his achievement that we only rarely feel that the glitter is for its own sake."

BIOGRAPHICAL/CRITICAL SOURCES: Time, September 20, 1968; Carolyn Riley, editor, *Contemporary Literary Criticism,* Gale, Volume II, 1973, Volume IV, 1975.

* * *

SHEERAN, James Jennings 1932-

PERSONAL: Born November 16, 1932, in Chicago, Ill.; son of Kieran F. (an executive) and Evelynne D. (Walsh) Sheeran; married Elayne Lane (died January 23, 1976); children: Suzanne Louise, Kathryn Lynne, Leslie Ann, Mary Elizabeth. *Education:* Georgetown University, B.S., 1953; Marquette University, Ph.B., 1954; Columbia University, M.A., 1958. *Home:* 315 East 72nd St., New York, N.Y. 10021. *Office:* Creative Marketing Management, 118 East 61st St., New York, N.Y. 10021; and 9100 Sunset Blvd., Hollywood, Calif. 90069.

CAREER: Helene Curtis Industries, Inc., Chicago, Ill., brand manager, 1955-60; Baton, Barton, Durston & Osborne Advertising, Inc., Chicago, account supervisor, 1960-64; Pepsi-Cola Co., New York, N.Y., advertising and promo-

tion director, 1964-67; Creative Marketing Management (consultants), New York, N.Y., owner and president, 1968—. *Military service:* U.S. Marine Corps Reserve, active duty, 1954-55; became captain. *Member:* American Marketing Association, Authors Guild of Authors League of America, Economic Club, Merchandising Executives Club (past member of board of directors), Sales Promotion Executives Association of New York (past member of board of directors), New York Criminal and Civil Courts Bar Association (honorary member).

WRITINGS: Five Figure Income, Fell, 1964; *The Opportunist* (novel), Fell, 1974; *How to Skyrocket Your Income,* Fell, 1976. Contributor of about fifty articles to travel trade magazines. Executive editor of *Showcase* (theatre magazine) and *Travel and Fashion;* marketing editor of *Travel Trade, Discover America,* and *Selling Travel in Canada.*

WORK IN PROGRESS: The Vigil, a novel about the "suicide penchant."

SIDELIGHTS: Sheeran writes that he is a painter who has had several shows, with "a new format of art expression—paintings that fit in the corner of a room; or are sculptured in the sense that they rise from the wall or floor." *Avocational interests:* Travel.

* * *

SHEFFIELD, Janet N. 1926-

PERSONAL: Born November 27, 1926, in Salt Lake, Utah; daughter of George S. (a civil engineer) and Virginia (Cannon) Nelson; married Fred J. Sheffield, June 25, 1946 (divorced, 1968); children: Laurey (Mrs. Edward J. Zayac), Sari, Flint. *Education:* University of Utah, student, 1944-46; San Francisco State University, B.A., 1968; University of Oregon, M.L.S., 1972. *Politics:* "Nothing pleases me at the moment." *Religion:* Church of Jesus Christ of Latter-day Saints (Mormons). *Home:* 800 24th Ave., Apt. 32, Santa Cruz, Calif. 95062.

CAREER: Writer. Has also worked as model, Yoga teacher, magician's assistant, and physical fitness instructor. *Awards, honors:* Utah Literary Society first prize, 1970, for children's picture book, *Our Maid Maud;* Utah State Institute of Fine Arts third prize, 1972, for juvenile novel, *Casey's Twin Brothers,* and first prize, 1973, for juvenile novel, *The Beginning of Me.*

WRITINGS: Not Just Sugar and Spice (juvenile novel), Morrow, 1975. Also author of *Our Maid Maud* (children's picture book), *Casey's Twin Brothers* (juvenile novel), and *The Beginning of Me* (juvenile novel). Contributor to magazines, including *Your New Baby, Young World, Friend, Jack and Jill,* and *Highlights for Children.*

WORK IN PROGRESS: On Her Way to the Fair, a juvenile novel; a mystery novel for adults.

SIDELIGHTS: Janet Sheffield writes: "I am a typical free-wheeling Saggitarian whose independence and fear of ties has led me to a life-style that includes virtually no material possessions but books and a Japanese bed. I am deeply into yoga at the moment, not only the physical but the mental aspects, and am currently interested in trying to combine some form of meditation with the more active sports. I jog almost every day, barefoot on the beach, and am beginning to study Tai Chi and Aikido and other Oriental disciplines.

"I have changed residences some twenty-six times in thirty years, living in such varied places as Taipei, Taiwan (where I learned to speak and write Mandarin Chinese) and London, England. . . .

"I have a deep affection for children, perhaps because I never really grew up, and I would like to write books for them that would make them feel warm and cozy and loved."

*   *   *

SHELLEY, Florence D(ubroff) 1921-

PERSONAL: Born January 21, 1921, in Baltimore, Md.; daughter of Nathan (a dentist) and Charlotte (a pharmacist; maiden name, Weisman) Dubroff; married Edwin F. Shelley (an engineer), August 29, 1941; children: Carolyn Jane (Mrs. Philip LeBel), William Edson. *Education:* Barnard College, A.B., 1940; Columbia University, M.S., 1941. *Home and office:* 339 Oxford Rd., New Rochelle, N.Y. 10804.

CAREER: J. Walter Thompson Co. (advertising agency), New York, N.Y., public relations writer and editor, 1941-47; free-lance writer, editor, and consultant, 1959—. Editorial and program consultant and member of board of directors, E. F. Shelley and Co., 1965-75. President of New Rochelle Council of Parent Teacher Association, 1963-66; writer and editor for New York State Citizens Committee for the Public Schools, 1964-68; president of Inwood Community School, 1951-52; member of advisory committee of New Rochelle Community Action Agency. Member of board of directors of Universal Solar Systems. Consultant to National Commission on Resources for Youth and National Committee on Citizens in Education.

MEMBER: American Academy of Political Science, American Educational Research Association, National Society for the Study of Education, Education Writers Association, Charter League (director), Institute for Responsive Action, Barnard Club (Westchester, N.Y.), Women's City Club (New York City), New Rochelle Board of Education.

WRITINGS: (With Jane Otten) *When Your Parents Grow Old,* Funk, 1976. Editor of *Education Training Market Report 1971-73.* Contributor of articles to *Newsday* and education periodicals. *Avocational interests:* Travel, music, modern dance, ballet.

*   *   *

SHEPARD, Ernest Howard 1879-1976

December 10, 1879—March 24, 1976; British artist, cartoonist, author, and illustrator of books, including *Winnie-the-Pooh.* Obituaries: *Bookseller,* April 3, 1976; *Publishers Weekly,* April 12, 1976; *School Library Journal,* May, 1976; *Current Biography,* May, 1976. (See index for previous *CA* sketch)

*   *   *

SHEPHERD, (Richard) David 1931-

PERSONAL: Born April 25, 1931, in London, England; son of Raymond and Joyce (Williamson) Shepherd; married Avril Gaywood, February 2, 1957; children: Melinda, Mandy, Melanie, Wendy. *Education:* Educated in Buckinghamshire, England. *Home:* Winkworth Farm, Hascombe, Surrey, England.

CAREER: Studied portrait painting under Robin Goodwin, 1950-53; began painting career as an aviation artist, London Airport, 1953-54; commissioned by British armed services to paint action pictures, 1954; African wildlife and portrait painter, 1962—. Work has been exhibited at several one-man shows, including Royal Academy, London, 1956, Tryon Galleries, London, 1962, 1965, 1972, and in Johannesburg, South Africa, 1966, 1969, and New York, 1967. *Awards, honors:* D.F.A., Pratt Institute, 1971; Order of Golden Ark

from the Prince of the Netherlands for services to conservation in Zambia and Operation Tiger, 1973.

WRITINGS: Artist in Africa, Collins, 1969; *The Man Who Loves Giants* (autobiography), David & Charles, 1975.

WORK IN PROGRESS: A book on preserved steam railways, for David & Charles; *Paintings of Africa and India* for Tryon Gallery.

SIDELIGHTS: Shepherd was able to present a helicopter to his personal friend, President Kaunda of Zambia, to combat poaching, raising the money at an auction of his paintings in the United States. All totaled, Shepherd has raised over 300,000 pounds for wildlife conservation.

Shepherd has a collection of steam locomotives and owns a full-scale steam railway, complete with an 1858 station, in Somerset. Open to the public, the money raised by the railway is donated to wildlife conservation. One of the locomotives, an 1896 Glasgow built steam engine, was presented to Shepherd by President Kaunda, who opened the border between Zambia and Rhodesia to enable the engine, exported during the reign of Queen Victoria, to return to England after 78 years. The journey of this locomotive was the subject of the 1973 B.B.C. television Film, "Last Train to Mulobezi."

Shepherd himself was the subject of the 1972 B.B.C. film, "The Man Who Loves Elephants." Several of his paintings are part of the National Collection in York Museum.

*   *   *

SHERWIN, Oscar 1902-1976

July 6, 1902—April 30, 1976; American educator, literary scholar, historian, and biographer. Obituaries: *New York Times,* May 2, 1976. (See index for previous *CA* sketch)

*   *   *

SHERWIN, Sidney 1920-

PERSONAL: Born October 29, 1920; son of David C. and Esther (Stiner) Rosetahl; married Jean Rabinowitz, November 19, 1944; children: Byron, Elliott. *Education:* Brooklyn College (now Brooklyn College of the City University of New York), B.A., 1942; Brooklyn Law School, J.D., 1948. *Religion:* Hebrew. *Residence:* Forest Hills, N.Y. *Office:* 169-12 Hillside Ave., Jamaica, N.Y. 11432.

CAREER: Attorney in private practice, 1948—. Sherwin Plan (finance institution), president, 1957—. *Military service:* U.S. Army, 1942-46. *Member:* American Bar Association, Queens County Bar Association.

WRITINGS: How to Collect a Money Judgment, Attorney's Aid Publications, 1965; *Debtors and Creditors: Rights and Remedies,* Attorney's Aid Publications, 1968; *How to Get Out of Debt Painlessly,* Books & Periodicals, 1969; *What to Do When Your Bills Exceed Your Paycheck: Everything You Need to Know About Getting Out of Debt,* Prentice-Hall, 1974. Writer of professional articles.

WORK IN PROGRESS: Rewriting plays involving trial drama.

*   *   *

SHIELDS, Allan (Edwin) 1919-

PERSONAL: Born July 3, 1919, in Columbus, Ohio; son of Richard Edwin and Eloessa (Smith) Shields; married Bernice Clark, August 2, 1941; children: Allan Oakley, Richard Minter, Larry Michael, Catherine Marie. *Education:* University of California, Berkeley, B.A., 1941; University of Southern California, M.A., 1947, Ph.D., 1951. *Politics:* Democrat. *Religion:* "No preference." *Home:* 8646 Washington Ave., La Mesa, Calif. 92041. *Office:* Department of Philosophy, San Diego State University, San Diego, Calif., 92182.

CAREER: San Diego State University, San Diego, Calif., assistant professor of philosophy and psychology, 1949-54, associate professor, 1954-59, professor of philosophy, 1959-68, chairman of department, 1956-59; University of Northern Iowa, Cedar Falls, professor of philosophy and dean of College of Humanities and Fine Arts, 1968-70; San Diego State University, professor of philosophy, 1970—. Seasonal ranger naturalist at Yosemite National Park, 1955-60. California State Fine Arts and Humanities Framework Committee, member, 1967-73, chairman, 1968; member of board of directors of San Diego Symphony Association, 1963-65; chairman of chamber music series of San Diego Fine Arts Gallery, 1963-65. *Military service:* U.S. Army Air Forces, 1942-45; became sergeant.

MEMBER: American Society for Aesthetics (trustee, 1969-72), Audubon Society, Phi Beta Kappa, Phi Kappa Phi, Phi Mu Alpha Sinfonia.

WRITINGS: Guide to Tuolumne Meadows Trails, Yosemite Natural History Association, 1959; (with son, Richard Shields) *Tuolumne Profile: Yosemite,* privately printed, 1967; (with Herbert Searles) *A Bibliography of the Works of F.C.S. Schiller, with an Introduction to Pragmatic Humanism,* San Diego State University Press, 1969; *The Tragedy of Tenaya* (novella), Montana Indian Publications Fund, 1974; *A Bibliography of Bibliographies in Aesthetics,* San Diego State University Press, 1974.

Author of columns, "Music" in *San Diego Magazine,* 1962-63, "Sound Judgment" in *Valley News and the Daily Californian,* 1963-65, and "Aesthetics for the Contemporary Artist" in *Leonardo,* 1973-74. Contributor to professional journals. *Leonardo,* corresponding editor, 1972—, member of editorial advisory board, 1974—; member of editorial board, *Journal of Aesthetic Education,* 1973—.

WORK IN PROGRESS: American Aestheticians, 1750-1940: Sketches.

SIDELIGHTS: Shields writes: "My contributions which I count most important have been made in the philosophy of art and aesthetics, though I do not wish to slight a constant professional concern with the problems of education at all levels." *Avocational interests:* Nature study, environmental concerns, music (plays violin; writes musical criticism), athletics (cross country running), mountaineering, gardening, wine making, wine aesthetics, horsemanship.

*   *   *

SHIPMAN, Harry L(ongfellow)   1948-

PERSONAL: Born February 20, 1948, in Hartford, Conn.; son of Arthur (a lawyer) and Mary (a painter; maiden name, Dana) Shipman; married Editha Davidson (a cellist), April 10, 1970. *Education:* Harvard University, B.A. (summa cum laude), 1969; California Institute of Technology, M.S., 1970, Ph.D., 1971. *Home:* 45 Augusta Dr., Newark, Del. 19713. *Office:* Department of Physics, University of Delaware, Newark, Del. 19711.

CAREER: Yale University, New Haven, Conn., J. Willard Gibbs Instructor in Astronomy, 1971-73; University of Missouri, St. Louis, assistant professor of physics, 1973-74; University of Delaware, Newark, assistant professor of physics, 1974—. Astronomer at McDonnell Planetarium,

1973-74. Harlow Shapley visiting lecturer of the American Astronomical Society, 1975—. *Member:* American Astronomical Society, Federation of American Scientists, American Association of University Professors, Phi Beta Kappa, Sigma Xi. *Awards, honors:* Grants from Research Corp., 1974-76, National Science Foundation, 1974-76, and National Aeronautics and Space Administration, 1976.

WRITINGS: Black Holes, Quasars, and the Universe (Library of Science Book Club selection), Houghton, 1976. Contributor of about twenty articles to scientific journals.

WORK IN PROGRESS: An introductory astronomy text; analyzing temperatures, masses, and sizes of some of the smallest known stars.

SIDELIGHTS: Shipman writes: "Is there life on Mars? When will the sun die? How does the universe evolve? Where did it all begin? These are the questions that excite the contemporary scientist. As a science writer, I seek to involve the intelligent reader in the pursuit of the answers to these and other questions of scientific research."

BIOGRAPHICAL/CRITICAL SOURCES: Wilmington News-Journal, July 25, 1976.

*   *   *

SHIPTON, Eric Earle   1907-

PERSONAL: Born August 12, 1907, in Ceylon; son of Cecil (a tea planter) and Alice (Earle) Shipton; married Diana Channer, December 16, 1942; children: Nicolas, John. *Home:* The Haye, Bridgnorth, Shropshire, England.

CAREER: British Consul-General at Kashgar, Sinkiang, China, 1940-42, 1946-48; Consular Liason Officer, Iran, 1943-44; Britain Military Mission, Hungary, technical advisor, 1945-46; British Consul-General at Kunming, Yunnan, China, 1949-57; advisor to the Chilson Government in Boundary Dispute, 1964-66. *Military service:* Served in Indian Army, 1940. *Awards, honors:* Gold Medal of Royal Geographical Society, 1938; Gold Medal of Royal Scottish Society, 1951; decorated Commander of the British Empire, 1955.

WRITINGS—Published by Hodder & Stoughton, except as indicated: *Nanda Devi,* 1935; *Blank on the Map,* 1938; *Upon that Mountain,* 1943; *Mountains of Tartary,* 1951; *Mount Everest Reconnaissance Expedition,* 1951; *Everest* (historical sketches), Frederick Muller, 1955; *The North Pole* (historical sketches), Frederich Muller, 1956; *Land of Tempest,* 1963; *Mountain Conquest* (historical sketches), American Heritage, 1966; *That Untravelled World* (autobiography), 1968; *Tierra Del Fuego* (history), Charles Knight (London), 1972.

WORK IN PROGRESS: Contributing further biographical work on the subject of the Bridges family in *Tierra Del Fuego.*

SIDELIGHTS: Shipton writes: "Most of my books are accounts of my experiences as a mountain explorer—a career which has occupied the main part of my life. I have stressed in particular the virtues of simple light travel."

*   *   *

SHOEMAKER, Lynn Henry   1939-

PERSONAL: Born March 31, 1939, in Racine, Wis.; son of William (an engineer) and Gretchen (a teacher and poet; maiden name, Gull) Shoemaker; divorced; children: Erica Zoe. *Education:* Harvard University, B.A., 1961; graduate study at University of South Dakota, 1962, and University of California, Davis, 1963-66. *Politics:* "Radical." *Religion:* "Radical Christian." *Home:* 211 Stewart, Ithaca, N.Y. 14850.

CAREER: Yankton College, Yankton, S.D., assistant professor of English, 1962-63; California State College, Los Angeles, lecturer in English, 1966-67; East Los Angeles Junior College, Los Angeles, Calif., lecturer in English, 1970-71; Beverly Hills High School, Beverly Hills, Calif., teacher of English, 1970-71; East Hill School, Ithaca, N.Y., teacher of wood shop, 1973—. *Member:* Ithaca Community Poets.

WRITINGS: Coming Home (poems), Ithaca House, 1973.

WORK IN PROGRESS—Poetry: *Curses and Blessings.*

* * *

SHORRIS, Earl 1936-

PERSONAL: Born June 25, 1936, in Chicago, Ill.; son of Samuel Robert and Betty (Mann) Shorris; married Sylvia Sasson (a writer), May 3, 1956; children: Anthony Ernest, James Sasson. *Education:* University of Chicago, student, 1950-53. *Home:* 444 East 82nd St., New York, N.Y. 10028. *Agent:* Lynn Nesbit, International Creative Management, 40 West 57th St., New York, N.Y. 10019.

CAREER: Has held various jobs as a journalist and in advertising in Texas, California, and New York; N. W. Ayer ABH International, New York, N.Y., currently senior vice-president. *Harper's,* New York, N.Y., contributing editor, 1972—.

WRITINGS: Ofay (novel), Delacorte, 1966; *The Boots of the Virgin* (novel), Delacorte, 1968; *The Death of the Great Spirit* (non-fiction), Simon & Schuster, 1971; *Villa* (novel based on the life of Pancho Villa), Knopf, in press. Contributor to magazines, including *Atlantic Monthly, Ramparts, Esquire, Antioch Review,* and *New York Times Sunday Magazine.*

WORK IN PROGRESS: A nonfiction book; research for a book on Aztec poetry.

* * *

SHORROCK, William I(rwin) 1941-

PERSONAL: Born June 16, 1941, in Milwaukee, Wis.; son of William J. (an editor) and Helen L. (a secretary; maiden name, Irwin) Shorrock; married Marjorie J. Brintnall (an office assistant), August 29, 1964; children: David W., Kimberly L. *Education:* Denison University, B.A., 1963; University of Wisconsin, Madison, M.A., 1965, Ph.D., 1968. *Home:* 3320 Glencairn Rd., Shaker Heights, Ohio 44122. *Office:* Department of History, Cleveland State University, Cleveland, Ohio 44115.

CAREER: University of Wisconsin, Wausau, instructor, 1967-68, assistant professor of history, 1968-69; University of Delaware, Newark, assistant professor of history, summer, 1969; Cleveland State University, Cleveland, Ohio, assistant professor, 1969-73, associate professor of history, 1973—. *Member:* American Historical Association, Ohio Academy of History, Cleveland Council on World Affairs, Common Cause, Phi Beta Kappa. *Awards, honors:* Woodrow Wilson fellowship, 1963.

WRITINGS: French Imperialism in the Middle East: The Failure of Policy in Syria and Lebanon, 1900-1914, University of Wisconsin Press, 1976. Contributor to European and Middle East studies journals.

WORK IN PROGRESS: Research on the origins of the French appeasement of Italian fascism.

SIDELIGHTS: Shorrock writes: "Most of my research is carried on in France. Consequently my family and I travel there quite frequently. We have also been active in hosting foreign students studying in this country. During the last several years, we have hosted foreign students from India, France, and Germany."

* * *

SHRIVER, Harry C(lair) 1904-

PERSONAL: Born October 2, 1904, in Gettysburg, Pa.; son of Edward Simpson (a farmer) and Minnie Bell (Snyder) Shriver; married Florence Basehoar, October 10, 1944; children: Ann Basehoar Shriver Bielot, Harry Clair, Florence Louise Shriver Armstrong. *Education:* Attended Dickinson College, 1925-26, and Gettysburg College, 1926-27; George Washington University, J.D., 1930, A.B., 1932. *Politics:* Republican. *Religion:* Lutheran. *Home:* 8409 Fox Run, Potomac, Md. 20854.

CAREER: School teacher in Adams County, Pa., 1924-25; Library of Congress, Washington, D.C., staff member, 1928-42; practiced law in Washington, D.C., 1932-35; 1947; Federal Trade Commission, Washington, D.C., attorney, 1942-44; War Shipping Administration, Washington, D.C., attorney, 1944-46; Maritime Commission, Washington, D.C., attorney, 1948-50; Maritime Administration, Washington, D.C., attorney, 1950-58; St. Lawrence Seaway Development Corp., assistant general counsel, 1958, general counsel, 1959-62; Federal Power Commission, Washington, D.C., hearing examiner, 1963-72, administration law judge, 1972—. Admitted to Bar of District of Columbia, 1931, U.S. Supreme Court, 1935, and Court of Claims, 1945. Staff member of Library of Congress, 1935, special agent, 1936.

MEMBER: American Bar Association, Federal Bar Association, American Society of International Law, Pennsylvania Historical Junto (president, 1968—), Phi Beta Gamma, Theta Chi, Rotary International, Old Georgetown Club (co-founder; member of board of directors).

WRITINGS: (Editor and author of notes) *Justice Oliver Wendell Holmes: His Book Notices and Uncollected Lettera and Papers,* Central Book Company, 1936, reprinted, Da Capo Press, 1973; *Judicial Opinions of Oliver Wendell Holmes,* Dennis, 1940; *How to Find the Law of Administrative Agencies,* West Publishing, 1940; (editor) *Proceedings of Section of International and Comparative Law,* American Bar Association, 1944, 1945.

A History of the Shriver Family, privately printed, 1962; *What Gusto: Stories and Anecdotes About Justice Oliver Wendell Holmes,* Fox Hills Press, 1970; *The Government Lawyer: Essays on Men, Books, and the Law,* Fox Hills Press, 1975. Contributor to law journals.

WORK IN PROGRESS: Research on censorship in World War Two and on the St. Lawrence Seaway.

SIDELIGHTS: Shriver told *CA:* "My opinion of Justice Holmes is that he was one of the great jurists of all time, and that present day judges can learn much from him. He had mastered the techniques of the jurist, but he was also a precursor. Since he had studied history and philosophy intensively he wanted to know the reasons for the law and all legal rules as a justification. He was never satisfied simply to hand down a decision based merely on precedent.

As a word about my own career, it is a bit ironic that I was reared in a home where there were few if any books (the Bible and one or two others) and I should spend so much time in the Library of Congress—14 years—and later be so concerned with books. My early schooling was quite inadequate. I was among the disadvantaged, to use a recently common phrase. I attended a one room rural school with all grades (1 to 8th) and with 65 students. One year we had three different teachers. After high school I was on my own. I worked my way through college and law school."

* * *

SHULMAN, Neil B(arnett) 1945-

PERSONAL: Born March 18, 1945, in Washington, D.C. *Education:* George Washington University, B.S., 1967; Emory University, M.D., 1971; also attended Harvard University, 1974, and Kennedy Institute, summer, 1976. *Office:* Medical School, Emory University, 69 Butler St., Atlanta, Ga. 30303.

CAREER: Intern at Emory University Hospital, Veterans Administration Hospital, and Grady Memorial Hospital, all in Atlanta, Ga., all 1972; Grady Memorial Hospital, fellow in nephrology and associate in department of medicine, 1972-74; Emory University, Atlanta, Ga., assistant professor of nephrology, 1974—. Director of local Inner City Medical Clinic; member of board of directors of Techwood Community Health Clinic and Central City Community Health Clinic. Project director for Atlanta Hypertension Program, 1972—, and Geogia Regional Medical Program, 1974—; member of National Patient Education Task Force on Hypertension, 1973. Host of daily program "Health Care U.S.A." on WATL-Television, 1976—. *Member:* American Heart Association. *Awards, honors:* Medal from Georgia Heart Association, 1974, for volunteer service.

WRITINGS: Finally I'm a Doctor, Scribner, 1976.

WORK IN PROGRESS: Novels on inner-city and rural health care; research on hypertension.

BIOGRAPHICAL/CRITICAL SOURCES: Atlanta, June, 1976; *Chicago Tribune,* August 16, 1976; *Philadelphia Inquirer,* August 23, 1976; *Atlanta Journal and Constitution,* September 19, 1976.

* * *

SICHEL, Peter M(ax) F(erdinand) 1922-

PERSONAL: Born September 12, 1922, in Germany; came to the United States in 1941, naturalized citizen, 1943; son of Eugene J.H.T. (a wine merchant) and Francesca (Loeb) Sichel; married Stella Spanoudaki, June 1, 1961; children: Bettina, Alexandra, Sylvia. *Education:* Attended elementary school in Germany and secondary school in England. *Politics:* Democrat. *Religion:* None. *Home:* 110 East 70th St., New York, N.Y. 10021. *Agent:* Russell & Volkening, Inc., 551 Fifth Ave., New York, N.Y. 10017. *Office:* H. Sichel Sons, 22 East 40th St., New York, N.Y. 10016.

CAREER: U.S. State Department, Washington, D.C., diplomat, 1946-59, consul in Hong Kong, 1956-59; H. Sichel Sons, Inc. (wine shippers, blenders, and bottlers), New York, N.Y., president, 1959—. *Military service:* U.S. Army, 1942-46; became captain. *Member:* Wine and Food Society. *Awards, honors:* Distinguished intelligence medal from Central Intelligence Agency, 1960; Andre Simon Silver Medal from Wine and Food Society, 1975.

WRITINGS: (With Judy Ley) *Which Wine,* Harper, 1975. Contributor to professional and consumer publications on food and wine.

WORK IN PROGRESS: Editing and revising *The Wines of Germany,* by Frank Schoonmaker, for Hastings House; a definitive book on German wine.

SIDEL, Victor W(illiam) 1931-

PERSONAL: Born July 7, 1931, in Trenton, N.Y.; son of Max A. (a pharmacist) and Ida (a pharmacist; maiden name Ring) Sidel; married Ruth Grossman (a psychiatric social worker and a writer), June 3, 1956; children: Mark, Kevin. *Education:* Princeton University, A.B. (cum laude), 1953; Harvard University, M.D. (with honors), 1957; postdoctoral study at Harvard University, 1964-66, and University of London, 1967-68. *Home:* 3614 Johnson Ave., Bronx, N.Y. 10463. *Office:* Montefiore Hospital and Medical Center, 111 East 210th St., Bronx, N.Y. 10467.

CAREER: Peter Bent Brigham Hospital, Boston, Mass., intern, 1957-58, junior assistant resident in medicine, 1958-59; National Institutes of Health, Bethesda, Md., clinical associate at National Heart Institute and senior assistant surgeon for U.S. Public Health Service, 1959-61; Peter Bent Brigham Hospital, senior assistant resident in medicine, 1961-62, junior associate in medicine, 1962-66; Harvard University, School of Medicine, Boston, Mass., instructor in biophysics, 1962-64, associate in preventive medicine, 1964-67, assistant professor of preventive medicine, 1968-69; Massachusetts General Hospital, Boston, chief of preventive medicine unit, 1964-67, chief of community medicine unit, 1968-69; Montefiore Hospital and Medical Center, Bronx, N.Y., chairman of department of social medicine, 1969—, also director of community health participation program, 1975—. Member of Center for Community Health and Medical Care, 1968-69; professor of social medicine at Albert Einstein College of Medicine, 1969—, chairman of department of community health, Montefiore Campus, 1972—; visiting professor at City College of the City University of New York, 1973—. United States-Soviet Union health exchange visitor, 1967-68. Member of Massachusetts Commission on Radiation Protection, 1963-64; member of board of directors and chairman of task force on research of Massachusetts Mental Retardation Planning, 1966-67; member of Metropolitan Boston 1970 Census Tract Committee, 1966-67; member of Technical Panel of Community Health Institute, 1971-74; member of Citizen's Committee for the Children of New York, 1971-75; project director of the First National House Staff Conference, 1971; member of National Committee on United States-China Relations, 1974—; temporary adviser to World Health Organization, 1974.

MEMBER: International Epidemiological Association, Pan American Community Health Association, American Association for the Advancement of Science, American College of Preventive Medicine, American Federation for Clinical Research, American Physiological Society, American Public Health Association (fellow), Association of Teachers of Preventive Medicine, Institute of Society, Ethics, and the Life Sciences, Scientists' Institute for Public Information, Society for Health and Human Values, Medical Society of the State of New York, New York Academy of Medicine, New York Academy of Sciences, Bronx County Medical Society (chairman of committee on community health, 1971-75.) Physicians Forum (member of board of directors, 1969—; chairman, 1971-72), Public Health Association of New York City, Phi Beta Kappa, Sigma Xi. *Awards, honors:* Advanced research fellowship from American Heart Association, 1962-64; research fellowship from Medical Foundation, 1964-68; faculty fellowship from Milbank Memorial Fund, 1964-71.

WRITINGS: (Editor with Saul Aronow and F. R. Ervin) *The Fallen Sky: Medical Consequences of Thermonuclear War,* Hill & Wang, 1963; (with wife, Ruth Sidel) *Serve the*

People: Observations on Medicine in the People's Republic of China, Josiah Macy, Jr. Foundation, 1973; (authro of foreword) Bernard Schoenberg and other editors, *Bereavement: Its Psychosocial Aspects,* Columbia University Press, 1975.

Contributor: Henry Eyring, editor, *Civil Defense,* American Association for the Advancement of Science, 1966; E. F. Torrey, editor, *Ethical Issues in Medicine: The Role of the Physician in Today's Society,* Little, Brown, 1968; Steven Rose, editor, *C.B.W.: Chemical and Biological Warfare,* Harrap, 1968; John Norman, editor, *Medicine in the Ghetto,* Appleton, 1969; Bonnie and vern Bullough, editors, *New Directions for Nurses,* Springer Publishing, 1971; Robert Eilers and Sue Moyerman, editors, *National Health Insurance,* Irwin, 1971; Everett Mendelsohn, Judith P. Swazey, and Irene Taviss, editors, *Human Aspects of Biomedical Innovation,* Harvard University Press, 1971; David Milton and other editors, *People's China: Social Experimentation, Politics, Entry onto the World Scene, 1966 Through 1972,* Vintage Books, 1974; J. R. Quinn, editor, *Medicine and Public Health in the People's Republic of Chaina,* U.S. Department of Health, Education and Welfare, 1972; Michel Oksenberg, editor, *China's Developmental Experience,* Academy of Political Science, Columbia University, 1973; Raymond G. Slavin and other editors, *Tice's Practice of Medicine,* Harper, 1973; Alan Gartner, Colin Green, and Frank Riessman, editors, *What Nixon Is Doing to Us,* Harper, 1973; John Z. Bowers and Elizabeth Purcell, editors, *Medicine and Society in China,* Josiah Macy, Jr. Foundation, 1974; Quinn, editor, *China Medicine as We Saw It,* U.S. Department of Health, Education and Welfare, 1974; K. W. Newell, editor, *Health by the People,* World Health Organization, 1975; Ethel Tobach and Harold M. Proshansky, editors, *Genetic Destiny: Scientific Controversy and Social Conflict,* AMS Press, in press.

Author of scientific abstracts and reports. Contributor to *Encyclopedia Americana.* Contributor of more than a hundred articles and reviews to scientific journals. Member of editorial board of *Postgraduate Medicine,* 1969—, *Update International,* 1972-74, *American Journal of Drug and Alcohol Abuse,* 1973—, and *American Journal of Chinese Medicine,* 1975—; member of editorial advisory board of *Hospital Practice,* 1966—; contributing editor of *New Physician,* 1971-76; editorial consultant to *International Journal of Health Services,* 1971—.

SIDELIGHTS: Sidel's involvement is in "community medicine" and "social medicine." He believes that physicians have to see environmental, political, and social influences upon their patients' health, and work with them accordingly. They must be aware of the world by which they are surrounded, and be prepared to try to change that world as much as possible in the interest of their patients and their communities.

He has traveled and studied in England, Scandinavia, and the Soviet Union; he visited the People's Republic of China at the invitation of the Chinese Medical Association in 1971 and 1972, went to Chile as the guest of the Chilean Ministry of Health in 1973, and visited Malaysia for the World Health Organization and Vietnam as representative of Medical Aid to Indochina, both in 1974.

BIOGRAPHICAL/CRITICAL SOURCES: Environment, June, 1972.

* * *

SIEGAN, Bernard H(erbert) 1924-

PERSONAL: Born July 28, 1924, in Chicago, Ill.; son of David and Jeanette (Seitz) Siegan; married Sharon Goldberg, June 15, 1952. *Education:* Attended Herzel Junior College, 1943, Carnegie Institute of Technology (now Carnegie-Mellon University), 1944, and Roosevelt College, 1946-47; University of Chicago, J.D., 1949. *Home:* 6005 Camino de la Costa, La Jolla, Calif. 92037. *Office:* School of Law, University of San Diego, Alcala Park, San Diego, Calif. 92110.

CAREER: Admitted to Bar of State of Illinois, and to Federal District Court, Chicago, Ill., 1950; Siegan & Karlin, Chicago, law partner, 1952-75; University of Chicago, Chicago, research fellow, 1968-69, consultant in law and economics, 1970-73; University of San Diego, San Diego, Calif., professor, 1974-75, distinguished professor of law, 1975—. President or secretary of various small corporations. *Military service:* U.S. Army, 1943-46.

MEMBER: American Bar Association, American Judicature Society, Chicago Bar Association. *Awards, honors:* Leander J. Monks Memorial Fund award from Institute for Humane Studies, 1972, for *Land Use Without Zoning;* Foundation for Research in Economics and Education grant, 1973; Council on Environment, Employment, Economy and Development award, 1975; Urban Land Institute research fellow, 1976.

WRITINGS: Zoning and Non-Zoning: Trends and Problems (monograph), University of Chicago, 1971; *Land Use Without Zoning,* Heath, 1972; *Costs and Consequences of Public Land Use Regulation* (monograph), Culver-Stockton College, 1975; *Other People's Property,* Heath, 1976. Author of "Land Use and the Law," weekly syndicated column, 1973—. Contributor to law and economics journals, and to newspapers.

* * *

SILBERSCHMIDT, Max 1899-

PERSONAL: Born January 29, 1899, in Zurich, Switzerland; son of William and Alice (Rueff) Silberschmidt; married Elisabeth Schreiber, April 2, 1927; children: Ines (Mrs. Peter Frey), Brigitta (Mrs. Juerg Rosenbusch). *Education:* Studied at University of Geneva, 1917-18, University of Leipzig, 1919-20, University of Berlin, 1920-21, Archives of Venice, 1921, University of Zurich, Dr. es lettres, 1923; University of Paris, additional study, 1925. *Religion:* Protestant. *Home:* Plattenstrasse 86, 8032 Zurich, Switzerland. *Office:* Swiss Churchill Foundation, Raamistrasse 33, 8001 Zurich, Switzerland.

CAREER: Academical Institution, Colraine, Northern Ireland, assistant master, 1924-25; Swiss National Bank, Zurich, assistant economics researcher, 1926; Technikum Winterthur, Canton of Zurich, Switzerland, professor of history and geography, 1926-45; University of Zurich, Zurich, Switzerland, lecturer, 1931-45, professor of modern European and American history, 1945-69, professor emeritus, 1969—, dean of faculty of arts and letters, 1960-62; Churchill Foundation, Zurich, Switzerland, vice-president and director of research center, 1966—. Member of board of directors, Swiss Institute for International Studies, 1950—, vice-president, Swiss Commission for World Colleges, 1972—. *Military service:* Swiss Army, 1940-45; served in press and radio section.

MEMBER: Swiss-British Society (member of board of directors, 1946), P.E.N., Swiss-American Historical Society, Swiss-American Society for Cultural Relations (vice-president, 1972—), Swiss Historical Society, European Association for American Studies (president, 1954-74), Zurich Antiquarian Society, Zurich Economic Society, Phi

Beta Kappa. *Awards, honors:* Rockefeller fellowship in the United States, 1932-34.

WRITINGS: Das orientalische Problem zur Zeit der Entstehung des tuerkischen Reiches, nach venezianischen Quellen: Ein Beitrag zur Geschichte der Beziehungen Venedigs zu Sultan Bajezid I., zu Byzanz, Ungarn und Genua und zum Reiche von Kiptschak (1381-1400), B. G. Teubner (Berlin), 1923, reprinted, Gerstenberg (Hildesheim), 1972; *Grossbritannien und die Vereinigten Staaten, ihr machtpolitisches Verhaeltnis vom amerikan:schen Unabhaengigkeitskrieg bis zum Weltkrieg: Ein Beitrag zur Geschichte des Weltstaatensystems,* B. G. Teubner, 1932; *Der Aufstieg der Vereinigten Staaten von Amerika zur Weltmacht: Staat und Wirtschaft der USA. im 20. Jahrhundert,* H. R. Sauerlaender (Aarau), 1941; *Staat und Wirtschaft in der Entwicklung der Vereinigten Staaten,* Schulthess (Zurich), 1944; *Praesidentschaft und Praesidenten in den Vereinigten Staaten,* Schulthess, 1946.

Die Bedeutung des Unternehmers in Weltgeschichtlicher Sicht (Zurich), 1956; *Amerikas industrielle Entwicklung, von der Zeit der Pioniere zur Aera von Big Business,* Francke (Bern), 1958; (editor) *Europa und der Kolonialismus,* Artemis Verlag (Zurich), 1969; *Beidseits des Atlantik: Studien ueber Wirtschaft, Gesellschaft und Staat,* edited by Max Mittler and Robert Schneebeli, Atlantis (Zurich), 1969; *Amerika-Europa, Freund und Rivale,* Eugen Rentsch (Stuttgart), 1970, translation by J. Maxwell Brownjohn published as *The United States and Europe: Rivals and Partners,* Harcourt, 1972.

WORK IN PROGRESS: Research in European-American intellectual and political relations and in American historiography.

* * *

SILLERY, Anthony 1903-1976

April 19, 1903—March 5, 1976; British colonial administrator, linguist, educator, and author of works on political science. Obituaries: *AB Bookman's Weekly,* April 12, 1976. (See index for previous *CA* sketch)

* * *

SILVER, Warren A. 1914-

PERSONAL: Born December 8, 1914, in Savannah, Ga.; son of Isaac E. (a businessman) and Kate (Wilensky) Silver; children: Marcelo. *Education:* University of California, Los Angeles, A.B.; Columbia University, J.D., 1940; also studied at University of Southern California. *Residence:* Washington, D.C. *Agent:* Jay Garon, Jay Garon-Brooke Associates, Inc., 415 Central Park W., New York, N.Y. 10025.

CAREER: National Labor Relations Board, Washington, D.C., field examiner, 1941-42; U.S. Department of State, Washington, D.C., economist, 1945-48; worked in civil transportation for U.S. Department of the Army, in Tokyo, Japan, 1948-50; staff member of the office of Secretary of State for International Security Affairs, Washington, D.C., 1950-51; U.S. Embassy, Tehran, Iran, special assistant to the American Ambassador, 1951-53; Department of State, Washington, D.C., supervisory international economic officer, 1953-56; worked in India, Laos, and Liberia for U.S. Foreign Service, 1956-65; U.S. Office of Economic Opportunity, Washington, D.C., consultant, 1965-66; International Development Services, Inc., Washington, D.C., vice-president, 1966-67, executive vice-president, 1968-69; in real

estate operations in Florida and Alaska, 1970—. *Military service:* U.S. Army, 1942-46; became captain. *Member:* District of Columbia Bar Association, Columbia Law School Alumni Association.

WRITINGS: The Green Rose (novel), Dial, 1977.

Plays: "Catherine de Medici" (three-act), first produced in New York, N.Y., at Columbia University, 1938; "The House on the Hill" (three-act), first produced in Westport, Conn., 1948; "Michael" (one-act), first produced in Tokyo, Japan, at Exchange Theatre, 1949; "The Little Pocket Picker" (one-act), first produced in Tokyo, Japan, at Waseda University, 1949.

* * *

SILVERT, Kalman H(irsch) 1921-1976

March 10, 1921—June 16, 1976; American social and political scientist, educator, and author of books on Latin American affairs. Obituaries: *New York Times,* June 16, 1976; *Washington Post,* June 16, 1976. (See index for previous *CA* sketch)

* * *

SILVERTON, Michael 1935-

PERSONAL: Born March 17, 1935, in White Plains, N.Y.; son of Jerry and Edith Louise (Smetana) Silverton; separated; children: Seth, Alexandra. *Education:* Brooklyn College (now of the City University of New York), B.A., 1957. *Politics:* None. *Religion:* None. *Home:* 60 East 17th St., Brooklyn, N.Y. 11226.

CAREER: High school teacher of English in New York, N.Y., 1960—. *Military service:* U.S. Army, 1958-60.

WRITINGS: Battery Park (poetry), Thing Press, 1966.

Poems represented in anthologies, *Eight Lines and Under: An Anthology of Short Short Poems,* edited by William Cole, Macmillan, 1967; *Pith and Vinegar: An Anthology of Short Humorous Poetry,* edited by Cole, Simon & Schuster, 1969; *Poetry Brief: An Anthology of Short Short Poems,* edited by Cole, Macmillan, 1971; and *Poems: One Line and Longer,* edited by Cole, Grossman, 1973. Contributor of poems to literary journals and popular magazines, including *Nation, Harper's, Prairie Schooner, Poetry Now, Wormwood Review,* and *Angel Hair.*

WORK IN PROGRESS: Mistress, a collection of related poems.

SIDELIGHTS: Silverton writes: "Friends tell me I'm a wonderful cook. (I concur.) I'm becoming increasingly interested in making visual art, though I've no formal training, nor feel the need. As for the poetry, my chiefmost interest, the horizon remains an intriguing place."

* * *

SIMMONS, Joseph Larry 1935-

PERSONAL: Born December 9, 1935, in Tylertown, Miss.; son of Richard Oliver and Nita (Packwood) Simmons; married Fleur Fuller (a teacher), April 25, 1964; children: Elizabeth Fuller, Jean Randle, Catherine Edna. *Education:* Florida State University, B.Mus., 1956; New York University, M.A., 1962; University of Virginia, Ph.D., 1967. *Religion:* Episcopalian. *Home:* 1304 Lowerline, New Orleans, La. 70118. *Office:* Department of English, Tulane University, New Orleans, La. 70118.

CAREER: North Texas State University, Denton, instructor in English, 1962-64; Tulane University, New Orleans, La., assistant professor, 1967-69, associate professor, 1969-74, professor of English, 1974—. *Member:* Shakespeare Association of America, Modern Language Association of America, South Atlantic Modern Language Association. *Awards, honors:* Huntington Library research fellowship, 1969; Folger Shakespeare Library research grants, 1970, 1972; National Endowment for the Humanities research grant, 1973-74; American Council of Learned Societies research fellowship, 1976-77.

WRITINGS: (Editor) *Tulane Studies in English,* Volume XX, 1972; *Shakespeare's Pagan World: The Roman Tragedies,* University Press of Virginia, 1973. Contributor to *Modern Language Quarterly, English Literary History, Renaissance Drama, Huntington Library Quarterly, Shakespeare Survey, Shakespeare Quarterly, Modern Language Review,* and *PMLA.*

WORK IN PROGRESS: A critical literary history of the revenge tragedy in the English Renaissance.

*   *   *

SIMONS, Howard, 1929-

PERSONAL: Born June 3, 1929, in Albany, N.Y.; son of Rubin (an insurance agent) and Mae (Chesler) Simons; married Florence Katz, 1956; children: Anna, Isabel, Julie, Rebecca. *Education:* Union College, Schenectady, N.Y., A.B., 1951; Columbia University, M.S., 1952; further study, Georgetown University, 1954-56. *Home:* 906 North Overlook Dr., Alexandria, Va. 22305. *Office: Washington Post,* 1150 15th St. N.W., Washington, D.C. 20071.

CAREER: Science Service, Washington, D.C., reporter, 1954-56, editor, 1956-59; *Washington Post,* Washington, D.C., science reporter, 1961-66, assistant managing editor, 1966-70, deputy managing editor, 1970-71, managing editor, 1971—. Spencer professor at Syracuse University, 1975. *Military service:* U.S. Army, Intelligence, 1952-54. *Member:* Council on Foreign Relations, American Society of Newspaper Editors, White House Correspondents Association. *Awards, honors:* Nieman fellow at Harvard University, 1958-59; Westinghouse awards from American Association for the Advancement of Science, 1962, 1964, both for science writing; Aviation/Space Writers award, 1964; Raymond Clapper Award, 1966; L.H.D., Union College, 1973; alumni award from Columbia University Graduate School of Journalism, 1974.

WRITINGS: (With Joseph A. Califano, Jr.) *The Media and the Law,* Praeger, 1976; *Simons' List Book,* Simon & Schuster, 1977. American columnist for *New Scientist* (London), 1963-67.

*   *   *

SIMONS, Robin 1951-

PERSONAL: Born July 1, 1951, in New York, N.Y.; daughter of Harry (an automotive parts dealer) and Sylvia (a dress buyer; maiden name, Gluck) Simons. *Education:* Attended University of Paris, 1970-71; Brandeis University, B.A., 1972; Lesley College, Master of Elem. Ed., 1976. *Home:* 428½ East San Miguel, Colorado Springs, Colo. 80903.

CAREER: Children's Museum, Boston, Mass., developer of Recycle Center, 1972-75; Colorado Springs School, Colorado Springs, Colo., fifth and sixth grade teacher, 1976—. Instructor at Greater Boston Teachers Center, 1972-75.

WRITINGS: Recycle Notes (pamphlet), privately printed, 1972, 4th edition, 1975; *Recyclopedia: Games, Science Equipment, and Crafts from Recycled Materials,* Houghton, 1976.

SIDELIGHTS: Simons writes: "Recycle, at the Boston Children's Museum, collects industrial scrap materials which form exciting and versatile raw materials for education. I worked with the materials we collected to develop curriculum materials for schools, day care centers and other children's programs. I devised math and language games, science equipment, social studies activities, and arts and crafts activities.

"In addition to working with the materials, I ran weekly workshops for the public and contract workshops for Boston-area public schools on possible uses for the materials. I worked closely with one of the Boston public schools under a federal grant, to develop a science curriculum using only recycled materials.

We have limited our vision of what is beautiful, useful or artistic to a very narrow range of items. I would like to help people expand that vision, to help them see new uses for old materials and new beauty and interest in familiar things."

AVOCATIONAL INTERESTS: Painting, drawing, crafts.

*   *   *

SIMPSON, Claude M(itchell), Jr. 1910-1976

July 29, 1910—April 6, 1976; American literary scholar, educator, college administrator, and editor. Obituaries: *Washington Post,* April 9, 1976. (See index for previous *CA* sketch)

*   *   *

SIMS, Mary Sophia Stephens 1886-1976

1885—May 22, 1976; American association administrator, sociologist, historian, and author. Obituaries: *New York Times,* May 25, 1976.

*   *   *

SINGER, Amanda
    See BROOKS, Janice Young

*   *   *

SINGER, Julia 1917-

PERSONAL: Born January 20, 1917, in New York; daughter of Samuel and Eleanor (Hamerschlag) Milch; married Simon H. Singer (a producer of audio-visual materials), July 10, 1946; children: Andrew M., Jul R. (Mrs. James Loche). *Education:* Attended New York School of Fine and Applied Art (now Parsons School of Design), 1933-35, and Yale University, 1935-36. *Politics:* "Not really a political thinker." *Religion:* Jewish. *Home:* 45 Phillies Bridge Rd., New Paltz, N.Y. 12561. *Office:* Julia Singer Associates, 315 West 57th St., New York, N.Y. 10019.

CAREER: Worked as production assistant and assistant in editing films to Paul Strand, Leo Hurwitz, Luis Bunnel, and Robert Flaherty, 1938-50; and United Nations, New York, N.Y., film editor in department of public information; member of staff of UNESCO in Patzcuaro, Mexico, 1951-53; free-lance film editor for motion pictures and editors, 1954-59; Julia Singer Associates (producers of audio-visual materials), New York, N.Y., founder and president, 1959—.

WRITINGS—For children: We All Come from Some Place: Children of Puerto Rico, Atheneum, 1976; *We Too Come from Puerto Rico,* Atheneum, in press.

Illustrator (with photographs): Henrietta Yurchenco, *Hablemos* (title means "We Speak"), Praeger, 1970. Contributor to UNESCO publications.

WORK IN PROGRESS: Books on East Germany and on Israel for children.

SIDELIGHTS: Julia Singer writes: "In most of my years of work whether in film or in photography my deepest concern has been people.... While working on *Hablemos* as the photographer I found myself at variance with the author in terms of what I saw and heard and responded to. I decided I wanted to do my own book on Puerto Rico. What I wanted to do was to find that common ground that children in one country could relate to in the lives of children living in a different cultural atmosphere.... My feeling being that children can find that common ground of acceptance and overcome the sickness of prejudice that most of us suffer from. Since we all do come from someplace this is just one little step."

* * *

SINGER, Marilyn 1948-

PERSONAL: Born October 3, 1948, in Bronx, N.Y.; daughter of Abraham (a photoengraver) and Shirley (Lax) Singer; married Steven Aronson (an association director), July 31, 1971. *Education:* Queens College of the City University of New York, B.A. (cum laude), 1969; New York University, M.A., 1972; also attended University of Reading, 1967-68. *Home and office:* 50 Berkeley Pl., Brooklyn, N.Y. 11217.

CAREER: Daniel S. Mead Literary Agency, New York, N.Y., editor, 1967; *Where* (magazine), New York City, assistant editor, 1969; teacher of English and speech in New York City, 1969-74; writer, 1974—. *Member:* Society of Children's Book Writers, American Civil Liberties Union, Audubon Society, Phi Beta Kappa.

WRITINGS: The Dog Who Insisted He Wasn't (juvenile), Dutton, 1976; (editor) *A History of Avant-Garde Cinema,* American Federation of Arts, 1976; (editor and contributor) *New American Filmmakers,* American Federation of Arts, 1976; *No Applause, Please* (juvenile), Dutton, in press. Author of scripts for the television series "The Electric Co." and of teaching guides. Contributor of poems to magazines, including *Yes, Encore, Corduroy, Tamesis,* and *Gyre.*

WORK IN PROGRESS: The Pickle Plan, juvenile, for Dutton; *It Can't Hurt Forever,* a novel; *The Fido Frame-Up,* a novel; a fantasy novel; writing the introduction to *Sources of Films on Art* for American Federation of Arts.

SIDELIGHTS: Marilyn Singer writes: "I write children's books because I want to write children's books. I do not write them in preparation for writing adult novels, nor because they are 'easier' to write. I write them because, corny as it sounds, 'the child is father to the man,' or, in my case, 'mother to the woman'.... I draw on a wealth of past and present events and fantasies and people I've known in New York—particularly Long Island where I grew up—, England, where I spent a year and many summers, and around the United States where I've travelled."

AVOCATIONAL INTERESTS: Avant-garde and independent film, bird watching and caring for animals, tap dancing, playing the piano, singing and playing the auto-harp.

* * *

SINGER, Samuel L(oewenberg) 1911-

PERSONAL: Born May 2, 1911, in Philadelphia, Pa.; son of Benjamin L. (a physician) and Hattie May (a piano teacher; maiden name, Loewenberg) Singer; married Betty Janet Levi, June 12, 1939; children: Ruth Babette, Samuel Lawrence, Robert Bookhammer. *Education:* Temple University, B.S.C., 1934. *Politics:* Independent Democrat. *Home:* 1431 Greywall Lane, Overbrook Hills, Philadelphia, Pa. 19151. *Office: Philadelphia Inquirer,* Philadelphia, Pa. 19101.

CAREER: Philadelphia Inquirer, Philadelphia, Pa., assistant arts editor, 1934-55, general assignment writer, 1948-51, music editor, 1955—, public service editor, 1973—, radio editor, 1973—; Temple University, Philadelphia, Pa., lecturer, 1946-71, adjunct professor of journalism, 1971—. Church organist, 1956—, conductor of "This Week's Music" on WDAS-FM, 1969-71, and on WUHY-Radio, 1971-73. *Military service:* U.S. Naval Reserve, chaplain's assistant, active duty, 1943-45.

MEMBER: Music Critics Association, American Guild of Organists, American Newspaper Guild, Philadelphia Press Association, Musical Fund Society of Philadelphia (director, 1970—), Pen and Pencil Club of Philadelphia, Sigma Delta Chi (life member).

WRITINGS: Reviewing the Performing Arts, Richards Rosen, 1974. Editor of *Crescendo,* 1970-76.

* * *

SINGH, Avtar 1929-

PERSONAL: Born January 9, 1929, in Patiala, India; son of Chanan (a government official) and Bishan (Kaur) Singh; married Harjeet Kaur, April 13, 1956; children: Gobind S. (son), Harsharan Kaur (daughter). *Education:* Delhi University, M.A., 1949; Punjab University, M.A. (economics), 1950, M.A. (sociology), 1962; Mississippi State University, Ph.D., 1967. *Religion:* Sikhism. *Residence:* Greenville, N.C. *Office:* Department of Sociology and Anthropology, East Carolina University, Greenville, N.C. 27834.

CAREER: Government of Punjab, Patiala, India, development officer, 1953-60; Mississippi State University, State College, assistant professor of sociology, 1967-70; East Carolina University, Greenville, N.C., associate professor, 1970-75, professor of sociology, 1975—. President of East West Fellowship. *Member:* Society for International Development, American Academy of Arts and Sciences, American Sociological Association, Rural Sociological Society (session chairman, 1974), Southern Sociological Society, North Carolina Sociological Association, Alpha Kappa Delta.

WRITINGS: Behavioral Approach to Agricultural Development, Social Science Research Center, Mississippi State University, 1965; *Town and Country Community,* Rutgers University, 1971; *Leadership Patterns and Village Structure,* Sterling, 1973; *Villages Upward Bound,* Editions Indian, 1976. Contributor to sociology and Indian studies journals.

WORK IN PROGRESS: Community Development: Continuity and Change in India, completion expected in 1978; *Karl Marx: The Prophet of Change.*

SIDELIGHTS: Singh writes: "My inspirations stem from the increasing trend toward decaying moral sense and spiritual values as observed during my travels in various parts of the world. The loss of traditional community through progressive industrialization is to me at the root of most personal and social problems of our times. Human progress and industrial or technological advances need not be coterminus;

and because of indiscriminate emphasis on 'Production Ethics' with little or no regard to 'personal-moral and consumption ethics' we, the masses, are helplessly drifting toward an unprecedented social and moral catastrophe and therefore alienation from the very life process distinctive to human beings.''

* * *

SISSMAN, L(ouis) E(dward)   1928-1976

January 1, 1928—March 10, 1976; American poet, columnist, and advertising copywriter. Obituaries: *New York Times,* March 11, 1976; *Time,* March 22, 1976; *Newsweek,* March 22, 1976; *Publishers Weekly,* March 29, 1976; *AB Bookman's Weekly,* May 17, 1976. (See index for previous *CA* sketch)

* * *

SIVE, Mary Robinson   1928-

PERSONAL: Born August 9, 1928, in Berlin, Germany; came to the United States in 1941, naturalized citizen, 1947; daughter of Morris (an editor) and Regina (a musician; maiden name, Hammer) Robinson; married David Sive (an attorney), July 23, 1948; children: Rebecca Anne Sive-Tomashefsky, Helen R., Alfred D., Walter D., Theodore P. *Education:* Connecticut College, B.A., 1948; Rutgers University, M.L.S., 1962. *Home:* 89 Lark St., Pearl River, N.Y. 10965.

CAREER: Brooklyn Public Library, Brooklyn, N.Y., assistant cataloger, 1948-50; librarian in elementary schools in New York City, N.Y., 1963-64, and Blauvelt, N.Y., 1965-69; Pearl River Public Library, Pearl River, N.Y., reference librarian, 1970-72; Environment Information Center, New York, N.Y., director of education and library department, 1973. *Member:* Sierra Club, Adirondack Mountain Club (chapter vice-president), Catskill Center for Conservation and Development (director).

WRITINGS: Educators Guide to Media Lists, Libraries Unlimited, 1975; *Environmental Legislation: A Sourcebook,* Praeger, 1976. Columnist, "Thriftips," *Media and Methods,* 1976—. Contributor of articles and reviews to library and educational magazines, including *Girl Scout Leader* and *Children's House.*

* * *

SIWEK, Manuel   1908-1976

June 23, 1908—February 21, 1976; American publisher. Obituaries: *New York Times,* February 23, 1976.

* * *

SJOEBERG, Leif   1925-

PERSONAL: Born December 15, 1925, in Boden, Sweden; son of Ernst Albert (a section master) and Maria Elisabeth (Falk) Sjoeberg; married Inger M. Wallervik (a secretary), January 31, 1959. *Education:* University of Uppsala, B.A., 1952, M.A., 1954, Ph.D., 1968. *Home:* 15 Claremont Ave., New York, N.Y. 10027. *Agent:* Curtis Brown Ltd., 60 East 56th St., New York, N.Y. 10022. *Office:* Department of German and Slavics, State University of New York, Stony Brook, N.Y. 11790.

CAREER: King's College, University of Newcastle, Newcastle-upon-Tyne, England, lecturer in Swedish, 1956-58; Columbia University, New York, N.Y., lecturer in Scandinavian languages and literature, 1958-69; State University of New York at Stony Brook, associate professor, 1968-72, professor of Scandinavian studies and comparative literature, 1972—. Trustee, Scandinavian Seminar in New York City, 1968—; governor, American Swedish Historical Museum, 1971-74; representative, The Emigrant Museum (Vaexjoe, Sweden), 1972—. *Military service:* Swedish Army, 1947-48, 1951.

MEMBER: Society for the Advancement of Scandinavian Study (member of publications committee, 1965—), American Association of University Professors, American-Scandinavian Foundation, American-Swedish Historical Foundation, Ibsen-foerbundet, Svenska Foerfattarfoerbundet, Islaendska Saellskapet. *Awards, honors:* Translation award from Swedish Academy, 1966, for *Selected Poems of Gunnar Ekeloef;* knighted, Royal Order of Vasa, 1972; National Book Award nomination, 1973, for translation *Windows and Stones.*

WRITINGS: A Reader's Guide to Gunnar Ekeloef's "A Mollna Elegy," Twayne, 1973; *Par Lagerkvist,* Columbia University Press, 1976.

Translator: Halldor Laxness, *The Flute Player* (stories), Raben & Sjoegren (Stockholm), 1955; (with W. H. Auden) Dag Hammarskjold, *Markings,* Knopf, 1964; (with Muriel Rukeyser, and author of introduction) *Selected Poems by Gunnar Ekeloef,* Twayne, 1967; (with May Swenson, and author of introduction) Tomas Transtroemer, *Windows and Stones,* Pittsburgh University Press, 1972; (with Auden) Par Lagkervist, *Evening Land,* Wayne State University Press, 1975.

Contributor of translations: *New Directions 21,* New Directions Press, 1969; (and author of foreword with W. H. Auden) *Penguin Modern European Poets,* edited by A. Alvarez, Penguin, 1971, Pantheon, 1972; *From Script to Stage: Eight Modern Plays,* edited by Randolph Goodman, Rinehart, 1971; *Focus on "The Seventh Seal,"* edited by Brigitta Steene, Prentice-Hall, 1972; *For W. H. Auden,* edited by Peter Salus, Random House, 1972. Contributor of articles, reviews and translations to *Malahat Review, Times Literary Supplement, Chelsea, New Statesman, Nimrod, Books Abroad,* and other American and European publications. Editor, Scandinavian Section, Twayne World Authors Series, 1965—; contributing editor and member of advisory board, *Studies in the Twentieth Century,* 1968-70.

WORK IN PROGRESS: Revising published essays for book; translating with William Jay Smith, Artur Lundkvist's *Agadir;* a catalogue for Charles Biederman's Retrospective, for Minneapolis Art Institute.

* * *

SJOEWALL, Maj   1935-

PERSONAL: Born September 25, 1935, in Stockholm, Sweden; daughter of Will and Margit (Trobaeck) Sjoewall; married Per Wahloo (a writer), 1962 (died June 22, 1975); children: Lena, Tetz, Jens. *Education:* Attended journalism and graphic schools in Stockholm. *Home:* Foreningsgat 53, 21152 Malmoe, Sweden.

CAREER: Worked for several newspapers and magazines in Sweden; full-time novelist, 1961—. *Awards, honors:* Sherlock award from Swedish newspaper *Expressen,* 1968, Edgar Allen Poe Award for best mystery novel from Mystery Writers of America, 1971, and Gran Giallo Citta di Cattolica, 1973, all for *The Laughing Policeman.*

WRITINGS—Martin-Beck detective series; all with husband, Per Wahloo; all published by Norstedt in Stockholm, except as noted: *Roseanna,* 1965, translation by Lois Roth published under same title, Pantheon, 1967; *Mannen som gick upp i roek,* 1966, translation by Joan Tate published as *The Man Who Went Up in Smoke,* Pantheon, 1969; *Mannen paa balkongen,* 1967, translation by Alan Blair published as *The Man on the Balcony,* Pantheon, 1968; *Den skrattande polisen,* 1968, translation by Alan Blair published as *The Laughing Policeman,* Pantheon, 1970; *Brandbilen som foersvann,* 1969, translation by Joan Tate published as *The Fire Engine that Disappeared,* Pantheon, 1970; *Polis, polis, potatismos!,* 1970, translation by Amy Knoespel and Ken Knoespel published as *Murder at the Savoy,* Pantheon, 1971; *Den vedervaerdige mannen fraan Saeffle,* 1971, translation by Thomas Teal published as *The Abominable Man,* Pantheon, 1972; *Det slutna rummet,* 1972, translation by Paul Britten Austin published as *The Locked Room,* Pantheon, 1973; *Polismoerdaren,* 1974, translation by Thomas Teal published as *The Cop Killer,* Pantheon, 1975; *Terroristerna,* 1975, translation by Joan Tate published as *The Terrorists,* Pantheon, 1976.

SIDELIGHTS: Haskel Frankel said of Maj Sjoewall and her late husband and co-author Per Wahloo: "The Wahloos are among the best—perhaps they are the best—writers of detective fiction today." Writing late at night after their children were asleep, the Wahloos created the "Martin Beck" detective series. Ten novels—or more precisely, ten parts of a single novel 300 chapters long—that were meant to describe the changing social, political, and economic background of Sweden as well as the changing personality of their main character over a ten year period. One book was written a year and the details were painstakingly accurate. "If you read of Martin Beck taking off on a certain flight," Maj Sjoewall said, "there was that flight, at that time, with those same weather conditions." Complimenting their success, a reviewer for *Book World* said: "The events [of the plot] . . . have a hard time competing with the absorbing details of their setting, and particularly with the delightful personality of their hero." The tenth and final book was completed just before her husband's death in 1975.

BIOGRAPHICAL/CRITICAL SOURCES: Book World, August 17, 1969; *Saturday Review,* February 27, 1971; *New York Times,* May 5, 1971, June 24, 1975.

*   *   *

SJOWALL, Maj
See SJOEWALL, Maj

*   *   *

SKLAR, Dusty   1928-

PERSONAL: Born March 11, 1928, in Poland; came to the United States in 1930, naturalized citizen, 1952; daughter of Max (a leather worker) and Lena (Charap) Kwalbrun; married David Sklar (a real estate executive), November 27, 1949; children: Steven, Lisa, Joseph. *Politics:* "Having read Machiavelli, I don't take politics seriously." *Religion:* "I believe that the universe is governed by natural laws, but dread organized religion." *Home:* 1043 Wilson Ave., Teaneck, N.J. 07666.

CAREER: Writer. *Member:* American Society of Journalists and Authors, Women in Communications, American Medical Writers Association, Society for Psychical Research.

WRITINGS: Gods and Beasts: The Nazis and Occultism, Crowell, 1977. Contributor of stories, articles, and reviews to magazines, including *Nation* and *Virginia Quarterly Review,* and to *New York Times.*

WORK IN PROGRESS: The Occult and Its Critics; The Fear of Being; The Decline of Productivity; The Welfare State Revisited; a biography of Henry George; a musical comedy on Madame Blavatsky.

SIDELIGHTS: Sklar told *CA:* "My personal and literary sympathies lie with Henry George, Tolstoy, Chekhov, Thoreau, and black humorists."

*   *   *

SKOGLUND, Goesta   1904-

PERSONAL: Born December 26, 1904, in Gothenburg, Sweden; son of Gustav (an engineer) and Emma (Andreasdotter) Skoglund; married Ella Karola Lenander, August 13, 1933; children: Kaj, Olle. *Education:* Attended Teacher Training School, Gothenburg, Sweden, 1928-32. *Home address:* Box 21013, 400 71 Gothenburg 21, Sweden.

CAREER: Sydsvenska Kredit A/B, Gothenburg, Sweden, bank clerk, 1920-25; Pellerins Margarin Factory, Gothenburg, clerk, 1925-28; free-lance journalist, 1931—. Teacher in elementary school in Gothenburg, 1932-67. *Awards, honors:* Swedish Editors Foundation fellowship, 1975; cultural activities award from town of Gothenburg, 1976.

WRITINGS: Fotolaerbok i bild (title means "How to Learn Photography by Photographs"), Nordisk Rotogravyr (Stockholm), 1952, 9th edition, Norstedt & Soener, 1975; *Colour in Your Camera: A Book of Colour Photographs to Show How to Make Colour Photographs,* Ziff Davis, 1960, 6th edition, American Photographic Book Publishing Co., 1975; *Radions fotokurs* (title means "Swedish Broadcasting Course in Photography"), [Stockholm], 1963; (translator) Harald Manthe, *Bildaufbau* (title means "Composition"), Norstedt & Soener, 1973. Also author of *Med lampa och blixt* (title means "By Flash and Bulb"), with Folke Soervik, 1955.

Writer of pamphlets for Hasselblad. Contributor to Swedish newspapers, *Goeteborgs-Posten* and *Goeteborgs-Tidningen,* and to *Foto* (photographic monthly).

SIDELIGHTS: Skoglund writes: "Beside my main work as a teacher at Gothenburg, Sweden, I started working in 1931 as a free-lance journalist and press photographer for a Gothenburg daily newspaper. There one day I began to write a series of articles on photography, illustrated by my own pictures, which were often taken as a comparison between this and that. Many of these pictures were transformed into slides, which we used as illustrations for photo courses arranged later on by the same newspaper. In the end I had more than six hundred slides for photographic instruction. The editor of *Foto,* the well-known photographic monthly in Stockholm, had a look at them, ordered a series on photography and wanted a book in black and white with about six hundred pictures, which was to have 'plenty of pictures and short explanations in the text.' This has always been my main idea when dealing with photography.

"I suppose my experiences as a press photographer, when I had to collect facts within the frame of the negatives, and what I had learned as a lecturer to grown up people and as a teacher of young people—that explanations can never be *too* simple—has helped me to write these books, which have sold edition after edition. An isolated case was a textbook for a broadcast series some years ago which sold 11,000 copies."

AVOCATIONAL INTERESTS: Travel (England, Scotland and northeast Atlantic isles).

SKRADE, Carl 1935-

PERSONAL: Born August 11, 1935, in Seneca, Wis.; son of Edwin P. (a carpenter) and Edith N. (Bonney) Skrade; married Carol J. Anderson (a Montessori teacher), June 4, 1960; children: Peter, Kristofer. *Education:* Lutheran College, Decorah, Iowa, B.A., 1957; Luther Theological Seminary, St. Paul, Minn., B.D., 1962; Union Theological Seminary, Th.M., 1963, Th.D., 1966. *Politics:* Independent. *Religion:* Lutheran. *Home:* 845 Pleasant Ridge, Columbus, Ohio 43209. *Office:* Department of Religion, Capital University, 2199 East Main St., Columbus, Ohio 43209.

CAREER: Capital University, Columbus, Ohio, assistant professor, 1968-72, associate professor of religion, 1972—.

WRITINGS: (With John C. Cooper) *Celluloid and Symbols*, Fortress, 1970; *God and the Grotesque*, Westminster, 1974. Contributor to journals.

WORK IN PROGRESS: The Meaning of Freedom; research on contemporary Scandinavian fiction and on "left-wing Freudianism."

SIDELIGHTS: Skrade writes: "The meaning of individualism, the relation of individual and group and the role of creativity in the health of the individual—these are driving motivational issues for me."

*   *   *

SLAPPEY, Sterling G(reene) 1917-

PERSONAL: Born June 18, 1917, in Fort Valley, Ga.; son of Jenkins Sterling and Elma Louise (Greene) Slappey; married Margaret Byne Sellers, January 13, 1945; children: Margaret Sterling, Charles Freeman. *Education:* Attended Alabama Polytechnic Institute (now Auburn University), 1937-38, and University of Georgia, 1938-39. *Politics:* "Ex-Liberal." *Religion:* "If anything, Protestant." *Home:* 121 Cameron Mews, Alexandria, Va. 22314. *Office: Nation's Business,* 1615 H St. N.W., Washington, D.C. 20006.

CAREER: Atlanta Georgian & Sunday American, Atlanta, Ga., general assignments reporter, 1938-40; National Youth Administration, Atlanta, director of field work, 1940; *Atlanta Constitution,* Atlanta, police reporter, 1940-41, general assignments reporter, 1945-46; Delta Air Lines, Atlanta, publicity representative, 1946; Associated Press, journalist in the United States, London, and Moscow, 1947-59; U.S. Golf Association, New York, N.Y., assistant executive director, 1959-60; *U.S. News & World Report,* Washington, D.C., reporter and photographer, 1960-63; *Los Angeles Times,* Los Angeles, Calif., central European bureau chief in Bonn, West Germany, 1963-65; journalist in Los Angeles, 1965-66; *Nation's Business,* Washington, D.C., associate editor, 1966-70, senior editor, 1970—. Has broadcast for Voice of America; secretary, part-owner, and member of board of directors of Iberian Imports Inc. *Military service:* U.S. Army, master gunner, 1941-45; served in Australia and New Guinea; became sergeant major; received several battle stars.

MEMBER: American Academy of Political Science, American Academy of Social and Political Science, National Trust for Historic Preservation, Overseas Writers Club, Overseas Press Club, Smithsonian Association, Association for the Preservation of Virginia Antiquities, Washington Independent Writers, Alexandria Assembly, Friends of Kennedy Center, Phi Delta Theta, International Club (Washington, D.C.).

WRITINGS: Exodus of the Damned (novel), New American Library, 1968; *Pioneers of American Business,* Gros-

set, 1973. Author of a business and financial column in *Washingtonian,* 1970-73. Contributor to magazines and newspapers, including *Smithsonian, Family Circle, Finance, Southwest Literary Review, Maclean's, Harvard Business Review,* and *Travel.* Consulting editor of *Jordan* magazine, 1975—.

WORK IN PROGRESS: Various magazine articles.

SIDELIGHTS: Slappey writes: "I've been writing for nearly forty years and so motivation is rather dimmed. Money and the requirement to earn a living are major motivations." His journalistic career has taken him nearly everywhere in the world; he has covered the death of Franklin D. Roosevelt, the coronation of Queen Elizabeth II, the launching of the "space age" in Moscow, rioting at the University of Mississippi, travels with Presidents Nixon and Kennedy and with Nikita Khrushchev in Europe, the Cyprus wars between Greeks and Turks, the assassination of Dominican dictator Trujillo, and other assignments in South America, the Middle East, and Europe.

*   *   *

SLATER, Charlotte (Wolpers) 1944-

PERSONAL: Born July 21, 1944, in Yakima, Wash.; daughter of Henry M. (a newspaper publisher) and Marianna (Knecht) Wolpers; married Robert M. Slater, August 21, 1965 (divorced, June, 1975). *Education:* University of Missouri, B.J., 1966. *Politics:* None. *Religion:* Protestant. *Agent:* Universal Press Syndicate, 6700 Squibb Rd., Mission, Kan. 66202. *Office: Detroit News,* 615 Lafayette, Detroit, Mich. 48231.

CAREER: Columbia Daily Tribune, Columbia, Mo., general assignment reporter, 1966-67; *Detroit News,* Detroit, Mich., general assignment feature writer, 1967—. *Member:* Detroit Press Club, Theta Sigma Phi.

WRITINGS: Things Your Mother Never Taught You, two volumes, Sheed, 1974; *All the Things Your Mother Never Taught You,* Sheed, 1975; *Things Your Mother Never Taught You About Car Care and Repair,* Sheed, 1975.

SIDELIGHTS: Charlotte Slater writes: "These books all deal with general repairs. . . . All grew out of syndicated columns I have done for the *Detroit News* and Universal Press Syndicate."

*   *   *

SLAYMAKER, R(edsecker) Samuel II 1923-

PERSONAL: Born January 1, 1923, in Lancaster, Pa.; son of Samuel C. and Martha (Fletcher) Slaymaker; married Elizabeth D. Schroeder, July 12, 1947 (divorced); married Sarah Hazzard, October 25, 1959; children: (first marriage) Elizabeth D., Caroline M. H.; (second marriage) Susan F., Samuel C. III. *Education:* Corpus Christi College, Cambridge, B.A., 1947. *Politics:* Republican. *Religion:* Presbyterian. *Home address:* White Chimneys, R.D. 1, Gap, Pa. 17527.

CAREER: Slaymaker Lock Co., Lancaster, Pa., executive vice-president and secretary, 1947—. *Military service:* U.S. Army Air Forces, 1943-44; served in England; received Air Medal with four oak leaf clusters. *Member:* Americans for Competitive Enterprises System (past member of board of directors), American Hardware Manufacturers Association, Society of the War of 1812, Pennsylvania Society of Sons of the Revolution, Pennsylvania Society of Colonial Wars, Maryland Society of the Sons of Cincinnati, Donegal Society, Lancaster Sales Executives Club (past member of board of directors), Lancaster County Manufacturers Association (past president), Lancaster County Historical Society, Union League Club. *Awards, honors:* Conservation award from Harrisburg Anglers Club.

WRITINGS: Simplified Fly Fishing, Harper, 1969; *Captives' Mansion* (family history; foreword by Sir Denis Brogan), Harper, 1973. Contributor to sport magazines, local history journals, and popular magazines, including *Esquire.*

AVOCATIONAL INTERESTS: Historical research, fly fishing, fly tying.

BIOGRAPHICAL/CRITICAL SOURCES: Book World, August 3, 1969.

* * *

SLAYTON, Mariette (Elizabeth) Paine 1908-

PERSONAL: Born May 31, 1908, in Danielson, Conn.; daughter of James Monroe (an educator) and Agnes Caroline (a teacher; maiden name, Haliday) Paine; married Ronald Alfred Slayton (an artist and teacher), April 15, 1961; children: (stepchildren) Thomas Kennedy, Peter Whitney, Helen Gail. *Education:* Student at Connecticut College for Women, 1925-26, Grand Central Art School, 1928-29, and Art Students League, 1928-29; also studied art privately. *Politics:* Independent. *Religion:* Christian Scientist. *Home address:* R.F.D. 2, Montpelier, Vt. 05602.

CAREER: Free-lance commercial artist in Danielson, Conn., 1935-60; teacher of private classes in American decorative arts, 1935-60; teacher at Fletcher Farm Crafts School, 1954-69, University of Connecticut, 1955-56, and Thousand Island Museum Crafts School, 1966-67. Has had one-woman shows in Vermont. Treasurer of Dog River Arts School, 1969-72; member of Montpelier Theatre Guild, 1971—; member of board of directors of Bugbee Memorial Library.

MEMBER: Historical Society of Early American Decoration, Montpelier League of Women Voters (vice-president, 1966-68). *Awards, honors:* Certificate of appreciation from New England Crafts Fair, 1967; Decorative Arts Book Award from American Life Foundation, 1972, for *Early American Decorating Techniques.*

WRITINGS: Early American Decorating Techniques, Macmillan, 1972.

SIDELIGHTS: Mariette Slayton writes: "I first studied Early American decoration as a hobby, but after a few years of recording historic designs from trays, furniture, glass, etc. it became a means of livelihood for a number of years. The hundreds of recorded designs are, I hope, a contribution to art history, but the greatest pleasure is in sharing these with others through teaching the craft in special classes over the country and in my studio at home. . . . Although these techniques have not been used extensively by painters and creative craftsmen of this period, the potential is there and may eventually be adapted to produce contemporary decorative art."

* * *

SLOAN, Pat(rick Alan) 1908-

PERSONAL: Born May 19, 1908, in Newcastle upon Tyne, England; son of Robert Patrick (a company chairman) and Inda A. L. (Ellis) Sloan; married Margaret Cohen (a nurse), October 23, 1944; children: Duncan, Robert, Daniel, Alan. *Education:* Cambridge University, first class honors in economics tripos, 1929. *Politics:* Communist. *Home:* 1 Bucks Cross Cottages, Chelsfield Village, Orpinstom, Kent BR6

7RN, England. *Office:* 134 Ballards Lane, London N3 2PD, England.

CAREER: British Soviet Friendship (magazine), London, England, editorial director, beginning 1960, *Labour Monthly* (magazine), London, editor, 1976—. Lived and worked in Russia, 1931-36, and has visited there six times since.

WRITINGS: Soviet Democracy, Gollancz, 1937; *Russia Without Illusions,* Muller, 1938; (editor) *John Cornford: A Memoir,* J. Cape, 1938; *Russia in Peace and in War,* Pilot Press, 1941; *How the Soviet State is Run,* Lawrence & Wishart, 1941; *Marx and the Orthodox Economists,* Rowman & Littlefield, 1973. Contributor to periodicals, including *Quarterly Review, Contemporary Review, Humanist,* and *Comment,* and to Soviet periodicals.

SIDELIGHTS: Pat Sloan's books have been issued in India, Spain, and the U.S.

* * *

SLOAN, Ruth Catherine 1898(?)-1976

1898(?)—July 29, 1976; American civil servant, foundation administrator, publisher, and author of books on African affairs. Obituaries: *Washington Post,* July 31, 1976.

* * *

SLOANE, Eugene A(nthony) 1926-

PERSONAL: Born August 17, 1926, in New York, N.Y.; son of Benjamin A. and Margaret (Fitzsimmons) Sloane; married Emily Cowan (an attorney), May 15, 1948; children: Peter, Nicholas, Todd. *Education:* Roosevelt University, M.A., 1976. *Politics:* Democrat. *Religion:* Unitarian Universalist. *Home and office:* 1032 Ridge Court, Evanston, Ill. 60202.

CAREER: Air Engineering, Detroit, Mich., editor, 1959-64; Maremont Corp., Chicago, Ill., director of public relations, 1964-72; Midwest Stock Exchange, Chicago, Ill., director of public relations, 1969-72; full time freelance writer in Evanston, Ill., 1972—.

WRITINGS: The Complete Book of Bicycling, Simon & Schuster, 1971, revised edition published as *The New Complete Book of Bicycling,* 1974; *The Complete Book of Locks, Keys, Burglar Alarms and Guard Dogs,* Morrow, in press.

WORK IN PROGRESS: Research on crime, on psychotherapy, on motorcycles, on camping, on tennis, and on health.

SIDELIGHTS: Sloane told *CA:* "I see writing as an essentially lonely experience which can be devastating and depressing. One simply does not have access to reinforcing feedback and interrelationships one has with extended family situations in industry. Ego satisfaction and money are not enough to compensate, so the writer has to work doubly hard at creating meaningful relationships if his work is not to suffer."

* * *

SLOBIN, Dan Isaac 1939-

PERSONAL: Born May 7, 1939, in Detroit, Mich.; son of Norval L. (a high school teacher) and Judith (a teacher; maiden name, Liepah) Slobin; married Ellen Wyzanski Holmes, December 23, 1962 (divorced, 1969); married Kathleen Gail Overin (a painter), May 23, 1969 (divorced); children: (second marriage) Heida Quisno Gordon (stepdaughter), Shem Alexander. *Education:* University of Michigan, B.A. (honors), 1960; Harvard University, M.A., 1962,

Ph.D., 1964. *Home:* 2323 Rose St., Berkeley, Calif. 94708. *Office:* Department of Psychology, University of California, Berkeley, Calif. 94720.

CAREER: Language Research, Inc., Cambridge, Mass., psycholinguistic consultant, 1961-62; Educational Services, Inc., Watertown, Mass., psychologist, 1962; University of California, Berkeley, assistant professor, 1963-67, associate professor, 1967-72, professor of psychology, 1972—, assistant research psychologist at Institute of Human Learning, 1963-67, associate research psychologist, 1967-72, research psychologist, 1972—.

MEMBER: International Association for the Study of Child Language (vice-president), International Association for Cross-Cultural Psychology, American Association for the Advancement of Science (fellow), Linguistic Society of America, Society for Research in Child Development, American Psychological Association, Society for the Psychological Study of Social Issues. *Awards, honors:* U.S. Office of Education fellowship, 1966-67; grants from Ford Foundation, 1968-69, National Institute of Mental Health, 1969-76, Grant Foundation, 1972-75, and National Science Foundation.

WRITINGS: (Editor and contributor) *A Field Manual for Cross-Cultural Study of the Acquisition of Communicative Competence,* Associated Students of the University of California Bookstore, University of California, 1967; (editor and contributor) *The Ontogenesis of Grammar: A Theoretical Symposium,* Academic Press, 1971; *Psycholinguistics,* Scott, Foresman, 1971; *Leopold's Bibliography of Child Language: Revised and Augmented Edition,* University of Indiana Press, 1972; (editor with Josef Brozek) *Fifty Years of Soviet Psychology: An Historical Perspective,* International Arts and Sciences Press, 1972; (editor with Charles A. Ferguson, and contributor) *Studies of Child Language Development,* Holt, 1973.

Contributor: Neil O'Connor, editor, *Present-Day Russian Psychology: A Symposium by Seven Authors,* Pergamon, 1966; Giovanni B. Flores d'Arcais and Wilhelm J. M. Levelt, editors, *Advances in Psycholinguistics,* North-Holland Publishing, 1970; Celia B. Lavatelli, editor, *Language Training in Early Childhood Education,* University of Illinois Press, 1971; William O. Dingwall, editor, *A Survey of Linguistic Science,* Linguistics Program, University of Maryland, 1971; Peter C. Dodwell, editor, *New Horizons in Psychology II,* Penguin, 1972; Serge Moscovici, editor, *The Psychosociology of Language,* Markham, 1972; David Krech, Richard S. Crutchfield, and Norman Livson, editors, *Elements of Psychology,* Knopf, 3rd edition (Slobin was not associated with earlier editions), 1974; Helen Leuninger, Max H. Miller and Frank Mueller, editors, *Linguistik und Psychologie,* Volume II, Athenaeum, 1974; *Developmental Psychology Today,* Random House, 2nd edition (Slobin was not associated with 1st edition), 1975; Eric H. Lenneberg and Elizabeth Lenneberg, editors, *Foundations of Language Development: A Multi-Disciplinary Approach,* Academic Press, 1975; Norman Kass and T. D. Spencer, editors, *Perspectives in Child Psychology: Research and Reviews,* McGraw, in press; Charles Schaefer, editor, *The Therapeutic Use of Child's Play,* Jason Aronson, in press; T. G. Bever and William Weksel, editors, *The Structure and Psychology of Language,* Holt, in press; Vladimir Honsa and M. J. Hardman-de-Bautista, editors, *Papers on Linguistics and Child Language: Ruth Hirsch Memorial Volume,* Mouton & Co., in press; John Macnamara, editor, *Language Learning and Thought,* Academic Press, in press; Lois Bloom, editor, *Selected Readings in*

Language Development, Wiley, in press; Ross D. Parke and E. Mavis Heatherington, editors, *Child Psychology: Contemporary Readings,* McGraw, in press.

Contributor of articles and reviews to language and psychology journals. Founding editor of *Soviet Psychology,* 1962-69; member of editorial board of *Cognition, Journal of Child Language, International Journal of Psycholinguistics, International Review of Slavic Linguistics, Journal of Verbal Learning and Verbal Behavior,* "Language, Thought, and Culture," a series, for Academic Press, and "Amsterdam Studies in the Theory and History of Linguistic Science."

WORK IN PROGRESS: Research on cross-linguistic investigation of early language and cognitive development, with a monograph expected to result.

SIDELIGHTS: Slobin's books and articles have been widely translated. He writes: "My basic interest is in the growth of the human mind, specifically in the child's ability to reconstruct on his own the structure of his language and culture. This has involved me in widespread cross-cultural research on early language and cognitive development (United States, Soviet Union, Finland, Hungary, Yugoslavia, Italy, Germany, Turkey, Kenya, Samoa, Mexico, Peru). . . . I have also spent much time in interpreting Soviet psychological research for American audiences. . . . I addressed the International Congress of Psychology in Russian, in Moscow in 1966. . . . I have spent several years doing research in Turkey, at the same time becoming deeply involved in ethnomusicology (learning to play a Turkish stringed instrument, the saz) and Byzantine and Islamic art history. My current interests are in the representation of time and temporal experiences, and I am beginning a new phase of research on personal autobiographical memory."

*   *   *

SLONIM, Marc   1894-1976

March 26, 1894—May 8, 1976; Russian-born American literary critic, editor, educator, and author. Obituaries: *New York Times,* May 13, 1976.

*   *   *

SLONIMSKI, Antoni   1895-1976

November 15, 1895—July 5, 1976; Polish poet, columnist, translator, and association official. Obituaries: *New York Times,* July 6, 1976; *Washington Post,* July 6, 1976; *AB Bookman's Weekly.* July 26, 1976.

*   *   *

SLOSSER, Bob G(ene)   1929-

PERSONAL: Born March 23, 1929, in Frederick, Okla.; son of John (an engineer) and Faye (Berry) Slosser: married Gloria Fisher, September 3, 1950; children: Cheryl, Brent, Lesley, Sarah. *Education:* University of Maine, B.A., 1950. *Religion:* Christian (Episcopal). *Home address:* Box 251, Bernardsville Road, Mendham, N.J. 07945. *Office:* Logos International, 201 Church St., Plainfield, N.J. 07060.

CAREER: New York World-Telegram and Sun, New York City, editor, 1955-59; *Keene Sentinel,* Keene, N.H., managing editor, 1957; *New York Times,* New York City, editor, 1959-66; New England Telephone Co., Boston, Mass., public relations supervisor, 1966-71; *New York Times,* editor, 1971-75; writer, 1975—. Instructor in journalism, Columbia University, 1965-66, 1973. *Member:* Christian Broadcasting Network (member of board of directors).

WRITINGS: (Editor) *The Pope's Journey to the U.S.,* Bantam, 1965; (editor) *The Night the Lights Went Out,* New American Library, 1965; (with others) *The Road to the White House,* McGraw, 1965; (editor) *The Watergate Hearings,* Bantam, 1973; (with Howard Norton) *The Miracle of Jimmy Carter,* Logos, 1976; *A Man Called Mr. Pentecost* (autobiography of evangelist David du Plessis as told to Bob Slosser), Logos, 1977. Founding editor, *National Courier,* 1975.

WORK IN PROGRESS: The life story of Susan Atkins, member of the Manson Family, publication by Logos expected in late 1977.

SIDELIGHTS: "My main area of expertise recently," Slosser told *CA,* "has been Christianity and those subjects to which Christianity offers a definite perspective. For example, the Carter book was set off by a desire to explore, in the context of politics, this presidential candidate's much discussed faith. My current work centers on a man very important to the ecumenical movement. In fact, there is hardly any subject falling outside this scope."

*   *   *

SMIRNOV, Sergei Sergeevich   1915-1976

1915—March 24, 1976; Russian novelist. Obituaries: *New York Times,* March 25, 1976; *AB Bookman's Weekly,* July 5, 1976.

*   *   *

SMITH, A(lbert) J(ames)   1924-

PERSONAL: Born November 5, 1924, in Cardiff, Wales; son of William John (a butcher) and Anne Laura (Davies) Smith; married Gwyneth Margaret Lane (a teacher), April 10, 1950; children: Geraint Owain. *Education:* University College of Wales, Aberystwyth, B.A., 1950, first class honors in English, 1951, M.A., 1954; graduate study at Oriel College, Oxford, 1953-54, and University of Florence, 1955-56. *Home:* 74 Holly Hill, Bassett, Southampton, England. *Office:* Department of English, University of Southampton, Highfield, Southampton SO9 5NH, England.

CAREER: English master in grammar school in East Barnet, England, 1954-55, and in Manchester, England, 1956-59; University of Wales, University College of Swansea, lecturer, 1959-68, senior lecturer in English, 1968-71; University of Keele, Keele, England, professor of English, 1971-74, head of department, 1972-74; University of Southampton, Southampton, England, professor of English and head of department, 1974—. *Military service:* Royal Air Force Volunteer Reserve, member of air crew, 1943-47. *Awards, honors:* Leverhulme fellowships, 1955-56, 1967-68; fellowship from British Academy and English-Speaking Union, 1974.

WRITINGS: (With W. H. Mason) *Short Story Study,* Edward Arnold, 1961; *Shakespeare's Stories,* Edward Arnold, 1962; *John Donne: The Songs and Sonnets,* Edward Arnold, 1964; (editor) *John Donne: The Complete English Poems,* Penguin, 1971, St. Martin's, 1974; (editor) *John Donne: Essays in Celebration,* Barnes & Noble, 1972; (editor) *John Donne: The Critical Heritage,* Routledge & Kegan Paul, 1976.

WORK IN PROGRESS: Essays on Renaissance love poetry; an edition of Donne's "divine poems;" a study of wit in Renaissance poetry.

AVOCATIONAL INTERESTS: Theater, music, cricket, rugby.

SMITH, Frederick Winston Furneaux   1907-1975 (Lord Birkenhead)

PERSONAL: Born December 7, 1907, in England; son of Frederick Edwin (first Earl of Birkenhead) and Margaret Eleanor (Furneaux) Smith; married Sheila Berry (an author), 1935; children: one son, one daughter. *Education:* Christ Church, Oxford. *Residence:* Oxford, England.

CAREER: Parliamentary private secretary to British secretary of state for foreign affairs, 1938-39; Lord-in-Waiting to King George VI, 1938-49 and 1951-52, to Queen Elizabeth II, 1952-55. Biographer, 1930-75. *Military service:* British Army, 1939-45; became major. *Member:* Royal Society of Literature (former chairman), Beefsteak Club, Buck's Club, White's Club, Royal Yacht Squadron.

WRITINGS: Frederick Edwin, Earl of Birkenhead (biography of father), foreword by Winston Churchill, Butterworth, Volume I, 1933, Volume II, 1935, published in one volume as *F. E.: The Life of F. E. Smith, First Earl of Birkenhead,* Ryerson, 1959; *Strafford* (biography of Thomas Wentworth, Earl of Strafford), Hutchinson, 1938; (editor) *More Famous Trials,* Hutchinson, 1938; *Lady Eleanor Smith: A Memoir,* Hutchinson, 1953; (compiler) *John Betjeman's Collected Poems,* J. Murray, 1958; *The Prof in Two Worlds: The Official Life of Professor F. A. Lindemann, Viscount Cherwell,* Collins, 1961, published as *The Professor and the Prime Minister: The Official Life oe Professor F. A. Lindemann, Viscount Cherwell,* Houghton, 1962; *Halifax: The Life of Lord Halifax* (biography of Edward Frederick Lindley Wood, Earl of Halifax), Hamish Hamilton, 1965, Houghton, 1966; *Walter Monckton: The Life of Viscount Monckton of Brenchley,* Weidenfeld & Nicolson, 1969.

Also author of a biography of Rudyard Kipling, which was never published, and of two lectures on Kipling, published by Royal Society of Literature.

WORK IN PROGRESS: Biography of Winston Churchill.*

(Died June 11, 1975, in Oxford, England)

*   *   *

SMITH, Gerald L(yman) K(enneth)   1898-1976

February 27, 1898—April 15, 1976; American clergyman and editor. Obituaries: *Time,* April 26, 1976; *Newsweek,* April 26, 1976; *Current Biography,* June, 1976.

*   *   *

SMITH, H(arry) Allen   1907-1976

December 19, 1907—February 24, 1976; American humorist, author, newsman, and editor. Obituaries: *New York Times,* February 25, 1976; *Detroit Free Press,* February 25, 1976; *Washington Post,* February 26, 1976; *Time,* March 8, 1976; *Publishers Weekly,* March 22, 1976; *AB Bookman's Weekly,* April 12, 1976; *Current Biography,* May, 1976; (See index for previous *CA* sketch)

*   *   *

SMITH, Hedrick   1933-

PERSONAL: Born July 9, 1933, in Scotland; son of Sterling L. (in management) and Phebe (an artist; maiden name, Hedrick) Smith; married Ann Bickford (an educator), June 29, 1957; children: Laurie, Jenny, Scott, Lesley. *Education:* Williams College, B.A., 1955; graduate study at Balliol College, Oxford, 1955-56. *Home:* 29 Hazel Lane, Larchmont, N.Y. 10538. *Agent:* Julian Bach, Jr., 3 East 48th St., New

York, N.Y. 10022. *Office: New York Times,* 229 West 43rd St., New York, N.Y. 10036.

CAREER: United Press International, New York City, reporter in Tennessee, 1959-61, Georgia, 1961-62, and at Cape Canaveral, 1962; *New York Times,* New York City, journalist in Washington, D.C., 1962-63, Saigon, 1963-64, Cairo, 1964-66, diplomatic correspondent in Washington, D.C., 1966-71, bureau chief in Moscow, 1971-74, deputy national editor in New York City, 1975-76, bureau chief in Washington, D.C., 1976—. *Military service:* U.S. Air Force, 1956-59. *Awards, honors:* Fulbright scholarship, 1955-56; Nieman Fellow at Harvard University, 1969-70; Pulitzer Prize for International Reporting, 1974.

WRITINGS: (With Neil Sheehan, E. W. Kenworthy, and others) *The Pentagon Papers,* Quadrangle, 1971; (contributor) Eugene Fodor, *Fodor's Soviet Union, 1974-1975: A Definitive Handbook of the U.S.S.R. for Foreign Visitors,* McKay, 1974; *The Russians,* Quadrangle, 1976. Contributor to magazines, including *Atlantic, Saturday Review,* and *Reader's Digest.*

AVOCATIONAL INTERESTS: Foreign travel, skiing, sailing, tennis, wine.

* * *

SMITH, Hobart M(uir) 1912-

PERSONAL: Born September 26, 1912, in Stanwood, Iowa; son of Charles Henry (a postal clerk) and Frances (Muir) Smith; married Rozella Blood (a research associate), August 26, 1938; children: Bruce Dyfrig, Sally Frances (Mrs. Ronald J. Nadvornik). *Education:* Kansas State University, A.B., 1932; University of Kansas, M.A., 1933, Ph.D., 1936. *Home:* 1393 Northridge Court, Boulder, Colo. 80302. *Office:* Department of Environmental, Population, and Organismic Biology, University of Colorado, Boulder, Colo. 80309.

CAREER: University of Rochester, Rochester, N.Y., instructor in biology, 1941-45; University of Kansas, Lawrence, assistant professor of zoology, 1945-46; Texas A & M College, College Station, associate professor of wildlife management, 1946-47; University of Illinois, Urbana, assistant professor, 1947-51, associate professor, 1951-57, professor of zoology, 1957-68, curator of herpetology at Museum of Natural History, 1947-68; University of Colorado, Boulder, professor of environmental, population, and organismic biology, 1968—, chairman of department, 1971-74. *Member:* German Herpetological Society, British Herpetological Society, American Society of Ichthyologists and Herpetologists (vice-president, 1938), Society for Systematic Zoology (president, 1967), Herpetologists League (president 1946-58), Society for Study of Amphibians and Reptiles. *Awards, honors:* National Research Council fellow at University of Michigan, 1936-37; assistantship at Chicago Academy of Science, 1937-38, at Chicago Museum of Natural History, 1938; Bacon traveling scholar at Smithsonian Institution, 1938-41.

WRITINGS: Handbook of Lizards of the United States and Canada, Cornell University Press, 1946; (with Herbert S. Zim) *Reptiles and Amphibians Golden Nature Guide,* Simon & Schuster, 1953, revised edition, 1956; *Snakes as Pets,* All-Pets Books, 1953, 3rd edition, T.F.H. Publications, 1965; *Lectures in Comparative Anatomy,* Hutner and Wroughton, 1954; *Pet Turtles,* All-Pets Books, 1954, 2nd edition, 1955; *Evolution of Chordate Structure,* Stipes, 1957, revised edition, Holt, 1960; *Laboratory Studies of Chordate Structure,* Stipes, 1957, 7th edition, 1973; *A Golden Stamp*

Book: Snakes, Turtles, and Lizards (juvenile), Simon & Schuster, 1958; (with Floyd Boys) *Poisonous Amphibians and Reptiles: Recognition and Bite Treatment,* C. C Thomas, 1959; *Glossary of Terms for Comparative Anatomy,* Stipes, 1961; (with Edward H. Taylor) *Herpetology of Mexico,* Eric Lundberg, 1966; *Turtles in Color,* T.F.H. Publications, 1967; (with wife, Rozella B. Smith) *Early Foundations of Mexican Herpetology: An Annotated and Indexed Bibliography of the Herpetological Publications of Alfredo Duges, 1826-1910,* University of Illinois Press, 1969; (with Jonathan C. Oldham and Sue Ann Miller) *A Laboratory Perspectus of Snake Anatomy,* Stipes, 1970; (with R. B. Smith) *Synopsis of the Herpetofauna of Mexico,* Volume I: *Analysis of the Literature on the Mexican Axolotl,* Eric Lundberg, 1971, Volume II: *Analysis of the Literature Exclusive of the Mexican Axolotl,* Eric Lundberg, 1973, Volume III: *Source Analysis and Index for Mexican Reptiles,* J. J. Johnson, 1976, Volume IV: *Source Analysis and Index for Mexican Amphibians,* J. J. Johnson, in press. Contributor to more than seventy-five professional journals. Member of editorial board of American Society of Ichthyology and Herpetology, 1958—, and Society for Study of Amphibian Reptiles, 1968—; editor for Herpetological League, 1957.

WORK IN PROGRESS: Handbook of Amphibians and Reptiles of North America, completion expected in 1978; *Synopsis of the Herpetofauna of Mexico,* Volumes V-IX, 1977-1982.

* * *

SMITH, Jean DeMouthe 1949-

PERSONAL: Born December 8, 1949, in Morristown, N.J.; daughter of Francis Edwin (a cost analyst) and Jean Adele (Kavanaugh) DeMouthe; married Theodore Cabot Smith (a geologist), July 8, 1972. *Education:* De Anza Community College, A.A., 1969; Humboldt State University, B.A., 1972; graduate study at Bakersfield State College, 1972-73, San Jose State University, 1973-74, and San Francisco State University, 1975—. *Residence:* Montara, Calif. *Office:* Department of Geology, California Academy of Sciences, Golden Gate Park, San Francisco, Calif. 94118.

CAREER: California Academy of Sciences, San Francisco, curatorial assistant in geology, 1973—. Associate of Burkland & Associates (engineering geologists), 1973—; volunteer curator of California Division of Mines and Geology Mineral Museum.

MEMBER: International Wildlife Federation, Association of Engineering Geologists, Geological Society of America, American Genetics Association, American Mineralogical Society, Friends of Mineralogy, California Malacozoological Society (business manager), California Academy of Sciences, Northern California Geological Society.

WRITINGS: A Horseman's Guide to Horse Coloration and Markings, (self-illustrated) A. S. Barnes, 1976. Author of "Museum Notes," a column in *California Geology.*

WORK IN PROGRESS: A Horseman's Guide to Horse Coloration and Markings, 2nd edition; a book on parti-colored horses, such as Appaloosas and pintos; a work on feline coloration and genetics; research on the use of the natural history museum as an educational tool; research on color perception and on the occurrence of color and pattern in the natural world.

SIDELIGHTS: Jean Smith writes: "My intellectual interests include geology, botany, Elizabethan history, and genetics. I am a cartographer and scientific illustrator. . . . My pen and ink and pencil drawings hang in several galleries in California, My subjects are mostly California plants and animals." *Avocational interests:* Horseback riding, photography, art, keyboard music.

BIOGRAPHICAL/CRITICAL SOURCES: Pacific Petroleum Geologist Newsletter, autumn, 1974.

* * *

SMITH, Joseph B(urkholder) 1921-

PERSONAL: Born June 16, 1921, in Harrisburg, Pa.; son of Robert Craighead (a businessman) and Margaret (Burkholder) Smith; married Jeanne Hoffman, December 19, 1942; children: Ruthven Smith Slawsky, Julie Smith Lenk, Andrew Craighead Smith. *Education:* Harvard University, A.B. (cum laude), 1944; University of Pennsylvania, M.A., 1950. *Home:* 1301 South First St., Jacksonville Beach, Fla. 32250. *Agent:* Anita Diamant, Writers' Workshop, Inc., 51 East 42nd St., New York, N.Y. 10017.

CAREER: Dickinson College, Carlisle, Pa., assistant professor in history and political science, 1946-51; Central Intelligence Agency (CIA), Washington, D.C., covert propagandist and political action specialist, 1951-73; writer, 1973—. Associate, Robert Benjamin y Asociados, Mexico City, Mexico, 1973-76; public relations consultant, Anderson Clayton Sociedad Anonima, Mexico City. *Military service:* U.S. Army, Military Intelligence Service, 1943-46. *Member:* Harvard Club of Mexico, University Club of Mexico City.

WRITINGS: Portrait of a Cold Warrior: Second Thoughts of a Top CIA Agent, Putnam, 1976. Contributor to *Pennsylvania History, Korean Review,* and to *Exportacion* (Mexico).

WORK IN PROGRESS: February, 1983, a novel about CIA and KGB confrontation; research on the Nazi espionage mission which landed by submarine at Ponte Vedra, Fla., during World War II.

SIDELIGHTS: Smith writes: *"Portrait of a Cold Warrior* was written to show that CIA officers were frequently unable to sort out priorities but really not trying to undermine the liberties of their countrymen. I also wanted to explain why the cold war was real and not a figment of Harry Truman's imagination." He adds, "in general, I like to write about the ironic connections between people and events—the unrealized coincidences, the unrecognized parallels, the unforeseen, inevitable future consequences of present acts."

AVOCATIONAL INTERESTS: Tennis, "helping my wife collect sharks' teeth."

* * *

SMITH, Liz 1923-

PERSONAL: Birth-given name, Mary Elizabeth; born February 2, 1923, in Ft. Worth, Tex.; daughter of Sloan (a cotton broker) and Sarah Elizabeth (McCall) Smith; married George E. Beeman (divorced); married Fred Lister (divorced). *Education:* University of Texas, Austin, B.J., 1948, graduate student, 1949. *Politics:* Democrat. *Religion:* Baptist. *Residence:* New York, N.Y. *Agent:* Gloria Safier, 667 Madison Ave., New York, N.Y.

CAREER: Columbia Broadcasting System (CBS), New York City, associate radio producer, 1952-54; National Broadcasting Co. (NBC), New York City, associate pro-

ducer of "Wide, Wide World" program, 1954-56; free-lance writer, 1956—; *Cosmopolitan* magazine, New York City, entertainment editor, 1964-66, film critic, 1966—; *Sports Illustrated* magazine, New York City, writer, 1966-67. *Member:* National Organization for Women (NOW), and many conservation, animal rescue, and wildlife organizations.

WRITINGS: The Mother Book, Doubleday, in press. Columnist, "Cholly Knickerbocker" column, 1957-62, "Instant Gotham" column in *Palm Beach Social Pictorial,* 1970—, and "Liz Smith" column appearing in more than sixty newspapers, including *New York Daily News, Detroit Free Press,* and *Chicago Tribune,* 1976—. Contributor of articles to *Vogue, Cosmopolitan, Esquire, New York, Redbook, Ladies Home Journal, Good Housekeeping, New York Times,* and other magazines and newspapers.

SIDELIGHTS: For the benefit of would-be writers, Liz Smith said: "I consider a well rounded liberal arts education important for people interested in working in media—read, write, learn and live. Never pass up the chance to have a love affair or open a book or do a favor. It never occurred to me not to write and writing every day was important to my development as a professional, even letter writing can be important. As well as typing well and fast. Helpful. Shorthand for interviewing. Magazine writing is an important fount of information and entertainment. I love magazines."

In a personal vein, she briefly told *CA:* "I have traveled widely but prefer to vacation in the Hamptons of Long Island. I return annually to my roots in Texas."

AVOCATIONAL INTERESTS: Reading, socializing with other writers, theatre, television, films and books—especially history and biography.

* * *

SMITH, Mary Elizabeth
See SMITH, Liz

* * *

SMITH, Michael P(eter) 1942-

PERSONAL: Born August 2, 1942, in Dunkirk, N.Y.; son of Peter J. and Rosalie (Lipka) Smith; married Patricia Anne Lendway (an artist and registered nurse), August 21, 1965. *Education:* St. Michael's College, A.B. (magna cum laude), 1964; University of Massachusetts, M.A., 1966, Ph.D., 1971. *Home:* 1230 Eighth St., New Orleans, La. 70115. *Office:* Department of Political Science, Tulane University, New Orleans, La. 70118.

CAREER: Dartmouth College, Hanover, N.H., instructor, 1968-70, assistant professor of government, 1970-71; Boston University, Boston, Mass., assistant professor of political science, 1971-74; Tulane University, New Orleans, La., associate professor of political science, 1974—. *Member:* International Political Science Association, American Political Science Association, American Society for Public Administration, Conference for the Study of Political Thought, Pi Sigma Alpha, Phi Kappa Phi.

WRITINGS: (Editor with Kenneth L. Deutsch, and contributor) *Political Obligation and Civil Disobedience,* Crowell, 1972; (editor and author of introduction) *American Politics and Public Policy,* Random House, 1973; (with Roger H. Davidson, Judson L. James, Gary Orfield, Edward W. Gude, and Mark V. Nadel) *Politics in America: Studies in Policy Analysis,* Random House, 1974; (contributor) Ralph A. Rossum and Allen Bent, editors, *Urban Administration:*

Political Processes, Dunellen, 1975; (contributor) Elinor Ostrom, editor, *Urban Policy Analysis: An Institutional Approach,* American Association for the Advancement of Science, 1975; (editor with G. David Garson, and contributor) *Organizational Democracy: Participation and Self-Management,* Sage Publications, 1976; (contributor) Ostrom, editor, *Delivery of Urban Services: Outcomes of Change,* Sage Publications, 1976. Contributor to political science journals, including *Journal of Politics, Public Administration Review,* and *Administration and Society.* Special co-editor of *Administration and Society,* May, 1975.

WORK IN PROGRESS: The City and Social Theory, for St. Martin's; research toward a theory of citizen participation in urban renewal.

*   *   *

SMITH, Paul C.   1908-1976

November 24, 1908—June 16, 1976; American newsman, publisher, magazine editor, and author. Obituaries: *New York Times,* June 17, 1976; *Current Biography,* September, 1976.

*   *   *

SMITH, R(eginald) C(harles)   1907-

PERSONAL: Born July 4, 1907, in Kenilworth, England; son of Harry (a coachbuilder) and Edith (a school teacher; maiden name, Warwick) Smith; married Marion Carter, August 2, 1941; children: Janet (Mrs. Bernard William Pascoe). *Education:* Borough Road College, teacher's certificate (with distinction), 1927. *Home:* Lowlands, Brent St., Brent Knoll, Somerset TA9 3DU, England.

CAREER: Assistant teacher at primary school in Middlesex County, England, 1927-42; science teacher and head of department at secondary school in Harrow, England, 1946-64; Harrow College of Further Education, Harrow, lecturer in physics, 1964-67; photographer and writer, 1967—. *Military service:* Royal Air Force, Signals Branch, 1942-46; became flight lieutenant. *Member:* Royal Photographic Society (associate; deputy chairman of museum committee, 1958-67; chairman, 1967-68). *Awards, honors:* Fellowship from Royal Photographic Society, 1968.

WRITINGS: Antique Cameras, David & Charles, 1975. Contributor to British photography journals and to *Teacher's World, Schoolmaster,* and *Look and Listen.*

WORK IN PROGRESS: Research for *Victorian Optical Entertainment* and *The Age of the Detective Camera: The Social Influence of Photography between 1880 and 1910.*

SIDELIGHTS: Smith writes that he spends "most of the summer months caravanning, taking pictorial colour photographs for magazine covers and calendars, sketching and painting in water colour." His winters are spent in research.

*   *   *

SMITH, Robert Charles   1938-
(Robert Charles, Charles Leader)

PERSONAL: Born May 10, 1938, in Cambridge, England; son of Cyril Charles (a sawyer) and Florence (Leader) Smith; married Elizabeth Marion Nicolson, April 29, 1975; children: Christopher, Andrew, Michelle. *Education:* Educated in Suffolk, England. *Politics:* "Conservative with social conscience." *Home:* 16 Heath Road, Brandon, Suffolk, England.

CAREER: Has worked as a laborer, merchant seaman, barman, and as a salesman; Suffolk Fire Service, fire fighter, Suffolk, England, 1972—. Novelist.

WRITINGS: All novels under pseudonym Robert Charles: *The Faceless Fugitive,* Hale, 1963; *Nothing to Lose,* Hale, 1963; *Dark Vendetta,* Hale, 1964; *One Must Survive,* Hale, 1964; *Mission of Murder,* Hale, 1965; *This Side of Hell,* Hale, 1965; *Arctic Assignment,* Hale, 1966; *The Fourth Shadow,* Hale, 1966; *Assassins for Peace,* Hale, 1967; *Stamboul Intrigue,* Hale, 1968; *Three Days to Live,* Hale, 1968; *Strikefast,* Hale, 1969; *The Big Fish,* Hale, 1969; *The Hour of the Wolf,* Hale, 1974, Pinnacle, 1975; *Sea Vengeance,* Hale, 1974, Pinnacle, 1976; *The Sun Virgin,* Hale, 1974; *A Clash of Hawks,* Pinnacle, 1974; *The Flight of the Raven,* Pinnacle, 1975; *The Scream of the Dove,* Pinnacle, 1975; *The Prey of the Falcon,* Pinnacle, 1976.

All novels under pseudonym Charles Leader; all published by Hale: *Frontier of Violence,* 1966; *Murder in Marrakech,* 1966; *The Golden Lure,* 1967; *Nightmare on the Nile,* 1967; *The Angry Darkness,* 1968; *Strangler's Moon,* 1968; *Cargo to Saigon,* 1969; *The Double M Man,* 1969; *Death of a Marine,* 1970; *The Dragon Roars,* 1970; *Salesman of Death,* 1971; *Scavengers of War,* 1974. *A Wreath of Poppies,* 1975; *A Wreath from Bangkok,* 1975.

WORK IN PROGRESS: Two books for Pinnacle, *The Power and the Dream* and *The Hammer and the Eagle.*

SIDELIGHTS: Smith returns to his boyhood home daily to write from 8:30 a.m. until 5:30 p.m., drawing ideas and information from his files of reference material and editorial cuttings. An avid traveler, he has sailed the coasts of New Zealand, Australia, South America and Africa, traveled overland to the Middle East, Far East and Africa, and completed a tour of Europe by motorcycle.

*   *   *

SMITH, William Gardner   1926-1974

PERSONAL: Born in 1926 in Philadelphia, Pa.; children: two. *Education:* Graduated from Temple University.

CAREER: Former reporter for newspapers *Afro-American* and *Pittsburgh Courier;* news editor of English Language Services, for Agence France-Presse, 1954-74. Director of Ghana Institute of Journalism during the 1960's. *Military service:* U.S. Army, served during World War II in Germany.

WRITINGS: Anger at Innocence (novel), Farrar, Straus, 1950, reprinted, Chatham Bookseller, 1973; *South Street* (novel), Farrar, Straus, 1954; *The Stone Face* (novel), Pocket Books, 1963; *Return to Black America,* Prentice-Hall, 1970. Also author of *Last of the Conquerors* (novel), 1948, reprinted, Chatham Bookseller, 1973; and *L'Amerique Noire* (title means "Black America"). Contributor to American magazines and newspapers.

OBITUARIES: New York Times, November 8, 1974; *Washington Post,* November 8, 1974; *Publishers Weekly,* November 25, 1974; *Black World,* February, 1975.*

(Died November 5, 1974, in Paris, France)

*   *   *

SMOKE, Richard   1944-

PERSONAL: Born October 21, 1944, in Huntingdon, Pa.; son of Kenneth L. (a college professor) and Lillian H. (a college librarian) Smoke. *Education:* Harvard University, B.A. (magna cum laude), 1965; Massachusetts Institute of Technology, Ph.D., 1972. *Home:* 312 Parnassus Ave., San Francisco, Calif. 94117. *Office:* Wright Institute, 2728 Durant Ave., Berkeley, Calif. 94704.

CAREER: Harvard University, Cambridge, Mass., lecturer in public policy and assistant dean for research, 1971-73; University of California, Berkeley, fellow at Institute of Personality Assessment and Research, 1973-74; Center for Advanced Study in the Behavioral Sciences, Palo Alto, Calif., fellow, 1974-75; Wright Institute, Berkeley, research fellow, 1975—. Consultant to Organization for Economic Cooperation and Development, Committee for Economic Development, and other organizations. *Awards, honors:* Bancroft Prize from Columbia University, 1974, for *Deterrence in American Foreign Policy: Theory and Practice.*

WRITINGS: (With Alexander L. George) *Deterrence in American Foreign Policy: Theory and Practice,* Columbia University Press, 1974; *Controlling Escalation,* Harvard University Press, in press. Contributor to *Handbook of Political Science.*

WORK IN PROGRESS: A book presenting "a new approach to temperament, personality, and personal 'worlds,'" with Humphry Osmond and Miriam Siegler; research on the psychology of decision-making, the psychology of cognition and personality, political leadership, public policy and policy-making, and world politics.

SIDELIGHTS: Smoke writes: "I started out mainly as an academic, a political scientist, interested in problems of peace, security and a sane world order, and in how U.S. foreign policy and military policies could contribute to them. This interest resulted in my first two books. Pretty quickly I became convinced that much of the essence of the problem lay in the way high-level policy-makers went about making decisions, and especially in the cognitive presuppositions, as specialists might term them, that formed the psychological context of decisions. I found myself, therefore, needing to take an increasingly psychological tack."

*   *   *

SMYSER, Jane Worthington   1914-1975

PERSONAL: Born August 1, 1914, in Johnstown, Pa.; married Hamilton M. Smyser (a professor of English), 1949. *Education:* Wells College, A.B., 1936; Yale University, A.M., 1941, Ph.D., 1944. *Residence:* New London, Conn.

CAREER: Connecticut College, New London, instructor, 1942-43, 1944-47, assistant professor, 1947-55, associate professor, 1956-62, professor of English, 1962-75, chairman of department, 1969-71. *Member:* Modern Language Association of America. *Awards, honors:* Ford Foundation fellowship, 1952-53; fellow of Fund for the Advancement of Education, 1952.

WRITINGS: Wordsworth's Reading of Roman Prose, Yale University Press, 1946; (editor with W.J.B. Owen) *The Prose Works of William Wordsworth,* three volumes, Clarendon Press, 1974. Contributor to literature journals.

OBITUARIES: New York Times, October 2, 1975; *AB Bookman's Weekly,* December 1, 1975.*

(Died October 2, 1975, in Norwich, Conn.)

*   *   *

SNOW, D(avid) W(illiam)   1924-

PERSONAL: Born September 30, 1924, in Windermere, England; son of Thomas William (a schoolmaster) and Margaret Catherine (Aspland) Snow; married Barbara Katharine Whitaker (an ornithologist), June 1, 1958; children: Stephen

Whitaker, Charles William. *Education:* Attended New College, Oxford, 1946-49. *Home:* Old Forge, Wingrave, Aylesbury, Buckinghamshire, England.

CAREER: Edward Grey Institute of Field Ornithology, Oxford, England, research officer, 1949-57; New York Zoological Society Research Station, Arima Valley, Trinidad, resident naturalist, 1957-61; Charles Darwin Research Station, Santa Cruz, Galapagos Islands, director, 1962-64; director of research at British Trust for Ornithology, 1964-68; British Museum (Natural History), Tring, England, staff member in subdepartment of ornithology, 1968—. *Military service:* Royal Navy Volunteer Reserve, 1943-46; served in western approaches and Pacific theater; became sub-lieutenant. *Member:* British Ornithologists' Union (vice-president). *Awards, honors:* Brewster Medal from American Ornithologists Union, 1972.

WRITINGS: A Study of Blackbirds, Allen & Unwin, 1958; *The Web of Adaptation: Bird Studies in the American Tropics,* Quadrangle, 1976. Editor of *Ibis,* 1968-72.

WORK IN PROGRESS: Continuing ornithological research.

*   *   *

SNOW, Russell E(lwin)   1938-

PERSONAL: Born October 14, 1938, in Port Jefferson, N.Y.; son of Russell J. (a worker) and Dorothy V. (Murdock) Snow; married Linda Michele, September 1, 1962; children: Russell, David, Christopher, Mary. *Education:* Hofstra University, B.A., 1967; State University of New York at Stony Brook, M.A., 1968, Ph.D., 1972. *Politics:* Democrat. *Religion:* Anglican. *Home:* 270 South Bayview Ave., Freeport, N.Y. 11520. *Office:* Hofstra University, Hempstead, N.Y. 11550.

CAREER: London Records, New York, N.Y., administrative assistant, 1962-67; Hofstra University, Hempstead, N.Y., instructor, 1969-72, assistant professor of history, 1972—. *Awards, honors:* Danforth fellowship, 1967-71.

WRITINGS: The Bolsheviks in Siberia, Fairleigh Dickinson University Press, 1977.

WORK IN PROGRESS: The Struggle for Siberia, publication expected in 1980; *The Russian Religious Renaissance; The Madonna in Art.*

SIDELIGHTS: Snow writes: "Since graduate school my interests have increasingly shifted and focused upon the Christian tradition and upon living the Christian life. I am especially interested in Russian Orthodoxy and the Anglican tradition." In addition to courses in history, Snow teaches courses in social science and religion.

*   *   *

SNYDER, Jerome   1915(?)-1976

1915(?)—May 2, 1976; American graphic designer, illustrator, and gourmet writer. Obituaries: *New York Times,* May 4, 1976; *Time,* May 17, 1976.

*   *   *

SOLOMON, Neil   1937-

PERSONAL: Born February 27, 1937, in Pittsburgh, Pa.; son of Max M. and Clara (Eisenstein) Solomon; married Frema Sindell, June 26, 1955; children: Ted, Scott, Clifford. *Education:* Western Reserve University (now Case Western Reserve University), A.B., 1954, M.D. and M.S., both 1961; University of Maryland, Ph.D., 1965. *Religion:* Jewish. *Office:* 201 West Preston St., Baltimore, Md. 21201.

CAREER: U.S. Public Health Service, Cleveland, Ohio, trainee in physiology at School of Medicine, Case Western Reserve University, 1955-61; Johns Hopkins Hospital, Baltimore, Md., intern, 1961-62, assistant resident, 1962-63, instructor in medicine, 1964-69, assistant professor of psychiatry and behavioral sciences, 1969—. Diplomate of National Board of Medical Examiners; licensed to practice medicine in Maryland and Ohio. Secretary of health and mental hygiene for the State of Maryland, 1969—; adviser to U.S. Secretary of Health, Education and Welfare. Assistant professor of medicine at University of Maryland, 1965-69, associate professor of physiology, 1965-69. Visiting physician at Baltimore City Hospital and assistant chief of medicine, 1963-68; senior assistant surgeon for U.S. Public Health Service, 1963-64, and National Institutes of Health, 1964-65; visiting physician at University of Maryland Hospital, 1965-68. Member of national advisory committee for the State of Maryland to the Selective Service System, 1970, Maryland governor's Commission on Environmental Pollution, 1970, and Environmental Council for Maryland, 1972; commissioner for Food and Drug Administration, 1975; member of board of trustees of Non-Profit Housing for Elderly People, 1965, and Homewood School, 1968; member of medical advisory board of American Joint Distribution Committee, 1972; member of board of advisers of Maryland Acupuncture Foundation, 1973, and St. Jude Volunteers, 1973.

MEMBER: American Federation for Clinical Research, American Heart Association, American Medical Association, American Physiological Society, American Public Health Association, Federation of American Societies for Experimental Biology, Association of Mental Health Administrators (honorary member), Authors Guild of Authors League of America, American Federation of Television and Radio Artists, Southern Medical Association, New York Academy of Science, Maryland Public Health Association, Maryland Society for Medical Research, Medical and Chirurgical Faculty of Maryland, Baltimore City Medical Society, Johns Hopkins Medical Society, Johns Hopkins Medical and Surgical Association, University of Maryland Alumni Association, Western Reserve University Alumni Association, Ohio Society of Washington, D.C., Phi Delta Epsilon, Alpha Omega Alpha.

AWARDS, HONORS: Lederle Award from American Geriatric Society, 1962; Schwentker Award from Johns Hopkins Hospital, 1963; American Heart Association fellowship, 1965-67; conservation communications award from National Wildlife Federation, 1971; Myrtle Wreath Award from Hadassah, 1973; Leader in Life Saving award from Safety First Club of Maryland, 1973; public health award from Maryland Optometric Association, 1973; award of honor for environmental improvements from American Institute of Architects, Potomac Valley chapter, 1973; first honor roll award from Izaak Walton League of America, 1974; presidential award from Maryland Public Health Association, 1974.

WRITINGS: (With Sally Sheppard) *The Truth About Weight Control: How to Lose Excess Pounds Permanently,* Stein & Day, 1972; (with Mary Knudson) *Dr. Soloman's Easy No Risk Diet,* Coward, 1974; *Dr. Soloman's Proven Master Plan for Total Body Fitness and Maintenance,* Putnam, 1976.

Contributor: *The Biology of Aging,* C. C Thomas, 1970; *Disorders of Metabolism: Obesity,* Saunders, 1971. Contributor of about fifty articles to professional journals.

SORENSEN, Andrew Aaron 1938-

PERSONAL: Born July 20, 1938, in Pittsburgh, Pa.; son of Albert A. (a minister) and Margaret (a director of religious education; maiden name, Lindquist) Sorensen; married Donna Ingemie (a nutritionist), August 4, 1968; children: Aaron Ashley. *Education:* University of Illinois, B.A., 1959; University of Michigan, M.P.H., 1966; Yale University, B.D., 1962, M.Ph., 1970, Ph.D., 1971. *Religion:* Presbyterian. *Office:* University of Rochester School of Medicine, 601 Elmwood Ave., Rochester, N.Y. 14642.

CAREER: Boston University Medical School, Boston, Mass., instructor in psychiatry, 1970-71; Cornell University, Ithaca, N.Y., assistant professor of community service education, 1971-73; University of Rochester, Rochester, N.Y., 1973—, began as assistant professor, became associate professor of preventive medicine. Visiting associate, Harvard University Medical School, 1975-77. Chairman of board of directors of Alpha House, 1971-73; member of citizen's advisory board, Ibero-American Action League; member of Monroe County Board of Mental Health, 1976—. *Military service:* U.S. Army Reserve, 1959-67; became captain. *Member:* Association of Teachers of Preventive Medicine, American Sociological Association, American Public Health Association, New York Academy of Sciences. *Awards, honors:* National Science Foundation faculty science fellow, 1975-76.

WRITINGS: (With Paul Conley) *The Staggering Steeple: The Story of Alcoholism and the Churches,* Pilgrim Press, 1971; (editor) *Confronting Drug Abuse,* Pilgrim Press, 1972; (editor) *Alcoholism in the United States,* Hoffman-La-Roche, 1973; *Alcoholic Priests,* Seabury, 1976.

* * *

SOUSA, Marion 1941-

PERSONAL Born September 11, 1941, in New York, N.Y.; daughter of Robert Remington (a tonal finisher of pipe organs) and Virginia (a teacher; maiden name, Galvin) Covell; married Paul Sousa (an Air Force major), October 10, 1964; children: Allison Erin, Marisabel, Milagros, Jennifer Lee, Jacqueline. *Education:* College of Mount St. Vincent, B.A., 1963; City College of the City University of New York, M.A., 1966. *Politics:* Independent. *Religion:* Roman Catholic. *Home address:* Rt. 3, Box 658, Seguin, Tex. 78155.

CAREER: Bow Beat, Bergstrom Air Force Base, Tex., assistant editor, 1966-67; junior high school English teacher in Bristol, R.I., 1967; kindergarten teacher in an American school in Spain, 1968-69; *Digame,* Torrejon Air Base, Madrid, Spain, editor, 1969-70; writer, 1973—. Has appeared on television and radio programs. Member of Sacramento Right to Life Committee; chairman of Sacramento Rally Committee.

WRITINGS: Childbirth at Home, Prentice-Hall, 1976.

WORK IN PROGRESS: Compiling an up-to-date list of American home delivery services.

SIDELIGHTS: Marion Sousa writes: "My husband and I had our fourth and fifth children at home because of negative reasons—i.e. lack of hospital facilities for natural childbirth. After experiencing the beauty of home birth, however, I decided to try to emphasize its many positive aspects. Having our last two babies at home, for example, has helped us assert our independence in other areas of our lives. I firmly believe that birth, like death, should be freed from government regulations, social pressures, and health-care delivery system profiteering. My next book will be written with these principles in mind.''

BIOGRAPHICAL/CRITICAL SOURCES: Sacramento Bee, March 21, 1976; *North Sacramento World,* March 31, 1976, April 7, 1976; *Providence Visitor,* May 20, 1976; *Marriage and Family Living,* May, 1976; *Bookmarks,* Spring-Summer, 1976.

* * *

SOUTHWICK, Charles H(enry) 1928-

PERSONAL: Born August 28, 1928, in Wooster, Ohio; son of Arthur F. and Faye (Motz) Southwick; married Heather Milne Beck (a medical abstractor), July 12, 1952; children: Steven Beck, Karen Leslie. *Education:* College of Wooster, B.A., 1949; University of Wisconsin, Madison, M.S., 1951, Ph.D., 1953. *Religion:* Presbyterian. *Home:* 6724 Glenkirk Rd., Baltimore, Md. 21239. *Office:* School of Hygiene and Public Health, Johns Hopkins University, 615 North Wolfe St., Baltimore, Md. 21205.

CAREER: Hamilton College, Clinton, N.Y., assistant professor of biology, 1953-54; Ohio University, Athens, assistant professor, 1955-59, associate professor of zoology, 1960-61; Johns Hopkins University, Baltimore, Md., associate professor, 1961-68, professor of pathobiology, 1968—. Member of advisory council of California Primate Center, 1973-77; member of Maryland governor's science advisory council, 1975-79; member of primate advisory committee of National Academy of Science-National Research Council, 1968-76. Member of primate research expeditions to Panama, India, Bolivia, Malaysia, and Kenya.

MEMBER: International Society of Primatologists, International Society for the Study of Aggression, American Association for the Advancement of Science (fellow), American Institute of Biological Sciences, Ecological Society of America, American Society of Zoologists, American Society of Mammalogists, Animal Behavior Society (president, 1968), Academy of Zoology (fellow), British Mammal Society, Atlantic Estuarine Society, Phi Beta Kappa, Sigma Xi. *Awards, honors:* National Science Foundation fellowship, Oxford University, 1954-55; Fulbright fellowship, Aligarh Muslim University, 1959-60.

WRITINGS: (Editor) *Primate Social Behavior,* Van Nostrand, 1963; (editor) *Animal Aggression,* Van Nostrand, 1970; *Ecology and the Quality of Our Environment,* Van Nostrand, 1972, 2nd edition, 1976; (editor) *Nonhuman Primates: Usage and Availability for Biomedical Programs,* National Academy of Sciences, 1975. Contributor of more than eighty articles to scientific journals.

WORK IN PROGRESS: Research on the population ecology of nonhuman primates, and on the comparative ethology of aggression.

SIDELIGHTS: Southwick has traveled extensively in Asia, and has been especially influenced by his residence in India.

* * *

SPAETH, Gerold 1939-

PERSONAL: Born October 16, 1939, in Rapperswil, Switzerland; son of Josef (an organ builder) and Martha (Ruegg) Spaeth; married Anita Baumann, 1964; children: Veit, Salome. *Education:* Attended commercial schools in Switzerland and England. *Home address:* Sternengraben, Rapperswil 8640, Switzerland. *Agent:* Scott Meredith Literary Agency, Inc., 580 Fifth Ave., New York, N.Y. 10036.

CAREER: Held various positions in international trade and advertising in Zurich, Vevey, Fribourg, and London; writer, 1968—. *Member:* International P.E.N., Gruppe Olten. *Awards, honors:* Conrad Ferdinand Meyer-Preis, 1970; Foederungspreis der Stiftung Pro Helvetia, 1972; Foederunspreis der Stiftung Schweizerische Landesausstellung, 1973; Foerderungspreis des Kantons Zurich, 1976.

WRITINGS: Unschlecht (novel), Verlag der Arche, 1970, translation by Rita Kimber and Robert Kimber published as *A Prelude to the Long Happy Life of Maximilian Goodman,* Little, Brown, 1975.

Other works: *Stimmgaenge* (novel; title means "To Tune a[n] Organ/Life"), Verlag der Arche, 1972; *Zwoelf Geschichten* (title means "Twelve Stories"), Verlag der Arche, 1973; *Die heile Hoelle* (novel; title means "The Hidden Hell"), Verlag der Arche, 1974; *Kings Insel* (novel; title means "King's Island"), Verlag der Arche, 1976. Author of radio plays for production in Switzerland and in Berlin.

WORK IN PROGRESS: A television play and a monodrama; a novel, *Als ich durchbrannte* (title means "As I Ran Away").

* * *

SPATH, Gerold
See SPAETH, Gerold

* * *

SPEER, Albert 1905-

PERSONAL: Born March 19, 1905, in Mannheim, Germany; son of Albert (an architect) and Wilhelmina Speer; married Margaret Weber, August 28, 1928; children: Albert, Hilde, Friedrich, Margaret, Arnold, Ernst. *Education:* Attended technical universities in Karlsruhe and Munich; Technical University of Berlin, diploma in engineering, 1927. *Politics:* "Skeptical of technocratic overdevelopment." *Religion:* Protestant. *Home:* Schloss-Wolfsbrunnenweg 50, 6900 Heidelberg 1, West Germany.

CAREER: Technical University of Berlin, Germany, assistant professor of architecture, 1927-31; free-lance architect in Mannheim, Germany, 1931-33; served as architect to Hitler, working on various projects, 1933-42; minister of war production, 1942-45; convicted by Nuremburg Tribunal and sentenced to 20 years in prison, 1946, released, 1966; writer, 1966—.

WRITINGS: Erinnerungen, Propylaen (Berlin), 1969, translation by Richard Winston and Clara Winston published as *Inside the Third Reich: Memoirs,* Macmillan, 1970; *Spandauer Tagebuecher,* Propylaen, 1975, translation by R. Winston and C. Winston published as *Spandau: The Secret Diaries,* Macmillan, 1976.

WORK IN PROGRESS: Notes to Armaments and War-Production.

SIDELIGHTS: As architect and war production minister in Nazi Germany, Speer was a member of Hitler's closest circle for almost twelve years. John Toland called *Inside the Third Reich* "not only the most significant personal German account to come out of the war but the most revealing document on the Hitler phenomenon yet written. It takes the reader inside Nazi Germany on four different levels: Hitler's inner circle, National Socialism as a whole, the area of wartime production and the inner struggle of Albert Speer. The author does not try to make excuses, even by implication, and is as unrelenting toward himself as to his associates.''

Speer had been motivated to give his side of the story when he read some irritating comments about that period while in prison. The book was written in Spandau, without permission, and smuggled out by a guard. The translation sold over a million copies in the United States.

When Speer's second book appeared, F. E. Hirsch commented on the different motivation. "Because Speer did not think of later publication while jotting down his notes, this volume may surpass his first book as a genuine historical source and human document. Speer describes the dreariness of prison life and his often very tense relationships with fellow inmates. His emotions about his past and his sense of personal guilt often change. But most important are the novel and penetrating observations about Hitler's personality that Speer wrote while his memory was still fresh."

AVOCATIONAL INTERESTS: Hiking.

BIOGRAPHICAL/CRITICAL SOURCES: Jack Fishman, *The Seven Men of Spandau,* Rinehart, 1954; *New York Times Book Review,* August 23, 1970, January 10, 1971; *Wall Street Journal,* September 22, 1970, March 19, 1976; *New York Review of Books,* January 7, 1971; *Library Journal,* March 15, 1976.

* * *

SPERBER, Al E(lias) 1916-

PERSONAL: Born February 14, 1916, in Boston, Mass.; son of Louis (a tailor) and Fannie (Firestone) Sperber; married Lilian Kliegman, September 15, 1946; children: Leslie (Mrs. Robert Cohen). *Education:* Educated in Bronx, N.Y. *Politics:* Liberal Party. *Religion:* Jewish. *Home and office:* 85-04 104th St., Richmond Hill, N.Y. 11418. *Agent:* Toni Mendez, 140 East 56th St., New York, N.Y. 10022.

CAREER: Musician and entertainer, 1936-50; Telephone Marketing Service, New York, N.Y., sales executive, 1960-75; moderator of "Out of Sight," on WHN-Radio, 1972—, nationally syndicated, 1977—. Member of board of directors of Jewish Braille Institute, 1976—.

WRITINGS: Out of Sight: Ten Stories of Victory over Blindness, Little, Brown, 1976.

SIDELIGHTS: Sperber writes: "Since I lost my sight I have personally given help to people who have lost their vision and needed strength, courage, and guidance. These newly blinded people did not receive any type of personal help from their doctors, therefore the reason for the book *Out of Sight.* The radio program now covers talks about all handicaps and has been heard around the country as well as overseas."

BIOGRAPHICAL/CRITICAL SOURCES: National Enquirer, June 29, 1976.

* * *

SPERO, Sterling D. 1896-1976

PERSONAL: Born November 20, 1896, in Brooklyn, N.Y.; son of Joseph and Sarah (Lewis) Spero; married Louise T. Rothschild, June 2, 1921; married second wife, Bertha Knappertsbusch, June 22, 1969; children: (first marriage) Robert, James Sterling, Ellen Louise Spero Roman. *Education:* Columbia University, A.B., 1918, A.M., 1920, Ph.D., 1924. *Residence:* Sarasota, Fla.

CAREER: Fellow of New School for Social Research, 1924-25, and Social Science Research Council, 1926-27; research associate of Columbia University's Council for Research in the Social Sciences, 1928-32, Twentieth Century Fund,

1934-35, and Columbia University's International Institute for Social Research, 1936-37; staff member of New York State Constitutional Convention Committee, 1938; New York University, New York, N.Y., professor of public administration, beginning 1939, acting dean of Graduate School of Public Administration and Social Service, 1959-60. Lecturer at Brooklyn College (now of the City University of New York), 1935-36, and at University of Sarasota. Chairman of New York-New Jersey regional trucking panel of War Labor Board, 1942-45; member of New York City Citizens Union; member of labor arbitrator's panel of New York Board of Mediation; member of New York mayor's Committee on Administration of Technical and Professional Personnel, 1958, and Committee on Technical, Scientific, and Professional Manpower Needs of New York, 1959-63. Consultant to state governments.

MEMBER: International Rescue Committee, American Society for Public Administration (director of New York chapter, 1952-53), American Political Science Association, Industrial Relations Research Association, Academy of Political Science, American Arbitration Association (member of labor arbitrators' panel), American Council for Emigres in the Professions, American Association of University Professors, Labor Education Service, League for Industrial Democracy, Consumers League for Fair Labor Practices, Civil Service Reform Association of New York, New York State Political Science Association (past director).

WRITINGS: The Labor Movement in a Government Industry: A Study of Employee Organization in the Postal Service—Unionism in a Government Industry, Doran Co., 1924, reprinted, Arno, 1971; (with Abram L. Harris) *The Balck Worker: A Study of the Negro and the Labor Movement,* Columbia University Press, 1931, reprinted, Atheneum, 1968; (editor) *Government Jobs and How to Get Them,* Lippincott, 1945; *Government as Employer,* Remsen Press, 1948, reprinted, Southern Illinois University Press, 1970; *Labor Relations in British Nationalized Industry,* New York University Press, 1955; (with John M. Capozzola) *The Urban Community and Its Unionized Bureaucracies: Pressure Politics in Local Government Labor Relations,* Dunellen, 1973. Contributor to *New York Times.*

OBITUARIES: New York Times, January 4, 1976.*

(Died January 2, 1976, in Sarasota, Fla.)

* * *

SPICKER, Stuart Francis 1937-

PERSONAL: Born May 14, 1937, in New York, N.Y.; son of Mark and Eleanor (Goldfaden) Spicker; married Judith Marcus (a special education teacher), July 18, 1959; children: Edana Lynn, Aaron Jon, Glenn David. *Education:* Queens College (now of the City University of New York), B.A., 1959; New School for Social Research, M.A., 1962; University of Colorado, Ph.D., 1968. *Home:* 17 Longlane Rd., West Hartford, Conn. 06117. *Office:* Department of Community Medicine and Health Care, School of Medicine, University of Connecticut, Farmington, Conn. 06032.

CAREER: University of Alabama, University, part-time instructor in philosophy, 1963-64; U.S. Air Force Academy, Colorado Springs, Colo., instructor in behavioral sciences, 1964-65, instructor in philosophy, 1965-66, assistant professor of philosophy, 1967; University of Wyoming, Laramie, assistant professor of philosophy, 1967-69; Lea College, Albert Lea, Minn., associate professor of philosophy and behavioral sciences, 1970-71; Coe College, Cedar Rapids, Iowa, associate professor of philosophy and chairman of department, 1971-73; University of Connecticut, Health Center, Farmington, associate professor of community medicine and philosophy, 1973—. Part-time instructor at University of Colorado, 1965-66, and Southern Colorado State College, 1966-67; visiting associate professor at University of Texas, Medical Branch, autumn, 1974. Chairman of human experimentation committee of Hartford, Conn., Department of Aging, 1976—. Consultant to Israel Ministry of Defense on Joint Clinical Research Project on Brain Injured Veterans. *Military service:* U.S. Air Force, 1962-67; became captain.

MEMBER: American Philosophical Association (Eastern division), American Association of University Professors, Aristotelian Society, Institute of Society, Ethics, and the Life Sciences; Metaphysical Society of America, Charles S. Peirce Society, Society for Health and Human Values, Society for the Neurosciences, Society for Phenomenology and Existential Philosophy, British Society for Phenomenology, Royal Institute of Philosophy, Southern Society for Philosophy and Psychology, Sigma Xi. *Awards, honors:* National Endowment for the Humanities fellowship, Cambridge, England, 1969-70; awards from Council for Philosophical Studies, 1968, 1974; fellowship from Institute on Human Values in Medicine, at University of Vermont, summer, 1973; National Endowment for the Humanities grant, 1974-75; Connecticut Humanities Council grants, 1974-75, 1975-76, 1976-77.

WRITINGS: (Editor and author of introduction) *The Philosophy of the Body: Rejections of Cartesian Dualism,* Quadrangle, 1970; (editor with H. T. Engelhardt, and contributor) *Evaluation and Explanation in the Biomedical Sciences,* D. Reidel, 1975; (contributor) I. R. Lawson and S. R. Ingman, editors, *The Language of Geriatric Care: Implications for Professional Review,* State of Connecticut, 1975; (editor with Engelhardt, and author of introduction) *Philosophical Dimensions of the Neuro-Medical Sciences,* D. Reidel, 1976; (editor with Engelhardt, and contributor) *Philosophical Medical Ethics: Its Nature and Significance,* D. Reidel, in press; (editor with Engelhardt, and author of introduction) *Mental Health: Philosophical Perspectives,* D. Reidel, in press; (editor and author of introduction) *Organism, Medicine, and Man: Natura Naturata–Essays in Honor of Hans Jonas on His Seventy-Fifth Birthday,* D. Reidel, in press; (editor with Engelhardt, and author of introduction) *Philosophical Foundations of Clinical Judgment,* D. Reidel, in press; (editor with F. C. Redlich, and author of introduction) *Proceedings of the New England Conference on Humanities in Clinical Medicine,* Society for Health and Human Values, in press.

Co-editor, "Philosophy and Medicine" series, D. Reidel, 1973—. Contributor to *Encyclopedia of Bioethics.* Contributor of articles and reviews to scholarly journals. Member of editorial advisory board of *Journal of Medicine and Philosophy,* 1976—; consulting editor of *Connecticut Medicine,* 1976—.

WORK IN PROGRESS: The Bounds of the Body: An Essay in the Philosophy of Medicine; research on the philosophical aspects of aging.

*   *   *

SPOTO, Donald 1941-

PERSONAL: Born June 28, 1941, in New Rochelle, N.Y.; son of Michael G. (an executive) and Anne (a public relations aide; maiden name, Werden) Spoto. *Education:* Iona College, B.A. (summa cum laude), 1963; Fordham University, M.A., 1966, Ph.D., 1970. *Religion:* Roman Catholic. *Agent:* Bertha Klausner, International Literary Agency, Inc., 71 Park Ave., New York, N.Y. 10016.

CAREER: Fairfield University, Fairfield, Conn., assistant professor of theology and humanities, 1966-68; College of New Rochelle, New Rochelle, N.Y., assistant professor of religious studies, 1968-74; City University of New York, New York City, assistant professor of classics, 1974-75; New School for Social Research, New York City, assistant professor of cinematic arts, 1975—. Adjunct professor at Iona College and Manhattanville College. *Member:* Authors Guild of Authors League of America, English-Speaking Union, American Film Institute.

WRITINGS: The Art of Alfred Hitchcock, Hopkinson & Blake, 1976. Contributor of articles and reviews to film journals. Contributing editor of *Audio.*

WORK IN PROGRESS: Screenplays; and two film books, expected date of publication, 1977.

SIDELIGHTS: Spoto told *CA,* "Critical appreciation and analysis of film is most exciting. Cinema is *the* medium of our time; its impact is deeper and wider than any other; it is a uniting form for peoples of disparate backgrounds, and, at its best, may be appreciated on several levels simultaneously. I have chosen to write about film, and to teach film, because I believe that filmmakers today are artists who are really asking the ultimate questions, are concerned with where we've been and where we're going. My background in languages, literature, music and theological studies serves me well in my profession as writer about film, and, on the completion of my current two books in progress, I look forward to expanding my work to include screenplays and a student textbook on film.

My favorite contemporary personalities include Simone Weil, Caryll Houselander, Francois Truffaut, Dag Hammarskjold, the smiling faces in stone on Chartres Cathedral (they are always contemporary!), Federico Fellini and Giulietta Masina, Juliana of Norwich, T. S. Eliot, and of course the great Alfred Hitchcock, about whom I wrote my first book. My favorite book? The Gospel according to St. Luke."

*   *   *

SPRIGG, June 1953-

PERSONAL: Born March 19, 1953, in Corpus Christi, Tex.; daughter of Rodney Searle (a U.S. Navy pilot) and Dorothy (a secretary; maiden name, Karabinus) Sprigg. *Education:* Lafayette College, A.B., 1974; University of Delaware, graduate study, 1975—. *Home:* 53 Elkton Rd., Newark, Del. 19711.

CAREER: Writer and illustrator. Trustee of Lafayette College. *Member:* Phi Beta Kappa.

WRITINGS: By Shaker Hands (self-illustrated), Knopf, 1975.

WORK IN PROGRESS: Research for a book on home life and women's work in eighteenth-century America, aimed at the general public, and self-illustrated with pencil drawings, for Knopf.

SIDELIGHTS: June Sprigg writes: "I've been fortunate to find my direction in life so young. When I was twenty, I spent a summer tour-guiding at the restored Shaker village in Canterbury, N.H., where several of America's few remaining Shakers still live. Because I owned neither a car nor a camera, I had plenty of free time, and began making pencil sketches to record the ingenious and elegantly simple things the Shakers created.

"I have considered myself a writer and illustrator," she added, "but the more I think about it, the more I'm sure that I'm in fact a teacher. The type of work I do is nonfiction aimed at the general educated public with an interest in history, crafts, and Americana. I happen to express myself better in . . . writing than in speaking. Furthermore, making a book is so much more efficient than teaching a single class: the work is done once, and then spread to a far broader range of people than would be possible by personal lecturing. That is the magic of books. If I turn to fiction, my intent would be far different; I think that's what separates my type of work from novelists, although we both can use imagination in distinct ways."

AVOCATIONAL INTERESTS: American decorative arts, crafts (both antique and contemporary), folklore studies, designing crewel embroidery, hiking, canoeing.

* * *

STADTLER, Bea 1921-

PERSONAL: Born June 26, 1921, in Cleveland, Ohio; daughter of David and Minnie (Gorelick) Horwitz; married Oscar Stadtler (a dentist), January 31, 1945; children: Dona (Mrs. Howard Rosenblatt), Sander, Miriam. *Education:* Attended Case Western Reserve University, 1953-62; Cleveland College of Jewish Studies, B.J.S., 1970. *Religion:* Jewish. *Home:* 24355 Tunbridge Lane, Beachwood, Ohio 44122. *Office:* 26500 Shaker Blvd., Beachwood, Ohio 44122.

CAREER: Teacher of Judaic studies in religious school in Cleveland, Ohio, 1950-55; Temple Beth Sholom, Cleveland, Ohio, supervisor, 1955-60; Cleveland College of Jewish Studies, Cleveland, Ohio, registrar, 1959—. Member of local Jewish Community Center; member of board of directors of Ethnic Heritage Committee, 1976—. *Member:* Society of Israel Philatelists, Pioneer Women (president, 1955-57). *Awards, honors:* Prize from Jewish Welfare Board, 1975, for *The Holocaust.*

WRITINGS—Juvenile: Once Upon a Jewish Holiday, KTAV, 1962; *The Adventures of Gluchel of Hamiln,* United Synagogue Book Service, 1967; *The Story of Dona Gracia,* United Synagogue Book Service, 1969; *Rescue from the Sky,* Jewish Agency, 1972; *The Holocaust: A History of Courage and Resistance,* Behrman, 1973, revised edition, 1974. Author of column "For the Young Reader," in *Cleveland Jewish News,* 1964—. Associate editor of *Israel Philatelist.*

WORK IN PROGRESS: A juvenile book on Zionism; a horse story; research on Hassidic legend.

* * *

STAHNKE, Arthur A(llan) 1935-

PERSONAL: Born April 9, 1935, in St. Paul, Minn.; son of Arthur Richard and Margaret (Payne) Stahnke; married Astrid Barbins, September 6, 1958; children: Lenora R., Karl W., Carma M., John E. *Education:* Bethel College, St. Paul, Minn., B.A., 1957; University of Minnesota, M.A., 1960; University of Iowa, Ph.D., 1966. *Home:* 10 Holiday Dr., Collinsville, Ill. 62234. *Office:* Department of Government, Southern Illinois University, Edwardsville, Ill. 62025.

CAREER: Southern Illinois University, Edwardsville, instructor, 1963-66, assistant professor, 1966-68, associate professor, 1968-74, professor of government, 1974—, chairman of department, 1972-76. *Member:* American Polit-

ical Science Association, Association of Asian Studies, Midwest Political Science Association. *Awards, honors:* American Philosophical Society travel grant, in Germany, 1971.

WRITINGS: (Contributor) *The Dynamics of China's Foreign Relations,* Harvard University Press, 1970; (editor and contributor) *China's Trade with the West: Political and Economic Analysis,* Praeger, 1972; (with John W. Ellsworth) *Politics and Political Systems: An Introduction to Political Science,* McGraw, 1976. Contributor to professional journals.

* * *

STANBURY, Walter A. 1910-1976

1910—May 11, 1976; American publisher, editor, educator, and author. Obituaries: *New York Times,* May 14, 1976.

* * *

STANFORD, Miles J(oseph) 1914-

PERSONAL: Born January 4, 1914, in Wheaton, Ill.; son of Arthur Joseph (an electrician) and Arline (Miles) Stanford; married Cornelia de Villiers Schwab, January 20, 1951. *Education:* Educated in Wheaton, Ill. *Religion:* Protestant. *Home and office:* Christian Correspondence, 3030 Wood Ave., Colorado Springs, Colo. 80907.

CAREER: H. F. Steinbrecher Co., Wheaton, Ill., cartographer, 1939-41; Christian Correspondence, Colorado Springs, Colo., owner and writer, 1947—. *Military service:* U.S. Army, cartographer with Corps of Engineers, 1942-45; served in Europe.

WRITINGS: The Green Letters, privately printed, 1964, published as *Principles of Spiritual Growth,* Back to the Bible Broadcast, 1967, published as *The Green Letters: Principles of Spiritual Growth,* Zondervan, 1975; *The Red Letters,* privately printed, 1965; *The Reckoning that Counts,* privately printed, 1966, published as *The Reckoning that Counts: The Realization of Spiritual Growth,* Zondervan, 1977; *The Principle of Position,* privately printed, 1967, Zondervan, 1976; *None But the Hungry Heart,* Volumes I-VI, privately printed, 1968-76; *Abide Above,* privately printed, 1970, Zondervan, in press; *The Ground of Growth,* privately printed, 1971, Zondervan, 1976; *The Line Drawn,* privately printed, 1972.

SIDELIGHTS: Stanford began his Christian counseling by mail in 1943, while he was still in the army. He writes that the purpose of his ministry by correspondence and publishing is mainly to help Christians become spiritually established.

* * *

STANGER, Ila (Ann) 1940-

PERSONAL: Born October 13, 1940, in New York, N.Y.; daughter of Jack Simon and Shirley Ruth (Nadelson) Stanger. *Education:* Brooklyn College of the City University of New York, B.A., 1961. *Home:* 115 West 71st St., New York, N.Y. 10023. *Office:* Travel & Leisure, 61 West 51st St., New York, N.Y. 10019.

CAREER: Harper's Bazaar, New York, N.Y., feature and travel editor, 1970-75; *Travel & Leisure,* New York City, senior editor, 1975—. *Member:* Society of American Travel Writers, New York Travel Writers Association.

WRITINGS: (Contributor) Betty Lyons, editor, *Three Women Alone,* Award Book, 1975. Contributor to popular magazines, including *Saturday Review.*

SIDELIGHTS: Ila Stanger has conducted interviews with entertainers and other well-known people, including Bette Davis, Lillian Hellman, Peter Ustinov, Peter O'Toole, Julia Child, Robert Redford, Beverly Sills, Julian Bond, Dr. Lee Salk.

* * *

STANNARD, David E(dward) 1941-

PERSONAL: Born June 11, 1941, in Teaneck, N.J.; son of David L. (a businessman) and Florence E. (Harwood) Stannard; married Valerie M. Nice (a translator), November 12, 1966; children: Timothy, Adam. *Education:* San Francisco State College (now University), A.B. (magna cum laude), 1971; Yale University, M.A., 1972, M.Phil., 1973, Ph.D., 1975. *Politics:* "Variations on a generally leftist theme." *Religion:* "Waiting to find out." *Home:* 1253 Trumbull College, Yale University, New Haven, Conn. 06520. *Office:* American Studies Program, Yale University, New Haven, Conn. 06520.

CAREER: Time, Inc., New York, N.Y., branch manager of several subsidiary company offices in California, Seattle, and Philadelphia, 1963-68; Connecticut College, New London, instructor in history, 1973; Yale University, New Haven, Conn., assistant professor of history and American studies, 1974—. Visiting assistant professor of religious studies at Stanford University, 1976; research associate of National Endowment for the Humanities. *Military service:* U.S. Air Force, 1960-62. *Member:* American Historical Association, American Studies Association.

WRITINGS: (Editor and contributor) *Death in America,* University of Pennsylvania Press, 1975; *The Puritan Way of Death: A Study in Religion, Culture, and Social Change,* Oxford University Press, 1976. Author of several novels under various pseudonyms. Contributor to history and American studies journals.

WORK IN PROGRESS: Editing *The Idea of National Character; Consciousness in Context: The Limits of Psychohistory* (tentative title); a book on sixteenth and seventeenth-century perceptions of the life cycle; essays on American slave religion and on childhood and old age in colonial and contemporary America.

SIDELIGHTS: Stannard writes: "While recognizing the danger this presents (paradoxically) in the pursuit of an academic career, I consider teaching to be the main focus of my working life. Fortunately, I also greatly enjoy research and writing. At present I am particularly concerned with the various ways cultures have of dealing with fundamental problems common to all human individuals and groups—such as growing up, growing old, and dying."

* * *

STANNUS, (James) Gordon (Dawson) 1902-
(Gordon Anthony, Jason)

PERSONAL: Born December 23, 1902, in Wicklow, Ireland; son of Thomas Robert Alexander (a British Army officer) and Lilith (Graydon-Smith) Stannus; married Frances Louise Haweis James, 1930 (divorced, 1933); married Jacqueline Compton, 1946 (divorced, 1948); children: (first marriage) John Paul James. *Education:* Attended school of Royal Architectural Association, 1919. *Politics:* "I dislike extremists (Fascists and Communists)." *Religion:* Church of England. *Home:* Garden Flat, Blue Willow, Landsdown Rd., Hove BN3 1FZ, England. *Agent:* Herbert van Thal, London Management, 235-241 Regent St., London W1A 2JT, England.

CAREER: Watney Combe Reid Ltd. (brewery), London, England, member of managerial staff, 1920-32; free-lance photographer, 1932-52, work exhibited at Shakespeare Festival, Stratford-on-Avon, 1934, Sadler's Wells Theatre, 1936, and at Royal Opera House, 1939; antique dealer in London, 1952-72. *Wartime service:* Official portrait photographer for the Air Ministry in London, 1943-45.

WRITINGS—All with photographs by author; all under pseudonym Gordon Anthony, except as noted: *Markova,* Chatto & Windus, 1935; *Ballet,* Bles, 1937; *Vic-Wells Ballet,* Routledge, 1938; *John Gielgud,* Routledge, 1938; *Massine,* Routledge, 1939; *Russian Ballet,* Bles, 1939; (under pseudonym Jason) *Blonde and Brunette* (nude figure study), Chapman & Hall, 1940; *Margot Fonteyn,* privately printed, 1941; *Sleeping Princess,* Routledge, 1942; *Sadler's Wells Ballet,* Bles, 1942; *Air Aces,* Home & Van Thal, 1944; *Ballerina,* Home & Van Thal, 1945; *Robert Helpman,* Home & Van Thal, 1946; (under real name) *Gordon Anthony,* Home & Van Thal, 1947; *Studies of Dancers* (text by Deryk Lynham), Home & Van Thal, 1948; *Margot Fonteyn,* Phoenix House, 1950; *Alicia Markova,* Phoenix House, 1951; *Beryl Grey,* Phoenix House, 1952; *A Camera at the Ballet: Pioneer Dancers of the Royal Ballet* (photographic autobiography), David & Charles, 1975. Illustrator of numerous other books. Contributor of photographs to magazines.

WORK IN PROGRESS: A book of collected articles, originally written for *Dancing Times,* to be called *Dancers To Remember;* an autobiography, to follow at a later date.

SIDELIGHTS: Gordon Stannus told *CA:* "I always wanted to be a dancer, and secondly a photographer, but family prejudice prevented this and I had to go into business for twelve miserable years. One of life's upheavals flung me into photography in 1933 and another in 1948 flung me out of it! During my life I've worked in a factory at night, been a companion, worked in a restaurant, been on dole, and worked as a 'char' during bad periods—a somewhat kaleidoscopic career of a cross between a Sagittarian and Capricornian." *Studies of Dancers* was the first book with color photographs to be published in England.

* * *

STANTON, Jessie Earl 1887-1976

1887—May 16, 1976; American educator, college administrator, and author. Obituaries: *New York Times,* May 18, 1976.

* * *

STAPPENBECK, Herb(ert) Louis (Jr.) 1935-

PERSONAL: Born February 5, 1935, in San Antonio, Tex.; son of Herbert Louis (a printer) and Gretchen (Weltner) Stappenbeck; married Barbara Ellen Pickard, August 2, 1958; children: Audrey Elaine, Gregory John, Stephen Charles. *Education:* St. Mary's University, San Antonio, Tex., B.A., 1956; University of Texas at Austin, M.A., 1958, Ph.D., 1968; postdoctoral study at University of Missouri, 1974—. *Home:* Route 4, Box 190, Columbia, Mo. 65201. *Office:* Lincoln University, Jefferson City, Mo. 65101.

CAREER: San Antonio College, San Antonio, Tex., assistant professor of English, 1958-65; University of Missouri, Columbia, assistant professor of English, 1969-75; Lincoln University, Jefferson City, Mo., coordinator of planning management, 1975—.

WRITINGS: A Catalogue of the Joseph Hergesheimer

Collection, University of Texas Press, 1974. Contributor to English journals.

WORK IN PROGRESS: A biography of Joseph Hergesheimer; articles on Jack London and Harold Frederic.

* * *

STAR, Shirley A(nn) 1918-1976

February 18, 1918—April 27, 1976; American sociologist, research institute official, public health consultant, and author. Obituaries: *Washington Post,* April 30, 1976. (See index for previous *CA* sketch)

* * *

STARKMAN, Miriam K(osh) 1916-

PERSONAL: Born May 31, 1916, in Poland; came to the United States in 1922, naturalized citizen, 1927; daughter of Abraham M. and Deborah (Halperin) Kosh; married Philip J. Starkman (deceased); children: Marjorie E. *Education:* Brooklyn College (now of the City University of New York), B.A., 1935; Columbia University, M.A. (honors), 1939, Ph.D., 1947. *Home:* 110-50 71st Rd., Forest Hills, N.Y. 11375. *Office:* Department of English, Queens College of the City University of New York, Flushing, N.Y. 11367.

CAREER: Queens College (now of the City University of New York), Flushing, N.Y., instructor, 1944-54, assistant professor, 1954-61, associate professor, 1961-65, professor of English, 1965—. Visiting assistant professor at Columbia University, 1957-58; visiting professor, Tel Aviv University, 1972; visiting professor at University of Wisconsin, Madison, summer, 1963. Delegate to Dublin Swift Tercentenary, 1967; member of Advisory Screening Committee on International Exchange of Persons, 1964-67, chairman, 1966-67.

MEMBER: Modern Language Association of America, American Association of University Professors, Milton Society of America, English Graduate Union (Columbia University). *Awards, honors:* Ford Foundation fellowship, 1956-57; Fulbright fellowship to Israel, 1962-63; Guggenheim fellowships, 1963-64.

WRITINGS: Swift's Satire on Learning, Princeton University Press, 1950; (editor) *Gullivers' Travels and Other Writings of Jonathan Swift,* Bantam, 1962; (contributor) Joseph Mazzeo and others, editors, *Reason and Imagination,* Columbia University Press, 1962; (editor) *Seventeenth Century Poetry,* two volumes, Knopf, 1967. Contributor of articles and reviews to literature and theology journals.

WORK IN PROGRESS: Studies in the Relationship of Poetry and Religion.

* * *

STARR, Cecile 1921-
Cecile Boyajian

PERSONAL: Born July 14, 1921, in Nashville, Tenn. daughter of Jacob and Carrie (Lightman) Starr; married Aram Boyajian (a documentary film producer and director), June 3, 1957; children: Marco Starr, Suzanne Helene. *Education:* Louisiana State University, B.A., 1941; Columbia University, M.A., 1952. *Residence:* New York, N.Y.

CAREER: Has worked for Australian News and Information Bureau, 1942-45; March of Time Forum Films, member of promotion staff, 1946-49; Columbia University, New York City, instructor in film and film history, 1955-61; Lincoln Center Education Department, New York City, creator and co-ordinator of school film program, 1967-68; New

School for Social Research, New York City, instructor in film and film history, 1973—. Instructor and consultant in film and film history at Hunter College (now of the City University of New York), New York Society of Ethical Culture, Metropolitan Museum of Art, and Walden High School, 1953-75; film consultant to United Nations, World Health Organization, and Mental Health Film Board. Film producer. *Member:* New York Film Council. *Awards, honors:* Blue Ribbon award from American Film Festival for "Fellow Citizen, A. Lincoln."

WRITINGS: How to Obtain and Screen Films for Community Use (pamphlet), Film Council of America, 1949; (editor) *Ideas on Film,* Funk, 1951; (editor) *Film Society Primer,* American Federation of Film Societies, 1956; *Discovering the Movies,* Van Nostrand, 1972; (with Robert Russett) *Experimental Animation,* Van Nostrand, 1976.

Documentary films: "Rembrandt and the Bible" released by ABC-TV, 1968; "In the Beginning" released by New York City Board of Education TV, 1970; "Islamic Carpets" released by Metropolitan Museum of Art, 1970; "Fellow Citizen, A. Lincoln," 1971-72; "Richter on Film," 1972; "A Talk with Carmen D'Avino," 1972; (with Maxine Haleff) "The Magic Lantern Movie," 1976.

Author of column "The Film Forum" in *Saturday Review,* 1949-59, and column in *House Beautiful,* 1953-59. Contributor to *Encyclopaedia Britannica* and to periodicals and film journals, including *New York Times, Consumer Reports,* and *Film Library Quarterly,* occasionally under name Cecile Boyajian. Associate editor of *Film Forum Review, 1946-48; New York editor of* Film Quarterly, *1953-57, and* Sight & Sound, *1958-61.*

* * *

STARR, Judy
See GELFMAN, Judith S(chlein)

* * *

STARR, Raymond 1937-

PERSONAL: Born August 7, 1937, in San Antonio, Tex.; son of John B. and Edith Nell (Buckelew) Starr. *Education:* Del Mar College, A.A., 1956; University of Texas at Austin, B.A., 1958, Ph.D., 1964; graduate study at Johns Hopkins University, 1958-59. *Politics:* Republican. *Home:* 5290 Remington Rd., San Diego, Calif. 92115. *Office:* Department of History, San Diego State University, San Diego, Calif. 92182.

CAREER: San Diego State University, San Diego, Calif., assistant professor, 1964-68, associate professor, 1968-74, professor of history, 1974—. *Member:* Organization of American Historians, American Civil Liberties Union, Southern Historical Association, Texas State Historical Association, South Carolina Historical Society, Phi Alpha Theta. *Awards, honors:* Woodrow Wilson fellow, 1958-59.

WRITINGS: (Contributor) Ronald Moe and William Schutze, editors, *American Government and Politics: Selected Readings,* C. E. Merrill, 1971; (contributor) Robert H. Ratcliffe, editor, *Vital Issues of the Constitution,* Houghton, 1971; (editor with Robert Detweiler) *Race, Prejudice and the Origins of Slavery in America,* Schenkman, 1975. Contributor of aritcles and reviews to history journals.

WORK IN PROGRESS: Historiographical articles on intellectual roots of American racism, new interpretations of slavery, and new interpretations of Reconstruction, 1863-1877; articles on Nathanael Greene and South Carolina, and South Carolina politics, 1776-1790.

SIDELIGHTS: Starr writes that most of his research and writing grow out of professional concerns as a historian, with a specialty in the American Revolution (emphasizing legal origins of the U.S. and the concept of liberty under law); and history of American racism, with special emphasis on slavery as a major institution developed in America's complicated race relations. He adds: "Current thrust of most work is toward study of racism, at least partially because I believe strongly that American racism is essentially a cultural phenomenon, and can best be attacked by identifying as such, and then attacking cultural means by which racism is transmitted."

*   *   *

STASHEFF, Christopher 1944-

PERSONAL: Born in January, 1944, in Mt. Vernon, N.Y.; son of Edward (a professor) and Evelyn (a teacher; maiden name, Maher) Stasheff; married Mary Miller, June 9, 1973; children: Isobel Marie, Edward James. *Education:* University of Michigan, B.A., 1965, M.A., 1966; University of Nebraska at Lincoln, Ph.D., 1972. *Politics:* Democrat. *Religion:* Roman Catholic. *Residence:* Montclair, N.J. *Office:* Department of Speech and Theater, Montclair State College, Valley Rd. at Normal Ave., Upper Montclair, N.J. 07043.

CAREER: University of Michigan, Ann Arbor, member of television floor crew, 1961-67; University of Nebraska, Lincoln, administrative assistant for CCTV-Nebraska Television Council for Higher Education, 1967-68; Montclair State College, Upper Montclair, N.J., instructor in radio and television, 1972—. Member of radio advisory committee to New Jersey Public Broadcasting Authority, 1973-74. *Member:* Speech and Theater Association of New Jersey.

WRITINGS: The Warlock in Spite of Himself (science fantasy), Ace, 1969; *King Kobold* (science fantasy), Ace, 1970.

Plays: "The Three-Legged Man," first produced in Lincoln, Neb., May 11, 1970; "Cotton-Eye Joe," first produced in Lincoln, Neb., December 16, 1970; "Joey Win," first produced in Lincoln, Neb., March 21, 1971.

WORK IN PROGRESS: Conventionalism for the Playwright; seven novels—*Sex of Hwun, The Kind of Man Who Reads "Playboy"; Golem in Limbo; The Closing of the Weird; The Wizard Who Wasn't; The Wizard Who Was; A Man in His Rumor,* an alternate-universe novel; research on the impact of media on society, the purpose of the artist in society, and the differences in kinds of dramatic media.

SIDELIGHTS: Stasheff writes: "In my boyhood, I was a puppeteer; I began to write my own scripts. In high school, I began writing for radio, and did my first original script which I adapted to short story form. I submitted it to *Fantasy and Science Fiction,* and got back a note explaining that it was very good, but too long for a first publication. Could they see something shorter? Oh, they certainly could!

"I may never make another sale, but I'll probably keep writing anyway—it sustains my belief in myself, and provides a much-needed escape into worlds I can control (usually). Also, there's always the possibility of another sale, and I need the money. Even more, I need the illusion, to keep me going. . . . A man without dreams loses youth, and must constantly fight off bitterness—which is why society needs fantasy and science fiction. Yes, and even the junk you see on prime-time television.

"I like SF—because it's the playground of ideas, one of the last places where a man can play with concepts for their own sake, without someone demanding he prove the validity of what he has written. Such a place is very important; a man must have a place to try a hypothesis per se. . . . In politics and culture, I'm a middle-of-the-road liberal—I look forward to new cultural aspects, but don't want to forsake the old ones." *Avocational interests:* Reading, "playing with my children (occasionally)."

BIOGRAPHICAL/CRITICAL SOURCES: Lester Del Ray, *Science Fiction: A Critical History,* Garland, 1975.

*   *   *

STEARNS, Pamela Fujimoto 1935-

PERSONAL: Born August 4, 1935, in Honolulu, Hawaii; daughter of James H. (a teacher) and Sybil Momi (a secretary; maiden name, Seong) Fujimoto; married Richard D. Stearns (a free-lance writer), April 3, 1956. *Education:* Antioch College, student, 1954-58. *Religion:* None. *Home:* 2153B Lombard, San Francisco, Calif. 94123.

CAREER: Writer and craftswoman, working in textiles.

WRITINGS: Into the Painted Bear Lair (juvenile), Houghton, 1976.

WORK IN PROGRESS: An adult historical novel; *The Gelsteen,* a juvenile fantasy; *The Ghost Who Would Hang by His Tree and Other Ghosts Who,* a book of ghost stories; a collection of humorous and bizarre narrative poetry.

*   *   *

STECHOW, Wolfgang 1896-1974

PERSONAL: Born June 5, 1896, in Kiel, Germany; came to the United States in 1936, naturalized U.S. citizen; married, 1931; children: three. *Education:* Attended University of Freiburg, 1914, and University of Berlin, 1920; University of Goettingen, Ph.D., 1921. *Residence:* Oberlin, Ohio.

CAREER: Kaiser Friedrich Museum, Berlin, Germany, assistant, 1921-22; University of Goettingen, Goettingen, Germany, instructor, 1926-31, assistant professor of art history, 1931-36; University of Wisconsin, Madison, acting assistant professor, 1936, associate professor of fine arts, 1937-40; Oberlin College, Oberlin, Ohio, professor of fine arts, 1940-63, professor emeritus, 1963-74, Charles B. Martin Lecturer, 1966, visiting professor, spring, 1972. Member of National Committee for the History of Art. Visiting professor at University of Michigan, 1963-64, Vassar College, 1969-70, Yale University, autumn, 1971, University of Goettingen, summer, 1972, University of Delaware, spring, 1973, and Princeton University, 1974; Sterling Clark Professor at Williams College, 1966-67; Mary Flexner Lecturer at Bryn Mawr College, 1967; adjunct professor at Case Western Reserve University, 1967; Neilson Professor at Smith College, spring, 1969; Kress Professor-in-Residence at National Gallery of Art, 1970-71; regents professor at University of California, Los Angeles, winter, 1974. Fellow of German Institute of Art History (Florence), 1927-28, and Bibliotheca Hertziana (Rome), 1931.

MEMBER: College Art Association (vice-president, 1945), Archaeological Institute of America, American Society for Aesthetics. *Awards, honors:* L.H.D. from University of Michigan, 1966; D.F.A. from Oberlin College, 1967, and Baldwin-Wallace College, 1973.

WRITINGS: Apollo und Daphne, B. G. Teubner, 1932, published as *Apollo und Daphne: Mit einem nachwort und nachtraegen zum neudruck,* Wissenschaftlish Buchgesellschaft, 1965; *Salomon van Ruysdael: Eine einfuehrung in seine kunst*, Mann, 1938; *Dutch Painting in the Seventeenth Century*, Rhode Island Museum Press, 1938; *Pieter Bruegel, the Elder (about 1525-1569)*, Abrams, 1954, reprinted, 1970; *Anthony van Dyck's "Betrayal of Christ,"* privately printed, 1960; (editor) *Northern Renaissance Art, 1400-1600: Sources and Documents*, Prentice-Hall, 1966; *Dutch Landscape Painting of the Seventeenth Century*, Phaidon, 1966, 2nd edition, 1968; *Rubens and the Classical Tradition*, Harvard University Press, for Oberlin College, 1968; *Duerer and America*, National Gallery of Art, 1971; (with others) *European Paintings Before 1500*, Kent State University Press, 1974. Editor-in-chief of *Art Bulletin*, 1950-52. Consultant to *Art Quarterly* and to *California Studies in the History of Art*.

OBITUARIES: New York Times, October 14, 1974.*

(Died October 12, 1974, in Princeton, N.J.)

* * *

STEIN, George P(hilip) 1917-

PERSONAL: Born September 16, 1917, in Newark, N.J.; son oe Isidor and Sarah (Geldzeiler) Stein; married Agnes Hippen (a writer), August 26, 1939; children: Katherine (Mrs. A. T. Cole), Elizabeth, Madeleine. *Education:* University of Michigan, B.A., 1938, M.A., 1939; Columbia University, Ph.D., 1953. *Home:* 440 South Mountain Rd., New City, N.Y. 10956. *Office:* Department of Philosophy, Bloomfield College, Bloomfield, N.J. 07003.

CAREER: City University of New York, New York, N.Y., lecturer in philosophy, 1953-59; Rutgers University, Newark, N.J., assistant professor of philosophy, 1959-64; Rockland Community College, Suffern, N.Y., director of arts and sciences, 1964-67; Bloomfield College, Bloomfield, N.J., professor of philosophy, 1967—. *Member:* American Philosophical Association, American Society for Aesthetics, American Association of Univeristy Professors.

WRITINGS: The Ways of Meaning in the Arts, Humanities Press, 1970; *The Forum of Philosophy*, McGraw, 1973; (with wife, Agnes Stein) *The Individual and Everybody Else*, Prentice-Hall, 1973. Contributor to *Journal of Aesthetic Education*.

WORK IN PROGRESS: Two books, *The Logic of Aesthetic Devices* and, with his wife, *The Arts: A Study in the Parallelism of Response;* also research in value expression and criticism in the arts.

* * *

STEIN, Herb 1928-

PERSONAL: Born March 3, 1928, in Pittsburgh, Pa.; son of David and Goldie Stein; married wife, Betsy L., July 14, 1972. *Education:* Pennsylvania State University, B.A., 1951; Columbia University, M.S., 1957. *Religion:* Jewish. *Home:* 4342 Centre Ave., Pittsburgh, Pa. 15213. *Office: Pittsburgh*, 4802 Fifth Ave., Pittsburgh, Pa. 15213.

CAREER: Oak Ridger, Oak Ridge, Tenn., reporter, 1951-56; *Pittsburgh Post-Gazette*, Pittsburgh, Pa., reporter, 1957-66; WQED-Television, Pittsburgh, Pa., city editor, 1969-74; *Pittsburgh*, Pittsburgh, Pa., editor, 1974—. Assistant professor at University of Pittsburgh, 1969—; lecturer at Chatham College, 1976. *Military service:* U.S. Army, 1946-47; became sergeant. *Member:* Pittsburgh Press Club, Sigma Delta Chi. *Awards, honors:* Pulitzer traveling fellowship from *Golden Quill*.

WRITINGS: Pittsburgh Magazine's Guide to Pittsburgh, Pittsburgh Magazine, 1976.

STEINBERG, Eleanor B(usick) 1936-

PERSONAL: Born July 25, 1936, in Washington, D.C.; married Robert M. Steinberg, August 26, 1962; children: David, Douglas. *Education:* Attended London School of Economics and Political Science, 1956-57; Oberlin College, B.A., 1958; Yale University, M.A., 1959. *Home:* 6203 Stratford Rd., Chevy Chase, Md. 20015. *Office:* Brookings Institution, 1775 Massachusetts Ave. N.W., Washington, D.C. 20036.

CAREER: U.S. Department of Commerce, Bureau of International Commerce, Washington, D.C., international economist, 1960-62; Brookings Institution, Washington, D.C., research assistant in economic studies program, 1962-67; member of transportation staff of Urban Institute, 1969-70; Brookings Institution, research associate on foreign policy staff, 1970-72; consultant to environmental adviser of World Bank, 1972; Brookings Institution, research associate, 1972—. *Awards, honors:* Woodrow Wilson fellowship, 1959-60.

WRITINGS: (with Edwin T. Haefele) *Government Controls on Transport: An African Case*, Brookings Institution, 1965; (with Joseph A. Yager) *Energy and U.S. Foreign Policy*, Ballinger, 1974; (contributor) Edward R. Fried and Charles L. Schultze, editors, *Higher Oil Prices and the World Economy*, Brookings Institution, 1975; (contributor) *Trade, Inflation, and Ethics*, Lexington Books, 1976. Contributor to history and technical journals.

WORK IN PROGRESS: Research for a book, setting up possible international taxes (as on trade) to pay for international programs (such as environmental programs), with Joseph A. Yager, for Brookings Institution.

* * *

STEPHENS, Meic 1938-

PERSONAL: Given name is pronounced Mike; born July 23, 1938, in Pontypridd, Glamorgan, Wales; son of Herbert Arthur Lloyd (an industrial worker) and Alma (Symes) Stephens; married Ruth Wynn Meredith, August 15, 1965; children: Lowri Angharad, Heledd Melangell, Brengain Gwenllian (daughters). *Education:* University of Rennes, diploma in French, 1960; University of Wales, B.A. (honors) from University College, Aberystwyth, 1961, diploma in education from University College of North Wales, Bangor, 1962. *Politics:* Plaid Cymru (Welsh Nationalist Party). *Religion:* "Calvinist Methodist." *Home:* 42 Heol yr Eglwys, Eglwys Newydd, Cardiff, Wales. *Office:* Welsh Arts Council, Museum Pl., Cardiff, Wales.

CAREER: Triskel Press, Merthyr Tydfil, Wales, director, 1962-67; Welsh Arts Council, Cardiff, Wales, assistant literature director, 1967-75, literature director, 1975—. French master in Ebbw Vale, 1962-66. *Member:* Yr Academi Gymreig (National Association of Welsh Writers; founding member of English section).

WRITINGS: (With Peter Gruffydd and Harri Webb) *Triad: Thirty-Three Poems*, Triskel Press, 1963; (editor with John Stuart Williams) *The Lilting House: An Anthology of Anglo-Welsh Poetry, 1917-1967*, Dent, 1969; (editor) *Artists in Wales*, three volumes, Gomer, 1971-76; *Exiles All* (poems), Christopher Davies, 1973; *A Reader's Guide to Wales: A Selective Bibliography*, National Book League, 1973; (editor) *The Welsh Language Today*, Gomer, 1973; *Linguistic Minorities in Western Europe*, Gomer, 1976; *The Arts in Wales Since 1950*, Welsh Arts Council, in press. Also translator of poems from French, Welsh, and Breton into English.

Editor, with R. Brinley Jones, of series "Writers of Wales," University of Wales Press, 1969-74. Staff journalist for *Western Mail,* 1966-67. Co-editor of *Poetry Wales,* 1965-72.

SIDELIGHTS: Stephens writes: "The culture of Wales is expressed mainly through the Welsh language, which is now spoken by only 520,000 people (20% of population of Wales). My interest is in conveying a sense of Welsh nationhood to English-speaking Welsh people. I have worked for a rapprochement between Welsh- and English-speaking writers. I am a Socialist who wants to see an autonomous, bilingual, progressive Wales, in a federal Europe."

* * *

STEPHENS, Otis H(ammond), Jr.   1936-

PERSONAL: Born September 20, 1936, in East Point, Ga.; son of Otis H. (a businessman) and Margaret (a businesswoman; maiden name, Fisher) Stephens; married Linda Duren (a certified public accountant), June 18, 1960; children: Ann Greer, Carol Ellen. *Education:* University of Georgia, A.B., 1957, M.A., 1958; Johns Hopkins University, Ph.D., 1963. *Politics:* Independent. *Home:* 2021 Kemper Lane, Knoxville, Tenn. 37920. *Office:* Department of Political Science, University of Tennessee, 1009 McClung Tower, Knoxville, Tenn. 37916.

CAREER: Georgia Southern College, Statesboro, assistant professor, 1962-63, associate professor, 1963-65, professor of political science, 1965-67; University of Tennessee, Knoxville, associate professor of political science, 1967—. Member of board of directors of American Council of the Blind, 1974—, and National Accreditation Council for Agencies Serving the Blind and Visually Handicapped, 1975—; liberal arts fellow in law and political science at Harvard Law School, 1975-76.

MEMBER: American Political Science Associaton, Law and Society Association, American Society for Legal History, American Civil Liberties Union (member of board of directors of East Tennessee chapter, 1970-72), Southern Political Science Association. *Awards, honors:* Russell Sage Foundation residency in law and social science, 1975-76.

WRITINGS: The Supreme Court and Confessions of Guilt, University of Tennessee Press, 1973; (contributor) Richard P. Claude, editor, *Comparative Human Rights,* Johns Hopkins Press, 1976. Contributor of articles and reviews to law and education journals and to *New England Quarterly.*

WORK IN PROGRESS: An Introduction to Law: Selected Readings and Original Essays; an essay on contours of due process of law in American Constitutional development; research for essay, "Judicial Values, Police Imperatives, and the Fifth Amendment," for inclusion in *The Constitution and the Rule of Law,* publication expected by University of Georgia Press.

SIDELIGHTS: Stephens writes: "I would not wish to overstate the influence of blindness on my decision to pursue a career as a teacher and writer in the academic profession. At the same time I must acknowledge that this factor provided direction and, in a very real way, motivation to my study of constitutional law within the political science discipline. For me the selection of an academic subject that is strongly analytical and at the same time manageable in scope has been personally and professionally challenging. I have never regretted the choice."

* * *

STERLAND, E(rnest) G(eorge)   1919-

PERSONAL: Born June 30, 1919, in Coventry, England; son of George Frederick and Frances Mary (White) Sterland; married Joyce Mary Davies, January 31, 1942; children: Martin John, Paul Rodney. *Education:* King's College, University of London, B.Sc., 1940; Cambridge University, M.A., 1946. *Home:* Seafield, 81 Nore Rd., Portishead, Bristol, England.

CAREER: English Electric Co., Rugby, England, graduate apprentice, 1940-42, assistant engineer in turbine engine department, 1942-46; Cambridge University, Engineering Laboratories, Cambridge, England, lecturer in engineering thermodynamics, 1946-53; has served as principal of Bristol Aeroplane Technical College, Filton, Bristol, England, during 1950s and as justice of the peace in Bristol, England, in 1960s.

MEMBER: Institution of Mechanical Engineers (member of council, 1955-58), Royal Aeronautical Society (fellow; member of Bristol branch committee, 1966—), Newcomen Society.

WRITINGS: Applied Heat, English Universities Press, 1964; *Energy into Power: The Story of Man and Machines* (juvenile), Doubleday, 1967. General editor of "Technical College Series," for English Universities Press.

SIDELIGHTS: Sterland writes that his special interest is in thermodynamics, "also in technological history as a vehicle for uniting technology and the arts." In 1956 he visited the Soviet Union as a member of a British team of engineering educators. *Avocational interests:* Sailing, photography, breeding and exhibiting dogs.

* * *

STERN, Harold S.   1923(?)-1976

1923(?)—May 25, 1976; American drama critic and magazine editor. Obituaries: *New York Times,* May 30, 1976.

* * *

STERN, Susan (Tanenbaum)   1943-1976

1943—July 31, 1976; American political activist and author. Obituaries: *Washington Post,* August 2, 1976; *New York Times,* August 2, 1976.

* * *

STETLER, Charles E(dward)   1927-

PERSONAL: Born September 12, 1927, in Pittsburgh, Pa.; son of Charles E. (a salesman) and Katherine (Seidel) Stetler; married Ellen Donovan (a typist and receptionist), June 25, 1955; children: Peter, Paul, Casey. *Education:* Duquesne University, B.A., 1950, M.A., 1961; Tulane University, Ph.D., 1966. *Politics:* Democrat. *Residence:* Los Alamitos, Calif. *Office:* Department of English, California State University, Long Beach, Calif. 90840.

CAREER: Rockwell Manufacturing, Pittsburgh, Pa., advertising copywriter, 1953-54; Gulf Oil Corp., Pittsburgh, advertising copywriter, 1954-57; *Pittsburgh Sun Telegraph,* Pittsburgh, reporter, 1957-61; Rollins College, Winter Park, Fla., instructor in English, 1961-62; Loyola University, New Orleans, La., assistant professor of English, 1962-67; California State University, Long Beach, assistant professor, 1967-70, associate professor, 1970-75, professor of English, 1975—. *Military service:* U.S. Navy, 1945-46, 1950-52.

WRITINGS: Roger, Karl, Rick, and Shane Are Friends of Mine (poems), Mag Press, 1973; (with Gerald Locklin and Ronald Koertge) *Tarzan and Shane Meet the Toad* (poems), Russ Haas Press, 1975.

Poems have been anthologized in *Anthology of Los Angeles Poets,* edited by Neeli, Charles Bukowski, Cherry, and Paul Vangelisti, Red Hill, 1972; *Holy Doors,* edited by William J. Robson, privately printed, 1972. Contributor of articles and reviews to journals, including *Wormwood Review,* and to newspapers.

WORK IN PROGRESS: Critical research on Ernest Hemingway.

* * *

STEVENS, Diane 1944-

PERSONAL: Born September 26, 1944, in Butte, Mont.; daughter of Edwin W. (a mining engineer) and Lucille (Barrett) Stevens. *Education:* University of Washington, Seattle, B.A., 1966, M.A., 1967; State University of New York at Stony Brook, further graduate study, 1967-70. *Politics:* "Liberal free-thinking Democrat." *Religion:* "Humanist." *Home:* 3949 19th St., San Francisco, Calif. 94114. *Agent:* Norma Lee Clark, Rollins, Joffe & Morra, 130 West 57th St., New York, N.Y. 10019.

CAREER: Finance, New York, N.Y., editorial assistant and assistant manager of circulation, 1970-71; Cahners Publishing Co., New York, N.Y., editorial secretary, 1971-73; University of Washington, Seattle, medical secretary, 1973-74; Veterans Administration, Seattle, Wash., administrative assistant in medical research, 1974-76; writer, 1976—. *Member:* Phi Beta Kappa.

WRITINGS: The Valley of the Shadows, Popular Library, 1976; *Labyrinth,* Doubleday, 1976; *Elves Chasm,* Popular Library, in press.

WORK IN PROGRESS: The Other Side of Silence, a novel dealing with relationships and loneliness; *The Janus Complex,* a novel dealing with the idea of androgyny; a gothic novel; a one-woman play, "A Woman of Genius," about Mary Austin.

SIDELIGHTS: Diane Stevens writes: "In my gothic and suspense novels I am interested in creating heroines who reflect the modern consciousness of women. That is they are capable, intelligent, able to deal with crises, danger and violence without fainting or falling apart. I see this as a necessary development in the so-called 'women's novels.' In addition I am working on ideas which deal with the difficulty of establishing and maintaining relationships. I want to write seriously about different types of relationships; e.g., heterosexual and homosexual, and show that regardless of the individuals involved the difficulties, emotions, and motivations are similar. I see myself first as a woman writer dealing with human experience and secondarily as a woman writing about women as individual human beings. I plan to explore these themes in a number of ways, including serious novels and 'entertainment' novels. I am an avid traveller and like to use unusual settings I discover in my travels for my gothic and suspense novels. I particularly like to use locales in the American West."

AVOCATIONAL INTERESTS: Skiing, backpacking, refinishing antique furniture, photography, the musical theater, "motion pictures as an art form."

* * *

STEVENSON, Augusta 1869(?)-1976

1869(?)—July 7, 1976; American author, playwright, and educator. Obituaries: *Washington Post,* July 10, 1976; (See index for previous *CA* sketch)

STEVENSON, Leslie (Forster) 1943-

PERSONAL: Born December 15, 1943, in England; son of Patric (an artist) and Betsy (a violinist; maiden name, Forster) Stevenson; married Pat Ryall, July 8, 1972. *Education:* Attended Campbell College, 1960-62; Corpus Christi College, Oxford, M.A., 1965, B.Phil., 1968. *Office:* Department of Logic and Metaphysics, University of St. Andrews, Fife, Scotland.

CAREER: University of St. Andrews, Fife, Scotland, lecturer in philosophy, 1968—.

WRITINGS: Seven Theories of Human Nature, Oxford University Press, 1974. Contributor to journals in his field.

WORK IN PROGRESS: Research in the philosophy of mind and human nature.

* * *

STEWART, Christina Duff 1926-

PERSONAL: Born November 6, 1926, in Scotland; daughter of James Duff (an engineer) and Matilda (Grant) Stewart. *Education:* City of London Library School, A.L.A., 1949; University of Toronto, B.A., 1966, M.A., 1968; Library Association of Great Britain, F.L.A., 1973. *Home:* 211 Roslin Ave., Toronto, Ontario M4N 1Z5, Canada. *Office:* Department of Book Selection, University of Toronto Library, Toronto, Ontario M4N 1Z5, Canada.

CAREER: Westminster City Libraries, London, England, librarian, 1947-48, 1949-50; Coulsdon and Purley Libraries, Surrey, England, librarian, 1950-54; Toronto Public Libraries, Toronto, Ont., librarian, 1955-63; University of Toronto Library, book selector for graduate research in English and drama, 1968—. *Military service:* Women's Royal Naval Service, 1944-46. *Member:* Library Association of Great Britain.

WRITINGS: (Author of preface) *Thomas Boreman: A Description of Three Hundred Animals* (first published in 1786), facsimile edition, Johnson Reprint, 1968; (author of preface) *Isaac Taylor: Scenes in America* (first published in 1821), facsimile edition, Johnson Reprint, 1968; *The Taylors of Ongar: An Analytical Bio-Bibliography,* two volumes, Garland Publishing, 1975; (author of introduction) Ann Taylor, Jane Taylor, and others, *Original Poems and Rhymes for the Nursery* (first published in 1804), facsimile edition, Garland Publishing, in press. Contributor to *Junior Bookshelf.*

WORK IN PROGRESS: Writing introduction and biographical notes for *Ann Taylor Gilberts Album.*

AVOCATIONAL INTERESTS: Theatre, music, children's literature, bird and animal watching, Georgian Bay.

* * *

STEWART, Robert G(ordon) 1931-

PERSONAL: Born May 5, 1931, in Baltimore, Md.; son of Kenneth Elsworth and Ruth (an art gallery executive; maiden name, Chambers) Stewart. *Education:* University of Pennsylvania, B.F.A., 1954. *Politics:* Republican. *Religion:* Episcopalian. *Home:* 2351 49th St. N.W., Washington, D.C. 20007. *Office:* National Portrait Gallery, Eighth and F Sts. N.W., Washington, D.C. 20007.

CAREER: Independence National Historical Park, Philadelphia, Pa., architect, 1954; National Park Service, Philadelphia, architect, 1956-57; Jefferson Barracks Historical Park, St. Louis, Mo., architect and curator, 1958-61; National Trust for Historic Preservation, Washington, D.C., director of properties, 1961-64; National Portrait Gallery, Washington, D.C., curator, 1964—. Director of landmarks of St. Louis, 1959-61; consultant to Loyalist Homestead, St. John's, New Brunswick, 1960—; lecturer at George Washington University, 1967-70; adjudicator at Jamaican National Art Competition, 1971. *Military service:* U.S. Army, Corps of Engineers, 1954-56. *Member:* American Association of Museums, College Art Association, American Institute of Architects, Maryland Historical Society, Dorchester County Historical Society, Lewes Historical Society, Zeta Psi.

WRITINGS: Nucleus for a National Collection, Smithsonian Institution Press, 1965; *Recent Acquisitions,* Smithsonian Institution Press, 1966; *A Nineteenth-Century Gallery of Distinguished Americans,* Smithsonian Institution Press, 1969; *Henry Benbridge, 1743-1812: American Portrait Painter,* Smithsonian Institution Press, 1971.

WORK IN PROGRESS: Robert Edge Pine: A British Artist Portrays the American Revolutionaries, completion expected in 1978.

*   *   *

STILES, John R.   1916(?)-1976

1916(?)—April 15, 1976; American business executive, political party official, presidential adviser, and author. Obituaries: *Washington Post,* April 16, 1976.

*   *   *

STILL, James   1906-

PERSONAL: Born July 16, 1906, in LaFayette, Ala.; son of J. Alex (a veterinarian) and Lonie (Lindsey) Still. *Education:* Lincoln Memorial University, A.B., 1929; Vanderbilt University, M.A., 1930; University of Illinois, B.S., 1931. *Home address:* Wolfpen Creek, Mallie, Ky. 41836. *Agent:* Phyllis Jackson, International Creative Management, 40 West 57th St., New York, N.Y. 10019. *Office address:* Drawer T, Hindman, Ky. 41822.

CAREER: Hindman Settlement School, Hindman, Ky., librarian, 1932-39; free-lance writer, 1939-41, 1945-52; Hindman Settlement School, librarian, 1952-62; Morehead State University, Morehead, Ky., associate professor of English, 1962-71; free-lance writer, 1971—. *Military service:* U.S. Army Air Forces, 1941-45; served in Africa and the Middle East; became technical sergeant.

MEMBER: American Civil Liberties Union. *Awards, honors:* MacDowell Colony fellowship, 1938; O. Henry Memorial Prize, 1939, for short story, "Bat Flight"; Southern Authors Award from Southern Women's National Democratic Organization, 1940, for *River of Earth;* Guggenheim fellowships, 1941-42, 1946-47; fiction award from American Academy of Arts and Letters, 1947; Litt.D. from Berea College, 1973; L.H.D. from Lincoln Memorial University, 1974.

WRITINGS: Hounds on the Mountain (poems), Viking, 1937, 1965; *River of Earth* (novel), Viking, 1940, University Press of Kentucky, 1977; *On Troublesome Creek* (stories), Viking, 1941; *Way Down Yonder on Troublesome Creek* (juvenile), Putnam, 1974; *The Wolfpen Rusties* (juvenile), Putnam, 1975; *Pattern of a Man* (stories), Gnomon Press, 1976; *Jack and the Wonder Beans* (juvenile), Putnam, 1976; *Sporty Creek* (novel), Putnam, 1977.

Work represented in anthologies, including *O. Henry Memorial Prize Stories,* edited by Harry Hanson, Doubleday, 1939; *O. Henry Memorial Prize Stories,* edited by Hershall

Brickell, Doubleday, 1941; *The Yale Review Anthology,* edited by Wilbur Cross and Helen MacAfee, Yale University Press, 1942; *The Best American Short Stories,* edited by Martha Foley, Houghton, 1950; *Twenty-Three Modern Stories,* edited by Barbara Howes, Random House, 1963; *The World of Psychoanalysis,* edited by C. B. Levitas, Braziller, 1966; and *From the Mountain,* edited by Helen White and Redding S. Sugg, Jr., Memphis State University Press, 1972. Contributor of stories and poems to popular magazines and literary journals, including *Atlantic, Esquire, Nation, New Republic, Saturday Evening Post, Yale Review, Poetry, Virginia Quarterly Review,* and *Sewanee Review.*

WORK IN PROGRESS: Journeys to the Sun, a travel book based on his five winters in Yucatan, Guatemala, and Honduras.

SIDELIGHTS: Still has lived for many years in an old log cabin connected to civilization by a long dirt road and a creek bed.

BIOGRAPHICAL/CRITICAL SOURCES: Thomas S. Ford, editor, *Southern Appalachian Region,* University of Kentucky Press, 1962; Frank N. Magill, editor, *Cyclopedia of Literary Characters,* Harper, 1963; *Yale Review,* winter, 1968.

*   *   *

STINE, G(eorge) Harry   1928-
(Lee Correy)

PERSONAL: Born March 26, 1928, in Philadelphia, Pa.; son of George Haeberle (an eye surgeon) and Rhea Matilda (O'Neil) Stine; married Barbara A. Kauth, June 10, 1952; children: Constance Rhea, Eleanor Ann, George Willard. *Education:* Attended University of Colorado, 1946-50; Colorado College, B.A., 1952. *Home:* 616 West Frier Dr., Phoenix, Ariz. 85021. *Agent:* Lurton Blassingame, 60 East 42nd St., New York, N.Y. 10017.

CAREER: White Sands Proving Ground, White Sands, N.M., chief of controls and instruments section in propulsion branch, 1952-55, chief of range operations division and Navy flight safety engineer, 1955-57; Martin Co., Denver, Colo., design specialist, 1957; Model Missiles, Inc., Denver, president and chief engineer, 1957-59; Stanley Aviation Corp., Denver, design engineer, 1959-60; Huyck Corp., Stamford, Conn., assistant director of research, 1960-65; consulting engineer and science writer in New Canaan, Conn., 1965-73; Flow Technology, Inc., Phoenix, Ariz., marketing manager, 1973-76; science writer and consultant, 1976—. *Member:* American Institute of Aeronautics and Astronautics (associate fellow), Instrument Society of America, Academy of Model Aeronautics, National Aeronautic Association, British Interplanetary Society (fellow), National Fire Protection Association, National Association of Rocketry (founder; president, 1957-67; honorary trustee), Science Fiction Writers of America, New York Academy of Sciences, Theta Xi, Explorers Club (New York City; fellow).

WRITINGS: (Under pseudonym Lee Correy) *Starship through Space,* Holt, 1954; (under pseudonym Lee Correy) *Contraband Rocket,* Ace, 1955; (under pseudonym Lee Correy) *Rocket Man,* Holt, 1956; *Rocket Power and Space Flight,* Holt, 1957; *Earth Satellites and the Race for Space Superiority,* Ace, 1957; *Man and the Space Frontier,* Knopf, 1962; (contributor) Frederick Pohl, editor, *The Expert Dreamers,* Doubleday, 1962; *The Handbook of Model Rocketry,* Follett, 1965, 4th edition, 1975; (contributor) George W. Early, editor, *Encounters with Aliens,* Sherbourne, 1969;

The Model Rocket Manual, Sentinel, 1969; *Model Rocket Safety,* Model Products Corp., 1970; (contributor) Ben Bova, editor, *The Analog Science Fact Reader,* Sherbourne, 1974; *The Third Industrial Revolution,* Putnam, 1975; (contributor) Ben Bova, editor, *A New View of the Solar System,* St. Martin's, 1976; *The New Model Rocketry Manual,* Arco, in press.

Also author of six technical papers and of five filmscripts. Science fiction short stories represented in anthologies, including *Science Fiction, '58: The Year's Greatest Science Fiction and Fantasy,* edited by Judith Merrill, Gnome, 1958; *The Sixth Annual of the Year's Best Science Fiction,* edited by Judith Merrill, Simon & Schuster, 1961; *Analog Six,* edited by John W. Campbell, Doubleday, 1968.

Contributor to *Collier's Encyclopedia;* contributor of over 150 science fiction stories and science fact and model rocketry articles to magazines, including *Saturday Evening Post, Astounding, Analog, Science Digest,* and *Magazine of Fantasy and Science Fiction;* writer of monthly column, "Conquest of Space," in *Mechanix Illustrated,* 1956-57. Editor, *Missile Away,* 1953-57, *The Model Rocketeer,* 1958-64, *Flow Factor,* 1973-76.

WORK IN PROGRESS: "Too many authors talk about the stories they are going to do tomorrow. I prefer to discuss only what I have done."

SIDELIGHTS: "I had the good fortune to grow up in Colorado Springs, Colorado on one of the last physical frontiers on the North American continent, the American West. I also had the good fortune to choose a father who was an eye surgeon, who was an amateur scientist, and who surrounded me with books from as early as I can remember. In concert with my father, a number of men instilled in me a consuming curiosity about the universe around me. Once I asked one of them what I could ever do to repay him. I have been repaying him ever since because he said, 'There is no way that you can repay me directly and personally. The only thing that you can do to repay me is to do the same thing for the next generation. The obligation is always toward the future.'

"I write the sort of thing that I would like to read. I write it the way I would like to read it. I write entertainment. I am competing for the reader's time and money; if he doesn't like what I write, he will not spend his time and plunk down his hard-earned money a second time."

Stine believes: "The human race is going to survive. We will use the accumulated knowledge of centuries plus our rational minds to solve the problems that seem to beset us at the moment . . . and they are really no worse than the problems that faced other generations in the past. The current problems seem worse because they are current and because we have not yet solved them. What is difficult to us was impossible to our parents and will be commonplace to our children. We will indeed slay the dragons of war, intolerance, and pollution. We will marry the princess of outer space. And we will live happily ever after among the stars. We now have or will soon have the capability to do anything we want to do; we must only be willing to pay for it and to live with all the consequences.

"Like it or not, we live in a technological reality. One can escape it only by regressing through centuries of human history. I have attempted to master or at least understand as much about technology as possible. I have operated or am at least aware of how to operate every possible human transportation machine, for example; I have operated railroad trains, horses, automobiles, boats, and airplanes. I am a licensed pilot, own an airplane, and fly regularly. I hope someday to fly in a rocket-powered space vehicle . . . or in any sort of space vehicle. I greatly admire the fictitious man who, when asked if he could fly a helicopter, replied, 'I don't know; I've never tried.'

"The human race has a long way yet to go, and there are a lot of things left to do. According to a recent U.N. survey, nearly half the people in the world cannot read or write their native language; in the 'literate' United States of America, there are 21,000,000 people who are illiterate. Over 100,-000,000 Americans have never been up in an airplane. 90% of the people on Earth have never been more than 25 miles from their birthplace, nor do they expect to travel beyond their village during their lifetimes."

* * *

STITES, Raymond S(omers) 1899-1974

PERSONAL: Born June 19, 1889, in Passaic, N.J.; married first wife, 1923; married second wife, M. Elizabeth, 1938; children: Gretel Stites Friedman, Nan Stites Thoenen, Mary Stites Mayer. *Education:* Brown University, B.S., 1921, A.M., 1922; University of Vienna, Ph.D., 1928; also studied at Rhode Island School of Design. *Religion:* Society of Friends (Quakers). *Residence:* Garrett Park, Md.

CAREER: Iowa State University, Ames, instructor in art history, 1928-29; University of Colorado, Boulder, instructor in art, 1929-30; Antioch College, Yellow Springs, Ohio, associate professor, 1930-35, professor of art and aesthetics and chairman of department, 1935-47; National Gallery of Art, Washington, D.C., curator in charge of education, 1948-66, assistant to director, 1966-69 (also founded Volunteer Guide Corps); Wesley Theological Seminary, Washington, D.C., adjunct professor of art, 1968-69. Museum director in Davenport, Iowa, 1928; instructor at University of Redlands, 1945-46; director of Cultural Films, Inc., 1950-65. Work has been exhibited in collections, including those at Metropolitan Museum of Art and American Museum of Natural History. *Military service:* U.S. Army, 1918, became lieutenant.

MEMBER: Archaeological Institute of America, College Art Association, American Society for Aesthetics, Society for the Psycho-Pathology of Expression, Ohio Valley Art Association.

WRITINGS: The Arts and Man, McGraw, 1940; (with wife, M. Elizabeth Stites, and Pierina Castiglione) *The Sublimations of Leonardo da Vinci, with a Translation of the Codex Trivulzianus,* Smithsonian Institution Press, 1970. Also author of *The Sculptures of Leonardo da Vinci,* 1930; *The Self Psychoanalysis of Leonardo da Vinci,* 1969; and *The Lost Sculptures of Leonardo.* Contributor to art magazines.

WORK IN PROGRESS: Stites was working on a film about Leonardo da Vinci to be used in schools.

OBITUARIES: New York Times, December 7, 1974; *Washington Post,* December 8, 1974; *AB Bookman's Weekly,* January 13, 1975.*

(Died December 6, 1974, in Garrett Park, Md.)

* * *

STOCK, Claudette 1934-

PERSONAL: Born September 22, 1934, in Denver, Colo.; daughter of Claude (a rancher) and Ethel (a rancher; maiden name, Jordan) Stock. *Education:* Colorado College, student, 1952-54; University of Kansas, B.A., 1956, M.A.,

1957; further graduate study at University of Denver, 1960-70, and Santa Clara University, 1976. *Home address:* R.R.1, Ridgway, Colo. 81432.

CAREER: Teacher of the orthopedically handicapped in public schools in Denver, Colo., 1957-60; University of Kansas, Medical Center, Children's Rehabilitation Unit, Kansas City, instructor and director of pre-school program for the multiple-handicapped, 1960-61; teacher of the perceptually handicapped pre-school child in public schools in Denver, Colo., 1961-65, special education teacher, 1966-67; J. F. Kennedy Child Development Center, Denver, Colo., pre-school director and teacher, 1967-69; private practice diagnosing and treating children with learning disabilities, 1969-71; education specialist in public schools in Craig, Colo., 1971-72, and Lakewood, Colo., 1972-75; Montrose County Public Schools, Montrose, Colo., education specialist, 1975—. Member of advisory board of Hope Center.

MEMBER: Council for Exceptional Children, Council for Children with Behavioral Disorders, national Association for Retarded Children, Colorado Education Association, Colorado Association for Children with Learning Disabilities, Colorado Association for Retarded Children (member of advisory board), Metropolitan Mental Health Association.

WRITINGS: Minimal Brain Dysfunction Child: Some Clinical Manifestations-Definition-Descriptions-Remediation Approaches, Pruett, 1969; *Learning Tasks for the Pre-Academic Child with Developmental Disabilities,* Pruett, 1971. Contributor to education journals.

* * *

STOEHR, C(arl) Eric 1945-

PERSONAL: Born January 25, 1945, in Englewood, N.J.; son of Richard G. (a textile firm executive) and Elizabeth (Jackson) Stoehr; married Gail Hanszen, February 11, 1967. *Education:* University of Miami, student, 1962-66 and 1970-71; University of New Mexico, B.F.A., 1972, M.Arch., 1974. *Home:* 4347 Dickason St. #217, Dallas, Tex. 75219. *Office:* Wong & Tung & Partners, Inc., 2215 N. Olive St., Dallas, Tex. 75201.

CAREER: Robert L. Torres & Associates (architects and planners), Albuquerque, N.M., architect, 1973-75; Wong & Tung & Partners, Inc. (architects and planners), Dallas, Tex., architect, 1975—. *Military service:* U.S. Air Force, security service in Brindisi, Italy, 1966-70.

WRITINGS: Bonanza Victorian: Architecture and Society in Colorado Mining Towns, University of New Mexico Press, 1975.

SIDELIGHTS: Stoehr told *CA:* "Bonanza Victorian was written to provide a record of the unique and vanishing architectural forms of nineteenth century Colorado mining towns. Many of the towns, which have stood for such a long time without significant change, are now being transformed in various ways. The natural deterioration of wood buildings and their vulnerability to fire have been constant factors in the disappearance of old towns. In addition, increasing vandalism and new booms in land development, such as the creation of ski areas and other recreational facilities, are contributing to the metamorphosis. Soon such transformation will make many of the original towns unrecognizable."

* * *

STOFFEL, Albert Law 1909-

PERSONAL: Born May 20, 1909, in Racine, Wis.; son of Albert John (a manufacturer) and Harriet (Law) Stoffel; married Catherine Williams, November 12, 1937; children: Catherine Ann (Mrs. Walter A. Bunnell), Albert Law, Jr. *Education:* University of Kentucky, B.A., 1931. *Politics:* Republican. *Religion:* Episcopal. *Home:* 231 23rd St., Santa Monica, Calif. 90402.

CAREER/WRITINGS: Wisconsin News, Milwaukee, Wis., reporter, 1931-36; Hamilton Wright Organization, New York, N.Y., news and feature writer in Italy, 1938-39; *Richmond News-Leader,* Richmond, Va., 1940-42; Western Publishing Co., Los Angeles, Calif., editor and manager, 1946-75; writer, 1975—. Author and producer of "Bugs Bunny" cartoon strip, syndicated daily and Sunday by Newspaper Enterprise Association to about seven hundred newspapers, 1946—. Author of books for Western Publishing. Member of board of directors of Beverly Hills Young Men's Christian Association (chairman of Athletic Club). *Military service:* U.S. Naval Reserve, active duty as communications officer on an aircraft carrier, 1942-46; became lieutenant. *Member:* University of Kentucky Southern California Alumni Club (president), Riviera Country Club, Businessmen's Athletic Club, Cave des Royes.

SIDELIGHTS: "I have always taken pride in the craft of being a writer," Stoffel told *CA,* "and always have given my best on any assignment. I feel that I am capable of producing anything that involves the written word in the realm of my experience. I have written books on such varied subjects as *How to Care for Your Dog* to a comprehensive rundown of the American space program." *Avocational interests:* Golf.

* * *

STOHLMAN, Martha Lou Lemmon 1913-

PERSONAL: Born October 25, 1913, in Springfield, Mo.; daughter of G. Bruce (a physician) and Mary (Horrell) Lemmon; married W. Frederick Stohlman (a professor), June 22, 1945 (deceased); children: Julie, Suzanne. *Education:* Sweet Briar College, A.B., 1934; Cornell University, A.M., 1935, Ph.D., 1937. *Politics:* Democrat. *Religion:* Presbyterian. *Home:* 11 Edgehill St., Princeton, N.J. 08540.

CAREER: Colorado College, Colorado Springs, assistant professor of psychology, 1937-44; U.S. Foreign Service, Washington, D.C., clerk at U.S. Embassy in Rome, 1945-46; Sweet Briar College, Sweet Briar, Va., visiting professor of psychology, 1957-58. Environmental commissioner for the Borough of Princeton.

WRITINGS: The Story of Sweet Briar College, Sweet Briar College, 1957; *John Witherspoon: Parson, Patriot, Politician,* Westminister, 1976.

Contributor to *Saturday Review* and *Presbyterian Life.*

WORK IN PROGRESS: Life in Springfield, Mo., 1913-1930.

SIDELIGHTS: Martha Stohlman writes: "Religion offers me more satisfying substance than psychology on the meaning of life and the mystery of death." *Avocational interests:* Reading, visiting friends, travel ("from the Galapagos to Narvik").

* * *

STOLOFF, Carolyn 1927-

PERSONAL: Born January 14, 1927, in New York, N.Y.; daughter of Charles I. (a dentist) and Irma (a sculptor; maiden name, Levy) Stoloff. *Eduation:* Attended University of Illinois, 1944-46; Columbia University, B.S., 1949; study at Art Students League and Atelier 17; private study of painting with Eric Isenburger and poetry with Stanley Kunitz. *Home:* 24 West 8th St., New York, N.Y. 10011. *Office:* 32 Union Sq. E., No. 911, New York, N.Y. 10003.

CAREER: Painter; has given group and solo shows. Manhattanville College, Purchase, N.Y., 1957-74, became assistant professor of painting, chairman of art department, 1960-65. Conducted poetry seminars, 1968-74. Teacher at a Quaker halfway house for drug addicts and at a women's house of detention. Has given readings from her works at public gatherings and on radio programs. *Awards, honors:* MacDowell Colony fellowships, 1961, 1962, 1970; Theodore Roethke Award from *Poetry Northwest,* 1967, for four poems; silver anniversary medal from Audubon Artists show, 1967; National Council on the Arts grant, 1968; Helene Wurlitzer Foundation residence grant, 1972, 1973, 1974; first prize for poetry from *Miscellany,* 1972.

WRITINGS—Poems: *Triptych* (broadside), Unicorn Press, 1970; *Stepping Out,* Unicorn Press, 1971; *In the Red Meadow* (chapbook), New Rivers Press, 1973; *Dying to Survive,* Doubleday, 1973.

Work has been anthologized in *The New Yorker Book of Poems,* Viking, 1969; *Our Only Hope Is Humor,* edited by Richard Snyder and Robert McGovern, Ashland Poetry Press, 1972; and *Rising Tides,* edited by Laura Chester and Sharon Barba, Washington Square Press, 1973. Contributor of poems to popular magazines and literary journals, including *New Yorker, Nation, Prairie Schooner, Antioch Review, Choice,* and *New England Review.*

SIDELIGHTS: Carolyn Stoloff, daughter of an artist and musician mother, studied Indian and Spanish dancing and developed a deep interest in the opera, but found the greatest personal satisfaction in painting and, later, in poetry. Travels in Europe and Mexico have enhanced her already broad interest in the arts.

AVOCATIONAL INTERESTS: Ethnic music and dance, ancient history, books on animals and insects, identifying flowers and trees, European and South American poets in translation, conservation, handcrafts, films, travel.

*　　*　　*

STONE, Vernon A(lfred)   1929-

PERSONAL: Born October 21, 1929, in Bowling Green, Ky.; son of Hughie H. (a farmer) and Mabel (Lothridge) Stone; married Saribenne Thomas (an artist), June 11, 1966; children: Hallie, Adam. *Education:* Western Kentucky University, B.A., 1951; University of Iowa, M.A., 1953; University of Wisconsin, Madison, Ph.D., 1966. *Home:* 4210 Old Lexington Rd., Athens, Ga. 30601. *Office:* School of Journalism, University of Georgia, Athens, Ga. 30602.

CAREER: WHAS-Television, Louisville, Ky., reporter, 1953-56, television news coordinator, 1956-62; University of Wisconsin, Madison, assistant professor, 1965-69, associate professor, 1969-73, professor of journalism and mass communication, 1973-74; University of Georgia, Athens, professor of journalism, 1974—. *Member:* International Society for Communication, Association for Education in Journalism (head of Radio-Television Division, 1972-74; member of advisory board, 1973-74), Radio Television News Directors Association (chairman of research and publications committee, 1972—), Society for Professional Journalists, Broadcast Education Association. *Awards, honors:* National Science Foundation grant, 1967-72.

WRITINGS: Careers in Broadcast News, Radio Television

News Directors Association, 1972; (with Bruce Hinson) *Television Newsfilm Techniques,* Hastings House, 1974. Contributor of about thirty articles to journalism and other communication journals.

WORK IN PROGRESS: Research on television and radio news operations, minorities and women in broadcast news, electronic news gathering, and source-message orientation.

SIDELIGHTS: Stone has conducted research on women in broadcast journalism and has produced and/or participated in public programs to discuss his research; he has also studied and discussed broadcast journalism education and careers, and has conducted experimental studies on source-message orientation and attitude change.

AVOCATIONAL INTERESTS: Gardening.

*　　*　　*

STOOP, Norma McLain

PERSONAL: Born in Panama Canal Zone; daughter of Harry Edward (a manufacturer) and Gladys (Brandon) McLain; married William J. Stoop, Jr. (died June, 1965). *Education:* Attended Penn Hall Junior College and Carnegie Institute of Technology (now Carnegie-Mellon University); additional study at Ivy House, Wimbledon, England, and in Paris at European branch of Finch College. *Politics:* Independent. *Religion:* Protestant. *Home:* 1 Lincoln Plaza, Apt. 23D, New York, N.Y. 10023. *Office:* Danad Publishing Co., 10 Columbus Cir., New York, N.Y. 10019.

CAREER: Poet, photographer, professional ballroom dancer, entertainment critic, and writer. *Dance* and *After Dark* magazines, New York, N.Y., contributing editor, 1969-71, associate editor, 1971—. Notable assignments include interviews of Christopher Isherwood, John Huston, Stanley Kramer, Ned Rorem, and Robert Redford. Has exhibited dance photographs at Harvard University and Tufts University. *Member:* National Society of Television Arts and Sciences, Poetry Society of America, Overseas Press Club of America, Dance Masters of America, Dance Critics Association. *Awards, honors:* Borestone Mountain Poetry Award, 1974.

WRITINGS: Work represented in *Best Poems of 1973: Borestone Mountain Poetry Awards, 1974,* edited by Lionel Stevenson, Pacific Books, 1974.

Writer of columns, "Films," 1972—, "TV Spotlight," 1975—, and "Behind Both Screens," 1976—, all in *After Dark,* and of "Dancevision: the TV Beat" in *Dance,* 1976—. Contributor of poetry, essays, fiction, reviews, and photography to magazines and newspapers, including *After Dark, Dance, Atlantic Monthly, Chicago Review, McCall's, Roanoke Review, La Depeche du midi, Stuttgarter Nachrichten, New York Times,* and *Christian Science Monitor.*

WORK IN PROGRESS: Two nonfiction books in the planning stage.

AVOCATIONAL INTERESTS: Travel.

BIOGRAPHICAL/CRITICAL SOURCES: Rock Scene, March, 1975; *Christian Science Monitor,* September 24, 1975.

*　　*　　*

STORY, Ronald   1946-

PERSONAL: Born February 12, 1946, in Joplin, Mo.; son of Raymond Christopher (a carpenter) and Willa (a licensed practical nurse; maiden name, Johnson) Story; married Rita

Lynn Motherway, October 30, 1969; children: Brenda Ann, Brian Alan. *Education:* University of Arizona, B.A. (with honors), 1970. *Politics:* Democrat. *Religion:* "Humanist." *Home:* 5309 East Glenn St., Apt. D, Tucson, Ariz. 85712. *Agent:* Albert Zuckerman, Writer's House, 132 West 31st St., New York, N.Y. 10001. *Office:* Tucson Gas and Electric Co., P.O. Box 711, Tucson, Ariz. 85702.

CAREER: Assistant manager of retail stores in Santa Maria, Calif., and Tucson, Ariz., 1970-72; Tucson Gas and Electric Co., Tucson, Ariz., buyer of electrical equipment, 1972—. *Military service:* U.S. Navy, 1963-69; served in Vietnam. *Member:* Aerial Phenomena Research Organization, Tucson Astronomical and Astronautical Association, Authors Guild.

WRITINGS: The Space Gods Revealed: A Close Look at the Theories of Erich von Daniken, Harper, 1976.

WORK IN PROGRESS: A U.F.O. catalog, with Walter H. Bowart, publication by Doubleday expected in 1978; editing bulletins of the Aerial Phenomena Research Organization for publication in book form.

SIDELIGHTS: Story's first book is a scientific rebuttal of the widely discussed theory that extraterrestrials have visited the earth in the distant past and left their marks in our archaeological record. "I was outraged with the fact so many publications, movies, and TV shows came out with such blatant inaccuracies," said Story. *The Space Gods Revealed* begins with a discussion of the topic in general and then, in detail, examines the speculative arguments of Erich von Daniken—the best selling author who has probably done the most to popularize the theory. Story said every important scientist he talked to rejected von Daniken's arguments, "however, most of our anthropologists, archaeologists, astronomers, theologians, and philosophers have remained [publicly] silent on the issue."

Andy Wickstrom said: "The publishers do not identify Story as a scientist; rather he appears to be a rather good journalist and researcher, and he is a bit annoyed with the academics who argue that they have better things to do with their time than refute the patently absurd Von Daniken books. It is their silence, argues Story, that is partly to blame for Von Daniken's popularity." Story believes an additional factor is that "people love theories that are overly simple. They're easier to understand. And another thing, people want to escape responsibility; von Daniken offers that, too—in effect, 'they'll come back and take care of our problems.'"

"What's more," says Barbara Ford, "millions of people believe him [von Daniken]. It's that belief that Story tries to shake and, in the opinion of this nonbeliever, he succeeds. He succeeds so well, in fact, that his method of attack might well serve as the model for future attacks on pseudo-science. Story's problems in handling his material were numerous. . . . Tracking down the origin of such details takes time, energy and patience. Most scientists—most writers, too—simply don't want to devote the time necessary to do the job well. Story, however, has reduced the task to manageable proportions."

Story told *CA:* "I believe in the power of three virtues: reason, honesty, and compassion, to solve human problems. I do not believe in blatant exploitation of human ignorance and gullibility. This is why I want to expose the pseudo-sciences by attempting to bring to light some of the many little-known facts in certain scientific areas. My principal goal is to reveal the truth and, at the same time, make academic science interesting to the general public."

BIOGRAPHICAL/CRITICAL SOURCES: Publishers Weekly, May 31, 1976; *Norfolk Virginian Pilot,* August 8, 1976; *Arizona Daily Star,* August 15, 1976; *Peninsula Living,* September 4, 1976; *Dallas Morning News,* October 7, 1976; *Science Digest,* December, 1976.

*　　*　　*

STOUT, Robert Joe 1936-
(Joe Pires)

PERSONAL: Born February 3, 1936, in Scotts Bluff, Neb.; son of Charles V. and Eunice (Diller) Stout; married Lynne Maier (a probation officer), August 11, 1962; children: Paul William, Emily Katherine, Ingrid, Deirdre Marie. *Education:* Mexico City College, B.A., 1960. *Home:* 1502 Citrus Ave., Chico, Calif. 95926.

CAREER: Western Publications, Austin, Tex., managing editor of *True West* and *Frontier Times,* 1960-63; typist, 1964; free-lance writer and editor, 1964-68; *Relics,* Austin, Tex., editor, 1968-73; secretary, bookkeeper, and accountant in San Francisco, Calif., 1974; property tax accountant for Butte County, Calif., 1975—. *Military service:* U.S. Air Force, 1954-58.

WRITINGS: Miss Sally (novel), Bobbs-Merrill, 1973; *Moving Out* (chapbook), Road Runner Press, 1973; *Trained Bears on Hoops* (chapbook), Thorp Springs Press, 1974; *Swallowing Dust* (poems), Red Hill Press, 1976; *The Trick* (chapbook), Juniper Press, 1976.

Work has been anthologized in *The New Breed,* edited by Dave Oliphant, Prickly Pear Press, 1973; *New Southern Poets,* edited by Guy Owen and Mary C. Williams, University of North Carolina Press, 1975; and *Survivors of the Invention,* edited by Bob Bonazzi, Latitudes Press, 1975.

Contributor of several dozen articles, stories, and poems, sometimes under pseudonym Joe Pires, to men's adventure magazines and to literary journals and newspapers, including *West Coast Review, Pageant, Nation, Twigs, Canadian Forum, Descant, South Dakota Review, Four Quarters, Kansas Quarterly,* and *Southwest Review.*

WORK IN PROGRESS: The November Campaign, a novel; a book of poems; a nonfiction series on contemporary welfare problems and the human beings that become involved in them.

SIDELIGHTS: Stout writes: "As a young man my father traveled throughout the world as an advance man for Chautauqua circuits and as a newspaperman. My mother was a Chautauqua actress, musician, and matinee entertainer. I was born after Chautauqua collapsed during the Depression. My father had taken a job as a sugar factory mechanic in a small town in Wyoming and never returned to writing or the arts. I quit high school to join the Air Force, worked my way into journalism as a non-combative sports writer and, after my discharge, took my G.I. Bill to Mexico, a land that is still the underside of my consciousness, a sort of alternate id."

*　　*　　*

STRAND, Paul 1890-1976

October 16, 1890—March 31, 1976; American-born French photographer and cinematographer. Obituaries: *Washington Post,* April 3, 1976; *Time,* April 12, 1976; *Newsweek,* April 12, 1976; *Current Biography,* May, 1976.

*　　*　　*

STRAND, Thomas 1944-

PERSONAL: Born March 7, 1944, in La Grande, Ore.; son

of Janette (a waitress) Strand; married Sheerie Lynn Mitchell, February 17, 1967 (divorced, 1972); children: David Carmony, Dylan Kell. *Education:* Eastern Oregon College, student, 1961-62; Southern Oregon State College, B.S., 1974. *Residence:* Portland, Ore. *Office:* C/O 407 Postal Bldg., 510 Southwest Third St., Portland, Ore. 97204.

CAREER: Writer; has worked as manager of a coffeehouse, security guard, and railway clerk. *Military service:* U.S. Army, paratrooper, 1963-66; served in Vietnam; received Purple Heart and Bronze Star with "V" device. *Member:* Poets and Writers, Inc.

WRITINGS: Questions to Brecht, Thorpe Springs Press, 1975. Contributor to literary journals, including *December, Cameo, Human Voice, Hyperion, Subterraneans, Desperado,* and *Grand Ronde Review.*

WORK IN PROGRESS: Night of the Horse and *The Heritage,* both autobiographical novels; *The Hanged Man,* a book of poems.

SIDELIGHTS: Strand comments: "I am very involved with the autobiographical form of prose since I am convinced that my own life is what I know best. Indeed, it may be all I know. Especially concerned with Vietnam and its aftermath. Currently trying to complete a novel dealing with this. Also, spent nearly two years in Europe which is also the genesis of a book."

* * *

STRATTON, Thomas
   See DeWEESE, (Thomas Eu)Gene

* * *

STREET, Margaret M(ary) 1907-

PERSONAL: Born May 20, 1907, in Toronto, Ontario, Canada; daughter of Louis J. (a civil engineer) and Amelia M. (Parkyn) Street. *Education:* University of Manitoba, B.A., 1928; Provincial Normal School, Winnipeg, Manitoba, collegiate certificate, 1929; Royal Victoria Hospital School of Nursing, diploma, 1936; McGill University, diploma in teaching and supervision, 1942; Boston University, M.Sc., 1961. *Home:* 3856 West Eighth Ave., Vancouver, British Columbia, Canada V6R 1Z4.

CAREER: High school teacher in Alonsa and Melita, Manitoba, 1929-33; St. Joseph's Hospital School of Nursing, Victoria, British Columbia, instructor in nursing, 1936-37; Vancouver General Hospital, Vancouver, British Columbia, general staff nurse, 1937-38, assistant to night supervisor, 1938-41; Misericordia Hospital School of Nursing, Winnipeg, Manitoba, instructor in nursing, 1942-43; Manitoba Association of Registered Nurses, Winnipeg, executive secretary, 1943-45; Royal Victoria Hospital School of Nursing, Montreal, Quebec, clinical instructor in nursing, 1945-49; Association of Nurses of the Province of Quebec, Montreal, executive secretary, 1949-52; University of British Columbia, Vancouver, instructor in nursing, 1952-53; Calgary General Hospital and School of Nursing, Calgary, Alberta, clinical coordinator, 1953-55, associate director of nursing, 1956-60; University of British Columbia, assistant professor, 1961-64, associate professor of nursing service administration, 1965-72; writer, 1972—.

MEMBER: Registered Nurses Association of Ontario (honorary member), Alberta Association of Registered Nurses (president, 1957-59; honorary life member). *Awards, honors:* Canada Council grants, 1969, 1970; grant from Humanities and Social Science Research Council of Canada, 1972;

Walter Stewart Baird Medal from University of British Columbia, 1974, for work in the history of health sciences; additional grants from Canadian Nurses Association, Association of Nurses of the Province of Quebec, Manitoba Association of Registered Nurses, Alberta Association of Registered Nurses, and Registered Nurses Association of British Columbia.

WRITINGS: Watch-Fires on the Mountains: The Life and Writings of Ethel Johns, University of Toronto Press, 1973. Contributor to nursing journals.

SIDELIGHTS: Royalties from Margaret Street's book are assigned to the Ethel Johns and Isabel Maitland Stewart Memorial Scholarship Fund at the University of British Columbia. This fund provides an annual scholarship for graduate studies in nursing.

* * *

STREETER, Edward 1891-1976

August 1, 1891—March 31, 1976; American banker, stock broker, and author of humorous fiction. Obituaries: *New York Times,* April 2, 1976; *Newsweek,* April 12, 1976. (See index for previous *CA* sketch)

* * *

STRICKLAND, Margot 1927-

PERSONAL: Born March 5, 1927, in Madrid, Spain; daughter of Heyworth (a linguist) and Ursula (a governess; maiden name, Johnstone) Spencer; married A. H. Strickland (a scientific civil servant), September 26, 1947; children: Diana Margaret Strickland Jackson, Simon Slade Strickland. *Education:* Educated in private schools in France and Spain. *Religion:* "Ecumenical Catholic." *Home:* 1 Brocket Hall, Welwyn, Hertfordshire AL8, England. *Agent:* Gerard Pollinger, 18 Maddox St., London W.C.1, England.

CAREER: Actress, has performed in theatres in England and Wales, and acted in three feature films; writer. Has worked as a teacher of Spanish and English; now teaching English as a second language. *Member:* Society of Authors, Byron Society, Anglo-Spanish, European-Atlantic Group.

WRITINGS: The Byron Women, P. Owen, 1974, St. Martin's, 1975; *"Mrs. Thirkell": The Portrait of a Lady Novelist,* Duckworth, 1977. Contributor to magazines, including *She, Private Eye, Lady, West African Review,* and *Time and Tide,* and to newspapers.

WORK IN PROGRESS: Memoirs of Sophia Baddeley; The Lambs, William and Caroline; I Want a Hero, a novel.

SIDELIGHTS: Margot Strickland writes: "My early years in the theatre have been of great value to me. Most human situations can be traced to a dramatic source. Twenty-five years living in an English village ws the spur to succeed as a writer, and the area, steeped in history, was my source."

* * *

STRINGER, William Henry 1908-1976

November 19, 1908—March 31, 1976; American news correspondent, editor, and government administrator. Obituaries: *Washington Post,* April 3, 1976.

* * *

STRONG, Bethany J(une)
   See McLAUGHLIN, Bethany J.

STROTHER, Elsie (Frances Warmoth Weitzel) 1912-

PERSONAL: Born June 15, 1912, in New York, N.Y.; daughter of Frank S. (a sugar planter) and Phyllis S. (Aitken) Warmoth; married George J. Weitzel, March 22, 1935 (died, 1959); married Dean C. Strother (a general in the U.S. Air Force), December 29, 1964; children: (first marriage) Carroll (Mrs. G.L.B. Rivers), Sallie (Mrs. Jamie Gough). *Education:* Attended New York School of Design, Grand Central Fine Arts School, and St. James Ecole in Paris, France. *Home:* 8 Polo Dr., Colorado Springs, Colo. 80906.

CAREER: Art teacher in private schools in Aiken, S.C., 1950-59, and in Charleston, S.C., 1959-62. Painter, especially of animals. *Member:* National League of American Pen Women (vice-president of local branch), Authors Guild of Authors League of America.

WRITINGS—For children: *The Royal Cheetah and the Untouchables,* Westminster, 1974; *Rendezvous at Live Oaks,* Avalon, 1975; *Island of Terror,* Avalon, 1976. Author of "The Children's Nook," a column in *Aitken Standard and Review,* 1951—. Contributor of stories and articles to children's magazines.

WORK IN PROGRESS: Four novels; a suspense-romance.

SIDELIGHTS: Elsie Strother writes that she was "Brought up in the West Indies with education acquired through governesses, tutors, and voluminous reading. I have traveled and lived all over the world and have painted and written about most of it." *Avocational interests:* Golfing, music.

*   *   *

STUCKEY, Gilbert B. 1912-

PERSONAL: Born August 5, 1912, in Platte County, Mo.; son of Arthur and Ethel (Searcy) Stuckey; married Mildred Onstott (a psychologist). *Education:* Chaffey College, student, 1930-32; University of Southern California, B.A., 1934, J.D., 1936. *Religion:* Methodist. *Home:* 21132 East Cloverland Dr., Covina, Calif. 91724. *Office:* Department of Public Safety and Service, Mount San Antonio College, Walnut, Calif. 91789.

CAREER: Federal Bureau of Investigation (FBI), Washington, D.C., special agent, 1938-62; Mount San Antonio College, Walnut, Calif., professor of public safety and service, 1962—, chairman of department, 1962-69. *Member:* Nebraska Bar Association.

WRITINGS: Evidence for the Law Enforcement Officer, McGraw, 1968, revised edition, 1974; *Procedures in the Justice System,* C. E. Merrill, 1976.

WORK IN PROGRESS: Evidence for the Law Enforcement Officer, 3rd edition; writing satire for family magazines.

SIDELIGHTS: Stuckey writes that his books are aimed at the community college student who may be planning a career in law enforcement or corrections. He has traveled to the Far East and the South Seas, studying aborigines and their mores, as well as their methods of handling offenders.

*   *   *

STUDER, Gerald C. 1927-

PERSONAL: Born January 31, 1927, in Smithville, Ohio; son of Martin G. (a farmer and tile maker) and Edna L. (Blough) Studer; married Marilyn R. Kreider (an elementary school teacher), June 16, 1950; children: Jerri Lynn, Maria Ann. *Education:* Goshen College, B.A., 1947; Goshen Biblical Seminary, Goshen, Ind., B.D., 1957; Goshen Biblical Seminary, Elkhart, Ind., M.Div., 1971. *Politics:* "Nonpartisan." *Home:* 1260 Orchard Lane, Lansdale, Pa. 19446. *Office:* Plains Mennonite Church, West Main St. and Orville Rd., Lansdale, Pa. 19446.

CAREER: Pastor of Mennonite churches in Smithville, Ohio, 1947-61, and Scottdale, Pa., 1961-73; Plains Mennonite Church, Lansdale, Pa., pastor, 1973—. Member of Mennonite Historical Committee; president of Mennonite Youth Fellowship of North America, 1947-50; member of Mennonite Church General Board, 1972-75.

WRITINGS: Frederick Goeb, Master Printer, privately printed, 1963; *Toward a Theology of Servanthood,* Association of Mennonite Aid Societies, 1965; (editor) *Over the Alleghenies,* privately printed, 1965; *Christopher Dock, Colonial Schoolmaster,* Herald Press, 1967; *After Death, What?,* Herald Press, 1976. Contributor to church magazines. Co-editor of *Mennonite Historical Bulletin,* 1961—, and *Bible Collector,* 1967—.

WORK IN PROGRESS: The Curious History of the Bible, (tentative title).

AVOCATIONAL INTERESTS: Collecting rare and different Bibles.

*   *   *

STUNTZ, Albert Edward 1902-1976

1902—May 25, 1976; American newsman, publisher, institute official, and author. Obituaries: *New York Times,* May 28, 1976.

*   *   *

STURM, Ernest 1932-

PERSONAL: Born August 21, 1932, in Vienna, Austria; naturalized U.S. citizen; son of Bernard B. (a businessman) and Annie (Gleicher) Sturm. *Education:* Attended University of Paris, 1953-54; Brown University, A.B., 1955; New York University, LL.B., 1959; Columbia University, M.A., 1962, Ph.D., 1967. *Office:* Department of French, University of California, Santa Barbara, Calif. 93106.

CAREER: Admitted to the bar of the State of New York, 1959; practicing attorney in New York, N.Y., 1959-60; Interstate Commerce Commission, Washington, D.C., legal examiner, 1960-61; Columbia University, New York, N.Y., lecturer in French, 1961-62; Lycee Buffon, Paris, France, lecturer in English and French, 1965-66; University of California, Santa Barbara, assistant professor, 1967-72, associate professor of French, 1972—. *Member:* New York State Bar Association, Phi Beta Kappa. *Awards, honors:* Fulbright fellowship, 1962-64; American Council of Learned Societies travel grant, 1970.

WRITINGS: Conscience et Impuissance chez Dostoievsky et Camus (title means "Consciousness and Impotence in Dostoievsky and Camus"), Nizet (Paris), 1967; *Crebillon fils et le libertinage au dix huitieme siecle* (title means "Crebillon fils and the Eighteenth Century Libertine Movement"), Nizet, 1970; (editor) Crebillon fils, *Lettres de la Marquise de M. au Comte de R.* (critical edition; title means "Letters from the Marquise of M—— to the Count of R——"), Nizet, 1970; (editor) Crebillon fils, *L'Ecumoire* (critical edition; title means "The Skimmer"), Nizet, 1976. Contributor of articles to *Diderot Studies, French Review, Sub-Stance,* and other publications.

WORK IN PROGRESS: Theoretical writings on human emotions and sensations, aiming at a fresh critical perspective to literary criticism.

* * *

SUGAR, Bert Randolph 1937-
(John Brooks, Suzanne Davis)

PERSONAL: Born June 7, 1937, in Washington, D.C.; son of Harold Randolph and Anne Edith (Rosensweig) Sugar; married Suzanne Davis (an art teacher and artist), November 22, 1960; children: Jennifer Anne, John-Brooks Randolph. Education: Attended Harvard University, 1956; University of Maryland, B.S., 1957; University of Michigan, M.B.A., 1959, LL.B., 1960, J.D., 1960; American University, Ph.D. candidate. Politics: Registered Republican. Religion: Congregationalist. Home: Six Southview Rd., Chappaqua, N.Y. 10514. Office: 6 Southview Rd., Chappaqua, N.Y. 10514.

CAREER: D'Arcy, MacManus & Masius (advertising agency), New York, N.Y., director of marketing and vice-president, 1967-70; Champion Sports (publishing firm), New York, N.Y., editor and publisher, 1970-73; Argosy, New York, N.Y., editor-in-chief, 1973-75; Baron, Costello & Fine (advertising agency), New York, N.Y., senior vice-president, 1975—. Member: American Political Items Collectors Society, Football Writers, Basketball Writers, Boxing Writers, Alpha Delta Sigma.

WRITINGS: (With Jackie Kannon) Where Were You When the Lights Went Out?, Kanrom Publishing, 1966; (with Jose Torres and Norman Mailer) . . . Sting Like a Bee, Abelard, 1971; (with Floyd Patterson) Inside Boxing, Regnery, 1972; The Sports Collectors Bible, Wallace-Homestead, 1975; (with Sybil Leek) The Assassination Chain, Sterling, 1976; Who Was Harry Steinfeldt? and Other Baseball Trivia Questions, Playboy Press, 1976; The Horseplayers' Guide to Winning Systems, Corwin, 1976; Houdini: His Life and Art, Grosset, 1976; Classic Baseball Cards, Dover, 1977. Contributor, sometimes under pseudonyms, to magazines.

WORK IN PROGRESS: The Thrill of Victory, The Agony of Defeat; Hit the Sign and Win a Free Suit of Clothes From Harry Finklestein; Ghosts and Things That Go Bump In the Night; George Washington's Love Letters.

AVOCATIONAL INTERESTS: Antiques.

* * *

SUGERMAN, Shirley 1919-

PERSONAL: Born July 24, 1919, in New York, N.Y.; daughter of Harry (an industrial adhesives manufacturer) and Leonora (a pianist; maiden name, Levy) Greene; married Morton M. Rosenberg (a university professor), July 24, 1970; children: Carol (Mrs. David Reck), Joan Olive, Andrew, Madeline (Mrs. William Jepson). Education: Barnard College, B.A., 1940; Drew University, Ph.D., 1970; Manhattan Center for Advanced Psychoanalytic Studies, postdoctoral study, 1971—. Home: 99 Whittredge Rd., Summit, N.J. 07901. Office: Drew University, Madison, N.J. 07940.

CAREER: Director of Rubber & Asbestos Corp., 1950-62; Drew University, Madison, N.J., academic director of Aquinas program, 1970—, lecturer in world religions and Asian psychology, 1972—. Individual and family therapist; president of Leonora Corp. (industrial real estate company), 1959-63. Member of Chester Township Juvenile Delinquency Commission, 1958-60; member Sculpture Center. Member: American Psychological Association, American Academy of Religion, American Philosophical Association, League of Women Voters (member of New Jersey board of directors, 1958-60); Chester Township president, 1958-60.

WRITINGS: (Editor and contributor) Evolution of Consciousness, Wesleyan University Press, 1976; Sin and Madness: Studies in Narcissism, Westminster, 1976. Contributor to Drew Gateway, Cross Currents, and Psychoanalytic Review.

WORK IN PROGRESS: Research on the psycho-ontological origins of religion, the subject-object problem in psychology, and contemporary narcissism.

SIDELIGHTS: Shirley Sugerman writes: "It occurs to me again and again in the course of my work in two fields considered to be diverse—psychology and theology—that both are concerned with a common fundamental human reality—the separateness, yet necessarily relaxedness, of each individual. To speak the languages of both disciplines interchangeably—to be 'bi-lingual'—seemed to be a path to understanding ourselves better; hence my interest in the core concepts of sin and madness—which point to that common reality."

AVOCATIONAL INTERESTS: Sculpture (carving in stone and wood).

* * *

SUHR, Elmer George 1902-1976

October 18, 1902—1976; American art historian, anthropologist, classical scholar, and author. Obituaries: AB Bookman's Weekly, June 7, 1976. (See index for previous CA sketch)

* * *

SUJATA, Anagarika 1948-

PERSONAL: Legal name, Windell Curry; born June 25, 1948, in Panama City, Fla.,; son of Daulton (an electrician) and Mildred (Sowell) Curry. Education: Attended Florida State University, 1967. Politics: "When one sees the truth, there is no need for opinions." Home and office: Stillpoint Institute, 604 South 15th St., San Jose, Calif. 95112.

CAREER: Performed in Europe as folk singer, 1967; traveled to Middle East and Asia, 1968; ordained Buddhist monk, 1968, studied in Ceylon, 1968-71; Stillpoint Institute, San Jose, Calif., teacher of Buddhist insight meditation, 1971—, lecturer at major American universities, 1972, lecturer in Europe, 1976. Lecturer in Asia.

WRITINGS: Beginning to See, Unity Press, 1975.

WORK IN PROGRESS: Translation of part of the Buddhist Canon, The Dhammapada.

SIDELIGHTS: Sujata traveled to the East where he met teachers who were not bound by the human enslavements of anger, attachment, and selfishness. While living as a Buddhist monk in Ceylon, he practiced the meditation of mindful awareness, recommended by these teachers as being the path leading to such freedom. His dynamic and open approach to living is directed toward the possibility of living freely with insight and awareness. Sujata presents alternatives to routine patterns of thought and desire, and attempts to bring about unexpected transformations through discovery of the nature of the mind. He writes: "We tend to believe life in all its parts to be permanent, satisfactory and in our control. When powerful mindfulness is cultivated, the truth unfolds itself. One realizes the impermanence: every thing is constantly changing, nothing remains the same. Because of this impermanent nature of life, all components are basically unsatisfactory: there can be no ultimate value in that which does not last."

* * *

SULLIVAN, Francis John 1892-1976
(Frank Sullivan)

September 22, 1892—February 19, 1976; American humorist and author. Obituaries: *New York Times,* February 20, 1976; *Washington Post,* February 21, 1976; *Time,* March 1, 1976; *Newsweek,* March 1, 1976; *Publishers Weekly,* March 5, 1976; *New Yorker,* March 8, 1976; *AB Bookman's Weekly,* April 12, 1976. (See index for previous *CA* sketch)

* * *

SULLIVAN, Frank 1912-1975

PERSONAL: Born June 6, 1912, in Denver, Colo.; married Majie Padberg, 1936; children: Raymond. *Education:* Regis College, Denver, Colo., A.B., 1934; St. Louis University, A.M., 1936; Yale University, Ph.D., 1940. *Residence:* Los Angeles, Calif.

CAREER: St. Louis University, St. Louis, Mo., instructor, 1936-41, assistant professor, 1941-44, associate professor of English, 1944-46; Loyola Marymount University, Los Angeles, Calif., associate professor, 1946-48, professor of English, 1948-74. *Member:* Modern Language Association of America, Mediaeval Academy of America, American Folklore Society, Bibliographical Society of America, National Council of Teachers of English, College English Association, Early English Text Society.

WRITINGS: Moreana: A Checklist of Material by and about St. Thomas More, Rockhurst College, 1946; *Syr Thomas More, a First Bibliographical Notebook, Wherin Betretyd Diuers Maters Compondyd and Divisyd by Frank Sullivan and Printed at the Costes and Charges of Loyola University of Los Angeles,* Loyola University of Los Angeles, 1953; (with wife, Majie Padberg Sullivan) *Moreana: Materials for the Study of Saint Thomas More,* Loyola University of Los Angeles, 1964, index, 1971. Also wrote seven other books on Thomas More.

OBITUARIES: New York Times, August 10, 1975; *AB Bookman's Weekly,* October 13, 1975.*

(Died August 7, 1975, in Los Angeles, Calif.)

* * *

SULLIVAN, Victoria 1943-
(Veronica Slater)

PERSONAL: Born April 16, 1943, in Philadelphia, Pa.; daughter of Martin J. (an executive) and Lenore (a civic volunteer; maiden name, Anderson) Brennan; married Daniel J. Sullivan (a lawyer), June 25, 1960 (separated); children: Monique, Gregory. *Education:* Radcliffe College, student, 1959-60; Barnard College, B.A., 1964; Columbia University, M.A., 1965, Ph.D., 1969. *Politics:* "Left/liberal (involved with civil rights and feminism)." *Home:* 620 West 116th St., Apt. 21, New York, N.Y. 10027. *Office:* Department of English, St. Peter's College, Jersey City, N.J. 07306.

CAREER: Columbia University, New York City, lecturer in English, 1969-70; City College of the City University of New York, New York City, assistant professor of English, 1970-75; St. Peter's College, Jersey City, N.J., assistant professor of English, 1976—. Has given drama and poetry readings; has directed and produced her own plays.

Member: Modern Language Association of America. *Awards, honors:* Woodrow Wilson fellowships, 1964-68.

WRITINGS: (Co-author of introduction and editor with James V. Hatch) *Plays By and About Women,* Random House, 1973; (contributor) Earl Rovit, editor, *Saul Bellow: A Collection of Critical Essays,* Prentice-Hall, 1974.

Plays: "They Don't Only Come Through Windows" (drama), first produced in New York at Hatch-Billops Studio, December, 1971; "A Modern Fable: The Man Who Wanted the Truth," first produced in New York at Off-Center Space Theater, March, 1974.

Also author of video-play, "The Need," aired on cable television, October 19, 1975. Contributor of articles and poems to literary journals, including *New Voices, Broadway Boogie, Poetry in Performance,* and *Event,* to television/movie magazines under pseudonym Veronica Slater, and to newspapers.

WORK IN PROGRESS: The Sexual Dialectic in Contemporary American Fiction, for Southern Illinois Press; *The Divided Bed,* with James V. Hatch, a collection of poems; a three-act play.

SIDELIGHTS: Victoria Sullivan writes: "I have been writing poetry since the age of seven. As poet and playwright my major concern seems to be the ever-shifting power struggles in male/female relations, the sexual dialectic. The more deeply I probe this area, the more I shun polemic. In readings around the city, I find my audience responds with both emotion and recognition to my sometimes half-ironic attempts to capture our present pain. My obsessive concern is the bedroom, symbolic and literal. I love to read as well as write, and have found the New York City poetry scene to be: sometimes supportive, frequently narcissistic, at times witty, occasionally phony, and at best alive and kicking."

BIOGRAPHICAL/CRITICAL SOURCES: Susan Brownmiller, *Against Our Will,* Simon & Schuster, 1975.

* * *

SUPONEV, Michael 1923-

PERSONAL: Born June 18, 1923, in Leningrad, U.S.S.R.; son of Nikolay and Olga (Swizchewsky) Suponev; married Cornelia Rammo (a teacher), 1948; children: Trina, Alexij, Vasily, Alexandre, *Education:* Attended Leningrad State University, 1951. *Home:* 46 Leninsky Avenue, Minsk, U.S.S.R. *Office: Soviet Sport,* Archipov Street, 8, Moscow, U.S.S.R.

CAREER: Velicolukskaja Prawda (newspaper), Velicy Luky, U.S.S.R., editor, 1951-57; *Soviet Sport* (newspaper), Moscow, U.S.S.R., staff correspondent for Belorussia, 1957—. *Member:* Journalist Association of the U.S.S.R.

WRITINGS: Olga Korbut: A Biographical Portrait, Doubleday, 1975.

WORK IN PROGRESS: Gymnastics of Belorussia.

* * *

SUPREE, Burt(on) 1941-

PERSONAL: Born March 20, 1941, in New York, N.Y.; son of William and Sarah (Harris) Supree. *Education:* City College of the City University of New York, B.A., 1961. *Home:* 60 East Seventh St., New York, N.Y. 10003. *Agent:* Arthur D. Zinberg, 11 East 44th St., New York, N.Y. 10017. *Office: Village Voice,* 80 University Pl., New York, N.Y. 10003.

CAREER: *Village Voice,* New York, N.Y., editor of entertainment listings, 1965—, author of columns "Kids," 1973—, and "Footlights," 1975—. Associate professor at Sarah Lawrence College, 1971-76. *Awards, honors:* Gold medal from Boys' Clubs of America, 1967, for *Mother, Mother, I Feel Sick, Send for the Doctor Quick, Quick, Quick;* Irma Simonton Black award from Bank Street College of Education, 1973, for *Harlequin and the Gift of Many Colors.*

WRITINGS: (With Remy Charlip) *Mother, Mother, I Feel Sick, Send for the Doctor Quick, Quick, Quick* (juvenile), Parents' Magazine Press, 1966; (with Charlip) *Harlequin and the Gift of Many Colors* (juvenile), Parents' Magazine Press, 1973; *Bear's Heart: Scenes from the Life of a Cheyenne Artist of a Hundred Years Ago,* Lippincott, in press. Contributor of poems to *St. Andrews Review* and *Weid,* and of articles and reviews to newspapers.

WORK IN PROGRESS: Research on Robert de Clari and his account of the Fourth Crusade; research on Japanese legends.

SIDELIGHTS: Supree worked as a dancer, choreographer, and actor from 1963 to 1970. Since 1970, he has taught workshops in making things up and ensemble theater at Sarah Lawrence College, a course focused on the development of personal material and community work, and other workshops in movement and sound for adults and children. He also presented "Costumes and Performing with Newspaper," in which visitors to the Museum of Contemporary Crafts made their own costumes and performed in them.

AVOCATIONAL INTERESTS: International travel (especially France; walking tour of Scotland and the Outer Hebrides; also South America, Central America, Japan, Cambodia, Nepal, and Afghanistan).

* * *

SUSANN, Jacqueline 1921-1974

PERSONAL: Born August 20, 1921, in Philadelphia, Pa.; daughter of Robert (a portrait artist) and Rose (a teacher; maiden name, Jans) Susann; married Irving Mansfield (a television and film producer); children: Guy. *Education:* Studied ballet and drama in New York, N.Y. *Home:* 112 Central Park S., New York, N.Y. 10019.

CAREER: Began as model, and later actress, appearing in more than twenty Broadway plays and road company productions, including "The Women," 1937, "She Gave Him All She Had" and "When We Are Married," 1939, "My Fair Ladies" and "Banjo Eyes," 1941, "Jackpot" and "The Lady Says Yes," 1944, and Off-Broadway in "The Madwoman of Chaillot," 1970; author and novelist, 1962-74. Made frequent appearances on television dramas, panels, and commercials.

WRITINGS: (With Beatrice Cole) "Lovely Me" (play), produced on Broadway, 1946; *Every Night, Josephine!* (nonfiction), Geis, 1963; *Valley of the Dolls: A Novel,* Geis, 1966; *The Love Machine* (novel), Simon & Schuster, 1969; *Once Is Not Enough* (novel), Morrow, 1973; *Dolores* (novel), Morrow, 1976. Also author of two unpublished books, *Bitter End,* and a science fiction work, *The Stars Scream.* Contributor to magazines.

WORK IN PROGRESS: *Good Night, Sweet Princess,* a sequel to *Every Night, Josephine!*

SIDELIGHTS: Jacqueline Susann was the first author to publish two number-one best sellers back to back, and simultaneously to face the nearly unanimous outrage of critics.

When asked if she read the reviews, the actress-turned-writer responded: "I'd like to have the critics like me, I'd like to have everybody like what I write. But when my book sells, I know people like the book. That's the most important thing, because writing is communication." Moreover, Susann contended, "The day is over when the point of writing is just to turn a phrase that critics will quote, like Henry James. *I'm* not interested in turning a phrase; what matters to *me* is telling a *story* that *involves* people. The hell with what critics say. I've made characters live, so that people talk about them at cocktail parties, and that, to me, is what counts. You have to have a divine conceit in your judgment. I have it."

When the author of *Valley of the Dolls* was criticized as being a writer of pornography, she explained such was not her motivation: "I don't think it is a dirty book," she told Roy Newquist. "I do believe, however, that you cannot define characters without identifying them with the sexual acts they would commit and the language they would use. For example, it is one sort of person who would say, 'Oh, for goodness' sake!' when a rehearsal went wrong. You would know that woman has restraint, a basic dignity, and is likely to be in command of a given situation. But when a performer blows sky-high, loses control of herself and her tongue, and lashes out at everyone in sight, then you are aware of the deficiencies in personality and character that will play themselves out in later events in the novel.... If I didn't sometimes show these characters at their more bestial, weaker moments, I'd have written a dishonest book. Frankly, I'd rather risk being called the author of a dirty book than the author of a weak or inaccurate one."

As Nora Ephron noted, "If Jacqueline Susann is no literary figure, she is nevertheless an extraordinary publishing phenomenon.... With the possible exception of *Cosmopolitan* magazine, no one writes about sadism in modern man and masochism in modern woman quite as horribly and accurately as Jacqueline Susann." In addition, Ephron was able to identify the reason behind the incredible success of Susann's first best seller: "*Valley* had a message that had a magnetic appeal for women readers: it described the standard female fantasy—of going to the big city, striking it rich, meeting fabulous men—and went on to show every reader that she was far better off than the heroines in the book—who took pills, killed themselves, and made general messes of their lives. It was, essentially, a morality tale. And despite its reputation, it was not really a dirty book. Most women, I think, do not want to read hard-core pornography. They do not even want to read anything terribly technical about the sex act. What they want to read about is lust. And Jacqueline Susann gave it to them...."

Susann's second best seller, *The Love Machine,* evoked another storm of criticism. Setting up the criterion for passing judgment on it, Christopher Lehmann-Haupt remarked that since it was going to "be devoured like popcorn at a Saturday matinee, ... it's irrelevant to judge it by any standard other than popcorn." He found it "salty (lots of four-letter words sprinkled into a morally square container). It dissolves in your mouth (the characters are so flat and interchangeable that at times I even forgot who Robin Stone was). It doesn't fill you up (I doubt if I've ever read a novel that made less of an impression). It goes down quickly and easily. It is the kernel of an idea, the seed of an inspiration, exploded into bite-sized nothingness."

To Jonathan Baumbach, "reading *The Love Machine* is a numbingly mindless experience. Its effect is narcotic. Miss Susann asks her readers not to think, not to feel, and, before all, not to see—nothing is asked and all is given. In a sense, the book is a collaboration—a shared inhuman cultural fantasy between author and readers, a reinforcement of culture-induced fantasies. Where real literature disturbs, books like *The Love Machine* comfort. It is only child's play to read but offers gratifyingly easy solutions.... The subliminal message of the novel is *stay as stupid as you are.*" He continued, "The main thrust of the novel is hedonistic—characters hop in and out of bed with one another in various combinations—but the novel opts finally for the middle-class puritan verities.... On the face of it, *The Love Machine* deplores the amoral world it describes.... Integrity and love triumph over hedonism and ambition. *The Love Machine* subscribes to cultural convention so successfully because it believes in it. There is no discernible vision in the novel outside popular culture's vision of itself, no higher intelligence, no other context." Baumbach concluded that "the novel is written in the very language of its world—a language wholly incapable of accounting for human experience, a language geared to genocide."

Both of Susann's best sellers were adapted as screenplays. "Valley of the Dolls" was released by Twentieth Century-Fox in 1967, and "The Love Machine" was released by Columbia, 1971.

BIOGRAPHICAL/CRITICAL SOURCES: Cosmopolitan, January, 1967; *Village Voice,* January 25, 1968; *Punch,* January 31, 1968; *Saturday Evening Post,* February 24, 1968; *New Statesman,* March 8, 1968; *New York Times Book Review,* May 11, 1969; *Life,* May 30, 1969; *Nation,* September 1, 1969; *Harper's,* October, 1969; Carolyn Riley, editor, *Contemporary Literary Criticism,* Volume III, Gale, 1975.*

(Died September 21, 1974, in New York, N.Y.)

* * *

SUTHERLAND, (Norman) Stuart 1927-

PERSONAL: Born March 26, 1927, in London, England; son of Norman MacLeod (a pharmacist) and Celia Dixon (Jackson) Sutherland; married Jose Louise Fogden (an antique dealer), June 30, 1956; children: Gay, Julia Claire. *Education:* Magdalen College, Oxford, B.A. (honors), 1949, D.Phil., 1957. *Politics:* None. *Religion:* Atheist. *Residence:* Brighton, England. *Agent:* Deborah Rogers, 29 Goodge St., London W.1, England. *Office:* Laboratory of Experimental Psychology, University of Sussex, Brighton, England.

CAREER: Oxford University, Oxford, England, lecturer in experimental psychology, 1957-64; University of Sussex, Brighton, England, professor of experimental psychology, 1964—. Visiting professor at Massachusetts Institute of Technology, 1961-62, 1964-65. Director of Schlackman Research Organization and Bond Street Antiques. *Military service:* Royal Air Force, 1949-51; became sergeant. *Member:* International Brain Research Organisation, Association for the Study of Artificial Intelligence and the Simulation of Behaviour, Association for the Study of Animal Behaviour, Experimental Psychology Society, American Psychological Association, Old Place Club.

WRITINGS: (Editor with R. M. Gilbert) *Animal Discrimination Learning,* Academic Press, 1969; (with N. J. Mackintosh) *Mechanisms of Animal Discrimination Learning,* Academic Press, 1971; *Breakdown: A Personal Crisis and a Medical Dilemma,* Weidenfeld & Nicolson, 1976; (editor) *Tutorial Essays in Psychology,* Erlbaum Associates, Volume I, 1977, Volume II, in press. Contributor to learned

journals and to newspapers. Editor of *Quarterly Journal of Experimental Psychology,* 1971.

WORK IN PROGRESS: Understanding the Mind.

SIDELIGHTS: Sutherland writes that after spending twenty years researching and writing on vision and learning processes in man and other animals, particularly the octopus, he "experienced a complete but comparatively short mental breakdown in 1973, the bizarre course of which is described in *Breakdown.* Fears of waning scientific creativity and the events that led up to my breakdown led me to change direction and concentrate on a more literary career including the exposition of psychological and philosophical ideas."

* * *

SUTTON, Eve(lyn Mary) 1906-

PERSONAL: Born September 14, 1906, in Preston, Lancashire, England; daughter of John James (a dentist) and Elizabeth (Clayton) Breakell; married Alfred Sutton (a pharmaceutical chemist), October 8, 1931; children: Richard John, Martin James. *Education:* Attended Goldsmiths College, University of London, 1925-27. *Home:* 84 Kohimarama Rd., Flat 1, Auckland 5, New Zealand.

CAREER: Teacher in primary level, Lancashire, England, 1927-31. Writer. *Member:* New Zealand Writers Society (Auckland chairman, 1971-72), Children's Literature Association (New Zealand), Auckland Museum Institute. *Awards, honors:* Esther Glen Award from New Zealand Library Association, 1975, for *My Cat Likes to Hide in Boxes.*

*WRITINGS—*All for children: *My Cat Likes to Hide in Boxes,* Parents' Magazine Press, 1974; *Green Gold,* Hamish Hamilton, 1976; *Tuppenny Brown,* Hamish Hamilton, 1977; *Johnny Sweep,* Hamish Hamilton, in press. Contributor of stories, poems, and articles to magazines in New Zealand, Australia, and England.

WORK IN PROGRESS: Moa Hunter, a novel for young people, for Hamish Hamilton.

SIDELIGHTS: Eve Sutton writes: "I now count myself almost exclusively a children's writer ... more interested in writing for older children.... I enjoy the story-telling, the plotting, the 'what happened next' element, and my self-involvement with the characters I create. If I *must* pontificate about my views on writing, I would say—respect your readers, don't write down to them, and 'only your *best* is good enough for children.'"

AVOCATIONAL INTERESTS: Golf, Braille transcription, reading.

BIOGRAPHICAL/CRITICAL SOURCES: Book World (New Zealand), February 21, 1976.

* * *

SUTTON, Howard 1930-

PERSONAL: Born October 28, 1930, in Youngstown, Ohio; son of Howard Ellis (a businessman) and Lucy (a teacher; maiden name, Dennison) Sutton; married Selden Womrath (a publicist), September 27, 1969. *Education:* University of Virginia, B.S., 1953; Columbia University, M.S., 1958. *Home:* 301 East 75th St., New York, N.Y. 10021.

CAREER: Needham, Harper & Steers (advertising agency), New York, N.Y., vice-president and associate research director, 1958-67; Grey Advertising, New York City, associate research director, 1967-68; free-lance filmmaker, 1969-

73, *Consumer Reports,* Mount Vernon, N.Y., economics writer, 1977—. *Military service:* U.S. Navy, 1953-56; became lieutenant junior grade.

WRITINGS: Contemporary Economics, Praeger, 1976

SIDELIGHTS: Sutton told *CA* about his book: "I had the advantage of ignorance. I knew almost nothing about economics before I started the book. So, by avoiding my predecessors' obvious errors of exposition, I figured I had a good chance of producing the clearest, most interesting introductory text on the market. I guess it's not for me to say whether it *is* that, but. . . ."

* * *

SWAN, Bradford Fuller 1908(?)-1976

American theatre and art critic, historian, and author. Obituaries: *AB Bookman's Weekly,* July 26, 1976.

* * *

SWANN, Lois 1944-

PERSONAL: Born November 17, 1944, in New York, N.Y.; daughter of Peter Joseph (a glove manufacturer) and Edith (an executive secretary; maiden name, De Rose) Riso; married Terrence Garth Swann (an executive producer of television commercials), August 15, 1964; children: Peter, Polly. *Education:* Marquette University, B.A., 1966. *Politics:* "Liberal—strong love of American Constitution." *Home:* 3634 Michigan Ave., Cincinnati, Ohio 45208.

CAREER: Actress, working in repertory, as well as community and university theater productions. Director of Children's Theatre for Santa Monica Recreation and Parks Department.

WRITINGS: The Mists of Manitto (novel), Scribner, 1976.

WORK IN PROGRESS: Toward Nonantum, a novel about a Massachusetts woman and native Americans during the American Revolution; *Sonata Blue,* a novel dealing with the structure of a modern marriage.

SIDELIGHTS: Lois Swann writes: "American culture, its formation and current strengths and weaknesses, forms the basis of my work. First-hand observation of sectional differences and beliefs and sub-cultures through living in many parts of America as well as research into native American language and history provide the groundwork. My personal predilection for conveying thought through character relationships and reliance on precise diction and poetical composition to reinforce meaning form the ideals of my style."

BIOGRAPHICAL/CRITICAL SOURCES: Cincinnati Enquirer, August 22, 1976; *Writer's Digest,* October, 1976.

* * *

SWEETING, George 1924-

PERSONAL: Born October 1, 1924, in Haledon, N.J.; son of William and Mary Sweeting; married Hilda Schnell, 1947; children: George, James, Donald, Robert. *Education:* Moody Bible Institute, Diploma, 1945; Gordon College, B.A., 1948; Gordon-Conwell Divinity School, D.D., 1970. *Home:* 550 Wilmot, Deerfield, Ill. 60015. *Office:* Moody Bible Institute, 820 North LaSalle St., Chicago, Ill. 60610.

CAREER: Pastor in Clifton, N.J., 1948-50; evangelist in South America, North America, and Europe, 1951-61; pastor in Paterson, N.J., 1961-66, and Chicago, Ill., 1966-71; Moody Bible Institute, Chicago, Ill., president, 1971—. *Awards, honors:* D.Hum., Azusa Pacific College, 1971; LL.D., Tennessee Temple College, 1971.

WRITINGS: How to Be a Chalk Artist, Zondervan, 1953; *The Jack Wyrtzen Story: The Personal Story of the Man, His Message, and His Ministry,* Zondervan, 1960; *And the Greatest of These: The Power of Christian Love,* Revell, 1968, revised edition published as *Love Is the Greatest,* Moody, 1974; *Living Stones: Guidelines for New Christians,* Baker Book, 1970; *The City: A Matter of Conscience, and Other Messages,* Moody, 1972; *How to Solve Conflicts,* Moody, 1973; *Living in a Dying World,* Moody, 1974. Also author of *Discovering the Will of God,* 1974, and *How to Begin the Christian Life,* 1975. Editor-in-chief of *Moody Monthly,* 1971—.

* * *

SYLVESTER, Arline 1914-

PERSONAL: Born April 13, 1914, in Iowa; daughter of Peter (a land owner) and Emily (a teacher; maiden name, Hanson) Hove; married Mark Harry Sylvester (a printer), January 12, 1934 (deceased); children: Peggy Lea Robertson, Douglas, Leslie Arnold (deceased). *Education:* Attended Iowa State College (now Iowa State University), 1931-32, and University of New Mexico, 1932-34. *Residence and office:* Albuquerque, N.M. *Agent:* Dorothy Davis, 1217 Valencia Dr. N.E., Albuquerque, N.M. 87110.

CAREER: U.S. Atomic Energy Commission, Albuquerque, N.M., clerk, 1955-57; Sylvester Printing Co., Albuquerque, secretary-bookkeeper, 1957-66; worked as nurse's aid in Albuquerque, 1964-66; ordained minister of the National Spiritualist Association of Churches, 1968; associate minister of church in El Paso, Tex., 1968-73.

WRITINGS: Who Me? Yes, You!, Branden Press, 1975.

WORK IN PROGRESS: Research and writing.

AVOCATIONAL INTERESTS: Handicrafts.

* * *

SZOVERFFY, Joseph 1920-

PERSONAL: Born June 19, 1920, in Clausenbourgh, Transylvania; came to United States, 1962, naturalized U.S. citizen; son of Louis (a businessman) and Anna Ilona (von Simkovith) de Szoeverffy. *Education:* St. Emeric College, Budapest, B.A., 1939; Budapest University, Ph.D., 1943; State Teachers College, Budapest, staatsexamen, 1944; University of Fribourg, Dr.Phil.Habil., 1950. *Religion:* Armenian Catholic. *Home:* 1514 Beacon St., Brookline, Mass. 02146. *Office:* Department of Comparative Literature, HU 227, State University of New York, 1400 Washington Ave., Albany, N.Y. 12222.

CAREER: Budapest University, Budapest, Hungary, assistant professor of German philology, 1943-48; Hungarian General Credit Bank, Budapest, assistant to the vice-president, 1944-48; University of Friborg, Friborg, Switzerland, visiting lecturer in medieval studies, 1949-50; Glenstal College, County Limerick, Ireland, professor of modern languages, 1950-52; Irish Folklore Commission, University College, Dublin, Ireland, archivist and special research librarian, 1952-57; University of Ottawa, Ottawa, Ontario, lecturer in classics, 1957-58, assistant professor of classical and medieval Latin literature, 1958-59; University of Alberta, Edmonton, assistant professor, 1959-61, associate professor of Germanic philology and German literature, 1961-62; Yale University, New Haven, Conn., associate professor of medieval German literature and philology, 1962-65, fellow of Calhoun College, 1962-65; Boston College, Chestnut Hill, Mass., professor of German and medieval studies, 1965-70; State University of New York, Albany, professor of comparative and world literature and of German, 1970—, chairman of department, 1972-75. Secretary-general, Foederatio Emericana in Budapest, 1943-46; member of board of directors, Institute for Early Christian Iberian Studies; visiting professor, University of Poitiers, 1961; Harvard University, James C. Loeb memorial lecturer, 1967, visiting professor, 1968, honorary research associate, 1975—; fellow, Center of Medieval and Renaissance Studies, 1973—.

MEMBER: Modern Language Association of America, Mediaeval Academy of America, International Platform Association, Comparative Literature Association, American Folklore Society, American Association of University Professors, American Association of Teachers of German, Canadian Linguistic Association, Internationale Vereinigung der Germanisten, Northeast Modern Language Association (chairman of Renaissance and Baroque Section, 1972-74), Connecticut Academy of Arts and Sciences. *Awards, honors:* University of Chicago folklore prize, 1954; Canada Council lecture grant, 1960-61; American Council of Learned Societies grants, 1960-61, 1964, and 1967; Guggenheim fellowships, 1961 and 1969-70, grants 1963, 1965, 1970, and 1975; American Philosophical Society fellowships, 1964-65 and 1973; Ella Lyman Cabot grant, 1965; Federal Republic of Germany grant, 1969; Government of Portugal grant, 1969; State University of New York Research Foundation fellowships, 1971 and 1972; State University of New York lifetime faculty exchange scholar, 1974—.

WRITINGS: Der heilige Christophorus und sein Kult (title means "St. Christopher and His Cult"), Budapest University Press, 1943; *Irisches Erzaehlgut im Abendland* (title means "Irish Literary Tradition in the Western World"), Erich Schmidt Verlag, 1957; *An Ungair* (title means "Hungary"), FAS (Dublin), 1958; *Annalen der lateinischen Hymnendichtung* (title means "Annals of Medieval Latin Hymnody"), Erich Schmidt Verlag, Volume I, 1965, Volume II, 1965; *A Mirror of Medieval Culture: Saint Peter Hymns of the Middle Ages,* Connecticut Academy of Arts and Sciences, 1965; *Weltliche Dichtungen des lateinischen Mittelalters* (title means "Secular Latin Lyrics of the Middle Ages"), Volume I, Erich Schmidt Verlag, 1970; *Iberian Hymnody: Survey and Problems,* Classical Folia Editions, 1971; (author of Volume I and of notes to text in Volume II) Peter Abelard, *Hymnarius Paraclitensis,* E. J. Brill, 1975.

Editor of the series "Medieval Classics: Text and Studies" and "Baroque, Romanticism and the Modern Mind." Contributor to *New Catholic Encyclopedia,* McGraw, 1967; contributor of articles and reviews to sixty international scholarly journals. Co-editor, *Mittellateinisches Jahrbuch,* 1970—; member of editorial board of *Mediaevalia.*

WORK IN PROGRESS: Researching German folklore, the lyric poetry of the Middle Ages, literature and politics, language minorities abroad, and cultural history of Transylvania.

SIDELIGHTS: Szoverffy has traveled in twenty-eight countries abroad and has acquaintance with fourteen languages. *Avocational interests:* Higher education reform in the United States; photography; journalism and public opinion; public lecturing on East-Central European affairs, folklore, mythology, and modern culture.

*   *   *

TABER, George M(cCaffrey)   1942-

PERSONAL: Born May 25, 1942, in Riverside, Calif.; son of Robert L. (a circus performer) and Marie (McCaffrey) Taber; married Jean Belden, September, 1967; children: Lara, Stephen, Jeffrey. *Education:* Georgetown University, B.A., 1964; College d'Europe, M.A., 1965. *Religion:* Roman Catholic. *Home and office:* 2118 North Blvd., Houston, Tex. 77006.

CAREER: United Press International, Charleston, W.Va., reporter, 1964; stringer for Time-Life, Inc. and *Washington Star* in Brussels, Belgium, 1966-67; *Time,* New York, N.Y., correspondent from Bonn, West Germany, 1967-71; European Economic Community, Brussels, Belgium, spokesman, 1971-73; *Time,* correspondent from Paris, France, and Houston, Tex., 1973—.

WRITINGS: John F. Kennedy and a Uniting Europe, College d'Europe, 1967; *Patterns and Prospects of Common Market Trade,* P. Owen, 1974.

*   *   *

TAHTINEN, Dale R(udolph)   1945-

PERSONAL: Born October 17, 1945, in Baraga, Mich.; son of Edwin (a merchant) and Priscilla (Bellaire) Tahtinen; married Jennifer Holmquist, February 20, 1967; children: Rana. *Education:* Northern Michigan University, B.S. (magna cum laude), 1967; University of Maryland, M.A., 1970, Ph.D., 1974. *Home:* 9014 Brook Ford Rd., Burke, Va. 22015.

CAREER: U.S. Department of Defense, Defense Intelligence Agency, Washington, D.C., writer and editor, 1967-72; assistant for research and legislative analysis to U.S. Senator Robert P. Griffin, in Washington, D.C., 1972-73; American Enterprise Institute for Public Policy Research, Washington, D.C., research associate, 1973-74, assistant director of foreign and defense policy studies, 1974—. Guest lecturer at University of Maryland, Henry Ford Community College, College of William and Mary, U.S. Marine Command and Staff College, University of Connecticut, University of Tel Aviv, World Institute, Gettysburg College, Northern Michigan University, University of Cairo, University of Delaware, Lehigh University, and University of South Florida. *Member:* Pi Sigma Alpha.

WRITINGS: The Arab-Israeli Military Balance Today, American Enterprise Institute for Public Policy Research, 1973; *Arms in the Persian Gulf,* American Enterprise Institute for Public Policy Research, 1974; *The Arab-Israeli Military Balance Since October, 1973,* American Enterprise Institute for Public Policy Research, 1974; (with Robert J. Pranger) *Toward a Realistic Military Assistance Program,* American Enterprise Institute for Public Policy Research, 1974; *A Comparative Framework for Analyzing Middle Eastern One-Party Systems,* Institute of Middle Eastern and North African Affairs, Maryland, 1975; (with Pranger) *Nuclear Threat in the Middle East,* American Enterprise Institute for Public Policy Research, 1975; *1976 Arab-Israeli Military Status,* American Enterprise Institute for Public Policy Research, 1976; (with Pranger) *Implications of the Arab-Israeli Military Status,* American Enterprise Institute for Public Policy Research, 1977. Contributor to *Journal of Conflict Resolution* and *Current History.*

WORK IN PROGRESS: Arms in the Indian Ocean, with John Lenczowski.

*   *   *

TAIT, Katharine   1923-

PERSONAL: Born December 29, 1923, in London, England; daughter of Bertrand (a mathematician, philosopher and writer) and Dora (a teacher and writer; maiden name, Black) Russell; married Charles W. Tait, February 24, 1948 (divorced, 1972); children: David, Anne, Jonathan, Andrew, Benjamin. *Education:* Radcliffe College, B.A., 1944, M.A., 1947; Harvard University, Ph.D., 1971. *Politics:* Democrat. *Religion:* Episcopal. *Residence:* Arlington, Va. *Agent:* Collins-Knowlton-Wing Inc., 60 East 56th St., New York, N.Y. 10022.

CAREER: Has worked as teacher, editor, tutor and translator. Free-lance writer, 1971—.

WRITINGS: My Father Bertrand Russell, Harcourt, 1975.

WORK IN PROGRESS: A book on motherhood.

SIDELIGHTS: Katharine Tait told *CA: "My Father Bertrand Russell* is a personal account of a relationship. It does not attempt to be a complete life of my father or myself, but the story of our affection for one another and the obstacles to its expression. It examines his ideas as they affected me and attempts to sort out those which I kept and which I rejected."

*　　*　　*

TAPIO, Pat Decker
　　See KINES, Pat Decker

*　　*　　*

TATGENHORST, John　1938-

PERSONAL: Born August 22, 1938; son of Donald and Margaret (Graham) Tatgenhorst; married Joan Mowry (a music editor), May 10, 1971. *Education:* Ohio State University, B.S., 1961. *Home and office:* 2415 Buckley Rd., Columbus, Ohio 43220.

CAREER: Capital University, Columbus, Ohio, instructor in percussion instruments and music arrangement, 1961-76; Cara Publications, Columbus, Ohio, president, 1972-76. Music composer and arranger for Warner Brothers and Columbia Pictures; has about thirty-five published musical compositions, including "Cubano Drums," "Mr. T's Rock," "Jazz Jubilee," "Soul Food," "Disco Rock," "Brother Funk," and "Nashville Country," as well as more standard works for band, clarinet, and drums.

MEMBER: American Society of Composers, Authors and Publishers, Music Educators National Conference, Percussive Arts Society, National Band Association, Columbus Rotary Club. *Awards, honors:* Governor's award for community action from state of Ohio, 1975.

WRITINGS: The Percussion, Allyn & Bacon, 1971; *The Slingerland Elementary Bell Method,* Slingerland Drum Co., 1972; *Music Through the Ages,* Heritage Press, 1976.

*　　*　　*

TAYLOR, (Frank Herbert) Griffin　1917-
　　(J. F. Schneyder)

PERSONAL: Born September 25, 1917, in Twickenham, England; came to the United States in 1949, son of Frank E. (an engineer) and Catherine (Griffin) Taylor; married Carolyn Elizabeth Dickinson (an anthropologist), October 1, 1945; children: Anne Elizabeth (Mrs. Richard Haimes), Mary Frances. *Education:* Educated in London, England. *Home:* 1850 Southwest 35th Pl., Gainesville, Fla. 32608. *Office:* 418 Little Hall, University of Florida, Gainesville, Fla. 32611.

CAREER: Price & Pierce (timber agents and importers), London, England, staff member in training for directorship in London and Finland, 1936-40; farmer in England, 1946-49, Virginia, 1949-51, and Florida, 1951-52; citrus grove worker in Florida, 1952-53; General Extension Division of Florida, Gainesville, writer in public relations, 1955-59; University of Florida, Gainesville, assistant professor, 1964-68, associate professor of humanities and English, 1968—. Worked with British Diplomatic Service in Helsinki, Finland, 1939; reporter for *Daily Express,* 1939; reporter and translator for British Broadcasting Corp., 1939; public relations writer and translator for Finnish Legation in London, 1939-40. Has participated in "Poems Aloud," a weekly series on WRUF-FM Radio, 1964—. *Military service:* Finnish Army, aide-decamp, 1940; became lieutenant. British Army, in Intelligence and later in Infantry, 1940-46; served in Norway and Western Europe; became major.

MEMBER: Modern Language Association of America, American Association of University Professors, South Atlantic Modern Language Association, Omicron Delta Kappa. *Awards, honors:* Fellowship for writing fiction from *Sewanee Review,* 1958-59.

WRITINGS: (Under pseudonym J. F. Schneyder) *Wiedergeburt der Demokratie* (title means "Rebirth of Democracy"), Verlag Ferdinand Schoeningh, 1946; *Mortlake* (novel), Houghton, 1960. Contributor of articles, stories, and reviews to literary journals, including *Sewanee Review, New Orleans Review,* and *Mill Mountain Review,* and to newspapers. Founding member of *Florida Quarterly,* member of advisory board, 1966-68, chairman of advisory board, 1968-76.

WORK IN PROGRESS: A novel, completion expected in 1978; a monograph on Flaubert's *Trois Contes;* poetry.

SIDELIGHTS: Taylor writes: "I began my career with a two-year immersion in Finland, its languages, its customs, its culture, its literature, its forests, and factories. The Finns were most kind to me and I grew to love them. On the first day of the Russo-Finnish War in November, 1939, before the war had begun, my best friend was killed. . . . His going was the loss of part of myself and I saw that if Finland went down before the chill and cynical power play of the Soviets, part of us all would go down with them." This was the original motivation for his devoted work during the war. Of his more recent activities he writes: "In order to know Nature, to know the land that is the Earth, I have worked that earth with my hands from Arctic Finland to Central Florida." And about his writing: "I hope that what I've done has in some measure the character of the greater mystery of Nature itself, for which Darwin's central metaphor was, in a phrase from Shakespeare, 'the tangled bank,' teeming with life, aglow with many flowers, some flamboyant, some not seeming flowers at all. I do not specially cultivate the flamboyants; I do not seek fame." Taylor speaks French, Finnish, and some German, Swedish and Norwegian.

AVOCATIONAL INTERESTS: Travel, studying the Dutch language, gardening.

*　　*　　*

TAYLOR, Zack　1927-

PERSONAL: Born March 27, 1927, in Philadelphia, Pa.; married Melissa Iszard; children: Melanie, Whitney, Zack. *Education:* Colgate University, B.A., 1951. *Home address:* Box 303, Canvasback Lane, Easton, Md. 21601.

CAREER: Sports Afield magazine, New York City, associate editor, 1955-59; Cunningham & Walsh, New York

City, copy chief, 1954-61; N. W. Ayer & Co., Philadelphia, Pa., copy chief, 1961-64; *Sports Afield,* boats editor, 1964—. *Awards, honors:* Evinrude awards for excellence in writing about boating, 1st place, 1970, 2nd place, 1972; National Association of Boat and Engine Manufacturing award for best boat writing of the year, 1976.

WRITINGS: A Thousand and One Ways to Go Boating for Less Than One Thousand Dollars, Funk, 1971; (with Bradford Augier) *Introduction to Canoeing,* Stackpole, 1972; *Successful Waterfowling,* Crown, 1975.

* * *

TEAFORD, Jon C(hristian) 1946-

PERSONAL: Born September 5, 1946, in Columbus, Ohio; son of Robert Eugene (an attorney) and Virginia (Hamilton) Teaford. *Education:* Oberlin College, B.A., 1969; University of Wisconsin, M.A., 1970, Ph.D., 1973. *Home:* 400 North River Rd., Apt. 1002, West Lafayette, Ind. 47907. *Office:* Department of History, Purdue University, West Lafayette, Ind. 47907.

CAREER: Iowa State University, Ames, visiting assistant professor of history, 1973-75; Purdue University, West Lafayette, Ind., assistant professor of history, 1975—. *Member:* American Historical Association, Phi Beta Kappa.

WRITINGS: The Municipal Revolution in America: The Origins of Modern Urban Rule 1650-1825, University of Chicago Press, 1975. Contributor to historical journals.

WORK IN PROGRESS: Researching the history of local government in metropolitan areas and the clash between central city and suburbs.

* * *

TEE-VAN, Helen Damrosch 1893-1976

May 26, 1893—July 29, 1976; American artist, illustrator, and author. Obituaries: *New York Times,* July 31, 1976. (See index for previous *CA* sketch)

* * *

TELANDER, Richard F(orster) 1948-

PERSONAL: Born December 24, 1948, in Peoria, Ill.; son of Richard Harry (an oilman) and Jeanne (a poet; maiden name Overstolz) Telander; children: Leo. *Education:* Northwestern University, B.A., 1971. *Politics:* "Reactionary conservative." *Home:* 1027 W. Dakin, Chicago, Ill. 60613. *Agent:* Lois Wallace, Wallace, Aitken & Sheil, 118 East 61 St., New York, N.Y. 10021.

CAREER: Worked as a gravedigger, farmer, merchant seaman, insurance salesman, dog breeder; Lakeview Beagle Fanciers Club, Chicago, Ill., vice-president, 1975-76; Del-Crustaceans Rock 'n Roll Band, Chicago, Ill., lead guitar player, 1971—. *Member:* Royal Order of Ex-Peorians (sergeant-at-arms, 1968-74), Tau Alpha Phi.

WRITINGS: Heaven Is a Playground, St. Martin's, 1976; *Joe Namath and the Other Guys,* Holt, 1976. Editor of *How to Write,* 1973—; associate editor of *Brown Eye* (a local newsletter for city animal owners), 1973—; contributor to magazines, including *Sports Illustrated,* and *Sport* (sometimes under pseudonyms).

WORK IN PROGRESS: A novel, entitled *If It's Not Your Mound of Venus, It Must Be Uranus,* about "absurd teenage love between two junior high school science fair students," in which the author recalls old experiences in junior high.

SIDELIGHTS: Telander lied to *CA:* "I never really felt I would become a real writer. I began writing after my leg was crushed in a pileup while playing for the Kansas City Chiefs. While recovering for 6 months in the hospital I wrote a 500 page autobiography (unpublished) entitled *I Fumbled at the Twenty.* Encouraged by the response from those who read the book, I wrote several screenplays, a history of pro football, several short stories, another novel and a rock opera (music included). None of these ever appeared in print but, undaunted, I continued my career in earnest. After two short articles appeared in *Dog World* magazine I finally published in *Sports Illustrated.* Today, after some success, I write at least 10 hours every day but Sunday."

* * *

TELFORD, Charles W(itt) 1903-

PERSONAL: Born July 15, 1903, in Bountiful, Utah; son of John Witt (an agricultural supervisor) and Martha (a nurse; maiden name, Rockwood) Telford; married Aldene E. Courtney, February 11, 1933; children: Jean A. (Mrs. William D. Nix), Janet E. (Mrs. Richard Olsen). *Education:* University of Idaho, B.S., 1926, M.S., 1927; George Peabody College for Teachers, Ph.D., 1929. *Home:* 230 South 17th St., San Jose, Calif. 95112.

CAREER: Elementary school teacher in Idaho, 1921-24; University of North Dakota, Grand Forks, assistant professor, 1929-33, associate professor, 1933-34, professor of psychology, 1934-47, chairman of department, 1933-47; University of Utah, Salt Lake City, professor of psychology and acting department head, 1947-48; San Jose State College (now University), San Jose, Calif., professor of psychology, 1948-72, professor emeritus, 1972—, chairman of Psychology and Philosophy Division, 1950-55; writer, 1972—. Diplomate in clinical psychology of American Board of Examiners in Professional Psychology; certified psychologist and school psychologist in California.

MEMBER: American Psychological Association, American Association on Mental Deficiency, Council for Exceptional Children (member of California State Federation), National Education Association, Western Psychological Association.

WRITINGS: (With P. F. Valentine) *Twentieth Century Education,* Philosophical Library, 1946; (with James M. Sawrey) *Educational Psychology,* Allyn & Bacon, 1958, 4th edition, 1973; (with John MacRae, Vernon Oulette, and Paul Ecker) *Handbook for Supervisors,* Prentice-Hall, 1959; (with Sawrey) *The Dynamics of Mental Health,* Allyn & Bacon, 1963, 2nd edition published as *Psychology of Adjustment,* 1967, 4th edition published as *Adjustment and Personality,* 1975; (with Walter Plant) *The Psychological Impact of the Public Two-Year College,* San Jose State College Press, 1963; (with Sawrey) *The Exceptional Individual,* Prentice-Hall, 1967, 3rd edition, in press; (with Sawrey) *Psychology: A Concise Introduction to the Fundamentals of Behavior,* Brooks-Cole, 1968, 2nd edition, 1973; *Studying Psychology,* Brooks-Cole, 1968, 2nd edition, 1973; (with Sawrey and A. T. Jersild) *Child Psychology,* Prentice-Hall, 7th edition (Telford was not associated with earlier editions), 1975. Contributor to psychology journals.

WORK IN PROGRESS: Revising previously published books.

* * *

TENNANT, Emma 1937-

PERSONAL: Born October 20, 1937, in London, England;

daughter of C. G. (a businessman) and Elizabeth Lenconner; married; children: Matthew, Daisy, Rose. *Education:* Educated in private school in London, England. *Home:* 60 Elgin Cres., London W.11, England. *Agent:* A. P. Watt & Son, 26 Bedford Row, London W.C.2, England. *Office: Bananas,* 2 Blenheim Cres., London W.11, England.

CAREER: Writer and editor; travel correspondent for *Queen,* 1963; features editor for *Vogue,* 1966; editor of *Bananas* (literary magazine of British Arts Council), 1975—.

WRITINGS: The Time of the Crack (novel), J. Cape, 1973; *The Last of the Country House Murders* (novel), J. Cape, 1975, Thomas Nelson, 1976; *Hotel de Dream* (novel), Gollancz, 1976. Fiction reviewer for *Listener.*

WORK IN PROGRESS: The Mothers-in-Law, a short story collection; *Violence,* a novel.

SIDELIGHTS: Emma Tennant describes her three novels as "political satire-fantasy" and adds that she dislikes "most contemporary 'realistic fiction.'" *Avocational interests:* Travel to France and Italy.

*   *   *

TERRACE, Vincent 1948-

PERSONAL: Born May 14, 1948, in Manhattan, N.Y.; son of Vincent (a printer) and Anne (Lauro) Terrace. *Education:* New York Institute of Technology, B.F.A., 1971. *Religion:* Roman Catholic. *Home and office:* 1830 Delancey Pl., Bronx, N.Y. 10462.

CAREER: Korvette's Department Store, New York, N.Y., salesman, 1971-75; writer, 1975—.

WRITINGS: The Complete Encyclopedia of Television Programs, 1947-1976, Volumes I and II, A. S. Barnes, 1976.

WORK IN PROGRESS: Charlie Chan: A Definitive Study, with Bert Stangler; *The Complete Encyclopedia on Radio Programs, 1920-1960; The Complete Encyclopedia of Television Programs,* Volume III, publication by A. S. Barnes expected in 1978; *The Films of Debbie Reynolds.*

SIDELIGHTS: Terrace writes: "The television book is the first of its kind and I hope it does what I had intended it to: help fellow researchers and provide an insight into television's past—the thousands of programs and performers that shaped more than a quarter century of American broadcasting history." *Avocational interests:* Sound and video tape recording, gardening, model railroading.

*   *   *

TERRIS, Virginia R(inaldy) 1917-

PERSONAL: Born August 26, 1917, in Brooklyn, N.Y.; daughter of Edward Sutherland (a motion picture engineer) and Edith (Staines) Rinaldy; married Albert Terris (an artist and college professor), February 14, 1942 (separated, July, 1969); children: Susan, Abby (Mrs. Mott Greene), David Rinaldy, Enoch Edward. *Education:* Rutgers University, B.A., 1938; Adelphi University, M.A., 1964; New York University, Ph.D., 1973. *Home:* 393 South Grove St., Freeport, N.Y. 11520. *Office:* Department of English, Adelphi University, Garden City, N.Y. 11530.

CAREER: Morristown National Historic Park, Morristown, N.J., translator of Hessian documents, 1939-41; Morris Junior College, Morristown, instructor in English and art, 1940-42; worked as laboratory assistant, newspaper writer, poll statistician, and editorial assistant, 1942-44; freelance editor for national publishing firms, 1944-62; Adelphi University, Garden City, N.Y., part-time instructor, 1962-

64, instructor, 1964-70, assistant professor, 1970-75, associate professor of English, 1975—. Gives readings of her poetry.

MEMBER: Modern Language Association of America, American Studies Association, American Association of University Professors (vice-president of Metropolitan Conference, 1976—), Common Cause, Women's Lobby, New York Public Interest Research Group.

WRITINGS: (Editor with Jacob Drackler) *The Many Worlds of Poetry,* Knopf, 1969; *Tracking* (poems), University of Illinois Press, 1976; (editor) *Woman in America: A Bibliography,* Gale, in press. Contributor of poems, articles, and reviews to literary journals, including *American Poetry Review, New Letters, Literary Review, Chelsea,* and *Poetry Now,* and to *Nation.*

WORK IN PROGRESS: Another book of poems; *Emily Dickinson and the Genteel Tradition.*

SIDELIGHTS: Virginia Terris writes: "Having been born and raised in a time when women's roles were much more restricted than they are now, I was first wife and mother, then college professor, and am now insisting on being what I set out to be in my extreme youth, that is, a poet." She made the tape recordings "Emily Dickinson As a Woman Poet" and "Muriel Rukeyser," both for Everett-Edwards in 1976.

AVOCATIONAL INTERESTS: "I love traveling when I have time and money, and gardening when I'm short of both."

*   *   *

TERWILLIGER, Robert E(lwin) 1917-

PERSONAL: Born August 28, 1917, in Cortland, N.Y.; son of Melville (a clergyman) and Ella May (Seaman) Terwilliger; married Viola Mae Carroll, December 27, 1942; children: Anne Elizabeth. *Education:* Syracuse University, B.A., 1939; Episcopal Theological School, B.D., 1943; Yale University, Ph.D., 1948; General Theological Seminary, S.T.M., 1949. *Office:* Episcopal Diocese of Dallas, 1630 Garrett, Dallas, Tex. 75206.

CAREER: Ordained Episcopal priest, 1943; curate of Episcopal church in Worcester, Mass., 1942-44, assistant in Hartford, Conn., 1944-47, rector of Episcopal churches in Poughkeepsie, N.Y., 1949-60, and Los Angeles, Calif., 1960-62, associate rector in New York, N.Y., 1963-67; Community of the Holy Spirit, New York City, chaplain, 1968-75; Bishop Suffragan of Episcopal Diocese of Dallas, Tex., 1975—. Chaplain at Vassar College, 1949-60, dean of Convocation of Dutchess, 1952-59; chaplain of St. Hilda's and St. Hugh's School, 1965-67; adjunct professor at General Theological Seminary and director of New York City's Trinity Institute, both 1967-75. Member of board of examining chaplains of Diocese of New York, 1966-73, member of Diocese's Ecumenical Commission, 1970—. Member of Episcopal Church's Council on Eastern Churches, 1969—, General Board of Examining Chaplains, 1970-73, International Anglican Theological Commission for Joint Doctrinal Discussion with the Orthodox Churches, 1971—, Joint Commission on Ecumenical Relations, 1971— (vice-chairman, 1971-73), and Anglican-Roman Catholic Consultation on the Ordination of Women, 1975—. Member of faith and order committee of National Council of Churches, 1970-73.

MEMBER: Society for the Promotion of Religion and Learning (trustee, 1956-60), Society for the Renewal of Christian Art (trustee, 1967-75; honorary member, 1975—), Anglican Society (president, 1976—), Episcopal Radio and

Television Foundation (trustee). *Awards, honors:* D.D. from Seabury Western Theological Seminary, 1970, and University of the South, 1976.

WRITINGS: Receiving the Word of God, Morehouse, 1960; (with Michael Ramsey and A. M. Allchin) *The Charismatic Christ,* Morehouse, 1973; *Christian Believing,* Morehouse, 1973; (editor with Urban T. Holmes) *To Be a Priest,* Seabury, 1975.

*   *   *

TETENS, Tete Harens 1899(?)-1976

1899(?)—February 29, 1976; German-born American government agency advisor and author of books on Germany. Obituaries: *New York Times,* March 4, 1976.

*   *   *

TEYTE, Maggie 1888-1976

April 17, 1888—May 26, 1976; British operatic soprano and author. Obituaries: *New York Times,* May 28, 1976; *Washington Post,* May 28, 1976; *Current Biography,* July, 1976.

*   *   *

THAYNE, Emma Lou 1924-

PERSONAL: Born October 22, 1924, in Salt Lake City, Utah; daughter of Homer C. (an automobile dealer) and Grace (an artist; maiden name, Richards) Warner; married Melvin E. Thayne (a real estate broker), December 27, 1949; children: Becky (Mrs. Paul Markosian), Rinda (Mrs. James Kilgore), Shelley (Mrs. Paul Rich), Diane, Megan. *Education:* University of Utah, B.A., 1945, M.A., 1970. *Politics:* "Best candidate." *Religion:* Church of Jesus Christ of Latter-day Saints (Mormon). *Home:* 1965 Saint Mary's Drive, Salt Lake City, Utah 84108. *Agent:* Carolyn Willyoung Stagg, Lester Lewis Associates, Inc., 15 East 48th St., New York, N.Y. 10017. *Office:* Department of English, University of Utah, Salt Lake City, Utah 84112.

CAREER: University of Utah, Salt Lake City, part-time instructor in English, 1946—, head coach for women's intercollegiate tennis team, 1966-71. Junior and senior high school English teacher, 1947-49. *Member:* University of Utah Alumni (member of board of directors, 1967-74; vice-president of board, 1970-74). *Awards, honors:* Poetry awards from American Academy of Poets, 1970, for "Fairy House" and other poems, Utah Poetry Society, 1971, for *Spaces in the Sage,* and from Utah Institute of Fine Arts, 1974, for "First Loss" and other poems.

WRITINGS: Spaces in the Sage (poems), Parliament, 1971; *Until Another Day for Butterflies* (poems), Parliament, 1973; *On Slim, Unaccountable Bones* (poems), Parliament, 1974; *With Love, Mother* (poems and prose), Deseret, 1975; *Never Past the Gate* (novel), Peregrine Smith, 1975. Author of church school material for young people. Contributor of stories, poems, and articles to national and local periodicals.

WORK IN PROGRESS: Come September, a novel; a series of vignettes, including poems, on a visit to Israel; collecting her own writing on sports and the out-of-doors.

SIDELIGHTS: Emma Thayne writes: "Out of a background of mountain living in a comradely athletic-aesthetic family has come the major part of my writing. Philosophically and culturally attached to Mormondom, I have found subject matter for writings about the enrichments as well as the contradictions of living in a world where family life is the basic 'given' in 'eternal progression.' Because of serving at the University and in the Church, I have inadvertently become a spokeswoman for the moderate Mormon woman who seeks professional satisfactions while attempting to maintain a lively and productive family life. Most of my writing deals with the dichotomies, frustrations, pleasures and harmonies tangled in the dailiness of expecting more than dogma and ritual in being a woman."

BIOGRAPHICAL/CRITICAL SOURCES: Lifestyle, August 17, 1975.

*   *   *

THEMERSON, Stefan 1910-

PERSONAL: Born January 25, 1910, in Poland; married Franciszka Weinles (an artist). *Education:* Educated in Poland. *Home:* 28 Warrington Crescent, London W.9, England.

CAREER: Writer. *Military service:* Polish Army, 1940-44; served in France and England. *Awards, honors:* Polish Order of Merit, 1976.

WRITINGS: Dno Nieba (poems; title means "On the Bottom of the Sky"), [London], 1943; *Croquis dans les tenebres* (poems; title means "Sketches in Darkness"), Hachette, 1944; *The Lay Scripture* (prose-poem), Froshaug, 1947; *Jankel Adler* (essay), Gaberbocchus, 1948; *Bayamus* (novel), Editions Poetry—London, 1949, revised edition, Gaberbocchus, 1965; *Adventures of Peddy Bottom* (juvenile), Editions Poetry—London, 1951, revised edition, Gaberbocchus, 1954; *Wooff Wooff Or Who Killed Richard Wagner?* (fiction), Gaberbocchus, 1951, revised edition, 1967; *Professor Mmaa's Lecture* (novel), Gaberbocchus, 1953, Overlook Press, 1976; *"Factor T" and "Semantic Sonata"* (essay), Gaberbocchus, 1956, revised edition, 1972; *Kurt Schwitters in England* (essay), Gaberbocchus, 1958.

Cardinal Polatuo (novel), Gaberbocchus, 1961; *Semantic Divertissements* (humor), Gaberbocchus, 1962; *Tom Harris* (novel), Gaberbocchus, 1967, Knopf, 1968; *Appollinaire's Lyrical Ideograms,* Gaberbocchus, 1968; *St. Francis and the Wolf of Gubbio* (opera), Gaberbocchus, 1972; *Special Branch* (essay), Gaberbocchus, 1972; *Logic Labels and Flesh* (philosophical essays), Gaberbocchus, 1974; *On Semantic Poetry,* Gaberbocchus, 1975; *General Piesc Or the Case of the Forgotten Mission* (fiction), Gaberbocchus, 1976.

Avant-garde films, with wife, Franciszka Themerson: "Apteka," 1931; "Europa," 1932; "Moment Musical," 1933; "Zwarcie," 1935; "The Adventures of a Good Citizen," 1937; "Calling Mr. Smith," 1943; "The Eye and the Ear," 1944.

Author of children's books, in Polish, 1930-37.

SIDELIGHTS: Themerson's books have been published in Polish, Italian, French, German, and Dutch.

*   *   *

THOMAN, Richard S(amuel) 1919-

PERSONAL: Born May 10, 1919, in Lamar, Colo.; son of Henry C. (a farmer) and Anna D. (Davis) Thoman; married Evelyn L. Zumwalt, November 28, 1942; children: Gordon Richard, Timothy Wilson Tillman. *Education:* University of Colorado, B.A., 1941, M.A., 1948; University of California, Los Angeles, graduate study, 1943; University of Chicago, Ph.D., 1953. *Home:* 3425 Oakes Dr., Hayward, Calif. 94542. *Office:* Department of Geography, California State University, Hayward, Calif. 94542.

CAREER: University of Alabama, Tuscaloosa, instructor in geography, 1943-44; Gorham State College, Gorham, Maine, instructor in geography, 1945-48; University of Missouri, Columbia, instructor in geography, 1948-51; University of Chicago, Chicago, Ill., research associate, 1954-55; University of Omaha, Omaha, Neb., associate professor of geography and head of department, 1955-57; consultant and writer in Alexandria, Va., 1957-61; Queen's University, Kingston, Ontario, associate professor, 1961-63, professor of geography, 1963-71, consultant and writer in Toronto, Ontario, 1971-72; California State University, Hayward, professor of geography, 1972—. Visiting professor at Northwestern University, 1959; director of regional development branch of Ontario Department of Treasury and Economics, 1967-71; member of Agricultural Rehabilitation and Development Directorate of Ontario, 1967-71; member of Canadian Council for Urban and Regional Research, 1971—. Chairman of board of trustees of Land Economics Foundation, 1973—. Consultant to Resources for the Future, Inc.

MEMBER: International Geographical Union (member of Commission on Regional Aspects of Development), Association of American Geographers (vice-president of New England Division, 1947-48), American Geographical Society, Canadian Association of Geographers, Canadian Association of American Studies (founding member; vice-president, 1964-67), Sigma Xi, Lambda Alpha (president of Simcoe chapter, 1969-71; international president, 1971-73), Alpha Pi Zeta. Awards, honors: U.S. Office of Naval Research grant, 1954-55; grants from Canadian Department of Labor and Ontario Department of Economics and Development, 1963-65, Ottawa Area Development Agency and Ontario Department of Economics and Development, 1965, and Canadian Department of Industry, 1966.

WRITINGS: The Changing Occupance Pattern of the Tri-State Area: Missouri, Kansas, and Oklahoma, Department of Geography, University of Chicago, 1953; (with Jesse H. Wheeler and J. Trenton Kostbade) Regional Geography of the World, Holt, 1955, 4th edition, 1975; Free Ports and Foreign Trade Zones, Cornell Maritime Press, 1956, reprinted, 1970; (contributor) Harvey Perloff, editor, Regions, Resources and Economic Growth, Johns Hopkins Press, 1960; The Geography of Economic Activity, McGraw, 1962, 3rd edition, 1974; (editor with Donald J. Patton) Focus on Geographic Activity: A Collection of Original Studies, McGraw, 1964; (editor with W. Donald Wood) Areas of Economic Stress in Canada, Industrial Relations Centre, Queen's University, 1965; (with Maurice H. Yeates) Delimitation of Development Regions in Canada, with Special Attention to the Georgian Bay Vicinity, Canadian Department of Industry, 1966; (with Edgar C. Conkling) The Geography of International Trade, Prentice-Hall, 1967; Design for Development in Ontario: The Initiation of a Regional Planning Program, privately printed, 1971; (editor) Proceedings of the First Colloquium of the Commission on Regional Aspects of Development, Volume I: Methodology and Case Studies, Commission on Regional Aspects of Development, International Geographical Union, 1974.

Contributor to International Encyclopaedia of the Social Sciences. Contributor of articles and reviews to academic journals. Member of editorial board of Queen's Quarterly: A Canadian Review, 1962-66, and Economic Geography, 1973—.

WORK IN PROGRESS: The United States and Canada: Present and Future, publication by C. E. Merrill expected in 1978.

SIDELIGHTS: Thoman writes: "Born and reared on a dust bowl farm during the depression of the 1930's, I am committed professionally to making such personal contributions as can be made in one lifetime to redressing excesses of man-land imbalance, regionally and worldwide."

*   *   *

THOMAS, A(ndrew) R(owland) B(enedick)   1904-

PERSONAL: Born October 11, 1904, in Liverpool, England; son of William Rowland (a teacher) and Ellen (Phillips) Thomas; married Elizabeth Ann Levo, September 2, 1967; children: Susan Elizabeth. Education: St. John's College, Cambridge, M.A., 1928. Religion: Christian. Home: 43 Old Rd., Tiverton, Devonshire, England.

CAREER: Blundell's School, Tiverton, England, teacher of mathematics, boarding housemaster, and president of Common Room, 1926-69; writer, 1969—.

WRITINGS: Chess for the Love of It, Routledge & Kegan Paul, 1973; Chess Techniques, Routledge & Kegan Paul, 1975.

WORK IN PROGRESS: The Life of Carl Schlechter.

SIDELIGHTS: Thomas has made several visits to the West Indies and the United States. He plans a trip to Austria in 1978, to conduct research for his book on Schlechter.

*   *   *

THOMAS, Charles W(ellington)   1943-

PERSONAL: Born February 20, 1943, in Oklahoma City, Okla.; son of Charles and Virginia (Peragory) Thomas; married; children: one. Education: McMurry College, B.Sc., 1966; University of Kentucky, M.A., 1969, Ph.D., 1971. Home: 128 North Maple St., Bowling Green, Ohio 43402. Office: Department of Sociology, Bowling Green State University, Bowling Green, Ohio 43403.

CAREER: Virginia Commonwealth University, Richmond, assistant professor of sociology, 1969-73; College of William and Mary, Williamsburg, Va., adjunct associate professor of sociology, 1973-75; Virginia Commonwealth University, adjunct professor of sociology, 1975; Bowling Green State University, Bowling Green, Ohio, associate professor of sociology, 1975—, research associate, 1975. Research associate, Survey Research Center, Virginia Commonwealth University, 1972-73; research director, Metropolitan Criminal Justice Center, College of William and Mary, 1973-75, director, 1975; senior research associate, Center for Policy Research, Inc., New York, N.Y., 1975-76. Chairman of board of directors, Fan Free Clinic, Inc., 1970-71. Military service: U.S. Air Force, 1961-65. Member: American Sociological Association, American Society of Criminology, Society for the Study of Social Problems, National Council on Crime and Delinquency, Pacific Sociological Association, Southern Sociological Society, Northcentral Sociological Association, Midwest Sociological Society.

WRITINGS: (Contributor) John G. Cull and Richard E. Hardy, editors, Fundamentals of Criminal Behavior and Correctional Systems, C. C Thomas, 1973; (editor with David M. Peterson) Corrections: Problems and Prospects, Prentice-Hall, 1975; (contributor) Hugo A. Bedau and Chester M. Pierce, editors, Capital Punishment in the United States, AMS Press, 1976; (contributor) P. A. Vales and Marc Reidel, editors, Treating the Offender: Problems and Issues, Praeger, 1977; (with Petersen) Prison Organization and Inmate Subcultures, Bobbs-Merrill, 1977. Writer of research reports; contributor of articles and reviews to criminological, legal, and sociological journals. Editorial reviewer for Addison-Wesley Publishers, 1971; editorial referee, *Sociological Quarterly*, 1973-74, *American Sociological Review*, 1974, and *Criminology: An Interdisciplinary Journal*, 1975—.

*   *   *

THOMAS, Daniel B.
See BLUESTEIN, Daniel Thomas

*   *   *

THOMAS, Dian 1945-

PERSONAL: Born May 19, 1945, in Moab, Utah; daughter of Julian and Norene (a teacher; maiden name, Richins) Thomas. *Education:* Brigham Young University, B.S., 1968, M.S., 1973. *Religion:* Church of Jesus Christ of Latter-day Saints (Mormons). *Home and office:* 3492 South 1200 E., Salt Lake City, Utah 84106.

CAREER: Brighton Latter-day Saints Camp, Brighton, Utah, director, 1962-68; junior high school teacher of home economics and arts and crafts in Orem, Utah, 1968-71; Brigham Young University, Provo, Utah, instructor in home economics, 1973-75. Writer. *Member:* American Home Economics Association, American Vocational Education Association, Utah Home Economics Association, Utah Vocational Association. *Awards, honors:* Outstanding service award from *Forecast*, 1975.

WRITINGS: Teaching Tips for Outdoor Trips, Brigham Young University Press, 1972; *Roughing It Easy*, Brigham Young University Press, 1974.

WORK IN PROGRESS: Roughing It Easy, II, expected date of publication by Warner Books, May 1977.

*   *   *

THOMAS, Gwyn 1913-

PERSONAL: Born July 6, 1913, in Cymmer, County of Glamorgan, South Wales; son of Walter (a miner) and Ziphorah (Davies) Thomas; married Eiluned Thomas (a secretary), May 1, 1938. *Education:* Attended Madrid University, 1933; St. Edmund Hall, Oxford, B.A. (with honors), 1934. *Politics:* Humanist. *Religion:* Humanist. *Home:* Cherry Trees, Wyndham Park, Peterston-Super-Ely, Cardiff CF5 6LR, Wales. *Agent:* Curtis Brown Ltd., 1 Craven Hill, London W2 3EW, England.

CAREER: University of Wales, Cathays Park, extension lecturer, 1934-40; school teacher in modern European languages in Barry, South Wales, 1940-62; full-time playwright and novelist, 1962—. *Awards, honors: Evening Standard* playwrighting award, 1962; *Western Mail* best performer on television award, 1966; Welsh Arts Council award, 1976.

WRITINGS—Novels: *The Dark Philosophers*, Dobson, 1946, Little, Brown, 1947; *The Alone to the Alone*, Nicholson & Watson, 1947, published as *Venus and the Voters*, Little, Brown, 1948; *All Things Betray Thee*, M. Joseph, 1949, published as *Leaves in the Wind*, Little, Brown, 1949; *The World Cannot Hear You: A Comedy of Ancient Desires* (British Book Society selection), Gollancz, 1951, Little, Brown, 1952; *Now Lead Us Home*, Gollancz, 1952; *A Frost on My Frolic*, Gollancz, 1953; *The Stranger at My Side*, Gollancz, 1954; *Point of Order* (British Book Society selection), Gollancz, 1956; *The Love Man* (British Book Society selection), Gollancz, 1958, published as *A Wolf at Dusk*, Macmillan, 1959; *The Sky of Our Lives*, Hutchinson, 1972.

Plays: *The Keep* (first produced in London at Royal Court Theatre, 1961), Elek, 1961; "Loud Organs," first produced in Blackpool, England, 1962; "Jackie the Jumper," first produced in London at Royal Court Theatre, 1963; "The Loot," first produced in schools, 1965; "Sap," first produced in Cardiff at Sherman Theatre, 1974; "The Breakers," first produced in Cardiff at Sherman Theatre, 1976.

Television plays: "The Slip," 1962; "The Dig," 19639 "The Keep," 1970; "Adelphi Terrace," 1975; "Up and Under," 1975.

Radio plays: "Gazooka," 1952; "Forenoon," 1953; "The Deep Sweet Roots," 1953; "The Singers of Meadow Prospect," 1954; "Vive L'Oompa," 1955; "Up the Handling Code," 1955; "To This One Place," 1956; "Merlin's Brow," 1957; "The Long Run," 1958; "Noise," 1960; "The Walk-Out," 1963; "The Entrance," 1964; "The Alderman," 1966; "The Giving Time," 1968; "He Knows, He Knows," 1972.

Other: *Where Did I Put My Pity?* (stories), Progress Publishing, 1946; *Gazooka and Other Stories*, Gollancz, 1957; *Ring Delirium 123* (stories), Gollancz, 1960; *A Welsh Eye* (essays), Stephen Greene, 1964; *A Hatful of Humors* (essays), Schoolmaster Publishing, 1965; *A Few Selected Exits: An Autobiography of Sorts*, Little, Brown, 1968; *The Lust Lobby: Stories*, Hutchinson, 1971.

Work represented in anthologies, including *Plays of the Year*, Volume 26, edited by J. C. Trewin, Ryerson Press, 1963, and *Eight Plays: Book 2*, edited by Malcolm Stuart Fellows, Cassell, 1965. Contributor to Canadian, British, and U.S. periodicals, including *Atlantic Advocate, Holiday, Travel and Camera, Punch*, and *Listener*.

WORK IN PROGRESS: A book on the devolutionary splitting of the United Kingdom, completion expected in 1977.

SIDELIGHTS: Thomas told *CA:* "My work is based on the humour of astonishment. That has been the prevailing mood of my life, the reaction to multiple shock of a community as sonorously sensitive as a drumskin. I was brought up in South Wales, an area of Britain, pulverised by a long and bitter slump in the years between the wars. The victims of this dislocation were people suckled on evangelical religion and radical politics. To them if any day dawned without the hot promise of heaven upon it, they blamed it on a failure of the post-office. From them I distilled a laughter of ravelling delusions, gallows-humor, scored for a horde of gifted hymn-singers. They lost simultaneously their aboriginal language (Welsh), their major industry (coal) and most of their religion. They recovered from the shock of this only when the 2nd World War came along with its promise of atomic power and cheaper funerals.

"Yet they remained sweet and, in a sardonic way, serene. That fact has given me my main interest today; the anatomy of those who forswear sweetness and reject serenity. The migrants, the fanatics, the bandits, the aberrants, the lurchers away from stability, courtesy and calm. Will we one day find a social anaesthetic that will keep people from being restless pests? Will it come from philosophic wisdom, lobectomy, overwhelming fear, or pellets in the water-supply?

"In pursuit of this thesis and through sheer physical interest I have paid much attention to the Moorish occupation of Spain. The years when Africa stormed into Europe and the Spanish reconquest made religious and racial violence an essential strand in European policy."

THOMAS, I(saac) D(avid) E(llis) 1921-

PERSONAL: Born April 30, 1921, in Wales; came to United States in 1972; son of David (a farmer) and Blodwen (in farming; maiden name, Thomas); married Mildred Stevenson (a cosmetologist), February 14, 1972. *Education:* University of Wales, B.A., 1943; North Wales Baptist Seminary, B.D., 1946; California Graduate School of Theology, Ph.D., 1971. *Home:* 2170 Century Park E., Century City, Calif. 90067. *Office:* First Baptist Church, Maywood, Calif. 90270.

CAREER: Ordained minister of Baptist Church, 1946; minister in Wales, 1958-62; special guest preacher in the United States, 1963-73; senior minister in Maywood, Calif., 1973—. Special correspondent for British Broadcasting Corp., 1968—; free-lance lecturer and writer. *Member:* Lion's Club.

WRITINGS: On Trial, Mercury, 1962; *God's Outsider,* Christopher Davies, 1968; *Astrology and the Bible,* Scripture Press, 1972; *The Golden Treasury of Puritan Quotations,* Moody, 1975. Contributor to religious journals.

WORK IN PROGRESS: Writing on the *Book of Proverbs.*

AVOCATIONAL INTERESTS: Travel.

*   *   *

THOMAS, Latta R(oosevelt) 1927-

PERSONAL: Born October 13, 1927, in Union, S.C., son of Pickett R. (a farmer) and Alsie (a farmer; maiden name, Crenshaw) Thomas; married Bessie Lowery (a teacher), May 22, 1958; children: Latta, Jr., Ronald Jerome; *Education:* Friendship Junior College, A.A., 1949; Benedict College, B.A., 1951; Colgate Rochester Divinity School, B.D., 1955; Andover Newton Theological Seminary, S.T.M., 1966, D.Min., 1973. *Politics:* Democrat. *Religion:* Baptist. *Home:* 711 Isaac St., Columbia, S.C. 29203. *Office:* Benedict College, Columbia, S.C. 29204.

CAREER: Pastor in Elmira, N.Y., 1952-63, Newport, R.I., 1963-65, Ridge Spring, S.C., 1967-74, Saluda, S.C., 1968-74; Second Calvary Baptist Church, Columbia, S.C., pastor, 1975—. Benedict College, Columbia, S.C., assistant professor, 1965-68, associate professor, 1968-73, professor of religion and philosophy, 1973—, acting dean of students, 1974-75; College minister at Benedict College 1965—. Member of board of trustees, Babcock Center, 1974-75. *Member:* National Education Association, National Association of College and University Chaplains, American Association of University Professors, National Association for the Advancement of Colored People (NAACP, president of Elmira, N.Y., branch, 1957-62), Gethsemane Baptist Association, South Carolina Academy of Religion (president, 1970).

WRITINGS: Biblical Faith and the Black American, Judson Press, 1976.

WORK IN PROGRESS: Research on the history and African elements of the Black American religious experience, and on current Black theologies; seven meditations for *The Upper Room Disciplines,* publication by The Upper Room expected February, 1978.

SIDELIGHTS: Thomas writes: "My philosophy of life is shaped by three strands of influence: The prophetic branch of the Judeo-Christian tradition, the Black American experience, and the extraordinary persons who took an interest in me. That philosophy is this: the creative, healing and liberating events and achieve of the human being with the providential potency of God. This is the meaning of the covenant concept in Judeo-Christian tradition. It is the core meaning of the Church-based Black liberation thrust. In the liberation quest, it is not the action of God alone, nor the action of man alone. The two must come together. God, for many legitimate reasons, will not liberate unilaterally; man cannot unilaterally and effectively liberate. God's active demand and man's active response produce liberation and redemption. History is littered with the aborted efforts of those who relied on one to the exclusion of the other."

AVOCATIONAL INTERESTS: Hunting, fishing, and analyzing propaganda.

*   *   *

THOMPSON, Charles Waters, Jr.
See THOMPSON, Toby

*   *   *

THOMPSON, (Harry) Harwood 1894-

PERSONAL: Born December 19, 1894, in Carnarvon, Wales, immigrated to Canada, 1955; son of Arthur George and Annie (Harwood) Thompson; married Mabel Eveline Boyle, March 28, 1921; children: Eileen Courtney (Mrs. Arthur Clarabut Soul). *Education:* Attended Friars School, Bangor, Wales. *Religion:* Christian. *Home:* 1014 Eighth Ave., New Westminster, British Columbia, Canada.

CAREER: Apprenticed in banking, 1913, retired as accountant, 1955; New Westminster Young Men's Christian Association, New Westminster, British Columbia, accountant, 1957-62; free-lance writer in New Westminster, British Columbia, 1962—. *Military service:* Royal Welch Fusiliers and Machine Gun Corps, 1914-18; Mermont Home Guard, 1939-45; lieutenant.

WRITINGS: Seeker at the Gate, Churches' Fellowship for Psychic and Spiritual Studies, 1971; *The Witch's Cat,* Blackie & Son, 1972, Addison-Wesley, 1975, produced by Australian Broadcasting Corp. Contributor of articles and stories to magazines since age 17. Writer of more than 50 scripts for radio and television.

AVOCATIONAL INTERESTS: Psychic phenomena, witchcraft, ghosts, folklore.

*   *   *

THOMPSON, J(ohn) Eric S(idney) 1898-1975

PERSONAL: Born December 31, 1898; son of George W. and Mary (Cullen) Thompson; married Florence L. Keens, 1930; children: Donald. *Education:* Educated at Cambridge University. *Residence:* Cambridge, England.

CAREER: Chicago Natural History Museum, Chicago, Ill., assistant curator in charge of Central and South American archaeology and ethnology, 1926-35, honorary curator of Middle American archaeology, 1945-75; Carnegie Institution of Washington, Washington, D.C., member of archaeological staff, 1935-58; Cambridge University, Cambridge, England, member of faculty of archaeology and anthropology, 1958-75. Honorary professor at Museo Nacional de Mexico, beginning 1941; professor at Seminario Maya, University of Mexico, 1960. President of Thirty-Second International Congress of Americanists, 1952; consejero, Centro de Investigaciones antropologicas mexicanas, 1953-75. *Military service:* Served with Coldstream Guards, 1918; became second lieutenant.

MEMBER: British Academy (fellow). *Awards, honors:* Rivers Memorial Medal from Royal Anthropological Institute, 1945; Viking Fund medal for anthropology, 1955; LL.D. from University of Yucatan, 1959; D.Lit. from University of Pennsylvania, 1962, and Tulane University, 1972; Encomienda de Isabel la Catolica, 1964; Order of the Aztec Eagle, 1965; Huxley Memorial Medal, 1966; Sahagun Medal, Mexico, 1972; Litt.D. from Cambridge University, 1973; honorary fellow of Fitzwilliam College, Cambridge, 1973; knighted in 1975.

WRITINGS: A Correlation of the Mayan and European Calendars, Field Museum of Natural History, 1927; *The Civilization of the Mayas,* Field Museum of Natural History, 1927, 6th edition, Chicago Natural History Museum, 1958; *Ethnology of the Mayas of Southern and Central British Honduras,* Field Museum of Natural History, 1930; *Archaeological Investigations in the Southern Cayo District, British Honduras,* Field Museum of Natural History, 1931; *The Solar Year of the Mayas at Quirigua, Guatemala,* Field Museum of Natural History, 1932, reprinted, Kraus Reprint, 1968; (with Harry E. D. Pollock and Jean Charlot) *A Preliminary Study of the Ruins of Coba, Quintana Roo, Mexico,* Carnegie Institution of Washington, 1932; *Mexico before Cortez: An Account of the Daily Life, Religion, and Ritual of the Aztecs and Kindred Peoples,* Scribner, 1933; *Archaeology of South America,* Field Museum of Natural History, 1936; *Excavations at San Jose, British Honduras,* Carnegie Institution of Washington, 1939.

Dating of Certain Inscriptions of Non-Maya Origin, [Cambridge, Mass.], 1941; *A Coordination of the History of Chichen Itza with Ceramic Sequences in Central Mexico,* [Mexico], 1941; *Pitfalls and Stimuli in the Interpretation of History through Loan Words,* Middle American Research Institute, Tulane University, 1943; *Maya Hieroglyphic Writing: An Introduction,* Carnegie Institution of Washington, 1950, 3rd edition, University of Oklahoma Press, 1971; *The Rise and Fall of Maya Civilization,* University of Oklahoma Press, 1954, 2nd edition, 1973; *Memoranda on Some Dates at Palenque, Chiapas,* Carnegie Institution of Washington, 1954; (with others) *Bonampak, Chiapas, Mexico,* Carnegie Institution of Washington, 1955; *Dieties Portrayed on Censers at Mayapan,* Carnegie Institution of Washington, 1957; *Symbols, Glyphs, and Divinatory Almanacs for Diseases in the Maya Dresden and Madrid Codices,* privately printed, 1958; (editor) Thomas Gage, *Travels in the New World,* new edition, University of Oklahoma Press, 1958, revised edition, 1970; *Systems of Hieroglyphic Writing in Middle America and Methods of Deciphering Them,* privately printed, 1959.

A Catalog of Maya Hieroglyphs, University of Oklahoma Press, 1962; *Maya Archaeologist,* University of Oklahoma Press, 1963; *Preliminary Decipherments of Maya Glyphs,* [Essex, England], 1965; (author of introduction and notes) Merle Greene, *Ancient Maya Relief Sculpture,* Museum of Primitive Art, 1967; (with Thomas S. Barthel) *Intentos de lectura de los afijos de los jeroglificos en Los Codices Mayas,* Coordinacion de Humanidades, Universidad Nacional Autonoma de Mexico, 1969; *Maya History and Religion,* University of Oklahoma Press, 1970; *Maya Hieroglyphs without Tears,* British Museum, 1972; *A Commentary on the Dresden Codex: A Maya Hieroglyphic Book,* American Philosophical Society, 1972; (author of introduction to reprinted edition) Henry C. Mercer, *Hill Caves of Yucatan,* University of Oklahoma Press, 1975.

Also: (With Thomas A. Joyce) *Report on the British Museum Expedition to British Honduras,* 1927; (with Thomas W. F. Gann) *The History of the Maya,* 1931; *Lunar Inscriptions in the Usumacintla Valley,* 1937; (editor and author of

introduction) Edward Herbert Thompson, *The High Priest's Grave, Chichen Itza, Yucatan, Mexico,* 1938, reprinted, Kraus Reprint, 1968; *Yokes or Ball Game Belts?,* 1941; *A Trial Survey of the Southern Maya Area,* 1943. Author of Spanish books: *Apuntes sobre las Supersticiones de los Mayas de Socotz, Honduras Britanica,* 1940; *Apuntes sobre la Estela Numero Cinco de Balakbal, Quintana Roo,* 1940; *Un Vistazo a las "Cuidades" Mayas: Su aspecto y funcion,* 1945. Contributor to professional journals. Editor of "Notes on Middle American Archaeology and Ethnology," for Carnegie Institution of Washington.

SIDELIGHTS: A leading authority on Mayan civilization, Thompson conducted excavations in British Honduras and at Chichen Itza. He was a member of the British Museum Expedition to British Honduras in 1927. He succeeded in deciphering Mayan hieroglyphic writing and calculating correlations between Mayan and Christian calendars, enabling scholars to place events from Mayan history in the larger perspective of world history.

OBITUARIES: New York Times, September 11, 1975; *Publishers Weekly,* October 13, 1975; *AB Bookman's Weekly,* December 1, 1975.*

(Died September 9, 1975, in Cambridge, England)

*   *   *

THOMPSON, Ken D(avid)   1926-

PERSONAL: Born August 14, 1926, in Lexington, Ky.; son of E. I. and Beulah (Ingram) Thompson; married Phyllis Valleau, September 21, 1947; children: Ann (Mrs. David Dogherty), Dorney Reed, Dan Logan, David W. *Education:* Attended University of Kentucky and University of Wisconsin, Madison. *Home:* 4400 Lincoln, Louisville, Ky. 40220. *Office:* Christ Church Cathedral, 421 South Second St., Louisville, Ky. 40202.

CAREER: Radio Station WLAP, Lexington, Ky., continuity editor, 1947-48; Begley Drug Co., Richmond, Ky., advertising manager, 1948-50; Time Finance Co., Louisville, Ky., advertising manager, 1950-53; M. R. Kopmeyer Co. (advertising agency), Louisville, vice-president, 1953-56; Fessell-Siegfriedt Advertising Agency, Louisville, vice-president, 1956-59; Citizens Fidelity Bank & Trust Co., Louisville, vice-president, 1959—. Ordained Episcopal priest; Episcopal priest-worker in Louisville, 1963—. Mayor of St. Regis Park, Ky., 1954-58. Co-founder of local drug abuse center and of Des Pres Park. Promotion chairman of Jefferson County Salk polio campaign and Sabin vaccine program. *Military service:* U.S. Army Air Forces, 1945-46.

WRITINGS: The Blue Shawl (inspirational short story), Brown & Bigelow, 1954; *The Story of Silent Night* (inspirational short story), Brown & Bigelow, 1955; *The Christmas Cradle* (inspirational short story), Brown & Bigelow, 1956; *Bless This Desk,* Abingdon, 1975. Contributor to *Louisville Courier-Journal.*

SIDELIGHTS: Thompson writes: "I am concerned that there exists such a gap between the sacred and secular. In being an ordained Episcopal priest yet earning my livelihood as a marketing executive in a large bank, I am attempting to bridge this gap for myself and others. I am very interested in enablement of the lay ministry, the building of a greater sense of Christian Community, and the evangelization of and by the Church."

*   *   *

THOMPSON, Thomas   1933-

PERSONAL: Born October 3, 1933, in Fort Worth, Tex.;

son of Clarence (a teacher) and Ruth (a high school principal) Thompson; married Joyce Alford, 1958 (divorced, 1969); children: Kirk M., Scott M. *Education:* University of Texas, B.A., 1955. *Residence:* Los Angeles, Calif. 90046.

CAREER: Houston Press, Houston, Tex., reporter and city editor, 1955-61; *Life,* New York, N.Y., worked as assistant editor, staff writer, entertainment editor, and Paris bureau chief, 1961-72; writer, 1972—. *Awards, honors:* National Headliner Award for investigative reporting for work at *Life;* Sigma Delta Chi national medallion for writing in *Life.*

WRITINGS—Nonfiction: *Hearts: Of Surgeons and Transplants, Miracles and Disasters Along the Cardiac Frontier,* McCall Publishing, 1971; *Richie: The Ultimate Tragedy Between One Decent Man and the Son He Loved,* Saturday Review Press, 1973; *Lost!,* Atheneum, 1974; *Blood and Money,* Doubleday, 1976. Contributor of several hundred articles to national magazines, including *McCall's, Ladies' Home Journal, New York Times, New Times, Cosmopolitan, New York,* and *New West.*

WORK IN PROGRESS: The Angel of Death (tentative title), a true story "about some violent events that took place in Asia and Europe."

SIDELIGHTS: Thompson writes: "*Hearts* was the account of the rivalry between the heart surgeons, Dr. Michael DeBakey and Dr. Denton Cooley, and a general look at the world of cardiac surgery, including a review (rather critical!) of the heart transplant era. *Richie* is the story of a drug tragedy on Long Island in which a father killed his addict son. It has just been made into a film for NBC-TV. *Lost!* is the true story of three people who were lost at sea for seventy-two days, and of their struggle against one another. *Blood and Money* is the true account of a series of unusual and violent events springing out of the death of a Houston socialite.

"I write exclusively in the non-fiction area, and my style is rather 'novelistic,' but at the same time staying within the framework of the truth. I draw my stories out of real life, for I feel that they are more vivid and more challenging than anything I could dream up as a novelist. My favorite theme, which I explore over and over again, is what happens to an ordinary man (or woman) when he or she is confronted with a difficult, even impossible situation. How does the person respond? Is the character changed? I shall go on writing of and around this theme for some time to come."

AVOCATIONAL INTERESTS: Tennis, gardening, walking on the beach, "planning ski trips to St. Moritz which never seem to come off."

*   *   *

THOMPSON, Toby 1944-

PERSONAL: Real name, Charles Waters Thompson, Jr.; born September 15, 1944, in Washington, D.C.; son of Charles Waters (a physician) and Elizabeth (Nichols) Thompson; married Corinne Collins (a registered nurse), November 9, 1974. *Education:* University of Delaware, B.A. (with distinction), 1966; University of Virginia, M.A., 1968. *Home:* 7906 Riverside Dr., Cabin John, Md. 20731. *Agent:* Ellen Levine, Curtis Brown Ltd., 60 East 56th St., New York, N.Y. 10022.

CAREER: Writer. Has worked as cowhand and professional guitarist.

WRITINGS: Positively Main Street: An Unorthodox View of Bob Dylan, Coward, 1971; *Saloon: A Guide to America's Great Bars, Pubs, Saloons, Taverns, Drinking Places, and*

Watering Holes, Grossman, 1976. Writer of rock music criticism for *Washington Post,* 1972-76.

WORK IN PROGRESS: Profiles of younger American writers; a novel.

SIDELIGHTS: Thompson writes: "In my journalism I have brought a highly personal approach to subjects usually treated in a pseudo-objective, if not offhand manner. . . . [That is] my reaction to that maddeningly impersonal time in which we live. Spent four years and over a hundred thousand land miles in research for *Saloon.* Was convinced I would find the Great American Bar. Perhaps I did."

*   *   *

THORPE, Elliott R(aymond) 1897-

PERSONAL: Born December 26, 1897, in Stonington, Conn.; son of Job (a sheet metal worker) and Amelia (Foster) Thorpe; married Mary E. Wilcox, March 12, 1917 (deceased); married Emily Linhoff, June 6, 1931; children: Elliott R., Jr., Donald K. *Education:* Attended University of Rhode Island, 1915-17. *Politics:* Republican. *Religion:* Episcopalian. *Home:* 7724 Westmoreland Dr., Sarasota, Fla. 33580. *Agent:* Curtis Brown Ltd., 575 Madison Ave., New York, N.Y. 10022.

CAREER: U.S. Army, career officer, 1917-50, served in France during World War I, in the Pacific, 1925-29, and in the Far East, 1940-46, commanding officer of Maui Military District, 1938-40, lend-lease commissioner in the Dutch East Indies, 1941, served in Malayan-Java campaign during World War II, chief of counter intelligence for General Douglas MacArthur, 1942-46, military attache at U.S. Embassy in Bangkok, 1948-50, retiring as brigadier general; writer, 1950—.

MEMBER: Siam Society (member of council). *Awards, honors*—Military: Distinguished Service Medal with oak leaf cluster, Legion of Merit, Bronze Star, Purple Heart. Other: L.H.D. from University of Rhode Island; named commander of the Order of Orange-Nassau (Netherlands) and knight commander of the Most Noble Order of the Crown of Thailand.

WRITINGS: Tapa Tactics (nonfiction), Hawaii Press, 1937; *East Wind, Rain* (nonfiction), Gambit, 1969; *Shipwrecks on the Shores of Westerly,* Westerly Historical Association, 1973. Author of studies on Southeast Asia for U.S. War Department and editor of a Malay-English dictionary.

WORK IN PROGRESS: A narrative of World War One and the Peace Conference; a tale of a small Hawaiian boy of fifty years ago, for children.

SIDELIGHTS: While working with General MacArthur, Thorpe was custodian of the Emperor of Japan and selected the Japanese war criminals who would be tried by the International Tribunal. He controlled the Japanese press and abolished the Thought Police. In 1946 Thorpe organized the Armed Forces Language School in Monterey, Calif.

*   *   *

THRELKELD, Richard 1937-

PERSONAL: Born November 30, 1937, in Cedar Rapids, Iowa; son of Robert Merle (a salesman) and Jane (Davis) Threlkeld; married Sharon A. Adams, June 11, 1960 (divorced, 1976). children: Susan Anne, Julia Lynne. *Education:* Ripon College, B.A., 1960; Northwestern University, M.S.J., 1961; Columbia University, M.A., 1965. *Agent:* N. S. Bienstock, Inc., 10 Columbus Cir., New York, N.Y.

10019. *Office:* CBS News, 2525 Van Ness, San Francisco, Calif. 94109.

CAREER/WRITINGS: Barrington Courier Review, Barrington, Ill., assistant editor, 1957-59; WHAS-TV, Louisville, Ky., writer and producer, 1961; WMT-TV, Cedar Rapids, Iowa, reporter, 1961-65; Columbia Broadcasting System (CBS) News, reporter and assignment editor in Los Angeles, 1966-68, correspondent in Indo-China, 1968-70, correspondent in San Francisco, 1970—. Notable assignments include assississation of Robert Kennedy, 1968, war in Indo-China, 1968-70 and 1972, Amchitka Island nuclear test controversy, 1971, Patricia Hearst kidnapping and trial, 1974-76, evacuations from Cambodia and Saigon, 1975. Lecturer. Author of scripts for television and radio broadcast by CBS News. *Member:* Radio and Television Directors Association, Deadline Club (New York City), Los Angeles Press Club, Sigma Delta Chi. *Awards, honors:* Columbia Broadcasting System news fellowship, 1964-65; Overseas Press Club awards, 1975, for coverage of Indo-China evacuations.

AVOCATIONAL INTERESTS: Ecology, conservation, English language usage, international affairs, domestic politics.

*   *   *

TICKLE, P(hyllis) A(lexander)   1934-

PERSONAL: Born March 12, 1934, in Johnson City, Tenn.; daughter of Philip Wade (an educator) and Katherine (Porter) Alexander; married Samuel Milton Tickle (a physician), June 17, 1955; children: Nora Katherine (Mrs. Devereaux D. Cannon, Jr.), Mary Gammon, Laura Lee, John Crockett II, Philip Wade (deceased), Samuel Milton, Jr., Rebecca Rutledge. *Education:* Shorter College, student, 1951-54; East Tennessee State University, B.A., 1955; Furman University, M.A., 1961. *Religion:* Episcopalian. *Home and office:* 1474 Harbert, Memphis, Tenn. 38104.

CAREER: Furman University, Greenville, S.C., instructor in psychology, 1960-62; Southwestern at Memphis, Memphis, Tenn., instructor in english, 1962-65; Memphis Academy of Arts, Memphis, Tenn., teacher and dean of humanities, 1965-71; writer, 1971—. Member of board of directors of Upward Bound at LeMoyne-Owen College, 1968-70, and Sunshine Day Care Center, 1970-71; member of board of trustees of Grace-St. Luke's Episcopal School, 1970-76.

WRITINGS: An Introduction to the Patterns of Indo-European Speech, Memphis Academy of Arts, 1968; *Figs and Fury* (a chancel play; first produced in Memphis, Tenn. at Grace-St. Luke Episcopal Church), St. Luke's Press, 1974, 2nd edition, 1976; *It's No Fun to Be Sick* (children), St. Luke's Press, 1976; *The Story of Two Johns* (for children facing the loss of a loved one), St. Luke's Press, 1976. Contributor of articles and poems to magazines.

WORK IN PROGRESS: A book of poems; several poems to be included in an anthology of erotica, publication expected, 1978.

SIDELIGHTS: Phyllis Tickle writes: "I lecture a great deal in colleges and schools and find this a most satisfying experience. I think of myself as a poetess by trade, but having had seven children has also given me some kind of background for enjoying children's literature and I am finding that rewarding also. Spanish is my language of choice and all things Mexican and/or Spanish are as natural to me as breathing.

"The women's movement comes at a time when being wife, mother, and writer is no longer regarded as natural, but rather as a social statement or a private protest. Within the framework of all these factors, I find myself drawn more and more toward the ancients—to the works and values of Sappho and Catullus, to Cavafy and Rilke in our own time, and always, to Eliot."

*   *   *

TILLINGHAST, B(urette) S(tinson), Jr.   1930-

PERSONAL: Born May 11, 1930, in Spartanburg, S.C.; son of Burette Stinson (a newspaperman) and Bessie Lee (a musician; maiden name, Farley) Tillinghast; married Josephine Wood (a librarian), August 31, 1952; children: Tom Wood, Sam Wood. *Education:* Davidson College, student; Wofford College, B.A., 1954; George Peabody College for Teachers, M.A., 1955; Florida State University, Ed.D., 1961. *Politics:* "I have no politics." *Religion:* "Skeptical, but hopeful." *Home:* 1011 Woodside Dr. E., Mobile, Ala. 36608. *Agent:* Ruth Cantor, 156 Fifth Ave., New York, N.Y. 10010. *Office:* Department of Education, University of South Alabama, Mobile, Ala. 36608.

CAREER: Teacher and guidance counselor in public schools in Nashville, Tenn., 1955-56; school psychologist for public schools in Melbourne, Fla., 1956-58; guidance counselor in public schools in Quincy, Fla., 1959-60, school psychologist, 1960-61, supervisor of guidance, 1961-62; University of Virginia, Charlottesville, assistant professor, 1962-65, associate professor of education, 1965-67; University of South Alabama, Mobile, professor of education in counseling, 1967—. Psychologist with Tennessee Department of Education, 1956. *Military service:* U.S. Navy, 1948-52.

MEMBER: American Psychological Association, American Personnal and Guidance Association, National Vocational Guidance Association, National Council on Measurement in Education, Association for Counselor Education and Supervision, Phi Beta Kappa, Pi Gamma Mu, Phi Delta Kappa.

WRITINGS: The Honey Man (novel), Dutton, 1976. Contributor to education journals and to *Nursing Outlook.*

WORK IN PROGRESS: The Bridge to Bonito Island (tentative title), a novel.

SIDELIGHTS: Tillinghast writes: "I had been submitting and receiving rejections for my fiction for twenty-four years before my first novel was published this year by Dutton. I wanted *The Honey Man* to be funny, interesting, and to contain some truths. I think it did."

*   *   *

TIPPETTE, Giles   1936-

PERSONAL: Born August 25, 1936, in Texas; son of O. B. and Mary Grace (Harpster) Tippette; married Mildred Ann Mebane, 1956; children: Shanna, Lisa. *Education:* Sam Houston University, B.S., 1959. *Politics:* "Despise all politics and politicians." *Religion:* No formal. *Residence:* Kerrville, Tex. *Agent:* Owne Laster, William Morris Agency, 1350 Avenue of the Americas, New York, N.Y. 10019.

CAREER: Held a variety of jobs, including rodeo contestant, diamond courrier, and gold miner in Mexico; now a writer. *Member:* Author's Guild.

WRITINGS: The Bank Robber (novel), Macmillan, 1970; *The Trojan Cow* (novel), Macmillan, 1971; *The Brave Man* (nonfiction), Macmillan, 1972; *Saturday's Children* (nonfiction), Macmillan, 1973; *The Survivalist* (novel), Macmillan,

1974; *Austin Davis* (novel), Dell, 1975; *Sunshine Killers* (novel), Dell, 1975; *The Mercanaries*, Delacorte, 1976. Contributor to magazines, including *Time, Sports Illustrated, Texas Monthly, Esquire, Newsweek,* and *Argosy.*

WORK IN PROGRESS: A novel, *The Texicans,* for Delacourt.

SIDELIGHTS: Two novels by Tippette, *Austin Davis* and *The Bank Robber,* have been made into movies. His manuscript, "Man of Ice," was adapted for a television movie, "Target Risk."

* * *

TOBEY, Mark 1890-1976

December 11, 1890—April 24, 1976; American artist, poet, and musician. Obituaries: *New York Times,* April 25, 1976; *Current Biography,* June, 1976.

* * *

TODD, Leonard 1940-

PERSONAL: Born February 10, 1940, in Greenville, S.C.; son of Leonard M. (a banker) and Lena-Miles (a poet; maiden name, Wever); *Education:* Sorbonne, University of Paris, student, 1959; Yale University, B.A. (cum laude), 1961, M.A., 1965. *Residence:* New York, N.Y. *Agent:* John Cushman Associates, 25 W. 43rd St., New York, N.Y. 10036.

CAREER: Sea Pines Plantation, Hilton Head Island, S.C., design director, 1967-71; one-man show of design work at American Museum of Natural History, 1975; free-lance writer, 1971—. Production and design director, *Coda,* 1976—. *Awards, honors:* Fulbright scholar, 1965-67.

WRITINGS: Trash Can Toys and Games, Viking, 1974. Contributor of articles to national magazines, including *Family Circle, Viva, Village Voice, Cosmopolitan, Americana,* and *Travel & Leisure.*

WORK IN PROGRESS: Paris in Black, a history of the cemetery of Pere Lachaise, illustrated with own photographs; a novel; a series of short stories.

SIDELIGHTS: Todd told *CA:* "Before becoming a writer, I studied and practiced architecture for more than a decade. The two disciplines couldn't be more different, yet I find they share a similar creative process. For me, designing a building and writing a novel both involve bringing order to disparate parts—establishing a form within which various needs and impulses can come together, find expression, take on life. The form I find most useful in my writing, for now at least, is the same that the early skyscraper architects employed; they always gave their buildings a beginning, a middle, and an end—like a column, they said. Within that simple framework wonders can happen."

* * *

TODD, Ruth Van Dorn 1889(?)-1976

1889(?)—March 16, 1976; American newswoman. Obituaries: *Washington Post,* March 18, 1976.

* * *

TODD, William Mills III 1944-

PERSONAL: Born August 15, 1944, in Newport News, Va.; son of William Mills, Jr. (a businessman) and Jeanette (Hofman) Todd; married Eva Andenaes, July 27, 1968; children: Karen Elizabeth. *Education:* Dartmouth College, A.B., 1966; Oxford University, B.A. and M.A., both 1968;

Columbia University, Ph.D., 1973. *Home:* 939 Valdez Pl., Stanford, Calif. 94305. *Office:* Department of Slavic Languages, Stanford University, Stanford, Calif. 94305.

CAREER: Stanford University, Stanford, Calif., assistant professor of Russian literature, 1972—. Visiting assistant professor at Yale University, spring, 1977. *Member:* Modern Language Association of America, American Association for the Advancement of Slavic Studies. *Awards, honors:* Fulbright-Hays grants, 1970-71, 1976.

WRITINGS: The Familiar Letter as a Literary Genre in the Age of Pushkin, Princteon University Press, 1976; (editor) *Literature and Society in Imperial Russia: 1800-1914,* Stanford University Press, in press. Contributor of translations, articles, and reviews to literature and Russian studies journals.

WORK IN PROGRESS: A book on the development of Russian fiction in the early nineteenth century.

SIDELIGHTS: Todd writes that his interests center around comparative and theoretical approaches to fiction and the sociology of literature. He adds that his literary criticism is based "on the idea that literature is both a social and an aesthetic phenomenon."

* * *

TOEPLITZ, Jerzy 1909-

PERSONAL: Born November 24, 1909, in Charkov, Russia; son of Teodor (a town planner) and Helen (Odrzywolska) Toeplitz; married Izabelle Stanislawa Gornicki, October 21, 1943; children: Elizabeth, Margaret (Mrs. Julian Winiewska), Suzanne. *Education:* University of Warsaw, M.Law, 1933, D.Phil., 1957. *Home:* 19-30 Archer St., Chatswood 2067, Australia. *Office:* Film and Television School, 13-15 Lyonpark Rd., North Ryde 2113, Australia.

CAREER: Toeplitz Film Productions Ltd., London, England, foreign sales manager, 1934-37; First Locomotive Works, Warsaw, Poland, secretary to general manager, 1937-39; teacher of English during German occupation, 1939-45; Polish Film (state enterprise), Lodz and Warsaw, secretary general, 1945, director of foreign department, 1946, assistant general director, 1947-48; Polish Film School, Lodz, director, 1949-52, professor of film history, 1952-57, rector, 1957-68; Institute of Art, Warsaw, director of film department, 1968-72; La Trobe University, Melbourne, Australia, visiting professor, 1972-73; Film and Television School, Sydney, Australia, foundation director, 1973—. President of International Federation of Film Archives, 1948-72; vice-president of International Film and Television Council, 1966-72; governor of Australian Film Institute. *Awards, honors:* Special award from Association of Polish Filmmakers, 1973, for "History of Cinematographic Art."

WRITINGS: Historia Sztuki Filmowej (title means "History of Cinematographic Art"), five volumes, Wydawnictwa Artystyczne i Filmowe (Warsaw), 1955-71; *My Meeting with the Tenth Muse* (in Polish), Wydawnictwa Artystyczne i Filmowe, 1960; *Film i Telewizja w U.S.A.* (title means "Film and Television in the U.S.A."), Wydawnictwa Artystyczne i Filmowe, 1964; *Twenty-Five Years of Film in Post-War Poland* (in Polish), Panstwowe Wydawnictwo Naukowe (Warsaw), 1969; *Geschichte des Films, 1895-1928* (title means "History of Film, 1895-1928"), Henschelverlag (Berlin), 1972; *Nowy Film Amerykanski* (title means "New American Film"), Wydawnictwa Artystyczne i Filmowe, 1973, English translation by Boleslaw Sulik published as

Hollywood and After: The Changing Face of Movies in America, Allen & Unwin, 1974, Regnery, 1975.

WORK IN PROGRESS: A Short History of the Cinema; volume VI of *Historia Sztuki Filmowej.*

SIDELIGHTS: Toeplitz's books have also been translated into German, Russian, Czech, and Slovak.

*   *   *

TOLBERT, Malcolm O(liver)   1924-

PERSONAL: Born August 4, 1924, in Alton, Ill.; son of Douglas M. (a carpenter) and Katie Lee (Davis) Tolbert; married Nell Sills, November 4, 1943; children: Sharon, Ellen, Laren, Anita. *Education:* Louisiana College, B.A., 1952; New Orleans Baptist Theological Seminary, B.D., 1952, Th.D., 1962. *Home:* 1660 Blue Ridge, Gainesville, Ga. 30501. *Office:* First Baptist Church, Gainesville, Ga. 30501.

CAREER: Minister of the Baptist Church; Foreign Mission Board (Southern Baptist Convention), missionary to Brazil, 1952-61; New Orleans Baptist Theological Seminary, New Orleans, La., professor of New Testament, 1961-76; First Baptist Church, Gainesville, Ga., pastor, 1976—. *Member:* Society of Biblical Literature, Association of Baptist Professors of Religion.

WRITINGS: "Luke" in *The Broadman Bible Commentary,* Broadman Press, 1969; *Walking with the Lord,* Broadman Press, 1970; *Speaking in Tongues,* Insight Press, 1972; *Good News from Matthew,* Broadman Press, 1975.

*   *   *

TOLSTOY, Alexandra L(vovna)   1884-

PERSONAL: Born July 1, 1884, in Yasnaya Polyana, Russia; came to United States 1931, became U.S. citizen, 1941; daughter of Leo N. (a writer) and Sophya (Bers) Tolstoy. *Education:* Educated privately. *Religion:* Eastern Orthodox. *Home:* Tolstoy Farm, Valley Cottage, N.Y. *Office:* Tolstoy Foundation Inc., 250 West 57th St., New York, N.Y. 10019.

CAREER: Secretary to father Leo N. Tolstoy at Yasnaya Polyana, Russia, 1901-1910; served as literary executor of her father's will, and edited manuscripts for posthumous publication, 1910-1914; worked as nurse in Moscow, East Prussia, and Turkish Armenia, 1914-15; represented Zemsky Unity on Western war front, with rank equivalent to colonel, co-founded schools and relief food centers for 10,000 children, and founded four military medical field detachments, 1916-17; returned to Moscow, 1918, and founded the Society for Dissemination and Study of Tolstoy's Works, for the purpose of completing a 91 volume edition of Tolstoy's writing; imprisoned by Soviets for political activities, 1920; after her release in 1921, was appointed curator of Leo Tolstoy Museum and Educational Center at Yasnaya Polyana, and founded schools and medical facilities, 1921-29; left Russia, 1929, for lecture tour in Japan; came to United States, 1931, as lecturer and farmer in New Square, Pa., 1931-33, and Haddan, Conn., 1933-39; founder and president of Tolstoy Foundation Inc., New York, N.Y., and Resettlement Center, Valley Cottage, N.Y., 1939—. Vice-president of CARE, 1946—; lecturer at colleges and universities, including University of Michigan, University of Illinois, Smith College, Michigan State University, Ohio State University, and Vassar College; also has appeared on radio and television programs.

AWARDS, HONORS: St. George medals (Russia), 1915,

and 1916, for World War I relief work; Presidential citation, 1946, for World War II relief work; Russian Red Cross in Exile citation, 1946; Kalmuk Society awards, 1952 and 1955; Chicago Civic Committee for World Refugees award, 1960; Order of Lafayette Freedom award, 1961; L.H.D. from Hobart and William Smith Colleges, 1962; U.S. Committee for Refugees award, 1966.

WRITINGS: The Tragedy of Tolstoy, Yale University Press, 1933; *I Worked for the Soviets,* Yale University Press, 1934; *Tolstoy: A Life of My Father,* Harper, 1953, reprinted, Octagon, 1973; *The Real Tolstoy: A Critique and Commentary,* H. S. Evans, 1968.

WORK IN PROGRESS: History of the Tolstoy Foundation, 1939-1976.

SIDELIGHTS: Alexandra Tolstoy is the youngest daughter of the thirteen children of Count Leo N. Tolstoy. A great admirer of her father's genius, Alexandra was named literary executor in Tolstoy's will. In order to fulfill the terms of the will, she edited and prepared her father's previously unpublished manuscripts. Also in accordance with Tolstoy's instructions, she used the proceeds of the publication (approximately $200,000) to buy back approximately 2,500 acres of land from the estate at Yasnaya Polyana, and distributed it among the peasants from neighboring villages.

Shortly after completing this project, Alexandra Tolstoy was licensed as a practical nurse. Since that time, she has dedicated her life to the aiding of refugees, first during the two world wars, and more recently in New York. As head of the Tolstoy Foundation she directs resettlement assistance programs for refugees or escapees from Communist bloc nations.

AVOCATIONAL INTERESTS: Fishing.

BIOGRAPHICAL/CRITICAL SOURCES: Alexandra L. Tolstoy, *The Tragedy of Tolstoy,* Yale University Press, 1933; *I Worked for the Soviets,* Yale University Press, 1934; *New Yorker,* March 22, 1952.

*   *   *

TOMLINSON, Kenneth Y(oung)   1944-

PERSONAL: Born August 3, 1944, in Grayson County, Va.; son of Young and Mattie (Wingate) Tomlinson; married Rebecca Moore (a Congressional aide), April 25, 1975. *Education:* Randolph-Macon College, B.A., 1966. *Home:* 4916 Flint Dr., Washington, D.C. 20016. *Office: Reader's Digest,* 1730 Rhode Island Ave. N.W., Washington, D.C. 20036.

CAREER: Richmond Times-Dispatch, Richmond, Va., reporter, 1965-68; *Reader's Digest,* Washington, D.C., associate editor, 1968—.

WRITINGS: (With John Hubbell) *POW* (nonfiction), Reader's Digest Press, 1976. Contributor to *Reader's Digest.*

*   *   *

TOOMAY, Patrick J(ay)   1948-

PERSONAL: Born May 17, 1948, in Pomona, Calif.; son of John C. (a major general in the U.S. Air Force) and Virginia (Sadler) Toomay; married Becky Bramblet, January 31, 1971; children: Seth Michael. *Education:* Vanderbilt University, B.E., 1971. *Agent:* Sterling Lord Agency, 550 Madison Ave., New York, N.Y.

CAREER: Tampa Bay Buccaneers, Tampa, Fla., professional football player, 1970—. Promotional director of country music for Warner Brothers Records, 1973—.

WRITINGS: The Crunch (nonfiction), Norton, 1975.

WORK IN PROGRESS: *Zebra,* a novel; a screenplay, with James Borrelli.

* * *

TOOMER, Derek 1946-

PERSONAL: Born February 8, 1946, in Weston-super-Mare, England; son of Arthur Edward (a carpenter) and Joan (Crandon) Toomer; married Janice Lesley Hunt (a teacher), September 21, 1968. *Education:* University of Bristol, B.S. (honors), 1968; University of Nottingham, Ph.D., 1971. *Home:* 43 Ridgeway Dr., Dunstable, Bedfordshire LU5 4QT, England. *Office:* Hemel Hempstead School, Heath Lane, Hemel Hempstead, Hertfordshire, England.

CAREER: University of Hull, Hull, England, research fellow in botany, 1971-72; College of Technology, Luton, England, lecturer in microbiology, 1972-75; Hemel Hempstead School, Hemel Heampstead, England, biology teacher, 1975—.

WRITINGS: (With Alan Cane) *Invisible World,* Audus Books, 1976. Contributor to scientific journals.

SIDELIGHTS: Toomer comments that he "developed a deep interest in natural history," and that his "concern for conservation in all aspects was increased by becoming interested in ornithology and doing a lot of voluntary work for the Royal Society for the Protection of Birds. I lead a local group of enthusiasts, and I am the local representative. . . ."

* * *

TOOTHAKER, Roy Eugene 1928-

PERSONAL: Born July 30, 1928, in Van Buren, Ark.; son of Vern Edward (a caller for a railroad company) and Birdie (Humphrey-Alcorn) Toothaker; married Norma Elnora Johnson, December 27, 1954 (divorced December 20, 1956). *Education:* Coffeyville Community Junior College, A.A., 1948; Pittsburg State College, B.S.Ed., 1952; Wichita State University, M.Ed., 1957; further graduate study at University of Kansas, University of California, Los Angeles, University of Missouri at Kansas City, University of Wisconsin—Platteville and Madison; University of Arkansas, Ed.D., 1970. *Politics:* Democrat. *Religion:* Protestant. *Home:* 864 North 11th St., DeKalb, Ill. 60115. *Office:* Department of Elementary Education, Northern Illinois University, DeKalb, Ill. 60115.

CAREER: Elementary school teacher in Kansas, 1945-46, 1948-52; Beech Aircraft Corp., Wichita, Kan., accounting clerk, 1952-57; elementary school teacher in California, 1957, and Kansas, 1958-65; University of Nebraska, Omaha, instructor in English and director of Reading Improvement Laboratory, 1965-67; elementary school teacher and high school teacher of English in Cherryvale, Kan., 1968-69; Coffeyville Community Junior College, Coffeyville, Kan., instructor in English, 1969-70; University of Wisconsin—Platteville, associate professor of education, 1970-72; University of Arkansas, Fayetteville, visiting associate professor of education, 1972-73; University of Miami, Coral Gables, Fla., visiting assistant professor of education, 1973-74; supervisor and staff development person for public schools of Marianna, Ark., 1974-75; Northern Illinois University, DeKalb, assistant professor of education, 1975—.

MEMBER: Association for Childhood Education International, International Reading Association (president of local chapters, 1963-64, 1965-66, 1971-72), National Council of Teachers of English, American Library Association, So-

ciety of Children's Book Writers, Children's Reading Round Table of Chicago, Phi Delta Kappa.

WRITINGS: *A Wild Goose Chase* (juvenile), Prentice-Hall, 1975.

Author of Spanish version of Barbara and Ed Emberley's, "Drummer Hoff" (juvenile sound filmstrip), Weston Woods Studio, 1976. Contributor of articles and reviews to literature and education journals. Editor of *Newsletter* of Kansas Council of International Reading Association, 1964-65; associate co-editor of *Journal for the Study of Perception,* 1967—.

WORK IN PROGRESS: *The Animal's Secret* (tentative title), a juvenile book, for Prentice-Hall; a historical novel for elementary school children; puzzles and quizzes for children; bibliographies of children's books; biographical essays of children's authors.

SIDELIGHTS: Toothaker writes: "Teaching and working with boys and girls bring me the greatest delight of all. . . . I like teaching others to write and have taught all grades, from first grade through graduate students. I am glad to have the opportunity to expose others to the beauty and versatility of the English language (and also Spanish and French)."

* * *

TORNEY, Judith V(ollmar) 1937-

PERSONAL: Born October 2, 1937, in Oakland, Calif.; daughter of Ralph C. (a chemist) and Anne (Flournoy) Vollmar; married E. Keith Torney (a minister), September 10, 1960; children: Susan M., Elizabeth A., Katherine D. *Education:* Stanford University, A.B. (with great distinction), 1959; Harvard University, graduate study, 1959-60; University of Chicago, M.A., 1962, Ph.D., 1965. *Office:* Department of Psychology, University of Illinois at Chicago Circle, Chicago, Ill. 60680.

CAREER: Illinois Institute of Technology, Chicago, assistant professor of psychology, 1967-69; University of Illinois at Chicago Circle, assistant professor, 1969-70, associate professor of psychology, 1970—. *Member:* International Studies Association, American Educational Research Association (secretary of Division G, 1976—), American Psychological Association, Society for Research in Child Development. *Awards, honors:* National Education Association award, 1967, for *The Development of Political Attitudes in Children;* educational specialist award from Government of Finland, 1976.

WRITINGS: (With R. D. Hess) *The Development of Political Attitudes in Children,* Aldine, 1967; (with A. N. Oppenheim and R. F. Farnen) *Civic Education in Ten Countries,* Wiley, 1975; (with Thomas Buergenthal) *International Human Rights and International Education,* U.S. National Commission for UNESCO, 1976. Associate editor of *International Studies Quarterly,* 1975—.

WORK IN PROGRESS: Additional writings on a ten-nation study of education.

SIDELIGHTS: Judith Torney studied more than thirty thousand young people for *Civic Education in Ten Countries.* These carefully selected students were tested for their knowledge and their attitudes toward government.

* * *

TOTH, Charles W(illiam) 1919-

PERSONAL: Born September 8, 1919, in Jersey City, N.J.; son of Gilbert and Rosina (Gassner) Toth; married Jane

Tucker (a librarian), November 26, 1948; children: Nathan Gilbert, Mathew Stuart, Pamela Wilson, Christopher Weston. *Education:* Bard College, B.A., 1946; University of Illinois, M.A., 1947. *Home:* K2 H8 (Cupey Alto), Rio Piedras, P.R. *Office:* University of Puerto Rico, Box 21795, University Station, Rio Piedras, P.R. 00931.

CAREER: New York University, New York, N.Y., instructor in American history, 1947-48; Inter-American University, San Juan, P.R., assistant professor of American history, 1949-54; University of Puerto Rico, Rio Piedras, assistant professor, 1954-64, associate professor, 1964-77, professor of American history, 1977—. External examiner for University of Guyana, 1967-68, 1974-76; member of board of directors of Caribbean Consolidated Schools. Chairman of organizing committee and member of executive committee for television production of "American Issues Forum." Director of historical section of San Juan Bicentennial Commission, 1974-76; special consultant to Puerto Rico Bicentennial Commission, 1975-76; member of Netherlands Antilles Bicentennial Commission. *Military service:* U.S. Army, 1942-44. *Member:* Caribbean Studies Association, Ateneo Puertorriqueno. *Awards, honors:* Ford Foundation grant, Institute of Caribbean Studies, 1964.

WRITINGS: El Mundo Contemporaneo (title means "The Contemporary World"), Editorial La Nueva Salamanca, 1954; (contributor) Norman Graebner, editor, *An Uncertain Tradition: American Secretaries of State in the Twentieth Century,* McGraw, 1961; (editor) *The American Revolution and the West Indies,* Kennikat, 1975; *Myth, Reality, and History: Selected Essays* (collection of his previously published journal articles), University of Puerto Rico Press, 1976. Contributor to history and political science journals in Spanish and English. Guest editor of *Revista/Review Interamericana,* Winter, 1975-76.

WORK IN PROGRESS: Editing *Liberte, Egalite, Fraternite: The American Revolution and the European Response; Anglo-American Diplomacy and the British West Indies, 1783-1830; Bulwark for Freedom: Samuel Gompers and the Pan American Federation of Labor,* a monograph.

*   *   *

TOWNSEND, Ralph M.   1901(?)-1976

1901(?)—January 25, 1976; American newsman, conservationist, and author. Obituaries: *Washington Post,* February 14, 1976.

*   *   *

TRACHTENBERG, Marvin (Lawrence)   1939-

PERSONAL: Born June 6, 1939, in Tulsa, Okla.; son of William (a businessman) and Leona (Fox) Trachtenberg; married Heidi Feldmeier (a medical technologist), November 10, 1961; children: Malcolm Blake, Gordon Charles. *Education:* Yale University, B.A. (magna cum laude), 1961; New York University, M.A., 1963, Ph.D., 1967. *Residence:* New York, N.Y. *Office:* Institute of Fine Arts, New York University, 1 East 78th St., New York, N.Y. 10021.

CAREER: New York University, Institute of Fine Arts, New York, N.Y., associate professor of art, 1967—. *Member:* Society of Architectural Historians, College Art Association, Renaissance Society of America, Phi Beta Kappa. *Awards, honors:* Woodrow Wilson fellow, 1961-62; Fulbright fellow in Florence, Italy, 1964-66; New York University Bernard Berenson fellowship, 1966-67, for study in Florence; Kress Foundation-National Gallery grant,

1970, for travel in France, Italy, Germany; Alice Davis Hitchcock prize from Society of Architectural Historians for outstanding book on architectural subject by North American scholar, 1972, 1973, and 1974; National Endowment for the Humanities senior fellowship, 1974-75, for study in Italy; Harvard University fellowship in Florence, 1974-76.

WRITINGS: The Campanile of Florence Cathedral: 'Giotto's Tower', New York University Press, 1971; (contributor) Otto von Simson, editor, *Propylaeen Kunstgeschichte* (title means "Propylaeen History of Art"), volume VI, Propylaeen Verlag (Berlin), 1972; *The Statue of Liberty,* Penguin, 1976. Contributor to *Dictionary of Architecture and Construction* and to professional journals.

WORK IN PROGRESS: With Heinrich Klotz, *History of Gothic Architecture in Tuscany,* publication of first volume by Kunsthistorisches Institut expected in 1977; research with Nicolai Rubenstein and Piero Micheli on the Palazzo Vecchio in Florence; *Brunelleschi Studies,* for 1979; research on the problem of the monument, on international relationships in Gothic architecture, and on origins of early Renaissance sculpture.

*   *   *

TRAISTER, Aaron   1904(?)-1976

1904(?)—March 30, 1976; American educator, editor, and writer. Obituaries: *New York Times,* April 1, 1976.

*   *   *

TRANTINO, Tommy   1938-

PERSONAL: Born February 11, 1938, in New York, N.Y.; son of Natale (a hatter) and Blanche (a clerk; maiden name, Stein) Trantino; married Charlee Irene Ganny (a college instructor in English), 1972. *Residence:* West Caldwell, N.J. *Agent:* Elaine Markson, 44 Greenwich Ave., New York, N.Y. 10011.

CAREER: Fifth World Press, West Caldwell, N.J., owner, 1975—. Member of Rahway Prisoners' Council, 1974; Leesburg Prison, chairman of ad hoc parole bill committee, 1975, member of prisoner's council, 1976.

WRITINGS: Lock the Lock (prose, poetry, and drawings), Knopf, 1974.

Work has been anthologized in *Imprisoned in America,* edited by Cynthia Owen Philip, Harper, 1973. Contributor to magazines, including *Choice,* and newspapers, including *Village Voice.*

WORK IN PROGRESS: A collection of poetry and/or prose, tentatively titled *Warguns.*

SIDELIGHTS: Tommy Trantino has been in New Jersey prisons since 1963. He began painting and writing in the Death House of Trenton State Prison. In 1972, the death penalty was rescinded and he was sentenced to life imprisonment. After political activities at Rahway State Prison, Trantino and another prisoner were removed from the prison in chains at midnight and taken to a unit for incorrigibles and the criminally insane at the New Jersey Psychiatric Hospital in Trenton. Three months later, he was sent by Federal Court order to Leesburg State Prison, a medium security institution. Trantino writes that the prison does not encourage self-rehabilitative efforts, will not provide prisoners with a work space for their painting and writing, and puts restrictions on materials they can be given to use. But his work continues.

BIOGRAPHICAL/CRITICAL SOURCES: Bergen

County Record, November 25, 1973; *University Review,* December, 1973; *Liberation,* February, 1975.

* * *

TRECKER, Janice Law 1941-
(Janice Law)

PERSONAL: Born June 10, 1941, in Sharon, Conn.; daughter of James Ord and Janet (Galloway) Law; married Jerrold B. Trecker (a teacher and sportswriter), June 9, 1962; children: James. *Education:* Syracuse University, B.A., 1962; University of Connecticut, M.A., 1967. *Home and office:* 33 Westfield Rd., West Hartford, Conn. 06119. *Agent:* Virginia Barber, 44 Greenwich Ave., New York, N.Y. 10011.

CAREER: Junior high school English teacher in Windsor, Conn., 1962-66; elementary school mathematics teacher in West Hartford, Conn., 1967; writer, 1967—. *Member:* Organization of American Historians, Authors Guild of Authors League of America, National Organization of Women, Phi Beta Kappa.

WRITINGS: Women on the Move, Macmillan, 1975; *Preachers, Rebels, and Traders,* Pequot Press, 1975; (under name Janice Law) *The Big Payoff* (fiction), Houghton, 1975. Author of "Women's Work in America," a filmstrip series, Schloat Productions, 1974. Contributor to academic journals and popular magazines, including *Saturday Review, Michigan Quarterly,* and *Take One.* Film reviewer for *West Hartford News,* 1967—.

WORK IN PROGRESS: Intentional Foul and *Gemini Trip,* mystery novels; research on the history of women's education in the United States and the impact of education of women on mass education in the United States.

AVOCATIONAL INTERESTS: Art, philosophy, music, birdwatching.

* * *

TREE, Ronald 1897-1976

1897—July 14, 1976; British diplomat, member of Parliament, journalist, and author. Obituaries: *New York Times,* July 15, 1976; *Newsweek,* July 26, 1976.

* * *

TRIMBLE, Vance H(enry) 1913-

PERSONAL: Born July 6, 1913, in Harrison, Ark.; son of Guy L. (an attorney) and Josie (Crump) Trimble; married Elzene Miller, January 9, 1932; children: Carol Ann Weisenfeld. *Education:* Educated in Wewoka, Okla., public schools. *Politics:* Independent. *Religion:* Baptist. *Home:* 1013 Sunset Ave., Covington, Ky. 41011. *Agent:* Aaron M. Priest, 150 East 35th St., New York, N.Y. 10016. *Office: Kentucky Post,* 421 Madison Ave., Covington, Ky. 41011.

CAREER: Reporter and telegraph editor on newspapers in Oklahoma and Texas, 1927-39; *Houston Press,* Houston, Tex., copy editor, 1939, city editor, 1939-50, managing editor, 1950-55; news editor of Washington bureau on the Scripps-Howard Newspapers, 1955-63; *Kentucky Post,* Covington, editor, 1963—. *Military service:* U.S. Army, Signal Corps, 1944-45; became staff sergeant. *Member:* American Society of Newspaper Editors, National Press Club, Authors Guild, Cincinnati Club, Sigma Delta Chi. *Awards, honors:* Pulitzer prize, Raymond Clapper award, and Sigma Delti Chi award, all 1960, for a series of articles exposing widespread payroll secrecy and nepotism in Congress; named to Oklahoma Journalism Hall of Fame.

WRITINGS: The Uncertain Miracle, Doubleday, 1974.

WORK IN PROGRESS: A nonfiction book on the operation of the U.S. Senate.

SIDELIGHTS: In 1958, Trimble began to investigate rumors of widespread nepotism in Congress by combing through Congressional payroll records, and conducting personal interviews. His research resulted in a series of articles, the first of which appeared early in 1959. Trimble's continued pursuit of the issue revealed further examples of abuse; public awareness was aroused, and his articles were inserted into the Congressional Record. He then filed suit to compel Congress to fully disclose payroll and expense records, and although the suit was dismissed, within a matter of months the Senate had adopted measures providing for the disclosure of these records.

* * *

TROMBLEY, Charles C(yprian) 1928-

PERSONAL: Born August 24, 1928, in Littleton, N.H.; son of Carroll Cyprian (a baker) and Beulah A. (Bradshaw) Trombley; married Gladys Allen (an executive secretary), January 27, 1951; children: David, Darlene, Deborah, Deanna. *Education:* Attended Immanuel Baptist College, 1969-72, and Moody Bible Institute, 1970. *Politics:* Republican. *Home:* 293 West Ithica, Broken Arrow, Okla. 74102. *Office:* Charles Trombley Ministries, 500 North Elm, Broken Arrow, Okla. 74012.

CAREER: Ordained minister of the Baptist Church; conference speaker at the Full Gospel Business Men's Fellowship International, 1959—; Gospel Light Telecast, Ottumwa, Iowa, director, 1970-72; Charismatic Teaching Ministries, Broken Arrow, Okla., director, 1973—. Executive secretary, Gospel Crusades, Sarasota, Fla., 1961-63; editor, The Expositor Publications, Tulsa, Okla., 1970—; instructor, Trinity Bible College, 1972; member of board of directors of The Way Out (a drug rehabilitation program), 1972-74. *Military service:* U.S. Coast Guard, 1946-49. U.S. Coast Guard Reserve, 1951-54.

WRITINGS: Visitation: Key to Church Growth, T.V.H. Publications, 1970; *Kicked Out of the Kingdom,* Whitaker House, 1974; *Christian Answers to J. W.,* Expositor Publications, 1975; *Guilty As Charged,* Expositor Publications, 1976; *How to Praise,* Fountain Press, 1976. Contributor to religious periodicals. Associate editor, *Harvest Time,* 1961-62.

WORK IN PROGRESS: A play.

BIOGRAPHICAL/CRITICAL SOURCES: Washington Star, March 16, 1969.

* * *

TROOBOFF, Peter D(ennis) 1942-

PERSONAL: Born June 22, 1942, in Baltimore, Md.; son of Benjamin Michael and Rebecca C. Trooboff; married Rhoda Morss, August 10, 1969. *Education:* Attended Institut d'Etudes Europeennes, 1962-63; Columbia University, A.B. (cum laude), 1964; Harvard University, LL.B. (cum laude), 1967; London School of Economics and Political Science, University of London, LL.M., 1968; Hague Academy of International Law, diploma (cum laude), 1968. *Home:* 4405 Yuma St. N.W., Washington, D.C. 20016. *Office:* Covington & Burling, 888 16th St. N.W., Washington, D.C. 20006.

CAREER: Admitted to Bar of State of New York, 1968, and

to Bar of District of Columbia, 1970; Covington & Burling, Washington, D.C., associate, 1969-75, law partner, 1975—. Law clerk at Denton, Hall & Burgin, London, England, summer, 1967; intern in office of Legal Adviser of U.S. Department of State, summer, 1966; assistant to executive editor of "The Advocates," WGBH-TV, summer, 1969; director of studies for English-speaking students at Hague Academy of International Law, summer, 1972; lecturer at University of Virginia, spring, 1973. *Member:* American Society of International Law (member of executive council, 1970-73), American Bar Association, District of Columbia Bar Association.

WRITINGS: (Contributor) *The United Nations: The Next Twenty-five Years,* U.N. Commission to Study the Organization of Peace, 1970; (editor) *Law and Responsibility in Warfare: The Vietnam Experience,* University of North Carolina Press, 1975. Contributor to professional journals.

* * *

TROPP, Martin 1945-

PERSONAL: Born July 10, 1945, in New York; son of Herman E. (a printer) and Eleanor (Holzer) Tropp; married Sandra Fehl (a teacher), August 30, 1969; children: Elena. *Education:* Brown University, B.A. (magna cum laude), 1966; Boston University, M.A., 1967, Ph.D., 1973. *Home:* 183 Mt. Vernon St., Malden, Mass. 02148.

CAREER: Northeastern University, Boston, Mass., instructor, 1970-73, assistant professor of English, 1973-74; part-time teacher at Babson College, Wellesley, Mass., Boston University, Boston, Mass., Northeastern University, and Massachusetts College of Pharmacy, Boston, all 1974-76; Babson College, assistant professor of liberal arts, 1976—. *Member:* Modern Language Association of America, Authors Guild of Authors League of America, Phi Beta Kappa.

WRITINGS: Mary Shelley's Monster: The Story of Frankenstein, Houghton, 1976.

WORK IN PROGRESS: Editing *The Literature of Fear,* a critical anthology of Gothic literature.

SIDELIGHTS: Tropp writes: "I am a teacher of literature to students who are not English majors. I also have long been interested in giving serious attention to subjects which are popular among average readers, but have not been accepted as fit subjects for literary research. Thus—*Frankenstein.*" *Avocational interests:* Reading science fiction and Gothic literature, travel, films, automobile repair, science and natural history.

* * *

TROWBRIDGE, Clinton W(hiting) 1928-

PERSONAL: Born January 14, 1928, in New York, N.Y.; son of George A. (a clergyman) and Jean (Whiting) Trowbridge; married Lucile Reeves (an artist), June 3, 1950; children: Tessa (adopted; Mrs. Harry Hooker), Paul, Patrick, Michele. *Education:* Princeton University, A.B., 1950; University of Florida, M.A., 1952, Ph.D., 1958. *Home:* 9 Scotts Cove Lane, East Setauket, N.Y. 11733. *Agent:* Francis Greenburger, 825 Third Ave., New York, N.Y. 10017. *Office:* Department of English, Dowling College, Oakdale, N.Y. 11769.

CAREER: University of Florida, Gainesville, instructor in English, 1955-57; Rollins College, Winter Park, Fla., assistant professor of English, 1957-61; College of Charleston, Charleston, S.C., associate professor of English, 1961-65;

Dowling College, Oakdale, N.Y., associate professor, 1965-68, professor of English, 1968—.

WRITINGS: The Crow Island Journal, Harper, 1970. Contributor to literary magazines, including *Sewanee Review, Cimarron Review, Critique, Modern Drama,* and *Mediterranean Review,* and to *Harper's.*

WORK IN PROGRESS: The Scatt II: A Love Story, with Francis Greenburger; *Island Dwellers on the Coast of Maine,* with Greenburger.

SIDELIGHTS: Trowbridge is the owner of "Crow Island," a small island off the coast of Maine, where he spends his summers quietly, without modern conveniences, and with a great deal of privacy. Out of his love for the island, its way of life, and the years he has spent there with his family came his first book. *Avocational interests:* Sailing, Maine, singing in the Long Island Symphonic Chorus.

BIOGRAPHICAL/CRITICAL SOURCES: Christian Science Monitor, August 8, 1975.

* * *

TROWELL, Kathleen Margaret 1904-

PERSONAL: Born February 27, 1904, in Ealing, Middlesex, England; daughter of Alfred John (a publisher) and Alice Elizabeth (Lord) Sifton; married Hugh Trowell (a physician); children: Elizabeth (Mrs. Jeremy Bray), *Education:* Slade School of Fine Art, diploma, 1932; London Institute of Education, further study, 1932-33. *Politics:* Liberal. *Religion:* Church of England. *Home:* Windhaven, Woodgreen, Fordingbridge, Hampshire, England.

CAREER: Makerere College, Kampala, Uganda, reader in fine art, 1944-59, became head of School of Art. *Awards, honors:* Member of the Order of the British Empire, 1944.

WRITINGS: African Arts and Crafts: Their Development in the School, Longmans, 1937; *Art Teaching in African Schools,* Longmans, 1952; (with K. P. Wachsmann) *Tribal Crafts of Uganda,* Oxford University Press, 1953; *Classical African Sculpture,* Praeger, 1954, 3rd edition, 1971; *African Tapestry* (autobiography), Faber, 1957; *Traditional African Sculpture,* Colonial Office Publication, for the Exhibition of Traditional Art, Imperial Institute, 1957; (editor) *A Handbook of the Museums and Libraries of Uganda,* Uganda Museum, 1957; *African Design,* Praeger, 1960; (with Hans Nevermann) *African and Oceanic Art,* Abrams, 1968.

SIDELIGHTS: Margaret Trowell is presently a painter, exhibiting regularly with the Royal Institute of Watercolour Painters. She has also had two solo shows. Mrs. Trowell has lived in East Africa.

* * *

TROYER, Byron L(eRoy) 1909-
(Dave Hamilton)

PERSONAL: Born June 3, 1909, in LaFontaine, Ind.; son of Chester E. (a seedman) and Cleo S. (Hamilton) Troyer; married Ina Holland Cranor, 1932 (divorced, 1949); married Iona Lloyd (a teacher), December 4, 1954; children: (first marriage) Bruce Alan and Arlene Kay (Mrs. Robert Apley)—twins. *Education:* Attended Indiana University, Purdue University, and Pennsylvania State University. *Politics:* Independent Republican. *Religion:* Christian. *Home:* 1344 Vesper Dr., Fort Myers, Fla. 33901. *Office address:* P.O. Box 932, Fort Myers, Fla. 33902.

CAREER: Marion Chronicle, Marion, Ind., reporter, 1928-29; *Indianapolis News,* Indianapolis, Ind., copy editor,

1929-30; assisted father, C. E. Troyer, in marketing hybrid corn seeds, 1930-33; *Marion Leader-Tribune,* Marion, Ind., telegraph editor, 1933; *South Bend News-Times,* South Bend, Ind., telegraph editor and acting managing editor, 1934-38; *South Bend Tribune,* South Bend, Ind., copy editor, 1938; C. E. Troyer (family hybrid corn business), La-Fontaine, Ind., assistant, 1939-47; *LaFontaine Herald,* LaFontaine, Ind., publisher and editor, 1947-48; KLAS-Radio, Las Vegas, Nev., news manager, 1948-49; *Marion Leader-Tribune,* Marion, Ind., reporter, 1949-52; *Fort Wayne Journal-Gazette,* Fort Wayne, Ind., copy editor, 1952-53; *Kalamazoo Gazette,* Kalamazoo, Mich., business-financial editor and music critic, 1953-59; Troyer Publishing Co., Bourbon-Plymouth, Ind., president, 1959-63; *Hoosierland* (magazine), Bourbon, Ind., publisher and editor, 1964-65; *Outdoor Indiana* (magazine), Indianapolis, Ind., planner and editor, 1966-67; Hoosierland Books, Indianapolis (now in Fort Myers, Fla.), proprietor, 1967—. Has made television and radio appearances. Copy editor of *Indianapolis News,* 1964-65. Member of Kalamazoo Bach Festival Executive Committee, 1958-59; member of executive committee of Museum of Indian Heritage.

MEMBER: National Writer's Club, Indiana Historical Society, American Hibiscus Society, Northern Indiana Historical Society, Collier County (Fla.) Historical Society, Fort Wayne (Ind.) Historical Society, Masons. *Awards, honors:* National and state awards for originating the first inbred-hybrid gladiolus and several miniature varieties.

WRITINGS: Touring Historic Indiana, Indiana Department of Commerce, 1966; (editor) T. S. Jesup, *Seminole Saga,* Island Press, 1973; (editor) *Colonel Evans of Kentucky: Fielding,* Hoosierland Books, 1974; *Yesterday's Indiana,* E. A. Seemann, 1975. Contributor, sometimes under pseudonym Dave Hamilton, to farm, business, and financial journals, and to juvenile and popular adult magazines.

WORK IN PROGRESS: They Walked Tall (tentative title), an intimate look at some of the men and women who opened America's frontiers; *The Fall Creek Massacre,* a factual account of the incidents on which Jessamyn West based her historical novel of similar name.

SIDELIGHTS: Troyer writes that he spent his early life on his father's farm, and was born in a farm home originally built for the Miami Indian Marshal Kilsoquah. This historic association stimulated an intense interest in history before he even entered school.

* * *

TU, Wei-ming 1940-

PERSONAL: Born February 26, 1940, in Kunming, China; came to United States, 1962; naturalized U.S. citizen, 1976; son of Shou-tsin (in government) and Shu-li (in business; maiden name, Ou-yang) Tu; married I-yu Hsiao (in university administration), August 24, 1963; children: Eugene Lung-sun Tu. *Education:* Tunghai University, B.A., 1961; Harvard University, M.A., 1963, Ph.D., 1968. *Politics:* "Humanist socialism." *Religion:* Confucianism. *Home:* 1729 Spruce, Berkeley, Calif. 94709. *Office:* Department of History, University of California, Berkeley, Calif. 94720.

CAREER: Tunghai University, Taichung, Taiwan, visiting lecturer in humanities, 1966-67; Princeton University, Princeton, N.J., lecturer, 1967-68, assistant professor of East Asian studies, 1968-71; University of California, Berkeley, assistant professor, 1971-73, associate professor of history, 1973—. Consultant, National Endowment for the Humanities. *Member:* American Historical Association,

Association for Asian Studies (member of board of directors, 1972-75), Society for Asian and Comparative Philosophy, Phi Tau Phi. *Awards, honors:* Fellowships from Harvard University, 1962-67, Princeton University, 1968, American Council of Learned Societies, 1970-71, Aspen Institute for Humanistic Studies, 1974, and University of California, 1974-75.

WRITINGS: (Editor with James T.VC. Liu, and contributor) *Traditional China,* Prentice-Hall, 1970; *San-nien ti hsu-ai* (essays; title means "Three Years of Cultivating the Moxa"), Chih-wen Book Co. (Taipei), 1970; (contributor) *Ch'ien Mu hsien-sheng pa-shih sui chi-nien lun-wen chi* (title means "Collected Essays in Honor of Mr. Ch'ien Mu's Eightieth Birthday"), New Asia Research Institute (Hong Kong), 1974; (contributor) William T. de Bary, editor, *The Unfolding of Neo-Confucianism,* Columbia University Press, 1975; (contributor) L. Carrington Goodrich and Chaoying Fang, editors, *Dictionary of Ming Biography,* Columbia University Press, 1976; *Centrality and Commonality: An Essay on Chung-yung* (monograph), University Press of Hawaii, 1976. (contributor) Charlotte Furth, editor, *The Limits of Change: Essays on Conservative Alternatives in Republican China,* Harvard University Press, 1976; *Jen-wen hsin-ling te chen-tang* (essays; title means "The Resonance of the Humanist Mind"), China Times Publication Co. (Taipei), 1976; *Neo-Confucian Thought in Action: Wang Yang-ming's Youth (1472-1509),* University of California Press, 1976.

Contributor to proceedings of International Seminar on World Philosophy and to journals, including *Philosophy East and West, Journal of Asian Studies, Eastern Buddhist, Daedalus,* and to Chinese-language journals.

WORK IN PROGRESS: A book-length monograph on the Neo-Confucian thinker Chu Hsi (1130-1200) and a general study on Chinese philosophy.

SIDELIGHTS: Tu told *CA:* "Although the issues I have been dealing with are broad, such as self-cultivation, human-relatedness, fiduciary community and religious truth, my approach has not been the construction of a general model of explanation but a process of analytical inquiry in which particular psychological conditions and cultural constraints are also taken into consideration. My published works so far are mainly concerned with the Confucian mode of thinking. To me, the study of the Confucian tradition in east Asia is not only the academic commitment of a professional intellectual historian but also the personal quest of a reflective human being."

* * *

TUCKER, Marcia 1940-

PERSONAL: Born April 11, 1940, in New York, N.Y.; daughter of Emmanuel and Dorothy (Wald) Silverman. *Education:* Connecticut College, B.A., 1961; New York University, M.A., 1965, doctoral course work, 1967-69. *Home:* 140 Sullivan St., New York, N.Y. 10012. *Office:* Whitney Museum, 945 Madison Ave., New York, N.Y. 10021.

CAREER: Museum of Modern Art, New York City, secretary, 1961-62; assistant to painter, Rene Bouche, 1962-63; curator of William N. Copley Collection, New York City, 1963-66; *ARTnews,* New York City, editorial associate, 1965-69; Whitney Museum of American Art, New York City, associate curator, 1969-73, curator, 1973—. Cataloger of private collections and Ferdinand Howald Collection of American Art at Columbus Gallery of Fine Art, 1966-69.

Instructor, University of Rhode Island, 1966-68, City University of New York Graduate Center, 1967-68, and School of Visual Arts, 1969-73; guest lecturer at art schools and universities. *Member:* International Art Critics Association (American section).

WRITINGS: Ferdinand Howald Collection of American Paintings (catalog), Columbus Gallery of Fine Art, 1969; *Robert Morris* (exhibition catalog), Praeger, 1970; *Bruce Nauman: Retrospective Exhibition* (catalog), Praeger, 1973; (author of preface) Cindy Nemser, *Art Talk: Conversations with Twelve Women Artists,* Scribner, 1975; (author of introduction) Spider Webb, *Heavily Tattooed Men and Women,* McGraw, 1976. Contributor to *Artforum, Art in America, ARTnews,* and *Ms.*

* * *

TUCKER, Nicholas 1936-

PERSONAL: Born November 13, 1936, in London, England; son of Archie (a professor) and Betty (Hills) Tucker; married Jacqueline Elizabeth Anthony (a teacher), 1964; children: Matthew, Emma, Lucy. *Education:* Kings College, Cambridge, B.A., 1958. *Politics:* Socialist. *Religion:* Atheist. *Home:* 56 Prince Edwards Rd., Lewes, Sussex, England. *Office:* University of Sussex, Falmer, Brighton, Sussex BN1 9QX, England.

CAREER: University of Sussex, Falmer, Brighton, lecturer in developmental psychology, 1969—.

WRITINGS: Understanding the Mass Media, Cambridge University Press, 1964; (editor) *One Hundred of the Best "Times Educational Supplement" Cartoons,* Penguin, 1968; (editor) *Mother Goose Lost,* Crowell, 1971; (editor) *Mother Goose Abroad,* Crowell, 1975; *The Look Book,* Penguin, 1975; (editor) *Suitable for Children: Controversies in Children's Literature,* University of California Press, 1976; *What is a Child?,* Open Books, 1977.

WORK IN PROGRESS: The Child and the Book, for Cambridge University Press, 1978.

* * *

TUCKER, Patricia 1912-

PERSONAL: Born October 29, 1912, in Red Lodge, Mont.; daughter of Royal Kenneth (an Episcopal clergyman) and Juliet (Luttrell) Tucker; married Nelson P. Jackson (a U.S. Air Force colonel), April 6, 1934 (deceased); married Edward Stuart (a consulting forester), July 16, 1958 (divorced, 1960); children: (first marriage) Lael Hollister (Mrs. Thomas Glenn Boyd). *Education:* Attended Tulane University, 1929-32, and Louisiana State University, 1932. *Politics:* Democrat. *Religion:* Episcopal. *Home:* 1272 New Hampshire Ave. N.W., Washington, D.C. 20036. *Agent:* Lael Wertenbaker, R.D., Marlborough, N.H.

CAREER: Air Reduction Co., Stamford, Conn., secretary, librarian, and assistant chemist, 1932-34; admitted to Texas bar, 1940; American Cyanamid Co., Stamford, Conn., assistant docket clerk in patent department, 1940-41; *Time,* New York, N.Y., researcher and reporter, 1941-44; *Fortune,* New York, N.Y., researcher and reporter, 1944; *Science Illustrated,* New York, N.Y., managing editor, 1944-45; free-lance public relations counsel and journalist, 1946—. Consultant on public information, Army Medical Department Research and Graduate School, 1951-54; member of board of directors and public relations officer of Dwight Corp., 1955-56, Eastern Forestry, Inc., 1956-60, and Craftsmen of Chelsea Court, 1972—; public relations and

legal counselor for Johnson-Crooks (Alaska), 1954-55. Member of Committee for Effective Use of the International Court, 1961; information officer of Central Florida Regional Planning Council, 1965-68. *Member:* Overseas Press Club, Mensa, Kappa Kappa Gamma.

WRITINGS: (With John Money) *Sexual Signatures: On Being a Man or a Woman,* Little, Brown, 1975. Contributor to *Encyclopedia Britannica Yearbook* and to magazines, including *Smithsonian* and *America Illustrated.* Stringer for *Time,* 1944—.

WORK IN PROGRESS: A book on sexual differentiation, with John Money, for Harvard University Press series to be called "The Developing Child."

* * *

TULLOCH, G(ertrude) Janet 1924-

PERSONAL: Born April 15, 1924, in New Haven, Conn.; daughter of Alexander B. (a golfer) and A. Muriel (a registrar; maiden name, Lawton) Tulloch. *Education:* Educated in Ottawa, Quebec and Washington, D.C. *Politics:* Liberal. *Religion:* Episcopalian. *Home:* 3720 Upton St. N.W., Washington, D.C. 20016.

CAREER: Free-lance writer. *Member:* Authors Guild of Authors League of America.

WRITINGS: (With Cynthia C. Wedel) *Happy Issue: My Handicap and the Church,* Seabury, 1962; *A Home Is Not a Home* (fiction), Seabury, 1975. Contributor of articles on nursing homes to *Harper's Weekly* and *Washingtonian.*

WORK IN PROGRESS: A novel on the elderly, "repeating life scripts."

SIDELIGHTS: Janet Tulloch writes: "Cerebral palsy made wielding a pencil difficult as a child, compositions an impossibility. Dreamed of being able to write profusely.... Pleasure in physical effort is foremost and do not know what will come out until it happens. Words fall together themselves."

* * *

TURNBULL, Ann (Christine) 1943-
(Ann Nicol)

PERSONAL: Born August 22, 1943, in Hertford, England; daughter of Harold Drysdale (a legal executive) and Muriel Violet (East) Turnbull; married Simon Thorne, August 6, 1966 (divorced, 1973); married Timothy Nicol (a landscape architect), August 3, 1973; children: (2nd marriage) David Ralf. *Education:* Attended Bexley Technical School, 1956-60, and Balls Park College of Education, 1971-74. *Religion:* None. *Home:* 6 Danesford, Hollinswood, Telford, Shropshire, England.

CAREER: Secretary in London and Reading, England, 1960-71, and Stevenage, England, 1974; writer.

WRITINGS: The Frightened Forest (juvenile), Kestrel, 1974; *The Wolf King* (juvenile), Kestrel, 1975.

WORK IN PROGRESS: Another book for juveniles.

AVOCATIONAL INTERESTS: Folk-lore, folk-singing, archaeology, ancient history.

* * *

TURNBULL, Gael Lundin 1928-

PERSONAL: Born April 7, 1928, in Edinburgh, Scotland; son of Ralph Gale (a minister) and Anne (Lundin) Turnbull; married Jonnie May Draper (a secretary), June 7, 1952; children: Christine, Julie, Sheri. *Education:* University of Cambridge, B.A., 1948; University of Pennsylvania, M.D., 1951. *Home:* 61 Belmont Road, Malvern, Worcestershire, England.

CAREER: Physician in general practice and anesthesiologist in Worcestershire, England, 1951—. *Awards, honors:* Union League Civic and Arts Foundation Prize, 1965; Alice Hunt Bartlett Prize, 1968.

WRITINGS—Poems: (With Eli Mandel and Phyllis Webb) *Trio,* Contact Press (Toronto), 1954; *The Knot in the Wood and Fifteen Other Poems,* Revision Press (London), 1955; *Bjarni Spike-Helgi's Son and Other Poems,* Origin Press (Ashland, Mass.), 1956; *A Libation,* The Poet (Glasgow), 1957; *With Hey, Ho. . . .,* Migrant Press (Birmingham, England), 1961; *To You, I Write,* Migrant Press, 1963; *A Very Particular Hill,* Wild Hawthorn Press, 1963; *Twenty Words, Twenty Days: A Sketchbook and a Morula,* Migrant Press, 1966; *Briefly,* Tarasque Press (Nottingham, England), 1967; *A Trampoline: Poems 1952-1964,* Cape Goliard Press, 1968; *I, Maksoud,* University of Exeter, 1969; *Scantlings: Poems 1964-69,* Cape Goliard Press, 1970; *Finger Cymbals,* Satis (Edinburgh), 1972; *A Random Sampling,* Pig Press (Newcastle-upon-Tyne, England), 1974; *Wulstan,* Blue Tunnel (Bradford, England), 1975; *Witley Court Revisited,* Migrant Press, 1975; *Residues,* Grosseteste (Staffordshire, England), 1976; *Thronging the Heart,* Aggie Weston, 1976.

SIDELIGHTS: Turnbull told *CA:* "Among various poems and also small pieces for the theatre, I am currently busy with a research project into the circumstances and people surrounding a famous early 19th century murder in a small Worcestershire village, Oddingley, which I hope eventually to make into a book.

I doctor to make a living, but quite enjoy it and try to do a good job at it. The chief problem is sheer competition of time and energy. There are undoubtedly American and Canadian influences in my work, although someone else might be better able to comment on that more objectively than I could. At the moment my life is very closely involved with people and events in Malvern and Worcestershire. I have written a number of things for direct performance in local clubs and in relation to things that other friends have been doing here."

* * *

UCHIDA, Tadao 1939-

PERSONAL: Born June 9, 1939, in Manila, Philippines; son of Yoshiharu (a businessman) and Shizue (Sekiguchi) Uchida; married Kazuko Hori, November 3, 1966 (marriage ended, November, 1975); married Kazuko Hashimoto, August 28, 1976. *Education:* Keio University, B.A., 1962. *Home and office:* 1155 North La Cienaga Blvd., Los Angeles, Calif. 90069.

CAREER: Yomiuri (newspaper), Tokyo, Japan, correspondent in Fukushima, 1962-64, sports writer in Tokyo, 1964-65, local edition editor, 1965-66, social affairs writer, 1966-75, Los Angeles correspondent, 1975—. Notable assignments include the airline hijacking to Seoul, the United Nations Conference on Human Environment, the Olympic events in Tokyo, Sapporo, and Montreal, and the investigation of Lockheed Aircraft and resignation of Prime Minister Tanaka. *Member:* International Correspondents Club, Japanese National Press Club, Greater Los Angeles Press Club, Tokyo Sports Writers Club.

WRITINGS: Man and Environment, Dai-Ichi Shobo, 1972.

SIDELIGHTS: Uchida told *CA:* "In Japan, we most often hear about America's problems; i.e., racism, smog, political corruption. But since I've been living in Los Angeles and travelling in the States, I've seen another side of America, a very healthy side. While I'm writing from L.A., I'd like to inform Japanese about the healthy aspects of American life and present a more accurate picture of the United States."

* * *

UDALL, Jan Beaney 1938-
(Jan Beaney)

PERSONAL: Born July 31, 1938, in Worcester Park, England; daughter of Jack and Audrey (Hames) Beaney; married John D. Hurman, July 31, 1961 (divorced, 1967); married Stephen James Nicholas Udall (a general manager), July 14, 1967; children: (second marriage) Nicholas Jason James, Victoria Emma. *Education:* Attended College of Art, Southampton, 1954-55; College of Art, West Sussex, N.D.D., 1958; College of Art, London, A.T.C., 1959. *Home:* 51 North Town Rd., Maidenhead, Berkshire 5L6 7JQ, England.

CAREER: Artist. Teacher of art and hand embroidery, and assistant mistress in grammar school in Middlesex, England, 1959-64; Whitelands College of Education, London, England, lecturer on creative embroidery, 1964-68; teacher of modern embroidery and design for Inner London Education Authority, 1966-69. Has exhibited work publicly and privately in shows in Great Britain and Australia, including in Victoria and Albert Museum and Commonwealth Institute, both London, and Museum of Wales, Cardiff. *Member:* Embroiderer's Guild (chairman of 62 Group, 1969-71).

WRITINGS—Published under name Jan Beaney: *The Young Embroiderer,* Nicholas Kaye, 1966, published as *The Young Embroiderer: A How-It-Is-Done Book of Embroidery,* Warne, 1970, revised edition published as *Fun with Embroidery,* Kaye & Ward, 1975; *Adventures with Collage,* Warne, 1970 (published in England as *Fun with Collage,* Kaye & Ward, 1970); *Landscapes,* Scroll Press, 1974 (published in England as *Landscape in Picture, Collage, and Design,* Pelham Books, in press); *Buildings,* Scroll Press, 1974 (published in England as *Buildings in Picture, Collage, and Design,* Pelham Books, in press; *Texture in Picture, Collage, and Design,* Pelham Books, in press. Contributor of articles to *Embroidery.*

WORK IN PROGRESS: A book, *Starting Creative Embroidery for Adults.*

SIDELIGHTS: Jan Udall comments: "I have written the books because I feel very strongly that if children are helped to look at things about them *properly* and then how to select, expand, emphasize certain aspects, their creative talents can be really stretched. I believe that everyone can achieve quite a high standard of work with real enjoyment. I remember with horror the number of parents at school open evenings who had already conditioned their children to think that they could not draw and that only a few have any talent!!

"As much as I enjoy teaching art and modern embroidery, working with children and adults and working on books," Mrs. Udall continues, "my first priority is my own creative embroidery in the form of wall panels. Although trained as a painter, I feel I can express my ideas more satisfactorily in fabrics and yarns. My sources of design for the last few years have been derived from all aspects of landscape. As I live in the Thames Valley, I am able to look at and draw on a variety of landscapes."

ULLMANN, Stephen   1914-1976

June 13, 1914—January 10, 1976; Hungarian-born British philologist and author of books on semantics and literature. Obituaries: *AB Bookman's Weekly,* March 1, 1976. (See index for previous *CA* sketch)

*   *   *

UNGER, Richard (Lawrence)   1939-

PERSONAL: Born March 11, 1939, in Springfield, Ill.; son of Lawrence B. (an industrial manager) and Elizabeth (Power) Unger. *Education:* St. Louis University, A.B. (honors), 1961; Cornell University, M.A., 1962, Ph.D., 1967; also attended University of Munich, 1963-64, and University of Zurich, 1965-66. *Home address:* P.O. Box 864, Athens, Ga. 30601. *Office:* Department of Comparative Literature, University of Georgia, Athens, Ga. 30602.

CAREER: University of Missouri, St. Louis, assistant professor of German, 1966-68; Emory University, Atlanta, Ga., assistant professor of English and comparative literature, 1968-71; Mississippi State University, State College, assistant professor of English, 1971-76; University of Georgia, Athens, associate professor of comparative literature, 1976—. *Member:* Modern Language Association of America, American Association of University Professors, American Civil Liberties Union, Hoelderlin-Gesellschaft.

WRITINGS: *Hoelderlin's Major Poetry: The Dialectics of Unity,* Indiana University Press, 1976.

WORK IN PROGRESS: Studies in English literature and in comparative literature of the romantic period; writing on the romantic ode and the Pindaric tradition, and on Shelley and Hegel as interpreters of the Gospel.

SIDELIGHTS: Unger writes: "My basic interest is in the accurate specification and analysis of the esthetic, philosophical, and religious ideas and attitudes of writers of the era around 1800; this interest is based on a conviction that an understanding of that era is essential to an understanding of our present situation, which is largely a result of the ideas and attitudes developed in that era."

AVOCATIONAL INTERESTS: European history and travel.

*   *   *

URY, Zalman F.   1924-

PERSONAL: Surname originally Fajwusowicz, name legally changed, 1955; born December 17, 1924, in Poland; came to United States in 1947, naturalized citizen, 1954; son of Abraham and Cypa (a merchant; maiden name, Borishansky) Fajwusowicz; married Eva Perl (a hospital administrator), August 30, 1945; children: Celia (Mrs. Hosea Rabinowitz), Natalie (Mrs. Moshe Amster), Ramma (Mrs. Robert Hoffnung), Israel. *Education:* Washington University, St. Louis, Mo., B.Sc., 1955; Loyola University, Los Angeles, Calif., M.A., 1962; University of California at Los Angeles, D.Ed. (honors), 1966. *Politics:* None. *Home:* 465 South Wetherly Dr., Beverly Hills, Calif. 90211. *Office:* Bureau of Jewish Education, Los Angeles, Calif. 90048.

CAREER: Teacher of Jewish subjects in Russia, 1941-45; elementary and high school teacher, principal, superintendent, and educational director in parochial schools in St. Louis, Mo., 1948-59; part-time parochial high school teacher of Judaica in Los Angeles, Calif., 1959-65; Jewish Federation-Council of Greater Los Angeles, Bureau of Jewish Education, Los Angeles, Calif., supervisor, 1959-65;

Yeshiva University, West Coast Teachers College, Los Angeles, part-time instructor in education and ethics, 1962—; Bureau of Jewish Education, Los Angeles, head consultant for orthodox schools, 1965—. Rabbi, part-time, Young Israel of Beverly Hills, 1968—. *Member:* National Council for Jewish Education, National Conference of Yeshiva Principals, Educators Council of America (West Coast vice-president, 1974—), National Council of Young Israel Rabbis, Association of Orthodox Jewish Scientists, Torah Umesorah, Doctor of Education Association (U.C.L.A.).

WRITINGS: (Editor) *Torat Elhanan* (title means "Teachings of Elhanan"), Twersky, 1954; (contributor) Norman Paris, editor, *Brakha LiMenahem* (a salute to Rabbi Menahem Eichenstein), Twersky, 1955; *The Musar Movement,* Yeshiva University Press, 1970; *The Story of Rabbi Yisroel Salanter,* Torah Umesorah, 1971; (contributor) Menahem Zohorietal, editor, *Hagut Ivrit Be-America* (studies on Jewish themes by contemporary American scholars), Volume 2, Yavneh Publishers, 1973. Also author of teachers' guides and pedagogis syllabi in history, bible, ethics and curricula; contributor to educational and religious journals.

*   *   *

UTTLEY, Alice Jane (Taylor)   1884-1976
(Alison Uttley)

December 17, 1884—May 7, 1976; British novelist and author of children's books. Obituaries: *New York Times,* May 9, 1976; *Bookseller,* May 22, 1976; *AB Bookman's Weekly,* June 7, 1976. (See index for previous *CA* sketch)

*   *   *

VALEN, Nanine   1950-

PERSONAL: Born November 7, 1950, in New York, N.Y.; daughter of Herbert (a writer) and Felice (a writer; maiden name, Holman) Valen. *Education:* Bryn Mawr College, B.A. (magna cum laude), 1971; Yale University, graduate study, 1971-73. *Home:* 158 Hillspoint Rd., Westport, Conn. 06880.

CAREER: Writer. Director of computer animation for "The Electric Co." for Children's Television Workshop, 1974-76.

WRITINGS—Juvenile: (With Felice Holman) *The Drac,* Scribner, 1975; *The Devil's Tail,* Scribner, in press.

Anthologized in *The Scribner Anthology for Young People,* Scribner, 1976. Created animated films for "The Electric Co." and filmstrips for "Sesame Street," Children's Television Workshop.

WORK IN PROGRESS: Another children's book.

SIDELIGHTS: Nanine Valen writes: "I spent the year preceding the publication of *The Drac* in the south of France researching the tales of these creatures of the 'fantastique' in libraries, archives, and attics. These tales made many trips across the Atlantic until Ms. Holman and I arrived at the completed manuscript, composed of five tales—five of the eeriest, most captivating creatures."

*   *   *

VALENTINE, Jean   1934-

PERSONAL: Born April 27, 1934, in Chicago, Ill.; daughter of John W. and Jean (Purcell) Valentine; divorced: children: Sarah Chace, Rebecca Chace. *Education:* Radcliffe College, B.A., 1956. *Home:* 527 West 110th St., New York, N.Y. 10025.

CAREER: Poet. Visiting poet at Sarah Lawrence College, Bronxville, N.Y., 1974—.

WRITINGS—Poetry: Dream Barker and Other Poems, Yale University Press, 1965; Pilgrims, Farrar, Straus, 1969; Ordinary Things, Farrar, Straus, 1974.

WORK IN PROGRESS: Poems.

* * *

VALERIANI, Richard (Gerard) 1932-

PERSONAL: Born August 29, 1932, in Camden, N.J.; son of Nicholas (a foundry foreman) and Christina (Camerota) Valeriani; married Coralee Hall, January 22, 1965 (separated). Education: Yale University, B.A., 1953; University of Pavia, graduate study, 1953-54. Home: 2737 Devonshire Pl., N.W., Washington, D.C. 20008. Office: NBC News, 4001 Nebraska Ave. N.W., Washington, D.C. 20016.

CAREER/WRITINGS: The Trentonian, Trenton, N.J., reporter, 1957; Associated Press, writer in New York City, 1957-59, in Havana, Cuba, 1959-61; National Broadcasting Corp. (NBC) News, reporter, 1961-64, correspondent in Washington, D.C., 1964—. Notable assignments include the Bay of Pigs invasion, 1961, civil rights movement throughout United States, 1962-65, Presidential campaigns, 1964, 1968, and 1972, civil war in Dominican Republic, 1965; White House, 1972-73, travels of Henry Kissinger, 1973-76. Presidential Debate panelist, 1976. Lecturer in American foreign policy. Author of scripts for television broadcast, including news and documentaries. Contributor to TV Guide, Ladies' Home Journal, Good Housekeeping, Penthouse and other periodicals. Military service: U.S. Army, 1955-56. Member: Overseas Writers, State Department Correspondents' Association (president, 1976-77), Yale Club (Washington, D.C.). Awards, honors: Overseas Press Club award for best radio reporting abroad, 1965, for work in Dominican Republic; Peabody award, 1965, for civil rights television special.

* * *

Van CLEVE, Thomas Curtis 1888-1976

May 1, 1888—February 10, 1976; American historian, educator, and author of books in his field. Obituaries: New York Times, February 11, 1976. (See index for previous CA sketch)

* * *

VAN DAHM, Thomas E(dward) 1924-

PERSONAL: Born February 20, 1924, in Chicago, Ill.; son of Thomas (a roofing contractor) and Sarah (Toren) Van Dahm; married Lois Stanton, March 17, 1951; children: Ruth. Education: Hope College, A.B., 1948; University of Michigan, M.A., 1949, Ph.D., 1959. Religion: Presbyterian. Home: 4103 Taft Rd., Kenosha, Wis. 53140. Office: Division of Business and Economics, Carthage College, 2001 Alford Dr., Kenosha, Wis. 53140.

CAREER: Central College, Pella, Iowa, assistant professor of business and economics, 1950-53; Hope College, Holland, Mich., assistant professor of business and economics, 1955-60; Southern Illinois University, Edwardsville, assistant professor of economics, 1960-64; Carthage College, Kenosha, Wis., professor of economics, 1964—, chairman of division of business and economics, 1964—. Military service: U.S. Army, 1943-46. Member: Midwest Economic Association, Kiwanis International.

WRITINGS: Money and Banking: An Introduction to the Financial System, Heath, 1975.

VAN LENTE, Charles R(obert) 1941-

PERSONAL: Born November 26, 1941, in Holland, Mich.; son of Lloyd R. (a clergyman) and Marion (Madderom) Van Lente; married Frances K. Vander Veen, January 19, 1963; children: Pamela, Deborah, Cynthia. Education: Attended Ferris State College, 1963-64, Central Michigan University, 1970-72, and Garrett Evangelical Seminary, 1972-75. Office: Eagle Boys Village, Route 1, Hersey, Mich. 49639.

CAREER: Pastor of United Methodist churches in Ashton, Mich., 1963-64, Niles, Mich., 1964-65; Michigan State Police, trooper in Alpena and Flint, 1966-70; pastor of United Methodist churches in St. Johns and Howard City, Mich., 1970-76; Eagle Boys Village, Hersey, Mich., chaplain, 1976—. Vice-president of Bread of Life Ministries, Inc. (executive producer of television series, 1974 and 1975). Member of Michigan Council of Churches radio and television committee. Mass media coordinator for West Michigan Conference of the United Methodist Church. Military service: U.S. Air Force, aircraft radio repairman, 1959-63, participated in United Nations Congo Action in Africa, 1961-62. Member: World Association for Christian Communication (North American Broadcast Section), John Wesley Association, Michigan State Police Troopers Association.

WRITINGS: Beyond Enforcement (autobiographical), Whitaker House, 1975. Author of television series scripts, "Fundamentals of the Christian Faith," 13 programs, and "Kingdom Principles," 13 programs. Contributor to magazines and newspapers.

WORK IN PROGRESS: The story of Eagle Boys Village and other institutions for children.

SIDELIGHTS: Van Lente writes: "Our society seems to be on a large merry-go-round that is spinning faster and faster. Every once in a while someone is unable to hang on anymore and lets go. Broken people are everywhere, and it is my firm conviction that more and more people are going to be needed in the years to come to help in the healing process. I look forward to when we can move into such relationships with our fellow man that we will not need huge amounts of police protection, or all the jails we presently have."

* * *

Van LHIN, Erik
See del REY, Lester 1915-

* * *

van LINT, June 1928-

PERSONAL: Born June 21, 1928, in Long Beach, Calif.; daughter of Walter (a real estate agent) and Mabel (Place) Woolhouse; married Victor A. J. van Lint (a physicist), June 10, 1950; children: Lawrence, Kenneth, Linda, Karen. Education: Educated in secondary school in Palm Springs, Calif. Religion: Presbyterian. Home: 1032 Skylark Dr., La Jolla, Calif. 92037.

CAREER: Writer.

WRITINGS: My New Life (memoirs), privately printed, 1975.

WORK IN PROGRESS: A sequel to My New Life.

SIDELIGHTS: Victor van Lint told CA: "Since 1966, June has been a quadriplegic, with serious speech disability. Her book, typed with one finger at about five words per minute, tells of her experiences in hospitals, at home, during trips, etc., and shows how much living a seriously disabled person can still experience."

van RJNDT, Philippe 1950-

PERSONAL: Born July 12, 1950, in Montreal, Canada; son of Pieter and Helena (Trubetskoy) van Rjndt. *Education:* Educated privately in Switzerland. *Politics:* "Pragmatic—believe in the powers behind the throne." *Religion:* None. *Residence:* Toronto, Ontario, Canada; and Ouchy, Switzerland. *Office:* 42 Charles Street East, Toronto M5R 1S7, Canada.

CAREER: Writer.

WRITINGS: The Tetramachus Collection (novel), Putnam, 1976; *Blueprint* (novel), Putnam, in press.

WORK IN PROGRESS: Preparing a film adaptation of *The Tetramachus Collection.*

SIDELIGHTS: Van Rjndt writes: "I had absolutely no idea of what was required to write a novel. . . . However, after leaving the intelligence service, I decided I had stories to tell and simply went to it. This was eighteen months ago. I find now that indeed there is plenty of material with which to work and I see my novels as a series of concentric circles, each becoming tighter and more defined as I work my way through to the centre. God knows what will be found there but the journey is marvelous."

*   *   *

VANSINA, Jan 1929-

PERSONAL: Born September 14, 1929, in Antwerp, Belgium; came to the United States in 1960; son of Dirk (a painter and writer) and Suzanne (a painter; maiden name, Verellen) Vansina; married Claudine Herman, September 3, 1954; children: Bruno. *Education:* Catholic University of Louvain, B.A., 1949, M.A., 1951, Ph.D., 1957; University of London, graduate study, 1951-52. *Home:* 2810 Ridge Rd., Madison, Wis. 53705. *Office:* Department of History, University of Wisconsin, 435 Park St., Madison, Wis. 53706.

CAREER: Institut pour la Recherche scientifique en Afrique Centrale, Zaire, researcher, officer, and head of social science, 1953-60; University of Wisconsin, Madison, assistant professor, 1960-63, associate professor, 1963-66, professor of history, 1966—. *Military service:* Belgian Army, infantry, 1954-56. *Member:* International African Institute (member of board of directors, 1968-76), Koninklijke Akademie voor Overzeese Wetenschappen. *Awards, honors:* Belgian National Prize in history, 1960-65; Herskovits Prize from African Studies Association, 1967, for *Kingdoms of the Savanna.*

WRITINGS: Tribus Ba-Kuba et les Peuplades Aparentees (title means "Ba-Kuba and Related Peoples"), International Publications Service, 1954; *Esquisse de grammaire Bushoong* (title means "Sketch of Bushoong Grammar"), Musee Royal de l'Afrique Centrale, 1959; (editor with R. Mauny and V. L. Thomas) *The Historian in Tropical Africa: Studies Presented and Discussed at the Fourth International Seminar at University of Dakar,* Oxford University Press, 1961; *De la tradition orale: Essai de methode historique,* Musee Royal de l'Afrique Centrale, 1961, English translation by H. M. Wright published as *Oral Tradition,* Aldine, 1965; *L'Evolution du royaume rwanda des origines a 1900* (title means "Evolution of the Kingdom of Rwanda From Its Beginnings to 1900"), Academie royale des sciences d'outre Mer, 1962, Johnson Reprint, 1969; *Geschiedenis van de Kuba* (title means "Kuba History"), Musee Royal de l'Afrique Centrale, 1963; *Le Royaume Kuba* (title means "The Kuba Kingdom"), Musee Royal de l'Afrique Centrale, 1964; *Introduction a l'ethnographie du Congo* (title means "Introduction to the Ethnography of Zaire"), Kinshasa, 1965; *Kingdoms of the Savanna,* University of Wisconsin Press, 1966; *La Legende du passe: Traditions orales du Burundi* (title means "Legend of the Part-Oral Traditions from Burundi"), Musee Royal de l'Afrique Centrale, 1972; *The Tio Kingdom of the Middle Congo: 1880-1892,* Oxford University Press, 1973; (with W. K. Foell, P. G. Hayes, J. M. Lang, and others) *Resources and Decisions,* Duxbury, 1975. Contributor of about a hundred articles to scholarly journals.

WORK IN PROGRESS: Time and the Red Halls: Essays in Kuba History; The Voice of Time, on oral history methods; *Central African Pre-Colonial History.*

SIDELIGHTS: Vansina has conducted field research in Zaire, Rwanda, Burundi, and Brazzaville. He speaks Dutch, French, German, and Bushoong, and is familiar with other European and Bantu languages.

*   *   *

van THAL, Herbert (Maurice) 1904-

PERSONAL: Born March 30, 1904, in London, England; married Phyllis Bayley. *Education:* Educated in private school in London, England. *Home:* 33 Queen's Gate Gardens, London S.W.7, England. *Office:* London Management, 235 Regent St., London W.1, England.

CAREER: London Management, London, England, literary agent, 1960—. *Member:* Society of Odd Volumes, Reform Club.

WRITINGS: Ernest Augustine, Duke of Cumberland and King of Hanover: A Brief Survey of the Man and His Times, Arthur Barker, 1936; *Recipe for Reading: A Letter to My Godsons,* Home & Van Thal, 1945, revised edition published as *Recipe for Reading: A Short Personal Guide,* Panther, 1967; *Fanfare for Ernest Newman,* Arthur Barker, 1955; (author of introduction) Charles Dickens and Wilkie Collins, *The Wreck of the Golden Mary,* Arthur Barker, 1955; *The Tops of the Mulberry Trees* (autobiography), Allen & Unwin, 1971.

Editor: *The Royal Letter Book: Being a Collection of Royal Letters from the Reign of William I to George V,* Cresset, 1937; Ernest Newman, *Testament of Music: Essays and Papers,* Putnam, 1962; Rhoda Broughton, *Not Wisely, but Too Well,* Cassell, 1967; Samuel Langhorne Clemens, *The Gilded Age,* Cassell, 1967; William Makepeace Thackeray, *Barry Lyndon,* Cassell, 1967, Herman Melville, *Typee,* Cassell, 1967; George Douglas, *House with the Green Shutters,* Cassell, 1967; Michael Arlen, *London Venture,* Cassell, 1968; Robert Louis Stevenson, *New Arabian Nights,* Cassell, 1968; Robert S. Surtees, *Jorrocks, Jaunts, and Jollities,* Dufour, 1969; Hilaire Belloc, *Belloc: A Biographical Anthology,* Knopf, 1970; (with Gervase Hughes) *The Music Lover's Companion,* Eyre & Spottiswoode, 1971; Michael Kelly, *Solo Recital: Memoirs of Michael Kelly,* Folio Society, 1972; Walter Savage Landor, *Landor: A Biographical Anthology,* Allen & Unwin, 1973; Anthony Trollope, *The Domestic Manners of Americans,* Folio Society, 1974; *Bedside Book of Strange Stories,* Arthur Barker, 1974; *The Bedside Book of Detective Stories,* Arthur Barker, 1975; *Tales of History,* Arthur Barker, 1976.

Editor of anthologies: *Victoria's Subjects Travelled: Being an Anthology from the Works of Explorers and Travellers between the Years 1850-1900,* Arthur Barker, 1951; *Oriental Splendour: An Anthology of Eastern Tales,* Arthur Barker, 1953; Edgar Allan Poe, *Tales of Mystery and Imagination,*

Folio Society, 1957; *Great Ghost Stories*, Hill & Wang, 1960; *Striking Terror!: A Selection of Great Horror Stories*, Arthur Barker, 1963; *Famous Land Battles*, Arthur Barker, 1964; *True Tales of Travel, Adventure, and Discovery*, Arthur Barker, 1964; *Famous Tales of the Fantastic*, Hill & Wang, 1965; *Tales of Kings and Queens: A Book of Fairy Tales*, Hamish Hamilton, 1965; *Lie Ten Nights Awake: Ten Tales of Horror*, Berkley, 1968; *Tales of Terror and the Supernatural*, Dover, 1972; *The Prime Ministers*, Stein & Day, 1975. Also editor of books published by Dufour: *Alton Locke*, by Charles Kingsley; *Cock and the Anchor*, by Joseph S. Le Fanu; and *Young Mistley*, by Henry S. Merriman.

WORK IN PROGRESS: The Girl of the Period, a biography of Mrs. E. Lynn Linton, for Allen & Unwin; editing *A Musical Miscellany*.

SIDELIGHTS: Of *The Prime Ministers* Philip Terzian wrote, "This is a delightful book. In spite of its massiveness, not to mention the massiveness of its intent, it is a pleasure to read—to dip into it at intervals, to follow from front to back and thereby obtain a political history of Britain from the early 18th century. Inevitably the quality is uneven . . . but it is a novel idea that works, and is a thorough, compact guide to information hitherto diffuse."

BIOGRAPHICAL/CRITICAL SOURCES: Herbert van Thal, *The Tops of the Mulberry Trees*, Allen & Unwin, 1971; *New Republic*, January 3 and 10, 1976.

*　　　*　　　*

VARANDYAN, Emmanuel P(aul) 1904-

PERSONAL: Born November 25, 1904, in Urumia, Iran; came to the United States in 1926, naturalized citizen, 1937; son of Paul Matevos and Shogat Der (Mardirossian) Varandyan. *Education:* Attended American Memorial School, Tabriz, Iran, Institute of Languages and Literatures, Teheran, Iran, and Ford's School of Technology; University of Michigan, A.B., 1932, A.M., 1934; State University of Iowa, Ph.D., 1938. *Home address:* Lake Shore Dr., Route 3, Dandridge, Tenn. 37725. *Office:* Department of English, Ohio State University, Columbus, Ohio 43210.

CAREER: University of Michigan, Ann Arbor, instructor in French, 1934-35, researcher in Turkish and Persian manuscripts at Clemens Library, 1936-37; State University of Iowa, Iowa City, instructor in English, 1945-48; Ohio State University, Columbus, instructor, 1948-49, assistant professor, 1950-56, postdoctoral research fellow, 1956-62, associate professor, 1962-70, professor of English and Middle Eastern culture, 1970-73, member of executive committee of Middle Eastern studies program, 1960-73. Cultural adviser to Office of Coordination of Cultural Information for the Middle East, 1942-45. *Military service:* 1938-45.

MEMBER: Modern Language Association of America, American Association of University Professors, Middle Eastern Institute (Washington, D.C.), Folklore Society of America, National Association for Armenian Studies and Research (honorary life member; past member of board of directors; member of national advisory board). *Awards, honors:* First prize from Avery Hopwood Literary Contest at University of Michigan, 1938, for *The Well of Ararat;* fellowship from Yaddo Writers and Artists Institute, 1949.

WRITINGS: The Well of Ararat (anthropological novel), Doubleday-Doran, 1938; (author of introduction) Armen Hovanesian, *The Crusades and Cilician Armenia*, Detroit Armenian Cultural Association, 1958; (translator) Avedic

Isahakian, *Abu Lala Mahary*, New World Weekly, 1963; *The Moon Sails*, Pinnacle Books, 1971. Contributor of poems, articles, novelettes, and reviews to literary magazines, including *University of Michigan Quarterly Review, Literature East and West, Comparative Literature, Books Abroad, Ararat*, and *New World*.

WORK IN PROGRESS: The Problems of Acculturation and Assimilation; The Contributions of the Ancient World to the New World.

SIDELIGHTS: Varandyan is competent in eight languages: Armenian, Persian, Turkish, Assyrian, Russian, German, French, and English.

*　　　*　　　*

VELLELA, Tony 1945-

PERSONAL: Born December 14, 1945, in Scranton, Pa.; son of William (a printer) and Caroline (a seamstress; maiden name, DeFrancesco) Vellela. *Education:* East Stroudsburg State College, B.A., 1967. *Residence:* New York, N.Y.

CAREER: Daily Record, Stroudsburg, Pa., theater critic, 1964-67; *Golf Magazine*, New York, N.Y., associate editor, 1967-68; *Motion Picture Daily*, New York, N.Y., film critic and reporter, 1968-69; free-lance writer. Producer-director, Court Players, summer 1968; member, Broadway Local (a food co-operative); board member, Direct Supply (federation of food co-operatives).

WRITINGS: Food Co-ops for Small Groups, Workman Publishing, 1975. Columnist for *Crawdaddy*, 1969-70, *Pop Scene*, 1970, and *College Magazine*, 1974. Contributor to magazines, including *Rolling Stone, Life, Christian Science Monitor* and *Pageant*.

SIDELIGHTS: Vellela wrote: "My work reflects the growth of the new culture in this country, one that considers its impact on the planet, and on the humanness of people. This culture touches every aspect of life, from entertainment and finance to food and health, and is not related to age, geographic location, sex, or economic background."

*　　　*　　　*

VENGROFF, Richard 1945-

PERSONAL: Born July 25, 1945, in New York, N.Y.; son of Ned (a contractor) and Alice Beth (a commercial artist; maiden name, Weber) Vengroff; married Linda Phyllis Krasilovsky, April 9, 1967; children: Darren Erik, Lisa Malaika. *Education:* State University of New York at Stony Brook, B.A. (magna cum laude), 1967; Syracuse University, M.S.Sc., 1970, Ph.D., 1972. *Religion:* Reformed Jewish. *Home:* 4616 62nd St., Lubbock, Tex. 79414. *Office:* Department of Political Science, Texas Tech University, Lubbock, Tex. 79409.

CAREER: Texas Tech University, Lubbock, assistant professor, 1972-76, associate professor of political science, 1976—. Conducted field research in Botswana and Niger. *Member:* International Studies Association, American Political Science Association, African Studies Association, American Society for Public Administration, Western Association of Africanists.

WRITINGS: (Contributor) Brian Larkin and Roy Price, editors, *Reforming American Education*, Syracuse University Press, 1974; *Botswana: Rural Development in the Shadow of Apartheid*, Associated University Presses, 1976. Contributor of fifteen articles and reviews to academic journals.

WORK IN PROGRESS: "Domestic Instability and the Foreign Conflict Behavior of Black African States"; "Dependency and Domestic Inequality in Black Africa"; "Small States in the United Nations: The Continuing Impact of the Ex-Colonial Power"; "Attitude Inconsistency: The Case of Women's Rights," with W. Vanderbok; "Sex and Social Change: Dimensions of the Women's Rights Movement," with Vanderbok; "Dependency and Inequality," with L. Sigelman; "Dependency and Foreign Policy Behavior"; *South Africa's Homelands: A Comparative Study;* "The Administration of Agricultural Development in Niger"; "The Ranking of Political Science Departments by the Quality of Their Publications," with Al Karnig.

* * *

VERCOURS

See BRULLER, Jean Marcel 1902-

* * *

VEREY, David (Cecil Wynter) 1913-

PERSONAL: Born September 9, 1913, son of Cecil Henry (a clergyman) and Constance Lindaraja Dearman (Birchall) Verey; married Rosemary Isabel Baird Sandilands, 1939; children: two sons, two daughters. *Education:* Trinity College, Cambridge, M.A.; Royal Institute of British Architects, A.R.I.B.A., 1940. *Home:* Barnsley House, Cirencester, Gloucester, England.

CAREER: Ministry of Housing and Local Government, London, England, senior investigator of historic buildings, 1946-65; high sheriff of the County of Gloucester, 1966; architectural historian and writer, 1966—. Chairman of Gloucester Diocesan Advisory Committee on Churches; member of Severn regional committee of the National Trust. *Military service:* British Army, Royal Fusiliers, 1939-45, special operations executive in North Africa and Italy, 1943; became captain.

MEMBER: Society of Antiquaries (fellow), Church Building Society, Bristol and Gloucestershire Archaeological Society (president, 1972), Cirencester Archaeological and Historical Society (president), Gloucestershire Society for Industrial Archaeology (president).

WRITINGS: (Editor) Anthony West, *Gloucestershire: A Shell Guide,* revised edition (Verey was not associated with original edition), Faber, 1952; *Herefordshire,* Faber, 1955; (editor) *Shell Guide to Wiltshire: A Series of Views of Castles, Seats of the Nobility, Mines, Picturesque Scenery, Towns, Public Buildings, Churches, Antiquities,* Faber, 1956; *A Shell Guide to Mid Wales: The Counties of Brecon, Radnor, and Montgomery,* Faber, 1960; *Gloucestershire,* Volume I: *The Cotswolds,* Volume II: *The Vale and the Forest of Dean,* Penguin, 1970; *Cutswold Churches,* Batsford, 1976; (contributor) Jane Fawcett, editor, *Seven Victorian Architects,* Thames & Hudson, 1977. Contributor to periodicals.

WORK IN PROGRESS: The City and County of Gloucestershire. *Avocational interests:* His private museum, gardening.

* * *

VERNEY, John 1913-

PERSONAL: Born September 30, 1913; son of Ralph and Janette (Walker) Verney; married Lucinda Musgrave, March 29, 1939; children: two sons (one deceased), five daughters. *Education:* Christ Church, Oxford, history de-

gree, 1935. *Home:* Runwick House, Farnham, Surrey, England.

CAREER: Painter, illustrator, and writer. Has had exhibits of his work at Royal Society of British Artists, London Group, and British galleries. Member of Franham Trust. *Military service:* British Army, served with North Somerset Yeomanry, Royal Armoured Corps, and Special Air Service Regiment; served in Middle East and Europe; received Military Cross, French Legion d'Honneur, mentioned in dispatches. *Awards, honors:* Created second baronet, 1959.

WRITINGS: Verney Abroad, Collins, 1954; *Going to the Wars,* Dodd, 1955 (published in England as *Going to the Wars: A Journey in Various Directions,* Collins, 1955); *Friday's Tunnel* (juvenile), Collins, 1959, Holt, 1966; *Look at Houses,* Hamish Hamilton, 1959; *Every Advantage,* Collins, 1961; *February's World* (juvenile), Collins, 1961, Holt, 1966; *The Mad King of Chichiboo,* F. Watts, 1963; *Ismo* (self-illustrated juvenile mystery novel), Collins, 1964, Holt, 1967; *A Dinner of Herbs* (memoirs of World War II), Collins, 1966; *Fine Day for a Picnic* (novel), Hodder & Stoughton, 1968; *Seven Sunflower Seeds* (self-illustrated juvenile mystery novel), Collins, 1968, Holt, 1969; *Samson's Hoard* (juvenile), Collins, 1973. Illustrator of books by others. Contributor to magazines, including *Cornhill, National Review, English Review,* and *Elizabethan.*

WORK IN PROGRESS: A diary in picture-form of a visit to New York; a novel about English local government; painting decorative pictures on furniture and other objects.

SIDELIGHTS: Verney explained: "More recently I have become mostly involved with painting decorative pictures on furniture, usually of people's towns or houses, which has become my specialty in the past ten years—though I take on anything that offers, such as a large mobile in the tower of Nuffield College, Oxford, or a glass-fired mural in the Fairlawn Primary School in the London Education Authority."

* * *

VIGNERAS, Louis-Andre 1903-

PERSONAL: Born May 28, 1903, in Paris, France; naturalized U.S. citizen; son of Paul Martial (an educator) and Esther (Jacquemin) Vigneras. *Education:* Earned Bach. es lettres from University of Portiers, and lic. es lettres from University of Bordeaux; Princeton University, B.A., 1920, M.A., 1921; Harvard University, Ph.D., 1934. *Politics:* Liberal. *Religion:* None. *Home address:* 7821 Custer Rd., Bethesda, Md. 20014.

CAREER: Has taught at Robert College (Istanbul, Turkey), Lycee Francais (Beirut, Lebanon), Ohio State University (Columbus), DePauw University (Greencastle, Ind.), Duquesne University (Pittsburgh, Pa.), and at University of Maine; George Washington University, Washington, D.C., professor of history until 1968; writer. *Military service:* French Army, liason officer, 1943-45. *Member:* Society for the History of Discoveries.

WRITINGS: (Editor) *The Journal of Christopher Columbus,* Orion Press, 1960; *The Discovery of South America and the Andalusian Voyages,* University of Chicago Press, 1976. Contributor to history journals in France, the United States, and other parts of the world.

WORK IN PROGRESS: The Search for Paradise and the Discovery of America.

* * *

VILLEGAS, Daniel Cosio 1898-1976

July 23, 1898—March 10, 1976; Mexican historian, economist, educator, and author. Obituaries: *New York Times,* March 12, 1976; *AB Bookman's Weekly,* May 17, 1976.

* * *

VINCENT, Charles 1945-

PERSONAL: Born October 19, 1945, in Hazlehurst, Mass.; son of Eddie, Sr. (a farmer) and Willie Mae (Holloway) Vincent; married Deloris Tillmon, December 24, 1971; children: Shari Delise, Charles Lerone. *Education:* Utica Junior College, diploma, 1964; Jackson State University, B.A., 1966; Louisiana State University, Baton Rouge, M.A., 1968, Ph.D., 1973. *Religion:* Baptist. *Home:* 2938 Fairfields Ave., Baton Rouge, La. 70802. *Office:* Department of History, Southern University, Baton Rouge, La. 70813.

CAREER: T. J. Harris Junior College, Meridian, Miss., instructor in social science, 1967-68; Southern University, Baton Rouge, La., instructor, 1968-69, assistant professor, 1969-70, 1973-75, associate professor of history, 1975—. *Member:* Organization of American Historians, National Social Studies Council, Association for the Study of Afro-American Life and History, Southern Historical Association, Louisiana Historical Association, Louisiana Social Studies Council.

WRITINGS: Black Legislators in Louisiana During Reconstruction, Louisiana State University Press, 1976.

WORK IN PROGRESS: A Centennial History of Southern University.

SIDELIGHTS: "In my opinion," Vincent wrote *CA,* "it is indispensable to set the records straight on the achievements of Blacks in history, not only American history but world history. To achieve this task, and to guarantee a measure of success, Black scholars should be in the vanguard as writers, custodians, and historians of the Black experience.

* * *

VINCENT, Howard Paton 1904-

PERSONAL: Born October 9, 1904, in Galesburg, Ill.; son of Clarence and Lucy Seymour (Hall) Vincent; married Mary Wilson Smith, September 4, 1931; children: Judith Hall, John Way. *Education:* Oberlin College, A.B., 1926; Harvard University, M.A., 1927, Ph.D., 1933; Pennsylvania School of Social Work, student, 1934-35. *Home:* 508 North Willow St., Kent, Ohio 44240.

CAREER: West Virginia University, Morgantown, instructor in composition and literature, 1927-28; Park School, Cleveland, Ohio, teacher, 1931-32; Blair County Relief Office, Pa., supervisor, 1935; Hillsdale College, Hillsdale, Mich., Ezra L. Koon Professor of English and head of department, 1935-42; Illinois Institute of Technology, Chicago, assistant professor, 1942-44, associate professor, 1944-47, professor of English and chairman of department of language, literature, and philosophy, 1947-62; Kent State University, Kent, Ohio, professor of English and American literature, 1962-69, university professor, 1969—. Fulbright lecturer on American civilization and literature in France, 1954-55, in Belgium, 1961-62, and in Italy, 1967; director of library service in France for U.S. Information Service, 1955-58.

MEMBER: National Council of Teachers of English, College English Association, English Institute, Modern Language Association of America, American Association of University Professors, Melville Society of America (past president; secretary, 1963-69), Keats-Shelley Association of America. *Awards, honors:* Fund for the Advancement of Education fellowship, 1951-52; Litt.D., Hillsdale College, 1958.

WRITINGS: (Editor and author of introduction) *Letters of Dora Wordsworth,* Packard & Co., 1944; (editor) *Collected Poems of Herman Melville: Complete Works,* Vol. XIV, Packard & Co., 1947; *The Trying-Out of Moby Dick,* Houghton, 1949, Southern Illinois University Press, 1965; (editor with Luther S. Mansfield) Herman Melville, *Moby Dick: Or, The Whale,* Hendricks House, 1952; (editor with Harrison Hayford) *Reader and Writer,* Houghton, 1954, 3rd edition, 1969.

(Editor) Henry A. Murray and others, *Bartleby the Scrivener: A Symposium,* Kent State University Press, 1966; (editor) Henry A. Murray and others, *Melville & Hawthorne in the Berkshires: A Symposium,* Kent State University Press, 1968; *Daumier and His World,* Northwestern University Press, 1968; (compiler) *The Merrill Checklist of Herman Melville,* C. E. Merrill, 1969; *The Merrill Guide to Herman Melville,* C. E. Merrill, 1969; (compiler) *The Merrill Studies in Moby Dick,* C. E. Merrill, 1969; *The Tailoring of Melville's White-Jacket,* Northwestern University Press, 1970; (editor) *Twentieth Century Interpretations of Billy Budd: A Collection of Critical Essays,* Prentice-Hall, 1971.

* * *

VIPOND, Don (Harry) 1932-

PERSONAL: Born July 26, 1932, in Toronto, Ontario, Canada; son of Harry K. and Allison (Bristol) Vipond; married Clare Angela Barker, August 24, 1963; children: Adam. *Education:* Attended University of Toronto. *Home:* 4853 Cherry Tree Bend, Victoria, British Columbia, Canada. *Agent:* Charles Neighbors, 240 Waverly Pl., New York, N.Y. 10014. *Office:* Victoria Press, 2621 Douglas St., Victoria, British Columbia, Canada.

CAREER: Victoria Times, Victoria, British Columbia, reporter, 1966—. *Military service:* Canadian Army, Royal Canadian Artillery, in supplementary reserve, 1950-52; became lieutenant.

WRITINGS: Night of the Shooting Star (suspense novel), Bobbs-Merrill, 1975.

* * *

VISCONTI, Luchino 1906-1976

November 2, 1906—1976; Italian film director. Obituaries: *Time,* March 29, 1976.

* * *

VOGEL, David 1947-

PERSONAL: Born April 14, 1947, in New York, N.Y.; son of Harry (an optician) and Charlotte (Rab) Vogel. *Education:* Queens College of the City University of New York, B.A., 1967; Princeton University, Ph.D., 1974. *Religion:* Jewish. *Home:* 1663 Euclid, Berkeley, Calif. 94709. *Office:* School of Business Administration, University of California, Berkeley, Calif. 94720.

CAREER: University of California, Berkeley, assistant professor of social, political, and legal environment of business, 1973—. *Member:* American Political Science Association, Phi Beta Kappa.

WRITINGS: (With Leonard Silk) *Ethics and Profits: The Crisis of Confidence in American Business,* Simon & Schuster, 1976. Contributor to business, popular and social sciences journals, including *Nation* and *Polity.*

WORK IN PROGRESS: The Citizen Challenge to Business (tentative title), for Basic Books.

*   *   *

von FURSTENBERG, George Michael   1941-

PERSONAL: Born December 3, 1941, in Germany; came to the United States in 1961, naturalized citizen, 1966; son of Kaspar and Elisabeth (von Boeselager) von Furstenberg; married Gabrielle von Koblitz, June 9, 1967. *Education:* Columbia University, B.S. (magna cum laude), 1963; Princeton University, Ph.D., 1967. *Home:* 837 Sheridan Rd., Bloomington, Ind. 47401. *Office:* Department of Economics, Indiana University, Bloomington, Ind. 47401.

CAREER: Cornell University, Ithaca, N.Y., assistant professor of economics, 1966-67; Brookings Institution, Washington, D.C., economic policy fellow, 1967-68; Cornell University, assistant professor of economics, 1968-70; Indiana University, Bloomington, associate professor, 1970-73, professor of economics, 1973—. Visiting professor at Augsburg University, autumn, 1972; senior staff economist for U.S. President's Council of Economic Advisers, 1973-76 (on leave from Indiana University); member of housing market research group of Federal Home Loan Bank Board.

MEMBER: Institut International de Finances Publiques, American Economic Association, National Tax Association, Association for Evolutionary Economics, Association for the Study of the Grants Economy, Western Economic Association, Western Finance Association, Indiana Academy of the Social Sciences, Phi Beta Kappa. *Awards, honors:* Brookings Institution fellow, 1965-66; research fellow of American Enterprise Institute, 1976.

WRITINGS: Technical Studies of Mortgage Default Risk (monograph), Urban Development Research Center, Cornell University, 1971; *The Economics of Mortgages with Variable Interest Rates* (monograph), Federal Home Loan Mortgage Corp., 1973; (editor with Bennett Harrison and Ann R. Horowitz) *Patterns of Racial Discrimination,* Volume I, *Housing,* Volume II, *Employment and Income,* Lexington Books, 1974.

*   *   *

VONNEGUT, Mark   1947-

PERSONAL: Born May 11, 1947, in Chicago, Ill.; son of Kurt, Jr. (an author) and Jane (a journalist; maiden name, Cox) Vonnegut; married Patricia O'Shea (an educator), May 24, 1975. *Education:* Swarthmore College, B.A., 1969; attended University of Massachusetts, Boston, 1973-75; Harvard Medical School, 1975—. *Politics:* Left. *Religion:* "Old Testament Agnostic." *Home:* 262 Kent St., Brookline, Mass., 02146. *Agent:* Knox Burger, Washington Square S., New York, N.Y.

CAREER: Boston State Hospital, Boston, Mass., administrative assistant in charge of security, 1969; lived and worked in alternative culture commune in Powell River, British Columbia, 1970-71; substitute teacher in high school in Barnstable, Mass., 1972; Wirtanen Associates (landscapers), Barnstable, landscape worker, 1972-73. Writer. Member of board of directors, Earth House (for recovering schizophrenics). *Member:* Huxley Institute. *Awards, honors:* Notable Book Award (in both adult and young adult categories) from American Library Association, 1976, for *The Eden Express*.

WRITINGS: The Eden Express, Praeger, 1975.

Contributor of articles to periodicals and journals, including,

Harper's, Village Voice, and *Journal of Orthomolecular Psychiatry.*

WORK IN PROGRESS: No More Double Talk: Thinking Straight About Mental Illness, completion expected, 1977.

SIDELIGHTS: The Eden Express reflects Mark Vonnegut's experiences with schizophrenia—a condition which has since been treated with prescribed drugs, shock-treatment, vitamin therapy, a high-protein diet, and a disciplined schedule. R. Z. Sheppard described the book as Vonnegut's "attempt to describe the slippage in and out of madness, to distinguish between the chaos in his head and the confusion in the world and, finally, to achieve a balance between the romantic myths about sick minds and the cold evidence that his own disorder is the product of abnormal body chemistry." Sheppard continued, saying that by the end of the book, "Vonnegut has found a truer, more subdued voice that reaches out of his agony and concern. It is not quite grace under pressure, but it is that necessary first step, growth under stress."

A.C.J. Bergman commented that Vonnegut's writing style is "By turns . . . vague, sentimental, rhapsodic, repetitious. It suffers from lank rumination and preachiness; its prose is often raw." Bergman allows, however, that *"The Eden Express* has its merits. Vonnegut catches the pulse of hippiedom, occasionally with droll self-deprecation. Much more important, he re-creates the pitch of riven sanity."

The book ends with Vonnegut's letter to a friend who fears mental illness. It says, in part, "your mental health is not dependent on the moral, socio-political health of the world. Thank God for little things like that. It also means that getting well doesn't involve our becoming any less angry with things as they are."

Vonnegut told *CA:* "Changing our outlook on mental illness would cut the pain and suffering at least in half. There is no basis for shame, blame, or romance. Mental illness is 99 percent biochemical. The problem is not so much the "crazy" behavior which gets all the attention, but the simple fact of being unable to take care of oneself. It's really painfully simple."

BIOGRAPHICAL/CRITICAL SOURCES: Atlantic, October, 1975; *Newsweek,* October 6, 1975; *Time,* October 6, 1975; *New York Times Book Review,* October 26, 1975.

*   *   *

von WUTHENAU, Alexander   1900-

PERSONAL: Born August 1, 1900, in Dresden, Germany; son of Carl Adam (a count) and Antoinette (a countess; maiden name, Choteck) von Wuthenau; married Rachelle von Catinelli, October 30, 1935 (died, 1945); married Beatriz von Pietsch, April 1, 1948; children: Maria, Francisca Fernanda, Alexander, Guadalupe, Antonio Carlota. *Education:* Attended University of Freiburg, 1919-20, and University of Munich, 1921; University of Kiel, Ph.D., 1925. *Religion:* Roman Catholic. *Home:* Ave. San Jeronimo 488, San Angel D. F. Mexico 20.

CAREER: German Legation, Buenos Aires, Argentina, secretary, 1928-30; German Embassy, Washington, D.C., secretary, 1930-34; University of the Americas (formerly Mexico City College), Mexico City, Mexico, assistant professor, 1945-50, associate professor, 1950-60, professor of art history, 1960-74. *Military service:* German Army, Leibkuerassier, 1918; became lieutenant. *Member:* American Epigraphic Society.

WRITINGS: The Military Chapel of Santa Fe, University

of Albuquerque, 1935; *Tepotzotlan: Art and Color in Mexico,* Fotocolor, 1941; *Altamerikanische Tonplastik: Das Menschenbild der Neuen Welt* (title means "Ancient American Clay Sculpture: The Human Image of the New World"), Holle Verlag, 1965; *Terrecuites Precolombiennes* (title means "Pre-Colombian Terracottas"), Albin Michel, 1969; *The Art of Terracotta Pottery,* Crown, 1970; *Unexpected Faces in Ancient America: The Historical Testimony of Pre-Colombian Artists,* Crown, 1975.

WORK IN PROGRESS: Central Photographic Archive of Human Representations in Ancient America.

*   *   *

WADSWORTH, Nelson B(ingham)   1930-

PERSONAL: Born September 27, 1930, in Martinez, Calif.; son of Claude Henry and Mable (Bingham) Wadsworth; married Gayle Forsyth (a nurse), March 28, 1958; children: Denise, Geri, Jon. *Education:* San Jose State College (now University), B.S., 1954; University of Utah, M.S., 1970. *Politics:* Democrat. *Religion:* Church of Jesus Christ of Latter-day Saints (Mormons). *Home:* 3278 Mohican Way, Provo, Utah 84601. *Office:* Department of Communications, Brigham Young University, Provo, Utah 84602.

CAREER: Salinas Californian, Salinas, Calif., valley editor, 1954-55; *Richmond Independent,* Richmond, Calif., news reporter, 1954-56; *Deseret News,* Salt Lake City, Utah, reporter, 1956-59; David W. Evans & Associates, Salt Lake City, Utah, writer, 1959-62; free-lance writer, 1962-64; Associated Press, Salt Lake City, Utah, writer and editor, 1964-66; University of Utah, Salt Lake City, instructor in photography, 1966-72 (also writer and editor for the university); Brigham Young University, Provo, Utah, assistant professor of communications, 1972—. *Military service:* U.S. Marine Corps Reserve, active duty, 1948-50, 1950-52; served in Korea. *Member:* National Press Photographers Association, Sigma Delta Chi. *Awards, honors:* Morris Rosenblat Award from Utah Historical Society, 1971.

WRITINGS: Through Camera Eyes, Brigham Young University Press, 1975. Contributor to popular magazines, including *Time, Life, National Observer,* and *People Weekly.*

WORK IN PROGRESS: Frontier photography; photojournalism; investigative reporting.

*   *   *

WAINHOUSE, David Walter   1900-1976

September 15, 1900—March 19, 1976; Lithuanian-born American lawyer, diplomat, foreign relations and defense expert, educator, and author of books in his field. Obituaries: *Washington Post,* March 22, 1976.

*   *   *

WAINWRIGHT, Nicholas Biddle   1914-

PERSONAL: Born July 12, 1914, in Saranac, N.Y.; son of Clement Reeves (a manufacturer) and Eugenia (Dixon) Wainwright; married Christine Henry, February 27, 1954; children: Christine. *Education:* Princeton University, A.B., 1936; University of Pennsylvania, M.A., 1949. *Home address:* Box 157, Gwynedd, Pa. 19436. *Office:* Historical Society of Pennsylvania, 1300 Locust St., Philadelphia, Pa. 19107.

CAREER: Historical Society of Pennsylvania, Philadelphia, research librarian, 1939-65, director, 1965-74. Member of board of directors of Library Company of Philadelphia,

1949—, president, 1951-66. *Member:* American Antiquarian Society, Massachusetts Historical Society, Walpole Society, Philadelphia Club, State Club (Schuykill, Pa.). *Awards, honors:* D.Litt. from Dickinson College, 1959; literary award from Athenaeum of Philadelphia, 1953, for *A Philadelphia Story;* special citation from Society of American Historians, 1958, for editorship of *The Pennsylvania Magazine of History and Biography.*

WRITINGS: A Philadelphia Story: The Philadelphia Contributionship for the Insurance of Houses from Loss by Fire, privately printed, 1952; *The History of the Philadelphia National Bank: A Century and a Half of Philadelphia Banking, 1803-1953,* privately printed, 1953; *Plan of Philadelphia,* Historical Society of Pennsylvania, 1956; *Philadelphia in the Romantic Age of Lithography: An Illustrated History of Early Lithography in Philadelphia, with a Descriptive List of Philadelphia Scenes Made by Philadelphia Lithographers Before 1866,* Historical Society of Pennsylvania, 1958; *George Croghan: Wilderness Diplomat,* University of North Carolina Press, 1959.

Augustus Kollner, Artist, privately printed, 1960; *History of the Philadelphia Electric Company,* privately printed, 1961; *The History of the Philadelphia Inquirer,* privately printed, 1962; *Colonial Grandeur in Philadelphia: The House and Furniture of General John Cadwalader,* Historical Society of Pennsylvania, 1964; *The Irvine Story,* Historical Society of Pennsylvania, 1964; *Commodore James Biddle and His Sketch Book,* Historical Society of Pennsylvania, 1966; *The History of the Church of the Messiah, Gwynedd: Its First Hundred Years, 1866-1966,* privately printed, 1966; (editor) *A Philadelphia Perspective: The Diary of Sidney George Fisher Covering the Years 1834-1871,* Historical Society of Pennsylvania, 1967; *Guide to the Microfilm Edition of the Thomas Penn Papers,* Historical Society of Pennsylvania, 1968.

(Editor) *Paintings and Miniatures at the Historical Society of Pennsylvania,* Historical Society of Pennsylvania, 1974; *One Hundred Years of Collecting by the Historical Society of Pennsylvania,* Historical Society of Pennsylvania, 1974; *Andalusia,* Historical Society of Pennsylvania, 1976. Editor of *Pennsylvania Magazine of History and Biography,* 1952—.

*   *   *

WAKEFIELD, Connie LaVon   1948-

PERSONAL: Born November 9, 1948, in Champaign, Ill.; daughter of Dale Scott (a businessman) and Nondus (Clutter) Wakefield. *Education:* Attended Danville Junior College, 1966-67, and Parkland College, 1967-68; University of Illinois, B.A., 1971, M.A., 1972. *Office:* Country Companies, P.O. Box 2020, Bloomington, Ill. 61701.

CAREER: Courier, Urbana, Ill., part-time reporter, 1970-72, women's editor, 1972-75; Country Companies, Bloomington, Ill., coordinator of consumer communications, 1975—. *Member:* Society of Professional Journalists (vice-president, Central Illinois Professional Chapter, 1973-73), International Association of Business Communicators, Illinois Agricultural Association Federal Credit Union (member of board of directors).

WRITINGS: (With Harold Kenneth Jones) *Sweetie Feetie* (juvenile), Follett, 1975.

*   *   *

WAKELIN, Martyn Francis   1935-

PERSONAL: Born September 5, 1935, in Wellingborough,

Northamptonshire, England; son of Ronald Francis (a general manager) and Doris (Bradshaw) Wakelin; married Diane King, September 10, 1966; children: Rebecca Jane, Julian Francis, Anna Louise. *Education:* University of Leeds, B.A., 1959, M.A. (with distinction), 1960, Ph.D., 1970; University of London, B.D., 1975. *Religion:* Anglican. *Home:* 60 Hythe Field Ave., Egham, Surrey, England. *Office:* Department of English, Royal Holloway College, Egham Hill, Egham, Surrey, England.

CAREER: Royal Holloway College, Egham, Surrey, England, lecturer in English, 1967—. *Military service:* Royal Air Force, 1954-56. *Member:* Society for Folk Life Studies, Yorkshire Dialect Society.

WRITINGS: (Reviser and editor) W. L. Renwick and Harold Orton, *The Beginnings of English Literature,* 3rd edition (Wakelin was not associated with earlier editions), Cresset Press, 1966; (with Orton) *Survey of English Dialects,* Volume IV, Arnold, 1967; (editor) *Patterns in the Folk Speech of the British Isles,* Athlone Press, 1972; *English Dialects: An Introduction,* Athlone Press, 1972; *Language and History in Cornwall,* Leicester University Press, 1975. Contributor to *Folk Life, Times Educational Supplement,* and professional and local journals.

WORK IN PROGRESS: A pamphlet, *Varieties of English,* for publication in Japan; a book on the theological background of medieval English literature; editing fifteenth-century documents from Cornwall and manuscripts of John Mirk's festival of English homilies written about 1400.

SIDELIGHTS: Wakelin has discussed English dialect on radio and television. His interests include Biblical studies and liturgy, Old Icelandic (which he teaches), Celtic languages and literatures, and comparative philology. He feels "the need for greater restraint in liturgical reform." *Avocational interests:* Piano, organ, cooking.

* * *

WALD, Carol 1935-

PERSONAL: Born January 21, 1935, in Detroit, Mich.; daughter of Peter B. (an accountant) and Rose (Smofsky) Wald. *Education:* Attended Society of Arts and Crafts, Detroit, Mich., 1954-58, and Cranbrook Academy of Art, 1968-69. *Home and studio:* 182 Grand St., New York, N.Y. 10013. *Agent:* Virginia Barber, 44 Greenwich Ave., New York, N.Y. 10011.

CAREER: Free-lance editorial illustrator; painter (work is represented in five major museums and several hundred private collections; solo exhibitions have been held in New York City and in Michigan). *Awards, honors:* Purchase awards from Henry Scripps Booth Collection, 1957, Detroit Institute of Arts, 1960, St. Paul Art Museum, 1968, and American Watercolor Society, 1969; Gold Medal Award from Society of Illustrators, 1975, for editorial illustration in *Viva International,* 1974-75; commission from National Bicentennial Competition, 1976, for painting "The New Spirit of '76."

WRITINGS: Myth America: Picturing Women, 1865-1945, Pantheon, 1975. Book jacket and cover illustrator. Contributor of articles and art work to magazines, including *Ms., Time, New Dawn, Penthouse,* and *Saturday Review,* and to newspapers.

WORK IN PROGRESS—Self-illustrated: *Art for People Who Can't Draw; The U.S. Male: The Popular Images of Men.*

SIDELIGHTS: Carol Wald is a painter, but works in several media, including photography and collage. She said, "I'm not interested in unique art works, and consider magazine illustration as legitimate as any other medium. If I mix pop images and bad taste with the Old Masters, it may sound campy, but the environment I grew up in was non-cultural—I never read a fine book or saw a fine painting—and while I developed a high regard for the art of the Old Masters later on, I see no reason to throw away a large part of my past. Anyway, we live in the first age where you can juxtapose a Rembrandt against a Diane Arbus or an advertising trademark and it would be foolish to waste the opportunity."

BIOGRAPHICAL/CRITICAL SOURCES: Art Gallery, February, 1975; *Detroit News Sunday Magazine,* June 29, 1975; *New Republic,* December, 1975; *Cleveland Plain Dealer Sunday Magazine,* February 22, 1976; *People,* May 17, 1976; *Ms.,* July, 1976; *New York Post,* July 17, 1976; *Detroit News,* July 30, 1976.

* * *

WALDER, (Alan) David 1928-

PERSONAL: Born November 13, 1928, in London, England; son of James (a civil servant) and Helen (McColville) Walder; married Elspeth Margaret Milligan (an economist), July 28, 1956; children: Robert, Isobel, Catherine, Alexandra. *Education:* Christ Church, Oxford, B.A., 1952, M.A., 1954. *Home:* White House, Grimsargh near Preston, Lancashire PR2 5JR, England; and 45 Courtenay St., London SE11 5PH, England.

CAREER: British Army, 1948-65, member of Fourth Queen's Own Hussars in Malaya, Germany, Aden, and Borneo, 1949-58, and Emergency Reserve, Queen's Royal Irish Hussars, 1958-65, leaving service as a major; called to the bar, Inner Temple, 1956; practiced as a barrister, 1956-66; conservative member of Parliament from High Peak, Derbyshire, 1961-66; conservative member of Parliament from Clitheroe, 1970—; Lexington International Public Relations Ltd., London, England, consultant, 1977—. Parliamentary private secretary to joint Under-Secretaries of State, Scottish Office, 1963-64, and to Minister for Trade, 1970-72; member of United Kingdom Parliamentary Delegation to the Republic of China, 1972, and to the Council of Europe and Assembly of Western European Union, 1973; vice-chairman of Conservative Home Affairs Committee, 1972; vice-chairman of Conservative Defence Committee, 1974. Member of court of University of Lancaster.

MEMBER: Institute for Strategic Studies, National Book League, Royal United Services Institute, Anglo-Omani Society, Wembley South Conservative Association (chairman, 1959), Cavalry and Guards Club, 1922 Committee. *Awards, honors:* Forster-Boulton Prize and Paul Methven scholarship from the Inner Temple, both 1956; Emergency Reserve decoration, 1965.

WRITINGS: Bags of Swank (novel), Hutchinson, 1963; *The Short List* (novel), Hutchinson, 1964; *The Gift Bearers* (novel), Coward, 1966; *The House Party* (novel), Hutchinson, 1966; *The Fair Ladies of Salamanca* (novel), Hutchinson, 1967; *The Chanak Affair* (nonfiction), Macmillan, 1969; *The Short Victorious War: the Russo-Japanese Conflict, 1904-05,* Hutchinson, 1973. Also author with Julian Critchley, *Stability and Survival,* 1961. Contributor to *Purnell's History of the First World War.*

WORK IN PROGRESS: A biography of Nelson, publication by Harper expected in 1977.

AVOCATIONAL INTERESTS: Shooting, ornithology, opera.

WALDMAN, Milton 1895-1976

October 4, 1895—March 6, 1976; American playwright, biographer, editor, and publisher. Obituaries: *New York Times,* March 13, 1976; *Publishers Weekly,* March 29, 1976; *AB Bookman's Weekly,* April 26, 1976.

* * *

WALKER, Eric Anderson 1886-1976

September 6, 1886—March, 1976; British historian, educator, biographer, and author of books in his field. Obituaries: *AB Bookman's Weekly,* March 22, 1976. (*CAP*-2; earlier sketch in *CA*-13/14)

* * *

WALL, Maggie 1937-
(Margaret Wall)

PERSONAL: Born April 3, 1937, in Boston, Mass.; daughter of William (an investment banker) and Margaret (Macgill) Bayne; married Wayne Watson Wall (in insurance), May 7, 1955; children: Margaret Macgill, Wayne Watson, Jr., Hillary Jennings. *Education:* Attended school in Pittsfield, Mass. *Home:* 145 Mountain Spring Rd., Farmington, Conn. 06032. *Office:* Barbara Eyre Ltd., 246 Main St., Farmington, Conn. 06032.

CAREER: Needleloft Inc. (needlepoint store), Farmington, Conn., co-owner, 1969-74; Barbara Eyre Ltd. (wholesale needlepoint outlet), Farmington, Conn., manager of wholesale business, 1974—.

WRITINGS: (Under name Margaret Wall with Muriel Baker, Barbara Eyre, and Charlotte Westerfield) *Needlepoint: Design Your Own,* Scribner, 1974; *Creative Needlepoint Borders,* Scribner, in press.

WORK IN PROGRESS: Co-authoring a needlepoint design book with Barbara Eyre.

* * *

WALL, Margaret
See WALL, Maggie

* * *

WALLACE, Mike 1918-

PERSONAL: Given name, Myron Leon; born May 9, 1918, in Brookline, Mass.; son of Frank (an insurance broker) and Zina (Sharfman) Wallace; married Norma Kaphan, August 27, 1940 (divorced, 1948); married Buff Cobb (an actress), 1949 (divorced, 1955); married Lorraine Perigord (an artist), August 21, 1955; children: Peter (deceased), Christopher; Anthony, Pauline (stepchildren). *Education:* University of Michigan, A.B., 1939. *Religion:* Jewish. *Home:* 133 East 74th St., New York, N.Y. 10021. *Office:* CBS News, Columbia Broadcasting System, 524 West 57th St., New York, N.Y. 10019.

CAREER: WOOD-WASH Radio, Grand Rapids, Mich., newscaster, announcer, continuity writer, 1939-40; WXYZ-Radio, Detroit, Mich., newscaster, narrator, announcer, 1940-41; worked as free-lance for various radio stations in Chicago, Ill., and as announcer on soap opera "Road of Life," 1941-42; *Chicago Sun-Times,* Chicago, reporter on "Air Edition," 1941-43 and 1946-48; Columbia Broadcasting System (CBS), New York City, presented "Mike and Buff," 1951-54, host of several radio and television programs and narrated documentaries, 1952-56; WABD-TV, New York City, anchorman in newscasts and interviewer on "Night-Beat," 1956-57; American Broadcasting Co. (ABC), New York City, "The Mike Wallace Interview," 1957-59; *New York Post,* New York City, columnist, 1957-58; WNTA-TV, New York City, anchorman of "News Beat," 1959-61; CBS News, staff correspondent, 1963—, co-editor of "Sixty Minutes," 1968—. Co-producer of Mary Drayton's comedy, "Debut," in Matunuck, R.I., at Theatre-by-the-Sea, 1955; actor on Broadway in "Reclining Figure," 1954. Chairman of U.S. State Department cultural exchange delegation concerning television to the Soviet Union, 1958. *Military service:* U.S. Naval Reserve, 1943-46; submarine force communications officer, later in charge of radio entertainment; served in Pacific theater; became lieutenant junior grade.

MEMBER: American Federation of Television and Radio Artists, Academy of Television Arts and Sciences (executive vice-president, 1960-61), Sigma Delta Chi (fellow). *Awards, honors:* Boston Headliners award, 1957; Robert E. Sherwood award, 1957; National Academy of Television Arts and Sciences (Emmy) awards, 1957, 1958, 1971, 1972, and 1973; George Foster Peabody awards, 1963 and 1971; Alfred DuPont Journalism award, Columbia University, 1971-72.

WRITINGS: Mike Wallace Asks, Simon & Schuster, 1958. Writer of column, "Mike Wallace Asks," *New York Post,* 1957-58.

WORK IN PROGRESS: Autobiography.

SIDELIGHTS: Wallace first became well-known in radio and television for his interview programs, presenting controversial guests and asking them controversial and often uncomfortable questions. His goal was to air ideas, to stimulate his audience to think. Despite some comments that he treated his guests unfairly, Wallace answers that many people welcomed an opportunity to discuss in public matters that they could not present in more conventional ways.

AVOCATIONAL INTERESTS: Current affairs, reading, tennis.

BIOGRAPHICAL/CRITICAL SOURCES: New York Daily Mirror, February 4, 1957; *New York Post,* February 13, 1957; *New York Times,* April 17, 1957.

* * *

WALLACE, Myron Leon
See WALLACE, Mike

* * *

WALLACE, Pat 1929-
(Pat Wallace Latner; Claudia Patrick)

PERSONAL: Born March 11, 1929, in Birmingham, Ala.; daughter of Claude Hunter (in real estate) and Gladys Eleanor (English) Wallace; married Lee Levitt (a public relations executive), June, 1951 (divorced, 1957); married David Latner, August, 1958 (divorced 1969). *Education:* Attended University of Tennessee, 1947-51, and Columbia University, 1962. *Politics:* Liberal Democrat. *Religion:* None. *Home:* 117 West 13th St., New York, N.Y. 10011. *Agent:* John Payne, Lenniger Literary Agency, 437 Fifth Ave., New York, N.Y. 10016.

CAREER: WGNS-Radio, Murfreesboro, Tenn., women's program director, 1951-52; WMAK-Radio, Nashville, Tenn., copy chief and announcer, 1952-54; International Brotherhood of Teamsters, Local Union 237, New York City, clerical worker and editorial assistant on union paper, 1954-57, secretary to president, 1957-62; Civic Center

Clinic, Brooklyn, N.Y., secretary, 1962-66; International Brotherhood of Teamsters, Local Union 237, secretary to the president, 1966-76.

WRITINGS: (Under name Pat Wallace) *House of Scorpio,* Avon, 1975; (under pseudonym Claudia Patrick) *The Wand and the Star,* Simon & Schuster, in press, Contributor of short stories, under name Pat Wallace Latner, and poems to popular magazines, including *Mademoiselle, Beloit Poetry Journal,* and *Canadian Forum.*

WORK IN PROGRESS: A sequel to *House of Scorpio;* gothic and comic novels.

SIDELIGHTS: Pat Wallace writes: "I started writing poetry at eleven, and this was my major interest until 1971, when I began writing novels, and invented the astrological novel genre. My interest in astrology goes back to 1963 when Ree Dragonette . . . introduced me to the subject. Though I am not a professional astrologer, my studies and observations have been intense, encompassing fourteen years."

*   *   *

WALSH, William 1916-

PERSONAL: Born February 23, 1916, in London, England; son of William and Elizabeth (Kennedy) Walsh; married Toosey May Watson, 1945; children: Margaret, Timothy. *Education:* Cambridge University, M.A., 1945; University of London, M.A., 1951. *Religion:* Church of England. *Home:* 27 Moor Dr., Headingley, Leeds, West Yorkshire LS6 4BY, England. *Office:* School of English, University of Leeds, Leeds, West Yorkshire LS2 9JT, England.

CAREER: Schoolmaster in England, 1943-51; University College of North Staffordshire, North Staffordshire, England, lecturer in education, 1951-53; University of Edinburgh, Edinburgh, Scotland, lecturer in education, 1953-57; University of Leeds, Leeds, England, professor of education, 1957-72, professor of Commonwealth literature, 1972—, head of department of education, 1957-72, chairman of School of Education, 1969-72, chairman of board of Combined Faculties of Arts, Economics, Social Studies, and Law, 1964-66, pro-vice-chancellor, 1965-67, chairman of board of adult education, 1966—. Director of Yorkshire Television, 1967—. Member of Independent Broadcasting Authority's Adult Education Committee, 1974-76, and Education Advisory Committee, 1976—. *Member:* Royal Society of Arts (fellow). *Awards, honors:* Austrailian Commonwealth visiting fellow, 1970.

WRITINGS: Use of Imagination, Chatto & Windus, 1959; *A Human Idiom,* Chatto & Windus, 1965; *Coleridge: The Work and the Relevance,* Chatto & Windus, 1967; *A Manifold Voice: Studies in Commonwealth Literature,* Chatto & Windus, 1970; *R. K. Narayan,* Longmans, 1971; *V. S. Naipaul,* Oliver & Boyd, 1973; *Commonwealth Literature,* Oxford University Press, 1973; (editor) *Readings in Commonwealth Literature,* Clarendon Press, 1973; *D. J. Enright: Poet of Humanism,* Cambridge University Press, 1974; *Patrick White: "Voss",* Edward Arnold, 1976. Contributor to journals, including *Encounter, Spectator, New Statesman, New Review, Listener, Notes and Queries,* and *Sewanee Review.*

WORK IN PROGRESS: Writing about Patrick White and John Keats.

*   *   *

WALTERS, Barbara 1931-

PERSONAL: Born September 25, 1931, in Boston, Mass.; daughter of Lou (founder of "Latin Quarter" nightclub chain and theatrical producer) and Dena (Selett) Walters; married Lee Guber (a theatrical producer), December 8, 1963 (divorced, 1975); children: Jacqueline Dena. *Education:* Sarah Lawrence College, B.A., 1953. *Office:* American Broadcasting Co., 1330 Avenue of the Americas, New York, N.Y. 10019.

CAREER: Television writer and journalist. Began work in television as writer and producer for New York television stations, WRCA and WPIX; writer and news and public affairs producer for Columbia Broadcasting System (CBS)-TV; National Broadcasting Co. (NBC)-TV, New York City, writer for "Today" show, 1961-64, regular panel member, 1964-74, co-host, 1974-76; American Broadcasting Co. (ABC)-TV, New York City, co-anchor on "Evening News," 1976—. Former moderator of syndicated television show, "Not for Women Only," and radio shows, "Emphasis" and "Monitor." *Awards, honors:* L.H.D., Ohio State University, 1971, Marymount College (New York), 1975; named broadcasting woman of the year by *Ladies Home Journal,* 1974; National Academy of Television Arts and Sciences (Emmy) award as outstanding hostess in a talk service or variety series, 1975; broadcaster of the year award from International Radio and Television Society, 1975.

WRITINGS: How to Talk with Practically Anybody about Practically Anything, Doubleday, 1970. Contributor to periodicals.

BIOGRAPHICAL/CRITICAL SOURCES: Life, February 18, 1966, June 23, 1972, July 14, 1972; *Newsweek,* May 19, 1969, July 2, 1973, May 6, 1974, May 3, 1976; *House Beautiful,* October, 1970; *Seventeen,* January, 1971; *Look,* February 9, 1971; *Time,* February 21, 1972, May 3, 1976; *Harper's Bazaar,* September, 1972, August, 1973; *New York Times Magazine,* September 10, 1972; Barbaralee Diamonstein, *Open Secrets,* Viking, 1972; *Ladies' Home Journal,* April, 1974; *Saturday Review,* June 12, 1976, June 26, 1976; *Progressive,* August, 1976.

*   *   *

WALTERS, Dorothy 1928-

PERSONAL: Born March 17, 1928, in Edmond, Okla.; daughter of R. A. and Lois E. (Jones) Walters. *Education:* Attended Central State College (now University), Edmond, Okla., 1944-46; University of Oklahoma, B.A., 1948, B.A.L.S., 1951, Ph.D., 1960. *Politics:* Democrat. *Home:* 3425 East English, Apt. 406, Wichita, Kan. 67218. *Office:* Office of Women's Studies, Wichita State University, Wichita, Kan. 67208.

CAREER: University of Colorado, Boulder, instructor, 1960-62, assistant professor of English, 1962-67; Wichita State University, Wichita, Kan., associate professor of English, 1967—, coordinator of women's studies, 1975—. *Member:* Modern Language Association of America, American Association of University Professors, American Civil Liberties Union, Women's Political Caucus, Kansans for ERA.

WRITINGS: Flannery O'Connor, Twayne, 1973; (editor with Carol Konek, and contributor) *I Hear My Sisters Saying: Poems by Twentieth-Century Women,* Crowell, 1976. Contributor to literature journals.

WORK IN PROGRESS: Editing *Women and Mysticism,* a book of essays; research on contemporary women writers in England.

SIDELIGHTS: Dorothy Walters writes: "My primary research interest is in writing by women, especially women poets today. I view the women's movement as an expression of the feminine principle manifest in earlier societies through the mother cults, then suppressed for centuries. The current vogue for the mystical and the occult likewise are attached to the revival of the feminine, as well as the infusion of the West by Eastern ideas."

AVOCATIONAL INTERESTS: "Studying the mystics who, in my view, transcend both sex and location."

* * *

WALTERS, Thomas N(oble) 1935-

PERSONAL: Born November 17, 1935, in Tarboro, N.C.; son of Thomas Edward (a farmer) and Vivian (Noble) Walters; married Linda Ball (a scriptwriter), August 9, 1974. *Education:* University of North Carolina, A.B. (honors), 1958; Duke University, M.A.T., 1963, Ed.D., 1968. *Home:* 5211 Melbourne Rd., Raleigh, N.C. 27606. *Office:* Department of English and English Education, North Carolina State University, Hillsborough, Raleigh, N.C. 27607.

CAREER: Teacher in public schools in Raleigh, N.C., 1962-64; North Carolina State University, Raleigh, instructor, 1964-68, assistant professor, 1968-72, associate professor of English and education, 1972—. Guest lecturer at Converse College, summer, 1969; chairman of North Carolina Writers Conference, 1975. Has given poetry readings at colleges and universities. *Military service:* U.S. Marine Corps, 1958-60; became second lieutenant.

MEMBER: National Council of Teachers of English, American Association of University Professors, North Carolina English Teachers Association, North Carolina Conservation Council, Kappa Delta Pi. *Awards, honors:* National Endowment for the Arts creative writing fellowship, 1973; North Carolina Poetry Society, first prize in contest, 1969, Special Awards Cup, 1973, for *Seeing in the Dark,* second prizes, 1970 and 1974.

WRITINGS: (Editor with Allen F. Stein) *The Southern Experience in Short Fiction* (anthology), Scott, Foresman, 1971; *Seeing in the Dark* (poems), Moore Publishing, 1972; *Always Next August* (juvenile novel), Moore Publishing, 1976; *The Loblolly Excalibur and a Crown of Shagbark* (poems), North Carolina Review Press, 1976.

Work has been anthologized in *Strange Things Happen,* edited by Bernice Kelly Harris, Johnson Publishing, 1971; *The Best Short Stories of 1971,* edited by Martha Foley, Houghton, 1972; *Poems for the Outer Banks,* edited by E. R. Platt, Loom Press, 1974. Contributor of articles, poems, and reviews to literary journals, including *Carolina Quarterly, Epos, Red Clay Reader, Southern Poetry Review, Crucible, Denver Quarterly,* and to newspapers.

WORK IN PROGRESS: Randolph Bourne: An American Radical; Carteret Island, a juvenile novel.

SIDELIGHTS: Walters has had one-man shows of his paintings, prints, and sculptures in Raleigh galleries.

* * *

WALTHAM, Antony Clive 1942-

PERSONAL: Born June 18, 1942, in Birmingham, England; son of Clive (a surveyor) and Mary (Platts) Waltham; married Janet Gore, December 16, 1963 (separated, 1975); children: Sam, Megan. *Education:* Earned B.Sc., D.I.C., and Ph.D. from Imperial College of Science and Technology, University of London. *Office:* Department of Civil Engi-

neering, Trent Polytechnic, Nottingham NG1 4BU, England.

CAREER: Trent Polytechnic, Nottingham, England, lecturer in geology, 1968—. *Member:* Royal Geographical Society (fellow), British Cave Research Association. *Awards, honors:* Winston Churchill Memorial Trust travel fellowship, 1970.

WRITINGS: (Editor) *Limestone and Caves of Northwest England,* David & Charles, 1974; *Caves,* Castle, 1974; *The World of Caves,* Putnam, 1976. Contributor to geology and cave research journals. Editor for British Cave Research Association, 1973—.

WORK IN PROGRESS: Geology of Catastrophe, publication by Macmillan (England) expected in 1978; research on the origins and development of limestone caves.

SIDELIGHTS: Waltham writes: "From schooldays I was interested in geography and travel, but then went to study geology because it seemed more promising career-wise than geography. While at University I was persuaded to go caving, on the principle of trying anything, but I got hooked on the sport of underground exploration. I drifted into teaching because it was the only occupation to give long summer vacations for travel, but then found teaching was my true vocation anyway, and I have developed it along the lines of practical and applied geology, well away from remote academic principles. My parallel interest in caving has developed to include geological research into cave development, but also has prompted very extensive travel.... Besides visiting nearly every country in Europe ... , I have led or joined expeditions to caves in Greece, Nepal, Iran, Canada, and Jamaica, but most of all I enjoy caving and consider myself fortunate to enjoy what is also my work."

* * *

WALTON, Ronald (Gordon) 1936-

PERSONAL: Born May 5, 1936, in Aldershot, England; son of Herbert (a policeman) and Phyllis (Underwood) Walton; married Pamela Denise Worrender, August 1, 1961; children: Susan, Catherine, Nancy. *Education:* University of Manchester, B.A., 1960, M.A., 1967, Ph.D., 1972. *Home:* 14 Beechwood Dr., Penarth, South Glamorganshire, Wales. *Office:* University College, University of Wales, Cardiff, South Glamorganshire, Wales.

CAREER: Child care worker and social worker in Oldham, England, 1960-65; University of Manchester, Manchester, England, lecturer in social work, 1965-72; University of Wales, University College, Cardiff, lecturer in social work, 1972—. Trustee of Riverside Community Center, 1975—. *Military service:* Royal Air Force, 1955-57. *Member:* British Association of Social Workers, Association of University Teachers.

WRITINGS: Women in Social Work, Routledge & Kegan Paul, 1975; (contributor) Howard Jones, editor, *Towards a New Social Work,* Routledge & Kegan Paul, 1975; (contributor) Kathleen Jones, editor, *Year Book of Social Policy in Britain, 1974,* Routledge & Kegan Paul, 1975.

WORK IN PROGRESS: Research on social work professions, organization of social work, and residential social work.

SIDELIGHTS: Walton writes: "I am particularly stimulated by trying to unravel the place of social work in society.... For the future I hope to see social work as a profession setting a new style of commitment from the traditional..."

WALTON, Vicki (Elizabeth) 1949-

PERSONAL: Born March 20, 1949, in Tacoma, Wash.; daughter of Willard Delefield (an Army major) and Bertha F. (a bookkeeper; maiden name, Petzke) Johnson; married Philip H. Walton (a technical representative), July 9, 19719 children: Alisa Victoria, Ami Michele, Tria Nicole. *Education:* University of Puget Sound, student, 1966-69; University of Washington, Seattle, B.A., 1975. *Religion:* Baptist. *Home:* 19316 3rd Ave. N.W., Seattle, Wash. 98177.

CAREER: Preparing Expectant Parents, Inc., Seattle, Wash., instructor in childbirth preparation, 1975—; Henry Philips Publishing Co., Seattle, Wash., senior editor, 1976—. Free-lance photographer and public relations representative. *Member:* Women in Communications.

WRITINGS: Have It Your Way: An Overview of Pregnancy, Labor and Postpartum Including Alternatives Available in the Hospital Childbirth Experience, Henry Philips Publishing, 1976. Contributor to local newspapers.

WORK IN PROGRESS: Research on childbirth practices in America and on how American obstetrics influences infant mortality and morbidity.

SIDELIGHTS: Vicki Walton writes: "It is extremely important for expectant parents to know about the alternatives available in childbirth—especially the alternatives available in the hospital setting. Many parents do not know enough to question the typical, traditional methods of giving birth. It is vitally important for expectant parents to be consumers of the care that they are getting. Childbirth is not an illness, nor a disease; it is something that can be safely handled in a multitude of ways. Some of these ways can make the experience more fulfilling. Many of the ways can also contribute to the safety and health of the child. Parents must be made aware of the alternatives available in order to make responsible choices."

*   *   *

WANG, Hao 1921-

PERSONAL: Born May 20, 1921, in Tsinan, Shantung, China; son of Chuchen and Tsecheng (Liu) Wang; married Yenking Kan, June 22, 1948 (separated March 1, 1972); children: Sanyu, Yiming, Jane Hsiaoching. *Education:* Southwestern Associated University (China), A.B., 1943; Tsing Hua Universsity (China), A.M., 1945; Harvard University, Ph.D., 1948; University of Zurich, postdoctoral study, 1950-51; Oxford University, M.A., 1956. *Home:* New York, N.Y. 10021. *Office:* Rockefeller University, 1230 York Ave., New York, N.Y. 10021.

CAREER: Teacher of mathematics in schools in China, 1943-46; Harvard University, Cambridge, Mass., fellow, 1948-51, assistant professor of philosophy, 1951-56; Oxford University, Oxford, England, reader in philosophy of mathematics, 1956-61; Harvard University, Cambridge, Mass., Gordon McKay Professor of Mathematical Logic and Applied Mathematics, 1961-67; Rockefeller University, New York, N.Y., professor of mathematics, 1967—. John Locke Lecturer in Philosophy, Oxford University, 1955. Research engineer, Burroughs Corp., 1953-54; member technical staff, Bell Telephone Laboratories, 1959-60; visiting scientist, I.B.M. Research Center, 1973-74; visiting scholar, Institute of Advanced Study, Princeton, 1975-76. *Member:* American Academy of Arts and Sciences (fellow), British Academy (foreign fellow), Association of Symbolic Logic. *Awards, honors:* Rockefeller Foundation fellow, 1954-55.

WRITINGS: A Survey of Mathematical Logic, Science Press (Peking), 1962, published as *Logic, Computers and Sets,* Chelsea, 1970; *Reflections on a Visit to China* (in Chinese), Seventies Publishing, 1973; *From Mathematics to Philosophy,* Routledge & Kegan Paul, 1974. Contributor of aritcles to mathematic and philosophic journals.

WORK IN PROGRESS: Presuppositions in the study of nature and society: "special attention will be paid to the contrast between formal and dialectical thinking, specialization and division of labor, technology and modernization, human nature and private property."

*   *   *

WANG Gungwu 1930-

PERSONAL: Born October 9, 1930, in Surabaya, Indonesia; son of Fo-wen (an educator) and Yen (Ting) Wang; married Margaret Ping-Ting Lim (a teacher), December 21, 1955; children: Shih-Chang (son), Lin-Chang and Hui-Chang (daughters). *Education:* Attended National Central University, Nanking, China, 1947-49; University of Malaya, B.A. (honors), 1953, M.A., 1955; School of Oriental and African Studies, London, Ph.D., 1957.*Home:* 77 Banambila St., Aranda, Canberra, Australian Capital Territory 2614, Australia. *Office:* Research School of Pacific Studies, Australian National University, Canberra, Australian Capital Territory 2600, Australia.

CAREER: University of Malaya (now University of Singapore), Singapore, lecturer in history, 1957-59; University of Malaya, Kuala Lumpur, Malaysia, began as lecturer, became professor of history, 1959-68; Australian National University, Canberra, professor of Far Eastern history, 1968—, head of department, 1968-75, director of Research School Pacific Studies, 1975—. Visiting senior fellow, School of Oriental and African Studies, London, 1971-72; visiting fellow, All Souls College, Oxford, 1974-75. Member of Commission of Inquiry on Singapore Riots, 1964-65; Chairman of Nanyang University Curriculum Review Committee, 1964-65. *Member:* International Association for Historians of Asia (president, 1964-68), American Oriental Society, Association for Asian Studies, Malaysian Branch Royal Asiatic Society (vice-president, 1952-68), Nanyang Hsueh-Hui (councillor, 1958-68), Australian Historical Society, Australian Academy of the Humanities (fellow, 1970—). *Awards, honors:* Rockefeller fellow, School of Oriental and African Studies, London, 1961-62.

WRITINGS: Pulse (verse), Beda Lim (Singapore), 1950; *The Nanhai Trade: A Study of the Early History of Chinese Trade in the South China Sea,* Malayan Branch Royal Asiatic Society (Singapore), 1958; *A Short History of the Nanyang Chinese,* Eastern Universities Press (Singapore), 1959; *Latar Belakang Kebudayaan Pendudok di-Tanah Melayu: Bahagian Kebudayaan China* (title means "The Cultural Background of the Peoples of Malaya: Chinese Culture"), Dewan Bahasa dan Pustaka (Kuala Lumpur), 1962; *The Structure and Power in North China during the Five Dynasties,* Stanford University Press, 1963, 2nd edition, 1967; (editor and author of introduction) *Malaysia: A Survey,* Praeger, 1964; (author of introduction) John Cameron, *Our Tropical Possessions in Malayan India,* Oxford University Press, 1965; *The Use of History,* Ohio University Center for International Studies, 1968; (author of introduction) Isabella Bird, *The Golden Chersonese and the Way Thither,* Oxford University Press, 1968; (editor with S. T. Alisjahbana and X. S. Thani Nayagam and contributor) *The Cultural Problems of Malaysia in the Context of Southeast Asia,* Malaysian Society of Orientalists (Kuala Lumpur),

1968; (editor with Donald Leslie and C. P. Mackerras and contributor) *Essays on the Sources for Chinese History,* Australian National University Press, 1974; (editor, contributor, and author of introduction) *Self and Biography: Essays on the Individual and Society in Asia,* Sydney University Press, 1976.

Contributor: Arthur F. Wright and Denis Twitchett, editors, *Confucian Personalities,* Stanford University Press, 1962; Margaret Grant, editor, *South Asia Pacific Crisis: National Development and the World Community,* Dodd, 1964; J. S. Bastin and Roelof Roolvink, editors, *Malayan and Indonesian Studies: Festschrift for Richard Winstedt,* Oxford University Press, 1964; Raghavan Iyer, editor, *The Glass Curtain between Europe and Asia,* Oxford University Press, 1965; Gehan Wijeyewardene, editor, *Leadership and Authority: A Symposium,* University of Malaya Press, 1968; J. K. Fairbank, editor, *The Chinese World Order: Traditional China's Foreign Relations,* Harvard University Press, 1968; Jerome Chen and Nicholas Tarling, editors, *Social History of China and Southeast Asia,* Cambridge University Press, 1970; Herbert Franke and others, *Saeculum Weltgeschichte,* Volume VI, Herder (Freiburg), 1971; G. C. Bolton, editor, *Everyman in Australia,* University of Western Australia Press, 1972; Bernard Grossmann, editor, *Southeast Asia in the Modern World,* Otto Harrassowitz (Wiesbaden), 1972; Arthur F. Wright and Denis Twitchett, editors, *Perspectives on the T'ang,* Yale University Press, 1973; Eugene Kamenka, editor, *Nationalism: The Nature and Evolution of an Idea,* Australian University Press, 1973; A. P. Elkin and N.W.G. McIntosh, editors, *Grafton Elliott-Smith: The Man and His Work,* Sydney University Press, 1974; C. D. Cowan and O. W. Wolters, editors, *Southeast Asian History and Historiography,* Cornell University Press, 1976; J.A.C. Mackie, editor, *The Chinese in Indonesia: Five Essays,* Nelson, 1976.

Work represented in anthologies, *Litmus One,* edited by Lloyd Fernando, University of Malaya, Raffles Society, 1958; *Compact,* edited by Herman Hochstadt, University of Malaya, Raffles Society, 1959; *Bunga Emas: An Anthology of Contemporary Malaysian Literature, 1930-1963,* edited by Thuraiappah Wignesan, Anthony Blond, 1964; and *Twenty-Two Malaysian Stories,* edited by Fernando, Heinemann (Hong Kong), 1968. Contributor to *Proceedings* of International Conference on Maritime History and of Second Asian Workshop on Higher Education; contributor to *Encyclopaedia of the Social Sciences;* contributor of poems, essays, and short stories to periodicals, including *Malayan Undergrad, New Cauldron,* and *Lydra;* contributor of articles to journals in his field.

General editor, "East Asian Historical Monographs" series, Oxford University Press, 1969—; editor with J.A.C. Mackie, "Studies in Contemporary Southeast Asia" series, Longman, 1973—; honorary editor, *Nanyang Hsueh-pao,* 1958-61, *Journal of the Malaysian Branch Royal Asiatic Society,* 1963-68.

WORK IN PROGRESS: A study on China and Southeast Asia during the Ming Dynasty; research on political life of the overseas Chinese in Southeast Asia, and on the transition to modern Chinese historiography.

* * *

WARD, Benedicta 1933-

PERSONAL: Born February 4, 1933, in Durham, England; daughter of Oswald Alleyn (a minister) and Florence Susannah (Linnet) Ward. *Education:* University of Manchester, B.A. (honors), 1955; St. Anne's College, Oxford, D.Phil., 1977. *Home:* Convent of the Incarnation, Fairacres, Oxford, England.

CAREER: Member of a contemplative enclosed order of women religious in the Church of England. Lecturer in England and the United States.

WRITINGS: Prayers and Meditations of St. Anselm, Penguin, 1973; *The Sayings of the Desert Fathers,* Mowbrays, 1975; *The Wisdom of the Desert Fathers,* SLG Press, 1975; (editor and contributor) *The Influence of St. Bernard,* SLG Press, 1976.

Contributor: M. Basil Pennington, editor, *Contemplative Community,* Cistercian Publication, 1972; Pennington, editor, *Bernard of Clairvaux,* Cistercian Publications, 1973; Pennington, editor, *One Yet Two,* Cistercian Publications, 1976. Also contributor to *Famulus Christi,* edited by G. Bonner, 1976.

WORK IN PROGRESS: Several religious articles and translations for Cistercian Publications; translating William of Malmesbury's *Gesta Pontificum.*

* * *

WARD, Stephen R(alph) 1938-

PERSONAL: Born October 24, 1938, in Elwood, Iowa; son of John Woodford (a teacher) and Eve (a teacher; maiden name, Vines) Ward; married Ann Kincaid, June 10, 1961; children: Stephen, Britton. *Education:* DePauw University, A.B., 1960; University of Cincinnati, M.A., 1964, Ph.D., 1969. *Home:* 623 East Main St., Vermillion, S.D. 57069. *Office:* Department of History, University of South Dakota, Vermillion, S.D. 57069.

CAREER: Lecturer in history at Wilmington College, Wilmington, Ohio, 1966, and University of Cincinnati, Cincinnati, Ohio, 1967; University of South Dakota, Vermillion, assistant professor, 1967-71, associate professor, 1971-76, professor of history, 1976—, chairman of department, 1973—. Member of Fulbright fellowship selection committee. *Member:* U.S. Air Force, 1960-63; became first lieutenant. *Member:* American Historical Association, Association of Contemporary Historians, Conference on British Studies. *Awards, honors:* American Council of Learned Societies grant, 1976.

WRITINGS: (Editor with Robert Sorey, Michael Ledeen, Donald Lisio, and James Diehl) *The War Generation: Veterans of the First World War,* Kennikat, 1975; (with Joseph Cash, Ramon Harris, and Herbert T. Hoover) *The Practice of Oral History,* Microfilming Corp., 1975.

WORK IN PROGRESS: A biography of J. Ramsay MacDonald, including research in England, completion expected in 1979.

* * *

WARE, Gilbert 1933-

PERSONAL: Born July 21, 1933, in Elkton, Va. *Education:* Morgan State University, B.A., 1955; Princeton University, M.A., 1961, Ph.D., 1962. *Residence:* Voorhees, N.J. *Office:* Department of History and Politics, Drexel University, Philadelphia, Pa. 19104.

CAREER: Morgan State University, Baltimore, Md., assistant professor of political science and assistant director of Institute for Political Education, 1962-63; University of Pennsylvania, Philadelphia, assistant professor of political science at Fels Institute, 1963-64; U.S. Commission on Civil

Rights, Washington, D.C., assistant director of Federal Programs Division, 1964-67; program executive on staff of the governor of Maryland, in Annapolis, 1967-68; Washington Technical Institute, Washington, D.C., executive assistant to the president, 1968-69; Urban Institute, Washington, D.C., member of senior research staff, 1969-70; Drexel University, Philadelphia, Pa., assistant professor of political science, 1970—. Executive director of Judicial Council of the National Bar Association. *Military service:* U.S. Army, Military Police, 1955-59; served in Germany; became first lieutenant.

MEMBER: American Academy of Political and Social Science, American Society of Criminology, Oral History Association, National Association for the Advancement of Colored People. *Awards, honors:* Fellow of Metropolitan Applied Research Center, 1972.

WRITINGS: From the Black Bar: Voices for Equal Justice, Putnam, 1976. Contributor of about fifteen articles to law and Black studies journals.

WORK IN PROGRESS: Continuing research on black lawyers and judges in American life and politics.

AVOCATIONAL INTERESTS: Photography, tennis, music.

* * *

WARMBRAND, Max 1896(?)-1976

1896(?)—June 2, 1976; Austrian-born American nutritionist and author. Obituaries: *New York Times,* June 3, 1976.

* * *

WARMINGTON, Brian Herbert 1924-

PERSONAL: Born August 19, 1924, in London, England; son of Eric Herbert (a professor) and Marian Eveline (Robertson) Warmington; married Suzanne Cowell, September 15, 1945; children: Sally, Rachel. *Education:* Cambridge University, B.A., 1948, M.A., 1950. *Home:* 178 Kingfisher Rd., Chipping Sodbury, Bristol, England. *Office:* Department of Classics, University of Bristol, Bristol BS8 1TH, England.

CAREER: University of Bristol, Bristol, England, assistant lecturer in classics, 1951-54, lecturer in ancient history, 1954-61, reader in ancient history, 1961—, deputy dean of Faculty of Arts, 1970-72. *Member:* Society for the Promotion of Roman Studies (member of executive council, 1961-63, 1967-70), Association of University Teachers (president of Bristol branch, 1967-70), Old Millhillians Club (London).

WRITINGS: The North African Provinces From Diocletian to the Vandal Conquest, Cambridge University Press, 1954; *Carthage,* Praeger, 1960, revised edition, 1969; *Nero: Reality and Legend,* Chatto & Windus, 1969, Norton, 1970. Contributor of articles to *Oxford Classical Dictionary, Encyclopaedia Britannica,* and to scholarly journals in his field.

WORK IN PROGRESS: Constantine and the Constantinian Dynasty.

AVOCATIONAL INTERESTS: European travel, music, conservation activities, spending time in the country.

* * *

WARNER, Kenneth Wilson, Jr. 1928-

PERSONAL: Born December 22, 1928, in Chicago, Ill.; son of Kenneth Wilson and Ann S. (Knapp) Warner; married Gail Marjorie Halling, March 30, 1968; children: Sara, Seth. *Education:* Northern Illinois University, B.S.Ed., 1950.

Home: 6510 Valley Court, Falls Church, Va. 22042. *Office:* National Rifle Association, 1600 Rhode Island Ave. N.W., Washington, D.C. 20036.

CAREER: Building Supply News, Chicago, Ill., staff editor, 1953-56; *Merchandising Week,* Chicago, regional editor, 1956-60; free-lance writer, 1960-66; *Gunsport,* Alexandria and Falls Church, Va., editor, 1966-67; *Funfacts,* Arlington, Va., editor and publisher, 1968-70; National Rifle Association, Washington, D.C., executive editor of *American Rifleman,* 1971—, assistant director of Publications Division, 1972—, editor of *American Hunter,* 1973—, executive editor of National Rifle Association publications, 1977—. *Military service:* U.S. Army, 1951-53. *Member:* National Rifle Association (life member), Outdoor Writers Association, American Knifemakers Guild Association (associate).

WRITINGS: The Practical Book of Knives, Winchester Press, 1976; (editor) Stuart Otteson, *The Bolt Action,* Winchester Press, 1976. Contributor to professional journals and popular magazines.

WORK IN PROGRESS: Guns and Gear for Survival, 1977; *The Practical Book of Guns;* a book on knives, completion expected in 1978; a novel, with a survival theme, 1978.

* * *

WARNER, Marina 1946-

PERSONAL: Born November 9, 1946, in London, England; daughter of Esmund (a bookseller) and Emilia (a teacher; maiden name Terzulli) Warner; married William Shawcross (a journalist), January 31, 1972. *Education:* Lady Margaret Hall, Oxford, M.A., 1967. *Religion:* None. *Agent:* A. D. Peters, 10 Buckingham St., London W.C. 2, England.

CAREER: Writer. *Awards, honors: Daily Telegraph* Young Writer of the Year Award, 1970.

WRITINGS: (Contributor) *Women,* Collins, 1971; (contributor) Margaret Laing, editor, *Woman on Woman,* Sidgwick & Jackson, 1972; *The Dragon Empress,* Macmillan, 1972; *Alone of All Her Sex: The Myth and the Cult of the Virgin Mary,* Knopf, 1976. Contributor to *New Statesman, Vogue,* and London *Daily Telegraph.*

WORK IN PROGRESS: In a Dark Wood, a novel for Knopf, publication expected, 1977; research on Joan of Arc.

SIDELIGHTS: Warner indicates that she is interested "especially in religious motives and in the pressure they can exert on societies not organised to listen to them."

* * *

WASHINGTON, Mary Helen 1941-

PERSONAL: Born January 21, 1941, in Cleveland, Ohio; daughter of David C. and Mary Catherine (Dalton) Washington. *Education:* Notre Dame College, B.A., 1962; University of Detroit, M.A., 1966, Ph.D., 1976. *Office:* Center for Black Studies, University of Detroit, Detroit, Mich. 48221.

CAREER: High school teacher of English in the public schools of Cleveland, Ohio, 1962-64; St. John College, Cleveland, Ohio, instructor in English, 1966-68; University of Detroit, Detroit, Mich., assistant professor of English, 1972-75, director of Center for Black Studies, 1975—. *Member:* National Council of Teachers of English, College Language Association, Michigan Black Studies Association.

WRITINGS: (Editor and author of introduction) *Black-Eyed Susans: Classic Stories By and About Black Women,*

Doubleday, 1975. Contributor of articles and reviews to *Negro Digest* and *Black World*.

WORK IN PROGRESS: Contributing to an anthology of women writers.

* * *

WASSERMAN, Sheldon 1940-

PERSONAL: Born December 17, 1940, in Boston, Mass.; son of Myer (a laborer) and Florence (Youngstein) Wasserman; married Pauline MacKenzie (a writer), April 17, 1963. *Education:* Attended schools in Providence, R.I. *Home and office:* 1 Liberty St., #63, Little Ferry, N.J. 07643.

CAREER: Honeywell Co., programmer analyst in Massachusetts and Colorado, 1963-65, programmer analyst in technical operations in Maryland, 1965, programmer analyst in computer applications in Massachusetts, 1966-67; RCA Corp., worked in Massachusetts, New Jersey, and Germany as systems designer analyst, systems programmer analyst, and regional systems specialist, 1967-71; Delta Resources, senior programmer analyst in New York, 1972-75; free-lance programmer and systems analyst, 1975—. *Military service:* U.S. Army Reserve, active duty, 1958-61. *Member:* Les Amis du Vin (regional director, 1972—).

WRITINGS: The Wines of Italy: A Consumers Guide, Stein & Day, 1976; *The Wines of the Cotes du Rhone,* Stein & Day, 1977; (with wife, Pauline Wasserman) *Don't Ask Your Waiter,* Stein & Day, in press. Contributor to *Cue* and *Free Interprise.* Associate editor, *Wine;* contributing editor, *Beverage Retailer Weekly.*

WORK IN PROGRESS: In Gold We Trust: Causes and Solution to Current International Monetary Mess; Zinfandel: A Grape and Its Wines, with wife, Pauline Wasserman.

SIDELIGHTS: Wasserman writes: "I am interested in writing a series of books on little-known wine areas, including Alsace and Loire Valley. I am also interested in economics, specifically monetary policy." *Avocational interests:* Travel "and related research with respect to food, wines, the people and their customs and history."

* * *

WATERHOUSE, Ellis Kirkham 1905-

PERSONAL: Born February 16, 1905; son of P. Leslie and Eleanor (Margetson) Waterhouse; married Helen Thomas, in 1949; children: two daughters. *Education:* New College, Oxford, M.A.; Princeton University, A.M. *Home:* Overshot, Hinksey Hill, Oxford, England.

CAREER: National Gallery, London, England, assistant, 1929-33; British School at Rome, Rome, Italy, librarian, 1933-36; selected and catalogued material for Royal Academy Exhibition of Seventeenth Century Art, 1937; temporary editor, *Burlington* (magazine), 1946; University of Manchester, Manchester, England, reader in history and art, 1947-48; National Galleries of Scotland, Edinburgh, director, 1949-52; University of Birmingham, Birmingham, England, Barber Professor of Fine Arts and director of Barber Institute, 1952-70; Paul Mellon Centre for Studies in British Art, director of studies, 1970-74. Fellow of Magdalen College, Oxford, 1938-47; Slade Professor of Fine Arts at Oxford University, 1953-55; Clark Visiting Professor at Williams College, 1962-63; Mellon Visiting Professor at University of Pittsburgh, 1967-68; Kren Professor, National Gallery, Washington, D.C., 1975-76. Served with His Majesty's

Foreign Service in the Middle East. Member of executive committee of National Art Collections Fund, 1972—. *Military service:* British Army.

MEMBER: British Academy (fellow), Royal Historical Association (fellow). *Awards, honors:* Commonwealth Fund fellow at Princeton University, 1927-29; member of the Order of the British Empire, 1943, commander, 1956; officer to the Order of Orange Nassau; Cavaliere ufficiale of Ordino al Merito della Repubblica italiana, 1961; D.Litt. from University of Nottingham, 1968, University of Leicester, 1970, and from University of Birmingham and Oxford University, 1976; Knight Bachelor, 1975.

WRITINGS: El Greco's Italian Period, Harvard & Princeton Art Studies, 1930; *Baroque Painting in Rome, the Seventeenth Century,* Macmillan, 1937, revised ed., Phaidon, 1976; *Sir Joshua Reynolds,* Kegan Paul & Co., 1941; *Titian's Diana and Actaeon,* Oxford University Press, 1952; *Painting in Britain, 1530-1790,* Penguin, 1953, 3rd edition, 1969; (editor) *Preliminary Check List of Portraits by Thomas Gainsborough,* Oxford University Press, 1953; *Italian Art and Britain,* Royal Academy of Arts, 1960; *Gainsborough,* E. Hulton, 1958, new edition, Spring Books, 1966; *The Collection of Pictures in Helmingham Hall,* privately printed, 1958.

Paintings: The James A. de Rothschild Collection at Waddesdon Manor, Shenval Press, 1962; *Italian Baroque Painting,* Phaidon, 1962, 2nd edition, 1969; *El Greco,* Purnell, 1965; *Three Decades of British Art, 1740-1770,* American Philosophical Society, 1965; *Reynolds's "Sitter Book" for 1755,* University of Glasgow Press, 1968; *Reynolds,* Phaidon, 1973. Author of catalogs; contributor to professional journals.

* * *

WATERS, Michael 1949-

PERSONAL: Born November 23, 1949, in New York, N.Y.; son of Raymond G. (a detective) and Dorothy (a professional tennis player; maiden name, Smith) Waters; married Robin Irwin (a dancer), May 13, 1972. *Education:* State University of New York College at Brockport, B.A., 1971, M.A., 1972; University of Nottingham, graduate study, 1970-71; University of Iowa, M.F.A., 1974; Ohio University, Ph.D., 1977. *Home:* 255 Albany Rd., Athens, Ohio 45701. *Office:* Department of English, Ohio University, Ellis Hall, Athens, Ohio 45701.

CAREER: Poet. South Carolina Arts Commission, Columbia, S.C., poet-in-residence, 1974-75; New York Arts Council, New York, N.Y., poet-in-the-schools, 1975. *Awards, honors:* National Young Poets award from London Poetry Society (England), 1971; award for excellence in poetry from Winthrop College, 1975, for *Fish Light.*

WRITINGS—Poems: A Rare Breed of Antelope, Byron Press, 1972; *Fish Light,* Ithaca House, 1975; *In Memory of Smoke,* Peaceweed Press, 1976.

Work has been anthologized in *The Ardis Anthology of New American Poetry,* edited by David Rigsbee, Ardis, 1976; *Holocaust,* edited by Lucy Steinitz, Bloch Publishing, 1976; *Bicentennial Anthology,* edited by James Scrimgeour, Illinois State University Press, 1976; *Intro,* edited by George Garrett, Doubleday, in press. Contributor to literary magazines, including *American Poetry Review, Modern Poetry Studies, Poetry Now, Sumac,* and *Southern Poetry Review,* and to *Rolling Stone.* Editorial assistant for *Ohio Review,* 1976-77.

WORK IN PROGRESS: Biography of a German mystic, *John Skoyles: His Mind and Logic* (tentative title).

*   *   *

WATKINS, Mark Hanna   1903-1976

November 23, 1903—February 24, 1976; American anthropologist, linguist, educator, and author of books in his field. Obituaries: *Washington Post,* February 27, 1976.

*   *   *

WATSON, Eunice L.   1932-

PERSONAL: Born March 21, 1932, in Puposky, Minn.; daughter of Roy M. (a carpenter) and Theo (a secretary; maiden name, Albano) Watson. *Education:* Boise Junior College, A.A., 1952; Lewis and Clark College, B.A., 1954; University of British Columbia, M.S.W., 1959. *Home:* 3357 Southwest Fir Ridge Rd., Lake Oswego, Ore. 97034. *Office:* Counseling Service, Reed College, Portland, Ore. 97202.

CAREER: State of Oregon, Public Welfare, social case worker in St. Helens, 1955-57, and Oregon City, 1959-61; social worker in elementary and secondary schools in Portland, Ore., 1961-65; day care consultant in Portland, Ore., 1965-69; Reed College, Portland, Ore., psychiatric social worker, 1969—. Liaison social worker for Child Welfare League of America, 1966-67; instructor for Oregon State Board of Higher Education, 1972-74, and Portland State University, 1972-75, spring, 1970; psychiatric social worker for Kaiser Foundation Hospitals, summer, 1972; private practice as a psychiatric social worker, 1974—. *Member:* National Association of Social Workers (board member of Oregon chapter, 1976-77), Academy of Certified Social Workers, Oregon Social Welfare Association.

WRITINGS: (With Alice H. Collins) *A Handbook for the Organization and Operation of a New Approach to Family Day Care,* privately printed, 1969; (with Arthur C. Emlen) *Matchmaking in Neighborhood Day Care: A Descriptive Study of the Day Care Neighbor Service,* privately printed, 1970; (with A. H. Collins) *Family Day Care: A Guide for Parents, Professionals, and Caregivers,* Beacon Press, 1976. Contributor to journals in the social sciences.

WORK IN PROGRESS: Analysis of data on student patients from Reed College.

AVOCATIONAL INTERESTS: Travel (Europe and the Far East), musical activities, reading.

*   *   *

WATSON, John A(rthur) F(ergus)   1903-

PERSONAL: Born July 24, 1903, son of J. G. Maitland (a captain in the Royal Artillery) and Mabel (Weir) Watson; married Joan Leigh, 1948; children: John George, Jane Margaret. *Education:* Attended private school in Rutland, England. *Home:* Elmdon Old Vicarage, Saffron Walden, Essex, England.

CAREER: Qualified as a chartered surveyor; partner in various firms in England, 1921-56; member of Lands Tribunal, 1957-69. Justice of the Peace and juvenile court magistrate, 1935-68; Chairman of Inner London Juvenile Courts, 1936-68; member of central housing advisory committee to Minister of Health, 1936-47, youth advisory council of Minister of Education, 1942-45; inter-departmental committee on new towns, 1945-46, and Prime Minister's Committee on Regent's Park Terraces, 1945-46; adviser to Control Commission of Germany on juvenile delinquency problems in the British Zone, 1947-48. Member of Royal Commission on Justices of the Peace, 1946-48, and national advisory council on the training of magistrates, 1967-73. Member of the Stevenage Development Corp., 1952-56. Has done volunteer work in prisons and borstals. *Member:* Royal Institution of Chartered Surveyors (president, 1949-50), National Association of Prison Visitors (vice-president, 1938—, chairman, 1941-44), Carlton Club, Pratt's Club. *Awards, honors:* Named Commander of the Order of the British Empire, 1965.

WRITINGS: Meet the Prisoner, J. Cape, 1939; *The Child and the Magistrate,* J. Cape, 1942, 3rd edition, 1965; *British Juvenile Courts,* Longman Group, 1948; *The Juvenile Court, Today and Tomorrow,* Clarke-Hall Fellowship, 1951; *Which is the Justice?* (memoirs), Allen and Unwin, 1969; *The Juvenile Court, 1970 Onward: A Guide to the Children and Young Persons Act 1969 for Magistrates, Police, Child-Care Officers and Others,* Shaw & Sons, 1970; *Nothing But the Truth: Expert Evidence in Principle and Practice for Surveyors, Valuers and Others,* Estates Gazette, 1971, revised edition, 1975; *The Incompleat Survevor* (memoirs) Estates Gazette, 1973; (with P. M. Austin) *The Modern Juvenile Court,* Shaw & Sons, 1975. *Sanills: A Family and a Firm, 1652-1977,* Hutchinson, 1977.

*   *   *

WATTS, Sarah Miles   1934-

PERSONAL: Born May 11, 1934, in Wellsville, N.Y.; daughter of Sydney Henderson and Evelyn (Gardner) Miles; married Ronald Alan Watts (a community relations officer), December 16, 1961; children: Valerie Louise, Sydney Evelyn, Alan Miles. *Education:* University of Rochester, B.A., 1956; Alliance Francaise, Brussels, Troisieme Degree, 1968. *Home:* 46 King St., Brockport, N.Y. 14420. *Office:* Community Relations Office, State University of New York College, Brockport, N.Y. 14420.

CAREER: Times-Union, Rochester, N.Y., reporter, 1956-62; *Journalists' World,* Brussels, Belgium, founder and editor, 1962-68; State University of New York College at Brockport, instructor, 1968—. Charter member of board of Brockport Symphony Association, 1972-74; consultant on journalism education to Genesee Community College, 1974-76. *Member:* Women in Communications, Inc. (president of Rochester chapter, 1973-74).

WRITINGS: The Art of Belgian Cooking, Doubleday, 1971.

WORK IN PROGRESS: The Sage, The Sun, and His Prejudices: The Monday Articles of H. L. Mencken.

*   *   *

WAYMAN, Dorothy G.   1893-1975
(Theodate Geoffrey)

PERSONAL: Born January 7, 1893, in San Bernardino County, Calif.; daughter of Charles Worthington and Sarah Lauretta Ida Vincent (Park) Godfrey; married Charles Stafford Wayman, July 10, 1915; children: John Godfrey, Charles Stafford, Richard Park. *Education:* Bryn Mawr College, graduated, 1914; attended Simmons School of Social Work, 1914. *Religion:* Roman Catholic. *Residence:* Olean, N.Y.

CAREER: Free-lance writer in Japan, 1918-22, and the United States; *Falmouth Enterprise,* Falmouth, Mass., managing editor, 1929-33; *Boston Globe,* Boston, Mass., member of editorial staff, 1933-53; St. Bonaventure University, St. Bonaventure, N.Y., reference librarian, 1955-62; most recently staff member of *Olean Times-Herald* (Olean, N.Y.). Member of Memorial Gallery of Living Catholic Authors.

MEMBER: Guild of Our Lady of Ransom (vice-president), American Catholic Historical Association (member of executive council), Falmouth Historical Society, Bryn Mawr Club. *Awards, honors:* Litt.D. from Holy Cross College, Worcester, Mass., 1954; gold medal from French Institute of Arts, for *An Immigrant in Japan.*

WRITINGS—Non-fiction: *Edward Sylvester Morse: A Biography,* Harvard University Press, 1942; *Bite the Bullet* (autobiography), Bruce Books, 1948; *David I. Walsh, Citizen-Patriot,* Bruce Books, 1952; *Cardinal O'Connell of Boston: A Biography of William Henry O'Connell, 1859-1944,* Farrar, Straus, 1955.

Under pseudonym Theodate Geoffrey: *An Immigrant in Japan,* Houghton, 1926; *Powdered Ashes: A Story of Modern Japan,* Houghton, 1926; *Suckanesset: Wherein May Be Read a History of Falmouth, Massachusetts,* Falmouth Publishing Co., 1930.

Also: (With V. H. Godfrey) *John Holmes at Annapolis,* 1927; (with Willis Fitch) *Wings in the Night,* 1938; *Dumaine of New England,* 1958; *Quaker Pioneers in Quaker History,* 1962; *Franciscan Illumination in John Rylands Library,* 1962; *Friends on the Frontier in Quaker History,* 1965. Contributor to magazines, including *American Heritage, Folklore,* and *Cord.*

OBITUARIES: New York Times, October 30, 1975; *AB Bookman's Weekly,* December 22-29, 1975.*

(Died October 27, 1975, in Olean, N.Y.)

* * *

WECHSLER, Herman J. 1904-1976

PERSONAL: Born August 21, 1904, in New York, N.Y.; married Rushelle Corman; children: Jane, Antonia, Richard. *Education:* New York University, B.S.; Harvard University, M.A.; also studied privately, and at Ecole Louvre (Paris). *Residence:* New York, N.Y.

CAREER: FAR Gallery, New York, N.Y., founder, president, and director, 1934-76. Former faculty member at New York University; lecturer and consultant.

WRITINGS: (Editor) *The Pocket Book of Old Masters: Containing Sixty-Four Reproductions of Paintings by Da Vinci* (juvenile), Pocket Books, 1949; *Gods and Goddesses in Art and Legend: Great Myths as Pictured by Great Masters,* Pocket Books, 1950; *French Impressionists,* Abrams, 1952; *Lives of Famous French Painters: From Ingres to Picasso,* Pocket Books, 1952; *French Impressionists and Their Circle,* Abrams, 1953; *An Introduction to Prints and Print-Making,* FAR Gallery, 1960; *A Portfolio of Twenty-Four Reproductions of Masterpieces of Graphic Art: Manet, Degas, Cezanne, Gauguin, Renoir, Lautrec, Bonnard, Vuillard, Morisot, Cassatt, Redon, Matisse, Braque, Maillol, Rouault, Utrillo, Segonzac, Picasso, Chagall, Miro,* Triton Press, 1961; *Great Prints and Printmakers,* Abrams, 1967. Also author of children's books *The Life and Art of Vincent Van Gogh* and *The French Impressionists.*

OBITUARIES: New York Times, January 14, 1976.*

(Died January 13, 1976, in New York, N.Y.)

* * *

WECHSLER, Louis K. 1905-

PERSONAL: Born August 7, 1905, in New York, N.Y.;

son of Adolph (a merchant) and Henrietta (Siegel) Wechsler; married Tatyana Podryska (a sculptor), September 1, 1929; children: Bruce. *Education:* College of the City of New York, B.A., 1925; Columbia University, M.A., 1928; also attended Harvard University. *Politics:* Democrat. *Religion:* Jewish. *Home:* 17 East 82nd St., New York, N.Y. 10028. *Office:* 299 Madison Ave., New York, N.Y. 10017.

CAREER: College of the City of New York (now City College of the City University of New York), New York, N.Y., instructor in Latin, 1925-30; high school English teacher in New York, N.Y., 1930-50, chairman of department, 1942-50; junior high school principal in Brooklyn, N.Y., 1950-52, high school principal in Brooklyn, 1952-59, and New York, N.Y., 1959-68; writer, 1968—. Principal of evening high school in New York, N.Y., 1941-42. Member of lay board of directors of Greenpoint Hospital; member of board of directors of Young Men's Hebrew Association (Williamsburg).

MEMBER: World Academy of Art and Science (fellow), National Association of Secondary School Principals, Poetry Society of America, Royal Society of Arts (fellow), New York Academy of Sciences, Phi Beta Kappa. *Awards, honors:* Medaille de Vermeil from Societe d'Encouragement au Progres, 1973.

WRITINGS: (With Martin Blum and Sidney Friedman) *College Entrance Counselor,* Barnes & Noble, 1960; (with Blum and Friedman) *College Entrance Examinations,* Barnes & Noble, 1960, 3rd edition, 1970; *Benjamin Franklin: American and World Educator,* Twayne, 1976.

WORK IN PROGRESS: New York Almanacs, 1694-1793: Their Significance and Influence; material for a book on schools of New York City seen from the inside, with implications for the future, completion expected in 1980.

SIDELIGHTS: Wechsler writes: "I have a great interest in the present condition and the future of public education in this country. I am also fascinated by the long history of man's foibles and follies and his accomplishments, which give me good reason to feel despair and hope when I contemplate his future, especially in the next hundred years. I lean toward hope, mainly because of his survival until now."

AVOCATIONAL INTERESTS: Literature and drama (American, English, Latin, Greek), astronomy, archaeology, music, international travel, golf, watching baseball, reading.

* * *

WEHRLE, Edmund S(heridan) 1930-

PERSONAL: Born January 18, 1930, in Chicago, Ill.; son of Edmund (an administrator) and Marion (a teacher; maiden name, O'Brien) Kelly; married Mary Louise Nelson, August 21, 1961; children: Margaret Marion, Edmund Francis, Matthew James. *Education:* University of Notre Dame, Ph.B., 1952, M.A., 1954; University of Chicago, Ph.D., 1961. *Politics:* Democrat. *Religion:* Roman Catholic. *Home:* 23 Ball Hill Rd., Storrs, Conn. 06268. *Office:* Department of History, University of Connecticut, Storrs, Conn. 06268.

CAREER: Indiana University, Bloomington, lecturer in history, 1961-62; Michigan State University, East Lansing, assistant professor of history, 1962-64; John Carroll University, University Heights, Ohio, assistant professor of history, 1964-66; University of Connecticut, Storrs, assistant professor, 1966-67, associate professor, 1967-75, professor of history, 1975—. *Military service:* U.S. Army, 1954-56. *Member:* American Historical Association, Association for Asian Studies, New England China Seminar. *Awards, honors:* American Philosophical Society grant for research in London, 1962.

WRITINGS: Britain, China, and the Antimissionary Riots, 1891-1900, University of Minnesota Press, 1966; (with Donald F. Lach) *International Politics in East Asia Since World War Two,* Praeger, 1975.

WORK IN PROGRESS: Research for *U.S. Policy in Asia, 1945-1972,* and *French Missionaries in China in the Nineteenth Century;* preparing, with Stephen Petersen, a microfilm edition on the English-language missionary press in mainland China in the nineteenth and twentieth centuries for Greenwood Press.

* * *

WEIDEGER, Paula 1939-

PERSONAL: Born July 6, 1939, in New York, N.Y.; daughter of Michael (a businessman) and Lillian (Topper) Weideger. *Education:* Antioch College, student, 1956-58; New York University, B.A., 1968, M.A., 1971. *Agent:* Claire Smith, Harold Ober Associates, 22 East 49th St., New York, N.Y. 10017.

CAREER: Scientific American (magazine), New York, N.Y., researcher, 1959-61; free-lance editor, 1962-70; New York University, New York, instructor in psychology, 1970-71; *Excerpta Medica,* Amsterdam, Netherlands, editor, 1971; Center for Reproductive and Sexual Health, New York, counselor, 1972; Women's Medical Center, New York, lecturer in women's health, 1972-74; Healthright, Inc., New York, staff associate, 1973—; State University of New York College at New Paltz, instructor in women's studies, 1975—. *Member:* Women's Ink. *Awards, honors:* Macdowell Colony fellowship, 1973.

WRITINGS: (With Geraldine Thorsten) *Travel with Your Pet,* Simon & Schuster, 1973; *Menstruation and Menopause,* Knopf, 1976.

* * *

WEIL, Joseph 1875-1976

1875—February 26, 1976; American confidence man, talking dog salesman, and author. Obituaries: *New York Times,* February 27, 1976; *Washington Post,* February 28, 1976; *Newsweek,* March 8, 1976.

* * *

WEINBERGER, Betty Kiralfy 1932-

PERSONAL: Born July 9, 1932, in Columbus, Ga.; daughter of Victor J. and Raye C. Kiralfy; married Stanley Robert Weinberger (an attorney), September 8, 1960; children: John, Beth. *Education:* Tulane University, B.A., 1953; Columbia University, graduate study, 1955-56; University of Chicago, M.A., 1958. *Home:* 5102 Jackson, Glencoe, Ill. 60022. *Agent:* Curtis Brown Ltd., 60 East 56th St., New York, N.Y. 10022. *Office:* Parents As Resources Project, 464 Central, Northfield, Ill. 60093.

CAREER: Muscogee County Children and Family Services, Columbus, Ga., child welfare worker, 1953-57; Michael Reese Hospital, Chicago, Ill., pediatric social worker, 1958-62; Parents As Resources Project, Northfield, Ill., consultant and partner, 1968—. Vice-president of Glencoe Human Relations Committee, 1973-74; member of board of directors of Glencoe Family Counseling Service, 1976. Consultant on television series "Look at Me!", produced by WTTW (Chicago).

WRITINGS: (With Ann Cole and Carolyn Buhai Haas) *Recipes for Fun* series (juvenile), Parents As Resources Project, 1970-76; (with Cole, Haas and Faith Bushnell) *I Saw a Purple Cow* (juvenile), Little, Brown, 1972; (with Cole, Haas and Elizabeth Heller) *A Pumpkin in a Pear Tree* (juvenile), Little, Brown, 1976; (with Cole, Haas and Heller) *Children Are Children Are Children,* Little, Brown, in press. Author with Haas and Cole, of column "Recipes for Fun," syndicated by *Register and Tribune,* (Des Moines).

Contributor to magazines, including *Synergist, LadyCom, Daycare* and *Early Education.*

WORK IN PROGRESS: A book for librarians, tentatively titled *Activities to Stimulate Book Enjoyment,* or *Be a Pre-School Bookworm;* a book about children's activities around the world.

SIDELIGHTS: Betty Weinberger writes that she is a "combination of parent who really enjoys her two children, a social worker with experience in Harlem and the Tobacco Roads areas of Georgia, and an English major who likes to write!"

* * *

WEINGARTEN, Violet (Brown) 1915-1976

February 23, 1915—July 17, 1976; American newspaper reporter, editor, advertising executive, novelist, and author of nonfiction. Obituaries: *New York Times,* July 18, 1976; *Publishers Weekly,* July 26, 1976. (See index for previous *CA* sketch)

* * *

WEINSTEIN, Fred 1931-

PERSONAL: Born October 19, 1931, in Brooklyn, N.Y.; son of Samuel (a teacher) and Sarah (Ginsberg) Weinstein; married Joan Berry, January 31, 1962; children: Samuel Noah; stepchildren: Blaine, Malcolm, Robert, Alison. *Education:* Brooklyn College (now of the City University of New York), B.A., 1954, M.A., 1957; University of California, Berkeley, Ph.D., 1962. *Home:* 3 Lotowana Lane, Stony Brook, N.Y. 11790. *Office:* Department of History, State University of New York at Stony Brook, Stony Brook, N.Y. 11794.

CAREER: University of California, Berkeley, lecturer and instructor of history, 1962-65; University of Oregon, Eugene, assistant professor of history, 1965-66; San Jose State College (now San Jose State University), San Jose, Calif., began as assistant professor, became associate professor of history and humanities; State University of New York, Stony Brook, began as associate professor, became professor of history, 1969—. *Military service:* U.S. Army, Adjutant General's Corps, 1954-56. *Member:* American Historical Association, Group for the Uses of Psychology in History (chairman). *Awards, honors:* Fellowships from Ford Foundation, 1961-62, Institute for Advanced Study, 1970-71, and American Council of Learned Societies, 1974.

WRITINGS: (With G. M. Platt) *The Wish to Be Free,* University of California Press, 1969; (with Platt) *Psychoanalytic Sociology,* Johns Hopkins Press, 1973. Member of board of advisors of *Psychoanalytic Review.* Contributor to scholarly journals.

WORK IN PROGRESS: Theories of Change.

* * *

WEIR, Alice M.
See McLAUGHLIN, Emma Maude

WEIR, Nancie MacCullough 1933-

PERSONAL: Born April 17, 1933, in Homewood, Ill.; daughter of Peter (a plumber) and Martha (a hotel manager; maiden name, Whitney) MacCullough; married Allan Kaufman (divorced, 1968); married Christopher Weir (a consultant), 1969; children: (first marriage) Noah MacCullough; (second marriage) Christina Whitney. *Education:* University of Illinois, student, 1951-53. *Home and office address:* West Meeting House Rd., South Kent, Conn. 06785. *Agent:* Harold Ober Associates, Inc., 40 East 49th St., New York, N.Y. 10017.

CAREER: Worked for advertising agencies in New York City, 1957-69, began as secretary, became copy supervisor; writer, 1969—. *Member:* Alpha Gamma Delta.

WRITINGS: Silver Spoons (novel), Putnam, 1976.

WORK IN PROGRESS: Another novel.

BIOGRAPHICAL/CRITICAL SOURCES: Ladies Home Journal, November, 1967.

* * *

WEISBORD, Marvin R(oss) 1931-

PERSONAL: Born June 11, 1931, in Philadelphia, Pa.; son of William W. (a businessman) and Ida (Rosen) Weisbord; married Dorothy Barclay (a teacher), December 23, 1956; children: Joseph, Nina, Robert, Dan. *Education:* University of Arizona, student, 1949-51; University of Illinois, B.S., 1953; State University of Iowa, M.A., 1955. *Home:* 252 Kent Rd., Wynnewood, Pa. 19096. *Agent:* John Schaffner, 425 East 51st St., New York, N.Y. 10022. *Office:* Block Petrella Associates, Organization Research and Development, 23 East Wynnewood Rd., Wynnewood, Pa. 19096.

CAREER: Pennsylvania State University, University Park, instructor in journalism, 1957-59; Regent Standard Forms, Philadelphia, Pa., executive vice-president, 1959-68; Block Petrella Associates, Wynnewood, Pa., director of Organization Research and Development Division, 1968—. Member of National Training Laboratories, 1972—. *Military service:* U.S. Navy, journalist, 1955-57. *Member:* International Association of Applied Social Scientists, National Organization Development Network, American Society of Journalists and Authors.

WRITINGS: Campaigning for President, Public Affairs Press, 1964; (editor) *A Treasury of Tips for Writers,* Writer's Digest, 1965; *A New Look at the Road to the White House,* Washington Square Press, 1966; *Some Form of Peace,* Viking, 1968; *Basic Photography,* Amphoto, 1972; (with Howard Lamb and Allan Drexler) *Improving Police Department Management,* Addison-Wesley, 1974. Associate editor of *Journal of Applied Behavioral Science,* 1973—.

WORK IN PROGRESS: Academic Medical Center Self-Study Guide: Practical Applications of Survey Diagnosis and Data Summaries from Nine Medical Centers, 1974, with Paul R. Lawrence and Martin P. Charns; *Organizational Diagnosis: A Workbook of Theory and Practice.*

* * *

WEISGERBER, Jean 1924-

PERSONAL: Born May 14, 1924, in Brussels, Belgium; son of Pierre (a businessman) and Yvonne (Mottard) Weisgerber; married Dina Dendoncker (a teacher), July 27, 1948. *Education:* University of Brussels, licencie en philosophie et lettres, 1946, Ph.D., 1951. *Home:* 17 Place Guy d'Arezzo, 1060 Brussels, Belgium. *Office:* Department of Germanic Philology, University of Brussels, 50 Avenue F. D. Roosevelt, 1050 Brussels, Belgium.

CAREER: University of Brussels, Brussels, Belgium, lecturer, 1952-54, professor of Dutch and comparative literature, 1954—. *Member:* Royal Academy (Dutch Language and Literature; fellow).

WRITINGS: Faulkner and Dostoevsky: Influence and Confluence (translated by Dean McWilliams), Ohio University Press, 1974. Contributor to literature journals.

WORK IN PROGRESS: The Avant-Garde in Literature, two volumes, for International Comparative Literature Association; research on the representation of space in the novel.

* * *

WEISMAN, Marilee 1939-

PERSONAL: Born January 26, 1939, in Toronto, Ontario, Canada; daughter of Abbey (a shopkeeper) and Anne (a shopkeeper; maiden name, Rappaport) Brown; children: Daniel, Naomi, David, Jerry. *Education:* University of Toronto, B.Sc.N., 1962. *Home and office:* 148 Collier St., Toronto, Ontario, Canada.

CAREER: Registered nurse; *Aurora Banner,* Ontario, columnist and feature writer, 1971-73; free-lance writer in Toronto, Ontario; feature writer, Scope Publications, Toronto.

WRITINGS: So Get On with It (nonfiction), Doubleday, 1976. Author of documentary film scripts, produced by Camera One Films, "A Motion Picture," 1975, and "Olympiad 1976", 1976. Contributor to Canadian newspapers.

WORK IN PROGRESS: A play for Canadian Broadcasting Corp.-Television; research for a television series and a theater short; feature writing for Scope Publications; a film script for Department of Culture and Recreation, Ontario.

* * *

WEISS, Leatie 1928-

PERSONAL: Born May 8, 1928, in New York; daughter of Abraham T. (a certified public accountant) and Amelia (a saleswoman and secretary; maiden name, Glass) Taber; married Jack Weiss (an accountant), August 27, 1949; children: Ellen, Gary. *Education:* Brooklyn College (now the City University of New York), B.A., 1949; Columbia University, M.A., 1951. *Religion:* Jewish. *Home:* 728 Bush Pl., Paramus, N.J. 07652. *Office:* Lincoln School, Hawthorne, N.J.

CAREER: Elementary school teacher in New York, N.Y., 1949-50; teacher in nursery school in New York City, 1951-52; substitute teacher in Paramus, N.J., 1963-65; Lincoln School, Hawthorne, N.J., kindergarten teacher, 1966—. *Member:* National Education Association, New Jersey Education Association, Hawthorne Teachers Association.

WRITINGS: Heather's Feathers (juvenile), F. Watts, 1976. Author of musical comedies for local Jewish Community Center.

WORK IN PROGRESS: An easy-to-read children's book about a pigeon-toed penguin, for F. Watts.

SIDELIGHTS: Leatie Weiss writes: "I think the most exciting things about *Heather's Feathers* is the teamwork involved between mother and daughter [her daughter illustrated the book]. We hope to do many more books together."

WELCH, George Patrick 1901-1976
(Patrick Welch)

April 10, 1901—May 5, 1976; American military officer, investment banker, novelist, and author of books on military history. Obituaries: *Washington Post,* May 7, 1976. (*CAP*-1; earlier sketch in *CA*-13/14)

*   *   *

WELCH, Jerome A. 1933-

PERSONAL: Born October 27, 1933, in Fort Wayne, Ind.; son of John Joseph and M. Florence (Giant) Welch. *Education:* Attended Indiana University, 1951-54, Our Lady of the Lake Seminary, Lake Wawasee, Ind., 1955, and St. Mary's College, St. Mary, Ky., 1955-57; St. Francis College, Fort Wayne, Ind., B.S., 1962, M.S., 1967. *Politics:* Democrat. *Religion:* Roman Catholic. *Home:* 2417 Hazelwood Ave., Fort Wayne, Ind. 46805. *Office:* Jewel Publications, 2417 Hazelwood Ave., Fort Wayne, Ind. 46805.

CAREER: Elementary school teacher in northeastern Indiana, 1959-70; writer. *Member:* Third Order of St. Francis, St. Charles Fraternity, Single Catholic Adult Club.

WRITINGS: Catholicism Today, Jewel Publications, 1977.

SIDELIGHTS: Welch writes that his book proposes an enlarged democratic base for the election of the pope and bishops, optional celibacy for the secular clergy, the permission of any medically safe form of contraception, the ordination of women, new vistas for Catholic education within the framework of the public school and the liturgy, polygenism as a tenable option regarding the origin of man, and the removal of the penalty of mortal sin for nonattendance at Mass on Sundays and Holy Days. Welch also includes a history of Catholicism in order to provide a foundation for reform and renewal. He emphasizes that he writes as a "dutiful son of the Church, with a deep reverence and love for the Catholic Faith."

*   *   *

WELCH, William A. 1915(?)-1976

1915(?)—February 2, 1976; American screenwriter, story-editor, and playwright. Obituaries: *New York Times,* February 4, 1976.

*   *   *

WELKE, Elton 1941-

PERSONAL: Born June 15, 1941, in Berkeley, Calif.; son of Elton G. (a physician) and Elsie (Shattuck) Welke; married Anna Lange, July 28, 1963; children: Allison, Erik. *Education:* University of California, Berkeley, A.B., 1962. *Home:* 1330 Channing, Palo Alto, Calif. 94301. *Office:* Lane Magazine and Book Co., 80 Willow Rd., Menlo Park, Calif. 94025.

CAREER: Sunset, Menlo Park, Calif., staff writer, 1962-66, assistant editor, 1966-68, associate editor, 1968-69; *Better Homes and Gardens,* Des Moines, Iowa, travel editor, 1970-71; *Apartment Life,* Des Moines, Iowa, managing editor, 1971-72; Lane Magazine and Book Co., Menlo Park, Calif., managing editor of "Sunset Special Interest Magazines," 1972-73, executive editor, 1973—. Member of board of directors of Olympic National Park Associates, 1968-70. *Member:* Society of American Travel Writers, Sierra Club.

WRITINGS: (With Donald L. Dudley) *How to Survive Being Alive,* Doubleday, 1977. Contributor to *Sunset Western Garden Book,* Lane, 1967.

WELLER, George (Anthony) 1907-
(Michael Wharf)

PERSONAL: Born July 13, 1907, in Boston, Mass.; son of George Joseph (a lawyer) and Matilda B. (McAleer) Weller; married Katherine Deupree, 1932 (divorced, 1944); married Charlotte Ebener, January 23, 1948; children: Ann Weller Tagge, Anthony. *Education:* Harvard University, B.A., 1929; graduate study at University of Vienna and Max Reinhardt School of Theatre, 1930-31. *Home:* Via Meropia 77, Rome, Italy; and, Via Vasca Moresca 20, San Felice di Circeo, Italy. *Agent:* Harold Ober Associates, Inc., 40 East 49th St., New York, N.Y. 10017. *Office:* Stampa Estera, Via della Mercede 55, Rome, Italy.

CAREER: Teacher in Tucson, Ariz., 1929-30; *New York Times,* New York, N.Y., correspondent for Greece and the Balkans, 1932-35; Homeland Foundation, New York, N.Y., director, 1937-40; *Chicago Daily News,* Chicago, Ill., correspondent, 1940-72 (covered news events in all parts of the world except western Africa). *Member:* Foreign Press Club of Rome, Stampa Estera (president, 1954-55; vice-president, 1973-74), Phi Beta Kappa. *Awards, honors:* Pulitzer Prize, for description of appendectomy aboard a submarine, 1943; Nieman fellow at Harvard University, 1947-48; George Polk prize, 1955; British drama contest awards, 1960, for "Second Saint of Cypress"; U.S. Navy public service citation, for volunteer work with U.S. Mediterranean Fleet, 1968.

WRITINGS: Not to Eat, Not for Love (novel), Smith & Haas, 1933; (translator under pseudonym Michael Wharf) Ignazio Silone, *Fontamara,* Random House, 1935; *Clutch and Differential* (novel), Random House, 1936; *Singapore Is Silent* (history), Harcourt, 1943; *Bases Overseas* (geopolitics), Harcourt, 1944; *The Crack in the Column* (novel), Random House, 1949; *The Story of the Paratroops* (history), Random House, 1958; *Story of the Submarine* (history), Random House, 1962. Author of plays: "Second Saint of Cyprus," and "Walking Time," 1965. Contributor of stories and articles to national magazines.

WORK IN PROGRESS: A geopolitical history.

*   *   *

WELLS, Harold P(hilmore) 1925-

PERSONAL: Born December 5, 1925, in Key West, Fla.; son of Samuel G. (a businessman) and Martha (Saunders) Wells; married Betty Monteith (a music director), December 19, 1950; children: Harold P., Jr., Douglas Monroe, Samuel Monteith. *Education:* Attended Florida Southern College, 1942-43; Bob Jones University, B.A., 1949; Western Reserve University (now Case Western Reserve University), graduate study, 1949; Southwestern Baptist Theological Seminary, diploma, 1952; Southern Lutheran Seminary, further graduate study, 1954-55; Protestant Episcopal University, Ph.D., 1963. *Religion:* Southern Baptist. *Home:* 1252 Everette Rd., Aberdeen Proving Ground-EA, Md. 21010. *Office:* Office of the Staff Chaplain, Aberdeen Proving Ground, Md. 21005.

CAREER: Ordained Baptist minister, 1949; pastor in Lugoff, S.C., 1951-53, and in Columbia, S.C., 1953-58; State of South Carolina, chaplain in Department of Corrections, 1958-60; pastor in Charleston, S.C., 1960-62; U.S. Army, staff chaplain, 1962—, present rank, lieutenant colonel. *Military service:* U.S. Navy, 1943-46. *Member:* Southeastern Magician's Association (president), Florida Association of Magical Entertainers (honorary member).

WRITINGS: *Sermons in Magic for Youngsters,* four volumes, Moody, Number 1, 1961, Number 2, 1963, Number 3, 1965, Number 4, 1968; *Sermons in Magic,* Moody, 1975; *You Can Be a Magician,* Moody, 1976.

Columnist, "Chaplain's Corner," a weekly column in *NACOM Chronicle,* 1963, and in *Traveler,* 1967-68; writer of monthly column in *European Life,* 1964-65. Contributor to magazines and newspapers, including *Christianity Today, Link* magazine, and *Pacific Stars and Stripes.*

WORK IN PROGRESS: *Crisis in Morality,* on the causes of juvenile delinquency; *A Biblical Panorama of the Places Christ Hallowed; A Spiritual Travelogue,* daily devotions; *Magic as a Medium of Visual Christian Education.*

AVOCATIONAL INTERESTS: Travel (western Europe, Greece, Lebanon, Syria, Jordan, Egypt, Japan, Philippines, Korea, Guam, Vietnam, Thailand), magic, woodworking, sailing.

* * *

WELLS, Harry Kohlsaat 1911-1976

February 28, 1911—February 8, 1976; American psychologist, philosopher, school administrator, and author of psychology books. Obituaries: *New York Times,* February 9, 1976. (See index for previous *CA* sketch)

* * *

WELLS, Louis T(ruitt), Jr. 1937-

PERSONAL: Born October 19, 1937, in Nashville, Tenn.; son of Louis Truitt Wells; married Margaret Landsberg, 1965; children: Karena S., Robin D. *Education:* Georgia Institute of Technology, B.S. (highest honors), 1960; Harvard University, M.B.A., 1963, D.B.A., 1966. *Home:* 72 Spruce Hill Rd., Weston, Mass. 02193. *Office:* Graduate School of Business Administration, Cotting 213, Harvard University, Boston, Mass.

CAREER: College of Aeronautics, Cranfield, England, member of staff, 1964; Harvard University, Graduate School of Business Administration, Boston, Mass., assistant professor, 1966-71, associate professor, 1971-75, professor of business administration, 1975—, faculty associate of Center for International Affairs. Consultant to the governments of Liberia, Ghana, Indonesia, Malaysia, Bolivia, Colombia, Peru, Egypt, and Papua New Guinea, and to private firms.

WRITINGS: (Contributor) Robert O. Keohane and Joseph S. Nye, Jr., editors, *Transnational Relations and World Politics,* Harvard University Press, 1971; (editor and contributor) *The Product Life Cycle and International Trade,* Division of Research, Graduate School of Business Administration, Harvard University, 1972; (with John M. Stopford) *Managing the Multinational Enterprise: Organization of the Firm and Ownership of the Subsidiary,* Basic Books, 1972; (contributor) Eliezer B. Ayal, editor, *Micro Aspects of Development,* Praeger, 1973; (with Walter A. Chudson) *The Acquisition of Technology from Multinational Corporations by Developing Countries,* United Nations Department of Economic and Social Affairs, 1974; (contributor) Raymond Vernon, editor, *Big Business and the State,* Harvard University Press, 1974; (with others) *The Choice of Technology in Developing Countries: Some Cautionary Tales,* Center for International Affairs, Harvard University, 1975; (with David N. Smith) *Negotiating Third World Mineral Agreements: Promises as Prologue,* Ballinger, 1976; (with Vernon) *The Manager in the International Economy,*

Prentice-Hall, 3rd edition (Wells not associated with earlier editions), 1976, teaching manual, 1968; (with Vernon) *The Economic Environment of International Business,* Prentice-Hall, 2nd edition (Wells not associated with earlier editions), 1976. Contributor to business and economic journals.

WORK IN PROGRESS: Research on investment by firms from developing countries in other developing countries.

* * *

WENDLAND, Michael F(letcher) 1946-

PERSONAL: Born February 2, 1946, in Bay City, Mich.; son of H. R. (a businessman) and Gertrude (Fletcher) Wendland; married Jennifer Jeffrey; children: Wendy, Scott, Jeffrey. *Education:* Attended Delta College, University Center, Mich., 1964-67. *Home:* 39775 Spitz Dr., Sterling Heights, Mich. 48078. *Office: Detroit News,* Detroit, Mich. 48231.

CAREER: WKNX-Radio/Television, Saginaw, Mich., reporter, 1964-67; *Bangor Beacon,* Bay City, Mich., writer, 1967-68; *Bay City Times,* Bay City, reporter, 1968-71; *Detroit News,* Detroit, Mich., reporter, 1971—. Foreign correspondent for *Toronto Star,* 1972—. Author of "CB Break," a weekly column syndicated by Universal Press Syndicate to about two hundred newspapers, 1976—. Has appeared on local and national television and radio programs. *Member:* Detroit Press Club. *Awards, honors:* Associated Press awards, 1970, for boating disaster story and series on bank failures, 1973, for stories on ship sinking, oil spill, and lake flooding, and 1976, for investigation of insurance fraud; United Press International awards, 1972, for Lake Erie storm story, and 1975, for investigation of Teamsters union and disappearance of James R. Hoffa; Detroit Press Club medallion, 1972, for work on series, "Voice of Detroit's Blacks"; Advancement of Justice award from Michigan Bar Association, 1973, for series on prison reform.

WRITINGS: *CB Update* (on citizens band radio), Sheed, Andrews & McMeel, 1976; *Complete CB Encyclopedia,* Sheed, Andrews & McMeel, 1977. Contributor to magazines and newspapers.

WORK IN PROGRESS: *Investigation of the Teamsters Union and the Underworld; Portrait of a Mafia Enforcer.*

SIDELIGHTS: Wendland claims organized crime and political corruption as his area of specialty. For six months (late 1976-early 1977) he was a member of the reporters and editors task force in Phoenix, Ariz., investigating the circumstances surrounding the bombing death of Phoenix reporter Don Bolles. Wendland is presently involved in the writing of several books based on his investigations.

He describes himself to *CA* as an avid organic gardener and an amateur radio operator.

* * *

WENHE, Mary B. 1910-

PERSONAL: Born August 10, 1910, in Poultney, Vt.; daughter of Chester Arthur (a merchant) and Grace (Young) Bixby; married Paul A. Wenhe (a general contractor), September 6, 1940 (died February 7, 1976); children: Paul A. II, Alice (Mrs. Stephen M. Harmon). *Education:* University of Washington, Seattle, B.A. (cum laude), 1931, M.A., 1936; summer graduate study at Northwestern University, 1938; graduate study at University of California Extension, San Diego, 1954, and San Diego State College (now University), 1957. *Politics:* Republican by registration. *Religion:* Evangelical Presbyterian. *Home:* 5130 July St., San Diego, Calif. 92110.

CAREER: Secretary, private tutor; high school teacher of English and speech in the public schools of Goldendale, Wash., 1931-32; Success Business University, Seattle, Wash., teacher of office skills and head of secretarial department, 1933-34; University of Washington, Seattle, instructor in speech, 1934-43; San Diego City College, San Diego, Calif., part time instructor in shorthand, 1950-61; Grossmont Adult School, Grossmont, Calif., instructor in shorthand and typing, 1951-53; Grossmont College, El Cajon, Calif., instructor in English and speech, 1965-67. *Member:* Phi Beta Kappa, Tau Kappa Alpha, Theta Alpha Delta, Zeta Phi Eta, Pi Lambda Theta.

WRITINGS: How To Pray for Healing, Revell, 1975. Contributor to professional journals.

WORK IN PROGRESS: A study of deeper Christian life.

AVOCATIONAL INTERESTS: Tape recording Bible studies, traveling.

*   *   *

WENNER, Lettie McSpadden 1937-

PERSONAL: Born April 9, 1937, in Battle Creek, Mich.; daughter of John Dean (a chiropodist) and Isma D. (a nurse; maiden name, Sullivan) McSpadden; married Manfred W. Wenner (a professor), April 3, 1961; children: Eric Alexis, Adrian Eduard. *Education:* University of Chicago, A.B., 1959; University of California, Berkeley, M.A., 1961; University of Wisconsin—Madison, Ph.D., 1971. *Home:* 124 Thrush Lane, Naperville, Ill. 60540. *Office:* Department of Political Science, University of Illinois, Box 4348, Chicago, Ill. 60680.

CAREER: University of Illinois at Chicago Circle, Chicago, Ill., assistant professor of political science, 1973—. *Member:* American political science Association, Law and Society Association, Midwest Political Science Association.

WRITINGS: One Environment Under Law, Goodyear Publishing, 1976. Contributor to law and political science journals.

WORK IN PROGRESS: Research on attitudes of judges toward their roles, the role of the courts in making environmental policy, and the effects of the National Environmental Policy Act.

SIDELIGHTS: "My interests," Wenner told *CA,* "include the way in which the law is used as a tool by all interests in a dispute to advance their own point of view, especially with regard to the environment, consumer protection, energy development and conservation, and women and minority employment opportunities."

*   *   *

WERE, Gideon S(aulo) 1934-

PERSONAL: Born October 27, 1934, in Kenya; son of Saulo (a teacher) and Abisage Wanzetse Omukofu; married Naomi Asoka (an education officer), September, 1964; children: Saulo, Abisage, Evaline, Masakha, Peres, Walter. *Education:* Royal Technical College of East Africa, G.C.E., 1959; London School of Oriental and African Studies, London, B.A. (honors), 1963; University of Wales, Ph.D., 1966. *Religion:* Anglican. *Home:* Kyuna Estate, Nairobi, Kenya. *Office:* Department of History, University of Nairobi, P.O. Box 30197, Nairobi, Kenya.

CAREER: University of Nairobi, Nairobi, Kenya, special lecturer, 1966-67, lecturer, 1967-70, senior lecturer, 1970-73, associate professor of history, 1973—, acting chairman of department, 1973-74, dean of Faculty of Arts, 1974—. Member of Kenya Secondary School History Panel, International History Panel of the Ministry of Education, and Public Archives Advisory Council. *Member:* Historical Association of Kenya (vice-chairman).

WRITINGS: A History of the Abaluyia of Western Kenya, circa 1500-1930, East African Publishing House, 1967; *Western Kenya Historical Texts,* East African Literature Bureau, 1967; *The Survivors,* Equatorial Publishers, 1968; (with Derek A. Wilson) *East Africa through a Thousand Years,* Evans Brothers, 1968, Holmes & Meier, 1970, revised edition, 1972; (contributor) B.A. Ogot and J. A. Kieran, editors, *Zamani,* Longmans, Green, 1968, revised edition, 1973; (author of introduction) S. G. Ayany, *A History of Zanzibar,* East African Literature Bureau, 1970; *A History of South Africa,* Holmes & Meier, 1974; *Essays in African Religion in Western Kenya,* East African Literature Bureau, in press; (with M. A. Ogutu) *Essays in the History of South-Central Africa,* East African Literature Bureau, in press; (contributor) *Circumcision Rites Among the Bamasaba,* Acta Musicologia et Linguistica, in press. Contributor to academic journals. Editor of *Journal of Eastern African Research and Development.*

WORK IN PROGRESS: Editing and writing material to be included in *A History of Kenya,* for Oxford University Press; "The Wanga Kingdom" to be included in *East African Kingdoms during the Nineteenth Century,* edited by M.S.M. Kiwanuka; research on the pre-colonial history of Bugisu and the role of religion in society.

*   *   *

WESTWOOD, Jennifer 1940-

PERSONAL: Born May 1, 1940, in England; daughter of Wilfrid James (a builder) and Beatrice (a teacher) Fulcher; married Trevor Frank Westwood in 1958 (divorced 1966), married Brian Herbert Chandler (a management consultant), 1968; children: (first marriage) Jonathan James. *Education:* St. Anne's College, Oxford, B.A., 1963, M.A., 1970; New Hall, Cambridge, B.A., 1965, M.A., 1972, M.Litt., 1973. *Religion:* Church of England. *Home:* 133 Shepherdess Walk, London N.1, England. *Agent:* Laura Cecil, Flat 10, Exeter Mansions, 106 Shaftesbury Ave., London, England.

CAREER: Cambridge University, Cambridge, England, university classes and tutorials in Old Norse and Anglo-Saxon, 1965-68; free-lance editor and publishing adviser, 1969—. *Member:* Viking Society for Northern Research, Children's Book History Society (British Branch of Osborne Society), Folklore Society, National Book League.

WRITINGS: (Compiler and translator) *Medieval Tales,* Hart-Davis, 1967, Coward, 1968; *Gilgamesh and Other Babylonian Tales,* Bodley Head, 1968, Coward, 1970; *The Isle of Gramarye,* Hart-Davis, 1970; *Tales and Legends,* Hart-Davis, 1971, Coward, 1971; *Stories of Charlemagne,* Bodley Head, 1972; *Alfred the Great,* Wayland, 1976.

SIDELIGHTS: Jennifer Westwood writes: "Read Old and Middle English course at Oxford, Anglo-Saxon Tripos at Cambridge. Became aware of fund of stories unavailable to children, or available only in Victorian retellings long out of print. Tried to retell in intelligible modern English whilst keeping flavour of style of originals—particularly *Gilgamesh* where semi-liturgical style aimed at.

"I speak French, some Danish and Icelandic. Read dead languages: Latin, Old Norse, Anglo-Saxon (Old English), and Old French. Have travelled extensively in Europe, and stayed for some time in Sweden, Denmark and Iceland for work purposes."

AVOCATIONAL INTERESTS: Fairy tales and folklore, mythology and legend; early children's books.

* * *

WEXLER, Jean Stewart 1921-

PERSONAL: Born June 12, 1921, in Charlotte, N.C.; daughter of Edvin M. (a professor) and Mary (a librarian; maiden name, Lindsay) Hoffman; married Stan Wexler (an editor), December 16, 1967; children: Michael A. Stewart. *Education:* Attended Oberlin College, 1938-41, Black Mountain College, New School for Social Research, and New York University. *Home:* 133 East 31st St., New York, N.Y. 10016.

CAREER: Worked as a secretary for *Time, Life,* and *House & Garden* in the early 1950's; McGraw-Hill, New York, N.Y., secretary to the art director, late 1950's; Random House, New York, copy editor and edit. seer, 1963-66; writer.

WRITINGS: (With Louise T. King) *The Martha's Vineyard Cook Book,* Harper, 1971, 2nd edition, 1975. Author of tape scripts for a series on famous Americans for use in inner city high schools. Contributor to *New York Times.*

WORK IN PROGRESS: A mystery, *One Guest Too Many; Journal of a Vineyard Gardner;* a compilation of articles on plants, to be published as a book; *Owl and Other Owl,* for children.

SIDELIGHTS: Jean Wexler told *CA:* "I am mainly interested in our struggle for survival in a technological age that I feel is destroying everything vital to the human spirit. I find plants—all aspects of our relations with them—a fascinating link to reality that it is essential for us to maintain; also an endless source of phenomenal instances of ingenuity related to survival in times when they have been threatened with extinction. I spend six months a year on Martha's Vineyard in our home there, the rest in New York where my husband works."

AVOCATIONAL INTERESTS: Mrs. Wexler and her husband are ardent anglophiles, and are especially fond of London and Scotland.

* * *

WHARF, Michael
See WELLER, George (Anthony)

* * *

WHEELER, Leslie A. 1945-

PERSONAL: Born August 21, 1945, in Pasadena, Calif.; daughter of John Leonard (a lawyer) and Helene (an interior decorator; maiden name, Albright) Wheeler; married Philip Lief (a graphic designer), October 2, 1976. *Education:* Stanford University, B.A., 1967; University of California, Berkeley, M.A., 1969. *Politics:* Liberal Democrat. *Home address:* Cagney Rd., New Marlborough, Mass., c/o Canaan, Conn. 06018.

CAREER: New York City Adult Training Center, New York, N.Y., teacher, 1969-71; Barron's Educational Series, Inc., Woodbury, N.Y., writer and editor, 1971-73; freelance writer, 1973—. *Member:* Phi Beta Kappa.

WRITINGS: Jimmy Who?, Barron's, 1976. Contributor to *Montana* and *Highlights for Children.*

WORK IN PROGRESS: Playground of the World, a pictorial history of Coney Island.

SIDELIGHTS: Leslie Wheeler writes: "Especial areas of interest are biography and history—the individual alone and in relation to a particular historical context." *Avocational interests:* Travel (especially in Europe), cooking, cross-country skiing, gardening.

* * *

WHEELER, Michael 1943-

PERSONAL: Born July 25, 1943, in Louisville, Ky.; son of Harry E. (an editor) and Erma (a painter; maiden name, Allen) Wheeler; married Candace Pullman (a planner), June 12, 1971. *Education:* Amherst College, B.A., 1965; Boston University, J.D., 1969; Harvard University, LL.M., 1974. *Agent:* David Otte, 9 Park St., Boston, Mass. 02108. *Office:* New England School of Law, 126 Newbury St., Boston, Mass. 02116.

CAREER: Private law practice in Boston, Mass., 1969-71; New England School of Law, Boston, Mass., assistant professor, 1971-74, associate professor, 1974-76, professor of law, 1976—. *Member:* Authors Guild of Authors League of America.

WRITINGS: No-Fault Divorce, Beacon Press, 1974; *Lies, Damn Lies, and Statistics,* Norton, 1976. Contributor to law journals, to *Atlantic* and *New Times,* and to newspapers.

* * *

WHEELER, (Robert Eric) Mortimer 1890-1976

September 10, 1890—July 22, 1976; British archaeologist, television and museum consultant, educator, and author of books in his field. Obituaries: *New York Times,* July 23, 1976; *Time,* August 2, 1976; *Current Biography,* September, 1976.

* * *

WHEELER-BENNETT, John 1902-1975

PERSONAL: Born October 13, 1902, in Keston, Kent, England; son of John Wheeler and Christina Hill (McNutt) Wheeler-Bennett; married Ruth Harrison Risher, March 26, 1945. *Education:* Educated at private school in England.

CAREER: League of Nations Union, assistant publicity secretary, 1923-24; *Bulletin of International News,* founder and editor, 1924-32; University of Virginia, Charlottesville, lecturer in international law and relations, 1938-39; British Library of Information, New York, N.Y., member of staff, 1939-40; British Press Service, New York City, assistant director, 1940-41; British Information Services in the United States, special assistant to director general, 1941-42; British Political Warfare Mission in the United States, New York City, head of New York office, 1942-44; British Foreign Office, European adviser to political intelligence department, 1944, assistant director general, 1945; member of British prosecuting team at Nuremberg war criminal trials, 1946; Oxford University, Oxford, England, lecturer in international politics at New College, 1946-50, fellow of St. Antony's College, 1950-57; historical adviser for Royal Archives, 1959-75. Leslie Stephen Lecturer at Cambridge University, 1955; Dance Memorial Lecturer at Virginia Military Institute, 1960; visiting lecturer at University of Arizona, 1964, 1966, 1968-70, 1972-73, 1973-74; Page-Barbour Lecturer at University of Virginia, 1966, scholar-in-residence, 1967-68, 1971-72; visiting professor at New York University, 1967, 1968-69, 1969-70, 1971. Founder and honorary secretary of Information Service on International Affairs, 1924-30; honorary information secretary of Royal Institute of International Affairs, 1927-31, member of council, 1930-38, 1959-67; assistant to political adviser to Supreme Headquarters, Allied Expeditionary Force, 1944-45; historical adviser to Foreign Office Project for publishing German Foreign Ministry Archives, 1948-56. Governor of Lord Williams's Grammar School, Radley College, 1955-67, and Cuddlesdon Theological College, 1955-72; member of council of Ditchley Foundation, 1961-72 (chairman, 1961-63), and Malvern College, 1955-72 (chairman, 1964-67); trustee of Imperial War Museum, beginning 1961.

MEMBER: Royal Society of Literature (fellow), British Academy (fellow), Beefsteak Club, Brooke's Club, Pratt's Club, Union Interalliee, Colonnade Club, University of Virginia Club, Brook Club, Century Club, New York University Club, Society of Fellows (University of Virginia; honorary member). *Awards, honors:* Order of the British Empire, 1946; named honorary citizen of New Orleans, La., 1949; companion of the Order of St. Michael & St. George, 1953; knight commander of the Royal Victorian Order, 1959; D.C.L. from Oxford University, 1960; honorary fellow of St. Antony's College, Oxford, 1961; D.Litt. from New York University, 1973, University of Birmingham, 1973, and University of Arizona, 1974.

WRITINGS: Information on the Permanent Court of International Justice, Association for International Understanding, 1924, supplements, 1925, 1926, 1927, 1928; *Information on the Reduction of Armaments,* Allen & Unwin, 1925; (with F. E. Langerman) *Information on the Problem of Security, 1917-1926,* Allen & Unwin, 1927, reprinted by Fertig; *Information on the Renunciation of War, 1927-1928,* Allen & Unwin, 1928, reprinted, Kennikat, 1973; (with Maurice Fanshawe) *Information on the World Court, 1918-1928,* Allen & Unwin, 1929; (editor with Stephen A. Heald) *Documents on International Affairs,* Royal Institute of International Affairs, 1929.

(With Hugh Latimer) *Information on the Reparation Settlement: Being the Background and History of the Young Plan and the Hague Agreements, 1929-1930,* Allen & Unwin, 1930, reprinted by Fertig; *Disarmament and Security since Locarno, 1925-1931: Being the Political and Technical Background of the General Disarmament Conference, 1932,* Allen & Unwin, 1932, reprinted, Fertig, 1973; *The Wreck of Reparations: Being the Political Background of the Lausanne Agreement, 1932,* Allen & Unwin, 1933, reprinted, Fertig, 1972; *Memorandum on Germany and Disarmament, 1918-1932,* Royal Institute of International Affairs, 1933; *The Disarmament Deadlock,* Routledge & Sons, 1934; *The Pipe Dream of Peace: The Story of the Collapse of Disarmament,* Morrow, 1935, reprinted, Fertig, 1971; *Wooden Titan: Hindenburg in Twenty Years of German History, 1914-1934,* Morrow, 1936, reprinted, Archon, 1963, reissued as *Hindenburg: The Wooden Titan,* St. Martin's, 1967; *Brest-Litovsk: The Forgotten Peace, March, 1918,* Macmillan, 1938, published as *The Forgotten Peace: Brest-Litovsk,* Morrow, 1939, reprinted edition of original title, Norton, 1971; *The Treaty of Brest-Litovsk and Germany's Eastern Policy,* Farrar & Rinehart, 1939, 3rd edition, Clarendon Press, 1940.

Munich: Prologue to Tragedy, Duell, Sloan & Pearce, 1948.

The Nemesis of Power: The German Army in Politics, 1918-1945, Macmillan, 1953, St. Martin's, 1954, 2nd edition, 1964; *Three Episodes in the Life of Kaiser Wilhelm II,* Cambridge University Press, 1956; *King George VI: His Life and Reign,* St. Martin's, 1958.

John Anderson, Viscount Waverley, St. Martin's, 1962; *A Wreath to Clio: Studies in British, American, and German Affairs,* St. Martin's, 1967; (editor and author of introduction) *Action This Day: Working with Churchill, Memoirs by Lord Normanbrook,* Macmillan, 1968, St. Martin's, 1969.

(With Anthony Nicholls) *The Semblance of Peace: The Political Settlement After the Second World War,* St. Martin's 1972; (editor with the Earl of Longford, and contributor) *The History Makers,* St. Martin's, 1974; *Knaves, Fools, and Heroes: Europe Between the Wars* (memoirs), Macmillan, 1974, St. Martin's, 1975; *Special Relationships: America in Peace and War* (memoirs), St. Martin's, in press. British editor-in-chief of captured German Foreign Ministry Archives, 1946-48. Contributor to *Encyclopaedia Britannica* and to journals.

OBITUARIES: New York Times, December 11, 1975; *Time,* December 22, 1975; *Publishers Weekly,* January 5, 1976; *AB Bookman's Weekly,* March 1, 1976.

(Died December 9, 1975, in London, England)

*   *   *

WHITAKER, Mary   1896(?)-1976

1896(?)—January 7, 1976; British writer of short stories under pseudonym Malachi Whitaker. Obituaries: *AB Bookman's Weekly,* March 1, 1976.

*   *   *

WHITE, Laurence B(arton), Jr.   1935-

PERSONAL: Born September 21, 1935, in Norwood, Mass.; son of Laurence B. (an engineer) and Anna (a teacher; maiden name, Dewhurst) White; married Doris E. Pickard (a teacher aide), September 10, 1961; children: William Oliver, David Laurence. *Education:* University of New Hampshire, B.A., 1958. *Home:* 12 Rockland St., Stoughton, Mass. 02192. *Office:* Needham Public Schools, Needham, Mass. 02072.

CAREER: Museum of Science, Boston, Mass., supervisor of programs and courses, 1958-65, acting director of Theatre of Electricity, 1960-65; Needham Public Schools, Needham, Mass., assistant director of Needham Science Center, 1965—. *Military service:* U.S. Army, Signal Corps, combat photographer, 1958-59. *Member:* Society of American Magicians, Mycological Society, Beekeepers Association. *Awards, honors: So You Want to Be a Magician* was chosen one of the children's books of the year, 1972, by Child Study Association of America.

WRITINGS—For children; all published by Addison-Wesley, except as indicated: Life in the Shifting Dunes, Boston Museum of Science, 1960; *Investigating Science with Coins,* 1969; *Investigating Science with Rubber Bands,* 1969; *Investigating Science with Nails,* 1970; *Investigating Science with Paper,* 1970; *So You Want to Be a Magician?,* 1972; *Science Games,* 1975; *Science Puzzles,* 1975; *Science Toys,* 1975; *Science Tricks,* 1975; *The Great Mysto: That's You,* 1975. Author of material for Eduquip-Macallaster Co. Contributor to children's magazines.

WORK IN PROGRESS: A magic book for first readers; a book on the human body, written in a "believe it or not" format, for elementary school and junior high school students.

SIDELIGHTS: White writes: "My entire life has revolved around the education of young children. I believe they are the salvation of our world. They must be taught to enjoy their curiosity and find delight and pleasure in new discoveries. The books that I have written have simply shared with my readers some of the magic tricks I have had fun with and the science I have enjoyed learning in hopes they will discover the same pleasure in life that I have!"

BIOGRAPHICAL/CRITICAL SOURCES: New York Times Book Review, August 20, 1972.

* * *

WHITE, Minor 1908-1976

July 9, 1908—June 24, 1976; American photographer, educator, and editor. Obituaries: *New York Times,* June 26, 1976. (See index for previous *CA* sketch)

* * *

WHITE, Poppy Cannon 1906(?)-1975

PERSONAL: Born in Cape Town, South Africa; came to United States, 1909; daughter of Robert and Marian (Raskin) Whitney; married Caesar Cannon (divorced); married Alf Askland (deceased); married Charles Claudius Phillipe (divorced); married Walter White (an NAACP executive), 1949; children: (third marriage) Claudia; (fourth marriage) Cynthia. *Education:* Vassar College, B.A.; also attended Columbia University. *Home:* 36 East 38th St., New York, N.Y. 10016; and Breakneck Hill, West Redding, Conn. 06896.

CAREER: Columnist. Former food editor for magazines, including, at various times, *Ladies Home Journal, Mademoiselle, House Beautiful,* and *Town and Country;* food editor of National Broadcasting Co.'s "Home Show"; commentator on radio and television. *Member:* P.E.N., Authors League, Overseas Press Club, Commanderie des Bordeaux. *Awards, honors:* Commandeur, Chevaliers des Tastevins; commandeur, Commanderie de Cordon Bleu.

*WRITINGS—*All under name Poppy Cannon—Cookbooks: *The Can-Opener Cookbook,* Crowell, 1952, published as *The New Can-Opener Cookbook,* 1959, as *The New New Can-Opener Cookbook,* 1968; *The Bride's Cookbook,* Holt, 1954; *Unforbidden Sweets: Delicious Desserts of One Hundred Calories Or Less,* Crowell, 1958; *The ABC's of Quick and Glamorous Cooking,* Dolphin, 1961; *Eating European Abroad and At Home,* Doubleday, 1961; *The Electric Epicure's Cookbook,* Crowell, 1961, published as *Cooking With Electric Appliances,* Macfadden-Bartell, 1968; *The Fast Gourmet Cookbook,* Fleet Press, 1964; *The Frozen-Foods Cookbook,* Crowell, 1964; (with Patricia Brooks) *The President's Cookbook: Practical Recipes From George Washington To the Present,* Funk, 1968; *Poppy Cannon's All-Time, No-Time, Any-Time Cookbook,* Crowell, 1974.

Other: *A Gentle Knight: My Husband, Walter White* (biography), Rinehart, 1956.

Also author of *Italian Cooking* volume in Grosset's "Good Life Books" series; writer of column, "The Fast Gourmet" for Los Angeles Times Syndicate; contributor of food articles to newspapers and magazines.*

(Died April 1, 1975, in New York City)

* * *

WHITEHEAD, E(dward) A(nthony) 1933-

PERSONAL: Born April 3, 1933, in Liverpool, England; son of Edward (a compositor) and Catherine (a factory worker; maiden name, Curran) Whitehead; married Kathleen Horton, December 6, 1958 (divorced, 1976); married Gwenda Bagshaw, June 5, 1976; children: Kathleen, Helen. *Education:* Christ's College, Cambridge, B.A. (honors), 1955. *Agent:* Margaret Ramsay, 14A Goodwins Ct., St. Martin's Lane, London W.C.2, England.

CAREER: Worked at various postions, including postman, milkman, bus conductor, sales promotion writer, and drug salesman, 1957-66; Brunning Advertising, Liverpool, England, advertising copywriter, 1966-71; full-time writer, 1971—. Fellow in creative writing, Bulmershe College, Reading, England, 1976. *Military service:* British Army, 1955-57, became corporal. *Awards, honors:* George Devine Award from English Stage Co. of Royal Court Theatre, and *Evening Standard* Award, both 1971, both for "The Foursome."

*WRITINGS—*Plays: *The Foursome* (three-act; produced in London at Royal Court Theatre, February, 1971), Faber, 1972; *Alpha Beta* (three-act; produced at Royal Court Theatre, January, 1972), Faber, 1972; *The Sea Anchor* (three-act; produced in Amsterdam at Centrum Theatre, March, 1974), Faber, 1975; *Old Flames* (two-act; first produced in Bristol at New Vic Theatre, 1975), Faber, 1976; *The Punishment* (one-act television play; released by British Broadcasting Corp. 2 TV 1972) Hutchinson, 1976; *Mecca,* Faber, 1977.

Television plays: "Under the Age" (one-act), released by BBC 2 TV, 1972; "The Proofing Session" (three-act), released by Thames TV, 1977. Also author of "The Peddler" (three-act), released by BBC 1TV.

Also author of screenplays, "Alpha Beta" (adapted from author's own play of the same title), 1976, and of "The Foursome" (based on author's own play of the same title), 1977. Contributor of weekly theatre reviews, *Spectator* magazine, 1976—.

BIOGRAPHICAL/CRITICAL SOURCES: Play and Players, May, 1971, *London Observer,* January 30, 1972.

* * *

WHITMAN, Wanda ?-1976

?—February 9, 1976; American editor, book club administrator, and author. Obituaries: *Publishers Weekly,* March 1, 1976.

* * *

WICKER, Thomas Grey 1926-
(Tom Wicker, Paul Connolly)

PERSONAL: Born June 18, 1926, in Hamlet, N.C.; son of Delancey David and Esta (Cameron) Wicker; married Neva Jewett McLean, August 20, 1949 (divorced, 1973); married Pamela Hill, March 9, 1974; children: Cameron McLean, Thomas Grey. *Education:* University of North Carolina, A.B., 1948. *Home:* 169 East 80th St., New York, N.Y. 10021. *Agent:* Paul R. Reynolds Inc., 12 East 41st St., New York, N.Y. 10007. *Office:* 229 West 43rd St., New York, N.Y. 10036.

CAREER: Southern Pines Chamber of Commerce, Southern Pines, N.C., executive director, 1948-49; *Sandhill Citizen,* Aberdeen, N.C., editor, 1949; *The Robesonian,* Lumberton, N.C., managing editor, 1949-50; North Carolina Board of Public Welfare, Raleigh, public information director, 1950-51; *Winston-Salem Journal,* Winston-Salem, N.C., copy editor, 1951-52, sports editor, 1954-55, Sunday feature editor, 1955-56, Washington correspondent, 1957, editorial writer and city hall correspondent, 1958-59; *Nashville Tennesseean,* Nashville, Tenn., associate editor, 1959; *New York Times,* Washington Bureau, Washington D.C., staff member, 1960-64, chief of bureau, 1964-68. *Military service:* U.S. Naval Reserve, 1952-54; became lieutenant (junior grade). *Member:* Society of Nieman Fellows. *Awards, honors:* Nieman fellow, Harvard University, 1957-58. Honorary degrees from over eleven colleges and universities, including Duke University, Dickinson College, Rutgers University, and Michigan State University.

WRITINGS—Novels: *The Kingpin,* Sloane, 1953; *The Devil Must,* Harper, 1957; *The Judgment,* Morrow, 1961; *Facing the Lions,* Viking, 1973.

Nonfiction: *Kennedy Without Tears: The Man Behind the Myth,* Morrow, 1964; (author of foreword) Neal R. Peirce, *The People's President: The Electoral College in American History and the Direct Vote,* Simon & Schuster, 1968; *JFK and LBJ: The Influence of Personality Upon Politics,* Morrow, 1968; (author of introduction) *U.S. Kerner Commission Report,* Dutton, 1968; *A Time to Die,* Quadrangle, 1975.

Novels under pseudonym Paul Connolly: *Get Out of Town,* Gold Medal, 1951; *Tears Are For Angels,* Gold Medal, 1952; *So Fair, So Evil,* Gold Medal, 1955.

Contributor of articles to national magazines.

*   *   *

WICKER, Tom
See WICKER, Thomas Grey

*   *   *

WILDEBLOOD, Peter 1923-

PERSONAL: Born May 19, 1923, in Alassio, Italy; son of Henry Seddon (a civil engineer) and Winifred (Evans) Wildeblood. *Education:* Trinity College, Oxford, B.A., 1947. *Home:* 30 St. Paul's Rd., Canonbury, London N.1., England. *Agent:* Mrs. Francis Head, 503 Carrington House, Hertford St., London W.1., England.

CAREER: Peter Wildeblood Co. Ltd. (literary and theatrical production), London, England, director, 1959—; Startgrove Properties Ltd. (property development firm), London, England, director, 1971—. Executive producer of plays for London Weekend Television Ltd., 1970-72. Playwright, novelist, television scriptwriter and producer, free-lance writer and journalist. *Military service:* Royal Air Force, 1941-45. *Member:* St. Paul's Conservation and Residents Society (honorary treasurer, 1972—). *Awards, honors:* Ivor Novello award from Songwriters Guild of Great Britain, 1960, for "The Crooked Mile."

WRITINGS: Against the Law (nonfiction), Weidenfeld & Nicolson, 1955, Messner, 1959; *A Way of Life* (nonfiction), Weidenfeld & Nicolson, 1956; *The Main Chance* (novel), Weidenfeld & Nicolson, 1957; *West End People* (novel), Weidenfeld & Nicolson, 1958.

Plays: "The Crooked Mile," first produced in London at Cambridge Theatre, 1959; "House of Cards," first produced in London at Phoenix Theatre, 1963; "The People's Jack," first produced in Manchester at Stables Theatre, 1969.

Writer and producer of television series "Six Shades of Black," six programs, 1964, and "Rogues Gallery," ten programs, 1968, both for Granada Television Ltd.; contributor of scripts to television series, "Adventures of Don Quick," "New Scotland Yard," "Upstairs, Downstairs", "Within These Walls", "Father Brown", "Crime of Passion", "Ten from the Twenties", "The Verdict Is Yours", and "Crown Court"; writer of television adaptations of stories and plays by Laurence Housman, Noel Coward, G. K. Chesterton, and Aldous Huxley.

WORK IN PROGRESS: A nonfiction book for Hutchinson, *Queen Victoria's Scandals;* a television play, "The Testament of Francois Villon."

*   *   *

WILKE, Ekkehard-Teja 1941-

PERSONAL: Born November 28, 1941, in Pritzwalk, Germany; came to the United States in 1953, naturalized citizen, 1961; son of Wilfried O.G. (a teacher) and Elisabeth (Kaufman) Wilke; married Carol Lee Search (a teacher and artist), June 8, 1968; children: Kirsten-Maja, Marc-Hanno. *Education:* University of Illinois, B.A., 1962, M.A., 1963, Ph.D., 1967; Indiana University, M.L.S., 1976. *Home:* 188 Lawton Road, Riverside, Ill. 60546.

CAREER: Indiana University, Bloomington, historian, 1966-74; Institute for the Study of Nineteenth Century Europe, Riverside, Ill., director, 1974—. *Member:* American Historical Association, American Association of Teachers of German, German Literary Society of Chicago.

WRITINGS: Political Decadence: Personnel-Political Aspects of the German Government Crisis, 1894-1897, University of Illinois Press, 1976. Editor of *Studies in Modern European History and Culture,* 1975—.

WORK IN PROGRESS: A biography of Chancellor Bernhard von Bulow.

SIDELIGHTS: Wilke writes: "The motivating force behind my dedication to higher education is my desire to achieve, maintain, and transmit the tradition of highest quality humanistic education. Among the forming influences I mention Ranke and Burckhardt, Thomas and Heinrich Mann, Aby Warburg and the Warburg Institute."

*   *   *

WILLANS, Jean Stone 1924-

PERSONAL: Born October 3, 1924, in Hillsboro, Ohio; daughter of Homer (a teacher) and Ella (Keys) Hammond; married Donald Stone (a lieutenant commander in the military; deceased); married second husband, Richard Willans (a writer and management consultant); children: Suzanne Jeanne. *Education:* Attended San Diego Junior College. *Home:* 12 Kotewall Rd., D4 Alpine Court, Hong Kong.

CAREER: Family Loan Co., Miami, Fla., assistant to vice-president, 1946-49; U.S. Air Force, General Officers Branch, Washington, D.C., civilian supervisor, 1953-55; *Trinity* (magazine), Los Angeles, Calif., editor, 1961-65; Society of Stephen, Altadena, Calif., vice-president and director of Asian Office in Hong Kong, 1967—. Has lectured in the United States. Founder of Blessed Trinity Society.

WRITINGS: (Editor with husband, Richard Willans) *Charisma in Hong Kong,* Society of Stephen, 1970; (editor with R. Willans) *Spiritual Songs,* Society of Stephen, 1970; *The Acts of the Green Apples,* Whitaker House, 1974.

WORK IN PROGRESS: Bad Apples (tentative title), a sequel to *The Acts of the Green Apples.*

SIDELIGHTS: Jean Willans' husband, Richard, writes: "Jean Willans . . . is one of the pioneers of the charismatic renewal, a movement in the historic churches which advocates glossolalia, or speaking in tongues. . . . In 1959 she received the experience while a member of an Episcopal church in Van Nuys, California, and the phenomenon was immediately written up in *Time* and *Newsweek* magazines. Through her instruction and prayer during that period, thousands of people, mainly professionals of the middle and upper middle class, experienced a personal conversion to Christianity and received the Gift of the Holy Spirit, evidenced by speaking in languages unknown to the speakers. The difference between this and the previous movement which formed the Pentecostal churches, was the low key approach, lack of emotionalism and the emphasis on order. . . .'' The Willanses' work includes helping drug addicts through withdrawal with no pain or discomfort, and without the use of medication. Jean Willans has traveled to England, Mexico, and the People's Republic of China.

BIOGRAPHICAL/CRITICAL SOURCES: People, September 8, 1975.

* * *

WILLCOCK, M(alcolm) M(aurice) 1925-

PERSONAL: Born October 1, 1925, in Leeds, England; son of Maurice Excel and Evelyn (Brooks) Willcock; married Sheena Gourlay, September 7, 1957; children: Sarah Jane, Clare Elizabeth, Georgina Kate, Sophie Amanda. *Education:* Pembroke College, Cambridge, B.A. (first class honors), 1950. *Home:* Moorside, Wyresdale Rd., Lancaster, England. *Office:* Department of Classics and Archaeology, University of Lancaster, Lancaster, England.

CAREER: Cambridge University, Sidney Sussex College, Cambridge, England, fellow, 1951-65; University of Lancaster, Lancaster, England, professor of classics, 1965—. *Military service:* Royal Air Force, flying officer, 1944-47. *Member:* Joint Association of Classical Teachers.

WRITINGS: (Author of revision) Samuel Butler, translator, *Homer's Iliad and Odyssey,* Washington Square Press, 1964; *A Commentary on Homer's Iliad,* Macmillan, Books I-VI, 1970, Books VI-XII, in press; *A Companion to the Iliad* (based on Richard Lattimore's translation), University of Chicago Press, 1976; (editor with W. T. MacCary) *Plautus: Casina,* Cambridge University Press, 1976. Contributor of articles and reviews to classical journals.

WORK IN PROGRESS: A Commentary on Homer's Iliad, Books XIII-XXIV, for Macmillan.

* * *

WILLIAM, D.
See RONALD, David William 1937-

* * *

WILLIAMS, Alice Cary 1892-

PERSONAL: Born July 16, 1892, in Nantucket, Mass.; daughter of Harold (dean of Tufts Medical School) and Alice (Cary) Williams. *Education:* Educated in Boston, Mass. *Religion:* Episcopalian. *Home:* 18 Cliff Rd., Nantucket, Mass. 02554.

CAREER: Cedar Lane Farm (dairy farm), Ridgefield, Conn., owner, 1920-50; writer, 1966—.

WRITINGS: Thru the Turnstile (a novel), Houghton, 1976. Contributor to magazines, including *House Beautiful, Yankee,* and *Fate.*

WORK IN PROGRESS: Two novels, *Farwell's Foresight* and *A Farming Story in World War Two.*

SIDELIGHTS: Alice Williams comments: ''My life has become increasingly vital since I began to write seriously in 1966.''

* * *

WILLIAMS, Carol M. 1917-

PERSONAL: Born December 1, 1917, in Detroit, Mich.; daughter of Ralph M. (an engineer) and Ethel Jeanette (Harris) Williams. *Education:* Wayne State University, B.A., 1940, M.A., 1945; currently attending University of Albuquerque for B.Th. *Religion:* Protestant. *Home:* 7819 Academy Trail N.E., Albuquerque, N.M. 87109.

CAREER: City of Detroit, Detroit, Mich., policewoman, 1941-51; U.S. Air Force, information officer serving in Alaska, France, and Hawaii, 1951-71, retired as major. Consultant in criminal investigation. *Member:* Zonta Club International.

WRITINGS: The Organization and Practices of Police Women's Divisions in the United States, National Training School of Public Service, 1946; *Make God Your Friend,* Zondervan, 1975. Contributor of poems and articles to *Christian Century* and *Detroit News.*

WORK IN PROGRESS: A book in the religious field; poetry.

AVOCATIONAL INTERESTS: Painting with oils and watercolors.

* * *

WILLIAMS, Edward Ainsworth 1907-1976

1907—June 21, 1976; American lawyer, economist, government official, and writer. Obituaries: *Washington Post,* June 27, 1976.

* * *

WILLIAMS, Frederick D(eForrest) 1918-

PERSONAL: Born May 13, 1918, in Braintree, Vt.; son of Frank Arthur (a steel executive) and Florence (Bigford) Williams; married Florence Green (a kindergarten teacher), April 8, 1944; children: Sandi (Mrs. Marty Jacobson), Craig Allen, Julianne (Mrs. Gary Masters), Kathy Marie. *Education:* Middlebury College, B.A., 1947; University of Connecticut, M.A., 1948; Indiana University, Ph.D., 1953. *Home:* 810 Larkspur Dr., East Lansing, Mich. 48823; 776 North Shore Dr., Walloon Lake, Mich. 49796. *Office:* Department of History, Michigan State University, East Lansing, Mich. 48824.

CAREER: Wayne State University, Detroit, Mich., instructor in history, 1950-54; Michigan State University, East Lansing, assistant professor, 1954-60, associate professor, 1960-68, professor of history, 1968—. Member, Michigan Civil War Centennial Commission, 1960-66; appointed by Secretary of the Army as member of advisory panel, Reserve Officers Training Corps Affairs, 1970—. *Military service:* U.S. Army Air Forces, 1942-46; became first lieutenant. *Member:* Organization of American Historians, American Historical Association, University Club of Michigan State University. *Awards, honors:* American Philosophical Society grants, 1957, 1958; Clarence M. Burton Memorial Lecturer Award from Michigan Historical Society, 1960.

WRITINGS: Michigan Soldiers in the Civil War, Michigan Historical Commission, 1960; (editor) *The Wild Life of the Army: Civil War Letters of James A. Garfield,* Michigan

State University Press, 1964; (editor with Harry James Brown) *The Diary of James A. Garfield,* Michigan State University Press, Volumes I and II, 1967, Volume III, 1973. Contributor to *Encyclopedia Americana;* contributor of articles and book reviews to professional journals.

WORK IN PROGRESS: Volume IV of *The Diary of James A. Garfield,* completion expected in 1977; articles on Civil War military history and biography.

* * *

WILLIAMS, John Stuart 1920-

PERSONAL: Born August 13, 1920, in Mountain Ash, Wales; son of Gwilym John (a shopkeeper) and Laura (Morgan) Williams; married Sheelagh Lee (a teacher), February 8, 1948; children: Michael, Gavin. *Education:* University of Wales, University College, Cardiff, B.A. (first class honors), 1942, M.A., 1957. *Home:* 52 Dan-y-Coed Rd., Cyncoed, Cardiff, Wales. *Office:* Cardiff College of Education, South Glamorgan Institute of Higher Education, Cyncoed Rd., Cardiff, Wales.

CAREER: High school English teacher in Whitchurch, Glamorgan, Wales, 1943-56, head of department, 1946-56; South Glamorgan Institute of Higher Education (now part of Cardiff College of Education), Cardiff, Wales, lecturer in English and drama, 1956—, head of department, 1956—. Composer; his work has been performed in England and has been broadcast by British Broadcasting Corp. Member of Welsh Arts Council literature committee and New Theatre (Cardiff) trust management committee, 1972—.

MEMBER: National Union of Teachers, Welsh Academy (English section). *Awards, honors:* Literature prize from Welsh Arts Council, 1971, for *Dic Penderyn and Other Poems.*

WRITINGS—Poetry: *Last Fall,* Outposts Publications, 1962; *Green Rain,* Christopher Davies, 1967; *Dic Penderyn and Other Poems,* Gomer, 1970; *Banna Strand,* Gomer, 1975.

Editor: (With Richard Milner) *Dragons and Daffodils,* Christopher Davies, 1960; (with Meic Stephens) *The Lilting House: An Anthology of Anglo-Welsh Poetry, 1917-1967,* Dent, 1969; *Poems '69,* Gomer, 1969. Contributor to literary journals, including *Anglo-Welsh Review, Decal International Review, Transatlantic Review, Spirit, Aquarius,* and *Planet.*

WORK IN PROGRESS: A book of verse; a book of stories; research on Anglo-Welsh poetry since 1945.

SIDELIGHTS: Williams writes: "I started as a composer, achieved some success but found it difficult to handle teaching and composition at the same time. I chose teaching. . . . In my writing the exploration of the ambiguity of reality remains a recurring theme. I have translated from Spanish and French and am able to read Welsh well enough, but speak it badly."

BIOGRAPHICAL/CRITICAL SOURCES: Outposts, winter, 1967; Raymond Garlick, *An Introduction to Anglo-Welsh Literature,* University of Wales Press, 1970.

* * *

WILLIAMS, L(eslie) Pearce 1927-

PERSONAL: Born September 8, 1927, in Harmon, N.Y.; son of George (in the theater) and Addie (a businesswoman; maiden name, Williams) Greenberg; married Sylvia Irene Alessandrini, September 3, 1949; children: David R., Alison

R., Adam J., Sarah L. *Education:* Cornell University, B.A., 1949, Ph.D., 1952. *Politics:* Democrat. *Religion:* Atheist. *Home address:* R.D. 3, Townline Rd., Ithaca, N.Y. 14850. *Office:* Department of History, Cornell University, Ithaca, N.Y. 14853.

CAREER: Yale University, New Haven, Conn., instructor in history, 1952-56; University of Delaware, Newark, assistant professor of history, 1956-59; Cornell University, Ithaca, N.Y., assistant professor, 1960-62, associate professor, 1962-65, professor, 1965-71, John Stambaugh Professor of History, 1971—. Associate historian for National Foundation for Infantile Paralysis, 1956-57. *Military service:* U.S. Navy, 1945-46. *Member:* Academie Internationale d'histoire des sciences, History of Science Society, American Historical Association, Royal Institution of Great Britain. *Awards, honors:* National Science Foundation fellowship, 1959-60; Pfizer Award from History of Science Society, 1965, naming *Michael Faraday, a Biography* best book on the history of science.

WRITINGS: Michael Faraday, a Biography, Basic Books, 1965; *The Origins of Field Theory,* Random House, 1967; (with Brian Tierney and Donald Kagan) *Great Issues in Western Civilization,* Random House, 1967; (editor) *Relativity Theory: Its Origins and Impact,* Wiley, 1968; (editor) *The Selected Correspondence of Michael Faraday,* two volumes, Cambridge University Press, 1971; *An Album of Science,* Scribner, 1976.

WORK IN PROGRESS: A textbook on Western civilization; a biography of A. M. Ampere.

SIDELIGHTS: Williams writes: "My major interest is in the genesis and development of scientific ideas. This means that I enjoy writing biographies for scientific ideas are uniquely individual in their nature." *Avocational interests:* Hunting (owns and operates a shooting preserve), raising and training Blue Weimaraners, gardening.

* * *

WILLIAMS, Mary Elizabeth 1909-1976

November 30, 1909—July 31, 1976; American mathematician, educator, and biographer. Obituaries: *New York Times,* August 1, 1976.

* * *

WILLIAMS, Phyllis S(awyer) 1931-

PERSONAL: Born January 27, 1931, in Brewer, Maine; daughter of Earle Linwood (a salesman) and Dorris (a registered nurse; maiden name, Wood) Sawyer; married Anthony Williams (a bridge inspector), February 15, 1958; children: Wesley, Jeremy, Bethany, Rowena. *Education:* Bates College, A.B., 1954; graduate study at St. Joseph College, Standish, Maine, summer, 1957, and University of Maine, 1958, 1965-66. *Home address:* R.F.D. 1, Box 204, Hampden Highlands, Maine 04445. *Office:* Maternal and Child Health Council, Inc., 611 Hammond, Bangor, Maine 04401.

CAREER: Junior high school teacher of English and science in Bangor, Maine, 1959-60; University of Maine, Orono, instructor in nursing, 1961-67; Eastern Maine Medical Center, Bangor, instructor in maternal and child health, 1968; self-employed as nutrition consultant in Penquis WIC program, 1968-76, and as health, education, and nursing consultant in Penquis family panning program, 1972-76; Maternal and Child Health Council, Bangor, Maine, coordinator of Child to Parent Health Education Project, 1976—, member of board of directors. Chairman of board of directors, Maternal and Child Health Council, 1964-69. Family Health Center, member of board of directors, vice-president, 1975—. Nutrition consultant, Illinois Association for Retarded Citizens. *Member:* International Childbirth Education Association, American Nurses' Association.

WRITINGS: (With Margaret Kenda) *The Natural Baby Food Cookbook,* Nash Publishing, 1972; *Nourishing Your Unborn Child,* Nash Publishing, 1974. Contributor to professional journals and popular magazines.

WORK IN PROGRESS: The Working Parents Handbook, with Margaret Kenda; a novel; continuing research on maternal and child health, nutrition, and counseling.

SIDELIGHTS: Phyllis Williams writes: "I live in a one hundred thirty-year-old farm house in the process of restoration. We have assorted animals—a regular McDonald's farm—and garden organically.... I am terribly provincial, being unable to conceive of living away from the East coast and especially New England, although I love to travel." She adds: "I have been writing since childhood. Somehow I got sidetracked into pre-med and then nursing from my original plans to become a journalist."

AVOCATIONAL INTERESTS: Drawing and painting, sewing and crafts, sports and dramatics, domestic European travel.

*   *   *

WILLIAMS, Rebecca (Yancy)   1899-1976

1899—April 6, 1976; American novelist. Obituaries: *New York Times,* April 7, 1976; *Washington Post,* April 10, 1976.

*   *   *

WILLIAMSON, H(enry) D(arvall)   1907-

PERSONAL: Born August 14, 1907, in Brisbane, Australia; son of Andrew (a merchant) and Cecile Deborah (Darvall) Williamson; married Marie Isabel Rea, December 22, 1934; children: Ann Moorea (Mrs. Leslie Michael Wilson), Sandra Mary (Mrs. Lancelot Charles Chapple). *Education:* Educated in Parramatta, Australia. *Religion:* Anglican. *Home:* 15 Fiddens Wharf Rd., Killara, New South Wales, Australia.

CAREER: Worked in family firm of Williamson, Croft Pty. Ltd., 1932-66, and with Dulux Pty. Ltd., 1966-69. *Military service:* Royal Australian Air Force, 1942-46. *Member:* Australian Society of Authors. *Awards, honors:* Second prize from *Sydney Morning Herald,* 1957, for the novel, *The Sunlit Plain.*

WRITINGS: The Sunlit Plain (novel), Angus & Robertson, 1958; *Sammy Anderson, Commercial Traveller* (novel), Angus & Robertson, 1959; *Fierce Encounter: Stories of Life and Death in the Australian Bush,* A. H. & A. W. Reed, 1970; *The Year of the Koala,* Scribner, 1975. Contributor of articles and stories to *Walkabout* and to Sydney newspapers.

SIDELIGHTS: Williamson left school at age seventeen to become a wool classer. The Depression came. During the years of the rabbit plague in central New South Wales he worked as a skin buyer, and his first book emerged from that experience. His main interests are the animals native to Australia and the effects of onrushes of land clearing. He feels that "Progress should be more truly scientific—that not only the main and immediate effect of a project be carefully considered but also the effects that are too often dismissed as minor."

WILLIAMSON, Norma (Goff)   1934-

PERSONAL: Born August 8, 1934, in Pascagoula, Miss.; daughter of Carey Wood (employed by a paper company) and Audrey (Broadus) Goff; married John Cecil Williamson (a clergyman), June 7, 1953; children: Sam, Lee Ann, Amos, Luke. *Education:* Mississippi University for Women, B.S. (cum laude), 1966. *Religion:* United Methodist. *Home:* 210 Woodlawn Rd., Starkville, Miss. 39759.

CAREER: High school teacher in Columbus, Miss., 1966-67; sometime writer, 1967-75; Mississippi State University, Starkville, instructor in English, 1975; part-time writer and speaker, 1975—. *Member:* Sigma Tau Delta, Phi Kappa Phi.

WRITINGS: Please Get Off the Seesaw Slowly, Revell, 1975. Author of "Sorting It Out," a column in *Mississippi United Methodist Advocate.*

SIDELIGHTS: Norma Williamson writes: "When I was in my mid-thirties, I gave birth to two little boys, one eighteen months after the other, and I saw right away that I was going to have to develop a sense of humor or go under. My writing began as therapy and a search for perspective. To my continuing amazement, others seem to identify with it and enjoy it." Her book and her column were described as being "at times purely inspirational, at times tongue-in-cheek inspirational, at times entertaining, rarely informative. Like their author, they do not lend themselves to neat, boxed-in descriptions." *Avocational interests:* Travel (Greece, Israel, Italy), skiing in New Mexico, reading, music, needlework, gardening "with great gusto and very little skill."

*   *   *

WILLIS, Irene   1929-

PERSONAL: Born May 27, 1929, in New York, N.Y.; daughter of George Sanford (a teacher) and Rhoda (in sales; maiden name, Unger) Jolley; married Richard Emerson Willis, June 12, 1949 (divorced, October, 1974); children: Grant Emerson. *Education:* St. Lawrence University, student, 1946-48; State University of New York College at Fredonia, B.S., 1953; New York University, M.A., 1963. *Politics:* "Usually vote Democratic." *Religion:* Unitarian-Universalist. *Home:* 500 East 85th St., New York, N.Y. 10028. *Agent:* Anita Diamant, Writer's Workshop, Inc., 51 East 42nd St., New York, N.Y. 10017. *Office:* Rye Neck High School, Mamaroneck, N.Y. 10543.

CAREER: High school English teacher and director of speech and dramatics in Valhalla, N.Y., 1961-71; Rye Neck Public Schools, Mamaroneck, N.Y., English teacher and chairman of department, 1971-73, director of alternative high school, 1974-76, coordinating teacher at the high school, 1976—. *Member:* Authors Guild of Authors League of America, Association for Humanistic Psychology, National Education Association, New York State United Teachers, New York Poets Cooperative, New York State English Council.

WRITINGS: (With Richard Willis) *Rosie's Josie* (juvenile), Children's Press, 1955; (with R. Willis and Walter Oliver) *New Worlds of Reading,* with reader's notebook, Harcourt, 1968; (with R. Willis) *New Worlds Ahead,* with reader's notebook, Harcourt, 1968; (with Arlene Kramer Richards) *How to Get It Together When Your Parents Are Coming Apart,* McKay, 1976.

Poetry is anthologized is *Love in New York,* edited by Donald Wigal, Alternative (New York City), 1976. Contributor of poems to *Cosmopolitan* and *New York Times.*

WORK IN PROGRESS: Research for a book on friendship, with Arlene Kramer Richards.

WILLKE, John Charles 1925-

PERSONAL: Born April 5, 1925, in Maria Stein, Ohio; son of Gerard T. (a physician) and Marie (Wuennemann) Willke; married Barbara Jean Hiltz (professor of nursing, author, and lecturer), June 5, 1948; children: Marie Margaret (Mrs. Robert Meyers), Theresa Ann, Charles Gerard, Joseph John, Anne Margaret, Timothy Edward. *Education:* Attended Xavier University, Cincinnati, Ohio, and Oberlin College; University of Cincinnati, M.D., 1948. *Religion:* Roman Catholic. *Home and office:* 7634 Pineglen Dr., Cincinnati, Ohio 45224.

CAREER: Good Samaritan Hospital, Cincinnati, Ohio, intern, 1948-49, resident, 1949-51; private practice in family medicine and counseling, 1950—, and in obstetrics, 1950-65. Certified sex educator. *Military service:* U.S. Air Force, Medical Corps, 1952-54; became captain.

MEMBER: World Federation of Physicians Who Respect Life (member of founding board of directors), International Birthright (member of founding board of directors), American Medical Association, National Right to Life Committee (member of founding board of directors; executive vice-president), American Academy of Family Practice, American Board of Family Practice, American Association of Sex Educators and Counselors, National Alliance for Family Life (founding member), National Institute of Family Relations, Ohio Right to Life Society (president), Ohio State Medical Association, Academy of Medicine of Cincinnati, Cincinnati Right to Life (co-chairman).

WRITINGS—All with wife, Barbara Willke: *The Wonder of Sex,* Hiltz Publishing, 1964; *Sex Education: The How-To for Teachers,* Hiltz Publishing, 1970; *Sex: Should We Wait,* Hiltz Publishing, 1970; *Handbook on Abortion,* Hayes Publishing, 1971; *Sex and Love,* Silver Burdett, 1972; *Marriage,* Silver Burdett, 1972; *How to Teach the Pro-Life Story,* Hiltz, 1973. Contributor to more than thirty magazines and professional journals.

WORK IN PROGRESS: Continued research on fetology, complications of induced abortion, viability and premature baby survival, as well as teaching methods for all these areas.

SIDELIGHTS: During the last dozen years, Willke has concentrated on preserving family life. He attempted to teach parents to love each other more and to raise stable children, to lead young adults toward mature decisions that would help them in permanent and satisfying marriages. His most recent conviction is that, if "the war on the unborn was won by the pro-abortionists, all other efforts at saving family life in America were doomed to failure."

*   *   *

WILSON, (Lindsay) Charles 1932-

PERSONAL: Born April 9, 1932, in Bristol, Va.; son of Crawford L. (a mining engineer) and Nancy (a teacher; maiden name, Rollins) Wilson; married Miriam Williams (a registered nurse and psychometrist), 1973; children: Nancy, Barrie, Rebecca, Patrick, Charles William. *Education:* University of Virginia, B.A., 1953; West Virginia University, M.S., 1956, Ph.D., 1958. *Home:* 1555 Renwood Dr., Wooster, Ohio 44691. *Office:* Ohio Agricultural Research and Development Center, Wooster, Ohio 44691.

CAREER: University of Arkansas, Fayetteville, assistant professor, 1958-60, associate professor, 1960-64, professor of biology, 1964-68; U.S. Department of Agriculture, Agricultural Research Service Shade Tree Laboratory, Dela-

ware, Ohio, investigations leader, 1968-74; Ohio Agricultural Research and Development Center, Wooster, Ohio, research plant pathologist, 1974—. *Member:* International Society of Arboriculture, American Association for the Advancement of Science, American Phytopathological Society, Mycological Society of America, Botanical Society of America.

WRITINGS: The World of Terrariums, Jonathan David, 1975; *Gardener's Hint Book,* Jonathan David, 1976.

WORK IN PROGRESS: A book entitled *The Sex Life of Plants;* research on the fundamental nature of diseased plant cells and on the biological control of Dutch Elm disease.

*   *   *

WILSON, Francis Graham 1901-1976

November 26, 1901—May 24, 1976; American political scientist, educator, news media expert, and author of books in his field. Obituaries: *New York Times,* May 27, 1976.

*   *   *

WILSON, G(lenn) D(aniel) 1942-

PERSONAL: Born December 29, 1942, in Christchurch, New Zealand; son of Daniel (an estate agent) and Dorothy (May) Wilson; married Judith Ann Holden (a graphic artist), February 28, 1967; children: Kirsten Lee. *Education:* University of Canterbury, M.A. (first class honors), 1966; University of London, Ph.D., 1970. *Home:* 24 Dorchester Dr., London S.E.24, England. *Office:* Institute of Psychiatry, University of London, De Crespigny Park, London S.E.5, England.

CAREER: University of London, London, England, lecturer in psychology, 1970—. Visiting professor at California State University, Los Angeles, summers, 1971, 1972, 1974, 1975. *Member:* British Psychological Society (associate member).

WRITINGS: (Editor) *The Psychology of Conservatism,* Academic Press, 1973; (with H. J. Eysenck) *The Experimental Study of Freudian Theories,* Methuen, 1973; *Improve Your IQ,* Futura, 1974; (editor with Eysenck) *A Textbook of Human Psychology,* University Park Press, 1976; (with Eysenck) *Know Your Own Personality,* Penguin, 1976; (with D.K.B. Nias) *The Mystery of Love,* Open Books, 1976; (with Diana Grylls) *Know Your Child's IQ,* Futura, 1977. Contributor of more than a hundred articles to professional journals.

WORK IN PROGRESS: A book on sexual fantasy.

SIDELIGHTS: Wilson writes that he is a part-time professional opera singer, commenting that he "claims the distinction of being the only British psychologist to have sung Don Giovanni in a Hollywood nightclub."

*   *   *

WILSON, Robert Anton 1932-

PERSONAL: Born January 18, 1932, in Brooklyn, N.Y.; son of John Joseph (a longshoreman) and Elizabeth (Milli) Wilson; married Arlen Riley (a free-lance writer), December 14, 1958; children: Karuna, Djoti, Graham, Luna. *Education:* Attended Brooklyn Polytechnical College, 1952-57, and New York University, 1957-58. *Politics:* "Anarcho-Technocrat." *Religion:* "Transcendental Atheist; Experimental Mystic." *Home and office:* 2510 College, Berkeley, Calif. 94704. *Agent:* Al Zuckerman, Writers House, 132 West 31st St., New York, N.Y. 10001.

CAREER: Ebasco Services, New York, N.Y., engineering aide, 1952-58; Antioch Bookplate, Yellow Springs, Ohio, assistant sales manager, 1962-65; *Playboy,* Chicago, Ill., associate editor, 1966-71. Educational director of School of Living, Brookville, Ohio, 1962. *Member:* World Esoteric Order (founding member, 1974—), Bavarian Illuminati, John Dillinger Died for You Society (treasurer, 1966—), Ordo Templi Celatus, New Reformed Orthodox Order of the Golden Dawn, Sociedad Magico de Chango.

WRITINGS: Playboy's Book of Forbidden Words, Playboy Press, 1973; *Sex and Drugs: Journey Beyond Limits,* Playboy Press, 1973; *The Sex Magicians* (novel), Ball Press, 1974; *Illuminatus!* (novel), three volumes, Dell, 1975; *Prometheus Rising: A Magick Manual for the Space Age,* Llewellyn, 1976. Editor of *Verbal Level,* 1957-59; associate editor of *Fact,* 1965, contributing editor, 1965-66.

WORK IN PROGRESS: The Starseed Signals, "a book on Dr. Timothy Leary and the biological mutation preparing us for starflight, contact with Higher Intelligence, and immortality," and *Death Shall Have No Dominion,* on current longevity and immortality research; a novel concerning modern physics, *The Universe Next Door.*

* * *

WINDLEY, Charles Ellis 1942-

PERSONAL: Name originally Irving Epps Jordan, Jr.; name legally changed, 1947; born June 20, 1942, in Norfolk, Va.; son of Irving Epps (a shipbuilder) and Betty (Ellis) Jordan; married Shirley Lee, November 22, 1963 (divorced September 22, 1970); married Lisa Tagatac, December 31, 1974; children: Saida Dawn. *Education:* Attended American University, 1960-61, and American Academy of Dramatic Arts, 1962; private study in mime, dance, and acting. *Home:* 2032 Sanford Ave. S.W., Roanoke, Va. 24014. *Office:* 1501 Broadway, Suite 2907, New York, N.Y. 10036.

CAREER: Actor, magician, and writer; served as apprentice to professional magicians; has performed on cruise ships, fairs, shopping malls, night clubs, amusement parks, circuses, and on tour; has performed in or directed seventeen plays in Virginia, Washington, D.C., and Indiana. *Member:* Australian Society of Magicians (honorary life member).

WRITINGS: Magic Master's Course in Magic, Magic Masters, Inc., 1970; *Teaching and Learning with Magic,* Acropolis Books, 1976.

WORK IN PROGRESS: Fleas and Floating Girls, an autobiography; a high school version of *Teaching and Learning with Magic.*

SIDELIGHTS: Windley writes: *Teaching and Learning with Magic* was written not as a text on the magic art but as a textbook to be used in elementary school education, as a teaching aid. The magic secrets are based on math or science skills."

He has performed in Mexico and Canada, in the Senate Dining Room of the U.S. Capitol, for Clyde Beatty-Cole Brothers Circus, and for Circus Bartok.

* * *

WINEGARTEN, Renee 1922-

PERSONAL: Born June 23, 1922, in London, England; daughter of Sidney (a sales manager) and Debbe (Tobias) Aarons; married Asher Winegarten (deputy director general of National Farmers Union), March 24, 1946. *Education:*

Girton College, Cambridge, B.A., 1943, M.A., 1945, Ph.D., 1950. *Politics:* "Liberalism with a small 'l'." *Religion:* Jewish. *Home:* 12 Heather Walk, Edgware, Middlesex HA8 9TS, England. *Agent:* Georges Borchardt, Inc., 145 East 52nd St., New York, N.Y. 10022.

CAREER: British Foreign Office, London, England, research assistant in Latin American section of research department, 1943-45; Cambridge University, Girton College, Cambridge, England, research scholar and supervisor, 1946-47; Westminster Tutors, London, tutor in French and Spanish, 1947-54; free-lance literary critic, 1954—. *Member:* Society of Authors.

WRITINGS: French Lyric Poetry in the Age of Malherbe, Manchester University Press, 1954; *Writers and Revolution: The Fatal Lure of Action,* F. Watts, 1974; (contributor) Leslie Field and Joyce Field, editors, *Bernard Malamud: A Collection of Critical Essays,* Prentice-Hall, 1975; (contributor) Henry A. Turner, Jr., editor, *Reappraisals of Fascism,* F. Watts, 1975. Contributor to literary and political journals. Member of editorial board of *Jewish Quarterly.*

WORK IN PROGRESS: A commissioned biography.

SIDELIGHTS: Renee Winegarten writes: "My chief interests now lie in the fields of French, English, and American writing, and more particularly, in the inter-relation of literature and politics." *Avocational interests:* Theatre, travel, gardening.

* * *

WINEK, Charles L(eone) 1936-

PERSONAL: Born January 13, 1936, in Erie, Pa.; married Mary Helen Newman (a registered nurse and pharmacist), September 10, 1960; children: Tracey, Duffy, Mike. *Education:* Duquesne University, B.S., 1957, M.S., 1959; Ohio State University, Ph.D., 1962. *Religion:* Roman Catholic. *Home:* 4223 Estate Court, Allison Park, Pa. 15101. *Office:* Allegheny County Coroner's Office, 542 Fourth Ave., Pittsburgh, Pa. 15219.

CAREER: Procter & Gamble Co., Miami Valley Laboratories, Cincinnati, Ohio, toxicologist, 1962-63; Duquesne University, Pittsburgh, Pa., assistant professor, 1963-65, associate professor, 1965-69, professor of toxicology, 1970—, adjunct professor of education, 1969—, guest lecturer at School of Law; chief toxicologist for Allegheny County Coroner's Office, 1965—. Visiting professor at Mount Mercy College, 1966-68; adjunct professor of toxicology at University of Pittsburgh, 1967—. Faculty member of Allegheny County Police and Fire Academy. Registered pharmacist in Pennsylvania and Ohio. Visiting scientist, Kirksville School of Osteopathic Medicine, University of Tennessee, University of Oklahoma, Northeast Louisiana State College, University of Arizona, St. Louis College of Pharmacy, University of Wisconsin, Madison, Xavier University of Louisiana, and University of Georgia. Past member of Pennsylvania governor's board on drugs, devices, and cosmetics; member of regional training council for governor's conference on alcohol and drug abuse and of advisory board of Pennsylvania State Department of Health, Bureau of Laboratories.

MEMBER: International Association of Forensic Toxicologists, International College of Pediatrics (fellow), Society of Toxicology, American Association for the Advancement of Science, American Pharmaceutical Association, Academy of Pharmaceutical Sciences, American Society for Clinical Pharmacology and Therapeutics, American Society of Pharmacognosy, American Association of Poison Control Centers (member of publications committee), Drug Information Association, American Academy of Forensic Sciences (fellow), American Association of University Professors, American Academy of Clinical Toxicology (charter member), Forum for the Advancement of Toxicology, Association of Official Analytical Chemists, Society of Forensic Toxicology, Association of Drug Detection Laboratories, American Association for Clinical Chemistry, Canadian Association for Research in Toxicology, Northeastern Association of Forensic Scientists, New York Academy of Sciences, Allegheny County Medical Society, Pittsburgh Institute of Legal Medicine, Pan American Medical Society, Dapper Dan Club of Pittsburgh, Sigma Xi, Rho Chi, Phi Delta Chi.

WRITINGS: Everything You Wanted to Know About Drug Abuse But Were Afraid to Ask, Dekker, 1974.

Technical works: (With Lucy Hoblitzelle) *Pharmacology Applied to Patient Care,* F. A. Davis, 1965, 3rd edition, 1969; (with S. P. Shanor, W. D. Collom, and F. W. Fochtman) *1971 Drug Abuse Reference,* BEK Technical Publications, 1971; (contributor) David Maurer and Victor Vogel, editors, *Narcotics and Narcotic Addiction,* C. C Thomas, 1970, 4th edition, 1974; (contributor) Andres Goth, editor, *Medical Pharmacology,* Mosby, 6th edition (Winek was not included in earlier editions), 7th edition, 1974; (editor) *The Toxicology Annual 1974,* Dekker, 1975; (contributor) I. L. Simmons and Galen W. Ewing, editors, *Progress in Analytical Chemistry,* Volume VII, Plenum, 1974; (with Shanor) *Clinical Pharmacology,* F. A. Davis, 1976.

Contributor to *Wecht's Legal Medicine Annual* and contributing editor to *Modern Drug Encyclopedia.* Contributor of more than fifty articles and reviews to professional journals. Editor of *Toxicology Newsletter, Poison Penletter* (of the American Association of Poison Control Centers), and *Toxicology Annual;* editor-at-large for Dekker; member of editorial board of *Clinical Toxicology* and *Forensic Science;* editorial consultant for *Physicians' Assistant* and *MXR-Malpractice X-Posure Reports.*

* * *

WINGATE, Gifford W(endel) 1925-

PERSONAL: Born November 29, 1925, in Valley Stream, N.Y.; son of Lester Brayton (a chemist) and Emily (Hinves) Wingate; married Jeanette Skavina, February 10, 1949 (divorced, May, 1965); married Elizabeth Neece (a university professor), June 23, 1967; children: Lynn Michael, Mark Lester, David Kean, Helen Lorraine. *Education:* State University of New York at Albany, B.A., 1949, M.A., 1950; Cornell University, Ph.D., 1954. *Home:* 1000 Madeline, El Paso, Tex. 79902. *Office:* Department of Drama and Speech, University of Texas, El Paso, Tex. 79999.

CAREER: Ithaca College, Ithaca, N.Y., instructor in speech and drama, 1953-54; Union College, Schenectady, N.Y., assistant professor, 1954-57, associate professor of speech and drama, 1957-64, director of theatre, 1954-57; University of Texas at El Paso, professor of drama and speech, 1964—. *Military service:* U.S. Army, Field Artillery, 1943-46. *Member:* Speech Communication Association of America, American Theatre Association, Southwest Theatre Association, Texas Educational Theatre Association, Phi Kappa Phi.

WRITINGS—Plays; all published by Samuel French: *The Lion Who Wouldn't* (juvenile), 1969; *The Tiger in Traction* (juvenile), 1970; *Family,* 1973; *How the Chicken Hawk Won the West* (juvenile), 1975.

WORK IN PROGRESS: A children's play; poems; a musical.

SIDELIGHTS: Wingate's two major literary concerns are "original children's plays not based on past children's stories and designed to be shared with adults; and plays with music which break with the traditions of American musical comedy in a new combination of poetry, action, and music."

* * *

WINSOR, Roy 1912-

PERSONAL: Born April 13, 1912, in Chicago, Ill.; son of Edward Arthur (a house painter) and Florence Louise (Williams) Winsaver; married Martha March Ricker, October 22, 1938; children: Ann, Mary, Ricker, Catherine. *Education:* Harvard University, A.B. (magna cum laude), 1936. *Politics:* Independent. *Religion:* Protestant. *Home:* 1007 Prospect Ave., Pelham Manor, N.Y. 10803.

CAREER: Columbia Broadcasting System (CBS), New York, N.Y., apprentice-in-training, 1936-37; WCCO-Radio, Minneapolis, Minn., assistant program-production manager, 1937-38; National Broadcasting Co. (NBC), Chicago, Ill., director of "Vic and Sade," 1938-39, Leo Burnett Co., Chicago, Ill., radio director and producer of "H.V. Kaltenbokn and the News," 1939-40; Blackett-Sample Hummert, Inc., Chicago, Ill., supervisor of eight Proctor & Gamble radio programs, including "Ma Perkins," "The Goldbergs," and "Kitty Keene," 1940-46, radio director, 1943, director of "Ma Perkins," 1944; free-lance writer, 1946-50; Biow Co., New York, N.Y., vice-president of television-radio, 1950-55; Roy Winsor Productions, New York City, president, 1955-69; free-lance television serial consultant, 1969-73; National Broadcasting Co., head writer of the serial "Somerset," 1974; New School for Social Research, New York City, instructor of television serial writing, 1974-75; novelist, 1976—. Summer stock actor in Provincetown, Mass., 1930-34.

MEMBER: Mystery Writers of America, Writers Guild of America (East), Pelham Country Club (past member of board of directors). *Awards, honors:* Edgar Award from Mystery Writers of America, 1974, for *The Corpse That Walked.*

WRITINGS—Mystery novels: *The Corpse That Walked,* Fawcett, 1974; *Three Motives for Murder,* Fawcett, 1976; *Always Lock Your Bedroom Door,* Fawcett, 1976. Television writer, 1946-74; presently contributing material for "CBS Radio Mystery Theatre."

WORK IN PROGRESS: A fourth mystery novel, *A Sweet Way to Die.*

SIDELIGHTS: Winsor writes: "I enjoy reading detective stories. That is why I write them." During his lengthy career in radio and television, Winsor has created "Hawkins Falls," and "Nothing But the Best"; created and produced "The Public Life of Cliff Norton," "Search for Tomorrow," "Love of Life," "The Secret Storm," "Ben Jerrod," and "Hotel Cosmopolitan"; served as executive producer of "Racket Squad," "I Love Lucy," "My Little Margie," "My Hero," "Sixty-Four Dollar Question" (radio), "Welcome Travellers" (radio), "Search for Tomorrow," "Love of Life," "The Secret Storm," and "Have Gun Will Travel"; he has also produced television commercials for major companies.

WISEMAN, Ann (Sayre) 1926-
(Ann Wiseman Denzer)

PERSONAL: Born July 20, 1926, in New York, N.Y.; daughter of Mark Huntington (a writer) and Eve Sayre (Norton) Wiseman; married Weyer Vermeer (a physician); married Peter W. Denzer. Children: (first marriage) Piet; (second marriage) Erik. *Education:* Attended Art Students League, New York City, and Grande Chaumiere, Paris, France. *Residence:* Cambridge, Mass.

CAREER: Museum of Modern Art, New York City, teacher of art classes for children, 1946-50; Lord & Taylor, New York City, display artist, 1946; chairman of art department at country day school in Princeton, N.J., 1964-68; Boston Children's Museum, Boston, Mass., program director, 1969-70; Lesley College, Cambridge, Mass., teacher of methods, materials, and art therapy at Graduate School, 1970—. Artist and writer. Conductor of Metropolitan Museum children's tapestry program, 1967-68, and Boston Bicentennial senior citizens' tapestry program, 1976. Her own tapestry, painting, and kinetic sandfountains have been exhibited in group shows at museums and galleries and are in private collections.

MEMBER: Society of Women Geographers, American Craftsmen's Council, New Jersey Designer-Draftsmen, Boston Visual Artists Union. *Awards, honors:* Karolyi Foundation fellowship in France, 1970.

WRITINGS: (Under name Ann Wiseman Denzer) *Tony's Flower* (children's book), Vanguard, 1959; *Rags, Rugs, and Wool Pictures,* Scribner, 1967; *Rag Tapestries and Wool Mosaics,* Van Nostrand, 1968; *Making Things: Handbook of Creative Discovery,* Little, Brown, Book I, 1973, Book II, 1975; *Bread Sculpture: The Edible Art,* 101 Productions, 1975; *Simple Cuts of Cloth,* Little, Brown, in press.

Film: "Rag Tapestry of New York City," International Film Foundation, 1968.

WORK IN PROGRESS: Hand Logic; Children's Tapestries; illustrated travel journals; *Garment Cores; Primitive Crafts; Dream Journals.*

SIDELIGHTS: Ann Wiseman has traveled in France, Italy, Greece, Portugal, Mexico, the Netherlands, and England.

*   *   *

WITT, Hubert 1935-

PERSONAL: Born June 20, 1935, in Breslau, Germany; son of August (a railroad employee) and Berta (Werner) Witt; married Sina Heins (a manuscript reader), March 5, 1960; children: Ines, Jan. *Education:* Attended University of Leipzig, 1953-57. *Home;* Fechnerstrasse 5, 7022 Leipzig, German Democratic Republic.

CAREER: Reclam Verlag, Leipzig, German Democratic Republic, manuscript reader of German philology, philosophy, and twentieth-century literature, 1959-75; free-lance editor, translator, and author in Leipzig, 1976—. *Member:* Schriftstellerverband der Deutschen Demokratischen Republik.

WRITINGS—Editor, except as noted: (And translator from he Yiddish) *Der Fiedler vom Getto* (poetry from Poland), Reclam, 1966, abridged edition published as *Meine juedischen Augen,* Claassen, 1969; (translator) Langston Hughes, editor, *Gedichte aus Afrika* (poetry), Reclam, 1972; (and translator) Oswald von Wolkenstein, *Um dieser Welten Lust* (poetry), Insel, 1968; Bertolt Brecht, *Erinnerungen an Brecht* (anthology), Reclam, 1964, revised edition, 1966,

translation of revised edition by John Peet published as *Brecht As They Knew Him,* International Book Publishers, 1974; Bertolt Brecht, *Von der Freundlichkeit der Welt* (poetry), Insel, 1971; (with Annie Voigtlaender) *Denkzettel* (anthology of political lyrics from West Germany and West Berlin), Roederberg, 1974.

Translator with others of the poetry of Carl Michael Bellman for Reclam, 1965—; translator with others of the poetry of Ossip Mandelstam, Reclam, 1975. Author of afterwords to books by Bertolt Brecht, Johann Peter Hebel, Joseph Roth, and Stephan Hermlin.

WORK IN PROGRESS: Editing and translating a collection of Walther von der Vogelweide's lyrics, a collection of Brecht's short stories to be called *Der Staedtebauer,* and Mendele Moicher-Sforim's *Fischke der Lahme;* editing the medieval lyrics of Neihart von Reuenthal, an anthology of East German short stories for English-speaking readers to be called *Thinking It Over,* and an anthology of West German lyrics from 1945-1975; writing poetry, stories, and a drama.

*   *   *

WITTLIN, Jozef 1896-1976

August 17, 1896—February 29, 1976; Polish-born American poet, translator, radio scriptwriter and broadcaster. Obituaries: *New York Times,* March 1, 1976; *AB Bookman's Weekly,* July 12, 1976. (See index for previous *CA* sketch)

*   *   *

WITTY, Paul 1898-1976

July 23, 1898—February 11, 1976; American educational psychologist, clinic director, educator, journal editor, and author of books in his field. Obituaries: *New York Times,* February 14, 1976; *Publishers Weekly,* March 22, 1976; *AB Bookman's Weekly,* April 26, 1976.

*   *   *

WOLCOTT, Harry F(letcher) 1929-

PERSONAL: Born February 28, 1929, in Oakland, Calif.; son of LeRoy O. (a dentist) and Alice (Fletcher) Wolcott. *Education:* University of California, Berkeley, B.S., 1951; San Francisco State College (now University), M.A., 1959; Stanford University, Ph.D., 1964. *Residence:* Eugene, Ore. *Office:* College of Education, University of Oregon, Eugene, Ore. 97403.

CAREER: Teacher in public schools in Richmond, Calif., 1955-56, and Carmel, Calif., 1956-59; University of Oregon, Eugene, assistant professor, 1964-67, associate professor, 1967-71, professor of education and anthropology, 1971—, research associate of Center for Educational Policy and Management, 1964—. *Military service:* U.S. Army, 1952-54. *Member:* American Anthropological Association (fellow), Society for Applied Anthropology (fellow), Council on Anthropology and Education (president, 1972-73), American Educational Research Association, Phi Delta Kappa.

WRITINGS: A Kwakiutl Village and School, Holt, 1967; *The Man in the Principal's Office: An Ethnography,* Holt, 1973; *The African Beer Gardens of Bulawayo: Integrated Drinking in a Segregated Society,* Center of Alcohol Studies, Rutgers University, 1974; *South Turkeyfoot Teachers versus the Technocrats: An Educational Innovation in Anthropological Perspective,* Center for Educational Policy and Management, University of Oregon, 1977.

Contributor: Raymond V. Wiman and Wesley Meierhenry, editors, *Educational Media: Theory into Practice*, C. E. Merrill, 1969; G. D. Spindler, editor, *Education and Cultural Process*, Holt, 1974; Clive Kileff and Wade Pendleton, editors, *Urban Man in Southern Africa*, Mambo Press, 1975; Joan Roberts and Sherrie Akinsanya, editors, *Schooling in the Cultural Context*, McKay, 1976. Contributor to education and anthropology journals. Guest editor of *Human Organization*, summer, 1975.

* * *

WOLFE, Don Marion 1902-1976

October 24, 1902—April 21, 1976; American educator, Milton scholar, editor, and author. Obituaries: *New York Times*, April 22, 1976; *Washington Post*, May 5, 1976; *AB Bookman's Weekly*, July 5, 1976.

* * *

WOLITZER, Hilma 1930-

PERSONAL: Born January 25, 1930, in Brooklyn, N.Y.; daughter of Abraham V. and Rose (Goldberg) Liebman; married Morton Wolitzer (a psychologist), September 7, 1952; children: Nancy, Margaret. *Education:* Attended Brooklyn Museum Art School, Brooklyn College of the City University of New York, and New School for Social Research. *Home:* 11 Ann Dr., Syosset, N.Y. 11791. *Agent:* McIntosh & Otis, Inc., 475 Fifth Ave., New York, N.Y.

CAREER: Writer and teacher of writing workshops. Has also worked as nursery school teacher and portrait artist at a resort. Staff assistant at Bread Loaf Writers Conference, 1975 and 1976. *Member:* International P.E.N., Authors Guild of Authors League of America. *Awards, honors:* Bread Loaf Writers Conference scholarship, 1970, fellowship, 1974; award from Great Lakes College Association, 1974-75, for *Ending*; Guggenheim fellowship, 1976-77.

WRITINGS: Ending (novel), Morrow, 1974; *Introducing Shirley Braverman* (juvenile), Farrar, Straus, 1975; *Out of Love* (juvenile), Farrar, Straus, 1976.

Work represented in anthologies, including *The Secret Life of Our Times*, edited by Gordon Lish, Doubleday, 1973; *Bitches and Sad Ladies*, edited by Pat Rotter, Harper Magazine Press, 1975; *All Our Secrets Are the Same*, edited by Gordon Lish, Norton, in press. Contributor of stories to *Saturday Evening Post, Esquire*, and *New American Review*.

WORK IN PROGRESS: In the Flesh, a novel.

* * *

WONG, Roderick 1932-

PERSONAL: Born November 12, 1932, in Vancouver, British Columbia, Canada; son of Ben (a laborer) and Pearl (a clerk; maiden name, Goon) Wong; married Bernice Yee Lan (a professor), May 29, 1968; children: Kristi Po Yin. *Education:* University of British Columbia, B.A., 1956; Western Michigan University, M.A., 1959; Northwestern University, Ph.D., 1963. *Home:* 5854 Ross St., Vancouver, British Columbia, Canada. *Office:* Department of Psychology, University of British Columbia, Vancouver 8, British Columbia, Canada, VGT 1W5.

CAREER: Dominion Bureau of Statistics, Ottawa, Ontario, statistician, 1956-60; Eastern Washington State College, Cheney, assistant professor of psychology, 1963-64; University of British Columbia, Vancouver, assistant professor,

1964-68, associate professor, 1969-77, professor of psychology, 1977—. *Member:* Canadian Psychological Association, American Psychological Association, Psychonomic Society, International Society for Developmental Psychobiology, Sigma Xi. *Awards, honors:* Grant from National Research Council of Canada, 1968-73.

WRITINGS: (Author of student guide) W. F. Hill, *Psychology: Principles and Problems*, Lippincott, 1970; *Motivation: A Biobehavioral Analysis of Consummatory Activities*, Macmillan, 1976. Contributor to psychology and biology journals in the United States, Canada, Germany, and England.

WORK IN PROGRESS: Research on fluid intake in rodents.

* * *

WOOD, (James) Lew(is) 1928-

PERSONAL: Born October 20, 1928, in Indianapolis, Ind.; son of James C. and Eleanor Shrewsbury (Wyatt) Wood; married Katherine Dittrich, February 2, 1952 (divorced, 1966); married Monick Cloutier, December 6, 1974; children: Robert L., Carole E., James D., Lara E., Brigitte M. *Education:* Purdue University, B.S., 1950; University of Notre Dame, M.A., 1958; additional study at Columbia University, 1959-60. *Religion:* Protestant. *Office:* NBC News, National Broadcasting Co., 30 Rockefeller Pl., New York, N.Y. 10020.

CAREER: WSBT-TV, South Bend, Ind., newsman, 1953-59; Columbia Broadcasting System (CBS), New York City, correspondent for CBS News, 1960-65; National Broadcasting Co. (NBC), New York City, correspondent for NBC News, 1966-71, newscaster on "Today" show, 1975—. Notable assignments include coverage of civil rights movement, John F. Kennedy assassination, 1964 Democratic convention, and Vietnam conflict. *Military service:* U.S. Marine Corps, 1950-52. U.S. Marine Corps Reserve, 1952-65; became major.

WRITINGS: Writer of newscasts for "Today" show, National Broadcasting Co. (NBC-TV), 1975—.

SIDELIGHTS: Wood writes: "I was inspired by Edward R. Murrow's example to become a broadcast journalist. I am truly a child of my medium, having grown up in radio's Golden Age of the 1930's and '40's, and grown with the television industry as it spread to the Midwest in the 1950's." *Avocational interests:* Yachting.

* * *

WOODSON, Meg
See BAKER, Elsie

* * *

WOODWARD, David B(rainerd) 1918-

PERSONAL: Born June 11, 1918, in Philippines; son of Frank J. (a missionary) and Marion (a missionary; maiden name, Wells) Woodward; married Elizabeth M. Gillman (a missionary), December 28, 1944; children: Marion (Mrs. Kenneth D. Shay), Ted, Edie, Susan. *Education:* Davidson College, B.A., 1939; Princeton Theological Seminary, M.Div., 1942; graduate study at Stanford University, 1952; Seattle Pacific College, M.A., 1969; currently D.Min. candidate at Fuller Theological Seminary. *Home:* Box 7-100 Taipei, Taiwan, China 106. *Office address:* The Evangelical Alliance Mission, Box 969, Wheaton, Ill. 60187.

CAREER: Ordained minister of United Presbyterian Church, 1942; Worldwide Evangelization Crusade, India and China, missionary, 1945-52; Overseas Missionary Fellowship, Taiwan and Hong Kong, missionary, 1952-57; Evangelical Alliance Mission, Taiwan and Korea, missionary, 1958—. Bible translation consultant in Asia.

WRITINGS: God, Men, and Missions, Gospel Light Publishers, 1962; *Aflame for God,* Moody, 1966; *Tsen-yang Wei Chu Hsieh-cho* (title means "How to Write for the Lord"), China Sunday School Association, 1963; *Detour from Tibet,* Moody, 1975; (editor with Harold Lovestrand) *Hostage in Djakarta,* Moody, 1967; (contributor) Donald Hoke, editor, *The Church in Asia,* Moody Press, 1975. Contributor to religious journals.

WORK IN PROGRESS: An autobiography of experiences in eastern Tibet; a biography of an American ex-soldier in the Philippines; children's stories.

* * *

WOODWARD, Herbert N(orton) 1911-

PERSONAL: Born December 16, 1911, in Altadena, Calif.; son of Arthur H. (a manufacturer) and Edith May (Norton) Woodward; married Nancy Thomas, October 2, 1948; children: Cynthia W. (Mrs. Gerould P. King), James L., Deborah W. (Mrs. Edwin F. Leach II). *Education:* Cornell University, B.A., 1933; University of Chicago, J.D., 1936. *Home:* 4 Golf Lane, Winnetka, Ill. 60093. *Agent:* Ray Freiman, 184 Brookdale Ave., Stamford, Conn. 06903. *Office:* International Science Industries, Inc., 100 West Monroe St., Chicago, Ill. 60603.

CAREER: Attorney in Chicago, Ill., 1937-42; DK Manufacturing Co., Batavia, Ill., 1946-68, began as secretary, became vice-president, chairman of board of directors, 1960-68; Printing Plate Supply Co., Chicago, chairman of board of directors, 1968-76; International Science Industries, Inc., Chicago, president, 1971-76, chairman of board, 1976—. Intermatic, Inc. (formerly International Register Co.), director, 1937-72, chairman of board, 1972—; member of board of directors of Vaughan-Jacklin Corp., Programming Technologies, Inc., ECM Motor Co., Astron Dental Corp., Ideal Roller & Graphics Co., and Printing Plate Supply Co.; former member of board of directors of Dunbar Kapple, Inc., Easterling Co., and GCO Optronics, Inc.; chairman of board of trustees of Blackburn College. *Military service:* U.S. Naval Reserve, active duty, 1942-45; became lieutenant.

MEMBER: Society of Midland Authors, Chicago Bar Association, Chicago Literary Club. *Awards, honors:* L.C.D. from Blackburn College, 1972.

WRITINGS: The Human Dilemma, Brookdale Press, 1971; *Capitalism Can Survive in a No-Growth Economy,* Walker & Co., 1976. Contributor to business journals.

WORK IN PROGRESS: A fictional book, completion expected in 1978.

SIDELIGHTS: Woodward writes: "I have always been interested in the future prospects for mankind. All my writing is concerned with this subject. Although mankind has many problems, the most serious, I believe, are the result of exponential population growth. Since the surface of our planet is limited and emigration into space will not alleviate our crowding, our human numbers must stop increasing—and soon. The problems of energy scarcities, environmental pollution and the stresses of crowding, would all be eased by reduction of population pressure. We are just beginning to recognize this—soon enough, I hope, to make plans to avoid disaster."

* * *

WORBOYS, Anne(tte) Isobel
(Annette Eyre, Vicky Maxwell)

PERSONAL: Born in Aukland, New Zealand; daughter of Thomas Edwardes (a property owner and sheep farmer) and Agnes Helen (Blair) Eyre; married Walter Brindy Worboys (a sales executive), September 20, 1946; children: Carolyn (Mrs. Derek Pretty), Robin. *Home:* The White House, Leigh, nr. Tonbridge, Kent, England. *Agent:* David Highman Associates, 5-8 Lower John Street, London W1R 4HA, England.

CAREER: Writer. *Military Service:* Royal New Zealand Air Force, 1942-45. *Member:* Society of Women Writers and Journalists; Crimewriters Association; Romantic Novelists Association; Tunbridge Wells & District Writers' Circle (chairman).

WRITINGS—Crime suspense novels: *Lion of Delos* (Book-of-the-Month Club alternate choice), Delacorte, 1974; *Every Man a King,* Scribner, 1976; *The Barrancourt Destiny,* Scribner, 1977.

All romantic novels under pseudonym Annette Eyre, all published by Hurst & Blackett: *Three Strings to a Fortune,* 1962; *Valley of Yesterday,* 1965; *A Net to Catch the Wind,* 1966; *Return to Bellbird Country,* 1966; *House of Five Pines,* 1967; *A River & Wilderness,* 1967; *A Wind from the Hill,* 1968; *Thorn-Apple,* 1968; *Tread Softly in the Sun,* 1969; *The Little Millstones,* 1970; *Dolphin Bay,* 1970; *Rainbow Child,* 1971; *The Magnolia Room,* 1972; *Venetian Inheritance,* 1973.

All suspense novels under pseudonym Vicky Maxwell: *Chosen Child,* Collins, 1973; *Flight to the Villa Mistra,* Collins, 1973; *The Way of the Tamarisk,* Collins, 1974, Delacorte, 1975; *High Hostage,* Collins, 1976.

WORK IN PROGRESS: Short stories for women's magazines.

SIDELIGHTS: "We travel a great deal," Worboys told *CA,* "just returned from a trek through the Himalayas with pack ponies and sherpas in search of background for a new novel. *Every Man a King* was written after riding a half-Arab, half-Andalusian horse over the Sierra Nevada, sleeping in centuries old mulemen's posadas, crossing the passes at 10,600 feet."

* * *

WORMSER, Sophie 1897-

PERSONAL: Born October 21, 1897, in Astoria, N.Y. *Education:* Attended City College of the City University of New York. *Home and office:* 3314 Waverly Dr., Los Angeles, Calif. 90027. *Agent:* Mrs. Ellen Stevenson & Associates, P.O. Box 219, Holyrood, Newfoundland, Canada AOA 2RO.

CAREER: Worked as supervisor and organizer for Hearst International Magazines in New York, as secretary in New York City, as residence manager in Morristown, N.J., and as manager at Rockefeller Center. Has taught remedial reading and creative writing, and English to speakers of foreign languages. Has done volunteer work in settlement houses, in hospitals, for the blind, and for political campaigns. *Military service:* U.S. Navy, World War I. *Awards, honors:* Many poetry prizes.

WRITINGS: About Silkworms and Silk, Melmont, 1961. Also author of *The Belted Kingfishers* and *Henry in a Hurry,* both to be published by Anthelion. Contributor of about sixty poems to magazines.

WORK IN PROGRESS: Monkey Baker, Mirands, the Garden Spider, My Brother Juan, and *A Family Is for Loving,* all for Oddo; *Make Me a World,* a novel.

*   *   *

WORTH, Douglas   1940-

PERSONAL: Born March 14, 1940, in Philadelphia, Pa.; son of C. Brooke (a naturalist and writer) and Merida (a bookstore operator; maiden name, Grey) Worth; married Karen Weisskopf (an educator), May 2, 1969; children: Colin, Danny. *Education:* Swarthmore College, B.A. (honors), 1962; Columbia University, M.A., 1964. *Home:* 66 Grove Hill Ave., Newton, Mass. 02160. *Office:* Meadowbrook Junior High School, Newton, Mass.

CAREER: Teacher of English at private schools in New York City, 1964-68; Meadowbrook Junior High School, Newton, Mass., English teacher, 1969—.

WRITINGS: Of Earth (poems), William Bauhan, 1974; *Invisibilities,* Apple-wood Press, 1977.

Work has been anthologized in *New American Poetry,* edited by Richard Monaco, McGraw, 1973. Contributor of poems to magazines, including *Nation, Prairie Schooner,* and *Massachusetts Review,* and to newspapers.

WORK IN PROGRESS: Poems.

SIDELIGHTS: Of his poetry Worth wrote, "I try to write as deeply and clearly as I can about the human condition and my experience of the world, to penetrate the surfaces of things and events in order to explore and reveal their inner morphologies and connections." Worth has won the attention and praise of many distinguished contemporary poets. A. R. Ammons wrote a poem in his honor:

> "Douglas Worth
> had too much
> to bring to
> appear quickly
> among us:
> others arrived
> early with a flashy
> branch or two:
> Mr. Worth is
> working
> the hardwood loads."

Denise Levertov said, "Worth strikes me as one of the most gifted and accomplished of the younger poets, having that care for the art of poetry that distinguishes the serious artist from the temporary self-expresser." Describing *Of Earth,* Hayden Carruth offers these comments: "Poems of gentle music, very apt for the loving concern that is their substance. I read them with lingering pleasure." Of Worth's newest book Richard Wilbur said: "I have truly enjoyed reading *Invisibilities.* Worth's form seems offhand and minimal, but his lines flow well and with authority, and when he abandons grammar he does so for a purpose and without confusing the reader. Almost all of his poems contain some fresh act of the imagination."

*   *   *

WORTHINGTON, Marjorie (Muir)   1898(?)-1976

1898(?)—February 17, 1976; American novelist, short story writer, and educator. Obituaries: *New York Times,* February 18, 1976. (See index for previous *CA* sketch)

*   *   *

WORTHY, Morgan   1936-

PERSONAL: Born March 8, 1936, in Spartanburg, S.C.; son of Buford Hood and Norma (Morgan) Worthy; married Linda Pauline Hammond, December 24, 1957; children: Bonnie Lyn, Steven Bruce. *Education:* North Greenville Junior College, A.A., 1956; Furman University, B.A., 1961; University of Florida, M.A., 1964, Ph.D., 1965. *Home:* 1257 Spring Valley Lane N.E., Atlanta, Ga. 30306. *Office:* Department of Psychology and Counseling Center, Georgia State University, University Plaza, Atlanta, Ga. 30303.

CAREER: Georgia State University, Atlanta, assistant professor, 1966-71, associate professor of psychology, 1971—. *Military service:* U.S. Air Force, 1957-60. *Member:* American Psychological Association, American Association for the Advancement of Science.

WRITINGS: Eye Color, Sex, and Race, Droke, 1974; *Aha! A Puzzle Approach to Creative Thinking,* Nelson-Hall, 1975.

*   *   *

WREN, M. K.
See RENFROE, Martha Kay 1938-

*   *   *

WRIGHT, D(avid) G(ordon)   1937-

PERSONAL: Born October 30, 1937, in Bradford, England; son of Stanley (a worker in a textile mill) and Beatrice Maud (a worker in a textile mill; maiden name, Sankey) Wright; married Valerie Lightowler (a kindergarten teacher), August 5, 1961; children: Timothy Stanley, Simon Charles, Victoria Lesley. *Education:* University of Manchester, B.A., 1959; University of Leeds, Ph.D., 1966. *Home:* 9 Victoria Park, Shipley, Bradford, Yorkshire BD18 4RL, England. *Office:* Department of History and Politics, Huddersfield Polytechnic, Queensgate, Huddersfield, Yorkshire HD1 3DH, England.

CAREER: High school teacher of history and English in Bradford, England, 1960-67; City of Leeds and Carnegie College, Leeds, England, lecturer in history, 1967-71; Huddersfield Polytechnic, Huddersfield, England, senior lecturer in history and politics, 1971—. Assistant staff tutor at Open University; member of education panel of Council for National Academic Awards. *Member:* Historical Association (president of Bradford branch), History of Education Society, Past and Present Society, Social History Society, Society for the Study of Labour History, Political Studies Association.

WRITINGS: Democracy and Reform, 1815-1885, Longman, 1970, revised edition, 1972; *Revolution and Terror in France, 1789-1795,* Longman, 1974. Contributor of articles and reviews to history journals and to *Sesame.*

WORK IN PROGRESS: Research on the response of established English literary figures to the outbreak of World War One.

SIDELIGHTS: Wright comments: "My books were written to help university and college teachers and students of history by summarizing recent research and providing both collections of primary documentary evidence and bibliographical guides to further study. They are largely aimed at introducing freshmen students to major historical subjects in relatively brief form."

* * *

WRIGHT, Elizabeth Atwell 1919-1976

1919—February 21, 1976; American educator, school administrator, and author of books in her field. Obituaries: *New York Times,* February 23, 1976.

* * *

WRIGHT, Francesca
See ROBINS, Denise (Naomi)

* * *

WRIGHT, Kenneth
See del REY, Lester 1915-

* * *

WRIGHT, (Mary) Patricia 1932-
(Mary Napier)

PERSONAL: Born May 10, 1932, in Surrey, England; daughter of Roy (a company chairman) and Violet Mary (Wilkinson) Matthews; married Richard M. Wright (an engineer), April 25, 1959; children: Katherine Mary, Penelope Diana. *Education:* Royal Institution of Chartered Surveyors, A.R.I.C.S., 1957; Chartered Land Agents' Society, Q.A.L.A.S., 1958; University of London, diploma (first class honors), 1966. *Politics:* "A liberal if the liberals were any good, which they aren't, so usually a conservative." *Religion:* "Church of England—up to a point." *Residence:* Sussex, England. *Agent:* Carol Smith Literary Agency, 2 John St., London W.C.1, England. *Office:* Turnbridge Wells Grammar School for Girls, Turnbridge Wells, Kent, England.

CAREER: Hughes & Wilbraham, Exeter, England, agricultural surveyor and agent, 1955-57; Alsop & Co., London, England, saleswoman, 1957-59; writer, 1959-66; Turnbridge Wells Grammar School for Girls, Turnbridge Wells, England, part-time teacher of history and economics, 1966—.

WRITINGS: (Under pseudonym Mary Napier) *Woman's Estate* (humorous account of trials of a female agricultural surveyor), Hart-Davis, 1959; *Conflict on the Nile* (study of Fashoda Incident, 1898-1901), Heinemann, 1971; *Space of the Heart* (novel), Doubleday, 1976; *Journey into Fire* (novel), Doubleday, in press. Contributor to *History Today.*

SIDELIGHTS: Patricia Wright comments: "Although no diehard in politics—in fact rather sceptical of all politicians and in favour of pragmatic approach to problems—I am very concerned about all issues of personal freedom and how easily it can be lost. This has been the chief motive for my writings over the past three or four years."

AVOCATIONAL INTERESTS: Travel (Western Europe and the Soviet Union).

* * *

WROBEL, Sylvia (Burroughs) 1941-

PERSONAL: Born April 2, 1941, in Bat Cave, N.C.; daughter of John Herbert (a teacher) and Elaine (a teacher; maiden name, Moore) Burroughs; married Arthur Wrobel, July 27, 1963 (divorced, 1976); children: Gabriel David Gunter. *Education:* Wake Forest University, student, 1959-62; University of North Carolina, B.A., 1963, M.A., 1968. *Politics:* Democrat. *Religion:* "Protestant—vaguely."

Home: 209 University Ave., Lexington, Ky. 40503. *Office:* Thomas Hunt Morgan Institute of Genetics, 628 North Broadway, Lexington, Ky. 40508.

CAREER: University of North Carolina, A & T State University, Greensboro, instructor in English, 1968; freelance writer and editor, 1968-72; University of Kentucky, Lexington, instructor in creative writing, 1972; Thomas Hunt Morgan Institute of Genetics, Lexington, Ky., writer and research associate, 1973—. *Member:* Authors Guild of Authors League of America, American League of Women Voters.

WRITINGS: The First Hundred Years: The University of Kentucky College of Pharmacy, University of Kentucky, 1971; (with George Grider) *Isaac Shelby: Kentucky's First Governor,* Cumberland Press, 1973; (with Ian B. Shine) *Thomas Hunt Morgan: Pioneer of Genetics,* University Press of Kentucky, 1976.

Work has been anthologized in *The Best from Descant,* edited by Betsy Colquitt, Texas Christian University, 1975. Contributor to magazines, including *Child Life, Seventeen, Good Housekeeping, Arizona Quarterly,* and *Colorado Quarterly,* and to newspapers.

WORK IN PROGRESS: A biography of Sewall Wright, a population geneticist, with Ian B. Shine.

SIDELIGHTS: Sylvia Wrobel writes: "My career has been haphazard, a bit of this, a bit of that, and constant time out for money to be earned or something to be cleaned. Now at least, I write for a living as well as pleasure. It's nice."

* * *

WUBBEN, John 1938-

PERSONAL: Surname is pronounced *Woo*-ben; born November 14, 1938, in Grand Junction, Colo.; son of Horace Jay (a college president) and Irene (a librarian; maiden name, Hazlett) Wubben; married Patsy Dyer, April 3, 1956; children: Andrea Gwen, Damon John. *Education:* Mesa College, A.A., 1959; Adams State College, B.A. and M.A., 1961. *Home:* Star Route, Box 106, Carbondale, Colo. 81623. *Office:* Division of Communications/Humanities, Colorado Mountain College, West Campus, Glenwood Springs, Colo. 81601.

CAREER: Teacher of English and social studies in Pueblo, Colo. high school, 1961-64; Northeastern Junior College, Sterling, Colo., instructor in English, 1964-67; Colorado Mountain College, West Campus, Glenwood Springs, assistant professor, 1967-68, associate professor, 1968-72, chairman of Division of Communications/Humanities, 1968—. President and member of board of directors of Crystal Community Theater Company, 1969-71. *Member:* Colorado Education Association (member of board of directors, 1975-77), Colorado Association of Higher Education (president and member of board of directors), Rocky Mountain Junior College English Association (member of board of directors), Phi Delta Kappa.

WRITINGS: Guided Writing, Random House, 1971.

WORK IN PROGRESS: An illustrated children's book, with wife, Patsy D. Wubben.

AVOCATIONAL INTERESTS: Crafts (especially wood working, metal working, and stained glass work), fishing.

* * *

WULIGER, Betty 1921-

PERSONAL: Born September 20, 1921, in Detroit, Mich.;

daughter of Jack (a realtor) and Lillian (Shapero) Stiglitz; married Frank Wuliger (a business executive), August 6, 1942; children: Betsy, Frank III. *Education:* Attended University of Michigan, 1938-39; University of Illinois, B.A. (honors), 1942. *Residence:* Rancho Mirage, Calif. *Agent:* Molson-Stanton, 10889 Wilshire Blvd., Los Angeles, Calif. 90024.

CAREER: Fashion model in Detroit, Mich., 1940; college editor, *Mademoiselle,* 1941-42; elementary school teacher in Memphis, Tenn., 1944; Joseph Mellon & Miller, Cleveland, Ohio, stock broker, 1960-65; business consultant in Cleveland, 1966-70; self-employed investment adviser in Los Angeles, Calif., 1976; writer. Actively involved in fundraising activities. *Member:* Cleveland Society for Financial Analysts, Phi Beta Kappa, Zeta Beta Tau, Mortar Board. *Awards, honors:* Award from Daughters of the American Revolution, 1938.

WRITINGS: Dollars and Sense: Protecting Your Money and Making It Grow, Random House, 1976. Contributor to *Harper's Bazaar.*

SIDELIGHTS: Betty Wuliger writes: "As a young girl, I realized it is just as important to know how to invest money wisely as it is to know how to earn money. I saw my dad, a wealthy retired wholesale grocer, lose his life savings in the stock market crash. What a struggle it is to make a comeback late in life!

"I was married in 1942. My husband and I decided he would earn the money and I would try my hand at investing it. I was so successful that an investment broker offered me a job in his firm's research department making recommendations to customers. I subsequently became a stockbroker, business consultant, and investment adviser.

"I feel particularly fortunate in having experienced investing from both sides—as an individual investor and also as a professional. I was motivated to write because I wanted to share with the general public my successful and safe way of investing money. I spent years relating investing to everyday life so that an individual with no previous investing experience can easily understand virtually all investment choices, how to buy them, when and where to buy them, and how to compare their values."

AVOCATIONAL INTERESTS: Golf, tennis, bridge, backgammon.

* * *

WUTHNOW, Robert 1946-

PERSONAL: Born June 23, 1946, in Kansas; son of Victor R. (a farmer) and Kathryn (a teacher; maiden name, Huey) Wuthnow; married Sara Wilcox (a nursing instructor), June 15, 1968; children: Robyn Beth, Kathryn Brooke. *Education:* University of Kansas, B.S., 1968; University of Northern Colorado, M.A., 1969; University of California, Berkeley, Ph.D., 1975. *Home:* 6 Allwood Dr., Lawrenceville, N.J. 08648. *Office:* Department of Sociology, Princeton University, Princeton, N.J. 08540.

CAREER: Princeton University, Princeton, N.J., assistant professor of sociology, 1976—. *Member:* American Sociological Association, Society for the Scientific Study of Religion, Religious Research Association.

WRITINGS: (With C. Y. Glock, J. A. Piliavin, and Metta Spencer) *Adolescent Prejudice,* Harper, 1975; *The Consciousness Reformation,* University of California Press, 1976. Contributor to sociology, psychology, education, and theology journals.

WORK IN PROGRESS: The Post-Christian Periphery, publication by University of California Press expected in 1978; historical research on moral community and world capitalism, focusing especially on the role of religion in forming the modern world-system.

SIDELIGHTS: Wuthnow writes that he has a "longstanding interest in exploring the meaning systems by which people make sense of their lives." He is "currently concerned with discovering ways in which the moral estrangement and loss of community which exists at the world level can be healed and an equitable world society can be constructed."

* * *

WYATT, B. D.
See ROBINSON, Spider

* * *

YANEY, Joseph P(aul) 1939-

PERSONAL: Born May 11, 1939, in Scranton, Pa.; son of Alexander and Mary Yaney; married wife, Barbara Ann (a designer), May 30, 1964; children: Paul, Monica. *Education:* University of Michigan, M.B.A., 1964, J.D., 1964, Ph.D., 1969. *Home:* 996 Kenley Ave., Columbus, Ohio 43220. *Office:* Department of Business, Ohio State University, 1775 South College Rd., Columbus, Ohio 43210.

CAREER: University of Michigan, Ann Arbor, program director, 1966-69; Ohio State University, Columbus, associate professor of business, 1969—. *Military service:* U.S. Army, 1964-66; became captain. *Member:* Academy of Management, Industrial Relations Research Association (president of Ohio chapter, 1972), State Bar of Michigan.

WRITINGS: Managing Instructional Progress Effort, University of Michigan Press, 1967; *Labor Relations,* Addison-Wesley, 1968; *Personnel Management,* C. E. Merrill, 1975.

WORK IN PROGRESS: Research on labor relations.

* * *

YARBRO, Chelsea Quinn 1942-

PERSONAL: Born September 15, 1942, in Berkeley, Calif.; daughter of Clarence Elmer (a cartographer) and Lillian (an artist; maiden name, Chatfield) Erickson; married Donald Paul Simpson (an artist and inventor), November 3, 1969. *Education:* Attended San Francisco State University, 1960-63. *Politics:* Democrat. *Religion:* Atheist. *Home and office:* 977 Kains St., Albany, Calif. 94706. *Agent:* Kirby McCauley, 220 East 26th St., New York, N.Y. 10010.

CAREER: C. E. Erickson & Associates, Oakland, Calif., cartographer, 1963-70; program director for Sampo Productions, 1970-71, 1973; Magic Cellar, San Francisco, Calif., tarot reader, 1974—. Voice teacher and composer. Counselor of mentally disturbed children, 1963-64. *Member:* Science Fiction Writers of America, Mystery Writers of America. *Awards, honors:* Mystery Writers of America scroll, 1973, for "The Ghosts at Iron River."

WRITINGS: (Editor with Thomas N. Scortia) *Two Views of Wonder* (science fiction anthology), Ballantine, 1974; *Ogilvie, Tallant, and Moon* (suspense novel), Putnam, 1976; *Time of the Fourth Horseman* (science fiction novel), Doubleday, 1976; *Hotel Transylvania,* Signet, in press.

Work has been anthologized in *Men and Malice,* edited by Dean W. Dickensheet, Doubleday.

Author of "The Little-Girl Dragon of Alabaster-on-Fenwick" (satiric fairy tale play), first produced in San Francisco, Calif. at the St. Francis Hotel, July, 1973. Composer of musical works including "Stabat Mater", "Sayre Cycle", and "Alpha and Omega".

WORK IN PROGRESS: Ximene of the Kites (tentative title), a historical novel of the twelfth century; a second Charlie Moon suspense novel for Putnam; a musical composition, "Nightpiece for Chamber Orchestra".

SIDELIGHTS: Ms. Yarbro told *CA:* "I've written since I've known how to read. I'm not trying to do anything other than entertain my reader. 'Entertain' is not a dirty word, by the way. Much of my work is quite grim, but that should not be taken as an indication that I am a grim person. Please do not confuse me with my work; it is not me and I am not it. I dislike being categorized as anything beyond writer. For me, clarity of writing is essential. The reader should not be aware of how the words are on the page, or with what pyrotechnics the language is thrown around. Language is not an end in itself, but a means, a channel that a writer must, by the nature of the art, use. Beyond that, the words should not get in the way of the reader building the story in his or her head.

"I have a strong dedication to writing, both words and music, but I don't want to limit it by being too rigorous in my view of my career. I want to branch out in new directions. I want to do historical novels and more suspense and science fiction. How this will work out, I don't know. My music is even more uncertain, though some of this comes from the problem of being a woman composer of serious music. Unfortunately the world of music is still too strongly male-oriented. Finding conductors and groups willing to do my compositions has proved to be difficult, but who knows? Things may improve, but I am not holding my breath."

* * *

YARTZ, Frank Joseph

PERSONAL: Born in Cleveland, Ohio; son of Frank James (a metalist) and Mary Josephine (Francis) Yartz. *Education:* Loyola University, Chicago, Ill., A.M., 1964; St. Louis University, Ph.D., 1968. *Home:* 701 North Michigan Ave., Chicago, Ill. 60611. *Office:* Department of Philosophy, Loyola University, 820 North Michigan Ave., Chicago, Ill. 60611.

CAREER: Loyola University, Chicago, Ill., instructor, 1965-68, assistant professor, 1968-75, associate professor of philosophy, 1976—. *Member:* American Philosophical Association, American Catholic Philosophical Association, Mediaeval Academy of America.

WRITINGS: (With Allan L. Larson and David J. Hassel) *Progress and the Crisis of Man,* Nelson-Hall, 1976. Contributor to philosophy and medieval studies journals.

WORK IN PROGRESS: Research on the philosophy of Plato and the history of ancient Greek philosophy.

* * *

YATES, Peter Bertram 1909-1976

November 30, 1909—February 25, 1976; American employment counselor, music critic, poet, educator, and author of books on music. Obituaries: *New York Times,* March 5, 1976.

* * *

YAW, Yvonne 1936-

PERSONAL: Born August 16, 1936, in Columbus, Ohio; daughter of James Benoni (an attorney) and Marguerite (a secretary; maiden name, Porter) Yaw; married Ralph B. Tucker, April 3, 1959 (separated, 1977); children: Anneke Megan. *Education:* Wellesley College, B.A., 1957; Radcliffe College, M.A., 1958; Harvard University, Ph.D., 1965. *Agent:* Elizabeth McKee, Harold Matson Co., Inc., 22 East 40th St., New York, N.Y. 10016.

CAREER: Quinnipiac College, Mt. Carmel, Conn., instructor in English, 1962-63; New Haven University, West Haven, Conn., instructor in English, 1963-65; Quinnipiac College, assistant professor, 1965-67, associate professor of English, 1967-69; free-lance writer, 1970—. Visiting lecturer in English at Yale University, 1968-70, and at Salem State College, 1976.

WRITINGS: (With Florence Haseltine) *Woman Doctor,* Houghton, 1976. Contributor to *Ms.* and *Young World.*

WORK IN PROGRESS: Revising a novel, for Houghton; another novel set in colonial New England; a manual on scenic design for amateur theater, with Richard Stayton; essays on the United States.

* * *

YOKEN, Melvin B(arton) 1939-

PERSONAL: Born June 25, 1939, in Fall River, Mass.; son of Albert B. (a teacher) and Sylvia (White) Yoken; married Cynthia Stein (a teacher), June 20, 1976. *Education:* University of Massachusetts, B.A., 1960; Brown University, M.A., 1961; Five-College Cooperative Program, Ph.D., 1972. *Home:* 4700 North Main St., Apt. IJ, Fall River, Mass. 02720. *Office:* Department of Modern Languages, Southeastern Massachusetts University, North Dartmouth, Mass. 02747.

CAREER: Southeastern Massachusetts University, North Dartmouth, instructor, 1966-72, assistant professor, 1972-76, associate professor of French, 1976—. *Member:* International Platform Association, Modern Language Association of America (life member), American Association of Teachers of French (life member), American Council on the Teaching of Foreign Languages, Big Brothers of America, New England Modern Language Association, Middlebury Amicale (life member), Friends of Fall River Public Library (founding member; chairman of board of directors and president, 1972—).

WRITINGS: Claude Tillier, Twayne, 1976; (contributor) Alfred F. Rosa, editor, *Essays in Honor of Charles Angoff,* Fairleigh Dickinson University Press, 1976. Contributor of translations, articles, and reviews to magazines and newspapers, including *Le Travailleur.*

WORK IN PROGRESS: Biographies of Jules Verne and Manuel Komroff; a book of translations of contemporary French poetry into English.

SIDELIGHTS: Yoken writes: "I love to write, and find it relaxing and stimulating. To me writing has to have a definite rime and reason, feeling and emotion. . . . My poetry, as life itself, must have a process and be constantly in flux, with an infinite number of possibilities. I like to relate both highly personal experiences and imaginative cogitations. . . . I have an incurable interest in life and people that continues to propel me into myriad literary endeavors."

AVOCATIONAL INTERESTS: Visiting France.

* * *

YOUMAN, Roger J(acob) 1932-

PERSONAL: Born February 25, 1932, in New York, N.Y.;

son of Robert H. (a businessman) and Ida (a teacher; maiden name, Kellner) Youman; married: Lillian Frank (a social worker), June 22, 1958; children: Nancy, Laura, Joshua, Andrew. *Education:* Swarthmore College, B.A., 1953. *Office: TV Guide,* Radnor, Pa. 19088.

CAREER: TV Guide, Radnor, Pa., held editorial positions, 1956-60, associate editor, 1960-65, assistant managing editor, 1965-72, managing editor, 1972-76, executive editor, 1976—. *Military service:* U.S. Army, 1953-55. *Member:* Academy of Television Arts and Sciences, American Society of Magazine Editors, Pennsylvania Society.

WRITINGS: (With Arthur Shulman) *How Sweet It Was* (history), Shorecrest, 1966; (with Shulman) *The Television Years* (history), Popular Library, 1973. Contributor to popular magazines.

WORK IN PROGRESS: Another television-history book; a children's book.

* * *

YOUNG, Anne P(atricia)   1921-

PERSONAL: Born July 25, 1921, in Cambridge, Mass.; daughter of Joseph L. (a businessman) and Mary T. (a teacher; maiden name, Shea) Moynahan; married Myrl M. Young (a professor), June 21, 1945; children: Joan, Constance. *Education:* Boston University, B.S.Ed., 1943, M.A., 1944; University of Chicago, Ph.D., 1951. *Residence:* West Newfield, Maine. *Office:* Department of History, University of Maine, Gorham, Maine 04038.

CAREER: High school teacher of history and social sciences in Peterborough, N.H., Jewett City, Conn., and Harrodsburg, Ky., 1943-47; University of Illinois, Urbana, instructor in history, 1947-48; Roosevelt University, Chicago, Ill., part-time instructor, 1948; Scott, Foresman & Co., Chicago, Ill., editor of college history textbooks, 1948-52; Ginn & Co., Boston, Mass., social science editor, 1952-65; University of Maine at Portland-Gorham, associate professor, 1965-67, professor of history, 1967—. *Member:* American Historical Association, American Association of University Professors, New England Historical Association.

WRITINGS: (With Daniel Roselle) *Our Western Heritage: A Cultural-Analytic History of Europe Since 1500,* Ginn, 1972, new edition, 1976. Also author of workbooks for Ginn, 1960, 1962.

WORK IN PROGRESS: The Germanies Since 1945; writing on Lenin and the French Revolution as myth and model.

SIDELIGHTS: Anne Young has lived and studied in Scandinavia, Germany, and Austria; she traveled in the Soviet Union in 1973. Presently she lives on a big farm in Maine, where her family raises vegetables and horses.

* * *

YOUNG, John Orr   1886-1976

1886—May 2, 1976; American advertising executive and author. Obituaries: *New York Times,* May 3, 1976.

* * *

YOUNGS, J. William T., Jr.   1941-

PERSONAL: Born February 18, 1941, in Columbus, Ohio; son of J.W.T. (a mathematician) and M.D.S. Youngs; married wife, Linda M. (a lawyer), June 24, 1967; children: J.W.T. III, Hope E. *Education:* Harvard University, B.A., 1963; University of California, Berkeley, M.A., 1966,

Ph.D., 1970. *Home:* 814 Sixth St., Cheney, Wash. 99004. *Office:* Department of History, Eastern Washington State College, Cheney, Wash. 99004.

CAREER: Kenyon College, Gambier, Ohio, assistant professor of history, 1970-72; Eastern Washington State College, Cheney, assistant professor, 1972-76, associate professor of history, 1976—. Visiting assistant professor at University of Washington, Seattle, summer, 1974. *Member:* American Historical Association, Organization of American Historians, American Society of Church History, Society for History Education, Association of Washington Historians (member of executive board). *Awards, honors:* Grants from National Endowment for the Humanities and American Philosophical Society, both 1973; Brewer Prize from American Society of Church History, 1974, for *God's Messengers.*

WRITINGS: God's Messengers: Religious Leadership in Colonial New England, 1700-1750, Johns Hopkins Press, 1976. Contributor to history journals, to *William and Mary Quarterly,* and to newspapers. Editor of *Pacific Northwest Forum.*

WORK IN PROGRESS: Two books on religion in early America, including the European backgrounds.

SIDELIGHTS: Youngs comments: "I am currently attempting to write a book about religious life in England and America that will combine the insights of theology (in describing the relationship between God and man), history (in describing the past accurately), and literature (in evoking a sense of the reality of a life once lived)."

* * *

YOUNKER, Lucas (a pseudonym)   1942-

PERSONAL: Born April 14, 1942; married Sadie Bogart. *Agent:* Julian Bach, Jr., 3 East 48th St., New York, N.Y. 10017. *Office:* 1905 Sunnycrest Dr., Fullerton, Calif. 92635.

CAREER: Veterinarian, caring for horses and small animals, in Fullerton, Calif, 1968—. Vice-president of Animal Health Foundation, 1975—; staff veterinarian for California State University, Fullerton. *Member:* International Veterinary Acupuncture Society, American Veterinary Medical Association, American Animal Hospital Association, American Association of Equine Practitioners, American Veterinarians for Israel, National Association for Veterinary Acupuncture (president, 1973—), California Veterinary Medical Association, Southern California Veterinary Medical Association.

WRITINGS: (With John Fried) *Animal Doctor,* Dutton, 1976. Editor of *Today's Animal Health/Animal Cavalcade,* 1976—.

WORK IN PROGRESS: A "book about animal care for laymen in a unique format that will make it easy for pet owners to know if they have a problem."

SIDELIGHTS: Younker writes: "I wrote *Animal Doctor* . . . mainly because I was offered an advance. I do feel though that there are vitally important topics which I can help to shed some light on. These are principally in the area of responsible pet ownership, animal health, and pet overpopulation."

* * *

YUILL, Phyllis Jean (Marquart)   1941-

PERSONAL: Born April 11, 1941, in Findlay, Ohio; daughter of Luther S. and Thelma (Winkler) Marquart. *Edu-*

cation: Valparaiso University, B.S., 1963; graduate study at Pratt Institute, 1967, and Queens College of the City University of New York, 1969; Columbia University, M.S. (honors), 1973. *Home:* 79-11 Jamaica Ave., Woodhaven, N.Y. 11421. *Office:* Glenwood Landing Elementary School, Glen Head, N.Y. 11545.

CAREER: Glenwood Landing Elementary School, Glen Head, N.Y., teacher, 1963-68, library media specialist, 1968—. Visiting summer professor at Central Michigan University, 1975, and Northern Michigan University, 1976. Bro-Dart Foundation, Newark, N.J., selector for *Elementary School Library Collection,* 1974—. *Member:* International Association of School Librarianship, International Institute for Children's, Juvenile and Popular Literature, American Library Association (Children's Services Division and American Association of School Librarians), American Federation of Teachers, New York State United Teachers, New York State Library Association, Nassau-Suffolk School Librarians Association, Long Island Educational Communications Council, Beta Phi Mu.

WRITINGS: Little Black Sambo: A Closer Look, Council on Interracial Books for Children, 1976. Contributor of articles and reviews to library journals.

WORK IN PROGRESS: A series of biographies of modern artists, for children.

SIDELIGHTS: Phyllis Yuill writes: "I'm most concerned at present about the seriously deteriorating state of affairs in the nation's school libraries due to cut-backs in funding and personnel, and about the need for national planning of children's literature research collections." *Avocational interests:* Ballet, classical music, experimental films.

* * *

YUSKO, A(aron) A(llen) 1935-

PERSONAL: Born January 7, 1935, in Chicago, Ill.; son of Irving and Frieda Yusko; married Kathleen Perdita, August 23, 1963. *Education:* Attended Phoenix Junior College and Art Institute of Chicago; Arizona State University, B.A., 1965; University of Oregon, M.A. (art education), 1968, M.S. (special education), 1970. *Residence:* Florence, Ore.

CAREER: Art teacher in public schools in Newhall, Calif., 1965-67; Siuslaw School District, Florence, Ore., special education and art teacher, 1970—. Member of curriculum design committee of Lane Co., 1972; assistant designer for National Broadcasting Co.-Television, 1957—; has designed theatrical productions and children's plays; has had one-man shows of paintings in Chicago and Phoenix. *Military service:* U.S. Air Force, 1957-60. *Member:* National Education Association, Council for Exceptional Children. *Awards, honors:* Regional and national awards for painting.

WRITINGS: Art: A Learning Experience for the Very Young, Pruett, 1974.

* * *

ZAKIA, Richard D(onald) 1925-

PERSONAL: Born December 12, 1925, in Rochester, N.Y.; son of Fuad M. (a tailor) and Rose E. (Karam) Zakia; married Lois Ann Arlidge (a registered nurse and educator), June 21, 1958; children: Renee Arlidge. *Education:* Attended University of Chicago, 1944; Rochester Institute of Technology, B.S., 1956; University of Rochester, Ed.D., 1960. *Politics:* Independent. *Religion:* Roman Catholic. *Home:* 44 Horseshoe Lane N., Henrietta, N.Y. 14467. *Office:* Department of Communications, Rochester Institute of Technology, 1 Lomb Dr., Rochester, N.Y. 14623.

CAREER: Eastman Kodak, Rochester, N.Y., photographic engineer, 1956-58; Rochester Institute of Technology, Rochester, N.Y., assistant professor, 1961-65, associate professor, 1965-69, professor of photography, 1969—, director of instructional development, 1969—. Member of board of directors of Photographic Sciences Corp., 1970—; consultant to Department of Defense, 1973—. *Military service:* U.S. Navy, 1944-46, 1950-52. *Member:* Photographic Scientists and Engineers, Association for Education Communications and Technology, American Association for Higher Education, Society for Photographic Education.

WRITINGS: (With Hollis Todd) *Photographic Sensitometry,* Morgan & Morgan, 1967; (with Todd) *One Thousand and One Experiments in Photography,* Morgan & Morgan, 1969; (with John J. Dowdell III) *Zone Systemizer,* Morgan & Morgan, 1973; (with Todd) *Color Primer I and II,* Morgan & Morgan, 1974; *Perception and Photography,* Prentice-Hall, 1975; (with Minor White and Peter Lorenz) *Zone System Manual,* Morgan & Morgan, 1976.

WORK IN PROGRESS: Visual Concepts for Photographers with Les Stroebel and Hollis Todd, for Hastings House, and *Literature, Perception, Photography* with George DeWolfe and wife, Lois A. Zakia.

* * *

ZALKIND, Sheldon S(tanley) 1922-

PERSONAL: Born December 29, 1922, in New York, N.Y.; son of Joseph and Minnie (Blauman) Zalkind. *Education:* Lehigh University, B.A., 1943; Columbia University, M.A., 1945; New York University, Ph.D., 1951. *Office:* Department of Psychology, Bernard M. Baruch College of the City University of New York, New York, N.Y. 10010.

CAREER: New York University, New York, N.Y., instructor in psychology, 1951; Brooklyn College (now of the City University of New York), Brooklyn, N.Y., instructor in psychology, 1953-55; New York University, began as assistant professor, became associate professor of psychology, 1956-61; Bernard M. Baruch College of the City University of New York, New York, N.Y., associate professor, 1961-67, professor of psychology, 1967—. Consultant in psychology for Richardson, Bellows & Henry Research Associates, 1951-59, and to private and governmental organizations.

MEMBER: International Association for Applied Psychology, American Psychological Association, Society for the Psychological Study of Social Issues, American Association for Public Opinion Research, Eastern Psychological Association, New York State Psychological Association (past president of Social Psychology Division), Metropolitan Association for Applied Psychology (past president), Phi Beta Kappa. *Awards, honors:* Grant from U.S. Office of Naval Research, 1967-69.

WRITINGS: (With D. H. Fryer and M. R. Feinberg) *Developing People in Industry,* Harper, 1956; (with T. W. Costello) *Psychology in Administration,* Prentice-Hall, 1963; (with Neil Kalt) *Urban Problems: Psychological Inquiries,* Oxford University Press, 1976. Contributor to social science and psychology journals. Special editor of *Journal of Social Issues,* 1975; member of editorial board of *Administrative Science Quarterly.*

* * *

ZEILIK, Michael 1946-

PERSONAL: Born September 26, 1946, in Bridgeport,

Conn.; son of Michael (an electrician) and Margaret (Sabo) Zeilik. *Education:* Princeton University, A.B. (honors), 1968; Harvard University, M.A., 1969, Ph.D., 1975. *Office:* Department of Physics and Astronomy, University of New Mexico, Albuquerque, N.M. 87131.

CAREER: Southern Connecticut State College, New Haven, instructor in astronomy, 1969-72; Harvard University, Cambridge, Mass., instructor in astronomy, 1974-75; University of New Mexico, Albuquerque, assistant professor of astronomy, 1975—. Research assistant at Smithsonian Astrophysical Observatory, summers, 1968-70, 1973; instructor at Cambridge Center for Adult Education, 1973; has discussed his field on Hartford and New Haven television and radio programs. *Member:* American Astronomical Association, American Association of Physics Teachers, National Science Teachers Association, Astronomical Society of the Pacific, Boothe Memorial Astronomical Society. *Awards, honors:* Woodrow Wilson fellowship, 1968; Bowdoin Prize in natural sciences, Harvard University, 1973; honorable mention from Griffith Observatory Writing Awards, 1976.

WRITINGS: Film Notes for Explorations in Space and Time, Houghton, 1974; *Astronomy: The Evolving Universe,* with study guide, Harper, 1976. Contributor to physics and astronomy journals. Astronomy consultant for Houghton.

WORK IN PROGRESS: Revising *Astronomy: The Evolving Universe,* completion expected in 1979; an astrophysics book for college-level science majors, with Charles Whitney.

SIDELIGHTS: Zeilik writes: "I wrote *Astronomy: The Evolving Universe* in part because of the awful writing found in most science textbooks. I've been trained as a poet and have a greater sensitivity to the language than do most scientists who write textbooks." *Avocational interests:* Photography, writing poetry.

* * *

ZENTNER, Carola 1927-
(Carola Mason)

PERSONAL: Born October 4, 1927, in Berlin, Germany; daughter of Carl E. (a pediatrician) and Gerda (Brasch) Mosse; married Donald C. Mason, 1955 (divorced); married Peter Zentner (a writer and consultant), 1963; children: Victoria, Adam, Laurence (twins), Marcus, Quentin (twins). *Education:* Received secondary school education in England. *Politics:* Liberal. *Home:* 38 Woodland Gardens, London, England.

CAREER: Economic Cooperation Administration, Paris, France, studio manager, 1950-54; Associated Rediffusion Television, London, England, research and program assistant, 1954-55; free-lance journalist and writer, 1955—.

WRITINGS: Twins (nonfiction), David & Charles, 1975. Author of "Make It a Better Buy," a column in *Housewife,* 1959-65, and "House Sense," in *Daily Mirror,* 1963, under name Carola Mason. Contributor to women's magazines, under name Carola Mason, including *Design, Home, Ideal Home,* and *Nursery World,* and to the *Times.*

WORK IN PROGRESS: More Value for Money, a consumer guide.

SIDELIGHTS: Carola Zentner writes that she "used to concentrate on practical consumer advice. Had two sets of twins within twenty-one months and decided to write about twins. Now writing more frequently about children for obvious reasons."

ZESMER, David M(ordecai) 1924-
PERSONAL: Born December 1, 1924, in Dallas, Tex.; son of Isadore (a merchant) and Jennie (Hesselson) Zesmer; married Suzanne Spector (a vocational counselor), August 14, 1949; children: Jennie (Mrs. Jerold Gorrell), Sarah. *Education:* Southern Methodist University, student, 1941-43, 1946; Columbia University, B.A., 1947, M.A., 1949, Ph.D., 1961. *Politics:* Liberal Democrat. *Religion:* Jewish. *Home:* 5302 South Cornell Ave., Chicago, Ill. 60615. *Office:* Illinois Institute of Technology, Chicago, Ill. 60616.

CAREER: Illinois Institute of Technology, Chicago, Ill., associate professor, 1962-67, professor of English, 1967—. Member of board of directors of Jewish Federation of Metropolitan Chicago and Drexel Home for the Aged; chairman of Educators Division of Jewish United Fund of Chicago, 1974, 1977. *Military service:* U.S. Army Air Forces, 1941-43; became sergeant. *Member:* Modern Language Association of America, Shakespeare Association of America, Milton Society of America, American Association of University Professors (past president of local chapter).

WRITINGS: Guide to English Literature from Beowulf Through Chaucer and Medieval Drama, Barnes & Noble, 1961; (editor) *Dryden: Poetry, Prose, Drama,* Bantam, 1967; *Guide to Shakespeare,* Barnes & Noble, 1976.

WORK IN PROGRESS: Research on Milton, *Romeo and Juliet,* and *Measure for Measure.*

SIDELIGHTS: Zesmer writes: "I believe that the unnatural gap between teaching and scholarship must be bridged; and I hope my writings on Chaucer, Shakespeare, and others contribute to this objective. I believe that literature, though it is a disciplined and specialized study, must enrich our lives and help us to understand the world better. I believe, as a humanist, that we English teachers and scholars must respect vocationalism and adapt to it, but must not surrender to it."

AVOCATIONAL INTERESTS: "My chief passion, aside from Shakespeare, is music. Perhaps getting paid to listen to and talk about *Don Giovanni* or the Beethoven quartets would be even more gratifying than being paid to read *Hamlet* and *The Miller's Tale.*"

* * *

ZIEMIAN, Joseph 1922-1971
PERSONAL: Born December 26, 1922, in Warsaw, Poland; emigrated to Israel in 1957; son of David (a music store owner) and Theophila (Judaszko) Ziemian; married Janina Brandwajn (a high school teacher), January 10, 1958; children: Rami. *Education:* Warsaw Polytechnic, certified engineer, 1956. *Religion:* Jewish.

CAREER: Direction of the Restoration of Warsaw, Poland, inspector, 1948-51; Metrobuilding, Warsaw, inspector of technical workmanship, 1951-53; United Fundament Works, Warsaw, inspector, 1953-55; Ministry of Motorized Industry, Warsaw, building inspector, 1955-56; Industrial Institute of Telecommunications, Warsaw, civil engineer, 1956-57; Shicun Ovdim, Histadruth, Israel, engineer, building housing projects, 1958-71. Worked as a volunteer in the absorption of Polish Jews into Israel. *Awards, honors:* Awards from the Government of Poland for his part in the Warsaw uprising of 1944; prize from American Jewish Congress, 1966.

WRITINGS: The Cigarette Sellers of Three Crosses Square (nonfiction, translated by Janina David), Yad Vshem, 1962, Lerner, 1975; *The Borders of the Warsaw Ghetto in Their Changes* (in Hebrew), Yad Vshem, 1971.

WORK IN PROGRESS: A book of Ziemian's articles, collected from Israeli periodicals, is being prepared by Yad Vshem.

SIDELIGHTS: Ziemian once lived in the Warsaw Ghetto and was a member of a Jewish underground movement; his writings are about those activities and the conditions in the ghetto during the years he spent there.

(Died January 30, 1971)

* * *

ZIKMUND, Joseph II 1937-

PERSONAL: Born December 3, 1937, in Chicago, Ill.; son of Joseph (an agriculturalist) and Dorothy (Barlow) Zikmund; married Barbara Brown (a professor), August 26, 1961; children: Brian. *Education:* Beloit College, B.A., 1959; University of Wisconsin, M.S., 1961; Duke University, Ph.D., 1965; postdoctoral study at Wayne State University, 1971-76. *Home:* 1360 East 58th St., Chicago, Ill. 60637. *Office:* Department of Social Science, Illinois Institute of Technology, Chicago, Ill. 60616.

CAREER: Temple University, Philadelphia, Pa., assistant professor of political science, 1965-69, acting director of Center for the Study of Federalism, 1968-69; Albion College, Albion, Mich., associate professor of political science, 1969-75; Illinois Institute of Technology, Chicago, associate professor of political science, 1975—. *Member:* American Political Science Association, American Society of Planning Officials, Midwest Political Science Association, Phi Beta Kappa.

WRITINGS: (Editor with Miriam Ershkowitz) *Black Politics in Philadelphia,* Basic Books, 1973; (editor with Daniel J. Elazar) *The Ecology of American Political Culture,* Crowell, 1975. Contributor to professional journals.

WORK IN PROGRESS: Politics of American Suburbia; Urban Planning in Communist Poland; Suburbs: A Guide to Information Sources, for Gale's Urban Studies Information Guide Series, completion expected in 1978.

* * *

ZILMER, Bertram G. 1899(?)-1976

1899(?)—June 24, 1976; American business writer and editor. Obituaries: *Washington Post,* July 1, 1976.

* * *

ZINK, Lubor Jan 1920-

PERSONAL: Born September 20, 1920, in Klapy, Czechoslovakia; son of Vilem (a teacher) and Bozena (Wohl) Zink; married Zora Nechvile (a librarian), April 1, 1942; children: Alec Guy. *Education:* Attended Prague University, 1937-39, 1945-46. *Politics:* Progressive Conservative. *Religion:* Protestant. *Home:* 47 Queensline Drive, Ottawa, Ontario, Canada K2H 7J3.

CAREER: Czechoslovak Foreign Office, Prague, press officer, 1945-48; British Broadcasting Corp., Foreign Service, Reading, England, monitor and script writer, 1948-58; *Brandon Sun,* Brandon, Manitoba, editor of editorial page, 1958-62; *Toronto Telegram,* Toronto, Ontario, author of daily syndicated political column "Comment," 1969-71; Toronto Sun Syndicate, Toronto, Ontario, author of syndicated political and economic column "Counterpoint," 1971—. Co-founder of International Students' Union and World Youth Organization, London, 1941-45; Progressive Conservative candidate for Canadian Parliament from Park-

dale Riding, 1972, 1974; has covered notable news assignments in Europe and the Far East, including Viet Nam. *Military service:* Czechoslovakian Armor Brigade, 1940-45; became first lieutenant; received Military Cross, Medal for Bravery, and Medal of Merit. *Awards, honors:* National Newspaper Award, 1961, for editorial writings in *Brandon Sun;* Bowater Award for Journalism, 1962, for a series of articles titled "The Unfinished Revolution."

WRITINGS: Dva Roky (poems in Czech), National Union of Czechoslovak Students (London), 1941; *Zhavy Dech* (poems in Czech), National Union of Czechoslovak Students, 1942; (with Viktor Fischl) *17 Listopad 1943* (poems in Czech), National Union of Czechoslovak Students, 1943; *The Uprooted* (novel), Longmans, 1962; *Under the Mushroom Cloud* (collected articles from *Brandon Sun*), Brandon Sun, 1962; *Trudeaucracy,* Toronto Sun, 1972. Also author of two novels in Czech, *Cestou Domu* (title means "On the Way Home"), 1948, and *Unor* (title means "February").

WORK IN PROGRESS: A book on Trudeau's second four years (1972-76), tentative title *Viva Fuddle Duddle.*

SIDELIGHTS: Zink's anti-Nazi underground activities forced him to flee Czechoslovakia in 1939 and he joined the Czech fighting forces in France. After World War Two he returned to Czechoslovakia, only to flee again following the Communist coup in 1948. He writes that he was "deeply influenced by Nazi and Communist takeovers of Czechoslovakia" and that he uses his column as a "fighting weapon against all forms of totalitarianism." He adds that he has a "consuming concern for survival of responsible freedom."

Zink's novel *Unor* was read in installments over Radio Free Europe in the mid-1950's.

* * *

ZIPES, Jack (David) 1937-

PERSONAL: Born June 7, 1937, in New York, N.Y.; son of Phillip P. (an investor) and Celia (Rifkin) Zipes. *Education:* Dartmouth College, B.A., 1959; Columbia University, M.A., 1960, Ph.D., 1965; graduate study at University of Munich, 1962, and University of Tuebingen, 1963. *Home:* 2847 North Shepard Ave., Milwaukee, Wis. 53211. *Office:* Department of German, University of Wisconsin, Milwaukee, Wis. 53201.

CAREER: University of Munich, Amerika-Institut, Munich, Germany, instructor in American literature, 1966-67; New York University, New York, N.Y., assistant professor of German, 1967-72; University of Wisconsin, Milwaukee, associate professor of German, 1972—. *Member:* Modern Language Association of America, American Association of Teachers of German, Brecht Society.

WRITINGS: The Great Refusal: Studies of the Romantic Hero in German and American Literature, Athenaeum, 1970; (translator and author of introduction) Hans Mayer, *Steppenwolf and Everyman,* Crowell, 1971; (with Michael Anderson, Jacques Guicharnaud, and Kristin Morrison) *Crowell's Handbook of Contemporary Drama,* Crowell, 1971; (contributor) Francelia Butler, editor, *Children's Literature: The Great Excluded,* volumes II and V, Temple University Press, 1973; (editor and author of introduction) Marianne Thalmann, *Romantik in Kritischer Perspektive* (title means "Romanticism in Critical Perspective"), Lothar-Stiehm Verlag, 1976; (editor and translator) *Political Plays for Children,* Telos, 1976; (translator) Mayer, *Richard Wagner in Bayreuth,* Rizzoli, 1976. Contributor to *Kindlers Literatur-Lexicon* and *Crowell's Encyclopedia of World*

Drama. Contributor of stories, articles, translations, and reviews to professional journals in the United States and Germany. Editor of *New German Critique,* 1973—.

WORK IN PROGRESS: A book on fairy tales.

SIDELIGHTS: Zipes writes: "Two major considerations have influenced my critical writings and translations: the need to develop a radical methodology based on Marxist aesthetics and the necessity to study popular forms of culture such as children's theater. Both are necessary to offset the commercial interests of the culture industry."

*   *   *

ZUBROW, Ezra B. W. 1945-

PERSONAL: Born January 14, 1945, in New Brunswick, N.J.; son of R. A. (a professor) and Ann W. (a teacher) Zubrow; married Marcia Lee Singal (a librarian), June 19, 1967; children: Alexis. *Education:* Harvard University, B.A., 1966; University of Arizona, M.A., 1967, Ph.D., 1971. *Residence:* Menlo Park, Calif. *Office:* Department of Anthropology, Stanford University, Stanford, Calif. 94305.

CAREER: Stanford University, Stanford, Calif., assistant professor of anthropology, 1971—. Conducted field research in Israel, Mexico, Italy, and the American Southwest. Member of Stanford Symphony, 1972-73, 1976. *Member:* American Anthropological Association, Society for American Archaeology, American Association for the Advancement of Science, Sigma Xi. *Awards, honors:* Travel grant from Sigma Xi, 1969.

WRITINGS: (Contributor) Mark Leone, editor, *Contemporary Archaeology: A Guide to Theory and Contributions,* Southern Illinois University Press, 1971; (contributor) Charles Redman, editor, *Research Theory in Current Anthropology,* Wiley, 1973; *Population, Climate, and Contact in the New Mexican Pueblos,* University of Arizona Press, 1974; (editor with Margaret Fritz and John Fritz) *New World Archaeology: Theoretical and Cultural Transformations,* W. H. Freeman, 1974; (editor with Andrew Willard, and contributor) *Models and Innovations: Archaeological and Regional Approaches to Guanajuato, Mexico,* Department of Anthropology, Stanford University, 1974; *Prehistoric Carrying Capacity: A Model,* Cummings, 1975; (editor and contributor) *Demographic Anthropology: Quantitative Approaches,* University of New Mexico Press, 1976. General editor of "Foundations of Archaeology," a series, Duxbury. Contributor to *Handbook of North American Indians* and to anthropology and archaeology journals.

WORK IN PROGRESS: Prehistoric Demography, for Academic Press; *Geological Archaeology,* with John Harbaugh, for Stanford University Press; research on theory and methods of prehistoric regionalization, carrying capacity models and prehistoric demography, the development of remote sensing with Stanford Research Institute, and aerial research on Guanajuato and Tuscany.

*   *   *

ZUCK, Lowell H(ubert) 1926-

PERSONAL: Born June 24, 1926, in Ephrata, Pa.; son of Abram W. (a railway mail clerk) and Verdie (Hibschman) Zuck; married Maya Stauch (a nursery school teacher), September 14, 1950; children: Peter Martin. *Education:* Elizabethtown College, B.A., 1947; Bethany Theological Seminary, B.D., 1950; Yale University, S.T.M., 1951, M.A., 1952, Ph.D., 1955. *Home:* 208 Oakwood Ave., Webster Groves, Mo. 63119. *Office:* Department of Church History,

Eden Theological Seminary, 475 East Lockwood Ave., Webster Groves, Mo. 63119.

CAREER: Ordained minister of the Church of the Brethren, 1946; summer pastor of churches in Pennsylvania, Maryland, and South Dakota, 1947-52; College of Idaho, Caldwell, visiting professor of philosophy and religion, 1954-55; Eden Theological Seminary, Webster Groves, Mo., assistant professor, 1955-57, associate professor, 1957-62, professor of church history, 1962—, librarian for Eden Archives, 1967—; ordained minister of the United Church of Christ, 1957. Instructor at Washington University, St. Louis, Mo., 1956-65. Member of board, Center for Reformation Research, 1976—.

MEMBER: American Society of Church History, American Society for Reformation Research (treasurer, 1969—), Sixteenth-Century Studies Conference (president, 1971-72), American Historical Association, Evangelical and Reformed Historical Society (vice-president, 1974—), Historical Council of the United Church of Christ (chairman, 1974-75). *Awards, honors:* Grant from American Association of Theological Schools, 1964-65, to attend University of Marburg.

WRITINGS: (Contributor) Franklin H. Littell, editor, *Reformation Studies,* John Knox, 1962; *Christianity and Revolution: Radical Christian Testimonies, 1520-1650,* Temple University Press, 1975; *European Roots of the United Church of Christ* (pamphlet), United Church Press, 1976.

WORK IN PROGRESS: A book on the European roots of the United Church of Christ (including the Congregational, Reformed, and Evangelical Churches); research on Reformation studies and Puritanism in the sixteenth and eighteenth centuries.

SIDELIGHTS: Zuck's main interests are "German history and culture from the Reformation to the present, Puritanism and Pietism, continental, English and American, Radical or Left-Wing Reformation, Lutheran and Reformed theology, and church history."

*   *   *

ZUCKERMAN, Solly 1904-

PERSONAL: Listed in some sources as Baron Zuckerman; born May 30, 1904, in Cape Town, South Africa; son of Moses (a merchant) and Rebecca (Glaser) Zuckerman; married Joan Rufus Isaacs, 1939; children: Paul, Stella. *Education:* University of Cape Town, B.S., 1923, M.A., 1925; University of London, D.Sc., 1932; University of Birmingham, M.D., 1946. *Address:* University of East Anglia, Norwich NR4 7TJ, England.

CAREER: University of Cape Town, Cape Town, South Africa, demonstrator in anatomy, 1923-25; University of London, University College, London, England, demonstrator in anatomy, 1928-32; Yale University, New Haven, Conn., research associate, 1933-34; Oxford University, Oxford, England, university lecturer and demonstrator in human anatomy, 1934-45; University of Birmingham, Birmingham, England, Sands Cox Professor of Anatomy, 1943-68, professor emeritus, 1968—; University of East Anglia, Norwich, England, professor emeritus at large, 1969—. Fellow Commoner, Christ Church, Cambridge; research anatomist to the Zoological Society of London, 1928-32. Hunterian Professor, Royal College of Surgeons, 1937; Gregnog Lecturer, University of Wales, 1956; Mason Lecturer, University of Birmingham, 1957; Lees Knowles Lecturer, Cambridge University, 1965; Romanes Lecturer,

Oxford University, 1975; Rhodes Lecturer, University of South Africa, 1975. Fellow of University College, London, 1955—; visitor, Bedford College, 1968—.

Member, British Agricultural Research Council, 1949-59; chairman of British Committee on Scientific Manpower, 1950-64, Natural Resources Committee, 1951-64, and Defence Research Policy Committee, 1960-64; deputy chairman, Advisory Council on Scientific Policy, 1948-64; chief scientific advisor to Her Majesty's government, 1964-71, and to British Secretary of State for Defense, 1960-66; chairman, Central Advisory Committee for Science and Technology, 1965-70; member of Royal Commission on Environmental Pollution, 1970—; president of Parliamentary and Scientific Committee, 1973-76; member of advisory committee on medical research, World Health Organization, 1973—; member of general advisory council, British Broadcasting Corp., 1957-62; trustee, British Museum, 1967—. *Military service:* Royal Air Force, scientific adviser on combined operations, 1939-46, honorary group captain, 1943-46; Supreme Headquarters, Allied Expeditionary Force, chief adviser on air planning, 1939-46.

MEMBER: Royal College of Physicians (fellow), Royal College of Surgeons (honorary fellow), Royal Society (fellow), Zoological Society of London (honorary secretary), Fauna Preservation Society (president), Association of Learned and Professional Society Publishers (president), American Philosophical Society, American Academy of Arts and Sciences (honorary member), Academia das Ciencias de Lisboa (honorary member), Beefsteak Club, Brook's Club. *Awards, honors:* Union research scholar, 1925; Rockefeller research fellow, 1933-34; Beit Memorial research fellow, 1934-37; William Julius Mickle fellow, 1935; Companion of the Bath, 1946; knighted, 1956; Knight Commander of the Bath, 1964; Order of Merit, 1968; Zoological Society of London gold medal, 1971; created Baron of Burnham Thorpe (life peer), 1971; received Medal of Freedom with silver palm (United States); Chevalier de la Legion d'Honneur (France); Companion D'Honneur (France); D.Sc. from University of Sussex, 1963, University of Jacksonville, 1964, and University of Bradford, 1966; LL.D. from University of Birmingham, 1970.

WRITINGS: The Social Life of Monkeys and Apes, Harcourt, 1932; *Functional Affinities of Man, Monkeys, and Apes: A Study of the Bearings of Physiology and Behavior on the Taxonomy and Phylogeny of Lemurs, Monkeys, Apes, and Man,* Harcourt, 1933; (author of foreword and postscript) Harrison Scott Brown, *The Next Hundred Years,* Weidenfeld & Nicolson, 1957; (author of introductory reading guide) *Biology: A Course of Selected Readings by Authorities,* International University Society, 1958, published as *Classics in Biology: A Course of Selected Readings by Authorities,* Philosophical Library, 1960.

Land Ownership and Resources, Department of Estate Management, Cambridge University, 1960; *A New System of Anatomy,* Oxford University Press, 1961; (with Alva R. Myrdal and Lester B. Pearson) *The Control of Proliferation: Three Views,* Institute of Strategic Studies, 1966; *Scientists and War: The Impact of Science on Military and Civil Affairs,* Hamish Hamilton, 1966, Harper, 1967; (contributor) Ashley Montague, editor, *Man and Aggression,* Oxford University Press, 1968.

Beyond the Ivory Tower: The Frontiers of Public and Private Science, Weidenfeld & Nicolson, 1970, Taplinger, 1971; *Cancer Research: A Report by Lord Zuckerman,* H.M.S.O., 1972.

Published lectures: *The Image of Technology,* Oxford University Press, 1967; *Attitudes to Enquiry and Understanding,* Middlesex Hospital Medical School, 1968; *Medicine and Tomorrow's Community,* University of Glasgow, 1969; *Technology and Society: A Challenge to Private Enterprise,* International Chamber of Commerce (Paris), 1971; *Doctors and Patients,* Royal Society of Medicine, 1974; *Advice and Responsibility,* Oxford University Press, 1975. Also contributor of lecture to *Experienta Supplementum 17,* Birkhauser Verlag (Stuttgart), 1972.

Editor: (With Peter Eckstein) *The Thyroid Gland: Proceedings of a Symposium Held Jointly by the Society for Endocrinology and the Endocrinological Section of the Royal Society of Medicine,* [London], 1953; (with Eckstein) *The Technique and Significance of Oestrogen Determinations,* Cambridge University Press, 1955; *The Ovary,* two volumes, Academic Press, 1962; *The Concepts of Human Evolution: The Proceedings of a Symposium Organized by the Anatomical Society of Great Britain and Ireland and the Zoological Society of London,* Academic Press, 1973.

Contributor of numerous articles to scientific journals.

WORK IN PROGRESS: Furthering the cause of the Zoological Society of London in writing, lecturing, and advising.

BIOGRAPHICAL/CRITICAL SOURCES: Guardian, April 7, 1967; April 12, 1971.

* * *

ZUMWALT, Eva 1936-

PERSONAL: Born June 8, 1936, in Eunice, N.M.; daughter of Ellis Otto (an oil lease foreman) and Elva (a poet; maiden name, Davidson) Beaty; married Ted L. Zumwalt (a hospital employee), February 21, 1954; children: Karyn Lisa (Mrs. Alan Charles Porter), Kathy Eve. *Education:* Attended high school in Artesia, N.M. *Residence:* Nogal, N.M. 88341. *Agent:* Miriam Gilbert, Authors' & Publishers' Service, 146-47 29th Ave., Flushing, N.Y. 11354.

CAREER: Free-lance writer.

WRITINGS: Masquerade of Evil (Gothic mystery), Ace Books, 1975; *Briarlea* (Gothic mystery), Ace Books, 1976; *Sun Dust* (young adult western), McKay, 1976; *The Deathday Song* (Gothic mystery), Major Books, in press. Contributor to *Progressive Farmer.*

WORK IN PROGRESS: A mystery novel; *Rebel Echo,* a horse story for teenagers.

SIDELIGHTS: Eva Zumwalt writes: "My background has been small town and country. My husband is a fine horseman and cowboy.... With him I have ridden a great deal over some of this state's most beautiful country. I am a confirmed nature-lover. I believe in solitude as a healer of troubled spirits, and I value privacy. The social life tempts me not at all. Happiness for me has always been found not among crowds but with my few most beloved people.... With no desire to preach, reform or make particular statements, social, political, etc., my purpose is to write what will entertain and give pleasure. I do have a deep belief in the potential beauty of each human spirit, the power of love and concern, and the need for strong family influence on children, and I hope this is reflected in my work."

AVOCATIONAL INTERESTS: Oil painting, horses and dogs, gardening.

* * *